TESTS IN PRINT VI

EARLIER PUBLICATIONS IN THIS SERIES

TESTS
IN PRINT VI

AN INDEX TO TESTS, TEST REVIEWS, AND THE LITERATURE ON SPECIFIC TESTS

Edited by

LINDA L. MURPHY
BARBARA S. PLAKE
JAMES C. IMPARA
ROBERT A. SPIES

The Buros Institute of Mental Measurements
The University of Nebraska-Lincoln
Lincoln, Nebraska

2002
Distributed by The University of Nebraska Press

LC 83-18866
ISBN 910674-56-6

Manufactured in the United States of America.

The paper used in this publication meets the minimum requirements of American National Standard for Information Sciences—Permanence of Paper for Printed Library Materials, ANSI Z39.48-1984.

Note to Users

TABLE OF CONTENTS

INTRODUCTION

Tests in Print (*TIP*) consists of descriptive listings of commercially published tests. It serves as a comprehensive index to all the *Mental Measurements Yearbooks* (*MMY*) published to date.

There are key differences between the *Tests in Print* series and the *Mental Measurements Yearbook* series. In contrast to *TIP*, the *MMY* series consists of both descriptive entries and critical reviews of commercially published tests available in the English language. Each *MMY*, of which there are now 14, includes reviews and descriptions of only those tests that are new or substantially revised since the previous *MMY*. The *MMY* series is, therefore, sequential in nature.

Each *TIP*, of which there are now six, is a comprehensive volume describing, to the best of our ability, every test that is currently commercially available. *TIP VI*, therefore, supersedes *TIP V*. Although it is necessary to have the entire *MMY* series to be sure of finding a review of a particular test, only the latest addition to the *TIP* series is needed for comprehensive coverage.

TIP VI can be a first strategy to locate and learn about a testing product. Because *TIP VI* indexes all 14 of the books in the *MMY* series (for tests still in print), it is an invaluable guide to both descriptive and analytical information.

In the Preface of the first *Tests in Print* volume, Oscar Buros noted that this work had been in preparation for over 20 years. The first two volumes of *The Mental Measurements Yearbook* were published in 1938 and 1940. It became increasingly apparent that a comprehensive bibliography

of tests was needed and an index to the contents of the *MMY* volumes was needed. The initial delay in *Tests in Print* was due to World War II, and then various other financial and production limitations postponed its publication. *Tests in Print II* was published in 1974. After the death of Oscar Buros, the Buros Institute was established at the University of Nebraska. The first publication from the new Institute was *Tests in Print III* in 1983. *Tests in Print IV* was published in 1994 and *Tests in Print V* was published in 1999.

The need for this comprehensive bibliography of tests continues. Because of the proliferation of commercially available tests we have adopted a new policy of reviewing in *The Mental Measurements Yearbook* only those tests with at least a minimum of technical and/or development information available for review. This new policy was implemented with tests reviewed in the *14th MMY*. Therefore, not all commercially available tests will be described and reviewed in the *MMY*. However, we continue to include descriptive information for all known in-print commercially available tests in *Tests in Print*. With the more frequent publication of *The Mental Measurements Yearbook* (approximately every 18 months), it is necessary to provide a comprehensive listing of commercially available tests on a more frequent basis. Beginning with *Tests in Print VI*, we have embarked on a plan to publish *TIP* every 3 years.

Our efforts within this massive enterprise have had the same purpose as proposed by Oscar K. Buros, that is, to improve testing products by offering valid information to consumers. *Tests in Print VI* (*TIP VI*) is a continuation of our efforts to provide useful data to people who develop, study, and/or buy testing products.

TESTS IN PRINT VI

The contents of *Tests in Print VI* include: (a) a comprehensive bibliography of commercially available tests published as separates for use with English-speaking individuals; (b) a test title index that includes all in-print tests, tests that have gone out of print since the publication of *TIP V*, and alternative or superseded titles for some tests; (c) a separate listing of the tests that have gone out of print since the publication of *TIP III* (1983); (d) a classified subject index that also describes the population for which each test is intended; (e) a publishers directory and index, including contact information and test listings by publisher; (f) a name index, which includes the names of all authors of tests or of reviews; (g) a score index listing all scores generated by tests listed in *TIP VI*; and (i) a list of contributing reviewers for the entire *MMY* series.

The organization of the volume is encyclopedic in nature, with tests being ordered alphabetically by title. Thus, if the title of a test is known, the reader can locate the test immediately without having to consult the Index of Titles. Test classifications appear in the Classified Subject Index.

The page headings reflect the encyclopedic organization. The page heading of the left-hand page cites the number and title of the first test listed on that page, and the page heading of the right-hand page cites the number and title of the last test listed on that page. All numbers presented in the various indexes are test numbers, not page numbers. Page numbers, important only for the Table of Contents, are indicated at the bottom of each page.

TESTS

Tests in Print VI contains 2,780 test entries. The in-print status of these tests was confirmed by direct correspondence with publishers. Table 1 presents the number of test entries included in each major classification of the Classified Subject Index. Any classification system is to some degree dependent on human judgment, but broad comparisons between categories are often useful. It is interesting to note, for example, that once again that the personality

TABLE 1

Test Entries in *TIP VI* by Major Classification

Classification	Number of Test Entries
Achievement	82
Behavior Assessment	127
Developmental	135
Education	99
English and Language	163
Fine Arts	18
Foreign Language	46
Intelligence and General Aptitude	210
Mathematics	69
Miscellaneous	244
Neuropsychological	97
Personality	629
Reading	110
Science	44
Sensory-Motor	52
Social Studies	35
Speech and Hearing	80
Vocations	540

test category continues to include the greatest number of tests of any category in *TIP VI*.

REVIEWS AND EXCERPTS

Tests in Print VI serves as a master index of in-print tests that refers the reader to all the original test reviews and excerpted test reviews that appeared for these tests in all of the *Mental Measurements Yearbooks* to date. In addition, it provides references to entries and reviews in earlier yearbooks for all tests that have gone out of print since *TIP III*. Authors of reviews and excerpts are named following the test entries in cross references to the appropriate *MMY*. Although *TIP VI* will serve a very useful function by providing a comprehensive bibliography of tests in print, the cross references to the critical reviews are also of great importance if tests are to be used wisely. Thus *TIP* and the *MMY*s are inseparable partners in the cause of promoting effective selection and use of tests.

To complement these two publications, *Tests Reviews Online* (www.unl.edu/buros) has been developed to permit users instant access to test descriptions and reviews from the Buros Institute of Mental Measurements. Information is available from *Tests Reviews Online* exactly as it appears in the *The Ninth* through *The Fourteenth Mental*

Measurements Yearbooks. In addition, regular updates are provided from our current database. For a small fee, users may download descriptive testing information and test critiques for over 2,000 tests.

A total of 2,894 individuals have contributed reviews to one or more *MMY*s. Because of their important contributions to the *Mental Measurements Yearbooks*, a complete listing of *MMY* test reviewers is presented in the index section of *TIP VI*.

REFERENCES

Previous volumes have included specific test references selected by Buros staff who searched through hundreds of professional journals. Because of the availability of online search features that allow users to do independent reference searches, it was our decision to discontinue providing these references in the *MMY* and *TIP* series. Cross references for a number of test descriptions will still indicate when references were provided in previous publications (e.g., "See T5:326 [10 references]").

INDEXES

As mentioned earlier, *TIP VI* includes seven indexes invaluable as aids to effective use: (a) Index of Titles, (b) Index of Recently-Out-of-Print Tests, (c) Index of Acronyms, (d) Classified Subject Index, (e) Publishers Directory and Index, (f) Index of Names, and (g) Score Index. Additional comment on these indexes is presented below.

Index of Titles. Because the organization of *TIP* is comprehensive in nature, with the tests ordered alphabetically by title throughout the volume, the test title index does not have to be consulted to find a test for which the title is known. However, the title index has some features that make it useful beyond its function as a complete title listing. First, it includes cross-reference information useful for tests with superseded or alternative titles or tests commonly (and sometimes inaccurately) known by multiple titles. Second, it lists the 469 tests that have gone out of print since being listed in *TIP V* or the *14th MMY*. To differentiate between in-print and out-of-print tests in the title index it is important to read carefully the instructions on the use of the test title index that precede the title listing. It is important to keep in mind that the numbers in this index, like those for all *TIP* and *MMY* indexes, are test numbers and not page numbers.

Index of Recently-Out-of-Print Tests. This index is a comprehensive listing of all tests that have gone out of print since the publication of *Tests in Print III* (1983). The number following the title indicates the last Buros publication in which the test was listed as an in-print test.

Index of Acronyms. Some tests seem to be better known by their acronyms than by their full titles. The Index of Acronyms can help in these instances; it refers the reader to the full title of the test and to the relevant descriptive information and reviews.

Classified Subject Index. The Classified Subject Index classifies all tests listed in *TIP VI* into 18 major categories: Achievement, Behavior Assessment, Developmental, Education, English and Language, Fine Arts, Foreign Languages, Intelligence and General Aptitude, Mathematics, Miscellaneous, Neuropsychological, Personality, Reading, Science, Sensory-Motor, Social Studies, Speech and Hearing, and Vocations. Each test entry includes test title, population for which the test is intended, and test number. The Classified Subject Index is of great help to readers who seek a listing of tests in given subject areas. The Classified Subject Index represents a starting point for readers who know their area of interest but do not know how to further focus that interest in order to identify the best test(s) for their particular purposes. A descriptive listing of the categories precedes the Classified Subject Index.

Publishers Directory and Index. The Publishers Directory and Index includes the names and addresses of the publishers of all tests included in *TIP VI* plus a listing of test numbers for each individual publisher. This index also includes telephone and FAX numbers and addresses for electronic access (email and web pages). Publishers were given an opportunity to provide this information as they wanted it listed. For those not providing contact information, only a mailing address is included. This index can be particularly useful in obtaining addresses for specimen sets or catalogs after the test descriptions have been read and evaluated. It can also be useful when a reader knows the publisher of a certain test but is uncertain about the test title, or when a reader is interested in the range of tests published by a given publisher. Several publishers are listed as "Status Unknown" because recent correspondence has been returned by the Post Office and we have been unable to obtain a current address.

Index of Names. The Index of Names provides a comprehensive list of names, indicating authorship of a test or a test review.

Score Index. The Score Index is an index to all scores generated by the tests in *TIP VI*. Test titles are sometimes misleading or ambiguous, and test content may be difficult to define with precision. Test scores represent operational definitions of the variables the test author is trying to measure, and as such they often define test purpose and content more adequately than other descriptive information. A search for a particular test is most often a search for a test that measures some specific variables. Test scores and their associated labels can often be the best definitions of the variables of interest. It is, in fact, a detailed subject index based on the most critical operational features of any test—the scores and their associated labels.

HOW TO USE TIP VI

A reference work like *TIP VI* can be of far greater benefit to a reader if a little time is taken to become familiar with what it has to offer and how one might use it most effectively to obtain the information wanted. The first step in this process is to read the Introduction to *TIP VI*. The second step is to become familiar with the seven indexes and particularly with the instructions preceding each index listing. The third step is to make actual use of the book by looking up needed information. This third step is simple if one keeps in mind the following possibilities:

1. If you know the title of the test, use the alphabetical page headings to go directly to the test entry.
2. If you do not know, cannot find, or are unsure of the title of a test, consult the Index of Titles for possible variants of the title or consult the appropriate subject area of the Classified Subject Index for other possible leads or for similar or related tests in the same area. (Other uses for both of these indexes were described earlier.)
3. If you know the author of a test but not the title or publisher, consult the Index of Names and look up the author's titles until you find the test you want.

4. If you know the test publisher but not the title or author, consult the Publishers Directory and Index and look up the publisher's titles until you find the test you want.
5. If you are looking for a test that yields a particular kind of score, but have no knowledge of which test that might be, look up the score in the Score Index and locate the test or tests that include the score variable of interest.
6. Once you have found the test or tests you are looking for, read the descriptive entries for these tests carefully so that you can take advantage of the information provided. A description of the information available in these test entries will be presented later in this section.
7. After you have read the descriptive information, you may want to order a specimen set for a particular test so that you can examine it firsthand. The Publishers Directory and Index has the address information needed to obtain specimen sets or catalogs.

Making Effective Use of the Test Entries. The test entries include extensive information. For each test, descriptive information is presented in the following order:

a) TITLES. Test titles are printed in boldface type. Secondary or series titles are set off from main titles by a colon.

b) PURPOSE. For each test we have included a brief, clear statement describing the purpose of the test. Often these statements are quotations from the test manual.

c) POPULATION. This is a description of the groups for which the test is intended. The grade, chronological age, semester range, or employment category is usually given. "Grades 1.5–2.5, 2–3, 4–12, 13–17" means that there are four test booklets: a booklet for the middle of first grade through the middle of the second grade, a booklet for the beginning of the second grade through the end of third grade, a booklet for Grades 4 through 12 inclusive, and a booklet for undergraduate and graduate students in colleges and universities.

d) PUBLICATION DATE. The inclusive range of publication dates for the various forms, accessories, and editions of a test is reported.

e) ACRONYM. When a test is often referred to by an acronym by the test publisher, the acronym is given in the test entry immediately following the publication date.

f) SCORES. The number of part scores is presented along with their titles or descriptions of what they are intended to represent or measure.

g) ADMINISTRATION. Individual or group administration is indicated. A test is considered a group test unless it may be administered only individually.

h) FORMS, PARTS, AND LEVELS. All available forms, parts, and levels are listed.

i) MANUAL. Notation is made if no manual is available. All other manual information is included under Price Data.

j) RESTRICTED DISTRIBUTION. This is noted only for tests that are put on a special market by the publisher. Educational and psychological restrictions are not noted (unless a special training course is required for use).

k) PRICE DATA. Price information is reported for test packages (usually 20 to 35 tests), answer sheets, all other accessories, and specimen sets. The statement "$17.50 per 35 tests" means that all accessories are included unless otherwise indicated by the reporting of separate prices for accessories. The statement also means 35 tests of one level, one edition, or one part unless stated otherwise. Because test prices can change very quickly, the year that the listed test prices were obtained is also given. Foreign currency is assigned the appropriate symbol. When prices are given in foreign dollars, a qualifying symbol is added (e.g., A$16.50 refers to 16 dollars and 50 cents in Australian currency). Along with cost, the publication date and number of pages on which print occurs is reported for manuals and technical reports (e.g., '95, 102 pages). All types of machine-scorable answer sheets available for use with a specific test are also reported in the descriptive entry. Scoring and reporting services provided by publishers are reported along with information on costs. In a few cases, special computerized scoring and interpretation services are given in separate entries immediately following the test.

l) FOREIGN LANGUAGE AND OTHER SPECIAL EDITIONS. This section concerns foreign language editions published by the same publisher who sells the English edition. It also indicates special editions (e.g., Braille, large type) available from the same or a different publisher.

m) TIME. The number of minutes of actual working time allowed examinees and the approximate length of time needed for administering a test are reported whenever obtainable. The latter figure is always enclosed in parentheses. Thus, "50(60) minutes" indicates that the examinees are allowed 50 minutes of working time and that a total of 60 minutes is needed to administer the test. A time of "40–50 minutes" indicates an untimed test that takes approximately 45 minutes to administer, or—in a few instances—a test so timed that working time and administration time are very difficult to disentangle. When the time necessary to administer a test is not reported or suggested in the test materials but has been obtained through correspondence with the test publisher or author, the time is enclosed in brackets.

n) COMMENTS. Some entries contain special notations, such as: "for research use only"; "revision of the ABC Test"; "tests administered monthly at centers throughout the United States"; "subtests available as separates"; and "verbal creativity." A statement such as "verbal creativity" is intended to further describe what the test claims to measure. Some of the test entries include factual statements that imply criticism of the test, such as "1990 test identical with test copyrighted 1970."

o) AUTHOR. For most tests, all authors are reported. In the case of tests that appear in a new form each year, typically only authors of the most recent forms are listed. Names are reported exactly as printed on test booklets. Names of editors generally are not reported.

p) PUBLISHER. The name of the publisher or distributor is reported for each test. Foreign publishers are identified by listing the country in brackets immediately following the name of the publisher. The Publishers Directory and Index must be consulted for a publisher's address and other contact information.

q) FOREIGN ADAPTATIONS. Revisions and adaptations of tests for foreign use are listed in a separate paragraph following the original edition.

r) SUBLISTINGS. Levels, editions, subtests, or parts of a test available in separate booklets are sometimes presented as sublistings with titles set in small capitals. Sub-sublistings are indented and titles are set in italic type.

s) CROSS REFERENCES. For tests that have been listed previously in a Buros Institute publication, a test entry includes—if relevant—a final paragraph containing a cross reference to the reviews, excerpts, and references for that test in those volumes. For example, in the cross references, "T3:467" refers to test 467 in *Tests in Print III*, "8:1023" refers to test 1023 in *The Eighth Mental Measurements Yearbook*, "T2:144" refers to test 144 in *Tests in Print II*, "7:637" refers to test 637 in *The Seventh Mental Measurements Yearbook*, "P:262" refers to test 262 in *Personality Tests and Reviews I*, "2:1427" refers to test 1427 in *The 1940 Yearbook*, and "1:1110" refers to test 1110 in *The 1938 Yearbook*. In the case of batteries and programs, the paragraph also includes cross references—from the battery to the separately listed subtests and vice versa—to entries in this volume and to entries and reviews in earlier editions of *TIP* and the *MMY*.

ACKNOWLEDGEMENTS

The publication of a volume of this kind is only accomplished with the effort and cooperation of many people. The editors are grateful to all who have given of their time and expertise in the publication process.

Staff members of the Buros Institute have been major contributors and vital to the success of gathering and compiling the information to be included in *TIP VI*. It has truly been a team effort. Gary Anderson, Assistant Editor, and Rosemary Sieck, Word Processing Specialist, have worked long and hard in helping to organize and present the information included. Their careful and conscientious efforts are very important. The administrative support of Rasma Strautkalns, Institute Secretary, has been very important and helpful also.

The Buros Institute is part of the Department of Educational Psychology of the University of Nebraska-Lincoln and many students from the department and the university have contributed to the publication of this volume. We thank the following graduate research assistants who helped with the preparation of *TIP VI*: Rene Ayers, Marta Coleman, Christine Gibbon, Jorge Gonzalez, Wei Huang, Sean Kitaoka, Brad Merker, Bo Ouyang, and Georgette Yetter. We also thank Elizabeth Murphy, student assistant, for her help.

Appreciation is also extended to our National Advisory Committee for their willingness to assist in the operation of the Buros Institute. The members of the National Advisory Committee during the time of preparation of this volume were Jane Close Conoley, Gail Latta, Larry Rudner, Paul Sackett, and Jeffrey Smith.

Most of the publishers of the tests listed have been extremely cooperative in providing us with materials and information to make the test listings comprehensive and accurate. We appreciate their input very much. A small minority of publishers refuse to provide information and materials. We sincerely regret that we were not able to list their products. Some others did not respond to our requests for an accuracy check of information, so we have included the information we have for their tests and addresses. We have tried very hard to stay aware of new tests, publishers, and publisher addresses. We apologize for any oversights and hope that the test authors or publishers will make us aware of omissions and discrepancies so this can be corrected in future editions.

And finally, we thank our friends and families for their patience and encouragement during the publication process.

Linda L. Murphy
Barbara S. Plake
James C. Impara
Robert A. Spies
August 2002

Tests in Print

[1]

A.I. Survey.

Purpose: "Screens for alienated attitudes that reduce performance and cause poor morale."
Population: Job applicants.
Publication Date: 1982.
Scores: Total score only.
Administration: Group or individual.
Price Data: Price information available from publisher for surveys and yearly license fee.
Time: Administration time not reported.
Comments: Also called Alienation Index Survey.
Authors: Alan L. Strand and others.
Publisher: Predictive Surveys Corporation.

[2]

AAMR Adaptive Behavior Scale—Residential and Community, Second Edition.

Purpose: To determine "an individual's strengths and weaknesses among adaptive domains and factors."
Population: Persons with disabilities in residential and community settings.
Publication Dates: 1969–1993.
Acronym: ABS-RC:2.
Scores, 23: 18 domain scores (10 part one domain scores: Independent Functioning, Physical Development, Economic Activity, Language Development, Numbers and Time, Domestic Activity, Prevocational/Vocational Activity, Self-Direction, Responsibility, Socialization; 8 part two domain scores: Social Behavior, Conformity, Trustworthiness, Stereotyped and Hyperactive Behavior, Sexual Behavior, Self-Abusive Behavior, Social Engagement, Disturbing Interpersonal Behavior); 5 factor scores (Personal Self-Sufficiency, Community Self-Sufficiency, Personal-Social Responsibility, Social Adjustment, Personal Adjustment).
Administration: Individual.
Price Data, 2001: $124 per complete kit including examiner's manual (1993, 76 pages), 25 examination booklets, and 25 profile/summary forms; $179 per 100 examination booklets; $24 per 25 profile/summary forms; $49 per examiner's manual.
Time: Administration time not reported.
Authors: Kazuo Nihira, Henry Leland, and Nadine Lambert.
Publisher: PRO-ED.
Cross References: For reviews by Karen T. Carey and Patti L. Harrison, see 13:1.

[3]

AAMR Adaptive Behavior Scale—School, Second Edition.

Purpose: "Used to assess adaptive behavior."
Population: Ages 3–21.
Publication Dates: 1981–1993.
Acronym: ABS-S:2.
Scores, 21: 16 domain scores (9 part one domain scores: Independent Functioning, Physical Development, Economic Activity, Language Development, Numbers and Time, Prevocational/Vocational Activity, Self-Direction, Responsibility, Socialization; 7 part two domain scores: Social Behavior, Conformity, Trustworthiness, Stereotyped and Hyperactive Behavior, Self-Abusive Behavior, Social Engagement, Disturbing Interpersonal Behavior), 5 factor scores (Personal Self-Sufficiency, Community Self-Sufficiency, Personal-Social Responsibility, Social Adjustment, Personal Adjustment).
Administration: Individual.
Price Data, 2001: $124 per complete kit including examiner's manual (1993, 118 pages), 25 examination booklets, and 25 profile/summary forms; $54 per 25 examination booklets; $24 per 25 profile/summary forms; $49 per examiner's manual.

Time: (15–30) minutes.
Comments: Previously called AAMD Adaptive Behavior Scale.
Authors: Nadine Lambert, Kazuo Nihira, and Henry Leland.
Publisher: PRO-ED.
Cross References: See T5:2 (2 references); for reviews by Robert G. Harrington and Terry A. Stinnett, see 13:2 (6 references); see also T4:2 (42 references); for a review of an earlier edition by Stephen N. Elliott, see 9:3 (9 references); see also T3:6 (55 references); for reviews of an earlier edition by Morton Bortner and C. H. Ammons and R. B. Ammons, see 8:493 (25 references); see also T2:1092 (3 references); for reviews of an earlier edition by Lovick C. Miller and Melvyn I. Semmel, see 7:37 (9 references).

[4]
The ABC Inventory to Determine Kindergarten and School Readiness.

Purpose: Measures kindergarten and school readiness and identifies children too immature for kindergarten or first grade before enrollment.
Population: Ages 3.5—6.5.
Publication Dates: 1965—1985.
Scores: Total score only.
Administration: Individual.
Price Data: Available from publisher.
Time: Administration time not reported.
Comments: An individualized computer-generated narrative report, The Learning Temperament Profile (based on child's ABC Inventory scores), available from publisher.
Authors: Normand Adair and George Blesch.
Publisher: Educational Studies & Development [No reply from publisher; status unknown].
Cross References: For reviews by Carl J. Dunst and J. Jeffrey Grill, see 10:1; see also T3:7 (2 references) and T2:1691 (2 references); for a review by David P. Weikart, see 7:739 (2 references).

[5]
Aberrant Behavior Checklist.

Purpose: Constructed to rate "inappropriate and maladaptive behavior of mentally retarded individuals in residential and community settings, and developmental centers."
Population: Mentally retarded adolescents and adults.
Publication Date: 1986.
Acronym: ABC.
Scores, 5: Irritability, Lethargy, Stereotypy, Hyperactivity, Inappropriate Speech.
Administration: Individual.
Price Data, 2002: $63 per Residential complete kit including manual (32 pages) and Community supplemental manual; $70 per Community complete kit in-

cluding manual, supplementary manual, and 50 Residential/Community forms/score sheets; $33 per 50 Residential/Community forms/score sheets; $33 per manual; $12 per Community supplemental manual.
Time: (5) minutes.
Comments: Ratings by direct care or professional staff member acquainted with individual.
Authors: Michael G. Aman and Nirbhay N. Singh.
Publisher: Slosson Educational Publications, Inc.
Cross References: See T5:4 (23 references); for reviews by Lena R. Gaddis and J. Jeffrey Grill, see 12:1 (5 references); see T4:4 (2 references).

[6]
Abortion Scale.

Purpose: To measure attitudes toward abortion.
Population: Older adolescents and adults.
Publication Dates: 1972–1988.
Score: Total score only.
Manual: No manual.
Price Data, 2002: $1 per scale.
Time: [10] minutes.
Comments: Supplementary article available.
Author: Panos D. Bardis.
Publisher: Donna Bardis.
Cross References: See T4:4 (2 references).

[7]
Abuse Risk Inventory for Women, Experimental Edition.

Purpose: To identify women who are current victims of abuse or who are at risk for abuse by their male intimate partners or ex-partners.
Population: Women seeking medical or mental health services.
Publication Date: 1989.
Acronym: ARNN.
Scores: Total score only.
Administration: Group and individual.
Price Data: Available from publisher.
Time: (10–15) minutes.
Comments: Test booklet title is Interpersonal Relationship Survey; self-administered.
Author: Bonnie L. Yegidis.
Publisher: Mind Garden, Inc.
Cross References: For reviews by Cynthia A. Rohrbeck and Janice G. Williams, see 11:1.

[8]
Academic Advising Inventory.

Purpose: "Designed to measure three aspects of academic advising: (1) the nature of advising relationships, seen along a developmental-prescriptive continuum, (2) the frequency of activities taking place during advising sessions, and (3) satisfaction with advising."

Population: Undergraduate students.
Publication Dates: 1984–1986.
Acronym: AAI.
Scores, 3: Developmental-Prescriptive Advising, Advisor-Advisee Activity Scales, Student Satisfaction with Advising.
Administration: Group.
Price Data: Available from publisher.
Time: (20) minutes.
Comments: Manual entitled Evaluating Academic Advising; scoring service available from publisher.
Authors: Roger B. Winston, Jr. and Janet A. Sandor.
Publisher: Student Development Associates, Inc. [No reply from publisher; status unknown].
Cross References: See T5:8 (1 reference) and T4:7 (2 references); for a review by Robert D. Brown, see 10:3.

[9]
Academic Aptitude Test: Non-Verbal Intelligence: Acorn National Aptitude Tests.

Purpose: "Designed to evaluate that aspect of intelligence related to the aptitude for abstract academic work required in mathematical, engineering, designing and other physical sciences."
Population: Grades 7—16 and adults.
Publication Dates: 1943—1957.
Scores, 4: Spatial Relations, Physical Relations, Graphic Relations, Total.
Administration: Group.
Price Data: Available from publisher.
Time: 26 minutes.
Authors: Andrew Kobal, J. Wayne Wrightstone, and Karl R. Kunze.
Publisher: Psychometric Affiliates.
Cross References: For a review by William B. Schrader, see 4:274.

[10]
Academic Aptitude Test: Verbal Intelligence: Acorn National Aptitude Tests.

Purpose: "Designed to evaluate mental abilities and capacities that are important in academic work."
Population: Grades 7–16 and adults.
Publication Dates: 1943–1952.
Scores, 4: General Information, Mental Alertness, Comprehension of Relations, Total.
Administration: Group.
Price Data: Available from publisher.
Time: 40 minutes.
Authors: Andrew Kobal, J. Wayne Wrightstone, and Karl R. Kunze.
Publisher: Psychometric Affiliates.
Cross References: For a review by William B. Schrader, see 4:275; for a review by Marion A. Bills, see 3:215.

[11]
Academic Competence Evaluation Scales.

Purpose: "Measures academic skills (reading/language arts, mathematics, critical thinking) as well as academic enablers (motivation, study skills, engagement, interpersonal skills)."
Population: Grades K–12, Grades 6–12, 2- or 4-year college.
Publication Date: 2000.
Acronym: ACES.
Scores, 9: Academic Skills (Reading/Language Arts, Mathematics, Critical Thinking, Total), Academic Enablers (Interpersonal Skills, Motivation, Study Skills, Engagement, Total).
Administration: Group.
Forms, 3: Teacher (Grades K–12), Student (Grades 6–12), College (2- or 4-year college).
Price Data, 2001: $119 per K–12 basic kit including manual, 25 each of student and teacher record forms, boxed; $195 per K–12 complete kit including manual (154 pages), 25 each of student and teacher record forms, scoring assistant (disk or CD-ROM version); $165 per college complete kit including manual, 25 college record forms, scoring assistant (disk or CD-ROM version); $65 per K–12 manual or college manual; $34 per 25 record forms (specify Student, Teacher, or College), quantity discounts available; $91 per scoring assistant software (disk or CD-ROM version).
Time: (10–15) minutes.
Comments: Standardized; indicates confidence intervals for each subscale; allows ranking of scale and subscale scores into one of three competence levels (developing, competent, advanced); Assistant software (version 2.0) scores, monitors change in scores over time, graphs data, generates descriptive reports; system requirements: Windows 95/98/2000/NT 4.0/Me, 32 MB RAM, 100 MHz processor or higher, CD-ROM and 3.5-inch floppy diskette drive (CD-ROM version) or 3.5-diskette drive only (diskette version), 2 MB video card, 800 x 600 resolution, 256 colors, 25 MB free disk space.
Authors: James C. DiPerna and Stephen N. Elliott.
Publisher: The Psychological Corporation.

[12]
Academic Freedom Survey.

Purpose: "Attempted to measure academic freedom" at college level.
Population: College students and faculty.
Publication Date: 1954.
Scores, 3: Student, Faculty, Total.
Administration: Group.
Price Data, 2001: $4 per specimen set.
Time: Administration time not reported.

Authors: Paul Slivnick and Academic Freedom Committee, Illinois Division, American Civil Liberties Union.
Publisher: Psychometric Affiliates.

[13]
Academic Perceptions Inventory [2000 Revision].

Purpose: "Developed to assess a profile of the academic self in various classrooms and in the learning environment ... with perceptions of the self as a person, as a student, and at school."
Population: Grades K–16.
Publication Dates: 1979–2000.
Acronym: API.
Administration: Group.
Price Data, 2002: $20 per packet of 25 scales (specify level); $25 per test manual (specify Primary Level [2000, 83 pages], Intermediate Level [2000, 76 pages], Advanced Level [2000, 79 pages], or College Level [2000, 73 pages]); $40 per composite test manual (2000, 146 pages); $.40 per answer sheet; $.30 per scale for scoring.
Foreign Language Editions: Also available in Spanish, Italian, and French.
Time: (5–20) minutes per test.
Comments: Ratings by self and others; previous edition entitled The Affective Perception Inventory.
Authors: Louise M. Soares and Anthony T. Soares.
Publisher: SOARES Associates.
    a) PRIMARY LEVEL.
    Population: Grades K–3.
    Scores: 9 Scales: Self Concept, Student Self, School, Reading, Social Studies, Science, Arithmetic, Fine Arts, Sports and Games.
    b) INTERMEDIATE LEVEL.
    Population: Grades 4–8.
    Scores: 11 Scales: Self Concept, Student Self, School, Language Arts, Reading, Foreign Languages, History and Geography, Science, Mathematics, Fine Arts, Physical Education.
    c) ADVANCED LEVEL.
    Population: Grades 9–12.
    Scores: 13 Scales: Self Concept, Student Self, School, English, Foreign Languages, American History, Mathematics, Biology, Chemistry, Earth Sciences, Physics, Fine Arts, Sports.
    d) COLLEGE LEVEL.
    Population: Grades 13–16.
    Scores: 15 Scales: Self Concept, Student Self, Campus, English, Foreign Languages, World History, Political Science, Business, Mathematics, Biology, Chemistry, Physics, Humanities, Fine Arts, Sports.
Cross References: See T4:130 (3 references); for reviews by Rosa A. Hagin and Gerald R. Smith of The Affective Perception Inventory, see 9:59.

[14]
Academic Proficiency Battery.

Purpose: To "aid in the selection of first-year students at universities and colleges."
Population: College entrants.
Publication Date: 1969.
Acronym: APB.
Scores, 5: Social Sciences, Commercial Sciences, Natural Sciences, Mathematical Sciences, Language (Afrikaans or English).
Administration: Group.
Price Data: Available from publisher.
Time: 85(110) minutes.
Comments: All test materials are in both English or Afrikaans; separate answer sheets (IBM 1230) must be used.
Authors: F. A. Fouche, N. F. Alberts, and C. L. J. Minnaar (test).
Publisher: Human Sciences Research Council [South Africa].

[15]
ACCESS—A Comprehensive Custody Evaluation Standard System.

Purpose: Constructed as a "total system for conducting child custody evaluations."
Population: Children, parents, and others involved in child custody evaluations.
Publication Date: 1997–2002.
Administration: Individual.
Price Data, 2002: $1,495 per complete kit including Bricklin Perceptual Scales Comprehensive Starting Kit with 3.5-inch unlimited use computer scoring profile, Perception-of-Relationships Test Comprehensive Starting Kit with 3.5-inch unlimited use computer scoring profile, Parent Awareness Skills Survey Comprehensive Starting Kit; Parent Perception-of-Child Profile Comprehensive Starting Kit, Custody Evaluation Questionnaires Kit, Custody Evaluation Interview Kit, Custody Evaluation Observation Kit, Custody Evaluation Aggregation Kit, Discipline Index Kit with 3.5-inch unlimited use computer scoring profiles, Home-Visit Kit, and Assessment of Parenting Skills: Infant and Preschooler.
Time: Administration time not reported.
Comments: Ratings by parents, children, teachers, and health/mental health professionals.
Authors: Barry Bricklin and Gail Elliot.
Publisher: Village Publishing.
    a) BRICKLIN PERCEPTUAL SCALES.
    Comments: See T5:334.
    b) PERCEPTION-OF-RELATIONSHIPS TEST.
    Comments: See T5:1917.
    c) PARENT AWARENESS SKILLS SURVEY.
    Comments: See T5:1879.

d) PARENT PERCEPTION OF CHILD PROFILE.
Comments: See T5:1886.

e) CUSTODY EVALUATION QUESTIONNAIRES KIT.
Purpose: "Designed to gather self-report data … in every single area that are considered important in model custody statutes."
Population: Children, parents, grandparents, and collateral informants involved in a custody evaluation.
Scores: No scores, ratings only.
Forms, 6: Parent Self-Report Questionnaire, "Would" Questionnaire, Child Data Questionnaire, Child Self-Report Questionnaire, Child's Access to Parental Strengths Questionnaire, Child's Sexual Abuse Questionnaire.

f) CUSTODY EVALUATION INTERVIEW KIT.
Purpose: Designed for conducting custody evaluation interviews.
Population: Professionals conducting custody evaluation interviews.
Scores: No scores, structured interviews only.
Forms, 5: Parent Interview, Physician Interview, Teacher Interview, Mental Health Professional Interview, Corroborative Source Interview.

g) CUSTODY EVALUATION OBSERVATION KIT.
Purpose: Constructed to "discriminate among the different ways, positive and negative, a child responds to parental communications."
Population: Professionals conducting custody evaluations.
Scores: No scores, ratings by observers.
Forms, 2: Adult Observation Form, Child Observation Form.

h) CUSTODY EVALUATION AGGREGATION KIT.
Purpose: "Designed to aggregate the enormous amount of information gathered" in custody evaluations.
Population: Professionals conducting custody evaluations.
Scores: No scores.
Comments: Also includes phone logs, critical targets forms, and model contracts.

i) DISCIPLINE INDEX.
Comments: See 826.

j) HOME-VISIT KIT.
Comments: See 1166.

k) ASSESSMENT OF PARENTING SKILLS: INFANT AND PRESCHOOLER.
Comments: See 208.
Cross References: For a review by Mark W. Roberts, see 14:1.

[16]
Access Management Survey.
Purpose: Designed to measure the extent to which a manager provides opportunities and support for employee involvement, and the necessary resources for people to influence work-life issues.
Population: Adults.
Publication Dates: 1989–1995.
Acronym: AMS.
Scores, 5: Access to the Problem, Access to People, Access to Information and Resources, Access to Support, Access to the Solution.
Administration: Group.
Price Data, 2001: $8.95 per instrument.
Time: Untimed.
Comments: Self-assessment survey.
Author: Jay Hall.
Publisher: Teleometrics International.
Cross References: For reviews by Thomas M. Haladyna and Mary A. Lewis, see 12:2.

[17]
Accounting Aptitude Test.
Purpose: Designed to assess aptitude for an accounting career.
Population: First-year college students.
Publication Dates: 1982–1992.
Scores, 3: Communication Skills, Quantitative Skills, Problem-Solving Skills.
Administration: Group or individual.
Price Data, 2002: $53 per examination kit including Form Z test booklet, Ready-Score answer document, and administrator's handbook (1992, 22 pages); $30 per 10 test booklets; $64 per 20 answer documents; $37.50 per administrator's handbook.
Time: 50(55) minutes.
Author: The Psychological Corporation.
Publisher: The Psychological Corporation.
Cross References: For reviews by JoEllen Carlson and Bikkar S. Randhawa, see 13:3.

[18]
Accounting Program Admission Test.
Purpose: Designed as "an objective measure of student achievement in elementary accounting."
Population: College level elementary accounting students.
Publication Date: 1988.
Acronym: APAT.
Scores, 3: Financial Accounting, Managerial Accounting, Total.
Administration: Group or individual.
Price Data: Available from publisher.
Time: 100(110) minutes.

Comments: Formerly called the AICPA Accounting Program Admission Test; no longer affiliated with the AICPA.
Author: American Institute of Certified Public Accountants.
Publisher: The Psychological Corporation.
Cross References: For reviews by JoEllen Carlson and William R. Koch, see 12:3.

[19]
ACCUPLACER: Computerized Placement Tests.

Purpose: Designed to assist colleges in determining student entry skills in reading, writing, mathematics, and levels of English proficiency; scores aid in the appropriate placement of students into entry level higher education courses.
Population: Entry level students in 2-year and 4-year institutions.
Publication Dates: 1985–2001.
Acronym: CPTs.
Administration: Individual.
Price Data: Price information for student fee available from publisher.
Time: Untimed.
Comments: Administered through the internet adaptively.
Author: The College Board.
Publisher: The College Board.
  a) READING COMPREHENSION.
  Scores: Total score only.
  Comments: Each student is administered a fixed number of items which are selected adaptively depending on student responses to prior items.
  b) SENTENCE SKILLS.
  Comments: Each student is administered a fixed number of items which are adaptively delivered; diagnostic information is available.
  c) ARITHMETIC.
  Scores: Total score only.
  Comments: Each student is administered a fixed number of items which are adaptively delivered.
  d) ELEMENTARY ALGEBRA.
  Scores: Total score only.
  Comments: Each student is administered a fixed number of items which are adaptively delivered.
  e) COLLEGE LEVEL MATHEMATICS.
  Comments: Each student is administered a fixed number of items covering the areas of College Algebra and Precalculus, which are adaptively delivered.
  f) LEVELS OF ENGLISH PROFICIENCY.
  Scores: 3 modules: Language Usage, Sentence Meaning, Reading Skills.

Comments: Designed to identify the English proficiency levels of students; each student takes a fixed number of items; the 3 tests are administered separately and adaptively delivered.
Cross References: For reviews by Martin A. Fischer and Steven V. Owen, see 13:4.

[20]
ACDI-Corrections Version and Corrections Version II.

Purpose: "Designed for troubled youth screening and assessment."
Population: Troubled youth between the ages of 12 and 18 years in juvenile probation, parole, and corrections programs.
Publication Dates: 1988–1995.
Acronym: ACDI.
Administration: Group.
Price Data: Available from publisher.
Time: (15–25) minutes.
Comments: Both computer version and paper-pencil format are scored on IBM-PC compatibles.
Author: Risk & Needs Assessment, Inc.
Publisher: Risk & Needs Assessment, Inc.
  a) VERSION I.
  Scores, 5: Truthfulness, Alcohol, Drug, Adjustment, Distress.
  b) VERSION II.
  Scores, 6: Truthfulness, Alcohol, Drug, Adjustment, Distress, Violence.
Cross References: For reviews by Carol Collins and Mark Pope, see 14:2.

[21]
ACER Advanced Test B40.

Purpose: "To measure general intelligence as demonstrated by the ability to see relationships and to solve problems."
Population: Ages 13 and over.
Publication Dates: 1945–1983.
Acronym: B40.
Scores: Total score only.
Administration: Group.
Price Data, 2002: A$11.55 per 10 test booklets; A$4.95 per scoring key; A$19 per manual (1983, 7 pages); A$24.20 per specimen set.
Time: 55(65) minutes.
Author: Australian Council for Educational Research Ltd.
Publisher: Australian Council for Educational Research Ltd. [Australia].
Cross References: For a review by Harriet C. Cobb, see 9:4; see also T2:323 (6 references) and 7:328 (4 references); for a review by C. Sanders, see 5:296 (3 references).

[22]
ACER Advanced Test B90: New Zealand Edition.

Purpose: "Designed to measure general intellectual ability."
Population: College students and adults.
Publication Date: 1991.
Scores: Total score only.
Administration: Group.
Price Data: Available from publisher for test materials including administrator's manual (5 pages).
Time: 50(55) minutes.
Comments: "Selected items from the ACER Advanced Test B40 and the ACER Test of Cognitive Ability."
Authors: Australian Council for Educational Research and manual by Neil Reid and Cedric Croft.
Publisher: New Zealand Council for Educational Research [New Zealand].
Cross References: For a review by John Rust, see 12:4; for a review of ACER Advanced Test B40 by Harriet C. Cobb, see 9:4; see also T2:323 (6 references) and 7:328 (4 references); for a review of ACER Advanced Test B40 by C. Sanders, see 5:296 (3 references).

[23]
ACER Advanced Test BL-BQ, New Zealand Revision.

Purpose: Designed to "measure broad aspects of general linguistic and quantitative abilities."
Population: College and superior adults.
Publication Dates: 1953–1986.
Scores, 3: Linguistic, Quantitative, Total.
Administration: Group.
Price Data: Available from publisher.
Time: 15(25) minutes for Section L (Linguistic), 20(30) minutes for Section Q (Quantitative).
Comments: Revision of ACER Advanced Test BL-BQ (9:5).
Authors: New Zealand Council for Educational Research, Neil Reid (norms supplement), Cedric Croft (norms supplement), Alison Gilmore (norms supplement), and David Philips (norms supplement).
Publisher: New Zealand Council for Educational Research [New Zealand].
Cross References: For reviews by Harriet C. Cobb and Leland K. Doebler of ACER Advanced Tests (Australian Edition), see 9:5; see also T3:21 (1 reference) and T2:324 (3 references); for a review by Duncan Howie, see 5:295.

[24]
ACER Advanced Tests AL and AQ (Second Edition) and BL-BQ.

Purpose: "To measure general intellectual ability."
Population: College and "superior adults."

Publication Dates: 1953–1982.
Acronyms: AL-AQ (2nd Edition), BL-BQ.
Administration: Group
Price Data, 2002: A$11.55 per 10 test booklets; A$4.95 per scoring key; A$24.80 per manual (1982, 22 pages); A$52.79 per specimen set.
Author: Australian Council for Educational Research Ltd.
Publisher: Australian Council for Educational Research Ltd. [Australia].
　a) TEST AL-BL.
　Scores: Linguistic.
　Forms, 2: A, B.
　Time: 15(25) minutes.
　b) TEST AQ-BQ.
　Scores: Quantitative.
　Forms, 2: A, B.
　Time: 20(30) minutes.
Cross References: See T5:23 (1 reference); for reviews by Harriet C. Cobb and Leland K. Doebler, see 9:5; see also T3:21 (1 reference) and T2:324 (3 references); for a review by Duncan Howie, see 5:295.

[25]
ACER Applied Reading Test.

Purpose: Designed to measure ability to read and understand technical material.
Population: Apprentices, trainees, technical and trade personnel.
Publication Dates: 1989–1990.
Scores: Total score only.
Administration: Group.
Forms, 2: A, B.
Price Data, 2002: A$7.69 per test booklet; A$7.69 per 10 answer sheets; A$5.50 per score key; A$24.70 per manual (1990, 24 pages); A$47.29 per specimen set.
Time: 40–45 minutes.
Authors: J. M. van den Berg and I. R. Woff.
Publisher: Australian Council for Educational Research Ltd. [Australia].
Cross References: For reviews by Mark H. Daniel and Michael S. Trevisan, see 12:5.

[26]
ACER Higher Test PL-PQ, New Zealand Revision.

Purpose: "Designed to measure general intellectual ability."
Population: Grades 9 and over.
Publication Dates: 1944–1986.
Scores, 3: Linguistic, Quantitative, Total.
Administration: Group.
Price Data: Available from publisher.
Time: 15(25) minutes for Section L (Linguistic); 20(30) minutes for Section Q (Quantitative).

Comments: Revision of ACER Higher Tests (9:11).
Authors: New Zealand Council for Educational Research, Neil Reid (norms supplement), Cedric Croft (norms supplement), Alison Gilmore (norms supplement), and David Philips (norms supplement).
Publisher: New Zealand Council for Educational Research [New Zealand].
Cross References: See T5:25 (1 reference); for reviews by Eric F. Gardner and Sharon L. Weinberg of ACER Higher Tests (Australian Edition), see 9:11; see also T3:28 (2 references), T2:325 (1 reference), and 6:432 (1 reference); for a review by C. Sanders, see 5:297.

[27]
ACER Intermediate Test F.

Purpose: "Designed to assess the general reasoning ability of students."
Population: Ages 10–15.
Publication Dates: 1980–1982.
Scores: Total score only.
Administration: Group.
Price Data, 2002: A$2.75 per test; $4.95 per scoring key; A$29.80 per manual (1982, 56 pages); A$36.29 per specimen set.
Time: 30(50) minutes.
Comments: Based upon a revision of ACER Intermediate Tests A and D.
Author: Marion M. de Lemos (manual).
Publisher: Australian Council for Educational Research Ltd. [Australia].
Cross References: See T5:26 (2 references).

[28]
ACER Intermediate Test G.

Purpose: "Designed to assess the general reasoning ability of students."
Population: Ages 10–15.
Publication Dates: 1980–1982.
Scores: Total score only.
Administration: Group.
Price Data, 2002: A$2.75 per test; A$4.95 per scoring key; A$29.80 per manual (1982, 48 pages); A$36.29 per specimen set.
Time: 30(50) minutes.
Comments: Based on a revision of the ACER Intermediate Tests A and D.
Author: Marion M. de Lemos (manual).
Publisher: Australian Council for Educational Research Ltd. [Australia].
Cross References: See T5:27 (1 reference); for a review by Don B. Oppenheim, see 9:13.

[29]
ACER Mechanical Comprehension Test.

Purpose: "Designed to test understanding of mechanical problems."

Population: Ages 13.5 and over.
Publication Dates: 1942–1956.
Scores: Total score only.
Administration: Group.
Price Data, 2002: A$3.84 per test booklet; A$4.95 per scoring key; A $7.69 per 10 answer sheets; A$18.70 per manual (1956, 6 pages); A$27 per specimen set.
Time: 30 minutes.
Author: Australian Council for Educational Research Ltd.
Publisher: Australian Council for Educational Research Ltd. [Australia].
Cross References: See T3:37 (1 reference); for reviews by John R. Jennings and Hayden S. Williams, see 5:874 (2 references); for a review by D. W. McElwain, see 4:756.

[30]
ACER Mechanical Reasoning Test [Revised 1997].

Purpose: "Designed to assess a person's aptitude for solving problems requiring the understanding of mechanical ideas."
Population: Ages 15 and over.
Publication Dates: 1951–1997.
Scores: Total score only.
Administration: Group.
Forms, 2: Parallel Forms A and B.
Price Data, 2002: A$10.45 per test booklet; A$8.25 per scoring key; A$17.05 per 10 answer sheets; A$50.59 per manual (1997, 58 pages); A$89.20 per specimen set.
Time: 20(25) minutes.
Comments: Abbreviated adaptation of ACER Mechanical Comprehension Test (29).
Author: Australian Council for Educational Research Ltd.
Publisher: Australian Council for Educational Research Ltd. [Australia].
Cross References: See T2:2238 (3 references); for reviews by John R. Jennings and Hayden S. Williams of an earlier edition, see 5:875.

[31]
ACER Short Clerical Test.

Purpose: Designed to measure aptitudes for routine clerical work.
Population: Age 15 and over.
Publication Dates: 1953–1984.
Scores, 2: Checking, Arithmetic.
Administration: Group.
Price Data, 2002: A$11.55 per 10 test booklets; A$5.50 per score key; A$29.80 per manual; A$42.89 per specimen set.
Time: 5(10) minutes per test.
Comments: Three parallel forms, Forms C and D only available for personnel selection and Form E only available to Commercial and TAFE Colleges.

Authors: Australian Council for Educational Research, J. Jenkinson (revised edition).
Publisher: Australian Council for Education Research Ltd. [Australia].

[32]
ACER Test of Employment Entry Mathematics.

Purpose: "A group test of basic mathematical ability … used for the selection of apprentices, trainees, and any other technical and trades personnel."
Population: Apprentice, trainee, technical and trade applicants.
Publication Date: 1992.
Acronym: TEEM.
Score: Total score only.
Administration: Group.
Price Data, 2002: A$6.59 per test booklet; A$5.50 per score key; A$7.69 per 10 answer sheets; A$67.09 per specimen set.
Time: 25 (40) minutes.
Comments: Can be hand scored or scored by testing service.
Authors: John Izard, Ian Woff, and Brian Doig.
Publisher: Australian Council for Educational Research Ltd. [Australia].

[33]
ACER Tests of Basic Skills—Orchid Series.

Purpose: Developed to assess skills in literacy and numeracy.
Population: Students, year 4 to 6 in Australian school system.
Publication Dates: 1990–1997.
Administration: Group.
Price Data, 2002: A$26.40 per 10 nonreusable Level A & B test booklets for Literacy; A$30.80 per 10 nonreusable Level A & B test booklets with press-out shapes and tiles for Numeracy; A$33 per stimulus material; A$22 per audio tape; A$66 per Level A manual (1997, 73 pages); A$66 per Level B manual (1997, 82 pages); A$93.50 per specimen set; A$26.40 per nonreusable Level C test booklets for Literacy; A$30.80 per 10 nonreusable Level C test booklets with press-out shape and tiles for Numeracy; A$33 per stimulus material; A$66 per Level C manual (1997, 60 pages); A$71.50 per specimen set.
Comments: Earlier versions called Blue and Green Series; requires a cassette tape player.
Authors: Australian Council for Educational Research, Joy McQueen, and Brian Doig.
Publisher: Australian Council for Educational Research Ltd. [Australia].
a) LEVEL A.
    Scores, 6: Aspects of Literacy (Reading, Proofreading and Editing, Listening, Writing), Aspects of Numeracy (Number, Measurement and Space).

Time: (222–245) minutes.
b) LEVEL B.
Scores, 6: Same as Level A.
Time: (248–271) minutes.
c) LEVEL C.
Scores, 4: Aspects of Literacy (Reading and Viewing, Proofreading and Editing, Writing), Aspects of Numeracy (Number/Measurement/Space).
Time: (165–181) minutes.
Cross References: For reviews by Lewis R. Aiken and Delwyn L. Harnisch of an earlier edition, see 12:88.

[34]
ACER Word Knowledge Test.

Purpose: Constructed to assess verbal skills and general reasoning ability.
Population: Australian years 9–11.
Publication Dates: 1984–1990.
Scores: Total score only.
Administration: Group.
Editions, 2: E, F.
Restricted Distribution: Distribution of Form E restricted to personnel use.
Price Data, 2002: A$5.50 per reusable test booklet; A$7.69 per 10 answer sheets; A$5.50 per score key; A$30 per manual (1990, 44 pages); A$41.30 per specimen set (specify Form E or F).
Time: 10(20) minutes.
Comments: Replacement for the ACER Adult Form B.
Author: Marion M. de Lemos.
Publisher: Australian Council for Educational Research Ltd. [Australia].
Cross References: See T5:34 (6 references); for reviews by Douglas Ayers and William R. Merz, Sr., see 11:2.

[35]
Achenbach System of Empirically Based Assessment.

Purpose: "An integrated … [approach] designed to provide standardized descriptions of … competencies, adaptive functioning, and problems."
Population: Ages 18 months to 30 years.
Publication Dates: 1980–2003.
Acronym: ASEBA.
Levels, 3: Preschool, School-Age, Young Adult.
Administration: Individual or group.
Price Data, 2002: $150 per Preschool hand-scoring starter kit including 50 each of CBCL/1 1/2–5 & LDS forms, C-TRF forms, CBCL/1 1/2–5 hand-scoring profiles, C-TRF hand-scoring profiles, LDS hand-scoring forms, CBCL/1 1/2–5 and C-TRF templates, and manual for the Preschool Forms & Profiles (2000, 189 pages); $230 per Preschool computer-scor-

ing starter kit including 50 CBCL/1 1/2–5 & LDS forms, 50 C-TRF forms, Ages 1 1/2–5 entry scoring module, manual for the Preschool Forms & Profiles; $325 per School-Age computer-scoring starter kit including 50 CBCL forms, 50 TRF forms, 50 YSR forms, Ages 6–18 entry scoring module, and manual for the School-Age Forms & Profiles (2001, 238 pages); $35 per manual for the Preschool Forms and Profiles, manual for the School-Age Forms and profiles, or manual for the SCICA (2001, 164 pages); $25 per manual for the YASR & YABCL (1997, 207 pages); $7 per Mental Health Practitioners' Guide for the ASEBA (2001, 39 pages), School-Based Practitioners' Guide for the ASEBA (2001, 47 pages), Child and Family Service Workers' Guide for the ASEBA (2001, 37 pages), or Medical Practitioners' Guide for the ASEBA (2001, 28 pages); $525 per full set of ADM Software Modules including Ages 1 1/2–5, 6–18, 18–30, and SCICA; $170 per ADM Software Modules for ages 1 1/2–5, 18–30, or SCICA; $250 per ADM Software Modules for Ages 6–18; $220 per Scanning Module or Client Entry Module for CBCL/6–18, TRF/6–18, and YSR/11–18; $220 per ASEBA Web-Link (following purchase of ADM Ages 6–18 Module for CBCL/6–18, YSR, and TRF) including E-package of 100 E-units; $25 per 50 CBCL/1 1/2–5 & LDS, C-TRF, CBCL/16–18, TRF/6–18, YSR, DOF, YASR, SCICA, or YABCL forms; $25 per 50 Profiles for hand scoring profiles for any of CBCL/1 1/2–5, C-TRF, CBCL/6–18 (specify gender), TRF (specify gender), YSR, DOF, SCICA, YASR, or YABCL; $25 per 50 forms for hand-scoring LDS; $25 per 50 Combined SCICA Observation and Self-Report scoring forms; $25 per 50 CBCL, TRF, YSR, or SCICA DSM-Oriented Profiles for Boys & Girls; $7 per reusable templates for hand scoring CBCL/1 1/2–5, C-TRF, CBCL/6–18, TRF, YSR, YASR, or YABCL Profiles.

Foreign Language Editions: One or more forms have been translated into 64 languages, check website (www.ASEBA.org for availability).

Comments: Revised version of the Child Behavior Checklist; includes both empirically based syndrome scales and DSM-oriented scales for scoring consistent with DSM-IV categories; designed to be usable in diverse contexts, including schools, mental health, medical, child and family service, and other settings; all forms except DOF and SCICA are parallel, facilitating comparisons across informants; hand- or computer-scorable; reusable hand-scoring templates available; data processed by Assessment Data Manager (ADM); minimum system requirements Windows 95/98/NT/2000, 64 MB RAM, 65 MB free hard disk space, Pentium recommended; can be completed using paper forms (hand- or machine-readable), by direct entry on computer, or via Web-Link; LDS, Preschool and School-Age manuals.

Authors: Thomas M. Achenbach (all forms and manuals), Leslie A. Rescorla (all forms and Mental Health Practitioners' Guide for the ASEBA), Stephanie H. McConaughy (SCICA, SCICA manual, and School-Based Practitioners' Guide for the ASEBA), Peter J. Pecora and Kathleen M. Wetherbee (Child and Family Service Workers' Guide for the ASEBA), and Thomas M. Ruffle (Medical Practitioners' Guide for the ASEBA).

Publisher: Research Center for Children, Youth, and Families at the University of Vermont.

a) PRESCHOOL FORMS AND PROFILES.

Purpose: To provide "systematic assessment of maladaptive behavior among preschoolers."

Comments: DSM-Oriented Scales rated as very consistent with the following DSM-IV categories: Affective Problems consistent with Dysthymia, Major Depressive Disorder; Anxiety Problems consistent with Generalized Anxiety Disorder, Separation Anxiety Disorder, Specific Phobia; Pervasive Developmental Problems consistent with Asperger's Disorder and Autistic Disorder; Attention Deficit/Hyperactivity Problems consistent with Hyperactive-Impulsive and Inattentive types of ADHD.

1) *Child Behavior Checklist for Ages 1 1/2–5.*

Population: Ages 18 months to 5 years.

Publication Dates: 1988–2000.

Acronym: CBCL/1 1/2–5.

Scores: 7 Syndrome scales (Emotionally Reactive, Anxious/Depressed, Somatic Complaints, Withdrawn, Sleep Problems, Attention Problems, Aggressive Behavior), plus Internalizing, Externalizing, Total Problems; Language Development Survey (LDS) score (for children age 18–35 months); 5 DSM-Oriented scales (Affective Problems, Anxiety Problems, Pervasive Developmental Problems, Attention Deficit/Hyperactivity Problems, Oppositional Defiant Problems).

Time: (10) minutes.

Comments: Designed to be completed by parents and others who see children in home-like settings; includes the Language Development Survey (LDS) for evaluating language delays in children under age 3 as well as those over age 3 suspected of having language delays.

2) *Caregiver-Teacher Report Form for Ages 1 1/2–5.*

Population: Ages 18 months to 5 years.

Publication Dates: 1997–2000.

Acronym: C-TRF.

Scores: 6 Syndrome scales (Emotionally Reactive, Anxious/Depressed, Somatic Complaints, Withdrawn, Attention Problems, Aggressive Behavior), plus Internalizing, Externalizing, Total Problems.

Time: (10) minutes.

Comments: Designed to be completed by daycare providers and preschool teachers who have known a child in daycare, preschool, or similar settings for at least 2 months.

b) SCHOOL-AGE FORMS AND PROFILES.

Comments: DSM-Oriented Scales rated as very consistent with the following DSM-IV categories: Affective Problems consistent with Dysthymia, Major Depressive Disorder; Anxiety Problems consistent with Generalized Anxiety Disorder, Separation Anxiety Disorder, Specific Phobia; Attention Deficit/Hyperactivity Problems consistent with Hyperactive-Impulsive and Inattentive types of ADHD; Somatic Problems consistent with Somatization Disorder and Somatoform Disorder.

1) *Child Behavior Checklist for Ages 6–18.*

Population: Ages 6–18.

Publication Dates: 1981–2001.

Acronym: CBCL/6–18.

Scores: 4 Competence scales (Activities, Social, School, Total Competence); 8 Syndrome scales (Anxious/Depressed, Withdrawn/Depressed, Somatic Complaints, Social Problems, Thought Problems, Attention Problems, Rule-Breaking Behavior, Aggressive Behavior), plus Internalizing, Externalizing, Total Problems; 6 DSM-Oriented scales (Affective Problems, Anxiety Problems, Somatic Problems, Attention Deficit/Hyperactivity Problems, Oppositional Defiant Problems, Conduct Problems).

Time: (15–20) minutes.

2) *Teacher's Report Form for Ages 6–18.*

Purpose: "Quickly obtain[s] a picture of children's functioning in school, as seen by teachers and other personnel."

Population: Teachers of children ages 6–18.

Publication Dates: 1981–2001.

Acronym: TRF.

Scores: 6 Adaptive Functioning scales (Academic Performance, Working Hard, Behaving Appropriately, Learning, Happy, Total); same Syndrome and DSM-Oriented scales as CBCL/6–18; yields separate scores for Inattention and Hyperactivity-Impulsivity.

Time: (15–20) minutes.

3) *Youth Self-Report for Ages 11–18.*

Purpose: To obtain youths' reports of their own problems and competencies in a standardized format.

Population: Ages 11–18.

Publication Dates: 1981–2001.

Acronym: YSR.

Scores: 2 Competence scales (Activities, Social) plus Total Competence; same Syndrome and DSM-Oriented scales as CBCL/6–18.

4) *Direct Observation Form for Ages 5–14.*

Purpose: "Used to record and rate behavior in group settings."

Publication Dates: 1983–1986.

Acronym: DOF.

Comments: Used to obtain 10-minute samples of children's behavior in classrooms and other group settings; enables users to compare an observed child with 2 control children for on-task, Internalizing, Externalizing, and Total Problems, averaged for up to 6 observation sessions; 6 syndrome scales available (computer-scored profiles only).

5) *Semistructured Clinical Interview for Children and Adolescents.*

Purpose: "Used to record and rate children's behavior and self-reports during an interview."

Population: Ages 6–18.

Publication Dates: 1989–2001.

Acronym: SCICA.

Scores: 8 Syndrome scales (Anxious, Anxious/Depressed, Withdrawn/Depressed, Language/Motor Problems, Aggressive/Rule-Breaking Behavior, Attention Problems, Self-Control Problems, Somatic Complaints (ages 12–18 only), plus Internalizing, Externalizing, Total Problems; same DSM-Oriented scales as CBCL/6–18.

Time: (60–90) minutes.

Comments: Designed for use by experienced clinical interviewers; protocol form includes topic questions and activities, such as kinetic family drawing and tasks for screening fine and gross motor functioning; observation and self-report form for rating what a child does and says during interview.

c) YOUNG ADULT FORMS AND PROFILES.

Publication Dates: 1997–2003.

1) *Young Adult Self-Report for Ages 18–30.*

Population: Ages 18–30.

Acronym: YASR.

Scores: 5 Adaptive Functioning scales (Education, Friends, Job, Family, Spouse or Partner), 3 Substance Use scales (Tobacco, Alcohol, Drugs) plus Mean Substance Use score, same Syndrome scales as CBCL/6–18 plus Internalizing, Externalizing, Total Problems.

Time: (15–20) minutes.

Comments: Upward extension of YSR.

2) *Young Adult Behavior Checklist for Ages 18–30.*

Population: Ages 18–30.

Publication Dates: 1997–2003.

Acronym: YABCL.
Time: (10–15) minutes.
Comments: Ratings by parents, surrogates and spouses of young adults.
Cross References: See T5:451 (292 references); for reviews by Beth Doll and by Michael J. Furlong and Michelle Wood of an earlier edition, see 13:55 (556 references); see also T4:433 (135 references); for reviews by Sandra L. Christenson and Stephen N. Elliott and R. T. Busse of the Teacher's Report Form and the Youth Self-Report, see 11:64 (216 references); for additional information and reviews by B. J. Freeman and Mary Lou Kelley, see 9:213 (5 references).

[36]
Achievement Identification Measure.

Purpose: "Determine the degree to which children exhibit the characteristics of underachievers so that preventative or curative efforts may be administered."
Population: School age children.
Publication Date: 1985.
Acronym: AIM.
Scores, 6: Competition, Responsibility, Control, Achievement, Communication, Respect.
Administration: Group.
Price Data, 2001: $100 per 30 tests, manual for administration (8 pages), manual for interpretation of scores (7 pages), and computer scoring of 30 tests; $15 per specimen set.
Foreign Language Edition: Spanish edition available.
Time: (20) minutes.
Comments: Parent report inventory.
Author: Sylvia B. Rimm.
Publisher: Educational Assessment Service, Inc.
Cross References: See T5:35 (1 reference); for reviews by Howard M. Knoff and Sharon B. Reynolds, see 10:5.

[37]
Achievement Identification Measure— Teacher Observation.

Purpose: Identify underachievers.
Population: "Students in all grades."
Publication Date: 1988.
Acronym: AIM-TO.
Scores: 5 dimension scores: Competition, Responsibility, Achievement Communication, Independence/Dependence, Respect/Dominance.
Administration: Individual.
Price Data, 2001: $100 per set of 30 test booklets/answer sheets (scoring by publisher included); $15 per specimen set.
Foreign Language Edition: Spanish edition available.
Time: (20) minutes.

Comments: Ratings by teacher.
Author: Sylvia B. Rimm.
Publisher: Educational Assessment Service, Inc.
Cross References: For reviews by William P. Erchul and Geoffrey F. Schultz, see 11:3.

[38]
Achievement Motivation Profile.

Purpose: "Designed to be a measure of a student's motivation to achieve" and related personality characteristics.
Population: Ages 14 and older in high school, junior college, and college.
Publication Dates: 1995–1996.
Acronym: AMP.
Scores, 18: Response style (Inconsistent Responding, Self-Enhancing, Self-Critical), Motivation for Achievement (Achiever, Motivation, Competitiveness, Goal Orientation), Inner Resources (Relaxed Style, Happiness, Patience, Self-Confidence), Interpersonal Strengths (Assertiveness, Personal Diplomacy, Extroversion, Cooperativeness), Work Habits (Planning and Organization, Initiative, Team Player).
Administration: Group.
Price Data, 2002: $99.50 per complete kit including 20 AutoScore™ forms, manual (1996, 93 pages), and 2-use disk for on-site computer scoring and interpretation and 2 PC answer sheets; $34.50 per 25 AutoScore™ forms; $49.50 per manual; $12.50 each for 1–9 AMP mail-in answer sheets; $10.90 each for 10+ AMP mail-in answer sheets; $199 per 25-use microcomputer disk (PC with Microsoft Windows); $15 per 100 microcomputer answer sheets; $10.50 per fax service scoring.
Time: (20–30) minutes.
Authors: Jotham G. Friedland, Harvey P. Mandel, and Sander I. Marcus.
Publisher: Western Psychological Services.

[39]
Achievement Test for Accounting Graduates.

Purpose: Constructed to assess achievement in accounting for use in selecting applicants or placing and training of current personnel.
Population: Accounting job applicants or employees.
Publication Dates: 1989–1992.
Acronym: ATAG.
Scores, 6: Financial Accounting, Auditing, Cost and Managerial Accounting, Information Systems, Taxation, Total.
Administration: Group or individual.
Forms, 2: T, V.
Restricted Distribution: Distribution restricted and test administered at licensed testing centers; details may be obtained from publisher.

Price Data, 2002: $53.50 per examination kit including Form V test booklet, Ready-Score answer document, and administrator's handbook (1992, 20 pages); $40.50 per 10 test booklets (specify Form T or V); $85.50 per 20 answer documents; $37.50 per administrator's handbook.
Time: 120(125) minutes.
Author: The Psychological Corporation.
Publisher: The Psychological Corporation.
Cross References: For reviews by JoEllen Carlson and Thomas F. Donlon, see 13:5.

[40]
Achieving Behavioral Competencies.

Purpose: To develop a program of instruction in social/emotional skills.
Population: "Students who are seriously emotionally disturbed, closed head injured, juvenile offenders, learning disabled, or at-risk for school drop-out" and "adults served by voc rehab programs."
Publication Date: 1992.
Acronym: ABC.
Scores, 24: Relating to Others (Building Friendships, Maintaining Friendships, Apologizing, Compromising/Negotiating, Giving/Accepting Praise or Criticism, Total), Personal Responsibility (Goal Setting, Decision Making, Assuming Responsibility, Promptness, Asking for Assistance, Total), Coping with Stress (Handling Frustration, Coping with Anger, Dealing with Stress, Accepting Authority, Resisting Peer Pressure, Total), Personal/Affective Development (Building Self-Esteem, Coping with Depression, Coping with Anxiety, Controlling Impulsivity, Sensitivity to Others, Total).
Administration: Group.
Editions, 2: Individual Student Report, Class Report.
Price Data, 2002: $137.50 per set including curriculum, 25 rating forms, and computer program (IBM/Compatibles, Macintosh, and Apple).
Time: Administration time not reported.
Comments: Computer reports generated from teacher ratings.
Authors: Lawrence T. McCarron, Kathleen McConnell Fad, and Melody B. McCarron.
Publisher: McCarron-Dial Systems.
Cross References: For reviews by Sally Kuhlenschmidt and Robert A. Leark, see 13:6.

[41]
Ackerman-Banks Neuropsychological Rehabilitation Battery.

Purpose: Designed as "a comprehensive screening instrument for the rehabilitation setting."
Population: Patients referred for psychological or neuropsychological assessment and/or cognitive rehabilitation.

Publication Dates: 1991–2000.
Acronym: A-BNRB.
Scores, 43: Alertness Scale (Attention/Concentration), Prosody Scales (Receptive Prosody, Expressive Prosody), Memory Scales (Long-Term Memory, Short-Term Interference Memory, Short-Term Input Memory, Short-Term Retrieval Memory), Sensorimotor Scales (Auditory Input, Auditory Discrimination, Tactile Input, Tactile Output, Visual Input, Visual Discrimination, Visual-Spatial Construction, Proprioception, Motor Quality, Motor Writing), Speech Scales (Speech Production, Dysarthria, Dysnomia/Neologisms, Confabulation, Perseveration, Lisping), Academic Abilities Scales (Mathematics, Reading, Writing), Cognitive Problem Solving Scales (Concreteness, Integration, Judgment, Speed), Organic Emotions Scales (Depression, Anxiety, Impulsivity), Laterality Scales (Left-Right Confusion, Left-Brain Controlled Balance, Right-Brain Controlled Balance, Left Hemisphere, Right Hemisphere, Neuropsychological Status), Treatment Problem Scales (Peripheral Damage, Awareness of Deficits, Socially Appropriate Comments, Frustration Tolerance).
Administration: Individual.
Price Data, 2002: $600 per complete kit including professional manual (1994, 206 pages), stimulus card book, 10 administration protocols, 10 response booklets, 10 scoring forms, and processing fee for web-based, mail-in, or faxed computer score submission; $450 per administration package including 10 administration protocols, 10 response booklets, 10 scoring forms, and processing fee for web-based, mail-in, or faxed computer score submission; $200 per professional manual; $125 per student training manual (2000, 85 pages); student, volume, and research discounts available.
Time: (45–120) minutes.
Authors: Rosalie J. Ackerman and Martha E. Banks.
Publisher: ABackans DCP, Inc.

[42]
Ackerman-Schoendorf Scales for Parent Evaluation of Custody.

Purpose: "A clinical tool designed to aid mental health professionals in making child custody recommendations."
Population: Parents engaged in a dispute over custody of their children.
Publication Date: 1992.
Acronym: ASPECT.
Scores: 3 scales (Observational, Social, Cognitive-Emotional) yielding 1 score: Parental Custody Index (PCI).
Administration: Individual.
Price Data, 2002: $125 per kit including 20 parent questionnaires, 10 AutoScore™ answer forms, manual

(77 pages), and 2 prepaid mail-in WPS test report answer sheets for computer scoring and interpretation; $32.50 per 20 answer forms; $25.80 per 20 parent questionnaires; $52.50 per manual; $17.50 or less per mail-in answer sheet; $12.50 each for test report fax service.

Time: Administration time not reported.

Comments: For complete set of information to score, need results of each parent's MMPI or MMPI-2, Rorschach, WAIS-R, and WRAT-R or NEAT tests.

Authors: Marc J. Ackerman and Kathleen Schoendorf.

Publisher: Western Psychological Services.

Cross References: See T5:41 (1 reference); for reviews by Joyce A. Arditti and Gary R. Melton, see 12:9.

[43]
ACS Cooperative Examination in General-Organic-Biological Chemistry.

Purpose: Designed to measure a student's achievement in general, organic, and biological chemistry.

Population: Nursing and other paramedical and home economics students.

Publication Dates: 1979–1985.

Scores, 10: General (Part A, Part B, Total), Organic (Part A, Part B, Total), Biological (Part A, Part B, Total), Part A Total.

Administration: Group.

Manual: No specific manual; general directions (no date, 4 pages).

Price Data: Available from publisher.

Time: 165(180) minutes.

Comments: ACS test program is continually updated by retiring an older form of the test upon publication of a new form; separate answer sheet must be used.

Author: ACS DivCHED Examinations Institute.

Publisher: ACS DivCHED Examinations Institute.

[44]
ACS Cooperative Examination in Physical Chemistry.

Purpose: Designed to measure a student's mastery of physical chemistry.

Population: 1 year college.

Publication Dates: 1946–1983.

Administration: Group.

Manual: No specific manual.

Price Data: Available from publisher.

Comments: ACS test program is continually updated by retiring an older form of the test upon publication of a new form; subtests may be administered separately or together; separate answer sheet must be used.

Author: ACS DivCHED Examinations Institute.

Publisher: ACS DivCHED Examinations Institute.

a) THERMODYNAMICS.

Scores, 3: Part A, Part B, Total.

Time: 90(100) minutes.

b) CHEMICAL DYNAMICS.

Scores, 3: Part A, Part B, Total.

Time: 90(100) minutes.

c) QUANTUM CHEMISTRY.

Scores, 3: Part A, Part B, Total.

Time: 100(110) minutes.

Cross References: For a review by Gerald R. Van Hecke of an earlier form, see 8:842 (2 references); see also T2:1826 (2 references), 7:833 (2 references), and 6:904 (1 reference); for a review by Alfred S. Brown, see 3:559.

[45]
ACS Examination in Analytical Chemistry.

Purpose: Designed to measure a student's achievement in analytical chemistry.

Population: 1 year college.

Publication Dates: 1944–1988.

Scores: Total score only.

Administration: Group.

Manual: No specific manual; general directions (no date, 4 pages).

Price Data: Available from publisher.

Time: 90(100) minutes.

Comments: ACS test program is continually updated by retiring an older form of the test upon publication of a new form; separate answer sheet must be used.

Author: ACS DivCHED Examinations Institute.

Publisher: ACS DivCHED Examinations Institute.

Cross References: See 7:836 (1 reference) and 6:907 (1 reference); for an excerpted review by H. E. Wilcox of an earlier form, see 5:735; for reviews by William B. Meldrum and William Rieman III, see 3:563.

[46]
ACS Examination in Biochemistry.

Purpose: Designed to measure a student's achievement in biochemistry.

Population: 1 year college.

Publication Dates: 1947–1982.

Scores: Total score only.

Administration: Group.

Manual: No specific manual; general directions (no date, 4 pages).

Price Data: Available from publisher.

Time: 120(130) minutes.

Comments: ACS test program is continually updated by retiring an older form of the test upon publication of a new form; separate answer sheet must be used.

Author: ACS DivCHED Examinations Institute.

Publisher: ACS DivCHED Examinations Institute.

Cross References: See 7:823 (1 reference); for an excerpted review by Wilhelm R. Frisell of an earlier form, see 6:898 (2 references).

[47]
ACS Examination in General Chemistry.

Purpose: Designed to measure a student's achievement in general chemistry.
Population: 1 year college.
Publication Dates: 1934–1989.
Scores: Total score only.
Administration: Group.
Manual: No specific manual; general directions (no date, 4 pages).
Price Data: Available from publisher.
Time: 110(120) minutes.
Comments: ACS test program is continually updated by retiring an older form of the test upon publication of a new form; separate answer sheet must be used.
Author: ACS DivCHED Examinations Institute.
Publisher: ACS DivCHED Examinations Institute.
Cross References: For a review by Frank J. Fornoff of an earlier edition, see 8:837 (3 references); see also T2:1819 (1 reference) and 7:826 (5 references); for reviews by J. A. Campbell and William Hered and an excerpted review by S. L. Burson, Jr., see 6:902 (3 references); for reviews by Frank P. Cassaretto and Palmer O. Johnson, see 5:732 (2 references); for a review by Kenneth E. Anderson, see 4:610 (1 reference); for reviews by Sidney J. French and Florence E. Hooper, see 3:557 (3 references); see also 2:1593 (5 references).

[48]
ACS Examination in General Chemistry (Brief Test).

Purpose: Designed to measure a student's achievement in general chemistry.
Population: 1 year college.
Publication Dates: 1981–1989.
Scores: Total score only.
Administration: Group.
Manual: No specific manual; general directions (no date, 4 pages).
Price Data: Available from publisher.
Time: 55(60) minutes.
Comments: ACS test program is continually updated by retiring an older form of the test upon publication of a new form; separate answer sheet must be used.
Author: ACS DivCHED Examinations Institute.
Publisher: ACS DivCHED Examinations Institute.

[49]
ACS Examination in High School Chemistry [Advanced Level].

Purpose: To measure achievement in high school chemistry.
Population: Advanced high school chemistry students.
Publication Dates: 1963–1984.
Scores: Total score only.
Administration: Group.
Price Data: Available from publisher.
Time: 110(120) minutes.
Comments: ACS test program is continually updated by retiring an older form of the test upon publication of a new form.
Author: ACS DivCHED Examinations Institute.
Publisher: ACS DivCHED Examinations Institute.
Cross References: See T5:48 (1 reference) and T4:57 (1 reference); for reviews by Peter A. Dahl and John P. Penna of an earlier form, see 8:844 (1 reference); for a review by Irvin J. Lehmann, see 7:838 (3 references); for reviews by Frank J. Fornoff and William Hered, see 6:909.

[50]
ACS Examination in High School Chemistry [Lower Level].

Purpose: To measure achievement in high school chemistry.
Population: High school first year chemistry students.
Publication Dates: 1957–1983.
Scores, 3: Part I, Part II, Total.
Administration: Group.
Price Data: Available from publisher.
Time: 80(90) minutes.
Comments: ACS test program is continually updated by retiring an older form of the test upon publication of a new form.
Author: ACS DivCHED Examinations Institute.
Publisher: ACS DivCHED Examinations Institute.
Cross References: See T5:49 (1 reference), T4:59 (1 reference) and 9:41 (1 reference); for a review by Edward F. DeVillafranca of an earlier form, see 8:845 (11 references); see also T2:1830 (3 references); for reviews by William R. Crawford and Irvin J. Lehmann, see 7:837 (9 references); for reviews by Frank J. Fornoff and William Hered and excerpted reviews by Christine Jansing and Joseph Schmuckler, see 6:908 (5 references); for reviews by Edward G. Rietz and Willard G. Warrington, see 5:729.

[51]
ACS Examination in Inorganic Chemistry.

Purpose: Designed to measure a student's achievement in inorganic chemistry.

Population: 1 year college.
Publication Dates: 1961–1985.
Scores: Total score only.
Administration: Group.
Manual: No specific manual; general directions (no date, 4 pages).
Price Data: Available from publisher.
Time: 120(130) minutes.
Comments: ACS test program is continually updated by retiring an older form of the test upon publication of a new form; separate answer sheet must be used.
Author: ACS DivCHED Examinations Institute.
Publisher: ACS DivCHED Examinations Institute.
Cross References: See T3:64 (1 reference), 8:838 (2 references), T2:1820 (1 reference), and 7:827 (2 references); for a review by Frank J. Fornoff and an excerpted review by George B. Kauffman of an earlier form, see 6:903 (1 reference).

[52]
ACS Examination in Instrumental Determinations.

Purpose: Designed to measure a student's achievement in instrumental determinations.
Population: 1 year college.
Publication Dates: 1966–1981.
Scores: Total score only.
Administration: Group.
Manual: No specific manual; general directions (no date, 4 pages).
Price Data: Available from publisher.
Time: 110(120) minutes.
Comments: ACS test program is continually updated by retiring an older form of the test upon publication of a new form; separate answer sheet must be used.
Author: ACS DivCHED Examinations Institute.
Publisher: ACS DivCHED Examinations Institute.
Cross References: See 7:830 (1 reference).

[53]
ACS Examination in Organic Chemistry.

Purpose: Designed to measure a student's achievement in organic chemistry.
Population: 1 year college.
Publication Dates: 1942–1986.
Scores: Total score only.
Administration: Group.
Manual: No specific manual; general directions (no date, 4 pages).
Price Data: Available from publisher.
Time: 115(125) minutes.
Comments: ACS test program is continually updated by retiring an older form of the test upon publication of a new form; separate answer sheet must be used.

Author: ACS DivCHED Examinations Institute.
Publisher: ACS DivCHED Examinations Institute.
Cross References: See 8:840 (3 references), 7:831 (3 references), and 6:905 (4 references); for a review by Shailer Peterson of an earlier form, see 3:558.

[54]
ACS Examination in Physical Chemistry for Life Sciences.

Purpose: Designed to measure a student's achievement in physical chemistry for life sciences.
Population: 1 year college.
Publication Date: 1982.
Scores: Total score only.
Administration: Group.
Manual: No specific manual; general directions (no date, 4 pages).
Price Data: Available from publisher.
Time: 100(110) minutes.
Comments: ACS test program is continually updated by retiring an older form of the test upon publication of a new form; separate answer sheet must be used.
Author: ACS DivCHED Examinations Institute.
Publisher: ACS DivCHED Examinations Institute.

[55]
ACS Examination in Polymer Chemistry.

Purpose: Designed to measure a student's achievement in polymer chemistry.
Population: 1 year college.
Publication Dates: 1978–1990.
Scores: Total score only.
Administration: Group.
Manual: No specific manual; general directions (no date, 4 pages).
Price Data: Available from publisher.
Time: 75(85) minutes.
Comments: ACS test program is continually updated by retiring an older form of the test upon publication of a new form; separate answer sheet must be used.
Author: ACS DivCHED Examinations Institute.
Publisher: ACS DivCHED Examinations Institute.

[56]
ACS Toledo Chemistry Placement Examination.

Purpose: Designed to measure a student's achievement in general chemistry.
Population: 1 year college.
Publication Dates: 1959–1981.
Scores, 4: General Mathematics, General Chemical Knowledge, Specific Chemical Knowledge, Total.
Administration: Group.
Manual: No specific manual; general directions (no date, 4 pages).

Price Data: Available from publisher.

Time: 55(65) minutes.

Comments: ACS test program is continually updated by retiring an older form of the test upon publication of a new form; separate answer sheet must be used.

Author: ACS DivCHED Examinations Institute.

Publisher: ACS DivCHED Examinations Institute.

Cross References: For a review by Frank J. Fornoff of an earlier form, see 8:853 (3 references); see also T2:1847 (2 references); for reviews by Kenneth E. Anderson and William R. Crawford, see 6:920 (1 reference).

[57]
ACT Assessment.

Purpose: "Contains four curriculum-based tests that measure academic achievement in English, mathematics, reading, and science reasoning as well as noncognitive components (high school course/grade information, ACT interest inventory, and the student profile section). Results of the cognitive section are used by high schools and post-secondary institutions to understand what students are likely to know and ready to learn next in preparation for, and the transition to, post-secondary education. Results from the ACT Assessment are used in admissions, scholarship determination, academic advising, course placement, and career counseling."

Population: Grades 10–12.

Publication Dates: 1959–1999.

Administration: Group.

Price Data: Available from publisher.

Time: 175(190) minutes.

Comments: Tests administered nationally 6 times per year (February, April, June, September [in some states], October, December) at centers established by the publisher; previous version entitled Enhanced ACT Assessment.

Author: ACT, Inc.

Publisher: ACT, Inc.

    a) ACT ENGLISH TEST.

    Purpose: "Measures the student's understanding of the conventions of standard written English."

    Scores, 3: Usage/Mechanics, Rhetorical Skills, Total.

    Time: 45 minutes.

    b) ACT MATHEMATICS TEST.

    Purpose: "Measures reasoning and mathematical skills."

    Scores, 4: Pre-Algebra/Elementary Algebra, Intermediate Algebra/Coordinate Geometry, Plane Geometry/Trigonometry, Total.

    Time: 60 minutes.

    c) ACT READING TEST.

    Purpose: "Measures reading comprehension as a product of skill in referring and reasoning."

    Scores, 3: Social Studies/Sciences, Arts/Literature, Total.

    Time: 35 minutes.

    d) ACT SCIENCE REASONING TEST.

    Purpose: "Measures the interpretation, analysis, evaluation, reasoning, and problem-solving skills required in the natural sciences."

    Scores: Total score only.

    Time: 35 minutes.

Cross References: See T5:56 (19 references); for reviews by A. Harry Passow and James S. Terwilliger of the Enhanced ACT Assessment, see 12:139 (35 references); see also T4:913 (71 references); for reviews by Lewis R. Aiken and Edward Kifer of the ACT Assessment Program, see 9:42 (27 references); see also T3:76 (76 references); for a review by John R. Hills, see 8:469 (208 references); see also T2:1044 (97 references); for a review by Wimburn L. Wallace of an earlier program, see 7:330 (265 references); for reviews by Max D. Engelhart and Warren G. Findley and an excerpted review by David V. Tiedeman, see 6:1 (14 references).

[58]
ACT Evaluation/Survey Service.

Purpose: A service " to assist educational institutions and agencies in the collection, interpretation, and use of student survey data" and to investigate the opinions, plans, goals, and impressions of students and/or prospective students, or graduates.

Population: High school and college students, prospective adult learners/students, graduates.

Publication Dates: 1979–2001.

Acronym: ESS.

Administration: Group or individual.

Comments: For measurement of groups, not individuals.

Author: ACT, Inc.

Publisher: ACT, Inc.

    a) SECONDARY SCHOOL LEVEL.

    Population: High school.

    Publication Dates: 1979–2001.

    Price Data, 2001: $12.15 per specimen set including one copy of each secondary-level instrument, sample report pages, user's guide (2001, 34 pages), sample subgroup form and ESS order form; $15 per 25 survey instruments; $7.45 per User's Guide; $37 per normative data reports; $7.45 per item catalog; $55 per institutional processing/handling fee; $54–$98.50 per report fee; $37.50 per diskette containing scoring data.

    Time: (15–25) minutes.

      1) *High School Student Opinion Survey.*

      Publication Dates: 1980–1994.

      Acronym: HSSOS.

      Scores: Student's perceptions in 6 areas: High School Environment, Occupational

Preparation, Educational Preparation, High School Characteristics, Additional Questions, Comments and Suggestions.

2) *Student Needs Assessment Questionnaire.*
Publication Dates: 1979–1989.
Acronym: SNAQ.
Scores: Student's personal and educational needs in 4 areas: Importance and Life Goals, Individual Growth/Development/Planning, Additional Questions, Comments and Suggestions.

3) *High School Follow-Up Survey.*
Publication Date: 1990–1998.
Acronym: HSFS.
Scores: Student's satisfaction with high school in 5 areas: Continuing Education, Employment History, High School Experiences, Additional Questions, Comments and Suggestions.
Comments: Administered to recent graduates.

b) POSTSECONDARY SCHOOL LEVEL.
Population: College.
Publication Dates: 1981–2001.
Price Data: $14.35 per specimen set including one copy of each post-secondary instrument, sample report pages, user's guide (2001, 41 pages), sample subgrouping form, and ESS order form; $13 per 25 four-page survey instruments; $10.90 per 25 two-page survey instruments; $8.30 per user's guide; $7.45 per item catalog; $37 per normative data reports; $47 per institutional processing/handling fee; $54–$98.50 report fee; $37.50 per diskette containing student data.
Time: (15–25) minutes.

1) *Adult Learner Needs Assessment Survey.*
Publication Date: 1981–1994.
Acronym: ALNAS.
Scores: Adult student's educational and personal needs in 4 areas: Personal and Educational Needs, Educational Plans and Preferences, Additional Questions, Comments and Suggestions.

2) *Alumni Survey.*
Publication Dates: 1981–1998.
Acronym: AS.
Scores: Impact of college on graduates in 5 areas: Continuing Education, College Experiences, Employment History, Additional Questions, Comments and Suggestions.

3) *Alumni Survey (2-Year College Form).*
Publication Dates: 1981–1989.
Scores: Same as 2 above but for 2-year colleges.

4) *Alumni Outcomes Survey.*
Publication Dates: 1993–1996.

Acronym: AOS.
Scores: Alumni outcomes in 7 areas: Employment History and Experiences, Educational Outcomes, Educational Experiences, Activities and Organizations, Additional Questions, Comments and Suggestions, Mailing Address.

5) *College Outcomes Survey.*
Publication Dates: 1992–1993.
Acronym: COS.
Scores: Student's perception of their college experience in 4 areas: College Outcomes, Satisfaction with Experiences at College, Additional Questions, Comments and Suggestions.

6) *College Student Needs Assessment Survey.*
Acronym: CSNAS.
Scores: Student's educational and personal needs in 4 areas: Career and Life Goals, Educational and Personal Needs, Additional Questions, Comments and Suggestions.

7) *Entering Student Survey.*
Publication Dates: 1982–1997.
Acronym: ESS.
Scores: Student's expectations for college in 4 areas: Educational Plans and Preferences, College Impressions, Additional Questions, Comments and Suggestions.

8) *Financial Aid Student Services Survey.*
Publication Date: 1997.
Acronym: FASSS.
Scores: Students' Perceptions of Financial Aid Services Received at Their College or University.

9) *Student Opinion Survey.*
Publication Dates: 1981–1997.
Acronym: SOS.
Scores: Student's perceptions of the institution in 4 areas: College Services, College Environment, Additional Questions, Comments and Suggestions.
Comments: Available via paper/pencil and online.

10) *Student Opinion Survey (2-Year College Form).*
Publication Dates: 1981–1997.
Scores: Student's perceptions of the 2-year college in 5 areas: College Impressions, College Services, College Environment, Additional Questions, Comments and Suggestions.
Comments: Available via paper/pencil and online.

11) *Survey of Academic Advising.*
Publication Date: 1990.
Acronym: SAA.
Scores: Student's perception of academic advising services in 6 areas: Advising Informa-

tion, Academic Advising Needs, Impressions of Your Advisor, Additional Advising Information, Additional Questions, Comments and Suggestions.
12) *Survey of Current Activities and Plans.*
Publication Dates: 1988–1996.
Acronym: SCAP.
Scores: Student's current educational status in 5 areas: Impressions of This College, Educational Plans and Activities, Employment Plans, Additional Questions, Comments and Suggestions.
13) *Survey of Postsecondary Plans.*
Publication Dates: 1982–1995.
Acronym: SPP.
Scores: Student's educational plans in 4 areas: Educational Plans After High School, Impressions of This College, Additional Questions, Comments and Suggestions.
14) *Withdrawing/Nonreturning Student Survey.*
Publication Dates: 1979–1990.
Acronym: WNSS.
Scores: Student's reasons for leaving an institution in 4 areas: Reasons for Leaving This College, College Services and Characteristics, Additional Questions, Comments and Suggestions.
15) *Withdrawing/Nonreturning Student Survey (short form).*
Publication Dates: 1981–1997.
Acronym: WNSS-Short Form.
Scores: Student's reasons for leaving an institution in 2 areas: Reasons for Leaving This College, Additional Questions.
16) *Faces of the Future.*
Publication Dates: 1998–2000.
Acronym: FFS.
Scores: 6 areas: Employment Background, Education Background, Current College Experience, ID Number, Additional Questions, Comments and Suggestions.
Cross References: For reviews by Marcia J. Belcher and Claudia J. Morner of an earlier edition, see 12:10; see T4:61 (5 references); for a review by Rodney T. Hartnett of an earlier edition, see 9:44.

[59]
AD/HD Comprehensive Teacher's Rating Scale, Second Edition [1998 Revision].
Purpose: "Designed to help identify attention disorder, with or without hyperactivity."
Population: Grades K–Adult.
Publication Dates: 1986–2000.
Acronym: ACTeRS.
Administration: Individual.
Editions, 2: Paper-and-pencil; microcomputer.

Price Data, 2001: $47 per Teacher and Parent Form examiner's kit including manual (2000, 31 pages) and 50 rating/profile forms; $32 per 50 rating/profile forms; $175 per microcomputer version for 100 administrations including manual, IBM-PC only; $100 per microcomputer version for 50 administrations including manual, IBM-PC only; $15 per introductory kit including manual, sample Parent rating/profile Form, sample Teacher rating/profile Form, sample Self-Report Form, and annotated bibliography of research; $15 per manual.
Time: [5–15] minutes.
Comments: IBM-PC necessary for administration of microcomputer edition; parent forms available in Spanish.
Authors: Rina K. Ullmann, Esther K. Sleator, Robert L. Sprague, and MetriTech staff.
Publisher: MetriTech, Inc.
a) ACTeRS TEACHER FORM.
Population: Grades K–8.
Scores, 4: Attention, Hyperactivity, SocialSkills, Oppositional Behavior.
Price Data: $47 including manual and 50 forms; $32 per 50 forms.
Time: Untimed.
b) ACTeRS PARENT FORM.
Scores, 5: Attention, Hyperactivity, Social Skills, Oppositional Behavior, Early Childhood.
Price Data: $47 including manual and 50 forms; $32 per 50 forms.
Time: Untimed.
c) ACTeRS SELF-REPORT.
Population: Adolescence through adulthood.
Scores, 3: Attention, Hyperactivity/Impulsivity, Social Adjustment.
Price Data: $51 including manual and 50 forms; $37 per 50 forms.
Time: Untimed [10–15 minutes].
Cross References: For reviews by Cederick O. Lindskog and Janet V. Smith and by Everett V. Smith, Jr., see 14:5; for reviews by Robert J. Miller and Judy Oehler-Stinnett of an earlier edition, see 12:15 (2 references); see also T4:89 (1 reference); for reviews by Ellen H. Bacon and Ayres G. D'Costa of an earlier edition, see 11:7 (2 references).

[60]
Adaptability Test.
Purpose: "Designed to measure mental adaptability or mental alertness."
Population: Job applicants.
Publication Dates: 1942–1994.
Scores: Total score only.
Administration: Individual or group.
Forms, 2: A, B.
Price Data, 2002: $79 per start-up kit including 25 test booklets (specify Form A or Form B) and examiner's

manual; $61 per 25 test booklets (specify Form A or Form B); $28 per examiner's manual.
Time: 15 minutes.
Authors: Joseph Tiffin and C. H. Lawshe.
Publisher: Reid London House.
Cross References: See T4:80 (2 references), T3:111 (1 reference), T2:337 (3 references), and 7:333 (6 references); for a review by John M. Willits, see 5:305 (13 references); for reviews by Anne Anastasi and Marion A. Bills, see 3:216 (3 references).

[61]
Adaptive Behavior Assessment System.

Purpose: "Measures adaptive skills in multiple environments including home, school, community, and work."
Population: Ages 5–21; 16–89.
Publication Date: 2000.
Acronym: ABAS.
Scores, 11: 10 Adaptive Skill Areas (Communication, Community Use, Functional Academics, Home/School Living, Health and Safety, Leisure, Self-Care, Self-Direction, Social, Work), General Adaptive Composite (GAC).
Administration: Individual.
Forms, 3: Teacher, Parent, Adult.
Price Data, 2002: $150 per School kit including manual (2000, 196 pages), 25 Teacher Forms, and 25 Parent Forms; $100 per Adult kit including manual and 25 Adult Forms; $43 per 25 Parent, Teacher, or Adult Forms (quantity discounts available); $195 per Scoring Assistant and PDA Application Complete kit including ABAS PDA Application preloaded with 10 e-record form Credits, and ABAS Scoring Assistant CD-ROM; $79 per ABAS for Palm OS CD-ROM; $153 per ABAS Scoring Assistant (CD-ROM or disk version); $41 per 25 e-record form Credits for PDA Application (Teacher, Parent, and/or Adult).
Time: (15–20) minutes.
Comments: Completed by adult informants (teacher, parent) for children aged 5–21; completed by self or informants for ages 16–89; consistent with both AAMR (1992) and DSM-IV definitions of mental retardation and with the IDEA (1997) special education and disability classification system; Scoring Assistant software scores responses, analyzes strengths and weaknesses, plots Skill Area Profile; Scoring Assistant system requirements: Windows 95/98/2000/NT 4.0, 100 MHz processor, 16 MB RAM, 2 MB video card, 800 x 600 resolution (256 colors), 20 MB free hard disk space, floppy drive; paper-and-pencil or electronic administration available using ABAS Personal Digital Assistant software; PDA system requirements: Palm OS version 3.0, 2 MB total RAM, 96K dynamic heap, Motorola Dragonball or Dragonball EZ chip, conduit software, cradle; desktop Scoring Assistant required to operate PDA application.

Authors: Patti L. Harrison and Thomas Oakland.
Publisher: The Psychological Corporation.

[62]
Adaptive Behavior Evaluation Scale, Revised.

Purpose: Designed to assist in "making diagnostic, placement, and programming decisions for mentally retarded and emotionally disturbed/behaviorally disordered children and adolescents."
Population: Ages 5-0 to 18-0.
Publication Dates: 1983–1995.
Acronym: ABES-R.
Scores, 10: Communication, Self-Care, Home Living, Social, Community Use, Self-Direction, Health and Safety, Functional Academics, Leisure, Work.
Administration: Individual.
Forms, 2: Adaptive Behavior Evaluation Scale, School Version; Adaptive Behavior Evaluation Scale, Home Version.
Price Data, 2002: $155 per complete kit including school (1995, 73 pages) and home (1995, 66 pages) versions of technical manuals, Adaptive Behavior Intervention Manual (1995, 316 pages), and 50 each school and home versions rating forms; $14 per technical manual (school or home); $35 per 50 rating forms (school, home in English or home in Spanish); $26 per Adaptive Behavior Intervention Manual; $35 per scoring disk (Windows); $149 per computerized Adaptive Behavior Intervention Manual (DOS).
Time: (15–20) minutes.
Author: Stephen B. McCarney.
Publisher: Hawthorne Educational Services, Inc.
Cross References: For reviews by John H. Kranzler and by Mark D. Shriver and Merilee McCurdy, see 14:4; for reviews by Mary Ross Moran and Harvey N. Switzky of an earlier edition, see 12:14.

[63]
Adaptive Behavior Inventory.

Purpose: Designed to evaluate functional daily living skills.
Population: Mentally retarded students ages 6-0 through 18-11 years and normal students ages 5-0 through 18-11 years.
Publication Date: 1986.
Acronym: ABI.
Scores, 6: Self-Care Skills, Communication Skills, Social Skills, Academic Skills, Occupational Skills, Composite Quotient.
Administration: Individual.
Price Data, 2001: $89 per complete kit including 25 profile and response sheets, 25 short form response sheets, and examiner's manual (69 pages); $34 per 25 profile and response sheets; $14 per 25 short form response sheets; $44 per examiner's manual.
Time: (20–25) minutes.

Comments: Inventory is completed by classroom teacher or other professional having regular contact with the student; ABI-Short Form available for research and screening purposes.
Authors: Linda Brown and James E. Leigh.
Publisher: PRO-ED.
Cross References: For a review by Corinne Roth Smith, see 10:9 (2 references).

[64]
Adaptive Behavior Inventory for Children.

Purpose: Designed to "measure the child's social role performance in the family, the peer group, and the community."
Population: Ages 5–11.
Publication Dates: 1977–1982.
Acronym: ABIC.
Scores, 6: Family, Community, Peer Relations, Nonacademic School Roles, Earner/Consumer, Self-Maintenance.
Administration: Individual.
Price Data, 2002: $149 per basic kit including manual (1982, 121 pages), 6 keys, and 25 record forms; $44 per 6 scoring keys; $40 per 25 record forms.
Time: (45) minutes.
Comments: A component of the System of Multicultural Pluralistic Assessment; the manual includes the ABIC questions in Spanish as well as in English.
Authors: Jane R. Mercer and June F. Lewis.
Publisher: The Psychological Corporation.
Cross References: See T5:61 (2 references) and T4:85 (10 references); for reviews by James E. Jirsa and Benson P. Low, see 9:48 (1 reference); see T3:2387 (9 references) for ABIC and related references.

[65]
Adaptive Behavior: Street Survival Skills Questionnaire.

Purpose: "To assess fundamental community living and prevocational skills of mentally disabled adolescents and adults."
Population: Ages 9.5 and over.
Publication Dates: 1979–1993.
Acronym: SSSQ.
Scores, 10: Basic Concepts, Functional Signs, Tools, Domestics, Health and Safety, Public Services, Time, Monetary, Measurements, Total.
Administration: Individual.
Price Data, 2002: $350 per complete kit including 9 picture volumes (1993, 50 pages each), 50 scoring forms, 50 planning charts, Curriculum Guide (1982, 272 pages), and manual (1993, 95 pages); $23 per 50 scoring forms; $15 per 50 planning charts; $51.25 per Curriculum Guide; $34.50 per manual; $225 per computer software offered by publisher.

Time: [45] minutes.
Authors: Dan Linkenhoker and Lawrence McCarron.
Publisher: McCarron-Dial Systems.
Cross References: See T4:139 (1 reference); for a review by Thomas G. Haring, see 11:6.

[66]
Adaptive Functioning Index.

Purpose: "Training and assessment tool to be used by those working with the developmentally handicapped adolescent and adult."
Population: Ages 14 and over in rehabilitation or special education settings.
Publication Dates: 1971–1978.
Acronym: AFI.
Administration: Individual.
Price Data: Price information available from publisher for complete kit, administration manual (1976, 43 pages), standardization manual (1977, 42 pages), program manual (1978, 198 pages), Program Workbooks (1977, 19 pages), and Target Workbooks (1977, 12 pages).
Time: Administration time not reported.
Comments: Ratings by staff; 3 subtests: Social Education Test, Vocational Check List, Residential Check List, plus Adaptive Functioning of the Dependent Handicapped; Training Package available, includes Training Manual, Program Workbook, and Target Workbook; Program manual and workbooks not necessary for test administration; no norms.
Authors: Nancy J. Marlett and E. Anne Hughson (Program Workbook and Target Workbook).
Publisher: Vocational and Rehabilitation Research Institute [Canada].
a) SOCIAL EDUCATION TEST.
Scores, 9: Reading, Writing, Communication, Concept Attainment, Number Concepts, Time, Money Handling, Community Awareness, Motor Movements.
b) VOCATIONAL CHECK LIST.
Scores, 12: Basic Work Habits (Independence, Making Decisions, Use and Care of Equipment and Materials, Taking Direction), Work Skills (Speed of Movement, Ability to Follow Instructions, Competence, Skill Level), Acceptance Skills (Appearance, Attendance/Punctuality, Self-Expressions, Relation with Co-workers).
c) RESIDENTIAL CHECK LIST.
Scores, 15: Personal Routines (Cleanliness, Appearance and Eating, Room Management, Time Management, Health), Community Awareness (Transportation, Shopping, Leisure, Budgeting, Cooking and Home Management), Social Maturity (Communication, Consideration, Getting Friends, Keeping Friends, Handling Problems).

d) ADAPTIVE FUNCTIONING OF THE DEPENDENT HANDICAPPED.
Population: Profoundly handicapped of all ages.
Scores, 20: Nursing Care (Medications, Body Tone, Medical Care, Observation for Injury, Feeding), Physical Development (Head, Legs, Body, Hands or Feet, Movement), Awareness (Eye Contact, Contact with His World, Contact with People, Communication, Contact with Things), Self Help (Feeding, Eating, Washing, Dressing, Toileting).
Cross References: See T5:63 (1 reference) and T4:87 (2 references); for reviews by Nadine M. Lambert and David J. Mealor, see 9:49 (1 reference).

[67]
Adaptive Style Inventory.

Purpose: "Designed to assess individuals' ability to adapt to different learning situations."
Population: Junior high through adult.
Publication Date: 1993.
Acronym: ASI.
Scores, 16: 4 scores: Concrete Experience, Reflective Observation, Abstract Conceptualization, Active Experimentation in each of 4 situations: Acting Situation, Deciding Situation, Thinking Situation, Valuing Situation.
Administration: Group or individual.
Price Data, 2001: $69 per complete kit including 10 questionnaires, 10 profiles and interpretive notes (14 pages), and 10 scoring booklets.
Time: [30–40] minutes.
Comments: Self-scored inventory.
Authors: Richard E. Boyatzis and David A. Kolb.
Publisher: Hay Group.
Cross References: For reviews by Thomas R. Knapp and Erich P. Prien, see 13:7.

[68]
Addiction Severity Index—Multimedia Version.

Purpose: "An interactive, multimedia administration of the Addiction Severity Index," "a measure of addiction severity."
Population: Adults seeking substance abuse treatment.
Publication Date: 1999.
Acronym: ASI-MV.
Scores, 7: Composite scores and severity ratings provided for 7 domains: Medical Status, Employment/Support Status, Alcohol Use, Drug Use, Legal Status, Family/Social Relationships, Psychiatric Status.
Administration: Individual or group.
Price Data: Available from publisher.
Time: (45) minutes.
Comments: Same clinical interview as Addiction Severity Index (5th edition) adapted for self-report, multimedia format; clients are guided through a series of on-screen offices and meet with virtual interviewers; produces narrative report, severity profile, utilization report; customized reports available; personal computer or mouse-driven computer kiosk versions available; PC system requirements: Windows 95/98/NT 4.0, 6 MB hard drive, 12 MB RAM, 100 MHz processor, SVGA monitor (256 colors), 4X CD-ROM, sound card, speakers with headphones, mouse, keyboard, printer; kiosk information available from publisher.
Author: Innovative Training Systems, Inc.
Publisher: The Psychological Corporation.

[69]
ADHD Rating Scale-IV.

Purpose: Designed to help identify the frequency of ADHD symptoms of a child as reported by a parent or educator.
Population: Ages 5–18 years.
Publication Date: 1998.
Scores, 3: Inattention, Hyperactivity-Impulsivity, Total.
Administration: Individual.
Forms, 2: Home, School.
Price Data, 2001: $29.75 per scale including manual (79 pages) and photocopiable scales.
Foreign Language Edition: Spanish questionnaires available.
Time: Administration time not reported.
Comments: Symptom criteria based on the DSM-IV; 18-item rating scale.
Authors: George J. DuPaul, Thomas J. Power, Arthur D. Anastopolous, and Robert Reid.
Publisher: Guilford Publications, Inc.

[70]
ADHD Symptom Checklist—4.

Purpose: Designed as "a screening instrument for the behavioral symptoms of attention-deficit/hyperactivity disorder (AD/HD) and oppositional defiant disorder (ODD)."
Population: Ages 3–18.
Publication Date: 1997.
Acronym: ADHD-SC4.
Scores, 3: Screening Cutoff, Symptom Count, Symptom Severity.
Administration: Individual.
Forms, 1: Same checklist completed by parent and teacher.
Price Data, 2001: $52 per kit including 50 checklists, 50 symptom count score sheets, 50 symptom severity profile score sheets, and manual (1997, 200 pages); $26 per 50 checklists.
Time: (5) minutes.
Authors: Kenneth D. Gadow and Joyce Sprafkin.
Publisher: Checkmate Plus, Ltd.

[71]
ADHD Symptoms Rating Scale.

Purpose: Designed "to assess behaviors symptomatic of Attention Deficit Hyperactivity Disorder in children and adolescents."
Population: Ages 5–18 years.
Publication Date: 2001.
Acronym: ADHD-SRS.
Scores, 4: Hyperactive, Impulsive, Inattentive, Total.
Administration: Individual.
Price Data, 2001: $72 per starter set including manual (100 pages), 25 English forms, 5 Spanish forms, and sample computer printout; $30 per 25 rating forms (specify English or Spanish); $42 per manual; $119 per IBM computer scoring program including CD ROM, and computer scoring guide.
Foreign Language and Other Special Editions: Spanish edition available.
Time: (20–15) minutes.
Authors: Melissa Lea Holland, Gretchen A. Gimpel, and Kenneth W. Merrell.
Publisher: Wide Range, Inc.

[72]
The Adjective Check List.

Purpose: Designed to identify personal characteristics of individuals.
Population: High school and over.
Publication Dates: 1952–1980.
Acronym: ACL.
Scores, 37: Number of Adjectives Checked, Number of Favorable Adjectives, Number of Unfavorable Adjectives, Commonality, Achievement, Dominance, Endurance, Order, Intraception, Nurturance, Affiliation, Heterosexuality, Exhibition, Autonomy, Aggression, Change, Succorance, Abasement, Deference, Counseling Readiness, Self-Control, Self-Confidence, Personal Adjustment, Ideal Self, Creative Personality, Military Leadership, Masculine Attributes, Feminine Attributes, Critical Parent, Nurturing Parent, Adult, Free Child, Adapted Child, High Origence-Low Intellectence, High Origence-High Intellectence, Low Origence-Low Intellectence, Low Origence-High Intellectence.
Administration: Group.
Price Data, 2001: $23 per 25 profiles; $72.10 per manual (1980, 110 pages); scoring service available from publisher; $106.7 per 10 prepaid profile/answer sheets; $26.70 per nonprepaid combined item booklet/answer sheet.
Foreign Language Edition: Spanish edition available.
Time: [15–20] minutes.
Authors: Harrison G. Gough and Alfred B. Heilbrun, Jr. (manual and bibliography).

Publisher: Consulting Psychologists Press, Inc.
Cross References: See T5:68 (62 references) and T4:93 (92 references); for reviews by Phyllis Anne Teeter and John A. Zarske, see 9:52 (39 references); see also T3:116 (117 references), 8:495 (202 references), and T2:1094 (85 references); for reviews by Leonard G. Rorer and Forrest L. Vance, see 7:38 (131 references); see also P:4 (102 references).

[73]
Adjustment Scales for Children and Adolescents.

Purpose: "Designed to assess through teacher observation behavior pathology in youths."
Population: Ages 5–17.
Publication Dates: 1993–1994.
Acronym: ASCA.
Scores, 10: Overactivity, Underactivity, Attention-Deficit Hyperactive, Solitary Aggressive-Provocative, Solitary Aggressive-Impulsive, Oppositional Defiant, Diffident, Avoidant, Delinquent, Lethargic-Hypoactive.
Administration: Individual.
Price Data, 2001: $84.95 per complete kit including 25 male and 25 female self-scoring forms and profiles and manual (1994, 68 pages); $21.95 per 25 self-scoring forms and profiles (specify male or female); $34.95 per manual.
Time: (10–20) minutes.
Comments: Behavior checklist to be completed by a teacher about a student; scored by a psychologist or assessment specialist.
Authors: Paul A. McDermott, Neville C. Marston, and Denis H. Stott.
Publisher: Ed & Psych Associates.
Cross References: For reviews by Gary L. Canivez and Richard V. Schowengerdt, see 14:6; see also T5:69 (1 reference).

[74]
Adolescent and Adult Psychoeducational Profile: Volume IV.

Purpose: Assesses skills and behaviors of moderately to severely retarded and autistic individuals.
Population: Adolescents and adults with moderate to severe mental retardation or autism.
Publication Date: 1988.
Acronym: AAPEP.
Scores: 3 scales (Direct Observation, Home, School/Work); 6 scores for each: Vocational Skills, Independent Functioning, Leisure Skills, Vocational Behavior, Functional Communication, Interpersonal Behavior.
Administration: Individual.
Price Data, 2001: $69 per manual (Vol. IV; 119 pages); price data for testing kit available from Residential Services, Inc., Day Program, P.O. Box 487, Carrboro, NC 27510.

Time: (60–90) minutes per scale.
Comments: Title on manual is Individualized Assessment and Treatment for Autistic and Developmentally Disabled Children, Volume IV; other materials (e.g., ball, magazines, playing cards) necessary for test administration may be supplied by examiner or purchased from Residential Services, Inc.
Authors: Gary Mesibov, Eric Schopler, Bruce Schaffer, and Rhoda Landrus.
Publisher: PRO-ED.
Cross References: See T5:70 (1 reference); for reviews by Lena R. Gaddis and J. Jeffrey Grill, see 11:8.

[75]
Adolescent Anger Rating Scale.

Purpose: Developed "to measure anger expression and specially differentiate among instrumental anger, reactive anger, and anger control."
Population: Ages 11–19.
Publication Date: 2001.
Acronym: AARS.
Scores, 4: Instrumental Anger, Reactive Anger, Anger Control, Total Anger.
Administration: Individual or group.
Price Data: Available from publisher for kit including professional manual (69 pages) and 50 test booklets.
Time: (5–10) minutes for individuals; (10–20) minutes per group.
Comments: Self-rating scale.
Author: DeAnna McKinnie Burney.
Publisher: Psychological Assessment Resources, Inc.

[76]
Adolescent Apperception Cards.

Purpose: "Intended to suggest themes and evoke narratives that include … family, sibling, and peer relationships; abuse and neglect."
Population: Ages 12–19.
Publication Date: 1993.
Acronym: AAC.
Scores: No scores.
Administration: Individual.
Forms, 2: Black, White.
Price Data, 2002: $98.50 per kit including Adolescent Apperception Cards (Black and White versions included); $49 per cards (specify version).
Time: [45–60] minutes.
Comments: Publisher recommends (a) training and experience in projective testing and in working with adolescents, and (b) that the test be used as one component of a comprehensive battery of measures.
Author: Leigh Silverton; illustrated by Laurie Harden.
Publisher: Western Psychological Services.
Cross References: For reviews by David M. Kaplan and Molly L. Vanduser and by Jody L. Swartz-Kulstad, see 14:7.

[77]
Adolescent Coping Scale.

Purpose: Assesses 18 possible coping strategies used by adolescents and young adults in dealing with stress.
Population: Ages 12–18.
Publication Date: 1993.
Acronym: ACS.
Scores, 18: Seek Social Support, Focus on Solving the Problem, Work Hard and Achieve, Worry, Invest in Close Friends, Seek to Belong, Wishful Thinking, Not Coping, Tension Reduction, Social Action, Ignore the Problem, Self-Blame, Keep to Self, Seek Spiritual Support, Focus on the Positive, Seek Professional Help, Seek Relaxing Diversions, Physical Recreation.
Administration: Group.
Price Data, 2002: A$121 per complete kit including manual (48 pages) and all required material in a notebook; A$24.70 per 10 questionnaires (short form); A$24.70 per 10 questionnaires (long form); A$11.55 per 10 scoring sheets; A$11.55 per 10 profile charts; A$51.80 per manual.
Time: 10 minutes for Long Form; 3 minutes for Short Form.
Authors: Erica Frydenberg and Ramon Lewis.
Publisher: Australian Council for Educational Research Ltd. [Australia].
Cross References: See T5:72 (3 references); for reviews by Frederick T. L. Leong and Judy J. Oehler-Stinnett, see 13:8.

[78]
Adolescent Diagnostic Interview.

Purpose: "Assesses psychoactive substance use disorders."
Population: Ages 12–18.
Publication Date: 1993.
Acronym: ADI.
Scores: 8 sections to indicate presence or absence of a DSM-III-R diagnosis of psychoactive substance use disorder: Sociodemographic Factors, Psychosocial Stressors, Substance Use/Consumption History, Alcohol Use Symptoms, Cannabis Use Symptoms, Additional Drug Use Symptoms, Level of Functioning Domains, Orientation and Memory Screen; plus 8 psychiatric status screens: Depression, Mania, Eating Disorder, Delusional Thinking, Hallucinations, Attention Deficit Disorder, Anxiety Disorder, Conduct Disorder.
Administration: Individual.
Price Data, 2002: $78 per complete kit including 5 administration booklets and manual (46 pages); $35 per 5 administration booklets; $45 per manual.
Time: (45–55) minutes.
Comments: Structured interview for use with adolescents; complements the Personal Experience Inventory (1854).

Authors: Ken C. Winters and George A. Henly.
Publisher: Western Psychological Services.
Cross Reference: See T5:73 (1 reference); for reviews by Tony Toneatto and Logan Wright, and by Donna Ford and Karyll Kiser, see 12:16.

[79]
Adolescent Dissociative Experiences Scale.
Purpose: Designed as a "screening measure for pathological dissociation during adolescence."
Population: Ages 11–17.
Publication Date: 1996.
Acronym: A-DES.
Scores, 5: Dissociative Amnesia, Absorption and Imaginative Involvement, Depersonalization and Derealization, Passive Influence, Total.
Administration: Individual or group.
Price Data, 1998: $12 per test.
Time: (10–15) minutes.
Comments: A 30-item self-report measure, derived from the Dissociative Experiences Scale (original adult version) (828).
Authors: Judith Armstrong, Frank Putnam, and Eve Carlson.
Publisher: The Sidran Foundation.
Cross References: For reviews by Rosemary Flanagan and Ramasamy Manikam, see 14:8.

[80]
Adolescent Drinking Index.
Purpose: Constructed to screen for alcohol abuse.
Population: Ages 12–17.
Publication Dates: 1985–1989.
Acronym: ADI.
Scores, 3: Self-Medicated Drinking (MED), Aggressive/Rebellious Behavior (REB), Total.
Administration: Group or individual.
Price Data: Available from publisher for complete kit including manual (1989, 34 pages) and 25 test booklets.
Time: (5) minutes.
Comments: Test booklet title is Drinking & You.
Authors: Adele V. Harrell and Philip W. Wirtz.
Publisher: Psychological Assessment Resources, Inc.
Cross References: See T5:75 (1 reference); for reviews by Thomas F. Donlon and Kevin J. McCarthy and Penelope W. Dralle, see 12:17.

[81]
Adolescent Language Screening Test.
Purpose: "Developed to screen for deficits in the dimensions of language use, content, and form" in adolescents.
Population: Ages 11–17.
Publication Date: 1984.
Acronym: ALST.

Scores: 7 subtests: Pragmatics, Receptive Vocabulary, Concepts, Expressive Vocabulary, Sentence Formulation, Morphology, Phonology.
Administration: Individual.
Price Data, 2001: $124 per complete kit including 50 test booklets, picture book, and examiner's manual (26 pages); $34 per 50 test booklets; $59 per picture book; $34 per examiner's manual.
Time: (10–15) minutes.
Authors: Denise L. Morgan and Arthur M. Guilford.
Publisher: PRO-ED.
Cross References: For reviews by Linda Crocker, Robert T. Williams, and Amy Finch-Williams, see 10:10.

[82]
Adolescent Psychopathology Scale.
Purpose: Designed to "evaluate symptoms of psychological disorders and distress in adolescents … measures psychopathology, personality, and social-emotional problems and competencies."
Population: Ages 12–19.
Publication Date: 1998.
Acronym: APS.
Scores: 40 scales in 4 domains: Clinical Disorders Domain (Attention-Deficit/Hyperactivity Disorder, Conduct Disorder, Oppositional-Defiant Disorder, Adjustment Disorder, Substance Abuse Disorder, Anorexia Nervosa, Bulimia Nervosa, Sleep Disorder, Somatization Disorder, Panic Disorder, Obsessive-Compulsive Disorder, Generalized Anxiety Disorder, Social Phobia, Separation Anxiety Disorder, Posttraumatic Stress Disorder, Major Depression, Dysthymic Disorder, Mania, Depersonalization Disorder, Schizophrenia); Personality Disorder Domain (Avoidant, Obsessive-Compulsive, Borderline, Schizotypal, Paranoid); Psychosocial Problem Content Domain (Self-Concept, Psycho-social Substance Use Difficulties, Introversion, Alienation-Boredom, Anger, Aggression, Interpersonal Problems, Emotional Lability, Disorientation, Suicide, Social Adaptation; Response Style Indicators (Lie, Consistency, Infrequency, Critical Item Endorsement); Factor Scales (Internalizing Disorder Factor, Externalizing Disorder Factor, Personality Disorder Factor).
Administration: Individual or group.
Price Data: Available from publisher.
Time: (45–60) minutes.
Comments: A 346-item self-report scale; developed to be consistent with the DSM-IV disorders; test form is entitled Adolescent Mental Health Questionnaire; software for computerized (Windows) scoring program included.
Author: William M. Reynolds.
Publisher: Psychological Assessment Resources, Inc.
Cross References: For reviews by Timothy R. Kanold and Wayne C. Piersel, see 14:9.

[83]
Adolescent Psychopathology Scale—Short Form.

Purpose: "Constructed as a brief self-report measure of psychopathology and problem behaviors in adolescents."
Population: Ages 12–19 years.
Publication Dates: 1998–2000.
Acronym: APS-SF.
Scores, 14: Defensiveness, Consistency Response, Conduct Disorder, Oppositional Defiant Disorder, Substance Abuse Disorder, Anger/Violence Proneness, Academic Problems, Generalized Anxiety Disorder, Posttraumatic Stress Disorder, Major Depression, Eating Disturbance, Suicide, Self-Concept, Interpersonal Problems.
Administration: Group or individual.
Price Data: Available from publisher for kit including scoring program with on-screen user's guide, 25 test booklets with 25-use key disk, and professional manual (2000, 137 pages).
Time: (15–20) minutes.
Comments: Derived from the Adolescent Psychopathology Scale (APS; 82).
Author: William M. Reynolds.
Publisher: Psychological Assessment Resources, Inc.

[84]
Adolescent Separation Anxiety Test.

Purpose: "Provides a measure of emotional and personality patterns which adolescents show in reaction to separation experiences."
Population: Ages 11–18.
Publication Dates: 1972–1980.
Scores, 28: 18 association responses (Rejection, Impaired Concentration, Phobic Feeling, Anxiety, Loneliness, Withdrawal, Somatic, Adaptive Reaction, Anger, Projection, Empathy, Evasion, Fantasy, Well-Being, Sublimation, Intrapunitive, Identify Stress, Total), plus 10 derived response patterns (Attachment, Individuation, Hostility, Painful Tension, Reality Avoidance, Concentration Impairment and Sublimation, Self-Love, Identity Stress, Absurd Responses, Attachment-Individuation Balance).
Administration: Individual.
Forms: Separate forms for boys and girls.
Price Data: Not available.
Time: Administration time not reported.
Comments: Formerly titled Separation Anxiety Test.
Author: Henry G. Hansburg.
Publisher: Krieger Publishing Company [No reply from publisher; status unknown].
Cross References: See T5:78 (1 reference) and T4:100 (1 reference); for reviews by Brenda Bailey-Richardson and Carolyn S. Hartsough, see 9:53.

[85]
Adolescent Symptom Inventory-4.

Purpose: Designed as a "screening instrument for the behavioral, affective, and cognitive symptoms of a variety of adolescent psychiatric disorders."
Population: Ages 12–18.
Publication Dates: 1997–1998.
Acronym: ASI-4.
Scores, 15: 11 scores shared on both Parent and Teacher Forms: AD/HD Inattentive, Hyperactive-Impulsive, Combined, Conduct Disorder, Oppositional Defiant, Generalized Anxiety Disorder, Schizoid Personality, Schizophrenia, Major Depressive Disorder, Dysthymic Disorder, Bipolar Disorder; 4 additional scores on the Parent Form: Antisocial Personality Disorder, Separation Anxiety, Anorexia Nervosa, Bulimia Nervosa.
Administration: Individual.
Forms, 2: Teacher Checklist, Parent Checklist.
Price Data, 2001: $102 per deluxe kit including 25 parent checklists, 25 teacher checklists, 50 symptom count score sheets, 50 parent and teacher symptom severity profile score sheets, , screening manual (1997, 145 pages), and norms manual (1998, 168 pages); $52 per 50 parent checklists; $38 per 50 teacher checklists.
Time: [10–15] minutes.
Comments: Checklists completed by teachers and caregivers about adolescents; scores are not intended for diagnostic purposes, only screening purposes.
Authors: Kenneth D. Gadow and Joyce Sprafkin.
Publisher: Checkmate Plus, Ltd.

[86]
Adult Attention Deficit Disorder Behavior Rating Scale.

Purpose: Designed to "identify behavior that will support a diagnosis of Attention Deficit Disorder (ADD)."
Population: Ages 16 and above.
Publication Date: 1993.
Acronym: AADDBRS.
Scores, 10: Inattention, Impulsivity, Hyperactivity, Anger Control, Academics, Anxiety, Confidence, Aggressiveness, Resistance, Social.
Administration: Individual.
Price Data: Not available.
Time: (15–30) minutes.
Comments: An extension of the Attention Deficit Disorder Behavior Rating Scales (218).
Authors: Ned Owens and Betty White Owens.
Publisher: Ned Owens, Inc. [No reply from publisher. Status unknown.]
Cross References: For reviews by Robert J. Miller and James C. Reed, see 13:9.

[87]

Adult Attention Deficit Disorders Evaluation Scale.

Purpose: Designed to provide a measure of inattention and hyperactivity-impulsivity in adults.
Population: Adults.
Publication Dates: 1996–1997.
Acronym: A-ADDES.
Scores, 3: Inattentive, Hyperactive-Impulsive, Total Percentile Rank.
Administration: Individual.
Price Data, 2002: $158 per complete kit including 50 self-report rating forms, 50 Home Version rating forms, 50 Work Version rating forms, Self-Report technical manual (1996, 43 pages), Home Version technical manual (1996, 41 pages), Work Version technical manual (1996, 40 pages), and Adult Attention Deficit Disorders Intervention manual (1997, 183 pages); $33 per 50 rating forms (specify Self-Report, Home Version, or Work Version); $22 per 50 ADDES/DSM-IV forms; $14 per technical manual (specify Self-Report, Home Version, or Work Version); $17 per Adult Attention Deficit Disorders Intervention manual; $2 per Comparing the Technical Aspects of Adult Attention-Deficit/Hyperactivity Disorder Rating Scales review.
Time: Untimed.
Comments: Behavioral rating system with three forms: Home, Work, and Self-Report; may be completed in one sitting or over a period of days.
Authors: Stephen B. McCarney and Paul D. Anderson.
Publisher: Hawthorne Educational Services, Inc.
   a) HOME VERSION.
   Comments: To be completed by a spouse or other close relative/friend who observes daily behavior in the home; best when used in conjunction with Work and Self-Report versions.
   b) WORK VERSION.
   Comments: To be completed by an employer, supervisor, or fellow employee who can closely observe the subject's work behaviors; best when used in conjunction with Work and Self-Report versions.
Cross References: For reviews by Helen Kitchens and James C. Reed, see 14:10.

[88]

Adult Basic Learning Examination, Second Edition.

Purpose: "Designed to measure the educational achievement of adults who may or may not have completed twelve years of schooling . . . also useful in evaluating efforts to raise the educational level of these adults."
Population: Adults with less than 12 years of formal schooling.

Publication Dates: 1986–1990.
Acronym: ABLE.
Administration: Group.
Levels, 3: 1, 2, 3 and placement test (SelectABLE).
Forms, 2: E, F (equivalent forms).
Price Data, 2002: $67 per examination kit containing test booklets and directions for administering for 1 form of each of the 3 levels, hand-scorable answer sheet, Ready Score® Answer Sheet and group record for Level 2, and SelectABLE Ready Score® Answer Sheet; $43.50 per Handbook of Instructional Techniques and Materials (1986, 67 pages); $51.90 per norms booklet (specify level); $13.80 per Reading Supplement.
Foreign Language Edition: Spanish edition (1990) ABLE Screening Battery available for Level 2 Reading and Mathematics subtests only.
Authors: Bjorn Karlsen and Eric F. Gardner.
Publisher: The Psychological Corporation.
   a) SELECTABLE.
   Purpose: A screening test to determine which level of ABLE is most suitable for use with a particular individual.
   Price Data: $72.60 per 25 Ready Score® Answer Sheets; $44.50 per 50 hand-scorable test sheets; $37.60 per scoring key; $12.70 per SelectABLE Handbook (1986, 15 pages).
   Time: (15) minutes.
   b) LEVEL 1.
   Population: Adults with 1–4 years of formal education.
   Scores, 5: Vocabulary, Reading Comprehension, Spelling, Number Operations, Problem Solving.
   Price Data: $89 per 25 hand-scorable test booklets and directions for administering including group record (specify Form E or F); $77.40 per scoring key (specify Form E or F); $10.60 per directions for administering (1986, 38 pages).
   Time: (130–165) minutes.
   c) LEVEL 2.
   Population: Adults with 5–8 years of formal education.
   Scores: Same as *b* plus Language.
   Price Data: $89 per 25 hand-scorable or reusable test booklets (specify Form E or F); $77.40 per scoring key (specify Form E or F); $79.50 per 25 Ready Score® Answer Sheets (specify Form E or F); $66.80 per 50 hand-scorable answer sheets and 2 group records; $10.60 per directions for administering Levels 2 and 3.
   Time: (175–215) minutes.
   d) LEVEL 3.
   Population: Adults with 9–12 years of formal schooling who may or may not have completed 12 years of schooling.

Scores: Same as *c* above.
Price Data: Same as *c* above.
Time: Same as *c* above.
Cross References: See T5:82 (1 reference); for reviews by Anne R. Fitzpatrick and Robert T. Williams, see 11:9 (1 reference); see also T3:121 (6 references), 8:2 (4 references), and T2:3 (3 references); for a review by A. N. Hieronymus of the earlier edition and excerpted reviews by Edward B. Fry and James W. Hall of Levels 1 and 2 of the earlier edition, see 7:3.

[89]
Adult Language Assessment Scales.

Purpose: "Designed to provide complete information about language proficiency of adults who speak English as a Second or Foreign Language.
Population: Adults.
Publication Date: 1991.
Acronym: A-LAS®.
Scores, 10: Listening (Conversations, Same/Different, Total), Speaking (Vocabulary, Making Sentences, Newscast, Sounds, Total), Pronunciation, Total.
Administration: Individual.
Forms, 2: A, B.
Price Data, 2002: $201.95 per complete kit (Form A) including oral administration manual (28 pages) (Forms A and B), oral scoring and interpretation manual (53 pages) (Forms A and B), cue picture book (Form A), audiocassette for the oral language component (Form A), audiocassette for the additional pronunciation section (Form A), audiocassette holder, and 50 answer booklets (Form A); $142.55 per augmentation kit (Form B including cue picture book (Form B), audiocassette for oral language component (Form B), audiocassette for pronunciation section (Form B), and 50 answer booklets (Form B); $110.15 per 25 reading and mathematics booklets (specify level and Form); $75.60 per 50 writing booklets (specify Form); $43.20 per 50 reading and mathematics answer sheets (specify level); $51.85 per 50 oral answer booklets (specify form); $45.35 per 50 oral profile sheets (specify form); $31.30 per oral administration manual; $32.40 per oral scoring and interpretation manual; $45.35 per cue picture book (specify form); $20.55 per audiocassette (specify form and story).
Time: (25–30) minutes.
Comments: Includes equivalent forms, A and B.
Authors: Sharon E. Duncan and Edward A. DeAvila.
Publisher: CTB/McGraw-Hill.
Cross References: For reviews by Roger A. Richards and Wayne H. Slater, see 14:11.

[90]
Adult Level of Care Index-2R.

Purpose: "To provide assessment summation and documentation for addictions treatment planning."

Population: Adults.
Publication Date: 2001.
Acronym: LOCI-2R.
Scores: 56 ratings: 5 Acute Intoxication/Withdrawal (Outpatient Detoxification, Ambulatory Detoxification with Extended On-Site Monitoring, Clinically Managed Residential Detoxification, Medically Monitored Inpatient Detoxification, Medically Managed Intensive Inpatient Detoxification); 8 Biomedical Conditions/Complications (Outpatient Treatment, Intensive Outpatient Treatment, Partial Hospitalization, Clinically Managed Low-/Medium-/High-Intensity Residential Treatment, Medically Monitored Intensive Inpatient, Medically Managed Inpatient Services); 9 Emotional, Behavioral, or Cognitive Conditions and Complications (Early Intervention, Outpatient Services, Intensive Outpatient, Partial Hospitalization, Clinically Managed Low-/Medium-/High-Intensity Residential Treatment, Medically Monitored Intensive Inpatient Services, Medically Managed Inpatient Services); 9 Readiness to Change (Early Intervention, Outpatient Services, Intensive Outpatient Treatment, Partial Hospitalization, Clinically Managed Low-/Medium-/High-Intensity Residential Treatment, Medically Monitored Inpatient Treatment, Medically Managed Inpatient Treatment); 9 Relapse, Continued Use, or Continued Problem Potential (Early Intervention, Outpatient Treatment, Intensive Outpatient Treatment, Partial Hospitalization, Clinically Managed Low-/Medium-/High-Intensity Residential Treatment, Medically Monitored Intensive Inpatient, Medically Managed Inpatient Treatment); 9 Recovery Environment (Early Intervention, Outpatient Treatment, Intensive Outpatient Treatment, Partial Hospitalization, Clinically Managed Low-/Medium-/High-Intensity Residential Treatment, Medically Monitored Inpatient Treatment, Medically Managed Inpatient Treatment); 6 Opioid Maintenance Therapy (Acute Intoxication/Withdrawal; Biomedical Conditions and Complications; Emotional, Behavioral, or Cognitive Conditions and Complications; Readiness to Change; Relapse, Continued Use, or Continued Problem Potential; Recovery Environment); Level of Care Indicated.
Administration: Individual.
Price Data: Available from publisher.
Time: Variable.
Comments: Not a psychometric instrument; summary checklist provides an estimate of the likelihood that an individual meets the criteria for substance abuse or dependency on six dimensions in accordance with the criteria of the American Society of Addiction Medicine; also indicates overall level of care needed.
Authors: Norman G. Hoffmann, David Mee-Lee, and Gerald D. Shulman.
Publisher: Evince Clinical Assessments.

[91]
Adult Personality Inventory [Revised].

Purpose: Designed as a "tool for analyzing and reporting differences in personality, interpersonal style, and career preferences."
Population: Ages 16–adult.
Publication Dates: 1982–1996.
Acronym: API.
Scores, 25: Personality Scores (Extroverted, Adjusted, Tough-Minded, Independent, Disciplined, Creative, Enterprising); Interpersonal Style Scores (Caring, Adapting, Withdrawn, Submissive, Uncaring, Non-Conforming, Sociable, Assertive); Career/Lifestyle Scores (Practical, Scientific, Aesthetic, Social, Competitive, Structured); Validity Scores (Good Impression, Bad Impression, Infrequency, Uncertainty).
Administration: Group or individual.
Time: (45–60) minutes.
Comments: Self-report; computer scored and interpreted.
Author: Samuel E. Krug.
Publisher: MetriTech, Inc.
  a) API NARRATIVE REPORTS.
  Purpose: "Oriented to the test taker, provides users with scores, extensive interpretive information in narrative form, and a series of questions that systematically guide the reader toward a practical application of assessment data."
  Price Data, 2001: $49 per Narrative Report kit including Interpretive and Technical Guide (1996, 53 pages), processing of 5 reports, 2 reusable test booklets, and 5 answer sheets; $48.75 per 5 reports; $89.50 per 10 reports; $196.25 per 25 reports; $337.50 per 50 reports; $16.50 per manual; $16 per 10 reusable test booklets.
  b) API/PC.
  Purpose: "Administers, scores, and generates immediate test results for the same 21 scales and validity checks as the API Narrative Report."
  Price Data: $54 per API/PC Introductory kit including manual (1996, 21 pages), and 5-report demo disk; $18 per manual; $105 per 10 administrations disk; $237.50 per 25 administrations disk; $400 per 50 administrations disk; [off-line assessment support materials: $16 per 10 reusable test booklets; $14 per 50 answer sheets; $20 per 50 scannable answer sheets; $36 per 50 decision model worksheets].
  Comments: Supports both on-line or off-line testing; IBM version only (5.25-inch HD or 3.5-inch DD); optional 189-item short version requires 25–35 minutes for administration.
  c) API/CAREER PROFILE.
  Purpose: Oriented to the test administrator and compares the individual test taker with Occupational Decision Models and user created models.

Forms, 2: Form E "includes expanded descriptions of the 6 career/lifestyle factors;" Form M offers "automatic comparisons of the individual test taker to each of the decision models."
Price Data: $59 per API/Career Profile Introductory Kit (Form E or M) including API/Career Profile manual (n.d., 71 pages), and 5-report demo disk; $120 per 10 administrations disk; $275 per 25 administrations disk; $475 per 50 administrations disk; $20 per manual.
Comments: Supports both on-line or off-line testing; IBM version only; optional 189-item short version requires 25–35 minutes for administration.
Cross References: For a review by Kevin Lanning, see 14:12; for a review by Rik Carl D'Amato of an earlier edition, see 12:20; see also T4:106 (4 references); for a review by Brian Bolton of an earlier edition, see 9:54.

[92]
Adult Rating of Oral English.

Purpose: "Designed to assess the oral English language skills of secondary and adult students" who speak English as a second language.
Population: Adult and secondary students in vocational education and employment training programs.
Publication Date: 1995.
Acronym: AROE.
Scores, 15: Pronunciation, Grammar, General Vocabulary, Vocational Vocabulary, Building Blocks Subscore; Listener and Speaker scores for Conversation, Instructions, Explanations, Clarification/Verification; Discourse Subscore; Mean Proficiency Score; Total Score.
Administration: Individual.
Price Data, 2002: $75 per training kit including 5 user's handbooks (43 pages) and 25 matrix scoring sheets; $20 per set of 25 matrix scoring sheets; $15 per user's handbook; $10 per technical manual (16 pages); $15 per supplementary video explaining use and purpose.
Time: Untimed.
Comments: A rating scale completed by teachers about individual students' skills; supplementary video explaining use and purpose is available.
Authors: Annette M. Zehler and Patricia A. DiCerbo.
Publisher: Development Associates, Inc.
Cross References: For reviews by Roger A. Richards and Gerald Tindal, see 14:13.

[93]
The Adult Self Expression Scale.

Purpose: Assesses the assertiveness level of the respondent.
Population: Adults.
Publication Dates: 1974-1975.
Acronym: ASES.

Scores: Total score only.
Administration: Group or individual.
Price Data: Available from publisher.
Time: Administration time not reported.
Authors: Melvin L. Gay, James G. Hollandsworth, Jr., and John P. Galassi.
Publisher: Adult Self Expression Scale.
Cross References: See T5:88 (2 references) and T4:107 (1 reference); for reviews by Philip H. Dreyer and Goldine C. Gleser, see 9:55 (15 references).

[94]
Adult Suicidal Ideation Questionnaire.

Purpose: "Designed to evaluate the presence and frequency of suicidal thoughts."
Population: Ages 18 and over.
Publication Dates: 1987–1991.
Acronym: ASIQ.
Scores: Total score only.
Administration: Individual or group.
Price Data: Available from publisher for complete kit including manual (1991, 62 pages) and 25 respondent forms.
Time: (5–10) minutes.
Author: William M. Reynolds.
Publisher: Psychological Assessment Resources, Inc.
Cross References: See T5:89 (1 reference); for reviews by Debra E. Cole and Isadore Newman, see 12:21.

[95]
Advanced Measures of Music Audiation.

Purpose: Developed to measure music aptitude.
Population: Junior high school through college.
Publication Date: 1989.
Scores, 3: Tonal, Rhythm, Total.
Administration: Group.
Price Data, 2001: $70 per complete kit including compact disc, 100 answer sheets, and manual (54 pages); $20 per 100 answer sheets; $10 per manual; $20 per set of scoring stencils (scoring stencils not part of complete kit); $25 per compact disc; scoring service available from publisher at $1 per student.
Time: 16(20) minutes.
Comments: Audiocassette recorder necessary for administration; upward extension of the Intermediate Measures of Music Audiation (1236).
Author: Edwin E. Gordon.
Publisher: G.I.A. Publications, Inc.
Cross References: For reviews by Rudolf E. Radocy and James W. Sherbon, see 12:22.

[96]
Advanced Placement Examination in Art History.

Purpose: Designed to measure college-level achievement of students in art history.

Population: High school students desiring credit for college-level courses and admission to advanced courses.
Publication Dates: 1972–2002.
Scores: Total score only.
Administration: Group.
Price Data: Available from publisher.
Time: 180 minutes.
Comments: Available to secondary schools for annual administration on specific days in May; inactive form and previous free-response questions available; program sponsored by the College Board with exams administered by Educational Testing Service.
Author: Educational Testing Service.
Publisher: The College Board.
Cross References: For additional information concerning an earlier edition, see 8:83. For reviews of the AP® Program, see 8:471 (2 reviews) and 7:662 (2 reviews).

[97]
Advanced Placement Examination in Biology.

Purpose: Designed to measure college-level achievement of students in biology.
Population: High school students desiring credit for college-level courses and admission to advanced courses.
Publication Dates: 1956–2002.
Scores: Total score only.
Administration: Group.
Price Data: Available from publisher.
Time: 180 minutes.
Comments: Available to secondary schools for annual administration on specific days in May; inactive form and previous free-response questions available; program sponsored by the College Board with exams administered by Educational Testing Service.
Author: Educational Testing Service.
Publisher: Educational Testing Service.
Cross References: See T5:92 (1 reference), T4:110 (1 reference), 8:381 (1 reference), and 7:807 (1 reference); for a review by Clarence H. Nelson of earlier forms, see 6:893 (1 reference); for a review by Clark W. Horton, see 5:724. For reviews of the AP® Program, see 8:471 (2 reviews) and 7:662 (2 reviews).

[98]
Advanced Placement Examination in Calculus.

Purpose: Designed to measure college-level achievement of students in calculus.
Population: High school students desiring credit for college-level courses and admission to advanced courses.
Publication Dates: 1954–2002.

Scores: Total score only.
Administration: Group.
Levels, 2: AB, BC (candidate elects only one).
Price Data: Available from publisher.
Time: 195 minutes.
Comments: Available to secondary schools for annual administration on specific days in May; inactive form and previous free-response questions available; program sponsored by the College Board with exams administered by Educational Testing Service.
Author: Educational Testing Service.
Publisher: The College Board.

a) CALCULUS AB.
Scores: Total score only.
Comments: Covers differential and integral calculus topics typically included in an introductory Calculus I college course.

b) CALCULUS BC.
Scores: Total score plus an AB subscore.
Comments: Covers the Calculus AB topics, as well as additional topics in differential and integral calculus, and series.

Cross References: See T5:93 (1 reference), 8:309 (1 reference), T2:742 (1 reference), 7:451 (2 references), and 6:570 (4 references); for a review by Paul L. Dressel of an earlier form, see 5:419. For reviews of the AP® Program, see 8:471 (2 reviews) and 7:662 (2 reviews).

[99]
Advanced Placement Examination in Chemistry.

Purpose: Designed to measure college-level achievement of students in chemistry.
Population: High school students desiring credit for college-level courses and admission to advanced courses.
Publication Dates: 1954–2002.
Scores: Total score only.
Administration: Group.
Price Data: Available from publisher.
Time: 180 minutes.
Comments: Available to secondary schools for annual administration on specific days in May; inactive form and previous free-response questions available; program sponsored by the College Board with exams administered by Educational Testing Service.
Author: Educational Testing Service.
Publisher: The College Board.
Cross References: See T5:94 (3 references) and T4:111 (1 reference); for a review by J. Arthur Campbell, see 8:846; see also T2:1832 (1 reference) and 6:915 (1 reference); for a review by Theo A. Ashford of an earlier form, see 5:743. For reviews of the AP® Program, see 8:471 (2 reviews) and 7:662 (2 reviews).

[100]
Advanced Placement Examination in Comparative Government and Politics.

Purpose: Designed to measure college-level achievement of students in comparative government and politics.
Population: High school students desiring credit for college-level courses and admission to advanced courses.
Publication Dates: 1987–2002.
Scores: Total score only.
Administration: Group.
Price Data: Available from publisher.
Time: 145 minutes.
Comments: Available to secondary schools for annual administration on specific days in May; inactive forms and previous free-response questions available; program sponsored by the College Board with exams administered by Educational Testing Service.
Author: Educational Testing Service.
Publisher: The College Board.

[101]
Advanced Placement Examination in Computer Science.

Purpose: Designed to measure college-level achievement of students in computer science.
Population: High school students desiring credit for college-level courses and admission to advanced courses.
Scores: Total score only.
Administration: Group.
Levels, 2: A, AB (candidate elects only one).
Price Data: Available from publisher.
Comments: Available to secondary schools for annual administration on specific days in May; inactive forms and previous free-response questions available; program sponsored by the College Board with exams administered by Educational Testing Service.
Author: Educational Testing Service.
Publisher: The College Board.

a) COMPUTER SCIENCE A.
Time: 180 minutes.
Publication Dates: 1988–2002.
Comments: Covers topics in a first-semester introductory college course in computer science; emphasizes programming in C++, programming methodology (including recursion), and procedural abstraction; also includes algorithms, data structures, and data abstraction.

b) COMPUTER SCIENCE AB.
Publication Dates: 1984–2002.
Time: 180 minutes.
Comments: Covers topics in a full-year introductory college course in computer science; includes all the topics in Computer Science A as well as more in-depth algorithm analysis (Big-Oh notation) and dynamic data structures.

[102]
Advanced Placement Examination in English (Language and Composition).

Purpose: Designed to measure college-level achievement of students in English (language and composition).
Population: High school students desiring credit for college-level courses and admission to advanced courses.
Publication Dates: 1981–2002.
Scores: Total score only.
Administration: Group.
Price Data: Available from publisher.
Time: 180 minutes.
Comments: Available to secondary schools for annual administration on specific days in May; inactive form and previous free-response questions available; program sponsored by the College Board with exams administered by Educational Testing Service.
Author: Educational Testing Service.
Publisher: The College Board.
Cross References: See T5:97 (1 reference); for additional information and a review by Ellis Batten Page of an earlier edition, see 8:39; see also T2:51 (2 references) and 7:184 (1 reference); for a review by Robert C. Pooley of an earlier form of the English composition test, see 5:205. For reviews of the AP® Program, see 8:471 (2 reviews) and 7:662 (2 reviews).

[103]
Advanced Placement Examination in English (Literature and Composition).

Purpose: Designed to measure college-level achievement of students in English (literature and composition).
Population: High school students desiring credit for college-level courses and admission to advanced courses.
Publication Dates: 1956–2002.
Scores: Total score only.
Administration: Group.
Price Data: Available from publisher.
Time: 180 minutes.
Comments: Available to secondary schools for annual administration on specific days in May; inactive form and previous free-response questions available; program sponsored by the College Board with exams administered by Educational Testing Service.
Author: Educational Testing Service.
Publisher: The College Board.
Cross References: See T4:112 (2 references); for a review by Ellis Batten Page of an earlier edition, see 8:39; see also T2:51 (2 references) and 7:184 (1 reference); for a review by Robert C. Pooley of an earlier form of the English composition test, see 5:205; for a review by John S. Diekhoff of an earlier form of the

literature test, see 5:211. For reviews of the AP® Program, see 8:471 (2 reviews) and 7:662 (2 reviews).

[104]
Advanced Placement Examination in Environmental Science.

Purpose: Designed to measure college-level achievement of students in environmental science.
Population: High school students desiring credit for college-level courses and admission to advanced courses.
Publication Dates: 1998–2002.
Scores: Total score only.
Administration: Group.
Price Data: Available from publisher.
Time: 180 minutes.
Comments: Available to secondary schools for annual administration on specific days in May; inactive forms and previous free-response questions available; program sponsored by the College Board with exams administered by Educational Testing Service.
Author: Educational Testing Service.
Publisher: The College Board.

[105]
Advanced Placement Examination in European History.

Purpose: Designed to measure college-level achievement of students in European history.
Population: High school students desiring credit for college-level courses and admission to advanced courses.
Publication Dates: 1956–2002.
Scores: Total score only.
Administration: Group.
Price Data: Available from publisher.
Time: 185 minutes.
Comments: Available to secondary schools for annual administration on specific days in May; inactive form and previous free-response questions available; program sponsored by the College Board with exams administered by Educational Testing Service.
Author: Educational Testing Service.
Publisher: The College Board.
Cross References: See T5:100 (1 reference), T4:114 (1 reference), 8:908 (1 reference), and 6:1001 (2 references). For reviews of the AP® Program, see 8:471 (2 reviews) and 7:662 (2 reviews).

[106]
Advanced Placement Examination in French Language.

Purpose: Designed to measure college-level achievement of students in the French language.
Population: High school students desiring credit for college-level courses and admission to advanced courses.
Publication Dates: 1971–2002.
Scores: Total score only.

Administration: Group.
Price Data: Available from publisher.
Time: 165 minutes.
Comments: Available to secondary schools for annual administration on apecific days in May; inactive form and previous free-response questions available; program sponsored by the College Board with exams administered by Educational Testing Service.
Author: Educational Testing Service.
Publisher: The College Board.
Cross References: See T3:131 (1 reference); for additional information and a review by Michio Peter Hagiwara, see 8:112. For reviews of the AP® Program, see 8:471 (2 reviews).

[107]
Advanced Placement Examination in French Literature.

Purpose: Designed to measure college-level achievement of students in French literature.
Population: High school students desiring credit for college-level courses and admission to advanced courses.
Publication Dates: 1954–2002.
Scores: Total score only.
Administration: Group.
Price Data: Available from publisher.
Time: 180 minutes.
Comments: Available to secondary schools for annual administration on specific days in May; inactive form and previous free-response questions available; program sponsored by the College Board with exams administered by Educational Testing Service.
Author: Educational Testing Service.
Publisher: The College Board.
Cross References: For additional information and reviews by Michio Peter Hagiwara and Joseph A. Murphy, see 8:113 (3 references); see also 7:268 (1 reference) and 6:368 (3 references). For a review of the AP® Program, see 8:471 (2 reviews) and 7:662 (2 reviews).

[108]
Advanced Placement Examination in German Language.

Purpose: Designed to measure college-level achievement of students in German language.
Population: High school students desiring credit for college-level courses and admission to advanced courses.
Publication Dates: 1956–2002.
Scores: Total score only.
Administration: Group.
Price Data: Available from publisher.
Time: 180 minutes.
Comments: Available to secondary schools for annual administration on specific days in May; inactive form and previous free-response questions available;

program sponsored by the College Board with exams administered by Educational Testing Service.
Author: Educational Testing Service.
Publisher: The College Board.
Cross References: For reviews of the AP® Program, see 8:471 (2 reviews) and 7:662 (2 reviews).

[109]
Advanced Placement Examination in Human Geography.

Purpose: Designed to measure college-level achievement of students in human geography.
Population: High school students desiring credit for college-level courses and admission to advanced courses.
Publication Dates: 2001–2002.
Scores: Total score only.
Administration: Group.
Price Data: Available from publisher.
Time: 120 minutes.
Comments: Available to secondary schools for annual administration on specific days in May; inactive form and previous free-response questions available; program sponsored by the College Board with exams administered by Educational Testing Service.
Author: Educational Testing Service.
Publisher: The College Board.

[110]
Advanced Placement Examination in International English Language.

Purpose: Designed to measure the non-native speaker's readiness to do university-level work conducted in English.
Population: High school students desiring credit or placement for English second language college courses.
Publication Dates: 1997–2002.
Scores: Total score only.
Administration: Group.
Price Data: Available from publisher.
Time: 180 minutes.
Comments: Available to secondary schools outside the U.S. only (as of 1/1/99) for administration on specific days each spring; inactive forms and previous free-response questions available; program sponsored by the College Board with exams administered by Educational Testing Service.
Author: Educational Testing Service.
Publisher: The College Board.

[111]
Advanced Placement Examination in Latin Literature.

Purpose: Designed to measure college-level achievement of students in Latin.
Population: High school students desiring credit for college-level courses and admission to advanced courses.

Publication Dates: 1980–2002.
Scores: Total score only.
Administration: Group.
Price Data: Available from publisher.
Time: 180 minutes.
Comments: Available to secondary schools for annual administration on specific days in May; inactive form and previous free-response questions available; program sponsored by the College Board with exams administered by Educational Testing Service.
Author: Educational Testing Service.
Publisher: The College Board.
Cross References: For additional information concerning an earlier edition of the Classics examination, see 8:144 (3 references). For reviews of the AP® Program, see 8:471 (2 reviews) and 7:662 (2 reviews).

[112]
Advanced Placement Examination in Latin (Vergil).

Purpose: Designed to measure college-level achievement of students in Latin.
Population: High school students desiring credit for college-level courses and admission to advanced courses.
Publication Dates: 1972–2002.
Scores: Total score only.
Administration: Group.
Price Data: Available from publisher.
Time: 180 minutes.
Comments: Available to secondary schools for annual administration on specific days in May; inactive form and previous free-response questions available; program sponsored by the College Board with exams administered by Educational Testing Service.
Author: Educational Testing Service.
Publisher: The College Board.
Cross References: For additional information concerning an earlier edition of the classics examination, see 8:144 (3 references). For reviews of the AP® Program, see 8:471 (2 reviews) and 7:662 (2 reviews).

[113]
Advanced Placement Examination in Macroeconomics.

Purpose: Designed to measure college-level achievement of students in macroeconomics.
Population: High school students desiring credit for college-level courses and admission to advanced courses.
Publication Dates: 1989–2002.
Scores: Total score only.
Administration: Group.
Price Data: Available from publisher.
Time: 120 minutes.
Comments: Available to secondary schools for annual administration on specific days in May; inactive forms and previous free-response questions available;

program sponsored by the College Board with exams administered by Educational Testing Service.
Author: Educational Testing Service.
Publisher: The College Board.

[114]
Advanced Placement Examination in Microeconomics.

Purpose: Designed to measure college-level achievement of students in microeconomics.
Population: High school students desiring credit for college-level courses and admission to advanced courses.
Publication Dates: 1989–2002.
Scores: Total score only.
Administration: Group.
Price Data: Available from publisher.
Time: 120 minutes.
Comments: Available to secondary schools for annual administration on specific days in May; inactive forms and previous free-response questions available; program sponsored by the College Board with exams administered by Educational Testing Service.
Author: Educational Testing Service.
Publisher: The College Board.

[115]
Advanced Placement Examination in Music Theory.

Purpose: Designed to measure college-level achievement of students in music theory.
Population: High school students desiring credit for college-level courses and admission to advanced courses.
Publication Dates: 1978–2002.
Scores, 3: Aural, Nonaural, Total.
Administration: Group.
Price Data: Available from publisher.
Time: 165 minutes.
Comments: Available to secondary schools for annual administration on specific days in May; inactive form and previous free-response questions available; program sponsored by the College Board with exams administered by Educational Testing Service.
Author: Educational Testing Service.
Publisher: The College Board.
Cross References: For additional information regarding an earlier edition of the Music Examination, see 8:90. For reviews of the AP® Program, see 8:471 (2 reviews).

[116]
Advanced Placement Examination in Physics.

Purpose: Designed to measure college-level achievement of students in physics.
Population: High school students desiring credit for college-level courses and admission to advanced courses.
Publication Dates: 1954–2002.

Administration: Group.
Levels, 2: B, C (candidate elects only one).
Price Data: Available from publisher.
Comments: Available to secondary schools for annual administration on specific days in May; inactive forms and previous free-response questions available; program sponsored by the College Board with exams administered by Educational Testing Service.
Author: Educational Testing Service.
Publisher: The College Board.

a) PHYSICS B.
Scores: Total score only.
Comments: Equivalent of 1-year terminal course in noncalculus-based college physics.
Time: 180 minutes.

b) PHYSICS C.
Scores: 1 or 2 scores: Mechanics (Part 1), Electricity and Magnetism (Part 2).
Comments: Equivalent of 1-year nonterminal course in calculus-based college physics; 2 parts in each test booklet (candidate elects either one or both parts).
Time: 90 minutes for each part.

Cross References: See T3:143 (1 reference); for a review by Mario Iona, see 8:862 (3 references); see also 6:927 (2 references); for a review by Leo Nedelsky of an earlier form, see 5:750. For reviews of the AP® Program, see 8:471 (2 reviews) and 7:662 (2 reviews).

[117]
Advanced Placement Examination in Psychology.

Purpose: Designed to measure college-level achievement of students in psychology.
Population: High school students desiring credit for college-level courses and admission to advanced courses.
Publication Dates: 1992–2002.
Scores: Total score only.
Administration: Group.
Price Data: Available from publisher.
Time: 120 minutes.
Comments: Available to secondary schools for annual administration on specific days in May; inactive forms and previous free-response questions available; program sponsored by the College Board with exams administered by Educational Testing Service.
Author: Educational Testing Service.
Publisher: The College Board.

[118]
Advanced Placement Examination in Spanish Language.

Purpose: Designed to measure college-level achievement of students in Spanish language.
Population: High school students desiring credit for college-level courses and admission to advanced courses.

Publication Dates: 1976–2002.
Scores: Total score only.
Administration: Group.
Price Data: Available from publisher.
Time: 170 minutes.
Comments: Available to secondary schools for annual administration on specific days in May; inactive form and previous free-response questions available; program sponsored by the College Board with exams administered by Educational Testing Service.
Author: Educational Testing Service.
Publisher: The College Board.
Cross References: See T3:139 (1 reference); for a review by George W. Ayer of an earlier edition, see 8:153 (1 reference); see also 7:313 (2 references) and 6:421 (1 reference). For reviews of the AP® Program, see 8:471 (2 reviews) and 7:662 (2 reviews).

[119]
Advanced Placement Examination in Spanish Literature.

Purpose: Designed to measure college-level achievement of students in Spanish literature.
Population: High school students desiring credit for college-level courses and admission to advanced courses.
Publication Dates: 1956–2002.
Scores: Total score only.
Administration: Group.
Price Data: Available from publisher.
Time: 180 minutes.
Comments: Available to secondary schools for annual administration on specific days in May; inactive form and previous free-response questions available; program sponsored by the College Board with exams administered by Educational Testing Service.
Author: Educational Testing Service.
Publisher: The College Board.
Cross References: For a review by George W. Ayer of an earlier edition, see 8:153 (1 reference); see also 7:313 (2 references) and 6:421 (1 reference). For reviews of the AP® Program, see 8:471 (2 reviews) and 7:662 (2 reviews).

[120]
Advanced Placement Examination in Statistics.

Purpose: Designed to measure college-level achievement of students in statistics.
Population: High school students desiring credit for college-level courses and admission to advanced courses.
Publication Dates: 1997–2002.
Scores: Total score only.
Administration: Group.
Price Data: Available from publisher.

Time: 180 minutes.
Comments: Available to secondary schools for annual administration on specific days in May; inactive forms and previous free-response questions available; program sponsored by the College Board with exams administered by Educational Testing Service.
Author: Educational Testing Service.
Publisher: The College Board.

[121]
Advanced Placement Examination in Studio Art.

Purpose: Designed to measure college-level achievement of students in studio art.
Population: High school students desiring credit for college-level courses and admission to advanced courses.
Publication Dates: 1972–2002.
Scores: Total score only.
Administration: Group.
Price Data: Available from publisher.
Comments: Candidate submits materials (original works, written commentary, slides) for evaluation of quality, concentration, and breadth; available to secondary schools for annual submission of materials on specific days in May; program sponsored by the College Board with exams administered by Educational Testing Service.
Author: Educational Testing Service.
Publisher: The College Board.
Cross References: For additional information concerning an earlier edition, see 8:83. For reviews of the AP® Program, see 8:471 (2 reviews).

[122]
Advanced Placement Examination in United States Government and Politics.

Purpose: Designed to measure college-level achievement of students in United States government and politics.
Population: High school students desiring credit for college-level courses and admission to advanced courses.
Publication Dates: 1987–2002.
Scores: Total score only.
Administration: Group.
Price Data: Available from publisher.
Time: 145 minutes.
Comments: Available to secondary schools for annual administration on specific days in May; inactive forms and previous free-response questions available; program sponsored by the College Board with exams by Educational Testing Service.
Author: Educational Testing Service.
Publisher: The College Board.

[123]
Advanced Placement Examination in United States History.

Purpose: Designed to measure college-level achievement of students in United States history.
Population: High school students desiring credit for college-level courses and admission to advanced courses.
Publication Dates: 1956–2002.
Scores: Total score only.
Administration: Group.
Price Data: Available from publisher.
Time: 185 minutes.
Comments: Available to secondary schools for annual administration on specific days in May; inactive form and previous free-response questions available; program sponsored by the College Board with exams administered by Educational Testing Service.
Author: Educational Testing Service.
Publisher: Educational Testing Service.
Cross References: See T5:117 (4 references), T4:127 (1 reference) and T2:1980 (1 reference); for a review by Harry D. Berg of an earlier form, see 6:1000 (1 reference); for reviews by James A. Field, Jr. and Christine McGuire, see 5:812. For reviews of the AP® Program, see 8:471 (2 reviews) and 7:662 (2 reviews).

[124]
Advanced Placement Examination in World History.

Purpose: Designed to measure college-level achievement of students in world history.
Population: High school students desiring credit for college-level courses and admission to advanced courses.
Publication Date: 2002.
Scores: Total score only.
Administration: Group.
Price Data: Available from publisher.
Time: 185 minutes.
Comments: Available to secondary schools for annual administration on specific days in May; inactive form and previous free-response questions available; program sponsored by the College Board with exams administered by Educational Testing Service.
Author: Educational Testing Service.
Publisher: The College Board.

[125]
Advanced Placement Examinations.

Purpose: Designed to measure college-level achievement of students in various subject areas.
Population: High school students desiring credit for college-level courses and admission to advanced courses.
Publication Dates: 1954–1999.

Acronym: AP®.

Scores: 32 tests in 18 subject areas: Art History, Studio Art (2 portfolios: Drawing and General), Biology, Calculus AB, Calculus BC, Chemistry, Computer Science A, Computer Science AB, English Language and Composition, English Literature and Composition, Environmental Science, European History, French Language, French Literature, German Language, Government & Politics—Comparative, Government & Politics—United States, International English Language, Latin Literature, Latin—Vergil, Macroeconomics, Microeconomics, Music Theory, Physics B., Physics C (2 tests: Electricity and Magnetism, Mechanics), Psychology, Spanish Language, Spanish Literature, Statistics, United States History.

Administration: Group.

Price Data: Available from publisher.

Time: 120–200 minutes.

Comments: Available to secondary schools for annual administration on specified days in May; inactive forms and previous essay/free-response sections available; program administered by the College Board and Educational Testing Service.

Author: Educational Testing Service.

Publisher: Educational Testing Service.

Cross References: See T5:118 (1 reference) and T3:124 (1 reference); for additional information and reviews by Paul L. Dressel and David A. Frisbie, see 8:471 (5 references); see also T2:1045 (4 references); for reviews by Warren G. Findley and Alexander G. Wesman of an earlier program, see 7:662 (3 references); see also 6:761 (5 references). For reviews of individual tests, see 8:112 (1 review), 8:113 (2 reviews), 8:126 (1 review), 8:153 (1 review), 8:846 (1 review), 8:862 (1 review), 6:893 (1 review), 6:1000 (1 review), 5:205 (1 review), 5:211 (1 review), 5:273 (1 review), 5:419 (1 review), 5:724 (1 review), 5:743 (1 review), 5:750 (1 review), and 5:812 (2 reviews).

[126]
Advanced Test Battery.

Purpose: "Designed for use in the selection, development, or guidance of personnel at graduate level or in management positions."

Population: Personnel at graduate level or in management positions.

Publication Dates: 1979–1983.

Acronym: ATB.

Administration: Group.

Levels, 2: Higher order aptitudes, Higher order aptitudes in a work setting.

Restricted Distribution: Restricted to persons who have completed the publisher's training course or members of the Division of Occupational Psychology of the British Psychological Society.

Price Data: Available from publisher.

Comments: Subtests available as separates; separate answer sheets must be used.

Authors: Roger Holdsworth (VA3, NA4, manual); Peter Saville (VA1, NA2, manual), Gill Nyfield (manual), Dave Hawkey (DA5, ST7, DT8), Steve Blinkhorn (VA3), and Alan Iliff (NA4).

Publisher: SHL Group plc [United Kingdom].

> *a)* LEVEL 1. 1979–1980; HIGHER ORDER APTITUDES, 3 TESTS.
>> 1) *Verbal Concepts.*
>> **Publication Date:** 1980.
>> **Acronym:** VA1.
>> **Time:** 15(20) minutes.
>> 2) *Number Series.*
>> **Publication Date:** 1980.
>> **Acronym:** NA2.
>> **Time:** 15(20) minutes.
>> 3) *Diagramming.*
>> **Publication Date:** 1980.
>> **Acronym:** DA5.
>> **Time:** 20(25) minutes.
> *b)* LEVEL 2. 1979–1980; HIGHER ORDER APTITUDES IN A WORK CONTEST; 4 TESTS.
>> 1) *Verbal Critical Reasoning.*
>> **Publication Date:** 1983.
>> **Acronym:** VA3.
>> **Time:** 30(35) minutes.
>> 2) *Numerical Critical Reasoning.*
>> **Publication Dates:** 1979–1983.
>> **Acronym:** NA4.
>> **Time:** 35(40) minutes.
>> 3) *Spatial Reasoning.*
>> **Publication Dates:** 1979–1981.
>> **Acronym:** ST7.
>> **Time:** 20(25) minutes.
>> 4) *Diagrammatic Reasoning.*
>> **Publication Dates:** 1979–1981.
>> **Acronym:** DT8.
>> **Time:** 15(20) minutes.

[127]
Age Projection Test.

Purpose: Designed as "an imagery test aimed at revealing self-images at various age [and self] levels and their associated structures of imagery functioning useful toward the understanding of a presented problem or a symptom."

Population: Adults.

Publication Date: 1988.

Acronym: APT.

Scores: No scores.

Administration: Individual.

Price Data: Available from publisher.

Time: [60–120] minutes.

Author: Akhter Ahsen.

Publisher: Brandon House, Inc.

Cross References: For reviews by Edward Aronow and Michael D. Botwin, see 12:23.

[128]
Ages and Stages Questionnaires (ASQ): A Parent-Completed, Child-Monitoring System, 2nd Edition.

Purpose: Designed to identify infants and young children who show potential developmental problems.
Population: Ages 4–48 months.
Publication Dates: 1995–1999.
Acronym: ASQ.
Scores, 5: Communication, Gross Motor, Fine Motor, Problem Solving, Personal-Social.
Administration: Group.
Price Data, 2002: $190 per complete system including 11 reproducible questionnaires, 11 reproducible, age-appropriate scoring sheets, and user's guide (165 pages).
Time: (10–30) minutes.
Comments: "A parent-completed, child-monitoring system."
Authors: Jane Squires, LaWanda Potter, and Diane Bricker.
Publisher: Paul H. Brookes Publishing Co., Inc.
Cross References: For reviews by Dorothy M. Singleton and Rhonda H. Solomon, see 14:14.

[129]
Aggression Questionnaire.

Purpose: Designed to aid in evaluating an individual's aggressive responses and ability to channel those responses in a safe and constructive manner.
Population: Ages 9–88.
Publication Date: 2000.
Scores, 7: Physical Aggression, Verbal Aggression, Anger, Hostility, Indirect Aggression, Inconsistent Responding, Total Score.
Administration: Individual or group.
Price Data, 2002: $89.50 per complete kit; $31.50 per 25 AutoScore™ answer forms; $158 per computer disk; $15 per 100 answer sheets; $45 per manual (2000, 95 pages).
Time: (10) minutes.
Comments: Updated version of the Buss-Durkee Hostility Inventory; computer scoring is available from publisher.
Authors: Arnold H. Buss and W. L. Warren.
Publisher: Western Psychological Services.

[130]
AGS Early Screening Profiles.

Purpose: Constructed to screen children for possible developmental problems or giftedness.
Population: Ages 2-0 to 6-11.
Publication Date: 1990.

Scores: 3 Profile Scores: Cognitive/Language, Motor, Self-Help/Social (Parent or Teacher), and 4 Survey scores: Articulation, Home, Behavior, Health History.
Administration: Individual.
Price Data, 2002: $314.95 per complete kit including test easel, 25 test records, 25 Self-Help/Social Profile questionnaires, Sample Home/Health History survey, 25 score summaries, tape measure, beads and string, Motor Profile administration manual (16 pages), manual (297 pages including reproducible Report to Parents and blackline masters for training examiners), and carry bag; $29.95 per 25 test records; $17.95 per 25 Self-Help/Social Profile questionnaires; $17.95 per 25 Home/Health History surveys; $11.95 per 25 score summaries; $55.95 per manual.
Time: [15—30] minutes.
Comments: Two levels of scoring: Level I scores are 6 "screening indexes" and 3 descriptive categories; Level II scores are standard scores, percentile ranks, normal curve equivalents (NCEs), stanines, and age equivalents; ecological assessment with ratings by parents and teachers as well as direct assessment of the child.
Authors: Patti L. Harrison (coordinating author and manual author), Alan S. Kaufman (Cognitive/Language Profile), Nadeen L. Kaufman (Cognitive/Language Profile), Robert H. Bruininks (Motor Profile), John Rynders (Motor Profile), Steven Ilmer (Motor Profile), Sara S. Sparrow (Self-Help/Social Profile), and Domenic V. Cicchetti (Self-Help/Social Profile).
Publisher: American Guidance Service, Inc.
Cross References: See T5:124 (1 reference); for reviews by David W. Barnett and Cathy Telzrow, see 12:24 (1 reference); see also T4:134 (2 references).

[131]
AH1 Forms X and Y.

Purpose: Designed to measure perceptual reasoning.
Population: Ages 7–11 for classroom purposes and 5–11 for research.
Publication Date: 1977.
Scores, 5: Series, Likes, Analogies, Differents, Total.
Administration: Group.
Price Data, 1993: £34.50 per 25 test booklets (specify Form X or Form Y); £9.20 per answer key; £19 per manual (28 pages); £29.90 per specimen set including booklets for Forms X and Y, manual, and scoring key.
Time: 12(40) minutes.
Comments: Downward extension of AH2/AH3.
Authors: A. W. Heim, K. P. Watts, and V. Simmonds.
Publisher: NFER-Nelson Publishing Co., Ltd. [England].
Cross References: For a review by Frank R. Yekovich, see 9:63.

[132]
AH2/AH3.

Purpose: Designed as parallel tests to measure general reasoning.
Population: Ages 9 and over.
Publication Dates: 1974–1978.
Scores, 4: Verbal, Numerical, Perceptual, Total.
Administration: Group.
Forms, 2: AH2, AH3.
Price Data: Price information available from publisher for AH2 or AH3 tests, answer sheets, marking key, AH2/3 key for examples, AH2/3 manual (1978, 47 pages), and specimen set.
Time: 28(45) or 42(65) minutes.
Authors: A. H. Heim, K. P. Watts, and V. Simmonds.
Publisher: NFER-Nelson Publishing Co., Ltd. [England].
Cross References: See T4:136 (2 references), 9:64 (1 reference), T3:149 (14 references), and 8:175 (1 reference).

[133]
AH4: Group Test of General Intelligence.

Purpose: "Designed as a group test of general intelligence."
Population: Ages 10 and over.
Publication Dates: 1955–1984.
Scores: Total score only.
Administration: Group.
Price Data: Price information available from publisher for tests, answer sheets, marking key, data supplement, manual (1970, 17 pages), and specimen set.
Time: 20(30–45) minutes.
Authors: A. W. Heim, K. P. Watts (test), V. Simmonds (test), and Anne Walters (data supplement).
Publisher: NFER-Nelson Publishing Co., Ltd. [England].
Cross References: See T5:127 (5 references), T4:137 (5 references), and T2:331 (20 references); for a review by John Nisbet, see 7:331 (12 references); for a review by John Liggett of the original edition, see 6:506; for a review by George A. Ferguson, see 5:390 (11 references).

[134]
AH5 Group Test of High Grade Intelligence.

Purpose: Designed as a test of general intelligence "for use with selected, highly intelligent subjects."
Population: "Highly intelligent pupils" ages 13 and over.
Publication Dates: 1968–1984.
Scores, 3: Verbal and Numeric, Diagrammatic, Total.
Administration: Group.
Price Data: Price information available from publisher for tests, answer sheets, manual (1983, 21 pages), and for specimen set including test, key, answer sheet, and manual.

Time: 40(60) minutes.
Author: A. W. Heim.
Publisher: NFER-Nelson Publishing Co., Ltd. [England].
Cross References: See T5:128 (3 references), T4:138 (2 references), and 9:66 (1 reference).

[135]
AH6 Group Tests of High Level Intelligence.

Purpose: Designed as tests for general reasoning ability, effecting discrimination among selected high ability groups.
Population: "Highly intelligent" individuals age 16 through college and university.
Publication Dates: 1970–1983.
Scores, 3: Verbal, Numerical Plus Diagrammatic, Total.
Administration: Group.
Price Data: Price information available from publisher for AG or SEM tests, set of 3 keys, AG or SEM answer sheets, AG/SEM manual (1983, 26 pages), and for specimen set including 1 each of AG and SEM tests.
Authors: A. W. Heim, K. P. Watts, and V. Simmonds.
Publisher: NFER-Nelson Publishing Co., Ltd. [England].
  a) SEM.
  Purpose: Intended for potential or qualified scientists, engineers, and mathematicians.
  Time: 40(70) minutes.
  b) AG.
  Purpose: Intended for historians, linguists, economists, philosophers, and all others not included for SEM.
  Time: 35(70) minutes.
Cross References: For reviews by Thomas J. Kehle and Paul Zelhart, see 10:11.

[136]
The Alcadd Test, Revised Edition.

Purpose: "Designed to: a) provide an objective measurement of alcoholic addiction that could identify individuals whose behavior and personality structure indicated that they were alcoholic addicts or had serious alcoholic problems; b) identify specific areas of maladjustment in alcoholics to facilitate therapeutic and rehabilitation activities; and c) obtain better insight into the psychodynamics of alcoholic addiction."
Population: Adults.
Publication Dates: 1949–1988.
Scores, 6: Regularity of Drinking, Preference for Drinking over Other Activities, Lack of Controlled Drinking, Rationalization of Drinking, Excessive Emotionality, Total.
Administration: Individual or group.
Editions, 2: Paper-and-pencil, microcomputer.

Price Data, 2002: $60 per complete kit including 25 AutoScore™ test/profile forms (1988, 4 pages) and manual (1988, 24 pages); $32.50 per 25 AutoScore™ test booklets; $32.50 per manual; $139.50 per microcomputer edition (IBM) including diskette (tests up to 25) and user's guide; $9.50 or less per mail-in answer sheet.
Time: (5–15) minutes.
Comments: Self-administered.
Authors: Morse P. Manson, Lisa A. Melcior, and G. J. Huba.
Publisher: Western Psychological Services.
Cross References: For reviews by William L. Curlette and Paul Retzlaff, see 11:12 (1 reference); see also T3:152 (3 references), T2:1098 (1 reference), and P:7 (3 references); for a review by Dugal Campbell, see 6:60 (6 references); for reviews by Charles H. Honzik and Albert L. Hunsicker, see 4:30.

[137]
Alcohol Dependence Scale.

Purpose: "Provides a brief measure of the extent to which the use of alcohol has progressed from psychological involvement to impaired control."
Population: Problem drinkers.
Publication Date: 1984.
Acronym: ADS.
Scores: Total score only.
Administration: Group.
Price Data: Available from publisher.
Foreign Language Edition: Questionnaire available in French.
Time: (5–10) minutes.
Comments: Test booklet title is Alcohol Use Questionnaire.
Authors: Harvey A. Skinner and John L. Horn.
Publisher: Centre for Addiction and Mental Health [Canada].
Cross References: See T5:134 (41 references) and T4:145 (5 references); for reviews by Robert E. Deysach and Nick J. Piazza, see 10:12 (1 reference).

[138]
Alcohol Use Disorders Identification Test.

Purpose: A screening procedure "to identify persons whose alcohol consumption has become hazardous or harmful to their health."
Population: Adults.
Publication Date: 1992–1993.
Acronym: AUDIT.
Scores: Total score only.
Administration: Individual or group.
Price Data, 2001: Test and manual (88 pages) are free; $75 per training module.
Foreign Language Editions: English, Japanese, Spanish, Norwegian, Romanian, Portuguese, German, Indian, French, Swedish, Russian, Catalan, and Italian.

Time: [2] minutes.
Comments: Developed by World Health Organization and validated on primary care patients in six countries.
Authors: Thomas F. Babor, Juan Ramon de la Fuente, John Saunders, O. G. Aasland, and Marcus Grant.
Publisher: World Health Organization [Switzerland].
Cross References: For reviews by Philip Ash and Herbert Bischoff, see 14:15; see T5:135 (6 references).

[139]
Alcohol Use Inventory.

Purpose: "To assess the nature of an individual's alcohol use pattern, and problems associated with that pattern."
Population: Adults and adolescents suspected of problem drinking.
Publication Date: 1987.
Acronym: AUI.
Scores, 24: Social Improvement, Mental Improvement, Manage Moods, Marital Coping, Gregarious, Compulsive, Sustained, Loss of Control, Role Maladaptation, Delirium, Hangover, Marital Problems, Quantity, Guilt and Worry, Help Before, Receptivity, Awareness, Enhanced, Obsessed, Disruption 1, Disruption 2, Anxious Concern, Receptive Awareness, Alcohol Involvement.
Administration: Group.
Price Data, 2002: $34 per 10 reusable test booklets; $33 per hand-scoring key; $50 per manual (1987, 95 pages); $27 per User's Guide: $145 per hand score starter kit including manual, test booklets, answer sheets, profile forms, and answer keys; $104 per Microtest Q preview package; $104 per mail-in scoring preview package; $15.50 per Microtest Q interpretive report; $7.50 per Microtest Q profile report; $17.50 per mail-in interpretive report; $9.50 per mail-in profile report.
Time: (35–60) minutes.
Comments: Reports are available via Microtest Q Assessment System Software as well as through a mail-in scoring service.
Authors: John L. Horn, Kenneth W. Wanberg, and F. Mark Foster.
Publisher: NCS Assessments (Minnetonka).
Cross References: See T5:136 (12 references); for reviews by Robert J. Drummond and Sharon McNeely, see 12:25 (3 references); see also T4:146 (6 references).

[140]
Algebra Test for Engineering and Science: National Achievement Tests.

Purpose: Designed to screen proficiency in trigonometry and geometry.
Population: College entrants.
Publication Dates: 1958–1961.

Scores, 2: Test 1, Total.
Administration: Group.
Price Data: Available from publisher.
Time: 50(55) minutes for Test 1; 80(85) minutes for total test.
Author: A. B. Lonski.
Publisher: Psychometric Affiliates.
Cross References: For a review by Peter A. Lappan, Jr., see 6:595.

[141]
Alleman Leadership Development Questionnaire.

Purpose: "Measures the amount of mentoring activity between individuals or in an organization or work unit."
Population: Mentors and protégés.
Publication Dates: 1982–1985.
Acronym: ALDQ.
Scores, 12: Teach the Job, Teach Politics, Assign Challenging Tasks, Career Counseling, General Counseling, Career Help, Demonstrated Trust, Endorse Acts/Views, Sponsor, Protect, Associate Socially, Friendship.
Administration: Group.
Restricted Distribution: Available for use only by those trained and certified by Leadership Development Consulting Co.
Price Data, 2002: $10 per manual (1985, 35 pages); $5 per questionnaire.
Time: (10–15) minutes.
Author: Elizabeth Alleman.
Publisher: Silverwood Enterprises, LLC.
Cross References: See T4:149 (1 reference).

[142]
Alleman Mentoring Activities Questionnaire.

Purpose: "Measures the amount, quality and impact of mentoring activity."
Population: Mentors and protégés.
Publication Dates: 1987–2000.
Acronym: AMAQ.
Scores, 10: Teach the Job, Provide Challenge, Teach Politics, Career Help, Protect, Sponsor, Counsel, Friendship, Demonstrate Trust, Total.
Administration: Group or individual.
Price Data, 2002: $10 per form; report costs and research discounts available from publisher.
Time: (10–15) minutes.
Comments: Previously listed as Alleman Mentoring Scales Questionnaire; available in paper-and-pencil or electronic format.
Author: Elizabeth Alleman and Diana Clarke
Publisher: Silverwood Enterprises, LLC.
Cross References: See T5:139 (1 reference).

[143]
Alleman Relationship Value Questionnaire.

Purpose: "Designed to measure the quality of mentoring activity."
Population: Mentors and protégés.
Publication Date: 1985.
Acronym: ARVQ.
Scores, 10: Information, Politics, Counsel, Tough Job, Career Moves, Trust, Achievements, Protection, Friendship, Overall Relationship.
Administration: Group.
Forms, 2: Mentor, Protégé.
Manual: No manual.
Price Data, 2002: $4 per questionnaire.
Time: Administration time not reported.
Author: Elizabeth Alleman.
Publisher: Silverwood Enterprises, LLC.

[144]
Allied Health Professions Admission Test.

Purpose: Developed to measure general academic ability and scientific knowledge.
Population: Applicants to 4-year allied health programs.
Publication Dates: 1979–1999.
Acronym: AHPAT.
Scores, 5: Verbal Ability, Quantitative Ability, Biology, Chemistry, Reading Comprehension.
Administration: Group.
Restricted Distribution: Distribution restricted and test administered at licensed testing centers; details may be obtained from publisher.
Price Data: Available from publisher.
Time: 165 minutes.
Author: The Psychological Corporation.
Publisher: The Psychological Corporation.
Cross References: For reviews by Alan C. Bugbee, Jr. and Richard C. Pugh, see 12:26

[145]
Alternate Uses.

Purpose: "Designed to represent an expected factor of 'flexibility of thinking' in an investigation of creative thinking."
Population: Grades 6–16 and adults.
Publication Dates: 1960–1978.
Scores: Total score only.
Administration: Group.
Forms, 2: Form B, C.
Price Data: Available from publisher.
Time: 12(20) minutes.
Authors: Paul R. Christensen, J. P. Guilford, Philip R. Merrifield, and Robert C. Wilson.
Publisher: Charlotte Mackley [No reply from publisher; status unknown].

Cross References: See T5:142 (8 references) and T4:154 (4 references); for a review by Edys S. Quellmalz, see 9:71 (3 references); see also T3:157 (21 references), 8:235 (32 references), T2:542 (94 references), and 6:542 (7 references).

[146]
The AMA DISC Survey.

Purpose: Personal styles survey that focuses on the ways in which people approach their work and relate to others within their organization.
Population: Adults.
Publication Date: 2000.
Scores: 4 styles of behavior: Directing, Influencing, Supportive, Contemplative.
Administration: Individual or group.
Price Data: Price data for test materials including Facilitator's Manual (84 pages) and Debriefing Guide (47 pages) available from Human Synergistics International.
Time: 20–25 minutes.
Author: Robert A. Cooke.
Publisher: American Management Association [distributed by Human Synergistics International].

[147]
The American Drug and Alcohol Survey.

Purpose: Designed to estimate levels of drug use in youth populations.
Population: Schools and school districts.
Publication Dates: 1989–1997.
Scores: Item scores, High/Moderate/Low Drug Involvement.
Administration: Group.
Levels, 2: Grades 4–6, Grades 6–12.
Price Data: Available from publisher.
Time: (20–30) minutes.
Comments: Results tabulated by publisher.
Authors: Eugene R. Oetting, Frederick Beauvais, and Ruth Edwards.
Publisher: Rocky Mountain Behavioral Science Institute, Inc.
Cross References: See T5:143 (1 reference); for reviews by Jeffrey Jenkins and Steven Schinke, see 12:27; see also T4:155 (1 reference).

[148]
American History: Junior High—Objective.

Purpose: Designed to assess students' general knowledge of American history.
Population: 1, 2 semesters Grades 7–9.
Publication Dates: 1963–1970.
Scores: Total score only for each test.
Administration: Group.
Scores: 12 tests: Exploration and Colonization, Revolutionary America, Foundation of a Strong Government, The Development of Democracy, Westward Expansion, First Semester Test, Division and Reunion, A Modern America, America Becomes a World Power, Post World War II, Second Semester Test, Final Test.
Manual: No manual.
Price Data, 1994: $9.95 per test book including tests and response key.
Time: Administration time not reported.
Comments: Formerly called Objective Tests in American History.
Author: John Barrett.
Publisher: Perfection Learning Corp.

[149]
American History: Senior High—Objective.

Purpose: To assess students' general knowledge of American history.
Population: 1, 2 semesters high school.
Publication Dates: 1960–1970.
Scores: Total score only for each of 13 tests: The Heritage of Colonial America, Background of the Revolutionary War/the Revolutionary War and Establishing a New Government (1763–1789), The United States Constitution, Washington's Administration Through the War of 1812, Expansion Westward and the Jacksonian Era (1815 thru 1841), Expansion/War and Reconstruction (1841–1868), First Semester Examination, The Emergence of Modern America, The United States Becomes a World Power (Spanish–American War/World War I/and Settlement 1896–1921), Prosperity and Depression (1920 thru 1940), World Leadership (1940–Present), Second Semester Examination, Final Examination.
Administration: Group.
Manual: No manual.
Price Data, 1994: $12.95 per test book including tests and response key.
Time: [50] minutes per unit test; [60] minutes per test for other tests.
Comments: Formerly called Objective Tests in American History.
Author: Earl Bridgewater.
Publisher: Perfection Learning Corp.

[150]
The American Home Scale.

Purpose: "Designed to measure the socioeconomic status of individuals and groups."
Population: Grades 8–16.
Publication Date: 1942.
Scores, 5: Cultural, Aesthetic, Economic, Miscellaneous, Total.
Administration: Group.
Price Data: Available from publisher.
Time: (35–50) minutes.
Author: W. A. Kerr.
Publisher: Psychometric Affiliates.
Cross References: See T2:1039 (5 references) and 5:596 (2 references); for reviews by Henry S. Maas and Verner M. Sims, see 3:417 (7 references).

[151]

American Invitational Mathematics Examination.

Purpose: "Provides challenge and recognition to high school students in the United States and Canada who have exceptional mathematical ability."

Population: American and Canadian high school students.

Publication Dates: 1983–2002.

Acronym: AIME.

Score: Total score only.

Administration: Group.

Manual: No manual.

Price Data: Price information available from publisher for practice examination set including past exam (specify year desired 1983–present) and solution pamphlet; other price data available from publisher.

Time: 180 minutes.

Comments: Administered annually, three weeks after the American Mathematics Competitions 12 (AMC12; 154) to students attaining a predetermined cutoff score on the AMC12.

Authors: Sponsored jointly by the Mathematical Association of America, Society of Actuaries, Mu Alpha Theta, National Council on Teachers of Mathematics, Casualty Actuarial Society, American Statistical Association, and American Mathematical Association of Two Year Colleges, and others.

Publisher: Mathematical Association of America; American Mathematics Competitions.

Cross References: For reviews by Robert W. Lissitz and Claudia R. Wright, see 11:14.

[152]

American Literacy Test.

Purpose: Constructed to assess literacy based on vocabulary.

Population: Adults.

Publication Date: 1962.

Scores: Total score only.

Administration: Group.

Price Data: Available from publisher.

Time: 4 minutes.

Author: John J. McCarty.

Publisher: Psychometric Affiliates.

Cross References: For a review by Victor H. Noll, see 6:328.

[153]

American Mathematics Competitions, Contest 8 (AMC8).

Purpose: "To increase interest in mathematics and to develop problem solving ability through a friendly competition."

Population: American and Canadian students in grade 8 or below.

Publication Dates: 1985–2001.

Acronym: AMC8.

Scores: Total score only.

Administration: Group.

Price Data, 2001: $25 per school registration fee; $10 per 10 exam booklets.

Special Edition: Braille and large-print editions available.

Time: 40 minutes.

Comments: Test administered annually in December at participating schools; test previously called American Junior High School Mathematics Examination.

Authors: Sponsored jointly by Mathematical Association of America, Society of Actuaries, Mu Alpha Theta, National Council of Teachers of Mathematics, Casualty Actuarial Society, American Statistical Association, and American Mathematical Association of Two Year Colleges.

Publisher: Mathematical Association of America; American Mathematics Competitions.

Cross References: For reviews by John M. Enger and Darrell Sabers, see 11:15.

[154]

American Mathematics Competitions, Contest 12.

Purpose: "To identify, through friendly competition, students with an interest and a talent for mathematical problem solving."

Population: High school students competing for individual and school awards.

Publication Dates: 1950–2002.

Acronym: AMC12.

Score: Total score only.

Administration: Group.

Price Data, 2002: $30 per school registration fee; $1.40 per exam (specify English or Spanish); $4 per 10 solutions pamphlets; $.51 per specimen set of prior year exams (specify year and English or Spanish); price data available from publisher for additional study aids and supplementary materials.

Foreign Language and Special Editions: Spanish, Braille, and large-print editions available.

Time: (75) minutes.

Comments: Test administered annually in February or March at participating secondary schools; test previously called American High School Mathematics Examination (AHSME).

Authors: Sponsored jointly by the Mathematical Association of America, Society of Actuaries, Mu Alpha Theta, National Council of Teachers of Mathematics, Casualty Actuarial Society, American Statistical Association, and American Mathematical Association of Two-Year Colleges, and others.

Publisher: Mathematical Association of America; American Mathematics Competitions.

Cross References: For reviews by Camilla Persson Benbow and Randy W. Kamphaus of the American High School Mathematics Examination, see 11:13; for a review by Thomas P. Hogan, see 8:252 (1 reference); see also T2:598 (3 references).

[155]
American Numerical Test.

Purpose: Designed to assess "numerical alertness and adaptation."
Population: Adults in "vocations which emphasize shop and white collar skills."
Publication Date: 1962.
Scores: Total score only.
Administration: Group.
Price Data: Available from publisher.
Time: 4 minutes.
Author: John J. McCarty.
Publisher: Psychometric Affiliates.
Cross References: For reviews by Marvin D. Glock and Richard T. Johnson, see 6:604.

[156]
The American Occupational Therapy Association, Inc. Fieldwork Evaluation for the Occupational Therapist.

Purpose: Constructed to evaluate "student competence at the completion of each Level II fieldwork experience."
Population: Occupational therapy students.
Publication Dates: 1973–1987.
Scores, 3: Performance, Judgment, Attitude.
Administration: Individual.
Price Data: Available from publisher.
Time: Administration time not reported.
Comments: Ratings by supervisor; revision of the Field Work Performance Report (T3:885).
Authors: The American Occupational Therapy Association, Inc.
Publisher: The American Occupational Therapy Association, Inc.
Cross References: For reviews by James T. Austin and Brian Bolton, see 12:28; for information on the Field Work Performance Report, see T3:885 (2 references) and 8:1107 (1 reference).

[157]
Analytic Learning Disability Assessment.

Purpose: Designed to match student learning style with instructional strategies.
Population: Ages 8-14.
Publication Date: 1982.
Acronym: ALDA.
Scores: Fail, Weak, or Solid in 77 unit skill subtests.
Administration: Individual.

Price Data, 2002: $158 per complete kit; $50 per 20 test forms including test score formulation sheet and student worksheets.
Time: (75) minutes.
Authors: Thomas D. Gnagey and Patricia A. Gnagey.
Publisher: Slosson Educational Publications, Inc.
Cross References: For a review by Marcia B. Shaffer, see 9:72.

[158]
Analytical Aptitude Skills Evaluation.

Purpose: To evaluate aptitude and potential for analyzing business problems.
Population: Entry-level and experienced candidates for positions requiring the ability to analyze business problems.
Publication Date: 1993.
Acronym: AASE.
Scores: Total Score, Narrative Evaluation, Rating, Recommendation.
Administration: Group.
Price Data, 2001: $235 per candidate; quantity discounts available.
Foreign Language Edition: French version available.
Time: (60) minutes.
Comments: Scored by publisher; must be proctored.
Author: Bruce A. Winrow.
Publisher: Walden Personnel Performance, Inc.

[159]
Analytical Reasoning Skills Battery.

Purpose: Measures high level analytical reasoning skills.
Population: Adults.
Publication Date: 1998.
Acronym: ANAL.
Scores: Total Score, Narrative Evaluation, Ranking, Recommendation.
Administration: Group.
Price Data, 2001: $150 per candidate; quantity discount available.
Time: (68) minutes.
Comments: Scored by publisher; must be proctored.
Author: Bruce A. Winrow.
Publisher: Walden Personnel Performance, Inc. [Canada].

[160]
Analytical Thinking Test.

Purpose: Designed as a self-assessment exercise in analytical thinking.
Population: Adults.
Publication Dates: 1992–1994.
Scores, 2: Situations, Proposals.
Administration: Group.
Manual: No manual.

Price Data: Available from publisher.
Time: [30–40] minutes.
Comments: Self-administered, self-scored.
Author: Training House, Inc.
Publisher: Training House, Inc.

[161]
Analyzing the Communication Environment.

Purpose: "An inventory of ways to encourage communication in functional activities."
Population: Preschool to adolescent children with severe disabilities.
Publication Date: 1993.
Acronym: ACE.
Scores: Total score only.
Administration: Individual.
Price Data, 1999: $99 per complete kit including 90-minutes VHS videotape and softbound instructor's guide (85 pages); $79 per videotape; $26.50 per manual.
Time: Administration time not reported.
Authors: Charity Rowland and Philip Schweigert.
Publisher: Communication Skill Builders—A Division of The Psychological Corporation.
Cross References: For reviews by Pat Mirenda and Sheila Pratt, see 14:16.

[162]
Ann Arbor Learning Inventory [1996 Edition].

Purpose: To evaluate competencies in visual, memory, auditory, and comprehension skills.
Publication Dates: 1977–1996.
Acronym: AALI.
Administration: Group.
Price Data, 2002: $20 per manual (specify Level A, B, or C); $15 per 10 student booklets (specify level); $8 per Level C stimulus cards.
Time: Administration time not reported.
Comments: Skill Level C in process of revision—information may be obtained from publisher; all levels available in Spanish.
Authors: Barbara Meister Vitale and Waneta B. Bullock.
Publisher: Academic Therapy Publications.
a) SKILL LEVEL A.
Population: Grades K–1.
Scores, 7: Body Image, Visual Discrimination, Visual Motor Coordination, Visual Sequential Memory, Auditory Discrimination, Auditory Sequential Memory, Auditory Conceptual Memory.
b) SKILL LEVEL B.
Population: Grades 2–4.
Scores, 6: Visual Discrimination, Visual Motor Coordination, Visual Sequential Memory, Audi-

tory Sequential Memory, Auditory Discrimination, Auditory Comprehension.
c) SKILL LEVEL C.
Population: Grades 5–8.
Comments: In process of revision; information available from publisher.
Cross References: For reviews by June Ellen Shepherd and Ruth E. Tomes of an earlier edition, see 11:16.

[163]
The ANSER System—Aggregate Neurobehavioral Student Health and Educational Review [Revised 1997].

Purpose: Designed as a system of collecting and integrating information from several sources about children suspected of having developmental and/or behavioral problems.
Population: Children ages 3+, suspected of having learning difficulties.
Publication Dates: 1980–1997.
Acronym: The ANSER System.
Scores: Not scored; questionnaires cover the following areas: Parent Questionnaires (Identifying Information, Initial Background Information, Possible Pregnancy Problems, Newborn Infant Problems, Health Problems or Conditions, Early Life Problems, Early Development, Family History), Attention Control Inventory (Skills and Interests, Attention Problems, Additional Behavior Traits, Behavioral Strengths, Open-Ended Comments), School Questionnaires (Identifying Information, Difficulties and Strengths, Specific Questions, School Facilities and Programs, Previous Reports and Assessments, Developmental Functions, Attention Control Inventory, Additional Behavior Traits, Open-Ended Comments), Self-Administered Student Profile (Attention, Language Function, Spatial Motor Function, Graphomotor Function, Gross Motor Function, Memory Function, Temporal-Sequential Ordering, Efficiency, Affect, Outlook, Academic Skills, Social Function, Weekend Activities, Strengths and Weaknesses, Open-Ended Comments), Self-Administered Follow-Up Profile ("How I Think I'm Doing").
Administration: Individual.
Forms, 6: Form 1 (Ages 3–5), Form 2 (Ages 6–11), Form 3 (Ages 12+), Form 4 (Ages 9+), Form 5 (All ages), Form 6 (Ages 9+).
Price Data, 2001: $16.65 per Interpreter's Guide (1997, 56 pages); $16.65 per specimen set; $32.75 each per Forms 1–3 (Parent Questionnaire); $27.25 each per Forms 1–3 (School Questionnaire); $26.25 each per Form 4; $26.45 per 24 edach of Forms 5P and 5S or Form 6; quantity discounts available.
Time: Administration time not reported.
Comments: A series of questionnaires to be completed by parents, school personnel, and students.
Author: Melvin D. Levine.

Publisher: Educators Publishing Service, Inc.
Cross References: For reviews by Robert G. Harrington and Kenneth W. Howell of an earlier edition, see 9:74.

[164]
Antisocial Psychopathy Screening Device.
Purpose: Designed to detect psychopathy or antisocial personality disorders in young populations.
Population: Ages 6–13.
Publication Date: 2001.
Acronym: APSD.
Scores, 4: Callous/Unemotional, Impulsivity, Narcissism, Total.
Administration: Individual.
Price Data, 2001: $105 per complete kit including manual (2001), 25 parent forms, 25 teacher forms, and 25 Quikscore forms; $37 per manual; $27 per 25 Quikscore forms; $45 per specimen set including manual, 1 parent form, 1 teacher form, and 1 Quikscore form.
Time: 10 minutes per rater for Parent and Teacher Forms.
Comments: Individual Parent and Teacher ratings.
Authors: Paul J. Frick and Robert D. Hare.
Publisher: Multi-Health Systems, Inc.

[165]
Aphasia Diagnostic Profiles.
Purpose: "Provides a systematic method of assessing language and communication impairment associated with aphasia."
Population: Adults with acquired brain damage.
Publication Date: 1992.
Acronym: ADP.
Scores: Behavioral Profile Score plus 9 subtests: Personal Information, Writing, Reading, Fluency, Naming, Auditory Comprehension, Repetition, Elicited Gestures, Singing.
Administration: Individual.
Price Data, 2001: $164 per complete kit including 25 record forms, manual (55 pages), stimulus cards/letterboard/pointer, and carrying case; $49 per 25 record forms; $64 per manual; $54 per stimulus cards/letterboard/pointer.
Time: (40–50) minutes.
Author: Nancy Helm-Estabrooks.
Publisher: PRO-ED.
Cross References: See T5:159 (2 references); for reviews by Wilfred G. Van Gorp and Richard G. Whitten, see 13:11.

[166]
Applicant Potential Inventory.
Purpose: Designed as a pre-employment screening assessment to help determine the employability of applicants.
Population: Job applicants.

Publication Date: 1996.
Acronym: API™.
Scores, 11: Candidness, Accuracy, Customer Service, Honesty, Drug Avoidance, Employee Relations, Safety Attitudes, Work Values, Supervision Attitudes, Tenure, Employability.
Administration: Group.
Price Data: Available from publisher.
Time: (15) minutes.
Author: National Computer Systems, Inc.
Publisher: Reid London House.

[167]
Appraise Your World.
Purpose: Constructed "to measure the complexity and richness of the way individuals develop their personal worlds and make life choices."
Population: Adults.
Publication Dates: 1983-2001.
Acronym: AYW.
Scores: 29 dimensions: Emphasis (Career, Economic, Community, Interpersonal, Recreation, Travel, Nature, Palate, Arts, Practical Arts, Home, Romance, Family, Intellectual, Ideological, Physical, Emotional, Spiritual), World Dynamics (Level of Security, Level of Insecurity, Level of Satisfaction, Level of Dissatisfaction, Internal Focus of World, External Focus of World, Flexibility of Boundaries, Level of Growth, Balance of World, Level of Public Success, Level of Present Support).
Administration: Group.
Price Data: Available from publisher.
Time: (45) minutes.
Comments: Purchase and use requires training by publisher.
Authors: James T. Mahoney, Joan W. Chadbourne (test), and Robert I. Kabacoff (manual).
Publisher: Management Research Group.

[168]
Apraxia Battery for Adults, Second Edition.
Purpose: Designed to "verify the presence of apraxia in the adult patient and to estimate the severity of the disorder."
Population: Adults.
Publication Dates: 1979–2000.
Acronym: ABA-2.
Scores: 6 subtests: Diadochokinetic Rate, Increasing Word Length, Limb Apraxia and Oral Apraxia, Latency Time and Utterance Time for Polysyllabic Words, Repeated Trials, Inventory of Articulation Characteristics of Apraxia.
Administration: Individual.
Price Data, 2002: $119 per complete kit; $39 per P/E record forms; $44 per manual (2000, 46 pages); $35 per picture book.
Time: (20) minutes.

Comments: Publisher states that the "vocabulary and conceptual structure of the six subtests allows administration of the battery to adolescents and children down to about age 9"; however, the norming group included only adults.
Author: Barbara L. Dabul.
Publisher: PRO-ED.
Cross References: See T5:163 (3 references) and T4:179 (4 references); for a review by Norma Cooke of an earlier edition, see 9:77 (1 reference).

[169]
Aprenda®: La prueba de logros en español— Segunda edición.

Purpose: Designed to measure the academic achievement of Spanish-speaking students.
Publication Dates: 1990–1998.
Acronym: Aprenda 2.
Administration: Group.
Price Data, 2002: $33.90 per multiple-choice assessment kit (Preprimer–Advanced) including test booklet and directions for administering (1997, 68 pages), practice test and directions, answer document, and reviewer's edition; $17.50 per 25 practice tests and directions (Preprimer–Intermediate 3); $5.30 per single copy directions for administering practice tests (Preprimer–Intermediate 3); $13.80 per directions for administering (Preprimer–Advanced); $102 per 25 reusable test booklets (Intermediate 1–Advanced); $42.90 each per overlay keys for scoring machine-scorable answer documents (Intermediate 1–Advanced); $28.60 each per response keys (Preprimer-Advanced); $125 per 25 machine-scorable test booklets (Preprimer-Primary 3); $79.50 per 100 type 1 machine-scorable answer documents (Intermediate 1–Advanced); $6.50 per package of 25 markers/rulers (Preprimer–Advanced); $64.60 per technical manual (1998, 331 pages); $71.55 per spring or fall multilevel norms book (all levels); $21.70 per 25 preview for parents (Preprimer–Advanced, in Spanish); $21.70 per 25 understanding test results (Preprimer–Advanced); $22.80 per compendium of instructional objectives (all levels); $33.40 per guide for classroom planning (all levels); $11 per open-ended assessment kit per level across Reading, Mathematics, and Writing (Primary 1–Advanced) including one open-ended directions for administering (1997, 68 pages), and reviewer's edition; $26 per 25 open-ended test booklets for Reading, Mathematics, or Writing (Primary 1–Advanced); $32.30 per single copy scoring guides for open-ended assessments for Reading, Mathematics (Primary 1–Advanced); $9 per single copy open-ended directions for administering Reading, Mathematics, Writing (Primary 1–Advanced); $23.30 per single copy manual for Interpreting Writing (Primary 1–Advanced); Information on optional score/reporting services, package services and electronic services can be obtained by contacting the publisher.

Foreign Language Edition: Test booklets written in Spanish; content mirrors Stanford Achievement Test Series (Stanford 9; 2357).
Author: Harcourt Brace Educational Measurement.
Publisher: Harcourt Educational Measurement.
  a) PREPRIMER (PREPRIMARIO).
Population: Grades K.5–1.5.
Scores, 6: Sounds and Letters, Word Reading, Sentence Reading, Total Reading, Mathematics, Listening to Words and Stories.
Time: (140) minutes.
  b) PRIMARY 1 (PRIMARIO 1).
Population: Grades 1.5–2.5
Scores, 11: 8 multiple-choice scores (Word Reading, Reading Comprehension, Total Reading, Mathematics: Problem Solving, Mathematics: Procedures, Total Mathematics, Language, Listening), and 3 open-ended scores (Reading, Mathematics, Writing).
Time: (265) minutes.
  c) PRIMARY 2 (PRIMARIO 2).
Population: Grades 2.5–3.5.
Scores, 11: 8 multiple-choice scores (Reading Vocabulary, Reading Comprehension, Total Reading, Mathematics: Problem Solving, Mathematics: Procedures, Total Mathematics, Language, Listening), and 3 open-ended scores (Reading, Mathematics, Writing).
Time: (260) minutes.
  d) PRIMARY 3 (PRIMARIO 3).
Population: Grades 3.5–4.5.
Scores, 11: 8 multiple-choice scores (Reading Vocabulary, Reading Comprehension, Total Reading, Mathematics: Problem Solving, Mathematics: Procedures, Total Mathematics, Language, Listening), and 3 open-ended scores (Reading, Mathematics, Writing).
Time: (280) minutes.
  e) INTERMEDIATE 1 (INTERMEDIO 1).
Population: Grades 4.5–5.5.
Scores, 12: 9 multiple-choice scores (Reading Vocabulary, Reading Comprehension, Total Reading, Mathematics: Problem Solving, Mathematics: Procedures, Total Mathematics, Language, Listening, English), and 3 open-ended scores (Reading, Mathematics, Writing).
Time: (320) minutes.
  f) INTERMEDIATE 2 (INTERMEDIO 2).
Population: Grades 5.5–6.5.
Scores, 12: 9 multiple-choice scores (Reading Vocabulary, Reading Comprehension, Total Reading, Mathematics: Problem Solving, Mathematics: Procedures, Total Mathematics, Language, Listening, English), and 3 open-ended scores (Reading, Mathematics, Writing).
Time: (330) minutes.

g) INTERMEDIATE 3 (INTERMEDIO 3).
Population: Grades 6.5–8.9.
Scores, 12: 9 multiple-choice scores (Reading Vocabulary, Reading Comprehension, Total Reading, Mathematics: Problem Solving, Mathematics: Procedures, Total Mathematics, Language, Listening, English), and 3 open-ended scores (Reading, Mathematics, Writing).
Time: (330) minutes.
h) ADVANCED (AVANZADO).
Population: Grades 9.0–12.9.
Scores, 9: 6 multiple-choice scores (Reading Vocabulary, Reading Comprehension, Total Reading, Mathematics, Language, English), and 3 open-ended scores (Reading, Mathematics, Writing).
Time: (265) minutes.
Cross References: For reviews by Joseph O. Prewitt and by Maria Prendes Lintel and Francisca Esteban Peterson, see 14:18; for reviews by Maria Medina-Diaz and Salvador Hector Ochoa of an earlier edition, see 13:12.

[170]

The APT Inventory.

Purpose: Designed to measure an individual's relative strength on each of ten personal traits.
Population: Adults.
Publication Date: 1992.
Scores, 10: Communication, Analytical Thinking, Administrative, Relating to Others, Influencing, Achieving, Empowering, Developing, Leadership, Ethics.
Administration: Individual or group.
Manual: No manual.
Price Data: Price information per set available from publisher (each set includes assessment, response sheet, and interpretation booklet).
Time: (40) minutes.
Comments: Self-administered; self-scored.
Author: Training House, Inc.
Publisher: Training House, Inc.
Cross References: For reviews by E. Scott Huebner and Jayne E. Stake, see 13:13.

[171]

Aptitude Assessment Battery: Programming.

Purpose: Designed to measure programming aptitude.
Population: Programmers and trainees.
Publication Date: 1967.
Acronym: AABP.
Scores: Total score only.
Administration: Group.
Restricted Distribution: Restricted to employers of programmers, not available to school personnel.
Price Data, 2001: $290 per candidate.

Foreign Language Edition and Other Special Editions: French, Spanish, Braille, and left-handed editions available.
Time: Untimed.
Comments: Percentile and qualitative information provided in detailed report.
Author: Jack M. Wolfe.
Publisher: Rose Wolfe Family Partnership LLP [Canada].
Cross References: See 7:1087 (1 reference).

[172]

Aptitude Interest Inventory.

Purpose: To develop a plan for career exploration.
Population: High school to adult.
Publication Dates: 1993–1996.
Acronym: Aii.
Administration: Group.
Restricted Distribution: Distribution restricted to licensed sites.
Price Data: Available from publisher.
Comments: Previously entitled Career Assessment Program; tests must be computer administered and scored (Windows format).
Author: Educational Technologies, Inc.
Publisher: Invest Learning. [No reply from publisher; status unknown].
a) APTITUDE BASED CAREER DECISION TEST.
Purpose: "Used to assist individuals in selecting a career based on their aptitudes."
Acronym: ABCD.
Scores, 7: Clerical Perception, Vocabulary, Numerical Computation, Numerical Reasoning, Spatial Visualization, Inductive Reasoning, Analytical Reasoning.
Time: (100) minutes.
b) INTEREST BASED CAREER DECISION TEST.
Purpose: "Used to assist individuals select a career based on their interests."
Acronym: IBCD.
Scores: Ratings grouped into 3 areas: Data, People, Things.
Time: (30–45) minutes.
Comments: Self-report survey.
Cross References: For reviews by Albert M. Bugaj and Donald Thompson, see 13:14.

[173]

Aptitude Profile Test Series.

Purpose: Designed to assess a range of core cognitive abilities relevant to and known to predict success in many occupations and areas of study.
Population: Years 9–11 in Australian school system to adults.
Publication Date: 2000.
Acronyms: APTS and APTS-E.

Scores, 4: Abstract Reasoning, Quantitative Reasoning, Spatial-Visual Reasoning, Verbal Reasoning.
Administration: Individual or group.
Price Data, 2002: A$11 per Abstract Reasoning test; A$9 per Quantitative Reasoning test; A$12 per Spatial-Visual Reasoning test; A$9 per Verbal Reasoning test; A$15 per scoring keys; A$9.90 per 10 answer sheets; A$99 per manual (specify APTS [79 pages] or APTS-E [90 pages]); A$155 per specimen set.
Time: 30(45) minutes per test.
Authors: George Morgan, Andrew Stephanou, and Brian Simpson.
Publisher: Australian Council for Educational Research Ltd. [Australia].
　　a) APTITUDE PROFILE TEST SERIES.
　　Purpose: "Developed for use ... with assessing people's abilities in relation to employment and to occupational needs of organisations and industry."
　　Population: Adults.
　　Acronym: APTS.
　　b) APTITUDE PROFILE TEST SERIES—EDUCATIONAL.
　　Purpose: "Developed for ... assessing students' abilities in an educational context."
　　Population: Years 9–11 in Australian school system.
　　Acronym: APTS-E.

[174]
Aptitude Tests for School Beginners.

Purpose: "Obtain a differentiated picture of certain aptitudes of school beginners."
Population: Grade 1 entrants.
Publication Dates: 1974–1994.
Acronym: ASB.
Scores, 8: Perception, Spatial, Reasoning, Numerical, Gestalt, Co-ordination, Memory, Verbal Comprehension.
Administration: Group.
Price Data: Available from publisher.
Time: (390–450) minutes for full battery, (180–240) minutes for abbreviated battery.
Comments: An abbreviated battery (Reasoning, Numerical, and Gestalt subtests) may be administered to obtain total score only; revised 1994 norms include norms for all South-Africans, norms for nonenvironmentally disadvantaged children, and norms for environmentally disadvantaged children.
Authors: D. J. Swart (manuals), T. M. Coetzee (manual), Margaretha Tredoux (manual), and N. M. Oliver (manual).
Publisher: Human Sciences Research Council [South Africa].
Cross References: See T5:169 (1 reference) and T4:186 (1 reference).

[175]
Aptitudes Associates Test of Sales Aptitude: A Test for Measuring Knowledge of Basic Principles of Selling, Revised.

Purpose: Designed to aid in the appraisal of one aspect of sales aptitude, understanding and appreciation of sales techniques.
Population: Applicants for sales positions and general population.
Publication Dates: 1947–1983.
Scores: Total score only.
Administration: Group.
Price Data, 2001: $94.20 per package; $52.20 per specimen set; $12.95 per manual; $3.75 per scoring key.
Time: (20–30) minutes.
Author: Martin M. Bruce.
Publisher: Martin M. Bruce, Ph.D.
Cross References: See 6:1169 (6 references); for reviews by Milton E. Hahn and Donald G. Paterson, see 4:824.

[176]
Arabic Proficiency Test.

Purpose: "Designed to measure the general proficiency in listening and reading attained by English-speaking learners of Arabic."
Population: Postsecondary to adult.
Publication Date: 1994.
Acronym: APT.
Scores, 2: Listening Comprehension, Reading Comprehension.
Administration: Group.
Price Data, 2002: $25 per test; quantity discounts available.
Time: (125) minutes.
Comments: Multiple-choice, machine-scorable test.
Authors: University of Michigan and Center for Applied Linguistics.
Publisher: Center for Applied Linguistics.

[177]
Arithmetic Skills Assessment Test.

Purpose: "Designed to quickly determine the approximate mathematical abilities of students with unknown math skills."
Population: High school and adults.
Publication Dates: 1993–1995.
Scores, 3: Whole Numbers, Fractions/Mixed Numbers, Decimals.
Administration: Group.
Price Data, 2001: $89 per computer application including 1 CD-ROM, management, and documentation.
Time: (15) minutes.
Comments: Computerized, self-administered; available in Macintosh Version and Windows Version.

Author: Howard Behrns.
Publisher: Educational Activities Software.
Cross References: For reviews by Michael B. Bunch and Kevin D. Crehan, see 14:19.

[178]
Arithmetic Test (Fundamentals and Reasoning): Municipal Tests: National Achievement Tests.

Purpose: Constructed to assess arithmetic skills.
Population: Grades 3–6, 6–8.
Publication Dates: 1938–1962.
Scores, 6: Computation, Number Comparisons, Comparisons, Problem Analysis, Problems, Total.
Administration: Group.
Forms, 2: A, B.
Price Data: Available from publisher.
Time: 60 minutes over 2 sessions.
Comments: Subtest of Municipal Battery.
Authors: Robert K. Speer and Samuel Smith.
Publisher: Psychometric Affiliates.
Cross References: For reviews by Foster E. Grossnickle and Charles S. Ross, see 4:406. For reviews of the complete battery, see 5:18 (1 review), 4:20 (1 review), and 2:1191 (2 reviews).

[179]
Arithmetic Test: National Achievement Tests.

Population: Grades 3–8.
Publication Dates: 1936–1961.
Administration: Group.
Forms, 2: A, B.
Manual: No manual.
Price Data: Available from publisher.
Authors: Robert K. Speer and Samuel Smith.
Publisher: Psychometric Affiliates.

a) FUNDAMENTALS.
   Purpose: Constructed to assess "speed, knowledge, and accuracy in computation."
   Scores, 4: Fundamentals-Speed, Number Comparisons, Fundamentals-Skills, Total.
   Time: (55–85) minutes.
b) REASONING.
   Purpose: Designed to measure ability to compare, comprehend, analyze, and solve problems.
   Scores, 5: Comparisons, Problem Analysis, Finding the Key to a Problem, Problems, Total.
   Time: (40) minutes.
Cross References: For reviews by R. L. Morton and Leroy H. Schnell, see 2:1449; for reviews by William A. Brownell and W. J. Osburn, see 1:889.

[180]
Arizona Articulation Proficiency Scale, Third Revision.

Purpose: An "assessment measure of articulatory proficiency in children, adolescents, and adults."
Population: Ages 1-6 through 18-11 years.
Publication Dates: 1963–2000.
Acronym: Arizona-3.
Scores: Total score only.
Administration: Individual.
Price Data, 2002: $124 per kit including 42 picture cards, 25 test booklets, and manual (2000, 60 pages); $62.50 per picture cards; $19.95 per 25 test booklets, quantity discounts available; $45 per manual.
Time: (3) minutes.
Comments: Replaces the Arizona Articulation Proficiency Scale, Second Edition (AAPS); has updated picture cards, new gender-specific norms.
Author: Janet Barker Fudala.
Publisher: Western Psychological Services.
Cross References: See T5:175 (12 references) and T4:191 (4 references); for reviews by Penelope K. Hall and Charles Wm. Martin of a previous edition, see 11:17 (12 references); see also T3:200 (8 references); for reviews by Raphael M. Haller and Ronald K. Sommers, and an excerpted review by Barton B. Proger, see 8:954 (6 references); see also T2:2065 (2 references), 7:948 (2 references), and 6:307a (2 references).

[181]
The Arizona Battery For Communication Disorders of Dementia.

Purpose: To measure "the effects and severity of Alzheimer's Disease."
Population: Alzheimer's patients.
Publication Dates: 1991–1993.
Acronym: ABCD.
Scores, 6: Mental Status, Episodic Memory, Linguistic Expression, Linguistic Comprehension, Visuospatial Construction, Total.
Administration: Individual.
Price Data, 2002: $198 per complete kit including manual (77 pages), scoring and interpretation card, 25 response record forms, stimulus book A, stimulus book B, and nail and envelope; $29 per 25 response record forms; $49 per stimulus book A; $59 per stimulus book B; $14 per scoring and interpretation card; $54 per manual.
Time: (45-90) minutes.
Authors: Kathryn A. Bayles and Cheryl K. Tomoeda.
Publisher: PRO-ED.
Cross References: For reviews by Charles J. Long and Kenneth Sakauye, see 12:31.

[182]
Arlin-Hills Attitude Surveys.

Purpose: Designed to measure the attitudes of a group of students "toward Teacher, Learning Processes, Language Arts, and Mathematics."
Population: Grades K–3, 4–6, 7–12.
Publication Date: 1976.
Scores: 4 subtests: Attitude Toward Language Arts, Attitude Toward Learning Processes, Attitude Toward Mathematics, Attitude Toward Teachers.
Administration: Group.
Price Data, 2002: $8.25 per 25 survey forms (specify subtest); $1.75 per administration/scoring card; $6.75 per manual (41 pages); $9 per specimen set including one survey each for 4 subtests, administration card, and manual.
Time: (10–15) minutes.
Comments: For measurement of groups, not individuals.
Author: Marshall Arlin.
Publisher: Psychologists and Educators, Inc.
Cross References: See T5:177 (2 references), T3:201 (2 references), and 8:499 (1 reference).

[183]
Arlin Test of Formal Reasoning.

Purpose: Designed to assess "individual's ability to use the eight specific concepts associated with (Piaget's) stages of formal operations"; profiles individual as "concrete, high concrete, transitional, low formal, or high formal."
Population: Grades 6-12 and adults.
Publication Date: 1984.
Acronym: ATFR.
Scores, 9: Volume, Probability, Correlations, Combinations, Propositions, Momentum, Mechanical Equilibrium, Frames of Reference, Total.
Administration: Group.
Price Data, 2002: $69 per complete kit; $37 per 35 test question booklets; $12 per 35 answer sheets; $5 per hand-scoring template; $15 per manual (28 pages).
Time: (45–50) minutes.
Author: Patricia Kennedy Arlin.
Publisher: Slosson Educational Publications, Inc.
Cross References: See T5:178 (1 reference) and T4:194 (3 references); for a review by Toni E. Santmire, see 9:80 (5 references).

[184]
Armed Services-Civilian Vocational Interest Survey.

Purpose: Designed to assess interest in careers in the armed-services and related civilian jobs.
Population: Grades 11—12.
Publication Date: 1983.
Acronym: ASCVIS.

Scores: Ratings in 8 occupational groups: Administrative/Clerical/Personnel, Communications, Computer and Data-Processing, Construction/Engineering/Craft, Mechanical/Repairer/Machining, Service and Transportation, Health and Health Care, Scientific/Technical/Electronic.
Administration: Group.
Price Data: Available from publisher.
Time: (30) minutes.
Comments: Self-administering and self-scoring; may be used in conjunction with the ASVAB (185).
Author: Robert Kauk.
Publisher: CFKR Career Materials [No reply from publisher; status unknown].
Cross References: For reviews by Bruce W. Hartman and Frederick A. Schrank, see 10:13.

[185]
Armed Services Vocational Aptitude Battery [Forms 18/19].

Purpose: Intended "for use in educational and vocational counseling and to stimulate interest in job and training opportunities in the Armed Forces."
Population: High school, junior college, and young adult applicants to the Armed Forces.
Publication Dates: 1967–1992.
Acronym: ASVAB.
Scores: 3 composite scores: Academic Ability, Verbal Ability, Math Ability.
Subtests, 10: General Science, Arithmetic Reasoning, Word Knowledge, Paragraph Comprehension, Numerical Operations, Coding Speed, Auto-Shop Information, Math Knowledge, Mechanical Comprehension, Electronics Information.
Administration: Group.
Price Data: Administered free of charge at participating high schools by Department of Defense personnel.
Time: 144(180) minutes.
Comments: Several supplemental publications provide support for counseling: Counselor Manual, an interpretive guide; Technical Manual; Exploring Careers: The ASVAB Workbook; Military Careers.
Author: United States Military Entrance Processing Command.
Publisher: United States Military Entrance Processing Command.
Cross References: See T5:180 (37 references) and T4:196 (27 references); for a review by R. A. Weitzman, see 9:81 (3 references); see also T3:202 (8 references); for a review by David J. Weiss, see 8:483 (4 references); see also T2:1067 (1 reference).

[186]
Arousal Seeking Tendency Scale.

Purpose: Designed to "assess individual differences in preference for change, novelty, and risk taking."

Population: Ages 15 and older.
Publication Dates: 1978–1994.
Acronym: MAST.
Scores: Total score only.
Administration: Group or individual.
Price Data: Available from publisher for test kit including scale, scoring directions, norms, and manual (1994, 6 pages).
Time: (10–15) minutes.
Comments: Previously listed as Measure of Arousal Seeking Tendency.
Author: Albert Mehrabian.
Publisher: Albert Mehrabian.
Cross References: For a review by Gregory J. Boyle, see 13:15; for reviews by Norman S. Endler and Jon D. Swartz of an earlier edition, see 9:677; see also T3:1438 (1 reference).

[187]
Ashland Interest Assessment.

Purpose: "A career interest inventory for individuals with restricted abilities developed in response to a need for a career measure to accommodate individuals with barriers to employment due to educational, physical, emotional, cognitive, or psychiatric conditions."
Population: Adults and adolescents.
Publication Date: 1997.
Acronym: AIA.
Scores: 12 scales: Arts and Crafts, Sales, Clerical, Protective Service, Food Service, Personal Service, Health Care, General Service, Plant or Animal Care, Construction, Transportation, Mechanical.
Administration: Group or individual.
Price Data, 2001: $54 per examination kit including manual (1997, 94 pages), 10 hand-scorable question and answer booklets, 10 profile sheets, 10 scoring sheets, one set of templates, and one machine-scorable question and answer booklet for an extended report; $2 per test manual; $18–$20.50 (depending on volume) per 25 hand-scorable question and answer booklets; $19–$22 (depending on volume) per 25 response sheets (including 25 scoring sheets and 25 profile sheets); $23 per set of templates; $59–$66 (depending on volume) per 10 machine-scorable question and answer documents for extended reports; $99 per software package including disks, software manual for Windows, test manual, and 10 coupons for computer report.
Time: (35) minutes.
Foreign Language Edition: Hand-scorable and machine-scorable question and answer booklets and extended reports available in French.
Comments: Scored by self, publisher, or computer.
Authors: Douglas N. Jackson and Connie W. Marshall.
Publisher: Sigma Assessment Systems, Inc.

Cross References: For reviews by Richard J. McCowan and Sheila C. McCowan and by Mary Roznowski, see 14:20.

[188]
ASIST: A Structured Addictions Assessment Interview for Selecting Treatment.

Purpose: To assess alcohol and drug use for the purpose of selecting treatment.
Population: Adults.
Publication Dates: 1984–1990.
Acronym: ASIST.
Scores: 12 sections: Identifying Information, Basic Information, Alcohol Use, Psychoactive Drug Use, Health Screening, Other Life Areas, Previous Treatment, Client Preference for Treatment, Treatment Assessment Summary, Treatment Plan, Actual Referrals, Assessment Worker's Observation.
Administration: Individual.
Price Data, 2002: C$25 per 10 questionnaires; C$35 per Assessment Handbook (1990, 200 pages).
Time: Administration time not reported.
Author: Addiction Research Foundation.
Publisher: Centre for Addiction and Mental Health [Canada].
Cross References: For reviews by Wesley E. Sime and by Nicholas A. Vacc and Gerald A. Juhnke, see 13:16.

[189]
Asperger Syndrome Diagnostic Scale.

Purpose: "Designed to assess individuals who manifest the characteristics of Asperger syndrome."
Population: Ages 5–18.
Publication Date: 2001.
Acronym: ASDS.
Scores, 6: Language, Social, Maladaptive, Cognitive, Sensorimotor, Total.
Administration: Individual.
Price Data, 2001: $89 per complete kit; $39 per 50 summary response forms; $52 per examiner's manual (2001, 39 pages).
Time: (10–15) minutes.
Comments: Ratings by parents, teachers, and professionals at home and school.
Authors: Brenda Smith Myles, Stacey Jones Bock, and Richard L. Simpson.
Publisher: PRO-ED.

[190]
The Assertiveness Skills Inventory.

Purpose: Developed to measure an individual's level of assertiveness.
Population: Adults.
Publication Date: 1997.
Acronym: ASI.

Scores: Total score only.
Administration: Group.
Manual: No manual; scoring/instruction sheet available.
Price Data: Available from publisher.
Time: Administration time not reported.
Author: Millard J. Bienvenu.
Publisher: Millard J. Bienvenu, Northwest Publications.

[191]
ASSESS Expert Assessment System Internet Version 1.3.

Purpose: "A web-based assessment system, which incorporates intellectual abilities and work personality characteristics for selection and development of professionals and managers."
Population: Potential employees and candidates for promotion in professional, managerial, and sales positions, as well as employee development applications.
Publication Date: 1997.
Scores: Updated and shortened versions of the Guilford Zimmerman Temperament Survey (GZTS) and Dynamic Factors Opinion Survey (DFOS) provide normative results on 23 characteristics grouped in the areas of Thinking, Working, and Relating; Intellectual Ability Tests: 7 possible scores: Watson-Glaser Critical Thinking, Raven's Standard Progressive Matrices (Abstract Reasoning), Thurstone Test of Mental Alertness, Arithmetic Reasoning, Employee Aptitude Survey 1 (EAS1)—Verbal Comprehension, EAS2—Numerical Ability, EAS7—Verbal Reasoning and SHL Numerical Critical Thinking Battery.
Administration: Group or individual.
Price Data, 2002: $1,095 per one-time purchase of the initial HASP key preloaded with units for 5 administrations, ASSESS software, user's guide (85 pages), technical manual (83 pages), 1 reusable personality survey booklet, 5 personality survey answer sheets, 1 Raven test booklet, 5 Raven answer sheets, 1 Watson-Glaser appraisal booklet, 5 Watson-Glaser answer sheets, 5 Thurstone self-scoring tests, scoring keys, samples of additional ability tests; report costs vary from $42.50 to $125 depending on report type and volume; additional consulting services available to customize the report.
Time: Administration time varies for each test.
Comments: "Detailed competency-based narrative reports or general assessment narrative reports provide profile level interpretation of personality and ability scores in comparison with a professional database of 33,000 people"; graphic profile results allow for additional comparison to specific subgroups; selection reports include interview and reference probes; developmental reports include specific developmental

suggestions; career manager reports provide job search and job fit suggestions; onsite scoring; administration via paper or Internet.
Author: Bigby, Havis, & Associates, Inc.
Publisher: Bigby, Havis, & Associates, Inc.
Cross References: For reviews by Peter F. Merenda and Stephen Olejnik of an earlier edition, see 14:21.

[192]
Assessing and Teaching Phonological Knowledge.

Purpose: Designed to assess children's reading readiness and diagnose a child's reading difficulty.
Population: Young children.
Publication Date: 1998.
Scores: 5 ratings: Acquiring Implicit Awareness of Sound Patterns in Words, Segmenting Words into Sounds, Sound Blending, Manipulating Sounds Within Words, Phonemic Recoding: Bridging to Written Words.
Administration: Individual.
Forms, 3: Screening Checklist, Parental Referral Form, Profile Sheet.
Price Data, 2002: A$89 per starter set including manual (144 pages), record book, checklist, and task sheets; A$49 per manual; A$20 per record book; A$16 per checklist; A$18 per task sheets.
Time: Administration time not reported.
Author: John Munro.
Publisher: Australian Council for Educational Research Ltd. [Australia].
Cross References: For reviews by Rebecca McCauley and Steven A. Stahl, see 14:22.

[193]
Assessing Motivation to Communicate.

Purpose: Designed to assess communication apprehension and willingness to communicate.
Population: Postsecondary students.
Publication Date: 1994.
Acronym: AMTC.
Scores, 5: Group Discussions, Meetings, Interpersonal Conversations, Public Speaking, Total.
Administration: Group.
Price Data: Available from publisher.
Time: Administration time not reported.
Comments: Instrument consists of two assessment tools (The Personal Report of Communication Apprehension and The Willingness to Communicate) administered on a Macintosh computer, Operating System 7.0 or higher.
Author: Speech Communication Association.
Publisher: National Communication Association.
Cross References: For reviews by Ric Brown and Claudia R. Wright, see 14:23.

[194]
Assessing Your Team: Seven Measures of Team Success.

Purpose: Intended to give insight and understanding in assessing a team.
Population: Teams.
Publication Date: 1994.
Scores, 7: Purpose, Role, Strategy, Processes, People, Feedback, Interfaces.
Administration: Group.
Price Data, 1997: $24.95 per package including Team Leader's manual (38 pages) and Team Member's manual (31 pages); $9.95 per Team Member's manual.
Time: [.5] day.
Authors: Dick Richards and Susan Smyth.
Publisher: Jossey-Bass, A Wiley Company.
Cross References: For a review by Peter F. Merenda, see 14:24.

[195]
Assessment for Persons Profoundly or Severely Impaired.

Purpose: Designed to measure the responsiveness of a preverbal individual's communicative functioning.
Population: Infants through adults who are preverbal and functioning with a mental age between approximately 0 and 8 months.
Publication Dates: 1984–1998.
Acronym: APPSI.
Administration: Individual.
Price Data, 2002: $149 per complete kit including examiner's manual (1998, 31 pages), 25 record booklets, 25 profile/summary forms, set of cards, and other manipulatives; $44 per examiner's manual; $44 per 25 record booklets; $24 per 25 profile/summary forms; $44 per object kit.
Time: Untimed.
Comments: A revision of the Preverbal Assessment—Intervention Profile (T4:2093).
Authors: Patricia Connard and Sharon Bradley-Johnson.
Publisher: PRO-ED.
a) STAGE I.
Population: Mental age 0–1 month.
Scores: 4 domains: Visual Responsiveness, Auditory Responsiveness, Tactile Responsiveness, Interaction with Others.
b) STAGE II.
Population: Mental age 1–4 months.
Scores: Same as *a* above.
c) STAGE III.
Population: Mental age 4–8 months.
Scores: 2 domains: Responsiveness to Objects, Interaction with Others.

Cross References: For reviews by Karen T. Carey and Joe Olmi of the earlier edition, see 11:301.

[196]
Assessment in Nursery Education.

Purpose: Designed to assess and evaluate development and performance of nursery children.
Population: Ages 3–5.
Publication Date: 1978.
Acronym: ANE.
Scores: Assessment in 5 areas: Social Skills and Social Thinking, Talking and Listening, Thinking and Doing, Manual and Tool Skills, Physical Skills.
Administration: Individual.
Price Data: Price information available from publisher for complete kit including 1 individual record form, 1 colour selection booklet, set of shapes and patterns, and manual (174 pages).
Time: Administration time not reported.
Comments: Two assessment methods: teacher's observation, children's performance tasks; accessories include video recordings.
Authors: Margaret Bate and Marjorie Smith.
Publisher: NFER-Nelson Publishing Co., Ltd. [England].
Cross References: For reviews by Robert P. Anderson and Phyllis L. Newcomer, see 9:85.

[197]
Assessment Inventory for Management.

Purpose: "For screening candidates for insurance field sales management positions."
Population: Managers.
Publication Dates: 1991–1993.
Acronym: AIM.
Scores, 19: 7 Job Task Areas [Basic Task Areas (Staffing/Recruiting and Selection, Training, Performance Management—Supervision, Total); Advanced Task Areas (Business Management, Field Office Development, Total)]; 12 Job Behaviors [Interpersonal Relations (Communicating, Counseling, Supporting), Leadership (Delegating, Motivating, Rewarding, Team Building, Networking), Organization (Coordinating, Monitoring, Planning, Problem-Solving and Decision-Making)].
Administration: Group.
Price Data: Available from publisher.
Foreign Language Edition: French Canadian edition (1992) available.
Time: (120–180) minutes.
Comments: Mail-in scoring.
Author: LIMRA International.
Publisher: LIMRA International.
Cross References: For reviews by Connie Kubo Della-Piana and Gabriel M. Della-Piana and by Cyril J. Sadowski, see 13:17.

[198]
Assessment of Adaptive Areas.

Purpose: Designed to identify deficits in 10 adaptive skill areas of mental retardation.
Population: Ages 3–60+ years.
Publication Date: 1996.
Acronym: AAA.
Scores: Communication, Self-Care, Home-Living, Social, Community Use, Self-Direction, Health and Safety, Functional Academics, Leisure, Work.
Administration: Individual.
Price Data, 2001: $98 per complete kit including examiner's manual (143 pages) and 25 Profile/Examiner Record Booklets; $46 per examiner's manual; $54 per 25 Profile/Examiner Record Booklets.
Time: (30) minutes.
Comments: The AAA is a system of reassigning the items from the AAMR Adaptive Behavior Scale—Residential and Community: Second Edition (2) and the AAMR Adaptive Behavior Scale—School: Second Edition (3) into the 10 adaptive skill areas delineated by the American Association on Mental Retardation.
Authors: Brian R. Bryant, Ronald L. Taylor, and Diane Pedrotty Rivera.
Publisher: PRO-ED.
Cross References: For reviews by Jack A. Cummings and by Mark D. Shriver and Merilee McCurdy, see 14:25.

[199]
The Assessment of Aphasia and Related Disorders, Second Edition.

Purpose: Provides "insight into the patient's functioning and [serves] as a bridge to relating test scores to the common aphasic syndromes recognized by neurologists."
Population: Aphasic patients, ages 5.5–59.
Publication Dates: 1972–1983.
Administration: Individual.
Price Data: Price data available from publisher for complete kit including both tests, scoring booklets, and manual (1983, 140 pages).
Publisher: Lippincott Williams & Wilkins.
   a) BOSTON DIAGNOSTIC APHASIA EXAMINATION.
   Scores, 45: Severity Rating, Fluency (Articulation Rating, Phrase Length, Melodic Line, Verbal Agility), Auditory Comprehension (Word Discrimination, Body-Part Identification, Commands, Complex Ideational Material), Naming (Responsive Naming, Confrontation Naming, Animal Naming), Oral Reading (Word Reading, Oral Sentence Reading), Repetition (Repetition of Words, High-Probability, Low-Probability), Paraphasia (Neologistic, Literal, Verbal, Extended), Automatic Speech (Automatized Sequences, Reciting), Reading Comprehension (Symbol Discrimination, Word Recognition, Comprehension of Oral Spelling, Word-Picture Matching, Reading Sentences and Paragraphs), Writing (Mechanics, Serial Writing, Primer-Level Dictation, Spelling to Dictation, Written Confrontation Naming, Sentences to Dictation, Narrative Writing), Music (Singing, Rhythm), Spatial and Computational (Drawing to Command, Stick Memory, 3-D Blocks, Total Fingers, Right-Left, Map Orientation, Arithmetic, Clock Setting); plus 8 ratings: Melodic Line, Phrase Length, Articulatory Agility, Grammatical Form, Paraphasia in Running Speech, Repetition, Word Finding, Auditory Comprehension.
   Price Data, 2001: $20 per 25 examination booklets (1983, 31 pages); $7.50 per set of 16 test stimulus cards.
   Time: (75–100) minutes.
   Authors: Harold Goodglass with the collaboration of Edith Kaplan.
   b) BOSTON NAMING TEST.
   Population: Ages 5.5–59.
   Scores: Total score only.
Price Data: $12.50 per test (1983, 64 pages); $10 per 25 scoring booklets (1983, 8 pages).
Time: Administration time not reported.
Authors: Edith Kaplan, Harold Goodglass, and Sandra Weintraub.
Cross References: See T5:199 (18 references) and T4:207 (105 references); for reviews by Rita Sloan Berndt and Malcolm R. McNeil of *a* only, see 10:15 (3 references); see 9:86 (2 references); see also T3:308 (28 references) of *a* only; for reviews by Daniel R. Boone and Manfred J. Meier of *a* only, see 8:955 (1 reference).

[200]
Assessment of Chemical Health Inventory.

Purpose: "Designed to evaluate the nature and extent of adolescent and adult chemical use and associated problems."
Population: Adolescents, adults.
Publication Dates: 1988–1992.
Acronym: ACHI.
Scores: 9 factors (Chemical Involvement, Alienation, Family Estrangement, Personal Consequence, Depression, Family Support, Social Impact, Self Regard, Family Chemical Use) yielding Total score.
Administration: Individual.
Price Data: Price available from publisher for starter set including microcomputer disk containing 25 administrations and user manual (1992, 119 pages); response forms; microcomputer disk (sold in multiples of 50) to administer and score ACHI; manual.
Time: (15–25) minutes.

Comments: Requires 4th grade reading level; may be taken and scored on computer (or administered on paper); mail-in service available.
Authors: Daniel Krotz, Richard Kominowski, Barbara Berntson, and James W. Sipe.
Publisher: RENOVEX Corporation.
Cross References: For reviews by Philip Ash and Betsy Waterman, see 13:18.

[201]
Assessment of Competencies for Instructor Development.

Purpose: To measure six competencies important to being an effective instructor in an industrial setting.
Population: Instructors in industrial settings.
Publication Date: 1986.
Scores, 7: Analyzing the Needs and "Entering Behavior" of the Learner, Specifying Outcomes and "Terminal Behaviors" for a Course, Designing Instructional Sequences and Learning Materials, Instructing in Both the Inductive and Deductive Modes, Maintaining Adult-to-Adult (not "Parent-Child") Relationships in Class, Staying Learner-Centered not Information-Centered, Overall Instructional Competency.
Administration: Individual or group.
Manual: No manual.
Price Data: Price information available from publisher for 20 tests, 20 interpretation brochures, and 20 response sheets.
Time: (45) minutes.
Comments: Self-administered, self-scored.
Author: Training House, Inc.
Publisher: Training House, Inc.
Cross References: For a review by Stephen F. Davis, see 11:20.

[202]
Assessment of Conceptual Organization (ACO): Improving Writing, Thinking, and Reading Skills.

Purpose: Developed to assess "understanding of conceptual organization in written language."
Population: Grades 4-6, 7-12, 10-adult.
Publication Date: 1991.
Acronym: ACO.
Scores: 3 criteria: Correct Superordinate Word Chosen, Appropriateness of Topic Sentence, Relatedness of Topic Sentence and Three Other Sentences.
Administration: Group.
Price Data, 2001: $4.99 per set of 20 assessment and 20 scoring forms (select level); $9.99 per manual (57 pages).
Time: (15-20) minutes.
Comments: Optional administration and scoring procedures available for "reluctant" writers.
Author: Christian Gerhard.

Publisher: Research for Better Schools, Inc.
Cross References: For reviews by Deborah L. Bandalos and Dale P. Scannell, see 12:34.

[203]
Assessment of Core Goals.

Purpose: Constructed to define core goals and to identify activities that will lead to satisfaction of these goals.
Population: High school and over.
Publication Date: 1991.
Acronym: ACG.
Scores: No scores.
Administration: Group or individual.
Price Data, 2001: $25 per sampler set including manual (33 pages) and workbook; $125 per one-year permission to reproduce up to 200 administrations of the workbook.
Time: (60-600) minutes.
Comments: Method and length of administration depends on desired depth of information.
Author: C. W. Nichols.
Publisher: Distributed by Mind Garden, Inc.
Cross References: For reviews by Gary J. Dean and Carol Kehr Tittle, see 12:35.

[204]
Assessment of Individual Learning Style: The Perceptual Memory Task.

Purpose: "To provide measures of the individual's perception and memory for spatial relationships; visual and auditory sequential memory; intermediate term memory; and discrimination of detail."
Population: Ages 4 and over.
Publication Dates: 1984–1993.
Acronym: PMT.
Scores: 7 scores, 3 alternate scores: Spatial Relations, Visual Designs Recognition, Visual Designs-Sequencing, Auditory-Visual Colors Recognition, Auditory-Visual Colors Sequencing, Discrimination Recall, Total PMT, Visual-Visual (alternate), Auditory-Auditory (alternate), Visual-Auditory (alternate).
Administration: Individual.
Price Data, 2002: $450 per complete kit including carrying case containing various subtest components, 25 scoring forms, 25 alternate forms, and manual (129 pages); $29 per 25 scoring forms; $17.50 per 25 alternate forms; $60 per manual; $350 per PMT computer report.
Time: (30–40) minutes.
Comments: PMT Computer Report (1993) is available for IBM or Macintosh and for use in profiling PMT scores for ages 14 through adult.
Author: Lawrence McCarron.
Publisher: McCarron-Dial Systems.
Cross References: For reviews by Steven Ferrara and Arlene Coopersmith Rosenthal, see 11:21 (1 reference).

[205]
Assessment of Intelligibility of Dysarthric Speech.

Purpose: Designed "to provide clinicians and researchers with a means of measuring intelligibility and speaking rate of dysarthric individuals."
Population: Adult and adolescent dysarthric speakers.
Publication Dates: 1981–1984.
Acronym: AIDS.
Scores, 6: Single Word Intelligibility (Transcription, Multiple Choice), Sentence Intelligibility (Transcription, Speaking Rate, Rate of Intelligible Speech, Communication Efficiency Ratio).
Administration: Individual.
Price Data, 2001: $98 per complete kit including examiner's manual (60 pages) and picture book of stimulus words and sentences.
Time: Administration time not reported.
Authors: Kathryn M. Yorkston, David R. Beukelman, and Charles Traynor.
Publisher: PRO-ED.
Cross References: See T5:209 (5 references) and T4:217 (3 references); for reviews by Katharine G. Butler and C. Dale Carpenter, see 10:19.

[206]
Assessment of Language-Related Functional Activities.

Purpose: Designed to answer the question, "Despite this person's impairment, is he or she able to integrate skills adequately to perform selected functional daily activities?"
Population: People with suspected language or cognitive compromise, aged 16 to 95.
Publication Date: 1999.
Acronym: ALFA.
Scores, 10: Telling Time, Counting Money, Addressing an Envelope, Solving Daily Math Problems, Writing a Check and Balancing a Checkbook, Understanding Medicine Labels, Using a Calendar, Reading Instructions, Using the Telephone, Writing a Phone Message.
Administration: Individual.
Price Data, 2001: $154 per complete kit; $34 per materials kit; $26 per profile/examiner record forms; $54 per picture book; $44 per examiner's manual (1999, 39 pages).
Time: (30–120) minutes.
Authors: Kathleen Anderson Baines, Heidi McMartin Heeringa, and Ann W. Martin.
Publisher: PRO-ED.

[207]
Assessment of Living Skills and Resources.

Purpose: Assesses "daily tasks that require a high level of cognitive function," or Instrumental Activities of Daily Living (IADLs), "in community-dwelling elders."

Population: Community-dwelling elders.
Publication Date: 1991.
Acronym: ALSAR.
Scores: 11 task scores: Telephoning, Reading, Leisure, Medication Management, Transportation, Shopping, Meal Preparation, Laundering, Housekeeping, Home Maintenance.
Administration: Individual.
Price Data, 1994: $5 per master of the reproducible ALSAR; $55 for each of two instructional videotapes ("An Overview of IADL Assessment" and "Administration of the ALSAR"); master of the ALSAR included in the latter videotape.
Time: (15–20) minutes.
Comments: Incorporates assessment of Instrumental Activities of Daily Living (IADL); administered by health professionals from any discipline.
Authors: Theresa J. K. Drinka, Jane H. Williams, Martha Schram, Jean Farrell-Holtan, and Reenie Euhardy.
Publisher: Madison Geriatric Research, Education, and Clinical Center, VA Medical Center.
Cross References: For reviews by Cameron J. Camp and Anita M. Hubley, see 13:20.

[208]
Assessment of Parenting Skills: Infant and Preschooler.

Purpose: Designed to "evaluate the parenting skills of parents of children between birth and five years of age."
Population: Parents of children between birth and 5 years of age.
Publication Dates: 1998–2002.
Acronym: APSIP.
Scores, 13: Discipline, Fears (Stranger Anxiety, Mobility Fears, Separation Fears, Nightmares and Night Terrors, Fears of Real Events, Abstract Fears, Doctors and Dentists), Tantrums, Crying, Individual Differences and Temperament, Daily Routine, Parental Strengths and Weaknesses.
Administration: Individual.
Price Data, 2002: $189 per complete kit including 8 booklets, 8 summary sheets, and instruction manual (21 pages); $99 per 8 booklets with summary sheets; $159 per 16 booklets with summary sheets; $199 per 24 booklets with summary sheets; $119 per instruction manual.
Time: [45] minutes.
Author: Gail Elliot.
Publisher: Village Publishing.
Cross References: For a review by T. Steuart Watson, see 14:26.

[209]
The Assessment of Phonological Processes—Revised.

Purpose: Designed to identify and evaluate the severity of phonological disorders.

Population: Ages 3-0 through 12-0.
Publication Date: 1986.
Acronym: APP-R.
Scores, 13: Phonological Omissions (Syllable Reduction, Consonant Sequence Reduction, Consonant Singleton Omissions [Prevocalic, Postvocalic]), Class Deficiencies (Stridents, Velar Obstruents, Liquid-l, Liquid-r, Nasals, Glides), Total, Phonological Deviancy Score, Severity Interval Rating for Phonology; Miscellaneous Error Patterns also available.
Administration: Individual.
Levels, 2: Preschool, Multisyllabic.
Price Data, 2001: $109 per complete kit including 50 Phonological Screening Forms—Preschool, 50 Phonological Screening Forms—Multisyllabic, 50 recording forms, 50 Analysis of Phonological Processes Forms, 50 Phonological Analysis Summary Forms, and examiner's manual (92 pages); $13 per 50 screening forms; $13 per 50 recording forms; $13 per 50 analysis forms; $13 per 50 analysis summary forms; $34 per examiner's manual; $36 per object kit.
Time: (15-20) minutes.
Author: Barbara Williams Hodson.
Publisher: PRO-ED.
Cross References: See T5:214 (19 references); for reviews by Allan O. Diefendorf, Michael K. Wynne, and Kathy Kessler and by Kathryn W. Kenney, see 12:36; also T4:220 (4 references); for a review by Sheldon L. Stick of an earlier version, see 9:91 (1 reference).

[210]
Assessment of Practices in Early Elementary Classrooms.

Purpose: "Designed to evaluate the use of developmentally appropriate practices in early elementary classrooms" "that include children with disabilities."
Population: Kindergarten through Grade 3 classrooms.
Publication Date: 2001.
Acronym: APEEC.
Scores: Total score only.
Administration: Group or individual.
Manual: No manual.
Price Data, 2002: $11.95 per booklet (39 pages).
Time: Administration time not reported.
Comments: Assesses three domains of classroom practices: physical environment, curriculum and instruction, social context.
Authors: Mary Louise Hemmeter, Kelly L. Maxwell, Melinda Jones Ault, and John W. Schuster.
Publisher: Teachers College Press.

[211]
Assessment of Qualitative and Structural Dimensions of Object Representations, Revised Edition.

Purpose: Designed to measure aspects of an individual's conceptualization of others.

Population: Adolescents and adults (patients and normals).
Publication Dates: 1981–1992.
Acronym: AQSDOR.
Scores: Ratings in 4 areas: Personal Qualities, Degree of Ambivalence in Description, Length of Description, Conceptual Level.
Administration: Group.
Price Data: Available from publisher.
Time: (5) minutes per description.
Comments: Subjects' descriptions of significant figures (e.g., parent) rated by judges; no reading by examinees.
Authors: Sidney J. Blatt, Eve S. Chevron, Donald M. Quinlan, Carrie E. Schaffer, and Steven Wein.
Publisher: Sidney J. Blatt.
Cross References: For a review by C. H. Swensen, see 9:92.

[212]
Assessment of School Needs for Low-Achieving Students: Staff Survey.

Purpose: Designed to measure "staff perceptions as to whether certain behaviors are occurring in their school."
Population: Teachers and administrators.
Publication Dates: 1988–1989.
Acronym: ASNLAS.
Scores, 9: School Programs and Policies, Classroom Management, Instruction, Teacher Expectations, Principal Leadership, Staff Development, Student Involvement in Learning, School Climate, Parent Involvement.
Administration: Group.
Price Data, 2001: $2 per survey booklet; $.25 per scoring form; $18.95 per manual (1989, 44 pages).
Time: (45–50) minutes.
Authors: Francine S. Beyer and Ronald L. Houston.
Publisher: Research for Better Schools, Inc.
Cross References: For a review by Dean H. Nafziger and Ann M. Muench, see 11:22.

[213]
Assessor Employment Values Inventory.

Purpose: "A measure of personal values associated with work and the working environment."
Population: Adults.
Publication Dates: 1988–2001.
Scores, 14: Work Ethic, Social Outgoingness, Risk-Taking, Stability, Responsibility, Need For Achievement, Task Orientation, Leadership, Training and Development, Innovation, Intellectual Demands, Status, Structure, Inclusion.
Administration: Individual or group.
Price Data: Available from publisher.
Time: (30–40) minutes.

Comments: Computer administration and scoring available; test previously listed as Employment Values Inventory.
Author: Selby MillSmith Limited.
Publisher: Penna Assessment [England].
Cross References: For reviews by Julie A. Allison and Nambury S. Raju, see 14:139.

[214]
Assessor Occupational Relationships Profile.

Purpose: Designed to assess a person's preferred styles of working with colleagues.
Population: Adults.
Publication Dates: 1991–2001.
Scores, 18: Core Scales (Contact at Work, Membership, Power, Responsiveness, Openness, Shyness); Composite Scales (Sociability, Proactivity); Special Scales (Team, Individual, Leadership Overall, Leadership-Coach, Leadership-Fighter, Leadership-Expert, Preferred Style of Leader Overall, Preferred Style of Leader-Coach, Preferred Style of Leader-Fighter, Preferred Style of Leader-Expert).
Administration: Individual or group.
Price Data: Available from publisher.
Time: (30) minutes.
Comments: Computer administration and scoring available; previously listed as Occupational Relationships Profile.
Author: Selby MillSmith, Ltd.
Publisher: Penna Assessment [England].
Cross References: For a review by Robert W. Hiltonsmith, see 13:215.

[215]
Assessor Occupational Type Profile.

Purpose: Designed to measure individual's preferences related to the manner in which they acquire information and make decisions based on that information.
Population: Adults.
Publication Dates: 1991–2001.
Scores, 5: Extraversion/Introversion, Sensing/Intuition, Thinking/Feeling, Judgement/Perception, Uncertainty.
Administration: Individual or group.
Price Data: Available from publisher.
Time: (20) minutes.
Comments: Computer administration and scoring available; previously listed as Occupational Type Profile.
Author: Selby MillSmith Ltd.
Publisher: Penna Assessment [England].
Cross References: For a review by Steven J. Lindner, see 14:261.

[216]
Association Adjustment Inventory.

Purpose: "Designed for use as a screening instrument for maladjustment and immaturity."

Population: Normal and institutionalized adults.
Publication Dates: 1959–1984.
Acronym: AAI.
Scores, 13: Juvenility, Psychotic Responses, Depressed-Optimistic, Hysteric-Non-Hysteric, Withdrawal-Sociable, Paranoid-Naive, Rigid-Flexible, Schizophrenic-Objective, Impulsive-Restrained, Sociopathic-Empathetic, Psychosomapathic-Physical Contentment, Anxious-Relaxed, Total.
Administration: Group.
Price Data, 2001: $72.05 per test package; $64.90 per IBM answer sheet/profile sheet package; $55 per set of IBM scoring stencils; $25 per set of fan type keys; $43.45 per manual (15 pages) and manuals supplement (1984, 17 pages); $76.50 per IBM format specimen set with keys; $26.50 per IBM format specimen set without keys; $49.50 per fan key specimen set.
Foreign Language Editions: Spanish and German editions available.
Time: (10) minutes.
Comments: Adaption of the Kent-Rosanoff Word List.
Author: Martin M. Bruce.
Publisher: Martin M. Bruce, Ph.D.
Cross References: For reviews by W. Grant Dahlstrom and Bertram R. Forer and an excerpted review by Edward S. Bordin, see 6:201.

[217]
Athletic Motivation Inventory.

Purpose: Constructed to measure the personality and motivation of athletes participating in competitive sports.
Population: Male and female athletes ages 13 and older and coaches.
Publication Dates: 1969–1995.
Acronym: AMI.
Scores, 14: Drive, Aggressiveness, Determination, Responsibility, Leadership, Self-Confidence, Emotional Control, Mental Toughness, Coachability, Conscientiousness, Trust, Validity Scales (Accuracy, Desirability, Completion Rate).
Administration: Group or individual.
Price Data: Available from publisher.
Foreign Language Editions: French and Spanish editions available.
Time: (40–50) minutes.
Authors: Thomas A. Tutko, Leland P. Lyon, and Bruce C. Oglive.
Publisher: Athletic Success Institute.
Comments: May be used for individual self-assessment.

a) ATHLETIC SUCCESS PROFILE.
 Publication Dates: 1968–1995.
 Acronym: ASP.
 Price Data: Available from publisher.
 Manual: No manual.

Time: (20) minutes.
Comments: Shortened version of the Athletic Motivation Inventory.
Cross References: For a review by John W. Shepard, see 12:37; for a review by Andrew L. Comrey of an earlier edition, see 8:409 (19 references).

[218]
Attention Deficit Disorder Behavior Rating Scales.

Purpose: Designed to help school personnel and psychologists make proper ADD referrals.
Population: School personnel and psychologists.
Publication Dates: 1982–1993.
Acronym: ADDBRS.
Scores, 10: Inattention, Impulsivity, Hyperactivity, Anger Control, Academics, Anxiety, Confidence, Aggressiveness, Resistance, Social.
Administration: Individual.
Editions, 2: Child, Adult.
Price Data: Not available.
Time: Administration time not reported.
Authors: Ned Owens and Betty White Owens.
Publisher: Ned Owens, Inc. [No reply from publisher. Status unknown.]
Cross References: For a review by E. Jean Newman, see 13:21.

[219]
Attention Deficit Disorder Checklist.

Purpose: Designed "to collect behavioral data" as a preliminary assessment for further in-depth evaluation.
Population: School-aged children.
Publication Date: 1990–1995.
Scores: Not scored.
Administration: Individual or group.
Manual: No manual.
Price Data, 2002: $10 per 25 checklists.
Time: Administration time not reported.
Comments: "This checklist is designed to collect behavioral data. It is not intended for diagnosis. It should be completed by adults familiar with the child's behavior in various settings—preferably the parent/guardian and the classroom teacher. It may be used for educational interveiont or as a prereferral tool for further in-depth testing."
Author: Academic Consulting & Testing Service.
Publisher: Academic Consulting & Testing Service.

[220]
Attention Deficit Disorders Evaluation Scale, Second Edition.

Purpose: Designed to provide a measure of inattention and hyperactivity-impulsivity.
Publication Dates: 1989–1995.
Acronym: ADDES.

Scores, 3: Inattentive, Hyperactive-Impulsive, Percentile Total.
Administration: Individual.
Price Data, 2002: $220 per complete kit; $27 per 50 pre-referral documentation forms; $14 per manual (School Version [1995, 44 pages] or Home Version [1995, 42 pages]); $33 per 50 School rating forms; $33 per 50 Home rating forms; $22 per 50 ADDES/DSM-IV forms; $149 per computerized manual (DOS); $35 per computerized QuickScore (Windows).
Authors: Stephen B. McCarney (test and manuals) and Angela Marie Bauer (Parent's Guide to Attention-Deficit Disorders manual).
Publisher: Hawthorne Educational Services, Inc.
a) ADDES—HOME VERSION.
Population: Ages 3–20 years.
Time: [12-15] minutes.
Comments: Child is rated by a parent/caregiver.
b) ADDES—SCHOOL VERSION.
Population: Ages 4–19 years.
Time: (15–20) minutes.
Comments: Student is rated by an educator.
Cross References: For reviews by Hugh W. Glenn and Beverly M. Klecker, see 14:27; for reviews by Deborah Collins and Stephen Olejnik of an earlier edition, see 12:38 (1 reference).

[221]
Attention Deficit Disorders Evaluation Scale: Secondary-Age Student.

Purpose: "Designed to provide a measure of those characteristics of Attention-Deficit/Hyperactivity Disorder."
Population: Ages 11.5–19.
Publication Date: 1996.
Acronym: ADDES-S.
Scores, 3: Inattentive, Hyperactive/Impulsive, Total Percentile Rank.
Administration: Individual or group.
Forms, 3: Home, School, DSM-IV.
Price Data, 2002: $171 per complete kit including 50 Pre-Referral Attention Deficit Checklists, 50 Intervention Strategies documentation forms, 50 School Version rating forms, 50 Home Version rating forms, 50 ADDES/DSM-IV forms, School Version technical manual, Home Version technical manual, Attention Deficit Disorders Intervention Manual: Secondary-Age Student, and Parent's Guide; $27 per 50 Pre-Referral Attention Deficit Checklists; $27 per 50 intervention Strategies documentation forms; $33 per 50 rating forms (specify School Version or Home Version); $22 per 50 ADDES/DSM-IV forms; $14 per technical manual (specify School Version or Home Version); $28 per Attention Deficit Disorders Intervention Manual: Secondary-Age Student; $20 per Parent's Guide; $35 per computerized Quick Score (Windows); $149 per

computerized (DOS) Parent's Guide to Attention Deficit Disorders.

Time: (15–20) minutes.

Comments: Ratings by parents/guardians and/or teachers.

Author: Stephen B. McCarney.

Publisher: Hawthorne Educational Services, Inc.

Cross References: For reviews by Helen Kitchens and Joseph G. Law, Jr., see 14:28.

[222]
Attention-Deficit Scales for Adults.

Purpose: Designed as an objective measure of attention deficit in adults.

Population: Adults.

Publication Date: 1996.

Acronym: ADSA.

Scores, 11: Attention-Focus/Concentration, Interpersonal, Behavior-Disorganized Activity, Coordination, Academic Theme, Emotive, Consistency/Long Term, Childhood, Negative-Social, Internal Consistency, Total.

Administration: Individual.

Price Data: Available from publisher.

Time: Untimed.

Comments: A 54-item, Likert-scale questionnaire to be administered in a clinical setting; self-report.

Authors: Santo James Triolo and Kevin Richard Murphy.

Publisher: Taylor & Francis [No reply from publisher; status unknown].

Cross References: For reviews by Joseph G. Law, Jr. and James C. Reed, see 14:29.

[223]
Attention-Deficit/Hyperactivity Disorder Test.

Purpose: Designed to "contribute to the diagnosis of students with Attention-Deficit/Hyperactivity Disorder."

Population: Ages 3–23.

Publication Date: 1995.

Acronym: ADHDT.

Scores: 3 subtests (Hyperactivity, Impulsivity, Inattention), plus ADHD Quotient.

Administration: Individual.

Price Data, 2001: $86 per complete kit including manual (46 pages) and 50 summary/response forms in storage box; $39 per 50 summary/response forms; $49 per manual.

Time: (5–10) minutes.

Comments: Ratings by teacher, teacher's aide, or parent.

Author: James E. Gilliam.

Publisher: PRO-ED.

Cross References: For reviews by Robert S. Miller and Anthony W. Paolitto, see 14:30.

[224]
Attention Disorders in Children: School-Based Assessment, Diagnosis, and Treatment.

Purpose: Designed to provide a rating "of the severity of the primary symptoms of [Attention Deficit Disorder]."

Population: Children with Attention Disorders.

Publication Date: 1996.

Administration: Group.

Price Data, 2002: $86.50 per complete kit including handbook (128 pages), 25 Attention Disorders Assessment Tools Forms, and 25 Attention Disorders Screening Summary Forms; $24.50 per 25 Attention Disorders Assessment Tools Forms; $19.95 per Attention Disorders Screening Summary Form; $49.50 per handbook.

Time: Administration time not reported.

Comments: Ratings by parents, teachers, and school psychologists.

Author: Richard Morriss.

Publisher: Western Psychological Services.

a) ATTENTION DISORDERS ASSESSMENT TOOLS.

Purpose: Designed to gather information regarding the primary symptoms of an attention disorder.

Acronym: ADAT.

Scores, 4: Distractibility, Impulsivity, Hyperactivity, Social Problems.

Forms, 3: School Psychologist, Parent, Teacher.

Comments: Also includes Teacher Reason for Referral Rating and Early ADD Symptoms Checklist.

b) ATTENTION DISORDERS SCREENING SUMMARY.

Purpose: Designed to "record and summarize" information to rule out Attention-Deficit Disorder.

Acronym: ADSS.

Scores: No scores.

[225]
The Attentional and Interpersonal Style Inventory.

Purpose: "Developed to measure the critical concentration and interpersonal determinants of performance."

Population: Adults and adolescents.

Publication Dates: 1993–1996.

Acronym: TAIS.

Scores: 18 scales: Attentional (Broad External Awareness, External Distractibility, Conceptual/Analytical, Internal Distractibility, Narrow/Focused, Reduced Flexibility), Interpersonal (Information Processing, Orientation Toward Rules and Risk/Impulse Control, Need for Control, Self Esteem, Physical Competitiveness,

Decision Making Speed, Extroversion, Introversion, Expression of Ideas, Expression of Criticism, Expression of Support, Self Critical).
Administration: Individual or group.
Price Data: Certification and test pricing available from publisher.
Time: [20–25] minutes.
Comments: Can be administered via pencil and paper, computer, or the internet.
Author: Robert M. Nideffer.
Publisher: Enhanced Performance Systems, Inc.
Cross References: For reviews by Phillip L. Ackerman and Eugene V. Aidman, see 14:31; see also T5:226 (2 references).

[226]
Attitudes Toward Mainstreaming Scale.

Purpose: "Developed to measure attitudes toward the integration of handicapped students into the regular classroom."
Population: Teachers.
Publication Dates: 1980–1989.
Acronym: ATMS.
Scores, 4: Learning Capability, General Mainstreaming, Traditional Limiting Disabilities, Total.
Administration: Group.
Price Data: Available from publisher.
Time: Administration time not reported.
Authors: Joan D. Berryman, W. R. Neal, Jr., and Charles Berryman.
Publisher: University of Georgia.
Cross References: For reviews by Ernest A. Bauer and Patricia B. Keith, see 12:39 (2 references); see also T4:228 (4 references); for reviews by Mary Elizabeth Hannah and Michael D. Orlansky, see 9:98 (1 reference); see also T3:224 (3 references).

[227]
Attitudes Toward Working Mothers Scale.

Purpose: "Designed to assess attitudes toward the . . . dual role of mother and worker."
Population: Adults.
Publication Date: No date on test materials.
Acronym: AWM.
Scores: Total score only.
Administration: Group.
Price Data: Free of charge for inventory, scoring instructions, and mimeographed paper on construction validation of scale (23 pages).
Time: Administration time not reported.
Authors: Toby J. Tetenbaum, Jessica Lighter, and Mary Travis.
Publisher: Toby J. Tetenbaum.
Cross References: See T4: 229 (1 reference); for reviews by Mark W. Roberts and Charles Wenar, see 9:99 (1 reference).

[228]
Attitudes Towards Guns and Violence Questionnaire.

Purpose: Designed to measure "attitudes concerning guns, physical aggression, and interpersonal conflict."
Population: Ages 6–29.
Publication Date: 2000.
Acronym: AGVQ.
Scores, 6: Total (Favorable or Unfavorable to Violence and Guns), Inconsistent Responding, Aggressive Response to Shame, Comfort with Aggression, Excitement, Power/Safety.
Administration: Group.
Price Data, 2002: $86 per kit including 25 score forms, manual, computer disk for on-site scoring, 2 PC answer sheets, 50 Aggressive Behavior checklists (25 teacher forms and 25 student forms); $32.50 per 25 answer forms; $39.50 per manual; $19.95 per 100 Aggressive Behavior checklists (teacher or student form); $85 per Windows scoring computer disk (good for 50 uses); $125 per Windows screening computer disk (good for 100 uses); $15 per 100 PC answer sheets.
Time: (5–10) minutes.
Author: Jeremy P. Shapiro.
Publisher: Western Psychological Services.

[229]
Auditory Continuous Performance Test.

Purpose: "Designed to help … identify children who have auditory attention disorders … Also yields information that will help diagnose children as having Attention Deficit/Hyperactivity Disorder."
Population: Ages 6 to 11.
Publication Date: 1994.
Acronym: ACPT.
Scores, 4: Inattention Errors, Impulsivity Errors, Total Error Score, Vigilance Decrement.
Administration: Individual.
Price Data, 2002: $109 per complete kit including examiner's manual (52 pages), test audiocassette, and 12 record forms; $16 per 12 record forms; $48 per examiner's manual; $59 per 1 test audiocassette.
Time: (15) minutes.
Author: Robert W. Keith.
Publisher: The Psychological Corporation.
Cross References: See T5:229 (1 reference); for reviews by Nadeen L. Kaufman and Alan S. Kaufman and by Joseph G. Law, Jr., see 13:22.

[230]
Auditory Memory Span Test.

Purpose: To measure a subject's ability to recall single syllable spoken words in progressively increasing series.
Population: Ages 5–8.
Publication Date: 1973.
Scores: Total score only.

Administration: Individual.
Price Data, 2002: $58.50 per kit including 200 tests, 100 each of Forms 1 and 2, and manual (6 pages); $25 per 100 copies of test (specify Form 1 or 2); $14.50 per manual.
Time: (5–7) minutes.
Comments: 2 equivalent forms: Forms 1 and 2.
Authors: Joseph M. Wepman and Anne Morency.
Publisher: Western Psychological Services.
Cross References: For a review by J. Joseph Freilinger, see 8:933.

[231]
Auditory Selective Attention Test.

Purpose: Designed as "a measure of auditory selective attention."
Population: Adults.
Publication Date: 1993.
Acronym: ASAT.
Scores: Total Errors.
Administration: Individual.
Price Data, 2002: $100 per test (cassette tape); $5 per manual (15 pages).
Time: 30(35) minutes.
Comments: Stereo tape player and a pair of stereo headphones must be supplied by the examiner.
Authors: Winfred Arthur, Jr., Gerald V. Barrett, and Dennis Doverspike.
Publisher: Barrett and Associates, Inc.
Cross References: See T5:231 (1 reference); for reviews by William W. Deardorff and Judy R. Dubno, see 13:23.

[232]
Auditory Sequential Memory Test.

Purpose: Designed to assess ability to repeat from immediate memory an increasing series of digits.
Population: Ages 5–8.
Publication Date: 1973.
Scores: Total score only.
Administration: Individual.
Price Data, 2002: $58.50 per kit including 200 tests, 100 each of Forms 1 and 2, and manual (6 pages); $25 per 100 test booklets; $14.50 per manual.
Time: (5–7) minutes.
Comments: 2 equivalent forms: Forms 1 and 2.
Authors: Joseph M. Wepman and Anne Morency.
Publisher: Western Psychological Services.
Cross References: See T4:233 (1 reference); for a review by J. Joseph Freilinger, see 8:934.

[233]
Australian Developmental Screening Checklist.

Purpose: Designed to "identify children who display signs of early developmental delay."

Population: Ages 3–60 months.
Publication Dates: 1968–1994.
Acronym: ADSC.
Scores, 5: Personal/Social, Language, Cognition, Fine Motor, Gross Motor.
Administration: Individual.
Price Data: Available from publisher.
Time: (10–15) minutes.
Author: Barry Burdon.
Publisher: The Psychological Corporation [Australia].

[234]
Australian Developmental Screening Test.

Purpose: Designed to provide a brief screening measure of early developmental delay.
Population: Ages 6–60 months.
Publication Date: 1993.
Acronym: ADST.
Scores, 5: Personal-Social, Language, Cognitive, Fine Motor, Gross Motor.
Administration: Individual.
Price Data, 2001: A$539.19 per complete kit including manual (135 pages), stimulus cards, 25 record forms, and a set of toys; A$91.51 per 25 record forms.
Time: (15–20) minutes.
Author: Barry Burdon.
Publisher: The Psychological Corporation [Australia].

[235]
Australian Second Language Proficiency Ratings.

Purpose: "Designed to measure general proficiency by matching observed language behavior against global descriptions."
Population: Adolescents and adults.
Publication Dates: 1982–1984.
Acronym: ASLPR.
Scores, 4: Speaking, Listening, Reading, Writing.
Administration: Individual.
Price Data: Available from publisher.
Foreign Language Editions: French, Italian, and Japanese versions available.
Time: Administration time not reported.
Authors: D. E. Ingram and Elaine Wylie.
Publisher: Australian Department of Immigration and Multicultural Affairs [Australia].
Cross References: See T5:233 (2 references).

[236]
Autism Screening Instrument for Educational Planning, Second Edition.

Purpose: "Designed to help professionals identify individuals with autism and to provide information needed to develop appropriate educational plans."
Population: Autistic individuals ages 18 months to adult.

Publication Dates: 1978–1993.
Acronym: ASIEP-2.
Administration: Individual.
Price Data, 2001: $198 per complete kit including examiner's manual (1993, 81 pages), 25 summary booklets, 25 Autism Behavior Checklist Forms, 25 Sample of Vocal Behavior Record Forms, 25 Interaction Assessment Record Forms, 25 Educational Assessment Forms, 25 Prognosis of Learning Rate Forms, toys, manipulatives, stand, and coding audiotape for Interaction Assessment; $24 per 25 summary booklets; $49 per toys, manipulatives, and stand; $14 per coding audiotape for Interaction Assessment; $49 per examiner's manual.
Time: Administration time varies.
Comments: Subtests administered depends on results of Autism Behavior Checklist and purpose of assessment.
Authors: David A. Krug, Joel R. Arick, and Patricia J. Almond.
Publisher: PRO-ED.

   a) AUTISM BEHAVIOR CHECKLIST.
   Scores, 6: Sensory, Relating, Body and Object Use, Language, Social and Self Help, Total.
   Price Data: $14 per 25 record forms.
   b) SAMPLE OF VOCAL BEHAVIOR.
   Scores, 5: Repetitive, Noncommunicative, Babbling, Unintelligible, Total.
   Price Data: $14 per 25 record forms.
   c) INTERACTION ASSESSMENT.
   Scores, 4: Interaction, Independent Play, No Response, Negative.
   Price Data: $14 per 25 record forms.
   d) EDUCATIONAL ASSESSMENT.
   Scores, 6: In Seat, Receptive Language, Expressive Language, Body Concept, Speech Imitation, Total.
   Price Data: $14 per 25 record forms.
   e) PROGNOSIS OF LEARNING RATE.
   Scores, 5: Hand-Shaping, Random Position–A, Fixed Position–B, Fixed Position–C, Random Position–D.
   Price Data: $14 per 25 record forms.
Cross References: See T5:234 (3 references); for reviews by D. Joe Olmi and Donald P. Oswald, see 13:24 (3 references); see also T4:235 (1 reference); for reviews by Lawrence J. Turton and Richard L. Wikoff of an earlier edition, see 9:105 (1 reference).

[237]

The Autistic Continuum: An Assessment and Intervention Schedule.

Purpose: Designed to indicate the presence of autistic features and to aid in developing educational and therapeutic programs.
Population: Ages 2–8.

Publication Dates: 1987–1992.
Scores: Item scores only in 8 areas: General Observations, Attention Control, Sensory Function, Non-Verbal Symbolic Function, Concept Formation, Sequencing and Rhythmic Abilities, Speech and Language, Educational Attainments and Intelligence.
Administration: Individual.
Price Data, 1998: £60 per manual (1992, 78 pages) incorporating schedule; sample sheets are free.
Time: Untimed.
Comments: Revision of Is This Autism? A Checklist of Behaviours and Skills for Children Showing Autistic Features.
Authors: Maureen Aarons and Tessa Gittens.
Publisher: NFER-Nelson Publishing Co., Ltd. [England].
Cross References: For reviews by William M. Bart and Doreen Ward Fairbank of the earlier edition, see 12:197.

[238]

Automated Office Battery.

Purpose: Aptitude tests designed for the selection of staff to work in offices with a high degree of automation.
Population: Student and employed clerical staff.
Publication Dates: 1985–1986.
Acronym: AOB.
Scores: 3 tests: Numerical Estimation, Computer Checking, Coded Instructions.
Administration: Group.
Price Data: Available from publisher.
Time: 40(60) minutes for entire battery.
Comments: "Tests may be used individually or as a complete battery as particular requirements dictate."
Authors: Bill Mabey and Hazel Stevenson.
Publisher: SHL Group plc [United Kingdom].

   a) NUMERICAL ESTIMATION.
   Purpose: A test to measure the ability to estimate the answer to a calculation.
   Acronym: NE-1.
   Time: 10(15) minutes.
   b) COMPUTER CHECKING.
   Purpose: A test to measure the ability to check machine input information with the corresponding output.
   Acronym: CC-2.
   Time: 12(17) minutes.
   c) CODED INSTRUCTIONS.
   Purpose: A test to measure the ability to comprehend and follow written instructions when a form of coded language is used.
   Time: 18(23) minutes.
Cross References: For a review by Philip Ash, see 11:24.

[239]
The Balanced Emotional Empathy Scale.

Purpose: To measure an individual's vicarious emotional response to perceived emotional experiences of others.
Population: Ages 15 and older.
Publication Dates: 1972–1996.
Acronym: BEES.
Scores: Total score only.
Administration: Group or individual.
Price Data: Available from publisher for test kit including scale, scoring directions, norms, manual (1996, 12 pages), and literature review.
Time: (10–15) minutes.
Comments: Replaces The Emotional Emphathic Tendency Scale.
Author: Albert Mehrabian.
Publisher: Albert Mehrabian.
Cross References: For reviews by Richard W. Johnson and Susana Urbina, see 13:25.

[240]
Ball Aptitude Battery.

Purpose: For vocational guidance ecisions.
Population: High school and adults.
Publication Date: 1981.
Acronym: BAB.
Scores: Profile of 16 ability/aptitude tests: Clerical, Idea Fluency, Inductive Reasoning, Word Association, Writing Speed, Paper Folding, Vocabulary, Ideaphoria, Finger Dexterity, Grip, Shape Assembly, Analytical Reasoning, Numerical Reasoning, Numerical Computation, Associative Memory, Auditory Memory Span.
Administration: Group.
Price Data: Price information for test materials including administration manual (40 pages), technical manual (120 pages), and counselor's manual available from publisher.
Time: (10–20) minutes for most tests; (260) minutes for battery.
Author: Ball Foundation.
Publisher: Ball Foundation.
Cross References: See T5:239 (1 reference) and T4:238 (5 references); for reviews by Philip G. Benson and Wilbur L. Layton, see 9:106 (5 references).

[241]
Bankson-Bernthal Test of Phonology.

Purpose: "Designed for use by speech-language clinicians to assess the phonology of preschool and school-age children."
Population: Ages 3–9.
Publication Dates: 1989–1990.
Acronym: BBTOP.
Scores, 3: Word Inventory, Consonants Composite, Phonological Processes Composite.

Administration: Individual.
Price Data, 2001: $154 per complete kit; $74 per picture book; $39 per 25 record forms; $44 per manual (1990, 111 pages).
Time: (10-15) minutes.
Authors: Nicholas W. Bankson and John E. Bernthal.
Publisher: PRO-ED.
Cross References: See T5:240 (4 references); for reviews by Lynn S. Bliss and Lawrence J. Turton, see 12:41.

[242]
Bankson Language Test—2.

Purpose: Constructed "to establish the presence of a language disorder and identify areas in need of further, in-depth testing."
Population: Ages 3-0 to 6-11.
Publication Dates: 1977–1990.
Acronym: BLT-2.
Scores, 4: Semantic Knowledge, Morphological and Syntactic Rules, Language Quotient, Pragmatic Knowledge (optional).
Administration: Individual.
Forms, 2: BLT-2; BLT-2 Screen.
Price Data, 2001: $139 per complete kit including 25 profile/examiner's record booklets, 25 screen record forms, picture book, and examiner's manual (1990, 32 pages); $49 per picture book; $34 per 25 profile/examiner's record booklets; $16 per 25 screen record forms; $44 per examiner's manual.
Time: (30) minutes.
Comments: Revision of Bankson Language Screening Test.
Author: Nicholas W. Bankson.
Publisher: PRO-ED.
Cross References: See T5:241 (4 references) and T4:241 (3 references); for reviews by Ronald B. Gillam and Roger L. Towne, see 11:26 (4 references); for a review of an earlier edition by Barry W. Jones, see 9:107 (1 reference).

[243]
Bar-Ilan Picture Test for Children.

Purpose: "A semi-projective device to pinpoint the child's perception of his place in society, in his formal educational setting, and in his home, as well as his perception of his weaker points and of his potential for coping with life."
Population: Ages 4–16.
Publication Dates: 1982–1989.
Scores: Guidelines for analysis in 8 areas: Emotional Makeup, Motivation, Interpersonal Behavior and Areas of Conflict, Attitudes of Teachers-Parents Toward Testee, Attitudes of Peers and Siblings Towards Testee, Degree of Mastery and Feeling of Competence, Quality of Thinking Process, Activity.
Administration: Individual.

Forms, 1: 9 drawings (6 of which have different versions for boys and girls).
Price Data, 2002: $35 per set of 15 drawings; $12 per manual (1982, 49 pages).
Time: Administration time not reported.
Comments: 1989 edition is identical to 1982 edition except Appendix II was added.
Authors: Rivkah Itskowitz and Helen Strauss.
Publisher: Dansk Psykologisk Forlag [Denmark].
Cross References: See T5:242 (1 reference) and T4:242 (1 reference).

[244]
BarOn Emotional Quotient Inventory.

Purpose: Designed to measure emotional intelligence.
Population: Ages 16 and older.
Publication Date: 1997.
Acronym: BarOn EQ-i.
Scores: 21 content scores: Composite Scale Scores (Total EQ, Intrapersonal EQ, Interpersonal EQ, Adaptability EQ, Stress Management EQ, General Mood EQ), Intrapersonal Subscale Scores (Self-Regard, Emotional Self-Awareness, Assertiveness, Independence, Self-Actualization), Interpersonal Subscale Scores (Empathy, Social Responsibility, Interpersonal Relationship), Adaptability Subscale Scores (Reality Testing, Flexibility, Problem Solving), Stress Management Subscale Scores (Stress Tolerance, Impulse Control), General Mood Subscale Scores (Optimism, Happiness), plus 4 validity indicators (Omission Rate, Inconsistency, Positive Impression, Negative Impression).
Administration: Individual or group.
Price Data, 2002: $16.50 per summary report; $27.50 per development report; $40 per group report (volume discounts available); $10 per 3 item booklets (volume discounts available); $77.50 per mail-in preview package including item booklet, development report, and user's manual; $150 per user's set including user's manual, administrator's guide, and facilitator's guide; $40 per user's manual; $15 per administrator's guide; $50per facilitator's guide; $60 per technical manual (234 pages).
Foreign Language Editions: Translations available in Afrikaans, Chinese, Czech, Dutch, French-Canadian, Korean, German, Hebrew, Norwegian, Russian, Spanish (South American), Swedish, Danish, Finnish, French (Euro), Hindi, Indonesian, Italian, Japanese, Portuguese, Slovakian, and Slovene.
Time: (30–40) minutes.
Comments: Paper-and-pencil and computer administrations available.
Author: Reuven Bar-On.
Publisher: Multi-Health Systems, Inc.
Cross References: For reviews by Andrew A. Cox and Robert M. Guion, see 14:32.

[245]
BarOn Emotional Quotient-Inventory: Short Development Version.

Purpose: Designed to measure emotionally intelligent behavior in situations where a more detailed assessment is not possible or required.
Population: Age 16 and older.
Publication Date: 2002.
Acronym: BarOn EQ-I:S.
Scores, 8: Intrapersonal, Interpersonal, Adaptability, Stress Management, General Mood, Positive Impression, Inconsistency Index, Total EQ.
Administration: Group or individual.
Price Data: Available from publisher.
Time: 10–15 minutes.
Comments: Self-report.
Author: Reuven Bar-On.
Publisher: Multi-Health Systems, Inc.

[246]
BarOn Emotional Quotient Inventory: Youth Version.

Purpose: "Designed to measure emotional intelligence in young people aged 7 to 18 years."
Population: Ages 7–18.
Publication Date: 2000.
Acronym: BarOn EQ-i: YV.
Scores, 8: Intrapersonal Scale, Interpersonal Scale, Adaptability Scale, Stress Management Scale, Total EQ, General Mood Scale, Positive Impression Scale, Inconsistency Index.
Administration: Group.
Forms, 2: BarOn EQ-i:YV Long Form; BarOn EQ-i:YV(S) Short Form.
Price Data, 2002: $60 per complete kit including manual (86 pages) and 25 score forms; $40 per manual; $30 per 25 score forms; $105 per 100 score forms; $45 per specimen set including manual, 3 score forms, and 3 short version score forms; $95 per EQ-i:YV/EQ-i: YV(S) complete kit including manual, 25 score forms, and 25 short version score forms; $30 per 25 short version score forms; $105 per 100 short version score forms.
Time: (20–25) minutes.
Comments: Self-report.
Authors: Reuven Bar-On and James D. A. Parker.
Publisher: Multi-Health Systems, Inc.

[247]
Barriers to Employment Success Inventory, 2nd Edition.

Purpose: Designed to help identify personal barriers to getting or keeping a job.
Population: Adult and teenage job seekers and career planners.

Publication Date: 2001.
Acronym: BESI.
Scores, 5: Personal and Financial, Emotional and Physical, Career Decision-Making and Planning, Job Seeking Knowledge, Training and Education.
Administration: Group or individual.
Price Data, 2001: $39.95 per 25 inventories including copy of instructor's guide.
Time: (10–15) minutes.
Comments: Self-administered and self-scored; revised version features simplified language, and color-coded response and scoring tables.
Author: John J. Liptak.
Publisher: JIST Publishing, Inc.

[248]
Barsch Learning Style Inventory.

Purpose: Designed to assess an individual's learning style.
Population: Students.
Publication Dates: 1980–1996.
Scores, 4: Visual Preference, Auditory Preference, Tactile Preference, Kinesthetic Preference.
Administration: Group.
Manual: No manual.
Price Data, 2002: $14 per 10 inventories.
Time: Administration time not reported.
Comments: Intended as an "informal survey, such as would be used by teachers or education specialists to guide them in setting up an appropriate educational plan."
Author: Jeffrey R. Barsch.
Publisher: Academic Therapy Publications.
Cross References: For reviews by John Biggs and Jayne A. Parker, see 9:11.

[249]
BASC Monitor for ADHD.

Purpose: Designed to survey the primary symptoms of ADHD in a format suited to repeated assessments in order to see relationships between treatments and symptoms over time.
Population: Ages 2.5–18.
Publication Date: 1998.
Acronym: BASC Monitor for ADHD.
Forms, 2: Teacher Monitor Ratings, Parent Monitor Ratings.
Scores: 4 scales: Attention Problems, Hyperactivity, Internalizing Problems, Adaptive Skills; plus Student Observation System (13 adaptive and maladaptive behavior categories).
Administration: Group.
Price Data, 2002: $104.95 per hand-scoring set including 25 Teacher Monitor rating forms, 25 Parent Monitor rating forms, scoring templates, and manual (112 pages); $24.95 per 25 Teacher Monitor rating forms or 25 Parent Monitor rating forms; $29.95 per 25 Student Observation System forms; $209.95 per single-user complete software kit including 25 Teacher Monitor rating forms, 25 Parent Monitor rating forms, manual, and software disks (network version also available).
Time: (5–10) minutes.
Comments: Instrument is designed to supplement the BASC (280) or to be used independently; questionnaires are completed by parents and teachers; Parent Monitor Ratings form available in Spanish; BASC Monitor software available for Windows 95 or Windows NT, single-user or network versions.
Authors: Randy W. Kamphaus and Cecil R. Reynolds.
Publisher: American Guidance Service, Inc.
Cross References: For reviews by Hugh W. Glenn and Kevin M. Jones, see 14:33.

[250]
Basic Achievement Skills Individual Screener.

Purpose: "Designed to provide norm-referenced and criterion-referenced information for reading, mathematics, and spelling."
Population: Grades 1–12 and post high school.
Publication Date: 1983.
Acronym: BASIS.
Scores, 3 or 4: Mathematics, Reading, Spelling, Writing Exercise (optional).
Administration: Individual.
Price Data, 2002: $92.20 per content booklet; $81 per 25 record forms; $92.20 per manual (1983, 232 pages); $181 per examiner's kit.
Time: (50–60) minutes.
Author: The Psychological Corporation.
Publisher: The Psychological Corporation.
Cross References: See T5:246 (7 references) and T4:244 (6 references); for reviews by Robert E. Floden and Richard E. Schutz, see 9:112.

[251]
Basic Economics Test, Second Edition

Purpose: "An updated economics achievement test for curriculum development, for the assessment of student understanding, and for determining the effectiveness of educational materials and teaching strategies."
Population: Grades 5–6.
Publication Dates: 1980–1990.
Acronym: BET.
Scores: Total score only.
Administration: Group.
Forms, 2: A, B.
Price Data, 2001: $19.95 per 25 test booklets (specify Form A or B); $14.95 per Examiner's Manual (1990, 54 pages) which includes scoring keys and model answer sheet which may be duplicated locally.

Time: 30 minutes.
Authors: William B. Walstad and Denise Robson
Publisher: National Council on Economic Education.
Cross References: For reviews by Irvin J. Lehmann and A. Harry Passow of an earlier edition, see 11:27; for reviews by Mary Friend Adams and James O. Hodges of an earlier edition, see 8:901 (1 reference).

[252]
Basic English Literacy Skills Test.

Purpose: To measure the skills needed for a basic knowledge of the English language.
Population: Candidates for any position requiring a basic knowledge of the English language.
Publication Date: 1996.
Acronym: ENGLIT.
Scores: Total Score, Narrative Evaluation, Rating, Recommendation.
Administration: Group.
Price Data, 2001: $130 per candidate; quantity discounts available.
Time: (77) minutes.
Comments: Scored by publisher; must be proctored.
Author: Walden Personnel Performance, Inc.
Publisher: Walden Personnel Performance, Inc.

[253]
Basic English Skills Test.

Purpose: Designed to test listening comprehension, speaking, reading, and writing skills at a basic level when information on the attainment of basic functional language skills is needed.
Population: Limited-English-speaking adults.
Publication Dates: 1982–1988.
Acronym: B.E.S.T.
Scores, 9: Oral Interview Section (Listening Comprehension, Communication, Fluency, Pronunciation, Reading/Writing, Total) and Literacy Skill Section (Reading Comprehension, Writing, Total).
Subtests, 2: Oral Interview Section, Literacy Skills Section.
Administration: Individual in part.
Parts: 4 forms (Forms B and C only in current circulation).
Price Data, 2002: $150 per complete test kit; $12 per picture cue book (1988, 15 pages); $13 per 5 interviewer's booklets (1988, 13 pages); $30 per 100 interview scoring sheets (1988, 2 pages); $45 per literacy skills testing package including 20 literacy skills test booklets (1988, 20 pages) and 20 literacy skills scoring sheets (1988, 2 pages); $25 per manual (1988, 79 pages); $50 per training video and guide.
Time: [75] minutes.
Comments: Orally administered in part; subtests available as separates; other test materials (e.g., 3 $1 bills, 2 dimes, etc.) must be supplied by examiner.

Authors: Center for Applied Linguistics (test), Dorry Kenyon (revised manual), and Charles W. Stansfield (revised manual) with assistance from Dora Johnson, Allene Grognet, and Dan Dreyfus.
Publisher: Center for Applied Linguistics.
Cross References: For reviews by Alan Garfinkel and Patsy Arnett Jaynes, see 11:28.

[254]
Basic Inventory of Natural Language.

Purpose: "To assess the language dominance, proficiency, and growth of students in school language arts and reading programs."
Population: Grades K–12.
Publication Dates: 1977–1979.
Acronym: BINL.
Scores, 3: Fluency, Level of Complexity, Average Sentence Length.
Administration: Individual.
Levels, 2: Forms A, B (grades K–6), Forms C, D (grades 7–12).
Price Data: Available from publisher.
Time: Administration time not reported.
Author: Charles H. Herbert.
Publisher: CHECpoint Systems, Inc. [No reply from publisher; status unknown].
Cross References: See T5:251 (2 references) and T4:248 (2 references); for a review by Thomas W. Guyette, see 9:115 (1 reference); see also T3:251 (1 reference).

[255]
Basic Mathematics Tests.

Purpose: Assesses children's understanding of basic mathematical relationships and processes.
Population: Ages 7-0 to 8-0, 8-0 to 9-0, 9-7 to 10-10, 10-0 to 12-6, 12-0 to 14-6.
Publication Dates: 1969–1972.
Score: Total score only.
Administration: Group.
Price Data: Price information available from publisher for tests (A, B, C, DE, or FG), and manual.
Author: The National Foundation for Educational Research.
Publisher: NFER-Nelson Publishing Co., Ltd. [England].
a) BASIC MATHEMATICS TEST A [ORAL].
Population: Ages 7-0 to 8-0.
Publication Date: 1971.
Time: (45) minutes.
b) BASIC MATHEMATICS TEST B [ORAL].
Population: Ages 8-0 to 9-0.
Publication Date: 1971.
Time: (45) minutes.
c) BASIC MATHEMATICS TEST C.
Population: Ages 9-7 to 10-10.

Publication Dates: 1970–1972.
Time: (50) minutes.
d) BASIC MATHEMATICS TEST DE.
Population: Ages 10-0 to 12-6.
Publication Dates: 1969–1972.
Time: (50) minutes.
e) BASIC MATHEMATICS TEST FG.
Population: Ages 12-0 to 14-6.
Publication Date: 1969.
Time: (50) minutes.
Cross References: See T4:251 (2 references) and T3:252 (2 references).

[256]
Basic Number Diagnostic Test [2001 Revision].

Purpose: Designed to "show what a child can do (and cannot do) so that teaching objectives for that child can be determined."
Population: Ages 5–7.
Publication Dates: 1980–2001.
Scores, 13: Reciting Numbers, Naming Numerals, Copying Over Numerals, Copying Underneath Numerals, Counting Bricks, Selecting Bricks, Writing Numerals in Sequence, Writing Numerals to Dictation, Addition with Objects, Addition with Numerals, Subtraction with Objects, Subtraction with Numerals, Total.
Administration: Individual.
Forms, 2: A, B.
Price Data, 2002: £9.99 per set of 20 copies (specify Form A or Form B); £10.99 per manual (2001, 30 pages); £11.99 per specimen set.
Time: (15–25) minutes.
Comments: "Criterion-referenced."
Author: Bill Gillham.
Publisher: Hodder & Stoughton Educational [England].
Cross References: For a review by Mary Montgomery Lindquist of an earlier edition, see 9:117.

[257]
Basic Number Screening Test [2001 Edition].

Purpose: "Quick assessment of a child's understanding of … number concepts and number skills."
Population: Ages 7–12.
Publication Dates: 1976–2001.
Forms, 2: A, B.
Scores: No scores.
Administration: Group.
Price Data, 2002: £9.99 per 20 tests (Form A or B); £10.99 per manual; £11.99 per specimen set.
Time: (20–35) minutes.
Comments: May be orally administered.
Authors: Bill Gillham and Kenneth Heese.
Publisher: Hodder & Stoughton Educational [England].

Cross References: For reviews by Mary Montgomery Lindquist and Marilyn N. Suydam of an earlier edition, see 9:118.

[258]
Basic Personality Inventory.

Purpose: Constructed to be a "measure of personality and psychopathology."
Population: Adult and adolescent.
Publication Dates: 1988-1997.
Acronym: BPI.
Scores, 12: Hypochondriasis, Depression, Denial, Interpersonal Problems, Alienation, Persecutory Ideas, Anxiety, Thinking Disorder, Impulse Expression, Social Introversion, Self Depreciation, Deviation.
Administration: Individual or group.
Price Data, 2001: $66 per examination kit including 5 reusable test booklets, scoirng template, 10 hand-scorable answer sheets, 10 profile sheets, answer sheet and coupon for BPI Basic Report, and manual (1996, 120 pages); $38 per manual; $30.50–$45 (depending on volume) per 25 test booklets; $10–$12 (depending on volume) per 25 hand-scorable answer sheets; $10–$12 (depending on volume) per 25 profile sheets (select adult or adolescent); $14 per scoring template; $59–$66 (depending on volume) per 10 machine-scorable answer sheets and coupons for Basic Reports; $99 per software package including disks, software manual for Windows, test manual, and 10 coupons for computer report.
Foreign Language Editions: Test booklets available in French and Spanish.
Time: [35] minutes.
Author: Douglas N. Jackson.
Publisher: Sigma Assessment Systems, Inc.
Cross References: See T5:256 (4 references); for reviews by Susana Urbina and Tamela Yelland, see 12:42 (1 reference); see also T4:254 (16 references).

[259]
Basic Reading Inventory, Eighth Edition.

Purpose: Designed as an informal measure of students' reading behavior.
Population: Pre-primer through Grade 12, Grades 3–12.
Publication Dates: 1978–2001.
Scores, 9–16: 3 reading scores (Independent, Instructional, Frustration, Word Recognition in Isolation, Word Recognition in Context, Comprehension—Oral, Comprehension—Silent, Listening Level); Rate of Reading (Optional); 9 informal Early Literacy Assessment ratings (Alphabet Knowledge, Writing, Literacy Knowledge, Wordless Picture Reading, Caption Reading, Auditory Discrimination, Phoneme Awareness, Phoneme Segmentation, Basic Word Knowledge).
Administration: Individual.

Levels, 2: Pre-primer through Grade 12; Grades 3–12.

Forms, 6: A, B, C, D, LN, LE.

Price Data: Price data available from publisher for manual with paper-and-pencil materials (2001, 472 pages), including CD-ROM (with videos, Performance Booklets, and Record Booklet, and demo disk for recording and tracking software); a training video is available to train administrators.

Time: [20] minutes.

Comments: Optional Basic Reading Inventory Tracking Software available to assist with advanced qualitative analysis available from publisher. System requirements: Windows or Macintosh, CD-ROM drive, 20 MB RAM, 20 MB hard drive, sound and video options.

Author: Jerry L. Johns.

Publisher: Kendall/Hunt Publishing Company.

Cross References: For reviews by Michael Harwell and Steven A. Stahl of the seventh edition, see 14:34 (6 references); see also T5:257 (4 references); for reviews by Jerrilyn V. Andrews and Robert T. Williams of the fifth edition, see 12:43 (3 references); see also T4:255 (4 references); for a review by Gus Plessas of the second edition, see 9:119.

[260]
Basic School Skills Inventory, Third Edition.

Purpose: Designed to locate children who are at-risk for school failure, who need more in-depth assessment, and who should be referred for additional study.

Population: Ages 4-0 to 8-11.

Publication Dates: 1975–1998.

Acronym: BSSI-3.

Scores, 7: Spoken Language, Reading, Writing, Mathematics, Classroom Behavior, Daily Living Skills, Overall Skill Level.

Administration: Individual.

Price Data, 2001: $86 per complete kit including examiner's manual (1998, 77 pages), and 25 profile/response forms; $49 per examiner's manual; $39 per 25 profile/response forms.

Time: (5–8) minutes.

Comments: Replaces the Basic School Skills Inventory—Diagnostic (T4:256).

Authors: Donald D. Hammill, James E. Leigh, Nils A. Pearson, and Taddy Maddox.

Publisher: PRO-ED

Cross References: For reviews by R. W. Kamphaus and Leah M. Nellis, see 14:35; see also T5:258 and T4:256 (1 reference); for a review by William J. Webster of the Basic School Skills Inventory—Diagnostic, see 9:120; for reviews by Byron R. Egeland and Lawrence M. Kasdon of an earlier edition, see 8:424 (2 references).

[261]
Basic Skills Locater Test.

Purpose: "Designed to assess a person's functional skill levels in math and language."

Population: Ages 15 to adult who are functioning below a 12th grade level.

Publication Date: 1998.

Scores, 2: Language, Math.

Administration: Group or individual.

Price Data, 2002: $195 per Basic Skills Locater Test (software version) including 1 guide, 1 reproducible test master, and software; $195 per Basic Skills Locater Test (print version) including 1 user's guide, 10 reusable test booklets, 100 answer sheets, 1 test key, and a Windows scoring disk; $995 per Network Version.

Time: (30–60) minutes.

Comments: Test results place test-takers into four levels corresponding to GED and grade levels: GED Level 1 (grades 1–3); GED Level 2 (grades 4–6); GED Level 3 (grades 7–8) and GED Level 4 (grades 9–12). Bar graphs representing competency in each level in the two domains of Language and Math yield 8 levels of competency for each test-taker.

Author: Helena Hendrix-Frye.

Publisher: Piney Mountain Press, Inc.

[262]
Basic Tests Series.

Purpose: To assess basic skills and knowledge relevant to the world of work or postsecondary education.

Population: High school seniors and college entrants and job applicants.

Publication Dates: 1981–1993.

Scores: Total scores only.

Administration: Group.

Restricted Distribution: Distribution restricted and tests administered at licensed testing centers.

Price Data, 2001: £9 entry fee per candidate per test; £1 per Basic Tests booklet containing syllabus and specimen papers (specify test); price data for additional supplementary materials available from publisher.

Comments: Tests administered each May at centers established by the publisher; tests available as separates.

Author: The Assessment and Qualifications Alliance.

Publisher: The Assessment and Qualifications Alliance [England].

a) BASIC TEST IN LIFE SKILLS.

Time: 90(100) minutes.

b) BASIC TEST IN GRAPHICACY.

Time: 90(100) minutes.

c) BASIC TEST IN HEALTH, HYGIENE AND SAFETY.

Time: 75(85) minutes.

Cross References: For reviews by Steven Ferrara and Anne R. Fitzpatrick, see 11:29.

[263]
BASIS-A Inventory [Basic Adlerian Scales for Interpersonal Success—Adult].

Purpose: Designed "to help understand how an individual's life-style, based on beliefs developed in early childhood, contributes to one's effectiveness in social, work, and intimate relationships."

Population: Adults.

Publication Dates: 1993–1997.

Acronym: BASIS-A.

Scores, 10: BASIS scales (Belonging-Social Interest, Taking Charge, Going Along, Wanting Recognition, Being Cautious); HELPS scales (Harshness, Entitlement, Liked By All, Striving for Perfection, Softness).

Administration: Group or individual.

Price Data, 2001: $95 per introductory kit including 15 test booklets, technical manual (1997, 87 pages), interpretive manual (1997, 61 pages), and 15 copies of interpretive guide; $85 per 25 test booklets; $34 per technical manual and interpretive manual; $7 per sampler kit including test booklet and BASIS-A interpretive guide; $35 per 25 BASIS-A interpretive guides.

Foreign Language Edition: Test items and instructions available in Spanish and German.

Time: (10–15) minutes.

Comments: Self-scored.

Authors: Mary S. Wheeler, Roy M. Kern, and William L. Curlette.

Publisher: TRT Associates, Inc.

Cross References: For reviews by James P. Choca and Peggy E. Gallaher, see 13:26.

[264]
Bass Orientation Inventory.

Purpose: Designed to measure kinds of satisfactions and rewards sought in jobs.

Population: College and industry.

Publication Dates: 1962–1977.

Acronym: RNVT.

Scores, 3: Self-Orientation, Interaction-Orientation, Task-Orientation.

Administration: Group.

Price Data, 2001: $25 per sampler set including inventory, scoring key, and manual (1977, 63 pages); $125 per permission set including sampler set plus permission to reproduce up to 200 copies of the inventory.

Time: (20–25) minutes.

Comments: Previously listed as The Orientation Inventory.

Author: Bernard M. Bass.

Publisher: Distributed by Mind Garden, Inc.

Cross References: See T3:1748 (1 reference); for a review by Thomas J. Bouchard, Jr., see 8:636 (15 references); see also T2:1306 (26 references) and P:187 (13 references); for reviews by Richard S. Barrett and H. Bradley Sagen, see 6:153 (2 references).

[265]
Batería Woodcock-Muñoz—Revisada.

Purpose: Designed to assess acognitive abilities and achievement in Spanish-speaking individuals.

Population: Spanish speaking ages 2 and over.

Publication Dates: 1982–1996.

Acronym: Batería-R.

Administration: Individual.

Scores: 7 standard battery test scores plus one cluster score: Memoria para Nombres, Memoria para Frases, Pareo Visual, Palabras Incompletas, Integración Visual, Vocabulario Sobre Dibujos, Análisis Síntesis, Amplia Habilidad Cognitiva; and 14 supplementary battery scores: Aprendizje Visual-Auditivo, Memoria para Palabras, Tachar, Integración de Sondidos, Reconocimiento de Dibujos, Vocabulario Oral, Formación de Conceptos, Memoria Diferida-Memoria para Nombres, Memoria Diferida-Aprendizaje Visual Auditivo, Inversión de Numeros, Configuración de Sonidos, Relaciones Especiales, Comprensión de Oraciones, Analogías Verbalis; plus 14 supplemental battery cluster scores derived from combinations of standard and supplemental scores: Recuperación a Largo Plazo (Glr), Memoria a Corto Plazo (Gsm), Rapidez en el Procesamiento (Gs), Procesamiento Auditivo (Ga), Procesamiento Visual (Gv), Comprensión Conocimiento (Gc), Razonamiento Fluido (Gf), Amplia Habilidad Cognitiva-Escala Extendida, Aptitud en Lectura, Aptitud en Matemáticas, Aptitud en Languaje Escrito, Aptitud en Concocimiento.

Administration: Individual.

Price Data: Available from publisher.

Time: (30–40) minutes for standard battery; (40) minutes additional for Supplemental battery.

Comments: Parallel Spanish version of the Woodcock-Johnson® (13:27).

Authors: Richard W. Woodcock and Ana F. Muñoz-Sandoval.

Publisher: Riverside Publishing.

Cross References: For reviews by Robert B. Frary and Maria Prendes Lintel, see 13:27. For reviews of the Woodcock-Johnson Psycho-Educational Battery—Revised by Jack A. Cummings and by Steven W. Lee and Elaine Flory Stefany, see 12:415 (36 references); see also T4:2973 (90 references) and T3:2639 (3 references); for reviews of an earlier edition of the Woodcock-Johnson Psycho-Educational Battery by Jack A. Cummings and Alan S. Kaufman, see 9:1387 (6 references).

[266]
Battelle Developmental Inventory.

Purpose: To identify the developmental strengths and weaknesses of handicapped and nonhandicapped children in infant, preschool, and primary programs.

Population: Birth to 8 years.

Publication Date: 1984.

Acronym: BDI.

Scores: 30 profile scores: Adult Interaction, Expression of Feeling/Affect, Self-Concept, Peer Interaction, Coping, Social Role, Personal-Social Total, Attention, Eating, Dressing, Personal Responsibility, Toileting, Adaptive Total, Muscle Control, Body Coordination, Locomotion, Gross Motor, Fine Muscle, Perceptual Motor, Fine Motor, Motor Total, Receptive, Expressive, Communication Total, Perceptual Discrimination, Memory, Reasoning and Academic Skills, Conceptual Development, Cognitive Total, Total.
Administration: Individual.
Price Data: Available from publisher.
Time: (60–120) minutes for complete inventory; (10–30) minutes for screening test.
Comments: Screening test available as a separate.
Authors: Initial development by Jean Newborg, John R. Stock, and Linda Wnek; pilot norming study by John Guidubaldi; completion and standardization by John Svinicki.
Publisher: Riverside Publishing.
Cross References: See T5:265 (15 references) and T4:263 (4 references); for reviews by Judy Oehler-Stinnett and Kathleen D. Paget, see 10:25 (1 reference).

[267]
Battelle Developmental Inventory Screening Test.

Purpose: For general screening, preliminary assessment, and/or initial identification of possible developmental strengths and weaknesses.
Population: Birth to age 8.
Publication Date: 1984.
Acronym: BDI Screening Test.
Scores, 10: Personal-Social, Adaptive, Motor (Gross Motor, Fine Motor, Total), Communication (Receptive, Expressive, Total), Cognitive, Total.
Administration: Individual.
Price Data: Available from publisher.
Time: (10–30) minutes.
Comments: Short form of the Battelle Developmental Inventory (267); other test materials must be supplied by examiner.
Authors: Initial development by Jean Newborg, John R. Stock, and Linda Wnek; pilot norming study by John Guidubaldi; completion and standardization by John Svinicki.
Publisher: Riverside Publishing.
Cross References: See T5:266 (4 references) and T4:264 (1 reference); for reviews by David W. Barnett and by Joan Ershler and Stephen N. Elliott, see 11:30.

[268]
Battery for Health Improvement.

Purpose: "Designed to identify factors that may interfere with a patient's normal course of recovery from a physical injury."

Population: Patients 18–65 who are being evaluated or treated for an injury.
Publication Date: 1996.
Acronym: BHI™.
Scores, 14: Psychological Factors (Depression, Anxiety, Hostility, Borderline, Symptom Dependency, Chronic Maladjustment, Substance Abuse, Perseverance), Environmental Factors (Family Dysfunction, Job Dissatisfaction, Doctor Dissatisfaction), Physical Factors (Somatic Complaints, Pain Complaints, Muscular Bracing).
Administration: Group or individual.
Price Data, 2002: $90 per preview package including manual (100 pages) and answer sheets with test items for three assessments (specify MICROTEST Q or mail-in scoring); $108 per hand scoring starter kit including manual, 10 test booklets, 50 answer sheets, and 50 profile forms; $26 per hand scoring test booklets, $19 per 25 MICROTEST Q answer sheets; $20 per MICROTEST Q interpretive report; $22 per mail-in interpretive report; $9.50 per MICROTEST Q profile report; $11.50 per mail-in profile report; $27 per manual; $54 per optional audiocassette; many items available in both English and Hispanic.
Time: (25–40) minutes.
Authors: Daniel Bruns and John Mark Disorbio with contributions by Julia Copeland.
Publisher: NCS Assessments (Minnetonka).
Cross References: For reviews by Gregory J. Boyle and Ephrem Fernandez, see 14:36.

[269]
Bay Area Functional Performance Evaluation, Second Edition.

Purpose: Developed to assess "general components of functioning that are needed to perform activities of daily living."
Population: Psychiatric patients.
Publication Dates: 1978–1987.
Acronym: BaFPE.
Administration: Individual.
Price Data: Available from publisher.
Comments: Task-Oriented Assessment and Social Interaction Scale may be used separately.
Authors: Susan Lang Williams and Judith Bloomer.
Publisher: Maddak, Inc.
a) TASK-ORIENTED ASSESSMENT.
Acronym: TOA.
Scores, 138: 16 Component scores: Cognitive (Memory for Written/Verbal Instruction, Organization of Time and Materials, Attention Span, Evidence of Thought Disorder, Ability to Abstract, Total), Performance (Task Completion, Errors, Efficiency, Total), Affective (Motivation/Compliance, Frustration Tolerance, Self-Confidence, General Affective Impression, Total), Total for the following 11 Parameters: Sorting Shells,

Money/Marketing, Home Drawing, Block Design, Kinetic Person Drawing, Total; also 11 Qualitative Signs and Referral Indicators ratings: Language, Comprehension, Hemispatial Neglect, Memory, Abstraction, Task-Specific Observations, Total for the above parameters.
Time: (30–45) minutes.
b) SOCIAL INTERACTION SCALE.
Acronym: SIS.
Scores, 13: Parameter scores (Verbal Communication, Psychomotor Behavior, Socially Appropriate Behavior, Response to Authority Figures, Degree of Independence/Dependence, Ability to Work with Others, Participation in Group Activities), Social Situations (One-to-One, Mealtime, Unstructured Group, Structured Task or Activity Group, Structured Verbal Group), Total Interaction.
Time: [50–60] minutes.
Cross References: See T5:268 (1 reference); for reviews by Deborah D. Roman and Orest E. Wasyliw, see 12:44; see also T4:265 (1 reference).

[270]
Bayley Infant Neurodevelopmental Screener.
Purpose: "Designed to identify infants between the ages of 3 and 24 months who are developmentally delayed or have neurological impairments."
Population: Ages 3–24 months.
Publication Dates: 1992–1995.
Acronym: BINS.
Scores: 4 areas: Basic Neurological Functions/Intactness, Auditory and Visual Receptive Functions, Verbal and Motor Expressive Functions, Cognitive Processes; total score for each level.
Administration: Individual.
Levels, 6: 3–4 months, 5–6 months, 7–10 months, 11–15 months, 16–20 months, 21–24 months.
Price Data, 2002: $265 per complete kit including 25 record forms, manual (1995, 105 pages), stimulus cards, and necessary manipulables in soft-sided carrying case; $33 per 25 record forms; 804 per manual; $17 per stimulus card; $50 per training video.
Time: (10–15) minutes.
Comments: Includes a subset of items from the Bayley Scales of Infant Development—Second Edition (BSID–II; 271), but is not an abbreviated form of the BSID–II.
Author: Glen P. Aylward.
Publisher: The Psychological Corporation.
Cross References: For reviews by James K. Benish and by Damon Krug and Brandon Davis, see 13:28.

[271]
Bayley Scales of Infant Development, Second Edition.
Purpose: "Assesses the current developmental functioning of infants and children."

Population: Ages 1–42 months.
Publication Dates: 1969–1993.
Acronym: BSID-II.
Scores, 2: Mental, Motor, plus 30 behavior ratings.
Administration: Individual.
Price Data, 2002: $950 per complete kit including 25 Mental Scale record forms, 25 Motor Scale record forms, 25 Behavior Rating Scale record forms, visual stimulus cards, map, manipulatives, carrying case, stimulus booklet, and manual (1993, 374 pages); $41 per 25 Mental Scale record forms, $35 per 25 Motor Scale record forms; $32 per 25 Behavior Rating Scale record forms; $80 per stimulus booklet; $80 per manual.
Time: (25–60) minutes.
Author: Nancy Bayley.
Publisher: The Psychological Corporation.
Cross References: See T5:270 (48 references); for reviews by Carl J. Dunst and Mark H. Fugate, see 13:29 (130 references); see also T4:266 (58 references); for reviews by Michael J. Roszkowski and Jane A. Rysberg of an earlier edition, see 10:26 (80 references); see also 9:126 (42 references) and T3:270 (101 references); for a review by Fred Damarin, see 8:206 (28 references); see also T2:484 (11 references); for reviews by Roberta R. Collard and Raymond H. Holden, see 7:402 (20 references).

[272]
Beck Anxiety Inventory [1993 Edition].
Purpose: "Measures the severity of anxiety in adults and adolescents."
Population: Adults and adolescents ages 17 and over.
Publication Dates: 1987–1993.
Acronym: BAI.
Scores: Total score only.
Administration: Group or individual.
Price Data, 2002: $66 per complete kit including 25 record forms and manual (1993, 23 pages); $34.50 per 25 record forms; $34 per manual.
Foreign Language Edition: Also available in Spanish.
Time: (5–10) minutes.
Comments: Computer scoring and interpretation available.
Authors: Aaron T. Beck and Robert A. Steer.
Publisher: The Psychological Corporation.
Cross References: See T5:271 (18 references); for reviews by E. Thomas Dowd and Niels G. Waller, see 13:30 (73 references); see also T4:267 (2 references).

[273]
Beck Depression Inventory—II.
Purpose: "Developed for the assessment of symptoms corresponding to criteria for diagnosing depressive disorders listed in the ... DSM IV."

Population: Ages 13 and over.
Publication Dates: 1961–1996.
Acronym: BDI-II.
Scores: Total score only.
Administration: Group or individual.
Price Data, 2002: $66 per complete kit including manual (1996, 38 pages) and 25 recording forms; $34 per manual; $34.50 per 25 recording forms; $130 per 100 recording forms; $34.50 per 25 Spanish recording forms; $130 per 100 Spanish recording forms.
Foreign Language Edition: Available in Spanish.
Time: (5–10) minutes.
Comments: Hand-scored or computer-based administration, scoring, and interpretation available; "revision of BDI based upon new information about depression."
Authors: Aaron T. Beck, Robert A. Steer, and Gregory K. Brown.
Publisher: The Psychological Corporation.
Cross References: For reviews by Paul A. Arbisi and Richard F. Farmer, see 14:37; see also T5:272 (384 references); for reviews by Janet F. Carlson and Niels G. Waller, see 13:31 (1026 references); see also T4:268 (660 references); for reviews by Collie W. Conoley and Norman D. Sundberg of an earlier edition, see 11:31 (286 references).

[274]
Beck Hopelessness Scale [Revised].

Purpose: Measures "the extent of negative attitudes about the future (pessimism) as perceived by adolescents and adults."
Population: Adolescents and adults ages 17 and over.
Publication Dates: 1978–1993.
Acronym: BHS.
Scores: Total score only.
Administration: Group or individual.
Price Data, 2002: $66 per complete kit including 25 record forms and manual (1993, 29 pages); $34.50 per 25 record forms; $34 per manual; $8.50 per scoring key.
Foreign Language Edition: Also available in Spanish.
Time: (5–10) minutes.
Comments: Computer scoring and interpretation available.
Authors: Aaron T. Beck and Robert A. Steer.
Publisher: The Psychological Corporation.
Cross References: See T5:273 (34 references); for a review by Ephrem Fernandez, see 13:32 (83 references); see also T4:269 (37 references); for reviews by E. Thomas Dowd and Steven V. Owen of an earlier edition, see 11:32 (13 references).

[275]
Beck Scale for Suicide Ideation.

Purpose: "To detect and measure the severity of suicidal ideation in adults and adolescents."
Population: Adults and adolescents ages 17 and over.
Publication Dates: 1991–1993.
Acronym: BSS.
Scores: Total score only; item score ranges.
Administration: Group or individual.
Price Data, 2002: $66 per complete kit including 25 record forms and manual (1993, 24 pages); $34.50 per 25 record forms; $34 per manual.
Foreign Language Edition: Spanish forms available.
Time: (5–10) minutes.
Comments: Computer scoring and interpretation available.
Authors: Aaron T. Beck and Robert A. Steer.
Publisher: The Psychological Corporation.
Cross References: For reviews by Karl R. Hanes and Jay R. Stewart, see 13:33 (14 references).

[276]
Beck Youth Inventories of Emotional & Social Impairment.

Purpose: To "evaluate children's emotional and social impairment."
Population: Ages 7–14.
Publication Date: 2001.
Forms, 5: Beck Depression Inventory for Youth, Beck Anxiety Inventory for Youth, Beck Anger Inventory for Youth, Beck Disruptive Behavior Inventory for Youth, Beck Self-Concept Inventory for Youth.
Administration: Group or individual.
Price Data, 2001: $108 per starter kit including manual (59 pages) and 25 combination inventory booklets: $70 per combination inventory including 25 booklets (quantity discounts available); $34.50 per 25 inventories (specify BDI-Y, BAI-Y, BANI-Y, BDBI-Y, or BSCI-Y) (quantity discounts available); $54 per manual.
Time: (5–10) minutes per inventory.
Comments: Brief self-report measures of behavior, cognitions, and feelings; consistent with IDEA requirements; inventories can be administered alone or in combination.
Authors: Judith S. Beck (tests and manual) and Aaron T. Beck (tests and manual) with John Jolly (manual).
Publisher: The Psychological Corporation.
a) BECK DEPRESSION INVENTORY FOR YOUTH.
Acronym: BDI-Y.
Score: Total.
Comments: Consistent with DSM-IV depression criteria.

b) BECK ANXIETY INVENTORY FOR YOUTH.
Acronym: BAI-Y.
Score: Total.
Comments: Reflects specific worries about school performance, the future, others' negative reactions; fears; physiological symptoms.
c) BECK ANGER INVENTORY FOR YOUTH.
Acronym: BANI-Y.
Score: Total.
Comments: Evaluates thoughts of being treated unfairly by others; feelings of anger, hatred.
d) BECK DISRUPTIVE BEHAVIOR INVENTORY FOR YOUTH.
Acronym: BDBI-Y.
Score: Total.
Comments: Identifies thoughts and behaviors associated with conduct disorder, oppositional-defiant behavior.
e) BECK SELF-CONCEPT INVENTORY FOR YOUTH.
Acronym: BSCI-Y.
Score: Total.
Comments: Taps cognitions of competence, potency, positive self-worth.

[277]

Becker Work Adjustment Profile.

Purpose: Provides "information about the work habits, attitudes and skills of individuals in sheltered and competitive work."
Population: Mentally retarded, physically disabled, emotionally disturbed, learning disabled, and economically disadvantaged, ages 13 and over.
Publication Date: 1989.
Acronym: BWAP.
Scores, 5: Work Habits/Attitudes, Interpersonal Relations, Cognitive Skills, Work Performance Skills, Broad Work Adjustment.
Administration: Individual.
Price Data: Available from publisher.
Time: (10–15) minutes for Short Scale; (20–25) minutes for Full Scale.
Comments: Ratings by teachers, counselors, or other vocational professionals; 2 forms: Short Scale, Full Scale.
Authors: Ralph L. Becker.
Publisher: Elbern Publications.
Cross References: See T5:275 (1 reference); for reviews by Brian Bolton and Elliot L. Gory, see 11:33.

[278]

Bedside Evaluation of Dysphagia, Revised.

Purpose: Designed to assess swallowing abilities and the factors that may influence those abilities.
Population: Adults neurologically impaired.
Publication Date: 1995.

Acronym: BED.
Scores, 13: Behavioral Characteristics, Cognition and Communication Screening (Cognition, Receptive Language, Expressive Language/Speech Production), Oral Motor Examination (Lips, Tongue, Soft Palate, Cheeks, Mandible, Larynx), Oral-Pharyngeal Dysphagia Symptoms Assessment (Oral State, Pharyngeal State, Additional Observations).
Administration: Individual.
Price Data, 2002: $35 per 25 evaluation forms; $69.75 per manual (54 pages), 25 standard evaluation forms, and 25 screening forms.
Time: (15–45) minutes.
Author: Edward Hardy.
Publisher: Imaginart International, Inc.
Cross References: For reviews by Carlos Inchaurralde and Steven B. Leder, see 14:38.

[279]

Bedside Evaluation Screening Test, Second Edition.

Purpose: "Designed to assess and quantify language disorders in adults resulting from aphasia."
Population: Patients with language deficits.
Publication Dates: 1987–1998.
Acronym: BEST-2.
Scores, 8: Conversational Expression, Naming Objects, Describing Objects, Repeating Sentences, Pointing to Objects, Pointing to Parts of a Picture, Reading, Total.
Administration: Individual.
Price Data, 2001: $139 per complete kit including examiner's manual (1998, 49 pages), picture book, 25 record forms, and 25 profile/summary sheets.
Time: (20–30) minutes.
Comments: Replaces the Bedside Evaluation and Screening Test of Aphasia (T4:272).
Authors: Joyce Fitch West, Elaine S. Sands, and Deborah Ross-Swain.
Publisher: PRO-ED.
Cross References: For reviews by Pamilla Morales and Carolyn Mitchell-Person, see 14:39; for a review by Malcolm R. McNeil of an earlier edition, see 11:34.

[280]

Behavior Assessment System for Children [Revised].

Purpose: Designed "to aid in the identification and differential diagnosis of emotional/behavior disorders in children and adolescents."
Population: Ages 2 1/2–18.
Publication Dates: 1992–1998.
Acronym: BASC.
Administration: Individual or group.
Forms, 10: Teacher Rating Scale—Preschool, Teacher Rating Scale—Child, Teacher Rating Scale—

Adolescent, Parent Rating Scale—Preschool, Parent Rating Scale—Child, Parent Rating Scale—Adolescent, Self-Report of Personality—Child, Self-Report of Personality—Adolescent, Structured Developmental History, Student Observation System.

Price Data, 2002: $89.95 per examination starter set including manual, one sample each of the hand-scored forms for all levels of the Teacher Rating Scale, Parent Rating Scale, and Self-Report of Personality, the Structured Developmental History, and the Student Observation Scale; $237.95 per PC Enhanced ASSIST software (unlimited use).

Comments: Subtests available as separates.

Authors: Cecil R. Reynolds and Randy W. Kamphaus.

Publisher: American Guidance Service, Inc.

a) TEACHER RATING SCALES.

Price Data: $27.95 per 25 hand-scored forms; $18.95 per 25 computer-scored forms.

Time: (10–20) minutes.

1) *Teacher Rating Scales—Preschool.*

Population: Ages 2 1/2–5.

Scores, 11: Externalizing Problems (Aggression, Hyperactivity), Internalizing Problems (Anxiety, Depression, Somatization), Attention Problems, Atypicality, Withdrawal, Adaptive Skills (Adaptability, Social Skills), Behavioral Symptoms Index.

2) *Teacher Rating Scales—Child.*

Population: Ages 6–11.

Scores, 19: Externalizing Problems (Aggression, Hyperactivity, Conduct Problems), Internalizing Problems (Anxiety, Depression, Somatization), School Problems (Attention Problems, Learning Problems), Atypicality, Withdrawal, Adaptive Skill (Adaptability, Leadership, Social Skills, Study Skills), Behavioral Symptoms Index.

3) *Teacher Rating Scales—Adolescent.*

Population: Ages 12–18.

Scores, 18: Externalizing Problems (Aggression, Hyperactivity, Conduct Problems), Internalizing Problems (Anxiety, Depression, Somatization), School Problems (Attention Problems, Learning Problems), Atypicality, Withdrawal, Adaptive Skills (Leadership, Social Skills, Study Skills), Behavioral Symptoms Index.

b) PARENT RATING SCALES.

Price Data: $27.95 per 25 hand-scored forms; $18.95 per 25 computer-scored forms.

Time: (10–20) minutes.

1) *Parent Rating Scales—Preschool.*

Population: Ages 2 1/2–5.

Scores, 14: Same as *a*-1 above.

2) *Parent Rating Scales—Child.*

Population: Ages 6–11.

Scores, 16: Externalizing Problems (Aggression, Hyperactivity, Conduct Problems), Internalizing Problems (Anxiety, Depression, Somatization), Attention Problems, Atypicality, Withdrawal, Adaptive Skills (Adaptability, Leadership, Social Skills), Behavioral Symptoms Index.

3) *Parent Rating Scales—Adolescent.*

Population: Ages 12–18.

Scores, 15: Externalizing Problems (Aggression, Hyperactivity, Conduct Problems), Internalizing Problems (Anxiety, Depression, Somatization), Attention Problems, Atypicality, Withdrawal, Adaptive Skills (Leadership, Social Skills), Behavioral Symptom Index.

c) SELF-REPORT OF PERSONALITY.

Price Data: $27.95 per 25 hand-scored forms; $18.95 per 25 computer-scored forms.

Time: (20–30) minutes.

1) *Self-Report of Personality—Child.*

Population: Ages 8–11.

Scores, 16: Clinical Maladjustment (Anxiety, Atypicality, Locus of Control, Social Stress), School Maladjustment (Attitude to School, Attitude to Teachers), Depression, Sense of Inadequacy, Personal Adjustment (Relations with Parents, Interpersonal Relations, Self-Esteem, Self-Reliance), Emotional Symptoms Index.

2) *Self-Report of Personality—Adolescent.*

Population: Ages 12–18.

Scores, 18: Clinical Maladjustment (Anxiety, Atypicality, Locus of Control, Social Stress, Somatization), School Maladjustment (Attitude to School, Attitude to Teachers, Sensation Seeking), Depression, Sense of Inadequacy, Personal Adjustment (Relations with Parents, Interpersonal Relations, Self-Esteem, Self-Reliance), Emotional Symptoms Index.

d) STRUCTURED DEVELOPMENTAL HISTORY.

Price Data: $36.95 per 25 history forms.

e) STUDENT OBSERVATION SYSTEM.

Price Data: $29.95 per 25 observation forms.

Time: [20] minutes.

Cross References: For reviews by James Clyde DiPerna and by Robert Spies and Christina Finley Jones, see 14:40; see also T5:280 (6 references); for reviews by Jonathon Sandoval and by Joseph C. Witt and Kevin M. Jones of an earlier edition, see 13:34 (4 reference).

[281]

Behavior Dimensions Rating Scale.

Purpose: Developed to screen for emotional/behavior disorders and for monitoring behavior change.

Population: Ages 5–adult.

Publication Date: 1989.
Acronym: BDRS.
Scores, 5: Aggressive/Acting Out, Irresponsible/Inattentive, Socially Withdrawn, Fearful/Anxious, Total.
Administration: Individual.
Price Data: Available from publisher.
Time: [5–10] minutes.
Comments: Ratings by teachers, parents, and psychologists.
Authors: Lyndal M. Bullock and Michael J. Wilson.
Publisher: Riverside Publishing.
Cross References: For reviews by Martha W. Blackwell and Rosemery O. Nelson-Gray, see 11:37 (1 reference).

[282]
Behavior Dimensions Scale.

Purpose: Designed to categorize and document existing behavior patterns into recognized areas of behavior disorders to assist in making diagnostic, placement, and programming decisions.
Population: Ages 3–19.
Publication Date: 1995.
Acronym: BDS.
Scores, 7: Inattentive, Hyperactive-Impulsive, Oppositional Defiant, Conduct, Avoidant Personality, Anxiety, Depression.
Administration: Individual.
Price Data, 2002: $157 per complete kit including School Version (59 pages) and Home Version (55 pages) manuals, 50 rating forms (School and Home), intervention manual (323 pages), and computerized scoring disk (Windows); $14 per manual (School or Home); $33 per 50 rating forms (School or Home); $33 per 50 Home Version Spanish rating forms; $28 per intervention manual; $35 per computerized scoring disk (Windows).
Time: (20–25) minutes.
Author: Stephen B. McCarney.
Publisher: Hawthorne Educational Services, Inc.
Cross References: For reviews by Kevin M. Jones and Beverly M. Klecker, see 14:41.

[283]
Behavior Disorders Identification Scale— Second Edition.

Purpose: "To document the existence of behaviors which meet the criteria for identifying the student as behaviorally disordered."
Population: Ages 4.5–21.
Publication Dates: 1988–2000.
Acronym: BDIS-2 SV (School Version); BDIS-2 HV (Home Version).
Scores, 5: Learning Problems, Interpersonal Relations, Inappropriate Behavior, Unhappiness/Depression, Physical Symptoms/Fears.

Administration: Individual.
Forms, 2: School Version, Home Version.
Price Data, 2001: $176 per complete kit including 50 Pre-Referral Behavior Checklists, 50 Intervention Strategies Documentation forms, 50 School Version Rating forms, 50 Home Version Rating forms, School Version Technical Manual, Home Version Technical Manual, and Teacher's Guide to Behavioral Interventions; $27 per 50 Pre-Referral Behavior Checklists; $27 per 50 Intervention Strategies Documentation forms; $14 per Technical Manual (School Version or Home Version); $33 per 50 rating forms (School Version, Home Version, or Home Version Spanish); $28 per Teacher's Guide to Behavioral Interventions; $35 per BDIS-2 Quick Score; $190 per Teacher's Guide to Behavioral Interventions computer version.
Time: [20] minutes for School Version; [15] minutes for Home Version.
Comments: Completed by adult observers; based on federal definitions of serious emotional disturbance (PL 94-142 and IDEA Amendments of 1997); available in paper or computer version; system requirements: IBM-compatible computer, 3 MB free hard disk space, MS DOS, 580K memory; Quick Score computer scoring of school and Home Versions available, system requirements Windows 95 or above, 8 MB RAM, 10 MB hard disk space, 2X CD-ROM drive; Quick Score provides individualized goals, objectives, interventions; Spanish language Home Version rating forms available.
Authors: Stephen B. McCarney and Tamara J. Arthaud (Technical Manuals, Home Version and School Version), and Kathy Cummins Wunderlich (Teacher's Guide to Behavioral Interventions).
Publisher: Hawthorne Educational Services, Inc.
Cross References: For reviews by Doreen Ward Fairbank and Harlan J. Stientjes of an earlier edition, see 12:46.

[284]
Behavior Evaluation Scale—2.

Purpose: To provide information about student behavior.
Population: Grades K-12.
Publication Dates: 1990–1993.
Acronym: BES-2.
Scores, 5: Learning Problems, Interpersonal Difficulties, Inappropriate Behaviors, Unhappiness/Depression, Physical Symptoms/Fears.
Administration: Individual.
Price Data, 2002: $240.50 per complete kit including 50 School Version rating forms, 50 Home Version rating forms, 50 Pre-Referral Behavior Evaluation Checklists—2, 50 Intervention Strategies documentation forms, 25 data collection forms, School Version technical manual, Home Version technical manual, Intervention manual (1993, 244 pages), and Parent's

Guide; $33 per 50 rating forms (specify Home Version or School Version); $33 per 50 Home Version Spanish rating forms; $27 per 50 Intervention Strategies documentation forms; $27 per 50 Pre-Referral Behavior Evaluation Checklists—2; $22 per 25 data collection forms; $14 per technical manual (specify School Version or Home Version); $26 per Intervention manual; $8.50 per Parent's Guide; $35 per computerized Quick Score program (DOS).
Time: (15-20) minutes.
Comments: "Criterion referenced"; ratings by teachers or other school personnel.
Authors: Stephen B. McCarney and James E. Leigh.
Publisher: Hawthorne Educational Services, Inc.
Cross References: See T5:284 (1 reference); for reviews by Bert A. Goldman and D. Joe Olmi, see 12:47; for reviews by J. Jeffrey Grill, Lester Mann, and Leonard Kenowitz of the earlier edition, see 9:128.

[285]
Behavior Rating Instrument for Autistic and Other Atypical Children, 2nd Edition.

Purpose: Designed to evaluate the status of autistic, atypical, and other developmentally delayed children by assessing their present levels of functioning and measuring changes in their behavior.
Population: Autistic children.
Publication Dates: 1977–1991.
Acronym: BRIAAC.
Scores, 9: Relationship to an Adult, Communication, Drive for Mastery, Vocalization and Expressive Speech, Sound and Speech Reception, Social Responsiveness, Psychobiological Development, Expressive Gesture and Sign Language, Receptive Gesture and Sign Language.
Administration: Individual.
Price Data, 2001: $130 per complete kit including manual (1991, 140 pages) and report form masters with permission to reproduce 50 copies; $50 per manual; $80 per reproducible masters and permission to make 50 copies.
Time: Untimed.
Authors: Bertram A. Ruttenberg, Enid G. Wolf-Schein, and Charles Wenar.
Publisher: Stoelting Co.
Cross References: For a review by Doreen Ward Fairbank, see 13:35; see also T4:280 (1 reference); for a review by Edward Workman of an earlier edition, see 9:129; see also T3:272 (1 reference).

[286]
Behavior Rating Inventory of Executive Function.

Purpose: Designed to assess impairment of executive function behaviors in the home and school environments.

Population: Ages 5–18.
Publication Dates: 1996–2000.
Acronym: BRIEF.
Administration: Individual or group.
Scores, 11: Inhibit, Shift, Emotional Control, Behavioral Regulation Index, Initiate, Working Memory, Plan/Organize, Organization of Materials, Monitor, Metacognition Index, Global Executive Composite.
Forms, 2: Parent Form, Teacher Form.
Price Data: Available from publisher for introductory kit including professional manual (2000, 150 pages), 25 Parent Form Questionnaires, 25 Teacher Form Questionnaires, 50 Parent Form Scoring Summary/Profile Forms, and 50 Teacher Form Scoring Summary/Profile Forms.
Time: (10–15) minutes.
Comments: Ratings by teachers, parents, or guardians.
Authors: Gerard A. Gioia, Peter K. Isquith, Steven C. Guy, and Lauren Kenworthy.
Publisher: Psychological Assessment Resources, Inc.

[287]
Behavior Rating Profile, Second Edition.

Purpose: "To evaluate students' behaviors at home, in school, and in interpersonal relationships."
Population: Ages 6-6 to 18-6.
Publication Dates: 1978–1990.
Acronym: BRP-2.
Scores: 5 checklists: Student Rating Scales (Home, School, Peers), Teacher Rating Scale, Parent Rating Scale, plus Sociogram score.
Administration: Individual.
Price Data, 2001: $198 per complete kit; $39 per 50 rating scale booklets (specify student, parent, or teacher form); $39 per 50 profile forms; $47 per examiner's manual (1990, 75 pages).
Time: (15–30) minutes per scale.
Authors: Linda Brown and Donald D. Hammill.
Publisher: PRO-ED.
Cross References: See T5:286 (3 references); for reviews by Sarah J. Allen and Lisa A. Bloom, see 12:48 (1 reference); see also T4:281 (1 reference); for reviews by Thomas R. Kratochwill and Joseph C. Witt of an earlier edition, see 9:130 (1 reference); see also T3:273 (1 reference).

[288]
Behavior Rating Scale.

Purpose: Designed to sample teachers' perceptions about their pupils' behavior in the classroom.
Population: Grades K–8.
Publication Dates: 1970–1975.
Score: Total score only.
Administration: Group.

Forms, 3: Forms differ only in number of rating categories.
Manual: No manual.
Price Data, 2001: Now free upon request from publisher.
Time: Administration time not reported.
Comments: Ratings by teachers; research instrument; may be used with or separately from Characteristics Scale (435).
Authors: Patricia B. Elmore and Donald L. Beggs.
Publisher: Patricia B. Elmore.
Cross References: See T5:287 (1 reference) and T4:282 (2 references); for a review by Jayne A. Parker, see 9:131 (2 references).

[289]
Behavior Status Inventory.

Purpose: Developed to rate patient behaviors in a psychiatric hospital setting.
Population: Psychiatric inpatients.
Publication Dates: 1969–1971.
Acronym: BSI.
Scores: Ratings in 7 areas (Personal Appearance, Manifest Behavior, Attitude, Verbal Behavior, Social Behavior, Work or School Behavior, Cognitive Behavior) and Total Patient Assets score.
Administration: Individual.
Manual: No manual.
Price Data, 2002: $15 per 25 rating forms (with instructions); $6.75 per 25 profile sheets; $5 per specimen set (with instructions).
Time: (5–10) minutes.
Author: William T. Martin.
Publisher: Psychologists and Educators, Inc.
Cross References: For a review by Alfred B. Heilbrun, Jr., see 8:505.

[290]
Behavioral Academic Self-Esteem.

Purpose: Constructed to measure "children's academic self-esteem by using direct observation of their classroom behaviors."
Population: Preschool–Grade 8.
Publication Dates: 1979–1982.
Acronym: BASE.
Scores, 6: Student Initiative, Social Attention, Success/Failure, Social Attraction, Self Confidence, Total.
Administration: Individual.
Price Data, 2001: $16 per 25 rating scales; $35.50 per manual (1982, 31 pages).
Time: (3–5) minutes.
Authors: Stanley Coopersmith and Ragnar Gilberts.
Publisher: Consulting Psychologists Press, Inc.
Cross References: See T5:289 (6 references) and T4:284 (2 references); for reviews by Herbert W. Marsh and Dale H. Schunk, see 9:132 (1 reference).

[291]
Behavioral Analysis Forms for Clinical Intervention.

Purpose: To gather client interview data in a structured manner.
Population: Behavior therapy clients.
Publication Dates: 1977–1981.
Scores: Volume 1: 36 plans, questionnaires, scales, forms, schedules, and data forms in areas such as Client History, Motivation for Change, Reinforcement, Social Performance; Volume 2: 59 questionnaires, scales, forms, schedules, and data forms in areas such as Reinforcers for Specific Populations, Survey of Phobic or Relationship Reactions, and Guidelines for Clients.
Administration: Group or individual.
Price Data, 2001: $79.95 for each volume.
Time: Administration times vary.
Author: Joseph R. Cautela.
Publisher: Cambridge Center for Behavioral Studies.
Cross References: For reviews by Mary Lou Kelley and Francis E. Lentz, Jr., see 9:127.

[292]
Behavioral and Emotional Rating Scale: A Strength-Based Approach to Assessment.

Purpose: "Designed to assess the behavioral and emotional strengths of children."
Population: Ages 5-0 to 18-11.
Publication Date: 1998.
Acronym: BERS.
Scores, 6: 5 subscales: Interpersonal Strength, Family Involvement, Intrapersonal Strength, School Functioning, Affective Strength, plus Strength Quotient.
Administration: Individual.
Price Data, 2001: $86 per complete kit; $49 per examiner's manual (60 pages); $39 per 50 summary/response forms.
Time: (10) minutes.
Comments: Normed for two separate groups: Children not identified with emotional or behavioral disorders and children diagnosed with emotional or behavioral disorders.
Authors: Michael H. Epstein and Jennifer M. Sharma.
Publisher: PRO-ED.
Cross References: For reviews by Beth Doll and D. Joe Olmi, see 14:42.

[293]
Behavioral Assessment of Pain Questionnaire.

Purpose: "Used for gaining a better understanding of factors which may be maintaining the subacute and chronic noncancerous pain experience."
Population: Subacute and chronic pain patients.

Publication Dates: 1990-1992.
Administration: Individual.
Price Data, 2001: $30 per sample kit including manual (1992, 44 pages); answer sheet and Mercury scoring with interpretive clinical profile, general information, scale descriptions, sample BAP clinical profile, and reprint of journal article; $10 per manual.
Foreign Language Edition: Spanish and French editions available.
Time: (60) minutes.
Authors: Michael J. Lewandowski and Blake H. Tearnan.
Publisher: Pain Assessment Resources.

a) BEHAVIORAL ASSESSMENT OF PAIN.
Acronym: BAP.
Scores, 34: Demographic Information, Activity Interference Scale (Domestic/Household Activities, Heavy Activities, Social Activities, Personal Care Activities, Personal Hygiene Activities), Avoidance Scale, Spouse/Partner Influence Scale (Reinforcement of Pain, Discouragement/Criticism of Pain, Reinforcement of Wellness, Discouragement/Criticism of Wellness), Physician Influence Scale (Discouragement/Criticism of Pain, Reinforcement of Wellness, Discouragement/Criticism of Wellness, Reinforcement of Pain), Physician Qualities Scale, Pain Beliefs Scale (Catastrophizing, Fear of Reinjury, Expectation for Cure, Blaming Self, Entitlement, Future Despair, Social Disbelief, Lack of Medical Comprehensiveness), Perceived Consequences Scale (Social Interference, Physical Harm, Psychological Harm, Pain Exacerbation, Productivity Interference), Coping Scale, Negative Mood Scale (Depression, Anxiety, Muscular Discomfort, Change in Weight).
Price Data: $21.50 per on-site scored interpretive report; $23.50 per Mercury scored interpretive report; $5 per BAP booklet.

b) POST BEHAVIORAL ASSESSMENT OF PAIN.
Acronym: P-BAP.
Scores, 23: Avoidance, Spouse/Partner Influence Scale (Reinforcement of Pain, Discouragement/Criticism of Pain, Reinforcement of Wellness, Discouragement/Criticism of Wellness), Pain Beliefs Scale (Catastrophizing, Fear of Reinjury, Expectation for Cure, Blaming Self, Entitlement, Future Despair, Social Disbelief, Lack of Medical Comprehensiveness), Perceived Consequences Scale (Social Interference, Physical Harm, Psychological Harm, Pain Exacerbation, Productivity Interference), Coping Scale, Negative Mood Scale (Depression, Anxiety, Muscular Discomfort, Change in Weight).
Price Data: $21.50 per on-site scored P-BAP report; $23.50 per Mercury scored P-BAP report; $5 per P-BAP booklet.

Cross References: For reviews by Gerald E. DeMauro and Ronald J. Ganellen, see 12:49.

[294]
Behavioral Characteristics Progression.

Purpose: Identifies specific skills exhibited during an individual's development.
Population: Physically and mentally handicapped children and adults.
Publication Date: 1973.
Acronym: BCP.
Scores: Item scores only.
Administration: Individual.
Price Data: Price information available from publisher for manual (1973, 205 pages), binder, and set of 5 method books (also available as separates).
Time: Administration time not reported.
Comments: "Criterion-referenced"; manual title is BCP Observation Booklet; also available in binder format.
Author: The Office of the Santa Cruz Superintendent of Schools.
Publisher: VORT Corporation.
Cross References: See T5:292 (1 reference); for reviews by Rosemery O. Nelson-Gray and Harvey N. Switzky, see 11:38.

[295]
Behavioral Objective Sequence.

Purpose: Designed to "assist special educators and other professionals assess behavioral competencies of students with emotional and behavioral disorders."
Population: Students (preschool through high school) with emotional and behavioral disorders.
Publication Date: 1998.
Acronym: BOS.
Scores, 6: Adaptive Behaviors, Self-Management Behaviors, Communication Behaviors, Interpersonal Behaviors, Task Behaviors, Personal Behaviors.
Administration: Individual.
Price Data, 2001: $39.95 per manual (1998, 104 pages), recording forms, and test.
Time: Administration time not reported.
Comments: "Can be used as a bank of (behavioral) objectives, as a rating scale, or as a structured observational system"; completed by educational/psychological professionals about a student; software program available.
Authors: Sheldon Braaten (test and software program) and John B. Merbler (software program).
Publisher: Research Press.

[296]
Behaviors and Experiences Inventory.

Purpose: "An initial screen for Attention-Deficit/ Hyperactivity Disorder (ADHD), Conduct Disorder (CD), and Antisocial Personality Disorder (ASPD)."

Population: Adults.
Publication Dates: 1998–1999.
Acronym: BEI.
Scores, 24: ADHD: Inattention (Difficulty Sustaining Attention, Fails to Finish Assignments, Inattention to Details/Careless, Difficulty Organizing Tasks/Activities, Tendency to Lose Things, Distractible), Hyperactivity, Impulsivity, Conduct Disorder as a Child/Adolescent (Aggression, Destruction of Property, Deceitfulness or Theft, Serious Violation of Rules, Cruelty to Animals and Fire-Setting), Antisocial Personality Disorder (Failure to Conform to Social Norms, Deceitfulness, Impulsivity, Irritability/Aggressiveness, Reckless Disregard for Safety, Irresponsibility, Lack of Remorse), History of Abuse as a Child/Adolescent (Physical, Sexual, Emotional).
Administration: Individual.
Price Data: Available from publisher.
Time: (15–20) minutes.
Comments: Can be administered as paper-and-pencil questionnaire or as a structured interview; screens for DSM-IV diagnostic criteria, providing an estimate of the likelihood that an individual meets the criteria for ADHD, CD, and ASPD; covers current problems only.
Authors: Norman G. Hoffmann, David Mee-Lee, and Gerald D. Shulman.
Publisher: Evince Clinical Assessments.

[297]
Behaviour Problems: A System of Management.

Purpose: "A systematic means of recording and analysing information on children's problem behaviour."
Population: Problem behavior children in a classroom situation.
Publication Date: 1984.
Scores: 8 areas of behavior: Classroom Conformity, Task Orientation, Emotional Control, Acceptance of Authority, Self-Worth, Peer Relationships, Self Responsibility/Problem Solving, Other.
Administration: Individual.
Price Data: Price information available from publisher for complete set including manual (15 pages), pad of 50 Daily Records, and pack of 10 Behaviour Checklist/Monthly Progress Charts.
Time: Administration time not reported.
Authors: Peter P. Galvin and Richard M. Singleton.
Publisher: NFER-Nelson Publishing Co., Ltd. [England].
Cross References: For reviews by Kathryn M. Benes and Terry Overton, see 11:39.

[298]
Behavioural Assessment of the Dysexecutive Syndrome.

Purpose: "A test battery aimed at predicting everyday problems arising from the Dysexecutive Syndrome."
Population: Ages 16 and above.
Publication Date: 1996.
Acronym: BADS.
Scores, 7: Rule Shift Card, Action Program, Key Search, Temporal Judgement, Zoo Map, Modified Six Elements, Total.
Administration: Individual.
Price Data: Available from publisher.
Time: Administration time not reported; some subtests timed.
Comments: Subtest scores "may be used individually, although validation studies have indicated that the overall battery score is the most sensitive predictor of executive problems"; useful with brain-injured and schizophrenic patients for identifying general or specific deficits in executive functions; supplemental information about patients can be gathered using the self-rating and caregiver rating forms included in the test kit.
Authors: Barbara A. Wilson, Nick Alderman, Paul W. Burgess, Hazel Elmslie, and Jonathan J. Evans.
Publisher: Thames Valley Test Company Ltd. [England].
Cross References: For reviews by Rik Carl D'Amato and Sandra D. Haynes, see 14:43.

[299]
Belbin Team-Roles Self-Perception Inventory.

Purpose: Designed to determine which contributions each team member can make best.
Population: Teams.
Publication Date: 1994.
Scores: 9 Profiles: Plant, Coordinator, Resource Investigator, Monitor Evaluator, Implementer, Team Worker, Completer-Finisher, Specialist, Shaper.
Administration: Group.
Price Data, 1996: $149 per package including Management Teams book (190 pages), Team Roles at Work book (158 pages), Team-Roles Package for 5-person team, and software (IBM); $24.95 per Management Teams book; $34.95 per Team Roles at Work book; $29.95 per team report; $9.95 per individual unit; $3.95 per observer unit.
Time: [1 day].
Author: Meredith Belbin.
Publisher: Jossey-Bass, A Wiley Company.
Cross References: For reviews by Keith Hattrup and by Kristin O. Prien and Erich P. Prien, see 14:44.

[300]
Bell Object Relations and Reality Testing Inventory.

Purpose: Designed to assess "dimensions of object relations and reality testing ego functioning."
Population: Ages 18 and older.
Publication Date: 1995.

Acronym: BORRTI.
Scores, 8: Object Relations (Alienation, Insecure Attachment, Egocentricity, Social Incompetence); Reality Testing (Reality Distortion, Uncertainty of Perception, Hallucinations and Delusions); Inconsistent Responding; plus two validity indexes: FREQ, INFREQ.
Administration: Group.
Price Data, 2002: $99.50 per complete kit including 2 prepaid Full Form mail-in answer sheets, 2-use clinical disk, 2 Full Form PC answer sheets, and manual; $47.50 per manual; $17.50 per Full Form mail-in answer sheet; $16.50 per Form O mail-in answer sheet; $215 per 20-use clinical disk (Full Form or Form O; PC with Microsoft Windows) including interpretive report; $72.50 per 20-use clinical disk for scoring only; $15 per 100 PC answer sheets (specify Full Form or Form O); $41.50 per FAX Scoring service for Full Form; $10.50 per FAX Scoring Service for Form O.
Time: (15–20) minutes.
Comments: Form O including only items measuring object relations also available.
Author: Morris D. Bell.
Publisher: Western Psychological Services.
Cross References: For reviews by Glen Fox and Steven I. Pfeiffer, see 14:45; see also T5:297 (2 references).

[301]
Bem Sex-Role Inventory.

Purpose: Designed to facilitate research on psychological androgyny.
Population: High school and college and adults.
Publication Dates: 1978-1981.
Acronym: BSRI.
Scores, 3: Femininity, Masculinity, Femininity-minus-Masculinity Differences.
Administration: Group.
Price Data: Available from publisher.
Time: (10-15) minutes.
Comments: Test is titled Bem Inventory; self-administered; short and long form available (short form consists of first 30 items only).
Author: Sandra Lipsitz Bem.
Publisher: Mind Garden, Inc.
Cross References: See T5:298 (167 references) and T4: 288 (204 references); for reviews by Richard Lippa and Frank D. Rayne, see 9:137 (121 references).

[302]
Bench Mark Measures.

Purpose: Measures a student's general knowledge of phonics.
Population: Ungraded.
Publication Date: 1977.
Scores: 3 levels in 4 areas: Alphabet and Dictionary Skills, Reading, Handwriting, Spelling.

Administration: Individual in part.
Price Data, 2001: $69.65 per complete kit including administrator's guide (16 pages), test booklet (26 pages), 24 summary sheets (6 pages), graph of concepts and multisensory introductions (16 pages), sheet of block capitals, set of three-dimensional letters, skeleton dictionary (Anna Gillingham and Bessie Stillman, 1956, 79 pages), test cards (56), spirit duplicating master (1 page); $16.25 per 12 summary sheets; $7.30 per graph; $8.65 per skeleton dictionary; quantity discounts available.
Time: (30–60) minutes.
Comments: "Criterion-referenced"; follows the sequence of the Alphabetic Phonics curriculum developed in the Language Research and Training Laboratory of the Texas Scottish Rite Hospital for its remedial language training program.
Author: Aylett R. Cox.
Publisher: Educators Publishing Service, Inc.
Cross References: For a review by David J. Carroll, see 9:138.

[303]
Benchmarks [Revised].

Purpose: "Assesses skills and perspectives that leaders can learn from experience; also, potential flaws that can derail a career."
Population: Middle- to upper-level managers and executives with at least 3–5 years of managerial experience.
Publication Dates: 1990–2001.
Scores, 21: 3 Skill Areas: Meeting Job Challenges (Resourcefulness, Doing Whatever It Takes, Being A Quick Study, Decisiveness), Leading People (Leading Employees, Confronting Problem Employees, Participative Management, Change Management), Respecting Self and Others (Building And Mending Relationships, Compassion And Sensitivity, Straightforwardness And Composure, Balance Between Personal Life And Work, Self-Awareness, Putting People At Ease, Differences Matter, Career Management), Potential for Derailment (Problems With Interpersonal Relationships, Difficulty Building And Leading A Team, Difficulty Changing Or Adapting, Failure To Meet Business Objectives, Too Narrow Functional Orientation).
Administration: Group.
Restricted Distribution: The publisher requires a 2-day certification program for those who wish to give feedback from Benchmarks in their own organization or as a consultant.
Price Data, 2002: $275 per set including 12 survey questionnaires, scoring of surveys, Feedback Reports, Developmental Learning Guides (paper-and-pencil or online version); $40 handling fee charged per set; quantity discounts available.
Foreign Language Editions: Available in French, French-Canadian, Dutch, French, German, Italian, and Spanish; document assisting non-English-speaking raters to complete the English observer form available in

Dutch, French, French-Canadian, German, Italian, and Spanish; normative comparisons available for Canada, and the United Kingdom.

Time: (30–40) minutes.

Comments: Available in paper-and-pencil and online formats; hard copy Feedback Report is generated providing mean scores and normative comparisons for all items and the 21 scores as rated by all observers, self, boss, superior, peer, direct report, other; Developmental Learning Guide "suggests strategies for change" including exercises to help analyze feedback, presentation of "tactics and strategies."

Authors: Michael Lombardo, Cynthia McCauley, Dana McDonald-Mann, and Jean Brittain Leslie.

Publisher: Center for Creative Leadership.

  a) BENCHMARKS GROUP PROFILE.

  Purpose: "To assess the caliber and potential of management to fulfill ... objectives, and to develop more appropriate and effective management and organizational development strategies."

  Price Data: $275 per group profile.

  Comments: Provides group-level mean scores and normative comparisons for the 21 scres as rated by all observers, self, boss/superior, peer, direct report, other.

Cross References: For a review by Sheldon Zedeck of an earlier edition, see 12:50.

[304]
[Bender-Gestalt Test.]

Purpose: Measures perceptual-motor abilities.

Scores: Scores vary depending on adaptation used.

Administration: Individual.

Price Data, 2002: $275 per comprehensive Bender Gestalt test material set including all materials needed to administer, score, and interpret the Bender Gestalt Test for Adults and for Children; $210 per set of materials for Bender Gestalt Test: Adults including 1 set of Design Cards, 100 test score sheets, A Visual Motor Gestalt Test and Its Clinical Use, and The Bender Gestalt Test: Quantification and Validity for Adults; $120 per set of materials for Bender Gestalt Test: Children including 1 set of Design Cards, 25 children's scoring booklets, 25 children's record forms, and Bender Visual Motor Gestalt Test of Children: A Manual.

Publisher: Western Psychological Services.

  a) BENDER VISUAL MOTOR GESTALT TEST DESIGN CARDS.

  Population: Ages 4 and over.

  Publication Dates: 1938–1946.

  Acronym: VMGT.

  Price Data: $49.95 per set of design cards (1946, 9 cards); $54 per manual entitled A Visual Motor Gestalt Test and Its Clinical Use (1938, 187 pages).

Time: (10) minutes.

Author: Lauretta Bender.

  b) THE BENDER GESTALT TEST.

  Population: Ages 4 and over.

  Publication Date: 1951.

  Acronym: BGT.

  Price Data: $14.50 per 100 scoring sheets (1 page); $99.50 per manual entitled The Bender Gestalt Test: Quantification and Validity for Adults (1951, 287 pages).

  Time: (10) minutes.

  Comments: Utilizes same test cards as *a*.

  Authors: Gerald R. Pascal and Barbara J. Suttell.

  c) THE BENDER VISUAL MOTOR GESTALT TEST FOR CHILDREN.

  Population: Ages 4–12.

  Publication Date: 1962.

  Price Data: $19.95 per 25 record forms; $22.50 per 25 scoring booklets; $44.50 per manual (1962, 92 pages).

  Time: (10) minutes without associations.

  Comments: Utilizes same test cards as *a*.

  Authors: Aileen Clawson and Charles J. Lagos (scoring booklet).

Cross References: See T5:301 (61 references) and T4:291 (34 references); for reviews by Jack A. Naglieri and John E. Obrzut and Carol A. Boliek, see 11:40 (92 references); for reviews by Kenneth W. Howell and Jerome M. Sattler, see 9:139 (65 references); see also T3:280 (159 references), 8:506 (253 references), and T2:1447 (144 references); for a review by Philip M. Kitay, see 7:161 (192 references); see also P:415 (170 references); for a review by C. B. Blakemore and an excerpted review by Fred Y. Billingslea, see 6:203 (99 references); see also 5:172 (118 references); for reviews by Arthur L. Benton and Howard R. White, see 4:144 (34 references); see also 3:108 (8 references).

[305]
Bennett Mechanical Comprehension Test, Second Edition.

Purpose: "Designed to measure the ability to perceive and understand the relationship of physical forces and mechanical elements in practical situations."

Population: Industrial employees and high school and adult applicants for mechanical positions or engineering schools.

Publication Dates: 1940–1994.

Acronym: BMCT.

Scores: Total score only.

Administration: Group.

Forms, 2: S, T (equivalent forms).

Price Data, 2002: $43 per complete examination kit including one test booklet per form, answer booklets for both forms, and manual; $149 per 25 test booklets;

$39 per hand-scoring keys; $41 per manual; $109 per taped recordings of test questions.

Time: (30) minutes.

Comments: Tape recordings of test questions read aloud are available for use with examinees who have limited reading abilities; Spanish version available.

Author: George K. Bennett.

Publisher: The Psychological Corporation.

Cross References: See T5:302 (4 references) and T4:292 (2 references); for a review by Hilda Wing of an earlier edition, see 11:41 (3 references); see also T3:282 (7 references) and T2:2239 (9 references); for reviews by Harold P. Bechtoldt and A. Oscar H. Roberts, and an excerpted review by Ronald K. Hambleton of the first edition, see 7:1049 (22 references); see also 6:1094 (15 references) and 5:889 (46 references); for a review by N. W. Morton of earlier forms, see 4:766 (28 references); for reviews by Charles M. Harsh, Lloyd G. Humphreys, and George A. Satter, see 3:683 (19 references).

[306]
Benton Visual Retention Test, Fifth Edition.

Purpose: "To assess visual perception, visual memory, and visuoconstructive abilities."

Population: Age 8–adults.

Publication Dates: 1946–1991.

Acronym: BVRT.

Scores, 9: Omissions, Distortions, Perseverations, Rotations, Misplacements, Size Errors, Total Left, Total Right, Total.

Administration: Individual.

Forms, 3: C, D, E in a single booklet.

Price Data, 2002: $168 per complete set including stimulus booklet (all 30 designs), scoring template, 25 response booklets, record form, and manual (1992, 108 pages); $76 per stimulus booklet; $45 per 25 response booklets-record form; $10 per scoring template; $67 per manual.

Time: (15–20) minutes.

Author: Arthur L. Benton.

Publisher: The Psychological Corporation.

Cross References: See T5:303 (32 references); for reviews by Anita M. Hubley and Cynthia A. Rohrbeck, see 13:36 (66 references); see also T4:293 (62 references), 9:140 (30 references), T3:283 (27 references), 8:236 (32 references), T2:543 (71 references), and 6:543 (22 references); for a review by Nelson G. Hanawalt, see 5:401 (5 references); for reviews by Ivan Norman Mensh, Joseph Newman, and William Schofield of the original edition, see 4:360 (3 references); for an excerpted review, see 3:297.

[307]
The Ber-Sil Spanish Test.

Purpose: Screening and evaluation of Spanish-speaking children.

Population: Ages 5–12, 13–17.

Publication Dates: 1972–1987.

Administration: Individual.

Price Data, 1993: $90 per combination elementary and secondary complete kits including 50 of each test booklet; $55 per elementary or secondary complete kit including 50 test booklets, 1 book of picture plates, 1 cassette tape; $31 per book of picture plates; $11 per cassette tape.

Author: Marjorie L. Beringer.

Publisher: Ber-Sil Co.

a) ELEMENTARY LEVEL.

Population: Ages 5–12.

Publication Date: 1987.

Scores, 7: Vocabulary, Response to Directions, Writing, Geometric Figures, Draw a Boy or Girl, Math Skills, English Vocabulary.

Price Data: $9 per 50 test booklets; $17 per manual (83 pages); $17 per translation for available languages.

Foreign Language Editions: Cantonese, Mandarin, Ilokano, Tagalog, Korean, and Persian translations available.

Time: (45–55) minutes.

b) SECONDARY LEVEL.

Population: Ages 13–17.

Publication Date: 1984.

Scores, 4: Vocabulary, Dictation in Spanish, Draw a Person, Mathematics.

Price Data: $9 per 50 test booklets; $17 per manual (69 pages).

Foreign Language Editions: Philippine, Tagalog, and Ilokano translations available.

Time: (45) minutes.

Cross References: For reviews by J. Manuel Casas and David Strand and by Giuseppe Costantino, see 10:30; for reviews by Giuseppe Costantino and Jaclyn B. Spitzer of an earlier edition, see 9:141.

[308]
BEST Instruments.

Purpose: A series of learning instruments designed to help managers and employees understand their behavior.

Population: Adults.

Publication Dates: 1989–1994.

Acronym: BEST.

Administration: Group.

Price Data, 1993: $25 per sample pack; $15 per user's guide (1989, 16 pages); $149 per user's kit.

Comments: Subtests available as separates.

Author: James H. Brewer.

Publisher: Associated Consultants in Education.

a) MY BEST PROFILE.

Purpose: "To promote positive interpersonal relations."

Publication Date: 1989.

Scores: 4 personality types: Bold, Expressive, Sympathetic, Technical.
Price Data: $4.95 per profile; $99.95 per computer software.
Time: (15–20) minutes.
b) MY BEST COMMUNICATION STYLE.
Purpose: "To improve communication skills."
Publication Dates: 1989–1990.
Scores: 4 styles: Bold, Expressive, Sympathetic, Technical.
Price Data: $2.95 per inventory.
Time: (15–20) minutes.
c) MY BEST LEADERSHIP STYLE.
Purpose: "To improve leadership skills."
Publication Dates: 1989–1994.
Scores: Same as *a* above.
Price Data: $4.95 per profile; $99.95 per computer software.
Time: (15–20) minutes.
d) LEADERSHIP/PERSONALITY COMPATIBILITY INVENTORY.
Purpose: "To promote more productive leadership in organizations."
Acronym: L/PCI.
Scores: Same as *a* above plus 4 Leadership Role Characteristics: Active/Competitive, Persuasive/Interactive, Precise/Systematic, Willing/Steady.
Publication Dates: 1990–1994.
Price Data: $5.95 per profile.
Time: (15–20) minutes.
e) WORKING WITH MY BOSS.
Purpose: "To improve the productive relationship between employee and supervisor."
Publication Date: 1989.
Scores: Same as *a* above.
Price Data: $4.95 per profile.
Time: (10–15) minutes.
f) PRE-EVALUATION PROFILE.
Purpose: "To prepare supervisors for performance evaluations of employees without personality type bias."
Acronym: PEP.
Publication Date: 1989.
Scores: Same as *a* above.
Price Data: $4.95 per profile.
Time: (15–20) minutes.
Comments: Supervisor completes profile for self and employee.
g) OUR BEST TEAM.
Purpose: "To build a more productive team."
Publication Date: 1989.
Scores: Same as *a* above.
Price Data: $6.95 per profile.
Time: (20–30) minutes.
Comments: Ratings of all team members are combined for a composite profile.

h) MY TIMESTYLE.
Purpose: "To develop more productive time usage."
Publication Date: 1990.
Scores: 4 timestyles: Road Runner, Race Horse, New Pup, Tom Cat.
Price Data: $2.95 per profile.
Time: (10–15) minutes.
i) MY BEST PRESENTATION STYLE.
Purpose: "To assist individuals in making more effective presentations."
Publication Date: 1989.
Scores: Same as *a* above.
Price Data: $4.95 per profile.
Time: (15–20) minutes.
j) SALES STYLE.
Purpose: "To sharpen sales skills."
Publication Date: 1990.
Scores: 4 sales styles: Quick-Sell, Persistent-Sell, Talkative-Sell, Precise-Sell.
Price Data: $2.95 per profile.
Time: (10–15) minutes.
k) MY TEACHING STYLE.
Purpose: "To help teachers understand learning style."
Publication Date: 1989.
Scores: Bold, Expressive, Sympathetic, Technical.
Price Data: $4.95 per profile.
Time: (15–20) minutes.
l) NEGOTIATING STYLE.
Purpose: "To build productive negotiating strategies."
Publication Date: 1991.
Scores: 4 negotiating styles: Pushy, Stand Pat, Buddy, Check All.
Price Data: $2.95 per profile.
Time: (10–15) minutes.
m) CAREER/PERSONALITY COMPATIBILITY INVENTORY.
Purpose: "To improve career selection."
Publication Date: No date on materials.
Acronym: C/PCI.
Scores: Bold, Expressive, Sympathetic, Technical.
Price Data: $5.95 per profile; $345 per computer software.
Time: (20–30) minutes.
Cross References: For reviews by Mary A. Lewis and Frank Schmidt, see 13:37.

[309]
Beta III.
Purpose: "Provides a quick ... measure of nonverbal intellectual ability."
Population: Ages 16–89.

Publication Dates: 1934–1999.
Scores, 6: Coding, Picture Completion, Clerical Checking, Picture Absurdities, Matrix Reasoning, IQ Score.
Administration: Individual.
Price Data, 2002: $145 per complete kit including manual (1999, 58 pages), 25 response booklets, and scoring key; $42 per manual; $104 per 25 response booklets; $299 per 100 response booklets; quantity discounts available; $16 per scoring key.
Time: 15(25–30) minutes including 10–15 minutes of instruction and practice.
Comments: Revision of the Revised Beta Examination, Second Edition.
Authors: C. E. Kellogg and N. W. Morton.
Publisher: The Psychological Corporation.
Cross References: For information regarding the previous edition, see T5:2212 (3 references) and T4:2255 (4 references); see also T2:447 (29 references); for a review by Bert A. Goldman, see 6:494 (13 references); see also 5:375 (14 references); for reviews by Raleigh M. Drake and Walter C. Shipley, see 3:259 (5 references); for reviews by S. D. Porteus and David Wechsler, see 2:1419 (4 references).

[310]
Bilingual Syntax Measure [medida de Sintaxis Bilingüe].

Purpose: Designed to measure second-language oral proficiency with respect to syntactic structures in English and Spanish.
Population: Grades PK–2, 3–12.
Publication Dates: 1975–1980.
Acronym: BSM I, BSM II.
Scores: Scores consist of assigned levels of proficiency.
Administration: Individual.
Editions, 2: English, Spanish (both of which may be administered as an indicator of language dominance).
Price Data, 2002: $476 per complete set including picture booklet, 35 English response booklets, 35 Spanish response booklets, class record, technical handbook, English manual, and Spanish manual (specify BSM I or BSM II); $133.50 per picture booklet (specify BSM I or BSM II); $118 per 35 BSM I response booklets (specify English or Spanish); $135 per 35 BSM II response booklets (specify English or Spanish); $10 per class record (specify BSM I or BSM II); $40.30 per BSM I technical handbook (1976, 53 pages); $40.30 per BSM II technical handbook (1980, 33 pages); $24.50 per BSM I manual (1975, 15 pages) (specify English or Spanish); $24.50 per BSM II manual (1978, 11 pages) (specify English or Spanish); $26 per English-Spanish reference handbook for educators.
Time: (10–15) minutes for each edition.
Comments: BSM II is an upward extension of the Bilingual Syntax Measure (BSM I).

Authors: Marina K. Burt, Heidi C. Dulay, and Eduardo Hernandez Ch.
Publisher: The Psychological Corporation.
Cross References: See T5:307 (3 references) and T4:298 (2 references); for reviews of BSM II by Eugene E. Garcia and Sylvia Shellenberger, see 9:147 (1 reference); for reviews of BSM I by Isaac I. Bejar and C. Ray Graham, and an excerpted review by John W. Oller, Jr., see 8:156 (4 references); for information on BSM I, see T3:290 (5 references).

[311]
Bilingual Two Language Battery of Tests.

Purpose: To assess Native and English language proficienceis and to establish language dominance.
Population: Students and adults having any level of language proficiency.
Publication Date: 1983.
Scores, 4 or 5: Phonetics, Comprehension, Writing, Total, Oral Proficiency (optional).
Tests, 5: English-Spanish, English-Italian, English-Portuguese, English-Vietnamese, English-French.
Administration: Group.
Price Data: Available from publisher.
Time: 21(31) minutes.
Comments: Test administered by tape cassette; "criterion-referenced"; each session is a Native Language Sitting followed by an English Language Sitting.
Author: Adolph Caso.
Publisher: Branden Publishing, Inc. [No reply from publisher; status unknown].

[312]
Bilingual Verbal Ability Tests.

Purpose: "Provides a measure of overall verbal ability, and unique combination of cognitive/academic language abilities for bilingual individuals."
Population: Ages 5 and over.
Publication Date: 1998.
Acronym: BVAT.
Scores, 5: Bilingual Verbal Ability, English Language Proficiency, Picture Vocabulary, Oral Vocabulary, Verbal Analogies.
Administration: Individual.
Price Data: Available from publisher.
Time: (20–30) minutes.
Comments: Yields an aptitude measure that can be used in conjunction with the WJ-R® Tests of Achievement (T5:2901); an optional training video with administration procedures is available.
Authors: Ana F. Muñoz-Sandoval, Jim Cummins, Criselda G. Alvarado, and Mary L. Ruef.
Publisher: Riverside Publishing.
Cross References: For reviews by Alan Garfinkel and Charles W. Stansfield, see 14:46.

[313]
Biofeedback Certification Examination.

Purpose: A certification examination covering "the knowledge needed by providers of biofeedback services at the time they begin practice."
Population: Entry-level biofeedback service providers.
Publication Dates: 1980–1984.
Scores: 11 Blueprint Areas: Introduction to Biofeedback, Preparing for Clinical Intervention, Neuromuscular Intervention: General, Neuromuscular Intervention: Specific, Central Nervous System Interventions: General, Autonomic Nervous System Interventions: General, Autonomic Nervous System Interventions: Specific, Biofeedback and Distress, Instrumentation, Adjunctive Techniques and Cognitive Interventions, Professional Conduct.
Administration: Group.
Manual: No manual.
Price Data: Available from BCIA.
Time: (180) minutes.
Comments: Administration schedule available from BCIA.
Author: Biofeedback Certification Institute of America.
Publisher: Biofeedback Certification Institute of America.

[314]
Biographical Inventory Form U.

Purpose: "To obtain and analyze information about an individual's characteristics and background."
Population: Grades 7–12.
Publication Dates: 1976–1978.
Acronym: BI.
Scores, 6: Academic Performance, Creativity, Artistic Potential, Leadership, Career Maturity, Educational Orientation.
Administration: Group.
Price Data: Available from publisher.
Time: (60–65) minutes.
Comments: Replaces earlier Alpha Biographical Inventory (7:975).
Author: Institute for Behavioral Research in Creativity.
Publisher: Institute for Behavioral Research in Creativity [No reply from publisher; status unknown].
Cross References: See T5:311 (1 reference); for reviews by Christopher Borman and Courtland C. Lee, see 9:150.

[315]
Birds of Different Feathers Work Style Assessment.

Purpose: Designed to provide "feedback and … tips on how to communicate effectively with others."
Population: Organization employees.
Publication Date: 1998.

Acronym: BDF.
Scores, 2: Personal Work Style, Organizational Work Style.
Administration: Group.
Price Data, 2001: $8.50 per test booklet including test and interpretive information.
Time: (20–30) minutes.
Authors: Barbara Hateley and Warren H. Schmidt.
Publisher: Consulting Psychologists Press, Inc.

[316]
Birmingham Object Recognition Battery.

Purpose: Designed to assess neuropsychological disorders of visual object recognition.
Population: Available from publisher.
Publication Date: 1993.
Acronym: BORB.
Scores: Available from publisher.
Administration: Individual.
Price Data, 2001: $250 per book.
Time: Administration time not reported.
Authors: M. Jane Riddoch and Glyn W. Humphreys.
Publisher: Psychology Press.

[317]
Birth to Three Assessment and Intervention System, Second Edition.

Purpose: Designed to "identify children who are developmentally at risk in the areas of language and learning."
Population: Birth to 3 years.
Publication Dates: 1986–2000.
Acronym: BTAIS-2.
Scores, 5: Language Comprehension, Language Expression, Nonverbal Thinking, Social/Personal Behaviors, Motor Behaviors.
Administration: Individual.
Price Data, 2001: $239 per complete kit including screening test kit, comprehensive test kit, and teaching manual (2000, 163 pages); $69 per teaching manual.
Time: Untimed.
Authors: Jerome J. Ammer and Tina E. Bangs.
Publisher: PRO-ED.
a) SCREENING TEST OF DEVELOPMENTAL ABILITIES.
Purpose: Designed "to identify young children who may have developmental delays."
Price Data: $79 per complete Screening Test kit including manual (2000, 93 pages) and 24 record forms; $47 per manual; $24 per 25 record forms.
b) COMPREHENSIVE TEST OF DEVELOPMENTAL ABILITIES.
Purpose: Designed "to identify each child's specific strengths and weaknesses and to guide the preparation of instructional plans."

Price Data: $98 per complete Comprehensive Test kit including manual (2000, 107 pages) and 25 record forms; $57 per manual; $44 per 25 record forms.

Cross References: See T5:315; for a review by Donna Spiker of an earlier edition, see 11:45; for a review by Bonnie W. Camp of an earlier edition, see 9:152.

[318]
Bloomer Learning Test—Neurologically Enhanced.

Purpose: Designed as a "diagnostic, focused process assessment of cognitive processes and neurological substrates underlying academic learning."

Population: Grades 1–11 and adults.

Publication Dates: 1978–1998.

Acronym: BLT-NE.

Scores: 56 scores in 5 domains: Cognitive Processing Speed (Activity Persistence, Automaticity, Arousal Need, Association Index, Language/Abstract Processing Ratio), Processing in Short Term Memory (Visual Short Term Memory, Auditory Short Term Memory, Visual Apprehension Span, Short Term Memory Composite, Stimulus Complexity Ratio, Working Memory for Letters, Working Memory for Words, Impulsivity, Rehearsal Effects, Cross Modal Efficiency, Stimulus Mode, Response Mode, Memory Response Sequencing, Working Memory Sequencing Stimulus Number Effects, Stimulus Number Sequencing Effects), Learning and Retention Processes (Serial Learning, Learning Set Ratio, Acquisition, Seriation, Auditory Serial Learning, Auditory Acquisition, Auditory Seriation, Free Association, Verbal Response Association, Verbal Written Association Ratio, Free Spelling Error Ratio, Idiosyncratic Language Ratio, Language Complexity Ratio, Cortical Arousal, Paired Associate Index, Paired Associate Learning, Paired Associate Decrement, Recall, Relearning, Recall Ratio, Savings Ratio), Complex Conceptual Processes (Concept Recognition, Concept Production, Concept Synthesis, Problem Solving, Familiarity, Multiordinality), Emotional Mediating Processes (Emotional Passivity, Intensity, Lability, Valence, Emotional Ratio, Verbal Emotional Ratio, Suppression Index).

Administration: Individual or group.

Price Data, 1998: $549 per complete kit.

Time: (10–25) minutes per domain; (70–95) minutes total.

Author: Richard H. Bloomer.

Publisher: Brador Publications, Inc.

Cross References: For a review by Edward Earl Gotts of an earlier edition, see 9:154.

[319]
Blox Test.

Purpose: Designed to measure the individual's perceptual ability for spatial relations.

Population: Job applicants with at least 10 years of education.

Publication Dates: 1961–1963.

Scores: Total score only.

Administration: Group.

Manual: No manual.

Price Data: Available from publisher.

Time: 30(35) minutes.

Comments: Test previously known as Perceptual Battery (T3:1777).

Author: National Institute for Personnel Research of the Human Sciences Research Council.

Publisher: Human Sciences Research Council [South Africa].

[320]
The Boder Test of Reading-Spelling Patterns.

Purpose: Designed as a diagnostic screening test for developmental dyslexia.

Population: Grades K–12 and adult.

Publication Date: 1982.

Scores, 5: Reading (Level, Age, Quotient), Spelling (Known Words/Correct, Unknown Words/Phonetic Equivalence).

Administration: Individual.

Price Data, 2002: $175 per complete kit including 25 reading test record forms, 25 spelling test record forms, 25 alphabet tasks record forms, 25 diagnostic summary record forms, and manual (175 pages); $55 per 25 reading test record forms; $39 per 25 spelling test record forms; $39 per 25 alphabet tasks record forms; $39 per 25 diagnostic summary forms; $82 per manual.

Time: (10–30) minutes.

Authors: Elena Boder and Sylvia Jarrico.

Publisher: The Psychological Corporation.

Cross References: See T5:322 (7 references) and T4:312 (5 references); for reviews by Frederick A. Schrank and Timothy Shanahan, see 9:155 (2 references).

[321]
Boehm Test of Basic Concepts—Third Edition.

Purpose: Designed to "assess ... [school] readiness or [to] identify students who may be at risk for learning difficulty."

Population: Grades K–2.

Publication Dates: 1967–2001.

Acronym: Boehm-3.

Scores: Total score only.

Administration: Group or individual.

Price Data, 2002: $57 per examination set including examiner's manual (2001, 145 pages), 1 Form E booklet, 1 Form F booklet, 1 Form E class key, 1 Form F class key, and 1 directions for administration (Forms

E and F, English and Spanish); $77 per testing kit (Form E or F) including directions for administration (English and Spanish), 1 package of 25 booklets, and 1 class key; $54 per examiner's manual (Fall norms manual); $5 per class key (Form E or F); $16 per directions for administration (English and Spanish).

Time: 30(45) minutes if administered in one session; 45(60) minutes if administered in two test sessions.

Comments: Revision of the Boehm Test of Basic Concepts—Revised.

Author: Ann E. Boehm.

Publisher: The Psychological Corporation.

Cross References: For information regarding previous editions, see T5:324 (12 references) and T4:314 (5 references); for reviews by Robert L. Linn, Colleen Fitzmaurice, and Joseph C. Witt, see 10:32 (16 references); see also T3:302 (18 references); for an excerpted review by Theodore A. Dahl, see 8:178 (22 references); se also T2:344 (1 reference); for reviews by Boyd R. McCandless and Charles D. Smock, and excerpted reviews by Frank S. Freeman, George Lawlor, Victor H. Noll, and Barton B. Proger, see 7:335 (1 reference).

[322]
Boehm-3 Preschool.

Purpose: "Designed to assess young children's understanding of the basic relational concepts" ("quality, spatial, temporal, quantity") "important for language and cognitive development."

Population: Ages 3-0 to 5-11.

Publication Dates: 1986–2001.

Scores: Total score only.

Administration: Individual.

Price Data, 2002: $129 per complete kit including picture book (1986, 112 pages), 35 individual record forms (1986, 5 pages), manual (1986, 35 pages), and class record form (1986, 5 pages); $85 per picture manual; $27 per 25 individual record forms; $41 per manual.

Foreign Language Edition: Spanish version available.

Time: (15–20) minutes.

Comments: Revision of Boehm Test of Basic Concepts—Preschool Version; norms extended upward; provides Parent Report Form, Ongoing Observation and Intervention Planning Form (Spanish versions included); includes directions for Spanish administration and scoring; both English and Spanish norms available.

Author: Ann E. Boehm.

Publisher: The Psychological Corporation.

Cross References: See T5:323 (1 reference) and T4:313 (1 reference); for reviews by Judy Oehler-Stinnett and Stephanie Stein of an earlier edition, see 11:46 (1 reference).

[323]
Booker Profiles in Mathematics: Numeration and Computation.

Purpose: "Designed to pinpoint strengths and weaknesses in basic mathematical knowledge."

Population: Ages 7–16.

Publication Date: 1994.

Scores, 2: Numeration, Computation.

Administration: Individual.

Price Data, 2002: A$132 per kit including manual; A$27.50 per manual.

Time: (45) minutes.

Author: George Booker.

Publisher: Australian Council for Educational Research Ltd. [Australia].

Cross References: For reviews by Richard C. Pugh and James P. Van Haneghan, see 13:38.

[324]
Booker Profiles in Mathematics: Problem Solving.

Purpose: Designed "to be used to gauge an individual's capacity to think, reason, and problem solve in mathematics."

Population: Early school learners through adults.

Publication Date: 2001.

Scores, 5: Relatively Obvious Answers, Less Obvious Answers, Too Much Information, Too Little Information, Strategic Thinking.

Administration: Individual or group.

Price Data, 2002: A$198 per kit including manual (2001, 60 pages), easel, and photocopy masters.

Time: Levels 1 and 2: 20–30 minutes depending on reading ability; Level 3: 20–30 minutes; Level 4: 30–40 minutes.

Authors: George Booker and Denise Bond.

Publisher: Australian Council for Educational Research Ltd. [Australia].

[325]
The Booklet Category Test, Second Edition.

Purpose: Designed to "measure concept formation and abstract reasoning."

Population: Ages 15 and older.

Publication Dates: 1979–1997.

Acronym: BCT.

Scores: Total score only.

Administration: Individual.

Price Data: Available from publisher.

Time: (30–60) minutes.

Authors: Nick A. DeFilippis and Elizabeth McCampbell.

Publisher: Psychological Assessment Resources, Inc.

Cross References: For reviews by Carolyn M. Callahan and David C. S. Richard, see 14:47; see also

T5:326 (10 references) and T4:315 (4 references); for reviews by Raymond S. Dean and Thomas A. Hammeke of an earlier edition, see 9:156.

[326]
Borromean Family Index.

Purpose: Developed to measure "attitudes and feelings about one's family."
Population: Adolescents and adults.
Publication Dates: 1975–1988.
Scores, 2: Internal (forces that attract toward family), External (forces that pull away).
Subtests, 2: For Married Persons, For Single Persons.
Administration: Group.
Manual: No manual.
Price Data, 2002: $1 per test.
Time: [10] minutes.
Comments: Supplementary article available.
Author: Panos D. Bardis.
Publisher: Donna Bardis.
Cross References: For additional information, see 8:332 (1 reference).

[327]
Boston Assessment of Severe Aphasia.

Purpose: Developed to identify "preserved abilities that might form the beginning steps of rehabilitation programs for severely aphasic patients."
Population: Aphasic adults.
Publication Date: 1989.
Acronym: BASA.
Scores, 5: Auditory Comprehension, Praxis, Oral-Gestural Expression, Reading Comprehension, Other.
Administration: Individual.
Price Data, 2001: $269 per complete kit; $64 per package of manipulatives; $44 per set of stimulus cards; $40 per custom aluminum clipboard; $39 per 25 record forms; $54 per manual (96 pages).
Time: (30–40) minutes.
Authors: Nancy Helm-Estabrooks, Gail Ramsberger, Alisa R. Morgan, and Marjorie Nicholas.
Publisher: PRO-ED.
Cross References: See T5:328 (1 reference); for reviews by Steven B. Leder and Roger L. Towne, see 12:52 (3 references).

[328]
The Boston Qualitative Scoring System for the Rey-Osterrieth Complex Figure.

Purpose: Designed as a quantifiable approach to rating the qualitative features of the ROCF (which was designed to assess visuoconstructional ability and visual memory performance in brain-impaired patients).
Population: Ages 18–94.
Publication Dates: 1994–1999.
Acronym: BQSS.

Scores, 23: Qualitative (Configural Presence, Configural Accuracy, Cluster Presence, Cluster Accuracy, Cluster Placement, Detail Presence, Detail Placement, Fragmentation, Planning, Neatness, Vertical Expansion, Horizontal Expansion, Reduction, Rotation, Perservation, Confabulation, Asymmetry), Summary (Copy Presence and Accuracy, Immediate Presence and Accuracy, Delayed Presence and Accuracy, Immediate Retention, Delayed Retention, Organization).
Administration: Individual.
Price Data: Available from publisher.
Time: (45) minutes, including a (20–30) minute delay interval.
Authors: Robert A. Stern, Debbie J. Javorsky, Elizabeth A. Singer, Naomi G. Singer Harris, Jessica A. Somerville, Lisa M. Duke, Jodi A. Thompson, and Edith Kaplan.
Publisher: Psychological Assessment Resources, Inc.

[329]
Botel Reading Inventory.

Purpose: To "determine the needed program of phonics and spelling instruction" by identifying "the word attack skills of each pupil."
Population: Grades 1–4, 1–6, 1–12.
Publication Dates: 1961–1970.
Acronym: BRI.
Scores, 9: Frustration Level, Instructional Level (Placement), and Free Reading Level scores for each of tests *a* and *b*.
Administration: Group.
Price Data: Available from publisher.
Time: Administration time not reported.
Author: Morton Botel.
Publisher: Modern Curriculum Press [No reply from publisher; status unknown].
  a) WORD RECOGNITION TEST.
  Population: Grades 1–4.
  Comments: Consists of 8 "graded" 20-word lists described as samples of reading materials at 8 levels.
  b) WORD OPPOSITES TEST.
  Population: Grades 1–12.
  Comments: Vocabulary test described as "an estimate of reading comprehension"; 10 "graded" 10-word lists at 10 levels.
Cross References: See T4:318 (1 reference), T3:309 (1 reference), T2:1658 (2 references), and 7:727 (5 references); for reviews by Ira E. Aaron and Charles M. Brown, see 6:834.

[330]
Bracken Basic Concept Scale—Revised.

Purpose: Designed to measure relevant educational concepts and receptive language skills.
Population: Ages 2 1/2 to 8.

Publication Dates: 1984–1998.

Acronym: BBCS-R.

Scores, 11: Colors, Letters, Numbers/Counting, Sizes, Comparisons, Shapes, Direction/Position, Self-/Social Awareness, Texture/Material, Quantity, and Time/Sequence.

Administration: Individual.

Price Data, 2002: $245 per complete program including examiner's manual (1998, 223 pages), stimulus manual (276 pages), 25 diagnostic scale record forms, and one screening test; $63 per examiner's manual; $195 per diagnostic scale stimulus manual; $19 per 15 English record forms; $57 per 50 English record forms; $19 per 15 Spanish record forms; $57 per 50 Spanish record forms.

Time: (30) minutes.

Comments: May be used diagnostically or as a screening test by scoring the first six subtests called the School Readiness Composite (SRC); may be used for norm-referenced, criterion referenced, or curriculum-based assessments.

Author: Bruce A. Bracken.

Publisher: The Psychological Corporation.

Cross References: See T5:331 (6 references) and T4:319 (4 references); for reviews by Timothy L. Turco and James E. Ysseldyke of an earlier edition, see 10:33.

[331]
Braille Assessment Inventory.

Purpose: Designed to assist educators "in determining whether Braille instruction is an appropriate intervention for students ... who are blind or visually impaired" in order to become more efficient learners as a result of using Braille as their primary reading mode.

Population: Ages 6–18.

Publication Date: 1996.

Acronym: BAI.

Scores, 5: Object Recognition, Visual Orientation, Tactual Orientation, Functional Considerations, Total.

Administration: Individual.

Price Data, 2002: $43.50 per complete kit including technical manual (28 pages) and 50 record forms; $12.50 per technical manual; $31 per 50 record forms.

Time: Untimed.

Authors: Michael N. Sharpe, Donna McNear, and Kevin S. McGrew.

Publisher: Hawthorne Educational Services, Inc.

Cross References: For reviews by John MacDonald and Robert G. Morwood, see 14:49.

[332]
Bricklin Perceptual Scales.

Purpose: Yields information on a child's unconscious or nonverbal perception of his or her parents; for determining which of the parents would make the better primary caretaker for a particular child in child-custody decisions.

Population: Ages 6 and over.

Publication Dates: 1984–2002.

Acronym: BPS.

Scores, 10: 5 scores each for mother and father: Perception of Competency, Perception of Supportiveness, Perception of Follow-Up Consistency, Perception of Admirable Character Traits, Total.

Administration: Individual.

Price Data, 2002: $199 per complete kit including 8 sets of response cards, 8 scoring sheets, stylus-pen, placement dots, test box with foam insert, manual (1992, 141 pages), instructions, and Bricklin Updates; $99 per 8 additional sets of response cards; $159 per 16 sets of response cards with summaries; $199 per 24 sets of response cards with summaries; $198 per IBM computer scoring profile (3.5-inch disk).

Time: (40) minutes.

Comments: IBM or compatible computer required for computer scoring profile (unlimited uses).

Author: Barry Bricklin.

Publisher: Village Publishing.

Cross References: For reviews by Rosa A. Hagin and Marcia B. Shaffer, see 11:48.

[333]
Brief Derogatis Psychiatric Rating Scale.

Purpose: To obtain clinical observors' ratings on nine personality dimensions.

Population: Psychiatric and medical patients.

Publication Dates: 1974–1978.

Acronym: B-DPRS™.

Scores: 9 dimensions: Somatization, Obsessive-Compulsive, Interpersonal Sensitivity, Depression, Anxiety, Hostility, Phobic Anxiety, Paranoid Ideation, Psychoticism.

Administration: Individual.

Manual: No manual.

Price Data, 2002: $42.75 per 100 tests.

Time: (5) minutes.

Comments: Formerly the Brief Hopkins Psychiatric Rating Scale; short form of the Derogatis Psychiatric Rating Scale; self-report; can also be used with Symptom Checklist-90-Revised or Brief Symptom Inventory.

Author: Leonard R. Derogatis.

Publisher: NCS Assessments (Minnetonka).

Cross References: See T5:335 (15 references) and T4:323 (5 references).

[334]
Brief Neuropsychological Cognitive Examination.

Purpose: Constructed as "an assessment of the severity and nature of cognitive impairment" for psychiatric and neurological patients.

Population: Ages 18 and older.

Publication Date: 1997.
Acronym: BNCE.
Scores, 4: Validity Index, Part I, Part II, Total.
Administration: Individual.
Price Data, 2002: $115 per complete kit including manual (58 pages), stimulus booklet, 20 response booklets, and 20 administration and scoring forms; $33.50 per 20 response booklets; $19.50 per 20 administration and scoring forms; $32.50 per stimulus booklet; $46 per manual.
Time: (30) minutes.
Author: Joseph Tonkonogy.
Publisher: Western Psychological Services.
Cross References: For reviews by Eugene V. Aidman and Sheila Mehta, see 14:50.

[335]
Brief Symptom Inventory.

Purpose: "Designed to reflect the psychological symptom patterns of psychiatric and medical patients as well as non-patients."
Population: Adults and adolescents age 13 or older.
Publication Date: 1975.
Acronym: BSI®.
Scores: 9 primary dimensions: Somatization, Obsessive-Compulsive, Interpersonal Sensitivity, Depression, Anxiety, Hostility, Phobic Anxiety, Paranoid Ideation, Psychoticism; plus 3 global indices: Global Severity Index, Positive Symptom Distress Index, Positive Symptom Total.
Administration: Group or individual.
Price Data, 2002: $111 per hand-scoring starter kit including manual, 50 answer sheets, 50 profile forms, 2 worksheets, and answer keys (specify Nonpatient Adult, Nonpatient Adolescent, Outpatient Psychiatric, or Inpatient Psychiatric); $41 per 50 hand-scoring answer sheets; $23.50 per answer keys; $22.25 per 50 profile forms and 2 worksheets (specify Nonpatient Adult, Nonpatient Adolescent, Outpatient Psychiatric, or Inpatient Psychiatric); $30 per manual; price information for Interpretive Report and Profile Report scoring and software available from publisher.
Time: (8–10) minutes.
Comments: Essentially the brief form of the Symptom Checklist-90-Revised (2674); self-report; useful in initial evaluation and measurement of patient progress during treatment to monitor change and after treatment for assessment of treatment outcome; companion clinician and observer rating forms are also available.
Author: Leonard R. Derogatis.
Publisher: NCS Assessments (Minnetonka).
Cross References: See T5:337 (198 references) and T4:324 (59 references); for reviews by Bert C. Cundick and Charles A. Peterson, see 10:35 (7 references); see also 9:160 (1 reference).

[336]
Brief Symptom Inventory 18.

Purpose: Designed to "screen for psychological distress and psychiatric disorders in medical and community populations."
Population: Age 18 and older.
Publication Dates: 2000–2001.
Acronym: BSI 18.
Scores, 4: Somatization, Depression, Anxiety, Total (General Severity Index).
Administration: Individual or group.
Price Data, 2002: $37 per preview package with profile reports including manual (2001, 54 pages), answer sheets with test items, and all materials necessary to conduct 3 assessments and receive profile reports using MICROTEST Q Assessment System software; $19 per 25 answer sheets (English or Hispanic); $3.65 per profile report (quantity discounts available); $86 per hand-scoring starter kit including manual, 50 answer sheets, and 50 profile forms (specify community or oncology norms); $41 per 50 answer sheets (English or Hispanic); $22.25 per 50 profile forms (community or oncology norms); $30 per manual.
Time: (4–5) minutes.
Comments: Abbreviated adaptation of Brief Symptom Inventory (335); self-report; may be administered in paper-and-pencil format or online.
Author: Leonard R. Derogatis.
Publisher: NCS Assessments [Minnetonka].
Cross References: For information on the Brief Symptom Inventory, see T5:337 (198 references); for reviews by Bert C. Cundick and Charles A. Peterson, see 10:35 (7 references); see also 9:160 (1 reference).

[337]
Brief Test of Attention.

Purpose: Designed "to assess the severity of attentional impairment among nonaphasic hearing adult patients."
Population: Ages 17–82.
Publication Date: 1997.
Acronym: BTA.
Scores: Total score only.
Administration: Individual.
Forms, 2: N (Numbers), L (Letters).
Price Data: Available from publisher for kit including manual (34 pages), and 50 scoring forms and for audio tape.
Time: (10) minutes.
Author: David Schretlen.
Publisher: Psychological Assessment Resources, Inc.

[338]
Brief Test of Head Injury.

Purpose: Designed to provide information about cognitive, linguistic, and communicative abilities of patients with severe head trauma.

Population: Acute and long-term head-injured adults.
Publication Dates: 1989–1991.
Acronym: BTHI.
Scores, 8: Orientation/Attention, Following Commands, Linguistic Organization, Reading Comprehension, Naming, Memory, Visual-Spatial Skills, Total.
Administration: Individual.
Price Data, 2001: $229 per complete kit including 25 record forms, examiner's manual (1991, 85 pages), manipulatives package, stimulus cards and letter board, and carrying case; $49 per 25 record forms; $34 per manipulatives package; $69 per stimulus cards and letter board; $74 per examiner's manual.
Time: (25–30) minutes.
Authors: Nancy Helm-Estabrooks and Gillian Hotz.
Publisher: PRO-ED.
Cross References: For reviews by Deborah D. Roman and Michael Lee Russell, see 13:39.

[339]
Brief Visuospatial Memory Test—Revised.

Purpose: Designed as an equivalent, multiple-test form assessment of visual memory.
Population: Ages 18–79.
Publication Dates: 1988–1997.
Acronym: BVMT-R.
Scores, 12: Trial 1, Trial 2, Trial 3, Total Recall, Learning, Delayed Recall, Percent Retained, Recognition Hits, Recognition False Alarms, Recognition Discrimination Index, Recognition Response Bias, Copy.
Administration: Individual.
Price Data: Available from publisher for kit including manual (1997, 131 pages), recognition stimulus booklet, recall stimulus booklet, and 10 response forms.
Time: (45) minutes including 25-minute delay.
Comments: Can be administered bed-side by appropriately trained personnel.
Author: Ralph H. B. Benedict.
Publisher: Psychological Assessment Resources, Inc.

[340]
BRIGANCE® Diagnostic Assessment of Basic Skills–Spanish Edition.

Purpose: Designed to indicate language dominance and to test for English oral language proficiency.
Population: Grades kindergarten–6.
Publication Date: 1984.
Scores: 102 tests in 10 areas: Readiness, Speech, Functional Word Recognition, Oral Reading, Reading Comprehension, Word Analysis, Listening, Writing and Alphabetizing, Numbers and Computation, Measurement.
Administration: Individual.
Price Data, 2001: $149 per complete set including manual (234 pages) with directions for administration

and scoring; $27.90 per 10 student record books; $12.95 per optional class record book.
Time: Administration time not reported.
Comments: "Criterion-referenced"; no suggested standards of memory.
Author: Albert H. Brigance.
Publisher: Curriculum Associates, Inc.

[341]
BRIGANCE® Diagnostic Comprehensive Inventory of Basic Skills, Revised.

Purpose: Designed for diagnostic and classroom assessment in basic reading skills, reading comprehension, math calculation, math reasoning, written language, listening comprehension, and information-processing.
Population: Ages 5–13.
Publication Dates: 1976–1999.
Acronym: CIBS-R.
Scores: 154 scores in 8 areas: Readiness, Speech, Listening, Research and Study Skills, Reading, Spelling, Writing, Math.
Administration: Individual and group.
Forms, 2: Form A (pretesting), Form B (posttesting).
Price Data, 2001: $185 per Inventory tests with standardization and validation manual (1999, 143 pages) (U.S. or Canadian versions); $159 per inventory only tests (U.S. or Canadian versions); $35 per 10 student record books; $329 per 100 student record books; $14 per class record book; $22 per 10 student profile test booklets; $40 per manual; $70 per 120 readiness or Grades 1–6 scoring sheets; $20 per 30 readiness of Grades 1–6 scoring sheets; conversion software available on CD-ROM.
Time: Specific time limits are listed for some normed/standardized tests.
Comments: "Criterion-referenced"; normed/standardized option for key tests; computer data program available.
Authors: Albert H. Brigance and Frances Page Glascoe (standardization and validation manual).
Publisher: Curriculum Associates, Inc.
Cross References: For reviews by Gregory J. Cizek and Mary J. McLellan, see 14:51; see also T5:340 (1 reference); for reviews by Craig N. Mills and Mark E. Swerdlik of an earlier edition, see 9:162.

[342]
BRIGANCE® Diagnostic Employability Skills Inventory.

Purpose: Designed to assess employability and basic skills in the "context of job-seeking or employment situations."
Population: Prospective job-applicants.
Publication Date: 1995.
Scores: 8 skills: Reading Grade-Placement Assessments; Career Awareness and Self-Understanding; Job-

Seeking Skills and Knowledge; Rating Scales; Reading Skills; Speaking and Listening Skills; Pre-Employment Writing; Math and Concepts.

Administration: Group.

Price Data, 2001: $89.95 per manual (233 pages); $24.95 per 10 Learner Record Books; $229 per 100 Learner Record Books; $12.95 per Program Record Book.

Time: Administration time varies.

Author: Albert H. Brigance.

Publisher: Curriculum Associates, Inc.

Cross References: For reviews by JoEllen V. Carlson and William C. Tirre, see 14:52.

[343]
BRIGANCE® Diagnostic Inventory of Essential Skills.

Purpose: Designed to assess skills seen as necessary for successful functioning as an adult.

Population: Grade 6-adult.

Publication Date: 1981.

Acronym: IES.

Scores: 191 tests in 26 areas: Word Recognition Grade Placement (1 test), Oral Reading (5 tests), Reading Comprehension (9 tests), Functional Word Recognition (6 tests), Word Analysis (9 tests), Reference Skills (5 tests), Schedules and Graphs (3 tests), Writing (7 tests), Forms (2 tests), Spelling (8 tests), Math Grade Placement (2 tests), Numbers (4 tests), Number Facts (4 tests), Computations of Whole Numbers (6 tests), Fractions (9 tests), Decimals (6 tests), Percents (4 tests), Measurement (15 tests), Metrics (16 tests), Math Vocabulary (3 tests), Health and Safety (6 tests), Vocational (23 tests), Money and Finance (11 tests), Travel and Transportation (10 tests), Food and Clothing (10 tests), Oral Communication and Telephone Skills (7 tests).

Administration: Individual in part.

Price Data, 2001: $169 per manual (391 pages); $36.95 per 10 student record books; $12.95 per class record book.

Time: Specific time limits are listed on many tests; others are untimed.

Author: Albert Brigance.

Publisher: Curriculum Associates, Inc.

Cross References: See T4: 329 (2 references); for reviews by Paula Matuszek and Philip A. Saigh, see 9:165.

[344]
BRIGANCE® Diagnostic Life Skills Inventory.

Purpose: Designed to evaluate "listening, speaking, reading, writing, comprehending, and computing skills within the context of everyday situations."

Population: Grades 2–8.

Publication Date: 1994.

Scores: 9 skills: Speaking and Listening Skills, Functional Writing Skills, Words on Common Signs and Warning Labels, Telephone Skills, Money and Finance, Food, Clothing, Health, Travel and Transportation.

Administration: Group.

Price Data, 2001: $89.95 per manual (239 pages); $24.95 per 10 Learner Record Books; $229 per 100 Learner Record Books; $12.95 per Program Record Book.

Time: Administration time varies.

Author: Albert H. Brigance.

Publisher: Curriculum Associates, Inc.

Cross References: For reviews by Cleborne D. Maddux and Rhoda Cummings and by james A. Wollack, see 14:53; see also T5:344 (1 reference).

[345]
BRIGANCE® Early Preschool Screen for Two-Year-Old and Two-and-a-Half-Year-Old Children.

Purpose: "Criterion-referenced" and normed referenced screen designed "to provide a sampling of a child's learning, development, and skills in a broad range of areas."

Population: Ages 2 to 2 1/2 years.

Publication Dates: 1990–2002.

Administration: Individual.

Price Data, 2001: $89 per manual (69 pages with building blocks); $49 per technical manual (2002, 246 pages); no charge for Spanish directions.

Foreign Language Edition: Spanish component available.

Time: (15–20) minutes.

Comments: Most skills included in the assessments were excerpted from the BRIGANCE® Diagnostic Inventory of Early Development.

Author: Albert H. Brigance.

Publisher: Curriculum Associates, Inc.

a) TWO-YEAR CHILD.

Scores, 9: Builds Tower with Blocks, Visual-Motor Skills, Identifies Body Parts, Picture Vocabulary, Identifies People in Picture by Pointing, Identifies Objects According to Use, Gross-Motor Skills, Verbal Fluency, Total.

Price Data: $31 per 30 data sheets ($90 per 120-pack).

b) TWO-AND-A-HALF-YEAR CHILD.

Scores, 10: Builds Tower with Blocks, Visual-Motor Skills, Identifies Body Parts, Picture Vocabulary, Identifies People in Picture by Naming, Knows Use of Objects, Quantitative Concepts, Gross-Motor Skills, Verbal Fluency, Total.

Price Data: $31 per 30 data sheets ($90 per 120-pack).

Cross References: For reviews by William M. Bart and Joseph M. Ryan, see 11:49.

[346]
BRIGANCE® Infant & Toddler Screen.

Purpose: Designed to obtain a broad sampling of a very young child's development and skills; ... enables professionals to monitor children's developmental progress, advise parents on how to promote a child's development, initiate individualized instruction, and recommend special services to facilitate learning needs and/or family adjustments.
Population: Infants (birth through 11 months) and toddler (12 months through 23 months).
Publication Date: 2002.
Administration: Individual or group.
Price Data, 2002: $110 per manual (89 pages); $31 per 30 Infant or Toddler data sheets (English or Spanish), volume discounts available; $39.90 per 10 Infant or Toddler record folders (English or Spanish); $59.95 per box of materials; $49 per technical report (232 pages); $29.95 per Screens Scoring Software; $15.95 per Screens Inservice Video (20 minutes) and Facilitator's Guide.
Time: (15) minutes.
Comments: Screens Scoring Software provides percentile ranks, standard scores, and age equivalent scores; includes directions in Spanish.
Authors: Albert H. Brigance (Screen) and Frances Page Glascoe (Screen and Technical Report).
Publisher: Curriculum Associates, Inc.
   a) INFANT.
      Scores, 7: Fine-Motor Skills, Receptive Language Skills, Expressive Language Skills, Gross Motor Skills, Self-Help Skills, Social-Emotional Skills, Total Score.
   b) TODDLER.
      Scores, 12: Fine-Motor Skills, Receptive Language Skills—General, Receptive Language Skills—Body Parts, Receptive Language Skills—Picture Naming, Receptive Language Skills—Environmental Sounds, Expressive Language Skills—General, Expressive Language Skills—Object Naming, Expressive Language Skills—Phrases, Gross Motor Skills, Self-Help Skills, Social-Emotional Skills, Total Score.

[347]
BRIGANCE® K & 1 Screen for Kindergarten and First Grade Children [Revised].

Purpose: Designed to screen for readiness for kindergarten or first grade.
Population: Grades K, 1.
Publication Dates: 1982–2002.
Administration: Individual.

Price Data, 2001: $89 per manual (1992, 88 pages); $49 per technical manual (2002, 246 pages).
Time: [15–20] minutes per child.
Comments: "Criterion-referenced" and normed referenced in key skill areas.
Author: Albert H. Brigance.
Publisher: Curriculum Associates, Inc.
   a) KINDERGARTEN.
      Scores, 13: Personal Data Response, Color Recognition, Picture Vocabulary, Visual Discrimination-Forms and Uppercase Letters, Visual-Motor Skills, Gross-Motor Skills, Rote Counting, Identifies Body Parts, Follows Verbal Directions, Numeral Comprehension, Prints Personal Data, Syntax and Fluency, Total.
      Price Data: $31 per 30 data sheets; $39 per 10 class summary folders; quantity discounts available.
   b) FIRST GRADE.
      Scores, 14: Personal Data Response, Color Recognition, Picture Vocabulary, Visual Discrimination-Lowercase Letters and Words, Visual-Motor Skills, Rote Counting, Recites Alphabet, Numeral Comprehension, Recognition of Lowercase Letters, Auditory Discrimination, Draw A Person, Prints Personal Data, Numerals in Sequence, Total.
      Price Data: $20.15 per 30 data sheets; $27.90 per 10 class summary folders; quantity discounts available.
Cross References: For reviews by Ronald A. Berk and T. Steuart Watson, see 12:53 (1 reference); see also T4:331 (3 references); for reviews of an earlier edition by Ann E. Boehm and Dan Wright, see 9:166.

[348]
BRIGANCE® Preschool Screen.

Purpose: Screens a child's basic "skills and behavior in order to identify the child who should be referred for more comprehensive evaluation."
Population: Ages 3–4.
Publication Dates: 1985–2002.
Acronym: BPS.
Administration: Individual.
Price Data, 2001: $89 per complete kit including building blocks and manual (88 pages); $49 per technical manual (2002, 246 pages).
Time: (10–20) minutes.
Comments: "Criterion-referenced" and normed referenced.
Author: Albert H. Brigance.
Publisher: Curriculum Associates, Inc.
   a) AGE 3.
      Scores: 11 skills: Personal Data Response, Identifies Body Parts, Gross Motor Skills, Identifies Objects, Repeats Sentences, Visual Motor Skills,

Number Concepts, Builds Tower with Blocks, Matches Colors, Picture Vocabulary, Plurals.

Price Data: $31 per 30 3-year data sheets; $90 per 120 3-year data sheets.

b) AGE 4.

Scores: 11 skills: Personal Data Response, Identifies Body Parts, Gross Motor Skills, Tells Use of Objects, Repeats Sentences, Visual Motor Skills, Number Concepts, Builds Tower with Blocks, Identifies Colors, Picture Vocabulary, Prepositions and Irregular Plural Nouns.

Price Data: $31 per 30 4-year data sheets; $90 per 120 4-year data sheets.

Cross References: For reviews by Edith S. Heil and Timothy L. Turco, see 10:36.

[349]
Bristol Achievement Tests.

Purpose: To assess school achievement.
Population: Ages 8-0 to 11-11.
Publication Dates: 1969–1982.
Administration: Group.
Levels, 3: 8-0 to 9-11, 9-0 to 10-11, 10-0 to 11-11.
Forms, 2: A, B.
Price Data: Price information available from publisher for test booklets (select level and form), profiles, teacher's set (without interpretive manual) of any one level (must be purchased to obtain administrative manual), and interpretive manual (1969, 84 pages).
Comments: Levels 4 and 5 out of print.
Publisher: NFER-Nelson Publishing Co., Ltd. [England].

  a) ENGLISH LANGUAGE.
  Scores, 6: Word Meaning, Paragraph Meaning, Sentence Organization, Organization of Ideas, Spelling and Punctuation, Total.
  Time: 50(55) minutes.
  Authors: Alan Brimer and Herbert Gross.
  b) MATHEMATICS.
  Scores, 6: Number, Reasoning, Space, Measurement, Arithmetic Laws and Processes, Total.
  Time: 55(60) minutes.
  Author: Alan Brimer.
  c) STUDY SKILLS.
  Scores, 6: Properties, Structures, Processes, Explanations, Interpretations, Total.
  Time: 50(55) minutes.
  Authors: Alan Brimer, Margaret Fidler, Wynne Harlen, and John Taylor.

Cross References: For a review by F. G. Brown of the complete battery, see 9:168; for a review by Roy A. Kress of the English test, see 9:169; for a review by F. G. Brown of the Mathematics test, see 9:170; for a review by Kenneth J. Smith of the Study Skills test, see 9:171; for reviews by G. A. V. Morgan and A. E. F. Pillner of an earlier edition of the complete battery, see

7:4; for a review by Ralph D. Dutch of an earlier edition of the English test, see 7:185; for a review by Kenneth Lovell of an earlier edition of the Mathematics test, see 7:453; for a review by Elizabeth J. Goodacre of an earlier edition of the Study Skills test, see 7:776.

[350]
British Ability Scales: Second Edition.

Purpose: Designed as a battery to assess "cognitive abilities and educational achievement."
Population: Ages 2.6 to 17.11.
Publication Dates: 1977–1996.
Acronym: BAS II.
Scores: 4 scales, 25 scores: Early Years Core Scales (Block Building, Verbal Comprehension, Picture Similarities, Naming Vocabulary, Recall of Objects—Immediate, Pattern Construction, Early Number Concepts, Recall of Objects—Delayed, Copying), School Age Core Scales (Recall of Designs, Word Definitions, Recall of Objects—Immediate, Pattern Construction, Matrices, Recall of Objects—Delayed, Verbal Similarities, Quantitative Reasoning), Diagnostic Scales (Speed of Information Processing, Recall of Digits Forward, Matching Letter-Like Forms, Recognition of Pictures, Recall of Digits Backward), Achievement Scales (Number Skills, Spelling, Word Reading).
Administration: Individual.
Forms, 2: Early Years, School Age.
Price Data, 1998: £695 per full age range complete set including stimulus books, 10 relevant record forms and consumable booklets; £495 per early years complete set including stimulus books, 10 record forms and consumable booklets; £425 per school age complete set including stimulus books, 10 record forms and consumable booklets; £35 per 25 early years record booklets; £45 per 25 school age record booklets; £10 per 10 Speed of Information Processing booklets A, B, or C; £10 per 10 Quantitative Reasoning booklets set A; £5 per 100 sheets copying paper; £5 per 100 recall of designs sheets; £15 per basic number skills/spelling worksheets; £75 per administration and scoring manual ('96, 544 pages); £60 per technical handbook; £27.50 per BAS Short-Form Record Booklet; £50 per 25 BAS Complete Record Booklet; £150 per BAS II Scoring and Reporting Software.
Time: Administration time varies.
Comments: Considerations for testing special populations detailed in manual.
Authors: Colin D. Elliott with Pauline Smith and Kay McCulloch.
Publisher: NFER-Nelson Publishing Co., Ltd. [England].
Cross References: See T5:349 (39 references) and T4:336 (25 references); for reviews by Susan Embretson (Whitely), Benjamin D. Wright, and Mark H. Stone of an earlier edition, see 9:172 (5 references); for reviews

by Steve Graham and William D. Schafer of an earlier edition of the British Ability Scales: Spelling Scale, see 12.55.

[351]
British Picture Vocabulary Scales.

Purpose: Designed "to screen for receptive language problems, to establish a child's level of receptive vocabulary, and to provide some indication of general ability."
Population: Ages 2.5–18.
Publication Date: 1982.
Acronym: BPVS.
Score: Total score only.
Administration: Individual.
Forms, 2: Long (156 items) for detailed assessment, short (38 items) for rapid screening.
Price Data: Price information available from publisher for complete kit including 25 each of long and short form test records, long and short form test plates, and manual (72 pages).
Time: (10–20) minutes for long form; (5–15) minutes for short form.
Authors: Lloyd M. Dunn, Leota M. Dunn, Chris Whetton, and David Pintillie.
Publisher: NFER-Nelson Publishing Co., Ltd. [England].
Cross References: See T5:350 (53 references) and T4:338 (16 references).

[352]
Brown Attention-Deficit Disorder Scales.

Purpose: Designed to "elicit cognitive and affective indications of Attention-Deficit Disorder."
Publication Dates: 1996–2001.
Acronym: Brown ADD Scales.
Scores, 6: Organizing and Activating to Work, Sustaining Attention and Concentration, Sustaining Energy and Effort, Managing Affective Interference, Utilizing "Working Memory" and Assessing Recall, Total.
Administration: Individual or group.
Price Data, 2002: $270 per complete kit for Children and Adolescents including 25 Ready Score® Parent and Teacher forms for ages 3–7, 25 Ready Score® Parent, Teacher and self-report forms for ages 8–12, 25 Ready Score® answer documents for ages 12–18, diagnostic forms (10 each, Children and Adolescents), and manual for Children and Adolescents; $160 per complete kit for Adolescents and Adults including treatment monitoring worksheet, 50 Ready Score® answer documents (25 each for ages 12–18 and 18+), diagnostic forms (10 each for ages 12–18 and 18+), and manual for Adolescents and Adults; $40 per 25 Ready Score® parent forms (specify ages 3–7 or ages 8–12); $40 per 25 Ready Score® teacher forms (specify ages 3–

7 or ages 8–12); $40 per 25 Ready Score® self-report forms/answer documents (specify ages 8–12, or ages 12–18, or ages 18+); $20 per 10 diagnostic forms (specify ages 3–12, ages 12–18, or ages 18+); $79 per manual for Children and Adolescents or manual for Adolescents and Adults; $150 per Scoring Assistant (3.5-inch diskette or CD-ROM Windows).
Time: (10–20) minutes.
Author: Thomas E. Brown.
Publisher: The Psychological Corporation.
 a) PRIMARY/PRESCHOOL.
 Population: Ages 3–7.
 b) SCHOOL-AGE.
 Population: Ages 8–12.
 c) ADOLESCENT SCALE.
 Population: Ages 12 to 18.
 d) ADULT SCALE.
 Population: Ages 18 and over.
Cross References: For reviews by Nadeen L. Kaufman and Alan S. Kaufman, by E. Jean Newman, and by Judy Oehler-Stinnett, see 14:54.

[353]
Brown Attention-Deficit Disorder Scales for Children and Adolescents.

Purpose: "Designed to elicit … [information] that may indicate impairment in executive functions related to Attention-Deficit/Hyperactivity Disorders (AD/HD)."
Population: Ages 3–18.
Publication Date: 2001.
Acronym: Brown ADD Scales for Children.
Scores, 7: 6 cluster scores (Organizing/Prioritizing/and Activating to Work, Focusing/Sustaining/and Shifting Attention to Tasks, Regulating Alertness/Sustaining Effort/and Processing Speed, Managing Frustration and Modulating Emotions, Utilizing Working Memory and Accessing Recall, Monitoring and Self-Regulating Action), Total Score.
Administration: Group or individual.
Price Data, 2001: $270 per complete kit including manual (149 pages), 25 each Ready Score Parent Forms and Teacher Forms (ages 3–7), 25 each Ready Score Parent Forms, Teacher Forms, and Self-Report Forms (ages 8–12), 25 Ready Score Answer Documents (ages 12–18), and 10 each Child Diagnostic Forms (ages 3–12) and Adolescent Diagnostic Forms (ages 12–18); $79 per manual; $40 per 25 Ready Score Parent Forms (ages 3–7 or 8–12); $40 per 25 Ready Score Teacher Forms (ages 3–7 or 8–12); $40 per 25 Ready Score Self-Report Forms/Answer Documents (child, ages 8–12; or adolescent, ages 12–18); $20 per 10 Diagnostic Forms (child, ages 3–12; or adolescent, ages 12–18); $350 per Scoring Assistant kit including manual, 25 each Parent Forms (ages 3–7 and 8–12), 25 each Teacher Forms (ages 3–7 and 8–12), 25 each Self-Report Forms (ages

8–12 and 12–18), Brown ADD Scoring Assistant CD-ROM (3.5-inch diskette version available); $40 per 25 Parent or Teacher Forms (ages 3–7 or 8–12); $40 per 25 Self-Report Forms/Answer Documents (child, ages 8–12; or adolescent, ages 12–18).

Time: (10–20) minutes.

Comments: Downward extension of the Brown Attention Deficit Disorder Scales (352); describes cognitive, affective, behavioral symptoms beyond DSM-IV diagnostic criteria to assess executive function impairments; optional Brown ADD Scales Scoring Assistant software scores, analyzes results, maintains records, generates graphical and narrative reports; system requirements: Windows 95/98/2000/Me/NT 4.0, 100 MHz Pentium processor, 32 MB RAM, 2 MB video card capable of 800 x 600 resolution (256 colors), 20 MB free hard disk space, 3.5-inch floppy drive, 50 MB temporary disk space.

Author: Thomas E. Brown.

Publisher: The Psychological Corporation.

a) PRIMARY/PRESCHOOL LEVEL.

Population: Ages 3–7.

Forms, 2: Parent Form, Teacher Form.

Comments: Elicits parent and teacher reports of symptoms.

b) SCHOOL-AGE LEVEL.

Population: Ages 8–12.

Forms, 3: Self-Report Form, Parent Form, Teacher Form.

Comments: Elicits parent, teacher and self-reports of symptoms.

c) ADOLESCENT LEVEL.

Population: Ages 13–18.

Form, 1: Ready-Score Answer Document.

Comments: Elicits parent and self-reports of symptoms.

[354]

Bruce Vocabulary Inventory.

Purpose: Constructed to measure vocabulary.

Population: Business and industry.

Publication Dates: 1959–1984.

Scores: Total score only.

Administration: Group.

Price Data, 2001: $62.50 per test package; $29.50 per IBM answer sheet package; $9.50 per set of IBM scoring stencils; $3.75 per set of fan keys; $28.50 per manual ('59, 4 pages) and manual supplement (1984, 17 pages); $37.50 per IBM specimen set; $32.50 per fan key specimen set.

Time: (15–20) minutes.

Author: Martin M. Bruce.

Publisher: Martin M. Bruce, Ph.D.

Cross References: See T5:352 (1 reference); for reviews by Fred H. Borgen and Robert Fitzpatrick, see 7:231.

[355]

Bruininks-Oseretsky Test of Motor Proficiency.

Purpose: Designed to measure gross and fine motor skills of children.

Population: Ages 4-6 through 14-5.

Publication Date: 1978.

Scores, 3: Gross Motor Composite, Fine Motor Composite, Battery Composite.

Administration: Individual.

Price Data, 2002: $524.95 per kit including 25 student booklets, 25 record forms for complete battery/ short form, and manual (153 pages); $30.95 per 25 record forms for complete battery/short form; $16.95 per 25 record forms for short form; $30.95 per 25 student booklets; $93.95 per manual; $93.95 per balance beam; $14.95 per response speed stick; $7.95 per target.

Time: (45–60) minutes for complete battery; (15–20) minutes for short form.

Comments: Revised edition of the Oseretsky Tests of Motor Proficiency.

Author: Robert H. Bruininks.

Publisher: American Guidance Service, Inc.

Cross References: See T5:353 (22 references) and T4:340 (18 references); for a review by David A. Sabatino, see 9:174 (7 references); see also T3:324 (3 references) and T2:1898 (15 references); for a review by Anna Espenschade, see 4:650 (10 references); for an excerpted review, see 3:472 (6 references).

[356]

Burks' Behavior Rating Scales.

Purpose: Identify "particular behavior problems and patterns of problems shown by children."

Population: Preschool–Grade 9.

Publication Dates: 1968–1977.

Acronym: BBRS.

Administration: Individual.

Price Data, 2002: $160 per set of 1 kit for each edition; $55 per revised handbook.

Time: Administration time not reported.

Comments: Ratings of problem children by teachers or parents.

Author: Harold F. Burks.

Publisher: Western Psychological Services.

a) PRESCHOOL AND KINDERGARTEN.

Population: Ages 3–6.

Scores, 18: Excessive Self-Blame, Excessive Anxiety, Excessive Withdrawal, Excessive Dependency, Poor Ego Strength, Poor Physical Strength, Poor Coordination, Poor Intellectuality, Poor Attention, Poor Impulse Control, Poor Reality Contact, Poor Sense of Identity, Excessive Suffering, Poor Anger Control, Excessive Sense of Persecution, Excessive Aggressiveness, Excessive Resistance, Poor Social Conformity.

Price Data: $65 per complete kit including 25 administration booklets and profile sheets and manual (1977, 41 pages); $32.50 per 25 administration booklets and profile sheets; $38 per manual.

b) GRADES 1–9.

Population: Grades 1–9.

Scores, 19: Same scores as *a* above plus Poor Academics.

Price Data: $120 per complete kit including 25 administration booklets and profile sheets, manual (1977, 53 pages), 2 parents' guides, 2 teacher's guides, and practitioner-oriented handbook; $32.50 per 25 administration booklets and profile sheets; $19.50 per 10 parents' guides; $26 per 10 teacher's guides; $368 per manual.

Cross References: See T5:355 (1 reference) and T4:342 (5 references); for reviews by Lisa G. Bischoff and by Leland C. Zlomke and Brenda R. Bush, see 11:50 (7 references); see also T3:328 (1 reference), T2:1115 (1 reference), and 7:46 (2 references).

[357]
Burns Brief Inventory of Communication and Cognition.

Purpose: Designed to "assist in determining which of a client's cognitive or communication skills are impaired as a result of a neurological lesion or other disease process, and to assist in selecting appropriate treatment targets and functional treatment goals."

Population: Adults with neurological impairment.

Publication Date: 1997.

Acronym: Burns Inventory.

Scores: Left Hemisphere Inventory: 16 scores in 5 domains: Auditory Comprehension (Yes/No Questions, Comprehension of Words and Sentences, Comprehension of Paragraphs), Verbal Expression (Automatic Speech, Verbal Repetition, Responsive Naming-Nouns, Responsive Naming-Verbs, Confrontation Naming), Reading (Oral Reading of Words and Sentences, Reading Comprehension of Words and Sentences, Reading Comprehension of Functional Paragraphs), Writing (Writing to Dictation, Functional Writing), Numerical Reasoning (Time, Money, Calculation); Right Hemisphere Inventory: 12 scores in 3 domains: Scanning and Tracking (Functional Scanning and Tracking, Scanning and Tracking of Single Words), Visuo-Spatial Skills (Functional Spatial Distribution of Attention, Spatial Distribution of Attention, Recognition of Familiar Faces, Gestalt Perception, Visuo-Spatial Construction-Clock, Visuo-Spatial Organization for Writing), Prosody and Abstract Language (Spontaneous Expressive Prosody, Receptive Prosody, Inferences, Metaphorical Language); Complex Neuropathology Inventory: 15 scores in 4 domains: Orientation to

Factual Memory (Orientation to Person/Place/Time, Factual Current and Remote Memory), Auditory Attention and Memory (Auditory Attention/Vigilance, Immediate Auditory Recall of Digits, Immediate Auditory Recall of Digits with Distractions, Immediate Auditory Recall of Functional Information); Visual Perception (Color Recognition, Picture Matching, Word Matching); Visual Attention and Memory (Functional Short-Term Recognition, Short-Term Recognition of Pictures, Short-Term Recognition of Words, Divided Visual Attention, Delayed Recognition of Pictures, Delayed Recognition of Words).

Administration: Individual.

Forms, 3: Inventories: Left Hemisphere Inventory, Right Hemisphere Inventory, Complex Neuropathology Inventory.

Price Data, 2002: $159 per complete kit; $23 per 15 Right Hemisphere record forms; $23 per 15 Complex Neuropathology record forms; $23 per 15 Left Hemisphere record forms; $52 per stimulus plates; $53 per examiner's manual (116 pages); $6 per 3-minute audiocassette.

Time: (30) minutes per inventory.

Comments: For use by speech pathologists; each inventory can be used separately or all three can be used as a battery.

Author: Martha S. Burns.

Publisher: The Psychological Corporation.

Cross References: For reviews by Joan C. Ballard and Richard I. Frederick, see 14:55.

[358]
Burns/Roe Informal Reading Inventory: Preprimer to Twelfth Grade, Sixth Edition.

Purpose: Provides information about the reading skills, abilities, and needs of individual students in order to plan an appropriate program of reading instruction.

Population: Beginning readers–grade 12.

Publication Dates: 1985–2002.

Acronym: IRI.

Scores, 2: Word Recognition, Comprehension.

Administration: Individual.

Levels, 14: Preprimer, Primer, First Reader, Second Grade, Third Grade, Fourth Grade, Fifth Grade, Sixth Grade, Seventh Grade, Eighth Grade, Ninth Grade, Tenth Grade, Eleventh Grade, Twelfth Grade.

Price Data: Available from publisher.

Time: (40–50) minutes.

Authors: Betty D. Roe and Paul C. Burns.

Publisher: Houghton Mifflin Company.

Cross References: For reviews by Felice J. Green and Timothy Shanahan of the Fifth Edition, see 14:56; see also T5:357 (1 reference) and T4:343; for reviews by Carolyn Colvin Murphy and Roger H. Bruning and by Edward S. Shapiro of an earlier edition, see 10:37.

[359]
Burt Word Reading Test, New Zealand Revision.

Purpose: Designed to provide an estimate of word recognition skills for 110 words.
Population: Ages 6-0 to 12-11 years.
Publication Date: 1981.
Scores: 1 overall performance score.
Administration: Individual.
Price Data, 2001: NZ$3.60 per 20 record forms; $.99 per test card; $6.30 per manual (10 pages); $8.10 per specimen set.
Time: [5] minutes.
Comments: Revision and New Zealand standardization of the Burt Word Reading Test; identical to 1974 revision except for word order.
Authors: Alison Gilmore, Cedric Croft, and Neil Reid.
Publisher: New Zealand Council for Educational Research [New Zealand].
Cross References: See T5:358 (13 references) and T4:344 (4 references); for reviews by Mark W. Aulls and John Elkins, see 9:175 (2 references).

[360]
Bury Infant Check.

Purpose: To aid in identifying children with special needs.
Population: Children in second term of infant school.
Publication Date: 1986.
Acronym: BIC.
Administration: Individual.
Price Data: Price information available from publisher for Full Check record booklets, Quick Check record forms, and for teacher's set including Full Check record booklet, Quick Check record form, and manual (36 pages).
Authors: Lea Pearson and John Quinn.
Publisher: NFER-Nelson Publishing Co., Ltd. [England].
a) QUICK CHECK.
Scores, 3: Language Expression, Learning Style, Total.
Time: (3–4) minutes.
Comments: Teacher-rated.
b) FULL CHECK.
Scores, 12: Language Skills (Comprehension, Expression, Total), Learning Style, Memory Skills (Visual, Auditory, Total), Number Skills, Perceptual Motor Skills (Copying Shapes, Visual Discrimination, Total), Total.
Time: (20) minutes.
Cross References: For a review by Stephan A. Henry, see 9:38.

[361]
Business Analyst Skills Evaluation [One-Hour].

Purpose: Measures practical and analytical skills for the position of Business Systems Analyst.
Population: Candidates for Business Analyst positions.
Publication Dates: 1984–1998.
Acronym: BUSAN.
Scores: Total Score, Narrative Evaluation, Ranking, Recommendation.
Administration: Group.
Price Data, 2001: $225 per candidate, quantity discounts available.
Foreign Language Edition: Available in French.
Time: (60) minutes.
Comments: Available in booklet and Internet formats; scored by publisher; must be proctored.
Author: Bruce A. Winrow.
Publisher: Walden Personnel Performance, Inc. [Canada].

[362]
Business Analyst Skills Evaluation—2 Hour.

Purpose: "Measures practical and analytical skills required for the position of Business Systems Analyst."
Population: Candidates for business analyst positions.
Publication Date: 1984.
Acronym: PRBUSAN.
Score: Total score, narrative evaluation, rating, recommendation.
Administration: Group.
Price Data, 2001: $350 per candidate; quantity discounts available.
Time: (120) minutes.
Comments: Also available with interpersonal skills; graded by publisher; must be proctored.
Author: Bruce A. Winrow.
Publisher: Walden Personnel Performance, Inc. [Canada].
Cross References: For a review by Lenore W. Harmon, see 10:39.

[363]
Business Judgment Test, Revised.

Purpose: "Designed to be a measure of empathy or 'feel' for the generally accepted ideas and opinions on desirable courses of action in interpersonal relationships."
Population: Adults.
Publication Dates: 1953–1984.
Acronym: BJT.
Scores: Total score only.
Administration: Group.

Price Data, 2001: $94.20 per test package; $3.45 per scoring key; $46.75 per manual (1965, 12 pages) and manual supplement (1984, 17 pages); $51.80 per specimen set.
Foreign Language Editions: French edition available.
Time: (10–20) minutes.
Author: Martin M. Bruce.
Publisher: Martin M. Bruce, Ph.D.
Cross References: See T2:2275 (1 reference); for a review by Jerome E. Doppelt, and an excerpted review by Kenneth D. Orton, see 7:1059 (1 reference); see also 6:1101 (4 references); for a review by Edward B. Greene, see 5:893.

[364]
Butcher Treatment Planning Inventory.

Purpose: Designed to provide psychotherapists with "relevant personality and symptomatic information early in the treatment process."
Population: Adults in therapy.
Publication Date: 1998.
Acronym: BTPI.
Administration: Individual or group.
Price Data, 2002: $147 per starter kit including manual (236 pages), 10 full form reusable question booklets, 25 full form answer/profile sheets, scoring templates, 1 free sample symptom monitoring form reusable question booklet, 1 free sample symptom monitoring ready score answer document; $74 per symptom monitoring supplement hand scoring kit including 10 reusable question booklets and 25 ready score answer booklets; $20 per 10 full form question booklets; $14 per 10 symptom monitoring form reusable question booklets; $32 per 25 full form answer sheets; $67 per 25 symptom monitoring ready score answer documents; $67 per manual; $39 per full form scoring templates.
Comments: Normed on ages 18 and over; hand- or computer-scored; paper-and-pencil or computerized administration; computer-generated interpretive reports available.
Author: James N. Butcher.
Publisher: The Psychological Corporation.
a) FULL FORM.
  Scores, 16: Validity Scales (Inconsistent Responding, Overly Virtuous Self-Views, Exaggerated Problem Presentation, Closed-Mindedness), Treatment Issues Scales (Problems in Relationship Formation, Somatization of Conflict, Low Expectation of Benefit, Self-Oriented/Narcissism, Perceived Lack of Environmental Support), Current Symptom Scales (Depression, Anxiety, Anger-Out, Anger-In, Unusual Thinking), General Pathology Composite, Treatment Difficulty Composite.
  Time: [30] minutes.

b) SYMPTOM MONITORING FORM.
  Scores: Includes only Current Symptom Scales from *a* above.
  Time: [12] minutes.
c) TREATMENT PROCESS/SYMPTOM FORM.
  Scores: Includes only Treatment Issues Scales and Current Symptom Scales from *a* above.
  Time: Administration time not reported.
d) TREATMENT ISSUES FORM.
  Scores: Includes only Validity Scales and Treatment Issues Scales from *a* above.
  Time: Administration time not reported.
Cross References: For reviews by William E. Hanson and Samuel Juni, see 14:57.

[365]
California Achievement Tests, Fifth Edition.

Purpose: "Designed to measure achievement in the basic skills taught in schools throughout the nation."
Population: Grades K.0–K.9, K.6–1.6, 1.6–2.2, 1.6–3.2, 2.6–4.2, 3.6–5.2, 4.6–6.2, 5.6–7.2, 6.6–8.2, 7.6–9.2, 8.6–10.2, 9.6–11.2, 10.6–12.9.
Publication Dates: 1957–1993.
Acronym: CAT/5.
Administration: Group.
Levels: 13 overlapping levels.
Forms, 4: Complete Battery A, B; Survey A, B.
Price Data, 2002: $34.65 per 30 locator tests with directions and answer sheets (specify Grades 1–6 or Grades 6–12); $20.85 per 30 practice tests; $16.50 per Form A Complete Battery Examiner's Manual (1993, 45 pages); $163.90 per 30 Form A Complete Battery reflective machine-scorable booklets including examiner's manual; $170.50 per 30 Form A Complete Battery (Trans-Optic) booklets including examiner's manual; $47.30 per 50 CompuScan answer sheets, Levels 14–21/22 (specify Complete Battery or Survey tests); $1,167 per 1,250 continuous form (Trans-Optic) answer sheets (specify form and indicate Level 14–21/22); $2.30 per class record sheet for hand-recording; $49.50 per test coordinator's handbook; $46.20 per technical report; $35.20 per Class Management Guide; $16.50 per Multi-Level Norms book (specify Fall, Winter, or Spring); scoring service available from publisher.
Comments: California Achievement Tests, Sixth Edition is now the same as TerraNova, The Second Edition (2510). CAT/5 is still available.
Author: CTB Macmillan/McGraw-Hill.
Publisher: CTB/McGraw-Hill.
a) LEVEL K.
  Population: Grades K.0–K.9.
  Scores, 5: Reading (Visual Recognition, Sound Recognition, Vocabulary, Comprehension), Mathematics Concepts and Applications.
  Time: (87) minutes.

b) LEVEL 10.
Population: Grades K.6–1.6.
Scores, 4: Reading (Word Analysis, Vocabulary, Comprehension), Mathematics Concepts and Applications.
Time: (88) minutes.
c) LEVEL 11.
Population: Grades 1.6–2.2.
Scores, 9: Reading (Word Analysis, Vocabulary, Comprehension), Language (Mechanics, Expression), Mathematics (Computation, Concepts and Applications), Science, Social Studies.
Time: (217) minutes.
d) LEVEL 12.
Population: Grades 1.6–3.2.
Scores, 10: Reading (Word Analysis, Vocabulary, Comprehension), Spelling, Language (Mechanics, Expression), Mathematics (Computation, Concepts and Applications), Science, Social Studies.
Time: (292) minutes.
e) LEVEL 13.
Population: Grades 2.6–4.2.
Scores, 10: Same as *d* above.
Time: (330) minutes.
f) LEVEL 14.
Population: Grades 3.6–5.2.
Scores, 10: Reading (Vocabulary, Comprehension), Spelling, Language (Mechanics, Expression), Mathematics (Computation, Concepts and Applications), Study Skills, Science, Social Studies.
Time: (330) minutes.
g) LEVEL 15.
Population: Grades 4.6–6.2.
Scores, 10: Same as *f* above.
Time: Same as *f* above.
h) LEVEL 16.
Population: Grades 5.6–7.2.
Scores, 10: Same as *f* above.
Time: Same as *f* above.
i) LEVEL 17.
Population: Grades 6.6–8.2.
Scores, 10: Same as *f* above.
Time: Same as *f* above.
j) LEVEL 18.
Population: Grades 7.6–9.2.
Scores, 10: Same as *f* above.
Time: Same as *f* above.
k) LEVEL 19.
Population: Grades 8.6–10.2.
Scores, 10: Same as *f* above.
Time: Same as *f* above.
l) LEVEL 20.
Population: Grades 9.6–11.2.
Scores, 10: Same as *f* above.
Time: Same as *f* above.

m) LEVEL 21/22.
Population: Grades 10.6–12.9.
Scores, 10: Same as *f* above.
Time: Same as *f* above.
Cross References: See T5:364 (28 references); for reviews by Anthony J. Nitko and by Robert F. McMorris, Wei-Ping Liu, and Elizabeth L. Bringsjord, see 13:40 (113 references); see also T4:352 (52 references); for reviews by Peter W. Airasian and James L. Wardrop of the 1985 edition, see 10:41 (68 references); for reviews by Bruce G. Rogers and Victor L. Willson of the 1978 edition, see 9:180 (19 references); see also T3:344 (68 references); for reviews by Miriam M. Bryan and Frank Womer of the 1970 edition, see 8:10 (33 references); for reviews by Jack C. Merwin and Robert D. North of the 1957 edition, see 6:3 (19 references); for a review by Charles O. Neidt, see 5:2 (10 references); for reviews by Warren G. Findley, Alvin W. Schindler, and J. Harlan Shores of the 1950 edition, see 4:2 (8 references); for a review by Paul A. Witty of the 1943 edition, see 2:1193 (1 reference); for a review by D. Welty Lefever and an excerpted review by E. L. Abell, see 7:876. For reviews of subtests, see 8:45 (2 reviews), 8:257 (1 review), 8:719 (2 reviews), see 6:251 (1 review), 5:177 (2 reviews), 5:468 (1 review), 4:151 (2 reviews), 4:411 (1 review), 4:530 (2 reviews, 1 excerpt), 2:1292 (2 reviews), 2:1459 (2 reviews), 2:1563 (1 review), 1:893 (1 review), and 1:1110 (2 reviews).

[366]
The California Child Q-Set.

Purpose: "Designed to describe a child's behavior and personality."
Population: Children.
Publication Date: 1980.
Acronym: CAQC.
Scores: Q-sort rating of children by teachers and counselors in 9 categories ranging from extremely uncharacteristic to extremely characteristic.
Administration: Group.
Price Data: Available from publisher.
Time: (35-60) minutes.
Comments: For an upward extension see The California Q-Sort (373).
Authors: Jeanne Block and Jack Block.
Publisher: Mind Garden, Inc.
Cross References: See T5:365 (11 references) and T4:354 (6 references); for a review by Alfred B. Heilbrun, Jr., see 9:181; see also T3:348 (2 references).

[367]
California Computerized Assessment Package.

Purpose: Designed as a "standardized assessment of reaction time and speed of information processing."
Population: Ages 10–90.

Publication Dates: 1986–1999.
Acronym: CalCAP.
Scores, 7: Simple Reaction Time, Choice Reaction Time for Single Digits, Serial Pattern Matching, Lexical Discrimination, Visual Selective Attention, Response Reversal and Rapid Visual Scanning, Form Discrimination.
Administration: Individual.
Forms, 2: Standard, Abbreviated.
Price Data, 1998: $495 per complete kit including manual (1996, 80 pages), standard battery and abbreviated battery; $10 per demonstration program; $15 per manual.
Time: (20–25) minutes.
Foreign Language Editions: Danish, Flemish, French, German, Norwegian, and Spanish editions available.
Comments: IBM AT or compatible, 512K RAM, color display or active color matrix laptop, and MS-DOS 3.1 or greater required.
Author: Eric N. Miller.
Publisher: Norland Software.
Cross References: For reviews by Howard A. Lloyd and by Goran Westergren and Ingela Westergren, see 14:58.

[368]
The California Critical Thinking Dispositions Inventory.

Purpose: "Measures one's disposition or inclination toward critical thinking."
Population: High school, college, and adult.
Publication Dates: 1992–1996.
Acronym: CCTDI.
Scores, 8: Truth-Seeking, Inquisitiveness, Open-Mindedness, Confidence, Analyticity, Systematicity, Cognitive Maturity, Total.
Administration: Group or individual.
Price Data, 2002: $60 per specimen kit including inventory, scoring templates, and manual (27 pages); $140 per 25 copies of inventory; quantity discounts available.
Foreign Language Editions: Available in English, Spanish, French, Japanese, and Hebrew.
Time: (15–20) minutes.
Authors: Peter A. Facione and Noreen C. Facione.
Publisher: Insight Assessment.
Cross References: For reviews by Carolyn M. Callahan and Salvador Hector Ochoa, see 12:57.

[369]
California Critical Thinking Skills Test.

Purpose: Designed to be "a standardized assessment instrument targeting core critical thinking skills at the post-secondary level."
Population: College and adult.

Publication Dates: 1990–1998.
Acronym: CCTST.
Scores, 6: Analysis, Evaluation, Inference, Inductive Reasoning, Deductive Reasoning, Total.
Administration: Group.
Forms, 2: A, B (alternate).
Price Data, 2002: $60 per specimen kit including Form A, Form B, Form 2000, and manual (1992, 20 pages); $140 per 25 copies of test (volume discounts available).
Time: 45 minutes.
Author: Peter A. Facione.
Publisher: Insight Assessment.
Cross References: For reviews by Robert F. McMorris and William B. Michael, see 12:58.

[370]
California Diagnostic Mathematics Tests.

Purpose: Developed to assess mathematics achievement for use in instructional planning and program evaluation.
Publication Date: 1988.
Acronym: CDMT.
Administration: Group.
Price Data, 2002: $20.55 per 35 practice tests (select Levels A, B–C, D–F); $35.55 per 35 locator tests (select Levels A–C, D–F); $30.15 per 50 locator test answer sheets (Levels D–F); $140.65 per 35 scannable test bookes (specify Level A, B, or C); $64.90 per 35 reusable test books (specify Level D, E, or F); $23.15 per 50 CompuScore or Scantron answer sheets (for use with scanning); $29.25 per 25 SCOREZE answer sheets (for use with handscoring); $16.90 per set of hand scoring stencils (select Levels D, E, F); $49.55 per 100 student diagnostic profiles; $2.70 per class report form; $11.20 per locator test directions; $14.65 per examiner's manual and answer keys (select level); $20.40 per teacher's guide (select Levels A–B, C–D, or E–F); $64.85 per specimen set; price information for norms book and technical report available from publisher; scoring service available from publisher.
Time: Administration time not reported.
Author: CTB/McGraw-Hill.
Publisher: CTB/McGraw-Hill.
 a) LEVEL A.
  Population: Grades 1.1–2.9.
  Scores, 3: Number Concepts, Computation, Applications.
 b) LEVEL B.
  Population: Grades 2.6–3.9.
  Scores, 3: Same as *a* above.
 c) LEVEL C.
  Population: Grades 3.6–4.9.
  Scores, 3: Same as *a* above.
 d) LEVEL D.
  Population: Grades 4.6–6.9.

Scores, 3: Same as *a* above.
e) LEVEL E.
Population: Grades 6.6–8.9.
Scores, 3: Same as *a* above.
f) LEVEL F.
Population: Grades 8.6–12.
Scores, 3: Same as *a* above plus Life Skills.
Cross References: For reviews by Michael B. Bunch and Jerry Johnson, see 11:52.

[371]
California Diagnostic Reading Tests.

Purpose: Developed to assess reading achievement for use in instructional planning and program evaluation.
Publication Date: 1989.
Acronym: CDRT.
Administration: Group.
Price Data, 2002: $20.55 per 35 practice books (select Levels A, B–C, D–F); $35.55 per 35 locator tests (select Levels A–C, D–F); $140.65 per 35 scannable test books (specify Level A, B, or C); $64.90 per 35 reusable test books (specify Level D, E, or F); $40.65 per 50 CompuScan answer sheets (use for scanning) (specify Level D, E, or F); $46.15 per 50 Scantron answer sheets (use for scanning) (specify Level D, E, or F); $58.50 per 25 SCOREZE answer sheets (use for handscoring) (specify Level D, E, or F); $30.15 per 50 locator test answer sheets (Levels D–F only); $50.95 per set of scoring stencils (Levels D–F only); $49.55 per 100 student diagnostic profiles; $2.70 per class record sheet for handscoring (select level); $11.20 per locator test directions; $14.55 per examiner's manual including answer keys (select level); $20.40 per teacher's guide (select Levels A–B, C–D, E–F); $14.55 per norms book (32 pages); $14.55 per technical report; $64.85 per review kit; scoring service available from publisher.
Time: Tests are untimed.
Author: CTB/McGraw-Hill.
Publisher: CTB/McGraw-Hill.
a) LEVEL A.
Population: Grades 1.1–2.9.
Scores, 3: Word Analysis, Vocabulary, Comprehension.
b) LEVEL B.
Population: Grades 2.6–3.9.
Scores, 3: Same as *a* above.
c) LEVEL C.
Population: Grades 3.6–4.9.
Scores, 3: Same as *a* above.
d) LEVEL D.
Population: Grades 4.6–6.9.
Scores, 4: Same as *a* above plus Applications.
e) LEVEL E.
Population: Grades 6.6–8.9.
Scores, 4: Same as *d* above.

f) LEVEL F.
Population: Grades 8.6–12.
Scores, 3: Vocabulary, Comprehension, Applications.
Cross References: For a review by T. Steuart Watson, see 11:53.

[372]
California Psychological Inventory™, Third Edition.

Purpose: Designed to assess personality characteristics and to predict what people will say and do in specified contexts.
Population: Ages 13 years and over.
Publication Dates: 1956–1996.
Acronym: CPI.
Scores, 36: 20 Folk Scales: Dominance (Do), Capacity for Status (Cs), Sociability (Sy), Social Presence (Sp), Self-Acceptance (Sa), Independence (In), Empathy (Em), Responsibility (Re), Socialization (So), Self-Control (Sc), Good Impression (Gi), Communality (Cm), Well-Being (Wb), Tolerance (To), Achievement via Conformance (Ac), Achievement via Independence (Ai), Intellectual Efficiency (Ie), Psychological-Mindedness (Py), Flexibility (Fx), Femininity/Masculinity (Fm); 3 Vector Scales: v. 1 (Internality/Externality), v. 2 (Norm Questioning/Norm Favoring), v. 3 (Self-Realization), plus 13 Special Purpose scales: Managerial Potential, Work Orientation, Creative Temperament, Leadership, Amicability, Law Enforcement Orientation, Tough-mindedness, Baucom Scale for Masculinity, Baucom Scale for Femininity, Leventhal Scale for Anxiety, Wink-Gough Scale for Narcissism, Dicken Scale for Social Desirability, Dicken Scale for Aquiescence.
Administration: Group.
Price Data, 2001: $18.50 per preview kit including prepaid answer sheet and item booklet; $70 per 25 reusable item booklets; $176.50 per 10 prepaid answer sheets (for mail-in scoring, for use with item booklets); $16.50 per 25 scannable answer sheets (specify for use with NCS Sentry 300 scanner or Scantron 8000 series scanners); $76 per manual (1996, 431 pages); $60.10 per A Practical Guide to CPI Interpretation, Third Edition.
Foreign Language Editions: French, German, Italian, and Spanish editions available in an earlier edition.
Time: (45–60) minutes.
Comments: Previous edition still available; 1 form; reports available: Narrative, Configural Analysis; Scoring Options: Prepaid (mail-in), CPP Software System, skillsone.com
Authors: Harrison G. Gough and Pamela Bradley (manual).
Publisher: Consulting Psychologists Press, Inc.

Cross References: See T5:372 (118 references) and T4:361 (57 references); for reviews by Brian Bolton and George Engelhard, Jr., see 11:54 (108 references); for reviews by Donald H. Baucom and H. J. Eysenck, see 9:182 (61 references); see also T3:354 (195 references); for a review by Malcolm D. Gynther, see 8:514 (452 references); see also T2:1121 (166 references); for reviews by Lewis R. Goldberg and James A. Walsh and an excerpted review by John O. Crites, see 7:49 (370 references); see also P:27 (249 references); for a review by E. Lowell Kelly, see 6:71 (116 references); for reviews by Lee J. Cronbach and Robert L. Thorndike and an excerpted review by Laurance F. Shaffer, see 5:37 (33 references).

[373]
California Q-Sort (Revised Adult Set).

Purpose: Designed as "a systematic way of comparing different [intra-individual] personalities with one another."

Population: Adults.

Publication Dates: 1961–1990.

Acronym: CAQR.

Scores: Ratings in 9 categories ranging from most uncharacteristic to most characteristic.

Administration: Individual.

Price Data, 2001: $25 per sampler set including instructions (1990, 5 pages), sorting guide (1990, 4 pages), and 100 cards.

Time: (30–40) minutes.

Comments: For an adaptation for children, see The California Child Q-Set (366).

Author: Jack Block.

Publisher: Mind Garden, Inc.

Cross References: For a review by George Domino, see 14:59; see also T5:373 (43 references); T4:362 (20 references), and T3:356 (1 reference); for reviews by Allen L. Edwards and David T. Lykken of an earlier edition and excerpted reviews by Samuel J. Beck and John E. Exner, Jr., see 6:72 (2 references); see also P:28 (1 reference).

[374]
California Verbal Learning Test, Children's Version.

Purpose: "Designed to assess multiple components of verbal learning and memory."

Population: Ages 5–16.

Publication Dates: 1989–1994.

Acronym: CVLT-C.

Scores: List A Trials 1–5 Total, List B Free-Recall Trial, Short Delay Free Recall, Short-Delay Cued Recall, Long-Delay Free Recall, Long-Delay Cued Recall, Semantic Cluster Ratio, Perseverations, Free-Recall Intrusions, Cued-Recall Intrusions, Recognition Hits, Discriminability, False Positives.

Administration: Individual.

Price Data, 2002: $145 per set including manual (1994, 147 pages) and 25 record forms; $48 per 25 record forms or $180 per 100 record forms; $110 per manual; $297 per scoring assistant including disk, user's guide, and keyboard overlay (Macintosh or Windows).

Time: (55) minutes.

Authors: Dean C. Delis, Joel H. Kramer, Edith Kaplan, and Beth A. Ober; Alan J. Fridlund, and Dean C. Delis (Scoring Assistant User's Guide).

Publisher: The Psychological Corporation.

Cross References: See T5:375 (8 references); for reviews by Billy T. Ogletree and LeAdelle Phelps, see 13:41 (2 references).

[375]
California Verbal Learning Test, Second Edition, Adult Version.

Purpose: To "obtain a detailed and comprehensive assessment of verbal learning and memory."

Population: 16–89 years.

Publication Dates: 1983–2000.

Acronym: CVLT-II (Standard); CVLT-II SF (Short Form).

Scores: Immediate Recall (Trial 1, Trials 2–5, Trials 1–5 Total), Learning Slope, Semantic Clustering, Serial Clustering, Subjective Clustering, Primacy/Recency Recall, Percentage of Recall Consistency, List B Trial, Proactive Interference, Short-Delay Free Recall, Retroactive Interference, Short-Delay Cued Recall, Long-Delay Free Recall, Long-Delay Free Recall Retention, Long-Delay Cued Recall, Repetition Errors, Synonym/Subordinate Intrusions, Across-List Intrusions, Categorical Intrusions, Non-Categorical Intrusions, Yes/No Recognition Testing, False-Positive Errors, Total Recognition Discriminability, Source Recognition Discriminability, Semantic Recognition Discriminability, Novel Recognition Discriminability, Response Bias, Critical Item Analysis, Forced-Choice Recognition [optional].

Administration: Individual.

Forms, 3: Standard Form, Alternate Form, Short Form.

Price Data, 2001: $464 per complete kit including software package (CD-ROM or diskette version), manual (2000, 287 pages), 25 Standard Record Forms, 1 Alternate Record Form, and 25 Short Record Forms; $96 per manual; $45 per 25 Standard or Alternate Record Forms (quantity discounts available); $33 per 25 Short Record Forms (quantity discounts available).

Time: (30) minutes plus 30 minutes of delay for Standard and Alternate Forms; (15) minutes plus 15 minutes of delay for Short Form.

Comments: Comprehensive Scoring System software generates Core Report (generates 27 scores), Expanded Report (generates 66 scores), Research Report

(generates over 260 scores); computer system requirements: Windows 95/98/NT 4.0, 100 MHz processor, 32 MB RAM, CD-ROM and 3.5-inch floppy diskette drive (CD-ROM version) or 3.5-inch diskette drive (diskette version), 2 MB video card with 800 x 600 resolution (256 colors), and 25 MB free disk space.
Authors: Dean C. Delis, Joel H. Kramer, Edith Kaplan, and Beth A. Ober.
Publisher: The Psychological Corporation.
Cross References: See T5:376 (35 references); for a review by Ray Fenton of the previous edition, see 13:42 (57 references); see also T4:364 (12 references).

[376]
Call Center Skills Test.

Purpose: Measures practical and intellectual skills for call center positions.
Population: Candidates for call center positions.
Publication Date: 2001.
Acronym: CCTR.
Scores: Total Score, Narrative Evaluation, Ranking, Recommendation.
Administration: Group.
Price Data, 2001: $150 per candidate; quantity discounts available.
Foreign Language Edition: Available in French.
Time: (60) minutes.
Comments: Available in booklet and Internet versions; scored by publisher; must be proctored.
Author: Bruce A. Winrow.
Publisher: Walden Personnel Performance, Inc. [Canada].

[377]
The Callier-Azusa Scale: G Edition.

Purpose: A developmental scale "designed to aid in the assessment of deaf-blind and severely and profoundly handicapped children."
Population: Deaf-blind and severely/profoundly handicapped children.
Publication Date: 1978.
Scores: 18 subscales in 5 areas: Motor Development (Postural Control, Locomotion, Fine Motor, Visual Motor), Perceptual Development (Vision, Auditory, Tactile), Daily Living Skills (Dressing, Personal Hygiene, Feeding, Toileting), Cognition, Communication and Language (Cognition, Receptive, Expressive, Speech), Social Development (Adults, Peers, Environment).
Administration: Individual.
Price Data: Available from publisher.
Time: Administration time not reported.
Comments: Criterion-referenced.
Author: Robert Stillman (Editor).
Publisher: Callier Center for Communication Disorders.
Cross References: See T5:377 (1 reference).

[378]
The Camden Memory Tests.

Purpose: Designed "to fulfill a clinical need that was not met by existing memory tests."
Population: Available from publisher.
Publication Date: 1996.
Scores: 5 tests: Pictorial Recognition Memory Test, Topographical Recognition Memory Test, Paired Associate Learning Test, Short Recognition Memory Test for Words, Short Recognition Memory Test for Faces.
Administration: Available from publisher.
Price Data, 2001: $182 per Pictorial Recognition Memory Test; $182 per Topographical Recognition Memory Test; $59.95 per Paired Associate Learning Test; $59.95 per Short Recognition Memory Test for Words; $59.95 per Short Recognition Memory Test for Faces; $21.95 per test manual; $395 per set of all 5 tests including 1 manual and 5 packs of scoring sheets; and $16.95 plus postage per 25 scoring sheets.
Time: Administration time not reported.
Author: Elizabeth Warrington.
Publisher: Psychology Press.

[379]
Campbell-Hallam Team Development Survey.

Purpose: "Designed to give teams standardized feedback on their strengths and weaknesses."
Population: Members of intact working teams.
Publication Date: 1994.
Acronym: TDS.
Scores, 19: Resources (Time and Staffing, Information, Material Resources, Organizational Support, Skills, Commitment), Efficiency (Mission Clarity, Team Coordination, Team Unity, Individual Goals, Empowerment), Improvement (Team Assessment, Innovation, Feedback, Rewards, Leadership), Success (Satisfaction, Performance, Overall Index).
Administration: Group.
Forms, 2: Observer, Member.
Price Data, 1999: $180 per preview package including 10 individual survey booklets, team report, individual report for each team member, manual (216 pages), administrator's guide (15 pages), and facilitator's guide (16 pages); $15 per individual survey and report; $10 per 10 observer survey forms; $60 per team report including scoring of one team report, narrative summary profile, miniature profile, and item response summary; $35 plus $10 per item per supplemental items summary reports; $30 per manual; $10 per administrator's guide; $20 per facilitator's guide; $50 per set of manual, administrator's guide, and facilitator's guide.
Time: (20–25) minutes.
Authors: Glenn Hallam and David Campbell.
Publisher: Reid London House.

Cross References: For reviews by Frederick T. L. Leong and Mary A. Lewis, see 14:60; see also T5:379 (1 reference).

[380]
Campbell™ Interest and Skill Survey.

Purpose: "Measures self-reported interests and skills."
Population: Ages 15 years to adult.
Publication Dates: 1989–1992.
Acronym: CISS™.
Scores, 99: 7 Orientation Scales (Influencing, Organizing, Helping, Creating, Analyzing, Producing, Adventuring), 29 Basic Scales (Leadership, Law/Politics, Public Speaking, Sales, Advertising/Marketing, Supervision, Financial Services, Office Practices, Adult Development, Child Development, Counseling, Religious Activities, Medical Practice, Art/Design, Performing Arts, Writing, International Activities, Fashion, Culinary Arts, Mathematics, Science, Mechanical Crafts, Woodworking, Farming/Forestry, Plants/Gardens, Animal Care, Athletics/Physical Fitness, Military/Law Enforcement, Risks/Adventure), 58 Occupational Scales (Attorney, Financial Planner, Hotel Manager, Manufacturer's Representative, Marketing Director, Realtor, CEO/President, Human Resources Director, School Superintendent, Advertising Account Executive, Media Executive, Public Relations Director, Corporate Trainer, Secretary, Bank Manager, Insurance Agent, Retail Store Manager, Hospital Administrator, Accountant/CPA, Bookkeeper, Child Care Worker, Guidance Counselor, Religious Leader, Teacher K–12, Social Worker, Psychologist, Nursing Administrator, Commercial Artist, Fashion Designer, Liberal Arts Professor, Librarian, Musician, Translator/Interpreter, Writer/Editor, Restaurant Manager, Chef, Physician, Chemist, Medical Researcher, Math/Science Teacher, Computer Programmer, Statistician, Systems Analyst, Carpenter, Electrician, Veterinarian, Airline Mechanic, Agribusiness Manager, Landscape Architect, Architect, Police Officer, Military Officer, Ski Instructor, Test Pilot, Athletic Coach, Athletic Trainer, Emergency Medical Technician, Fitness Instructor), 2 Special Scales (Academic Focus, Extraversion), 3 Procedural Checks (Response Percentage Check, Inconsistency Check, Omitted Items Check).
Administration: Group.
Price Data, 2002: $2.49 per Career Planner; $43 per hardcover (ring-binder) manual; $29 per softcover manual; $11 per 50 interest/skill pattern worksheets; $19 per 25 Microtest Q System answer sheets; $7.20 per Microtest Q System report; $27 per 100 report cover sheets; $47.50 per preview package including soft cover manual and 3 reports; $8.75 per mail-in answer sheet/report.
Time: (35) minutes.

Comments: Each scale contains both an interest and a skill score; combined gender scales allow for broadest interpretation of survey results; workshops available.
Author: David Campbell.
Publisher: NCS Assessments (Minnetonka).
Cross References: See T5:380 (1 reference); for reviews by Richard C. Pugh and Michael J. Roszkowski, see 13:43; see also T4:368 (1 reference).

[381]
Campbell Leadership Index.

Purpose: "An adjective checklist designed to be used in the assessment of leadership characteristics."
Population: Leaders.
Publication Date: 1991.
Acronym: CLI.
Scores, 22: Ambitious, Daring, Dynamic, Enterprising, Experienced, Farsighted, Original, Persuasive, Energy, Affectionate, Considerate, Empowering, Entertaining, Friendly, Credible, Organized, Productive, Thrifty, Calm, Flexible, Optimistic, Trusting.
Administration: Group or individual.
Price Data: Available from publisher.
Time: (45–60) minutes.
Comments: Self-ratings plus 3–5 observer ratings.
Author: David Campbell.
Publisher: Reid London House.
Cross References: See T5:381 (1 reference); for reviews by George Domino and Charles Houston, see 12:59; see also T4:369 (1 reference).

[382]
Campbell Organizational Survey.

Purpose: Designed to measure attitudes of employees regarding the organization.
Population: Working adults.
Publication Dates: 1988–1990.
Acronym: COS.
Scores, 14: The Work Itself, Working Conditions, Freedom from Stress, Co-Workers, Supervision, Top Leadership, Pay, Benefits, Job Security, Promotional Opportunities, Feedback/Communications, Organizational Planning, Support for Innovation, Overall Satisfaction Index.
Administration: Group.
Price Data: Available from publisher.
Time: (15–25) minutes.
Comments: A component of Campbell Development Surveys (CDS); scoring and reporting discounts for 50, 250, 1,000 or 2,500+ examinees.
Author: David Campbell.
Publisher: Reid London House.
Cross References: For reviews by Ralph O. Mueller and Kevin R. Murphy, see 12:60; see T4:370 (1 reference).

[383]

Canadian Achievement Survey Tests for Adults.

Purpose: "Designed to measure achievement in reading, language, and mathematics ... subject areas commonly found in adult basic education curricula."

Population: Adults.

Publication Date: 1994.

Acronym: CAST.

Scores, 6: Reading (Vocabulary, Comprehension), Language (Language Mechanics, Language Expression), Mathematics (Mathematics Computation, Mathematics Concepts and Applications).

Administration: Group.

Levels, 3: Completed up to Grade 6, completed Grades 7 to 9, completed Grades 10 and above.

Price Data, 1997: $63 per 25 test booklets (specify level); $32 per 25 hand-scorable answer sheets; $58 per 50 machine scorable answer sheets; $44 per manual (53 pages); $21 per review kit including brochure, 1 copy each of Levels 1, 2, and 3 test booklets, hand-scorable answer sheet, machine-scorable answer sheet, and directions for administering.

Time: (90) minutes.

Author: Canadian Test Centre.

Publisher: Canadian Test Centre, Educational Assessment Services [Canada].

Cross References: For reviews by John O. Anderson and Mark H. Daniel, see 14:61.

[384]

Canadian Achievement Tests, Third Edition.

Purpose: Designed to measure achievement in the basic skills of reading, language, spelling, mathematics, and writing.

Population: Grades 1.6–postsecondary.

Publication Dates: 1981–2002.

Acronym: CAT-3.

Administration: Group.

Parts, 3: Basic Battery, Supplemental Tests, Constructed-Response Tests.

Levels, 10: 11 (Grades 1.6–2.5), 12 (Grades 2.6–3.5), 13 (Grades 3.6–4.5), 14 (Grades 4.6–5.5), 15 (Grades 5.6–6.5), 16 (Grades 6.6–7.5), 17 (Grades 7.6–8.5), 18 (Grades 8.6–9.5), 19 (Grades 9.6–11.5), 20 (Grades 11.6–postsecondary).

Price Data, 2002: C$205 per Teacher Resource Kit including 3 Student Books at each of Levels 11–13, 1 Student Book at each of Levels 14–19/20, 1 Test Directions for Teachers for each level, 3 Practice Tests for each level, 3 U-Score answer sheets each (Levels 14–19/20), 3 Student Diagnostic Profiles for each level, 9 each of Locator Tests 1 and 2, 1 Locator Test Directions, 18 Locator Test answer sheets, 1 scoring key at each of Levels 11–13, 1 scoring mask at each of Levels 14–18, 1 Norms Book (2001, 101 pages), 1 Teacher Resource Manual for CAT-3 (2002, 242 pages), 1 Parents' Guide to Understanding CAT Results, and 1 carrying bag; $105 per 30 Basic Battery Plus test books (Levels 11–13, specify level); $120 per 30 Basic Battery Plus test books (Levels 14–19/20, specify level); $90 per 30 Basic Battery test books (Levels 12, 13, specify level); $65 per 50 machine-scorable answer sheets (Levels 14–19/20, specify level); $42 per 30 hand-scorable answer sheets (Levels 14–19/20, specify level); $1 per machine-scoring Directions for Test Co-ordinators; $8 per Test Directions for Teachers (Levels 11–18) or Administering Directions (Levels 19/20), specify level; $40 per Norms Book; $48 per Technical Manual (2002, 156 pages); $35 per Teacher Resource Manual for CAT-3; $1.50 per Parents' Guide to CAT Results; $15 per 30 Student Diagnostic Profiles (Levels 11–19/20, specify level); $12 per 30 Practice Tests (Levels 11–19/20, specify level); $1.50 per scoring key (Levels 11–19/20, specify level); $21 per Locator Test 1 or 2 (specify Test 1 or 2) including directions and 35 answer sheets; $8 per additional directions for Locator Tests 1–2; $21 per 50 additional answer sheets for Locator Tests 1–2; $1.50 per Constructed Response Dictation Worksheet Photocopy Master (Levels 14–16, specify level); $22.50 per Constructed Response Writing Directions including 30 Student Worksheets Narrative Prompts (Levels 12–16), Informational Prompts (Levels 14–16), Letter Prompts (Levels 17–19/20), or Persuasive Prompts (Levels 17–19/20), specify level and prompt; $22.50 per Constructed Response Mathematics directions including 30 Student Worksheets (Levels 11–18), specify level and task; $50 per scoring binder for Constructed-Response Writing or Mathematics including blackline masters for scoring manual, rubrics, and anchor papers (Levels 12–19/20, specify level); $.44 per Administrator's Summary/Graphic Frequency Distribution (per student); $2.90 per Class Record Sheet (per student, Level 11); $4 per Class Record Sheet (per student, Levels 12–13, specify level), $2.10 per Class Record Sheet (per student, Levels 14–19/20, specify level); $.61 per Objective Competency Report (per student); $.91 per Parent Report or Student Test Record (per student); additional price information available from publisher.

Time: Varies by level; (85–115) minutes for Basic Battery, (55–75) minutes for Supplemental Tests, (40–230) minutes for Constructed Response Test.

Comments: Revision of the CAT/2; hand- or machine-scored by the Canadian Test Centre; machine-scoring recommended when testing 30 or more students; Supplemental and Constructed Response Tests optional.

Author: Canadian Test Centre, Educational Assessment Services.

Publisher: Canadian Test Centre, Educational Assessment Services [Canada].

a) LOCATOR TESTS.
Population: Grades 2–12.
Scores, 2: Vocabulary, Mathematics.
Levels, 2: 1 (Grades 2–6), 2 (Grades 6–12).
Time: (10) minutes.

b) LEVEL 11.
Population: Grades 1.6–2.5.
Scores, 6: 2 Basic Battery Tests (Reading/Language, Mathematics), 3 Supplemental Tests (Word Analysis, Vocabulary, Computation), 1 Constructed Response Test (Mathematics).
Time: (85) minutes for Basic Battery, (55) minutes for Supplemental Tests, (40) minutes for Constructed Response Test.

c) LEVEL 12.
Population: Grades 2.6–3.5.
Scores, 9: 2 Basic Battery Tests (Reading/Language, Mathematics), 4 Supplemental Tests (Word Analysis, Vocabulary, Language/Writing, Computation), 3 Constructed Response Tests (Dictation, Mathematics, Writing-Narrative).
Time: (115) minutes for Basic Battery, (70) minutes for Supplemental Tests, (110) minutes for Constructed Response Test.

d) LEVEL 13.
Population: Grades 3.6–4.5.
Scores, 9: 2 Basic Battery Tests (Reading/Language, Mathematics), 4 Supplemental Tests (Word Analysis, Vocabulary, Language/Writing, Computation), 3 Constructed Response Tests (Dictation, Mathematics, Writing-Narrative).
Time: (110) minutes for Basic Battery, (70) minutes for Supplemental Tests, (110) minutes for Constructed Response Test.

e) LEVEL 14.
Population: Grades 4.6–5.5.
Scores, 10: 2 Basic Battery Tests (Reading/Language, Mathematics), 4 Supplemental Tests (Vocabulary, Spelling, Language/Writing, Computation), 4 Constructed Response Tests (Dictation, Mathematics, Writing-Narrative, Writing-Informational).
Time: (110) minutes for Basic Battery, (75) minutes for Supplemental Tests, (230) minutes for Constructed Response Test.

f) LEVEL 15.
Population: Grades 5.6–6.5.
Scores, 10: 2 Basic Battery Tests (Reading/Language, Mathematics), 4 Supplemental Tests (Vocabulary, Spelling, Language/Writing, Computation), 4 Constructed Response Tests (Dictation, Mathematics, Writing-Narrative, Writing-Informational).

Time: (110) minutes for Basic Battery, (75) minutes for Supplemental Tests, (220) minutes for Constructed Response Test.

g) LEVEL 16.
Population: Grades 6.6–7.5.
Scores, 10: 2 Basic Battery Tests (Reading/Language, Mathematics), 4 Supplemental Tests (Vocabulary, Spelling, Language/Writing, Computation), 4 Constructed Response Tests (Dictation, Mathematics, Writing-Narrative, Writing-Informational).
Time: (110) minutes for Basic Battery, (75) minutes for Supplemental Tests, (220) minutes for Constructed Response Test.

h) LEVEL 17.
Population: Grades 7.6–8.5.
Scores, 10: 2 Basic Battery Tests (Reading/Language, Mathematics), 4 Supplemental Tests (Vocabulary, Spelling, Language/Writing, Computation), 3 Constructed Response Tests (Mathematics, Writing-Letter, Writing-Persuasive).
Time: (110) minutes for Basic Battery, (75) minutes for Supplemental Tests, (220) minutes for Constructed Response Test.

i) LEVEL 18.
Population: Grades 8.6–9.5.
Scores, 10: 2 Basic Battery Tests (Reading/Language, Mathematics), 4 Supplemental Tests (Vocabulary, Spelling, Language/Writing, Computation), 3 Constructed Response Tests (Mathematics, Writing-Letter, Writing-Persuasive).
Time: (110) minutes for Basic Battery, (75) minutes for Supplemental Tests, (220) minutes for Constructed Response Test.

j) LEVEL 19.
Population: Grades 9.6–11.5.
Scores, 10: 2 Basic Battery Tests (Reading/Language, Mathematics), 4 Supplemental Tests (Vocabulary, Spelling, Language/Writing, Computation), 2 Constructed Response Tests (Writing-Letter, Writing-Persuasive).
Time: (110) minutes for Basic Battery, (75) minutes for Supplemental Tests, (180) minutes for Constructed Response Test.

k) LEVEL 20.
Population: Grades 11.6-postsecondary.
Scores, 10: 2 Basic Battery Tests (Reading/Language, Mathematics), 4 Supplemental Tests (Vocabulary, Spelling, Language/Writing, Computation), 2 Constructed Response Tests (Writing-Letter, Writing-Persuasive).
Time: (110) minutes for Basic Battery, (75) minutes for Supplemental Tests, (180) minutes for Constructed Response Test.

Cross References: See T5:384; for reviews by John Hattie and Leslie Eastman Lukin of the second edition, see 13:44 (2 references); see also T4:371 (3 references); for a review by L. A. Whyte of an earlier edition, see 9:187.

[385]
Canadian Cognitive Abilities Test, Form K.

Purpose: "Designed to assess the development of cognitive abilities related to verbal, quantitative, and nonverbal reasoning and problem solving."
Population: Grades K–2, 3–12.
Publication Dates: 1970–1997.
Acronym: CCAT.
Scores, 3: Verbal, Quantitative, Non-Verbal.
Administration: Group.
Time: Administration time not reported.
Comments: Canadian version of Cognitive Abilities Test, Form 4 (T4:537); CCAT, Form 7 still available from publisher.
Authors: Original edition by Robert L. Thorndike and Elizabeth P. Hagen; Canadian version by Edgar N. Wright.
Publisher: Nelson Thomson Learning [Canada].
   a) PRIMARY BATTERIES.
   Population: Grades K–1, 2–3.
   Levels, 2: 1, 2.
   Price Data, 2001: $3.45 per test booklet; $6.90 per Guide for Administration; $7.50 per scoring key; $33 per norms booklet; $33 per teacher's handbook; $9.65 per class record folder; $33 per assessment coordinator's handbook; $155 per score conversion software; $11 per preview kit.
   b) MULTILEVEL EDITION.
   Population: Grades 3–12.
   Levels, 8: A, B, C, D, E, F, G, and H.
   Price Data: $4.20 per test booklet; $25.80 per 35 answer sheets; $62.95 per 100 answer sheets; $6.90 per Guide for Administration; $17.95 per scoring mask; $33 per norms booklet; $33 per teacher's handbook; $9.65 per class record folder; $32 per assessment coordinator's handbook; $210 per score conversion software; $12.20 per preview kit.
Cross References: See T5:385 (3 references); for reviews by John O. Anderson and John Hattie of an earlier edition, see 12:61 (3 references); for reviews by Giuseppe Costantino and Jack A. Cummings of an earlier edition, see 10:42 (3 references); see also T3:361 (5 references) and 8:180 (2 references).

[386]
Canadian Dental Aptitude Test.

Purpose: "Designed to measure general academic achievement, comprehension of scientific information, and perceptual ability."
Population: Canadian dental school applicants.
Publication Dates: 1946-2002.

Scores, 7: Reading Comprehension, Natural Sciences (Biology, General Chemistry, Total), Perceptual Ability Test, Chalk Carving Test, Academic Average.
Administration: Group.
Price Data: Available from publisher.
Time: 235(330) minutes in 2 sessions.
Comments: Based on the Dental Admission Testing program (733).
Author: Department of Testing Services, American Dental Association.
Publisher: American Dental Association.

[387]
Canadian Occupational Interest Inventory.

Purpose: Developed to help identify types of employment from which clients may derive the most satisfaction.
Population: High school or college students.
Publication Dates: 1981-1982.
Acronym: COII.
Scores, 5: Things/People, Business Contact/Scientific, Routine/Creative, Social/Solitary, Prestige/Production.
Administration: Group.
Price Data, 2001: $85.90 per 25 test booklets; $23.35 per 35 answer sheets; $13.95 per set of scoring stencils; $23.35 per 35 profile sheets; $23.35 per 35 profile and charts; $41.35 per administrator's manual (1982, 50 pages); $41.35 per technical manual (1982, 30 pages); $79.50 per glossary of interests (1982, 118 pages); $42.40 per examination kit.
Foreign Language Edition: French edition available.
Time: [40] minutes.
Authors: Luc Begin, Luc Lavallee (test and technical manual), and J. A. Gordon Booth (manuals).
Publisher: Nelson Thomson Learning [Canada].
Cross References: For a review by Richard W. Johnson, see 9:188.

[388]
Canadian Test of Cognitive Skills.

Purpose: Designed to assess the academic aptitude important for scholastic success of students in grades 2 through 12.
Population: Grades 2–12.
Publication Dates: 1992–1996.
Acronym: Canadian TCS.
Scores, 4: Sequences, Memory, Analogies, Verbal Reasoning.
Administration: Group.
Levels, 5: Level 1 (Grades 2–3); Level 2 (Grades 4–5); Level 3 (Grades 6–7); Level 4 (Grades 8–9); Level 5 (Grades 10–12+).
Price Data, 1996: C$75 per 35 consumable test booklets (Level 1); $95 per 35 reusable test booklets

(specify Level 2–5); $12 per 35 practice tests including directions; $58 per 50 machine-scorable answer sheets (specify level); $28 per 25 U-Score answer sheets; $1 per scoring keys (specify level); $17 per 50 individual record sheets; $1.50 per class record sheet; $8 per examiner's manual (1992, 26 pages; specify level); $32 per norms book (1992, 154 pages); $21 per handbook and technical bulletin (1996, 87 pages); $48 per Multi-Level specimen set; $21 per Primary, Junior, or Senior specimen set.

Time: (52) minutes for Level 1; (55) minutes for Level 2–5.

Comments: A Practice Test (15–20 minute administration time) is available and is recommended to be administered at least one day prior to the actual testing session; adapted from Test of Cognitive Skills, Second Edition (T5:2677).

Author: Canadian Test Centre, Educational Services.

Publisher: Canadian Test Centre, Educational Assessment Services [Canada].

Cross References: For reviews by Martine Hébert and Susan J. Maller, see 13:45.

[389]
Canadian Tests of Basic Skills, Forms K and L.

Purpose: Constructed to measure growth in the fundamental skills crucial to day-to-day learning.

Population: Grades K–2, 3–8, and 9–12.

Publication Dates: 1955–1997.

Acronym: CTBS.

Scores, 7: Vocabulary, Reading, Language, Sources of Information, Mathematics, Science, Maps and Diagrams.

Administration: Group.

Time: Administration time not reported.

Comments: Canadian Tests of Basic Skills, Forms 7 and 8 still available from publisher.

Authors: A. N. Hieronymus, H. D. Hoover, E. F. Lindquist, and others (original Level 5–14 tests); Dale P. Scannell and others (original Level 15–18 tests); Ethel King-Shaw and others (Canadian adaptation).

Publisher: Nelson Thomson Learning [Canada].

a) PRIMARY BATTERY FORM K.

Population: Grades K.1–1.5, K.8–1.9, 1.7–2.6, 2.5–3.5.

Levels, 4: 5, 6, 7, 8.

Price Data, 2001: $3.35 per test booklet; $9 per Guide for Administration; $11 per scoring key and skill guide; $33 per norms booklet; $33 per teacher's handbook; $9.65 per 10 class record folders; $9.65 per 10 profile charts; $12.95 per 35 student profile charts (K and L); $48 per Assessment Coordinator's Handbook; $155 per score conversion software; $11 per preview kit.

b) LEVELS 9–14 FORM K.

Population: Grades 3–8.

Levels, 6: 9, 10, 11, 12, 13, 14.

Price Data: $3.35 per test booklet (Language Arts or Math & Science); $25.80 per 35 answer sheets; $6.90 per Guide for Administration; $17.95 per scoring mask; $33 per norms booklet; $33 per teacher's handbook; $9.65 per 10 class record folders; $8.95 per 10 profile charts; $12.95 per 35 student profile charts; $48 per Assessment Coordinator's Handbook; $210 per score conversion software; $17 per preview kit.

c) LEVELS 15–18 FORM K.

Population: Grades 9–12.

Levels, 3: 15, 16, 17/18.

Price Data: $3.35 per test booklet (English or Math & Science); $25.80 per 35 answer sheets; $6.90 per Guide for Administration; $17.95 per scoring mask; $33 per norms booklet; $33 per teacher's handbook; $9.65 per 10 class record folders; $8.95 per 10 profile charts; $12.95 per 35 student profile charts; $48 per Assessment Coordinator's Handbook; $149 per score conversion software; $14 per preview kit.

d) LEVELS 9–14 FORM L.

Population: Grades 3–8.

Levels, 6: 9, 10, 11, 12, 13, 14.

Price Data: $4.20 per test booklet; $25.80 per 35 answer sheets; $6.90 per Guide for Administration; $17.95 per scoring mask; $32 per norms booklet; $33 per teacher's handbook; $9.65 per 10 class record folders; $9.65 per 10 profile charts; $13.95 per 35 student profile charts; $9.65 per Assessment Coordinator's Handbook; $199 per score conversion software; $12.20 per preview kit.

Cross References: See T5:389 (14 references) and T4:375 (5 references); for reviews by John O. Anderson and by Jean-Jacques Bernier and Martine Hébert of an earlier edition, see 11:55 (9 references); see also T3:363 (15 references) and 8:11 (1 reference); for a review by L. B. Birch of an earlier edition, see 7:6.

[390]
Canfield Instructional Styles Inventory.

Purpose: Constructed to identify instructional preferences.

Population: Instructors.

Publication Dates: 1976–1988.

Acronym: ISI.

Scores, 21: Conditions for Instruction (Peer, Organization, Goal Setting, Competition, Instructor, Detail, Independence, Authority), Areas of Interest (Numeric, Qualitative, Inanimate, People), Modes of Instruction (Lecturing, Readings, Iconic, Direct Experience), Influence (A-influence, B-influence, C-influence, D-influence, Total Influence).

Administration: Group or individual.

Price Data, 2002: $65 per complete kit including 5 inventory booklets and manual (1988, 55 pages); $39.50 per 10 inventory booklets; $48 per manual.
Time: (30–40) minutes for individual administration; (35–40) minutes for group administration.
Comments: May be self-administered.
Authors: Albert A. Canfield and Judith S. Canfield.
Publisher: Western Psychological Services.
Cross References: See T4:377 (1 reference); for reviews by Nancy L. Allen and Jerrilyn V. Andrews, see 11:56; for reviews by Thomas B. Bradley and C. Dean Miller of an earlier edition, see 9:514.

[391]
Canfield Learning Styles Inventory.

Purpose: Designed to assess learning preferences.
Population: Junior High School, High School, College, Adults in business settings.
Publication Dates: 1976–1988.
Acronym: LSI.
Scores, 21: Conditions for Learning (Peer, Organization, Goal Setting, Competition, Instructor, Detail, Independence, Authority), Area of Interest (Numeric, Qualitative, Inanimate, People), Mode of Learning (Listening, Reading, Iconic, Direct Experience), Expectation for Course Grade (A-expectation, B-expectation, C-expectation, D-expectation, Total expectation).
Administration: Group.
Forms, 4: A (College), B (High School), C (Junior High School), E (College-Easy).
Price Data, 2002: $99.50 per complete kit including 2 each of Forms A, B, C, and E inventory booklets, 1 Form ABC computer-scorable booklet, 1 Form E computer-scorable booklet, 2 prepaid mail-in booklets for computer scoring and interpretation, and manual (1988, 76 pages); $49.95 per 10 inventory booklets (specify form); $12.50 per computer-scorable booklet (price depends on quantity ordered and includes scoring service by publisher); $47.50 per manual; $199.50 per 25-use computer disk (PC with DOS).
Time: (15–20) minutes.
Author: Albert A. Canfield.
Publisher: Western Psychological Services.
Cross References: See T5:392 (2 references) and T4:378 (5 references); for a review by Stephen L. Benton, see 11:57 (2 references); for reviews by John Biggs and C. Dean Miller of an earlier edition, see 9:609 (1 reference).

[392]
Cardall Test of Practical Judgement— Revised

Purpose: To measure problem-solving ability in everyday life.

Population: Adults in business and industry.
Publication Dates: 1942–1999.
Scores, 3: Factual, Empathetic, Total.
Administration: Group.
Price Data, 2001: $20 per review set including manual (1961, 4 pages); $50 per 25 test booklets.
Foreign Language Edition: French edition available.
Time: (30) minutes.
Author: Alfred J. Cardall.
Publisher: Institute of Psychological Research, Inc. [Canada].
Cross References: See 6:1102 (4 references) and 4:784 (6 references); for reviews by Glen U. Cleeton and Howard R. Taylor of an earlier edition, see 3:694.

[393]
Career Ability Placement Survey.

Purpose: Designed to measure abilities as they relate to careers.
Population: Junior high, high school, college, and adults.
Publication Dates: 1976–1995.
Acronym: CAPS.
Scores: Scores in 14 COPSystem Career Clusters: Science-Professional, Science-Skilled, Technology-Professional, Technology-Skilled, Consumer Economics, Outdoor, Business-Professional, Business-Skilled, Clerical, Communication, Arts-Professional, Arts-Skilled, Service-Professional, Service-Skilled; and 8 ability scores: Mechanical Reasoning, Spatial Relations, Verbal Reasoning, Numerical Ability, Language Usage, Word Knowledge, Perceptual Speed and Accuracy, Manual Speed and Dexterity.
Administration: Group.
Price Data, 1999: $75.75 per 25 self-scoring test booklets [$280.25 per 100, $945.50 per 500]; $12.50 per 25 Self-Interpretation Profile and Guides [$44.50 per 100, $206.75 per 500]; $44.50 per 25 machine-scoring test booklets [$150 per 100, $710.25 per 500]; $7.25 per 25 CAPS tests (by each test) [$96.50 per 500]; $1.60 each scoring by publisher; $14.75 per hand-scoring keys; $2.75 per examiner's manual (1992, 22 pages); $8.25 per technical manual (1992, 59 pages); $10.50 per administration tape; $22.75 per CAPS Visuals; $10 per specimen set.
Time: (5) minutes per test; (50) minutes for entire battery.
Authors: Lila F. Knapp and Robert R. Knapp.
Publisher: EdITS/Educational and Industrial Testing Service.
Cross References: See T5:395 (1 reference) and T4:382 (1 reference).

[394]
Career Anchors: Discovering Your Real Values, Revised Edition.

Purpose: Designed to help a person identify their career anchor, uncover their real values, and use them to make better career choices.
Population: Adults.
Publication Date: 1990.
Scores, 8: Technical/Functional Competence, General Managerial Competence, Autonomy/Independence, Security/Stability, Entrepreneurial Creativity, Service/Dedication to a Cause, Pure Challenge, Lifestyle.
Administration: Group.
Price Data: Price information available from publisher for complete kit including instrument (67 pages) and trainer's manual (20 pages).
Time: (180–240) minutes.
Comments: Self-rating plus interview with a partner.
Author: Edgar H. Schein.
Publisher: Jossey-Bass, A Wiley Company.
Cross References: See T5:396 (1 reference); for reviews by Michael B. Bunch and Gary J. Robertson, see 13:46.

[395]
Career Assessment Inventory™—The Enhanced Version.

Purpose: A vocational interest assessment tool focusing on careers requiring "various amounts of post-secondary education."
Population: Grade 9 through adult.
Publication Dates: 1975–1994.
Scores, 142: 6 themes (Realistic, Investigative, Artistic, Social, Enterprising, Conventional), 25 basic interest (Mechanical/Fixing, Electronics, Carpentry, Manual/Skilled Trades, Protective Service, Athletics/Sports, Nature/Outdoors, Animal Service, Mathematics, Scientific Research/Development, Medical Science, Writing, Creative Arts, Performing/Entertaining, Educating, Community Service, Medical Service, Religious Activities, Public Speaking, Law/Politics, Management/Supervision, Sales, Office Practices, Clerical/Clerking, Food Service), 111 occupational (Accountant, Advertising Artist/Writer, Advertising Executive, Aircraft Mechanic, Architect, Athletic Trainer, Author/Writer, Auto Mechanic, Bank Manager, Bank Teller, Barber/Hairstylist, Biologist, Bookkeeper, Bus Driver, Buyer/Merchandiser, Cafeteria Worker, Camera Repair Technician, Card/Gift Shop Manager, Carpenter, Caterer, Chef, Chemist, Child Care Assistant, Chiropractor, Computer Programmer, Computer Scientist, Conservation Officer, Cosmetologist, Counselor-Chemical Dependency, Court Reporter, Data Input Operator, Dental Assistant, Dental Hygienist, Dental Lab Technician, Dentist, Dietitian, Drafter, Economist, Elected Public Official, Electrician, Electronic Technician, Elementary School Teacher, Emergency Medical Technician, Engineer, Executive Housekeeper, Farmer/Rancher, Firefighter, Florist, Food Service Manager, Forest Ranger, Guidance Counselor, Hardware Store Manager, Hospital Administrator, Hotel/Motel Manager, Insurance Agent, Interior Designer, Janitor/Janitress, Lawyer, Legal Assistant, Librarian, Machinist, Mail Carrier, Manufacturing Representative, Mathematician, Math-Science Teacher, Medical Assistant, Medical Lab Technician, Military Enlisted, Military Officer, Musical Instrument Repair, Musician, Newspaper Reporter, Nurse Aide, Nurse/LPN, Nurse/RN, Occupational Therapist, Operating Room Technician, Orthotist/Prosthetist, Painter, Park Ranger, Personnel Manager, Pharmacist, Pharmacy Technician, Photographer, Physical Therapist, Physician, Piano Technician, Pipefitter/Plumber, Police Officer, Printer, Private Investigator, Psychologist, Purchasing Agent, Radio/TV Repair, Radiologic Technician, Real Estate Agent, Religious Leader, Reservation Agent, Respiratory Therapy Technician, Restaurant Manager, Secretary, Security Guard, Sheet Metal Worker, Surveyor, Teacher Aide, Telephone Repair Technician, Tool and Die Maker, Travel Agent, Truck Driver, Veterinarian, Waiter/Waitress.
Administration: Group or individual.
Price Data, 2002: $45 per preview package mail-in reports (including 3 interpretive reports and a manual); $40.50 per preview package Microtest Q System reports preview package (including 3 interpretive reports and a manual); $19 per 25 answer sheets including test items to be used with Microtest Q; $25 per manual; $8–$6.50 per Microtest Q interpretive report; $9.50–$8 per mail-in interpretive report; $4.95–$4.10 per Microtest Q profile report; $6.50–$5.75 per mail-in profile report.
Time: (35–40) minutes.
Author: Charles B. Johansson.
Publisher: NCS Assessments (Minnetonka).
Cross References: See T5:398 (4 references); for a review by James B. Rounds, see 10:43 (2 references); see also T3:367 (1 reference); for reviews by Jack L. Bodden and Paul R. Lohnes of an earlier edition, see 8:993.

[396]
Career Assessment Inventory™—Vocational Version.

Purpose: "A vocational interest assessment tool for individuals planning to enter occupations requiring 0-2 years of post-secondary training."
Population: Grade 9 through adult.
Publication Dates: 1973–1994.
Scores, 125: 2 Administrative Indices (Total Responses, Response Patterning), 4 Nonoccupational (Fine Arts-Mechanical, Occupational Extroversion-Introver-

sion, Educational Orientation, Variability of Interests), 6 General Themes (Realistic, Investigative, Artistic, Social, Enterprising, Conventional), 22 Basic Interest Area Scales (Mechanical/Fixing, Electronics, Carpentry, Manual/Skilled Trades, Agriculture, Nature/Outdoors, Animal Service, Science, Numbers, Writing, Performing/Entertaining, Arts/Crafts, Social Service, Teaching, Child Care, Medical Service, Religious Activities, Business, Sales, Office Practices, Clerical/Clerking, Food Service), 91 Occupational Scales (Aircraft Mechanic, Auto Mechanic, Bus Driver, Camera Repair Technician, Carpenter, Conservation Officer, Dental Laboratory Technician, Drafter, Electrician, Emergency Medical Technician, Farmer/Rancher, Firefighter, Forest Ranger, Hardware Store Manager, Janitor/Janitress, Machinist, Mail Carrier, Musical Instrument Repair, Navy Enlisted, Orthodontist/Prosthetist, Painter, Park Ranger, Pipefitter/Plumber, Police Officer, Printer, Radio/TV Repair, Security Guard, Sheet Metal Worker, Telephone Repair, Tool/Die Maker, Truck Driver, Veterinary Technician, Chiropractor, Computer Programmer, Dental Hygienist, Electronic Technician, Math-Science Teacher, Medical Laboratory Technician, Radiological Technician, Respiratory Therapeutic Technician, Surveyor, Advertising Artist/Writer, Advertising Executive, Author/Writer, Counselor-Chemical Dependency, Interior Designer, Legal Assistant, Librarian, Musician, Newspaper Reporter, Photographer, Piano Technician, Athletic Trainer, Child Care Assistant, Cosmetologist, Elementary School Teacher, Licensed Practical Nurse, Nurse Aide, Occupational Therapist Assistant, Operating Room Technician, Physical Therapist Assistant, Registered Nurse, Barber/Hairstylist, Buyer/Merchandiser, Card/Gift Shop Manager, Caterer, Florist, Food Service Manager, Hotel/Motel Manager, Insurance Agent, Manufacturing Representative, Personnel Manager, Private Investigator, Purchasing Agent, Real Estate Agent, Reservation Agent, Restaurant Manager, Travel Agent, Accountant, Bank Teller, Bookkeeper, Cafeteria Worker, Court Reporter, Data Entry Operator, Dental Assistant, Executive Housekeeper, Medical Assistant, Pharmacy Technician, Secretary, Teacher Aide, Waiter/Waitress).

Administration: Group.

Price Data, 2002: $25 per manual (1984, 152 pages); $45 per preview package mail-in reports including 3 interpretive reports and a manual; $45 per preview package Microtest Q system reports including 3 interpretive reports and a manual; $19 per 25 interpretive report answer sheets ; $6.50–$8 per Microtest Q interpretive report; $8–$9.50 per mail-in interpretive report; $12 per 25 Microtest Q profile report answer sheets; $4.10–$4.95 per Microtest Q and Microtest profile report; $5.75–$6.50 per mail-in profile report; $7.70–$5.65 per Microtest Q interpretive report; $8–$6.50 per mail-in interpretive report; $4.95–$4.10 per Microtest Q profile report; $6.50–$5.75 per mail-in profile report.

Foreign Language Editions: Spanish and French editions available.

Time: (30–45) minutes.

Author: Charles B. Johansson.

Publisher: NCS Assessments (Minnetonka).

Cross References: See T5:399 (5 references) and T4:385 (4 references); for reviews by Jerard F. Kehoe and Nicholas A. Vacc, see 11:59 (1 reference); see also T3:367 (1 reference); for reviews by Jack L. Bodden and Paul R. Lohnes of an earlier edition, see 8:993.

[397]
Career Attitudes and Strategies Inventory: An Inventory for Understanding Adult Careers.

Purpose: "Developed to assess some common attitudes, feelings, experiences, and obstacles that influence the careers of employed and unemployed adults."

Population: Adults seeking vocational counseling.

Publication Dates: 1992–1994.

Acronym: CASI.

Scores: 9 scales: Job Satisfaction, Work Involvement, Skill Development, Dominant Style, Career Worries, Interpersonal Abuse, Family Commitment, Risk-Taking Style, Geographical Barriers.

Administration: Individual.

Price Data: Available from publisher for kit including manual (1994, 53 pages), 25 inventory booklets, 25 handscorable answer sheets, and 25 interpretive summary booklets.

Time: (35) minutes.

Comments: Also includes Career Obstacles Checklist designed to assess "personal problems that may influence an individual's job situation."

Authors: John L. Holland and Gary D. Gottfredson.

Publisher: Psychological Assessment Resources, Inc.

Cross References: For reviews by Michael B. Brown and Richard T. Kinnier, see 13:47.

[398]
Career Beliefs Inventory.

Purpose: Designed to assist people to identify career beliefs that may influence their career goals.

Population: 13 years and above.

Publication Dates: 1991–1998.

Acronym: CBI.

Scores, 26: Administrative Index, Employment Status, Career Plans, Acceptance of Uncertainty, Openness, Achievement, College Education, Intrinsic Satisfaction, Peer Equality, Structured Work Environment, Control, Responsibility, Approval of Others, Self-Other Comparisons, Occupation/College Variation, Career Path Flexibility, Post-Training Transition, Job Experi-

mentation, Relocation, Improving Self, Persisting While Uncertain, Taking Risks, Learning Job Skills, Negotiating/Searching, Overcoming Obstacles, Working Hard.
Administration: Group.
Price Data, 2001: $60.60 per 25 test booklets; $78.20 per 10 prepaid answer sheets (price includes scoring by publisher); $49.40 per 10 self-scorable booklets; $47.80 per manual (46 pages); $69.60 per preview kit including item booklet, answer sheet, manual, and Exploring Your Career Beliefs workbook.
Time: (20–30) minutes.
Comments: Available in self-scorable booklets.
Author: John D. Krumboltz.
Publisher: Consulting Psychologists Press, Inc.
Cross References: See T5:401 (3 references); for reviews by David L. Bolton and Robert M. Guion, see 12:64 (9 references).

[399]
Career Counseling Personal Data Form.
Purpose: "Designed to provide [background] information useful in career counseling."
Population: Vocational counselees.
Publication Date: 1962.
Scores: No scores.
Administration: Group.
Manual: No manual.
Price Data, 2001: $94.20 per package of forms; $42.90 per specimen set.
Time: (30-40) minutes.
Author: John B. Ahrens.
Publisher: Martin M. Bruce, Ph.D.

[400]
Career Decision Scale.
Purpose: Developed to provide "an estimate of career indecision."
Population: Grades 9–12 and college.
Publication Dates: 1976–1987.
Scores, 2: Certainty, Career Decision.
Administration: Group or individual.
Price Data: Available from publisher for complete kit including 50 test booklets and manual (1987, 28 pages).
Time: (10-15) minutes.
Authors: Samuel H. Osipow, Clarke G. Carney (test), Jane Winer (test), Barbara Yanico (test), and Maryanne Koschier (test).
Publisher: Psychological Assessment Resources, Inc.
Cross References: See T5:404 (47 references) and T4:390 (49 references); for reviews by Lenore W. Harmon and David O. Herman, see 9:194 (4 references).

[401]
Career Decision Self-Efficacy Scale.
Purpose: "Measures an individual's degree of belief that he/she can successfully complete tasks necessary to making career decisions."

Population: College students.
Publication Dates: 1983–1994.
Acronym: CDMSE.
Scores, 6: Self-Appraisal, Occupational Information, Goal Selection, Planning, Problem Solving, Total.
Administration: Group.
Price Data: Available from publisher.
Time: Administration time not reported.
Comments: A 25-item short form is also available.
Authors: Nancy E. Betz and Karen M. Taylor.
Publisher: Nancy E. Betz (the author).
Cross References: For reviews by James K. Benish and Richard W. Johnson, see 14:62; see also T5:403 (1 reference).

[402]
Career Directions Inventory.
Purpose: Designed as an "easily read interest inventory emphasizing technical, sales, and service occupations."
Population: High school and college and adults.
Publication Dates: 1986-2001.
Acronym: CDI.
Scores: 15 Basic Interest scales: Administration, Art, Clerical, Food Service, Industrial Arts, Health Service, Outdoors, Personal Service, Sales, Science & Technology, Teaching/Social Service, Writing, Assertive, Persuasive, Systematic.
Administration: Group or individual.
Price Data, 2001: $35 per examination kit including manual (2001, 94 pages) and machine-scorable question and answer document for an Extended Report; $30 per test manual; $79–$89 (depending on volume) per 10 machine-scorable Extended Reports; $99 per software package including disks, software manual for Windows, test manual, and 10 coupons for computer report.
Foreign Language Editions: Question/answer documents and Extended Reports available in French.
Time: (30-50) minutes.
Comments: Must be computer scored through mail-in scoring service or CDI software.
Author: Douglas N. Jackson.
Publisher: Sigma Assessment Systems, Inc.
Cross References: For reviews by Darrell L. Sabers and Fredrick A. Schrank, see 9:44.

[403]
Career Exploration Inventory: A Guide for Exploring Work, Leisure, and Learning, Second Edition.
Purpose: To help participants explore and plan three major areas of their lives—work, leisure activities, and education or learning.
Population: Employed and unemployed youth and adults.

Publication Dates: 1992–2001.
Acronym: CEI.
Scores: 15 occupational categories: Arts, Entertainment, and Media; Physical and Life Sciences; Math, Engineering, and Technology; Plants and Animals; Law, Law Enforcement, and Public Safety; Mechanics, Installers, Repairers, and Construction; Transportation; Industrial Production; Business Detail; Sales and Marketing; Recreation, Travel, and Personal Services; Education and Social Service; General Management and Support; Financial Detail; Medical and Health Services.
Administration: Group or individual.
Price Data, 2001: $34.95 per 25 inventories including Tips for Counselors and Other Professionals booklet (4 pages); price information for Professional manual (82 pages) and Workshop manual (48 pages) available from publisher.
Time: (30–45) minutes.
Comments: Twelve-panel foldout; self-scoring and self-interpreting; no other components needed.
Author: John J. Liptak.
Publisher: JIST Publishing, Inc.
Cross References: For reviews by Bert A. Goldman and Douglas J. McRae of an earlier edition, see 13:49.

[404]
Career Exploration Series, 1992 Revision.

Purpose: Designed for career guidance using "a series of six job interest inventories that focus on specific occupational fields."
Population: Grades 7–12 and college and adults.
Publication Dates: 1979–1992.
Acronym: CES.
Scores: 6 areas: Agriculture–Forestry–Conservation, Science–Mathematics–Health, Business, Industrial, Consumer Economics, Design–Art–Communications.
Administration: Group.
Price Data: Available from publisher.
Time: (50–60) minutes.
Comments: Self-administered and self-scored interest inventories.
Authors: Arthur Cutler, Francis Ferry, Robert Kauk, and Robert Robinett.
Publisher: CFKR Career Materials [No reply from publisher; status unknown].
Cross References: For a review by Herbert C. Rudman, see 13:50; for reviews by Mark Pope and William I. Sauser, Jr. of an earlier edition, see 11:60; for reviews by Bruce R. Fretz and Robert B. Slaney of the original edition, see 9:196.

[405]
Career Factors Inventory.

Purpose: Designed to provide an understanding of career decision-making readiness.

Population: Ages 13 and over.
Publication Date: 1997.
Acronym: CFI.
Scores, 4: Need for Career Information, Need for Self-Knowledge, Career Choice Anxiety, Generalized Indecisiveness.
Administration: Group.
Price Data, 2001: $33.30 per kit including self-scorable item booklet and answer sheet, interpretation, and Applications and Technical Guide (37 pages); $19.10 per 10 self-scorable booklets; $2.70 per single self-scorable booklet; $34.50 per Applications and Technical Guide.
Time: (5–10) minutes.
Comments: Inventory is untimed; also part of the skillsone.com website.
Authors: Judy M. Chartrand, Steven B. Robbins, and Weston H. Morrill.
Publisher: Consulting Psychologists Press, Inc.
Cross References: For a review by Ayres D'Costa, see 14:63.

[406]
Career Guidance Inventory.

Purpose: "Designed to provide measures of relative interest in postsecondary instructional programs."
Population: Students and prospective students at trade, vocational, or technical school, or at community college.
Publication Dates: 1972–1989.
Acronym: CGI.
Scores, 47: Agribusiness and Agricultural Production, Renewable Natural Resources, Business (Accounting and Finance, Data Processing, Clerical/Typing/Word Processing, Office Supervision and Management, Secretarial), Marketing and Distribution (General Marketing, Financial Services, Hospitality/Recreation/Tourism, Real Estate), Communications and Communications Technologies, Computer and Information Sciences, Cosmetology and Barbering, Engineering and Related Technologies (Architectural, Civil, Electrical and Electronic, Environmental Control, Industrial Production, Mechanical Engineering, Mining and Petroleum), Allied Health (Dental Services, Diagnostic and Treatment Services, Miscellaneous Services, Medical Laboratory Technologies, Mental Health/Human Services, Nursing and Related Services, Rehabilitation Services), Vocational Home Economics (Child Care and Guidance, Clothing/Apparel/Textiles, Food Production/Management/Services, Institutional/Home Management/Supporting Services), Protective Services, Construction Trades (Brickmason/Stonemason/Tile Setting, Carpentry, Electrical and Power Transmission Installation, Plumbing/Pipefitting/Steamfitting), Mechanics and Repairers (Electrical and Electronic Equipment Repair, Heating/Air Condition-

ing/Refrigeration Mechanics, Industrial Equipment Maintenance and Repair, Vehicle and Mobile Equipment), Precision Production (Drafting, Graphic and Printing Communications, Precision Metal Work, Woodworking), Transportation and Material Moving, Visual Arts (Fine Arts).

Administration: Group.

Price Data: Price information available from publisher for reusable test booklet, answer sheet/interpretation guides, administrator's manual (1989, 43 pages), and specimen set of all Career Guidance Inventory and Educational Interest Inventory (859) components.

Time: [45–60] minutes.

Comments: Self-administered, self-scored.

Author: James E. Oliver.

Publisher: Wintergreen/Orchard House, Inc.

Cross References: For reviews by E. Jack Asher, Jr., and Michael B. Bunch, see 11:61; for a review by James B. Rounds, Jr., of an earlier edition, see 9:197; for a review by Bert W. Westbrook, see 8:996.

[407]

Career Interest Inventory.

Purpose: "Designed to assist students in making decisions concerning their educational and vocational plans."

Publication Dates: 1989–1996.

Administration: Group or individual.

Price Data, 2002: $18 per examination kit including Level 1 machine-scorable answer document, Level 2 hand-scorable booklet, directions for administering, and student profile; $51 per counselor's manual (1991, 120 pages); $18 per 25 Exploring Interests: An Introduction to the Career Interest Inventory; $7 per directions for administering 1990, 29 pages); $2.65 scoring charge per Level 1 answer document; $1 for first copy and $.27 per each additional copy of individual report; $.92 for first copy and $.06 per each additional copy of counselor's report (by Teacher/Counselor or School); $.86 for first copy and $.28 per each additional copy of student record label; $.68 for first copy and $.16 per each additional copy of occupational interest report (by School); $.44 for first copy and $29.75 per set of career planning summary (by Teacher/Counselor); $.35 for first copy and $26.50 per set of career planning summary (by School); $.24 for first copy and $22.05 per set of career planning summary (by District); $.61 per pupil for student data diskette; $25 for first 1,000 and $10 per each additional 1,000 for return of test booklets; $25 for first 1,000 plus $10 per each additional 1,000 for return of answer documents; $25 for first 1,000 plus $10 per each additional 1,000 for return of mixed documents.

Time: (30–40) minutes.

Author: The Psychological Corporation.

Publisher: The Psychological Corporation.

a) LEVEL 1.

Population: Grades 7–9.

Scores, 47: 15 Occupational Interests (Social Science, Clerical Services, Health Services, Agriculture, Customer Services, Fine Arts, Mathematics and Science, Building Trades, Educational Services, Legal Services, Transportation, Sales, Management, Benchwork, Machine Operation), 16 High School Subject Interests (Speech or Drama, Metal Shop or Woodworking, Mathematics, Auto Repair, Science, Cooking or Sewing, Art or Music, Farming or Livestock Care, Newspaper Writing, Typing or Office Machines, Social Studies, Health Care, Creative Writing, Computers, English or Literature, Bookkeeping or Office Practices), 16 High School Activity Interests (Mathematics Club, Farming Club, Speech or Debate Team, School Library Aide, School Play, Automobile Club, Science Fair, Teacher's Aide, Student Government, Office Helper or Assistant, School Literary Magazine, School Officer, Photography Club, Business Club, School Newspaper, Computer Club).

Price Data: $59 per 25 hand-scorable booklets; $59 per 25 Type 1 machine-scorable answer documents; Type 2 machine-scorable answer documents available from publisher by special arrangement.

b) LEVEL 2.

Population: Grades 10–12 and adults.

Scores, 35: 15 Occupational Interests (same as Level 1), 20 Post-High School Course Interests (Marketing or Sales, Computer Programming, Electronics or Electrical Trades, Plumbing or Welding, Automotive Repair, Carpentry or Home Building, Word Processing or Typing, Haircutting or Styling, Bookkeeping or Office Practices, Cooking or Sewing, Music or Art, Farming or Livestock Care, Mathematics or Science, English or Foreign Language, Business Law or Management, Creative Writing, Speech or Drama, Photography, Health Care, Newspaper Writing).

Price Data: $64 per 25 hand-scorable booklets; $64 per 25 Type 1 machine-scorable answer documents; Type 2 machine-scorable answer documents available from publisher by special arrangement.

Cross References: For reviews by William D. Schafer and Sheldon Zedeck, see 13:51.

[408]

Career IQ Test.

Purpose: "Developed to assist individual in self exploration, vocational exploration, and career development."

Population: Ages 13–adults.

Publication Date: 1997.

Scores, 18: Aptitude (Verbal, Numerical, Spatial, Perceptual, Manual Dexterity, General Ability); Interest (Artistic, Scientific, Nature, Protective, Mechanical, Industrial, Business Detail, Selling, Accommodating, Humanitarian, Leading-Influencing, Physical Performing).

Administration: Group.

Price Data: Available from publisher.

Time: Administration time not reported.

Comments: Computer administered; Windows 3.1 or higher or Windows 95, MS-DOS Version 5.0 or later, or Macintosh System 7.0 or higher required.

Author: Virtual Knowledge.

Publisher: Virtual Knowledge [No reply from publisher; status unknown].

Cross References: For reviews by Wayne Camara and Donald Thompson, see 14:64.

[409]
Career Maturity Inventory.

Purpose: "Constructed to measure the maturity of attitudes and competencies that are critical in realistic career decision making."

Population: Grades 6–12.

Publication Dates: 1973–1978.

Acronym: CMI.

Administration: Group.

Price Data, 1993: $19.50 per 50 hand-scorable answer sheets; $37.40 per set of hand-scoring stencils; $1 per hand-scoring stencil; $30 per 100 profile sheets; $7.15 per administration manual (1978, 52 pages); $10.05 per theory and research handbook (1978, 44 pages); $17.98 per specimen set; $30.38 or less per 10 Compuscan answer sheets (includes prepaid computer scoring).

Comments: Formerly entitled Vocational Development Inventory (VDI).

Author: John O. Crites.

Publisher: Chronicle Guidance Publications, Inc.

a) ATTITUDE SCALE, SCREENING FORM A-2.

Price Data: $46.90 per 35 tests (1978, 7 pages).

Time: (30) minutes.

b) ATTITUDE SCALE, COUNSELING FORM B-1.

Scores, 5: Decisiveness, Involvement, Independence, Orientation, Compromise.

Price Data: $46.90 per 35 tests (1978, 7 pages).

Time: (40) minutes.

c) COMPETENCE TEST.

Scores, 5: Self-Appraisal, Occupational Information, Goal Selection, Planning, Problem Solving.

Price Data: $77.35 per 35 tests (1978, 38 pages).

Time: (120) minutes.

Cross References: See T5:413 (30 references), T4:398 (30 references), 9:199 (12 references), and

T3:374 (48 references); for reviews by Martin R. Katz and Donald G. Zytowski, and an excerpted review by Garth Sorenson, see 8:997 (152 references); see also T2:2103 (35 references).

[410]
Career Occupational Preference System, Interest Inventory, Form R.

Purpose: Designed to measure interests as they relate to careers using simplified language.

Population: Grade 6 through high school.

Publication Dates: 1984–1992.

Acronym: COPS-R.

Scores: Scores in the 14 COPSystem Career Clusters: Science-Professional, Science-Skilled, Technology-Professional, Technology-Skilled, Consumer Economics, Outdoor, Business-Professional, Business-Skilled, Clerical, Communication, Arts-Professional, Arts-Skilled, Service-Professional, Service-Skilled.

Administration: Group.

Price Data, 1998: $25.25 per 25 self-scoring forms [$91 per 100, $427.25 per 500]; $13.50 per 25 machine-scoring forms [$47.50 per 100, $223.50 per 500]; $1.60 each scoring by publisher; $5 per technical manual (1989, 34 pages); $2.75 per examiner's manual (1989, 14 pages); $7.25 per specimen set; $35 per 25 COPS-R Comprehensive Career Guides [$117 per 100, $549.50 per 500]; $5.50 per 25 COPS-R Summary Guides [$20.75 per 100, $91.25 per 500]; $22.75 per COPS-R Visuals.

Time: (20) minutes.

Authors: Lila F. Knapp and Robert R. Knapp.

Publisher: EdITS/Educational and Industrial Testing Service.

Cross References: See T5:414 (2 references and T4:399 (12 references).

[411]
Career Occupational Preference System, Intermediate Inventory.

Purpose: To measure career interests and provide a rating of interests based on knowledge of school subjects and activities familiar to elementary and intermediate grade students.

Population: Elementary through high school with 4th grade reading level.

Publication Dates: 1981–1997.

Acronym: COPS-II.

Scores: Scores in 14 COPSystem Career Clusters: Science-Professional, Science-Skilled, Technology-Professional, Technology-Skilled, Consumer Economics, Outdoor, Business-Professional, Business-Skilled, Clerical, Communication, Arts-Professional, Arts-Skilled, Service-Professional, Service-Skilled.

Administration: Group.

Price Data, 1998: $26.50 per 25 self-scoring test booklets [$96.50 per 100, $454.75 per 500]; $4 per examiner's manual (1992, 23 pages); $5.50 per specimen set; $7.25 per 25 pocket size cluster charts [$16.75 per 100]; $5.50 per 25 COPS-II Summary Guide [$20.75 per 100, $91.25 per 500]; $22.75 per COPS-II Visuals.

Time: (15–20) minutes.

Authors: Robert R. Knapp and Lila F. Knapp.

Publisher: EdITS/Educational and Industrial Testing Service.

Cross References: See T5:415 (1 reference).

[412]
Career Occupational Preference System—Professional Level Interest Inventory.

Purpose: Designed to measure career interest for those wanting to focus on the professional level careers.

Population: College and adult professionals, college-bound senior high school students.

Publication Dates: 1982–1989.

Acronym: COPS-P.

Scores: Scores in the 16 COPSystem Career Clusters: Service-Social, Service-Instructional, Science-Physical, Science-Medical/Life, Technology-Civil, Technology-Electrical, Technology-Mechanical, Outdoor-Agribusiness, Outdoor-Nature, Business-Management, Business-Finance, Computation, Communication-Written, Communication-Oral, Arts-Design, Arts-Performing.

Administration: Group.

Price Data, 1998: $13 per 25 self-scoring forms [$46.75 per 100, $220.50 per 500]; $12.50 per 25 Self-Interpretation Profiles and Guide [$44.50 per 100, $206.75 per 500]; $13.50 per 25 machine-scoring forms [$47.50 per 100, $223.50 per 500]; $1.60 each scoring by publisher; $22.25 per hand-scoring keys; $5 per technical manual (1989, 37 pages); $2.75 per examiner's manual (1989, 15 pages); $22.75 per set of COPS-P Visuals; $9 per specimen set.

Time: (15–20) minutes.

Authors: Lisa Knapp-Lee, Lila F. Knapp, Robert R. Knapp.

Publisher: EdITS/Educational and Industrial Testing Service.

Cross References: For reviews by Mark A. Albanese and Jeffrey A. Jenkins, see 14:65; see also T5:416 (1 reference). [Editor's Note: The reviews in the *14th MMY* are based on materials received prior to January 2000. The publisher advises that a revision was done in 2000.]

[413]
Career Orientation Placement and Evaluation Survey.

Purpose: Designed to measure values having a demonstrated effect on vocational motivation.

Population: Grade 7 through high school, college, and adult.

Publication Dates: 1981–1995.

Acronym: COPES.

Scores: Scores in 8 work values dimensions: Investigative v. Accepting, Practical v. Carefree, Independence v. Conformity, Leadership v. Supporting, Orderliness v. Flexibility, Recognition v. Privacy, Aesthetic v. Realistic, Social v. Reserved; and 14 COPSystem Career Clusters: Science-Professional, Science-Skilled, Technology-Professional, Technology-Skilled, Consumer Economics, Outdoor, Business-Professional, Business-Skilled, Clerical, Communication, Arts-Professional, Arts-Skilled, Service-Professional, Service-Skilled.

Administration: Group.

Price Data, 1998: $13 per 25 self-scoring test booklets [$46.75 per 100, $220.50 per 500]; $4.75 per 25 Self-interpretation Profiles and scoring test booklets [$12.50 per 100, $59.50 per 500]; $13.50 per 25 machine-scoring test booklets [$47.50 per 100, $223.50 per 500]; $1.60 each scoring by publisher; $7 per specimen set including manual (1990, 13 pages); $2.75 per examiner's manual; $22.75 per COPES visuals.

Time: (15–20) minutes.

Authors: Robert R. Knapp and Lila F. Knapp.

Publisher: EdITS/Educational and Industrial Testing Service.

[414]
Career Planning Survey.

Purpose: Intended "to help students in grades 8–10 identify and explore personally relevant occupations and high school courses … to provide students with a general sense of direction for career exploration … show students how occupations relate to each other, thus providing them with a context in which to explore their career options."

Population: Grades 8–10.

Publication Dates: 1997–2001.

Scores, 4: (UNIACT) Interest Inventory, Inventory of Work-Relevant Abilities, and 2 ability measures (Reading Skills, Numerical Skills).

Administration: Group.

Price Data, 2001: $3.80 per Assessment Set Option A (with ability measures); $3.25 per Assessment Set Option B (without ability measures) (each set includes an answer sheet [scored by ACT], a student guidebook, prepaid scoring, and two copies of the student report); $12.50 per examination kit (with detailed information and sample materials for the preview of Career Planning Survey, including test booklet, Directions for Administration, Counselor's Manual [2001, 48 pages], and student guidebook [2001, 24 pages]); $.65 per reusable test booklet; $8.25 per Counselor's Manual; $2.25 per Directions for Administration; volume discounts available.

Time: (90) minutes (Option A); (45) minutes (Option B).
Author: ACT, Inc.
Publisher: ACT, Inc.

[415]
Career Problem Check List.

Purpose: "Developed to help career teachers, career officers, and counsellors ... identify the problems secondary school or college students may be experiencing in making career plans."
Population: Ages 14–17.
Publication Date: 1983.
Acronym: CPCL.
Scores: 7 areas: Problems at School or College, Problems in Making Decisions, Problems at Home, Problems in Obtaining Specific Occupational Information, Problems in Applying for a Job or for a Course, Problems in Starting Work, Problems Outside Work.
Administration: Group.
Price Data: Price information available from publisher for checklists and manual (16 pages).
Time: (10–15) minutes.
Author: A. D. Crowley.
Publisher: NFER-Nelson Publishing Co., Ltd. [England].
Cross References: For a review by Nicholas A. Vacc and James Pickering, see 9:200.

[416]
The Career Profile System, Second Edition.

Purpose: "Predicts an individual's probability of success in an insurance sales career."
Population: Insurance sales representatives and candidates for insurance.
Publication Dates: 1983–1992.
Administration: Individual.
Price Data: Available from publisher.
Foreign Language Editions: English-speaking Canada and French-speaking Canada editions available; U.S. Spanish edition of Initial Career Profile available in 1994.
Time: (55–65) minutes.
Comments: Profiles processed by publisher.
Author: Life Insurance Marketing and Research Association, Inc.
Publisher: LIMRA International.
  a) STUDENT CAREER PROFILE.
  Population: High school—college.
  Scores: Total score and ratings in 3 areas: Industry Contacts, Achievement Orientation, Economic Maturity.
    1) Candidate Self-Assessment.
    Scores: 11 areas: Motivating Goals (External Goals, Internal Goals, Nonwork Goals),

Knowledge and Expectations of the Career (Knowledge of the Career, Expectations of the Commitment Required, Expectations of Sales Process, Income Expectations), The Candidate's Concerns (Acceptance as a Sales Representative, Potential Drawbacks of Career, Impact on Social Relationships, Income).
  b) INITIAL CAREER PROFILE.
  Population: Inexperienced candidates.
  Scores: Total score and ratings in 6 areas: Commitment to Present Situation, Belief in the Value of Insurance, Financial Situation, Income Expectations, Career Expectations, Work History.
    1) Candidate Self-Assessment.
    Scores: Same as *a*-1 above.
  c) ADVANCED CAREER PROFILE.
  Population: Experienced candidates.
  Scores: Total score and ratings in 5 areas: Position Familiarity, Professional Involvement, Belief in the Value of Insurance, Insurance Earnings, Income Needs and Expectations.
    1) Candidate Self-Assessment.
    Scores: 11 areas: Satisfaction with Present Insurance Sales Career (Training and Support, Compensation, Evaluation of Products, Evaluation of Current Agency, Administrative Issues), Sales Results (Number of Sales, Total Annualized Premiums, Persistency), Insurance Income (Income History, Income Needs, Income Expectations).
Cross References: For reviews by Ayres G. D'Costa and Michael S. Trevisan, see 13:52.

[417]
Career Thoughts Inventory.

Purpose: Constructed to assess "dysfunctional thinking in career problem solving and decision making."
Population: Adults, college students, and high school students.
Publication Dates: 1994–1996.
Acronym: CTI.
Scores, 4: Decision Making Confusion, Commitment Anxiety, External Conflict, Total.
Administration: Group.
Price Data: Available from publisher for introductory kit including manual (1996, 99 pages), 25 test booklets, and 10 workbooks (1996, 39 pages).
Time: (7–15) minutes.
Authors: James P. Samson, Jr., Gary W. Peterson, Janet G. Lenz, Robert C. Reardon, and Denise E. Saunders.
Publisher: Psychological Assessment Resources, Inc.
Cross References: For a review by Janet H. Fontaine, see 14:66.

[418]
Career Transitions Inventory.

Purpose: "Designed to assess the resources and barriers" experienced "in making a career transition."
Population: Adults.
Publication Date: 1991.
Acronym: CTI.
Scores, 5: Readiness, Confidence, Personal Control, Support, Independence.
Administration: Group.
Manual: No manual.
Price Data: Available from author.
Time: Administration time not reported.
Author: Mary J. Heppner.
Publisher: Mary J. Heppner (the author).

[419]
Career Values Card Sort.

Purpose: Defines factors that affect career satisfaction, the intensity of feelings about these factors, determines areas of value conflict and congruence, helps make career decisions.
Population: Adults.
Publication Dates: 1993–2002.
Scores: No scores.
Administration: Group or individual.
Price Data: Available from publisher
Time: (20–30) minutes.
Comments: Self-administered.
Author: Richard L. Knowdell.
Publisher: Career Research & Testing, Inc.
Cross References: For reviews by Esther E. Diamond and Richard T. Kinnier, see 13:53.

[420]
Caregiver-Teacher Report Form.

Purpose: Designed "to assess behavioral/emotional problems and identify syndromes of problems that tend to occur together."
Population: Ages 2–5.
Publication Date: 1997.
Acronym: C-TRF.
Scores, 10: Anxious/Obsessive, Depressed/Withdrawn, Fears, Somatic Problems, Immature, Attention Problems, Aggressive Behavior, Internalizing, Externalizing, Total.
Administration: Group.
Price Data: Available from publisher
Time: Administration time not reported.
Comments: Ratings by daycare providers and preschool teachers.
Author: Thomas M. Achenbach.
Publisher: Research Center for Children, Youth, and Families.
Cross References: For reviews by Karen T. Carey and by Michael Furlong and Renee Pavelski, see 14:67.

[421]
Carey Temperament Scales.

Purpose: Designed to assess "temperamental characteristics in infants and children."
Population: Ages 0-1 to 12-11.
Publication Dates: 1996–1998.
Acronym: CTS.
Scores, 9: Activity, Rhythmicity, Approach, Adaptability, Intensity, Mood, Persistence, Distractibility, Threshold.
Administration: Individual.
Price Data: Available from publisher.
Time: [15–20] minutes.
Comments: IBM computer scoring software and internet scoring available.
Authors: William B. Carey, Sean C. McDevitt, Barbara Medoff-Cooper, William Fullard, and Robin L. Hegvik.
Publisher: Behavioral-Developmental Initiatives.
Cross References: For reviews by Aimée Langlois and E. Jean Newman, see 14:68.

[422]
Caring Relationship Inventory.

Purpose: Designed to "measure the … elements of love or caring in human relationships."
Population: Premarital and marital counselees.
Publication Dates: 1966–1975.
Acronym: CRI.
Scores, 7: Affection, Friendship, Eros, Empathy, Self-Love, Being Love, Deficiency Love.
Administration: Individual.
Price Data, 1998: $18.25 per 25 tests (specify male or female form); $11.75 per 50 profile sheets; $20 per 7 hand-scoring keys; $4 per manual (1975, 15 pages); $7.75 per specimen set including manual and 1 copy of all forms.
Time: (40) minutes.
Author: Everett L. Shostrom.
Publisher: EdITS/Educational and Industrial Testing Service.
Cross References: See T4:408 (3 references); for reviews by Donald L. Mosher and Robert F. Stahmann, see 8:333 (5 references); for a review by Albert Ellis, see 7:561; see also P:31 (1 reference).

[423]
Carlson Psychological Survey.

Purpose: Developed to assess and classify offenders quickly and accurately.
Population: Adult and adolescent offenders.
Publication Dates: 1982–1997.
Acronym: CPS.
Scores: 5 scale scores: Chemical Abuse, Thought Disturbance, Anti-Social Tendencies, Self-Depreciation, Validity.

Administration: Group or individual.

Price Data, 2001: $41 per examination kit including manual (1982, 28 pages), 10 question and answer booklets, 10 scoring sheets, 10 profile sheets, and one machine-scorable question-and-answer document for an Extended Report; $21 per test manual; $30.50–$45 (depending on volume) per 25 question-and-answer booklets; $21-$24 (depending on volume) per 25 response sheets (including 25 scoring sheets and 25 profile sheets); $43–$49 (depending on volume) per 10 machine-scorable question-and-answer booklets for Extended Reports; $99 per software package including disks, software manual for Windows, test manual, and 10 coupons for computer reports.

Foreign Language Editions: Psicologico Texto (PT) designed specifically for use with Spanish-literate offenders; question and answer booklets available in French.

Time: [10–20] minutes.

Author: Kenneth A. Carlson.

Publisher: Sigma Assessment Systems, Inc.

Cross References: See T4:409 (2 references); for a review by H. C. Ganguli, see 9:203.

[424]
Carolina Picture Vocabulary Test (for Deaf and Hearing Impaired).

Purpose: "To measure the receptive sign vocabulary in individuals where manual signing [is] the primary mode of communication."

Population: Deaf and hearing-impaired children ages 4–11.5 years.

Publication Date: 1985.

Acronym: CPVT.

Scores: Total score only.

Administration: Individual.

Price Data, 2001: $129 per complete program; $64 per picture book; $29 per 50 record forms; $39 per manual (38 pages).

Time: (10-15) minutes.

Authors: Thomas L. Layton and David W. Holmes.

Publisher: PRO-ED.

Cross References: For additional information, see 11:62 (1 reference).

[425]
Carroll Depression Scales.

Purpose: Designed as a measure of depression; providing diagnostic as well as level of severity information.

Population: 18 years and over.

Publication Date: 1998.

Scores, 5: Major Depression, Dysthymic Disorder, Melancholic and Atypical Features, HDRS, Total.

Administration: Group.

Price Data, 2002: $93 per complete kit including 25 CDS-R QuikScore™ forms and technical manual (96 pages); $35 per CDS-R 25 QuikScore™ forms

(English or French-Canadian); $28 per 25 Brief QuikScore™ forms (English or French-Canadian); $45 per technical manual; $57 per specimen set including 3 CDS-R QuikScore™ forms, 3 Brief CDS-R QuikScore™ forms, and technical manual.

Comments: Interpretation by qualified professionals only.

Foreign Language Editions: French-Canadian QuikScore™ forms available.

Author: Bernard Carroll.

Publisher: Multi-Health Systems, Inc.

a) CARROLL DEPRESSION SCALES.
   Acronym: CDS-R.
   Time: (20) minutes.
   Comments: A 52-item self-report measure.
b) CARROLL DEPRESSION SCALE—REVISED.
   Acronym: CDS-R.
   Time: (10) minutes.
   Comments: A 52-item self-report measure; includes diagnostic index in addition to severity score provided by CDS.
c) BRIEF CARROLL DEPRESSION INVENTORY.
   Acronym: Brief CDS-R.
   Time: (2) minutes.
   Comments: A 12-item self-report rapid screening measure of depressive symptoms.

Cross References: For a review by Susan M. Swearer, see 14:69.

[426]
CAT/5 Listening and Speaking Checklist.

Purpose: "Designed to help the teacher in evaluating two important aspects of the reading/language arts domain: listening and speaking."

Population: Grades K–12.

Publication Date: 1993.

Scores: Overall Rating Index.

Administration: Group.

Levels, 3: Grades K–3, 4–8, 9–12.

Price Data, 2002: $35.75 per classroom package including 30 checklists, teacher's guide (28 pages), and class summary folder (specify level); $16.50 per teacher's guide; $3.30 per class summary folder.

Time: Administration time not reported.

Comments: Student self-evaluation forms, a checklist assessment plan, and a letter to parents are also available.

Authors: CTB Macmillan/McGraw-Hill.

Publisher: CTB/McGraw-Hill.

Cross References: For reviews by Gerald S. Hanna and Richard M. Wolf, see 13:54.

[427]
The Category-Specific Names Test.

Purpose: Designed to detect category-specific deficits both in naming and in comprehension of the spoken or written name within four semantic categories: animals, fruits and vegetables, praxic objects, and non-praxic objects.

Population: Children and adults.
Publication Date: Unavailable.
Scores: Available from publisher.
Administration: Individual.
Price Data, 2001: $415 per complete test.
Time: Administration time not reported.
Author: Pat McKenna.
Publisher: Psychology Press.

[428]
Cattell Infant Intelligence Scale.

Purpose: Designed to measure the infant's developmental progress.
Population: Ages 3–30 months.
Publication Dates: 1946–1960.
Acronym: CIIS.
Scores: Ratings in 4 areas: Willingness, Self-Confidence, Social-Confidence, Attention.
Administration: Individual.
Price Data, 2002: $795 per basic set including all necessary equipment, 25 record forms, and carrying case (manual not included); $113 per manual entitled The Measurement of Intelligence of Infants and Young Children (1960, 274 pages); $40 per 25 record forms.
Time: (20-30) minutes.
Comments: Downward extension of Stanford-Binet Intelligence Scale, Second Revision.
Author: Psyche Cattell.
Publisher: The Psychological Corporation.
Cross References: See T5:433 (14 references), T4:423 (13 references) and T3:381 (19 references); for a review by Fred Damarin, see 8:209 (7 references); see also T2:487 (27 references) and 6:515 (22 references); for reviews by Florence M. Teagarden and Beth L. Wellmann and excerpted reviews by Rachel Stutsman Ball, C. M. Louttit, T. L. McCulloch, Norma V. Schneidmann, and Helen Speyer, see 3:281.

[429]
CERAD (Consortium to Establish a Registry for Alzheimer's Disease) Assessment Battery.

Purpose: "To develop brief, standardized instruments for the assessment of patients with probable Alzheimer's disease."
Population: Patients with mild to moderate dementia.
Publication Date: 1987.
Acronym: CERAD.
Scores: Information gathered in 19 areas: Demographic, Drug Inventory, Informant History (Clinical, Blessed Dementia Rating Scale), Subject History, Short Blessed Test, Depression and Calculation and Language), Examinations (Physical, Neurological), Laboratory Studies, Diagnostic Impression, Neuropsychological Battery (Neuropsychology Battery Status, Verbal Fluency Categories, Boston Naming Test, Mini-Mental State Exam, Word List Memory, Constructional Praxis, Word List Recall, Word List Recognition), Constructional Praxis Recall.
Administration: Individual.
Restricted Distribution: Current use only with permission of CERAD.
Price Data: Price information available from publisher.
Foreign Language Editions: Forms available in French, Spanish, Italian, Chinese, Japanese, and Korean.
Time: [50–70] minutes.
Comments: Manual title is Instruction Manual for Assessment of Patient and Control Subjects Entered into the CERAD Study.
Author: Consortium to Establish a Registry for Alzheimer's Disease, Albert Heyman (Principal Investigator).
Publisher: CERAD Administrative CORE, Duke University Medical Center.
Cross References: For reviews by Frank M. Bernt and Gabrielle Stutman, see 12:66 (1 reference).

[430]
Certified Picture Framer Examination.

Purpose: "To provide professional recognition to competent individuals who are engaged in the business of picture framing."
Population: Individuals actively involved in the business of picture framing for one year.
Publication Dates: 1986–1993.
Acronym: CPF.
Scores: Total score only.
Administration: Group.
Price Data, 1994: Registration fee $200 for members of PPFA or $300 for nonmembers.
Time: (210) minutes.
Comments: Test administered on specific dates at centers established by the publisher.
Author: Certification Board of the Professional Picture Framers Association.
Publisher: Professional Picture Framers Association.

[431]
Change Abilitator.

Purpose: Designed to identify six types of concerns people experience when change is introduced into their organization.
Population: Teams.
Publication Date: 1995.
Scores, 6: Information, Personal, Operational, Impact, Collaboration, Transforming.
Administration: Group.

Price Data, 1998: $7.95 per questionnaire; $34.95 per Leader's Guide (149 pages).
Time: (15) minutes.
Comments: Revision of the Stages of Concern Questionnaire.
Author: LHE, INC.
Publisher: Human Resource Development Press.
Cross References: For a review by Cynthia A. Larson-Daugherty, see 14:70.

[432]
Change Agent Questionnaire.

Purpose: Assesses "the underlying assumptions and practical strategies employed by agents of change as they seek to influence others."
Population: Adults.
Publication Dates: 1969-1995.
Acronym: CAQ.
Scores, 20: Client-Centered Change (Philosophy, Strategy, Evaluation, Total), Charismatic Change (Philosophy, Strategy, Evaluation, Total), Custodial Change (Philosophy, Strategy, Evaluation, Total), Compliance Change (Philosophy, Strategy, Evaluation, Total), Credibility Change (Philosophy, Strategy, Evaluation, Total).
Administration: Group.
Manual: No manual.
Price Data, 2001: $8.95 per instrument.
Time: Administration time not reported.
Authors: Jay Hall and Martha S. Williams.
Publisher: Teleometrics International.

[433]
Change Readiness Survey.

Purpose: Designed to observe an "organization's readiness to effectively endure organizational change."
Population: Organizations.
Publication Date: 1999.
Acronym: CRS.
Scores, 5: Leadership, Performance, Communication, Customer Focus, Total.
Administration: Individual.
Price Data: Available from publisher.
Time: [15–20] minutes.
Comments: Can be administered online via the Internet.
Author: Lore International Institute.
Publisher: Lore International Institute.

[434]
Chapin Social Insight Test.

Purpose: Designed to "assess the perceptiveness and accuracy with which an individual can appraise others and forecast what they might say and do."
Population: Ages 13 and over.
Publication Dates: 1967–1993.
Acronym: SCLT.

Scores: Total score only.
Administration: Group.
Price Data, 2001: $25 per sampler set including situations booklet, response booklet, and manual (1968, 18 pages); $100 per permissions set including sampler set plus permission to reproduce up to 200 copies of the test.
Time: (20–30) minutes.
Authors: F. Stuart Chapin (test) and Harrison G. Gough (manual).
Publisher: Mind Garden, Inc.
Cross References: See T3:384 (5 references); for reviews by Richard I. Lanyon and David B. Orr, see 7:51; see also P:34 (3 references).

[435]
Characteristics Scale.

Purpose: To determine teachers' views of important pupil characteristics and behaviors.
Population: Grades K-8.
Publication Dates: 1970-1975.
Scores: Total score only.
Administration: Group.
Manual: No manual.
Price Data, 2001: Now free upon request from publisher.
Time: Administration time not reported.
Comments: Ratings by teachers; research instrument; may be used with or separately from Behavior Rating Scale.
Authors: Patricia B. Elmore and Donald L. Beggs.
Publisher: Patricia B. Elmore.

[436]
Chart of Initiative and Independence.

Purpose: Designed as "an assessment of environmental opportunities available to clients and ... of their current and potential use of those resources."
Population: Mentally handicapped adults.
Publication Date: 1980.
Acronym: CII.
Scores: No scores.
Administration: Individual.
Price Data: Price information available from publisher for individual assessment forms, Development Programme forms, Residential Policy form, Preliminary Assessment forms, manual of activities (10 pages), preliminary assessment manual (9 pages), and complete manual (67 pages).
Time: Administration time not reported.
Comments: 4 formats: Individual Assessment Format (assesses present behavior), Development Programme Format (assesses future behavior), Residential Policy Format (assesses residential policy), Preliminary Assessment Format (short form of individual assessment to be used by social workers).

Authors: I. Macdonald and T. Couchman.
Publisher: NFER-Nelson Publishing Co., Ltd. [England].
Cross References: For reviews by Morton Bortner and Wayne C. Piersel, see 9:209.

[437]
Checklist for Child Abuse Evaluation.

Purpose: "Provides a standard format for evaluating abuse in children and adolescents."
Population: Children and adolescents.
Publication Dates: 1988–1990.
Acronym: CCAE.
Scores: 24 sections: Identification and Case Description, The Child's Status, Accuracy of Allegations by the Reporter, Interview with the Child (Physical/Behavioral Observations, Disclosure, Emotional Abuse, Sexual Abuse, Physical Abuse, Neglect), Events Witnessed or Reported by Others (Neglect, Emotional Abuse, Sexual Abuse, Physical Abuse), The Child's Psychological Status, History and Observed/Reported Characteristics of the Accused, Credibility of the Child—Observed/Reported, Competence of the Child—Observed/Reported, Conclusions (Consistency of Other Information, Allegation Motives, Substantiation of Allegations, Competence of the Child as a Witness, Level of Stress Experienced by the Child, Protection of the Child), Treatment Recommendations.
Administration: Individual.
Price Data: Available from publisher for complete kit including manual (1990, 19 pages), and 10 checklists.
Time: Untimed.
Author: Joseph Petty.
Publisher: Psychological Assessment Resources, Inc.
Cross References: For reviews by Denise M. DeZolt and Janice G. Williams, see 12:68.

[438]
Checklist of Adaptive Living Skills.

Purpose: "A criterion-referenced measure of adaptive living skills and a tool for program planning."
Population: Infants to adults.
Publication Date: 1991.
Acronym: CALS.
Scores: 4 areas: Personal Living Skills, Home Living Skills, Community Living Skills, Employment Skills; and 24 subscales: Socialization, Eating, Grooming, Toileting, Dressing, Health Care, Sexuality, Clothing Care, Meal Planning and Preparation, Home Cleaning and Organization, Home Maintenance, Home Safety, Home Leisure, Social Interaction, Mobility and Travel, Time Management, Money Management and Shopping, Community Safety, Community Leisure, Community Participation, Job Search, Job Performance and Attitudes, Employee Relations, Job Safety.
Administration: Individual.

Price Data: Available from publisher.
Time: [60] minutes.
Comments: "Designed to be completed by a respondent who has had the opportunity to observe the learner in natural environments for a period of three or more months"; conceptually and statistically linked to two normative measures of adaptive behavior: Scales of Independent Behavior—Revised (SIB-R; 2189) and Inventory for Client and Agency Planning (ICAP; 1250); companion publication is the Adaptive Living Skills Curriculum.
Authors: Lanny E. Morreau and Robert H. Bruininks.
Publisher: Riverside Publishing.
Cross References: See T5:443 (1 reference); for reviews by Patricia A. Bachelor and James P. Van Haneghan, see 12:69.

[439]
Chelsea Diagnostic Mathematics Tests.

Purpose: "Designed as diagnostic instruments to be used both for ascertaining a child's level of understanding and to identify the incidence of errors."
Population: Ages 10–15.
Publication Dates: 1984–1985.
Scores: 10 tests: Algebra, Fractions 1, Fractions 2, Graphs, Measurement, Number Operations, Place-Value and Decimals, Ratio and Proportion, Reflection and Rotation, Vectors.
Administration: Group.
Price Data: Price information available from publisher for complete kit including 10 each of test booklets, set of marking overlays, and teacher's guide (1985, 154 pages); tests (Algebra, Fractions 1, Fractions 2, Number Operations, Ratio and proportion, Graphs, Place-Value and Decimals, Reflection and Rotation, Vectors, or Measurement), Reflection and Rotation marking overlays, teacher's guide, and for specimen set including 1 each of tests and teacher's guide.
Time: (30–70) minutes per test.
Authors: Kathleen Hart, Margaret Brown, Daphne Kerslake, Dietmar Kuchemann, and Graham Ruddock.
Publisher: NFER-Nelson Publishing Co., Ltd. [England].

[440]
Child Abuse/Husband Abuse/Wife Abuse.

Purpose: Designed to compile an individual's history of abuse.
Population: Children, husbands, wives.
Publication Date: 1991.
Administration: Individual or group.
Forms, 3: Child Abuse, Husband Abuse, Wife Abuse.
Manual: No manual.
Price Data, 2001: $10 per 20 record forms (specify Child, Husband, or Wife).

Time: Administration time not reported.
Author: Allan Roe.
Publisher: Diagnostic Specialists, Inc.

[441]
The Child Abuse Potential Inventory, Form VI.

Purpose: "To assist in the screening of suspected physical child abuse cases."
Population: Male and female parents or primary caregivers who are suspected of physical child abuse.
Publication Dates: 1980–1993.
Acronym: CAP Inventory.
Scores: 12 scale scores: Abuse scale (Distress, Rigidity, Unhappiness, Problems With Child and Self, Problems With Family, Problems With Others, Total Physical Child Abuse), Validity scales (Lie Scale, Random Response Scale, Inconsistency Scale), Loneliness, Ego-Strength, and 3 Response Distortion Indexes (Faking-Good, Faking-Bad, Random Response).
Administration: Individual administration recommended.
Price Data: Available from publisher.
Time: (12–20) minutes.
Author: Joel S. Milner.
Publisher: Psytec Inc.
Cross References: See T5:448 (30 references) and T4:429 (10 references); for reviews by Stuart N. Hart and Gary B. Melton, see 10:50 (5 references).

[442]
Child and Adolescent Adjustment Profile [Revised].

Purpose: Designed to "measure five factor-analyzed areas of adjustment."
Population: Children and adolescents seen in mental health programs, outpatient and inpatient, health care programs, and schools.
Publication Dates: 1977–1998.
Acronym: CAAP Scale.
Scores, 5: Dependency, Hostility, Peer Relations, Productivity, Withdrawal.
Administration: Individual.
Price Data, 2002: $10 per 25 scales; $5 per 25 profiles; $25 per manual (1998, 28 pages).
Time: (10) minutes.
Comments: Pre- and posttreatment ratings by parents, teachers, and counselors, or any adult who knows the child.
Authors: Robert B. Ellsworth and Shanae L. Ellsworth.
Publisher: Ellsworth Krebs Incorporated.
Cross References: See T5:449 (4 references) and T4:430 (1 reference); for reviews by Robert H. Deluty and David R. Wilson of an earlier edition, see 9:211.

[443]
Child Care Inventory.

Purpose: Developed to evaluate child care programs in order to improve program effectiveness or to determine the level of program implementation.
Population: Child care programs.
Publication Date: 1986.
Scores: 11 performance areas: Classroom Arrangement, Safety, Curriculum, Interacting, Scheduling, Child Assessment, Health, Special Needs, Parent Involvement, Outdoor Play, Infant Programs.
Administration: Individual.
Price Data, 2002: $22.95 per complete kit including test booklet and manual (32 pages); 11.95 per test booklet; $12.95 per manual.
Time: Administration time not reported.
Authors: Martha S. Abbott-Shim and Annette M. Sibley.
Publisher: Humanics Learning.
Cross References: For reviews by Lisa G. Bischoff and Annette M. Iverson, see 12:71.

[444]
Child Development Inventory.

Purpose: "Designed to provide systematic ways of obtaining in depth developmental information from parents."
Population: Ages 1–3 to 6–3.
Publication Dates: 1968–1992.
Acronym: CDI.
Scores, 9: Social, Self Help, Gross Motor, Fine Motor, Expressive Language, Language Comprehension, Letters, Numbers, General Development.
Administration: Individual.
Price Data, 2001: $65 per complete set including 10 test booklets, 25 answer sheets, 25 CDI profiles, and manual (1992, 44 pages) with scoring template; $15 per 10 test booklets; $10 per 25 answer sheets; $10 per 25 CDI profiles; $30 per manual with scoring template; $32 per specimen set.
Time: [30–50] minutes.
Comments: Parent-completed questionnaire; formerly called the Minnesota Child Development Inventory.
Author: Harold Ireton.
Publisher: Behavior Science Systems, Inc.
Cross References: For reviews by Jean Powell Kirnan and Diana Crespo and by Stephanie Stein, see 13:56; see also T4:436 (14 references); for a review of an earlier edition by Jane A. Rysberg, see 9:712; see also T3:1492 (6 references); for a review by William L. Goodwin, see 8:220 (3 references).

[445]
Child Development Review.

Purpose: A brief screening inventory "designed to help identify children with developmental, behavioral, or health problems."

Population: 18 months to age 5.
Publication Date: 1994.
Acronym: CDR.
Scores, 5: Development (Social, Self-Help, Gross Motor, Fine Motor, Language), Possible Problems, Child Description, Parents' Questions/Concerns, Parents' Functioning.
Administration: Individual.
Price Data, 2001: $10 per 25 parent questionnaire/child development charts; $10 per manual (22 pages).
Time: Administration time not reported.
Comments: Parent-completed questionnaire; scores reflect parents' report of child's present functioning-development.
Author: Harold Ireton.
Publisher: Behavior Science Systems, Inc.
Cross References: For reviews by Terry Overton and Gary J. Stainback, see 14:71.

[446]
Child Language Ability Measures.

Purpose: "Designed to measure language development."
Population: Ages 2–8.
Publication Date: 1979.
Acronym: CLAM.
Scores: 6 tests: Vocabulary Comprehension, Grammar Comprehension, Inflection Production, Grammar Imitation, Grammar Formedness Judgment, Grammar Equivalence Judgment.
Administration: Individual.
Price Data: Available from publisher.
Time: (15) minutes per test.
Comments: Tests may be administered separately or in any of 11 combinations.
Authors: Christy Moynihan and Albert Mehrabian.
Publisher: Albert Mehrabian.
Cross References: For a review by Allen Jack Edwards, see 10:51.

[447]
Child Sexual Behavior Inventory.

Purpose: Designed as a "measure of sexual behavior in children"; used in the identification of sexual abuse.
Population: Ages 2–12.
Publication Dates: 1986–1997.
Acronym: CSBI.
Scores, 3: Developmentally Related Sexual Behaviors, Sexual Abuse Specific Items, Total.
Administration: Individual.
Price Data: Available from publisher for introductory kit including manual (1997, 61 pages) and 50 test booklets.
Time: [10–15] minutes.
Comments: Completed by a child's primary caregiver.

Author: William N. Friedrich.
Publisher: Psychological Assessment Resources, Inc.
Cross References: For reviews by Frank M. Bernt and Thomas McKnight, see 14:72; see also T5:457 (1 reference).

[448]
Child Symptom Inventory 4.

Purpose: Designed as a "screening instrument for the behavioral affective, and cognitive symptoms" of childhood psychiatric disorders.
Population: Ages 5–12.
Publication Dates: 1994–1998.
Acronym: CSI-4.
Scores, 13: AD/HD Inattentive, AD/HD Hyperimpulsive, AD/HD Combined, Oppositional Defiant Disorder, Conduct Disorder, Generalized Anxiety Disorder, Schizophrenia, Major Depressive Disorder, Dysthymic Disorder, Autistic Disorder, Asperger's Disorder, Social Phobia, Separation Anxiety Disorder.
Administration: Individual.
Forms, 2: Parent Checklist, Teacher Checklist.
Price Data, 2001: $98 per deluxe kit including screening manual (1998, 123 pages), norms manual (1997, 158 pages), 25 parent checklists, 25 teacher checklists, 50 symptom count score sheets, and 50 symptom severity profile score sheets; $22 per screening manual or norms manual; $32 per 50 parent checklists; $60 per 100 parent checklists; $20 per 25 Spanish parent checklists; $32 per 50 teacher checklists; $60 per 100 teacher checklists; $13 per 50 profiles for parent or teacher checklists; $225 per computer scoring and report writing software.
Time: [10–15] minutes.
Comments: Instrument is designed to correspond to the DSM-IV classification system.
Authors: Kenneth D. Gadow and Joyce Sprafkin.
Publisher: Checkmate Plus Ltd.

[449]
Child Well-Being Scales and Rating Form.

Purpose: Designed for the assessment of children's welfare.
Population: Child welfare practitioners.
Publication Date: 1987.
Scores: No scores.
Administration: Group.
Manual: No manual.
Price Data, 1997: $10 per test booklet.
Time: Administration time not reported.
Comments: Ratings by child welfare practitioners.
Authors: Stephen Magura and Beth Silverman Moses.
Publisher: Child Welfare League of America, Inc.
Cross References: See T5:458 (2 references).

[450]
The Childhood Autism Rating Scale.

Purpose: "To identify children with autism, and to distinguish them from developmentally handicapped children without the autism syndrome."
Population: Ages 2 and over.
Publication Dates: 1986–1988.
Acronym: CARS.
Scores: 16 rating scores: Relating to People, Imitation, Emotional Response, Body Use, Object Use, Adaptation to Change, Visual Response, Listening Response, Taste/Smell/Touch Response and Use, Fear or Nervousness, Verbal Communication, Nonverbal Communication, Activity Level, Level and Consistency of Intellectual Response, General Impressions, Total.
Administration: Individual.
Price Data, 2002: $65 per complete kit including 25 rating scales and manual (1988, 20 pages); $22.50 per 25 rating scales; $45 per manual; $182.50 per training video (Demonstration tape using the CARS or Practice Tape on Using the CARS).
Time: Administration time not reported.
Comments: Revision of the Childhood Psychosis Rating Scale; ratings by professionals trained to administer the CARS.
Authors: Eric Schopler, Robert J. Reichler, and Barbara Rochen Renner.
Publisher: Western Psychological Services.
Cross References: See T5:459 (40 references) and T4:439 (6 references); for reviews by Barry M. Prizant and J. Steven Welsh, see 11:65 (4 references).

[451]
Childhood Trauma Questionnaire.

Purpose: Designed as a self-report inventory for "screening for histories of abuse and neglect."
Population: Ages 12 and up.
Publication Dates: 1997–1998.
Acronym: CTQ.
Scores, 5: Emotional Abuse, Physical Abuse, Sexual Abuse, Emotional and Physical Neglect and Minimization/Denial of Abuse.
Administration: Individual.
Price Data, 2002: $99 per complete kit including 25 READYSCORE answer documents and manual (1998, 76 pages); $40 per 25 READYSCORE answer documents; $73 per manual.
Time: (5) minutes.
Comments: A 28-item, self-report inventory.
Authors: David P. Bernstein and Laura Fink.
Publisher: The Psychological Corporation.
Cross References: For reviews by Michael Furlong and Renee Pavelski and by Jonathan Sandoval, see 14:73; see also T5:460 (2 references).

[452]
Children of Alcoholics Screening Test.

Purpose: Measures children's and adults' attitudes, feelings, perceptions, and experiences related to their parents' drinking behavior; also identifies probable children of alcoholics (CoAs) and adult children of alcoholics (ACoAs).
Population: School-age children through adults.
Publication Dates: 1981–1993.
Acronym: CAST.
Scores: Total score only.
Administration: Group or individual.
Price Data: Not available.
Time: (5–10) minutes.
Comments: Reduced rate is available for additional forms used in research or mass testing.
Author: John W. Jones.
Publisher: Camelot Unlimited.
Cross References: See T5:462 (33 references) and T4:440 (8 references); for reviews by Stuart N. Hart and Steven P. Schinke, see 10:52; for reviews by Susanna Maxwell and Barrie G. Stacey, see 9:217.

[453]
Children's Abilities Scales.

Purpose: Designed as a broad assessment of a pupil's abilities as the pupil enters a secondary school.
Population: Ages 11-0 to 12-6.
Publication Dates: 1982–1984.
Acronym: CAS.
Scores, 10: Verbal (Word Pairs, Word Overlap, Total), Spatial (Flags [Part 1], Flags [Parts 1 and 2], Dice, Total), Non-Verbal (Symbols, Shapes, Total).
Administration: Group.
Price Data: Price information available from publisher for introductory pack including class set of 30 pupil's books, 3 answer sheet packs, and manual (1984, 39 pages); reusable pupil's book, scoring keys, answer sheet pack, manual, and for specimen set including pupil's book, 10 answer sheets, and manual.
Time: (140) minutes for the battery, (15–35) minutes for any one test.
Authors: Chris Whetton and Roy Childs.
Publisher: NFER-Nelson Publishing Co., Ltd. [England].
Cross References: For reviews by Stephen N. Elliott and Stephan A. Henry, see 10:53.

[454]
Children's Academic Intrinsic Motivation Inventory.

Purpose: "To measure academic intrinsic motivation … defined as enjoyment of school learning characterized by an orientation toward mastery, curiosity, persistence, and the learning of challenging, difficult, and novel tasks."

Population: Grades 4–8.
Publication Date: 1986.
Acronym: CAIMI.
Scores: 5 scales: Reading, Math, Social Studies, Science, General.
Administration: Individual or group.
Price Data: Available from publisher for complete kit including 50 test booklets, 50 profile forms, and manual (24 pages).
Time: (20–30) minutes for individual administration; (60) minutes for group administration.
Comments: Self-report inventory.
Author: Adele Gottfried.
Publisher: Psychological Assessment Resources, Inc.
Cross References: See T5:464 (5 references); for a review by C. Dale Posey, see 10:54.

[455]
Childrens Adaptive Behavior Scale, Revised.

Purpose: Provides a means to gather information on the relevant knowledge and concepts requisite to adaptive functioning.
Population: Ages 5–11.
Publication Dates: 1980–2002.
Acronym: CABS.
Scores, 6: Language Development, Independent Functioning, Family Role Performance, Economic-Vocational Activity, Socialization, Total.
Administration: Individual.
Price Data, 2002: $1 per student booklet; $14.95 per manual (1983, 42 pages); $35.95 per specimen set including 5 student booklets, picture book, and manual.
Time: (45–50) minutes.
Comments: Other test materials (e.g., coins, blocks, scissors, paper) must be supplied by examiner.
Authors: Richard H. Kicklighter and Bert O. Richmond.
Publisher: Humanics Learning.
Cross References: See T4:442 (1 reference); for reviews by Kenneth A. Kavale and Esther Sinclair, see 10:55 (1 reference); for reviews by Thomas R. Kratochwill and Corinne R. Smith of the original edition, see 9:218; see also T3:395 (1 reference).

[456]
Children's Apperception Test [1991 Revision].

Purpose: A projective "method of investigating personality by studying the dynamic meaningfulness of the individual differences in perception of standard stimuli."
Population: Ages 3–10.
Publication Dates: 1949–1992.
Acronym: C.A.T.
Scores: No scores.
Administration: Individual.

Editions, 3: Animal, Human, Supplement, plus Short Form.
Price Data, 2001: $95 per C.A.T.–A, C.A.T.–S, C.A.T.–H, manual (1991, 24 pages), 25 recording and analysis blanks (short form), and 10 copies of Haworth's Schedule of Adaptive Mechanisms in C.A.T. Responses; $86 per C.A.T.–A or C.A.T.–H; $32 per C.A.T.–S; $9.25 per 25 recording and analysis blanks (short form); $9 per 30 Haworth's Schedules; $9 per 10 psychodiagnostic test reports.
Time: (15–20) minutes.
Authors: Leopold Bellak and Sonya Sorel Bellak.
Publisher: C.P.S., Inc.
Cross References: See T5:466 (1 reference); for reviews by Howard M. Knoff and Robert C. Reinehr, see 13:58 (4 references); see also T4:444 (4 references); for reviews by Clifford V. Hatt and Marcia B. Shaffer of an earlier edition, see 9:219 (1 reference); see also T3:396 (1 reference), T2:1451 (23 references), and P:419 (18 references); for reviews by Bernard L. Murstein and Robert D. Wirt, see 6:206 (19 references); for reviews by Douglas T. Keeny and Albert I. Rabin, see 5:126 (15 references); for reviews by John E. Bell and L. Joseph Stone and excerpted reviews by M. M. Genn, Herbert Herman, Robert R. Holt, Laurance F. Shaffer, and Adolf G. Woltmann, see 4:103 (2 references).

[457]
Children's Articulation Test.

Purpose: Designed to "assess child's ability to produce consonants, vowels and diphthongs in an in-depth relationship to other consonants and vowels."
Population: Ages 3–11.
Publication Date: 1989.
Acronym: CAT.
Scores, 7: Medial Vowels/Diphthongs, Final Consonants, Initiating Consonants, Abutting Consonants, Abutting Consonants and Vowels/Diphthongs, Connected Speech, Language Concepts.
Administration: Individual.
Price Data: Available from publisher.
Time: [15] minutes.
Author: George S. Haspiel.
Publisher: Dragon Press.
Cross References: For reviews by Kathryn W. Kenney and Lawrence J. Turton, see 12:74.

[458]
Children's Attention and Adjustment Survey.

Purpose: "Designed to measure the diagnostic criteria of inattention, impulsivity, hyperactivity, and aggressiveness or conduct problems."
Population: Ages 5–13.
Publication Date: 1990.
Acronym: CAAS.

Scores, 7: Inattention, Impulsivity, ADD, Hyperactivity, ADHD, Conduct Problems, DSM III-R ADHD.
Administration: Individual.
Editions, 2: School, Home.
Price Data, 2002: $39.95 per 25 self-scorable booklets (select School or Home form); $19.95 per 25 scoring profiles; $27.95 per manual (75 pages); $127.95 per starter set including manual and 25 each of Home Form, School Form, and Scoring Profile.
Time: (5–10) minutes per form.
Comments: Ratings by teacher or parent.
Authors: Nadine Lambert, Carolyn Hartsough, and Jonathan Sandoval.
Publisher: American Guidance Service, Inc.
Cross References: See T5:469 (3 references); for reviews by Claire B. Ernhart and Stephen L. Koffler, see 12:75 (1 reference).

[459]
Children's Auditory Verbal Learning Test-2.

Purpose: Constructed to assess the presence and severity of learning and memory impairment in children.
Population: Ages 6-6 to 17-11.
Publication Dates: 1988–1993.
Acronym: CAVLT-2.
Scores, 7: Immediate Memory Span, Level of Learning, Interference Trial, Immediate Recall, Delayed Recall, Recognition Accuracy, Total Intrusions.
Administration: Individual.
Price Data: Available from publisher for complete kit including 25 test booklets and manual (1993, 68 pages).
Time: (25–30) minutes.
Comments: Orally administered.
Author: Jack L. Talley.
Publisher: Psychological Assessment Resources, Inc.
Cross References: For reviews by John O. Anderson and Sherwyn Morreale, see 12:76.

[460]
Children's Category Test.

Purpose: "Designed to assess non-verbal learning and memory, concept formation, and problem-solving abilities."
Population: Ages 5-0 to 16-11.
Publication Date: 1993.
Acronym: CCT.
Scores, 6: Subtest I, Subtest II, Subtest III, Subtest IV, Subtest V, Total.
Administration: Individual.
Levels, 2: Level 1 (Ages 5 to 8), Level 2 (Ages 9 to 16).
Price Data, 2002: $339 per complete kit including manual (72 pages), 25 Level 1 record forms, 25 Level 2 record forms, stimulus booklets, and color response

cards (1 for each level); $28 per 25 record forms; $57 per manual.
Time: (15–20) minutes.
Author: Thomas Boll.
Publisher: The Psychological Corporation.
Cross References: For reviews by Mark D. Shriver and Nicholas A. Vacc, see 13:59.

[461]
Children's Depression Inventory.

Purpose: A self-rating assessment of children's depression.
Population: Ages 7-17.
Publication Dates: 1977-1992.
Acronym: CDI.
Scores, 6: Negative Mood, Interpersonal Problems, Ineffectiveness, Anhedonia, Negative Self-Esteem, Total.
Administration: Individual and small groups.
Price Data: Available from publisher for test, manual, instructions for administration, Quikscore form, computerized version, reference list, and alternate versions.
Foreign Language Editions: Translations available in Arabic, Bulgarian, Italian, Hungarian, Hebrew, Spanish, Swedish, German, French, Portuguese, Russian, and several Chinese and Indian languages.
Time: [10-15] minutes.
Comments: A 10-item screening version is also available (10 minutes to complete).
Author: Maria Kovacs.
Publisher: Multi-Health Systems, Inc.
Cross References: See T5:472 (235 references) and T4:450 (71 references); for reviews by Michael G. Kavan and Howard M. Knoff, see 11:66 (63 references).

[462]
Children's Depression Rating Scale, Revised.

Purpose: Constructed as a "screening instrument, diagnostic tool, and severity measure of depression in children."
Population: Ages 6–12.
Publication Date: 1996.
Acronym: CDRS-R.
Scores: Total score only.
Administration: Group.
Price Data, 2002: $72 per complete kit including manual (91 pages), and 25 administration booklets; $27.50 per 25 administration booklets; $49.50 per manual.
Time: (15–20) minutes.
Comments: Ratings by health care professionals.
Authors: Elva O. Poznanski and Hartmut B. Mokros.
Publisher: Western Psychological Services.

Cross References: For reviews by E. Thomas Dowd and Donald Lee Stovall, see 14:74; see also T5:473 (8 references).

[463]
Children's Interview for Psychiatric Syndromes.

Purpose: Designed to identify "symptoms of 20 common Axis I psychiatric disorders in children and adolescents."
Population: Ages 6–18.
Publication Date: 1999.
Acronym: ChIPS.
Scores, 20: Attention-Deficit/Hyperactivity Disorder, Oppositional Defiant Disorder, Conduct Disorder, Substance Abuse, Specific Phobia, Social Phobia, Separation Anxiety Disorder, Generalized Anxiety Disorder, Obsessive-Compulsive Disorder, Acute Stress Disorder, Posttraumatic Stress Disorder, Anorexia, Bulimia, Depressive Episode, Dysthymic Disorder, Manic Episode, Hypomanic Episode, Enuresis, Encopresis, Schizophrenia/Psychosis.
Administration: Individual.
Price Data, 2002: $44.95 per interview administration booklet (1999, 32 pages).
Time: Administration time not reported.
Authors: Marijo Teare Rooney, Mary A. Fristad, Elizabeth B. Weller, and Ronald A. Weller.
Publisher: American Psychiatric Publishing, Inc.

[464]
Children's Inventory of Anger.

Purpose: Designed "to measure aspects of a youngster's experience of anger."
Population: Ages 6–16.
Publication Date: 2000.
Acronym: CIA.
Scores, 5: Frustration, Physical Aggression, Peer Relationship, Authority Relations, Total.
Administration: Group or individual.
Price Data: Available from publisher.
Time: (10–15) minutes.
Comments: Self-report inventory.
Authors: W. Michael Nelson III and A. J. Finch, Jr.
Publisher: Western Psychological Services.

[465]
Children's Inventory of Self-Esteem, Second Edition.

Purpose: "Provides … a quick way to assess the relative strength of a child's self-worth."
Population: Ages 5–12.
Publication Dates: 1987–2001.
Acronym: CISE.
Scores, 7: 4 components of self-esteem: Belonging (B), Purpose (P), Control (C), Self (S); Total (T); 2 favored coping styles: Defensive (TD), Aggressive (TA).
Administration: Group.
Price Data, 2001: $99 per an individual lifetime license for individuals, including examiner's manual (2001, 24 pages), CISE for girls, CISE for boys, answer form, Exploring Your Child's Self-Esteem form, Your Child's Sense of Self form, Your Child's Sense of Purpose form, Your Child's Sense of Control form, Your Child's Sense of Belonging form (all forms personalized with unlimited copying privileges); $125 per school or agency lifetime license; $110 per lifetime license for each school when purchased by school district (minimum 2 schools); $4.95 shipping/handling fee.
Time: (10) minutes.
Comments: 64-item behavior rating scale completed by parents and teachers of child; provides strategies for helping improve self-esteem.
Author: Richard A. Campbell.
Publisher: Brougham Press.
Cross References: For reviews by Kathy E. Green and Nicholas A. Vacc of a previous edition, see 12:78.

[466]
Children's Memory Scale.

Purpose: "Designed to evaluate learning and memory functioning" in children and adolescents.
Population: Ages 5–16.
Publication Dates: 1997–1998.
Acronym: CMS.
Scores, 34: 14 Core Battery Subtest scores: Dot Locations (Learning, Total Score, Long Delay); Stories (Immediate, Delayed, Delayed Recognition); Faces (Immediate, Delayed); Word Pairs (Learning, Total Score, Long Delay, Delayed Recognition); Numbers (Total Score); Sequences (Total Score); 6 supplemental scores: Dot Locations (Short Delay), Stories (Immediate Thematic, Delayed Thematic), Word Pairs (Immediate), Numbers (Forward, Backward); 6 Supplemental scores from 3 Supplemental Subtests: Word Lists (Learning, Delayed, Delayed Recognition), Picture Locations (Total Score), Family Pictures (Immediate, Delayed); 8 Indexes: Visual Immediate, Visual Delayed, Verbal Immediate, Verbal Delayed, General Memory, Attention/Concentration, Learning, Delayed Recognition.
Administration: Individual.
Levels, 2: 5–8, 9–16.
Price Data, 2003: $395 per complete kit including manual (1997, 288 pages), 25 record forms for both age levels, 2 stimulus booklets, 5 family picture cards and response grid in a box along with 8 chips in a pouch; $449 per complete kit available in soft-sided carrying case; $42 per record forms (specify level); $103 per manual (1997, 288 pages); $98 per computer Scoring Assistant (available for Windows or Macintosh); $445 per complete kit with Scoring Assistant.

Time: (20–50) minutes.
Author: Morris J. Cohen.
Publisher: The Psychological Corporation.
Cross References: For reviews by Scott A. Napolitano and Margot B. Stein, see 14:75.

[467]
Children's Personality Questionnaire.

Purpose: Designed to measure personality traits to predict and evaluate the course of personal, social, and academic development.
Population: Ages 8–12.
Publication Dates: 1959–1992.
Acronym: CPQ.
Scores, 14 to 18: 14 primary factors [Cool vs. Warm (A), Concrete Thinking vs. Abstract Thinking (B), Affected by Feelings vs. Emotionally Stable (C), Phlegmatic vs. Excitable (D), Obedient vs. Dominant (E), Sober vs. Enthusiastic (F), Expedient vs. Conscientious (G), Shy vs. Bold (H), Tough-Minded vs. Tender-Minded (I), Vigorous vs. Guarded (J), Forthright vs. Shrewd (N), Self-Assured vs. Apprehensive (O), Undisciplined Self-Conflict vs. Controlled (Q3), Relaxed vs. Tense (Q4)]; 4 optional secondary factors (Extraversion, Anxiety, Tough Poise, Independence).
Administration: Group or individual.
Forms, 4: A, B, C, D.
Price Data, 2002: $40 per handscoring introductory kit including test booklet (Form A), technical handbook (1992, 84 pages) with norms, answer/profile sheet, second-order worksheet, and scoring keys; $20 per technical handbook; $20 per 25 reusable test booklets (Form A or B); $25 per 25 reusable test booklets (Form C or D); $18 per 50 handscoring answer sheets; $20 per 50 answer-profile sheets; $15 per 50 second-order worksheets; $18 per scoring key (separate scoring keys required for Forms A/C and B/D); $22 per 25 machine-scorable answer sheets; $23 per computer interpretation introductory kit including test booklet (Form A), technical handbook, machine-scorable answer sheet, and report processing form; $6.50 to $30 per computer interpretation.
Foreign Language Editions: Information regarding several non-English-language adaptations available from publisher.
Time: (30–60) minutes per form.
Comments: Test booklet is entitled "What You Do and What You Think."
Authors: Rutherford B. Porter and Raymond B. Cattell.
Publisher: Institute for Personality and Ability Testing, Inc.
Cross References: For reviews by Rosa A. Hagin and Terry A. Stinnett, see 13:60 (3 references); see also T4:454 (9 references); for reviews by Steven Klee and Howard M. Knoff of an earlier edition, see 9:222 (11

references); for a review by Harrison G. Gough, see 8:520 (46 references); see also T3:1129 (60 references) and P:38 (14 references); for reviews by Anne Anastasi, Wilbur L. Layton, and Robert D. Wirt of the 1963 edition, see 6:122 (2 references).

[468]
Children's Problems Checklist.

Purpose: "To identify relevant problems, establish rapport, and provide written documentation of presenting problems consistent with community standards of care."
Population: Ages 5-12.
Publication Date: 1985.
Acronym: CPC.
Scores: 11 areas: Emotions, Self-Concept, Peers and Play, School, Language and Thinking, Concentration and Organization, Activity Level and Motor Control, Behavior, Values, Habits, Health.
Administration: Individual or group.
Manual: No manual.
Price Data: Available from publisher.
Time: (10-20) minutes.
Comments: Ratings by parent or guardian.
Author: John A. Schinka.
Publisher: Psychological Assessment Resources, Inc.
Cross References: For a review by Wayne C. Piersel, see 10:56.

[469]
The Children's Test of Nonword Repetition.

Purpose: To assess short term memory in children.
Population: Ages 4–8.
Publication Date: 1996.
Acronym: CNRep.
Scores: Total score only.
Administration: Individual.
Price Data, 2002: $94.39 per complete set including scoring sheets, cassette tape, and manual (29 pages).
Time: [15] minutes.
Authors: Sue Gathercole and Alan Baddeley.
Publisher: The Psychological Corporation Europe [United Kingdom].

[470]
Children's Version of the Family Environment Scale.

Purpose: "Provides a measure of young children's subjective appraisal of their family environment."
Population: Ages 5–12.
Publication Date: 1984.
Acronym: CV/FES.
Scores, 10: Cohesion, Expressiveness, Conflict, Independence, Achievement Orientation, Intellectual-Cultural Orientation, Active-Recreational Orientation, Moral-Religious Emphasis, Organization, Control.

Administration: Group.
Price Data, 2002: $64 per complete kit; $14 per manual (15 pages); $34 per 10 (reusable) test answer booklets; $19 per 50 profiles; $19 per 50 examiner's worksheets; $19 per 50 individual student answer sheets.
Time: Administration time not reported.
Comments: Downward extension of the Family Environment Scale (9:408).
Authors: Christopher J. Pino, Nancy Simons, and Mary Jane Slawinowski.
Publisher: Slosson Educational Publications, Inc.
Cross References: For a review by Nancy A. Busch-Rossnagel, see 10:57.

[471]
Chinese Proficiency Test.

Purpose: "Designed to evaluate the proficiency in Chinese listening and reading comprehension attained by Americans and other English-speaking learners of Chinese."
Population: Postsecondary to adults.
Publication Dates: 1986–1992.
Scores, 4: Listening Comprehension, Structure, Reading Comprehension, Total.
Administration: Group.
Price Data, 2002: $25 per test (quantity discounts available); $6 per official score report.
Time: 120(180) minutes.
Comments: Mail-in scoring.
Author: Center for Applied Linguistics.
Publisher: Center for Applied Linguistics.
a) PRELIMINARY CHINESE PROFICIENCY TEST.
  Publication Date: 1991.
  Acronym: Pre-CPT.
  Comments: "Designed to be most appropriate for students who are completing at least one year of language study at the college level or three or four years of instruction at the high school level.
b) CHINESE PROFICIENCY TEST.
  Publication Dates: 1986–1992.
  Acronym: CPT.
  Comments: Available in Cantonese and Mandarin; "designed to be most appropriate for students who have completed two or more years of study at the college level."
Cross References: For reviews by Chi-wen Kao and Antony John Kunnan, see 13:62.

[472]
Choosing Outcomes and Accommodations for Children (COACH): A Guide to Educational Planning for Students with Disabilities, Second Edition.

Purpose: A tool to assist in educational planning.

Population: Preschool and school-aged learners with moderate, severe, or profound handicap.
Publication Date: 1998.
Acronym: COACH.
Scores: Item scores only.
Administration: Individual.
Price Data, 2002: $23.95 per 3 student record forms; $39.95 per manual (1998, 400 pages).
Time: (60) minutes (part 1 of 3 parts).
Comments: "Criterion-referenced"; ratings by a team including a parent, student (where appropriate), educators, related service personnel, and family advocate; previous versions available on microfiche from ERIC; previously listed as C.O.A.C.H.: Cayuga-Onondaga Assessment for Children with Handicaps.
Authors: Michael F. Giangreco, Chigee J. Cloninger, and Virginia S. Iverson.
Publisher: Paul H. Brookes Publishing Co., Inc.
Cross References: See T5:553 (1 reference); for a review by Jay Kuder and David E. Kapel, see 11:73.

[473]
Christensen Dietary Distress Inventory.

Purpose: Designed to provide an objective assessment of the probability of diet contributing to emotional distress.
Population: Ages 18 and above.
Publication Date: 1990.
Acronym: CDDI.
Scores: Total score only.
Administration: Group.
Price Data: Available from publisher.
Time: (10–15) minutes.
Comments: Self-report inventory.
Author: Larry Christensen.
Publisher: Larry Christensen.
Cross References: For reviews by Richard F. Farmer and Sandra D. Haynes, see 13:64 (1 reference); see also T4:460 (1 reference).

[474]
Chronic Pain Battery.

Purpose: Constructed to assess chronic pain by collecting "medical, psychological, behavioral, social, demographic and pain data."
Population: Patients ages 18 and over.
Publication Dates: 1983–1986.
Acronym: CPB.
Scores: 10 topics: Demographic and Social History, Past and Present Pain History, Past Treatment, Medications, Medical History, Personality-Pain Coping Style, Patient Expectations and Goals, Behavioral-Learning Factors, Psychosocial Factors, Patient Problem Ratings.
Administration: Group or individual.
Manual: No manual.

Price Data, 1994: $20 per specimen set including question book, answer sheet, and sample report.
Time: (30–60) minutes.
Comments: Comprises the Pain Assessment Questionnaire—Revised and the Symptom Checklist 90—Revised (2464); self-administered; self-report; symptom inventory questionnaire.
Author: Stephen R. Levitt.
Publisher: Pain Resource Center, Inc.

[475]
Chronicle Career Quest©.

Purpose: Designed to "help individuals identify careers related to personal interests and preferences."
Publication Dates: 1989–1993.
Acronym: CCQ.
Scores: 12 G.O.E. clusters: Artistic, Scientific, Plants and Animals, Protective, Mechanical, Industrial, Business Detail, Selling, Accommodating, Humanitarian, Leading Influencing, Physical Performing.
Administration: Group or individual.
Forms, 2: S and L.
Price Data, 1994: $3.50 per specimen set including 1 each Form S and L, Interest Inventory, Interpretation Guide (1993, 20 pages), Administrator's Guide (1992, 20 pages), and Career Paths; $8 per 100 Occupational Profiles; $5.50 per 50 summary sheets; $4 per 50 Career Paths Chart; $10 per Technical Manual (1992, 30 pages); $12 per Career Crosswalk.
Time: (10–15) minutes for Interest Inventory (Form S and Form L); (10–15) minutes for Interpretation Guide (Form S and Form L); (20–45) minutes for Career Paths (Form S); (180–240) minutes for Career Paths (Form L).
Author: Chronicle Guidance Publications, Inc.
Publisher: Chronicle Guidance Publications, Inc.
a) FORM S.
  Population: Grades 7–10.
  Price Data: $40.50 per kit including 25 Interest Inventories, 25 Interpretation Guides, and Administrator's Guide; $18.75 per 25 reusable Career Paths (Form S).
b) FORM L.
  Population: Grades 9–16 and adult.
  Price Data: $59.50 per kit of 25 Interest Inventories, 25 Interpretation Guides, and Administrator's Guide; $20.75 per 25 reusable Career Paths (Form L).
Cross References: For reviews by Larry G. Daniel and Donald Thompson, see 12:79.

[476]
CID Phonetic Inventory.

Purpose: To evaluate the hearing-impaired "child's speech ability at the phonetic level."
Population: Hearing-impaired children.

Publication Date: 1988.
Scores, 7: Suprasegmental Aspects, Vowels and Diphthongs, Initial Consonants, Consonants with Alternating Vowels, Final Consonants, Alternating Consonants, Average.
Administration: Individual.
Price Data, 2002: $50 per complete kit including manual (24 pages), 25 rating forms, and 166 stimulus cards; $12 per 25 rating forms.
Time: (30-35) minutes.
Author: Jean S. Moog.
Publisher: Central Institute for the Deaf.
Cross References: See T5:486 (3 references); for a review by Vincent J. Samar, see 11:67.

[477]
CID Picture SPINE (SPeech INtelligibility Evaluation).

Purpose: To "provide a measure of speech intelligibility for severely and profoundly hearing-impaired children and adolescents."
Population: Hearing-impaired children ages 6–13.
Publication Date: 1988.
Scores: Total score only.
Administration: Individual.
Price Data, 2002: $110 per complete kit including 300 picture cards, 25 response forms (4 pages), and test manual (31 pages); $12 per 25 response forms.
Time: (20-30) minutes.
Authors: Randall Monsen, Jean S. Moog, and Ann E. Geers.
Publisher: Central Institute for the Deaf.
Cross References: See T5:487 (2 references) and T4:465 (1 reference); for a review by Vincent J. Samar, see 11:68.

[478]
CID Preschool Performance Scale.

Purpose: Designed to measure the intelligence of hearing-impaired and language-impaired children.
Population: Hearing- and language-impaired and normal children ages 2 to 5-5.
Publication Date: 1984.
Scores, 7: Manual Planning, Manual Dexterity, Form Perception, Perceptual-Motor Skills, Preschool Skills, Part/Whole Relations, Total.
Administration: Individual.
Price Data, 2001: $850 per complete kit including manipulatives for subtests, manual (29 pages), and 30 recording booklets; $25 per manual; $30 per 30 recording booklets.
Time: (40) minutes.
Comments: Adaptation of the Randall's Island Performance Series.
Authors: Ann E. Geers, Helen S. Lane, and Central Institute for the Deaf.

Publisher: Stoelting Co.
Cross References: For reviews by Bruce A. Bracken and Albert C. Oosterhof, see 12:80.

[479]
The City University Colour Vision Test, Second Edition 1980.

Purpose: To assess defects of color vision.
Population: Adults and children.
Publication Date: 1980.
Scores, 3: Chroma Four, Chroma Two, Overall.
Administration: Individual.
Manual: No manual (introductory notes and instructions included in binder of test plates).
Price Data, 2001: $268 per complete kit including profile sheets, 10 test pages, and instructions.
Time: Administration time not reported.
Author: Robert Fletcher.
Publisher: Keeler Instruments Inc.
Cross References: For a review by Karen T. Carey, see 13:65.

[480]
The Clark Wilson Group Multi-Level Feedback Instruments and Development Programs.

Purpose: Designed to identify group or individual training needs, assess the effects of training, support interactive and participatory management, and to be used in organizational and management studies.
Population: Organizations, executives, managers, and employees.
Publication Dates: 1973–2002.
Administration: Group.
Price Data: Available from publisher.
Time: (12–18) minutes.
Comments: Paper-and-pencil or web-based administration; publisher suggests allowing 6 weeks to administer surveys and give feedback.
Authors: Clark L. Wilson and others noted below.
Publisher: The Clark Wilson Group.

a) LEADERSHIP SERIES.
1) *Executive Leadership.*
Purpose: Assesses executive competencies such as strategic foresight and oversight.
Population: Executives.
Publication Date: 1988.
Acronym: EXEC.
Scores, 17: Leadership Vision, Risk-Taking, Financial and Operational Analysis, Marketplace Savvy, Organizational Savvy, Judgement, Decisiveness, Team Growth and Development, Cultural Appreciation, Standards of Performance, Executive Energy, Push/Pressure, Coping with Stress, Sharing Credit, Effectiveness/Outcomes, Temporary Sources of Power, Lasting Sources of Power.
Authors: Paul M. Connolly and Clark L. Wilson.
2) *Leadership Practices.*
Purpose: Designed to provide feedback on an individual's vision, influence, and drive for change.
Population: Managers and executives.
Publication Date: 1986.
Acronym: SLP.
Scores, 17: Vision/Imagination, Risk-Taking, Organizational Sensitivity, Encouraging Participation, Persuasiveness, Teaming, Standards of Performance, Perseverance, Push/Pressure, Effectiveness/Outcomes, Coping with Stress, Feedback, Energy, Sharing Credit, Trustworthiness, Temporary Sources of Power, Lasting Sources of Power.
Authors: Clark L. Wilson and Paul M. Connolly.
3) *Project Leadership Practices.*
Purpose: Designed to assess leadership skills for project managers.
Population: Project managers and project leaders.
Publication Date: 1995.
Acronym: PLP.
Scores, 19: Clarification of Goals and Objectives, Organization Courage, Judgement, Planning, Adaptation, Problem Solving, Teaming, Coaching, Manager Relations, Customer Relations, Feedback, Push/Pressure, Delegation/Permissiveness, Recognition/Reinforcement, Approachability, Building Trust, Sources of Power, Effectiveness, Belief in Project.
Authors: Clark L. Wilson, Paul M. Connolly, and David B. Gillespie
4) *Leadership in Health Services.*
Purpose: Designed to assess leadership and management skills for health administration.
Population: VPs, directors, senior and middle administrators.
Acronym: LHS.
Scores, 21: Vision and Imagination, Strategic and Operational Goals, Understanding the Changing Environment, Managing Financial Drivers, Expertise, Risk-Taking, Empowering Employees, Building a Team Environment, Coaching for Performance, Openness to Feedback, Valuing Diversity, Standards of Performance, Clarity of Communications, Persuasiveness, Managing Conflict, Delegation/Permissiveness, Goal Pressure, Recognizing and Reqarding Others, Building Trust, Tension Level, Overall Effectiveness.

Authors: Eugene P. Buccini, Richard L. Dowall, and Clark L. Wilson.

b) MANAGEMENT SERIES.

1) *Management Practices.*

Purpose: Assesses basic managerial competencies.

Population: Managers.

Publication Date: 1973.

Acronym: SMP.

Scores, 23: Clarification of Goals and Objectives, Upward Communication, Orderly Work Planning, Expertise, Work Facilitation, Feedback, Time Emphasis, Control of Details, Goal Pressure, Delegation (Permissiveness), Recognition for Good Performance, Approachability, Teambuilding, Interest in Subordinate Growth, Building Trust, Work Involvement, Coworker Competence, Team Atmosphere, Opportunity for Growth, Tension Level, Organization Climate, General Morale, Commitment.

Author: Clark L. Wilson.

2) *Peer Relations.*

Purpose: Assesses organizational skills for specialists.

Population: Managers and individual contributors.

Publication Date: 1974.

Acronym: SPR.

Scores, 22: Clarity of Your Own Goals, Clarity of Communications, Encouraging Peer Participation, Orderly Work Planning, Problem Solving, Expertise, Teamwork/Cooperation, Feedback to Peers, Time Emphasis, Attention to Details, Pressure on Peers, Acknowledging Peer Contributions, Approachability, Dependability, Work Involvement, Coworker Competence, Team Atmosphere, Opportunity for Growth, Tension Level, Organization Climate, General Morale, Commitment.

Author: Clark L. Wilson.

3) *Working with Others.*

Purpose: Assesses supervisory skills for the first-time or prospective manager.

Publication Date: 1991.

Acronym: WWO.

Scores, 13: Commitment to Work, Assertiveness, Problem Solving/Resourcefulness, Teamwork, Willingness to Listen, Attention to Details, Push/Pressure, Recognizing Co-worker Performance, Effectiveness/Outcomes, Friendliness, Dependability, Working with Diversity, Future Promise.

Author: Clark L. Wilson.

4) *Coaching Practices.*

Purpose: Assesses coaching and appraising skills for performance management.

Population: Managers and executives.

Publication Date: 1993.

Acronym: SCP.

Scores, 14: Commitment to Coaching, Planning for Personal Growth, Coaching Skills, Coaching for Teamwork, Technical/Functional Expertise, Organization Awareness, Assessment Skills, Responding to Defensiveness, Control of Details, Delegation (Permissiveness), Recognizing Good Performance, Approachability, Trust, Overall Effectiveness.

Authors: Richard L. Dowall and Clark L. Wilson.

5) *Leadership Competencies for Managers.*

Population: Managers.

Publication Date: 1998.

Acronym: LCM.

Scores, 21: Vision/Imagination, Clarification of Goals, Risk-Taking, Decision Making/Problem Solving, Managing Costs, Encouraging Participation, Clarity of Communications, Teambuilding, Coaching, Managing Conflict, Feedback, Standards of Performance, Personal Drive, Persuasiveness, Delegation, Goal Pressure, Recognition for Good Performance, Building Trust, Managing Diversity, Tension Level, Overall Effectiveness.

Authors: Clark L. Wilson, Paul Connolly, and Richard L. Dowell.

c) SALES SERIES.

1) *Sales Management Practices.*

Purpose: Assesses managerial competencies for field sales managers.

Population: Sales managers.

Publication Date: 1975.

Acronym: SSMP.

Scores, 23: Clarification of Goals and Objectives, Upward Communication, Orderly Work Planning, Expertise, Work Facilitation, Feedback, Time Emphasis, Control of Details, Goal Pressure, Delegation (Permissiveness), Recognition of Good Performance, Approachability, Teambuilding, Interest in Subordinate Growth, Building Trust, Work Involvement, Coworker Competence, Team Atmosphere, Opportunity for Growth, Tension Level, Organization Climate, General Morale, Commitment.

Author: Clark L. Wilson.

2) *Sales Relations.*

Purpose: Provides feedback on skills of sales representatives from customers and prospects.

Population: Sales representatives.

Publication Date: 1975.

Acronym: SSR.

Scores, 11: Understanding Us, Communicating Effectively, Account Service, Analyzing

Needs, Presenting Benefits, Asking for the Order, Answering Objections, Selling Pressure, Professionalism, Approachability, Overall Satisfaction.
Author: Clark L. Wilson.

3) *Client Relations.*
Purpose: Assesses internal and external consulting skills.
Population: Consultants and client service representatives.
Publication Date: 1998.
Acronym: SCR.
Scores, 13: Understanding Us, Communicating Effectively, Account Service, Analyzing Needs, Presenting Benefits, Making Recommendations, Answering Objections, Personal Enthusiasm, Personal Pressure, Acknowledging Client Responses, Professionalism, Approachability, Overall Satisfaction.

d) TEAM SERIES.

1) *Executive Team.*
Purpose: Coordinates efforts of top management groups.
Population: Executive teams.
Publication Date: 1993.
Acronym: XT.
Scores, 16: Clarity of Mission/Strategic Goals, Leadership for Growth/Productivity, Resistance to Change, Marketing Focus, Organization Awareness, Consensus Planning, Team Atmosphere, Information/Data Support, Human Resource Development, Organization Stretch, Monitoring Executive Plans, Satisfying, Internal Problems, Sharing Credit, Coping with Stress, Effectiveness/Outcomes.
Authors: Paul M. Connolly and Clark L. Wilson.

2) *Our Team.*
Purpose: Provides feedback from team members on team negotiating skills and conflict resolution.
Population: Teams (Work Groups, Task Forces, Quality Circles, Project Teams, Design Teams, Teams with or without Leaders).
Publication Date: 1989.
Acronym: OT.
Scores, 14: Clarity of Goals and Priorities, Coworker Competence, Consensus Planning, Team Atmosphere, Newcomer Support, Conflict Resolution, Management Support, Management Feedback, Monitoring the Team's Work, Tension/Stress Level, Domination, Satisfying, Recognition/Satisfaction, Effectiveness/Outcomes.
Author: Clark L. Wilson.

3) *My Team Mates.*
Purpose: Provides feedback from team mates on a member's teaming skills.
Population: Team members.
Publication Date: 1989.
Acronym: MTM.
Scores, 13: Clarity of Personal Goals, Innovativeness, Functional Expertise, Teamwork, Leadership for Consensus, Negotiating Skills, Monitoring Personal Output, Coping with Stress and Ambiguity, Personal Drive, Pressure on Team Mates, Acknowledging Others' Efforts, Personal Values, Personal Effectiveness.
Author: Clark L. Wilson.
Cross References: See T4:469 (1 reference).

[481]
Clarke Sexual History Questionnaire.
Purpose: Designed "to evaluate a sex offender's sexual preference profile as well as evaluating their potential for sexually conventional behavior."
Population: Sex offenders.
Publication Date: 1999.
Acronym: SHQ-R.
Scores: 20 content scores assessing different types of sexual behavior, 2 validity scores.
Administration: Individual.
Price Data, 2002: $50 per preview kit including manual, 1 item booklet, and 1 summary report; $10 per 3 item booklets; $30 per 10 item booklets; $40 per technical manual; $10 per mail-in or fax-in individual summary report.
Time: Administration time not reported.
Comments: Publisher advises this instrument is a valuable adjunct for use in the area of sexual offense but is insufficient on its own for examining behavior in sex offenders.
Authors: Ron Langevin and Dan Paitche.
Publisher: Multi-Health Systems, Inc.

[482]
The Class Activities Questionnaire.
Purpose: Developed to provide "a measure of the instructional climate."
Population: Students and teachers Grades 6–12.
Publication Date: 1982.
Acronym: CAQ.
Scores: 5 dimensions: Lower Thought Processes, Higher Thought Processes, Classroom Focus, Classroom Climate, Student Opinions.
Administration: Group.
Price Data: Available from publisher.
Time: (20–30) minutes.
Author: Joe M. Steele.
Publisher: Creative Learning Press, Inc.

Cross References: See T5:493 (1 reference); for a review by Robert W. Hiltonsmith, see 9:226 (1 reference).

[483]
The Classroom Communication Skills Inventory: A Listening and Speaking Checklist.

Purpose: Evaluates "oral communication skills that have been determined to be important for listening and speaking in the school setting and are essential for classroom learning."
Population: Students.
Publication Date: 1993.
Acronym: CCSI.
Scores: 10 ratings: Basic Speech and Hearing Processes (Auditory Perception, Speech), Classroom Communication (Attention, Class Participation), Language Content and Structure (Vocabulary, Grammar, Organization of Language), Interpersonal Classroom Communication (Using Language for a Variety of Purposes, Conversing Effectively, Using Appropriate Nonverbal Communication Skills).
Administration: Individual.
Price Data, 2002: $40.30 per teacher's manual (51 pages) and 25 record forms.
Time: (10–15) minutes.
Author: The Psychological Corporation.
Publisher: The Psychological Corporation.
Cross References: For reviews by Linda Crocker and Dolores Kluppel Vetter, see 13:66.

[484]
Classroom Environment Scale, Second Edition.

Purpose: Designed to "assess the social climate of junior high and high school classrooms. It focuses on teacher-student and student-student relationships and on the organizational structure of a classroom."
Population: Junior high and senior high teachers and students.
Publication Dates: 1974–1987.
Acronym: CES.
Scores, 9: Relationship dimensions (Involvement, Affiliation, Teacher Support), Personal Growth/Goal Orientation dimensions (Task Orientation, Competition), System Maintenance and Change dimensions (Order and Organization, Rule Clarity, Teacher Control, Innovation).
Administration: Group.
Forms, 3: Real Form (Form R), Ideal Form (Form I), Expectations Form (Form E), and a Short Form (Form S) by administering and scoring the first 36 items of Form R.
Price Data, 2001: $74.50 per preview kit including item booklet, profile, nonprepaid answer sheets, scoring

keys, and manual (42 pages); $38.20 per 25 reusable item booklets; $24.30 per 25 nonprepaid sheets for handscoring for use with item booklets; $10 per 25 profiles for hand scoring; $11.30 per scoring key; $64.60 per manual.
Time: [15–20] minutes.
Comments: One of ten Social Climate Scales (T5:2445).
Authors: Rudolf H. Moos and Edison J. Trickett.
Publisher: Consulting Psychologists Press, Inc.
Cross References: See T5:495 (16 references) and T4:475 (5 references); for reviews by Richard A. Saudargas and Corinne Roth Smith, see 10:60 (16 references); see also T3:409 (9 references); for reviews by Maurice J. Eash and C. Robert Pace of an earlier edition, see 8:521 (3 references). For a review of the Social Climate Scales, see 8:681.

[485]
Classroom Reading Inventory, Seventh Edition.

Purpose: To identify the student's reading skills and/or abilities.
Population: Grades 2–8, high school and adults.
Publication Dates: 1965–1994.
Acronym: CRI.
Scores, 6: Word Recognition, Comprehension, Independent Reading Level, Instructional Reading Level, Frustration Reading Level, Hearing Capacity Level.
Administration: Individual in part.
Forms: Form A (elementary, subskills format); Form B (elementary, literature format); Form C (junior high or middle school students); Form D (for use with high school and adults).
Price Data: Available from publisher.
Time: (24) minutes.
Author: Nicholas J. Silvaroli.
Publisher: Brown and Benchmark Publishers, a Division of Wm. C. Brown Communications [No reply from publisher; status unknown].
Cross References: See T5:496 (4 references) and T4:476 (4 references); for reviews by Ira E. Aaron and Sylvia M. Hutchinson and Janet A. Norris, see 10:61 (4 references); for a review of an earlier edition by Marjorie S. Johnson, see 8:749; see also T2:1618 (1 reference); for an excerpted review by Donald L. Cleland, see 7:715.

[486]
CLEP Examination in American Government.

Purpose: For college accreditation, advanced placement, or assessment of educational attainment.
Population: Persons entering college or already in college.
Publication Dates: 1965–2002.

Scores: Total score only.
Administration: Group.
Price Data: Available from publisher.
Time: (90) minutes.
Comments: Tests administered at centers throughout the United States and internationally; program administered by the College Board and Educational Testing Service.
Author: Educational Testing Service.
Publisher: Educational Testing Service.
Cross References: For additional information and a review by Howard D. Mehlinger, see 8:919. For reviews of the CLEP program, see 8:473 (3 reviews) and 7:664 (3 reviews).

[487]
CLEP Examination in American Literature.

Purpose: For college accreditation, advanced placement, or assessment of educational attainment.
Population: Persons entering college or already in college.
Publication Dates: 1971–2002.
Scores: Total score only; optional essay, locally scored.
Administration: Group.
Price Data: Available from publisher.
Time: (90) minutes.
Comments: Tests administered at centers throughout the United States and internationally; program administered by the College Board and Educational Testing Service.
Author: Educational Testing Service.
Publisher: Educational Testing Service.
Cross References: For additional information and a review by Leo P. Ruth, see 8:64. For reviews of the CLEP program, see 8:473 (3 reviews).

[488]
CLEP Examination in Analyzing and Interpreting Literature.

Purpose: For college accreditation, advanced placement, or assessment of educational attainment.
Population: Persons entering college or already in college.
Publication Dates: 1964–2002.
Scores: Total score only; optional essay, locally scored.
Administration: Group.
Price Data: Available from publisher.
Time: (90) minutes.
Comments: Tests administered at centers throughout the United States and internationally; program administered by the College Board and Educational Testing Service.
Author: Educational Testing Service.
Publisher: Educational Testing Service.
Cross References: For additional information and a review by John C. Sherwood, see 8:65 (1 reference).

For reviews of the CLEP program, see 8:473 (3 reviews) and 7:664 (3 reviews).

[489]
CLEP Examination in Calculus with Elementary Functions.

Purpose: For college accreditation, advanced placement, or assessment of educational attainment.
Population: Persons entering college or already in college.
Publication Dates: 1974–2002.
Scores: Total score only.
Administration: Group.
Price Data: Available from publisher.
Time: (90) minutes.
Comments: Tests administered at centers throughout the United Statesand internationally; program administered by the College Board and Educational Testing Service.
Author: Educational Testing Service.
Publisher: Educational Testing Service.
Cross References: For a review by J. Phillip Smith, see 8:255. For reviews of the CLEP program, see 8:473 (3 reviews).

[490]
CLEP Examination in College Algebra.

Purpose: For college accreditation, advanced placement, or assessment of educational attainment.
Population: Persons entering college or already in college.
Publication Dates: 1968–1999.
Scores: Total score only.
Administration: Group.
Price Data: Available from publisher.
Time: (90) minutes.
Comments: Tests administered at centers throughout the United States and internationally; program administered by the College Board and Educational Testing Service.
Author: Educational Testing Service.
Publisher: Educational Testing Service.
Cross References: For additional information and a review by J. Philip Smith, see 8:297. For reviews of the CLEP program, see 8:473 (3 reviews) and 7:664 (3 reviews).

[491]
CLEP Examination in College Algebra–Trigonometry.

Purpose: For college accreditation, advanced placement, or assessment of educational attainment.
Population: Persons entering college or already in college.
Publication Dates: 1968–1999.
Scores: Total score only.

Administration: Group.
Price Data: Available from publisher.
Time: (90) minutes.
Comments: Tests administered at centers throughout the United States and internationally; program administered by the College Board and Educational Testing Service.
Author: Educational Testing Service.
Publisher: Educational Testing Service.
Cross References: For a review by Peter A. Lappan, Jr., see 8:256 (1 reference); for a review by Carl G. Willis, see 7:454. For reviews of the CLEP program, see 8:473 (3 reviews) and 7:664 (3 reviews).

[492]
CLEP Examination in College-Level French Language, Levels 1 and 2.

Purpose: For college accreditation, advanced placement, or assessment of educational attainment.
Population: Persons entering college or already in college.
Publication Dates: 1975–2002.
Scores, 3: Reading Comprehension, Listening Comprehension, Total.
Administration: Group.
Price Data: Available from publisher.
Time: (90) minutes.
Comments: Tests administered at centers throughout the United States and internationally; program administered by the College Board and Educational Testing Service.
Author: Educational Testing Service.
Publisher: Educational Testing Service.
Cross References: For a review by Michio Peter Hagiwara, see 8:115. For reviews of the CLEP program, see 8:473 (3 reviews).

[493]
CLEP Examination in College-Level German Language, Levels 1 and 2.

Purpose: For college accreditation, advanced placement, or assessment of educational attainment.
Population: Persons entering college or already in college.
Publication Dates: 1975–2002.
Scores, 3: Reading Comprehension, Listening Comprehension, Total.
Administration: Group.
Price Data: Available from publisher.
Time: (90) minutes.
Comments: Tests administered at centers throughout the United States and internationally; program administered by the College Board and Educational Testing Service.
Author: Educational Testing Service.
Publisher: Educational Testing Service.

Cross References: For reviews by Stefan R. Fink and Herbert Lederer, see 8:127. For reviews of the CLEP program, see 8:473 (3 reviews).

[494]
CLEP Examination in College-Level Spanish Language, Levels 1 and 2.

Purpose: For college accreditation, advanced placement, or assessment of educational attainment.
Population: Persons entering college or already in college.
Publication Dates: 1975–2002.
Scores, 3: Reading Comprehension, Listening Comprehension, Total.
Administration: Group.
Price Data: Available from publisher.
Time: (90) minutes.
Comments: Tests administered at centers throughout the United States and internationally; program administered by the College Board and Educational Testing Service.
Author: Educational Testing Service.
Publisher: Educational Testing Service.
Cross References: For reviews of the CLEP program, see 8:473 (3 reviews).

[495]
CLEP Examination in Educational Psychology.

Purpose: For college accreditation, advanced placement, or assessment of educational attainment.
Population: Persons entering college or already in college.
Publication Dates: 1967–2002.
Scores: Total score only.
Administration: Group.
Price Data: Available from publisher.
Time: (90) minutes.
Comments: Tests administered at centers throughout the United States and internationally; program administered by the College Board and Educational Testing Service.
Author: Educational Testing Service.
Publisher: Educational Testing Service.
Cross References: For reviews of the CLEP program, see 8:473 (3 reviews) and 7:664 (3 reviews).

[496]
CLEP Examination in English Literature.

Purpose: For college accreditation, advanced placement, or assessment of educational attainment.
Population: Persons entering college or already in college.
Publication Dates: 1970–2002.
Scores: Total score only; optional essay, locally scored.
Administration: Group.

Price Data: Available from publisher.
Time: (90) minutes.
Comments: Tests administered at centers throughout the United States and internationally; program administered by the College Board and Educational Testing Service.
Author: Educational Testing Service.
Publisher: Educational Testing Service.
Cross References: For additional information and a review by Edward M. White, see 8:66. For reviews of the CLEP program, see 8:473 (3 reviews).

[497]
CLEP Examination in Freshman College Composition.
Purpose: For college accreditation, advanced placement, or assessment of educational attainment.
Population: Persons entering college or already in college.
Publication Dates: 1994–2002.
Scores: Total score only; optional essay, scored locally.
Administration: Group.
Price Data: Available from publisher.
Time: (90) minutes.
Comments: Tests administered at centers throughout the United States and internationally; program administered by the College Board and Educational Testing Service; replaces College Composition (T4:491) and Freshman English (T4:498) examinations.
Author: Educational Testing Service.
Publisher: Educational Testing Service.
Cross References: For a review by Leonard S. Feldt of the CLEP Freshman English Examination, see 8:44 (1 reference). For a review by Charlotte Croon Davis of the CLEP College Composition Examination, see 8:43 (2 references).

[498]
CLEP Examination in General Biology.
Purpose: For college accreditation, advanced placement, or assessment of educational attainment.
Population: Persons entering college or already in college.
Publication Dates: 1970–2002.
Scores: Total score only.
Administration: Group.
Price Data: Available from publisher.
Time: (90) minutes.
Comments: Tests administered at centers throughout the United States and internationally; program administered by the College Board and Educational Testing Service.
Author: Educational Testing Service.
Publisher: Educational Testing Service.
Cross References: For additional information and a review by Clarence H. Nelson, see 8:832. For reviews

of the CLEP program, see 8:473 (3 reviews) and 7:664 (3 reviews).

[499]
CLEP Examination in General Chemistry.
Purpose: For college accreditation, advanced placement, or assessment of educational attainment.
Population: Persons entering college or already in college.
Publication Dates: 1964–2002.
Scores: Total score only.
Administration: Group.
Price Data: Available from publisher.
Time: (90) minutes.
Comments: Tests administered at centers throughout the United States and internationally; program administered by the College Board and Educational Testing Service.
Author: Educational Testing Service.
Publisher: Educational Testing Service.
Cross References: For additional information and a review by J. Arthur Campbell, see 8:847. For reviews of the CLEP program, see 8:473 (3 reviews) and 7:664 (3 reviews).

[500]
CLEP Examination in History of the United States: Early Colonizations to 1877.
Purpose: For college accreditation, advanced placement, or assessment of educational attainment.
Population: Persons entering college or already in college.
Publication Dates: 1980–2002.
Scores: Total score only.
Administration: Group.
Price Data: Available from publisher.
Time: (90) minutes.
Comments: Tests administered at centers throughout the United States and internationally; program administered by the College Board and Educational Testing Service.
Author: Educational Testing Service.
Publisher: Educational Testing Service.

[501]
CLEP Examination in History of the United States II: 1865 to the Present.
Purpose: For college accreditation, advanced placement, or assessment of educational attainment.
Population: Persons entering college or already in college.
Publication Dates: 1980–2002.
Scores: Total score only.
Administration: Group.
Price Data: Available from publisher.
Time: (90) minutes.

Comments: Tests administered at centers throughout the United States and internationally; program administered by the College Board and Educational Testing Service.
Author: Educational Testing Service.
Publisher: Educational Testing Service.

[502]
CLEP Examination in Human Growth and Development.

Purpose: For college accreditation, advanced placement, or assessment of educational attainment.
Population: Persons entering college or already in college.
Publication Dates: 1969–2002.
Scores: Total score only.
Administration: Group.
Price Data: Available from publisher.
Time: (90) minutes.
Comments: Tests administered at centers throughout the United States and internationally; program administered by the College Board and Educational Testing Service.
Author: Educational Testing Service.
Publisher: Educational Testing Service.
Cross References: For reviews of the CLEP program, see 8:473 (3 reviews) and 7:664 (3 reviews).

[503]
CLEP Examination in Information Systems and Computer Applications.

Purpose: For college accreditation, advanced placement, or assessment of educational attainment.
Population: Persons entering college or already in college.
Publication Dates: 1968–2002.
Scores: Total score only.
Administration: Group.
Price Data: Available from publisher.
Time: (90) minutes.
Comments: Tests administered at centers throughout the United States and internationally; program administered by the College Board and Educational Testing Service; previously entitled CLEP Subject Examination in Computers and Data Processing.
Author: Educational Testing Service.
Publisher: Educational Testing Service.
Cross References: For reviews of the CLEP program, see 8:473 (3 reviews) and 7:664 (3 reviews).

[504]
CLEP Examination in Introductory Business Law.

Purpose: For college accreditation, advanced placement, or assessment of educational attainment.

Population: Persons entering college or already in college.
Publication Dates: 1970–2002.
Scores: Total score only.
Administration: Group.
Price Data: Available from publisher.
Time: (90) minutes.
Comments: Tests administered at centers throughout the United States and internationally; program administered by the College Board and Educational Testing Service.
Author: Educational Testing Service.
Publisher: Educational Testing Service.
Cross References: For reviews of the CLEP program, see 8:473 (3 reviews) and 7:664 (3 reviews).

[505]
CLEP Examination in Introductory Psychology.

Purpose: For college accreditation, advanced placement, or assessment of educational attainment.
Population: Persons entering college or already in college.
Publication Dates: 1967–2002.
Scores: Total score only.
Administration: Group.
Price Data: Available from publisher.
Time: (90) minutes.
Comments: Tests administered at centers throughout the United States and internationally; program administered by the College Board and Educational Testing Service; previously entitled CLEP Subject Examination in General Psychology.
Author: Educational Testing Service.
Publisher: Educational Testing Service.
Cross References: See T3:442 (2 references); for additional information and a review by Alfred E. Hall of an earlier edition, see 8:460. For reviews of the CLEP program, see 8:473 (3 reviews) and 7:664 (3 reviews).

[506]
CLEP Examination in Introductory Sociology.

Purpose: For college accreditation, advanced placement, or assessment of educational attainment.
Population: Persons entering college or already in college.
Publication Dates: 1965–2002.
Scores: Total score only.
Administration: Group.
Price Data: Available from publisher.
Time: (90) minutes.
Comments: Tests administered at centers throughout the United States and internationally; program

administered by the College Board and Educational Testing Service.
Author: Educational Testing Service.
Publisher: Educational Testing Service.
Cross References: For reviews of the CLEP program, see 8:473 (3 reviews) and 7:664 (3 reviews).

[507]
CLEP Examination in Principles of Accounting.

Purpose: For college accreditation, advanced placement, or assessment of educational attainment.
Population: Persons entering college or already in college.
Publication Dates: 1970–2002.
Scores: Total score only.
Administration: Group.
Price Data: Available from publisher.
Time: (90) minutes.
Comments: Tests administered at centers throughout the United States and internationally; program administered by the College Board and Educational Testing Service.
Author: Educational Testing Service.
Publisher: Educational Testing Service.
Cross References: For reviews of the CLEP program, see 8:473 (3 reviews).

[508]
CLEP Examination in Principles of Macroeconomics.

Purpose: For college accreditation, advanced placement, or assessment of educational attainment.
Population: Persons entering college or already in college.
Publication Dates: 1974–2002.
Scores: Total score only.
Administration: Group.
Price Data: Available from publisher.
Time: (90) minutes.
Comments: Tests administered at centers throughout the United States and internationally; program administered by the College Board and Educational Testing Service.
Author: Educational Testing Service.
Publisher: Educational Testing Service.
Cross References: For reviews of the CLEP program, see 8:473 (3 reviews).

[509]
CLEP Examination in Principles of Management.

Purpose: For college accreditation, advanced placement, or assessment of educational attainment.
Population: Persons entering college or already in college.

Publication Dates: 1969–2002.
Scores: Total score only.
Administration: Group.
Price Data: Available from publisher.
Time: (90) minutes.
Comments: Tests administered at centers throughout the United States and internationally; program administered by the College Board and Educational Testing Service.
Author: Educational Testing Service.
Publisher: Educational Testing Service.
Cross References: For reviews of the CLEP program, see 8:473 (3 reviews) and 7:664 (3 reviews).

[510]
CLEP Examination in Principles of Marketing.

Purpose: For college accreditation, advanced placement, or assessment of educational attainment.
Population: Persons entering college or already in college.
Publication Dates: 1968–2002.
Scores: Total score only.
Administration: Group.
Price Data: Available from publisher.
Time: (90) minutes.
Comments: Tests administered at centers throughout the United States and internationally; program administered by the College Board and Educational Testing Service.
Author: Educational Testing Service.
Publisher: Educational Testing Service.
Cross References: For reviews of the CLEP program, see 8:473 (3 reviews) and 7:664 (3 reviews).

[511]
CLEP Examination in Principles of Microeconomics.

Purpose: For college accreditation, advanced placement, or assessment of educational attainment.
Population: Persons entering college or already in college.
Publication Dates: 1974–2002.
Scores: Total score only.
Administration: Group.
Price Data: Available from publisher.
Time: (90) minutes.
Comments: Tests administered at centers throughout the United States and internationally; program administered by the College Board and Educational Testing Service.
Author: Educational Testing Service.
Publisher: Educational Testing Service.
Cross References: For reviews of the CLEP program, see 8:473 (3 reviews).

[512]
CLEP Examination in Trigonometry.

Purpose: For college accreditation, advanced placement, or assessment of educational attainment.
Population: Persons entering college or already in college.
Publication Dates: 1968–2002.
Scores: Total score only.
Administration: Group.
Price Data: Available from publisher.
Time: (90) minutes.
Comments: Tests administered at centers throughout the United States and internationally; program administered by the College Board and Educational Testing Service.
Author: Educational Testing Service.
Publisher: Educational Testing Service.
Cross References: For reviews of the CLEP program, see 8:473 (3 reviews) and 7:664 (3 reviews).

[513]
CLEP Examination in Western Civilization I: Ancient Near East to 1648.

Purpose: For college accreditation, advanced placement, or assessment of educational attainment.
Population: Persons entering college or already in college.
Publication Dates: 1964–2002.
Scores: Total score only.
Administration: Group.
Price Data: Available from publisher.
Time: (90) minutes.
Comments: Tests administered at centers throughout the United States and internationally; program administered by the College Board and Educational Testing Service.
Author: Educational Testing Service.
Publisher: Educational Testing Service.
Cross References: For reviews of the CLEP program, see 8:473 (3 reviews) and 7:664 (3 reviews).

[514]
CLEP Examination in Western Civilization II: 1648 to Present.

Purpose: For college accreditation, advanced placement, or assessment of educational attainment.
Population: Persons entering college or already in college.
Publication Dates: 1964–2002.
Scores: Total score only.
Administration: Group.
Price Data: Available from publisher.
Time: (90) minutes.
Comments: Tests administered at centers throughout the United States and internationally; program administered by the College Board and Educational Testing Service.
Author: Educational Testing Service.
Publisher: Educational Testing Service.
Cross References: For reviews of the CLEP program, see 8:473 (3 reviews) and 7:664 (3 reviews).

[515]
CLEP Examinations in English Composition and English Composition Test with Essay.

Purpose: For college accreditation, advanced placement, or assessment of educational attainment.
Population: Persons entering college or already in college.
Publication Dates: 1964–2002.
Scores: Total score only.
Administration: Group.
Price Data: Available from publisher.
Time: (45) minutes per composition test; (45) minutes per essay.
Comments: English Composition Test with Essay administered via computer at any time per a test site's schedule; English Composition test administered at centers throughout the United States and internationally; program administered by the College Board and Educational Testing Service.
Author: Educational Testing Service.
Publisher: Educational Testing Service.
Cross References: See T3:412 (1 reference); for additional information, see 8:42 (4 references) and T2:58 (1 reference); for reviews of the CLEP program, see 8:473 (3 reviews) and 7:664 (3 reviews).

[516]
CLEP Examinations in Humanities.

Purpose: For college accreditation, advanced placement, or assessment of educational attainment.
Population: Persons entering college or already in college.
Publication Dates: 1964–2002.
Scores: Total score only.
Administration: Group.
Price Data: Available from publisher.
Time: (90) minutes.
Comments: Tests administered at centers throughout the United States and internationally; program administered by the College Board and Educational Testing Service.
Author: Educational Testing Service.
Publisher: Educational Testing Service.
Cross References: For additional information and a review by William E. Kline, see 8:254 (1 reference); for reviews of the CLEP program, see 8:473 (3 reviews) and 7:664 (3 reviews).

[517]
CLEP Examinations in Mathematics.

Purpose: For college accreditation, advanced placement, or assessment of educational attainment.
Population: Persons entering college or already in college.
Publication Dates: 1964–2002.
Scores: Total score only.
Administration: Group.
Price Data: Available from publisher.
Time: (90) minutes.
Comments: Tests administered at centers throughout the United States and internationally; program administered by the College Board and Educational Testing Service.
Author: Educational Testing Service.
Publisher: Educational Testing Service.
Cross References: For a review by William E. Kline, see 8:254 (1 reference).

[518]
CLEP Examinations in Natural Sciences.

Purpose: For college accreditation, advanced placement, or assessment of educational attainment.
Population: Persons entering college or already in college.
Publication Dates: 1964–2002.
Scores: Total score only.
Administration: Group.
Price Data: Available from publisher.
Time: (90) minutes.
Comments: Tests administered at centers throughout the United States and internationally; program administered by the College Board and Educational Testing Service.
Author: Educational Testing Service.
Publisher: Educational Testing Service.
Cross References: For additional information by George G. Mallinson, see 8:824 (2 references); for reviews of the CLEP program, see 8:473 (3 reviews) and 7:664 (3 reviews).

[519]
CLEP Examinations in Social Sciences and History.

Purpose: For college accreditation, advanced placement, or assessment of educational attainment.
Population: Persons entering college or already in college.
Publication Dates: 1964–2002.
Scores: Total score only.
Administration: Group.
Price Data: Available from publisher.
Time: (90) minutes.
Comments: Tests administered at centers throughout the United States and internationally; program administered by the College Board and Educational Testing Service.
Author: Educational Testing Service.
Publisher: Educational Testing Service.
Cross References: For additional information and a review by Richard E. Gross, see 8:886 (1 reference); for reviews of the CLEP program, see 8:473 (3 reviews) and 7:664 (3 reviews).

[520]
Clerical Abilities Battery.

Purpose: Assesses clerical abilities "for use in hiring and promoting clerical personnel."
Population: Clerical applicants and employees and business school students.
Publication Dates: 1985–1987.
Acronym: CAB.
Scores: 7 tests: Filing, Comparing Information, Copying Information, Using Tables, Proofreading, Addition and Subtraction, Reasoning with Numbers.
Administration: Group or individual.
Forms, 2: A, B.
Restricted Distribution: Distribution of Form A restricted to personnel departments in business and industry.
Price Data, 2002: $158 per complete kit including 5 test booklets of each test, 7 keys, and manual (1987, 22 pages); $48 per 25 test booklets (Filing [1987, 7 pages], Copying Information [1987, 6 pages], Comparing Information [1987, 5 pages], Using Tables [1987, 6 pages], Proofreading [1987, 6 pages], Addition and Subtraction [1987, 7 pages], Reasoning with Numbers [1987, 7 pages]); $73 per set of scoring stencils; $36 per manual.
Time: 70(105) minutes for the battery; 5(10) minutes each for first four tests, 15(20) minutes each for next two tests, 20(25) minutes for last test.
Comments: Tests available as separates.
Author: The Psychological Corporation.
Publisher: The Psychological Corporation.
Cross References: For reviews by Joseph C. Ciechalski and Bikkar S. Randhawa, see 11:71.

[521]
Clerical Aptitude Test: Acorn National Aptitude Tests.

Purpose: Designed to measure qualities associated with good clerical performance.
Population: Grades 7–12 and adult clerks.
Publication Dates: 1943–1950.
Scores, 4: Business Practice, Number Checking, Date and Name and Address Checking, Total.
Administration: Group.
Price Data: Available from publisher.
Time: 40(50) minutes.
Authors: Andrew Kobal, J. Wayne Wrightstone, and Karl R. Kunze.

Publisher: Psychometric Affiliates.
Cross References: See T3:464 (2 references); see also 5:847 (1 reference); for reviews by Marion A. Bills, Donald G. Paterson, Henry Weitz, and E. F. Wonderlic, see 3:623.

[522]
Clerical Aptitudes.

Purpose: "Designed to indicate ability to learn the tasks usually performed in various clerical jobs."
Population: Applicants for office personnel positions.
Publication Dates: 1947–1992.
Scores, 4: Office Vocabulary, Office Arithmetic, Office Checking, Total.
Administration: Individual or group.
Price Data: Available from publisher.
Time: 25 minutes.
Comments: Previously listed as SRA Clerical Aptitudes.
Author: Richardson, Bellows, Henry & Co., Inc.
Publisher: Reid London House.
Cross References: See T2:791 (2 references); for reviews by Edward N. Hay and G. A. Satter, see 4:732.

[523]
Clerical Skills Series.

Purpose: "Designed to measure proficiency in paper work tasks typical of . . . clerical occupations."
Population: Clerical workers.
Publication Dates: 1966-1986.
Administration: Group.
Price Data, 2001: $64.35 per complete kit; $32.45 per profile sheet package; $47.85 per manual (1966, 20 pages) and manuals supplement (1984, 17 pages).
Author: Martin M. Bruce.
Publisher: Martin M. Bruce, Ph.D.
   a) ALPHABETIZING-FILING.
   Time: 8(13) minutes.
   Price Data: $38.50 per specimen set; $43.50 per test package; $3.15 per scoring key.
   b) ARITHMETIC.
   Time: 8(13) minutes.
   Price Data: Same as *a* above.
   c) CLERICAL SPEED AND ACCURACY.
   Time: 3(5) minutes.
   Price Data: Same as *a* above.
   d) CODING.
   Time: 2(7) minutes.
   Price Data: Same as *a* above.
   e) EYE-HAND ACCURACY.
   Time: 5(10) minutes.
   Price Data: $38.50 per specimen set; $43.50 per test package; no key required.
   f) GRAMMAR AND PUNCTUATION.
   Time: (5-10) minutes.
   Price Data: Same as *a* above.

   g) SPELLING.
   Time: (15-20) minutes.
   Price Data: Same as *a* above.
   h) SPELLING-VOCABULARY.
   Time: (15-20) minutes.
   Price Data: Same as *a* above.
   i) VOCABULARY.
   Time: (10-15) minutes.
   Price Data: Same as *a* above.
   j) WORD FLUENCY.
   Time: 5(10) minutes.
   Price Data: Same as *e* above.
Cross References: For a review by Robert Fitzpatrick, see 7:988.

[524]
Clerical Skills Test Series [Scored By Client].

Purpose: Measures 16 different clerical-administrative skills.
Population: Adults.
Publication Date: 1990.
Scores: 16 skills: Alphabetizing—Filing, Attention to Detail With Words & Numbers, Bookkeeping Skills, Coding, Grammar & Punctuation, Manual Dexterity, Mechanical Comprehension, Numerical Skills, Problem Solving, Proofreading Skills, Reading Comprehension, Receptionist Skills, Spatial Perception, Spelling, Verbal Fluency, English Vocabulary, plus Total Score.
Administration: Group.
Price Data, 2001: $300 per 20 of the same test; quantity discounts available.
Time: (5) minutes per subtest.
Comments: Scored by the client; includes scoring keys; must be proctored.
Author: Stephen Berke.
Publisher: Walden Personnel Performance, Inc. [Canada].

[525]
Client/Server Skills Test.

Purpose: To evaluate the candidate's general client/server knowledge.
Population: Information technology professionals who possess some basic knowledge or experience in a client/server environment.
Publication Date: 1994.
Scores: Total Score, Narrative Evaluation, Ranking, Recommendation.
Administration: Group.
Price Data, 2001: $240 per candidate.
Time: (80) minutes.
Comments: Scored by publisher; must be proctored.
Author: Bruce A. Winrow.
Publisher: Walden Personnel Performance, Inc.

[526]
Clifton Assessment Procedures for the Elderly.

Purpose: Designed to assess cognitive and behavioral competence of the elderly.
Population: Ages 60 and over.
Publication Dates: 1979–1981.
Acronym: CAPE.
Administration: Group.
Price Data, 2002: £8.99 per 20 report forms; £9.50 per manual (1979, 34 pages); £11.99 per specimen set.
Time: Administration time not reported.
Comments: Distributed in the U.S.A. by The Psychological Corporation; 2 tests plus combination short version; authors recommend administering both tests concurrently, however, they can be used separately.
Authors: A. H. Pattie and C. J. Gilleard.
Publisher: Hodder & Stoughton Educational [England].

a) COGNITIVE ASSESSMENT SCALE.
Acronym: CAS.
Scores, 4: Information/Orientation, Mental Ability, Psychomotor (adaptation of Gibson Spiral Maze), Total.
Price Data: £8.99 per 20 tests (CAS); £13.99 per 20 mazes.
b) BEHAVIOUR RATING SCALE.
Acronym: BRS.
Scores, 5: Physical Disability, Apathy, Communication Difficulties, Social Disturbance, Total.
Price Data: £8.99 per 20 tests.
Comments: Shortened version of Stockton Geriatric Rating Scale.
Cross References: See T5:537 (4 references) and T4:518 (19 references); for reviews by Alicia Skinner Cook and K. Warner Schaie, see 9:231 (2 references); see also T3:471 (1 reference).

[527]
Clinical Analysis Questionnaire.

Purpose: Designed to assess both normal and pathological personality traits.
Population: Ages 16 and over.
Publication Dates: 1949–1997.
Acronym: CAQ.
Administration: Group or individual.
Price Data, 2002: $60 per hand-scoring introductory kit including test booklet, scoring keys, answer sheet, individual record folder, and manual (1997, 98 pages); $28 per computer interpreted introductory kit including test booklet, answer sheet, prepaid processing form, and manual; $40 (Standard Form) or $35 (Short Form) per 25 reusable test booklets; $32 per 2 short form scoring keys or 4 standard form scoring keys; $15 per 25 hand-scorable or 25 machine-scorable answer sheets (specify short or standard form); $18 per 25

individual record folders (specify short or standard form); $19 to $30 per report for scoring and interpretive services.
Foreign Language Edition: Information regarding several non-English-language adaptations available from publisher.
Time: (120) minutes for both parts of standard form; (100) minutes for both parts of short form.
Authors: Samuel E. Krug and Raymond B. Cattell.
Publisher: Institute for Personality and Ability Testing, Inc.

a) PART I (NORMAL PERSONALITY TRAITS).
Scores, 21: 16 primary factor scores: Warmth (A), Intelligence (B), Emotional Stability (C), Dominance (E), Impulsivity (F), Conformity (G), Boldness (H), Sensitivity (I), Suspiciousness (L), Imagination (M), Shrewdness (N), Insecurity (O), Radicolism (Q), Sufficiency (Q2), Self-Discipline (Q3), Tension (Q4), plus 5 second-order factor scores: Extraversion (Ex), Anxiety (Ax), Tough Poise (C+), Independence (In), Super-ego Strength (Se).
Comments: Normal personality traits from the 16PF.
b) PART II (THE CLINICAL FACTORS).
Scores, 16: 12 primary factor scores: Hypochondriasis (D1), Suicidal Depression (D2), Agitation (D3), Anxious Depression (D4), Low Energy Depression (D5), Guilt and Resentment (D6), Boredom and Withdrawal (D7), Paranoia (Pa), Psychopathic Deviation (Pp), Schizophrenia (Sc), Psychasthenia (As), Psychological Inadequacy (Ps), plus 4 second-order factor scores: Socialization (So), Depression (D), Psychoticism (P), Neuroticism (Ne).
Cross References: See T5:538 (8 references) and T4:519 (7 references); for a review by George Guthrie, see 9:232 (4 references); see also T3:472 (11 references); for a review by Douglas McNair, see 8:522 (7 references); see also T2:1131 (1 reference) and 7:54 (1 reference).

[528]
Clinical Assessment Scales for the Elderly and Clinical Assessment Scales for the Elderly—Short Form.

Population: Ages 55–90.
Publication Dates: 1999–2001.
Scores, 10: Anxiety, Cognitive Competence, Depression, Fear of Aging, Mania, Obsessive-Compulsive, Paranoia, Psychoticism, Somatization, Substance Abuse.
Administration: Group.
Forms, 2: R (caregiver rating), S (self-rating).
Price Data, 2001: $235 per combination kit including professional manual (2001, 140 pages), 25

Short Form R test booklets, 25 Short Form S test booklets, 25 Form R item booklets, 25 Form S item booklets, 25 Form R hand-scorable answer sheets, 25 Form S hand-scorable answer sheets, and 100 profile forms; $20 per 50 profile forms; $40 per professional manual.

Comments: Addresses selected DSM-IV Axis I disorders.

Authors: Cecil R. Reynolds (test and manual) and Erin D. Bigler (test).

Publisher: Psychological Assessment Resources, Inc.

a) CLINICAL ASSESSMENT SCALES FOR THE ELDERLY.

Purpose: "A comprehensive measure of acute psychopathology in the elderly."

Acronym: CASE.

Price Data: $150 per introductory kit including professional manual (2001, 140 pages), 25 Form R item booklets, 25 Form S item booklets, 25 Form R hand-scorable answer sheets, 25 Form S hand-scorable answer sheets, and 50 profile forms; $20 per 25 reusable item booklets (Form R or S); $39 per 25 hand-scorable answer sheets (Form R or S) (discount available for 50 or more).

Time: 20–40 (30–50) minutes.

b) CLINICAL ASSESSMENT SCALES FOR THE ELDERLY—SHORT FORM.

Purpose: To "screen for acute psychopathology in the elderly."

Acronym: CASE-SF.

Price Data: $110 per Short Form introductory kit including professional manual (2001, 140 pages), 25 Form R item booklets, 25 Form S item booklets, and 50 profile forms; $39 per 25 test booklets (Forms R or S) (discount available for 50 or more).

Time: 10–20 (20–30) minutes.

[529]
Clinical Evaluation of Language Fundamentals—Preschool.

Purpose: "Measures a broad range of expressive and receptive language skill in preschool-aged children."

Population: Preschool and early elementary.

Publication Dates: 1991–1992.

Acronym: CELF-Preschool.

Scores, 9: Receptive Language (Linguistic Concepts, Sentence Structure, Basic Concepts, Total), Expressive Language (Recalling Sentences in Context, Formulating Labels, Word Structure, Total), Total.

Administration: Individual.

Price Data, 2002: $249 per complete kit including examiner's manual (1992, 120 pages), 25 record forms, and 3 stimulus manuals; $52 per examiner's manual;

$45 per 25 record forms; $138 per stimulus manual 1; $36 per stimulus manual 2 or stimulus manual 3.

Time: (30–45) minutes.

Comments: A downward extension of the Clinical Evaluation of Language Fundamentals—Revised (T5:540).

Authors: Elisabeth H. Wiig, Wayne Secord, and Eleanor Semel.

Publisher: The Psychological Corporation.

Cross References: See T5:539 (2 references); for reviews by Janet A. Norris and Nora M. Thompson, see 13:67 (2 references).

[530]
Clinical Evaluation of Language Fundamentals, Third Edition.

Purpose: Constructed as a "clinical tool for the identification, diagnosis, and follow-up evaluation of language skill deficits."

Population: Ages 6.0–21.11.

Publication Dates: 1980–1995.

Acronym: CELF—3.

Administration: Individual.

Price Data, 2002: $360 per complete kit; $28.50 per 12 record forms; $99 per 50 record forms; $189 per set of 2 stimulus manuals; $80 per examiner's manual; $84 per technical manual.

Time: (30–45) minutes.

Authors: Eleanor Semel, Elisabeth H. Wiig, and Wayne A. Secord.

Publisher: The Psychological Corporation.

a) CELF—3, AGES 6–21.

Population: Ages 6–8.

Scores, 12: Receptive Language (Sentence Structure, Concepts and Directions, Word Classes); Expressive Language (Word Structure, Formulated Sentences, Recalling Sentences); Total Language; Supplementary Subtests (Word Associations, Listening to Paragraphs); Rapid/Automatic Naming [optional].

b) CELF—3, AGES 6–21.

Population: Ages 9–21.11.

Scores, 12: Receptive Language (Concepts and Directions, Word Classes, Semantic Relationships); Expressive Language (Formulated Sentences, Recalling Sentences, Sentence Assembly); Total Language; Supplementary Subtests (Word Associations, Listening to Paragraphs); Rapid/Automatic Naming [optional].

Cross References: See T5:540 (26 references); for reviews by Ronald B. Gillam and John MacDonald, see 13:68 (38 references); see also T4:521 (5 references); for reviews by Linda Crocker and David A. Shapiro of an earlier edition, see 11:72; for a review by Dixie D. Sanger of an earlier edition, see 9:233 (2 references); see also T3:474.

[531]
Clinical Evaluation of Language Fundamentals, Third Edition—Observational Rating Scales.

Purpose: Designed to measure "a student's classroom communication and language learning difficulties."
Population: Ages 6–21.
Publication Date: 1996.
Acronym: CELF-3ORS.
Scores: 4 sections: Listening, Speaking, Reading, Writing.
Administration: Individual or group.
Forms, 4: Parent, Teacher, Student, Summary.
Price Data, 2002: $59 per complete kit including rating scales, summary forms, and guide (86 pages); $15 per Teacher rating forms; $15 per Parent rating forms; $20 per summary forms; $27 per guide.
Time: Administration time not reported.
Comments: Ratings by parents, teachers, and students.
Authors: Eleanor Semel, Elisabeth H. Wiig, and Wayne A. Secord.
Publisher: The Psychological Corporation.
Cross References: For reviews by Robert R. Haccoun and David P. Hurford, see 14:76; see also T5:541 (1 reference).

[532]
Clinical Evaluation of Language Fundamentals—3 Screening Test.

Purpose: "Designed to screen school age children, adolescents, and young adults for language disorders."
Population: Ages 6-0 to 21-11.
Publication Dates: 1995–1996.
Acronym: CELF-3 Screening Test.
Scores: Total score only.
Administration: Individual.
Price Data, 2002: $185 per kit including examiner's manual (1996, 55 pages), stimulus manual, and 25 record forms; $62 per examiner's manual; $119 per stimulus manual; $41 per 25 record forms; $137 per 100 record forms.
Time: (10–15) minutes.
Comments: A test in the CELF series of language testing instruments; administered orally with visual stimuli; not for diagnostic use; "criterion-referenced."
Authors: Eleanor Semel, Elisabeth H. Wiig, and Wayne A. Secord.
Publisher: The Psychological Corporation.
Cross References: See T5:542 (2 references); for reviews by Billy T. Ogletree and Marcel O. Ponton, see 13:69 (1 reference); for reviews by Linda M. Crocker and Jon F. Miller of an earlier edition, see 9:234.

[533]
Clinical Experience Record for Nursing Students.

Purpose: Evaluates the "performance and progress of nursing students."
Population: Nursing students and nurses.
Publication Dates: 1960–1975.
Acronym: CERNS.
Scores: No scores.
Administration: Individual.
Price Data: Available from publisher.
Time: Administration time not reported.
Comments: Two assessment areas: Clinical Performance Record, Performance/Progress Record.
Authors: John C. Flanagan, Angeline C. Marchese, Grace Fivars, and Shirley A. Tuska (manual).
Publisher: Grace Fivars.
Cross References: For additional information, see 8:1120 (1 reference).

[534]
Clinical Rating Scale.

Purpose: Designed to type marital and family systems and identify intervention targets.
Population: Couples and families.
Publication Dates: 1980–1990.
Acronym: CRS.
Scores: 3 ratings (Cohesion, Change, Communication) yielding Family System Type.
Administration: Group (couple or family).
Price Data, 1998: $10 per manual (includes unlimited copying privileges).
Time: Administration time not reported.
Author: David H. Olson.
Publisher: Life Innovations, Inc.
Cross References: For reviews by Stuart N. Hart and Steven W. Lee, see 12:81 (4 references).

[535]
The Clock Test.

Purpose: Measures an individual's level of cognitive impairment and helps differentiate between normal elderly and thos suffering from dementia.
Population: Ages 65 and older.
Publication Date: 1995.
Scores, 3: Clock Reading, Clock Drawing, Clock Setting.
Administration: Individual.
Price Data, 2002: $165 per test kit including 25 QuikScore™ forms, 25 profile sheets, administration test, and manual (85 pages); $65 per 25 QuikScore™ forms; $13 per 25 profile sheets; $63 per administration tent; $42 per manual.
Time: [15–30] minutes.
Authors: H. Tuokko, T. Hadjistavropoulos, J. A. Miller, A. Horton, and B. L. Beattie.

Publisher: Multi-Health Systems, Inc.
Cross References: For reviews by Howard A. Lloyd and Antony M. Paolo, see 14:78.

[536]
Closed Head Injury Screener.

Purpose: "Designed to help medical doctors and psychologists assess whether patient symptoms are suggestive of closed-head injuries."
Population: English-speaking adults.
Publication Date: 1994.
Acronym: CHIS.
Scores: 3 ratings: Medical Facts, Presenting Complaints, Response Validity.
Administration: Individual.
Price Data, 2001: $25 per sampler set including manual (20 pages), questionnaire/answer sheet, and scoring directions; $125 per permission set including sampler set plus permission to reproduce up to 200 copies of the instrument.
Time: Approximately 30 minutes.
Comments: To be used as a supplement to a full face-to-face patient interview; partial paper and pencil/partial oral interview; results interpreted by administrator; not to be used with patients with cognitive deficits that are explainable by a previous diagnosis.
Author: Michael Ivan Friedman.
Publisher: Mind Garden, Inc.
Cross References: For reviews by Thomas J. Cullen, Jr. and Scott A. Napolitano, see 14:79.

[537]
Closed High School Placement Test.

Purpose: Designed as a measure of cognitive and basic skills to assist in placement decisions for entering freshmen.
Population: Eighth grade students.
Publication Dates: 1985–2001.
Acronym: HSPT.
Scores, 8: Cognitive Skills (Verbal, Quantitative, Total), Basic Skills (Reading, Mathematics, Language, Total), Composite.
Administration: Group.
Price Data, 2002: Available only through Lease/Score program including school rental of test materials and scoring service; $5.70 per student, minimum scoring service charge of $42.35 required.
Time: (140) minutes plus (15–25) minutes per optional test.
Comments: Optional tests include science, mechanical aptitude, and Catholic religion.
Author: Scholastic Testing Service, Inc.
Publisher: Scholastic Testing Service, Inc.
Cross References: For Reviews by George Engelhard, Jr. and Ernest Kimmel, see 14:80; see also T5:547 (1 reference) and T3:2324 (1 reference); for

reviews by Leonard S. Cahen and Irvin J. Lehmann of an earlier edition, see 8:26 (1 reference); see also 7:21 (2 references); for reviews by Marion F. Shaycoft and James R. Hayden of an earlier series, see 6:6; for reviews by William C. Cottle and Robert A. Jones of the 1955 "open" test, see 5:15.

[538]
Closure Flexibility (Concealed Figures).

Purpose: "To measure the ability to hold a configuration in mind despite distracting irrelevancies."
Population: Wide range of higher level occupations personnel.
Publication Dates: 1956–1965.
Scores: Total score only.
Administration: Individual or group.
Price Data, 2002: $91 per start-up kit including 25 test booklets, score key, and interpretation and research manual (1965, 20 pages); $54 per 25 tests (quantity discounts available); $20 per score key; $28 per interpretation and research manual.
Time: (10) minutes.
Authors: L. L. Thurstone and T. E. Jeffrey.
Publisher: Reid London House.
Cross References: See T5:548 (1 reference), T3:477 (5 references), T2:547 (9 references), and 7:435 (9 references); for a review by Leona E. Tyler, see 6:545 (4 references).

[539]
Closure Speed (Gestalt Completion).

Purpose: "To measure the ability to see apparently disorganized or unrelated parts as a meaningful whole."
Population: Employees in wide range of occupations.
Publication Date: 1959.
Scores: Total score only.
Administration: Individual or group.
Price Data, 2002: $91 per start-up kit including 25 test booklets, score key, and interpretation and research manual (1966, 18 pages); $54 per 25 test booklets (quantity discounts available); $20 per score key; $28 per interpretation and research manual.
Time: 3 minutes.
Authors: L. L. Thurstone and T. E. Jeffrey.
Publisher: Reid London House.
Cross References: See T4:530 (2 references), T3:478 (2 references), T2:548 (1 reference), and 7:436 (2 references); for a review by Leona E. Tyler, see 6:546 (3 references).

[540]
Cloze Reading Tests 1-3, Second Edition.

Purpose: Designed to provide a method of testing reading skills.
Population: Ages 8-0 to 10-6, 8-5 to 11-10, 9-5 to 12-6.

Publication Date: 1982–1992.
Scores: Overall performance score.
Administration: Individual or group.
Levels, 3: Level 1 (Ages 8-0 to 10-6), Level 2 (Ages 8-5 to 11-10), Level 3 (Ages 9-5 to 12-6).
Price Data, 2002: £5.99 per 10 tests (specify Test 1, 2, or 3); £11.99 per manual (16 pages); £12.99 per specimen set.
Time: 35(45) minutes.
Author: D. Young.
Publisher: Hodder & Stoughton Educational [England].
Cross References: See T5:550 (5 references) and T4:531 (3 references); for a review by Esther Geva, see 9:237.

[541]
Coaching Effectiveness Survey.

Purpose: "Designed to help managers and others who coach people on the job to assess their effectiveness."
Population: Managers, supervisors, coaches.
Publication Date: 1997.
Scores, 5: Coaching Behavior, Coaching Attitude, Coaching Process, Coaching Style, Coaching Effectiveness.
Administration: Group.
Forms, 2: Coach Questionnaire, Coachee Questionnaire.
Price Data, 2002: $49 per complete kit including questionnaires and answer sheets for 1 self-assessment, 12 coachees, and 1 feedback report.
Time: (30) minutes.
Comments: Diagnostic recommendations are provided; can be administered online via the Internet.
Authors: Terry R. Bacon (manual) and International LearningWorks®.
Publisher: Lore International Institute.

[542]
Coaching Process Questionnaire.

Purpose: "Provides managers with an assessment of their coaching ability."
Population: Managers and employees.
Publication Date: 1992.
Acronym: CPQ.
Administration: Group or individual.
Time: [30–40] minutes.
Foreign Language Edition: Available in French and Spanish.
Comments: Self-scored instrument.
Author: Hay Group.
Publisher: Hay Group.
   a) PARTICIPANT VERSION.
   Population: Managers.
   Scores, 5: Diagnostic Skills, Coaching Techniques, Coaching Qualities, Coaching Model, Overall CPQ score.

Price Data, 2001: $69 per complete kit including 10 questionnaires, and 10 profiles and interpretive notes.
   b) EMPLOYEE VERSION.
   Population: Employees.
   Scores, 5: Diagnostic Skills, Coaching Techniques, Coaching Qualities, Coaching Model, Overall Employee score.
   Price Data: $29 per 10 questionnaires.
Cross References: For reviews by Patricia A. Bachelor and Geneva D. Haertel, see 13:70.

[543]
Coaching Skills Inventory.

Purpose: Identifies and evaluates "success in performing coaching functions" for organizational leaders.
Population: Adults.
Publication Date: 1991.
Acronym: CSI.
Scores, 5: Contact and Core Skills, Counseling, Mentoring, Tutoring, Confronting and Challenging.
Administration: Group.
Forms, 2: Self, Other.
Price Data, 1997: $7.95 per self-inventory; $3.95 per "other" inventory.
Time: Administration time not reported.
Comments: Self-administered; self-scored.
Author: Dennis C. Kinlaw.
Publisher: Jossey-Bass, A Wiley Company.

[544]
Coddington Life Events Scales.

Purpose: Designed "to assess the influence of life events and change in a young person's life, and help determine how these events affect their personal growth and ability to adjust."
Population: Ages 5 and under, ages 6–10, ages 11–19.
Publication Dates: 1981–1999.
Acronym: CLES.
Scores: Total Life Change Unit score only.
Administration: Group.
Forms, 3: Preschool (CLES-P), Child (CLES-C), Adolescent (CLES-A).
Price Data, 2002: $114 per complete kit including technical manual and 25 Quikscore forms for the CLES-P, CLES-C, and CLES-A; $37 per technical manual (1999, 58 pages); $30 per 25 Quikscore forms (specify CLES-P, CLES-C, or CLES-A); $38 per specimen set including technical manual and 3 of each Quikscore forms for the CLES-P, CLES-C, CLES-A.
Time: (15) minutes.
Comments: Self-report, assisted self-report.
Author: R. Dean Coddington.
Publisher: Multi-Health Systems, Inc.
Cross References: See T5:557 (7 references) and T4:1453 (3 references).

[545]
Cognistat (The Neurobehavioral Cognitive Status Examination).

Purpose: Designed to assess intellectual functioning.
Population: Adults.
Publication Dates: 1983–1995.
Acronym: Cognistat.
Scores, 11: Level of Consciousness, Orientation, Attention, Language (Comprehension, Repetition, Naming), Constructional Ability, Memory, Calculations, Reasoning (Similarities, Judgment).
Administration: Individual.
Price Data: Available from publisher.
Time: Administration time not reported.
Authors: R. J. Kiernan, J. Mueller, and J. W. Langston.
Publisher: Northern California Neurobehavioral Group, Inc.
Cross References: For reviews by Charles J. Long and Faith Gunning-Dixon and by Steven R. Shaw, see 14:81.

[546]
Cognitive Abilities Scale—Second Edition.

Purpose: Developed to assess the cognitive abilities of infants and young children and to identify children who have delays in cognitive development.
Publication Dates: 1987–2001.
Acronym: CAS-2.
Administration: Individual.
Price Data, 2001: $69 per examiner's manual (2001, 83 pages); $39 per 25 Profile/Examiner Record Booklets (Infant Form); $39 per 25 Profile/Examiner Record Booklets (Preschool Form); $14 per 25 Symbol Reproduction Forms; $39 per 25 Mikey's Favorite Things Book; $29 per Picture Cards; $9 per Ramp; $198 per Manipulatives Kit; $424 per complete kit including examiner's manual, 25 Profile/Examiner Record Booklets (Infant Form), 25 Profile/Examiner Record Booklets (Preschool Form), 25 Symbol Reproduction Forms, 25 copies of "Mikey's Favorite Things," Picture Cards, Ramp, and Manipulatives Kit.
Time: (20–30) minutes.
Authors: Sharon Bradley-Johnson and C. Merle Johnson.
Publisher: PRO-ED.
a) INFANT FORM.
Population: Ages 3–23 months.
Scores, 3: Exploration of Objects, Communication with Others, Initiation and Imitation.
b) PRESCHOOL FORM.
Population: Ages 24–47 months.
Scores, 5: Oral Language, Reading, Math, Writing, Enabling Behaviors.

Cross References: See T5:559 (1 reference); for reviews by A. Dirk Hightower and Gary J. Robertson of the original edition, see 10:65.

[547]
Cognitive Abilities Test™, Form 5.

Purpose: "To assess students' abilities in reasoning and problem solving using verbal, quantitative, and spatial (nonverbal) symbols."
Population: Grades K–12.
Publication Dates: 1954–1993.
Acronym: CogAT.
Administration: Group.
Price Data: Available from publisher.
Comments: Scoring service available from publisher.
Authors: Robert L. Thorndike and Elizabeth P. Hagen.
Publisher: Riverside Publishing.
a) PRIMARY BATTERY.
Population: Grades K–3.
Publication Dates: 1979–1993.
Scores, 4: Verbal, Quantitative, Nonverbal, Composite.
Levels, 2: Primary Battery, Level 1 and Primary Battery, Level 2.
Time: Untimed, approximately 90 minutes.
b) MULTILEVEL EDITION
Population: Grades 3–12.
Publication Dates: 1979–1993.
Scores, 4: Verbal, Quantitative, Nonverbal, Composite.
Levels: 8 overlapping levels: Level A through Level H.
Time: Approximately 90 minutes.
Cross References: See T5:560 (4 references); for reviews by Bert A. Goldman and Stephen H. Ivens, see 13:71 (23 references); see also T4:537 (19 references); for reviews by Anne Anastasi and Douglas Fuchs of an earlier edition, see 10:66 (13 references); for a review by Charles J. Ansorge of an earlier edition, see 9:240 (5 references); see also T3:483 (32 references); for reviews by Kenneth D. Hopkins and Robert C. Nichols, see 8:181 (12 references); for reviews by Marcel L. Goldschmid and Carol K. Tittle and an excerpted review by Richard C. Cox of the primary batteries, see 7:343.

[548]
Cognitive Abilities Test, Second Edition [British Edition].

Purpose: Measures "the individual's ability to use and manipulate abstract and symbolic relationships."
Population: Ages 7–15.
Publication Dates: 1973–1986.
Acronym: CAT.
Scores, 3: Verbal, Quantitative, Nonverbal.

Administration: Group.
Levels, 6: 6 overlapping levels (A—F) in a single booklet.
Price Data: Price information available from publisher for pupil's booklet, practice tests, answer sheets (specify level), handscoring overlays, circular profiles, administration manual (1986, 96 pages), and for specimen set; scoring service offered by publisher.
Time: 20(40) minutes for practice test; 32(60) minutes per battery.
Authors: Robert L. Thorndike, Elizabeth Hagen, and Norman France (manual).
Publisher: NFER-Nelson Publishing Co., Ltd. [England].
Cross References: See T5:561 (2 references); for reviews by Anne Anastasi and Douglas Fuchs of the U.S. edition, see 10:66 (13 references); for a review by Charles J. Ansorge of an earlier edition, see 9:240 (5 references); see also T3:483 (32 references); for reviews by Kenneth D. Hopkins and Robert C. Nichols, see 8:181 (12 references); for reviews by Marcel L. Goldschmid and Carol K. Tittle and an excerpted review by Richard C. Cox of the primary batteries, see 7:343.

[549]
Cognitive Behavior Rating Scales.

Purpose: "To allow a family member, or other reliable observer, to rate the presence and severity of cognitive impairment, behavioral deficits, and observable neurological signs."
Population: Patients with possible neurological impairment.
Publication Date: 1987.
Acronym: CBRS.
Scores: 9 scales: Language Deficit, Apraxia, Disorientation, Agitation, Need for Routine, Depression, Higher Cognitive Deficits, Memory Disorder, Dementia.
Administration: Individual.
Price Data: Available from publisher for complete kit including manual, 25 reusable item booklets, and 50 rating booklets.
Time: (15-20) minutes.
Comments: Completed by significant others.
Author: J. Michael Williams.
Publisher: Psychological Assessment Resources, Inc.
Cross References: For reviews by Ron Edwards and David J. Mealor, see 11:74.

[550]
Cognitive Distortion Scales.

Purpose: Designed to measure cognitive distortions (dysfunctional thinking patterns).
Population: Ages 18 and over.
Publication Date: 2000.

Acronym: CDS.
Scores, 5: Self-Criticism, Self-Blame, Helplessness, Hopelessness, Preoccupation with Danger.
Administration: Individual or group.
Price Data: Available from publisher for kit including manual (2000, 40 pages), 25 booklets, and 25 profile forms.
Time: (10–15) minutes.
Author: John Briere.
Publisher: Psychological Assessment Resources, Inc.

[551]
Cognitive Linguistic Quick Test.

Purpose: "To assess the relative status of five cognitive domains in adults with known or suspected neurological dysfunction."
Population: Adults ages 18–89 with known or suspected acquired neurological dysfunction.
Publication Date: 2001.
Acronym: CLQT.
Scores, 7: 5 Cognitive Domain Scores (Attention, Memory, Language, Executive Functions, Visuospatial Skills), Total Composite Severity Rating, Clock Drawing Severity Rating.
Administration: Individual.
Price Data, 2002: $150 per complete kit including examiner's manual (146 pages), stimulus manual, 15 English record forms, and 15 response forms; $71 per examiner's manual; $61 per stimulus manual; $53 per 25 English record response forms; $32 per 15 Spanish record/response forms.
Foreign Language Editions: Available in English and Spanish versions.
Time: (15–30) minutes.
Comments: Test is composed of 10 tasks (Personal Facts, Symbol Cancellation, Confrontation Naming, Clock Drawing, Story Retelling, Symbol Trails, Generative Naming, Design Memory, Mazes, Design Generation); includes 5 tasks with minimal language demands; hand-scored.
Author: Nancy Helm-Estabrooks.
Publisher: The Psychological Corporation.

[552]
Cognitive Skills Assessment Battery, Second Edition.

Purpose: "To provide teachers with information regarding children's progress relative to teaching goals in the cognitive and physical-motor areas."
Population: PreK–K.
Publication Dates: 1974–1981.
Acronym: CSAB.
Scores: 98 item scores (49 consist of plus or minus) in 18 areas: Basic Information (4 scores), Identification of Body Parts (4 scores), Color Identification (4 scores), Shape Identification (4 scores), Symbol Discrimination

(10 scores), Visual-Auditory Discrimination (5 scores), Auditory Discrimination (6 scores), Number Knowledge (10 scores), Letter Naming (2 scores), Vocabulary (6 scores), Information from Pictures (4 scores), Picture Comprehension (4 scores), Story Comprehension (4 scores), Multiple Directions (4 scores), Large Muscle Coordination (4 scores), Visual-Motor Coordination (6 scores), Memory (8 scores), Response During Assessment (8 scores).

Administration: Individual.

Price Data, 2002: $51.95 per testing materials including 30 response sheets (1981, 4 pages); $8.95 per refill (1 class record, 30 pupil response sheets); $3.50 per assessors manual (1981, 61 pages); $3.95 per specimen set (including 1 sample easel page).

Time: (20-25) minutes.

Comments: "Criterion-referenced."

Authors: Ann E. Boehm and Barbara R. Slater.

Publisher: Teachers College Press.

Cross References: See T5:565 (1 reference) and T4:542 (3 references); for reviews by Esther E. Diamond and Susan Embretson (Whitely), see 9:242; see also T3:484 (2 references); for reviews by Kathryn Hoover Calfee and Barbara K. Keogh, see 8:797.

[553]
Cognitive Symptom Checklists.

Purpose: "Developed to assist in the identification and treatment of problems in five basic cognitive areas."

Population: Ages 16 and older.

Publication Date: 1993.

Acronym: CSC.

Scores: 5 checklists: Attention/Concentration, Memory, Visual Processes, Language, Executive Functions.

Administration: Individual or group.

Price Data: Available from publisher for complete kit including manual (26 pages), and 10 each of Attention/Concentration, Memory, Visual Processes, Language, and Executive Functions checklists.

Time: (10–20) minutes per checklist.

Comments: Checklists can be used separately or in any combination.

Authors: Christina O'Hara, Minnie Harrell, Eileen Bellingrath, and Katherine Lisicia.

Publisher: Psychological Assessment Resources, Inc.

Cross References: For reviews by Thomas J. Cullen, Jr. and Michael Lee Russell, see 14:82.

[554]
CogScreen Aeromedical Edition.

Purpose: "Designed to rapidly assess deficits or changes in" various cognitive abilities associated with flying.

Population: Aviators ages 25–73 with 12 or more years of education.

Publication Date: 1995.

Acronym: CogScreen-AE.

Scores, 65: 19 Speed Measures (Math Speed, Visual Sequence Comparison Speed, Matching-to-Sample Speed, Manikin Speed, Divided Attention Sequence Comparison Speed, Divided Attention Indicator Alone Speed, Divided Attention Indicator Dual Speed, Auditory Sequence Comparison Speed, Pathfinder Number Speed, Pathfinder Letter Speed, Pathfinder Combined Speed, Shifting Attention Arrow Direction Speed, Shifting Attention Arrow Color Speed, Shifting Attention Instruction Speed, Shifting Attention Discovery Speed, Dual Task Previous Number Alone Speed, Dual Task Previous Number Dual Speed, Dual Task Tracking Alone Error, Dual Task Tracking Dual Error), 19 Accuracy Measures (Backward Digit Span Accuracy, Math Accuracy, Visual Sequence Comparison Accuracy, Symbol Digit Coding Accuracy, Symbol Digit Coding Immediate Recall Accuracy, Symbol Digit Coding Delayed Recall Accuracy, Matching-to-Sample Accuracy, Manikin Accuracy, Divided Attention Sequence Comparison Accuracy, Auditory Sequence Comparison Accuracy, Pathfinder Number Accuracy, Pathfinder Letter Accuracy, Pathfinder Combined Accuracy, Shifting Attention Arrow Direction Accuracy, Shifting Attention Arrow Color Accuracy, Shifting Attention Instruction Accuracy, Shifting Attention Discovery Accuracy, Dual Task Previous Number Alone Accuracy, Dual Task Previous Number Dual Accuracy), 16 Thruput Measures (Math Thruput, Visual Sequence Comparison Thruput, Symbol Digit Coding Thruput, Matching-to-Sample Thruput, Manikin Thruput, Divided Attention Sequence Comparison Thruput, Auditory Sequence Comparison Thruput, Pathfinder Number Thruput, Pathfinder Letter Thruput, Pathfinder Combined Thruput, Shifting Attention Arrow Direction Thruput, Shifting Attention Arrow Color Thruput, Shifting Attention Instruction Thruput, Shifting Attention Discovery Thruput, Dual Task Previous Number Alone Thruput, Dual Task Previous Number Dual Thruput), 11 Process Measures (Divided Attention Indicator Alone Premature Responses, Divided Attention Indicator Dual Premature Responses, Pathfinder Number Coordination, Pathfinder Letter Coordination, Pathfinder Combined Coordination, Shifting Attention Discovery Rule Shifts Completed, Shifting Attention Discovery Failures to Maintain Set, Shifting Attention Discovery Nonconceptual Responses, Shifting Attention Discovery Perseverative Errors, Dual Task Tracking Alone Boundary Hits, Dual Task Tracking Dual Boundary Hits).

Administration: Individual.

Price Data, 1996: $849 per software kit including manual (148 pages), quick start guide, internal light pen package, and Testkey with 10 administrations (specify 3.5-inch or 5.25-inch disk); $69 per manual; $29.50 per

administration with Testkey unlock; $75 per extra Testkey (with no administration); $375 per internal light pen package.
Time: (45–60) minutes.
Comments: Requires IBM or compatible 640K, EGA or VGA graphics card, color monitor, and light pen.
Author: Gary G. Kay.
Publisher: CogScreen LLC [No reply from publisher; status unknown].
Cross References: For reviews by Robert W. Elliott and Hilda Wing, see 14:83.

[555]
Coitometer.

Purpose: Designed to "measure knowledge of the physical aspects of human coitus."
Population: Adults.
Publication Dates: 1974–1988.
Scores: Total score only.
Administration: Group.
Manual: No manual.
Price Data, 2002: $1 per test.
Time: [10] minutes.
Comments: Supplementary article available.
Author: Panos D. Bardis.
Publisher: Donna Bardis.

[556]
College Adjustment Scales.

Purpose: Identifies developmental and psychological problems experienced by college students.
Population: College and university students.
Publication Date: 1991.
Acronym: CAS.
Scores, 9: Anxiety, Depression, Suicidal Ideation, Substance Abuse, Self-Esteem Problems, Interpersonal Problems, Family Problems, Academic Problems, Career Problems.
Administration: Individual or group.
Price Data: Available from publisher for complete kit including manual (25 pages), 25 reusable item booklets, and 25 answer sheets.
Time: (15–20) minutes.
Authors: William D. Anton and James R. Reed.
Publisher: Psychological Assessment Resources, Inc.
Cross References: For reviews by William E. Martin, Jr. and Edward R. Starr, see 13:72 (3 references); see also T4:544 (1 reference).

[557]
College Basic Academic Subjects Examination.

Purpose: Designed to assess skills and competencies typically achieved through the general education component of a college curriculum.

Population: College students having completed the general education component of a college curriculum (i.e., late sophomores or early juniors).
Publication Dates: 1989–2002.
Acronym: College BASE.
Administration: Group.
Scores, 40: Competency (Interpretive Reasoning, Strategic Reasoning, Adaptive Reasoning), Skill (Social Science Procedures, Political/Economic Structures, Geography, Significance of U.S. Events, Significance of World Events, Physical Sciences, Life Sciences, Interpreting Results, Laboratory/Field Techniques, Observation/Experimental Design, Geometrical Calculations, 2- & 3-Dimensional Figures, Equations & Inequalities, Evaluating Expressions, Using Statistics, Properties and Notations, Practical Applications, Expository Writing Sample, Conventions of Written English, Writing as a Process, Understanding Literature, Reading Analytically, Reading Critically), Cluster (Social Sciences, History, Fundamental Concepts, Laboratory & Field Work, Geometry, Algebra, General Mathematics, Writing, Reading & Literature), Subject (Social Studies, Science, Mathematics, English), Composite.
Price Data, 2003: $65 per 50 test booklets; $44 per 50 answer booklets (includes examiner's manual); Scoring: $19.800 per student for four subjects with essay, and $9.30 per student for four subjects without essay. Includes institutional summary and student score report.
Time: 220 minutes with writing exercise; 180 minutes without writing exercise; plus 20 minutes for administration time.
Comments: "Criterion-referenced"; 180 multiple-choice items, optional essay assignment.
Author: Steven J. Osterlind.
Publisher: Assessment Resource Center, University of Missouri-Columbia.
Cross References: See T5:570 (1 reference); for reviews by William E. Coffman and Delwyn L. Harnisch, see 11:76.

[558]
College Board Descriptive Tests System.

Purpose: Designed to help college personnel determine the placement levels and remediation requirements of incoming as well as continuing students; helps secondary school personnel determine college readiness of and identify areas in need of remediation of upper grade students.
Population: Entering and continuing college students and upper level high school students.
Publication Dates: 1989–1999.
Acronym: DTS (previously DTLA/DTMS).
Scores: Total test scores and skill cluster scores in Reading Comprehension, Critical Reasoning, Conven-

tions of Written English, Sentence Structure, Arithmetic, Elementary Algebra, Intermediate Algebra, and Functions and Graphs (Calculus Readiness).
Administration: Individual or group.
Price Data: Available from publisher.
Time: Administration time not reported.
Comments: The Descriptive Tests System is part of the College Board On-Campus Testing Program, formerly called the Multiple Assessments Programs and Services (MAPS) of the College Board; each test title (Reading Comprehension, Critical Reasoning, Conventions of Written English, Sentence Structure, Arithmetic, Elementary Algebra, Intermediate Algebra, and Functions and Graphs (Calculus Readiness) is printed in individual reusable booklets. Either DTS self-scoring answer sheets or DTS-designed scannable answer sheets for use with the DTS MicroScore software are required. (Previously known as the Descriptive Test of Language Skills [T4:749] and the Descriptive Tests of Mathematical Skills [T4:750]).
Author: Educational Testing Service.
Publishers: Educational Testing Service and the College Board.
Cross References: See T5:571 (6 references) and T4:749 (4 references) or information about the Descriptive Tests of Language Skills (DTLS); for a review by Francis X. Archambault, Jr. of the DTLS, see 11:108 (4 references); see also T3:685 (1 reference). See T4:750 (2 references) for information about the Descriptive Tests of Mathematics Skills (DTMS); for reviews by Stephen B. Dunbar and John R. Hester of the DTMS, see 11:109.

[559]
College Board Institutional SAT II: American History and Social Studies Subject Test.

Purpose: To measure content knowledge in American History and Social Studies.
Population: Entering college freshmen.
Publication Dates: 1965–1999.
Scores: Total (200–800).
Administration: Group or individual.
Price Data: Rental fee per student available from publisher.
Time: (60) minutes.
Comments: Available for local administration and scoring by higher educational institutions; previously known as College Board One-Hour Achievement Test in American History and Social Studies.
Author: Educational Testing Service.
Publisher: The College Board.
Cross References: For a review by Howard R. Anderson of an earlier form, see 6:966; for a review by Ralph W. Tyler, see 5:786; for a review by Robert L.

Thorndike, see 4:662; for a review of an earlier form of the program, see 7:665.

[560]
College Board Institutional SAT II: Biology E/M Subject Test.

Purpose: To measure content knowledge in biology.
Population: Entering college freshmen.
Publication Dates: 1962–1999.
Scores: Total (200–800).
Administration: Group or individual.
Price Data: Rental fee per student available from publisher.
Time: (60) minutes.
Comments: Available for local administration and scoring by higher educational institutions; student chooses an Ecological (E) or Molecular (M) emphasis; previously known as College Board One-Hour Achievement Test in Biology.
Author: Educational Testing Service.
Publisher: The College Board.
Cross References: See T5:573 (1 reference) and 8:834 (1 reference); for a review by Elizabeth Hagen of an earlier form, see 5:723; for a review by Clark W. Horton of an earlier form, see 4:600; for a review of an earlier form of the program, see 7:665.

[561]
College Board Institutional SAT II: Chemistry Subject Test.

Purpose: To measure content knowledge in chemistry.
Population: Entering college freshmen.
Publication Dates: 1962–1999.
Scores: Total (200–800).
Administration: Group or individual.
Price Data: Rental fee per student available from publisher.
Time: (60) minutes.
Comments: Available for local administration and scoring by higher educational institutions; previously known as College Board One-Hour Achievement Test in Chemistry.
Author: Educational Testing Service.
Publisher: The College Board.
Cross References: See T5:574 (1 reference); for a review by William Hered of earlier forms, see 6:914; for a review by Max D. Engelhart of an earlier form, see 5:742; for a review by Evelyn Raskin of an earlier form, see 4:617; for a review of an earlier form of the program, see 7:665.

[562]
College Board Institutional SAT II: Chinese with Listening Subject Test.

Purpose: To measure content knowledge in Chinese.

Population: Entering college freshmen.
Publication Dates: 1997–1999.
Scores, 4: Subscores in Listening, Usage, Reading (20–80), and Total (200–800).
Administration: Group or individual.
Price Data: Rental fee per student available from publisher.
Time: (60) minutes.
Comments: Available for local administration and scoring by higher educational institutions; program previously known as College Board One-Hour Achievement Test.
Author: Educational Testing Service.
Publisher: The College Board.
Cross References: For a review of an earlier form of the program, see 7:665.

[563]
College Board Institutional SAT II: English Language Proficiency Test.

Purpose: To measure spoken and written standard American English, and the ability to use English in the classroom and in daily life.
Population: Entering college freshmen.
Publication Dates: 1997–1999.
Acronym: ELPT.
Scores, 3: Listening, Reading (1–50), and Total (901–999).
Administration: Group or individual.
Price Data: Rental fee per student available from publisher.
Time: (60) minutes.
Comments: Available for local administration and scoring by higher educational institutions.
Author: Educational Testing Service.
Publisher: The College Board.
Cross References: For a review of an earlier form of the program, see 7:665.

[564]
College Board Institutional SAT II: French Subject Test.

Purpose: To measure content knowledge in French.
Population: Entering college freshmen.
Publication Dates: 1962–1999.
Scores: Total (200–800).
Administration: Group or individual.
Price Data: Rental fee per student available from publisher.
Time: (60) minutes.
Comments: Available for local administration and scoring by higher educational institutions; previously known as College Board One-Hour Achievement Test in French Reading.
Author: Educational Testing Service.
Publisher: The College Board.

Cross References: For a review of an earlier form of the program, see 7:665.

[565]
College Board Institutional SAT II: French with Listening Subject Tests.

Purpose: To measure content knowledge in French.
Population: Entering college freshmen.
Publication Dates: 1971–1999.
Scores, 3: Subscores in Listening, Reading (20–80), Total (200–800).
Administration: Group or individual.
Price Data: Rental fee per student available from publisher.
Time: (60) minutes.
Comments: Available for local administration and scoring by higher educational institutions; cassette required; previously known as College Board One-Hour Achievement Test in French with Listening and College Placement Test.
Author: Educational Testing Service.
Publisher: The College Board.
Cross References: For a review of an earlier form of the program, see 7:665.

[566]
College Board Institutional SAT II: German Subject Test.

Purpose: To measure content knowledge in German.
Population: Entering college freshmen.
Publication Dates: 1962–1999.
Scores: Total (200–800).
Administration: Group or individual.
Price Data: Rental fee per student available from publisher.
Time: (60) minutes.
Comments: Available for local administration and scoring by higher educational institutions; previously known as College Board One-Hour Achievement Test in German Reading and College Placement Test.
Author: Educational Testing Service.
Publisher: The College Board.
Cross References: See 7:285 (2 references); for a review by Gilbert C. Kettelkamp of earlier forms, see 6:383; for a review by Harold B. Dunkel, see 5:272; for a review by Herbert Schueler, see 4:244. For a review of an earlier form of the program, see 7:665.

[567]
College Board Institutional SAT II: German with Listening Subject Test.

Purpose: To measure content knowledge in German.
Population: Entering college freshmen.
Publication Dates: 1971–1999.
Scores, 3: Subscores in Listening, Reading (20–80), Total (200–800).

Administration: Group or individual.
Price Data: Rental fee per student available from publisher.
Time: (60) minutes.
Comments: Available for local administration and scoring by higher educational institutions; cassette required; previously known as College Board One-Hour Achievement Test in German with Listening and College Placement Test.
Author: Educational Testing Service.
Publisher: The College Board.
Cross References: See 8:130 (1 reference). For a review of an earlier form of the program, see 7:665.

[568]
College Board Institutional SAT II: Italian Subject Test.

Purpose: To measure content knowledge in Italian.
Population: Entering college freshmen.
Publication Dates: 1962–1999.
Scores: Total (200-800) score only.
Administration: Group or individual.
Price Data: Rental fee per student available from publisher.
Time: (60) minutes.
Comments: Available for local administration and scoring by higher educational institutions; previously known as College Board One-Hour Achievement Test in Italian and College Placement Test.
Author: Educational Testing Service.
Publisher: The College Board.
Cross References: For a review by Paolo Valesio of earlier forms, see 7:300. For a review of an earlier form of the program, see 7:665.

[569]
College Board Institutional SAT II: Japanese with Listening Subject Test.

Purpose: To measure content knowledge in Japanese.
Population: Entering college freshmen.
Publication Dates: 1997–1999.
Scores, 4: Subscores in Listening, Usage, Reading (20–80), and Total (200–800).
Administration: Group or individual.
Price Data: Rental fee per student available from publisher.
Time: (60) minutes.
Comments: Active forms of College Board SAT II: Subject Tests in Japanese with Listening available for local administration and scoring by colleges, universities, and other appropriate organizations; program previously known as College Board One-Hour Achievement Test.
Author: Educational Testing Service.
Publisher: The College Board.
Cross References: For a review of an earlier form of the program, see 7:665.

[570]
College Board Institutional SAT II: Latin Subject Test.

Purpose: To measure content knowledge in Latin.
Population: Entering college freshmen.
Publication Dates: 1962–1999.
Scores: Total (200–800).
Administration: Group or individual.
Price Data: Rental fee per student available from publisher.
Time: (60) minutes.
Comments: Available for local administration and scoring by higher educational institutions; previously known as College Board One-Hour Achievement Test in Latin Reading and College Placement Test.
Author: Educational Testing Service.
Publisher: The College Board.
Cross References: For a review by Konrad Gries of an earlier form, see 5:280; for a review by Harold B. Dunkel, see 4:250. For a review of an earlier form of the program, see 7:665.

[571]
College Board Institutional SAT II: Literature Subject Test.

Purpose: To measure content knowledge in literature.
Population: Entering college freshmen.
Publication Dates: 1968–1999.
Scores: Total (200–800).
Administration: Group or individual.
Price Data: Rental fee per student available from publisher.
Time: (60) minutes.
Comments: Available for local administration and scoring by higher educational institutions; previously known as College Board One-Hour Achievement Test in Literature.
Author: Educational Testing Service.
Publisher: The College Board.
Cross References: For a review of an earlier form of the program, see 7:665.

[572]
College Board Institutional SAT II: Mathematics Level IC Subject Tests, and SAT II: Mathematics Level IIC Subject Tests.

Purpose: To measure content knowledge in mathematics.
Population: Entering college freshmen.
Publication Dates: 1964–1999.
Scores: Total (200–800).
Administration: Group or individual.
Price Data: Rental fee per student available from publisher.

Time: (60) minutes for each level.
Comments: Available for local administration and scoring by higher educational institutions; a calculator at least at the level of a scientific calculator is required to solve some, but not all of the questions; previously known as College Board One-Hour Achievement Test in Mathematics.
Author: Educational Testing Service.
Publisher: The College Board.
Cross References: See T5:585 (1 reference); for a review of an earlier form of the program, see 7:665.

[573]
College Board Institutional SAT II: Modern Hebrew Subject Test.

Purpose: To measure content knowledge in Hebrew.
Population: Entering college freshmen.
Publication Dates: 1962–1999.
Scores: Total (200–800) score only.
Administration: Group or individual.
Price Data: Rental fee per student available from publisher.
Time: (60) minutes.
Comments: Available for local administration and scoring by higher educational institutions; previously known as College Board One-Hour Achievement Test in Modern Hebrew and College Placement Test.
Author: Educational Testing Service.
Publisher: The College Board.
Cross References: For a review of an earlier form of the program, see 7:665.

[574]
College Board Institutional SAT II: Physics Subject Test.

Purpose: To measure content knowledge in physics.
Population: Entering college freshmen.
Publication Dates: 1962–1999.
Scores: Total (200–800).
Administration: Group or individual.
Price Data: Rental fee per student available from publisher.
Time: (60) minutes.
Comments: Available for local administration and scoring by higher educational institutions; previously known as College Board One-Hour Achievement Test in Physics.
Author: Educational Testing Service.
Publisher: The College Board.
Cross References: See T5:587 (1 reference); for a review of an earlier form of the program, see 7:665.

[575]
College Board Institutional SAT II: Spanish Subject Test.

Purpose: To measure content knowledge in Spanish.

Population: Entering college freshmen.
Publication Dates: 1962–1999.
Scores: Total (200–800).
Administration: Group or individual.
Price Data: Rental fee per student available from publisher.
Time: (60) minutes.
Comments: Available for local administration and scoring by higher educational institutions; previously known as College Board One-Hour Achievement Test in Spanish Reading.
Author: Educational Testing Service.
Publisher: The College Board.
Cross References: See 8:161 (1 reference) and 7:316 (1 reference); for a review of an earlier form of the program, see 7:665.

[576]
College Board Institutional SAT II: Spanish with Listening Subject Test.

Purpose: To measure content knowledge in Spanish.
Population: Entering college freshmen.
Publication Dates: 1971–1999.
Scores, 3: Subscores in Listening, Reading (20–80), Total (200–800).
Administration: Group or individual.
Price Data: Rental fee per student available from publisher.
Time: (60) minutes.
Comments: Available for local administration and scoring by higher educational institutions; cassette required; previously known as College Board One-Hour Achievement Test in Spanish with Listening and College Placement Test.
Author: Educational Testing Service.
Publisher: The College Board.
Cross References: For a review of an earlier form of the program, see 7:665.

[577]
College Board Institutional SAT II: World History Subject Test.

Purpose: To measure content knowledge in World History.
Population: Entering college freshmen.
Publication Dates: 1963–1999.
Scores: Total (200–800).
Administration: Group or individual.
Price Data: Rental fee per student available from publisher.
Time: (60) minutes.
Comments: Available for local administration and scoring by higher educational institutions; previously known as College Board One-Hour Achievement Test in World History.
Author: Educational Testing Service.

Publisher: The College Board.
Cross References: For a review by David K. Heenan of an earlier form, see 6:967; for a review of an earlier form of the program, see 7:665.

[578]
College Board Institutional SAT II: Writing Subject Test.

Purpose: To measure students' writing skills.
Population: Entering college freshmen.
Publication Dates: 1962–1999.
Scores: Subscores in Multiple Choice, Writing Sample (20–80), Total (200–800).
Administration: Group or individual.
Price Data: Rental fee per student available from publisher.
Time: (60) minutes (20-minute essay and 40-minute multiple-choice).
Comments: Administration and scoring by higher educational institutions; previously known as College Board One-Hour Achievement Test in Writing and College Placement Test; includes a writing sample and multiple-choice questions.
Author: Educational Testing Service.
Publisher: The College Board.
Cross References: See 8:48 (20 references); for a review by John C. Sherwood of an earlier form, see 7:190 (3 references); for reviews by Charlotte Croon Davis, Robert C. Pooley, and Holland Roberts of earlier forms, see 6:287; for a review by Charlotte Croon Davis with Frederick B. Davis, see 4:178. For a review of an earlier form of the program, see 7:665.

[579]
College Board On-Campus Tests.

Purpose: A portfolio of assessments, programs, and services designed to help higher education personnel determine the placement levels and remediation requirements of incoming, as well as continuing, students.
Population: Entering and continuing college students.
Publication Dates: 1989–2001.
Scores: Provides data in the following assessment areas: Course Placement, Remediation, Selection, Instruction, Guidance, and Counseling. Also used for Exemption by some institutions of higher education
Administration: Group or individual.
Price Data: Available from publisher.
Comments: Through its On-Campus Testing Program, the College Board offers institutions of higher education the following: Descriptive Tests System (DTS) (558), Institutional SAT Program (2175), Test of Standard Written English (two forms), Essay Reading Service, and special contracts for state departments of education and consortia of higher education institu-

tions; previously entitled Multiple Assessments, Programs, and Services (MAPS) of the College Board.
Author: Educational Testing Service.
Publisher: Educational Testing Service and the College Board.
Cross References: See T5:1746 (1 reference).

[580]
College Board SAT I Reasoning Test.

Purpose: To measure "the developed verbal and mathematical reasoning abilities related to successful performance in college."
Population: Candidates for college entrance.
Publication Dates: 1926–1999.
Acronym: SAT I.
Scores, 2: Verbal, Math (reported on the College Board 200–800 scale).
Administration: Group.
Forms: Forms issued annually.
Price Data: Examination fees per candidate available from publisher. Price data for guidelines on the uses of College Board test scores and related data, guide to the College Board Admitted Student Evaluation Service (formerly the Validity Study Service), technical handbook, SAT Program handbooks, student bulletins, Taking the SAT I, test and technical data, SAT I Question and Answer Service, SAT I Student Answer Service, SAT Score Verification Service, and clerical scoring service are all available from the publisher.
Time: (180) minutes.
Comments: The SAT I is administered 7 times annually (January, March or April, May, June, October, November, and December) at centers established by the publisher. The SAT I: Reasoning Test replaced the College Board Scholastic Aptitude Test and Test of Standard Written English in 1994. Scores are reported for Verbal and Mathematical sections of the SAT I. Performance data by item type/content are available for Verbal and Math beginning in 1994. The SAT I scale was rescaled in 1995; equivalence tables are available for converting scores from one scale to another. SAT I forms are available for local administration and scoring through the College Entry-Level Assessment (CELA) Program. Special administration arrangements available for students with disabilities, including Braille, cassette tape, regular type and large-type formats, individualized testing, and additional testing time.
Authors: The College Board and Educational Testing Service.
Publisher: The College Board.
Cross References: See T5:592 (107 references) and T4:564 (167 references); for reviews by Sanford J. Cohn and Lee J. Cronbach of an earlier edition, see 9:244 (31 references); see T3:501 (152 references), 8:182 (217 references), and T2:357 (148 references); for reviews by Philip H. Dubois and Wimburn L.

Wallace of an earlier form, see 7:344 (298 references); for reviews by John E. Bowers and Wayne S. Zimmerman, see 6:449 (79 references); for a review by John T. Dailey, see 5:318 (20 references); for a review by Frederick B. Davis, see 4:285 (22 references). For reviews of the testing program, see 6:760 (2 reviews).

[581]
College Board SAT II: American History and Social Studies Subject Test.

Purpose: To measure content knowledge in American history and social studies.
Population: Candidates for college entrance with one-year American history course at the college-preparatory level.
Publication Dates: 1937–1999.
Scores: Total scores reported on the College Board 200–800 scale, subscores reported on a 20–80 scale; ELPT total score reported on a 901–999 scale; ELPT subscores reported on a 1–50 scale.
Administration: Group.
Price Data: Available from publisher.
Time: Administration time not reported.
Comments: Test administered 6 times annually (January, May, June, October, November, December) at centers established by publisher; available for local administration and scoring by higher educational institutions through the College Entry-Level Assessment (CELA) programs; replaces College Board Achievement Test in American History and Social Studies.
Authors: Program administered by The College Board and Educational Testing Service.
Publisher: The College Board.
Cross References: See T4:565 (1 reference) and T2:1939 (1 reference); for a review by Howard R. Anderson of earlier forms, see 6:966; for a review by Ralph W. Tyler, see 5:786 (3 references); for a review by Robert L. Thorndike, see 4:662 (6 references). For reviews of an earlier form of the testing program, see 6:760 (2 reviews).

[582]
College Board SAT II: Biology E/M Subject Test.

Purpose: To measure content knowledge in biology.
Population: Candidates for college entrance with one-year courses in biology and algebra.
Publication Dates: 1998–1999.
Scores: Total score only.
Administration: Group.
Price Data: Available from publisher.
Time: Administration time not reported.
Comments: Administered 6 times annually beginning in 1999 (October, November, December, January, May, and June) at centers established by publisher; candidates take a core set of questions and then select

a specialized section of questions in either ecological or molecular biology; available for local administration and scoring by higher educational institutions through the College Entry-Level Assessment (CELA) Program; replaces College Board SAT II: Subject Test in Biology.
Authors: Program administered by the College Board and Educational Testing Service.
Publisher: The College Board.

[583]
College Board SAT II: Biology Subject Test.

Purpose: To measure content knowledge in biology.
Population: Candidates for college entrance with one-year courses in biology and algebra.
Publication Dates: 1915–1999.
Scores: Total (200–800).
Administration: Group.
Price Data: Available from publisher.
Time: Administration time not reported.
Comments: Test administered for the last time in May 1999 at centers established by publisher; available for local administration and scoring by higher educational institutions through the College Entry-Level Assessment (CELA) Program; replaces College Board Achievement Test in Biology.
Authors: Program administered by the College Board and Educational Testing Service.
Publisher: The College Board.
Cross References: See 8:833 (1 reference), 7:813 (2 references), and 6:892 (3 references); for a review by Elizabeth Hagen of an earlier form, see 5:723; for a review by Clark W. Horton, see 4:600. For reviews of an earlier form of the testing program, see 6:760 (2 reviews).

[584]
College Board SAT II: Chemistry Subject Test.

Purpose: To measure content knowledge in chemistry.
Population: Candidates for college entrance with one-year course in introductory chemistry at the college-preparatory level.
Publication Dates: 1937–1999.
Scores: Total (200–800) score only.
Administration: Group.
Price Data: Available from publisher.
Time: Administration time not reported.
Comments: Test administered 6 times annually (January, May, June, October, November, December) at centers established by publisher; available for local administration and scoring by higher educational institutions through the College Entry-Level Assessment (CELA) Program.
Authors: Program administered by the College Board and Educational Testing Service.

Publisher: The College Board.
Cross References: See T4:567 (1 reference and 7:844 (3 references); for a review by William Hered of earlier forms, see 6:914 (4 references); for a review by Max D. Engelhart, see 5:742 (2 references); for a review by Evelyn Raskin, see 4:617 (4 references). For reviews of an earlier form of the testing program, see 6:760 (2 reviews).

[585]
College Board SAT II: English Language Proficiency Test.

Purpose: To measure understanding of spoken and written standard American English and ability to use English in the classroom and in daily life.
Population: Candidates for college entrance who attend American high schools and who are not native speakers of English, but have completed two to four years of English Language instruction in an English as Second Language program or English enrichment courses and/or whose best language is not English and/or who usually speak a language other than English at home or at work.
Publication Dates: 1997–1999.
Acronym: ELPT.
Scores: 3 subscores in Listening, Reading (1–50), and Total (901–999); in addition proficiency ratings (below intermediate to advanced high or higher) are provided for Listening and Reading.
Administration: Group.
Price Data: Available from publisher.
Time: Administration time not reported.
Comments: Test administered once annually (November) at centers established by the publisher; also administered once annually (April) in participating high schools; test takers are required to bring a cassette player with earphones for use on the Listening section of the test; available for local administration and scoring by higher-educational institutions through the College Entry-Level Assessment (CELA) Program.
Authors: Program administered by the College Board and Educational Testing Service.
Publisher: The College Board.

[586]
College Board SAT II: French Subject Test.
Purpose: To measure content knowledge in French.
Population: Candidates for college entrance with 3–4 years high school French.
Publication Dates: 1937–1999.
Scores: Total (200–800) score only.
Administration: Group.
Price Data: Available from publisher.
Time: Administration time not reported.
Comments: Test administered 5 times annually (January, May, June, October, December) at centers established by publisher; available for local administra-

tion and scoring by higher educational institutions through the College Entry-Level Assessment (CELA) Program; replaces College Board Achievement Test in French
Authors: Program administered by the College Board and Educational Testing Service.
Publisher: The College Board.
Cross References: For a review by Helen L. Jorstad of an earlier form, see 8:116; see also 6:366 (4 references) and 5:263 (2 references); for a review by Walter V. Kaulfers of earlier forms, see 4:237 (7 references). For reviews of an earlier form of the testing program, see 6:760 (2 reviews).

[587]
College Board SAT II: French with Listening Subject Test.
Purpose: To measure content knowledge in French.
Population: Candidates for college entrance with 3–4 years high school French.
Publication Dates: 1994–1999.
Scores: 3 subscores in Listening, Reading (20–80), and Total (200–800).
Administration: Group.
Price Data: Available from publisher.
Time: Administration time not reported.
Comments: Test administered once annually (November) at centers established by publisher; test takers are required to bring a cassette player with earphones for use on the Listening section of the test; available for local administration and scoring by higher educational institutions through the College Entry-Level Assessment (CELA) Program.
Authors: Program administered by the College Board and Educational Testing Service.
Publisher: The College Board.

[588]
College Board SAT II: German Subject Test.
Purpose: To measure content knowledge in German.
Population: Candidates for college entrance with 2–4 years high school German.
Publication Dates: 1937–1999.
Scores: Total (200–800) score only.
Administration: Group.
Price Data: Available from publisher.
Time: Administration time not reported.
Comments: Test administered once annually (June) at centers established by publisher; available for local administration and scoring by higher educational institutions through the College Entry-Level Assessment (CELA) Program; replaces College Board Achievement Test in German.
Authors: Program administered by the College Board and Educational Testing Service.

Publisher: The College Board.
Cross References: For a review by Randall L. Jones of an earlier form, see 8:128; for a review by Gilbert C. Kettelkamp of earlier forms, see 6:383; for a review by Harold B. Dunkel, see 5:272 (3 references); for a review by Herbert Shueler, see 4:244 (3 references). For reviews of an earlier form of the testing program, see 6:760 (2 reviews).

[589]
College Board SAT II: German with Listening Subject Test.

Purpose: To measure content knowledge in German.
Population: Candidates for college entrance with 2–4 years in high school German.
Publication Dates: 1994–1999.
Scores: 3 subscores in Listening, Reading (20–80), and Total (200–800).
Administration: Group.
Price Data: Available from publisher.
Time: Administration time not reported.
Comments: Test administered once annually (November) at centers established by publisher; test takers are required to bring a cassette player with earphones for use on the Listening section of the test; available for local administration and scoring by higher educational institutions through the College Entry-Level Assessment (CELA) Program.
Authors: Program administered by the College Board and Educational Testing Service.
Publisher: The College Board.

[590]
College Board SAT II: Korean with Listening Subject Test.

Purpose: To measure content knowledge in Korean.
Population: Candidates for college entrance with 2–4 years high school Korean.
Publication Dates: 1994–1999.
Scores: 4 subscores: Usage, Listening, Reading (20–80), Total (200–800).
Administration: Group.
Price Data: Available from publisher.
Time: Administration time not reported.
Comments: Test administered once annually (November) at centers established by publisher; test takers are required to bring a cassette player with earphones for use on the Listening section of the test.
Authors: Program administered by the College Board and Educational Testing Service.
Publisher: The College Board.

[591]
College Board SAT II: Latin Subject Test.

Purpose: To measure content knowledge in Latin.

Population: Candidates for college entrance with 2–4 years high school Latin.
Publication Dates: 1937–1999.
Scores: Total score only.
Administration: Group.
Price Data: Available from publisher.
Time: Administration time not reported.
Comments: Test administered 2 times annually (January, December) at centers established by publisher; available for local administration and scoring by higher educational institutions through the College Entry-Level Assessment (CELA) Program; replaces College Board Achievement Test in Latin.
Authors: Program administered by the College Board and Educational Testing Service.
Publisher: The College Board.
Cross References: For a review by Konrad Gries of an earlier form, see 5:280 (1 reference); for a review by Harold B. Dunkel, see 4:250 (2 references). For reviews of an earlier form of the testing program, see 6:760 (2 reviews).

[592]
College Board SAT II: Literature Subject Test.

Purpose: To measure content knowledge in Literature.
Population: Candidates for college entrance.
Publication Dates: 1968–1999.
Scores: Total (200–800) score only.
Administration: Group.
Price Data: Available from publisher.
Time: Administration time not reported.
Comments: Test administered 6 times annually (January, May, June, October, November, December) at centers established by publisher; available for local administration and scoring by higher educational institutions through the College Entry-Level Assessment (CELA) Program; replaces College Board Achievement Test in Literature.
Authors: Program administered by the College Board and Educational Testing Service.
Publisher: The College Board.
Cross References: See T5:604 (1 reference) and 7:217 (2 references). For reviews of an earlier form of the testing program, see 6:760 (2 reviews).

[593]
College Board SAT II: Mathematics Level IC and SAT II: Mathematics Level IIC.

Purpose: To measure content knowledge in mathematics.
Population: Candidates for college entrance.
Publication Dates: 1937–1999.
Scores: Total (200–800) score only.
Administration: Group.

Price Data: Available from publisher.

Time: Administration time not reported.

Comments: For Math Level IC, administered to candidates with 3 years of college-preparatory math (2 years algebra, 1 year of geometry); for Math Level IIC, administered to candidates with more than 3 years of college-preparatory Math (2 years algebra, 1 year geometry, and precalculus and/or trigonometry); test administered 6 times annually (January, May, June, October, November, December) at centers established by publisher; a calculator at least at the level of a scientific calculator is required to solve some, but not all, of the questions; available for local administration and scoring by higher educational institutions through the College Entry-Level Assessment (CELA) Program; replaces College Board Achievement Tests in Mathematics, the final administration of the Math Level 2 test was January 1994; it was replaced by the Math Level IIC Subject Test at all administrations beginning in May 1994; the final administration of Math Level 1 test was January 1998; it was replaced by the Math Level IC Subject Test at all administrations beginning May 1998.

Authors: Program administered by the College Board and Educational Testing Service.

Publisher: The College Board.

Cross References: See T4:578 (2 references); for reviews by Jeremy Kilpatrick and Peter A. Lappan, Jr. of Level 1, see 8:258 (4 references); see also 7:456 (4 references). For additional information concerning Level 2, see 8:259 (1 reference); see also 7:457 (1 reference). For reviews of an earlier form of the testing program, see 6:760 (2 reviews).

[594]
College Board SAT II: Modern Hebrew Subject Test.

Purpose: To measure content knowledge in Modern Hebrew.

Population: Candidates for college entrance with 2–4 years high school Hebrew.

Publication Dates: 1989–1999.

Scores: Total (200–800) score only.

Administration: Group.

Price Data: Available from publisher.

Time: Administration time not reported.

Comments: Test administered once annually (June) at centers established by publisher; available for local administration and scoring by higher educational institutions through the College Entry-Level Assessment (CELA) Program; replaces College Board Achievement Test in Hebrew.

Authors: Program administered by the College Board and Educational Testing Service.

Publisher: The College Board.

Cross References: For reviews of an earlier form of the testing program, see 6:760 (2 reviews).

[595]
College Board SAT II: Physics Subject Test.

Purpose: To measure content knowledge in physics.

Population: Candidates for college entrance with one-year course in introductory physics at the college-preparatory level.

Publication Dates: 1937–1999.

Scores: Total (200–800) score only.

Administration: Group.

Price Data: Available from publisher.

Time: Administration time not reported.

Comments: Test administered 6 times annually (January, May, June, October, November, December) at centers established by publisher; available for local administration and scoring by higher educational institutions through the College Entry-Level Assessment (CELA) Program; replaces College Board Achievement Test in Physics.

Authors: Program administered by the College Board and Educational Testing Service.

Publisher: The College Board.

Cross References: See T4:574 (2 reference, 8:863 (1 reference), 7:855 (2 references), and 6:926 (4 references); for a review by Theodore G. Phillips of an earlier form, see 5:749 (2 references); for a review by Palmer O. Johnson, see 4:633 (3 references). For reviews of an earlier form of the testing program, see 6:760 (2 reviews).

[596]
College Board SAT II: Spanish Subject Test.

Purpose: To measure content knowledge in Spanish.

Population: Candidates for college entrance with 3–4 years high school Spanish.

Publication Dates: 1937–1999.

Scores: Total (200–800) score only.

Administration: Group.

Price Data: Available from publisher.

Time: Administration time not reported.

Comments: Test administered 5 times annually (January, May, June, October, December) at centers established by publisher; available for local administration and scoring by higher educational institutions through the College Entry-Level Assessment (CELA) Program; replaces College Board Achievement Test in Spanish.

Authors: Program administered by the College Board and Educational Testing Service.

Publisher: The College Board.

Cross References: See 6:419 (1 reference), 5:287 (1 reference), and 4:259 (3 references) for information on earlier forms. For reviews of an earlier form of the testing program, see 6:760 (2 reviews).

[597]
College Board SAT II: Spanish with Listening Subject Test.

Purpose: To measure content knowledge in Spanish.
Population: Candidates for college entrance with 3–4 years high school Spanish.
Publication Dates: 1994–1999.
Scores: 3 subscores in Listening, Reading (20–80), Total (200–800).
Administration: Group.
Price Data: Available from publisher.
Time: Administration time not reported.
Comments: Test administered once annually (November) at centers established by publisher; test takers required to bring a cassette player with earphones for use on the Listening section of the test; available for local administration and scoring by higher educational institutions through the College Entry-Level Assessment (CELA) Program.
Authors: Program administered by the College Board and Educational Testing Service.
Publisher: The College Board.

[598]
College Board SAT II: Subject Test in Chinese with Listening.

Purpose: To measure content knowledge in Chinese.
Population: Candidates for college entrance with 2–4 years high school Chinese (Mandarin).
Publication Dates: 1994–1999.
Scores, 4: Usage, Listening, Reading, Total.
Administration: Group.
Price Data: Available from publisher.
Comments: Test administered once annually (November) at centers established by publisher; test takers are required to bring a cassette player with earphones for use on the Listening section of the test; available for local administration and scoring by higher educational institutions through the College Entry-Level Assessment (CELA) Program.
Authors: Program administered by the College Board and Educational Testing Service.
Publisher: The College Board.

[599]
College Board SAT II: Subject Test in Italian.

Purpose: To measure content knowledge in Italian.
Population: Candidates for college entrance with 2–4 years high school Italian.
Publication Dates: 1990–1999.
Scores: Total score only (200–800).
Administration: Group.
Price Data: Available from publisher.
Comments: Test administered once annually (December) at centers established by publisher; available for local administration and scoring by higher educational institutions through the College Entry-Level Assessment (CELA) Program; replaces College Board Achievement Test in Italian.
Authors: Program administered by the College Board and Educational Testing Service.
Publisher: The College Board.

[600]
College Board SAT II:Subject Test in Japanese with Listening.

Purpose: To measure content knowledge in Japanese.
Population: Candidates for college entrance with 2–4 years high school Japanese.
Publication Dates: 1993–1999.
Scores, 4: Usage, Listening, Reading, Total.
Administration: Group.
Price Data: Available from publisher.
Comments: Test administered once annually (November) at centers established by the publisher; test takers required to bring a cassette player with earphones for use on the Listening section of the test; available for local administration and scoring by higher educational institutions through the College Entry-Level Assessment (CELA) Program.
Authors: Program administered by the College Board and Educational Testing Service.
Publisher: The College Board.

[601]
College Board SAT II: World History Subject Test.

Purpose: To measure content knowledge in world history.
Population: Candidates for college entrance with one-year course in world or global history, world cultures or area studies, or European history taught against a global background.
Publication Dates: 1937–1999.
Scores: Total (200–800) only.
Administration: Group.
Price Data: Available from publisher.
Time: Administration time not reported.
Comments: Test administered 2 times annually (June, December) at centers established by publisher; available for local administration and scoring by higher educational institutions through the College Entry-Level Assessment (CELA) Program; replaces College Board Achievement Test in European History and World Cultures.
Authors: Program administered by the College Board and Educational Testing Service.
Publisher: The College Board.
Cross References: For a review by David K. Heenan of an earlier form, see 6:967. For reviews of an earlier form of the testing program, see 6:760 (2 reviews).

[602]
College Board SAT II: Writing Subject Test.

Purpose: To measure students' writing skills.
Population: Candidates for college entrance.
Publication Dates: 1943–1999.
Scores: 3 subscores: Multiple Choice, Writing Sample (20–80), Total (200–800).
Administration: Group.
Price Data: Available from publisher.
Time: Administration time not reported.
Comments: Test administered 6 times annually (January, May, June, October, November, December) at centers established by publisher; test consists of 40 minutes of multiple-choice questions and 20 minutes writing on an assigned topic; available for local administration and scoring by higher educational institutions through the College Entry-Level Assessment (CELA) Program; replaces College Board English Composition Test.
Authors: Program administered by the College Board and Educational Testing Service.
Publisher: The College Board.
Cross References: See T5:614 (1 reference) and T4:580 (2 references); for reviews by Dale P. Scannell and John C. Sherwood of an earlier form, see 9:243. For reviews on the College Board Achievement Test in English Composition (without essay) by David P. Harris and Leo P. Ruth, see 8:46 (2 references); see also T2:64 (1 reference) and 7:188 (10 references); for reviews by Charlotte Croon Davis, Robert C. Pooley, and Holland Roberts of earlier forms, see 6:287 (6 references); see also 5:204 (14 references); for a review by Charlotte Croon Davis with Frederick B. Davis, see 4:178 (6 references). For reviews of an earlier form of the testing program, see 6:760 (2 reviews).

[603]
College Board SAT Program.

Purpose: To provide "tests and related educational services for students who plan to continue their education beyond high school."
Population: Candidates for college entrance.
Publication Dates: 1901–1999.
Acronym: SAT Program.
Administration: Group.
Price Data: Price data is available from the publisher for priced and free materials including technical report (1984, 225 pages), supervisor's manual (1998, 69 pages), student bulletins, test familiarization material for students, score use and interpretation booklets for counselors and admissions officers, summary report guides for high schools and for colleges, state and national reports on college-bound seniors, guide to the College Board Admitted Student Evaluation Service (formerly Validity Study Service), and test and technical data; examination fees include reporting of scores to the candidate's secondary school and 1–4 colleges and/or scholarship services.
Comments: Formerly called the College Board Admissions Testing Program; the SAT I: Reasoning Test is administered 7 times annually (January, March or April, May, June, October, November, December) at centers established by the publisher; The SAT II: Subject Tests are administered 6 times annually (January, May, June, October, November, December) at centers established by the publisher, though not all tests are available at each administration; English Language Proficiency Test (ELPT) is also offered in April in participating secondary schools; Student Descriptive Questionnaire provides background information to colleges and scholarship services; special administration arrangements available for students with disabilities, including Braille, cassette tape, regular type, and large-type formats, individualized testing, and additional testing time. The SAT I and SAT II score scales were rescaled in 1995; equivalence tables are available for converting scores from the original scale to the new recentered scale. SAT I and SAT II forms are available for local administration and scoring by higher educational institutions through the College Entry-Level Assessment (CELA) Program.
Author: Educational Testing Service.
Publisher: Educational Testing Service and the College Board.

a) COLLEGE BOARD SAT I: REASONING TEST.
Publication Dates: 1926–1999.
Acronym: SAT I.
Price Data: Examination fee per candidate available from publisher. Price data for guidelines on the uses of College Board test scores and related data, guide to the College Board Admitted Student Evaluation Service (formerly the Validity Study Service), Technical Handbook, SAT Program Handbooks, Student Bulletins, Taking the SAT I, test preparation materials and software, SAT I Question and Answer Service, SAT I Student Answer Service, SAT Score Verification Service, and clerical scoring service are all available from the publisher.
Time: (180) minutes.
Comments: The SAT I: Reasoning Test replaced the College Board Scholastic Aptitude Test and the Test of Standard Written English in 1994. Scores are reported for Verbal and Mathematical sections of the SAT I. No subscores are provided. Performance data by item type/content available for Verbal and Mathematics beginning in 1994.

b) COLLEGE BOARD SAT II: SUBJECT TESTS.
Publication Dates: 1901–1999.
Scores: 21 tests in 18 subjects: Writing (including an essay at every national administration), Literature, American History & Social Studies,

World History, Mathematics [Math Level IC, Math Level IIC], Biology E/M [Ecological/Molecular], Chemistry, Physics, French (reading only), French (reading and listening), German (reading only), German (reading and listening), Spanish (reading only), Spanish (reading and listening), Modern Hebrew, Italian, Latin, Japanese (reading and listening), Chinese (reading and listening), Korean (reading and listening), and English Language Proficiency.

Price Data: Examination fees per candidate available from publisher. Price data for guidelines on the uses of College Board test scores and related data, guide to the College Board Admitted Student Evaluation Service (formerly the Validity Study Service), Writing Sample Copy Service, technical handbook, SAT Program Handbooks, student bulletins, Taking the SAT II, test and preparation materials, and clerical scoring service are all available from the publisher.

Time: (60) minutes.

Comments: Formerly called the College Board Achievement Tests; candidate elects 1 to 3 tests as specified by individual college or scholarship program requirements; candidates have the option of reviewing their SAT II scores prior to deciding whether or not to have these scores reported to colleges or scholarship services. The administration schedule of each Subject Test is available from the publisher.

Cross References: See T5:615 (55 references), T3:500 (3 references), 8:472 (6 references), T2:1048 (9 references), and 7:663 (16 references); for reviews by Benno G. Fricke and Dean K. Whitla of an earlier program, see 6:760 (12 references); see also 5:599 (3 references) and 4:526 (9 references). For reviews of individual tests, see 8:46 (2 reviews), 8:128 (1 review), 8:147 (1 review), 8:258 (2 reviews), 7:344 (2 reviews), 6:287 (3 reviews, 6:289 (1 review), 6:383 (1 review), 6:384 (2 reviews), 6:449 (2 reviews), 6:568 (1 review), 6:569 (1 review), 6:914 (1 review), 6:966 (1 review), 6:967 (1 review), 5:272 (1 review), 5:277 (1 review), 5:280 (1 review), 5:318 (1 review), 5:723 (1 review), 5:742 (1 review), 5:749 (1 review), 5:786 (1 review), 4:178 (1 review), 4:237 (1 review), 4:244 (1 review), 4:250 (1 review), 4:285 (1 review), 4:367 (1 review), 4:368 (1 review), 4:600 (1 review), 4:617 (1 review), 4:633 (1 review), and 4:662 (1 review).

[604]
College English Test: National Achievement Tests.

Purpose: Designed to measure the student's mastery of elements of the English language.

Population: High school and college freshmen.

Publication Dates: 1937–1943.

Scores, 7: Punctuation, Capitalization, Language Usage, Sentence Structure, Modifiers, Miscellaneous Principles, Total.

Administration: Group.

Forms, 2: A, B.

Price Data: Available from publisher.

Time: 45(50) minutes.

Author: A. C. Jordan.

Publisher: Psychometric Affiliates.

Cross References: For a review by Osmond E. Palmer, see 5:178; for reviews by Constance M. McCullough and Robert W. Howard, see 2:1269.1.

[605]
College Level Examination Program.

Purpose: Designed as a way for college accreditation, advanced placement, or assessment of educational attainment.

Population: 1–2 years of college or equivalent.

Publication Dates: 1964–2002.

Acronym: CLEP.

Price Data: Available from publisher.

Time: (90) minutes per test.

Comments: Tests administered at 1,100 centers throughout the United States as well as internationally; as of July, 2001 administered as a computer-based program; program administered by the College Board and Educational Testing Service.

Author: Educational Testing Service.

Publisher: Educational Testing Service.

a) BUSINESS.
    1) *Information Systems and Computer Applications.*
    2) *Principles of Management.*
    3) *Principles of Accounting.*
    4) *Introductory Business Law.*
    5) *Principles of Marketing.*

b) COMPOSITION AND LITERATURE

Comments: Composition and Literature tests have optional essay supplement that is scored by the college.
    1) *American Literature.*
    2) *Analyzing and Interpreting Literature.*
    3) *Freshman College Composition.*
    4) *English Literature.*
    5) *English Composition (with and without essay).*
Comments: English Composition with Essay scored by faculty for CLEP.
    6) *Humanities.*

c) FOREIGN LANGUAGES
    1) *College French, Levels 1 and 2.*
    2) *College German, Levels 1 and 2.*
    3) *College Spanish, Levels 1 and 2.*

d) HISTORY AND SOCIAL SCIENCES
    1) *American Government.*
    2) *History of the United States I: Early Colonization to 1877.*

3) *History of the United States II: 1865 to the Present.*
4) *Educational Psychology.*
5) *Introductory Psychology.*
6) *Human Growth and Development.*
7) *Principles of Macroeconomics.*
8) *Principles of Microeconomics.*
9) *Introductory Sociology.*
10) *Western Civilization I: Ancient Near East to 1648.*
11) *Western Civilization II: 1648 to the Present.*
12) *Social Sciences and History.*
e) SCIENCE AND MATHEMATICS.
1) *Calculus with Elementary Functions.*
2) *College Algebra.*
3) *College Algebra—Trigonometry.*
4) *General Biology.*
5) *General Chemistry.*
6) *Trigonometry.*
7) *Mathematics.*
8) *Natural Sciences.*

Cross References: See 9:245 (1 reference) and T3:506 (7 references); for reviews by Paul L. Dressel, David A. Frisbie, and Wimburn L. Wallace of an earlier program, see 8:473 (15 references); for reviews of the General Examinations, see 8:8 (2 reviews); for reviews of the separate Subject Examinations, see 8:43 (1 review), 8:44 (1 review), 8:64 (1 review), 8:65 (1 review), 8:66 (1 review), 8:255 (1 review), 8:256 (1 review), 8:297 (1 review), 8:365 (1 review), 8:460 (1 review), 8:832 (1 review), 8:847 (1 review), 8:911 (1 review), , 8:919 (1 review), 8:1119 (1 review), and 8:1120 (1 review); see also T2:1050 (4 references); for reviews by Alexander W. Astin, Benjamin S. Bloom, and Warren G. Findley, see 7:664 (7 references).

[606]
College Student Expectations Questionnaire, Second Edition.

Purpose: Designed to evaluate new students' expectations for college including their goals, motivations, and future plans for college experiences.
Population: Precollege students and first-year students early in the first semester.
Publication Dates: 1997–2002.
Acronym: CSXQ.
Scores, 16: Background Information, College Activities Scales (Library and Information Technology, Experiences with Faculty, Course Learning, Writing, Campus Facilities, Clubs, Organizations, Service Projects, Student Acquaintances, Scientific and Quantitative Experiences, Conversations), Reading/Writing, Satisfaction, The College Environment, Additional Questions.
Administration: Group.

Price Data, 2002: $.75 per questionnaire; $1.50 per questionnaire processing; $125 participation fee including student responses, scores, and a summary report of the results; $100 per hour for special additional analysis.
Time: (10–15) minutes.
Comments: Adapted from the College Student Experiences Questionnaire (SEQ; 607); longitudinal assessments are possible by comparing results from the CSXQ with data from the CSEQ completed by the same students near the end of the first year or later in the college experience.
Authors: George D. Kuh and C. Robert Pace.
Publisher: Indiana University Center for the Study of Postsecondary Research and Planning, Bloomington.

[607]
College Student Experiences Questionnaire, Fourth Edition.

Purpose: Designed to measure (a) the quality of effort undergraduate students invest in using educational resources and opportunities provided for their learning and development, (b) the students' perceptions of how much the campus environment emphasizes a diverse set of educational priorities, and (c) how the students' efforts and perceptions relate to personal estimates of progress made toward a holistic set of learning outcomes.
Population: Undergraduate college students.
Publication Dates: 1979–2002.
Acronym: CSEQ.
Scores, 19: Background Information, College Activities Scales (Library, Computer and Information Technology, Course Learning, Writing Experiences, Experiences with Faculty, Art, Music and Theater, Campus Facilities, Clubs and Organizations, Personal Experiences, Student Acquaintances, Scientific and Quantitative Experiences, Conversations), Reading/Writing, Satisfaction, The College Environment, Estimate of Gains, Additional Questions.
Administration: Group.
Price Data, 2002: 2002 price data: $.75 per questionnaire; $1.50 per questionnaire processing; $125 participation fee (including student responses, scores, and a summary report of the results); $15 per Norms and Psychometric Properties for the Four Edition (2002, 120 pages); $100 per hour for special additional analysis.
Time: (30–40) minutes.
Authors: C. Robert Pace and George D. Kuh.
Publisher: Indiana University Center for the Study of Postsecondary Research and Planning, Bloomington.
Cross References: See T5:620 (6 references) and T4:588 (4 references); for reviews by David A. Decoster and Susan McCammon of an earlier edition, see 10:67; for reviews by Robert D. Brown and John K. Miller, see 9:246 (1 reference).

[608]
College Student Inventory [part of the Retention Management System].

Purpose: Designed to assess "a variety of motives and background information related to college success," improved student retention, and enhancing student advising effectiveness.
Population: Candidates for college entrance.
Publication Date: 1988.
Acronym: CSI.
Scores: 4 Domains: Academic Motivation (Study Habits, Intellectual Interests, Academic Confidence, Desire to Finish College, Attitude Toward Educators), Social Motivation (Self-Reliance, Sociability, Leadership), General Coping Ability (Ease of Transition, Family Emotional Support, Openness, Career Planning, Sense of Financial Security), Receptivity to Support Services (Academic Assistance, Personal Counseling, Social Enhancement, Career Counseling).
Administration: Group.
Price Data: Available from publisher.
Time: (60) minutes.
Author: Michael L. Stratil.
Publisher: Noel-Levitz.

[609]
Collegiate Assessment of Academic Proficiency.

Purpose: Designed to assess selected academic skills typically obtained in a core general education curriculum.
Population: Freshmen–Seniors in college.
Publication Dates: 1989–2991.
Acronym: CAAP.
Administration: Group.
Restricted Distribution: Available to institutions signing a participation agreement and paying a participation fee.
Price Data, 2001: $330 per year institutional participation fee; test module prices (including scoring and reporting) available from publisher.
Time: 40 minutes per test.
Author: ACT, Inc.
Publisher: ACT, Inc.
a) WRITING SKILLS.
Publication Date: 1998.
Scores, 3: Usage/Mechanics, Rhetorical Skills, Total.
b) MATHEMATICS.
Publication Date: 1989.
Scores, 3: Basic Algebra, College Algebra, Total.
c) READING.
Publication Date: 1989.
Scores, 3: Arts/Literature, Social Studies/Sciences, Total.

d) CRITICAL THINKING.
Publication Date: 1989.
Scores: Total score only.
e) SCIENCE REASONING.
Publication Date: 1989.
Scores: Total score only.
f) WRITING (ESSAY).
Publication Date: 1990.
Scores: Total score only.
Comments: Total of 3 individual essays.
Cross References: See T5:621 (2 references); for reviews by Steven V. Owen and Jeffrey K. Smith, see 13:74 (3 references); see also T4:589 (1 reference).

[610]
Collis-Romberg Mathematical Problem Solving Profiles.

Purpose: Assesses student progress through a variety of mathematical problem-solving skills.
Population: Ages 9–13, 13–17.
Publication Date: 1992.
Scores, 6: Number, Algebra, Space, Measurement, Chance and Data, Total.
Administration: Group.
Levels, 2: Junior, Senior.
Price Data, 2002: A $66 per complete set including profiles A and B, and manual (72 pages); A$20.90 per manual.
Time: (40–50) minutes.
Comments: Junior version (ages 9–13) uses Parts A to C of each question; Senior version (ages 13–17) uses Parts A to D of each question.
Authors: K. F. Collis and T. A. Romberg.
Publisher: Australian Council for Educational Research Ltd. [Australia].
Cross References: For reviews by John W. Fleenor and Judith A. Monsaas, see 12:85.

[611]
Color Trails Test.

Purpose: Designed as a test of sustained visual attention and simple sequencing.
Population: Ages 18 and over.
Publication Dates: 1994–1996.
Acronym: CTT.
Scores, 10: Color Trails 1, Color Trails 1 Errors, Color Trails 1 Near-Misses, Color Trails 1 Prompts, Color Trails 2, Color Trails 2 Color Errors, Color Trails 2 Number Errors, Color Trails 2 Near-Misses, Color Trails 2 Prompts, Interference Index.
Administration: Individual.
Forms, 8: Color Trails 1: A, B, C, D; Color Trails 2: A, B, C, D.
Price Data: Available from publisher for kit including manual (1996, 88 pages) and 50 record forms (25 each of Form A for CTT1 and CTT2).

Time: (10) minutes.
Comments: The CTT was developed to be free from the influence of language, and is an analogue of the Trail Making Test (TMT). Administration instructions in Spanish and English are provided in the manual. Respondents must be able to recognize Arabic numerals 1–25.
Authors: Louis F. D'Elia, Paul Satz, Craig Lyons Uchiyama, and Travis White.
Publisher: Psychological Assessment Resources, Inc.

[612]
Colored Overlay Assessment Kit.

Purpose: Designed to help determine the effectivenss of each colored overlay in reading.
Population: Individuals experiencing reading and writing problems due to suspected visual perception problems.
Publication Date: 1993.
Scores: Not scored.
Administration: Individual.
Price Data, 1993: $29.95 per complete pack including 8 assorted colored overlays (blue, aquamarine, gray, peach, pink, pale rose, turquoise, yellow); $14.95 per pack of 4 colored overlays of one color.
Time: Administration time not reported.
Author: Marie Carbo.
Publisher: National Reading Styles Institute, Inc.

[613]
Columbia Mental Maturity Scale, Third Edition.

Purpose: Designed to provide "an estimate of the general reasoning ability of children."
Population: 3.5–10 years.
Publication Dates: 1954–1972.
Acronym: CMMS.
Scores: Total score only.
Administration: Individual.
Price Data, 2002: $678 per complete kit including 95 item cards, Guide for Administering and Interpreting (1972, 61 pages); $72 per 35 individual record forms; $25 per English-Spanish Reference Handbook for Educators; $75 per Guide for Administering and Interpreting including Spanish Directions.
Time: (15-20) minutes.
Comments: Requires no verbal response and a minimal motor response.
Authors: Bessie B. Burgemeister, Lucille Hollander Blum, and Irving Lorge.
Publisher: The Psychological Corporation.
Cross References: See T5:624 (31 references), T4:591 (20 references), and T3:534 (15 references); for reviews by Byron R. Egeland and Alan S. Kaufman, and an excerpted review by Joseph M. Petrosko, see 8:210 (18 references); see also T2:489 (43 references);

for reviews by Marshall S. Hiskey and T. Earnest Newland of the 1959 edition, see 6:517 (22 references); see also 5:402 (13 references).

[614]
The Columbus: Picture Analysis of Growth Towards Maturity.

Purpose: Designed "as an aid in exploring and analyzing developmental processes in children."
Population: Ages 5–18.
Publication Dates: 1969–1981.
Scores: No scores.
Administration: Individual.
Price Data: Price information available from publisher for complete kit including manual (1969, 76 pages) and 24 picture cards.
Time: [30–60] minutes.
Author: M. J. Langeveld.
Publisher: S. Karger, AG [Switzerland].
Cross References: For excerpted reviews by C. H. Ammons (with R. B. Ammons) and Steven G. Vandenberg, see 7:164 (1 reference).

[615]
Combined Cognitive Preference Inventory.

Purpose: Designed to measure how a student processes information intellectually.
Population: Students.
Publication Date: [no date on materials].
Acronym: CCPI.
Scores: 4 cognitive preference areas: Recall, Principles, Questioning, Application.
Administration: Group.
Manual: No manual.
Price Data: Available from publisher.
Time: (20) minutes.
Author: Pinchas Tamir.
Publisher: Israel Science Teaching Center [Israel] [No reply from publisher; status unknown].
Cross References: See T5:626 (1 reference).

[616]
The Common-Metric Questionnaire.

Purpose: "Designed to describe, analyze, and evaluate jobs of all types from both public and private sector organizations."
Population: Job incumbents, supervisors, job analysts.
Publication Dates: 1990–1992.
Acronym: CMQ.
Scores: 6 sections: General Background, Contacts With People, Making Decisions, Physical and Mechanical Activities, Work Setting, Selection Test Scores.
Administration: Group.
Price Data: Available from publisher.
Time: (180–240) minutes.

Comments: When individually administered, the CMQ is mailed to the rater who completes it on his/her own time and returns it; The CMQ should only be individually administered to executive, managerial, and professional level employees; small group administration is recommended.
Authors: Robert J. Harvey (questionnaire) and The Psychological Corporation (manuals).
Publisher: Robert J. Harvey (the author) [No reply from publisher; status unknown].
Cross References: For a review by Gerald A. Rosen, see 13:75.

[617]
Communication Activities of Daily Living, Second Edition.

Purpose: "To assess the functional communication skills of adults with neurogenic communication disorders."
Population: Aphasic adults.
Publication Dates: 1980–1999.
Acronym: CADL-2.
Scores: Total score only.
Administration: Individual.
Price Data, 2001: $177 per complete kit; $24 per patient response forms; $39 per examiner record booklets; $69 per picture book; $49 per examiner's manual.
Time: (25–35) minutes.
Comments: Previous edition entitled Communicative Abilities in Daily Living.
Authors: Audrey Holland, Carol Frattali, and David Fromm.
Publisher: PRO-ED.
Cross References: For reviews by Carolyn Mitchell Person and Katharine Snyder, see 14:84; for a review by Rita Sloan Berndt of an earlier edition, see 10:69 (2 references).

[618]
Communication and Symbolic Behavior Scales.

Purpose: "A standardized method of examining communicative and symbolic behaviors of children."
Population: 6 months to 24 months.
Publication Date: 1993.
Acronym: CSBS.
Scores, 7: Communicative Functions, Gestural Communicative Means, Vocal Communicative Means, Verbal Communicative Means, Reciprocity, Social-Affective Signaling, Symbolic Behavior.
Administration: Individual.
Price Data, 2002: $599 per complete kit.
Time: (60–70) minutes.
Comments: Assessments videotaped for analysis.
Authors: Amy M. Wetherby and Barry M. Prizant.
Publisher: Brookes Publishing Co., Inc.

Cross References: See T5:630 (1 reference); for reviews by Steven H. Long and Dolores Kluppel Vetter, see 13:76 (3 references).

[619]
Communication Response Style: Assessment.

Purpose: To assess an individual's communication response style.
Population: Adults.
Publication Dates: 1981–1987.
Scores, 4: Empathic Response Score, Critical Response Score, Searching Response Score, Advising Response Score.
Administration: Group or individual.
Manual: No manual.
Price Data: Price information available from publisher for set including test, answer sheets, and interpretation sheets.
Time: (20) minutes.
Comments: Self-administered, self-scored.
Author: Madelyn Burley-Allen.
Publisher: Training House, Inc.
Cross References: For reviews by Janet Norris and Gargi Roysircar Sodowsky, see 11:78.

[620]
Communication Skills Profile.

Purpose: "Designed to help people who want to gain a thorough knowledge of the processes of communication and to improve their effectiveness as communicators."
Population: Individuals or teams within organizations.
Publication Date: 1997.
Scores: 6 scales: Slowing My Thought Processes, Making Myself Understood, Testing My Conclusions, Listening Constructively, Getting to the Essence, Exploring Disagreement.
Administration: Group.
Price Data, 1997: $12.95 per test booklet.
Time: Administration time not reported.
Author: Elena Tosca.
Publisher: Jossey-Bass, A Wiley Company.
Cross References: For reviews by Robert Brown and Thomas P. Hogan, see 14:86.

[621]
Community-Based Social Skill Performance Assessment Tool.

Purpose: Designed to assess students' social skill performance in the home and in the community.
Population: Ages 14–21 years, with emotional or behavioral disorders.
Publication Date: Not dated.
Acronym: CBSP.

Scores, 5: Positive Social Behavior, Social Skills Mechanics, Anti-Social Behavior, Self-Control, Total.
Administration: Group.
Forms, 2: Male, Female.
Price Data, 2000: $99 per set including teaching guide and script (no date, 34 pages), male and female testing materials, response form, and response interpretation/scoring guide.
Time: (45) minutes.
Author: Michael Bullis.
Publisher: James Stanfield Co., Inc.

[622]
Community College Student Experiences Questionnaire, Second Edition.

Purpose: Designed to assess community college students' "quality of effort" toward maximizing college opportunities and achieving their goals.
Population: Community college students.
Publication Dates: 1990–2001.
Acronym: CCSEQ-2.
Scores: 9 scales: Quality of Effort (Course Activities, Library Activities, Faculty-Student Acquaintances, Art, Music and Theater, Writing Activities, Science Activities, Vocational Skills), Satisfaction.
Administration: Group.
Price Data, 2002: $.75 per copy of questionnaire; $1.50 per copy for scoring and processing; $12 per test manual (2001, 111 pages); $125 per diskette containing results and summary computer report.
Time: (20–30) minutes.
Comments: For use with students fluent in English.
Authors: C. Robert Pace, Patricia H. Murrell, Jack Friedlander, Penny W. Lehman; Corinna A. Ethington, Anne Marie Guthrie, and Penny W. Lehman (test manual, 3rd edition).
Publisher: Center for the Study of Higher Education, The University of Memphis.
Cross References: For reviews by Candice Haas Hollingsead and James P. Van Haneghan, see 14:87; for reviews by Charles Houston and by Rosemary E. Sutton and Hinsdale Bernard of the original edition, see 12:87.

[623]
Community Improvement Scale.

Purpose: Designed as "a device for measuring neighborhood morale" and "obtaining a diagnostic analysis of principal areas of neighborhood morale maintenance."
Population: Citizens in a neighborhood.
Publication Date: No date.
Scores: Total score only.
Administration: Individual or group.
Price Data, 2001: $3 per specimen set.
Time: (10) minutes.
Author: Inez Fay Smith.
Publisher: Psychometric Affiliates.

[624]
Community Opinion Inventory, Revised Edition.

Purpose: "To identify areas the public sees as being done well, and areas seen as not done well" in the local school.
Population: Adults who do not have children enrolled in school.
Publication Dates: 1990–1995.
Scores: 6 subscales: Quality of the Instructional Program, Program Awareness, Responsiveness to the Community, Support for Student Learning, Environment for Learning, Resource Management.
Administration: Group.
Parts, 2: A (Likert-scale items), B (customize up to 20 local questions).
Price Data, 1998: $15 per 25 inventories; $6.50 per administrator's manual (26 pages).
Time: Untimed.
Author: National Study of School Evaluation.
Publisher: National Study of School Evaluation.

[625]
Community Oriented Programs Environment Scale, Third Edition.

Purpose: Designed to "assess the social environments of community-based psychiatric treatment programs, day programs, sheltered workshops, rehabilitation centers and community care homes."
Population: Patients and staff of community oriented psychiatric facilities.
Publication Dates: 1974–1996.
Acronym: COPES.
Scores, 10: Involvement, Support, Spontaneity, Autonomy, Practical Orientation, Personal Problem Orientation, Anger and Aggression, Order and Organization, Program Clarity, Staff Control.
Administration: Group.
Price Data: Available from publisher.
Time: Administration time not reported.
Comments: A part of the Social Climate Scales (T5:2445).
Author: Rudolf H. Moos.
Publisher: Mind Garden, Inc.
Cross References: See T5:637 (3 references), T4:605 (11 references) and T3:542 (6 references); for a review by Richard I. Lanyon, see 8:525 (17 references). For a review of the Social Climate Scales, see 8:681.

[626]
Competency-Based Performance Improvement: Organizational Assessment Package.

Purpose: Used to assess an organization(s) performance improvement program/s and to improve planning for future programs.

Population: Business managers.
Publication Date: 1995.
Scores, 7: 6 categories (Strategic Goals and Business Objectives, Needs Analysis/Assessment/Planning, Competency Modeling, Curriculum Planning, Learning Intervention Design and Development, Evaluation), Total.
Administration: Group.
Price Data, 1996: $59.95 per Administrator's Handbook (61 pages), and 10 data collection instruments; $34.95 per Administrator's Handbook; $2.95 per data collection instrument (volume discounts available).
Time: Administration time not reported.
Author: David D. Dubois.
Publisher: Human Resource Development Press.
Cross References: For reviews by Stephen F. Davis and Jerry M. Lowe, see 14:88.

[627]
The Competent Speaker Speech Evaluation Form.

Purpose: Designed to measure public speaking competency.
Population: Post-secondary students.
Publication Date: 1993.
Scores, 9: Chooses and Narrows a Topic Appropriately for the Audience and Occasion, Communicates the Thesis/Specific Purpose in a Manner Appropriate for Audience and Occasion, Uses an Organizational Pattern Appropriate to Topic/Audience/Occasion and Purpose, Provides Appropriate Supporting Material Based on the Audience and Occasion, Uses Language That is Appropriate to the Audience/Occasion and Purpose, Uses Vocal Variety in Rate/Pitch and Intensity to Heighten and Maintain Interest, Uses Pronunciation/Grammar and Articulation Appropriate to the Designated Audience, Uses Physical Behaviors that Support the Verbal Message, Total.
Administration: Individual.
Price Data: Available from publisher.
Time: Administration time not reported.
Author: Speech Communication Association.
Publisher: National Communication Association.
Cross References: For reviews by Sandra M. Ketrow and Julia Y. Porter, see 14:89.

[628]
Complex Figure Test.

Purpose: To serve as an index of brain damage.
Population: Ages 16 and over.
Publication Dates: 1970–1973.
Acronym: CFT.
Scores, 4: Interruption, Omission, Sequence, Total.
Administration: Individual.
Price Data: Available from publisher.

Time: Administration time not reported.
Comments: Originally published in Dutch in 1970 as a revision of Test de Copie d'une Figure Complexe (1959) by André Rey.
Author: R. S. H. Visser.
Publisher: Swets Test Publishers [The Netherlands].
Cross References: See T5:641 (8 references) and T4:606 (8 references); for an excerpted review by C. H. Ammons and R. B. Ammons, see 8:528 (1 reference).

[629]
Composite International Diagnostic Interview.

Purpose: "For use in epidemiological studies of mental disorders."
Population: Adults.
Publication Date: 1993.
Acronym: CIDI.
Scores, 18: Demographics, Tobacco Use Disorder, Somatoform Disorders, Panic Disorder, Generalized Anxiety, Phobic Disorders, Major Depressive Episode and Dysthymia, Manic Episode, Schizophrenic and Schizophreniform Disorders, Eating Disorders, Alcohol Abuse and Dependence, Obsessive Compulsive Disorder, Drug Abuse and Dependence, Organic Brain Syndrome, Psychosexual Dysfunctions, Comments by the Respondent and the Interviewer, Interviewer Observations, Interviewer Rating.
Administration: Individual.
Price Data: Available from publisher.
Time: (75–95) minutes.
Author: World Health Organization.
Publisher: American Psychiatric Publishing, Inc.
Cross References: For reviews by Mary Mathai Chittoran and Janice G. Williams, see 13:77 (17 references).

[630]
Comprehensive Ability Battery.

Purpose: "Features 20 tests, each designed to measure a single primary ability factor ... important in industrial settings and career and vocational counseling."
Population: Ages 15 and over.
Publication Dates: 1975–1982.
Acronym: CAB.
Administration: Group or individual.
Price Data, 2002: $25 per 10 test booklets (CAB-1, CAB-2, CAB-3/4 are reusable; CAB-5 is not reusable); $18 per 50 answer sheets (CAB-1/2, CAB-3/4); $15 per 50 profile sheets; $20 per audio cassette tape (required for AA and Ms tests); $18 per scoring key and instructions (specify Level CAB-1/2/3/4); $32 per 2 scoring keys and instructions (CAB-5).
Foreign Language Editions: Contact publisher regarding non-English-language versions.

Authors: A. Ralph Hakstian and Raymond B. Cattell.
Publisher: Institute for Personality and Ability Testing, Inc.

a) CAB-1.

Scores: 4 test scores: Verbal Ability (V), Numerical Ability (N), Spatial Ability (S), Speed of Closure (Cs).

Time: 21.75(30) minutes.

b) CAB-2.

Scores: 5 test scores: Perceptual Speed and Accuracy (P), Inductive Reasoning (I), Flexibility of Closure (Cf), Associative Memory (Ma), Mechanical Ability (Mk).

Time: 28(35) minutes.

c) CAB-3/4.

Scores: 5 test scores: Memory Span (Ms), Meaningful Memory (Mm), Spelling (Sp), Auditory Ability (AA), Esthetic Judgment (E).

Time: (25–30) minutes.

Comments: MS and AA administered by audio cassette tape.

d) CAB-5.

Scores: 6 test scores: Spontaneous Flexibility (Fs), Ideational Fluency (Fi), Word Fluency (W), Originality (O), Aiming (A), Representational Drawing (RD).

Time: 32(40) minutes.

Comments: Test booklets are reusable for Batteries 1, 2, and 3/4; not reusable for Battery 5; non-machine-scorable tests.

Cross References: See T5:644 (7 references) and T4:609 (11 references); for reviews by Robert C. Nichols and Karl R. White, see 9:255; see also T3:547 (5 references); for reviews by John B. Carroll and Robert M. Thorndike, see 8:484 (3 references).

[631]
Comprehensive Adult Student Assessment System.

Purpose: Used for "assessing adult basic skills within a functional context" to "place learners into appropriate instructional levels, diagnose learners' needs, monitor progress, and certify mastery of functional basic skills."

Population: Adults.
Publication Dates: 1980–2001.
Acronym: CASAS.
Administration: Group.
Restricted Distribution: Agency training is required before tests can be provided.
Price Data: Available from publisher.
Time: Administration times vary.
Comments: The CASAS system "currently offers more than 80 standardized assessment instruments including multiple choice, written response, and performance-based assessment ... has the capacity to customize assessment to measure specific competencies and learner outcomes."

Author: CASAS.
Publisher: CASAS.

a) APPRAISAL TESTS.

1) *Life Skills Appraisal.*

Scores: 2 tests: Reading, Math.

2) *ESL Appraisal (English as a Second Language).*

Scores: 4 tests: Reading, Listening, Writing, Oral.

Comments: Places students into Levels A, B, or C of the CASAS Life Skills Series pretests.

3) *ECS Appraisal (Employability Competency System).*

Scores: 2 tests: Reading, Math.

Comments: Places students into Levels A, B, or C of the CASAS Basic Skills for Employability pretests; also available in computer-based format.

4) *Workplace Appraisal.*

Scores: 2 tests: Reading, Reading/Math.

Comments: Not a pre-employment test; designed to be used at worksite to provide an initial assessment of workers' functional reading skills of materials encountered at the worksite.

b) CASAS TESTS FOR MONITORING PROGRESS.

Comments: All tests serve as pre/post-tests.

1) *Life Skills Survey Achievement Tests.*

(a) Reading.

Levels: 4 levels (A, B, C, D), each with 2 forms.

(b) Math.

Levels: 4 levels (A, B, C, D), each with 2 forms.

(c) Listening Comprehension (for ESL students).

Levels: 3 levels (A, B, C), each with 2 forms.

2) *Basic Skills for Employability Tests.*

(a) Reading.

Levels: 4 levels (A, B, C, D), A and D each with 2 forms, B and C each with 3 forms.

(b) Math.

Levels: 4 levels (A, B, C, D), each with 2 forms.

(c) Listening Comprehension (for ESL students).

Levels: 3 levels (A, B, C), each with 2 forms.

3) *Life and Work Tests.*

(a) Reading.

Levels: 2 levels (A, C) each with 2 forms.

c) CASAS TESTS FOR SPECIAL NEEDS.
Population: Developmentally disabled students.
Levels: 4 levels (AA, AAA, AAAA, each with 2 forms, AAAAA with 1 form).
Comments: Tests serve as pre/post-tests.
1) *Adult Life Skills Tests.*
2) *Workplace and Employability Skills Summary.*
Acronym: WESS.
Comments: Performance-based assessment, component of POWER System (Providing Options for the Workplace, Education and Rehabilitation).
d) CASAS CERTIFICATION TESTS.
Comments: "Designed to determine if a student is ready to move to a higher level of instruction or to be certified as completing a program of instruction."
1) *Life Skills Certification (Exit) Tests.*
Scores: 1 test: Reading.
Levels: 3 levels (A, B, with 1 form, c with 3 forms).
2) *Employability Certification (Exit) Tests.*
Scores: 2 tests: Reading, Math.
Levels: 2 levels (B, C), each with 1 form for each test.
3) *Workforce Skills Certification System.*
  (a) Reading/Math.
  (b) Critical Thinking and Problem Solving.
  Areas: Banking, Health, Telecommunications, High-Tech.
  (c) Applied Performance.
  Areas: Banking, Health, Telecommunications.
  (d) Portfolio Assessment System.
e) CASAS TEST FOR WRITING ASSESSMENT.
Purpose: "Measures a student's functional writing skill abilities within a life skills context."
Comments: Pretest and posttest are available.
f) OCCUPATION SPECIFIC TESTS.
Purpose: "Assess whether a person is ready to enter an occupational training program."
Scores: 5 areas: Auto Mechanic, Clerical, Food Service, Health Occupations Level B, Health Occupations Level C.
g) CASAS SECONDARY DIPLOMA TESTS.
Scores: 8 areas: Math, Economics, American Government, United States History, English/Language Arts, World History, Biological Science, Physical Science.
Comments: Tests are available for pretesting and posttesting.
Cross References: See T5:645 (1 reference); for reviews by Ralph O. Mueller and Patricia K. Freitag and by William D. Schafer, see 13:78 (2 references).

[632]
Comprehensive Affair Worksheets.

Purpose: Designed to "analyze the reasons for the affair, the affair behaviors and relationship, the impact on the marriage and all the individuals involved, decisions that need to be made and what needs to be done to solve the problems caused by the affair."
Population: Individuals who have had an affair.
Publication Date: 1995.
Scores: 19 sections: Therapy, Marriage Before the Affair, Pre-Affair Involvement, Activities, Relationship, Religion, Communication, Feelings, Sex, Cheating Opinions, Keeping It Secret, Spouse's Reaction, Effects on the Person, Effects on the Spouse, Others Finding Out, Decisions and Planning, Repairing the Marriage, Marital Sex, Other Problems.
Administration: Individual.
Manual: No manual.
Price Data, 2001: $16 per 5 worksheets.
Time: Administration time not reported.
Author: Allan Roe.
Publisher: Diagnostic Specialists, Inc.

[633]
Comprehensive Assessment of Mathematics Strategies.

Purpose: Designed to "identify and assess a student's level of mastery in each of 12 mathematics strategies."
Population: Grades 2–8.
Publication Date: 2000.
Acronym: CAMS.
Scores, 12: Building Number Sense, Using Estimation, Applying Addition, Applying Subtraction, Applying Multiplication, Applying Division, Converting Time and Money, Converting Customary and Metric Measures, Using Algebra, Using Geometry, Determining Probability and Averages, Interpreting Graphs and Charts.
Administration: Group.
Levels, 7: Grade 2, Grade 3, Grade 4, Grade 5, Grade 6, Grade 7, Grade 8.
Price Data, 2001: $23.90 per 10 student books; $3.95 per teacher guide (for each level, 14 pages); $19.95 per CD-ROM management software.
Time: (60) minutes.
Comments: Testing materials include practice lessons, self-assessments, and teacher assessments; self-assessments (both of which are completed after the student is exposed to and practices lessons 1–5, and again after the student is exposed to each practices lessons 6–10); class performance chart available; Teacher Assessment 1 "assesses a student's performance for each of the 12 mathematics' strategies"; Teacher Assessment 2 compares a student's level of mastery in the criteria for the 12 mathematics' strategies.
Author: Robert G. Forest.
Publisher: Curriculum Associates, Inc.

[634]
Comprehensive Assessment of Reading Strategies.

Purpose: Designed to "identify and assess a student's level of mastery with each of 12 reading strategies."
Population: Grades 3–8.
Publication Date: 1998.
Acronym: CARS.
Scores, 13: Finding Main Idea, Recalling Facts and Details, Understanding Sequence, Recognizing Cause and Effect, Comparing and Contrasting, Making Predictions, Finding Word Meaning in Context, Drawing Conclusions and Making Inferences, Distinguishing Between Fact and Opinion, Identifying Author's Purpose, Interpreting Figurative Language, Distinguishing Between Real and Make-Believe [Books 3–4], Summarizing [Books 5–8].
Administration: Group.
Levels, 6: Grade 3, Grade 4, Grade 5, Grade 6, Grade 7, Grade 8.
Price Data, 2001: $23.90 per 10 student book;s $4.95 per teacher's guide.
Time: (45) minutes.
Comments: Testing materials include practice lessons, self-assessments, and teacher assessments; self-assessment and teacher assessment are completed after student is exposed to and practices the lessons presented in the test materials; class performance charts available; computer software available for generating interpretive reports; assessment consists of 2 assessments to be given at separate times.
Authors: Deborah Adcock and Courtney Bolser (contributing author to test booklet).
Publisher: Curriculum Associates, Inc.

[635]
Comprehensive Assessment of School Environments.

Purpose: Developed to assess perceptions of the school climate and student, teacher, and parent satisfaction with each individual's personal environment in order "to foster data-based decision making for school improvement."
Population: Junior and senior high schools.
Publication Dates: 1986–1989.
Acronym: CASE.
Administration: Group.
Price Data, 1998: $15 per sampler kit including one of each form and examiner's manual (1987, 36 pages); $10 per 35 surveys (specify form) and manual; $8 per examiner's manual; $17 per technical manual; ; scoring service available from Western Michigan University [The Evaluation Center, Kalamazoo, MI 49008; (616) 387-5917]).
Time: Administration time not reported.

Comments: Test booklet titles are School Climate Survey, Parent Satisfaction Survey, Teacher Satisfaction Survey, and Student Satisfaction Survey.
Authors: Cynthia Halderson (manuals and climate survey), Edgar A. Kelley (manuals and climate survey), James W. Keefe (manuals and climate survey), Paul S. Berge (technical manual), John A. Glover (climate survey), Carrie Sorenson (climate survey), Carol Speth (climate survey), Neal Schmitt (satisfaction surveys), and Brian Loher (satisfaction surveys).
Publisher: National Association of Secondary School Principals.
a) SCHOOL CLIMATE SURVEY.
Scores: Student, Teacher, and Parent scores for the following 10 subscales: Teacher-Student Relationships, Security and Maintenance, Administration, Student Academic Orientation, Student Behavioral Values, Guidance, Student-Peer Relationships, Parent & Community-School Relationships, Instructional Management, Student Activities.
b) PARENT SATISFACTION SURVEY.
Scores, 9: Parent Involvement, Curriculum, Student Activities, Teachers, Support Services, School Building/Supplies/Maintenance, Student Discipline, School Administrators, School Information Services.
c) TEACHER SATISFACTION SURVEY.
Scores, 9: Administration, Compensation, Opportunities for Advancement, Student Responsibility & Discipline, Curriculum and Job Tasks, Co-workers, Parents and Community, School Building/Supplies/Maintenance, Communication.
d) STUDENT SATISFACTION SURVEY.
Scores, 8: Teachers, Fellow Students, Schoolwork, Student Activities, Student Discipline, Decision-Making Opportunities, School Building/Supplies/Upkeep, Communication.
Cross References: For reviews by Nancy L. Allen and Frederick T. L. Leong, see 11:80.

[636]
Comprehensive Assessment of School Environments Information Management System.

Purpose: Designed to facilitate and encourage the use of data-based planning for school improvement projects.
Population: Secondary schools.
Publication Dates: 1991–1995.
Acronym: CASE-IMS.
Scores, 9: Principal Questionnaire, Teacher Report Form, Student Report Form, Teacher Satisfaction Survey, Student Satisfaction Survey, Parent Satisfaction Survey (optional), School Climate Survey for Teachers, School Climate Survey for Students, School Climate Survey for Parents (optional).

Administration: Group.
Price Data, 1995: $175 per MS/DOS 3.5-inch or 5.25-inch software and user's manual; $49 per Version 1.2 add-on disk and manual (1996, 87 pages); $195 per Version 1.5 scoring package update with scanner interface; $395 per Version 1.5 enhancement and scoring package update; $395 per Macintosh version; $6 per 35 surveys (specify School Climate, Student Satisfaction, Teacher Satisfaction or Parent Satisfaction); $5 per 35 answer sheets (specify NCS or Scantron); $5 per examiner's manual; $15 per technical manual; $5 per Climate/Satisfaction sampler kit including examiner's manual and one of each form; $135 per Mainframe scoring package; $95 per MS/DOS or Apple II/e scoring package; $1.50 per 35 Principal Questionnaire and Report Forms (specify NCS or Scantron); $7 per 35 Teacher or Student Report Forms (specify NCS or Scantron); $5 per computer demo disk.
Time: Administration time not reported.
Comments: Computer administered; available in MS/DOS (3.5-inch or 5.25-inch disks) or Macintosh (3.5-inch disk) format.
Author: National Association of Secondary School Principals Task Force on Effective School Environments.
Publisher: National Association of Secondary School Principals.
Cross References: For reviews by Joseph R. Manduchi and Daniel L. Yazak, see 14:90.

[637]
Comprehensive Assessment of Spoken Language.

Purpose: Designed to measure the processes of comprehension, expression, and retrieval in oral language.
Population: Ages 3–21.
Publication Date: 1999.
Acronym: CASL.
Scores: 15 tests: Basic Concepts, Antonyms, Synonyms, Sentence Completion, Idiomatic Language, Syntax Construction, Paragraph Comprehension, Grammatical Morphemes, Sentence Comprehension, Grammaticality Judgment, Nonliteral Language, Meaning from Context, Inference, Ambiguous Sentences, and Pragmatic Judgment; plus Core Composite scores, Category Index scores (Lexical/Semantic, Syntactic, Supralinguistic); Processing Index scores (Expressive, Receptive).
Forms, 2: 1, 2.
Administration: Individual.
Price Data, 2002: $299.95 per complete kit including manual (164 pages), three test books, 12 record Forms 1 and 2, norms book (168 pages), and carry bag; $20.95 per 12 record Form 1; $26.95 per 12 record Form 2; $199.95 per AGS computer ASSIST™ CD for CASL (Mac/Win).

Author: Elizabeth Carrow-Woolfolk.
Publisher: American Guidance Service, Inc.

[638]
Comprehensive Assessment of Symptoms and History.

Purpose: "Designed as a structured interview and recording instrument for documenting the signs, symptoms, and history of subjects evaluated in research studies of the major psychoses and affective disorders."
Population: Psychiatric patients.
Publication Date: 1987.
Acronym: CASH.
Scores: Interview divided into 3 major sections: Present State (Sociodemographic Data, Evaluation of Current Condition, Psychotic Syndrome, Manic Syndrome, Major Depressive Syndrome, Treatment, Cognitive Assessment, Global Assessment Scale, Diagnosis for Current Episode), Past History (History of Onset and Hospitalization, Past Symptoms of Psychosis, Characterization of Course, Past Symptoms of Affective Disorder), Lifetime History (History of Somatic Therapy, Alcoholism, Drug Use and Abuse and Dependence, Modified Premorbid Adjustment Scale, Premorbid or Intermorbid Personality, Functioning During Past Five Years, Global Assessment Scale, Diagnosis for Lifetime).
Administration: Individual.
Price Data: Available from publisher.
Time: [60–180] minutes.
Comments: The CASH is one component of a modular assessment battery available from the publisher.
Author: Nancy C. Andreasen.
Publisher: Nancy C. Andreasen.
Cross References: See T5:650 (16 references); for reviews by Patricia A. Bachelor and Barbara J. Kaplan, see 12:88 (12 references); see also T4:612 (4 references).

[639]
Comprehensive Behavior Rating Scale for Children.

Purpose: A teacher rating scale designed to measure various dimensions of a child's school functioning.
Population: Ages 6–14.
Publication Date: 1990.
Acronym: CBRSC.
Scores: 9 scales: Inattention-Disorganization, Reading Problems, Cognitive Deficits, Oppositional-Conduct Disorders, Motor Hyperactivity, Anxiety, Sluggish Tempo, Daydreaming, Social Competence.
Administration: Individual.
Price Data, 2002: $118 per complete kit including manual (10 pages), 25 profile and questionnaire forms, and scoring key; $26 per 25 profile and questionnaire forms; $65 per manual; $39 per scoring key.

Time: (10–15) minutes.
Authors: Ronald Neeper, Benjamin B. Lahey, and Paul J. Frick.
Publisher: The Psychological Corporation.
Cross References: See T5:651 (2 references); for a review by Wayne C. Piersel, see 13:79 (1 reference).

[640]
Comprehensive Identification Process [Revised].

Purpose: "Designed to identify children who may have problems that could interfere with their success in school."
Population: Ages 2–6.5.
Publication Dates: 1975–1997.
Acronym: CIP.
Administration: Individual.
Price Data, 2002: $278.60 per complete kit including Symbol booklet, Screening booklet, Parent Interview forms, Observation of Behavior forms, Speech and Expressive Language Record forms, Child Record Folders, Interviewer's manual (1997, 40 pages), Administrator's Manual (1997, 54 pages,) and manipulatives in carrying case.
Foreign Language Edition: Earlier edition available in Spanish.
Time: (25–35) minutes.
Comments: CIP screening team should include at least one member who has a background in early childhood education of the disabled and is skilled in screening and evaluation; alternatives to the standard screening, such as in-home screening or bilingual screening available.
Authors: R. Reid Zehrbach (test), and Joan Good Erickson (Speech and Expressive Language Record Form).
Publisher: Scholastic Testing Service, Inc.
  a) CHILD: RECORD FOLDER.
  Scores, 5: Hearing, Vision, Perceptual Motor, Cognitive-Verbal, Gross Motor.
  Comment: Materials for hearing and vision screening must be obtained locally.
  b) SPEECH AND EXPRESSIVE LANGUAGE RECORD FORM.
  Scores, 6: Articulation/Phonology, Voice, Fluency, Expressive Language, Associated Factors, Total.
  Author: Joan Good Erickson.
  c) OBSERVATION OF BEHAVIOR FORM.
  Scores, 7: Hearing, Vision, Physical/Motor Speech and Expressive Language, Social Behavior (Responses, Interaction), Affective Behavior.
  d) PARENT INTERVIEW FORM.
  Scores, 7: Pregnancy/Birth/Hospitalization, Walking/Toilet Training, Hearing, Vision, Speech and Expressive Language, Medical, Social Affect.
  Comment: History and ratings by parent.

Cross References: For a review by J. Jeffrey Grill, see 14:91; see also T4:616 (1 reference); for reviews by Robert P. Anderson and Phyllis L. Newcomer of an earlier version, see 8:425 (1 reference).

[641]
Comprehensive Personality Profile.

Purpose: "To identify individuals with personality traits that are compatible with both occupational and organizational demands."
Population: Adults.
Publication Dates: 1985–1998.
Acronym: CPP.
Scores, 17: Primary Scales (Emotional Intensity, Intuition, Recognition Motivation, Sensitivity, Assertiveness, Trust, Exaggeration), Secondary Traits (Ego Drive, Interpersonal Warmth, Stability, Empathy, Objectivity, Independence, Aggressiveness, Decisiveness, Tolerance, Efficiency).
Administration: Group or individual.
Price Data, 2001: $125 per 5 kits including manual (1999, 105 pages), 5 questionnaires (quantity discounts available), and PC compatible scoring software or fax scoring.
Time: (15–25) minutes.
Comments: Also available in French and Spanish; title on questionnaire is CPP Compatibility Questionnaire.
Authors: Wonderlic Personnel Test, Inc. and Larry L. Craft (questionnaire).
Publisher: Wonderlic, Inc.
Cross References: For reviews by Sanford J. Cohn and Ira Stuart Katz, see 14:92; see also T4:617 (1 reference).

[642]
Comprehensive Receptive and Expressive Vocabulary Test—Second Edition.

Purpose: "To identify ... deficiencies in oral vocabulary ... discrepancies between receptive and expressive vocabulary, [and] ... progress in instructional programs."
Population: Ages 4-0 through 89-11 (Receptive Vocabulary), ages 5-0 through 89-11 (Expressive Vocabulary).
Publication Dates: 1994–2002.
Acronym: CREVT-2.
Scores, 3: Receptive Vocabulary, Expressive Vocabulary, General Vocabulary.
Administration: Individual.
Forms, 2: A, B.
Price Data, 2001: $219 per complete kit; $39 per forms (A or B); $76 per photo album picture book; $69 per examiner's manual (2002, 141 pages).
Time: Untimed.
Comments: Combines the CREVT and CREVT-A; old editions still available.
Authors: Gerald Wallace and Donald D. Hammill.

Publisher: PRO-ED.
Cross References: See T5:655 (CREVT, 1 reference) and T5:656 (CREVT); for reviews by Alan S. Kaufman and Mary J. McLellan of the CREVT, see 13:80 (1 reference); for reviews by Margaret E. Malone and Wayne H. Slater of the CREVT-A, see 14:93 (1 reference).

[643]
Comprehensive Scales of Student Abilities: Quantifying Academic Skills and School-Related Behavior Through the Use of Teacher Judgments.

Purpose: To provide "a quick teacher rating scale of student ability."
Population: Ages 6–0 to 17–0.
Publication Date: 1994.
Acronym: CSSA.
Scores, 9: Verbal Thinking, Speech, Reading, Writing, Handwriting, Mathematics, General Facts, Basic Motor Generalizations, Social Behavior.
Administration: Individual.
Price Data, 2001: $86 per complete kit including 100 profile/record forms and examiner's manual (52 pages); $39 per 50 profile/record forms; $49 per examiner's manual.
Time: (5–10) minutes.
Authors: Donald D. Hammill and Wayne P. Hresko.
Publisher: PRO-ED.
Cross References: For reviews by Jennifer J. Fager and by Blaine R. Worthen and Xitao Fan, see 13:81.

[644]
Comprehensive Sex History.

Purpose: Designed to compile an individual's complete sexual history.
Population: Adults.
Publication Date: 1995.
Administration: Individual.
Forms, 2: Male, Female.
Manual: No Manual.
Price Data, 2001: $12 for one set of reusable question sheets for all 5 parts (specify Male or Female).
Time: Administration time not reported.
Author: Allan Roe.
Publisher: Diagnostic Specialists, Inc.
   a) SEXUAL EXPERIENCES.
   Population: General adult.
   b) DATING EXPERIENCES.
   Population: Those who have dated.
   c) NON-MARITAL INTERCOURSE.
   Population: Those who have had intercourse outside of marriage.

   d) MARITAL OR LIVING TOGETHER SEXUAL EXPERIENCES.
   Population: Those who have been married or lived together.
   e) INAPPROPRIATE SEXUAL BEHAVIORS.
   Population: Those who have done inappropriate criminal sexual activities.

[645]
Comprehensive Spouse's Worksheets.

Purpose: Designed to "analyze the spouse's reaction to [an] affair, the impact on the marriage and everyone involved, decisions that need to be made and what needs to be done to solve the problems caused by the affair."
Population: Spouses of persons who had an affair.
Publication Date: 1996.
Scores: 14 sections: Therapy, Marriage Before the Affair, Pre-Affair, Spouse's Relationship with the Lover, Cheating Opinions, Keeping It Secret, Reaction to the Affair, Others Finding Out, Spouse's Reaction, Effects on the Person, Sex After the Affair, Decisions and Planning, Repairing the Marriage, Other Problems.
Administration: Individual.
Manual: No manual.
Price Data, 2001: $10 per 5 worksheets.
Time: Administration time not reported.
Author: Allan Roe.
Publisher: Diagnostic Specialists, Inc.

[646]
Comprehensive Test of Adaptive Behavior.

Purpose: "Evaluates how well a retarded student is functioning independently in the environment."
Population: Birth–age 60.
Publication Date: 1984.
Acronym: CTAB.
Scores: 31 scores in 6 skill areas: 5 self-help skills (Toileting, Grooming, Dressing, Eating, Subtotal), 7 home living skills (Living Room, Kitchen-Cooking, Kitchen-Cleaning, Bedroom, Bath and Utility, Yard Care, Subtotal), 7 independent living skills (Health, Telephone, Travel, Time-Telling, Economic, Vocational, Subtotal), 4 social skills (Self-Awareness, Interaction, Leisure Skills, Subtotal), 3 sensory and motor skills (Sensory Awareness, Motor, Subtotal), 4 language and academic skills (Language Concepts, Math Skills, Reading and Writing, Subtotal), Total.
Administration: Individual.
Price Data: Available from publisher.
Time: Administration time not reported.
Comments: More comprehensive version of the Normative Adaptive Behavior Checklist (1719).
Authors: Gary L. Adams and Jean Hartleben (Parent/Guardian Survey).

Publisher: Gary L. Adams (the author) [No reply from publisher; status unknown].
Cross References: See T4:621 (1 reference).

[647]
Comprehensive Test of Nonverbal Intelligence.

Purpose: Constructed to measure "nonverbal intellectual abilities."
Population: Ages 6-0 to 90-11.
Publication Date: 1996.
Acronym: CTONI.
Scores, 9: 6 subtest scores (Pictorial Analogies, Geometric Analogies, Pictorial Categories, Geometric Categories, Pictorial Sequences, Geometric Sequences), 3 composite scores (Nonverbal Intelligence Quotient, Pictorial Nonverbal Intelligence Quotient, Geometric Nonverbal Intelligence Quotient).
Administration: Individual.
Price Data, 2001: $314 per complete kit including examiner's manual (92 pages), analogies picture book, categories picture book, sequences picture book, and 25 profile/examiner record forms in storage box; $34 per 25 profile/examiner record forms; $79 per examiner's manual; $69 per picture book (specify Analogies, Categories, or Sequences).
Time: (40–60) minutes.
Authors: Donald D. Hammill, Nils A. Pearson, and J. Lee Wiederholt.
Publisher: PRO-ED.
Cross References: See T5:662 (1 reference); for reviews by Glen P. Aylward and Gabriele van Lingen, see 13:82.

[648]
Comprehensive Test of Phonological Processing.

Purpose: Designed to measure "phonological awareness, phonological memory, and rapid naming."
Population: Ages 5 to 24.
Publication Date: 1999.
Acronym: CTOPP.
Administration: Individual.
Price Data, 2001: $224 per complete kit including manual (159 pages), 25 each profile/examiner record booklets for ages 5 to 6 and ages 7 to 24, picture book, and audiocassette; $44 per 25 profile/examiner record booklets for ages 5 to 6; $54 per 25 profile/examiner record booklets for ages 7 to 24; $34 per picture book; $79 per manual; $19 per audiocassette.
Time: (30) minutes.
Authors: Richard K. Wagner, Joseph K. Torgesen, and Carol A. Rashotte.
Publisher: PRO-ED.
  a) 5- AND 6-YEAR-OLD VERSION.
  Population: Ages 5–6.

Scores, 11: Phonological Awareness (Elision, Blending Words, Sound Matching), Phonological Memory (Memory for Digits, Nonword Repetition), Rapid Naming (Rapid Color Naming, Rapid Object Naming), Blending Nonwords (Supplemental Subtest).
  b) 7- THROUGH 24-YEAR-OLD VERSION.
  Population: Ages 7–24.
  Scores, 17: Phonological Awareness (Elision, Blending Words), Phonological Memory (Memory for Digits, Nonword Repetition), Rapid Naming (Rapid Digit Naming, Rapid Letter Naming), Alternate Phonological Awareness (Blending Nonwords, Segmenting Nonwords), Alternate Rapid Naming (Rapid Color Naming, Rapid Object Naming), Phoneme Reversal (Supplemental Subtest), Segmenting Words (Supplemental Subtest).

[649]
Comprehensive Test of Visual Functioning.

Purpose: Designed to identify and differentiate type of visual perceptual dysfunction.
Population: Ages 8 and over.
Publication Date: 1990.
Acronym: CTVF.
Scores, 9: Visual/Letter Integration, Visual/Writing Integration, Nonverbal Visual Closure, Nonverbal Visual Reasoning/Memory, Spatial Orientation/Memory/Motor, Spatial Orientation/Motor, Visual Design/Motor, Visual Design/Memory/Motor, Total.
Administration: Individual.
Price Data, 2002: $108 per complete kit including manual (64 pages), stimulus cards/easel, and stimulus items; $28 per manual; $42 per examiner's directions and scoring protocol (18 pages); $29 per 25 examinee test booklets; $29 per stimulus cards/easel.
Time: (25) minutes.
Comments: "Norm-referenced"; includes 4 additional subtests (Visual Acuity, Visual Processing/Figure-Ground, Visual Tracking, Reading Word Analysis) which do not contribute to the overall visual performance quotient.
Authors: Sue L. Larson, Evelyn Buethe, and Gary J. Vitali.
Publisher: Slosson Educational Publications, Inc.
Cross References: For reviews by Stephen R. Hooper and Douglas J. McRae, see 12:89.

[650]
Comprehensive Testing Program III.

Purpose: "Designed to measure attainment of major educational objectives regardless of particular curriculum programs and methods."
Population: Grades 1–2, 2–3, 3–4, 4–6, 6–8, 8–12.
Publication Dates: 1974–1996.
Acronym: CTPIII.

Administration: Group.
Forms, 2: 1, 2 (2 parallel forms at each level).
Price Data: Available from publisher.
Comments: "All quantitative ability and mathematics tests are written to the NCTM standards; where applicable, items intended to tap higher-order thinking skills are included and are identified on reports"; previously listed as ERB Comprehensive Testing Program.
Author: Educational Records Bureau.
Publisher: Educational Records Bureau.
  a) ACHIEVEMENT TESTS, LEVEL A.
  Population: Grades 1–2.
  Scores, 4: Auditory Comprehension, Reading Comprehension, Word Analysis, Mathematics.
  Time: (155–235) minutes in several sessions.
  b) ACHIEVEMENT TESTS, LEVEL B.
  Population: Grades 2–3.
  Scores, 5: Auditory Comprehension, Reading Comprehension, Word Analysis, Writing Mechanics, Mathematics.
  Time: (190–290) minutes in several sessions.
  c) ABILITY/ACHIEVEMENT TEST, LEVEL C.
  Population: Grades 3–4.
  Scores, 7: Ability (Verbal, Quantitative), Auditory Comprehension, Reading Comprehension, Writing Mechanics, Writing Process, Mathematics.
  Time: 310(330) minutes in several sessions.
  d) ABILITY/ACHIEVEMENT TEST, LEVEL D.
  Population: Grades 4–6.
  Scores, 7: Ability (Verbal, Quantitative), Vocabulary, Reading Comprehension, Writing Mechanics, Writing Process, Mathematics.
  Time: (290) minutes in several sessions.
  e) ABILITY/ACHIEVEMENT TEST, LEVEL E.
  Population: Grades 6–8.
  Scores, 8: Ability (Verbal, Quantitative), Vocabulary, Reading Comprehension, Writing Mechanics, Writing Process, Mathematics, Algebra I [optional end-of-course test].
  f) ABILITY/ACHIEVEMENT TEST, LEVEL F.
  Population: Grades 8–12.
  Scores, 10: Ability (Verbal, Quantitative), Vocabulary, Reading Comprehension, Writing Mechanics, Writing Process, Mathematics (Algebra I, Algebra II, Geometry [optional end-of-course tests]).
Cross References: For reviews by Steven J. Osterlind and Darrell L. Sabers, see 13:83; for a review by Kathleen Barrows Chesterfield of an earlier edition, see 9:397.

[651]
Comprehensive Trail-Making Test.

Purpose: Developed for the evaluation and diagnosis of brain injury and other forms of central nervous system compromise.

Population: Ages 11 to 74-11.
Publication Date: 2002.
Acronym: CTMT.
Scores, 6: Trail 1, Trail 2, Trail 3, Trail 4, Trail 5, Composite Index.
Administration: Individual.
Price Data, 2002: $87 per complete kit; $40 per 10 record booklets; $49 per examiner's manual (79 pages).
Time: (5–12) minutes.
Author: Cecil R. Reynolds.
Publisher: PRO-ED.

[652]
Computer-Based Test of English as a Foreign Language and Test of Written English.

Purpose: "To evaluate the English proficiency of people whose native language is not English."
Population: University and college applicants.
Publication Dates: 1964–1999.
Acronym: TOEFL, TWE.
Scores, 5: Listening, Structure, Reading, Writing, Test of Written English Score.
Administration: Group.
Price Data, 1999: (The following prices apply to quantities of 1–9 items; quantity discounts available on larger orders): $15 each for TOEFL Sampler CD ROM; $47 each for Test Preparation Kit, 2nd Edition; $16 each for Volume 1 paper-based Practice Tests; $24 each for Volume 2 paper-based Practice Tests; $14 each for Volume 2 computer-based Practice Tests; $32 each for Volume 2 computer-based Practice Tests; $8 each for TOEFL Sample Test, 6th Ed.; $100 fee for taking Computer-Based TOEFL test.
Time: (155–205) minutes for TOEFL; 30 (35) minutes for TWE.
Comments: Tests administered at centers designated by the publisher; computer-based testing available throughout the year by appointment at centers in the U.S. and most countries; candidates may take the test not more than once a month; TOEFL may be administered separately but TWE given only in conjunction with TOEFL test at specific annually determined combined administrations; as of July 1998, the TOEFL program has gone to a computer-based delivery; the paper-based TOEFL/TWE is currently offered in limited areas (primarily in Asia); the paper-based TOEFL/TWE will be phased out (target date: 2000).
Authors: Jointly sponsored by College Entrance Examination Board, Graduate Records Examination Board, and Educational Testing Service.
Publisher: Educational Testing Service.
Cross References: For reviews by R. J. DeAyala and Alan Solomon, see 14:94; see also T5:666 (15 references) and T4:2757 (12 references); for reviews by Brenda H. Loyd and Kikumi K. Tatsuoka of an earlier edition of the TOEFL, see 9:1257 (1 reference); see also T3:2441 (9

references), 8:110 (15 references), and T2:238 (4 references); for reviews by Clinton I. Chase and George Domino of earlier forms, see 7:266 (10 references).

[653]
Computer Career Assessment Test.

Purpose: Measures aptitude for work in the computer field.
Population: Any adult without prior computer experience.
Publication Date: 2000.
Acronym: CCAT.
Scores: Total Score, Narrative Evaluation, Ranking.
Administration: Group.
Price Data, 2001: $99 for industry; $65 for educational institutions; quantity discounts available.
Time: (60) minutes.
Comments: Available in booklet and internet versions; scored by publisher; must be proctored.
Author: Bruce A. Winrow.
Publisher: Walden Personnel Performance, Inc. [Canada].

[654]
The Computer Category Test.

Purpose: Designed for neuropsychological screening via computer.
Population: Ages 9–14, adult.
Publication Dates: 1994–1999.
Acronym: CAT, ACAT.
Scores: Information available from publisher.
Administration: Individual or group.
Levels, 2: Adult, Intermediate.
Price Data, 2002: $360 per MS DOS computer program on 3.5-inch disk including manual (1994, 98 pages); $45 per MS DOS computer program preview (3 uses) on 3.5-inch disk.
Time: (30–40) minutes; up to 90 minutes for impaired patients.
Comments: A computerized version of the Halstead Category Test including the Adaptive Category Test (ACAT); requires MS DOS compatible computer, a graphics card, and a disk drive.
Authors: James Choca, Linda Laatsch, Dan Garside, and Carl Arnemann.
Publisher: Multi-Health Systems, Inc.

[655]
Computer Literacy Skills Profile.

Purpose: To evaluate computer literacy potential.
Population: Candidates whose job responsibilities will include utilizing common software packages.
Publication Date: 1996.
Acronym: COMPLIT.
Scores: Total Score, Narrative Evaluation, Ranking, Recommendation.
Administration: Group.

Price Data, 2001: $235 per candidate; quantity discounts available.
Time: (110) minutes.
Comments: Scored by publisher; must be proctored.
Author: Bruce A. Winrow.
Publisher: Walden Personnel Performance, Inc.

[656]
Computer Operator Aptitude Battery.

Purpose: Predict "ability to perform computer operator job and potential for learning computer programming."
Population: Experienced computer operators and trainees.
Publication Dates: 1973–1974.
Acronym: COAB.
Scores, 4: Sequence Recognition, Format Checking, Logical Thinking, Total.
Administration: Individual or group.
Price Data, 2002: $193 per Start-up kit including 5 test booklets, 25 answer sheets, and examiner's manual (1974, 19 pages); $112 per 5 test booklets; $76 per 25 answer sheets (quantity discounts available); $28 per examiner's manual.
Time: 45 minutes.
Author: Science Research Associates.
Publisher: Reid London House.

[657]
Computer Programmer Aptitude Battery.

Purpose: To "measure abilities related to success in computer programmer and systems analysis fields."
Population: Students, programmer trainees, entry-level and experienced.
Publication Dates: 1964–1993.
Acronym: CPAB.
Scores, 6: Verbal Meaning, Reasoning, Letter Series, Number Ability, Diagramming, Total.
Administration: Individual or group.
Forms, 2: A, B.
Foreign Editions: British Version (1964–1991) available.
Price Data, 2002: $193 per start-up kit including 5 test reusable booklets (specify Form A or Form B), 25 answer sheets (specify Form A or Form B) and examiner's manual; $166 per Short Form start-up kit; $158 per 25 Short Form A tests (with carbon answer sheets); $112 per 5 test booklets (quantity discount available; specify Form A or Form B); $76 per 25 answer sheets (quantity discount available; specify Form A or Form B); $28 per examiner's manual.
Time: 79 minutes; 55 minutes for short form.
Comments: Short form contains the Reasoning and Diagramming sections and can be used for all levels of programmers but norms for short form available only for entry level.

Author: Science Research Associates.
Publisher: Reid London House.
Cross References: For reviews by Roderick K. Mahurin and William D. Schafer, see 11:85; see also T3:557 (1 reference); for additional information and a review by Nick L. Smith, see 8:1079 (3 references); see also T2:2334 (2 references); for reviews by Richard T. Johnson and Donald J. Veldman, see 7:1089 (2 references).

[658]
Computerized Assessment of Response Bias: Revised Edition.

Purpose: "To quantitatively assess a given patient's attitude (response bias) in taking neuropsychological or neurocognitive tests."
Population: Severely impaired neurologic patients, mild traumatic brain injury patients, non-neurologic simulators.
Publication Dates: 1992–2000.
Acronym: CARB.
Scores, 24: 4 actions (Block 1, 2, 3, Total) each with 6 scores: Total Correct, Number of Correct Responses Obtained with Left Hand, Number of Correct Responses Obtained with Right Hand, Reaction Time Average, Reaction Time Average for Correct Responses, Reaction Time Average for Incorrect Responses.
Administration: Individual.
Forms, 4: Standard or Quick form, each with or without item-specific feedback.
Price Data, 2002: $300 for disk and comprehensive manual (63 pages).
Foreign Language Edition: Spanish language version available.
Time: (22–40) minutes.
Comments: Typically, this is a test of motivation, not ability or impairment; instructions for installing and operating CARB (DOS based) software are included in the manual.
Authors: Robert L. Conder, Jr., Lyle M. Allen, III, David R. Cox, and Carol M. King.
Publisher: CogniSyst, Inc.
Cross References: For reviews by M. Allan Cooperstein and Edward E. Gotts, see 14:95.

[659]
Computerized Lifestyle Assessment.

Purpose: Designed to identify lifestyle behaviors such as substance use, health maintenance, preventive activities, social issues, and emotional well-being to provide a basis for individuals to discuss their lifestyles with a health professional.
Population: 14 years and older.
Publication Date: 1994.
Scores, 16: Nutrition, Eating Habits, Caffeine Use, Physical Activity, Body Weight, Sleep, Social Relationships, Family Interactions, Tobacco Use, Alcohol Use, Non-Medical Drug Use, Medical/Dental Care, Motor Vehicle Safety, Sexual Activities, Work & Leisure, Emotional Health.
Administration: Individual.
Price Data, 2002: $195 per MS-DOS disk for 100 uses; $895 per MS-DOS disk for 500 uses; $25 per Previous Version MS-DOS for 3 uses.
Time: (20–30) minutes.
Comments: Self-Report; designed to run on most IBM-compatible computers; minimum requirements include a color graphics adapter card (CGA, EGA, VGA, or SVGA), DOS ver. 3.3 or later, 640K free RAM, and 2 floppy drives or 1 hard disk and 1 floppy disk drive; registered users receive all program upgrades free for the first year after purchase.
Author: Harvey A. Skinner.
Publisher: Multi-Health Systems, Inc.

[660]
Comrey Personality Scales.

Purpose: Developed to measure major personality characteristics.
Population: Ages 16 and over.
Publication Date: 1970.
Acronym: CPS.
Scores, 10: Trust vs. Defensiveness (T), Orderliness vs. Lack of Compulsion (O), Social Conformity vs. Rebelliousness (C), Activity vs. Lack of Energy (A), Emotional Stability vs. Neuroticism (S), Extraversion vs. Introversion (E), Mental Toughness vs. Sensitivity (M), Empathy vs. Egocentrism (P), Validity Check (V), Response Bias (R).
Administration: Group.
Price Data, 1998: $20.75 per 25 reusable test booklets; $14 per 50 answer sheets [$125 per 500]; $15.25 per 50 answer sheets for use in machine scoring for optical scanning with computer input [$131.50 per 500]; $11.75 per 50 profile sheets [$96.50 per 500]; $24.50 per manual (40 pages) and handbook of interpretations; $4 per hand-scoring instructions; $32 per specimen set including manual and 1 copy of all forms.
Time: (35–50) minutes.
Comments: Comrey Personality Scales, Short Form is also available with same scales and prices.
Author: Andrew L. Comrey.
Publisher: EdITS/Educational and Industrial Testing Service.
Cross References: See T5:672 (6 references), T4:628 (21 references), 9:261 (8 references), and T3:558 (22 references); for a review by Edgar Howarth, see 8:527 (27 references); for reviews by R. G. Demaree and M. Y. Quereshi, see 7:59 (20 references).

[661]
Comrey Personality Scales—Short Form.

Purpose: To provide a comprehensive, multidimensional assessment instrument for measuring eight personality dimensions.
Population: High school, college, and adults.
Publication Dates: 1993–1995.
Acronym: CPS Short Form.
Scores, 10: Trust vs. Defensiveness, Orderliness vs. Lack of Compulsion, Social Conformity vs. Rebelliousness, Activity vs. Lack of Energy, Emotional Stability vs. Neuroticism, Extraversion vs. Introversion, Mental Toughness vs. Sensitivity, Empathy vs. Egocentrism, Validity Check, Response Bias.
Administration: Group.
Price Data, 1998: $61.50 per 50 test booklets and answer sheets combined [$86 per 100, $307 per 500]; $5.25 per hand-scoring instructions; $14 per 50 profile sheets [$25.75 per 100, $117 per 500].
Time: Administration time not reported.
Comments: Includes same scales as the Comrey Personality Scales (550) but has fewer items per scale.
Author: Andrew L. Comrey.
Publisher: EdITS/Educational and Industrial Testing Service.

[662]
Concept Assessment Kit—Conservation.

Purpose: To "determine child's level of conservation by his conservation behavior and his comprehension of the principle involved."
Population: Ages 4–7.
Publication Date: 1968.
Acronym: CAK.
Administration: Individual.
Price Data, 1998: $57.25 per complete kit including Forms A, B, and C, and manual (29 pages); $11 per 25 tests [$37.75 per 100 tests, $143.75 per 500 tests] (specify Form A or B); $11 per 25 Form C tests [$33.75 per 100, $137.25 per 500]; $4 per manual.
Authors: Marcel L. Goldschmid and Peter M. Bentler.
Publisher: EdITS/Educational and Industrial Testing Service.

  a) FORMS A AND B.
  Scores, 13: 2 scores (Behavior, Explanation) in each of 6 areas (2-Dimensional Space, Number, Substance, Continuous Quantity, Weight, Discontinuous Quantity), Total.
  Time: (15) minutes per form.
  b) FORM C.
  Scores, 13: 2 scores (Behavior, Explanation) in each of 3 areas and 3 lengths, Total.
Cross References: See T5:674 (5 references), T4:630 (11 references), T3:559 (17 references), 8:238 (32 references), and T2:549 (5 references); for a review by J. Douglas Ayers, and excerpted reviews by Rheta

DeVries (with Lawrence Kohlberg), Vernon C. Hall (with Michael Mery), and Charles D. Smock, see 7:437 (5 references).

[663]
Conditional Reasoning Test of Aggression.

Purpose: "To identify people who have a high probability of engaging in aggressive, harmful behavior."
Population: Employees ages 18 and over.
Publication Date: 2000.
Acronym: CRTA.
Scores: Total score only.
Administration: Group or individual.
Price Data, 2002: $162 per complete kit including manual (63 pages), 25 test booklets, answer sheet, scoring key, and score interpretation; $37 per manual; $132 per 25 test booklets, answer sheet, and score interpretation.
Time: (25) minutes.
Comments: Provides an indirect measure of "potential for aggressive tendencies"; paper-and-pencil format only; hand-scored.
Authors: Lawrence R. James and Michael D. McIntyre.
Publisher: The Psychological Corporation.

[664]
Conduct Disorder Scale.

Purpose: "To identify persons with Conduct Disorder by evaluating the characteristic behaviors that define this condition."
Population: Ages 5–22 years.
Publication Date: 2002.
Acronym: CDS.
Scores, 5: 4 subscales (Aggressive Conduct, Hostility, Deceitfulness/Theft, Rule Violations), Conduct Disorder Quotient.
Administration: Group or individual.
Price Data, 2002: $86 per complete kit including examiner's manual (41 pages), 50 summary/response forms, and storage box; $49 per examiner's manual; $39 per 50 summary/response forms.
Time: (5–10) minutes.
Comments: Based on the diagnostic criteria for conduct disorder specified by the Diagnostic and Statistical Manual of Mental Disorders—Fourth Edition—Text Revision (DSM-IV-TR); provides interpretation guide for classifying degree of severity of conduct disorder (severe, moderate, mild, not applicable).
Author: James E. Gilliam.
Publisher: PRO-ED.

[665]
Conference Meeting Rating Scale.

Purpose: Designed as "an overall rating procedure for observers in evaluating both the effectiveness of the conference leader and the conference group, conferees

in evaluating leader portion of the meeting, and for the conference leader in measuring the reactions of the conference group."
Population: Employees.
Publication Date: No date.
Scores: Total score only.
Administration: Group.
Price Data: Available from Publisher.
Time: Administration time not reported.
Author: B. J. Speroff.
Publisher: Psychometric Affiliates.

[666]
Conflict Management Appraisal.

Purpose: "Designed to provide information about the various ways people react to and try to manage the differences between themselves and others."
Population: Adults.
Publication Dates: 1986–1995.
Acronym: CMA.
Scores, 20: 5 conflict management styles (9/1 Win-Lose, 1/9 Yield-Lose, 1/1 Lose-Leave, 5/5 Compromise, 9/9 Synergistic) for each of 4 contexts (Personal Orientation, Interpersonal Relationships, Small Group Relationships, Intergroup Relationships).
Administration: Individual.
Price Data, 2001: $7.95 per instrument.
Time: (30) minutes.
Comments: Adaptation of the Conflict Management Survey (667); to be used in conjunction with the Conflict Management Survey; ratings by person well acquainted with subject.
Author: Jay Hall.
Publisher: Teleometrics International.
Cross References: For reviews by William L. Curlette and David N. Dixon, see 12:90.

[667]
Conflict Management Survey.

Purpose: "Designed to provide information about the various ways people react to and try to manage the differences between themselves and others."
Population: Adults.
Publication Dates: 1969–1996.
Acronym: CMS.
Scores, 20: 5 conflict management styles (9/1 Win-Lose, 1/9 Yield-Lose, 1/1 Lose-Leave, 5/5 Compromise, 9/9 Synergistic) for each of 4 contexts (Personal Orientation, Interpersonal Relationships, Small Group Relationships, Intergroup Relationships).
Administration: Group.
Price Data, 2001: $8.95 per instrument.
Time: Administration time not reported.
Comments: Self-ratings.
Author: Jay Hall.
Publisher: Teleometrics International.

Cross References: For reviews by Frederick Bessai and Douglas J. McRae, see 12:91; for a review by Frank J. Landy of an earlier edition, see 8:1173 (2 references).

[668]
Conflict Style Inventory.

Purpose: Designed to assess an individual's approach to conflict resolution.
Population: Adults.
Publication Dates: 1990–1995.
Acronym: CSI.
Scores, 15: Total Score, Individual [one-on-one] Conflict Situations, Group/Team Conflict Situations on 5 styles: (Avoiding, Smoothing, Bargaining, Forcing, Problem Solving).
Administration: Group.
Price Data, 1995: $24.95 per trainer's guide (1994, 47 pages); $6.50 per inventory; $4.95 per Managing Conflict Constructively Participant Handout.
Time: (20) minutes.
Comments: Self-scored.
Author: Marshall Sashkin.
Publisher: Human Resource Development Press.
Cross References: For reviews by Trenton R. Ferro and Scott T. Meier, see 14:96.

[669]
Conners Adult ADHD Diagnostic Interview for DSM-IV.

Purpose: Empirically based structured interview that assists the process of diagnosing ADHD.
Population: Age 18 and older.
Publication Date: 2001.
Acronym: CAADID.
Scores: Childhood and Adult ADHD Diagnosis (specifies Inattentive vs. Hyperactive Impulsive).
Administration: Individual.
Price Data, 2002: $85 per complete kit including manual, 25 patient history forms, and 25 diagnostic criteria forms; $35 per specimen set including manual, 1 patient history form, and 2 diagnostic criteria form.
Time: (60–90) minutes for Interview; (30–60) minutes for Self-Report.
Comments: Interview format.
Authors: C. Keith Conners, Jeff Epstein, and Diane Johnson.
Publisher: Multi-Health Systems, Inc.

[670]
Conners' Adult ADHD Rating Scales.

Purpose: Designed to assess "psychopathology and problem behaviors associated with adult ADHD."
Population: Ages 18 and over.
Publication Date: 1999.
Acronym: CAARS.
Administration: Individual.

Forms, 6: Self-Report: Long (CAARS-S:L); Self-Report: Short (CAARS-S:S); Self-Report: Screening (CAARS-S:SV); Observer: Long (CAARS-O:L); Observer: Short (CAARS-O:S); Observer: Screening (CAARS-O: SV).

Price Data, 2002: $192 per complete kit including manual (144 pages) and 25 QuikScore™ forms for each of the 6 forms; $40 per manual; $29 per 25 QuikScore™ forms for either Long form; $29 per 25 QuikScore™ forms for either Short form or either Screening form; quantity discounts available; $45 per specimen set including manual, and 1 QuikScore™ form for each of the 6 forms.

Authors: C. Keith Conners, Drew Erhardt, and Elizabeth Sparrow.

Comments: Observer rating and/or self-report.

Publisher: Multi-Health Systems, Inc.

a) CAARS—SELF-REPORT: LONG; CAARS—OBSERVER: LONG.

Scores, 9: Inattention/Memory Problems, Hyperactivity/Restlessness, Impulsivity/Emotional Lability, Problems with Self-Concept, DSM-IV Inattentive Symptoms, DSM-IV Hyperactive-Impulsive Symptoms, DSM-IV Total ADHD Symptoms, ADHD Index, Inconsistency Index.

Time: (30) minutes.

b) CAARS—SELF-REPORT: SHORT; CAARS—OBSERVER: SHORT.

Scores, 6: Inattentive/Memory Problems, Hyperactivity/Restlessness, Impulsivity/Emotional Lability, Problems with Self-Concept, ADHD Index, Inconsistency Index.

Time: (10) minutes.

c) CAARS—SELF-REPORT: SCREENING; CAARS—OBSERVER: SCREENING.

Scores, 4: DSM-IV Inattentive Symptoms, DSM-IV Hyperactive/Impulsivity Symptoms, DSM-IV Total ADHD Symptoms, ADHD Index.

Time: (10) minutes.

[671]

Conners' Continuous Performance Test for Windows: Kiddie Version.

Purpose: Software program designed to identify attention problems and measure treatment effectiveness in very young children.

Population: Age 4–5.

Publication Date: 2001.

Acronym: K-CPT.

Scores: Omissions, Comissions, Hit RT, Hit RT Standard Error, Variability, Detectability (d'), Response Style, Perseverations, Hit RT Block Change, Hit SE Block Change, Hit RT ISI Change, Hit SE ISI Change, and Confidence Index.

Administration: Individual.

Price Data, 2002: $200 per manual and PsychManager software kit; $45 per preview version.

Time: 7.5 minutes.

Comments: Self-completed.

Authors: C. Keith Conners and Multi-Health Systems, Inc. staff.

Publisher: Multi-Health Systems, Inc.

[672]

Conners' Continuous Performance Test II.

Purpose: A computerized assessment tool used to assess attention problems and to measure treatment effectiveness.

Population: Ages 6 to adult.

Publication Dates: 1992–1996.

Acronym: CPT II.

Scores, 12: Omissions, Commissions, Hit Reaction Time, Hit Reaction Time Standard Error, Variability of Standard Error, Attentiveness (d prime), Perseverations, Hit Reaction Time Block Change (Vigilance Measure), Hit Standard Error Block Change (Vigilance Measure), Hit Reaction Time Inter-Stimulus Interval Change (Adjusting to Presentation Speed), Hit Standard Error Inter-Stimulus Change (Adjusting to Presentation Speed), Confidence Index.

Administration: Individual

Price Data, 2002: $495 per Psychmanager Lite CD kit and Correction Manager CD kit with manual; $45 per preview version.

Time: (14) minutes.

Comments: Self-report performance measure; includes CD-ROM and 3.5-inch disk; requires Windows 95 or higher.

Authors: C. Keith Conners and the MHS staff.

Publisher: Multi-Health Systems, Inc.

Cross References: For a review by James Ysseldyke, see 14:97; see also T5:679 (2 references).

[673]

Conners-March Developmental Questionnaire.

Purpose: To gather personal history information about a child from the parents prior to meeting with a physician or psychologist.

Population: Children.

Publication Date: 1994.

Scores: Not scored.

Administration: Group.

Manual: No manual.

Price Data, 2002: $27 per 25 questionnaires; $90 per 100 questionnaires.

Time: Administration time not reported.

Comments: Completed by parent.

Authors: C. Keith Conners and John S. March.

Publisher: Multi-Health Systems, Inc.

[674]
Conners' Rating Scales—Revised.

Purpose: Constructed to assess psychopathology and problem behaviors.

Population: Ages 3–17; self-report scales can be completed by 12- to 17-year-olds.

Publication Dates: 1989–1997.

Acronym: CRS-R.

Administration: Group.

Price Data, 2002: $425 per complete kit including manual (1997, 226 pages), 25 feedback forms for each of the CPRS-R:L, CPRS-R:S, CTRS-R:L, CTRS-R:S, CASS:L, CASS:S, CADS-Parent, CADS-Teacher, CADS-Self-Report, 25 Global Index-Teacher Forms, 25 Global Index-Parent Forms, 15 CRS-R Treatment Progress Color Plot, and 100 Teacher Information Forms; $26 per 25 Quick Score forms (specify test and version); $22 per feedback forms (specify test and version); $46 per technical manual; $40 per user's manual; $45 per Windows preview version including 3 administrations/interpretive reports, and user's manual; $10 per computer interpretive report; $4 per computer profile report.

Comments: Ratings by parents and teachers and adolescent self-report.

Author: C. Keith Conners.

Publisher: Multi-Health Systems, Inc.

a) CONNERS' PARENT RATING SCALE—REVISED.

Acronym: CPRS-R.

Scores, 13: Oppositional, Cognitive Problems/Inattention, Hyperactivity, Anxious-Shy, Perfectionism, Social Problems, Psychosomatic, ADHD Index, Conners' Global Index: Restless-Impulsive and Emotional Lability, DSM-IV Inattentive, DSM-IV Hyperactive-Impulsive, DSM-IV Total.

Forms, 2: Long, Short.

Time: (15–20) minutes.

b) CONNERS' TEACHER RATING SCALE—REVISED.

Acronym: CTRS-R.

Scores: Same as *a* above.

Forms, 2: Long, Short.

Time: (15) minutes.

c) CONNERS-WELLS' ADOLESCENT SELF-REPORT SCALE.

Acronym: CASS.

Scores, 10: Conduct Problems, Cognitive Problems/Inattention, Hyperactivity, ADHD Index, Family Problems, Anger Control Problems, Emotional Problems, DSM-IV Inattentive, DSM-IV Hyperactive-Impulsive, DSM-IV Total.

Forms, 2: Long, Short.

Time: (15–20) minutes.

d) CONNERS' GLOBAL INDEX.

Acronym: CGI.

Scores, 3: Emotional Lability, Restless-Impulsive, Total.

Forms, 2: Parent, Teacher.

Time: (5) minutes.

e) CONNERS' ADHD/DSM-IV™ SCALES.

Acronym: CADS.

Scores, 4: Conners' ADHD Index, DSM-IV: Inattentive, DSM-IV: Hyperactive/Impulsive, DSM-IV Total.

Forms, 3: Parent, Teacher, Adolescent.

Time: (5–10) minutes.

Cross References: For reviews by Allen K. Hess and Howard M. Knoff, see 14:98; see also T5:681 (99 references) and T4:636 (50 references); for reviews by Brian K. Martens and Judy Oehler-Stinnett of the original edition, see 11:87 (83 references).

[675]
Consequences.

Purpose: Measure ideational fluency and originality.

Population: Grades 9–16.

Publication Date: 1958.

Scores, 2: Originality, Ideational Fluency.

Administration: Group.

Forms, 2: A1, A2.

Price Data: Available from publisher.

Time: 10(13) minutes.

Comments: Mimeographed manual, third edition (8 pages); Form A1 consists of first 5 items and Form A2 consists of last 5 items of the original 1958 (single-form) 10-item test.

Authors: Paul R. Christensen, P. R. Merrifield, and J. P. Guilford.

Publisher: Charlotte Mackley [No reply from publisher; status unknown].

Cross References: See T5:682 (5 references), T4:637 (2 references) and T2:551 (71 references); for a review by Goldine C. Gleser of the 10-item test, see 6:547 (13 references).

[676]
Constructive Thinking Inventory.

Purpose: "Evaluates an individual's experiential intelligence and coping skills."

Population: Ages 18–80 years.

Publication Date: 2001.

Acronym: CTI.

Scores, 24: Emotional Coping (Self-Acceptance, Absence of Negative Overgeneralization, Nonsensitivity, Absence of Dwelling, Total), Behavioral Coping (Positive Thinking, Action Orientation, Conscientiousness, Total), Personal Superstitious Thinking, Categorical Thinking (Polarized Thinking, Distrust of Others, Intolerance, Total), Esoteric Thinking (Belief in the Unusual, Formal Superstitious Thinking, Total), Naive Optimism (Over-Optimism, Stereotypical Thinking,

Polyanna-ish Thinking, Total), Defensiveness, Validity, Global Constructive Thinking.
Administration: Individual or group.
Price Data, 2001: $125 per introductory kit (3.5-inch disk) including scoring program with on-screen user's manual, professional manual (59 pages), 25 test booklets, and 25-use key disk; $30 per professional manual; $99 per 25 test booklets with 25-use key disk.
Time: (15–30) minutes.
Comments: Administered in paper-and-pencil format only; responses are manually entered into scoring program; software generates *T*-scores, report, and profile; system requirements: Windows 95/98/NT/2000/ME; 8 MB hard disk, 16 MB RAM (Windows 95/98/ME) or 24 MB RAM (Windows NT/2000), 3.5-inch disk drive.
Author: Seymour Epstein.
Publisher: Psychological Assessment Resources, Inc.

[677]
Contextual Memory Test.

Purpose: Designed to assess awareness of memory capacity, strategy use, and recall in adults with memory dysfunction.
Population: Adults.
Publication Date: 1993.
Acronym: CMT.
Scores, 12: Recall Score (Immediate Recall, Delayed Recall, Total Recall), Cued Recall, Recognition, Awareness Score (Prediction, Estimation of Performance Following Recall, Response to General Questioning [Prior to Recall, Following Recall]), Strategy Use (Effect of Context, Order of Recall, Total Strategy Score).
Administration: Individual.
Price Data, 2002: $105 per complete kit including manual (138 pages), 2 test cards, 14 cut-apart sheets of 80 picture cards, 25 score sheets (12 pages), and carrying case; $37 per 25 score sheets.
Time: (10–20) minutes.
Author: Joan P. Toglia.
Publisher: Therapy Skill Builders—A Division of The Psychological Corporation.
Cross References: For reviews by Karen Mackler and Alan J. Raphael, see 14:99.

[678]
Continuous Visual Memory Test [Revised].

Purpose: Constructed to assess visual memory.
Population: Ages 7–80+.
Publication Dates: 1983–1997.
Acronym: CVMT.
Scores, 6: Acquisition (Hits, False Alarms, d-Prime, Total), Delayed Recognition, Visual Discrimination.
Administration: Individual.
Price Data: Available from publisher for complete kit including manual (1988, 22 pages), norms manual (1997, 51 pages), stimulus cards, and 50 scoring forms.

Time: (45–50) minutes.
Authors: Donald E. Trahan and Glenn J. Larrabee.
Publisher: Psychological Assessment Resources, Inc.
Cross References: For reviews by Michael B. Brown and Alice J. Corkill, see 14:100; see also T5:687 (4 references); for reviews by Nancy B. Bologna and Stephen F. Davis of an earlier edition, see 12:93; see also T4:642 (4 references).

[679]
Controller Staff Selector.

Purpose: To evaluate the bookkeeping and analytical reasoning skills necessary for the position of controller.
Population: Candidates for the position of controller.
Publication Date: 1988.
Acronym: COCON.
Scores: Total Score, Narrative Evaluation, Ranking, Recommendation.
Administration: Group.
Price Data, 2001: $500 per candidate; quantity discounts available.
Time: (319) minutes.
Comments: Scored by publisher; must be proctored; previously listed as Controller/Accountant Staff Selector.
Author: Walden Personnel Performance, Inc.
Publisher: Walden Personnel Performance, Inc.

[680]
The Conversational Skills Rating Scale: An Instructional Assessment of Interpersonal Competence.

Purpose: "To assess the skills domain of conversational competence."
Population: Secondary and post-secondary students.
Publication Date: 1995.
Acronym: CSRS.
Scores, 5: Altercentricism, Composure, Expressiveness, Interaction Management, Total.
Administration: Group.
Forms, 7: Rating of Partner Form, Rating of Self Form, Instructor Rating of Student Form, Self Frequency Version, Partner Frequency Version, Self Trait Rating Form, Other Trait Rating Form.
Price Data: Available from publisher.
Time: (5–15) minutes.
Author: Brian H. Spitzberg.
Publisher: National Communication Association.
Cross References: For reviews by Sandra M. Ketrow and Julia Y. Porter, see 14:101.

[681]
Coolidge Assessment Battery.

Purpose: Designed to assess personality disorders and neuropsychological functioning.
Population: Ages 15 and over.

Publication Date: 1999.

Acronym: CAB.

Scores, 46: 7 Axis I scales (Anxiety, Depression, Post-Traumatic Stress, Psychotic Thinking, Schizophrenia, Social Phobia, Withdrawal); 14 Axis II scales (Antisocial, Avoidant, Borderline, Dependent, Depressive, Histrionic, Narcissistic, Obsessive-Compulsive, Paranoid, Passive-Aggressive, Sadistic, Schizoid, Schizotypal, Self-Defeating); 4 Neuropsychological Dysfunction scales (Overall Neuropsychological, Language Functions, Memory and Concentration, Neurosomatic Functions); 4 Executive Functions of the Frontal Lobe scales (Overall Executive Functions, Decision Difficulty, Planning Problems, Task Completion Difficulty); 5 Personality Change due to Medical Condition scales (Aggression, Apathy, Disinhibition, Emotional Lability, Paranoid); 3 Hostility scales (Anger, Dangerousness, Impulsiveness); 5 Normative scales (Apathy, Emotional Lability, Indecisiveness, Maladjustment, Introversion-Extroversion); 4 Validity scales (Answer Choice Frequency, Random Responding, Tendency to Look Good or Bad, Tendency to Deny Blatant Pathology).

Administration: Group or individual

Price Data, 2001: $38 per manual (1999, 54 pages); $12 per narrative report (Self Rating or Other Rater); $9 per brief report (Self Rating or Other Rater); $99 per Windows software package including disks, software manual, and test manual.

Time: (40) minutes.

Comments: Originally published as the Coolidge Axis II Inventory (14:102); mail-in or software scoring.

Author: Frederick L. Coolidge.

Publisher: Sigma Assessment Systems, Inc.

Cross References: For reviews by Kevin L. Moreland and Paul Retzlaff of an earlier edition, see 14:102; see also T5:690 (3 references).

[682]
The Cooperative Institutional Research Program.

Purpose: "A national longitudinal study of the American higher educational system" based on freshman survey data.

Population: First-time, full-time entering college freshmen.

Publication Dates: 1966–1994.

Acronym: CIRP.

Scores: No scores.

Administration: Group.

Price Data: Available from publisher.

Time: (40) minutes.

Comments: Test entitled Student Information Form (T3:2333); national norms reported annually.

Authors: Alexander W. Astin, William S. Korn, and Ellyne R. Riggs.

Publisher: Higher Education Research Institute, University of California-Los Angeles [No reply from publisher; status unknown].

Cross References: See T5:692 (1 reference) and T4:645 (8 references); for a review by Harvey Resnick, see 9:266. For a review by Albert B. Hood of the Student Information Form, see 8:397 (15 references).

[683]
Coopersmith Self-Esteem Inventories.

Purpose: "Designed to measure evaluative attitudes toward the self in social, academic, family, and personal areas of experience."

Population: Ages 8–15, 16 and above.

Publication Date: 1981.

Acronym: SEI.

Administration: Group.

Price Data, 2001: $31.50 per School preview kit including School Form, School key, and manual; $31.50 per Adult preview kit including Adult Form, Adult key, and manual; $16 per 25 nonreusable School form item booklets; $14.40 per 25 nonreusable Adult form item booklets; $12.60 per scoring key (specify School or Adult form); $20.10 per manual.

Time: (10) minutes.

Author: Stanley Coopersmith.

Publisher: Consulting Psychologists Press, Inc.

  a) SCHOOL FORM.

  Population: Ages 8–15.

  Scores, 6: General Self, Social Self-Peers, Home-Parents, School-Academic, Total Self Score, Lie.

  Comments: Separate answer sheets may be used; school short form also available.

  b) ADULT FORM.

  Population: Ages 16 and above.

Cross References: See T5:694 (134 references) and T4:647 (106 references); for reviews by Christopher Peterson and James T. Austin and Trevor E. Sewell, see 9:267 (32 references).

[684]
Coping Inventory: A Measure of Adaptive Behavior.

Purpose: "Assess the behavior patterns and skills to meet personal needs and to adapt to the demands of the environment."

Population: Ages 3–16, adults.

Publication Date: 1985.

Scores, 9: 3 scores (Productive, Active, Flexible) for Coping with Self, Coping with Environment, plus Adaptive Behavior Index.

Administration: Individual.

Levels: 2.

Time: Administration time not reported.

Author: Shirley Zeitlin.

Publisher: Scholastic Testing Service, Inc.

a) SELF-RATED FORM.
Population: Adult.
Price Data, 2002: $34.50 per starter set including manual (6 pages) and 10 forms; $17.70 per 10 inventories; $16.40 per manual; $15.75 per sample set
Comments: Self-report ratings of adaptive behavior.
b) OBSERVATION FORM.
Population: Ages 3–16.
Price Data: $53 per starter set including manual (75 pages) and 20 forms; $34.50 per 20 inventories; $28.30 per manual; $25.95 per sample set.
Comments: Ratings of adaptive behavior by adult informant.
Cross References: See T5:695 (3 references) and T4:648 (1 reference).

[685]
Coping Inventory for Stressful Situations, Second Edition.

Purpose: Designed as a "scale for measuring coping styles."
Population: Adolescents ages 13–18, adults age 18 and over.
Publication Dates: 1990–1999.
Acronym: CISS.
Scores, 5: Task, Emotion, Avoidance, Distraction, Social Diversion.
Administration: Individual or group.
Forms, 2: Adult, Adolescent.
Price Data, 2002: $45 per complete kit including 25 QuikScore™ forms, and manual (1999, 87 pages) (specify Adult or Adolescent Form); $30 per specimen set including 3 Adult QuikScore™ forms, 3 Adolescent QuikScore™ forms, 3 Situation Specific QuikScore™ forms, and manual; $24 per 25 QuikScore™ forms (specify Adult or Adolescent); $26 per manual.
Foreign Language Editions: French (Canadian), Spanish (U.S.), Dutch, Icelandic, and Polish forms available.
Time: (10) minutes.
Comments: Self-report.
Authors: Norman S. Endler and James D. A. Parker.
Publisher: Multi-Health Systems, Inc.
Cross References: For reviews by E. Thomas Dowd and Stephanie Stein, see 14:104, see also T5:696 (2 references).

[686]
Coping Resources Inventory.

Purpose: Developed to assess a person's resources for coping with stress.
Population: Middle school-age to adult.
Publication Dates: 1987–1988.
Acronym: CRI.

Scores, 6: Cognitive, Social, Emotional, Spiritual/Philosophical, Physical, Total.
Administration: Group.
Price Data, 2001: $95 per preview kit including item booklet, prepaid answer sheet, scoring keys, CRI profile, and manual (1988, 30 pages); $34 per 25 item booklets; $51.70 per 25 nonprepaid answer sheets for hand scoring; $76.30 per scoring keys for hand scoring; $20.90 per 25 profiles for hand scoring; $22.50 per manual.
Time: (10) minutes.
Comments: For research use only; also available as part of www.careerhub.org website; mail-in or hand scoring available.
Authors: Allen L. Hammer and M. Susan Marting.
Publisher: Consulting Psychologists Press, Inc.
Cross References: See T5:697 (6 references); for reviews by Roger A. Boothroyd and Larry Cochran, see 12:95 (1 reference); see also T4:649 (2 references).

[687]
Coping Resources Inventory for Stress.

Purpose: "Designed to measure coping resources which are believed to help lessen the negative effects of stress."
Population: Adults.
Publication Dates: 1988–1993.
Acronym: CRIS.
Scores, 16: Self-Disclosure, Self-Directedness, Confidence, Acceptance, Social Support, Financial Freedom, Physical Health, Physical Fitness, Stress Monitoring, Tension Control, Structuring, Problem Solving, Cognitive Restructuring, Functional Beliefs, Social Ease, Coping Resource Effectiveness.
Administration: Group or individual.
Price Data, 1997: $2.95 per test booklet; $16.95 per manual (1993, 65 pages); $19.95 per interpretive report; $8.95 per profile report; $29.95 per specimen set including test booklet, manual, pre-paid answer sheet, and interpretive report; $399 per PC-CRIS test administration and scoring program (with PC-CRIS manual); $5.95 to $11.95 per PC-CRIS Interpretive or Profile report (depending on quantity purchased); $9.95 per PC-CRIS test administration program.
Foreign Language Editions: Spanish, French, Russian, Chinese, Portugese, and Korean editions available.
Time: (45–90) minutes.
Comments: Computer (PC-CRIS) administration and software package available.
Authors: Kenneth B. Matheny, William L. Curlette, David W. Aycock, James L. Pugh, and Harry F. Taylor.
Publisher: Health Prisms, Inc.
Cross References: See T5:698 (1 reference); for reviews by Sharon L. Weinberg and Paul D. Werner, see 13:84; see also T4:650 (3 references).

[688]
Coping Responses Inventory—Adult and Youth.

Purpose: Constructed as "a measure of ... types of coping responses to stressful life circumstances."
Population: Ages 12–18, 18 and older.
Publication Date: 1993.
Acronym: CRI.
Scores: 8 scales: Logical Analysis, Positive Reappraisal, Seeking Guidance and Support, Problem Solving, Cognitive Avoidance, Acceptance or Resignation, Seeking Alternative Rewards, Emotional Discharge.
Administration: Group.
Levels, 2: Adult and Youth.
Forms, 2: Ideal, Actual.
Price Data: Available from publisher for complete kit including manual (44 pages), 10 reusable item booklets (actual form and 50 answer sheets (specify adult or child).
Time: (10–15) minutes.
Comments: Computer scoring system available from publisher.
Author: Rudolf H. Moos.
Publisher: Psychological Assessment Resources, Inc.
Cross References: For reviews by Ashraf Kagee and Everett V. Smith, Jr., see 14:105; see also T5:699 (5 references).

[689]
Coping Scale for Adults.

Purpose: Designed as a self-report inventory that examines coping behavior.
Population: Ages 18 and over.
Publication Date: 1997.
Acronym: CSA.
Forms, 2: Short Form, Long Form.
Scores, 19: Seek Social Support, Focus on Solving the Problem, Work Hard, Worry, Improve Relationships, Wishful Thinking, Tension Reduction, Social Action, Ignore the Problem, Self-Blame, Keep to Self, Seek Spiritual Support, Focus on the Positive, Seek Professional Help, Seek Relaxing Diversions, Physical Recreation, Protect Self, Humor, Not Cope.
Administration: Group.
Price Data, 2002: A$121 per complete kit; A$24.70 per 10 short forms; A$24.70 per 10 long forms; A$11.55 per 10 scoring sheets; A$11.55 per 10 profile charts; A$51.80 per manual (60 pages).
Time: Administration time not reported.
Authors: Erica Frydenberg and Ramon Lewis.
Publisher: Australian Council for Educational Research Ltd. [Australia].

[690]
Coping With Health Injuries and Problems.

Purpose: Designed to assess coping with physical health problems.

Population: Adults.
Publication Dates: 1992–2000.
Acronym: CHIP.
Scores: 4 dimensions: Distraction, Palliative, Instrumental, Emotional Preoccupation.
Administration: Group.
Price Data, 2002: $48 per complete kit including technical manual (2000, 76 pages) and 25 Quikscore forms; $24 per 25 Quikscore forms; $86 per 100 Quickscore forms; $30 per technical manual; $32 per specimen set including technical manual and 3 Quikscore forms.
Time: (10) minutes.
Comments: Self-report.
Authors: Norman S. Endler and James D. A. Parker.
Publisher: Multi-Health Systems, Inc.

[691]
Coping With Stress.

Purpose: Constructed as a self-assessment tool to identify sources of stress and responses to stress.
Population: Adults.
Publication Date: 1989.
Scores, 9: Reaction to Stress (Obsessive, Hysteria, Anxiety, Phobia, Total, Normal), Adjustment to Stress (Healthy, Unhealthy), Sources of Stress.
Administration: Group.
Price Data: Price information available from publisher for complete kit including 20 test folders, 20 response sheets, and 20 interpretation sheets.
Time: [20] minutes administration; [10] minutes scoring; [30] minutes interpretation.
Comments: Self-administered, self-scored.
Author: Training House, Inc.
Publisher: Training House, Inc.
Cross References: For a review by Bert W. Westbrook and Suzanne Markel-Fox, see 12:96.

[692]
COPSystem Picture Inventory of Careers.

Purpose: To measure career interest for persons with reading or language difficulties.
Population: Elementary through adult-non-verbal.
Publication Date: 1993.
Acronym: COPS-PIC.
Scores: Interest scores in 14 COPSystem Career Clusters: Science—Professional, Science—Skilled, Technology—Professional, Technology—Skilled, Consumer Economics, Outdoor, Business—Professional, Business—Skilled, Clerical, Communication, Arts—Professional, Arts—Skilled, Service—Professional, Service—Skilled.
Administration: Group.
Price Data, 1998: $29.75 per 25 booklets and answer sheets combined including profile and guide [$105.50 per 100, $491.75 per 500]; $22.75 per set of

hand-scoring keys; $1.60 each scoring by publisher; $2.75 per manual (6 pages); $2.75 per specimen set.
Time: (30) minutes.
Author: Lisa Knapp-Lee.
Publisher: EdITS/Educational and Industrial Testing Service.

[693]
The Cornell Class-Reasoning Test, Form X.
Purpose: "A multiple-choice deductive logic class-reasoning test."
Population: Grades 4–12.
Publication Date: 1964.
Scores: Deductive Logic.
Administration: Group.
Manual: No manual.
Price Data: Available from publisher.
Time: Untimed.
Comments: Subtitle on test booklet is Cornell Critical Thinking Test Series.
Authors: Robert H. Ennis, William L. Gardiner, Richard Morrow, Dieter Paulus, and Lucille Ringel.
Publisher: Illinois Critical Thinking Project.
Cross References: See T2:1753 (1 reference).

[694]
The Cornell Conditional-Reasoning Test.
Purpose: Designed as "a multiple-choice deductive logic conditional-reasoning test."
Population: Grades 4–12.
Publication Date: 1964.
Scores: Deductive Logic.
Administration: Group.
Manual: No manual.
Price Data: Available from publisher.
Time: Untimed.
Comments: Subtitle on test booklet is Cornell Critical Thinking Test Series.
Authors: Robert H. Ennis, William L. Gardiner, John Gazzetta, Richard Morrow, Dieter Paulus, and Lucille Ringel.
Publisher: Illinois Critical Thinking Project.
Cross References: See T2:1754 (1 reference).

[695]
Cornell Critical Thinking Tests.
Purpose: Assesses general critical thinking ability including "induction, deduction, evaluation, observation, credibility (of statements made by others), assumption identification, and meaning."
Publication Dates: 1961–1985.
Acronym: CCTT.
Scores: Total score only for each level.
Administration: Group.
Levels, 2: X, Z.
Price Data, 2001: $21.99 per 10 test booklets (specify level); $8.99 per 10 machine-gradable answer

sheets; $8.99 per manual (1985, 32 pages); $17.99 per specimen set including both tests, answer sheet, and manual; $39.99 per software (specify Level X or Level Z and Macintosh or Windows; quantity licenses available); includes 10 free tests (any combination of X and Z levels); $.99 per additional per student license.
Time: (50) minutes.
Comments: Identical to 1971 edition except for minor format and wording changes and 1999 publication of software; 1 form.
Authors: Robert H. Ennis, Jason Millman, and Thomas N. Tomko (manual).
Publisher: Critical Thinking Books & Software.
   a) LEVEL X.
   Population: Grade 5–college.
   Comments: Software version for Grade 7–college population.
   b) LEVEL Z.
   Population: Advanced and gifted high school students and college students and adults.
Cross References: See T5:705 (10 references) and T4:655 (1 reference); for reviews by Jan N. Hughes and Koressa Kutsick Malcolm, see 11:88 (3 references); see also 9:269 (1 reference), T3:606 (7 references), T2:1755 (2 references), and 7:779 (10 references).

[696]
Cornell Index—Form N2.
Purpose: For collecting pertinent medical and psychiatric data from patients.
Population: Ages 14 and over.
Publication Dates: 1949–1956.
Acronym: C.I.
Scores: Total score only.
Administration: Group or individual.
Price Data, 2002: $60 per 100 copies; $30 per specimen set.
Foreign Language Edition: French Canadian and Spanish editions available.
Time: (5–15) minutes.
Comments: Title on test is C.I. Form N2.
Authors: Arthur Weider.
Publisher: Arthur Weider.
Cross References: See T5:708 (9 references), T4:658 (16 references), 9:270 (15 references), T3:609 (33 references), 8:530 (46 references), and T2:1145 (42 references); for reviews by Eugene E. Levitt and David T. Lykken, see 7:61 (32 references); see also P:49 (77 references).

[697]
The Cornell Inventory for Student Appraisal of Teaching and Courses.
Purpose: "Provides teachers with feedback of student opinion."
Population: College teachers.

Publication Dates: 1972–1973.
Scores: Item norms only.
Administration: Group.
Price Data: Not available.
Time: (15–20) minutes.
Authors: James B. Maas and Thomas R. Owen (manual).
Publisher: James B. Maas [No reply from publisher; status unknown].
Cross References: For a review by Wilbert J. McKeachie, see 8:367.

[698]
The Cornell Learning and Study Skills Inventory.

Purpose: To identify "specific competencies that are requisite for effective learning at the secondary school and college levels of instruction."
Population: Grades 7–13, 13–16.
Publication Date: 1970.
Acronym: CLASSIC.
Scores, 9: Goal Orientation, Activity Structure, Scholarly Skills, Lecture Mastery, Textbook Mastery, Examination Mastery, Self Mastery, Total, Reading Validity Index.
Administration: Group.
Price Data, 2002: $20 per 25 Secondary Form test booklets; $27.50 per 25 College Form test booklets; $6.75 per scoring key; $6.75 per 25 answer sheets; $5 per hand scoring stencils (College Form); $6.75 per 25 profiles (junior high, senior high, junior college, and senior college, graduate level); $6.75 per manual (31 pages); $9 per specimen set including manual and forms; specify Secondary Form or College Form for all test materials.
Time: (30–50) minutes.
Comments: Self-administered.
Authors: Walter Pauk and Russell Cassel.
Publisher: Psychologists and Educators, Inc.
a) SECONDARY SCHOOL FORM.
Population: Grades 7–13.
b) COLLEGE FORM.
Population: Grades 13–16.
Cross References: See T4:657 (1 reference); for reviews by Allen Berger and Richard D. Robinson, see 8:815 (1 reference); see also T2:1756 (2 references).

[699]
Cornell Word Form 2.

Purpose: "To assess mental health adjustment using a forced choice word association technique."
Population: Adults.
Publication Dates: 1946–1955.
Acronym: C.W.F.-2.
Scores: Total score only.
Administration: Group or individual.

Price Data, 2002: $60 per 100 copies; $30 per specimen set.
Time: [5–15] minutes.
Comments: Title on test is C.W.F.
Author: Arthur Weider.
Publisher: Arthur Weider.
Cross References: See T2:1146 (1 reference), P:50 (2 references), and 5:44 (11 references); for a review by S. B. Sells, see 6:80 (1 reference).

[700]
Correctional Institutions Environment Scale, Second Edition.

Purpose: Designed to measure the "social climate of juvenile and adult correctional programs."
Population: Residents and staff of correctional facilities.
Publication Dates: 1974–1987.
Acronym: CIES.
Scores, 9: Involvement, Support, Expressiveness, Autonomy, Practical Orientation, Personal Problem Orientation, Order and Organization, Clarity, Staff Control.
Administration: Group.
Forms, 4: Real (R), Ideal (I), Expectations (E), Short (S).
Price Data, 2001: $25 per sampler set including manual (1987, 64 pages), test booklet (R, E, I, S) and scoring key; $125 per permission set.
Foreign Language Editions: Versions adapted for use in French Quebec, Slovenia, Sweden, Spain, and the United Kingdom.
Time: Administration time not reported.
Comments: Part of the Social Climate Scales (T5:2445).
Author: Rudolf H. Moos.
Publisher: Mind Garden, Inc.
Cross References: For reviews by Kevin J. McCarthy and M. David Miller, see 14:106; see also T4:660 (3 references) and T3:612 (1 reference); for a review by Kenneth A. Carlson of an earlier version, see 8:531 (16 references). For a review of the Social Climate Scales, see 8:681.

[701]
Correctional Officer's Interest Blank.

Purpose: Designed for research in the development of selection techniques for correctional officers.
Population: Correctional officer applicants.
Publication Dates: 1953-2001.
Acronym: COIB.
Scores: 19 scales: Dominance, Capacity for Status, Sociability, Social Presence, Self-Acceptance, Well-Being, Responsibility, Socialization, Self-Control, Tolerance, Good Impression, Communality, Achievement via Conformance, Achievement via Independence, Intellectual Efficiency, Psychological-Mindedness, Flexibility, Femininity, Empathy.

Administration: Group or individual.
Price Data, 2002: $25 per sample set, and $1 per copy for COIBB bulk permission.
Time: (10) minutes.
Author: Harrison G. Gough.
Publisher: Mind Garden, Inc.
Cross References: For reviews by Robert J. Howell and R. Lynn Richards and Samuel Roll, see 10:75.

[702]
Correctional Policy Inventory: A Survey of Correctional Philosophy and Characteristic Methods of Dealing with Offenders.

Purpose: Developed to identify the correctional philosophies utilized in particular situations.
Population: Correctional managers.
Publication Date: 1970.
Scores, 4: Reintegration, Rehabilitation, Reform, Restraint.
Administration: Group.
Price Data: Available from publisher.
Time: [20] minutes.
Author: Vincent O'Leary.
Publisher: National Council on Crime and Delinquency [No reply from publisher; status unknown].
Cross References: See 8:1092 (2 references).

[703]
Cotswold Junior Ability Tests.

Purpose: Measures intelligence, understanding of numbers, mastery of the vocabulary, arithmetic processes, and the comprehension and use of English.
Population: Ages 8.5–9.5, 9.5–10.5.
Publication Dates: 1949–1969.
Administration: Group.
Price Data: Not available.
Comments: Tests A, B, C, and E are out of print.
Author: C. M. Fleming.
Publisher: Gibson (Robert) & Sons, Glasgow, Ltd. [Scotland] [No reply from publisher; status unknown].
a) JUNIOR MENTAL ABILITY, D.
  Population: Ages 8.5–9.5.
  Publication Dates: 1967–1969.
  Scores: Total score only.
  Time: 30(40) minutes.
b) JUNIOR MENTAL ABILITY, F.
  Population: Ages 9.5–10.5.
  Publication Dates: 1967–1969.
  Scores: Total score only.
  Time: 30(40) minutes.

[704]
Cotswold Personality Assessment P.A. 1.

Purpose: "Devised as an aid to the assessment of the personal characteristics of boys and girls."
Population: Ages 11–16.

Publication Date: 1960.
Scores, 6: 3 Preferences (Things, People, Ideas), and 3 Attitudes (Using One's Hands, Being with Other People, Talking About School).
Administration: Group.
Price Data: Not available.
Time: Administration time not reported.
Comments: Manual (6 pages) subtitle is A Study of Preferences and Values for Use in School and Clubs.
Author: C. M. Fleming.
Publisher: Gibson (Robert) & Sons, Glasgow, Ltd. [Scotland] [No reply from publisher; status unknown].
Cross References: For reviews by Ralph D. Dutch and G. A. V. Morgan, see 6:81 (1 reference).

[705]
Counselor and Client Verbal Response Category Systems.

Purpose: To "provide a standardized method for analyzing counselor and client verbal behavior."
Population: Counselors in training.
Publication Date: 1981.
Scores: 23 categories: Counselor (Minimal Encourager, Silence, Approval/Reassurance, Information, Direct Guidance, Closed Question, Open Question, Restatement, Reflection, Interpretation, Confrontation, Verbal Referent, Self Disclosure, Other), Client (Simple Responses, Requests, Description, Experiencing, Exploration of Counselor-Client Relationship, Insight, Discussion of Plans, Silence, Other).
Administration: Group.
Price Data: Available from publisher.
Time: Administration time not reported.
Comments: 2 systems: Counselor, Client; interaction must be taped and transcribed.
Authors: Clara E. Hill, Carole Greenwald, Kathryn G. Reed, Darlene Charles, Mary K. O'Farrell, and Jean A. Carter.
Publisher: Marathon Consulting and Press.
Cross References: See T5:716 (2 references) and T4:667 (1 reference).

[706]
Course Finder.

Purpose: Assesses "students' interests and preferences, and identifies suitable higher education courses at appropriate universities/colleges in Great Britain."
Population: Students entering higher education.
Publication Dates: 1992–1993.
Acronym: CF.
Administration: Group.
Price Data: Available from publisher.
Time: (45–60) minutes.
Comments: For use in Great Britain; was listed in a previous MMY as Course Finder 2000, however, is updated each year.

Authors: Malcolm Morrisby, Glen Fox, and Mark Parkinson.
Publisher: The Morrisby Organisation [England].
Cross References: For a review by Colin Cooper, see 13:85.

[707]
CPF [Second Edition].

Purpose: "To assess extroversion and preference for social contact."
Population: Ages 16–adult.
Publication Dates: 1954–1992.
Acronym: CPF.
Scores, 3: Validity Scores (Uncertainty, Good Impression), Total Extroversion.
Administration: Group or individual.
Price Data, 2001: $30 per introductory kit including manual (1992, 10 pages), 20 test booklets, and scoring key; $26 per 20 test booklets; $10 per manual.
Time: (5–10) minutes.
Comments: Previously listed as a subtest of the Employee Attitude Series of the Job-Tests Program (T3:1219).
Author: Samuel E. Krug.
Publisher: Industrial Psychology International, Ltd.
Cross References: For reviews by Michael R. Harwell and Allen K. Hess, see 12:97.

[708]
C-R Opinionaire.

Purpose: Measures degree of "conservatism" and "radicalism" on a number of issues.
Population: Grades 11–16 and adults.
Publication Dates: 1935–1950.
Scores: Conservatism-Radicalism.
Administration: Group.
Forms, 2: J, K.
Price Data: Available from publisher.
Time: Administration time not reported.
Author: Theodore F. Lentz.
Publisher: Lentz Peace Research Laboratory [No reply from publisher; status unknown].
Cross References: See T5:363 (1 reference), T4:676 (1 reference), T2:1116 (7 references), and P:21 (3 references); for a review by George W. Hartmann, see 4:39 (5 references); for a review by Goodwin Watson, see 2:1212 (5 references); for a review by H. H. Remmers, see 1:899.

[709]
Crane Oral Dominance Test: Spanish/ English.

Purpose: "To determine if the student has a dominant language, if the student is bilingual ..., or if the student needs concentrated language, concept, and memory development to function adequately in either language."
Population: Ages 4-8.
Publication Date: 1976.
Acronym: CODT.
Scores, 4: Spanish Dominant, English Dominant, Bilingual, Indeterminable.
Administration: Individual.
Price Data, 2001: $34.64 per 30 test booklets and manual (11 pages).
Time: (20) minutes.
Comments: Both English and Spanish used in administration and in pupil responses.
Author: Barbara J. Crane.
Publisher: Bilingual Educational Services, Inc.
Cross References: For excerpted reviews by Protase E. Woodford and Porfirio Sanchez, see 8:162 (1 reference).

[710]
Crawford Small Parts Dexterity Test.

Purpose: "A performance test designed to measure fine eye-hand coordination."
Population: High school and adults.
Publication Dates: 1946–1981.
Acronym: CSPDT.
Scores, 2: Pins and Collars, Screws.
Administration: Individual.
Price Data, 2002: $446 per complete set including manual (1981, 22 pages) and spare parts; $18 per manual; replacement parts are available by calling the publisher.
Time: (8–15) minutes.
Authors: John E. Crawford and Dorothea M. Crawford.
Publisher: The Psychological Corporation.
Cross References: See T4:679 (2 references), T3:627 (4 references), and T2:2223 (12 references); for a review by Neil D. Warren, see 5:871 (8 references); for a review by Raymond A. Katzell, see 4:752; for a review by Joseph E. Moore, see 3:667.

[711]
Creative Behavior Inventory.

Purpose: Designed to measure "behavioral characteristics associated with creativity."
Population: Grades 1–6, 7–12.
Publication Date: 1989.
Acronyms: CBI1, CBI2.
Scores, 5: Contact, Consciousness, Interest, Fantasy, Total.
Administration: Individual.
Levels, 2: I (elementary), II (secondary).
Price Data: Price data for materials including manual (70 pages) available from publisher.
Time: Administration time not reported.
Comments: Ratings by teachers; manual title is Understanding the Creative Activity of Students.
Author: Robert J. Kirschenbaum.

Publisher: Creative Learning Press, Inc.
Cross References: For a review by Richard M. Clark, see 11:93.

[712]
Creativity Assessment Packet.

Purpose: To assess creative potential.
Population: Ages 6 through 18.
Publication Date: 1980.
Acronym: CAP.
Administration: Group.
Price Data, 2001: $109 per complete kit including 25 of each test and manual (1980, 24 pages); $29 per manual.
Author: Frank Williams.
Publisher: PRO-ED.

  a) TEST OF DIVERGENT THINKING.
  Scores, 6: Fluency, Flexibility, Originality, Elaboration, Titles, Total.
  Forms, 2: A, B.
  Price Data: $21 per 25 tests (specify Form A or Form B).
  Time: 20(25) minutes for grades 6-12; 25(30) minutes for grades 3-5.
  b) TEST OF DIVERGENT FEELING.
  Scores, 5: Curiosity, Imagination, Complexity, Risk-Taking, Total.
  Price Data: $24 per 25 tests.
  Time: 10(20) minutes.
  c) THE WILLIAMS SCALE.
  Scores, 9: Fluency, Flexibility, Originality, Elaboration, Curiosity, Imagination, Complexity, Risk-Taking, Total.
Price Data: $21 per 25 tests.
Time: Administration time not reported.
Comments: Ratings by parents and teachers.
Cross References: See T5:724 (6 references) and T4:682 (3 references); for reviews by Fred Damarin and Carl L. Rosen, see 9:280.

[713]
Creativity Attitude Survey.

Purpose: Designed to assess attitudes toward creative behaviors and oneself as a creative thinker.
Population: Grades 4–6.
Publication Date: 1971.
Acronym: CAS.
Scores: Total score only.
Administration: Group.
Price Data, 2002: $15 per 25 tests; $4.50 per manual (8 pages); $5 per specimen set.
Time: (10) minutes.
Author: Charles E. Schaefer.
Publisher: Psychologists and Educators, Inc.
Cross References: For reviews by Philip V. Vernon and Kaoru Yamamoto, see 8:240 (1 reference); see also T2:553 (1 reference).

[714]
Creativity Tests for Children.

Purpose: To measure different aspects of divergent production ability.
Population: Grades 4–6.
Publication Dates: 1971–1976.
Administration: Group.
Price Data: Available from publisher.
Authors: J. P. Guilford and others listed.
Publisher: SOI Systems.

  a) ADDING DECORATIONS.
  Time: 6(10) minutes.
  Authors: Arthur Gershon, Sheldon Gardner, and Philip R. Merrifield.
  b) DIFFERENT LETTER GROUPS.
  Time: 8(12) minutes.
  Author: Arthur Gershon.
  c) HIDDEN LETTERS.
  Time: 5(8) minutes.
  d) KINDS OF PEOPLE.
  Time: 6(10) minutes.
  Author: Arthur Gershon.
  e) MAKE SOMETHING OUT OF IT.
  Time: 5(8) minutes.
  f) MAKING OBJECTS.
  Time: 5(8) minutes.
  Authors: Sheldon Gardner, Arthur Gershon, and Philip K. Merrifield.
  g) NAMES FOR STORIES.
  Time: 8(12) minutes.
  h) SIMILAR MEANINGS.
  Time: 6(10) minutes.
  Author: Philip R. Merrifield.
  i) WHAT TO DO WITH IT.
  Time: 7(11) minutes.
  Authors: Philip R. Merrifield (Form A), Robert C. Wilson (Form B), and Paul R. Christensen (Form B).
  j) WRITING SENTENCES.
  Time: 7(11) minutes.
Cross References: See T3:630 (1 reference); for reviews by John W. French and Kaoru Yamamoto, see 8:241 (1 reference).

[715]
The Creatrix Inventory.

Purpose: "To help people identify their levels of creativity as well as their orientations toward risk taking."
Population: Members of organizations.
Publication Dates: 1971–1986.
Acronym: C&RT.
Scores, 2: Creativity, Risk Taking; plotted on matrix to determine 1 of 8 styles: Reproducer, Modifier, Challenger, Practicalizer, Innovator, Synthesizer, Dreamer, Planner.

Administration: Group.
Price Data: Price information available from publisher for manual (1986, 26 pages) including inventory and scoring instructions plus administrator's guide (2 pages).
Time: Administration time not reported.
Comments: Catalog uses the title Creativity and Risk-Taking.
Author: Richard E. Byrd.
Publisher: Jossey-Bass, A Wiley Company.
Cross References: For reviews by Harrison G. Gough and John F. Wakefield, see 11:95.

[716]
Cree Questionnaire.

Purpose: "To measure an individual's overall creative potential."
Population: Individuals in a variety of occupations; clients in vocational and career counseling.
Publication Dates: 1957–1995.
Acronym: CQ.
Scores, 11: Overall Creative Potential, plus 10 factorially determined dimension scores grouped under 4 broad headings: Social Orientation, Work Orientation, Internal Functioning, and Interests.
Administration: Individual or group.
Price Data, 2002: $114 per start-up kit including 25 test booklets, 25 score sheets, and interpretation and research manual; $54 per 25 test booklets (quantity discounts available); $45 per 25 score sheets; $28 per interpretation and research manual.
Time: No limit (approximately 20 minutes).
Authors: T. G. Thurstone and J. Melinger.
Publisher: Reid London House.
Cross References: See T5:728 (1 reference); for a review by Janet M. Stoppard, see 9:282; see also T2:1149 (1 reference) and P:53 (3 references); for reviews of an earlier edition by Allyn Miles Munger and Theodor F. Naumann, see 6:84.

[717]
Crichton Vocabulary Scale.

Purpose: Designed to provide an index of a child's "acquired fund of verbal information."
Population: Ages 4.5–11.
Publication Dates: 1950–1988.
Acronym: CVS.
Scores, 3: Definitions of Set One, Definitions of Set Two, Total.
Administration: Individual.
Price Data: Available from publisher.
Time: Administration time not reported.
Comments: Designed for use with Raven's Progressive Matrices (2064).
Author: J. C. Raven.
Publisher: Oxford Psychologists Press, Ltd. [England].

Cross References: See T4:687 (3 references), T3:632 (2 references), and T2:491 (3 references); for a review by Morton Bortner, see 6:518 (1 reference); for reviews by Charlotte Banks and W. D. Wall, see 4:337.

[718]
Criterion Test of Basic Skills.

Purpose: "Developed to assess the basic reading and arithmetic skills of individual students."
Population: Age 6 through 11-11.
Publication Dates: 1976–2000.
Administration: Individual.
Price Data, 2002: $112 per test kit including manual, 25 arithmetic recording forms, 25 reading recording forms, 25 math problem sheets, and test plates in vinyl folder; $25 per 25 arithmetic recording forms; $25 per 25 reading recording forms; $12 per 25 math problem sheets; $25 per test plates; $25 per manual.
Time: (15–20) minutes.
Comments: "Criterion-referenced."
Authors: Keith Lundell, William Brown, and James Evans.
Publisher: Academic Therapy Publications.
a) READING.
 Scores: Letter Recognition, Letter Sounds, Blending, Sequencing, Decoding of Common Spelling Patterns and Multisyllable Words, Sight Word Recognition.
b) ARITHMETIC.
 Scores: Counting, Number Concepts and Numerical Recognition, Addition, Subtraction, Multiplication, Division, Measurement Concepts, Fracts, Decimals, Percents, Geometric Concepts, Pre-Algebra, Rounding and Estimation.
Cross References: See T3:635 (1 reference).

[719]
Criterion Validated Written Test for Emergency Medical Practitioner.

Purpose: Intended for the selection of paramedic personnel.
Population: Prospective paramedics.
Publication Date: 1995.
Scores: 7 subtests and total: Interest, Teamwork, Problem Solving—Common Sense, Problem Solving—Map Reading, Problem Solving—Logical Thinking, Problem Solving—Relevancy, Attentiveness, Total.
Administration: Group.
Form, 1: ESV-90 EMP (90 items).
Restricted Distribution: Distribution restricted to civil service commissions and qualified municipal officials.
Price Data: Available from publisher.
Time: 110 minutes.

Comments: Practice test and candidate study guide available.
Author: McCann Associates, Inc.
Publisher: McCann Associates, Inc.

[720]
Criterion Validated Written Test for Fire Medic.

Purpose: Intended for the selection of cross-trained firefighter/fire medic candidates.
Population: Prospective firefighter/fire medic candidates.
Publication Date: 1995.
Scores: 7 subtests and total: Interest, Teamwork, Problem Solving—Common Sense, Problem Solving—Mechanical, Problem Solving—Logical Thinking, Problem Solving—Relevancy, Attentiveness, Total.
Administration: Group
Form, 1: ESV-100 Fire Medic (100 items).
Restricted Distribution: Distribution restricted to civil service commissions and qualified municipal officials.
Price Data: Available from publisher.
Time: 135 minutes.
Comments: Practice test and candidate study guide available.
Author: McCann Associates, Inc.
Publisher: McCann Associates, Inc.

[721]
Criterion Validated Written Tests for Firefighter.

Purpose: For the selection of firefighter candidates.
Population: Prospective firefighters.
Publication Dates: 1976–1998.
Scores: 7 subtests and total: Interest in Firefighting, Compatibility, Map Reading, Spatial Visualization, Visual Pursuit, Understanding and Interpreting Table and Text Material About Firefighting, Mechanical Aptitude, Total.
Administration: Group.
Forms, 2: Form ESV-100 (100 items), ESV M-100 (100 items).
Restricted Distribution: Distribution restricted to civil service commissions and qualified municipal officials.
Price Data: Available from publisher.
Time: 131(141) minutes.
Comments: Practice test and candidate study guide available.
Author: McCann Associates, Inc.
Publisher: McCann Associates, Inc.

[722]
Criterion Validated Written Tests for Police Officer.

Purpose: Designed for the selection of police officer candidates.

Population: Prospective police officers.
Publication Dates: 1980–1993.
Time: 170(180) minutes.
Administration: Group.
Restricted Distribution: Distribution restricted to civil service commissions and qualified municipal officials.
Forms, 2: Form 100, Form N-100.
Price Data: Available from publisher.
Scores: 7 subtests and total: Observational Ability, Ability to Exercise Judgment and Common Sense, Interest in Police Work, Ability to Exercise Judgment-Map Reading, Ability to Exercise Judgment-Dealing With People, Ability to Read and Comprehend Police Test Material, Reasoning Ability, Total.
Comments: Practice test and candidate study guide available.
Author: McCann Associates, Inc.
Publisher: McCann Associates, Inc.

[723]
Critical Reasoning Test Battery.

Purpose: To assist students in subject and career choices and employers with the selection of job candidates.
Population: Students and employees ages 15 and over.
Publication Dates: 1981–1983.
Acronym: CRTB.
Administration: Group.
Restricted Distribution: Distribution restricted to persons who have completed the publisher's training course or members of the Division of Occupational Psychology of the British Psychological Society.
Price Data: Available from publisher.
Comments: 3 subtests available as separates.
Authors: Peter Saville, Roger Holdsworth, Gill Nyfield, David Hawkey, Susan Bawtree, and Ruth Holdsworth.
Publisher: SHL Group plc [United Kingdom].
  a) VERBAL EVALUATION.
  Publication Dates: 1982–1983.
  Acronym: VC1.
  Time: 30(35) minutes.
  b) INTERPRETING DATA.
  Publication Dates: 1982–1983.
  Acronym: NC2.
  Time: 30(35) minutes.
  c) DIAGRAMMATIC SERIES.
  Publication Dates: 1982–1983.
  Acronym: DC3.
  Time: 20(25) minutes.

[724]
Critical Reasoning Tests.

Purpose: Assesses intellectual skills needed for a managerial level post.

Population: Prospective managers.
Publication Date: 1992.
Acronym: CRT.
Administration: Group.
Price Data: Available from publisher.
Authors: Pauline Smith and Chris Whetton.
Publisher: NFER-Nelson Publishing Co., Ltd. [England].

a) VERBAL TEST.
Purpose: "Assesses how well a candidate can cope with different reasoning tasks."
Scores: Total score only.
Time: (28–33) minutes.
b) NUMERICAL TEST.
Purpose: "Assesses how well the candidate interprets numerical information."
Scores: Total score only.
Time: (30–35) minutes.
Cross References: For reviews by Timothy Z. Keith and Harold Takooshian, see 12:98.

[725]
Cross-Cultural Adaptability Inventory.

Purpose: "Designed to provide information to an individual about his or her potential for cross-cultural effectiveness."
Population: Trainers and professionals who work with culturally diverse and cross-culturally oriented populations.
Publication Dates: 1987–1995.
Acronym: CCAI.
Scores: 4 scales: Emotional Resilience, Flexibility/ Openness, Perceptual Acuity, Personal Autonomy.
Administration: Group.
Price Data: Available from publisher.
Time: [15–30] minutes.
Comments: Observer-rating survey is optional.
Authors: Colleen Kelley and Judith Meyers.
Publisher: Reid London House.
Cross References: For reviews by Lynn L. Brown and Wendy Naumann, see 14:107.

[726]
Cross Reference Test.

Purpose: Constructed to assess "skill in routine checking tasks."
Population: Clerical job applicants.
Publication Date: 1959.
Scores: Total score only.
Administration: Group.
Price Data: Available from publisher.
Time: 5(10) minutes.
Author: James W. Curtis.
Publisher: Psychometric Affiliates.
Cross References: For a review by Philip H. Kriedt, see 6:1039.

[727]
CRS Placement/Diagnostic Test.

Purpose: Designed to diagnose and locate the student's CRS (Crane Reading System) level.
Population: Grades Preprimer–2.
Publication Dates: 1977–1978.
Scores: Total score only.
Administration: Group.
Price Data: Price information for test materials including general directions (1977, 7 pages) available from publisher.
Foreign Language Edition: Spanish version available.
Time: Administration time not reported.
Author: Barbara J. Crane.
Publisher: Bilingual Educational Services, Inc.

a) ENGLISH VERSION.
1) *Level A.*
Population: Grade Preprimer.
Subtests, 4: Rhyming, Words That Begin Alike, Long Vowel Recognition, Consonant Sounds.
2) *Levels B, C, and D (Beginning Consonant Sounds).*
Population: Preprimer-primer.
Comments: Levels determined by number of errors.
3) *Level E (Blends).*
Population: Grade 1.
4) *Level F (Vowel Recognition).*
Population: Grade 1.
5) *Level G (Digraphs).*
Population: Grade 1.
6) *Levels H, I, and J (Special Vowel Patterns).*
Population: Grades 1-2.
Comments: Levels determined by number of errors.

b) SPANISH VERSION.
1) *Level A.*
Subtests, 2: Rhyming, Words That Begin Alike.
2) *Level B (Beginning Consonant Sounds—S, M, F, R, N, L, Z).*
3) *Level C (Beginning Consonant Sounds—B, P, T, D, V, CH).*
4) *Level D (Beginning Consonant Sounds—C, G, LL, Q, J, Y).*
5) *Level E (Special Patterns).*

[728]
CTB Performance Assessment.

Purpose: Designed to measure student ability in reading comprehension, vocabulary, language, spelling, study skills, mathematics, science and social studies by allowing students to construct their own responses.
Population: Grades 2–11.

Publication Date: 1994.
Scores, 4: Language Arts, Mathematics, Science, Social Studies.
Administration: Group.
Levels, 9: 12/13, 13/14, 14/15, 15/16, 16/17, 17/18, 18/19, 19/20, 20/21.
Price Data: Available from publisher.
Time: (150–180) minutes.
Comments: "The test is designed primarily for use with two of CTB's norm-referenced, selected-response achievement tests, CAT/5 (365) or CTBS/4 (T5:665), with correlated results reported in terms of Integrated Outcomes. The CTB Performance Assessment also works as a stand-alone test that yields both student and class reports." The mathematics section complies with NTCM standards. Response tests for each subject area (Reading/Language Arts, Mathematics, Science, Social Studies) may be administered and scored separately from the complete Performance Assessment. Scoring services provided at an additional cost for administrations tailored to the needs of the test user: administration of all four areas of the CTB Performance Assessment along with all subtests from either the CAT/5 or CTBS/4; administration of only the Reading/Language Arts section of the CTB Performance Assessment along with all the Reading, Language, Spelling, and Study Skill subtests of the CAT/5 or CTBS/4; or administration of CTB Performance Assessment independent of a selected-response achievement test. The CTB Performance Assessment may be scored locally.
Author: CTB Macmillan/McGraw-Hill.
Publisher: CTB/McGraw-Hill.

[729]
CTB Writing Assessment System.
Purpose: "Includes direct and indirect writing measures to aid educators in evaluating writing programs and students' writing abilities."
Population: Grades 2.0–12.9.
Publication Date: 1993.
Scores, 6: Holistic, Analytic (Content, Organization, Sentence Construction, Vocabulary/Grammar, Spelling/Capitalization).
Administration: Group.
Levels, 4: 12–13 (grades 2.0–4.2), 14–16 (grades 3.6–7.2), 17–19 (grades 6.6–10.2), and 20–22 (grades 9.6–12.9 and adults).
Price Data, 2002: $53.35 per 30 consumable Writing books including administration and scoring manual (specify Narrative, Descriptive, Informative, or Persuasive and specify level); $41.80 per 30 Writing books with independent prompts only (Specify Narrative, Descriptive, Informative, or Persuasive and specify level); $23.10 per 50 Student Information and Score Sheets; additional price information

and information regarding scoring services available from publisher.
Comments: Includes books 1–32 with a writing assignment called a "prompt"; each book comes with its own manual; books are available as separates; overall guide is entitled Writing Assessment Guide.
Author: CTB Macmillan/McGraw-Hill.
Publisher: CTB/McGraw-Hill.
　a) LEVEL 12–13.
　Population: Grades 2.0–4.2
　Time: 30–35 (35–40) minutes.
　Comments: 4 books (Personal Expression—Descriptive [Books 1 & 4], Personal Expression—Narrative [Books 2 & 3]) available as separates.
　b) LEVEL 14–16.
　Population: Grades 3.6–7.2.
　Time: 30–35 (35–40) minutes.
　Comments: 8 books (Personal Expression—Descriptive [Books 5 & 8], Personal Expression—Narrative [Books 6 & 7], and Informative [Books 9–12]) available as separates.
　c) LEVEL 17–19.
　Population: Grades 6.6–10.2.
　Time: 40–45 (45–50) minutes.
　Comments: 10 books (Personal Expression—Narrative [Books 13 & 14], Informative [Books 15–18], Persuasive [Books 19–22]) available as separates.
　d) LEVEL 20–22.
　Population: Grades 9.6–12.9.
　Time: 40–45 (45–50) minutes.
　Comments: 10 books (Personal Expression—Narrative [Books 23 & 24], Informative [Books 25–28], Persuasive [Books 29–32]) available as separates.
Cross References: For reviews by George Engelhard, Jr. and Joe B. Hansen, see 13:88.

[730]
Cultural Competence Self-Assessment Instrument.
Purpose: Designed "to help agencies measure their cultural competency in agency policymaking, administrative procedures, and practices."
Population: Business staff and clients of child welfare agencies.
Publication Date: 1993.
Scores: Not scored.
Administration: Group.
Price Data, 2000: $24.95 per instrument including manual (48 pages).
Time: Administration time not reported.
Author: Child Welfare League of America, Inc.
Publisher: Child Welfare League of America, Inc.

[731]
Culture Fair Intelligence Test.

Purpose: Designed to measure individual intelligence with minimal influence from verbal fluency, educational level, and ethnic/racial group membership.
Publication Dates: 1950–1973.
Acronym: CFIT.
Scores: Total scores only.
Administration: Group or individual.
Foreign Language Edition: Information regarding many non-English-language adaptations available from publisher.
Comments: Formerly called Culture Free Intelligence Test; test booklet title is Test of "g": Culture Fair.
Authors: Raymond B. Cattell and A. Karen S. Cattell (Scales 2 and 3).
Publisher: Institute for Personality and Ability Testing, Inc.
a) SCALE 1.
Population: Ages 4–8 and educable mentally retarded adults.
Publication Dates: 1933–1969.
Administration: Individual in part.
Price Data, 2002: $61 per introductory kit including 25 test booklets, scoring key, reusable classification cards, and handbook (1950, 15 pages); $25 per 25 test booklets; $8 per scoring key: $22 per reusable classification test cards; $6 per handbook; $16 per specimen set including test booklet, scoring key, and handbook.
Time: (22–60) minutes.
Comments: Identical to Cattell Intelligence Tests, Scale O: Dartington Scale; materials for Test 5 (Following Directions) must be assembled locally.
b) SCALE 2.
Population: Ages 8–14 and average IQ adults.
Publication Dates: 1949–1973.
Forms, 2: A, B.
Price Data: $55 per introductory kit including test booklet, scoring keys, answer sheets, manual (1973, 27 pages), and technical supplement (1973, 30 pages); $25 per 25 test booklets (specify Form A or B); $8 per scoring keys for answer sheets; $8 per scoring keys for test booklets; $18 per 50 answer sheets; $33 per cassette tape recording of Scale 2 instructions; $15 per manual; $15 per technical supplement.
Time: 12.5 (30) minutes.
Comments: Cassette recording available for individual untimed administration of Form A.
c) SCALE 3.
Population: Senior high, college, and high IQ adults.
Publication Dates: 1950–1973.
Forms, 2: A, B.

Price Data: Same as *b* above.
Time: 12.5 (30) minutes.
Cross References: See T5:745 (25 references), T4:699 (34 references), 9:290 (13 references), T3:643 (51 references), 8:184 (38 references), and T2:364 (61 references); for reviews by John E. Milholland and Abraham J. Tannenbaum, see 6:453 (15 references); for a review by I. MacFarlane Smith of *a*, see 5:343 (11 references); for reviews by Raleigh M. Drake and Gladys C. Schwesinger, see 4:300 (2 references).

[732]
Culture-Free Self-Esteem Inventories, Third Edition.

Purpose: "A set of self-report inventories used to determine the level of self-esteem in students ages 6-0 through 18-11."
Population: Ages 6-0 through 18-11.
Publication Dates: 1981–2002.
Acronym: CFSEI-3.
Administration: Group.
Levels, 3: Primary, Intermediate, Adolescent.
Price Data, 2002: $179 per complete kit including manual (2002, 60 pages), 50 primary examiner record forms, 50 intermediate profile/scoring forms, 50 intermediate student response forms, 50 adolescent profile/scoring forms, and 50 adolescent student response forms in a storage box; $49 per manual.
Time: (15–20) minutes.
Comments: Newly normed revision of Culture-Free Self-Esteem Inventories, Second Edition; all levels include Defensiveness Score (a lie scale); previous editions entitled Culture-Free Self-Esteem Inventories for Children and Adults; derivative entitled North American Depression Inventories for Children and Adults.
Author: James Battle.
Publisher: PRO-ED.
a) PRIMARY.
Population: Ages 6–8.
Score: Global Self-Esteem Quotient.
Price Data: $27 per 50 primary examiner record forms.
b) INTERMEDIATE.
Population: Ages 9–12.
Scores, 5: Academic, General, Parental/Home, Social, Global Self-Esteem Quotient.
Price Data: $27 per 50 intermediate profile/scoring forms; $27 per 50 intermediate student response forms.
c) ADOLESCENT.
Population: Ages 13–18.
Scores, 6: Academic, General, parental/Home, Social, Personal, Global Self-Esteem Quotient.
Price Data: $27 per 50 adolescent profile scoring forms, $27 per 50 adolescent student response forms.

Cross References: See T5:746 (4 references); for reviews by Michael G. Kavan and Michael J. Subkoviak of a previous edition, see 12:100 (7 references); see also T4:700 (9 references); for reviews by Gerald R. Adams and Janet Morgan Riggs of the original edition, see 9:291 (1 reference); see also T3:644 (1 reference). For reviews by Patricia A. Bachelor and Michael G. Kavan of the North American Depression Inventories for Children and Adults, see 11:265 (1 reference).

[733]
Curtis Interest Scale.

Purpose: Developed to identify vocational interest patterns.
Population: Grades 9–16 and adults.
Publication Date: 1959.
Scores, 10: Business, Mechanics, Applied Arts, Direct Sales, Production, Science, Entertainment, Interpersonal, Computation, Farming; 1 rating: Desire for Responsibility.
Administration: Group.
Price Data: Available from publisher.
Time: (6–12) minutes.
Comments: Self-administered.
Author: James W. Curtis.
Publisher: Psychometric Affiliates.
Cross References: See T2:2177 (1 reference); for reviews by Warren T. Norman and Leona E. Tyler, see 6:1052.

[734]
[Curtis Object Completion and Space Form Tests].

Purpose: "Devised to provide estimates of individual competence in two basic areas of mechanical aptitude and pattern visualization."
Population: Applicants for mechanical and technical jobs.
Publication Dates: 1960–1961.
Scores: Total scores only.
Administration: Group.
Price Data: Available from publisher.
Time: 1(6) minutes per test.
Author: James W. Curtis.
Publisher: Psychometric Affiliates.
  a) OBJECT-COMPLETION TEST.
  b) SPACE FORM TEST.
Cross References: For reviews by Richard S. Melton and I. Macfarlane Smith, see 6:1085.

[735]
Curtis Verbal-Clerical Skills Tests.

Purpose: "Devised to provide estimates of individual competence in … verbal skill usually identified with office and clerical work."
Population: Applicants for clerical positions.

Publication Dates: 1963–1965.
Acronym: CVCST.
Scores: 4 tests: Computation, Checking, Comprehension, Capacity.
Administration: Group.
Price Data: Available from publisher.
Time: 8(10) minutes.
Author: James W. Curtis.
Publisher: Psychometric Affiliates.

[736]
Customer Reaction Survey.

Purpose: Assesses customers' perceptions of salespeople's interpersonal skills.
Population: Salespeople.
Publication Dates: 1972–1995.
Acronym: CRS.
Scores, 4: Observed Exposure, Observed Feedback, Preferred Exposure, Preferred Feedback.
Administration: Group.
Price Data, 2001: $7.95 per instrument.
Time: Administration time not reported.
Comments: Ratings by customers; also called Customer Reaction Index; based on the Johari Window Model of interpersonal relations.
Authors: Jay Hall and C. Leo Griffith.
Publisher: Teleometrics International.

[737]
Customer Service Applicant Inventory.

Purpose: "Evaluates skills and attitudes to help hire customer service oriented, honest, safe, and productive employees."
Population: Job applicants.
Publication Date: 1996.
Acronym: CSAI.
Scores, 12: Validity Scales (Candidness, Accuracy), Interpersonal Scales (Customer Service, Teamwork, Communication, Stress Tolerance), Core Values (Honesty, Drug Avoidance, Safety), Supplemental Scales (Applied Math, Training Readiness), Composite (Employability Index).
Administration: Group or individual.
Price Data: Available from publisher.
Time: (45) minutes.
Comments: Paper-and-pencil or computer administration available.
Author: NCS London House.
Publisher: Reid London House.

[738]
Customer Service Simulator.

Purpose: "Designed to identify individuals who can project responsiveness and sensitivity in dealing with customers, independent of any particular job classification."
Population: Any position requiring public contact.

Publication Dates: 1993–2002.
Acronym: CSS.
Scores, 2: Customer Service Orientation, Interpersonal Sensitivity.
Administration: Group or individual.
Forms, 2: Private and public sector forms: Worker Version, Supervision Version.
Restricted Distribution: Clients must pay a one-time overhead/sign-up fee of $100.
Price Data, 2002: $60 per candidate for rental/scoring, bar chart, and feedback report.
Time: 90 minutes.
Author: Richard C. Joines.
Publisher: Management & Personnel Systems, Inc.

[739]
Customer Service Skills Test.

Purpose: To evaluate technical and interpersonal skills of persons for the customer service position; available also to measure computer use skills.
Population: Candidates for customer service positions.
Publication Date: 1992.
Acronym: BASLCUS.
Scores: Total Score, Narrative Evaluation, Ranking, Recommendation.
Administration: Group.
Foreign Language Edition: Available in French.
Price Data, 2001: $150 per candidate; quantity discounts available.
Time: (700) minutes.
Comments: Scored by publisher; available in booklet and internet versions; must be proctored.
Author: Walden Personnel Performance, Inc.
Publisher: Walden Personnel Performance, Inc. [Canada].

[740]
d2 Test of Attention.

Purpose: Designed as "a psychodiagnostic instrument for measuring concentration, and in particular visual attention."
Population: Adults.
Publication Date: 1998.
Acronym: d2 Test.
Scores: Score information available from publisher.
Administration: Individual.
Price Data, 2001: $64 per complete test including 20 recording blanks, set of 2 scoring keys, and manual (1998, 80 pages); $12.50 per 50 recording blanks; $9.50 per set of 2 scoring keys; $45 per manual.
Time: (8) minutes.
Comments: Originally conceived to assess individuals' suitability for driving, the test has also been used as a part of personnel selection in other workplace environments where high levels of visual attention and concentration are demanded.

Authors: Rolf Brickenkamp and Eric Zillmer.
Publisher: Hogrefe & Huber Publishers.

[741]
DABERON-2: Screening for School Readiness, Second Edition.

Purpose: Developed to provide a standardized assessment of school readiness.
Population: Ages 3-0 to 7-11.
Publication Dates: 1972–1991.
Scores: Total score only.
Administration: Individual.
Price Data, 2001: $129 per complete kit including 24 presentation cards, 25 screen forms, 25 readiness reports, 5 classroom summary forms, object kit of manipulatives, and administration manual (1991, 38 pages); $8 per set of presentation cards; $24 per 25 screen forms; $24 per 25 readiness reports; $9 per 5 classroom summary forms; $34 per object kit of manipulatives; $36 per administration manual.
Time: (20-40) minutes.
Authors: Virginia A. Danzer, Mary Frances Gerber, Theresa M. Lyons, and Judith K. Voress.
Publisher: PRO-ED.
Cross References: For reviews by Stephen N. Axford and Selma Hughes, see 11:100 (1 reference).

[742]
Dallas Pre-School Screening Test.

Purpose: "Designed to screen the primary learning areas for children from three to six years of age."
Population: Ages 3-6.
Publication Date: 1972.
Scores, 6: Psychological, Auditory, Visual, Language, Motor, Articulation Development (optional).
Administration: Individual.
Foreign Language Edition: Spanish edition available.
Price Data, 2001: $36.60 per 25 pupil record forms, stimuli card book, and manual (42 pages); $12 per stimuli cards; $17 per 25 record forms & profile sheets (quantity discounts available); $12 per manual; Spanish edition prices are equivalent (specify which edition).
Time: (15-20) minutes.
Authors: Robert R. Percival and Suzanne C. Poxon (stimuli book).
Publisher: Dallas Educational Services.
Cross References: For a review by James E. Ysseldyke, see 11:102.

[743]
Das•Naglieri Cognitive Assessment System.

Purpose: "To provide a cognitive processing measure of ability that is fair to minority children, effective for differential diagnosis, and related to intervention."
Population: Ages 5 to 17-11.

Publication Date: 1997.
Acronym: CAS.
Levels, 2: Ages 5–7, ages 8–17.
Price Data: Available from publisher.
Comments: PASS theory reconceptualizes intelligence as cognitive processes.
Authors: Jack A. Naglieri and J. P. Das.
Publisher: Riverside Publishing.

a) STANDARD BATTERY.
Scores: 4 scales with 13 subtests: Planning (Matching Numbers, Planned Codes, Planned Connections), Simultaneous (Nonverbal Matrices, Verbal-Spatial Relations, Figure Memory), Attention (Expressive Attention, Number Detection, Receptive Attention), Successive (Word Series, Sentence Repetition, Speech Rate, Sentence Questions).
Time: [60] minutes.

b) BASIC BATTERY.
Scores: 4 scales with 8 subtests: Planning (Matching Numbers, Planned Codes), Simultaneous (Nonverbal Matrices, Verbal-Spatial Relations), Attention (Expressive Attention, Number Detection), Successive (Word Series, Sentence Repetition).
Time: [40] minutes.
Cross References: For reviews by Joyce Meikamp and Donald Thompson, see 14:109; see also T5:763 (5 references).

[744]
Database Analyst Staff Selector.

Purpose: To evaluate the analytical reasoning and detail skills necessary for successful performance as a database analyst.
Population: Candidates for database positions.
Publication Date: 1992.
Acronym: DBPRDF.
Scores: Total Score, Narrative Evaluation, Ranking, Recommendation.
Administration: Group.
Price Data, 2001: $340 per candidate.
Time: (85) minutes.
Comments: Scored by publisher; must be proctored.
Author: Walden Personnel Performance, inc.
Publisher: Walden Personnel Performance, Inc. [Canada].

[745]
A Dating Scale.

Purpose: To measure "liberalism of attitudes toward dating."
Population: Adolescents and adults.
Publication Dates: 1962–1988.
Scores: Total score only.
Administration: Group.
Manual: No manual.

Price Data, 2001: $1 per scale.
Time: [10] minutes.
Comments: Supplementary article available.
Author: Panos D. Bardis.
Publisher: Donna Bardis.
Cross References: For additional information and a review by Charles F. Warnath, see 8:335 (3 references).

[746]
Davidson Trauma Scale.

Purpose: Developed to assess post traumatic stress disorder (PTSD) symptoms and aid in treatment.
Population: Adults who have been exposed to a serious trauma.
Publication Date: 1996.
Acronym: DTS.
Scores, 4: Intrusion, Avoidance/Numbing, Hyperarousal, Total.
Administration: Individual or group.
Price Data, 2002: $50 per complete kit including manual (42 pages), and 25 QuikScore™ forms; $25 per 25 QuikScore™ forms; $31 per manual.
Foreign Language Edition: French-Canadian QuikScore™ forms available.
Time: (10) minutes.
Comments: Self-report.
Author: Jonathan Davidson.
Publisher: Multi-Health Systems, Inc.
Cross References: For reviews by Janet F. Carlson and William E. Martin, Jr., see 14:110.

[747]
DCS—A Visual Learning and Memory Test for Neuropsychological Assessment.

Purpose: Designed as "a learning and memory test for detecting memory deficits resulting from neurological disorders."
Population: Ages 6–70.
Publication Date: 1998.
Scores: Score information available from publisher.
Administration: Individual.
Price Data, 2001: $89 per complete kit including folder, 50 record and evaluation sheets, 18 test cards, 5 wooden sticks, and manual (1998, 48 pages); $15 per 50 record and evaluation sheets; $30 per set of 18 test cards and 5 wooden sticks; $39.50 per manual.
Time: (20–60) minutes.
Authors: Georg Lamberti and Sigrid Weidlich.
Publisher: Hogrefe & Huber Publishers.

[748]
Decision Making Inventory.

Purpose: "Designed to assess an individual's preferred style of decision making."
Population: High school and college, working adults.

Publication Dates: 1983–1986.
Acronym: DMI.
Scores, 4: Information Gathering Style (Spontaneous, Systematic), Information Processing Style (Internal, External).
Administration: Group.
Forms, 2: H, I.
Price Data: Available from publisher.
Time: (10) minutes.
Authors: William C. Coscarelli, Richard Johnson (test), and JaDean Johnson (test).
Publisher: Marathon Consulting and Press.
Cross References: See T5:768 (2 references); for reviews by George Domino and Barbara A. Kerr, see 10:77 (3 references).

[749]
Defendant Questionnaire.

Purpose: "Designed for defendant (misdemeanor or felony) assessment in court settings."
Population: Defendants (misdemeanor or felony).
Publication Date: 1997.
Acronym: DQ.
Scores: 7 scales: Truthfulness, Alcohol, Drugs, Substance Abuse/Dependency, Violence (Lethality), Antisocial, Stress Coping Abilities.
Administration: Group.
Price Data: Available from publisher.
Foreign Language Edition: Available in English and Spanish.
Time: Administration time not reported.
Comments: Can be administered via paper and pencil test booklet, directly on computer screen, optically scanned answer sheet, human voice audio via headset and computer.
Author: Risk & Needs Assessment, Inc.
Publisher: Risk & Needs Assessment, Inc.

[750]
Defense Mechanisms Inventory [Revised].

Purpose: To "measure and predict responses to conflict and threat."
Population: Adults and college students.
Publication Dates: 1968–1993.
Acronym: DMI.
Scores, 5: Turning Against Object, Projection, Principalization, Turning Against Self, Reversal.
Administration: Individual.
Forms: 2 forms (Male, Female) for each of 3 versions (Adolescent, Adult, Elderly).
Price Data: Available from publisher for DMI Introductory Kit including administration manual (1993, 147 pages), clinical manual (1993, 126 pages), 20 reusable adult test booklets (10 male and 10 female), 25 answer sheets, set of 5 scoring keys, 25 adult profile forms, and the supplementary bibliography.

Time: (30–45) minutes.
Comments: Title of administration manual is Defense Mechanisms: Their Classification, Correlates, and Measurement with the Defense Mechanisms Inventory; title of clinical manual is Defenses in Psychotherapy: The Clinical Application of the Defense Mechanisms Inventory.
Authors: David Ihilevich and Goldine C. Gleser.
Publisher: Psychological Assessment Resources, Inc.
Cross References: See T5:770 (1 reference); for reviews by Kevin D. Crehan and Lizanne DeStefano, see 13:89 (12 references); see also T4:723 (15 references); for a review by James J. Hennessy of the earlier edition, see 10:79 (8 references); see also T3:665 (14 references), 8:534 (30 references), and T2:1152 (5 references); for a review by James A. Walsh, see 7:63 (4 references).

[751]
Defining Issues Test.

Purpose: "Gives information about the process by which people judge what ought to be done in moral dilemmas."
Population: Grades 9-12 and college and adults.
Publication Dates: 1979-1987.
Acronym: DIT.
Scores, 12: Consistency Check, M (meaningless items) score, P (principled moral thinking) score, U (utilizer) score, D (composite) score, A (antiestablishment) score, and stage scores (2, 3, 4, 5A, 5B, and 6).
Administration: Group.
Forms, 2: Short form, long form.
Price Data, 2001: $25 per manual including both forms and scoring information (1986, 96 pages); scoring service available from publisher; $1.90 or less per prepaid scoring sheet including all reports, handling costs, etc.
Time: (30-40) minutes for short form; (40-50) minutes for long form.
Comments: 2 optional companion booklets available: Development in Judging Moral Issues from the Center for the Study of Ethical Development, and Moral Development: Advances in Theory and Research from Praeger Press.
Authors: James R. Rest, with model computer scoring programs by Steve Thoma, Mark Davison, Stephen Robbins, and David Swanson.
Publisher: Center for the Study of Ethical Development.
Cross References: See T5:771 (28 references) and T4:724 (10 references); for reviews by Rosemary E. Sutton and by Bert W. Westbrook and K. Denise Bane, see 11:104 (34 references); for reviews by Robert R. McCrae and Kevin L. Moreland, see 9:304 (22 references); see also T3:666 (8 references).

[752]
DeGangi-Berk Test of Sensory Integration.

Purpose: "Designed to overcome problems in detecting sensory integrative dysfunction in the early years."
Population: Ages 3–5.
Publication Date: 1983.
Acronym: TSI.
Scores, 4: Postural Control, Bilateral Motor Integration, Reflex Integration, Total.
Administration: Individual.
Price Data, 2002: $175 per complete kit including set of test materials, 25 star design sheets, 25 protocol booklets, and manual (48 pages) in a carrying case; $22.50 per 100 star designs; $23.50 per 25 record booklets; $38.50 per manual.
Time: (30) minutes.
Comments: Other test materials (e.g., stopwatch, carpeted scooter board, hula hoop) must be supplied by examiner.
Authors: Georgia A. DeGangi and Ronald A. Berk.
Publisher: Western Psychological Services.
Cross References: See T5:772 (2 references); for a review by R. A. Bornstein, see 10:80.

[753]
Degrees of Reading Power [Revised].

Publication Dates: 1979–1995.
Acronym: DRP.
Scores: Total score only.
Administration: Group.
Price Data, 1998: $40 per Primary/Standard DRP Examination set including 1 copy each of test forms, practice exercises, and manuals); $35 per Advanced DRP examination set; $130 per classroom set of Primary DRP; $126 per classroom set of Standard DRP; $123 per classroom set of Advanced DRP (classroom sets include all manuals and testing materials for 30 students).
Time: (45–50) minutes.
Comments: Practice tests may be used to select appropriate test form for student; also provides readability analysis of instructional material in print; machine or hand-scored; group profiles available.
Author: Touchstone Applied Science Associates (TASA), Inc.
Publisher: Touchstone Applied Science Associates (TASA), Inc.

a) PRIMARY.
  Purpose: Constructed to measure "how well students are able to construct meaning from prose material."
  Population: Grades 1–3.
  Forms, 2: G, H.
  Levels, 3: 0, 9, 8.
  Price Data: $90 per 30 machine-scorable test booklets (select form); $11.50 per 30 practice booklets.

b) STANDARD.
  Purpose: Same as *a* above.
  Population: Grades 3–12 and over.
  Forms, 2: G, H.
  Levels, 5: 8, 7, 6, 4, 2.
  Price Data: $68 per 30 test booklets (select level and form); $12.50 per 30 practice booklets (select level S1 or S2); $16 per 30 NCS answer sheets.
c) ADVANCED.
  Purpose: Constructed to measure "how well students are able to reason with text."
  Population: Grades 6–12 and over.
  Forms, 2: T, U.
  Levels, 2: 2, 4.
  Price Data: $75 per 30 test booklets (select level and form); $14.50 per 30 practice booklets; $16 per 30 NCS answer sheets.
Cross References: For reviews by Felice J. Green and Howard Margolis, see 14:111; see also T5:773 (5 references); for reviews by Darrell N. Caulley, Elaine Furniss, and Michael McNamara and by Lawrence Cross of an earlier edition, see 12:101 (9 references); see also T4:726 (14 references); for reviews of an earlier edition by Roger Bruning and Gerald S. Hanna, see 9:305 (1 reference).

[754]
Degrees of Word Meaning.

Purpose: Developed to "assess the size of students' reading vocabularies by measuring their understanding of the meaning of words in naturally occurring contexts."
Population: Grades 3–8+.
Publication Date: 1993.
Acronym: DWM.
Scores: Total score only.
Administration: Group.
Levels: 6 overlapping levels.
Price Data, 1998: $32 per user's manual (96 pages); $17 per 5 test administration procedures; $50 per 30 test booklets (select level); $12.50 per 30 practice booklets; $16 per 30 NCS answer sheets; $14 per scoring key (select level).
Time: Untimed.
Author: Touchstone Applied Science Associates (TASA), Inc.
Publisher: Touchstone Applied Science Associates (TASA), Inc.
Cross References: For reviews by David P. Hurford and Judith A. Monsaas, see 13:90.

[755]
Delaware County Silent Reading Test, Second Edition.

Purpose: "Designed to measure pupil achievement in typical . . . reading materials."
Population: Grades 1.5, 2, 2.5, 3, 3.5, 4, 5, 6, 7, 8.

Publication Date: 1965.
Scores, 5: Interpretation, Organization, Vocabulary, Structural Analysis, Total.
Administration: Group.
Levels, 10: Grades 1.5, 2, 2.5, 3, 3.5, 4, 5, 6, 7, 8.
Manual: No manual.
Price Data: Available from publisher.
Time: Administration time not reported.
Comments: Teacher's guide for each level.
Authors: Judson E. Newburg and Nicholas A. Spennato.
Publisher: Delaware County Intermediate Unit.
Cross References: For a review by Allen Berger, see 7:686.

[756]
Delis-Kaplan Executive Function System.

Purpose: To "comprehensive assess ... the key components of executive functions believed to be mediated primarily by the frontal lobe."
Population: 8–89 years.
Publication Date: 2001.
Acronym: D-KEFS.
Scores: 9 tests: Trail Making Test, Verbal Fluency Test, Design Fluency Test, Color-Word Interference Test, Sorting Test, 20 Questions Test, Word Context Test, Tower Test, Proverb Test.
Administration: Individual.
Price Data, 2001: $415 per complete kit in box including manual (388 pages), stimulus booklet, sorting cards (3 sets of 6 cards each), 1 tower stand with 5 color disks, 25 record forms, 25 Design Fluency Response booklets, 25 Trail Making response booklet sets (each set contains 25 response booklets for the 5 Trail Making conditions; $470 per complete kit with soft-side case; $520 per complete kit in box with Scoring Assistant (CD-ROM or diskette, Windows only); $575 per complete kit in a soft-side case with Scoring Assistant; $155 per D-KEFS Scoring Assistant (CD-ROM or diskette); $68 per examiner's and technical manual; $53 per examiner's manual; $42 per technical manual (144 pages); $37 per 25 record forms; $21 per 25 Sorting or Color-Word Interference test record forms; $55 per 25 sets of Trail Making Test response booklets (each set contains 25 different response booklets for the 5 Trail Making conditions); $15 per 25 Trail Making or Design Fluency Test record forms; $22 per 25 Verbal Fluency, 20 Questions, or Word Context test record forms; $18 per 25 Tower or Proverb test record forms; $21 per 25 alternate record forms for Sorting, Verbal Fluency, 20 Questions Tests; $42 per Sorting Test set of cards including 2 sets of standard sorting cards, and 2 practice set; $42 per Sorting Test alternate set of cards including 3 sets of 6 cards each.
Time: (90) minutes for all 9 tests.
Comments: Each test assesses a different executive-function domain; tests may be administered alone or in combination; hand-scorable; D-KEFS Scoring Assistant software available; scoring software generates reports in table or graphical format; for system requirements contact publisher.
Authors: Dean C. Delis, Edith Kaplan, and Joel H. Kramer.
Publisher: The Psychological Corporation.

a) D-KEFS TRAIL MAKING TEST.
Purpose: Assesses "flexibility of thinking on a visual-motor task".
Form, 1: Standard Record Form.
Scores, 6: Visual Scanning, Number Sequencing, Letter Sequencing, Number-Letter Switching, Motor Speed, Composite Score.

b) D-KEFS VERBAL FLUENCY TEST.
Purpose: Assesses "fluent productivity in the verbal domain."
Forms, 2: Standard Record Form, Alternate Record Form.
Scores, 3: Letter Fluency, Category Fluency, Category Switching.

c) D-KEFS DESIGN FLUENCY TEST.
Purpose: Assesses "fluent productivity in the spatial domain."
Form, 1: Standard Record Form.
Scores, 3: Filled Dots, Empty Dots Only, Switching.

d) D-KEFS COLOR-WORD INTERFERENCE TEST.
Purpose: Assesses "verbal inhibition."
Form, 1: Standard Record Form.
Scores, 4: Color Naming, Word Reading, Inhibition, Inhibition/Switching.

e) D-KEFS SORTING TEST.
Purpose: Assesses "problem-solving, verbal and spatial concept formation, flexibility of thinking on a conceptual task."
Forms, 2: Standard Record Form, Alternate Record Form.
Scores, 2: Free Sorting, Sort Recognition.
Comments: Alternate set of scoring cards available.

f) D-KEFS TOWER TEST.
Purpose: Assesses "planning and reasoning in the spatial modality [and] impulsivity."
Form, 1: Standard Record Form.
Score: Total Achievement Score.

g) D-KEFS 20 QUESTIONS TEST.
Purpose: Assesses "hypothesis testing, verbal and spatial abstract thinking, [and] impulsivity."
Forms, 2: Standard Record Form, Alternate Record Form.
Score: Initial Abstraction Score.

h) D-KEFS WORD CONTEXT TEST.
Purpose: Assesses "deductive reasoning [and] verbal abstract thinking."

Form, 1: Standard Record Form.
Score: Total Consecutively Correct.
i) D-KEFS PROVERB TEST.
Purpose: Assesses "metaphorical thinking, generating versus comprehending abstract thought."
Form, 1: Standard Record Form.
Scores, 2: Total Achievement scores: Free Inquiry, Multiple Choice.

[757]
Dementia Rating Scale—2.

Purpose: To measure and track "mental status in adults with cognitive impairment."
Population: Adults ages 35–89+ years.
Publication Dates: 1973–2001.
Acronym: DRS-2.
Scores, 6: Attention, Initiation/Perseveration, Construction, Conceptualization, Memory, Total.
Administration: Individual.
Price Data: Available from publisher for introductory kit including professional manual (2001, 47 pages), 50 scoring booklets, and set of 32 stimulus cards.
Time: (15–30) minutes.
Comments: Revised version of the DRS; DRS-2 stimulus cards same as for original DRS; can be administered bedside by appropriately trained personnel.
Authors: Steven Mattis (professional manual, stimulus cards, scoring booklet), Paul J. Jurica, and Christopher L. Leitten (professional manual).
Publisher: Psychological Assessment Resources, Inc.
Cross References: See T5:776 (63 references); for a review by R. A. Bornstein of an earlier edition, see 11:107 (2 references).

[758]
The Dennis Test of Child Development.

Purpose: Assess developmental status of children at kindergarten or first grade in "five major areas of child growth."
Population: Kindergarten–grade 1.
Publication Dates: 1966–1974.
Acronym: DCD.
Scores, 7: Gross Motor, Fine Motor, Visual Perception, Attention (Auditory), Language, Mental Age Development, Developmental Quotient.
Administration: Group.
Price Data: Not available.
Time: (22) minutes.
Author: William H. Dennis.
Publisher: William H. Dennis [No reply from publisher; status unknown].

[759]
Dennis Test of Scholastic Aptitude.

Purpose: Measures scholastic aptitude.
Population: Grades 4–8, 5–8.

Publication Dates: 1961–1963.
Acronym: DTSA.
Scores: 5 subtests: Arithmetic Reasoning, Verbal Concepts, Memory, Abstract Reasoning, General Information.
Administration: Group.
Levels, 2: Form 2, Form 3.
Price Data: Not available.
Time: (40) minutes.
Author: William H. Dennis.
Publisher: William H. Dennis [No reply from publisher; status unknown].

[760]
Dental Admission Test.

Purpose: "Designed to measure general academic achievement, comprehension of scientific information, and perceptual ability."
Population: Dental school applicants.
Publication Dates: 1946–2002.
Acronym: DAT.
Scores, 8: Natural Sciences (Biology, General Chemistry, Organic Chemistry, Total), Reading Comprehension, Quantitative Reasoning, Perceptual Ability, Academic Average.
Administration: Group.
Price Data: Available from publisher.
Time: 255(270) minutes.
Comments: Formerly called Dental Aptitude Testing Program; computer-based test administered throughout the year at centers approved by publisher.
Author: Department of Testing Services.
Publisher: American Dental Association.
Cross References: For reviews by Janet Baldwin and Jerry S. Gilmer, see 12:102; for reviews by Henry M. Cherrick and Linda M. DuBois of an earlier edition, see 9:308; see also T3:673 (2 references); for reviews by Robert L. Linn and Christine H. McGuire of an earlier edition, see 8:1085 (7 references); see also T2:2337 (8 references), 7:1091 (28 references), 5:916 (6 references), and 4:788 (2 references).

[761]
Dental Assistant Test.

Purpose: Developed to help screen for dental assistant positions.
Population: Dental assistant applicants.
Publication Date: 1975.
Scores: 8 tests: Attention to Details, Organization Skills, Perception of Objects in Space, Perception of Spatial Perspective, Following Directions, Detail Judgments, Dexterity, Logic and Reasoning.
Administration: Group.
Price Data: Available from publisher.
Time: (40-45) minutes.
Comments: Self-administered.

Authors: Mary Meeker and Robert Meeker.
Publisher: SOI Systems.

[762]
Dental Receptionist Test.

Purpose: Developed to help screen for dental receptionist positions.
Population: Dental receptionist applicants.
Publication Date: 1975.
Scores: 8 tests: Attention to Details, Vocabulary, Verbal Reasoning, Following Directions, Management of Details, Management of Numerical Information, Dexterity, Logic and Reasoning.
Administration: Group.
Price Data: Available from publisher.
Time: (45-50) minutes.
Comments: Self-administered.
Authors: Mary Meeker and Robert Meeker.
Publisher: SOI Systems.

[763]
Denver Articulation Screening Exam.

Purpose: Designed to identify significant developmental delay in the acquisition of speech sounds.
Population: Ages 2.5 to 7.0.
Publication Dates: 1971–1973.
Acronym: DASE.
Scores, 2: DASE Word Score, Intelligibility Rating.
Administration: Individual.
Price Data, 2001: $8 per 25 test forms; $8 per set of picture cards for use with "shy or immature" children; $230 per training videotape; $19 per manual/workbook (1973, 42 pages).
Time: (10–15) minutes.
Comments: Orally administered.
Authors: Amelia F. Drumwright and William K. Frankenburg (manual).
Publisher: Denver Developmental Materials, Inc.
Cross References: See T3:675 (1 reference); for a review by Harold A. Peterson, see 8:958.

[764]
Denver Audiometric Screening Test.

Purpose: Constructed to identify children who have a serious hearing loss.
Population: Ages 3–6.
Publication Date: 1973.
Acronym: DAST.
Scores: 3 ratings for each ear: Pass, Fail, Uncertain.
Administration: Individual.
Price Data, 2001: $5 per 25 test forms; $230 per training videotape; $28 per manual/workbook (30 pages); $23.50 per reference manual.
Time: [5–10] minutes.
Authors: William K. Frankenburg, Marion Downs, and Elynor Kazuk.

Publisher: Denver Developmental Materials, Inc.
Cross References: See T5:784 (1 reference); for a review by Lear Ashmore, see 9:309.

[765]
Denver Eye Screening Test.

Purpose: Developed to detect problems in visual acuity and screen for eye diseases.
Population: Ages 6 months and over.
Publication Date: 1973.
Acronym: DEST.
Scores: 3 ratings for each eye: Normal, Abnormal, Untestable.
Administration: Individual.
Price Data, 2001: $6 per 25 test forms; $16.50 per set of test materials including picture cards, cord, and spinning toy; $9.50 per set of picture cards; $2.25 per cord; $4.75 per spinning toy; $180 per training videotape; $20 per manual/workbook (37 pages); $17 per reference manual.
Time: (5-10) minutes.
Comments: "Criterion-referenced."
Authors: William K. Frankenburg, Arnold D. Goldstein, and John Barker.
Publisher: Denver Developmental Materials, Inc.
   a) VISION TESTS.
   1) *Fixation.*
   Population: Ages 6 months to 2.5 years.
   2) *Picture Card.*
   Population: Ages 2.5 to 3.
   3) *"E."*
   Population: Ages 3 and over.
   b) TESTS FOR NON-STRAIGHT EYES.
   Population: Ages 6 months and over.

[766]
Denver Prescreening Developmental Questionnaire II.

Purpose: "To facilitate earlier identification of children whose development may be delayed."
Population: Ages 0-9 months, 9-24 months, 2-4 years, 4-6 years.
Publication Dates: 1975–1998.
Acronym: PDQII.
Scores: Item scores only.
Administration: Individual.
Levels, 4: Ages 0-9 months, 9-24 months, 2-4 years, 4-6 years.
Manual: No manual.
Price Data, 2001: $19–$22 per 100 questionnaires (specify level).
Time: [12.5] minutes.
Comments: Ratings by parents; previous edition entitled Revised Denver Prescreening Developmental Questionnaire.
Author: William K. Frankenburg.

Publisher: Denver Developmental Materials, Inc.
Cross References: See T5:787 (4 references); for reviews by Stephen N. Axford and William B. Michael of the Revised Denver Prescreening Developmental Questionnaire, see 12:327 (1 reference).

[767]
Denver II (Denver Developmental Screening Test).

Purpose: Designed to screen for developmental delays.
Population: Birth to age 6.
Publication Dates: 1967–1992.
Scores: Item scores in 4 areas (Personal-Social, Fine Motor-Adaptive, Language, Gross Motor) and 5 test behavior ratings (Typical, Compliance, Interest in Surroundings, Fearfulness, Attention Span).
Administration: Individual.
Price Data, 2001: $84 per complete package; $48 per test kit; $23 per 100 test forms; $215 per training videotape (rental price $90); $25 per training manual (1990, 50 pages); $28 per technical manual (1990, 91 pages).
Time: (10–15) minutes for abbreviated version; (20–25) minutes for entire test.
Comments: Revision is intended to be used as a developmental chart designed to give a broad overview of general development in a minimum amount of time.
Authors: W. K. Frankenburg, Josiah Dodds, Phillip Archer, Beverly Bresnick, Patrick Maschka, Norma Edelman, and Howard Shapiro.
Publisher: Denver Developmental Materials, Inc.
Cross References: See T5:788 (3 references); for reviews by Selma Hughes and Pat Mirenda, see 12:103 (3 references); see also T4:740 (18 references).

[768]
Depression and Anxiety in Youth Scale.

Purpose: Designed to help professionals identify depression and anxiety in children and youth.
Population: Ages 6-0 to 19-0.
Publication Date: 1994.
Acronym: DAYS.
Administration: Group.
Price Data, 2001: $139 per complete kit including 50 student rating scales, 50 teacher rating scales, 50 parent rating scales, 50 profile/record forms, scoring keys, and manual (39 pages); $24 per 50 record forms; $24 per 50 profile/record forms; $49 per manual.
Authors: Phyllis L. Newcomer, Edna M. Barenbaum, and Brian R. Bryant.
Publisher: PRO-ED.
　　a) STUDENT SELF-REPORT SCALE (SCALE S).
　　Scores, 2: Depression, Anxiety.
　　Time: (15–20) minutes.
　　b) TEACHER RATING SCALE (SCALE T).
　　Scores, 2: Depression, Anxiety.

Time: (5–10) minutes.
　　c) PARENT RATING SCALE (SCALE P).
　　Scores, 3: Depression, Anxiety, Social Maladjustment.
　　Time: (6–10) minutes.
Cross References: For reviews by Gloria Maccow and Janet V. Smith, see 13:91.

[769]
Depressive Experiences Questionnaire.

Purpose: Designed to assess an individual's depressive experience.
Population: Adolescents and adults (patients and normals).
Publication Dates: 1976–1989.
Acronym: DEQ.
Scores, 3: Dependency, Self-Criticism, Efficacy.
Administration: Group.
Manual: No manual.
Forms, 2: DEQ, DEQ-A.
Price Data: Available from publisher.
Time: Administration time not reported.
Authors: Sidney J. Blatt, Carrie E. Schaffer, Susan A. Bers, and Donald M. Quinlan.
Publisher: Sidney J. Blatt.
Cross References: See T5:790 (29 references), T4:744 (30 references), 9:316 (2 references), and T3:682 (1 reference).

[770]
Derogatis Affects Balance Scale [Revised].

Purpose: Designed as a multidimensional mood and affects inventory to "measure the affects profile of community, medical, and psychiatric respondents."
Population: Adults.
Publication Dates: 1975–1996.
Acronym: DABS.
Scores, 13: Joy, Contentment, Vigor, Affection, Anxiety, Depression, Guilt, Hostility, Positive Score Total, Negative Score Total, Affects Balance Index, Affects Expressiveness Index, Positive Affects Ratio.
Administration: Individual.
Forms, 2: DABS, DABS-SF (Short Form).
Price Data, 2002: $50 per 50 tests; $25 per 50 profiles; $29.50 per manual (1996, 58 pages).
Time: (5) minutes (DABS); (2–3) minutes (Short Form).
Comments: Self-report inventory, for clinical or research uses; formerly published as the Affects Balance Scale (ABS); scoring is available online at www.derogatis-tests.com.
Author: Leonard R. Derogatis.
Publisher: Clinical Psychometric Research, Inc.
Cross References: For reviews by Mark J. Atkinson and Carlen Hennington, see 14:112; see also T5:791 (16 references), T4:132 (6 references), and 9:61 (6 references).

[771]
Derogatis Interview for Sexual Functioning.
Purpose: "A brief semistructured interview designed to provide an estimate of the quality of an individual's current sexual functioning in quantitative terms."
Population: Adults.
Publication Dates: 1987–1989.
Scores, 6: Sexual Cognition/Fantasy, Sexual Arousal, Sexual Behavior/Experience, Orgasm, Sexual Drive/Relationship, Total Score.
Administration: Individual.
Price Data, 2002: $50 per 50 DISF or DISF-SR (specify gender); $25 per 50 DISF or DISF-SR score sheets (specify gender); additional shipping charges apply.
Foreign Language Editions: Danish, Dutch, English, French, German, Italian, Norwegian, and Spanish editions available.
Time: (15–20) minutes for DISF; (10–15) minutes for DISF-SR.
Author: Leonard R. Derogatis.
Publisher: Clinical Psychometric Research, Inc.
  a) DEROGATIS INTERVIEW FOR SEXUAL FUNCTIONING.
  Acronym: DISF.
  Time: (15–20) minutes.
  Comments: Semistructured interview format using a 4-point Likert scale.
  b) DEROGATIS INTERVIEW FOR SEXUAL FUNCTIONING—SELF REPORT.
  Acronym: DISF-SR.
  Time: (10–15) minutes.
  Comments: Paper-and-pencil format using Likert scales; may be used to gain evaluations of patient's sexual functioning by the patient or the patient's spouse.

[772]
Derogatis Psychiatric Rating Scale.
Purpose: Multidimensional psychiatric rating scale for use by clinician to assist in validating patient-reported results.
Population: Adults and adolescents.
Publication Dates: 1974–1992.
Acronym: DPRS.
Administration: Individual.
Comments: Formerly called Hopkins Psychiatric Rating Scale (9:483).
Author: Leonard R. Derogatis.
Publisher: NCS (Minnetonka).
  a) BRIEF DEROGATIS PSYCHIATRIC RATING SCALE.
  Acronym: B-DPRS.
  Scores, 10: Primary Dimensions (Somatization, Obsessive-Compulsive, Interpersonal Sensitivity, Depression, Anxiety, Hostility, Phobic Anxi-

ety, Paranoid Ideation, Psychoticism) and Global Pathology Index.
Price Data, 1994: $30 per 100 forms; $50 per 50 scannable forms.
Time: (1–2) minutes.
  b) DEROGATIS PSYCHIATRIC RATING SCALE.
  Acronym: DPRS.
  Scores, 18: Same as brief edition plus Sleep Disturbance, Psychomotor Retardation, Hysterical Behavior, Abjection-Disinterest, Conceptual Dysfunction, Disorientation, Excitement, Euphoria.
  Price Data: $32 per 100 forms.
  Time: (2–5) minutes.
Cross References: For reviews by Samuel Juni and Paul Retzlaff, see 13:92 (1 reference); see also T4:745 (6 references) and 9:483 (1 reference).

[773]
Derogatis Sexual Functioning Inventory.
Purpose: Multidimensional assessment of sexual functioning.
Population: Adults.
Publication Dates: 1975–1979.
Acronym: DSFI.
Scores, 12: Information, Experience, Drive, Attitudes, Psychological Symptoms, Affects, Gender Role, Definition, Fantasy, Body Image, Sexual Satisfaction, Total, Patient's Evaluation of Current Functioning.
Administration: Individual.
Price Data, 2002: $3 per nonreusable test (1978, 8 pages); $12.50 per manual (1979, 36 pages); $.50 per profile form (specify male or female).
Time: (45–60) minutes.
Comments: Scoring is available online at www.derogatis-tests.com.
Author: Leonard R. Derogatis.
Publisher: Clinical Psychometric Research, Inc.
Cross References: See T5:793 (24 references) and T4:746 (10 references); for reviews by Edward S. Herold and David L. Weis, see 9:317 (3 references); see also T3:683 (6 references).

[774]
Derogatis Stress Profile.
Purpose: "Designed to assess and represent stress at three distinct but related levels of measurement."
Population: Adults.
Publication Dates: 1984–1986.
Acronym: DSP.
Scores: 3 domains: Environmental Events, Emotional Response, Personality Mediators; 11 dimensions: Time Pressure, Driven Behavior, Attitude Posture, Relaxation Potential, Role Definition, Vocational Satisfaction, Domestic Satisfaction, Health Posture, Hostility, Anxiety, Depression; 2 global scores: Subjective Stress, Total Stress.

Administration: Individual.
Price Data, 2002: $55 per 50 tests; $25 per 50 score profile forms; $12.50 per summary report and scoring instructions (1986, 14 pages).
Time: 10(15) minutes.
Comments: Scoring available online at www.derogatis-tests.com.
Author: Leonard R. Derogatis.
Publisher: Clinical Psychometric Research, Inc.
Cross References: See T5:794 (2 references); for reviews by Mariela C. Shirley and Paul D. Werner, see 13:93 (4 references); see also T4:747 (1 reference).

[775]
Detailed Assessment of Posttraumatic Stress.

Purpose: Designed as a comprehensive diagnostic measure of trauma exposure and posttraumatic stress and associated functions, including dissociative symptoms, substance abuse, and suicidality.
Population: Adults 18 and over who have undergone a significant psychological stressor.
Publication Date: 2001.
Acronym: DAPS.
Scores: 2 validity scales (Positive Bias and Negative Bias) and 11 scales in 3 clusters: Trauma Specification (Relative Trauma Exposure, Peritraumatic Distress, Peritraumatic Dissociation), Posttraumatic Stress (Reexperiencing, Avoidance, Hyperarousal, Posttraumatic Stress—Total, Posttraumatic Impairment), Associated Features (Trauma-Specific Dissociation, Substance Abuse, Suicidality).
Administration: Individual or group.
Price Data: Available from publisher for kit including professional manual (56 pages), 10 item booklets, 50 hand-scorable answer sheets, and 50 male/female profile forms.
Time: (20–30) minutes.
Comments: Self-administered.
Author: John Briere.
Publisher: Psychological Assessment Resources, Inc.

[776]
Detention Promotion Tests—Complete Service.

Purpose: Designed as a custom-made test to fit duties and responsibilities for promotion of detention personnel.
Population: Detention workers under consideration for promotion.
Publication Dates: 1990–1998.
Scores: 6 subtests: Detention-Related Technical Knowledges, Knowledge of the Behavioral Sciences and Human Relations, Supervisory and Managerial Knowledges, Administrative Knowledges, Knowledge of Inmate Legal Rights, Comprehension Ability, Total.
Administration: Group.

Price Data: Available from publisher.
Time: [210] minutes.
Comments: Candidate study guide available.
Author: McCann Associates, Inc.
Publisher: McCann Associates, Inc.

[777]
Detroit Tests of Learning Aptitude—Adult.

Purpose: Designed to measure both general intelligence and discrete mental ability areas.
Population: Ages 16-0 and over.
Publication Date: 1991.
Acronym: DTLA-A.
Scores, 20: 12 subtest scores: Word Opposites, Story Sequences, Sentence Imitation, Reversed Letters, Mathematical Problems, Design Sequences, Basic Information, Quantitative Relations, Word Sequences, Design Reproduction, Symbolic Relations, Form Assembly and 8 composite scores (Linguistic Verbal, Linguistic Nonverbal, Attention-Enhanced, Attention-Reduced, Motor-Enhanced, Motor-Reduced, General Mental Ability, Optimal).
Administration: Individual.
Price Data, 2001: $279 per complete kit including picture book 1, picture book 2, 25 response forms, 25 examiner record booklets, 25 profile/summary forms, and manual (120 pages); $57 per picture book 1; $26 per picture book 2; $24 per 25 response forms; $49 per 25 examiner record booklets; $24 per 25 profile/summary forms; $49 per manual; $49 per manipulatives; $109 per microcomputer scoring and report system software (IBM).
Time: (90–150) minutes.
Comments: Upward extension of the Detroit Tests of Learning Aptitude (Second Edition) (10:85) and (Third Edition) (12:107).
Authors: Donald D. Hammill and Bryan R. Bryant.
Publisher: PRO-ED.
Cross References: For reviews by Thomas E. Dinero and Cynthia Ann Druva-Roush, see 12:105.

[778]
Detroit Tests of Learning Aptitude, Fourth Edition.

Purpose: Designed to measure both general intelligence and discrete ability areas.
Population: Ages 6-0 to 17-11.
Publication Dates: 1935–1998.
Acronym: DTLA-4.
Scores: 10 subtest scores: Word Opposites, Design Sequences, Sentence Imitation, Reversed Letters, Story Construction, Design Reproduction, Basic Information, Symbolic Relations, Word Sequences, Story Sequences; and 16 composite scores: General Mental Ability Composite, Optimal Composite, Domain Composites (Verbal, Nonverbal, Attention-Enhanced, At-

tention-Reduced, Motor-Enhanced, Motor-Reduced, Total), Theoretical Composites (Fluid Intelligence, Crystallized Intelligence, Associative Level, Cognitive Level, Simultaneous Processing, Successive Processing, Verbal Scale, Performance Scale, Total).

Administration: Individual.

Price Data, 2001: $329 per complete kit including examiner's manual (1998, 247 pages), Picture Books 1 and 2, 25 Profile/Summary forms, 25 Examiner Record Booklets, 25 response forms, Story Sequence Chips, and Design Sequence Cubes; $79 per examiner's manual; $94 per Picture Book 1 (for Design Sequences, Design Reproduction and Symbolic Relations); $34 per Picture Book 2 (for Story Sequences and Story Construction); $24 per 25 Profile/Summary forms; $44 per 25 Examiner Record Booklets; $24 per 25 response forms; $20 per Story Sequence Chips; $29 per Design Sequence Cubes; $109 per software scoring and report system (Windows).

Time: (40–120) minutes.

Author: Donald D. Hammill.

Publisher: PRO-ED.

Cross References: For reviews by Jeffrey K. Smith and Ross E. Traub, see 14:113; see also T5:798 (27 references); for reviews by William A. Mehrens and Michael Poteat of an earlier edition, see 12:107 (4 references); see also T4:752 (7 references); for reviews by Arthur B. Silverstein and Joan Silverstein of an earlier edition, see 10:85 (15 references); see also 9:320 (11 references), and T3:691 (20 references); for a review by Arthur B. Silverstein of an earlier edition, see 8:213 (14 references); see also T2:493 (3 references), and 7:406 (10 references); for a review by F. L. Wells, see 3:275 (1 reference); for reviews by Anne Anastasi and Henry Feinburg and an excerpted review by D. A. Worcester (with S. M. Corey), see 1:1058.

[779]
Detroit Tests of Learning Aptitude—Primary, Second Edition.

Purpose: Constructed to identify strengths and weaknesses in mental abilities and to identify "children who are markedly deficient in general mental ability."

Population: Ages 3–9.

Publication Dates: 1986–1991.

Acronym: DTLA-P:2.

Scores, 7: Linguistic (Verbal, Nonverbal), Attentional (Enhanced, Reduced), Motoric (Enhanced, Reduced), General Mental Ability.

Administration: Individual.

Price Data, 2001: $159 per complete kit including picture book, 25 response forms, 25 profile/examiner record forms, and manual (1991, 106 pages); $49 per picture book; $29 per 25 response forms; $39 per 25 profile/examiner record forms; $46 per manual; $109 per microcomputer scoring and report system software (IBM).

Time: (15–45) minutes.

Comments: Downward extension of the Detroit Tests of Learning Aptitude (Second Edition) (10:85) and (Third Edition) (12:107).

Authors: Donald D. Hammill and Bryan R. Bryant.

Publisher: PRO-ED.

Cross References: See T5:799 (2 references); for reviews by Terry A. Ackerman and Robert T. Williams, see 12:106 (1 reference); for reviews of an earlier edition by Cathy F. Telzrow and Stanley F. Vasa, see 10:84 (1 reference).

[780]
Developing Skills Checklist.

Purpose: Designed to measure skills and behaviors that children typically develop between prekindergarten and the end of kindergarten.

Population: Ages 4–6.8.

Publication Date: 1990.

Acronym: DSC.

Scores: 9 scales: Mathematical Concepts and Operations, Language, Memory, Auditory, Print Concepts, Motor, Visual, Writing and Drawing Concepts, Social-Emotional.

Administration: Individual.

Price Data, 2002: $357.10 per complete kit; $14.50 per 50 Writing and Drawing books; $40.800 per 50 Social-Emotional Observational Records; $41.20 per 50 score sheets (specify hand-recording or machine-scoring); $40.80 per 50 Parent Conference Forms; $4 per Class record book; $76.20 per set of 3 DSC item books; $9.60 per A Day at School; $20.20 per administration and score interpretation manual; $14.80 per Concepts of Print and Writing administration manual; $14.80 per Social-Emotional Administration manual; $16.30 per norms book and technical manual (90 pages); $42.60 per training video (entitled How to Administer and Score DSC); $29.80 per 5 replacement bunnies; $4.10 per student scoring service available from publisher; $188.70 per La Lista test kit.

Foreign Language Editions: Spanish adaptation entitled Lista de Destrezas en Desarrollo (La Lista) available as an all-in-Spanish supplement to the DSC. English DSC kit is also required in order to administer La Lista.

Time: (10–15) minutes per session (untimed).

Author: CTB Macmillan/McGraw-Hill.

Publisher: CTB/McGraw-Hill.

Cross References: For reviews by Elaine Clark and Claire B. Ernhart, see 12:108 (2 references).

[781]
Developing the High-Performance Workplace.

Purpose: "Created to give organizational members a tool for assessing employee opinions about the status of

high-performance workplace characteristics in their work environments."
Population: Organizational employees.
Publication Date: 1996.
Scores, 18: Importance Ratings (Training and Continuous Learning, Information Sharing, Employee Participation, Organization Structure, Worker-Management Partnerships, Compensation Linked to Performance and Skills, Employment Security, Supportive Work Environment, Overall HPW Rating), Quality Ratings (Training and Continuous Learning, Information Sharing, Employee Participation, Organization Structure, Worker-Management Partnerships, Compensation Linked to Performance and Skills, Employment Security, Supportive Work Environment, Overall HPW Rating).
Administration: Group.
Price Data, 1996: $64.95 per complete kit including administrator's handbook (77 pages), and 10 collection instruments; $2.95 per collection instrument; $39.95 per administrator's handbook.
Time: Administration time not reported.
Authors: David D. Dubois and William J. Rothwell.
Publisher: Human Resource Development Press.
Cross References: For reviews by M. David Miller and Deniz S. Ones, see 14:114.

[782]
Developing the Leader Within.

Purpose: Assessment of leadership skills by self and others.
Population: Management personnel.
Publication Date: 1995.
Scores: 4 dimensions: Developing Within, Helping Others Excel, Improving Critical Processes, Showing Commitment to the Team.
Administration: Group.
Forms, 4: Leader Form, Direct Manager Form, Higher Manager Form, Colleague Form.
Manual: No manual.
Price Data, 2001: $80 per Multi-Rater (7 forms); $20 per Self-Rater (1 form); $25 per Leadership General Workbook.
Time: Administration time not reported.
Comments: Basic assessment includes leader self-rating and up to six ratings by colleagues; Direct Manager and Higher Manager Forms are optional.
Author: L. Phillips-Jones.
Publisher: Mind Garden, Inc.

[783]
Developmental Activities Screening Inventory, Second Edition.

Purpose: "Designed to provide early detection of developmental difficulties."
Population: Ages birth to 60 months.

Publication Dates: 1977–1984.
Acronym: DASI-II.
Scores: Total score only.
Administration: Individual.
Price Data, 2001: $89 per complete kit including 50 record forms, 37 Picture Cards, 5 Set-Configuration Cards, 2 pairs of Numeral Cards, 3 pairs of Word Cards, 4 Shape Cards, and examiner's manual (1984, 103 pages); $24 per 50 record forms; $34 per 56 Picture Cards; $34 per examiner's manual.
Time: (25-30) minutes.
Comments: Behavior checklist; same test materials (form board, bell) must be supplied by examiner.
Authors: Rebecca R. Fewell and Mary Beth Langley.
Publisher: PRO-ED.
Cross References: See T5:803 (3 references); for reviews by Dennis C. Harper and William B. Michael, see 10:87; see also 9:323 (1 reference).

[784]
A Developmental Assessment for Individuals with Severe Disabilities—Second Edition.

Purpose: Designed to aid "in identifying discrete changes in behavior … in five areas of development."
Population: Individuals of all ages who are functioning within the birth to 7-year developmental range.
Publication Dates: 1980–1999.
Acronym: DASH-2.
Scores, 6: Social-Emotional, Language, Sensory-Motor, Activities of Daily Living, Basic Academics, Overall Developmental Age.
Administration: Individual.
Forms: 5 pinpoint scales: Social-Emotional (17 pages), Language (30 pages), Sensory-Motor (35 pages), Activities of Daily Living (21 pages), Basic Academics (25 pages).
Price Data, 2001: $189 per complete kit including manual (23 pages), 5 each of 5 pinpoint scales, 50 priority intervention worksheets, 50 comprehensive program record forms, and 50 cumulative summary sheets; $45 per 10 pinpoint scales (specify area); $14 per 50 priority intervention worksheets; $14 per 50 comprehensive program record forms; $14 per 50 cumulative summary sheets; $39 per manual.
Time: (120–180) minutes.
Comments: Previously titled Developmental Assessment for the Severely Handicapped; also listed as A Developmental Assessment for Students with Severe Disabilities, Second Edition in Tests in Print V; may administer all or any combination of the pinpoint scales; "criterion-referenced"; criterion performance levels 1–5; ratings by developmental professionals.
Authors: Mary K. Dykes and Jane N. Erin.
Publisher: PRO-ED.

Cross References: See T5:804 (1 reference); for reviews by Harvey N. Switzky and David P. Wacker of the original edition, see 9:324.

[785]
Developmental Assessment of Life Experiences (2000 Edition).

Purpose: Developed to assess daily living, intellectual, and adaptive skills of persons with disabilities.
Population: Individuals with developmental disabilities.
Publication Dates: 1974–2000.
Acronym: D.A.L.E. System.
Scores: 8 categories: Personal Hygiene, Daily Living Skills, Community Skills/Safety Skills, Language and Educational Skills, Personal Management, Gender Specific—Female, Gender Specific—Male, Leisure Skills.
Administration: Individual.
Price Data, 2000: $10.50 per complete set including manual (2000, 64 pages).
Time: Administration time not reported.
Authors: Gertrude A. Barber, Vincent Olewnik, Joanne Haughey, Traci Gardner, Michelle Sosnowski, Jennifer Lawrence, Nia Bell, Daneen Engel, Pam Johns, and Nadine Hornyak.
Publisher: The Barber Center Press, Inc.
Cross References: For reviews by Martie E. Block and Linda K. Bunker and Elizabeth L. Jones of an earlier edition, see 12:109; for a review by Frank M. Gresham of an earlier edition, see 9:295.

[786]
Developmental Assessment of Young Children.

Purpose: Designed to measure "developmental abilities."
Population: Birth to age 5-11.
Publication Date: 1998.
Acronym: DAYC.
Scores: General Development Quotient.
Administration: Individual.
Price Data, 2001: $174 per complete kit including examiner's manual (67 pages), 25 each of Adaptive, Cognitive, Communication, Physical, and Social-Emotional scoring forms, and 25 profile/summary forms; $24 per 25 scoring forms (specify domain); $14 per 25 profile/summary forms; $49 per manual.
Time: (10–20) minutes per subtest.
Comments: Rating by examiner; subtests may be used alone or in any combination.
Authors: Judith K. Voress and Taddy Maddox.
Publisher: PRO-ED.
a) COGNITIVE SUBTEST.
Purpose: Designed to measure "skills and abilitiess that are conceptual in nature."
Scores: Total score only.

b) COMMUNICATION SUBTEST.
Purpose: Constructed to assess "the exchange of ideas, information, and feelings."
Scores: Total score only.
c) SOCIAL-EMOTIONAL SUBTEST.
Purpose: Designed to measure "social awareness, social relationships, and social competence."
Scores: Total score only.
d) PHYSICAL DEVELOPMENT SUBTEST.
Purpose: Designed to measure "motor development."
Scores: Total score only.
e) ADAPTIVE BEHAVIOR SUBTEST.
Purpose: Designed to assess "independent functioning."
Scores: Total score only.
Cross References: For reviews by Billy T. Ogletree and T. Steuart Watson, see 14:115.

[787]
Developmental Assessment Resource for Teachers (DART) English.

Purpose: Designed to "assist teachers of upper primary and middle primary in their assessment of students' viewing, reading, listening, speaking and writing skills."
Population: Australian students in years 3–4, 5–6.
Publication Dates: 1994–1997.
Acronym: DART ENGLISH.
Scores, 5: Viewing, Reading, Listening, Speaking, Writing.
Administration: Group.
Forms, 2: Form A, Form B.
Publisher: Australian Council for Educational Research Ltd. [Australia].
a) DART MIDDLE PRIMARY ENGLISH.
Population: Students in years 3–4 in Australian classrooms.
Publication Date: 1997.
Price Data, 2002: A$132 per specimen set including 1 of each test component; A$49.50 per manual (1997, 152 pages); A$18.65 per 10 Viewing answer booklets; A$53.90 per Viewing video; A$21.95 per 10 reusable Reading stimulus booklets (specify Form A or Form B); A$10.95 per 10 Reading answer booklets A; A$14.25 per 10 Reading answer booklets B; A$7.65 per 10 Listening answer booklets; A$14.25 per audio cassette; A$10.95 per 10 reusable Character Review Speaking Guides; A$10.95 per 10 Writing answer booklets.
Time: (40–190) minutes per section.
Authors: Wendy Bodey, Lynne Darkin, Margaret Forster, and Geoff Masters.
b) DART UPPER PRIMARY ENGLISH.
Population: Students in years 5–6 in Australian classrooms.
Publication Date: 1994.

Price Data: A$120 per specimen set including 1 of each test component; A$45 per manual (1994, 159 pages); A$16.95 per 10 Viewing answer booklets; A$49 per Viewing video; A$5 per Viewing poster; A$19.95 per 10 reusable Reading stimulus booklets (specify Form A or Form B); A$9.95 per 10 Reading answer booklets A; A$12.95 per 10 Reading answer booklets B; A$6.95 per 10 Listening answer booklets; A$12.95 per audio cassette; A$9.95 per 10 reusable Speaking poetry booklets; A$9.95 per 10 Writing answer booklets; A$295 per complete package including testing materials for 30 students.
Time: (40–190) minutes per section.
Authors: Margaret Forster, Juliette Mendelovits, and Geoff Masters.

[788]
Developmental Assessment Resource for Teachers (DART) Mathematics.

Purpose: "Provides an estimate of a student's level of achievement on each of four strands of the [Australian] national mathematics profile ... and on each of three strands of the national benchmark framework."
Population: Australian students in years 5–6.
Publication Date: 1998.
Acronym: DART MATHEMATICS.
Scores, 5: Number, Space, Measurement, Chance and Data, Data Sense.
Administration: Group.
Forms, 2: Form A, Form B.
Price Data, 2002: A$273.90 per kit including video, manual (160 pages), 30 grid sheets, 30 measurement sheets, and photocopy master answer booklet and stimulus for all tests; A$54.95 per manual; A$54.95 per video; A$21.95 per each photocopy master answer booklet and stimulus (specify Number, Space, Measurement, Chance and Data or Data Sense; also specify Form A or Form B); A$14.25 per 30 grid sheets; A$14.255 per 30 measurement sheets.
Time: (60) minutes per section.
Authors: Eve Recht, Margaret Forster, and Geoff Masters.
Publisher: Australian Council for Educational Research Ltd. [Australia].

[789]
Developmental History Checklist for Children.

Purpose: To document the developmental history of children.
Population: Ages 5–12.
Publication Date: 1989.
Scores: 7 Content Areas: Presenting Information, Personal Information/Family Background, Early Developmental History, Educational History, Medical History/Health Status, Family History, Current Behavior/Relationships.
Administration: Individual.
Manual: No manual.
Price Data: Available from publisher.
Time: Administration time not reported.
Comments: Designed to be completed by a parent, guardian, or clinician.
Authors: Edward H. Dougherty and John A. Schinka.
Publisher: Psychological Assessment Resources, Inc.

[790]
Developmental Indicators for the Assessment of Learning, Third Edition.

Purpose: A developmental screening test for identifying young children in need of further diagnostic assessment.
Population: Ages 3-0 to 6-11.
Publication Dates: 1983–1998.
Acronym: DIAL-3.
Scores, 7: Motor, Concepts, Language, DIAL-3 Total, Self-Help Development, Social Development, Speed DIAL.
Administration: Individual.
Subtests, 5: Motor, Concepts, Language, Self-Help Development, Social Development.
Price Data, 2002: $388.95 per complete kit including manual (1998, 126 pages), 50 record forms (English), 1 record form (Spanish), 50 cutting cards, 50 parent questionnaires (English), manipulatives, dials, operator's handbooks in English and Spanish for motor, concepts and language areas, Speed DIAL, and training packet; $388.95 per complete kit in Spanish; $55.95 per DIAL-3 administration forms (specify English or Spanish) including 50 record forms, 50 cutting cards, and 50 parent questionnaires; $39.95 per 50 cutting cards and 50 record forms (specify English or Spanish); $25.95 per 50 parent/child activity forms (specify English or Spanish); $78.95 per training video; $199.95 per computer program (specify Windows or Macintosh).
Foreign Language Editions: Spanish edition available.
Time: (30) minutes; Speed DIAL: (15–20) minutes.
Comments: In contrast to DIAL-R, the DIAL-3 has two formats: the full version and the short version (called the Speed DIAL).
Authors: Carol Mardell-Czudnowski and Dorothea S. Goldenberg.
Publisher: American Guidance Service, Inc.
Cross References: For reviews by Gregory J. Cizek and Doreen Ward Fairbank, see 14:116; see also T5:809 (2 references); for reviews by Darrell L. Sabers and Scott Spreat of an earlier edition, see 12:110 (1 reference); see also T4:762 (6 references); for reviews by David W. Barnett and G. Michael Poteat of an earlier version, see 10:89 (6 references); see also 9:326 (1

reference) and T3:696 (2 references); for reviews by J. Jeffrey Grill and James J. McCarthy of an earlier edition, see 8:428 (3 references).

[791]
Developmental Observation Checklist System.

Purpose: "For the assessment of very young children with respect to general development (DC), adjustment behavior (ABC), and parent stress and support (PSSC)."
Population: Birth to age 6.
Publication Date: 1994.
Acronym: DOCS.
Scores, 12: Developmental Checklist (Cognition, Language, Social, Motor, Total); Adjustment Behavior Checklist (Mother, Father, Both Parents, Teacher); Parental Stress and Support Checklist (Mother, Father, Both Parents).
Administration: Individual.
Parts, 3: Developmental Checklist, Adjustment Behavior Checklist, Parental Stress and Support Checklist.
Price Data, 2001: $129 per complete kit including manual (91 pages), 25 profile/record forms, 25 DC profile/record forms, 25 ABC profile/record forms, and 25 PSSC profile/record forms; $49 per manual; $14 per 25 profile/record forms; $44 per 25 DC profile/record forms; $14 per ABC or PSSC profile/record forms.
Time: Administration time not reported.
Authors: Wayne P. Hresko, Shirley A. Miguel, Rita J. Sherbenou, and Steve D. Burton.
Publisher: PRO-ED.
Cross References: For reviews by Frank M. Bernt and Gene Schwarting, see 13:95.

[792]
Developmental Profile II.

Purpose: "Designed to assess a child's functional, developmental age level."
Population: Birth to age 9.5.
Publication Dates: 1972–1986.
Acronym: DP-II.
Scores: Ratings in 5 areas: Physical Age, Self-Help Age, Social Age, Academic Age, Communication Age.
Administration: Group.
Price Data, 2002: $129 per kit including 25 scoring/profile forms, and manual (1986, 95 pages); $48.50 per 25 scoring/profile forms; $58.50 per manual; $205 per 25-use disk (PC with DOS) for administration, scoring, and interpretation; $13.50 per mail-in answer sheet.
Time: (20–40) minutes.
Authors: Gerald Alpern, Thomas Boll, and Marsha Shearer.
Publisher: Western Psychological Services.

Cross References: See T5:811 (14 references) and T4:764 (1 reference); for reviews by A. Dirk Hightower and E. Scott Huebner, see 10:90 (3 references); for reviews by Dennis C. Harper and Sue White, see 9:327; see also T3:698 (5 references); for a review by Jane V. Hunt of the original edition, see 8:215 (1 reference).

[793]
Developmental Readiness Scale—Revised.

Purpose: Designed as a screening instrument for school readiness.
Population: Ages 3–6.
Publication Dates: 1982–1993.
Acronym: DRS-R.
Scores, 9: Fine Motor, Visual Motor, Numbers, Concepts, Body Image, Language, Personal-Social, Gross Motor, Reading.
Administration: Individual.
Price Data, 2002: $90 per starter set including manual (1993, 117 pages), test kit, stimulus cards, 25 test forms, and 25 report forms; $30 per manual; $20 per test kit, $16 per set of stimulus cards; $24 per 25 test forms; $24 per 25 report forms; quantity discounts available.
Time: (30–40) minutes.
Author: Barbara Ball.
Publisher: Academic Consulting & Testing Service.

[794]
Developmental Tasks for Kindergarten Readiness—II.

Purpose: Designed to provide "objective data about the school-readiness of pre-kindergarten children so that effective educational programming can be planned for them."
Population: Pre-kindergarten children.
Publication Dates: 1978–1994.
Acronym: DTKR-II.
Scores, 19: Composite Score (Social Interaction, Name Printing, Body Concepts—Awareness, Body Concepts—Use, Auditory Sequencing, Auditory Association, Visual Discrimination, Visual Memory, Visual Motor, Color Naming, Relational Concepts, Number Counting, Number Use, Number Naming, Alphabet Knowledge), Acquired Knowledge, Verbal-Conceptual, Visual Skills.
Administration: Individual.
Price Data, 2001: $114 per kit including manual (1994, 97 pages), materials book (cards), and 25 test booklets; $39 per 25 test booklets; $29 per materials book; $49 per test manual.
Time: (20–40) minutes.
Comments: Administered by school personnel for diagnostic-remedial purposes.
Authors: Walter J. Lesiak and Judi Lucas Lesiak.
Publisher: PRO-ED.

Cross References: For reviews by Joseph O. Prewitt and Theresa Graham, see 14:117; see also T4:766 (1 reference); for reviews by Carol A. Gray and Sue White of an earlier edition, see 9:328.

[795]
Developmental Teaching Objectives and Rating Form—Revised.

Purpose: Designed "for assessing social and emotional development of children and youth."
Population: Ages 0–16 years.
Publication Dates: 1992–1999.
Acronym: DTORF-R.
Scores, 5: Behavior, Communication, Socialization, Academics/Cognition, Total.
Administration: Individual.
Price Data, 2002: $60 per kit including 4 subscale booklets, user's manual (63 pages), technical report (29 pages), and rating forms; $25 per additional packet of 4 subscale booklets; software in revision.
Time: Administration time not reported.
Comments: Rating form filled out by people familiar with the child, following observations; older students (and also their parents) participate in their own team ratings.
Authors: Mary M. Wood; Developmental Therapy Institute, Inc.
Publisher: Developmental Therapy Institute, Inc.
Cross References: For a review by Sharon H. deFur, see 14:118.

[796]
Developmental Test of Visual-Motor Integration, 4th Edition, Revised.

Purpose: "Designed to assess the extent to which individuals can integrate their visual and motor abilities."
Population: Ages 3-0 to 17-11.
Publication Dates: 1967–1997.
Acronym: VMI.
Scores, 3: VMI, Visual, Motor.
Administration: Group.
Price Data: Available from publisher.
Time: Administration time not reported.
Authors: Keith E. Beery (test and manual) and Norman A. Buktenica (test).
Publisher: Modern Curriculum Press [No reply from publisher; status unknown].
Cross References: For a review by Jan Visser, see 14:119; see also T5:815 (52 references); for reviews by Darrell L. Sabers and James E. Ysseldyke of the Third Revision, see 12:111 (25 references); see also T4:768 (42 references), 9:329 (15 references), and T3:701 (57 references); for reviews by Donald A. Leton and James A. Rice of an earlier edition, see 8:870 (24 references); see also T2:1875 (6 references); for a review by Brad S. Chissom of an earlier edition, see 7:867 (5 references).

[797]
Developmental Test of Visual Perception—Adolescent and Adult.

Purpose: "To document the presence and degree of visual perceptual or visual-motor difficulties in individual adolescents and adults."
Population: Ages 11-0 to 74-11 years.
Publication Date: 2002.
Acronym: DTVP-A.
Scores, 9: Motor-Reduced Visual Perception (Figure-Ground, Visual Closure, Form Constancy, Motor-Reduced Visual Perception Index), Visual-Motor Integration (Copying, Visual-Motor Search, Visual-Motor Speed, Visual-Motor Integration Index), General Visual Perception Index.
Administration: Individual.
Price Data, 2002: $164 per complete kit including examiner's manual (135 pages), picture book, 25 profile/examiner record forms, 25 response booklets, and storage box; $59 per examiner's manual; $46 per picture book; $39 per 25 profiler/examiner record forms; $24 per 25 response booklets.
Time: (20–30) minutes.
Comments: Upward extension and redevelopment of the Developmental Test of Visual Perception, Second Edition (DTVP-2; 798); designed to identify candidates for referral to special education, cognitive rehabilitation, or occupational therapy; may be used to distinguish true visual-perception deficits from problems solely with complex eye-hand or perceptual-motor actions; may assist in differential diagnosis of various dementias.
Authors: Cecil R. Reynolds, Nils A. Pearson, and Judith K. Voress.
Publisher: PRO-ED.

[798]
Developmental Test of Visual Perception, Second Edition.

Purpose: Measures visual-perceptual and visual-motor integration skills.
Population: Ages 4-0 to 10-11.
Publication Dates: 1961–1993.
Acronym: DTVP-2.
Scores, 8: Motor-Reduced Visual Perception (Position in Space, Figure Ground, Visual Closure, Form Constancy), Visual-Motor Integration (Eye-Hand Coordination, Copying, Spatial Relations, Visual-Motor Speed), General Visual Perception.
Administration: Individual.
Price Data, 2001: $174 per complete kit including examiner's manual (1993, 73 pages), picture book, 25 profile/examiner record forms, and 25 response booklets; $49 per examiner's manual; $46 per picture book; $24 per 25 profile/examiner record forms; $59 per 25 response booklets.

Time: (35–45) minutes.
Comments: 1993 revision of the Marianne Frostig Developmental Test of Visual Perception (DTVP).
Authors: Donald D. Hammill, Nils A. Pearson, and Judith K. Voress.
Publisher: PRO-ED.
Cross References: See T5:816 (1 reference); for reviews by Nancy B. Bologna and Gerald Tindal, see 12:112 (1 reference); see also T4:767 (2 references); for reviews by Richard E. Darnell and David A. Sabatino of the earlier edition, see 9:650 (4 references); see also T3:1371 (25 references), 8:882 (72 references), and T2:1921 (43 references); for reviews by Brad S. Chissom, Newell C. Kephart, and Lester Mann, see 7:871 (117 references); for reviews by James M. Anderson and Mary C. Austin, see 6:553 (7 references).

[799]
Devereux Behavior Rating Scale—School Form.

Purpose: To evaluate "behaviors typical of children and adolescents with moderate to severe emotional disturbance."
Population: Ages 5–18.
Publication Dates: 1990–1993.
Acronym: BRSS.
Scores, 4: Interpersonal Problems, Inappropriate Behaviors/Feelings, Depression, Physical Symptoms/Fears.
Administration: Individual or group.
Forms, 2: Children, Adolescents.
Price Data, 2002: $149 per complete kit including manual (1993, 142 pages), 25 answer documents 5–12, and 25 ready score answer documents 13–18; $80 per manual; $36 per 25 ready score answer documents 5–12; $36 per 25 ready score answer documents 13–18.
Time: (5–10) minutes.
Comments: Ratings by parents and teachers.
Authors: Jack A. Naglieri, Paul A. LeBuffe, and Steven I. Pfeiffer.
Publisher: The Psychological Corporation.
Cross References: See T5:817 (1 reference); for additional information on the Devereux Adolescent Behavior Rating Scale, see T3:702 (1 reference); for a review by Carl F. Jesness, see 7:66; see also P:60 (1 reference). For reviews by Lisa Bloom and Richard F. Farmer, see 13:96 (8 references). For additional information on the Devereux Child Behavior Rating Scale, see T3:203 (6 references); see also T2:1158 (1 reference); for a review by Allan G. Barclay, see 7:67; see also P:61 (3 references).

[800]
Devereux Early Childhood Assessment.

Purpose: "To assess preschool children's protective factors and behavioral concerns."
Population: Ages 2–5.

Publication Date: 1999.
Acronym: DECA.
Scores, 5: Initiative, Self-Control, Attachment, Total Protective Factors, Behavioral Concerns.
Administration: Individual.
Price Data, 2002: $199.95 per kit including 40 record forms, user's guide (65 pages), technical manual (42 pages), classroom strategies guide, 20 parent guides, and classroom observation journal in a carrying case.
Foreign Language Edition: Parent guides and record forms also available in Spanish.
Time: (10) minutes.
Comments: Ratings by teachers and parents.
Authors: Paul A. LeBuffe and Jack A. Naglieri.
Publisher: Kaplan Early Learning Company.

[801]
Devereux Scales of Mental Disorders.

Purpose: Constructed for "evaluating behaviors associated with psychopathology."
Population: Ages 5–12, 13–18.
Publication Dates: 1993–1996.
Acronym: DSMD.
Scores, 10: Conduct, Attention/Delinquency, Anxiety, Depression, Autism, Acute Problems, Internalizing Composite, Externalizing Composite, Critical Pathology Composite, Total.
Administration: Group or individual.
Forms, 2: Child Form, Adolescent Form.
Price Data, 2002: $195 per complete kit including manual (1994, 300 pages), and 25 ReadyScore™ answer documents for each Child Form and Adolescent Form; $64 per ReadyScore™ answer documents (specify form); $80 per manual; $242 per DSMD Scoring Assistant including user's guide (1996, 77 pages), 2 disks, 5 child's record forms, and 5 adolescent record forms.
Time: (15) minutes.
Comments: Revision of Devereux Child Behavior Rating Scale (T3:703) and Devereux Adolescent Behavior Rating Scale (T3:702); ratings by parents, teachers, or other professionals; Scoring Assistant available to provide narrative interpretive reports and other information.
Authors: Jack A. Naglieri, Paul A. LeBuffe, and Steven I. Pfeiffer.
Publisher: The Psychological Corporation.
Cross References: For reviews by Colin Cooper and Charles A. Peterson, see 14:120; see also T5:818 (1 reference).

[802]
The Devine Inventory.

Purpose: Designed to assist "in the selection, deployment and development of individuals" in job settings.
Population: Employees and prospective employees.
Publication Date: 1989.

Scores, 3: Problem Solving, Self Description, Personal Choices.
Administration: Group or individual.
Price Data: Available from publisher.
Time: Administration time not reported.
Author: Donald W. Devine.
Publisher: Donald W. Devine & Associates [No reply from publisher; status unknown].
Cross References: For reviews by Philip Benson and William L. Deaton, see 12:113.

[803]
Diagnosing Organizational Culture.

Purpose: "Designed to help consultants and organizational members identify the shared values and beliefs that constitute an organization's culture."
Population: Adults.
Publication Dates: 1992–1993.
Scores: 5 scores (Power, Role, Achievement, Support, Total) in each of two areas: Existing Culture, Preferred Culture.
Administration: Group.
Price Data: Price information available from publisher for complete kit including trainer's manual (1993, 58 pages) and instrument (1992, 30 pages).
Time: (45–60) minutes.
Authors: Roger Harrison and Herb Stokes (instrument only).
Publisher: Jossey-Bass, A Wiley Company.
Cross References: For a review by John W. Fleenor, see 13:97.

[804]
Diagnostic Achievement Battery, Third Edition.

Purpose: Designed "to assess children's abilities in listening, speaking, reading, writing, and mathematics."
Population: Ages 6-0 to 14-11.
Publication Dates: 1984–2001.
Acronym: DAB-3.
Scores, 22: 14 subtest scores (Story Comprehension, Characteristics, Synonyms, Grammatic Completion, Alphabet/Word Knowledge, Reading Comprehension, Capitalization, Punctuation, Spelling, Writing: Contextual Language, Writing: Story Construction, Mathematics Reasoning, Mathematics Calculation, Phonemic Analysis) and 8 composite scores (Listening, Speaking, Reading, Writing, Mathematics, Spoken Language, Written Language, Total Achievement).
Administration: Individual.
Price Data, 2001: $244 per complete kit including manual (2001, 152 pages), student booklet, 25 profile/examiner's record booklets, 25 student response booklets, and audiotape; $109 per software kit including manual and CD-ROM; $69 per manual; $39 per 25 student response booklets; $54 per 25 profile/examiner's

record booklets; $39 per student booklet; $14 per audiotape; $34 per assessment probes.
Time: (90–120) minutes.
Author: Phyllis Newcomer.
Publisher: PRO-ED.
Cross References: See T5:821 (2 references); for reviews by Jean-Jacques Bernier and Martine Hébert and by Ric Brown of an earlier edition, see 12:114 (2 references); see also T4:774 (1 reference); for a review by William J. Webster of the original edition, see 9:333.

[805]
Diagnostic Achievement Test for Adolescents, Second Edition.

Purpose: To measure the spoken language ability and academic achievement levels of students.
Population: Ages 12–0 to 18–11.
Publication Dates: 1986–1993.
Acronym: DATA-2.
Scores, 22: 13 subtest scores (Receptive Vocabulary, Receptive Grammar, Expressive Grammar, Expressive Vocabulary, Word Identification, Reading Comprehension, Spelling, Writing Composition, Math Calculation, Math Problem Solving, Science, Social Studies, Reference Skills) and 9 composite scores (Listening, Speaking, Reading, Writing, Math, Spoken Language, Written Language, Achievement Screener, Total Achievement).
Administration: Individual.
Price Data, 2001: $149 per complete kit including examiner's manual (1993, 73 pages), 25 student response forms, 25 profile/examiner record forms, and a student booklet; $49 per examiner's manual; $24 per 25 student response forms; $49 per 25 profile/examiner record forms; $31 per student booklet.
Time: (60–120) minutes.
Authors: Phyllis L. Newcomer and Brian R. Bryant.
Publisher: PRO-ED.
Cross References: For reviews by Jerrilyn V. Andrews and Gerald E. DeMauro, see 13:98 (1 reference); for reviews by Randy W. Kamphaus and James E. Ysseldyke of an earlier edition, see 10:92.

[806]
Diagnostic Assessments of Reading.

Purpose: Assesses skills in reading and language.
Population: Grades 1–12.
Publication Date: 1992.
Acronym: DAR.
Scores: Mastery level scores in 6 areas: Word Recognition, Word Analysis, Oral Reading, Silent Reading Comprehension, Spelling, Word Meaning.
Administration: Individual.
Price Data: Available from publisher.
Time: Untimed; approximately 20–30 minutes.

Comments: Part of the DARTTS testing and teaching program.
Authors: Florence G. Roswell and Jeanne S. Chall.
Publisher: Riverside Publishing.
Cross References: For reviews by Kevin D. Crehan and Gene Schwarting, see 12:115.

[807]
Diagnostic English Language Tests.

Purpose: Designed to measure "ability to cope with the English language demands of upper secondary school in Australia."
Population: Non-English-speaking students entering Australian secondary schools at years 10 and 11.
Publication Date: 1994.
Acronym: DELTA.
Scores, 3: Reading, Writing, Listening.
Administration: Group.
Price Data, 2002: A$195 per complete set; A$21.95 per 10 copies Reading Test; A$21.95 per 10 copies Listening Test.
Time: (180) minutes.
Authors: Joy McQueen and Cecily Aldous.
Publisher: Australian Council for Educational Research Ltd. [Australia].

[808]
Diagnostic Interview for Borderline Patients.

Purpose: Designed to discriminate borderline patients from patients with schizophrenia, neurotic depression, and mixed diagnoses.
Population: Patients.
Publication Dates: [1982–1983].
Scores, 6: Social Adaptation, Impulse Action Patterns, Affects, Psychosis, Interpersonal Relations, Total.
Administration: Individual.
Price Data: Available from publisher.
Time: (50–90) minutes.
Authors: John G. Gunderson (interview), Pamela S. Ludolph (manual), Kenneth R. Silk (manual), Naomi E. Lohr (manual), and Dewey G. Cornell (manual).
Publisher: Pamela S. Ludolph [No reply from publisher; status unknown].
Cross References: See T5:824 (6 references) and T4:779 (19 references); for reviews by Robert E. Deysach and Charles A. Peterson, see 10:95 (12 references).

[809]
Diagnostic Mathematics Profiles.

Purpose: Constructed to diagnose problems in addition, subtraction, multiplication, and division.
Population: Australian school years 3–6.
Publication Date: 1990.
Scores: Item scores only.
Administration: Group or individual.
Parts, 4: Addition, Subtraction, Multiplication, Division.

Price Data, 2002: A$40.70 per test package including 30 copies of each part; A$15.29 per manual (23 pages).
Time: Administration time not reported.
Author: Brian Doig.
Publisher: Australian Council for Educational Research Ltd. [Australia].
Cross References: For reviews by John M. Enger and Arlen R. Gullickson, see 12:116.

[810]
Diagnostic Screening Test: Achievement.

Purpose: Designed "for estimating practical data about student's overall school achievement level in general, and achievement in Science, Social Studies, and Literature and the Arts more specifically."
Population: Grades K–12.
Publication Date: 1977.
Acronym: DSTA.
Scores, 5: Science, Social Studies, Literature and the Arts, Practical Knowledge, Total Achievement.
Administration: Group.
Price Data, 2002: $58 per complete kit including manual (12 pages) and 50 test forms; $33 per 50 test forms.
Time: (5–10) minutes.
Authors: Thomas D. Gnagey and Patricia A. Gnagey.
Publisher: Slosson Educational Publications, Inc.
Cross References: For a review by Edward F. Iwanicki, see 9:339.

[811]
Diagnostic Screening Test: Language, Second Edition.

Purpose: Designed "for estimating over-all achievement level in written language."
Population: Grades 1–12.
Publication Date: 1977.
Acronym: DSTL.
Scores, 8: Punctuation, Grammar, Spelling Rules, Sentence Structure, Capitalization, Formal Knowledge of Language, Applied Knowledge of Language, Total Language.
Administration: Group.
Price Data, 2002: $58 per complete kit including manual (12 pages) and 50 test forms; $33 per 50 test forms.
Time: (5–10) minutes.
Authors: Thomas D. Gnagey and Patricia A. Gnagey.
Publisher: Slosson Educational Publications, Inc.
Cross References: For reviews by Janice Arnold Dole and Edward J. Iwanicki, see 9:340.

[812]
Diagnostic Screening Test: Math, Third Edition.

Purpose: Designed for estimating practical data about students' mathematical skills.

Population: Grades 1–11.
Publication Date: 1980.
Acronym: DSTM.
Scores, 31: Basic Process Scores (Addition, Subtraction, Multiplication, Division, Total), Specialized Process Scores (Money, Time, Percent, U.S. Measurement, Metric Measurement, Total), Concept Scores (Process, Sequencing, Simple Computation, Complex Computation, Special Manipulations, Use of Zero, Decimals, Simple Fractions, Manipulation in Fractions), 11 consolidation index scores.
Administration: Group.
Price Data, 2002: $58 per complete kit including manual (17 pages), 25 test Form A, and 25 test Form B; $29 per 50 test Form A; $29 per 50 test Form B.
Time: (5–20) minutes.
Author: Thomas D. Gnagey.
Publisher: Slosson Educational Publications, Inc.
Cross References: For reviews by Edward F. Iwanicki and Stanley F. Vasa, see 9:341.

[813]
Diagnostic Screening Test: Reading, Third Edition.

Purpose: Designed "for estimating practical data about students' reading skills."
Population: Grades 1–12.
Publication Date: 1979.
Acronym: DSTR.
Scores, 16: Comfort Reading Level, Instructional Reading Level, Frustration Reading Level, Comprehension Reading Level, Listening Level, Phonics/Sight Ratio, Word Attack Skill Analysis (c-v/c, v-r, v-l, v-v, c-v-c, Silent e, Mix, Sight, Total), Consolidation Index.
Administration: Individual.
Price Data, 2002: $58 per complete kit including manual (13 pages), 25 test Form A, and 25 test Form B; $29 per 50 test Form A; $29 per 50 test Form B.
Time: (5–10) minutes.
Authors: Thomas D. Gnagey and Patricia A. Gnagey.
Publisher: Slosson Educational Publications, Inc.
Cross References: For a review by Edward F. Iwanicki, see 9:342; for a review by P. David Pearson of an earlier edition, see 8:755.

[814]
Diagnostic Screening Test: Spelling, Third Edition.

Purpose: Designed to gather diagnostic information regarding spelling skills.
Population: Grades 1–12.
Publication Date: 1979.
Acronym: DSTS.
Scores, 12: 3 scores (Verbal, Written, Total) for each of 3 categories (Phonics, Sight, Total); 3 Consolidation Index scores (Phonics Written, Sight Written, Total Spelling Written).
Administration: Group.
Price Data, 2002: $58 per complete kit including manual (13 pages), 25 test Form A, and 25 test Form B; $29 per 50 test Form A; $29 per 50 test Form B.
Time: (5–10) minutes.
Author: Thomas D. Gnagey.
Publisher: Slosson Educational Publications, Inc.
Cross References: For reviews by Edward F. Iwanicki and Robert E. Schafer, see 9:343 (4 references).

[815]
Diagnostic Spelling Test.

Purpose: "Designed for the identification and diagnosis of spelling difficulty."
Population: Ages 8–12.
Publication Dates: 1981–1982.
Acronym: DST.
Scores, 9: Homophones, Common Words, Proof-Reading, Letter Strings, Nonsense Words, Dictionary Use, Dictation, Total, Self-Concept.
Administration: Group.
Forms, 2: A, B.
Price Data: Price information available from publisher for pupil's booklets (Form A or Form B), teacher's manual (1982, 18 pages), and for specimen set.
Time: (50–60) minutes.
Authors: Denis Vincent and Jenny Claydon.
Publisher: NFER-Nelson Publishing Co., Ltd. [England].
Cross References: For reviews by Gwyneth M. Boodoo and Philip L. Smith, see 9:346.

[816]
Differential Ability Scales.

Purpose: Designed to measure cognitive abilities and achievement.
Population: Ages 2-6 to 17-11.
Publication Date: 1990.
Acronym: DAS.
Administration: Individual.
Price Data, 2002: $750 per complete kit with briefcase; $46 per 20 preschool forms; $46 per 20 school-age record forms; $15 per 20 basic number skills and spelling worksheets; $15 per 10 speed of information processing booklets (select A, B, C); $25 per 10 sequential and quantitative reasoning booklets; $94 per administration and scoring manual (1990, 445 pages); $43 per introductory and technical handbook (1990, 379 pages).
Author: Colin D. Elliott.
Comments: Based on the British Ability Scales (350).
Publisher: The Psychological Corporation.

a) COGNITIVE BATTERY.

1) *Preschool.*

Population: Ages 2-6 to 7-11.

Time: (25–65) minutes.

(a) Ages 2-6 to 3-5.

Scores, 7: Block Building, Verbal Comprehension, Picture Similarities, Naming Vocabulary, Total General Conceptual Ability, Recall of Digits, Recognition of Pictures.

(b) Ages 3-6 to 5-11.

Scores, 14: Verbal Ability (Verbal Comprehension, Naming Vocabulary, Total), Nonverbal Ability (Picture Similarities, Pattern Construction, Copying, Total), Early Number Concepts, Total General Conceptual Ability, Block Building, Matching Letter-Like Forms, Recall of Digits, Recall of Objects, Recognition of Pictures.

2) *School-Age.*

Population: Ages 6-0 to 17-11.

Scores, 13: Verbal Ability (Word Definitions, Similarities, Total), Nonverbal Reasoning Ability (Matrices, Sequential and Quantitative Reasoning, Total), Spatial Ability (Recall of Designs, Pattern Construction, Total), Total General Conceptual Ability, Recall of Digits, Recall of Objects, Speed of Information Processing.

Time: (40–65) minutes.

b) SCHOOL ACHIEVEMENT.

Population: Ages 6-0 to 17-11.

Scores, 3: Basic Number Skills, Spelling, Word Reading.

Time: (15–25) minutes.

Cross References: See T5:837 (14 references) and T4:800 (3 references); for reviews by Glen P. Aylward and Robert C. Reinehr, see 11:111 (1 reference).

[817]
Differential Aptitude Tests—Australian and New Zealand Editions [Forms V and W].

Purpose: Provides a standardized procedure for measuring the abilities of males and females for the purpose of educational and vocational guidance.

Population: Grades 8–12.

Publication Dates: 1973–1989.

Scores, 9: Verbal Reasoning, Numerical Ability, Abstract Reasoning, Clerical Speed and Accuracy, Mechanical Reasoning, Space Relations, Spelling, Language Use, Verbal Reasoning + Numerical Ability. Subtests: Available as separates.

Administration: Group.

Price Data, 1999: A$163.95 per 25 Test 1 (Abstract Reasoning, Numerical Reasoning, Abstract Reasoning); A$69.95 per 25 Test 2 (Clerical Speed and Accuracy); A$142.95 per 25 Test 3 (Mechanical Rea-

soning); A$116.95 per 25 Test 4 (Space Relations); A$95.95 per 25 Test 5 (Spelling and Language Usage); A$19.95 per score keys; A$15 per 10 answer sheets; A$59 per exam kit; A$84.95 per manual (1989, 160 pages).

Time: (225) minutes for entire battery.

Comments: New Zealand manual information included; Australian manual same as that for the American version of the Differential Aptitude Tests with norms and revisions for the Australian and New Zealand population.

Authors: Marion M. de Lemos (Australian manual), George K. Bennett, Harold G. Seashore, and Alexander G. Wesman.

Publisher: The Psychological Corporation [Australia] and Australian Council for Educational Research Ltd. [Australia].

[818]
Differential Aptitude Tests, Fifth Edition.

Purpose: "Designed to measure students' ability to learn or to succeed in a number of different areas."

Population: Grades 7–9, grades 10–12 and adults.

Publication Dates: 1947–1992.

Acronym: DAT.

Scores: 9 tests (Verbal Reasoning, Numerical Reasoning, Abstract Reasoning, Perceptual Speed and Accuracy [Part 1, Part 2], Mechanical Reasoning, Space Relations, Spelling, Language Usage) and Total Scholastic Aptitude.

Administration: Group.

Levels, 2: 1, 2.

Price Data, 2002: $59 per 25 Form C partial battery test booklets (Levels 1 or 2) including Directions for Administering (1990, 47 pages); $128 per 25 Form C complete battery test booklets (Levels 1 or 2) including Directions for Administering; $128 per 100 Type 1 machine-scorable answer documents with DAT (Levels 1 or 2, Form C), $152 per 100 Type 1 machine-scorable answer documents with DAT (Levels 1 or 2, Form C) and Level 1 or Level 2 Career Interest Inventory; $67 per Ready-Score answer documents with 25 Perceptual Speed and Accuracy—Part 1 answer sheets, Profile Your DAT scores pamphlet, and Levels 1 or 2 of Form C; $34.50 per norms booklet (Fall or Spring); $34.50 per Using the DAT with Adults; $28 per 25 Practice Tests including a practice test for the Career Interest Inventory and Directions; $108.70 per Guide to Careers Student Workbook; $19 per 25 Exploring Aptitudes: An Introduction to the Differential Aptitude Tests; $19 per 25 Using Test Results for Decision-Making; $34.50 per Technical Manual (1992, 192 pages); $5.30 per Directions for Practice Test; $7 per Directions for Administering; price information for scoring and reporting services available from publisher.

Time: 90(150) minutes.

Comments: 2 forms (C, D) per level; partial battery includes only 2 subtests (Verbal Reasoning and Numerical Reasoning); can be used in conjunction with Career Interest Inventory (407).
Authors: G. K. Bennett, H. G. Seashore, and A. G. Wesman.
Publisher: The Psychological Corporation.
Cross References: See T5:838 (23 references); for reviews by Keith Hattrup and Neal Schmitt, see 12:118 (16 references); see also T4:802 (31 references); for reviews of Forms V and W by Ronald K. Hambleton and Daryl Sander, see 9:352 (19 references); see also T3:732 (26 references); for reviews by Thomas J. Bouchard, Jr., and Robert L. Linn and an excerpted review by Gerald S. Hanna of earlier forms, see 8:485 (56 references); see also T2:1069 (64 references); for a review by M. Y. Qureshi and an excerpted review by Jack C. Merwin of earlier forms, see 7:673 (139 references); for reviews by J. A. Keats and Richard E. Schutz, see 6:767 (52 references); for reviews by John B. Carroll and Norman Frederiksen, see 5:605 (49 references); for reviews by Harold Bechtoldt, Ralph F. Berdie, and Lloyd G. Humphreys, see 4:711 (27 references); for an excerpted review, see 3:620.

[819]
Differential Aptitude Tests for Personnel and Career Assessment.

Purpose: Designed to measure ability to learn in eight aptitude areas.
Population: Adult.
Publication Dates: 1972–1991.
Acronym: DAT for PCA.
Scores, 8: General Cognitive Abilities Tests (Verbal Reasoning, Numerical Ability, Total), Perceptual Abilities Tests (Abstract Reasoning, Mechanical Reasoning, Space Relations), Clerical and Language Tests (Spelling, Language Usage, Clerical Speed and Accuracy).
Administration: Group or individual
Price Data, 2002: $146 per 25 General Cognitive Abilities Battery tests; $146 per 25 Perceptual Abilities Battery tests; $146 per 25 Clerical/Language Battery tests; $74 per 25 tests (select Verbal Reasoning, Numerical Reasoning, Abstract Reasoning, Spelling, Language Usage, or Clerical Speed and Accuracy); $74 per 25 tests (select Mechanical Reasoning or Space Relations); $57 per 25 ready-score answer sheets (select battery); $38 per 50 General Cognitive Abilities Battery hand-scorable answer sheets; $38 per 50 Perceptual Abilities Battery or Clerical/Language Battery hand-scorable answer sheets; $38 per 50 specific test hand-scorable answer sheets (select test); $32 per set of General Cognitive Abilities Battery scoring keys; $32 per set of Perceptual Abilities Battery or Clerical/Language Battery scoring keys; $19 per set of scoring keys for specific tests (select test); $45 per directions for

administering (includes norms); $45 per technical manual; $62 per examination kit.
Time: 114(144) minutes.
Comments: Abbreviated form of the Differential Aptitude Tests, Form V/W.
Authors: George K. Bennett, Harold G. Seashore, and Alexander G. Wesman.
Publisher: The Psychological Corporation.
Cross References: For reviews by Victor L. Willson and Hilda Wing, see 12:119.

[820]
The Differential Diagnostic Technique.

Purpose: "A projective drawing test" designed to "provide an indication of an individual's ego functioning and organization."
Publication Date: 1995.
Acronym: DDT.
Scores, 30: 6 scores (Personality Rigidity, Intellectual Control, Energy Output, Impulsiveness, Dissociation Summary) in 5 areas (Total-Area, H-Area, P-Area, H-P Area, Memory).
Administration: Group.
Forms, 2: Adult, Children's.
Price Data, 2001: $35 per test (specify Adult or Children's form); $20 per scoring stencils; $10 per scoring charts; $50 per manual (1995, 135 pages).
Time: Untimed.
Authors: Otto Weininger (test and scoring manual) and D. Barry Cook (scoring manual).
Publisher: Otto Weininger (the author).
   a) DDT—ADULT FORM.
   Population: Age 12 and over.
   b) DDT—CHILDREN'S FORM.
   Population: Ages 6–12 years.
Cross References: For a review by Sandra A. Loew, see 14:121.

[821]
Differential Test of Conduct and Emotional Problems.

Purpose: "Designed to effect differentiations between conduct problem, emotionally disturbed and noninvolved populations."
Population: Grades K–12.
Publication Dates: 1990–1991.
Acronym: DT/CEP.
Scores, 2: Emotional Disturbance Scale, Conduct Problem Scale.
Administration: Group.
Price Data, 2002: $78 per complete set including manual (1990, 58 pages), score forms, and scoring template; $29 per 50 score forms; $9 per set of 2 scoring templates.
Time: (15–20) minutes.
Comments: Ratings by teachers.

Author: Edward J. Kelly.
Publisher: Slosson Educational Publications, Inc.
Cross References: For reviews by Richard Brozovich and Alida S. Westman, see 12:120; see also T4:804 (1 reference).

[822]
Digit Vigilance Test.

Purpose: Designed to measure vigilance during rapid visual tracking and accurate selection of target stimuli.
Population: Ages 20–80.
Publication Date: 1995.
Acronym: DVT.
Scores, 2: Total Time, Total Errors.
Administration: Individual.
Forms, 2: 6s, 9s.
Price Data: Available from publisher for introductory kit including Professional User's Guide (12 pages), 25 test booklets, and set of 4 scoring templates.
Time: (10) minutes.
Author: Ronald F. Lewis.
Publisher: Psychological Assessment Resources, Inc.
Cross References: For reviews by Raymond S. Dean and Scott Kristian Hill and by Daniel C. Miller, see 14:122.

[823]
Dimensions of Excellence Scales [1991 Edition].

Purpose: Designed to identify, describe and validate successful programs and practices of a school district, as well as to forecast future needs.
Population: Schools or districts.
Publication Dates: 1988–1990.
Acronym: DOES.
Administration: Group.
Price Data, 2001: $2 per school staff survey; $1.25 per parent survey; $1.25 per student survey; $23.95 per manual (1990, 71 pages).
Comments: Ratings by students, parents, and school staff.
Authors: Russel A. Dusewicz and Francine S. Beyer.
Publisher: Research for Better Schools, Inc.
   a) STUDENT SCALE.
   Scores: 4 dimensions: School Climate, Teacher Behavior, Monitoring and Assessment, Student Discipline and Behavior.
   Time: (30) minutes.
   b) PARENT SCALE.
   Scores, 8: Same as *a* above plus Leadership, Curriculum, Staff Development, Parent Involvement.
   Time: (20–30) minutes.
   c) SCHOOL STAFF SCALE.
   Scores, 8: Same as *b* above.
   Time: (45) minutes.

Cross References: For a review by Andrew A. McConney, see 14:123; for reviews by Janet F. Carlson and William P. Erchul of an earlier edition, see 11:112.

[824]
Dimensions of Self-Concept.

Purpose: Designed to "measure non-cognitive factors associated with self-esteem or self-concept in a school setting."
Publication Dates: 1976–1989.
Acronym: DOSC.
Administration: Group.
Price Data, 1998: $10.75 per 25 tests (specify form) [$38 per 100 tests, $143.50 per 500 tests]; $4.25 per technical manual (1989, 23 pages); $7.75 per specimen set; $1.60 per test for scoring by publisher.
Comments: Self-report instrument.
Authors: William B. Michael, Robert A. Smith, and Joan J. Michael.
Publisher: EdITS/Educational and Industrial Testing Service.
   a) FORM E.
   Population: Grades 4–6.
   Scores, 5: Level of Aspiration, Anxiety, Academic Interest and Satisfaction, Leadership and Initiative, Identification vs. Alienation.
   Time: (20–40) minutes.
   b) FORM S.
   Population: Grades 7–12.
   Scores: Same as for *a* above.
   Time: (15–35) minutes.
   c) FORM H.
   Population: College.
   Scores: Same as for *a* above.
   Time: (15–35) minutes.
   d) FORM W.
   Population: Adult workers.
   Scores, 5: Aspiration, Anxiety, Job Interest and Satisfaction, Identification vs. Alienation, Level of Job Stress.
   Time: Administration time not reported.
Cross References: See T5:844 (6 references) and T4:806 (1 reference); for a review by Sharon Johnson-Lewis, see 11:113 (10 references); for reviews by Herbert G. W. Bischoff and Alfred B. Heilbrun, Jr., see 9:353 (4 references); see also T3:734 (5 references).

[825]
The Diplomacy Test of Empathy.

Purpose: Constructed to measure empathic ability.
Population: Business and industrial personnel.
Publication Dates: 1960–1962.
Scores: Total score only.
Administration: Group.
Price Data: Available from publisher.
Time: (20–25) minutes.

Comments: Revision of Primary Empathic Abilities; title on test is Diplomacy Test of Empathic Ability.
Author: Willard A. Kerr.
Publisher: Psychometric Affiliates.
Cross References: See T2:1160 (1 reference) and P:64 (2 references); for reviews by Arthur H. Brayfield and Richard S. Hatch, see 6:85 (1 reference); for a review by Robert L. Thorndike of the earlier test, see 5:99.

[826]
The Discipline Index.

Purpose: "Systematically obtains information from a child about the child's overall perceptions of each parent's disciplinary practices."
Population: Ages 6–17.
Publication Dates: 1999–2002.
Acronym: DI.
Scores, 6: Mother and Father scores for: Clear Expectations, Effectively Monitors, Consistently Enforces, Fairness, Attunement, Moderates Anger, plus Mother Total, Father Total.
Administration: Individual.
Price Data, 2002: $199 per complete kit including handbook (2000, 140 pages), 8 sets response cards, 8 scoring summaries, stylus-pen, placement dots, updates, and 3-year update service; $99 per 8 response cards with summaries; $159 per 16 response cards with summaries; $199 per 24 response cards with summaries; $198 per computer scoring program (half price when purchased with kit); $129 per handbook.
Time: (35 minutes).
Authors: Anita K. Lampel, Barry Bricklin, and Gail Elliot.
Publisher: Village Publishing.

[827]
Dissemination Self-Inventory.

Purpose: "To help people involved in NIDRR-funded disability research and development projects bridge the gap between the creation of disability research outcomes and their use."
Population: Organizations.
Publication Date: 2002.
Scores, 4: Organizational Structure and Policies, Research Design, Dissemination Plan, Evaluation.
Administration: Individual.
Price Data, 2002: $10 per Dissemination Self-Inventory (2002, 24 pages).
Time: [20–35] minutes.
Author: Southwest Educational Development Laboratory.
Publisher: Southwest Educational Development Laboratory.

[828]
Dissociative Experiences Scale.

Purpose: "Developed to serve as a clinical tool to help identify patients with dissociative psychopathology and as a research tool to provide a means of quantifying dissociative experiences."
Population: Late adolescent–adult.
Publication Date: 1986.
Acronym: DES.
Scores: Total score only.
Administration: Group or individual.
Price Data, 1998: $12 per complete test.
Foreign Language Editions: Available in French, Spanish, Italian, Dutch, Hindi, Cambodian, Czech, Swedish, Norwegian, Japanese, Hebrew, Chinese (Mandarin, Traditional Character, and Simplified Character), Finnish, Korean, Polish, and Turkish.
Time: [10] minutes.
Comments: Self-report inventory; translation also in progress for version of the DES in German; test is in the public domain and is available from publisher for cost of copying, handling, and mailing.
Authors: Eve Bernstein Carlson and Frank W. Putnam.
Publisher: The Sidran Foundation.
Cross References: See T5:846 (26 references); for reviews by Samuel Juni and Niels G. Waller, see 12:122 (16 references); see also T4:809 (1 reference).

[829]
Dissociative Features Profile.

Purpose: Developed to "help uncover dissociative pathology in children and adolescents."
Population: Children and adolescents.
Publication Date: 1996.
Acronym: DFP.
Scores, 22: Part I: Evidence of Amnesia, Staring Episodes, Odd Movements, Fluctuations/Relatedness, Fluctuations/Language, Fearfulness, Anger, Physical Complaints, Dividedness (1), Dividedness (2), Total; Part II: Multiplicity, Malevolent Religiosity, Dissociative Coping, Depersonalized Humans, Explicit Emotional Confusion, Categories of Good and Bad, Mutilation, Torture, Magical Transformations, Total; Combined Part I and Part II Total.
Administration: Individual.
Parts, 2: Behaviors, Markers.
Price Data, 1998: $10 per set of 5 preliminary DFP forms and scoring manual/reference guide (1996, 4 pages).
Time: Untimed.
Comments: "Developed to be used with a typical psychological testing battery" (at least 2 other psychological tests given in conjunction with this test); profile completed by psychological professionals about juvenile clients.

Author: Joyanna L. Silberg.
Publisher: The Sidran Foundation.

[830]
Diversity Awareness Profile.

Purpose: "Designed to assist people in becoming aware of ways in which they discriminate against, judge, or isolate others."
Population: Employees or managers.
Publication Date: 1991.
Acronym: DAP.
Scores: Total score only.
Administration: Group.
Forms, 2: Employee, Manager.
Price Data: Price information available from publisher.
Time: (90) minutes.
Author: Karen Grote.
Publisher: Jossey-Bass, A Wiley Company.
Cross References: For reviews by Donald B. Pope-Davis and Jonathan G. Dings and by Gargi Roysircar Sodowsky, see 12:123.

[831]
Domestic Violence Inventory.

Purpose: "Designed specifically for risk and needs assessment of people who have committed physical, emotional and verbal abuse."
Population: Ages 12–18, adults.
Publication Dates: 1991–1995.
Acronym: DVI.
Scores: 6 scales: Truthfulness, Violence, Alcohol, Drugs, Control, Stress Coping Ability.
Administration: Group.
Forms, 2: Adult, Juvenile.
Price Data: Available from publisher.
Time: (30) minutes.
Comments: Available in English and Spanish; both computer version and paper-pencil format are scored on IBM-PC compatibles.
Author: Risk & Needs Assessment, Inc.
Publisher: Risk & Needs Assessment, Inc.
Cross References: For reviews by Carol Collins and by David M. Kaplan and Molly L. Vanduser, see 14:125.

[832]
Dos Amigos Verbal Language Scales.

Purpose: Designed to assess the level of both English and Spanish language development in children.
Population: Ages 5-0 to 13-5.
Publication Dates: 1973–1996.
Scores, 3: English, Spanish, Dominant Language.
Administration: Individual.
Price Data, 2002: $45 per complete test kit including manual (1996, 17 pages), and 25 test forms; $20 per 25 test forms.

Time: (20) minutes.
Comments: No reading by examinees; examiner must read and speak Spanish and English; the 1996 edition is a criterion-referenced test with scoring based on previous normative material used in earlier test editions.
Author: Donald E. Critchlow.
Publisher: Academic Therapy Publications.
Cross References: For reviews by Robert B. Frary and Maria Del R. Medina-Diaz, see 14:126.

[833]
Draw A Person: A Quantitative Scoring System.

Purpose: "To meet the need for a modernized, recently normed, and objective scoring system to be applied to human figure drawings produced by children and adolescents."
Population: Ages 5–17.
Publication Date: 1988.
Acronym: Draw A Person: QSS.
Scores, 4: Man, Woman, Self, Total.
Administration: Group.
Price Data, 2002: $146 per complete kit including 25 student record/response forms, scoring chart, and manual (1988, 100 pages); $101 per scoring chart and manual; $47 per 25 student record/response forms.
Time: 15(25) minutes.
Author: Jack A. Naglieri.
Publisher: The Psychological Corporation.
Cross References: See T5:854 (2 references) and T4:814 (3 references); for reviews by Merith Cosden and W. Grant Willis, see 11:114 (1 reference).

[834]
Draw A Person: Screening Procedure for Emotional Disturbance.

Purpose: Designed to screen for children who may have emotional disorders and require further evaluation.
Population: Ages 6–17.
Publication Date: 1991.
Acronym: DAP:SPED.
Scores: Total score only.
Administration: Group and individual.
Price Data, 2001: $104 per complete kit including 25 record forms and manual (77 pages); $39 per 25 record forms; $49 per manual; $19 per 10 scoring templates.
Time: 15(20) minutes.
Authors: Jack A. Naglieri, Timothy J. McNeish, and Achilles N. Bardos.
Publisher: PRO-ED.
Cross References: See T5:852 (1 reference); for reviews by Merith Cosden and Gale M. Morrison, see 12:124 (2 references); see also T4:816 (1 reference).

[835]
The Draw-A-Person.

Purpose: To provide clinical interpretations of the DAP.
Population: Ages 5 and over.
Publication Date: 1963.
Acronym: DAP.
Scores: Total score only.
Administration: Group.
Price Data, 2002: $39.50 per manual (72 pages, catalogue for interpretative analysis).
Time: [5–10] minutes.
Author: William H. Urban.
Publisher: Western Psychological Services.
Cross References: See T5:853 (25 references), T4:813 (40 references), 9:358 (23 references), and T3:751 (44 references); for reviews by Dale B. Harris and Phillip M. Kitay, see 7:165.

[836]
Draw-a-Story: Screening for Depression and Age or Gender Differences.

Purpose: Designed to identify depression.
Population: Ages 5 and over.
Publication Dates: 1987–1998.
Acronym: DAS.
Scores: 2 task scores: Draw-A-Story, Stimulus Drawing Task.
Administration: Group or individual.
Forms, 2: A, B.
Price Data, 2001: $25 per test including manual (1993, 111 pages); $15 per manual entitled "Updating the Silver Drawing Test and Draw A Story Manuals" (1998, 32 pages).
Time: (5–15) minutes.
Comments: Previous edition titled Draw-a-Story: Screening for Depression and Emotional Needs.
Author: Rawley Silver.
Publisher: Ablin Press Distributors.
Cross References: For reviews by Dennis C. Harper and by Joseph C. Witt and Frank M. Gresham, see 13:103 (1 reference); see also T4:817 (1 reference); for reviews by Walter Katkovsky and David Lachar of the earlier edition, see 11:115.

[837]
Driver Risk Inventory—II.

Purpose: "Designed for DUI/DWI offender screening."
Population: Convicted DUI and DWI offenders.
Publication Dates: 1986–1997.
Acronym: DRI-II.
Scores, 6: Truthfulness, Alcohol, Driver Risk, Drug, Stress Coping, Dependency.
Price Data: Available from publisher.
Time: (30–35) minutes.

Comments: Self-administered, computer-scored test.
Author: Behavior Data Systems Ltd.
Publisher: Behavior Data Systems Ltd.
Cross References: For reviews by Tony Cellucci and Kevin J. McCarthy, see 14:127; for a review by Frank Gresham of an earlier version, see 12:125.

[838]
Drug Abuse Screening Test.

Purpose: To assess "potential involvement with drugs."
Population: Clients of addiction treatment.
Publication Date: 1982.
Acronym: DAST-20.
Scores: Total score only.
Administration: Group.
Price Data, 2002: C$9.05 in Ontario (C$12.95 outside Ontario) per test.
Foreign Language Edition: Available in French.
Time: (5–10) minutes.
Comments: Self-report inventory; manual is entitled "Directory of Client Outcome Measures for Addiction Treatment Programs"; has also been listed as Drug Use Questionnaire.
Author: Harvey A. Skinner.
Publisher: Centre for Addiction and Mental Health [Canada].
Cross References: For reviews by Philip Ash and Jeffrey S. Rain, see 13:104.

[839]
Drug-Taking Confidence Questionnaire.

Purpose: "As an assessment tool, the DTCQ identifies a client's coping self-efficacy in relation to 50 drinking or drug-taking situations."
Population: Clients of addiction treatment.
Publication Date: 1997.
Acronym: DTCQ.
Scores: Situation profiles in two areas: Personal States, Situations Involving Other People; 8 subscales: Unpleasant Emotions, Physical Discomfort, Pleasant Emotions, Testing Personal Control, Urges and Temptations to Use, Conflict with Others, Social Pressure to Use, Pleasant Times with Others.
Administration: Group.
Price Data, 2002: C$34.95 per user's guide; C$14.95 per 30 questionnaires (specify alcohol or drug); C$39.95 per sample pack including user's guide and 40 questionnaires (10 alcohol and 30 drug); C$75 per 50 uses of computer-administration software (DOS format); C$100 per 50 uses of software with user's guide; C$250 per 200 uses of software; C$275 per 200 uses of software with user's guide.
Time: (15) minutes.
Comments: User's guide written in both English (160 pages) and French (69 pages); "French versions of DTCQ have not been scientifically validated."

Authors: Helen M. Annis, Sherrilyn M. Sklar, and Nigel E. Turner.
Publisher: Centre for Addiction and Mental Health [Canada].
Cross References: For reviews by Michael H. Campbell and Glenn B. Gelman, see 14:128.

[840]
DSST/DANTES Subject Standardized Tests.

Purpose: Gives colleges and universities the opportunity ...to offer non-traditional learners college credit for knowledge acquired outside the traditional classroom.
Population: Non-traditional students wishing to earn college credit by examination.
Publication Dates: 1983–2002.
Acronym: DSST.
Administration: Group.
Price Data, 2002: $40 per exam; test centers may also require an administration fee for each examination; scoring by publisher included in price.
Time: Untimed, requiring approximately (90) minutes per test.
Comments: Paper-and-pencil administration; additional information available at www.getcollegecredit.com.
Author: The Chauncey Group International.
Publisher: The Chauncey Group International.

a) MATHEMATICS.
Scores: Total score for each of 2 tests:
    1) *Fundamentals of College Algebra.*
    2) *Principles of Statistics.*
b) SOCIAL SCIENCE.
Scores: Total score for each of 14 tests:
    1) *Western Europe Since 1945.*
    2) *Introduction to the Modern Middle East.*
    3) *A History of the Vietnam War.*
    4) *Human/Cultural Geography.*
    5) *Lifespan Developmental Psychology.*
    6) *General Anthropology.*
    7) *Introduction to Law Enforcement.*
    8) *Criminal Justice.*
    9) *Fundamentals of Counseling.*
    10) *Art of the Western World.*
    11) *Drug and Alcohol Abuse.*
    12) *The Civil War and Reconstruction.*
    13) *Foundations of Education.*
    14) *Rise and Fall of the Soviet Union.*
c) PHYSICAL SCIENCE.
Scores: Total score for each of 5 tests:
    1) *Astronomy.*
    2) *Here's to Your Health.*
    3) *Environment and Humanity: The Race to Save the Planet.*
    4) *Principles of Physical Science I.*
    5) *Physical Geology.*

d) BUSINESS.
Scores: Total score for each of 12 tests:
    1) *Principles of Finance.*
    2) *Principles of Financial Accounting.*
    3) *Human Resource Management.*
    4) *Organizational Behavior.*
    5) *Introduction to Computing.*
    6) *Introduction to Business.*
    7) *Money and Banking.*
    8) *Business Mathematics.*
    9) *Business Law II.*
    10) *Principles of Supervision.*
    11) *Personal Finance.*
    12) *Management Information Systems.*
e) FOREIGN LANGUAGE.
f) APPLIED TECHNOLOGY.
    1) *Technical Writing.*
g) HUMANITIES.
Scores: Total score for each of 3 tests:
    1) *Ethics in America.*
    2) *Principles of Public Speaking.*
    3) *Introduction to World Religions.*
Cross References: For reviews by Laura L. B. Barnes and William A. Mehrens, see 11:103.

[841]
Durrell Analysis of Reading Difficulty, Third Edition.

Purpose: Designed to screen for reading problems.
Population: Grades 1–6.
Publication Dates: 1937–1980.
Acronym: DARD.
Scores, 16 to 21: Oral Reading, Silent Reading, Listening Comprehension, Word Recognition, Word Analysis, Listening Vocabulary, Sounds in Isolation (Letters, Blends and Digraphs, Phonograms, Initial Affixes, Final Affixes), Spelling, Phonic Spelling of Words, Visual Memory of Words (Primary, Secondary), Identifying Sounds in Words, Prereading Phonics Abilities Inventories (Optional, Including Syntax Matching, Letter Names in Spoken Words, Phonemes in Spoken Words, Naming Lower Case Letters, Writing Letters from Dictation).
Administration: Individual.
Price Data, 2002: $137 per examiner's kit including tachistoscope, reading booklet, 5 record booklets, and manual (1980, 63 pages); $45.60 per reading booklet; $43 per tachistoscope; $81.60 per 35 record booklets; $23 per manual.
Time: (35–50) minutes.
Authors: Donald D. Durrell and Jane H. Catterson.
Publisher: The Psychological Corporation.
Cross References: See T5:861 (5 references) and T4:822 (14 references); for reviews by Nancy L. Roser and Byron H. Van Roekel, see 9:360 (3 references); see also T3:766 (14 references) and T2:1628 (18 refer-

ences); for reviews by James Maxwell and George D. Spache of an earlier edition, see 5:660; for a review by Helen M. Robinson of the original edition, see 4:561 (2 references); for reviews by Guy L. Bond and Miles A. Tinker, see 2:1533; for a review by Marion Monroe, see 1:1098.

[842]
Dvorine Color Vision Test.
Purpose: Designed as a "method of identifying individuals with defective color vision."
Population: Ages 3 and over.
Publication Dates: 1944–1958.
Scores, 2: Nomenclature, Color Perception.
Administration: Individual.
Price Data, 2002: $335 per booklet of color plates (1953, 33 pages, manual and 24 color plates); 297 per 35 record forms.
Time: [2] minutes.
Comments: Revision of Dvorine Color Perception Testing Charts; also called Dvorine Pseudo-Isochromatic Plates.
Author: Israel Dvorine.
Publisher: The Psychological Corporation.
Cross References: See T4:823 (1 reference), T3:767 (1 reference), T2:1911 (13 references), and 6:955 (12 references); for excerpted reviews by Elsie Murray, Laurance F. Shaffer, and Miles A. Tinker, see 5:773 (13 references); for excerpted reviews by Knight Dunlap, Carel C. Koch, Elsie Murray (reply by Israel Dvorine), and Miles A. Tinker, see 3:462 (4 references).

[843]
Dyadic Adjustment Scale.
Purpose: Designed to measure the quality of adjustment in marriage and similar dyadic relationships.
Population: People who have any committed couple relationship including unmarried cohabitation.
Publication Date: 1989.
Acronym: DAS.
Scores, 5: Dyadic Consensus, Dyadic Satisfaction, Affectional Expression, Dyadic Cohesion, Total.
Administration: Group or individual.
Price Data, 2002: $40 per complete kit including test manual (55 pages) and 20 QuikScore™ forms; $29 per 20 QuikScore™ forms(for 10 couples); 20 per manual; $5 each for Windows software profile reports (with Psychmanager platform).
Time: (5-10) minutes.
Comments: Self-report.
Author: Graham B. Spanier.
Publisher: Multi-Health Systems, Inc.
Cross References: See T5:863 (94 references) and T4:824 (37 references); for reviews by Karen S. Budd and Nancy Heilman and Richard B. Stuart, see 11:117 (17 references).

[844]
Dyadic Parent-Child Interaction Coding System: A Manual.
Purpose: "For use in assessing the quality of parent-child social interaction."
Population: Children ages 2–10 and their parents.
Publication Date: 1981.
Acronym: DPICS.
Scores: 24 behavioral frequency scores in 4 general areas: Parent Behaviors, Child Behaviors, Child Responses to Commands, Parent Responses to Deviant Child Behaviors.
Administration: Individual.
Price Data: Price data including manual (87 pages) available from publisher.
Time: 15(20) minutes.
Comments: Behavioral ratings by clinician in 3 standard situations.
Authors: Sheila M. Eyberg and Elizabeth A. Robinson.
Publisher: Sheila M. Eyberg, Ph.D. [No reply from publisher; status unknown].
Cross References: See T5:864 (3 references) and T4:825 (11 references); for reviews by Robert J. McMahon and Phillip S. Strain, see 9:361 (1 reference); see also T3:768 (1 reference).

[845]
Dynamic Factors Survey.
Purpose: Measurement of motivational factors related to personality and interest research, personnel selection, and vocational assessment.
Population: Grades 12–16 and adults.
Publication Dates: 1954–1956.
Acronym: DFOS.
Scores, 10: Need for Attention, Liking for Thinking, Adventure vs. Security, Self-Reliance vs. Dependence, Aesthetic Appreciation, Cultural Conformity, Need for Freedom, Realistic Thinking, Need for Precision, Need for Diversion.
Administration: Group.
Price Data: Available from publisher.
Time: (45) minutes.
Authors: J. P. Guilford, Paul R. Christensen, and Nicholas A. Bond, Jr.
Publisher: Mind Garden, Inc.
Cross References: See T2:1151 (7 references) and P:54 (12 references); for reviews by Andrew R. Baggaley, John W. French, and Arthur W. Meadows, see 5:45.

[846]
Dysarthria Examination Battery.
Purpose: Designed to "assess motor speech disorders."
Population: Children and adults.
Publication Date: 1993.

Scores, 5: Respiration, Phonation, Resonation, Articulation, Prosody.
Administration: Individual.
Price Data, 1999: $68 per complete kit including test booklet, 3 stimulus cards, 20 scoring forms, and manual (48 pages); $18 per 20 scoring forms.
Time: (60) minutes.
Author: Sakina S. Drummond.
Publisher: Communication Skill Builders—A Division of The Psychological Corporation.
Cross References: For reviews by Steven B. Leder and Malcolm R. McNeil, see 14:129.

[847]
Dyslexia Adult Screening Test.

Purpose: To assess strengths and weaknesses often associated with dyslexia.
Population: 16 years 5 months to adult.
Publication Date: 1998.
Acronym: DAST.
Scores, 12: Rapid Naming, One Minute Reading, Postural Stability, Nonverbal Reasoning, Phonemic Segmentation, Two Minute Spelling, Backwards Span, Verbal Fluency, Semantic Fluency, Nonsense Passage Reading, One Minute Writing, Total.
Administration: Individual.
Price Data, 2002: $180.46 per complete kit.
Time: 30 minutes.
Authors: Angela J. Fawcett and Rod I. Nicholson.
Publisher: The Psychological Corporation Europe.

[848]
Dyslexia Determination Test, Second Edition.

Purpose: To identify individuals who exhibit dyslexic patterns of responding in the areas of reading, writing, and spelling.
Population: Grades 2–12.
Publication Dates: 1980–1987.
Acronym: DDT.
Scores: 6 subtests: Dysnemkinesia (Writing of Numbers, Writing of Letters), Dysphonesia (Decoding, Encoding), Dyseidesia (Decoding, Encoding).
Administration: Individual.
Price Data: Available from publisher.
Time: (15–20) minutes.
Authors: John R. Griffin and Howard N. Walton.
Publisher: I-MED, Instructional Materials & Equipment Distributors.
Cross References: For a review by Fred M. Grossman, see 9:362.

[849]
Dyslexia Early Screening Test.

Purpose: A battery of tests to "provide ... a simple 'at risk' index for dyslexia."

Population: Ages 1 to 6-5.
Publication Date: 1996.
Acronym: DEST.
Scores, 11: 2 Tests of Attainment (Digit Naming, Letter Naming), 8 Diagnostic Tests (Rapid Naming, Bead Threading, Phonological Discrimination, Postural Stability, Rhyme Detection, Forwards Digit Span, Sound Order, Shape Copying), At Risk Quotient.
Administration: Individual.
Price Data, 2002: $119 per complete kit including manual (1996, 65 pages), score keys, subtests, sample permission letter, 50 record forms, blindfold, balance tester, Forwards Digit Span tape, Sound Order test tape, and carrying case; $55 per 50 record forms.
Time: (30) minutes for entire battery.
Comments: Downward extension of the Dyslexia Screening Test (851); normed in the United Kingdom.
Authors: Rod I. Nicolson and Angela J. Fawcett.
Publisher: The Psychological Corporation Europe [United Kingdom]; distributed by The Psychological Corporation.

[850]
Dyslexia Screening Instrument.

Purpose: Designed to identify students with dyslexia.
Population: Grades 1–12, ages 6–21.
Publication Date: 1994.
Scores, 4: Passed, Failed, Inconclusive, Cannot Be Scored.
Administration: Individual.
Price Data, 2002: $85 per complete kit including teacher rating scale, manual (40 pages), and scoring program software; $16 per 50 rating forms.
Time: (15–20) minutes.
Comments: Rating form is completed by student's teacher; computer scored, DOS 3.0 or higher.
Authors: Kathryn B. Coon, Mary Jo Polk, and Melissa McCoy Waguespack.
Publisher: The Psychological Corporation.
Cross References: For reviews by Janet E. Spector and Betsy Waterman, see 14:130.

[851]
Dyslexia Screening Test.

Purpose: "A screening instrument ... for profil[ing] the strengths and weaknesses often associated with dyslexia."
Population: Ages 6-6 to 16-5.
Publication Date: 1996.
Acronym: DST.
Scores, 11: 3 Tests of Attainment (One Minute Reading, Two Minute Spelling, One Minute Writing), 8 Diagnostic Tests (Rapid Naming, Bead Threading, Postural Stability, Phonemic Segmentation, Backwards Digit Span, Nonsense Passage Reading, Semantic Fluency, Verbal Fluency), At Risk Quotient.

Administration: Individual.
Price Data, 2002: $119 per complete kit including manual (1996, 63 pages), score keys, Backwards Digit Span audiocassette, Sound Order test tape, and carrying case; $55 per 50 record forms.
Time: (30) minutes for entire battery.
Comments: Normed in the United Kingdom.
Authors: Angela J. Fawcett and Rod I. Nicolson.
Publisher: The Psychological Corporation Europe [United Kingdom]; distributed by The Psychological Corporation.

[852]
Dysphagia Evaluation Protocol.

Purpose: Developed to "assist in evaluating swallowing functioning in adult patients."
Population: Adult patients.
Publication Date: 1997.
Acronym: DEP.
Scores: 14 ratings: History and Observations (Feeding History, Nutritional Status, Respiratory Status), Clinical Evaluation of Swallowing (Observations, Oral Control, Primitive and Abnormal Reflexes, Pharyngeal Control), Feeding Trial (Appetite/Willingness to Participate, Ability to Swallow Without Food Bolus, Oral State, Pharyngeal Stage), Impressions (Summary, Functional Level, Recommendations/Plan).
Administration: Individual.
Price Data, 2002: $72 per complete kit including 15 record forms, pocket manual (40 pages), and manual (64 pages), $13 per 15 record forms; $36 per pocket manual; $36 per manual.
Time: (30) minutes.
Authors: Wendy Avery-Smith, Abbey Brod Rosen, and Donna M. Dellarosa.
Publisher: Therapy Skill Builders—A Division of The Psychological Corporation.
Cross References: For a review of Maynard D. Filter, see 14:131.

[853]
E. S. Survey.

Purpose: "Screens applicants and employees for emotional stability and control."
Population: Job applicants and employees.
Publication Date: 1970.
Scores: Overall score, "Fake Good" Index.
Administration: Group.
Price Data: Price information available from publisher for surveys and yearly license fee.
Time: (5–10) minutes.
Authors: Alan L. Strand and others.
Publisher: Predictive Surveys Corporation.
Cross References: For reviews by Jeanette N. Cleveland and James W. Pinkney, see 9:364.

[854]
Early Child Development Inventory.

Purpose: "A brief screening inventory ... designed to help identify children with developmental, behavioral, or health problems."
Population: Ages 1-3 to 3-0.
Publication Date: 1988.
Acronym: ECDI.
Scores: General Development Score, Possible Problems List (24), Child Description, Parent's Questions/Concerns, Parent's Functioning.
Administration: Individual or group.
Price Data, 2001: $10 per 25 Parent Questionnaires; $10 per manual (15 pages).
Time: (15) minutes.
Comments: Parent-completed questionnaire; scores reflect parent's report of child's present functioning.
Authors: Harold Ireton.
Publisher: Behavior Science Systems, Inc.
Cross References: For a review by Robert W. Hiltonsmith, see 11:119.

[855]
Early Childhood Attention Deficit Disorders Evaluation Scale.

Purpose: Designed to document behaviors and measure the characteristics of ADHD in school and home environments.
Population: Males ages 24–84 months; Females ages 24–83 months.
Publication Date: 1995.
Acronym: ECADDES.
Scores, 3: Inattentive, Hyperactive-Impulsive, Total Percentile Rank.
Administration: Individual.
Forms, 3: Home, School, ECADDES/DSM-IV.
Price Data, 2002: $154 per complete kit including 50 School Version rating forms, 50 Home Version rating forms, 50 ECADDES/DSM-IV forms, School Version technical manual (42 pages), Home Version technical manual (42 pages), ECADDES Intervention manual (147 pages), and Parent's Guide (134 pages); $33 per 50 rating forms (specify School Version or Home Version); $33 per 50 Home Version Spanish rating forms; $22 per 50 ECADDES/DSM-IV forms; $14 per technical manual (specify School Version or Home Version); $24 per ECADDES Intervention manual; $14 per Parent's Guide; $35 per computerized Quick Score program (DOS).
Time: (15–20) minutes.
Comments: Ratings by persons familiar with the child's behavior patterns in home or school settings.
Authors: Stephen B. McCarney and Nancy W. Johnson (Intervention Manual and Parent's Guide).

Publisher: Hawthorne Educational Services, Inc.
Cross References: For reviews by Libby G. Cohen and Harold R. Keller, see 14:132.

[856]
The Early Childhood Behavior Scale.

Purpose: Designed to assess behaviors related to early childhood emotional disturbance and behavior disorder.
Population: 36–72 months.
Publication Dates: 1991–1994.
Acronym: ECBS.
Scores, 4: Academic Progress, Social Relationships, Personal Adjustment, Total Percentile Rank.
Administration: Individual.
Price Data, 2002: $96 per complete kit including technical manual (1992, 36 pages), intervention manual (1991, 130 pages), and 50 ratings forms; $14 per technical manual; $20 per intervention manual; $33 per 50 rating forms.
Time: (15–20) minutes.
Comments: Ratings by teachers.
Author: Stephen B. McCarney.
Publisher: Hawthorne Educational Services, Inc.
Cross References: For reviews by Kathleen D. Paget and Jonathan Sandoval, see 13:105.

[857]
Early Childhood Environment Rating Scale—Revised Edition.

Purpose: Designed to measure the quality of the environments in early childhood programs.
Population: Early childhood programs or classrooms (excluding infant and toddler programs).
Publication Dates: 1980–1998.
Acronym: ECERS-R.
Scores, 8: Space and Furnishings, Personal Care Routines, Language-Reasoning, Activities, Interaction, Program Structure, Parents and Staff, Total.
Administration: Group.
Price Data, 2002: $11.95 per complete test.
Foreign Language Editions: Translations of the original ECERS in Italian, Swedish, German, Portugese, Spanish, and Icelandic.
Time: (140) minutes.
Comments: Can be completed by an outside observer or as a self-assessment by program staff.
Authors: Thelma Harms, Richard M. Clifford, and Debbie Cryer.
Publisher: Teachers College Press.
Cross References: For reviews by Kathleen D. Paget and Gene Schwarting, see 14:133; see also T5:875 (11 references) and T4:833 (7 references); for reviews by Richard Elardo and Cathy Fultz Telzrow of the original version, see 9:365.

[858]
Early Childhood Inventory–4.

Purpose: Constructed to assess the "behavioral, affective, and cognitive symptoms of childhood psychiatric disorders."
Population: Ages 3–6.
Publication Dates: 1996–1997.
Acronym: ECI-4.
Scores, 25: AD/HD Inattentive, AD/HD Hyperactive-Impulsive, AD/HD Combined, Oppositional Defiant Disorder, Conduct Disorder, Peer Conflict Scale, Separation Anxiety Disorder, Specific Phobia, Obsessions, Compulsions, Motor Tics, Vocal Tics, Generalized Anxiety Disorder, Selective Mutism, Major Depressive Disorder, Dysthymic Disorder, Adjustment Disorder, Social Phobia, Sleep Problems, Elimination Problems, Posttraumatic Stress Disorder, Feeding Problems, Reactive Attachment Disorder, Autistic Disorder, Asperger's Disorder.
Administration: Individual.
Forms, 2: Parent Checklist, Teacher Checklist.
Price Data, 2001: $102 per deluxe kit including screening manual (2000, 117 pages), norms manual (1997, 184 pages), 25 parent checklists, 25 teacher checklists, 50 parent score sheets, and 50 teacher score sheets; $52 per 50 parent checklists and score sheets; 38 per 50 teacher checklists and score sheets; $22 per screening manual; $22 per norms manual.
Time: (10–15) minutes.
Comments: Instrument is designed to correspond to the DSM-IV classification system.
Authors: Kenneth D. Gadow and Joyce Sprafkin.
Publisher: Checkmate Plus, Ltd.
Cross References: For a review by Robert C. Reinehr, see 14:134.

[859]
Early Childhood Physical Environment Observation Schedules and Rating Scales.

Purpose: "Intended for the systematic assessment of the quality of the physical environment of child care centers and related early childhood environments."
Population: Directors and staff of child care centers, early childhood teachers.
Publication Dates: 1982–1994.
Scores: 9 scales: Early Childhood Teacher Style and Dimensions of Education Rating Scales (Early Childhood Teacher Style Rating Scale, Early Childhood Dimensions of Education Rating Scale, Teacher Style and Dimensions of Education Validity Check), Early Childhood Physical Environment Scales (Pattern 905: Spatial Organization, Pattern 908: Behavior Settings), Playground and Neighborhood Observation Behavior Maps (Playground Observation Behavior Map, Neighborhood Observation Behavior Map, Neighborhood Observation Supplementary Coding Sheet), Environ-

ment/Behavior Observation Schedule for Early Childhood Environments.
Administration: Group.
Price Data, 2002: $12 per complete kit including manual (1994, 80 pages, technical report, and specimen sets.
Time: [10–30] minutes per scale.
Comments: For research purposes only.
Author: Gary T. Moore.
Publisher: Center for Architecture and Urban Planning Research, University of Wisconsin—Milwaukee.
Cross References: For reviews by Lisa G. Bischoff and Patricia B. Keith, see 13:106.

[860]
Early Coping Inventory.

Purpose: Measures adaptive behavior.
Population: Ages 4–36 months.
Publication Date: 1988.
Scores, 4: Sensorimotor Organization, Reactive Behavior, Self-Initiated Behavior, Total.
Administration: Individual.
Price Data, 2002: $53 per complete kit including manual (62 pages) and 20 inventories (9 pages); $34.50 per 20 inventories; $28.30 per manual; $25.95 per sample set.
Time: Administration time varies.
Comments: Downward extension of the Coping Inventory (684); ratings of adaptive behavior by an adult.
Authors: Shirley Zeitlin and G. Gordon Williamson with Margery Szczepanski.
Publisher: Scholastic Testing Service, Inc.
Cross References: See T5:878 (1 reference); for reviews by Harlan J. Stientjes and Logan Wright and Wade L. Hamil, see 11:120.

[861]
Early Intervention Developmental Profile.

Purpose: Designed to yield information for planning comprehensive developmental programs for children with all types of handicaps.
Population: Children with handicaps who function at the 0–35 month age level.
Publication Dates: 1977–1991.
Scores, 8: Perceptual/Fine Motor, Cognition, Language, Social/Emotional, Self-Care (Feeding, Toileting, Dressing), Gross Motor.
Administration: Individual.
Price Data: Available from publisher.
Time: (50–60) minutes.
Comments: Stimulation activities manual included; see Preschool Developmental Profile (1962) for extended ages.
Authors: D. Sue Schafer, Martha S. Moersch, Sally J. Rogers, Diane B. D'Eugenio, Sara L. Brown, Carol M. Donovan, and Eleanor Whiteside Lynch.

Publisher: University of Michigan Press.
Cross References: For reviews by Barbara A. Rothlisberg and Gary J. Stainback, see 13:107 (1 reference); see also T4:835 (1 reference).

[862]
Early Language Milestone Scale, Second Edition.

Purpose: To assess speech and language development during infancy and early childhood.
Population: Birth to 36 months.
Publication Dates: 1983–1993.
Acronym: ELM Scale-2.
Scores, 4: Auditory Expressive, Auditory Receptive, Visual, Global Language.
Administration: Individual.
Price Data, 2001: $139 per complete kit including manual (1993, 95 pages), object kit, and 100 records; $49 per manual; $44 per 100 record forms; $49 per object kit.
Time: (1–10) minutes.
Author: James Coplan.
Publisher: PRO-ED.
Cross References: See T5:880 (1 reference) for reviews by Philip Backlund and Sherwyn Morreale and by Betsy Waterman, see 13:108; for a review by Ruth M. Noyce of an earlier edition, see 10:99 (2 references).

[863]
Early Language Skills Checklist.

Purpose: Designed as an observation-based checklist for children "whose language development is causing concern."
Population: Ages 3–5.
Publication Date: 1998.
Acronym: ELS.
Scores: No scores; 4 areas: Attention and Listening Skills, Receptive Language, Expressive Language, Social and Intellectual Use of Language.
Administration: Individual.
Price Data, 2002: £9.99 per 10 checklists; £16.99 per specimen set; £15.99 per handbook.
Time: (5–20) minutes.
Authors: James Boyle and Elizabeth McLellan.
Publisher: Hodder & Stoughton Educational [England].

[864]
Early Mathematics Diagnostic Kit.

Purpose: "To provide the teacher with an effective means of diagnosing early difficulties in the learning of mathematics."
Population: Ages 4–8.
Publication Dates: 1977–1987.
Acronym: EMDK.

Scores: 10 areas: Number, Shape, Representation, Length, Weight, Capacity, Memory, Money, Time, Foundation.
Administration: Individual.
Price Data: Price information available from publisher for complete kit including record booklets, book of test items, set of coloured cubes, set of 3 small boxes, and manual (1987, 32 pages).
Time: 30(35) minutes.
Comments: Item checklist.
Authors: David Lumb and Margaret Lumb.
Publisher: NFER-Nelson Publishing Co., Ltd. [England].
Cross References: For reviews by John M. Enger and G. Michael Poteat, see 11:121.

[865]
Early Memories Procedure.

Purpose: "Method of exploring personality organization, especially current life concerns, based on an individual's memory of the past."
Population: Ages 10 and over with at least a fourth-grade reading level.
Publication Dates: 1989–1992.
Scores: No scores.
Administration: Group.
Price Data: Available from publisher.
Time: (90–240) minutes.
Comments: Instrument may be interpreted according to a Freudian, Adlerian, Ego-Psychological or Cognitive-Perceptual model.
Author: Arnold R. Bruhn.
Publisher: Arnold R. Bruhn and Associates.
Cross References: For reviews by Karl R. Hanes and LeAdelle Phelps, see 13:109; see also T4:840 (1 reference).

[866]
Early School Assessment.

Purpose: Designed to measure prereading and mathematics skills.
Population: End of prekindergarten to middle of kindergarten, middle of kindergarten to beginning of grade 1.
Publication Date: 1990.
Acronym: ESA.
Scores, 7: Prereading (Language, Visual [also used in Mathematics total], Auditory, Memory, Total), Mathematics Concepts and Operations (Visual [also used in Prereading total], Total).
Administration: Group.
Levels, 2: 1, 2.
Price Data, 2002: $25.60 per multi-level test review kit; $190 per 35 scannable test books (specify level); $114.20 per 35 handscorable test bookes (specify level); $16 per 35 practice books; $51.10 per 35 parent conference forms (specify level); $2.60 per class record sheet for handscoring (specify level); $2.10 per scoring key (specify level); $15 per examiner's manual (81 pages, specify level); $30.50 per teacher's guide (51 pages, specify level); $15 per norms book; $15 per technical bulletin; information for scoring service available from publisher.
Time: 229 (Level 2) to 239 (Level 1) minutes over 8 sessions.
Author: CTB MacMillan/McGraw-Hill.
Publisher: CTB/McGraw-Hill.
Cross References: For reviews by Sonya Blixt and Christine F. Strauss, and Herbert C. Rudman, see 12:127.

[867]
Early School Inventory.

Population: Ages 5–7.
Publication Dates: 1986–1987.
Acronym: ESI.
Price Data: Available from publisher.
Time: Administration time not reported.
Authors: Joanne R. Nurss and Mary E. McGauvran.
Publisher: Pearson Early Learning [No reply from publisher; status unknown).
a) EARLY SCHOOL INVENTORY—DEVELOPMENTAL.
Purpose: "Provides a systematic method for gathering information about a child's development for use in planning effective instruction."
Acronym: ESI-D.
Scores, 4: Physical Development, Language Development, Cognitive Development, Social-Emotional Development.
Administration: Group.
b) EARLY SCHOOL INVENTORY—PRELITERACY.
Purpose: Provides information about "a child's progress in acquiring the preliteracy skills needed when learning to read and write."
Acronym: ESI-P.
Scores, 3: Print Concepts, Writing Concepts, Story Structure.
Administration: Individual.
Cross References: For reviews by Damon Krug and Brandon Davis and by Carol Westby, see 13:110.

[868]
Early School Personality Questionnaire.

Purpose: Measures personality dimensions of young children; useful in the treatment of emotional and conduct problems.
Population: Ages 6–8.
Publication Dates: 1966–1982.
Acronym: ESPQ.
Scores: 13 primary factors (Reserved vs. Warm-hearted, Dull vs. Bright, Affected by Feelings vs.

Emotionally Stable, Undemonstrative vs. Excitable, Obedient vs. Dominant, Sober vs. Enthusiastic, Disregards Rules vs. Conscientious, Shy vs. Venturesome, Tough-Minded vs. Tender-Minded, Vigorous vs. Circumspect Individualism, Forthright vs. Shrewd, Self-Assured vs. Guilt-Prone, Relaxed vs. Tense), and 4 second-order factors (Extraversion, Anxiety, Tough Poise, Independence).

Administration: Group or individual.

Price Data, 2002: $37 per introductory kit including manual with test questions, 2 answer booklets, profile sheet, and scoring keys; $15 per manual with test questions; $14 per 25 child's answer booklets (2 answer booklets needed for each child); $20 per 50 profile sheets/second-order worksheets; $20 per tape recording of items; $18 per scoring keys.

Foreign Language Edition: Information regarding several non-English-language adaptations available from publisher.

Time: (30–50) minutes for each of two parts (untimed).

Authors: Richard W. Coan and Raymond B. Cattell.

Publisher: Institute for Personality and Ability Testing, Inc.

Cross References: See T4:843 (3 references and T3:772 (4 references); for reviews by Jacob O. Sines and Robert L. Thorndike, see 8:540 (8 references); see also T2:1163 (3 references); for a review by Lovick C. Miller, see 7:71 (8 references); see also P:66 (7 references).

[869]
Early Screening Inventory—Revised.

Purpose: Designed to identify children at risk for possible school failure.

Population: Ages 3–6.

Publication Dates: 1976–1997.

Acronym: ESI-R.

Scores, 3: Visual-Motor/Adaptive, Language and Cognition, Gross Motor.

Administration: Individual.

Levels, 2: Preschool (3 to 4 1/2 years old), Kindergarten (4 1/2 to 6 years old).

Price Data, 1997: $96 per complete kit including examiner's manual (1997, 195 pages), 30 score sheets, 30 parent questionnaires, screening materials, tote; $75 per package including trainer's manual (1997, 91 pages), introductory and training videos; $44.50 per examiner's manual $19.50 per trainer's manual; $19.50 per 30 score sheets; $29.50 per introductory video (25 minutes); $39.50 per training video (60 minutes); $17.50 per package of screening materials.

Foreign Language Edition: All screening materials available in Spanish.

Time: (15–20) minutes.

Comments: Originally introduced as the Eliot-Pearson Screening Inventory.

Authors: Samuel J. Meisels, Dorothea B. Marsden, Martha Stone Wiske, and Laura W. Henderson.

Publisher: Rebus Inc.

Cross References: For reviews by Ernest Kimmel and Kathleen D. Paget, see 14:135; see also T5:889 (1 reference); for reviews by Denise M. Dezolt and Kevin Menefee of an earlier edition, see 11:122 (1 reference).

[870]
Early Screening Project.

Purpose: "Allows for the cost-effective screening of problem behaviors to aid in the early remediation of behavior disorders."

Population: Ages 3–6.

Publication Date: 1995.

Acronym: ESP.

Scores, 4: Critical Events Index, Aggressive Behavior Scale [Externalizers], Social Interaction Scale [Internalizers], Combined Frequency Index Adaptive Behavior, Combined Frequency Index Maladaptive Behavior.

Administration: Individual and group.

Price Data, 2002: $95 per complete kit including manual (103 pages), instrument packet, social observation training video, and a stopwatch.

Time: [60] minutes total/group.

Authors: Hill M. Walker, Herbert H. Severson, and Edward G. Feil.

Publisher: Sopris West.

Cross References: For a review by J. Jeffrey Grill, see 14:136.

[871]
Early Speech Perception Test.

Purpose: "Developed to obtain increasingly more accurate information about speech discrimination skills as the profoundly hearing-impaired child's verbal abilities develop."

Publication Date: 1990.

Acronym: ESP.

Administration: Individual.

Price Data, 2002: $200 per ESP kit including manual (32 pages), scoring forms, box of toys, full-color picture cards, and audio cassette tape; $25 per IBM computer diskette; $15 per alternate randomization audiotape.

Time: (15–20) minutes.

Comments: Information regarding specialized hardware and software equipment necessary for administering the computerized version of the ESP test battery can be found in the test manual.

Authors: Jean S. Moog and Ann E. Geers.

Publisher: Central Institute for the Deaf.

a) ESP STANDARD VERSION.

Population: Ages 6–15.

Scores, 4: Pattern Perception, Spondee Identification, Monosyllable Identification, Total.
Price Data: $10 per 25 standard version scoring forms.
b) ESP LOW-VERBAL VERSION.
Population: Ages 3–6.
Scores, 4: Pattern Perception Test, Word Identification Test (Spondee Identification, Monosyllable Identification), Total.
Price Data: $10 per 25 low-verbal version scoring forms.
Cross References: See T5:891 (1 reference); for a review by Arlene E. Carney, see 12:128.

[872]
Early Years Easy Screen.
Purpose: Constructed to screen for strengths and weaknesses in the areas of physical and cognitive development.
Population: Ages 4–5.
Publication Date: 1991.
Acronym: EYES.
Scores, 6: Level of Performance in 6 areas: Pencil Coordination, Active Body, Number, Oral Language, Visual Reading, Auditory Reading.
Administration: Group.
Price Data: Available from publisher.
Time: (160–194) minutes over several sessions.
Comments: Other test materials (e.g., bean bag, beads) must be supplied by examiner.
Authors: Joan Clerehugh, Kim Hart, Rosalind Pither, Kay Rider, and Kate Turner.
Publisher: NFER-Nelson Publishing Co., Ltd. [England].
Cross References: For a review by Martin J. Wiese, see 12:129.

[873]
Eating Disorder Inventory-2.
Purpose: Constructed as a self-report measure of psychological features commonly associated with anorexia nervosa and bulimia nervosa.
Population: Ages 12 and over.
Publication Dates: 1984–1991.
Acronym: EDI.
Scores, 11: Drive for Thinness, Bulimia, Body Dissatisfaction, Ineffectiveness, Perfectionism, Interpersonal Distrust, Interoceptive Awareness, Maturity Fears, Asceticism (provisional), Impulse Regulation (provisional), Social Insecurity (provisional).
Administration: Group or individual.
Price Data: Available from publisher for complete kit including 25 item booklets, 25 symptom checklists, 25 answer sheets, 25 profile forms, and manual (1991, 74 pages).
Time: (20) minutes.
Comments: Computer version available.

Author: David M. Garner.
Publisher: Psychological Assessment Resources, Inc.
Cross References: See T5:893 (54 references); for reviews by Philip Ash and Steven Schinke, see 12:130 (38 references); see also T4:847 (38 references); for a review by Cabrini S. Swassing of an earlier edition, see 10:100 (16 references).

[874]
Eating Inventory.
Purpose: To assess "three dimensions of eating behavior found to be important in recognizing and treating eating-related disorders: cognitive control of eating, disinhibition, and hunger."
Population: Ages 17 and older.
Publication Dates: 1983–1988.
Scores, 3: Cognitive Restraint of Eating, Disinhibition, Hunger.
Administration: Group or individual.
Price Data, 2002: $160 per complete kit including 25 questionnaires, 25 answer sheets, and manual (1988, 37 pages); $46 per 25 questionnaires; $67 per 25 answer sheets; $67 per manual.
Time: (15–20) minutes.
Authors: Albert J. Stunkard and Samuel Messick.
Publisher: The Psychological Corporation.
Cross References: For reviews by Lisa Bloom and Sandra D. Haynes, see 13:111 (3 references); see also T4:848 (1 reference).

[875]
Eckstein Audiometers.
Purpose: For the measurement and evaluation of hearing losses.
Population: All ages.
Publication Dates: 1961–1973.
Subtests: 7 models (solid state).
Administration: Individual.
Price Data: Available from publisher.
Time: Administration time not reported.
Author: Eckstein Bros., Inc.
Publisher: Eckstein Bros., Inc.
a) EB-47 MICROPROCESSOR SCREENING AUDIOMETER.
Publication Date: 1998.
Comments: For screening in schools and medical offices; 4 frequencies; 4 hearing classifications.
b) MINIATURE AUDIOMETER MODEL 60.
Publication Date: 1961.
Comments: For air conduction screening and threshold testing in schools and medical offices; 7 frequencies.
c) AUDIOMETER MODEL 350-I.
Publication Dates: 1964–1972.
Comments: Air conduction threshold testing in industry.

d) FULL RANGE PORTABLE AUDIOMETERS.
Publication Dates: 1970–1972.
Comments: 2 models (may be AC operated).
1) *Model 390.*
   Comments: For pure tone air conducting testing.
2) *Model 390 MB.*
   Comments: Diagnostic Model for pure tone air and bone conducting testing.
e) DIAGNOSTIC AUDIOMETER, MODEL 400.
Publication Date: 1969.
Comments: Air and bone conduction; calibrated speech and pure tone.
f) EB-23-NOISESTIK II - PEDIATRIC HEARING SCREENER.
Publication Date: 1998.
Comments: A hearing screener for testing of infants, toddlers, and older persons not able to respond manually to auditory stimulus.

[876]
[Economics/Objective Tests].

Purpose: To assess students' general knowledge of high school economics.
Population: 1 semester high school.
Publication Date: 1970.
Scores: Total score only for each test.
Administration: Group.
Tests, 5: Concepts in Economics, Price/Income and Personal Growth, Money/Banking and Insurance, International Trade, Final Test.
Manual: No manual.
Price Data, 1994: $7.95 per test book including tests and response key.
Time: Administration time not reported.
Comments: Formerly called Economics Tests.
Author: Perfection Learning Corp.
Publisher: Perfection Learning Corp.

[877]
Edinburgh Picture Test.

Purpose: To assess reasoning ability in young children.
Population: Ages 6-6 to 8-3.
Publication Dates: 1985–1991.
Scores, 6: Doesn't Belong, Classification, Reversed Similarities, Analogies, Sequences, Total.
Administration: Group.
Price Data, 2002: £8.99 per specimen set; £12.99 per 20 test booklets; £6.99 per manual (1988, 15 pages).
Time: (30–60) minutes.
Author: Godfrey Thomson Unit, University of Edinburgh.
Publisher: Hodder & Stoughton Educational [England].
Cross References: For reviews by Carole M. Krauthamer and Bruce G. Rogers, see 12:133.

[878]
The Edinburgh Questionnaires (1982 Edition).

Purpose: Constructed to measure "personal interests and organisational climate."
Population: Adults.
Publication Date: 1982.
Scores: 3 sections: Quality of Working Life (Working Conditions, Type of Work Wanted, Relationships, General), Important Activities, Consequences (Compatibility, Perceptions of Task and Personal Reactions, Reactions of Superiors, Reactions of Colleagues and Workmates, Benefits and Disbenefits to Others, Competencies Engaged).
Administration: Group.
Price Data: Available from publisher.
Time: Administration time not reported.
Comments: Research use only.
Author: John Raven.
Publisher: NFER-Nelson Publishing Co., Ltd. [England].
Cross References: See T5:900 (5 references); for a review by Bruce Shertzer, see 10:102.

[879]
Edinburgh Reading Tests.

Purpose: To assess pupil progress in reading.
Population: Ages 7-0 to 9-0, 8-6 to 10-6, 10-0 to 12-6, 12-0 to 16-6.
Publication Dates: 1972–2002.
Administration: Group.
Levels, 4: Stages 1, 2, 3, 4.
Publisher: Hodder & Stoughton Educational [England].
a) STAGE 1 [THIRD EDITION].
   Population: Ages 7-0 to 9-0.
   Publication Dates: 1977–2002.
   Scores, 5: Vocabulary, Syntax, Sequences, Comprehension, Total.
   Forms, 2: A, B.
   Price Data, 2002: £9.99 per 10 copies of test (specify Form A or Form B); £14.99 per manual; £16.99 per specimen set.
   Time: (30–55) minutes.
   Author: Educational Assessment Unit, University of Edinburgh.
b) STAGE 2 [FOURTH EDITION].
   Population: Ages 8-6 to 10-6.
   Publication Dates: 1972–2002.
   Scores, 5: Vocabulary, Comprehension of Sequences, Use of Context, Comprehension of Essential Ideas, Total.
   Price Data: £9.99 per 10 copies of test booklet; £14.99 per manual; £15.99 per specimen set; £39.99 per scorer/profiler CD-ROM.

Time: (40) minutes for part I; (35) minutes for part II.
Authors: Educational Assessment Unit, University of Edinburgh
c) STAGE 3 [FOURTH EDITION].
Population: Ages 10-0 to 12-6.
Publication Dates: 1973–2002.
Scores, 5: Reading for facts and Comprehension of Sequences, Main Ideas, Comprehension of Points of View, Vocabulary, Total.
Price Data: £9.99 per 10 test booklets; £14.99 per manual; £15.99 per specimen set; £39.99 per scorer/profiler CD-ROM.
Time: (40) minutes for part I; (35) minutes for part II.
Author: Educational Assessment Unit, University of Edinburgh.
d) STAGE 4 [THIRD EDITION].
Population: Ages 11-7 to 16+.
Publication Dates: 1977–2002
Scores, 6: Skimming, Vocabulary, Reading for Facts, Points of View, Comprehension, Total.
Price Data: £10.99 per 10 test booklets; £15.99 per manual; £16.99 per specimen set; £39.99 per scorer/profiler CD-ROM.
Time: 60(70) minutes.
Author: Educational Assessment Unit, University of Edinburgh.
e) SHORTENED EDINBURGH READING TEST.
Purpose: Designed as a survey and screening instrument of written language attainment.
Population: Ages 10-0 to 11-6.
Scores, 3: Vocabulary, Syntax and Sequence, Comprehension.
Time: (40) minutes.
Price Data: £15.99 per 20 copies of test; £14.99 per manual; £15.99 per specimen set.
Comments: Questions selected from items in the full Edinburgh Reading Tests.
Authors: Godfrey Thomson Unit for Educational Research, Moray House Institute of Education, and the Child Health and Education Study, University of Bristol.
Cross References: See T5:901 (2 references) and T4:855 (1 reference); for reviews by Nancy L. Roser and Byron H. Van Roekel of previous editions, see 9:374 (1 reference); see T3:775 (2 references); for reviews by Douglas A. Pidgeon and Earl F. Rankin of the first editions of Stages 2 and 3, see 8:724.

[880]
Educational Abilities Scales.

Purpose: "Designed to yield additional information to assist with the selection of options subjects in the final two years of compulsory schooling."
Population: Ages 13–15.

Publication Dates: 1982–1983.
Acronym: EAS.
Scores: 10 tests yielding 5 scales: Clerical Aptitude, Mechanical Comprehension, Symbolic Reasoning, Spatial Reasoning, Science Reasoning.
Administration: Group.
Price Data: Price information available from publisher for reusable student book, answer booklets, profiles, developer pens, manual (1983, 45 pages), and scoring stencil, and for specimen set.
Time: 150(200) minutes in 2 sessions.
Authors: Andy Stillman and Chris Whetton.
Publisher: NFER-Nelson Publishing Co., Ltd. [England].
Cross References: See T5:902 (2 references) and T4:856 (1 reference).

[881]
Educational Development Series (2000 Edition).

Purpose: A battery of ability and achievement tests and questions on interests and plans.
Population: Grades K–12.
Publication Dates: 1963–2000.
Acronym: EDS.
Administration: Group.
Levels: 13.
Price Data, 2002: $51.70 per 10 test booklets (Levels 13G–16H) and manual (1999, 15–20 pages); $59.45 per 10 test booklets (Levels 17G–18H) and manual; $35.60 per 50 answer sheets (Levels 13G–18H); $4 per student for complete battery standard scoring; $35.60 per sample set of specified grades (K–2, 3–5, 6–8, 9–12).
Authors: O. F. Anderhalter, R. H. Bauernfeind, V. M. Cashew, Mary E. Greig, Walter M. Lifton, George Mallinson, Jacqueline Mallinson, Joseph F. Papenfuss, and Neil Vail.
Publisher: Scholastic Testing Service, Inc.
a) LEVEL 10G.
Population: Grade K.
Publication Date: 2002.
Scores, 8: Cognitive Skills (Verbal, Nonverbal, Total), Basic Skills (Reading, Language, Mathematics, Total), Battery Average.
Price Data: $6.50 per student for rental and scoring service.
Time: (190) minutes in 5 sessions.
b) LEVEL 11G.
Population: Grade 1.
Publication Date: 1999.
Scores, 11: Cognitive Skills (Verbal, Quantitative, Total), Basic Skills (Reading, Language, Mathematics, Total), Reference Skills, Science, Social Studies, Battery Average.

Price Data: $7.05 per student for rental and scoring service.
Time: (280-300) minutes in 5 sessions.
c) LEVEL 12G.
Population: Grade 2.
Publication Date: 1999.
Scores, 11: Cognitive Skills (Verbal, Quantitative, Total), Basic Skills (Reading, Language Arts, Mathematics, Total), Reference Skills, Science, Social Studies, Battery Average.
Price Data: $7.05 per student for rental and scoring service.
Time: (310) minutes in 5 sessions.
d) LEVEL 13G.
Population: Grade 3.
Publication Date: 1999.
Scores, 11: Same as for *c* above.
Price Data: $5.70 per student for rental and scoring service.
Time: (360) minutes in 5 sessions.
e) LEVEL 14G.
Population: Grade 4.
Publication Date: 1999.
Scores, 14: Cognitive Skills (Verbal, Quantitative, Total), Basic Skills (Reading, Language Arts, Mathematics, Total), Reference Skills, Science, Social Studies, Battery Average, Career Interests, School Plans, School Interests.
Price Data: Same as for *d* above.
Time: (400) minutes in 3 sessions.
f) LEVEL 15G.
Population: Grade 5.
Publication Date: 1999.
Scores, 14: Same as for *e* above.
Price Data: Same as for *d* above.
Time: (400) minutes in 3 sessions.
g) LEVEL 15H.
Population: Grade 6.
Publication Date: 1999.
Scores, 14: Same as for *e* above.
Price Data: Same as for *d* above.
Time: (400) minutes in 3 sessions.
h) LEVEL 16H.
Population: Grade 7.
Publication Date: 1999.
Scores, 14: Same as for *e* above.
Price Data: Same as for *d* above.
Time: (400) minutes in 3 sessions.
i) LEVEL 16H.
Population: Grade 8.
Publication Date: 1999.
Scores, 14: Same as for *e* above.
Price Data: Same as for *d* above.
Time: (400) minutes in 3 sessions.
j) LEVEL 17G.
Population: Grade 9.

Publication Date: 1999.
Scores, 14: Same as for *e* above.
Price Data: Same as for *d* above.
Time: (410) minutes in 3 sessions.
k) LEVEL 17H.
Population: Grade 9.
Publication Date: 1999.
Details: Same as for *j* above.
l) LEVEL 18G.
Population: Grade 10.
Publication Date: 1999.
Details: Same as for *j* above.
m) LEVEL 18H.
Population: Grade 11.
Publication Date: 1999.
Details: Same as for *j* above.
Cross References: See T4:858 (2 references); for a review by Esther E. Diamond of an earlier edition, see 9:376; see also T3:2325 (1 reference); for reviews by Samuel T. Mayo and William A. Mehrens of forms copyrighted 1976 and earlier see 8:27; see also T2:33 (1 reference); for a review by Robert D. North of forms copyrighted 1968 and earlier see 7:22.

[882]
Educational Interest Inventory.

Purpose: Designed to identify personal preference for different college educational programs.
Population: Prospective college students.
Publication Date: 1989.
Acronym: EII.
Scores: 47 scales: Agriculture (Agribusiness/Agricultural Production, Agricultural Sciences, Renewable Natural Resources), Architecture and Environmental Design, Area/Ethnic Studies, Business/Management (Accounting and Finance, Administration and Management, Human Resources Management, Marketing/Distribution), Communications, Computer and Information Sciences, Education (Pre-Elementary and Elementary, Secondary and Post-Secondary, Special Education, Physical Education, Industrial Arts), Engineering (Chemical, Civil, Electrical/Electronic, Mechanical), Foreign Languages, Health Sciences (General Medicine, Dentistry, Nursing, Pharmacy, Medical Laboratory), Home Economics, Law, Letters, Library and Archival Sciences, Life Sciences/General Biology, Mathematics, Philosophy and Religion, Theology, Physical Sciences (Chemistry, Geological Sciences, Physics), Psychology, Protective Services, Public Affairs/Social Work, Social Sciences (Economics, History, Political Sciences/Government, Sociology), Visual and Performing Arts (Fine Arts, Drama, Music).
Administration: Group.
Price Data: Price information available from publisher for reusable test booklet, answer sheets and profile guides, manual (43 pages), and for specimen set of

all Educational Interest Inventory and Career Guidance Inventory components.
Time: [45–60] minutes.
Comments: Self-administered; self-scored; manual is for the EII and the Career Guidance Inventory (406).
Author: James E. Oliver.
Publisher: Wintergreen/Orchard House, Inc.
Cross References: For reviews by Lois T. Strauss and David E. Kapel and Jim Fortune and Javaid Kaiser, see 11:123.

[883]
Educational Process Questionnaire.

Purpose: "To aid teachers in their own self-development by providing objective information about the processes used in the teacher's own actual classroom."
Population: Grades 4–12.
Publication Dates: 1973–1987.
Acronym: EPQ.
Scores: 5 scale scores: Reinforcement of Self-Concept, Academic Learning Time, Feedback, Expectations, Development of Multiple Talents.
Administration: Group.
Price Data: Available from publisher.
Time: 35(45) minutes.
Comments: Ratings by students.
Author: Institute for Behavioral Research in Creativity.
Publisher: Institute for Behavioral Research in Creativity [No reply from publisher; status unknown].
Cross References: For a review by William L. Curlette, see 11:125.

[884]
Edwards Personal Preference Schedule.

Purpose: Developed to measure "a number of relatively independent normal personality variables."
Population: College and adults.
Publication Dates: 1953–1959.
Acronym: EPPS.
Scores, 16: Achievement, Deference, Order, Exhibition, Autonomy, Affiliation, Intraception, Succorance, Dominance, Abasement, Nurturance, Change, Endurance, Heterosexuality, Aggression, Consistency.
Administration: Group or individual.
Price Data, 2002: $91 per 25 schedule booklets; $50 per 50 hand-scorable answer documents; $65 per 50 NCS machine-scorable answer documents; $65 per 50 IBM answer documents; $47 per scoring template for hand-scorable answer documents including manual (1959, 27 pages); $86.50 per keys for IBM answer documents including manual; $42 per manual; $50 per examination kit.
Time: (40–50) minutes.
Author: Allen L. Edwards.
Publisher: The Psychological Corporation.

Cross References: See T5:908 (12 references), T4:862 (44 references), 9:378 (16 references), T3:780 (70 references), 8:542 (334 references), and T2:1164 (226 references); for reviews by Alfred B. Heilbrun, Jr., and Michael G. McKee, see 7:72 (391 references); see also P:67 (363 references); for reviews by John A. Radcliffe and Lawrence J. Stricker and an excerpted review by Edward S. Bordin, see 6:87 (284 references); for reviews by Frank Barron, Ake Bjerstedt, and Donald W. Fiske and excerpted reviews by John W. Gustad and Laurance F. Shaffer, see 5:47 (50 references).

[885]
Effectiveness Motivation Scale.

Purpose: To assess levels of motivation in specific environments.
Population: Ages 3–5.
Publication Dates: 1973–1976.
Scores, 3: E (Strength of Effectiveness Motivation), W (Withdrawal), Q (Inconsequence).
Administration: Individual.
Price Data: Available from publisher.
Time: Administration time not reported.
Comments: Manual title is Stott-Sharp Effectiveness Motivation Scale; test booklet title is Scale of Effectiveness Motivation; ratings by teachers.
Authors: John D. Sharp, D. H. Stott, J. B. Albin (manual), and H. L. Williams (manual).
Publisher: NFER-Nelson Publishing Co., Ltd. [England].

[886]
The Egan Bus Puzzle Test.

Purpose: "Designed to assess language development and some performance skills of young children."
Population: 20 months to 4 years.
Publication Date: No date on test materials.
Scores, 6: Expressive Verbal Labels, Comprehension (Verbal Labels, Recognition of Shape, Orientation of Piece to Recess), Comprehension of Sentences, Expressive Language.
Administration: Individual.
Price Data, 2001: £89.50 per complete set including manual (no date, 36 pages), board, and 25 forms; £73.50 per board and manual; £22.50 per 25 forms.
Time: (7-8) minutes.
Authors: Dorothy F. Egan and Rosemary Brown.
Publisher: The Test Agency Limited [England].
Cross References: For a review by Sheldon L. Stick, see 10:105.

[887]
Ego Function Assessment.

Purpose: Designed as a "mental status examination" to assess ego function.
Population: Adults.
Publication Date: 1989.

Acronym: EFA.

Scores, 12: Reality Testing, Judgment, Sense of Reality, Regulation and Control of Drives, Object Relations, Thought Processes, Adaptive Regression in the Service of the Ego, Defensive Functions, Stimulus Barrier, Autonomous Functions, Synthetic Functions, Mastery-Competence.

Administration: Individual.

Price Data, 2001: $12 per manual (64 pages); $9.50 per 10 blanks.

Time: Administration time not reported.

Author: Leopold Bellak.

Publisher: C.P.S., Inc.

Cross References: For reviews by Beth Doll and Samuel Juni, see 13:112.

[888]
The Ego Strength Q-Sort Test.

Purpose: Designed to "assess the general strength of one's ego."

Population: Grades 9–16 and adults.

Publication Dates: 1956–1958.

Acronym: ESQST.

Scores, 6: Ego-Status, Social Status, Goal Setting and Striving, Good Mental Health, Physical Status, Total.

Administration: Individual or group.

Price Data: Available from publisher.

Time: (50–90) minutes.

Author: Russell N. Cassel.

Publisher: Psychometric Affiliates.

Cross References: See T5:913 (1 reference) and T2:1167 (1 reference); for reviews by Allen L. Edwards and Harrison G. Gough, see 6:88 (3 references).

[889]
Eidetic Parents Test.

Purpose: To provide stimuli meant to arouse eidetic images of parents to aid in exploring emotional attachments that affect current functioning.

Population: Clinical patients and marriage and family counselees.

Publication Date: 1972.

Acronym: EPT.

Scores: No scores; verbal reporting by individuals of subjective visual images (called eidetics) of increasingly surrealistic situations.

Administration: Individual.

Price Data: Available from publisher.

Time: (60) minutes for brief report; "many hours" for comprehensive report.

Author: Akhter Ahsen.

Publisher: Brandon House, Inc.

Cross References: For additional information and a review by Charles Warnath and excerpted reviews by Gregory Sarmousakis, Barry Bricklin, and Manas Raychaudhuri, see 8:546 (8 references).

[890]
Einstein Assessment of School-Related Skills.

Purpose: "To identify children who are at risk for, or are experiencing, learning difficulties; and who therefore should be referred for a comprehensive evaluation."

Population: Grades K–5.

Publication Date: 1988.

Administration: Individual.

Levels, 6: Kindergarten, First Grade, Second Grade, Third Grade, Fourth Grade, Fifth Grade.

Price Data: Available from publisher.

Time: (10) minutes.

Authors: Ruth L. Gottesman and Frances M. Cerullo.

Publisher: Modern Curriculum Press [No reply from publisher; status unknown].

a) KINDERGARTEN LEVEL.

Scores, 5: Language/Cognition, Letter Recognition, Auditory Memory, Arithmetic, Visual-Motor Integration.

b) FIRST GRADE LEVEL.

Scores, 7: Language/Cognition, Word Recognition, Oral Reading, Reading Comprehension, Auditory Memory, Arithmetic, Visual-Motor Integration.

c) SECOND GRADE LEVEL.

Scores: Same as *b* above.

d) THIRD GRADE LEVEL.

Scores: Same as *b* above.

e) FOURTH GRADE LEVEL.

Scores: Same as *b* above.

f) FIFTH GRADE LEVEL.

Scores: Same as *b* above.

Cross References: See T5:916 (1 reference) and T4:871 (1 reference); for a review by Gloria A. Galvin, see 11:126 (1 reference).

[891]
Ekwall/Shanker Reading Inventory—Third Edition.

Purpose: "Designed to assess the full range of students' reading abilities."

Population: Grades 1–9.

Publication Dates: 1979–1993.

Acronym: ESRI.

Administration: Individual.

Price Data: Available from publisher.

Authors: Eldon E. Ekwall and James L. Shanker.

Publisher: Allyn & Bacon.

a) GRADED WORD LIST.

Purpose: "To obtain a quick estimate of the student's independent, instructional, and frustration reading levels."

Acronym: GWL.

Scores, 3: Independent Reading Level, Instructional Reading Level, Frustration Level.
Time: (5–10) minutes
b) ORAL AND SILENT READING.
Purpose: To obtain an assessment of the student's independent, instructional, and frustration reading levels in oral and silent reading.
Scores, 3: 3 scores (Independent Reading Level, Instructional Reading Level, Frustration Level) in each of two areas (Oral, Silent Reading).
Time: (10–30) minutes.
c) LISTENING COMPREHENSION.
Purpose: "To obtain the level at which a student can understand material when it is read to him or her."
Score: Listening Comprehension Level.
Time: (5–10) minutes.
d) THE BASIC SIGHT WORDS AND PHRASES TEST.
Purpose: To determine basic sight words and basic sight word phrases that can be recognized and pronounced instantly by the student.
Scores, 2: Basic Sight Words, Basic Sight Phrases.
Time: (5–12) minutes.
e) LETTER KNOWLEDGE.
Purpose: "To determine if the student can associate the letter symbols with the letter names."
Scores, 2: Letters (Auditory), Letters (Visual).
Time: Administration time not reported.
f) PHONICS.
Purpose: "To determine if the student has mastered letter-sound (phonics)."
Scores, 9: Initial Consonants, Initial Blends and Digraphs, Ending Sounds, Vowels, Phonograms, Blending, Substitution, Vowel Pronunciation, Application in Context.
Time: Administration time not reported.
g) STRUCTURAL ANALYSIS.
Purpose: "To determine if the student can use structural analysis skills to aid in decoding unknown words."
Scores, 10: Hearing Word Parts, Inflectional Endings, Prefixes, Suffixes, Compound Words, Affixes, Syllabication, Application in Context (Part I, Part II, Total).
Time: Administration time not reported.
h) KNOWLEDGE OF CONTRACTIONS TEST.
Purpose: "To determine if the student has knowledge of contractions."
Scores, 3: Number of Words Pronounced, Number of Words Known, Total.
Time: Administration time not reported.
i) EL PASO PHONICS SURVEY.
Purpose: "To determine if the student has the ability to pronounce and blend 90 phonic elements."

Scores, 4: Initial Consonant Sounds, Ending Consonant, Initial Consonant Clusters, Vowels, Vowel Teams, and Special Letter Combinations.
Time: Administration time not reported.
j) QUICK SURVEY WORD LIST.
Purpose: "To determine quickly if the student has mastered phonics and structural analysis."
Score: Comments.
Time: Administration time not reported.
k) READING INTEREST SURVEY.
Purpose: "To assess the student's attitude toward reading and school, areas of reading interest, reading experiences, and conditions affecting reading in the home."
Score: Comments.
Time: Administration time not reported.
Cross References: For reviews by Koressa Kutsick Malcolm and by Blaine R. Worthen and Richard R. Sudweeks, see 13:113 (2 references); see also T4:872 (3 references); for reviews by Lynn S. Fuchs and Mary Beth Marr of an earlier edition, see 9:380.

[892]
Electrical and Electronics Test.

Purpose: "Examines knowledge of fundamental laws, symbols and definitions and requires the application of them to familiar equipment."
Population: Students in electrical or electronics programs ages 15 and over.
Publication Date: No date on test materials.
Scores: Total score only.
Administration: Group.
Price Data, 2001: £6.50 per test booklet; £8.50 per answer key; £12.50 per manual; £27 per specimen set.
Time: (15-30) minutes.
Author: The Test Agency Ltd.
Publisher: The Test Agency Limited [England].

[893]
Electrical Maintenance Trainee—Form UKE-1C.

Purpose: "To measure the knowledge and skills required for electrical maintenance."
Population: Applicants for jobs requiring electrical knowledge and skills.
Publication Dates: 1991–2001.
Scores, 12: Motors, Digital and Analog Electronics, Schematics and Electrical Print Reading, Control, Power Supplies, Basic AC/DC Theory, Construction Installation and Distribution, Test Instruments, Mechanical/Equipment Operation/Hand and Power Tools, Computers and PLC, Electrical Maintenance, Total.
Administration: Group.
Price Data, 2002: $16 per consumable self-scoring test booklet (20 minimum order); $24.95 per manual (2001, 18 pages).

Time: (60) minutes.
Comments: Self-scoring instrument.
Author: Roland T. Ramsay.
Publisher: Ramsay Corporation.
Cross References: For a review by David C. Roberts of an earlier edition, see 13:114.

[894]
Electrical Sophistication Test.

Purpose: "Intended to discriminate between persons with substantial knowledges of electricity and those with no, little, and merely chance knowledge."
Population: Job applicants.
Publication Dates: 1963–1965.
Scores: Total score only.
Administration: Group.
Price Data: Available from publisher.
Time: (5–10) minutes.
Author: Stanley G. Ciesla.
Publisher: Psychometric Affiliates.
Cross References: For a review by Charles F. Ward, see 7:1125.

[895]
Electromechanical Vocational Assessment Manuals.

Purpose: Designed to evaluate a variety of work abilities (tasks) of blind or visually impaired persons.
Population: Blind or visually impaired adults.
Publication Date: 1983.
Scores, 6: Fine Finger Dexterity Work Task Unit, Foot Operated Hinged Box Work Task Unit, Hinged Box Work Task Unit, Index Card Work Task Unit, Multifunctional Work Task Unit, Revolving Assembly Table Work Task Unit.
Administration: Individual.
Price Data: Available from publisher.
Time: 50(60) minutes for any one task unit.
Comments: Special administration equipment required.
Author: Rehabilitation Research and Training Center on Blindness and Low Vision.
Publisher: Rehabilitation Research and Training Center on Blindness and Low Vision.
Cross References: For reviews by John Geisler and Robert Johnson, see 13:115.

[896]
Electron Test—Form H-C.

Purpose: "To measure the knowledge and skills required for electronics jobs."
Population: Electronics employees and applicants for electronics jobs.
Publication Dates: 1987–2001.
Scores: 7 areas: Digital & Analog Electronics; AC/DC Theory, Schematics & Print Reading; Motors/

Regulators/Electronic Equipment/Power Distribution; Power Supplies; Test Instruments; Computers and PLC; Total.
Administration: Group.
Price Data, 2002: $16 per consumable self-scoring test booklets (20 minimum order); $24.95 per manual (2001, 15 pages).
Time: (60) minutes.
Comments: Self-scoring instrument.
Author: Roland T. Ramsay.
Publisher: Ramsay Corporation.
Cross References: For reviews by Keith Hattrup and Eugene (Geno) Pichette, see 13:116.

[897]
Electronics and Instrumentation Technician —Form A2.

Purpose: "To evaluate the knowledge of electronics and instrumentation workers in specific subject areas."
Population: Applicants or incumbents for jobs where electronics and instrumentation knowledge is a necessary part of training or job activities.
Publication Dates: 1984–1994.
Acronym: E&ITT.
Scores, 8: Motor Control, Digital Electronics/Computers, Analog/Radio, Schematics/Test Instruments, Power Supplies/Power Distribution, AC & DC Theory, Mechanical Maintenance, Total.
Administration: Group.
Price Data, 2002: $498 per complete kit including 10 reusable test booklets, 100 answer sheets, manual (1994, 16 pages), and scoring key.
Time: (190) minutes.
Author: Roland T. Ramsay.
Publisher: Ramsay Corporation.
Cross References: For a review by Alan R. Suess, see 10:106.

[898]
Elementary Program Implementation Profile.

Purpose: Designed as an instrument for "evaluating the appropriateness of elementary school programs and for rating the level of implementation of the High/Scope educational approach in a variety of program settings."
Population: Elementary schools.
Publication Date: 1997.
Acronym: PIP.
Scores, 6: Physical Environment, Daily Schedule, Adult-Child Interaction, Instructional Methods/Content and Assessment, Staff Development and Non-School Collaboration, Total.
Administration: Individual.
Price Data, 2001: $6.95 per manual (7 pages); $14.95 per 25 assessment forms.

Time: Administration time not reported.
Comments: Can also be used with non-High/Scope programs.
Author: High/Scope Educational Research Foundation.
Publisher: High/Scope Educational Research Foundation.

[899]
Eliot-Price Perspective Test.

Purpose: "Designed to measure the ability to perceive and to imagine object arrangments from different viewpoints."
Population: Grades 2 and over.
Publication Dates: 1974–1975.
Scores: Total score only.
Administration: Group.
Price Data: Available from publisher.
Time: (20) minutes.
Comments: For research use only.
Authors: John Eliot and Lewis Price.
Publisher: John Eliot (the author) [No reply from publisher; status unknown].
Cross References: See T3:792 (1 reference).

[900]
Embedded Figures Test.

Purpose: A perceptual test designed to reflect competence at perceptual disembedding.
Population: Ages 10 and over.
Publication Dates: 1950–1971.
Acronym: EFT.
Scores: Total score only.
Administration: Individual.
Forms, 2: A, B.
Price Data, 2001: $142.64 per complete kit including Card Set (Forms A and B), stylus, and 25 recording sheets; $121.30 per Card Sets (Forms A and B); $8.90 per stylus; $21 per 25 recording sheets; $33.80 per manual (1971, 32 pages).
Time: (10–45) minutes.
Comments: 3 minutes-per-figure Forms A and B estimated from the original 24-figure, 5-minutes-per-figure test; combined manual for this and Group Embedded Figures Test (1091); colored versions of the original black-and-white figures by K. Gottschaldt (1926).
Author: Herman A. Witkin.
Publisher: Consulting Psychologists Press, Inc.
Cross References: See T5:926 (22 references), T4:882 (48 references), 9:382 (23 references), T3:794 (88 references), 8:548 (134 references), T2:1169 (149 references), and P:71 (47 references); for reviews by Harrison G. Gough and Leona E. Tyler, see 6:89 (24 references); see also 5:49 (9 references).

[901]
Emo Questionnaire.

Purpose: "Designed to assess an individual's personal-emotional adjustment."
Population: Clinical and research applications.
Publication Dates: 1958–1998.
Scores: 10 diagnostic dimensions: Rationalization, Inferiority Feelings, Hostility, Depression, Fear and Anxiety, Organic Reaction, Projection, Unreality, Sex Problems, Withdrawal, 3 key adjustment factors: Internal, External, Somatic, and 4 normative level adjustment factors: Internal, External, Somatic, General.
Administration: Individual or group.
Forms, 2: A, B.
Price Data, 2002: $97 per start-up kit including 25 test booklets (specify Form A or Form B), 25 score sheets, and interpretation and research manual; $52 per 25 test booklets (quantity discounts available; specify Form A or Form B); $29 per 25 score sheets; $28 per interpretation and research manual.
Time: No limit (approximately 20 minutes).
Authors: George O. Baehr and Melany E. Baehr.
Publisher: Reid London House.
Cross References: See T5:927 (1 reference) and T4:883 (1 reference); for reviews by Allan L. Lavoie and Paul McReynolds, see 9:383; see also T2:1170 (1 reference); for reviews by Bertram D. Cohen and W. Grant Dahlstrom, see 6:90 (1 reference).

[902]
Emotional and Behavior Problem Scale— Second Edition.

Purpose: "Developed to contribute to the early identification and service delivery for students with behavior disorders/emotional disturbance."
Population: Ages 5–18.
Publication Dates: 1989–2001.
Acronym: EBPS-2.
Scores, 10: Theoretical (Learning Problems, Interpersonal Relations, Inappropriate Behavior, Unhappiness/Depression, Physical Symptoms/Fears); Empirical (Social Aggression/Conduct Disorder, Social-Emotional Withdrawal/Depression, Learning/Comprehension Disorder, Avoidance/Unresponsiveness, Aggressive/Self-Destructive).
Administration: Individual.
Price Data, 2002: $119 per complete kit including technical manual (2001, 47 pages), 50 school version rating forms, 50 home version rating forms, and IEP and intervention manual (2001, 205 pages); $14 per technical manual (specify Home or School); $33 per 50 rating forms; $25 per IEP and intervention manual; $25 per computerized quick score (Windows); $149 per computerized IEP and intervention manual (DOS).
Time: (15) minutes.

Comments: Ratings by teachers and/or parents/guardians.
Authors: Stephen B. McCarney and Tamara J. Arthaud.
Publisher: Hawthorne Educational Services, Inc.
Cross References: For reviews by J. Jeffrey Grill and Robert C. Reinehr of the original edition, see 12:134.

[903]
Emotional Behavioral Checklist.

Purpose: To assess an individual's overt emotional behavior.
Population: Ages 16 and over.
Publication Date: 1986.
Acronym: EBC.
Scores, 8: Impulsivity-Frustration, Anxiety, Depression-Withdrawal, Socialization, Self-Concept, Aggression, Reality Disorientation, Total EBC.
Administration: Individual.
Manual: No manual.
Price Data, 2002: $25.25 per 25 checklists.
Time: Administration time not reported.
Comments: Included in the Auxiliary Component of the McCarron-Dial System (1535).
Authors: Jack G. Dial, Carolyn Mezger, Theresa Massey, and Lawrence T. McCarron.
Publisher: McCarron-Dial Systems.
Cross References: For reviews by William A. Stock and Hoi K. Suen, see 11:130.

[904]
Emotional Competence Inventory

Purpose: "Designed to assess emotional intelligence (the ability to recognize and manage emotions [yours and other])."
Population: Coaches, executive coaches, mid to senior level managers.
Publication Dates: 1999–2001.
Acronym: ECI.
Scores: 4 clusters, 20 competencies: Self-Awareness (Emotional Self-Awareness, Accurate Self-Assessment, Self-Confidence); Self-Management (Self-Control, Trustworthiness, Conscientiousness, Adaptability, Achievement Orientation, Initiative); Social Awareness (Empathy, Organizational Awareness, Service Orientation); Social Skills (Developing Others, Leadership, Influence, Communication, Change Catalyst, Conflict Management, Building Bonds, Teamwork & Collaboration).
Administration: Group or individual.
Manual: No manual.
Price Data, 2001: $3,000 Accreditation (2-day program); once accredited internet assessments are $135 per participant (this includes unlimited raters).
Time: (50–60) minutes.

Comments: Accreditation required; multirater assessment to be administered by accredited consultants only; accreditation programs run approximately every second month.
Authors: Daniel Goleman, Richard Boyatzis, and the Hay Group.
Publisher: Hay Group.

[905]
Emotional or Behavior Disorder Scale.

Purpose: Designed to identify behavior problems of students in the home or school environment.
Population: Ages 4.5 to 21.
Publication Dates: 1991–1992.
Acronym: EBDS.
Scores, 3: Academic, Social Relationships, Personal Adjustment.
Administration: Individual.
Price Data, 2002: $118 per complete kit including School Version technical manual (1992, 33 pages) and 50 School Version rating forms, Home Version technical manual (1992, 31 pages) and 50 Home Version rating forms, and intervention manual (1991, 202 pages); $14 per technical manual (specify School Version or Home Version); $33 per 50 rating forms (specify School Version or Home Version); $24 per intervention manual.
Time: (15–20) minutes.
Author: Stephen B. McCarney.
Publisher: Hawthorne Educational Services, Inc.
 a) SCHOOL VERSION.
 b) HOME VERSION.
Cross References: For reviews by Patti L. Harrison and Steven W. Lee, see 13:117.

[906]
Emotional Problems Scales.

Purpose: "To assess emotional and behavioral problems in individuals with mild mental retardation or borderline intelligence."
Population: Ages 14 and over.
Publication Dates: 1984–1991.
Acronym: EPS.
Price Data: Available from publisher for complete kit including manual (1991, 31 pages), 25 BRS test booklets, 25 SRI test booklets, SRI scoring keys, and 25 profile forms.
Comments: Previous editions titled Prout-Strohmer Personality Inventory and Strohmer-Prout Behavior Rating Scale.
Authors: H. Thompson Prout and Douglas C. Strohmer.
Publisher: Psychological Assessment Resources, Inc.
 a) BEHAVIOR RATING SCALES.
 Acronym: BRS.
 Scores, 12: Thought/Behavior Disorder, Verbal Aggression, Physical Aggression, Sexual Mal-

adjustment, Distractibility, Hyperactivity, Somatic Concerns, Depression, Withdrawal, Low Self-Esteem, Externalizing Behavior Problems, Internalizing Behavior Problems.
Administration: Individual.
Time: [20–50] minutes.
b) SELF-REPORT INVENTORY.
Acronym: SRI.
Scores, 7: Positive Impression, Thought/Behavior Disorder, Impulse Control, Anxiety, Depression, Low Self-Esteem, Total Pathology.
Administration: Individual.
Time: (30–35) minutes.
Cross References: For reviews by S. Alvin Leung and John A. Mills, see 13:118. For reviews by Richard Brozovich and Ernest A. Bauer and by Peter F. Merenda of the Prout-Strohmer Personality Inventory, see 11:311.

[907]
Emotions Profile Index.
Purpose: Designed as a measure of personality traits.
Population: College and adults.
Publication Date: 1974.
Acronym: EPI.
Scores, 9: Timid, Aggressive, Trustful, Distrustful, Controlled, Dyscontrolled, Gregarious, Depressed, Bias.
Administration: Group or individual.
Price Data, 2002: $45 per kit including 25 tests, profile sheets, and manual (13 pages plus test and profile); $22.50 per 25 tests and profile sheets; $25 per manual.
Time: (10–15) minutes.
Authors: Robert Plutchik and Henry Kellerman.
Publisher: Western Psychological Services.
Cross References: See T3:796 (2 references); for a review by Douglas N. Jackson, see 8:549 (33 references).

[908]
The Empathy Test.
Purpose: Constructed to assess empathy.
Population: Junior high school and over.
Publication Dates: 1947–1962.
Scores: Total score only.
Administration: Group.
Forms, 3: A, B, C.
Price Data: Available from publisher.
Time: (6-15) minutes.
Authors: W. A. Kerr and B. J. Speroff.
Publisher: Psychometric Affiliates.
Cross References: See T4:890 (2 references), T2:1171 (10 references), and P:73 (1 reference); for a review by Wallace B. Hall, see 6:91 (9 references); for a review by Robert L. Thorndike, see 5:50 (20 references).

[909]
Employability Maturity Interview.
Purpose: "Developed to assess readiness for the vocational rehabilitation planning process."
Population: Rehabilitation clients.
Publication Date: 1987.
Acronym: EMI.
Scores: Total score only.
Administration: Individual.
Price Data, 1994: $10 per complete kit; $7.50 per 50 test forms; $10 per 100 test forms; $5 per manual (29 pages).
Time: (15–20) minutes.
Comments: Based upon the Adult Vocational Maturity Assessment Interview.
Authors: Richard Roessler and Brian Bolton.
Publisher: The National Center on Employment & Disability.
Cross References: See T5:936 (1 reference); for a review by William R. Koch, see 11:132.

[910]
Employee Aptitude Survey, Second Edition.
Purpose: Designed to predict future job performance.
Population: Ages 16 to adult.
Publication Dates: 1952–2000.
Acronym: EAS.
Administration: Group.
Price Data: Price data available from publisher for test materials including Technical Manual (1994, 91 pages), Technical addendum: Fairness of the EAS (2000, 11 pages); Examiner's Manual (1994, 66 pages), and Supplemental Norms Report (1995, 92 pages).
Time: (5–10) minutes.
Comments: Tests available separately.
Authors: G. Grimsley (*a–b*), F. L. Ruch (*a–g, i, j*), N. D. Warren (*a–g*), and J. S. Ford (*a, c, e–g*).
Publisher: Psychological Services, Inc.
   a) TEST 1, VERBAL COMPREHENSION.
   Publication Dates: 1956–1984.
   Scores: Total score only.
   b) TEST 2, NUMERICAL ABILITY.
   Publication Dates: 1952–1963.
   Scores: Total score only.
   c) TEST 3, VISUAL PURSUIT.
   Publication Date: 1956.
   Scores: Total score only.
   d) TEST 4, VISUAL SPEED AND ACCURACY.
   Publication Dates: 1952–1980.
   Scores: Total score only.
   e) TEST 5, SPACE VISUALIZATION.
   Publication Dates: 1952–1980.
   Scores: Total score only.
   f) TEST 6, NUMERICAL REASONING.
   Publication Dates: 1957–1985.
   Scores: Total score only.

g) TEST 7, VERBAL REASONING.
Publication Dates: 1952–1963.
Scores: Total score only.
h) TEST 8, WORD FLUENCY.
Publication Dates: 1953–1963.
Scores: Total score only.
i) TEST 9, MANUAL SPEED AND ACCURACY.
Publication Dates: 1953–1963.
Scores: Total score only.
j) TEST 10, SYMBOLIC REASONING.
Publication Dates: 1957–1985.
Scores: Total score only.
Cross References: For reviews by Brian Engdahl and Paul M. Muchinsky, see 14:137; see also T5:937 (4 references), T4:894 (1 reference), T3:799 (4 references), and T2:1071 (14 references); for reviews by Paul F. Ross and Erwin K. Taylor, and an excerpted review by John O. Crites of an earlier edition, see 6:769 (4 references); for reviews by Dorothy C. Adkins and S. Rains Wallace of an earlier edition, see 5:607.

[911]
Employee Assistance Program Inventory.

Purpose: "Designed as an intake or screening tool for professionals in Employee Assistance Programs (EAP's)."
Population: Adults seeking vocational counseling.
Publication Date: 1994.
Acronym: EAPI.
Scores: 10 scales: Anxiety, Depression, Self-Esteem Problems, Marital Problems, Family Problems, External Stressors, Interpersonal Conflict, Work Adjustment, Problem Minimization, Effects of Substance Abuse.
Administration: Group.
Price Data: Available from publisher for introductory kit including manual (44 pages), 25 reusable item booklets, and 25 answer sheet/profiles.
Time: (20) minutes.
Authors: William D. Anton and James R. Reed.
Publisher: Psychological Assessment Resources, Inc.
Cross References: For reviews by Michael G. Kavan and David J. Pittenger, see 14:138.

[912]
Employee Effectiveness Profile.

Purpose: "Designed to assist managers in identifying the overall effectiveness of individual employees."
Population: Managers.
Publication Date: 1986.
Scores: Total score only.
Administration: Individual.
Price Data: Price information available from publisher for profiles (24 pages) or short forms.
Time: No time limit.
Author: J. William Pfeiffer.
Publisher: Jossey-Bass, A Wiley Company.

Cross References: For reviews by Lawrence M. Aleamoni and Daniel E. Vogler, see 12:136.

[913]
Employee Involvement Status Survey.

Purpose: Measures the presence and status of employee involvement in work situations.
Population: Employees.
Publication Date: 1988.
Scores, 3: Belief in Employee Involvement, Barriers to Employee Involvement, Total.
Administration: Group.
Price Data: Price information available from publisher for Survey Response Sheets.
Time: Administration time not reported.
Author: Training House, Inc.
Publisher: Training House, Inc.

[914]
Employee Involvement Survey.

Purpose: Assesses employees' actual and desired opportunities for personal involvement and influence in the workplace.
Population: Business and industry employees.
Publication Date: 1988.
Acronym: EIS.
Scores, 5: Basic Creature Comfort, Safety and Order, Belonging and Affiliation, Ego-Status, Actualization and Self-Expression.
Administration: Group.
Price Data, 2001: $7.95 per instrument (14 pages).
Time: Administration time not reported.
Comments: Self-administered, self-scored.
Author: Jay Hall.
Publisher: Teleometrics International.

[915]
Employee Performance Appraisal.

Purpose: "Designed as a tool to aid in performance appraisal and merit review."
Population: Business and industry.
Publication Dates: 1962-1984.
Acronym: EPA.
Scores: 7 merit ratings: Quantity of Work, Quality of Work, Job Knowledge, Initiative, Interpersonal Relationships, Dependability, Potential.
Administration: Group.
Manual: No manual; included in Manuals Supplement (1984) along with 13 tests from this publisher.
Price Data, 2001: $35.20 per package of forms; $19.25 per specimen set.
Time: [10-20] minutes.
Comments: Ratings by supervisors.
Author: Martin M. Bruce.
Publisher: Martin M. Bruce, Ph.D.
Cross References: For a review by Jean Maier Palormo, see 6:1116.

[916]
Employee Reliability Inventory.

Purpose: Designed to be used as a preemployment instrument assessing a number of different dimensions of reliable and productive work behavior.
Population: Prospective employees.
Publication Dates: 1986–1998.
Acronym: ERI.
Scores, 7: Freedom from Disruptive Alcohol and Illegal Drug Use, Emotional Maturity, Conscientiousness, Trustworthiness, Long Term Job Commitment, Safe Job Performance, Courtesy.
Administration: Group.
Price Data, 2002: $14 or less (volume discounts available) per questionnaire including User's Manual (1998, 52 pages), all documentation, training, toll-free (or in-house computer) scoring, technical support, and consultation; $55 per Americans With Disabilities Act Kit including User's Manual Addendum (1992, 19 pages), Audio version, Braille version, and Large Print version.
Special Editions: Braille, Large Print, and Audio versions available.
Time: (12–15) minutes.
Author: Gerald L. Borofsky.
Publisher: Bay State Psychological Associates, Inc.; distributed by Wonderlic Personnel Test, Inc.
Cross References: See T5:944 (1 reference); for reviews by Robert M. Guion and Lawrence M. Rudner, see 12:137 (3 references); see also T4:899 (2 references).

[917]
Employee Safety Inventory.

Purpose: Designed to "assess the safety attitudes of job applicants and current employees."
Population: Job applicants and employees.
Publication Dates: 1989–1994.
Acronyms: ESI.
Scores, 7: Survey Scales (Safety Control, Risk Avoidance, Stress Tolerance), Validity Scales (Validity/Distortion, Accuracy), Composite Score (Safety Index), Supplemental Scale (Driver Attitude).
Administration: Group or individual.
Price Data: Price information for Quanta Touch Test administration and scoring and for Windows administration and scoring available from publisher.
Time: (45) minutes.
Comments: Paper-and-pencil or computer administration available.
Author: London House.
Publisher: Reid London House.

[918]
Empowerment Inventory.

Purpose: To identify actions that individuals, managers, and work teams can take to raise one's level of empowerment.
Population: Work team members/employees.
Publication Date: 1993.
Acronym: EI.
Scores, 4: Choice, Competence, Meaningfulness, Progress.
Administration: Group or individual.
Price Data, 2001: $8.50 per inventory.
Time: (20) minutes.
Comments: Self-scored.
Authors: Kenneth W. Thomas and Walter G. Tymon.
Publisher: Consulting Psychologists Press, Inc.
Cross References: For reviews by Leslie Eastman Lukin and Patricia Schoenrade, see 13:119.

[919]
Endeavor Instructional Rating System.

Purpose: Student ratings of courses and instructors.
Population: College.
Publication Dates: 1973–1979.
Acronym: EIRS.
Scores, 9: 7 item scores (Hard Work, Advanced Planning, Class Discussion, Personal Help, Presentation Clarity, Grade Accuracy, Increased Knowledge), and 2 composite scores (Student Perception of Achievement, Student-Instructor Rapport).
Administration: Group.
Price Data: Available from publisher.
Time: (5–10) minutes.
Author: Peter W. Frey.
Publisher: Endeavor Information Systems, Inc. [No reply from publisher; status unknown].
Cross References: See 9:386 (1 reference), and T3:818 (2 references); for a review by Kenneth O. Doyle, Jr., see 8:370 (5 references).

[920]
Endicott Work Productivity Scale.

Purpose: "Designed to describe types of behavior and subjective feelings that are highly likely to reduce productivity and efficiency in work activities."
Population: Adults.
Publication Dates: 1994–1997.
Acronym: EWPS.
Scores: Total score only.
Administration: Individual.
Manual: No manual.
Price Data, 2001: $1 per questionnaire.
Time: [3–5] minutes.
Author: Jean Endicott.
Publisher: Department of Research Assessment and Training.
Cross References: For reviews by Andrew A. Cox and William C. Tirre, see 14:140.

[921]
Endler Multidimensional Anxiety Scales.

Purpose: Developed to assess state and trait anxiety and the respondent's perception of threat in the immediate situation.
Population: Ages 15 and over.
Publication Date: 1991.
Acronym: EMAS.
Administration: Group.
Price Data, 2002: $82.50 per complete kit including 10 EMAS-S AutoScore™ test forms, 10 EMAS-T/EMAS-P AutoScore™ test forms, 2 EMAS-S prepaid mail-in answer sheets, 2 EMAS-T/EMAS-P prepaid answer sheets, and manual; $25 per 25 test forms (select EMAS-S or EMAS-T/EMAS-P); $12.50 per prepaid test report answer sheets (select EMAS-S or EMAS-T/EMAS-P); $48 per manual; $140 per 20-use computer disk (PC with MS Windows); $18 per 100 PC answer booklets; $10 per FAX service scoring charge.
Time: (25) minutes.
Comments: Tests may be used separately.
Authors: Norman S. Endler, Jean M. Edwards, and Romeo Vitelli.
Publisher: Western Psychological Services.
  a) EMAS-STATE.
  Acronym: EMAS-S.
  Scores, 3: Cognitive-Worry, Autonomic-Emotional, Total.
  b) EMAS-TRAIT.
  Acronym: EMAS-T.
  Scores, 4: Social Evaluation, Physical Danger, Ambiguous, Daily Routines.
  c) EMAS-PERCEPTION.
  Acronym: EMAS-P.
  Scores: Item scores only.
Cross References: See T5:950 (6 references); for reviews by Deborah L. Bandalos and Steven D. Spaner, see 12:138 (2 references); see also T4:905 (7 references).

[922]
English as a Second Language Oral Assessment, Second Edition.

Purpose: Measures the "learner's ability to speak and understand English."
Population: Adult nonnative speakers of English.
Publication Dates: 1978–1996.
Acronym: ESLOA.
Scores, 4: Auditory Comprehension, Basic Vocabulary and Grammatical Structures, Complex Grammatical Structures and Communicating Meaning and Comprehension, Comprehension and Fluency and Pronunciation.
Administration: Individual.
Levels, 4: 1, 2, 3, 4.

Price Data, 1999: $3.50 per 50 answer sheets; $13.50 per manual (1996, 80 pages).
Time: Administration time not reported.
Authors: Joye Coy Shaffer and Teri McLean.
Publisher: Literacy Volunteers of America, Inc.
Cross References: For reviews by James D. Brown and Charlene Rivera of an earlier edition, see 11:136.

[923]
English Picture Vocabulary Test.

Purpose: "Designed to assess levels of listening vocabulary."
Publication Dates: 1962–1968.
Scores: Total score only.
Time: Administration time not reported.
Authors: M. A. Brimer and Lloyd M. Dunn.
Publisher: Educational Evaluations [England].
  a) FULL RANGE VERSION.
  Population: Ages 3-0 and over.
  Administration: Individual.
  Price Data, 2002: £33.40 per complete kit including test book, 50 record sheets, and manual; £18.20 per test book; £10.20 per 50 record sheets; £5 per manual.
  b) TEST 1.
  Population: Ages 5-0 to 8-11.
  Administration: Individual.
  Price Data: £21per complete kit; £5.80 per test book; £10.20 per 50 record sheets; £5 per manual.
  c) TEST 2.
  Population: Ages 7-0 to 11-11.
    1) *Individual.*
    Price Data: Same as *b* above.
    2) *Group.*
    Price Data: £7.45 per complete kit; £5.25 per 25 test booklets; £2.20 per manual and key.
  d) TEST 3.
  Population: Ages 11-0 and over.
  Administration: Group.
  Price Data: Same as *c-2* above.
Cross References: See T5:952 (1 reference), T4:907 (10 references), T3:823 (15 references), and T2:495 (3 references); for a review by Kenneth Lovell of Tests 1-2, see 7:408 (5 references); for reviews by L. B. Birch and Philip M. Levy, see 6:520.

[924]
English Placement Test.

Purpose: Place students into homogeneous ability levels as they enter an intensive English language course.
Population: Entrants to courses in English as a second language.
Publication Dates: 1972–1993.
Acronym: EPT.
Score: Total score only.
Administration: Group.

Forms, 3: A, B, C (equivalent forms).
Price Data, 2002: $65 per complete kit including 20 tests of 1 form, 100 answer sheets, stencil, manual, and cassette tape; $20 per 20 tests (specify form); $10 per 100 answer sheets; $10 per scoring stencil; $20 per cassette (contains all 3 forms); $5 per manual.
Time: (75) minutes.
Comments: Tape recording available for administration.
Authors: A. Corrigan, B. Dobson, E. Kellman, M. Spaan, L. Strowe, and S. Tyma.
Publisher: English Language Institute, University of Michigan.
Cross References: See T4:908 (3 references); for a review by John L. D. Clark of an earlier form, see 8:102.

[925]
English Progress Test.

Purpose: "Designed to provide a continuous assessment of English skill."
Population: Ages 7-3 to 15-6.
Publication Dates: 1952–1972.
Scores: Total score only for each of 13 subtests.
Administration: Group.
Price Data: Price information available from publisher for tests (specify level), manual (specify level), primary specimen set, and secondary specimen set.
Time: (40–50) minutes per test.
Comments: Tests B, C, D, and F are out of print.
Publisher: NFER-Nelson Publishing Co., Ltd. [England].

a) ENGLISH PROGRESS TEST A.
Population: Ages 8-0 to 9-0.
Publication Dates: 1952–1960.
Author: A. F. Watts.
b) ENGLISH PROGRESS TEST E.
Population: Ages 12-0 to 13-0.
Publication Date: 1956.
Authors: M. A. Brimer and A. F. Watts.
c) ENGLISH PROGRESS TEST G.
Population: Ages 13-0 to 15-6.
Publication Date: 1962.
Author: S. M. Unwin.
d) ENGLISH PROGRESS TEST A2.
Population: Ages 7-3 to 8-11.
Publication Dates: 1962–1966.
Authors: M. A. Brimer and A. F. Watts.
e) ENGLISH PROGRESS TEST B2.
Population: Ages 8-6 to 10-0.
Publication Dates: 1959–1960.
Author: Manuals by Valerie C. Land.
f) ENGLISH PROGRESS TEST C2.
Population: Ages 9-6 to 11-0.
Publication Date: 1961.
Author: Valerie Land.

g) ENGLISH PROGRESS TEST D2.
Population: Ages 10-6 to 12-0.
Publication Dates: 1963–1964.
Author: Jennifer Henchman.
h) ENGLISH PROGRESS TEST E2.
Population: Ages 11-0 to 13-0.
Publication Dates: 1962–1972.
Author: S. M. Unwin.
i) ENGLISH PROGRESS TEST F2.
Population: Ages 12-0 to 13-6.
Publication Dates: 1963–1972.
Authors: Test by Jennifer Henchman and Elsa Hendry.
j) ENGLISH PROGRESS TEST B3.
Population: Ages 8-0 to 9-6.
Publication Dates: 1970–1972.
k) ENGLISH PROGRESS TEST C3.
Population: Ages 9-0 to 10-9.
Publication Dates: 1970–1972.
l) ENGLISH PROGRESS TEST D3.
Population: Ages 10-0 to 11-8.
Publication Dates: 1970–1972.
m) ENGLISH PROGRESS TEST F3.
Population: Ages 12-0 to 13-6.
Publication Date: 1969.
Cross References: See T4:909 (4 references); for reviews by Neil Gourlay and Stanley Nisket of Tests *a–f,* see 5:187.

[926]
English Skills Assessment.

Purpose: ACER adaptation of STEP Series and DTLS by Educational Testing Service and The College Board.
Population: Grades 11-12 and first year of postsecondary education.
Publication Dates: 1969-1982.
Acronym: ESA.
Scores, 11: Part I (Spelling, Punctuation and Capitalization, Comprehension I, Total), Part II (Comprehension II, Usage, Vocabulary, Sentence Structure, Logical Relationships [optional], Total), Total.
Administration: Group.
Price Data, 2002: A$3.52 per Part I test booklet; A$3.85 per Part II test booklet; A$24.20 per 10 answer sheets; A$4.95 per score key; A$22 per manual; A$34.10 per specimen set.
Time: 50(70) minutes for Part I; 60(70) minutes for Part II.
Author: Australian Council for Educational Research (adaptation).
Publisher: Australian Council for Educational Research Ltd. [Australia].
Cross References: See T4:910 (1 reference); for a review by John C. Sherwood, see 9:389.

[927]
English Test: Municipal Tests: National Achievement Tests.

Purpose: "To test ... mastery in language usage (words and sentences), punctuation and capitalization, and expression of ideas."
Population: Grades 3–8.
Publication Dates: 1938–1956.
Scores, 5: Language Usage-Words, Language Usage-Sentences, Punctuation and Capitalization, Expressing Ideas, Total.
Administration: Group.
Forms, 2: A, B.
Levels, 2: Grades 3-6, Grades 6-8.
Price Data: Available from publisher.
Time: 30(35) minutes.
Comments: Subtest of the formerly published Municipal Battery (see 4:20).
Authors: Robert K. Speer and Samuel Smith.
Publisher: Psychometric Affiliates.
Cross References: See T2:77 (1 reference) and 5:190. For reviews of the complete battery, see 5:18 (1 review), 4:20 (1 review), and 2:1191 (2 reviews).

[928]
English Test: National Achievement Tests.

Purpose: To test skills in English language usage.
Population: Grades 3–12.
Publication Dates: 1936–1957.
Administration: Group.
Levels, 2: Grades 3–8, Grades 7–12.
Forms, 2: A, B.
Price Data: Available from publisher.
Time: (40) minutes.
Authors: Robert K. Speer and Samuel Smith.
Publisher: Psychometric Affiliates.
a) GRADES 3–8.
Publication Dates: 1936–1938.
Scores, 7: Capitalization, Punctuation, Language Usage (Sentences), Language Usage (Words), Expressing Ideas, Letter Writing, Total.
b) GRADES 7–12.
Publication Dates: 1936–1957.
Scores, 7: Word Usage, Punctuation, Vocabulary, Language Usage (Sentences), Expressing Ideas, Expressing Feeling, Total.
Cross References: See T2:78 (1 reference) and 5:191; for a review by Winifred L. Post, see 4:162; for a review by Harry A. Greene, see 3:126.

[929]
Enneagram Personality Portraits Inventory and Profile.

Purpose: Designed to identify an individual's personality type, work style, and leadership style.
Population: Work team members.
Publication Date: 1997.
Scores, 9: Ones—Perfecters/Quality Performers/Stabilizers, Twos—Carers/Helpers/Supporters, Threes—Achievers/Producers/Motivators, Fours—Creators/Expressionists/Individualists, Fives—Observers/Thinkers/Systematizers, Sixes—Groupists/Relaters/Teamsters, Sevens—Cheerers/Animators/Cheerleaders, Eights—Challengers/Asserters/Directors, Nines—Accepters/Receptionists/Reconcilers.
Administration: Group.
Price Data, 1997: $12.95 per inventory and profile; quantity pricing available.
Time: Administration time not reported.
Comments: Classifies respondents into one of nine "types."
Authors: Patrick J. Aspell and Dee Dee Aspell.
Publisher: Jossey-Bass, A Wiley Company.

[930]
The Ennis-Weir Critical Thinking Essay Test.

Purpose: "To help evaluate a person's ability to appraise an argument and to formulate in writing an argument in response, thus recognizing a creative dimension in critical thinking ability."
Population: High school and college.
Publication Dates: 1983-1985.
Scores: Critical Thinking Ability.
Administration: Group.
Price Data, 1993: $9.95 per set including 1 reproducible test, scoring sheet, scoring directions, and manual (1985, 16 pages).
Time: (40) minutes.
Authors: Robert H. Ennis and Eric Weir.
Publisher: Robert H. Ennis (the author).
Cross References: See T5:959 (2 references); for reviews by James A. Poteet and Gail E. Tompkins, see 10:107.

[931]
The Enright Forgiveness Inventory.

Purpose: "To measure the degree to which one person forgives another who has hurt him or her deeply and unfairly."
Population: High school and college and adults.
Publication Date: 2000.
Acronym: EFI.
Scores, 10: 3 Affect scores (Positive Affect, Negative Affect, Total Affect), 3 Behavior scores (Positive Behavior, Negative Behavior, Total Behavior), 3 Cognition scores (Positive Cognition, Negative Cognition, Total Cognition), Total.
Administration: Group or individual.
Price Data, 2001: $35 per manual (70 pages); $75 copying privileges of less than 100 copies; student discount available; additional price information available at www.forgiveness-institute.org.

Time: (40) minutes.
Authors: Robert D. Enright, Julio Rique, and Catherine T. Coyle.
Publisher: International Forgiveness Institute.

[932]
Entrance Examination for Schools of Nursing [RN Entrance Examination].

Purpose: Constructed to assess academic achievement for use in selection and placement of students.
Population: Applicants to schools of registered nursing.
Publication Dates: 1938–1991.
Acronym: RNEE.
Scores, 6: Verbal Ability, Numerical Ability, Life Sciences, Physical Sciences, Reading Skill, Composite.
Administration: Group.
Restricted Distribution: Distribution restricted and test administered at licensed testing centers; details may be obtained from publisher.
Price Data: Available from publisher.
Time: (210) minutes.
Comments: Title on test is RN Entrance Examination for Schools of Nursing.
Author: The Psychological Corporation.
Publisher: The Psychological Corporation.
Cross References: For reviews by Anita S. Tesh and Larry Weber, see 12:140; for reviews by Carolyn Dawson and Christine H. McGuire of an earlier edition, see 8:1121; see also T2:2379 (1 reference), 7:1115 (3 references), and 6:1156 (2 references).

[933]
Entrance Examination for Schools of Practical/Vocational Nursing.

Purpose: "Designed to measure achievement in areas critical for success in the basic practical/vocational nursing curriculum."
Population: Applicants to practical/vocational nursing schools.
Publication Dates: 1942–1991.
Acronym: PNEE.
Scores, 5: Verbal Ability, Numerical Ability, Science, Reading Comprehension, Composite.
Administration: Group.
Restricted Distribution: Distribution restricted and test administered at licensed testing centers; details may be obtained from publisher.
Price Data: Available from publisher.
Time: (180) minutes.
Author: The Psychological Corporation.
Publisher: The Psychological Corporation.
Cross References: For reviews by George Engelhard, Jr. and James W. Pinkney, see 12:141; see also 7:1116 (2 references).

[934]
Entrepreneurial Style and Success Indicator.

Purpose: Assesses variables thought to be related to entrepreneurial success and increase understanding of entrepreneurial style.
Population: Adults.
Publication Dates: 1988–1989.
Acronym: ESSI.
Scores, 4: Behavioral Action, Cognitive Analysis, Interpersonal Harmony, Affective Expression; plus 28 Success Factors.
Administration: Group.
Price Data, 1993: $15 per test booklet; $10 per interpretations booklet (1988, 42 pages); $15 per audiotape (Business With Style); $35 per professional's guide (1989, 73 pages).
Time: (120–180) minutes for Basic; (360–720) minutes for Advanced.
Comments: May be self-administered.
Authors: Howard L. Shenson, Terry D. Anderson, Jonathan Clark, and Susan Clark.
Publisher: Consulting Resource Group International, Inc.
Cross References: For a review by Stephen F. Davis, see 13:120.

[935]
Eosys Word Processing Aptitude Battery.

Purpose: For use in selection, allocation, and development of word processor operators.
Population: Job candidates for work processor operator positions.
Publication Date: 1983.
Acronym: WPAB.
Scores, 5: Verbal Skills (WP1), Checking Skills (WP2), Written Instructions (WP3), Coded Information (WP4), Numerical Computation (WP5).
Administration: Group.
Price Data: Available from publisher.
Time: (10) minutes per WP1, WP2, WP5; (12) minutes per WP3; (15) minutes per WP4.
Authors: Gill Nyfield, Susan Bawtree, Michael Pearn (test), David Hawkey (test), and Emma Bird (manual).
Publisher: SHL Group plc [United Kingdom].

[936]
EQ Questionnaire.

Purpose: "To measure entrepreneurial and executive effectiveness to be used as a personal and organizational development tool."
Population: Adults.
Publication Dates: 1993–1998.
Acronym: EQ Questionnaire.
Scores, 12: Adaptability, Managerial Traits (Risk Tolerance, Time Management, Creativity, Strategic Thinking, Planning, Goal-Orientation), Personality

Traits (Extroversion, Intuition, Thinking, Perceiving), EQ Index.

Administration: Group.

Price Data, 1998: $75 per 5 questionnaires including user's manual (1995, 32 pages) and scoring software; volume discounts available.

Time: [25–35] minutes.

Comments: Test booklet title is EQ Questionnaire; manual title is Entrepreneurial Quotient; administered with paper and pencil and scored using PC or administered and scored using PC (requires IBM or compatible computer).

Authors: Wonderlic Personnel Test, Inc. and Edward J. Fasiska.

Publisher: Wonderlic, Inc.

Cross References: For reviews by James T. Austin and Paul M. Muchinsky, see 14:141.

[937]
ERB Writing Assessment.

Purpose: "Provides a direct measure of writing ability."

Population: Grades 3–6, 7–9, 10–12.

Publication Date: 1989.

Scores, 7: Topic Development, Organization, Support, Sentence Structure, Word Choice, Mechanics, Total.

Administration: Group.

Price Data, 2001: $6.60 per student for test materials in packages of 5, 10, and 20 plus shipping; $27 per computer disk (IBM only); $50 per data tape; $5 per additional set of anchor papers; $1 per additional analytic scoring guide; $7.75 per perusal set (per level); $140 per written analysis of overall results by class or grade; price information for technical manual available from publisher.

Comments: Writing samples scored by Measurement Incorporated.

Author: Educational Records Bureau.

Publisher: Educational Records Bureau.

   a) PRIMARY LEVEL.
   Purpose: To assess student's narrative writing.
   Population: Grade 3.
   b) LEVEL I.
   Purpose: To assess student's descriptive writing.
   Population: Grades 4–6.
   Time: (35–40) minutes (2 sessions).
   c) LEVEL II.
   Purpose: To assess student's expository writing.
   Population: Grades 7–9.
   Time: (45–50) minutes (2 sessions).
   d) LEVEL III.
   Purpose: To assess student's persuasive writing.
   Population: Grades 10–12.
   Time: (45–50) minutes (2 sessions).

Cross References: For reviews by G. Michael Poteat and Wayne H. Slater, see 13:122.

[938]
Erotometer: A Technique for the Measurement of Heterosexual Love.

Purpose: Designed to measure attitudes toward heterosexual love.

Population: Adults.

Publication Dates: 1971–1988.

Scores: Total score only.

Administration: Group.

Manual: No manual.

Price Data, 2002: $1 per test.

Time: [10] minutes.

Comments: Supplementary article available.

Author: Panos D. Bardis.

Publisher: Donna Bardis.

Cross References: For additional information, see 8:337 (1 reference).

[939]
ESL/Adult Literacy Scale.

Purpose: Developed to identify "the appropriate starting level for ESL and literacy instruction."

Population: Adults.

Publication Date: 1989.

Scores, 6: Listening, Grammar, Life Skills, Reading, Composition, Total.

Administration: Individual.

Manual: No manual.

Price Data, 2002: $16 per 25 test booklets; $25 per scoring overlay; $5 per instruction sheet.

Time: [15–20] minutes.

Author: Michael Roddy.

Publisher: Academic Therapy Publications.

Cross References: See T5:971 (2 references); for reviews by Anne L. Harvey and Dianna L. Newman and Kathleen T. Toms, see 11:138.

[940]
Essential Skills Assessments: Information Skills.

Purpose: "Broad measures of achievement set within the Essential skills of the New England Curriculum Framework ... [for the purpose of] formative assessment."

Population: Ages 9–14.

Publication Date: 2001.

Acronym: ESA:IS.

Levels, 3: Primary, Intermediate, Secondary.

Administration: Group.

Price Data, 2002: NZ$36 per full specimen set including 1 each of primary, intermediate, and secondary tests, and teacher's manual (71 pages); NZ$22.50 per specimen set including all tests and teacher's manual (primary level); NZ$27 per specimen set including all tests and teacher's manual (intermediate level); NZ$22.95 per specimen set including all tests and teacher's manual (secondary level); NZ$450 per CD-ROM pack including CD-ROM with all tests (PDF format), teacher's manual, 1 set of printed tests, and help sheet; NZ$18 per teacher's manual; NZ$9.90 per 10 Finding Information in Books (all levels, specify level); NZ$9.90 per 10 Finding Information in Graphs and Tables (primary level); NZ$12.60 per 10 Finding Information in Graphs and Tables (intermediate level); NZ$11.70 per 10 Finding Information in Graphs and Tables (secondary level); NZ$9.90 per 10 Finding Information in a Library (primary and intermediate levels, specify level); NZ$12.60 per 10 finding Information in a Library (secondary level); NZ$9.90 per 10 Finding Information in Reference Sources (primary and intermediate levels, specify level); NZ$9.90 per 10 Evaluating Information in Text (intermediate level); NZ12.60 per 10 Evaluating Information in Text (secondary level); NZ$12.60 per 10 finding Information in Prose Text (intermediate and secondary levels, specify level).

Time: (30) minutes per test.

Comments: Replaces the Progressive Achievement Tests of Study Skills (T5:2095); tests include both constructed-response and selected-response format items; normed on children living in New Zealand; available in print or CD-ROM format; CD-ROM system requirements: 600 dpi laser or inkjet printer, Adobe Acrobat reader version 3 or 4.

Authors: Cedric Croft, Karyn Dunn, and Gavin Brown.

Publisher: New Zealand Council for Educational Research [New Zealand].

   a) FINDING INFORMATION IN BOOKS.

   Levels, 2: Primary, Intermediate.

   Scores: Total score only.

   b) FINDING INFORMATION IN GRAPHS AND TABLES.

   Levels, 3: Primary, Intermediate, Secondary.

   Scores: Total score only.

   c) FINDING INFORMATION IN A LIBRARY.

   Levels, 3: Primary, Intermediate, Secondary.

   Scores: Total score only.

   d) FINDING INFORMATION IN PROSE TEXT.

   Levels, 2: Intermediate, Secondary.

   Scores: Total score only.

   e) FINDING INFORMATION IN REFERENCE SOURCES.

   Levels, 2: Primary, Intermediate.

   Scores: Total score only.

   f) FINDING INFORMATION IN TEXT.

   Levels, 2: Intermediate, Secondary.

   Scores: Total score only.

Cross References: See T5:2095 (1 reference); for reviews by Michael D. Hiscox and Ronald C. Rodgers of an earlier edition, see 9:1006; see also T3:1913 (1 reference).

[941]
ETS Tests of Applied Literacy Skills.

Purpose: To measure adult literacy.

Population: Adults.

Publication Date: 1991.

Scores, 3: Total score for each of 3 subtests: Quantitative Literacy, Document Literacy, Prose Literacy.

Administration: Group.

Forms, 2: Forms A and B for each test.

Price Data: Available from publisher.

Time: 6(20) minutes for the battery; 2(20) minutes of any one subtest.

Authors: Educational Testing Service, Irwin J. Kirsch (manual), Anne Jungeblut (manual), and Anne Campbell (manual), with contributions from Norman E. Freeberg, Robert J. Mislevy, Donald A. Rock, and Kentaro Yamamoto.

Publisher: Prentice Hall [No reply from publisher; status unknown].

Cross References: For reviews by Roger A. Richards and Herbert C. Rudman, see 13:124.

[942]
ETSA Tests.

Purpose: Designed to measure aspects of intelligence, specific abilities or aptitudes, and certain personality characteristics to supplement other factors in decisions of hiring, placement, training, and promotion.

Population: Employment applicants.

Publication Dates: 1959–1998.

Scores: 8 tests: General Mental Ability, Office Arithmetic, General Clerical Ability, Office Skills, Mechanical Familiarity, Mechanical Knowledge, Sales Aptitude, Personal Adjustment Index.

Administration: Individual or group.

Time: 45–90 minutes.

Price Data: Available from publisher.

Comments: Electronic tests available at www.etsatests.com; publisher recommends use of General mental Ability Test with other tests dependant upon nature of employment tasks.

Authors: S. Trevor Hadley, George A. W. Stouffer, and Psychological Services Bureau, Inc.

Publisher: Employers' Tests and Services Associates.

Cross References: For reviews by Roland H. Good, III and Hilda Wing, see 11:139; for additional information, see 9:399 and T3:846; for reviews by Marvin D. Dunnette and Raymond A. Katzell of an earlier edition, see 6:1025.

[943]
Evaluating Courses for Inclusion of New Scholarship on Women.

Purpose: A student evaluation questionnaire designed to evaluate course content in terms of information presented about women.

Population: Post-secondary students.
Publication Date: 1988.
Scores: 4 ratings: Evaluation of Course Readings, Evaluation of the Syllabus, Evaluation of the Class, Overall Course Evaluation.
Administration: Group.
Manual: No manual.
Price Data: Available from publisher.
Time: Administration time not reported.
Author: Women's Studies Program, Duke University.
Publisher: Association of American Colleges and Universities.

[944]
Evaluating Diversity Training.

Purpose: "Designed to help diversity-training managers evaluate the effectiveness of training, instructors, and vendors."
Population: Diversity-training managers.
Publication Date: 1996.
Scores: 17 checklists: Participant Reactions (rating scale, open ended), Self-Assessment of Learning, Learning Self-Assessment, Knowledge of Diversity Issues, Learning Outcomes Role-Play, Participant Post-Training (open ended, short version, rating scale), Manager's Post training (open ended, satisfaction measure, application estimate), Diversity Behavior, Organizational Results, Vendor Evaluation, Instructor/Facilitator Effectiveness, Experiential Training Evaluation.
Administration: Group.
Price Data, 1998: $89.95 per loose-leaf binder (105 pages).
Time: Untimed.
Authors: John M. Keller, Andrea Young, and Mary Riley.
Publisher: Jossey-Bass, A Wiley Company.

[945]
Evaluating Movement and Posture Disorganization in Dyspraxic Children.

Purpose: Designed to determine and analyze the normal and disorganized components of movement and posture.
Population: Learning disabled children ages 5 and above.
Publication Date: 1989.
Scores, 2: Total Quality Performance, Total Problem Performance.
Subtests, 10: Supine to Stand, Supine to Flexion Hold, Prone Reach, Alternating Prone Reach, Kneel Walk Forward and Back, Alternating One Foot Kneel, Alternating Half Kneel-Stand, One Foot Balance, Squat Pick-up, Unilateral/Bilateral Toss.
Administration: Individual.

Price Data: Available from publisher.
Time: Administration time not reported.
Comments: "Criteria-referenced" test; full-color videotape (30 minutes) shows examples of normal and disorganized movement responses for each subtest.
Author: W. Michael Magrun.
Publisher: Clinician's View [No reply from publisher; status unknown].
Cross References: For reviews by Randy W. Kamphaus and Barbara Rothlisberg, see 12:144.

[946]
Evaluation Aptitude Test.

Purpose: Constructed to assess deductive reasoning.
Population: Candidates for college and graduate school entrance.
Publication Dates: 1951–1952.
Acronym: EAT.
Scores, 5: Neutral Syllogisms, Emotionally Toned Syllogisms, Total, Emotional Bias, Indecision.
Administration: Group.
Price Data: Available from publisher.
Time: 50(55) minutes.
Author: DeWitt E. Sell.
Publisher: Psychometric Affiliates.
Cross References: For reviews by J. Thomas Hastings and Walker H. Hill, see 5:691.

[947]
Evaluation Disposition Toward the Environment.

Purpose: Evaluates "value orientation used to approach environmental experiences and responsibilities."
Population: High school and college.
Publication Date: 1976.
Acronym: EDEN.
Scores, 7: Aesthetic, Experiential, Knowledge Seeking, Prudent, Active, Responsible, Practical.
Administration: Group.
Price Data: Not available.
Time: (45) minutes.
Comments: Scoring must be done by publisher.
Author: Norman J. Milchus.
Publisher: Person-O-Metrics, Inc.

[948]
Evaluation Modality Test.

Purpose: Developed to analyze the characteristics of "the mode in which an individual valuates."
Population: Adults.
Publication Date: 1956.
Acronym: EMT.
Scores, 4: Realism, Moralism, Individualism, Total.
Administration: Individual or group.
Price Data: Available from publisher.
Time: (25–35) minutes.

Author: Hugo O. Engelmann.
Publisher: Psychometric Affiliates.
Cross References: For a review by Wilson H. Guertin, see 5:51.

[949]
Evaluation of Basic Skills.

Purpose: Designed to provide a concept-based measurement of reading, writing, and mathematics.
Population: Ages 3 to 18.
Publication Dates: 1995–1996.
Scores, 3: Reading, Writing, Mathematics.
Administration: Individual.
Price Data, 2002: $49.95 per complete start-up kit including administration manual (1995, 27 pages), 50 test forms, and 25 pre-test/post-test word tests; $15.95 per administration manual; $12 per 2-tape audio cassette set "Administering the Test"; $95 per application fee as test administrator; $25 per 50 test forms; $20 per 50 pre-test/post-test word tests.
Time: (10) minutes for Mathematics section; untimed for Reading and Writing sections.
Author: Lee Havis.
Publisher: Trust Tutoring.
Cross References: For reviews by Eleanor E. Sanford and Loraine J. Spenciner, see 14:142.

[950]
Everyday Life Activities: Photo Series.

Purpose: Designed as a photo series for "language training, teaching, testing and remediation of word-, sentence-, and text/discourse-level abilities."
Population: Children with delay in language development, autistic children, and adults with a language or speech impairment sequel to brain damage.
Publication Date: 1994.
Acronym: ELA.
Scores: Available from publisher.
Administration: Individual.
Price Data, 2001: $743 per book.
Time: Administration time not reported.
Author: Jacqueline Stark.
Publisher: Psychology Press.

[951]
Examination for the Certificate of Competency in English.

Purpose: "Intended for learners who have acquired an intermediate competence in English language use" who may wish some "external measure of their competence in English for documentation for employment or promotion purposes" in their native countries.
Population: Nonnative speakers of English.
Publication Dates: 1995–2002.
Acronym: ECCE.

Scores, 4: Listening, Grammar/Vocabulary/Reading, Writing, Speaking.
Administration: Group.
Price Data, 2002: $40 per candidate to publisher plus local administrative fees.
Time: (160–180) minutes for complete battery; (25) minutes for Listening; (90) minutes for Grammar/Vocabulary and Reading; (30) minutes for Writing; (10–15) minutes for Speaking.
Comments: Administrative manual for local test centers includes Speaking criteria; not "an academically oriented examination, though it may be a bridge to such an examination, for instance, the ECPE"; 2 forms per year; "administered once a year at approved test centers outside the U.S."; "examinees who pass all sections of the ECCE receive the Michigan Certificate of Competency in English."
Author: The English Language Institute of the University of Michigan, Testing and Certification Division.
Publisher: English Language Institute, University of Michigan.

[952]
Examination for the Certificate of Proficiency in English.

Purpose: Designed to assess language proficiency for advanced English-as-a-Second-Language speakers.
Population: Adults who are advanced level English-as-a-Second-Language speakers and who wish documentation for academic or employment purposes.
Publication Dates: 1953–2002.
Acronym: ECPE.
Scores, 5: Writing, Listening Comprehension, Cloze, Grammar/Vocabulary/Reading, Speaking.
Administration: Group.
Forms: 3 Preliminary, 1 Final each year.
Price Data, 2002: $50 per candidate to publisher plus local administrative fees.
Comments: Administrative manual for local test centers includes Speaking criteria.
Author: English Language Institute of the University of Michigan.
Publisher: English Language Institute, University of Michigan.
a) PRELIMINARY ECPE.
Time: 30 minutes.
Comments: A 35-item preliminary test designed to familiarize the examinee with the examination and serve as an indicator of how they might perform on the Final ECPE.
b) FINAL ECPE.
Time: (160–180) minutes for Final Battery; (10–15) minutes for Speaking; (30) minutes for Writing; (25–30) minutes for Listening; (25) minutes for Cloze; (60) minutes for Grammar/Vocabulary/Reading.

Comments: "Administered once a year, at approved test centers" throughout the world; "an entirely new ECPE is produced every year"; "examinees who pass all sections of the ECPE receive the Michigan Certificate of Proficiency in English. The CPE is not awarded in recognition of academic studies, nor teaching ability," it is only a recognition of language proficiency. It may be used for entrance to U.S. or Canadian universities, for advanced placement in local university English courses, for evidence of English language ability for teachers of English.

[953]
Examining for Aphasia, Third Edition.

Purpose: "For evaluating possible aphasic language impairments and other acquired impairments that are often closely related to language functions."
Population: Adolescents and adults.
Publication Dates: 1946–1994.
Acronym: EFA-3.
Scores, 41: Agnosias (Common Objects, Pictures, Colors, Geometric Forms, Numerals, Letters, Printed Words, Almost Alike Pictures, Printed Sentences, Nonverbal Noises, Object Identification, Total); Aphasias (Word Identification, Comprehension of Sentences, Comprehension of Multiple Choice, Oral Paragraphs, Silent Reading Sentences, Silent Reading Paragraphs, Total); Apraxias (Body Parts, Simple Skills, Pretend Action, Numerals, Words, Sentences, Total), Aphasios (Automatic Speech, Writing Numerals, Writing Letters, Spelling, Writing from Dictation, Naming Body Parts, Word Finding, Arithmetic Computations, Arithmetic Problems, Total); Composites (Receptive, Expressive, Subaphasic, Aphasia, Total).
Administration: Individual.
Price Data, 2001: $169 per complete kit including 25 examiner record books, 25 Profile/Response forms, picture book, examiner's manual (1994, 35 pages), and object kit; $44 per 25 examiner record booklets; $24 per 25 Profile/Response forms; $41 per picture book; $39 per examiner's manual; $16 per object kit.
Time: (30–120) minutes.
Comments: Shortened version of test may be administered for screening purposes.
Author: Jon Eisenson.
Publisher: PRO-ED.
Cross References: For a review by Helen Kitchens, see 13:124: see also T4:940 (2 references), T2:2071 (3 references), and P:76 (2 references); for excerpted reviews by Louis M. DiCarlo and Laurance F. Shaffer, see 5:52 (3 references); for a review by D. Russell Davis and excerpted reviews by Nolan D. C. Lewis and one other, see 4:42; for a review by C. R. Strother and an excerpted review, see 3:39.

[954]
Executive Administrative Assistant Skills Test.

Purpose: To evaluate the suitability of candidates for the position of executive administrative assistant.
Population: Candidates with all levels of experience for the position of executive administrative assistant.
Publication Date: 1977.
Acronym: PRSECTY.
Scores: Total Score, Narrative Evaluation, Ranking, Recommendation.
Administration: Group.
Price Data, 2001: $355 per candidate.
Time: (45) minutes.
Comments: Scored by publisher; must be proctored.
Author: Walden Personnel Performance, Inc.
Publisher: Walden Personnel Performance, Inc.

[955]
The Executive Control Battery.

Purpose: "To document the presence and extent of the 'executive dyscontrol' or 'frontal lobe' syndrome."
Population: Adults.
Publication Date: 1999.
Acronym: ECB.
Administration: Individual.
Price Data: Available from publisher.
Comments: Neuropsychological battery; subtests can be administered independently.
Authors: Elkhonon Goldberg, Kenneth Podell, Robert Bilder, and Judith Jaeger.
Publisher: Psych Press [Australia].
 a) THE GRAPHICAL SEQUENCES TEST.
 Purpose: "Designed to elicit perseverations ... and various behavioural stereotypies."
 Scores, 7: Hyperkinetic Motor Perseverations (Occurrences), Perseveration of Elements (Occurrences, Repetitions), Perseveration of Features (Occurrences, Repetitions), Perseverations of Activities (Occurrences, Repetitions).
 Time: (15–20) minutes.
 b) COMPETING PROGRAMS TEST.
 Purpose: "Designed to elicit various types of echopraxia, behavioural stereotypies, and disinhibition."
 Scores, 8: Simple Go/No-Go (Random, Simple Stereotype, Alternating Stereotype, Total Errors), Simple Conflict—Visual (Random, Simple Stereotype, Alternating Stereotype, Total Errors).
 Time: (12–15) minutes.
 c) MANUAL POSTURES TEST.
 Purpose: "Designed to elicit various types of echopraxia."
 Scores: 3 ratings: Correct, Full Mirroring, Other.
 Time: (10–15) minutes.

d) MOTOR SEQUENCES TEST.
Purpose: "Designed to elicit various types of motor perseverations, stereotypies, and other deficits of sequential motor organisation."
Parts, 2: Dynamic Praxis, Bimanual Coordination.
Time: (10–15) minutes.
  1) *Dynamic Praxis.*
    Scores, 6: Two Stage Movement (Imitation, Continuation, Without Model), Reversal of Two State Movement (Imitation, Continuation Without Model), Three Stage Movement (Imitation, Continuation Without Model.
  2) *Bimanual Coordination.*
    Scores, 6: Distal (Imitation, Continuation Without Model), Proximal (Imitation, Continuation Without Model), Mixed (Imitation, Continuation Without Model).

[956]
Executive Profile Survey.

Purpose: Constructed to assess "self-attitudes, self-beliefs, and value patterns" needed for executive-level jobs.
Population: Prospective executives.
Publication Dates: 1967–1983.
Scores: 11 dimensions: Ambitious, Assertive, Enthusiastic, Creative, Spontaneous, Self-Focused, Considerate, Open-Minded, Relaxed, Practical, Systematic.
Administration: Group or individual.
Price Data, 2002: $22 per 10 reusable test booklets; $15 per 10 answer sheets; $25 per manual (1983, 79 pages); $28 per introductory kit; $16 to $30 per reports.
Time: (60) minutes.
Comments: Self-administered; manual title is Perspectives on the Executive Personality.
Authors: Virgil R. Lang and Samuel E. Krug (manual).
Publisher: Institute for Personality and Ability Testing, Inc.
Cross References: For reviews by S. David Kriska and Gregory J. Marchant, see 12:146; for a review of an earlier edition by William I. Sauser, Jr., see 9:401.

[957]
Expectations Edition of the Personal Values Inventory.

Purpose: To identify role expectations and compare them with the motivational values of the person in the role.
Population: Adolescents and adults reading at or above sixth grade (U.S.) reading level.
Publication Date: 2001.
Acronym: EE/PVI.
Scores: Blue Motivation, Red-Blue Motivation, Red Motivation, Red-Green Motivation, Green Motivation, Blue-Green Motivation.

Administration: Group or individual.
Manual: No manual.
Price Data, 2002: $4.50 per inventory.
Time: (15–30) minutes.
Comments: For use with the Personal Values Inventory (1876); scores reflect expectations of the person in the role when things are going well and the expected responses when there is conflict or opposition.
Author: Elias H. Porter.
Publisher: Personal Strengths Publishing.

[958]
Expectations Edition of the Strength Development Inventory.

Purpose: To identify role expectations and compare them with the motivational values of the person in the role.
Population: Adults.
Publication Date: 2001.
Acronym: EE/SDI.
Scores: Altruistic-Nurturing Motivation, Assertive-Nurturing Motivation, Assertive-Directing Motivation, Judicious-Competing Motivation, Analytic-Autonomizing Motivation, Cautious-Supporting Motivation.
Administration: Group or individual.
Manual: No manual.
Price Data, 2002: $4.50 per inventory.
Foreign Language Edition: French edition available entitled Édition sur les attentes de l'inventaire du déploiement des forces de la personnalité.
Time: (15–30) minutes.
Comments: For use with the Strength Deployment Inventory (2380); supersedes the Job Interactions Inventory (14:474); scores reflect expectations of the person in the role when things are going well and the expected responses when there is conflict or opposition.
Author: Elias H. Porter.
Publisher: Personal Strengths Publishing.

[959]
Experience and Background Inventory (Form S).

Purpose: "Provides quantitative measures of past performance and experience."
Population: Adults (Industry).
Publication Dates: 1980–1996.
Acronym: EBI.
Scores: 9 factors: School Achievement, Choice of a College Major, Aspiration Level, Drive/Career Progress, Leadership and Group Participation, Vocational Satisfaction, Financial Responsibility, General Responsibility, Relaxation Pursuits.
Administration: Group.
Price Data, 2002: $102 per start-up kit including 25 test booklets, 25 score sheets, and interprettion and research manual (1996, 15 pages); $54 per 25 test

booklets; $32 per 25 score sheets; $28 per interpretation and research manual.
Time: Administration time not reported.
Authors: Melany E. Baehr and Ernest C. Froemel.
Publisher: Reid London House.

[960]
The Experiencing Scale.

Purpose: Assess the degree to which a patient communicates and employs a personal, phenomenological perspective in a therapy session.
Population: Counselors and counselor trainees, patients in any form of psychotherapy.
Publication Date: 1969.
Acronym: EXP.
Scores, 2: Mode, Peak; based on a 7-point rating scale.
Administration: Individual.
Price Data, 2001: $26 per Volumes I and II; $42 per Volume III.
Time: Administration time not reported.
Comments: "Evaluating the quality of patient self-involvement in psychotherapy directly from tape recordings or typescripts of the therapy session"; tape or transcript of session required; rated by trained raters from tapes (audio or video).
Authors: M. H. Klein, P. L. Mathieu, E. T. Gendlin, and D. J. Kiesler.
Publisher: Marjorie H. Klein (the author).
Cross References: See T5:991 (3 references) and T4:943 (1 reference).

[961]
EXPLORE.

Purpose: Measures the academic progress of eighth and ninth graders in four areas: English, mathematics, reading, and science reasoning; helps students explore the range of career options; and assists them in developing a high school coursework plan.
Population: Grades 8–9.
Publication Dates: 1995–2000.
Administration: Group.
Price Data, 2001: $52.50 per 30 reusable test booklets; $135 per 30 consumable student assessment sets; volume discounts available.
Time: (120) minutes for four academics tests; (45–60) minutes for interest inventory, plans and background information, and needs assessment.
Comments: The initial component of ACT's Educational Planning and Assessment System (EPAS), which also includes PLAN (1916), the ACT Assessment (57), and Work Keys (2749).
Author: ACT, Inc.
Publisher: ACT, Inc.
a) EXPLORE ENGLISH TEST.
   Purpose: Measures understanding of the conventions of standard written English.

Scores, 3: Usage/Mechanics (Punctuation, Grammar and Usage, Sentence Structure), Rhetorical Skills (Strategy, Organization, Style), Total.
Time: 30 minutes.
b) EXPLORE MATHEMATICS TEST.
Purpose: Measures level of mathematics achievement.
Scores: Total score only.
Time: 30 minutes.
c) EXPLORE READING TEST.
Purpose: Measures reading comprehension as a product of referring and reasoning skills.
Scores: Total score only.
Time: 30 minutes.
d) EXPLORE SCIENCE REASONING TEST.
Purpose: Measures scientific reasoning skills.
Scores: Total score only.
Time: 30 minutes.

[962]
Explore the World of Work.

Purpose: Designed to stimulate job awareness and exploration for jobs requiring up to 2 years of training.
Population: Elementary and special education.
Publication Dates: 1989–1991.
Acronym: E-WOW.
Scores, 6: Business/Office/Sales, Industry/Mechanics/Transportation/Construction, Art/Communications/Design, Health/Education/Social Service, Forestry/Agriculture/Natural Resources, Scientific/Technical/Health.
Administration: Group.
Price Data: Available from publisher.
Time: (40–70) minutes.
Comments: Children's Occupational Outlook Handbook suggested to complete follow-up activities on the questionnaire; self-scored.
Authors: Lori Constantino, Bob Kauk, and CFKR Career Materials, Inc. (manuals).
Publisher: CFKR Career Materials [No reply from publisher; status unknown].

[963]
Expressive One-Word Picture Vocabulary Test [2000 Edition].

Purpose: Designed to measure an individual's English-speaking vocabulary.
Population: Ages 2–18.
Publication Dates: 1979–2000.
Acronym: EOWPVT.
Scores: Total score only.
Administration: Individual.
Price Data, 2002: $140 per kit including manual (2000, 128 pages), 25 record forms, and test plates in a vinyl portfolio; $75 per test plates; $25 per 25 record forms; $40 per manual.

Time: (10–15) minutes.
Comments: The editor combines the lower and upper levels in previous editions and extends the use of the test through age 18-11.
Author: 1990 and earlier edition by Morrison F. Gardner; later edition prepared by publisher.
Publisher: Academic Therapy Publications.
Cross References: See T5:994 (53 references) and T4:946 (23 references); for reviews by Gregory J. Cizek and Larry B. Grantham of an earlier edition, see 12:147 (6 references); for reviews by Jack A. Cummings and Gilbert M. Spivak of the Lower Level, see 9:403 (2 references).

[964]
Expressive Vocabulary Test.

Purpose: Designed to assess expressive vocabulary and word retrieval.
Population: Ages 2.5–90+ years.
Publication Date: 1997.
Acronym: EVT.
Scores: Total score only.
Administration: Individual.
Price Data, 2002: $146.95 per complete kit including test easel, 25 record forms, and manual (176 pages); $28.95 per 25 record forms; $199.95 per AGS Computer ASSIST™ for the EVT (IBM or Macintosh).
Time: (15) minutes.
Comments: Conormed with the Peabody Picture Vocabulary Test—III; comparison between EVT and PPVT-III standard scores yields an evaluation of word retrieval; ; scoring ASSIST™ provides extended norms below 40 and includes vocabulary-building exercises.
Author: Kathleen T. Williams.
Publisher: American Guidance Service, Inc.
Cross References: For reviews by Frederick Bessai and Orest Eugene Wasyliw, see 14:143.

[965]
Eyberg Child Behavior Inventory and Sutter-Eyberg Student Behavior Inventory—Revised.

Purpose: Designed "to measure conduct problems in children ages 2 through 16 years."
Population: Ages 2–16 years.
Publication Dates: 1978–1999.
Acronym: ECBI; SESBI-R.
Scores, 2: Intensity, Problem.
Administration: Group or individual.
Forms, 2: Eyberg Child Behavior Inventory; Sutter-Eyberg Student Behavior Inventory—Revised.
Price Data: Available from publisher for introductory kit including professional manual (1999, 64 pages), 50 ECBI test sheets, and 50 SESBI-R test sheets.
Time: (10) minutes.

Comments: ECBI is a rating form completed by parents; SESBI-R is a rating form completed by teachers.
Authors: Sheila Eyberg (SESBI-R, ECBI, and professional manual), Joseph Sutter (SESBI-R), and Donna Pincus (professional manual).
Publisher: Psychological Assessment Resources, Inc.
Cross References: For information on the Eyberg Child Behavior Inventory, see T5:997 (30 references) and T4:948 (26 references); for a review by Michael L. Reed of an earlier edition, see 9:404 (6 references); see also T3:858 (2 references). For information on the Sutter-Eyberg Student Behavior Inventory, see T5:2595 (2 references) and T4:2668 (1 reference); for a review by T. Steuart Watson of an earlier edition, see 11:410 (2 references).

[966]
Eysenck Personality Inventory.

Purpose: Measures two independent dimensions of personality: Extraversion-Introversion and Neuroticism-Stability.
Population: Adults.
Publication Dates: 1963–1969.
Acronym: EPI.
Scores, 3: Extraversion, Neuroticism, Lie.
Administration: Group.
Time: (10–15) minutes.
Comments: Revision of Maudsley Personality Inventory; for revised edition of EPI, see Eysenck Personality Questionnaire—Revised (967); no reliability data for Lie scores; authors recommend use of both forms to obtain adequate reliability for individual measurements; U.S. and British Editions are identical except for three words and directions.
Authors: H. J. Eysenck and Sybil B. G. Eysenck.
a) UNITED STATES EDITION.
    Population: Grades 9–16 and adults.
    Publication Dates: 1963–1969.
    Forms, 2: A, B.
    Price Data: Available from publisher.
    Foreign Language Edition: Spanish edition (1972) available.
    Comments: A printing with the title Eysenck Personality Inventory is available for industrial use.
    Publisher: EdITS/Educational and Industrial Testing Service.
b) BRITISH EDITION.
    Population: Adults.
    Publication Dates: 1963–1964.
    Forms, 2: A, B.
    Price Data, 1999: £10.99 per 20 inventories (Form A or Form B); £8.99 per scoring key; £10.99 per manual (1964, 24 pages); £11.99 per specimen set.

Comments: This test is now superseded by Eysenck Personality Questionnaire [Revised] (967) except where parallel forms are required.

Publisher: Hodder & Stoughton Educational [England].

Cross References: See T5:998 (135 references), T4:949 (226 references), 9:405 (91 references), and T3:859 (245 references); for a review by Auke Tellegen, see 8:553 (405 references); see also T2:1174 (140 references); for reviews by Richard I. Lanyon and excerpted reviews by A. W. Heim and James Linder, see 7:776 (121 references); see also P:77 (52 references); for a review by James C. Lingoes, see 6:93 (1 reference).

[967]
Eysenck Personality Questionnaire [Revised].

Publication Dates: 1975–1994.
Acronym: EPQ-R.
Scores, 5: Psychotocism or Tough-Mindedness, Extraversion, Neuroticism or Emotionality, Lie, Addiction.
Administration: Group.
Time: (10–15) minutes.
Comments: Revision of the still-in-print Eysenck Personality Inventory (986).
Authors: H. J. Eysenck and Sybil B. G. Eysenck.
  a) UNITED STATES EDITION.
  Purpose: Designed to measure four dimensions of personality in adults.
  Population: College and general adults including those with lower education levels.
  Publication Dates: 1975–1994.
  Price Data, 1998: $14 per 25 tests [$55.75 per 100, $209.25 per 500]; $36.75 per hand-scoring keys; $23.50 per manual; $30.75 per specimen set including manual and one copy of each form.
  Publisher: EdITS/Educational and Industrial Testing Service.
  b) BRITISH EDITION.
  Purpose: Measures three main personality factors: Psychotocism, Extraversion, and Neuroticism.
  Population: Ages 7–15, 16 and over.
  Publication Dates: 1975–1991.
  Price Data, 1994: £29.99 per specimen set; £7.99 per 20 questionnaires; £13.99 per scoring keys; £16.99 per manual.
  Publisher: Hodder & Stoughton Educational [England].

Cross References: See T5:999 (195 references), T4:950 (190 references), 9:406 (32 references), and T3:860 (72 references); for reviews by Jack Block, Paul Kline, Lawrence J. Stricker, and Auke Tellegen, see 8:554 (84 references).

[968]
FACES II & FACES III.

Purpose: To determine the structure of the family, in terms of the Circumplex Model.
Population: Families.
Publication Date: 1985.
Acronym: FACES II & FACES III.
Scores: 2 dimensions: Family Cohesion, Family Adaptability.
Administration: Group.
Price Data, 1998: $30 per set of inventory materials including FACES II or III scale, which may be copied for use after obtaining permission, and manual (49 pages).
Special Edition: Couple version available for couples without children.
Time: [15] minutes.
Comments: Also known as Family Adaptability & Cohesion Evaluation Scales; self-report instrument.
Authors: David H. Olson, Joyce Portner, and Yoav Lavee.
Publisher: Life Innovations, Inc.
Cross References: See T5:1000 (110 references), T4:951 (31 references), and 11:140 (26 references).

[969]
Facial Action Coding System.

Purpose: Constructed to assess facial movements or expressions.
Population: Adults.
Publication Date: 1978.
Acronym: FACS.
Scores: 66 Action Units.
Administration: Individual.
Price Data, 1999: $320 per complete kit including 10 scoring sheets, 146 illustrative facial photographs, VHS videocassette, manual (341 pages), and investigator's guide Part 1 (42 pages) and Part 2 (149 pages).
Time: Administration time not reported.
Authors: Paul Ekman and Wallace V. Friesen.
Publisher: Paul Ekman (the author).
Cross References: See T5:1001 (17 references); for reviews by Kathryn M. Benes and Thomas F. Donlon, see 12:149 (7 references); see also T4:952 (11 references).

[970]
Faculty Morale Scale for Institutional Improvement.

Purpose: Designed "as a diagnostic instrument—an attitudinal fact-finding device."
Population: Faculty members.
Publication Date: No date.
Scores: Total score only.
Administration: Group.

Price Data, 2001: $3 per specimen set.
Time: Administration time not reported.
Author: A Local Chapter Committee, American Association of University Professors.
Publisher: Psychometric Affiliates.

[971]
A Familism Scale.

Purpose: Measures attitudes related to family.
Population: Adolescents and adults.
Publication Dates: 1959–1988.
Scores, 3: Nuclear, Extended, Total.
Administration: Group.
Manual: No manual.
Price Data, 2002: $1 per scale.
Time: [8] minutes.
Comments: Supplementary article available.
Author: Panos D. Bardis.
Publisher: Donna Bardis.
Cross References: See T4:957 (1 reference).

[972]
Family Adjustment Test.

Purpose: "Designed to measure feelings of intrafamily homeyness-homelessness."
Population: Ages 12 and over.
Publication Dates: 1952–1954.
Acronym: FAT.
Scores, 11: Attitudes Toward Mother, Attitudes Toward Father, Father-Mother Attitude Quotient, Oedipal, Struggle for Independence, Parent-Child Friction-Harmony, Interparental Friction-Harmony, Family Inferiority-Superiority, Rejection of Child, Parental Qualities, Total.
Administration: Group.
Price Data: Available from publisher.
Time: (35–40) minutes.
Comments: Title on test is Elias Family Opinion Survey.
Author: Gabriel Elias.
Publisher: Psychometric Affiliates.
Cross References: See T4:958 (1 reference), T2:1181 (12 references), and P:80 (1 reference); for a review by John Elderkin Bell, see 6:95; for a review by Albert Ellis, see 5:53 (6 references).

[973]
Family Apperception Test.

Purpose: Designed to assess family system variables.
Population: Ages 6 and over.
Publication Dates: 1985–1991.
Acronym: FAT.
Scores, 35 to 40: Obvious Conflict (Family Conflict*, Marital Conflict*, Other Conflict, Absence of Conflict), Conflict Resolution (Positive Resolution, Negative or No Resolution*), Limit Setting (Appropri-ate/Compliance, Appropriate/Noncompliance*, Inappropriate/Compliance*, Inappropriate/Noncompliance*), Quality of Relationships (Mother=Ally, Father=Ally, Sibling=Ally, Spouse=Ally, Other=Ally, Mother=Stressor*, Father=Stressor*, Sibling=Stressor*, Spouse=Stressor*, Other=Stressor), Boundaries (Enmeshment*, Disengagement*, Mother/Child Coalition*, Father/Child Coalition*, Other Adult/Child Coalition*, Open System, Closed System*), Dysfunctional Circularity*, Abusive Remarks (Physical Abuse*, Sexual Abuse*, Neglect/Abandonment*, Substance Abuse*), Unusual Responses*, Refusals, Total Dysfunctional Index (total of scores with *) plus 5 optional Emotional Tone scores: Sadness/Depression, Anger/Hostility, Worry/Anxiety, Happiness/Satisfaction, Other.
Administration: Individual.
Price Data, 2002: $125 per complete kit including set of test pictures, 100 scoring sheets, and manual (1991, 36 pages); $62.50 per set of test pictures; $22.50 per 100 scoring sheets; $45 per manual.
Time: (30–35) minutes.
Comments: Projective test.
Authors: Alexander Julian III, Wayne M. Sotile, Susan E. Henry, and Mary O. Sotile.
Publisher: Western Psychological Services.
Cross References: For reviews by Mark J. Benson and Merith Cosden, see 12:150.

[974]
Family Assessment Form: A Practice-Based Approach to Assessing Family Functioning.

Purpose: Constructed to "standardize the assessment of family functioning and service planning for families receiving home-based services."
Population: Families receiving home-based services.
Publication Date: 1997.
Acronym: FAF.
Scores: 6 scales: Parent-Child Interactions, Living Conditions, Caregiver Interactions, Supports for Parents, Financial Conditions, Developmental Stimulation.
Administration: Group.
Price Data, 1997: $18.95 per test booklet/manual (79 pages).
Time: (60–90) minutes.
Comments: Ratings by child welfare practitioners.
Author: Children's Bureau of Southern California.
Publisher: Child Welfare League of America, Inc.
Cross References: For reviews by Cindy Carlson and Mary Lou Kelley, see 14:144; see also T5:1007 (1 reference).

[975]
Family Assessment Measure Version III.

Purpose: "Provides quantitative indices of family strengths and weaknesses."

Population: Families.
Publication Dates: 1993–1995.
Acronym: FAM-III.
Scores, 26: General scale (Task Accomplishment, Role Performance, Communication, Affective Expression, Involvement, Control, Values and Norms, Social Desirability, Defensiveness, Total), Dyadic Relationships (Task Accomplishment, Role Performance, Communication, Affective Expression, Involvement, Control, Values and Norms, Total), Self-Rating (Task Accomplishment, Role Performance, Communication, Affective Expression, Involvement, Control, Values and Norms, Total).
Administration: Individual.
Price Data, 2002: $135 per starter kit including manual (1995, 90 pages), 25 General Scale QuikScore™ forms, 25 Dyadic Relationship Scale QuikScore™ forms, 25 Self-Rating Scale QuikScore™ forms, and 15 MHS ColorPlot Profile of Family Perceptions; $28 per 25 General Scale QuikScore™ forms (English, Spanish, or French-Canadian); $28 per 25 Dyadic Relationship Scale QuikScore™ forms (English, Spanish, or French-Canadian); $28 per 25 Self-Rating Scale QuikScore™ forms (English, Spanish, or French-Canadian); $24 per 15 Progress Color Plot Profiles; $24 per 15 MHS ColorPlot Profile of Family Perceptions; $42 per manual; $47 per specimen set including 5 General Scale QuikScore™ forms, 10 Dyadic Relationship Scale QuikScore™ forms, 1 MHS ColorPlot Profile of Family Perceptions, and 1 Progress ColorPlot; software also available; $6 per long profile report; $4 per brief profile report; $45 per preview version including 3 profile reports and manual.
Foreign Language Editions: Spanish and French-Canadian QuikScore™ forms available.
Time: (30–40) minutes.
Authors: Harvey A. Skinner, Paul D. Steinhauer, and Jack Santa-Barbara.
Publisher: Multi-Health Systems, Inc.
Cross References: For reviews by Kenneth J. Manges and Stephen A. Spilland, see 14:145; see also T5:1008 (3 references).

[976]
Family Day Care Rating Scale.
Purpose: Assesses the quality of family day care.
Population: Consumers of day care services, day care providers, agency supervisors, and researchers.
Publication Date: 1989.
Acronym: FDCRS.
Scores, 6: Space and Furnishings for Care and Learning, Basic Care, Language and Reasoning, Learning Activities, Social Development, Adult Needs.
Administration: Group.
Price Data, 2002: $11.95 per manual (48 pages); $8.95 per 30 scoring sheets.

Time: (2) hours.
Authors: Thelma Harms and Richard M. Clifford.
Publisher: Teachers College Press.
Cross References: For a review by Annette M. Iverson, see 11:141.

[977]
Family Environment Scale [Third Edition Manual].
Purpose: Designed to assess family members' perceptions of their social environment.
Population: Ages 11–adult.
Publication Dates: 1974–1994.
Acronym: FES.
Scores, 11: Cohesion, Expressiveness, Conflict, Independence, Achievement, Intellectual-Cultural, Active-Recreational, Moral-Religious, Organization, Control, Incongruence.
Administration: Group.
Forms, 4: Real (Form R), Ideal (Form I), Expectations (Form E), Children's Version.
Price Data, 2001: $56.80 per preview kit including Form R item booklet, self-scorable answer sheet, interpretive report form, and third edition manual (1994, 96 pages); $32.30 per 25 Form R reusable item booklets; $48.40 per 25 Form I or Form E reusable item booklets; $16 per 25 nonprepaid answer sheets for use with item booklets; $10 per 25 profiles; $34 per 25 interpretive report forms; $15.40 per scoring key; $40.50 per 25 self-scorable answer sheets for use with item booklets; 56.40 per third edition manual; $32.30 per Social Climate Scales user's guide, revised.
Time: (15–20) minutes.
Comments: One component of the Social Climate Scales (T5:2445).
Authors: Rudolf H. Moos and Bernice S. Moos.
Publisher: Consulting Psychologists Press, Inc.
Cross References: For reviews by Jay A. Mancini and Michael J. Sporakowski, see 14:146; see also T5:1010 (138 references); for reviews by Julie A. Allison and Brenda H. Loyd of an earlier edition, see 12:151 (76 references); see also T4:961 (136 references); for reviews by Nancy A. Busch-Rossnagel and Nadine M. Lambert of an earlier edition, see 9:408 (18 references); see also T3:872 (14 references); for a review by Philip H. Dreyer, see 8:557 (4 references). For a review of the Social Climate Series, see 8:681.

[978]
Family Relations Test.
Purpose: "Designed to give concrete representation of the subject's childhood family."
Publication Dates: 1965–1978.
Acronym: FRT.

Scores: Nobody, Self, Father, Mother, Siblings, and Others scores for 2 areas: Outgoing Feelings, Incoming Feelings.
Administration: Individual.
Time: (20–25) minutes.
Publisher: NFER-Nelson Publishing Co., Ltd. [England].

  a) CHILDREN'S VERSION.
  Price Data, 1999: £180 per complete set; £98 per set of figures; £36 per manual (1978, 56 pages).
  Authors: Eva Bene and James Anthony.
    1) *Younger Children.*
    Population: Ages 7–12.
    Price Data: £18 per 25 record/score sheets.
    2) *Older Children.*
    Population: Ages 13–17.
    Price Data: £31 per 25 record/score sheets.
  b) ADULT VERSION.
  Population: Adults.
  Price Data: £216 per complete set; £51.50 per 25 record/score sheets.
  Author: Eva Bene.
  c) MARRIED COUPLES VERSION.
  Population: Married couples.
  Price Data: Same as for *b* above.
  Authors: Eva Bene and James Anthony (test).
Cross References: See T5:1011 (4 references), T4:962 (1 reference), 9:409 (3 references), T3:874 (33 references), 8:558 (18 references), and T2:1182 (4 references); for an excerpted review by B. Semeonoff of *a* and *b*, see 7:79 (7 references); see also P:81 (2 references); for reviews by John E. Bell, Dale B. Harris, and Arthur R. Jensen of *a*, see 5:132 (1 reference).

[979]
Family Relations Test: Children's Version.

Purpose: "To assess the relative importance that different family members have for children" and to explore the child's emotional relations with his family.
Population: Ages 3–15.
Publication Date: 1976.
Administration: Individual.
Levels, 2: Form for Young Children, Form for Older Children.
Price Data, 1999: £180 for complete set including manual (1985, 59 pages), test figures and item cards, scoring and record sheets for older children, and record/score sheets for young children.
Time: 25(40) minutes.
Authors: Eva Bene (test and revised manual) and James Anthony (test).
Publisher: NFER-Nelson Publishing Co., Ltd. [England].

  a) FORM FOR YOUNG CHILDREN.
  Population: Ages 3–7.

Scores, 8: Outgoing Feelings (Positive Total, Negative Total), Incoming Feelings (Positive Total, Negative Total), Dependency Feelings, Sum of Positive, Sum of Negative, Total Involvement.
  b) FORM FOR OLDER CHILDREN.
  Population: Ages 7–15.
  Scores, 12: Sum of Outgoing Positive, Sum of Outgoing Negative, Sum of Incoming Positive, Sum of Incoming Negative, Total Involvement, Sum of Positive Mild, Sum of Positive Strong, Sum of Negative Mild, Sum of Negative Strong, Maternal Overprotection, Paternal Overindulgence, Maternal Overindulgence.
Cross References: See T5:1012 (2 references); for reviews by Cindy I. Carlson and Steven I. Pfeiffer, see 11:142; for information on the complete test, see 9:409 (3 references), T3:874 (33 references), 8:558 (18 references), and T2:1182 (4 references); for an excerpted review by B. Semeonoff of the Children's Version and the Adult Version, see 7:79 (7 references); see also P:81 (2 references); for reviews by John E. Bell, Dale B. Harris, and Arthur R. Jensen of the Children's Version, see 5:132 (1 reference).

[980]
Family Relationship Inventory.

Purpose: "Method of examining family relationships, designed to clarify individual feelings and interpersonal behavior."
Population: Young children, adolescents, and adults.
Publication Dates: 1972–1984.
Acronym: FRI.
Scores, 2: Positive, Negative, for each family member.
Administration: Individual or family groups.
Price Data, 2002: $99 per complete kit including item cards, 25 scoring forms, 50 tabulating forms, 50 individual relationship wheel forms, 25 familygram forms, and test manual (1982, 36 pages); $43 per set of item cards; $23 per 100 scoring forms; $23 per 100 tabulating forms; $23 per 100 individual relationship wheels; $20 per 100 familygrams.
Time: Administration time not reported.
Comments: Based upon Family Relationship Scale.
Authors: Ruth B. Michaelson, Harry L. Bascom, Louise Nash, W. Lee Morrison, and Robert M. Taylor.
Publisher: Psychological Publications, Inc.
Cross References: See T5:1013 (2 references) and T4:964 (2 references); for a review by Mary Henning-Stout, see 10:112.

[981]
Family Satisfaction Scale.

Purpose: Designed to measure satisfaction on the dimensions of family cohesion and family adaptability.
Population: Families.

Publication Date: 1982.
Scores, 3: Family Cohesion, Family Adaptability, Total Family Satisfaction.
Administration: Group.
Price Data, 1998: $20 (plus postage) per manual (7 pages) and scale.
Time: Administration time not reported.
Authors: David H. Olson and Marc Wilson.
Publisher: Life Innovations, Inc.
Cross References: See T5:1014 (7 references).

[982]
Family System Test.
Purpose: Designed "for representing emotional bonds (cohesion) and hierarchical structures in the family or similar social systems."
Population: Individuals and families.
Publication Dates: 1993–1998.
Acronym: FAST.
Scores: Score information available from publisher.
Administration: Individuals or group.
Price Data, 2001: $298 per complete test including 20 recording blanks, board and schematic figures, and manual (1998, 80 pages); $19.50 per 20 recording blanks; $39.50 per manual.
Time: (5–10) minutes for individuals; (10–30) minutes for groups.
Comments: A "figural technique"; "language independent"; authorized English translation of the 1993 German edition "Familiensystemtest" (FAST).
Author: Thomas Gehring; translated from the German edition by Anita Arnone-Reitezle.
Publisher: Hogrefe & Huber Publishers.

[983]
A Family Violence Scale.
Purpose: To indicate the occurrence of family violence in one's childhood.
Population: Adolescents and adults.
Publication Dates: 1973–1988.
Scores: Total Family Violence Score.
Administration: Group.
Manual: No manual.
Price Data, 2002: $1 per scale.
Time: Administration time not reported.
Comments: Supplementary article available.
Author: Panos D. Bardis.
Publisher: Donna Bardis.
Cross References: See 8:340 (1 reference).

[984]
The Farnum String Scale: A Performance Scale for All String Instruments.
Purpose: Measurement of ability to play a stringed instrument.
Population: Grades 7–12.

Publication Date: 1969.
Scores, 4: Total score only for each test (Violin, Viola, Cello, String Bass).
Administration: Individual.
Price Data: Available from publisher.
Time: Administration time not reported.
Author: Stephen E. Farnum.
Publisher: Hal Leonard Publishing Corporation.
Cross References: For additional information and a review by Walter L. Wehner, see 8:94.

[985]
Fast Health Knowledge Test, 1986 Revision.
Purpose: "To measure discrimination and judgment in matters of health."
Population: High school and college.
Publication Date: 1986.
Scores, 11: Personal Health, Exercise-Relaxation-Sleep, Nutrition, Consumer Health, Contemporary Health Problems, Substance of Abuse, Safety and First Aid, Disease Control, Mental Health, Family Life and Sex Education, Total.
Administration: Group.
Price Data: Available from publisher.
Time: 40(50) minutes.
Author: Charles G. Fast.
Publisher: Charles G. Fast.
Cross References: For a review by Linda K. Bunker, see 10:113.

[986]
Fear of Appearing Incompetent Scale.
Purpose: Designed "to identify if individuals are concerned about maintaining or saving face around others to the extent of sacrificing tangible rewards in order to do so."
Population: Adults and college-age.
Publication Date: No date.
Scores: Total score only.
Administration: Group.
Price Data, 2001: $3 per specimen set.
Time: Administration time not reported.
Authors: L. R. Good and K. C. Good.
Publisher: Psychometric Affiliates.

[987]
Fear of Powerlessness Scale.
Purpose: Developed as "a self-report measure of the motive to avoid powerlessness."
Population: College-age and adults.
Publication Date: No date.
Scores: Total score only.
Administration: Group.
Price Data, 2001: $3 per specimen set.
Time: Administration time not reported.

Authors: L. R. Good, K. C. Good, and S. B. Golden, Jr.
Publisher: Psychometric Affiliates.

[988]
Fear of Success Scale.

Purpose: Designed as a self-report measure of fear of success.
Population: College students.
Publication Date: No date.
Scores: Total score only.
Administration: Group.
Price Data, 2001: $3 per specimen set.
Time: Administration time not reported.
Authors: L. R. Good and K. C. Good.
Publisher: Psychometric Affiliates.

[989]
Fear Survey Schedule.

Purpose: "Designed to identify and quantify patients' reactions to a variety of sources of maladaptive emotional reactions."
Population: College and adults.
Publication Dates: 1964–1977.
Acronym: FSS.
Scores: Total score only.
Administration: Group.
Price Data, 1998: $12.50 per 25 response forms and manual (1977, 11 pages); $36 per 100 response forms and manual.
Time: (15) minutes.
Comments: Self-rating.
Authors: Joseph Wolpe and Peter J. Lang.
Publisher: EdITS/Educational and Industrial Testing Service.
Cross References: See T5:1021 (48 references), T4:974 (30 references), 9:411 (23 references), and T3:883 (53 references); for a review by Charles D. Spielberger, see 8:559 (32 references); see also T2:1185 (14 references); for a review by R. G. Demaree, see 7:80 (17 references).

[990]
Feedback Edition of the Strength Deployment Inventory.

Purpose: Designed to elicit feedback to describe how a person uses his/her personal strengths in relationships.
Population: Adults.
Publication Dates: 1973–1996.
Acronym: SDI/PVI.
Scores, 20: 7 Motivational Values (Altruistic-Nurturing, Assertive-Directing, Analytic-Autonomizing, Flexible-Cohering, Assertive-Nurturing, Judicious-Competing, Cautious-Supporting), plus 13 scores reflecting Progression through Conflict.

Administration: Individual or group.
Price Data, 2001: $4.50 per test booklet; $30 per manual (1996, 146 pages).
Time: (20–40) minutes.
Comments: Uses self-ratings and ratings of a significant other person; manual is entitled Relationship Awareness Theory Manual of Administration and Interpretation (9th Ed.).
Author: Elias H. Porter.
Publisher: Personal Strengths Publishing.

[991]
Feedback Portrait of Overdone Strengths.

Purpose: Designed to elicit feedback to describe how a person uses his/her personal strengths.
Population: Adults.
Publication Date: 1997.
Scores, 3: Profile, Top Overdone Strengths, Least Overdone Strengths.
Administration: Individual or group.
Price Data, 2001: $5.50 per test booklet; $100 per manual.
Time: (20–40) minutes.
Author: Personal Strengths Publishing.
Publisher: Personal Strengths Publishing.

[992]
Feedback Portrait of Personal Strengths.

Purpose: Designed to elicit feedback to describe how a person uses his/her personal strengths in relationships.
Population: Adults.
Publication Date: 1997.
Scores, 3: Profile, Top Strengths, Least Deployed Strengths.
Administration: Individual or group.
Price Data, 2001: $5.50 per test booklet; $100 per manual.
Time: (20–40) minutes.
Author: Personal Strengths Publishing.
Publisher: Personal Strengths Publishing.

[993]
Feelings, Attitudes, and Behaviors Scale for Children.

Purpose: "Designed to assess a range of emotional and behavioral problems."
Population: Ages 6–13.
Publication Date: 1996.
Acronym: FAB-C.
Scores, 7: Conduct Problems, Self Image, Worry, Negative Peer Relationships, Antisocial, Lie, Problem Index.
Administration: Group.
Price Data, 2002: $60 per complete kit including manual (59 pages), and 25 QuikScore™ forms; $30 per

25 QuikScore™ forms; $37 per manual; $38 per specimen set including manual and 3 QuikScore™ forms.
Time: (10) minutes.
Comments: Self-report.
Author: Joseph H. Beitchman.
Publisher: Multi-Health Systems, Inc.
Cross References: For reviews by Patti L. Harrison and Mary Lou Kelley, see 14:147.

[994]
50 Grammar Quizzes for Practice and Review.
Purpose: Designed to "guide students to learn correct grammar, improve their writing skills, and write clearly and effectively."
Population: Students.
Publication Date: 1985.
Scores: No scores.
Administration: Group.
Parts, 6: Part I: Writing Clear, Complete Sentences (15 quizzes); Part II: Correcting Errors in Agreement: Pronouns and Antecedents, Subjects and Verbs (3 study guides and 9 quizzes); Part III: Correcting
Pronoun and Verb Shifts (2 sets of instructions and 5 quizzes); Part IV: Correcting Errors in the Use of Modifiers (4 quizzes); Part V: Correcting Errors in the Use of Parallel Structure (study guide and 3 quizzes); Part VI: Writing Precise, Effective Sentences (3 study guides and 14 quizzes).
Price Data: Price information available form publisher for complete set of display copy.
Time: Administration time not reported.
Comments: Reproduction rights limited to purchaser of masters and a single classroom teacher.
Author: Joan R. Markos.
Publisher: J. Weston Walch, Publisher.

[995]
Figure Classification Test.
Purpose: Designed to "measure abstract reasoning ability."
Population: Applicants for industrial work with 7 to 9 years of schooling.
Publication Date: 1976.
Scores: Total score only.
Administration: Group.
Price Data: Price information available from publisher for test materials including manual (21 pages).
Foreign Language Edition: Manual written in both English and Afrikaans.
Time: 60(70) minutes.
Comments: Separate answer sheets must be used.
Author: T. R. Taylor.
Publisher: Human Sciences Research Council [South Africa].
Cross References: See T4:978 (1 reference).

[996]
The Filipino Work Values Scale.
Purpose: "Constructed to measure work values."
Population: Filipino employees and students.
Publication Dates: 1987–1988.
Acronym: FWVS.
Scores, 10: Environmental, Familial, Intellectual-Achievement Oriented, Interpersonal, Managerial, Material, Occupational, Organizational, Religious, Variety.
Administration: Group.
Forms, 2: Employee, Student.
Price Data, 2001: $130 per employee edition complete kit including manual (1987, 39 pages), 25 scale booklets, 25 answer sheets, and manual scoring keys; $140 per student edition complete kit including manual, 25 scale booklets, 25 answer sheets, and manual scoring keys.
Foreign Language Editions: English, Tai; Philippine languages editions: Cebuano, Filipino, Pangasinense.
Time: (15–20) minutes.
Author: Vicentita M. Cervera.
Publisher: Vicentita M. Cervera [Philippines].
Cross References: For reviews by Gary J. Dean and William I. Sauser, Jr., see 14:148.

[997]
Fine Dexterity Test.
Purpose: To provide "a measure of manual dexterity using a fine test task."
Population: Applicants for jobs involving fine motor dexterity.
Publication Date: 1983.
Acronym: FDT.
Scores, 2: Finger Dexterity, Fine Tool Dexterity.
Administration: Group.
Price Data: Available from publisher.
Time: 6(8) minutes.
Author: Educational & Industrial Test Services Ltd.
Publisher: Educational & Industrial Test Services Ltd. [England].

[998]
Fire Promotion Tests—Complete Service.
Purpose: Custom-made test to fit duties and responsibilities for promotion of firefighters.
Population: Firefighters.
Publication Dates: 1979–1998.
Scores: 8 subtests: Knowledge of Fire Protection/ Prevention Practices, Fire Investigation Knowledge, Fire Attack-Related Technical Knowledge, Extinguishment-Related Technical Knowledge, Emergency Medical Care Knowledge, Supervisory and Managerial Knowledge, Administrative Knowledge, Comprehension Ability, Total.

Administration: Group.
Price Data: Available from publisher.
Time: (210) minutes.
Comments: Candidate study guide available.
Author: McCann Associates, Inc.
Publisher: McCann Associates, Inc.

[999]
Firefighter Learning Simulation.
Purpose: Designed to "simulate the learning process required of entry-level firefighters in Fire Academies."
Population: Applicants for firefighter trainee positions.
Publication Date: 1998.
Acronym: FLS.
Scores: Total score only.
Administration: Group.
Price Data: Price information available from publisher for test material including administration guide and technical manual (11 pages), and training manual (26 pages).
Time: 90 minutes.
Comments: Simulated training manual is provided to examinees in advance of the test.
Author: Psychological Services, Inc.
Publisher: Psychological Services, Inc.

[1000]
Firefighter Selection Test [Revised].
Purpose: "To rank-order applicants according to their probability of success in training and success on the job" as a firefighter.
Population: Applicants for firefighter trainee positions.
Publication Dates: 1983–1998.
Acronym: FST.
Scores: Total score only.
Administration: Group.
Price Data: Price data available from publisher for test material including Technical Manual (1998, 22 pages), Administrator's Guide (1998, 6 pages), and Study Guide (1998, 16 pages).
Time: 150 (170) minutes.
Comments: Measures mechanical comprehension, reading comprehension, and report interpretation.
Author: Psychological Services, Inc.
Publisher: Psychological Services, Inc.
Cross References: For reviews by David O. Anderson and Cynthia Ann Druva-Roush of an earlier edition, see 11:143.

[1001]
Firestone Assessment of Self-Destructive Thoughts.
Purpose: Constructed "for the clinical assessment of a patient's suicidal potential."
Population: Ages 16–80.
Publication Date: 1996.

Acronym: FAST.
Scores: No scores.
Administration: Group.
Price Data, 2002: $142 per complete kit including manual (176 pages) and 25 ReadyScore® response booklets; $61 per 25 response booklets, $86 per manual.
Time: (20) minutes.
Comments: Includes 11 levels of progressively self-destructive thoughts on a continuum ranging from Social Isolation, Eating Disorders, Substance Abuse, Self-Mutilation, and Suicide.
Authors: Robert W. Firestone and Lisa A. Firestone.
Publisher: The Psychological Corporation.
Cross References: For reviews by William E. Martin and Robert C. Reinehr, see 14:149.

[1002]
FIRO-B™ [Fundamental Interpersonal Relations Orientation–Behavior™].
Purpose: Designed "to measure behavior that derives from interpersonal needs."
Population: Age 13 and over.
Publication Dates: 1957–2000.
Acronym: FIRO-B™.
Scores, 7: 2 Overall Behavior scores (Expressed, Wanted) for each of 3 dimensions (Inclusion, Control, Affection) plus Overall Need score.
Administration: Individual or group.
Price Data, 2001: $60 per 10 FIRO-B™ self-scorable forms; $38 per 10 FIRO-B™ technical guides (2000, 77 pages); $9.35 per Introduction to the FIRO-B™; $160 per 10 prepaid Leadership Reports; $100 per 10 FIRO-B™ Interpretive Reports for Organizations.
Time: (10–15) minutes.
Comments: May be administered via paper-pencil or online at skillsone.com; earlier versions entitled FIRO Awareness Scales.
Authors: Will Schutz (original test), Allen L. Hammer (technical guide), and Eugene R. Schnell (technical guide).
Publisher: Consulting Psychologists Press, Inc.
Cross References: See T5:1036 (13 references) and T4:982 (18 references); for a review by Peter D. Lifton of an earlier edition, see 9:416 (12 references); see also T3:890 (45 references), 8:555 (147 references), and T2:1176 (58 references); for a review by Bruce Bloxom, see 7:78 (70 references); see also P:79 (30 references) and 6:94 (15 references).

[1003]
First Year Algebra Test: National Achievement Tests.
Purpose: Designed to measure the student's knowledge of first year algebra.
Population: One year high school.
Publication Dates: 1958–1962.

Scores: Total score only.
Administration: Group.
Forms, 2: A, B.
Price Data: Available from publisher.
Time: (40–45) minutes.
Authors: Ray Webb and Julius H. Hlavaty.
Publisher: Psychometric Affiliates.
Cross References: For a review by Donald L. Meyer, see 6:600.

[1004]
FirstSTEP: Screening Test for Evaluating Preschoolers.

Purpose: "Designed to identify preschool children who are at risk for developmental delays in the five areas mandated by IDEA (PL 99-457)."
Population: Preschool children.
Publication Dates: 1990–1993.
Scores, 7: Cognitive, Language, Motor, Composite, Social-Emotional, Adaptive Behavior, Parent/Teacher.
Administration: Individual.
Levels, 3: Ages 1–2, Ages 3–4, Ages 5–7.
Price Data, 2002: $195 per complete kit including 5 record forms each for levels 1, 2, and 3, 25 Social-Emotional/Adaptive Behavior booklets, 25 Parent booklets, manipulatives in a plastic case, and manual (1993, 166 pages); $34 per 25 record forms (specify level); $34 per 25 Social-Emotional Scale/Adaptive Behavior checklists; $17 per 25 Parent/Teacher Scales.
Time: (15–20) minutes.
Author: Lucy J. Miller.
Publisher: The Psychological Corporation.
Cross References: For a review by Terry Overton, see 13:126.

[1005]
The Fisher-Logemann Test of Articulation Competence.

Purpose: "Designed to ... facilitate ... analysis and categorization of articulation errors."
Population: Preschool to adult.
Publication Date: 1971.
Acronym: F-LTOAC.
Scores: No scores.
Administration: Individual.
Price Data, 2001: $164 per complete kit; $24 per manual; $89 per test portfolio; $29 per Picture Test or Sentence Articulation Test record forms.
Time: (40-45) minutes.
Authors: Hilda B. Fisher and Jerilyn A. Logemann.
Publisher: PRO-ED.
   a) PICTURE TEST.
   Population: Preschool to adult.
   Comments: 3 areas are covered: Singleton Consonants, Consonant Blends, Vowel Phonemes and Diphthongs; a shortened screening form consist-

ing of 11 of the Singleton Consonants may be administered.
   b) SENTENCE ARTICULATION TEST.
   Population: Grade 3 to adult.
   Comments: 5 areas are covered: Consonant Pairs, Singleton Consonants, Nasals, Vowel Phonemes, Diphthongs.
Cross References: See T5:1040 (11 references), T4:986 (6 references), and T3:896 (9 references); for reviews by Marie C. Fontana and Lawrence J. Turton, see 8:961.

[1006]
The Five P's (Parent/Professional Preschool Performance Profile) [Revised].

Purpose: Constructed to collect teacher and parent ratings of child's observed performance across all domains of development to produce a comprehensive profile of child's current level of functioning, to link assessment to goal setting and remediation, to monitor change over time, and to promote home/school collaboration.
Population: Children with disabilities functioning between the ages of 6 and 60 months.
Publication Dates: 1982–2001.
Scores: Index and percentile scores for 5 areas of development: Self Help Skills (Toileting and Hygiene, Mealtime Behaviors, Dressing), Language Development (Communicative Competence, Receptive Language, Expressive Language), Social Development (Classroom Adjustment, Emerging Self, Relationships to Adults, Relationships to Children), Motor Development (Gross Motor/Balance/Coordination Skills, Perceptual/Fine Motor Skills), Cognitive Development.
Administration: Individual.
Price Data, 2001: $135 per materials for class of 10 children including 10 sets of scales, 1 user manual, 10 Information & Directions, 10 graphic profiles, 1 bound copy of The Five P's Preschool Annual Goals and Short-Term Instructional Objectives; $45 per training video (25 minutes); $7.50 per set of research papers (2 papers—Validity and Reliability); $85 per sample packet including assessment packet, training video, research papers, and The Five P's Preschool Annual Goals and Short-Term Instructional objectives; $25 per The Five P's Preschool Annual Goals and Short-Term Instructional Objectives (bound copy); $25 per index and percentile scores tables; $10 per user manual; $2 per Information and Directions; $35 per technical manual.
Foreign Language Edition: Spanish edition available.
Time: (60) minutes.
Comments: Tool for parent education and staff development.
Authors: Judith Simon Bloch, John S. Hicks, and Janice L. Friedman.
Publisher: Variety Child Learning Center.

Cross References: For reviews by Annie W. Ward and Steven Zucker, see 13:127; for a review by Barbara Perry-Sheldon of an earlier edition, see 10:116.

[1007]
Flanagan Aptitude Classification Tests.

Purpose: Measurement of aptitudes for sixteen on-the-job skills.
Population: Individuals in a variety of lower-level industrial or mechanical positions.
Publication Dates: 1951–1994.
Acronym: FACT.
Scores: Total score only for each test.
Administration: Individual or group.
Price Data, 2002: $85 per start-up kit including 25 test booklets (specify test) and examiner's manual; $67 per 25 test booklets (quantity discounts available; specify test); $28 per examiner's manual.
Author: John C. Flanagan.
Publisher: Reid London House.
　a) FACT 1A, INSPECTION.
　Publication Dates: 1953–1956.
　Time: 6 minutes.
　b) FACT 2A AND 2B, CODING.
　Publication Dates: 1953–1956.
　Forms, 2: A, B.
　Time: 10 minutes.
　c) FACT 3A AND 3B, MEMORY.
　Publication Dates: 1953–1956.
　Forms, 2: A, B.
　Time: 4 minutes.
　d) FACT 4A, PRECISION.
　Publication Dates: 1953–1956.
　Time: 8 minutes.
　e) FACT 5A, ASSEMBLY.
　Publication Dates: 1953–1956.
　Time: 12 minutes.
　f) FACT 6A, SCALES.
　Publication Dates: 1953–1956.
　Time: 16 minutes.
　g) FACT 7A, COORDINATION.
　Publication Dates: 1953–1956.
　Time: 2 minutes, 40 seconds.
　h) FACT 8A, JUDGEMENT AND COMPREHENSION.
　Publication Dates: 1953–1956.
　Time: No limit (approximately 35 minutes).
　i) FACT 9A, ARITHMETIC.
　Publication Dates: 1953–1956.
　Time: 10 minutes.
　j) FACT 10A, PATTERNS.
　Publication Dates: 1953–1956.
　Time: 20 minutes.
　k) FACT 11A, COMPONENTS.
　Publication Dates: 1953–1956.
　Time: 20 minutes.

　l) FACT 12A, TABLES.
　Publication Dates: 1953–1956.
　Time: 10 minutes.
　m) FACT 13A AND 13B, MECHANICS.
　Publication Dates: 1953–1956.
　Forms, 2: A, B.
　Time: 20 minutes.
　n) FACT 14A, EXPRESSION.
　Publication Dates: 1953–1956.
　Time: No limit (approximately 30 minutes).
　o) FACT 15A, REASONING.
　Publication Dates: 1957–1960.
　Time: 24 minutes.
　p) FACT 16A, INGENUITY.
　Publication Dates: 1957–1960.
　Time: 24 minutes.
Cross References: See T3:899 (2 references), and T2:1072 (1 reference); for an excerpted review by Harold D. Murphy (with John P. McQuary), see 7:675 (10 references); for reviews by Norman Frederiksen and William B. Michael, see 6:770 (7 references); for reviews by Harold P. Bechtoldt, Ralph F. Berdie, and John B. Carroll, see 5:608.

[1008]
Flanagan Industrial Tests.

Purpose: Measurement of aptitudes for eighteen on-the-job skills.
Population: Supervisory, technical, office, skilled labor, and other industrial positions.
Publication Dates: 1960–1975.
Acronym: FIT.
Scores: Total score only for each test.
Administration: Individual or group.
Price Data, 2002: $99 per start-up kit including 25 test booklets, scoring stencil, and examinee's manual (1975, 36 pages); $63 per 25 test booklets (quantity discounts available); $20 per scoring stencil; $28 per examiner's manual.
Author: John C. Flanagan.
Publisher: Reid London House.
　a) ARITHMETIC.
　Time: 5(7) minutes.
　b) ASSEMBLY.
　Time: 10(13) minutes.
　c) COMPONENTS.
　Time: 10(12) minutes.
　d) COORDINATION.
　Price Data: $82 per start-up kit.
　Time: 5(7) minutes.
　e) ELECTRONICS.
　Time: 15(17) minutes.
　f) EXPRESSION.
　Time: 5(8) minutes.
　g) INGENUITY.
　Time: 15(18) minutes.

h) INSPECTION.
Price Data: $117 per start-up kit; $39 per scoring stencil.
Time: 5(9) minutes.
i) JUDGMENT AND COMPREHENSION.
Time: 15(17) minutes.
j) MATHEMATICS AND REASONING.
Time: 15(18) minutes.
k) MECHANICS.
Time: 15(18) minutes.
l) MEMORY.
Time: 10(19) minutes.
m) PATTERNS.
Time: 5(7) minutes.
n) PLANNING.
Time: 15(18) minutes.
o) PRECISION.
Price Data: $82 per start-up kit.
Time: 5(8) minutes.
p) SCALES.
Time: 5(7) minutes.
q) TABLES.
Time: 5(8) minutes.
r) VOCABULARY.
Time: 15(17) minutes.

Cross References: See T5:1043 (1 reference) and T4:989 (1 reference); for reviews by David O. Herman and Arthur C. MacKinney, see 8:981 (3 references); for reviews by C. J. Adcock and Robert C. Droege and an excerpted review by John L. Horn, see 7:977 (1 reference).

[1009]

Fleishman Job Analysis Survey [Revised].

Purpose: "A means for analyzing the knowledge, skills and abilities needed to perform jobs."
Population: Adults.
Publication Dates: 1992–1996.
Acronym: F-JAS.
Scores: 52 Abilities Scales: Cognitive (Oral Comprehension, Written Comprehension, Oral Expression, Written Expression, Fluency of Ideas, Originality, Memorization, Problem Sensitivity, Mathematical Reasoning, Number Facility, Deductive Reasoning, Inductive Reasoning, Information Ordering, Category Flexibility, Speed of Closure, Flexibility of Closure, Spatial Orientation, Visualization, Perceptual Speed, Selective Attention, Time Sharing), Psychomotor (Control Precision, Multilimb Coordination, Response Orientation, Rate Control, Reaction Time, Arm-Hand Steadiness, Manual Dexterity, Finger Dexterity, Wrist-Finger Speed, Speed of Limb Movement), Physical (Static Strength, Explosive Strength, Dynamic Strength, Trunk Strength, Extent Flexibility, Dynamic Flexibility, Gross Body Coordination, Gross Body Equilibrium, Stamina), Sensory/Perceptual (Near Vision, Far Vision, Visual

Color Discrimination, Night Vision, Peripheral Vision, Depth Perception, Glare Sensitivity, Hearing Sensitivity, Auditory Attention, Sound Localization, Speech Recognition, Speech Clarity).
Administration: Group.
Levels, 3: Job-Level Analysis, Job Dimension-Level Analysis, Task-Level Analysis.
Price Data, 1999: $160 per kit of 10 rating scale booklets (60 pages), self-scorable answer sheets, and tally sheets; $80 per additional packets of 5 booklets and administrator's guide; $40 per Handbook of Human Abilities (132 pages).
Time: (40) minutes.
Comments: Previously referred to as the Task Assessment Scales, Ability Requirement Scale, Manual for the Ability Requirement Scales (MARS); Handbook of Human Abilities brings together ability definitions, tasks, and jobs requiring each ability, and test descriptions and tests available to measure each ability.
Authors: Edwin A. Fleishman, Maureen E. Reilly, and David P. Costanza.
Publisher: Management Research Institute, Inc.
  a) SOCIAL/INTERPERSONAL ABILITIES.
Publication Date: 1996.
Acronym: F-JAS-2.
Scores: 21 Social/Interpersonal Skill Scales: Agreeableness, Behavior Flexibility, Coordination, Dependability, Assertiveness, Negotiation, Persuasion, Sociability, Social Conformity, Social Sensitivity, Self Control, Social Confidence, Coaching, Oral Fact Finding, Achievement Striving, Openness to Experience, Self Sufficiency, Perseverance, Resistance to Premature Judgment, Oral Defense, Resilience.
Price Data: $65 per 5 rating scale booklets including self-scoring answer sheets and tally sheets.
Time: (20) minutes.
  b) KNOWLEDGES/SKILLS.
Publication Date: 1992.
Acronym: F-JAS-3.
Scores: 33 Knowledge Scales: Administration and Management, Clerical, Economics and Accounting, Sales and Marketing, Customer and Personal Service, Personnel and Human Resources, Production and Processing, Food Production, Computers and Electronics, Engineering and Technology, Design, Building and Construction, Mechanical, Mathematics, Physics, Chemistry, Biology, Psychology, Sociology and Anthropology, Geography, Medicine and Dentistry, Therapy and Counseling, Education and Training, English Language, Foreign Language, Fine Arts, History and Archeology, Philosophy and Theology, Public Safety and Security, Law/Government and Jurisprudence, Telecommunications, Communications and Media, Transportation.

Price Data: $75 per 5 rating scale booklets including answer sheets and tally sheets.
Time: (25) minutes.

[1010]
Flex Style Negotiating.

Purpose: Designed to profile participants' preferred negotiation styles and to define legitimate versus illegitimate behaviors.
Population: Employees and managers.
Publication Date: 1997.
Scores, 3: Social Dimension, Emotional Dimension, Cognitive Dimension.
Administration: Group.
Price Data, 1998: $7.95 per self-assessment; $7.95 per 3 "other" assessments; $14.95 per assessment set consisting of 1 self- and 3 other assessments; $3.95 per situational strategy selector; $49.95 per instructor's manual (137 pages); $19.95 per participant workbook.
Time: (25) minutes.
Author: Alexander Watson Hiam.
Publisher: Human Resource Development Press.

[1011]
Fluharty Preschool Speech and Language Screening Test—Second Edition.

Purpose: Designed to identify preschool children whose speech and language skills warrant a comprehensive communication evaluation.
Population: Ages 3-0 to 6-11.
Publication Dates: 1978–2001.
Acronym: FLUHARTY-2.
Scores, 8: Articulation, Repeating Sentences, Following Directives and Answering Questions, Describing Actions, Sequencing Events, Receptive Language, Expressive Language, General Language.
Administration: Individual.
Price Data, 2001: $149 per complete kit; $29 per profile/examiner record forms; $26 per 2 blocks; $49 per picture book; $49 per examiner's manual (2001, 65 pages).
Time: (10) minutes.
Author: Nancy Buono Fluharty.
Publisher: PRO-ED.
Cross References: See T5:1047 (7 references) and T4:993 (2 references); for reviews by Nicholas W. Bankson and Harold A. Peterson of an earlier edition, see 9:422 (1 reference).

[1012]
Food Protection Certification Test.

Purpose: "To test persons who have ongoing on-site responsibility for protecting the consumer from foodborne illness in food preparation, serving, or dispensing establishments."
Population: Food industry personnel.

Publication Dates: 1985–1993.
Scores, 3: Purchasing/Receiving/Storing Food, Processing/Serving/Dispensing Food, Employees/Facilities/Equipment.
Administration: Group.
Price Data: Price information available from publisher for registration fee providing for administration and scoring of the test and mailing of results to examinee and for practice test.
Time: (120) minutes.
Comments: Tests administered per request of certified site examiner.
Author: Center for Occupational and Professional Assessment.
Publisher: Educational Testing Service.

[1013]
The Forer Structured Sentence Completion Test.

Purpose: Designed to measure personality variables and attitudes that may be of some value in treatment planning.
Population: Ages 10–18 and adults.
Publication Dates: 1957–1967.
Acronym: FSSCT.
Scores: No scores; 100 items in 18 areas: Interpersonal Figures (Mother, Males, Females, Groups, Father, Authority), Wishes, Causes of Own (Aggression, Anxiety/Fear, Giving Up [Adolescents] or Depression [Adults], Failure, Guilt, Inferiority Feelings [Adolescents]), Reactions To (Aggression, Rejection, Failure, Responsibility, School [Adolescents], Sexual Stimuli [Adults], Love and Marriage [Adults]).
Administration: Group.
Editions, 4: Separate editions for boys, girls, men, and women.
Price Data, 2002: $75 per kit including 10 tests, 10 checklists, and manual (1957, 34 pages) for any of each level; $16.50 per 25 tests (specify edition); $16.50 per 25 checklists (specify edition); $29.50 per manual.
Time: [30–45] minutes.
Author: Bertram R. Forer.
Publisher: Western Psychological Services.
Cross References: See T5:1049 (2 references), T2:1461 (3 references), and P:429 (4 references); for reviews by Charles N. Cofer and Percival M. Symonds, see 5:134 (5 references).

[1014]
Forms for Behavior Analysis with Children.

Purpose: A collection of assessment measures "designed to provide a comprehensive portrait of childhood problems with an eye to how the information can be used to design behavioral treatments."
Population: Children.
Publication Date: 1983.

Scores: 21 measures: Behavior Analysis History Questionnaire, Behavior Status Checklist, Reinforcement Survey Schedules, Assertive Behavior Survey Schedule, Bodily Cues for Tension and Anxiety, Fear Inventory, Medical History Inventory, Parental Reaction Survey Schedule, Physical Complaint Survey Schedule, School Behavior Status Checklist, Self-Evaluation Scale, Parents' and Children's Reinforcement Survey Schedule, Reinforcement Menu, Response Cost Survey Schedule, School Reinforcement Survey Schedule, Behavior Record Form, Home Visit Observation Form, Behavior Rating Card, Motivation Assessment of Parents and Children, Progress Chart, Session Report.
Administration: Group.
Forms, 5: C (child), A (adolescent), P (parent), S (school personnel), T (therapist).
Price Data, 2001: $39.95 per manual (208 pages) including reproducible forms.
Time: Administration time not reported.
Comments: Forms (C, A, P, S, T) refer to the person who is to complete the form; "Different assessment formats are encompassed, ranging from direct observations and interviews to informant ratings and self-report."
Authors: Joseph R. Cautela, Julie Cautela, and Sharon Esonis.
Publisher: Research Press.
Cross References: For reviews by Sarah J. Allen and Karen T. Carey, see 11:144.

[1015]
Four Picture Test, Third Revised Edition.

Purpose: A projective technique "of the Thematic Apperception type" requiring written, rather than verbal, responses.
Population: Ages 10 and over.
Publication Dates: 1948–1983.
Acronym: FPT.
Scores: No scores.
Administration: Group.
Price Data: Price information available from publisher for materials including manual (1983, 26 pages).
Time: (30–45) minutes.
Comments: Projective analysis guidelines provided in manual.
Author: D. J. van Lennep.
Publisher: Swets Test Publishers [The Netherlands].
Cross References: See P:431 (3 references); for a review by S. G. Lee and Johann M. Schepers of an earlier edition, see 6:213 (3 references); for reviews by John E. Bell, E. G. Bradford, and Ephraim Rosen of the original edition, see 4:105 (3 references, 1 excerpt).

[1016]
Fox in a Box: An Adventure in Literacy.

Purpose: "A diagnostic classroom assessment … measur[ing] literacy development as defined by specific, observable end-of-semester benchmarks … to inform teachers' instructional planning."
Population: Grades K–2.
Publication Date: 1998.
Administration: Individual.
Levels, 6: 1 (midyear Kindergarten), 2 (end of Kindergarten), 3 (midyear Grade 1), 4 (end of Grade 1), 5 (midyear Grade 2), 6 (end of Grade 2).
Price Data, 2002: $295 per complete kit including 12 Leveled Readers, Individual Literacy Progress Reports and Student Folders, Teacher Tools and Child Cards, Teacher's Guide (48 pages), Training Video, Fox Puppet, and flip-top storage box; $25 per 25 Literacy Progress Reports; $25 per 25 Student Folders; $28.50 per Teacher's Guide; $32 per set of Child Cards; $32 per set of Teacher Tools; $108.10 per 12 Readers; $30 per Training Video; $28.50 per Fox Puppet.
Time: (35) minutes per child for individual activities; 80 minutes collectively for small group activities.
Comments: Test is administered over a 2–3 week period of time; includes individual and 3 group activities; online Fox in a Box e-Management and Reporting System reports, aggregates, and archives each student's literacy progress, allowing teachers to enter student data into a PC or Mac, or on a handheld PDA device and into a secure web-based environment; website manages data and generates multiple reports including class, grade, school, district, state, and individualized home reports.
Author: CTB McGraw-Hill.
Publisher: CTB McGraw-Hill.

a) LEVEL 1.
Scores, 6: Measures attainment of 6 benchmarks in 4 learning strands: Phonemic Awareness, Phonics (Alphabet Recognition, Alphabet Writing, Spelling), Reading and Oral Expression, Listening and Writing.

b) LEVEL 2.
Scores, 8: Measures attainment of 8 benchmarks in 4 learning strands: Phonemic Awareness, Phonics (Alphabet Recognition, Alphabet Writing, Spelling, Decoding), Reading and Oral Expression (Sight Words, Reading), Listening and Writing.

c) LEVEL 3.
Scores, 5: Measures attainment of 5 benchmarks in 3 learning strands: Phonics (Spelling, Decoding), Reading and Oral Expression (Sight Words, Reading), Listening and Writing.

d) LEVELS 4–6.
Scores, 6: Measures attainment of 6 benchmarks in 3 learning strands: Phonics (Spelling, Decoding), Reading and Oral Expression (Sight Words, Reading, Reading Fluency), Listening and Writing.

[1017]
Frenchay Dysarthria Assessment.
Purpose: Developed to diagnose dysarthria.
Population: Ages 12 and over.
Publication Date: 1983.
Scores, 11: Reflex, Respiration, Lips, Jaw, Palate, Laryngeal, Tongue, Intelligibility, Rate, Sensation, Associated Factors.
Administration: Individual.
Price Data, 2001: $54 per complete kit including examiner's manual (59 pages) and scoring form; $29 per 25 scoring forms.
Time: [20] minutes.
Comments: Tongue depressor, stop watch, tape recorder, glass of water, and word cards needed for administration.
Author: Pamela M. Enderby.
Publisher: PRO-ED.
Cross References: See T5:1056 (2 references); for reviews by Steven B. Leder and Malcolm R. McNeil, see 12:154; see also T4:1007 (2 references).

[1018]
Friedman Well-Being Scale.
Purpose: "Designed to assess the level of well-being of an individual."
Population: Adults.
Publication Dates: 1992–1994.
Acronym: FWBS.
Scores, 6: Composite/Total, Sociability, Self-Esteem, Joviality, Emotional Stability, Happiness.
Administration: Group.
Price Data, 2001: $25 per sampler set including manual (1992, 62 pages), questionnaire, and scoring materials; $125 per permission set including sampler set plus permission to reproduce up to 200 copies of the questionnaire.
Time: (2–3) minutes.
Comments: Scale for rating perception of others or for self-rating; self-administered, administrator scored.
Author: Phillip H. Friedman.
Publisher: Mind Garden, Inc.
Cross References: For a review by John W. Fleenor, see 14:152.

[1019]
Frontal Systems Behavior Scale.
Purpose: "Provides a means ... to quantify behavioral change due to frontal lobe lesions."
Population: Ages 18–95.
Publication Date: 2001.
Acronym: FrSBe.
Scores, 4: Apathy (subscale A), Disinhibition (subscale D), Executive Dysfunction (subscale E), Total Score.
Administration: Individual or group.
Forms, 2: Family Rating Form, Self-Rating Form.
Price Data, 2002: $145 per introductory kit including professional manual (109 pages), 25 hand-scorable Self-Rating test booklets, 25 hand-scorable Family Rating test booklets, 25 Self-Rating profile forms, and 25 Family Rating profile forms; $40 per professional manual; $49 per 25 hand-scorable test booklets (Self-Rating or Family Rating); $15 per 25 profile forms (Self-Rating or Family Rating).
Time: 10 minutes to administer; 10–15 minutes to score.
Comments: Revision of the Frontal Lobe Personality Scale; available in paper-and-pencil form only; obtains ratings of patients's behavior before and after an injury or illness.
Authors: Janet Grace and Paul F. Malloy.
Publisher: Psychological Assessment Resources, Inc.

[1020]
Fuld Object-Memory Evaluation.
Purpose: Designed to "evaluate memory and learning under conditions that virtually guarantee attention and minimize anxiety."
Population: Ages 70–90 regardless of language and sensory handicaps.
Publication Date: 1977.
Acronym: FOME.
Scores, 5: Total Recall, Storage, Consistency of Retrieval, Ability to Benefit from Reminding, Ability to Say Words in Categories.
Administration: Individual.
Forms, 2: Record Form I, II.
Price Data, 2001: $75 per complete kit; $25 per 30 record forms; $25 per manual (24 pages).
Time: Administration time not reported.
Author: Paula Altman Fuld.
Publisher: Stoelting Co.
Cross References: See T5:1058 (9 references) and T4:1009 (6 references); for a review by Eric F. Gardner, see 9:427.

[1021]
The Fullerton Language Test for Adolescents, Second Edition.
Purpose: Constructed to "distinguish normal from language-impaired adolescents."
Population: Ages 11–18.
Publication Dates: 1980–1986.
Scores, 8: Auditory Synthesis, Morphology Competency, Oral Commands, Convergent Production, Divergent Production, Syllabication, Grammatic Competency, Idioms.
Administration: Individual.
Price Data, 2002: $76 per complete kit including stimulus items, 25 scoring forms and profiles, and manual (1986, 55 pages); $29 per set of stimulus items; $24 per 25 scoring forms and profiles; $34 per manual.

Time: (45) minutes.
Author: Arden R. Thorum.
Publisher: PRO-ED.
Cross References: See T5:1060 (7 references) and T4:1011 (3 references); for a review by Diane J. Sawyer of the experimental edition, see 10:122; for a review by Margaret C. Byrne, see 9:428.

[1022]
Functional Communication Profile.

Purpose: Designed to measure functional language performance in aphasic patients.
Population: Aphasic adults.
Publication Dates: 1956–1969.
Acronym: FCP.
Scores, 6: Movement, Speaking, Understanding, Reading, Other, Total.
Administration: Individual.
Price Data: Available from publisher.
Time: (15–30) minutes for interview.
Comments: Ratings by experienced clinician following nonstructured interview.
Author: Martha Taylor Sarno.
Publisher: Institute of Rehabilitation Medicine, New York University Medical Center [No reply from publisher; status unknown].
Cross References: See T5:1061 (1 reference), T4:1012 (3 references), and T3:925 (3 references); for reviews by Raphael M. Haller and Harvey Halpern, see 8:962 (11 references).

[1023]
Functional Fitness Assessment for Adults Over 60 Years, Second Edition.

Purpose: Developed as a field test to determine the functional capacity of older adults.
Population: Adults over age 60.
Publication Dates: 1990–1996.
Scores, 7: Body Composition (Body Weight, Standing Height Measurement), Flexibility, Agility/Dynamic Balance, Coordination, Strength/Endurance, Endurance.
Administration: Group.
Price Data, 2001: $12 per manual (1996, 60 pages).
Time: Administration time not reported.
Authors: Wayne H. Osness, Marlene Adrian, Bruce Clark, Werner Hoeger, Dianne Raab, and Robert Wiswell.
Publisher: American Association for Active Lifestyles and Fitness.
Cross References: For reviews by Matthew E. Lambert and Cecil R. Reynolds of an earlier edition, see 13:128.

[1024]
Functional Grammar Test.

Purpose: To assess student mastery of English grammar.
Population: High school and college.
Publication Date: 1970.
Acronym: FGT.
Scores: Total score only.
Administration: Group.
Forms, 2: A, B.
Price Data: Available from publisher.
Time: (15–20) minutes.
Author: Joyce E. Lackey.
Publisher: Psychometric Affiliates.

[1025]
Functional Linguistic Communication Inventory.

Purpose: "Designed to quantify the functional linguistic communication skills of moderately and severely demented individuals."
Population: Adults diagnosed with Alzheimer's disease.
Publication Date: 1994.
Acronym: FLCI.
Scores, 11: Greeting and Naming, Question Answering, Writing, Comprehension of Signs and Object-to-Picture Matching, Word Reading and Comprehension, Reminiscing, Following Commands, Pantomime, Gesture, Conversation, Total.
Administration: Individual.
Price Data, 2002: $169 per complete kit including manual (31 pages), 25 response record forms, 25 score forms, stimulus book (50 pages), and 3 objects (comb, pencil, mask); $19 per 25 response record forms; $9 per 25 score sheets; $49 per manual; $89 per stimulus book; $9 per kit including comb, pencil, and mask.
Time: (30) minutes.
Authors: Kathryn A. Bayles and Cheryl K. Tomoeda.
Publisher: PRO-ED.
Cross References: For reviews by Cameron J. Camp and Jennifer A. Brush and by Wilfred G. Van Gorp, see 13:129.

[1026]
Functional Performance Record.

Purpose: "For recording the observable actions and behaviours of people whose physical, social or psychological functioning is impaired."
Population: Individuals of all ages with disabilities.
Publication Date: 1989.
Acronym: FPR.
Scores: 27 topic areas: Activity Level, Aggression, Attention Span, Domestic/Survival Skills, Dressing Female/Male, Feeding, Fits and Faints, Hearing, Incontinence, Memory, Mobility, Motor Co-ordination and

Loss of Balance, Movement of Limbs and Trunk, Number Skills, Personal Hygiene, Personal Safety, Reading Skills, Social Behaviour, Socially Unacceptable Behaviour, Speech and Language Reception, Speech and Language Production, Toileting, Touch, Temperature and Hypothermia, Transportation, Vision, Writing Skills.

Administration: Individual.

Price Data, 1999: £67 per administration manual (33 pages); £25.75 per 5 checklists; £299 per software starter set, 3.5-inch version; £87.50 per paper-and-pencil starter set.

Time: Untimed.

Author: David J. Mulhall.

Publisher: NFER-Nelson Publishing Co., Ltd. [England].

Cross References: See T5:1066 (1 reference); for reviews by Delwyn L. Harnisch and Deborah D. Roman, see 12:156.

[1027]
Functional Skills Screening Inventory.

Purpose: "To be used in natural settings to assess critical living and working skills in persons with moderate to severe handicapping conditions."

Population: Age 6 through adult.

Publication Dates: 1984–1986.

Acronym: FSSI.

Scores, 9: Categorized into 3 priority levels: Basic Skills and Concepts, Communication, Personal Care, Homemaking, Work Skills and Concepts, Community Living, Social Awareness, Functional Skills Subtotal, Problem Behaviors.

Administration: Individual.

Price Data, 2001: $125 per master print copy including assessment booklet for unlimited assessments, hand-scoring sheets, and user guide (1986, 117 pages); $450 per Windows interactive computer program; web site provides demo with documentation.

Time: [60–120] minutes per assessment.

Comment: A domain-referenced behavioral checklist.

Authors: Heather Becker, Sally Schur, Michele Paoletti-Schelp, and Ed Hammer.

Publisher: Functional Resources.

Cross References: See T5:1067 (1 reference); for reviews by Diane Browder and G. Michael Poteat, see 10:123 (3 references).

[1028]
GAINS: A Pre-test and Post-test for Measuring Career Development Competency Progress.

Purpose: A diagnostic tool for assessing level of competency accrued from career development studies.

Population: Grades 4–7, 8–11.

Publication Date: 1995.

Acronym: GAINS I, GAINS II.

Scores, 2: Pre-Test Total, Post-Test Total, Modified Percent Gain.

Administration: Group.

Price Data, 1995: $55 per classroom set including 30 tests and teacher's guide (specify GAINS I or GAINS II; volume discounts available).

Time: Testing time specified by teacher based on reading ability; pre-test and post-test must use the same time limit.

Author: Norene Lindsay.

Publisher: Wintergreen/Orchard House, Inc.

[1029]
The Gardner Children's Projective Battery.

Purpose: Designed to elicit themes in a child's psychodynamics.

Population: Children who are able to respond verbally to questions about their thoughts and perceptions.

Publication Date: 1999.

Acronym: GCPB.

Scores: Not quantitatively scored.

Administration: Individual.

Price Data, 1999: $114.95 + $10.35 shipping per test kit; $89.95 + $8.50 shipping per battery only; $25 + $5.50 shipping per book only (entitled Clinical Utilization of the Gardner Children's Projective Battery).

Time: (180–240) minutes.

Comments: Respondents' answers are evaluated qualitatively based on guidelines provided by the author; 17-item test given over several sessions.

Author: Richard A. Gardner.

Publisher: Creative Therapeutics, Inc.

[1030]
Gates-MacGinitie Reading Tests, 2nd Canadian Edition.

Purpose: Constructed to assess reading achievement.

Publication Dates: 1978–1992.

Administration: Group.

Forms, 2: 3, 4.

Price Data, 2001: $49.95 per 35 test booklets (select level); $7.40 per scoring key (select level); $11.20 per 10 class record sheets; $37.50 per manual (select level); $30 per out-of-level norms booklet; $38.20 per examination kit; scoring service available from publisher.

Comments: 1981 edition still available.

Authors: Walter H. MacGinitie and Ruth K. MacGinitie.

Publisher: Nelson Thomson Learning [Canada].

a) LEVEL PRE.

Population: Grades K.7–1.2.

Scores: Total score only.

Price Data: $46.95 per test booklets.

Time: (90) minutes

b) LEVEL R.
Population: Grades 1.0–1.9.
Scores: Total score only.
Time: (70) minutes.
c) LEVEL A.
Population: Grades 1.3–1.9.
Scores, 3: Vocabulary, Comprehension, Total.
Price Data: $7.90 per decoding skills analysis forms.
Time: 55 minutes.
d) LEVEL B.
Population: Grade 2.
Scores, 3: Same as for *c* above.
Price Data: Same as for *c* above.
Time: Same as for *c* above.
e) LEVEL C.
Population: Grade 3.
Scores, 3: Same as for *c* above.
Time: Same as for *c* above.
f) LEVEL D 4.
Population: Grade 4.
Scores, 3: Same as for *c* above.
Price Data: $30.75 per 35 hand-scorable answer sheets; $73.70 per 100 hand-scorable answer sheets; $320 per 250 machine-scorable answer sheets; $15.10 per set of scoring stencils.
Time: Same as for *c* above.
g) LEVEL D 5/6.
Population: Grades 5–6.
Scores, 3: Same as for *c* above.
Price Data: Same as for *f* above.
h) LEVEL E.
Population: Grades 7–9.
Scores, 3: Same as for *c* above.
Price Data: Same as for *f* above.
Time: Same as for *c* above.
i) LEVEL F.
Population: Grades 10–12.
Scores, 3: Same as for *c* above.
Price Data: Same as for *f* above.
Time: Same as for *c* above.
Cross References: See T5:1071 (5 references) and T4:1021 (6 references); for reviews by Mariam Jean Dreher and Susanna W. Pflaum of an earlier edition, see 9:431.

[1031]
Gates-MacGinitie Reading Tests, Third Edition.

Purpose: Measures reading achievement.
Population: Grades K.6–12.
Publication Dates: 1926–1989.
Acronym: GMRT.
Scores, 11: Literacy Concepts, Reading Instruction Relational Concepts, Oral Language Concepts, Letters and Letter-Sound Correspondences, Initial Consonants, Final Consonants, Vowels, Use of Context, Vocabulary, Comprehension, Total.
Administration: Group.
Levels: 9.
Forms, 2: K, L.
Price Data, 2002: $17.50 per scoring booklet for any one level; $18.50 per 35 class summary sheets; $21.50 per technical report (1989, 92 pages); $12 per administrator's summary; $additional prince information available from publisher.
Time: (55–105) minutes.
Authors: Walter H. MacGinitie and Ruth K. MacGinitie.
Publisher: Riverside Publishing.

[1032]
Gates-McKillop-Horowitz Reading Diagnostic Test, Second Edition.

Purpose: "Assess the strengths and weaknesses in reading and related areas of a particular child."
Population: Grades 1–6.
Publication Dates: 1962–1981.
Scores, 23: Omissions, Additions, Repetitions, Mispronunciations (Directional Errors, Wrong Beginning, Wrong Middle, Wrong Ending, Wrong in Several Parts, Accent Errors, Total), Reading Sentences, Words-Flash, Words-Untimed, Word-Attack (Syllabication, Recognizing and Blending Common Word Parts, Reading Words, Giving Letter Sounds, Naming Capital Letters, Naming Lower-Case Letters), Vowels, Auditory (Blending, Discrimination), Spelling.
Administration: Individual.
Price Data, 2002: $2.50 per test materials; $7.50 per 30 pupil record booklets; $1 per manual of directions (1981, 16 pages); $3.95 per manual of directions kit (includes test materials, 1 pupil record booklet, manual of directions).
Time: Administration time not reported.
Comments: Revision of Gates-McKillop Reading Diagnostic Tests.
Authors: Arthur I. Gates, Anne S. McKillop, and Elizabeth Cliff Horowitz.
Publisher: Teachers College Press.
Cross References: See T5:1072 (3 references) and T4:1023 (3 references); for reviews by Priscilla A. Drum and P. David Pearson and Patricia Herman, see 9:432 (2 references); for a review by Harry Singer of an earlier edition, see 8:759 (8 references); see also T2:1629 (11 references); for reviews by N. Dale Bryant and Gabriel M. Della-Piana, see 6:824 (2 references); for a review by George D. Spache of the earlier edition, see 5:662; for a review by T. L. Torgerson, see 3:510 (3 references).

[1033]
The Geist Picture Interest Inventory.

Purpose: Designed to "assess quantitatively eleven male and twelve female general interest areas and identify motivating forces behind occupational choice."
Population: Grades 8–16 and adults.
Publication Dates: 1959–1971.
Acronym: GPII.
Scores: 18 (males) or 19 (females) scores: 11 or 12 Interest scores (Persuasive, Clerical, Mechanical, Musical, Scientific, Outdoor, Literary, Computational, Artistic, Social Service, Dramatic, Personal Service—females only), and 7 Motivation scores (Family, Prestige, Financial, Intrinsic and Personality, Environmental, Past Experience, Could Not Say).
Administration: Group or individual.
Forms, 2: M (male), F (female).
Price Data, 2002: $79.95 per kit including 10 tests of each form (male or female), and manual (1971, 42 pages plus tests and motivation questionnaires); $34.50 per 20 tests of male form; $32.50 per 20 tests of female form; $52 per manual; $13.50 per 20 motivation questionnaires of male form; $10.50 per 20 motivation questionnaires of female form.
Time: (40–65) minutes.
Author: Harold Geist.
Publisher: Western Psychological Services.
Cross References: See T2:2180 (18 references); for reviews by Milton E. Hahn and Benjamin Shimberg, and an excerpted review by David V. Tiedeman, see 6:1054 (12 references).

[1034]
General Ability Measure for Adults.

Purpose: "Designed to evaluate intellectual ability using abstract designs."
Population: Ages 18–96.
Publication Date: 1997.
Acronym: GAMA.
Scores, 5: Matching, Analogies, Sequences, Construction, GAMA IQ Score.
Administration: Individual and/or group.
Price Data: Available from publisher.
Time: (25) minutes.
Comments: May be self-administered.
Authors: Jack A. Naglieri and Achilles N. Bardos.
Publisher: NCS (Minnetonka).
Cross References: For reviews by Robert Fitzpatrick and Bert A. Goldman, see 14:153.

[1035]
General Chemistry Test: National Achievement Tests.

Purpose: Designed to measure students' knowledge in three areas of general chemistry.
Population: Grades 10–16.
Publication Dates: 1958–1959.
Scores, 4: Uses-Processes-Results, Formulae and Valence, Miscellaneous Facts, Total.
Administration: Group.
Manual: No manual.
Price Data: Available from publisher.
Time: 40(45) minutes.
Authors: Lester D. Crow and Roy S. Cook.
Publisher: Psychometric Affiliates.
Cross References: See T4:1025 (1 reference); for a review by J. A. Campbell, see 6:918.

[1036]
General Clerical Ability Test: ETSA Test 3A.

Purpose: Measures the general skills required of clerical office work.
Population: Employment applicants.
Publication Dates: 1960–1998.
Scores: Total score only.
Administration: Group or individual.
Price Data, 2002: $10 per electronic test; $10 each per test booklet and answer sheet (scoring and reporting); $20 per administrator's manual; $20 per technical manual.
Time: 30 minutes.
Comments: Electronic tests available at www.etsatests.com.
Author: Psychological Services Bureau, Inc.
Publisher: Employers' Tests and Services Associates.
Cross References: For reviews by Marvin D. Dunnette and Raymond A. Katzell of an earlier version of the ETSA Tests, see 6:1025.

[1037]
General Clerical Test.

Purpose: Developed to assess clerical speed and accuracy, numerical skills, and language-related skills.
Population: Clerical applicants and workers.
Publication Dates: 1972–1988.
Acronym: GCT.
Scores, 4: Clerical, Numerical, Verbal, Total.
Administration: Group or individual.
Price Data, 2002: $133 per 25 Clerical/Numerical/Verbal test booklets; $88 per 25 Clerical/Numerical test booklets; $63 per 25 Verbal test booklets; $492 per 100 Clerical/Numerical/Verbal test booklets; $318 per 100 Clerical/Numerical test booklets; $190 per 100 Verbal only test booklets; $45 per set of handscoring keys; $40.50 per manual (1988, 68 pages); $50 per examination kit.
Time: 60 minutes.
Author: The Psychological Corporation.
Publisher: The Psychological Corporation.

Cross References: See T5:1078 (1 reference); for reviews by Dianna L. Newman and Alfred L. Smith, Jr., see 12:158.

[1038]
General Health Questionnaire.

Purpose: Designed to screen for nonpsychotic psychiatric disorders.
Population: Adolescents to adults.
Publication Dates: 1969–1988.
Scores: Total scores only for GHQ-60 and GHQ-30; Total and scale scores for GHQ-28: Somatic Symptoms, Anxiety/Insomnia, Social Dysfunction, Severe Depression.
Administration: Group.
Forms, 4: GHQ-60, GHQ-30 (short form), GHQ-28 (research form), GHQ-12.
Price Data, 1999: £46.50 per user's guide; £18 per 25 GHQ-60 record forms; £12 per 25 GHQ-30 record forms; £41.50 per 100 GHQ-28 record sorms; £12 per 25 GHQ-28 record forms; $28.50 per 100 GHQ-12 record forms.
Time: [3–8] minutes.
Comments: Self-administered.
Authors: David Goldberg and Paul Williams (user's guide).
Publisher: NFER-Nelson Publishing Co., Ltd. [England].
Cross References: See T5:1079 (112 references); for reviews by Steven G. LoBello and Cecil R. Reynolds, see 12:159 (88 references); see also T4:1028 (183 references); for a review by John D. Black of an earlier edition, see 9:434 (50 references); see also T3:941 (34 references) and 8:565 (15 references).

[1039]
General Management In-Basket.

Purpose: "Designed to assess supervisory/managerial skills independent of any particular job classification; may be used for selection and/or career development."
Population: Supervisors and managers.
Publication Dates: 1986–2002.
Acronym: GMIB.
Scores, 5: Leadership Style and Practices, Handling Priorities and Sensitive Situations, Managing Conflict, Organizational Practices/Management Control, Total.
Administration: Group or individual.
Forms, 4: Private and public sector forms include Executive Version, Police Versions, Fire Versions, and Engineer Versions.
Restricted Distribution: Clients must pay a one-time overhead/sign-up fee of $300.
Price Data, 2002: $145 per candidate for rental/scoring and bar chart; $75 per optional Career Development Report.
Time: 165 (175) minutes.

Author: Richard C. Joines.
Publisher: Management & Personnel Systems, Inc.
Cross References: For reviews by S. David Kriska and William J. Waldron, see 12:160.

[1040]
General Mental Ability Test: ETSA Test 1A.

Purpose: Measurement of "ability to learn."
Population: Employment applicants.
Publication Dates: 1960–1998.
Scores: Total score only.
Administration: Group or individual.
Price Data, 2002: $10 per test booklet and answer sheet (scoring and reporting); $10 per electronic test; $20 per administrator's manual; $20 per technical manual.
Time: (45) minutes.
Comments: Electronic tests available at www.etsatests.com.
Author: Psychological Services Bureau, Inc.
Publisher: Employers' Tests and Services Associates.
Cross References: See T3:942 (1 reference); for reviews by Marvin D. Dunnette and Raymond A. Katzell of an earlier version of the ETSA Tests, see 6:1025.

[1041]
General Physics Test: National Achievement Tests.

Purpose: "Constructed to test the student's basic knowledge of Physics and his ability to apply that knowledge."
Population: Grades 10–16.
Publication Dates: 1958–1962.
Scores, 3: Uses and Application of Principles, Miscellaneous Facts and Scientists, Total.
Administration: Group.
Manual: No manual.
Price Data: Available from publisher.
Time: 40(45) minutes.
Authors: Lester D. Crow and Roy S. Cook.
Publisher: Psychometric Affiliates.
Cross References: For a review by Theodore G. Phillips, see 6:930.

[1042]
General Processing Inventory.

Purpose: Designed to identify learning disabilities.
Population: Ages 5–75 years.
Publication Dates: 1986–1996.
Acronym: GPI.
Scores, 7: Graphomotor, Short Term Memory Retrieval, Long Term Memory Retrieval, Visual (Dyslexia), Auditory, Speech (Dysphasia), Total.
Subtests, 2: General Elementary Inventory of Language Skills (GEILS), General Elementary Inventory of Mathematics and Numeration (GEIMAN).

Administration: Individual.
Levels, 4: One (5 years old), Two (Above 6 years), Three (Above 8 years), Four (Above 10 years).
Price Data, 1999: $350 per test kit; $400 for training required to administer test.
Time: (60–180) minutes.
Comments: Training required; psychologists and other licensed test administrators will learn to tabulate errors and may send their results to publisher for report writing. There is a fee for report writing dependent on volume.
Author: Ruth M. Geiman.
Publisher: Ruth M. Geiman, Ph.D.
Cross References: For reviews by Sherry K. Bain and Stephen A. Spillane, see 14:154.

[1043]
General Science Test: National Achievement Tests.

Purpose: Designed to measure students' knowledge of general science.
Population: Grades 7–9.
Publication Dates: 1936–1950.
Scores, 7: General Concepts, Identifications, Men of Science, Definitions, Uses of Objects, Miscellaneous Facts, Total.
Administration: Group.
Manual: No manual.
Price Data: Available from publisher.
Time: (30–45) minutes.
Authors: Robert K. Speer, Lester D. Crow, and Samuel Smith.
Publisher: Psychometric Affiliates.
Cross References: For a review by Robert M. W. Travers, see 5:712; for reviews by Francis D. Curtis and G. W. Hunter, see 2:1602.

[1044]
The Gesell Developmental Observation.

Purpose: Assesses a child's developmental age to aid in grade placement and development of instructional programs.
Population: Ages 4.5–9.
Publication Dates: 1964–1980.
Administration: Individual.
Price Data, 2001: $30.95 per Gesell Assessment Kit including right and left assessments, Monroe Visual III, Monroe Visual I, copy form, cylinder and cube, cubes, and cube assessment direction booklet; $22.95 per School Readiness text: manual (1978, 238 pages); $21.50 per manual (Spanish Edition).
Foreign Language Edition: Also available in Spanish.
Comments: Manual title is School Readiness; test formerly called The Gesell School Readiness Test.

Authors: Frances L. Ilg, Louise Bates Ames, Jacqueline Haines, and Clyde Gillespie.
Publisher: Modern Learning Press, Inc.
   a) KINDERGARTEN ASSESSMENT.
   Population: Ages 4.5–6.
   Subtests, 6: Interview, Cube Test, Paper and Pencil Test, Copy Forms, Incomplete Man, Animals and Interests Test.
   Price Data: $99.50 per kindergarten start-up package; $38.75 per 50 kindergarten assessment recording sheets.
   Time: (20) minutes.
   b) SCHOOL-AGE ASSESSMENT.
   Population: Ages 5–9 years.
   Subtests, 9: Interview, Cube Test, Paper and Pencil Test, Copy Forms, Incomplete Man, Right and Left, Monroe Visual I Test, Animals and Interests Test, Monroe Visual III Test.
   Price Data: $115 per school-age start-up package; $45 per 50 school-age assessment recording sheets.
   Time: (40) minutes.
Cross References: See T5:1085 (4 references) and T4:1035 (13 references); for reviews by Robert H. Bradley and Everett Waters, see 9:438; see also T3:953 (6 references) and T2:1703 (4 references); for excerpted reviews by L. J. Borstelmann and Edith Meyer Taylor, see 7:750 (5 references).

[1045]
Gesell Preschool Test.

Purpose: "Designed to measure . . . relative maturity ratings in four basic fields of behavior."
Population: Ages 2.5–6.
Publication Date: 1980.
Scores: Ratings in 4 areas: Motor, Adaptive, Language, Personal-Social.
Administration: Group.
Price Data, 2001: $127.30 per kit (reusable materials only); $29 per formboard; $28 per picture vocabulary cards; $10 per color forms; $9 per letters and numbers; $5.50 per pellets and bottles; $12.50 per copy forms; $14.95 per manual (72 pages); $5 per 25 developmental schedules; $9.50 per 10 one-inch cubes; $13.75 per typical response cards for incomplete man test.
Time: (30-45) minutes.
Comments: Abbreviated adaptation of the Gesell Developmental Schedules (see 6:522) and the Gesell Developmental Tests (see 7:750).
Authors: Jacqueline Haines, Louise Bates Ames, and Clyde Gillespie.
Publisher: Modern Learning Press, Inc.
Cross References: See T5:1086 (4 references); for reviews by Nadeen L. Kaufman and Jack A. Naglieri, see 9:437 (8 references).

[1046]
Gibson Spiral Maze, Second Edition.
Purpose: Measures "the speed, accuracy, and general style of people's muscular reactions in response to carefully controlled stimuli."
Population: Children and adults.
Publication Dates: 1961–1965.
Scores, 2: Time score, Error score.
Administration: Individual.
Price Data, 2002: £13.99 per test 20 copies; manual and specimen set are now out of print.
Time: (2) minutes.
Comments: Forms part of the Clifton Assessment Procedures for the Elderly (526).
Author: H. B. Gibson.
Publisher: Hodder & Stoughton Educational [England].
Cross References: For reviews by William K. Wilkinson and James Ysseldyke, see 14:155; see also T4:1037 (3 references), T3:955 (1 reference), T2:1191 (3 references), 7:82 (3 references), and P:90 (2 references).

[1047]
Gifted Evaluation Scale, Second Edition.
Purpose: Designed to help identify gifted students.
Population: Ages 5–18.
Publication Dates: 1987–2000.
Acronym: GES-2.
Scores, 8: 6 subscales (Intellectual, Creativity, Specific Academic Aptitude, Leadership Ability, Performing and Visual Arts, Motivation [optional]), Quotient Score, Percentile Score.
Administration: Individual.
Price Data, 2002: $69 per complete kit including technical manual (1998, 60 pages), 50 rating forms, and Gifted Intervention Manual (1990, 107 pages); $10 per 50 motivation scoring forms; $14 per technical manual; $33 per 50 rating forms; $22 per Gifted Intervention Manual; $4 per subscale percentile tables.
Time: (15–20) minutes.
Comments: Ratings by "anyone familiar with the student's behavior patterns and specific skills ... (e.g., teacher, counselor, etc.)."
Authors: Diana Henage (The Gifted Intervention Manual), Stephen B. McCarney and Paul D. Anderson (technical manual and subscale percentile tables).
Publisher: Hawthorne Educational Services, Inc.
Cross References: For reviews by Douglas K. Smith and John W. Young, see 14:156; see also T5:1089 (2 references); for reviews by Carolyn M. Callahan and Ross E. Traub of an earlier edition, see 12:162 (1 reference).

[1048]
Gilliam Asperger's Disorder Scale.
Purpose: Designed to evaluate children with unique behavioral problems who may have Asperger's Disorder.

Population: Ages 3–22 years.
Publication Date: 2001.
Acronym: GADS.
Scores, 4: Social Interaction, Restricted Patterns of Behavior, Cognitive Patterns, Pragmatic Skills.
Administration: Individual.
Price Data, 2001: $89 per complete kit including examiner's manual (52 pages) and 25 summary/response forms; $52 per examiner's manual; $39 per 25 summary/response booklets.
Time: (5–10) minutes.
Author: James E. Gilliam.
Publisher: PRO-ED.

[1049]
Gilliam Autism Rating Scale.
Purpose: Constructed to "help professionals diagnose autism" and estimate the severity of the problem.
Population: Ages 3–22.
Publication Date: 1995.
Acronym: GARS.
Scores: 4 subscales (Stereotyped Behaviors, Communication, Social Interaction, Developmental), plus Autism Quotient.
Administration: Individual.
Price Data, 2001: $86 per complete kit includingexaminer's manual (45 pages) and 25 summary/response forms in storage box; $39 per 25 summary/response forms; $49 per examiner's manual.
Time: (5–10) minutes.
Comments: Ratings by teacher, teacher's aide, or parent.
Author: James E. Gilliam.
Publisher: PRO-ED.
Cross References: For reviews by Donald P. Oswald and Steven Welsh, see 13:130.

[1050]
Gilmore Oral Reading Test.
Purpose: "Developed to provide ... a means of analyzing the oral reading performance of pupils."
Population: Grades 1–8.
Publication Dates: 1951–1968.
Acronym: GORT.
Scores, 3: Accuracy, Comprehension, Rate.
Administration: Individual.
Forms, 2: C, D.
Price Data, 2002: $24.50 per examination kit including manual (1968, 31 pages) and record blank; $41.25 per reading paragraphs (both forms); $70 per 35 record blanks (specify Form C or D); $22 per manual.
Time: (15–20) minutes.
Author: John V. Gilmore and Eunice C. Gilmore.
Publisher: Harcourt Educational Measurement.
Cross References: See T5:1092 (18 references), T4:1042 (21 references), and T3:958 (13 references);

for an excerpted review by Jerry Stafford, see 8:785 (17 references); see also T2:1679 (5 references); for reviews by Albert J. Harris and Kenneth J. Smith, see 7:737 (17 references); for reviews by Lydia A. Duggins and Maynard C. Reynolds of the original edition, see 5:671.

[1051]

Giotto.

Purpose: To provide a wide-ranging measure of personal integrity for use in staff selection.
Population: Adults.
Publication Dates: 1996–1997.
Scores: 7 scales: Prudence, Fortitude, Temperance, Justice, Faith, Charity, Hope.
Administration: Group or individual.
Price Data, 2002: $361.94 per complete set including answer booklet, scoring software, and manual (1997, 79 pages).
Time: (5–20) minutes.
Comments: Must be scored by computer on Giotto software using Windows 3.1 or Windows 95.
Author: John Rust.
Publisher: The Psychological Corporation Europe [United Kingdom].

[1052]

Global Assessment Scale.

Purpose: "For evaluating the overall functioning of a subject during a specified time period on a continuum from psychological or psychiatric sickness to health."
Population: Psychiatric patients and possible psychiatric patients.
Publication Dates: 1976-1985.
Acronym: GAS.
Scores: Mental Health-Illness rating of individual on a continuum of 1 to 100.
Administration: Individual.
Price Data, 2001: $.50 per scale; $2.50 per case vignettes and keys (1985, 17 pages); $1 per instructions (1978, 8 pages).
Authors: Robert L. Spitzer, Miriam Gibbon, and Jean Endicott.
Publisher: Department of Research Assessment and Training.
Cross References: See T5:1093 (116 references) and T4:1043 (62 references); for a review by Michael J. Subkoviak, see 11:147 (22 references).

[1053]

GOALS®: A Performance-Based Measure of Achievement.

Purpose: A measure of student achievement using open-ended questions requiring reasoning skills.
Population: Grades 1–12.
Publication Dates: 1992–1994.
Administration: Group.

Forms, 3: A, B, C (Form C is secure and not available through the catalog).
Levels, 11: 1–11.
Price Data, 2002: $23.90 per 25 test booklets including directions for administering; $11.70 per scoring guide; $8 per directions for administering; $26.50 per 1991 norms booklet (separate by content area); $80 per 1992 norms booklet (all content areas); $53 per technical manual (1994, 114 pages); $26.50 per interpretive manual; $4.50 per Option 1 computer scoring by publisher of one domain including scoring and two copies of the Student Performance Roster; $3.40 per each additional domain; $.22 per additional copy of Student Performance Roster); $760 set-up charge for Option 2 computer scoring by publisher including scoring and recording of scores in test booklets; $3.41 per domain scored; $.62 per class profile ($43.25 per order each additional copy); $.51 per school profile ($34.25 per order each additional copy); $.44 per district profile ($25.50 per order each additional copy); $.79 per administrator's data summary-school ($34.50 per order each additional copy); $.79 per administrator's data summary-district ($25.50 per order each additional copy); $1.03 per administrator's data summary-school and district ($43.25 per each additional copy); $.87 per student profile ($.25 per additional copy); $.68 per student record label; $.68 per master list of test results ($.22 per additional copy); $.68 per student performance roster ($.22 per additional copy); $.44 per student data diskette; $760 per set-up charge for customer data input (plus cost of additional optional reports ordered).
Time: Approximately one class period.
Comments: Produces norm-referenced and holistic-analytic scores.
Author: Harcourt Brace Educational Measurement.
Publisher: Harcourt Educational Measurement.
a) MATHEMATICS.
Scores, 5: Content (Problem Solving [All Levels], Procedures [All Levels]), Process (Applying Mathematical Skills and Concepts to Solve Problems [Levels 1–2], Drawing Conclusions Using Mathematical Skills and Concepts [Levels 1–4], Integrating Mathematical Concepts and Skills to Solve Problems [Levels 1–8], Analyzing Problems Using Mathematical Skills and Concepts [Levels 3–11], Creating Solutions Through Synthesis of Mathematical Concepts and Skills [Levels 5–11], Evaluating Problems Using Mathematical Skills and Concepts [Levels 9–11]).
b) LANGUAGE.
Scores, 5: Content (Narrative Writing, Expository Writing), Process (Skill in Composing, Understanding of Usage, Application in Mechanics).
c) READING.
Scores, 5: Content (Narrative Text, Informational Text), Process (Global Understanding, Iden-

tification and Application of Strategies, Critical Analysis).

d) SCIENCE.

Scores, 6: Content (Life Science, Physical Science, Earth/Space Science), Process (Collecting and Recording Scientific Data, Applying Science Concepts, Drawing Conclusions).

e) SOCIAL SCIENCE.

Scores, 5: Content (Geographic/Economic/and Cultural Foundations of Society, Historical and Political Bases of Society), Process (Understanding of Basic Conceptual Social Science Frameworks, Creative Thinking and Problem-Solving Skills, Inquiry and Decision Making Using Social Science Tools).

Cross References: For reviews by C. Dale Carpenter and Darrell L. Sabers, see 13:131.

[1054]
Goldman Fristoe Test of Articulation—Second Edition.

Purpose: Designed as "a systematic means of assessing an individual's articulation of the consonant sounds of Standard American English."

Population: Ages 2–21.

Publication Dates: 1969–2000.

Acronym: GFTA-2.

Scores: 3 subtests: Sounds-in-Words, Sounds-in-Sentences, Stimulability.

Administration: Individual.

Price Data, 2002: $189.95 per complete kit including manual (2000, 146 pages), test easel, 25 response forms, canvas carrying bag, and supplemental developmental norms booklet; $26.95 per 25 response forms; $35.95 per manual.

Time: 5–15 minutes.

Authors: Ronald Goldman and Macalyne Fristoe.

Publisher: American Guidance Service, Inc.

Cross References: See T5:1095 (48 references) and T4:1045 (15 references); for a review by Donald E. Mowrer of an earlier edition, see 10:126 (7 references); see also T3:960 (21 references); for reviews by Margaret C. Byrne and Ralph L. Shelton, and an excerpted review by Dorothy Sherman, see 7:952 (4 references).

[1055]
Goldman-Fristoe-Woodcock Test of Auditory Discrimination.

Purpose: "Designed to provide measures of speech-sound discrimination ability."

Population: Ages 3-8 years and up.

Publication Date: 1970.

Acronym: GFW.

Scores: 2 subtests: Quiet, Background Noise.

Administration: Individual.

Price Data, 2002: $111.95 per kit including easel-kit containing test plates, 50 response forms, test audio-cassette, and manual (31 pages); $17.95 per 50 response forms; $11.95 per manual.

Time: [20–30] minutes.

Authors: Ronald Goldman, Macalyne Fristoe, and Richard W. Woodcock.

Publisher: American Guidance Service, Inc.

Cross References: See T5:1096 (13 references), T4:1046 (8 references), and T3:962 (14 references); for an excerpted review by Alex Bannatyne, see 8:938 (18 references); see also T2:2037 (4 references); for reviews by Eugene C. Sheeley and Ralph L. Shelton and an excerpted review by Barton B. Proger, see 7:938.

[1056]
Goodenough-Harris Drawing Test.

Purpose: Developed for use "as a measure of intellectual maturity."

Population: Ages 3-15.

Publication Dates: 1926-1963.

Scores: Total score only.

Administration: Group or individual.

Price Data, 2002: $70 per 35 test booklets; $67 per set of quality scale cards; $62 per manual (1963, 80 pages); $131 per examiner's kit.

Time: (10-15) minutes.

Comments: Revision and extension of the Goodenough Draw-a-Man Test.

Authors: Florence L. Goodenough and Dale B. Harris (test).

Publisher: The Psychological Corporation.

Cross References: See T5:1097 (14 references), T4:1049 (20 references), 9:441 (6 references), T3:964 (52 references), 8:187 (87 references), and T2:381 (93 references); for reviews by Anne Anastasi and James A. Dunn, and excerpted reviews by M. L. Kellmer Pringle, Marjorie P. Honzik, Carol Hunter, Adolph G. Woltmann, Marvin S. Kaplan, and Mary J. Rouse, see 7:352 (158 references); see also 6:460 (43 references) and 5:335 (34 references); for a review by Naomi Stewart of the original edition, see 4:292 (60 references).

[1057]
The Gordon Diagnostic System.

Purpose: Aids in the evaluation of Attention Deficit Hyperactivity Disorder. Is also used in the neuropsychological assessment of disorders such as subclinical hepatic encephalopathy, AIDS dementia complex, post concussion syndrome, closed head injury, and neurotoxicity.

Population: Children, adolescents, and adults.

Publication Dates: [1982–1996].

Acronym: GDS.

Scores: 11 tests: Standard Vigilance Task, Standard Distractibility Test, Delay Task, Preschool Delay Task,

Preschool Vigilance "0" Task, Preschool Vigilance "1" Task, Vigilance "3/5" Task, Adult Vigilance Task, Adult Distractibility Task, Auditory Vigilance Task, Auditory Interference Task.

Administration: Individual.

Price Data, 1996: $1,595 per GDS III microprocessor-based portable unit including all tasks, capacity for automatic output to a printer, instruction manual (1996, 102 pages), interpretive guide, 50 record forms, 4 issues of ADHD/Hyperactivity Newsletter, and 1-year warranty; $200 plus shipping per 2-month trial rental; $299 plus shipping per GDS compatible printer; $30 per 50 GDS record forms; $399 plus shipping per optional auditory module.

Time: (9) minutes per task.

Author: Michael Gordon.

Comments: A micro-processor-based unit that administers tests of attention and impulse control.

Publisher: Gordon Systems, Inc.

Cross References: See T5:1099 (5 references); for reviews by Robert G. Harrington and Judy J. Oehler-Stinnett, see 13:132 (6 references); see also T4:1051 (6 references).

[1058]
Gordon Occupational Check List II.

Purpose: "Designed for persons seeking education and job training below the college level."

Population: Grades 8–12 and adults.

Publication Dates: 1961–1981.

Acronym: GOCL II.

Scores, 6 or 12: Business, Outdoor, Arts, Technology (Mechanical, Industrial), Service, and 6 optional summarization scores (preceding 6 areas).

Administration: Group or individual.

Price Data, 2002: $105 per 35 check lists including manual (1982, 19 pages) and 35 job title supplements; $29 per manual; $36.50 per examination kit including check list, manual, and job title supplement.

Time: (20-25) minutes.

Author: Leonard V. Gordon.

Publisher: The Psychological Corporation.

Cross References: For a review by Donald G. Zytowski, see 9:443; for reviews by John N. McCall and Bert W. Westbrook of an earlier edition, see 7:1019; for reviews by John O. Crites and Kenneth B. Hoyt of an earlier edition, see 6:1056.

[1059]
Gordon Personal Profile—Inventory™ [Revised].

Purpose: Constructed to assess "eight important factors in the personality domain."

Population: Grades 9–12 and college and adults.

Publication Dates: 1951–1993.

Acronym: GPP-I.

Administration: Group.

Price Data, 2002: $66 per examination kit including handscorable booklet, machine-scorable booklet, and manual (1993, 119 pages); $70 per 25 handscorable booklets; $100 per 25 machine-scorable booklets; $54 per manual; $37 per keys for hand scoring.

Time: (20–25) minutes.

Comments: Combination of Gordon Personal Profile and Gordon Personal Inventory; separate booklet editions still available.

Author: Leonard V. Gordon.

Publisher: The Psychological Corporation.

a) GORDON PERSONAL PROFILE.

Scores, 5: Ascendancy, Responsibility, Emotional Stability, Sociability, Self-Esteem (Total).

b) GORDON PERSONAL INVENTORY.

Scores, 4: Cautiousness, Original Thinking, Personal Relations, Vigor.

Cross References: See T5:1101 (2 references); for reviews by Robert M. Guion and Allen K. Hess, see 13:133 (4 references); see also T4:1053 (2 references); for reviews by Douglas Fuchs and Alfred B. Heilbrun, Jr. of an earlier edition, see 10:128 (4 references); see also 9:444 (1 reference), T3:966 (6 references), 8:568 (34 references), 8:569 (52 references), T2:1194 (56 references), and P:93 (23 references); for reviews by Charles F. Dicken and Alfred B. Heilbrun, Jr., see 6:102 (13 references) and 6:103 (25 references); for reviews by Benno G. Fricke and John A. Radcliffe and excerpted reviews by Laurance F. Shaffer and Laurence Siegel, see 5:58 and 5:59 (16 references).

[1060]
Goyer Organization of Ideas Test, Form S (Revised).

Purpose: Intended to assess the ability to organize ideas.

Population: College and adults.

Publication Dates: 1966–1993.

Acronym: GOIT, Form S (Rev.).

Scores: Total score only.

Administration: Individual or group.

Manual: No manual.

Price Data: Available from publisher.

Time: [20–40] minutes.

Author: Robert S. Goyer.

Publisher: Robert S. Goyer.

Cross References: For reviews of an earlier edition by Ric Brown and Robert B. Frary, see 9:445; see also 8:817 (1 reference).

[1061]
Graded Arithmetic-Mathematics Test.

Purpose: Designed to assess overall mathematical attainment.

Population: Ages 5–12.

Publication Dates: 1949–1998.
Scores: Total score only.
Administration: Group.
Price Data, 2002: £9.99 per 20 tests; £9.99 per manual; £10.99 per specimen set.
Time: (30) minutes.
Comments: Oral administration instructions provided.
Authors: P. E. Vernon and K. M. Miller.
Publisher: Hodder & Stoughton Educational [England].
Cross References: See T3:972 (3 references) and T2:618 (8 references); for a review by Stanley Nisbet of the original edition, see 5:476.

[1062]
Graded Naming Test.

Purpose: Constructed to detect "minor degrees of naming difficulty … in patients with left hemisphere lesions."
Population: Ages 20 and over.
Publication Date: 1983.
Scores: Total score only.
Administration: Individual.
Price Data, 1999: £11.50 per 25 record sheets; £33 per object/picture books; £16.50 per manual.
Time: Administration time not reported.
Authors: Pat McKenna and Elizabeth K. Warrington.
Publisher: NFER-Nelson Publishing Co., Ltd. [England].
Cross References: See T5:1104 (14 references) and T4:1055 (7 references).

[1063]
Graded Word Spelling Test, Second Edition.

Purpose: Designed to measure spelling achievement.
Population: Ages 6-0 to adults.
Publication Dates: 1977–1998.
Scores: Total Words Correct.
Administration: Group.
Price Data, 2002: £8.99 per test booklet/manual.
Time: (20–30) minutes.
Author: P. E. Vernon.
Publisher: Hodder & Stoughton Educational [England].
Cross References: For a review by Deborah L. Bandalos, see 14:157; see also T5:1105 (1 reference); for a review by Carol E. Westby of an earlier edition, see 12:165 (3 references); see also T4:1056 (2 references).

[1064]
Graduate and Managerial Assessment.

Purpose: Constructed to assess numerical skills needed in finance-related occupations.
Population: Undergraduate and graduate students.
Publication Date: 1985.
Acronym: GMA.

Scores: 3 tests: Numerical, Abstract, Verbal.
Administration: Group.
Forms, 2: A, B.
Price Data: Price information available from publisher for reference set, Numerical test booklets, VErbal test booklets, Abstract test booklets, self-scoring answer sheets, administrator's test records, set of instruction cards, and manual (59 pages).
Time: 30(35) minutes per test.
Author: Psychometric Research Unit, The Hatfield Polytechnic.
Publisher: NFER-Nelson Publishing Co., Ltd. [England].
Cross References: See T5:1106 (1 reference); for reviews by Philip G. Benson and Rhonda L. Gutenberg, see 10:129.

[1065]
Graduate Management Admission Test.

Purpose: Designed to measure "general verbal and mathmatical skills important in the study of management at the graduate level."
Population: Applicants to study in graduate management education.
Publication Dates: 1954–1994.
Acronym: GMAT.
Scores, 3: Verbal, Quantitative, Total.
Administration: Group.
Price Data, 1993: $52 per student (fee includes reporting of scores to 5 schools).
Time: 180(210) minutes; 210(235) minutes including Writing Assessment.
Comments: Test administered 4 times annually (January, March, June, October) at centers established by publisher; Analytical Writing Assessment added October 1994.
Author: Graduate Management Admission Council.
Publisher: Educational Testing Service.
Cross References: See T5:1107 (10 references) and T4:1058 (6 references); for reviews by Lawrence A. Crosby and James Ledvinka, see 9:447 (1 reference); see also T3:973 (6 references), 8:1074 (11 references), and T2:2325 (5 references); for reviews by Jerome E. Doppelt and Gary R. Hanson of earlier forms, see 7:1080 (10 references).

[1066]
Graduate Program Self-Assessment Service.

Purpose: "To assist colleges and universities that are carrying out departmental or program reviews at the graduate level."
Population: Faculty members, students majoring in the department, and recent graduates.
Publication Date: 1986.
Acronym: GPSA.
Scores, 16: Environment for Learning, Scholarly Excellence, Quality of Teaching, Faculty Concern for Students, Curriculum, Departmental Procedures, Avail-

able Resources, Student Satisfaction with Program, Internship/Fieldwork/Clinical Experiences, Resource Accessibility, Employment Assistance, Faculty Work Environment, Faculty Program Involvement, Faculty Research Activities, Faculty Professional Activities, Student Accomplishments.
Administration: Group.
Forms, 6: Faculty, Student, Alumni for both Masters and Doctoral Programs.
Price Data: Available from publisher.
Time: (30–45) minutes.
Author: Educational Testing Service.
Publisher: Educational Testing Service.

[1067]
The Graduate Record Examinations Biochemistry, Cell and Molecular Biology.

Purpose: Designed to assess the qualifications of graduate school applicants for advanced study and for fellowships in biochemistry, cell biology, molecular biology, and genetics, along with related programs in microbiology and genetics.
Population: Graduate school candidates.
Publication Dates: 1990–2002.
Acronym: GRE.
Scores, 4: Biochemistry, Cell Biology, Molecular Biology and Genetics, Total.
Administration: Group.
Price Data: Available from publisher.
Time: (170) minutes.
Comments: Test administered 3 times annually (April, November, December) at centers established by publisher.
Author: Educational Testing Service.
Publisher: Educational Testing Service.
Cross References: For reviews of the GRE program, see 7:667 (1 review) and 5:601 (1 review).

[1068]
The Graduate Record Examinations Biology Test.

Purpose: Designed to assess the qualifications of graduate school applicants for advanced study and for fellowships in cellular and molecular biology, organismal biology, and ecology and evolution.
Population: Graduate school candidates.
Publication Dates: 1939–2002.
Acronym: GRE.
Scores, 4: Cellular and Molecular Biology, Organismal Biology, Ecology and Evolution, Total.
Administration: Group.
Price Data: Available from publisher.
Time: (170) minutes.
Comments: Test administered 3 times annually (April, November, December) at centers established by publisher.

Author: Educational Testing Service.
Publisher: Educational Testing Service.
Cross References: See T5:1110 (1 reference); for a review by Clark W. Horton of an earlier form, see 5:727. For reviews of the GRE program, see 7:667 (1 review) and 5:601 (1 review).

[1069]
The Graduate Record Examinations Chemistry Test.

Purpose: Designed to assess the qualifications of graduate school applicants for advanced study and for fellowships in chemistry.
Population: Graduate school candidates.
Publication Dates: 1939–2002.
Acronym: GRE.
Scores: Total score only.
Administration: Group.
Price Data: Available from publisher.
Time: (170) minutes.
Comments: Test administered 3 times annually (April, November, December) at centers established by publisher.
Author: Educational Testing Service.
Publisher: Educational Testing Service.
Cross References: See T4:1060 (1 reference), 8:852 (1 reference), and 7:848 (1 reference); for a review by Max D. Engelhart of an earlier form, see 6:919. For reviews of the GRE program, see 7:667 (1 review) and 5:601 (1 review).

[1070]
The Graduate Record Examinations Computer Science Test.

Purpose: Designed to assess the qualifications of graduate school applicants for advanced study and for fellowships in computer science.
Population: Graduate school candidates.
Publication Dates: 1976–2002.
Acronym: GRE.
Scores: Total score only.
Administration: Group.
Price Data: Available from publisher.
Time: (170) minutes.
Comments: Test administered 3 times annually (April, November, December) at centers established by publisher.
Author: Educational Testing Service.
Publisher: Educational Testing Service.

[1071]
The Graduate Record Examinations— General Test.

Purpose: "Designed to assess the Verbal, Quantitative and Analytical reasoning abilities of graduate school applicants."

Population: Graduate school candidates.
Publication Dates: 1949–2002.
Acronym: GRE.
Scores, 3: Verbal Reasoning, Quantitative Reasoning, Analytical Reasoning.
Administration: Individual
Price Data: Available from publisher.
Time: (270) minutes for computer-based test.
Comments: Computer-adaptive tests administered daily by appointment. Beginning in October 2002, the General Test will be composed of verbal, quantitative sections will be unchanged from their present content. The analytical writing section is new and measures critical thinking and analytical writing. The analytical section will no longer be part of the General Test.
Author: Educational Testing Service.
Publisher: Educational Testing Service.
Cross References: See T5:1115 (29 references) and T4:1076 (31 references); for reviews by Sanford J. Cohn and Richard M. Jaeger, see 9:448 (9 references); see also T3:995 (26 references), 8:188 (45 references), T2:382 (15 references), and 7:353 (43 references); for reviews by Robert L. French and Warren W. Willingham of an earlier edition, see 6:461 (17 references); for a review by John T. Dailey, see 5:336 (7 references); for reviews by J. P. Guilford and Carl I. Hovland, see 4:293 (2 references). For reviews of the GRE program, see 7:667 (1 review) and 5:601 (1 review).

[1072]
The Graduate Record Examinations Literature in English Test.

Purpose: Designed to assess the qualifications of graduate school applicants for advanced study and for fellowships in literature in English.
Population: Graduate school candidates.
Publication Dates: 1939–2002.
Acronym: GRE.
Scores: Total score only.
Administration: Group.
Price Data: Available from publisher.
Time: (170) minutes.
Comments: Test administered 3 times annually (April, November, December) at centers established by publisher.
Author: Educational Testing Service.
Publisher: Educational Testing Service.
Cross References: See T5:1118 (1 reference); for a review by Edward M. White, see 8:69; see also 7:219 (1 reference); for a review by Robert C. Pooley of an earlier form, see 5:215. For reviews of the GRE program, see 7:667 (1 review) and 5:601 (1 review).

[1073]
The Graduate Record Examinations Mathematics Test.

Purpose: Designed to assess the qualifications of graduate school applicants for advanced study and for fellowships in mathematics.
Population: Graduate school candidates.
Publication Dates: 1939–2002.
Acronym: GRE.
Scores: Total score only.
Administration: Group.
Price Data: Available from publisher.
Time: (170) minutes.
Comments: Test administered 3 times annually (April, November, December) at centers established by publisher.
Author: Educational Testing Service.
Publisher: Educational Testing Service.
Cross References: See T4:1069 (1 reference) and 8:272 (1 reference); for a review by Paul C. Rosenbloom of an earlier form, see 6:578; for a review by Eric F. Gardner, see 5:427 (1 reference). For reviews of the GRE program, see 7:667 (1 review) and 5:601 (1 review).

[1074]
The Graduate Record Examinations Physics Test.

Purpose: Designed to assess the qualifications of graduate school applicants for advanced study and for fellowships in physics.
Population: Graduate school candidates.
Publication Dates: 1939–2002.
Acronym: GRE.
Scores: Total score only.
Administration: Group.
Price Data: Available from publisher.
Time: (170) minutes.
Comments: Test administered 3 times annually (April, November, December) at centers established by publisher.
Author: Educational Testing Service.
Publisher: Educational Testing Service.
Cross References: See 8:866 (1 reference); for a review by Theodore G. Phillips, see 6:931; for a review by Leo Nedelsky, see 5:754. For reviews of the GRE program, see 7:667 (1 review) and 5:601 (1 review).

[1075]
The Graduate Record Examinations Psychology Test.

Purpose: Designed to assess the qualifications of graduate school applicants for advanced study and for fellowships in psychology.
Population: Graduate school candidates.

Publication Dates: 1939–2002.
Acronym: GRE.
Scores, 3: Experimental Psychology, Social Psychology, Total.
Administration: Group.
Price Data: Available from publisher.
Time: (170) minutes.
Comments: Test administered 3 times annually (April, November, December) at centers established by publisher.
Author: Educational Testing Service.
Publisher: Educational Testing Service.
Cross References: See T5:1122 (2 references), T4:1073 (3 references), 8:461 (3 references), T2:1005 (2 references), and 7:644 (9 references); for a review by Harold Seashore of an earlier form, see 5:583. For reviews of the GRE program, see 7:667 (1 review) and 5:601 (1 review).

[1076]
Graduate Record Examinations: Subject Tests.

Purpose: Designed to assess the qualifications of graduate school applicants in specific fields of study.
Population: Graduate school candidates.
Publication Dates: 1939–2002.
Acronym: GRE.
Scores: 8 subtests: Biochemistry/Cell and Molecular Biology, Biology, Chemistry, Computer Science, Literature in English, Mathematics, Physics, Psychology.
Administration: Group.
Price Data: Available from publisher.
Time: (170) minutes.
Comments: Test administered 3 time annually (April, November, December) at centers established by publisher.
Author: Educational Testing Service.
Publisher: Educational Testing Service.
Cross References: See T4:1075 (2 references), T3:994 (5 references), and 8:476 (6 references); for a review by Leona E. Tyler of an earlier program, see 7:667 (10 references); see also 6:762 (1 reference); for a review by Harold Seashore, see 5:601 (12 references); see also 4:527 (24 references).

[1077]
Grammatical Analysis of Elicited Language—Pre-Sentence Level.

Purpose: Designed to provide in-depth grammatical analysis of children's expressive language.
Population: Hearing-impaired children ages 3–6.
Publication Date: 1983.
Acronym: GAEL-P.
Scores: 3 sections (Readiness Skills, Single Words, Word Combinations) yielding 3 scores: Comprehension, Prompted Production, Imitated Production.

Administration: Individual.
Price Data, 2002: $400 per complete kit including manual (81 pages), scoring forms, videotape, and toys; $10 per videotape; $19.95 per manual; $12 per 25 record forms.
Time: [60] minutes.
Comments: Simple Sentence Level (GAEL-S; 1077) and Complex Sentence Level (GAEL-C) also available.
Authors: Jean S. Moog, Victoria J. Kozak, and Ann E. Geers.
Publisher: Central Institute for the Deaf.
Cross References: See T5:1126 (3 references) and T4:1078 (1 reference).

[1078]
Grandparent Strengths and Needs Inventory.

Purpose: "To help grandparents recognize their favorable qualities and identify aspects of their family relationships in which further growth is needed."
Population: Grandparents of children 6 and over.
Publication Date: 1993.
Acronym: GSNI.
Scores, 6: Satisfaction, Success, Teaching, Difficulty, Frustration, Information Needs.
Administration: Group.
Price Data, 2002: $78.75 per complete kit including 20 identification forms and 20 inventory booklets each: grandparent, parent, and grandchild versions, 20 profiles, and manual (20 pages).
Foreign Language Edition: Spanish version available.
Time: Administration time not reported.
Comments: Parent and grandchild inventories included for comparison purposes.
Authors: Robert D. Strom and Shirley K. Strom.
Publisher: Scholastic Testing Service, Inc.
Cross References: See T5:1128 (4 references); for reviews by Roger A. Boothroyd and Dianna L. Newman, see 13:134 (2 references).

[1079]
Gravidometer.

Purpose: Measures knowledge about human pregnancy.
Population: Adolescents and adults.
Publication Dates: 1974–1988.
Scores: Total score only.
Administration: Group.
Manual: No manual.
Price Data, 2002: $1 per test.
Time: [10] minutes.
Comments: Supplementary article available.
Author: Panos D. Bardis.
Publisher: Donna Bardis.

[1080]
Gray Oral Reading Tests—Diagnostic.

Purpose: Developed to assess oral reading proficiency in students having difficulties in reading continuous print.
Population: Ages 5-6 to 12-11.
Publication Date: 1991.
Acronym: GORT-D.
Scores, 4: Total Reading, Meaning Cues, Graphic/Phonemic Cues, Function Cues.
Administration: Individual.
Forms, 2: A, B.
Price Data, 2001: $169 per complete kit including student book, 25 each Form A and B record forms, and examiner's manual (78 pages); $36 per student book; $44 per 25 record forms; $49 per manual.
Time: (50-90) minutes.
Comments: Expanded edition of the Gray Oral Reading Tests—Third Edition (12:166).
Authors: Brian R. Bryant and J. Lee Wiederholt.
Publisher: PRO-ED.
Cross References: See T5:1130 (2 references); for reviews by William R. Merz, Sr. and Steven A. Stahl, see 11:149 (1 reference).

[1081]
Gray Oral Reading Tests, Fourth Edition.

Purpose: Designed "to provide a measure of growth in oral reading and an aid in the diagnosis of oral reading difficulties."
Population: Ages 6-0 to 18-11.
Publication Dates: 1967–2001.
Acronym: GORT-4.
Scores, 4: Rate, Accuracy, Fluency, Comprehension.
Forms, 2: A, B.
Administration: Individual.
Price Data, 2001: $189 per kit including 25 profile/examiner record forms (specify A or B), student book, and examiner's manual (2001, 146 pages); $39 per 25 record forms (specify A or B); $46 per student book; $69 per examiner's manual.
Time: (20–30) minutes.
Authors: J. Lee Wiederholt and Brian R. Bryant.
Publisher: PRO-ED.
Cross References: See T5:1131 (18 references); for reviews by John D. King and Deborah King Kundert of an earlier edition, see 12:166 (5 references); see also T4:1084 (9 references); for reviews by Julia A. Hickman and Robert J. Tierney of an earlier edition, see 10:131 (15 references).

[1082]
Gray Silent Reading Tests.

Purpose: "Designed to assess silent reading comprehension."
Population: Ages 7–25.
Publication Date: 2000.
Acronym: GSRT.
Score: Silent Reading Quotient.
Administration: Group.
Forms, 2: A, B.
Price Data, 2001: $134 per complete kit; $14 per profile/response forms; $28 per reading book (Form A or B); $69 per manual.
Time: (15–30) minutes.
Comments: Developed to be used as an adjunct to the Gray Oral Reading Test (1081) or independently.
Authors: J. Lee Wiederholt and Ginger Blalock.
Publisher: PRO-ED.

[1083]
Gregorc Style Delineator.

Purpose: "Designed to aid an individual to recognize and identify the channels through which he/she receives and expresses information."
Population: Adults.
Publication Dates: 1982–2002.
Scores, 4: Concrete Sequential score, Abstract Sequential score, Abstract Random score, Concrete Random score.
Administration: Group.
Price Data, 2002: $69.95 per sample set including An Adult's Guide to Style (2002, 110 pages), Mind Styles Model: Theory Principles and Practice (1998, 28 pages), Mind Styles FAQs Book (2001, 152 pages), Relating with Style (1997, 170 pages), test, Extends Charts, Phoenix bookmark, and Careful Us audio tape; $15.95 per technical manual (1982, 46 pages); $59.50 per 25 instrument packets or $29.95 per 10 instrument packets including guidelines for group administration; $9.95 per audiocassette on careful use; $17.95 per An Adult's Guide to Style; $19.95 per Mind Styles FAQs Book; $19.95 per Relating with Style; $7.50 per Mind Styles Model: Theory, Principles, and Practice.
Time: 3 minutes.
Comments: Self-assessment instrument.
Author: Anthony F. Gregorc.
Publisher: Gregorc Associates, Inc.
Cross References: See T5:1132 (1 reference); for reviews by Stephen L. Benton and Trenton R. Ferro, see 12:167 (3 references); see also T4:1086 (2 references).

[1084]
Grid Test of Schizophrenic Thought Disorder.

Purpose: "Developed to detect the presence of schizophrenic thought disorder."
Population: Adults.
Publication Date: 1967.
Acronym: GTSTD.

Scores, 2: Intensity, Consistency.
Administration: Individual.
Price Data: Available from publisher.
Time: (15–25) minutes.
Comments: 1 form (set of 8 photographs).
Authors: D. Bannister and Fay Fransella.
Publisher: Psychological Test Publications [England] [No reply from publisher; status unknown].
Cross References: See T4:1087 (4 references) and T3:1009 (3 references); for a review by Robert W. Payne, see 8:571 (30 references); see also T2:1198 (8 references); for a review by David Jones, see 7:84 (7 references); see also P:96 (8 references).

[1085]
Griffiths Mental Development Scales [Revised].

Purpose: Designed to measure trends of development that are indicative of intelligence/mental growth.
Publication Dates: 1951–1996.
Administration: Individual.
Forms, 2: Scale 1 (0–2 years), Scale 2 (2–8 years).
Restricted Distribution: Restricted to persons who qualify by attending an approved course; details available from distributor.
Price Data, 2001: £260 per Scale 1; £315 per Scale 2; £2.20 per Scale 2 record book; £1.65 per Scale 1 record form; £24.50 per The Abilities of Babies (1976, 239 pages); £24.50 per The Abilities of Young Children (1996, 114 pages); £39.50 per Scale 1 manual; £29.50 for 8 additional test items for 1996 Revised Scale 1.
Authors: Ruth Griffiths and Michael Huntley (Birth–2 years Scale [Scale 1] and manual, 1996 Revision).
Publisher: The Test Agency Limited [England].
   a) SCALE 1: BIRTH TO 2 YEARS.
   Population: Ages 0–2 years.
   Publication Dates: 1951–1996.
   Scores, 6: Locomotor, Personal-Social, Hearing and Speech, Eye and Hand, Performance, Total.
   Time: (20–40) minutes.
   b) SCALE 2: (2 TO 8 YEARS).
   Population: Ages 2–8 years.
   Publication Dates: 1951–1978.
   Scores, 7: Same as Scale 1 above plus Practical Reasoning.
   Time: Administration time not reported.
Cross References: See T5:1134 (8 references), T4:1088 (10 references), and 9:450 (1 reference); for a review by C. B. Hindley of an earlier version of Scale 2, see 6:523 (4 references); for a review by Nancy Bayley of Scale 1, see 5:404 (3 references).

[1086]
Grooved Pegboard Test.
Purpose: To assess manipulative dexterity.

Population: Ages 5 to 8-12, 9 to 14-12, 15 to adult.
Publication Date: 1989.
Scores, 3: Total Time, Number of "Drops," Total Pegs Correctly Placed.
Administration: Individual.
Price Data: Available from publisher.
Time: Trial discontinued after 5 minutes.
Comments: Ages 5 to 8-12 only complete first two rows of the Pegboard.
Author: Ronald Trites (manual).
Publisher: Lafayette Instrument.
Cross References: See T5:1135 (27 references); for reviews by Roderick K. Mahurin and Erin McClure and Richard K. Stratton, see 12:170 (14 references); see also T4:1089 (2 references).

[1087]
Group Achievement Identification Measure.
Purpose: "To determine the degree to which children exhibit the characteristics of underachievers so that preventative or curative efforts may be administered."
Population: Grades 5–12.
Publication Date: 1986.
Acronym: GAIM.
Scores, 6: Competition, Responsibility, Achievement Communication, Independence/Dependence, Respect/Dominance, Total.
Administration: Group.
Price Data, 2001: $15 per specimen set; $100 per class set of 30 inventories including prepaid computer scoring by publisher; manual for administration and interpretation (12 pages) included with test orders.
Time: (30) minutes.
Comments: Self-report inventory.
Author: Sylvia B. Rimm.
Publisher: Educational Assessment Service, Inc.
Cross References: See T5:1136 (1 reference); for reviews by Robert K. Gable and Jeffrey Jenkins, see 11:151.

[1088]
Group Cohesiveness: A Study of Group Morale.
Purpose: Designed to assess group cohesiveness.
Population: Adults.
Publication Dates: 1957–1958.
Acronym: GC.
Scores, 5: Satisfaction of Individual Motives, Satisfaction of Interpersonal Relations, Homogeneity of Attitude, Satisfaction With Leadership, Total.
Administration: Group.
Price Data: Available from publisher.
Time: (10–15) minutes.
Comments: Self-administered.
Author: Bernard Goldman.
Publisher: Psychometric Affiliates.

Cross References: See T2:1199 (1 reference) and P:97; for reviews by Eric F. Gardner and Cecil A. Gibb, see 6:104 (1 reference).

[1089]
Group Diagnostic Reading Aptitude and Achievement Tests.

Purpose: Diagnose whether children need remedial work in reading.
Population: Grades 3–9.
Publication Date: 1939.
Scores, 15: Reading (Paragraph Understanding, Speed), Word Discrimination (Vowels, Consonants, Reversals, Additions and Omissions), Arithmetic, Spelling, Visual Ability (Letter Memory, Form Memory), Auditory Ability (Letter Memory, Discrimination and Orientation), Motor Ability (Copying Text, Crossing Out Letters), Vocabulary.
Administration: Group.
Manual: No manual.
Price Data, 1997: $150 per lifetime privilege to use test.
Time: (60–70) minutes.
Authors: Marion Monroe and Eva Edith Sherman.
Publisher: C. H. Nevins Printing Co.
Cross References: See T5:1138 (2 references) and T4:1092 (1 reference).

[1090]
Group Diagnostic Reading Aptitude and Achievement Tests, Intermediate Form.

Purpose: Designed to assess reading achievement and to diagnose reading problems.
Population: Grades 3–9.
Publication Date: [Orig. 1937].
Scores, 13: Achievement [Reading (Paragraph Understanding, Speed, Word Discrimination), Arithmetic, Spelling], Diagnostic [Word Discrimination Errors, Visual (Letter Memory, Form Memory), Auditory (Letter Memory, Discrimination and Orientation), Motor (Copying Text, Cross Out Letters), Language-Vocabulary].
Administration: Group.
Price Data, 1997: $150 per lifetime privilege to use test.
Time: (40) minutes (includes both timed and untimed tests).
Authors: Marion Monroe and Eva Edith Sherman.
Publisher: C. H. Nevins Printing Co.
Cross References: For reviews by Deborah King Kundert and Margaret R. Rogers, see 12:170.

[1091]
Group Embedded Figures Test.

Purpose: Developed to evaluate field-dependence.
Population: Older children, adolescents, adults.
Publication Date: 1971.
Acronym: GEFT.
Scores: Total score only.
Administration: Group.
Price Data, 2001: $44.55 per preview kit including item booklet, scoring key, and manual (32 pages); $51.70 per 25 item booklets; $11.30 per scoring key.
Time: (20) minutes.
Comments: Adaptation of the individually administered Embedded Figures Test (900); manual is a combined manual for this test and the Embedded Figures Test.
Authors: Philip K. Oltman, Evelyn Raskin, Herman A. Witkin, and Stephen A. Karp (manual).
Publisher: Consulting Psychologists Press, Inc.
Cross References: See T5:1140 (60 references), T4:1094 (95 references), 9:452 (41 references), and T3:1013 (88 references); for reviews by Leonard D. Goodstein and Alfred E. Hall, see 8:572 (47 references); see also T2:1201 (3 references); for references to reviews of the individual test, see 8:548.

[1092]
Group Environment Scale, Second Edition.

Purpose: Designed to "measure the social-environmental characteristics of task-oriented, social, and psychotherapy and mutual support groups."
Population: Group members and leaders.
Publication Dates: 1974–1986.
Acronym: GES.
Scores, 10: Cohesion, Leader Support, Expressiveness, Independence, Task Orientation, Self-Discovery, Anger and Aggression, Order and Organization, Leader Control, Innovation.
Administration: Group.
Forms, 3: Real (R), Ideal (I), Expectation (E).
Price Data, 2001: $52 per 25 item booklets; $18.30 per 25 answer sheets; $10.90 per scoring key; $10 per 25 profiles; $60.30 per manual (1986, 43 pages).
Time: (15-20) minutes.
Comments: A component of the Social Climate Scales (T5:2445).
Author: Rudolf H. Moos.
Publisher: Consulting Psychologists Press, Inc.
Cross References: See T5:1141 (5 references) and T4:1095 (5 references); for a review by Arthur M. Nezu, see 10:132 (6 references); for reviews by Michael J. Curtis and Robert J. Illback, see 9:453 (4 references); for reviews by David P. Campbell and Robyn M. Dawes, see 8:573; see also T3:1015 (1 reference); for a review of the Social Climate Scales, see 8:681.

[1093]
Group Inventory for Finding Creative Talent.

Purpose: "Identify students with attitudes and values usually associated with creativity."

Population: Grades K–2, 3–4, 5–6.
Publication Dates: 1976–1980.
Acronym: GIFT.
Scores, 4: Imagination, Independence, Many Interests, Total.
Administration: Group or individual.
Levels, 3: Primary, Elementary, Upper Elementary.
Price Data, 2001: $90 per 30 test booklets and scoring service (scoring must be done by publisher); $15 per specimen set.
Foreign Language Edition: Spanish edition available.
Time: (20-45) minutes.
Author: Sylvia B. Rimm.
Publisher: Educational Assessment Service, Inc.
Cross References: See T5:1142 (5 references); for reviews by Patricia L. Dwinell and Dan Wright, see 9:454 (1 reference); see also T3:1016 (1 reference).

[1094]
Group Inventory For Finding Interests.
Purpose: "Identify students with attitudes and interests usually associated with creativity."
Population: Grades 6–12.
Publication Dates: 1979–1980.
Acronym: GIFFI.
Scores: 5 dimensional scores: Creative Arts and Writing, Challenge-Inventiveness, Confidence, Imagination, Many Interests.
Administration: Group or individual.
Levels, 2: Level 1: Grades 6-9; Level 2: Grades 9-12.
Price Data, 2001: $100 per 30 test booklets and scoring service (scoring must be done by publisher); $15 per specimen set.
Foreign Language Edition: Spanish edition available.
Time: (20–40) minutes.
Authors: Sylvia B. Rimm and Gary A. Davis.
Publisher: Educational Assessment Service, Inc.
Cross References: See T5:1143 (2 references); for a review by M. O'Neal Weeks, see 9:455 (1 reference).

[1095]
Group Literacy Assessment.
Purpose: To sample children's overall skills level with written material.
Population: End of junior school and beginning of secondary school.
Publication Dates: 1981–1999.
Acronym: GLA.
Scores, 3: Proof-Reading, Fill the Gaps, Total.
Administration: Group.
Price Data, 2002: £8.50 per 20 tests; £8.99 per manual (16 pages); £9.99 per specimen set.

Time: 16(30) minutes.
Author: Frank A. Spooncer.
Publisher: Hodder & Stoughton Educational [England].
Cross References: For a review by Gail E. Tompkins of an earlier edition, see 9:456.

[1096]
Group Mathematics Test, Third Edition.
Purpose: General assessment of mathematical understanding.
Population: Ages 6.5–8.10 and older underachieving students.
Publication Dates: 1970–1996.
Acronym: GMT.
Scores, 3: Oral, Computation, Total.
Administration: Group.
Forms, 2: A, B.
Price Data, 2002: £7.99 per 20 tests (Form A or B); £8.99 per manual; £9.99 per specimen set.
Time: (40–50) minutes.
Author: D. Young.
Publisher: Hodder & Stoughton Educational [England].
Cross References: See T5:1145 (2 references) and T4:1049 (1 reference); for reviews by Mary Kay Corbitt and Douglas H. Crawford, see 9:457; for a review by John Cook of an earlier edition, see 8:273.

[1097]
Group Process Questionnaire.
Purpose: "Designed to help groups assess how effective they are."
Population: Adults.
Publication Date: 1988.
Scores, 29 to 145: My Rating, Group Rating, and How I Did scores for Behavior Scale (Task Behavior, Maintenance Behavior), for Total Scale, and for 12 optional categories (Initiating, Seeking Information or Opinions, Giving Information or Opinions, Clarifying and Elaborating, Summarizing, Consensus-Testing, Listening, Harmonizing, Gatekeeping, Encouraging, Compromising, Standard Setting/Testing), and My Rating and Group Rating scores for 5 additional optional categories (Leadership, Time Utilization, Results, Acceptance, Inclusion).
Administration: Group.
Price Data: Available from publisher.
Time: (60) minutes.
Comments: Scale for ratings by group members and for self-ratings.
Authors: Richard Hill, D. Joseph Fisher, Tom Webber, and Kathleen A. Fisher.
Publisher: Aviat.

[1098]

Group Reading Assessment and Diagnostic Evaluation.

Purpose: "A diagnostic tool to see what pre-reading or reading skills individuals have and what skills they need to be taught."

Population: Grades Pre-K and higher.

Publication Date: 2001.

Acronym: GRADE.

Administration: Individual or group.

Levels, 11: P (pre-kindergarten and kindergarten), K (kindergarten and first grade), 1 (kindergarten through second grade), 2, 3, 4, 5, 6, M (middle school, grades 5–9), H (high school, grades 9–12), A (grades 11 to postsecondary).

Forms, 2: Form A, Form B.

Price Data, 2002: $899.95 per Elementary Resource Specialist set (Levels P–6) including 10 each of Form A and Form B student booklets per Elementary Level, 1 teacher's administration manual—Form A and B—per Elementary Level (22–81 pages), 1 scoring and interpretative manual per elementary level (59–90 pages), 1 set of hand-scoring templates, and 20 answer sheets for each of Levels 4, 5, and 6; $429.95 per Secondary Resource Specialist set (Levels M—A) including 10 each of Form A and Form B student booklets per Secondary Level, 1 teacher's administration manual per Secondary Level (22–24 pages each), 1 scoring and interpretative manual per Secondary Level (72–90 pages), 1 set of hand-scoring templates, and 20 answer sheets per secondary level; $209.95 per Levels P or K Classroom Set with Forms A and B including 30 each of Form A and For B student booklets, 1 teacher's administration manual (Forms A and B), and 1 scoring and interpretative manual; $189.95 per Levels 1, 2, or 3 Classroom Set with Forms A and B including 30 each of Form A and Form B student booklets, 1 teacher's administration manual, and 2 scoring and interpretative manual; $279.95 per Levels 4, 5, 6, M, H, or A Classroom Set with Forms A and B including 30 each of Form A and Form B student booklets, 1 teacher's administration manual, 1 scoring and interpretative manual, 1 set of hand-scoring templates, and 60 answer sheets; $122.95 per Levels P, K, 1, 2, or 3 Classroom Set with Form A including 30 of Form A student booklets, 2 teacher's administration manual, and 1 scoring and interpretative manual; $169.95 per Levels 4, 5, 6, M, H, or A Classroom Set with Form A including 30 of Form A student booklets, 1 teacher's administration manual, 1 scoring and interpretative manual, 2 set of hand-scoring templates, and 30 answer sheets; $26.95 per 10 student booklets (all levels); $9.95 per 10 answer sheets (Levels 4–A); $39.95 per Forms a and B hand-scoring templates (each of Levels 4–A); $11.95 per teacher's administration manual (each of Levels P or K); $9.95 per teacher's administration manual (each of Levels 1–A); $39.95 per scoring and interpretative manual (each of Levels P–A); $49.95 per technical manual (Levels P–A); $99.95 per GRADE Resource Library (each of Levels P–A); $299.95 per GRADE Scoring and Reporting Software (single-user version); $9,995 per GRADE Scoring and Reporting Software (network version).

Time: (45–90) minutes.

Comments: May be hand scored or computer scored; scoring system requirements: OS 7.0 or later, 16 MB RAM, 68030 CPU or higher (Macintosh); Microsoft Windows, Version 3.1 or better, 6 MB RAM (Windows), 4 MB hard drive space; computer-generated report options include group and individual score summaries, diagnostic analyses for each subtest, reports to parents and students; networked version of the GRADE scoring software available; GRADE Resource Library (GRL) software on CD-ROM contains teaching activities and reproducible worksheets.

Author: Kathleen T. Williams.

Publisher: American Guidance Service, Inc.

a) LEVEL P.

Scores, 8: Picture Matching, Picture Differences, Verbal Concepts, Picture Categories, Sound Matching, Rhyming, Listening Comprehension, Total Score.

b) LEVEL K.

Scores, 9: Sound Matching, Rhyming, Print Awareness, Letter Recognition, Same and Different Words, Phoneme-Grapheme Correspondence, Word Reading, Listening Comprehension, Total Score.

c) LEVEL 1, 2.

Scores, 6: Word Reading, Word Meaning, Sentence Comprehension, Passage Comprehension, Listening Comprehension, Total Score.

d) LEVEL 3.

Scores, 6: Word Reading, Vocabulary, Sentence Comprehension, Passage Comprehension, Listening Comprehension, Total Score.

e) LEVEL 4–A.

Scores, 5: Vocabulary, Sentence Comprehension, Passage Comprehension, Listening Comprehension, Total Score.

[1099]

Group Reading Test, Fourth Edition.

Purpose: Designed to measure "the reading of single words and of simple sentences."

Population: Ages 6:4 to 8:11 and less able children 8:0 to 11:11.

Publication Dates: 1968–1999.

Acronym: GRT.

Scores: Total score only.

Administration: Group.

Forms, 2: A, B
Price Data, 2002: £7.99 per 20 Form A or Form B; £9.99 per manual (1999, 27 pages); £4.99 per template A or B; £10.99 per specimen set.
Time: (20) minutes.
Author: Dennis Young.
Publisher: Hodder & Stoughton Educational [England].
Cross References: For reviews by Gretchen Owens and John W. Young, see 14:158; for reviews by William R. Merz, Sr., and Diane J. Sawyer of an earlier edition, see 12:171 (1 reference); see also T4:1102 (4 references); for reviews by Patrick Groff and Douglas A. Pidgeon of the Second Edition, see 9:458 (1 reference); for a review by Ralph D. Dutch of the original edition, see 8:729.

[1100]
Group Shorr Imagery Test.
Purpose: Designed as a projective measure of personality conflict.
Population: Adults.
Publication Date: 1977.
Acronym: GSIT.
Scores, 6: Item scores in 5 areas (Human, Animal, Inanimate, Botanical, Others) plus Total score for Conflict.
Administration: Group.
Price Data: Available from publisher.
Time: Administration time not reported.
Comments: Tape cassette used for administration; group form of the Shorr Imagery Test (2279).
Author: Joseph E. Shorr.
Publisher: Institute for Psychoimagination Therapy.

[1101]
Group Styles Inventory.
Purpose: Designed to "assess the particular style or styles of your work group following a simulated or real problem-solving session or meeting."
Population: Group members.
Publication Dates: 1990–1993.
Acronym: GSI.
Scores: 12 styles in 3 general clusters: Constructive (Achievement, Self-Actualizing, Humanistic-Encouraging, Affiliative), Passive/Defensive (Approval, Conventional, Dependent, Avoidance), Aggressive/Defensive (Oppositional, Power, Competitive, Perfectionistic).
Administration: Group.
Price Data: Price information for test materials including Participant Guide (50 pages) and Leader's Guide (53 pages) available from publisher.
Time: [10–15] minutes.
Authors: Robert A. Cooke and J. Clayton Lafferty.
Publisher: Human Synergistics International.
Cross References: For reviews by Lawrence M. Aleamoni and Bert A. Goldman, see 12:172.

[1102]
Group Test 82.
Purpose: Designed to assess spatial perception.
Population: Ages 15 and over.
Publication Dates: 1959–1974.
Scores: Total score only.
Administration: Group.
Manual: No manual.
Price Data: Price information available from publisher for test booklets, answer sheets, marking key, and instruction card.
Time: 24 minutes.
Comments: Subtest of N.I.I.P. Engineering Apprentice Selection Test Battery.
Author: National Institute of Industrial Psychology.
Publisher: NFER-Nelson Publishing Co., Ltd. [England].

[1103]
Group Tests 70 and 70B.
Purpose: To assess reasoning ability or nonverbal intelligence.
Population: Ages 15 and over.
Publication Dates: 1939–1970.
Acronyms: GT 70 and GT 70B.
Scores: Total score only.
Administration: Group.
Forms, 2: 70, 70B.
Price Data: Available from publisher.
Time: 18(35) minutes.
Author: National Institute of Industrial Psychology.
Publisher: NFER-Nelson Publishing Co., Ltd. [England].
Cross References: See T2:388 (9 references) and 7:355 (5 references); for a review by George Westby of Form 70, see 4:297 (5 references).

[1104]
Group Tests 90A and 90B.
Purpose: Designed as "tests of intelligence and verbal aptitude."
Population: Ages 15 and over.
Publication Dates: 1950–1970.
Scores: Total score only.
Administration: Group.
Price Data: Available from publisher.
Time: 20(30) minutes.
Comments: Subtest of N.I.I.P. Engineering Apprenticeship Selection Test Battery.
Author: National Institute of Industrial Psychology.
Publisher: NFER-Nelson Publishing Co., Ltd. [England].
Cross References: See T3:1038 (1 reference), T2:390 (2 references), and 7:357 (1 reference); for a review by John Liggett of Form 90A, see 5:340.

[1105]
Group Tests of Musical Abilities.
Purpose: Developed to measure an individual's musical ability level.
Population: Ages 7–14.
Publication Date: 1988.
Scores, 2: Pitch, Pulse.
Administration: Group.
Price Data: Price information available from publisher for starter pack including cassette tape, 25 answer sheets, and manual (25 pages).
Time: [15–20] minutes.
Comments: A good quality audiocassette player is needed to administer test.
Author: Janet Mills.
Publisher: NFER-Nelson Publishing Co., Ltd. [England].
Cross References: For reviews by J. David Boyle and Annabel J. Cohen, see 12:173.

[1106]
Guide for Occupational Exploration Interest Inventory, Second Edition.
Purpose: Designed to help people identify their interests, then use this information to explore career, learning, and lifestyle alternatives.
Population: High school through adult.
Publication Date: 2001.
Acronym: GOEII.
Scores, 14: Arts, Entertainment, and Media; Science, Math, and Engineering; Plants and Animals; Law, Law Enforcement, and Public Safety; Mechanics, Installers, and Repairers; Construction, Mining, and Drilling; Transportation; Industrial Production; Business Detail; Sales and Marketing; Recreation, Travel, and Other Personal Services; Education and Social Service; General Management and Support; Medical and Health Services.
Administration: Group or individual.
Price Data, 2001: $29.95 per 25 inventories.
Time: Administration time not reported.
Comments: Self-administered and self-scored.
Author: J. Michael Farr.
Publisher: JIST Publishing, Inc.

[1107]
Guide to the Assessment of Test Session Behavior for the WISC-III and the WIAT.
Purpose: Assesses "whether a child's behavior during WISC-III and/or WIAT testing differs substantially from the behavior of other children of the same age."
Population: Ages 6–16.
Publication Date: 1992.
Acronym: GATSB.
Scores: 4 scales: Avoidance, Inattentiveness, Uncooperative Mood, Total Score.

Administration: Individual.
Price Data, 2002: $80 per complete kit including 25 ready-score answer forms and manual (88 pages); $36 per 25 ready-score answer documents; $140 per 100 ready-score answer documents; $44 per manual.
Time: (5–10) minutes.
Authors: Joseph J. Glutting and Tom Oakland.
Publisher: The Psychological Corporation.
Cross References: See T5:1155 (1 reference); for reviews by Alice J. Corkill and Eleanor E. Sanford, see 13:135.

[1108]
The Guilford-Zimmerman Aptitude Survey.
Purpose: Measurement of verbal and abstract intelligence, numerical facility, and perception.
Population: Grades 9-16 and adults.
Publication Dates: 1947–1956.
Acronym: GZAS.
Administration: Group.
Price Data, 2001: $379 per complete kit; $22.70 per 25 answer sheets (needed only for parts 1, 2, 5, & 6); $11 per 25 profiles; $32.40 per manual (1956, 7 pages).
Authors: J. P. Guilford and Wayne S. Zimmerman.
Publisher: Consulting Psychologists Press, Inc.
    a) PART 1, VERBAL COMPREHENSION.
    Price Data: $53.50 per 25 tests; $18.30 per scoring key; $51. per preview kit.
    Time: 25(30) minutes.
    b) PART 2, GENERAL REASONING.
    Price Data: $64.40 per 25 tests; $18.30 per scoring key; $51 per preview kit.
    Time: 35(40) minutes.
    c) PART 3, NUMERICAL OPERATIONS.
    Price Data: $53.30 per 25 tests; $18.30 per scoring key; $51 per preview kit.
    Time: 8(13) minutes.
    d) PART 4, PERCEPTUAL SPEED.
    Price Data: $53.30 per 25 tests; $18.30 per scoring key; $51 per preview kit.
    Time: 5(10) minutes.
    e) PART 5, SPATIAL ORIENTATION.
    Price Data: $91.20 per 25 tests; $18.30 per scoring key; $52 per preview kit.
    Time: 10(20) minutes.
    f) PART 6, SPATIAL VISUALIZATION.
    Price Data: $91.20 per 25 tests; $18.30 per scoring key; $52 per preview kit.
    Time: 10(15) minutes.
Cross References: See T5:1156 (4 references), T4:1113 (3 references), and T3:1044 (4 references); for a review by M. Y. Qureshi, see 8:486 (9 references); see also T2:1074 (19 references) and 6:772 (17 references); for reviews by Anne Anastasi, Harold Bechtoldt, John B. Carroll, and P. E. Vernon, see 4:715 (15 references).

[1109]
The Guilford-Zimmerman Interest Inventory.

Purpose: A vocational interest measure.
Population: College and adults.
Publication Dates: 1962–1989.
Acronym: GZII.
Scores, 10: Natural, Mechanical, Scientific, Creative, Literary, Artistic, Service, Enterprising, Leadership, Clerical.
Administration: Group or individual.
Price Data, 2001: $29.20 per 25 test booklets; $47.20 per 25 answer sheets; $38.20 per 25 report forms; $47.20 per manual (1989, 11 pages); $48.40 per preview kit including item booklet, single self-scorable answer sheet, report form, and manual.
Time: (20–30) minutes.
Comments: Self-report and self-scorable.
Authors: Joan S. Guilford and Wayne S. Zimmerman.
Publisher: Consulting Psychologists Press, Inc.
Cross References: For reviews by Bruce H. Biskin and Gary L. Marco, see 12:174; see also T2:2185 (7 references); for a review by Kenneth B. Hoyt of a previous edition, see 6:1057.

[1110]
The Guilford-Zimmerman Temperament Survey.

Purpose: To assess multiple facets of personality.
Population: Ages 16 through adult.
Publication Dates: 1949–1978.
Acronym: GZTS.
Scores, 10: General Activity, Restraint, Ascendancy, Sociability, Emotional Stability, Objectivity, Friendliness, Thoughtfulness, Personal Relations, Masculinity/Femininity.
Administration: Individual or group.
Price Data, 2001: $52 per preview kit including item booklet, non prepaid answer sheet, scoring keys, profile, and manual (1978, 19 pages); $62.50 per 25 test booklets; $32.40 per set of scoring keys; $27.70 per 25 non-prepaid answer sheets for hand scoring; $17.50 per 25 profiles; $42.40 per GZTS handbook; $17.50 per 25 interpretation worksheets (specify male or female); $19.30 per manual; $42.40 per interpretation system manual.
Time: (45) minutes.
Comments: Revision and condensation of 3 tests: Inventory of Factors, Guilford-Martin Personnel Inventory, and Inventory of Factors STDCR.
Authors: J. P. Guilford and Wayne S. Zimmerman.
Publisher: Consulting Psychologists Press, Inc.
Cross References: See T5:1158 (3 references) and T4:1115 (18 references); for a review by John B. Gormly, see 9:460 (4 references); see also T3:1046 (24 references), 8:574 (72 references), T2:1207 (188 references), P:104 (132 references), and 6:110 (120 references); for a review by David R. Saunders, see 5:65 (48 references); for reviews by William Stephenson and Neil Van Steenberg and an excerpted review by Lawrence F. Shaffer, see 4:49 (5 references).

[1111]
Hahnemann Elementary School Behavior Rating Scale.

Purpose: Designed "to provide a standard system for identifying and measuring classroom behaviors of elementary school students in both regular and open classrooms."
Population: Elementary school students in both regular and open classrooms.
Publication Date: 1975.
Acronym: HESB.
Scores, 14: Originality, Independent Learning, Involvement, Productive with Peers, Intellectual Dependency with Peers, Failure Anxiety, Unreflectiveness, Irrelevant Talk, Disruptive Social Environment, Negative Feelings, Holding Back/Withdrawn, Critical-Competitive, Blaming, Approach to Teacher, plus 2 added items: Inattention, Academic Achievement.
Administration: Individual.
Price Data: Available from publisher.
Time: [10] minutes.
Comments: Ratings by teachers.
Authors: George Spivack and Marshall Swift.
Publisher: Hahnemann Medical College & Hospital, Department of Mental Health Sciences [No reply from publisher; status unknown].
Cross References: See T5:1161 (2 references) and T4:1116 (5 references).

[1112]
Hahnemann High School Behavior Rating Scale.

Purpose: Designed to "identify and measure classroom behaviors of junior and senior high school students."
Population: Grades 7–12.
Publication Dates: 1971–1972.
Acronym: HHSB.
Scores, 13: Reasoning Ability, Originality, Verbal Interaction, Rapport with Teacher, Anxious Producer, General Anxiety, Quiet-Withdrawn, Poor Work Habits, Lack Intellectual Independence, Dogmatic-Inflexible, Verbal Negativism, Disturbance-Restless, Expressed Inability.
Administration: Individual.
Price Data: Available from publisher.
Time: Administration time not reported.
Comments: Ratings by teachers.
Authors: George Spivack and Marshall Swift.

Publisher: Hahnemann Medical College & Hospital, Department of Mental Health Sciences [No reply from publisher; status unknown].

Cross References: See T4:1117 (3 references); for a review by Bert O. Richmond, see 9:462 (2 references); see also T3:1050 (2 references).

[1113]
Hall Occupational Orientation Inventory, Fourth Edition.

Purpose: Designed to help individuals understand their values, needs, interests, and preferred life-styles, and how these relate to career goals and future educational plans.

Population: Grades 3–7, 8–16 and adults, low-literate adults, junior high students–adults.

Publication Dates: 1968–2000.

Administration: Group or individual.

Price Data, 2002: $18.65 per Choosing: Your Way, a supplementary career reader (2000, 40 pages); $18.65 per Counselor/User's manual (2000, 59 pages); $15 per sample set (specify Intermediate, YA/C/A, and Adult Basic Forms); $21.75 per sample set with Choosing: Your Way; $21.75 per sample set with Counselor/User's manual; $39.75 per sample set with both Choosing: Your Way and Counselor/User's manual; $19 per sample set (Form II); $25.75 per sample set with Professional Manual (Form II).

Time: (45–60) minutes.

Author: Lacy G. Hall.

Publisher: Scholastic Testing Service, Inc.

   a) INTERMEDIATE FORM.

   Population: Grades 3–7.

   Publication Dates: 1968–1976.

   Scores, 22: Free Choice, Chance Game, Effort to Learn, Belonging, Being Safe, Goals, Being Important, Being Yourself, Being Proud, Order, Working Alone, Working with Your Hands, Working with People, Places, Ready to Learn, Rewards, Physical Fitness, The World Around You, Others, Skills, Use of Time, Being on Guard.

   Price Data: $33.90 per 20 inventory booklets; $24.55 per 20 interpretive folders; $24.55 per 20 response sheets.

   b) YOUNG ADULT/COLLEGE/ADULT FORM.

   Population: Grades 8–16 and adults.

   Publication Dates: 1968–2000.

   Scores, 29: Creativity-Independence, Information-Knowledge, Belongingness, Security, Aspiration, Esteem, Self-Actualization, Personal Satisfaction, Routine-Dependence, People-Social-Accommodating, Data-Information, Things-Physical, People-Business-Influencing, Ideas-Scientific, Aesthetics-Arts, Geographic Location, Abilities, Monetary-Compensation, Workplace, Coworkers, Time, Qualifications, Risk, Subjective External Authority, Objective External Authority, Subjective Internal Authority, Shaping/Autonomy/ and Self-Empowerment, Interdependent, Procrastination.

   Price Data: $36.15 per 20 inventory booklets; $25.65 per 20 self-interpretive folders; $24.55 per 20 response sheets.

   c) ADULT BASIC FORM.

   Population: Low-literate adults.

   Publication Dates: 1968–2000.

   Scores, 29: Same as for *b* above.

   Price Data: $33.85 per 20 inventory booklets; $24.55 per 20 self-interpretive folders; $24.55 per 20 response sheets.

   d) FORM II.

   Population: Junior high students–adults.

   Publication Dates: 1968–1989.

   Scores, 15: Creativity-Independence, Information-Knowledge, Belongingness, Security, Aspiration, Esteem, Self-Actualization, Personal Satisfaction, Routine-Dependence, People-Social-Accommodating, Data-Information, Things-Physical, People-Business-Influencing, Ideas-Scientific, Aesthetics-Arts.

   Price Data: $35.80 per 20 inventory booklets; $105.20 per 20 For self-interpretive digests; $24.85 per 20 response sheets.

Cross References: For reviews by Gregory Schraw and Hilda Wing of an earlier edition, see 12:175 (1 reference); see T3:1051 (4 references); for reviews by Robert H. Dolliver and Austin C. Frank of an earlier edition, see 8:1003 (5 references); see also T2:2187 (3 references); for a review by Donald G. Zytowski of the original edition, see 7:104 (4 references).

[1114]
Halstead-Reitan Neuropsychological Test Battery.

Purpose: "Developed to evaluate the brain-behavior functioning of individuals."

Population: Ages 5–8, 9–14, 15 and over.

Publication Dates: 1979-1993.

Scores: 1 combined score for each battery and for areas of function, plus scores for individual tests.

Price Data: Available from publisher.

Comments: Consists of three neuropsychological test batteries, one for each age level; each battery includes a Neuropsychological Deficit Scale, which provides normative ranges for each test, for areas of function, and for the entire battery in addition to cut-off scores (brain impairment versus normal brain status) for each variable, area, and summary score.

Author: Ralph M. Reitan.

Publisher: Reitan Neuropsychology Laboratory/Press.

   a) REITAN-INDIANA NEUROPSYCHOLOGICAL TEST BATTERY FOR YOUNG CHILDREN.

   Population: Ages 5–8.

1) *Category.*
Comments: Projection box with slide projector and slides necessary for administration.
2) *Tactual Performance.*
Scores, 3: Total Time, Memory, Localization.
Comments: 6-figure board.
3) *Finger Tapping.*
Comments: Electronic finger tapper necessary for administration.
4) *Matching Pictures.*
5) *Individual Performance.*
Subtests, 4: Matching Figures, Star, Matching V's, Concentric Squares.
6) *Marching.*
7) *Progressive Figures.*
8) *Color Form.*
Scores, 2: Total Time, Errors.
9) *Lateral Dominance Examination.*
10) *Target.*
11) *Aphasia Screening.*
12) *Sensory Perceptual.*
Subtests, 6: Imperception (Tactile, Auditory, Visual), Tactile Finger Recognition, Finger-Tip Symbol Writing and Recognition, Tactile Form Recognition.
13) *Grip Strength.*
Scores, 2: Preferred Grip, Nonpreferred Grip.
Comments: Hand dynamometer necessary for administration.
14) *Name Writing.*
b) HALSTEAD-REITAN NEUROPSYCHOLOGICAL TEST BATTERY FOR OLDER CHILDREN.
Population: Ages 9–14.
1) *Category.*
Comments: Similar to *a* above.
2) *Tactual Performance.*
Comments: Same as *a* above.
3) *Seashore Rhythm Test.*
4) *Speech–Sounds Perception.*
5) *Trail Making.*
6) *Finger Tapping.*
Comments: Manual finger tapping apparatus necessary for administration.
7) *Aphasia Screening.*
8) *Sensory–Perceptual.*
Subtests, 5: Sensory Imperception (Tactile, Auditory, Visual), Finger Agnosia, Finger-Tip Number Writing.
9) *Tactile Form Recognition.*
10) *Grip Strength.*
Scores, 2: Preferred Grip, Nonpreferred Grip.
Comments: Hand dynamometer necessary for administration.

11) *Lateral Dominance.*
12) *Name Writing.*
c) HALSTEAD-REITAN NEUROPSYCHOLOGICAL TEST BATTERY FOR ADULTS.
Population: Ages 15 and over.
Comments: Battery has 11 tests same as *b* above with a number of changes in equipment, administration, and scoring forms for this level.
Cross References: See T5:1164 (187 references) and T4:1119 (159 references); for reviews by Raymond S. Dean and Manfred J. Meier, see 9:463 (79 references); see also T3:1052 (4 references).

[1115]
Halstead Russell Neuropsychological Evaluation System.

Purpose: Provides "comprehensive measures of the functions relevant to neuropsychological assessment."
Population: Neuropsychological patients.
Publication Date: 1993.
Acronym: HRNES.
Scores, 3: Percent Impaired Score, Average Index Score, Lateralization Key.
Administration: Individual.
Price Data, 2002: $450 per complete kit including manual (99 pages), 10 recording booklets, and 3.5-inch IBM unlimited use microcomputer disk; $49.50 per 10 recording booklets; $52 per manual.
Time: Administration time not reported.
Comments: HRNES computer program compiles raw scores from up to 22 tests, corrects them for age and education, and converts them to scaled scores; includes unlimited use disk.
Authors: Elbert W. Russell and Regina I. Starkey.
Publisher: Western Psychological Services.
Cross References: For reviews by Roderick K. Mahurin and Paul Retzlaff, see 12:176 (1 reference).

[1116]
Hamilton Depression Inventory.

Purpose: "Designed for the evaluation of the severity of depressive symptomatology."
Population: Adults.
Publication Date: 1995.
Acronym: HDI.
Scores: Total score only.
Administration: Group or Individual.
Forms, 2: HS and Short Form.
Price Data: Available from publisher for complete kit including manual (140 pages), 5 reusable item booklets, 25 summary sheets, 25 answer sheets, and 5 short form test booklets.
Time: (10) minutes.
Comments: Self-report version of the Hamilton Depression Rating Scale; computer scoring system available from publisher.

Authors: William M. Reynolds and Kenneth A. Kobak.
Publisher: Psychological Assessment Resources, Inc.
Cross References: See T5:1166 (230 references); for reviews by Ephrem Fernandez and Carl Isenhart, see 13:136 (43 references).

[1117]
Hammill Multiability Achievement Test.

Purpose: Designed as a "measure of school achievement."
Population: Ages 7-0 to 17-11.
Publication Date: 1998.
Acronym: HAMAT.
Scores, 5: Reading, Writing, Arithmetic, Facts, General Achievement Quotient.
Administration: Individual.
Forms, 2: A, B.
Price Data, 2001: $189 per complete kit including examiner's manual (116 pages), 25 each Form A and Form B response booklets, and 25 each Form A and Form B record forms; $39 per student response booklets (Form A or B); $24 per profile/examiner record forms; $69 per examiner's manual.
Time: (30–60) minutes.
Authors: Donald D. Hammill, Wayne P. Hresko, Jerome J. Ammer, Mary E. Cronin, and Sally S. Quinby.
Publisher: PRO-ED.
Cross References: For reviews by Jeffrey A. Jenkins and Eleanor E. Sanford, see 14:159.

[1118]
The Hand Test [Revised].

Purpose: Designed as "a diagnostic technique that uses pictures of hands as the projective medium."
Population: Ages 5 and older.
Publication Dates: 1959–1991.
Scores, 41: 24 quantitative scores: Interpersonal (Affection, Dependence, Communication, Exhibition, Direction, Aggression, Total), Environmental (Acquisition, Active, Passive, Total), Maladjustive (Tension, Crippled, Fear, Total), Withdrawal (Description, Bizarre, Failure, Total), Experience Ratio, Acting Out Ratio, Pathological, Average Initial Response Time, High Minus Low Score, plus 17 qualitative scores: Ambivalent, Automatic Phrase, Cylindrical, Denial, Emotion, Gross, Hiding, Immature, Inanimate, Movement, Oral, Perplexity, Sensual, Sexual, Original, Repetition.
Administration: Individual.
Price Data, 2002: $134 per complete kit including manual (1983, 94 pages), manual supplement: Interpreting Child and Adolescent Responses (1991, 41 pages), 25 scoring booklets, and 1 set of picture cards; $18 per 25 scoring booklets; $35 per set of picture cards; $48 per manual; $44.50 per manual supplement: Interpreting Child and Adolescent Responses.

Time: (10) minutes.
Author: Edwin E. Wagner.
Publisher: Western Psychological Services.
Cross References: For reviews by Colin Cooper and Susana Urbina, see 14:161; see also T5:1169 (6 references) and T4:1121 (17 references); for a review by Marcia B. Shaffer of an earlier edition, see 10:134 (5 references); see also 9:464 (16 references), T3:1053 (21 references), 8:575 (29 references), T2:1470 (15 references), and P:438 (12 references); for a review by Goldine C. Gleser and an excerpted review by Irving R. Stone of an earlier edition, see 6:216 (6 references).

[1119]
Hand-Tool Dexterity Test.

Purpose: Intended to "provide a measure of proficiency in using ordinary mechanic's tools."
Population: Adolescents and adults.
Publication Dates: 1946–1981.
Acronym: HTDT.
Scores: Total score only.
Administration: Individual.
Price Data, 2002: $348 per complete set including all necessary equipment and manual (1981, 19 pages); $37 per manual.
Time: (5–10) minutes.
Comments: Examinee's score based on time it takes to finish test.
Author: George K. Bennett.
Publisher: The Psychological Corporation.
Cross References: See T3:1054 (1 reference) and 7:1044 (4 references); for reviews by C. H. Lawshe, Jr. and Neil D. Warren, see 3:649 (2 references).

[1120]
Hanes Sales Selection Inventory.

Purpose: Designed "to help select potentially successful insurance, printing and closely allied salesmen."
Population: Applicants for sales positions.
Publication Date: No date.
Scores: Part II, Part III, Drive Score.
Administration: Group.
Price Data: Price data available from publisher.
Time: (30) minutes.
Author: Bernard Hanes.
Publisher: Psychometric Affiliates.

[1121]
Hare P-Scan.

Purpose: Designed as a "tool for assessing psychopathy and managing risk for antisocial, criminal, and violent behavior."
Population: Ages 13 and older.
Publication Date: 1999.
Scores, 4: Interpersonal Facet, Affective Facet, Lifestyle Facet, Total.

Administration: Individual.

Price Data, 2002: $57 per complete kit including 25 QuikScore™ forms, manual, and book "Without Conscience"; $24 per 25 QuikScore™ forms; $20 per manual; $22 per specimen set including 3 QuikScore™ forms and manual.

Time: (10–15) minutes.

Comments: Ratings by evaluator.

Author: Robert D. Hare.

Publisher: Multi-Health Systems, Inc.

[1122]
Hare Psychopathy Checklist—Revised.

Purpose: "Designed to assess psychopathic (antisocial) personality disorders in forensic populations."

Population: Prison inmates, forensic patients ages 18 and older.

Publication Dates: 1990–1991.

Acronym: PCL-R.

Scores, 3: Factor 1, Factor 2, Total.

Administration: Individual.

Price Data, 2002: $250 per complete hardcover kit including manual (1991, 77 pages), 1 rating booklet, 25 QuikScore™ forms, and 25 interview guides; $215 per softcover kit; $100 per manual; $40 per reusable hardcover rating booklet; $50 per 25 QuikScore™ forms; $100 per 25 interview guides; $30 per rating criteria clipboard.

Time: (90–180) minutes.

Comments: Structured interview; time includes interview and review of available collateral information; Factor 1 description: Selfish, callous, and remorseless use of others; Factor 2 description: Chronically unstable and antisocial lifestyle, social deviance.

Author: Robert D. Hare.

Publisher: Multi-Health Systems, Inc.

Cross References: See T5:1174 (1 reference); for reviews by Solomon M. Fulero and Gerald L. Stone, see 12:177 (5 references); see also T4:1127 (3 references).

[1123]
Hare Psychopathy Checklist: Screening Version.

Purpose: To screen for psychopathy in forensic and nonforensic settings.

Population: Adults age 18 and over.

Publication Date: 1995.

Acronym: PCL:SV.

Scores, 3: Part 1, Part 2, Total.

Administration: Individual.

Price Data, 2002: $120 per kit including 25 interview guides, 25 QuikScore™ forms, and manual (82 pages); $90 per 25 interview guides/QuikScore™ forms; $45 per 25 interview guides; $45 per 25 QuikScore™ forms; $40 per manual; $30 per optional

rating criteria clipboard; $42 per specimen set including manual, 3 interview guides, and 3 QuikScore™ forms.

Time: (30–60) minutes; case history review and scoring require further (20–30) minutes.

Comments: Interview format; shortened version of Hare Psychopathy Checklist—Revised (1122).

Authors: S. D. Hart, D. N. Cox, and R. D. Hare.

Publisher: Multi-Health Systems, Inc.

Cross References: For reviews by Ronald J. Ganellen and by Nathaniel J. Pallone and James J. Hennessy, see 14:162.

[1124]
Harmonic Improvisation Readiness Record and Rhythm Improvisation Readiness Record.

Purpose: Designed to "help determine objectively whether individual students have the necessary harmonic and rhythmic readiness to learn to improvise" music.

Population: Grades 3 through music graduate school.

Publication Date: 1998.

Scores, 2: Harmonic Readiness, Rhythmic Readiness.

Administration: Group.

Price Data, 2001: $110 per complete kit including 100 harmonic answer sheets, 100 rhythm answer sheets, scoring masks, compact disc, and manual (1998); $20 per 100 answer sheets (specify harmonic or rhythm); $20 per scoring masks; $25 per compact disc.

Time: (20) minutes per test.

Comments: Can be machine scored.

Author: Edwin E. Gordon.

Publisher: G.I.A. Publications, Inc.

[1125]
The Harrington-O'Shea Career Decision-Making System Revised.

Purpose: An interest inventory that provides an assessment of career interests, job choices, school subjects, future plans, values, and abilities.

Population: Grade 7 and over.

Publication Dates: 1976–2000.

Acronym: CDM.

Administration: Group or individual.

Price Data, 2002: $52.95 per Level I or Level II hand-scored edition; $29.95 per manual.

Foreign Language Edition: Hand-scored version of original CDM also available in Spanish.

Authors: Thomas F. Harrington and Arthur J. O'Shea.

Publisher: American Guidance Service, Inc.

a) LEVEL 1.

Publication Dates: 1992–2000.

Scores: 6 scores: Crafts, Scientific, The Arts, Social, Business, Office Operations, used to iden-

tify occupational areas from among 18 career clusters: Manual, Skilled Crafts, Technical, Math-Science, Medical-Dental, Literary, Art, Music, Entertainment, Customer Service, Personal Service, Social Service, Education, Sales, Management, Legal, Clerical, Data Analysis.
Time: (20–25) minutes.
Comments: Hand-scored.
b) LEVEL 2.
Publication Dates: 1976–2000.
Scores: Same as *a* above and questions in 5 areas: Job Choices, School Subjects, Future Plans, Values, Abilities.
Time: (30–35) minutes.
Comments: Hand-scored edition and computer-scored edition (individual and group summary reports available).
Cross References: See T5:1177 (2 references); for reviews by Debra Neubert and Marcia B. Shaffer, see 12:179; see also T4:1128 (1 reference); for a review by Caroline Manuele-Adkins of an earlier edition, see 10:136 (1 reference); see also T3:1054 (3 references); for a review by Carl G. Willis of an earlier edition, see 8:1004.

[1126]
Hassles and Uplifts Scales, Research Edition.
Purpose: To identify sources of stress and positive aspects of daily living that help counteract the damaging effects of stress.
Population: Adults.
Publication Date: 1989.
Acronym: HSUP.
Administration: Group.
Price Data: Available from publisher.
Time: (10-15) minutes per test.
Comments: Self-administered; tests available as separates.
Authors: Richard S. Lazarus and Susan Folkman.
Publisher: Mind Garden, Inc.
a) THE DAILY HASSLES SCALE.
Scores, 2: Frequency, Severity.
b) THE UPLIFTS SCALE.
Scores, 2: Frequency, Intensity.
c) THE COMBINED HASSLES AND UPLIFTS SCALES.
Scores, 2: Hassles, Uplifts.
Cross References: See T5:1178 (17 references) and T4:1132 (2 references); for reviews by Karen S. Budd and Nancy Heilman and by Barbara A. Reilly, see 11:155 (6 references).

[1127]
Hay Aptitude Test Battery [Revised].
Purpose: "Helps select applicants with the ability to work quickly and accurately with numerical and alphabetical detail."

Population: Applicants for positions that place a heavy emphasis on information processing for speed and accuracy.
Publication Dates: 1947–1999.
Scores, 3: Number Perception, Name Finding, Number Series Completion.
Administration: Group or individual.
Price Data, 2001: $385 per test battery including all 4 tests, user's manual (1999, 32 pages), and scoring key; $65 per 25 Warm-Up Tests; $85 per 25 tests (specify Number Perception Test, Name Finding Test, or Number Series Completion Test); quantity discounts available.
Foreign Language Editions: French and Spanish versions available.
Time: 4 minutes per test; 1 minute per Warm-Up Test.
Author: Edward N. Hay.
Publisher: Wonderlic, Inc.
Cross References: For reviews by Mark A. Albanese and Michael Kane, see 14:164; for reviews by Sue M. Legg and M. David Miller of an earlier edition, see 12:179; for a review by Robert P. Vecchio of an earlier edition, see 9:470; see also T2:2132 (2 references) and 5:849 (2 references); for reviews by Reign H. Bittner and Edward E. Cureton, see 4:725 (8 references).

[1128]
HCR-20: Assessing Risk for Violence.
Purpose: Designed as "a broad-band violence risk assessment instrument with potential applicability to a variety of settings."
Population: Adults (Psychiatric and Correctional Settings).
Publication Date: 1997.
Scores, 4: Final Risk Judgment, Historical Items, Clinical Items, Risk Management Items.
Administration: Individual.
Price Data: Available from publisher.
Time: Administration time not reported.
Comments: "Research instrument."
Authors: Christopher D. Webster, Kevin S. Douglas, Derek Eaves, and Stephen D. Hart.
Publisher: Mental Health, Law, and Policy Institute, Simon Fraser University [Canada].

[1129]
Health and Daily Living Form, Second Edition.
Purpose: To examine the influence of extratreatment factors on treatment outcome as well as to explore the social resources and coping processes people use to prevent and adapt to stressful life circumstances.
Publication Dates: 1984–1990.
Acronym: HDLF.
Administration: Group.
Forms, 2: Youth Form, Adult Form B.

Price Data, 2001: $25 per sampler set; $125 per 1-year use permission for up to 200 administrations.
Time: (30–45) minutes.
Comments: May be administered as an interview or as a questionnaire.
Authors: Rudolf H. Moos, Ruth C. Cronkite, and John W. Finney.
Publisher: Mind Garden, Inc.
a) YOUTH FORM.
Population: Students ages 12–18.
Scores: 9 indices: Health-Related (Self-Confidence, Positive Mood, Distressed Mood, Physical Symptoms, Medical Conditions, Health—Risk Behaviors), Social Functioning (Family Activities, Activities with Friends, Social Integration in School).
b) ADULT FORM B.
Population: Adults.
Scores: 41 indices: Health-Related Functioning (Self-Confidence, Physical Symptoms, Medical Conditions, Global Depression, Depressive Mood and Ideation, Endogenous Depression, Depressive Features, Depressed Mood/Past 12 Months, Alcohol Consumption—Quantity, Alcohol Consumption—Quantity/Frequency, Drinking Problems, Smoking Symptoms, Medication Use), Social Functioning and Resources (Social Activities with Friends, Network Contacts, Number of Close Relationships, Quality of Significant Relationship), Family Functioning and Home Environment (Family Social Activities, Family Task Sharing, Tasks Performed by Self, Tasks Performed by Partner, Family Arguments, Negative Home Environment), Children's Health and Functioning (Children's Physical Health Problems, Children's Psychological Health Problems, Children's Total Health Problems, Children's Behavioral Problems, Children's Health—Risk Behaviors), Life Change Events (Negative Life Change Events, Exit Events, Positive Life Change Events), Help-Seeking (Mental Health Professional [past 12 months], Mental Health Professional [ever gone], Non-Mental Health Professional [past 12 months], Non-Mental Health Professional [ever gone]), Family Level Composite (Quality of Conjugal Relationship, Family Social Activities, Family Agreement on Task Sharing, Family Agreement on Household Tasks, Family Arguments, Negative Home Environment).
Cross References: See T5:1181 (28 references) and T4:1135 (19 references); for reviews by Arthur M. Nezu and Steven P. Schinke, see 10:137 (8 references).

[1130]
Health and Safety Education Test: National Achievement Tests.
Purpose: Designed to measure students' knowledge of health and safety.

Population: Grades 3–6.
Publication Dates: 1947–1960.
Scores, 5: Good Habits, Cause and Effect, Facts, Application of Rules, Total.
Administration: Group.
Manual: No manual.
Price Data: Available from publisher.
Time: 40(45) minutes.
Authors: Lester D. Crow and Loretta C. Ryan.
Publisher: Psychometric Affiliates.
Cross References: For a review by Clarence H. Nelson, see 5:555.

[1131]
Health Attribution Test.
Purpose: Constructed to measure "beliefs about the causes and cures of illness."
Population: High school and college and adult patients.
Publication Date: 1990.
Acronym: HAT.
Scores, 3: Internal Scale, Powerful Others Scale, Chance Scale.
Administration: Group or individual.
Price Data, 2002: $27 per complete kit including 10 combination test booklets/answer sheets/scoring keys, and manual (20 pages); $30 per 25 combined test booklets/answer sheets/scoring keys; $15 per manual.
Foreign Language Edition: Spanish edition available.
Time: (10) minutes.
Authors: Jeanne Achterberg and G. Frank Lawlis.
Publisher: Institute for Personality and Ability Testing, Inc.
Cross References: For reviews by Dianna L. Newman and Stephen Olejnik, see 11:156.

[1132]
Health Care Reading Test–Form HC-1.
Purpose: "To measure the reading skills required for health care workers."
Population: Adults.
Publication Date: 1992.
Scores: Total score only.
Administration: Group.
Price Data, 2002: $200 per complete kit including 10 reusable test booklets, 100 answer sheets, manual (13 pages), and scoring key.
Time: (30) minutes.
Author: Roland T. Ramsay.
Publisher: Ramsay Corporation.
Cross References: For reviews by Betty Bergstrom and Craig S. Shwery, see 13:252.

[1133]
Health Education Test: Knowledge and Application: Acorn National Achievement Tests, Revised Edition.

Purpose: Constructed to measure the student's knowledge and application of health information.
Population: Grades 7–13.
Publication Dates: 1946–1956.
Scores, 3: Knowledge, Application, Total.
Administration: Group.
Manual: No manual.
Price Data: Available from publisher.
Time: 40(45) minutes.
Authors: John H. Shaw and Maurice E. Troyer.
Publisher: Psychometric Affiliates.
Cross References: See T2:928 (1 reference) and 5:557 (1 reference); for reviews by H. H. Remmers and Mabel E. Rugen, see 3:421.

[1134]
Health Knowledge Test for College Freshmen: National Achievement Tests.

Purpose: Designed to measure the health knowledge of college freshmen.
Population: College freshmen.
Publication Date: 1956.
Scores: Total score only.
Administration: Group.
Price Data: Available from publisher.
Time: 40(45) minutes.
Author: A. Frank Bridges.
Publisher: Psychometric Affiliates.
Cross References: For a review by James E. Bryan, see 5:558 (3 references).

[1135]
Health Occupations Basic Entrance Test.

Purpose: "A diagnostic instrument [designed] to assist Health Occupation schools evaluate the academic and counseling skills of new applicants to their programs."
Population: Adult applicants to health occupation schools or programs.
Publication Dates: 2000–2001.
Acronym: HOBET.
Scores, 28: 7 Essential Math Skills scores (Whole Numbers, Number System Conversions, Algebra Equations, Percent Operations, Decimal Operations, Fractions Operations, Composite), 3 Reading Comprehension scores (Reading Rate, Reading Rate Placement, Composite), 3 Critical Thinking Appraisal scores (Main Idea of Passage, Inferential Reading, Predicting of Outcomes), Testtaking Skills score, 2 Social Interaction Profile scores (Passive, Aggressive), 5 Stress Level Profile scores (Family, Social, Money/Time, Academic,

Work Place), 6 Learning Styles (Auditory Learner, Solitary Learner, Visual Learner, Social Learner, Oral Dependent Learner, Writing Dependent Learner), Composite Percentage.
Administration: Group.
Forms, 2: A, B.
Price Data, 2002: $17 per test by computer; $10.50 per test booklet (36 pages); $8 per answer sheet; $27.50 per Study Guide (150 pages); quantity discounts available.
Time: 150 minutes.
Comments: Generates a Diagnostic Report including Group Report, and individual Student Reports; Group Report provides group-level mean percentages and normative comparisons for the 28 scores; optional Study Guide offers test-taking strategy tips and practice tests.
Author: Michael D. Frost.
Publisher: Educational Resources, Inc.

[1136]
Health Problems Checklist.

Purpose: To facilitate "the rapid assessment of the health status and potential health problems of clients typically seen in psychotherapy settings."
Population: Adults.
Publication Dates: 1984–1989.
Scores: Items in 13 areas: General Health, Cardiovascular/Pulmonary, Endocrine/Hematology, Gastrointestinal, Dermatological, Visual, Auditory/Olfactory, Mouth/Throat/Nose, Orthopedic, Neurological, Genitourinary, Habits, History; no formal scoring procedure.
Administration: Individual or group.
Manual: No manual.
Price Data: Available from publisher.
Time: (10–20) minutes.
Author: John A. Schinka.
Publisher: Psychological Assessment Resources, Inc.
Cross References: See T5:1186 (1 reference); for a review by Robert M. Kaplan and Michelle T. Toshima of an earlier version, see 10:138.

[1137]
Health Status Questionnaire 2.0.

Purpose: Designed "to measure physical and social functioning and emotional well-being."
Population: Ages 14 and older.
Publication Date: 1994.
Acronym: HSQ® 2.0.
Scores, 8: Health Perception, Physical Functioning, Role Limitations-Physical, Role Limitations-Emotional, Social Functioning, Mental Health, Bodily Pain, Energy/Fatigue.
Administration: Group.
Price Data, 2002: $19 per 25 answer sheets; $26 per user's guide (48 pages); $1.20 per MICTOTEST Q

Assessment System Software single administration report; price data available from publisher for MICROTEST Q Assessment System Software Progress Report.

Time: (5–10) minutes.

Comments: Self-administered; may be administered in paper-and-pencil format or online; contains all items found on the SF-36 Questionnaire (MOS 36-Item Short Form Health Survey; 2273) and SF-36 scores are included in the HSQ 2.0 report; scoring via MICROTEST Q Assessment System Software.

Authors: Health Outcomes Institute and the RAND Health Services Program.

Publisher: NCS Assessments [Minnetonka].

[1138]
Health Test: National Achievement Tests.

Purpose: To assess students' information, judgment, and evaluation of health knowledge and habits.

Population: Grades 3–8.

Publication Dates: 1937–1957.

Scores, 5: Recognizing Best Habits, Health Comparisons, Causes and Effects, Health Facts, Total.

Administration: Group.

Forms, 2: A, B.

Manual: No manual.

Price Data: Available from publisher.

Time: (40) minutes.

Authors: Robert K. Speer and Samuel Smith.

Publisher: Psychometric Affiliates.

Cross References: For a review by Benno G. Fricke, see 5:560; for a review by Jacob S. Orleans, see 4:485.

[1139]
Healthcare Customer Service Test.

Purpose: Selects customer service oriented workers for hospitals and healthcare settings.

Population: Hospital employees (service, skilled, professional, nursing, administrative, physician, technicians, environmental services).

Publication Dates: 1996–1997.

Acronym: HCST.

Scores: Collaborate, Accommodate, Respect, Engage, Total.

Administration: Group.

Price Data: Available from publisher.

Time: (25–35) minutes, untimed.

Comments: Used for selection; subtests can be used for interview probes.

Author: Healthcare Testing, Inc.

Publisher: Silverwood Enterprises, LLC.

[1140]
HELP CHECKLIST (Hawaii Early Learning Profile).

Purpose: Assesses developmental skills/behaviors.

Population: Ages birth–3.

Publication Dates: 1984–1988.

Acronym: HELP Checklist.

Scores: Item scores only; 6 developmental areas: Cognitive, Language, Gross Motor, Fine Motor, Social, Self-Help.

Administration: Individual.

Price Data: Available from publisher.

Time: Administration time not reported.

Comments: Ratings by professionals.

Authors: Setsu Furuno, Katherine A. O'Reilly, Carol M. Hosaka, Takayo T. Inatsuka, Barbara Zeisloft-Falbey, and Toney Allman.

Publisher: VORT Corporation.

Cross References: For reviews by William Steven Lang and Koressa Kutsick Malcolm, see 11:157.

[1141]
Help Desk Support Staff Selector.

Purpose: To evaluate essential skills for the Help Desk position.

Population: Candidates for Help Desk positions.

Publication Date: 1993.

Acronym: HEDCO.

Scores: Total Score; Narrative Evaluation, Ranking, Recommendation.

Administration: Group.

Price Data, 2001: $300 per candidate; quantity discounts available.

Time: (180) minutes.

Comments: Scored by publisher; must be proctored.

Authors: Walden Personnel Testing & Training, Inc. and R. Label.

Publisher: Walden Personnel Performance, Inc. [Canada].

[1142]
Help for Special Preschoolers ASSESSMENT CHECKLIST: Ages 3-6.

Purpose: Comprehensive screening and assessment of developmentally delayed children.

Population: Ages 2-6 to 6-0.

Publication Date: 1987.

Scores: Ratings in 5 developmental areas: Self Help, Motor Development, Communication, Social Skills, Learning/Cognitive; 28 goals areas: Self-Help (Eating and Drinking, Toileting, Grooming, Dressing, Undressing, Oral and Nasal Hygiene, Self-Identification), Motor Development (Sensory Perception, Fine Motor, Gross Motor, Wheelchair, Swimming), Communication (Auditory Perception, Language Comprehension, Language, Sign Language, Speechreading), Social Skills (Adaptive Behaviors, Responsible Behaviors, Interpersonal Relationships, Personal Welfare, Social Manners), Learning/Cognitive (Attention Span, Basic Reading, Math, Writing Skills, Reasoning Skills, Music/Rhythm).

Administration: Individual.

Price Data: Price information for test booklet (20 pages) available from publisher.

Time: Administration time not reported.

Comments: Adaptation of Behavioral Characteristics Progression (BCP); upward extension of Hawaii Early Learning Profile (1140); "criterion-referenced."

Author: The Santa Cruz County Office of Education.

Publisher: VORT Corporation.

Cross References: For reviews by Harlan J. Stientjes and Gerald Tindal, see 11:158.

[1143]
Henmon-Nelson Ability Test, Canadian Edition.

Purpose: "Designed to measure those aspects of cognitive ability which are important for success in academic work and in similar endeavors outside the classroom."

Population: Grades 3–6, 6–9, 9–12.

Publication Dates: 1957–1990.

Scores: Total score only.

Administration: Group.

Price Data, 2001: $58.30 per 35 reusable or consumable test booklets (specify level); $68.90 per 100 answer sheets (hand/machine scorable); $18 per scoring mask (all levels); $21.20 per examiner's manual (1990, 44 pages); $9.95 per 10 class record sheets; $21.20 per examination kit.

Time: (30) minutes.

Comments: Adapted from the now out-of-print 1973 U.S. edition of the test (The Henmon-Nelson Tests of Mental Ability, 3:1073).

Authors: Tom A. Lamke, M. J. Nelson, and Joseph L. French.

Publisher: Nelson Thomson Learning [Canada].

Cross References: For reviews by John O. Anderson and David J. Bateson, see 12:180; see T3:1073 (13 references); for a review by Eric F. Gardner of an earlier edition, see 8:190 (14 references); see also T2:391 (52 references); for a review by Norman E. Wallen and an excerpted review by John O. Crites of an earlier edition, see 6:462 (11 references); for reviews by D. Welty Lefever and Leona E. Tyler and an excerpted review by Laurance F. Shaffer, see 5:342 (14 references); for a review by H. M. Fowler, see 4:299 (25 references); for reviews by Anne Anastasi, August Dvorak, Howard Easley, and J. P. Guilford and an excerpted review by Francis N. Maxfield, see 2:1398.

[1144]
Herrmann Brain Dominance Instrument [Revised].

Purpose: Designed to measure "a person's preference both for right-brained or left-brained thinking and for conceptual or experiential thinking."

Population: Adults.

Publication Dates: 1981–1995.

Acronym: HBDI.

Scores, 12: Left Mode Dominance, Right Mode Dominance, Quadrant (Upper Left, Lower Left, Upper Right, Lower Right), Adjective Pairs (subset of 4 Quadrant Scores), Cerebral Mode Dominance, Limbic Mode Dominance.

Administration: Group.

Manual: No manual.

Price Data, 1998: $52 per scored survey form including interpretation package.

Time: (15–20) minutes.

Comments: Self-administered; must be scored by publisher or certified practitioner.

Author: Ned Herrmann.

Publisher: Herrmann International.

Cross References: For reviews by F. Felicia Ferrara and Gabriele van Lingen, see 14:165; see also T5:1197 (1 reference); for a review by Rik Carl D'Amato of an earlier edition, see 11:159 (7 references).

[1145]
High Level Battery: Test A/75.

Purpose: To provide "measures of general intelligence, arithmetical ability and certain language abilities."

Population: Adults with at least 12 years of education.

Publication Dates: 1960–1972.

Scores: Total scores only for 4 tests in a single booklet: Mental Alertness, Arithmetic Problems, Reading Comprehension (English, Afrikaans), Vocabulary (English, Afrikaans).

Administration: Group.

Price Data: Available from publisher.

Time: 197 (215) minutes.

Comments: Formerly listed as National Institute for Personnel Research High Level Battery.

Author: D. P. M. Beukes (manual).

Publisher: Human Sciences Research Council [South Africa].

Cross References: See 6:778 (1 reference).

[1146]
High Level Figure Classification Test.

Purpose: Designed to assess intellectual ability.

Population: Grades 10–12.

Publication Date: 1983.

Acronym: HL FCT.

Scores: Total score only.

Administration: Group.

Price Data: Available from publisher.

Foreign Language Edition: Test printed in both English and Afrikaans.

Time: 30(40) minutes.

Authors: M. Werbeloff and T. R. Taylor.
Publisher: Human Sciences Research Council [South Africa].

[1147]
High School Career-Course Planner.

Purpose: Designed "to develop a high school course plan that is consistent with self-assessed career goals."
Population: Grades 8 and 9.
Publication Dates: 1983–1990.
Acronym: HSCCP.
Scores: Total score only.
Administration: Group.
Price Data: Available from publisher.
Time: (50) minutes; (5–8) minutes for computer version.
Comments: Computer version also available.
Author: CFKR Career Materials, Inc.
Publisher: CFKR Career Materials [No reply from publisher; status unknown].
Cross References: For reviews by Mary Henning-Stout and James W. Pinkney, see 12:181.

[1148]
High School Personality Questionnaire.

Purpose: Measures primary personality characteristics in adolescents.
Population: Ages 12–18.
Publication Dates: 1958–1984.
Acronym: HSPQ.
Scores, 18: 14 primary factor scores (Warmth, Abstract Thinking, Emotional Stability, Excitability, Dominance, Enthusiasm, Conformity, Boldness, Sensitivity, Withdrawal, Apprehension, Self-Sufficiency, Self-Discipline, Tension), 4 second-order factor scores (Extraversion, Anxiety, Tough Poise, Independence).
Administration: Group or individual.
Price Data, 2002: $25 per 25 reusable test booklets; $18 per scoring keys; $15 per 25 machine-scorable answer sheets; $18 per 50 hand-scoring answer sheets; $20 per 50 hand-scoring answer-profile sheets; $15 per 50 profile sheets; $15 per 50 second-order worksheets; $20 per manual (1984, 98 pages); $23 per computer interpretation introductory kit including manual, reusable test booklet, answer sheet, and prepaid processing form for computer interpretive report; $41 per hand-scoring introductory kit including test booklet, scoring keys, answer sheet, and profile sheet; computer scoring and interpretive services available from publisher for $6.50 to $30 per individual report depending upon quantity requested.
Foreign Language Edition: Information regarding several non-English-language adaptations available from publisher.
Time: (45-60) minutes.
Comments: Previously listed as Jr.–Sr. High School Personality Questionaire.

Authors: Raymond B. Cattell, Mary D. Cattell, and Edgar Johns (manual and norms).
Publisher: Institute for Personality and Ability Testing, Inc.
Cross References: See T5:1201 (6 references) and T4:1159 (4 references); for reviews by Richard I. Lanyon and Steven V. Owen, see 11:188 (17 references); see also 9:559 (8 references), T3:1233 (22 references), 8:597 (68 references), and T2:1253 (37 references); for reviews by Robert Hogan and Douglas N. Jackson, see 7:97 (53 references); see also P:136 (29 references); for reviews by C. J. Adcock and Philip E. Vernon of an earlier edition, see 6:131 (17 references); see also 5:72 (4 references).

[1149]
High School Placement Test—Open Edition.

Purpose: Designed as a measure of cognitive and basic skills to assist in placement decisions for entering freshmen.
Population: Eighth grade students.
Publication Dates: 1982–1995.
Acronym: HSPT.
Scores, 5: Verbal Skills, Quantitative Skills, Reading, Mathematics, Language.
Administration: Group.
Restricted Distribution: Available for school purchase only.
Price Data, 2002: $114.05 per starter set including manual (1995, 15 pages), and 35 test booklets; $41.35 per 35 optional test booklets (specify subject); $5 per large-print test booklet; $28.34 per 50 answer sheets; $22.94 per scoring kit including manual for hand scoring and interpreting results, 1 answer key, and 2 class record sheets; $5.83 per manual; $6.33 per manual for handscoring and interpreting results; $7.96 per technical supplement; $.42 per pressure sensitive label; $.31 per student score folder; $18 per audio-cassette; $8.18 per 20 practice tests; $19.48 per specimen set.
Time: (135) minutes plus (15–25) minutes per optional test.
Comments: Optional tests available including Science, Mechanical Aptitude, and Catholic Religion.
Author: Scholastic Testing Service, Inc.
Publisher: Scholastic Testing Service, Inc.
Cross References: For reviews by John O. Anderson and Geneva D. Haertel, see 14:166.

[1150]
High School Reading Test: National Achievement Tests.

Purpose: Designed to measure the student's mastery and application of factual material in English, reading, literature, and vocabulary.
Population: Grades 7–12.

Publication Dates: 1939–1952.
Scores, 6: Vocabulary, Word Discrimination, Sentence Meaning, Noting Details, Interpreting Paragraphs, Total.
Administration: Group.
Forms, 2: A, B.
Price Data: Available from publisher.
Time: (40) minutes.
Authors: Robert K. Speer and Samuel Smith.
Publisher: Psychometric Affiliates.
Cross References: For a review by Victor H. Noll, see 5:634; for a review by Holland Roberts, see 4:536; for a review by Robert L. McCaul, see 3:488.

[1151]
High/Scope Child Observation Record for Ages 2 1/2–6.

Purpose: Designed to assess children's development, learning, and interests.
Population: Ages 2 1/2–6 years.
Publication Date: 1992.
Acronym: COR.
Scores, 6: Initiative, Social Relations, Creative Representation, Music and Movement, Language and Literacy, Logic and Mathematics.
Administration: Group.
Price Data: Available from publisher.
Time: Administration time not reported.
Comments: Ratings by teachers.
Author: High/Scope Educational Research Foundation.
Publisher: High/Scope Educational Research Foundation.
Cross References: For reviews by Glen P. Aylwood and Mary Mathai Chittooran, see 14:167.

[1152]
Higher Education Learning Profile.

Purpose: "Designed primarily as a diagnostic instrument to assist educational programs evaluate the academic processing skills of new applicants."
Population: Adult applicants to college automotive, business, computer, electronics, legal, technology, and telecommunication programs.
Publication Date: 2001.
Acronym: HELP.
Scores, 28: Essential Math Skills (Whole Numbers, Number System Conversions, Algebra Equations, Percent Operations, Decimal Operations, Fractions Operations, Composite), Reading Comprehension (Reading Rate, Reading Rate Placement, Composite), Critical Thinking Appraisal (Main Idea of Passage, Inferential Reading, Predicting of Outcomes), Testtaking Skills, Social Interaction Profile (Passive, Aggressive), Stress Level Profile (Family, Social, Money/Time, Academic, Work Place), Learning Styles (Auditory Learner, Solitary Learner, Visual Learner, Social Learner, Oral Dependent Learner, Writing Dependent Learner), Composite Percentage.
Administration: Group.
Forms, 3: A, B, C.
Price Data, 2002: $17 per test by computer; $10.50 per test booklet; $8 per answer sheet; $27.50 per Student Study Guide; quantity discounts available.
Time: (150) minutes.
Comments: Generates a Diagnostic Report including the test Group Report, and Individual Student Reports; Group Report provides group-level mean percentages and normative comparisons for the 28 scores; optional Study Guide offers test-taking strategy tips and practice tests.
Author: Educational Resources, Inc.
Publisher: Educational Resources, Inc.

[1153]
Hill Interaction Matrix.

Purpose: "To study group development, group composition, and therapist style."
Population: Prospective members, members, and leaders of psychotherapy groups.
Publication Dates: 1954–1994.
Acronym: HIM.
Scores: Matrix of 4 columns (Topics, Groups, Personal, Relationship) and 4 rows (Conventional, Assertive, Speculative, Confrontive) produces 16 scores, 8 marginal Total scores, Grand Total, and other derivative scores.
Administration: Group or individual.
Price Data: Available from publisher.
Time: (20) minutes.
Author: Wm. Fawcett Hill [No reply from publisher; status unknown].
Publisher: Howdah Press.
   a) HIM A AND B.
   Population: Prospective members and members of psychotherapy groups.
   Publication Dates: 1954–1968.
   Editions, 2: HIM-A, HIM-B.
   b) HIM-G.
   Population: Observers and leaders of psychotherapy groups.
   Publication Dates: 1967–1968.
   Manual: No manual.
Cross References: See T5:1205 (1 reference), T4:1162 (25 references), T3:1099 (9 references), 8:577 (35 references), and T2:1214 (29 references).

[1154]
Hilson Adolescent Profile.

Purpose: "Designed as a screening tool to assess the presence and extent of adolescent behavior patterns and problems."
Population: Ages 10 to 19.

Publication Dates: 1984–1987.

Acronym: HAP.

Scores, 16: Guarded Responses, Alcohol Use, Drug Use, Educational Adjustment Difficulties, Law Violations, Frustration Tolerance, Antisocial/Risk-Taking, Rigidity/Obsessiveness, Interpersonal/Assertiveness Difficulties, Homelife Conflicts, Social/Sexual Adjustment, Health Concerns, Anxiety/Phobic Avoidance, Depression/Suicide Potential, Suspicious Temperament, Unusual Responses.

Administration: Group.

Price Data: Available from publisher.

Special Edition: Audiotape edition available.

Time: (45–55) minutes.

Comments: Self-administered; computer-scored.

Author: Robin E. Inwald.

Publisher: Hilson Research, Inc. [No reply from publisher; status unknown].

Cross References: See T5:1207 (1 reference); for a review by Allen K. Hess, see 11:161.

[1155]
Hilson Adolescent Profile—Version S.

Purpose: "Designed as a screening tool to identify adolescent emotional difficulties, depression and/or suicidal tendencies, homelife conflicts, and other behavior patterns."

Population: Ages 10–19.

Publication Date: 1993.

Acronym: HAP-S.

Scores, 7: Guarded Responses, Educational Adjustment Difficulties, Frustration Tolerance, Homelife Conflicts, Social/Sexual Adjustment, Depression/Suicide Potential, Unusual Responses.

Administration: Group.

Price Data: Available from publisher.

Time: (15–25) minutes.

Comments: Short version of the Hilson Adolescent Profile (1154).

Author: Robin Inwald.

Publisher: Hilson Research, Inc. [No reply from publisher; status unknown].

[1156]
Hilson Career Satisfaction Index.

Purpose: To aid in employee "fitness-for-duty" evaluations, promotion, and special assignment decisions.

Population: Public safety/security officers.

Publication Date: 1989.

Acronym: HCSI.

Scores, 13: Stress Patterns, Stress Symptoms, Drug/Alcohol Abuse, Interpersonal Support, Anger/Hostility Patterns, Disciplinary History, Excusing Attitudes, Aggression/Hostility, Dissatisfaction with Career, Dissatisfaction with Supervisor, Relationship with Co-Workers, Dissatisfaction with Job, Defensiveness.

Administration: Group.

Price Data: Available from publisher.

Time: (25–35) minutes.

Author: Robin Inwald.

Publisher: Hilson Research, Inc. [No reply from publisher; status unknown].

Cross References: See T4:1166 (1 reference).

[1157]
Hilson Personnel Profile/Success Quotient.

Purpose: To identify individual "strengths," behavior patterns, and personality characteristics "leading to success in a variety of work settings."

Population: High school through adult.

Publication Date: 1988.

Acronym: HPP/SQ.

Scores, 13: Candor, Achievement History, Social Ability (Extroversion, Popularity/"Charisma," Sensitivity to Approval), "Winner's" Image (Competitive Spirit, Self-Worth, Family Achievement Expectations), Initiative (Drive, Preparation Style, Goal Orientation, Anxiety About Organization), Success Quotient.

Administration: Group.

Price Data: Available from publisher.

Time: (20–30) minutes.

Author: Robin E. Inwald.

Publisher: Hilson Research, Inc. [No reply from publisher; status unknown].

Cross References: For a review by Joseph G. Law, Jr., see 11:162.

[1158]
Hogan Development Survey.

Purpose: "Designed to assess eleven common dysfunctional dispositions."

Population: Ages 16 and older.

Publication Dates: 1995–1997.

Acronym: HDS.

Scores: 11 scales: Excitable, Skeptical, Cautious, Reserved, Leisurely, Bold, Mischievous, Colorful, Imaginative, Diligent, Dutiful.

Administration: Group.

Price Data, 1998: $2 per test booklet; $12.50 per 25 answer sheets; $45 per manual (1997, 74 pages); $30 per interpretive profile; $15 per graph or data file profile.

Time: (20) minutes.

Authors: Robert Hogan and Joyce Hogan (manual).

Publisher: Hogan Assessment Systems, Inc.

Cross References: For reviews by Glen Fox and E. Scott Huebner, see 14:168.

[1159]
Hogan Personality Inventory [Revised].

Purpose: Measure of normal personality designed for use in personnel selection, individualized assessment, and career-related decision making.

Population: College students and adults.

Publication Dates: 1985–1995.

Acronym: HPI.

Scores: 7 primary scale scores (Intellectance, Adjustment, Ambition, Sociability, Likeability, Prudence, School Success), 6 occupational scale scores (Service Orientation, Stress Tolerance, Reliability, Clerical Potential, Sales Potential, Managerial Potential), and Validity scale score.

Administration: Group.

Price Data, 1998: $2 per 5 reusable test booklets; $12.50 per 25 answer sheets; $45 per technical manual (1995, 126 pages); $40 per specimen set including manual, sample report, reusable test booklet, and answer sheet; scoring services producing interpretive and/or graphic reports available from publisher ($30 per interpretive Personality Report; $15 per graphic; $15 per data file; $.50 per faculty research; $10 per interpretive report for Occupational Scale and Clerical, Sales, or Managerial Scales; $5 per graphic).

Time: (15–20) minutes.

Authors: Robert Hogan and Joyce Hogan (manual).

Publisher: Hogan Assessment Systems, Inc.

Cross References: See T5:1212 (1 reference); for reviews by Stephen N. Axford and Steven G. LoBello, see 13:138 (2 references); see also T4:1169 (7 references); for reviews by James J. Hennessy and Rolf A. Peterson of an earlier edition, see 10:140.

[1160]
Holden Psychological Screening Inventory.

Purpose: "To provide a very brief measure of psychiatric symptomatology, social symptomatology, and depression."

Population: Ages 14 and older.

Publication Date: 1996.

Acronym: HPSI.

Scores, 4: Psychiatric Symptomatology, Social Symptomatology, Depression, Total.

Administration: Individual or group.

Price Data, 2002: $53 per complete kit including manual (50 pages) and 25 QuikScore™ forms; $27 per 25 QuikScore™ forms (English or French-Canadian); $32 per manual; $33 per specimen set including manual and 3 QuikScore™ forms.

Comments: Windows™ version computer administration and scoring available on CD or 3.5-inch disk.

Foreign Language Editions: French-Canadian QuikScore™ forms available.

Time: [5–7] minutes.

Comments: Self-report.

Author: Ronald R. Holden.

Publisher: Multi-Health Systems, Inc.

Cross References: For reviews by Stephen N. Axford and Janet F. Carlson, see 14:169; see also T5:1213 (1 reference).

[1161]
Holtzman Inkblot Technique.

Purpose: Designed as a projective personality test.

Population: Ages 5 and over.

Publication Dates: 1958–1972.

Acronym: HIT.

Scores, 20–22: Reaction Time (a only), Rejection, Location, Space, Form Definiteness, Form Appropriateness, Color, Shading, Movement, Pathognomic Verbalization, Integration, Content (Human, Animal, Anatomy, Sex, Abstract), Anxiety, Hostility, Barrier, Penetration, Balance (a only), Popular.

Administration: Group or individual.

Price Data, 2002: $11 per 25 or $40 per 100 Hill clinical summary forms; $31.50 per Workbook for the Holtzman Inkblot Technique.

Author: Wayne H. Holtzman.

Publisher: The Psychological Corporation.

a) INDIVIDUAL TEST.

Publication Dates: 1958–1972.

Forms, 2: A, B.

Price Data: $687 per complete set for Forms A and B combined including 47 inkblots, 25 record forms with summary sheets, and scoring guide; $369 per complete set (specify Form A or B).

b) GROUP TEST.

Publication Dates: 1958–1972.

Manual: No manual.

Price Data: $21 per 50 Gorham-Holtzman group record forms; $11 per normative item statistics.

Comments: Administration slides for either form must be constructed locally.

Author: Donald R. Gorham (record form).

Cross References: See T4:1170 (12 references); for reviews by Bert P. Cundick and David M. Dush, see 9:480 (17 references); see also T3:1106 (25 references); for a review by Rolf A. Peterson, see 8:578 (96 references); see also T2:1471 (42 references); for excerpted reviews by Raymond J. McCall and David G. Martin, see 7:169 (106 references); see also P:439 (90 references); for reviews by Richard N. Coan, H. J. Eysenck, Bertram R. Forer, and William N. Thetford, see 6:217 (22 references).

[1162]
Home and Community Social Behavior Scales.

Purpose: Provides rating of both social skills and antisocial behaviors.

Population: Ages 5–18.

Publication Date: 2002.

Acronym: HCSBS.

Scores, 6: Peer Relations, Self-Management/Compliance, Social Competence Total, Defiant/Disruptive, Antisocial/Aggressive, Antisocial Behavior Total.

Administration: Individual.

Price Data, 2002: $47 per user's guide (116 pages); $32 per 25 test forms.
Time: (5–10) minutes.
Comments: Rated by parent or other home-based rater.
Authors: Kenneth W. Merrell and Paul Caldarella.
Publisher: Assessment-Intervention Resources.

[1163]
Home Environment Questionnaire, HEQ-2R and HEQ-1R.

Purpose: Measures "dimensions of the child's psychological environment that exert specific types of pressure on the child."
Population: Grades 4–6.
Publication Date: 1983.
Acronym: HEQ.
Scores, 10: P(ress) Achievement, P Aggression-External, P Aggression-Home, P Aggression-Total, P Supervision, P Change, P Affiliation, P Separation, P Sociability, P Socioeconomic Status.
Administration: Individual or Group.
Forms, 2: HEQ-2R for use with two-parent families and HEQ-1R for use with single-parent families.
Price Data: Available from publisher.
Time: Administration time not reported.
Comments: Ratings by child's mother.
Author: Jacob O. Sines.
Publisher: Jacob O. Sines (the author).
Cross References: See T5:1215 (4 references) and T4:1171 (1 reference); for a review by Steven I. Pfeiffer and Julia Pettiette-Doolin, see 10:141 (1 reference).

[1164]
Home Observation for Measurement of the Environment.

Purpose: Screen for sources of potential environmental retardation or environmental risk.
Population: Birth to age 3, early childhood, middle childhood.
Publication Dates: 1978–2001.
Acronym: HOME.
Administration: Individual.
Price Data, 2001: $30 per manual; $90 per 50 Infant Toddler scoring sheets; $.50 each per Early Childhood form or Middle Childhood form.
Time: (60) minutes.
Authors: Bettye M. Caldwell and Robert H. Bradley.
Publisher: Home Inventory LLC.
a) INFANT/TODDLER HOME INVENTORY.
Population: Birth–3 years.
Scores, 7: Responsivity, Acceptance, Organization, Learning Materials, Involvement, Variety, Total.
b) EARLY CHILDHOOD HOME INVENTORY.
Population: 3–6 years.

Scores, 9: Learning Materials, Language Stimulation, Physical Environment, Responsivity, Academic Stimulation, Modeling, Variety, Acceptance, Total.
c) MIDDLE CHILDHOOD HOME INVENTORY.
Population: 6–10 years.
Scores, 8: Responsivity, Encouragement of Maturity, Acceptance, Learning Materials, Enrichment, Family Companionship, Paternal Involvement, Total.
Cross References: See T5:1216 (113 references), T4:1172 (42 references), 9:481 (13 references), and T3:1108 (14 references).

[1165]
Home Screening Questionnaire.

Purpose: Constructed to screen the home environment for factors related to the child's growth and development.
Population: Birth to age 3, ages 3–6.
Publication Date: 1981.
Acronym: HSQ.
Scores, 3: Questions, Toy Checklist, Total.
Administration: Individual.
Price Data, 2001: $15 per 25 questionnaires; $15 per reference manual (29 pages).
Time: (15–20) minutes.
Comments: Ratings by parents; abbreviated adaptation of the Home Observation for Measurement of the Environment (1164).
Authors: Cecilia E. Coons, Elizabeth C. Gay, Alma W. Fandal, Cynthia Ker, and William K. Frankenburg.
Publisher: Denver Developmental Materials, Inc.
Cross References: See T5:1217 (1 reference).

[1166]
Home-Visit Kit.

Purpose: Yields information regarding home safety and life-style issues necessary in child custody evaluations.
Population: Families involved in child custody situations.
Publication Dates: 1997–2002.
Scores: Unscored.
Administration: Group.
Price Data, 2002: $189 per kit including 8 Home-Visit booklets, instruction booklet (42 pages), and update service; $99 per 8 Home-Visit booklets; $159 per 16 Home-Visit booklets; $199 per 24 Home-Visit booklets; $119 per Home-Visit instruction booklet.
Time: Administration time not reported.
Comments: Previously listed as The Bricklin/Elliot Child Custody Evaluation.
Authors: Barry Bricklin and Gail Elliot.
Publisher: Village Publishing.

[1167]

The Hooper Visual Organization Test.

Purpose: Measures an individual's ability to organize visual stimuli.
Population: Ages 13 and over.
Publication Dates: 1957–1983.
Acronym: VOT.
Scores: Total score only.
Administration: Group or individual.
Price Data, 2002: $180 per complete kit including 4 reusable test pictures booklets, manual (1983, 39 pages), 25 test booklets, 100 answer sheets, and scoring key; $19.95 per 25 test booklets; $30 per reusable test pictures booklet; $14 per scoring key; $19.50 per 100 answer sheets; $37.50 per manual.
Time: (10–15) minutes.
Author: H. Elston Hooper.
Publisher: Western Psychological Services.
Cross References: See T5:1218 (19 references); for reviews by Kathy E. Green and Wilfred G. VanGorp, see 12:182 (7 references); see also T4:1174 (28 references), T3:1109 (6 references), T2:1216 (5 references), and P:111 (7 references); for reviews by Ralph M. Reitan and Otfried Spreen of an earlier edition, see 6:116 (4 references).

[1168]

Hopkins Verbal Learning Test—Revised.

Purpose: A "brief assessment of verbal memory (immediate recall, delayed recall, delayed recognition)."
Population: Ages 16 years and older.
Publication Dates: 1991–2001.
Acronym: HVLT-R.
Scores, 4: Total Recall, Delayed Recall, Retention, Recognition Discrimination Index.
Administration: Individual.
Forms, 6: 1–6.
Price Data, 2001: $199 per introductory kit including professional manual (2001, 59 pages) and 25 each of 6 test booklets (Forms 1–6); $30 per 25 test booklets (any of Forms 1–6); $45 per professional manual.
Time: (5–10) minutes with a 25-minute delay.
Comments: Forms 1–6 are very similar psychometrically and can be used to eliminate practice effects on repeated administration.
Authors: Jason Brandt and Ralph H. B. Benedict.
Publisher: Psychological Assessment Resources, Inc.

[1169]

The Hospital Anxiety and Depression Scale with the Irritability-Depression-Anxiety Scale and the Leeds Situational Anxiety Scale.

Purpose: Designed to detect and distinguish "between anxiety and depression and measures the severity of emotional disorder."
Population: Adults.
Publication Date: 1994.
Acronym: HADS.
Scores, 3: Irritability, Anxiety, Depression.
Administration: Group.
Price Data: Available from publisher.
Time: (5) minutes.
Authors: R. P. Snaith and A. S. Zigmond.
Publisher: NFER-Nelson Publishing Co., Ltd. [England]

[1170]

House-Tree-Person and Draw-A-Person as Measures of Abuse in Children: A Quantitative Scoring System.

Purpose: "Developed to assess personality/emotional characteristics of sexually abused children."
Population: Ages 7–11.
Publication Date: 1994.
Acronym: H-T-P/D-A-P.
Scores, 4: Preoccupation with Sexually Relevant Concepts, Aggression and Hostility, Withdrawal and Guarded Accessibility, Alertness for Danger/Suspiciousness and Lack of Trust.
Administration: Individual.
Price Data: Available from publisher for complete kit including manual (140 pages) and 10 scoring booklets.
Time: Administration time not reported.
Comments: A projective drawing instrument; for related instruments see The Draw-A-Person (835), Draw A Person: A Quantitative Scoring System (833), Draw-A-Person Quality Scale, and Draw A Person: Screening Procedure for Emotional Disturbance (834).
Author: Valerie Van Hutton.
Publisher: Psychological Assessment Resources, Inc.
Cross References: See T5:1219 (1 reference); for reviews by E. Thomas Dowd and Howard M. Knoff, see 13:139 (2 references).

[1171]

How Am I Doing? A Self-Assessment for Child Caregivers.

Purpose: Designed to identify areas of strength and skill development needs of caregivers of children with disabilities.
Population: Caregivers of children with disabilities.
Publication Date: 1993.
Scores: 8 sections: Arrival and Departure, Free Choice Play, Structured Group Activities, Outside Play, Meal Time, Toileting, Nap Time, Throughout the Day.
Administration: Group.
Price Data: Price data available from publisher.
Time: Administration time not reported.
Author: Irene Carney.

Publisher: Child Development Resources.
Cross References: For reviews by Lisa G. Bischoff and by Frederic J. Medway and Karen Fay, see 13:140.

[1172]
How I Think Questionnaire.

Purpose: Designed to "measure self-serving cognitive distortion."
Population: Ages 12–21.
Publication Date: 2001.
Acronym: HIT.
Scores, 11: Hit Questionnaire, Overt, Covert, Self-Centered, Blaming Others, Minimizing/Mislabeling, Assuming the Worst, Opposition-Defiance, Physical Aggression, Lying, Stealing, Anomalous Responding.
Administration: Group.
Price Data, 2001: $25.95 per 20 questionnaires and manual (49 pages).
Time: (5–15) minutes.
Authors: Alvaro Q. Barriga, John C. Gibbs, Granville Bud Potter, and Albert K. Kiau.
Publisher: Research Press.

[1173]
How Supervise?

Purpose: Designed to assess the knowledge of practices affecting worker efficiency.
Population: Supervisors.
Publication Dates: 1943–1971.
Scores: Total score only.
Administration: Group or individual.
Forms, 3: A, B, M.
Price Data, 2002: $77 per 25 test booklets (specify form); $26 per manual (1971, 17 pages); $30 per examination kit including test booklets for all three forms and manual.
Time: [40] minutes.
Authors: Quentin W. File and H. H. Remmers.
Publisher: The Psychological Corporation.
Cross References: See T4:1177 (2 references) and T2:2448 (11 references); for a review by Joel T. Campbell, see 6:1189 (9 references); see also 5:926 (18 references); for a review by Milton M. Mandell, see 4:774 (8 references); for reviews by D. Welty Lefever, Charles I. Moiser, and C. H. Ruedisili, see 3:687 (5 references).

[1174]
How Well Do You Know Your Interests?

Purpose: Designed to identify "an individual's attitudes of liking, disliking, or apathy toward … work activities."
Population: Grades 9–12, college, adults.
Publication Dates: 1957–1975.
Scores, 54: Numerical, Clerical, Retail Selling, Outside Selling, Selling Real Estate, One-Order Selling, Sales Complaints, Selling Intangibles, Buyer, Labor Management, Production Supervision, Business Management, Machine Operation, Repair & Construction, Machine Design, Farm or Ranch, Gardening, Hunting, Adventure, Social Service, Teaching Service, Medical Service, Nursing Service, Applied Chemistry, Basic Chemical Problems, Basic Biological Problems, Basic Physical Problems, Basic Psychological Problems, Philosophical, Visual Art (Appreciative, Productive, Decorative), Amusement (Appreciative, Productive, Managerial), Literary (Appreciative, Productive), Musical (Appreciative, Performing, Composing), Sports (Appreciative, Participative), Domestic Service, Unskilled Labor, Disciplinary, Power Seeking, Propaganda, Self-Aggrandizing, Supervisory Initiative, Bargaining, Arbitrative, Persuasive, Disputatious, Masculinity (for males only) or Femininity (for females only).
Administration: Group.
Levels, 3: Secondary School, College, Personnel.
Price Data: Price information available from publisher forr complete kit including 3 test booklets of each edition, scoring keys, and manual (1974, 24 pages) and for handbook on interpretation (1975, 19 pages).
Time: (15–20) minutes.
Authors: Thomas N. Jenkins (test booklets, manual), John H. Coleman (manual, handbook), and Harold T. Fagin (manual).
Publisher: Psychologists and Educators, Inc.
Cross References: See 7:1022 (2 references); for a review by John R. Hills and an excerpted review by Gordon V. Anderson, see 6:1059 (1 reference); for reviews by Jerome E. Doppelt and Henry S. Dyer, see 5:859.

[1175]
How Well Do You Know Yourself?

Purpose: Developed to assess personality characteristics.
Population: Grades 9–12, college, office and factory workers.
Publication Dates: 1959–1976.
Scores, 19: Irritability, Practicality, Punctuality, Novelty-Loving, Vocational Assurance, Cooperativeness, Ambitiousness, Hypercriticalness, Dejection, General Morale, Persistence, Nervousness, Seriousness, Submissiveness, Impulsiveness, Dynamism, Emotional Control, Consistency, Test Objectivity.
Administration: Group.
Levels, 3: Secondary School, College, Personnel.
Price Data, 2002: $11 per complete kit including test booklets (3 of each level) and manual (1974, 30 pages); $20 per 25 test booklets (select level); $6.75 per set of scoring keys; $6.75 per manual.
Time: Administration time not reported.
Authors: Thomas N. Jenkins, John H. Coleman (manual), and Harold T. Fagin (manual).
Publisher: Psychologists and Educators, Inc.

Cross References: See 11:166 (1 reference) and T2:1220 (2 references); for reviews by Lee J. Cronbach and Harrison G. Gough and excerpted reviews by Edward S. Bordin and Laurence Siegel, see 6:118 (2 references).

[1176]
H.R.R. Pseudoisochromatic Plates for Detecting, Classifying and Estimating the Degree of Defective Color Vision.

Purpose: Designed to test for color vision.
Population: People who may have color vision deficiency.
Publication Date: 1991.
Scores, 3: Normal Color Vision, Defective Color Vision (Red-Green Deficiency, Blue-Yellow Deficiency).
Administration: Individual.
Price Data, 2001: $197 per H.R.R. book including 4 demonstration plates, 20 test pages, and score sheet.
Time: (1–3) minutes.
Authors: Richmond Products, Inc.; LeGrand H. Hardy (manual), Gertrude Rand (manual), and M. Catherine Rittler (manual).
Publisher: Richmond Products, Inc.

[1177]
H-T-P: House-Tree-Person Projective Drawing Technique.

Purpose: "To provide psychologists and psychiatrists … with an examining procedure with which to acquire diagnostically and prognostically significant data concerning a subject's total personality."
Population: Ages 3 and over.
Publication Dates: 1946–1993.
Acronym: H-T-P.
Scores: Total score only.
Administration: Individual.
Price Data, 2002: $168 per complete kit including 1 copy of The House-Tree-Person Projective Drawing Technique: Manual and Interpretive Guide (1993, 165 pages), 1 copy of H-T-P Drawings: An illustrated Diagnostic Handbook (108 pages), 1 copy of Catalog for the Qualitative Interpretation of the H-T-P (191 pages), 25 interpretation booklets, and 25 drawing forms; $37.50 per interpretive catalogue; $39.50 per diagnostic handbook; $65 per revised manual (1993).
Time: (60–90) minutes.
Authors: John N. Buck, W. L. Warren (revision), Isaac Jolles (interpretive catalog), L. Stanley Wenck (diagnostic handbook), and Emmanuel F. Hammer (clinical research manual).
Publisher: Western Psychological Services.
Cross References: See T5:1160 (4 references), T4:1183 (6 references), T2:1469 (61 references), and P:437 (24 references); for a review by Mary R. Haworth of an earlier edition, see 6:215 (32 references); for a review by Philip L. Harriman, see 5:139 (61 references); for reviews by Albert Ellis and Ephraim Rosen and an excerpted review, see 4:107 (14 references); for reviews by Morris Krugman and Katherine N. Wilcox, see 3:47 (5 references).

[1178]
Hughes Basic Gross Motor Assessment.

Purpose: Designed to detect disorders in motor performance.
Population: Ages 6–12 believed to have minor motor dysfunctions.
Publication Date: 1979.
Acronym: BGMA.
Scores: 8 subtests: Static Balance, Stride Jump, Tandem Walking, Hopping, Skipping, Target, Yo-Yo, Ball Handling Skills.
Administration: Individual.
Price Data: Available from publisher.
Time: Administration time not reported.
Author: Jeanne E. Hughes.
Publisher: Nancy Hughes [No reply from publisher; status unknown].
Cross References: See 9:487 (1 reference).

[1179]
Human Figure Drawing Test.

Purpose: "Designed to provide an objective approach" to human figure drawings.
Population: Clients in psychotherapy.
Publication Date: 1993.
Acronym: HFDT.
Scores, 4: Impairment, Distortion, Simplification, Organic Factors Index.
Administration: Individual.
Price Data, 2002: $75 per complete kit including handbook (189 pages), 25 drawing forms, and 25 AUTOSCORE™ forms; $15 per 25 drawing forms; $29.50 per 25 AUTOSCORE™ forms; $49.50 per handbook.
Time: (5–20) minutes.
Authors: Jerry Mitchell, Richard Trent, and Roland McArthur.
Publisher: Western Psychological Services.
Cross References: For reviews by Charles A. Peterson and William K. Wilkinson, see 14:170; see also T5:1226 (4 references).

[1180]
Human Information Processing Survey.

Purpose: "Assesses processing preference—left, right, integrated, or mixed [brain functioning]."
Population: Adults.
Publication Date: 1984.
Acronym: HIP Survey.
Scores, 3: Right, Left, Integrated.

Administration: Group.
Editions, 2: Research Edition, Professional Edition.
Price Data, 2002: $56.90 per professional edition starter set including administrator's manual (44 pages), 10 survey forms, and 10 strategy and tactics profiles booklets; $43.85 per 10 survey forms and strategy and tactics profiles; $22 per manual (professional and research editions); $75.50 per research edition starter set including administrator's manual, 20 reusable survey forms, 20 profile forms, and 20 response sheets; $22.65 per 20 profile forms and response sheets (research edition); $23.10 per sample set for each edition.
Time: [40] minutes.
Authors: E. Paul Torrance, William Taggart (manual), and Barbara Taggart.
Publisher: Scholastic Testing Service, Inc.
Cross References: See T5:1227 (2 references) and T4:1186 (1 reference); for a review by J. P. Das, see 10:144 (1 reference).

[1181]
Human Loyalty Expressionaire.
Purpose: "Measures human loyalty and global awareness" for use in peace and global studies courses.
Population: College and university students.
Publication Date: No date on test materials.
Scores: Total score only.
Administration: Group.
Price Data: Available from publisher.
Time: Administration time not reported.
Author: Theodore J. Lentz.
Publisher: Lentz Peace Research Laboratory [No reply from publisher; status unknown].

[1182]
Human Relations Inventory.
Purpose: Designed to measure social conformity.
Population: Grades 9–16 and adults.
Publication Dates: 1954–1959.
Acronym: HRI.
Scores: Total score only.
Administration: Group.
Price Data: Available from publisher.
Time: (20) minutes.
Author: Raymond E. Bernberg.
Publisher: Psychometric Affiliates.
Cross References: See T2:1221 (4 references), P:114 (1 reference), and 6:119 (6 references); for reviews by Raymond C. Norris and John A. Radcliffe, see 5:68.

[1183]
Humanics National Child Assessment Form [Revised].
Purpose: To serve as developmental checklists of skills and behavior that occur during the first 9 years of life.
Population: Ages 0–3, 3–6, 6–9.

Publication Dates: 1981–2002.
Administration: Group.
Levels, 3: Birth to age 3, ages 3 to 6, ages 6 to 9.
Price Data, 2002: $34.95 per 25 assessment forms (specify level).
Time: Administration time varies.
Comments: Behavior checklists to be completed by parents or teachers.
Publisher: Humanics Learning.
  a) BIRTH TO THREE.
  Scores, 5: Social-Emotional, Language, Cognitive, Gross Motor, Fine Motor.
  Price Data: $23.95 per handbook and 5 assessment forms; $18.95 per handbook.
  Authors: Marsha Kaufman (checklist), T. Thomas McMurrain (checklist), Jane A. Caballero (handbook), and Derek Whordley (handbook).
  b) AGES THREE TO SIX.
  Scores, 5: Same as *a* above.
  Price Data: $39.95 per handbook and 5 assessment forms; $18.95 per handbook.
  Authors: Derek Whordley (handbook) and Rebecca J. Doster (handbook).
  c) AGES SIX TO NINE.
  Scores, 5: Same as *a* above.
  Authors: Jackson Rabbit (checklist), Sylvia B. Booth (checklist), and Marilyn L. Perling (checklist).
  Comments: Age level 6 to 9 is not accompanied by a handbook; behavior checklists to be completed by parents or teachers.
Cross References: For reviews by Arthur S. Ellen and David MacPhee of an earlier edition, see 11:170.

[1184]
The Hundred Pictures Naming Test.
Purpose: "A confrontation naming test designed to evaluate rapid naming ability."
Population: Ages 4-6 to 11-11.
Publication Date: 1992.
Acronym: HPNT.
Scores, 3: Error, Accuracy, Time.
Administration: Individual.
Price Data, 2002: A$104.50 per complete kit including manual (84 pages), test book, and 25 response forms; A$10 per 25 response forms.
Time: (6) minutes.
Authors: John P. Fisher and Jennifer M. Glenister.
Publisher: Australian Council for Educational Research Ltd. [Australia].
Cross References: For reviews by Jeffrey A. Atlas and Stephen Jurs, see 12:183.

[1185]
Hunter-Grundin Literacy Profiles.
Purpose: Designed to monitor the written and spoken language skills of children.

Population: Ages 6.5–8, 7.10–9.3, 9–10, 9.10–11.5, 10.10–12.7.
Publication Dates: 1979–1989.
Scores: 6 tests: Attitude to Reading (Levels 1 and 2 only), Reading for Meaning, Spelling, Free Writing, Spoken Language, Profile of Personal Interests (Levels 4 and 5 only).
Administration: Individual and group.
Levels: 5 overlapping levels.
Manual: Separate manual for each level.
Price Data: Available from publisher.
Time: (3-10) minutes per test at any one level.
Comments: Ratings by teacher in part.
Authors: Elizabeth Hunter-Grundin and Hans U. Grundin.
Publisher: The Test Agency Limited [England].
  a) LEVEL 1.
  Population: Ages 6.5–8.
  b) LEVEL 2.
  Population: Ages 7.10–9.3.
  c) LEVEL 3.
  Population: Ages 9–10.
  d) LEVEL 4.
  Population: Ages 9.10–11.5.
  e) LEVEL 5.
  Population: Ages 10.10–12.7.
Cross References: For reviews by Martha C. Beech and Patricia H. Kennedy of a previous edition, see 9:491.

[1186]
I Can Do Maths.

Purpose: Designed "to inform teachers and parents about children's development in numeracy in the early years of schooling."
Population: Children in years 1–3 of Australian and New Zealand school systems.
Publication Date: 2000.
Scores, 4: Number, Measurement, Space, Total.
Administration: Group.
Price Data, 2002: A$58.30 per specimen set including one Level A test booklet, one Level B test booklet, one Level A Ezi-guide, one Level B Ezi-guide, and teacher's guide (36 pages).
Time: (30–40) minutes.
Authors: Brian Doig and Marion de Lemos.
Publisher: Australian Council for Educational Research Ltd. [Australia].
  a) LEVEL A.
  Population: Children in years 1 and 2.
  Price Data: $27.50 per 10 Level A test booklets.
  b) LEVEL B.
  Population: Children in end of year 2 and year 3.
  Price Data: Same as Level A above.

[1187]
I-SPEAK Your Language™: A Survey of Personal Styles.

Purpose: Designed to teach employees how to identify and modify their communication style to work best with others in a variety of situations.
Population: Employees.
Publication Dates: 1972–1999.
Scores, 8: Favorable Conditions (Intuitor, Thinker, Feeler, Senser), Stress Conditions (Intuitor, Thinker, Feeler, Senser).
Administration: Group or individual.
Price Data, 2002: $50 per 10 questionnaires; $12.95 per Self-Development Exercises manual (1992, 59 pages); $12.95 per manual (1993, 46 pages); $25 per specimen set including questionnaire, manual, and Self-Development Exercises manual.
Time: (20) minutes.
Comments: Also available (except Self-Development Exercises manual) in Spanish, French, German, Portugese, Arabic, Norwegian, Bhasa Indonesian.
Author: Drake Beam Morin, Inc.
Publisher: DBM Publishing.
Cross References: For reviews by Mary Anne Bunda and Kimberly A. Lawless, see 13:141.

[1188]
IDEA Feedback for Department Chairs.

Purpose: Designed to diagnose administrative performance and discover ways to effectively improve it.
Population: College and university department chairpersons.
Publication Dates: 1977–1998.
Scores: 17 scores in 3 areas: Overall Ratings (Summary Judgement, Effectiveness in Performance, Five Types of Administrative Responsibilities); Effectiveness in Performing Twenty Specific Administrative Responsibilities (Administrative Support, Personnel Management, Program Leadership/Support, Building Image/Reputation, Developing Positive Climate); Description of Administrative Methods and Personal Characteristics (Democratic/Humanistic, Goal-Oriented/Structured, Supports Faculty, Promotes Positive Climate, Promotes Department Advancement, Ability to Resolve Issues, Communication Skills, Steadiness, Trustworthiness, Openness).
Administration: Group.
Price Data: Available from publisher.
Time: (15–30) minutes.
Comments: Available for online administration; previous version entitled Departmental Evaluation of Chairperson Activities for Development; publisher scores and generates interpretive reports; online inventory completed by faculty about their department chairs.
Authors: IDEA Center and Donald D. Hoyt (Technical Report, 1998).

Publisher: The IDEA Center.
Cross References: See T4:741 (1 reference).

[1189]
IDEA Oral Language Proficiency Test.

Purpose: To "assist in the initial identification designation and redesignation of a student as being NES, LES, or FES (Non-Limited-Fluent English Speaking)."
Population: Preschool–grade 12.
Publication Dates: 1983–2001.
Acronym: IPT.
Scores, 4: Vocabulary, Comprehension, Syntax, Verbal Expression.
Administration: Individual.
Price Data: Available from publisher.
Foreign Language Edition: English and Spanish versions available for each level.
Publisher: Ballard & Tighe Publishers.
  a) PRE-IPT.
  Population: Ages 3–5.
  Publication Date: 1999.
  Time: (8–13) minutes.
  Authors: Constance O. Williams, Enrique F. Dalton, and Phyllis L. Tighe.
  b) IPT-I.
  Population: Grades K–6.
  Publication Date: 2001.
  Time: (14–19) minutes.
  Authors: Wanda S. Ballard, Phyllis L. Tighe, and Enrique F. Dalton.
  c) IPT-II.
  Population: Grades 7–12.
  Publication Date: 1998.
  Time: (15–20) minutes.
  Authors: Enrique F. Dalton and Beverly A. Amori.
Cross References: For reviews by Emilia C. Lopez and Salvador Hector Ochoa, see 14:171; see also T5:1234 (5 references).

[1190]
IDEA Reading and Writing Proficiency Test.

Purpose: To provide "comprehensive assessment for the initial identification and redesignation of Limited English Proficient (LEP) students."
Population: Grades 2–12.
Publication Dates: 1992–2001.
Acronym: IPT R & W.
Scores, 20: Reading (Vocabulary, Vocabulary in Context, Reading for Understanding, Reading for Life Skills, Language Usage), Writing (Conventions, Write a Story, Write Your Own Story), Early Literacy (Visual Recognition, Letter Recognition, Phonemic Awareness, Phonics, Reading Vocabulary, Reading for Life Skills, Reading for Understanding, Sentences and Stories, Copy Letters, Write Name and Copy Sentence, Descriptive/Narrative Writing, Spelling).
Administration: Group.
Levels, 4: Grades K–1, Grades 2–3, Grades 4–6, Grades 7–12.
Price Data: Available from publisher.
Foreign Language Editions: English and Spanish versions available for each level.
Time: (70–115) minutes.
Comments: Used in conjunction with the IPT Oral Language Proficiency Test (1189).
Authors: Beverly A. Amori, Enrique F. Dalton, and Phyllis L. Tighe.
Publisher: Ballard & Tighe Publishers.
Cross References: For reviews by James Dean Brown and Alan Garfinkel, see 13:142.

[1191]
IDEA Student Ratings of Instruction.

Purpose: Designed to provide student ratings of college instructors.
Population: College faculty.
Publication Dates: 1975–1998.
Scores: 5-part report compiled from ratings data: Overall Measures of Teaching Effectiveness, Student Ratings of Progress in Specific Objectives, Teaching Methods/Style, Course Description/Context, Statistical Detail.
Administration: Group.
Price Data: Available from publisher.
Time: (10–20) minutes.
Comments: Available for use in the classroom and in online classes.
Authors: Donald P. Hoyt, William H. Pallett, Amy B. Gross, Richard E. Owens, William E. Cashin (technical reports), Glenn R. Sixbury (technical reports, numbers 7–10), Yih-Fen Chen (technical report number 11).
Publisher: The IDEA Center.
Cross References: For reviews by Raoul A. Arreola and Jennifer J. Fager, see 14:172; see also T4:1195 (1 reference); for a review by John C. Ory of an earlier edition, see 9:493 (2 references).

[1192]
IDEAS: Interest Determination, Exploration and Assessment System™.

Purpose: "To be used as an introduction to career exploration for students and adults."
Population: Grades 7–12 and adults.
Publication Dates: 1977–1994.
Acronym: IDEAS™.
Scores, 16: Mechanical/Fixing, Protective Services, Nature/Outdoors, Mathematics, Science, Medical, Creative Arts, Writing, Community Service, Educating, Child Care, Public Speaking, Business, Sales, Office Practices, Food Service.

Administration: Group or individual.
Price Data, 2002: $64.50 per 50 booklets; $17 per manual (1990, 80 pages); $18.50 per preview package.
Time: (40–45) minutes.
Comments: Self-administered, self-scored.
Author: Charles B. Johansson.
Publisher: NCS Assessments (Minnetonka).
Cross References: For a review by Robert J. Miller, see 11:172; for a review by M. O'Neal Weeks of an earlier edition, see 9:516.

[1193]
Illinois Test of Psycholoinguistic Abilities, Third Edition.

Purpose: Designed "to help children who have weakness in various linguistic processes including spoke or written language."
Population: Ages 5-0 to 12-11.
Publication Dates: 1961–2001.
Acronym: ITPA-3.
Scores, 12: Spoken Analogies, Spoken Vocabulary, Morphological Closure, Syntactic Sentences, Sound Deletion, Rhyming Sequences, Sentence Sequencing, Written Vocabulary, Sight Decoding, Sound Decoding, Sight Spelling, Sound Spelling.
Administration: Individual.
Price Data, 2001: $159 per kit including 25 profile/examiner record booklets, 25 student response booklets, manual (2001, 165 pages), and an audio cassette; $44 per 25 profile/examiner record booklets; $39 per 25 student response booklets; $69 per examiner's manual; $12 per audio cassette; $109 per software scoring and report system.
Time: (45–60) minutes.
Authors: Donald D. Hammill, Nancy Mather, and Rhia Roberts.
Publisher: PRO-ED.
Cross References: See T5:1240 (51 references), T4:1201 (53 references), 9:496 (37 references), and T3:1126 (145 references); for reviews by James Lumsden and J. Lee Wiederholt of an earlier edition, and an excerpted review by R. P. Waugh, see 8:431 (269 references); see also T2:981 (113 references); for reviews by John B. Carroll and Clinton I. Chase, see 7:442 (239 references); see also 6:549 (22 references).

[1194]
Illness Behaviour Questionnaire, Third Edition.

Purpose: "To record aspects of illness behaviour, particularly those attitudes that suggest or are associated with inappropriate or maladaptive modes of responding to one's state of health."
Population: Pain clinic, psychiatric, and general practice patients.
Publication Dates: 1983–1994.

Acronym: IBQ.
Scores, 9: 7 factors (General Hypochondriasis, Disease Conviction, Psychological vs. Somatic Perception of Illness, Affective Inhibition, Affective Disturbance, Denial, Irritability) and Discriminant Function Score and Whitely Index of Hypochondriasis.
Administration: Individual or group.
Price Data, 1999: $40 per manual (1994, 95 pages) including test.
Time: (10) minutes.
Comments: Self-report instrument; the Discriminant Function Score indicates likelihood of conversion disorder.
Authors: Issy Pilowsky and Neil Spence.
Publisher: I. Pilowsky [South Australia].
Cross References: See T5:1241 (6 references) and T4:1203 (6 references).

[1195]
Impact Message Inventory, Research Edition.

Purpose: "Designed to measure . . . interpersonal style."
Population: College.
Publication Dates: 1975–1987.
Acronym: IMI.
Scores, 15: Dominant, Competitive, Hostile, Mistrustful, Detached, Inhibited, Submissive, Succorant, Abasive, Deferent, Agreeable, Nurturant, Affiliative, Sociable, Exhibitionistic.
Administration: Group.
Forms, 2: Male Targets, Female Targets.
Price Data: Available from publisher.
Time: [15] minutes.
Comments: Self-report inventory; includes original and octant version.
Author: Donald J. Kiesler.
Publisher: Mind Garden, Inc.
Cross References: See T4:1205 (13 references); for reviews by Stephen L. Benton and Steven G. LoBello, see 12:186 (4 references); for reviews by Fred H. Borgen and Stanley R. Strong of an earlier edition, see 9:500 (1 reference); see also T3:1130 (1 reference).

[1196]
Incentives Management Index.

Purpose: Designed to make explicit sales managers' "assumptions, theories, and practices in the realm of sales motivation."
Population: Sales managers.
Publication Dates: 1972–1995.
Acronym: IMI.
Scores, 5: Basic Creative Comfort, Safety and Order, Belonging and Affiliation, Ego-Status, Actualization and Self-Expression.
Administration: Group.

Price Data, 2001: $8.95 per instrument (1995, 24 pages).
Time: Administration time not reported.
Comments: Self-administered; self-scored.
Authors: Jay Hall and Norman J. Seim.
Publisher: Teleometrics International.
Cross References: For reviews by Leslie H. Krieger and Patricia H. Wheeler, see 14:173.

[1197]
Independent Living Scales.

Purpose: Designed to assess adults' competence in instrumental activities of daily living.
Population: Adults with cognitive impairments.
Publication Date: 1996.
Acronym: ILS.
Scores, 6: Memory/Orientation, Managing Money, Managing Home and Transportation, Health and Safety, Social Adjustment, Total.
Administration: Individual.
Price Data, 2002: $248 per complete kit including manual (119 pages), 25 record forms, stimulus booklet, and a pouch containing a facsimile of a driver's license, credit card, and key; $37 per 25 record forms.
Time: (45) minutes.
Comments: Four screening items are used to determine whether the examinee has a vision, speech, or hearing impairment; the stimulus booklet is designed for adults who can hear and those with a hearing impairment.
Author: Patricia Anderten Loeb.
Publisher: The Psychological Corporation.
Cross References: For reviews by Libby G. Cohen and Jack A. Cummings, see 14:174.

[1198]
Independent Mastery Testing System for Math Skills.

Purpose: "To monitor the student's mastery of basic mathematics skills, to diagnose specific student weaknesses, to recommend a program of further study, and to provide the teacher with a comprehensive record of student progress."
Population: Adult students.
Publication Date: 1984.
Acronym: IMTS.
Scores: 13 tests: Adding and Subtracting Whole Numbers, Multiplying and Dividing Whole Numbers, Adding and Subtracting Fractions, Multiplying and Dividing Fractions, Adding and Subtracting Decimals, Multiplying and Dividing Decimals, Percents Skills, Charts and Graphs Skills, Measurement Skills, The Language of Algebra, The Uses of Algebra, Geometry—Angles, Geometry—Plane and Solid Figures.
Administration: Individual.
Forms: 3 parallel forms of each test.

Price Data: Not available.
Time: Administration time not reported.
Comments: Computer-administered instructional management system; Apple II, Apple II+, Apple IIe, or Apple IIc computer necessary for administration.
Authors: Cambridge, The Adult Education Company in association with Moravian College, Bethlehem, PA.
Publisher: Prentice Hall [No reply from publisher; status unknown].
Cross References: For a review by Richard M. Jaeger, see 10:147.

[1199]
Independent Mastery Testing System for Writing Skills.

Purpose: "To monitor the student's mastery of basic grammar and writing skills, to diagnose specific student weaknesses, to recommend a program of further study, and to provide the teacher with a comprehensive record of student progress."
Population: Adult students.
Publication Date: 1984.
Acronym: IMTS.
Scores: 15 tests: Recognizing Sentences, Verb Tenses, Subject-Verb Agreement—Part A, Subject-Verb Agreement—Part B, Pronouns—Part A, Pronouns—Part B, Plurals and Possessives, Adjectives and Adverbs—Part A, Adjectives and Adverbs—Part B, Sentence Structure, Prepositions and Conjunctions, Logic and Organization, Capitalization, Punctuation, Spelling.
Administration: Individual.
Forms: 3 parallel forms (1, 2, 3) of each test.
Price Data: Not available.
Time: Administration time not reported.
Comments: Computer-administered instructional management system; Apple II, Apple II+, Apple IIe, or Apple IIc computer necessary for administration.
Authors: Cambridge, The Adult Education Company, in association with Moravian College, Bethlehem, PA.
Publisher: Prentice Hall [No reply from publisher; status unknown].
Cross References: For a review by Pamela A. Moss, see 11:173.

[1200]
Independent School Entrance Examination.

Purpose: Developed to assess verbal ability, quantitative ability, reading comprehension, and mathematics achievement for use in admissions into independent schools and to provide independent schools with a candidate's writing sample given under standard conditions.
Population: Grades 4–11, or candidates for grades 5–12.

Publication Dates: 1989–1999.
Acronym: ISEE.
Scores, 4: Verbal Ability, Quantitative Ability, Reading Comprehension, Mathematics Achievement.
Administration: Group.
Levels, 3: Lower, Middle, Upper.
Forms, 2: A, B.
Price Data: Price data including technical manual (1999, 104 pages) available from publisher.
Time: 130 minutes; 30 minutes for essay component.
Comments: Test book name is ISEE; essay component is not scored but is sent to schools.
Author: Educational Records Bureau, Inc.
Publisher: Educational Records Bureau.
Cross References: For reviews by Mary Anne Bunda and Joyce R. McLarty, see 11:174.

[1201]
Indiana Student Scale: A Measure of Self-Esteem.

Purpose: Designed to "identify a profile of self-esteem dimensions for individuals to be used for research, counseling, and education."
Population: Middle school, high school, and university students.
Publication Dates: 1997–1998.
Scores: 8 dimensions: Appearance, Academic Competence (Efficacy), Kinesthetic Competence (Efficacy), Power, Destiny Control, Ethics, Social Affiliation, General Self.
Administration: Group.
Price Data, 2002: $50 per 50 test booklets; $10 per specimen set; manual free with order; $2 per subject (minimum of 25) for scoring.
Time: (40) minutes.
Comments: Manual provides rationale for dimensions, reliability, and validity information.
Author: Meryl E. Englander.
Publisher: Meryl E. Englander.

[1202]
Individual Directions Inventory™.

Purpose: Designed to provide insight into a wide range of personal motivations; useful in individual and organizational development.
Population: Adults.
Publication Dates: 1988–2001.
Acronym: IDI.
Scores: 17 dimensions: Types of Emotional Satisfaction (Giving, Receiving, Belonging, Expressing, Gaining Stature, Entertaining, Creating, Interpreting, Excelling, Enduring, Structuring, Maneuvering, Winning, Controlling, Stability, Independence, Irreproachability).
Administration: Individual or group.
Price Data: Available from publisher.
Time: (30) minutes.

Comments: Purchase and use requires training by publisher or credential review.
Authors: James T. Mahoney (test) and Robert I. Kabacoff (manual).
Publisher: Management Research Group.

[1203]
Individual Employment Plan with 84-Item Employability Assessment.

Purpose: To help service organizations gather information about clients' employability status and assist clients in creating and completing a training and services plan.
Population: Participants in employment programs.
Publication Date: 2001.
Acronym: IEP.
Scores: Personal Issues and Considerations, Health and Physical Considerations, Work Orientation, Career and Life Planning Skills, Job Seeking Skills, Job Adaptation Skills, Education and Training.
Administration: Individual.
Price Data, 2001: $34.95 per 25 inventories including administrator's guide (8 pages).
Time: (30) minutes.
Comments: Eight-panel foldout.
Authors: LaVerne L. Ludden and Bonnie Maitlen.
Publisher: JIST Publishing, Inc.

[1204]
Individual Outlook Test.

Purpose: Designed to assess codependent orientation.
Population: Adults.
Publication Date: 1993.
Acronym: IOT.
Scores, 6: Codependent Orientation, Externally Derived Sense of Self Worth, Anxiety, Dysfunctional Family of Origin, Dependency within Relationships, Dysfunctional Relationships.
Administration: Group or individual.
Price Data: Available from publisher.
Time: (15–20) minutes.
Authors: Laurie A. Sim and Eugene E. Fox (test and manual); Michelle J. Worth and Donald Macnab (manual).
Publisher: Psychometrics Canada Ltd. [Canada].

[1205]
Individual Service Strategy Portfolio.

Purpose: Designed to help human service organizations gather information about clients' employability status and assist clients in creating and completing a training and services plan.
Population: Participants in employment programs.
Publication Date: 1993.
Acronym: ISSP.
Scores: Employability assets and barriers for 7 categories: Personal Considerations, Health, Work Ori-

entation, Career Planning Skills, Job Seeking Skills, Job Adaptation Skills, Education and Training.
Administration: Individual.
Price Data, 2001: $34.95 per 25 copies plus instruction booklet.
Time: Administration time not reported.
Authors: LaVerne L. Ludden (manual and portfolio), Bonnie R. Maitlen (manual and portfolio), and J. Michael Farr (portfolio).
Publisher: JIST Publishing, Inc.
Cross References: For reviews by Javaid Kaiser and Albert Oosterhof, see 13:143.

[1206]
Individual Style Survey.
Purpose: "Intended to be an educational tool for self and interpersonal development."
Publication Dates: 1989–1990.
Administration: Group.
Price Data: Available from publisher.
Time: (60–90) minutes.
Comments: Self-administered, self-scored survey.
Author: Norman Amundson.
Publisher: Psychometrics Canada Ltd. [Canada] [No reply from publisher; status unknown].
a) INDIVIDUAL STYLE SURVEY.
Population: Adults.
Publication Date: 1989.
Acronym: ISS.
Scores, 14: 8 categories of behavior (Forceful, Assertive, Outgoing, Spontaneous, Empathetic, Patient, Reserved, Analytical) yielding 4 styles (Dominant, Influencing, Harmonious, Cautious) that combine to form 2 summary scores (People/Task Orientation, Introspective/Interactive Stance).
b) MY PERSONAL STYLE.
Population: Ages 10–18.
Publication Date: 1990.
Acronym: MPS.
Scores, 14: 8 categories (Carefree, Outgoing, Straight Forward, Forceful, Precise, Reserved, Patient, Sensitive) yielding 4 styles (Influencing, Strong Willed, Cautious, Peaceful) that combine to form 2 summary scores (People/Task Orientation, Expressive/Thoughtful Stance).
Comments: Simplified version of the Individual Style Survey for use with young people.
Cross References: For reviews by Jeffrey A. Atlas and William I. Sauser, see 13:144.

[1207]
Individualised Classroom Environment Questionnaire.
Purpose: "An instrument for measuring perceptions of the classroom environment among secondary school students or their teachers."

Population: Junior and senior high school students and teachers.
Publication Date: 1990.
Acronym: ICEQ.
Scores, 5: Personalisation, Participation, Independence, Investigation, Differentiation.
Administration: Group.
Forms, 4: Actual Classroom-Long Form, Actual Classroom-Short Form, Preferred Classroom-Long Form, Preferred Classroom-Short Form.
Price Data, 2002: A$49.50 per complete materials including manual (39 pages).
Time: (10–15) minutes for short form; (15–30) minutes for long form.
Comments: Test forms contained in manual may be photocopied by purchaser.
Author: Barry J. Fraser.
Publisher: Australian Council for Educational Research Ltd. [Australia].
Cross References: See T5:1254 (1 reference); for a review by Lawrence M. Aleamoni, see 11:176.

[1208]
Industrial Test Battery.
Purpose: Intended to assess an individual's conceptual reasoning and spatial abilities.
Population: Individuals with less than 7 years of formal schooling.
Publication Date: 1986.
Acronym: ITB.
Scores: Total score only for each test.
Subtests, 3: Anomalous Concept Test (ACT), Anomalous Figure Test (AFT), Series Induction Test (SIT).
Administration: Group.
Price Data: Available from publisher.
Foreign Language Edition: Tests printed in both English and Afrikaans.
Time: 20(30) minutes for ACT; 25(35) minutes for AFT; 30(40) minutes for SIT.
Author: T. R. Taylor.
Publisher: Human Sciences Research Council [South Africa].

[1209]
The Infanib.
Purpose: Designed to provide a systematic scorable method to assess the neurological status of infants, especially infants who are premature or have special conditions.
Population: Infants from 4 to 18 months corrected gestational age.
Publication Date: 1994.
Scores, 20: Hands Open, Hands Closed, Scarf Sign, Heel-To-Ear, Popliteal Angle, Leg Abduction, Dorsiflexion of the Foot, The Foot Grasp, Tonic Labyrinthine Supine, Asymmetric Tonic Neck Reflex, Pull-

To-Sitting, Body Denotative, Body Rotative, All-Fours, Tonic Labyrinthine Prone, Sitting, Sideways Parachute, Backwards Parachute, Standing-Positive Support Reaction, Forward Parachute.
Administration: Individual.
Price Data, 2002: $94 per complete kit including 50 screening forms and manual (131 pages); $28 per 50 screening forms.
Time: Untimed.
Comments: "Criterion-referenced" test with ratings determined by therapist.
Author: Patricia H. Ellison.
Publisher: Therapy Skill Builders—A Division of The Psychological Corporation.
Cross References: For reviews by Jill Ann Jenkins and John J. Vacca, see 14:175.

[1210]
Infant Development Inventory.
Purpose: Designed "for screening the development of infants in the first eighteen months."
Population: Birth to 18 months.
Publication Dates: 1980–1995.
Acronym: IDI.
Scores, 5: Social, Self-Help, Gross Motor, Fine Motor, Language.
Administration: Individual.
Manual: Brief Instructions only.
Price Data, 2001: $10 per 25 parent questionnaires.
Time: Administration time not reported.
Comments: New version of the Minnesota Infant Development Inventory (T4:1642); observations by mother.
Author: Harold Ireton.
Publisher: Behavior Science Systems, Inc.
Cross References: For reviews by Alan S. Kaufman and John J. Vacca, see 14:176; see also T5:1259 (2 references); for information on the earlier edition, see T4:1642 (1 reference); for a review by Bonnie W. Camp of the earlier edition, see 9:714.

[1211]
Infant Index.
Purpose: Designed as a screening tool "to identify and monitor children at risk of having or developing, special educational needs."
Population: Students entering infant school (ages approximately 4–5 years).
Publication Date: 1995.
Scores, 7: Literacy Skills, Mathematical Skills, Social Behaviour, Independent Learning, Basic Skills Composite Score, Behaviour Composite Score, Total Score.
Administration: Individual.
Price Data, 2002: £8.99 per set of 20 checklists; £9.99 per teacher's handbook; £10.99 per specimen set.

Time: Administration time not reported.
Comments: Checklist completed by educator.
Authors: Martin Desforges and Geoff Lindsay.
Publisher: Hodder & Stoughton Educational [England].

[1212]
The Infant Reading Tests.
Population: Ages 4-7 to 7.
Publication Date: 1979.
Administration: Group.
Time: (20) minutes.
Authors: Alan Brimer and Birdie Raban.
Publisher: Educational Evaluations [England].
a) PRE-READING TESTS.
Purpose: Developed to assess "linguistic competence; the ability to use printed symbols; the recognition of speech sounds; and the discrimination of printed shapes varying in orientation."
Price Data, 2002: £11.12 per introductory set including manual (12 pages) and 8 of each of 3 tests; £25 per 25 test booklets.
1) *Test 1.*
Scores: Total score only.
2) *Test 2.*
Scores, 3: Beginning Sounds, Middle Sounds, End Sounds.
3) *Test 3.*
Scores: Total score only.
b) READING TESTS.
Purpose: Constructed to assess "contributory skills of word recognition, sentence completion and reading comprehension."
Scores: Total score only.
Levels, 3: Test 1, Test 2, Test 3.
Price Data: £9 per introductory set including manual and 8 of each of 3 tests; £18.45 per 25 test booklets.
Cross References: For a review by Carl J. Dunst, see 9:505.

[1213]
The Infant-Toddler and Family Instrument.
Purpose: Designed as "a relatively short survey of family and child functioning" to "help in making a judgment about whether a child and family need further services and referrals."
Population: Families with infants and toddlers 6–36 months.
Publication Date: 2001.
Acronym: ITFI.
Scores, 4: Caregiver Interview, Developmental Map, Checklist for Evaluating Concern, Plan for the Child and Family.
Administration: Individual.
Price Data: Available from publisher.

Time: (150–165) minutes.
Authors: Nancy H. Apfel and Sally Provence.
Publisher: Paul H. Brookes Publishing Co.

[1214]
Infant-Toddler Developmental Assessment.

Purpose: Constructed as "an integrated family-centered assessment process that addresses the health and development of children."
Population: Birth to 36 months.
Publication Date: 1995.
Acronym: IDA.
Scores: 8 developmental domains: Gross Motor, Fine Motor, Relationship to Inanimate Objects (Cognitive), Language Communication, Self-Help, Relationship to Persons, Emotions and Feeling States (Affects), Coping.
Administration: Individual.
Price Data: Available from publisher.
Time: Varies.
Comments: Ratings by multidisciplinary team.
Authors: Sally Provence, Joanna Erikson, Susan Vater, and Saro Palmeri.
Publisher: Riverside Publishing.
Cross References: For reviews by Melissa M. Groves and E. Jean Newman, see 13:146.

[1215]
Infant/Toddler Environment Rating Scale.

Purpose: Developed to assess "the quality of center-based child care for children up to 30 months of age."
Population: Infant/toddler day care centers.
Publication Date: 1990.
Acronym: ITERS.
Scores, 8: Furnishings and Display for Children, Listening and Talking, Personal Care Routines, Learning Activities, Interaction, Program Structure, Adult Needs, Total.
Administration: Individual.
Price Data, 2002: $11.95 per rating scale; $8.95 per 30 scoring sheets.
Time: (120) minutes to observe and rate.
Comments: Adaptation of the Early Childhood Environment Rating Scales (9:365) and the Family Day Care Rating Scale (976).
Authors: Thelma Harms, Debby Cryer, and Richard M. Clifford.
Publisher: Teachers College Press.
Cross References: See T5:1264 (6 references).

[1216]
Infant/Toddler Symptom Checklist.

Purpose: Designed as a screening instrument for infants and toddlers with regulatory and sensory-integrative disorders.
Population: 7–30 months.
Publication Date: 1995.

Scores, 9: Self-Regulation, Attention, Sleep, Eating or Feeding, Dressing/Bathing or Touch, Movement, Listening and Language, Looking and Sight, Attachment/Emotional Functioning.
Administration: Individual.
Levels, 6: 7–9 months, 10–12 months, 13–18 months, 19–24 months, 25–30 months, General Screening Version (when age specific administration is inconvenient).
Price Data, 2002: $63 per Infant/Toddler Symptom Checklist including manual (58 pages) and 6 sets of 5 score sheets in 25-page pads in a vinyl storage portfolio; $37 per additional score sheets available in 6 sets of five sheets in 25-page pads.
Time: (10) minutes.
Comments: "Criterion-referenced"; checklist completed by parents or caregiver.
Authors: Georgia A. DeGangi, Susan Poisson, Ruth Z. Sickel, and Andrea Santman Wiener.
Publisher: Therapy Skill Builders—A Division of The Psychological Corporation.
Cross References: For reviews by Deborah Erickson and Ruth E. Tomes, see 14:178.

[1217]
Influence Strategies Exercise.

Purpose: Designed to identify various influence strategies used by individuals.
Population: Managers and employees.
Publication Date: 1990.
Acronym: ISE.
Scores, 9: Empowerment, Interpersonal Awareness, Bargaining, Relationship Building, Organizational Awareness, Common Vision, Impact Management, Logical Persuasion, Coercion.
Administration: Group.
Parts, 2: Participant Version, Employee Version (optional).
Price Data, 2001: $69 per complete kit including 10 exercises and 10 profiles and interpretive notes (19 pages); $29 per 10 employee version exercises.
Time: (20–25) minutes.
Comments: Self-administered questionnaire.
Author: Hay Group.
Publisher: Hay Group.
Cross References: For reviews by Collie W. Conoley and Paul M. Muchinsky, see 13:147.

[1218]
The Influence Styles Inventory.

Purpose: Designed to identify and examine the styles and strategies used in "day-to-day problems managers face."
Population: Managers.
Publication Dates: 1997–1998.
Scores, 3: Aggressive, Assertive, Passive.
Administration: Group.

Price Data: Available from publisher.
Time: (20) minutes.
Author: Marshall Sashkin.
Publisher: Human Resource Development Press.

[1219]
Informal Reading Comprehension Placement Test [Revised].

Purpose: "Assesses the instructional and independent comprehension levels of students from pre-readiness (grade 1) through level twelve plus (grade 12)."
Population: Grades 1–8 for typical learners and grades 8–12 remedially; adult education students.
Publication Dates: 1983–1993.
Scores, 3: Word Comprehension, Passage Comprehension, Total Comprehension.
Administration: Individual.
Price Data, 2001: $59.95 per test including Mac/Win CD ROM, management, and guide.
Time: (35–50) minutes for the battery; (15–20) minutes for Part 1; (20–30) minutes for Part 2.
Comments: Automatically administered, scored, and managed; for use with adults, the placements are correlated with Tests of Adult Basic Education (2583); test administered in two parts; microcomputer (IBM Windows or MAC) necessary for administration.
Authors: Ann Edson and Eunice Insel.
Publisher: Educational Activities Software.
Cross References: For reviews by Diane I. Sawyer and Gabrielle Stutman, see 13:148; for reviews by Gloria A. Galvin and Claudia R. Wright of an earlier edition, see 11:178.

[1220]
Information System Skills.

Purpose: Constructed to predict "a person's success in operating terminal based information systems."
Population: Information processing job applicants.
Publication Date: 1983.
Acronym: ISS.
Scores, 4: Reasoning, Form Recognition, Document Checking, Speed.
Administration: Group.
Price Data: Available from publisher.
Time: 36 minutes and 30 seconds (45 minutes).
Author: Malcolm Morrisby.
Publisher: Educational & Industrial Test Services Ltd. [England].

[1221]
Informeter: An International Technique for the Measurement of Political Information.

Purpose: Designed to measure political information.
Population: Adults.
Publication Date: 1972.

Scores, 5: Local, National, International, Miscellaneous, Total.
Administration: Group.
Manual: No manual.
Price Data, 2002: $1 per scale.
Time: [15] minutes.
Comments: Supplementary article available.
Author: Panos D. Bardis.
Publisher: Donna Bardis.

[1222]
INSIGHT Inventory [Revised].

Purpose: Designed to determine how an individual differs from other individuals in his or her style of influencing others, relating to others, responding to people, making decisions and taking action, and structuring time and handling details.
Population: Adults age 21 and over, students age 16–21.
Publication Dates: 1988–2000.
Scores: 4 traits: Getting Your Way (Direct, Indirect), Responding to People (Reserved, Outgoing), Pacing Activity (Urgent, Steady), Dealing with Details (Unstructured, Precise).
Administration: Group or individual.
Forms, 6: A (Adult Team-Building), B (Adult Communications), F (Adult Feedback/Others), I (Adult Job Interviewing), C (Student Leadership and Self-Esteem), D (Student Feedback/Others).
Price Data, 2002: $7.50 per Forms B and I; $9.95 per Form A; $12 per Form F, 360 Feedback set; $6 per Forms C and D; $250 per Training Kit for adult version including video, training guide, technical manual, and CD with digital slides; $150 per Teaching Kit for student version including video, teaching guide, technical manual, transparency masters, and CD with digital slides; quantity discounts available for all materials.
Time: (15–20) minutes.
Comments: Users get two profiles, one reflecting how they see themselves in their work (school) environment and the other reflecting how they see themselves in their personal (at home) environment; "has field theory base which takes into account that participants may change their behavior from one environment (field) to another"; utilizes self-perception; supporting feedback sets provide perceptions of how five others see the user; 1993 revision based on a second collection of norms and a factor analysis of the items; online version available at www.insightinstitute.com.
Author: Patrick Handley.
Publisher: Insight Institute, Inc.
Cross References: For reviews by Sanford J. Cohen and Elizabeth L. Jones, see 14:179; for a review by Susana Urbina of an earlier edition, see 13:149.

[1223]
The Instructional Environment System—II: A System to Identify a Student's Instructional Needs (Second Edition).

Purpose: "Designed to assist education professionals in a systematic analysis of a target student's instructional environment, which includes both school and home contexts."

Population: Grades K–12.

Publication Dates: 1987–1993.

Acronym: TIES-II.

Scores: 12 Instructional Environment Components (Instructional Match, Teacher Expectations, Classroom Environment, Instructional Presentation, Cognitive Emphasis, Motivational Strategies, Relevant Practice, Informed Feedback, Academic Engaged Time, Adaptive Instruction, Progress Evaluation, Student Understanding), 5 Home Support for Learning Components (Expectations and Attributions, Discipline Orientation, Home Affective Environment, Parent Participation, Structure for Learning).

Administration: Individual.

Forms, 4: Instructional Needs Checklist, Parent Interview Record, Home Support for Learning Form, Instructional Environment Form.

Price Data, 2002: $55 per TIES-II Program Kit including manual (1993, 199 pages).

Time: Administration time not reported.

Comments: Observational and interview data from teachers, parents, and students is gathered by an education professional; can be used in regular classrooms, homes, special education, and in different content areas; publisher advises that a revision entitled Functional Assessment of Academic Behavior will be published in February 2002.

Authors: James Ysseldyke and Sandra Christenson.

Publisher: Sopris West.

Cross References: See T5:1275 (1 reference); for reviews by Michael J. Furlong and Jennifer A. Rosenblatt and by Jerry Tindal, see 13:150; for reviews by Kenneth W. Howell and by William T. McKee and Joseph C. Witt of an earlier form, see 10:149.

[1224]
Instructional Leadership Evaluation and Development Program (ILEAD).

Population: School climates and leadership.

Publication Dates: 1985–1988.

Acronym: ILEAD.

Administration: Individual or group.

Price Data: Available from publisher.

Time: Administration time varies with form.

Authors: Larry A. Braskamp (School Climate Inventories, School Administrator Assessment Survey), Martin L. Maehr (same material as above), and MetriTech, Inc. (manual and Instructional Leadership Inventory).

Publisher: MetriTech, Inc.

a) SCHOOL CLIMATE INVENTORY (FORM T).

Purpose: "Designed to assess instructional leadership behavior, job satisfaction and commitment, and school culture or climate from the teachers' perspective."

Scores, 12: Instructional Leadership (Defines Mission, Manages Curriculum, Supervises Teaching, Monitors Student Progress, Promotes Instructional Climate), Climate (Satisfaction, Commitment, Strength, Accomplishment, Recognition, Power, Affiliation).

Comments: Ratings by teachers.

b) SCHOOL CLIMATE INVENTORY (FORM S).

Purpose: "Designed to assess school climate from the student perspective."

Scores, 5: Strength of Climate, Accomplishment, Recognition, Power, Affiliation.

Comments: Ratings by students in grades 3–12.

c) SCHOOL ADMINISTRATOR ASSESSMENT SURVEY.

Purpose: "Designed to simultaneously assess the person, the job, and the culture or climate of the setting in which the person works."

Scores, 19: Personal Incentive (Accomplishment, Recognition, Power, Affiliation), Self-Concept (Self-Reliance, Self-Esteem, Goal-Directedness), Job Opportunity (Accomplishment, Recognition, Power, Affiliation, Advancement), Organizational Culture (Accomplishment, Recognition, Power, Affiliation, Satisfaction, Strength of Culture, Commitment).

Comments: Adaptation of SPECTRUM; self-ratings by administrators.

d) INSTRUCTIONAL LEADERSHIP INVENTORY.

Purpose: "Designed to assess instructional leadership behavior."

Scores, 8: Instructional Leadership (Defines Mission, Manages Curriculum, Supervises Teaching, Monitors Student Progress, Promotes Instructional Climate), Contextual (Staff, School, Community).

Comments: Self-ratings by principals.

Cross References: For reviews by David L. Bolton and Donna L. Sundre, see 12:190; see also T4:1240 (1 reference).

[1225]
Instructional Skills Assessment.

Purpose: Designed to give instructors a better view of their strengths and weaknesses in class.

Population: Instructors.

Publication Date: 1994.
Scores, 7: 6 dimensions: Instructor's Role as Catalyst and Facilitator and Mediator of Learning, Instructor's Ability to Teach on "Adult-to-Adult" Basis and not Become Parent, Instructor's Ability to Keep a Good Balance Between Stimulus-Response-Feedback, Instructor's Organizational Skills in Pacing and Managing the Instructional Sequence, Instructor's Ability to Teach Effectively in Both the Inductive and Deductive Modes, Instructor's Effectiveness as a Communicator, Total.
Administration: Group.
Price Data: Price information available from publisher for booklet/manuals (4 pages).
Time: [20] minutes.
Comments: Self-administered; self-scored.
Author: Training House, Inc.
Publisher: Training House, Inc.

[1226]
Instrument for Disability Screening [Developmental Edition].
Purpose: To screen for learning disabilities.
Population: Primary grade children.
Publication Date: 1980.
Acronym: IDS.
Scores, 9: Hyperactive/Aggression, Visual, Speech/Auditory, Reading, Drawing/Writing, Inactivity, Concepts, Psychomotor Development, Total.
Administration: Individual.
Manual: No manual.
Price Data: Not available.
Time: (5-15) minutes.
Author: James R. Beatty.
Publisher: James R. Beatty [No reply from publisher; status unknown].
Cross References: See T3:1161 (3 references); for reviews by Norman A. Buktenica and Stephen J. Pfeiffer, see 9:515.

[1227]
Instrument Technician Test—Form IPO-I.
Purpose: Developed to measure knowledge and skills required for instrument technician jobs.
Population: Applicants and incumbents for jobs requiring technical knowledge of instrumentation.
Publication Dates: 1989–1996.
Scores, 12: Mathematics, Digital Electronics, Analog Electronics, Schematics and Electrical Print Reading, Process Control, Power Supplies, Basic AC/DC Theory, Test Instruments, Mechanical, Computer and PLC, Chemical Processes, Total.
Administration: Group.
Price Data, 2002: $498 per complete kit including 10 reusable test booklets, 100 answer sheets, manual (1996, 16 pages), and answer key.

Time: (120) minutes.
Author: Roland T. Ramsay.
Publisher: Ramsay Corporation.
Cross References: For reviews by Phillip L. Ackerman and Alan C. Bugbee, Jr., see 13:151.

[1228]
Instrument Timbre Preference Test.
Purpose: "To act as an objective aid to the teacher and the parent in helping a student choose an appropriate woodwind or brass instrument to learn to play in beginning instrumental music and band."
Population: Grades 4–12.
Publication Dates: 1984–1985.
Acronym: ITPT.
Scores, 7: Flute, Clarinet, Saxophone and French Horn, Oboe/English Horn/Bassoon, Trumpet and Cornet, Trombone/Baritone/French Horn, Tuba and Sousaphone.
Administration: Group.
Price Data, 2001: $59 per complete kit including 100 test sheets, scoring masks, compact disc, and manual (1984, 53 pages); $14.50 per 100 test sheets; scoring service available from publisher.
Time: (30) minutes.
Author: Edwin E. Gordon.
Publisher: G.I.A. Publications, Inc.
Cross References: For reviews by Richard Colwell and Paul R. Lehman, see 10:150.

[1229]
Integrated Assessment System®.
Purpose: "A series of performance tasks that can be used independently or in combination with a norm-referenced achievement test to offer a comprehensive view of student achievement."
Population: Grades 1–9.
Publication Dates: 1990–1992.
Acronym: IAS®.
Subtests: 3.
Administration: Group.
Authors: Roger Farr and Beverly Farr (Language Arts and Spanish only).
Publisher: The Psychological Corporation.
  a) IAS-LANGUAGE ARTS.
  Population: Grades 1–8.
  Scores, 3: Response to Reading, Management of Content, Command of Language.
  Price Data, 2002: $160.60 per complete grade 1 package including 25 each of three student booklets and one directions for administering; $280.40 per complete grades 2–8 package including 25 each of three reading passages, three sets of guided-writing-activity blackline masters, directions for administering, three packages of 25 response forms, and response form directions; $28.10

per grade 1 examination kit including student booklet, directions for administering, and one passage-specific scoring rubric; $35.50 per grades 2–8 examination kit including one each of reading passage, guided-writing-activity blackline master, response form, response form directions, directions for administering, and one passage-specific scoring rubric; $40.30 per grade 1 activity package including 25 of one student booklet and directions for administering; $100.20 per grades 2–8 activity package including 25 of one reading passage, one directions for administering, and one guided-writing activity blackline master; $9 per grades 2–8 response form package; $10.60 per grades 1–8 directions for administering; $23.30 per grades 1–8 scoring guides; $37.10 per 25 grade 1 reading passage only; $91.20 per 25 grades 2–8 reading passage only; $20.10 per grades 2–8 guided-writing-activity blackline masters; $55 per technical report (1991, 53 pages); $324.90 per scoring workshop kit including videotape, trainer's manual, 25 overhead transparencies, and blackline masters of model papers and training papers; $200.30 per portfolio starter kit including classroom storage box, 25 student portfolios, and teacher's manual; $64.10 per 25 student portfolio folders; $64.10 per teacher's manual; $98.60 per introductory videotape and viewer's guide; $6.60 per basic scoring service including list report and summary.

Time: (120–240) minutes.

1) *IAS—Language Arts, Spanish Edition.*

Scores: Same as *a* above.

Price Data: $28 per grade 1 examination kit including student booklet, directions for administering, and a passage-specific scoring rubric; $33 per grades 2–8 examination kit including one each of reading passage, guided-writing-activity blackline master, response form, response form directions, directions for administering, and passage-specific scoring rubric; $38.70 per grade 1 activity package including 25 copies of one student booklet and one directions for administering; $97 per grades 2–8 activity package including 25 copies of one reading passage, one directions for administering, and one guided-writing-activity blackline master; $9 per grades 2–8 response form package including 25 response forms and one response form directions; $10.60 per grades 1–8 directions for administering; $22.80 per grades 1–8 scoring guides; $36 per 25 grade 1 reading passage; $88 per 25 grades 2–8 reading passage; $18.60 per grades 2–8 guided-writing-activity blackline masters; $6.60 per basic scoring service including list report and summary.

b) IAS-MATHEMATICS.

Population: Grades 1–9.

Scores, 4: Reasoning, Conceptual Knowledge, Communication, Procedures.

Price Data: $28.10 per examination kit including one of each student booklet, directions for administering, and scoring rubric; $40.90 per activity package including 25 student booklets and one directions for administering; $11.70 per directions for administering; $24.40 per scoring guides; $180.70 per scoring training kit including binder and overhead transparencies; $8 per basic scoring service (holistic only).

Time: (80–90) minutes.

c) IAS-SCIENCE.

Population: Grades 1–8.

Scores, 4: Experimenting, Collecting Data, Drawing Conclusions, Communicating.

Price Data: $27 per examination kit including one each of student booklet, directions for administering, and scoring rubric; $40.90 per activity package including 25 student booklets and one directions for administering; $11.70 per directions for administering; $24.40 per scoring guides; $45.60 per manipulative materials; $179 per scoring workshop kit including trainer's manual; $8 per basic scoring service (holistic only).

Time: (80–90) minutes.

Cross References: For reviews by Gabriel M. Della-Piana and Bikkar S. Randhawa, see 13:152.

[1230]
Integrated Visual and Auditory Continuous Performance Test.

Purpose: Designed to assess visual and auditory response control, attention, and hyperactivity, providing data to help the clinician diagnose and differentiate between the four subtypes of Attention-Deficit/Hyperactivity Disorder outlined in the DSM-IV.

Population: Age 6 to adult.

Publication Dates: 1993–2002.

Acronym: IVA.

Scores, 28: Attention Quotient Auditory, Attention Quotient Full-Scale, Attention Quotient Visual, Balance, Comprehension Auditory, Comprehension Visual, Consistency Auditory, Consistency Visual, Fine Motor Regulation, Focus Auditory, Focus Visual, Persistence Auditory, Persistence Visual, Readiness Auditory, Readiness Visual, Response Control Quotient Auditory, Response Control Quotient Full-Scale, Response Control Quotient Visual, Sensory/Motor Auditory, Sensory/Motor Visual, Speed Auditory, Speed Visual, Stamina Auditory, Stamina Visual, Vigilance Auditory, Vigilance Visual.

Administration: Individual.

Price Data, 2002: Three options: Option 1: $295 per Starter Kit including software, Administration & Interpretation manual (2002, on the CD), and 10 tests (licensed for use at 1 computer, CD-ROM); $99 per 10 additional tests; or Option 2: $598 per Registration Kit including software, Administration & Interpretation manual, and 10 tests (licensed for use at 1 computer, CD-ROM); $89 per 25 additional tests; or Option 3: $1,495 per unlimited use version including software, Administration & Interpretation manual, and unlimited tests (licensed for use at 1 computer, CD-ROM); $495 per unlimited use version for schools.
Time: 13 minutes.
Comments: Computer administered; requires Windows 98 or higher computer.
Authors: Joseph A. Sandford and Ann Turner.
Publisher: BrainTrain.
Cross References: For reviews by Harrison Kane and Susan C. Whiston and by Martin J. Wiese, see 14:180.

[1231]
Integrated Writing Test.

Purpose: "Designed to evaluate major components of good writing in students' writing samples."
Population: Grades 2–12.
Publication Date: 1993.
Acronym: IWT.
Scores, 7: Productivity, Clarity, Vocabulary, Spelling, Punctuation, Legibility, Total Test Language Quotient.
Administration: Group.
Levels, 5: Grades 2/3, Grade 4, Grades 5/6, Grades 7 to 9, Grades 10 to 12.
Price Data, 2001: $131.95 per kit including manual (66 pages) and 35 booklets for each grade level; $22.95 per package of 35 booklets; $22.95 per manual.
Time: 15(20) minutes.
Comments: Academic extension of the Developmental Test of Visual-Motor Integration (119); also based upon the National Assessment of Educational Progress Writing Test.
Authors: Keith E. Beery with assistance from the Integrated Teaching Team.
Publisher: Golden Educational Center.
Cross References: For reviews by C. Dale Carpenter and Richard M. Wolf, see 14:181.

[1232]
INteraction CHecklist for Augmentative Communication, Revised Edition.

Purpose: Designed to assess features of interaction between augmentative system users and their partners.
Population: Augmentative system users.
Publication Dates: 1984–1991.
Acronym: INCH.

Scores, 13: Strategies (Initiation, Facilitation, Regulation, Termination); Modes (Linguistic, Paralinguistic, Kinesic, Proxemic, Chronemic); Contexts (Familiar-Trained, Familiar-Untrained, Unfamiliar-Trained, Unfamiliar-Untrained).
Administration: Individual.
Price Data, 2002: $38 per complete kit including manual (1991, 74 pages) and 25 checklists; $13 per 25 checklists.
Time: Administration time not reported.
Comments: Behavior checklist.
Authors: Susan Oakander Bolton and Sallie E. Dashiell.
Publisher: Imaginart International, Inc.
Cross References: For reviews by Anthony J. Nitko and Kenneth G. Shipley, see 13:153 (1 reference).

[1233]
Interest Explorer.

Purpose: Designed "to explore interests combined with academic skills for the purpose of career and educational planning.
Population: Grades 8–12.
Publication Date: 1999.
Scores: Interest Levels in 14 career areas: Animals and Plants, Arts, Business Services, Computer Technology, Customer Services, Educational and Social Services, Engineering Technology, Legal Services, Management and Administration, Mechanical and Craft Technology, Medical Sciences, Physical and Life Sciences and Mathematics, Protective Services, Sales.
Administration: Group.
Levels, 2: 1, 2.
Price Data: Available from publisher.
Time: (235) minutes for complete battery; (90) minutes for survey.
Comments: The Interest Explorer is designed to be used in conjunction with The Iowa Tests (1268; 1269).
Author: Riverside Publishing.
Publisher: Riverside Publishing.

[1234]
Interference Learning Test.

Purpose: Designed "for detecting and characterizing mild and moderate as well as severe levels of" neuropsychological impairment.
Population: Ages 16–93.
Publication Date: 1999.
Scores: Learning Performance (List 1 Total Recall, Best Recall, List 2 Total Recall, Added Words, Lost Words, Middle Recall, Recency Minus Primary, Subjective Organization, Category Clustering, Seriation, Intertrial Consistency, New Word Priority, Repeats, Source Errors, Confabulations), Delayed Recall Performance (Short Delay Recall, Long Delay Recall, Cued

Recall, Retroactive Inhibition, Cueing Facilitation, Encoding, Rebound), Recognition Performance (Recognition Correct, Overlap Correct, Novel Foil Correct, Indirect Correct), Total.
Administration: Individual.
Price Data, 2002: $150 per kit including manual (186 pages), 5 Response Record Forms, a stimulus booklet, 5-use disk for computer scoring and interpretation; $50 per stimulus booklet; $50 per manual; $32.50 per 20 Response Record Forms; $240 per 20-use disk.
Time: (20–30) minutes.
Comments: Computer administration option available.
Authors: Michael M. Schmidt and Frederick L. Coolidge.
Publisher: Western Psychological Services.

[1235]
Intermediate Booklet Category Test.
Purpose: Designed as a "test of higher order cognitive functions" to assess brain damage.
Population: Ages 9–14.
Publication Dates: 1985–1987.
Acronym: IBCT.
Scores: Total Error Score.
Administration: Individual.
Price Data: Available from publisher for complete kit including IBCT in 2 volumes, manual (1987, 19 pages), and 50 scoring forms.
Time: (30–60) minutes.
Author: Paul B. Byrd.
Publisher: Psychological Assessment Resources, Inc.
Cross References: For reviews by James K. Benish and Vincent J. Samar, see 14:182.

[1236]
Intermediate Measures of Music Audiation.
Purpose: "To identify children with exceptionally high music aptitude … who can profit from the opportunity to participate in additional group study and special private instruction … to evaluate the comparative tonal and rhythm aptitudes of each child with exceptionally high music aptitude."
Population: Grades 1–4.
Publication Dates: 1978–1982.
Acronym: IMMA.
Scores, 3: Tonal, Rhythm, Composite.
Administration: Group.
Price Data, 2001: $100 per complete kit containing 1 tonal and rhythm compact disc, 100 tonal answer sheets, 100 rhythm answer sheets, 2 sets of scoring masks, 100 profile cards, 4 class record sheets, research monographs, and test manual (1982, 44 pages); $25 per CD; $41.50 per 500 tonal answer sheets; $41.50 per 500 rhythm answer sheets; $5 per

set of tonal or rhythm scoring masks; $15.50 per 100 profile cards; $2 per 10 class record sheets; $20 per manual.
Time: (20) minutes per Tonal test; (20) minutes per Rhythm test.
Comments: Advanced version of the Primary Measures of Music Audiation (1976); tests administered by 7 1/2 ips tape recordings.
Author: Edwin E. Gordon.
Publisher: G.I.A. Publications, Inc.

[1237]
Internalized Shame Scale.
Purpose: Developed to measure an individual's feelings of shame and the negative response patterns that result from internalized chance.
Population: Age 13 and older.
Publication Date: 2001.
Acronym: ISS.
Scores, 2: Shame, Self-Esteem.
Administration: Individual.
Price Data, 2002: $73 per complete kit including manual, 25 Quikscore forms, and 25 brochure handouts; $36 per specimen set including manual, 3 Quikscore forms, and 3 brochure handouts; $32 per technical manual.
Time: 15 minutes.
Comments: Self-completed.
Author: David R. Cook.
Publisher: Multi-Health Systems, Inc.

[1238]
Internalizing Symptoms Scale for Children.
Purpose: Developed to provide a screening and assessment self-report tool for research and clinical evaluation of internalizing symptoms associated with depression, anxiety, somatic problems, social withdrawal, and various types of affect in children.
Population: Ages 8–13.
Publication Date: 1998.
Acronym: ISSC.
Scores, 3: Negative Affect/General Distress, Positive Affect, Total.
Administration: Group or individual.
Levels, 3: Normal, At-Risk, High Risk.
Price Data, 2001: $74 per complete kit; $19 per response sheets; $19 per summary sheets; $39 per manual.
Time: (20) minutes.
Authors: Kenneth W. Merrell and Amy S. Walters.
Publisher: PRO-ED.
Cross References: For reviews by Robert Christopher and Suzanne G. Martin, see 14:183; see also T5:1288 (2 references).

[1239]
International Personality Disorder Examination.

Purpose: To "identify those traits and behaviors that are relevant to an assessment of the criteria for personality disorders in the ICD-10 and DSM-IV classification systems."

Population: Adults.

Publication Dates: 1988–1999.

Acronym: IPDEE.

Scores: 11 scores for DSM-IV version: Paranoid, Schizoid, Schizotypal, Antisocial, Borderline, Histrionic, Narcissistic, Avoidant, Dependent, Obsessive-Compulsive, Not Otherwise Specified; 10 scores for ICD-10 version: Paranoid, Schizoid, Dissocial, Emotionally Unstable/Impulsive Type, Emotionally Unstable/Borderline Type, Histronic, Anankastic, Anxious (Avoidant), Dependent, Unspecified.

Administration: Individual.

Parts, 2: DSM-IV Module, ICD-10 Module.

Price Data: Available from publisher for introductory kit including 25 screening questionnaires (specify for DSM-IV or ICD-10), 15 scoring booklets (specify DSM-IV or ICD-10), and 50 answer sheets (specify DSM-IV or ICD-10), and for manual (1999, 240 pages).

Time: [60–120] minutes.

Comments: Complete administration includes a self-administered questionnaire as well as a clinical interview with client/subject.

Author: Armand W. Loranger.

Publisher: Psychological Assessment Resources, Inc.

[1240]
Interpersonal Adjective Scales.

Purpose: "A self-report instrument designed to measure two important dimensions of interpersonal transactions: Dominance and Nurturance."

Population: Ages 18 and up.

Publication Date: 1995.

Acronym: IAS.

Scores, 10: Assured-Dominant, Arrogant-Calculating, Cold-hearted, Aloof-Introverted, Unassured-Submissive, Unassuming-Ingenious, Warm-Agreeable, Gregarious-Extraverted, Dominance, Nurturance.

Administration: Individual or group.

Price Data: Available from publisher for introductory kit including manual (143 pages), 25 test booklets, 25 scoring booklets, and 25 glossaries.

Time: (15–20) minutes.

Comments: Separate norms are available for college students and adults; glossary is included to be used by subjects during testing.

Author: Jerry S. Wiggins.

Publisher: Psychological Assessment Resources, Inc.

Cross References: For reviews by Steven J. Lindner and Gerald R. Schneck, see 14:184; see also T5:1288 (2 references).

[1241]
Interpersonal Behavior Survey.

Purpose: "Developed to distinguish assertive behaviors from aggressive behaviors."

Population: Grades 9–16 and adults.

Publication Date: 1980.

Acronym: IBS.

Scores, 21: Denial, Infrequency, Impression Management, General Aggressiveness—Rational, Hostile Stance, Expression of Anger, Disregard for Rights, Verbal Aggressiveness, Physical Aggressiveness, Passive Aggressiveness, General Assertiveness—Rational, Self-Confidence, Initiating Assertiveness, Defending Assertiveness, Frankness, Praise, Requesting Help, Refusing Demands, Conflict Avoidance, Dependency, Shyness, plus additional scores (General Aggressiveness—Empirical, General Assertiveness—Empirical) and 10 short-form scores.

Administration: Group.

Price Data, 2002: $110 per complete kit including 5 reusable administration booklets, 50 profile forms, 50 answer sheets, set of scoring keys, and manual (78 pages); $22.50 per 10 administration booklets; $29.50 per set of scoring keys; $22.50 per 100 answer sheets; $22.50 per 100 profiles; $47.50 per manual.

Time: (40–50) minutes.

Comments: Self-report inventory.

Authors: Paul A. Mauger, David R. Adkinson, Suzanne K. Zoss (test), Gregory Firestone (test), and J. David Hook (test).

Publisher: Western Psychological Services.

Cross References: See T5:1290 (4 references) and T4:1251 (5 references); for reviews by Stephen L. Franzoi and Robert R. Hutzell, see 9:518.

[1242]
Interpersonal Check List.

Purpose: "To obtain self-descriptions and descriptions of, or by, others with respect to an interpersonal domain of personality."

Population: Adults.

Publication Date: 1955.

Acronym: ICL.

Scores, 24: 16 interpersonal scores, 4 intensity scores, plus 4 summary scores: Number of Items Checked, Average Intensity, Dominance, Love.

Administration: Group.

Price Data, 1998: Single reproducible list of 134 items available for cost of postage and handling.

Time: (15–20) minutes.

Comments: For research by qualified users only.

Authors: Rolfe LaForge and Robert Suczek (test).

Publisher: Rolfe LaForge.
Cross References: See T5:1291 (5 references), T4:1252 (18 references), T3:1170 (16 references), T2:1240 (115 references), and P:127 (70 references); for a review by P. M. Bentler, see 6:127 (39 references).

[1243]
Interpersonal Communication Inventory.
Purpose: To assess "a client's interpersonal communication as it provides clues to communication difficulties outside of the family relationship."
Population: Grade 9 to adult.
Publication Dates: 1969-1976.
Acronym: ICI.
Scores, 12: Self-Disclosure, Awareness, Evaluation and Acceptance of Feedback, Self-Expression, Attention, Coping with Feelings, Clarity, Avoidance, Dominance, Handling Differences, Perceived Acceptance, Total.
Administration: Group.
Price Data, 1993: $.75 per inventory; $3.50 per guide (1976, 15 pages).
Time: (20) minutes.
Author: Millard J. Bienvenu.
Publisher: Millard J. Bienvenu, Northwest Publications.
Cross References: See T5:1292 (1 reference), T4:1253 (3 references), and T3:1171 (2 references); see also 8:589 (3 references) and T2:1241 (1 reference).

[1244]
Interpersonal Relations Questionnaire.
Purpose: "To identify specific problems in connection with interpersonal relations and identity formation".
Population: "White pupils" in Standards 5–7 in South African schools.
Publication Dates: 1981–1988.
Acronym: IRQ.
Scores, 13: Self-Confidence, Self-Esteem, Self-Control, Nervousness, Health, Family Influences, Personal Freedom, Sociability A, Sociability T, Sociability D, Moral Sense, Formal Relations, Lie Scale.
Administration: Group.
Price Data: Available from publisher.
Time: (105–120) minutes.
Comments: Supplementary manual in English and Afrikaans.
Authors: Marianne Joubert and Dawn Schlebusch (supplementary manual).
Publisher: Human Sciences Research Council [South Africa].

[1245]
Interpersonal Style Inventory.
Purpose: To measure "an individual's characteristic ways of relating to other people ... also evaluates style

of impulse control and characteristic modes of dealing with work and play."
Population: Ages 14 and over.
Publication Dates: 1977–1986.
Acronym: ISI.
Scores: 15 in 5 areas: Interpersonal Involvement (Sociable, Help Seeking, Nurturant, Sensitive), Socialization (Conscientious, Trusting, Tolerant), Autonomy (Directive, Independent, Rule Free), Self-Control (Deliberate, Orderly, Persistent), Stability (Stable, Approval Seeking).
Administration: Group.
Price Data, 2002: $125 per complete kit including 2 reusable administration booklets, 10 AutoScore™ answer forms, manual (1986, 69 pages), 2 prepaid mail-in answer sheets for computer scoring and interpretation, and 2-use disk and 2 PC answer sheets for on-site computer scoring and interpretation; $21.50 per 10 administration booklets; $45 per manual; $32.50 per 20 AutoScore™ answer forms; $18.50 per 20 profile sheets for adolescents; $199.50 per 25-use computer disk (PC with DOS); $12.50 per mail-in answer sheet; $15 per 100 PC answer sheets; $15 per FAX service scoring charge.
Time: (40–45) minutes.
Authors: Maurice Lorr and Richard P. Youniss.
Publisher: Western Psychological Services.
Cross References: See T5:1294 (4 references) and T4:1256 (6 references); for reviews by Randy W. Kamphaus and Gerald L. Stone, see 10:151 (4 references); for reviews by John Duckitt and Stuart A. Karabenick of an earlier edition, see 9:521; see also T3:1173 (1 reference).

[1246]
Interpersonal Style Questionnaire.
Purpose: Designed "to help educators determine their primary interpersonal style."
Population: Educators at grades K–12.
Publication Dates: 1987–1998.
Scores, 4: Achiever, Persuader, Supporter, Analyst.
Administration: Group.
Manual: No manual.
Price Data, 2002: $25 per 20 test booklets.
Time: Administration time not reported.
Comments: Can be used alone or with Working Together, a tool for collaborative teaching, available from publisher.
Author: Anita DeBoer.
Publisher: Sopris West.

[1247]
Interpersonal Trust Surveys.
Purpose: Designed to measure an individual's "propensity to trust and to build trust with other people."
Population: Adults.

Publication Dates: 1996–1997.
Acronym: ITS; ITS-O; OTS.
Forms, 3: Interpersonal Trust Survey, Interpersonal Trust Survey—Observer, Organizational Trust Survey.
Scores, 6: Shares Information, Reduces Control, Allows for Mutual Influences, Clarifies Expectations, Meets Others' Expectations, Total.
Administration: Group.
Price Data, 1998: $59.95 per kit including Interpersonal Trust Survey—Observer, Interpersonal Trust Survey, Organizational Trust Survey, scoring software, and facilitator's guide (1996, 172 pages); $5.95 per Interpersonal Trust Survey; $3.95 per Iterpersonal Trust Survey-Observer; $3.95 per Organizational Trust Survey.
Time: Administration time not reported.
Comments: Scored for "My Behavior" and "Others' Behavior"; can be used as part of an educational workshop in interpersonal trust or as a tool for counseling; based on the "behavioral model of interpersonal trust"; scoring software available (must be run with Microsoft Excel).
Author: Guy L. DeFuria.
Publisher: Jossey-Bass, A Wiley Company.
Cross References: For a review by Mark E. Sibicky, see 14:185.

[1248]
Intra- and Interpersonal Relations Scale.

Purpose: Identify children's attitudes toward themselves and their relationships with their parents.
Population: Bantu pupils in Forms IV and V in South African schools.
Publication Dates: 1973–1975.
Acronym: IIPS.
Scores, 4: Self-Image, Mother-Child Relationship, Father-Child Relationship, Ideal Self.
Administration: Group.
Price Data: Available from publisher.
Time: (40–60) minutes.
Comments: Test materials in both English and Afrikaans.
Author: G. G. Minnaar.
Publisher: Human Sciences Research Council [South Africa].
Cross References: See T5:1297 (1 reference).

[1249]
Intuitive Mechanics (Weights & Pulleys).

Purpose: "To measure the ability to understand mechanical relationships, to visualize internal movement in a mechanical system."
Population: Industrial positions.
Publication Dates: 1956–1984.
Scores: Total score only.
Administration: Individual or group.

Price Data, 2002: $91 per start-up kit including 25 test booklets, score key, and interpretation and research manual; $54 per 25 test booklets (quantity discounts available); $20 per score key; $28 per interpretation and research manual.
Time: (3) minutes.
Authors: L. L. Thurstone and T. E. Jeffrey.
Publisher: Reid London House.
Cross References: For a review by William A. Owens, see 9:523.

[1250]
Inventory for Client and Agency Planning.

Purpose: Developed "to assess the status, adaptive functioning, and service needs of clients."
Population: Infant to adult.
Publication Date: 1986.
Acronym: ICAP.
Scores, 10: Maladaptive Behavior Indexes (Internalized, Asocial, Externalized, General), Adaptive Behavior (Motor Skills, Social and Communication Skills, Personal Living Skills, Community Living Skills, Total), Service Level Index.
Administration: Individual.
Price Data: Available from publisher.
Time: (20–30) minutes.
Comments: Statistically related to the Scales of Independent Behavior (2189) and the Woodcock-Johnson Psycho-Educational Battery (2732); to be completed by "a respondent who has known a client for at least 3 months and who sees him or her on a day-to-day basis."
Authors: Robert H. Bruininks, Bradley K. Hill, Richard F. Weatherman, and Richard W. Woodcock.
Publisher: Riverside Publishing.
Cross References: See T5:1300 (11 references) and T4:1260 (3 references); for reviews by Ronn Johnson and Richard L. Wikoff, see 10:152.

[1251]
Inventory of Altered Self-Capacities.

Purpose: Designed to assess difficulties in relatedness, identity, and affect control.
Population: Age 18 and above.
Publication Dates: 1998–2000.
Acronym: IASC.
Scores, 11: Interpersonal Conflicts, Idealization—Disillusionment, Abandonment Concerns, Identity Impairment, Self-Awareness, Identity Diffusion, Susceptibility to Influence, Affect Dysregulation, Affect Skill Deficits, Affect Instability, Tension Reduction Activities.
Administration: Group or individual.
Price Data: Available from publisher for kit including 25 reusable item booklets, 50 hand-scorable answer sheets, 50 profile forms, and professional manual (2000, 49 pages).

Time: [10–15] minutes.
Author: John Briere.
Publisher: Psychological Assessment Resources, Inc.

[1252]
Inventory of Anger Communication.
Purpose: "To identify the subjective and interactional aspects of anger in assessing how one communicates around anger."
Population: High school and adults.
Publication Dates: 1974-1976.
Acronym: IAC.
Scores: Total score only.
Administration: Group.
Price Data, 1993: $.75 per inventory; $2 per manual (1976, 10 pages).
Time: [15-20] minutes.
Author: Millard J. Bienvenu.
Publisher: Millard J. Bienvenu, Northwest Publications.
Cross References: For additional information, see 8:591 (1 reference).

[1253]
Inventory of Drinking Situations.
Purpose: "Designed to assess situations in which a client drank heavily over the past year."
Population: Ages 18 to 75.
Publication Date: 1987.
Acronym: IDS.
Scores, 8: Personal Status (Unpleasant Emotions, Physical Discomfort, Pleasant Emotions, Testing Personal Control, Urges and Temptations), Situations Involving Other People (Conflict with Others, Social Pressure to Drink, Pleasant Times with Others).
Administration: Group.
Forms, 2: IDS-100, IDS-42 (Brief Version).
Price Data, 2002: C$25 per specimen set including user's guide (53 pages), 25 questionnaires, 25 answer sheets, 25 profiles; C$13.50 per user's guide; C$12.75 per 25 IDS-42 (Brief Version) questionnaires, 25 answer sheets, and 25 profile sheets; C$14.75 per 25 IDS-100 questionnaires, 25 answer sheets, and 25 profile sheets.
Foreign Language Edition: Both forms available in French.
Time: (20–25) minutes.
Comments: IDS-42 (Brief Version) is for research use only.
Authors: Helen M. Annis, J. Martin Graham, and Christine S. Davis.
Publisher: Centre for Addiction and Mental Health [Canada].
Cross References: See T5:1304 (1 reference); for reviews by Merith Cosden and Kevin L. Moreland, see 13:155 (3 references); see also T4:1265 (2 references).

[1254]
Inventory of Drug Taking Situations.
Purpose: "Designed primarily as an assessment instrument, the IDTS generates an individualized profile detailing situations in which a client has used alcohol and/or other drugs over the past year."
Population: Drug or alcohol users.
Publication Date: 1997.
Acronym: IDTS.
Scores: Situation profiles in three areas: Negative Situations, Positive Situations, Temptation Situations; 8 subscales: Unpleasant Emotions, Physical Discomfort, Pleasant Emotions, Testing Personal Control, Urges/Temptations to Use, Conflict with Others, Social Pressure to Use, Pleasant Times with Others.
Administration: Group.
Price Data, 2002: C$34.95 per user's guide; C$14.95 per 30 questionnaires (specify alcohol or drug); C$39.95 per sample pack including user's guide, and 40 questionnaires (10 alcohol and 30 drug);C$75 per 50 uses of computer-administration software (DOS format); C$100 per 50 uses of software with user's guide; C$250 per 200 uses of software; C$275 per 200 uses of software with user's guide.
Time: (15) minutes per each drug class.
Comments: User's guide written in both English (150 pages) and French (72 pages); French version of IDTS have not been scientifically validated; "The IDTS is administered separately for each of the client's major substances of abuse, not once for the client's overall use of drugs."
Authors: Helen M. Annis, Nigel E. Turner, and Sherrilyn M. Sklar.
Publisher: Centre for Addiction and Mental Health [Canada].
Cross References: For reviews by Tony Cellucci and Glenn B. Gelman, see 14:186.

[1255]
Inventory of Interpersonal Problems.
Purpose: "A self-report instrument that identifies a person's most salient interpersonal problems."
Population: Adults ages 18 and over.
Publication Date: 2000.
Acronym: IIP.
Scores, 9: Domineering/Controlling, Vindictive/Self-Centered, Cold/Distant, Socially Inhibited, Nonassertive, Overly Accommodating, Self-Sacrificing, Intrusive/Needy, Total.
Administration: Individual or group.
Price Data, 2002: $111 per complete kit including manual (2000, 98 pages), 25 64-item question sheets, 25 64-item scoring sheets, and 25 32-item question scoring sheets; $48 per manual; $42 per 64-item question/scoring sheet combination including 25 64-item

question sheets, and 25 64-item scoring sheets; $33 per 25 32-item question/scoring sheets.
Time: (10–15) minutes for Full Version; (5–10) minutes for Short Version.
Comments: Full version (IIP-64) contains 64 items; short version (IIP-32), intended for screening, contains 32 items.
Authors: Leonard M. Horowitz, Lynn E. Alden, Jerry S. Wiggins, and Aaron L. Pincus.
Publisher: The Psychological Corporation.

[1256]
Inventory of Learning Processes—R.
Purpose: To measure learning styles of college and university students.
Population: College and university students.
Publication Dates: 1977–1992.
Acronym: ILP-R.
Scores, 14: Academic Self-Concept (Intrinsic Motivation, Self-Efficacy, Non-reiterative Processing, Self-Esteem, Total), Reflective Processing (Deep Processing, Elaborative Processing, Self-Expression, Total), Agentic Processing (Conventional, Serial Processing, Fact Retention, Total), Methodical Study.
Administration: Group.
Price Data: Price information available from publisher for test booklet (includes answer sheets).
Time: Administration time not reported.
Authors: Ronald R. Schmeck and Elke Geisler-Bernstein.
Publisher: Ronald R. Schmeck (the author).
Cross References: For reviews by Kusum Singh and Gerald L. Stone, see 13:156 (5 references).

[1257]
Inventory of Perceptual Skills.
Purpose: "Assesses visual and auditory perceptual skills."
Population: Ages 5–10.
Publication Date: 1983.
Acronym: IPS.
Scores, 11: Visual Perception Skills (Visual Discrimination, Visual Memory, Object Recognition, Visual-Motor Coordination, Total), Auditory Perception Skills (Auditory Discrimination, Auditory Memory, Auditory Sequencing, Auditory Blending, Total), Total.
Administration: Individual.
Price Data, 2001: $45 per complete kit including manual (16 pages), stimulus cards, student workbook, and record books; $20 per 10 student record books; $15 per manual; $15 per stimulus cards; $6 per student workbook.
Time: (15) minutes.
Author: Donald R. O'Dell.
Publisher: Stoelting Co.

Cross References: For reviews by Donna Spiker and by Logan Wright, Tim Eck, and Natasha Gwartney, see 12:193.

[1258]
Inventory of Positive Thinking Traits.
Purpose: "Designed to assess the attitudes of individuals in terms of their positivity and negativity."
Population: Adults and adolescents.
Publication Date: 1992.
Scores: Total score only.
Administration: Individual and group.
Price Data, 1998: $.50 per inventory; $1 per guide.
Time: (10) minutes.
Author: Millard J. Bienvenu.
Publisher: Millard J. Bienvenu, Northwest Publications.
Cross References: For a review by Peggy E. Gallaher, see 13:157.

[1259]
An Inventory of Religious Activities and Interests.
Purpose: "Measures interest in activities performed by persons employed in a variety of church-related occupations."
Population: High school and college.
Publication Dates: 1967–1970.
Acronym: IRAI.
Scores: 11 scales: Counselor, Administrator, Teacher, Scholar, Evangelist, Spiritual Guide, Preacher, Reformer, Priest, Musician, Check Scale.
Administration: Group.
Price Data: Available from publisher.
Time: (40–45) minutes for both forms.
Comments: For research use only.
Authors: Sam C. Webb and Richard A. Hunt.
Publisher: Ministry Inventories.
Cross References: See T2:1025A (2 references); for a review by Donald G. Zytowski, see 7:1023.

[1260]
Inventory of Suicide Orientation-30.
Purpose: "To assess and help identify adolescents who are at risk for suicide orientation by measuring the strength of their suicide orientation."
Population: Adolescents.
Publication Dates: 1988–1994.
Acronym: ISO-30.
Scores, 2: Final Raw Score, Final Critical Item Score.
Administration: Group.
Price Data, 2002: $86 per 50 handscoring answer sheets (reorder); $19 per 25 Microtest Q answer sheets; $3.25 per Microtest Q profile report; $38 per Microtest Q preview package; $48 per handscoring starter kit; $32.50 per manual.

Foreign Language Edition: Hispanic edition also available.
Time: [10] minutes.
Authors: John D. King and Brian Kowalchuk.
Publisher: NCS Assessments (Minnetonka).
Cross References: For a review by George Domino, see 13:158.

[1261]
Inventory of Vocational Interests: Acorn National Aptitude Tests.

Purpose: Designed to provide evidence of vocationally significant interests.
Population: Grades 7–16 and adults.
Publication Dates: 1943–1960.
Scores, 5: Mechanical, Academic, Artistic, Business and Economic, Farm-Agricultural.
Administration: Group.
Price Data, 2001: $4 per specimen set.
Time: (35) minutes.
Authors: Andrew Kobal, J. Wayne Wrightstone, and Karl R. Kunze.
Publisher: Psychometric Affiliates.
Cross References: For a review by John W. French, see 6:1060; for reviews by Marion A. Bills, Edward S. Bordin, Harold D. Carter, and Patrick Slater, see 3:638.

[1262]
InView.

Purpose: "A cognitive abilities test ... measur[ing] selected verbal, nonverbal, and quantitative reasoning abilities ... important for success in an educational program."
Population: Grades 2–12.
Publication Date: 2000.
Scores, 8: 5 subtest scores (Sequences, Analogies, Quantitative Reasoning, Verbal Reasoning—Words, Verbal Reasoning—Context); 3 composite scores (Verbal Composite, Nonverbal Composite, Total Test Scale Score).
Administration: Group.
Levels, 6: 1 (Grades 2–3), 2 (Grades 4–5), 3 (Grades 6–7), 4 (Grades 8–9), 5 (Grades 10–11), 6 (Grades 11–12).
Price Data, 2002: $84.80 per 25 InView-1 consumable test books; $66.25 per 25 InView 2–6 reusable test books (specify level); $28.60 per 50 InView 2–6 answer sheets; $1,115 per 2,500 InView continuous form answer sheets; $21.20 per InView 2–6 stencil set (specify level); $18 per examiner's manual, specify level); $31.80 per Teacher's Guide to InView, Technical Bulletin 1, Technical Report (CD-ROM version), or Norms Book (all levels); $2.10 per Class Record Sheet for Handscoring.
Time: 95 minutes.
Comments: Replaces the Test of Cognitive Skills, Second Edition (TCS/2); conformed with the Primary Test of Cognitive Skills (PTCS) (see 1978) and with TerraNova, The Second Edition (see 2510); Level 1 students record answers in test books; Levels 2–6 students use separate answer sheets; variety of score report formats available; on-line feedback on test performance available, contact publisher for details.
Author: CTB/McGraw-Hill.
Publisher: CTB/McGraw-Hill.
Cross References: See T5:2677 for information on the Test of Cognitive Skills, Second Edition; for a review by Randy W. Kamphaus of an earlier edition, see 13:325 (8 references); see also T4:2745 (4 references); for reviews by Timothy Z. Keith and Robert J. Sternberg of an earlier edition, see 9:1248; for a review by Lynn H. Fox and an excerpted review by David M. Shoemaker of the Short Form Test of Academic Aptitude, see 8:202 (9 referen

[1263]
Inwald Personality Inventory [Revised].

Purpose: "To aid public safety/law enforcement and security agencies in selecting new officers."
Population: Public safety, security, and law enforcement applicants (post-conditional job offer only).
Publication Dates: 1980–1992.
Acronym: IPI.
Scores, 26: Guardedness, Externalized Behavior Measures (Actions [Alcohol, Drugs, Driving Violations, Job Difficulties, Trouble with the Law and Society, Absence Abuse], Attitudes [Substance Abuse, Antisocial Attitudes, Hyperactivity, Rigid Type, Type A]), Internalized Conflict Measures (Illness Concerns, Treatment Programs, Anxiety, Phobic Personality, Obsessive Personality, Depression, Loner, Unusual Experiences/Thoughts), Interpersonal Conflict Measures (Lack of Assertiveness, Interpersonal Difficulties, Undue Suspiciousness, Family Conflicts, Sexual Concerns, Spouse/Mate Conflicts).
Administration: Group.
Price Data: Available from publisher.
Time: (30–45) minutes.
Author: Robin Inwald.
Publisher: Hilson Research, Inc. [No reply from publisher; status unknown].
Cross References: See T5:1313 (2 references) and T4:1275 (1 reference); for reviews by Brian Bolton and Richard I. Lanyon, see 12:194; for reviews by Samuel Juni and Niels G. Waller of an earlier edition, see 11:183 (2 references); for reviews by Brian Bolton and Jon D. Swartz of an earlier edition, see 9:530.

[1264]
Inwald Survey 5.

Purpose: "To aid in employee selection."
Population: All occupations including public safety/security, clerical, managerial, sales, and entry-level.

Publication Dates: 1992–1993.
Acronym: IS5.
Scores, 11: Lack of Insight/Candor, Frustration/Anger Patterns, Distrust of Others, Work Adjustment Difficulties, Attitudes (Antisocial Behaviors), Behavior Patterns (Integrity Concerns), Lack of Competitive Motivation, Work Effort Concerns, Lack of Sensitivity, Leadership Avoidance, Introverted Personality Style.
Administration: Group.
Price Data: Available from publisher.
Time: (25–30) minutes.
Comments: "Appropriate under ADA and can be administered pre-employment."
Author: Robin Inwald.
Publisher: Hilson Research, Inc. [No reply from publisher; status unknown].

[1265]
Iowa Algebra Aptitude Test, Fourth Edition.

Purpose: "To assess student readiness for Algebra I."
Population: Grades 7–8.
Publication Dates: 1931–1993.
Acronym: IAAT.
Scores, 5: Interpreting Mathematical Information, Translating to Symbols, Finding Relationships, Using Symbols, Total.
Administration: Group.
Price Data: Available from publisher.
Time: (50) minutes.
Authors: Harold L. Schoen, Timothy N. Ansley, H. D. Hoover, Beverly S. Rich, Sheila I. Barron, and Robert A. Bye. (Earlier edition by Harry A. Greene and Darrell Sabers.)
Publisher: Riverside Publishing.
Cross References: For reviews by John W. Fleenor and Judith A. Monsaas, see 12:195; see T2:681 (7 references); for reviews by W. L. Bashaw and Cyril J. Hoyt, and an excerpted review by Russell A. Chadbourn of an earlier edition, see 7:505 (8 references); for reviews by Harold Gulliken and Emma Spaney of an earlier edition, see 4:393; for a review by David Segel, see 3:327 (2 references); for reviews by Richard M. Drake and M. W. Richardson, see 2:1441 (1 reference).

[1266]
Iowa Parent Behavior Inventory.

Purpose: Designed "to measure parental behavior in relation to a child."
Population: Parents.
Publication Dates: 1976–1979.
Acronym: ITBI.
Administration: Group.
Price Data: Price information available from publisher for test and manual (1979, 41 pages including both forms and score sheet).

Time: Administration time not reported.
Authors: Sedahlia Jasper Crase, Samuel G. Clark, and Damaris Pease.
Publisher: Iowa State University Research Foundation, Inc. [No reply from publisher; status unknown].
a) MOTHER FORM.
Publication Date: 1977.
Scores, 6: Parental Involvement, Limit Setting, Responsiveness, Reasoning Guidance, Free Expression, Intimacy.
b) FATHER FORM.
Publication Date: 1977.
Scores, 5: Parental Involvement, Limit Setting, Responsiveness, Reasoning Guidance, Intimacy.
Cross References: See T5:1316 (2 references) and T4:1278 (3 references); for reviews by Verna Hart and Richard L. Wikoff, see 9:531 (1 reference).

[1267]
Iowa Social Competency Scales.

Purpose: To provide an "easily administered and objectively scored individual rating instrument for parents relative to the social behavior (competencies) of normal children."
Population: Ages 3–12.
Publication Dates: 1976–1982.
Acronym: ISCS.
Administration: Group.
Price Data: Available from publisher.
Time: Administration time not reported.
Comments: Ratings by parents.
Authors: Damaris Pease, Samuel G. Clark, and Sedahlia Jasper Crase.
Publisher: Iowa State University Research Foundation, Inc. [No reply from publisher; status unknown].
a) PRESCHOOL.
Population: Ages 3–6.
  1) *Mother*.
  Scores, 5: Social Activator, Hypersensitivity, Reassurance, Uncooperativeness, Cooperativeness.
  2) *Father*.
  Scores, 5: Social Activator, Hypersensitivity, Reassurance, Social Ineptness, Attentiveness.
  3) *Combined*.
  Scores, 3: Social Activator, Hypersensitivity, Reassurance.
b) SCHOOL-AGE.
Population: Ages 6–12.
Comments: Adaptation of Devereux Elementary School Behavior Rating Scale.
  1) *Mother*.
  Scores, 6: Task Oriented, Disruptive, Leader, Physically Active, Affectionate Toward Parent, Apprehensive.

2) *Father.*

Scores, 5: Capable, Defiant, Leader, Active with Peers, Affectionate Toward Parent.

Cross References: For a review by Gloria E. Miller, see 10:154; see also 9:532 (2 references).

[1268]

Iowa Tests of Basic Skills®, Forms K, L, and M.

Purpose: "To provide a comprehensive assessment of student progress in the basic skills."

Population: Grades K–9.

Publication Dates: 1955–1996.

Acronym: ITBS®.

Administration: Group.

Levels, 10: 5–14.

Forms, 3: K, L, and M; 3 batteries: Core, Complete, and Survey.

Price Data: Available from publisher.

Special Editions: Braille and large-print editions available.

Comments: Provides norm-referenced scores and national performance standards scores.

Authors: H. D. Hoover, A. N. Hieronymus, D. A. Frisbie, and S. B. Dunbar.

Publisher: Riverside Publishing.

a) LEVEL 5.

Population: Grade K.1–1.5.

Scores, 7: Vocabulary, Listening, Language, Language Total, Mathematics, Total, Word Analysis (optional).

Time: Untimed, approximately 110–130 minutes.

b) LEVEL 6.

Population: Grade K.8–1.9.

Scores, 10: Vocabulary, Listening, Language, Language Total, Mathematics Advanced Skills, Mathematics Total, Core Total, Word Analysis (optional), Reading Advanced Skills, Reading Total.

Time: Untimed, approximately 153–173 minutes.

c) LEVELS 7 AND 8.

Population: Grade 1.7–2.6; Grade 2.5—3.5.

Scores: Complete Battery: 16 scores: Vocabulary, Reading, Reading Total, Listening, Language, Language Total, Mathematics Concepts, Mathematics Problems, Mathematics Computation (optional), Mathematics Total, Core Total, Social Studies, Science, Sources of Information, Composite, Word Analysis (optional); Survey Battery: 7 scores: Reading, Advanced Skills, Reading Total, Language Advanced Skills, Language Total, Mathematics Advanced Skills, Mathematics Total, Survey Battery Total.

Time: Untimed, approximately 260–275 minutes for Complete Battery; approximately 90–100 minutes for Survey Battery.

d) LEVELS 9–14.

Population: Grades 3–8.

Scores: Complete Battery: 19 scores: Vocabulary, Reading Comprehension, Reading Total, Spelling, Capitalization, Punctuation, Usage and Expression, Language Total, Mathematics Concepts and Estimation, Mathematics Problem Solving and Data Interpretation, Mathematics Total, Mathematics Computation (optional), Core Total, Social Studies, Science, Maps and Diagrams, Reference Materials, Sources of Information Total, Composite; Survey Battery: 7 scores: Reading Advanced Skills, Reading Total, Language Advanced Skills, Language Total, Mathematics Advanced Skills, Mathematics Total, Survey Battery Total.

Time: 290 minutes for Complete Battery; (310 minutes with optional test); 90 minutes for Survey Battery (100 minutes with optional test).

Cross References: See T5:1318 (24 references); for reviews by Susan M. Brookhart and Lawrence H. Cross, see 13:159 (110 references); see also T4:1280 (33 references); for reviews by Suzanne Lane and Nambury S. Raju of Form J, see 11:184 (24 references); for reviews by Robert L. Linn and Victor L. Willson of Forms G and H, see 10:155 (45 references); for reviews by Peter W. Airasian and Anthony J. Nitko of Forms 7 and 8, see 9:533 (29 references); see also T3:1192 (97 references); for reviews by Larry A. Harris and Fred Pyrczak of Forms 5–6, see 8:19 (58 references); see T2:19 (87 references) and 6:13 (17 references); for reviews by Virgil E. Herrick, G. A. V. Morgan, and H. H. Remmers, and an excerpted review by Laurence Siegel of Forms 1–2, see 5:16. For reviews of the modern mathematics supplement, see 7:481 (2 reviews).

[1269]

Iowa Tests of Educational Development®, Forms K, L, and M.

Purpose: "To provide objective, norm-referenced information about high school students' development in the skills that are the long-term goals of secondary education—skills that constitute a major part of the foundation for continued learning."

Population: Grades 9–12.

Publication Dates: 1942–1996.

Acronym: ITED®.

Levels, 3: 15, 16, 17/18.

Scores: Complete Battery, 13 scores: Vocabulary, Content Area Reading, Reading Total, Correctness and Appropriateness of Expression Advanced Skills, Expression Total, Ability to Do Quantitative Thinking Advanced Skills, Quantitative Thinking Total, Core Total, Ability to Interpret Literary Materials, Analysis of Social Studies Materials, Analysis of Science Materials, Use of Sources of Information Composite; Survey

Battery, 7 scores: Reading Advanced Skills, Reading Total, Correctness and Appropriateness of Expression Advanced Skills, Expression Total, Ability to Do Quantitative Thinking Advanced Skills, Quantitative Thinking Total, Survey Battery Total.

Administration: Group.

Forms, 3: K, L, and M; editions: Complete and Survey Batteries.

Price Data: Available from publisher.

Time: 235 minutes for Complete Battery; 90 minutes for Survey Battery.

Comments: Provides norm-referenced scores and national performance standards scores.

Authors: Leonard S. Feldt, Robert A. Forsyth, Timothy N. Ansley, and Stephanie D. Alnot.

Publisher: Riverside Publishing.

Cross References: For reviews by William A. Mehrens and Michael J. Subkoviak, see 13:160 (7 references); see also T4:1281 (4 references); for a review by S. E. Phillips of an earlier edition, see 10:156 (3 references); for reviews by Edward Kifer and James L. Wardrop of an earlier form, see 9:534 (5 references); see also T3:1193 (14 references); for reviews by C. Mauritz Lindvall and John E. Milholland of an earlier form, see 8:20 (15 references); see T2:20 (85 references); for reviews by Ellis Batton Page and Alexander G. Wesman of earlier forms, see 6:14 (23 references); for reviews by J. Murray Lee and Stephen Wiseman, see 5:17 (9 references); for a review by Eric Gardner, see 4:17 (3 references); for reviews by Henry Chauncey, Gustav J. Froelich, and Lavone A. Hanna, see 3:12.

[1270]
Iowa Tests of Music Literacy, Revised.

Purpose: Assesses "a student's comparative strengths and weaknesses in six dimensions of tonal and rhythm audiation and notational audiation" and compares these scores to the student's "music aptitude."

Population: Grades 4–12.

Publication Dates: 1970–1991.

Scores, 9: Tonal Concepts (Audiation/Listening, Audiation/Reading, Audiation/Writing, Total), Rhythm Concepts (Audiation/Listening, Audiation/Reading, Audiation/Writing, Total), Total.

Administration: Group.

Price Data, 2001: $350 per complete kit for all six levels including manual, six cassette tapes, 50 answer sheets, six record folders, and scoring masks; $90 per complete kit for Level One Only including manual, one cassette tape, scoring masks, 50 answer sheets, and 6 record folders; $8 per 50 tonal answer sheets; $8 per 50 rhythm answer sheets; $15 per 50 cumulative record folders; $3 per 6 class record sheets; $15 per manual; $15 per cassette tape (specify level).

Time: 36(45) minutes for Tonal Concepts; 36(45) minutes for Rhythm Concepts.

Author: Edwin E. Gordon.

Publisher: G.I.A. Publications, Inc.

Cross References: For a review by Rudolf E. Radocy, see 13:161; for a review by Paul R. Lehman of an earlier edition, see 8:97 (16 references); see also T2:199 (5 references) and 7:245 (2 references).

[1271]
IPI Job-Tests Program.

Purpose: "Screening, selection, and promotion of job applicants and employees."

Population: Job applicants and employees in industry.

Publication Dates: 1948–1997.

Administration: Group or individual.

Price Data, 2001: $18 per 20 scoring worksheets.

Foreign Language Editions: French and Spanish editions available.

Comments: Program is composed of 19 tests "used in different combinations to form specific batteries for each of the job-test fields"; job fields include Sales Personnel, Medical Office Personnel, Clerical Staff, Dental Technician, and Factory/Mechanical.

Author: Industrial Psychology International, Ltd.

Publisher: Industrial Psychology International, Ltd.

a) OFFICE TERMS.

Price Data: $26 per 20 test booklets; $30 per introductory kit including 20 test booklets, technical manual, and scoring key.

Time: (6) minutes.

b) NUMBERS.

Price Data: Same as *a* above.

Time: (6) minutes.

c) PERCEPTION.

Price Data: Same as *a* above.

Time: Same as *a* above.

d) JUDGMENT.

Price Data: Same as *a* above.

Time: Same as *a* above.

e) FLUENCY.

Price Data: Same as *a* above.

Time: Same as *a* above.

f) PARTS.

Price Data: Same as *a* above.

Time: Same as *a* above.

g) MEMORY.

Price Data: $40 per 20 test booklets; $44 per introductory kit including 20 test booklets, technical manual, and scoring key.

Time: Same as *a* above.

h) BLOCKS.

Price Data: Same as *a* above.

Time: Same as *a* above.

i) DEXTERITY.

Price Data: Same as *a* above.

Time: (3) minutes.

j) DIMENSION.
Price Data: Same as *a* above.
Time: Same as *a* above.
k) PRECISION.
Price Data: Same as *a* above.
Time: Same as *a* above.
l) TOOLS.
Price Data: Same as *a* above.
Time: Same as *a* above.
m) MOTOR.
Price Data: $26 per 20 record booklets; $30 per introductory kit including 20 record booklets and technical manual; $150 per motor board.
Time: Same as *a* above.
n) SALES TERMS.
Price Data: Same as *a* above.
Time: (5) minutes.
o) APPLIED MATH.
Price Data: Same as *a* above.
Time: (12) minutes.
p) READING COMPREHENSION.
Price Data: $18 per 10 reusable test booklets; $28 per 20 answer/score sheets; $38 per introductory kit including 5 reusable test booklets, 20 answer/score sheets, and technical manual.
Time: Same as *o* above.
q) CPF SECOND EDITION.
Acronym: CPF.
Price Data: Same as *a* above.
Time: (5–10) minutes.
Author: Samuel E. Krug.
r) NPF SECOND EDITION.
Acronym: NPF.
Price Data: Same as *a* above.
Time: Same as *q* above.
Author: Same as *q* above.
Cross References: For reviews by Laura L. B. Barnes and Mary A. Lewis, see 11:185; see also T2:1078 (12 references); for reviews by William H. Helme and Stanley I. Rubin, see 6:774; for a review by Harold P. Bechtoldt of the Factored Aptitude Series, see 5:602; for a review by D. Welty Lefever and an excerpted review by Laurance F. Shaffer of an earlier edition of this series, see 4:712 (1 reference).

[1272]
IPMA Correctional Officer Test.

Purpose: To assess skills and abilities needed in an entry-level correctional officer position.
Population: Prospective correctional personnel.
Publication Date: 1991.
Administration: Group.
Parts: 1 test: Entry-Level Correctional Officer.
Restricted Distribution: Restricted to public personnel agencies who have completed a Test Security Agreement and returned it to the publisher.

Price Data, 1994: $40 basic rental fee; $10 per test booklet (agency member); $11.50 per test booklet (non-agency member); $15 per manual; $30 per set scoring fee plus $.25 per answer sheet.
Time: (120) minutes.
Author: International Personnel Management Association.
Publisher: International Personnel Management Association.

[1273]
IPMA Fire Service Tests.

Purpose: To assess skills and abilities needed in fire service positions.
Population: Prospective Fire Service personnel.
Publication Dates: 1973–1994.
Scores: Varies by test.
Administration: Group.
Parts: 10 tests: Entry-Level Firefighter (4 exams); Study Guides (for 2 entry-level exams); Fire Supervisor (Sergeant/Lieutenant); Fire Administrator (Captain); Fire Administrator (Battalion Chief); Fire Administrator (Deputy Chief); Fire Administrator (Chief); Fire Engineer.
Restricted Distribution: Restricted to public personnel agencies who have completed a Test Security Agreement and returned it to the publisher.
Price Data, 1994: $40 basic rental fee; $10 per test booklet (agency member); $11.50 per test booklet (non-agency member); $15 per manual; $30 per set scoring fee plus $.25 per answer sheet.
Time: (120–195) minutes; varies by test.
Author: International Personnel Management Association.
Publisher: International Personnel Management Association.
Cross References: For a review by Lawrence Allen, see 9:538.

[1274]
IPMA Police Service Tests.

Purpose: To assess skills and abilities needed in police service positions.
Population: Prospective police service personnel.
Publication Dates: 1983–1992.
Administration: Group.
Parts: 15 tests: Entry-Level Police Officer Background Data Questionnaire; Entry-Level Police Officer (5 exams); Study Guides (for 2 entry-level exams); Police Radio Dispatcher; Police Supervisor (Corporal/Sergeant) (4 exams); Police Administrator (Lieutenant); Police Administrator (Captain); Police Administrator (Assistant Chief); Police Administrator (Chief).
Restricted Distribution: Restricted to public personnel agencies who have completed a Test Security Agreement and returned it to the publisher.

Price Data, 1994: $40 basic rental fee; $10 per test booklet (agency member); $11.50 per test booklet (non-agency member); $15 per manual; $30 per set scoring fee plus $.25 per answer sheet.
Time: (60–210) minutes depending on test.
Author: International Personnel Management Association.
Publisher: International Personnel Management Association.

[1275]
Irenometer.
Purpose: Measures attitudes toward peace.
Population: Adults.
Publication Dates: 1984–1985.
Scores: Total score only.
Administration: Group.
Manual: No manual.
Price Data, 1998: $1 per scale.
Time: [12] minutes.
Comments: Supplementary article available.
Author: Panos D. Bardis.
Publisher: Donna Bardis.

[1276]
IS Manager/Consultant Skills Evaluation.
Purpose: To assess essential skills needed for the position of IS Manager or IS Consultant.
Population: Candidates for IS Manager or IS Consultant positions.
Publication Date: 1992.
Acronym: BAEDPMC.
Scores: Total Score, Narrative Evaluation, Ranking, Recommendation.
Administration: Group.
Price Data, 2001: $500 per candidate; quantity discounts available.
Time: Administration time not reported.
Comments: Scored by publisher; must be proctored.
Author: Bruce A. Winrow.
Publisher: Walden Personnel Performance, Inc. [Canada].

[1277]
IT Consultant Skills Evaluation.
Purpose: Designed "to evaluate technical, intellectual and supervisory skills required for a senior level IT Consultant, Data Processing Consultant, or IT Trainer."
Population: Candidates for the position of senior level IT Consultant, Data Processing Consultant, or IT Trainer.
Publication Dates: 1988–2002.
Scores, 7: Technical-Analytical Skills (Procedural Ability, Error Recognition, Problem Solving, Business Analysis, Project Management, Planning), Management-Related Skills (Business Judgment).
Administration: Group.

Price Data: Available from publisher.
Foreign Language Edition: Available in French and English.
Time: (180) minutes.
Author: Walden Personnel Performance, Inc.
Publisher: Walden Personnel Performance, Inc. [Canada].

[1278]
Jackson Personality Inventory—Revised.
Purpose: Designed as a "modern measure of normal personality, useful in counseling and business settings."
Population: Adolescents and adults.
Publication Dates: 1976–1997.
Acronym: JPI-R.
Scores: 15 scales in 5 clusters: Analytical (Complexity, Breadth of Interest, Innovation, Tolerance), Emotional (Empathy, Anxiety, Cooperativeness), Extroverted (Sociability, Social Confidence, Energy Level), Opportunistic (Social Astuteness, Risk Taking), Dependable (Organization, Traditional Values, Responsibility).
Administration: Group or individual.
Price Data, 2001: $62 per examination kit including manual (1994, 138 pages), 5 test booklets, 10 Quick Score answer sheets, 10 profile sheets, and coupon and machine-scorable answer sheet for one Basic Report; $40 per manual; $30.50–$34.50 (depending on volume) per 25 test booklets; $20–$23 (depending on volume) per 25 Quick Score answer sheets; $10–$12 (depending on volume) per 25 profile sheets; $48–$56 (depending on volume) per 10 machine-scorable answer sheets and coupons for Basic Reports; $99 per software package including disks, software manual for Windows, test manual, and 10 coupons for computer reports.
Foreign Language Edition: Available in French (booklets only).
Time: (35–45) minutes.
Author: Douglas N. Jackson.
Publisher: Sigma Assessment Systems, Inc.
Cross References: See T5:1333 (8 references); for reviews by David J. Pittenger and Peter Zachar, see 13:162 921 references); see also T4:1296 (28 references) and T3:1203 (6 references); for reviews by Lewis R. Goldberg and David T. Lykken of an earlier edition, see 8:593 (6 references).

[1279]
Jackson Vocational Interest Survey [1999 Revision].
Purpose: "Designed to yield ... a set of scores representing interests and preferences relevant to work ..., conceptualized as work roles and work styles."
Population: High school and above.
Publication Dates: 1977–2000.
Acronym: JVIS.

Scores, 50: 34 Basic Interest Scales (Creative Arts, Performing Arts, Mathematics, Physical Science, Engineering, Life Science, Social Science, Adventure, Nature—Agriculture, Skilled Trades, Personal Service, Family Activity, Medical Service, Dominant Leadership, Job Security, Stamina, Accountability, Teaching, Social Service, Elementary Education, Finance, Business, Office Work, Sales, Supervision, Human Relations Management, Law, Professional Advising, Author—Journalism, Academic Achievement, Technical Writing, Independence, Planfulness, Interpersonal Confidence); 10 General Occupational Themes (Expressive, Logical, Inquiring, Practical, Assertive, Socialized, Helping, Conventional, Enterprising, Communicative); 3 Administrative Indices (Unscorable Responses, Response Consistency Index, Infrequency Index); Academic Satisfaction; Similarity to College Students; Similarity to Occupational Classifications.

Administration: Group.

Price Data, 2002: $79 per examination kit including manual (2000, 149 pages), applications handbook, occupations guide, machine-scorable answer sheet for Extended Report, reusable test booklet, hand-scorable answer and profile sheets, and jvis.com password; $32 per test manual; $36 per applications handbook; $22.95 per Occupations Guide–2000; $34.50 per 25 reusable test booklets, quantity discounts available; $12 per 25 hand-scorable answer sheets, scannable answer sheets, or profile sheets, quantity discounts available; $11 per Extended Report including machine-scorable answer sheet and laser-printed report; $8 per Basic Report including machine-scorable answer sheet; report in duplicate; quantity discounts available on both reports; $99 per SigmaSoft JVIS for Windows start-up package including disks, software manual, test manual, and 10 coupons; $1.75 per SigmaSoft Coupon, quantity discounts available; cost per report: 2 coupons per Data Report, 4 coupons per Basic Report, 6 coupons per Extended Report.

Foreign Language Editions: Available in Spanish (booklets only) and in French (booklets and extended reports); also, online administration using SigmaSoft JVIS for Windows and reports).

Time: (45)55 minutes.

Comments: Former edition no longer available; available in paper-and-pencil format (hand scoring or mail-in scoring), Basic and Extended Reports online administration and scoring available using SigmaSoft JVIS for Windows software; system requirements: SigmaSoft JVIS for Windows also can be used for scoring data scanned by an optical mark reader using SigmaSoft Scanning Utility; SigmaSoft JVIS for Windows produces Basic Report, Extended Report, and Data Report.

Authors: Douglas N. Jackson and Marc Verhoeve (applications handbook).

Publisher: Sigma Assessment Systems, Inc.

Cross References: See T5:1334 (5 references and T4:1297 (1 reference); for reviews by Douglas T. Brown and John W. Shepard of a previous edition, see 10:158 (1 reference); for reviews by Charles Davidshofer and Ruth G. Thomas, see 9:542; see also T3:1204 (1 reference).

[1280]
Jail Inmate Inventory.

Purpose: "Designed for inmate risk assessment and needs identification"; provides information to "help determine inmate risk, establish supervisory levels and identify readiness for classification or status changes."

Population: Jail inmates with a sixth grade or above reading level.

Publication Dates: 1991–1995.

Acronym: JII.

Scores, 6: Truthfulness, Violence, Antisocial, Adjustment, Alcohol, Drugs.

Administration: Group.

Price Data: Available from publisher.

Foreign Language Edition: Spanish Edition available.

Time: (15–20) minutes.

Comments: Can be administered by paper and pencil or by computer; all scoring is done by computer.

Author: Risk & Needs Assessment, Inc.

Publisher: Risk & Needs Assessment, Inc.

[1281]
Jansky Diagnostic Battery.

Purpose: To provide a profile of reading weaknesses and strengths.

Population: Kindergarten.

Publication Date: No date on test materials.

Scores: Ratings in 4 areas: Oral Language, Pattern Matching, Pattern Memory, Visuo Motor Organization.

Administration: Individual.

Manual: No manual.

Price Data: Available from publisher.

Time: Administration time not reported.

Author: Jeannette Jansky.

Publisher: Jeannette Jansky [No reply from publisher; status unknown].

[1282]
Jansky Screening Index.

Purpose: Designed to identify children who are at risk of failing in reading.

Population: Kindergarten.

Publication Date: 1972.

Acronym: JSI.

Scores, 5: Letter Naming, Picture Naming, Gates Matching, Bender, Sentence Memory.
Administration: Individual.
Price Data: Available from publisher.
Time: (15-20) minutes.
Comments: Appendix E (pp. 150–159) of *Preventing Reading Failure* (1972) can be used as a manual.
Authors: Jeannette Jansky and Katrina de Hirsch.
Publisher: Jeannette Jansky [No reply from publisher; status unknown].
Cross References: See T5:1337 (2 references), T3:1205 (1 reference), and 8:800 (14 references).

[1283]
Jesness Behavior Checklist.

Purpose: Designed as "a multiple rating scale to be used by self and others that measures individuals at risk for antisocial behavior."
Population: Delinquents ages 13–20.
Publication Dates: 1970–1971.
Scores, 14: Unobtrusiveness/Obtrusiveness, Friendliness/Hostility, Responsibility/Irresponsibility, Considerateness/Inconsiderateness, Independence/Dependence, Rapport/Alienation, Enthusiasm/Depression, Sociability/Poor Peer Relations, Conformity/Non-Conformity, Calmness/Anxiousness, Effective Communications/Inarticulateness, Insight/Unawareness and Indecisiveness, Social Control/Attention-Seeking, Anger Control/Hypersensitivity.
Administration: Individual.
Editions, 2: Observer, Self-Appraisal.
Price Data, 2002: $110 per complete kit including 10 Observer item booklets, 25 Observer QuikScore™ forms, 10 Self-Appraisal item booklets, 25 Self-Appraisal QuikScore™ forms, and manual (1971, 32 pages); $15 per 10 Observer item booklets; $27 per 25 Observer QuikScore™ forms; $24 per 10 Self-Appraisal item booklets; $27 per 25 Self-Appraisal QuikScore™ forms; $15.50 per manual; $23 per specimen set including 1 Observer and 1 Self-Appraisal item booklet, 1 Observer and 1 Self-Appraisal QuikScore™ form, and manual.
Time: (15-20) minutes.
Comments: Self-report and observer rating; Windows™ or MS DOS computer administration and scoring software available on CD or 3.5-inch disk.
Author: Carl F. Jesness.
Publisher: Multi-Health Systems, Inc.
Cross References: See T5:1340 (5 references); for reviews by Dorcas Susan Butt and Edwin I. Megargee, see 8:594 (3 references).

[1284]
The Jesness Inventory.

Purpose: Designed as a classification system for delinquent and conduct disordered youths.

Population: Ages 8 and older.
Publication Dates: 1962–1996.
Acronym: JI.
Scores, 22: Conventional Scales (Social Maladjustment, Value Orientation, Immaturity, Autism, Alienation, Manifest Aggression, Withdrawal-Depression, Social Anxiety, Repression, Denial, Asocial Index), Validity Scales (Lie, Random Response), Subtype Classification (Undersocialized—Active, Undersocialized—Passive, Immature Conformist/Conformist, Cultural Conformist/Group-Oriented, Manipulator/Pragmatist, Neurotic—Acting-out/Autonomy-Oriented, Neurotic—Anxious/Introspective, Situational/Inhibited, Cultural Identifier/Adaptive).
Administration: Individual or group.
Price Data, 2002: $75 per complete kit including manual, 10 test booklets, and 25 QuikScore™ forms; $13 per 10 reusable test booklets (specify English, Spanish or French-Canadian); $30 per 25 QuikScore™ forms (specify English or Spanish); $40 per manual; $42 per specimen set including manual, 1 test booklet, and 3 QuikScore™ forms; $75 per set of scoring templates; computer version also available.
Foreign Language Edition: Spanish and French-Canadian forms available.
Time: Administration time not reported.
Comments: Self-report; "Originally developed for use in the assessment and classification of male delinquent youths."
Author: Carl F. Jesness.
Publisher: Multi-Health Systems, Inc.
Cross References: For reviews by Robert M. Guion and Susana Urbina, see 14:188; see also T5:1341 (3 references) and T3:1209 (9 references); for a review by Dorcas Susan Butt of an earlier edition, see 8:595 (14 references); see also T2:1249 (5 references); for a review by Sheldon A. Weintraub of the Youth Edition of the earlier edition, see 7:94 (10 references); see also P:133 (3 references).

[1285]
Job Activity Preference Questionnaire.

Purpose: To obtain a measure of job interests or preferences.
Population: Adults.
Publication Dates: 1972–1981.
Acronym: JAPQ.
Scores, 16: Making Decisions/Communicating and Having Responsibility, Operating Vehicles, Using Machines-Tools-Instruments, Performing Physical Activities, Operating Keyboard and Office Equipment, Monitoring and/or Controlling Equipment and/or Processes, Working Under Uncomfortable Conditions, Working with Art-Decor/Entertainment, Performing Supervisory Duties, Performing Estimating Activities, Processing Written Information,

Working With Buyers-Customers-Salespersons, Working Under Hazardous Conditions, Performing Paced and/or Repetitive Activities, Working with Aerial and Aquatic Equipment, Catering/Serving/Smelling/Tasting.
Administration: Group.
Price Data: Available from publisher.
Time: Administration time not reported.
Comments: Restructured and simplified version of Position Analysis Questionnaire (1931).
Authors: Robert C. Mecham, Alma F. Harris (test), Ernest J. McCormick (test), and P. R. Jeanneret (test).
Publisher: PAQ Services, Inc.
Cross References: For reviews by Norman G. Peterson and Paul R. Sackett, see 9:547.

[1286]
Job Attitude Analysis.
Purpose: Devised to "reveal a person's underlying attitudes pertinent for success and satisfaction in his work."
Population: Production and clerical workers.
Publication Dates: 1961–1970.
Acronym: JAA.
Scores: Total score only.
Administration: Group.
Price Data: Available from publisher.
Time: Administration time not reported.
Comments: An inventory for employment interviewing and vocational counseling.
Author: P. L. Mellenbruch.
Publisher: Psychometric Affiliates.
Cross References: For additional information, see 7:980 (1 reference).

[1287]
Job Attitude Scale.
Purpose: Designed to assess intrinsic and extrinsic job orientations.
Population: Adults.
Publication Dates: 1971–1988.
Acronym: JAS.
Scores, 17: Praise and Recognition, Growth in Skill, Creative Work, Responsibility, Advancement, Achievement, Salary, Security, Personnel Policies, Competent Supervision, Relations-Peers, Relations-Subordinates, Relations-Supervisor, Working Conditions, Status, Family Needs-Salary, Total Intrinsic.
Administration: Group.
Forms, 2: Full, Abbreviated.
Price Data: Available from publisher.
Time: (15–20) minutes.
Author: Shoukry D. Saleh.
Publisher: Shoukry D. Saleh [Canada] [No reply from publisher; status unknown].

Cross References: For a review by Gregory J. Boyle, see 11:186; see also 8:1049 (9 references).

[1288]
Job Challenge Profile.
Purpose: "Designed to help managers better understand and see their job assignments as opportunities for learning and growth."
Population: Managers, leaders, and executives.
Publication Date: 1999.
Acronym: JCP.
Scores, 10: Unfamiliar Responsibilities, New Directions, Inherited Problems, Problems with Employees, High Stakes, Scope and Scale, External Pressure, Influence Without Authority, Work Across Cultures, Work Group Diversity.
Administration: Group.
Price Data, 2002: $27 per Facilitator's Guide (76 pages); $14 per Participant's Workbook/Survey (49 pages); quantity discounts available.
Time: 15(25) minutes.
Comments: Revision of the Developmental Challenge Profile (DCP; no longer available); self-scored; Facilitator's Guide includes details of workshop procedures, reproducible overheads, and handout masters; Participant's Workbook contains test items and action guide.
Authors: Cynthia D. McCauley (Facilitator's Guide, Participant Workbook/Survey), Patricia J. Ohlott (Facilitator's Guide, Survey), and Marian N. Ruderman (Facilitator's Guide, Survey).
Publisher: Center for Creative Leadership.
Cross References: For reviews by Jean Powell Kirnan and Kristen Wojcic and by Eugene P. Sheehan of The Developmental Challenge Profile, see 13:94 (2 references).

[1289]
A Job Choice Decision-Making Exercise.
Purpose: Serves as a behavioral decision theory measurement approach to need for affiliation, need for power, and need for achievement.
Population: High school and college and adults.
Publication Dates: 1981–1986.
Acronym: JCE.
Scores, 3: Affiliation, Power, Achievement.
Administration: Group.
Price Data, 2002: $4 per exercise booklet; $35 per Managerial and Technical Motivation book (1986, 178 pages, available from Praeger Publishers, in lieu of manual).
Time: [15–20] minutes.
Authors: Michael J. Stahl and Anil Gulati (scoring software and scoring manual).
Publisher: Assessment Enterprises.
Cross References: For a review by Nicholas A. Vacc and J. Scott Hinkle, see 11:187.

[1290]
Job Descriptive Index (1997 Revision) and The Job in General Scales.

Purpose: Designed as measures of job satisfaction to be useful for diverse organizations and employee groups.

Population: Employees.

Publication Dates: 1969–1997.

Acronym: JDI; JIG.

Scores, 6: Work on Present Job, Pay, Opportunities for Promotion, Supervision, People on Your Present Job, Job in General.

Administration: Group or individual.

Price Data, 2001: $100 per 100 test booklets; $350 per paper user's manual (1997, 275 pages); $40 per electronic manual (pdf format 340 KB).

Time: (60) minutes.

Authors: Patricia C. Smith, Lorne M. Kendall, and Charles L. Hulin (earlier edition); William K. Balzer, Jenifer A. Kihm, Patricia C. Smith, Jennifer L. Irwin, Peter D. Bachiochi, Chet Robie, Evan F. Sinar, and Luis F. Parra.

Publisher: Bowling Green State University, Department of Psychology.

Cross References: See T5:1348 (16 references); for reviews by Charles K. Parsons and Norman D. Sundberg for an earlier edition of the Job Descriptive Index and Retirement Descriptive Index, see 12:199 (33 references); see also T4:1312 (63 references); for reviews by John O. Crites and Barbara A. Kerr of an earlier edition of the Job Descriptive Index, see 9:550 (49 references).

[1291]
JOB-O.

Purpose: "To facilitate self-awareness, career-awareness, and career exploration."

Publication Dates: 1981–1992.

Administration: Group.

Price Data: Price information available from publisher.

Comments: Also known as Judgement of Occupational Behavior-Orientation.

Authors: Arthur Cutler, Francis Ferry, Robert Kauk, and Robert Robinett.

Publisher: CFKR Career Materials [No reply from publisher; status unknown].

a) JOB-O (ELEMENTARY).

Population: Grades 4–7.

Scores: 6 ratings: Mechanical/Construction/Agriculture, Scientific/Technical, Creative/Artistic, Social/Legal/Educational, Managers/Sales, Administrative Support.

Time: Administration time not reported.

b) JOB-O.

Population: Junior high school through adult.

Scores, 8: Education, Interest, Inclusion, Control, Affection, Physical Activity, Hands/Tools/Machinery, Problem-Solving, Creative-Ideas.

Foreign Language Editions: Spanish and Vietnamese test booklets and answer sheets available.

Time: (60–65) minutes.

c) JOB-O A (ADVANCED).

Population: Grades 10–12 and adult.

Scores, 16: Occupational Interest, Training Time, Reasoning Skills, Mathematical Skills, Language Skills, Working with Data, Working with People, Working with Things, Working Conditions, Physical Demands, Leadership, Helping People, Problem-Solving, Initiative, Team Work, Public Contact.

Time: [50–55] minutes.

Comments: May be self-administered.

Cross References: For reviews by F. Marion Asche and Lawrence H. Cross, see 12:200; for a review by James W. Pinkney of an earlier edition, see 10:160; for a review by Bruce J. Eberhardt of an earlier edition, see 9:560.

[1292]
Job Observation and Behavior Scale.

Purpose: Designed as "a work performance evaluation for supported and entry level employees."

Population: Ages 15 and above.

Publication Dates: 1998–2000.

Acronym: JOBS.

Scores, 4: Work-Required Daily Living Activities, Work-Required Behavior, Work-Required Job Duties, Quality of Performance Composite/Total.

Administration: Individual.

Price Data, 2001: $75 per complete kit including 25 record forms and manual (1998, 28 pages); $30 per 25 record forms; $50 per job manual.

Time: (30) minutes.

Authors: Howard Rosenberg and Michael Brady.

Publisher: Stoelting Co.

[1293]
Job Readiness Skills Pre- and Post-Assessment.

Purpose: Designed to assess examinees on skills related to employability and work maturity/job retention.

Population: Individuals seeking employment.

Publication Dates: 1984–2000.

Administration: Group or individual.

Manual: No manual.

Price Data, 2002: $18 per specimen set including 5 copies each of Pre- and Post-Assessment forms; $52 per set of 25 assessments (specify Pre- or Post-Assessment).

Time: (45–55) minutes.
Comments: Earlier version entitled Assessing Specific Competencies.
Author: Education Associates, Inc.
Publisher: Education Associates.
   a) PRE-ASSESSMENT.
   Scores: 9 areas: Career Goals, Finding a Job, Resumes, Job Applications, Interviews, Positive Attitudes, Good Appearance, Communication, Written Communication.
   b) POST-ASSESSMENT.
   Scores: Same as *a* above.
Cross References: For reviews by Robert Fitzpatrick and Robert C. Reinehr of an earlier edition, see 12:33.

[1294]
Job Search Attitude Inventory, 2nd Edition.

Purpose: Helps identify personal attitudes about looking for a job.
Population: Adult and teen job seekers and career planners.
Publication Date: 2001.
Acronym: JSAI.
Scores, 4: Luck vs. Planning, Uninvolved vs. Involved, Help from Others vs. Self-Help, Passive vs. Active.
Administration: Group or individual.
Price Data, 2001: $39.95 per 25 inventories including copy of administrator's guide.
Time: (10–15) minutes.
Comments: Self-administered and self-scored; revised edition features simplified language and directions, plus added practical advice for becoming more self-directed in a job search.
Author: John J. Liptak.
Publisher: JIST Publishing, Inc.

[1295]
Job Seeking Skills Assessment.

Purpose: "For assessing clients' ability to complete a job application form and participate in the employment interview, and to serve as a guide for integrating the results into program planning."
Population: Vocational rehabilitation clients.
Publication Date: 1988.
Acronym: JSSA.
Scores, 2: Job Application, Employment Interview.
Administration: Group.
Price Data, 1994: $10 per manual (96 pages).
Time: Administration time not reported.
Comments: Designed as a component of the Diagnostic Employability Profile (DEP).
Authors: Suki Hinman, Bob Means, Sandra Parkerson, and Betty Odendahl.
Publisher: The National Center on Employment & Disability.

Cross References: For reviews by Paul M. Muchinsky and William I. Sauser, Jr., see 12:201.

[1296]
Job Skills Tests.

Purpose: "Evaluate the ability of industrial workers to perform (various) operations."
Population: Job applicants and industrial workers.
Publication Dates: 1981–1991.
Administration: Group or individual.
Price Data: Available from publisher.
Author: Roland T. Ramsay.
Publisher: Ramsay Corporation.
   a) READING.
   Purpose: "Ability to read a passage and answer questions about the passage."
   Publication Dates: 1983–1991.
   Time: 30(35) minutes.
   b) ORAL DIRECTIONS.
   Purpose: "Ability to follow directions."
   Publication Date: 1983.
   Time: (20) minutes.
   c) MEASUREMENT.
   Purpose: "Ability to measure."
   Publication Dates: 1981–1983.
   Time: [20] minutes.
   d) ARITHMETIC.
   Purpose: "Arithmetic skills."
   Publication Dates: 1983–1991.
   Time: 20(25) minutes.

[1297]
Job Stress Survey.

Purpose: "Designed to assess generic sources of occupational stress encountered by men and women employed in a variety of work settings."
Population: Adults ages 18 and older.
Publication Dates: 1991–1999.
Acronym: JSS.
Scores, 9: Job Stress Index, Job Stress Severity, Job Stress Frequency, Job Pressure Index, Job Pressure Severity, Job Pressure Frequency, Lack of Organizational Support Index, Lack of Organizational Support Severity, Lack of Organizational Support Frequency.
Administration: Group.
Forms, 2: Form HS (Hand-Scorable), Form SP (Scoring Program).
Price Data: Available from publisher for introductory kit including professional manual (1999, 72 pages), 25 test booklets, 25 profile forms, and 3.5-inch disk with 5 free uses of the scoring program.
Time: (10–15) minutes.
Comments: Computer scoring program available; Forms HS and SP are identical in content.
Authors: Charles D. Spielberger and Peter R. Vagg.
Publisher: Psychological Assessment Resources, Inc.

[1298]

Job Style Indicator.

Purpose: Analyzes how employers and their staff perceive a job.
Population: Adults.
Publication Date: 1988.
Acronym: JSI.
Scores, 4: Behavioral, Cognitive, Interpersonal, Affective.
Administration: Group.
Price Data, 1993: $6 per test booklet; $35 per leader's manual (80 pages); $15 per audiotape (Living and Working With Style).
Time: (30–60) minutes.
Comments: May be used in conjunction with Personal Style Indicator (1873).
Authors: Terry D. Anderson and Everett T. Robinson (JSI and PSI/JSI Leader's Manual), Jonathon Clark and Susan Clark (audiotape).
Publisher: Consulting Resource Group International, Inc.
Cross References: For reviews by Neal Schmitt and David M. Williamson, see 13:164.

[1299]

Johnston Informal Reading Inventory.

Purpose: "To assess the reading comprehension of junior and senior high school students."
Population: Grades 7–12.
Publication Date: 1982.
Acronym: JIRI.
Scores, 2: Vocabulary Screening, Reading Comprehension.
Administration: Group or individual.
Price Data: Available from publisher.
Time: (20) minutes.
Comments: Forms B and C are approximately parallel and Form L is longer; "high-interest materials utilized."
Author: Michael C. Johnston.
Publisher: Educational Publications [No reply from publisher; status unknown].
Cross References: For reviews by Margaret R. Rogers and Claudia R. Wright, see 12:202.

[1300]

Joliet 3-Minute Preschool Speech and Language Screen.

Purpose: "Differentiates individuals with intact skills from those with suspected problems in phonology, semantics, and grammar."
Population: 2.5–4.5 years.
Publication Date: 1992.
Scores: 3 areas: Grammar, Semantics, Phonology.
Administration: Individual.

Price Data, 1999: $66 per complete kit including 12 vocabulary plates on card stock, 2 reproducible scoring sheets, recordkeeping manual, and manual (57 pages).
Time: (3) minutes.
Author: Mary C. Kinzler.
Publisher: Communication Skill Builders—A Division of The Psychological Corporation.
Cross References: For a review by Carlos Inchaurralde, see 14:189.

[1301]

Joliet 3-Minute Speech and Language Screen (Revised).

Purpose: To "identify children with age-appropriate phonological, grammatical, and semantic structures."
Population: Grades K, 2, 5.
Publication Dates: 1983–1992.
Scores, 5: Receptive Vocabulary, Grammar (Evoked Sentences), Phonology, Voice, Fluency.
Administration: Individual.
Levels, 3: Grades K, 2, 5.
Price Data, 1999: $66 per complete kit including manual (1992, 39 pages), vocabulary plates on card stock, recordkeeping manual (15 pages), and 2 reproducible scoring sheets.
Time: (2–5) minutes.
Authors: Mary C. Kinzler and Constance Cowing Johnson.
Publisher: Communication Skill Builders—A Division of The Psychological Corporation.
Cross References: For reviews by Martin A. Fischer and by Malcolm R. McNeil and Thomas F. Campbell, see 13:165; for a review by Robert E. Owens, Jr. of the original edition, see 9:555 (1 reference).

[1302]

The Jones-Mohr Listening Test.

Purpose: "To provide feedback on listening efficiency and to measure the effect of skill building in this area."
Population: Persons in educational and training programs.
Publication Date: 1976.
Scores: Total score only.
Administration: Group.
Forms, 2: A, B.
Price Data: Price informatin available from publisher for kit including 50 test forms, audiocassette, and facilitator's guide (26 pages); 25 test forms (specify form).
Time: (25–30) minutes.
Authors: John E. Jones and Lawrence Mohr.
Publisher: Jossey-Bass, A Wiley Company.
Cross References: For reviews by Lear Ashmore and John F. Schmitt, see 9:556 (1 reference).

[1303]
Jordan Left-Right Reversal Test (1990 Edition).

Purpose: Constructed "to measure letter and number reversals in the area of visual receptive functioning."
Population: Ages 5–12.
Publication Dates: 1973–1990.
Scores: Total score only.
Administration: Individual or group.
Levels: 2 overlapping levels (ages 5-12, 9-12) in a single booklet.
Price Data, 2002: $90 per complete kit including 50 test forms, 50 laterality checklists, 50 remedial checklists, and manual (1990, 64 pages); $30 per 50 test forms; $15 per 50 laterality checklists; $15 per 50 remedial checklists; $30 per manual; $30 per specimen set including manual and sample forms.
Time: (20) minutes.
Comments: "Norm-referenced."
Author: Brian T. Jordan.
Publisher: Academic Therapy Publications.
Cross References: For reviews by Christine W. Burns and Jeffrey H. Snow, see 12:203 (1 reference); see also T4:1326 (4 references); for reviews by Mary S. Poplin and Joseph Torgesen, see 9:557; see also T3:1224 (2 references); for reviews by Barbara K. Keogh and Richard J. Reisboard, and excerpted reviews by Alex Bannatyne and Alan Krichev, see 8:434 (5 references).

[1304]
Joseph Pre-School and Primary Self-Concept Screening Test.

Purpose: Constructed as an early screen for learning problems.
Population: Ages 3-6 to 9-11.
Publication Date: 1979.
Scores: Global Self Concept.
Administration: Individual.
Price Data, 2001: $150 per complete kit including manual (66 pages), 56 stimulus cards, 100 identity reference drawings, and 100 record forms; $30 per 50 record forms; $80 per set of stimulus cards; $35 per set of identity drawings; $25 per manual.
Time: (5–7) minutes.
Comments: May be used with non-verbal children.
Author: Jack Joseph.
Publisher: Stoelting Co.
Cross References: See T5:1363 (2 references); for reviews by Kathryn Clark Gerken and Cathy Fultz Telzrow, see 9:558.

[1305]
Jung Personality Questionnaire.
Purpose: "To assist pupils in choosing a career."

Population: Standards 7 and 8 and 10 in South African school system.
Publication Date: 1983.
Acronym: JPQ.
Scores, 4: Extraversion vs. Introversion, Thinking vs. Feeling, Sensation vs. Intuition, Judgement vs. Perception.
Administration: Group.
Price Data: Available from publisher.
Foreign Language Edition: Afrikaans edition available.
Time: (25–35) minutes.
Comments: "Criterion-referenced."
Author: L. B. H. duToit.
Publisher: Human Sciences Research Council [South Africa].

[1306]
Jungian Type Survey: The Gray-Wheelwrights Test (16th Revision).

Purpose: "Designed to delineate types of personality structure."
Population: Adults.
Publication Date: 1964.
Scores, 6: Introversion, Extraversion, Intuition, Sensation, Thinking, Feeling.
Administration: Group.
Price Data, 1998: $.50 per reusable question sheet; $.50 per answer sheet; $5 per manual (8 pages).
Time: (20) minutes.
Authors: Horace Gray (test only), Joseph B. Wheelwright (test and manual), Jane H. Wheelwright (test and manual), and John A. Bueler (manual only).
Publisher: C. G. Jung Institute of San Francisco.

[1307]
Junior Eysenck Personality Inventory.
Purpose: "Designed to measure ... neuroticism or emotionality, and extraversion-introversion in children."
Population: Ages 7–16.
Publication Dates: 1963–1970.
Acronym: JEPI.
Scores, 3: Extraversion, Neuroticism, Lie.
Administration: Group.
Price Data, 1998: $11 per 25 inventories [$38 per 100, $143.50 per 500]; $8.50 per scoring key; $4 per manual (1963, 11 pages); $7.25 per specimen set including manual and 1 copy of all forms.
Foreign Language Edition: Spanish edition available.
Time: [15–20] minutes.
Author: Sybil B. G. Eysenck.
Publisher: EdITS/Educational and Industrial Testing Service.
Cross References: See T5:1367 (7 references), T4:1331 (13 references), 9:561 (10 references), T3:1229

(24 references), 8:596 (36 references), and T2:1252 (14 references); for reviews by Maurice Chazan and Robert D. Wirt and excerpted reviews by Gertrude H. Keir and B. Semeonoff, see 7:96 (19 references); see also P:135 (7 references).

[1308]

Junior High School Mathematics Test: Acorn Achievement Tests.

Purpose: Designed to test the pupil's knowledge of junior high level mathematics concepts, skills, and insights.
Population: Grades 7–9.
Publication Dates: 1942–1952.
Scores, 4: Concepts, Problem Analysis, Problems, Total.
Administration: Group.
Price Data: Available from publisher.
Time: 52(57) minutes.
Author: Harry Eisner.
Publisher: Psychometric Affiliates.
Cross References: For a review by Myron F. Rosskopf, see 5:429; for a review by William Betz, see 3:310.

[1309]

Junior Rating Scale.

Purpose: Designed to provide teachers with a framework to record and display visually ratings of pupils' strengths and needs.
Population: Ages 8–11.
Publication Date: 1990.
Acronym: JRS.
Scores: 5 subscale scores: Language/Education, Motor Skills, Behaviour, Social Integration, General Development.
Administration: Individual.
Price Data: Available from publisher.
Time: Untimed.
Comments: Developed from Infant Rating Scale.
Authors: J. A. Abraham and G. A. Lindsay.
Publisher: NFER-Nelson Publishing Co., Ltd. [England].

[1310]

Junior South African Individual Scales.

Purpose: Measures general intellectual level.
Population: South African children ages 3.0–7.11.
Publication Dates: 1981–1988.
Acronym: JSAIS.
Scores, 27: Verbal (Vocabulary, Reading Knowledge, Story Memory, Picture Riddles, Word Association, Social Reasoning, Picture Analogies, Word Fluency), Numerical (Number and Quantity A, Number and Quantity B, Number and Quantity A & B, Memory for Digits A, Memory for Digits B, Memory for Digits

A & B), Visual-Spatial (Form Board, Block Designs, Absurdities A, Absurdities B, Form Discrimination A & B, Grouping, Gestalt Completion, Picture Series, Picture Puzzles, Visual Memory A, Visual Memory B, Visual Memory A & B, Copying).
Administration: Individual.
Price Data: Available from publisher.
Foreign Language Edition: Afrikaans edition available.
Time: (60–90) minutes.
Authors: Elizabeth M. Madge (manuals, Parts 1-3), A. R. vandenBerg (manual, Part 3), Maryna Robinson (manual, Part 3), and J. Landman (appendix to manuals).
Publisher: Human Sciences Research Council [South Africa].
Cross References: See T5:1370 (1 reference) and T4:1335 (1 reference).

[1311]

Just-in-Time Training Assessment Instrument.

Purpose: "Intended to measure ... perceptions of how frequently and how effectively [an] organization has created a work environment that supports JITT."
Population: Adults.
Publication Date: 1996.
Acronym: JITT.
Scores, 2: Frequency, Effectiveness.
Administration: Group.
Price Data: Available from publisher.
Time: (15–20) minutes.
Author: William J. Rothwell.
Publisher: Human Resource Development Press.

[1312]

Juvenile Automated Substance Abuse Evaluation.

Purpose: Intended to "measure adolescent alcohol and drug use/abuse ... attitudes and life-stress issues."
Population: Adolescents.
Publication Dates: 1989–1997
Acronym: JASAE.
Scores, 6: Test Taking Attitude, Life Circumstance Evaluation, Drinking Evaluation Category, Alcohol Addiction Evaluation, Drug Use Evaluation, Summary.
Administration: Individual or group.
Price Data: Available from publisher.
Manual: No manual; Reference Guide available.
Time: (20) minutes.
Comments: Self-administered; computer scored, IBM compatible with either DOS or Windows required; provides DSM–IV classification for alcohol and drug use and ASAM patient placement criteria for

treatment recommendations; available in English and Spanish.
Author: ADE Incorporated.
Publisher: ADE Incorporated.
Cross References: For reviews by Mark Pope and Jody L. Swartz-Kulstad, see 14:190.

[1313]
Juvenile Justice Policy Inventory.

Purpose: "Designed to assess both individual attitudes toward juvenile justice policies and characteristic methods of dealing with juvenile offenders."
Population: Juvenile justice professionals.
Publication Date: 1973.
Scores, 4: Reintegration, Rehabilitation, Reform, Restraint.
Administration: Group.
Price Data: Available from publisher.
Time: Administration time not reported.
Author: Vincent O'Leary.
Publisher: National Council on Crime and Delinquency [No reply from publisher; status unknown].

[1314]
Kaplan Baycrest Neurocognitive Assessment.

Purpose: "Test of neurocognitive functioning."
Population: Ages 20–89.
Publication Date: 2000.
Acronym: KBNA.
Scores: 8 index scores: Attention/Concentration, Immediate Memory Recall, Delayed Memory Recall, Delayed Memory Recognition, Spatial Processing, Verbal Fluency, Reasoning/Conceptual Shifting, Total Index.
Administration: Individual.
Price Data, 2002: $239 per complete kit including manual (188 pages), stimulus book (94 pages), 8 response chips, cassette, 25 response booklets, 25 record forms, and response grid (packaged in a box); $70 per manual; $70 per stimulus book; $43 per 25 response booklets; $43 per 25 record forms; $11 per response grid.
Time: (60–90) minutes.
Comments: Test contains 25 subtests (Orientation, Sequences, Numbers, Word Lists 1, Complex Figure 1, Motor Programming, Auditory Signal Detection, Symbol Cancellation, Clocks, Word Lists 2, Complex Figure 2, Picture Naming, Sentence Reading—Arithmetic, Reading Single Words, Spatial Location, Verbal Fluency, Praxis, Picture Recognition, Expression of Emotion, Practical Problem Solving, Conceptual Shifting, Picture Description—Oral, Auditory Comprehension, Repetition, Picture Description—Written); detailed analysis of neurocognitive functioning can be obtained through examination of 94 component Process Scores; Process Scores are categorized as below average, equivocal, or average.

Authors: Larry Leach, Edith Kaplan, Dmytro Rewilak, Brian Richards, and Guy-B. Proulx.
Publisher: The Psychological Corporation.

[1315]
Kaufman Adolescent and Adult Intelligence Test.

Purpose: Designed as a "measure of general intelligence."
Population: Ages 11 to 85+.
Publication Date: 1993.
Acronym: KAIT.
Scores, 9 to 14: Crystallized Scale (Definitions, Auditory Comprehension, Double Meanings, Famous Faces [alternate subtest], Total), Fluid Scale (Rebus Learning, Logical Steps, Mystery Codes, Memory for Block Designs [alternate subtest], Total), Measures of Delayed Recall [optional] (Rebus Delayed Recall, Auditory Delayed Recall), Mental Status [supplementary subtest], Total.
Administration: Individual.
Price Data, 2002: $577.95 per complete kit; $52.95 per record set including 25 each, record booklets and mystery code booklets; $58.95 per manual (161 pages); $199.95 per KAIT ASSIST (IBM); $89.95 per KAIT training video.
Time: (58–73) minutes for Core Battery; (83-102) minutes for Expanded Battery.
Authors: Alan S. Kaufman and Nadeen L. Kaufman.
Publisher: American Guidance Service, Inc.
Cross References: See T5:1378 (14 references); for reviews by Dawn P. Flanagan and Timothy Z. Keith, see 12:204 (6 references); see also T4:1342 (1 reference).

[1316]
Kaufman Assessment Battery for Children.

Purpose: Designed as a clinical instrument for assessing cognitive development.
Population: Ages 2.5 to 12.5.
Publication Date: 1983.
Acronym: K-ABC.
Scores: 16 subtests with a maximum of 13 administered to any particular child: 10 mental processing subtests: Magic Window (Ages 2.6–4.11), Face Recognition (Ages 2.6–4.11), Hand Movements (Ages 2.6–12.5), Gestalt Closure (Ages 2.6–12.5), Number Recall (Ages 2.6–12.5), Triangles (Ages 4.0–12.5), Word Order (Ages 4.0–12.5), Matrix Analogies (Ages 5.0–12.5), Spatial Memory (Ages 5.0–12.5), Photo Series (Ages 6.0–12.5) plus 6 achievement subtests: Expressive Vocabulary (Ages 2.6–4.11), Faces and Places (Ages 2.6–12.5), Arithmetic (Ages 3.0–12.5), Riddles (Ages 3.0–12.5), Reading/Decoding (Ages 5.0–12.5), Reading/Understanding (Ages 7.0–12.5).
Administration: Individual.

Price Data, 2002: $412.95 per complete kit including all test materials, 25 individual test records, administrative and scoring manual (272 pages), and interpretive manual (352 pages); $499.95 per complete kit with briefcase; $38.95 per 25 individual test records; $35.95 per administration and scoring manual; $35.95 per interpretive manual.

Time: (35) minutes for age 2.5; (40–45) minutes for age 3; (45–55) minutes for age 4; (50–60) minutes for age 5; (60–70) minutes for age 6; (75–85) minutes for ages 7.0–12.5.

Comments: Nonverbal scale available for hearing impaired, speech- and language-disordered, and non-English speaking children ages 4.0–12.5 (an adaptation that examiners can make when verbal concerns are present).

Authors: Alan S. Kaufman and Nadeen L. Kaufman.

Publisher: American Guidance Service, Inc.

Cross References: See T5:1379 (103 references) and T4:1343 (114 references); for reviews by Anne Anastasi and William E. Coffman, see 9:562 (3 references).

[1317]
Kaufman Brief Intelligence Test.

Purpose: Intended as a brief measure of verbal and nonverbal intelligence.

Population: Ages 4–90.

Publication Date: 1990.

Acronym: K-BIT.

Scores, 3: Vocabulary, Matrices, IQ Composite.

Subtests, 2: Vocabulary (including Part A, Expressive Vocabulary and Part B, Definitions) and Matrices.

Administration: Individual.

Price Data, 2002: $136.95 per complete kit including easel, manual (123 pages), and 25 individual test records; $29.95 per 25 individual test records; $41.95 per manual.

Time: (15–30) minutes.

Comments: Definitions task not administered to children ages 4-7 years; examiners are encouraged to teach individuals, using teaching items, how to solve the kinds of items included in both subtests.

Authors: Alan S. Kaufman and Nadeen L. Kaufman.

Publisher: American Guidance Service, Inc.

Cross References: See T5:1380 (21 references); for reviews by M. David Miller and John W. Young, see 12:205 (9 references); see also T4:1344 (4 references).

[1318]
Kaufman Developmental Scale.

Purpose: Designed to assess the "level of development … and an overall level of functioning."

Population: Birth to age 9 and mentally retarded of all ages.

Publication Dates: 1972–1975.

Acronym: KDS.

Scores, 7: Gross Motor, Fine Motor, Receptive, Expressive, Personal Behavior, Inter-Personal Behavior, Total.

Administration: Individual.

Price Data, 2001: $425 per complete kit including test materials, manual (1974, 83 pages), 25 record forms, and carrying case; $55 per 25 evaluation booklets; $30 per 25 record forms; $55 per manual.

Time: Administration time not reported.

Author: H. Kaufman.

Publisher: Stoelting Co.

Cross References: For a review by Dorothy H. Eichorn, see 8:218.

[1319]
Kaufman Functional Academic Skills Test.

Purpose: "Measure of an adolescent's or adult's ability to demonstrate competence in reading and mathematics as applied to daily life situations."

Population: Ages 15–85 and over.

Publication Date: 1994.

Acronym: K-FAST.

Scores, 3: Arithmetic Subtest, Reading Subtest, Functional Academic Skills Composite.

Administration: Individual.

Price Data, 2002: $111.95 per complete kit including manual (110 pages), test easel, and 25 record forms; $83.95 per test easel; $26.95 per 25 record forms; $30.95 per manual.

Time: (15–25) minutes.

Comments: Examinees may respond in any language.

Authors: Alan S. Kaufman and Nadeen L. Kaufman.

Publisher: American Guidance Service, Inc.

Cross References: See T5:1382 (1 reference); for reviews by Steven R. Shaw and Robert T. Williams, see 13:166 (2 references).

[1320]
Kaufman Infant and Preschool Scale.

Purpose: Designed to measure "early, high-level cognitive thinking, and indicates possible need for intervention."

Population: Ages 1 month–48 months and mentally retarded individuals whose preacademic functioning age does not exceed 48 months.

Publication Date: 1979.

Acronym: KIPS.

Scores: Tasks in 3 areas: General Reasoning, Storage, Verbal Communication.

Administration: Individual.

Price Data, 2001: $300 per complete kit including all manipulatives, stimulus cards, and 10 evaluation booklets; $33 per 10 evaluation booklets; $20 per set of stimulus cards; $28 per manual (40 pages).

Time: (20-30) minutes.
Author: H. Kaufman.
Publisher: Stoelting Co.
Cross References: For reviews by Roy A. Kress and Phyllis Anne Teeter, see 9:563.

[1321]
Kaufman Short Neuropsychological Assessment Procedure.

Purpose: Constructed to assess the "ability to demonstrate intact mental functioning."
Population: Ages 11 to 85.
Publication Date: 1994.
Acronym: K-SNAP.
Scores, 5: Gestalt Closure, Number Recall, Four-Letter Words, Recall/Closure Composite, K-SNAP Composite.
Administration: Individual.
Price Data, 2002: $173.95 per complete kit including manual (128 pages), easel, and 25 record forms; $26.95 per 25 record forms.
Time: (30) minutes.
Authors: Alan S. Kaufman and Nadeen L. Kaufman.
Publisher: American Guidance Service, Inc.
Cross References: See T5:1384 (2 references); for reviews by Karen Geller and Martine Hebert, see 13:167 (2 references).

[1322]
Kaufman Survey of Early Academic and Language Skills.

Purpose: A measure of children's language skills, pre-academic skills, and articulation.
Population: 3-0 to 6-11.
Publication Date: 1993.
Acronym: K-SEALS.
Subtests, 3: Vocabulary; Numbers, Letters, and Words; Articulation Survey.
Administration: Individual.
Price Data, 2002: $199.95 per complete kit including manual (109 pages), easel, 25 test records, and carrying bag; $28.95 per 25 record booklets.
Time: (15–25) minutes.
Comments: The Early Academic Scales can be interpreted only for ages 5-0 to 6-11.
Authors: Alan S. Kaufman and Nadeen L. Kaufman.
Publisher: American Guidance Service, Inc.
Cross References: For reviews by Phillip L. Ackerman and Laurie Ford and Kerri Turk, see 12:206.

[1323]
Kaufman Test of Educational Achievement [1998 Normative Update].

Purpose: "Provides an analysis of a child's educational strengths and weaknesses in reading, mathematics, and spelling, to identify possible skill areas (e.g.,

reading comprehension, mathematics computation) needing remediation or enrichment."
Population: Grades 1 through 12, ages 6–22.
Publication Dates: 1985–1998.
Acronym: K-TEA.
Administration: Individual.
Price Data, 2002: $274.95 per complete kit including brief form and comprehensive form, 2 test easels, 2 manuals, 50 record booklets, 2 sample reports to parents, and carry bag; $373.95 per complete kit with comprehensive form with ASSIST.
Authors: Alan S. Kaufman and Nadeen L. Kaufman.
Publisher: American Guidance Service, Inc.

a) BRIEF FORM.
Purpose: "Screening of student on global achievement skills to determine the need for follow-up testing and evaluation."
Scores, 4: Reading, Mathematics, Spelling, Battery Composite.
Price Data: $122.95 per Brief Form kit including 77 test plates in easel, 25 record booklets, sample reports to parents, carry bag, and manual (1998, 288 pages); $30.95 per 25 record booklets; $20.95 per 25 reports to parents; $80.95 per manual.
Time: (30) minutes.
b) COMPREHENSIVE FORM.
Purpose: "Provides an analysis of a child's educational strengths and weaknesses in reading, mathematics, and spelling, to identify possible skill areas (e.g., reading comprehension, mathematics computation) needing remediation or enrichment."
Scores, 8: Reading Decoding, Reading Comprehension, Reading Composite, Mathematics Applications, Mathematics Computation, Mathematics Composite, Spelling, Battery Composite.
Price Data: $195.95 per Comprehensive Form kit including 133 test plates in easel, 25 record booklets (including error analyses), sample report to parents, carry bag, and manual (1998, 591 pages); $41.95 per 25 record booklets; $25.95 per 25 reports to parents (available in Spanish); $91.95 per manual; $199.95 per software package ASSIST to Windows or Macintosh.
Time: (60–75) minutes.
Cross References: For reviews by John Poggio and William D. Schafer, see 14:191; see also T5:1386 (26 references) and T4:1348 (5 references); for reviews by Elizabeth J. Doll and Jerome M. Sattler of an earlier edition, see 10:161.

[1324]
Keegan Type Indicator.

Purpose: Measures perception, judgment, and attitude (extraversion/introversion) based on C. G. Jung's theory of psychological types.
Population: Adults.

Publication Dates: 1980–1982.
Acronym: KTI.
Scores, 3: Extraversion vs. Introversion, Sensation vs. Intuition, Thinking vs. Feeling.
Administration: Group.
Price Data: Price data, including user's manual (1980, 12 pages) and instructor's manual (1980, 21 pages), available from publisher.
Time: [20] minutes.
Author: Warren J. Keegan.
Publisher: Warren Keegan Associates Press.
Cross References: For a review by Arlene C. Rosenthal, see 10:162.

[1325]
Keele Pre-School Assessment Guide.

Purpose: Developed to plot the progress of individual children and to be a curriculum guide for preschoolers.
Population: Children in nursery school.
Publication Date: 1980.
Acronym: KPAG.
Scores: Ratings by teachers or counselors in 5 areas: Social Behavior, Cognition, Physical Skills, Socialization, Language.
Administration: Individual.
Price Data: Price information available from publisher for record forms and manual (36 pages).
Time: Administration time not reported.
Comments: Experimental form; criterion-referenced.
Author: Stephen Tyler.
Publisher: NFER-Nelson Publishing Co., Ltd. [England].
Cross References: For reviews by Cathy W. Hall and Robert F. McMorris, see 9:565.

[1326]
Kelvin Measurement of Ability in Infant Classes.

Purpose: Provides information on young children's abilities.
Population: Ages 8–12.
Publication Dates: 1935–1956.
Scores: Total score only.
Administration: Group.
Price Data: Not available.
Time: Administration time not reported.
Author: C. M. Fleming.
Publisher: Gibson (Robert) & Sons, Glasgow, Ltd. [Scotland] [No reply from publisher; status unknown].
Cross References: See T2:395 (1 reference).

[1327]
Kendrick Assessment Scales of Cognitive Ageing.

Purpose: Designed "to provide an accurate and flexible means of screening for and predicting possible dementia."

Population: Ages 40–92.
Publication Dates: 1979–1999.
Administration: Individual.
Price Data, 1999: £125 per complete set including 10 record forms, manual (1999), and material for the four subtests; £15 per 10 record forms.
Time: Untimed.
Comments: Revision of Kendrick Cognitive Tests for the Elderly (T4:1352).
Authors: Don Kendrick and Geoff Watts.
Publisher: NFER-Nelson Publishing Co., Ltd. [England].
a) OBJECT LEARNING TEST.
Acronym: KOLT.
Scores: Total score only.
Forms, 2: A, B (4 cards).
Comments: Test of recall of everyday objects.
b) DIGIT COPYING TEST.
Acronym: KDCT.
Scores: Total score only.
Comments: Test of speed performance.
c) WATTS VISUO-SPATIAL TEST.
Acronym: WVST.
Scores: Total score only.
Comments: Test of visuo-spatial ability.
d) KENDRICK ATTENTION AND REASONING TEST.
Acronym: KART.
Scores: Total score only.
Comments: Test of reasoning and attention.
Cross References: See T5:1390 (7 references), T4:1352 (1 reference), and 11:189 (2 references); for reviews by Joseph D. Matarazzo and K. Warner Schaie of an earlier edition, see 9:566 (2 references).

[1328]
Kent Inventory of Developmental Skills [1996 Standardization].

Purpose: Designed to assess the developmental status and progress of healthy infants, infants at risk, and young children with developmental disabilities.
Population: Infants up to 15 months of age and young children whose developmental age is less than 15 months.
Publication Dates: 1978–1999.
Acronym: KIDS.
Scores, 12: Developmental Ages and Standard Scores for: Cognitive, Motor, Language, Self-Help, Social Domains, Full Scale.
Administration: Individual.
Price Data: Price information available from publisher for complete kit including 25 profile sheets, 25 answer sheets, reusable administration and scoring booklet, 5 scoring templates, set of developmental timetables, manual, and 2-use disk for on-site computer scoring and interpretation.

Time: (45) minutes.

Comments: Relies on caregiver report; also yields individualized developmental timetables; includes hand-scoring materials and an expanded computer report, including a list of developmentally appropriate activities selected to match each child's specific competencies; earlier editions entitled The Kent Infant Development Scale.

Authors: Jeanette Reuter with Lewis Katoff and Jeffrey Wozniak (3rd edition of the test manual and user's guide) and James Whiteman (computer-scoring disk).

Publisher: Western Psychological Services.

Cross References: For reviews by Diane J. Sawyer and Gary J. Stainback, see 14:192; see also T5:1391 (2 references); for reviews by Candice Feiring and Edward S. Shapiro of an earlier edition, see 10:163 (2 references); for a review by Candice Feiring of an earlier version, see 9:567; see also T3:1246 (1 reference).

[1329]
Kent Visual Perceptual Test.

Purpose: Designed to "identify and characterize visual processing deficits in school or neuropsychological settings."

Population: Ages 5–11, 18–22, 55–91.

Publication Dates: 1995–2000.

Acronym: KVPT.

Administration: Individual.

Price Data: Available from publisher for kit including 10 copy tests, memory test stimuli, discrimination test stimuli, 10 scoring and error analysis booklets, and manual (2000, 128 pages).

Time: (25–30) minutes.

Author: Lawrence E. Melamed.

Publisher: Psychological Assessment Resources, Inc.

a) KENT VISUAL PERCEPTION TEST—DISCRIMINATION.

Purpose: Designed to assess visual discrimination skills.

Acronym: KVPT-D.

Scores, 2: Error Analysis, Total.

b) KENT VISUAL PERCEPTION TEST—COPY.

Purpose: Designed to assess visual reproduction skills.

Acronym: KVPT-C.

Scores, 4: KVPT-C1, KVPT-C2, KVPT-C3, Total.

c) VISUAL PERCEPTION TESTS—IMMEDIATE MEMORY.

Purpose: Designed to assess immediate memory.

Acronym: KVPT-M.

Scores, 2: Error Analysis, Total.

Cross References: For a review by Annie W. Ward, see 14:193.

[1330]
KeyMath Revised: A Diagnostic Inventory of Essential Mathematics [1998 Normative Update].

Purpose: Designed to assess understanding and applications of mathematics concepts and skills.

Population: Grades K–9, ages 5-0 to 22-11.

Publication Dates: 1971–1998.

Acronym: KeyMath-R.

Scores, 17: Basic Concepts (Numeration, Rational Numbers, Geometry, Total), Operations (Addition, Subtraction, Multiplication, Division, Mental Computation, Total), Applications (Measurement, Time and Money, Estimation, Interpreting Data, Problem Solving, Total), Total.

Administration: Individual.

Forms, 2: A, B.

Price Data, 2002: $445.95 per complete kit including Form A and Form B test easels, 25 each Form A and Form B test records, sample report to parents, and normative update manual (1998, 255 pages); $245.95 per single form (A or B) kit including test easels, 25 test records, sample reports to parents, manual, and carry bag; $41.95 per 25 test records (select A or B); $21.95 per 25 reports to parents; $95.95 per manual; $199.95 per complete ASSIST™ reporting software (Macintosh or Windows).

Time: (30–50) minutes.

Comments: Revision of KeyMath Diagnostic Arithmetic Test; computerized reporting software available.

Author: Austin J. Connolly.

Publisher: American Guidance Service, Inc.

Cross References: For reviews by G. Gage Kingsbury and James A. Wollack, see 14:194; see also T5:1392 (15 references) and T4:1355 (5 references); for reviews by Michael D. Beck and Carmen J. Finley of an earlier edition, see 11:191 (26 references); see also T3:1250 (12 references); for an excerpted review by Alex Bannatyne of an earlier edition, see 8:305 (10 references).

[1331]
Keynotes Music Education Software Kit.

Purpose: Designed to "provide the classroom teacher with a profile of students' strengths and weaknesses in domains considered to be important for most kinds of music learning" and to provide instrumental music teachers and their students with information that may be used to help student select an instrument.

Population: Ages 9–14.

Publication Date: 2000.

Scores, 3: Pitch Discrimination, Patterns Recognition, Music Reading.

Administration: Individual.

Price Data, 2002: A$199.95 per complete kit; A$99.95 per 5 copies CD-ROM.
Time: Administration time not reported.
Comments: Software does not operate on Macintosh computers; requires Windows 95 or higher.
Authors: Jennifer Bryce and Margaret Wu.
Publisher: Australian Countil for Educational Research Ltd. [Australia].

[1332]
KEYS® to Creativity.
Purpose: Designed to measure how "employees perceive stimulants and barriers to creativity."
Population: Employees.
Publication Date: 1995.
Scores, 10: 8 environment scales (6 environmental stimulants to creativity: Organizational Encouragement of Creativity, Supervisory Encouragement of Creativity, Work Group Supports, Freedom, Sufficient Resources, Challenging Work; 2 obstacles to creativity: Organizational Impediments, Workload Pressure); 2 outcome scales (Creativity, Productivity).
Administration: Group.
Price Data, 2002: $20 per survey booklet (5–50 booklets); quantity discounts available.
Time: (15–20) minutes.
Comments: Costs of survey booklets includes scoring, standard feedback results, one KEYS User's Guide (205 pages), and one KEYS: Interpreting the Results.
Authors: Teresa M. Amabile and Center for Creative Leadership.
Publisher: Center for Creative Leadership.
Cross References: For a review by Carolyn M. Callahan, see 14:195; see also T5:1393 (1 reference).

[1333]
Khan-Lewis Phonological Analysis—Second Edition.
Purpose: "Recommended for use in the diagnosis and description of articulation or phonological disorders."
Population: Ages 2-0 to 21-11.
Publication Dates: 1986–2002.
Acronym: KLPA-2.
Scores, 11: 5 Reduction Processes (Deletion of Final Consonants, Syllable Reduction, Stopping of Fricatives and Affricates, Cluster Simplification, Liquid Simplification), 3 Place and Manner Processes (Velar Fronting, Palatal Fronting, Deaffrication), 2 Voicing Processes (Initial Voicing, Final Devoicing), Total Score.
Administration: Individual.
Price Data, 2002: $114.95 per kit including manual (2002, 206 pages), 25 analysis forms, Sound Change booklet, and 25 Phonological Summary and Progress Report worksheets; $59.95 per manual; $21.95 per analysis forms.

Time: [10–30] minutes.
Comments: Revision of the Khan-Lewis Phonological Analysis (KLPA), old edition still available; supplements the Goldman-Fristoe Test of Articulation—Second Edition (GFTA-2; 1054); scores based on responses to the Sounds-in-Words subtest of the GFTA-2; to complete the KLPA-2, examiner needs both complete KLPA-2 kit and complete GFTA-2 kit.
Authors: Linda M. L. Khan and Nancy P. Lewis.
Publisher: American Guidance Service, Inc.
Cross References: See T5:1394 (13 references) and T4:1356 (1 reference); for a review by Donald E. Mowrer of an earlier edition, see 10:164.

[1334]
Khatena-Morse Multitalent Perception Inventory.
Purpose: Identifies giftedness in music, art, and leadership.
Population: Grade 5–adult.
Publication Dates: 1985–1998.
Acronym: KMMPI.
Scores, 6: Artistic, Musical, Creative Imagination, Initiative, Leadership, Versatility.
Administration: Group.
Forms, 2: A, B.
Price Data, 2002: $56.60 per starter set including 35 questionnaires and 35 profile charts (specify Form A or B) and manual (1994, 101 pages); $27.75 per 35 questionnaires and 35 profile charts (specify Form A or B); $31.10 per manual; $30 per sample set.
Time: (30–45) minutes.
Authors: Joe Khatena and David T. Morse.
Publisher: Scholastic Testing Service, Inc.
Cross References: For reviews by Carolyn M. Callahan and William Steve Lang, see 13:169.

[1335]
Khatena-Torrance Creative Perception Inventory.
Purpose: Developed as measures of creative personality.
Population: Age 10–adult.
Publication Dates: 1976–1998.
Acronym: KTCPI.
Administration: Group.
Price Data, 2001: $57.65 per starter set including instruction manual (1998, 96 pages), 35 SAM checklists, 35 WKOPAY checklists, and 35 scoring worksheets; $32.75 per instruction manual; $38 per package of 35 SAM checklists, 35 WKOPAY checklists, and 35 scoring worksheets; $18.90 per specimen set including instruction manual (abridged), 1 SAM checklist, and 1 WKOPAY checklist.
Time: (10–20) minutes per checklist.

Comments: Includes 2 self-report checklists designed to identify candidates for creativity programs.

Publisher: Scholastic Testing Service, Inc.

a) WHAT KIND OF PERSON ARE YOU?

Purpose: Designed to "yield an index of the individual's disposition or motivation to function in creative ways."

Acronym: WKOPAY.

Scores: 5 factors: Acceptance of Authority, Self-Confidence, Inquisitiveness, Awareness of Others, Disciplined Imagination.

Author: E. Paul Torrance.

b) SOMETHING ABOUT MYSELF.

Purpose: Designed as an autobiographical "screening device for the identification of creative people."

Acronym: SAM.

Scores: 6 factors: Environmental Sensitivity, Initiative, Self-Strength, Intellectuality, Individuality, Artistry.

Author: Joe Khatena.

Cross References: See T5:1396 (5 references); for reviews by David L. Bolton and William Steve Lang of a previous edition, see 13:168 (2 references); for a review by Philip E. Vernon of an earlier edition, see 9:569 (3 references).

[1336]
Kilmann-Saxton Culture-Gap Survey [Revised].

Purpose: Assesses "actual versus desired cultural norms."

Population: Work team members, employees.

Publication Dates: 1983–1991.

Acronym: CGS.

Scores, 4: Task Support, Social Relationships, Task Innovation, Personal Freedom.

Administration: Group.

Price Data, 2001: $8.50 per survey.

Time: (30) minutes.

Authors: Ralph H. Kilmann and Mary J. Saxton.

Publisher: Consulting Psychologists Press, Inc.

Cross References: For reviews by Russell N. Carney and Norman D. Sundberg, see 13:170; for reviews by Andres Barona and Gargi Roysircar Sodowsky of an earlier edition, see 11:192.

[1337]
Kilmanns Organizational Belief Survey.

Purpose: Assesses beliefs about one's level of control in their organizational surroundings.

Population: Employees.

Publication Date: 1991.

Scores, 8: Control Score, My Work Group, My Department, My Organization, Individual Profile, Work Group Profile, Department Profile, Organizational Profile.

Administration: Group.

Price Data, 2001: $8.50 each questionnaire/booklet.

Time: Administration time not reported.

Comments: A component of the Workshop for Implementing the Five Tracks, part of a completely integrated set of materials for creating and maintaining long-term organizational success; self-scored.

Authors: Ralph H. Kilmann and Ines Kilmann.

Publisher: Consulting Psychologists Press, Inc.

[1338]
Kindergarten Diagnostic Instrument— Second Edition.

Purpose: "Designed to assess developmental readiness skills in children."

Population: Children ages 4–6 years or older children with known or suspected developmental delays.

Publication Date: 2000.

Acronym: KDI-2.

Scores, 22: 13 subtest scores (Body Awareness, Concept Mastery, Form/Letter Identification, General Information, Gross Motor, Memory for Sentences, Number Skills, Phonemic Awareness, Verbal Associations, Visual Discrimination, Visual Memory, Visual-Motor Integration, Vocabulary), 6 subskills (Form Identification, Letter Identification, Verbal Associations—Similarities, Verbal Associations—Opposites, Visual Discrimination—Similarities, Visual Discrimination—Differences), Nonverbal Factor Score, Verbal Factor Score, Total Test Score.

Administration: Individual.

Price Data, 2002: $165 per complete test kit including administration manual (146 pages), 3 stimulus booklets, 13 1-inch wooden blocks, and 25 student response booklets in a carrying case; $450 per assessment bundle including complete test kit, 50 student response booklets, 50 My Kindergarten Fun Books-II (40 pages), and scoring program for Windows; $32 per 25 student response booklets; $2 per My Kindergarten Fun Book-II; $250 per KDI-2 Scoring Program for Windows (one-time license fee, additional cost applies for sites screening more than 300 children annually); $40 per training video; quantity discounts available on all items.

Time: (35–45) minutes.

Comments: KDI-2 Scoring Program for Windows stores students' pre-kindergarten and kindergarten data, generates local schoolwide norms, assesses performance compared to local norms, generates individual reports, test-retest reports; contact publisher for KDI-2 Scoring Program system requirements.

Authors: Daniel C. Miller (KDI-2, Training Video, My Kindergarten Fun Book-II) and Michie A. Miller (Training Video, My Kindergarten Fun Book-II).

Publisher: Kindergarten Interventions and Diagnostic Services, Inc.

[1339]
Kindergarten Inventory of Social-Emotional Tendencies.

Purpose: "Designed to screen for social skill deficits and signs of emotional immaturity in preschool and kindergarten aged children."

Population: Ages 4–6.

Publication Date: 1997.

Acronym: KIST.

Scores: 7 domains: Communication Skills, Daily Living Skills, Hyperactive/Inattentive Behaviors, Maladaptive Behaviors, Separation Anxiety Behaviors, Socialization or Peer Relation Skills, Sleeping & Eating Behaviors.

Administration: Individual.

Price Data: Available from publisher.

Time: (10) minutes.

Comments: Ratings by child's primary caregiver, or by a teacher who knows the child well.

Authors: Daniel C. Miller and Michie A. Miller.

Publisher: Kindergarten Interventions and Diagnostic Services, Inc.

[1340]
Kindergarten Language Screening Test, Second Edition.

Purpose: Designed to help identify children "who need further diagnostic testing to determine whether or not they have language deficits that will accelerate academic failure."

Population: Ages 4-0 through 6-11.

Publication Dates: 1978–1998.

Acronym: KLST-2.

Scores: Total score only.

Administration: Individual.

Price Data, 2001: $109 per complete kit including examiner's manual (1998, 30 pages), 50 profile/examiner record forms, picture book, and 3 picture cards; $34 per examiner's manual; $39 per 50 profile/examiner record forms; $34 per picture book; $6 per 3 picture cards.

Time: (5) minutes.

Authors: Sharon V. Gauthier and Charles L. Madison.

Publisher: PRO-ED.

Cross References: For reviews by Timothy R. Konold and Leslie Eastman Lukin, see 14:196; see also T4:1359 (2 references).

[1341]
Kindergarten Readiness Test.

Purpose: Determines the readiness of children to begin kindergarten.

Population: Ages 4–6.

Publication Date: 1988.

Acronym: KRT.

Scores: Total score only.

Administration: Individual.

Price Data, 2002: $118 per complete kit; $38 per manual (39 pages); $55 per 25 test booklets; $14 per 25 performance grid sheets; $14 per 25 letter to parent; $14 per 25 scoring interpretation; $21 per stimulus items.

Time: (15) minutes.

Authors: Sue L. Larson and Gary J. Vitali.

Publisher: Slosson Educational Publications, Inc.

Cross References: For reviews by Michael D. Beck and Rosemary E. Sutton and Catharine C. Knight, see 12:207.

[1342]
Kinetic Drawing System for Family and School: A Handbook.

Purpose: Designed "as a projective technique which assesses a child's perceptions of relationships among the child, peers, family, school, and significant others."

Population: Ages 5–20.

Publication Date: 1985.

Acronym: KDS.

Scores: 5 diagnostic categories: Actions of and Between Figures, Figure Characteristics, Position/Distance/Barriers, Style, Symbols.

Administration: Individual.

Price Data, 2002: $65 per complete kit including 25 scoring booklets and handbook (65 pages); $28.50 per 25 scoring booklets; $39.95 per handbook (including scoring booklet).

Time: (20–40) minutes.

Comments: A combination of the Kinetic Family Drawing and Kinetic School Drawing.

Authors: Howard M. Knoff and H. Thompson Prout (handbook).

Publisher: Western Psychological Services.

Cross References: See T5:1401 (4 references) and T4:1362 (2 references); for reviews by Bert P. Cundick and Richard A. Weinberg, see 10:166 (4 references).

[1343]
Kipnis-Schmidt Profiles of Organizational Influence Strategies.

Purpose: To "measure how people use influence in their organizations."

Population: Organizational members.

Publication Date: 1982.

Acronym: POIS.

Scores, 12 or 14: Friendliness, Bargaining, Reason, Assertiveness, Sanctions (Form S only), Higher Authority, Coalition scores for each of 2 areas (First Attempt to Influence, Attempts to Overcome Resistance to Influence).

Administration: Group.

Forms, 3: M (Influencing Your Manager), C (Influencing Your Co-Workers), S (Influencing Your Subordinates).

Price Data: Price information available from publisher for set of 10 forms (specify Form M, C, S, or respondent's guides); trainer's package including 1 copy of each instrument, respondent's guide, and manual (16 pages).
Time: (20–30) minutes.
Authors: David Kipnis and Stuart M. Schmidt.
Publisher: Jossey-Bass, A Wiley Company.
Cross References: See T5:1402 (3 references) and T4:1363 (2 references).

[1344]

The Kirkpatrick Management and Supervisory Skills Series.

Purpose: Designed to assess "Key management skills and practices."
Publication Date: 1995.
Scores: Total score only.
Administration: Group.
Price Data: Available from publisher.
Time: (20) minutes per inventory.
Author: Donald L. Kirkpatrick.
Publisher: Donald L. Kirkpatrick (the author).
a) COMMUNICATION INVENTORY.
Purpose: Constructed to "improve knowledge, attitudes, and skills" related to communication.
Population: Supervisors and all levels of managers.
Acronym: CI.
b) HUMAN RELATIONS INVENTORY.
Purpose: Constructed to assess "the relationships that exist between supervisor and subbordinate."
Population: Same as *a* above.
Acronym: HRI.
c) MANAGING CHANGE INVENTORY.
Purpose: Designed to "cover principles, facts, and attitudes that are basic to managing change effectively."
Population: All levels of managers.
Acronym: MCI.
d) MODERN MANAGEMENT INVENTORY.
Purpose: Designed to measure "philosophy, principles, and approaches related to the effective performance of managers."
Population: Same as *c* above.
Acronym: MMI.
e) COACHING AND PERFORMANCE APPRAISAL INVENTORY.
Purpose: Constructed to assess "concepts, principles, and techniques that are important ingredients" of on-the-job coaching.
Population: Same as *c* above.
Acronym: CPAI.
f) TIME MANAGEMENT INVENTORY.
Purpose: Constructed to measure "Key factors in better time utilization and delegation."

Population: Same as *c* above.
Acronym: TMI.
g) LEADERSHIP, MOTIVATION, AND DECISION-MAKING INVENTORY.
Purpose: Constructed to "make managers more conscious of their need to be leaders."
Population: Same as *c* above.
Acronym: LMDMI.
Cross References: For a review by L. Carolyn Pearson and Lee Droegemueller, see 14:197.

[1345]

Kirton Adaption-Innovation Inventory [1998 Edition].

Purpose: A measure of a person's preference for, or style of, creativity, problem solving, and decision making.
Population: British and U.S. adults and teenagers over age 14.
Publication Dates: 1976–1998.
Acronym: KAI.
Scores, 4: Sufficiency v. Proliferation of Originality, Efficiency, Rule/Group Conformity, Total.
Administration: Individual or group.
Price Data: Available from publisher.
Time: (5–10) minutes.
Comments: Translations available for Italian, Slovak, French, and Dutch adults and teenagers.
Author: Michael Kirton.
Publisher: Occupational Research Centre [England].
Cross References: For reviews by Lynn L. Brown and Ric Brown, see 14:198; see also T5:1404 (15 references) and T4:1364 (9 references); for reviews by Gregory J. Boyle and Gerald E. DeMauro of an earlier edition, see 11:193 (8 references).

[1346]

Kit of Factor Referenced Cognitive Tests.

Purpose: "To provide research workers with a means of identifying certain aptitude factors in factor-analytic studies."
Population: Various grades 6–college level.
Publication Dates: 1954–1978.
Administration: Group.
Price Data, 2002: $30 per complete set including 72 tests and manual (1976, 230 pages); $10 per manual; a license agreement is required for the use of the tests ($.10 a copy with a minimum of $35 for graduate students, $.20 a copy with a minimum of $50 for other researchers).
Time: Administration time given separately for each test.
Comments: Formerly called the Kit of Reference Tests for Cognitive Factors.
Authors: Tests and manual written by Ruth B. Ekstrom, John W. French, Harry H. Harman, and Diran Dermen.
Publisher: Educational Testing Service.

a) FACTOR CF: FLEXIBILITY OF CLOSURE.
  1) *Hidden Figures Test.*
  2) *Hidden Patterns Test.*
  3) *Copying Test.*
b) FACTOR CS: SPEED OF CLOSURE.
  1) *Gestalt Completion Test.*
  2) *Concealed Words Test.*
  3) *Snowy Pictures.*
c) FACTOR CV: VERBAL CLOSURE.
  1) *Scrambled Words.*
  2) *Hidden Words.*
  3) *Incomplete Words.*
d) FACTOR FA: ASSOCIATIONAL FLUENCY.
  1) *Controlled Associations Test.*
  2) *Opposites Test.*
  3) *Figures of Speech.*
e) FACTOR FE: EXPRESSIONAL FLUENCY.
  1) *Making Sentences.*
  2) *Arranging Words.*
  3) *Rewriting.*
f) FACTOR FF: FIGURAL FLUENCY.
  1) *Ornamentation Test.*
  2) *Elaboration Test.*
  3) *Symbols Test.*
g) FACTOR FI: IDEATIONAL FLUENCY.
  1) *Topics Test.*
  2) *Theme Test.*
  3) *Thing Categories Test.*
h) FACTOR FW: WORD FLUENCY.
  1) *Word Endings Test.*
  2) *Word Beginnings Test.*
  3) *Word Beginnings and Endings Test.*
i) FACTOR I: INDUCTION.
  1) *Letter Sets Test.*
  2) *Locations Test.*
  3) *Figure Classifications.*
j) FACTOR IP: INTEGRATIVE PROCESSES.
  1) *Calendar Test.*
  2) *Following Directions.*
k) FACTOR MA: ASSOCIATIVE MEMORY.
  1) *Picture–Number Test.*
  2) *Object–Number Test.*
  3) *First and Last Names Test.*
l) FACTOR MS: MEMORY SPAN.
  1) *Auditory Number Span Test.*
  2) *Visual Number Span Test.*
  3) *Auditory Letter Span Test.*
m) FACTOR MV: VISUAL MEMORY.
  1) *Shape Memory Test.*
  2) *Building Memory.*
  3) *Map Memory.*
n) FACTOR N: NUMBER.
  1) *Addition Test.*
  2) *Division Test.*
  3) *Subtraction and Multiplication Test.*
  4) *Addition and Subtraction Correction.*

o) FACTOR P: PERCEPTUAL SPEED.
  1) *Finding A's Test.*
  2) *Number Comparison Test.*
  3) *Identical Pictures Test.*
p) FACTOR RG: GENERAL REASONING.
  1) *Arithmetic Aptitude Test.*
  2) *Mathematics Aptitude Test.*
  3) *Necessary Arithmetic Operations Test.*
q) FACTOR RL: LOGICAL REASONING.
  1) *Nonsense Syllogisms Test.*
  2) *Diagramming Relationships.*
  3) *Inference Test.*
  4) *Deciphering Languages.*
r) FACTOR S: SPATIAL ORIENTATION.
  1) *Card Rotations Test.*
  2) *Cube Comparisons Test.*
s) FACTOR SS: SPATIAL SCANNING.
  1) *Maze Tracing Speed Test.*
  2) *Choosing a Path.*
  3) *Map Planning Test.*
t) FACTOR V: VERBAL COMPREHENSION.
  1) *Vocabulary Test I.*
  2) *Vocabulary Test II.*
  3) *Extended Range Vocabulary Test.*
  4) *Advanced Vocabulary Test I.*
  5) *Advanced Vocabulary Test II.*
u) FACTOR VZ: VISUALIZATION.
  1) *Form Board Test.*
  2) *Paper Folding Test.*
  3) *Surface Development Test.*
v) FACTOR XF: FIGURAL FLEXIBILITY.
  1) *Toothpicks Test.*
  2) *Planning Patterns.*
  3) *Storage Test.*
w) FACTOR XU: FLEXIBILITY OF USE.
  1) *Combining Objects.*
  2) *Substitute Uses.*
  3) *Making Groups.*
  4) *Different Uses.*

Cross References: See T5:1405 (40 references), T4:1365 (92 references), 9:572 (27 references), T3:1257 (78 references), and T2:561 (103 references).

[1347]

Knowledge of Occupations Test.

Purpose: "To measure the extent to which high school students have knowledge of occupations."
Population: High school.
Publication Date: 1974.
Acronym: KOT.
Scores, 9: Earnings, Licensing and Certification, Job Descriptions, Employment Trends, Training, Terminology, Graphs, Tools, Total.
Administration: Group.
Price Data, 2002: $20 per 25 tests; $2.75 per answer key; $8.25 per 25 answer sheets; $8.25 per 25

profiles; $6.75 per manual (8 pages); $9 per specimen set including manual and forms (keys not included).
Time: 40(45) minutes.
Author: Leroy G. Baruth.
Publisher: Psychologists and Educators, Inc.
Cross References: For reviews by David O. Herman and Dean H. Nafziger, see 8:1008 (1 reference).

[1348]
Knox's Cube Test.

Purpose: A nonverbal mental test designed to measure "the attention span and short-term memory of children and adults."
Population: Ages 3–8, 9 and over.
Publication Date: 1980.
Acronym: KCT.
Scores: Total score only.
Administration: Individual.
Levels, 2: Junior Test Form, Senior Test Form.
Price Data, 2001: $95 per complete kit (specify level); $22 per 15 tests and report forms (specify level); $75 per set of blocks; $28 per manual (53 pages).
Time: Administration time not reported.
Authors: Mark H. Stone and Benjamin D. Wright.
Publisher: Stoelting Co.
Cross References: See T5:1407 (5 references) and T4:1367 (7 references); for reviews by Raymond S. Dean and Jerome M. Sattler, see 9:574 (2 references).

[1349]
Kohlberg's Moral Judgment Interview.

Purpose: To identify stages of moral development.
Population: Ages 10 and over.
Publication Date: 1983.
Scores: Moral Development Stages.
Price Data: Available from publisher.
Time: Administration time not reported.
Authors: Anne Colby and Lawrence Kohlberg.
Publisher: Cambridge University Press.
Cross References: See T5:1408 (9 references), T4:1368 (9 references), and T3:1262 (2 references).

[1350]
The Kohlman Evaluation of Living Skills.

Purpose: "An occupational therapy evaluation that is designed to determine a person's ability to function in basic living skills."
Population: Occupational therapy clients with living skill deficits.
Publication Dates: 1981–1992.
Acronym: KELS.
Scores: 5 areas: Self-care, Safety and Health, Money Management, Transportation and Telephone, Work and Leisure.
Administration: Individual.
Price Data, 1998: $35 per administration booklet.

Time: (30–45) minutes.
Comments: Evaluation combines interview questions and tasks; can be used with the elderly, with persons who have cognitively disabling conditions, in court for the determination of commitment, and in discharge planning at acute-care hospitals.
Author: Linda Kohlman Thomson.
Publisher: The American Occupational Therapy Association, Inc.
Cross References: For a review by Gabriele van Lingen, see 14:199.

[1351]
The Kohs Block-Design Test.

Purpose: Designed as "performance tests that have been standardized to measure intelligence."
Population: Mental ages 5–20.
Publication Date: [1919].
Scores: Total score only.
Administration: Individual.
Price Data, 2001: $140 per complete kit including cubes, cards, manual (20 pages), and 50 record blanks; $25 per 50 record blanks; $20 per set of design cards; $100 per set of blocks; $25 per manual.
Time: (30–40) minutes.
Comments: Formerly called The Block-Design Test; modifications appear in Arthur Point Scale of Performance Tests, New Guinea Performance Scales, Ohwaki-Kohs Tactile Block Design Intelligence Test for the Blind, and Pacific Design Construction Test.
Author: S. C. Kohs.
Publisher: Stoelting Co.
Cross References: See T5:1410 (4 references), T4:1370 (5 references), T3:1265 (4 references), and T2:545 (74 references).

[1352]
Kolbe Conative Index.

Purpose: Designed to focus on the "predisposition of a subject to respond to specific behavioral settings with certain patterns of behavior."
Publication Dates: 1987–1997.
Administration: Group or individual.
Price Data: Available from publisher.
Comments: A series of instruments designed to enhance personnel selection and increase self-awareness about instructive talent and potential.
Author: Kathy Kolbe.
Publisher: Kolbe Corp.
   a) KOLBE A™ INDEX.
   Purpose: Designed to measure conative style.
   Population: Adults.
   Acronym: KCI-A.
   Scores, 4: Fact Finder, Follow Thru, Quick Start, Implementor.
   Time: (25) minutes.

b) KOLBE B™ INDEX.
Purpose: Designed to "identify the characteristics perceived as necessary to succeed in a given job."
Population: Job applicants.
Acronym: KCI-B.
Time: (15–20) minutes.
c) KOLBE C™ INDEX.
Purpose: Designed to "identify the characteristics necessary to function successfully in a specific job."
Population: Supervisors.
Acronym: KCI-C.
d) KOLBE R™ INDEX.
Purpose: Designed to identify "how you (the respondent) wish another person would take action."
Population: Adults.
Acronym: KCI-R.
e) KOLBE Y™ INDEX.
Purpose: Designed to assist the respondent in identifying his/her "talent for certain types of activities."
Population: Youth (5th grade reading level).
Acronym: KCI-Y.
Cross References: For reviews by Raoul A. Arreola and Chockalingam Visweswaran, see 14:200; for reviews by Collie Wyatt Conoley and Frank Gresham of an earlier edition, see 12:208.

[1353]
Krantz Health Opinion Survey.
Purpose: "To measure attitudes toward different treatment approches."
Population: College, healthy adults, and chronic disease populations.
Publication Date: 1980.
Acronym: KHOS.
Scores, 3: Information, Behavioral Involvement, Total.
Administration: Group.
Manual: No manual.
Price Data: Test materials now available free of charge from author.
Time: (10-15) minutes.
Authors: David S. Krantz, Andrew Baum, and Margaret V. Wideman.
Publisher: David S. Krantz.
Cross References: See T5:1412 (4 references) and T4:1373 (1 reference); for a review by James A. Blumenthal, see 9:578 (1 reference); see also T3:1267 (1 reference).

[1354]
Kuder Career Search.
Purpose: Assesses activity preferences to suggest possible satisfying occupations.

Population: Middle school through adult.
Publication Date: 1999.
Acronym: KCS.
Scores, 6: Outdoor/Mechanical, Science/Technical, Arts/Communication, Social/Personal Services, Sales/Management, Business Operations.
Administration: Individual or group.
Price Data: Available from publisher.
Time: (20–25) minutes including scoring.
Comments: Uses preference profile to find best matches from a database of approximately 2,000 employed adults and yields first-person accounts of their occupations/jobs; with Kuder Skills Assessment (1357) and Super's Work Values Inventory—Revised (2436), plus the Kuder Electronic Career Portfolio constitutes the Kuder Career Planning System.
Authors: Frederic Kuder and Donald G. Zytowski.
Publisher: National Career Assessment Services, Inc.

[1355]
Kuder General Interest Survey, Form E.
Purpose: Constructed to assess "broad interest areas" related to occupational choices.
Population: Grades 6–12.
Publication Dates: 1963–1991.
Scores, 11: Outdoor, Mechanical, Computational, Scientific, Persuasive, Artistic, Literary, Musical, Social Service, Clerical, Verification.
Administration: Group.
Price Data: Available from publisher.
Time: [45–60] minutes.
Comments: Extension of the Kuder vocational interest inventories series.
Author: G. Frederic Kuder.
Publisher: National Career Assessment Services.
Cross References: See T5:1413 (1 reference); for reviews by Mark Pope and Donald Thompson, see 12:209; see also T4:1374 (4 references), T3:1269 (4 references), and 8:1009 (16 references); for reviews by Barbara A. Kirk, Paul R. Lohnes, and John N. McCall of an earlier edition, and excerpted reviews by T. R. Husek and Robert F. Stahmann, see 7:1024 (8 references).

[1356]
Kuder Occupational Interest Survey, Revised (Form DD).
Purpose: Measures individual interests in order to "suggest promising occupations and college majors in rank order, based on examinee's interest pattern."
Population: Grade 10 through adult.
Publication Dates: 1956–1985.
Acronym: KOIS.
Scores, 4: Dependability, Vocational Interest Estimates (10 areas), Occupational Scales (approximately 100), College Major Scales (approximately 40).

Administration: Group.
Price Data: Available from publisher.
Time: (30–45) minutes.
Comments: Includes Vocational Interest Estimate scales identical in content to those of the Kuder Preference Record, Form C and the Kuder General Interest Survey, Form E.
Authors: Frederic Kuder, Esther E. Diamond, and Donald G. Zytowski (manual supplement).
Publisher: National Career Assessment Services, Inc.
Cross References: See T4:1375 (1 reference); for reviews by Edwin L. Herr and Mary L. Tenopyr, see 10:167 (3 references); see also T3:1270 (12 references), 8:1010 (41 references), and T2: 2194 (13 references); for reviews by Robert H. Dolliver and W. Bruce Walsh, and excerpted reviews by Frederick G. Brown and Robert F. Stahmann, see 7:1025 (19 references).

[1357]
Kuder Skills Assessment.

Purpose: Assesses self-efficacy in six skill areas.
Population: Middle school through adult.
Publication Date: 2001.
Acronym: KSA.
Scores, 6: Outdoor/Mechanical, Science/Technical, Arts/Communication, Social/Personal Services, Sales Management, Business Operations.
Administration: Individual or group.
Price Data: Available from publisher.
Time: (15–20) minutes.
Comments: Online administration; instant scoring; combined report with Kuder Career Search (1354) available; with Kuder Career Search and Super's Work Values Inventory—Revised (2435), plus the Kuder Electronic Career Portfolio, constitutes the Kuder Career Planning System.
Authors: Donald G. Zytowski and Darrell Luzzo.
Publisher: National Career Assessment Services, Inc.

[1358]
Kuhlmann-Anderson Tests, Eighth Edition.

Purpose: "Designed to provide a measure of an individual's academic potential through assessing cognitive skills related to the learning process."
Population: Grades K, 1, 2–3, 3–4, 5–6, 7–9, 9–12.
Publication Dates: 1927–1982.
Acronym: KA.
Scores, 6: 3 raw scores (Verbal, Nonverbal, Full) and 3 derived scores.
Administration: Group.
Levels, 7: K, A, BC, CD, EF, G, and H.
Manual: Separate manual of directions for each level.
Authors: F. Kuhlmann (fourth and earlier editions) and Rose G. Anderson.
Publisher: Scholastic Testing Service, Inc.

a) LEVEL K.
Population: Kindergarten.
Price Data, 2002: $37.70 per starter set including manual of directions and 20 machine-scorable test booklets; $31.30 for starter set including manual of directions, 20 hand-scorable test booklets, class record shee, and answer key; $5.10 per student for scoring service.
Time: 28(50–75) minutes in 2 days.
b) LEVEL A.
Population: Grade 1.
Price Data: Same as for *a* above.
Time: 28(50–75) minutes in 2 days.
c) LEVEL BC.
Population: Grades 2, 3.
Price Data: Same as for *a* above.
Time: 28(50–75) minutes in 2 days.
d) LEVEL CD.
Population: Grades 3, 4.
Price Data: $31.30 per starter set including manual of directions, 20 test booklets, and class record sheet, $3.90 per student for scoring service.
Time: 35(50–75) minutes.
e) LEVEL EF.
Population: Grades 5, 6.
Price Data: Same as for *d* above.
Time: 40(50–75) minutes.
f) LEVEL G.
Population: Grades 7–9.
Price Data: Same as for *d* above.
Time: 40(50–75) minutes.
g) LEVEL H.
Population: Grades 9–12.
Price Data: Same as for *d* above.
Time: 40(50–75) minutes.
Cross References: See T4:1377 (2 references); for reviews by Michael D. Hiscox and Ronald C. Rodgers, see 9:579 (2 references); see T3:1272 (13 references) and T2:398 (53 references); for reviews by William B. Michael and Douglas A. Pidgeon, and an excerpted review by Frederick B. Davis of the seventh edition, see 6:466 (11 references); see also 5:348 (15 references); for reviews by Henry E. Garrett and David Segel of an earlier edition, see 5:302 (10 references); for reviews by W. G. Emmett and Stanley S. Maryolf, see 3:236 (25 references); for a review by Henry E. Garrett, see 2:1404 (15 references); for reviews by Psyche Cattell, S. A. Courtis, and Austin H. Turney, see 1:1049.

[1359]
Kundu Introversion Extraversion Inventory.

Purpose: Designed to obtain a measure of the introversion-extraversion dimension of adult behavior to be used for diagnosis, selection, or career guidance.
Population: Adults.
Publication Date: 1976.

Scores: Total score only.
Administration: Group.
Price Data: Available from publisher.
Time: (20–40) minutes.
Author: Ramanath Kundu.
Publisher: Ramanath Kundu [India] [No reply from publisher; status unknown].

[1360]
Kundu Neurotic Personality Inventory.
Purpose: Designed to measure neurotic tendencies.
Population: Adults.
Publication Dates: 1965–1987.
Acronym: KNPI.
Scores: Item scores only.
Administration: Individual or group.
Price Data: Available from publisher.
Foreign Language Edition: Bengali edition available.
Time: (20–30) minutes.
Author: Ramanath Kundu.
Publisher: Ramanath Kundu [India] [No reply from publisher; status unknown].
Cross References: See T2:1257 (2 references) and P:140 (5 references).

[1361]
La Monica Empathy Profile.
Purpose: "To measure and improve a person's ability to care, manage, and provide the empathy needed for optimum performance in fields where personal interaction is intense and frequent."
Population: Managers/helpers/teachers in industry, education, and health care.
Publication Dates: 1980–1986.
Acronym: LEP.
Scores, 5: Nonverbal Behavior, Perceiving Feelings and Listening, Responding Verbally, Respect of Self and Others, Openness/Honesty and Flexibility.
Administration: Group or individual.
Price Data, 2001: $7.50 or less per instrument (1986, 21 pages includes profile, instructions, and scoring information).
Time: [15] minutes.
Comments: Self-administered; self-scored.
Author: Elaine L. La Monica.
Publisher: Consulting Psychologists Press, Inc.
Cross References: For reviews by Susan McCammon and LeAdelle Phelps, see 10:168.

[1362]
The Lake St. Clair Incident.
Purpose: To examine group and individual decision-making processes, help individuals and groups perceive and evaluate their interactions and styles of communicating, and utilize the instrument to simply have fun or create an environment.

Population: Adults.
Publication Dates: 1977–1978.
Acronym: LSC.
Scores, 3: Autocratic, Consultative, Consensual.
Administration: Individual in part.
Price Data, 2002: $39.95 per 25 test booklets; $25 per manual (1977, 22 pages); $39.95 per kit including 10 test booklets and manual.
Time: (65–80) minutes.
Author: Albert A. Canfield.
Publisher: Western Psychological Services.
Cross References: For a review by Jack L. Bodden, see 9:582.

[1363]
Language Arts Objective Sequence.
Purpose: "Helps evaluate students' current [language arts] performance levels and identify specific goals and objectives."
Population: Grades pre-K–9.
Publication Date: 2001.
Scores: 9 ratings/objectives: Readiness (Level 3), Listening (Levels 3, 2), Speaking (Levels 3, 2, 1), Reading—Word Recognition (Level 3), Reading—Comprehension (Levels 3, 2, 1), Writing—Handwriting (Level 3), Writing—Spelling (Levels 3, 2), Writing Process (Levels 3, 2, 1), Writing—Grammar (Levels 3, 2, 1).
Administration: Individual.
Levels, 3: 1, 2, 3.
Price Data, 2001: $39.95 per assessment manual (120 pages) including 24 reproducible forms and checklists.
Time: Administration time not reported.
Comments: Intended to be used by teachers as an informal "curriculum guide, bank of objectives, rubric guide, or structured observation system"; some objectives do not include all 3 levels.
Authors: Jacqueline Robertson and Sheldon Braaten.
Publisher: Research Press.

[1364]
Language Assessment Scales—Oral.
Purpose: Designed to "measure those English and language skills necessary for functioning in a mainstream academic environment."
Population: Grades 1–6, 7–12.
Publication Dates: 1987–1991.
Acronym: LAS-O.
Scores, 6: Vocabulary, Listening Comprehension, Story Retelling, Minimal Sound Pairs, Phonemes, Total.
Administration: Individual.
Levels, 2: 1, 2.
Forms, 2: C, D.
Parts, 2: Oral Language (for Level 1 & 2), Pronunciation (for Grades 2–12).
Price Data, 2002: $61 per test review kit including administration manual, scoring and interpretation

manual, student test booklet or multicopy scoresheet, and cue picture booklet along with test reviewer's guide (specify level and form); $42.65 per 50 answer documents; $45.35 per reusable cue picture booklet; $20.55 per audiocassette (specify level and form); $33.50 per administration manual (specify level); $35.65 per scoring and interpretation manual (specify level); $33.50 per technical report (1991, 144 pages); $162 per examiner's kit (specify level).

Foreign Language Edition: Spanish edition (1990) available.

Time: [15] minutes.

Authors: Edward A. DeAvila and Sharon E. Duncan.

Publisher: CTB/McGraw-Hill.

Comments: Language Proficiency Score also incorporates Language Assessment Scales, Reading and Writing (1365).

Cross References: See T5:1420 (1 references); for reviews by Natalie L. Hedberg and Pamela S. Tidwell, se 12:210 (1 reference); for a review of the Language Assessment Scales by Lyn Haber, see 9:584 (1 reference).

[1365]
Language Assessment Scales, Reading and Writing.

Purpose: Designed to measure "English language skills in reading and writing necessary for functioning in a mainstream academic environment."

Population: Language-minority students in Grades 2–3, 4–6, 7–11.

Publication Date: 1988.

Acronym: LAW R/W.

Scores, 3: Reading, Writing, Total.

Administration: Group.

Levels, 3: 1, 2, 3.

Forms, 2: A, B.

Price Data, 2002: $106.90 per 35 Level 1 Reading test booklets and examiner's manual (67 pages); $68.05 per 35 Level 2 or Level 3 Reading test booklets and Reading/Writing examiner's manual (Level 2, 79 pages; Level 3, 73 pages); $51.85 per 35 Writing test booklets (specify level); $44.30 per 50 student answer documents (sepecify Level 2 or Level 3); $160.95 per 9 Level 1 scoring stencils (Reading only); $18.35 per Level 2 or Level 3 scoring stencil (Reading only); $16.20 per administration manual (specify level); materials also available in Spanish; $23.75 per technical manual (98 pages); $714 (with $170.10 charge for technical support) for LASSCORE site license.

Time: (50–75) minutes for Level 1; (49–87) minutes for Level 2; (53–86) minutes for Level 3.

Comments: May be used in conjunction with LAS Oral (1364).

Authors: Sharon E. Duncan and Edward A. DeAvila.

Publisher: CTB/McGraw-Hill.

Cross References: See T5:1421 (4 references); for reviews by C. Dale Carpenter and Thomas W. Guyette, see 12:211; see also T4:1386 (5 references).

[1366]
Language Facility Test.

Purpose: Measures language and grammar skills in both English or Spanish.

Population: Ages 3 and over.

Publication Dates: 1965–1980.

Acronym: LFT.

Scores: 2 scoring systems: (9 point qualitative scale for evaluating communication in primary language, error analysis for standard English) for verbal responses to 12 pictures.

Administration: Individual.

Price Data: Not available.

Time: (10–15) minutes.

Author: John T. Dailey.

Publisher: The Allington Corporation [No reply from publisher; status unknown].

Cross References: For a review by Charles Stansfield, see 9:585; see also T3:1282 (1 reference); for a review by Nicholas Anastasiow of an earlier form, see 7:955 (1 reference).

[1367]
Language Imitation Test.

Purpose: "Developed for use as a language assessment technique, specifically for the severely educational subnormal."

Population: Educationally subnormal children.

Publication Date: No date on test materials.

Acronym: LIT.

Scores: 6 subtest scores: Sound Imitation, Word Imitation, Syntactic Control 1, Syntactic Control 2, Word Organization Control, Sentence Completion.

Administration: Individual.

Price Data: Price information available from publisher for specimen set, record forms, and manual (no date, 41 pages).

Time: Administration time not reported.

Authors: Paul Berry and Peter Mittler.

Publisher: NFER-Nelson Publishing Co., Ltd. [England].

Cross References: See T5:1423 (1 reference); for a review by Rita Sloan Berndt, see 9:586 (1 reference).

[1368]
Language Processing Test.

Purpose: Designed to identify "students' language processing strengths and weaknesses in a hierarchical framework."

Population: Ages 5-0 to 11-11.

Publication Date: 1985.

Acronym: LPT.

Scores, 8: Labeling, Stating Functions, Associations, Categorization, Similarities, Differences, Multiple Meanings, Attributes.
Administration: Individual.
Price Data: Available from publisher.
Time: (30) minutes.
Authors: Gail J. Richard and Mary Anne Hanner.
Publisher: LinguiSystems, Inc. [No reply from publisher; status unknown].
Cross References: See T5:1424 (5 references); for reviews by Thomas W. Guyette and Lyn Haber, see 10:169.

[1369]
Language Proficiency Test.

Purpose: Developed to "assess oral/aural, reading, and writing skills."
Population: Grades 9 and over.
Publication Date: 1981.
Acronym: LPT.
Scores, 6–9: Aural/Oral (Commands, Short Answers [optional], Comprehension [optional]), Reading (Vocabulary, Comprehension), Writing (Grammar, Sentence Response, Paragraph Response, Translation [optional]).
Administration: Individual in part.
Price Data, 2002: $50 per complete kit including 20 test booklets and manual (29 pages); $20 per manual.
Time: (80–100) minutes.
Authors: Joan Gerard and Gloria Weinstock.
Publisher: Academic Therapy Publications.
Cross References: See T5:1425 (1 reference); for a review by John M. Keene, Jr., see 9:588.

[1370]
Language Proficiency Test Series.

Purpose: Designed to aid in student placement and the evaluation of student language proficiency in reading, writing, listening, and speaking.
Population: Grades K–12, specifically LEP students.
Publication Dates: 1998–2001.
Acronym: LPTS.
Scores, 3: Reading, Writing, Listening/Speaking.
Administration: Individual or group.
Forms, 24: Listening/Speaking: L/S 1—Grades K–2, L/S 2—Grades 3–5, L/S 3—Grades 6–8, L/S 4—Grades 9–12, Reading: R1—Grades K–2, R2—Grades 3–5, R3—Grades 6–8, R4—Grades 9–12, Writing: W1—Grades K–2, W2—Grades 3–5, W3—Grades 6–8, W4—Grades 9–12; alternate forms available for all subjects and grade clusters.
Price Data, 2002: $32 per administrator's sample set including Administration and Scoring Guide plus one test booklet each for Reading, Writing, and Listening/Speaking at grade level of choice (K-2, 3–5, 6–8, or

9–12); $59.50 per 25 Grades K–2 or for Grades 3–5 (For A or B) Reading Test booklets; $51.50 per 25 Grades 6–8 or Grades 9–12 (Form A or B) Reading Test booklets; $12.50 per 25 scannable answer sheets for Reading Test (Grades 6–12 only); $1.25 each for Scoring Reading Test booklet; $26.50 per 25 Writing Test booklets (Grades K-2, 3–5, 6–8, or 9–12, Form A or B); $2.30 each for Scoring Writing Test booklet; $26.50 per 25 Listening/Speaking Test booklets (Grades K-2, 3–5, 6–8, or 9–12, Form A or B); $1.25 each for Scoring Listening/Speaking Test booklet; $59.50 per technical manual (2001, 41 pages).
Time: (25) minutes average per test.
Author: MetriTech, Inc.
Publisher: MetriTech, Inc.

[1371]
Language Sampling, Analysis, and Training—Third Edition.

Purpose: "Designed to analyze the syntax and morphology of children who are producing a significant number of utterances containing at least three morphemes."
Population: Children with language delay.
Publication Dates: 1974–1999.
Acronym: LSAT-3.
Scores, 39: Word Morpheme (Sentences Total, Words Total, Morphemes Total, Words/Sentences Means, Morphemes/Sentence Means, Word-Morpheme Index), Noun Phrase Constituents (Pronouns, Prepositions, Possessive Marker, Demonstratives, Articles, Plurals, Locatives, Conjunctions), Verb Phrase Constituents (Modals, Particles, Copula, Present Progressive Tense, Present Tense-3rd Singular, Past Tense, Irregular), Simple Sentence Constructions (Noun Phrase, Verb Phrase, Verb Phrase + Noun Phrase, Noun Phrase + Verb Phrase + [Noun Phrase], Noun Phrase + Copula + N/Adj, Unclassifiable Constructions), Complex Sentences (Coordination, Subordination-Infinitives, Adverbials, Indirect Questions, Verb + [that] + Sentence, Relatives, Direct Quotations, Complex in More Than One Way, Unclassifiable, Percentage Complex), Questions, Negatives.
Administration: Individual.
Price Data, 2001: $89 per complete kit including manual (1999, 163 pages), analysis forms, and transcription sheets; $34 per manual; $34 per analysis forms; $24 per transcription sheets.
Time: Administration time varies.
Comments: Visual and verbal stimuli for eliciting language sample determined by examiner; tape recording recommended for recording responses; a detailed tutorial with self-checking exercises covering all steps in the procedure, multicultural issues, setting targets, training, measuring and reporting change are new inclusions in the third edition handbook.

Authors: Dorothy Tyack and Gail Portnuff Venable.
Publisher: PRO-ED.
Cross References: For a review by Sheila Pratt, see 14:201; for a review by Margaret C. Byrne of an earlier edition, see 9:590.

[1372]
Law Enforcement Assessment and Development Report.

Purpose: Intended to evaluate personality implications for performance in law enforcement jobs.
Population: Applicants and incumbents for law enforcement and other public safety positions.
Publication Dates: 1967–1987.
Acronym: LEADR.
Scores, 37: 4 personality dimensions (Emotional Adjustment, Integrity/Control, Intellectual Efficiency, Interpersonal Relations); 16 normal personality primary factor scores; 12 pathological characteristics; Performance Index; Tough Poise; Independence; Leadership, Accident Proneness.
Administration: Group or individual.
Price Data, 2002: $40 per 25 reusable test booklets; $15 per 25 answer sheets; $20 per manual (1987, 43 pages); $23 per introductory kit including manual, test booklet, answer sheet, and prepaid processing form; $19 to $30 per individual score report.
Time: (120) minutes.
Comments: Test represents a computer-based analysis from the Clinical Analysis Questionnaire (527); onsite software scoring and report options available.
Author: IPAT staff.
Publisher: Institute for Personality and Ability Testing, Inc.
Cross References: For a review by David S. Hargrove, see 10:170; for a review by Lawrence Allen of the earlier edition, see 9:593.

[1373]
The LAW-PSI Adult Life History Questionnaire.

Purpose: Designed to gather a defendant's summary of life history prior to legal investigation or polygraph examination.
Population: Adults.
Publication Date: 1986.
Scores: 17 areas: Personal History, Developmental History, Family History, Educational History, Employment History, Dating History, Marital History, Driving History, Legal History, Financial History, Drug History, Alcohol History, Mental Health History, Health History, Sexual History, Military History, Daily Activity History.
Administration: Individual.
Price Data, 2001: $24.50 each questionnaire booklet (66 pages).

Time: Administration time not reported.
Author: Stephen B. Lawrence.
Publisher: California Counseling Centers.

[1374]
The LAW-PSI Child/Adolescent Life History Questionnaire.

Purpose: Individual life history information gathered prior to verification either by legal investigation or polygraph examination.
Population: Children/adolescents.
Publication Date: [1986].
Scores: 14 areas: Personal History, Developmental History, Family History, Educational History, Employment History, Dating History, Driving History, Legal History, Financial History, Drug History, Alcohol History, Mental Health History, Daily Activity History, Health History.
Administration: Individual.
Price Data, 2001: $24.50 each questionnaire/booklet.
Time: Untimed.
Author: Stephen B. Lawrence.
Publisher: California Counseling Centers.

[1375]
The LAW-PSI Sexual History Questionnaire.

Purpose: "To obtain a comprehensive, accurate sexual history in a wide variety of individuals."
Population: Adults.
Publication Date: 1994.
Scores: 16 areas: Total Sexual Partners, Primary Sexual Partners, Locations for Sex, Use of Erotic Materials, Masturbation History, Visiting Erotic Locations, Commercial Sex Experiences, Sexual Victim History, Sexual Disorders, Homosexual Experiences, Physical Sexual Problems, Sexual Dysfunctions, Child Pornography, Sexual Fantasies, Sexual Offenses, Current Sexual Allegations/Offenses.
Administration: Individual.
Price Data, 2001: $24.50 per sexual history questionnaires; $15 per 5 sexual history worksheets; $35 per sexual offender reports; $24.50 per manual (72 pages); $25 per 15 minutes for forensic consultation via telephone with author.
Time: Administration time not reported.
Author: Stephen B. Lawrence.
Publisher: California Counseling Centers.

[1376]
Law School Admission Test.

Purpose: "To measure skills that are considered essential for success in law school."
Population: Law school entrants.
Publication Dates: 1948–1998.
Acronym: LSAT.

Scores: Total score plus unscored writing sample.
Administration: Group.
Price Data, 1998: $86 per LSAT; $52 per late registration; $26 per test center change; $26 per test date change; $190 per nonpublished test center (U.S.A., Canada, Puerto Rico); $255 per nonpublished test center (all other countries); $32 per hand scoring; $35 per reporting renewal; $32 per former registrants score report; $91 per LSDAS subscription (12 months plus one law school report); $9 per law school report ordered at time of subscription; $11 per law school report ordered after initial subscription; $54 per LSDAS subscription renewal.
Time: 175(200) minutes per LSAT; 30(40) minutes per writing sample.
Comments: Test administered 4 times annually (June, October, December, February) at centers established by the publisher.
Authors: Law School Admission Council, administered by Law School Admission Service.
Publisher: Law School Admission Council/Law School Admission Service.
Cross References: See T5:1434 (2 references); for reviews by James B. Erdmann and by Robert F. McMorris, Elizabeth L. Bringsjord, and Wei-Ping Liu, see 13:174 (8 references); see also T4:1400 (4 references); for a review by Gary B. Melton of an earlier edition, see 9:594 (2 references); see also T3:1292 (6 references), 8:1093 (7 references), and T2:2349 (7 references); for a review by Leo A. Munday of earlier forms, see 7:1098 (23 references); see also 5:928 (7 references); for a review by Alexander G. Wesman, see 4:815 (6 references).

[1377]
The Lawrence Psychological Forensic Examination.

Purpose: "A guide for comprehensive psychological assessments and report writing with clients in the criminal, juvenile and civil justice systems."
Population: Juvenile, criminal, and civil justice clients.
Publication Dates: 1978–1983.
Acronym: LAW-PSI.
Scores: No scores as such; ratings and judgments.
Administration: Individual.
Price Data: Available from publisher.
Comments: Ratings by mental health professional; handbook contains descriptive legal information for report writing, and 3 tests.
Author: Stephen B. Lawrence.
Publisher: California Counseling Centers.
   a) LAWRENCE PSYCHOLOGICAL FORENSIC EXAMINATION.
   Comments: Guided forensic interview to determine precise mental states of mind, life history, or prediction of future client behavior.

   b) LAWRENCE MENTAL COMPETENCY TEST.
   Acronym: LAW-COMP.
   Comments: To aid clinicians in making judgments needed to determine a client's present legal mental competency to stand trial.
   c) LAWRENCE PSYCHOLOGICAL FORENSIC EXAMINATION REPORT EVALUATION.
   Acronym: LAW-PSI/EVAL.
   Comments: A rating instrument (175 pages) for evaluating written forensic reports.
Cross References: For a review by Samuel Roll, see 10:171.

[1378]
Leader Behavior Analysis II.

Purpose: Developed to assess leadership style.
Population: Middle and upper level managers.
Publication Date: 1991.
Acronym: LBAII.
Scores, 6: Style Flexibility, Style Effectiveness, Directing Style, Coaching Style, Supporting Style, Delegating Style.
Administration: Group.
Editions, 2: Self, Other.
Price Data: Price information available from publisher for complete kit including 1 LBAII-Self instrument, 8 LBAII-Other instruments, data summary sheet, and scoring instructions.
Time: [15-20] minutes.
Comments: Ratings by employees and self-ratings.
Authors: Drea Zigarmi, Douglas Forsyth, Kenneth Blanchard, and Ronald Hambleton (tests).
Publisher: Blanchard Training & Development, Inc.
Cross References: See T5:1436 (1 reference); for reviews by H. John Bernardin and Donna K. Cooke and Sharon McNeely, see 12:212; see also T4:1402 (1 reference).

[1379]
Leader Behavior Questionnaire, Revised.

Purpose: Constructed as a measure of "organizational leadership."
Population: Managers and employees.
Publication Dates: 1988–1996.
Acronym: LBQ.
Scores: Visionary Leadership Behavior Scales (Clear Leadership, Communicative Leadership, Consistent Leadership, Caring Leadership, Creative Leadership) Visionary Leadership Characteristics Scales (Confident Leadership, Empowered Leadership, Visionary Leadership), Visionary Culture Building Scales (Organizational Leadership, Cultural Leadership).
Administration: Group.
Forms, 2: Self, Other.
Price Data, 1996: $7.95 per self questionnaire; $2.95 per other questionnaire; $24.95 per trainer's guide (1996, 63 pages).

Time: (10–20) minutes.
Author: Marshall Sashkin.
Publisher: Human Resource Development Press.
Cross References: For reviews by Janet Barnes-Farrell and Hilda Wing, see 14:202.

[1380]
Leadership and Self-Development Scale.

Purpose: Measurement of the effectiveness of a leadership workshop for college women.
Population: College.
Publication Dates: 1976–1979.
Scores, 9: Assertiveness, Risk Taking, Self-Concept, Setting Goals, Decision Making, Obtaining a Followership, Conflict Resolution, Group Roles, Evaluation.
Administration: Group.
Manual: No manual; mimeographed research report (1976, 20 pages).
Price Data, 2001: Now free upon request from publisher.
Time: Administration time not reported.
Authors: Virginia Hoffman and Patricia B. Elmore.
Publisher: Patricia B. Elmore.
Cross References: For a review by Robert R. McCrae, see 9:597; see also T3:1298 (2 references).

[1381]
Leadership Appraisal Survey.

Purpose: "An assessment of leadership practices and attitudes as viewed through the eyes of others."
Population: Adults.
Publication Dates: 1971–1997.
Scores, 5: Philosophy, Planning, Implementation, Evaluation, Total.
Administration: Group.
Manual: No manual.
Price Data, 2001: $7.95 per instrument.
Time: Administration time not reported.
Comments: Self-administered survey.
Author: Jay Hall.
Publisher: Teleometrics International.
Cross References: See T3:2351 (1 reference); for a review by Abraham K. Korman of the Styles of Leadership and Management, see 8:1185 (8 references).

[1382]
Leadership Competency Inventory.

Purpose: Measures an individual's use of four competencies related to leadership.
Population: Adults.
Publication Dates: 1993–1996.
Acronym: LCI.
Scores, 4: Information Seeking, Conceptual Thinking, Strategic Orientation, Service Orientation.
Administration: Group or individual.

Price Data, 2001: $69 per complete kit including 10 profiles and interpretive notes (25 pages), and 10 questionnaires; $29 per 10 (employee version) questionnaires; $55 per 10 Development Assistant booklets.
Time: [30–40] minutes.
Comments: Self-scored questionnaire.
Author: Hay Group.
Publisher: Hay Group.
Cross References: For a review by L. Carolyn Pearson, see 13:175.

[1383]
Leadership Development Report.

Purpose: "An expert system provid[ing] insight into how a manager's personality affects his or her performance and how to modify a manager's behavior within his or her natural limits."
Population: Adults.
Publication Dates: 1996–2000.
Acronym: LDR.
Scores, 34: Impulsivity, Understanding, Complexity, Risk Taking, Breadth of Interests, Innovation, Endurance, Cognitive Structure, Order, Organization, Play, Self-Esteem, Anxiety, Tolerance, Change, Achievement, Aggression, Responsibility, Abasement, Value Orthodoxy, Energy Level, Harm Avoidance, Affiliation, Dominance, Exhibition, Interpersonal Affect, Succorance, Social Participation, Social Adroitness, Conformity, Defendence, Social Recognition, Nurturance, Autonomy.
Administration: Group.
Price Data, 2001: $90 per report including test administration materials and return by courier; volume discounts available.
Time: Untimed.
Comments: Includes items from the Jackson Personality Inventory—Revised (1278), The Personality Research Form (1885), and The Survey of Work Styles (2456) (all still available); answer sheets are faxed to publisher; bound reports returned via courier; email delivery available.
Authors: Richard A. Hagberg and Douglas N. Jackson.
Publisher: Sigma Assessment Systems, Inc.

[1384]
Leadership Effectiveness Analysis.

Purpose: Developed to identify leadership skills and behaviors in a 360 degree context.
Population: Managers, supervisors, individual contributors at all levels.
Publication Dates: 1981–2001.
Acronym: LEA.
Scores, 23: Conservative, Innovative, Technical, Self, Strategic, Persuasive, Outgoing, Excitement, Restraint, Structuring, Tactical, Communication, Delegation, Control, Feedback, Management Focus, Domi-

nant, Production, Cooperation, Consensual, Authority, Empathy, Exaggeration.
Administration: Group.
Price Data: Available from publisher.
Time: (45) minutes.
Comments: Requires training by publisher before purchase and use.
Authors: James T. Mahoney (test) and Robert I. Kabacoff (manual).
Publisher: Management Research Group.

[1385]
Leadership/Impact.

Purpose: Provides people in leadership with information about their current performance as well as insights into ways they can enhance their effectiveness through the leadership strategies they employ and the impact they have on others.
Population: Leaders at the executive level.
Publication Date: 1996.
Acronym: L/I.
Scores: 3 Dimensions of Effectiveness: Organizational Effectiveness, Personal Effectiveness, Balance; 12 Types of Impact on Others: Constructive Impact (Achievement, Self-Actualizing, Humanistic-Encouraging, Affiliative), Passive/Defensive (Approval, Conventional, Dependent, Avoidance), Aggressive/Defensive (Oppositional, Power, Competitive, Perfectionistic); 10 Domains of Leadership: Personal Focus (Envisioning, Role Modeling), Interpersonal Focus (Mentoring, Stimulating Thinking, Referring, Monitoring, Providing Feedback), Organizational Focus (Reinforcing, Influencing, Creating a Setting).
Administration: Individual or group.
Price Data: Price data for test materials including Facilitator's Guide available from publisher.
Time: Administration time not reported.
Comments: Ratings by self and at least three co-workers.
Author: Robert A. Cooke.
Publisher: Human Synergistics International.

[1386]
Leadership Opinion Questionnaire.

Purpose: To measure supervisory leadership dimensions.
Population: Supervisors and prospective supervisors.
Publication Dates: 1960–1989.
Acronym: LOQ.
Scores, 2: Structure, Consideration.
Administration: Individual or group.
Price Data, 2002: $72 per start-up kit including 25 test booklets and examiner's manual; $53 per 25 test booklets (quantity discounts available); $28 per examiner's manual; price data available from publisher for Quanta Computer Administration and Scoring software (Windows); $72 per Quanta start-up kit includ-

ing examiner's manual and 25 administrations and scoring (does not include Quanta software).
Time: No limit (approximately 10–15 minutes).
Author: Edwin A. Fleishman.
Publisher: Reid London House.
Cross References: See T5:1444 (4 references), T4:1409 (7 references), T3:1300 (10 references), 8:1177 (52 references), and T2:2454 (15 references); for a review by Cecil A. Gibb, see 7:1149 (41 references); for reviews by Jerome E. Doppelt and Wayne K. Kirchner, see 6:1190 (6 references).

[1387]
Leadership Practices Inventory—Individual Contributor [Second Edition].

Purpose: "Designed to assist a nonmanagerial leader in assessing the extent to which he or she engages in certain leadership behaviors."
Population: Nonmanagerial leaders.
Publication Dates: 1990–1997.
Acronym: LPI-IC.
Scores, 5: Challenging, Inspiring, Enabling, Modeling, Encouraging.
Administration: Group.
Forms, 2: Self, Observer.
Price Data, 1999: $49.95 per kit including workbook, Self and Other forms, and scoring software; $12.95 per Self form plus workbook; $3.95 per Other form.
Time: Administration time not reported.
Comments: Nonmanagerial version of the Leadership Practices Inventory (1388); a 30-item Self or Observer rating; hand or computer scored (computer scoring recommended); computer scoring software available.
Authors: James M. Kouzes and Barry Z. Posner.
Publisher: Jossey-Bass, A Wiley Company.
Cross References: For reviews by John M. Enger and L. Carolyn Pearson, see 14:204; for reviews by Frederick T. L. Leong and Mary A. Lewis of an earlier edition of the Leadership Practices Inventory, see 12:213; see also T4:1411 (2 references).

[1388]
Leadership Practices Inventory .

Purpose: Designed to provide ratings of five leadership behaviors.
Population: Managers.
Publication Dates: 1990–1992.
Acronym: LPI.
Scores, 5: Challenging the Process, Inspiring a Shared Vision, Enabling Others to Act, Modeling the Way, Encouraging the Heart.
Administration: Group.
Editions, 2: Self, Other.
Price Data: Price information available from publisher for trainer's package including LPI: Self-Assessment book-

let and inventory, LPI: Other inventory, technical manual (1992, 31 pages) and trainer's manual (1990, 39 pages); LPI: Self-Assessment booklet and inventory; LPI: Other inventory; IBM-PC (or compatible) scoring software.
Time: Administration time not reported.
Comments: Scale for ratings by employees and for self-ratings.
Authors: James M. Kouzes and Barry Z. Posner.
Publisher: Jossey-Bass, A Wiley Company.
Cross References: See T5:1448 (1 reference); for reviews by Frederick T. L. Leong and Mary A. Lewis, see 12:213; see also T4:1411 (2 references).

[1389]
The Leadership Q-Sort Test (A Test of Leadership Values).

Purpose: Designed to "assess an individual's values with respect to the leadership role."
Population: Adults.
Publication Date: 1958.
Acronym: LQST.
Scores, 7: Personal Integrity, Consideration of Others, Mental Health, Technical Information, Decision Making, Teaching and Communication, Total.
Administration: Individual or group.
Price Data: Available from publisher.
Time: (40–45) minutes.
Author: Russell N. Cassel.
Publisher: Psychometric Affiliates.
Cross References: For reviews by Joel T. Campbell, Cecil A. Gibb, and William Stephenson, see 6:134 (6 references).

[1390]
Leadership Skills Inventory [Consulting Resource Group].

Purpose: Helps individuals develop the ability to handle the "people" side of enterprise.
Population: Adults.
Publication Date: 1992.
Acronym: LSI.
Scores, 7: Transforming Leadership Principles, Awareness and Self-Management Skills, Interpersonal Communication Skills, Counseling and Problem Management Skills, Consulting Skills for Developing Groups and Organizations, Style/Role and Skill Shifting for Developing Versatility, Grand Total.
Administration: Group.
Editions, 2: Self Assessment, Other.
Price Data, 1993: $10 per test booklet (Other); $12 per test booklet (Self Assessment).
Time: (40–50) minutes.
Comments: Self-administered and self-scored; book entitled Transforming Leadership: New Skills for an Extraordinary Future serves as manual.
Author: Terry D. Anderson.

Publisher: Consulting Resource Group International, Inc.
Cross References: For reviews by Mary Henning-Stout and George C. Thornton, III, see 13:176.

[1391]
Leading Edge Portrait.

Purpose: Designed as "an assessment of preferences for nine distinctive leadership roles."
Population: Age 13 and over.
Publication Date: 1997.
Scores, 9: Sage, Visionary, Magician, Globalist, Mentor, Ally, Sovereign, Guide, Artisan.
Administration: Group.
Manual: No manual.
Price Data, 2001: $15.25 per client kit; $138.70 per 10 item booklet/answer sheets; $106 per facilitator's guide.
Time: (30) minutes.
Comments: Self-scored instrument; can be accompanied by PowerPoint® software product facilitator's guide.
Author: Stuart Wells.
Publisher: Consulting Psychologists Press, Inc.

[1392]
Learned Behaviors Profile—Self/Other.

Purpose: "Designed to help people explore their patterns of behavior."
Population: Adults.
Publication Date: 1990.
Acronym: LBP.
Scores, 6: Caretaker, People-Pleaser, Workaholic, Martyr, Perfectionist, Tap Dancer.
Administration: Group.
Editions, 2: Self, Other.
Price Data: Price information available from publisher for LBP: Self inventory (31 pages); LBP: Other inventory (6 pages); each includes administrator's guide (no date, 2 pages).
Time: Administration time not reported.
Comments: Self-administered, self-scored.
Authors: J. William Pfeiffer and Judith A. Pfeiffer.
Publisher: Jossey-Bass, A Wiley Company.
Cross References: For reviews by Diane Billings Findley and John R. Graham, see 11:197.

[1393]
Learning Accomplishment Profile Diagnostic Edition.

Purpose: "Designed to provide the teacher of the young child with a simple criterion-referenced tool for systematic assessment of the child's existing skills."
Publication Dates: 1992–1997.
Administration: Individual or group.
Parts, 4: LAP-D Normed Assessment, LAP-D Screen, LAP (Revised Edition), Early LAP.

Comments: May be administered in station or individual format.

Publisher: Kaplan.

a) LEARNING ACCOMPLISHMENT PROFILE DIAGNOSTIC EDITION NORMED ASSESSMENT.

Purpose: "Facilitates standardized, norm referenced assessment ... of developmental skills."

Population: Ages 30–60 months.

Publication Date: 1992.

Acronym: LAP-D.

Scores, 8: 4 development areas: Fine Motor (Writing, Manipulation), Language (Comprehension, Naming), Gross Motor (Body Movement, Object Movement), Cognitive (Counting, Matching).

Price Data, 2001: $624.95 per Normed Assessment including examiner's manual (62 pages), technical report, scoring booklets, and training manual (55 pages); $25.95 per 20 scoring protocols; $19.95 per technical report; $9.95 per examiner's manual; $12.95 per 10 Partial Person pads; $9.95 per 10 Plain Paper pads or 10 Diamond Design Cutting pads; $199.95 per single-user software (diskette or CD-ROM); $899.95 per 5-user site license (diskette); $1,799.95 per 10-user site license (diskette).

Time: (45–90) minutes.

Comments: "Designed to assist in making relevant educational decisions with regard to young children and to enable the teacher to develop developmentally appropriate instructional objectives and strategies"; hand or computer scoring available; LAP-D Windows software Version 3.5 system requirements: Windows 3.1, 3.51, or 98, 80486 or higher microprocessor, VGA or higher resolution screen supported by Windows, 8MB or more RAM, Windows-compatible printer.

Authors: Aubrey D. Nehring, Ema F. Nehring, John R. Bruni, Jr., and Patricia L. Randolph.

b) LEARNING ACCOMPLISHMENT PROFILE DIAGNOSTIC EDITION NORMED SCREEN.

Purpose: "Quick initial developmental instruments designed as entry level to the diagnostic process."

Population: Ages 3–5 years.

Publication Date: 1997.

Acronym: LAP-D Screen.

Scores, 6: 4 developmental areas: Fine Motor (Writing, Manipulation), Language (Comprehension, Naming), Gross Motor, Cognitive.

Price Data: $124.95 per Screen kit (specify age 3, age 4, or Kindergarten) including examiner's manual, 25 scoring booklets, 3 Kindergarten Progress Charts, and screening items (specify English or Spanish); $349.95 per ages 3/4/5 Screen package (specify English or Spanish); $9.95 per 30 scoring profiles (specify age 3, age 4, or Kindergarten, specify English or Spanish); $52.95 per Screen manuals for ages 3, 4, and 5 (specify English or Spanish).

Time: (12–15) minutes, untimed.

Comments: Designed to be completed by the child's classroom teacher; items selected from LAP-D Standardized Assessment.

Author: Kaplan Press.

c) LEARNING ACCOMPLISHMENT PROFILE— REVISED EDITION.

Purpose: "A systematic, ongoing, criterion-referenced assessment of a child's existing skills in fine and gross motor, cognitive/language, personal/social, and self-help skills."

Population: Ages 3–6 years.

Publication Date: 1995.

Acronym: LAP-R.

Ratings, 7: Gross Motor, Fine Motor, Pre-Writing, Cognitive, Language, Self-Help, Personal/Social.

Price Data: $274.95 per kit including manipulatives, supplies, toys for use during assessment, 380 Learning Activities for Young Children cards, 20 scoring booklets, instruction manual (132 pages), and IEP forms; $89.95 per 10 manuals (specify English or Spanish); $6.50 per Social or Self-Help Observation Checklist.

Time: Administration time not reported.

Authors: Anne R. Sanford and Janet G. Zelman.

d) EARLY LEARNING ACCOMPLISHMENT PROFILE.

Purpose: "An ongoing, criterion-referenced assessment system covering gross motor, fine motor, cognitive, language, self-help, and social/emotional domains."

Population: Birth to 36 months.

Publication Date: 1995.

Acronym: E-LAP.

Ratings, 6: Gross Motor, Fine Motor, Cognitive, Language, Self-Help, Social/Emotional.

Price Data: $334.95 per Early Learning kit including manipulatives, toys, supplies, 20 scoring booklets, Early Learning Activity Cards, and instruction manual (111 pages); $89.95 per 10 manuals (specify English or Spanish); $22.95 per 20 scoring booklets (specify English or Spanish); $9.95 per manual.

Time: Administration time not reported.

Authors: M. Elayne Glover, Jodi L. Preminger, and Anne R. Sanford.

[1394]
Learning and Memory Battery.

Purpose: Used for assessing both specificity and sensitivity to diverse memory problems.

Population: Ages 20 to 80.

Publication Date: 1995.

Acronym: LAMB.

Scores: 7 subtests: Paragraph Learning, Word List, Word Pairs, Digit Span, Supraspan Digit, Simple Figure, Complex Figure.

Administration: Individual.

Price Data, 2002: $315 per complete kit including 25 recording forms, 25 profile/summary sheets, 100 Simple and Complex Figure drawing forms, administration tents, standard score conversion booklet, and manual (171 pages); $559 per manual; $70 per 25 recording forms; $12 per Standard Score Conversion Booklet; $10 per 100 Simple and Complex Figure Drawing Forms; $193 per administration tents (set of 2); $295 per LAMB Score Windows™ CD or 3.5-inch disk (unlimited use); price information available from publisher for Administration Windows™ 3.5-inch (per usage).

Time: (45–60) minutes.

Authors: James P. Schmidt and Tom N. Tombaugh.

Publisher: Multi-Health Systems, Inc.

Cross References: For reviews by Charles J. Long and Michelle L. Ries and by Wilfred G. Van Gorp, see 14:205.

[1395]
Learning and Study Strategies Inventory.

Purpose: "To measure students' use of learning and study strategies and methods."

Population: College students.

Publication Date: 1987.

Acronym: LASSI.

Scores, 10: Attitude, Motivation, Time Management, Anxiety, Concentration, Information Processing, Selecting Main Ideas, Study Aids, Self Testing, Test Strategies.

Administration: Group or individual.

Price Data: Price information available from publisher for packet including test booklet, manual (15 pages), and score interpretation information; information regarding computer administration and volume discounts also available from publisher.

Time: (30) minutes.

Comments: Manual title is LASSI User's Manual; Apple II and IBM PC microcomputer versions available.

Author: Claire E. Weinstein.

Publisher: H & H Publishing Co., Inc.

Cross References: See T5:1455 (13 references) and T4:1417 (1 reference); for reviews by Martha W. Blackwell and Steven C. Hayes, see 11:198 (3 references).

[1396]
Learning and Study Strategies Inventory—High School Version.

Purpose: Designed to assist high school students "in determining their study skills strategies, problems and attitudes, and learning practices."

Population: Grades 9–12.

Publication Date: 1990.

Acronym: LASSI-HS.

Scores, 10: Attitude, Motivation, Time Management, Anxiety, Concentration, Information Processing, Selecting Main Ideas, Study Aids, Self Testing, Test Strategies.

Administration: Group.

Price Data, 1994: $2.25 per self-scored form; $2.50 per computer scored form.

Time: (25–30) minutes.

Authors: Claire E. Weinstein and David R. Palmer.

Publisher: H & H Publishing Co., Inc.

Cross References: For reviews by Kenneth A. Kiewra and Robert T. Williams, see 13:177 (4 references).

[1397]
Learning/Behavior Problems Checklist.

Purpose: Designed "to identify children at risk of or already experiencing behavior problems of learning disorders."

Population: Students in the primary grades.

Publication Date: 1990.

Scores: Not scored.

Administration: Individual.

Price Data, 2002: $10 per 25 checklists.

Time: [5–10] minutes.

Comments: Ratings by teachers.

Author: Academic Consulting & Testing Service.

Publisher: Academic Consulting & Testing Service.

[1398]
Learning Disabilities Diagnostic Inventory.

Purpose: Designed to identify specific learning disabilities and to help diagnose dysphasia, dyslexia, dysgraphia, dyscalculia, and disorders in executive function.

Population: Ages 8-0 to 17-11.

Publication Date: 1998.

Acronym: LDDI.

Scores, 6: Listening, Speaking, Reading, Writing, Mathematics, Reasoning.

Administration: Individual.

Price Data, 2001: $109 per complete kit including examiner's manual (106 pages) and 50 rating summary booklets; $42 per examiner's manual; $69 per 50 rating summary booklets.

Time: (10–20) minutes.

Authors: Donald D. Hammill and Brian R. Bryant.

Publisher: PRO-ED.

Cross References: For reviews by Terry B. Gutkin and John MacDonald, see 14:206.

[1399]
Learning Disability Evaluation Scale (Renormed).

Purpose: "Developed to aid in diagnosis, placement, and planning for learning disabled children and adolescents."

Population: Grades K–12.
Publication Dates: 1983–1996.
Acronym: LDES.
Scores, 7: Listening, Thinking, Speaking, Reading, Writing, Spelling, Mathematical Calculations.
Administration: Individual.
Price Data, 2002: $144 per complete kit including 50 Pre-Referral Learning Problem Checklist forms, 50 Pre-Referral Intervention Strategies Documentation forms, 50 LDES rating forms, LDES technical manual (1996, 71 pages), Learning Disability Intervention manual (1995, 223 pages), and Parents' Guide to Learning Disabilities (1991, 200 pages); $27 per 50 Pre-Referral Learning Problem Checklist forms; $27 per 50 Pre-Referral Intervention Strategies Documentation forms; $33 per 50 LDES rating forms; $14 per technical manual; $25 per Learning Disability Intervention manual; $19 per Parents' Guide to Learning Disabilities; $25 per computerized Quick Score (DOS); $149 per computerized manual (DOS).
Time: (15–20) minutes.
Comments: Ratings by teacher; the 1996 edition is renormed but content is not revised.
Authors: Stephen B. McCarney (test and manual) and Angela Marie Bauer (manual).
Publisher: Hawthorne Educational Services, Inc.
Cross References: For reviews by Patricia B. Keith and Loraine J. Spenciner, see 14:207; for reviews by Glen P. Aylward and Scott W. Brown or an earlier edition, see 12:214 (1 reference).

[1400]
Learning Efficiency Test-II (1992 Revision).

Purpose: "Yields information about a person's preferred modality for learning and provides insights about the impact of interference on memory storage and retrieval, and the kinds of metacognitive strategies used during learning."
Population: Ages 5–75.
Publication Dates: 1981–1992.
Acronym: LET-II.
Scores, 15: Visual Ordered Recall (Immediate Recall, Short Term Recall, Long Term Recall) Visual Unordered Recall (Immediate Recall, Short Term Recall, Long Term Recall), Auditory Ordered Recall (Immediate Recall, Short Term Recall, Long Term Recall), Auditory Unordered Recall (Immediate Recall, Short Term Recall, Long Term Recall), Total Visual Memory, Total Auditory Memory, Global Memory.
Administration: Individual.
Price Data, 2002: $92 per test kit including manual (1992, 159 pages), stimulus cards, and 50 record forms; $40 per specimen set including manual and sample forms.
Time: (10–15) minutes.
Author: Raymond E. Webster.

Publisher: Academic Therapy Publications.
Cross References: See T5:1462 (3 references); for reviews by Alice J. Corkill and Gregory Schraw, see 12:215; see also T4:1423 (1 reference); for a review by Robert G. Harrington of an earlier form, see 9:601.

[1401]
Learning Organization Practices Profile.

Purpose: Designed "to facilitate a diagnostic process by which an organization can measure its capacity as a learning organization."
Population: Organizations.
Publication Date: 1994.
Acronym: LOPP.
Scores, 12: Vision and Strategy, Executive Practices, Managerial Practices, Climate, Organizational and Job Structure, Information Flow, Individual and Team Practices, Work Processes, Performance Goals and Feedback, Training and Education, Rewards and Recognition, Individual and Team Development.
Administration: Group.
Price Data, 1997: $24.95 per set including manual (43 pages) and 1 profile booklet; $7.95 per profile; quantity pricing available.
Time: Administration time not reported.
Author: Michael J. O'Brien.
Publisher: Jossey-Bass, A Wiley Company.
Cross References: For reviews by Neil P. Lewis and Michael J. Zickar, see 14:208.

[1402]
Learning Process Questionnaire.

Purpose: "To assess the extent to which a secondary school student endorses different approaches to learning and the more important motives and strategies comprising those approaches."
Population: Secondary students.
Publication Dates: 1985–1987.
Acronym: LPQ.
Scores, 9: Surface Motive, Surface Strategy, Deep Motive, Deep Strategy, Achieving Motive, Achieving Strategy, Surface Approach, Deep Approach, Achieving Approach.
Administration: Individual or group.
Price Data, 2002: A$11.50 per 10 questionnaires; A$7.69 per 10 answer sheets; A$5.50 per score key; A$34.10 per monograph entitled Student Approaches to Learning and Studying (1987, 151 pages); A$29.80 per manual (1987, 36 pages); A$51.80 per starter set.
Time: 20(40) minutes.
Comments: Tertiary counterpart of the Study Process Questionnaire (2417).
Author: John Biggs.
Publisher: Australian Council for Educational Research Ltd. [Australia].

Cross References: See T5:1466 (9 references); for reviews by Robert D. Brown and Cathy W. Hall, see 11:202 (1 reference); for a review by Cathy W. Hall of the Study Process Questionnaire, see 11:389.

[1403]
Learning Skills Profile.

Purpose: To assess the gap between personal aptitudes and critical skills required by a job.
Population: Junior high to adults.
Publication Date: 1993.
Acronym: LSP.
Scores, 36: 3 scores: Personal Learning Skill, Job Skill Demand, and Learning Gap in each of 12 skill areas: Interpersonal Skills (Leadership Skill, Relationship Skill, Help Skill), Analytical Skills (Theory Skill, Quantitative Skill, Technology Skill), Information Skills (Sense-Making Skill, Information-Gathering Skill, Information Analysis Skill), Behavioral Skills (Goal Setting Skill, Action Skill, Initiative Skill).
Administration: Group or individual.
Price Data, 2001: $50 per complete kit including 10 workbooks and profiles, and 1 set of reusable LSP cards and instructions; $40 per 10 workbooks; $15 per reusable LSP cards, instructions, and profiles; also available online at $10 per person.
Time: [45–60] minutes.
Comments: Self-scored profile.
Authors: Richard E. Boyatzis and David A. Kolb.
Publisher: Hay Group.
Cross References: See T5:1467 (1 reference); for a review by David O. Herman, see 13:179.

[1404]
Learning Style Inventory [Price Systems, Inc.].

Purpose: Identifies "the conditions under which an individual is most likely to learn, remember, and achieve."
Population: Grades 3–12.
Publication Dates: 1976–1996.
Acronym: LSI.
Scores: 22 areas: Noise Level, Light, Temperature, Design, Motivation, Persistent, Responsible, Structure, Learning Alone/Peer Oriented, Authority Figures Present, Learn in Several Ways, Auditory, Visual, Tactile, Kinesthetic, Requires Intake, Evening/Morning, Late Morning, Afternoon, Needs Mobility, Parent Figure Motivated, Teacher Motivated, plus a Consistency score.
Administration: Group.
Price Data, 2001: $22.50 per 10 answer sheets for grades 3 & 4 or for grade 5 (includes scoring); $7.50 or less per group and subscale summaries available from publisher only in addition to individual profiles; $.40 per individual interpretive booklet; $12.50 per manual (1997, 100 pages); $3.25 per research report; $395 per computerized self-administered inventory program with 100 administrations ($60 per 100 additional administrations) (PC); $495 per Scan Win program permitting schools to scan and profile forms on site; $.60 per answer form to use with Scan Win.
Time: (20–30) minutes.
Comments: IBM or IBM-compatible computer required for (optional) computerized administration; 3000, NCS, OPScan 5, Scrantron 8000, 8200, 8400, or Scanning System 380 scanner required for (optional) Scan Win.
Authors: Rita Dunn, Kenneth Dunn, and Gary E. Price.
Publisher: Price Systems, Inc.
Cross References: See T5:1470 (5 references); for reviews by Thomas R. Knapp and Craig S. Shwery, see 13:180 (9 references); see also T4:1432 (3 references); for reviews by Jan N. Hughes and Alida S. Westman of an earlier edition, see 11:203 (6 references).

[1405]
Learning Style Inventory, Version 3.

Purpose: Designed to describe the ways an individual learns and deals with day-to-day situations.
Population: Ages 18–60.
Publication Dates: 1976–2000.
Acronym: LSI3.
Scores: 4 scores: Concrete Experience, Active Experimentation, Reflective Observation, Abstract Conceptualization; 4 learning styles: Accommodating, Diverging, Converging, Assimilating.
Administration: Group or individual.
Price Data, 2001: $79 per 10 self-scoring booklets; $50 per facilitator's guide to learning (2000, 81 pages); $38 per 15 transparancies; also available online at $15 per person.
Foreign Language Editions: French and Spanish versions available.
Time: [20–30] minutes.
Author: David A. Kolb.
Publisher: Hay Group.
Cross References: See T5:1469 (13 references) and T4:1438 (12 references); for a review by Noel Gregg of an earlier edition, see 10:173 (17 references); see also 9:607 (7 references).

[1406]
Learning Style Profile.

Purpose: Designed to evaluate student learning style as the basis for student advisement and placement, instructional strategy, and the evaluation of learning.
Population: Grades 6–12.
Publication Dates: 1986–1990.
Acronym: LSP.
Scores, 23: Cognitive Skills (Analytic, Spatial, Discrimination, Categorizing, Sequential Processing,

Memory), Perceptual Responses (Visual, Auditory, Emotive), Persistence Orientation, Verbal Risk Orientation, Study and Instructional Preferences (Verbal-Spatial, Manipulative, Study Time [Early Morning, Late Morning, Afternoon, Evening], Grouping, Posture, Mobility, Sound, Lighting, Temperature).
Administration: Group.
Foreign Language Edition: Spanish version available.
Price Data, 1998: $8 per sampler kit including one each of profile, answer sheet, and examiner's manual; $40 per 35 profiles with examiner's manual; $7 per 35 answer sheets (specify NCS, Scantron, or Scantron 8000); $7 per examiner's manual; $20 per technical manual (1988, 105 pages); $40 per 35 Spanish version profiles with Sapnish instruction sheet and examiner's manual; $7 per 35 Spanish answer sheets (specify NCS, Scantron, or Scantron 8000); $275 per scoring software package and user's manual (available on Macintosh 3.5-inch disk, IBM/Windows 3.5-inch disk, IBM/MS-DOS 3.5-inch disk, Fortran tape, Fortran disk, or Windows 2-disk student computer keyboard scoring).
Time: (50–60) minutes.
Authors: James W. Keefe (test, Handbook II), John S. Monk (test), Charles A. Letteri (test, Handbook I), Marlin Languis (test), Rita Dunn (test), John M. Jenkins (Handbook I), and Patricia Rosenlund (Handbook I).
Publisher: National Association of Secondary School Principals.
Cross References: For reviews by Sonya Blixt and James A. Jones and Philip Nagy, see 12:217 (1 reference); see also T4:1433 (1 reference).

[1407]
Learning Style Questionnaire.

Purpose: Developed to "help individuals measure their preferences for learning."
Population: Adults.
Publication Date: 1999.
Acronym: LSQ.
Scores, 4: Participation, Reflecting, Structuring, Experiencing.
Administration: Group.
Price Data, 2001: $6.50 per questionnaire; $29.95 per leader's guide (24 pages).
Time: (20–30) minutes.
Author: Chris Hutcheson.
Publisher: Human Resource Development Press.

[1408]
Learning Styles Inventory [Creative Learning Press, Inc.].

Purpose: "Designed to measure student attitudes toward nine general modes of instruction."
Population: Grades 4–12 and teachers.
Publication Date: 1978.

Acronym: LSI.
Scores: 9 factor scores: Projects, Drill and Recitation, Peer Teaching, Discussion, Teaching Games, Independent Study, Programmed Instruction, Lecture, Simulation.
Administration: Group.
Forms, 2: Student, Teacher.
Price Data: Availalbe from publisher.
Time: (30) minutes.
Comments: "A measure of student preference for instructional techniques."
Authors: Joseph S. Renzulli and Linda H. Smith.
Publisher: Creative Learning Press, Inc.
Cross References: See T5:1474 (2 references) and T4:1435 (1 reference); for a review by Benson P. Low, see 9:608.

[1409]
Learning Styles Inventory [Educational Activities, Inc.].

Purpose: Designed to assess an individual's learning style of receiving and expressing information.
Population: Intermediate and secondary level students.
Publication Date: 1993.
Acronym: LSI.
Scores, 9: Visual Language, Visual Numeric, Auditory Language, Auditory Numeric, Tactile Concrete, Social Individual, Social Group, Oral Expressiveness, Written Expressiveness.
Administration: Group.
Price Data, 2001: $98 per 2 CD-ROM, management, and documentation; $588 per site license.
Foreign Language Editions: Available in English and Spanish with audio.
Time: Administration time not reported.
Comments: Pencil-and-paper or computer (Apple/MS-DOS/Windows/Mac) administered.
Authors: Jerry F. Brown and Richard M. Cooper.
Publisher: Educational Activities Software.
Cross References: For reviews by Robert Brown and Robert J. Drummond, see 14:209.

[1410]
Learning Styles Inventory [Piney Mountain Press, Inc.].

Purpose: Designed to identify learning needs of students.
Population: Grades 6–12.
Publication Dates: 1988–2000.
Scores: 9 subtopics in 2 areas: Learning (Auditory Language, Visual Language, Auditory Numerical, Visual Numerical, Auditory-Visual-Kinesthetic), Working (Group Learner, Individual Learner, Oral Expressive, Written Expressive).
Administration: Individual or group.

Price Data, 2002: $195 per single station software; $395 per multistation software including instructor guide, software, multimedia CD, video, and response sheets; $995 for Network version.
Time: [11] minutes.
Author: Al Babich.
Publisher: Piney Mountain Press, Inc.
Cross References: For reviews by Kevin D. Crehan and Mark H. Fugate, see 12:218.

[1411]
Learning Tactics Inventory.
Purpose: "Provides … individuals with information about how they learn and illustrates behaviors that they can adopt to become more versatile learners."
Population: Managers, leaders, executives.
Publication Date: 1999.
Acronym: LTI.
Scores: 4 learning tactics: Action, Thinking, Feeling, Accessing Others.
Administration: Group.
Price Data, 2002: $27 per Facilitator's Guide (41 pages); $14 per Participant's Workbook/Survey; quantity discounts available.
Time: 15 minutes.
Comments: An inventory of the behaviors individuals have reported using when engaged in the task of learning from experience; self-scored; Facilitator's Guide includes details of workshop procedures, reproducible overheads, and handout masters.
Author: Maxine Dalton.
Publisher: Center for Creative Leadership.

[1412]
Learning/Working Styles Inventory.
Purpose: "Developed to assess learning styles and preferred working conditions."
Population: Grades 7–12 and adults.
Publication Date: 1989–2000.
Scores: 25 subtopics in 5 areas: Physical Domain (Kinesthetic, Visual, Tactile, Auditory), Social Domain (Group, Individual), Environmental Domain (Formal Design, Informal Design, Bright Lights, Dim Lights, Warm Temperature, Cool Temperature, With Sound, Without Sound), Mode of Expression Domain (Oral Expressive, Written Expressive), Work Characteristics Domain (Outdoors, Indoors, Sedentary, Non-Sedentary, Lifting, Non-Lifting, Data, People, Things).
Administration: Group and individual.
Price Data, 2002: $195 per single station software, $395 per multistation software including instructor guide, software, multimedia CD, video, and response sheets; $995 for Network version.
Time: [15] minutes.
Comments: Previously entitled Vocational Learning Styles.

Author: Helena Hendrix-Frye.
Publisher: Piney Mountain Press, Inc.
Cross References: For reviews by Leo M. Harvill and Craig N. Mills of the earlier edition, see 12:410.

[1413]
Leatherman Leadership Questionnaire [Revised].
Purpose: "To aid in selecting leaders, providing specific feedback to participants on their leadership knowledge for career counseling, conducting accurate needs analysis, and screening for assessment centers or giving pre/post assessment feedback."
Population: Managers, supervisors, team leaders, and potential leaders.
Publication Dates: 1987–1992.
Acronym: LLQ.
Scores, 28: Assigning Work, Career Counseling, Coaching Employees, Oral Communication, Managing Change, Handling Employee Complaints, Dealing with Employee Conflicts, Counseling Employees, Helping an Employee Make Decisions, Delegating, Taking Disciplinary Action, Handling Emotional Situations, Setting Goals/Planning with Employees, Handling Employee Grievances, Conducting Employee Meetings, Giving Positive Feedback, Negotiating, Conducting Performance Appraisals, Establishing Performance Standards, Persuading/Influencing Employees, Making Presentations to Employees, Problem Solving with Employees, Conducting Selection Interviews, Team Building, Conducting Termination Interviews, Helping an Employee Manage Time, One-on-One Training, Total.
Subtests, 2: May be administered in separate parts.
Administration: Group.
Price Data, 2002: $1,500 per administrator's kit including administrator's manual (1992, 52 pages), overhead transparencies, 10 sets of reusable questionnaire booklets, and 10 sets of answer sheets with scoring service; $65 per additional answer sheets and scoring service including development manual (1992, 347 pages); $55 per additional answer sheets and scoring service; $20 per additional sets of questionnaire booklets; $1 each for "confidential service" (participant's scoring sheet sealed in an envelope), $100 per extra administrator's kit; testing materials and service will be provided without charge for qualified, not-for-profit college or university research.
Time: (300–325) minutes for battery; (150–165) minutes per part.
Comments: Complete test administered in 2 parts; machine scored by publisher.
Author: Richard W. Leatherman.
Publisher: International Training Consultants, Inc.
Cross References: For reviews by Jeffrey S. Rain and Lawrence M. Rudner, see 12:219; for reviews by

Walter Katkovsky and William D. Porterfield of an earlier edition, see 11:205.

[1414]
Leatherman Leadership Questionnaire: 360 Degree Leadership Profile.

Purpose: "To provide specific feedback to individuals, groups, and organizations about their leadership behaviors."
Population: Leaders, managers, supervisors, team leaders, potential leaders, supervisors, and executives.
Publication Dates: 1987–1996.
Acronym: LLQ-360.
Scores, 28: Assigning Work, Career Counseling, Coaching Employees, One-on-One Oral Communication, Managing Change, Handling Employee Complaints, Dealing with Employee Conflicts, Counseling on Attendance, Performance and Work Habits, Helping an Employee Make Decisions, Delegating, Taking Disciplinary Action, Handling Emotional Situations, Setting Goals and Objectives and Planning with Employees, Handling Employee Grievances, Conducting Employee Meetings, Giving Positive Feedback, Negotiating, Conducting Performance Appraisals, Establishing Performance Standards, Persuading/Influencing Employees, Making Presentations to Employees, Problem Solving with Employees, Conducting Selection Interviews, Team Building, Conducting Termination Interviews, Helping an Employee Manage Time, One-on-One Training, Total.
Administration: Group.
Price Data, 2002: $1,500 per Basic LLQ 360 Degree administrator's kit including administrator's manual (1996, 207 pages), overhead transparencies (43), rater's booklets, 10 answer sheets for participants, 50 answer sheets for "others," scoring service for 10 participants which includes group summary reports in hardcopy and overhead transparencies, development manual (1992, 365 pages), and self-development action planner; $75 per additional answer sheets and scoring service with development manual; $55 per additional answer sheets and scoring service without development manual; $5 per additional answer sheet for "Others"; $10 per additional rater's booklet (1996, 24 pages); $10 per self-development action planners (1996, 16 pages); $29.95 per additional self-development manual; $750 per additional administrator's kit (no scoring service).
Time: (30) minutes.
Comments: Machine-scored by publisher; related to but separate from the Leatherman Leadership Questionnaire (1413).
Author: Richard W. Leatherman.
Publisher: International Training Consultants, Inc.
Cross References: For reviews by Claudia J. Morner and William Verdi, see 14:210.

[1415]
Leeds Scales for the Self-Assessment of Anxiety and Depression.

Purpose: Self-assessment measure of the severity of symptoms of clinical anxiety and depression.
Population: Psychiatric patients.
Publication Date: 1976.
Scores, 4: Depression (General, Specific), Anxiety (General, Specific).
Administration: Group or individual.
Price Data: Available from publisher.
Time: Administration time not reported.
Comments: Self-rating scale.
Authors: R. P. Smith, G. W. K. Bridge, and Max Hamilton.
Publisher: Psychological Test Publications [England] [No reply from publisher; status unknown].
Cross References: See T5:1481 (4 references) and T4:1440 (11 references); for reviews by John Duckitt and H. J. Eysenck, see 9:611 (4 references).

[1416]
Leisure Interest Inventory.

Purpose: Designed to assess "preferred leisure activities."
Population: College students.
Publication Date: 1969.
Acronym: LII.
Scores, 5: Sociability, Games, Art, Mobility, Immobility.
Administration: Group.
Price Data: Available from publisher.
Time: (20-25) minutes.
Author: Edwina E. Hubert.
Publisher: Edwina E. Hubert, Ph.D.

[1417]
Leisure to Occupations Connection Search.

Purpose: Designed to allow the user to explore career options based on leisure-time interests.
Population: Seventh-grade students through adults.
Publication Date: 1998.
Acronym: LOCS.
Scores: Scores interests in 100 leisure activities.
Administration: Individual.
Manual: No manual.
Price Data, 2001: $29.95 per 25 inventories.
Time: (45) minutes.
Comments: Lists related occupations for each leisure activity; 12-panel foldout; self-scoring and self-interpreting; consumable; no other components needed.
Authors: Carl McDaniels and Sue Mullins.
Publisher: JIST Publishing, Inc.

[1418]
Leisure/Work Search Inventory.
Purpose: To help identify employment opportunities related to their leisure interests.
Population: High school students through adults.
Publication Date: 1994.
Acronym: LSI.
Scores: 12 occupational clusters: Artistic, Scientific, Plants and Animals, Protective, Mechanical, Industrial, Business Detail, Selling, Accommodating, Humanitarian, Leading-Influencing, Physical Performing.
Administration: Group.
Manual: No manual.
Price Data, 2001: $2.95 per 25 copies.
Time: [30] minutes.
Comments: Self-administered and self-scored; previously listed as Leisure Search Inventory.
Author: John J. Liptak.
Publisher: JIST Publishing, Inc.
Cross References: For reviews by Leo M. Harvill and Ellen Weissinger, see 13:181.

[1419]
Leiter International Performance Scale—Revised.
Purpose: Constructed as a "nonverbal cognitive assessment."
Population: Ages 2.0–20.11, adults.
Publication Dates: 1936–1998.
Acronym: Leiter-R.
Scores, 31: Visualization and Reasoning (Figure Ground, Design Analogies, Form Completion, Matching, Sequential Order, Repeated Patterns, Picture Context, Classification, Paper Folding, Figure Rotation), VR Composite (Fluid Reasoning, Brief IQ, Fundamental Visualization, Spatial Visualization, Full IQ), Attention and Memory Associated Pairs, Immediate Recognition, Forward Memory, Attention Sustained, Reverse Memory, Visual Coding, Spatial Memory, Delayed Pairs, Delayed Recognition, Attention Divided), AM Composite (Memory Screen, Associative Memory, Memory Span, Attention, Memory Process, Recognition Memory).
Administration: Individual.
Price Data, 2001: $850 per complete kit (in cloth carrying case) including manual (1997, 378 pages), 3 easel books, VR response cards, AM response cards, manipulatives, 20 each VR and AM record forms, Attention Sustained booklets A, B, and C, and the Growth Profile Booklet and the rating scales; $25 per 20 record forms (specify battery); $15 per 20 Attention Sustained booklets (specify form); $10 per 20 rating scale record forms (specify form); $25 per 20 Growth Profile booklets, $75 per manual.
Time: (90) minutes.

Comments: May calculate growth scores (criterion-referenced scores) to assess improvement in cognitive skills; computer scoring software available requiring Windows 3.1, Windows 95 or Windows 98 operating systems.
Authors: Gale H. Roid and Lucy J. Miller.
Publisher: Stoelting Co.
Cross References: For reviews by Gary L. Marco and Terry A. Stinnett, see 14:211; see also T5:1485 (64 references), T4:1446 (33 references), T3:1319 (16 references), and T2:505 (18 references); for a review by Emmy E. Werner of the original version, see 6:526 (10 references); see also 5:408 (17 references); for a review by Gwen F. Arnold and an excerpted review by Laurance F. Shaffer, see 4:349 (25 references).

[1420]
Level of Service Inventory—Revised: Screening Version.
Purpose: Designed to provide "a risk/needs assessment important to offender treatment planning."
Population: Ages 16 and older.
Publication Date: 1998.
Acronym: LSI-R:SV.
Scores: Total score only.
Administration: Individual.
Price Data, 2002: $85 per complete kit including 25 interview guides, 25 QuikScore™ forms, and manual (1998, 26 pages); $50 per 25 interview guides/QuikScore™ forms; $22 per 25 interview guides; $37 per 25 QuikScore™ forms; $40 per manual; $45 per specimen set including 3 interview guides, 3 QuikScore™ forms, and manual; computer version also available.
Time: (10–15) minutes.
Authors: Don Andrews and James Bonta.
Publisher: Multi-Health Systems, Inc.

[1421]
The Level of Service Inventory—Revised.
Purpose: Constructed as "a quantitative survey of attributes of offenders and their situations relevant to level of supervision and treatment decisions."
Population: Ages 16 and older.
Publication Date: 1995.
Acronym: LSI-R.
Scores: Total score only.
Administration: Individual.
Price Data, 2002: $130 per complete kit including manual (53 oages), 25 interview guides, 25 QuikScore™ forms, and 25 ColorPlot profiles; $60 per 25 interview guides; $35 per 25 QuikScore™ forms; $18 per 25 ColorPlot profiles; $45 per manual; $55 per specimen set including manual, 3 interview guides, 3 QuikScore™ forms, and 3 ColorPlot profiles.
Time: (30–45) minutes.

Foreign Language Editions: Spanish guides and forms available; information for French-Canadian version available from publisher.

Comments: Ratings by probation officers, parole officers, and/or correctional workers to provide a comprehensive risk/needs assessment important to offender treatment planning; Windows™ computerized version available on CD or 3.5-inch disk.

Authors: D. A. Andrews and James L. Bonta.

Publisher: Multi-Health Systems, Inc.

Cross References: For reviews by Solomon M. Fulero and Romeo Vitelli, see 14:212.

[1422]
Levine-Pilowsky [Depression] Questionnaire.

Purpose: A questionnaire technique for classifying depression.

Population: Adults.

Publication Date: 1979.

Acronym: LPD.

Scores: 9 subscales: Insomnia (Initial), Sleep (General), Paranoia, Appetite, Insomnia (Late), Crying, Diurnal Variation, Hopelessness, Intensity of Depression.

Administration: Individual or group.

Manual: No manual.

Price Data: Available from publisher.

Time: (10) minutes.

Author: I. Pilowsky.

Publisher: I. Pilowsky [South Australia].

Cross References: See T4:1448 (3 references).

[1423]
Lewis Counselling Inventory.

Purpose: Designed as an "instrument for identifying those pupils most in need of guidance and counselling."

Population: Adolescents in school.

Publication Date: 1978.

Scores, 8: Relationship With Teachers, Relationship With Family, Irritability, Social Confidence, Relationship With Peers, Health, Total, Lie Scale.

Administration: Group.

Parts, 2: 1, 2 (optional supplementary questionnaire).

Price Data: Price information available from publisher for inventories (Part 1), questionnaires (Part 2), 6 keys, manual (29 pages), and specimen set; automated version available.

Time: (10–15) minutes for each part.

Authors: D. G. Lewis and P. D. Pumfrey.

Publisher: NFER-Nelson Publishing Co., Ltd. [England].

Cross References: For reviews by Deborah N. Bauserman and Gerald L. Stone, see 9:614.

[1424]
Lexington Developmental Scales.

Purpose: To "provide an individual graph or profile which depicts the child's developmental age level."

Population: Ages birth–6 years.

Publication Dates: 1973–1977.

Acronym: LDS.

Scores: Contains behavioral and experimental items rated by examiner in 4 areas: Motor, Language, Cognitive, Personal and Social.

Administration: Individual administration to ages birth-2 years.

Price Data: Not available.

Time: (60) minutes in children birth-2 years; time varies for older children.

Comments: Long and Short Forms; may be used by parents and volunteers; "particularly helpful in pre- and post-testing"; additional testing materials must be supplied by the examiner.

Authors: United Cerebral Palsy of the Bluegrass, John V. Irwin, Margaret Norris Ward, Ann B. Greis, Carol C. Deen, Valerie C. Cooley, Alice A. Auvenshine, Rhea A. Taylor, C. A. Coleman.

Publisher: Child Development Centers of the Bluegrass, Inc. [No reply from publisher; status unknown].

Cross References: See T5:1490 (2 references) and T4:1450 (1 reference); for reviews by Michael J. Roznowski and Zona R. Weeks, see 9:615 (1 reference); see also T3:1322 (1 reference).

[1425]
The Life Adjustment Inventory.

Purpose: Developed to survey "the extent to which a secondary school curriculum meets the needs of all its pupils."

Population: Grades 9–12.

Publication Date: 1951.

Scores, 14: General Feeling of Adjustment to the Curriculum, Reading and Study Skills, Communication and Listening Skills, General Social Skills and Etiquette, Boy-Girl Relationships, Religion/Morals/Ethics, Functional Citizenship, Vocational Orientation and Preparation, Education for Physical and Mental Health, Education for Family Living, Orientation to Science, Consumer Education, Development of Appreciation for and Creativity in the Arts, Education for Wise Use of Leisure Time.

Administration: Group.

Price Data: Available from publisher.

Time: (20–25) minutes.

Authors: Ronald C. Doll and J. Wayne Wrightstone.

Publisher: Psychometric Affiliates.

Cross References: See P:145 (1 reference); for reviews by John W. M. Rothney and Helen Schacter, see 4:67.

[1426]
Life Stressors and Social Resources Inventory—Adult Form.

Purpose: "Provides an integrated picture of an individual's current life context" including "stable life stressors and social resources."

Population: Healthy adults, psychiatric patients, and medical patients.

Publication Dates: 1988–1994.

Acronym: LISRES-A.

Scores: 16 scales: 9 Life Stressor Scales (Physical Health, Home/Neighborhood, Financial, Work, Spouse or Partner, Children, Extended Family, Friends, Negative Life Events); 7 Social Resources Scales (Financial, Work, Spouse or Partner, Children, Extended Family, Friends, Positive Life Events).

Administration: Individual or group.

Price Data: Available from publisher for complete kit including manual (1994, 40 pages), 10 reusable item booklets, and 25 handscorable answer/profile forms.

Time: [10] minutes.

Comments: May be administered using either a self-report or a structured interview format.

Authors: Rudolf H. Moos (instrument and manual) and Bernice S. Moos (manual).

Publisher: Psychological Assessment Resources, Inc.

Cross References: See T5:1495 (1 reference); for reviews by M. Allan Cooperstein and Richard B. Stuart, see 13:184 (1 reference).

[1427]
Life Stressors and Social Resources Inventory—Youth Form.

Purpose: "Provides an integrated picture of a youth's current life context ... assesses stable life stressors and social resources as well as changes in them over time."

Population: Ages 12–18.

Publication Dates: 1990–1994.

Acronym: LISRES-Y.

Scores, 16: 9 Life Stressors Scales (Physical Health, Home and Money, Parents, Siblings, Extended Family, School, Friends, Boyfriend/Girlfriend, Negative Life Events); 7 Social Resources Scales (Parents, Siblings, Extended Family, School, Friends, Boyfriend/Girlfriend, Positive Life Events).

Administration: Individual or Group.

Editions, 2: Youth, Adult.

Price Data: Available from publisher for introductory kit including manual (1994, 38 pages), 10 item booklets, and 25 profile forms.

Time: (45) minutes for self-report; (45–90) minutes for structured interview.

Comments: Available as self-report or structured interview; structured interview "allows an interviewer to use the inventory with youths whose reading and comprehension skills are below a sixth-grade level."

Authors: Rudolf H. Moos and Bernice S. Moos.

Publisher: Psychological Assessment Resources, Inc.

Cross References: See T5:1496 (1 reference); for reviews by Kevin D. Crehan and Albert Oosterhof, see 13:185 (1 reference).

[1428]
Life Style Questionnaire.

Purpose: To provide information regarding vocational interests and attitudes.

Population: Ages 14 and over.

Publication Date: No date on test materials.

Acronym: LSQ.

Scores: 13 scales: Expressive/Imaginative, Logical/Analytical, Managerial/Enterprising, Precise/Administrative, Active/Concrete, Supportive/Social, Risk Taking/Uncertainty, Perseverance/Determination, Self Evaluation, Sensitivity/Other Awareness, Affiliation, Degree to Which a Vocation is Associated with Self Fulfillment, Degree of Certainty.

Administration: Group or individual.

Price Data, 2001: £35 per specimen set; £4 per answer sheet and graph; £6.50 per questionnaire booklet; £25 per manual (26 pages); £459 per computer software version.

Time: Administration time not reported.

Author: James S. Barrett.

Publisher: The Test Agency Limited [England].

Cross References: For a review by Robert B. Slaney, see 9:169.

[1429]
Life Styles Inventory.

Purpose: Designed to assess an individual's thinking and behavioral styles.

Population: Adults.

Publication Dates: 1973–1990.

Acronym: LSI.

Administration: Individual.

Price Data: Price data for test materials including Leader's Guide (1989, 211 pages), Self-Development Guide (1989, 75 pages), and Description by Others Self-Development Guide (1990, 123 pages) available from publisher.

Time: (20-25) minutes.

Author: J. Clayton Lafferty.

Publisher: Human Synergistics International.

a) LSI1: LIFE STYLES INVENTORY (SELF DESCRIPTION).

Scores, 12: Constructive Styles (Achievement, Self-Actualizing, Humanistic-Encouraging, Affiliative), Passive/Defensive Styles (Approval, Conventional, Dependent, Avoidance), Aggressive/Defensive Styles (Oppositional, Power, Competitive, Perfectionistic).

b) LSI2: LIFE STYLES INVENTORY (DESCRIPTION BY OTHERS).

Scores, 12: Same as for *a* above.

Comments: Administered to manager and 4 or 5 others.

Cross References: For reviews by Gregory J. Boyle and Patricia Schoenrade, see 12:222; see also T4:1459 (6 references); for reviews by Henry M. Cherrick and Linda M. DuBois, see 9:620 (1 reference).

[1430]
Lifestyle Assessment Questionnaire.

Purpose: Provides individuals with a measurement of their lifestyle status in various wellness categories, offers a health risk appraisal component that lists the individual's top ten risks of death, projects an achievable health age, makes suggestions for lifestyle improvement, and offers a stimulus for positive lifestyle change by providing a guide to successful implementation of that change.

Population: Adults ages 18–60 with a minimum of 12th grade education.

Publication Dates: 1978–1989.

Scores, 16: Physical (Exercise, Nutrition, Self-Care, Vehicle Safety, Drug Usage), Social/Environmental, Emotional (Emotional Awareness and Acceptance, Emotional Management), Intellectual, Occupational, Spiritual, Actual Age, Appraised Health Age, Achievable Health Age, Top 10 Risks of Death, Lifestyle Improvement Suggestions.

Administration: Group.

Price Data, 1998: $10 per individual National Wellness Processing Center scoring; $50 per group report.

Time: (45–60) minutes.

Comments: Scoring by National Wellness Institute; information on up to four wellness areas included in scoring report; individual and group reports available.

Authors: Dennis Elsenrath, Bill Hettler, and Fred Leafgren.

Publisher: National Wellness Institute, Inc.

Cross References: For reviews by Michael B. Brown and William E. Martin, Jr., see 13:186 (3 references); see also T4:1461 (3 references).

[1431]
Light's Retention Scale [Revised Edition 1998].

Purpose: Aids the school professional in determining whether the student would benefit from grade retention.

Population: Grades K–12.

Publication Dates: 1981–1998.

Acronym: LRS.

Scores, 20: Sex of Student, Student's Age, Knowledge of English Language, Physical Size, Present Grade Placement, Previous Grade Retentions, Siblings, Parents' School Participation, Experiential Background, Transiency, School Attendance, Estimate of Intelligence, History of Learning Disabilities, Present Level of Academic Achievement, Student's Attitude About Possible Retention, Motivation to Complete School Tasks, Immature Behavior, Emotional Problems, History of Delinquency, Total.

Administration: Individual.

Price Data, 2002: $85 per complete test kit including manual (1991, 78 pages), 50 recording forms, and 50 parent guides; $32 per manual; $25 per 50 recording forms; $25 per 50 parent guides; $20 per 25 parent consent forms; $32 per specimen set.

Time: (10–15) minutes.

Comments: Ratings by teachers and parents; a nonpsychometric instrument used as a counseling tool with a specific retention candidate.

Author: H. Wayne Light.

Publisher: Academic Therapy Publications.

Cross References: For reviews by Bruce K. Alcorn and Frederic J. Medway, see 11:208 (2 references); for reviews by Michael J. Hannafin and Patti L. Harrison of an earlier edition, see 9:622; see also T3:1328 (1 reference).

[1432]
The Lincoln-Oseretsky Motor Development Scale.

Purpose: "Designed to test the motor ability of children."

Population: Ages 6–14.

Publication Dates: 1948-1956.

Scores: Total score only.

Administration: Individual.

Price Data, 2001: $235 per complete kit including 50 record blanks and manual (1948, 79 pages); $20 per 50 record blanks; $20 per 50 mazes; $20 per 50 concentric circles; $25 per manual.

Time: Administration time not reported.

Comments: Revision of Oseretsky Tests of Motor Proficiency.

Author: William Sloan.

Publisher: Stoelting Co.

Cross References: See T4:1464 (5 references), T3:1331 (5 references), and T2:1895 (27 references); for a review by Anna Espenschade, see 5:767 (10 references).

[1433]
Lindamood Auditory Conceptualization Test, Revised Edition.

Purpose: "To discriminate one speech sound or phoneme from another and segment a spoken word into its constituent phonemic units."

Population: All ages.

Publication Dates: 1971–1979.
Acronym: LAC.
Scores, 3: Isolated Sounds in Sequence, Sounds Within a Syllable Pattern, Total.
Administration: Individual.
Forms, 2: A, B.
Price Data, 2001: $98 per complete kit including 50 each of tests A and B, 2 examiner's cue sheets (English and Spanish), 24 wooden blocks, cassette, and manual (1971, 80 pages); $29 per 50 each of tests A and B; $24 per block kit.
Time: (10-35) minutes.
Comments: No reading by examinees.
Authors: Charles H. Lindamood and Patricia C. Lindamood.
Publisher: PRO-ED.
Cross References: See T5:1503 (16 references) and T4:1465 (2 references); for reviews by Nicholas G. Bountress and James R. Cox, see 9:623 (1 reference).

[1434]
Linguistic Awareness in Reading Readiness.

Purpose: Designed for determining individual strengths and weaknesses "with regard to their understanding of the linguistic concepts that they need for reasoning about the tasks of reading instruction."
Population: Grades K–1.
Publication Date: 1983.
Acronym: LARR.
Scores: Total scores only.
Administration: Group.
Forms, 2: A, B.
Parts, 3: Recognizing Literacy Behaviour, Understanding Literacy Functions, Technical Language of Literacy.
Price Data: Price information available from publisher for 10 booklets and 1 class record form for Part 1, Form A or B, 10 booklets and 1 class record form for Parts 2 or 3, Form A or B, class record forms for Parts 1, 2, and 3, manual (36 pages), and specimen set including 1 each of the 3 Form A booklets, the 3 Form B booklets, the 3 record forms, and manual).
Time: (20–25) minutes for each part.
Authors: John Downing, Douglas Ayers, and Brian Schaefer.
Publisher: NFER-Nelson Publishing Co., Ltd. [England].
Cross References: See T4:1466 (3 references).

[1435]
Listen Up: Skills Assessment.

Purpose: Designed to measure listening comprehension, interpretation, and ability to follow directions.
Population: Grades 7–12 and adults.
Publication Dates: 1985–1995.

Scores, 6: Evaluating Message Content, Understanding Meaning in Conversations, Understanding and Remembering Lectures, Evaluating Emotional Meanings in Messages, Following Instructions and Directions, Total.
Administration: Group.
Price Data, 1998: $295 per one-day program including facilitator's guide (1995, 48 pages), two 40-minute videos (Forms A and B), and 25 answer sheets (Forms A and B); $195 per half-day program including facilitator's guide (1995, 32 pages), one 20-minute video, and 25 answer sheets; $24.95 per 25 answer sheets (Forms A or B).
Time: [40–80] minutes.
Authors: Kittie W. Watson and Larry L. Barker.
Publisher: Jossey-Bass, A Wiley Company.
Cross References: For reviews by Cleborne D. Maddux and Sandra J. Wanner, see 14:213.

[1436]
Listening Comprehension Test.

Purpose: To estimate a student's ability to comprehend orally presented basic English structures.
Population: Nonnative speakers of English who wish to pursue academic work at universities where English is the medium of instruction.
Publication Dates: 1972–1986.
Acronym: LCT.
Scores: Total score only.
Administration: Group.
Forms, 3: 4, 5, 6 (equivalent forms).
Price Data, 2002: $70 per complete kit including 20 test booklets, 3 scoring stencils, 100 answer sheets, cassette tape, and manual (17 pages); $5 per 20 test booklets; $10 per scoring stencil; $10 per 100 answer sheets; $20 per cassette; $10 per manual; no charge for specimen set.
Time: 15(20) minutes.
Comments: Created for use as one of the component tests of the former Michigan Battery II.
Authors: J. Upshur, H. Koba, M. Spaan, and L. Strowe.
Publisher: English Language Institute, University of Michigan.
Cross References: See T5:1506 (1 reference); for reviews by James Dean Brown and Phyllis Kuehn, see 12:113.

[1437]
The Listening for Meaning Test.

Purpose: Constructed as a measure of receptive language through the recognition of pictures.
Population: Ages 3-0 to 18-11.
Publication Dates: 1981–2002.
Acronym: LFMT
Scores: Total score only.
Administration: Individual.

Price Data, 2002: £27.50 per complete kit including book of plates, 50 record sheets, and manual (2002, 6 pages); £13.20 per book of plates; £8 per 50 record sheets; £3.50 per manual.
Time: Administration time not reported.
Author: Alan Brimer.
Publisher: Educational Evaluations [England].

[1438]
Listening Practices Feedback Report—360 Degrees.

Purpose: Designed "to provide self-knowledge about a person's listening behaviors at work."
Population: Adults.
Publication Dates: 1987–1999.
Acronym: LPFR-360°.
Scores, 7: Attention, Empathy, Respect, Response, Memory, Open Mind, Overall Listening Practices.
Administration: Individual or group.
Forms, 2: Self, Observer.
Price Data, 2002: $299 per complete packet including administrator's guide (1999, 36 pages), computer disk for compiling data, facilitator's guide (1999, 25 pages), and reproducible participant's guide (1999, 17 pages) and questionnaires; $30 per psychometric properties report (1996, 15 pages); $10 per packet of 1 self questionnaire and 6 observer questionnaires; $50 per 10 questionnaires; discount for dissertations.
Time: Untimed.
Comments: Compares participant's and associates' reports of extent of use of 28 "good listening practices"; may be used as part of a listening training program for workers in business, industry, and government; system requirements: Windows 3.1/95/98.
Authors: Richard C. Brandt (LPFR), Janice D. Brandt (LPFR, "Psychometric Properties of the LPFR"), Victoria Emmert ("Psychometric Properties of the LPFR"), and Philip Emmert ("Psychometric Properties of the LPFR").
Publisher: Brandt Management Group.

[1439]
The Listening Skills Test.

Purpose: Designed to measure "comprehension monitoring and message appraisal."
Population: 3 years 6 months to 6 years 11 months.
Publication Date: 2001.
Acronym: LIST.
Scores: 4 subtests: Referent Identification, Message Appraisal, Comprehension of Directions, Verbal Message Evaluation.
Administration: Individual.
Price Data, 2002: $103.98 per complete test kit including record forms, stimulus manual, and manual (101 pages).
Time: (20–30) minutes.

Authors: Peter Lloyd, Ian Peers, and Caroline Foster.
Publisher: The Psychological Corporation Europe [United Kingdom].

[1440]
Listening Styles Profile.

Purpose: "Designed to identify habitual listening responses and to encourage participants to think about how preference traits might be expressed in actual settings."
Population: Adults.
Publication Date: 1995.
Scores, 4: People Oriented, Action Oriented, Content Oriented, Time Oriented.
Administration: Group.
Price Data, 1998: $19.95 per trainer's package including facilitator's guide (24 pages), profile, and answer sheet; $69.95 per complete kit; quantity discounts available.
Time: (5–10) minutes.
Comments: Can be used to evaluate self or another person.
Authors: Kittee W. Watson and Larry L. Barker.
Publisher: Jossey-Bass, A Wiley Company.
Cross References: For reviews by Mildred Murray-Ward and Sandra Ward, see 14:214.

[1441]
Literature Tests/Objective and Essay.

Purpose: To assess students' literal and interpretive comprehension of over 200 works of contemporary and classical literature.
Population: Middle school and high school.
Publication Dates: 1929–1990.
Scores: Total score only.
Administration: Group.
Manual: No manual.
Price Data, 1994: $2.50 per 50-question test; $3.50 per 100-question test; $3.50 per essay test.
Time: Administration time not reported.
Comments: Over 700 tests on specific literary works; formerly called Book Review Tests and Objective Tests in English.
Author: Perfection Learning Corp.
Publisher: Perfection Learning Corp.

[1442]
Living in the Reader's World: Locator Test.

Purpose: Diagnose nonproficient reader's appropriate starting point in a 4-book adult education reading program.
Population: Adults at reading grade levels 2.0–6.0.
Publication Date: 1983.
Administration: Group.
Price Data: Not available.

Time: Administration time not reported.
Comments: Upward extension of the Maryland/Baltimore County Design for Adult Basic Education (1513).
Author: Cambridge, The Adult Education Co.
Publisher: Prentice Hall [No reply from publisher; status unknown].

[1443]
Living Language.
Purpose: "Remedial teaching programme, concentrating on spoken language, for use with all children who are failing to develop adequate language skills"; includes assessment of prelanguage/language skills for placement in this program.
Population: Language-impaired children.
Publication Date: 1985.
Scores: No scores.
Administration: Individual.
Levels, 3: Pre-Language, Starter, Main Programme.
Manual: No manual.
Price Data: Price information available from publisher for complete kit including general manual (57 pages), subtest manuals (Before Words [31 pages], First Words [16 pages], Putting Words Together [67 pages]), set of 10 record booklets (Pre-Language [8 pages], Starter Programme [8 pages], Main Programme [12 pages]), and assessment pictures (50 pages).
Time: Administration time variable.
Comments: General manual title is Teaching Spoken Language; subtest manual titles are Before Words, First Words, and Putting Words Together; test booklet titles are Pre-Language Record Booklet, Starter Programme Record Booklet, and Main Programme (Level I) Record Booklet; subtests available as separates.
Author: Ann Locke.
Publisher: NFER-Nelson Publishing Co., Ltd. [England].

[1444]
LOCO (Learning Opportunities Coordination): A Scale for the Assessment of Coordinated Learning Opportunities in Living Units for People with a Handicap.
Purpose: Designed "for indicating to what extent a Living Unit for people with handicaps is able to contribute significantly to their social and personal development and to maintain a level of reasonable independence."
Population: Residents of any type of living units where people with a handicap live with the assistance of care givers.
Publication Date: 1987.
Acronym: LOCO.

Scores, 4: Basic Training Conditions, Essential Items, Additional Items, Total.
Administration: Group.
Price Data, 1993: $20 (U.S.) per complete test.
Time: Administration time not reported.
Comments: Can be used in conjunction with P-A-C (Progress Assessment Chart) (2005).
Authors: H. C. Gunzburg and A. L. Gunzburg.
Publisher: SEFA (Publications) Ltd. [England].

[1445]
Loewenstein Occupational Therapy Cognitive Assessment.
Purpose: "A cognitive battery of tests for both primary assessments and ongoing evaluation in the occupational therapy treatment of brain-injured patients."
Population: Ages 6 to 12 and brain-injured adults.
Publication Date: 1990.
Acronym: LOTCA.
Scores: 21 tests in 4 areas: Orientation (Orientation for Place, Orientation for Time), Visual and Spatial Perception (Object Identification, Shapes Identification, Overlapping Figures, Object Constancy, Spatial Perception, Praxis), Visual Motor Organization (Copying Geometric Forms, Reproduction of a Two-Dimensional Model, Pegboard Construction, Colored Block Design, Plain Block Design, Reproduction of a Puzzle, Drawing a Clock), Thinking Operations (Categorization, ROC Unstructured, ROC Structured, Pictorial Sequence A, Pictorial Sequence B, Geometric Sequence).
Administration: Individual.
Price Data, 1993: $198 per complete kit including manual (56 pages), test booklet, and other materials packed in a plastic carrying case.
Time: (30–45) minutes.
Authors: Loewenstein Rehabilitation Hospital; Malka Itzkovich (manual), Betty Elazar (manual), Sarah Averbuch (manual), Naomi Katz (principal researcher), and Levy Rahmani (advisor).
Publisher: Maddak, Inc.
Cross References: For reviews by Elaine Clark and Stephen R. Hooper, see 13:187.

[1446]
Logical Reasoning.
Purpose: Designed to measure sensitivity to logical necessity, consistency and inconsistency, and relationships.
Population: Grades 9–16 and adults.
Publication Date: 1955.
Scores: Total score only.
Administration: Group.
Parts, 2: 1, 2.
Price Data: Available from publisher.
Time: 20(25) minutes.

Comments: Two parallel parts may be administered separately or together.
Authors: Alfred F. Hertzka and J. P. Guilford.
Publisher: Charlotte Mackley [No reply from publisher; status unknown].
Cross References: See T5:1514 (1 reference), T4:1476 (3 references), and T2:1761 (10 references); for reviews by Duncan Howie and Charles R. Langmuir, see 5:694 (1 reference).

[1447]
The Lollipop Test: A Diagnostic Screening Test of School Readiness—Revised.

Purpose: "A screening test to identify the child's deficits (and strengths) in readiness skills."
Population: First grade entrants.
Publication Dates: 1981–2002.
Scores, 5: Identification of Colors and Shapes and Copying Shapes, Picture Description and Position and Spatial Recognition, Identification of Numbers and Counting, Identification of Letters and Writing, Total.
Administration: Individual.
Price Data, 2002: $59.95 per complete kit including 25 test booklets, stimulus cards, and manual (1989, 35 pages); $34.95 per 25 test booklets; $14.95 per set of stimulus cards; $15.95 per manual.
Foreign Language Edition: Available in Spanish.
Time: (15–20) minutes.
Author: Alex L. Chew.
Publisher: Humanics Learning.
Cross References: See T5:1515 (1 reference) and T4:1477 (2 references); for reviews by Sylvia T. Johnson and Albert C. Oosterhof, see 11:210 (5 references); for reviews by Isabel L. Beck and Janet A. Norris of an earlier edition, see 9:629.

[1448]
London Reading Test.

Purpose: Constructed to assess "reading attainment."
Population: Ages 10-7 to 12-4.
Publication Dates: 1978–1980.
Acronym: LRT.
Scores: Total score only.
Administration: Group.
Forms, 2: A, B.
Price Data: Available from publisher.
Time: (60) minutes.
Authors: Margaret Biscoe, Ced Bradshaw, Sheila Clarke, Miles Halliwell, David Morgan, Theresa Nunn, Helen Quigley, and Irene Zelickman.
Publisher: NFER-Nelson Publishing Co., Ltd. [England].
Cross References: See T4:1479 (1 reference); for reviews by Amos L. Hahn and David M. Memory, see 9:632.

[1449]
Looking at MySELF.

Purpose: Designed to help students "build self-esteem."
Population: Grades 3–6, Grades 7–12.
Publication Dates: 1991–1993.
Scores: Total score only.
Administration: Group.
Forms, 2: Form I, Form II.
Price Data: Available from publisher.
Time: (120–180) minutes or in steps in a weekly program.
Author: CFKR Career Materials, Inc.
Publisher: CFKR Career Materials [No reply from publisher; status unknown].

[1450]
Lore Leadership Assessment II.

Purpose: Designed to "measure behaviors, skills, and impacts desirable in a leader."
Population: Adults working in organizations.
Publication Dates: 1998–2001.
Scores, 6: Overall Leadership Effectiveness, Moral Leadership, Intellectual Leadership, Courageous Leadership, Collaborative Leadership, Visionary/Inspirational Leadership.
Administration: Group.
Forms, 2: Self-Assessment, Assessment of Other.
Manual: No manual.
Price Data, 2002: $49 per set including questionnaires and answer sheets.
Time: [30] minutes.
Comments: Test forms are mailed to publisher for scoring and interpretation or can be administered online via the Internet.
Authors: Terry R. Bacon and International LearningWorks.
Publisher: Lore International Institute.
Cross References: For a review by Connie Kubo Della-Piana of the original edition, see 14:215.

[1451]
Lorimer Braille Recognition Test: A Test of Ability in Reading Braille Contractions.

Purpose: Designed to test blind children's performance in reading Braille contractions.
Population: Students (ages 7–13) in Grade 2 Braille.
Publication Date: 1962.
Scores: Total score only.
Administration: Group.
Price Data: Price data, including manual (27 pages) (available in printed form or Braille), available from publisher.
Time: Administration time not reported.
Author: John Lorimer.

Publisher: Association for the Education and Welfare of the Visually Handicapped [England] [No reply from publisher; status unknown].
Cross References: See 6:854 (1 reference).

[1452]
LOTE Reading and Listening Tests.

Purpose: Designed to assess achievement in a foreign language.
Population: Secondary school students in their second year of learning another language.
Publication Dates: 1990–1991.
Scores, 2: Listening, Reading.
Administration: Group.
Editions, 3: French, Japanese, Modern Greek.
Price Data, 2002: A$31.90 per test pack including 10 test booklets, 10 magazines, photocopy master for answer/profile sheet, and score key (select French, Japanese, or Modern Greek); A$13.75 per cassette (select French, Japanese, or Modern Greek); A$25 per manual (1991, 23 pages); A$34.65 per specimen set (select French, Japanese, or Modern Greek).
Time: 42(50) minutes.
Comments: Cassette recorder necessary for administration.
Author: Susan A. Zammit.
Publisher: Australian Council for Educational Research Ltd. [Australia].
Cross References: For reviews by John Hattie and Ian C. Palmer, see 12:224.

[1453]
Louisville Behavior Checklist.

Purpose: "Designed to help parents conceptualize and communicate concerns about their children."
Population: Ages 4–6, 7–12, 13–17.
Publication Dates: 1977–1984.
Acronym: LBC.
Administration: Group.
Price Data, 2002: $125 per complete kit including materials for all 3 forms; $12.50 per 10 reusable questionnaires (specify Form E1, E2, or E3); $15 per scoring keys (specify Form E1, E2, or E3); $19.50 per 100 answer-profile sheets; $30 per manual (1984, 124 pages); $125 per 25-use disk (PC with DOS); $11 per mail-in answer sheet.
Time: Administration time not reported.
Author: Lovick C. Miller.
Publisher: Western Psychological Services.
a) FORM E1.
   Population: Ages 4–6.
   Scores: 20 scales: Infantile Aggression, Hyperactivity, Antisocial Behavior, Aggression, Social Withdrawal, Sensitivity, Fear, Inhibition, Intellectual Deficit, Immaturity, Cognitive Disability, Normal Irritability, Prosocial Deficit, Rare Devi-

ance, Neurotic Behavior, Psychotic Behavior, Somatic Behavior, Sexual Behavior, School Disturbance Predictor, Severity Level.
b) FORM E2.
   Population: Ages 7–12.
   Scores: 19 scales: Infantile Aggression, Hyperactivity, Antisocial Behavior, Aggression, Social Withdrawal, Sensitivity, Fear, Inhibition, Academic Disability, Immaturity, Learning Disability, Normal Irritability, Prosocial Deficit, Rare Deviance, Neurotic Behavior, Psychotic Behavior, Somatic Behavior, Sexual Behavior, Severity Level.
c) FORM E3.
   Population: Ages 13–17.
   Scores: 13 scales: Egocentric-Exploitive, Destructive-Assaultive, Social Delinquency, Adolescent Turmoil, Apathetic Isolation, Neuroticism, Dependent-Inhibited, Academic Disability, Neurological or Psychotic Abnormality, General Pathology, Longitudinal, Severity Level, Total Pathology.
Cross References: See T5:1522 (3 references) and T4:1484 (2 references); for a review by Francis E. Lentz, Jr., see 10:176 (6 references); for a review by Betty N. Gordon, see 9:635 (5 references); see also T3:1343 (1 reference).

[1454]
LSI Conflict.

Purpose: Enables individuals to identify and understand how their thinking patterns and coping behaviors influence their ability to deal with conflict situations.
Population: Adults.
Publication Date: 1990.
Scores: 12 patterns of thinking and behavior: Constructive (Pragmatist, Self-Empowered, Conciliator, Relationship Builder), Passive/Defensive (Accommodator, Regulator, Insulator, Avoider), Aggressive/Defensive (Escalator, Dominator, Competitor, Perfectionist).
Administration: Individual or group.
Price Data: Price data for test materials including Self-Development Guide and Leader's Guide available from publisher.
Time: Administration time not reported.
Author: J. Clayton Lafferty.
Publisher: Human Synergistics International.

[1455]
Luria-Nebraska Neuropsychological Battery: Children's Revision.

Purpose: "To diagnose general and specific cognitive deficits, including lateralization and localization of focal brain impairments, and to aid in the planning and evaluation of rehabilitation programs."
Population: Ages 8–12.
Publication Date: 1987.

Acronym: LNNB-C.

Scores, 16: Clinical scales (Motor Functions, Rhythm, Tactile Functions, Visual Functions, Receptive Speech, Expressive Speech, Writing, Reading, Arithmetic, Memory, Intellectual Processes), Optional scales (Spelling, Motor Writing), Summary scales (Pathognomonic, Left Sensorimotor, Right Sensorimotor).

Administration: Individual.

Price Data, 2002: $459.50 per complete kit including manual (266 pages) and all required materials in a carrying case; $24.50 per 10 patient response booklets; $54.50 per 10 administration and scoring booklets; $85 per manual; $19.50 per prepaid WPS Test Report answer sheet; $280 per 25-use computer disk (PC with DOS); $13.50 each per FAX scoring service.

Time: (90–120) minutes.

Comments: Uses the same stimulus materials, with the addition of 3 extra cards and an audiotape, as Form I of the adult version of the Luria-Nebraska Neuropsychological Battery (1455); other test materials (e.g., tape recorder, stopwatch, eraser, door key) must be supplied by examiner.

Author: Charles J. Golden.

Publisher: Western Psychological Services.

Cross References: See T5:1524 (2 references) and T4:1487 (2 references); for a review by Stephen R. Hooper, see 11:211 (3 references).

[1456]
Luria-Nebraska Neuropsychological Battery: Forms I and II.

Purpose: Designed "to diagnose general and specific cognitive deficits, including lateralization and localization of focal brain impairments, and to aid in the planning and evaluation of rehabilitation programs."

Population: Ages 15 and over.

Publication Dates: 1980–1985.

Acronym: LNNB.

Scores, 27: Clinical and Summary scales (Motor Functions, Rhythm, Tactile Functions, Visual Functions, Receptive Speech, Expressive Speech, Writing, Reading, Arithmetic, Memory, Intellectual Processes, Intermediate Memory [Form II only], Pathognomonic, Left Hemisphere, Right Hemisphere, Profile Elevation, Impairment), Localization scales (Left Frontal, Left Sensorimotor, Left Parietal-Occipital, Left Temporal, Right Frontal, Right Sensorimotor, Right Parietal-Occipital, Right Temporal), Optional scales (Spelling, Motor Writing), plus 28 Factor scales.

Administration: Individual.

Forms, 2: I, II.

Price Data, 2002: $499.50 per Form I set including manual (1985, 423 pages), test materials, 10 administration and scoring booklets, 10 patient response book-

lets, and 2 prepaid mail-in computer-scored answer sheets; $440 per Form II set; $54.50 per 10 administration and scoring booklets (Form I); $49.95 per 10 administration and scoring booklets (Form II); $19.95 per 10 patient response booklets (Forms I and II); $135 per manual; $19.50 per computer-scored answer sheet; $280 per 25-use (PC with DOS) disk for LNNB, Forms I, II, and Children's Revision; $13.50 per FAX service scoring charge.

Time: (90–150) minutes.

Comments: Uses cards adapted from Luria's Neuropsychological Investigation by Anne-Lise Christensen (Form II includes improved, spiral-bound stimulus cards); tape provided for rhythm subtest; Form I can be scored by hand or computer; Form II is computer scored only.

Authors: Charles J. Golden, Arnold D. Purisch, and Thomas A. Hammeke.

Publisher: Western Psychological Services.

Cross References: See T5:1525 (25 references) and T4:1488 (16 references); for reviews by Jeffrey H. Snow and Wilfred G. van Gorp, see 11:212 (105 references); for a review by Russell L. Adams, see 9:637 (41 references); see also T3:1346 (8 references).

[1457]
MAC Checklist for Evaluating, Preparing, and/or Improving Standardized Tests for Limited English Speaking Students.

Purpose: Aids in the review, critique, or preparation of ESL assessment instruments.

Population: ESL test developers, reviewers, and users.

Publication Date: 1981.

Scores: 5 criterion categories: Evidence of Validity, Evidence of Examinee Appropriateness, Evidence of Proper Item Construction, Evidence of Technical Merit, Evidence of Administrative Excellence.

Administration: Group.

Price Data: Available from publisher.

Time: Administration time not reported.

Author: Jean D'Arcy Maculaitis.

Publisher: Jean D'Arcy Maculaitis [No reply from publisher; status unknown].

Cross References: For reviews by Eugene E. Garcia and Charles W. Stansfield, see 10:177.

[1458]
MacArthur Communicative Development Inventories.

Purpose: "Evaluates young children's communication skills with norm-referenced parent checklists."

Population: 8–30 months.

Publication Date: 1993.

Acronym: CDI.

Scores, 16: Words and Gestures [Early Words (First Signs of Understanding, Phrases, Starting to Talk, Vocabulary Checklist), Actions and Gestures (First Communicative Gestures, Games and Routines, Actions with Objects, Pretend To Be a Parent, Imitating Other Adult Actions, Pretend Gestures)], Words and Sentences [Words Children Use (Vocabulary Checklist, How Children Use Words), Sentences and Grammar (Word Endings/Part I, Word Forms, Word Endings/Part II, Examples of the Child's Three Longest Sentences)].
Administration: Individual.
Price Data: Available from publisher.
Time: (20–30) minutes.
Comments: CDI Words and Gestures is for ages 8 months through 16 months; CDI Words and Sentences is for ages 16 months through 30 months; both inventories can be used with older children who have developmental delays.
Authors: Larry Fenson, Philip S. Dale, J. Steven Reznick, Donna Thal, Elizabeth Bates, Jeffery P. Hartung, Steve Pethick, and Judy S. Reilly.
Publisher: Singular Publishing Group [No reply from publisher; status unknown].
Cross References: See T5:1528 (8 references); for a review by Carol Westby, see 13:188 (14 references).

[1459]
Machinist Test—Form AC.

Purpose: "To measure the knowledge and skills required in the area of machine shop jobs."
Population: Machinist job applicants.
Publication Dates: 1981–1999.
Scores, 10: Heat Treating, Layout/Cutting and Assembly, Print Reading, Steel/ Metals and Materials, Rigging, Mechanical Principles and Repair, Machine Tools, Tools/Material and Equipment, Machine Shop Lubrication, Total.
Administration: Group.
Price Data, 2002: $16 per consumable self-scoring booklet (20 minimum order); $24.95 per manual (1999, 17 pages).
Time: (60) minutes.
Comments: Self-scoring instrument.
Author: Roland T. Ramsay.
Publisher: Ramsay Corporation.
Cross References: For reviews by John Peter Hudson, Jr. and James W. Pinkney, see 13:253.

[1460]
Maculaitis Assessment of Competencies II.

Purpose: "A comprehensive assessment of English Language proficiency for students … whose first language is not English."
Population: Grades K–12.
Publication Dates: 1982–2001.

Acronym: MAC II.
Scores, 5: 4 subtests (Speaking, Listening, Reading, Writing), Total Battery.
Forms, 2: A, B.
Price Data: Available from publisher.
Comments: Updated and revised version of Maculaitis Assessment of Competencies (MAC), subtests can be administered separately; hand- or machine-scorable; machine scoring performed by publisher; variety of score reports available including Roster Reports, Individual Student Labels, Individual Student Record Form Reports, Summary Reports; Green 10-minute screening test for new students also available.
Author: Jean D'Arcy Maculaitis.
Publisher: Touchstone Applied Science Associates, Inc.

a) RED LEVEL.
Population: Grades K–1.
Administration: Individual.
Time: (25) minutes.
b) BLUE LEVEL.
Population: Grades 2–3.
Administration: Individual or group.
Time: (75) minutes.
c) ORANGE LEVEL.
Population: Grades 4–5.
Administration: Individual or group.
Time: (121) minutes.
d) IVORY LEVEL.
Population: Grades 6–8.
Administration: Individual or group.
Time: (126) minutes.
e) TAN LEVEL.
Population: Grades 9–12.
Administration: Individual or group.
Time: (131) minutes.
Cross References: For reviews by J. Manuel Casas, David Strand, and Eugene G. Garcia of the previous edition, see 10:180.

[1461]
MainTest—Forms NL-1, B, C.

Purpose: "Developed to measure the mechanical and electrical knowledge and skills required for maintenance jobs."
Population: Applicants and incumbents for jobs requiring practical mechanical and electrical knowledge.
Publication Dates: 1991–1999.
Scores, 22: Hydraulics, Pneumatics, Welding, Power Transmission, Lubrication, Pumps, Piping, Rigging, Mechanical Maintenance, Shop Machines/Tools/ Equipment, Combustion, Motors, Digital Electronics, Schematics and Print Reading, Control Circuits, Power Supplies, Basic AC and DC Theory, Power Distribu-

tion, Test Instruments, Computers and PLC, Electrical Maintenance, Total.
Administration: Group.
Price Data, 2002: $500 per 10 instruments including manual (17 pages).
Time: (150–160) minutes.
Comments: Tests scored by publisher; percentile ranks given for local and national norms.
Author: Roland T. Ramsay.
Publisher: Ramsay Corporation.
Cross References: For reviews by Nambury S. Raju and William J. Waldron, see 13:189.

[1462]
Major Field Tests.

Purpose: Designed to reflect the basic knowledge and understanding gained in the undergraduate major curriculum.
Population: Undergraduate students completing an academic major program.
Publication Dates: 1988–2002.
Acronym: MFT.
Scores: Total score only.
Administration: Group.
Price Data: Available from publisher.
Time: (120) minutes.
Comments: Objective, end-of-program content tests in 16 disciplines; yields individual scores and subscores, group mean scores, and "assessment indicators" (group reliable subscores).
Authors: Educational Testing Service and the Graduate Records Examination Board.
Publisher: Educational Testing Service.

[1463]
The Major-Minor-Finder, 1986–1996 Edition.

Purpose: Designed to assist students in selecting a college major.
Population: High school and college.
Publication Dates: 1978–1987.
Acronym: MMF.
Scores: No scores; decisions based on number of matches for each major.
Administration: Group.
Price Data: Available from publisher.
Time: (40) minutes per printed version; (10) minutes per microcomputer version.
Authors: Arthur Cutler, Francis Ferry, Robert Kauk, and Robert Robinett.
Publisher: CFKR Career Materials [No reply from publisher; status unknown].
Cross References: For a review by James W. Pinkney, see 10:181; for reviews by Rodney L. Lowman and Daryl Sander of an earlier edition, see 9:643.

[1464]
Make a Picture Story.

Purpose: "A projective psychological test" intended "as an aid in inferring psychodynamic interpretations and structural aspects of personality."
Population: Age 6 and over.
Publication Dates: 1947–1952.
Acronym: MAPS.
Scores: Not scored.
Administration: Individual.
Price Data, 2002: $90 per complete kit including manual (1952, 92 pages), 22 stimulus cards, 67 cut-out figures, and 25 Location sheets; $19.50 per 100 Location sheets.
Time: Untimed.
Comments: A projective test similar to the Thematic Apperception Test (2593); best when used as a component of a battery of psychological tests; guidelines for qualitative interpreting of subjects' responses provided.
Author: Edwin S. Shneidman.
Publisher: Western Psychological Services.
Cross References: See T3:1361 (66 references), T2:1482 (10 references) and P:452 (4 references); for a review by Arthur R. Jensen, see 6:230 (10 references); see also 5:149 (18 references); for reviews by Albert Rabin and Charles R. Strother, see 4:113 (19 references).

[1465]
Making a Terrific Career Happen.

Purpose: For use in guiding examinees in self-evaluation and exploration of careers.
Population: High school graduates, college students, and adults.
Publication Date: 1992.
Acronym: MATCH.
Scores: Science-Professional, Science-Skilled, Technology-Professional, Technology-Skilled, Consumer Economics, Outdoor, Business-Professional, Business-Skilled, Clinical, Communication, Arts-Professional, Arts-Skilled, Service-Professional, Service-Skilled.
Administration: Group.
Price Data, 1998: $11.75 per MATCH self-scoring form (includes COPSystem booklets and Narrative Report) [$104.75 per 10].
Time: Administration time varies.
Comments: Self-administered and interpreted.
Author: Lisa Knapp-Lee.
Publisher: EdITS/Educational and Industrial Testing Service.

[1466]
Making Work Teams Work.

Purpose: A self-inventory to assess the level of empowerment of work teams.

Population: Employees.
Publication Date: 1992.
Scores, 18: Relevancy, Effort Required, Total Score for each (Organizational Behavior, Supervision and Management, Membership and Leadership, Training and Development, Goals and Responsibilities), Total Relevancy, Total Effort Required, Total Score.
Administration: Group.
Price Data: Price information available from publisher for test booklet/manual (volume discounts available).
Time: [30–40] minutes.
Author: Scott B. Parry.
Publisher: Training House, Inc.

[1467]
Malingering Probability Scale.

Purpose: Designed to "assess whether an individual is attempting to produce false evidence of psychological distress."
Population: Ages 17 and over.
Publication Date: 1998.
Acronym: MPS.
Scores, 6: Depression and Anxiety, Dissociative Disorders, Post-Traumatic Stress, Schizophrenia, Inconsistency, Malingering.
Administration: Individual.
Price Data, 2002: $132.50 per kit for mail-in computer scoring including reusable administration card, 5 prepaid mail-in answer sheets, and manual; $365 per kit for on-site computer scoring including reusable administration card, 20-use disk, 100 PC answer sheets, and manual; $4.95 per reusable administration card; $49.50 per manual; $19.95 per mail-in answer sheet; $315 per 20-use disk (PC with Microsoft Windows); $15 per 100 PC answer sheets; $16 per FAX Service Scoring charge.
Time: (20) minutes.
Comments: May be administered by paper and pencil or personal computer; computer scored (only) and interpreted locally or by publisher FAX or mail-in service.
Authors: Leigh Silverton and Chris Gruber (manual).
Publisher: Western Psychological Services.
Cross References: For reviews by Solomon M. Fulero and Radhika Krishnamurthy, see 14:216.

[1468]
Management and Graduate Item Bank.

Purpose: "For use in the selection, development or guidance of personnel at graduate level or in management positions."
Population: Graduate level and senior management applicants for the following areas: finance, computing, engineering, corporate planning, purchasing, personnel, and marketing.

Publication Dates: 1985–1987.
Acronym: MGIB.
Scores, 2: Verbal Critical Reasoning, Numerical Critical Reasoning.
Administration: Group.
Price Data: Available from publisher.
Time: 60(65) minutes.
Comments: Abbreviated adaptation of the Advanced Test Battery (126); subtests available as separates.
Authors: Saville & Holdsworth Ltd. and Linda Espey (supplementary norms manual).
Publisher: SHL Group plc [United Kingdom].
Cross References: For reviews by James T. Austin and H. John Bernardin and by R. W. Faunce, see 11:213.

[1469]
Management & Leadership Systems.

Purpose: Designed to assess management and leadership skills and team effectiveness.
Population: Management personnel.
Publication Dates: 1992–2001.
Acronym: MLS.
Administration: Group.
Price Data, 2001: $495 per Facilitator's kit including User's Manual (2001, 230 pages), Guide to Management & Leadership, High-Performing Teams Action Planning Workbook, 6 Management & Leadership Profiles, 6 Team Effectiveness Profiles, 6 Management Candidate Profiles, and transparency masters; $35 per Guide to Management & Leadership; $35 per High-Performing Teams Action Planning workbook; $195 annual licensing fee for scoring software.
Foreign Language Editions: Available in English, Spanish, French, and Portuguese.
Time: (20) minutes per test.
Comments: Inventories may be completed via paper-and-pencil, or on-line via the internet; microcomputer software requirements are Windows 98 or newer, 32 MB RAM, and 10 MB free on hard drive; the option to have the publisher generate the MLP, TEKP, MCP, and SIP is available, thus eliminating licensing of the scoring software; reports can be printed in different languages.
Author: Curtiss S. Peck.
Publisher: Assessment Systems International, Inc.
a) MANAGEMENT & LEADERSHIP PROFILE.
Purpose: Designed to measure "both present behavior and desired behavior based on the needs and expectations of the people who are evaluating the manager."
Acronym: MLP.
Scores, 15: Clarity of Purpose (Goals, Communication), Planning and Problem Avoidance (Planning, Involvement, Decision Making), Task Accomplishment (Competence, Motivation, Work

Facilitation), Providing Feedback (Feedback), Exercising Control (Managing Performance, Accountability, Delegation), Individual & Team Relationships (Relationships, Linking, Teamwork).

b) TEAM EFFECTIVENESS PROFILE.

Purpose: "Provides a way of measuring and giving feedback to teams on how they manage their processes and projects."

Acronym: TEP.

Scores, 15: Clarity of Purpose (Goals, Communication), Planning and Problem Avoidance (Planning, Involvement, Innovation/Risk, Decision Making), Task Accomplishment (Values, Competence, Motivation, Quality/Continuous Improvement), Providing Feedback (Feedback), Exercising Control (Control, Delegation), Individual & Team Relationships (Linking, Teamwork).

c) MANAGEMENT CANDIDATE PROFILE.

Purpose: "Measures day-to-day behavior that is correlated with effective management and leadership behavior. The MCP helps people understand the skills required to become effective managers and provides a clear picture of the candidate's strengths and softspots in ten important areas."

Acronym: MCP.

Scores, 10: Goals, Communication, Planning, Innovation/Risk, Decision Making, Motivation, Quality/Continuous Improvement, Feedback, Control, Relationships.

d) SELLING WITH INTEGRITY PROFILE.

Purpose: "Measure the perceptions of current behavior and desired behavior of internal and external sales people. The SIP is completed by customers, sales manager, and sales person."

Acronym: SIP.

Scores, 7: Professionalism, Identification of Needs, Partnering, Competence, Negotiation, Close, Service.

Cross References: For reviews by Stephen F. Davis and William J. Waldron, see 14:217.

[1470]
Management Appraisal Survey.

Purpose: "An assessment of managerial practices and attitudes as viewed through the eyes of employees."

Population: Employees.

Publication Dates: 1967-1996.

Scores, 5: Overall Leadership Style, Philosophy, Planning, Implementation, Evaluation.

Administration: No manual.

Price Data, 2001: $7.95 per instrument.

Time: Administration time not reported.

Comments: Self-administered survey.

Authors: Jay Hall, Jerry B. Harvey, and Martha S. Williams.

Publisher: Teleometrics International.

Cross References: See T3:2351 (1 reference); for a review by Abraham K. Korman of the Styles of Leadership and Management, see 8:1185 (8 references).

[1471]
Management Development Questionnaire.

Purpose: A personal competence assessment instrument "designed to help managers identify their weakness and strengths and decide what they need to do to develop themselves."

Population: Managers.

Publication Date: 1997.

Acronym: MDQ.

Scores, 20: Initiative, Risk Taking, Innovation, Flexibility/Adaptability, Analytical Thinking, Decision Making, Planning, Quality Focus, Oral Communication, Sensitivity, Relationships, Teamwork, Achievement, Customer Focus, Business Awareness, Learning Orientation, Authority/Presence, Motivating Others, Developing People, Resilience.

Administration: Individual.

Price Data, 1998: $20 per assessment and narrative report; $9.95 per questionnaire; $24.45 per user's manual (52 pages).

Time: (35) minutes.

Author: Alan Cameron.

Publisher: Human Resource Deveopment Press.

[1472]
Management Effectiveness Profile System.

Purpose: "Identifies managers' current strengths and weaknesses and provides direction for individual development."

Population: Managers and coworkers.

Publication Dates: 1983–1993.

Acronym: MEPS.

Scores: 2 scores (Self, Other) in 14 management skill areas: Problem Solving, Time Management, Planning, Goal Setting, Performance Leadership, Organizing, Team Development, Delegation, Participation, Integrating Differences, Providing Feedback, Stress Processing, Maintaining Integrity, Commitment.

Administration: Individual or group.

Forms, 2: Self Description, Description by Others.

Price Data: Available from publisher.

Comments: Originally called Management Practices Audit; administered to manager and 4 or 5 coworkers.

Author: Human Synergistics International.

Publisher: Human Synergistics International.

[1473]
Management Interest Inventory.

Purpose: "To assist both organizations and individuals in making decisions relating to selection, placement, and career development at management level."

Population: Managers.
Publication Dates: 1983–1986.
Scores, 54: Management Functions Preference Scores and Experience Scores (Production Operations, Technical Services, Research and Development, Distribution, Purchasing, Sales, Marketing Support, Personnel and Training, Data Processing, Finance, Legal and Secretarial, Administration, Total, Spread Across Functions); Management Skills Preference Scores and Experience Scores (Information Collecting, Information Processing, Problem-Solving, Decision-Making, Modelling, Communicating Orally, Communicating in Writing, Organising Things, Organising People, Persuading, Developing, Representing, Total).
Administration: Group.
Price Data: Available from publisher.
Time: (20–40) minutes.
Authors: Roger Holdsworth (test), Ruth Holdsworth (test), Lisa Cramp (test), and Miranda Blum (manual).
Publisher: SHL Group plc [United Kingdom].
Cross References: For a review by David M. Saunders, see 11:216.

[1474]
Management Inventory on Leadership, Motivation and Decision-Making.

Purpose: Designed for use in the training and selection of managers.
Population: Managers and manager trainees.
Publication Date: 1991.
Acronym: MILMD.
Scores: Total score only.
Administration: Group.
Price Data, 2001: $40 per 20 test and answer booklets; $5 per Instructor Manual (1991, 8 pages); $10 per Review Set including one test, one answer booklet, and Instructor Manual.
Time: (15-20) minutes.
Author: Donald L. Kirkpatrick.
Publisher: Donald L. Kirkpatrick (the author).
Cross References: For reviews by Kevin R. Murphy and Eugene P. Sheehan, see 12:226.

[1475]
Management Inventory on Managing Change.

Purpose: To assess managers' attitudes, knowledge, and opinions regarding principles and approaches for facilitating change.
Population: Managers.
Publication Dates: 1978-1983.
Acronym: MIMC.
Scores: Total score only.
Administration: Group or individual.
Price Data, 2001: $40 per 20 tests and answer booklets; $5 per instructor's manual (1983, 8 pages);

$10 per review set (includes test, answer booklet, and manual).
Time: (15-25) minutes.
Author: Donald L. Kirkpatrick.
Publisher: Donald L. Kirkpatrick (the author).

[1476]
Management Inventory on Modern Management.

Purpose: "Developed to cover eight different topics of importance to managers."
Population: Managers.
Publication Date: 1984.
Acronym: MIMM.
Scores: 8 areas: Leadership Styles, Selecting and Training, Communicating, Motivating, Managing Change, Delegating, Decision Making, Managing Time; Total score is sum of the 8 areas.
Administration: Group or individual.
Price Data, 2001: $40 per 20 tests and answer booklets; $5 per manual (12 pages); $10 per specimen set.
Time: (20) minutes.
Comments: Self-scored training tool.
Author: Donald L. Kirkpatrick.
Publisher: Donald L. Kirkpatrick (the author).
Cross References: For a review by Lenore W. Harmon, see 10:183.

[1477]
Management Inventory on Performance Appraisal and Coaching.

Purpose: "To determine the need for training in "performance appraisal and coaching.'"
Population: Managers.
Publication Date: 1990.
Acronym: MIPAC.
Scores: Total score only.
Administration: Group.
Price Data, 2001: $40 per 20 tests and answer booklets; $10 per optional audiocassette; $5 per manual (7 pages); $10 per specimen set.
Time: (20-25) minutes.
Comments: Self-administered, self-scored.
Author: Donald L. Kirkpatrick.
Publisher: Donald L. Kirkpatrick (the author).

[1478]
Management Inventory on Time Management.

Purpose: Tests time management ability of managerial personnel.
Population: Managers.
Publication Date: 1980.
Acronym: MITM.
Scores: Total score only.

Administration: Group or individual.
Price Data, 2001: $40 per 20 tests and answer booklets; $5 per instructor's manual (8 pages); $10 per review set (includes test, answer booklet, and manual).
Time: (15-25) minutes.
Author: Donald L. Kirkpatrick.
Publisher: Donald L. Kirkpatrick (the author).

[1479]
Management of Differences Inventory.

Purpose: To provide feedback to an individual concerning his/her manner of handling differences in managerial situations.
Population: Business managers.
Publication Dates: 1981–1994.
Acronym: MODI.
Scores, 9: Maintain, Smooth, Dominate, Decide by Rule, Coexist, Bargain, Yield, Release, Collaborate.
Administration: Group.
Forms, 2: Self, Feedback.
Price Data, 2002: $8.95 per Self form; $8.95 per Feedback form; minimum of 20 (volume discounts available).
Time: (20) minutes.
Comments: Self-administered; self-scored.
Author: Herbert S. Kindler.
Publisher: The Center for Management Effectiveness, Inc.

[1480]
Management Practices Update.

Purpose: To provide individuals with information about managerial behavior in areas of interpersonal relationships, the management of motivation, and personal "style" of management.
Population: Individuals involved in the management of others.
Publication Date: 1987.
Acronym: MPU.
Scores, 12: Section I (Exposure, Feedback), Section II (Basic, Safety, Belonging, Ego Status, Actualization), Section III (Team Management, Middle-of-the-Road Management, Task Management, Country Club Management, Impoverished Management).
Administration: Group.
Levels: 3 parts: I (Interpersonal Relationships), II (Management of Motivation), III (Analysis of Management Style).
Price Data, 2001: $8.95 per instrument (25 pages).
Time: Administration time not reported.
Comments: Represents a shortened version of Personnel Relations Survey (1891), Management of Motives Index, and Styles of Management Inventory (2424).
Author: Jay Hall.
Publisher: Teleometrics International.

[1481]
Management Relations Survey.

Purpose: To assess employees' perceptions of their practices toward their managers.
Population: Subordinates to managers.
Publication Dates: 1970-1995.
Acronym: MRS.
Scores, 2: Exposure, Feedback.
Administration: Group.
Price Data, 2001: $7.95 per instrument.
Time: Administration time not reported.
Comments: Companion instrument to Personnel Relations Survey (1891); based on the Johari Window Model of interpersonal relations.
Author: Jay Hall.
Publisher: Teleometrics International.
Cross References: For a review by Walter C. Borman, see 8:1178 (1 reference).

[1482]
Management Situation Checklist.

Purpose: Designed to help determine how management style matches management demands, to define vulnerabilities from management style and develop strategies for improving vulnerabilities.
Population: Managers.
Publication Date: 1986.
Acronym: MSC.
Scores, 6: Coercive, Authoritative, Affiliative, Democratic, Pacesetting, Coaching.
Administration: Group or individual
Price Data, 2001: $33 per 10 booklets.
Time: [20–30] minutes.
Comments: Self-rating checklist; self-scored; is a companion to the Managerial Style Questionnaire (1497).
Author: Hay Group.
Publisher: Hay Group.

[1483]
Management Style Inventory [Training House, Inc.].

Purpose: "This exercise is designed to give you some insights into your management style and how it affects others."
Population: Industry.
Publication Dates: 1986–1987.
Scores, 5: Team Builder, Soft, Hard, Middle of Road, Ineffective.
Administration: Group or individual.
Price Data: Price information available from publisher for complete sets including test, answer sheet, and interpretation sheet.
Time: (20) minutes.
Comments: Self-administered, self-scored.
Author: Training House, Inc.

Publisher: Training House, Inc.
Cross References: For reviews by Ernest J. Kozma and Charles K. Parsons, see 11:220.

[1484]
Management Styles Inventory.

Purpose: Assesses individual management style under a variety of conditions.
Population: Adults.
Publication Dates: 1964–1995.
Scores, 5: Philosophy, Planning and Goal Setting, Implementation, Performance Evaluation, Total.
Administration: Group.
Price Data, 2001: $8.95 per instrument.
Time: Untimed.
Comments: Self-administered survey.
Authors: Jay Hall, Jerry B. Harvey, and Martha S. Williams.
Publisher: Teleometrics International.
Cross References: For reviews by Ralph F. Darr, Jr. and Charles K. Parsons, see 12:227.

[1485]
Management Success Profile.

Purpose: "Provides a standardized measure of potential for success in management and is an ideal instrument for selecting supervisors, unit managers, and team leaders. The MSP assesses the individual's interest in, motivation toward, and knowledge about management positions."
Population: Adults (management position candidates).
Publication Date: 1996.
Acronym: MSP.
Scores: Validity (Candidness, Accuracy), Management Focus (Work Background, Leadership), Motivation and Attitudes (Management Responsibility, Productivity, Customer Service Orientation), Management Style (Practical Thinking, Adaptability, Coaching), Stability and Risk (Business Ethics, Job Commitment), Overall Management Profile Index.
Administration: Group.
Price Data: Available from publisher.
Time: [45] minutes.
Comments: Toll free customer service hotline for immediate assistance with Profile (1-800-221-8378).
Author: London House.
Publisher: Reid London House.

[1486]
Management Team Roles—Indicator.

Purpose: "A team roles model and questionnaire [that] identifies the contribution ... made by each individual to the success of [his or her work] team" and "indicates which [of 8 distinct] Jungian function-attitudes are primarily being used at present."
Population: Adults.
Publication Date: 2000.
Acronym: MTR-i.

Scores: 8 team roles: Coach, Crusader, Explorer, Innovator, Sculptor, Curator, Conductor, Scientist.
Administration: Group.
Price Data, 2001: £49.50 per specimen set including technical manual (2000, 95 pages), question card, answer sheet, report, and 360 Degree feedback form; £35 per 10 self-score answer sheets; £35 per 10 report and 360 Degree feedback forms; £42.50 per technical manual.
Time: (10–15) minutes.
Comments: Can be completed online.
Author: Stephen P. Myers.
Publisher: The Test Agency Limited [England].

[1487]
Management Transactions Audit.

Purpose: Assesses "ones interpersonal transactions and their implications for managerial effectiveness."
Population: Managers.
Publication Dates: 1973–1997.
Acronym: MTA.
Scores, 9: Transaction Scores (Parent Subsystem, Adult Subsystem, Child Subsystem); Tension Index Scores (Subordinates [Disruptive, Constructive], Colleagues [Disruptive, Constructive], Superiors [Disruptive, Constructive]).
Administration: Group.
Manual: No manual.
Price Data, 2001: $8.95 per instrument.
Time: [15-30] minutes.
Comments: Self-administered survey.
Authors: Jay Hall and C. Leo Griffith.
Publisher: Teleometrics International.
Cross References: For reviews by Stephan J. Motowidlo and Ronald N. Taylor, see 8:1180.

[1488]
Manager Style Appraisal.

Purpose: A measure of managerial style.
Population: Adults.
Publication Dates: 1967–1995.
Scores, 5: Philosophy, Planning and Goal Setting, Implementation, Performance Evaluation, Total.
Administration: Group.
Price Data, 2001: $7.95 per instrument.
Time: Untimed.
Comments: Self-administered survey.
Authors: Jay Hall, Jerry B. Harvey, and Martha S. Williams.
Publisher: Teleometrics International.
Cross References: For reviews by Kenneth N. Anchor and Claudia J. Morner, see 12:228.

[1489]
Manager/Supervisor Staff Selector.

Purpose: "Measures important intellectual and personality characteristics needed for the successful manager/supervisor."

Population: Candidates for managerial and supervisory positions.
Publication Dates: 1976–1984.
Scores: 10 tests: Problem Solving Ability, Numerical Skills, Fluency, Business, Judgment, Supervisory Practices, CPF (interest in working with people), NPF (emotional stability), Adult Personality Inventory, Work Motivation Inventory.
Administration: Group.
Price Data, 2001: $500 per person; quantity discounts available.
Foreign Language Edition: French edition available.
Time: (240) minutes.
Comments: Graded by publisher; comprehensive report prepared for each candidate; must be proctored.
Authors: Tests from various publishers compiled, distributed, and scored by Walden Personnel Testing.
Publisher: Walden Personnel Performance, Inc. [Canada].
Cross References: For a review by Eric F. Gardner, see 10:186.

[1490]
Managerial and Professional Job Functions Inventory.

Purpose: "For defining the basic dimensions of jobs and assessing their relative importance for the job" and "assessing one's ability to perform them."
Population: Middle and upper level managers and higher-level professionals.
Publication Dates: 1978–1997.
Acronym: MPJFI.
Scores, 16: Setting Organizational Objectives, Financial Planning and Review, Improving Work Procedures and Practices, Interdepartmental Coordination, Developing and Implementing Technical Ideas, Judgment and Decision-Making, Developing Teamwork, Coping with Difficulties and Emergencies, Promoting Safety Attitudes and Practices, Communications, Developing Employee Potential, Supervisory Practices, Self-Development and Improvement, Personnel Practices, Promoting Community-Organization Relations, Handling Outside Contacts.
Administration: Individual or group.
Forms, 2: Ability Rating, Importance Rating.
Price Data, 2002: $101 per start-up kit including 25 test booklets (specify Importance or Ability), 25 score sheets, and interpretation and research manual; $54 per 25 test booklets (specify Importance or Ability); $31 per 25 score sheets; $28 per interpretation and research manual.
Time: No limit (approximately 40–60 minutes).
Authors: Melany E. Baehr, Wallace G. Lonergan, and Bruce A. Hunt.
Publisher: Reid London House.

Cross References: For reviews by L. Alan Witt and Sheldon Zedeck, see 11:222.

[1491]
Managerial Assessment of Proficiency MAP™.

Purpose: "Shows a participant's strengths and weaknesses in twelve areas of managerial competency and two dimensions of management style."
Population: Managers.
Publication Dates: 1985–1988.
Acronym: MAP.
Scores, 19: Administrative Competencies (Time Management and Prioritizing, Setting Goals and Standards, Planning and Scheduling Work, Administrative Composite), Communication Competencies (Listening and Organizing, Giving Clear Information, Getting Unbiased Information, Communication Composite), Supervisory Competencies (Training/Coaching/Delegating, Appraising People and Performance, Disciplining and Counseling, Supervisory Composite), Cognitive Competencies (Identifying and Solving Problems, Making Decisions/Weighing Risk, Thinking Clearly and Analytically, Cognitive Composite), Proficiency Composite, Theory X Style (Parent-Child), and Theory Y Style (Adult-Adult).
Administration: Group.
Price Data, 1998: $20,000 initial investment for purchase with licensing agreement (for high-volume users) including set of 12 videocassettes, 50 sets of participant materials including workbook (1988, 60 pages) and booklet entitled Interpreting Your Scores (1988, 24 pages), personal computer floppy disk for in-house scoring, scoring by publisher of first 25 participants, 1 1/2-day training and pilot cycle by senior instructor from publisher; $80 per person for additional participant materials; $30 per person for additional (optional) scoring by publisher; $400 per person (minimum 12 persons) for contracting for in-house program including materials, scoring, and instructor/consultant time; $200-$250 per person for registration at public workshop held in Princeton, NJ by publishers.
Time: (360–420) minutes.
Comments: May be purchased with licensing agreement, contracted for in-house administration, or used by attending a public workshop provided by publisher; administered in part by videocassette.
Author: Scott B. Parry.
Publisher: Training House, Inc.
Cross References: For a review by Jerard F. Kehoe, see 11:223.

[1492]
Managerial Competence Index.

Purpose: "To assess the probable competence of one's approach to management."

Population: Individuals who manage or are being assessed for their potential to manage others.
Publication Dates: 1980-1989.
Acronym: MCI.
Scores, 5: Team Management, Middle-of-the-Road Management, Task Management, Country Club Management, Impoverished Management.
Administration: Group.
Price Data, 2001: $8.95 per instrument (1989, 21 pages).
Time: Administration time not reported.
Author: Jay Hall.
Publisher: Teleometrics International.
Cross References: For a review by Kurt F. Geisinger, see 11:224.

[1493]
Managerial Competence Review.

Purpose: To identify a manager's preferred managerial style and assess the relative competence of his/her approach to management.
Population: Subordinates to managers.
Publication Dates: 1980–1989.
Acronym: MCR.
Scores, 5: Relative measures of concern for people and concern for production ("9/9," "1/9," "5/5," "9/1," "1/1").
Administration: Group.
Price Data, 2001: $7.95 per instrument (1989, 17 pages).
Time: Administration time not reported.
Comments: Companion instrument for Managerial Competence Index (1492).
Author: Jay Hall.
Publisher: Teleometrics International.

[1494]
Managerial Competency Questionnaire.

Purpose: "Developed to measure the use of seven competencies that have been found to be critical for effective managers."
Population: Managers.
Publication Date: 1997.
Acronym: MCQ.
Scores, 7: Achievement Orientation, Developing Others, Directiveness, Impact and Influence, Interpersonal Understanding, Organizational Awareness, Team Leadership.
Administration: Group.
Price Data, 2001: $69 per 10 questionnaire, and interpretive notes (24 pages); $29 per 10 questionnaires only; $55 per 10 Development Assistant booklets.
Time: [30–40] minutes.
Comments: Self-report questionnaire.
Author: Hay Group.
Publisher: Hay Group.

[1495]
Managerial Philosophies Scale.

Purpose: Surveys the "manager's assumptions and working theories about the nature of those whose activities he or she coordinates."
Population: Managers.
Publication Dates: 1975–1995.
Acronym: MPS.
Scores, 2: Theory X (Reductive Management Beliefs), Theory Y (Developmental Management Beliefs).
Administration: Group.
Manual: No manual.
Price Data, 2001: $8.95 per instrument.
Time: [15-30] minutes.
Comments: Self-administered survey.
Authors: Jacob Jacoby and James R. Terborg.
Publisher: Teleometrics International.
Cross References: See T3:1366 (1 reference).

[1496]
Managerial Scale for Enterprise Improvement.

Purpose: Designed "to measure management morale."
Population: Managers.
Publication Date: No date.
Scores: Total score only.
Administration: Group.
Price Data, 2001: $2 per specimen set.
Time: (12) minutes.
Author: Herbert A. Kaufman.
Publisher: Psychometric Affiliates.

[1497]
Managerial Style Questionnaire.

Purpose: Measures individuals' perception of how they manage based on the assessment of six managerial styles.
Population: Persons in managerial situations.
Publication Dates: 1980–1996.
Acronym: MSQ.
Scores, 6: Coercive, Authoritative, Affiliative, Democratic, Pacesetting, Coaching.
Administration: Group or individual.
Forms, 2: Participant, Employee.
Price Data, 2001: $69 per 10 Participant version questionnaires, profiles, and interpretive notes; $29 per 10 Employee version questionnaires; $28 per 6 transparencies; $25 per trainer's guide (1994, 28 pages).
Foreign Language Edition: Available in Spanish and French.
Time: [30–40] minutes.
Comments: Self-scored instrument.
Author: Hay Group.
Publisher: Hay Group.

Cross References: For a review by H. John Bernardin and Joan E. Pynes, see 10:185; for a review by Frank L. Schmidt of an earlier edition, see 8:1182 (1 reference).

[1498]
Manchester Personality Questionnaire.

Purpose: Designed to provide an occupational personality test with a focus on traits relevant to creative and innovative behavior.
Population: Adults.
Publication Dates: 1993–1996.
Acronym: MPQ.
Administration: Group.
Author: CIM Test Publishers.
Publisher: The Test Agency Limited [England]; North American Distributor: Human Resource Development Press.

a) MPQ FACTOR 14.
Purpose: An assessment of 14 personality traits covering the Big Five personality factors.
Scores, 19: Big Five Factors (Creativity, Agreeableness, Achievement, Extroversion, Resilience), Originality, Rule Consciousness, Openness to Change, Assertiveness, Social Confidence, Empathy, Communicativeness, Independence, Rationality, Competitiveness, Conscientiousness, Perfectionism, Decisiveness, Apprehension.
Price Data, 2001: £65 per administration set including user's manual (1996, 72 pages), reusable questionnaire, answer sheet, and profile chart; £55 per user's manual; £6.50 per reusable question booklet; £62.50 per 25 answer sheets; £25 per 25 profile charts; £450 per MPQ Expert System.
Time: (20) minutes.

b) MANCHESTER CREATIVITY QUESTIONNAIRE FACTOR 7.
Purpose: An assessment of the personality attributes of creativity.
Scores, 9: Global Factor (Creativity), Originality, Rule Consciousness, Openness to Change, Assertiveness, Independence, Achievement, Radicalness, Response Style.
Price Data: £65 per 10 combined question/answer booklets.
Time: Administration time not reported.
Cross References: For reviews by Jack E. Gebart-Eaglemont and Carl Isenhart, see 13:191.

[1499]
Manifestation of Symptomatology Scale.

Purpose: Designed "to identify problems of children and adolescents."
Population: Ages 11–18.
Publication Date: 1999.
Acronym: MOSS.

Scores, 20: Validity Scores (Inconsistent Responding, Random Responding, Faking Good, Faking Bad), Summary Index (Affective State, Home, Acting Out), Content Scales (Sexual Abuse, Alcohol and Drugs, Suspiciousness, Thought Process, Self-Esteem, Depression, Anxiety, Mother, Father, Home Environment, Impulsivity, School, Compliance).
Administration: Group or individual.
Price Data, 2002: $106 per kit including 25 AutoScore forms, manual (69 pages), 2-use disk and 2 PC answer sheets for on-site computer scoring and interpretation, $42.50 per 25 AutoScore forms; $49.95 per manual.
Time: (15–20) minutes.
Comments: Self-report inventory.
Author: Neil L. Mogge.
Publisher: Western Psychological Services.

[1500]
The Manson Evaluation, Revised Edition.

Purpose: Identifies alcoholics and potential alcoholics.
Population: Adults.
Publication Dates: 1948–1987.
Scores, 8: Anxiety, Depressive Fluctuations, Emotional Sensitivity, Resentfulness, Incompleteness, Aloneness, Interpersonal Relations, Total.
Administration: Individual or group.
Editions, 2: Paper-and-pencil, microcomputer.
Price Data, 2002: $60 per complete kit including 25 AutoScore™ test profile forms and manual (1987, 28 pages); $32.50 per 25 AutoScore™ test booklets/profiles (1987); $32.50 per manual; $139.50 per 25-use disk (PC with DOS) to administer, score, and interpret Manson Evaluation or Alcadd Test; $9.50 per mail-in answer sheet.
Time: (10–20) minutes.
Comments: Self-administered; computer program and mail-in answer sheets can be used for both the Manson Evaluation and the Alcadd Test (136).
Authors: Morse P. Manson and George J. Huba.
Publisher: Western Psychological Services.
Cross References: For reviews by Tony Toneatto and Jalie A. Tucker, see 11:226; see also T2:1271 (2 references) and P:152 (1 reference); for a review by Dugal Campbell, see 6:137 (5 references); for reviews by Charles H. Honzik and Albert L. Hunsicker, see 4:68 (4 references).

[1501]
Manual Dexterity Test.

Purpose: Designed to provide "a measure of manual speed and skill."
Population: Ages 16 and over.
Publication Date: No date.
Acronym: MDT.
Scores, 4: Speed, Speed and Skill, Manual Speed (average scale score of Speed, Speed and Skill), Manual

Skill (difference between Speed, Speed and Skill scale scores).
Administration: Group.
Price Data: Available from publisher.
Time: 2 minutes and 15 seconds (8 minutes).
Author: Educational & Industrial Test Services Ltd.
Publisher: Educational & Industrial Test Services Ltd. [England].

[1502]
MAPP: Motivational Appraisal of Personal Potential.

Purpose: Intended to measure "an individual's potential and motivation for given areas of work."
Population: Employees at all levels.
Publication Date: 1995.
Acronym: MAPP.
Scores, 13: Interest in Job Content, Temperament for the Job, Aptitude for the Job, Orientation to People, Affinity for Objects and Things, Approach to Data and Information, Reasoning and Thinking Style, Mathematical Capability, Language Levels, Personal Style, Personal Traits, Interpersonal and Social Tendencies, Learning Style.
Administration: Group.
Price Data, 1997: $350 per job profile (direct or composite); $10 per database input; $200 per personal appraisal; $150 per executive appraisal; $40 per job match summary; $80 per job match analysis; $120 per work team; $30 per people to job match; $30 per job to people match; $950 per corporate training; $1,800 per consultant training.
Time: (20–25) minutes.
Comments: Available as paper-and-pencil or computerized version.
Author: International Assessment Network.
Publisher: International Assessment Network.
Cross References: For reviews by Martha E. Hennen and Abbot Packard, see 14:218.

[1503]
A Marital Communication Inventory.

Purpose: Designed to assess the communications dimension of a marital relationship for purposes of counseling and marriage enrichment.
Population: Married couples.
Publication Dates: 1968–1979.
Acronym: MCI.
Scores: Total score only.
Administration: Group.
Price Data, 1993: $1.50 per inventory; $2 per manual (1978, 8 pages).
Time: (20) minutes.
Author: Millard J. Bienvenu.
Publisher: Millard J. Bienvenu, Northwest Publications.

Cross References: See T5:1580 (5 references) and T4:1536 (4 references); for a review by Joseph P. Stokes, see 9:651 (1 reference).

[1504]
Marital Evaluation Checklist.

Purpose: "Provides a brief yet comprehensive survey of the most common characteristics and problem areas in a marital relationship."
Population: Married couples in counseling.
Publication Date: 1984.
Acronym: MEC.
Scores: 3 areas: Reasons for Marrying, Problems of the Current Relationship, Motivation for Counseling.
Administration: Group.
Price Data: Available from publisher.
Time: (30-40) minutes.
Comments: Self-administered checklist.
Author: Leslie Navran.
Publisher: Psychological Assessment Resources, Inc.
Cross References: See T5:1581 (1 reference); for a review by Richard B. Stuart, see 10:187.

[1505]
Marital Satisfaction Inventory—Revised.

Purpose: Designed to "identify, separately for each partner in a relationship, the nature and extent of distress along several key dimensions of their relationship."
Population: Couples who are married or living together.
Publication Dates: 1979–1998.
Acronym: MSI-R.
Scores, 13: Conventionalization, Global Distress, Affective Communication, Problem-Solving Communication, Aggression, Time Together, Disagreement About Finances, Sexual Dissatisfaction, Role Orientation, Family History of Distress, Dissatisfaction with Children, Conflict over Child Rearing, Inconsistency.
Administration: Group.
Price Data, 2002: : $99.50 per complete kit including 20 AutoScore™ answer forms, 2-use disk and 2 PC answer sheets for on-site computer scoring and interpretation, and manual (1997, 126 pages); $34.50 per 20 AutoScore™ answer forms; $48 per manual; $12.50 per 6 Spanish research administration booklets; $17 per mail-in answer booklet; $210 per 20-use disk (PC with Microsoft Windows); $15 per 100 PC answer sheets; $11.50 per FAX Service Scoring charge.
Foreign Language Edition: Spanish research edition administration booklet available but without separate norms.
Time: (25) minutes.
Comments: 150-item self-report inventory; hand or computer scoring available; computer-generated interpretation available.

Author: Douglas K. Snyder.
Publisher: Western Psychological Services.
Cross References: For reviews by Frank Bernt and Mary Lou Bryant Frank, see 14:219; see also T5:1582 (15 references) and T4:1538 (7 references); for reviews by David N. Dixon and E. M. Waring of an earlier edition, see 9:652 (2 references).

[1506]
The Maroondah Assessment Profile for Problem Gambling.

Purpose: Designed as "an instrument that assists counselors in developing treatment intervention for their clients with gambling problems."
Population: People with gambling problems.
Publication Date: 1999.
Acronym: G-MAP.
Scores, 17: Beliefs About Winning (Control, Prophecy, Uninformed), Feelings (Good Feelings, Relaxation, Boredom, Numbness), Situations (Oasis, Transition, Desperation, Mischief), Attitudes to Self (Low Self-Image, "Winner," Entrenchment, Harm to Self), Social (Shyness, Friendship).
Administration: Group or individual.
Price Data: Price data available from publisher for kit including 10 questionnaires, manual (2000, 234 pages), 10 answer sheets, 18 photocopiable action sheet masters, 10 profile sheets, 10 response reports, and computer scoring program disk.
Time: (20) minutes.
Comments: Self-report inventory.
Authors: Tim Loughnan, Mark Pierce, and Anastasia Sagris-Desmond.
Publisher: Australian Council for Educational Research Ltd. [Australia].

[1507]
The Marriage and Family Attitude Survey.

Purpose: "A diagnostic and educational instrument for understanding relationship attitudes" in marriage and family life.
Population: Adolescents and adults.
Publication Date: No date.
Scores: 10 areas: Cohabitation and Premarital Sexual Relations, Marriage and Divorce, Childhood and Child Rearing, Division of Household Labor and Professional Employment, Marital and Extramarital Sexual Relations, Privacy Rights and Social Needs, Religious Needs, Communication Expectations, Parental Relationships, Professional Counseling Services.
Administration: Group.
Price Data, 2002: $15 per 25 test forms; $4.50 per examiner's manual (no date, 8 pages); $5 per specimen set.
Time: (4–10) minutes.
Authors: Donald V. Martin and Maggie Martin.

Publisher: Psychologists and Educators, Inc.
Cross References: For reviews by Mark W. Roberts and by Donald U. Robertson and Virginia L. Brown, see 11:227.

[1508]
Marriage Scale (For Measuring Compatibility of Interests).

Purpose: To identify attitudes toward a variety of relationship issues.
Population: Premarital and marital counselees.
Publication Dates: 1970–1973.
Scores: Item scores only.
Administration: Group.
Price Data, 2002: $15 per 25 rating folders; $5 per specimen set with instructions.
Time: (10–15) minutes.
Comments: Self-administered.
Author: J. Gustav White.
Publisher: Psychologists and Educators, Inc.

[1509]
Martin and Pratt Nonword Reading Test.

Purpose: Designed to "investigate the [phonological] recoding skills of students."
Population: Ages 6–16.
Publication Date: 2001.
Scores: Total score only.
Administration: Individual.
Forms, 2: A, B.
Price Data, 2002: A$120 per starter set including record booklet, stimulus book, and manual (60 pages); A$16.50 per 10 record booklets (A or B); A$35 per stimulus book; A$60 per manual.
Time: (5–10) minutes.
Authors: Frances Martin and Chris Pratt.
Publisher: Australian Council for Educational Research Ltd. [Australia].

[1510]
Martin S-D Inventory.

Purpose: Constructed to assess depression and suicide-proneness.
Population: Clients and patients.
Publication Dates: 1970–1971.
Scores: Total score only.
Administration: Group.
Price Data, 2002: $8.25 per 25 test forms; $2.75 per set of score templates; $4.50 per pamphlet on suicide and depression (1971, 12 pages); $9 per specimen set.
Time: [15] minutes.
Comments: Self-ratings.
Author: William T. Martin.
Publisher: Psychologists and Educators, Inc.
Cross References: See T4:1548 (1 reference).

[1511]
Martinek-Zaichkowsky Self-Concept Scale for Children.
Purpose: "Designed to measure the global self-concept of children."
Population: Grades 1–8.
Publication Date: 1977.
Acronym: MZSCS.
Scores: Total score only.
Administration: Group or individual.
Price Data, 2002: $35 per 25 tests; $6.75 per manual (25 pages); $10 per specimen set.
Time: (10-15) minutes.
Comments: "A non-verbal, culture-free instrument."
Authors: Thomas J. Martinek and Leonard D. Zaichkowsky.
Publisher: Psychologists and Educators, Inc.
Cross References: See T5:1586 (2 references) and T4:1549 (6 references); for reviews by George M. Guthrie and David R. Wilson, see 9:656 (4 references); see also T3:1386 (3 references).

[1512]
Maryland Addictions Questionnaire.
Purpose: Intended to survey "issues relevant to the severity of patients' alcohol and drug abuse history."
Population: Ages 17 and older.
Publication Date: 1997.
Acronym: MAQ.
Scores, 15: Validity (Response Inconsistency, Defensiveness), Summary (Emotional Distress, Resistance to Treatment, Admission of Problems), Substance Abuse (Alcoholism Severity, Drug Abuse Severity, Craving, Substance Abuse Control, Resentment), Treatment (Motivation for Treatment, Social Anxiety, Antisocial Behaviors, Cognitive Symptoms, Affective Disturbance).
Administration: Group.
Price Data, 2002: $99.50 per complete kit including manual (102 paages), 20 AutoScore™ answer sheets, 2 prepaid mail-in answer sheets for computer scoring and interpretation, and 2-use disk and 2 PC answer sheets for on-site computer scoring and interpretation; $36.50 per 25 AutoScore™ answer sheets; $13.50 per mail-in answer sheet; $15 per 100 microcomputer answer sheets; $48 per manual; $250 per microcomputer disk good for 25 uses (3.5-inch, Microsoft Windows required); $10.50 per FAX Scoring Service.
Time: (15–20) minutes.
Comments: Author suggests should be administered as an intake measure for individuals entering addiction treatment programs.
Authors: William E. O'Donnell, Clinton B. DeSoto, and Janet L. DeSoto.
Publisher: Western Psychological Services.
Cross References: For reviews by Carl Isenhart and John A. Mills, see 14:220.

[1513]
Maryland/Baltimore County Design for Adult Basic Education.
Purpose: "Diagnoses a student's strengths, weaknesses, and deficiencies in skill areas that are prerequisite to literacy."
Population: Adult nonreaders.
Publication Date: 1982.
Scores: 21 subtest scores in 5 areas: Background Knowledge, Alphabet Recognition and Reproduction, Auditory Perception and Discrimination, Visual Perception and Discrimination, Sight Vocabulary.
Administration: Group and individual.
Price Data: Not available.
Time: (120–180) minutes.
Comments: Commonly called the "BCD Test."
Author: Baltimore County Public Schools Office of Adult Education.
Publisher: Prentice Hall [No reply from publisher; status unknown].
Cross References: For reviews by Mary M. Dupuis and Sharon L. Smith, see 9:658.

[1514]
Maryland Parent Attitude Survey.
Purpose: Designed to measure child-rearing attitudes.
Population: Parents.
Publication Dates: [1957–1966].
Acronym: MPAS.
Scores, 4: Disciplinarian, Indulgent, Protective, Rejecting.
Administration: Group.
Price Data, 2001: $5 per complete package including test, scoring instructions and tables, T scores, and copy of article.
Time: [2--60] minutes.
Comments: For research use only; tests may be reproduced locally.
Author: Donald K. Pumroy.
Publisher: Donald K. Pumroy.
Cross References: See T4:1551 (1 reference).

[1515]
Maslach Burnout Inventory, Third Edition.
Purpose: Constructed to measure three aspects of burnout.
Population: Members of the helping professions including educators and human service professionals.
Publication Dates: 1981–1996.
Scores, 3: Emotional Exhaustion, Depersonalization, Personal Accomplishment.
Administration: Group.
Price Data, 2001: $65 per review kit including Human Services Survey booklet, Educators Survey booklet, General Survey booklet, set of scoring keys, and manual (1996, 56 pages); $28 per 25 nonreusable survey

booklets (specify Human Services, Educators, or General); $17.50 per 25 Human Services Survey or Educators Survey demographic data sheets; $14 per 25 scoring keys; $42 per manual.
Authors: Wilmar B. Schaufeli, Michael P. Leiter, Christina Maslach, and Susan E. Jackson.
Publisher: Consulting Psychologists Press, Inc.
a) HUMAN SERVICES SURVEY.
Acronym: MBI-HSS.
Population: Staff members in the Human Services profession.
Time: (10–15) minutes.
b) EDUCATORS SURVEY.
Acronym: MBI-ES.
Population: Educators.
Time: (5–10) minutes.
c) GENERAL SURVEY.
Acronym: MBI-GS.
Population: Other workers in the service professions.
Time: (10-15) minutes.
Cross References: See T5:1590 (69 references) and T4:1552 (30 references); for reviews by David S. Hargrove and Jonathan Sandoval of an earlier edition, see 10:189 (34 references).

[1516]
Matching Assistive Technology & CHild.

Purpose: A series of instruments designed to assess "infants' and childrens' need for assistive technology" to determine the most appropriate child-technology match.
Population: Children with disabilities, ages 0–5; children older than age 5 depending on developmental level.
Publication Date: 1997.
Acronym: MATCH.
Administration: Individual.
Price Data: Available from publisher.
Time: (120) minutes for entire battery.
Comments: To be used by Early Intervention and Special Education professionals with parents.
Author: Marcia J. Scherer.
Publisher: The Institute for Matching Person & Technology, Inc.
a) TECHNOLOGY UTILIZATION WORKSHEET FOR MATCHING ASSISTIVE TECHNOLOGY & CHILD.
Purpose: Designed to "review technologies the child is currently using, has used in the past, and needs."
Scores: No formal scores; examines perceptions in 10 areas: Communication, Mobility/Gross Motor, Vision, Hearing, Fine Motor Skills, Daily Living, Health Maintenance, Play, Self-Care, Learning/Cognition.
Comments: Completed by parent and/or educator.

b) WORKSHEET FOR MATCHING ASSISTIVE TECHNOLOGY & CHILD.
Purpose: Designed to "obtain parent perspectives of a child's particular limitations, goals, and interventions as well as strengths which can be bulit upon in planning interventions."
Scores: No scores; examines perceptions of 10 areas: Communication, Mobility/Gross Motor, Vision, Hearing, Fine Motor Skills, Daily Living, Health Maintenance, Play, Self-Care, Learning/Cognition.
Comments: Completed by the child's parent.
c) SURVEY OF TECHNOLOGY USE.
Purpose: Designed to "help identify technologies and technology functions/features a child is likely to feel comfortable or successful in using."
Acronym: SOTU.
Scores: No formal scores.
Comments: Completed by educator and/or parent.
d) MATCHING ASSISTIVE TECHNOLOGY & CHILD.
Purpose: Designed to help "select the most appropriate assistive technology for a child's use while pinpointing areas for training and further assessment."
Acronym: MATCH.
Scores: No formal scores.
Comments: Completed by caregiver or educator.

[1517]
Matching Familiar Figures Test.

Purpose: Measurement of constructs of reflection and impulsivity.
Population: Ages 5–12, 13 and over.
Publication Date: 1965.
Acronym: MFF.
Scores: Total score only.
Administration: Individual.
Levels, 2: Elementary, Adolescent/Adult.
Manual: No manual.
Price Data: Available from publisher.
Time: Administration time not reported.
Authors: Jerome Kagan (test) and Neil J. Salkind (norms booklet).
Publisher: Jerome Kagan [No reply from publisher; status unknown].
Cross References: See T5:1592 (28 references), T4:1553 (106 references), and 9:662 (71 references).

[1518]
Matching Person and Technology.

Purpose: Designed for "selecting and evaluating technologies used in rehabilitation, education, the workplace and other settings."
Population: Clients, students, or employees.

Publication Dates: 1991–1994.
Acronym: MPT.
Administration: Group.
Forms, 2: Consumer, Professional.
Price Data: Available from publisher.
Time: (15) minutes per test.
Author: Marcia J. Scherer.
Publisher: The Institute for Matching Person & Technology, Inc.

a) SURVEY OF TECHNOLOGY USE.
Purpose: Constructed to measure "the consumer's present experiences and feelings toward technological devices."
Acronym: SOTU.
Scores: 4 categories: Experience with Current Technologies, Perspectives on Technologies, Typical Activities, Personal/Social Characteristics.
b) ASSISTIVE TECHNOLOGY DEVICE PREDISPOSITION ASSESSMENT.
Purpose: Designed to "help individuals select appropriate assistive technologies."
Acronym: ATD PA.
Scores: 5 categories: Disability, Environment, Temperament, Device, Degree of Match.
c) EDUCATIONAL TECHNOLOGY PREDISPOSITION ASSESSMENT.
Purpose: Designed "for teachers who are helping students use technology to reach educational goals."
Acronym: ET PA.
Scores: 4 categories: Educational Goal, The Student, Educational Technology, Educational Environment.
d) WORKPLACE TECHNOLOGY PREDISPOSITION ASSESSMENT.
Purpose: "Designed to assist employers in identifying factors that might inhibit the acceptance or use of a new technology in the workplace."
Acronym: WT PA.
Scores: 4 categories: The Technology, The Employee Being Trained to Use the Technology, The Workplace Environment, Match Between Person and Technology.
e) HEALTH CARE TECHNOLOGY PREDISPOSITION ASSESSMENT.
Purpose: "Developed to assist health care professionals in identifying factors that might inhibit the acceptance or appropriate use of health care technologies."
Acronym: HCT PA.
Scores: 5 categories: Health Problem, Consequences of HCT Use, Characteristics of the Health Care Technology, Personal Issues, Attitudes of Others.
Cross References: For reviews by Patricia A. Bachelor and by Laura L. B. Barnes and Carrie L. Winterowd, see 14:221.

[1519]
MATE [Marital ATtitude Evaluation].

Purpose: "Designed to explore the relation between two people who have close contact with each other."
Population: Couples.
Publication Date: 1989.
Acronym: MATE.
Scores: 5 scales: Inclusion Behavior, Inclusion Feelings, Control Behavior, Control Feelings, Affection.
Administration: Group.
Manual: Information included in manual of FIRO Awareness Scales (1002).
Price Data: Available from publisher.
Time: Administration time not reported.
Comments: Based on FIRO Awareness Scales (1002).
Author: Will Schutz.
Publisher: Mind Garden, Inc.

[1520]
Mathematical Olympiads.

Purpose: Constructed "to discover and challenge secondary school students with outstanding mathematical talent."
Population: Secondary school.
Publication Dates: 1972–2001.
Scores: Total score only.
Administration: Group.
Manual: No manual.
Price Data: Available from publisher.
Author: Committee on the American Mathematics Competitions.
Publisher: Mathematical Association of America; American Mathematics Competitions.

a) USA MATHEMATICAL OLYMPIAD.
Acronym: USAMO.
Time: (10–20) minutes over 2 sessions.
Comments: Test administered annually in April; selection to participate... is based on both the AMC12 and AIME scores.
b) INTERNATIONAL MATHEMATICAL OLYMPIAD.
Acronym: IMO.
Time: (10–20) minutes over 2 sessions.
Comments: Test administered annually in July; selection to participate is based on USAMO scores and other scores obtained during the training session.
Cross References: For reviews by Phillip L. Ackerman and William R. Koch, see 11:228.

[1521]
Mathematics Attainment Test C1.

Purpose: Designed to concentrate on children's mathematical understanding.
Population: Ages 9–12.
Publication Dates: 1965–1969.

Scores: Total score only.
Administration: Group.
Price Data: Price information available from publisher for test booklets and manual.
Time: (50) minutes.
Author: National Foundation for Educational Research.
Publisher: NFER-Nelson Publishing Co., Ltd.
Cross References: See T5:1596 (1 references); for a review by John Cook, see 7:470.

[1522]
Mathematics Attainment Test DE2.
Purpose: Designed to assess "children's mathematical understanding rather than their skill at computation."
Population: Ages 10–12.
Publication Dates: 1967–1970.
Scores: Total score only.
Administration: Group.
Price Data: Price information available from publisher for test booklets and manual (1970, 8 pages).
Time: (50–60) minutes.
Comments: Formerly called Intermediate Mathematics Test I; Mathematics Attainment Test DE1 is no longer available.
Author: National Foundation for Educational Research in England and Wales.
Publisher: NFER-Nelson Publishing Co., Ltd. [England].

[1523]
Mathematics Attainment Test EF.
Purpose: Used to identify pupils who have learning difficulties in the area of mathematical understanding.
Population: Ages 11-0 to 13-6.
Publication Date: 1972.
Scores: Total score only.
Administration: Group.
Price Data: Price information available from publisher for reusable test booklets, answer sheets, marking stencis, and manual.
Time: (50) minutes.
Author: NFER-Nelson Publishing Co., Ltd.
Publisher: NFER-Nelson Publishing Co., Ltd. [England].

[1524]
Mathematics Attitude Inventory.
Purpose: "To measure the attitudes toward mathematics of secondary school students."
Population: Grades 7–12.
Publication Date: 1979.
Acronym: MAI.
Scores, 6: Perception of the Mathematics Teacher, Anxiety Toward Mathematics, Value of Mathematics in Society, Self-Concept in Mathematics, Enjoyment of Mathematics, Motivation in Mathematics.

Administration: Group.
Price Data: Price information available from publisher for tests, scoring key, and manual (26 pages).
Time: (20–30) minutes.
Comments: Tests may be reproduced locally.
Author: Richard S. Sandman.
Publisher: Psychological Foundations of Education [No reply from publisher; status unknown].
Cross References: See T5:1599 (6 references); for reviews by Harvey Resnick and Richard F. Schmid, see 9:664 (3 references); see also T3:1410 (1 reference).

[1525]
Mathematics Competency Test.
Purpose: Constructed to assess "mathematics achievement."
Population: Ages 11 to adult.
Publication Date: 1996.
Scores: Total score only.
Administration: Group.
Price Data: Available from publisher.
Time: (40) minutes.
Authors: P. E. Vernon, K. M. Miller, and J. F. Izard.
Publisher: Australian Council for Educational Research Ltd. [Australia] and Hodder & Stoughton Educational [England].
Cross References: For reviews by Joseph C. Ciechalski and G. Michael Poteat, see 14:222.

[1526]
Mathematics 8–12.
Purpose: Designed "to assess the extent to which children have acquired the mathematical skills and concepts covered by each year's curriculum."
Population: Ages 8–12.
Publication Dates: 1983–1985.
Scores, 5: Understanding, Computation, Application, Factual Recall, Total.
Administration: Group.
Levels, 5: Mathematics 8, Mathematics 9, Mathematics 10, Mathematics 11, Mathematics 12.
Price Data: Price information available from publisher for test booklets (specify Mathematics 8, 9, 10, 11, or 12), Teacher's Guide, and specimen set including 1 each of 8–12 test booklets, teacher's guide, and group record sheet.
Time: (60–80) minutes for each level.
Authors: Alan Brighouse, David Godber, and Peter Patilla.
Publisher: NFER-Nelson Publishing Co., Ltd. [England].

[1527]
Mathematics Self-Efficacy Scale.
Purpose: Intended to measure beliefs regarding ability to perform various math-related tasks and behaviors.
Population: College freshmen.

Publication Date: 1993.
Acronym: MATH.
Scores, 3: Mathematics Task Self-Efficacy, Math-Related School Subjects Self-Efficacy, Total Mathematics Self-Efficacy Score.
Administration: Group.
Forms, 2: A, B.
Price Data, 2001: $25 per sampler set including manual (22 pages); $125 per one-year permission to reproduce up to 200 administrations of the test.
Time: (15) minutes.
Authors: Nancy E. Betz and Gail Hackett.
Publisher: Mind Garden, Inc.
Cross References: For reviews by Joseph C. Ciechalski and Everett V. Smith, Jr., see 14:223; see also T5:1602 (1 reference).

[1528]
Mathematics 7.

Purpose: "Assess the mathematics attainment of children near the end of the school year in which they reach their seventh birthday."
Population: Ages 6-10 to 7-9.
Publication Date: 1987.
Scores: 1 individual total score, 4 item analysis categories: Understanding, Computational Skill, Application, Factual Recall.
Administration: Group.
Price Data: Price information available from publisher for specimen set including Teacher's Guide (24 pages), test booklet, and group record sheet.
Time: (30–50) minutes.
Comments: Downward extension of Mathematics 8–12 Series (1526); no norms for categories; orally administered.
Author: Test Development Unit of the Foundation for Educational Research in England and Wales.
Publisher: NFER-Nelson Publishing Co., Ltd. [England].
Cross References: For reviews by Camilla Persson Benbow and Kevin Menefee, see 11:230.

[1529]
A Mathematics Test for Grades Four, Five and Six.

Purpose: Designed to measure "achievement in modern mathematics."
Population: Grades 4–6.
Publication Date: 1969.
Scores, 13: Understanding Numeration Systems, Set Terminology, Mathematical Structure, Addition and Subtraction of Whole Numbers, Multiplication of Whole Numbers, Division of Whole Numbers, Common Fractions, Decimal Fractions and Per Cent, Measurements, Geometry, Solving Problems with the Use of Number Sentences, Graphs and Scale Drawings, Total.

Administration: Group.
Price Data: Available from publisher.
Time: (120–180) minutes in 2 sessions.
Author: Stanley J. LeJeune.
Publisher: Psychometric Affiliates.
Cross References: For a review by William H. Nibbelink, see 8:280; for a review by Arthur Mittman, see 7:476.

[1530]
Mather-Woodcock Group Writing Tests.

Purpose: "Designed for early identification of problems/weaknesses, measurement of growth in writing skills, instructional planning, and curriculum evaluation."
Population: Grades 2.0–16.9.
Publication Date: 1997.
Acronym: GWT.
Scores: 3 clusters (Total Writing, Basic Writing Skills, Expressive Writing Ability), and 4 subtests (Dictation Spelling, Writing Samples, Editing, Writing Fluency).
Administration: Group.
Price Data: Available from publisher.
Time: (60) minutes or less.
Authors: Nancy Mather and Richard W. Woodcock.
Publisher: Riverside Publishing.
Cross References: For a review by Bruce Thompson, see 14:224.

[1531]
Matrix Analogies Test.

Purpose: Developed to "measure nonverbal reasoning ability."
Population: Ages 5-0 to 17-11.
Publication Date: 1985.
Author: Jack A. Naglieri.
Publisher: The Psychological Corporation.
a) SHORT FORM.
Acronym: MAT-SF.
Administration: Group.
Scores: Total score only.
Price Data, 2002: $105 per 15 test booklets; $58 per 25 answer sheets; $43 per manual (1985, 45 pages); $51 per examination kit.
Time: 25(30) minutes.
b) EXPANDED FORM.
Acronym: MAT-EF.
Administration: Individual.
Scores, 5: Pattern Completion, Reasoning by Analogy, Serial Reasoning, Spatial Visualization, Total.
Price Data: $218 per complete kit including stimulus book, 50 answer sheets, manual (1985, 82 pages) and case; $98 per stimulus manual; $58 per 50 answer sheets; $73 per examiner's manual.
Time: (20–25) minutes.

Cross References: See T5:1607 (15 references) and T4:1566 (8 references); for a review by Robert F. McMorris, David L. Rule, and Wendy J. Steinberg, see 10:191 (1 reference).

[1532]
Mayer-Salovey-Caruso Emotional Intelligence Test.

Purpose: Designed to assess emotional intelligence, measuring a person's capacity for reasoning with emotional information.
Population: Age 17 and older.
Publication Date: 2002.
Acronym: MSCEIT.
Scores, 4: Managing Emotions, Understanding Emotions, Using Emotions, Perceiving Emotions.
Administration: Individual or group.
Price Data, 2002: $50 per user kit including user's manual (100 pages), 1 profile summary report, and 1 item booklet; $40 per user's manual; $30 per mail-in/fax-in report
Time: 25–35 minutes.
Comments: Self-completed.
Authors: John D. Mayer, Peter Salovey, David R. Caruso.
Publisher: Multi-Health Systems, Inc.

[1533]
The MbM Questionnaire: Managing by Motivation, Third Edition.

Purpose: Designed for "helping managers understand their own needs" … and "to identify the needs of their employees."
Population: Managers and supervisors.
Publication Dates: 1986–1996.
Acronym: The MbM Questionnaire.
Scores: 4 scales: Safety/Security, Social/Belonging, Self-Esteem, Self-Actualization.
Administration: Group.
Price Data: Available from publisher.
Time: (10) minutes.
Author: Marshall Sashkin.
Publisher: Human Resource Development Press.
Cross References: For reviews by John W. Fleenor and Robert K. Gable, see 14:225.

[1534]
McCall-Crabbs Standard Test Lessons in Reading.

Purpose: Measurement of reading progress.
Population: Reading level grades 3-8.
Publication Dates: 1926–1979.
Scores: Item and grade equivalent scores.
Administration: Group.
Levels, 6: Overlapping levels labeled A, B, C, D, E, F.

Price Data, 2002: $2.95 per test booklet (any level); $6.95 per 30 answer sheets; $1.50 per manual/answer key (1979, 16 pages).
Time: 3 minutes for any one test; 180 minutes for each booklet (60 tests per booklet).
Comments: Fourth edition.
Authors: William A. McCall and Lelah Crabbs Schroeder; revision by Robert P. Starr.
Publisher: Teachers College Press.
Cross References: See T4:1568 (1 reference); for a review by Brendan John Bartlett, see 9:669.

[1535]
McCarron-Dial System.

Purpose: A battery of neurometric and behavioral measures to be used for vocational, educational, and neuropsychological assessment particularly in meeting the programming needs of handicapped persons.
Population: Normal and handicapped individuals ages 3 to adult.
Publication Dates: 1973-1986.
Acronym: MDS.
Scores: 5 factors: Verbal-Spatial-Cognitive, Sensory, Motor, Emotional, Integration-Coping.
Administration: Individual.
Parts: 3 components (Auxiliary Component, Haptic Visual Discrimination Test [HVDT], McCarron Assessment of Neuromuscular Development [MAND]).
Price Data, 2002: $2,825 per complete System including Auxiliary, HVDT, and MAND Components; price data for software for computer-assisted programs supporting the MDS available from publisher; price information for workshops and training available from publisher.
Comments: "A commitment to receive training is required for all purchasers of the McCarron-Dial System"; components available as separates.
Authors: Lawrence McCarron and Jack G. Dial.
Publisher: McCarron-Dial Systems.
a) AUXILIARY COMPONENT.
    Publication Dates: 1973-1986.
    Price Data: $525 per set of materials in carrying case; $42 per 25 forms for Peabody Form A; $25.25 per 50 IEP forms; $26.25 per 25 IPP forms; $105 per manual (1986, 259 pages).
    Comments: Manual title is Revised McCarron-Dial Evaluation System Manual; kit includes Peabody Picture Vocabulary Test-III (1997), Bender Visual Motor Gestalt Test, and Koppitz Scoring Manual for The Bender Gestalt Test for Young Children, the McCarron-Dial System Individual Evaluation Profile (IEP), the McCarron-Dial Individual Program Plan (IPP), the Observational Emotional Inventory, the Emotional Behavioral Checklist, and the Dial Behavior Rating Scale.

1) *Dial Behavior Rating Scale.*
Purpose: To provide an abbreviated assessment of essential personal, social, and work adjustment behaviors that relate to vocational placement, adjustment to work, and personal-social adjustment.
Publication Dates: 1973–1986.
Acronym: BRS.
Price Data: $25.25 per 25 forms.
Author: Jack G. Dial.
2) *Observational Emotional Inventory.*
Publication Date: 1986.
Acronym: OEI.
Price Data: $25.25 per 25 forms.
Time: 120 minutes on each of 5 days.
Comments: Behavior checklist.
3) *Emotional Behavioral Checklist.*
Purpose: To assess an individual's overt emotional behavior.
Publication Date: 1986.
Acronym: EBC.
Price Data: $25.25 per 25 forms.
Comments: Behavior Checklist (alternate to OEI).
b) HAPTIC VISUAL DISCRIMINATION TEST.
Purpose: To measure an individual's haptic-visual integration skills.
Publication Dates: 1976–1979.
Acronym: HVDT.
Scores, 4: Shape, Size, Texture, Configuration.
Price Data: $1,040 per complete kit including score forms, photographic plates, folding screen, sets of shapes, sizes, textures, and configurations, manual (1988, 261 forms) in a carrying case; $28 per 50 score forms; $45 per manual.
Time: (10-15) minutes per hand.
Comments: Manual title is Sensory Integration: The Haptic Visual Processes.
c) McCARRON ASSESSMENT OF NEUROMUSCULAR DEVELOPMENT.
Purpose: "A standardized and quantitative procedure for assessing fine and gross motor abilities."
Population: Ages 3.5 to adult.
Publication Dates: 1976–1986.
Acronym: MAND.
Scores, 3: Fine Motor, Gross Motor, Total.
Price Data: $1,260 per complete kit including score forms, a dynamometer, stopwatch-timer, components for fine and gross motor testing, and manual (1982, 221 pages) in carrying case; $336 per 25 score forms; $57.75 per manual.
Time: (15) minutes.
Comments: Manual title is Revised McCarron Assessment of Neuromuscular Development Manual.
Author: Lawrence T. McCarron.

Cross References: For reviews by Calvin P. Garbin and David C. Solly, see 11:231 (1 reference).

[1536]
McCarthy Scales of Children's Abilities.
Purpose: Developed to "determine . . . general intellectual level as well as . . . strengths and weaknesses in important abilities."
Population: Ages 2.6–8.6.
Publication Dates: 1970–1972.
Acronym: MSCA.
Scores, 6: Verbal, Perceptual-Performance, Quantitative, Composite (General Cognitive), Memory, Motor.
Administration: Individual.
Price Data, 2002: $583 per complete set including all necessary equipment, 25 drawing booklets, 25 record forms, and manual (1972, 217 pages); $57 per 25 drawing booklets; $220 per 100 drawing booklets; $43 per 25 record forms; $157 per 100 record forms; $66 per manual.
Time: (45–60) minutes.
Author: Dorothea McCarthy.
Publisher: The Psychological Corporation.
Cross References: See T5:1612 (101 references) and T4:1571 (97 references); for reviews by Kathleen D. Paget and David L. Wodrich, see 9:671 (29 references); see also T3:1424 (60 references); for reviews by Jane V. Hunt, Jerome M. Sattler, and Arthur B. Silverstein, and excerpted reviews by Everett E. Davis, Linda Hufano and Ralph Hoepfner, R. B. Ammons and C. H. Ammons, and Alan Krichev, see 8:219 (29 references).

[1537]
McCarthy Screening Test.
Purpose: Designed to "identify children who are likely to encounter difficulty in coping with school-work."
Population: Ages 4–6.5.
Publication Dates: 1970–1978.
Acronym: MST.
Scores, 6: Right-Left Orientation, Verbal Memory, Draw-A-Design, Numerical Memory, Conceptual Grouping, Leg Coordination.
Administration: Individual.
Price Data, 2002: $225 per complete set including all necessary equipment, manual (1978, 71 pages), 25 record forms, 25 drawing booklets, and carrying case: $58 per 25 drawing booklets; $230 per 100 drawing booklets; $37 per 25 record forms; $152 per 100 record forms; $52 per manual.
Time: (20) minutes.
Comments: Adaptation of the McCarthy Scales of Children's Abilities; criterion-referenced; percentile cutoff scores provided for classification as "at risk" for learning problems.

Author: Dorothea McCarthy.
Publisher: The Psychological Corporation.
Cross References: See T5:1613 (2 references) and T4:1572 (9 references); for reviews by Nadeen L. Kaufman and Jack A. Naglieri, see 9:672 (3 references); see also T3:1425 (2 references).

[1538]
McDowell Vision Screening Kit.

Purpose: "Designed for screening children's vision problems."
Population: Birth to age 21.
Publication Date: 1994.
Scores, 15: Distance Vision, Near Point Vision, Ocular Alignment/Motility (Cover/Uncover, Light Reflex), Color Perception, Ocular Function (Pupils, Scanning, Shifts Attention, Blink, Tracking, Convergence, Conjugate Gaze, Visual Fields, Distant/Near Accommodation, Nystagmus).
Administration: Individual.
Price Data, 2002: $125 per kit including all test materials, 100 recording forms, and manual (40 pages); $22.50 per 100 recording forms; $40 per manual.
Time: (10–20) minutes.
Comments: Recording form for use in screening young children or disabled students; administrator scored.
Authors: P. Marlene McDowell and Richard L. McDowell.
Publisher: Western Psychological Services.
Cross References: For a review by Cynthia A. Rohrbeck, see 14:226.

[1539]
MD5 Mental Ability Test.

Purpose: "To assess mental ability quickly, easily and over a wide range of educational and ability levels, in staff selection, placement and counselling."
Population: Supervisors to managers.
Publication Date: No date on test materials.
Scores: Total score only.
Administration: Group.
Price Data, 2001: £3.25 per question/answer book; £5 per scoring key; £19.50 per technical manual; £300 per computer system version.
Time: (15) minutes.
Author: The Test Agency.
Publisher: The Test Agency Limited [England].
Cross References: For reviews by M. Harry Daniels and David J. Mealor, see 10:193.

[1540]
MDS Vocational Interest Exploration System.

Purpose: "A computer-assisted interest exploration process that facilitates the discovery of personal preferences and job opportunities."

Population: High school–adults.
Publication Date: 1991.
Acronym: VIE.
Scores: 3 steps: Selection of Jobs Based on Work Preferences, Occupational Exploration, Job Review Comparison.
Administration: Individual.
Price Data, 2002: $350 per set including computer program (IBM/Compatibles, Macintosh, and Apple), 4 VIE job manuals, instructor's manual (135 pages), 25 VIE system guides with work preference questionnaires and job review forms.
Time: Administration time not reported.
Comments: Three supplementary forms are also provided with materials: Pre-Post Job Knowledge Form, Understanding of Self and Job Questionnaire, and Vocational Goal Planning Exercise.
Authors: Lawrence T. McCarron and Harriette P. Spires.
Publisher: McCarron-Dial Systems.
Cross References: For reviews by Douglas J. McRae and Myra N. Womble, see 13:194.

[1541]
Meadow-Kendall Social-Emotional Assessment Inventory for Deaf and Hearing Impaired Students.

Purpose: "Can be used to flag students who need extra attention in particular areas . . . . useful in communicating with parents who are reluctant to admit that their child needs special attention ... helpful in implementing an individualized program so that social and emotional areas are emphasized in the curriculum for the child who needs them."
Population: Ages 3–6, 7–21.
Publication Date: 1983.
Acronym: SEAI.
Administration: Group.
Levels: 2 levels.
Price Data, 2001: $8 per 10 forms; $15 per manual (37 pages).
Time: Administration time not reported.
Comments: Behavior checklist to be completed by adult informant.
Authors: Kathryn P. Meadow and others listed below.
Publisher: Laurent Clerc National Deaf Education Center.
  a) PRE-SCHOOL.
    Population: Ages 3-6.
    Scores, 5: Sociable/Communicative Behaviors, Impulsive Dominating Behaviors, Developmental Lags, Anxious/Compulsive Behaviors, Special Items.
    Authors: Kathryn P. Meadow, Pamela Getson, Chi K. Lee, Linda Stamper, and the Center for Studies in Education and Human Development.

b) SCHOOL-AGE.
Population: Ages 7–21.
Scores, 3: Social Adjustment, Self Image, Emotional Adjustment.
Authors: Kathryn P. Meadow, Michael A. Karchmer, Linda M. Petersen, and Lawrence Rudner.
Cross References: See T5:1618 (3 references) and T4:1579 (2 references); for reviews by Marilyn E. Demorest and Kenneth L. Sheldon, see 10:194 (1 reference).

[1542]
Means-Ends Problem-Solving Procedure.
Purpose: Designed to measure real-life problem-solving.
Population: Adults.
Publication Date: 1975.
Acronym: MEPS.
Scores, 2: Relevancy Scores, Relevant Means.
Administration: Group.
Forms, 2: Form 1-F for females, Form 1-M for males.
Price Data: Available from publisher.
Time: [30–60] minutes.
Comments: May be orally administered.
Authors: Jerome J. Platt and George Spivack.
Publisher: Hahnemann Medical College & Hospital, Department of Mental Health Sciences [No reply from publisher; status unknown].
Cross References: See T5:1619 (11 references), T4:1580 (24 references), T3:1436 (6 references), and 8:612 (11 references).

[1543]
Measure of Achieving Tendency.
Purpose: Developed to assess achievement motivation.
Population: Ages 15 and older.
Publication Dates: 1969–1993.
Acronym: MACH.
Scores: Total score only.
Administration: Group or individual.
Price Data: Available from publisher for complete kit including scales, scoring directions, norms, manual (1994, 8 pages), and literature review.
Time: (10–15) minutes.
Comments: Current revision also based on previous edition entitled A Questionnaire Measure of Individual Differences in Achieving Tendency.
Author: Albert Mehrabian.
Publisher: Albert Mehrabian.
Cross References: For reviews by James T. Austin and E. Scott Huebner, see 13:195 (1 reference); for a review by Timothy S. Hartshorne of an earlier edition, see 10:301; for a review by Jayne E. Stake of an earlier edition, see 9:682; see also T3:1442 (1 reference).

[1544]
Measure of Child Stimulus Screening and Arousability.
Purpose: Designed to assess child individual differences in positive and/or negative emotionality, emotional sensitivity, or emotional reactivity.
Population: Ages 3 months to 7 years.
Publication Date: 1978.
Scores: Total score only.
Administration: Group or individual.
Manual: No manual.
Price Data: Available from publisher for test kit including scale, scoring directions, norms, and descriptive material.
Time: [15] minutes.
Comments: Ratings by parents.
Authors: Albert Mehrabian and Carol A. Falender.
Publisher: Albert Mehrabian.
Cross References: See T5:1621 (1 reference); for a review by Steven Klee, see 9:678; see also T3:1439 (2 references).

[1545]
Measure of Existential Anxiety.
Purpose: Designed as a measure of existential anxiety.
Population: Adults and college-age.
Publication Date: No date.
Scores: Total score only.
Administration: Group.
Price Data, 2001: $3 per specimen set.
Time: Administration time not reported.
Authors: L. R. Good and K. C. Good.
Publisher: Psychometric Affiliates.

[1546]
Measure of Individual Differences in Dominance-Submissiveness.
Purpose: Constructed as a "general measure of trait dominance-submissiveness—the general feeling of control and influence versus lack of control over one's surroundings and life situations."
Population: Ages 15 and older.
Publication Dates: 1978–1994.
Scores: Total score only.
Administration: Group or individual.
Price Data: Available from publisher for test kit including scale, scoring directions, norms, and manual (1994, 7 pages).
Time: (10–15) minutes.
Authors: Albert Mehrabian and Melissa Hines (original edition).
Publisher: Albert Mehrabian.
Cross References: For reviews by Robert H. Deluty and Douglas N. Jackson of an earlier edition, see 9:679.

[1547]
Measure of Questioning Skills.
Purpose: Designed "to measure the quantity and quality of questions."
Population: Grades 3–10.
Publication Dates: 1986–1993.
Scores, 4: Gathering Information, Organizing Information, Extending Information, Composite.
Administration: Group.
Forms, 2: A, B.
Price Data, 2002: $42.85 per complete kit including manual (1993, 61 pages), 20 activity booklets, 20 tally sheets, 20 result forms, 20 individual profile charts, and 1 class record sheet (specify form); $28 per 20 activity booklets, 20 tally sheets, and 1 class record sheet (specify form); $16.55 per manual; $18.80 per sample set.
Time: (20) minutes.
Authors: Ralph Himsl and Garnet Miller.
Publisher: Scholastic Testing Service, Inc.
Cross References: For a review by Darrell R. Sabers, see 14:228.

[1548]
A Measure of Self-Esteem.
Purpose: Designed as a "measure of self-esteem ... that was constructed on the assumption that low self-esteem is indicated when someone feels inferior, inadequate, unworthy, disliked, helpless, etc."
Population: College-age and adults.
Publication Date: No date.
Scores: Total score only.
Administration: Group.
Price Data, 2001: $3 per specimen set.
Time: Administration time not reported.
Authors: L. R. Good and K. C. Good.
Publisher: Psychometric Affiliates.

[1549]
Measure of Self-Evaluation.
Purpose: Developed to measure an individual's need for self-evaluation.
Population: Adults.
Publication Date: No date.
Scores: Total score only.
Administration: Group.
Price Data, 2001: $3 per specimen set.
Time: Administration time not reported.
Comments: Manual is entitled An Objective Measure of the Self-Evaluation Motive.
Authors: L. R. Good and K. C. Good.
Publisher: Psychometric Affiliates.

[1550]
Measure of Vindication.
Purpose: Designed to measure the vindication motive.

Population: College-age and adults.
Publication Date: No date.
Scores: Total score only.
Administration: Group.
Price Data, 2001: $3 per specimen set.
Time: Administration time not reported.
Authors: L. R. Good and K. C. Good.
Publisher: Psychometric Affiliates.

[1551]
The Measurement of Moral Judgment.
Purpose: Measures moral judgment through dilemma interviews.
Population: Ages 10 and over.
Publication Date: 1984.
Scores: 1 score dichotomized as moral stage (I to V) and moral type (A: Heteronomous or B: Autonomous).
Administration: Individual.
Forms, 3: Parallel Forms A, B, and C consist of 3 standard dilemmas each.
Price Data: Available from publisher.
Time: (10–15) minutes.
Authors: Anne Colby, Lawrence Kohlberg, John Gibbs, and Marcus Lieberman.
Publisher: Cambridge University Press.
Cross References: See T5:1625 (1 reference), 9:681 (9 references), and T3:1262 (2 references).

[1552]
Measures in Post Traumatic Stress Disorder: A Practitioner's Guide.
Purpose: A set of tests that may be used to assist in identifying post traumatic stress disorder.
Population: Adults.
Publication Date: 1998.
Administration: Individual and group.
Price Data, 1998: £95 per practitioner's guide (77 pages); sample sheets are free.
Time: Administration time not reported.
Comments: Some of these tests may also have other uses and may be available separately from other sources.
Authors: Stuart Turner and Deborah Lee.
Publisher: NFER-Nelson Publishing Co., Ltd. [England].
a) GENERAL HEALTH QUESTIONNAIRE—28.
  Publication Date: 1981.
  Acronym: GHQ-28.
  Scores: 4 subscales; Somatic Symptoms, Anxiety and Insomnia, Social Dysfunction, Severe Depression.
  Comments: Self-report measure; see 1038.
b) HOSPITAL ANXIETY AND DEPRESSION SCALE.
  Purpose: Designed to detect anxiety and depressive states.
  Publication Dates: 1983–1994.

Acronym: HADS.
Scores: 2 subscales; Anxiety, Depression.
Comments: Self-report.
c) THE IMPACT OF EVENT SCALE.
Purpose: Designed as a measure of specific responses to trauma.
Acronym: IES.
Scores: 2 subscales; Intrusion, Avoidance.
Comments: Self-report.
d) DISSOCIATIVE EXPERIENCES SCALE II.
Purpose: A measure of dissociation.
Publication Date: 1993.
Acronym: DES-II.
Comments: Self-report; see 828.
e) INTERNALISED SHAME SCALE.
Purpose: Developed to measure the extent to which respondents have internalised shame feelings.
Publication Date: 1990.
Acronym: ISS.
Scores, 2: Shame, Positive Self-Esteem.
Comments: Self-administered.
f) TRAUMA, ATTITUDES AND BELIEFS SCALE.
Purpose: A descriptive measure intended to identify feelings of personal change and alienation.
Acronym: TABS.
Comments: Self-administered.
g) TRAUMA INTERVIEW SCHEDULE.
Acronym: TIS.
Comments: A structured interview.
h) CLINICIAN-ADMINISTERED PTSD SCALE FOR DSM-IV.
Acronym: CAPS.
Comments: A structured interview designed to assess the 17 symptoms of PTSD outlined in the DSM-IV.

[1553]
Measures of Affiliative Tendency and Sensitivity to Rejection.

Population: Ages 15 and older.
Publication Dates: 1976–1994.
Administration: Group or individual.
Price Data: Available from publisher for complete kit including scales, scoring directions, norms, manual (1994, 13 pages), and literature review.
Time: (10–15) minutes.
Author: Albert Mehrabian.
Publisher: Albert Mehrabian.
a) AFFILIATIVE TENDENCY.
Purpose: "Designed to measure friendliness, sociability, and social skills conducive to positive and comfortable social exchanges."
Score: Total score only.
b) SENSITIVITY TO REJECTION.
Purpose: "Designed to assess social submissiveness."
Scores: Total score only.

Cross References: For reviews by Sheila Mehta and Scott T. Meier, see 13:196; for a review by Peter D. Lifton of an earlier edition, see 9:683; see also T3:1443 (1 reference).

[1554]
Measures of Individual Differences in Temperament.

Purpose: Provides three basic temperament scores (Trait Pleasure-Displeasure, Trait Arousability, Trait Dominance-Submissiveness) for a comprehensive description of temperament; includes formulas that can employ these basic temperament scores to compute a variety of personality-scale scores (e.g., Trait Anxiety, Neuroticism, Depression, Exuberance, Dependency, Achievement, Affiliation, Shyness, Dependency).
Population: Ages 15 and older.
Publication Dates: 1978–1994.
Scores: Total scores only.
Administration: Group or individual.
Price Data: Available from publisher for complete kit including scales, scoring directions, norms, computational formulas, four manuals (1994, 10 pages, 8 pages, 7 pages, 5 pages), and literature review.
Time: (30–45) minutes.
Author: Albert Mehrabian.
Publisher: Albert Mehrabian.
Cross References: For a review by John B. Gormly of an earlier edition, see 9:684; see also T3:1444 (1 reference).

[1555]
Measures of Musical Abilities.

Purpose: Constructed to "measure the kinds of basic judgements that are necessarily involved in music-making."
Population: Ages 7–14.
Publication Dates: 1966–1985.
Scores: 4 tests: Pitch Discrimination, Tonal Memory, Chord Analysis, Rhythmic Memory.
Administration: Group.
Price Data: Price information available from publisher for complete set, audiocassette tape, answer sheets, and manual (1985, 8 pages) and scoring key.
Time: 21(30) minutes.
Comments: Self-administered by cassette tape.
Author: Arnold Bentley.
Publisher: NFER-Nelson Publishing Co., Ltd. [England].
Cross References: For a review by Richard Colwell, see 10:196; see also T3:1446 (1 reference) and T2:206 (3 references); for reviews by Richard Colwell and John McLeish, and excerpted reviews by Richard R. Bentley and Paul R. Farnsworth, see 7:247 (13 references).

[1556]

Measures of Pleasure-, Arousal-, and Dominance-Inducing Qualities of Parental Attitudes.

Purpose: Constructed for "a comprehensive measurement of the emotional climate parents create for their children."

Population: Parents of children ages 3 months to 7 years.

Publication Date: 1980.

Scores, 3: Pleasure-Inducing Parental Attitude, Arousal-Inducing Parental Attitude, Dominance-Inducing Parental Attitude.

Administration: Individual.

Manual: No manual.

Price Data: Available from publisher for complete kit including scale, scoring directions, norms, and descriptive material.

Time: [20] minutes.

Authors: Carol Ann Falender and Albert Mehrabian.

Publisher: Albert Mehrabian.

Cross References: For reviews by Douglas N. Jackson and Charles Wenar, see 9:686; see also T3:1448 (1 reference).

[1557]

Measures of Psychosocial Development.

Purpose: "Provides a measure of the positive and negative attitudes, or attributes of personality, associated with each developmental stage, the status of conflict resolution at each stage, and overall psychosocial health."

Population: Ages 13–50 years and older.

Publication Dates: 1980–1988.

Acronym: MPD.

Scores, 27: 8 Positive scores (Trust [P1], Autonomy [P2], Initiative [P3], Industry [P4], Identity [P5], Intimacy [P6], Generativity [P7], Ego Integrity [P8]), 8 Negative scores (Mistrust [N1], Shame and Doubt [N2], Guilt [N3], Inferiority [N4], Identity Confusion [N5], Isolation [N6], Stagnation [N7], Despair [N8]), 8 Resolution scale scores (R1, R2, R3, R4, R5, R6, R7, R8), 3 Total scores (Total Positive [TP], Total Negative [TN], Total Resolution [TR]).

Administration: Individual or group.

Price Data: Available from publisher for complete kit including 25 reusable item booklets, 50 answer sheets, 25 male profile forms, 25 female profile forms, and manual (1988, 31 pages).

Time: (15–20) minutes.

Comments: Based upon Erikson's theory of human development.

Author: Gwen A. Hawley.

Publisher: Psychological Assessment Resources, Inc.

Cross References: See T5:1631 (4 references); for reviews by James C. Carmer and Robert K. Gable, see 11:233.

[1558]

Mechanic Evaluation Test—Forms AI-C, BI-C, CI-C.

Purpose: To measure the knowledge and skills required for mechanics.

Population: Mechanic job applicants.

Publication Dates: 1992–2001.

Administration: Group.

Levels, 3: C Mechanic, B Mechanic, A Mechanic.

Price Data, 2002: $16 per consumable self-scoring booklet (20 minimum order); $24.95 per manual (A: 2001, 20 pages; B: 2001, 18 pages; C: 2001, 18 pages).

Time: [60] minutes.

Comments: Self-scoring instrument.

Author: Roland T. Ramsay.

Publisher: Ramsay Corporation.

a) A MECHANIC.

Scores: 6 areas: Welding & HVAC; Pneumatics amd Lubrication; Print Reading and Shop; Electrical; Mechanical & Miscellaneous; Total.

b) B MECHANIC.

Scores: 5 areas: Welding, Plumbing & HVAC; Pneumatics and Lubrication; Print Reading, Mechanical & Shop; Electrical; Total.

c) C MECHANIC.

Scores: 6 areas: Welding, Plumbing & HVAC; Pneumatics and Lubrication; Mechanical & Print Reading; Electrical; Shop, Tools & Machines; Rigging & Miscellaneous; Total.

Cross References: For reviews by David O. Anderson and Alan C. Bugbee, see 13:254.

[1559]

Mechanical Aptitude Test: Acorn National Aptitude Tests.

Purpose: Designed to measure interests and abilities associated with aptitudes for skilled trades.

Population: Grades 7–16 and adults.

Publication Dates: 1943–1952.

Scores, 5: Verbal (Comprehension of Mechanical Tasks, Use of Tools and Materials, Matching Tools and Operations), Nonverbal (Use of Tools and Materials), Total.

Administration: Group.

Price Data: Available from publisher.

Time: 45(50) minutes.

Authors: Andrew Kobal, J. Wayne Wrightstone, and Karl R. Kunze.

Publisher: Psychometric Affiliates.

Cross References: For reviews by Reign H. Bittner, James M. Porter, Jr., and Alec Rodger, see 3:669.

[1560]
Mechanical Aptitudes.

Purpose: Measures ability to learn and succeed in an industrial, mechanical or maintenance position.
Population: Applicants for industrial positions, training programs, and vocational counseling.
Publication Dates: 1947–1995.
Scores, 4: Mechanical Knowledge, Space Relations, Shop Arithmetic, Total.
Administration: Individual or group.
Price Data, 2002: $177 per start-up kit including 5 test booklets, 25 answer sheets, 100 profile sheets, and examiner's manual; $91 per 5 test booklets (quantity discounts available); $41 per 25 answer sheets (quantity discounts available); $37 per 100 profile sheets (quantity discounts available); $28 per examiner's manual.
Time: 35 minutes.
Comments: Previously listed as SRA Mechanical Aptitudes.
Author: Richardson, Bellows, Henry & Co., Inc.
Publisher: Reid London House.
Cross References: See T2:2267 (8 references); for reviews by Alec Rodger and Douglas G. Schultz, see 4:764.

[1561]
Mechanical Familiarity Test: ETSA Test 5A.

Purpose: Measures ability to recognize common tools and instruments.
Population: Employment applicants.
Publication Dates: 1959–1998.
Scores: Total score only.
Administration: Group or individual.
Price Data, 2002: $10 per electronic test; $10 each per test booklet and answer sheet (scoring and reporting); $20 per technical manual; $20 per administrator's manual.
Time: (60) minutes.
Comments: Electronic tests available at www.etsatests.com.
Authors: George A. W. Stouffer, Jr., and Psychological Services Bureau, Inc.
Publisher: Employers' Tests and Services Associates.
Cross References: For reviews by Marvin D. Dunnette and Raymond A. Katzell of an earlier version of the ETSA Tests, see 6:1025.

[1562]
Mechanical Knowledge Test: ETSA Test 6A.

Purpose: Designed to measure mechanical insight and understanding.
Population: Employment applicants.
Publication Dates: 1984—1998.
Scores: Total score only.
Administration: Group or individual.
Price Data, 2002: $10 per electronic test; $10 each per test booklet and answer sheet (scoring and report-

ing); $20 per technical manual; $20 per administrator's manual.
Time: (60) minutes.
Comments: Electronic tests available at www.etsatests.com.
Authors: S. Trevor Hadley and George A. W. Stouffer, Jr., and Psychological Services Bureau, Inc.
Publisher: Employers' Tests and Services Associates.
Cross References: For reviews by Marvin D. Dunnette and Raymond A. Katzell of an earlier version of the ETSA Tests, see 6:1025.

[1563]
Mechanical Movements.

Purpose: Assesses the ability to visualize a mechanical system where there is internal movement or displacement of parts.
Population: Employees and potential employees in industrial positions.
Publication Dates: 1959–1963.
Scores: Total score only.
Administration: Individual or group.
Price Data, 2002: $91 per start-up kit including 25 test booklets, score key, and interpretation and research manual (1963, 14 pages); $54 per 25 test booklets (quantity discounts available); $20 per score key; $28 per interpretation and research manual.
Time: 14 minutes.
Authors: L. L. Thurstone and T. E. Jeffrey.
Publisher: Reid London House.
Cross References: For a review by William A. Owens, see 6:1089.

[1564]
MecTest (A Test for Maintenance Mechanics)—Form AU-C.

Purpose: "Developed to measure the mechanical knowledge and skills required for maintenance jobs."
Population: Applicants and incumbents for maintenance jobs.
Publication Dates: 1991–1998.
Scores, 9: Hydraulics and Pneumatics, Print Reading, Welding and Rigging, Power Transmission, Lubrication, Pumps and Piping, Mechanical Maintenance, Machines/Tools/Equipment, Total.
Administration: Group.
Price Data, 2002: $16 each per 20–99 self-scoring booklets (20 minimum order); $24.95 per manual (1998, 17 pages).
Time: (60) minutes.
Comments: Self-scoring instrument.
Author: Roland T. Ramsay.
Publisher: Ramsay Corporation.
Cross References: For a review by Robert J. Drummond, see 13:197.

[1565]
Medical College Admission Test.

Purpose: "Designed primarily to aid members of admissions committees in the . . . selection of applicants" for medical colleges.

Population: Applicants for admission to member colleges of the Association of American Medical Colleges and to other participating institutions.

Publication Dates: 1946–1994.

Acronym: MCAT.

Scores, 4: Verbal Reasoning, Physical Sciences, Biological Sciences, Writing Sample.

Administration: Group.

Price Data, 1994: $15 per student manual; $150 examination fee.

Time: (345) minutes.

Comments: Administered 2 times annually (April, August) at centers established by publisher.

Author: Constructed under the direction of the Association of American Medical Colleges.

Publisher: Administered at the direction of the Association of American Medical Colleges.

Cross References: See T5:1638 (3 references), T4:1600 (11 references), 9:691 (9 references), T3:1576 (40 references), 8:1101 (40 references), and T2:2355 (30 references); for reviews by Nancy S. Cole and James M. Richards, Jr. of earlier forms, see 7:1100 (57 references); for reviews by Robert L. Ebel and Philip H. DuBois, see 6:1137 (43 references); for a review by Alexander G. Wesman, see 5:932 (4 references); for a review by Morey J. Wantman, see 4:817 (11 references).

[1566]
Medical Ethics Inventory.

Purpose: Designed to provide "profiles of the value preferences of medical students regarding medical ethical dilemmas."

Population: First year medical students.

Publication Date: 1982.

Acronym: MEI.

Scores, 6: Social, Economic, Theoretical, Political, Religious, Aesthetic.

Administration: Group.

Price Data: Available from publisher.

Time: [30-40] minutes.

Authors: Cynthia J. Stolman and Rodney L. Doran.

Publisher: Rodney L. Doran [No reply from publisher; status unknown].

Cross References: For reviews by Joseph D. Matarazzo and Gary B. Melton, see 10:197.

[1567]
Meeker Behavioral Correlates.

Purpose: Assesses "major dimensions of intellectual abilities and personality characteristics" for management matching of teams.

Population: Industry.

Publication Date: 1981.

Scores: Ratings by self in 6 areas: Comprehension, Memory, Leadership, Convergent Production Skills, Creativity, Team Contributions.

Administration: Group.

Price Data: Available from publisher.

Time: [20] minutes.

Comments: Self-ratings.

Author: Mary Meeker.

Publisher: SOI Systems.

[1568]
Memory and Behavior Problems Checklist and The Burden Interview.

Publication Dates: 1983–1990.

Administration: Individual.

Price Data, 2001: $5.25 per manual including the instruments.

Authors: Steven H. Zarit and Judy M. Zarit.

Publisher: Gerontology Center, The Pennsylvania State University.

a) MEMORY AND BEHAVIOR PROBLEMS CHECKLIST.

Purpose: Designed to "determine how frequently a dementia patient engages in problematic behaviors and which problems are especially upsetting for family members."

Population: Dementia patients and their families.

Acronym: MBPC.

Scores, 3: Frequency of Problems, Severity of Functional Behavior Problems, Mean Distress.

Comments: Administered by an interviewer to family members of a demential patient.

b) THE BURDEN INTERVIEW.

Purpose: "Designed to assess the stresses experienced by family caregivers of elderly and disabled persons."

Population: Caregivers of elderly and disabled persons.

Scores, 2: Personal Strain, Role Strain.

Comments: Administered by an interviewer or self-administered.

Cross References: For reviews by Sally Kuhlenschmidt and Richard A. Wantz, see 14:229; see also T5:1643 (2 references).

[1569]
Memory Assessment Scales.

Purpose: Developed to provide a comprehensive battery that assesses short- and long-term verbal and visual (nonverbal) memory.

Population: Ages 18 and over.

Publication Date: 1991.

Acronym: MAS.

Scores, 16: Short-Term Memory (Verbal Span, Visual Span, Total), List Acquisition, Delayed List Recall, Delayed Prose Recall, Global Memory Scale (Verbal Memory [List Recall, Immediate Prose Recall, Total], Visual Memory [Visual Reproduction, Immediate Visual Recognition, Total], Total), Delayed Visual Recognition, Names-Faces (Immediate, Delayed) and 7 Verbal Process scores: Total Intrusions, List Clustering (Acquisition, Recall, Delayed Recall), Cued List Recall (Recall, Delayed Recall), List Recognition.
Administration: Individual.
Price Data: Available from publisher for complete kit including stimulus card set, 25 record forms, manual (131 pages), and attache case.
Time: [40–45] minutes.
Author: J. Michael Williams.
Publisher: Psychological Assessment Resources, Inc.
Cross References: See T5:1644 (1 reference); for reviews by Ronald A. Berk and John W. Young, see 12:229.

[1570]
Menometer.
Purpose: Designed to measure "knowledge of the physical aspects of human menstruation."
Population: Adolescents and adults.
Publication Dates: 1974–1988.
Scores: Total score only.
Administration: Group.
Manual: No manual.
Price Data, 2002: $1 per scale.
Time: [10] minutes.
Comments: For a supplementary source, see Panos D. Bardis, "Research Instruments for Population Studies," Society and Culture, July 1974, 5(2), 177-191.
Author: Panos D. Bardis.
Publisher: Donna Bardis.

[1571]
Menstrual Distress Questionnaire.
Purpose: Designed as "a self-report inventory for use in the diagnosis and treatment of premenstrual and menstrual distress."
Population: Women who experience strong to severe premenstrual or menstrual distress.
Publication Dates: 1968–1991.
Acronym: MDQ.
Scores, 8: Pain, Water Retention, Autonomic Reactions, Negative Affect, Impaired Concentration, Behavior Change, Arousal, Control.
Administration: Group or individual.
Forms, 2: Form C, Form T.
Price Data, 2002: $75 per complete kit including 10 questionnaires (Form C), manual (1991, 125 pages), and 2 prepaid Form C mail-in answer sheets for computer scoring and interpretation; $19.50 per 10 Form C

questionnaires; $49 per 50 Form T questionnaires; $11 per Form C prepaid mail-in answer sheet; $27.50 per 50 Form T prepaid mail-in answer sheets; $47.50 per manual; $125 per 20-use Form C disk (PC with DOS).
Time: (15) minutes for Form C; (5) minutes for Form T.
Author: Rudolph H. Moos.
Publisher: Western Psychological Services.
Cross References: See T5:1647 (4 references); for reviews by Jennifer J. Fager and Donna L. Sundre, see 12:230 (12 references); see T4:1608 (7 references), 9:695 (6 references), and T3:1466 (4 references).

[1572]
Mental Status Checklist for Adolescents.
Purpose: To assist professionals in the assessment of adolescents' mental status.
Population: Ages 13–17.
Publication Date: 1988.
Scores: Item scores only.
Administration: Individual.
Price Data: Available from publisher.
Time: Administration time not reported.
Comments: Reliability and validity data not reported; problems checklist.
Authors: Edward H. Dougherty and John A. Schinka.
Publisher: Psychological Assessment Resources, Inc.
Cross References: For a review by Julian Fabry, see 11:234.

[1573]
Mental Status Checklist for Adults, 1988 Revision.
Purpose: "Surveys items that are commonly included in a comprehensive mental status examination."
Population: Adults.
Publication Dates: 1986–1988.
Scores: 10 Content Areas: Presenting Problems, Behavioral/Physical Descriptions, Emotional State, Mental Status, Health and Habits, Legal Issues, Current Living Situation, Diagnoses, Treatment Recommendations, Disposition.
Administration: Individual.
Manual: No manual.
Price Data: Available from publisher.
Time: Administration time not reported.
Author: John A. Schinka.
Publisher: Psychological Assessment Resources, Inc.

[1574]
Mental Status Checklist for Children.
Purpose: Assess childhood problems and plan for treatment approaches.
Population: Ages 5–12.
Publication Date: 1989.
Scores: Item scores only.

Administration: Individual.
Manual: No manual.
Price Data: Available from publisher.
Time: (10–20) minutes.
Comments: Downward extension of the Mental Status Checklist–Adult (1573); scale for ratings by parents, caregivers, or self-ratings; Computer Report package using item responses requires 256K and two disk drives.
Authors: Edward H. Dougherty and John A. Schinka.
Publisher: Psychological Assessment Resources, Inc.
Cross References: For reviews by David Lachar and Marcia B. Shaffer, see 11:235.

[1575]
Mentoring Skills Assessment.

Purpose: Constructed to assess mentoring/coaching skills and mentee skills.
Population: Mentors, coaches, and mentees.
Publication Dates: 1995–1998.
Acronym: MSA.
Scores, 27: Importance, Quality, Frequency on each of the following scales: Listening, Encouraging, Inspiring/Instilling Vision, Coaching, Instructing, Managing Risks, Opening Doors, Demonstrating Personal Mastery, Giving Constructive Feedback.
Administration: Group.
Forms, 2: Mentor/Colleague or Mentee/Colleague.
Manual: No manual.
Price Data, 2001: $100 per set; additional price information available from publisher.
Time: Administration time not reported.
Author: Linda Phillips-Jones.
Publisher: Mind Garden, Inc.

[1576]
Merrill-Palmer Scale of Mental Tests.

Purpose: Designed as a measure of children's intellectual ability.
Population: Ages 24–63 months.
Publication Dates: 1926–1948.
Scores: Overall Performance.
Administration: Individual.
Tests, 33: Action Agent Test (modification of Action-Agent Association Test ['11] by R. S. Woodworth and F. L. Wells), Simple Questions, Repetition of Words and Word Groups, Obeying Simple Commands, Throwing a Ball, Straight Tower, Crossing Feet, Standing On One Foot, Counting Two Blocks, Folding Paper, Making a Block Walk, Drawing Up String, Identification of Self in Mirror, Cutting With Scissors, Matching Colors, Closing Fist and Moving Thumbs, Opposition of Thumb and Fingers, Copying a Circle, Copying a Cross, Copying a Star, Sequin Form Board, Mare and Foal Picture Completion, Manikin, Stutsman Picture Formboard (1, 2, 3), Decroly Matching Game, Wallin Peg Boards, Fitting Sixteen Cubes in a Box, Stutsman Nested Cubes, Stutsman Pyramid Test, Stutsman Buttoning Test, Little Pink Tower Test.

Price Data, 2001: $750 per complete kit including manual, 50 record blanks, and carrying case; $35 per manual; $25 per 50 record blanks; price data for replacement pieces for component tests available from publisher.
Time: Administration time not reported.
Comments: The publisher advised in January 2002 that a revision is in development.
Author: Rachel Stutsman.
Publisher: Stoelting Co.
Cross References: See T5:1653 (29 references) and T4:1614 (19 references); for a review by Jack A. Naglieri, see 9:697 (4 references).

[1577]
Meta-Motivation Inventory.

Purpose: Designed to measure personal and managerial style.
Population: Managers and persons in leadership positions.
Publication Date: 1979.
Acronym: MMI.
Scores, 32: Motivation for Achievement, Perfection, Assertiveness, Independence, Achievement, Meta-Achievement, Deterministic, Approval, Conventional, Dependent, Avoidance, Helplessness, Need for Control, Persuasiveness, Manipulation, Reactive, Authoritarian, Exploitive, Concern for People, Cooperation, Affiliation, Humanistic, Synergy, Meta-Humanistic, Self-Actualization, Stress, Repression, Anger, Judgemental, Creativity, Growth Potential, Fun Scale.
Administration: Group.
Price Data: Available from publisher.
Time: Administration time not reported.
Comments: Self-administered.
Author: John A. Walker.
Publisher: Meta-Visions.
Cross References: For reviews by John K. Butler, Jr. and Denise M. Rousseau, see 9:698.

[1578]
Metaphon.

Purpose: Designed to be "a complete assessment and therapy programme for children with phonological disorders."
Population: Ages 3.5–7.
Publication Date: 1990.
Scores: Total score only.
Administration: Individual.
Parts, 4: Screening, Probing, Intervention, Monitoring.

Price Data, 1999: £257.50 per complete set; £34 per manual (48 pages); £26.75 per 25 screening forms; £34 per 10 probe record books; £49 per screening picture book; £87.50 per probe picture book; £38.50 per set of monitoring pictures.

Time: (15) minutes.

Authors: Elizabeth Dean, Janet Howell, Ann Hill, and Daphne Waters.

Publisher: NFER-Nelson Publishing Co., Ltd. [England].

Cross References: For a review by Allan O. Diefendorf, Kathy Kessler, and Michael K. Wynne, see 12:231.

[1579]
Metropolitan Achievement Tests, Eighth Edition.

Purpose: Designed to provide assessment of students' achievement in reading, mathematics, language arts, science, and social studies at appropriate levels.

Publication Dates: 1931–2001.

Acronym: METROPOLITAN8.

Forms, 2: Complete Battery, Short Form.

Administration: Group.

Price Data, 2002: $31.50 per multiple-choice Complete Battery examination kit (for preview only) including Complete Battery test booklet, directions for administering, practice test with directions (Preprimer through Intermediate 4 only), separate answer document (Elementary 1 through Secondary 3 only), and open-ended assessment preview brochure (specify level); $16 per multiple-choice Complete Battery 25 practice tests (specify Level Preprimer through Intermediate 2/3/4); $7 per directions for administering practice tests; $122.50 per 25 machine-scorable multiple-choice Complete Battery test booklets (specify preprimer–Elementary 1); $93 per 25 reusable multiple-choice Complete Battery test booklets (specify Elementary 1–Secondary 3); $76 per 100 Complete Battery machine-scorable answer documents (specify Elementary 1–Secondary 3); $11.50 per directions for administering (specify level); $7 per 25 test booklet place markers; $31.50 per multiple-choice Complete Battery response key-list of correct responses (specify level); $16 per 25 multiple-choice Short Form practice tests (specify Primary 1–Intermediate 2/3/4); $7 per directions for administering Short Form practice tests; $104 per 25 multiple-choice Short Form machine-scorable test booklets (specify Primary 1–Elementary 1); $83 per 25 multiple-choice Short Form reusable test booklets (specify Elementary 2–Secondary 3); $11.50 per directions for administering (specify Primary 1–Secondary); $69 per 100 multiple-choice Short Form machine-scorable answer documents (specify Elementary 1–Secondary 3); $31.50 per multiple-choice Short Form response key-list of correct responses (specify level); $14 per 25 Parent Guide to METROPOLITAN8 (specify English or Spanish); $66 per norms book (specify Fall or Spring); $60 per technical manual; $40 per Compendium of Instructional Objectives (also available in CD-ROM version); $25 per Guide for Classroom Planning (specify Primary 1/2, Elementary 1/2, Intermediate 1/2/3/4, or Secondary 1/2/3); $21 per Understanding Test Results (specify Primary 1/2–Secondary 1/2/3); price information for scoring and reporting services available from publisher.

Author: Harcourt Educational Measurement.

Publisher: Harcourt Educational Measurement.

a) PREPRIMER.

Population: Grades K.0–K.5.

Scores, 4: Sounds and Print, Mathematics, Language, Complete Battery.

Time: (90–100) minutes.

b) PRIMER.

Population: Grades K.5–1.5.

Scores, 4: Same as for Preprimer.

Time: (90–100) minutes.

c) PRIMARY 1.

Population: Grades 1.5–2.5.

Scores, 12: Sounds and Print, Reading Vocabulary, Reading Comprehension, Total Reading, Mathematics Concepts and Problem Solving, Mathematics Computation, Total Mathematics, Language, Spelling, Science, Social Studies, Complete Battery.

Time: (265–292) minutes.

d) PRIMARY 2.

Population: Grades 2.5–3.5.

Scores, 12: Same as for Primary 1.

Time: (270–296) minutes.

e) ELEMENTARY 1.

Population: Grades 3.5–4.5.

Scores, 12: Same as for Primary 1.

Time: (275–328) minutes.

f) ELEMENTARY 2.

Population: Grades 4.5–5.5.

Scores, 11: Same as for Primary 1 minus Sounds and Print.

Time: (255–298) minutes.

g) INTERMEDIATE 1.

Population: Grades 5.5–6.5.

Scores, 11: Same as Elementary 2.

Time: (275–316) minutes.

h) INTERMEDIATE 2.

Population: Grades 6.5–7.5.

Scores, 11: Same as for Elementary 2.

Time: (275–316) minutes.

i) INTERMEDIATE 3.

Population: Grades 7.5–8.5.

Scores, 11: Same as for Elementary 2.

Time: (275–316) minutes.

j) INTERMEDIATE 4.
Population: Grades 8.5–9.5.
Scores, 11: Same as for Elementary 2.
Time: (275–316) minutes.
k) SECONDARY 1.
Population: Grade 9.
Scores, 9: Reading Vocabulary, Reading Comprehension, Sounds and Print/Total Reading, Mathematics, Language, Spelling, Science, Social Studies, Complete Battery.
Time: (240–288) minutes.
l) SECONDARY 2.
Population: Grade 10.
Scores, 9: Same as for Secondary 1.
Time: (240–288) minutes.
m) SECONDARY 3.
Population: Grades 11–12.
Scores, 9: Same as for Secondary 1.
Time: (240–288) minutes.
Cross References: See T5:1657 (25 references); for reviews by Carmen J. Finley and Ronald K. Hambleton, see 12:232 (37 references); see also T4:1618 (31 references); for reviews by Anthony J. Nitko and Bruce G. Rogers of an earlier edition, see 10:200 (44 references); for reviews by Edward H. Haertel and Robert L. Linn, see 9:699 (30 references); see also T3:1473 (89 references); for reviews by Norman E. Gronlund and Richard M. Wolf and an excerpted review by Joseph A. Wingard and Peter M. Bentler of an earlier edition, see 8:22 (41 references); see also T2:22 (20 references) and 7:14 (25 references); for reviews by Henry S. Dyer and Warren G. Findley of an earlier edition, see 6:16 (16 references); for a review by Warren G. Findley, see 4:18 (10 references); see also 3:13 (7 references); for reviews by E. V. Pullias and Hugh B. Wood, see 2:1189 (3 references); for reviews by Jack W. Dunlap, Charles W. Odell, and Richard Ledgerwood, see 1:874. For reviews of subtests, see 8:283 (1 review), 8:732 (2 reviews), 6:627 (2 reviews), 6:797 (1 review), 6:877 (2 reviews), 6:970 (2 reviews), 4:416 (1 review), 4:543 (2 reviews), 2:1458.1 (2 reviews), 2:1551 (1 review), 1:892 (2 reviews), and 1:1105 (2 reviews).

[1580]
Metropolitan Performance Assessment: Integrated Performance Tasks.

Purpose: Designed to show progression in the "acquisition of concepts, strategies, and skills needed to perform language/literacy and quantitative/mathematics tasks" usually taught through kindergarten.
Population: Ages 4-4 to 6-3; ages 5-5 to 7-0.
Publication Date: 1995.
Acronym: MPA.
Scores, 3: Holistic, Analytic (Language/Literacy, Quantitative/Mathematics).

Administration: Group.
Levels, 2: 1, 2.
Price Data, 2002: $40 per examination kit including task booklet, set of manipulative sheets, directions for administering, scoring guide, and teacher observation form (Level 1 or Level 2); $49 per task package including 25 booklets, 25 sets of manipulative sheets, directions for administering, and teacher observation form (Level 1 or Level 2); $26.50 per scoring guide (Level 1 or Level 2); $6.40 per directions for administering (Level 1 or Level 2); $57 per preliteracy inventory including 25 record forms, Homer the Goose Storybook, and directions for administering; $23.85 per developmental inventory; $13.25 per portfolio assessment guidelines with information for interpreting preliteracy and devlopmental inventories; $17 per literacy environment inventory; $65.75 per Handbook of Early Childhood Activities.
Time: Untimed.
Comments: Handbook of Early Childhood Activities covers many areas assessed in the MPA, but may also be used independently of the program.
Author: Joanne R. Nurss.
Publisher: The Psychological Corporation.
Cross References: For reviews by Theodore Coladarci and Delwyn L. Harnisch, see 14:230.

[1581]
Metropolitan Readiness Tests®, Sixth Edition.

Purpose: Designed to assess basic and advanced skills important in beginning reading and mathematics.
Population: PreKindergarten through grade 1.
Publication Dates: 1933–1995.
Acronym: MRT®6.
Administration: Individual (Level 1) or Group (Level 2).
Price Data, 2002: $19 per 25 parent-teacher conference reports (specify level); $19 per story comprehension big book.
Time: (85) minutes per level; (10) minutes for the practice items for each level.
Authors: Joanne R. Nurss and Mary E. McGauvran.
Publisher: The Psychological Corporation.
a) LEVEL 1.
Population: PreKindergarten and beginning Kindergarten.
Administration: Individual
Scores: 5 tests: Beginning Reading Skill Area (Visual Discrimination, Beginning Consonants, Sound-Letter Correspondence), Story Comprehension, Quantitative Concepts and Reasoning, plus Prereading Composite.
Price Data: $121 per complete kit including stimulus manual, story comprehension big book, manual (1995, 43 pages), 25 parent-teacher con-

ference reports, and 25 student record forms; $32 per 25 student record forms; $31 per manual; $57.25 per stimulus manual; $29 per exam kit including Level I flyer, story comprehension big book flyer, manual, student record form, and parent-teacher conference report.

b) LEVEL 2.

Population: Middle and end of kindergarten and beginning of grade 1.

Administration: Group.

Scores: 5 tests: Beginning Reading Skill Area (Beginning Consonants, Sound-Letter Correspondence, Aural Cloze with Letter), Story Comprehension, Quantitative Concepts and Reasoning, plus Prereading Composite.

Price Data: $164 per starter kit including 25 test booklets, directions for administering, story comprehension big book, 25 practice booklets, class record and analysis chart, norms book, answer keys, parent-teacher conference reports, 25 Birthday Surprise Task booklets, 25 Birthday Surprise manipulative sheets, Birthday Surprise directions for administering, scoring guide, and teacher observation form; $82 per 25 handscorable test booklets also including directions for administration, 25 practice booklets, and class record and analysis chart; $29.50 per answer keys; $41 per manual; $31 per norms book (1995, 72 pages); $17 per exam kit including test booklet, directions for administering, practice booklet, class record and analysis chart, and parent-teacher conference report.

Cross References: For reviews by Randy W. Kamphaus and Christine Novak, see 14:231; see also T5:1659 (14 references) and T4:1619 (35 references); for a review by Michael M. Ravitch of an earlier edition, see 9:700 (11 references); see also T3:1479 (73 references), 8:802 (111 references), and T2:1716 (55 references); for reviews by Robert Dykstra and Harry Singer of an earlier edition, see 7:757 (124 references); for a review by Eric F. Gardner and an excerpted review by Fay Griffith, see 4:570 (3 references); for a review by Irving H. Anderson, see 3:518 (5 references); for a review by W. J. Osburn, see 2:1552 (10 references).

[1582]
Meyer-Kendall Assessment Survey.

Purpose: Constructed to assess work-related personality style.

Population: Business employees and job applicants.

Publication Dates: 1986–1991.

Acronym: MKAS.

Scores, 12: Objectivity, Social Desirability Bias, Dominance, Extraversion, People Concerns, Attention to Detail, Anxiety, Stability, Psychosomatic Tenden-

cies, Determination, Achievement Motivation, Independence.

Administration: Group or individual.

Price Data, 2002: $92.50 per complete kit including 2 prepaid assessment sheets, 2 prepaid pre-assessment sheets, and manual (1991, 72 pages); $29.50 per mail-in assessment sheet (price includes scoring and report by publisher); $8.50 per pre-assessment sheet; $45 per manual.

Time: (15–20) minutes.

Authors: Henry D. Meyer and Edward L. Kendall.

Publisher: Western Psychological Services.

Cross References: For reviews by Mark H. Daniel and Gregory H. Dobbins, see 12:234.

[1583]
Michigan Alcoholism Screening Test.

Purpose: Designed as a screening test for assessing alcohol abuse.

Population: Adults.

Publication Dates: 1971–1980.

Acronym: MAST.

Scores: Total score only.

Administration: Group or individual.

Manual: No manual available.

Price Data, 2001: $40 per copy, which includes scoring key and permission to duplicate the test.

Foreign Language Editions: French, Japanese, Spanish, and Vietnamese versions available.

Time: (10) minutes.

Comments: Can be self-administered.

Author: Melvin L. Selzer.

Publisher: Melvin L. Selzer.

Cross References: For reviews by Jane Close Conoley and Jeff Reese and by Janice W. Murdoch, see 14:232; see also T5:1661 (85 references).

[1584]
Michigan English Language Assessment Battery.

Purpose: Designed "to evaluate the advanced level English language proficiency of adult non-native speakers of English."

Population: Adult non-native speakers of English.

Publication Dates: 1985–2002.

Acronym: MELAB.

Scores, 5: Writing, Listening, GCVR [includes Grammar, Cloze Reading, Vocabulary Synonym, Vocabulary Completion, Reading] Final Score, Speaking Test (optional).

Administration: Group or individual.

Forms: Multiple equivalent forms.

Price Data, 2002: $35 per registration for Standard Individual MELAB; $25 per examiner's fee; $15 per Oral Interview; additional price information available from publisher.

Time: (135–150) minutes for complete battery; (30) minutes for Writing; (30) minutes for Listening; (75) minutes for Grammar/Cloze/Vocabulary/Reading; (15) minutes for optional oral interview.

Comments: "Used primarily to draw inferences about a test-taker's ability to study in an institution where English is the medium of instruction" or for test takers who require evidence of English language ability for professional purposes; candidates register to take exam through the publisher, which authorizes every examination (at a group test center or by certified examiner), marks all papers, and issues official score report directly to institutions selected by examinee.

Author: The English Language Institute Testing and Certification Division.

Publisher: English Language Institute, The University of Michigan.

Cross References: For reviews by Ayres D'Costa and Alan Garfinkel, see 14:233.

[1585]
Michigan English Language Institute College English Test—Grammar, Cloze, Vocabulary, Reading.

Purpose: "To provide educational institutions and researchers with information about the English language competencies of their own students, employees, or research participants."

Population: Adult nonnative speakers of English.

Publication Date: 2001.

Acronym: MELICET-GCVR.

Scores: Total score only.

Administration: Group.

Forms, 2: AA, BB.

Price Data, 2001: $75 per complete testing package (specify Form AA or BB) including 20 test booklets, 100 answer sheets, stencil, and user's manual (32 pages); $30 per 20 test booklets (specify Form AA or BB); $10 per 100 answer sheets; $10 per plastic scoring stencil (specify Form AA or BB); $25 per user's manual.

Time: 75(90) minutes.

Comments: Consists of retired forms of grammar, cloze, vocabulary, and reading components of the Michigan English Language Assessment Battery, Part 3 (MELAB, see 1584); administered and scored by educational institutions or researchers who have purchased the test for use within their institution; test is nonsecure; all items are of multiple-choice format; scoring by punched stencil, purchasers may use their own scannable answer sheets.

Author: The English Language Institute Testing and Certification Division.

Publisher: English Language Institute, The University of Michigan.

[1586]
Michigan Prescriptive Program in English.

Purpose: Designed to identify student strengths and weaknesses in preparation for the high school equivalency GED English Test.

Population: Persons striving to obtain 10th grade equivalency or pass the GED Test.

Publication Dates: 1973–1996.

Scores: Total score only.

Administration: Individual or group.

Manual: No manual (instructions packaged with Scoring Template).

Price Data 2002: $10 per English Study Guide; $15 per 10 pretest booklets; $8 per 10 response sheets; $3 per scoring template.

Time: Administration time not reported.

Comments: Separate answer sheets must be used.

Author: William E. Lockhart.

Publisher: Academic Therapy Publications.

Cross References: For a review by Gail E. Tompkins, see 9:702.

[1587]
Michigan Test of English Language Proficiency.

Purpose: "To screen non-native speakers of English who wish to study at universities where English is the medium of instruction."

Population: College applicants from non-English-language countries.

Publication Dates: 1961–1979.

Acronym: MTELP.

Scores: Total score only.

Administration: Group.

Forms, 8: G, H, J, K, L, P, Q, R.

Price Data, 2002: $47–$50 per complete kit including 20 tests of 1 form, 100 answer sheets, stencil, and manual (1977, 24 pages); $20 per 20 tests (specify form); $10 per 100 answer sheets; $10 per scoring stencil (specify form); $10 per manual (all forms).

Time: 75(90) minutes.

Comments: Forms A, B, D, E, and F no longer available; a component test of the former "Michigan Battery."

Authors: J. Upshur, A. Palmer, M. Spaan, J. Peterson, A. Corrigan, B. Dobson, E. Kellman, L. Strowe, and S. Tyma (tests), and Division of Testing and Certification (manual).

Publisher: English Language Institute, University of Michigan.

Cross References: See T5:1664 (6 references), T4:1623 (5 references), and T3:1484 (7 references); for a review by Edward J. Cervenka, see 8:106 (5 references); see also T2:233 (1 reference) and 7:264 (2 references); for a review by John B. Carroll, see 6:360.

[1588]
MicroCog: Assessment of Cognitive Functioning.

Purpose: "Assesses important neurocognitive functions in adults."
Population: Ages 18–89.
Publication Dates: 1993–1996.
Scores: 9 areas: Attention/Mental Control, Memory, Reasoning/Calculation, Spatial Processing, Reaction Time, Information Processing Accuracy, Information Processing Speed, General Cognitive Functioning, General Cognitive Proficiency.
Administration: Individual.
Price Data, 2002: $184 per MicroCog kit including user's guide (120 pages), technical manual (211 pages), 3.5-inch high-density diskettes, and 10 report credits on PsyTest Use Counter; $125 per 10 report credits ($261 per 25 and $829 per 100).
Time: (50–60) minutes for Standard form; (30) minutes for Brief form.
Comments: Computer administered and scored; must be used with PsyTest Assessment Management System.
Authors: Douglas Powell, Edith Kaplan, Dean Whitla, Sandra Weintraub, Randolph Catlin, and Harris Funkenstein.
Publisher: The Psychological Corporation.
Cross References: For reviews by Charles J. Long and Stephanie L. Cutlan and by Cynthia A. Rohrbeck, see 13:199.

[1589]
The MIDAS: Multiple Intelligence Developmental Assessment Scales.

Purpose: "Designed to provide an objective measure of the multiple intelligences."
Population: Age 14 to adult.
Publication Dates: 1994–1996.
Acronym: MIDAS.
Scores: 10 scales with 27 subscales: Musical (Appreciation, Instrument, Vocal, Composer), Kinesthetic (Athletic, Dexterity), Logical-Mathematical (School Math, Science, Logic Games, Everyday Math, Everyday Problem-Solving), Spatial (Spatial Awareness, Art Design, Working with Objects), Linguistic (Expressive, Rhetorical, Written/Reading), Interpersonal (Persuasion, Sensitivity, Working with People), Intrapersonal (Personal Knowledge, Calculations, Spatial Problem-Solving, Effectiveness), Leadership (Communication, Management, Social), General Logic, Innovative.
Administration: Group.
Price Data: Available from publisher.
Time: (30) minutes.
Comments: May be group administered via self-completion or individually as a structured interview; based on Howard Gardner's theory of Multiple Intelligences.

Author: C. Branton Shearer.
Publisher: Multi-Health Systems, Inc.
Cross References: For reviews by Abbot Packard and Michael S. Trevisan, see 14:234.

[1590]
Milani-Comparetti Motor Development Screening Test.

Purpose: "The test provides the clinician with a synopsis of the child's motor development by systematically examining the integration of primitive reflexes and the emergence of volitional movement against gravity."
Population: Ages 1–16 months.
Publication Dates: 1977–1992.
Scores, 27: Body Lying Supine, Hand Grasp, Foot Grasp, Supine Equilibrium, Body Pulled Up From Supine, Sitting Posture, Sitting Equilibrium, Sideways Parachute, Backward Parachute, Body Held Vertical, Head Righting, Downward Parachute, Standing, Standing Equilibrium, Locomotion, Landau Response, Forward Parachute, Body Lying Prone, Prone Equilibrium, All Fours, All Fours Equilibrium, Symmetric Tonic Neck Reflex, Body Derotative, Standing Up From Supine, Body Rotative, Asymmetrical Tonic Neck Reflex, Moro Reflex.
Administration: Individual.
Price Data: Price data for test including manual (1992, 48 pages) available from publisher.
Time: (10–15) minutes.
Comments: Behavior checklist.
Authors: Wayne Stuberg (Project Director), Pam Dehne, Jim Miedaner, and Penni White (Content Consultants).
Publisher: Munroe-Meyer Institute for Genetics & Rehabilitation.
Cross References: See T5:1668 (1 reference); for reviews by Linda K. Bunker and Ruth E. Tomes, see 11:236.

[1591]
MILCOM Patient Data Base System.

Purpose: Designed to record a patient's medical history.
Population: Medical patients.
Publication Dates: 1971–1985.
Scores: Item scores only.
Administration: Individual.
Manual: No manual.
Price Data: Available from publisher.
Foreign Language Edition: Spanish version available.
Time: Administration time not reported.
Comments: Questionnaire includes health questionnaire and 18-part physical exam; Spanish version available.
Author: MILCOM Systems, A Division of Hollister, Inc.

Publisher: MILCOM Systems, A Division of Hollister, Inc.

[1592]
Military Environment Inventory.

Purpose: "Asesses the social environment of varied types of military contexts."
Population: Military personnel.
Publication Date: 1986.
Acronym: MEIN.
Scores, 7: Involvement, Peer Cohesion, Officer Support, Personal Status, Order and Organization, Clarity, Officer Control.
Administration: Group.
Forms, 4: Real Form (Form R), Short Form (Form S), Ideal Form (Form I), Expectations Form (Form E).
Price Data: Available from publisher.
Time: Administration time not reported.
Comments: One of 10 Social Climate Scales.
Author: Rudolf H. Moos.
Publisher: Mind Garden, Inc.
Cross References: For reviews by David O. Herman and Alfred L. Smith, Jr., see 11:237 (1 reference).

[1593]
Mill Hill Vocabulary Scale.

Purpose: Provides a measure of acquired verbal knowledge.
Publication Dates: 1943–1998.
Acronym: MHV.
Scores: Total score only.
Administration: Group or individual.
Forms, 2: A, B.
Price Data: Price information available from publisher for test booklets and for specimen set including one of each test booklet, scoring key, and appropriate sections of the Raven's manuals (Section 1–1998, 119 pages; Section 5–1998, 124 pages).
Time: (15–40) minutes.
Comments: To be used in conjunction with the Raven's Progressive Matrices (2064); short-form also available.
Authors: J. C. Raven, J. H. Court, and J. Raven.
Publisher: Oxford Psychologists Press, Ltd. [England].
  a) JUNIOR.
    Population: Ages 6.5–16.5.
  b) SENIOR.
    Population: Ages 18–adult.
Cross References: See T5:1671 (8 references); for reviews by Theodore L. Hayes and William K. Wilkinson, see 13:200 (30 references); see also T4:1629 (51 reference), 9:705 (8 references), T3:1485 (29 references), and T2:402 (32 references); for a review by Morton Bortner of an earlier edition, see 6:471 (16

references); see also 4:303 (7 references); for a review by David Wechsler, see 3:239 (3 references).

[1594]
Miller Analogies Test.

Purpose: Constructed to assess mental ability for use in selecting graduate students.
Population: Applicants for graduate schools.
Publication Dates: 1926–1992.
Acronym: MAT.
Scores: Total score only.
Administration: Group.
Restricted Distribution: Distribution restricted and test administered at licensed testing centers; details may be obtained from publisher.
Price Data: Available from publisher.
Time: 65 minutes.
Author: W. S. Miller (test).
Publisher: The Psychological Corporation.
Cross References: See T5:1672 (5 references); for reviews by Robert B. Frary and Stephen H. Ivens, see 12:235 (2 references); see also T4:1630 (1 reference), T3:1486 (16 references), 8:192 (31 references), T2:404 (15 references), and 7:363 (57 references); for reviews by Lloyd G. Humphreys, William B. Schrader, and Warren W. Willingham, see 6:472 (26 references); for a review by John T. Dailey, see 5:352 (28 references); for reviews by J. P. Guilford and Cart I. Hovland, see 4:304 (16 references).

[1595]
Miller Assessment for Preschoolers.

Purpose: Designed "to identify children who exhibit moderate 'preacademic' problems."
Population: Ages 2-9 to 5-8.
Publication Date: 1982.
Acronym: MAP.
Scores, 6: Foundations, Coordination, Verbal, Non-Verbal, Complex Tasks, Total.
Administration: Individual.
Levels: 6 developmental levels (ages 2-9 to 3-2, 3-3 to 3-8, 3-9 to 4-2, 4-3 to 4-8, 4-9 to 5-2, 5-3 to 5-8).
Price Data, 2002: $695 per complete kit including manual (220 pages), score sheets, and all items needed for administration and scoring; $100 per examiner's manual; $299 per training tape; $99 per training tape rental; $72 per workshop set; $36 per 6 cue sheets; $34 per 25 score sheets; $34 per 25 drawing booklets; $34 per 25 record booklets.
Time: (20–30) minutes.
Author: Lucy Jane Miller.
Publisher: The Psychological Corporation.
Cross References: See T5:1673 (11 references) and T4:1631 (6 references); for reviews by Dennis J. Deloria and William B. Michael, see 9:706.

[1596]
Miller Common Sense Scale.

Purpose: "Designed to permit the individual to compare his/her level of common sense with other individuals … and to determine changes that should be made as a result of this information."
Population: Ages 15 to adult.
Publication Date: 1997.
Scores: Total score only.
Administration: Group.
Price Data, 2001: $35 per administration via webpage (Visa or MasterCard are required to use this test).
Time: (15) minutes.
Comments: Administered and scored on the internet (webpage URL is http://www.metadevelopment.com); printout of results is provided.
Author: Harold J. Miller.
Publisher: Meta Development LLC [Canada].

[1597]
Miller Depression Scale.

Purpose: Designed to "measure an individual's depression level."
Population: Ages 15 years and over.
Publication Date: 1997.
Scores: Total score only.
Administration: Individual or group.
Manual: No manual.
Price Data, 2001: $35 per administration via webpage (Visa or MasterCard are required to use this test).
Time: (15) minutes.
Comments: "Designed to be given and scored over the internet" (webpage URL is http://www.metadevelopment.com); printout of results provided; can be used to monitor treatment effectiveness.
Author: Harold J. Miller.
Publisher: Meta Development LLC [Canada].

[1598]
Miller Emotional Maturity Scale.

Purpose: Designed to "measure the individual's emotional maturity."
Population: Adults with reading levels at 7th grade or above.
Publication Date: 1991.
Scores, 8: Secure, Stable, Independent, Optimistic, Responsible, Assertive, Social, Honest.
Administration: Individual or group.
Manual: No manual.
Price Data, 2001: $35 per administration via webpage (Visa or MasterCard are required to use this test).
Time: (30–45) minutes.
Comments: "Designed to be administered and scored on the internet" (webpage URL is http://

www.metadevelopment.com); printout of results is provided.
Author: Harold J. Miller.
Publisher: Meta Development LLC [Canada].

[1599]
Miller Forensic Assessment of Symptoms Test.

Purpose: Designed to "provide information regarding the probability that an individual is malingering psychiatric illness."
Population: Ages 18 and over.
Publication Dates: 1995–2001.
Acronym: M-FAST.
Scores, 8: Reported vs. Observed, Extreme Symptomatology, Rare Combinations, Unusual Hallucinations, Unusual Symptom Course, Negative Image, Suggestibility, Total.
Administration: Individual.
Price Data: Available from publisher.
Time: (5–10) minutes.
Author: Holly A. Miller.
Publisher: Psychological Assessment Resources, Inc.

[1600]
Miller Getting Along With People Scale.

Purpose: "Designed to help individuals determine how well they get along with other people."
Population: Ages 15 to adult.
Publication Date: 1996.
Scores: Total score only.
Administration: Group.
Price Data, 2001: $35 per administration via webpage (Visa or MasterCard are required to use this test).
Time: (15) minutes.
Comments: Administered and scored on the internet (webpage URL is http://www.metadevelopment.com); printout of results provided.
Author: Harold J. Miller.
Publisher: Meta Development LLC [Canada].

[1601]
Miller Happiness Scale.

Purpose: "Designed to measure eight areas of an individual's happiness."
Population: Grade 7 reading level or higher.
Publication Date: 1998.
Scores, 8: Personal Happiness, Health Happiness, Spiritual Happiness, Intimate Relationship Happiness, Family Happiness, Friendship Happiness, Work Happiness, Leisure Happiness.
Administration: Group.
Price Data, 2001: $35 per administration via webpage (Visa or MasterCard are required to use this test).

Time: (30–45) minutes.
Comments: Administered and scored on the internet (webpage URL is http://www.metadevelopment.com); printout of results is provided.
Author: Harold J. Miller.
Publisher: Meta Development LLC [Canada].

[1602]
Miller Love Scale.

Purpose: "Designed to measure eight areas of love."
Population: Ages 16 to adult.
Publication Date: 1998.
Scores, 8: Self-Love, Love Motivation, Value, Perception of Partner, Love Thoughts, Love Feelings, Love Behavior, Spiritual Love.
Administration: Group.
Price Data, 2001: $35 per administration via webpage (Visa or MasterCard are required to use this test)
Time: (30–45) minutes.
Comments: Administered and scored on the internet (webpage URL is http://www.metadevelopment.com); printout of results is provided.
Author: Harold J. Miller.
Publisher: Meta Development LLC [Canada].

[1603]
Miller Marriage Satisfaction Scale.

Purpose: "Designed to compare one's level of marriage satisfaction to the marriage satisfaction of other married people."
Population: Individuals who are dating, living together or who are married.
Publication Date: 1997.
Scores: Total score only.
Administration: Group.
Price Data, 2001: $35 per administration via webpage (Visa or MasterCard are required to use this test).
Time: (15) minutes.
Comments: Administered and scored on the internet (webpage URL is http://www.metadevelopment.com); printout of results is provided.
Author: Harold J. Miller.
Publisher: Meta Development LCC [Canada].

[1604]
Miller Motivation Scale.

Purpose: "Designed to measure positive and negative aspects of the individual's motivation."
Population: Individuals who have a grade seven reading level or greater.
Publication Dates: 1986–1988.
Scores, 8: Creative, Innovative, Productive, Cooperative, Attention, Power, Revenge, Give-Up.
Administration: Group.

Price Data, 2001: $35 per administration via webpage (Visa or MasterCard are required to use this test).
Time: (30–45) minutes.
Comments: Administered and scored on the internet (webpage URL is http://www.metadevelopment.com); printout of results is provided.
Author: Harold J. Miller.
Publisher: Meta Development LLC [Canada].

[1605]
Miller Psychological Independence Scale.

Purpose: Designed to "measure the individual's psychological independence in a dependent-independent continuum."
Population: High school students and athletes.
Publication Date: 1996.
Scores, 8: Independent Behavior, Independence in Relationships, Perfection, Effectiveness, Egocentric, Independent Thoughts, Independent Feelings, Control.
Administration: Group.
Price Data, 2001: $35 per administration via webpage (Visa or MasterCard are required to use this test).
Time: (30–45) minutes.
Comments: "Designed to be given on the internet" (webpage URL is http://www.metadevelopment.com); results immediately available in a six-page printout.
Author: Harold J. Miller.
Publisher: Meta Development LLC [Canada].

[1606]
Miller Self-Concept Scale.

Purpose: Designed to "measure components of the individual's self-concept."
Population: Individuals with a seventh-grade or higher reading level.
Publication Date: 1989.
Scores, 8: Intrapsychic, Family, Friendship Self-Concept, Work/School Self-Concept, Locus of Control, Attribution, Courage, Flexibility.
Administration: Group.
Price Data, 2001: $35 per administration via webpage (Visa or MasterCard are required to use this test).
Time: (30–45) minutes.
Comments: "Designed to be given and scored on the internet" (webpage URL is http://www.metadevelopment.com); results are immediately available in a six-page printout.
Author: Harold J. Miller.
Publisher: Meta Development LLC [Canada].

[1607]
Miller Stress Scale.

Purpose: "Designed to measure the individual's stress in several areas of the individual's life."

Population: Individuals with reading level at or above the 7th grade.
Publication Date: 1992.
Scores, 8: Stressful Behavior, Relationship Stress, Family Stress, Work Stress, Physical Stress, Stressful Thoughts, Stressful Feelings, Coping.
Administration: Group.
Price Data, 2001: $35 per administration via webpage (Visa or MasterCard are required to use this test).
Time: (30–45) minutes.
Comments: "Designed to be given and scored on the internet" (webpage URL is http://www.metadevelopment.com); results are available immediately in a six-page printout.
Author: Harold J. Miller.
Publisher: Meta Development LLC [Canada].

[1608]
Millon Adolescent Clinical Inventory.

Purpose: Designed to assess "an adolescent's personality, along with self-reported concerns and clinical syndromes."
Population: Ages 13–19.
Publication Date: 1993.
Acronym: MACI.
Scores: 27 scales: Personality Patterns (Introversive, Inhibited, Doleful, Submissive, Dramatizing, Egotistic, Unruly, Forceful, Conforming, Oppositional, Self-Demeaning, Borderline Tendency), Expressed Concerns (Identify Diffusion, Self-Devaluation, Body Disapproval, Sexual Discomfort, Peer Insecurity, Social Insensitivity, Family Discord, Childhood Abuse), Clinical Syndromes (Eating Dysfunctions, Substance Abuse Proneness, Delinquent Predisposition, Impulsive Propensity, Anxious Feelings, Depressive Affect, Suicidal Tendency), and 3 Modifying Indices (Disclosure, Desirability, Debasement).
Administration: Individual or group.
Price Data, 2002: $90 per mail-in starter kit; $90 per MICROTEST Q starter kit; $24.25 per mail-in interpretive report; $24.25 per mail-in Spanish interpretive report; $17.25 per mail-in profile report; $17.25 per Spanish profile report; $19 per 25 MICROTEST Q answer sheets; $19 per 25 Spanish MICROTEST Q answer sheets; $22.25 per MICROTEST Q interpretive reports; ›15.25 per MICROTEST Q profile reports; $69 per audio cassette (specify English or Hispanic); $27.25 per 10 handscoring test booklets; $37 per manual (123 pages); $299 per handscoring starter kit including manual, handscoring user's guide, 10 test booklets, 50 answer sheets, 50 work sheets, and 50 profile forms and keys; $100 per reorder kit including 50 answer sheets, 50 worksheets, and 50 profile sheets.
Time: (30) minutes.

Comments: Self-report personality inventory replacing the Millon Adolescent Personality Inventory (9:707); available in paper-and-pencil and on-line administration; MICROTEST Q, mail-in scoring, and handscoring available.
Authors: Theodore Millon with Carrie Millon and Roger Davis.
Publisher: NCS Assessments (Minnetonka).
Cross References: See T5:1685 (2 references); for reviews by Paul Retzlaff and Richard B. Stuart, see 12:236 (6 references); see also T4:1633 (14 references); for reviews by Douglas T. Brown and Thomas A. Widiger of the Millon Adolescent Personality Inventory, see 9:707.

[1609]
Millon Behavioral Medicine Diagnostic.

Purpose: Designed to "assess psychological factors that can influence the course of treatment of medically ill patients ... especially for patients in which psychosocial factors may play a role in the course of the disease and treatment outcome."
Population: Clinical and rehabilitation patients ages 18–85.
Publication Date: 2001.
Acronym: MBMD.
Scores, 39: Validity Indicator, Response Patterns (Disclosure, Desirability, Debasement), Negative Health Habits (Alcohol, Drug, Eating, Caffeine, Inactivity, Smoking), Psychiatric Indications (Anxiety-Tension, Depression, Cognitive Dysfunction, Emotional Lability, Guardedness), Coping Styles (Introversive, Inhibited, Dejected, Cooperative, Sociable, Confident, Nonconforming, Forceful, Respectful, Oppositional, Denigrated), Stress Moderators (Illness Apprehension, Functional Deficits, Pain Sensitivity, Social Isolation, Future Pessimism, Spiritual Absence), Treatment Prognostics (Interventional Fragility, Medication Abuse, Information Discomfort, Utilization Excess, Problematic Compliance), Management Guides (Adjustment Difficulties, Psych Referral).
Administration: Individual or group.
Price Data, 2002: $298 per hand-scoring starter kit including manual (183 pages), hand-scoring user's guide, 10 test booklets, 50 answer sheets, 50 worksheets, and 50 profile forms and answer keys; $28 per 10 hand-scoring test booklets (English or Hispanic); $100 per MICROTEST Q Assessment System Software starter kit with Interpretive Reports including manual and answer sheets with test items and all materials necessary to conduct 3 assessments and receive interpretive reports using assessment system software; $19 per 25 software answer sheets including test items (English or Hispanic); $22.95 per software interpretive report; $15 per software profile report; $100 per mail-in scoring service starter kit with Interpretive Reports including

manual and answer sheets with test items and all materials necessary to conduct 3 assessments and receive interpretive reports using mail-in scoring service; $24.95 per mail-in interpretive report (test items and answer sheets included) (specify English or Hispanic); $17 per mail-in profile reports (test items and answer sheets included) (English or Hispanic); $48 per manual; $60 per audiocassette (English or Hispanic); $19 per 25 large print answer sheets; quantity discounts available.
Time: (20–25) minutes.
Comments: Available in Spanish and in large-print paper-and-pencil version; upgrading of the Millon Behavioral Health Inventory (T5:1686); self-administered; may be administered in paper-and pencil format, online, or via audiocassette; interpretive reports with healthcare provider summary and profile available; scoring options include handscoring, mail-in, MICROTEST Q Assessment System software.
Authors: Theodore Millon, Michael Antoni, Carrie Millon, Sarah Meagher, and Seth Grossman.
Publisher: NCS Assessments [Minnetonka].
Cross References: For information regarding the original Millon Behavioral Health Inventory, see T5:1686 (7 references) and T4:1634 (6 references); for reviews of the Millon Behavioral Health Inventory by Mary J. Allen and Richard I. Lanyon, see 9:708 (1 reference).

[1610]
Millon Clinical Multiaxial Inventory—III [Manual Second Edition].

Purpose: Designed to provide diagnostic and treatment information to clinicians in the areas of personality disorders and clinical syndromes.
Population: "Adults [18+] who are seeking [or in] mental health treatment and who have eighth-grade reading skills."
Publication Dates: 1976–1997.
Acronym: MCMI-III.
Scores, 28: Modifying Indices (Disclosure, Desirability, Debasement, Validity), Clinical Personality Patterns (Schizoid, Avoidant, Depressive, Dependent, Histrionic, Narcissistic, Antisocial, Aggressive (Sadistic), Compulsive, Passive-Aggressive (Negativistic), Self-Defeating), Severe Personality Pathology (Schizotypal, Borderline, Paranoid), Clinical Syndromes (Anxiety, Somatoform, Bipolar: Manic, Dysthymia, Alcohol Dependence, Drug Dependence, Post-Traumatic Stress Disorder), Severe Clinical Syndromes (Thought Disorder, Major Depression, Delusional Disorder).
Administration: Individual or group.
Price Data, 2002: $123.75 per starter kit (specify mail-in or MICROTEST Q); $307 per handscoring starter kit including manual (1997, 216 pages), handscoring user's guide (1994, 9 pages), 10 test booklets, 50 answer sheets, 50 worksheets, 50 profile forms,

and answer keys; $34.50 per prepaid interpretive mail-in answer sheet (specify English or Hispanic); $32 per prepaid corrections interpretive mail-in answer sheet (specify English or Hispanic); $17.25 per prepaid profile mail-in answer sheet (specify English of Hispanic); $19 per 25 MICROTEST Q answer sheets (specify English or Hispanic); $32.50 per interpretive MICROTEST Q report; $30 per corrections interpretive MICROTEST Q report; $15.25 per profile MICROTEST Q report; $27.50 per 10 handscoring test booklets; $46 per manual; $18 per Corrections Report User's Guide (1998, 56 pages); $66 per audiocassette (specify English of Hispanic).
Time: [25] minutes.
Comments: Designed to coordinate with DSM-IV categories of clinical syndromes and personality disorders; revision of the Millon Clinical Multiaxial Inventory—III (13:201); includes optional Corrections Report for use with correctional inmates.
Authors: Theodore Millon, Roger Davis, and Carrie Millon.
Publisher: NCS Assessments (Minnetonka).
Cross References: For reviews by James P. Choca and Thomas A. Widiger, see 14:236; see also T5:1687 (47 references); for reviews by Allen K. Hess and Paul Retzlaff of the third edition, see 13:201 (81 references); see also T4:1635 (104 references); for reviews by Thomas M. Haladyna and Cecil K. Reynolds of the second edition, see 11:239 (74 references); for reviews by Allen K. Hess and Thomas A. Widiger of the original edition, see 9:709 (1 reference); see also T3:1488 (3 references).

[1611]
Millon Index of Personality Styles.

Purpose: "Designed to measure personality styles of normally functioning adults."
Population: Adults.
Publication Date: 1994.
Acronym: MIPS.
Scores, 27: Enhancing, Preserving, Modifying, Accommodating, Individuating, Nurturing, Extraversing, Introversing, Sensing, Intuiting, Thinking, Feeling, Systematizing, Innovating, Retiring, Outgoing, Hesitating, Asserting, Dissenting, Conforming, Yielding, Controlling, Complaining, Agreeing, Positive Impression, Negative Impression, Consistency.
Administration: Group or individual.
Price Data, 2002: $93 per complete kit including manual (182 pages), 2 mail-in profile booklets, 2 mail-in interpretive booklets, and mailing labels; $114 per 10 mail-in profile booklets; $170 per 10 interpretive booklets; $9 per 10 scannable test booklets; $25 per 25 scannable test booklets; $95 per 100 scannable test booklets; $56 per scoring template; $21 per 25 answer sheets; $56 per technical manual; $188 per Psy Test Kit

including manual, user's guide, 3.5-inch diskette, and 2 scannable booklets; $66 per 10 profile report credits; $123 per 10 interpretive report credits.

Time: (30) minutes.

Comments: Measure may be scored by hand, through mail-in service, or by personal computer.

Author: Theodore Millon.

Publisher: The Psychological Corporation.

Cross References: See T5:1688 (1 reference); for reviews by James P. Choca and Peter Zachar, see 13:202.

[1612]
The Milwaukee Evaluation of Daily Living Skills.

Purpose: "To assess basic daily living skills for use with the chronically mentally ill."

Population: Ages 18 and over.

Publication Date: 1989.

Acronym: MEDLS.

Scores, 20: Basic Communication Skills, Bathing, Brushing Teeth, Denture Care, Dressing, Eating, Eyeglass Care, Hair Care, Maintenance of Clothing, Makeup Use, Medication Management, Nail Care, Personal Health Care, Safety in Community, Safety in Home, Shaving, Time Awareness, Use of Money, Use of Telephone, Use of Transportation.

Administration: Individual.

Price Data: Available from publisher.

Time: (80) minutes.

Author: Carol A. Leonardelli.

Publisher: SLACK Incorporated.

[1613]
Miner Sentence Completion Scale.

Purpose: Intended for use in "selection, vocational and career guidance, identifying talent supplies, and evaluating training primarily."

Population: Workers and prospective workers in management, professional, and entrepreneurial or task-oriented occupations.

Publication Dates: 1961–1986.

Acronym: MSCS.

Administration: Group.

Forms, 3: Form H (Management domain), Form P (Professional domain), Form T (Task domain).

Price Data, 2002: $30 per 50 tests with scoring sheets; $10 per scoring guide (Form H, 1964, 64 pages, with 1977 supplement, 15 pages, and 1989 supplement, 4 pages; Form P, 1981, 49 pages; Form T, 1986, 56 pages).

Time: (20–30) minutes.

Comments: Form H available as free-response or multiple-choice version; directions included for scoring rare response patterns.

Author: John B. Miner.

Publisher: Organizational Measurement Systems Press.

a) FORM H.

Scores, 9: Authority Figures, Competitive Games, Competitive Situations, Assertive Role, Imposing Wishes, Standing Out from Group, Routine Administrative Functions, Supervisory Job, Total.

b) FORM P.

Scores, 6: Acquiring Knowledge, Independent Action, Accepting Status, Providing Help, Professional Commitment, Total.

c) FORM T.

Scores, 6: Self Achievement, Avoiding Risks, Feedback of Results, Personal Innovation, Planning for the Future, Total.

Cross References: See T5:1689 (4 references) and T4:1637 (1 reference); for reviews by Frederick T. L. Leong and Linda F. Wightman, see 11:241 (2 references); see also T2:1484 (4 references); for a review by C. J. Adcock, see 7:172 (2 references); see also P:450 (3 references) and 6:230a (2 references).

[1614]
Mini-Battery of Achievement.

Purpose: Constructed as a brief, wide-range test of basic skills and knowledge.

Population: Ages 4–adult..

Publication Date: 1994.

Acronym: MBA.

Scores, 5: Basic Skills (Reading, Writing, Mathematics, Total), Factual Knowledge.

Administration: Individual.

Price Data:

Time: (20–30) minutes.

Comments: Previously listed as Woodcock-McGrew-Weider Mini-Battery of Achievement.

Authors: Richard W. Woodcock, Kevin S. McGrew, and Judy K. Werder.

Publisher: Riverside Publishing.

Cross References: See T5:2903 (2 references); for reviews by William B. Michael and Eleanor E. Sanford, see 13:363.

[1615]
Mini Inventory of Right Brain Injury, Second Edition.

Purpose: Designed for "screening neurocognitive deficits associated with right hemisphere lesions."

Population: Ages 20–80.

Publication Dates: 1989–2000.

Acronym: MIRBI-2.

Scores, 10: Visual Scanning, Integrity of Gnosis, Integrity of Body Image, Visuoverbal Processing, Visuosymbolic Processing, Integrity of Visuomotor Praxis, Higher-Level Language Skills, Expressing Emotion, General Affect, General Behavior.

Administration: Individual.
Price Data, 2001: $134 per complete kit; $29 per examiner record booklets; $29 per response forms; $14 per response sheets; $14 per caliper; $34 per manual.
Time: (15–30) minutes.
Authors: Patricia A. Pimental and Jeffrey A. Knight.
Publisher: PRO-ED.
Cross References: For reviews by R. A. Bornstein and by John E. Obrzut and Carol A. Boliek, see 11:242.

[1616]
Mini-Mental State Examination.

Purpose: Designed to "measure cognitive status in adults."
Population: Adults.
Publication Dates: 1975–2001.
Acronym: MMSE.
Scores: Total score only with items in 11 sections: Orientation to Time, Orientation to Place, Registration, Attention and Calculation, Recall, Naming, Repetition, Comprehension, Reading, Writing, Drawing.
Administration: Individual.
Price Data: Available from publisher for introductory kit including 50 test forms and user's guide (2001, 11 pages).
Time: (5–10) minutes.
Authors: Marshal F. Folstein, Susan E. Folstein, and Paul R. McHugh, and Gary Fanjiang (manual only).
Publisher: Psychological Assessment Resources, Inc.

[1617]
Minnesota Clerical Assessment Battery.

Purpose: "Designed to assess knowledge and skills required for a number of clerical jobs."
Population: Secretaries and other clerical workers.
Publication Dates: 1988–1995.
Acronym: MCAB.
Scores: 3 composite scores: Secretaries, Clerk-Typists, Generalists.
Administration: Group.
Price Data, 1995: $260 per complete system, limited-use license administration units; $1,495 per single machine, unlimited-use license; $5,995 per single building site license; additional license and volume discount information available from publisher.
Comments: Composite scores are derived from two or more subtests; requires MS-DOS or PC-DOS computer to administer.
Author: Assessment Systems Corporation.
Publisher: Assessment Systems Corporation.
a) TYPING/KEYBOARDING.
Scores, 3: Gross Speed, Accuracy, Net Speed.
Time: (2–4) minutes.
b) PROOFREADING.
Scores, 3: Initially Incorrect, Initially Correct, Total.
Time: (45) minutes.

c) FILING.
Scores, 3: Alphabetical, Numerical, Total.
Time: (50) minutes.
d) BUSINESS VOCABULARY.
Scores: Total score only.
Time: (25) minutes.
e) BUSINESS MATH.
Scores: Total score only.
Time: (60) minutes.
f) CLERICAL KNOWLEDGE.
Scores: Total score only.
Time: (25) minutes.
Cross References: For reviews by Robert Fitzpatrick and Bikkar S. Randhawa, see 14:237.

[1618]
Minnesota Clerical Test.

Purpose: Designed to measure speed and accuracy in clerical work.
Population: Grades 8–12 and adults.
Publication Dates: 1933–1979.
Acronym: MCT.
Scores, 2: Number Comparison, Name Comparison.
Administration: Group or individual
Price Data, 2002: $78 per 25 test booklets including key and manual (1979, 22 pages); $25 per key for hand scoring test booklets; $26 per manual; $32 per examination kit.
Time: 15(20) minutes.
Authors: Dorothy M. Andrew, Donald G. Paterson, and Howard P. Longstaff.
Publisher: The Psychological Corporation.
Cross References: See T5:1693 (3 references) and T4:1640 (3 references); for reviews by Michael Ryan and Ruth G. Thomas, see 9:713 (2 references); see also T3:1493 (5 references), T2:2135 (23 references), and 6:1040 (10 references); for a review by Donald E. Super, see 5:850 (46 references); for reviews by Thelma Hunt, R. B. Selover, Erwin K. Taylor, and E. F. Wonderlic, see 3:627 (22 references); for a review by W. D. Commins, see 2:1644 (18 references).

[1619]
Minnesota Handwriting Assessment.

Purpose: "Used to assess manuscript and D'Nealian handwriting of students."
Population: Grades 1–2.
Publication Date: 1999.
Acronym: MHA.
Scores, 6: Rate, Legibility, Form, Alignment, Size, Spacing.
Administration: Group or individual.
Price Data, 2002: $56 per kit including 25 manuscript sheets, 25 D'Nealian sheets, and manual (99 pages).
Time: (2.5–10) minutes.

Author: Judith Reisman.
Publisher: Therapy Skill Builders—A Division of The Psychological Corporation.

[1620]
Minnesota Importance Questionnaire.

Purpose: "To measure twenty psychological needs and six underlying values that have been found to be relevant to work adjustment, specifically to satisfaction with work."
Population: Ages 16 and over.
Publication Dates: 1967–1981.
Acronym: MIQ.
Scores, 21: Ability Utilization, Achievement, Activity, Independence, Variety, Compensation, Security, Working Conditions, Advancement, Recognition, Authority, Social Status, Co-workers, Social Services, Moral Values, Company Policies, Supervision-Human Relations, Supervision-Technical, Creativity, Responsibility, Autonomy (ranked form only).
Administration: Group.
Forms, 2: Ranked form (1975, 9 pages), paired form (1975, 18 pages).
Price Data, 2001: $39.50 per complete kit including 50 answer sheets, 10 reusable booklets, manual (1981, 73 pages), and Occupational Reinforcer Patterns (1986); $.70 or less per reusable booklet ($7 minimum); $.12 or less per answer sheet ($6 minimum); $8.50 per manual; scoring service offered by publisher.
Foreign Language Edition: Spanish edition available.
Time: (15–25) minutes for ranked form; (30–40) minutes for paired form.
Authors: James B. Rounds, Jr., George A. Henly, René V. Dawis, Lloyd H. Lofquist, and David J. Weiss.
Publisher: Vocational Psychology Research.
Cross References: See T5:1694 (10 references) and T4:1641 (3 references); for reviews by Barbara Lachar and Wilbur L. Layton, see 11:243 (4 references); for reviews by Lewis E. Albright and Sheldon Zedeck, see 8:1050 (40 references); see also T3:1495 (14 references), T2:2283 (8 references), and 7:1063 (29 references).

[1621]
Minnesota Job Description Questionnaire.

Purpose: "Designed to measure the reinforcer characteristics of jobs."
Population: Employees and supervisors.
Publication Dates: 1967–1968.
Acronym: MJDQ.
Scores: 21 reinforcer dimensions: Ability Utilization, Achievement, Activity, Advancement, Authority, Company Policies and Practices, Compensation, Co-Workers, Creativity, Independence, Moral Values, Recognition, Responsibility, Security, Social Service, Social

Status, Supervision—Human Relations, Supervision—Technical, Variety, Working Conditions, Autonomy.
Administration: Group.
Forms, 2: E (for employees), S (for supervisors).
Price Data, 2001: $.73-$.75 per copy (Form S); $.78-$.80 per copy (Form E); $6 per manual (1968, 96 pages); $1.75 per person for scoring service.
Time: [20] minutes.
Comments: For research use only; 20 scores parallel scores of the Minnesota Importance Questionnaire (1620) and Minnesota Satisfaction Questionnaire (1626).
Authors: Fred H. Borgen, David J. Weiss, Howard E. A. Tinsley, René V. Dawis, and Lloyd H. Lofquist.
Publisher: Vocational Psychology Research.
Cross References: See T5:1695 (2 references), T4:1643 (3 references), and T3:1497 (4 references); for a review by Sheldon Zedeck, see 8:1051 (15 references); see also T2:2284 (8 references).

[1622]
Minnesota Manual Dexterity Test.

Purpose: "Measures capacity for simple but rapid eye-hand-finger movement."
Population: Ages 13–adult.
Publication Date: [Undated].
Scores: Total time for each of two tests.
Administration: Group.
Tests, 2: Placing Test, Turning Test.
Price Data: Available from publisher.
Time: Administration time not reported.
Author: Lafayette Instrument.
Publisher: Lafayette Instrument.
Cross References: For reviews by Deborah Erickson and Alida S. Westman, see 12:237.

[1623]
Minnesota Multiphasic Personality Inventory-2.

Purpose: "Designed to assess a number of the major patterns of personality and emotional disorders."
Population: Ages 18 and over.
Publication Dates: 1942–1990.
Acronym: MMPI-2.
Scores, 75: 7 Validity Indicators: Cannot Say (?), Lie (L), Infrequency (F), Correction (K), Back F (FB), Variable Response Inconsistency (VRIN), True Response Inconsistency (TRIN); 10 Clinical Scales: Hypochondriasis (Hs), Depression (D), Conversion Hysteria (Hy), Psychopathic Deviate (Pd), Masculinity-Femininity (Mf), Paranoia (Pa), Psychasthenia (Pt), Schizophrenia (Sc), Hypomania (Ma), Social Introversion (Si); 15 Supplementary Scales: Anxiety (A), Repression (R), Ego Strength (Es), MacAndrew Alcoholism Scale-Revised (MAC-R), Overcontrolled Hostility (O-H), Dominance (Do), Social Responsibil-

ity (Re), College Maladjustment (Mt), Gender Role-Masculine (GM), Gender Role-Feminine (GF), 2 Post-Traumatic Stress Disorder Scales (PK & PS); Marital Distress Scale (MDS), Addiction Potential Scale (APS), Addiction Admission Scale (AAS); 15 Content Scales: Anxiety (ANX), Fears (FRS), Obsessiveness (OBS), Depression (DEP), Health Concerns (HEA), Bizarre Mentation (BIZ), Anger (ANG), Cynicism (CYN), Antisocial Practices (ASP), Type A (TPA), Low Self-Esteem (LSE), Social Discomfort (SOD), Family Problems (FAM), Work Interference (WRK), Negative Treatment Indicators (TRT); 3 Si subscales: Shyness/Self-Consciousness (Si1), Social Avoidance (Si2), Alienation-Self and Others (Si3); 28 Harris-Lingoes Subscales: Subjective Depression (D1), Psychomotor Retardation (D2), Physical Malfunctioning (D3), Mental Dullness (D4), Brooding (D5), Denial of Social Anxiety (Hy1), Need for Affection (Hy2), Lassitude-Malaise (Hy3), Somatic Complaints (Hy4), Inhibition of Aggression (Hy5), Familial Discord (Pd1), Authority Problems (Pd2), Social Imperturbability (Pd3), Social Alienation (Pd4), Self-Alienation (Pd5), Persecutory Ideas (Pa1), Poignancy (Pa2), Naivete (Pa3), Social Alienation (Sc1), Emotional Alienation (Sc2), Lack of Ego Mastery, Cognitive (Sc3), Conative (Sc4), Defective Inhibition (Sc5), Bizarre Sensory Experiences (Sc6), Amorality (Ma1), Psychomotor Acceleration (Ma2), Imperturbability (Ma3), Ego Inflation (Ma4).

Administration: Group or individual.

Price Data, 1999: $27 per 10 reusable softcover test booklets (English or Hispanic); $36 per reusable hardcover test booklet (English); $77 per 100 hand-scorable answer sheets and profile forms; $78 per audiocassette (English or Hispanic); $38.50 per 50 profile forms (specify Supplementary Scales, Content Scales, Content Component Scales, or Harris-Lingoes Subscales); $67 per answer keys (specify scale and for softcover or hardcover test booklets); $43 per manual for administration and scoring (1989, 166 pages); $18 per Adult Clinical System User's Guide (1989, 71 pages); $18 per Revised Personnel System User's Guide (1989, 76 pages); price data available from publisher for IBM compatible microcomputer edition based on type of score or interpretive report desired; price data available from publisher for scoring service by publisher based on type of score or interpretive report desired.

Time: (90) minutes.

Comments: Revision of the Minnesota Multiphasic Personality Inventory; may be administered by audiocassette or microcomputer.

Authors: James N. Butcher, W. Grant Dahlstrom, John Graham, Auke Tellegen, and Beverly Kaemmer.

Publisher: Published by University of Minnesota Press; distributed by NCS [Minnetonka].

Cross References: See T5:1697 (600 references) and T4:1645 (504 references); for reviews by Robert P.

Archer and David S. Nichols, see 11:244 (637 references); see also 9:715 (339 references) and T3:1498 (749 references); for reviews by Henry A. Alker and Glen D. King of the original version, see 8:616 (1,188 references); see also T2:1281 (549 references); for reviews by Malcolm D. Gynther and David A. Rodgers, see 7:104 (831 references); see also P:166 (1,066 references); for a review by Arthur L. Benton, see 4:71 (211 references); for reviews by Arthur L. Benton, H. J. Eysenck, L. S. Penrose, and Julian B. Rotter, and an excerpted review, see 3:60 (76 references).

[1624]
Minnesota Multiphasic Personality Inventory–Adolescent.

Purpose: Designed for use with adolescents to assess a number of the major patterns of personality and emotional disorders.

Population: Ages 14–18.

Publication Date: 1992.

Acronym: MMPI-A.

Scores, 68: 16 Basic Scales [6 Validity Scales (Cannot Say (?), Lie, Infrequency, Defensiveness, Variable Response Inconsistency, True Response Inconsistency); 10 Clinical Scales (Hypochondriasis, Depression, Hysteria, Psychopathic Deviate, Masculinity-Femininity, Paranoia, Psychasthenia, Schizophrenia, Hypomania, Social Introversion); 28 Harris-Lingoes Subscales (Subjective Depression, Psychomotor Retardation, Physical Malfunctioning, Mental Dullness, Brooding, Denial of Social Anxiety, Need for Affection, Lassitude-Malaise, Somatic Complaints, Inhibition of Aggression, Familial Discord, Authority Problems, Social Imperturbability, Social Alienation, Self-Alienation, Persecutory Ideas, Poignancy, Naivete, Social Alienation, Emotional Alienation, Lack of Ego Mastery-Cognitive, Lack of Ego Mastery-Conative, Lack of Ego Mastery-Defective Inhibition, Bizarre Sensory Experiences, Amorality, Psychomotor Acceleration, Imperturbability, Ego Inflation); 3 Si Subscales (Shyness/Self-Consciousness, Social Avoidance, Alienation); 15 Adolescent Content Scales (Anxiety, Obsessiveness, Depression, Health Concerns, Alienation, Bizarre Mentation, Anger, Cynicism, Conduct Problems, Low Self-Esteem, Low Aspirations, Social Discomfort, Family Problems, School Problems, Negative Treatment Indicators); 6 Supplementary Scales (Anxiety, Repression, MacAndrew Alcoholism Scale—Revised, Alcohol/Drug Problem Acknowledgment, Alcohol/Drug Problem Proneness, Immaturity).

Administration: Group or individual.

Price Data, 1992: Microtest Reports ($20 per Adolescent Interpretive System, $14 per Extended Score Report, $8 per Basic Service Profile); Prepaid Mail-In Reports ($21 per Adolescent Interpretive System; $15 per Extended Score Report; $9 per Basic Service Profile); $40 per manual; $15 per Adolescent Interpretive System User's Guide; $25 per 10 softcover test booklets; $25 per hardcover test booklet; $75 per audiocassette; $60 per 100 Content/Supplementary Scales Profile Forms; $60 per 100 Harris-Lingoes Subscales Profile Forms; $50 per Basic Scales answer keys; $50 per Content/Supplementary Scales answer keys; $50 per Harris-Lingoes Subscales answer keys; $385 per hand-scoring starter kit including manual, test booklets, Basic Scales keys, Harris-Lingoes Subscales keys, Content/Supplementary Scale keys, 100 hand-scoring answer sheets, 100 Basic Scale Profile Forms, Harris-Lingoes Profile Forms, 100 Content/Supplementary Profile Forms.

Time: Administration time not reported.

Comments: May be administered by audiocassette or microcomputer.

Authors: James N. Butcher, Carolyn L. Williams, John R. Graham, Beverly Kaemmer, Robert P. Archer (manual); Auke Tellegen (manual), and Yossef S. Ben-Porath (manual).

Publisher: University of Minnesota Press; distributed by NCS [Minnetonka]).

Cross References: See T5:1698 (28 references); for reviews by Charles D. Claiborn and Richard I. Lanyon, see 12:238 (4 references); see also T4:1646 (4 references).

[1625]
Minnesota Percepto-Diagnostic Test, Revised Edition.

Purpose: "Designed to assess visual perception and visual abilities" for the purpose of identifying brain damages and emotional disturbances.

Population: Ages 5–16 and adults.

Publication Dates: 1962–1986.

Acronym: MPDT.

Scores: Overall Performance Score.

Administration: Individual.

Price Data: Available from publisher.

Time: (5-20) minutes.

Authors: Gerald B. Fuller and J. T. Laird (test).

Publisher: Multi-Health Systems, Inc.

Cross References: See T5:1699 (2 references), T4:1647 (6 references), 9:719 (3 references), 8:872 (22 references), T2:1485 (17 references), and P:475 (19 references); for reviews by Richard W. Coan and Eugene E. Levitt of the original edition, see 6:231 (2 references).

[1626]
Minnesota Satisfaction Questionnaire.

Purpose: "Designed to measure an employee's satisfaction with his/her job."

Population: Business and industry.

Publication Dates: 1963–1977.

Acronym: MSQ.

Administration: Group.

Price Data, 2001: $.38 to $.39 per questionnaire for Short Form; $.64 to $.66 per questionnaire for Long Form; $4.95 per manual (1967, 130 pages); $6.60 per specimen set including MSQ Long Form, MSQ Long Form (1967 revision), MSQ Short Form, and manual; $1.10 per booklet for scoring service (Short Form); $1.65 per booklet for scoring service (Long Form).

Authors: David J. Weiss, René V. Dawis, George W. England, and Lloyd H. Lofquist.

Publisher: Vocational Psychology Research.

　　a) LONG FORM.

　　Scores, 21: Ability Utilization, Achievement, Activity, Advancement, Authority, Company Policies and Practices, Compensation, Coworkers, Creativity, Independence, Moral Values, Recognition, Responsibility, Security, Social Service, Social Status, Supervision-Human Relations, Supervision-Technical, Variety, Working Conditions, General Satisfaction.

　　Editions, 2: 1967 revision, 1977 edition.

　　Time: (15–20) minutes.

　　b) SHORT FORM.

　　Scores, 3: Intrinsic, Extrinsic, General.

　　Time: (5–10) minutes.

Cross References: See T5:1701 (56 references), T4:1649 (49 references), 9:721 (21 references), and T3:1508 (27 references); for a review by Robert M. Guion, see 8:1052 (82 references); see also T2:2285 (11 references); for reviews by Lewis E. Albright and John P. Foley, Jr., see 7:1064 (18 references).

[1627]
Minnesota Satisfactoriness Scales.

Purpose: "Designed to measure an employee's satisfactoriness on a job."

Population: Employees.

Publication Dates: 1965–1970.

Acronym: MSS.

Scores, 5: Performance, Conformance, Dependability, Personal Adjustment, General Satisfactoriness.

Administration: Group.

Price Data, 2001: $.33-$.35 per test; manual (1970, 53 pages plus test) no longer in print, photocopies available for $3.50; $1.25 per person for scoring service.

Time: (5) minutes.

Comments: Ratings by supervisors.

Authors: Dennis L. Gibson, David J. Weiss, René V. Dawis, and Lloyd H. Lofquist.

Publisher: Vocational Psychology Research.

Cross References: See T5:1702 (4 references), T4:1650 (6 references), and T3:1509 (2 references); for a review by Jerome E. Doppelt, see 8:1061 (9 references).

[1628]
Mirror Edition of the Personal Values Inventory.

Purpose: Designed to describe how a person uses his/her personal strengths in relationships.
Population: Adolescents and adults reading at sixth grade level or above.
Publication Dates: 1973–1997.
Scores, 20: 7 Motivational Values.
Administration: Individual or group..
Price Data, 2001: $4.50 per test booklet; $30 per manual (1996, 146 pages).
Time: (20–40) minutes.
Comments: Manual is entitled Relationship Awareness Theory Manual of Administration and Interpretation (9th Ed.).
Author: Elias H. Porter.
Publisher: Personal Strengths Publishing.

[1629]
Mirror-Couple Relationship Inventory.

Purpose: To reflect to a couple how each partner sees self and other partner.
Population: Engaged and married couples.
Publication Date: 1980.
Scores: 24 scales: 11 content scales (Parents, Lifestyle, Career, Money, Sex, Leisure, Friends, Religion, Children, Future, Rank Importance), 12 process scales (Personality, Awareness, OK Alone, Freedom, Problem Solving, Fight/Flight, Values Self, Values Partner, Positive Communication, Negative Communication, Stress, Satisfaction), and 1 Attitude scale.
Administration: Group or individual.
Price Data: Available from publisher.
Time: Administration time not reported.
Authors: Joan A. Hunt and Richard A. Hunt.
Publisher: Ministry Inventories.
Cross References: See T5:1705 (4 references).

[1630]
The Missouri Children's Picture Series.

Purpose: Assessment of personality.
Population: Ages 5–16.
Publication Dates: 1971, c1963–1964.
Acronym: MCPS.
Scores, 8: Conformity, Masculinity-Femininity, Maturity, Aggression, Inhibition, Activity Level, Sleep Disturbance, Somatization.
Administration: Group.
Price Data: Available from publisher.
Time: (25–35) minutes.
Authors: Jacob O. Sines, Jerome D. Pauker, and Lloyd K. Sines.
Publisher: Jacob O. Sines (the author).
Cross References: See T5:1706 (3 references), T4:1655 (6 references), and T3:1515 (3 references); for

reviews by Dale B. Harris and Lovick C. Miller, and an excerpted review by George Gilmore, see 8:625 (11 references); see also T2:1287 (4 references).

[1631]
Missouri Kindergarten Inventory of Developmental Skills, Alternate Form.

Purpose: A screening battery providing a comprehensive assessment measure to use at or before kindergarten entrance.
Population: Ages 48–72 months.
Publication Dates: 1978–1982.
Acronym: KIDS.
Scores: 6 areas: Number Concepts, Auditory Skills, Language Concepts, Paper and Pencil Skills, Visual Skills, Gross Motor Skills.
Administration: Individual.
Price Data, 2001: $.50 per answer sheet; $15 per specimen set including sample test materials, answer sheet, administration and scoring manual (1980, 78 pages), and instructional guide book (1981, 45 pages).
Time: (35) minutes.
Comments: Can be given anytime within the year preceding kindergarten as well as at kindergarten entrance.
Author: Missouri Department of Elementary and Secondary Education.
Publisher: Assessment Resource Center, University of Missouri-Columbia.
Cross References: For reviews by Mary Henning-Stout and James E. Ysseldyke, see 11:246.

[1632]
MKM Binocular Preschool Test.

Purpose: To evaluate "the near point performance of preschool and other nonreading children."
Population: Preschool.
Publication Dates: 1963–1965.
Scores: Item scores only.
Administration: Individual.
Price Data: Available from publisher.
Time: [1–2] minutes.
Comments: Stereoscope necessary for administration.
Authors: Leland D. Michael, James W. King, and Arlene Moorhead (instructions).
Publisher: MKM.

[1633]
MKM Monocular and Binocular Reading Test.

Purpose: "To detect children who are likely to have reading problems associated with poor binocular coordination and macular suppression."
Population: Grades 1–2, 3 and over.

Publication Dates: 1963–1964.
Scores: Item scores only.
Administration: Individual.
Levels, 2: 1, 2.
Price Data: Available from publisher.
Time: [3–10] minutes.
Comments: Stereoscope necessary for administration.
Authors: Leland D. Michael, James W. King, and Arlene Moorhead (instructions).
Publisher: MKM.
Cross References: See T2:1920 (1 reference).

[1634]
MKM Picture Arrangement Test.

Purpose: Tests directionality.
Population: Grades K–6.
Publication Dates: 1963–1965.
Scores: No scores.
Administration: Individual.
Price Data: Available from publisher.
Time: [1–2] minutes.
Authors: Leland D. Michael and James W. King.
Publisher: MKM.

[1635]
Mobile Vocational Evaluation.

Purpose: "Computer assisted testing system that measures vocationally related abilities and interests."
Population: Adults.
Publication Date: 1983.
Acronym: MVE.
Scores, 29: 17 ability factors (Finger Dexterity, Wrist-Finger Speed, Arm-Hand Steadiness, Manual Dexterity, Two-Arm Coordination, Two-Hand Coordination, Perceptual Accuracy, Spatial Perception, Aiming, Reaction Time, Abstract Reasoning, Numerical Reasoning, Verbal Reasoning, Reading and Arithmetic Grade Levels, Leadership Structure and Consideration, Following Directions, Sales Attitude); 12 interest categories (Artistic, Scientific, Plants and Animals, Protective, Mechanical, Industrial, Business Detail, Selling, Accommodating, Humanitarian, Leading-Influencing, Physical Performing).
Administration: Group and individual.
Price Data, 2001: $4,195 for the entire system including 10 each of nine standardized paper-and-pencil tests with manuals, scoring keys, and oral directions, cassette tape with cassette tape player, 10 interest inventory test booklets with scoring forms, system manual, software (IBM or MAC), data processing user's guide, and professional consultation.
Time: (180) minutes.
Author: Edward J. Hester.
Publisher: Hester Evaluation Systems, Inc.

[1636]
Modern Occupational Skills Tests.

Purpose: Developed to assess skills in checking, numeracy, verbal skills, and office administration skills for use in "recruitment, selection and development of clerical and related staff."
Population: Potential and current office employees.
Publication Dates: 1989–1990.
Acronym: MOST.
Scores: Total score only for each test.
Administration: Group.
Editions, 2: British, Australian.
Price Data: Price information available from publisher for administration pack including task inventory, 10 question and answer booklets, 10 profile sheets, 10 test taker's guides, scoring key, test record sheet, and administration and scoring instructions (select area), and for reference set including one each of question and answer booklets and test taker's guides, a profile sheet, task inventory, administration and scoring instructions, and user's guides (1989 and 1990, 77 pages).
Authors: Charles Johnson, Steve Blinkhorn, Robert Wood, and Jonathan Hall.
Publisher: NFER-Nelson Publishing Co., Ltd. [England].
Foreign Adaptation: Australian Edition available from Australian Council for Educational Research Ltd. [Australia].
  a) NUMERICAL ESTIMATION.
  Time: 12 minutes.
  b) NUMERICAL AWARENESS.
  Time: 8 minutes.
  c) NUMERICAL CHECKING.
  Time: 8 minutes.
  d) TECHNICAL CHECKING.
  Time: 12 minutes.
  e) WORD MEANINGS.
  Time: 12 minutes.
  f) VERBAL CHECKING.
  Time: 8 minutes.
  g) DECISION MAKING.
  Time: 15 minutes.
  h) SPELLING AND GRAMMAR.
  Time: 8 minutes.
  i) FILING.
  Time: 12 minutes.
Cross References: For reviews by Joseph C. Ciechalski and Bikkar S. Randhawa, see 12:239.

[1637]
Modern Photography Comprehension Test.

Purpose: Developed to assess knowledge of photography.
Population: Photography students.
Publication Dates: 1953–1969.
Scores: Total score only.

Administration: Group.
Price Data, 2001: $49.50 per test package; $2.25 per key; $2 per direction sheet; $9.50 per specimen set.
Time: (15-20) minutes.
Comments: Revision of What Do You Know About Photography?
Author: Martin M. Bruce.
Publisher: Martin M. Bruce, Ph.D.
Cross References: For a review by David P. Campbell, see 7:547.

[1638]
Modified Vygotsky Concept Formation Test.

Purpose: "Measures an individual's ability to think in abstract concepts."
Population: Older children and adolescents and adults.
Publication Dates: 1940–1984.
Scores, 2: Convergent Thinking, Divergent Thinking.
Administration: Individual.
Price Data, 2001: $195 per Kasanin-Hanfmann test kit; $35 per modified manual (1984, 75 pages); $28 per 30 record forms.
Time: (30) minutes.
Comments: Modified manual used in conjunction with Kasanin-Hanfmann Concept Formation Test (Vigotsky Test) (T3:1239).
Author: Paul L. Wang (modified manual).
Publisher: Stoelting Co.
Cross References: For reviews by Kathryn A. Hess and Gregory Schraw, see 12:240; for information on the Kasanin-Hanfmann Concept Formation Test, see also T3:1239 (1 reference), T2:1140 (9 references), P:47 (7 references), and 6:78 (11 references); for a review of an earlier edition by Kate Levine Kogan (with William S. Kogan), see 4:35 (8 references); for a review of an earlier edition by O. L. Zangwill, see 3:27 (21 references).

[1639]
Monitoring Basic Skills Progress—Second Edition.

Purpose: "Designed to monitor students' acquisition of basic skills in one of three academic areas" using curriculum-based measurements.
Publication Dates: 1990–1999.
Administration: Group, via individual personal computers.
Price Data, 2001: $329 per complete program including Basic Reading, Basic Math Computation, and Basic Math Concepts and Applications; $119 per Basic Reading—Second Edition; $229 per Math Complete kit; $119 per Basic Math Computation—Second Edition; $129 per Math Concepts and Applications; $19 per Basic Math Computation, Second Edition

blackline masters; $39 per Math Concepts and Applications blackline masters.
Comments: "Derived from the curriculum-based measurement (CBM) model of student monitoring"; for use in general or special education classrooms; computer administered and scored (requires Macintosh 68020 or higher CPU with System 7.1 or later).
Authors: Lynn S. Fuchs, Carol L. Hamlett, and Douglas Fuchs.
Publisher: PRO-ED.

a) BASIC READING.
Purpose: Designed to "monitor student progress, identify students who require intervention, and improve instructional programs" in reading.
Population: Grades 1–7.
Scores: Total score only.
Time: (2.5) minutes.

b) BASIC MATH COMPUTATION.
Purpose: Designed to "monitor student progress, identify students who require intervention, and improve instructional programs" in mathematics.
Population: Grades 1–6.
Scores: Total score only.
Time: (2–6) minutes.

c) MATH CONCEPTS AND APPLICATIONS.
Population: Grades 1–6.
Cross References: For reviews by Mary J. McLellan and Jeffrey K. Smith of *a* and *b*, see 14:238; for a review by Joseph C. Witt and Kevin M. Jones of an earlier edition, see 12:241.

[1640]
The Mooney Problem Check Lists, 1950 Revision.

Purpose: "Intended to help individuals express their personal problems."
Population: Junior high–adults.
Publication Dates: 1941–1950.
Acronym: MPCL.
Administration: Group.
Price Data, 2002: $36 per combined levels examination kit (for use without separate answer documents) including Check Lists and manual (1950, 15 pages); $12 per combined examination kit (for use with separate answer documents) including Check List, answer document, and manual; $4 per 25 checklists (for use without separate answer documents) and manual (specify level); $151 per 100 checklists (for use without separate answer documents) and manual (specify level).
Time: (35) minutes.
Authors: Ross L. Mooney and Leonard V. Gordon (manuals, *c*, and *d*).
Publisher: The Psychological Corporation.

a) JUNIOR HIGH SCHOOL FORM.
Population: Grades 7–9.
Publication Dates: 1942–1950.

Scores, 7: Health and Physical Development, School, Home and Family, Money-Work-The Future, Boy and Girl Relations, Relations to People in General, Self-Centered Concerns.
b) HIGH SCHOOL FORM.
Population: Grades 9–12.
Publication Dates: 1941–1950.
Scores, 11: Health and Physical Development, Finances-Living Conditions-Employment, Social and Recreational Activities, Social-Psychological Relations, Personal-Psychological Relations, Courtship-Sex-Marriage, Home and Family, Morals and Religion, Adjustment to School Work, The Future-Vocational and Educational, Curriculum and Teaching Procedure.
c) COLLEGE FORM.
Population: Grades 13–16.
Publication Dates: 1941–1950.
Scores, 11: Same as for High School Form.
d) ADULT FORM.
Population: Adults.
Publication Date: 1950.
Scores, 9: Health, Economic Security, Self-Improvement, Personality, Home and Family, Courtship, Sex, Religion, Occupation.
Cross References: See T5:1716 (5 references), T4:1667 (14 references), T3:1531 (19 references), 8:626 (48 references), T2:1289 (92 references), and P:173 (55 references); for a review by Thomas C. Burgess, see 6:145 (25 references); see also 5:89 (26 references); for reviews by Harold E. Jones and Morris Krugman, see 4:73 (13 references); for reviews by Ralph C. Bedell and Theodore F. Lentz of an earlier form of *a-c,* see 3:67 (17 references).

[1641]
Morrisby Profile.

Purpose: "Designed to give a complete statement, in objective terms, about the basic mental structure of a person."
Population: Age 14–adults.
Publication Dates: 1955–1992.
Acronym: MP.
Scores: 12 tests: Compound Series, General Abilities-Verbal, General Abilities-Numerical, General Abilities-Perceptual, Shapes, Mechanical Ability, Speed Tests 1–4 (Modal Profile), Speed Tests 5–6 (Dexterity).
Administration: Group.
Price Data: Available from publisher.
Time: 180 (210) minutes.
Comments: Previously called the Differential Test Battery.
Author: The Morrisby Organisation.
Publisher: The Morrisby Organisation [England].
Cross References: For information on the Differential Test Battery, see T3:733 (2 references), T2:1070

(6 references); for reviews by E. A. Peel, Donald E. Super, and Philip E. Vernon, see 5:606.

[1642]
Mossford Assessment Chart for the Physically Handicapped.

Purpose: Designed as a "checklist of daily living activities."
Population: Ages 5–18.
Publication Date: 1983.
Acronym: MACPH.
Scores: 12 scales: Sitting and Walking, Mobility, Bathing and Dressing, Personal Hygiene, Health, Leisure and Social Activities, Reading and Writing, Mathematics, Financial Skills, Domestic Skills, Manipulative and Perceptual Skills, Communication and Aids.
Administration: Individual.
Price Data: Price information available from publisher for record forms, chart transparencies, and manual (20 pages).
Time: Administration time not reported.
Author: Janet Whitehouse.
Publisher: NFER-Nelson Publishing Co., Ltd. [England].

[1643]
Motivated Skills Card Sort.

Purpose: To identify skills that are central to personal and career satisfaction and success by rank ordering skills on two dimensions: Competency and Motivation.
Population: Adults.
Publication Dates: 1981–2002.
Scores: Skills Ratings Matrix.
Administration: Group or individual.
Price Data: Available from publisher.
Time: (45–60) minutes.
Author: Richard L. Knowdell.
Publisher: Career Research & Testing, Inc.
Cross References: For reviews by Albert M. Bugaj and Gary J. Robertson, see 13:204.

[1644]
Motivated Strategies for Learning Questionnaire.

Purpose: "To assess college students' motivational orientations and their use of different learning strategies for a college course."
Population: College students.
Publication Date: 1991.
Acronym: MSLQ.
Scores, 15: 3 Motivation Scales [Value Component (Intrinsic Goal Orientation, Extrinsic Goal Orientation, Task Value), Expectancy Component (Control of Learning Beliefs, Self-Efficacy for Learning and Performance), Affective Component (Test Anxiety)]; 2

Learning Strategies Scales [Cognitive and Metacognitive Strategies (Rehearsal, Elaboration, Organization, Critical Thinking, Metacognitive Self-Regulation), Resource Management Strategies (Time and Study Environment, Effort Regulation, Peer Learning, Help Seeking)].
Administration: Group.
Price Data: Available from publisher.
Time: (20–30) minutes.
Authors: Paul R. Pintrich, David A. F. Smith, Teresa Garcia, and Wilbert J. McKeachie.
Publisher: National Center for Research to Improve Postsecondary Teaching and Learning.
Cross References: See T5:1720 (5 references); for reviews by Jeri Benson and Robert K. Gable, see 13:205 (5 references).

[1645]
Motivation Assessment Scale.
Purpose: Designed to assess the motivation underlying problem behaviors so as to curb those behaviors.
Population: People with mental disabilities.
Publication Date: 1992.
Scores, 4: Sensory, Escape, Attention, Tangible.
Administration: Individual.
Price Data: Available from publisher.
Time: Administration time not reported.
Comments: A rating tool to be completed by someone in close contact with the target individual; can be completed by paper and pencil or as an interview.
Authors: V. Mark Durand and Daniel B. Crimmins.
Publisher: Monaco and Associates, Inc.
Cross References: For reviews by Roger A. Boothroyd and James P. Van Haneghan, see 14:239; see also T5:1722 (2 references).

[1646]
Motivational Patterns Inventory.
Purpose: "Designed to help members of an organization explore dominant motivations that can affect the way they contribute to the success of that organization."
Population: Organizational members.
Publication Date: 1990.
Scores, 3: Farmer, Hunter, Shepherd.
Administration: Group.
Price Data: Price information available from publisher for inventory (33 pages) including administrator's guide (2 pages).
Time: Administration time not reported.
Comments: Self-scored.
Authors: Richard E. Byrd and William R. Neher.
Publisher: Jossey-Bass, A Wiley Company.
Cross References: For reviews by Larry G. Daniel and Barbara A. Reilly, see 12:245.

[1647]
Motivational Styles Questionnaire.
Purpose: "Designed to define the kind of work situation to which individuals are suited and the way in which they will most willingly exert effort."
Population: Job applicants.
Publication Date: 1998.
Acronym: MSQ.
Scores: 10 scales: Work Style Preferences (Achievement, Independence, Structure, Affiliation, System Power, People Power, Person Power), Work and Life Attitudes (Central Orientation, Medium-term Striving, Short-term Striving).
Administration: Individual.
Price Data: Available from publisher.
Time: [20–30] minutes.
Author: Roland Tarleton.
Publisher: The Psychological Corporation Europe [United Kingdom].

[1648]
Motive to Attain Social Power.
Purpose: Designed to evaluate one's "probable enjoyment or dislike (motivational preference) for a variety of socialized power activities."
Population: Undergraduates.
Publication Date: No date.
Scores: Total score only.
Administration: Group.
Price Data, 2001: $3 per specimen set.
Time: Administration time not reported.
Authors: L. R. Good and K. C. Good.
Publisher: Psychometric Affiliates.

[1649]
Motives, Values, Preferences Inventory.
Purpose: Designed to assess "the fit between an individual and the organizational culture" and "a person's motives."
Population: Adults.
Publication Dates: 1987–1996.
Acronym: MVPI.
Scores, 10: Aesthetic, Affiliation, Altruistic, Commercial, Hedonistic, Power, Recognition, Scientific, Security, Tradition.
Administration: Group.
Price Data, 1998: $2 per test booklet; $12.50 per 25 answer sheets; $45 per manual (1996, 90 pages); $75 per software starter kit; $30 per interpretive profile; $15 per graph or data file.
Time: (20) minutes.
Authors: Joyce Hogan and Robert Hogan.
Publisher: Hogan Assessment Systems, Inc.
Cross References: For reviews by Brent W. Roberts and Sheldon Zedeck, see 14:240.

[1650]
Motor-Free Visual Perception Test—Revised.

Purpose: Designed as a test of visual perception that avoids any motor involvement.
Population: Ages 4–11, adults.
Publication Dates: 1972–1996.
Acronym: MVPT-R.
Scores, 2: Perceptual Quotient, Perceptual Age.
Administration: Individual.
Price Data, 2002: $85 per test kit including manual (1996, 40 pages), test plates, and 50 recording forms in vinyl volder; $27 per manual; $40 per test plates; $15 per 50 recording forms; $9 per pad of 50 remedial checklists (optional); $27 per specimen set including manual and sample form.
Time: (10) minutes.
Comments: The publisher advises that a revision will be available in 2002.
Authors: Ronald P. Colarusso and Donald D. Hammill.
Publisher: Academic Therapy Publications.
Cross References: For reviews by Nancy B. Bologna and Theresa Volpe-Johnstone, see 14:241; see also T5:1725 (8 references) and T4:1677 (6 references); for a review by Carl L. Rosen of an earlier edition and an excerpted review by Alan Krichev, see 8:883 (9 references).

[1651]
Motor-Free Visual Perception Test—Vertical.

Purpose: Designed to assess problems in visual perception in individuals with hemispatial visual neglect.
Population: People with brain injuries.
Publication Date: 1997.
Acronym: MVPT-V.
Scores: Total score only.
Administration: Individual
Price Data, 2002: $80 per complete test kit including manual (35 pages), test plates, and 50 recording forms; $16 per 50 recording forms; $38 per test plates; $23 per manual.
Time: (10) minutes.
Comments: Contents of test based on the Motor-Free Visual Perception Test (1650).
Authors: Louisette Mercier, Rejean Hebert, Ronald Colarusso, and Donald Hammill.
Publisher: Academic Therapy Publications.
Cross References: For a review by Matthew E. Lambert, see 14:242.

[1652]
Motor Skills Acquisition Checklist.

Purpose: "Helps identify the proper milestones ... of [motor] development."

Population: Birth to 12 months.
Publication Date: 2000.
Scores: 47 behavior ratings.
Administration: Individual.
Price Data, 2002: $9 per checklist (48 pages); $40 per 10 checklists
Time: Untimed.
Comments: Companion to "Motor Skills Acquisition in the First Year."
Author: Lois Bly.
Publisher: Therapy Skill Builders—A Division of the Psychological Corporation.

[1653]
Movement Assessment Battery for Children.

Purpose: Designed to assess motor skills and motor development difficulties.
Population: Ages 4–12 years.
Publication Dates: 1972–1992.
Acronym: Movement ABC.
Administration: Individual.
Price Data, 1999: $463.50 per complete kit including checklist, manual (1992, 250 pages), record forms, and all necessary manipulatives in an attaché case; $14 per 50 checklists; $40 per 50 record forms (specify level).
Authors: Sheila E. Henderson and David A. Sugden.
Publisher: The Psychological Corporation Limited [United Kingdom]; distributed by The Psychological Corporation.

a) MOVEMENT ABC.
  Scores, 3: Manual Dexterity, Ball Skills, Static and Dynamic Balance.
  Administration: Individual.
  Levels, 4: Age Band 1 (Ages 4–6); Age Band 2 (Ages 7–8); Age Band 3 (Ages 9–10); Age Band 4 (Ages 11–12).
  Time: (20–30) minutes.
  Comments: Developed from the Test of Motor Impairment (9:1265).
b) MOVEMENT ABC CHECKLIST.
  Scores, 5: Child Stationary/Environment Stable, Child Moving/Environment Stable, Child Stationary/Environment Changing, Child Moving/Environment Changing, Behavioral Problems Related to Motor Difficulties.
  Administration: Group or individual.
  Time: Administration time not reported.
  Comments: Behavior Checklist used by teachers, parents, and other professionals.
Cross References: For reviews by Larry M. Bolen and Carol E. Kessler, see 14:243; see also T5:1725 (8 references); for a review by Jerome D. Pauker of an earlier edition, see 8:881 (2 references); see also T2:1904 (4 references).

[1654]
Mullen Scales of Early Learning: AGS Edition.

Purpose: A comprehensive measure of cognitive functioning for infants and preschool children.
Population: Birth to 68 months.
Publication Dates: 1984–1995.
Scores, 6: Gross Motor Scale, Cognitive Scales (Visual Reception, Fine Motor, Receptive Language, Expressive Language), Early Learning Composite.
Administration: Individual.
Price Data, 2002: $635.95 per complete kit; $28.95 per 25 record forms; $199.95 per Mullen ASSIST (Macintosh/Windows CD-ROM).
Time: (15–60) minutes.
Comments: Previous editions entitled Infant Mullen Scales of Early Learning and Preschool Mullen Scales of Early Learning.
Author: Eileen M. Mullen.
Publisher: American Guidance Service, Inc.
Cross References: For reviews by Mary Mathai Chittooran and Carol E. Kessler, see 14:244; see also T5:1728 (2 references); for a review by Verna Hart of the earlier edition, see 11:177.

[1655]
The Multidimensional Addictions and Personality Profile.

Purpose: Designed as "an objective measure of substance abuse and personal adjustment problems."
Population: Adolescents and adults experiencing substance abuse and mental health disorders.
Publication Dates: 1988–1996.
Acronym: MAPP.
Scores, 15: Substance Abuse Subscales (Psychological Dependence, Abusive/Secretive/Irresponsible Use, Interference, Signs of Withdrawal, Total), Personal Adjustment Subscales (Frustration Problems, Interpersonal Problems, Self-Image Problems, Total), Defensiveness and Inconsistency Scores (Defensiveness, Inconsistency, Total); Minimizing Response Pattern Scales (Substance Abuse, Personal Adjustment, Total).
Administration: Group and individual.
Price Data: Availalbe from publisher.
Foreign Language Edition: French and Spanish translation package available (including printed questions with audio tape).
Time: (20–25) minutes.
Comments: Previous edition entitled The COM-PASS; IBM or compatible with 2 disk drives and at least 640K RAM, monitor, and printer required for computer scoring option.
Authors: John R. Craig and Phyllis Craig.
Publisher: Diagnostic Counseling Services, Inc.

Cross References: For reviews by Carl Isenhart and Keith F. Widaman, see 14:245.

[1656]
Multidimensional Anxiety Questionnaire.

Purpose: Designed "for the evaluation of anxiety symptoms in adults."
Population: Ages 18–89.
Publication Date: 1999.
Acronym: MAQ.
Scores, 5: Physiological-Panic, Social Phobia, Worry-Fears, Negative Affectivity, Total.
Administration: Group or individual.
Price Data: Available from publisher for introductory kit including 25 hand-scorable booklets, professional manual (94 pages), and 50 profile forms.
Time: (10) minutes.
Author: William M. Reynolds.
Publisher: Psychological Assessment Resources, Inc.

[1657]
Multidimensional Anxiety Scale for Children.

Purpose: "Designed to assess a variety of anxiety dimensions in children and adolescents."
Population: Ages 8–19.
Publication Date: 1997.
Administration: Group.
Price Data, 2002: $60 per MASC complete kit including manual (62 pages) and 25 QuikScore™ forms; $32 per MASC specimen set including manual, 3 MASC QuikScore™ forms, and 3 MASC-10 QuikScore™ forms; $37 per manual; $39 per 25 MASC QuikScore™ forms; $86 per MASC-10 complete kit including 25 MASC QuikScore™ forms and 25 MASC-10 QuikScore™ forms; $28 per 25 MASC-10 QuikScore™ forms.
Comments: Self-report.
Author: John March.
Publisher: Multi-Health Systems, Inc.
  a) MULTIDIMENSIONAL ANXIETY SCALE FOR CHILDREN.
Acronym: MASC.
Scores, 13: Physical Symptoms (Tense Symptom Subscale, Somatic Symptoms Subscale, Total), Harm Avoidance (Perfectionism Subscale, Anxious Coping Subscale, Total), Social Anxiety (Humiliation Fears Subscale, Performance Fears Subscale, Total), Separation/Panic, Total Anxiety, Anxiety Disorders Index, Inconsistency Index.
Time: (15) minutes.
Comments: Self-report measure; can be orally administered to young children or poor readers; for use only by psychology professionals with training in assessment.

b) MASC-10: MULTIDIMENSIONAL ANXIETY SCALE FOR CHILDREN—10 ITEM.
Acronym: MASC-10.
Scores, 4: Physical Symptoms, Harm Avoidance, Social Anxiety, Separation/Panic.
Time: (2–5) minutes.
Comments: A shortened, 10-item version of the MASC tapping the four basic anxiety scales.
Cross References: For reviews by John C. Caruso and Robert Christopher, see 14:246.

[1658]
Multidimensional Aptitude Battery—II.

Purpose: Designed "to provide a measure of general cognitive ability or intelligence."
Population: Ages 16 and over.
Publication Dates: 1984–1998.
Acronym: MAB-II.
Scores, 13: Verbal (Information, Comprehension, Arithmetic, Similarities, Vocabulary, Total); Performance (Digit Symbol, Picture Completion, Spatial, Picture Arrangement, Object Assembly, Total), Total.
Administration: Group or individual.
Price Data, 2001: $45 per machine scoring examination kit including Verbal and Performance booklets, manual (1998, 107 pages), Verbal and Performance answer sheets, and one coupon for computerized scoring; $62 per hand-scoring examination scoring kit including Verbal and Performance booklets, manual, Verbal and Performance answer sheets, record form, and set of scoring templates; $33 per 10 Verbal or Performance test booklets; $17–$19.50 per 25 Verbal or Performance answer sheets; $10–$12 per 25 record forms.; $24 per scoring templates; $48–$56 (depending on volume) per 10 machine-scorable answer sheets and coupons for extended reports; $83–$92 (depending on volume) per 10 machine-scorable answer sheets and coupons for clinical reports; $99 per software package including disks, software manual for Windows, test manual, and 10 coupons for computer reports.
Time: (100) minutes.
Comments: Paper-and-pencil or computer administration available.
Author: Douglas N. Jackson.
Publisher: Sigma Assessment Systems, Inc.
Cross References: See T5:1731 (3 references), and T4:1678 (13 references); for reviews by Sharon B. Reynolds and Arthur B. Silverstein of an earlier edition, see 10:202 (5 references).

[1659]
Multidimensional Health Profile.

Purpose: Developed to provide a brief but comprehensive assessment of psychosocial and health functioning for general use in health-related settings.
Population: Ages 18–90.

Publication Dates: 1992–1998.
Acronym: MHP.
Administration: Group or Individual.
Forms, 2: Health Functioning, Psychosocial Functioning.
Price Data: Available from publisher.
Time: (15) minutes for either form.
Authors: Linda S. Ruehlman, Richard I. Lanyon, and Paul Karoly.
Publisher: Psychological Assessment Resources, Inc.
  a) MULTIDIMENSIONAL HEALTH PROFILE—PSYCHOSOCIAL FUNCTIONING.
Acronym: MHP-P.
Scores, 17: Number of Stressful Events, Perceived Stress, Coping Skills, Total Social Support, Emotional Support, Informational Support, Tangible Support, Negative Social Exchange, Total Psychological Distress, Depressed Affect, Guilt, Motor Retardation, Anxious Affect, Somatic Complaints, Cognitive Disturbance, Life Satisfaction, Global Stress.
Comments: 58-item self-report questionnaire to assess psychosocial functioning.
  b) MULTIDIMENSIONAL HEALTH PROFILE—HEALTH FUNCTIONING.
Acronym: MHP-H.
Scores, 20: Self-Help, Professional Help, Help from Friends, Spiritual Help, Positive Health Habits, Negative Health Habits, Self-Efficacy, Health Vigilance, Health Values, Trust in Health Care Personnel, Trust in Health Care System, Hypochondriasis, Overall Health, Recent Health, Presence of a Chronic Illness, Impairment Due to a Chronic Illness, Office Visits, Overnight Hospital Treatment, Emergency Room Treatment, Over the Counter Medication.
Comments: 69-item self-report questionnaire to assess health functioning.
Cross References: For reviews by Wendy Naumann and Terri L. Weaver, see 14:247.

[1660]
Multidimensional Self Concept Scale.

Purpose: Designed to provide a multidimensional assessment of self concept in clinical and research settings.
Population: Grades 5–12.
Publication Date: 1992.
Acronym: MSCS.
Scores, 7: Social, Competence, Affect, Academic, Family, Physical, Total.
Administration: Group or individual.
Price Data, 2001: $94 per complete set; $49 per 50 record booklets; $47 per examiner's manual (82 pages).
Time: (20) minutes.
Author: Bruce A. Bracken.

Publisher: PRO-ED.
Cross References: See T5:1734 (6 references); for reviews by Francis X. Archambault, Jr. and W. Grant Willis, see 12:246 (1 reference); see also T4:1682 (1 reference).

[1661]
The Multidimensional Self-Esteem Inventory.

Purpose: "Provides measures of the components of self-esteem."
Population: College students.
Publication Dates: 1983–1988.
Acronym: MSEI.
Scores, 11: Competence, Lovability, Likability, Self-control, Personal Power, Moral Self-approval, Body Appearance, Body Functioning, Identity Integration, Defensive Self-enhancement, Global Self-esteem.
Administration: Individual or group.
Price Data: Available from publisher for complete kit including manual [1988, 22 pages], 25 reusable test booklets, 50 rating forms, and 50 profile forms.
Time: (15-30) minutes.
Comments: Originally called Self-Report Inventory.
Authors: Edward J. O'Brien and Seymour Epstein.
Publisher: Psychological Assessment Resources, Inc.
Cross References: See T5:1735 (12 references) and T4:1683 (2 references); for reviews by Barbara J. Kaplan and Joseph G. Ponterotto, see 11:250 (1 reference).

[1662]
Multifactor Leadership Questionnaire for Research.

Purpose: Designed to access the full range of leadership styles.
Population: Management personnel.
Publication Dates: 1985–2000.
Acronym: MLQ.
Scores, 12: Idealized Influence (Attributed to You), Idealized Influence (Behaviors You Display), Inspirational Motivational, Intellectual Stimulation, Individualized Consideration, Contingent Reward, Management-by-Exception (Active), Management-by-Exception (Passive), Laissez-Faire, Extra Effort, Effectiveness, Satisfaction.
Administration: Group.
Forms, 2: Leader, Rater.
Price Data, 2001: $25 per Sampler set including manual (1995, 41 pages), and one each of the components used to administer, score, and interpret the MLQ; $125 per Permission set including the Sampler set along with an agreement to reproduce up to 200 copies of the instrument for personal and non-commercial use for one year.

Time: Administration time not reported.
Authors: Bernard M. Bass and Bruce J. Avolio.
Publisher: Mind Garden, Inc.
Cross References: For a review by David J. Pittenger, see 14:248; see also T5:1736 (5 references); for reviews by Frederick Bessai and Jean Powell Kirnan and Brooke Snyder of an earlier edition, see 12:247 (5 references); see also T4:1684 (5 references).

[1663]
Multifactor Leadership Questionnaire for Teams for Research.

Purpose: To assess and develop a plan for enhancing team leadership.
Population: Management personnel.
Publication Date: 1996.
Acronym: MLQT.
Scores, 6: Transformational Leadership, Transactional Leadership, Non-Transactional Leadership, Outcomes of Leadership Styles (Extra Effort, Effectiveness, Satisfaction).
Administration: Group.
Price Data, 2001: $25 per sampler set including manual (35 pages); $125 per one-year permission to reproduce up to 200 administrations of the test.
Time: Administration time not reported.
Comments: Same instrument as MLQTR (1664) but packaged for researchers only.
Authors: Bernard M. Bass and Bruce J. Avolio.
Publisher: Mind Garden, Inc.

[1664]
Multifactor Leadership Questionnaire for Teams Report.

Purpose: To assess and develop a plan for enhancing team leadership.
Population: Management personnel.
Publication Date: 1996.
Acronym: MLQTR.
Scores, 6: Transformational Leadership, Transactional Leadership, Non-Transactional Leadership, Outcomes of Leadership Styles (Extra Effort, Effectiveness, Satisfaction).
Administration: Group.
Price Data, 2001: $150 per Team Report for up to 10 team members; $10 per additional team member form.
Time: Administration time not reported.
Comments: Questionnaires from up to five team members are faxed or mailed to the publisher for compilation of a final report.
Authors: Bernard M. Bass and Bruce J. Avolio.
Publisher: Mind Garden, Inc.

[1665]
Multilevel Academic Survey Test.

Purpose: Developed "for use by school personnel who make decisions about student performance in reading and mathematics."

Population: K–8 and high school students with reading or mathematics skills deficits.

Publication Date: 1985.

Acronym: MAST.

Scores: Total score only for each test.

Price Data, 2002: $79 per examination kit including Grade Level test booklet, answer sheet, Curriculum Level record form, and manual (189 pages); $52 per 25 grade 1 evel test booklets; $33 per 25 grade level self-scoring answer sheets; $51 per 25 curriculum level record forms.

Authors: Kenneth W. Howell, Stanley H. Zucker, and Mada Kay Morehead.

Publisher: The Psychological Corporation.

   a) GRADE LEVEL TEST.

     1) *Primary.*

     Population: Grades K–2.

     Administration: Individual.

     Time: (10–15) minutes.

     2) *Short.*

     Population: Grades 3–12.

     Administration: Group.

     Time: 22(27) minutes.

     3) *Extended.*

     Population: Grades 3-12.

     Administration: Group.

     Time: 30(35) minutes.

     Comments: Administered to students who have taken the short form when a larger sample of performance is required.

   b) CURRICULUM LEVEL TEST.

   Population: Grades K–8.

   Administration: Group.

   Time: 1–5 minutes per test.

   Comments: "Criterion-referenced."

     1) *Reading.*

     Tests, 4: Graded Oral Reading, Graded Comprehension, Diagnostic Oral Reading, Comprehension Problem Profile.

     2) *Mathematics.*

     Tests, 8: Basic Facts Screening, Addition, Multiplication, Division, Fractions, Decimals/Ratios/Percents, Problem Solving, Applications Content.

Cross References: See T5:1738 (1 reference) and T4:1685 (1 reference); for reviews by Ellen H. Bacon and Thomas G. Haring, see 10:203.

[1666]
Multilingual Aphasia Examination, Third Edition.

Purpose: Designed to evaluate the presence, severity, and qualitative aspects of aphasic disorder.

Population: Ages 6–69.

Publication Dates: 1978–1994.

Acronym: MAE.

Scores, 11: Visual Naming, Sentence Repetition, Controlled Word Association, Oral Spelling, Written Spelling, Block Spelling, MAE Token Test, Aural Comprehension of Words and Phrases, Reading Comprehension of Words and Phrases, Rating of Articulation, Rating of Praxic Features of Writing.

Administration: Individual.

Price Data: Not available.

Foreign Language Edition: Spanish edition available.

Time: Administration time not reported.

Authors: A. L. Benton, deS. Hamsher, and A. B. Sivan.

Publisher: AJA Associates [No reply from publisher; status unknown].

Cross References: For reviews by Nancy B. Bologna and by Malcolm R. McNeil and Wiltrud Fassbinder, see 14:249; see also T5:1740 (36 references).

[1667]
Multimodal Life History Questionnaire.

Purpose: To provide "therapists with an in-depth assessment tool for adult counseling."

Population: Adult counseling clients.

Publication Date: 1980.

Scores: No scores.

Administration: Group.

Manual: No manual.

Price Data, 2001: $25.95 per set of 20 inventories.

Time: Administration time not reported.

Comments: Self-report to be completed in the client's "own time."

Author: Arnold A. Lazarus.

Publisher: Research Press.

[1668]
Multiphasic Environmental Assessment Procedure.

Purpose: Characterizes the "physical and social environments of residential care settings for older adults."

Population: Nursing home residents, residential care facilities, congregate apartments.

Publication Dates: 1979–1998.

Acronym: MEAP.

Administration: Individual.

Price Data: Available from publisher.

Time: [4–8] hours.

Comments: Administration time dependent on size and complexity of facility.

Authors: Rudolf H. Moos and Sonne Lemke.

Publisher: SAGE Publications [No reply from publisher; status unknown].

a) PHYSICAL AND ARCHITECTURAL FEATURES CHECKLIST.
Acronym: PAF.
Scores, 8: Community Accessibility, Physical Amenities, Social-Recreational Aids, Prosthetic Aids, Orientational Aids, Safety Features, Staff Facilities, Space Availability.
b) POLICY AND PROGRAM INFORMATION FORM.
Acronym: POLIF.
Scores, 9: Expectations for Functioning, Acceptance of Problem Behavior, Policy Choice, Resident Control, Policy Clarity, Provision for Privacy, Availability of Health Services, Availability of Daily Living Assistance, Availability of Social-Recreational Activities.
c) RESIDENT AND STAFF INFORMATION FORM.
Acronym: RESIF.
Scores, 6: Resident Social Resources, Resident Heterogeneity, Resident Functional Abilities, Resident Activity Level, Resident Activities in the Community, Staff Resources.
d) SHELTERED CARE ENVIRONMENT SCALE.
Acronym: SCES.
Scores, 7: Cohesion, Conflict, Independence, Self-Disclosure, Organization, Resident Influence, Physical Comfort.
e) RATING SCALE.
Acronym: RS.
Scores, 4: Physical Attractiveness, Environmental Diversity, Resident Functioning, Staff Functioning.
Cross References: See T5:1743 (2 references); for reviews by Julian Fabry and Kenneth Sakauye, see 12:248; see also T4:1688 (4 references), 9:733 (1 reference), and T3:1546 (4 references).

[1669]
Multiphasic Sex Inventory.

Purpose: "To assess a wide range of psychosexual characteristics of the sexual offender."
Publication Date: 1984.
Acronym: MSI.
Administration: Group.
Price Data, 1998: $100 per kit (specify Juvenile or Adult form) including 5 test booklets, 25 answer sheets, 25 profile forms, scoring templates, and manual (50 pages); $5 per 5 test booklets (specify form); $10 per 25 answer and profile forms; $35 per set of scoring templates; $25 per cassette tape; $25 per manual.
Time: (45–50) minutes.
Authors: H. R. Nichols and Ilene Molinder.
Publisher: Nichols & Molinder Assessments.
a) JUVENILE FORM.
Population: Juvenile males.

Scores, 19: Validity Scales (Parallel Items Scale, Social/Sexual Desirability Scale, Sexual Obsessions Scale, Lie Scale), Accountability Scales (Cognitive Distortion and Immaturity Scale, Justifications Scale, Treatment Attitudes Scale), Sex Deviance Scales (Child Molest Scale, Rape Scale, Exhibitionism Scale), Paraphilias Scales (Fetish, Voyeurism, Obscene Call, Bondage and Discipline, Sado-Masochism), Sexual Dysfunction Scales (Physical Disabilities, Impotence), Sex Apprehension/Confidence Scale, Sex Knowledge and Beliefs Scale.
b) ADULT FORM.
Population: Adult males.
Scores, 20: Same as *a* above plus Sexual Dysfunction Scales (Sexual Inadequacies, Premature Ejaculation) and excluding Sex Apprehension/Confidence Scale.
Cross References: See T5:1744 (8 references) and T4:1689 (2 references).

[1670]
Multiple Affect Adjective Check List—Revised.

Purpose: "To measure both states and affect traits."
Population: Ages 20–79.
Publication Dates: 1960–1999.
Acronym: MAACL-R.
Scores, 7: Anxiety, Depression, Hostility, Positive Affect, Sensation Seeking, Dysphoria, Positive Affect and Sensation Seeking.
Administration: Group.
Price Data, 1998: $9.50 per 25 hand-scoring or machine-scoring lists (specify State or Trait) [$36 per 100, $143.50 per 500]; $14.25 per scoring key; $5.75 per recording form; $14.50 per manual (1999, 71 pages); $23.50 per bibliography (1,000 references); $8 per specimen set including manual and 1 copy of all forms.
Time: 5(10) minutes.
Comments: Previous edition still available.
Authors: Marvin Zuckerman and Bernard Lubin.
Publisher: EdITS/Educational and Industrial Testing Service.
Cross References: See T5:1745 (89 references) and T4:1690 (96 references); for a review by John A. Zarske of an earlier edition, see 10:205 (84 references); see also 9:734 (47 references), T3:1547 (108 references), 8:628 (102 references), and T2:1293 (56 references); for reviews by E. Lowell Kelly and Edwin I. Megargee of an earlier edition, see 7:112 (60 references); see also P:176 (28 references).

[1671]
Multiscore Depression Inventory.

Purpose: "To provide an objective measure of the severity of self-reported depression."

Population: Ages 13 through adult.
Publication Date: 1986.
Acronym: MDI.
Scores, 11: Low Energy Level, Cognitive Difficulty, Guilt, Low Self-Esteem, Social Introversion, Pessimism, Irritability, Sad Mood, Instrumental Helplessness, Learned Helplessness, Total.
Administration: Group.
Forms, 2: Short Form version available by administering first 47 items of questionnaire.
Price Data, 2002: $115 per kit including scoring keys, 25 hand-scored test/answer sheets, 25 profile forms, 2-use disk, 2 PC answer sheets, and manual (111 pages); $18.50 per set of scoring keys; $19.95 per 100 hand-scored test/answer sheets; $16.50 or less per prepaid mail-in WPS Test Report answer sheet; $19.95 per 100 profile forms; $48.50 per manual; $299 per 25-use disk (PC with DOS) for administration, scoring, and interpretation; $15 per 100 PC answer sheets; $13.50 per FAX service scoring charge.
Time: (20–25) minutes; (10) minutes for Short Form.
Comments: Self-report format; IBM PC, XT, or AT or compatible computer required for optional computer administration or scoring.
Author: David J. Berndt.
Publisher: Western Psychological Services.
Cross References: See T5:1748 (1 reference) and T4:1693 (2 references); for reviews by David N. Dixon and Stephen G. Flanagan, see 11:251.

[1672]
Multiscore Depression Inventory for Children.

Purpose: Designed to assess depression and "features related to depression."
Population: Ages 8–17.
Publication Date: 1996.
Acronym: MDI-C.
Scores, 9: Anxiety, Self-Esteem, Sad Mood, Instrumental Helplessness, Social Introversion, Low Energy, Pessimism, Defiance, Total.
Administration: Group.
Price Data, 2002: $118 per complete kit including manual (54 pages), 25 AutoScore™ test forms, 25 profile forms, 2-use disk, and 2 PC answer sheets for on-site computer scoring and interpretation; $34.50 per 25 AutoScore™ test forms; $17.50 per mail-in answer sheet; $19.95 per 50 profile forms; $46 per manual; $299 per MDI-C microcomputer disk including 25 uses (IBM or compatible and Microsoft Windows 3.1 or above; 3.5-inch); $15 per 100 microcomputer answer sheets; $13.50 per FAX service scoring.
Time: (10–20) minutes.
Authors: David J. Berndt and Charles F. Kaiser.
Publisher: Western Psychological Services.

Cross References: For reviews by Jill Ann Jenkins and Michael G. Kavan, see 14:250.

[1673]
Murphy-Meisgeier Type Indicator for Children.

Purpose: Designed to assess "how an individual child best perceives and processes information and how that child prefers to interact socially and behaviorally with others."
Population: Ages 7–12.
Publication Date: 1987.
Acronym: MMTIC.
Scores, 4: Extraversion/Introversion, Sensing/Intuition, Thinking/Feeling, Judging/Perceiving.
Administration: Group.
Price Data, 2001: $42.50 per preview kit including item booklet, prepaid answer sheet, and manual (45 pages); $39.20 per 25 item booklets; $80.30 per 10 prepaid answer sheets for mail-in scoring; $23.40 per 25 nonprepaid answer sheets for template scoring (for use with item booklets); $20 per 25 Professional's Report Forms for template scoring; $20 per 25 Student Profile Sheets for template scoring; $73.10 per scoring keys for template scoring; $32.90 per manual.
Time: (30) minutes.
Comments: Modeled after the Myers-Briggs Type Indicator™ (1678); scoring options: template (hand) score or prepaid mail-in score.
Authors: Charles Meisgeier and Elizabeth Murphy.
Publisher: Consulting Psychologists Press, Inc.
Cross References: See T5:1750 (1 reference); for reviews by Joanne Jensen and Norman A. Constantine and Hoi K. Suen, see 12:249.

[1674]
Music Achievement Tests 1, 2, 3, and 4.

Purpose: Constructed to measure musical achievement.
Publication Dates: 1968–1986.
Acronym: MAT.
Administration: Group.
Price Data: Available from publisher.
Comments: Record player necessary for administration.
Author: Richard Colwell.
Publisher: MAT [No reply from publisher; status unknown].
a) TEST 1.
Population: Grades 3–12.
Scores, 4: Pitch Discrimination, Interval Discrimination, Meter Discrimination, Total.
Time: (18) minutes.
b) TEST 2.
Population: Grades 4–12.

Scores, 6: Major-Minor Mode Discrimination, Feeling for Tonal Center, Auditory-Visual Discrimination (Pitch, Rhythm, Total), Total.
Time: (28) minutes.
c) TEST 3.
Population: Grades 4–12.
Scores, 5: Tonal Memory, Melody Recognition, Pitch Recognition, Instrument Recognition, Total.
Time: (32) minutes.
d) TEST 4.
Population: Grades 5–12.
Scores, 7: Musical Style (Composers, Texture, Total), Auditory-Visual Discrimination, Chord Recognition, Cadence Recognition, Total.
Time: (38) minutes.
Cross References: For reviews by J. David Boyle and Rudolf E. Radocy, see 12:250; see also T2:207 (5 references); for a review by Paul R. Lehman, see 7:248 (5 references).

[1675]
Musical Aptitude Profile [1995 Revision].
Purpose: Designed to evaluate music aptitude.
Population: Grades 5–12.
Publication Dates: 1965–1995.
Scores, 11: Tonal Imagery (Melody, Harmony, Total), Rhythm Imagery (Tempo, Meter, Total), Musical Sensitivity (Phrasing, Balance, Style, Total), Total.
Administration: Group.
Price Data, 2001: $140 per complete kit; $25 per 100 answer sheets; $30 per 100 profile cards; $2 per class record sheet; $25 per sensitivity compact disc; $25 per tonal and rhythm compact disc; $20 per scoring masks (with school purchase order only; $20 per manual (1995).
Time: (210) minutes.
Comments: Test must be scored manually.
Author: Edwin E. Gordon.
Publisher: G.I.A. Publications, Inc.
Cross References: See T5:1752 (1 reference); for reviews by Annabel J. Cohen and James W. Sherbon of an earlier edition, see 12:251; see also T4:1697 (2 references); T3:1552 (4 references); 8:98 (25 references), and T2:209 (11 references); for reviews by Robert W. Lundin and John McLeish, see 7:249 (33 references).

[1676]
Musical Aptitude Test.
Purpose: Measures musical aptitude.
Population: "White people" in standards 1–10 in South African schools.
Publication Dates: 1977–1988.
Comments: All test materials available in English and Afrikaans.

Administration: Group.
Levels: 2 forms.
Price Data: Available from publisher.
Authors: A. W. Wegelin and J. J. Wolmarans.
Publisher: Human Sciences Research Council [South Africa].
a) JUNIOR MUSICAL APTITUDE TEST.
Population: Standards 1–5.
Acronym: MUSAT J.
Scores, 10: Time Aspect (Rhythm, Duration, Speed, Counting, Total), Short Test (Rhythm, Interval, Harmony, Total), Timbre, Total.
Time: 46(61) minutes.
b) SENIOR MUSICAL APTITUDE TEST.
Population: Standards 6–10.
Acronym: MUSAT S.
Scores, 13: Musical Aptitude (Interval, Harmony, Rhythm, Total), Time Aspect (Rhythm, Duration, Speed, Counting, Total), Timbre, Loudness, Intonation, Selective Listening, Total.
Time: 62(78) minutes.

[1677]
My Vocational Situation.
Purpose: Designed to diagnose difficulties in vocational decision-making.
Population: High school and college and adult.
Publication Date: 1980.
Acronym: MVS.
Scores, 3: Vocational Identity, Occupational Information, Barriers.
Administration: Group.
Price Data, 2001: $14.50 per 25 item booklets (for hand scoring); $5.50 per manual (8 pages).
Time: (5–10) minutes.
Authors: John L. Holland, Denise Daiger, and Paul G. Power.
Publisher: Consulting Psychologists Press, Inc.
Cross References: See T5:1754 (27 references) and T4:1701 (24 references); for a review by Bert W. Westbrook, see 9:738 (1 reference).

[1678]
Myers-Briggs Type Indicator™, Form M.
Purpose: Designed for "the identification of basic preferences on each of the four dichotomies specified or implicit in Jung's theory" and "the identification and description of the 16 personality types that result from interactions among the preferences."
Population: Ages 14 and older.
Publication Dates: 1943–1998.
Acronym: MBTI™.
Scores, 4: Extraversion vs. Introversion, Sensing vs. Intuition, Thinking vs. Feeling, Judging vs. Perceiving.
Administration: Group.

Foreign Language Edition: Spanish (Form M Template scoring) edition available.

Price Data, 2001: $70 per 10 MBTI Form M self-scorable; $75 per manual (1998, 420 pages); $6.50 per Introduction to Type, Sixth Edition (1998, 43 pages); $9 per Introduction to Type in Organizations, Third Edition; $90 per 10 Form M prepaid profile combined item booklet/answer sheets; $230 per 10 Form M prepaid interpretive report combined item booklet/answer sheets; $180 per 10 Form M prepaid Interpretive Report for Organizations combined item booklet/answer sheets; $170 per 10 Form M prepaid Team Report answer sheets; $105 per 10 Form M prepaid Career Report combined item booklet/answer sheets; $82.50 per Form M item booklets; $22.50 per 25 nonprepaid answer sheets; $67 per 8 templates (for nonprepaid answer sheets); $90 per 10 prepaid workstyles report.

Time: (15–25) minutes.

Comments: Scoring options: Self-scorable, template scoring, software on-site scoring, mail-in scoring; administration also available via software and internet; Spanish (Form M template scoring) edition available; based on personality theory of C. G. Jung; Forms F and G still available.

Authors: Katharine C. Briggs, Isabel Briggs Myers, Mary H. McCaulley (revised manual), Naomi L. Quenk (revised manual), and Allen L. Hammer (revised manual).

Publisher: Consulting Psychologists Press, Inc.

Cross References: For reviews by John W. Fleenor and Paul M. Mastrangelo, see 14:251; see also T5:1755 (78 references) and T4:1702 (45 references); for a review by Jerry S. Wiggins of an earlier edition, see 10:206 (42 references); for a review by Anthony J. DeVito of an earlier edition, see 9:739 (19 references); see also T3:1555 (42 references); for a review by Richard W. Coan, of an earlier edition, see 8:630 (115 references); see also T2:1294 (120 references) and P:177 (56 references); for reviews by Gerald A. Mendelson and Norman D. Sundberg and an excerpted review by Laurence Siegel, see 6:147 (10 references).

[1679]
Myers-Briggs Type Indicator® Step II (Form Q).

Purpose: "Provides an in-depth personalized account of personality preferences."

Population: Ages 18 and over.

Publication Date: 2001.

Acronym: MBTI Step II—Form Q.

Scores, 24: Four dichotomies (Extraversion vs. Introversion, Sensing vs. Intuition, Thinking vs. Feeling, Judging vs. Perceiving), 20 facets: 5 Extraversion—Introversion facets (Initiating—Receiving, Expressive—Contained, Gregarious—Intimate, Active—Reflective, Enthu-

siastic—Quiet), 5 Sensing—Intuition facets (Concrete—Abstract, Realistic—Imaginative, Practical—Conceptual, Experiential—Theoretical, Traditional—Original), 5 Thinking—Feeling facets (Logical—Empathetic, Reasonable—Compassionate, Questioning—Accommodating, Critical—Accepting, Tough—Tender), 5 Judging—Perceiving facets (Systematic—Casual, Planful—Open-Ended, Early Starting—Pressure-Prompted, Scheduled—Spontaneous, Methodical—Emergent).

Administration: Individual or group.

Price Data, 2001: $85 per preview kit including item booklet, prepaid profile answer sheet, and manual (2001, 202 pages); $97 per interpretive (Form Q) preview kit including item booklet, prepaid interpretive answer sheet, and manual; $50 per 25 item booklets; $150 per 10 profile answer sheets; $110 per 5 interpretive answer sheets; $15 per profile web administration; $22 per interpretive web administration; $65 per manual.

Time: (25–35) minutes.

Comments: Includes all items comprising Step I, Form M of MBTI® (1678); can be used to generate all reports produced by Step I, Form M of MBTI®; provides advice for enhancing communication, conflict and change management, and decision making skills; computer or web-administered scoring available.

Authors: Katharine C. Briggs, Isabel Briggs Myers, Naomi L. Quenk (Profile Form, Interpretive Form, MBTI Step II Manual), Jean Kummerow (Profile Form, Interpretive Form), Allen L. Hammer (MBTI Step II Manual), and Mark S. Major (MBTI Step II Manual).

Publisher: Consulting Psychologists Press, Inc.

Cross References: For information about other components of this program, see T5:1755 (78 references) and T4:1702 (45 references); for reviews by John W. Fleenor and Paul M. Mastrangelo of Form M, see 14:251 (1 reference); for a review by Jerry S. Wiggins, see 10:206 (42 references); for a review by Anthony J. DeVito, see 9:739 (19 references); see also T3:1555 (42 references); for a review by Richard Coan, see 8:630 (115 references); see also T2:1294 (120 references) and P:177 (56 references); for reviews by Gerald A. Mendelsohn and Norman D. Sundberg and an excerpted review by Laurence Siegel, see 6:147 (10 references).

[1680]
Naglieri Nonverbal Ability Test.

Purpose: A "measure of nonverbal reasoning and problem solving independent of educational curricula and cultural or language background."

Population: Grades K–12.

Publication Dates: 1996–1997.

Acronym: NNAT.

Scores, 5: Pattern Completion (PC), Reasoning by Analogy (RA), Serial Reasoning (SR), Spatial Visualization (SV), Total (Nonverbal Ability Index—NAI).
Administration: Group.
Levels, 7: A (Kindergarten), B (Grade 1), C (Grade 2), D (Grades 3–4), E (Grades 5–6), F (Grades 7–9), G (Grades 10–12).
Price Data, 2002: $24.90 per examination kit (specify Level A–G) including one copy each machine-scorable or reusable test booklets, multilevel directions for administration, and machine-scorable answer documents (for Levels E–G); $92.80 per 25 machine-scorable test booklets including directions for administering and order for scoring services (specify Level A–D); $67.30 per 25 reusable test booklets for use with machine-scorable and hand-scorable answer documents (specify Level E–G); $67.30 per 25 hand-scorable test booklets including directions and 1 multilevel class record (specify Level A–D); $26 per 25 combined D/E/F/G machine-scorable answer documents; $26 per 25 combined D/E/F/G hand-scorable answer documents; $44.50 per side by side keys for hand-scorable test booklets (specify Level A–D); $22 per stencil keys for hand-scorable answer documents (specify Level D–G); $30 per response keys for all levels (list of correct responses); $60 per fall or spring norms book; $78.50 per technical manual; $9 per additional copy of directions for administering (all levels); price information for scoring and reporting services available from publisheer.
Time: 30(45) minutes.
Comments: An extension and revision of the Matrix Analogies Test (1531); appropriate for non-English-speaking students, students with hearing, language, or motor impairment, and impaired color vision; a general measure of ability or identification of students with learning problems.
Author: Jack A. Naglieri.
Publisher: Harcourt Educational Measurement.
Cross References: For reviews by Terry A. Stinnett and Michael S. Trevisan, see 14:252.

[1681]
NASA Moon Survival Task.

Purpose: To explore the performance characteristics of a decision-making group and the significance of member contributions to the quality of group production.
Population: Individuals who work, or anticipate working, in a group setting.
Publication Dates: 1963–1989.
Scores, 4: Commitment, Conflict, Creativity, Consensus.
Administration: Individual in part.
Price Data, 2001: $8.95 per instrument (1989, 21 pages).
Time: Administration time not reported.

Author: Jay Hall.
Publisher: Teleometrics International.
Cross References: See T5:1757 (2 references).

[1682]
National Adult Reading Test, Second Edition.

Purpose: Developed to estimate "the premorbid intelligence levels of adult patients suspected of suffering from intellectual deterioration."
Population: Ages 20–70.
Publication Dates: 1982–1991.
Acronym: NART.
Scores: Total score only.
Administration: Individual.
Price Data, 1999: £67 per complete set; £15.50 per 25 answer sheets; £31 per Word Booklet.
Time: Administration time not reported.
Authors: Hazel E. Nelson and Jonathan Willison (manual).
Publisher: NFER-Nelson Publishing Co., Ltd. [England].
Cross References: See T5:1758 (104 references); for a review by Janet F. Carlson, see 12:252 (77 references); see also T4:1705 (80 references); for reviews by Kathryn H. Au and John M. Bradley of an earlier edition, see 9:741.

[1683]
National Assessment of Educational Progress—Released Exercises.

Purpose: "A continuing, congressionally mandated national survey of knowledge, skills, and understanding, of young Americans" in the fields of mathematics, science, reading, writing, U.S. history, geography, and other subject areas.
Population: Grades 4, 8, and 12 (main NAEP); Ages 9, 13, and 17 (Long-Term Trend NAEP).
Publication Dates: 1983–2002.
Acronym: NAEP.
Scores: No individual scores, scaled results (average proficiency) are provided for designated reporting subgroups.
Administration: Group.
Price Data: Released items available on the NAEP web-site.
Comments: Released-exercise set, which is approximately one-third to one-half of the complete assessment package; administered to national samples of specified age groups biennially since 1969 (1969–1998 now out of print); released exercises are in the public domain and may be copied without restriction following receipt of permission from the author (NCES); student, teacher, and school questionnaires are also available; details of the assessments, procedures, analyses, and results can be found in a series of

reports available from the author and publisher; ETS has served as the primary NAEP contractor since 1983. Available on the web at NCES.ed.gov/nationsreportand/itmrls.

Authors: National Assessment of Educational Progress; National Center for Education Statistics; Office of Educational Research and Improvement; U.S. Dept. of Education.

Publisher: Educational Testing Service.

a) MATHEMATICS.

Scores: 5 content areas (Numbers and Operations, Measurement, Geometry, Data Analysis/Statistics and Probability, Algebra and Functions), Estimation Skills; 3 process areas (Conceptual Understanding, Procedural Knowledge, Problem Solving).

Comments: Assessment dates: 1986, 1990, 1992, 1996.

b) SCIENCE.

Scores: 3 content areas (Life Sciences, Physical Sciences, Earth & Space Sciences); 3 thinking skills/areas (Conducting Inquiries, Solving Problems, Knowing Science).

Comments: Assessment dates: 1986, 1990.

c) READING.

Scores: 3 purposes (Reading for Literary Experience, Reading to Gain Information, Reading to Perform a Task); 4 stances (Initial Understanding, Developing Interpretation, Personal Reflection and Response, Demonstrating a Critical Stance).

Comments: Assessment dates: 1984, 1986, 1988, 1990, 1992, 1994, 1998, 2000, 2002.

d) WRITING.

Scores: 3 purposes (Informative, Narrative, Persuasive).

Comments: Assessment dates: 1984, 1988, 1992, 1998, 2002.

e) U.S. HISTORY.

Scores: 4 themes (Change and Continuity in American Democracy, The Gathering and Interaction of Peoples/Cultures/and Ideas, Economic and Technological Changes and Their Relation to Society/Ideas/and the Environment, The Changing Role of America in the World).

Comments: Assessment dates: 1988, 1994, 2001.

f) GEOGRAPHY.

Scores: 3 content areas (Space and Place, Environment and Society, Spatial Dynamics and Dimensions).

Comments: Assessment dates: 1988, 1994, 2001.

g) FINE ARTS.

Scores: 4 content areas (Music, Dance, Theatre, Visual Arts).

Comments: Assessment date: 1997.

Cross References: See T5:1759 (18 references).

[1684]
National Educational Development Tests.

Purpose: To provide students with information in their development of skills that are necessary to do well on college admissions tests and in college work itself.

Population: Grades 9–10.

Publication Dates: 1983–1984.

Acronym: NEDT.

Scores, 6: English Usage, Mathematics Usage, National Sciences Reading, Social Studies Reading, Composite Score, Educational Ability.

Administration: Group.

Price Data: Available from publisher for combined test materials and standard scoring services, student materials consist of test booklets and answer sheets, Student Handbook, Certificates of Educational Development, and Student Information Bulletin; administrative materials consist of identification sheets, Supervisor's and Examiner's Manuals (1984, 14 pages), and Interpretive Manuals.

Time: 150(180) minutes.

Comments: Tests administered 2 times annually (October and February).

Authors: Science Research Associates, Inc.

Publisher: CTB/McGraw-Hill.

Cross References: See T4:1707 (1 reference); for reviews by Patti L. Harrison and Howard M. Knoff, see 11:255.

[1685]
National German Examination for High School Students.

Purpose: To evaluate students' achievement in German study, may be used as a diagnostic tool.

Population: 2, 3, or 4 years high school.

Publication Dates: 1960–1994.

Scores: Total score only.

Administration: Group.

Levels, 3: 2nd year, 3rd year, 4th year.

Price Data, 2001: $4 per test, includes scoring service; Interpretive data (17 pages) available; test booklets, tapes, and answer sheets are to be returned to Software, Inc.

Time: 60(65) minutes.

Comments: Also called AATG National Standardized Testing Program; formerly called AATG German Test and National German Contest for High School Students; tests administered annually in January under auspices of high school guidance departments or centers established by the publisher.

Author: American Association of Teachers of German.

Publisher: American Association of Teachers of German, Inc.

Cross References: For reviews by Gilbert C. Kettelkamp and Theodor F. Naumann of an earlier edition, see 6:382.

[1686]
National Institute for Personnel Research Normal Battery.

Purpose: "Designed as a selection device for use mainly with Bantu clerks in various industrial and government organizations."

Population: South African Standards 6–10 and job applicants with 8–11 years of education.

Publication Dates: 1960–1973.

Subtests, 5: Mental Alertness, Reading Comprehension, Vocabulary, Spelling, Computation.

Administration: Group.

Price Data: Price information available from publisher for test materials including manual (1969, 129 pages).

Author: S. M. A. Waterhouse (manual).

Publisher: Human Sciences Research Council [South Africa].

Cross References: See T2:1085 (2 references) and 6:779.

[1687]
National Police Officer Selection Test.

Purpose: Measures skills critical to the successful performance of entry-level officers.

Population: Police officer candidates.

Publication Dates: 1991–1992.

Acronym: POST.

Partial Batteries: POST III or POST IV.

Administration: Group.

Restricted Distribution: Available to authorized police personnel only.

Price Data: Price information available from publisher for administration guide (1991, 12 pages), examiner's manual (1992, 13 pages; required with first purchase), and study guide.

Comments: Test may be self-scored or scored by Stanard & Associates, Inc.

Author: Stanard & Associates, Inc.

Publisher: Stanard & Associates, Inc.

a) POST III.

Scores, 4: Mathematics, Reading Comprehension, Grammar, Total.

Price Data: Price information available from publisher for 1-250 POST III (scored by publisher) and 1–250 POST III (self-scored).

Time: 66(71) minutes.

b) POST IV.

Scores, 5: Mathematics, Reading Comprehension, Grammar, Incident Report Writing, Total.

Price Data: Price information available from publisher for 1-250 POST IV (scored by publisher) and 1–250 POST IV (self-scored).

Time: 83(88) minutes.

Cross References: See T5:1763 (1 reference); for reviews by Jim C. Fortune and Abbot Packard and by Kurt F. Geisinger, see 12:253.

[1688]
National Spanish Examinations.

Purpose: Designed as a motivational extracurricular contest for students of members of the American Association of Teachers of Spanish and Portuguese (AATSP) and chapters.

Population: Second semester of 1, 2, 3, 4–6 year Spanish students.

Publication Dates: 1957–2002.

Acronym: NSE.

Scores: Total score only.

Administration: Group.

Levels, 6: 01, 1, 2, 3, 4, 5 (3, 4, and 5 include a Bilingual/Native Supplement).

Manual: Directions for Administering, 2002, 10 pages (revised annually).

Restricted Distribution: Available only to current members of AATSP.

Price Data, 2001: $1 per test; $5 per accompanying cassette.

Time: 60 minutes.

Comments: New form constructed annually for administration in February and March at local secondary schools or centers established by local chapters of the AATSP; summary of results of top three scorers in each level published in Hispania in September following the completion of the testing program.

Author: Test Development Committees, American Association of Teachers of Spanish and Portuguese.

Publisher: National Spanish Exam.

Cross References: See 8:168 (2 references); for a review by Walter V. Kalfers of earlier forms, see 7:323 (1 reference); see also 6:428 (8 references).

[1689]
National Survey of Student Engagement.

Purpose: Designed to provide colleges and universities information about the student experience and institutional performance to use to improve undergraduate education, inform accountability and accreditation efforts, and facilitate national and sector benchmarking efforts.

Population: Undergraduate students at 4-year colleges and universities.

Publication Dates: 2000–2002.

Acronym: NSSE.

Scores, 7: Level of Academic Challenge, Active and Collaborative Learning, Student Interactions with Faculty Members, Enriching Educational Experiences, Supportive Campus Environment, Background Information, Consortium Questions.

Administration: Group.

Price Data, 2002: $275 institutional participation fee and $2,700 to $6,000 student sampling fee (includes customized institutional report with means and frequency distribution by item, along with sector and

national comparisons, response rates and sampling error, student response data on a CD-ROM, national report and institutional benchmarks of effective educational practice, and a sample presentation); $6 each for paper oversampling; $2 each for web-only mode oversampling for first 1,000 students and $1.50 each for additional students over 1,000; $1.50 for locally administered oversampling; additional fees for participating in consortium or special analyses; $30 per Technical and Norms Report (2000, 288 pages); $300 special peer comparison reports that compares institution against select group of 8–10 other participating institutions.
Time: (10–15) minutes.
Author: George D. Kuh.
Publisher: Indiana University Center for Postsecondary Research and Planning, Bloomington.

[1690]
Neale Analysis of Reading Ability, Revised British Edition.

Purpose: "To assess the reading attainment of individuals and to provide diagnostic information about reading difficulties."
Population: Ages 6–13.
Publication Dates: 1957–1989.
Scores, 3: Rate, Accuracy, Comprehension; plus 4 supplementary diagnostic scores (Discrimination of Initial and Final Sounds, Names and Sounds of the Alphabet, Graded Spelling, Auditory Discrimination and Blending).
Administration: Individual.
Forms, 2: 1, 2.
Levels, 6: 1–6.
Price Data: Available from publisher.
Time: (10–15) minutes.
Comments: Demonstration cassette available for familiarization with administration procedure.
Authors: Marie D. Neale, British adaptation and standardization by Una Christophers and Chris Whetton.
Publisher: NFER-Nelson Publishing Co., Ltd. [England].
Cross References: See T5:1765 (36 references) and T4:1714 (7 references); for reviews by Cleborne D. Maddux and G. Michael Poteat, see 11:257 (41 references); see also T3:1567 (13 references) and T2:1683 (7 references); for reviews by M. Alan Brimer and Magdalen D. Vernon, and an excerpted review, see 6:843.

[1691]
Neale Analysis of Reading Ability, 3rd Edition [Australian Standardisation].

Purpose: Designed to "assess reading progress objectivity [and] to obtain structured diagnostic observations of an individual's reading behaviour."
Population: Ages 6 to 12.

Publication Dates: 1958–1999.
Scores, 3: Accuracy, Comprehension, Rate.
Administration: Individual.
Forms, 2: 1, 2.
Price Data, 2002: A$35 per test booklet; A$1.50 per individual record standardised test (specify form); A$1.50 per individual record diagnostic tutor (specify form); A$49.50 per manual (1999, 141 pages); A$19.95 per audio cassette tape; A$89 per specimen set including test booklet, 1 each individual record standarised test form 1 and 2, 1 each individual record diagnostic tutor form A and B, and manual.
Time: Administration time not reported.
Comments: Includes six supplementary diagnostic tests (Discrimination of Initial and Final Sounds, Names and Sounds of the Alphabet, Graded Spelling, Auditory Discrimination and Blending, Word Lists, and Silent Reading/Writing).
Authors: Marie D. Neale, Michael McKay, and John Barnard.
Publisher: Australian Council for Educational Research Ltd. [Australia].

[1692]
NEEDS Survey.

Purpose: Designed "to provide a concise but comprehensive profile of an individual's functioning" relative to the treatment of substance abuse.
Population: Adults.
Publication Date: 1994.
Acronym: NEEDS.
Scores, 10: Test Taking Attitude, Basic Problem Solving and Reading, Emotional Stability, Substance Abuse, Employment, Personal Relationship and Support System, Physical Health, Education, Criminal History, Overall "Needs."
Administration: Individual or group.
Manual: No manual; Reference Guide available.
Price Data: Available from publisher.
Time: (26) minutes.
Comments: Self-administered; computer-scored, IBM compatible with either DOS or Windows required; provides DSM-IV classification for alcohol and drug abuse and ASAM patient placement criteria for treatment recommendations; available in English or Spanish.
Author: ADE Incorporated.
Publisher: ADE Incorporated.
Cross References: For reviews by Anita M. Hubley and Paul M. Mastrangelo, see 14:253.

[1693]
Nelson-Denny Reading Test, Forms G and H.

Purpose: "To assess student achievement and progress in vocabulary, comprehension, and reading rate."

Population: Grades 9–16 and adult.
Publication Dates: 1929–1993.
Scores, 4: Vocabulary, Comprehension, Total, Reading Rate.
Administration: Group.
Price Data: Available from publisher.
Time: 35 minutes.
Comments: Computer-administered version is available on CD-ROM in Windows format.
Authors: James I. Brown, Vivian Vick Fishco, and Gerald S. Hanna.
Publisher: Riverside Publishing.
Cross References: See T5:1767 (9 references); for reviews by Mildred Murray-Ward and Douglas K. Smith, see 13:206 (52 references); see also T4:1715 (30 references); for reviews by Robert J. Tierney and James E. Ysseldyke of Forms E and F, see 9:745 (12 references); see also T3:1568 (38 references); for reviews by Robert A. Forsyth and Alton L. Raynor of Forms C and D, see 8:735 (31 references); see also T2:1572 (46 references); for reviews by David B. Orr and Agatha Townsend and an excerpted review by John O. Crites of Forms A and B, see 6:800 (13 references); for a review by Ivan A. Booker, see 4:544 (17 references); for a review by Hans C. Gordon, see 2:1557.

[1694]
NEO-4.

Purpose: Designed as a four-factor version of the Revised NEO Personality Inventory (2110).
Population: Ages 17 and older.
Publication Date: 1998.
Scores, 28: Extraversion (Warmth, Gregariousness, Assertiveness, Activity, Excitement-Seeking, Positive Emotions, Total); Openness to Experience (Fantasy, Aesthetics, Feelings, Actions, Ideas, Values, Total); Agreeableness (Trust, Straightforwardness, Altruism, Compliance, Modesty, Tender-Mindedness, Total); Conscientiousness (Competence, Order, Dutifulness, Achievement Striving, Self-Discipline, Deliberation, Total).
Administration: Group or individual.
Forms, 2: Form S (self-reports), Form R (observer ratings).
Price Data: Available from publisher for comprehensive kit including NEO PI-R manual (101 pages), NEO-4 manual supplement (19 pages), 10 each Form S and Form R reusable item booklets, 25 hand-scorable answer sheets, 25 profile forms, 25 style graph booklets, 25 summary forms, and set of 8 overhead transparencies; and for the introductory kit including all items in tje comprehensive kit except the NEO PI-R manual.
Time: [25–35] minutes.
Comments: Questionnaire items, scoring keys, and scale norms are identical to those found in the Revised NEO Personality Inventory (NEO PI-R; 2110) for the four factors of Extraversion, Openness to Experience, Agreeableness, and Conscientiousness and users are encouraged to consult the professional manual for the NEO PI-R.
Authors: Paul T. Costa and Robert R. McCrae.
Publisher: Psychological Assessment Resources, Inc.
Cross References: For reviews by Theresa M. Bahns and Carlen Hennington, see 14:254.

[1695]
Neonatal Behavioral Assessment Scale, 3rd Edition.

Purpose: Designed to evaluate an infant's behavioral and neurological status.
Population: Ages 3 days through 2 months.
Publication Dates: 1973–1995.
Acronym: NBAS.
Scores, 53: (Each item represents a score) in 3 domains: Behavioral (28 items), Supplementary (7 items), Reflex (18 items).
Administration: Individual.
Price Data, 1998: $33.95 per assessment.
Time: (20–30) minutes.
Comments: Previous version entitled Brazelton Neonatal Behavioral Assessment Scale-380; a 53-item rating scale of infant behavior and reflexes; not for use with infants recovering from illness or premature birth; to be administered by clinicians trained in neonatal behavior.
Authors: T. Berry Brazelton and J. Kevin Nugent.
Publisher: Cambridge University Press.
Cross References: For reviews by Carol M. McGregor and Hoi K. Suen, see 14:255; see also T5:1770 (17 references), T4:321 (9 references), 9:157 (9 references), and T3:311 (31 references); for a review by Anita Miller Sostek of an earlier edition, and an excerpted review by Stephen Wolkind of an earlier edition, see 8:208 (15 references).

[1696]
NEPSY: A Developmental Neuropsychological Assessment.

Purpose: "Designed to assess neuropsychological development."
Population: Ages 3–12.
Publication Date: 1998.
Acronym: NEPSY.
Scores, 32: Attention/Executive (Tower, Auditory Attention and Response Set, Visual Attention, Statue, Design Fluency, Knock and Tap, Total), Language (Body Part Naming, Phonological Processing, Speeded Naming, Comprehension of Instructions, Repetition of Nonsense Words, Verbal Fluency, Oromotor Sequences, Total), Sensorimotor (Fingertip Tapping, Imitating Hand Positions, Visuomotor Precision, Manual Motor Sequences, Finger Discrimination, Total), Visuospatial

(Design Copying, Arrows, Block Construction, Route Finding, Total), Memory and Learning (Memory for Faces, Memory for Names, Narrative Memory, Sentence Repetition, List Learning, Total).

Administration: Individual.

Forms, 2: Ages 3–4, Ages 5–12.

Price Data, 2002: $575per complete kit including manual (464 pages), 10 record forms for both Ages 3–4 version and Ages 5–12 version, 10 response booklets for both Ages 3–4 version and Ages 5–12 version, scoring templates and manipulables packaged in a bright nylon bag; $26 per 25 Ages 3–4 response booklets; $32 per 25 Ages 5–12 response booklets; $29 per 25 Ages 3–4 record forms; $34 per 25 Ages 5–12 record forms; $96 per manual; $112 per stimulus booklet; $96 per tower (with 3 balls).

Time: (45–60) minutes for preschool-aged children; (65–120) minutes for school-aged children.

Comments: Also includes optional qualitative behavioral observations and supplemental scores.

Authors: Marit Korkman, Ursula Kirk, and Sally Kemp.

Publisher: The Psychological Corporation.

Cross References: For reviews by Sandra D. Haynes and Daniel C. Miller, see 14:256.

[1697]
Network Analyst Staff Selector.

Purpose: To evaluate essential skills needed for the network analyst.

Population: Candidates for technical network positions.

Publication Date: 1992.

Acronym: NETAL.

Scores: Total Score, Narrative Evaluation, Ranking, Recommendation.

Administration: Group.

Price Data, 2001: $340 per candidate; quantity discounts available.

Time: (150) minutes.

Comments: Scored by publisher; must be proctored.

Author: Bruce A. Winrow.

Publisher: Walden Personnel Performance, Inc. [Canada].

[1698]
Network Technician Staff Selector.

Purpose: To measure network knowledge and analytical skills.

Population: Candidates for the position of network technician.

Publication Date: 1992.

Acronym: NETECH.

Scores: Total Score, Narrative Evaluation, Ranking, Recommendation.

Administration: Group.

Price Data, 2001: $340 per candidate.

Time: (107) minutes.

Comments: Scored by publisher; must be proctored.

Author: Bruce A. Winrow.

Publisher: Walden Personnel Performance, Inc.

[1699]
Neurobehavioral Functioning Inventory.

Purpose: "Designed to measure the frequency of neurobehavioral problems associated with traumatic brain injury and other neurological disorders."

Population: Patients ages 17 and older.

Publication Date: 1999.

Acronym: NFI.

Scores, 6: Depression, Somatic, Memory/Attention, Communication, Aggression, Motor.

Administration: Individual or group.

Price Data, 2002: $137 per complete kit including manual (120 pages), 25 Family record forms, and 25 Patient record forms; $79 per manual; $39 per 25 record forms (Family or Patient).

Time: (30) minutes.

Comments: Self-scoring self-report forms.

Authors: Jeffrey S. Kreutzer, Ronald T. Seel, and Jennifer H. Marwitz.

Publisher: The Psychological Corporation.

[1700]
The Neuropsychological Impairment Scale.

Purpose: Designed to screen for "neuropsychological symptoms."

Population: Ages 18 and older.

Publication Date: 1994.

Acronym: NIS.

Scores, 14: Defensiveness, Affective Disturbance, Response Inconsistency, Subjective Distortion Index, Global Measure of Impairment, Total Items Circled, Symptom Intensity Measure, Critical Items, Cognitive Efficiency, Attention, Memory, Frustration Tolerance, Learning-Verbal, Academic Skills.

Administration: Group.

Forms, 3: Self-Report, Observer Report, Senior Interview.

Price Data, 2002: $129.50 per complete kit including 25 self-report AutoScore™ answer forms, 25 observer-report AutoScore™ answer forms, and manual (71 pages) with Senior Interview Supplement and Response Card; $36.50 per 25 self-report AutoScore™ answer forms; $36.50 per 25 observer-report AutoScore™ answer forms; $56 per manual; $85 per Senior Interview kit including 25 Senior Interview AutoScore™ answer forms, 1 manual with Senior Interview Supplement and Response Card, and 25 Mini Mental Status Exam record forms; $36.50 per 25 Senior Interview AutoScore™ answer forms; $15 per 100 Mini Mental Status Exam record forms.

Time: (15–20) minutes.
Comments: Self-Report form and Observer-Report form both utilize the 14 scores listed above, Senior Interview provides Global Measure of Impairment and scores for Defensiveness, Affective Disturbance, and Inconsistency.
Authors: William E. O'Donnell, Clinton B. DeSoto, Janet L. DeSoto, and Don McQ. Reynolds.
Publisher: Western Psychological Services.
Cross References: For a review by Robert A. Leark, see 14:257; see also T5:1775 (3 references).

[1701]
Neuropsychological Status Exam.

Purpose: Designed to organize data useful in neuropsychological assessment.
Population: Neuropsychological patients.
Publication Date: 1983.
Acronym: NSE.
Scores: Checklists in 13 areas: Patient Data, Referral Data, Tentative Findings, Neuropsychological Symptom Checklist, Premorbid Status, Physical Status, Emotional Status, Cognitive Status, Test Administration, Results of Neuropsychological Testing, Diagnostic Comments, Effects on Patient Functioning, Treatment Recommendations.
Administration: Individual.
Price Data: Available from publisher for complete kit including 25 forms and manual (13 pages).
Time: Administration time not reported.
Author: John A. Schinka.
Publisher: Psychological Assessment Resources, Inc.

[1702]
Neuropsychology Behavior and Affect Profile.

Purpose: Designed to assess psychological changes in personality that accompany selective neurological disorders.
Population: Brain-impaired individuals ages 15 and over.
Publication Dates: 1989–1994.
Acronym: NBAP.
Scores, 5: Indifference, Inappropriateness, Pragnosia, Depression, Mania.
Administration: Individual.
Forms, 2: Form S, Form O.
Price Data, 2001: $25 per sampler set including manual (1994, 65 pages); $125 per one-year permission to reproduce up to 200 administrations of the test.
Time: Administration time not reported.
Comments: Form S is self-administered by patients judged capable of accurate self-report; Form O is filled out by significant other when Form S is deemed inappropriate.

Authors: Linda Nelson, Paul Satz, and Louis F. D'Elia.
Publisher: Mind Garden, Inc.
Cross References: For a review by Surendra P. Singh, see 14:258.

[1703]
New Jersey Test of Reasoning Skills—Form B.

Purpose: Assesses elementary reasoning and inquiry skills.
Population: Reading level grade 5 and over.
Publication Dates: 1983–1985.
Scores: 22 skill areas: Converting Statements, Translating into Logical Form, Inclusion/Exclusion, Recognizing Improper Questions, Avoiding Jumping to Conclusions, Analogical Reasoning, Detecting Underlying Assumptions, Eliminating Alternatives, Inductive Reasoning, Reasoning with Relationships, Detecting Ambiguities, Discerning Causal Relationships, Identifying Good Reasons, Recognizing Symmetrical Relationships, Syllogistic Reasoning (Categorical), Distinguishing Differences of Kind and Degree, Recognizing Transitive Relationships, Recognizing Dubious Authority, Reasoning with 4-Possibilities Matrix, Contradicting Statements, Whole-Part and Part-Whole Reasoning, Syllogistic Reasoning (Conditional).
Administration: Group.
Manual: No manual.
Price Data, 2001: $2.40 per test booklet.
Time: (30–45) minutes.
Author: Virginia Shipman.
Publisher: Institute for the Advancement of Philosophy for Children.
Cross References: See T4:1723 (1 reference); for reviews by Arthur S. Ellen and Rosemary E. Sutton, see 11:259 (1 reference).

[1704]
New Technology Tests: Computer Commands.

Purpose: To "provide a measure of aptitude for those entering employment or training in occupations where computers are used as basic operational tools ... it focuses on skills relating to the rapid identification of differences between two pieces of information, and the use of commands to bring about change."
Population: Applicants for computer-related jobs.
Publication Date: 1987.
Scores: Total score only.
Administration: Group.
Price Data: Price information available from publisher for test booklets (20 pages), set of answer sheets including 25 answer sheets, 25 command lists, 1 test record for, and 1 data collection form, and specimen set including user's guide (34 pages), test booklet, com-

mand list, answer key, test record form, data collection form, and administration cards.

Time: 20[25] minutes.

Comments: New Technology Tests: Computer Rules (1705) also available.

Author: NFER-Nelson Publishing Co., Ltd.

Publisher: NFER-Nelson Publishing Co., Ltd. [England].

Cross References: For a review by Bruce W. Hall, see 11:260.

[1705]
New Technology Tests: Computer Rules.

Purpose: To "provide a measure of aptitude for those entering employment or training in occupations where computers are used as a basic operational tool … the emphasis in this test is primarily on following rules."

Population: Applicants for computer-related jobs.

Publication Date: 1987.

Scores: Total score only.

Administration: Group.

Price Data: Price information available from publisher for test booklets (30 pages), set of answer sheets including 25 answer sheets, 25 command lists, 1 test record form, and 1 data collection form, and for specimen set including user's guide (30 pages), test booklet, answer sheet, test record form, data collection form, and administration cards.

Time: 30[35] minutes.

Comments: New Technology Tests: Computer Commands (1704) also available.

Author: NFER-Nelson Publishing Co., Ltd.

Publisher: NFER-Nelson Publishing Co., Ltd. [England].

Cross References: For a review by Bruce W. Hall, see 11:261.

[1706]
NewGAP.

Purpose: Constructed to assess reading comprehension using Cloze technique.

Population: Grades 2–5.

Publication Date: 1990.

Scores: Total score only.

Administration: Group or individual.

Forms, 2: I, II.

Price Data, 2002: $55 per complete kit including 25 each Forms I/II, scoring template, and manual (39 pages); $22 per 50 test forms (25 each form); $6 per scoring template; $22 per manual; $22 per specimen set.

Time: 15(20) minutes.

Comments: "Norm-referenced."

Authors: John McLeod and Rita McLeod.

Publisher: Academic Therapy Publications.

Cross References: For reviews by Terry A. Ackerman and Ruth Johnson, see 12:254.

[1707]
N.I.I.P. Engineering Apprenticeship Selection Test Battery.

Purpose: "For use in personnel selection and assessment."

Population: Engineering apprentices.

Publication Dates: 1936–1972.

Scores, 8: 7 subtest scores plus battery total.

Administration: Group.

Price Data: Available from publisher.

Time: 116(180) minutes.

Comments: Subtests available only as separates.

Author: National Institute of Industrial Psychology.

Publisher: NFER-Nelson Publishing Co., Ltd. [England].

a) GROUP TEST 82.

Purpose: Designed as a measure of spatial perception.

b) GROUP TEST 90 A/B.

Purpose: Designed as a measure of intelligence.

c) GROUP TEST 70/70B.

Purpose: Designed as a measure of nonverbal intelligence.

d) TEST EA2A.

Purpose: Designed as a measure of arithmetic attainment.

Population: Ages 14.5 and over.

Publication Dates: 1947–1971.

Comments: Decimalized version of Test EA2; 1971 test identical to test copyrighted 1947 except for 1 revised item.

e) TEST EA4.

Publication Date: 1972.

Comments: Metricated version of *d.*

f) VINCENT MECHANICAL DIAGRAMS TEST.

Purpose: Designed to measure mechanical ability.

g) MECHANICAL INFORMATION.

Cross References: See 7:1096 (1 reference).

[1708]
NIIP Engineering Arithmetic Test EA4.

Purpose: Used as a selection instrument for courses, apprenticeships, and occupations.

Population: Age 15–adult.

Publication Dates: 1936–1980.

Scores: Total score only.

Administration: Group.

Price Data: Available from publisher.

Time: 20(25) minutes.

Comments: One of five subtests of the NIIP Engineering Selection Test Battery.

Author: National Institute of Industrial Psychology.

Publisher: NFER-Nelson Publishing Co., Ltd. [England].

[1709]

19 Field Interest Inventory.

Purpose: Measure vocational interests in 19 broad vocational areas.

Population: Standards 8–10 in South African school system and college and adults.

Publication Dates: 1970–1971.

Acronym: 19FII.

Scores, 21: Fine Arts, Performing Arts, Language, Historical, Service, Social Work, Sociability, Public Speaking, Law, Creative Thought, Science, Practical-Male, Practical-Female, Numerical, Business, Clerical, Travel, Nature, Sport, Work-Hobby, Active-Passive.

Administration: Group.

Price Data: Available from publisher.

Time: (45) minutes.

Authors: F. A. Fouche and N. F. Alberts.

Publisher: Human Sciences Research Council [South Africa].

Cross References: For additional information, see 7:1027.

[1710]

NOCTI Experienced Worker Assessments.

Purpose: "Designed to measure an individual's knowledge of higher-level concepts, theories and applications in the related occupation."

Population: Technical teachers and potential teachers and journey workers.

Publication Dates: 1973–1999.

Scores: Duty category scores and total scores are reported for 54 Written and Performance tests: Advertising and Design, Air Cooled Gas Engine Repair, Appliance Repair, Architectural Drafting, Audio Visual Communications Technology, Automotive Technician, Building and Home Maintenance Services, Building Construction Occupations, Building Trades Maintenance, Cabinetmaking and Millwork, Carpentry, Child Care and Guidance, Collision Repair, Collision Repair/Refinishing Technology, Computer Programming, Computer Technology, Cosmetology, Diesel Engine Repair, Diesel Mechanics, Electrical Construction and Maintenance, Electrical Installation, Electromechanical Technology, Electronic Product Servicing, Electronics Communications, Electronics Technology, Graphic Imaging Technology, Heating/Ventilation & Air Conditioning (HVAC), Heating/Ventilation/Air Conditioning & Refrigeration (HVAC/R), Heavy Equipment Mechanics, Hospitality Management—Food & Beverage, Hospitality Management—Lodging, Industrial Electrician, Industrial Electronics, Industrial Technology, Marine Mechanics, Masonry, Materials Handling, Mechanical Technology, Metal-

working Occupations, Microcomputer Repair, Motorcycle Mechanics, Painting and Decorating, Plumbing, Precision Machining, Quantity Food Preparation, Quantity Foods, Refinishing Technology, Retail Commercial Baking, Retail Trades, Scientific Data Processing, Sheet Metal, Technical Drafting, Tool and Die Making, Welding.

Administration: Group.

Parts, 2: Written, Performance.

Price Data, 2002: $180 per complete test including written and performance part, instructions for administration, scoring and reporting services and certificates of completion, if applicable.

Time: (180) minutes for all written tests; (1.5–6) hours for performance tests.

Comments: In 1995 names was changed from NOCTI TOCT to NOCTI Experienced Worker tests; a list of approved NOCTI Test Centers is available from publisher; all teacher tests must be administered through an approved test center.

Author: National Occupational Competency Testing Institute.

Publisher: National Occupational Competency Testing Institute.

Cross References: For a review of an earlier version of the NOCTI program, see 8:1153 (6 references). Reviews and references for previous separate NOCTI TOCT tests: Appliance Repair: For reviews by Geneva D. Haertel and Cyril J. Sadowski, see 13:208; for a review by Richard C. Erickson, see 10:227; Architectural Drafting: See 9:776 (1 reference); for a review by Gary E. Lintereur, see 8:1131; Audio-Visual Communications Technology: For reviews by JoEllen V. Carlson and Anne L. Harvey, see 11:262; for reviews by Patricia A. Bachelor and Connie Kubo Della-Piana, see 13:209; Auto Body Repair: For reviews by Robert J. Drummond and Dale P. Scannell, see 13:210; see also 9:777 (1 reference); Automotive Technician: For reviews by Dale P. Scannell and George C. Thornton III, see 13:211; see also 9:778 and T3:1595 (1 reference); for a review by Charles W. Pendleton, see 8:1133; Brick Masonry: For a review by Thomas S. Baldwin, see 10:229; Building and Home Maintenance Services: For a review by Gary E. Lintereur, see 10:230; Cabinet Making and Millwork: See 9:782 (1 reference); for a review by Gary E. Lintereur, see 8:1134; Carpentry: See 9:783 (1 reference); for a review by Daniel L. Householder, see 8:1535; Child Care and Guidance: For reviews by Patricia B. Keith and by Jean Powell Kirnan and Jennifer DeNicolis, see 12:255; Commercial Art: For a review by Gary E. Lintereur, see 10:231; Diesel Engine Repair: See 9:786 (1 reference); for a review by Charles W. Pendleton, see 8:1138; Electrical Installation: See 9:788 (1 reference) and T3:1601 (1 reference); for a review by Alan R. Suess, see 8:1139 (1 reference); Electronics Communications: See 9:789 (1 reference);

for a review by Emil H. Hoch, see 8:1140; Industrial Electrician: See 9:792 (1 reference); for a review by Alan R. Suess, see 8:1141; Industrial Electronics: See 9:793 (1 reference); for a review by Emil H. Hoch, see 8:1142; Machine Drafting: See 9:794 (1 reference); for a review by Tim L. Wentling, see 8:1143; Machine Trades: For a review by Thomas S. Baldwin, see 10:239; see also 9:795 (1 reference) and 8:1144 (1 reference); Masonry: See 9:797 (1 reference); Mechanical Technology: For reviews by Bruce K. Alcorn and David O. Anderson, see 12:256; Microcomputer Repair: For reviews by Kurt F. Geisinger and David O. Herman, see 12:257; Plumbing: See 9:801 (1 reference); for a review by Richard C. Erickson, see 8:1147; Quantity Food Preparation: See 9:804 (1 reference); Scientific Data Processing: For reviews by Jim C. Fortune and Myra N. Womble, see 13:212; for a review by William M. Bart, see 11:263; Sheet Metal; See 9:807 (1 reference) and T3:1612 (1 reference); for a review by Daniel L. Householder, see 8:1150; Small Engine Repair: See 9:808 (1 reference); for a review by Kenneth E. Poucher, see 8:1151; Welding: See 9:809 (1 reference); for a review by Richard C. Erickson, see 8:1152.

[1711]
NOCTI Industrial Assessments.

Purpose: "Designed to measure an individual's knowledge of competencies related specifically to industrial occupations."

Population: Industrial employees and potential employees.

Publication Dates: 1998–1999.

Scores: Duty support scores and total scores are reported for 19 tests: Die Making, Electrical/Electronics, Electrical/Electronics Maintenance, General Industrial/Mechanical, General Technical Skills, Industrial Maintenance Technician, Instrumentation and Control, Instrumentation and Electrician Technician, Lead Maintenance, Machine Repair, Maintenance, Maintenance Mechanic, Maintenance Technician, Master Machine Repair, Mechanical, Mechanical and Fluid Power Maintenance, Mechanical Maintenance, Pipefitter, Toolmaker.

Administration: Group.

Price Data, 2002: $75 per complete test including instructions for administration, scoring, and reporting services.

Time: (180) minutes per test.

Comments: Consists of only a written portion; intended for evaluating individuals with a combination of education, training, and work experience.

Author: National Occupational Competency Testing Institute.

Publisher: National Occupational Competency Testing Institute.

[1712]
NOCTI Job Ready Assessments.

Purpose: "Designed to measure an individual's knowledge of basic processes including the identification and use of terminology and tools."

Population: Students in vocational and technical programs.

Publication Dates: 1983–2000.

Scores: Duty category and total scores are reported for 74 Written and Performance tests: Accounting, Administrative Assisting, Advertising Design, Agriculture Mechanics, Air Cooled Gas Engine Repair, Appliance Repair, Architectural Drafting, Audio-Visual Communications, Auto Diesel Mechanics, Automotive Technician, Building Construction Occupations, Building Trades Maintenance, Business and Information Processing, CAD/CAM, Cabinet Making, Carpentry, Clothing and Textiles Management and Production, Collision Repair, Collision Repair/Refinishing Technology, Commercial Foods, Computer Programming, Computer Technology, Construction Electricity, Construction Masonry–Blocklaying, Construction Masonry—Bricklaying, Construction Masonry–Stone, Cosmetology, Dental Assisting, Diesel Engine Mechanics, Early Childhood Care & Education, Electrical Construction, Electrical Occupations, Electronic Product Servicing, Electronic Technology, Electronics, Food Production Management and Services, Forestry Products and Processing, General Drafting and Design, Graphic Communications Tech, Health Assisting, Heating/Ventilation & Air Conditioning, Heating/Ventilation/Air Conditioning & Refrigeration, Heavy Equipment Maintenance and Repair, Home Health Aide, Horticulture—Floriculture, Horticulture-Landscaping, Horticulture—Olericulture, Hospitality Management—Food & Beverage, Hospitality Management—Lodging, Industrial Electricity, Industrial Electronics, Industrial Maintenance Mechanic, Law Enforcement, Marine Mechanics, Medical Assisting, Metalworking and Fabrication, Microcomputer Repair, Motorcycle Mechanics, Nursing Assisting, Office Assisting, Painting and Decorating, Plumbing, Practical Nursing, Precision Machining, Production Agriculture, Refinishing Technology, Retail Commercial Baking, Retail Trades, Robotics Technology, Technical Drafting, Truck and Bus Mechanics, Warehousing Services, Welding, Workplace Readiness.

Administration: Group.

Parts, 2: Written, Performance.

Price Data, 2002: $20 per complete test (Written and Performance) including instructions for administration, scoring and reporting services and certificates of completion, if applicable; $17.50 if purchased separately (Written only or Performance only).

Time: (180) minutes for all written tests; (1–5) hours for performance tests.

Comments: In 1995 name was changed from NOCTI SOCAT tests to NOCTI Job Ready tests; "standardized tools for assessing and improving entry-level performance ... based on national standards and are designed to support high-quality educational and training programs"; can be used for both secondary and postsecondary education as well as business and industry applications.
Author: National Occupational Competency Testing Institute.
Publisher: National Occupational Competency Testing Institute.

[1713]
Noncognitive Variables and Questionnaire.

Purpose: To aid in admission decisions and advising regarding minority college student applicants.
Population: Minority college student applicants.
Publication Dates: 1978–1998.
Acronym: NCQ.
Scores, 8: Positive Self-Concept or Confidence, Realistic Self-Appraisal, Understands and Deals with Racism, Prefers Long-Range Goals to Short-Term or Immediate Needs, Availability of Strong Support Person, Successful Leadership Experience, Demonstrated Community Service, Knowledge Acquired in a Field.
Administration: Group.
Manual: No manual.
Price Data, 1998: $20 per packet including copies of research reports and/or journal article reprints, admission reference list, copy of NCQ questionnaire, and scoring key; $35 per subscription to Counseling Center Report Series for the academic year.
Time: [20] minutes.
Author: William E. Sedlacek.
Publisher: University of Maryland, University Counseling Center [No reply from publisher; status unknown].
Cross References: For reviews by Gregory J. Marchant and Lisa F. Smith, see 14:259.

[1714]
Non-Language Multi-Mental Test.

Purpose: Designed to estimate intelligence of individuals "who do not speak English, or who are illiterate, or who are deaf."
Population: Grades 3–8 and adults.
Publication Dates: 1942–1969.
Scores: Total score only.
Administration: Group.
Price Data, 2001: $8 per specimen set including directions (1967, 4 pages) and Forms A and B; $28 per 25 Form A or Form B.
Foreign Language Edition: French edition available.
Time: 30 minutes.

Authors: E. L. Terman, William A. McCall, and Irving Lorge.
Publisher: Institute of Psychological Research, Inc. [Canada].
Cross References: For a review by Carroll A. Whitmer, see 3:243 (1 reference).

[1715]
Non-Reading Intelligence Tests, Levels 1–3.

Purpose: Measures "aspects of language and thinking that are not fully represented in the earlier stages of learning in reading and mathematics."
Population: Ages 6-4 to 8-3, 7-4 to 9-3, 8-4 to 10-11.
Publication Dates: 1989–1992.
Acronym: NRIT.
Scores, 5: Total score for each of four subtests (A, B, C, D), Grand Total.
Administration: Group.
Levels: 3 overlapping levels.
Price Data, 2002: £16.99 per specimen set including manual (1989, 48 pages) and one copy each of the three test forms; £11.99 per manual; £7.99 per 20 Level 1, Level 2 or Level 3 test sheets; £5.99 per marking template.
Time: (60) minutes for Levels 1 and 2; (45–60) minutes for Level 3.
Comments: Incorporates the Non-Readers Intelligence Test (9:811) as Level 1 and the Oral Verbal Intelligence Test (8:197) as Level 3, along with a newer intermediate test as Level 2.
Author: Dennis Young.
Publisher: Hodder & Stoughton Educational [England].
Cross References: For reviews by Carole M. Krauthamer and Esther E. Diamond, see 12:258; see also T4:1816 (1 reference). For a review by A. E. G. Pilliner of the Oral Verbal Intelligence Test, see 8:197; for reviews by Calvin O. Dyer and Steven I. Pfeiffer of the Non-Readers Intelligence Test, Third Edition, see 9:811.

[1716]
Nonverbal Form.

Purpose: Measures general learning ability independent of language and reading skills.
Population: Individuals in a wide variety of occupations and vocational counseling.
Publication Dates: 1946–1986.
Scores: Total score only.
Administration: Individual or group.
Price Data: Available from publisher.
Time: 10 minutes.
Comments: Previously listed as SRA Nonverbal Form.
Authors: Robert N. McMurray and Joseph E. King.

Publisher: Reid London House.

Cross References: See T2:449 (12 references); for a review by W. D. Commins, see 4:318; for an excerpted review, see 3:261 (incorrectly listed under 3:260 in the first printing of *The Third Mental Measurements Yearbook*).

[1717]

Nonverbal Reasoning.

Purpose: "To measure the capacity to reason logically as indicated by solutions to pictoral problems."

Population: Individuals in a variety of occupations.

Publication Dates: 1957–1986.

Scores: Total score only.

Administration: Individual or group.

Price Data, 2002: $94 per start-up kit including 25 test booklets, score key, and interpretation and research manual; $58 per 25 test booklets (quantity discounts available); $20 per score key; $28 per interpretation and research manual.

Time: No limit (approximately 20 minutes).

Author: Raymond J. Corsini.

Publisher: Reid London House.

Cross References: See T4:1817 (1 reference) and T2:414 (2 references); for reviews by James E. Kennedy and David G. Ryans, see 6:478.

[1718]

Non-Verbal Tests.

Purpose: "Measures non-verbal reasoning ability."

Population: Ages 8–11, 10–15.

Publication Dates: 1947–1965.

Administration: Group.

Publisher: NFER-Nelson Publishing Co. [England].

a) NON-VERBAL TEST BD.

Population: Ages 8–11.

Scores, 5: Cypher, Similarities, Analogies, Series, Total.

Price Data: Price information available from publisher for manual (1965, 15 pages) and test booklets.

Time: (40) minutes.

Author: D. A. Pidgeon.

b) NON-VERBAL TEST DH.

Population: Ages 10–15.

Scores: Total score only.

Price Data: Price information available from publisher for manual (1958, 8 pages), test booklets, and answer sheets.

Time: (35–50) minutes.

Author: B. Calvert.

Cross References: See T5:1800 (1 reference), T2:415 (12 references), and 7:367 (1 reference); for reviews by T. R. Miles and John Nisbet, see 6:479 (1 reference); for a review by Cyril A. Rogers, see 5:356 (1 reference); for a review by E. A. Peel of the original edition, see 4:307 (3 references).

[1719]

Normative Adaptive Behavior Checklist.

Purpose: Assesses "how well a child compares to peers of his/her age (birth to 21 years) in performing skills needed for independent living."

Population: Birth–21 years.

Publication Date: 1984.

Scores, 7: Self-Help, Home Living, Independent Living, Social Skills, Sensory Motor, Language Concepts, Total.

Administration: Individual.

Price Data: Available from publisher.

Time: (20) minutes.

Comments: Condensed version of the Comprehensive Test of Adaptive Behavior (646).

Author: Gary L. Adams.

Publisher: Gary L. Adams (the author) [No reply from publisher; status unknown].

[1720]

Norris Educational Achievement Test.

Purpose: Designed to assess educational ability.

Publication Dates: 1991–1992.

Acronym: NEAT.

Administration: Individual.

Forms, 2: A, B.

Price Data, 2002: $128.50 per complete kit including 10 test booklets (5 Form A, 5 Form B), administration and scoring manual (1992, 234 pages), and technical manual (1992, 86 pages); $38.50 per 25 test booklets (select Form A or B); $65 per administration and scoring manual; $49.95 per technical manual.

Authors: Janet Switzer and Christian P. Gruber (manuals).

Publisher: Western Psychological Services.

a) READINESS.

Population: Ages 4-0 to 6-11.

Scores, 4: Fine Motor Coordination, Math Concepts, Letters, Total.

Time: (10–15) minutes.

b) ACHIEVEMENT.

Population: Ages 6-0 to 17-11.

Scores, 4-6: Word Recognition, Spelling, Arithmetic, Total plus 2 supplemental scores (Oral Reading and Comprehension, Written Language).

Time: (20–30) minutes for basic battery; (30–40) minutes for entire battery.

Cross References: See T5:1802 (1 reference); for reviews by A. Harry Passow and Michael S. Trevisan, see 12:260.

[1721]

NPF [Second Edition].

Purpose: "To assess stress tolerance and overall adjustment."

Population: Ages 1–adult.

Publication Dates: 1955–1992.
Acronym: NPF.
Scores, 3: Validity Scores (Uncertainty, Good Impression), Total Adjustment.
Administration: Group or individual.
Price Data, 2001: $30 per introductory kit including manual (1992, 10 pages), 20 test booklets, and scoring key; $26 per 20 test booklets; $10 per manual.
Time: (5–10) minutes.
Comments: Previously listed as a subtest of the Employee Attitude Series of the Job-Tests Program (T3:1219).
Author: Samuel E. Krug.
Publisher: Industrial Psychology International, Ltd.
Cross References: For reviews by Charles D. Claiborn and Howard M. Knoff, see 12:261.

[1722]
NSight Aptitude/Personality Questionnaire.

Purpose: A "method for measuring a person's work-related characteristics ... [that can be used] for hiring and promoting people who are similar to those already successful in the job."
Population: Adults.
Publication Dates: 1990–2002.
Acronym: NAPQ.
Scores, 26: 3 Cognitive Characteristics (Verbal Reasoning/Comprehension, Numerical Reasoning, Word Knowledge); 1 Achievement Characteristic (Visual Perception); 19 Personality Characteristics measured along 6 subtopics: Thinking Style (Emotional Decision Maker, Analytical Thinker, Logical Thinker, Practical), Drives (Security Oriented, Cooperative, Rule Bound), Stress (Anxious, Tolerant, Apprehensive), Communication (Serious, Reserved, Assuming), Leadership (Passive, Submissive, Suspicious), Reliability (Indifferent, Changeable, Expedient); 3 Validity Scales (Lie, Faking Bad, Faking Good).
Administration: Group.
Price Data, 2002: $168 per assessment including 11-page report and telephone consultation; quantity discounts available.
Time: (120) minutes for Cognitive Characteristics Inventory; Personality Inventory untimed.
Author: Stephen Overcash.
Publisher: Directional Insight International, Inc.

[1723]
Number Test DE.

Purpose: "To provide a measure of the child's understanding of the four number processes (addition, subtraction, multiplication and division)."
Population: Ages 10-6 to 12-6.
Publication Date: 1965.
Scores: Total score only.

Administration: Group.
Price Data: Available from publisher.
Time: (50–60) minutes.
Comments: Formerly called Number Test 1.
Author: E. L. Barnard.
Publisher: NFER-Nelson Publishing Co., Ltd. [England].
Cross References: See T3:1652 (1 reference).

[1724]
Nurse Entrance Test.

Purpose: "Designed ... as a diagnostic instrument to assist nursing programs evaluate the academic and social skills of new applicants to their programs."
Population: Adult applicants to nursing schools.
Publication Dates: 1998–2001.
Acronym: NET.
Scores, 28: 7 Essential Math Skills scores (Whole Numbers, Number System Conversions, Algebra Equations, Percentage Operations, Decimal Operations, Fraction Operations, Essential Math Skills), 3 Reading Comprehension scores (Reading Rate, Reading Rate Placement, Reading Comprehension), 3 Critical Thinking Appraisal scores (Main Idea of Passage, Inferential Reading, Predicting of Outcomes); Testtaking Skills score, 2 Social Interaction Profile scores (Passive, Aggressive), 5 Stress Level Profile scores (Family, Social, Money/Time, Academic, Work Place), 6 Learning Styles (Auditory Learner, Solitary Learner, Visual Learner, Social Learner, Oral Dependent Learner, Writing Dependent Learner), Composite Percentage.
Administration: Group.
Price Data, 2002: $17 per test by computer; $10.50 per test; $8 per answer sheet; $27.50 per Study Guide.
Time: (150) minutes.
Comments: Generates a Diagnostic Report including NET Group Report, individual Student Reports; Group Report provides group-level mean percentages and normative comparisons for the 28 scores; optional Study Guide offers testtaking strategy tips and practice tests.
Author: Michael D. Frost.
Publisher: Educational Resources, Inc.

[1725]
OARS Multidimensional Functional Assessment Questionnaire.

Purpose: Designed to assess individual functioning in the elderly.
Population: Ages 65 and over.
Publication Dates: 1975–1988.
Acronym: OARS MFAQ.
Scores: One of 6 ratings (Excellent, Good, Mildly Impaired, Moderately Impaired, Severely Impaired, Totally Impaired) for 5 scales: Social Resources, Eco-

nomic Resources, Mental Health, Physical Health, Activities of Daily Living.

Administration: Individual.

Price Data: Price data for test materials including manual (1988, 191 pages) available from publisher.

Time: (45) minutes.

Comments: Orally administered to the subject or to someone who knows the subject well.

Author: Center for the Study of Aging and Human Development.

Publisher: Center for the Study of Aging and Human Development, Duke University Medical Center.

Cross References: See T5:1808 (3 references) and T4:1855 (9 references); for reviews by Keith S. Dobson and Bruce R. Fretz, see 9:847 (4 references); see also T3:1659 (1 reference).

[1726]
Oaster Stressors Scales.

Purpose: Designed to index an individual's level of stressors by using derived trait scales.

Population: Adults.

Publication Date: 1983.

Scores: 4 profiles: Classic/Overload Stressor Pattern of Type A Behavior, Overload Stressor Pattern, Underload Stressor Pattern/Goal-Blocked Type A, Type B Behavior Pattern.

Administration: Group.

Price Data: Available from publisher.

Time: Administration time not reported.

Author: Thomas R. Oaster.

Publisher: Thomas R. Oaster.

[1727]
Object-Oriented Programmer Analyst Staff Selector.

Purpose: To measure knowledge of object-oriented terminology and C++.

Population: Candidates for the position of object-oriented programmer analyst.

Publication Date: 1994.

Acronym: OOPS.

Scores: Total Score, Narrative Evaluation, Ranking, Recommendation.

Administration: Group.

Price Data, 2001: $350 per candidate; quantity discounts available.

Time: (120) minutes.

Comments: Scored by publisher.

Author: Bruce A. Winrow.

Publisher: Walden Personnel Performance, Inc. [Canada].

[1728]
The Object Relations Technique.

Purpose: Developed as a projective technique designed to assess ways "of conducting human relationships."

Population: Counselees ages 11 and over.

Publication Dates: 1955–1973.

Acronym: ORT.

Scores: No scores.

Administration: Individual.

Editions, 3: A Series, B Series, C Series.

Price Data, 1999: £71 per set of 12 plates; £15.50 per Handbook.

Time: Administration time not reported.

Author: Herbert Phillipson.

Publisher: NFER-Nelson Publishing Co., Ltd. [England].

Cross References: See T4:1857 (1 reference), T2:1486 (5 references), and P:458 (5 references); for a review by H. R. Beech and an excerpted review by Leopold Bellak, see 6:233 (7 references); for a review by George Westby, see 5:151 (6 references).

[1729]
Observation Ability Test for the Police Service.

Purpose: As a supplement for other testing instruments for police jobs, such as Investigator and Detective, and other jobs with high observational requirements.

Population: Candidates for police entry-level and promotional positions.

Publication Date: 1993.

Scores, 1: Observation Ability.

Administration: Group.

Restricted Distribution: Distribution restricted to civil service commissions and qualified municipal officials.

Price Data: Available from publisher.

Time: (45) minutes.

Author: McCann Associates, Inc.

Publisher: McCann Associates, Inc.

[1730]
Observation of Type Preference.

Purpose: Designed to help one identify how others perceive one's personality preferences.

Population: Adults.

Publication Date: 1995.

Acronym: OTP.

Scores, 8: Introversion, Extraversion, Intuitive, Sensate, Thinking, Feeling, Judging, Perceiving.

Administration: Group.

Manual: Manual not available.

Price Data, 2002: $49 per complete set including questionnaires and answer sheets.

Time: [30] minutes.

Comments: Complements the Myers-Briggs Type Indicator (MBTI; 1678); can be administered online via the Internet.

Authors: Terry R. Bacon, Barbara Singer, and International LearningWorks.

Publisher: Lore International Institute.

[1731]

Observational Assessment of Temperament.

Purpose: Assesses temperamental characteristics, primarily in industrial/organizational settings.
Population: Higher level specialized and managerial personnel.
Publication Dates: 1979–1996.
Acronym: OAT.
Scores: 3 behavior factors: Extroversive/Impulsive vs. Introversive/Reserved, Emotional/Responsive vs. Nonemotional/Controlled, Self-Reliant/Individually Oriented vs. Dependent/Group Oriented.
Administration: Group.
Price Data, 2002: $54 per 25 tests (including background research, scoring iinstructions, and norms).
Time: [10] minutes.
Comments: Can be used as a self-assessment or for the assessment of the observed behavior of others; assesses the three behavior factors measured by the Temperament Comparator (2506).
Author: Melany E. Baehr.
Publisher: Reid London House.

[1732]

Observational Emotional Inventory—Revised.

Purpose: "Provides a stucture for observing and rating overt emotional behaviors which interfere with educational or vocational potential."
Population: Students and adults.
Publication Date: 1986.
Acronym: OEI-R.
Scores, 8: Impulsivity-Frustration, Anxiety, Depression-Withdrawal, Socialization, Self-Concept, Aggression, Reality Disorientation, Total Score.
Administration: Group.
Price Data, 2002: $38 per package of 25 inventories.
Time: 120 minutes each day for 5 days.
Comments: Problems checklist.
Authors: Lawrence T. McCarron and Jack G. Dial.
Publisher: McCarron-Dial Systems.
Cross References: For a review by Joseph G. Ponterotto, see 11:266.

[1733]

Occupational Aptitude Survey and Interest Schedule—Third Edition.

Purpose: To assist in career development.
Population: Grades 8–12.
Publication Dates: 1983–2002.
Administration: Group or individual.
Time: (30–45) minutes per survey.
Comments: Machine scoring is available.
Author: Randall M. Parker.
Publisher: PRO-ED.

a) APTITUDE SURVEY.
Acronym: OASIS-3:AS.
Scores, 6: General Ability, Verbal Aptitude, Numerical Aptitude, Spatial Aptitude, Perceptual Aptitude, Manual Dexterity.
Price Data, 2002: $159 per complete kit including 10 student test booklets, 50 handscorable answer sheets, 50 profile sheets, and examiner's manual (2002, 45 pages); $39 per 10 student test booklets; $39 per 50 handscorable answer sheets; $27 per 50 profile sheets; $54 per examiner's manual.
b) INTEREST SCHEDULE.
Acronym: OASIS-3:IS.
Scores, 12: Artistic, Scientific, Nature, Protective, Mechanical, Industrial, Business Detail, Selling, Accommodating, Humanitarian, Leading-Influencing, Physical Performing.
Price Data: $169 per complete kit including 25 student test booklets, 50 handscorable answer sheets, 50 profile sheets, 50 scoring forms, and examiner's manual (2002, 53 pages); $39 per 25 student test booklets; $27 per 50 handscorable answer sheets; $27 per 50 profile sheets; $27 per scoring forms; $54 per examiner's manual.
Cross References: For reviews by Laura L. B. Barnes and Thomas E. Dinero of an earlier version of the Aptitude Survey, see 12:263 (2 references); see also T4:1862 (2 references). For reviews by Robert J. Miller and Donald G. Zytowski of an earlier version of the Interest Schedule, see 12:264; see also T4:1863 (2 references); for reviews by Christopher Borman and Ruth G. Thomas of an earlier edition, see 20:244 (1 reference).

[1734]

Occupational Interest Inventories.

Purpose: Interest assessment to be used in career guidance, placement, selection, and counseling.
Population: Adults.
Publication Date: 1982.
Administration: Group.
Price Data: Available from publisher.
Time: (25–45) minutes per inventory.
Authors: Ruth Holdsworth and Lisa Camp (manual and user's guide).
Publisher: SHL Group plc [United Kingdom].
a) GENERAL OCCUPATIONAL INTEREST INVENTORY.
Population: Adults of average educational level.
Acronym: GOII.
Scores, 18: Medical, Welfare, Personal Services, Selling Goods, Selling Services, Supervision, Clerical, Office Equipment, Control, Leisure, Art and Design, Crafts, Plants, Animals, Transport, Construction, Electrical, Mechanical.

b) ADVANCED OCCUPATIONAL INTEREST INVENTORY.
Population: Adults of above average educational level.
Acronym: AOII.
Scores, 19: Medical, Welfare, Education, Control, Commercial, Managerial, Administration, Legal, Financial, Data Processing, Information, Media, Art and Design, Biological Sciences, Physical Sciences, Process, Mechanical, Electrical/Electronic, Construction.

[1735]
The Occupational Interest Rating Scale.
Purpose: Designed to measure the individual's occupational interests and preferences for modes of interaction within occupations.
Population: Ages 14 and over.
Publication Date: 2002.
Acronym: OIRS.
Scores, 12: 7 occupational interests (Business, Technical, Care, Aesthetic, Scientific, Numerical, Field) and 5 directions of involvement (Persuasive, Operational, Empathic, Making, Intellectual).
Administration: Group.
Price Data, 2002: £17.55 per complete set; £3 per test book; £10.20 per 50 record sheets; £4.35 per manual (2002, 12 pages) and keys; £28 per on-screen kit 3.5-inch disk (self-administering and scoring), manual, administration rates, and guide to profile interpretation; £23 per replacement disk.
Time: (35–45) minutes.
Author: Alan Brimer.
Publisher: Educational Evaluations [England].

[1736]
Occupational Interests Card Sort.
Purpose: To identify and rank occupational interests.
Population: Adults.
Publication Dates: 1993–2002.
Scores: Interests Summary Sheet.
Administration: Group or individual.
Price Data: Available from publisher.
Time: (20–30) minutes.
Author: Richard L. Knowdell.
Publisher: Career Research & Testing, Inc.
Cross References: For reviews by Michael B. Bunch and Donald Thompson, see 13:213.

[1737]
Occupational Personality Assessment.
Purpose: Designed as a "computer simulation of a vocational assessment."
Population: Individuals seeking vocational counseling.
Publication Date: 1993.

Acronym: OPA.
Administration: Individual.
Price Data, 1996: $100 per start up trial set including 5 administrations and multipart manual (54 pages); $175 per complete set including 25 administrations; $100 per each additional 20 administrations.
Time: Administration time not reported.
Comments: Self-administered computerized test requires IBM or compatible Windows for administration.
Authors: Don Schaeffer and Joyce Schaeffer.
Publisher: Measurement for Human Resources.
a) INTEREST TEST.
Purpose: "Designed to assess what kinds of things a person would enjoy doing."
Scores, 3: Interest Profile, Experience Profile, How Much Interest and Experience Match.
Comments: Scores are based on Holland's RIASEC occupational codes.
b) COMMERCIAL ORIENTATION.
Purpose: Designed to measure "skills and attitudes related to commercial business."
Scores, 4: Focus on Making Money, Tactical Orientation, Reading Business Tables, Total.
c) MOTIVATION.
Purpose: Constructed to assess "motivational preferences."
Scores, 8: Personal Motives (Peaceful, Sensory, Acquisitive, Work Driven), Work Motives (Intellect, Beauty, Independent Authority, Pleasing Others).
d) MANAGEMENT.
Purpose: Designed to assess "management style."
Scores, 7: Aggressiveness, Field Independence, Toughness, Determination, Fluctuating Salary, Fluctuating Income Tolerance, Management Style Preference.
Cross References: For a review by Peter F. Merenda, see 13:214.

[1738]
Occupational Stress Indicator.
Purpose: To clarify the nature of stress in organisations by identifying sources of stress, intervening factors, and the effects of stress on employees.
Population: Employees.
Publication Date: 1988.
Acronym: OSI.
Scores, 28: Sources (Intrinsic to Job, Managerial Role, Relationships with Other People, Career and Achievement, Organisational Structure and Climate, Home-Work Interface), Individual Characteristics (Attitude to Living, Style of Behavior, Ambition, Broad View Type A, Organisational Forces, Management Processes, Individual Influences, Broad View of Control), Coping (Social Support, Task Strategies, Logic, Home and Work Relationship, Time, Involvement),

Effects (Achievement Value and Growth, Job Itself, Organisational Design and Structure, Organisational Processes, Personal Relationships, Broad View of Job Satisfaction, Mental Ill Health, Physical Ill Health).

Administration: Group.

Price Data: Price information available from publisher for complete Management Set kit including 15 questionnaires (Indicators), 15 biographical questionnaires, score sheet, scoring stencils, administration card, and Management Guide (71 pages), Group Profiling Pack including 15 questionnaires (Indicators), and for Disk Pack-IBM PC compatible, 50 administrations (to be used in conjunction with the complete kit).

Time: 45(55) minutes.

Authors: Cary L. Cooper, Stephen J. Sloan, and Stephen Williams.

Publisher: NFER-Nelson Publishing Co., Ltd. [England].

Cross References: See T5:1824 (7 references); for reviews by Mark Pope and L. Alan Witt, see 11:268.

[1739]
Occupational Stress Inventory—Revised Edition.

Purpose: Designed as a "measure of three dimensions of occupational adjustment: occupational stress, psychological strain, and coping resources."

Population: Age 18 years and over.

Publication Dates: 1981–1998.

Acronym: OSI-R.

Scores, 14: Occupational Roles Questionnaire (Role Overload, Role Insufficiency, Role Ambiguity, Role Boundary, Responsibility, Physical Environment); Personal Strain Questionnaire (Vocational Strain, Psychological Strain, Interpersonal Strain, Physical Strain); Personal Resources Questionnaire (Recreation, Self-Care, Social Support, Rational Cognitive Coping).

Administration: Individual or group.

Price Data: Available from publisher.

Time: (30) minutes.

Comments: Self-administered.

Author: Samuel H. Osipow.

Publisher: Psychological Assessment Resources, Inc.

Cross References: For reviews by Patricia K. Freitag and Robert Wall, see 14:260; see also T5:1825 (7 references) and T4:1870 (4 references); for reviews by Mary Ann Bunda and Larry Cochran of an earlier edition, see 11:269 (1 reference).

[1740]
Occupational Test Series-Basic Skills Tests.

Purpose: Designed for the "assessment of current levels of skill in comprehension, writing and dealing with numbers."

Population: New trainees and employees.

Publication Date: 1988.

Scores, 7: Literacy (Reading Comprehension and Information-Seeking, Writing [optional], Total), Numeracy (Calculating, Approximating, Problem-Solving, Total).

Administration: Group.

Price Data: Price information available from publisher for Reference Set, reusable Literacy Newspapers, Literacy Administration pack, Numeracy Administration pack, and reusable Numeracy Question Booklets.

Time: 35(45) minutes for Literacy Test (both sections); 20(30) minutes for Reading section of Literacy Test; (35) minutes for Numeracy Test.

Authors: Pauline Smith and Chris Whetton.

Publisher: NFER-Nelson Publishing Co., Ltd. [England].

Cross References: For reviews by Phyllis Kuehn and Mark Pope, see 12:267.

[1741]
Occupational Test Series: General Ability Tests.

Purpose: "Assessing persons without previous work experience; selection for supervisory and similar management posts."

Population: Employees and candidates for employment.

Publication Date: 1988.

Scores: 4 tests: Verbal, Non-Verbal, Numerical, Spatial.

Administration: Group.

Price Data: Price information available from publisher for Reference Set, test booklet (specify Verbal, Non-Verbal, Numerical, or Spatial), Administration Pack (specify Non-Verbal, Numerical, or Spatial), and Test Taker's Guide.

Time: 25(30) minutes for Verbal; 30(35) minutes for each (Non-Verbal, Numerical, Spatial).

Comments: Tests may be administered separately.

Authors: Pauline Smith and Chris Whetton.

Publisher: NFER-Nelson Publishing Co., Ltd. [England].

Cross References: For reviews by Philip G. Benson and Michael S. Trevisan, see 11:270.

[1742]
Oetting Michaels Anchored Ratings for Therapists.

Purpose: Designed for use by supervisors to rate therapists in training.

Population: Graduate students and interns in counseling and clinical training.

Publication Date: 1989.

Acronym: OMART.

Scores: Developmental ratings on 34 dimensions of therapist effectiveness: Interviewing (Relationship with the Client, Dealing with Therapist Identification Issues, Personal Style, Exploration of Client Goals, Exploration of Issues, Exploration of Feelings, Time During the Interview, Responsiveness to Nonverbal Cues, Use of Language), Conceptualization of Therapy (Knowledge of Personality Theory, Applying Psychotherapy Theory, Knowledge of DSM III, Ability to Analyze Course of Therapy, Treatment Plans), Reaction to Supervision (Interaction During Supervision, Openness to Feedback, Confidence, Self Evaluation), Sensitivity to Client Issues (Dealing with Dependency, Dealing with Client/Therapist Sexual Feelings, Awareness of Environmental Influences, Sensitivity to Cultural Differences, Sensitivity to Sex-Role Stereotypes, Handling of Conflicts of Client/Therapist Values), Trainee Issues (Management of Personal Stress, Interference Because of Therapist's Adjustment Problems, Self-Direction of Professional Development), Other (Dealing with Ambiguity, Therapist's Attitudes to Authority, Writing Reports, General Test Interpretation, Intellective Assessment, Appropriate Handling of Sexual Material).

Administration: Individual.

Price Data: Available from publisher (license to reproduce provided for Ph.D.s or Ed.D.s).

Time: [20–30] minutes.

Comments: Completed by supervisor.

Authors: E. R. Oetting and Laurie Michaels.

Publisher: E. R. Oetting, Colorado State University.

Cross References: For a review by John S. Geisler, see 14:262.

[1743]
Oetting's Computer Anxiety Scale.

Purpose: Developed "to provide a general measure of computer anxiety."

Population: Entering college freshmen.

Publication Date: 1983.

Acronym: COMPAS.

Scores, 8: Hand Calculator, Trust, General Attitude, Data Entry, Word Processing, Business Operations, Computer Science, Total; Total score only for short form.

Administration: Group.

Price Data: License to reproduce for Ph.D.s or Ed.D.s available from publisher.

Time: [15] minutes.

Author: E. R. Oetting.

Publisher: E. R. Oetting, Colorado State University.

Cross References: For reviews by Benjamin Kleinmuntz and Steven L. Wise, see 10:245.

[1744]
Offer Self-Image Questionnaire for Adolescents, Revised.

Purpose: Designed to measure the self-image of adolescents.

Population: Ages 13–18.

Publication Dates: 1971–1992.

Acronym: OSIQ-R.

Scores, 13: Emotional Tone, Impulse Control, Mental Health, Social Functioning, Family Functioning, Vocational Attitudes, Self-Confidence, Self-Reliance, Body Image, Sexuality, Ethical Values, Idealism, Total Self-Image.

Administration: Group or individual.

Price Data, 2002: $99.50 per complete kit including manual (1992, 75 pages), 2 reusable administration booklets, and 5 WPS Test Report prepaid mail-in answer sheets; $29.50 per 10 reusable administration booklets; $45 per manual; $15.95 per mail-in answer sheet; $229 per 25-use WPS Test Report IBM Microcomputer scoring disk; $15 per 100 answer sheets for use with Microcomputer disk; $10.50 per FAX scoring.

Time: [30–45] minutes.

Comments: Computer scored via disk or prepaid mail-in answer sheet.

Authors: Daniel Offer (test/manual), E. Ostrov (manual), K. I. Howard (manual), and S. Dolan (manual).

Publisher: Western Psychological Services.

Cross References: See T5:1832 (17 references); for reviews by Sarah J. Allen and Michael Furlong and Mitchell Karno, see 12:268 (9 references); see also T4:1877 (6 references); for reviews of an earlier edition by Robert Hogan and Roy P. Martin, see 9:855 (5 references); see also T3:1673 (1 reference) and 8:633 (10 references).

[1745]
Office Arithmetic Test: ETSA Test 2A.

Purpose: Designed to assess basic arithmetic skills used in office work.

Population: Employment applicants.

Publication Dates: 1960–1998.

Scores: Total score only.

Administration: Group or individual.

Price Data, 2002: $10 per electronic test; $10 each per test booklet and answer sheets (scoring and reporting); $20 per administrator's manual; $20 per technical manual.

Time: 60 minutes.

Comments: Electronic tests available at www.etsatests.com.

Author: Psychological Services Bureau, Inc.

Publisher: Employers' Tests and Services Associates.

Cross References: For reviews by Marvin D. Dunnette and Raymond A. Katzell of an earlier version of the ETSA Tests, see 6:1025.

[1746]
Office Arithmetic Test—Form CA.

Purpose: "To measure the arithmetic skills required to perform office and clerical jobs."

Population: Adults.

Publication Date: 1990.
Scores: Total score only.
Administration: Group.
Price Data, 2002: $200 per complete kit including 10 test booklets, 100 answer sheets, manual (10 pages), and scoring key.
Time: (30) minutes.
Author: Roland T. Ramsay.
Publisher: Ramsay Corporation.
Cross References: For reviews by Frederick Bessai and Anita Tesh, see 13:255.

[1747]
Office Proficiency Assessment and Certification [OPAC System].

Purpose: "Assess[es] the knowledge, skills, and abilities of ... job candidates [and students]" "for both the corporate and educational environments."
Population: Ages 18 and over.
Publication Dates: 1994–2002.
Acronym: OPAC System.
Scores, 41: 28 office skills scores [Computer Applications (Windows, Editing/Formatting from a Rough Draft, Spreadsheet, Intermediate Excel, Database, PowerPoint), Keyboarding Skills (Keyboarding, 10-Key, Data Entry—Vendor, Data Entry—Inventory, Data Entry—Invoice), Clerical Skills (Formatting a Letter, Transcription, Alphabetic Filing, Minutes Composition, Numeric Filing, Proofreading 1, Proofreading 2, Content Proofreading Practice), Financial Skills (Bank Deposit, Bank Reconciliation, Petty Cash, Basic Math), Professional Skills (Legal and Medical Keyboarding, Legal and Medical Proofreading, Legal and Medical Terminology, Legal and Medical Transcription)]; 13 Hogan Personality Inventory scores [7 primary scale scores (Intellectance, Adjustment, Ambition, Sociability, Likeability, Prudence, School Success), 6 occupational scale scores (Service Orientation, Stress Tolerance, Reliability, Clerical Potential, Sales Potential, Managerial Potential)].
Administration: Individual or group.
Price Data, 2002: $2,295 per Single-User OPAC including CD-ROM, administrator manual (2001, 200 pages), candidate manual (2001, 92 pages), one test station packet per station, and 3 dictation cassette tapes; $4,295 per Multi-User OPAC (up to 5 test stations); $6,295 per Multi-User OPAC (up to 10 test stations, plus $200 for each test station over 10); all packages include one year OPAC Plus Customer Support offering unlimited technical support, free updates, and free upgrades; $50 per administrator manual; $30 per Test Station Pack; price information available from publisher for additional site licenses and OPAC Plus subscriptions available.
Time: Time limits for OPAC tests set by user; (15–20) minutes for Hogan Personality Inventory.

Comments: Computer administered; System requirements: Windows 95, 98, or ME (16 MB additional RAM, 32 MB recommended), Windows 2000, XKP, NT 4.0 (128 MB RAM, 256 MB recommended), 16-bit color SVGA monitor, Pentium 133 or higher; self-administered, self-scored; user selects tests to be administered; test writer provides custom test development inhouse enabling user to create additional tests in other content areas; assists user in determining cutoff scores and examining content validity; includes Hogan Personality Inventory (HPI).
Author: International Association of Administrative Professionals.
Publisher: OPAC Testing Software.

[1748]
Office Reading Test—Form G.

Purpose: "To measure the reading skills required for office workers."
Population: Adults.
Publication Dates: 1990–1999.
Scores: Total score only.
Administration: Group.
Price Data, 2002: $200 per complete kit including 10 test booklets, 100 answer sheets, manual (1999, 15 pages), and scoring key.
Time: (30) minutes.
Author: Roland T. Ramsay.
Publisher: Ramsay Corporation.
Cross References: For reviews by Laura L. B. Barnes and Steven J. Osterlind, see 13:256 (1 reference).

[1749]
Office Skills Achievement Test.

Purpose: Constructed to assess office skills.
Population: Office employees.
Publication Dates: 1962–1963.
Scores, 7: Business Letter, Grammar, Checking, Filing, Arithmetic, Written Directions, Total.
Administration: Group.
Price Data: Available from publisher.
Time: 20(25) minutes.
Author: P. L. Mellenbruch.
Publisher: Psychometric Affiliates.
Cross References: For reviews by Douglas G. Schultz and Paul W. Thayer, see 6:1043.

[1750]
Office Skills Series.

Purpose: "Designed to measure the basic skills and aptitudes required in office and commercial occupations."
Population: Applicants for clerical positions.
Publication Dates: 1983–1993.
Acronym: OSS.
Administration: Group.

Price Data: Available from publisher.
Comments: Formerly called E.I.T.S. Clerical Tests.
Author: The Morrisby Organisation.
Publisher: The Morrisby Organisation [England].
a) SPEED AND ACCURACY.
Scores, 3: Number Checking, Name Checking, Total.
Time: 5(10) minutes.
b) ARITHMETIC.
Scores, 3: Simple Calculation, Problems, Total.
Time: 10(15) minutes.
c) ENGLISH USAGE.
Scores, 3: Spelling, Grammar, Total.
Time: 4(9) minutes.
Cross References: For reviews by Gregory J. Cizek and Eugene P. Sheehan, see 13:216.

[1751]
Office Skills Test: ETSA Test 4A.

Purpose: Designed to measure typing and/or keyboard skills required of office work.
Population: Employment applicants.
Publication Dates: 1960–1998.
Scores: Total score only.
Administration: Group or individual.
Price Data, 2002: $10 per electronic test; $10 each per test booklet and answer sheet (scoring and reporting); $20 per administrator's manual; $20 per technical manual.
Time: 45 minutes.
Comments: Previously listed as Stenographic Skills Test; electronic tests available at www.etsatests.com.
Author: Psychological Services Bureau, Inc.
Publisher: Employers' Tests and Services Associates.
Cross References: For reviews by Marvin D. Dunnette and Raymond A. Katzell of an earlier version of the ETSA Tests, see 6:1025.

[1752]
Office Skills Tests.

Purpose: Designed for measurement of aptitudes for twelve on-the-job skills.
Population: Applicants for clerical positions.
Publication Dates: 1977–1984.
Acronym: OST.
Scores: Total score only for each of 12 tests: Checking, Coding, Filing, Forms Completion, Grammar, Numerical Skills, Oral Directions, Punctuation, Reading Comprehension, Spelling, Typing, Vocabulary.
Administration: Individual or group.
Forms, 2: A, B for each test.
Price Data, 2002: $93 per start-up kit including 25 test booklets, scoring stencil, and examiner's manual (specify test; $126 per start-up kit including Oral Directions audiocassette; $56 per 25 test booklets (specify test; quantity discounts available); $20 per scoring sten-

cil (specify test); $28 per examiner's manual; $37 per Oral Directions audiocassette.
Time: (3–10) minutes per test.
Author: Science Research Associates.
Publisher: Reid London House.
Cross References: See T5:1836 (1 references); for reviews by Benjamin Shimberg and Paul W. Thayer, see 9:857.

[1753]
Office Systems Battery.

Purpose: Designed to measure an individual's clerical skills in a way that examines how those skills are integrated; provides an overall picture of the way in which information is learned and processed.
Population: Applicants for clerical positions.
Publication Date: [1993].
Acronym: OSB.
Scores: 6 subtests: Visual Judgement, Information Access and Checking, Numerical Estimation, Numerical Calculation, Problem Analysis, Memory.
Administration: Group or individual.
Price Data, 2001: £30 per administrator's manual; £25 per set of scoring keys; £12.50 per set of 3 data cards; £15 per question booklet; £40 per 50 answer sheets.
Time: (127) minutes for full battery.
Author: Roy Childs.
Publisher: The Test Agency Limited [England].

[1754]
Official GED Practice Test.

Purpose: To help candidates determine their readiness to take the full-length GED tests.
Population: Candidates preparing for the full-length GED.
Publication Dates: 1979–1983.
Scores, 5: Writing Skills, Social Studies, Science, Reading Skills, Mathematics.
Administration: Group.
Forms, 2: A, B.
Price Data: Not available.
Foreign Language Edition: Spanish edition available.
Time: 202.5(227.5) minutes for complete test.
Comments: Suggested standards of mastery for full length GED given for each state.
Author: American Council on Education [No reply from publisher; status unknown].
Publisher: Prentice Hall [No reply from publisher; status unknown].

[1755]
The Ohio Penal Classification Test.

Purpose: Developed to assess mental abilities of penal populations.
Population: Penal institutions.

Publication Dates: 1952–1954.
Acronym: OPCT.
Scores, 5: Block Counting, Digit-Symbol, Number Series, Memory Span, Total.
Administration: Group.
Price Data: Available from publisher.
Time: (25–30) minutes.
Comments: Also available for industrial use under the title Ohio Classification Test (1957).
Authors: DeWitt E. Sell, Robert W. Scollay, and Leroy N. Vernon (manual for industrial edition).
Publisher: Psychometric Affiliates.
Cross References: See T2:418 (2 references); for a review by Norman Eagle, see 5:358.

[1756]
Older Persons Counseling Needs Survey.

Purpose: To assess the needs of older persons and their desires for counseling.
Population: Ages 60 and over.
Publication Date: 1993.
Scores, 3: Needs, Desires, Total.
Administration: Group or individual.
Price Data, 2001: $25 per sampler set including manual (16 pages) and test booklet; $125 per one-year permission to reproduce up to 200 administrations of the test.
Time: (10–15) minutes.
Author: Jane E. Myers.
Publisher: Mind Garden, Inc.
Cross References: For reviews by Dennis C. Harper and Lawrence J. Ryan, see 14:264.

[1757]
Oliver Organization Description Questionnaire.

Purpose: Describes occupational organizations along four dimensions.
Population: Adults.
Publication Date: 1981.
Acronym: OODQ.
Scores, 4: H (Hierarchy), P (Professional), T (Task), G (Group).
Administration: Group.
Price Data, 2002: $30 per 50 tests with scoring sheets; $5 per scoring guide (1981, 13 pages).
Time: (15–20) minutes.
Author: John E. Oliver, Jr.
Publisher: Organizational Measurement Systems Press.
Cross References: For a review by Peter Villanova and H. John Bernardin, see 11:271.

[1758]
OMNI Personality Inventory and OMNI-IV Personality Disorder Inventory.

Purpose: "Comprehensive self-report instruments for measuring normal and abnormal personality traits."

Population: Ages 18–74 years.
Publication Date: 2001.
Administration: Individual or group.
Price Data, 2001: $245 per OMNI/OMNI-IV combination kit (3.5-inch disk) including professional manual (75 pages), 25 OMNI test booklets, OMNI software system with on-screen manual, 5 free on-screen administrations of OMNI, 25 OMNI-IV test booklets, OMNI-IV software system with on-screen manual, and 5 free on-screen administrations of OMNI-IV.
Comments: Paper-and-pencil and computer administration available; computer-scored only (cannot be hand-scored); scoring software generates interpretive report; system requirements: Windows only, Windows 95/98/NT/2000/ME, 8 MB hard drive, 16 MB RAM (Windows 95/98/ME) or 24 MB RAM (Windows, NT/2000), 3.5-inch floppy disk drive.
Author: Armand W. Loranger.
Publisher: Psychological Assessment Resources, Inc.
   a) OMNI PERSONALITY INVENTORY.
   Acronym: OMNI.
   Scores, 44: 2 Validity Scales: Variable Response Inconsistency (VRIN), Current Distress (CD); 25 Normal Scales: Aestheticism (AE), Ambition (AM), Anxiety (AN), Assertiveness (AS), Conventionality (CO), Depression (DE), Dutifulness (DU), Excitement (EC), Exhibitionism (EH), Energy (EN), Flexibility (FL), Hostility (HS), Impulsiveness (IM), Intellect (IT), Irritability (IR), Modesty (MD), Moodiness (MO), Orderliness (OR), Self-Indulgence (SI), Sincerity (SN), Sociability (SO), Self-Reliance (SR), Tolerance (TO), Trustfulness (TR), Warmth (WR); 10 Personality Disorder Scales: Paranoid (PAR), Schizoid (SCH), Schizotypal (SCT), Antisocial (ANT), Borderline (BOR), Histrionic (HIS) Narcissistic (NAR), Avoidant (AVD), Dependent (DEP), Obsessive-Compulsive (OBC); 7 Personality Factor Scales: Agreeableness (AGRE), Conscientiousness (CONC), Extraversion (EXTR), Narcissism (NARC), Neuroticism (NEUR), Openness (OPEN), Sensation-Seeking (SENS).
   Price Data: $145 per OMNI introductory kit (3.5-inch disk) including professional manual, 25 OMNI test booklets, OMNI software system with on-screen manual, unlimited-use scoring and interpretation, 5 free on-screen administrations of OMNI: $40 per professional manual; $125 per 25 test booklets; $125 per OMNI key disk (25 on-screen administrations).
   Time: (60–90) minutes.
   Comments: 375-item self-report inventory; measure both normal and abnormal personality traits as specified in DSM-IV.

b) OMNI-IV PERSONALITY DISORDER INVENTORY.

Acronym: OMNI-IV.

Scores, 12: 2 Validity Scales: Variable Response Inconsistency (VRIN), Current Distress (CD); 10 Personality Disorder Scales: Paranoid (PAR), Schizoid (SCH), Schizotypal (SCT), Antisocial (ANT), Borderline (BOR), Histrionic (HIS), Narcissistic (NAR), Avoidant (AVD), Dependent (DEP), Obsessive-Compulsive (OBC).

Price Data: $120 per OMNI-IV introductory kit (3.5-inch disk) including professional manual, 25 OMNI-IV test booklets, OMNI-IV software system with on-screen manual, 5 free on-screen administrations of OMNI-IV; $100 per 25 OMNI-IV test booklets; $100 per OMNI-IV key disk (25 on-screen administrations).

Time: (35–45) minutes.

Comments: 210 items taken from the OMNI; assesses personality disorders as specified in DSM-IV.

[1759]

O*NET Career Interests Inventory: Based on the "O*NET Interest Profiler" developed by the U.S. Department of Labor.

Purpose: To allow users to rank six career interest areas and relate them to specific careers

Population: Youth and adults.

Publication Date: 2001.

Scores: 6 interest categories: Realistic, Investigative, Artistic, Social, Enterprising, Conventional.

Administration: Group or individual.

Price Data, 2001: $29.95 per 25 inventories including copy of administrator's guide (8 pages).

Time: (20–60) minutes.

Comments: Twelve-panel foldout; a compact, shorter, and less expensive version of the Department of Labor's "O*NET Interest Profiler"; based on the "O*NET Interest Profiler" developed by the U.S. Department of Labor.

Author: JIST Publishing, Inc.

Publisher: JIST Publishing, Inc.

[1760]

O*NET Career Values Inventory: Based on the "O*NET Work Importance Locator" developed by the U.S. Department of Labor.

Purpose: To allow users to rank six work values and relate them to specific careers.

Population: Youth and adults.

Publication Date: 2001.

Scores: Achievement, Independence, Recognition, Relationships, Support, Working Conditions.

Administration: Group or individual.

Price Data, 2001: $29.95 per 25 inventories including administrator's guide (8 pages).

Time: (20–60) minutes.

Comments: Twelve-panel foldout; a compact, shorter, and less expensive version of the Department of Labor's "O*NET Work Importance Locator"; based on the "O*NET Work Importance Locator" developed by the U.S. Department of Labor.

Author: JIST Publishing, Inc.

Publisher: JIST Publishing, Inc.

[1761]

O*NET Interest Profiler.

Purpose: "Provides ... self-knowledge about [one's] ... vocational personality type ... [and] fosters career awareness."

Population: Age 14 and older.

Publication Dates: 1985–2000.

Acronym: IP.

Scores, 11: Interest Areas (Realistic, Investigative, Artistic, Social, Enterprising, Conventional), Job Zones (Little or No Preparation Needed, Some Preparation Needed, Medium Preparation Needed, Considerable Preparation Needed, Extensive Preparation Needed).

Administration: Group.

Price Data: Available from publisher.

Time: (20–60) minutes.

Comments: Replaces the Job Search Inventory (T5:1351); self-administered and self-scored; pencil-and-paper format; Computerized Interest Profile is administered and scored on computer; part of the O*NET Career Exploration Tools; intended for career exploration, planning, and counseling purposes only; results should not be used for employment or hiring decisions.

Author: U.S. Department of Labor, Employment and Training Administration.

Publisher: U.S. Department of Labor, Employment and Training Administration.

Cross References: For reviews by Ralph O. Mueller and Sheldon Zedeck of the Job Search Inventory, see 13:163.

[1762]

O*NET Work Importance Locator.

Purpose: "Helps users identify what is important to them in a job."

Population: Ages 16 and older.

Publication Date: 2000.

Acronym: WIL.

Scores, 6: Achievement, Independence, Recognition, Relationships, Support, Working Conditions.

Administration: Group.

Price Data: Available from publisher.

Time: (15–45) minutes.

Comments: Available in paper-and-pencil format only; related Work Importance Profiler is adminis-

tered and scored on computer; part of O*NET Career Exploration Tools; intended for career exploration, planning, and counseling purposes only; results should not be used for employment or hiring decisions.
Author: U.S. Department of Labor, Employment and Training Administration.
Publisher: U.S. Department of Labor, Employment and Training Administration.

[1763]
Opinions About Deaf People Scale.
Purpose: To measure hearing adults' beliefs about the capabilities of deaf adults.
Population: Adults.
Publication Date: Undated.
Scores: Total score only.
Administration: Group.
Price Data, 1995: $11.50 per development and validation manual (127 pages); $1 per administration guide including reproducible copy of the scale; $5 per disk of both.
Time: Administration time not reported.
Authors: Paul James Berkay, J. Emmett Gardener, and Patricia L. Smith.
Publisher: National Clearinghouse of Rehabilitation Training Materials.
Cross References: For reviews by Jeffery P. Braden and by Vincent J. Samar and Ila Parasnis, see 14:265.

[1764]
Opinions Toward Adolescents.
Purpose: Measures ideas and attitudes toward adolescents.
Population: College and adults.
Publication Dates: 1971–1972.
Acronym: OTA.
Scores: 8 subscales: Liberal-Conservative, Punitive-Permissive, Restrictive-Accepting, Authoritarian-Democratic, Mistrust-Trust, Prejudice-Acceptance, Understanding-Misunderstanding, Skepticism-Sincerity (test taking attitude).
Administration: Group.
Price Data, 2002: $40 per examiner's set including manual (1972, 11 pages), keys, 25 test booklets, 25 answer sheets, and 25 profile sheets; $15 per 25 tests; $6.75 per 8 scoring keys; $6.75 per 25 answer sheets; $8.25 per 25 profile sheets; $4.50 per manual; $12 per specimen set.
Time: [20] minutes.
Author: William T. Martin.
Publisher: Psychologists and Educators, Inc.
Cross References: For a review by W. Grant Dahlstrom, see 8:635.

[1765]
OPQ32.
Purpose: "Designed to give information on individual styles or preferences at work."
Population: Employees and employee candidates.
Publication Dates: 1984–1999.
Acronym: OPQ32.
Scores: 32 scales: Relationships with People (Persuasive, Controlling, Outspoken, Independent Minded, Outgoing, Affiliative, Socially Confident, Modest, Democratic, Caring), Thinking Style (Data Rational, Evaluative, Behavioural, Conventional, Conceptual, Innovative, Variety Seeking, Adaptable, Forward Thinking, Detail Conscious, Conscientious, Rule Following), Feelings and Emotions (Relaxed, Worrying, Tough Minded, Optimistic, Trusting, Emotionally Controlled, Vigorous, Competitive, Achieving, Decisive).
Administration: Group.
Forms, 2: OPQ32n, OPQ32i.
Price Data: Available from publisher.
Time: Untimed; administration time not reported.
Comments: May be administered via Palm-top (PSION) Personal Questionnaire Administrator, personal computer, booklet and answer sheet, or on the internet; previous version was listed as Occupational Personality Questionnaire.
Author: SHL Group plc.
Publisher: SHL Group plc [United Kingdom].
Cross References: See T5:1822 (7 references; for a review by Thomas M. Haladyna of the earlier edition, see 11:267.

[1766]
Optometry Admission Testing Program.
Purpose: "Designed to measure general academic ability and comprehension of scientific information."
Population: Optometry school applicants.
Publication Dates: 1987-2002.
Acronym: OAT.
Scores, 8: Natural Sciences (Biology, General Chemistry, Organic Chemistry, Total), Reading Comprehension, Quantitative Reasoning, Physics, Academic Average.
Administration: Group.
Price Data: Available from publisher.
Time: 260(275) minutes in 2 sessions.
Comments: Supplants the Optometry College Admission Test.
Author: Optometry Admission Testing Program.
Publisher: Optometry Admission Testing Program.
Cross References: For reviews by Alan C. Bugbee, Jr. and James E. Carlson, see 12:269; for a review by Penelope Kegel-Flom of the Optometry College Admission Test, see 8:1104 (3 references).

[1767]

Oral and Written Language Scales: Listening Comprehension and Oral Expression.

Purpose: Designed to assess "receptive and expressive ... language."

Population: Ages 3–21.

Publication Date: 1995.

Acronym: OWLS LC/OE.

Scores, 3: Listening Comprehension, Oral Expression, Oral Composite.

Administration: Individual.

Price Data, 2002: $199.95 per complete kit including manual (212 pages), Listening Comprehension Easel, Oral Expression easel, and 25 record forms; $28.95 per 25 record forms; $199.95 per AGS Computer ASSIST™ for OWLS LC/OE (IBM or Macintosh).

Time: (5–15) minutes for LC; (10–25) minutes for OE.

Author: Elizabeth Carrow-Woolfolk.

Publisher: American Guidance Service, Inc.

Cross References: For reviews by Steve Graham and Koressa Kutsick Malcolm, see 14:266.

[1768]

Oral and Written Language Scales: Written Expression.

Purpose: Constructed as an "assessment of written language."

Population: Ages 5–21.

Publication Date: 1996.

Acronym: OWLS WE.

Scores, 2: Written Expression, Language Composite (when used with OWL Listening Comprehension and Oral Expression Scales).

Administration: Individual or group.

Price Data, 2002: $100.95 per complete kit including manual (255 pages), response booklets, record forms, and administration card; $26.95 per 25 response booklets; $21.95 per 25 record forms; $73.95 per manual; $199.95 per AGS Computer ASSIST™ for OWLS WE (IBM or Macintosh).

Time: (10–40) minutes.

Comments: May be used alone or in combination with OWLS Listening Comprehension and Oral Expression (1767).

Author: Elizabeth Carrow-Woolfolk.

Publisher: American Guidance Service, Inc.

Cross References: For reviews by C. Dale Carpenter and Koressa Kutsick Malcolm, see 14:267.

[1769]

Oral English/Spanish Placement Test.

Purpose: A measure of bilingualism to aid in placing children properly for efficient instruction.

Population: Ages 4–20.

Publication Dates: 1974–1976.

Acronym: OE/SPPT.

Scores: Total score and grade level equivalents.

Administration: Individual.

Tests, 2: English, Spanish.

Price Data, 1998: $20 per packet (includes manual and 1 English and 1 Spanish rating/answer sheets); permission to copy answer sheets is included.

Time: (1–2) minutes for children with little or no proficiency; (2–5) minutes for children with slightly better proficiency.

Comments: Performance rated by examiner; no reading by examinees.

Author: Steve Moreno.

Publisher: Moreno Educational Co.

Cross References: For a review by Stephen Powers, see 9:902.

[1770]

Oral-Motor/Feeding Rating Scale.

Purpose: Constructed to assess "oral-motor movement/feeding dysfunction."

Population: Ages 1 and over.

Publication Date: 1990.

Scores: Item scores only.

Administration: Individual.

Price Data, 2002: $40 per complete kit including 25 progress charts and manual (26 pages); $23 per 25 progress charts.

Time: (60) minutes or less.

Comments: Ratings by professional.

Author: Judy Michels Jelm.

Publisher: Therapy Skill Builders—A Division of The Psychological Corporation.

Cross References: For reviews by Glen E. Ray and Donna Spiker, see 12:271.

[1771]

Oral Speech Mechanism Screening Examination, Third Edition.

Purpose: "To provide the speech-language pathologist and other professionals with a method for assessing the adequacy of the oral mechanism for speech and related functions."

Population: Age 5 through adults.

Publication Dates: 1981–2000.

Acronym: OSMSE-3.

Scores: 9 areas: Lips, Tongue, Jaw, Teeth, Hard Palate, Soft Palate, Pharynx, Breathing, Diadochokinesis.

Administration: Individual.

Price Data, 2001: $98 per complete kit; $$27 per scoring forms; $19 per audio cassette; $54 per examiner's manual.

Time: (10–15) minutes.

Authors: Kenneth O. St. Louis and Dennis M. Ruscello.
Publisher: PRO-ED.
Cross References: For a review by Roger L. Towne, see 14:268; see also T5:1852 (6 references) and T4:1900 (4 references); for reviews by Charles Wm. Martin and Malcolm R. McNeil of an earlier edition, see 11:272.

[1772]
Organic Dysfunction Survey Schedules.

Purpose: To assist in discovering psychological and medical factors that may contribute to treatment.
Population: Adult clients.
Publication Date: 1981.
Acronym: ODSS.
Scores: 22 survey schedules: Arthritis, Asthma, Cancer, Cardiac, Covert Thermal, Cues for Tension and Anxiety, Dysmenorrhea, Gastrointestinal, Guidelines for Cardiac Rehabilitation, Headache, Hypertension, Nutrition, Organic Dysfunction-Medical, Organic Dysfunction-Psychological, Pain, Physical Complaint, Reactions Toward Illness, Renal Failure, Seizure, Stress, Stroke, Vomiting.
Administration: Group or individual.
Manual: No manual.
Price Data, 2001: $79.95 per set of schedules.
Time: Administration time not reported.
Author: Joseph R. Cautela.
Publisher: Cambridge Center for Behavioral Studies.
Cross References: See T5:1853 (1 reference); for reviews by Julian Fabry and George N. Prigitano, see 9:909.

[1773]
Organizational Assessment Survey.

Purpose: Designed to help businesses identify problems leading to low productivity and employee dissatisfaction.
Population: Adult.
Publication Date: 1985.
Acronym: OAS.
Scores, 4: Accomplishment, Recognition, Power, Affiliation.
Administration: Group or individual.
Price Data, 2002: $49.50 per OAS Report Kit including manual, reusable test booklets, and processing of 2 reports; $15.75–$21 each per individual report; $8.50–$12 each per group report.
Time: Untimed.
Authors: Larry A. Breskamp and Martin L. Maehr.
Publisher: MetriTech, Inc.

[1774]
Organizational Behavior Profile.

Purpose: Designed to detect signs of codependency in organizations.

Population: Organizations.
Publication Date: 1993.
Acronym: OBP.
Scores, 4: Closed/Open, Denial/Collusion, Excessive Changes/Crisis Management/Confusion, Excessive Promises.
Administration: Group.
Price Data: Available from publisher.
Time: Administration time not reported.
Comments: Self-scored inventory; completed by members to measure the organization.
Authors: Jeanette Goodstein and Earnie Larsen.
Publisher: Jossey-Bass/Pfeiffer.

[1775]
Organizational Beliefs Questionnaire.

Purpose: "Intended to give concerned managers a deeper understanding of their own organization's culture."
Population: Organizations.
Publication Date: 1997.
Acronym: OBQ.
Scores, 10: Work Can Be As Much Fun As Play, Seek Constant Improvement, Accept Specific And Difficult Goals, Accept Responsibility For Your Actions, Care About One Another, Quality Is Crucially Important, Work Together To Get The Job Done, Have Concern For Measures Of Our Success, There Must Be Hands-On Management, A Strong Set Of Shared Values And Beliefs Guide Our Actions.
Administration: Group.
Price Data, 1997: $195 per basic assessment package; $49.95 per additional reports; $99.95 per 50 additional answer sheets.
Time: Administration time not reported.
Comments: Computerized interpretive information provided by publisher, including scale summaries and individual item analyses.
Author: Marshall Sashkin.
Publisher: Human Resource Development Press.
Cross References: For reviews by Cynthia A. Larson-Daugherty and Mary Roznowski, see 14:269.

[1776]
Organizational Change-Readiness Scale.

Purpose: Constructed "to analyze the ability of an organization to manage change effectively and to plan improvement actions."
Population: Employees.
Publication Date: 1996.
Acronym: OCRS.
Scores: 5 scales: Structural Readiness, Technological Readiness, Climatic Readiness, Systemic Readiness, People Readiness.
Administration: Group.
Price Data, 1996: $6.50 per assessment inventory; $24.95 per facilitator's guide (24 pages).

Time: (20) minutes.
Comments: Redevelopment of Organizational Change-Readiness Survey.
Authors: John E. Jones and William L. Bearley.
Publisher: Human Resource Development Press.
Cross References: For reviews by Gary J. Dean and Eugene P. Sheehan, see 14:270.

[1777]
Organizational Climate Exercise II.

Purpose: "Designed to evaluate the internal environment of an organization."
Population: Work groups.
Publication Dates: 1991–1993.
Acronym: OCE.
Scores, 12: Actual Organizational Climate and Ideal Organizational Climate on 6 dimensions: Flexibility, Responsibility, Standards, Rewards, Clarity, Team Commitment.
Administration: Group or individual.
Price Data, 2001: $69 per complete kit including 10 questionnaires and 10 profiles and interpretive notes (11 pages); $29 per 10 Feedback Version questionnaires; $15 per Trainer's Guide (1993, 31 pages).
Foreign Language Editions: French and Spanish editions available.
Time: [30] minutes.
Comments: Self-scored instrument.
Author: Hay Group.
Publisher: Hay Group..
Cross References: For reviews by Mary Anne Bunda and Erich P. Prien, see 13:217.

[1778]
Organizational Culture Inventory.

Purpose: Designed to measure an organization's current and ideal norms and expectations.
Population: Organizational members.
Publication Dates: 1987–1989.
Acronym: OCI.
Scores: 12 culture styles: Constructive Cultures (Achievement, Self-Actualizing, Humanistic-Encouraging, Affiliative), Passive/Defensive Cultures (Approval, Conventional, Dependent, Avoidance Style), Aggressive/Defensive Cultures (Oppositional, Power, Competitive, Perfectionistic).
Administration: Group or individual.
Forms, 2: OCI Ideal, OCI Current.
Price Data: Price information available from publisher for test materials including Leader's Guide (1989, 74 pages).
Time: [15–20] minutes.
Authors: Robert A. Cooke and J. Clayton Lafferty.
Publisher: Human Synergistics International.
Cross References: See T5:1862 (2 references); for reviews by Charlene M. Alexander and Gargi Roysircar Sodowsky, see 12:272 (1 reference).

[1779]
Organizational Description Questionnaire.

Purpose: Designed to "measure how often each member of the organization perceives the culture of their unit/department/organization to be using a full range of specific leadership factors."
Population: Organizations.
Publication Date: 1992.
Acronym: ODQ.
Scores, 2: Transactional, Transformational.
Administration: Group.
Price Data, 2001: $200 per report including 100 forms; $25 per sampler set (1992, 35 pages); $125 per permission set; $20 per web review set; $80 per web permission set.
Time: (20–25) minutes.
Comments: Time required for entire training module, including questionnaire, is 180–250 minutes.
Authors: Bernard M. Bass and Bruce J. Avolio.
Publisher: Mind Garden, Inc.

[1780]
Organizational Effectiveness Inventory.

Purpose: Determines the impact of organizational, group, and job level factors on organizational effectiveness.
Population: Organization members.
Publication Date: 1997.
Acronym: OEI.
Scores: 41 Outcomes and Causal Factors: Mission and Philosophy (Articulation of Mission, Customer-Service Focus), Structures (Empowerment, Employee Involvement), Systems (Selection /Placement, Training and Development, Respect for Members, Fairness of Appraisals, Use of Rewards, Use of Punishment, Goal Clarity, Goal Challenge, Participative Goal Setting, Goal Acceptance), Technology (Autonomy, Skill Variety, Feedback, Task identity, Significance, Interdependence), Skills/Qualities (Upward Communication, Downward Communication, Communication for Learning, Interaction Facilitation, Task Facilitation, Goal Emphasis, Consideration, Personal Bases of Power, Organizational Bases of Power), Individual Outcomes—Positive Indices (Role Clarity, Motivation, Satisfaction, Intention to Stay), Individual Outcomes—Negative Indices (Role Conflict, Job Insecurity, Stress), Group Outcomes (Intra-Unit Cooperation, Inter-Unit Coordination, Departmental—Level Quality), Organizational Outcomes (Organizational—Level Quality, External Adaptability).
Administration: Individual or group.
Price Data: Available from publisher.
Time: Administration time not reported.
Author: Robert A. Cooke.
Publisher: Human Synergistics International.

[1781]
Orleans-Hanna Algebra Prognosis Test, Third Edition.

Purpose: Designed as a predictor of student success in first-year algebra.
Population: Grades 7 and over.
Publication Dates: 1928–1998.
Scores: Total score only.
Administration: Group.
Price Data, 2002: $75.50 per 25 test booklets and manual; $24.90 per hand-scorable key; $30.75 per 25 answer documents (specify hand-scorable or NCS machine-scorable); $9.50 per class record; $24.90 per manual; $2.25 per pupil for basic NCS scoring service which includes 1 copy of the master list with summary by class, school, or district; optional services are also available.
Time: 40(55–60) minutes.
Authors: Gerald S. Hanna and Joseph B. Orleans.
Publisher: The Psychological Corporation.
Cross References: See T4:1910 (3 references); for reviews by Dietmar Kuchemann and Charles Secolsky, see 9:912 (1 reference); see also T2:688 (11 references); for reviews by W. L. Bashaw and Cyril J. Hoyt of an earlier edition, see 7:510 (3 references); for reviews by Harold Gulliksen and Emma Spany, see 4:396 (1 reference); for a review by S. S. Wilks, see 2:1444 (4 references).

[1782]
Orpheus.

Purpose: To assess work-based personality for use in selection, team building, and personal development.
Population: Adults.
Publication Date: 1996.
Scores: Total score only.
Administration: Group or individual.
Price Data, 2002: $361.94 per complete kit.
Time: (20) minutes.
Author: John Rust.
Publisher: The Psychological Corporation Europe [United Kingdom].

[1783]
The "Orton" Intelligence Test, No. 4.

Purpose: Determines children's mental age.
Population: Ages 9–14.
Publication Date: 1931.
Scores: Total score only.
Administration: Group.
Manual: No manual.
Price Data: Not available.
Time: 60(70) minutes.
Author: Gibson (Robert) & Sons, Glasgow, Ltd.
Publisher: Gibson (Robert) & Sons, Glasgow, Ltd. [Scotland] [No reply from publisher; status unknown].

[1784]
OSOT Perceptual Evaluation.

Purpose: Designed to identify perceptual impairment in adults.
Population: Adults.
Publication Date: 1991.
Scores, 19: Scanning, Spatial Neglect, Motor Planning, Copying 2 Dimensional Designs, Copying 3 Dimensional Designs, Body Puzzle, Draw-a-Person, Right/Left Discrimination, Clock, Peg Board, Draw-a-House, Shape Recognition, Colour Recognition, Size Recognition, Figure Ground Discrimination, Proprioception, Stereognosis R, Stereognosis L, Total.
Administration: Individual.
Price Data, 2001: 725 per test kit; $75 per manual (60 pages).
Time: Administration time not reported.
Authors: Pat Fisher, Marian Boys, and Claire Holzberg.
Publisher: Nelson Thomson Learning [Canada].
Cross References: For a review by Raoula Arreola, see 12:274.

[1785]
Otis-Lennon School Ability Test®, Seventh Edition.

Purpose: "Designed to measure abstract thinking and reasoning ability."
Population: Grades K–12.
Publication Dates: 1977–1996.
Acronym: OLSAT®.
Scores, 3: Verbal, Nonverbal, Total.
Administration: Group.
Levels, 7: A, B, C, D, E, F, G.
Forms, 3: 1, 2, 3.
Price Data, 2002: $25.50 per examination kit including one test booklet and directions for administering (Form 3, Levels A-G); $95 per 25 Type 1 machine-scorable test booklets including 1 directions for administering (Form 3, Levels AD); $70 per 25 test booklets (specify reusable or hand scorable, and level); $29 per 25 Type 1 machine-scorable answer documents; $29 per 25 hand-scorable answer documents; $70 per technical manual; $14.50 per separate directions for administering; $49 per side-by-side keys for hand-scorable test booklets; $25 per stencil keys for hand-scorable answer documents; $25 per overlay keys for Type 1 machine-scorable answer documents; $6 per response keys (Form 3, specify level); $14.50 per 25 practice tests, including 1 directions for administering (Form 3, specify level); $6 per separate directions for administering practice tests; $75 per norms book (specify spring or fall); $6.50 per class records (Form 3, specify level).
Comments: Originally titled Otis-Lennon Mental Ability Test.

Authors: Arthur S. Otis and Roger T. Lennon.
Publisher: Harcourt Educational Measurement.
   a) LEVEL A.
   Population: Grade K.
   Time: (70) minutes over 2 sessions.
   Comments: Orally administered.
   b) LEVEL B.
   Population: Grade 1.
   Time: Same as *a* above.
   Comments: Orally administered.
   c) LEVEL C.
   Population: Grade 2.
   Time: Same as *a* above.
   Comments: Partially self-administered.
   d) LEVEL D.
   Population: Grade 3.
   Time: (60) minutes.
   Comments: Self-administered.
   e) LEVEL E.
   Population: Grades 4–5.
   Time: Same as *d* above.
   Comments: Self-administered.
   f) LEVEL F.
   Population: Grades 6–8.
   Time: Same as *d* above.
   Comments: Self-administered.
   g) LEVEL G.
   Population: Grades 9–12.
   Time: Same as *d* above.
   Comments: Self-administered.
Cross References: For reviews by Lizanne DeStefano and Bert A. Goldman, see 14:271; see also T5:1866 (45 references) and T4:1913 (8 references); for reviews by Anne Anastasi and Mark E. Swerdlik of an earlier edition, see 11:274 (48 references); for reviews by Calvin O. Dyer and Thomas Oakland of an earlier edition, see 9:913 (7 references); see also T3:1754 (64 references); 8:198 (35 references), and T2:424 (10 references); for a review by John E. Milholland and excerpted reviews by Arden Grotelueschen and Arthur E. Smith of an earlier edition, see 7:370 (6 references).

[1786]
Our Class and Its Work.

Purpose: "To measure those teaching behaviors believed to contribute to student achievement in the classroom."
Population: Grades 3–12.
Publication Date: 1983.
Acronym: OCIW.
Scores, 9: Didactic Instruction, Enthusiasm, Feedback, Instructional Time, Opportunity to Learn, Pacing, Structuring Comments, Task Orientation, Total.
Administration: Group.
Price Data: Available from publisher.
Time: Administration time not reported.
Comments: Self-report instrument.
Authors: Maurice J. Eash and Hersholt C. Waxman.
Publisher: Maurice J. Eash [No reply from publisher; status unknown].
Cross References: See T4:1914 (1 reference); for reviews by James R. Barclay and F. Charles Mace, see 10:269 (1 reference).

[1787]
Outcomes: Planning, Monitoring, Evaluating.

Purpose: "A tool for monitoring student progress toward selected goals."
Population: Grades K–12.
Publication Date: 2001.
Acronym: PME.
Scores, 8: Concern Description, Goals and Benchmarks, Benchmark Sealing, Social-Validation Criteria, Intervention Planning, Progress-Monitoring Procedures, Progress Chart, Progress Analysis.
Administration: Individual.
Price Data, 2002: $85 per complete kit including manual (2002, 139 pages), binder, and 25 record forms; $50 per manual; $40 per 25 record forms.
Time: Administration time not reported.
Comments: Provides a framework for documenting education professionals' problem-solving efforts; helps identify concerns, describe context of problem, rate baseline performance, operationalize goals, plan intervention, monitor and graph student progress, evaluate intervention outcomes, plan next steps.
Authors: Karen Callan Stoiber and Thomas R. Kratochwill.
Publisher: The Psychological Corporation.

[1788]
Pain Assessment Battery, Research Edition.

Purpose: Constructed as "a comprehensive assessment tool for evaluating and documenting the physical, experiential, behavioral, and psychological dimensions of chronic pain."
Population: Patients with chronic pain.
Publication Dates: 1993–1999.
Acronym: PAB-RE.
Scores: 7 tests: Pain History and Status Interview, Pain Imagery Interview, Pain Experience Scale, Pain Coping Interview—Research Edition, Stress Symptoms Checklist, Coping Style Profile, Interview Behavior Checklist.
Administration: Individual.
Price Data, 2002: $400 per test.
Time: (10–120) minutes.
Comments: Research instrument; computer-administered (DOS version only).
Authors: Bruce N. Eimer and Lyle M. Allen, III.
Publisher: CogniSyst, Inc.

Cross References: For reviews by M. Allan Cooperstein and F. Felicia Ferrara, see 14:272.

[1789]
Pain Patient Profile.

Purpose: "Designed to identify patients who are experiencing emotional distress associated with primary complaints of pain and assess the severity of distress in comparison to community and pain patient population national sample.

Population: Pain patients aged 17–76.
Publication Dates: 1992–1995.
Acronym: P-3®.
Scores, 4: Depression, Anxiety, Somatization, Validity Index.
Administration: Group.
Price Data, 2002: $57.50 per preview package including manual (1995, 89 pages), and answer sheets with test items for three assessments (specify Microtest or mail-in scoring); $86 per 50 hand-scorable answer sheets; $10 per MICROTEST Q interpretive report; $12 per mail-in interpretive report includihng answer sheet with test items; $30 per manual.
Time: (10–15) minutes.
Authors: C. David Tollison and Jerry C. Langley.
Publisher: NCS Assessments (Minnetonka).
Cross References: For reviews by Gregory J. Boyle and Ronald J. Ganellen, see 14:273.

[1790]
Pair Attraction Inventory.

Purpose: "Designed to measure both complementarity and symmetry in pair relationships."
Population: College and adults.
Publication Dates: 1970–1971.
Acronym: PAI.
Scores, 7: Mother-Son, Daddy-Doll, Bitch-Nice Guy, Master-Servant, Hawks, Doves, Person-Person.
Administration: Individual.
Price Data, 1998: $20.25 per 25 test booklets (specify male or female); $12.50 per 50 answer sheets; $11.75 per 50 profile sheets; $4 per manual; $20.25 per kit of materials for individual administration including 3 male booklets, 3 female booklets, 50 answer sheets, 50 profiles, and manual.
Time: (20-30) minutes.
Author: Everett L. Shostrom.
Publisher: EdITS/Educational and Industrial Testing Service.
Cross References: For a review by James R. Clopton, see 8:349 (10 references).

[1791]
Panic and Agoraphobia Scale.

Purpose: "Determine[s] the severity of panic disorder with or without agoraphobia and ... monitor[s] treatment efficacy."

Population: Age 16 and older.
Publication Dates: 1999–2000.
Acronym: PAS.
Scores, 6: Panic Attacks, Agoraphobic Avoidance, Anticipatory Anxiety, Disability, Worries About Health, Total.
Administration: Group.
Forms, 2: Observer-rated, self-rated.
Price Data, 2001: $79.50 per kit including manual (1999, 88 pages), 50 observer-rated scales, and 50 patient questionnaires; $14.50 per 50 patient questionnaires; $12 per 50 observer-rated scales; $49 per manual; $4 per folder.
Time: (5–10) minutes for observer-rated scale.
Comments: Self-administered; computerized version of self-rated scale in preparation; compatible with DSM-IV and ICD-10 classifications.
Author: Borwin Bandelow.
Publisher: Hogrefe & Huber Publishers.

[1792]
Paper and Pencil Games.

Purpose: Constructed to measure "figural, quantitative and verbal skills closely related to scholastic achievement."

Population: Pupils in their second, third and fourth years in South African school system.
Publication Date: 1996.
Acronym: PPG.
Administration: Group.
Levels, 2: 2, 3.
Price Data, 2002: R5.13 per test booklet (specify level); R3.99 per Level 2 short version test booklet; R1.14 per practice test; R39.90 per manual (90 pages) (English only); R28.50 per directions for administration (specify language).
Time: (150–180) minutes including 20-minute break.
Comments: Available in Afrikaans, Ndebele, Northern Sotho, Swati, Southern Sotho, Tsonga, Tswana, Venda, Xhosa, and Zulu.
Author: N. C. W. Claassen.
Publisher: Human Sciences Research Council [South Africa].

a) LEVEL 2.
Population: School years 2–3.
Scores, 5: Classification, Verbal and Quantitative Reasoning, Figure Series, Comprehension, Pattern Completion.

b) LEVEL 3.
Population: School years 3–4.
Scores, 5: Figure Series, Verbal and Quantitative Reasoning, Pattern Completion, Comprehension, Number Series.

Cross References: For a review by Gary L. Marco, see 14:274.

[1793]
PAR: Proficiency Assessment Report.

Purpose: Developed to identify proficiency in 22 abilities associated with effective management.
Population: Supervisors and managers.
Publication Date: 1989.
Scores, 24: 22 Ability Scores, 2 Style Scores.
Administration: Group or individual.
Manual: No manual.
Price Data: Available from publisher.
Time: (30) minutes.
Comments: Ratings by manager and self; administered prior to training program and then discussed in pairs.
Author: Training House, Inc.
Publisher: Training House, Inc.
Cross References: For reviews by Stephen F. Davis and S. Alvin Leung, see 12:276.

[1794]
Parallel Spelling Tests, Second Edition.

Purpose: Designed to help "chart children's progress in spelling."
Population: Ages 6 to 13 years.
Publication Dates: 1983–1998.
Scores: Total score only.
Administration: Group.
Price Data, 2002: £16.99 per test booklet/manual (1998, 40 pages).
Time: (20) minutes per test.
Comments: Teachers create tests from two banks of items: A (for ages 6 to 10) and B (for ages 9 to 13).
Author: Dennis Young.
Publisher: Hodder & Stoughton Educational [England].
Cross References: For reviews by Theresa G. Siskind and Lisa F. Smith, see 14:275; for reviews by Steven R. Shaw and Mark E. Swerdlik and by Claudia R. Wright of an earlier edition, see 12:277.

[1795]
A Parent-Adolescent Communication Inventory.

Purpose: "Designed to measure the parent's perceived communication with the adolescent."
Population: Parents and adolescents.
Publication Dates: 1968–1979.
Acronym: PACI.
Scores: Total score only.
Administration: Group.
Price Data: Price information available from publisher for parent or adolescent form and user's guide (1969, 4 pages).
Time: (20) minutes.
Author: Millard J. Bienvenu.
Publisher: Millard J. Bienvenu, Northwest Publications.

Cross References: See T5:1876 (1 reference) and T4:1929 (1 reference); for a review by Mark W. Roberts, see 9:916 (12 references); see also T3:1761 (2 references) and T2:1310 (1 reference); for a review by David B. Orr of an earlier edition, see 7:119 (3 references).

[1796]
Parent-Adolescent Communication Scale.

Purpose: Designed to assess "the views of adolescents and their parents regarding their perceptions and experience of communication with each other."
Population: Adolescents and their parents.
Publication Date: 1982.
Scores, 3: 2 subscale scores (Open Family Communication, Problems in Family Communication), Total Communication.
Administration: Group.
Price Data, 1998: $20 per manual (16 pages) including scale.
Time: (5–10) minutes.
Authors: Howard Barnes and David H. Olson.
Publisher: Life Innovations, Inc.
Cross References: See T5:1877 (2 references); for reviews by Allen Jack Edwards and Steven Ira Pfeiffer, see 12:278 (7 references); see also T4:1930 (3 references).

[1797]
Parent as a Teacher Inventory [Revised].

Purpose: "Intended to help mothers and fathers of preschool and primary grade children ... recognize their favorable qualities and identify realms in which further personal growth is needed."
Population: Mothers and fathers of children ages 3–9.
Publication Dates: 1978–1995.
Acronym: PAAT.
Scores, 6: Creativity, Frustration, Control, Play, Teaching/Learning, Total.
Administration: Group.
Price Data, 2002: $58.45 per starter set including manual (1995, 29 pages), 20 inventory booklets/identification questionnaires, and 20 profiles (specify English or Spanish); $22.15 per 20 inventory booklets/identification questionnaires; $21.20 per 20 profiles; $18.85 per manual; $20.90 per sample set.
Foreign Language Edition: Spanish edition available.
Time: (30–45) minutes.
Author: Robert D. Strom.
Publisher: Scholastic Testing Service, Inc.
Cross References: See T5:1878 (1 reference); for reviews by Alice J. Corkill and Ralph F. Darr, Jr., see 13:218 (4 references); see also T4:1922 (6 references); for a review by Elizabeth A. Robinson of an earlier edition, see 9:917 (1 reference).

[1798]
Parent Awareness Skills Survey.

Purpose: Constructed to identify strengths and weaknesses in a parent's sensitivity to typical child care situations.
Population: Parents involved in custody decisions.
Publication Dates: 1990–2002.
Acronym: PASS.
Scores, 18: 6 categories (Awareness of Critical Issues, Awareness of Adequate Solutions, Awareness of Communicating in Understandable Terms, Awareness of Acknowledging Feelings, Awareness of the Importance of Relevant Aspects of a Child's Past History, Awareness of Feedback Data) for each of the following conditions (Spontaneous Level, Probe Level One, Probe Level Two).
Administration: Individual.
Price Data, 2002: $189 per complete kit including 8 booklets, 8 scoring summaries, answer pen, updates, and manual and scoring guide; $99 per 8 booklets; $159 per 16 booklets; $199 per 24 booklets; $129 per manual and scoring guide
Time: [30–60] minutes.
Comments: Orally administered.
Author: Barry Bricklin.
Publisher: Village Publishing.
Cross References: For reviews by Lisa G. Bischoff and Debra E. Cole, see 12:279.

[1799]
Parent Behavior Form.

Purpose: "Designed to assess ... dimensions of perceived parent behavior."
Population: Parents; ratings by ages 8–12, 12–18 and adults.
Publication Date: No date.
Acronym: PBF.
Scores, 15: Acceptance, Active Involvement, Egalitarianism, Cognitive Independence, Cognitive-Understanding, Cognitive Competence, Lax Control, Conformity, Achievement, Strict Control, Punitive Control, Hostile Control, Rejection, Inconsistent Responding, Social Desirability.
Administration: Group or individual.
Forms, 5: PBF, PBF-S, PBF Elementary, Form A, Form C-B.
Price Data: Available from publisher.
Time: Administration time not reported.
Comments: Ratings of parent behavior by their children; form for parent self-rating available.
Authors: Leonard Worell and Judith Worell.
Publisher: Judith Worell, Ph.D.
Cross References: See T5:1881 (3 references) and T4:1925 (1 reference); for reviews by JoEllen V. Carlson and Stephen Olejnik, see 11:277 (1 reference).

[1800]
Parent-Child Communication Inventory.

Purpose: "To better understand how parents and their children communicate."
Population: Children and parents.
Publication Date: 1974.
Acronym: PCCI.
Scores, 2: Total Child, Total Parent.
Administration: Group.
Manual: No manual.
Price Data: Price information available from publisher for child form, parent form, and guide.
Time: Administration time not reported.
Author: Millard J. Bienvenu.
Publisher: Millard J. Bienvenu, Northwest Publications.

[1801]
Parent-Child Relationship Inventory.

Purpose: "Assesses parents' attitudes toward parenting and toward their children."
Population: Parents of 3–15-year-old children.
Publication Date: 1994.
Acronym: PCRI.
Scores, 9: 7 content scales (Parental Support, Satisfaction With Parenting, Involvement, Communication, Limit Setting, Autonomy, Role Orientation), 2 validity indicators (Social Desirability, Inconsistency).
Administration: Group.
Price Data, 2002: $104 per complete kit including manual (57 pages), 25 AutoScore™ answer sheets, 2-use disk, and 2 PC answer sheets for on-site computer scoring and interpretation; $38.50 per 25 AutoScore™ answer sheets; $48 per manual; $15 per each mail-in computer scored and interpreted answer sheet; $285 per 25-use disk (PC with Microsoft Windows); $15 per 100 microcomputer answer sheets; $15 each for FAX service scoring.
Time: (15) minutes.
Comments: Self-report; microcomputer edition available.
Author: Anthony B. Gerard.
Publisher: Western Psychological Services.
Cross References: See T5:1883 (1 reference); for reviews by Roger A. Boothroyd and Gregory J. Marchant, see 13:220.

[1802]
Parent/Family Involvement Index.

Purpose: "Measure of the extent to which parents are involved in their child's special education program."
Population: Parents with children in special education programs.
Publication Dates: 1984–1985.
Acronym: P/FII.

Scores, 13: Contact with Teacher, Participation in the Special Education Process, Transportation, Observations at School, Educational Activities at Home, Attending Parent Education/Consultation Meetings, Classroom Volunteering, Involvement with Administration, Involvement in Fund Raising Activities, Involvement in Advocacy Groups, Disseminating Information, Involvement Total, Total.
Administration: Group.
Price Data, 1998: $5 per index and mimeographed paper (1985, 21 pages).
Time: (12–15) minutes.
Comments: Ratings by teachers.
Authors: John D. Cone, David D. DeLawyer, and Vicky V. Wolfe.
Publisher: John D. Cone.
Cross References: For reviews by Marilyn Friend and Koressa Kutsick, see 10:270.

[1803]
Parent Opinion Inventory, Revised Edition.

Purpose: Designed "to provide the school personnel or administrator(s) with the opinions of parents in regard to how they believe the school is meeting the needs of students."
Population: Parents of school children.
Publication Dates: 1976–1995.
Scores: 4 subscales: Parent/School/Community Relations, Quality of the Instructional Program, Support for Student Learning, School Climate/Environment for Learning.
Administration: Group.
Parts, 2: A (Likert-scale items), B (customize up to 20 local questions).
Foreign Language Edition: Available in Spanish.
Price Data, 1998: $15 per 25 inventories; $6.50 per manual (1995, 26 pages).
Time: Untimed.
Author: National Study of School Evaluation.
Publisher: National Study of School Evaluation.

[1804]
Parent Perception of Child Profile.

Purpose: Designed to elicit a parent's knowledge and understanding of a child.
Population: Parents.
Publication Dates: 1991–2002.
Acronym: PPCP.
Scores, 13: Interpersonal Relations, Daily Routine, Health History, Developmental History, School History, Fears, Communication Style, Depth of Knowledge, Scope of Knowledge, Emotional Tone, Value/Philosophy, Areas Needing Attention, Recall.
Administration: Individual.

Price Data, 2002: $189 per comprehensive starting kit including directions (1991, 11 pages), 8 Q-books, 8 recall worksheets, 8 summary forms, "answer" pen (black), "other source" pen (red), and updates; $99 per 8 Q-books with recall worksheets and summary sheets; $159 per 16 Q-books with recall worksheets and summary sheets; $199 per 24 Q-books with recall worksheets and summary sheets; $109 per directions.
Time: (60) minutes.
Comments: Self- or evaluator-administered.
Authors: Barry Bricklin and Gail Elliot.
Publisher: Village Publishing.
Cross References: For reviews by Robert W. Hiltonsmith and Mary Lou Kelley, see 12:280.

[1805]
Parent/Teacher Conference Checklist.

Purpose: Designed "to provide a self-evaluation of the teacher's role in the parent/teacher conference."
Population: Teachers.
Publication Date: 1988.
Scores: Not scored.
Administration: Individual.
Manual: No manual.
Price Data, 2002: $10 per 25 forms.
Time: [5–10] minutes.
Comments: Self-report inventory; title on checklist is Parent Conference Evaluation Form.
Author: Academic Consulting & Testing Service.
Publisher: Academic Consulting & Testing Service.

[1806]
The Parenthood Questionnaire.

Purpose: Designed to obtain information from youth concerning their opinions and knowledge of parenting and child development.
Population: Youth who are prospective parents or who may work with children in the future.
Publication Dates: 1977–1978.
Scores: 9 subsections: Opinions About Marriage and Having Children, Feelings About Parenthood, Feelings About Myself, Opinions About Children, Understanding of Children, Child Care Skills, Before Birth, Family Life Situations, Knowledge and Opinions About Sex.
Administration: Group.
Price Data: Available from publisher.
Foreign Language Edition: Spanish version available.
Time: Administration time not reported.
Comments: Intended for use in parent-training or child care training programs; manual title is Education for Parenthood: A Program, Curriculum, and Evaluation Guide.
Authors: James C. Petersen, Jean M. Baker, Larry A. Morris, and Rachel Burkholder.
Publisher: The Assessment and Development Centre.

[1807]
Parenting Alliance Measure.

Purpose: "Measures the strength of the perceived alliance between parents of children ages 1 to 19 years"; and "reflects the parents' ability to cooperate with each other in meeting the needs of the child."

Population: Parents of children ages 1–19 years.

Publication Dates: 1988–1999.

Acronym: PAM.

Scores: Total score only.

Administration: Group.

Price Data: Available from publisher for introductory kit; $30 per 25 test forms; $30 per professional manual (1999, 58 pages).

Time: (5–15) minutes.

Authors: Richard R. Abidin (test) and Timothy R. Konold (manual and test).

Publisher: Psychological Assessment Resources, Inc.

[1808]
Parenting Satisfaction Scale™.

Purpose: Designed to assess "parents' attitudes toward parenting."

Population: Adults with dependent children.

Publication Date: 1994.

Acronym: PSS.

Scores, 3: Satisfaction with Spouse/Ex-Spouse Parenting Performance, Satisfaction with the Parent-Child Relationship, Satisfaction with Parenting Performance.

Administration: Group.

Price Data, 2002: $119 per comprehensive kit including manual (47 pages) and 25 ReadyScore® answer documents; $37 per 25 ReadyScore® answer documents; $87 per manual.

Time: (30) minutes.

Authors: John Guidubaldi and Helen K. Cleminshaw.

Publisher: The Psychological Corporation.

Cross References: For reviews by Ira Stuart Katz and Janet V. Smith, see 14:276; see also T5:1888 (1 reference).

[1809]
Parenting Stress Index, Third Edition.

Purpose: To identify stressors experienced by parents that are related to dysfunctional parenting.

Population: Parents of children 12 years old or younger.

Publication Dates: 1983–1995.

Acronym: PSI.

Scores, 15: Child Domain (Adaptability, Acceptability, Demandingness, Mood, Hyperactivity and Distractibility, Reinforces Parent), Parent Domain (Depression, Attachment, Restrictions of Role, Sense of Competence, Social Isolation, Relationship with Spouse, Parental Health), Life Stress, Total Score.

Administration: Group.

Forms, 2: Full Length, Short Form.

Price Data: Available from publisher.

Time: (20–30) minutes.

Comments: Self-scoring; also can be computer administered (requires Windows 95/98/NT/2000/ME; 8 MB hard drive space; 16 MB RAM for Windows 95/98/ME or 24 MB RAM for Windows NT 4.0 and Windows 2000; Standard 3-5-inch 1.44 MB floppy drive for installation.

Authors: Richard R. Abidin, and PAR Staff (Software Portfolio).

Publisher: Psychological Assessment Resources, Inc.

Cross References: See T5:1889 (20 references); for reviews by Julie A. Allison and by Laura L. B. Barnes and Judy J. Oehler-Stinnett, see 13:221 (51 references); see also T4:1933 (22 references); for reviews by Frank M. Gresham and Richard A. Wantz of an earlier edition, see 10:271 (2 references).

[1810]
Parents' Evaluation of Developmental Status.

Purpose: Designed to help "identify children at risk for school problems and those with undetected developmental and behavioral disabilities"; "helps providers decide when to refer, reassure, advise, wait and see versus screen."

Population: Birth–8 years.

Publication Dates: 1997–1998.

Acronym: PEDS.

Scores, 3: Low Risk, Medium Risk, High Risk.

Administration: Individual.

Price Data: Available from publisher.

Foreign Language Edition: Spanish version available.

Time: (2–5) minutes.

Comments: Questionnaire for parents about children; can be administered as an interview or in paper and pencil form.

Author: Frances Page Glascoe.

Publisher: Ellsworth & Vandermeer Press, Ltd.

Cross References: For reviews by Lisa Bischoff and Mark W. Roberts, see 14:277.

[1811]
Parents' Observation of Study Behaviors Survey.

Purpose: To measure students' improvement in study habits and behaviors.

Population: Grades 6–13.

Publication Date: 1991.

Scores, 4: Positive Attitudes, Useful Work Habits, Efficient Learning Tools, Effective Test Taking.

Administration: Individual.

Price Data, 2001: $3 per survey.

Time: Administration time not reported.

Comments: Ratings by parents.

Author: The Cambridge Stratford Study Skills Institute.
Publisher: The Cambridge Stratford Study Skills Institute.

[1812]
Parker Team Player Survey.
Purpose: "Helps individuals identify their primary team player styles."
Population: Employees.
Publication Date: 1991.
Acronym: PTPS.
Scores, 4: Contributor, Collaborator, Communicator, Challenger.
Administration: Group or individual.
Time: (15) minutes.
Comments: Self-scored.
Author: Glenn M. Parker.
Publisher: Consulting Psychologists Press, Inc.
   a) PARKER TEAM PLAYER SURVEY.
   Price Data, 2001: $9 per test booklet/manual (23 pages).
   b) PTPS: STYLES OF ANOTHER PERSON.
   Price Data: $6.75 per test booklet/manual (12 pages).
Cross References: For reviews by Gary J. Dean and Richard B. Stuart, see 13:222 (1 reference).

[1813]
A Partial Index of Modernization: Measurement of Attitudes Toward Morality.
Purpose: Designed to measure attitudes toward morality issues.
Population: Children and adults.
Publication Date: 1972.
Scores: Total score only.
Administration: Group.
Manual: No manual.
Price Data, 2002: $1 per scale.
Time: [8] minutes.
Comments: Supplementary article available.
Author: Panos D. Bardis.
Publisher: Donna Bardis.
Cross References: See 8:464 (1 reference).

[1814]
Participative Management Survey.
Purpose: To assess the extent to which a leader provides opportunities and support for employee involvement.
Population: Individuals involved in a leadership capacity with others.
Publication Date: 1988.
Acronym: PMS.
Scores, 5: Basic Creature Comfort, Safety, Belonging, Ego-Status, Actualization.
Administration: Group or individual.

Price Data, 2001: $8.95 per instrument (17 pages).
Time: Administration time not reported.
Author: Jay Hall.
Publisher: Teleometrics International.

[1815]
PASAT 2000 [Poppleton Allen Sales Aptitude Test].
Purpose: "Designed to measure those personality attributes which have a direct relevance to success in sales roles."
Population: Adults.
Publication Date: 1999.
Acronym: PASAT 2000.
Scores: 11 scales: Motivational, Emotional, Social, Adaptability, Conscientious, Emotional Stability, Social Control, Self-Assurance, Attentive Distortion, Adaptive Distortion, Social Distortion.
Administration: Group.
Price Data: Available from publisher.
Time: (20) minutes.
Authors: Steve Poppleton and Peter Jones
Publisher: The Test Agency Limited [England].
Cross References: For reviews by Larry Cochran and David O. Herman of an earlier edition of the Poppleton Allen Sales Aptitude Test, see 10:285.

[1816]
Pathways to Independence, Second Edition.
Purpose: Assess skills that contribute to personal and social independence.
Population: Disadvantaged school-aged children and mentally and otherwise handicapped teenagers and adults and rehabilitating brain-damaged and geriatric patients.
Publication Dates: 1982–1998.
Scores: Checklists for recording behavior in 11 areas: Eating and Drinking, Domestic Tasks, Cleanliness and Health, Clothing, Giving Information, Use of Information, Time, Money, Freedom of Movement, Use of Amenities, Leisure.
Administration: Individual.
Manual: No manual.
Price Data, 2002: £22.99 per 10 checklists, including instructions and profile sheet; £4.99 per specimen copy.
Time: Administration time not reported.
Authors: Dorothy M. Jeffree and Sally Cheseld'
Publisher: Hodder & Stoughton Educationa' gland].
Cross References: See T5:1897 (1 refe' T4:1940 (2 references).

[1817]
The Patterned Elicitation Syr Morphonemic Analysis.
Purpose: Designed to determ'
expressive grammatical skills a'

Population: Ages 3–0 to 7–6.
Publication Dates: 1981–1993.
Acronym: PEST.
Scores, 13: Articles, Adjectives, Auxilaries/Modals/Copulas, Conjunctions, Negatives, Plurals, Possessives, Pronouns, Questions, Verbs, Subject/Verb Agreement, Embedded Elements, Total.
Administration: Individual.
Price Data, 1998: $61 per complete kit including manual (1993, 18 pages), stimulus picture book, and 10 data form booklets; $20 per 10 data form booklets.
Time: (15–20) minutes.
Comments: Previously titled The Patterned Elicitation Syntax Test.
Authors: Edna Carter Young and Joseph J. Perachio.
Publisher: Communication Skill Builders—A Division of The Psychological Corporation.
Cross References: For reviews by Clinton W. Bennett and Sheila R. Pratt, see 13:223 (2 references); for a review by Carolyn Peluso Atkins of an earlier edition, see 9:921.

[1818]
Paulhus Deception Scales: Balanced Inventory of Desirable Responding Version 7.

Purpose: Designed to measure the tendency to give socially desirable responses to tests.
Population: Ages 16 and older.
Publication Dates: 1998–1999.
Acronym: PDS.
Scores, 2: Impression Management, Self-Deceptive Enhancement.
Administration: Group.
Price Data, 1999: $50 per complete kit including 25 QuikScore™ forms and manual; $25 per 25 QuikScore™ forms; $30 per manual.
Time: (5–7) minutes.
Comments: Self-report; computerized version for Windows™ available on CD.
Author: Delroy L. Paulhus.
Publisher: Multi-Health Systems, Inc.
Cross References: See T5:1898 (1 reference).

[1819]
P.C. User Aptitude Test.

Purpose: To evaluate the practical and analytical skills required for the effective use of microcomputers.
Population: Applicants for positions involving the use of microcomputers.
Publication Date: 1986.
Acronym: WMICRO.
Scores: Total Score, Narrative Evaluation, Ranking, Recommendation.
Administration: Group.
Price Data, 2001: $235 per candidate; quantity discounts available.

Foreign Language Edition: French edition available.
Time: 75 minutes.
Comments: Graded by publisher; must be proctored; previously listed as Microcomputer User Aptitude Test.
Author: Richard Label.
Publisher: Walden Personnel Performance, Inc. [Canada].
Cross References: For a review by Robert Fitzpatrick, see 11:473.

[1820]
PDI Employment Inventory and PDI Customer Service Inventory.

Purpose: Designed to identify job applicants most likely to display positive employee traits.
Population: Job applicants.
Publication Dates: 1985–1993.
Administration: Group.
Price Data: Available from publisher.
Time: (30) minutes.
Comments: Paper and pencil inventories of attitudes and self-descriptions; oral instructions; computer-scored.
Authors: George E. Paajanen, Timothy L. Hansen, and Richard A. McLellan.
Publisher: Personnel Decisions, Inc.

a) PDI EMPLOYMENT INVENTORY.
Purpose: Designed to identify job applicants who will be likely to be productive and to stay on the job at least 3 months.
Publication Dates: 1985–1993.
Acronym: PDI-EI.
Scores, 2: Performance, Tenure.
Foreign Language and Other Special Editions: Foreign and bilingual editions available include American Spanish/English, French-Canadian English, Mexican Spanish, British English, and Vietnamese/English.
b) PDI CUSTOMER SERVICE INVENTORY.
Purpose: Designed to identify job applicants most likely to exhibit helpful and positive behaviors in interacting with customers.
Publication Dates: 1991–1993.
Acronym: PDI-CSI.
Score: Customer Service Knowledge and Skills (Total).
Foreign Language Edition: Spanish-English edition available.
Cross References: For reviews by Gordon C. Bruner II and Annie W. Ward, see 14:278.

[1821]
Peabody Developmental Motor Scales—Second Edition.

Purpose: Designed "to assess gross motor skills and fine motor skills."

Population: Birth to 72 months.
Publication Dates: 1983–2000.
Acronym: PDMS-2.
Scores, 9: Reflexes, Stationary, Locomotion, Object Manipulation, Grasping, Visual-Motor Integration, Gross Motor, Fine Motor, Total Motor.
Administration: Individual.
Price Data, 2001: $389 per complete kit; $309 per complete test; $59 per examiner record booklets; $24 per profile summary forms; $79 per motor activities program; $49 per object kit; $9 per shape cards/BLM kit; $89 per guide to item administration; $79 per examiner's manual (2000, 234 pages); $18 per color chart; $109 per software CD (PC; Windows 95/98).
Time: (45–60) minutes.
Authors: M. Rhonda Folio and Rebecca R. Fewell.
Publisher: PRO-ED.
Cross References: See T5:1901 (19 references) and T4:1943 (3 references); for a review by Homer B. C. Read, Jr. of an earlier edition, see 9:922.

[1822]
Peabody Individual Achievement Test—Revised [1998 Normative Update].

Purpose: Designed to measure academic achievement.
Population: Grades K–12.
Publication Dates: 1970–1998.
Acronym: PIAT-R.
Scores, 9: General Information, Reading Recognition, Reading Comprehension, Total Reading, Mathematics, Spelling, Total Test, Written Expression, Written Language.
Administration: Individual.
Levels: 2 for Written Expression subtest (Level I: Grades K–1; Level II: Grades 2–12).
Price Data, 2002: $325.95 per complete kit including 50 combined test record and written response booklets, and manual (1998, 271 pages); $73.95 per 50 combined record/response booklets; $94.95 per manual; $16.95 per pronunciation guide cassette; $199.95 per software package (specify DOS 3.5-inch or 5.25-inch, Windows, or Macintosh).
Time: (60) minutes.
Comments: This test (PIAT-R [1998 Normative Update]) is the same as the PIAT-R (1989) but with new norms.
Author: Frederick C. Markwardt, Jr.
Publisher: American Guidance Service, Inc.
Cross References: For reviews by Lawrence H. Cross and Jennifer J. Fager, see 14:279; see also T5:1902 (103 references) and T4:1944 (33 references); for reviews by Kathryn M. Benes and Bruce G. Rogers of an earlier version, see 11:280 (125 references); see also 9:923 (39 references), T4:1944 (33 references), and T3:1769 (67 references); for excerpted reviews by Alex

Bannatyne and Barton B. Proger of the original edition, see 8:24 (36 references); see also T2:26 (2 references); for a review by Howard B. Lyman of the original edition, see 7:17.

[1823]
Peabody Picture Vocabulary Test—III.

Purpose: Designed to measure receptive vocabulary and can also be used as a screening test of verbal ability.
Population: Ages 2.5–90.
Publication Dates: 1959–1997.
Acronym: PPVT-III.
Scores: Total score only.
Administration: Individual.
Forms, 2: IIIA, IIIB.
Price Data, 2002: $249.95 per complete kit including all testing materials for Forms IIIA and IIIB, 2 norms booklets (1997, 48 pages), 2 examiner's manuals (1997, 78 pages), 25 performance records for Form IIIA, and 25 performance records for Form IIIB; $146.95 per PPVT-IIIA test kit; $146.95 per PPVT-IIIB test kit; $28.95 per 25 performance records; $199.95 per AGS Computer ASSIST™ for the PPVT-III (IBM or Macintosh); $37.95 per Technical References to the PPVT-III.
Time: (10–15) minutes.
Comments: Orally administered, norm-referenced test; only for use with standard-English-speaking individuals.
Authors: Lloyd M. Dunn, Leota M. Dunn, Kathleen T. Williams (technical supplement), and Jing-Jen Wang (technical supplement).
Publisher: American Guidance Service, Inc.
Cross References: For reviews by Frederick Bessai and Orest Eugene Wasyliw, see 14:280; see also T5:1903 (585 references) and T4:1945 (426 references); for reviews by R. Steve McCallum and Elisabeth H. Wiig of an earlier edition, see 9:926 (117 references); see also T3:1771 (301 references), 8:222 (213 references), T2:516 (77 references), and 7:417 (201 references); for reviews by Howard B. Lyman and Ellen V. Piers, see 6:530 (21 references).

[1824]
Peacock Profile.

Purpose: Constructed to measure "how comfortable that individual feels in their department, team, work group or organization."
Population: Employees.
Publication Dates: 1995.
Acronym: PP.
Scores: 6 scales: Work Style, Relationships, Mastery, Career Optimism, Policies and Operations, Total.
Administration: Group.
Price Data, 2001: $8.50 per test booklet.
Time: Administration time not reported.

Comments: May be used alone or in combination with the Penguin Index (1832).
Authors: Barbara Hateley and Warren H. Schmidt.
Publisher: Consulting Psychologists Press, Inc.

[1825]
Pediatric Early Elementary Examination [PEEX2].

Purpose: Designed to "enable health care and other professionals to derive an empirical description of a child's development and functional neurologic status."
Population: Ages 6–9.
Publication Dates: 1983–1996.
Acronym: PEEX-2.
Scores, 6: Fine Motor/Graphomotor Functions, Attention Checkpoints, Language Functions, Gross Motor Functions, Memory Functions, Visual Processing Functions.
Administration: Individual.
Price Data, 2001: $100 per complete set including all materials except observer's guide and video; $16.65 per manual (1998, 65 pages); $66.40 per record form and response book; $19.45 per stimulus book; $34.10 per observer's guide; $21.10 per specimen set including observer's guide, record form, and examiner's manual; $48.70 per clinician's training video tape; quantity discounts available.
Time: (60) minutes.
Comments: Recommended for use as part of a multifaceted assessment process.
Authors: Developed under the direction of Melvin D. Levine and Adrian D. Sandler.
Publisher: Educators Publishing Service, Inc.
Cross References: For reviews by Denise M. DeZolt and Carl J. Dunst of an earlier edition, see 13:224 (1 reference); for reviews by J. Jeffrey Grill and Neil H. Schwartz of another earlier edition, see 10:272.

[1826]
Pediatric Evaluation of Disability Inventory.

Purpose: Designed as a "comprehensive clinical assessment instrument that samples key functional capabilities and performance."
Population: Ages 6 months to 7.5 years.
Publication Date: 1992.
Acronym: PEDI.
Scores, 9: Self-Care (Functional Skills, Caregiver Assistance, Modification Frequencies), Mobility (Functional Skills, Caregiver Assistance, Modification Frequencies), Social Function (Functional Skills, Caregiver Assistance, Modification Frequencies).
Administration: Individual.
Price Data: Available from publisher.
Time: (45–60) minutes.

Comments: Should be completed by the person or group of persons familiar with the child's typical performance in the domains surveyed; software program (IBM-compatible) available for data entry, scoring, and generation of individual summary score profiles.
Authors: Stephen M. Haley, Wendy J. Coster, Larry H. Ludlow, Jane T. Haltiwanger, and Peter J. Andrellos.
Publisher: Center for Rehabilitation Effectiveness, Boston University.
Cross References: For a review by Billy T. Ogletree, see 14:281.

[1827]
Pediatric Examination of Educational Readiness at Middle Childhood.

Purpose: Constructed to enable "health care and other professionals to derive an empirical description of a child's development and neurological status."
Population: Ages 9 to 15.
Publication Dates: 1984–1996.
Acronym: PEERAMID-2.
Scores: 6 major sections: Fine Motor/Graphomotor Function, Attention Checkpoints, Language Functions, Gross Motor Functions, Memory Functions, Visual Processing Functions.
Administration: Individual.
Price Data, 2001: $118.25 per complete kit including manual (1996, 80 pages), stimulus booklet, PEERAMID 2 kit, 12 record forms, and 12 response booklets; $77.50 per 12 record forms and 12 response booklets; $19.45 per stimulus booklet; $4.85 per PEERAMID 2 kit including cup and ball; $16.65 per examiner's manual (1996, 80 pages); $21.10 per specimen set including observer's guide, record form, and examiner's manual; $38.45 observer's guide; $48.70 per clinician's training video; quantity discounts available.
Time: (60) minutes.
Comments: Publisher suggests should only be used as a part of a multifaceted evaluation.
Author: Melvin D. Levine.
Publisher: Educators Publishing Service, Inc.
Cross References: For reviews by Joseph C. Kush and Robert G. Morwood, see 14:282; see also T5:1908 (1 reference); for reviews by Cathy W. Hall and Jan N. Hughes of the original edition, see 10:273.

[1828]
Pediatric Examination of Educational Readiness (PEER).

Purpose: "A combined neurodevelopmental, behavioral, and health assessment" that generates descriptive observations to be used in planning health, education, and developmentally oriented services.
Population: Ages 4–6.
Publication Dates: 1982–1988.
Acronym: PEER.

Scores: 27 or 28 rating scores: Developmental Attainment (Orientation, Gross Motor, Visual-Fine Motor, Associated Observations, Sequential, Linguistic, Preacademic Learning), Associated Observations (Selective Attention/Activity, Processing Efficiency, Adaptation), Neuromaturation (Associated Movements, Other Minor Neurological Signs), Other Physical Findings (General Physical Examination, Neurological Examination, Auditory and Vision Testing, Dressing and Undressing [optional]), Task Analysis (Visual, Verbal, Sequential, Somesthetic, Total, Short-Term Memory, Experiential Acquisition, Total, Fine Motor, Motor Sequential, Verbal Sequential, Verbal Expressive, Total).

Administration: Individual.

Price Data, 2001: $93.45 per complete set including examiner's manual, stimulus booklet, PEER kit, and 24 record forms; $36 per 24 record forms; $13.90 per stimulus booklet; $17.35 per PEER kit including ball, plastic sticks, wooden blocks, key, and rubber band; $26.40 per examiner's manual (80 pages); $27.10 per specimen set including record form and examiner's manual; quantity discounts available.

Time: (40–50) minutes excluding physical examination.

Authors: Developed under the direction of Melvin D. Levine and Elizabeth A. Schneider (manual).

Publisher: Educators Publishing Service, Inc.

Cross References: See T4:1947 (1 reference).

[1829]
Pediatric Extended Examination at Three (PEET).

Purpose: "To aid in the early detection and clarification of problems with learning, attention, and behavior in three- to four-year-old children."

Population: Ages 3-4.

Publication Date: 1986.

Acronym: PEET.

Scores, 20: Developmental Attainment (Gross Motor, Language, Visual-Fine Motor, Memory, Intersensory Integration), Assessment of Behavior Rating Scale (Initial Adaptation, Reactions during Assessment), Global Language Rating Scale, Physical Findings (General Physical Examination, Neurological Examination, Auditory and Vision Testing), Task Analysis (Reception, Discrimination, Sequencing, Memory, Fine Motor Output, Gross Motor Output, Expressive Language, Instructional Output, Experiential Application).

Administration: Individual.

Price Data, 2001: $136.25 per complete kit including 24 record booklets, PEET kit (ball, target, key, wooden blocks, plastic sticks, car, crayon, doll, buttoning strip, checkers, and objects for stereognosis task), stimulus booklet (40 pages), and examiner's manual (64 pages); $29.50 per 24 record forms; $19.45 per stimulus

booklet; $14.90 per examiner's manual; $73.05 per PEET kit; $15.75 per specimen set including examiner's manual and record form; quantity discounts available.

Time: Administration time not reported.

Authors: James A. Blackman, Melvin D. Levine, and Martha Markowitz.

Publisher: Educators Publishing Service, Inc.

Cross References: For reviews by William B. Michael and Hoi K. Suen, see 11:281.

[1830]
PEEK—Perceptions, Expectations, Emotions, and Knowledge About College.

Purpose: "Designed to assess prospective student's expectations about what college will be like."

Population: Prospective college students.

Publication Date: 1995.

Acronym: PEEK.

Scores, 3: Academic Expectations, Personal Expectations, Social Expectations.

Administration: Group.

Price Data, 1996: $1.75 per publisher scored form; $1.25 per software scored form (volume discounts available); $10 per software scoring kit (one-time purchase).

Time: (15–25) minutes.

Comments: Self-report questionnaire; can be machine scored by publisher, locally via software, or by hand in classroom settings.

Authors: Claire E. Weinstein, David R. Palmer, and Gary R. Hanson.

Publisher: H & H Publishing Co., Inc.

Cross References: For reviews by David Gillespie and Daniel L. Yazak, see 14:283.

[1831]
Peg Board.

Purpose: Developed to measure manual dexterity.

Population: Applicants for electrical and light engineering assembly jobs.

Publication Date: 1983.

Scores, 4: Preferred Hand, Non-Preferred Hand, Both Hands, Assemblies.

Administration: Group.

Price Data: Available from publisher.

Time: 3 minutes and 50 seconds (7 minutes).

Author: Educational & Industrial Test Services Ltd.

Publisher: Educational & Industrial Test Services Ltd. [England].

[1832]
Penguin Index.

Purpose: Designed to assess respondents' observations "about how their leaders manage people with diverse ethnic backgrounds, gender, work styles, personality characteristics, etc."

Population: Employees.

Publication Date: 1995.
Acronym: PI.
Scores: 6 scales: Pluralism, Openness, Participation, Support, Fairness, Total.
Administration: Group.
Price Data, 2001: $8.50 per test booklet.
Time: Administration time not reported.
Comments: May be used alone or in combination with the Peacock Profile (1824).
Authors: Warren H. Schmidt and Barbara Hateley.
Publisher: Consulting Psychologists Press, Inc.

[1833]
Penna Assessor Adaptive Ability Tests.

Purpose: "For use in the selection, training, and career development of personnel in the UK."
Population: Junior school–adult.
Publication Dates: 1988–1990.
Administration: Individual.
Price Data: Available from publisher.
Time: [15] minutes per subtest.
Comments: All subtests are computer administered; previously listed as Selby MillSmith Adaptive Ability Tests.
Author: Selby MillSmith Ltd.
Publisher: Penna Assessment [England].
  a) NUMERIC ABILITY TEST.
  Purpose: "To assess basic numeracy and numerical skills at all levels of the organisation."
  Scores: Total score only.
  b) LANGUAGE ABILITY TEST.
  Purpose: "Assesses the individual's range and clarity in the use of vocabulary."
  Scores: Total score only.
  c) ADMINISTRATIVE ABILITY TEST.
  Purpose: "To assess the speed and accuracy of an individual's administrative capabilities."
  Scores, 3: Numbers, Addresses, Codes.
Cross References: For reviews by Colin Cooper and Glen Fox, see 13:279.

[1834]
Penna Assessor Values Indices.

Purpose: "A measure of personal values associated with work and the working environment."
Population: Adults.
Publication Dates: 1985–1991.
Administration: Individual or group.
Editions, 2: Management Values Index, Supervisory Values Index.
Price Data: Available from publisher.
Comments: Test may be paper-and-pencil or computer administered; previously listed as Selby MillSmith Values Indices.
Author: Adrian W. Savage.
Publisher: Penna Assessment [England].

a) MANAGEMENT VALUES INDEX.
Purpose: "For selection, assessment and training and development at managerial and senior levels within an organisation."
Population: Managers.
Acronym: MVI.
Scores, 27: Core Scales [Achievement Values (Work Ethic, Responsibility, Risk Taking, Task Orientation, Leadership, Activity, Need for Status, Self Esteem), Expertise Values (Need for Mental Challenge, Innovation, Analysis, Attention to Detail), Consolidation Values (Need for Stability, Need for Structure, Career Development), Interpersonal Values (Sociability, Inclusion, Personal Warmth, Tactfulness, Tolerance)], [Second Order Indices (Executive Index, Stability Index, Conscientiousness Index, Expert Orientation Index, Team Orientation Index, Empathy Index, Motivational Distortion Index)].
Time: (30–45) minutes.
b) SUPERVISORY VALUES INDEX.
Purpose: "For selection, assessment and training and development at supervisory and 'A' level standard."
Scores, 26: Core Scales [Achievement Values (Work Ethic, Responsibility, Risk Taking, Task Orientation, Leadership, Activity, Need for Status, Self Esteem), Expertise Values (Need for Mental Challenge, Innovation, Analysis, Attention to Detail), Consolidation Values (Need for Stability, Need for Structure, Career Development), Interpersonal Values (Sociability, Inclusion, Personal Warmth, Tactfulness, Tolerance)], Second Order Indices (Initiative Index, Team Orientation Index, Stability Index, Enquiry Index, Conscientiousness Index, Motivational Distortion Index).
Time: (30–45) minutes.
Cross References: For reviews by Peter Miles Berger and Gerald R. Schneck, see 14:343.

[1835]
People Performance Profile.

Purpose: Designed to determine how employees perceive their organization, their work team, and themselves.
Population: Organization members.
Publication Date: 1985.
Acronym: PPP.
Scores, 20: Organizational Performance (Planning, Management Procedures, Motivational Climate, Physical Environment, Organizational Stress Factors), Work-Team Performance (Supervision, Role Clarity, Communications, Conflict Management, Problem Solving, Meeting Effectiveness, Job Satisfaction, Group Productivity), Personal Fitness (Health, Exercise, Nutri-

tion, Alcohol and Drug Use, Interpersonal Support, Time Management, Personal Stress Management).
Administration: Group.
Price Data: Available from publisher.
Time: Administration time not reported.
Authors: Bob Crosby, John Scherer (survey, leader's guide), and Gil Crosby (work-team guide).
Publisher: Jossey-Bass, A Wiley Company.
Cross References: For reviews by Seymour Adler and Larry Cochran, see 10:274.

[1836]
The People Process.

Purpose: Designed to help determine personalities and assist in relating to people "of the same or different personality traits."
Population: Adults.
Publication Date: 1992.
Scores: 4 processes: Energy, Information, Decisions, Actions.
Administration: Group.
Price Data, 1997: $69.95 per complete trainer's package including 1 trainer's guide (90 pages), 1 participant's booklet (63 pages), 1 cardboard wheel, and 16 profile sheets; $19.95 per complete participant's package including 1 participant's booklet, 1 cardboard wheel, and 16 profile sheets.
Time: (120–240) minutes.
Author: Pam Hollister.
Publisher: Jossey-Bass, A Wiley Company.

[1837]
People Smarts: Behavioral Profiles.

Purpose: Designed to reveal perceptions of behavioral styles in the workplace.
Population: Adults.
Publication Date: 1994.
Scores: 4 profiles: Relater, Socializer, Thinker, Director.
Administration: Group.
Price Data: Price information available from publisher for trainer's package including trainer's guide (100 pages), 1 self-assessment, 1 observer assessment, 1 scoring matrix, 1 reminder card, 1 45-minute videocassette, and 1 People Smarts book (224 pages); participant's package including 1 workbook, 1 self-assessment, 1 scoring matrix, and 5 observer assessments; 1 self-assessment or 1 observer assessment; scoring matrix; reminder card; participant workbook; People Smarts book.
Time: Administration time not reported.
Author: Tony Alessandra.
Publisher: Jossey-Bass, A Wiley Company.

[1838]
Perception of Ability Scale for Students.

Purpose: "Designed to assess children's feelings about their academic abilities and school-related achievement."

Population: Grades 3–6.
Publication Date: 1992.
Acronym: PASS.
Scores, 7: General Ability, Math, Reading/Spelling, Penmanship and Neatness, School Satisfaction, Confidence, Total.
Administration: Group or individual.
Price Data, 2002: $68 per complete kit including manual (88 pages), 2 prepaid mail-in answer sheets, and 10 AutoScore™ answer forms; $29.50 per 25 AutoScore™ answer forms; $40 per manual; $10.50 per test report answer sheet.
Time: (15) minutes.
Comments: Self-report inventory.
Authors: Frederic J. Boersma and James W. Chapman.
Publisher: Western Psychological Services.
Cross References: See T5:1916 (3 references); for reviews by Michael R. Harwell and Michael J. Subkoviak, see 12:282; see also T4:1953 (1 reference).

[1839]
Perception-Of-Relationships-Test.

Purpose: Constructed to measure the degree to which a child seeks psychological "closeness" with each parent; and the types of behaviors the child has had to develop to permit or accommodate interaction with each parent.
Population: Children age 3 and over.
Publication Dates: 1964–2002.
Acronym: PORT.
Scores: No scores.
Administration: Individual.
Price Data, 2002: $199 per complete kit including 8 test/scoring booklets, handbook (1990, 179 pages); pen, eraser, and updates; $99 per 8 test/scoring booklets; $159 per 16 test/scoring booklets; $199 per 24 test/scoring booklets; $149 per handbook; $198 per IBM computer scoring profile (3.5-inch disk).
Time: [30] minutes.
Comments: Projective test for use in custody decisions.
Author: Barry Bricklin.
Publisher: Village Publishing.
Cross References: For reviews by Janet F. Carlson and Judith Conger, see 12:283.

[1840]
Perceptions of Parental Role Scales.

Purpose: "To measure perceived parental role responsibilities."
Population: Parents.
Publication Date: 1982.
Acronym: PPRS.
Scores: 13 areas in 3 domains: Teaching the Child (Cognitive Development, Social Skills, Handling of Emotions, Physical Health, Norms and Social Values, Personal Hygiene, Survival Skills), Meeting the Child's Basic Needs

(Health Care, Food/Clothing/Shelter, Child's Emotional Needs, Child Care), Family as an Interface With Society (Social Institutions, the Family Unit Itself).
Administration: Group.
Price Data: Available from publisher.
Time: (15) minutes.
Comments: Self-administered.
Authors: Lucia A. Gilbert and Gary R. Hanson.
Publisher: Marathon Consulting and Press.
Cross References: For reviews by Cindy I. Carlson and Mark W. Roberts, see 11:282.

[1841]
Perceptual-Motor Assessment for Children & Emotional/Behavioral Screening Program.

Purpose: "Designed for screening visual, auditory and haptic perception; fine and gross motor abilities; and perceptual memory in children."
Population: Ages 4-0-15-11.
Publication Date: 1988.
Acronym: P-MAC/ESP.
Scores, 12: 3 scores for the Perceptual Memory Task-Abbreviated (PMT-A): Spatial Relations, Auditory-Visual Colors Recognition, Auditory-Visual Colors Sequence; 3 scores for Haptic Visual Discrimination Test-Abbreviated (HVDT-A): Shape, Size, Texture; 6 scores for McCarron Assessment of Neuromuscular Development-Abbreviated (MAND-A): Beads in Box, Finger Tapping, Nut and Bolt, Hand Strength, Standing on One Foot, Finger-Nose-Finger. Subtests, 3: PMT-A, HVDT-A, MAND-A.
Administration: Individual.
Price Data, 1999: $1,745 per P-MAC including P-MAC battery, computer program, manual (219 pages), 25 Protocol/Data Entry Forms, and 5 GEM volumes; $250 per ESP including 25 Behavioral Checklists for Students, computer program, and manual; $1,995 per combined P-MAC & ESP; $44.50 per each of 5 GEM volumes; $37.75 per 25 P-MAC Protocol/Data Entry Forms; $27.75 per 25 Behavioral Checklists for Students; $65 per P-MAC manual; $26.50 per separate ESP manual.
Time: (45) minutes.
Comments: P-MAC battery consists of selected subtests from the MAND, HVDT, and PMT; 5 age-specific volumes of Guides for Educational Management (GEM) that provide expanded recommendations and functional implications; computer software included; Behavioral Checklist for Students for ESP program.
Authors: Jack G. Dial (P-MAC and ESP), Lawrence McCarron (P-MAC), and Garry Amann (P-MAC and ESP).
Publisher: McCarron-Dial Systems.
Cross References: See T5:1919 (1 reference); for reviews by Barbara A. Rothlisberg and E. W. Testut, see 12:284.

[1842]
Perceptual Speed (Identical Forms).

Purpose: Designed to assess "the ability to rapidly compare visual configurations and identify two figures as similar or identical or to identify some particular detail that is buried in distracting material."
Population: Visual inspectors, proofreaders, clerical personnel.
Publication Dates: 1984–1996.
Scores: Total score only.
Administration: Group or individual.
Price Data, 2002: $51 per 25 tests; $28 per interpretation and research manual (1959, 10 pages); $20 per score key.
Time: 5 minutes.
Comments: Primarily used in industry and governmental organizations (norms provided for these personnel).
Authors: L. L. Thurstone and T. E. Jeffrey
Publisher: Reid London House.

[1843]
Per-Flu-Dex Tests.

Purpose: Developed to test "a variety of abilities to cope with the needs for effective performance."
Population: High school and college and industry.
Publication Date: 1955.
Administration: Group.
Price Data: Available from publisher.
Time: 7(25) minutes; 1(5) minutes for any one test.
Author: Frank J. Holmes.
Publisher: Psychometric Affiliates.
   a) PER-SYMB TEST.
   Purpose: Symbol number substitution.
   b) PER-VERB TEST.
   Purpose: Letter perception and counting.
   c) PER-NUMB TEST.
   Purpose: Number counting and perception.
   d) FLU-VERB TEST.
   Purpose: Word completion and verbal fluency.
   e) FLU-NUMB TEST.
   Purpose: Arithmetic computation.
   f) THE DEX-MAN SCALE.
   Purpose: Manual speed of movement.
   g) DEX-AIM TEST.
   Purpose: Aiming accuracy and speed.
Cross References: See T2:2286 (2 references); for reviews by Andrew L. Comrey and John W. French, see 5:901.

[1844]
[Performance Review Forms].

Purpose: To provide a format to accomplish an appraisal of managerial performance in relation to accountability and personal characteristics.
Publication Dates: 1960–1961.

Scores: Ratings in 3 areas: Accountability, Performance, Developmental Program.
Administration: Individual.
Author: Seymour Levy.
Publisher: Martin M. Bruce, Ph.D.

a) COUNSELING INTERVIEW SUMMARY.
Purpose: For summarizing a performance review interview.
Population: Employees, managers.
Publication Date: 1960.
Forms, 2: Employee, Management.
Price Data, 2001: $5.95 per employee forms; $3.45 per employee specimen set; $8.25 per management forms; $4.95 per management specimen set; $9.75 per guide to counseling.
Time: (10) minutes.

b) MANAGERIAL PERFORMANCE REVIEW.
Purpose: Ratings by supervisors preparatory to performance review interview.
Population: Managers.
Publication Date: 1961.
Price Data: $51.50 per forms; $26.50 per specimen set.
Time: (40-50) minutes.

[1845]
Performance Skills Leader.

Purpose: Designed to identify "leadership strengths and developmental needs."
Population: Employees in leadership positions.
Publication Date: 1996.
Acronym: PS Leader.
Scores, 24: Strategic Focus (Vision, Business Knowledge, Change Management), Business Focus (Quality Centered, Planning and Executing, Budgeting, Technology Management and Application), Work Force Focus (Coaching, Team Leadership, Creativity and Innovation, Commitment to Work Force Diversity, Human Resource Management), Interpersonal Focus (Interpersonal Skills, Oral Communication, Influencing, Writing, Conflict Resolution and Negotiation), Personal Focus (Self-Development, Action Orientation, Results Focus, Flexibility, Problem Solving and Decision Making, Role Modeling, Time Management).
Administration: Group.
Price Data, 1996: $65 per assessment disk per leader; $800 per half-day seminar plus $65 per leader for assessment disk; $1,500 per full-day seminar plus $65 per leader for assessment disk (also includes Insight Inventory); $150 per group report; $49.95 per administrator's manual (110 pages).
Time: Administration time not reported.
Author: Human Technology, Inc.
Publisher: Human Resource Development Press.
Cross References: For reviews by Trenton R. Ferro and George C. Thornton III, see 14:284.

[1846]
Personal Achievement Formula.

Purpose: Constructed to identify an individual's managerial strategy and his/her view of the organizational culture.
Population: Managers.
Publication Dates: 1976–1997.
Scores: 4 scores (Personal Achievement Formula, Organizational Culture, Group Achievement Formula, Group Assessment of Organization) each falling in one of 4 domains (Human Relations Specialist, Low Achiever, Average Achiever, High Achiever).
Administration: Group.
Price Data, 2001: $8.95 per instrument.
Time: Administration time not reported.
Author: Jay Hall.
Publisher: Teleometrics International.

[1847]
Personal Adjustment Index: ETSA Test 8A.

Purpose: Designed to facilitate person-vocation match through assessment of feelings and attitudes.
Population: Employment applicants.
Publication Dates: 1960–1998.
Scores, 8: Community Spirit, Teamwork, Optimism, Cooperative Spirit, Self Confidence, Leadership, Dependability, Total.
Administration: Group or individual.
Price Data, 2002: $10 per electronic test; $10 each per test booklet and answer sheet (scoring and reporting); $20 per administrator's manual; $20 per technical manual.
Time: (45) minutes.
Comments: Electronic tests available at www.etsatests.com.
Author: Psychological Services Bureau, Inc.
Publisher: Employers' Tests and Services Associates.
Cross References: For reviews by Marvin D. Dunnette and Raymond A. Katzell of an earlier version of the ETSA Tests, see 6:1025.

[1848]
Personal Assessment of Intimacy in Relationships.

Purpose: "Measures the expected (ideal) versus the realized (perceived) degree of intimacy" in a relationship.
Population: Couples.
Publication Date: 1981.
Acronym: PAIR.
Scores, 6: Emotion, Social, Sexual, Intellectual, Recreational, Conventionality.
Administration: Group.
Price Data, 1998: $30 per complete test including item booklet, answer sheet, scoring template, couple feedback sheet, and procedure manual (14 pages).

Time: (20–30) minutes.
Comments: Self-report measure; forms may be photocopied after obtaining permission by submitting Abstract on Proposed Study.
Authors: David H. Olson and Mark T. Schaefer.
Publisher: Life Innovations, Inc.
Cross References: See T5:1927 (9 references) and T4:1966 (2 references); for a review by Richard M. Wolf, see 11:283.

[1849]

Personal Audit.

Purpose: Assess individual personality characteristics.
Population: Individuals in a variety of professional occupations.
Publication Dates: 1941–1992.
Administration: Individual or group.
Price Data: Available from publisher.
Authors: Clifford R. Adams and William M. Lepley.
Publisher: Reid London House.

a) FORM SS (SHORT FORM).
Scores, 6: Seriousness, Firmness, Frankness, Tranquility, Stability, Tolerance.
Time: No limit (approximately 40 minutes).
b) FORM LL (LONG FORM).
Scores, 9: 6 scores listed in *a* above plus Steadiness, Persistence, Contentment.
Time: No limit (approximately 50 minutes).
Cross References: See T2:1314 (4 references) and P:192 (6 references); for a review by William Seeman, see 4:75 (3 references); for a review by Percival M. Symonds, see 3:64 (10 references).

[1850]

Personal Creativity Assessment.

Purpose: Designed "to allow individuals to determine how they measure up in the realm of creativity."
Population: Age 18 and above.
Publication Date: 1999.
Acronym: PCA.
Scores, 2: Enabler, Barrier.
Administration: Group or individual.
Price Data, 2001: $29.95 per Creativity by Design leader's guide (73 pages).
Time: (20–25) minutes.
Author: Alexander Watson Hiam.
Publisher: Human Resource Development Press.

[1851]

Personal Directions®.

Purpose: An executive coaching tool designed to aid in the structured exploration of an individual's personal choices regarding life balance issues, career planning, feelings of satisfaction and security, and opportunities for growth and development.
Population: Adults.

Publication Dates: 1997–2001.
Scores: 46 dimensions: Types of Emotional Satisfaction (Giving, Receiving, Belonging, Expressing, Gaining Stature, Entertaining, Creating, Interpreting, Excelling, Enduring, Structuring, Maneuvering, Winning, Controlling, Stability, Independence, Irreproachability), Areas of Emphasis (Career, Economic, Community, Interpersonal, Recreation, Travel, Nature, Palate, Arts, Practical Arts, Home, Romance, Family, Intellectual, Ideological, Physical, Emotional, Spiritual), World Outcomes (Level of Satisfaction, Level of Dissatisfaction, Level of Security, Level of Insecurity, Level of Growth, Balance of World, Level of Present Support, Internal Focus of World, External Focus of World, Flexibility of Boundaries, Level of Public Success).
Administration: Individual or group.
Price Data: Available from publisher.
Time: (45) minutes.
Comments: Purchase and use requires training by publisher.
Authors: James T. Mahoney, Joan W. Chadbourne (test), and Robert I. Kabacoff (manual).
Publisher: Management Research Group.

[1852]

Personal Dynamics Profile.

Purpose: Designed to measure "personality characteristics relevant to success," and "to assist organizations in hiring the best available applicants and developing employees to their potential," and to "assist individuals in achieving career success and personal contentment."
Population: Current personnel and potential employees.
Publication Dates: 1995–1998.
Acronym: PDP.
Scores, 26: Assessment Validity (Objectivity, Accuracy), Interpersonal Traits (Sociability, Recognition, Conscientiousness, Exhibition, Trust, Nurturance); Organizational Traits (Alertness, Structure, Order, Flexibility, Creativity, Responsibility); Dedication Traits (Ambition, Endurance, Assertiveness, Boldness, Coachability, Leadership); Self-Control Traits (Self-Confidence, Composure, Tough-Mindedness, Autonomy, Contentment, Control).
Administration: Individual or group.
Price Data, 1998: $195 per report including participant's report, manager's report, executive profiles, position compatibility report, group profiles, subgroup profiles, group profile overlays, success profile overlays, and position analyses report; group discounts available.
Time: [60] minutes.
Authors: Denis Waitley, Lem Burnham, Charles C. Kaufman, J. Michael Priddy, Joan L. Francis, Thomas A. Tutko, Bruce C. Ogilvie, and Leland P. Lyon.
Publisher: Winslow Research Institute.

[1853]
Personal Effectiveness Inventory.

Purpose: Provides insights into attitudes, beliefs, and behavior, and increases skills for effectiveness.
Population: Adults.
Publication Date: 1996.
Acronym: PEI.
Scores, 15: Self-Development (Self-Image, Control, Approval, Amicability), Relationship Building (Trust, Cooperation, Interpersonal, Inclusion), Goal Achievement (Satisfaction, Directedness, Expectations, Effectiveness), Time Orientation (Past, Present, Future).
Administration: Individual.
Price Data: Price data for test materials including Self-Development Guide (70 pages) available from publisher.
Time: Administration time not reported.
Author: Human Synergistics International.
Publisher: Human Synergistics International.

[1854]
Personal Experience Inventory.

Purpose: "To identify problems associated with adolescent chemical involvement."
Population: Ages 12–18.
Publication Dates: 1988–1989.
Acronym: PEI.
Scores: 45 scores/screens: Chemical Involvement Problem Severity Section: Basic Scales (Personal Involvement with Chemicals, Effects from Drug Use, Social Benefits of Drug Use, Personal Consequences of Drug Use, Polydrug Use), Clinical Scales (Social-Recreational Drug Use, Psychological Benefits of Drug Use, Transsituational Drug Use, Preoccupation with Drugs, Loss of Control), Validity Indicators (Infrequent Responses, Defensiveness, Pattern Misfit), Drug Use Frequency/Duration/Age of Onset (Alcohol, Marijuana, LSD, Psychedelics, Cocaine, Amphetamines, Quaaludes, Barbiturates, Tranquilizers, Heroin, Opiates, Inhalants); Psychosocial Section: Personal Risk Factor Scales (Negative Self-Image, Psychological Disturbance, Social Isolation, Uncontrolled, Rejecting Convention, Deviant Behavior, Absence of Goals, Spiritual Isolation), Environmental Risk Factor Scales (Peer Chemical Environment, Sibling Chemical Use, Family Pathology, Family Estrangement), Problem Screens (Psychiatric Referral, Eating Disorder, Sexual Abuse, Physical Abuse, Family Chemical Dependency, Suicide Potential), Validity Indicators (Infrequent Responses, Defensiveness).
Administration: Group.
Parts, 2: Chemical Involvement Problem Severity Section, Psychosocial Section.
Price Data, 2002: $150 per kit for mail-in computer scoring including 5 prepaid mail-in answer booklets for computer scoring and interpretation and manual (1989, 103 pages); $120 per kit for on-site computer scoring including 5-use disk (PC with Windows), 5 PC answer booklets, and manual; $50 per manual; $24.50 per mail-in answer booklet; $299 per 25-use disk (PC with Windows); $22.50 per 10 PC answer booklets; $18.50 per FAX service scoring.
Time: (45–55) minutes.
Authors: Ken C. Winters and George A. Henly.
Publisher: Western Psychological Services.
Cross References: See T5:1931 (1 reference) and T4:1971 (2 references); for reviews by Tony Toneatto and Jalie A. Tucker, see 11:284.

[1855]
Personal Experience Inventory for Adults.

Purpose: Designed to yield "comprehensive information about an individual's substance abuse patterns and problems."
Population: Age 19 and older.
Publication Dates: 1995–1996.
Acronym: PEI-A.
Scores, 37: Problem Severity Scales (Personal Involvement with Drugs, Physiological Dependence, Effects of Use, Social Benefits of Use, Personal Consequences of Use, Recreational Use, Transsituational Use, Psychological Benefits of Use, Preoccupation, Loss of Control, Infrequency—1, Self-Deception, Social Desirability—1, Treatment Receptiveness), Psychosocial Scales (Negative Self-Image, Psychological Disturbance, Social Isolation, Uncontrolled, Rejecting Convention, Deviant Behavior, Absence of Goals, Spiritual Isolation, Peer Drug Use, Interpersonal Pathology, Estrangement in the Home, Infrequency—2, Social Desirability—2), Problem Screens (Suicide Risk, Work Environment Risk, Past Family Pathology, Other Impulse-Related Problems, Significant Other Drug Problem, Sexual Abuse Perpetrator, Physical Abuse Perpetrator, Physical/Sexual Abuse Victim, Need for Psychiatric Referral, Miscellaneous).
Administration: Group.
Parts, 2: Problem Severity Scales, Psychosocial Scales.
Price Data, 2002: $150 per kit for mail-in computer scoirng including 5 prepaid mail-in answer booklets and manual (1996, 100 pages); $120 per kit for on-site computer scoring including 5-use disk, 5 PC answer booklets, and manual; $24.50 or less per mail-in answer booklet; $299 or less per 25-use (PC with Windows) scoring disk; $22.50 or less per 10 PC answer booklets for use with computer disk; $50 per manual.
Time: (45–60) minutes.
Comments: Untimed self-report inventory; computer scored only.
Author: Ken C. Winters.
Publisher: Western Psychological Services.

Cross References: For reviews by Mark D. Shriver and Claudia R. Wright, see 13:225.

[1856]
Personal Experience Screening Questionnaire.

Purpose: "Designed as a brief screening tool to aid . . . in the identification of teenagers likely to need a drug abuse assessment referral."
Population: Adolescents.
Publication Date: 1991.
Acronym: PESQ.
Scores, 3: Infrequency, Defensiveness, Problem Severity.
Administration: Group.
Price Data, 2002: $78 per complete kit including 25 AutoScore™ test forms and manual (30 pages); $36 per 25 AutoScore™ test forms; $48 per manual.
Time: (10) minutes.
Author: Ken C. Winters.
Publisher: Western Psychological Services.
Cross References: For reviews by Stuart N. Hart and Richard W. Johnson, see 12:286 (1 reference).

[1857]
Personal History Checklist for Adults.

Purpose: To obtain historical information during routine intake procedures.
Population: Adult clients of mental health services.
Publication Date: 1989.
Scores: Item scores only.
Administration: Individual.
Manual: No manual.
Price Data: Available from publisher.
Time: Administration time not reported.
Comments: Checklist can be completed by client or clinician.
Author: John A. Schinka.
Publisher: Psychological Assessment Resources, Inc.
Cross References: For a review by Thomas A. Widiger, see 11:285.

[1858]
Personal Inventory of Needs.

Purpose: Designed as a self-assessment tool to identify the strengths of basic needs.
Population: Employees.
Publication Date: 1990.
Scores, 3: Achievement, Affiliation, Power.
Administration: Group or individual.
Price Data: Price information available from publisher for complete kit including 20 inventories, 20 response sheets, and 20 interpretation sheets.
Time: [30] minutes administration; [30] minutes interpretation.

Comments: Self-administered, self-scored; based on David McClelland's research at MIT.
Author: Training House, Inc.
Publisher: Training House, Inc.
Cross References: For reviews by Gary J. Dean and Trenton R. Ferro, see 12:287.

[1859]
Personal Opinion Matrix.

Purpose: Surveys the impressions and reactions of those who are managed.
Population: Employees.
Publication Dates: 1977-1983.
Scores, 2: Managerial Review, Climate.
Administration: Group.
Manual: No manual.
Price Data, 2001: $7.95 per instrument.
Time: Administration time not reported.
Comments: Self-administered survey.
Author: Jay Hall.
Publisher: Teleometrics International.
Cross References: For a review by Gregory H. Dobbins, see 10:276 (7 references).

[1860]
Personal Orientation Dimensions.

Purpose: Designed to "measure attitudes and values in terms of concepts of the actualizing person."
Population: High school, college, and adults.
Publication Dates: 1975–1977.
Acronym: POD.
Scores, 13: Orientation (Time Orientation, Core Centeredness), Polarities (Strength, Weakness, Anger, Love), Integration (Synergistic Integration, Potentiation), Awareness (Being, Trust in Humanity, Creative Living, Mission, Manipulation Awareness).
Administration: Group.
Price Data, 1998: $20.25 per 25 reusable test booklets; $13.75 per 50 answer sheets (machine-scoring) [$136.25 per 500]; $1.60 for EdITS scoring; $8 per specimen set; $4 per manual (1977, 14 pages).
Time: Administration time not reported.
Comments: A refinement and extension of concepts first measured by the Personal Orientation Inventory (1861); self-administering.
Author: Everett L. Shostrom.
Publisher: EdITS/Educational and Industrial Testing Service.
Cross References: For reviews by Gloria Maccow and Claudia R. Wright, see 14:285; see also T5:1938 (1 reference) and T4:1977 (1 reference).

[1861]
Personal Orientation Inventory.

Purpose: Designed as a "measure of values and behavior seen to be of importance in the development of the self-actualizing person."

Population: High school, college, and adults.
Publication Dates: 1962–1996.
Acronym: POI.
Scores, 12: Time Ratio, Support Ratio, Self-Actualizing Value, Existentiality, Feeling Reactivity, Spontaneity, Self-Regard, Self-Acceptance, Nature of Man, Synergy, Acceptance of Aggression, Capacity for Intimate Contact.
Administration: Group.
Price Data, 1998: $20.50 per 25 reusable tests; $41 per 14 scoring stencils; $14 per 50 answer sheets (hand scoring); $13.75 per 50 answer sheets (NCS for EdITS processing); $11.75 per 50 profiles; $22.50 per POI handbook (1990); $4.75 per manual with 1980 supplementation (1974, 56 pages); $8.25 per specimen set (manual and all forms); $1.60 per test NCS scoring service.
Time: (30–40) minutes.
Comments: Self-administered.
Author: Everett L. Shostrom.
Publisher: EdITS/Educational and Industrial Testing Service.
Cross References: See T5:1939 (15 references), T4:1978 (42 references), 9:943 (24 references), and T3:1789 (98 references); for an excerpted review by Donald J. Tosi and Cathy A. Lindamood, see 8:641 (433 references); see also T2:1315 (80 references); for reviews by Bruce Bloxom and Richard W. Coan, see 7:121 (97 references); see also P:193 (26 references).

[1862]
Personal Problems Checklist-Adult.

Purpose: "To facilitate the rapid assessment of an individual's problems as seen from that person's point of view."
Population: Adults.
Publication Date: 1985.
Scores: 13 areas: Social, Appearance, Vocational, Family and Home, School, Finances, Religion, Emotions, Sex, Legal, Health and Habits, Attitude, Crises.
Administration: Individual or group.
Manual: No manual.
Price Data: Available from publisher.
Time: (10) minutes.
Author: John A. Schinka.
Publisher: Psychological Assessment Resources, Inc.
Cross References: See T5:1941 (1 reference); for a review by Harold R. Keller, see 10:278.

[1863]
Personal Problems Checklist for Adolescents.

Purpose: "To identify relevant problems, establish rapport, and provide written documentation of presenting problems consistent with community standards of care."
Population: Adolescents.

Publication Dates: 1985–1989.
Acronym: PPC.
Scores: 13 problem areas: Social and Friends, Appearance, Job, Parents, Family and Home, School, Money, Religion, Emotions, Dating and Sex, Health and Habits, Attitudes and Opinions, Crises.
Administration: Individual or group.
Manual: No manual.
Price Data: Available from publisher.
Time: (10–20) minutes.
Comments: Adolescent version of the Personal Problems Checklist (1863).
Author: John A. Schinka.
Publisher: Psychological Assessment Resources, Inc.
Cross References: See T5:1942 (1 reference); for reviews by Brian K. Martens and Toni E. Santmire, see 10:279.

[1864]
Personal Questionnaire Rapid Scaling Technique.

Purpose: Developed to monitor "fluctuations in the intensity of personal experiences such as feelings, beliefs, symptoms etc."
Population: Psychiatric patients.
Publication Dates: 1977–1980.
Acronym: PQRST.
Scores: Total score only.
Administration: Group.
Editions, 2: PQ10, PQ14.
Price Data: Price information available from publisher for question booklet, PQ10 scoring key, PQ14 scoring key, answer sheets, manual (1980, 31 pages), and specimen set.
Time: (10–15) minutes for short form (PQ10); (15–20) minutes for long form (PQ14).
Author: David J. Mulhall.
Publisher: NFER-Nelson Publishing Co., Ltd. [England].
Cross References: See T5:1944 (1 reference) and T4:1984 (4 references); for a review by Auke Tellegen, see 9:945.

[1865]
Personal Reaction Index.

Purpose: Assesses how people feel regarding the aspects of their work environment.
Population: Employees.
Publication Dates: 1974–1995.
Scores, 6: Degree of Participation, Feelings of Satisfaction, Feelings of Responsibility, Feelings of Commitment, Feelings of Frustration, Perceived Decision Quality.
Administration: Group.
Manual: No manual.
Price Data, 2001: $2.95 per instrument.

Time: Administration time not reported.
Comments: Self-administered survey.
Author: Jay Hall.
Publisher: Teleometrics International.
Cross References: For reviews by Ralph M. Alexander and Daniel G. Spencer, see 9:946.

[1866]
Personal Relationship Inventory.

Purpose: "Designed to assess one's capacity to love and engage in intimate interpersonal relationships."
Population: Ages 15 and over.
Publication Dates: 1988–1991.
Acronym: PRI.
Scores, 13: Compassion, Friendship, Intimacy, Masculine/Feminine, Primitive Self, Psychological Adjustment, Romantic Love, Self-Respect, Sensitivity, Spirituality, Trust, Love Capacity (Total), Persona.
Administration: Group or individual.
Price Data: Price information available from publisher for test booklets, prepaid answer sheet for scoring by publisher, answer sheet (on-site scoring by computer), manual (1991, 91 pages), A Guide to Using The Love Factor, and computer program for on-site processing.
Comments: Originally published as the Love Factor Inventory.
Time: (20–30) minutes.
Author: Ronald L. Mann.
Publisher: Mann Consulting Group.
Cross References: For reviews by Bradley Elison and William K. Wilkinson, see 12:288.

[1867]
Personal Resource Questionnaire.

Purpose: Provides information about adults' social networks and perceived levels of social support.
Population: Ages 18–80.
Publication Dates: 1981–1987.
Acronym: PRQ-85.
Scores: Part I, 3 scores: Size of Network, Number of Problems Experienced, Degree of Satisfaction with Help Received; Part II, total score only.
Administration: Group.
Parts, 2: I, II.
Manual: No manual.
Price Data: Price information available from publisher for instructions and Questionnaire; additional copies may be photocopied locally.
Time: (10–15) minutes.
Comments: May be self-administered; Parts I and II can be administered independently of each other.
Authors: Patricia Brandt and Clarann Weinert.
Publisher: Patricia Brandt and Clarann Weinert.
Cross References: See T5:1947 (8 references); for a review by Esther E. Diamond, see 11:286.

[1868]
Personal Skills Map.

Purpose: "Offers a means for the self-assessment of personal skills."
Population: Ages 13–19.
Publication Date: 1993.
Acronym: PSM.
Scores: 14 scales: Self-Esteem, Growth Motivation, Change Orientation, Interpersonal Assertion, Interpersonal Aggression, Interpersonal Deference, Interpersonal Awareness, Empathy, Drive Strength, Decision Making, Time Management, Sales Orientation, Commitment Ethic, Stress Management.
Administration: Group or individual.
Forms, 3: The Personal Skills Map, The Personal Skills Survey, Teacher Observation Test.
Price Data, 1994: $125 per 10 Personal Skills Map; $62.50 per 25 Personal Skills Survey (specify grades 3–5 or 6–12); $60 per 25 Teacher Observation Test.
Time: (30–40) minutes for Personal Skills Map; (20–25) minutes for Personal Skills Survey; (10–15) minutes for Teacher Observation Test.
Comments: Part of Becoming a Champion program; Personal Skills Survey and Teacher Observation Test are components derived from the Personal Skills Map.
Author: People Builders International, Inc.
Publisher: Chronicle Guidance Publications, Inc.
Cross References: For a review by Delwyn L. Harnisch, see 13:226 (1 reference).

[1869]
Personal Stress Assessment Inventory.

Purpose: A self-assessment instrument designed to identify those who would most likely benefit from participation in stress-management training.
Population: Adults.
Publication Dates: 1981–1993.
Acronym: PSAI.
Scores, 6: Predisposition, Resilience, Sources of Stress, Overall Stress Factor, Health Symptoms, Personal Reactions.
Administration: Group or individual.
Price Data, 2002: $8.95 per inventory; minimum of 20 (volume discounts available).
Time: (20–30) minutes.
Comments: Self-administered; self-scored.
Author: Herbert S. Kindler.
Publisher: The Center for Management Effectiveness, Inc.
Cross References: For reviews by E. Scott Huebner and Norman D. Sundberg, see 14:286.

[1870]
Personal Stress Inventory.

Purpose: Measure a patient's current concerns, emotional status, life stresses, and personal functioning.

Population: Ages 16 and over.
Publication Dates: 1980–1981.
Acronym: PI.
Scores: No scores.
Administration: Group or individual.
Price Data: Available from publisher.
Time: (10–15) minutes.
Comments: Self-rating scale; previously listed as A Personal Inventory.
Author: Harold Ireton.
Publisher: Behavior Science Systems, Inc.
Cross References: For reviews by Fred M. Grossman and Randall M. Jones, see 9:941 (1 reference).

[1871]
Personal Style Assessment.

Purpose: To assess an individual's personal style of communication.
Population: Adults.
Publication Dates: 1980–1987.
Scores, 4: Thinker, Intuitor, Sensor, Feeler.
Administration: Group.
Manual: No manual.
Price Data: Price information available from publisher for tests and interpretation sheets.
Time: (15–25) minutes.
Comments: Self-administered, self-scored.
Author: Training House, Inc.
Publisher: Training House, Inc.
Cross References: For reviews by Cathy W. Hall and Gerald L. Stone, see 11:287.

[1872]
Personal Style Assessment, Jung-Parry Form.

Purpose: To assess an individual's relative strength on Jung's four personal styles, or "psychological types."
Population: Adults.
Publication Date: 1992.
Scores, 4: Thinker, Intuitor, Sensor, Feeler.
Administration: Group or individual.
Manual: No manual.
Price Data: Price information available from publisher for set including tests, answer sheets, and interpretation folder.
Time: (20–30) minutes.
Comments: Self-administered; self-scored.
Author: Scott B. Parry.
Publisher: Training House, Inc.
Cross References: For a review by Vicki S. Packman, see 13:227.

[1873]
Personal Style Indicator.

Purpose: Designed to increase mutual understanding, acceptance and communication among people and to increase self-awareness.

Population: Adults.
Publication Dates: 1988–1989.
Acronym: PSI.
Scores, 4: Behavioral Action, Cognitive Analysis, Interpersonal Harmony, Affective Expression.
Administration: Group.
Price Data, 1993: $12 per test booklet; $10 per interpretations booklet (1989, 32 pages); $15 per audiotape (Living with Style); $35 per PSI/JSI Leader's manual (1988, 75 pages).
Time: (90) minutes.
Comments: Self-administered, -scored, -interpreted.
Authors: Terry D. Anderson (test and audiotape), Everett T. Robinson, Jonathan Clark (audiotape), and Susan Clark (audiotape).
Publisher: Consulting Resource Group International, Inc.
Cross References: For reviews by James T. Austin and Kusum Singh, see 13:228.

[1874]
Personal Styles Inventory [PSI-120] [1999 Revision].

Purpose: Provides a comprehensive assessment of normal personality characteristics.
Population: Adults.
Publication Dates: 1990–2001.
Acronym: PSI-120.
Scores, 24: Styles of Expressing Emotions (Sympathetic, Enthusiastic, Expansive, Confronting, Self-Willed, Reserved, Modest, Patient), Styles of Doing Things (Agreeing, Sociable, Excitement-Seeking, Venturing, Restless, Self-Directed, Self-Motivated, Organizing), Styles of Thinking (Traditional, Dedicated, Imaginative, Inquiring, Individualistic, Analytical, Practical, Focused).
Administration: Group or individual.
Price Data: Available from publisher.
Time: (20–30) minutes.
Comments: Computerized interpretation report is available.
Authors: Joseph T. Kunce, Corrine S. Cope, and Russel M. Newton.
Publisher: Educational & Psychological Consultants, Inc.
Cross References: See T5:1954 (1 reference); for reviews by Paul A. Arbisi and Mary Henning-Stout of an earlier edition, see 13:229 (2 references); see also T4:1993 (4 references).

[1875]
Personal Success Profile.

Purpose: Designed "to measure the personality characteristcs of individuals, to assist organizations in hiring the best available applicants and developing current employees to their potential, and to assist individuals in achieving career success and personal contentment."

Population: Current personnel and potential employees.

Publication Dates: 1968–1996.

Scores, 16: AssessmentValidity (Objectivity, Accuracy), Competitiveness Traits (Drive, Assertiveness, Determination, Leadership), Self-Control Traits (Self-Confidence, Emotional Control, Mental Toughness), Dedication Traits (Coachability, Conscientiousness, Responsibility, Trust), Composite Traits (Competitiveness, Self-Control, Dedication), Ambition.

Administration: Individual and group.

Price Data, 1998: $95 per report including participant's report, manager's report, executive profiles, group profiles, subgroup profiles, and group profile overlays; group discounts available.

Time: (45) minutes.

Comments: Derivation of the Athletic Motivation Inventory (217).

Authors: Denis Waitley, Lem Burnham, Charles C. Kaufman, J. Michael Priddy, Linda G. Griggs, Joan L. Francis, Thomas A. Tutko, Leland P. Lyon, and Bruce C. Ogilvie.

Publisher: Winslow Research Institute.

    a) PERSONAL SUCCESS SURVEY.

    Publication Dates: 1990–1995.

    Scores, 3: Ambition, Self-Confidence, Mental Toughness.

    Price Data: Available from publisher.

    Time: (10) minutes.

    Comments: Shortened version of the Personal Success Profile; derivation of the Athletic Motivation Inventory (217).

[1876]
Personal Values Inventory [Personal Strengths Publishing].

Purpose: Designed to facilitate self-discovery of personal style of approaching tasks, conflicts, decision-making, and relationships.

Population: Adolescents and adults with sixth grade or above reading levels.

Publication Dates: 1973–1997.

Acronym: PVI.

Scores: 7 Motivational Values (a set of values that helps a person decide how to act when things are going well); 13 scores reflecting predictable progressive responses to conflict and opposition.

Administration: Group or individual.

Editions, 2: Personal Values Inventory; Mirror Edition of the Personal Values Inventory.

Price Data, 2001: $10 per self-scorable inventory; $30 per manual (1996, 146 pages).

Time: (20–40) minutes.

Comments: Highest scores represent motivational values and valued relating style for an individual; self-scorable; for corporate (e.g., training workshops), and clinical (e.g., individual and group counseling) uses; can be self-administered, but trained administrators and interpreters recommended; Mirror Edition uses self-ratings and ratings from a significant other person.

Authors: Elias H. Porter and Sara E. Maloney.

Publisher: Personal Strengths Publishing.

[1877]
Personal Values Questionnaire.

Purpose: Measures individuals' "values related to achievement, affiliation, and power."

Population: Adults.

Publication Date: 1991.

Acronym: PVQ.

Scores, 3: Achievement, Affiliation, Power.

Administration: Group or individual.

Price Data, 2001: $69 per complete kit including 10 questionnaires and 10 profiles and interpretive notes (10 pages).

Time: [30] minutes.

Comments: Self-scored profile; also available online.

Author: Hay Group.

Publisher: Hay Group.

Cross References: For reviews by Brian F. Bolton and Gary J. Dean, see 13:230.

[1878]
Personality Adjective Check List.

Purpose: "Developed primarily as a self-report instrument for measuring personality in counseling clients and normal adults."

Population: Ages 16–adult.

Publication Dates: 1987–1991.

Acronym: PACL.

Scores, 9: Introversive, Inhibited, Cooperative, Sociable, Confident, Forceful, Respectful, Sensitive, PI (indicator of potential personality problems).

Administration: Group.

Price Data, 2001: $79 per start-up kit including manual (92 pages), scoring keys, 50 test sheets, and 50 profile sheets; $30 per manual; $30 per 50 test sheets; $25 per 50 profile sheets; $15 per scoring key set; $425 per WinPACL and AutoPACL software with narrative interpretations.

Time: (10–15) minutes.

Comments: Conceived as a tool for measuring the personality styles outlined by Theodore Millon among counseling clients and normal adults.

Author: Stephen Strack.

Publisher: 21st Century Assessment.

Cross References: See T5:1958 (1 reference); for reviews by Allen K. Hess and Howard M. Knoff, see 12:289 (1 reference); see also T4:1996 (3 references).

[1879]
Personality Advantage Questionnaire.

Purpose: Designed to "identify personality strengths, and set those strengths in a work context."
Population: Employees.
Publication Date: 1998.
Acronym: PAQ.
Scores, 5: Communication Style, Emotions, Drive and Determination, Relationships with People, Thinking Style.
Administration: Individual.
Manual: No manual.
Price Data, 2001: $14.95 per diskette.
Time: Administration time not reported.
Author: Human Resource Development Press.
Publisher: Human Resource Development Press.

[1880]
Personality Assessment Inventory.

Purpose: Designed to provide information relevant to clinical diagnosis, treatment planning, and screening for psychopathology.
Population: Ages 18–adult.
Publication Date: 1991.
Acronym: PAI.
Scores, 53: Inconsistency, Infrequency, Negative Impression, Positive Impression, Somatic Complaints (Conversion, Somatization, Health Concerns, Total), Anxiety (Cognitive, Affective, Physiological, Total), Anxiety-Related Disorders (Obsessive-Compulsive, Phobias, Traumatic Stress, Total), Depression (Cognitive, Affective, Physiological, Total), Mania (Activity Level, Grandiosity, Irritability, Total), Paranoia (Hypervigilance, Persecution, Resentment, Total), Schizophrenia (Psychotic Experiences, Social Detachment, Thought Disorder, Total), Borderline Features (Affective Instability, Identity Problems, Negative Relationships, Self-Harm, Total), Antisocial Features (Antisocial Behaviors, Egocentricity, Stimulus-Seeking, Total), Alcohol Problems, Drug Problems, Aggression (Aggressive Attitude, Verbal Aggression, Physical Aggression, Total), Suicidal Ideation, Stress, Nonsupport, Treatment Rejection, Dominance, Warmth.
Administration: Individual or group.
Price Data: Available from publisher for comprehensive kit including professional manual (193 pages), 2 reusable item booklets, 2 administration folios, 25 Form HS handscorable answer sheets, 25 adult profile forms, and 25 critical items forms.
Time: [50–60] minutes.
Comments: Self-report inventory of adult psychopathology.
Author: Leslie C. Morey.
Publisher: Psychological Assessment Resources, Inc.
Cross References: See T5:1959 (8 references); for reviews by Gregory J. Boyle and Michael G. Kavan, see 12:290 (8 references); see also T4:1997 (3 references).

[1881]
Personality Assessment Screener.

Purpose: "Designed to identify individuals in need of further assessment for emotional problems, behavioral problems, or both."
Population: Ages 18 and older.
Publication Dates: 1991–1997.
Acronym: PAS.
Scores, 11: Negative Affect, Acting Out, Health Problems, Psychotic Features, Social Withdrawal, Hostile Control, Suicidal Thinking, Alienation, Alcohol Problem, Anger Control, Total.
Administration: Individual or group.
Price Data, 2001: $70 per complete kit including manual (1997, 69 pages) and 25 hand-scorable response forms, and the PAI Software Portfolio.
Time: (5) minutes.
Comments: Screening version of the Personality Assessment Inventory (1880).
Author: Leslie C. Morey.
Publisher: Psychological Assessment Resources, Inc.
Cross References: For a review by Matthew Burns, see 14:288.

[1882]
Personality Disorder Interview—IV: A Semistructured Interview for the Assessment of Personality Disorders.

Purpose: Constructed to "facilitate reliable and valid interview assessments of ... personality disorders."
Population: Ages 18 and older.
Publication Date: 1995.
Acronym: PDI—IV.
Scores, 21: 12 Personality Disorder Scores (Antisocial, Avoidant, Borderline, Dependent, Histrionic, Narcissistic, Obsessive-Compulsive, Paranoid, Schizoid, Schizotypal, Depressive, Passive-Aggressive); 9 Thematic Content Area Scores (Attitudes Toward Self, Attitudes Toward Others, Security/Comfort with Others, Friendships and Relationships, Conflicts and Disagreements, Work and Leisure, Social Norms, Mood, Appearance and Perception).
Administration: Individual.
Price Data: Available from publisher for complete kit including hardcover manual (1995, 277 pages), Personality Disorders Interview Booklet, Thematic Content Areas Interview Booklet, and 10 profile booklets.
Time: [120] minutes.
Comments: Corresponds with DSM—IV Personality Disorder diagnosis criteria.
Authors: Thomas A. Widiger, Steve Mangine, Elizabeth M. Corbitt, Cynthia G. Ellis, and Glenn V. Thomas.
Publisher: Psychological Assessment Resources, Inc.
Cross References: For reviews by Samuel Juni and Paul Retzlaff, see 14:289.

[1883]
Personality Inventory for Children, Second Edition.

Purpose: "Assesses both broad and narrow dimensions of behavioral, emotional, cognitive, and interpersonal adjustment."

Population: Ages 5–19 years (Kindergarten–Grade 12).

Publication Dates: 1977–2001.

Acronym: PIC-2.

Forms, 2: Standard Form, Behavioral Summary.

Administration: Group.

Price Data, 2002: $175 per kit including 2 reusable administration booklets, 50 answer sheets, 1 set of scoring templates, 25 Behavioral Summary AutoScore forms, 50 Standard Form profile sheets, manual (2001, 212 pages), 25 Behavioral Summary profile sheets, and 50 Critical Items summary sheets; $50 per manual; $25 per reusable administration booklet, quantity discount available; $19.50 per 5 Spanish translation administration booklets, quantity discount available; $19.50 per 100 answer sheets; $32.50 per set of scoring templates.

Foreign Language Editions: Spanish editions available for both forms.

Comments: Complete revision and restandardization of Personality Inventory for Children, Revised (PIC-R); old edition no longer available; coordinates with Personality Inventory for Youth (PIY, 1884) and Student Behavior Survey (SBS, 2404).

Authors: David Lachar and Christian P. Gruber.

Publisher: Western Psychological Services.

a) STANDARD FORM.

Scores, 33: 9 Adjustment Scales and 21 Adjustment Subscales: Cognitive Impairment (Inadequate Abilities, Poor Achievement, Developmental Delay), Impulsivity and Distractibility (Disruptive Behavior, Fearlessness), Delinquency (Antisocial Behavior, Dyscontrol, Noncompliance), Family Dysfunction (Conflict Among Members, Parent Maladjustment), Reality Distortion (Developmental Deviation, Hallucinations and Delusions), Somatic Concern (Psychosomatic Preoccupation, Muscular Tension and Anxiety), Psychological Discomfort (Fear and Worry, Depression, Sleep Disturbance/Preoccupation with Death), Social Withdrawal (Social Introversion, Isolation), Social Skill Deficits (Limited Peer Status, Conflict With Peers), 3 Response Validity Scales (Defensiveness, Dissimulation, Inconsistency).

Price Data: $19.50 per 100 Standard Form profiles or 100 Critical Items summary sheets.

Time: (40) minutes.

Comments: Hand-scored; computer scoring option will be available 2003 and will include mail, fax, or computer disks; system requirements DOS 3.0 or above, 512K memory, 286 processor, 1 MB free disk space, 3.5-inch high-density floppy drive.

b) BEHAVIORAL SUMMARY.

Scores, 12: 8 Short Adjustment Scales (Impulsivity and Distractibility—Short, Delinquency—Short, Family Dysfunction—Short, Reality Distortion—Short, Somatic Concern—Short, Psychological Discomfort—Short, Social Withdrawal—Short, Social Skill Deficits—Short), 3 Composite Scales (Externalization—Composite, Internalization—Composite, Adjustment—Composite), Total Score.

Price Data: $29.95 per 25 Behavioral Summary AutoScore answer forms, quantity discount available; $19.50 per 100 Behavioral Summary profiles.

Time: (15) minutes.

Comments: "A quick screening version of the Standard Form; focuses on current behavior that can support the development of a treatment plan; can be administered using standard PIC-2 test materials"; hand-score only.

Cross References: See T5:1962 (23 references) and T4:1998 (21 references); for a review by Howard M. Knoff of an earlier edition, see 10:281 (20 references); for reviews by Cecil R. Reynolds and June M. Tuma of an earlier editions, see 9:949 (5 references); see also T3:1796 (5 references).

[1884]
Personality Inventory for Youth.

Purpose: "Assesses emotional and behavioral adjustment, family character and interaction, and school adjustment and academic ability."

Population: Ages 9–18.

Publication Date: 1995.

Acronym: PIY.

Scores, 37: Validity, Inconsistency, Dissimulation, Defensiveness, Cognitive Impairment (Poor Achievement and Memory, Inadequate Abilities, Learning Problems, Total), Impulsivity and Distractibility (Brashness, Distractibility and Overactivity, Impulsivity, Total), Delinquency (Antisocial Behavior, Dyscontrol, Noncompliance, Total), Family Dysfunction (Parent-Child Conflict, Parent Maladjustment, Marital Discord, Total), Reality Distortion (Feelings of Alienation, Hallucinations and Delusions, Total), Somatic Concern (Psychosomatic Syndrome, Muscular Tension and Anxiety, Preoccupation with Disease, Total), Psychological Discomfort (Fear and Worry, Depression, Sleep Disturbance, Total), Social Withdrawal (Social Introversion, Isolation, Total), Social Skill Deficits (Limited Peer Status, Conflict with Peers, Total).

Administration: Group.

Price Data, 2002: $220 per complete kit including administration and interpretation guide, technical guide, 100 answer sheets, 1 set of scoring templates, 100 profile forms (male and female), 100 critical items summary sheets (male and female), 2 WPS TEST REPORT mail-in answer sheets for computer scoring, 2 reusable administration booklets, audiotape, and 2-use disk for on-site computer scoring and interpretation; $450 per kit for on-site computer scoring including 2 reusable administration booklets, 100 answer sheets, administration and interpretation guide and technical guide, audiotape, and 25-use disk; $25 per reusable administration booklet; $19.50 per Spanish Research Edition reusable administration booklet; $19.50 per 100 answer sheets; $22.50 per 100 profile forms; $22.50 per 100 critical items summary sheets; $18.50 per mail-in answer sheet; $299.50 per 25-use disk (PC with Microsoft Windows); $12 per FAX service scoring charge; $32.50 per set of scoring templates; $15 per audiotape; $45 per administration and interpretation guide; $49.50 per technical guide.

Time: (45) minutes.
Authors: David Lachar and Christian P. Gruber.
Publisher: Western Psychological Services.
Cross References: For reviews by Lizanne DeStefano and by Gregory J. Marchant and T. Andrew Ridenour, see 13:231.

[1885]
Personality Research Form, 3rd Edition.

Purpose: Designed as an "extensively validated comprehensive measure of normal personality."
Population: Grade 6–college, adults.
Publication Dates: 1964–1997.
Acronym: PRF.
Administration: Group or individual.
Levels, 2: Grades 6-16 and adults, college.
Price Data, 2001: $59 per examination kit including manual (1984, 72 pages), 5 test booklets, scoring template, 10 hand-scorable answer sheets, 10 profile sheets, and one machine-scorable answer sheet and coupon for an Extended Report; $29 per test manual; $30.50–$34.50 (depending on volume) per 25 test booklets; $10–$12 (depending on volume) per 25 hand-scorable answer sheets; $10–$12 (depnding on volume) per 25 profile sheets; $14 per scoring template; $79–$89 (depending on volume) per 10 machine-scorable answer sheets and coupons for Extended Report; $40–$45 (depending on volume) per 10 machine-scorable answer sheets and coupons for Basic Report; $28 per audio presentation cassette tape; $99 per software package including disks, software manual for Windows, test manual, and 10 coupons for computer reports; (limited quantities available for Forms A, B, AA, and BB; contact publishers for availability and prices).
Foreign Language Editions: Available in Spanish and French (Form E test booklets only).
Comments: Cassette tape available for audio presentation of Form E.

Author: Douglas N. Jackson.
Publisher: Sigma Assessment Systems, Inc.
  a) FORM A.
  Population: Ages 16–adult.
  Publication Dates: 1965–1985.
  Scores, 15: Achievement, Affiliation, Aggression, Autonomy, Dominance, Endurance, Exhibition, Harmavoidance, Impulsivity, Nurturance, Order, Play, Social Recognition, Understanding, Infrequency.
  Time: (30–45) minutes.
  b) FORM B.
  Comments: Parallel form to Form A.
  c) FORM AA.
  Population: College students.
  Publication Dates: 1965–1985.
  Scores, 22: Same as Form A and Form B plus Abasement, Change, Cognitive Structure, Defendence, Sentience, Succorance, Desirability.
  Time: (40–70) minutes.
  d) FORM BB.
  Comments: Parallel form to Form AA.
  e) FORM E.
  Population: Grade 6–adult.
  Publication Dates: 1974–1987.
  Scores, 22: Same as Form AA.
  Comments: Cassette tape available for administration to individuals with limited verbal skills.
  Time: (30-45) minutes.
Cross References: See T5:1965 (86 references) and T4:2000 (45 references); for reviews by Robert Hogan and Jerry S. Wiggins, see 10:282 (68 references); see also 9:950 (42 references) and T3:1798 (116 references); for a review by Robert Hogan of an earlier edition, see 8:643 (132 references); see also T3:1322 (23 references); for reviews by Anne Anastasi, E. Lowell Kelly, and Jerry Wiggins, and excerpted reviews by John O. Crites, Lonnie D. Valentine, Jr., and Ruth Wessler with Jane Loevinger of an earlier edition, see 7:123 (27 references); see also P:201 (13 references).

[1886]
Personalysis®.

Purpose: Constructed "to inventory personality characteristics of individuals at five different levels" yielding information on "how to maximize personal, interpersonal, and group effectiveness in the work place."
Population: Leaders, employees, families, individuals.
Publication Dates: 1975–2001.
Scores, 32: Preferred Style—Rational Self (Authoritative, Democratic, Structured, Self Directed), Communication Expectations—Socialized Self (Direction, Involvement, Methodology, Input), Motivational Needs—Instinctive Self (Authority, Influence, Control, Understanding), Defensive Self (Coerce, Provoke,

Resist, Reject), Irrational Self (Hostile, Rebellious, Stubborn, Withdrawn); Act, Adapt, Analyze, and Assess scores for Preferred Style—Rational Self, Back-Up Style—Socialized Self, and Functional Stress—Instinctive.
Administration: Individual or group.
Price Data: Available from publisher.
Time: Untimed.
Comments: Self-administered.
Author: James R. Noland.
Publisher: Personalysis Corporation.
Cross References: For reviews by George Engelhard, Jr. and L. Alan Witt of an earlier edition, see 12:291.

[1887]
Personnel Assessment Selection System.

Purpose: To "screen out potential problem employees" before hiring, by screening for trust risk, alienation, and emotional stability.
Population: Retail and business applicants, and applicants for police/fire/security positions.
Publication Dates: 1970–1986.
Acronym: PASS.
Scores: Total score only.
Administration: Group.
Price Data: Available from publisher for test materials including validity/reliability information booklet (1986, 5 pages), information booklet (no date, 13 pages), and validity manual (no date, 95 pages).
Comments: The PASS series are various combinations of the T.A., A.I., E.S., and D.A. Surveys to serve the specific requirements of organizations (PASS includes T.A., A.I., and E.S. Surveys; PASS II includes T.A. and A.I. Surveys; PASS III includes condensation of T.A., A.I., and D.A. Surveys); 4 surveys may be administered separately or in combination.
Author: Alan L. Strand.
Publisher: Predictive Surveys Corporation.
a) ALIENATION INDEX.
Purpose: "A method of determining pre-employment alienated attitudes toward work, employees, work conditions, and fellow employees."
Publication Date: 1982.
Time: (15) minutes.
Comments: Test booklet title is A.I. Survey.
b) TRUSTWORTHINESS ATTITUDE.
Purpose: A trust prediction instrument based purely on attitudinal questions.
Publication Dates: 1970–1983.
Time: (15) minutes.
Comments: Test booklet title is T.A. Survey.
c) EMOTIONAL STABILITY.
Purpose: Self-report questionnaire to indicate emotional status.
Population: Applicants for police and security positions.

Time: (5–10) minutes.
Comments: Test booklet title is E.S. Survey.
d) DRUG ATTITUDE.
Purpose: Evaluates an applicant's attitude toward illegal drug usage and abuse of alcohol.
Time: Administration time not reported.
Comments: Test booklet title is D.A. Survey.
Cross References: For a review by Michael B. Bunch, see 11:288; for reviews by John K. Butler, Jr., and Denise M. Rousseau of the T.A. Survey, see 9:1223.

[1888]
[Personnel Interviewing Forms].

Purpose: Designed to help business and industry to obtain various information from interviewees.
Population: Business and industry.
Publication Dates: 1956–1984.
Administration: Individual.
Manual: No manual.
Time: (20–30) minutes.
Author: Judd-Safian Associates.
Publisher: Martin M. Bruce, Ph.D.
a) INITIAL INTERVIEW TABULATION.
Scores: For recording ratings in 10 areas: Appearance, Voice and Speech, Poise, Health, Education, Manner, Responsiveness, Experience, Job Stability, Motivation.
Price Data, 2001: $5.40 per specimen set; $9.35 per package of forms.
b) DEPTH INTERVIEW PATTERN.
Scores: For interviewing in 5 areas: Work Evaluation, Educational and Social Evaluation, Economic Evaluation, Personality Evaluation, Ambitions Evaluation.
Price Data: $13.75 per specimen set; $26.40 per package of forms.
c) EMPLOYMENT REFERENCE INQUIRY.
Purpose: For securing employee evaluation from previous employers.
Price Data: $4.40 per specimen set; $9.35 per package of forms.

[1889]
Personnel Performance Problems Inventory.

Purpose: To "help supervisors identify the areas of job clarification most likely to improve delegation effectiveness."
Population: Management and administrative personnel.
Publication Dates: 1977–1980.
Acronym: PPPI.
Scores, 5: Responsibility, Authority, Accountability, Results, Conditions.
Administration: Group.
Price Data, 2002: $24.50 per 10 inventories; $16.50 per manual (1980, 16 pages); $38.50 per kit including 10 inventories and manual.

Time: (20–30) minutes.
Author: Albert A. Canfield.
Publisher: Western Psychological Services
Cross References: For a review by Jeffrey H. Greenhaus, see 9:951.

[1890]
Personnel Reaction Blank.

Purpose: "Aids in hiring dependable, conscientious employees."
Population: Ages 15 to adult.
Publication Dates: 1972–1988.
Acronym: PRB.
Scores: Total score only.
Administration: Group.
Price Data, 2001: $56.50 per preview kit; $33.80 per 25 item booklets; $28.60 per scoring key; $35.60 per manual (1972, 12 pages).
Restricted Distribution: "Sold only to companies that employ personnel psychologists or retain consultants qualified to use and interpret psychological tests."
Time: (10–15) minutes.
Authors: Harrison G. Gough and Richard Arvey.
Publisher: Consulting Psychologists Press, Inc.
Cross References: For a review by Donna L. Sundre, see 13:232.

[1891]
Personnel Relations Survey [Revised].

Purpose: "Designed to assess the understanding and behavior of managers in their interpersonal relationships."
Population: Managers.
Publication Dates: 1967–2000.
Acronym: PRS.
Scores, 6: Relationships with Employees (Exposure, Feedback); Relationships with Colleagues (Exposure, Feedback); Relationships with Superiors (Exposure, Feedback).
Administration: Group.
Manual: No manual.
Price Data, 2001: $8.95 per instrument.
Time: Administration time not reported.
Comments: Self-administered, self-scored; based on the Johari Window Model of interpersonal relationships.
Authors: Jay Hall and Martha S. Williams.
Publisher: Teleometrics International.
Cross References: For a review by Matthew E. Lambert, see 14:29.

[1892]
Personnel Selection Inventory.

Purpose: Helps identify job applicants who are likely to be honest and have positive attitudes toward work, safety and customer service and provides a valid, fair,

and cost effective means of identifying applicants who are likely to be productive and responsible.
Population: Job applicants.
Publication Dates: 1975–1980.
Acronym: PSI.
Scores: 21 scales: Honesty, Supervision Attitudes, Tenure, Drug Avoidance Scale, Nonviolence Scale, Employee/Customer Relations Scale, Risk Avoidance Scale, Stress Tolerance Scale, Safety Scale, Work Values Scale, Math Scale, Responsibility, Productivity, Customer Service Aptitude Scale, Customer Service Attitude Scale, Sales Aptitude Scale, Customer Service Index, Candidness Validity Scale, Employability Index, Detailed Personal and Behavioral History.
Administration: Individual or group.
Forms: 20 versions available including non-integrity test versions.
Price Data: Available from publisher.
Time: Varies based on version.
Comments: Previously listed as London House Personnel Selection Inventory.
Author: London House.
Publisher: Reid London House.
Cross References: See T5:1972 (1 reference) and T4:1478 (1 reference); for a review by William I. Sauser, see 9:631; see also T3:1339 (2 references).

[1893]
Personnel Test Battery.

Purpose: Designed to assess numerical skills, language proficiency, and perceptual accuracy.
Population: Office and sales groups.
Publication Dates: 1979–1981.
Acronym: PTB.
Subtests: Available as separates.
Administration: Group.
Levels, 2: 1, 2.
Restricted Distribution: Restricted to persons who have completed the publisher's training course or members of the Division of Occupational Psychology of the British Psychological Society.
Price Data: Available from publisher.
Authors: Peter Saville, Gill Nyfield, Roger Holdsworth (test), and Ruth Holdsworth (manual).
Publisher: SHL Group plc [United Kingdom].
   a) LEVEL 1.
   Comments: "Basic skills and comprehension"; 3 tests plus 2 optional tests for Levels 1 and 2.
     1) Verbal Usage.
     Acronym: VPI.
     Time: 10(15) minutes.
     2) Numerical Comprehension.
     Acronym: NP2.
     Time: 7(12) minutes.
     3) Checking.
     Acronym: CP3.

Time: 7(12) minutes.
4) *Basic Checking.*
Acronym: CP7.
Time: 5(10) minutes.
Comments: Optional test for Levels 1 and 2.
5) *Audio Checking.*
Acronym: CP8.
Time: (15) minutes.
Comments: Optional test for Levels 1 and 2; test administered by cassette tape.
b) LEVEL 2.
Comments: "Higher-order reasoning skills"; 3 tests plus 2 optional tests for Levels 1 and 2.
1) *Classification.*
Acronym: CP4.
Time: 7(12) minutes.
2) *Verbal Meaning.*
Acronym: VP5.
Time: 10(15) minutes.
3) *Numerical Reasoning.*
Acronym: NP6.
Time: 10(15) minutes.

[1894]
Personnel Tests for Industry.

Purpose: To assist in the selection, placement, training, and promotion of individuals in industrial settings.
Population: Trade school and adults.
Publication Dates: 1945–1974.
Acronym: PTI.
Scores: Total score only.
Administration: Group or individual.
Publisher: The Psychological Corporation.
a) PTI-VERBAL TEST.
Publication Dates: 1952–1969.
Acronym: PTI-V.
Forms, 2: A, B.
Price Data, 2002: $41 per examination kit including all forms of Verbal and Numerical booklets and manual (1969, 23 pages); $70 per 25 test booklets (manual, booklets, key) (specify Form A or B); $260 per 100 test booklets (includes manual, booklet, key).
Time: 5(15) minutes.
Author: Alexander G. Wesman.
b) PTI-NUMERICAL TEST.
Publication Dates: 1952–1969.
Acronym: PTI-N.
Forms, 2: A, B.
Price Data: Same as for *a* above.
Time: 20(25) minutes.
Author: Jerome E. Doppelt.
c) PTI-ORAL DIRECTIONS TEST.
Publication Dates: 1945–1974.
Acronym: PTI-ODT.
Forms, 2: S, T.

Price Data: $160 per complete set including script, recording, 100 answer documents, key, and manual (1954, 8 pages); $40 per examination kit including scripts, answer documents for both forms, and manual (does not include scoring keys); $118 per replacement cassette recording (specify form); $95 per 100 answer documents.
Time: (15) minutes.
Author: Charles R. Langmuir.
Cross References: See T5:1974 (1 reference), T4:2008 (5 references), T3:1808 (3 references), T2:433 (5 references), and 7:373 (3 references); for a review by Erwin K. Taylor, see 5:366; see also 4:309 (1 reference); for reviews by Charles D. Flory, Irving Lorge, and William W. Turnbull on the Oral Directions Test, see 3:245.

[1895]
Pharmacy College Admission Test.

Purpose: Designed to measure general academic ability and scientific knowledge needed to begin the study of "pharmacy school curriculum."
Population: Pharmacy college applicants.
Publication Dates: 1976–1994.
Acronym: PCAT.
Scores, 6: Verbal Ability, Quantitative Ability, Biology, Chemistry, Reading Comprehension, Composite.
Administration: Group.
Restricted Distribution: Distribution restricted and test administered at licensed testing centers; details may be obtained from publisher.
Price Data: Available from publisher.
Time: (210) minutes.
Author: The Psychological Corporation.
Publisher: The Psychological Corporation.
Cross References: For reviews by Mark Albanese and Leo M. Harvill, see 13:233.

[1896]
Phelps Kindergarten Readiness Scale.

Purpose: Constructed to assess the academic strengths and weaknesses of children prior to enrolling in kindergarten or shortly after starting school.
Population: Pre-kindergarten and early kindergarten.
Publication Dates: 1991–1997.
Acronym: PKRS.
Scores, 4: Verbal Processing, Perceptual Processing, Auditory Processing, Total Readiness.
Administration: Individual.
Price Data: Available from publisher.
Time: (15) minutes.
Author: LeAdelle Phelps.
Publisher: Psychology Press Inc.
Cross References: For a review by Theresa H. Elofson, see 12:292.

[1897]
Philadelphia Head Injury Questionnaire.

Purpose: Developed for use in gathering the history of individuals with head injuries.
Population: Head trauma patients.
Publication Date: 1991.
Acronym: PHIQ.
Scores: No scores; 6 sections: Identifying Information, Cognitive Aspects, Accident Description, Personality Changes, Persistent Symptoms, Pertinent Personal/Medical History.
Administration: Individual.
Price Data, 2002: $28 per complete kit including 100 questionnaires and manual (2 pages).
Time: [20] minutes.
Authors: Lucille M. Curry, Richard G. Ivins, and Thomas L. Gowen.
Publisher: Western Psychological Services.
Cross References: For reviews by Mark Albanese and William W. Deardorff, see 12:293.

[1898]
Phonemic-Awareness Skills Screening.

Purpose: "The PASS is a quick screening that pinpoints" three "specific areas of phonological weakness": to identify students with problems, to determine strengths and weaknesses, to document progress.
Population: Grades 1–2.
Publication Date: 2000.
Acronym: PASS.
Scores: 8 subtests: Rhyming, Sentence Segmentation, Blending, Syllable Segmentation, Deletion, Phoneme Isolation, Phoneme Segmentation, Substitution, Total.
Administration: Individual.
Price Data, 2001: $29 per complete kit; $19 per 25 record forms; $12 per examiner's manual (2000, 16 pages).
Time: (15) minutes.
Comments: Can be administered by a teacher or assistant, requires "no specialized training in testing"; subtests may be administered separately.
Authors: Linda Crumrine and Helen Lonegan.
Publisher: PRO-ED.

[1899]
Phonological Abilities Test.

Purpose: "A screening test for the identification of children at risk of reading difficulties and as a diagnostic test to assess the nature and extent of phonological difficulties in older children with recognized reading problems."
Population: Ages 5–7.
Publication Date: 1997.
Acronym: PAT.
Scores, 8: Rhyme Detection, Rhyme Production, Word Completion—Syllables, Word Completion—

Phonemes, Phoneme Deletion—Beginning Sounds, Phoneme Deletion—End Sounds, Speech Rate, Letter Knowledge.
Administration: Individual.
Price Data, 2002: $119 per complete kit including examiner's manual (45 pages), stimulus manual, alphabet cards, and 25 record forms in carrying case; $42 per 25 record forms; $49 per examiner's manual; $59 per stimulus manual.
Time: (5) minutes per subtest; (30) minutes per entire battery.
Comments: Normed in the U.K.; tests can be given individually or in combination; normative data are also available for 4-year-olds.
Authors: Valerie Muter, Charles Hulme, and Margaret Snowling.
Publisher: The Psychological Corporation Europe [United Kingdom].

[1900]
Phonological Assessment Battery [Standardised Edition].

Purpose: Designed to identify "those children who need special help by providing an individual assessment of the child's phonological skills."
Population: Ages 6–15.
Publication Date: 1997.
Acronym: PLAB.
Scores: 6 tests: Alliteration, Naming Speed, Rhyme, Spoonerisms, Fluency, Non-Word Reading.
Administration: Individual.
Price Data, 1998: £75 per complete set including 10 record booklets and manual (130 pages); £10 per 10 record booklets; sample sheets are free.
Time: (30–40) minutes.
Comments: Is also appropriate for children whose first language is not English.
Authors: Norah Frederickson, Uta Frith, and Rea Reason.
Publisher: NFER-Nelson Publishing Co., Ltd. [England].

[1901]
The Phonological Awareness Skills Program Test.

Purpose: "Designed to provide a means for placing students at the appropriate entry points in the Phonological Awareness Skills Program Curriculum."
Population: Ages 4 to 10.
Publication Date: 1999.
Acronym: PASP Test.
Scores: Total score only.
Administration: Individual.
Price Data, 2001: $79 per complete kit; $15 per record forms..
Time: (2–4) minutes.

Author: Jerome Rosner.
Publisher: PRO-ED.

[1902]
Phonovisual Diagnostic Tests [1975 Revision].

Purpose: "Designed to test phonetic skills as taught by the Phonovisual Method."
Population: Grades 3–12.
Publication Date: 1975.
Scores: Total score only.
Administration: Group.
Tests: 6 tests consisting of 24 words each.
Price Data, 2001: $9.50 per set of tests and instructions.
Time: Administration time not reported.
Authors: Edna B. Smith and Mazie C. Lloyd.
Publisher: Phonovisual Products, Inc.
Cross References: For reviews by Charles M. Brown and George D. Spache of an earlier edition, see 6:829.

[1903]
Photo Articulation Test, Third Edition.

Purpose: Constructed as a "systematic method for eliciting speech sounds from children and identifying errors in articulation."
Population: Ages 3–8.
Publication Dates: 1969–1997.
Acronym: PAT-3.
Scores: Total score only.
Administration: Individual.
Price Data, 2001: $154 per complete kit; $39 per summary/response forms; $39 per examiner's manual; $55 per photo album picture book; $25 per picture card deck.
Time: (20) minutes.
Authors: Barbara A. Lippke, Stanley E. Dickey, John W. Selmar, and Anton L. Sodor.
Publisher: PRO-ED.
Cross References: For a review by David P. Hurford, see 14:291; see also T5:1982 (15 references), T4:2017 (12 references), 9:957 (2 references), and T3:1814 (5 references); for a review by Lawrence D. Shriberg of an earlier edition, see 8:969 (1 reference); see also 7:962 (2 references).

[1904]
PHSF Relations Questionnaire.

Purpose: Constructed "to measure … the personal, home, social and formal relations of high school pupils, students and adults, in order to determine the level of adjustment."
Population: Standards 6–10 in South African school system, college, and adults.
Publication Dates: 1969–1971.

Acronym: PHSF.
Scores, 12: Personal (Self-Confidence, Self-Esteem, Self-Control, Nervousness, Health), Home (Family Influences, Personal Freedom), Social (Sociability-Group, Sociability-Specific Person, Moral Sense), Formal Relations, Validity Scale.
Administration: Group.
Price Data: Available from publisher.
Time: (30) minutes.
Comments: Test materials in both English and Afrikaans.
Authors: F. A. Fouche and P. E. Grobbelaar.
Publisher: Human Sciences Research Council [South Africa].

[1905]
Picha-Seron Career Analysis.

Purpose: "Provides a description and analysis of an individual's workstyle and relates this workstyle to 178 selected technical, managerial and professional occupations (career profile and occupational profile) or to an in-depth workstyle analysis (personnel profile)."
Population: Middle school-adult.
Publication Dates: 1991–1993.
Acronym: PSCA.
Administration: Individual or group.
Price Data: Not available.
Time: [10–15] minutes.
Author: Merron S. Seron.
Publisher: International Career Planning Services, Inc. [No reply from publisher; status unknown].
a) PSCA-CAREER PROFILE.
Population: Middle school-secondary school.
Acronym: PSCA-CP.
Scores, 16: Workstyle Graph Interpretations (Dominance, Influence, Adaptance, Compliance), Occupational Strengths (Practical, Analytical, Creative, Service, Managerial, Supportive), Learning Styles (Cognitive Organization, Internality, Time Orientation), Occupational Scales (178).
b) PSCA-OCCUPATIONAL PROFILE.
Population: College-adult.
Acronym: PSCA-OP.
Scores, 18: Workstyle Graphs (Ideal Self, Pressure Self, Usual Self), other scores same as *a* above.
c) PSCA-PERSONNEL PROFILE.
Population: Adults.
Acronym: PSCA-PP.
Scores, 18: Verification Score, Workstyle Graphs (Ideal Self, Pressure Self, Usual Self), Workstyle Graph Interpretations (Dominance, Influence, Adaptance, Compliance), Strength of Occupational Area (Practical, Analytical, Creative, Service, Managerial, Supportive), Learning Styles (Internality, Cognitive Organization, Time Orientation), Major Workstyles.

Cross References: For reviews by Michael B. Bunch and Bertram C. Sippola, see 12:295.

[1906]
Pictographic Self Rating Scale.

Purpose: Designed to assess pupils' attitudes toward their academic subjects and classroom activities.
Population: High school and college.
Publication Dates: 1955–1957.
Scores: Total score only.
Administration: Group.
Price Data: Available from publisher.
Time: (35) minutes.
Author: Einar R. Ryden.
Publisher: Psychometric Affiliates.
Cross References: For reviews by Stanley E. Davis and John D. Krumboltz, see 6:701 (2 references).

[1907]
Pictorial Reasoning Test.

Purpose: Assesses general learning ability independent of language and reading skills.
Population: Entry-level positions in a variety of occupations.
Publication Dates: 1966–1994.
Acronym: PRT.
Scores: Total score only.
Administration: Individual or group.
Price Data: Available from publisher.
Time: 15 minutes.
Comments: Previously listed as SRA Pictorial Reasoning Test.
Authors: Robert N. McMurry and Phyllis D. Arnold (test), and Bruce A. Campbell (manual).
Publisher: Reid London House.
Cross References: For reviews by Raymond A. Katzell and John E. Milholland, and an excerpted review by John L. Horn, see 7:381.

[1908]
The Pictorial Scale of Perceived Competence and Social Acceptance for Young Children.

Purpose: Measures "perceived competence and perceived social acceptance" in young children.
Population: Preschool through second grade.
Publication Dates: 1980–1983.
Scores, 4: Cognitive Competence, Peer Acceptance, Physical Competence, Maternal Acceptance.
Administration: Individual.
Forms, 2: Preschool/Kindergarten, First/Second Grade.
Price Data: Available from publisher.
Time: Administration time not reported.
Comments: Downward extension of the Perceived Competence Scale for Children.
Authors: Susan Harter and Robin Pike in collaboration with Carole Efron, Christine Chao, and Beth Ann Bierer.

Publisher: Susan Harter, University of Denver.
Cross References: See T5:1987 (23 references) and T4:2022 (6 references); for reviews by William B. Michael and Susan M. Sheridan, see 11:292 (9 references).

[1909]
Pictorial Test of Intelligence, Second Edition.

Purpose: Designed to "provide a test of general intelligence for children with or without disabilities."
Population: Ages 3–8.
Publication Dates: 1964–2001.
Acronym: PTI-2.
Scores, 4: Verbal Abstractions, Form Discrimination, Quantitative Concepts, Pictorial Intelligence Quotient.
Administration: Individual.
Price Data, 2001: $139 per kit including examiner's manual (2001, 87 pages), picture book, and 25 profile/examiner record booklets; $39 per 25 record booklets; $44 per manual; $59 per picture book.
Time: (15–30) minutes.
Author: Joseph L. French.
Publisher: PRO-ED.
Cross References: See T3:1823 (3 references); for an excerpted review by Thomas A. Smith, see 8:223 (11 references); see also T2:517 (1 reference); for reviews by Philip Himelstein and T. Ernest Newland, see 7:418 (17 references); see also 6:531 (2 references).

[1910]
Picture Identification Test.

Purpose: "Designed to measure judgments, attitudes, sex-of picture differences, organizing principle strength, and need ego relationships associations pertaining to 22 needs based on the Murray need system."
Population: 12 years and older.
Publication Dates: 1959–1979.
Acronym: PIT.
Scores: 4 scores (Judgment Problem, Ego Problem, Organizing Principle, Sex-of-Picture) for each of 22 needs (Abasement, Achievement, Affiliation, Aggression, Autonomy, Blame Avoidance, Counteraction, Deference, Dependence, Dominance, Exhibition, Gratitude, Harm Avoidance, Inferiority Avoidance, Nurturance, Order, Play, Rejection, Sentience, Sex, Succorance, Understanding), plus scores for 3 need dimensions (Combative, Personal-Social, Competitive), 6 Dimension Confusion scores, 3 Dimension Weight scores, 9 Sex-of-Picture Dimension Attitude score, scores for 10 need clusters (Friendliness, Intimacy, Inhibition, Competition, Dominance, Sociability, Independence, Aggression, Performance, Failure Avoidance), 10 Cluster Problem scores, 10 Combative Dimension Cluster Problem scores, 10 Personal-Social Dimension Cluster Problem scores, 10 Competitive Dimension Cluster Problem scores, 20 Combative

Dimension Cluster Conflict score, 9 Personal-Social Dimension Cluster Conflict scores, 10 Competitive Dimension Cluster Conflict scores, 13 Averaged Set Problem scores, 1 General Motivation System Function score.
Administration: Group or individual
Price Data: Available from publisher.
Time: [40] minutes.
Author: Jay L. Chambers.
Publisher: Jay L. Chambers.
Cross References: See T4:2026 (2 references), T3:1825 (3 references), T2:1490 (2 references), and P:463 (17 references).

[1911]

Picture Test A.

Purpose: Developed to assess intelligence.
Population: Ages 6-9 to 8-3.
Publication Dates: 1955–1970.
Scores: Total score only.
Administration: Group.
Price Data: Available from publisher.
Time: 22(27) minutes.
Comments: Formerly called Picture Test 1.
Author: Joan E. Stuart.
Publisher: NFER-Nelson Publishing Co., Ltd. [England].
Cross References: For reviews by Charlotte E. K. Banks and M. L. Kellmer Pringle, see 5:367.

[1912]

Picture Vocational Interest Questionnaire for Adults.

Purpose: "To measure the interest ... in certain occupational activities."
Population: Long-term South African prisoners who have passed Standard 5.
Publication Date: 1981.
Acronym: PVI.
Scores: 11 raw score groupings: Clerical Work, Higher Engineering Trades, Lower Engineering Trades, Wood-Work, Painting, Building, Domestic Work, Food Preparation, Agriculture, Tailoring, Leather-Work.
Administration: Group.
Price Data: Available from publisher.
Time: (45–60) minutes.
Comments: Manual is in English and Afrikaans.
Authors: J. J. Taljaard and J. S. Gericke (test).
Publisher: Human Sciences Research Council [South Africa].

[1913]

Piers-Harris Children's Self-Concept Scale (The Way I Feel About Myself).

Purpose: "Designed to aid in the assessment of self-concept in children and adolescents."
Population: Grades 4–12.

Publication Dates: 1969–1984.
Acronym: PHCSCS.
Scores: Total score plus 6 cluster scores: Behavior, Intellectual and School Status, Physical Appearance and Attributes, Anxiety, Popularity, Happiness and Satisfaction.
Administration: Group.
Foreign Language Edition: Spanish boolets are available.
Price Data, 2001: $99.50 per complete kit including 20 AutoScore™ answer forms, manual (1984, 113 pages), and 2 prepaid mail-in answer sheets for computer scoring and interpretation; $29.50 per 20 AutoScore™ answer forms; $49.50 per manual; $17.50 per 20 Spanish test booklets; $19.50 per scoring key for Spanish test booklet; $22.50 per profile form for Spanish test booklet; $15.50 per mail-in answer sheet; $230 per 25-use disk (PC with DOS); $15 per 100 PC answer sheets; $9.50 per FAX service scoring.
Time: (15–20) minutes.
Comments: The publisher advised in January 2002 that this test is in revision.
Authors: Ellen V. Piers and Dale B. Harris (test).
Publisher: Western Psychological Services.
Cross References: See T5:1991 (108 references) and T4:2030 (123 references); for reviews by Jayne H. Epstein and Patrick J. Jeske, see 9:960 (38 references); see also T3:1831 (107 references), 8:646 (95 references), and T2:1326 (10 references); for a review by Peter M. Bentler, see 7:124 (8 references).

[1914]

A Pill Scale.

Purpose: Designed to measure attitudes toward oral contraception.
Population: Adults.
Publication Dates: 1969–1988.
Scores: Total score only.
Administration: Group.
Manual: No manual.
Price Data, 2002: $1 per scale.
Time: [10] minutes.
Comments: Supplementary article available.
Author: Panos D. Bardis.
Publisher: Donna Bardis.
Cross References: See 8:350 (3 references).

[1915]

PIP Developmental Charts, Second Edition.

Purpose: Assess behaviors to establish several developmental levels.
Population: Mentally handicapped children birth to age 5.
Publication Dates: 1976–1998.
Scores: Profile of 5 areas of development: Physical, Social, Eye-Hand, Development of Play, Language.

Administration: Individual.
Manual: No manual (instructions for administration and scoring included on test).
Price Data, 2002: £12.99 per 10 charts; £3.99 per specimen copy.
Time: Administration time not reported.
Authors: Dorothy M. Jeffree and Ray McConkey.
Publisher: Hodder & Stoughton Educational [England].
Cross References: For reviews by Joan F. Goodman and Robert L. Slonaker, see 9:961.

[1916]
PLAN.

Purpose: Measures knowledge and skills attained early in secondary education in four curriculum areas: English, mathematics, reading, and science reasoning, to provide students "with information they will need to plan and prepare for future academic and career success."
Population: Grade 10.
Publication Dates: 1989–2001.
Administration: Group.
Price Data: Available from publisher.
Time: 115 minutes for 4 academic tests; (60–70) minutes for student information, Interest Inventory, Study Power Assessment, and High School Course information.
Comments: Formerly called P-ACT+.
Author: ACT, Inc.
Publisher: ACT, Inc.
a) PLAN ENGLISH TEST.
Purpose: Measures understanding of the conventions of standard written English.
Scores, 7: Usage/Mechanics (Punctuation, Basic Grammar, Sentence Structure), Rhetorical Skills (Strategy, Organization, Style), Total.
Time: 30 minutes.
b) PLAN MATHEMATICS TEST.
Purpose: Measures level of mathematical reasoning and achievement.
Scores, 5: Algebra (Pre-Algebra, Elementary Algebra), Geometry (Coordinate Geometry, Plane Geometry), Total.
Time: 40 minutes.
c) PLAN READING TEST.
Purpose: Measures reading comprehension as a product of referring and reasoning skills.
Scores: Total score only.
Time: 20 minutes.
d) PLAN SCIENCE REASONING TEST.
Purpose: Measures scientific reasoning skills.
Scores: Total score only.
Time: 25 minutes.

Cross References: See T5:1997 (1 reference); for reviews by Martha Blackwell and Mary Henning-Stout, see 12:296.

[1917]
Plane Geometry: National Achievement Tests.

Purpose: To measure students' knowledge of plane geometry.
Population: High school.
Publication Dates: 1958–1960.
Scores: Total score only.
Administration: Group.
Forms, 2: A, B.
Price Data: Available from publisher.
Time: 40(45) minutes.
Authors: Ray Webb and Julius H. Hlavaty.
Publisher: Psychometric Affiliates.
Cross References: For a review by Dorothy L. Jones, see 7:540.

[1918]
Plane Trigonometry: National Achievement Tests.

Purpose: To measure students' knowledge of plane trigonometry.
Population: Grades 10–16.
Publication Dates: 1958–1960.
Scores: Total score only.
Administration: Group.
Forms, 2: A, B.
Price Data: Available from publisher.
Time: 40(45) minutes.
Authors: Ray Webb and Julius H. Hlavaty.
Publisher: Psychometric Affiliates.

[1919]
The Play Observation Scale.

Purpose: To assess children's free play preferences.
Population: Preschool children.
Publication Date: 1989.
Acronym: POS.
Scores: 27 possible ratings: 6 Non-Play (Transition, Unoccupied, Onlooker, Aggression, Teacher Conversation, Peer Conversation); 18 Play, 6 ratings (Functional, Exploratory, Reading, Constructive, Dramatic, Games) in each of 3 areas (Solitary, Parallel, Group); 3 Affective (Positive, Negative, Neutral).
Administration: Individual.
Price Data: Price available from publisher for complete kit including manual (19 pages).
Time: (4–5) minutes per observation.
Author: Kenneth H. Rubin.
Publisher: Kenneth H. Rubin (the author).
Cross References: For reviews by Denise M. DeZolt and Mark H. Fugate, see 13:234.

[1920]
Police Promotion Tests—Complete Service.

Purpose: "Custom-made test to fit duties and responsibilities for promotion of Police Officers."

Population: Police officers.

Publication Dates: 1979–1998.

Scores: 6 subtests: Technical Police Knowledge, Investigative Knowledge, Legal Knowledge, Supervisory and Managerial Knowledge, Administrative Knowledge, Comprehension Ability, Total.

Administration: Group.

Restricted Distribution: Distribution restricted to civil service commissions and qualified municipal officials.

Price Data: Available from publisher.

Time: (210) minutes.

Comments: Candidate study guide available.

Author: McCann Associates, Inc.

Publisher: McCann Associates, Inc.

[1921]
Police Selection Test.

Purpose: "Designed to measure abilities important for successful performance in training and on-the-job" as a police officer.

Population: Police officer applicants.

Publication Dates: 1989–1995.

Acronym: PST.

Scores: Total score only.

Administration: Group.

Price Data: Price information available from publisher for test material including Technical manual (1990, 17 pages), Administrator's Guide (1990, 8 pages), and Study Guide and sample questions (1990, 21 pages).

Time: (120) minutes.

Comments: Measures reading comprehension, quantitative problem solving, data interpretation, writing skills, and verbal problem solving.

Author: Psychological Services, Inc.

Publisher: Psychological Services, Inc.

Cross References: For reviews by Jim C. Fortune and Deniz S. Ones, see 14:292.

[1922]
Polish Proficiency Test.

Purpose: "Designed to evaluate the level of proficiency in Polish attained by American and other English-speaking learners of Polish."

Population: Postsecondary to adult.

Publication Date: 1992.

Acronym: PPT.

Scores, 3: Listening Comprehension, Reading Comprehension, Structure.

Administration: Group.

Price Data, 2002: $25 per test; quantity discounts available.

Time: (150) minutes.

Comments: Machine-scorable.

Author: Center for Applied Linguistics.

Publisher: Center for Applied Lingusistics.

[1923]
Politte Sentence Completion Test.

Purpose: To elicit information from individuals concerning their immediate environments, especially the people in the environments.

Population: Grades 1–8, 7–12, and adults functioning at elementary school level.

Publication Dates: 1970–1971.

Acronym: PSCT.

Scores: No scores.

Administration: Individual or group.

Price Data, 2002: $8.25 per 25 tests (specify form) and manual (1971, 1 page); $4.50 per specimen set.

Time: (15) minutes.

Comments: Subjective scoring.

Author: Alan J. Politte.

Publisher: Psychologists and Educators, Inc.

a) ELEMENTARY SCHOOL FORM.
Population: Grades 1–8.
Publication Dates: 1970–1971.
b) INTERMEDIATE AND SECONDARY FORM.
Population: Grades 7–12.
Publication Date: 1971.
c) ADULT FORM.
Population: Adults functioning at elementary school level.
Publication Date: Not reported.

[1924]
Polyfactorial Study of Personality.

Purpose: Developed "to offer diagnostic profiles approximating those which would be obtained with projective instruments."

Population: Adults.

Publication Dates: 1959–1984.

Acronym: PSP.

Scores, 11: Hypochondriasis, Sexual Identification, Anxiety, Social Distance, Sociopathy, Depression, Compulsivity, Repression, Paranoia, Schizophrenia, Hyperaffectivity.

Administration: Group.

Price Data, 2001: $54.50 per test package; $59 per IBM answer sheet/profile sheet package; $39 per set of IBM scoring stencils; $41.50 per manual (1959, 11 pages) and manuals supplement (1984, 17 pages); $53.50 per specimen set.

Time: (45-50) minutes.

Authors: Ronald H. Stark and Martin M. Bruce.

Publisher: Martin M. Bruce, Ph.D.

Cross References: For reviews by Bertram D. Cohen and Donald R. Peterson and an excerpted review by Edward S. Bordin, see 6:160.

[1925]
Portable Tactual Performance Test.

Purpose: Designed to assess the speed of movement, tactile perception, and problem solving ability.
Population: Ages 5 to adult.
Publication Date: 1984.
Acronym: P-TPT.
Scores, 3: Dominant Hand, Non-dominant Hand, Both Hands.
Administration: Individual.
Price Data: Available from publisher for test kit including 50 record forms, 6-hole and 10-hole form boards in case, and manual (8 pages).
Time: (10-15) minutes per trial (three trial limit).
Comments: A portable alternative to the original Tactual Performance Test for use with the Halstead-Reitan Neuropsychological Test Battery (1114).
Author: Psychological Assessment Resources, Inc.
Publisher: Psychological Assessment Resources, Inc.
Cross References: For a review by Calvin P. Garbin, see 11:296.

[1926]
Porteus Mazes.

Purpose: "Designed to examine the individual's ability or ... tendency to use planning capacity, prudence and mental alertness in a new situation of a concrete nature."
Publication Dates: 1914–1965.
Scores, 2: Quantitative, Qualitative.
Administration: Group.
Price Data, 2002: $19 per 100 score sheets; $56 per manual (1965, 324 pages).
Comments: Formerly called The Porteus Maze Test.
Author: S. D. Porteus.
Publisher: The Psychological Corporation.
a) VINELAND REVISION.
Population: Ages 3–12, 14, adult.
Price Data: $225 per basic set including mazes and 100 score sheets.
Time: Administration time not recorded.
b) PORTEUS MAZE EXTENSION.
Population: Ages 7–12, 14, adult.
Price Data: $165 per basic set including mazes and 100 score sheets.
Time: [25] minutes.
Comments: For use only as a practice-free retest of *a*.
c) PORTEUS MAZE SUPPLEMENT.
Population: Ages 7–12, 14, adult.
Price Data: $155 per basic set including 100 each of 8 mazes.
Time: [25] minutes.
Comments: For use only as a third retest after *a* and *b*.
Cross References: See T5:2010 (24 references), T4:2051 (25 references), 9:965 (19 references), T3:1853

(34 references), 8:224 (25 references), and T2:518 (52 references); for reviews by Richard F. Docter and John L. Horn, and excerpted reviews by William D. Altus, H. B. Gibson, D. C. Kendrick, and Laurance F. Shaffer, see 7:419 (67 references); see also 6:532 (38 references) and 5:412 (28 references); for reviews by C. M. Louttit and Gladys C. Schwesinger, see 4:356 (56 references).

[1927]
Portland Digit Recognition Test.

Purpose: "Designed for neuropsychological assessment of exaggeration and malingering."
Population: Adults.
Publication Dates: 1989–1992.
Acronym: PDRT.
Scores, 3: Easy Items, Hard Items, Total.
Administration: Individual.
Price Data: Available from publisher.
Time: (40-50) minutes.
Author: Laurence M. Binder.
Publisher: Laurence M. Binder (the author).
Cross References: For reviews by Charles J. Long and Stephanie Western and Orest E. Wasyliw, see 12:297 (1 reference); see also T4:2052 (1 reference).

[1928]
Portland Problem Behavior Checklist—Revised.

Purpose: "Developed to aid school and mental health personnel to identify problem behaviors, make classification or diagnostic decisions, and evaluate counseling, intervention, or behavior consultation procedures."
Population: Grades K–12.
Publication Dates: 1980–1992.
Acronym: PPBC-R.
Administration: Individual.
Price Data, 2001: $45 per complete kit; $20 per 25 male or female forms.
Time: Untimed.
Comments: Respondents are professionals working with children; scoring form also includes opportunity to report on "other" problems (those not specifically included as a subscale).
Author: Steven A. Waksman.
Publisher: Enrichment Press.
a) FORM FOR FEMALES, GRADES K–6.
Scores, 4: Conduct Problems, Peer Problems, Personal Problems, Total.
b) FORM FOR FEMALES, GRADES 7–12.
Scores, 5: Academic Problems, Personal Problems, Conduct Problems, Anxiety Problems, Total.
c) FORM FOR MALES, GRADES K–6.
Scores, 5: Conduct Problems, Academic Problems, Anxiety Problems, Peer Problems, Total.

d) FORM FOR MALES, GRADES 7–12.

Scores, 6: Academic Problems, Anxiety Problems, Peer Problems, Conduct Problems, Personal Problems, Total.

Cross References: For reviews by Thomas McKnight and Robert Spies, see 14:293; for reviews by Terry A. Stinnett and John G. Svinicki of an earlier edition, see 10:287 (1 reference).

[1929]
Portrait of Overdone Strengths.

Purpose: Designed to demonstrate how one may "overdo or misapply" personal strengths, thereby contributing to unwarranted conflict in relationships.

Population: Adults.

Publication Dates: 1973–1996.

Scores, 3: Profile, Most Overdone Strengths, Least Overdone Strengths.

Administration: Group or individual

Price Data, 2001: $5.50 per test booklet; $100 per facilitation guide.

Time: (20–40) minutes.

Comments: To be used with the Strength Deployment Inventory (2380); self-report using Q Sort; Feedback Edition of the Portrait of Overdone Strengths uses self-ratings and ratings from a significant other person.

Author: Personal Strengths Publishing.

Publisher: Personal Strengths Publishing.

[1930]
Portrait of Personal Strengths.

Purpose: "Designed to help you see how you use your strengths when things are going well in your relationships."

Population: Adults.

Publication Dates: 1973–1996.

Scores, 3: Profile, Top Strengths (6), Least Deployed Strengths (6).

Administration: Group or individual.

Price Data, 2001: $5.50 per test booklet; $100 per facilitation guide.

Time: (20–40) minutes.

Comments: To be used with the Strength Deployment Inventory (2380); self-report by Q Sort; Feedback Edition of the Portrait of Personal Strengths uses self-rating and ratings from a significant other person.

Author: Personal Strengths Publishing.

Publisher: Personal Strengths Publishing.

[1931]
Position Analysis Questionnaire.

Purpose: Constructed to analyze "jobs in terms of work activities and work-situation variables."

Population: Business and industrial jobs.

Publication Dates: 1969–1989.

Acronym: PAQ.

Scores: 45 dimensions in 7 divisions: Information Input, Mental Processes, Work Output, Relationships with Other Persons, Job Context, Other Job Characteristics, Overall Dimensions.

Administration: Individual.

Price Data: Available from publisher.

Time: Administration time not reported.

Comments: Ratings by 2 or more analysts; also provides estimates of selected employment tests useful for personnel selection and job evaluation points.

Authors: Ernest J. McCormick, Robert C. Mecham, and P. R. Jeanneret.

Publisher: PAQ Services, Inc.

Cross References: See T5:2016 (2 references); for reviews by Ronald A. Ash and George C. Thornton III, see 12:299 (2 references); see also T4:2054 (17 references) and T3:1855 (12 references); for a review by Alan R. Bass, see 8:983 (17 references).

[1932]
Positive and Negative Syndrome Scale.

Purpose: Designed to assist in the assessment of schizophrenia.

Population: Psychiatric patients.

Publication Dates: 1986–1992.

Acronym: PANSS.

Scores: 9 clinical dimensions: Positive Syndrome, Negative Syndrome, Composite Index, General Psychopathology, Anergia, Thought Disturbance, Activation, Paranoid Belligerence, Depression.

Administration: Individual.

Price Data, 2002: $135 per complete kit including manual (1986, 59 pages), 25 QuikScore™ forms, and 25 Structured Clinical Interview forms; $30 per manual, $32 per 25 QuikScore™ forms; $55 per 25 SCI-PANSS Structured Clinical Interview forms.

Time: (30–40) minutes.

Comments: Completed by clinician.

Authors: Stanley R. Kay, Lewis A. Opler, and Abraham Fiszbein.

Publisher: Multi-Health Systems, Inc.

Cross References: See T5:2017 (17 references); for reviews by Barbara J. Kaplan and Cecil R. Reynolds, see 12:300 (15 references); see also T4:2055 (1 reference).

[1933]
Post-Assault Traumatic Brain Injury Interview and Checklist.

Purpose: "Designed to assist in treatment planning for neuropsychological and neurological evaluation, treatment, and rehabilitation."

Population: Assault victims.

Publication Date: 1997.

Acronym: P-TBI-IC.

Scores: 13 symptom areas: Hallmarks of Brain Injury Alertness, Prosody, Memory, Sensorimotor Functions,

Speech, Academic Abilities, Cognitive Problem Solving, Organic Depression, Organic Anxiety, Organic Impulsivity, Laterality, Treatment Problems.
Administration: Group or individual.
Price Data, 2002: $75 per complete kit including manual (11 pages), and 10 test booklets; $50 per 10 test booklets; $30 per manual; student, volume, and research discounts available.
Time: Administration time not reported.
Comments: Ratings by health care professionals, shelter personnel, sexual assault center personnel, and from data obtained from client, significant others, and other health care professionals.
Authors: Martha E. Banks and Rosalie J. Ackerman.
Publisher: ABackans DCP, Inc.

[1934]
Posttraumatic Stress Diagnostic Scale.

Purpose: "Designed to aid in the diagnosis of posttraumatic stress disorder."
Population: Ages 17–65.
Publication Date: 1995.
Acronym: PDS.
Scores, 5: Symptom Severity Score, Number of Symptoms Endorsed, Symptom Severity Rating, Level of Impairment in Functioning, PTSD Diagnosis.
Administration: Group.
Price Data, 2002: $53 per hand scoring starter kit including manual (54 pages), 10 answer sheets, 10 scoring worksheets, and 1 scoring sheet; $120 per hand scoring reorder kit including 50 answer sheets, 50 scoring worksheets, and 1 scoring sheet; $19 per 25 MICROTEST Q answer sheets; $5 per MICROTEST Q profile report; $30 per manual; $42 per MICROTEST Q preview package including manual, answer sheets, and materials for 3 assessments.
Time: (10–15) minutes.
Author: Edna B. Foa.
Publisher: NCS Assessments (Minnetonka).
Cross References: For reviews by Stephen N. Axford and Beth Doll, see 14:294; see also T5:2018 (1 reference).

[1935]
Posture and Fine Motor Assessment of Infants.

Purpose: Designed to identify motor delays in infants and to monitor progress in the first year of life.
Population: Ages 2–12 months.
Publication Date: 2000.
Acronym: PFMAI.
Scores, 2: Posture, Fine Motor.
Administration: Individual.
Price Data, 2001: $55 per manual (99 pages).
Time: (25–30) minutes.
Authors: Jane Case-Smith and Rosemarie Bigsby.

Publisher: Therapy Skill Builders—A Division of The Psychological Corporation.

[1936]
Power and Performance Measures.

Purpose: Battery of nine aptitude and ability tests designed to measure both potential and achievement in a wide range of occupational settings.
Population: Ages 16 and over.
Publication Date: 1990.
Acronym: PPM.
Scores: Verbal Reasoning, Verbal Comprehension, Perceptual Reasoning, Spatial Ability, Numerical Reasoning, Numerical Computation, Mechanical Understanding, Clerical Speed and Accuracy, Applied Logic.
Administration: Group or individual.
Price Data, 2001: £55 per technical manual; £6,59 per question booklet; £2.75 per answer sheet; £133 per specimen set.
Time: (3–12) minutes.
Author: James S. Barrett.
Publisher: The Test Agency Limited [England].

[1937]
Power Base Inventory.

Purpose: Assesses the techniques individuals use to influence others.
Population: Work team members, leaders, managers, supervisors.
Publication Dates: 1985–1991.
Acronym: PBI.
Scores, 6: Information, Expertise, Goodwill, Authority, Reward, Discipline.
Administration: Group or individual.
Price Data, 2001: $8.50 per inventory.
Time: (15) minutes.
Comments: Self-scored.
Authors: Kenneth W. Thomas and Gail Fann Thomas.
Publisher: Consulting Psychologists Press, Inc.
Cross References: For a review by Judy L. Elliott, see 13:235.

[1938]
Power Management Inventory.

Purpose: "Designed to assess a manager's characteristic management of influence dynamics; that is, how a given manager prefers to handle situations calling for the exercise of power and authority."
Population: Managers.
Publication Dates: 1981–2000.
Acronym: PMI.
Scores, 4: Power Motive (Personalized, Socialized, Affiliative), Power Style.
Administration: Group.
Manual: No manual.
Price Data, 2001: $8.95 per instrument.

Time: Administration time not reported.
Comments: Self-administered survey; companion to Power Management Profile (1939).
Authors: Jay Hall and James Hawker.
Publisher: Teleometrics International.
Cross References: For reviews by Philip G. Benson and William A. Owens, see 9:967.

[1939]
Power Management Profile.

Purpose: Assesses "the methods and reasons which most characterize your manager's handling of power situations."
Population: Managers.
Publication Dates: 1981–1995.
Acronym: PMP.
Scores, 5: Power Motive (Personalized, Socialized, Affiliative), Power Style, Moral.
Administration: Group.
Manual: No manual.
Price Data, 2001: $8.95 per instrument.
Time: Administration time not reported.
Comments: Self-administered survey; companion to Power Management Inventory (1938).
Authors: Jay Hall and James Hawker.
Publisher: Teleometrics International.
Cross References: For a review by Rhonda L. Gutenberg, see 9:968.

[1940]
The Power of Influence Test.

Purpose: Designed as an instrument that "records the attitudes of pupils toward each other and tells which pupils have friendship capacity."
Population: Grade 5 and over.
Publication Date: No date.
Scores: Total score only.
Administration: Group.
Price Data: Available from publisher.
Time: (5) minutes.
Comments: Also referred to as The Sociometric Test.
Authors: Roy Cochrane and Wesley Roeder.
Publisher: Psychometric Affiliates.

[1941]
Practical Adolescent Dual Diagnostic Interview.

Purpose: "To elicit information relevant to the identification and diagnosis of mental health and substance use disorders in adolescents."
Population: Ages 12–18.
Publication Date: 2000.
Acronym: PADDI.
Scores, 17: Major Depressive Episode, Manic Episode, Mixed Episode, Psychotic Symptoms, Panic At-tacks, Anxiety and Phobias, Posttraumatic Stress Disor-der, Obsessions/Compulsions, Conduct Disorder, Oppo-sitional Defiant Disorder, Personality Disorders, Paranoid Personality Traits, Dependent Personality Traits, Sexual Orientation, Substance Abused Disorders, Dangerousness to Self or Others, Child Abuse—Victimization.
Administration: Individual.
Price Data: Available from publisher.
Time: (20–40) minutes.
Comments: A structured diagnostic interview com-patible with the DSM-IV diagnostic criteria; can be administered by paraprofessionals as a screening device.
Authors: Todd W. Estroff and Norman G. Hoffmann.
Publisher: Evince Clinical Assessments.

[1942]
Practical Maths Assessments.

Purpose: Designed to assess knowledge and skills in practical mathematics.
Publication Date: 1990.
Administration: Group.
Price Data: Available from publisher.
Time: Administration time not reported.
Comments: Other test materials (e.g., dice, calcula-tors) must be supplied by examiner.
Authors: Derek Foxman, Neil Hagues, and Graham Ruddock.
Publisher: NFER-Nelson Publishing Co., Ltd. [En-gland].
  a) TEST A.
  Population: Age 9.
  Scores, 4: Dice, Calculator, Length, Squares and Counters.
  Comments: Orally administered.
  b) TEST B.
  Population: Ages 10–11.
  Scores, 4: Same as *a* above.
  c) TEST C.
  Population: Ages 12–13.
  Scores, 4: Making Lengths, Area, Calculator, Making Boxes.
Cross References: For reviews by Anthony J. Nitko and Michael S. Trevisan, see 12:301.

[1943]
Pragmatics Profile of Everyday Communica-tion Skills in Adults.

Purpose: Developed as a means of obtaining struc-tured, descriptive information about an individual's communication.
Population: Adolescents and adults.
Publication Date: 1997.
Acronym: PPA.
Scores: 3 focus areas: Communicative Functions, Re-sponse to Communication, Interaction and Conversation.

Administration: Individual.
Price Data, 1998: £50 per complete set including manual and photocopiable profile sheets; sample sheets are free.
Time: (20) minutes.
Authors: H. Dewart and S. Summers.
Publisher: NFER-Nelson Publishing Co., Ltd. [England].

[1944]

Pragmatics Profile of Everyday Communication Skills in Children.

Purpose: Developed to provide a descriptive and qualitative analysis of a child's communication skills in everyday situations by means of a structured interview with a parent or other caregiver and teacher.
Population: Ages 9 months to 10 years.
Publication Dates: 1988–1995.
Acronym: PPC.
Scores: 3 focus areas: Communicative Functions, Response to Communication, Interaction and Conversation.
Administration: Individual.
Price Data, 1998: £36.50 per complete set including manual and photocopiable profile sheets; sample sheets are free.
Time: (20) minutes.
Comments: Revision of the Pragmatics Profile of Early Communication Skills.
Authors: H. Dewart and S. Summers.
Publisher: NFER-Nelson Publishing Co., Ltd. [England].
Cross References: For reviews by David MacPhee and Sherwyn Morreale of the earlier edition, see 12:302.

[1945]

The Praxis Series: Professional Assessments for Beginning Teachers®.

Purpose: "Provide measures of academic achievements and proficiencies for students entering or completing college or provisional teacher preparation programs and for individuals in professional areas."
Population: Beginning and experienced teachers.
Publication Dates: 1993–1998.
Administration: Group.
Restricted Distribution: Secure instruments administered at centers established by the publisher.
Comments: Tests administered 5 to 6 times annually; earlier versions previously available as NTE Programs (1940–1992).
Author: Educational Testing Service.
Publisher: Educational Testing Service.
  a) PRAXIS I: ACADEMIC SKILLS ASSESSMENTS.
  Purpose: Designed to be taken early in a student's college career to measure reading, writing and mathematical skills.

Price Data, 1999: PPST tests: $18 per test; CBT tests: $70 for one test, $90 for two tests, $110 for three tests.
Time: PPST tests: 60 minutes per test; PI-CBT tests: 120 minutes per test.
Comments: Includes the paper-based Pre-Professional Skills Test (PPST®) and the Praxis I Computer-Based Tests (PI-CBT) in Reading, Writing, and Mathematics.
  b) PRAXIS II: SUBJECT ASSESSMENTS.
  Purpose: Measures a student's knowledge of subjects he or she will teach and his or her general and subject-specific pedagogical skills and knowledge.
  Price Data: Core Battery Tests: $60 examination fee per test; MSAT: Content Knowledge: $60 examination fee; MSAT: Content Area Exercises: $95 examination fee; PLT tests: $65 examination fee per test; One-hour multiple-choice Subject Assessment/Specialty Area tests: $45 examination fee per test; One-hour constructed-response Subject Assessment/Specialty Area tests: $50 examination fee per test; Two-hour multiple-choice Subject Assessment/Specialty Area tests: $60 examination fee per test; Two-hour constructed-response Subject Assessment/Specialty Area tests: $65 examination fee per test; Two-hour combined multiple-choice and constructed-response Subject Assessment/Specialty Area tests: $65 examination fee per test.
  Time: Core Battery Tests: 120 minutes per test; MSAT: Content Knowledge: 120 minutes; MSAT: Content Area Exercises: 180 minutes; PLT tests: 120 minutes per test; Subject Assessment/Specialty Area tests: 60–120 minutes per test.
  Comments: Includes Core Battery Tests, Multiple Subjects Assessment for Teachers (MSAT), Principles of Learning and Teaching (PLT) Tests, and Subject Assessments/Specialty Area Tests. Core Battery tests include General Knowledge, Communication Skills and Professional Knowledge. MSAT tests include one multiple-choice and one constructed-response assessment covering Literature and Language Studies, Mathematics, Visual and Performing Arts, Physical Education, Human Development, History/Social Studies, and Science. PLT tests include assessments for grade levels K–6, 5–9, and 7–12 in Organizing Content Knowledge for Student Learning, Creating an Environment for Student Learning, Teaching Student Learning, and Teacher Professionalism. Subject Assessments/Specialty Area Tests include the following 134 tests: Accounting (PA); Agriculture; Agriculture (CA); Art Education; Art Making; Art: Content Knowledge; Art: Content, Traditions, Criticism, Aesthetics; Athletic Trainer;

Audiology; Biology; Biology and General Science; Biology: Content Essays; Biology; Content Knowledge; Biology: Content Knowledge, Part 1; Biology: Content Knowledge, Part 2; Biology: Pedagogy; Business Education; Chemistry; Chemistry, Physics and General Science; Chemistry: Content Essays; Chemistry: Content Knowledge; Chemistry: Content Knowledge (CT); Communication; Computer Literacy/Data Processing; Cooperative Education; Data Processing (PA); Driver Education (WV); Early Childhood Education; Earth Science: Content Knowledge; Earth/Space Science; Economics; Educational Leadership: Administration and Supervision; Education of Deaf and Hard of Hearing Students; Education of Students with Mental Retardation; Elementary Education: Content Area Exercises; Elementary Education: Curriculum, Instruction and Assessment; Elementary Education: Curriculum, Instruction and Assessment (CBT); Elementary Education: Curriculum, Instruction and Assessment K–5 (GA); Elementary School: Content Knowledge; English Language, Literature and Composition: Content Knowledge; English Language, Literature and Composition: Essays; English Language, Literature and Composition: Pedagogy; Environmental Education; Foreign Language Pedagogy; French; French: Content Knowledge; French: Linguistic, Literary and Cultural Analysis; French: Productive Language Skills; General Mathematics; General Science; General Science: Content Essays; General Science: Content Knowledge (CT); General Science: Content Knowledge, Part 1; General Science: Content Knowledge, Part 2; Geography; German; German: Content Knowledge; German: Productive Language Skills; Gifted Education; Government/Political Science; Health and Physical Education; Health and Physical Education: Content Knowledge; Health Education; Home Economics Education; Introduction to the Teaching of Reading; Italian; Latin; Library Media Specialist; Marketing (PA); Marketing Education; Mathematics; Mathematics: Content Knowledge; Mathematics: Pedagogy; Mathematics: Proofs, Models and Problems, Part 1; Mathematics: Proofs, Models and Problems, Part 2; Middle School English Language Arts; Middle School Mathematics; Middle School Mathematics: Content Knowledge; Middle School Science; Middle School Social Studies; Middle School: Content Knowledge (GA); Music Education; Music: Analysis (CR-LC); Music: Concepts and Processes; Music; Content Knowledge; Office Technology (PA); Physical Education; Physical Education: Content Knowledge; Physical Education: Movement Forms—Analysis and Design; Physical Education: Movement Forms—Video Evaluation; Physical Science: Content Essays; Physical Science: Content Knowledge; Physical Science: Pedagogy; Physics; Physics: Content Essays; Physics: Content Knowledge; Physics: Content Knowledge (CT); Pre-Kindergarten Education; Psychology; Reading Specialist; Safety/Driver Education; School Guidance and Counseling (MC-LC); School Leaders Licensure Assessment; School Psychologist; School Social Worker; Secretarial (PA); Social Studies: Analytical Essays; Social Studies: Content Knowledge; Social Studies: Interpretation of Materials; Social Studies: Pedagogy; Sociology; Spanish; Spanish: Content Knowledge: Spanish: Linguistic, Literary, and Cultural Analysis; Spanish: Pedagogy; Spanish: Productive Language Skills; Special Education; Special Education: Application of Core Principles; Special Education: Knowledge-Based Core Principles; Special Education: Preschool/Early Childhood; Special Education: Teaching Students with Learning Disabilities; Special Education: Teaching Students with Mental Retardation; Special Education: Teaching Students with Behavioral Disorders/Emotional Disturbance; Speech-Language Pathology; Speech Communication; Teaching English as a Second Language; Teaching Speech to Students with Language Impairments; Teaching Students with Emotional Disturbance; Teaching Students with Learning Disabilities; Teaching Students with Orthopedic Impairments; Teaching Students with Visual Impairments; Technology Education; Theatre; Vocational General Knowledge; World and U.S. History.

c) PRAXIS III: CLASSROOM PERFORMANCE ASSESSMENT.

Comments: Developed to assess teachers' classroom performance for licensure needs of some states. To determine whether required in a particular state, please contact that state's department of education.

Cross References: For information on earlier editions of the NTE Core Battery, see T4:1824 (5 references), T3:1624 (1 reference), and 8:382 (2 references). For information on earlier editions of the Pre-Professional Skills Test, see T4:2071 (6 references); for reviews by Don B. Oppenheim and Edys S. Quellmalz of an earlier edition, see 9:975.

[1946]
Predictive Ability Test, Adult Edition.

Purpose: Measures "the ability to predict" as the basis for determining intelligence.
Population: Ages 17 and over.
Publication Date: 1974.
Acronym: PAT.

Scores: Overall performance score.
Administration: Group.
Price Data: Available from publisher.
Time: [30–40] minutes.
Author: Myles I. Friedman.
Publisher: Myles I. Friedman.
Cross References: For a review by Arthur R. Jensen, see 9:971.

[1947]
Pre-Kindergarten Screen.

Purpose: Designed "to be a quick screening instrument for children between the ages of 4 years 0 months and 5 years 11 months who may be at risk for early academic difficulty."
Population: Ages 4–6.
Publication Date: 2000.
Acronym: PKS.
Scores, 10: Gross Motor Skills, Fine Motor Skills, Following Directions, Block Tapping, Visual Matching, Visual Memory, Imitation, Basic Academic Skills, Delayed Gratification, Total.
Administration: Individual.
Price Data, 2002: $65 per test kit including 50 record forms, test plates, and manual (56 pages); $25 per 50 record forms; $18 per test plates; $22 per manual.
Time: [15] minutes.
Authors: Raymond E. Webster and Angela Matthews.
Publisher: Academic Therapy Publications.

[1948]
PRE-LAS English.

Purpose: "To measure young children's expressive and receptive abilities in three linguistic components of oral language: morphology, syntax, and semantics."
Population: Ages 4–6.
Publication Date: 1985–1987.
Acronym: PRE-LAS.
Scores, 8: Simon Says, Choose A Picture, What's in the House, Say What You Hear, Finishing Stories, Let's Tell Stories, Total, Level.
Administration: Individual.
Price Data, 2002: $181.45 per complete kit including 50 test booklets (1985, 4 pages), Cue Picture Booklet and House, audio cassette, scoring and interpretation manual (1987, 28 pages), and administration manual (1986, 16 pages); $28.10 per Technical Report (1985, 47 pages).
Foreign Language Edition: Spanish edition available.
Time: (10–20) minutes.
Comments: 2 forms: A, B; downward extension of the Language Assessment Scales (LAS; 1365).
Authors: Sharon E. Duncan and Edward A. De Avila.

Publisher: CTB/McGraw-Hill.
Cross References: See T5:2029 (2 references) and T4:2065 (1 reference); for reviews by Patsy Arnett Jaynes and Kikumi Tatsuoka, see 11:296. For a review by Lyn Haber of the Language Assessment Scales, see 9:584 (1 reference); see also T3:1281 (4 references).

[1949]
PreLAS 2000.

Purpose: Designed to "assess oral language proficiency in young children"; the PreLAS2000 "assesses receptive language and expressive language, which requires all the processing capacities of comprehension plus cognitive organization and the performance of appropriate motor behavior to make the requisite speech sounds."
Population: Ages 4–6.
Publication Date: 1998.
Scores, 12: Oral Language Component (Simon Says, Art Show, Say What You Hear, Human Body, Story #1, Story #2); Pre-Literacy Component (Letters, Numbers, Colors, Shapes, Reading, Writing).
Administration: Individual.
Parts, 2: Oral Language Component, Pre-Literacy Component.
Price Data, 2002: $181.45 per examiner's kit including manual (79 pages); $28.10 per technical report.
Time: (15–25) minutes.
Authors: Sharon E. Duncan and Edward A. De Avila.
Publisher: CTB/McGraw-Hill.

[1950]
Preliminary SAT/National Merit Scholarship Qualifying Test.

Purpose: "Measures reasoning, math problem-solving, and writing skills generally associated with academic achievement in college—for guidance in grades 10-11 and entry to scholarship programs in grade 11."
Population: Grades 10–11.
Publication Dates: 1959–1998.
Acronym: PSAT/NMSQT.
Scores, 4: Verbal, Mathematical, Writing Skills, Section Index (for scholarship consideration by NMSC).
Administration: Group.
Price Data: Available from publisher.
Special Editions: Braille, cassette, script, and large-type editions available.
Time: [140] minutes.
Comments: A shortened version of SAT I (2175); administered in October at participating secondary schools; testing accommodations available for students with disabilities.
Authors: Administered for the College Board and National Merit Scholarship Corporation by Educational Testing Service.

Publisher: Educational Testing Service.
Cross References: See T5:2031 (11 references), T4:2067 (6 references), and T3:1866 (7 references); for reviews by Jerome E. Doppelt and J. Thomas Hastings, see 8:199 (15 references); see also T2:436 (4 references) and 7:375 (10 references); for a review by Wayne S. Zimmerman of earlier forms, see 6:487 (2 references).

[1951]
Preliminary Test of English as a Foreign Language.

Purpose: Measures "the English proficiency of non-native speakers."
Population: College and other institutional applicants, grade 11 and over, from non-English-language countries.
Publication Dates: 1983–1989.
Acronym: Pre-TOEFL®.
Scores, 4: Listening Comprehension, Structure and Written Expression, Reading Comprehension and Vocabulary, Total.
Administration: Group.
Price Data: Price information available from publisher for examination fee per institution per administration; fee includes machine scoring by publisher, test results, and use of booklets and administrative materials which must be returned to publisher.
Time: 70 minutes.
Comments: A shorter test measuring the same components of language proficiency as the regular TOEFL; 2 forms per year; offered only through the TOEFL Institutional Testing Program.
Authors: Jointly sponsored by College Entrance Examination Board, Graduate Record Examination Board, and Educational Testing Service.
Publisher: Educational Testing Service.
Cross References: For reviews by Roger A. Richards and Charlene Rivera, see 11:298. For reviews by Brenda H. Loyd and Kikumi K. Tatsuoka of the Test of English as a Foreign Language, see 9:1257 (1 reference); see also T3:2441 (9 references), 8:110 (15 references), and T2:238 (4 references); for reviews by Clinton I. Chase and George Domino of the TOEFL, see 7:266 (10 references).

[1952]
Pre-Literacy Skills Screening.

Purpose: Provides a quick look at the reading readiness skills of children beginning school.
Population: Kindergarten.
Publication Date: 1999.
Acronym: PLSS.
Scores, 11: Rhyme, Sentence Repetition, Naming Accuracy, Naming Time, Blending, Sentence Segmentation, Letter Naming, Syllable Segmentation, Deletion, Multisyllabic Word Repetition, Overall Score.
Administration: Individual.

Price Data, 2001: $49 per complete kit; $19 per record forms; $32 per examiner's manual (30 pages).
Time: (15) minutes.
Authors: Linda Crumrine and Helen Lonegan.
Publisher: PRO-ED.

[1953]
A Premarital Communication Inventory.

Purpose: "To help counselors assess the marriageability of a couple."
Population: Premarital couples.
Publication Dates: 1968–1982.
Acronym: PCI.
Scores: Total score only.
Administration: Group.
Price Data, 1993: $.75 per inventory; $2.50 per manual (1982, 6 pages).
Time: (20) minutes.
Author: Millard J. Bienvenu.
Publisher: Millard J. Bienvenu, Northwest Publications.
Cross References: For a review by James R. Clopton, see 8:351.

[1954]
PREPARE/ENRICH.

Purpose: Designed as a series of tests for use in assessing couples' relationships.
Population: Couples.
Scores: 17 scores common to all four tests: Idealistic Distortion, Personality Issues, Communication, Conflict Resolution, Financial Management, Leisure Activities, Sexual Expectations, Role Relationship, Spiritual Beliefs, Couple Closeness, Couple Flexibility, Family Closeness, Family Flexibility, Self-Confidence, Assertiveness, Avoidance, Partner Dominance.
Administration: Group.
Price Data: Available from publisher.
Time: Administration time not reported.
Comments: Available as a compiled series of 4 tests with one manual.
Publisher: Life Innovations, Inc.
　a) PREMARITAL PERSONAL AND RELATIONSHIP EVALUATION.
　Purpose: Designed to help couples getting reading for marriage (who do not have children) assess their relationship.
　Population: Couples planning to marry who do not have children.
　Acronym: PREPARE.
　Publication Dates: 1978–1998.
　Scores, 20: 17 scores common to all 4 tests plus Marital Expectations, Children and Parenting, Family and Friends.
　Authors: David H. Olson, David G. Fournier, and Joan M. Druckman.

b) PREMARITAL PERSONAL AND RELATION-SHIP EVALUATION—MARRIED WITH CHIL-DREN.

Purpose: Designed to help couples who are planning to marry (and who already have children) assess their relationship and identify important issues.

Population: Couples planning to marry who have children.

Publication Dates: 1981–1998.

Acronym: PREPARE-MC.

Scores, 20: Same as *a* above.

Authors: David H. Olson, David G. Fournier, and Joan M. Druckman.

c) ENRICHING RELATIONSHIP ISSUES, COM-MUNICATION AND HAPPINESS.

Purpose: Designed to assess relationship strengths and areas for growth.

Population: Married couples or couples who have cohabitated for 2 or more years.

Publication Dates: 1981–1998.

Acronym: ENRICH.

Scores, 19: 17 scores common to all 4 tests plus: Marital Satisfaction, Children and Parenting.

Authors: David H. Olson, David G. Fournier, and Joan M. Druckman.

d) MATURE AGE TRANSITION EVALUATION.

Purpose: Designed to help mature couples who are preparing for marriage assess their relationships.

Population: Couples over 50 planning marriage.

Publication Dates: 1995–1998.

Acronym: MATE.

Scores, 20: 17 scores common to all 4 tests plus: Life Transitions, Intergenerational Issues, Health Issues.

Authors: David H. Olson and Elinor Adams.

Cross References: For reviews by Corine Fitzpatrick and Jay A. Mancini, see 14:295; see also T5:2034 (7 references).

[1955]
Pre-Referral Intervention Manual [Revised and Updated Second Edition].

Purpose: To provide appropriate intervention strategies for learning and behavior problems.

Population: K–12 students.

Publication Dates: 1988–1993.

Acronym: PRIM.

Scores: Not scored.

Administration: Individual.

Price Data, 2002: $96 per complete kit including pre-referral intervention manual (1993, 504 pages), 50 pre-referral checklist forms, and 50 pre-referral intervention strategies documentation forms; $36 per pre-referral intervention manual; $33 per 50 learning and behavior problem checklists; $27 per 50 pre-referral

intervention strategies documentation forms; $225 per computerized pre-referral intervention manual (WIN).

Comments: Ratings in 13 areas: Memory/Abstractions/Generalizations/Organization, Listening, Speaking, Reading, Writing, Spelling, Mathematical Calculations, Academic Performance, Interpersonal Relationships, Depression/Motivation, Inappropriate Behavior Under Normal Circumstances, Rules and Expectations, Group Behavior.

Author: Stephen B. McCarney.

Publisher: Hawthorne Educational Services, Inc.

Cross References: For reviews by Anthony W. Paolitto and Gabriele van Lingen, see 13:236.

[1956]
Preschool and Kindergarten Behavior Scales.

Purpose: "A behavioral rating instrument for use in evaluating social skills and problem behavior patterns of preschool and kindergarten-aged children."

Population: Ages 3–6.

Publication Date: 1994.

Acronym: PKBS.

Scores, 12: Social Cooperation, Social Interaction, Social Independence, Social Skills Total, Self-Centered/Explosive, Attention Problems/Overactive, Antisocial/Aggressive, Externalizing Problems, Social Withdrawal, Anxiety/Somatic Problems, Internalizing Problems, Problem Behavior Total.

Administration: Group.

Price Data, 2001: $76 per complete kit including manual (1994, 65 pages) and 20 test forms; $39 per 50 test forms; $39 per test manual; $37 per specimen set including test manual and 1 test form.

Time: (8–12) minutes.

Comments: Ratings by individual who has interacted with and known child for at least 3 months; optional additional information section.

Author: Kenneth W. Merrell.

Publisher: PRO-ED.

Cross References: See T5:2036 (1 reference); for reviews by David MacPhee and T. Steuart Watson, see 13:237.

[1957]
Preschool and Kindergarten Interest Descriptor.

Purpose: "Identify children with attitudes and interests usually associated with preschool and kindergarten creativity."

Population: Ages 3–6.

Publication Date: 1983.

Acronym: PRIDE.

Scores: 4 dimension scores: Originality, Imagination-Playfulness, Independence-Perseverance, Many Interests.

Administration: Group.

Price Data, 2001: $100 per complete set including manual (10 pages) and 30 scales; $15 per specimen set.
Time: (20-35) minutes.
Comments: Downward extension of the Group Inventory for Finding Creative Talent (1093); scale for rating by parents.
Author: Sylvia B. Rimm.
Publisher: Educational Assessment Service, Inc.
Cross References: For reviews by Gloria A. Galvin and Sue White, see 10:289.

[1958]
Preschool and Primary Inventory of Phonological Awareness.

Purpose: "Designed to identify children who have poor phonological awareness" and are at risk for literacy problems.
Population: Ages 3 to 6-11.
Publication Date: 2000.
Acronym: PIPA.
Scores: 6 subtests: Syllable Segmentation, Rhyme Awareness, Alliteration Awareness, Phoneme Isolation, Phoneme Segmentation, Letter Knowledge.
Administration: Individual.
Price Data, 2002: $118.47 per complete kit including record forms, stimulus booklet, and manual (54 pages).
Time: (25–30) minutes; (5) minutes per subtest.
Authors: Barbara Dodd, Sharon Crosbie, Beth McIntosh, Tania Teitzel, and Anne Ozanne.
Publisher: The Psychological Corporation Europe [United Kingdom].

[1959]
Pre-School Behavior Checklist.

Purpose: "To help identify children with emotional and behavioral problems by providing a tool for the systematic and objective description of behavior."
Population: Ages 2–5.
Publication Date: 1988.
Acronym: PBCL.
Scores: Total score only.
Administration: Group.
Price Data, 2002: ATP prices: $67 per test kit including 25 recording forms, scoring acetate, 50 Developmental Activities Checklist forms, and manual; $14 per 25 recording forms; $10 per scoring acetate; $15 per 50 Developmental Activities Checklist forms; $22 per manual; $15 per specimen set including manual and sample forms; NFER-Nelson prices: Available from publisher.
Time: (8–10) minutes.
Comments: Behavior checklist.
Authors: Jacqueline McGuire and Naomi Richman.
Publisher: Academic Therapy Publications [U.S. Distributor]; NFER-Nelson Publishing Co., Ltd. [England].

Cross References: See T5:2038 (5 references); for reviews by Roger D. Carlson and Gary Stoner, see 11:299.

[1960]
The Preschool Behavior Questionnaire.

Purpose: Designed as a screening tool to identify emotional/behavioral problems in children.
Population: Ages 3–6.
Publication Date: 1974.
Acronym: PBQ.
Scores, 4: Hostile-Aggressive, Anxious-Fearful, Hyperactive-Distractible, Total.
Administration: Group.
Price Data, 1998: $20 per 50 questionnaires, 50 scores sheets, and manual (16 pages).
Time: [5–10] minutes.
Comments: Modification of Michael A. Rutter's 1967 unpublished Children's Behavior Questionnaire.
Authors: Lenore Behar and Samuel Stringfield.
Publisher: Lenore Behar.
Cross References: See T5:2039 (24 references) and T4:2077 (15 references); for a review by Robert A. Fox, see 9:978 (6 references).

[1961]
Preschool Development Inventory.

Purpose: A brief screening inventory "designed to help identify children with developmental, behavioral, or health problems."
Population: Ages 3–6.
Publication Dates: 1984–1998.
Acronym: PDI.
Scores: General Development Score, Possible Problems List (24); 4 ratings: Child Description, Special Problems or Handicaps, Parent's Questions/Concerns, Parent's Functioning.
Administration: Individual.
Price Data, 2001: $10 per manual (1998, 25 pages); $10 per 25 parent questionnaires.
Time: (15) minutes.
Comments: Parent-completed questionnaire; replaces the Minnesota Preschool Inventory (aka Minnesota PreKindergarten Inventory) (9:720) and the Preschool Developmental Inventory (10:291).
Author: Harold Ireton.
Publisher: Behavior Science Systems, Inc.
Cross References: For reviews by Lena R. Gaddis and Diane J. Sawyer, see 13:238; see also T4:2079 (1 reference); for a review by R. A. Bornstein of an earlier edition, see 10:291.

[1962]
Preschool Developmental Profile.

Purpose: "Designed to be used to write an individualized education program and to serve as a way of measuring a child's developmental progress."

Population: Children with handicaps who function at the 3–6 year age level.
Publication Dates: 1977–1991.
Scores, 10: Perceptual/Fine Motor, Cognition (Classification, Number, Space, Seriation, Time), Speech and Language, Social Emotional, Self-Care, Gross Motor.
Administration: Individual.
Price Data: Available from publisher.
Time: (50–60) minutes.
Comments: See Early Intervention Developmental Profile (861) for younger ages.
Authors: Diane B. D'Eugenio, Martha S. Moersch, Sara L. Brown, Judith E. Drews, B. Suzanne Haskin, Eleanor Whiteside Lynch, and Sally J. Rogers.
Publisher: University of Michigan Press.
Cross References: For reviews by Doreen Ward Fairbank and David MacPhee, see 13:239.

[1963]
Preschool Evaluation Scale.

Purpose: Designed to assess behavior related to developmental delays.
Population: Birth–72 months.
Publication Dates: 1991–1992.
Acronym: PES.
Scores, 6: Large Muscle Skills, Small Muscle Skills, Cognitive Thinking, Expressive Language Skills, Social/Emotional, Self-Help Skills.
Administration: Individual.
Levels, 2: Birth–35 months, 36–72 months.
Price Data, 2002: $80 per complete kit including technical manual (1992, 41 pages), 50 birth–35 months rating forms, and 50 36–72 months rating forms; $33 per 50 birth–35 months ratings forms; $33 per 50 36–72 months rating forms; $20 per computerized quick score (DOS); $14 per technical manual.
Time: (20–25) minutes.
Comments: Ratings by parents or child care providers.
Author: Stephen B. McCarney.
Publisher: Hawthorne Educational Services, Inc.
Cross References: For reviews by Mary Mathai Chittooran and Lena R. Gaddis, see 13:240.

[1964]
Preschool Language Assessment Instrument.

Purpose: "Designed to assess young children's skills in coping with the language demands of the teaching situation."
Population: Ages 2.9 through 5.8.
Publication Date: 1978.
Acronym: PLAI.
Scores: 4 areas: Matching Perception, Selective Analysis of Perception, Reordering Perception, Reasoning About Perception [15 items per area scored numerically using a four-level criterion system and qualitatively using a seven-level criterion system].
Administration: Individual.
Price Data, 2002: $48 per 50 English record forms; $48 per 50 Spanish record forms; $99 per English test manual; $99 per Spanish test manual.
Foreign Language Edition: Spanish edition available.
Time: (20–30) minutes.
Authors: Marion Blank, Susan A. Rose, and Laura J. Berlin.
Publisher: The Psychological Corporation.
Cross References: See T5:2044 (6 references) and T4:2083 (2 references); for reviews by William O. Haynes and Kenneth G. Shipley, see 9:979.

[1965]
Preschool Language Scale—3.

Purpose: "Measures young children's receptive and expressive language ability."
Population: Ages birth to 6–11.
Publication Dates: 1969–1992.
Acronym: PLS-3.
Scores, 3: Auditory Comprehension, Expressive Communication, Total Language Score.
Administration: Individual.
Price Data, 2002: $185 per complete kit including 12 record forms, picture book, and manual (1992, 177 pages); $33 per 12 record forms (English or Spanish); $105 per picture book; $58 per English examiner's manual; $58 per Spanish examiner's manual; $119 per 50 record forms.
Foreign Language Edition: Spanish edition available.
Time: (20–50) minutes.
Authors: Irla Lee Zimmerman, Violette G. Steiner, and Roberta Evatt Pond.
Publisher: The Psychological Corporation.
Cross References: See T5:2045 (6 references); for reviews by J. Jeffrey Grill and Janet A. Norris, see 13:241 (26 references); see also T4:2084 (24 references); for an excerpted review by Barton B. Proger of an earlier edition, see 8:929 (3 references); see also T2:2024 (1 reference); for a review by Joel Stark and an excerpted review by C. H. Ammons, see 7:965.

[1966]
Preschool Motor Speech Evaluation & Intervention.

Purpose: To assess oral motor and motor speech abilities of children from 18 to 60 months who are exhibiting significant speech delays.
Population: Ages 18–60 months.
Publication Date: 2000.
Scores: No scores.
Administration: Individual.

Price Data, 2000: $44 per complete kit including spiral-bound soft cover manual with an assessment form and several reproducible pages.
Time: (75–160) minutes.
Comments: Parent interview/observation.
Author: Margaret M. Earnest.
Publisher: Imaginart International, Inc.

[1967]
Preschool Screening Instrument.

Purpose: Designed to identify potential learning problems in prekindergarten children.
Population: Ages 3-0 to 5-3.
Publication Date: 1979.
Acronym: PSSI.
Scores, 6: Human Figure Drawing, Visual Motor Perception/Fine Motor, Gross Motor, Language Development, Speech, Behavior.
Administration: Individual.
Price Data, 2001: $75 per complete kit including 25 student record forms, 25 parental questionnaires, story card, manipulatives, and manual (40 pages); $30 per 25 student record forms; $20 per 25 parental questionnaires; $20 per manual.
Time: (5–8) minutes.
Author: Stephen Paul Cohen.
Publisher: Stoelting Co.
Cross References: For a review by Gene Schwarting, see 9:981.

[1968]
Preschool Screening System.

Purpose: For identifying children with special needs.
Population: Ages 2-6 to 5-9.
Publication Date: 1980.
Acronym: PSS.
Scores: Child Record Form: 7 skills areas: Body Awareness and Control Skills, Visual-Perceptual-Motor Skills, Language Skills, Imitation, Learned Skills, Behavioral Characteristics, Total; Parental Questionnaire: 3 area profiles: Developmental History, Medical History, Behavioral History.
Administration: Individual.
Parts: Child Record Form; Parental Questionnaire.
Price Data: Available from publisher.
Time: 20(25) minutes.
Authors: Peter K. Hainsworth and Marion L. Hainsworth.
Publisher: ERISys [No reply from publisher; status unknown].
Cross References: See T4:2086 (1 reference).

[1969]
The Pre-School Screening Test.

Purpose: To screen children for special educational needs.
Population: 3 years 6 months to 4 years 5 months.

Publication Date: 2001.
Acronym: PREST.
Scores, 14: PREST 1 (Rapid Naming, Bead Threading & Paper Cutting, Digits & Letters, Repetition, Shape Copying, Corsi Frog, At-Risk Total), PREST 2 (Balance, Phonological Discrimination, Digit Span, Rhyme, Sound Order, Teddy and Form Matching, At-Risk Total).
Administration: Individual.
Price Data, 2001: $120.28 per complete kit including score sheets, card sets, beads, sound order audiotape, training videotape, and manual (98 pages).
Time: (10–30) minutes.
Authors: Angela Fawcett, Rod Nicholson, and Ray Lee.
Publisher: The Psychological Corporation Europe [United Kingdom].

[1970]
Preschool Skills Test.

Purpose: "Designed to assess the [developmental] skills of preschool-aged, early elementary or mentally handicapped children."
Population: Age 2 through Grade 2 level children.
Publication Dates: 1983–1993.
Scores: 7 developmental areas: Fine Motor, Personal/Social, Visual, Visual Identification, Number Concepts, Discrimination/Matching, Readiness/Academic.
Administration: Individual.
Price Data, 1998: $225 per complete kit; $35 per 50 answer sheets; $50 per 50 fine motor drawing sheets.
Time: [20–30] minutes.
Comments: Previous edition entitled Preschool Screening Test.
Author: Carol Lepera.
Publisher: Preschool Skills Test.
Cross References: For reviews by Doreen Ward Fairbank and Mark E. Swerdlik, see 14:296; for a review by Ruth Tomes of an earlier edition, see 12:303.

[1971]
Present State Examination.

Purpose: Clinical interview questionnaire for ratings of psychiatric symptoms reported by patient during preceding month.
Population: Adult psychiatric patients.
Publication Dates: 1967–1974.
Acronym: PSE.
Scores: 38 syndrome scores and various derived scores.
Administration: Individual.
Price Data: Available from publisher.
Time: (45–60) minutes.
Comments: No scoring instructions except description of computer scoring program.
Authors: J. K. Wing, J. E. Cooper, and N. Sartorius.
Publisher: Cambridge University Press.

Cross References: See T5:2050 (142 references), T4:2091 (237 references), 9:985 (71 references), and T3:1883 (70 references); for a review by Jack Zusman, Isabel C. A. Moyes, Clive A. Sims, and David Goldberg, see 8:649.

[1972]
The Press Test.

Purpose: Measures how well an individual performs tasks when experiencing stress.
Population: Managers and high-level professionals.
Publication Dates: 1959–1987.
Scores, 5: Reading Speed, Color-Naming Speed, Color-Naming Speed With Distraction, Difference Between Color-Naming Speed With and Without Distraction, Difference Between Reading Speed and Color-Naming Speed.
Administration: Individual or group.
Price Data: Available from publisher.
Time: (6–10) minutes.
Authors: Melany E. Baehr and Raymond J. Corsini.
Publisher: Reid London House.
Cross References: For a review by Robert P. Vecchio, see 9:986; see also T3:1884 (2 references), T2:1333 (1 reference), and P:213 (1 reference); for reviews by William H. Helm and Allyn Miles Munger, see 6:163.

[1973]
Pre-Verbal Communication Schedule.

Purpose: "The Schedule is aimed mainly at assessing existing non-verbal and vocal communication skills and other abilities which may be relevant in programme development."
Population: Children and adolescents and adults.
Publication Date: 1987.
Acronym: PVCS.
Administration: Individual.
Forms, 2: Full Form, Short Form.
Price Data, 1999: £48.75 per complete set including 10 scoring sheets and manual (20 pages); £31 per 10 checklists.
Time: (120–150) minutes.
Comments: Behavior checklist.
Authors: Chris Kiernan and Barbara Reid.
Publisher: NFER-Nelson Publishing Co., Ltd. [England].
a) SCORE SHEET 1.
  Scores: 27 sections: Needs and Preferences, Vision and Looking, Use of Visual Cues, Control of Hands and Arms, Social Interaction Without Communication, Hearing and Listening, Development of Sounds, Control of Speech Musculature, Consistent Use of Noise, Expression of Emotion (Non-Communicative), Music and Singing, Motor Imitation, Vocal Imitation, Giving, Communication Through Pictures or Objects, Communication Through Whole Body Action, Communication Through Gestures, Communication Through Manipulation, Communication Through Pointing, Communication Through Looking, Communicative Use of Sounds, Expression of Emotion (Communicative), Manipulation of Emotion, Understanding of Non-Vocal Communication, Understanding of Vocalization and Speech, Understanding of Emotion, Use of Communication Through Symbols/Signs or Speech.
b) SCORE SHEET 2 (SHORT FORM PVCS).
  Scores: 6 category scores: Attention Seeking, Need Satisfaction, Simple Negation, Positive Interaction, Negative Interaction, Shared Attention.
Cross References: See T5:2052 (2 references); for reviews by E. W. Testut and Susan Ellis Weismer, see 11:302.

[1974]
The Prevocational Assessment and Curriculum Guide.

Purpose: Designed to "assess and identify the prevocational training needs of handicapped persons."
Population: Mentally retarded individuals.
Publication Dates: 1978–1993.
Acronym: PACG.
Scores: 9 categories: Attendance/Endurance, Independence, Production, Learning, Behavior, Communication, Social Skills, Grooming/Eating, Toileting.
Administration: Individual.
Price Data, 2002: $12 per complete kit including inventory, summary profile sheet, manual (6 pages), and curriculum guide.
Time: [15–20] minutes.
Comments: Ratings by professional acquainted with individual; title on test is PACG Inventory.
Authors: Dennis E. Mithaug, Deanna K. Mar, and Jeffrey E. Stewart.
Publisher: Exceptional Education.
Cross References: For reviews by Richard A. Wantz and Jean M. Williams, see 12:304.

[1975]
Prevocational Assessment Screen.

Purpose: "Designed to assess a student's motor and perceptual abilities in relation to performance requirements within a local vocational training program."
Population: Grades 8-12.
Publication Date: 1985–2000.
Acronym: PAS.
Scores, 16: Time and Error scores for 8 modules: Alphabetizing, Etch A Sketch Maze, Calculating, Small Parts, Pipe Assembly, O Rings, Block Design, Color Sort.

Administration: Individual.
Price Data, 2002: $1,195 per complete kit including manual (50 pages) and computer software for use in scoring and reporting.
Time: (50) minutes.
Author: Michele Rosinek.
Publisher: Piney Mountain Press, Inc.
Cross References: For reviews by Stephen L. Koffler and James B. Rounds, see 12:305.

[1976]
Primary Measures of Music Audiation.

Purpose: To assess basic music aptitudes.
Population: K-3.
Publication Date: 1979.
Acronym: PMMA.
Scores, 3: Tonal, Rhythm, Composite.
Administration: Group.
Price Data, 2001: $100 per complete kit including 1 tonal and rhythm compact disc, 100 total answer sheets and 100 rhythm answer sheets, 1 set of scoring masks, 100 profile cards, 4 class record sheets, and test manual (107 pages); $25 per CD ; $41.50 per 100 tonal or rhythm answer sheets; $5 per set of scoring masks; $15.50 per 100 profile cards; $2 per 10 class record sheets; $20 per manual.
Time: (20) minutes per tonal tape and (20) minutes per rhythm tape.
Comments: For upward extension, see Intermediate Measures of Music Audiation (1236); test administered by 7.5 ips tape recordings.
Author: Edwin E. Gordon.
Publisher: G.I.A. Publications, Inc.
Cross References: See T4:2099 (2 references); for reviews by Paul R. Lehman and Walter L. Wehner, see 9:988; see also T3:1891 (1 reference).

[1977]
Primary Reading Test.

Purpose: To "provide an overall assessment of the ability to apply reading skills for the understanding of words and simple sentences."
Publication Dates: 1978-1981.
Acronym: PRT.
Scores: Total score only.
Administration: Group.
Forms, 2: A, B.
Price Data: Price information available from publisher for pupil's booklets Level 1 or Level 2, Level 1A or Level 2A, teacher's guide (1981, 18 pages), and for specimen set including pupil's booklets for Levels 1, 1A, 2, and 2A, and teacher's guide.
Time: (35) minutes.
Author: Norman France.
Publisher: NFER-Nelson Publishing Co., Ltd. [England].

a) LEVEL 1.
Population: Ages 6–10.
Comments: May be administered as a word recognition test.
b) LEVEL 2.
Population: Ages 7–12.
Cross References: See T4:2101 (1 reference).

[1978]
Primary Test of Cognitive Skills.

Purpose: Designed to "measure verbal, spatial, memory, and conceptual abilities."
Population: Grades K–1.
Publication Date: 1990.
Acronym: PTCS.
Scores, 5: Spatial, Memory, Concepts, Verbal, Total.
Administration: Group.
Price Data: Price information available from publisher for test materials including manual (70 pages), norms book (82 pages), and technical bulletin (23 pages); scoring service available from publisher.
Time: (30) minutes per subtest; (120) minutes total test.
Authors: Janellen Huttenlocher and Susan Cohen Levine.
Publisher: CTB/McGraw-Hill.
Cross References: For reviews by Sherry K. Bain and Laura L. B. Barnes and David E. McIntosh, see 12:307.

[1979]
Principles of Adult Mentoring Inventory.

Purpose: Designed "to provide a self-assessment instrument for those who have assumed the role of mentor in their contact with adult learners."
Population: Adults.
Publication Date: 1998.
Acronym: PAMI.
Scores, 7: Relationship Emphasis/Trust, information Emphasis/Advice, Facilitative Focus/Alternatives, Conforntive Focus/Challenge, Mentor Model/Motivation, Employee Vision/Initiative, Total.
Administration: Individual.
Price Data, 2001: $39.95 per leader's guide (51 pages); $4.95 per critique form.
Time: Administration time not reported.
Author: Norman H. Cohen.
Publisher: Human Resource Development Press.

[1980]
PrinTest—Forms A-C and B-C.

Purpose: To measure the the skills required to learn and perform jobs involving reading mechanical prints and drawings.
Population: Adults.
Publication Dates: 1990–1998.
Acronym: RCJS-PrinTest.

Scores: Total score only.
Administration: Group.
Price Data, 2002: $16 per consumable, self-scoring booklet; $24.95 per manual (1998, 15 pages).
Time: (35) minutes.
Comments: Self-scoring instrument.
Author: Roland T. Ramsay.
Publisher: Ramsay Corporation.
Cross References: For reviews by James W. Pinkney and Nambury S. Raju, see 13:258.

[1981]
Prison Inmate Inventory.

Purpose: "Designed for inmate risk assessment and needs identification."
Population: Prison inmates.
Publication Date: 1996.
Acronym: PII.
Scores: 10 scales: Truthfulness, Violence, Antisocial, Adjustment, Self-Esteem, Alcohol, Drugs, Judgment, Distress, Stress Coping Abilities.
Administration: Group.
Price Data: Available from publisher.
Time: (35) minutes.
Comments: Available in English and Spanish; both computer version and paper-pencil format are scored on IBM-PC compatibles.
Author: Risk & Needs Assessment, Inc.
Publisher: Risk & Needs Assessment, Inc.
Cross References: For reviews by R. J. DeAyala and John A. Mills, see 14:297.

[1982]
Problem Behavior Inventory [Adult & Adolescent Screening Forms].

Purpose: Designed to help "clinicians structure and focus the diagnostic interview."
Population: Adults and adolescents.
Publication Date: 1991.
Scores: No scores.
Administration: Group.
Forms, 2: Adult, Adolescent.
Price Data, 2002: $34.50 per 25 forms (specify Adult or Adolescent).
Time: (10–20) minutes.
Author: Leigh Silverton.
Publisher: Western Psychological Services.

[1983]
Problem Experiences Checklist.

Purpose: Developed for use prior to the initial intake interview to identify potential problems for further discussion.
Population: Adolescents, adults.
Publication Date: 1991.
Scores: No scores.

Administration: Individual.
Editions, 2: Adolescent, Adult.
Manual: No manual.
Price Data, 2002: $19.95 per 25 checklists (specify Adult or Adolescent).
Time: [10–15] minutes.
Author: Leigh Silverton.
Publisher: Western Psychological Services.
Cross References: For reviews by Mark H. Daniel and Michael J. Sporakowski, see 12:309.

[1984]
Problem-Solving Decision-Making Style Inventory.

Purpose: Provides feedback on one's perception of problem-solving and decision-making styles of self or others.
Population: High school and college and adults in organizational settings.
Publication Date: 1982.
Scores, 4: Delegative, Facilitative, Consultative, Authoritative.
Administration: Group.
Forms, 2: Self, Other.
Manual: No manual (administrative and scoring directions included in instrument).
Price Data: Price information available from publisher.
Time: Administration time not reported.
Comments: Self-administered ratings questionnaire.
Authors: Paul Hersey and Walter E. Natemeyer.
Publisher: Jossey-Bass/Pfeiffer.
Cross References: For reviews by David N. Dixon and Paul McReynolds, see 10:295.

[1985]
The Problem Solving Inventory.

Purpose: "To assess an individual's perceptions of his or her own problem-solving behaviors and attitudes."
Population: Age 16 and above.
Publication Date: 1988.
Acronym: PSI.
Scores, 4: Problem-Solving Confidence, Approach-Avoidance Style, Personal Control, Total.
Administration: Group and individual.
Price Data, 2001: $31.25 per 25 test booklets; $13.50 per scoring key; $32 per manual (23 pages); $47 per preview kit including manual, test booklet, and scoring key.
Time: (10–15) minutes.
Comments: Self-ratings scale.
Author: P. Paul Heppner.
Publisher: Consulting Psychologists Press, Inc.
Cross References: See T5:2065 (35 references) and T4:2108 (26 references); for reviews by Cameron J. Camp and Steven G. LoBello, see 11:303 (11 references).

[1986]

Process Assessment of the Learner: Test Battery for Reading and Writing.

Purpose: "Designed for assessing the development of reading and writing processes in children in kindergarten through grade 6."

Population: Grades K–6.

Publication Date: 2001.

Acronym: PAL.

Administration: Individual.

Levels, 3: Kindergarten, Grades 1–3, Grades 4–6.

Price Data, 2002: $260 per complete kit in a box including examiner's manual (180 pages), 2 stimulus booklets, 25 record forms, 25 response forms, stylus-wood, word card, audiotape, and shield; $285 per complete kit in a bag including examiner's manual, 2 stimulus booklets, 25 record forms, 25 response forms, stylus-wood, word card, audiotape, and shield; $150 per PAL Scoring Assistant for Windows (CD ROM or 3.5-inch diskette); $64 per manual; $48 per 25 record forms or response forms; $80 per stimulus book (specify Book 1 or Book 2); $11 per word card and audiotape; PAL Test Battery Training Video available (contact publisher for price information); quantity discounts available.

Time: (30–60) minutes if all subtests for a specific grade are administered; (1–6) minutes per subtest.

Comments: Subtests may be administered separately; PAL Scoring Assistant for Windows available.

Author: Virginia Wise Berninger.

Publisher: The Psychological Corporation.

a) KINDERGARTEN.
Scores, 10: Alphabet Writing, Receptive Coding—Tasks A and B, Rapid Automatized Naming (RAN)—Letters, RAN—Digits, Rhyming—Tasks A and B, Syllables, Phonemes—Tasks A and B, Story Retell, Finger Sense, Copying—Task A.

b) GRADES 1–3.
Scores, 14: Alphabet Writing; Receptive Coding—Tasks A, B, and C; Rapid Automatized Naming (RAN)—Letters; RAN—Words; RAN—Digits; RAN—Words and Digits; Syllables; Phonemes—Tasks A, B, and C; Rimes—Task A; Word Choice; Pseudoword Decoding; Finger Sense; Sentence Sense; Copying—Tasks A and B.

c) GRADES 4–6.
Scores, 17: Alphabet Writing; Receptive Coding—Tasks C, D, and E; Expressive Coding—Tasks A, B, and C; Rapid Automatized Naming (RAN)—Letters; RAN—Words; RAN—Digits; RAN—Words and Digits; Note-Taking—Task A; Syllables; Phonemes—Task D; Rimes—Task B; Word Choice; Pseudoword Decoding; Finger Sense; Sentence Sense; Copying—Tasks A and B; Note-Taking—Task B.

[1987]

Production and Maintenance Technician Test—Form A.

Purpose: "To evaluate the knowledge and skill of industrial production and maintenance workers in specific subject areas."

Population: Applicants or incumbents for jobs where production and maintenance knowledge is a necessary part of training or job activities.

Publication Date: 1985.

Scores: 9 areas: Pneumatics/Hydraulics, Piping/Pumps, Lubrication/Bearings/Power Transmission, Print Reading, Mechanical Maintenance/Tools/Shop Mechanics, Rigging, Welding, Chemical Processes/Instrumentation & Control, yielding 1 Total Score.

Administration: Group.

Price Data, 2002: $498 per complete kit including 10 reusable test booklets, 100 answer sheets, manual (18 pages), and scoring key.

Time: 120(130) minutes.

Author: Roland T. Ramsay.

Publisher: Ramsay Corporation.

Cross References: For a review by Bruce K. Alcorn, see 11:304.

[1988]

Productive Practices Survey.

Purpose: "To assess, describe, and pinpoint specific practices of the manager which support—or fail to support—organizational productivity."

Population: Managers.

Publication Dates: 1987–1996.

Acronym: PPS.

Scores, 12: Dimension I (Management Values, Support Structure, Managerial Credibility, Total), Dimension II (Impact, Relevance, Community, Total), Dimension III (Task Environment, Social Context, Problem Solving, Total).

Administration: Group.

Price Data, 2001: $8.95 per instrument.

Time: (30–35) minutes.

Comments: Based on model of organizational functioning called Competence Theory; self ratings; self scored.

Author: Jay Hall.

Publisher: Teleometrics International.

[1989]

Productivity Environmental Preference Survey.

Purpose: Identifies "how adults prefer to function, learn, concentrate and perform in their occupational or educational activities."

Population: Adults.

Publication Dates: 1979–1996.

Acronym: PEPS.

Scores, 20: Sound, Light, Temperature, Design, Motivated/Unmotivated, Persistent, Responsible, Structure, Learning Alone/Peer-Oriented Learner, Authority-Oriented Learner, Several Ways, Auditory Preferences, Visual Preferences, Tactile Preferences, Kinesthetic Preferences, Requires Intake, Evening/Morning, Late Morning, Afternoon, Needs Mobility.
Administration: Group.
Price Data, 2001: $22.50 per 10 answer sheets for adults (includes scoring); $7.50 or less per group and subscale summary available from publisher only in addition to individual profiles; $.40 per individual interpretative booklet; $9 per manual (1996, 66 pages); $395 per computerized self-administered inventory program with 100 administrations ($60 per 100 additional administrations) (PC); $495 per Scan Win program permitting schools and businesses to scan and profile forms on site; $.60 per answer form to use with Scan Win.
Time: (20–30) minutes.
Comments: Computer scored.
Authors: Gary E. Price, Rita Dunn, and Kenneth Dunn.
Publisher: Price Systems, Inc.
Cross References: See T5:2069 (3 references); for reviews by Javaid Kaiser and Thaddeus Rozecki, see 13:242 (6 references); see also T4:2114 (2 references); for reviews by Craig N. Mills and Bertram C. Sippola of an earlier edition, see 11:306 (9 references).

[1990]
Productivity Profile.

Purpose: Designed to identify areas in which organizational productivity plans need improvement.
Population: Employees.
Publication Date: 1989.
Scores, 10: Supporting Worker Participation, Setting Goals and Standards, Measuring Output, Providing Incentives and Recognition, Simplifying the Work Methods, Maintaining Supply Lines, Investing in New Equipment, Installing Flexible Hours, Consulting with Experts, Building a Healthier Company.
Administration: Group.
Price Data: Price information available from publisher for self-assessment booklets and answer sheets.
Time: Administration time not reported.
Author: Diane Roemer Yarosz.
Publisher: Training House, Inc.

[1991]
Professional and Managerial Position Questionnaire.

Purpose: Constructed for use in analyzing professional and managerial jobs.
Population: Professional and managerial jobs.
Publication Dates: 1980–1992.
Acronym: PMPQ.

Scores: 3 categories: Job Functions, Personal Requirements, Other Information.
Administration: Group.
Price Data: Available from publisher.
Time: Administration time not reported.
Authors: J. L. Mitchell, E. J. McCormick, S. Morton McPhail (manual), P. Richard Jeanneret (manual), and Robert C. Mecham (manual).
Publisher: PAQ Services, Inc.
Cross References: For reviews by Mary Anne Bunda and William I. Sauser, Jr., see 12:311; for reviews of an earlier edition by Gregory H. Dobbins and George Thornton, see 9:993.

[1992]
Professional Employment Test.

Purpose: Designed to measure reading comprehension, reasoning, quantitative problem solving, and data interpretation for use in selecting personnel for professional, administrative, and managerial occupations.
Population: Potential managerial, administrative, and professional employees.
Publication Dates: 1986–1988.
Acronym: PET.
Scores: Total score only.
Administration: Group.
Forms, 3: A, A-1, B-1.
Price Data: Price information available from publisher for test material including Technical Manual (1987, 31 pages), Administration Instructions (1986, 7 pages), Supplemental Technical Manual for Form A-1 (1988, 9 pages), and Administration Instructions for Form A-1 (1988, 8 pages).
Time: 80(85) minutes for long form; 40(45) minutes for short form.
Authors: William W. Ruch, Richard H. McKillip, and Ricki Buckly.
Publisher: Psychological Services, Inc.
Cross References: For reviews by Gregory J. Cizek and Jayne E. Stake, see 12:312.

[1993]
Profile of Adaptation to Life.

Purpose: Designed to measure adjustment and life style behaviors associated with adjustment.
Population: Adults seen in mental health and self-development programs.
Publication Dates: 1979–2002.
Acronym: PAL Scale.
Scores, 11: Adjustment (Alcohol/Drug Use, Close Relationships, Income Management, Negative Emotions, Psychological Well Being, Physical Symptoms, Relationships with Children), Life Style Behaviors (Nutrition and Exercise, Personal Growth, Self Nurturing Activity, Social Activity).
Administration: Individual.

Price Data, 2002: $10 per 25 scales; $5 per 25 profiles; $25 per manual (2002, 28 pages).
Time: (10) minutes.
Comments: Self-report ratings of pre- and post-treatment adjustment.
Authors: Robert B. Ellsworth and Shanae L. Ellsworth.
Publisher: Ellsworth Krebs Incorporated.
Cross References: See T5:2074 (1 reference); for information about earlier editions see T4:2119 (1 reference) and T4:2120 (1 reference); for reviews by Robert Deluty of the PAL-Clinical Scale and PAL-Holistic Scale, see 9:995 and 9:996.

[1994]
Profile of Aptitude for Leadership.

Purpose: To measure an individual's relative strength in each of four leadership styles (or types of leader).
Population: Adults.
Publication Date: 1991.
Acronym: PAL.
Scores, 4: Manager (Administrator), Supervisor (Coach), Entrepreneur (Leader), Technician (Specialist).
Administration: Group or individual.
Manual: No manual.
Price Data: Price information available from publisher for test, answer sheet, and interpretation folder.
Time: (20) minutes.
Comments: Self-administered; self-scored.
Author: Training House, Inc.
Publisher: Training House, Inc.
Cross References: For reviews by Jack E. Gebart-Eaglemont and Neal Schmitt, see 13:243.

[1995]
Profile of Mood States.

Purpose: "Developed to measure mood or affective states."
Population: College and psychiatric outpatients.
Publication Dates: 1971–1992.
Acronym: POMS.
Scores, 6: Tension-Anxiety, Depression-Dejection, Anger-Hostility, Vigor-Activity, Fatigue-Inertia, Confusion-Bewilderment.
Administration: Individual or group.
Price Data, 1998: $9.50 per 25 inventories [$36 per 100, $143.50 per 500]; $7.25 per profile sheet (specify college or outpatient) [$11.75 per 50, $104.25 per 500]; $17.50 per hand-scoring key; $9 per specimen set including manual (1981, 28 pages) and all forms; $5.80 per manual; $24.50 per POMS bibliography; $843 per on-site scoring software; $16.75 per 25 on-site inventories [$63.75 per 100, $287.25 per 500].
Time: (3–5) minutes.

Comments: Earlier experimental forms called Lorr Outpatient Mood Scale and Psychiatric Outpatient Mood Scale; self-administering.
Authors: Douglas M. McNair, Maurice Lorr, and Leo F. Droppleman.
Publisher: EdITS/Educational and Industrial Testing Service.
Cross References: See T5:2076 (187 references) and T4:2122 (191 references), 9:998 (46 references), and T3:1904 (84 references); for reviews by William J. Eichman and Thaddeus E. Weckowicz, see 8:651 (33 references); see also T2:1337 (17 references).

[1996]
Profile of Mood States, Bi-Polar Form.

Purpose: Developed to measure mood dimensions in terms of six bipolar affective states.
Population: Ages 18–adult.
Publication Dates: 1984–1988.
Acronym: POMS-BI.
Scores, 6: Composed—Anxious, Elated—Depressed, Agreeable—Hostile, Energetic—Tired, Clearheaded—Confused, Confident—Unsure.
Administration: Group.
Price Data, 1998: $9.50 per 25 inventories [$36 per 100, $143.50 per 500]; $7.25 per 25 profile sheets [$11.75 per 50, $104.25 per 500]; $17.50 per hand-scoring keys; $5.50 per manual (1988, 10 pages); $9 per specimen set including manual and one copy of all forms.
Time: (5) minutes.
Authors: Maurice Lorr and Douglas M. McNair.
Publisher: EdITS/Educational and Industrial Testing Service.
Cross References: See T5:2077 (9 references).

[1997]
Profile of Nonverbal Sensitivity.

Purpose: "Designed to measure ability to decode nonverbal cues conveyed by the face, body, and tone of voice."
Population: Grades 3–16 and adults.
Publication Date: 1979.
Acronym: PONS.
Scores: Total score only.
Administration: Group.
Price Data, 1993: $12.95 per manual (1979, 90 pages); $25 per 50 question sheets; $55 per 50 child's version question sheets.
Authors: Robert Rosenthal, Judith Hall, Dane Archer, Robin DiMatteo, and Peter Rogers.
Publisher: Irvington Publishers, Inc.
　　a) THE FULL PONS TEST.
　　Purpose: Matching facial expressions, body movements, and tone of voice to situations.
　　Price Data: $215 per VHS video cassette.
　　Time: 45(50) minutes.

b) AUDIO CASSETTE VERSION.
Purpose: To test sensitivity to tone of voice.
Price Data: $8.95 per audio cassette.
Time: 60(65) minutes.
Comments: Cassette tape includes the audio sections of the Full PONS, male, female, and child speakers.
c) FACE AND BODY PONS.
Price Data: $185 per VHS video cassette.
Time: 8(13) minutes.
Comments: Visual-only-no-sound test; contains 20 face-only and 20 body-only items from the Full PONS test.
d) BRIEF EXPOSURE PONS.
Price Data: $185 per VHS video cassette.
Time: 8(13) minutes.
Comments: Contains same 40 items as *c* but the exposure times are shortened to from 2 seconds to 1/24, 3/24, 9/24, and 27/24 seconds.
e) NON-VERBAL DISCREPANCY TEST.
Purpose: Measures how well the viewer detects discrepant audio versus visual signals.
Price Data: $185 per VHS video cassette.
Time: 30(35) minutes.
Cross References: See T5:2078 (7 references) and T4:2124 (7 references).

[1998]
Program for Assessing Youth Employment Skills.

Purpose: Measures attitudes concerning job-holding skills and supervision, self-confidence, cognitive measures, and vocational interest for persons with low verbal skills.
Population: Adolescents and young adults with low verbal skills.
Publication Dates: 1967–1979.
Acronym: PAYES.
Scores: 7 subtests: Job-Holding Skills, Attitudes Toward Supervision, Self-Confidence, Job Knowledge, Job-Seeking Skills, Practical Reasoning, Vocational Interest Inventory.
Administration: Group.
Forms: 1 form in 3 booklets: Booklet 1 (1979, 18 pages), Booklet 2 (1979, 31 pages), Booklet 3 (1979, 11 pages).
Price Data: Not available.
Time: (75) minutes.
Comments: May be orally administered.
Authors: Simon & Schuster Higher Education Group.
Publisher: Prentice Hall [No reply from publisher; status unknown].
Cross References: For reviews by Shirley A. White and Dan Zakay, see 9:1001.

[1999]
Program Quality Assessment.

Purpose: Designed "to evaluate the quality of early childhood programs and identify staff-training needs."
Population: Early childhood programs.
Publication Date: 1998.
Acronym: PQA.
Scores: Total score only.
Administration: Individual.
Price Data, 2001: $22.85 per package including administration manual (11 pages), Head Start user guide (16 pages), and assessment form; $7 per administration manual; $7 per Head Start user guide; $10.85 per assessment form.
Time: Untimed.
Author: High/Scope Educational Research Foundation.
Publisher: High/Scope Educational Research Foundation.

[2000]
Program Self-Assessment Service.

Purpose: "To assist colleges and universities that are carrying out departmental or program reviews at the undergraduate level."
Population: Faculty members, students majoring in the department, and recent graduates.
Publication Date: 1986.
Acronym: PSAS.
Scores, 16: Environment for Learning, Scholarly Excellence, Quality of Teaching, Faculty Concern for Students, Curriculum, Departmental Procedures, Available Resources, Student Satisfaction With Program, Internship/Fieldwork/Clinical Experiences, Resource Accessibility, Employment Assistance, Faculty Work Environment, Faculty Program Involvement, Faculty Research Activities, Faculty Professional Activities, Student Accomplishments.
Administration: Group.
Forms, 3: Faculty, Student, Alumni.
Price Data: Available from publisher.
Time: (30-45) minutes.
Author: Educational Testing Service.
Publisher: Educational Testing Service.
Cross References: For a review by Darrell L. Sabers, see 10:298.

[2001]
Programmer Analyst Aptitude Test [One-Hour Version].

Purpose: To evaluate the candidate's aptitude and potential for programming and analyzing business problems.
Population: Entry-level and experienced applicants for programmer analyst positions.

Publication Date: 1997.
Acronym: PROGANI.
Scores: Total Score, Narrative Evaluation, Ranking, Recommendation.
Administration: Group.
Price Data, 2001: $235 per person; quantity discounts available.
Foreign Language Edition: Available in French.
Time: (60) minutes.
Comments: Available in booklet and Internet versions; scored by publisher; must be proctored.
Author: Bruce A. Winrow.
Publisher: Walden Personnel Performance, Inc.

[2002]
Programmer Analyst Aptitude Test [Two-Hour Version].

Purpose: "To evaluate the candidate's aptitude and potential for programming and analyzing business problems."
Population: Applicants for programmer analyst positions.
Publication Date: 1984.
Acronym: PAAT.
Scores: Programming, Analytical, Total, Narrative Evaluation, Ranking, Recommendation.
Administration: Group.
Price Data, 2001: $350 per candidate; quantity discounts available.
Time: (120) minutes.
Comments: Tests scored by publisher only; must be proctored.
Author: Bruce Winrow.
Publisher: Walden Personnel Performance, Inc. [Canada].
Cross References: For reviews by Frederick Bessai and Ralph F. Darr, Jr., see 11:308.

[2003]
Programmer Aptitude Battery.

Purpose: Designed to assess aptitude for programming.
Population: Adults naive to programming task.
Publication Date: 1988.
Acronym: PAB.
Scores, 4: Procedures, Matrices I, Matrices II, Grand Total.
Administration: Group.
Price Data: Available from publisher.
Foreign Language Edition: Test printed in both English and Afrikaans.
Time: 100(135) minutes.
Author: T. R. Taylor.
Publisher: Human Sciences Research Council [South Africa].

[2004]
Programmer Aptitude Series.

Purpose: Assess skills needed in the data processing environment.
Population: Computer programming personnel.
Publication Dates: 1979–1983.
Acronym: PAS.
Administration: Group or individual.
Restricted Distribution: Distribution restricted to persons who have completed the publisher's training course or members of the Division of Occupational Psychology of the British Psychological Society.
Price Data: Available from publisher.
Comments: Consists of tests from within the Advanced, Personnel, and Technical Test Batteries; subtests available as separates.
Authors: Peter Saville (VA1, NA2, manual), Gill Nyfield (CP7, manual), Roger Holdsworth (VA3, NA4), David Hawkey (DA5, ST7, DT8, ST9), Sue Bawtree (CP7), Steve Blinkhorn (VA3), and Alan Iliffe (NA4).
Publisher: SHL Group plc [United Kingdom].
  a) LEVEL 1.
  Publication Dates: 1979–1981.
  Purpose: Basic programming.
    1) *Number Series.*
    Publication Date: 1980.
    Acronym: NA2.
    Time: 15(20) minutes.
    2) *Diagramming.*
    Publication Date: 1980.
    Acronym: DA5.
    Time: 20(25) minutes.
    3) *Verbal Concepts.*
    Publication Date: 1980.
    Acronym: VA1.
    Time: 15(20) minutes.
    4) *Basic Checking.*
    Publication Dates: 1980–1981.
    Acronym: CP7.
    Time: 10(15) minutes.
    5) *Spatial Recognition.*
    Publication Dates: 1980–1981.
    Acronym: ST9.
  Time: 15(20) minutes.
  b) LEVEL 2.
  Publication Dates: 1979–1983.
  Purpose: Complex programming skills.
    1) *Number series.*
    Details same as for Level 1.
    2) *Diagramming.*
    Details same as for Level 1.
    3) *Verbal Critical Reasoning.*
    Publication Date: 1983.
    Acronym: VA3.
    Time: 30(35) minutes.

4) *Basic Checking.*
Details same as for Level 1.
5) *Special Reasoning.*
Publication Dates: 1979–1981.
Acronym: ST7.
Time: 20(25) minutes.
c) LEVEL 3.
Publication Dates: 1979–1983.
Population: Systems analysts and management.
1) *Verbal Concepts.*
Details same as for Level 1.
2) *Number Series.*
Details same as for Level 1.
3) *Verbal Reasoning.*
Details same as for Level 2.
4) *Numerical Critical Reasoning.*
Publication Dates: 1979–1983.
Acronym: NA4.
Time: 35(40) minutes.
5) *Diagrammatic Reasoning.*
Publication Dates: 1979–1981.
Acronym: DT8.
Time: 15(20) minutes.

[2005]
Progress Assessment Chart of Social and Personal Development.

Purpose: Constructed to assess progress in social development.
Publication Dates: 1966–1982.
Administration: Individual.
Price Data: Available from publisher.
Foreign Language Editions: Dutch, French, German, Portuguese, and Spanish editions available.
Time: Administration time not reported.
Comments: Behavior checklist.
Author: H. C. Gunzburg.
Publisher: SEFA (Publications) Ltd. [England].
a) PRIMARY PROGRESS ASSESSMENT CHART OF SOCIAL DEVELOPMENT, FORM P.
Population: Young mentally handicapped children, severely handicappted young children, and profoundly handicapped adults, very young normal children.
Acronym: P-PAC.
Scores: 4 areas: Self-Help, Communication, Occupation, Socialisation.
b) PROGRESS ASSESSMENT CHART OF SOCIAL AND PERSONAL DEVELOPMENT, FORM 1.
Population: Handicapped children and adolescents.
Acronym: PAC-1.
Scores: 5 areas: Same as *a* above plus Personal Assessment.

c) PROGRESS ASSESSMENT CHART OF SOCIAL AND PERSONAL DEVELOPMENT, FORM A1.
Population: Same as *b* above.
Acronym: A-PAC1.
Scores: Same as *b* above.
Comments: Extension of PAC-1.
d) PROGRESS ASSESSMENT CHART OF SOCIAL AND PERSONAL DEVELOPMENT, FORM 2.
Population: Mentally handicapped adolescents and adults.
Acronym: PAC-2.
Scores: Same as *b* above.
e) PROGRESS ASSESSMENT CHART OF THE SOCIAL DEVELOPMENT OF CHILDREN WITH DOWN'S SYNDROME, FORM 1.
Population: Mentally handicapped children with Down's Syndrome.
Acronym: M-PAC1.
Scores: Same as *a* above.
Authors: H. C. Gunzberg and Janice Sinson.
f) ELEMENTARY PROGRESS ASSESSMENT CHART, FORM S/E.
Population: Profoundly and severely handicapped persons.
Acronym: S/E PAC.
Scores: Same as *a* above.
g) PROGRESS ASSESSMENT CHART S1 OF SOCIAL AND PERSONAL DEVELOPMENT, FORM S1.
Population: Same as *f* above.
Acronym: S-PAC1.
Scores: Same as *b* above.
h) PROGRESS ASSESSMENT CHART OF SOCIAL AND PERSONAL DEVELOPMENT, FORM S2.
Population: Same as *f* above.
Acronym: S-PAC2.
Scores: Same as *b* above.
Cross References: See T5:2088 (1 reference); for reviews by Betty N. Gordon and Joel Hundert, see 9:1003; see also T3:1908 (1 reference), T2:1338 (3 references), 7:125 (1 reference), and P:216 (5 references).

[2006]
Progressive Achievement Test of Mathematics [Revised].

Purpose: To assist classroom teachers in determining the mathematics skills of their students.
Population: Ages 8-0 to 14-11.
Publication Dates: 1974–1994.
Acronym: PAT Mathematics.
Scores: Total score only.
Administration: Group.

Levels: 7 overlapping levels called Parts 2 (Standard 2), 3(3), 4(4), 5(Form 1), 6(2), 7(3), 8(4) in three booklets (Primary, Parts 2-4; Intermediate, Parts 5 and 6; Secondary, Parts 7 and 8); 2 forms: A and B.

Price Data, 2001: NZ$6.75 per teacher's manual (1993, 46 pages); $1.80 per test booklet (Primary (S2-S4), Intermediate (F1 & F2), Secondary (F3 & F4); $.99 per marking key (Parts 2-8); $1.44 per answer sheet (Parts 2-8).

Time: (45-55) minutes.

Author: Neil A. Reid.

Publisher: New Zealand Council for Educational Research [New Zealand].

Cross References: For reviews by Linda E. Brody and Suzanne Lane, see 12:313; see also T3:1911 (1 reference); for a review by Harold C. Trimble of an earlier edition, see 8:288; for reviews by James C. Impara and A. Harry Passow of an earlier Australian edition, see 11:309.

[2007]
Progressive Achievement Tests in Mathematics—Revised.

Purpose: Designed "to provide information to teachers about the level of achievement attained by their students in the skills and understanding of mathematics."

Population: Australian students in years 4–9.

Publication Dates: 1983–1998.

Acronym: PATMaths Revised.

Scores: Total score only.

Administration: Group.

Forms, 2: Form A, Form B.

Price Data, 2002: A$3.90 per test booklet; A$66 per specimen set including booklet, teacher's manual (1997, 21 pages), answer sheet, and score key; A$49.95 per teacher's manual; A$5 per scoring key; A$7.50 per 10 answer sheets; A$99.95 per combined specimen set including components from each level plus teacher's manual; price data for norming manual (1998, 18 pages) available from publisher.

Time: (45) minutes.

Author: Australian Council for Educational Research Press.

Publisher: Australian Council for Educational Research Ltd. [Australia].

    a) LEVEL 1.

    Population: Years 4–6.

    b) LEVEL 2.

    Population: Years 6–9.

    c) LEVEL 3.

    Population: Years 7–9.

Cross References: See T5:2091 (5 references); for reviews by James C. Impara and A. Harry Passow of an earlier edition, see 11:309 (2 references). For information on the New Zealand edition, see T3:1911 (1 reference); for additional information and a review by Harold C. Trimble, see 8:288.

[2008]
Progressive Achievement Tests in Reading: Comprehension and Vocabulary—Third Edition.

Purpose: "Tests designed to assist teachers in their assessment of students' reading comprehension skills and vocabulary knowledge."

Population: Years 3–9 in Australian school system.

Publication Dates: 1973–2001.

Acronym: PAT-R.

Scores, 2: Reading Comprehension, Reading Vocabulary.

Administration: Individual or group.

Parts, 2: PAT-R: Comprehension, PAT-R: Vocabulary.

Levels, 4: 4 levels for Comprehension and for Vocabulary: Test Form 1 (Years 3–5), Test Form 2 (Years 4–6), Test Form 3 (Years 6–8), Test Form 4 (Years 7–9).

Price Data, 2001: A$130 per specimen set including revised teacher's manual with score keys (2001, 79 pages), Comprehension test forms 1–4 (reusable), Comprehension answer sheets (10 each for Forms 1–4), Vocabulary test forms 1–4 (reusable), Vocabulary answer sheets (10 each for Forms 1–4); $85 per revised manual with score keys; $6.30 per Comprehension test form (any of Levels 1–4); $3.85 per Vocabulary test for (any of Levels 1–4); $11 per 10 Comprehension answer sheets or 10 Vocabulary answer sheets (any of Levels 1–4).

Time: 40(55) minutes (Comprehension); 25 minutes (Vocabulary).

Comments: Developed especially, but not exclusively, for use in Australian schools; hand- or machine-scorable; machine scoring performed by publisher; two types of reports available (PAT-R Report, PAT-R Diagnostic Report).

Author: Australian Council for Educational Research, Ltd.

Publisher: Australian Council for Educational Research, Ltd. [Australia].

Cross References: For information on an earlier edition, see T5:2092 (4 references); for reviews by Paul C. Burnett and Richard Lehrer of an earlier edition, see 11:310 (4 references); see also T3:1912 (4 references); for a review by Douglas A. Pidgeon of an earlier edition, see 8:738 (1 reference); see also T2:1579 (1 reference); for excerpted reviews by Milton L. Clark and J. Elkins, see 7:699.

[2009]
Progressive Achievement Test of Listening Comprehension [Revised].

Purpose: "Intended … to assist teachers in determining levels of development attained by their students in the basic skills of listening comprehension."

Population: Ages 7–14.
Publication Dates: 1971–1994.
Acronym: PAT: Listening Comprehension.
Scores: Total score only.
Administration: Group.
Levels: 8 overlapping levels labeled Parts 1–8: Primary: Parts 1–4 (Standards 1–4); Intermediate: Parts 5–6 (Forms 1–2); Secondary: Parts 7–8 (Forms 3–4).
Price Data, 2001: NZ$1.80 per Primary, Intermediate, or Secondary test booklet; $4.50 per Primary, Intermediate, or Secondary teacher's script; $.99 per scoring key; $1.44 per 10 answer sheets; $9 per Intermediate audiotape; $9.90 per Secondary audiotape; $9 per teacher's manual (1994, 32 pages).
Time: (55) minutes.
Comments: 2 forms (A & B) available (Form A is used in odd-numbered years and Form B is used in even-numbered years); this test was specifically developed for use in New Zealand schools.
Authors: Neil A. Reid, Ian C. Johnston, and Warwick B. Elley.
Publisher: New Zealand Council for Educational Research [New Zealand].
Cross References: For a review by Sherwyn Morreale and Philip Backlund, see 13:245 (1 reference); see also T4:2140 (2 references) and T3:1910 (1 reference); for a review by Roger A. Richards of an earlier edition, see 8:453 (2 references).

[2010]
Progressive Achievement Tests of Reading [Revised].

Purpose: Designed to assess the skills and abilities of the students in reading with a view to providing instruction adapted to their present stages of development.
Population: Ages 8–14.
Publication Dates: 1969–1991.
Scores, 2: Reading Comprehension, Reading Vocabulary.
Administration: Group.
Levels, 3: Primary, Intermediate, Secondary.
Forms, 2: A, B.
Price Data: Available from publisher.
Time: 45 minutes for Comprehension part, 30 minutes for Vocabulary part.
Comments: Raw scores convert to the Level scores (1–10), age percentile rank, and class percentile rank.
Authors: Neil A. Reid and Warwick B. Elley.
Publisher: New Zealand Council for Educational Research [New Zealand].
Cross References: See T5:2094 (3 references); for a review by Herbert C. Rudman, see 12:314 (3 references); see also T4:2141 (7 references) and T3:1912 (2 references); for a review by Douglas A. Pidgeon, see 8:738 (1 reference); see also T2:1579 (1 reference); for excerpted reviews by Milton L. Clark and J. Elkins, see 7:699.

[2011]
Project Leader Skills Evaluation.

Purpose: To assess essential skills needed for the position of Project Leader.
Population: Candidates for Project Leader position.
Publication Date: 1993.
Acronym: BALEADS.
Scores: Total Score, Narrative Evaluation, Ranking, Recommendation.
Administration: Group.
Price Data, 2001: $235 per candidate; quantity discounts available.
Foreign Language Edition: Available in French.
Time: [60] minutes.
Comments: Scored by publisher; available in booklet and Internet versions; must be proctored.
Author: Bruce A. Winrow.
Publisher: Walden Personnel Performance, Inc. [Canada].

[2012]
Project Management Competency Assessment.

Purpose: Designed to assess project manager competencies.
Population: Project managers.
Publication Date: 1996.
Scores, 18: Project Definition, Organization Awareness, Team Leadership, Time Management, Resource Management, Lost Management, Quality Management, Risk Management, Team Facilitation, Managing Conflict, Negotiating Changes, Communication Management, Project Integration, Receiving Feedback, Results Focus, Goal Pressure, Delegation, Recognition.
Administration: Group.
Manual: No manual.
Price Data: Available from publisher.
Time: Administration time not reported.
Comments: Ratings by self and/or coworkers; can be used alone or in conjunction with Project Management Knowledge & Skills Assessment (14:298).
Author: Clark L. Wilson.
Publisher: The Clark Wilson Group for the exclusive use of Educational Services Institute.

[2013]
Proof-Reading Tests of Spelling.

Purpose: Constructed to measure a child's ability to discriminate between words spelled correctly and incorrectly in the context of meaningful paragraphs.
Population: Ages 8–13.
Publication Date: 1981.
Acronym: PRETOS.
Scores, 2: Production, Recognition.
Administration: Group.

Levels, 5: Test 2, Test 3, Test 4, Test 5, Test 6.
Price Data: Available from publisher
Time: 30 minutes.
Authors: Cedric Croft, Alison Gilmore, Neil Reid, and Peter Jackson.
Publisher: New Zealand Council for Educational Research [New Zealand].
Cross References: See T4:2146 (2 references); for a review by Sally Anita Whiting, see 9:1009.

[2014]
Prospector: Discovering the Ability to Learn and to Lead.

Purpose: "Designed to assess openness to learning from experience."
Population: Managers and executives.
Publication Date: 1996.
Scores, 11: Seeks Opportunities to Learn, Has the Courage to Take Risks, Seeks Broad Business Knowledge, Adapts to Cultural Differences, Acts with Integrity, Is Committed to Making a Difference, Brings Out the Best in People, Is Insightful: Sees Things from New Angles, Seeks and Uses Feedback, Learns from Mistakes, Is Open to Criticism.
Administration: Group.
Price Data, 2002: $195 per 1–10 complete prospector sets including one self survey, 10 "other" surveys, one feedback report, one learning guide, and one user's guide (96 pages); quantity discounts available.
Time: [10–15] minutes.
Authors: Morgan W. McCall, Gretchen M. Spreitzer, and Joan Jay Mahoney.
Publisher: Center for Creative Leadership.
Cross References: For reviews by Theodore L. Hayes and Neil P. Lewis, see 14:299.

[2015]
PSB Aptitude for Practical Nursing Examination.

Purpose: Designed as a method of selection, placement, guidance, and counseling of incoming practical/vocational nursing students.
Population: Applicants for admission to practical and vocational nursing schools.
Publication Dates: 1961–1999.
Scores, 7: Academic Aptitude (Verbal, Arithmetic, Nonverbal), Spelling, Information in the Natural Sciences, Judgment and Comprehension in Practical Nursing Situations, Vocational Adjustment Index.
Administration: Individual or group.
Price Data, 2002: $10 per test booklet; $20 per technical manual; $20 per administrator's manual; $10 per answer sheet (scoring and reporting); $15 per electronic test.

Time: (135) minutes.
Comments: Electronic tests available at www.psb.tests.com.
Authors: Anna S. Evans, Phyllis G. Roumm, and George A. W. Stouffer, Jr., with technical assistance from Psychological Services Bureau, Inc.
Publisher: Psychological Services Bureau, Inc.
Cross References: For reviews by Mark Albanese and Anita Tesh of the Revised PSB—Aptitude for Practical Nursing Examination, see 13:264.

[2016]
PSB Health Occupations Aptitude Examination.

Purpose: Measures "abilities, skills, knowledge, and attitudes important for successful performance of students in the allied health education programs."
Population: Candidates for admission to programs of study in the allied health occupations.
Publication Dates: 1978–1999.
Scores, 7: Academic Aptitude (Verbal, Arithmetic, Nonverbal), Spelling, Reading Comprehension, Information in the Natural Sciences, Vocational Adjustment Index.
Administration: Group or individual.
Price Data, 2002: $10 per test booklet; $10 per answer sheet (scoring and reporting); $20 per technical manual; $20 per administrator's manual; $15 per electronic test.
Time: (135) minutes.
Comments: Electronic tests available at www.psbtests.com.
Authors: Psychological Services Bureau, Inc. with consultant contributions.
Publisher: Psychological Services Bureau, Inc.
Cross References: For reviews by Betty Bergstrom and Hilda Wing of the Revised PSB—Health Occupations Apptitude Examination, see 13:265; for reviews by Stephen B. Dunbar and Lawrence M. Rudner of an earlier edition, see 11:312.

[2017]
PSB Nursing School Aptitude Examination (RN).

Purpose: Predicts readiness or suitability for specialized instruction in a school/program of professional nursing.
Population: Applicants for admission to programs of study in professional nursing.
Publication Dates: 1978–1998.
Scores, 7: Academic Aptitude (Verbal, Arithmetic, Nonverbal), Spelling, Reading Comprehension, Information in the Natural Sciences, Vocational Adjustment Index.
Administration: Individual or group.
Price Data, 2002: $10 per test booklet; $10 per answer sheet (scoring and reporting); $20 per technical

manual; $20 per administrator's manual; $15 per electronic test..

Time: (105) minutes.

Comments: Electronic tests available at www.psbtests.com.

Authors: Anna S. Evans, Phyllis G. Roumm, and George A. W. Stouffer, Jr.

Publisher: Psychological Services Bureau, Inc.

Cross References: For reviews by Mark H. Daniel and William B. Michael of the Revised PSB—Nursing School Aptitude Examination (R.N.), see 13:266; for reviews by Kurt F. Geisinger and James C. Impara of an earlier edition, see 11:313.

[2018]
PSB Reading Comprehension Examination.

Purpose: To reveal the examinee's comprehension or understanding of what is read.

Population: Secondary and postsecondary students applying or enrolled in terminal vocational or occupational programs, general population.

Publication Dates: 1978–2000.

Scores: Total score only.

Administration: Group or individual.

Price Data, 2002: $10 per test booklet; $8 per answer sheet (scoring and reporting); $20 per technical manual; $20 per administrator's manual; $15 per electronic test.

Time: (60) minutes.

Comments: Electronic tests available at www.psbtests.com

Authors: Psychological Services Bureau, Inc., with consultant contributions.

Publisher: Psychological Services Bureau, Inc.

Cross References: For reviews by Ray Fenton and Felice J. Green of the Revised PSB—Reading Comprehension Examination, see 13:267; for reviews by Joseph C. Ciechalski and by Brandon Davis and John A. Glover of an earlier edition, see 11:314.

[2019]
PSC-Survey ADT.

Purpose: "Evaluates a job applicant's attitudes toward companies, business, work and trust attitudes."

Population: Job applicants.

Publication Date: 1987.

Scores, 4: Alienation, Trustworthiness, Total, False Positives.

Administration: Group or individual.

Price Data, 1994: $7.50 (or less) per survey.

Time: (15–20) minutes.

Comments: On-site scoring available.

Authors: Alan L. Strand and Mark L. Strand.

Publisher: Predictive Surveys Corporation.

Cross References: For a review by Chantale Jeanrie, see 13:247.

[2020]
PSC Survey-SA.

Purpose: "Measures attitudes toward the position of supervisor for selection or promotion."

Population: Job applicants or current employees.

Publication Date: 1987.

Scores, 6: Attitudes Toward Companies and Business, Attitudes Toward Managers and Executives, Attitudes Toward Peers and Associates, Attitudes Toward Being a Supervisor, Attitudes Toward Subordinates, Total.

Administration: Group or individual.

Price Data, 1994: $7.50 (or less) per survey.

Time: (10–15) minutes.

Authors: Alan L. Strand and Mark L. Strand.

Publisher: Predictive Surveys Corporation.

Cross References: For reviews by L. Carolyn Pearson and E. Lea Witta, see 13:248.

[2021]
PSI Basic Skills Tests for Business, Industry, and Government.

Purpose: "Designed to assess abilities and skills that are important for clerical, Administrative, and customer service positions."

Population: Prospective administrative, customer service, and clerical employees.

Publication Dates: 1981–1984.

Acronym: BST.

Scores: 15 subtest scores: Language Skills, Reading Comprehension, Vocabulary, Computation, Problem Solving, Decision Making, Following Oral Directions, Following Written Directions, Forms Checking, Reasoning, Classifying, Coding, Filing Names, Filing Numbers, Visual Speed and Accuracy.

Administration: Group.

Price Data: Price information available from publisher for test material including administrator's guide (1982, 48 pages), validation report (1982, 93 pages), and technical manual (1984, 78 pages).

Time: 1.5-10(5-15) minutes for each test.

Comments: Tests available separately; computerized versions available; transportability procedure available.

Authors: William W. Ruch, Allen N. Shub, Sheryl M. Moinat, and David A. Dye.

Publisher: Psychological Services, Inc.

Cross References: See T5:2105 (1 reference); for reviews by Michael J. Stahl and Sheldon Zedeck, see 9:1010.

[2022]
Psychiatric Content Analysis and Diagnosis.

Purpose: "For measuring the magnitude of various psychological states and traits from the content analysis of verbal behavior."

Population: Children and adults.

Publication Dates: 1993–2000.
Acronym: PCAD.
Scores, 13: Anxiety Scale, Hostility Scales (Hostility Directed Outward, Hostility Directed Inward, Ambivalent Hostility), Social Alienation—Personal Disorganization Scale, Cognitive and Intellectual Impairment Scale, Depression Scale, Hope Scale, Health-Sickness Scale, Achievement Striving Scale, Human Relations Scale, Dependency Strivings Scale, Quality of Life Scale.
Administration: Individual or group.
Price Data, 2001: $299.95 per software license including media and manual (2000, 83 pages).
Time: (5) minutes; more if multiple speakers.
Comments: Earlier version listed in previous Buros publications as Psychologic and Neuropsychiatric Assessment Manual.
Authors: Louis A. Gottschalk and Robert Bechtel.
Publisher: GB Software LLC.
Cross References: For a review by William M. Reynolds, see 14:300.

[2023]
Psychiatric Diagnostic Interview—Revised.

Purpose: "Designed to determine if an individual is suffering, or has ever suffered, from a major psychiatric disorder."
Population: Ages 18 and older.
Publication Date: 1989.
Acronym: PDI-R.
Scores, 21: 17 basic syndromes: Organic Brain Syndrome (OB), Alcoholism (Al), Drug Abuse (Dr), Depression (De), Mania (Ma), Schizophrenia (Sc), Antisocial Personality (As), Somatization Disorder (So), Anorexia Nervosa (AN), Bulimia (Bu), Post-Traumatic Stress Disorder (PS), Obsessive-Compulsive Disorder (OC), Phobic Disorder (Ph), Panic Disorder (Pa), Generalized Anxiety (GA), Mental Retardation (MR), Adjustment Disorder (Ad), and 4 derived syndromes: Polydrug Abuse (Poly), Schizoaffective Disorder (Sc-Af), Manic-Depressive Disorder (Ma-De), Bulimarexia (Bu-AN).
Administration: Individual.
Price Data, 2002: $99.50 per complete kit including reusable administration booklet, 25 recording booklets, and manual (174 pages); $47.50 per administration booklet; $19.50 per 25 recording booklets; $42.50 per manual; $195 per microcomputer disk (IBM).
Time: (15–30) minutes for normals; (60) minutes for those with 2 or more syndromes.
Comments: Computer-assisted interview is available along with scoring and recording instructions.
Authors: Ekkehard Othmer, Elizabeth C. Penick, Barbara J. Powell, Marsha R. Read, and Sieglinde C. Othmer.
Publisher: Western Psychological Services.

Cross References: See T5:2107 (2 references) and T4:2152 (2 references); for reviews by Brian Bolton and Peter F. Merenda, see 11:316 (3 references).

[2024]
Psychiatric Evaluation Form.

Purpose: Designed "to record scaled judgments of a subject's functioning during a one week period" on dimensions of psychopathology.
Population: Psychiatric patients and nonpatients.
Publication Dates: 1967–1968.
Acronym: PEF.
Scores, 28: 20 psychopathological scores in Part I (Narcotics-Drugs, Agitation-Excitement, Suicide-Self Mutilation, Grandiosity, Somatic Concerns, Anti-Social Attitudes-Acts, Speech Disorganization, Hallucinations, Social Isolation, Belligerence-Negativism, Disorientation-Memory, Alcohol Abuse, Anxiety, Inappropriate, Suspicion-Persecution, Daily Routine-Leisure Time, Denial of Illness, Depression, Retardation-Lack of Emotion, Overall Severity of Illness), 3 occupational roles and 2 social roles; 3 admission scores (Duration, Stress, Reason for Admission).
Administration: Individual.
Price Data, 2001: $3.50 per booklet including score sheet; $1 per instruction manual; $4 per teaching tape/key; additional price data available from publisher.
Time: (20–40) minutes.
Authors: Robert L. Spitzer, Jean Endicott, Alvin Mesnikoff, and George Cohen.
Publisher: Department of Research Assessment and Training.
Cross References: See T5:2108 (5 references) and T4:2153 (9 references); for reviews by Goldine C. Gleser and Jerome D. Paulker, see 7:126 (1 reference); see also T3:1922 (15 references) and T2:1339 (4 references).

[2025]
Psychiatric Self-Assessment & Review.

Purpose: "To assist psychiatrists in keeping abreast of new knowledge and scientific developments in the field of psychology."
Population: Physicians.
Publication Date: 1999.
Acronym: PSA-R.
Scores: Total score only.
Administration: Individual.
Price Data, 1999: $175 (member) or $225 (nonmember) per examination book with answer sheet, syllabus (in print and CD-ROM formats), and personal score report and accompanying critique and reference book and performance interpretation guidelines.

Time: Administration time not reported.
Comments: Self-administered and self-scored; information regarding obtaining Continuing Medical Education credit for this examination available from publisher.
Authors: American Psychiatric Association.
Publisher: American Psychiatric Association.

[2026]
The Psychiatric Status Schedule: Subject Form, Second Edition.

Purpose: Designed to evaluate social and role functioning as well as mental status.
Population: Psychiatric patients and nonpatients.
Publication Dates: 1966–1968.
Acronym: PSS-2.
Scores, 43: 18 symptom scores (Inappropriate Affect—Appearance—Behavior, Interview Belligerence—Negativism, Agitation—Excitement, Retardation—Lack of Emotion, Speech Disorganization, Grandiosity, Suspicion—Persecution—Hallucinations, Reported Overt Anger, Depression—Anxiety, Suicide—Self-Mutilation, Somatic Concerns, Social Isolation, Daily Routine—Leisure Time Impairment, Antisocial Impulses or Acts, Alcoholic Abuse, Drug Abuse, Disorientation Memory, Denial or Illness), 5 role functioning scores (Wage Earner, Housekeeper, Student or Trainee, Mate, Parent), 5 summary symptom and role scales (Subjective Distress, Behavioral Disturbance, Impulse Control Disturbance, Reality Testing Disturbance, Summary Role), 20 supplemental scores (Anxiety, Auditory Hallucinations, Catatonic Behavior, Conversion Reaction, Delusions—Hallucinations, Depression—Suicide, Disassociation, Elated Mood, Guilt, Lack of Emotion, Obsessions—Compulsions, Persecutory Delusions, Phobia, Psychomotor Retardation, Sex Deviation, Silliness, Somatic Delusions or Hallucinations, Visual Hallucinations, Miscellaneous, Validity Check).
Administration: Individual.
Price Data: Available from publisher.
Time: (30–50) minutes.
Comments: Most sections dealing with signs and symptoms of psychiatric disorder are from Mental Status Schedule.
Authors: Robert L. Spitzer, Jean Endicott, and George M. Cohen.
Publisher: Department of Research Assessment and Training.
Cross References: See T5:2109 (1 reference), T4:2154 (14 references), T3:1923 (18 references), and T2:1340 (6 references); for a review by Hans H. Strupp, see 7:127 (5 references).

[2027]
Psychodiagnostic Test Report Blank.

Purpose: Organizes client information from a battery of tests.

Population: Psychologists.
Publication Dates: 1965-1974.
Price Data, 2001: $9 per 10 forms.
Time: Administration time not reported.
Author: Leopold Bellak.
Publisher: C.P.S., Inc.
Cross References: See 8:463 (1 reference).

[2028]
Psychoeducational Profile Revised.

Purpose: Designed "to assess skills and behaviors of autistic and communication-handicapped children who function between the ages of 6 months and 7 years."
Population: Autistic or communication-handicapped children whose chronological age is less than 12 years.
Publication Dates: 1979–1990.
Acronym: PEP-R.
Scores, 12: Behavioral (Relating, Materials, Sensory, Language); Developmental (Imitation, Perception, Fine Motor, Gross Motor, Eye-Hand, Cognitive Performance, Cognitive Verbal, Total).
Administration: Individual.
Price Data, 2001: $74 per complete program; $62 per manual (1990, 182 pages); $14 per 10 Profile sheets; materials kit available from Orange Interpr., 500 Valley Forge Rd., Hillsborough, NC 27278.
Time: (45–90) minutes.
Authors: Eric Schopler, Robert Jay Reichler, Ann Bashford, Margaret D. Lansing, and Lee M. Marcus.
Publisher: PRO-ED.
Cross References: See T5:2111 (2 references); for reviews by Pat Mirenda and Gerald Tindal, see 12:316 (2 references); for reviews by Gerald S. Hanna and Martin J. Wiese of an earlier edition, see 11:317.

[2029]
Psycho-Epistemological Profile.

Purpose: "Designed to provide a profile of an individual's epistemological hierarchy."
Population: College and adults.
Publication Dates: 1968–1980.
Acronym: PEP.
Scores, 3: Metaphoric, Rational, Empirical.
Administration: Group.
Price Data: Available from publisher.
Foreign Language Edition: French edition available.
Time: (20–30) minutes.
Comments: Experimental form.
Authors: J. R. Royce and L. P. Mos.
Publisher: Psychometric Affiliates.
Cross References: See T5:2112 (1 reference) and T4:2157 (2 references); for reviews by Bruce A. Bracken and Thomas J. Kehle, see 9:1013; see also 8:653 (2 references).

[2030]
Psycholinguistic Assessments of Language Processing in Aphasia.

Purpose: Designed as "an assessment of language processing in adult acquired aphasia."
Population: Adults with aphasia.
Publication Date: 1992.
Acronym: PALPA.
Scores: Available from publisher.
Administration: Individual.
Price Data, 2001: $397 per box file including 60 tests.
Time: Administration time not reported.
Authors: Janice Kay, Ruth Lesser, and Max Coltheart.
Publisher: Psychology Press.

[2031]
Psychological Screening Inventory.

Purpose: Developed to screen for mental health problems.
Population: Ages 16 and over.
Publication Dates: 1973–1978.
Acronym: PSI.
Scores, 5: Alienation, Social Nonconformity, Discomfort, Expression, Defensiveness.
Administration: Group or individual.
Price Data, 2001: $54 per examination kit including manual (1978, 44 pages), 10 question-and-answer sheets, set of 10 scoring templates, and 10 profile sheets; $18 per test manual; $29 per set of 10 scoring templates; $20–$23 (depending on volume) per testing kit (including 25 question-and-answer sheets and 25 profile sheets).
Foreign Language Edition: Available in Spanish (question and answer sheets only).
Time: (15) minutes.
Author: Richard I. Lanyon.
Publisher: Sigma Assessment Systems, Inc.
Cross References: See T5:2115 (6 references), T4:2159 (20 references), 9:1015 (2 references), and T3:1931 (18 references); for a review by Stephen L. Golding, see 8:654 (32 references); see also T2:1342 (7 references).

[2032]
Psychometric Behavior Checklist.

Purpose: For recording unusual test taking behavior.
Population: Adults.
Publication Date: 1960.
Acronym: PBC.
Score: Total score only.
Administration: Group.
Price Data: Available from publisher.
Time: Administration time not reported.
Comments: Also called Maryland Test Behavior Checklist.

Authors: Bernard G. Berenson, Kathryn C. Biersdorf, Thomas M. Magoon, Martha J. Maxwell, Donald K. Pumroy, and Marjorie H. Richey.
Publisher: University of Maryland, University Counseling Center [No reply from publisher; status unknown].
Cross References: See 6:166 (1 reference).

[2033]
Psychosocial Adjustment to Illness Scale.

Purpose: "Designed to assess the quality of a patient's psychosocial adjustment to a current medical illness or its residual effects."
Population: Medical patients or their immediate relatives.
Publication Date: 1983.
Acronym: PAIS.
Scores, 8: Health Care Orientation, Vocational Environment, Domestic Environment, Sexual Relationship, Extended Family, Social Environment, Psychological Distress, Total.
Administration: Individual.
Editions, 2: Interview, Self-Report.
Price Data, 2002: $3 per reusable booklet (interview); $1 per self-report booklet; $.70 per score/profile sheet (select edition); $.25 per score sheet; $29 per manual (56 pages).
Time: (20–30) minutes.
Comments: Scoring is available online at www.derogatis-tests.com.
Author: Leonard R. Derogatis.
Publisher: Clinical Psychometric Research, Inc.
Cross References: See T5:2117 (5 references) and T4:2161 (3 references); for a review by Cabrini S. Swassing, see 10:299.

[2034]
Psychosocial Pain Inventory [Revised].

Purpose: "Provides a standardized method of evaluating psychosocial factors important in maintaining and exacerbating chronic pain problems."
Population: Adults with chronic pain.
Publication Dates: 1980–1985.
Acronym: PSPI.
Scores: Item scores only.
Administration: Individual.
Price Data: Available from publisher for complete kit including manual (1985, 38 pages) and 50 forms.
Time: [60–120] minutes.
Authors: R. K. Heaton, R. A. W. Lehman, and C. J. Getto.
Publisher: Psychological Assessment Resources, Inc.
Cross References: For reviews by Julie A. Allison and Dennis C. Harper, see 14:301; see also T4:2162 (1 reference).

[2035]
Psychotherapy Outcome Kit (Including Quality of Emotional Life Self-Report).

Purpose: Designed to assist mental health care providers in collecting treatment outcome data. **Publication Date:** 1994. **Acronym:** PSOK. **Scores:** Total score only. **Administration:** Individual. **Price Data, 2001:** $25 per sampler set including QELSR, data sheet, clinical summary form, clinical summary end of treatment form, Psychotherapy Outcome Profile, and manual (52 pages, including sample forms) for child and adult versions; $125 per permission set including sampler set and permission to reproduce 200 copies of the test. **Time:** Administration time not reported. **Author:** David P. Isenberg. **Publisher:** Mind Garden, Inc.

a) CHILD VERSION.
Population: Age 15 and under.
Comments: Child Version QELSR completed by parent/guardian.
b) ADULT VERSION.
Population: Age 16 and older.
Comments: Adult Version QELSR completed by patient.
Cross References: For reviews by Matthew Burns and George Domino, see 14:302.

[2036]
Psypercept-170.

Purpose: "Designed to measure work-related personality and interest variables among managers." **Population:** Managers. **Publication Date:** 1996. **Acronym:** Psypercept-170. **Scores, 17:** Directive, Inclusive, Expressive, Persuasive, Persistent, Accommodating, Calming, Inventive, Discerning, Aspiring, Urgent, Materialistic, Numerical, Altruistic, Technological, Artistic, Procedural. **Administration:** Individual or group. **Price Data, 2001:** $300 per assessment set including 5 reusable test booklets, 50 answer sheets, 50 data summary sheets, 1 set of hand-scoring keys, and manual (66 pages); $75 per 5 reusable test booklets; $75 per 50 answer sheets; $50 per 50 data summary sheets; $60 per set of hand-scoring keys; $75 per manual. **Time:** (35–45) minutes. **Comments:** A 170-item self-administered questionnaire; "For use in assessing and developing the talents of executives, managers, and supervisors." **Author:** Joseph Hartman. **Publisher:** Joseph Hartman Consulting Psychology, Inc.

[2037]
The Pupil Rating Scale Revised: Screening for Learning Disabilities.

Purpose: To identify students with deficits in learning. **Population:** Grades K–6. **Publication Dates:** 1971–1981. **Scores, 8:** Verbal (Auditory Comprehension, Spoken Language, Total), Nonverbal (Orientation, Motor Coordination, Personal-Social Behavior, Total), Total. **Administration:** Individual. **Price Data, 2002:** $53 per 50 record forms; $49 per manual (1981, 84 pages). **Time:** (10–15) minutes. **Comments:** Ratings by teachers. **Author:** Helmer R. Myklebust. **Publisher:** The Psychological Corporation. **Cross References:** See T5:2123 (1 reference) and T4:2165 (2 references); for a review by Shavaun M. Wall, see 9:1019 (3 references); see also T3:1934 (8 references); for a review by Nicholas J. Anastasiow of an earlier edition and an excerpted review by Barton B. Proger, see 8:439 (5 references).

[2038]
Purdue Interest Questionnaire.

Purpose: To help students identify an appropriate specialization within or outside of engineering. **Population:** Freshmen engineering students. **Publication Dates:** 1976–1980. **Acronym:** PIQ. **Scores:** 18 scale scores: 11 engineering, 5 transfer, 2 general. **Administration:** Group. **Price Data:** Available from publisher. **Time:** Administration time not reported. **Comments:** Separate answer sheets (machine scored) must be used. **Authors:** William K. LeBold and Kevin D. Shell (manual). **Publisher:** Purdue Research Foundation [No reply from publisher; status unknown]. **Cross References:** See T4:2167 (1 reference) and 9:1020 (1 reference).

[2039]
Purdue Pegboard.

Purpose: Measures an individual's ability to move hands, fingers, and arms (gross movement) and to control movements of small objects (finger tip dexterity). **Population:** Assembly, general factory and various industrial positions and vocational rehabilitation. **Publication Dates:** 1941–1992. **Scores, 5:** Right Hand, Left Hand, Both Hands, Right plus Left plus Both Hands, Assembly.

Administration: Individual or group.
Price Data, 2002: $346 per start-up kit including 100 profile sheets, pegboard with complete set of washers, collars, and pegs, and examiner's manual; $70 per 100 profile sheets (quantity discounts available); $47 per replacement set of pegs, washers, and collars; $28 per examiner's manual.
Time: [3–9] minutes.
Author: Purdue Research Foundation.
Publisher: Reid London House.
Cross References: See T5:2125 (30 references), T4:2168 (34 references), T3:948 (13 references), T2:2234 (51 references), and 6:1081 (15 references); for a review by Neil D. Warren, see 5:873 (11 references); see also 4:751 (12 references); for reviews by Edwin F. Ghiselli, Thomas W. Harrell, and Albert Gibson Packard, see 3:666 (3 references).

[2040]
The Purpose in Life Test.

Purpose: To detect "existential vacuum."
Population: Adults.
Publication Dates: 1962–1981.
Acronym: PIL.
Scores: Total score only.
Administration: Individual or group.
Price Data: Available from publisher.
Time: (10–15) minutes.
Comments: 1976 form identical to 1969 version except for minor format changes; 1981 manual identical to 1969 version.
Authors: James C. Crumbaugh and Leonard T. Maholick.
Publisher: Psychometric Affiliates.
Cross References: See T5:2126 (16 references), T4:2169 (17 references), 9:1021 (9 references), T3:1960 (21 references), 8:656 (54 references), and T2:1350 (4 references); for reviews by John R. Braun and George Domino, see 7:130 (7 references).

[2041]
The Pyramid Scales.

Purpose: "Assesses adaptive behavior in handicapped persons of all ages."
Population: Handicapped persons ages birth to 78.
Publication Date: 1984.
Scores, 20: Sensory (Tactile Responsiveness, Auditory Responsiveness, Visual Responsiveness), Primary (Gross Motor, Eating, Fine Motor, Toileting, Dressing, Social Interaction, Washing/Grooming, Receptive Language, Expressive Language), Secondary (Recreation/Leisure, Writing, Domestic Behavior, Reading, Vocational, Time, Numbers, Money).
Administration: Individual.
Price Data, 1993: $11.40 per 50 answer/profile sheets; $17.40 per manual.

Time: (30–45) minutes.
Comments: "Criterion-referenced"; behavior checklist for measuring adaptive behavior by directly observing client or by interviewing adult informant.
Author: John D. Cone.
Publisher: John D. Cone.
Cross References: See T5:2127 (2 references) and T4:2170 (1 reference); for a review by John G. Svinicki, see 10:300.

[2042]
The Q-Tags Test of Personality.

Purpose: "Designed to enquire into the self-development influences."
Population: Ages 6 and over.
Publication Dates: 1967–1969.
Acronym: Q-TTP.
Administration: Group or individual.
Price Data, 2001: $20 per 25 answer sheets; $40 per specimen set (including 4 series of 54 tags, 4 paper boards, manual ['69, 27 pages], list of directions, and 25 answer sheets).
Time: (60–80) minutes in 2 sessions.
Comments: Self-administering.
Authors: Arthur G. Storey and Louise I. Masson.
Publisher: Institute of Psychological Research, Inc. [Canada].
   a) [BIOGRAPHICAL FORM].
   Population: Ages 6 and over.
   Scores, 13: 6 factor scores (Affective, Assertive, Effective, Hostility, Reverie, Social) in each of 2 areas (He or She Is, He or She Should Be), Correlation of Self and Ideal Self.
   b) [AUTOBIOGRAPHICAL FORM].
   Population: Ages 12 and over.
   Scores, 13: 6 factor scores (same as *a* above) in each of 2 areas (I Am, I Wish I Were), Correlation of Self and Ideal Self.
Cross References: See T4:2171 (1 reference) and T2:1351 (2 references); for a review by Joan Preston, see 7:131 (2 references); see also P:225 (5 references).

[2043]
Quality Culture Assessment.

Purpose: Designed to assess and evaluate organizational practices, policies, and procedures.
Population: Managers and personnel.
Acronym: QCA.
Administration: Group.
Manual: No manual.
Price Data: Available from publisher.
Time: Administration time not reported.
Authors: Juran Institute and Teleometrics International.
Publisher: Teleometrics International.

a) QUALITY POTENTIAL ANALYSIS.
Publication Dates: 1982–1995.
Acronym: QPA.
Scores, 2: As It Is Now, As I Would Like It To Be.
b) QUALITY CULTURE ANALYSIS.
Publication Date: 1995.
Acronym: QCA.
Scores, 9: Quality Values (Senior Leadership, Goals and Objectives, Rewards and Recognition), Empowered Employees (Self-Control, Recovery, Participation), Customer Focus (Individual Customer Focus, Managerial Customer Focus, Organizational Customer Focus).

[2044]
Quality of Life Enjoyment and Satisfaction Questionnaire.

Purpose: Designed to measure the "degree of enjoyment and satisfaction experienced by subjects in various areas of daily functioning."
Population: Adults with mental or medical disorders.
Publication Date: 1990.
Acronym: Q-LES-Q.
Forms, 2: Regular Form, Short Form.
Scores, 9: 6 scores (Physical Health, Subjective Feelings, Leisure Time Activities, Social Relationships, General Activities, Overall Life Enjoyment and Satisfaction); 3 optional scores (Work, Household Duties, School/Coursework).
Administration: Group.
Price Data, 2001: $1.50 per regular form; $.50 per short form; $1.50 per summary scale scores.
Time: Regular Form: [5–15] minutes; Short Form: [3–5] minutes.
Comments: Self-report measure.
Author: Jean Endicott.
Publisher: Department of Research Assessment and Training.
Cross References: For reviews by John C. Caruso and Mary Lou Bryant Frank, see 14:303.

[2045]
Quality of Life Inventory.

Purpose: Developed to provide a measure of a person's quality of life and their satisfaction with life.
Population: Ages 18 and over.
Publication Date: 1994.
Acronym: QOLI®.
Scores: 17 scales: Health, Self-Esteem, Goals-and-Values, Money, Work, Play, Learning, Creativity, Helping, Love, Friends, Children, Relatives, Home, Neighborhood, Community, Overall Quality of Life.
Administration: Group or individual.
Price Data, 2002: $86.50 per starter kit for handscoring including manual (84 pages), 50 answer sheets, and 50 worksheets; $52 per preview package for computer scoring including manual, 10 answer sheets, materials needed for 10 assessments, and 10 profile reports; $69 per reorder kit for handscoring including 50 answer sheets and 50 worksheets; $19 per 25 computer answer sheets; $1.85 per profile report, $36 per manual.
Time: (5) minutes.
Comments: Useful for outcomes measurement as well as individual counseling.
Author: Michael B. Frisch.
Publisher: NCS Assessments (Minnetonka).
Cross References: For reviews by Laura L. B. Barnes and Richard W. Johnson, see 14:304.

[2046]
Quality of Life Questionnaire.

Purpose: "Developed to assess the quality of an individual's life across a broad range of specific areas."
Population: Ages 18 and over.
Publication Date: 1989.
Acronym: QLQ.
Scores, 17: Material Well-Being, Physical Well-Being, Personal Growth, Marital Relations, Parent-Child Relations, Extended Family Relations, Extra-marital Relations, Altruistic Behavior, Political Behavior, Job Characteristics, Occupational Relations, Job Satisfiers, Creative/Aesthetic Behavior, Sports Activity, Vacation Behavior, Social Desirability, Total Quality of Life.
Administration: Group.
Price Data, 2002: $51 per complete kit including 25 QuikScore™ answer forms, 10 question booklets, and manual (43 pages); $17 per 10 reusable question booklets; $19 per 25 QuikScore™ answer forms; $21 per manual; $28 per specimen set including 1 question booklet, 3 QuikScore™ answer forms, and manual.
Time: (30) minutes.
Comments: Self-report; MS-DOS computer software program available for administration, scoring, and to generate narrative report.
Authors: David R. Evans and Wendy E. Cope.
Publisher: Multi-Health Systems, Inc.
Cross References: See T5:2132 (4 references) and T4:2172 (1 reference); for reviews by Gary B. Seltzer and Richard B. Stuart, see 11:318.

[2047]
Quality Potential Assessment.

Purpose: "Designed to provide information about an organization, such as data on its policies, practices, and logistics, and the degree to which the data contribute to encouraging staff to give their best to the organization."
Population: Adults.
Publication Dates: 1992–1995.
Acronym: QPA.

Scores: Actual and Desired ratings in 10 areas: Collaboration (Management Values, Support Structure, Managerial Credibility, Climate), Commitment (Impact, Relevance, Community), Creativity (Task Environment, Social Context, Problem Solving).
Administration: Group.
Price Data: Available from publisher.
Time: Administration time not reported.
Author: Jay Hall.
Publisher: Teleometrics International.
Cross References: For reviews by Theodore L. Hayes and Michael J. Zickar, see 14:305.

[2048]
QUEST.

Purpose: A screening, diagnostic, and remediation kit designed to identify reading and number difficulties.
Population: Ages 7–8.
Publication Dates: 1983–1991.
Administration: Group.
Price Data: Price information available from publisher for teacher's set including manual (1991, 144 pages), spirit masters, test cards, posters, starter workbooks, reading skills workbooks, number skills workbooks, and diagnostic testing equipment.
Time: (30–40) minutes per test.
Comments: Teacher's manual includes information on remedial and individualized learning programs.
Authors: Alistair H. Robertson, Anne Henderson, Ann Robertson, Joanna Fisher, and Mike Gibson.
Publisher: NFER-Nelson Publishing Co., Ltd. [England].
a) READING SCREENING TEST.
Scores, 3: Word Identification, Reading Comprehension, Total.
Price Data: Price information available from publisher for spirit masters.
b) NUMBER SCREENING TEST.
Scores: Total score only.
Price Data: Price information available from publisher for posters.
c) DIAGNOSTIC READING TEST.
Scores, 11: Pre-reading (Auditory Discrimination, Visual Discrimination, Auditory Sequential Memory, Visual Sequential Memory, Visuo-motor Coordination), Word Attack Skills (Sight Vocabulary, Letter Recognition, Simple Blends, Beginnings and Endings, Diagraphs and the Silent e Rule, Reversals).
Price Data: Price information available from publisher for diagnostic test cards and diagnostic testing equipment.
d) DIAGNOSTIC NUMBER TEST.
Scores, 10: Pre-number (Visual Perception, Visuo-motor Coordination, Auditory Sequential

Memory), Early Number Concepts (Sorting, Conservation, Ordering), Number Concepts (Addition, Subtraction); Number Skills (Ordering, Computation).
Price Data: Same as *c* above.
Cross References: See T5:2134 (1 reference); for reviews by G. Gage Kingsbury and Christine Novak, see 12:317.

[2049]
Questionnaire Measure of Trait Arousability (Or Its Converse, Stimulus Screening).

Purpose: Designed to measure individual differences in positive and/or negative emotionality, emotional sensitivity, or emotional reactivity.
Population: Ages 15 and older.
Publication Dates: 1976–1994.
Scores: Total score only.
Administration: Group or individual.
Price Data: Available from publisher for specimen set including manual (1994, 8 pages) and literature review.
Time: (10–15) minutes.
Comments: Previously known as Questionnaire Measure of Stimulus Screening and Arousability.
Author: Albert Mehrabian.
Publisher: Albert Mehrabian.
Cross References: For a review by Robert A. Leark, see 13:249; for a review by James J. Jupp of the earlier edition, see 9:1025.

[2050]
QUESTS: A Life-Choice Inventory.

Purpose: To assess outcomes of substance abuse prevention education.
Population: Grades 9–12.
Publication Dates: 1974–1976.
Acronym: QUESTS.
Scores, 6: Needs Recognition, Values Classification, Adaptive Autonomy, Perception of Reality, Self-Worth, Total.
Administration: Group.
Price Data: Not available.
Time: (23–30) minutes.
Comments: Scoring must be done by publisher.
Authors: Norman J. Milchus, Omar D. Numey, and David N. Rodwell.
Publisher: Person-O-Metrics, Inc.

[2051]
QUIC Tests.

Purpose: Designed "to establish or verify the functional level of proficiency in the areas of either mathematics or the communicative arts."
Population: Grades 2–12.
Publication Dates: 1989–1990.

Scores, 8: Mathematics (Computation, Concepts, Problem Solving, Total), Communicative Arts (Reading, Reference Skills, Language Arts, Total).
Administration: Individual or group.
Forms, 2: A, B.
Price Data, 2002: $59.80 per starter set including 20 tests (specify content area of Mathematics or Communicative Arts and Form A or B), 20 response forms, and examiner's manual; $26.75 per 20 response forms; $16.90 per examiner's manual; $18 per sample set including 1 test and response form for each of content areas and examiner's manual.
Time: (30) minutes or less.
Comments: Self-administered; competency-based interpretation.
Author: Scholastic Testing Service, Inc.
Publisher: Scholastic Testing Service, Inc.
Cross References: For a review by Delwyn L. Harnisch, see 11:320.

[2052]
Quick Informal Assessment.

Purpose: To "informally assess a student's stage of language acquisition."
Population: Grades K–12.
Publication Date: 1997.
Acronym: QIA.
Scores: Total score only.
Administration: Individual.
Forms, 6: 6 alternate forms A–F.
Price Data: Available from publisher.
Time: (5) minutes.
Comments: Students classified into one of four stages of language acquisition (a) preproduction, (b) early production, (c) speech emergence, (d) intermediate fluency.
Author: Constance Olivia Williams.
Publisher: Ballard & Tighe Publishers.
Cross References: For reviews by Alan Garfinkel and Alfred P. Longo of an earlier edition, see 13:250.

[2053]
Quick Language Assessment Inventory.

Purpose: Designed to provide information about student's English and Spanish language background.
Population: Grades K–6.
Publication Date: 1974.
Scores: Total score and grade level equivalents.
Administration: Individual.
Price Data: Available from publisher.
Time: (1–2) minutes.
Comments: Designed for children suspected of needing English as a second language; parents or guardians provide information about child's English and Spanish background.
Author: Steve Moreno.

Publisher: Moreno Educational Co.
Cross References: For reviews by Giuseppe Costantino and Beth L. Evard, see 9:1026.

[2054]
Quick Neurological Screening Test, 2nd Revised Edition.

Purpose: "Designed to assess areas of neurological integration as they relate to learning."
Population: Ages 5–18.
Publication Dates: 1974–1998.
Acronym: QNST-II.
Scores, 15: Hand Skill, Figure Recognition and Production, Palm Form Recognition, Eye Tracking, Sound Patterns, Finger to Nose, Thumb and Finger Circle, Double Simultaneous Stimulation of Hand and Cheek, Rapidly Reversing Repetitive Hand Movements, Arm and Leg Extensions, Tandem Walk, Standing on One Leg, Skipping, Left-Right Discrimination, Behavioral Irregularities.
Administration: Individual.
Price Data, 2002: $85 per test kit including manual (93 pages), 25 scoring forms, 25 geometric form reproduction sheets, 25 remedial guideline forms, and cue cards; $27 per manual; $20 per 25 scoring forms; $10 per 25 geometric form reproduction sheets; $12 per 25 remedial guideline forms; $15 per directions for administration and scoring printed on 20 cue cards; $35 per specimen set inclufing manual and sample forms.
Time: (20–30) minutes.
Comments: Screening for early identification of learning disabilities; 1998 edition provides extensive literature reviews, clarified directions for administration, and reformatted test protocol sheets.
Authors: Margaret C. Mutti, Harold M. Sterling, Nancy A. Martin, and Norma V. Spalding.
Publisher: Academic Therapy Publications.
Cross References: For a review by Edward E. Gotts, see 14:306; see also T5:2141 (1 reference) and T4:2183 (3 references); for a review by Russell L. Adams of an earlier edition, see 9:1027.

[2055]
Quick Phonics Survey.

Purpose: Designed to "assess a child's understanding of sound/symbol relationships, transfers, and associations."
Population: Grades 1–4.
Publication Date: 1976.
Acronym: QPS.
Scores: Total score only.
Administration: Individual.
Manual: No manual.
Price Data, 2002: $15 per plasticized reading card and 50 recording forms with directions.
Time: Administration time not reported.

Author: Bob Wright.
Publisher: Academic Therapy Publications (High Noon Division).
Cross References: For reviews by Beth D. Bader and Dawn P. Flanagan, see 12:318.

[2056]
Quick Quizzes for U.S. History Classes.

Purpose: To be used as pre- or post-tests, self-tests, or study guides for 52 U.S. History topics.
Population: Grades 6–12.
Publication Date: 1989.
Scores: Total score only.
Administration: Group.
Manual: No manual.
Price Data: Price information available from publisher for 52 blackline master quiz forms and answer booklet.
Time: Administration time not reported.
Authors: E. Richard Churchill and Linda R. Churchill.
Publisher: J. Weston Walch, Publisher.

[2057]
Quick Spelling Inventory.

Purpose: To "identify the grade level at which a student can function in spelling."
Population: Grades 1–6.
Publication Date: 1988.
Acronym: QSI.
Scores: Total score only.
Administration: Group or individual.
Manual: No manual.
Price Data, 2002: $15 per 50 recording forms and plasticized word list with directions.
Time: Administration time not reported.
Author: Bob Wright.
Publisher: Academic Therapy Publications (High Noon Division).
Cross References: For reviews by Kevin D. Crehan and Dale P. Scannell, see 11:322.

[2058]
The Quick Test.

Purpose: Designed to assess intelligence based on verbal-perceptual performance.
Population: Ages 2 and over.
Publication Dates: 1958–1962.
Acronym: QT.
Scores: Total score only.
Administration: Individual.
Forms, 3: 1, 2, 3.
Price Data: Price data available from publisher for complete kit including 3 plates, 100 record sheets, instruction card, and item card, and provisional manual (1962, 54 pages).
Time: (3-10) minutes.
Authors: R. B. Ammons and C. H. Ammons.

Publisher: Psychological Test Specialists.
Cross References: See T5:2146 (20 references), T4:2191 (44 references), 9:1028 (19 references), T3:1969 (44 references), 8:225 (33 references), and T2:522 (15 references); for excerpted reviews by Peter F. Merenda and B. Semeonoff, see 7:422 (30 references); for reviews by Boyd R. McCandless and Ellen V. Piers, see 6:534 (3 references).

[2059]
Quickview Social History.

Purpose: Assists in the collection and reporting of client information.
Population: Ages 16 and older.
Publication Dates: 1983–1992.
Administration: Group or individual.
Price Data, 2002: $74 per MICROTEST Q preview package including user's guide (1992, 33 pages), hardcover test booklet, 3 answer sheets, and 3 assessments; $49 per hardcover test booklet; $43 per 10 reusable soft cover test booklets; $11 per MICROTEST Q report.
Time: (30–45) minutes.
Author: Ronald A. Giannetti.
Publisher: NCS Assessments (Minnetonka).

a) BASIC REPORT.

Scores: 9 areas of inquiry: Demographic Data, Developmental History, Family of Origin, Educational History, Marital History, Occupational History/Financial Status, Legal History, Military History, Symptom Screen.

Comments: The report also has a follow-up summary that includes contradictory responses, indeterminate responses, and client-requested follow-up sections.

b) CLINICAL SUPPLEMENT.

Scores: Includes 8 areas of inquiry listed in Basic Report, plus Physical and Psychological Symptom Screens including: Adult Problems (Substance Use, Psychotic Symptoms, Mood Symptoms, Anxiety Disorders, Somatoform Symptoms, Psychosexual Disorders, Sleep and Arousal, Antisocial Personality, Other Current or Past Potential Adult Problems/Stressors), Developmental Problems (Activity Level/Lability, Conduct Problems, Anxious/Avoidant, Eating/Weight, Tic/Elimination/Sleep, Other Disorders/Delays, Other Potential Developmental Problems/Stressors).

Cross References: For reviews by David N. Dixon and Edward R. Starr, see 13:251.

[2060]
Racial Attitude Test.

Purpose: Measures attitudes toward an examiner selected group of people using a generic semantic differential method.

Population: Adults.
Publication Date: 1989.
Scores, 8: Physical, Ego Strength (Dominance, Control, Anxiety, Ethics, General Social, On the Job), You Would Object.
Administration: Group.
Price Data, 1998: $29.95 per test booklet which may be photocopied for local use with NCS scan sheets; price information for SPSS statistics (reliability and norms) available from publisher.
Time: Administration time not reported.
Comments: Part of the Cultural Diversity Test by the same author; can also be taken online at www.nov.com.
Author: Thomas J. Rundquist.
Publisher: Nova Media, Inc.
Cross References: For reviews by Richard I. Lanyon and Steven G. LoBello, see 11:323.

[2061]
Rahim Organizational Conflict Inventories.

Purpose: "Designed to measure three independent dimensions of organizational conflict: Intrapersonal, Intragroup, Intergroup" (ROCI-I) and "designed to measure five independent dimensions that represent styles of handling interpersonal conflict: Integrating, Obliging, Dominating, Avoiding, and Compromising" (ROCI-II).
Population: Managers, employees, supervisors.
Publication Date: 1983.
Acronym: ROCI.
Administration: Group.
Price Data, 2001: $34.70 per manual (27 pages); $46.60 per preview kit including manual, test booklets I and II, and answer sheets I and II.
Comments: Self-administering; separate answer sheets must be used.
Author: M. Afzalur Rahim.
Publisher: Consulting Psychologists Press, Inc.
  a) RAHIM ORGANIZATIONAL CONFLICT INVENTORY I.
  Acronym: ROCI-I.
  Scores: 3 subscales: Intrapersonal, Intragroup, Intergroup.
  Price Data: $34 per 25 inventories; $30.50 per 25 answer sheets.
  Time: (10–12) minutes.
  b) RAHIM ORGANIZATIONAL CONFLICT INVENTORY II.
  Acronym: ROCI-II.
  Scores, 5: Integrating, Obliging, Dominating, Avoiding, Compromising.
  Price Data: $51.25 per 25 each Forms A, B, and C inventories; $52 per 25 answer sheets.
  Time: (10–12) minutes.
Cross References: See T5:2149 (5 references) and T4:2195 (1 reference); for a review by George C. Thornton III, see 10:303 (3 references).

[2062]
RAND-36 Health Status Inventory.

Purpose: Designed to assess "general health status."
Population: Adults.
Publication Date: 1998.
Acronym: R-36 HSI.
Scores, 10: Physical Functioning, Role Limitations Due to Physical Health Problems, Pain, General Health Perceptions, Emotional Well-Being, Role Limitations Due to Emotional Problems, Social Functioning, Energy/Fatigue/Physical Health Composite, Mental Health Composite, Global Health Composite.
Administration: Group or individual.
Forms, 2: RAND-36, RAND-12 (a short form).
Price Data, 2002: $60 per complete kit including manual (126 pages), 25 question/answer sheets, and 25 hand-scoring worksheets; $8 per 25 question/answer sheets; $8 per 25 hand-scoring worksheets; $8 per 25 RAND-12 HSI question/answer sheets; $50 per manual.
Time: Administration time not reported.
Comments: Paper-and-pencil or computer administered; hand-scoring forms also available.
Author: Ron D. Hays.
Publisher: The Psychological Corporation.
Cross References: For reviews by Corine Fitzpatrick and Richard I. Frederick, see 14:307.

[2063]
Randt Memory Test.

Purpose: Designed "as a global survey and evaluation of patients' complaints concerning their memory."
Population: Ages 20–90.
Publication Dates: 1983–1989.
Acronym: RMT.
Scores, 10: Acquisition Recall (Five Items Acquisition, Paired Words Acquisition, Short Story Verbatim, Digit Span, Incidental Learning), Delayed Recall (Five Items Recall, Paired Words Recall, Picture Recall, General Information), Memory Index.
Administration: Individual.
Forms, 5: Alternative forms for repeated measures.
Price Data, 2001: $95 per complete test including 10 administration booklets, 5 sets of picture cards, and manual (1989, 36 pages); $45 per 50 administration booklets.
Time: (20–25) minutes.
Authors: C. T. Randt and E. R. Brown.
Publisher: Life Science Associates.
Cross References: See T5:2159 (4 references) and T4:2204 (2 references); for a review by Joseph D. Matarazzo, see 10:304 (1 reference).

[2064]
Raven's Progressive Matrices.

Purpose: Constructed as a nonverbal assessment of perception and thinking skills.

Publication Dates: 1938–2000.
Acronym: RPM.
Scores: Total score only.
Price Data: Available from publisher.
Comments: Formerly called Progressive Matrices; may be used with Crichton Vocabulary Scale (717) or Mill Hill Vocabulary Scale (1593).
Authors: J. C. Raven, J. H. Court (manual), and J. Raven (manual).
Publisher: Oxford Psychologists Press, Ltd. [England].

a) STANDARD.
Population: Ages 6–65.
Acronym: SPM.
Administration: Group.
Time: (45) minutes.
Comments: Includes Classic, Parallel, and Plus Versions.

b) COLOURED.
Population: Ages 5–11 and people with mental defects and elderly people.
Acronym: CPM.
Administration: Individual.
Forms, 2: Board, Book.
Time: (15–30) minutes.

c) ADVANCED.
Population: Ages 11 and over with average or high intellectual ability.
Acronym: APM.
Administration: Group.
1) *Set I.*
Time: (10) minutes.
2) *Set II.*
Time: 40(45) or 60(65) minutes.

Cross References: See T5:2163 (356 references), T4:2208 (260 references), 9:1007 (67 references), T3:1914 (200 references), 8:200 (190 references), T2:439 (122 references), and 7:376 (194 references); for a review by Morton Bortner, see 6:490 (78 references); see also 5:370 (62 references); for reviews by Charlotte Banks, W. D. Wall, and George Westby, see 4:314 (32 references); for reviews by Walter C. Shipley and David Wechsler of the 1938 edition, see 3:258 (13 references); for a review by T. J. Keating, see 2:1417 (8 references).

[2065]
Reading Ability Series.

Purpose: To provide an assessment of reading skills children need at school and at home as well as diagnostic information concerning reading difficulties.
Population: Ages 7-0 to 8-11, 8-0 to 9-11, 9-0 to 10-11, 10-0 to 11-11, 11-0 to 12-11, 12-0 to 13-11.
Publication Date: 1989.
Scores, 6: Narrative, Expository, Total, Percentile, Standardised Score, Scale Score.

Administration: Group.
Price Data: Price information available from publisher for specimen set including Teacher's Handbook (1989, 76 pages), reading booklets, Levels A–C and F (1989, 8 pages), Level D (1989, 12 pages), Level E (1987, 11 pages), work booklets, Levels A–D (1988, 12 pages), Levels E and F (1988, 16 pages).
Authors: Anne Kispal, Tom Gorman, and Chris Whetton.
Publisher: NFER-Nelson Publishing Co., Ltd. [England].

a) LEVEL A.
Population: Ages 7-0 to 8-11.
Price Data: Price information available from publisher for pack of 5 reading booklets, and answer key.
Time: 60(70) minutes.

b) LEVEL B.
Population: Ages 8-0 to 9-11.
Parts, 2: Narrative, Expository.
Price Data: Same as Level A.
Time: 45(55) minutes per part.
Comments: Parts 1 and 2 need to be administered at least 1 day and not more than 7 days apart.

c) LEVEL C.
Population: Ages 9-0 to 10-11.
Comments: Parts, Price Data, and Time same as Level B.

d) LEVEL D.
Population: Ages 10-0 to 11-11.
Comments: Parts, Price Data, and Time same as Level B.

e) LEVEL E.
Population: Ages 11-0 to 12-11.
Comments: Parts, Price Data, and Time same as Level B.

f) LEVEL F.
Population: Ages 12-0 to 13-11.
Comments: Parts, Price Data, and Time same as Level B.

Cross References: For reviews by Cleborne D. Maddux and Howard Stoker, see 11:324.

[2066]
Reading and Arithmetic Indexes.

Population: Age 14–adult applicants for entry level jobs and special training programs.
Publication Dates: 1968–1996.
Administration: Group.
Forms, 2: Reading Index, Arithmetic Index.
Price Data, 1998: $53 per 25 tests (specify Arithmetic Index or Reading Index); $19.75 per examiner's manual.
Comments: Self-scoring booklets.
Author: Science Research Associates.
Publisher: Reid London House.

a) READING–ARITHMETIC INDEX.

Purpose: "Measures level of development in reading and math."

Acronym: RAI.

Scores, 11: Reading Index (Picture-Word Association, Word Decoding, Comprehension of Phrases, Comprehension of Sentences, Comprehension of Paragraphs, Total), Arithmetic Index (Addition and Subtraction of Whole Numbers, Multiplication and Division of Whole Numbers, Basic Operations Involving Fractions, Basic Operations Involving Decimals and Percentages, Total).

Time: (25) minutes per Index.

b) READING AND ARITHMETIC INDEXES (12).

Purpose: "Assesses proficiency levels in reading and math."

Acronym: RAI-12.

Scores, 14: Reading Index (Picture-Word Association, Word Decoding, Comprehension of Phrases, Comprehension of Sentences, Comprehension of Paragraphs I, Comprehension of Paragraphs II, Total), Arithmetic Index (Addition and Subtraction of Whole Numbers, Multiplication and Division of Whole Numbers, Basic Operations Involving Fractions, Basic Operations Involving Decimals and Percentages, Basic Operations Involving Square Roots and Powers, Basic Operations Involving Geometry and Word Problems, Total).

Time: (35) minutes per Index.

Cross References: For a review by Dorothy C. Adkins of an earlier edition, see 7:20. See T4:2538 (1 reference) and 8:813 (3 references) for information regarding the Reading Index. See T5:171 (2 references) and 8:307 (3 references) for information regarding the Arithmetic Index.

[2067]

Reading Comprehension Battery for Aphasia, Second Edition.

Purpose: "Designed to provide systematic evaluation of the nature and degree of reading impairment in adolescents and adults with aphasia."

Population: Pre-adolescent to geriatric aphasic people.

Publication Dates: 1979–1998.

Acronym: RCBA-2.

Scores, 19: Word–Visual, Word–Auditory, Word–Semantic, Functional Reading, Synonyms, Sentence–Picture, Paragraph–Picture, Paragraph–Factual, Paragraph–Inferential, Morpho–Syntax, Overall Score of Core Subtests, Letter Discrimination, Letter Naming, Letter Recognition, Lexical Decision, Semantic Categorization, Oral Reading: Words, Oral Reading: Sentences, Overall Score of Supplemental Subtests.

Administration: Individual.

Price Data, 2001: $159 per complete kit including examiner's manual (1998, 38 pages), picture book, supplementary picture book, and 25 profile/summary record forms; $26 per examiner's manual, $49 per picture book or supplementary picture book; $39 per 25 profile/summary record forms.

Time: (30) minutes.

Comments: Instrument is criterion-referenced.

Authors: Leonard L. LaPointe and Jennifer Horner.

Publisher: PRO-ED.

Cross References: For reviews by Candice Haas Hollingsead and Robert Wall, see 14:308; see also T5:2172 (1 reference), T4:2220 (5 references), and 9:1033 (1 reference).

[2068]

Reading Comprehension Test DE.

Purpose: Designed to assess reading by means of passages rather than sentences.

Population: Ages 10-0 to 12-10.

Publication Dates: 1970–1976.

Scores: Total score only.

Administration: Group.

Price Data: Available from publisher.

Time: (50) minutes.

Comments: A component of the Reading Tests Series.

Authors: E. L. Barnard and the National Foundation for Educational Research in England and Wales.

Publisher: NFER-Nelson Publishing Co., Ltd. [England].

Cross References: For a review by Douglas K. Smith, see 10:306.

[2069]

Reading Efficiency Tests.

Purpose: Designed to provide measures of reading rate, comprehension, and efficiency.

Population: Grades 7–16 and adults.

Publication Dates: 1966–1974.

Acronym: MRET.

Scores, 3: Rate, Comprehension Accuracy, Reading Efficiency.

Administration: Group.

Price Data: Available from publisher.

Time: [30–40] minutes.

Comments: Formerly called Maintaining Reading Efficiency Tests.

Author: Lyle L. Miller.

Publisher: Developmental Reading Distributors [No reply from publisher; status unknown].

a) TEST 1, HISTORY OF BRAZIL, 1970 REVISION.

Publication Dates: 1966–1970.

b) TEST 2, HISTORY OF JAPAN, 1970 REVISION.

Publication Dates: 1966–1970.

c) TEST 3, HISTORY OF INDIA.
Publication Date: 1970.
d) TEST 4, HISTORY OF NEW ZEALAND.
Publication Date: 1970.
e) TEST 5, HISTORY OF SWITZERLAND.
Publication Date: 1970.
Cross References: See T4:2222 (1 reference); for a review by Alton L. Raygor, see 8:731.

[2070]
Reading Electrical Drawings & Schematics—Form A.

Purpose: "To measure the skills required to learn and perform jobs involving electrical print reading skills."
Population: Adults.
Publication Date: 1992–1996.
Acronym: RCJS—Reading Electrical Drawings & Schematics.
Scores: Total score only.
Administration: Group.
Price Data, 2002: $200 per complete kit including 10 test booklets, 100 answer sheets, manual (1994, 11 pages), and scoring key.
Time: (35) minutes.
Author: Roland T. Ramsay.
Publisher: Ramsay Corporation.
Cross References: For a review by David O. Anderson, see 13:257.

[2071]
Reading Evaluation Adult Diagnosis, Fifth Edition.

Purpose: Designed for assessing existing reading competencies.
Population: Illiterate adult students.
Publication Dates: 1972–1999.
Acronym: READ.
Scores: 3 parts, 21 scores: Sight Words (List 1, List 2, List 3, List 4), Word Analysis Skills (Letter Sound Relationships, Letter Names [Upper-Case], Letter Names [Lower-Case], Reversals, CVC, CV[CC], Final Digraphs, Initial Digraphs, Final Blends, Initial Blends, Multi-Syllabic Words, Silent Letters, Soft C & G, Suffixes), Reading/Listening Inventory (Word Recognition, Reading Comprehension, Listening Comprehension).
Administration: Individual.
Price Data, 1999: $8 per test booklet/manual (1999, 51 pages); $2.50 per answer pad.
Time: Administration time not reported.
Authors: Original test by Ruth J. Colvin and Jane H. Root; 1999 revision by Kathleen A. Hinchman and Rebecca Schoultz.
Publisher: Literacy Volunteers of America, Inc.
Cross References: For reviews by Howard Margolis and Timothy Shanahan, see 14:309; for reviews by

Mary E. Huba and Diane J. Sawyer of an earlier edition, see 11:326 (1 reference).

[2072]
Reading Evaluation and Diagnostic Screen.

Purpose: An evaluative and diagnostic tool to determine sensory deficiencies relating to reading and spelling.
Population: Ages 4–15.
Publication Date: 1983.
Acronym: READS.
Scores, 4: Letter Memory, Say Words, Distal Quadrant, Total.
Administration: Individual.
Price Data, 2001: $100 per test.
Time: (20) minutes.
Comments: Experimental form.
Author: Alvin H. Shapiro.
Publisher: Psychogenics, Inc. [Canada].
Cross References: For reviews by Edith S. Heil and Diane J. Sawyer, see 10:308.

[2073]
Reading-Free Vocational Interest Inventory: 2.

Purpose: "To measure the vocational interest of the special needs student/adult and regular classroom students."
Population: Ages 12 to 62.
Publication Dates: 1975–2000.
Acronym: RFVII:2.
Scores: 11 scales: Automotive, Building Trades, Clerical, Animal Care, Food Service, Patient Care, Horticulture, Housekeeping, Personal Service, Laundry Service, Materials Handling, plus 5 cluster scores: Mechanical, Outdoor, Mechanical—Outdoor, Food Service—Handling Operations, Clerical—Social Service.
Administration: Individual.
Price Data, 2001: $89.50 per complete kit including 20 test booklets, manual (2000, 123 pages), and Occupational Title Lists 2 (2001, 42 pages); $47.75 per sample set including 10 test booklets and manual; $34.50 per examination set including 1 test booklet and manual; $36.50 per 20 test booklets (discounts available for orders of 40 or more); $33 per manual.
Time: 20(30) minutes.
Comments: Revision of Reading-Free Vocational Interest Inventory; earlier edition listed as AAMD-Becker Reading-Free Vocational Interest Inventory; self-administered; hand-scorable only.
Author: Ralph L. Becker.
Publisher: Elbern Publications.
Cross References: For information on an earlier edition, see T4:2177; for a review by Robert J. Miller of an earlier edition, see 11:327; see also T3:1996 (2

references); for reviews by Esther E. Diamond and George Domino of an earlier edition, see 8:988 (6 references).

[2074]
Reading-Level Indicator.

Purpose: Designed "to identify individual reading at a second-to-sixth-grade level and functional nonreaders."
Population: Upper elementary to college students.
Publication Date: 2000.
Scores, 5: Sentence Comprehension Score, Vocabulary Score, Total Raw Score, Instructional Reading Level, Independent Reading Level.
Administration: Group or individual.
Forms, 2: Blue Form, Purple Form.
Price Data: Available from publisher.
Time: (4–20) minutes.
Author: Kathleen T. Williams.
Publisher: American Guidance Service, Inc.

[2075]
Reading Progress Tests.

Purpose: Designed to "provide a continuous measure of individual and group progress in reading comprehension."
Population: Ages 5-0 to 12-2.
Publication Dates: 1996–1997.
Acronym: RPT.
Scores: Total score only.
Administration: Group.
Price Data, 2002: £12.99 per Stage One manual (1996, 48 pages); £13.50 per Stage Two manual (1997, 47 pages); £14.99 per Stage One specimen set; £16.99 per Stage Two specimen set.
Time: (20) minutes per test.
Authors: Denis Vincent, Mary Crumpler, and Mike de la Mare.
Publisher: Hodder & Stoughton Educational [England}.

a) STAGE ONE.
1) *Literacy Baseline.*
Purpose: "To provide a 'baseline' from which to measure subsequent progress."
Population: Children in first term of their first year of compulsory schooling (ages 5-0 to 6-4).
Price Data: £6.99 per 10 copies.
2) *RPT Test 1.*
Purpose: Constructed to "assess developing reading skills."
Population: Year 1 (ages 5-8 to 7-2).
Price Data: £6.99 per 10 copies.
Time: (45–50) minutes.
3) *RPT Test 2.*
Population: Year 2 (ages 6-8 to 8-1).
Price Data: £6.99 per 10 copies.

b) STAGE TWO.
1) *RPT Test 3.*
Population: Year 3 (ages 7-8 to 9-2).
Price Data: £6.99 per 10 copies; £11.50 per 10 Test 3 broadsheets.
2) *RPT Test 4.*
Population: Year 4 (ages 8-8 to 10-2).
Price Data: £6.99 per 10 copies; £11.50 per 10 Test 4 broadsheets.
3) *RPT Test 5.*
Population: Year 5 (ages 9-8 to 11-2).
Price Data: £6.99 per 10 copies; £11.50 per 10 Test 5 broadsheets.
4) *RPT Test 6.*
Population: Year 6 (ages 10-8 to 12-2).
Price Data: £6.99 per 10 copies; £11.50 per 10 Test 6 broadsheets.

[2076]
Reading Skills Diagnostic Test III, Level 4.

Purpose: Assesses "three areas in encoding/decoding" of reading including content, processes, and basic capacity.
Population: Grades 2.5–12.
Publication Dates: 1967–1983.
Acronym: RSDT-III.
Scores, 12: Letter Writing, Short Term Memory—Letters, Simple Phonics, Open Syllable Writing, Syllable Writing, Word Writing, Short Term Memory—Words, Long Vowels, Consonant Diphthongs, Vowel Diphthongs, Sight Word Writing (2 parts), Context Clues.
Administration: Group.
Price Data, 1998: $115 per complete kit.
Time: (40–60) minutes.
Author: Richard H. Bloomer.
Publisher: Brador Publications, Inc.
Cross References: For reviews by Ira E. Aaron and Edward R. Sipay, see 8:772; see also T2:1644 (1 reference).

[2077]
Reading Style Inventory.

Purpose: "To identify the individual reading style preferences and strengths of youngsters when they read."
Population: Grades 1–12.
Publication Dates: 1980–1987.
Acronym: RSI.
Scores: 30 elements: Environmental Stimuli (Sound-Quiet, Sound-Music/Talking, Light, Temperature, Design-Formal/Informal, Design-Organization), Emotional Profile (Peer-Motivated, Adult-Motivated, Self-Motivated, Persistence, Responsibility, Structure-Choices, Structure-Directions, Structure-Work Checked When, Structure-Work Checked by Whom), Sociological Preferences (Prefers Reading to a Teacher,

With Peers, Alone, With Peers and the Teacher, With One Peer, Intake, Prefers Reading in the Morning, Prefers Reading in Early Afternoon, Prefers Reading in Late Afternoon, Prefers Reading in the Evening, Mobility), Perceptual Strengths/Preferences (Auditory Strengths, Visual Strengths, Tactual Preferences, Kinesthetic Preferences).

Administration: Group; individual for first grade.
Price Data, 1993: $10 per 25 test booklets; $8 per 30 answer sheets; $12 per manual (1984, 76 pages); $14 per specimen set including test booklet, sample profiles, Research Supplement (1983, 39 pages), manual, and free processing of 1 RSI; $59 per RSI Starter set (including manual and disk that produces 50 RSI reports); $159 per RSI Group Profile Disk (produces 3 types of RSI group reports).

Foreign Language Edition: Spanish edition available.

Time: (20–40) minutes.

Comments: Based upon learning style model; scoring service offered by publisher; also available on software for IBM, IBM compatibles, and Apple 2e and 2gs.

Author: Marie Carbo.
Publisher: National Reading Styles Institute, Inc.
Cross References: See T5:2181 (2 references); for reviews by Jeri Benson and Alice J. Corkill, see 11:328 (1 reference).

[2078]
Reading Test AD.

Purpose: Designed to test reading comprehension.
Population: Ages 8-0 to 10-7.
Publication Dates: 1970–1978.
Scores: Total score only.
Administration: Group.
Price Data: Price information available from publisher for test booklets and manual (1978, 8 pages).
Time: 15(20) minutes.
Authors: A. F. Watts and the National Foundation for Educational Research in England and Wales.
Publisher: NFER-Nelson Publishing Co., Ltd. [England].
Cross References: For reviews by Peter W. Airasian and Anthony J. Nitko, see 10:310.

[2079]
Reading Test (Comprehension and Speed): Municipal Tests: National Achievement Tests.

Purpose: Measures reading comprehension and speed.
Population: Grades 3–6, 6–8.
Publication Dates: 1938–1957.
Scores, 5: Following Directions, Sentence Meaning, Paragraph Meaning, Reading Speed, Total.
Administration: Group.

Price Data: Available from publisher.
Time: (32) minutes.
Comments: Subtest of Municipal Battery; 2 forms: A, B.
Authors: Robert K. Speer and Samuel Smith.
Publisher: Psychometric Affiliates.
Cross References: For a review by Larry A. Harris, see 8:741. For reviews of the complete battery, see 5:18 (1 review), 4:20 (1 review), and 2:1191 (2 reviews).

[2080]
Reading Test SR-A & SR-B.

Purpose: "Designed to provide a means of estimating the reading attainment of primary school children."
Population: Ages 7-6 to 11-11.
Publication Dates: 1970–1982.
Scores: Total score only.
Administration: Group.
Editions, 2: SR-A, SR-B.
Price Data: Price information available from publisher for test booklets and manual (1971, 17 pages).
Time: 20(25) minutes.
Authors: Brian Pritchard and the National Foundation for Educational Research in England and Wales.
Publisher: NFER-Nelson Publishing Co., Ltd. [England].
Cross References: For reviews by Robert C. Calfee and Marian Jean Dreher, see 10:311.

[2081]
Reading Tests A and BD.

Purpose: Designed as a "test of reading comprehension of the sentence completion type."
Population: 1, 2–4 years primary school.
Publication Dates: 1967-1973.
Scores: Total score only.
Administration: Group.
Price Data: Price information available from publisher for test booklets (specify Test A or Test BD), and for Test A manual (1973, 8 pages) or Test BD manual (1969, 16 pages).
Time: (20–30) minutes per level.
Author: National Foundation for Educational Research in England and Wales.
Publisher: NFER-Nelson Publishing Co., Ltd. [England].
  a) READING TEST A.
  Comments: Formerly called Primary Reading Test 1.
  b) READING TEST BD.
  Comments: Formerly called Primary Reading Test 2.
Cross References: See T4:2234 (1 reference) and T3:2003 (1 reference).

[2082]
Reading Tests EH 1-2.

Purpose: Provides a measure of reading ability.
Population: Ages 11-0 to 15-1.
Publication Dates: 1961–1966.
Scores: 2 tests: Vocabulary, Comprehension.
Administration: Group.
Price Data: Price information available from publisher for test booklets (specify EH1 [Vocabulary] or EH2 [Comprehension]) and for manual.
Time: (15–20) minutes for EH1; (40–45) minutes for EH2.
Author: S. M. Bate.
Publisher: NFER-Nelson Publishing Co., Ltd. [England].
Cross References: See T3:2004 (1 reference).

[2083]
The Reading Vocabulary Tests.

Purpose: Developed as a measure or reading comprehension.
Population: Ages 7–12.
Publication Dates: 1979–2002.
Scores: Total score only.
Administration: Group.
Forms, 2: A, B.
Price Data, 2002: £16.10 per complete set; £7.50 per 25 test forms (A or B); £1.10 per administrative manual and scoring key (2002, 6 pages).
Time: 30(35) minutes.
Authors: Alan Brimer and Herbert Gross.
Publisher: Educational Evaluations [England].
Cross References: See T5:2187 (1 reference).

[2084]
Reality Check Survey.

Purpose: Assesses "how managerial actions serve employee needs."
Population: Adults.
Publication Dates: 1989–1995.
Acronym: RCS.
Scores: Total score only.
Administration: Group.
Price Data, 2001: $7.95 per instrument.
Time: Untimed.
Comments: Self-administered survey.
Author: Jay Hall.
Publisher: Teleometrics International.
Cross References: For reviews by S. Alvin Leung and Sheldon Zedeck, see 12:322.

[2085]
Receptive-Expressive Emergent Language Test, Second Edition.

Purpose: Designed to identify children who have specific language problems.

Population: Children from birth to 3 years of age.
Publication Dates: 1971–1991.
Acronym: REEL-2.
Scores, 3: Expressive Language Age, Receptive Language Age, Combined Language Age.
Administration: Individual.
Price Data, 2001: $109 per complete kit; $39 per 50 profile/test forms; $34 per examiner's manual (1991, 50 pages).
Time: Administration time not reported.
Authors: Kenneth R. Bzoch and Richard League.
Publisher: PRO-ED.
Cross References: See T5:2189 (7 references); for reviews by Lyle F. Bachman and Lynn S. Bliss, see 12:323 (2 references); see also T4:2238 (3 references) and T3:338 (5 references); for excerpted reviews by Alex Bannatyne, Dale L. Johnson and Barton B. Proger, see 8:956 (5 references); see also T2:2067 (2 references).

[2086]
Receptive One-Word Picture Vocabulary Test [2000 Edition].

Purpose: Designed to assess an individual's English hearing vocabulary.
Population: Ages 2–18.
Publication Dates: 1985–2000.
Acronym: ROWPVT.
Scores: Total score only.
Administration: Individual.
Price Data, 2002: $140 per kit including manual (2000, 110 pages), 25 record forms, and test plates; $25 per 25 record forms; $75 per test plates; $40 per manual.
Time: (10–15) minutes.
Comments: Lower and upper levels have been combined into this edition.
Authors: 1985 edition by Morrison F. Gardner; later edition prepared by publisher.
Publisher: Academic Therapy Publications.
Cross References: See T5:2190 (9 references); T4:2239 (1 reference); for reviews by Janice A. Dole and Janice Santogrossi of an earlier edition, see 10:312; for reviews by Laurie Ford and William D. Schaffer of an earlier edition of the upper level, see 11:329.

[2087]
Recognition Memory Test.

Purpose: Developed "to detect minor degrees of memory deficit."
Population: Adult patients referred for neuropsychological assessment.
Publication Date: 1984.
Acronym: RMT.
Scores, 2: Words, Faces.
Administration: Individual.

Price Data, 1999: £87.75 per complete kit; £62 per set of 3 booklets and word card; £15.50 per 25 record forms; £16.50 per manual (16 pages).
Time: Administration time not reported.
Author: Elizabeth K. Warrington.
Publisher: NFER-Nelson Publishing Co., Ltd. [England].
Cross References: See T5:2193 (59 references) and T4:2241 (12 references); for a review by Russell L. Adams, see 10:313 (1 reference).

[2088]
Recovery Attitude and Treatment Evaluator.

Purpose: Intended for use after diagnosis of alcohol or other drug dependency to determine the "patient's level of resistance to treatment and other important information" to be considered in treatment planning.
Population: Adults.
Publication Dates: 1987–1996.
Acronym: RAATE–CE; RAATE–QI.
Scores: 5 dimensions: Resistance to Treatment, Resistance to Continuing Care, Acuity of Biomedical Problems, Acuity of Psychiatric/Psychological Problems, Social/Family Environmental Status.
Administration: Individual.
Forms, 2: Clinical Evaluation, Initial Questionnaire.
Price Data: Available from publisher.
Time: (30–45) minutes for Clinical Evaluation; [20–30] minutes for Initial Questionnaire.
Authors: David Mee-Lee, Norman G. Hoffmann, and Maurice B. Smith (manual).
Publisher: Evince Clinical Assessments.
Cross References: For reviews by Philip Ash and Tony Toneatto, see 14:311.

[2089]
REHAB: Rehabiliation Evaluation Hall and Baker.

Purpose: "Designed to assess people with a major psychiatric handicap."
Population: Psychiatric patients who live in residential care.
Publication Dates: 1984–1994.
Acronym: REHAB.
Scores, 8: Deviant Behaviour, General Behaviour (Social Activity, Speech Disturbance, Self Care, Community Skills, Overall Rating), Speech Skills.
Administration: Individual.
Price Data, 2001: $405 (£215) per complete set including 50 assessment forms, 5 rater guides, 1 scoring key, 25 score sheets, 25 individual presentation sheets, 25 group presentation sheets, manual (1994, 136 pages), and carrying case; $33 (£17.50) per 25 assessment forms; $44 (£23) per 5 raters guides; $34 (£17.50) per scoring key; $19.50 (£10.50) per 25 score sheets; $27.50

(£14.50) per 25 individual presentation sheets; $46 (£26) per 25 group presentation sheets; $88 (£45.50) per manual; $105 (£60) per carrying case.
Time: (1) week.
Comments: A multipurpose behavior rating scale requiring observation of the target client over a period of one week; raters can include any direct care staff.
Authors: Roger Baker and John N. Hall.
Publisher: Dr. Baker Partnership [England].
Cross References: For reviews by James P. Choca and Pamilla Morales, see 14:312; see also T5:2195 (2 references).

[2090]
Rehabilitation Checklist.

Purpose: Designed to help determine the needs of clients recovering from serious physical injuries.
Population: Adults.
Publication Dates: 1998–1999.
Acronym: RCL.
Scores: 7 scales (Physical, Cognitive, Emotional Psychosocial, Employability, Job), plus Total and Total Rehabilitation subscale.
Administration: Group.
Price Data, 2002: $82 per complete kit including 25 QuikScore™ forms and manual; $48 per 25 QuikScore™ forms; $43 per manual (1998, 54 pages).
Time: (15) minutes.
Comments: Self-report.
Author: J. Douglas Salmon, Jr.
Publisher: Multi-Health Systems, Inc.

[2091]
Rehabilitation Compliance Scale.

Purpose: Intended to provide a measurement of compliance to a rehabilitation program in the severely injured musculoskeletal patient.
Population: Severely injured patients ages 17–85 years.
Publication Date: 1994.
Administration: Group.
Price Data, 2001: $25 per sampler set including manual, test, and scoring sheets; $125 per one-year permission to reproduce up to 200 administrations of the test.
Time: Administration time not reported.
Author: Neil W. Rheiner.
Publisher: Mind Garden, Inc.
    a) REHABILITATION COMPLIANCE SCALE.
    Acronym: RHAB.
    Scores, 3: Appointment Compliance, Participation in Therapy, Progress in Therapy.
    Forms, 2: A, B.
    b) PATIENT EXPERIENCE QUESTIONNAIRE.
    Score: Total score only.
Cross References: For reviews by Michael P. Gamache and Robert A. Leark, see 14:313.

[2092]

Reid Report.

Purpose: "The Report consists of a customized set of scales and questionnaires which focus on key, business-related employee behaviors. Measures attitudes toward conscientiousness and counterproductivity in the workplace and predicts overall work performance and counterproductive acts (turnover, absenteeism, tardiness, theft and inappropriate substance use)."
Population: Job applicants.
Publication Dates: 1969–1992.
Scores: 1 of 4 possible evaluations (Recommended, Qualified, Not Recommended, No Opinion) in 4 parts (Integrity Attitude, Antisocial History, Recent Drug Use, Work History) and overall evaluation.
Administration: Group.
Price Data: Price information available from publisher for test materials including examiner's manual (1989, 39 pages).
Time: (15–60) minutes.
Comments: Overall evaluation established by client organization, based upon specific organizational requirements.
Authors: Reid Psychological Systems, Paul Brooks (manual), and David Arnold (manual).
Publisher: Reid Psychological Systems [No reply from publisher; status unknown].
Cross References: For reviews by George Domino and Kevin R. Murphy, see 12:324 (2 references); see also T4:2243 (1 reference); for a review by Stanley L. Brodsky, see 8:658 (3 references); for integrated version of Reid Report/Reid Survey, see T2:1353 (1 reference) and 7:132 (1 reference).

[2093]

Reiss-Epstein-Gursky Anxiety Sensitivity Index.

Purpose: To measure the fear of anxiety in order to "identify patients with high anxiety sensitivity" and "to obtain information relevant to the diagnosis of panic disorder or posttraumatic stress disorder; to evaluate treatment outcomes; to assess soldiers at risk to panic under stress."
Population: Adults and adolescents.
Publication Date: 1987.
Acronym: ASI.
Scores: Total Anxiety Sensitivity.
Administration: Individual or group.
Price Data: Not available.
Time: [5] minutes.
Comments: Translated into 18 languages: Catalan, Chinese, Dutch, Farsi, French, German, Greek, Icelandic, Italian, Japanese, Polish, Portuguese, Russian, Spanish, Swedish, Turkish.
Authors: Steven Reiss and Rolf A. Peterson.

Publisher: IDS Publishing Inc.
Cross References: See T5:2199 (14 references) and T4:2244 (2 references); for a review by Harrison G. Gough, see 11:330.

[2094]

A Religion Scale.

Purpose: Measures attitudes toward religion.
Population: Adolescents and adults.
Publication Date: 1961.
Scores: Total score only.
Administration: Group.
Manual: No manual.
Price Data, 2002: $1 per scale.
Time: [10] minutes.
Comments: Supplementary article available.
Author: Panos D. Bardis.
Publisher: Donna Bardis.
Cross References: See 8:465 (2 references).

[2095]

The Renfrew Bus Story.

Purpose: Designed as a "test of narrative recall."
Population: Ages 3.6–7.0.
Publication Date: 1994.
Scores, 4: Information, Sentence Length, Complexity, Independence.
Administration: Individual.
Price Data, 2001: $45 per complete kit including manual (56 pages), 15 record forms, and story booklet; $10 per 15 record forms.
Time: Administration time not reported.
Comments: American adaptation of original British version.
Authors: Judy Cowley and Cheryl Glasgow.
Publisher: Centreville School.
Cross References: For reviews by Sherry K. Bain and Robert R. Haccoun, see 14:314.

[2096]

Repeatable Battery for the Assessment of Neuropsychological Status.

Purpose: Designed to measure "attention, language, visuospatial/constructional abilities, and immediate and delayed memory."
Population: Ages 20–89.
Publication Date: 1998.
Acronym: RBANS.
Scores, 18: Immediate Memory (List Learning, Short Memory, Total), Visuospatial/Constructional (Figure Copy, Line Orientation, Total), Language (Picture Naming, Semantic Fluency, Total), Attention (Digit Span, Coding, Total), Delayed Memory (List Recall, List Recognition, Story Memory, Figure Recall, Total), Total.
Administration: Individual.

Forms, 2: A, B.
Price Data, 2002: $149 per primary form kit including manual, record form A, stimulus book A, and coding scoring template A; $125 per alternative form kit including 25 record form B, stimulus book B, and coding scoring template B; $44 per 25 record forms (specify form); $81 per stimulus book (specify form); $13 per coding scoring template (specify form); $37 per manual.
Time: (20–30) minutes.
Author: Christopher Randolph.
Publisher: The Psychological Corporation.
Cross References: For reviews by Stephen J. Freeman and Timothy J. Makatura, see 14:315.

[2097]
Research Personnel Review Form.

Purpose: Designed "to provide a means for the periodic review of scientific, engineering, and technical personnel, and the environment in which they work."
Population: Research and engineering and scientific firms.
Publication Dates: 1959–1960.
Acronym: RPRF.
Scores: No scores.
Administration: Group.
Price Data: Available from publisher.
Time: Administration time not reported.
Author: Morris I. Stein.
Publisher: The Mews Press.

[2098]
Responsibility and Independence Scale for Adolescents.

Purpose: Measures adolescents' adaptive behaviors.
Population: Ages 12.0–19.11.
Publication Date: 1990.
Acronym: RISA.
Scores, 3: Responsibility, Independence, Adaptive Behavior Total.
Subscales, 9: Self-Management, Social Maturity, Social Communication, Domestic Skills, Money Management, Citizenship, Personal Organization, Transportation Skills, Career Skills.
Administration: Individual.
Price Data: Available from publisher.
Time: (30–45) minutes.
Comments: Administered in a standardized interview format to a respondent who is familiar with the adolescent.
Authors: John Salvia, John T. Neisworth, and Mary W. Schmidt.
Publisher: Riverside Publishing.
Cross References: For reviews by D. Joe Olmi and James P. Van Haneghan, see 13:325 (2 references).

[2099]
Retail Sales Skills Test.

Purpose: To evaluate the knowledge necessary for successful performance as a retail salesperson.
Population: Candidates for the position of retail salesperson.
Publication Date: 1994.
Acronym: RETSALES.
Scores: Total Score, Narrative Evaluation, Ranking, Recommendation.
Administration: Group.
Price Data, 2001: $150 per candidate; quantity discounts available.
Time: (70) minutes.
Comments: Scored by publisher; must be proctored.
Author: Walden Personnel Performance, Inc.
Publisher: Walden Personnel Performance, Inc.

[2100]
Retail Store Manager Staff Selector.

Purpose: To evaluate the knowledge necessary for successful performance in retail store management.
Population: Candidates for the position of store manager or assistant manager.
Publication Date: 1996.
Acronym: RSALES.
Scores: Total Score, Narrative Evaluation, Ranking, Recommendation.
Administration: Group.
Price Data, 2001: $500 per candidate; quantity discounts available.
Time: (255) minutes.
Comments: Scored by publisher; must be proctored.
Author: Walden Personnel Performance, Inc.
Publisher: Walden Personnel Performance, Inc.

[2101]
Retirement Activities Card Sort Planning Kit.

Purpose: "To introduce a new perspective on adult development and a model of understanding the process of change as it relates to retirement; to stimulate personal thinking on handling retirement; and to assist participants to identify and begin planning for avenues of new growth or expanded satisfaction in retirement living."
Population: Retired adults or adults who plan to retire.
Publication Dates: 1992–1994.
Scores: Item scores only.
Administration: Group or individual.
Price Data: Available from publisher.
Time: (75–120) minutes.
Comments: 8 supplementary activities included.
Author: Richard L. Knowdell.
Publisher: Career Research & Testing, Inc.

Cross References: For reviews by M. Allan Cooperstein and Robert B. Frary, see 13:262.

[2102]
Retirement Descriptive Index.

Purpose: Designed to measure satisfaction with facets of retirement and global retirement satisfaction (i.e., Retirement in General [RIG] Scale).
Population: Retirees.
Publication Dates: 1969–1993.
Acronym: RDI.
Scores, 5: Present Work and Activities, Financial Situation, Present Health, People You Associate With, Retirement in General.
Administration: Group or individual.
Price Data, 2001: $34 per 100 test booklets; $5 per handscoring key.
Time: Administration time not reported.
Comments: Previously listed with the Job Descriptive Index (1290).
Authors: Patricia C. Smith, Lorne M. Kendall, and Charles L. Hulin.
Publisher: Bowling Green State University, Department of Psychology.
Cross References: For reviews by Charles K. Parsons and Norman D. Sundberg of the Job Descriptive Index and Retirement Descriptive Index, see 12:199 (33 references); see also T4:1312 (63 references).

[2103]
The Reversals Frequency Test.

Purpose: "To assess objectively number and letter reversals frequency."
Population: Ages 5-0 to 15-11.
Publication Date: 1978.
Scores, 3: Execution, Recognition, Matching.
Administration: Individual.
Price Data: Price information available from publisher for complete kit including 3 subtests and manual (21 pages).
Time: [10–15] minutes.
Author: Richard A. Gardner.
Publisher: Creative Therapeutics, Inc.
Cross References: See T5:2210 (1 reference); for reviews by Frank M. Gresham and David J. Mealor, see 11:331 (1 reference).

[2104]
Revised Behavior Problem Checklist.

Purpose: Developed as a screening measurement of dimensions of behavior problems.
Population: Ages 5–18.
Publication Dates: 1979–1987.
Acronym: RBPC.
Scores, 6: Conduct Disorder, Socialized Aggression, Attention Problems-Immaturity, Anxiety-Withdrawal, Psychotic Behavior, Motor Tension-Excess.

Administration: Individual.
Price Data: Available from publisher for complete kit including 50 checklists, scoring templates, and manual (1987, 45 pages).
Time: 20 (30) minutes.
Comments: Ratings by teachers, parents, and child care staff.
Authors: Herbert C. Quay and Donald R. Peterson.
Publisher: Psychological Assessment Resources, Inc.
Cross References: See T5:2211 (52 references) and T4:2254 (45 references); for reviews by Denise M. Dezolt and by Edward S. Shapiro and Stewart M. Shear, see 11:332 (80 references); for a review by Anthony A. Cancelli, see 9:1043 (31 references); see also T3:2012 (6 references).

[2105]
Revised BRIGANCE® Diagnostic Inventory of Early Development.

Purpose: Constructed to "determine the developmental or performance level of the infant or child."
Population: Birth to age 7.
Publication Dates: 1978–1991.
Scores: 11 areas: Preambulatory Motor Skills and Behaviors, Gross-Motor Skills and Behaviors, Fine-Motor Skills and Behaviors, Self-Help Skills, Speech and Language Skills, General Knowledge and Comprehension, Social and Emotional Development, Readiness, Basic Reading Skills, Manuscript Writing, Basic Math.
Administration: Individual.
Price Data, 2001: $124 per manual with tests (1991, 298 pages); $26.90 per 10 record books; $12.95 per group record book; $35.95 per classroom testing kit.
Time: [15–20] minutes per child.
Comments: "Criterion-referenced."
Author: Albert H. Brigance.
Publisher: Curriculum Associates, Inc.
Cross References: For reviews by C. Dale Carpenter and Douglas A. Penfield, see 12:326; see also T4:2256 (3 references); for reviews by Stephen J. Bagnato and Elliot L. Gory of an earlier edition, see 9:164.

[2106]
Revised Children's Manifest Anxiety Scale.

Purpose: "Designed to assess the level and nature of anxiety in children and adolescents."
Population: Ages 6–19.
Publication Date: 1985.
Acronym: RCMAS.
Scores, 5: Physiological Anxiety, Worry/ Oversensitivity, Social Concerns/Concentration, Total Anxiety, Lie.
Administration: Group.
Foreign Language Edition: Spanish version available.

Price Data, 2002: $94.50 per kit including 50 AutoScore™ answer forms, and manual (106 pages); $29.50 per 25 AutoScore™ answer forms; $49 per manual; $59.95 per Spanish language kit including 15 test forms, scoring key, and manual (all in Spanish); $15 per 15 Spanish test forms; $10 per scoring key for Spanish test forms; $48 per Spanish manual.
Time: (10–15) minutes.
Comments: Revision and published version of the Children's Manifest Anxiety Scale (CMAS).
Authors: Cecil R. Reynolds and Bert O. Richmond.
Publisher: Western Psychological Services.
Cross References: See T5:2214 (140 references) and T4:2257 (47 references); for a review by Frank M. Gresham, see 10:314 (7 references).

[2107]
Revised Evaluating Acquired Skills in Communication.

Purpose: Constructed to assess communication skills in the areas of semantics, syntax, morphology, and pragmatics.
Population: Children 3 months to 8 years with severe language impairments.
Publication Dates: 1984–1991.
Acronym: EASIC.
Scores: Ratings in 10 areas: Labels/Nouns and Pronouns, Verbs and Action Commands, Comprehension of Three-Word Phrases, Affirmation and Negation, Prepositional Location Commands, Comprehension of Singular and Plural, Adjectives and Attributes, Money Concepts, Categorization and Association, Interrogatives.
Administration: Individual.
Price Data, 1999: $99 per complete kit including manual (1991, 54 pages).
Time: Administration time not reported.
Author: Anita Marcott Riley.
Publisher: Communication Skill Builders—A Division of The Psychological Corporation.
Cross References: For reviews by William O. Haynes and John H. Kranzler, see 12:329; for reviews by Barry W. Jones and Robert E. Owens, Jr. of an earlier edition, see 10:109.

[2108]
Revised Hamilton Rating Scale for Depression.

Purpose: Designed as a clinician-rated scale for evaluating individuals already diagnosed with depressive illness.
Population: Depressed individuals.
Publication Date: 1994.
Acronym: RHRSD.
Scores, 22: General Screening, Depressed Mood, Feelings of Guilt, Suicide, Insomnia, Nocturnal Wak-

ing, Early Morning Waking, Work and Activities, Sexual Symptoms, Loss of Insight, Retardation, Agitation, Worry, Somatic Anxiety, Gastrointestinal Somatic Symptoms, General Somatic Symptoms, Hypochondriasis, Loss of Weight, Diurnal Variation, Obsessive-Compulsive Symptoms, Paranoid Symptoms, Depersonalization/Derealization.
Administration: Individual.
Price Data, 2002: $94.50 per kit including 10 AutoScore™ clinican forms, 10 AutoScore™ self-report problem inventories, manual (62 pages), and 2-use disk plus 4 PC answer sheets for on-site computer scoring and interpretation; $34.50 per 25 AutoScore™ clinician forms; $34.50 per 25 AutoScore™ self-report problem inventories; $49.95 per manual; $185 or less per 20-use IBM scoring interpretive software; $15 per 100 microcomputer answer sheets; $9.50 each per FAX report service.
Time: (5–10) minutes.
Comments: A self-report scale is also provided.
Author: W. L. Warren.
Publisher: Western Psychological Services.
Cross References: For reviews by Paul C. Burnett and Barbara J. Kaplan, see 13:263 (382 references); see also T4:2261 (10 references).

[2109]
Revised Minnesota Paper Form Board Test, Second Edition.

Purpose: "Designed to measure aspects of mechanical ability requiring the capacity to visualize and manipulate objects in space."
Population: Grade 9 and over.
Publication Dates: 1934–1995.
Acronym: RMPFBT.
Scores: Total score only.
Administration: Group.
Forms, 4: Series AA, BB, MA, MB.
Price Data, 2002: $49 per examination kit including test booklets for 4 forms and manual (1995, 91 pages); $79 per 25 Form AA or BB test booklets for booklet scoring; $101 per 25 test booklets for Forms MA and MB for use with scannable or hand-scorable answer document; $8 per key for Forms AA and BB; $40 per key for hand scoring scannable answer document for Forms MA and MB; $64 per 50 scannable answer documents for use with Form MA or MB; $39 per manual.
Time: 20(40) minutes.
Authors: Rensis Likert and W. H. Quasha.
Publisher: The Psychological Corporation.
Foreign Adaptations: Australian edition: 1981; revised edition prepared by J. Jenkinson; Australian Council for Education Research [Australia]; British norms supplement: 1978; Gil Nyfield, NFER-Nelson Publishing Co. [England].

Cross References: For reviews by L. Carolyn Pearson and Michael J. Roszkowski, see 14:316; see also T5:2217 (3 references) and T4:2262 (2 references); for a review by Paul W. Thayer of an earlier edition, see 9:1045 (2 references); see also T3:2015 (19 references), T2:2266 (37 references), 7:1056 (19 references), and 6:1092 (16 references); for a review by D. W. McElwain, see 5:885 (29 references); for reviews by Clifford E. Jurgensen and Raymond A. Katzell, see 4:763 (38 references); for a review by Dewey B. Stuit, see 3:677 (48 references); for a review by Alec Rodger, see 2:1673 (9 references).

[2110]
Revised NEO Personality Inventory.

Purpose: To measure five major dimensions or domains of normal adult personality.
Population: Ages 17 and older.
Publication Dates: 1978–1992.
Administration: Group.
Price Data: Available from publisher.
Authors: Paul T. Costa, Jr. and Robert R. McCrae.
Publisher: Psychological Assessment Resources, Inc.

a) REVISED NEO PERSONALITY INVENTORY.
Acronym: NEO PI-R.
Forms, 2: Form S (self-reports), Form R (observer ratings).
Scores, 35: 30 facets in 5 domains: Neuroticism (Anxiety, Angry Hostility, Depression, Self-Consciousness, Impulsiveness, Vulnerability, Total), Extraversion (Warmth, Gregariousness, Assertiveness, Activity, Excitement-Seeking, Positive Emotions, Total), Openness (Fantasy, Aesthetics, Feelings, Actions, Ideas, Values, Total), Agreeableness (Trust, Straightforwardness, Altruism, Compliance, Modesty, Tender-Mindedness, Total), Conscientiousness (Competence, Order, Dutifulness, Achievement Striving, Self-Discipline, Deliberation, Total).
Time: [35–45] minutes.
Comments: Form R has two parallel versions: male and female.

b) NEO FIVE-FACTOR INVENTORY.
Acronym: NEO-FFI.
Scores, 5: Neuroticism, Extraversion, Openness, Agreeableness, Conscientiousness.
Time: (10-15) minutes.
Comments: Shortened version of Form S.
Cross References: See T5:2218 (135 references); for reviews by Michael D. Botwin and Samuel Juni, see 12:330 (50 references); see also T4:2263 (49 references; for reviews by Allen K. Hess and Thomas A. Widiger of an earlier edition see 11:258 (5 references); for a review by Robert Hogan of an earlier edition of *a*, see 10:214 (6 references).

[2111]
Revised Pre-Reading Screening Procedures [1997 Edition].

Purpose: Designed to "find among children of average to superior intelligence the ones who show difficulties in Auditory, Visual, and/or Kinesthetic modalities that often indicate Specific Language Disability (SLD)."
Population: First grade entrants.
Publication Dates: 1968–1997.
Scores: 7 areas: Visual, Visual-Kinesthetic-Motor, Auditory, Auditory-Visual, Auditory-Visual-Kinesthetic-Motor, Language, Letter Knowledge.
Administration: Group.
Price Data, 2001: : $58.85 per test booklet (32 pages) including 12 Teacher Observation/Summary sheets, 12 Practice Pages, and 12 cardboard markers); $19.45 per Teacher's Manual (1997, 94 pages) including instructions plus detachable key; $21.85 per Teacher's Cards and Chart (2 sets of 5 x 10 cards and 2 copies of a wall chart used in giving the tests); $21.10 per specimen set including Teacher's Manual and 1 test booklet; quantity discounts available.
Time: Administration time not reported.
Authors: Beth H. Slingerland and Marty Aho.
Publisher: Educators Publishing Service, Inc.
Cross References: For a review by Maurine A. Fry of an earlier edition, see 9:1046; see also T2:1721 (1 reference); for reviews by Colleen B. Jamison and Roy A. Kress of an earlier edition, see 7:732 (1 reference).

[2112]
The Revised Sheridan Gardiner Test of Visual Acuity.

Purpose: To measure visual acuity.
Population: Age 5 and over.
Publication Dates: 1970–c1993.
Scores, 2: Distance Vision, Near Vision.
Administration: Individual.
Manual: No manual.
Price Data, 2001: $36 per test.
Time: Administration time not reported.
Authors: Mary D. Sheridan and Peter A. Gardiner.
Publisher: Keeler Instruments Inc. (U.S. Distributor).
Cross References: See T2:1926 (1 reference).

[2113]
Revised Token Test.

Purpose: Designed as a quantitative and descriptive test for "auditory disorders associated with aphasia and brain damage."
Population: Preliminary normative data based on the following standardization samples: non-brain-damaged, left hemisphere brain-damaged, right hemisphere brain-damaged.

Publication Date: 1978.
Acronym: RTT.
Scores, 22: 10 Subtest mean scores, Overall mean score, 11 Linguistic Element mean scores.
Administration: Individual.
Price Data, 2001: $149 per complete kit including 25 scoring forms, 25 profile forms, administration manual, 24 tokens, and manual (118 pages); $36 per profile forms; $34 per administration manual and scoring forms; $36 per tokens; $49 per manual.
Time: Administration time varies with condition.
Comments: Reconstruction of the Token Test.
Authors: Malcolm Ray McNeil and Thomas E. Prescott.
Publisher: PRO-ED.
Cross References: See T5:2225 (21 references) and T4:2270 (5 references); for reviews by Michael D. Franzen and Charles J. Golden and by Thomas Hammeke, see 9:1048; see also T3:2017 (5 references).

[2114]
Rey Auditory Verbal Learning Test: A Handbook.
Purpose: Designed to measure "verbal learning and memory."
Population: Ages 7–89.
Publication Date: 1996.
Acronym: RAVLT.
Scores, 3: Learning, Recall, Recognition.
Administration: Individual.
Price Data, 2002: $72.50 per complete kit including handbook (148 pages) and 25 record sheets and score summaries; $19.95 per 25 record sheets and score summaries; $58 per handbook.
Time: (15) minutes.
Author: Michael Schmidt.
Publisher: Western Psychological Services.
Cross References: For reviews by Karen Mackler and Steven R. Shaw, see 14:317; see also T5:2226 (42 references).

[2115]
Rey Complex Figure Test and Recognition Trial.
Purpose: Designed to assess "visuospatial constructional ability and visual memory."
Population: Ages 6–89.
Publication Dates: 1995–1996.
Acronym: RCFT.
Scores, 9: Immediate Recall, Delayed Recall, Recognition Total Correct, Copy, Time to Copy, Recognition True Positives, Recognition False Positives, Recognition True Negatives, Recognition False Negatives.
Administration: Individual.
Price Data: Available from publisher for complete kit including manual (1995, 126 pages), 25 test book-

lets, stimulus card, and supplemental norms for children and adolescents (1996, 21 pages).
Time: (45) minutes, including a 30-minute delay interval.
Authors: John E. Meyers and Kelly R. Meyers.
Publisher: Psychological Assessment Resources, Inc.
Cross References: For reviews by D. Ashley Cohen and Deborah D. Roman, see 14:318; see also T5:2227 (62 references).

[2116]
Reynell Developmental Language Scales: Third Edition [British Edition].
Purpose: Developed for use by speech and language therapists in assessing children with suspected language problems.
Population: 15 months to 7 years.
Publication Dates: 1969–1997.
Acronym: RDLS III.
Scores: 2 scales; Comprehension Scale, Expressive Scale.
Administration: Individual.
Price Data, 1998: £375 per complete set including 35 record forms, manual (1997, 74 pages), and all stimulus items and pictures required for Comprehension and Expressive Scales; £42 per 35 record forms.
Time: (35–40) minutes
Authors: Susan Edwards, Paul Fletcher, Michael Garman, Arthur Hughes, Carolyn Letts, and Indra Sinka.
Publisher: NFER-Nelson Publishing Co., Ltd. [England].
Cross References: For a review by Carol M. McGregor, see 14:319; see also T5:2228 (24 references) and T4:2271 (18 references); for reviews by Doris V. Allen and Diane Nelson Bryen of an earlier edition, see 9:1049 (6 references); see also T3:2018 (16 references); for reviews by Katharine G. Butler and Joel Stark, see 8:974 (3 references); see also T2:2025 (3 references).

[2117]
Reynell Developmental Language Scales [U.S. Edition].
Purpose: Developed to measure verbal comprehension and expressive language skills.
Population: Ages 1-0 to 6-11.
Publication Dates: 1977–1990.
Acronym: RDLS.
Scores, 2: Verbal Comprehension, Expressive Language.
Administration: Individual.
Price Data, 2002: $499 per complete kit including a set of stimulus materials, 10 record forms, and manual (1990, 91 pages) in carrying case; $49.50 per 25 record forms; $60 per manual.
Time: (30) minutes.

Comments: Two Verbal Comprehension scales available to accommodate simple oral responses or pointing responses; British version available.
Authors: Joan K. Reynell and Christian P. Gruber.
Publisher: Western Psychological Services.
Cross References: See T5:2229 (16 references); for reviews by Dawn P. Flanagan and Rebecca J. McCauley, see 12:331 (3 references); see also T4:2272 (2 references); for reviews by Doris V. Allen and Diane Nelson Bryen of the British version, see 9:1049 (5 references); see also T3:2018 (16 references); for reviews by Katharine G. Butler and Joel Stark of the British version, see 8:974 (3 references); see also T2:2025 (3 references).

[2118]
Reynolds Adolescent Adjustment Screening Inventory.

Purpose: Designed as "a screening measure of adolescent adjustment."
Population: Ages 12–19.
Publication Dates: 1998–2001.
Acronym: RAASI.
Scores, 5: Antisocial Behavior, Anger Control Problems, Emotional Distress, Positive Self, Adjustment Total Score.
Administration: Individual or group.
Price Data: Available from publisher for kit including 50 test booklets and professional manual (2001, 134 pages).
Time: (5) minutes.
Author: William M. Reynolds.
Publisher: Psychological Assessment Resources, Inc.

[2119]
Reynolds Adolescent Depression Scale.

Purpose: "To assess depressive symptomatology in adolescents."
Population: Grades 7–12.
Publication Dates: 1986–1987.
Acronym: RADS.
Scores: Total score only.
Administration: Individual or group.
Price Data: Available from publisher.
Time: (5–10) minutes.
Comments: Self-report measure; hand-scored.
Author: William M. Reynolds.
Publisher: Psychological Assessment Resources, Inc.
Cross References: See T5:2230 (21 references) and T4:2274 (11 references); for reviews by Barbara J. Kaplan and Deborah King Kundert, see 11:333 (6 references).

[2120]
Reynolds Child Depression Scale.

Purpose: Provides screening for and a measure of depressive symptomatology.

Population: Grades 3–6.
Publication Dates: 1981–1989.
Scores: Total score only.
Administration: Group or individual.
Price Data: Available from publisher for complete kit including 25 test booklet/answer sheets (Form HS), scoring key, and manual (1989, 55 pages).
Time: (10–15) minutes.
Comments: Test booklet title is About Me; self-ratings.
Author: William M. Reynolds.
Publisher: Psychological Assessment Resources, Inc.
Cross References: See T5:2231 (7 references) and T4:2275 (3 references); for reviews by Janet F. Carlson and Cynthia A. Rohrbeck, see 11:334 (1 reference).

[2121]
Reynolds Depression Screening Inventory.

Purpose: Constructed as a "self-report measure of the severity of depressive symptoms."
Population: Ages 18–89.
Publication Date: 1998.
Acronym: RDSI.
Scores: Total score only.
Administration: Individual or group.
Price Data: Available from publisher for introductory kit including manual (64 pages) and 25 booklets.
Time: (5–10) minutes.
Authors: William M. Reynolds and Kenneth A. Kobak.
Publisher: Psychological Assessment Resources, Inc.
Cross References: For reviews by Michael H. Campbell and Rosemary Flanagan, see 14:320.

[2122]
Rhode Island Test of Language Structure.

Purpose: "Provides a measure of English language development—a profile of the child's understanding of language structure—and assessment data."
Population: Hearing-impaired children ages 3–20, hearing children ages 3–6.
Publication Date: 1983.
Acronym: RITLS.
Scores: Measures syntax response errors for 20 sentence types, both simple and complex, including Relative and Adverbial Clauses, Subject and Other Complements, Reversible and Nonreversible Passives, Datives, Deletions, Negations, Conjunctives, Embedded Imperatives.
Administration: Individual.
Price Data, 2001: $139 per complete kit including 10 analysis sheets, 10 response sheets, test booklet, and manual (114 pages); $29 per 10 response and 10 analysis sheets; $64 per test booklet; $49 per manual.
Time: (25–35) minutes.
Authors: Elizabeth Engen and Trygg Engen.

Publisher: PRO-ED.
Cross References: See T5:2233 (4 references) and T4:2276 (1 reference); for reviews by Lynn S. Bliss and Joan I. Lynch, see 10:315.

[2123]
Richmond Tests of Basic Skills: Edition 2.

Purpose: "Comprehensive and continuous measurement of the growth of an individual child in the fundamental skills."
Population: Ages 8-0 to 13-11.
Publication Dates: 1975–1988.
Acronym: RTBS: Edition 2.
Scores: 11 tests: Vocabulary, Reading Comprehension, Language Skills (Spelling, Use of Capital Letters, Punctuation, Usage), Work-Study Skills (Map Reading, Reading Graphs and Tables, Knowledge and Use of Reference Materials), Mathematics Skills (Mathematics Concepts, Mathematics Problem Solving).
Administration: Group.
Levels: 6 overlapping levels (ages 8-0 to 8-11, 9-0 to 9-11, 10-0 to 10-11, 11-0 to 11-11, 12-0 to 12-11, 13-0 to 13-11) in a single reusable booklet.
Price Data: Price information available from publisher for pupil's book, answer sheets (specify level), scoring overlay (specify level), pupil profile charts, circular profiles, administration manual (1988, 96 pages), and specimen set; scoring service offered by publisher.
Time: (60) minutes per test.
Comments: British adaptation of Iowa Tests of Basic Skills (1268).
Authors: A. N. Hieronymus, E. F. Lindquist, and Norman France.
Publisher: NFER-Nelson Publishing Co., Ltd. [England].
Cross References: See T5:2234 (2 references); for a review by Carmen J. Finley, see 11:335 (3 references); for reviews by Michael Berger and Thomas Kellaghan of an earlier edition, see 8:25.

[2124]
The Riley Articulation and Language Test, Revised.

Purpose: To identify children in need of speech therapy.
Population: Grades K–2.
Publication Dates: 1966–1971.
Acronym: RALT.
Scores, 3: Language Proficiency and Intelligibility, Articulation Function, Language Function.
Administration: Individual.
Price Data, 2002: $45 per complete kit including 25 tests and manual (1971, 7 pages); $22.50 per 25 tests; $25 per manual.

Time: (3–5) minutes.
Author: Glyndon D. Riley.
Publisher: Western Psychological Services.
Cross References: For reviews by Ralph L. Shelton and Lawrence D. Shriberg, see 8:975 (1 reference); for a review by Raphael M. Haller of the original edition, see 7:967 (1 reference).

[2125]
Risk Taking Inventory & Guide.

Purpose: Designed to "help respondents see the filters through which they assess risk" and "also guides them in improving the likelihood of gains while reducing uncertainty and the likelihood of losses."
Population: Managers.
Publication Date: 1997.
Scores, 3: Risk-Preference Pattern, Risk-Avoidance Pattern, Risk-Neutral Pattern.
Administration: Group.
Manual: No manual.
Price Data, 2002: $8.95 per inventory and guide; minimum of 20 (volume discounts available).
Time: [15] minutes including self-scoring.
Author: Herbert S. Kindler.
Publisher: The Center for Management Effectiveness, Inc.

[2126]
The Rivermead Behavioural Memory Test [Second Edition].

Purpose: "Developed to detect impairment of everyday memory functioning and to monitor change following treatment for memory difficulties."
Publication Dates: 1985–1991.
Acronym: RBMT.
Administration: Individual.
Price Data: Available from publisher.
Time: Administration time not reported.
Publisher: Thames Valley Test Company Ltd. [England].
a) THE RIVERMEAD BEHAVIOURAL MEMORY TEST.
Population: Brain-damaged persons, ages 11 to elderly adult.
Publication Dates: 1985–1991.
Scores, 2: Screening Score, Standardized Profile Score.
Comments: For multiple administrations with the same subject, four parallel versions available.
Authors: Barbara Wilson (test, manual, supplementary manual 2), Janet Cockburn (test, manual, supplementary manuals 2 and 3), Alan Baddely (test, manual, supplementary manual 2), Robert Hiorns (supplementary manual 2), and Phillip T. Smith (supplementary manual 3).

b) THE RIVERMEAD BEHAVIOURAL MEMORY TEST FOR CHILDREN.
Population: Brain-damaged children, ages 5–10.
Publication Date: 1991.
Score: Standardized Profile Score.
Comments: Materials from adult version used for most subtests, but some additional materials needed.
Authors: Barbara A. Wilson (test and manual), Rebecca Ivani-Chalian (test and manual), Frances Aldrich (manual).
Cross References: For reviews by Anthony M. Paolo and by Goran Westergren and Ingela Westergren, see 14:321; see also T5:2239 (35 references).

[2127]
Rivermead Perceptual Assessment Battery.

Purpose: "To assess deficits in visual perception following a stroke or head injury."
Population: Adult stroke and head injury patients.
Publication Date: 1985.
Acronym: RPAB.
Scores, 16: Picture Matching, Object Matching, Colour Matching, Size Recognition, Series, Animal Halves, Missing Article, Figure Ground Discrimination, Sequencing/Pictures, Body Image, R/L Copying Shapes, R/L Copying Words, 3D Copying, Cube Copying, Cancellation, Body Image/Self Identification.
Administration: Individual.
Price Data, 1999: £592.50 per complete set containing all items for each subtest, layout guide, 25 record forms, and manual (83 pages) in a carrying case; £16 per 25 record forms; £41.50 per manual.
Time: (49–59) minutes.
Authors: S. Whiting, N. Lincoln, G. Bhavnani, and J. Cockburn.
Publisher: NFER-Nelson Publishing Co., Ltd. [England].
Cross References: See T5:2240 (3 references) and T4:2283 (1 reference); for a review by Jeffery P. Braden, see 11:336.

[2128]
Riverside Performance Assessment Series.

Purpose: "To assess students' strategic thinking and process skills, and problem-solving strategies" in reading, mathematics, and writing.
Population: Grades 1–12.
Publication Date: 1993.
Acronym: R-PAS.
Scores, 3: Reading, Mathematics, Writing.
Administration: Group.
Levels, 6: A (Grades 1–3), B (Grades 2–4), C (Grades 3–5), D (Grades 4–6), E (Grades 6–9), F (Grades 9–12).
Price Data: Available from publisher.

Foreign Language Edition: Selected student booklets in each subject area available in Spanish.
Time: (50–120) minutes per test.
Comments: Criterion-referenced, constructed response assessments; each assessment begins with a pre-assessment activity.
Author: Riverside Publishing.
Publisher: Riverside Publishing.

[2129]
Roberts Apperception Test for Children [with new Interpretive Handbook].

Purpose: Constructed to "assess children's perceptions of common interpersonal situations."
Population: Ages 6–15.
Publication Dates: 1982–1994.
Acronym: RATC.
Scores, 13: 8 Adaptive Profile Scales (Reliance on Others, Support—Other, Support—Child, Limit Setting, Problem Identification, Resolution 1, Resolution 2, Resolution 3), 5 Clinical Profile Scales (Anxiety, Aggression, Depression, Rejection, Unresolved Problems), 3 Indicators (Atypical Responses, Maladaptive Outcome, Refusal), and 3 Supplemental Measures (Ego Functioning, Aggression, Levels of Projection).
Administration: Individual.
Price Data, 2002: $128 per kit including manual (1982, 129 pages), 1 set of pictures (does not include test pictures for black children), and 25 record booklets; $22.50 per 25 record booklets; $59.95 per test pictures; $59.95 per test pictures for black children; $49.95 per manual; $59.50 per interpretive handbook (1994, 270 pages).
Time: (20–30) minutes.
Authors: Dorothea S. McArthur and Glen E. Roberts.
Publisher: Western Psychological Services.
Cross References: For reviews by Merith Cosden and Niels G. Waller, see 14:322; see also T5:2242 (8 references) and T4:2285 (5 references); for a review by Jacob O. Sines of an earlier edition, see 9:1054.

[2130]
Rockford Infant Developmental Evaluation Scales.

Purpose: Developed as a developmental checklist offering an informal assessment of developmental function.
Population: Birth–4 years.
Publication Date: 1979.
Acronym: RIDES.
Scores, 5: Personal-Social/Self-Help, Fine Motor/Adaptive, Receptive Language, Expressive Language, Gross Motor.
Administration: Individual.
Price Data, 2002: $41 per 20 checklists; $58.50 per manual (150 pages); $80.65 per manual and 20 checklists.

Time: Administration time varies; author recommends administration in several sessions in one week.
Comments: 3 ways of administering items: ask parents for information, observe spontaneous actions and informal play, present specific tasks or set up situation that will elicit a particular kind of response.
Author: Developed by PROJECT RHISE, Children's Development Center, Rockford, IL.
Publisher: Scholastic Testing Service, Inc.
Cross References: See T5:2243 (1 reference); for a review by Dennis C. Harper, see 9:1055.

[2131]
Roeder Manipulative Aptitude Test.

Purpose: Measures manual and finger dexterity and hand-eye coordination.
Population: Elementary school to adult.
Publication Date: 1967.
Scores, 1 to 3: Left Hand Dexterity (optional), Right Hand Dexterity (optional), Total.
Administration: Group.
Price Data: Available from publisher.
Time: 5(10) minutes.
Author: Wesley S. Roeder.
Publisher: Lafayette Instrument.
Cross References: For reviews by Jean Powell Kirnan and Shauna Faltin and Suzanne Lane, see 12:333.

[2132]
Rogers Criminal Responsibility Assessment Scales.

Purpose: "To quantify essential psychological and situational variables at the time of the crime and to implement criterion-based decision models for criminal responsibility."
Population: Criminals.
Publication Date: 1984.
Acronym: R-CRAS.
Scores: 5 scales: Patient Reliability, Organicity, Psychopathology, Cognitive Control, Behavioral Control.
Administration: Individual.
Price Data: Available from publisher for complete kit including 25 booklets and manual (62 pages).
Time: Administration time not reported.
Comments: "Criterion-referenced."
Author: Richard Rogers.
Publisher: Psychological Assessment Resources, Inc.
Cross References: See T4:2288 (1 reference); for a review by Robert J. Howell and R. Lynn Richards, see 10:316.

[2133]
Rokeach Value Survey.

Purpose: Constructed to identify values of importance to the respondent.

Population: Ages 11 and over.
Publication Dates: 1967–1983.
Scores: No scores.
Administration: Group.
Price Data, 2001: $67 per 25 test booklets; $32.95 per manual (322 pages).
Time: (10–20) minutes.
Comments: Rankings of 18 terminal values ("end-states of existence") and 18 instrumental values ("modes of behavior"); manual title is Understanding Human Values.
Author: Milton Rokeach.
Publisher: Consulting Psychologists Press, Inc.
Cross References: See T5:2246 (14 references); for reviews by Susan M. Brookhart and Eleanor E. Sanford, see 12:334 (14 references); see also T4:2290 (28 references), 9:1058 (17 references), and T3:2029 (49 references); for reviews by Jacob Cohen and Tom Kitwood, see 8:660 (155 references); see also T2:1355 (39 references).

[2134]
Rorschach.

Purpose: A projective technique for clinical assessment and diagnosis.
Population: Ages 5 and over.
Publication Dates: 1921–1998.
Scores: Many variations of scoring and interpretation are in use with no single method generally accepted.
Administration: Individual.
Price Data, 2001: $75 per set of 10 plates; $17 per 100 recording sheets; $32 per set of 5 location charts; $66 per manual (1998, 228 pages).
Time: (20–30) minutes.
Comments: Variously referred to by such titles as Rorschach Method, Rorschach Test, Rorschach Psychodiagnostics.
Author: Hermann Rorschach.
Publisher: Hogrefe & Huber Publishers.
Cross References: For a review by Allen K. Hess, Peter Zachar, and Jeffrey Kramer, see 14:323; see also T5:2247 (136 references), T4:2292 (273 references), 9:1059 (79 references), and T3:2030 (155 references); for reviews by Richard H. Dana and Rolf A. Peterson, see 8:661 (360 references); see also T2:1499 (376 references); for reviews by Alvin G. Burstein, John F. Knutson, Charles C. McArthur, Albert I. Rabin, and Marvin Resnikoff, see 7:175 (455 references); see also P:470 (719 references); for reviews by Richard H. Dana, Leonard D. Eron, and Arthur R. Jensen, see 6:237 (734 references); for reviews by Samuel J. Beck, H. J. Eysenck, Raymond J. McCall, and Laurance F. Shaffer, see 5:154 (1078 references); for a review by Helen Sargent, see 4:117 (621 references); for reviews by Morris Krugman and J. R. Wittenborn, see 3:73 (452 references); see also 2:1246 (147 references).

[2135]
The Rosenzweig Picture-Frustration Study.

Purpose: Designed to measure patterns of aggressive responding to everyday stress.
Population: Ages 4–13, 12–18, 18 and over.
Publication Dates: 1944–1988.
Scores, 15: Directions of Aggression (Extraggression, Intraggression, Imaggression), Types of Aggression (Obstacle-Dominance, Ego [Etho]-Defense, Needs-Persistence), 9 combinations of the preceding categories.
Administration: Group.
Price Data: Available from publisher for P-F study kit including basic manual (1978, 66 pages), manual supplement, 25 test booklets, and 25 scoring sheets (specify level).
Time: (15-20) minutes.
Comments: Basic manual necessary for administration of any or all levels.
Author: Saul Rosenzweig.
Publisher: Psychological Assessment Resources, Inc.
  a) FORM FOR CHILDREN-C.
  Population: Ages 4–13.
  Publication Dates: 1948–1988.
  Comments: Supplement to basic manual (1981, 47 pages).
  b) REVISED FORM FOR ADOLESCENTS-T.
  Population: Ages 12–18.
  Publication Date: 1964.
  Comments: Supplement to basic manual (1987, 40 pages).
  c) REVISED FORM FOR ADULTS-A.
  Population: Ages 18 and over.
  Publication Dates: 1944–1978.
  Comments: Supplement to basic manual (1978, 48 pages).
Cross References: See T5:2248 (7 references) and T4:2293 (12 references); for reviews by Donald J. Viglione, Jr. and Edwin E. Wagner, see 9:1060 (6 references); see also T3:2031 (7 references), 8:662 (39 references), T2:1500 (106 references), and P:471 (63 references); for a review of *a* and *c* by Ake Bjerstedt, see 6:238 (61 references); for reviews by Richard H. Dana and Bert R. Sappenfield, see 5:155 (109 references); for reviews by Robert C. Challman and Percival M. Symonds, see 4:129 (77 references).

[2136]
Ross Information Processing Assessment—Geriatric.

Purpose: A clinical instrument designed to identify, describe, and quantify cognitive-linguistic deficits in the geriatric population following traumatic brain injury.
Population: Geriatric patients.
Publication Date: 1996.
Acronym: RIPA-G.

Scores, 12: Immediate Memory, Recent Memory, Temporal Orientation, Spatial Orientation, Orientation to Environment, Recall of General Information, Problem Solving and Abstract Reasoning, Organization of Information, Auditory Processing and Comprehension, Problem Solving and Concrete Reasoning, Naming Common Objects, Functional Oral Reading.
Administration: Individual.
Price Data, 2001: $213 per complete kit; $49 per examiner's manual (77 pages); $54 per 25 response record forms; $24 per 25 profile summary forms; $49 per picture book; $41 per Geriatric Treatment Manual.
Time: (45–60) minutes.
Comments: 10 core subtests, 2 supplemental subtests.
Authors: Deborah Ross-Swain and Paul T. Fogle.
Publisher: PRO-ED.
Cross References: For reviews by Surendra P. Singh and Wilfred G. Van Gorp, see 14:324.

[2137]
Ross Information Processing Assessment—Primary.

Purpose: Designed to "assess information processing skills in children ages 5-0 through 12-11 who have acquired or developmental problems involving the brain."
Population: "Ages 5-0 through 12-11 who have acquired or developmental problems involving the brain."
Publication Date: 1999.
Acronym: RIPA-P.
Scores, 12: 8 subtests (Immediate Memory, Recent Memory, Recall of General Information, Spatial Orientation, Temporal Orientation, Organization, Problem Solving, Abstract Reasoning); 4 composite scores (Memory, Orientation, Thinking and Reasoning, Information Processing).
Administration: Individual.
Price Data, 2001: $114 per complete kit including manual (61 pages), 25 record booklets, and 25 profile forms; $54 per manual; $39 per 25 record booklets; $24 per 25 profile forms.
Time: (45) minutes for complete battery.
Comments: Certain subtests not administered to younger children.
Author: Deborah Ross-Swain.
Publisher: PRO-ED.

[2138]
Ross Information Processing Assessment, Second Edition.

Purpose: Designed to assess "cognitive-linguistic deficits following traumatic brain injury."
Population: Ages 15–90.
Publication Dates: 1986–1996.
Acronym: RIPA—2.
Scores, 20: 10 Subtest scores (Immediate Memory, Recent Memory, Temporal Orientation [Recent

Memory, Remote Memory], Spatial Orientation, Orientation to Environment, Recall of General Information, Problem Solving and Abstract Reasoning, Organization, Auditory Processing and Retention); 10 Diacritical scores (Errors, Perseveration, Repeat Instructions/Stimulus, Denial/Refusal, Delayed Response, Confabulation, Partially Correct, Irrelevant, Tangential, Self-Corrected).
Administration: Individual.
Price Data, 2001: $119 per complete kit including examiner's manual (1996, 68 pages), 25 record forms, and 25 profile/summary forms in storage box; $44 per 25 record forms; $24 per 25 profile/summary forms; $54 per examiner's manual.
Time: (60) minutes.
Author: Deborah Ross-Swain.
Publisher: PRO-ED.
Cross References: For a review by Stephen R. Hooper, see 14:325; see also T4:2294; for a review by Jonathan Ehrlich of an earlier edition, see 11:337.

[2139]
Roswell-Chall Auditory Blending Test.

Purpose: "Developed to evaluate a student's ability to blend sounds to form words when the sounds are presented orally."
Population: Grades 1–4 and "older students with reading difficulties."
Publication Dates: 1963–1997.
Scores: Total score only.
Administration: Individual.
Price Data, 2001: $15.90 per packet of 24 test forms; $5.70 per manual of instructions (1995, 5 pages); quantity discounts available.
Time: Administration time not reported.
Comments: Oral administration; useful for judging the ease with which students will learn phonics.
Authors: Florence G. Roswell and Jeanne S. Chall.
Publisher: Educators Publishing Service, Inc.
Cross References: For reviews by Joyce R. McLarty and Janet Norris, see 14:326; see also T5:2253 (2 reeferences), T4:2296 (1 reference), and T2:1674 (7 references); for reviews by Ira E. Aaron and B. H. Von Roekel of an earlier edition, see 6:830 (2 references).

[2140]
Roswell-Chall Diagnostic Reading Test of Word Analysis Skills.

Purpose: "Designed to evaluate the basic word analysis (decoding) and word recognition skills."
Population: Reading levels grades 1–4.
Publication Dates: 1956–1997.
Scores, 15: Words (High Frequency Words), Decoding Test (Consonant Sounds, Consonant Digraphs, Consonant Blends, Short Vowel Sounds, Short and Long Vowel Sounds, Rule of Silent e, Vowel Digraphs, Diphthongs and Vowels Controlled by r, Syllabication, Total), Letter Names (Naming Capital Letters, Naming Lower Case Letters), Encoding (Encoding Single Consonants, Encoding Regular Words).
Administration: Individual.
Forms, 2: A, B.
Price Data, 2001: $15.90 per 24 test forms including 12 each Form A and B; $5,45 per manual of instructions (1997, 14 pages); $6.05 per technical supplement (1997, 16 pages); quantity discounts available.
Time: (10) minutes.
Comments: Republication of 1978 version.
Authors: Florence G. Roswell and Jeanne S. Chall.
Publisher: Educators Publishing Service, Inc.
Cross References: For a review by Thomas P. Hogan, see 14:327; for reviews by John Wills Lloyd and Ira E. Aaron of an earlier edition, see 9:1062 (1 reference); see also T3:2034 (3 references) and T2:1643 (2 references); for reviews by Ira E. Aaron and Albert Betts of an earlier edition, see 6:831 (1 reference); for a review by Byron H. Van Roekel of the original edition, see 5:667.

[2141]
Rothwell Miller Interest Blank (Revised).

Purpose: "Designed primarily to give an assessment of vocational interests as an aid to a career interview . Other applications include company selection and promotion, and clinical and rehabilitation counselling."
Population: Ages 13 and over.
Publication Dates: 1958–1994.
Acronym: RMIB.
Scores, 12: Outdoor, Mechanical, Computational, Scientific, Persuasive, Aesthetic, Literary, Musical, Social Service, Clerical, Practical, Medical.
Forms, 3: A, B, and C.
Administration: Individual or group.
Price Data: Available from publisher.
Foreign Language and Other Special Editions: Culturally adapted editions (English language): Australian, New Zealand, Philippine, Singapore, South African editions; Foreign language editions: French and Greek language editions available (Afrikaans, German, Hungarian, Icelandic, and Romanian editions in progress).
Time: (15–30) minutes.
Comments: In addition to main task of ranking occupations in order of preference, there is an opportunity for free choice responses; can be used in conjunction with the complementary measure Rothwell Miller Values Blank (2143).
Authors: J. W. Rothwell (original test), K. M. Miller (original test and revision), and B. Tyler (1994 revision).
Publisher: Miller & Tyler, Limited [England].

Cross References: For reviews by Richard E. Harding and William K. Wilkinson, see 13:269; for reviews by A. W. Heim and Clive Jones of an earlier edition, see 7:1034 (2 references).

[2142]
Rothwell-Miller Interest Blank.

Purpose: Designed to assess vocational interests.
Population: Ages 12 and over.
Publication Date: 1986.
Acronym: RMIB.
Scores, 12: Outdoor, Mechanical, Computational, Scientific, Persuasive, Artistic, Literary, Musical, Social Service, Clerical, Practical, Medical.
Administration: Group.
Price Data: Available from publisher.
Foreign Language Edition: Test printed in English and Afrikaans.
Time: 30(40) minutes.
Authors: B. A. Hall, M. E. Halstead, and T. R. Taylor.
Publisher: Human Sciences Research Council [South Africa].

[2143]
Rothwell Miller Values Blank.

Purpose: "Designed as a measure of work related values to be used primarily in career guidance, in conjunction with an occupational interests measure. Other applications include company selection (with school leavers or older basic level staff) and clinical and rehabilitation counselling."
Population: Ages 15 and older.
Publication Dates: 1968–1994.
Acronym: RMVB.
Scores, 5: Rewards, Interest, Security, Pride in Work, Autonomy.
Administration: Individual or group.
Price Data: Available from publisher.
Foreign Language Editions: French and Greek language editions available; Afrikaans, German, Hungarian, Icelandic, and Romanian editions in progress.
Time: [10–20] minutes.
Comments: Previously entitled Choosing a Career; developed as a complementary measure to be used with the Rothwell Miller Interest Blank (2143).
Authors: J. W. Rothwell, K. M. Miller, and B. Tyler.
Publisher: Miller & Tyler, Limited [England].
Cross References: For reviews by John S. Geisler and William I. Sauser, Jr., see 14:328.

[2144]
Rotter Incomplete Sentences Blank, Second Edition.

Purpose: Primarily used "as a screening instrument of overall adjustment."

Population: College students, adults, high-school students.
Publication Dates: 1950–1992.
Acronym: RISB.
Score: Index of Overall Adjustment.
Administration: Individual or group.
Forms, 3: College, Adult, High School.
Price Data, 2002: $34 per 25 response sheets or $127 per 100 response sheets(specify High School, College, or Adult; $82 per manual (1992, 256 pages).
Time: (20–40) minutes.
Authors: Julian B. Rotter, Michael I. Lah, and Janet E. Rafferty.
Publisher: The Psychological Corporation.
Cross References: See T5:2258 (6 references); for reviews by Gregory J. Boyle and Mary J. McLellan, see 12:335 (3 references); see also T4:2300 (11 references), T3:2037 (11 references), 8:663 (21 references), T2:1501 (48 references), P:472 (35 references), 6:239 (17 references), and 5:156 (18 references); for reviews by Charles N. Cofer and William Schofield of an earlier edition and an excerpted review by Adolf G. Woltmann, see 4:130 (6 references).

[2145]
Roughness Discrimination Test.

Purpose: Measures the tactual discrimination ability of children for predicting Braille reading readiness.
Population: Blind children in grades Kgn–1.
Publication Date: 1965.
Acronym: RDT.
Scores: Total score only.
Administration: Individual.
Price Data: Not available.
Time: (15) minutes.
Comments: Test may be given by any sighted teacher.
Authors: Carson Y. Nolan and June E. Morris.
Publisher: American Printing House for the Blind, Inc.
Cross References: For additional information, see 7:551 (4 references).

[2146]
Ruff Figural Fluency Test.

Purpose: Developed with the "aim of providing clinical information regarding nonverbal capacity for fluid and divergent thinking, ability to flexibly shift cognitive set, planning strategies, and executive ability to coordinate this process."
Population: Ages 16–70.
Publication Dates: 1988–1996.
Acronym: RFFT.
Scores, 3: Unique Designs, Perseverative Errors, Index of Planning Efficiency (Error Ratio).
Administration: Individual

Price Data: Available from publisher for complete kit including 25 test booklets and manual (1996, 43 pages).
Time: 5 minutes.
Comments: Especially useful in neuropsychological applications.
Author: Ronald M. Ruff.
Publisher: Psychological Assessment Resources, Inc.

[2147]
Ruff-Light Trail Learning Test.

Purpose: "To assess visuospatial learning and memory."
Population: Ages 16–70.
Publication Date: 1999.
Acronym: RULIT.
Scores, 7: Learning (Total Correct, Total Step Errors, Trials to Completion), Immediate Memory (Trials 2 Correct, Trials 2 Errors), Delayed Memory (Delayed Correct, Delayed Errors).
Administration: Individual.
Price Data: Available from publisher.
Time: (5–15) minutes with a 60-minute delay.
Comments: Two alternate versions of a 15-step trail; llong-term memory is evaluated by having the respondent retrace the trail after a 60-minute delay.
Authors: Ronald M. Ruff and C. Christopher Allen.
Publisher: Psychological Assessment Resources, Inc.

[2148]
Ruff 2 & 7 Selective Attention Test.

Purpose: Developed to "measure two overlapping aspects of visual attention: sustained attention, and selective attention."
Population: Ages 16–70 years.
Publication Dates: 1995–1996.
Acronym: 2 & 7 Test.
Scores, 11: Automatic Detection Speed, Automatic Detection Errors, Automatic Detection Accuracy, Controlled Search Speed, Controlled Search Errors, Controlled Search Accuracy, Total Speed, Total Accuracy, Speed Difference, Accuracy Difference, Total Difference.
Administration: Individual.
Price Data: Available from publisher for kit including manual and 50 test booklets.
Time: (5) minutes.
Authors: Ronald M. Ruff and C. Christopher Allen.
Publisher: Psychological Assessment Resources, Inc.

[2149]
Rust Advanced Numerical Reasoning Appraisal.

Purpose: Measures the ability to recognize, understand, and apply mathematical and statistical reasoning abilities.
Population: Adults.

Publication Dates: 2001–2002.
Acronym: RANRA.
Scores: Total score only.
Administration: Group or individual.
Price Data, 2002: $251.20 per complete kit.
Time: (40) minutes.
Author: John Rust.
Publisher: The Psychological Corporation Europe [United Kingdom].

[2150]
Rust Inventory of Schizotypal Cognitions.

Purpose: For assessment of risk of schizotypal symptoms.
Population: Age 16 and over.
Publication Date: 1989.
Acronym: RISC.
Scores: Total score only.
Administration: Individual or group.
Price Data, 2002: $86.55 per complete kit including record forms and manual (57 pages).
Time: (10) minutes.
Author: John Rust.
Publisher: The Psychological Corporation Europe [United Kingdom].
Cross References: For reviews by Gregory J. Boyle and George Domino, see 13:270 (3 references); see also T4:2303 (3 references).

[2151]
The Rutgers Drawing Test.

Purpose: A nonverbal "test of perception through motor response."
Population: Ages 4–6, 6–9.
Publication Dates: 1961–1973.
Scores: Total score only.
Administration: Group.
Price Data, 2001: $22 per specimen set; $40 per 25 test forms (specify Form A or Form B).
Time: Administration time not reported.
Author: Anna Spiesman Starr.
Publisher: Institute of Psychological Research, Inc. [Canada].
    a) FORM A.
    Population: Ages 4–6.
    b) FORM B.
    Population: Ages 6–9.
Cross References: For a review by Melvyn I. Semmel, see 7:446 (6 references); see also 6:559 (2 references).

[2152]
Safran Student's Interest Inventory, Third Edition.

Purpose: Developed to identify occupational interests.
Population: Grades 5–9, 9–12.

Publication Dates: 1960–1985.
Scores, 7: Economic, Technical, Outdoor Service, Humane, Artistic, Scientific.
Administration: Group.
Levels, 2: One, Two.
Price Data, 2001: $59 per 35 test booklets (select level); $35 per student's manual (1985, 8 pages); $33.95 per counsellor's manual (1985, 39 pages); $35 per examination kit.
Time: Administration time not reported.
Comments: Self-administered.
Authors: Carl Safran, Douglas W. Feltham, and Edgar N. Wright.
Publisher: Nelson Thomson Learning [Canada].
Cross References: For reviews by Albert M. Bugaj and Caroline Manuele-Adkins, see 12:336; for a review by Thomas T. Frantz of an earlier edition, see 7:1035; see also 6:1069 (1 reference).

[2153]
Sales Achievement Predictor.

Purpose: Constructed to assess "characteristics that are critical for success in sales."
Population: Adults.
Publication Date: 1995.
Acronym: Sales AP.
Scores, 21: Validity Scores (Inconsistent Responding, Self-Enhancing, Self-Critical), Special Scores (Sales Disposition, Initiative-Cold Calling, Sales Closing), Basic Domain Scores (Achievement, Motivation, Competitiveness, Goal Orientation, Planning, Initiative-General, Team Player, Managerial, Assertiveness, Personal Diplomacy, Extroversion, Cooperativeness, Relaxed Style, Patience, Self-Confidence).
Administration: Group.
Price Data, 2002: $180 per kit including manual (73 pages), 2 mail-in answer sheets, 2-use disk for onsite computer scoring, and 2 PC answer sheets; $48 per mail-in answer sheet; $55 per manual; $385 per 10-use computer disk (PC with Windows); $15 per 100 PC answer sheets; $40 per FAX service scoring.
Time: (20–25) minutes.
Comments: Microsoft Windows 3.1 or above required for computer scoring.
Authors: Jotham G. Friedland, Sander I. Marcus, and Harvey P. Mandel.
Publisher: Western Psychological Services.
Cross References: For reviews by Gordon C. Bruner II and Brent W. Roberts, see 14:329.

[2154]
Sales Aptitude Test.

Purpose: "To measure an individual's sales aptitude."
Population: Sales people and sales managers.
Publication Dates: 1993–1996.
Score: Total score only.

Administration: Group.
Price Data, 2002: $106 per start-up kit including 25 test booklets and examiner's manual (1996, 11 pages); $91 per 25 tests; $28 per examiner's manual; price information for Quanta scoring software available from publisher.
Time: (30) minutes.
Comments: Paper-and-pencil or computer administration available.
Author: Science Research Associates.
Publisher: Reid London House.

[2155]
Sales Aptitude Test: ETSA Test 7A.

Purpose: Designed to measure likelihood of success in sales positions.
Population: Employmnet applicants.
Publication Dates: 1960–1998.
Scores: Total score only.
Administration: Group or individual.
Price Data, 2002: $10 per electronic test: $10 each per test booklet and answer sheet (scoring and reporting); $20 per administrator's manual; $20 per technical manual.
Time: (60) minutes.
Comments: Electronic tests available at www.etsatests.com.
Author: Psychological Services Bureau, Inc.
Publisher: Employers' Tests and Services Associates.
Cross References: For reviews by Marvin D. Dunnette and Raymond A. Katzell of an earlier version of the ETSA Tests, see 6:1025.

[2156]
Sales Attitude Check List.

Purpose: To measure attitudes toward selling and habits in the sales situation.
Population: Applicants for sales positions.
Publication Dates: 1960–1992.
Acronym: SACL.
Scores: Total score only.
Administration: Individual or group.
Price Data, 2002: $97 per start-up kit including 25 test booklets and examiner's manual; $81 per 25 test booklets (quantity discounts available); $28 per examiner's manual.
Time: No limit (approximately 10–15 minutes).
Author: Erwin K. Taylor.
Publisher: Reid London House.
Cross References: For reviews by Walter C. Borman and Stephan J. Motowidlo, see 9:1066 (1 reference); for a review by John P. Foley, Jr., see 6:1177.

[2157]
Sales Competency Inventory.

Purpose: Designed to measure the frequency with which respondents display certain competencies associated with effective sales performance.

Population: Salespeople.
Publication Date: 1996.
Scores, 5: Achievement Orientation, Customer Service Orientation, Impact and Influence, Initiative, Interpersonal Understanding.
Administration: Group.
Price Data, 2001: $69 per 10 Profile and Interpretive Notes (22 pages) and 10 questionnaires; $29 per 10 Employee Version questionnaires; $55 per 10 Development Assistant booklets.
Time: [30–40] minutes.
Comments: Self-scoring and interpretive information provided.
Author: Hay Group.
Publisher: Hay Group.

[2158]
Sales Comprehension Test.

Purpose: "Designed to aid in the appraisal of sales ability and potential."
Population: Sales applicants.
Publication Dates: 1947–1994.
Acronym: SCT.
Scores: Total score only.
Administration: Group.
Price Data, 2001: $94.20 per test; $3.75 per key; $35.40 per profiles; $52.65 per manual (1976, 20 pages), manuals supplement (1984, 17 pages), manual supplement (1985, 4 pages), and norms supplement (1994, 4 pages); $4.20 per norms supplement (1988, 1 page); $55.95 per specimen set.
Foreign Language Editions: Spanish, Dutch, French, German, and Italian editions available.
Time: (15–20) minutes.
Comments: Revision of the Aptitudes Associates Test of Sales Aptitude.
Author: Martin M. Bruce.
Publisher: Martin M. Bruce, Ph.D.
Cross References: See T2:2406 (3 references) and 6:1178 (7 references); for a review by Raymond A. Katzell, see 5:947 (10 references).

[2159]
Sales Effectiveness Analysis.

Purpose: Designed to identify an individual's strengths and weaknesses in the area of sales.
Population: Salespeople.
Publication Dates: 1985–2001.
Acronym: SEA.
Scores, 25: Market Awareness, Technical, Strategic, Structure, Sales Focus, Prospecting, Entrepreneurship, Communication, Outgoing, Optimistic, Excitement, Persuasive Negotiation, Insight, Aggressiveness, Tactical, Empathy, Customer Identification, Team Player, Persistence, Production, Management Focus, Idealism, Ego Drive, Materialism, Exaggeration.

Administration: Group.
Price Data: Available from publisher.
Time: (45) minutes.
Comments: Purchase and use requires training by publisher.
Authors: James T. Mahoney (test) and Management Research Group Staff (manual).
Publisher: Management Research Group.

[2160]
Sales Effectiveness Survey.

Purpose: "Designed to help salespeople and others responsible for business development assess their effectiveness."
Population: Sales and business development professionals.
Publication Date: 1996.
Scores, 7: Overall Sales Effectiveness, Comparative Sales Effectiveness, Personal Sales Characteristics, Basic Sales Skills, Selling Skills, Account Management Skills, Opportunity Management Skills.
Administration: Group.
Manual: No manual.
Price Data, 2002: $49 per set including questionnaires and answer sheets for 1 self-assessment, 6 others, 6 customers, and 1 feedback report.
Time: [30] minutes.
Comments: Can be administered online via the Internet.
Author: Terry R. Bacon.
Publisher: Lore International Institute.

[2161]
Sales Motivation Inventory, Revised.

Purpose: Designed for "assessment of interest in, and motivation for, sales work."
Population: Prospective and employed salespeople.
Publication Dates: 1953–1988.
Acronym: SMI.
Scores: Total score only.
Administration: Group.
Price Data, 2001: $94.20 per test package; $52.65 per manual/manuals supplement; $4.20 per norms supplement; $35.40 per profile sheet package; $3.75 per scoring key; $55.95 per specimen set.
Foreign Language Editions: French edition also available.
Time: (20–30) minutes.
Author: Martin M. Bruce.
Publisher: Martin M. Bruce, Ph.D.
Cross References: For a review by Leo M. Harvill, see 11:338; for reviews by Robert M. Guion and Stephan J. Motowidlo of an earlier edition, see 9:1067; see also T2:2408 (5 references); for a review by S. Rains Wallace, see 5:948 (2 references).

[2162]
Sales Motivation Survey.

Purpose: Designed to assess the kinds of needs and values salespeople see as important considerations in making decisions about their work.
Population: Salespeople.
Publication Dates: 1972–1995.
Scores, 5: Basic Creative Comfort, Safety and Order, Belonging and Affiliation, Ego-Status, Actualization and Self-Expression.
Administration: Group.
Price Data, 2001: $7.95 per instrument.
Time: Administration time is not reported.
Comments: Self-administered; self-scored.
Authors: Jay Hall and Norman J. Seim.
Publisher: Teleometrics International.
Cross References: For reviews by Leslie H. Krieger and Sheldon Zedeck, see 14:330.

[2163]
Sales Personality Questionnaire.

Purpose: Developed to assess personality characteristics necessary for sales success.
Population: Sales applicants.
Publication Dates: 1987–1990.
Acronym: SPQ.
Scores, 12: Interpersonal (Confidence, Empathy, Persuasive), Administration (Systematic, Conscientious, Forward Planning), Opportunities (Creative, Observant), Energies (Relaxed, Resilient, Results Oriented), Social Desirability.
Administration: Group.
Price Data: Available from publisher.
Time: (20-30) minutes.
Author: Saville & Holdsworth Ltd.
Publisher: SHL Group plc [United Kingdom].
Cross References: For reviews by Wayne J. Camara and Michael J. Roszkowski, see 12:337.

[2164]
Sales Professional Assessment Inventory.

Purpose: Designed "to assess the individual's interest, motivation and skills needed for success in the sales profession."
Population: Salespeople.
Publication Dates: 1989–1992.
Acronym: SPAI.
Scores, 15: Validity (Candidness, Accuracy), Sales Motivation (Sales/Work Experience, Sales Interest, Sales Responsibility, Sales Orientation, Energy Level, Self Development), Sales Readiness (Sales Skills, Sales Understanding, Sales Arithmetic, Customer Service), Dependability (Business Ethics, Job Stability), Overall Index (Sales Potential).
Administration: Group or individual.

Price Data: Price information for Quanta Touch Test administration and scoring and for Windows administration and scoring available from publisher.
Time: (45) minutes.
Comments: Paper-and-pencil or computer administration available.
Author: London House.
Publisher: Reid London House.

[2165]
Sales Relations Survey.

Purpose: Designed to assess the interpersonal practices and customer orientation of salespeople.
Population: Salespeople.
Publication Dates: 1972–1995.
Scores, 2: Exposure, Feedback.
Administration: Group.
Price Data, 2001: $8.95 per instrument.
Time: Administration time not reported.
Comments: Self-administered; self-scored.
Author: Jay Hall.
Publisher: Teleometrics International.

[2166]
The Sales Sentence Completion Blank.

Purpose: "Designed to aid in the selection of competent sales personnel."
Population: Applicants for sales positions.
Publication Dates: 1961–1982.
Acronym: SSCB.
Scores: Total score only.
Administration: Group.
Price Data, 2001: $65.95 per test package; $19.50 per manual (1961, 25 pages); $28.05 per specimen set.
Time: (20–35) minutes.
Author: Norman Gekoski.
Publisher: Martin M. Bruce, Ph.D.
Cross References: For a review by William E. Kendall, and an excerpted review by John O. Crites, see 6:1181.

[2167]
Sales Staff Selector.

Purpose: "Evaluates the suitability of candidates of all levels of experience for the position of Sales Representative."
Population: Candidates for sales representative positions.
Publication Date: 1984.
Scores: Total score, Narrative Evaluation, Ranking, Recommendation.
Administration: Group.
Price Data, 2001: $150 per candidate; quantity discounts available.
Foreign Language Edition: French edition available.
Time: (65) minutes.

Comments: Scored by publisher; available in booklet and internet versions.
Author: Walden Personnel Performance, Inc.
Publisher: Walden Personnel Performance, Inc.
Cross References: For reviews by Philip G. Benson and Richard W. Johnson, see 10:319.

[2168]
Sales Style Indicator.

Purpose: To assist individuals and sales teams to identify strengths and weaknesses, and to help develop a plan to increase sales style flexibility.
Population: Sales personnel.
Publication Date: 1991.
Acronym: SSI.
Scores, 4: Behavioral Action, Cognitive Analysis, Interpersonal Harmony, Affective Expression.
Administration: Group.
Price Data, 1993: $15 per test booklet; $10 per interpretations booklet (41 pages).
Time: (90) minutes.
Comments: Self-administered, self-scored, self-interpreted.
Authors: Terry D. Anderson and Bruce R. Wares.
Publisher: Consulting Resource Group International, Inc.
Cross References: For reviews by Wayne J. Camara and Gerald A. Rosen, see 13:271.

[2169]
Sales Transaction Audit.

Purpose: Intended as an assessment of sales style and its impact on salesperson-customer transactions.
Population: Salespeople.
Publication Dates: 1972–1980.
Acronym: STA.
Scores, 3: Parent, Adult, Child.
Administration: Group.
Manual: No manual.
Price Data, 2001: $8.95 per instrument.
Time: Administration time not reported.
Authors: Jay Hall and C. Leo Griffith.
Publisher: Teleometrics International.
Cross References: For a review by Chantale Jeanrie, see 14:331; for a review by Stephen L. Cohen of an earlier edition, see 8:1127.

[2170]
SalesMax System Internet Version.

Purpose: Designed as a pre-employment assessment for the selection of top performing sales people for professional, consultative sales positions.
Population: Potential employees for consultative sales positions.
Publication Date: 1998.

Scores, 25: Sales Personality (Energetic, Follows Through, Optimistic, Resilient, Assertive, Social, Expressive, Serious-Minded, Self-Reliant, Accommodating, Positive About People), Sales Knowledge (Prospecting/Pre-qualifying, First Meetings/First Impressions, Probing/Presenting, Overcoming Objections, Influencing/Convincing, Closing), Sales Motivations (Recognition/Attention, Control, Money, Freedom, Developing Expertise, Affiliation, Security/Stability, Achievement).
Administration: Group or individual.
Price Data, 2002: $995 per one-time purchase of the web-based system including units for 10 administrations; subsequent report costs vary from $74 to $98 depending on volume purchase.
Time: (90) minutes.
Comments: Administered via the web.
Author: Bigby, Havis & Associates, Inc.
Publisher: Bigby, Havis & Associates, Inc.

[2171]
Salford Sentence Reading Test (Revised).

Purpose: To assess level of oral reading achievement.
Population: Ages 6-0 to 10-6.
Publication Dates: 1976–2000.
Acronym: SSRT (R).
Scores: Reading Age.
Administration: Individual.
Forms, 2: X and Y.
Price Data, 2002: £8.99 per set of 2 test cards (X and Y); £8.99 per manual (2000, 16 pages); £6.99 per 20 record sheets; £17.99 per specimen set including one each of test cards X and Y, record sheet, and manual.
Time: [2–3] minutes.
Authors: G. E. Bookbinder; revision by Denis Vincent and Mary Crumpler.
Publisher: Hodder & Stoughton Educational [England].
Cross References: See T4:2320 (1 reference); for a review by J. Douglas Ayers of an earlier edition, see 8:791.

[2172]
SAQ-Adult Probation III.

Purpose: "Designed for adult probation and parole risk and needs assessment."
Population: Adult probationers and parolees.
Publication Dates: 1985–1997.
Acronym: SAQ.
Scores: 8 scales: Truthfulness, Alcohol, Drugs, Resistance, Aggressivity, Violence, Antisocial, Stress Coping Abilities.
Administration: Group.
Price Data: Available from publisher.
Time: (30) minutes.

Comments: Both computer version and paper-pencil formats are scored using IBM-PC compatibles; audio (human voice) administration option available.
Author: Risk & Needs Assessment, Inc.
Publisher: Risk & Needs Assessment, Inc.
Cross References: For reviews by John R. Hays and by Robert Spies and Mark Cooper, see 14:332; for a review by Tony Toneatto of an earlier edition, see 12:338.

[2173]
SAQS Chicago Q Sort.

Purpose: Developed to "describe people to be sorted out in terms of continuum of applicability about self or others" to obtain a measure of similarity.
Population: College and adults.
Publication Dates: 1956–1957.
Acronym: SAQS.
Scores: Total score only.
Administration: Group.
Price Data: Available from publisher.
Time: (10–15) minutes.
Author: Raymond Corsini.
Publisher: Psychometric Affiliates.
Cross References: See T2:1358 (5 references) and P:232 (2 references); for reviews by William Stephenson and Clifford H. Swenson, Jr., see 5:103 (2 references).

[2174]
SASB [Structural Analysis of Social Behavior] Intrex Questionnaires.

Purpose: Designed to measure the patient's perceptions of self and others, based on trait x state x situational philosophy and Structural Analysis of Social Behavior.
Population: Psychiatric patients and normals.
Publication Dates: 1980–2000.
Acronym: SASB Intrex.
Scores: Pattern Coefficient Scores, cluster profiles, and weighted affiliation and autonomy scores for each of 3 areas: Interpersonal Transitive-Focus on Other, Interpersonal Intransitive-Focus on Self, Intrapsychic Introjection; 3 forms (short, medium, long), 6 subtests: Self (Best, Worst), He/I Present Tense (Best, Worst), She/I Present Tense (Best, Worst), Mother/I Past Tense, Father/I Past Tense, Mother with Father/Father with Mother Past Tense.
Administration: Individual or group.
Price Data, 2000: $120 (research use) or $160 (clinical use) per questionnaire and coding software package including all 3 forms of Intrex questionnaire (short, medium, long), electronic forms, questionnaire user's manual (2000, 56 pages), SASBWorks coding programs (Process, Content, Complex, Markov), and coding reference manual (2000, 59 pages); $80 (re-search use) or $120 (clinical use) per all 3 forms of Intrex questionnaire with electronic forms and questionnaire user's manual; $80 per all 4 SASBWorks coding programs with coding reference manual; $.20 (research use, $10 minimum) or $2 (clinical use, $20 minimum) royalty fee per administration; $25 per questionnaire user's manual; $15 per coding reference manual; miscellaneous specialized SASB coding programs also available (contact Benjamin@Xmission.com for details).
Time: (60) minutes for complete battery, short form.
Comments: PC systems with DOS or Windows 95/98/2000 and Microsoft Access2000, Excel (1997 version or later), and Word necessary to process SASBWorks coding programs.
Author: Lorna Smith Benjamin.
Publisher: University of Utah, Department of Psychology.
Cross References: See T5:1298 (1 reference); for a review by Scott T. Meier of an earlier edition, see 12:192; see also T4:1258 (2 references).

[2175]
SAT On-Campus Program (Institutional SAT I: Reasoning Test and SAT II: Subject Tests).

Purpose: To place students at the appropriate level of study in college, and/or to help determine admission status.
Population: Entering college freshmen.
Publication Dates: 1962–2001.
Scores: SAT I: Reasoning Test provides a Verbal and a Mathematics score on the College Board 200 to 800 scale. SAT II: Subject Tests provide total test scores on the College Board's 200 to 800 score scale, except for the English Language Proficiency Test that is on a score scale from 901 to 999. Some SAT II: Subject Tests also provide subscores.
Administration: Group or individual.
Tests: SAT I: Reasoning Test and SAT II: Subject Tests. Subject Tests include: English Language Proficiency; Literature; Writing; Mathematics Levels IC and Mathematics IIC; Biology, Biology E/M (Ecological/Molecular); Chemistry, Physics; Reading Language Tests in French, German, Hebrew, Italian, Latin, and Spanish; and Reading and Listening Language Tests in Chinese, French, German, Japanese, Korean, and Spanish.
Price Data: Available from publisher.
Comments: Available for local administration and scoring by higher educational institutions. The Institutional SAT tests are offered through the College Board's SAT On-Campus Testing Program. Institutional SAT I test answer sheets are scored locally with MicroScore software; Institutional SAT II test answer sheets are scored using clear scoring tem-

plates. The Institutional SAT II: Subject Tests were previously known as the College Placement Tests and the One-Hour Achievement Tests. The Institutional SAT I: Reasoning Test was previously known as the Scholastic Aptitude Test and SAT.

Author: Educational Testing Service.

Publisher: The College Board.

Cross References: See T5:1274 (2 references) and T3:507 (2 references); for a review by John R. Hills of the College Placement Tests, see 7:665.

[2176]
Scale for Assessing Emotional Disturbance.

Purpose: Designed to assist in "the identification of children who qualify for the federal special education category of emotional disturbance."

Population: Students ages 5-0 to 18-11.

Publication Date: 1998.

Acronym: SAED.

Scores, 7: Inability to Learn, Relationship Problems, Inappropriate Behavior, Unhappiness or Depression, Physical Symptoms or Fears, Socially Maladjusted, Overall Competence.

Administration: Individual.

Price Data, 2001: $86 per complete kit; $49 per manual (66 pages); $39 per 50 S/R forms.

Time: (10) minutes.

Comments: Should be "completed … by teachers or other school personnel who have had substantial contact with the student."

Authors: Michael H. Epstein and Douglas Cullinan.

Publisher: PRO-ED.

Cross References: For reviews by Sandra J. Carr and Gretchen Owens, see 14:333.

[2177]
Scale for the Assessment of Negative Symptoms.

Purpose: To assess negative symptoms of schizophrenia.

Population: Psychiatric inpatients and outpatients of all ages.

Publication Dates: 1981–1984.

Acronym: SANS.

Scores: 25 behavioral rating scores within 5 areas: Affective Flattening or Blunting, Alogia, Avolition-Apathy, Anhedonia-Asociality, Attention.

Administration: Individual.

Price Data: Available from publisher.

Foreign Language Editions: Available in Spanish, French, Italian, German, Portuguese, Japanese, Chinese, and Greek.

Time: [15–30] minutes.

Comments: May be used in conjunction with the Scale for the Assessment of Positive Symptoms (SAPS; 2178).

Author: Nancy C. Andreasen.

Publisher: Nancy C. Andreasen.

Cross References: See T5:2288 (85 references); for reviews by Suzanne King and Niels G. Waller, see 12:339 (75 references); see also T4:2325 (37 references); for information on an earlier edition, see 9:1069 (2 references).

[2178]
Scale for the Assessment of Positive Symptoms.

Purpose: "Designed to assess positive symptoms, principally those that occur in schizophrenia."

Population: Psychiatric inpatients and outpatients of all ages.

Publication Date: 1984.

Acronym: SAPS.

Scores: 35 behavior ratings within 5 areas: Hallucinations, Delusions, Bizarre Behavior, Positive Formal Thought Disorder, Inappropriate Affect.

Administration: Individual.

Price Data: Available from publisher.

Time: [15–30] minutes.

Comments: Intended to serve as a complementary instrument to the Scale for the Assessment of Negative Symptoms (SANS; 2177).

Author: Nancy C. Andreasen.

Publisher: Nancy C. Andreasen.

Cross References: See T5:2289 (69 references); for reviews by John D. King and Suzanne King, see 12:340 (44 references); see also T4:2326 (24 references).

[2179]
Scale for the Assessment of Thought, Language, and Communication.

Purpose: Designed to assess clinical and pathological characteristics of language behavior.

Population: Manics, depressives, and schizophrenics.

Publication Date: 1980.

Acronym: TLC.

Scores: 19 ratings: Poverty of Speech, Poverty of Content of Speech, Pressure of Speech, Distractible Speech, Tangentiality, Derailment, Incoherence, Illogicality, Clanging, Neologisms, Word Approximations, Circumstantiality, Loss of Goal, Perseveration, Echolalia, Blocking, Stilted Speech, Self-Reference, Global Rating.

Administration: Individual.

Price Data: Price data for materials including manual (19 pages) available from publisher.

Time: [45–60] minutes.

Author: Nancy C. Andreasen.

Publisher: Nancy C. Andreasen.

Cross References: See T5:2290 (2 references) and T4:2327 (4 references).

[2180]
Scale of Feelings and Behavior of Love: Revised.

Purpose: Designed to "identify the patterns of behavior and feelings people exhibit and experience in their love relationships."
Population: College and adults.
Publication Dates: 1973–1992.
Scores, 8: Verbal Expression of Affection, Self-Disclosure, Toleration of Loved Ones' Bothersome Aspects, Moral Support/Encouragement and Interest, Feelings Not Expressed, Material Evidence of Affection, Total Love Scale, Love Scale Index.
Administration: Group.
Price Data: Available from publisher.
Time: (30) minutes.
Comments: Separate answer sheets may be used; current edition now included in Innovations in Clinical Practice: A Source Book (Vol. II).
Authors: Clifford H. Swensen, Michele Killough Nelson, Jan Warner, and David Dunlap.
Publisher: Clifford H. Swensen.
Cross References: See T4:2328 (1 reference); for a review by H. Thompson Prout of an earlier edition, see 9:1072.

[2181]
Scale of Job-Related Social Skill Performance.

Purpose: Designed to assess the strengths and weaknesses of a student's social skill performance in various work settings.
Publication Date: [Undated].
Administration: Individual.
Price Data, 2000: $99 per complete kit including teaching guide and script, response form, and interpretation/scoring guide.
Authors: Michael Bullis, Vicki Nishioka-Evans, H. D. Bud Fredericks, and Cheryl D. Davis.
Publisher: James Stanfield Co., Inc.
a) SCALE OF JOB-RELATED SOCIAL SKILLS KNOWLEDGE.
Population: Ages 15–25.
Acronym: SSSK.
Scores: Total score only.
Time: (45) minutes.
Comments: Administered using a verbal role playing method.
b) SCALE OF JOB-RELATED SOCIAL SKILL PERFORMANCE.
Population: Ages 14–21.
Acronym: SSSP.
Scores: 6 scales: Positive Social Behaviors, Self Control, Personal Issues, Body Movements, Personal Appearance, Negative Social Behaviors.
Time: Administration time not reported.

[2182]
Scale of Marriage Problems: Revised.

Purpose: Designed to measure marital conflicts.
Population: Couples.
Publication Dates: 1975–1992.
Scores, 7: Problem-Solving, Childrearing, Relatives, Personal Care, Money, Outside Relationships, Total.
Administration: Group.
Price Data: Available from publisher.
Time: Administration time not reported.
Comments: Current edition now included in Innovations in Clinical Practice: A Source Book (Vol. II).
Authors: Clifford H. Swensen, Michele Killough Nelson, Jan Warner, and David Dunlap.
Publisher: Clifford H. Swensen.
Cross References: For reviews by Cindy Carlson and Delores D. Walcott, see 14:334.

[2183]
Scaled Curriculum Achievement Levels Test.

Purpose: Assesses individual and group achievement in mathematics computation, reading, and language usage.
Population: Grades 3–8.
Publication Date: 1992.
Acronym: SCALE.
Administration: Group.
Levels: 9 levels in each of 3 subtests: Mathematics Computation (M1-M9), Reading (R1-R9), Language Usage (L1-L9).
Price Data, 2002: $95 per complete kit including 6 reusable administration booklets (2 each for Mathematics Computation, Reading, and Language Usage), 10 class placement/record sheets; 30 answer forms (10 each for Mathematics Computation, Reading, and language Usage), and manual (135 pages); $15 per 100 class placement/record sheets; $47.50 per manual.
Authors: Victor W. Doherty and Gale H. Roid.
Publisher: Western Psychological Services.
a) MATHEMATICS COMPUTATION.
Scores: Total score only.
Price Data: $24.50 per 10 reusable administration booklets; $15 per 10 AutoScore™ answer forms.
Time: (20–25) minutes.
b) READING.
Scores: Same as *a* above.
Price Data: $34.50 per 10 reusable administration booklets; $15 per 10 AutoScore™ answer forms.
Time: Same as *a* above.
c) LANGUAGE USAGE.
Scores: Sames as *a* above.
Price Data: $31.50 per 10 reusable administration booklets; $15 per 10 AutoScore™ answer forms.
Time: (15–20) minutes.

Cross References: For reviews by Russell N. Carney and Robert K. Gable, see 12:341.

[2184]
Scales for Diagnosing Attention-Deficit/Hyperactivity Disorder.

Purpose: "To help identify children and adolescents who have attention-deficit/hyperactivity disorder (ADHD)."

Population: Ages 5-0 through 18-11.

Publication Date: 2002.

Acronym: SCALES.

Scores, 4: Inattention, Hyperactivity, Impulsivity, Total.

Administration: Individual

Forms, 2: Summary/School Rating Scale Form (SRS), Home Rating Scale Form (HRS).

Price Data, 2001: $84 per complete kit including examiner's manual (78 pages), 25 Summary/School Rating Scale forms, 25 Home Rating Scale forms, and storage box; $49 per examiner's manual; $24 per 25 Summary/School Rating Scale forms; $14 per 25 Home Rating Scale forms.

Time: Administration time not reported.

Comments: Completed by parents and teachers of target child; designed as part of a comprehensive ADHD assessment; identifies specific behavioral targets for intervention; allows for ratings on DSM-IV-TR criterion for ADHD.

Authors: Gail Ryser and Kathleen McConnell.

Publisher: PRO-ED.

[2185]
Scales for Predicting Successful Inclusion.

Purpose: Designed to identify students with disabilities for potential for success in general education classes.

Population: Ages 5–18.

Publication Date: 1997.

Acronym: SPSI.

Scores: 4 scales: Work Habits, Coping Skills, Peer Relationships, Emotional Maturity.

Administration: Group.

Price Data, 2001: $86 per complete kit including examiner's manual (47 pages) and 50 summary/response forms; $39 per 50 summary/response forms; $49 per examiner's manual.

Time: (5–10) minutes.

Comments: Ratings by teachers, parents, and/or assistants.

Authors: James E. Gilliam and Kathleen S. McConnell.

Publisher: PRO-ED.

Cross References: For reviews by David Gillespie and Joseph R. Manduchi, see 14:335.

[2186]
Scales for Rating the Behavioral Characteristics of Superior Students.

Purpose: Designed to aid teachers in the identification of gifted children.

Population: Population unspecified, developed from research with students in Grades 4–6.

Publication Date: 1976.

Acronym: SRBCSS.

Scores, 10: Learning, Motivational, Creativity, Leadership, Artistic, Musical, Dramatics, Communication (Precision, Expressiveness), Planning.

Administration: Group.

Price Data: Available from publisher.

Time: Administration time not reported.

Comments: Scales for rating by teachers.

Authors: Joseph S. Renzulli, Linda H. Smith, Alan J. White, Carolyn M. Callahan, and Robert K. Hartman.

Publisher: Creative Learning Press, Inc.

Cross References: See T5:2295 (9 references); for reviews by Edward N. Argulewicz and James O. Rust, see 9:1073 (1 reference).

[2187]
Scales of Cognitive Ability for Traumatic Brain Injury.

Purpose: To "provide a systematic method of assessing cognitive deficits associated with traumatic brain injury."

Population: Patients with acquired brain damage.

Publication Date: 1992.

Acronym: SCATBI.

Scores, 46: Perception and Discrimination (Sound Recognition, Shape Recognition, Word Recognition [no distraction], Word Recognition [with distraction], Color Discrimination, Shape Discrimination, Size Discrimination, Discrimination of Color/Shape/Size, Discrimination of Pictured Objects, Auditory Discrimination [real words], Auditory Discrimination [nonsense], Total); Orientation (Premorbid Questions, Postmorbid Questions, Total); Organization (Identifying Pictured Categories, Identifying Pictured Category Members, Word Associations, Sequencing Objects [size], Sequencing Words [alphabetical], Sequencing Events [time of year], Sequencing Events [pictured task steps], Sequencing Events [recall task steps], Total); Recall (Memory for Graphic Elements, Naming Pictures, Immediate Recall of Word Strings, Delayed Recall of Word Strings, Cued Recall of Words, Cued Recall of Words in Discourse, Word Generation, Immediate Recall of Oral Directions, Recall of Oral Paragraphs, Total); Reasoning (Figural Reasoning: Matrix Analogies, Convergent Thinking: Central Theme, Deductive Reasoning: Elimination, Inductive Reasoning: Opposites, Inductive Reasoning: Analogies, Divergent Thinking: Homographs, Divergent Thinking: Idioms, Divergent Thinking: Proverbs, Divergent Thinking: Verbal Absurdities, Multiprocess Reasoning: Task Insight, Multiprocess Reasoning: Analysis, Total).

Administration: Individual.

Price Data, 2001: $269 per complete kit; $54 per 25 record forms; $55 per stimulus card set; $69 per stimulus manual; $69 per examiner's manual; $29 per audiocassette.

Time: Administration time not reported.

Authors: Brenda Adamovich and Jennifer Henderson.

Publisher: PRO-ED.

Cross References: For reviews by Charles J. Long and Faith Gunning and by Deborah D. Roman, see 13:273.

[2188]
Scales of Early Communication Skills for Hearing-Impaired Children.

Purpose: "Designed to evaluate speech and language development of hearing-impaired children between the ages of two and eight years."

Population: Ages 2-0 to 8-11.

Publication Date: 1975.

Acronym: SECS.

Scores, 4: Receptive Language Skills, Expressive Language Skills, Nonverbal Receptive Skills, Nonverbal Expressive Skills.

Administration: Individual.

Price Data, 2002: $14.95 per manual (42 pages); $12 per 25 rating forms.

Time: [60] minutes (through observation).

Comments: Ratings by teachers.

Authors: Jean S. Moog and Ann E. Geers.

Publisher: Central Institute for the Deaf.

Cross References: See T5:2298 (3 references); for reviews by Vincent J. Samar and Marc Marschark and by E. W. Testut, see 12:342.

[2189]
Scales of Independent Behavior—Revised.

Purpose: "Designed to measure functional independence and adaptive functioning in school, home, employment, and community settings."

Population: Infants to adults, with or without developmental disabilities.

Publication Dates: 1984–1996.

Acronym: SIB-R.

Scores, 24: Full Scale (Gross-Motor Skills, Fine Motor Skills, Social Interaction, Language Comprehension, Language Expression, Eating and Meal Preparation, Toileting, Dressing, Personal Self-Care, Domestic Skills, Time and Punctuality, Money and Value, Work Skills, Home/Community Orientation), Problem Behavior Scale [optional] (Hurtful to Self, Unusual or Repetitive Habits, Withdrawal or Inatten-

tive Behavior, Socially Offensive Behavior, Uncooperative Behavior, Hurtful to Others, Destructive to Property, Disruptive Behavior).

Administration: Individual.

Forms, 3: Full Scale, Short Form, Early Development.

Price Data: Available from publisher.

Time: (45–60) minutes for Full Scale; (15–20) minutes for Short Form; (15–20) minutes for Early Development.

Comments: SIB-R in conjunction with the Woodcock-Johnson® Psychoeducational Battery—Revised can be used as a comprehensive diagnostic system for measuring adaptive behavior, problem behavior, cognitive ability, language proficiency, and achievement; can be administered either via interview or checklist; short and early development forms available as part of test kit; computerized scoring system available in Windows or Macintosh.

Authors: Robert H. Bruininks, Richard W. Woodcock, Richard F. Weatherman, and Bradley K. Hill.

Publisher: Riverside Publishing.

Cross References: For reviews by Gloria Maccow and Leland C. Zlomke, see 14:337; see also T5:2299 (7 references) and T4:2335 (6 references); for reviews by Bonnie W. Camp and Louis J. Heifetz of the earlier version, see 10:321.

[2190]
SCAN-A: A Test for Auditory Processing Disorders in Adolescents and Adults.

Purpose: Used to identify adolescents and adults who have auditory processing disorders and who may benefit from intervention.

Population: Ages 12 to 50.

Publication Dates: 1986–1994.

Acronym: SCAN-A.

Scores, 6: Filtered Words, Auditory Figure-Ground, Competing Words, Competing Sentences, Total Test, Competing Words Ear Advantage.

Administration: Individual.

Price Data, 2002: $129 per audiocassette complete kit including examiner's manual (1994, 69 pages), test audiocassette, and 12 record forms; $19 per 12 record forms; $60 per examiner's manual; $80 per test audiocassette; $129 per CD-ROM complete kit including examiner's manual, Test CD-ROM, and 12 record forms; $80 per Test CD-ROM; $160 per Scanware™-A 5.0.

Time: (20–25) minutes.

Comments: SCAN-A requires an audiocassette player, two sets of stereo headphones, and a "Y" adapter.

Author: Robert W. Keith.

Publisher: The Psychological Corporation.

Cross References: For reviews by William R. Merz, Sr., and Jaclyn B. Spitzer, see 13:275.

[2191]
SCAN-C: Test for Auditory Processing Disorders in Children—Revised.

Purpose: Designed to identify children who have auditory processing disorders.
Population: Ages 5-0 to 11-11.
Publication Dates: 1986–1999.
Acronym: SCAN-C.
Scores, 5: Filtered Words, Auditory Figure-Ground, Competing Words, Competing Sentences, Composite.
Administration: Individual.
Price Data, 2002: $149 per kit including 25 record forms, compact disc in a vinyl album, and examiner's manual (2000, 129 pages); $34 per 25 record forms; $58 per examiner's manual.
Time: (30) minutes.
Author: Robert W. Keith.
Publisher: The Psychological Corporation.
Cross References: See T5:2300 (1 reference); for a review by Sami Gulgoz of an earlier edition, see 11:341 (2 references).

[2192]
SCC Clerical Skills Series.

Purpose: Assess clerical skills needed in various public service positions.
Population: Job applicants.
Publication Dates: 1975–1976.
Scores: 6 tests in series: 361.1 Clerical Skills Series (Punctuation, Vocabulary, Filing, Reading Skills, Grammar, Spelling); 362.1 Clerical Skills Series (Name and Number Checking, Vocabulary, Reading Skills, Numerical Skills, Coding Part I, Coding Part II); 363.1 Clerical Skills Series (Name and Number Checking, Vocabulary, Filing, Coding Part I, Coding Part II); Oral Instructions; Typing Test; Dictation/Transcription.
Administration: Group.
Restricted Distribution: Restricted to public personnel agencies who have completed a Test Security Agreement and returned it to the publisher.
Price Data, 1994: $40 basic rental fee; $8.25 per test booklet (agency member); $8.50 per test booklet (non-agency member); $9.75 per manual (member); $30 per manual; $30 per set scoring fee plus $.25 per answer sheet.
Time: (5–87) minutes; varies by test.
Author: Selection Consultation Center.
Publisher: International Personnel Management Association.
Cross References: For a review by Lorraine D. Eyde, see 9:1074.

[2193]
The Scenotest: A Practical Technique for Understanding Unconscious Problems and Personality Structure.

Purpose: A projective instrument intended "to help very quickly assess emotional problems in children."
Population: Children and adolescents.
Publication Dates: 1971–1998.
Scores: Score information available from publisher.
Administration: Individual.
Price Data, 2001: $775 per complete test kit and manual (1998, 110 pages).
Time: Administration time not reported.
Comments: Material in the test kit consists of flexible human figures and accessories including animals, trees, symbolic figures, and items from everyday life.
Author: G. von Staabs (original edition) and Joseph A. Smith (translated from the German edition and adapted).
Publisher: Hogrefe & Huber Publishers.

[2194]
Schaie-Thurstone Adult Mental Abilities Test.

Purpose: Designed to "measure the mental abilities of adults."
Population: Ages 22–84.
Publication Date: 1985.
Acronym: STAMAT.
Scores: 7 scale scores: Recognition Vocabulary (V), Figure Rotation (FR), Object Rotation (OR, Form OA only), Letter Series (LS), Word Series (WS, Form OA only), Number Addition (N), Word Fluency (W).
Administration: Group.
Forms, 2: Form A (for "Adult," essentially the Thurstone Primary Mental Abilities Test Form II-17 (PMA) with new adult norms), Form OA (for "Older Adult," large-type version of the original plus two additional scales for adults over age 55).
Price Data: Price information available from publisher for Form OA expendable test booklets, Form A booklets, Form A answer sheets, Form A scoring key, profiles for both OA and A, manual (86 pages), and specimen set.
Time: (50–60) minutes.
Author: K. Warner Schaie.
Publisher: K. Warner Schaie (the author).
Cross References: See T5:2304 (4 references) and T4:2339)3 references); for a review by Eric F. Gardner, see 10:322.

[2195]
Schedule for Affective Disorders and Schizophrenia, Third Edition.

Purpose: "To record information regarding a subject's functioning and psychopathology."

Population: Adults.
Publication Dates: 1977-1988.
Acronym: SADS.
Administration: Individual.
Price Data, 2001: $.50 per SADS/SADS-L suggested procedures; $2.50 per SADS/SADS-L instructions and clarifications (1985, 24 pages).
Time: [30–120] minutes.
Authors: Robert L. Spitzer, Jean Endicott, Jo Ellen Loth (SADS-LB, SADS-LI), Patricia McDonald-Scott (SADS-LI), and Patricia Wasek (SADS-LI).
Publisher: Department of Research Assessment and Training.

a) SCHEDULE FOR AFFECTIVE DISORDERS AND SCHIZOPHRENIA.
Scores, 24: Current Syndromes (Depressive Mood/Ideation, Endogenous Features, Depressive-Associated Features, Suicidal Ideation/Behavior, Anxiety, Manic Syndrome, Delusions-Hallucinations, Formal Thought Disorder, Impaired Functioning, Alcohol or Drug Abuse, Behavioral Disorganization, Miscellaneous Psychopathology, GAS [worst period], Extracted Hamilton); Past Week Functioning (Depressive Syndrome, Endogenous Features, Manic Syndrome, Anxiety, Delusions-Hall-Disorganization, GAS rating, Extracted Hamilton, Miscellaneous Psychopathology); Past Other than Diagnosis (Social Functioning, Suicidal Behavior).
Price Data: $3 per SADS booklet; $.50 per SADS score sheet; $1.50 per SADS summary scales scores; $.50 per editing and coding instructions; $2.50 per instructions/clarifications.

b) SCHEDULE FOR AFFECTIVE DISORDERS AND SCHIZOPHRENIA LIFETIME (VARIOUS VERSIONS).
   1) *SADS-L.*
   Purpose: To record information regarding a subject's functioning and psychopathology; includes current disturbance.
   Price Data: $2 per SADS-L booklet; $.50 per SADS-L score sheet.
   2) *SADS-LB.*
   Purpose: To record information regarding a subject's functioning and psychopathology; includes current disturbance and additional items related to bipolar affective disorder.
   Price Data: $2 per SADS-LB booklet; $.50 per SADS-LB score sheet.
   3) *SADS-LI.*
   Purpose: To record information regarding a subject's functioning and psychopathology; specifies follow-up interval.
   Price Data: $2 per SADS-LI booklet; $.50 per SADS-LI score sheet.

Cross References: See T5:2305 (248 references); for reviews by Paul A. Arbisi and James C. Carmer, see 12:343 (414 references); see also T4:2340 (152 references).

[2196]
Schedule for Nonadaptive and Adaptive Personality.

Purpose: "Designed to assess trait dimensions in the domain of personality disorders."
Population: Ages 18 and older.
Publication Date: 1993.
Acronym: SNAP.
Scores: 34 scales: Trait (Mistrust, Manipulativeness, Aggression, Self-harm, Eccentric Perceptions, Dependency, Exhibitionism, Entitlement, Detachment, Impulsivity, Propriety, Workaholism), Temperament (Negative Temperament, Positive Temperament, Disinhibition), Diagnostic (Paranoid, Schizoid, Schizotypal, Antisocial, Borderline, Histrionic, Narcissistic, Avoidant, Dependent, Obsessive-Compulsive, Passive-Aggressive, Sadistic, Self-Defeating), Validity (Variable Response Inconsistency, True Response Inconsistency, Desirable Response Inconsistency, Deviance, Rare Virtues, Invalidity Index).
Administration: Individual or group.
Price Data, 2001: $55 per starter kit including 10 test booklets, 100 answer sheets, set of scoring keys, 25 profile forms, and manual for administration, scoring, and interpretation (92 pages); $10 per 10 test booklets; $15 per 100 answer sheets; $35 per set of 34 scoring keys; $5 per 25 profile forms (specify diagnostic scales or validity trait, and temperament scales); $15 per manual for administration, scoring, and interpretation; price data for scoring disks available from publisher.
Time: Administration time not reported.
Author: Lee Anna Clark.
Publisher: University of Minnesota Press, Test Division.
Cross References: For reviews by Lizanne DeStefano and Niels G. Waller, see 14:338; see also T5:2306 (1 reference) and T4:2341 (1 reference).

[2197]
A Schedule of Adaptive Mechanisms in CAT Response.

Purpose: "Designed to aid in qualitative evaluation of C.A.T. stories."
Population: Children.
Publication Date: [ca. 1963].
Scores: 12 categories: Defense Mechanisms (Reaction-Formation, Undoing and Ambivalence, Isolation, Repression and Denial, Deception, Symbolization, Projection and Introjection, Fear and Anxiety, Regression, Controls Weak or Absent), Identification (Adequate/Same-Sex, Confused/or Opposite Sex).

Administration: Individual.
Manual: No manual.
Price Data, 2001: $9 per 30 forms.
Time: Administration time not reported.
Comments: See Children's Apperception Test (456).
Author: Mary Haworth.
Publisher: C.P.S., Inc.

[2198]
The Schedule of Growing Skills: Second Edition.

Purpose: Designed as an assessment of child development.
Population: Ages 0–5 years.
Publication Dates: 1987–1996.
Acronym: SGS II.
Scores, 9: Passive Postural, Active Postural, Locomotor, Manipulative, Visual, Hearing and Language, Speech and Language, Interactive Social, Self-Care Social.
Administration: Individual.
Price Data, 1998: £120 per starter set including 10 child records, 50 profiles, user's guide (1996, 109 pages), and all stimulus materials; £40 per conversion kit including user's guide, picture book, shape formboard, fish formboard, pegboard and pegs, STYCAR distant vision card B and key card, pom pom, and baby rattle; £65 per 10 record forms; £40 per 50 profiles; £30 per reference manual.
Time: (20) minutes.
Authors: Martin Bellman, Sundara Lingam, and Anne Aukett.
Publisher: NFER-Nelson Publishing Co., Ltd. [England].
Cross References: See T5:2308 (1 reference); for reviews by Michelle M. Creighton and Scott R. McConnell and by Donna Spiker of an earlier edition, see 11:342.

[2199]
Scholastic Abilities Test for Adults.

Purpose: "Designed to be a general measure of scholastic accomplishment."
Population: Ages 16 through 70.
Publication Date: 1991.
Acronym: SATA.
Scores: 9 subtest scores: Verbal Reasoning, Nonverbal Reasoning, Quantitative Reasoning, Reading Vocabulary, Reading Comprehension, Math Calculation, Math Application, Writing Mechanics, Writing Composition, and 9 composite scores: Scholastic Abilities, General Aptitude, Total Achievement, Verbal, Quantitative, Reading, Mathematics, Writing, Achievement Screener.
Administration: Group.
Price Data, 2001: $159 per complete kit including 10 test books, 25 response booklets, 25 profile/exam-

iner record forms, and examiner's manual (102 pages); $51 per 10 test books; $39 per 25 response booklets; $24 per 25 profile/examiner record forms; $49 per examiner's manual.
Time: (60-120) minutes.
Authors: Brian R. Bryant, James R. Patton, and Caroline Dunn.
Publisher: PRO-ED.
Cross References: See T5:2309 (2 references); for reviews by Nambury S. Raju and Douglas K. Smith, see 12:344.

[2200]
School-Age Care Environment Rating Scale.

Purpose: Designed to assess the quality of center-based child care for school-aged children.
Population: Child care programs.
Publication Dates: 1980–1996.
Acronym: SACERS.
Scores, 7: Space and Furnishings, Health and Safety, Activities, Interactions, Program Structure, Staff Development, Total.
Administration: Group.
Price Data, 2002: $11.95 per rating scale (1996, 44 pages); $8.95 per 30 scoring sheets.
Time: (120) minutes.
Comments: An adaptation of the Early Childhood Environment Rating Scale (857); for use with center-based care (not family child care homes); respondents cue evaluators of the child-care environment; "Also includes a set of 6 supplementary items for centers that include children with special needs."
Authors: Thelma Harms, Ellen Vineberg Jacobs, and Donna Romano White.
Publisher: Teachers College Press.
Cross References: For reviews by Patricia B. Keith and Hillary Michaels, see 14:339.

[2201]
School Archival Records Search.

Purpose: ""Designed to overlay existing school records so that they can be coded and quantified systematically."
Population: Grades 1–12.
Publication Date: 1991.
Acronym: SARS.
Scores: 11 archival variables: Demographics, Attendance, Achievement Test Information, School Failure, Disciplinary Contacts, Within-School Referrals, Certification for Special Education, Placement Out of Regular Classroom, Receiving Chapter I Services, Out-of-School Referrals, Negative Narrative Comments.
Administration: Group.
Price Data, 2002: $35 per complete kit including user's guide, technical manual (86 pages), and 50 instrument packets.
Time: Administration time varies.

Authors: Hill M. Walker, Alice Block-Pedego, Bonnie Todis, and Herbert H. Severson.
Publisher: Sopris West.
Cross References: For reviews by John Crawford and Robert Fitzpatrick, see 13:275 (1 reference).

[2202]
School Assessment Survey.

Purpose: "Designed to measure schoolwide characteristics."
Population: Elementary through senior high school teachers and administrators.
Publication Date: 1985.
Acronym: SAS.
Scores, 9: Goal Consensus, Facilitative Leadership, Centralization of Influence: Classroom Instruction, Centralization of Influence: Curriculum and Resources, Vertical Communication, Horizontal Communication, Staff Conflict, Student Discipline, Teaching Behavior.
Administration: Group.
Price Data, 2001: $9.99 per kit including manual (69 pages).
Time: [30–40] minutes.
Authors: Bruce L. Wilson and William A. Firestone.
Publisher: Research for Better Schools, Inc.
Cross References: See T5:2312 (1 reference); for reviews by LeAnn M. Gamache and Dean Nafziger and Joanne L. Jensen, see 12:345 (1 reference); see also T4:2355 (1 reference).

[2203]
School Effectiveness Questionnaire.

Purpose: Assesses variables that have an impact on school effectiveness.
Population: Students, teachers, parents.
Publication Date: 1993.
Acronym: SEQ.
Scores, 11: Effective Instructional Leadership, Clear and Focused Mission, Safe and Orderly Environment, Positive School Climate, High Expectations, Frequent Assessment/Monitoring of Student Achievement, Emphasis on Basic Skills, Maximum Opportunities for Learning, Parent/Community Involvement, Strong Professional Development, Teacher Involvement in Decision Making.
Administration: Group.
Forms, 4: Level 1 Students (Elementary), Level 2 Students (High School), Teachers, Parents.
Price Data, 2002: $13 per 10 reusable questionnaires (Teacher Form); $33 per 10 reusable questionnaires (Level 1, Level 2, Parent Forms); $18 per manual (45 pages); $85 per 100 Type 2 machine-scorable answer documents; $22 per examination kit including manual, one each of all four questionnaires, and one answer document.
Time: (15–20) minutes.

Comments: Optional data analysis software available from publisher.
Authors: Lee Baldwin, Freeman Coney III, Diane Färdig, and Roberta Thomas.
Publisher: The Psychological Corporation.
Cross References: For reviews by Robert Fitzpatrick and Michael Harwell, see 13:276.

[2204]
School Environment Preference Survey.

Purpose: "Designed to measure the student's commitment to the set of attitudes, values and behaviors that have been characteristically fostered and rewarded in traditional school environments."
Population: Grades 4–12.
Publication Date: 1978.
Acronym: SEPS.
Scores, 5: Self-Subordination, Traditionalism, Rule Conformity, Uncriticalness, Structured Role Orientation.
Administration: Group.
Price Data, 1998: $9 per 25 SEPS forms (machine form for hand scoring or computer processing by EdITS) [$35.75 per 100, $143.75 per 500]; $14.75 per hand-scoring keys; $4 per manual (17 pages); $7.50 per specimen set.
Time: (10–15) minutes.
Author: Leonard V. Gordon.
Publisher: EdITS/Educational and Industrial Testing Service.
Cross References: See T5:2315 (1 reference) and T4:2360 (1 reference); for a review by Joan Silverstein, see 10:324.

[2205]
School Function Assessment.

Purpose: Designed to "measure a student's performance of functional tasks that support his or her participation in the academic and social aspects of an elementary school program."
Population: Grades K–6.
Publication Date: 1998.
Acronym: SFA.
Scores, 26: Participation, Task Supports (Physical Tasks Assistance, Physical Tasks Adaptations, Cognitive/Behavioral Tasks Assistance, Cognitive/Behavioral Tasks Adaptations), Activity Performance (Travel, Maintaining and Changing Positions, Recreational Movement, Manipulation with Movement, Using Materials, Setup and Cleanup, Eating and Drinking, Hygiene, Clothing Management, Up/Down Stairs, Written Work, Computer and Equipment Use, Functional Communication, Memory and Understanding, Following Social Conventions, Compliance with Adult Directives and School Rules, Task Behavior/Completion, Positive Interaction, Behavior Regulation, Personal Care Awareness, Safety).

Administration: Individual.
Price Data, 2002: $149 per complete kit including 25 record forms with 3 rating scale guides and user's manual (136 pages); $59 per 25 record forms with 3 rating scale guides.
Time: Untimed; (5–10) minutes per scale.
Comments: Ratings to be completed by an educational and therapeutic professional who is familiar with the child's typical performance.
Authors: Wendy Coster, Theresa Deeney, Jane Haltiwanger, and Stephen Haley.
Publisher: Therapy Skills Builders—A Division of The Psychological Corporation.
Cross References: For reviews by Wayne C. Piersel and William D. Schafer, see 14:340.

[2206]
School Leaders Licensure Assessment.

Purpose: To provide an assessment for states to use as part of the licensure process for school principals.
Population: Prospective school principals.
Publication Date: 1998.
Scores: Total score only.
Administration: Group.
Restricted Distribution: Secure instruments administered three time annually at centers established by the publiser.
Price Data, 1999: $400 examination fee.
Time: 360 minutes in three 120-minute modules.
Comments: State department of education for a particular state should be consulted to determine whether the School Leaders Licensure Assessment is required.
Author: Educational Testing Service.
Publisher: Educational Testing Service.

[2207]
School Readiness Checklist.

Purpose: Designed "to involve the parent in planning the child's educational program."
Population: Kindergarten entrants.
Publication Date: 1989.
Scores: Not scored.
Administration: Individual.
Manual: No manual.
Price Data, 2002: $10 per 25 checklists.
Time: [5–10] minutes.
Comments: Ratings by parents.
Author: Academic Consulting & Testing Service.
Publisher: Academic Consulting & Testing Service.

[2208]
School-Readiness Evaluation by Trained Teachers.

Purpose: To screen all school entrants to identify different levels of school-readiness.
Population: South African school beginners.
Publication Date: 1984.
Acronym: SETT.
Scores, 9: Language and General Development (Basic Level, Potential Level, Total), Physical Motor Development (Motor Ability, Integration, Total), Emotional Social Development (Sociability, Emotionality, Total).
Administration: Individual.
Price Data: Available from publisher.
Time: (30) minutes.
Comments: Parent Questionnaire for the Evaluation of School-Readiness and Nursery-School Questionnaire for the Evaluation of School-Readiness may be used in conjunction with this test.
Author: Marianne Joubert.
Publisher: Human Sciences Research Council [South Africa].

[2209]
School Readiness Test.

Purpose: Designed to test the student's readiness for first grade academics.
Population: End of kindergarten through first 3 weeks of Grade 1.
Publication Dates: 1974–1990.
Acronym: SRT.
Scores, 9: Vocabulary, Identifying Letters, Visual Discrimination, Auditory Discrimination, Comprehension and Interpretation, Number Knowledge, Handwriting Ability, Developmental Spelling Ability, Total.
Administration: Group.
Price Data, 2002: $59.45 per 35 test booklets, scoring key, class record sheet, and manual (1990, 26 pages); $6.75 per scoring key; $14.25 per manual; $3.45 per class record sheet; $21 per sample set.
Time: (90) minutes.
Comments: Subtest scores convert to "OK," "Probably Needs Help," "Definitely Needs Help"; total score converts to "Gifted Ready," "Superior Ready," "Average Ready," "Marginal Delay," "Short Delay," and "Long Delay."
Authors: O. F. Anderhalter and Jan Perney.
Publisher: Scholastic Testing Service, Inc.
Cross References: For reviews by Esther Stavrou Toubanos and Larry Weber, see 12:346; for a review of an earlier edition by Thorsten R. Carlson of an earlier edition, see 8:808.

[2210]
School Situation Survey.

Purpose: Designed to measure "school-related student stress."
Population: Grades 4–12.
Publication Date: 1989.
Acronym: SSS.
Scores, 7: Sources of Stress (Teacher Interactions, Academic Stress, Peer Interactions, Academic Self-

Concept), Manifestations of Stress (Emotional, Behavioral, Physiological).

Administration: Group.

Price Data, 2001: $25 per sampler set containing each test component: $125 per permission set including sampler set along with agreement that allows purchaser to reproduce up to 200 copies of the instrument in one year; $25 per 25 test booklets; $10 per scoring key.

Time: (10–15) minutes.

Authors: Barbara J. Helms and Robert K. Gable.

Publisher: Mind Garden, Inc.

Cross References: For reviews by Theodore Coladarci and LeAdelle Phelps, see 12:347; see also T4:2368 (1 reference).

[2211]
School Social Behavior Scales.

Purpose: Provides rating of both social skills and antisocial problem behaviors.

Population: Grades K–12.

Publication Date: 1993.

Acronym: SSBS.

Scores, 8: Social Competence (Interpersonal Skills, Self-Management Skills, Academic Skills, Total), Antisocial Behavior (Hostile-Irritable, Antisocial-Aggressive, Disruptive-Demanding, Total).

Administration: Individual.

Price Data, 2002: $35 per manual (58 pages); $19 per 20 test booklets.

Time: (5–10) minutes.

Comments: Rated by teacher or other school personnel.

Author: Kenneth W. Merrell.

Publisher: Assessment-Intervention Resources.

Cross References: For reviews by Stephen R. Hooper and Lesley A. Welsh, see 13:277 (2 references); see also T4:2369 (1 reference).

[2212]
School Social Skills.

Purpose: Developed to assess social skills exhibited in a school setting.

Population: Elementary school and junior high school and high school.

Publication Date: 1984.

Acronym: S3.

Scores: Ratings in 4 categories: Adult Relations, Peer Relations, School Rules, Classroom Behaviors.

Administration: Individual.

Price Data, 2002: $58 per complete kit including manual (25 pages); $38 per 50 rating scales; $25 per manual.

Time: (10) minutes.

Comments: Ratings by teachers.

Authors: Laura J. Brown, Donald D. Black, and John C. Downs.

Publisher: Slosson Educational Publications, Inc.

Cross References: For reviews by Beth D. Bader and William K. Wilkinson, see 12:348; see also T4:2370 (1 reference).

[2213]
Schubert General Ability Battery.

Purpose: Developed as a test of an individual's ability to understand and think in terms of words, numbers, and ideas.

Population: Grades 12–16 and adults.

Publication Dates: 1946–1965.

Acronym: SGAB.

Scores, 5: Vocabulary, Analogies, Arithmetic Problems, Syllogisms, Total.

Administration: Group.

Price Data, 2002: $63 per complete kit including 25 tests and manual (1965, 24 pages); $41 per 25 tests.

Time: 16(25) or 32(40) minutes.

Authors: Herman J. P. Schubert and Daniel S. P. Schubert (test).

Publisher: Slosson Educational Publications, Inc.

Cross References: See 7:386 (1 reference); for a review by William B. Schrader, see 5:382.

[2214]
SCID Screen Patient Questionnaire and SCID Screen Patient Questionnaire—Extended.

Purpose: "An Axis I symptoms and disorders screening tool."

Population: Psychiatric or general medical patients ages 18 or older.

Publication Dates: 1991–1999.

Acronym: SSPQ, SSPQ-X.

Scores, 6: Mood Disorders, Anxiety Disorders, Substance Use Disorders, Somatoform Disorders, Eating Disorders, Schizophrenia and Other Psychotic Disorders.

Administration: Individual.

Price Data, 2002: $395 per SCID Screen PQ for Windows including 3 report options: Summary of Responses, Concise Report, Long Report; SCID Screen PQ and SCID Screen PQ Extended Software Manual (1999, 108 pages), and PsychManager Lite CD Kit (PsychManager Lite CD, Quick Start Guide, Key Diskette); $45 per SCID Screen PQ for Windows Preview Version (3 uses); Price data available from publisher for SSPQ-X including 2 report options: Summary of Response, Diagnostic Report.

Time: (20) minutes SSPQ; (30–45) minutes for SSPQ-X.

Comments: SSPQ is an abbreviated computer-administered screening version of the Structured Clinical

Interview for DSM-IV (SCID-I) and an adaptation of the MiniSCID for DSM-IIIR; SSPQ-X is an extended adaptation of the SSPQ; System requirements: Pentium 120 MB hard drive, VGA or SVGA color monitor, 16 MB RAM, 3.5-inch floppy disk drive, CD-ROM drive, Windows 95 or higher.
Authors: Michael B. First, Miriam Gibbon, Janet B. W. Williams, and Robert L. Spitzer.
Publisher: Multi-Health Systems, Inc. and American Psychiatric Association.
Cross References: For reviews by Paul D. Werner and Thomas A. Widiger of the clinician version, see 14:373 (9 references); see also T5:2519 (56 references).

[2215]
Scientific Orientation Test.
Purpose: "Designed to measure a range of affective outcomes for students of science or science-related subjects."
Population: Students in school years 5 to 12.
Publication Date: 1995.
Acronym: S.OR.T.
Scores, 4: Interest in Science, Scientific Attitude, Attitude to School Science, Total.
Administration: Group or individual.
Price Data: Available from publisher.
Time: (40) minutes.
Comments: Includes 5 subtests yielding 13 subscores; formerly titled A Test of Interests.
Author: G. Rex Meyer.
Publisher: GRM Educational Consultancy [Australia].
Cross References: For reviews by Bruce G. Rogers and Herbert C. Rudman, see 14:341.

[2216]
SCL-90 Analogue™.
Purpose: A brief rating scale "for collecting observer data on a patient's psychological symptomatic distress."
Population: Adults and adolescents.
Publication Date: 1976.
Scores, 10: Primary Dimensional Scales (Somatization, Obsessive Compulsive, Interpersonal Sensitivity, Depression, Anxiety, Hostility, Phobic Anxiety, Paranoid Ideation, Psychoticism), Global Psychopathology Scale.
Administration: Group.
Price Data, 2002: $41.25 per 100 forms.
Time: (1–3) minutes.
Comments: Designed for use by health professionals without in-depth training or knowledge of psychopathology.
Author: Leonard R. Derogatis.
Publisher: NCS Assessments (Minnetonka).
Cross References: See T5:2326 (3 references).

[2217]
Screening Assessment for Gifted Elementary and Middle School Students, Second Edition.
Purpose: "Used to identify students who are gifted in academics and reasoning."
Population: Ages 5–14.
Publication Dates: 1987–2001.
Acronym: SAGES-2.
Scores, 3: Mathematics/Science, Language Arts/Social Studies, Reasoning.
Administration: Group.
Price Data, 2001: $179 per kit including 10 K–3 mathematics/science student response booklets, 10 K–3 language arts/social studies student response booklets, 10 K–3 reasoning student response booklets, 10 4–8 mathematics/science student response booklets, 10 4–8 language arts/social studies student response booklets, 10 4–8 reasoning response booklets, manual (2001, 128 pages), 50 K–3 profile/scoring sheets, 50 4–8 profile/response sheets, and a 4–8 scoring transparency; $14 per 10 K–3 mathematics/science student response booklets; $14 per 10 K–3 language arts/social studies student response booklets; $14 per 10 K–3 reasoning student response booklets; $14 per 10 4–8 mathematics/science student response booklets; $17 per 10 4–8 language arts/social studies student response booklets; $14 per 10 4–8 reasoning student response booklets; $49 per manual; $24 per 50 K–3 profile/scoring sheets; $4 per 50 4–8 profile/response sheets; $5 per 4–8 scoring transparency.
Time: (30–45) minutes.
Comments: This edition replaces both the earlier Screening Assessment for Gifted Elementary Students (T5:2328) and the Screening Assessment for Gifted Elementary Students—Primary (T5:2329).
Authors: Susan K. Johnsen and Anne L. Corn.
Publisher: PRO-ED.
Cross References: See T5:2328 (1 reference); for reviews by Lewis R. Aiken and Susana Urbina of an earlier edition, see 12:349; for a review by E. Scott Huebner of an earlier edition, see 10:327.

[2218]
Screening Kit of Language Development.
Purpose: Assesses preschool language development in order to identify language disorders/delays.
Population: Ages 2–5.
Publication Dates: 1983–2002.
Acronym: SKOLD.
Scores, 6: Vocabulary, Comprehension, Story Completion, Individual and Paired Sentence Repetition with Pictures, Individual Sentence Repetition without Pictures, Comprehension of Commands.
Administration: Individual.

Editions, 2: Standard English, Black English.

Price Data, 2002: $93 per complete kit including manual (37 pages), stimulus book, and 1 set of standard English scoring forms or 1 set of Black English scoring forms; $42 per 25 standard English scoring forms; $42 per 25 Black English scoring forms; $30 per stimulus materials and scoring guidelines; $26 per examiner's manual.

Time: (15) minutes.

Authors: Lynn S. Bliss and Doris V. Allen.

Publisher: Slosson Educational Publications, Inc.

Cross References: See T4:2381 (1 reference).

[2219]
Screening Test for Developmental Apraxia of Speech—Second Edition.

Purpose: Developed "to screen for the potential presence of developmental apraxia of speech in children."

Population: Ages 4-0 to 12-11.

Publication Dates: 1980–2001.

Acronym: STDAS-2.

Scores, 3: Prosody, Verbal Sequencing, Articulation.

Administration: Individual.

Price Data, 2001: $86 per complete kit; $39 per profile/examiner record forms; $49 per examiner's manual (2001, 37 pages).

Time: (10–15) minutes.

Author: Robert W. Blakeley.

Publisher: PRO-ED.

Cross References: See T5:2332 (2 references) and T4:2383 (3 references); for a review by Ronald K. Sommers of an earlier edition, see 11:347.

[2220]
Screening Test for Educational Prerequisite Skills.

Purpose: Developed to screen for skills needed for beginning kindergarten.

Population: Ages 4-0 to 5-11.

Publication Dates: 1976–1990.

Acronym: STEPS.

Scores: 5 areas: Motor Skills, Intellectual Skills, Verbal Information Skills, Cognitive Strategies, Attitudes.

Administration: Individual.

Price Data, 2002: $145 per complete kit including test materials (pictures, bears, pencil), 25 AutoScore™ forms, 25 AutoScore™ home questionnaires, and manual (1990, 68 pages); $38 per set of test materials; $49.95 per 25 AutoScore™ forms; $29.95 per 25 AutoScore™ home questionnaires; $39.50 per manual; $99.95 per 50-use IBM microcomputer disk; $15 per 100 microcomputer answer sheets for use with disk.

Time: (8–10) minutes.

Author: Frances Smith.

Publisher: Western Psychological Services.

Cross References: For reviews by John Christian Busch, M. Elizabeth Graue, and Jeffrey K. Smith, see 12:351.

[2221]
Screening Test for the Luria-Nebraska Neuropsychological Battery: Adult and Children's Forms.

Purpose: Screening tests for "predicting which individuals would probably show 'normal' or 'clinical' patterns if they were administered the appropriate form of the full Luria-Nebraska Neuropsychological Battery."

Population: Ages 8–12, 13 and older.

Publication Date: 1987.

Acronym: ST-LNNB-C, ST-LNNB-A.

Scores: Running total score.

Administration: Individual.

Forms, 2: Children's Form, Adult Form.

Price Data, 2002: $139.50 per complete set including 25 administration and scoring booklets for children, 25 administration and scoring booklets for adults, set of stimulus cards, and manual; $27 per 25 administration and scoring booklets (specify adult or children's form); $48.50 per set of stimulus cards; $48 per manual.

Time: (20) minutes.

Comments: For screening purposes only.

Author: Charles J. Golden.

Publisher: Western Psychological Services.

Cross References: For reviews by Arlene Coopersmith Rosenthal and W. Grant Willis, see 11:348.

[2222]
S-D Proneness Checklist.

Purpose: "Intended to be used for the measurement of depression and suicide-proneness."

Population: Depressed or suicidal clients.

Publication Dates: 1970–1972.

Scores, 3: Suicide, Depression, Total.

Administration: Individual.

Price Data, 2002: $8.25 per 25 rating forms; $5 per specimen set.

Time: (5) minutes.

Comments: Checklist completed by interviewer.

Author: William T. Martin.

Publisher: Psychologists and Educators, Inc.

Cross References: For a review by Charles Neuringer, see 8:664.

[2223]
Search Institute Profiles of Student Life: Attitudes and Behaviors.

Purpose: Designed to "assist ... communities in measuring 40 developmental assets related to youth well-being."

Population: Grades 6–12.
Publication Dates: 1989–1996.
Scores: Total score only.
Administration: Group.
Price Data, 2001: $55 per 25 copies of survey; $700 per 80-page report.
Time: (50) minutes.
Author: Search Institute.
Publisher: Search Institute.
Cross References: For reviews by Ernest A. Bauer and Sharon Johnson-Lewis of an earlier edition, see 11:350.

[2224]
Secondary Level English Proficiency Test.

Purpose: "A measure of ability in two primary areas: understanding spoken English and understanding written English."
Population: Grades 7–12.
Publication Dates: 1980–1994.
Acronym: SLEP.
Scores, 3: Listening Comprehension, Reading Comprehension, Total.
Administration: Group.
Forms, 3: 1, 2, 3.
Price Data, 1998: $155 per complete set including 20 tests, 100 answer sheets, cassette tape, test manual (1997, 31 pages); $55 per 10 testbooks; $55 per 100 2-play answer sheets; $10 per cassette tape; $6 per test manual.
Time: 85(90) minutes.
Author: Educational Testing Service.
Publisher: Educational Testing Service.
Cross References: See T4:2393 (2 references); for reviews by Brenda H. Loyd and Michael J. Subkoviak, see 9:1090.

[2225]
Secondary-School Record.

Purpose: "Designed to present a summary of the student's academic record and summarize ratings by several teachers."
Population: Grades 9–12.
Publication Dates: 1941–1964.
Acronym: SSR.
Price Data: Available from publisher.
Time: Administration time not reported.
Comments: Transcript form only still available.
Author: National Association of Secondary School Principals.
Publisher: National Association of Secondary School Principals.
Cross References: See 4:516 (1 reference).

[2226]
Secondary Screening Profiles.

Purpose: Designed to help "identify pupils' individual strengths and weaknesses upon entry to sec-ondary school (junior high)," and also as a "standardised basis for screening special education needs."
Population: Junior high students, ages 10–13 years.
Publication Dates: 1995–1999.
Acronym: SSP.
Scores, 3: Reasoning, Reading, Mathematical.
Administration: Group.
Forms, 6: Reading, Forms A and B; Mathematics, Forms A and B; Reasoning, Forms A and B.
Price Data, 2002: £12.99 per 20 test forms; £16.99 per manual; £16.99 per specimen set.
Time: (20–40) minutes for each form.
Author: Centre for Research on Learning and Instruction, University of Edinburgh.
Publisher: Hodder & Stoughton Educational [England].

[2227]
The Seeking of Noetic Goals Test.

Purpose: Constructed "to measure the strength of motivation to find life meaning."
Population: Adolescents and adults.
Publication Date: 1977.
Acronym: SONG.
Scores: Total score only.
Administration: Group.
Price Data: Available from publisher.
Time: (10) minutes.
Comments: Complementary scale to the Purpose in Life Test.
Author: James C. Crumbaugh.
Publisher: Psychometric Affiliates.
Cross References: For reviews by Brenda Bailey-Richardson and Kevin L. Moreland, see 9:1092, see also T3:2124 (1 reference).

[2228]
Seguin-Goddard Formboards.

Purpose: Designed for testing spatial perception and motor coordination.
Population: Age 4 to adult.
Publication Date: [1911].
Scores: No scores.
Price Data, 2001: $185 per "flush" formboard; $340 per "raised" formboard.
Time: [5–10] minutes.
Comments: Used in the Halstead-Reitan Neuropsychological Test Battery (1114), Merrill-Palmer Scale of Mental Tests (1576), and Arthur Point Scale of Performance Tests (T5:182).
Authors: E. Seguin, H. H. Goddard, and N. Norsworthy.
Publisher: Stoelting Co.
Cross References: See T4:2397 (1 reference), T3:2125 (1 reference), and T2:578 (25 references).

[2229]
SELECT Associate Screening System—Internet Version.

Purpose: Designed to assist organizations in making effective employee selection decisions at the associate level.

Publication Dates: 1995–2002.

Acronym: SELECT.

Administration: Individual or group.

Price Data, 2002: $489 per one-time purchase of Initial System including units for 10–12 surveys, SELECT software, and user's guide (1998, 90 pages); $8–$22 per report.

Time: (20–45) minutes depending on survey.

Author: Bigby, Havis, & Associates, Inc.

Publisher: Bigby, Havis, & Associates, Inc.

Comments: A software platform that combines 17 screening tools validated for specific jobs or industries; web-based administered, scored, and interpreted; reports include results, recommendations, and interview questions.

a) SELECT FOR CONVENIENCE STORES.

Purpose: Designed to "measure characteristics and abilities important in most convenience store jobs."

Population: Applicants for positions in convenience stores.

Scores, 3: Provides Overall Performance, Integrity, and Retail Math indices with recommended ranges; subscale results for Energy, Frustration Tolerance, Self-Control, Accommodation to Others, Acceptance of Diversity, Positive Service Attitude; also includes self-report of Counterproductive Work Behaviors, Willingness to Do Common C-Store Tasks.

b) SELECT FOR CUSTOMER SERVICE.

Purpose: Designed as an associate-level pre-employment test for positions in customer service.

Population: Job Applicants for customer service positions.

Scores, 2: Provides Overall Performance and Integrity indices with recommended ranges; subscale results for Energy, Frustration Tolerance, Accommodation to Others, Acceptance of Diversity, and Positive Service Attitude; optional modules available for Counterproductive Behaviors, Retail Math.

c) SELECT FOR HEALTH CARE.

Purpose: Designed to "measure characteristics important in most health care provider jobs."

Population: Applicants for health care positions.

Scores, 2: Provides Overall Performance and Integrity indices with recommended ranges; subscale results for Energy, Frustration Tolerance, Accommodation to Others, Acceptance of Diversity, Positive Service Attitude, Accountability, Rapport, Empathy, Multi-Tasking.

d) SELECT FOR PRODUCTION AND DISTRIBUTION.

Purpose: Designed to "measure characteristics important to team-oriented manufacturing and distribution jobs."

Population: Applicants for production and distribution positions.

Scores, 2: Provides Overall Performance and Integrity indices with recommended ranges; subscale results for Energy, Frustration Tolerance, Acceptance of Diversity, Self-Control, Acceptance of Structure, Productive Attitude; optional module is available for Counterproductive Behaviors.

e) SELECT FOR ADMINISTRATIVE SUPPORT.

Purpose: Designed "as a personality-based survey for measuring characteristics that have been found to predict job effectiveness in administrative or clerical positions."

Population: Applicants for administrative support positions.

Scores, 2: Provides Overall Performance and Integrity indices with recommended ranges; subscale results for Energy, Multi-Tasking, Attention to Detail, Self-Reliance, Task Focus, Interpersonal Insight, Criticism Tolerance, Acceptance of Diversity, Self-Control, Productive Attitude.

f) SELECT FOR PERSONAL SERVICES.

Purpose: Designed "as a personality-based survey for measuring characteristics that have been found to predict job effectiveness for those employed in personal-care-type positions."

Population: Applicants for personal services positions (i.e., hairstylists/photographers).

Scores, 2: Provides Overall Performance and Integrity indices with recommended ranges; subscale results for Energy, Frustration Tolerance, Accommodation to Others, Acceptance of Diversity, Socially Outgoing, Positive Service Attitude.

g) SELECT FOR CALL CENTERS—INBOUND SERVICE.

Purpose: Designed to help screen applicants for inbound service positions at call centers.

Population: Applicants for inbound service positions at call centers.

Scores, 2: Provides Overall Performance and Integrity indices with recommended ranges; subscale results for Energy, Frustration Tolerance, Accommodation to Others, Acceptance of Diversity, Positive Service Attitude.

h) SELECT FOR CALL CENTERS—INBOUND SALES.

Purpose: Designed to help screen applicants for inbound sales positions at call centers.

Population: Applicants for inbound sales positions at call centers.

Scores, 2: Provides Overall Performance and Integrity indices with recommended ranges; subscale results for Energy, Frustration Tolerance, Accountability, Preference for Structure, Influence, Social Comfort, Productive Attitude.

i) SELECT FOR CALL CENTERS—OUTBOUND SALES.

Purpose: Designed to help screen applicants for outbound sales positions at call centers.

Population: Applicants for outbound sales positions at call centers.

Scores, 2: Provides Overall Performance and Integrity indices with recommended ranges; subscale results for Energy, Multi-Tasking Ability, Accountability, Assertiveness, Social Comfort, Diplomacy, Acceptance of Diversity, Frustration Tolerance, Criticism Tolerance, Productive Attitude.

j) SELECT FOR HELP DESK AGENTS.

Purpose: Designed to help screen applicants for help desk agents.

Population: Applicants for help desk agent positions.

Scores, 2: Provides Overall Performance and Integrity indices with recommended ranges; subscale results for Energy, Problem Solving, Multi-Tasking, Accountability, Assertiveness, Collaboration, Frustration Tolerance, Criticism Tolerance, Acceptance of Diversity.

k) SELECT FOR CONVENIENCE STORE MANAGERS.

Purpose: Designed to help identify people who will manage a small team of associates to serve and sell to customers in convenience stores and gas stations.

Population: Applicants for convenience store management positions.

Scores, 3: Provides Overall Performance, Integrity, and Retail Math indices with recommended ranges: subscale results for Positive Sales Attitude, Leadership, Persuasiveness, Energy, Good Judgment, Organization and Attention to Detail, Frustration Tolerance.

l) SELECT FOR RETAIL SALES ASSOCIATES.

Purpose: Designed to help identify people who enjoy selling and dealing with customers in a retail store.

Population: Applicants for retail sales positions in a retail store.

Scores, 3: Provides Overall Performance, Integrity, and Retail Math indices with recommended ranges; subscale results for Positive Sales Attitude, Persuasiveness, Energy, Initiative, Good Judgment, Frustration Tolerance.

m) SELECT FOR RETAIL CLERK/CASHIERS.

Purpose: Designed to help identify people who enjoy serving others in a retail store in positions where active selling is not required.

Population: Applicants for clerk or cashier positions in a retail store.

Scores, 3: Provides Overall Performance, Integrity, and Retail Math indices with recommended ranges; subscale results for Energy, Frustration Tolerance, Accommodation to Others, Acceptance of Diversity, Positive Service Attitude.

n) SELECT FOR ENTRY LEVEL RETAIL MANAGERS.

Purpose: Designed to help identify people who can manage associates to serve and sell in small format stores or department managers in large format stores.

Population: Applicants for entry level retail management positions.

Scores: Provides Overall Performance, Integrity, and Retail Math indices with the recommended ranges; subscale results for Energy, Positive Sales Attitude, Leadership, Persuasiveness, Good Judgment, Organization and Attention to Detail, Frustration Tolerance.

o) SELECT FOR HOSPITALITY.

Purpose: Designed to help identify people who have a positive and engaging service attitude.

Population: Applicants for wait staff or host positions in restaurants, hotels, and other hospitality positions.

Scores, 2: Provides Overall Performance and Integrity indices with recommended ranges; subscale results for Energy, Frustration Tolerance, Accommodation to Others, Acceptance of Diversity, Positive Service Attitude, Socially Outgoing.

p) SELECT FOR LEASING AGENTS.

Purpose: Designed to help identify people who will be positive service providers and are able to influence people to lease or rent apartments.

Population: Applicants for leasing agent positions.

Scores, 3: Provides Overall Performance, Integrity, and Leasing Agent Math indices with recommended ranges; subscale results for Energy, Assertiveness, Positive Sales Attitude, Social Comfort, Accommodation to Others, Frustration Tolerance, Criticism Tolerance, Self-Reliance, Acceptance of Diversity.

q) SELECT FOR RECEPTIONISTS.

Purpose: Designed to identify people who are socially engaging and enjoy serving the needs of the customer.

Population: Applicants for receptionist positions.

Scores, 2: Provides Overall Performance and Integrity indices with recommended ranges; subscale results for Energy, Frustration Tolerance, Accommodation to Others, Acceptance of Diversity, Positive Service Attitude, Socially Outgoing.
Cross References: For reviews by James T. Austin and Vicki S. Packman, see 14:344.

[2230]
[Selection Interview Forms].

Purpose: Designed to help interviewers obtain appropriate and valid information from job applicants.
Population: Business and industry.
Publication Date: 1962.
Scores: Ratings in 8 areas (Motivation for the Job, Adequacy of Work Experience, Supervisory Experience and Ability, Achievements at School, Vocational Adjustment, Family Background and Personal Adjustments, Wife's and Family's Role, Health) plus Total.
Administration: Individual.
Author: Benjamin Balinsky.
Publisher: Martin M. Bruce, Ph.D.
 a) SELECTION INTERVIEW FORM.
 Price Data, 2001: $13.75 per specimen set; $26.40 per package of forms.
 Time: [60-90] minutes.
 b) INTERVIEW RATING FORM.
 Price Data: $10.45 per specimen set; $19.80 per package of forms.
 Time: [15] minutes.

[2231]
Self-Assessment in Writing Skills.

Purpose: Developed as a self-assessment tool to assess writing skills.
Population: Clerical, managerial, and sales employees.
Publication Date: 1990.
Scores, 3: Content and Style, Organization and Format, Total.
Administration: Group or individual.
Price Data: Price information available from publisher for complete kit including 20 inventories, 20 scoring sheets for part 1, and 20 scoring sheets for part 2.
Time: [90–120] minutes.
Comments: Self-administered, self-scored.
Author: Training House, Inc.
Publisher: Training House, Inc.
Cross References: For reviews by Gabriel M. Della-Piana and Stephen Jurs, see 12:352.

[2232]
Self-Awareness Profile.

Purpose: "This self-assessment provides insight into the basic personality attributes that influence the way we behave."
Population: Industry.

Publication Dates: 1980–1987.
Scores, 4: Dominance, Influence, Conformity, Evenness.
Administration: Individual or group.
Price Data: Price information available from publisher for complete sets including 16-item inventory, interpretation sheet, planning sheet, and 20 sets of cards containing profiles on 10 different personalities, to be sorted by participants ("most like me, next most," etc.).
Time: (80–100) minutes.
Author: Scott B. Parry.
Publisher: Training House, Inc.
Cross References: For a review by Timothy M. Osberg, see 11:353.

[2233]
Self-Concept Adjective Checklist.

Purpose: Developed to assess self-concept.
Population: Grades K–8.
Publication Dates: 1971–1972.
Acronym: SCAC.
Scores: Total score only.
Administration: Group.
Price Data, 2002: $15 per 25 rating checklists including manual (1972, 4 pages); $5 per specimen set.
Time: [10] minutes.
Author: Alan J. Politte.
Publisher: Psychologists and Educators, Inc.

[2234]
The Self-Concept and Motivation Inventory: What Face Would You Wear?

Purpose: To assess motivation and academic self-concept.
Population: Age 4–kindergarten, grades 1–3, 3–6, 7–12.
Publication Dates: 1967–1977.
Acronym: SCAMIN.
Administration: Group.
Price Data: Not available.
Authors: Norman J. Milchus, George A. Farrah, and William Reitz.
Publisher: Person-O-Metrics, Inc.
 a) PRE-SCHOOL/KINDERGARTEN FORM.
 Population: Age 4–kindergarten.
 Scores, 14: Motivation (Goal and Achievement Needs, Achievement Investment, Self-Concept), Total (optional).
 Time: (25–30) minutes.
 b) EARLY ELEMENTARY FORM.
 Population: Grades 1-3.
 Scores, 5: Motivation (Goal and Achievement Needs, Achievement Investment), Self-Concept (Role Expectations, Self-Adequacy), Total (optional).
 Time: (25–30) minutes.

c) LATER ELEMENTARY FORM.
Population: Grades 3–6.
Scores, 10: Same as *b* above plus 6 optional Sources of Support Climate scores (Parents, Teachers, Peers and Siblings, Academic Self, Academic Activity Climate, School Climate), Total (optional).
Time: (30–35) minutes.
d) SECONDARY FORM.
Population: Grades 7–12.
Scores, 20: Same as *b* above plus 16 optional scores: Sources of Support Climate (Parents, Teachers, Peers, Academic Self, Physical and Social Self, Adults and Counselors, Academic Activity Climate, School Climate), Immediate-Intrinsic Orientation (Evaluated Competition, Tasks and Projects, Discovery and Creativity, Skills), Fulfillment Orientation (Aspiration, Cooperation and Conformity, Responsibility, Acceptance and Praise).
Time: (40) minutes.
Cross References: See T5:2355 (3 references) and T4:2408 (3 references); for a review by Lorrie Shepard, see 8:670 (4 references).

[2235]

Self Concept Scale, Secondary Level.

Purpose: To measure self concepts in basic living skills.
Population: Grades 7–12.
Publication Dates: 1980–1982.
Scores, 6: Decision Making, Interpersonal Relationships, Responsibility, Citizenship, Career Planning, Total.
Administration: Group.
Price Data, 2001: $35.80 per kit including manual (1982, 14 pages), 35 pupil record forms and profile sheets; $35.75 per 50 pupil record forms/profile sheets; $3.85 per manual; $1 per pupil for machine scoring.
Time: (15-20) minutes.
Author: Bob Percival.
Publisher: Dallas Educational Services.

[2236]

Self-Description Questionnaire—I, II, III.

Purpose: To measure aspects of self-concept.
Population: Ages 5–12, 13–17, 16–Adult.
Publication Dates: 1987–1992.
Acronym: SDQ.
Administration: Group.
Price Data, 1998: A$150 per complete kit including SDQ-I manual (1992, 171 pages), SDQ-II manual (1992, 118 pages), and SDQ-III manual (1989, 114 pages), master copy of each instrument, master copy of each scoring profile, and scoring program; A$120 per materials for two instruments; A$75 per materials for one instrument.

Comments: Self-report measures.
Author: Herbert W. Marsh.
Publisher: SDQ Instruments, Publication Unit [Australia].
a) SELF-DESCRIPTION QUESTIONNAIRE—I.
Population: Ages 8–12.
Scores, 11: Academic (Mathematics, Reading, General—School, Total), Non-Academic (Physical Abilities, Physical Appearance, Peer Relations, Parent Relations, Total), Global (General—Self, Total—Self).
Time: (15–20) minutes.
b) SELF-DESCRIPTION QUESTIONNAIRE—II.
Population: Ages 13–17.
Scores, 12: Academic (Mathematics, Verbal, General—School), Non-Academic (Physical Abilities, Physical Appearance, Same Sex Peer Relations, Opposite Sex Peer Relations, Parent Relations, Emotional Stability, Honesty/Trustworthiness), Global (General—Self, Total—Self).
Time: (20–25) minutes.
c) SELF-DESCRIPTION QUESTIONNAIRE—III.
Population: Ages 16–Adult.
Scores, 14: Academic (Mathematics, Verbal, Problem-Solving, General—Academic), Non-Academic (Physical Abilities, Physical Appearance, Same Sex Peer Relations, Opposite Sex Peer Relations, Parent Relations, Spiritual Values/Religion, Honesty/Trustworthiness, Emotional Stability), Global (General—Self, Total—Self).
Time: (20–25) minutes.
Cross References: See T5:2358 (17 references); for reviews by Jeffrey A. Atlas, Robert K. Gable, and Steven Isonio, see 13:280 (42 references); see also T4:2412 (10 references).

[2237]

Self-Directed Learning Readiness Scale.

Purpose: Assesses "learning preferences and attitudes towards learning, which result in readiness for self-directed learning."
Population: Age 14 and over.
Publication Dates: 1977–1982.
Acronym: SDLRS.
Scores: Total score only.
Administration: Individual or group.
Price Data, 2001: $4.95 each scale; quantity discounts available.
Time: [25] minutes.
Comments: A self-scoring form, entitled the Learning Preference Assessment, is available for use in workshops; an elementary form is available for Grades 3–7.
Author: Lucy M. Guglielmino.
Publisher: Guglielmino & Associates.
Cross References: See T5:2359 (2 references).

[2238]
Self-Directed Search, 4th Edition [Forms R, E, CE, and CP].

Purpose: A vocational inventory designed to identify "a person's particular activities, competencies, and self-estimates compared with various occupational groups."
Population: Ages 12 and above.
Publication Dates: 1970–1997.
Acronym: SDS.
Scores, 6: Realistic, Investigative, Artistic, Social, Enterprising, Conventional.
Administration: Group.
Editions, 4: Form R (Regular), Form E (Easy), Form CP (Career Planning), Form CE (Career Explorer).
Price Data: Available from publisher for kit (Form R) including manuals, 25 booklets and occupational finders, 25 "You and Your Career" booklets, 10 leisure activity finders, and 10 educational opportunities finders; for kit (Form E) including manuals, 25 assessment booklets, 25 job finders, and 25 "You and Your Job" booklets; for kit (Form CP) including manuals, 25 assessment booklets, 25 career options finders, and 25 exploring career options booklets; for kit (Career Explorer) including manual, teacher's guide, 35 self-assessment booklets, 35 careers booklets, and 35 Exploring Your Future with the SDS booklets; various combinations of components available in varied-priced kits; price information for additional versions and computer software also available from publisher.
Foreign Language Editions: "Adaptations available in the following countries/continents: Australia, Canada, China, Finland, France, Greece, Guyana, Hungary, Indonesia, Israel, Italy, Japan, Netherlands, New Zealand, Nigeria, Norway, Poland, Portugal, Russia, Saudi Arabia, Slovenia, South Africa, South America, Spain, Switzerland"; English-Canadian, Spanish, Vietnamese, and Braille editions also available.
Time: (30–50) minutes.
Comments: Self-administered, -scored, and -interpreted; computer software available; based on the Holland typology of vocational preferences.
Authors: John L. Holland (test and manuals), Amy B. Powell (manuals), and Barbara A. Fritzsche (manuals).
Publisher: Psychological Assessment Resources, Inc.
Cross References: For a review by Michael B. Brown, see 14:345; see also T5:2360 (13 references); for reviews by Joseph C. Ciechalski and Esther E. Diamond of an earlier edition, see 13:281 (48 references); see also T4:2414 (23 references); for reviews by M. Harry Daniels and Caroline Manuele-Adkins, see 10:330 (19 references); for a review by Robert H. Dolliver, see 9:1098 (12 references); see also T3:2134 (55 references); for a review by John O. Crites and excerpted reviews by Fred Brown, Richard Seligman, Catherine C. Cutts, Robert H. Dolliver, and Robert N. Hanson, see 8:1022 (88 references); see also T2:2211 (1 reference).

[2239]
Self-Directed Search—Second Australian Edition.

Purpose: Designed as an instrument "for students and adults wishing to explore their career options."
Population: Ages 15 and over.
Publication Dates: 1970–2001.
Acronym: SDS.
Scores: 4 scales: Activities, Competencies, Occupations, Summary.
Administration: Group or individual.
Price Data: Available from publisher.
Foreign Language and Other Special Editions: Spanish, Vietnamese, French, and Braille editions available.
Time: (50) minutes.
Authors: John L. Holland, Meredith Shears (Australian Manual), and Adrian Harvey-Beavis (Australian Manual).
Publisher: Australian Council for Educational Research Ltd. [Australia].

[2240]
Self-Esteem Index.

Purpose: "Designed to measure the way individuals perceive themselves."
Population: Ages 7-0 to 18-11.
Publication Dates: 1990–1991.
Acronym: SEI.
Scores, 5: Familial Acceptance, Academic Competence, Peer Popularity, Personal Security, Self-Esteem Quotient.
Administration: Group.
Price Data, 2001: $124 per complete kit including 50 student response booklets, 50 profile/record forms, and manual (1991, 51 pages); $39 per 50 student response booklets; $39 per 50 profile/record forms; $49 per examiner's manual.
Time: (30–35) minutes.
Authors: Linda Brown and Jacquelyn Alexander.
Publisher: PRO-ED.
Cross References: See T5:2361 (4 references); for reviews by E. Scott Huebner and by Ralph O. Mueller and Paula J. Dupuy, see 11:354.

[2241]
The Self-Esteem Inventory.

Purpose: Developed to examine an individual's self-esteem.
Population: Adolescents and adults.
Publication Date: 1995.

Scores: Total score only.
Administration: Group.
Manual: No manual.
Price Data: Available from publisher.
Time: Administration time not reported.
Author: Millard J. Bienvenu.
Publisher: Millard J. Bienvenu, Northwest Publications.

[2242]
Self-Esteem Questionnaire.

Purpose: Measures self esteem and satisfaction with self esteem.
Population: Ages 9 and over.
Publication Dates: 1971–1976.
Acronym: SEQ.
Scores, 2: Self-Esteem, Self-Other Satisfaction.
Administration: Group.
Price Data: Not available.
Time: (15–20) minutes.
Author: James K. Hoffmeister.
Publisher: Test Analysis & Development Corporation.
Cross References: See T4:2416 (3 references).

[2243]
The Self Image Profiles.

Purpose: To quickly assess self image and self esteem in children and adolescents.
Publication Date: 2001.
Acronym: SIP.
Administration: Group or individual.
Price Data, 2002: $93.71 per complete kit including Adolescent Profiles, Child Profiles, and manual (43) pages.
Author: Richard J. Butler.
Publisher: The Psychological Corporation Europe [United Kingdom].
    a) THE SELF IMAGE PROFILE FOR CHILDREN.
    Population: Ages 7–11.
    Acronym: SIP-C.
    Scores, 11: Positive Self Image, Negative Self Image, Sense of Difference, Self Esteem, Aspects of Self (Behaviour, Social, Emotional, Outgoing, Academic, Resourceful, Appearance).
    Time: (12–25) minutes.
    b) THE SELF IMAGE PROFILE FOR ADOLESCENTS.
    Population: Ages 12–16.
    Acronym: SIP-A.
    Scores, 14: Positive Self Image, Negative Self Image, Sense of Difference, Self Esteem, Aspects of Self (Expressive, Caring, Outgoing, Academic, Emotional, Hesitant, Feel Different, Inactive, Unease, Resourceful).
    Time: (9–17) minutes.

[2244]
Self-Motivated Career Planning Guide.

Purpose: To help the individual develop vocational objectives through self-administered exercises.
Population: High school and college and adults.
Publication Dates: 1978–1984.
Acronym: SMCP.
Scores: 7 pencil/paper exercises (Personal Orientation Survey, Education Summary, Career Experience Summary, Personal Career Life Summary, Career Strengths and Interests, Next Career Steps, Personal Development Summary) plus a 16PF personality assessment and interpretive report (Personal/Career Development Profile).
Administration: Group or individual.
Price Data, 2002: $25 per self-motivated Career Planning Guide (1984, 88 pages).
Time: (50–120) minutes per exercise.
Authors: Verne Walter and Melvin Wallace.
Publisher: Institute for Personality and Ability Testing, Inc.
Cross References: For reviews by Larry Cochran and Samuel Juni, see 11:355; for reviews by Robert H. Dolliver and Kevin W. Mossholder of an earlier edition, see 9:1099.

[2245]
Self Observation Scales.

Purpose: Designed as a measure of self-concept.
Population: Grades K–3, 4–6, 7–9, 10–12.
Publication Dates: 1974–1979.
Acronym: SOS.
Administration: Group.
Forms: 1 or 2 for each of 4 levels.
Price Data: Available from publisher.
Time: (20–30) minutes.
Comments: Publisher recommends use of local norms; self-report; interactive computer version of the SOS available.
Authors: A. Jackson Stenner and William G. Katzenmeyer.
Publisher: NTS Research Corporation [No reply from publisher; status unknown].
    a) PRIMARY LEVEL.
    Population: Grades K–3.
    Scores: 4 scales: Self Acceptance, Self Security, Social Maturity, School Affiliation.
    Forms, 2: A, C.
    Comments: Orally administered.
    b) INTERMEDIATE LEVEL.
    Population: Grades 4–6.
    Scores: 7 scales: Same as *a* above plus Social Confidence, Teacher Affiliation, Peer Affiliation.
    Forms, 2: A, C.
    c) JUNIOR HIGH LEVEL.
    Population: Grades 7–9.

Scores: 7 scales: Same as *a* above except include Self Assertion in place of Social Maturity.
d) SENIOR HIGH LEVEL.
Population: Grades 10–12.
Scores: 7 scales: Same as *c* above.
Cross References: See T4:2418 (2 references); see 9:1100 (3 references).

[2246]
Self Perception Inventory.

Purpose: Designed to determine subject's perceptions of self, how other perceive him/her, and perceptions others have of him/her.
Population: Ages 12 and over.
Publication Dates: 1967–1969.
Acronym: SPI.
Scores, 12: General Adjustment (Consistency, Self-Actualization, Supervision, Total), General Maladjustment (Uncommon Response, Rigidity-Dogmatism, Authoritarianism, Anxiety, Depression, Paranoia, Total), Time.
Administration: Group.
Price Data, 2002: $27.50 per 25 tests; $9 per 9 score keys; $6.75 per 25 answer sheets; $6.75 per 25 profile sheets; $40 per examiner's set including 10 tests, 25 answer sheets, 25 profile sheets, score keys, and manual (1969, 14 pages); $12 per specimen set.
Time: (5–20) minutes.
Author: William T. Martin.
Publisher: Psychologists and Educators, Inc.
Cross References: For additional information and a review by John R. Braun, see 8:674 (1 reference); see also 7:136 (3 references).

[2247]
Self-Perception Profile for College Students.

Purpose: To measure college students' self-concept.
Population: College students.
Publication Date: 1986.
Scores: 13 domains: Creativity, Intellectual Ability, Scholastic Competence, Job Competence, Athletic Competence, Appearance, Romantic Relationships, Social Acceptance, Close Friendships, Parent Relationships, Finding Humor in One's Life, Morality, Global Self-Worth.
Administration: Group.
Price Data: Available from publisher.
Time: 30(40) minutes.
Authors: Jennifer Neemann and Susan Harter.
Publisher: Susan Harter, University of Denver.
Cross References: See T5:2369 (12 references); for reviews by Robert D. Brown and Stephen F. Davis, see 11:357 (1 reference).

[2248]
Self-Perceptions Inventory [1999 Revision].

Purpose: To describe "the present affective dimension of children and adults primarily in regard to themselves and their relationships with others."

Publication Dates: 1965–1999.
Acronym: SPI.
Administration: Group.
Price Data, 2002: $20 per 25 forms; $25 per separate test manual (specify for Student Forms, Adult Forms, Teacher Forms, Nursing Forms, or Educational Leadership Forms [1999, 50 pages each]; $40 per composite manual (1999, 150 pages).
Foreign Language and Other Special Editions: Spanish, Italian, and French Editions available.
Time: (5–20) minutes per test.
Authors: Louise M. Soares and Anthony T. Soares.
Publisher: SOARES Associates.
a) STUDENT FORMS.
Population: Grades 1–12.
Scores: 11 scales: Self Concept, Ideal Concept, Reflected Self/Classmates, Reflected Self/Friends, Reflected Self/Teachers, Reflected Self/Parents, Reflected Self/Others, Perceptions of Others/Males, Perceptions of Others/Females, Student Self, Perceptions of Others/Students.
b) ADULT FORMS.
Population: Grades 9–12 and adults.
Scores: 11 scales: Self Concept ["masculine" first], Self Concept ["feminine" first], Ideal Concept, Reflected Self/Friends, Reflected Self/Teachers/Professors, Reflected Self/Parents, Reflected Self/Partners, Reflected Self/Others, Perceptions of Others, Student Self, Perceptions of Others/Students.
c) TEACHER FORMS.
Population: Student teachers and other instructors.
Scores: 7 scales: Self as a Teacher, Ideal as a Teacher, Self as a College Professor, Self as a Student Teacher, Self as an Intern, Reflected Self, Perceptions of Others/Teachers.
d) NURSING FORMS.
Population: Nurses and nursing students.
Scores: 5 scales: Self Concept, Self as a Nurse, Ideal as a Nurse, Reflected Self, Perceptions of Others/Nurses.
e) EDUCATIONAL LEADERSHIP.
Population: Administrators and Coordinators.
Scores: 9 scales: Self Concept, Self as an Educational Leader, Ideal Educational Leader, Self as an Educational Manager, Reflected Self/Leader, Reflected Self/Manager, Perceptions of Others/Leaders, Perceptions of Others/Managers, Ideal Educational Manager.
Cross References: See T4:2421 (1 reference); for a review by Janet Morgan Riggs of an earlier edition, see 9:1101; for a review by Lorrie Shepard of an earlier edition, see 8:673 (2 references). For reviews by Gerald E. DeMauro and Michael R. Harwell of an earlier edition of the Nursing forms, see 11:356.

[2249]
Self Profile Q-Sort.
Purpose: Designed to assess self-concepts of children.
Population: Grades 2–8.
Publication Dates: 1972–1974.
Acronym: SPQS.
Scores: No scores; examiners may develop their own criteria for evaluation of items.
Administration: Individual or group.
Price Data, 2002: $6.75 per 25 forms and manual (1972, 1 page); $4.50 per specimen set.
Time: [5–10] minutes.
Author: Alan J. Politte.
Publisher: Psychologists and Educators, Inc.
Cross References: For a review by Stanley E. Ridley, see 9:1102.

[2250]
Self Worth Inventory.
Purpose: "Helps respondents increase their understanding of self-worth and how it is developed."
Population: Adults.
Publication Date: 1990.
Acronym: SWI.
Scores, 8: Self, Family, Peers, Work, Projected Self, Self-Concept, Self-Esteem, Self-Worth.
Administration: Group.
Manual: No manual.
Price Data, 1993: $10 per inventory.
Time: Administration time not reported.
Comments: May be self-administered.
Author: Everett Robinson.
Publisher: Consulting Resource Group International, Inc.
Cross References: For reviews by Jayne E. Stake and Norman D. Sundberg, see 13:282.

[2251]
The Senior Apperception Technique [1985 Revision].
Purpose: A projective instrument to gather information on forms of depression, loneliness, or rage in the elderly.
Population: Ages 65 and over.
Publication Dates: 1973–1985.
Acronym: S.A.T.
Scores: No scores.
Administration: Individual.
Price Data, 2001: $22 per manual (1985, 12 pages) and set of picture cards.
Time: Administration time not reported.
Author: Leopold Bellak.
Publisher: C.P.S., Inc.
Cross References: For reviews by Paul A. Arbisi and Michael G. Kavan, see 13:283; see also T3:2148 (2 references); for a review by K. Warner Schaie of an earlier edition, see 8:676 (1 reference).

[2252]
Senior Aptitude Tests.
Purpose: Constructed "to measure a number of aptitudes of pupils . . . for the purpose of guidance and selection."
Population: Standards 8–10 in South African schools, college, and adults.
Publication Dates: 1969–1970.
Acronym: SAT.
Scores, 12: Verbal Comprehension, Numerical Fluency, Word Fluency, Visual Perception Speed, Reasoning (Deductive, Inductive), Spatial Visualization (2 Dimensional, 3 Dimensional), Memory (Paragraphs, Symbols), Psychomotor Coordination, Writing Speed.
Administration: Group.
Price Data: Available from publisher.
Time: 88(120) minutes.
Comments: Test materials in English and Afrikaans.
Authors: F. A. Fouche and N. F. Alberts.
Publisher: Human Sciences Research Council [South Africa].
Cross References: See T5:2373 (1 reference) and T4:2430 (1 reference).

[2253]
Senior South African Individual Scale— Revised.
Purpose: Measures general intelligence.
Population: Ages 7-0 to 16-11.
Publication Dates: 1964–1991.
Acronym: SSAIS-R.
Scores: 11 tests: Verbal (Vocabulary, Comprehension, Similarities, Number Problems, Story Memory, Memory for Digits), Nonverbal (Pattern Completion, Block Designs, Missing Parts, Form Board, Coding).
Administration: Individual.
Price Data: Available from publisher.
Time: Tests 1–9: (75) minutes; Tests 10–11: (10) minutes; Tests 3, 4, 7, and 8 (Abbreviated Scale): (45) minutes.
Comments: Developed for Afrikaans-speaking and English-speaking South African students.
Author: Human Sciences Research Council.
Publisher: Human Sciences Research Council [South Africa].
Cross References: See T3:2153 (1 reference) and 7:413 (1 reference).

[2254]
Sensory Evaluation Kit.
Purpose: "Designed to increase functional performance through the primary use of smell."

Population: Ages 2 to adult.
Publication Date: 1991.
Scores, 20: Motor, Tactile, Visual, Auditory, Olfactory, Gustatory, Problem Solving, Attention Span, Directions (2-Step, No Cuing), Interpretation of Signs/Symbols, Memory, Body Scheme (Body Parts, R/L Discrimination), Motor Planning, Stereognosis, Figure/Ground, Color Perception, Form Constancy, Position in Space.
Administration: Individual.
Price Data: Available from publisher.
Time: Administration time not reported.
Author: Bonnye S. Klein.
Publisher: Maddak, Inc.
Cross References: For reviews by J. Jeffrey Grill and Ellen Weissinger, see 13:284.

[2255]
Sensory Integration and Praxis Tests.

Purpose: Designed to assess several practic abilities, various aspects of sensory processing status, and behavioral manifestations of deficits in integration of sensory inputs from these systems.
Population: Ages 4–8.11.
Publication Date: 1989.
Acronym: SIPT.
Scores: 17 tests: Space Visualization, Figure-Ground Perception, Standing and Walking Balance, Design Copying, Postural Praxis, Bilateral Motor Coordination, Praxis Verbal Command, Constructional Praxis, Postrotary Nystagmus, Motor Accuracy, Sequencing Praxis, Oral Praxis, Manual Form Perception, Kinesthesia, Finger Identification, Graphesthesia, Localization of Tactile Stimuli.
Administration: Individual.
Price Data, 2002: $1,15 per set for mail-in scoring including all test materials, 25 copies of each consumable test form, 10 complete sets of all 17 computer-scored answer sheets with 10 transmittal sheets, manual (307 pages), and carrying case; $1,150 per set for PC scoring including all test materials, 25 copies of each consumable test form, 1 disk, 10 PC answer booklets, manual, and carrying case; $29.50 per one each of 17 test answer sheets and 1 transmittal sheet; $14.50 per transmittal sheet; $3.90 per individual test answer sheet; $255 per 10-use disk (PC with Microsoft Windows) with 10 PC answer booklets; $18.50 per 25 test booklets (specify Design Copying, Motor Accuracy, or Kinesthesia); $70 per manual; $132.50 per training administration video (VHS); $179.50 per training administration 2 CD-ROM set.
Time: (10) minutes or less per individual test.
Comments: Extension and revision of the Southern California Sensory Integration Tests (SCSIT) and the Southern California Postrotary Nystagmus Test (SCPNT); computer-scoring only; stopwatch capable of recording 1/10 seconds needed (available from publisher).
Author: A. Jean Ayres.
Publisher: Western Psychological Services.
Cross References: See T5:2377 (4 references); for a review by James E. Ysseldyke, see 12:353 (18 references); see also T4:2433 (9 references). For a review by Byron P. Rourke of the SCPNT, see 9:1157 (20 references); for information on the SCSIT, see 9:1158 (5 references) and T3:2244 (21 references); for reviews by Homer B. C. Reed, Jr. and Alida S. Westman of the SCSIT, see 8:875 (5 references); see also T2:1887 (18 references).

[2256]
Sensory Integration Inventory—Revised for Individuals with Developmental Disabilities.

Purpose: "Designed to screen for [occupational therapy] clients who might benefit from a sensory integration treatment approach."
Population: Developmentally disabled occupational therapy clients school aged to adults, including autism spectrum and PDD.
Publication Dates: 1990–1992.
Acronym: SI Inventory.
Scores: Item scores in each of 4 sections interpreted individually: Tactile, Vestibular, Proprioception, General Reactions.
Administration: Individual.
Price Data: Available from publisher.
Time: Administration time not reported.
Comments: A semistructured interview of a person who works/lives closely with the client (e.g., parent or therapeutic staff member); space also provided for qualitative comments.
Authors: Judith E. Reisman and Bonnie Hanschu.
Publisher: P.D.P. Press, Inc.
Cross References: For a review by William Verdi, see 14:346.

[2257]
Sensory Profile.

Purpose: "To measure a child's sensory processing abilities."
Publication Dates: 1999–2002.
Administration: Individual or group.
Levels, 2: Infant/Toddler Sensory Profile—Clinical Edition, Sensory Profile.
Price Data, 2002: $150 per software kit including user's manual (1999, 146 pages), e-record forms, and 1-year subscription; $105 per software stand-alone including 1-year subscription for e-record forms; $65 per manual; $45 per e-record forms including subscription renewal for 1-year.
Foreign Language Editions: Also available in Spanish.

Comments: Profiles completed by child's caregiver; can be administered and scored electronically using personal computer or PDA (Windows and Palm OS), contact publisher for details.
Publisher: The Psychological Corporation.

a) INFANT/TODDLER SENSORY PROFILE—CLINICAL EDITION.
Population: Birth to 36 months.
Publication Date: 2002.
Scores, 6: General Processing, Auditory Processing, Visual Processing, Tactile Processing, Vestibular Processing, Oral Sensory Processing.
Price Data: $119 per Infant/Toddler Sensory Profile complete kit including user's manual (2002, 21 pages), 25 English caregiver questionnaires, and 25 summary score sheets; $75 per user's manual; $31.50 per 25 caregiver questionnaires (English or Spanish); $16.50 per 25 summary score sheets.
Time: 15(25) minutes.
Comments: Ages birth to 6 months: 5 scores (General Processing, Auditory Processing, Visual Processing, Tactile Processing, Vestibular Processing).
Author: Winnie Dunn.

b) SENSORY PROFILE.
Population: Ages 3–10.
Forms, 2: Sensory Profile, Short Sensory Profile.
Scores, 23: 6 Sensory Processing categories (Auditory Processing, Visual Processing, Vestibular Processing, Touch Processing, Multisensory Processing, Oral Sensory Processing); 5 Modulation categories (Sensory Processing Related to Endurance/Tone, Modulation Related to Body Position and Movement, Modulation of Movement Affecting Activity Level, Modulation of Sensory Input Affecting Emotional Responses, Modulation of Visual Input Affecting Emotional Responses and Activity Level); 3 Behavioral and Emotional Responses categories (Emotional/Social Responses, Behavioral Outcomes of Sensory Processing, Items Indicating Thresholds for Response); 9 Factor Scores (Sensory Seeking, Emotionally Reactive, Low Endurance/Tone, Oral Sensitivity, Inattention/Distractibility, Poor Registration, Sensory Sensitivity, Sedentary, Fine Motor/Perceptual).
Time: (15–30) minutes.
Comments: 125-question profile.
Author: Winnie Dunn.

c) SHORT SENSORY PROFILE.
Purpose: "To help service providers in screening settings quickly identify children with sensory processing difficulties."
Population: Ages 5–10.
Acronym: SSP.

Scores, 8: Tactile Sensitivity, Taste/Smell Sensitivity, Movement Sensitivity, Underresponsive/Seeks Sensation, Auditory Filtering, Low Energy/Weak, Visual/Auditory Sensitivity, Total.
Time: (10) minutes.
Authors: Daniel N. McIntosh, Lucy Jane Miller, Vivian Shyu, and Winnie Dunn.

[2258]
Sentence Completion Series.

Purpose: Constructed as a "semiprojective method of gathering client information" for personality and psychodiagnostic assessment.
Population: Adolescents and adults.
Publication Dates: 1991–1992.
Acronym: SCS.
Scores: No scores.
Administration: Individual or group.
Forms, 8: Adult, Adolescent, Family, Marriage, Parenting, Work, Illness, Aging.
Price Data: Available from publisher for complete kit including manual and 15 of each form
Time: [10–45] minutes.
Comments: Forms may be administered alone or in any combination.
Authors: Larry H. Brown and Michael A. Unger.
Publisher: Psychological Assessment Resources, Inc.
Cross References: For reviews by Kevin L. Moreland and Paul D. Werner, see 14:347.

[2259]
Sentence Completion Test.

Purpose: Developed to assess examinee's feelings, urges, beliefs, attitudes, and desires.
Population: High school and college.
Publication Date: 1972.
Acronym: SCT.
Scores: 35 item scores in 6 areas: Self Concept, Parental Attitude, Peer Attitude, Need for Achievement, Learning Attitude, Body Image.
Administration: Group or individual.
Price Data, 2002: $8.25 per 25 tests; $6.75 per specimen set.
Time: [15] minutes.
Author: Floyd S. Irvin.
Publisher: Psychologists and Educators, Inc.
Cross References: See T5:2380 (11 references), T4:2434 (19 references), T3:2155 (9 references), and T2:1057 (5 references).

[2260]
Sentence Completion Tests.

Purpose: "These tests provide a projective technique for individuals to express in their own way their own unique feelings, behaviors, attitudes, assets, needs, problems, thoughts, opinions of self, relationships, likes, dislikes, moods, frustrations, inhibitions, fantasies, backgrounds, responses from others, desires, mistakes, habits, secrets, idiosyncrasies, dreams, attitudes toward the test, etc."

Publication Dates: 1989–1995.

Administration: Group.

Price Data, 2001: $10 per 20 tests; $95 for 2 copies of all tests and Lifetime License to copy for personal or institutional use.

Time: Administration time not reported.

Comments: Master List includes sentence completion stems and alternatives used in the development of all the tests.

Author: Allan Roe.

Publisher: Diagnostic Specialists, Inc.

a) GENERAL INCOMPLETE SENTENCES TEST.

Population: General including college, clinical, hospitalized, and private practice adults.

Acronym: GIST.

Foreign Language Editions: Spanish GIST is available.

b) SHORT INCOMPLETE SENTENCES.

Population: Adult and adolescent clients.

Acronym: SIS.

c) FULL INCOMPLETE SENTENCES TEST.

Purpose: To be used for courts, custody, and diagnostic decisions.

Acronym: FIST.

d) FULL I AM TEST.

Purpose: "Helpful for eliciting identity problems."

Acronym: FIAT.

e) KIDS INCOMPLETE SENTENCES TEST.

Population: Ages 5–12.

Acronym: KIST.

f) TEENAGE SENTENCE COMPLETION.

Population: Ages 13–19.

Acronym: TASC.

g) MARRIAGE INCOMPLETE SENTENCES TEST.

Population: Married couples.

Acronym: MIST.

h) RELATIONSHIP INCOMPLETE SENTENCES TEST.

Population: Any relationship.

Acronym: RIST.

i) FULL LENGTH ALCOHOL SENTENCE COMPLETION.

Population: Alcohol users.

Acronym: FLASC.

j) DRUG INQUIRY SENTENCE COMPLETION.

Population: Drug users.

Acronym: DISC.

k) TALKING HONESTLY AND OPENLY ABOUT OUR RELATIONSHIP.

Population: Sex offenders.

Acronym: THOR.

l) SEXUAL ABUSE SURVIVOR'S TEST.

Population: Sex abuse victim.

Acronym: SAST.

[2261]

Sequenced Inventory of Communication Development, Revised Edition.

Purpose: Designed as a diagnostic assessment to evaluate the communication abilities of normal and retarded children.

Population: Ages 4 months through 4 years.

Publication Dates: 1975–1984.

Acronym: SICD-R.

Administration: Individual.

Price Data, 2002: $390 per complete kit (includes instruction manual [1984, 79 pages], test manual [1984, 117 pages], 50 record booklets/profile forms, and over 100 items used in the test administration); $48 per 25 scales (Expressive and Receptive); $32.50 per instruction manual; $32.50 per test manual.

Foreign Language Editions: Cuban-Spanish edition available; Spanish translation included in test manual and separate Spanish-language forms with pictures are available.

Time: (30–75) minutes.

Comments: Some test accessories (e.g., paper, coins, and picture book) must be assembled locally.

Authors: Dona Lea Hedrick, Elizabeth M. Prather, and Annette R. Tobin, with contributions by Doris V. Allen, Lynn S. Bliss, and Lillian R. Rosenberg.

Publisher: Western Psychological Services.

a) RECEPTIVE SCALE.

Scores, 3: Awareness, Discrimination, Understanding.

b) EXPRESSIVE SCALE.

Scores, 4: Imitating, Initiating, Responding, Verbal Output.

Cross References: See T5:2382 (40 references) and T4:2438 (21 references); for reviews by Carol Mardell-Czudnowski and Mary Ellen Pearson, see 10:331 (6 references); for reviews by Barbara W. Hodson and Joan I. Lynch of the earlier edition, see 9:1109 (4 references); see also T3:2159 (4 references).

[2262]

Service Animal Adaptive Intervention Assessment.

Purpose: Constructed for "evaluating predispositions to and outcomes of service animal use."

Population: Occupational, physical, and recreational therapists, assistive technology professionals, and animal assisted therapy specialists.

Publication Date: 1998.

Acronym: SAAIA.

Scores, 5: Knowledge and Experience of Animals, Typical Activities/Skills, Personal/Social Characteris-

tics, Requirements of Service Animal Compared to Resources of Person, Total Predisposition Score.
Administration: Group or individual.
Price Data, 2001: $29.95 per complete kit including all assessments as masters for photocopying and manual (10 pages).
Time: (90–120) minutes.
Comments: Ratings by professionals; also includes qualitative information.
Author: Susan A. Zapf.
Publisher: The Institute for Matching Person & Technology, Inc.

[2263]
ServiceFirst.
Purpose: Constructed to measure "customer service orientation or potential."
Population: Employees in service-oriented positions.
Publication Dates: 1990–2001.
Scores, 5: Active Customer Relations, Polite Customer Relations, Helpful Customer Relations, Personalized Customer Relations, Total.
Administration: Group.
Price Data, 2001: $30 per test kit including sample test booklet, sample answer sheet, test manual (2001, 47 pages), administration and scoring manual, and demonstration administration and scoring manual; $10 per administrator's manual; $10 per reusable test booklet; scoring service $11.50 to $15 per applicant.
Time: (20) minutes.
Comments: Internet-based administration and scoring is available at www.peoplefocus.com; paper-and-pencil and PC administration also available with scoring via telephone or fax by publisher, or onsite with a DOS-compatible disk.
Author: Larry Fogli.
Publisher: People Focus.
Cross References: For reviews by Michael B. Bunch and Mary A. Lewis, see 14:348.

[2264]
Severe Cognitive Impairment Profile.
Purpose: Designed to measure and monitor the cognitive performance of patients previously diagnosed with dementia.
Population: Severely demented patients.
Publication Dates: 1995–1998.
Acronym: SCIP.
Scores, 9: Comportment, Attention, Language, Memory, Motor, Conceptualization, Arithmetic, Visuospatial, Total.
Administration: Individual.
Price Data: Available from publisher for complete kit including manual (1998, 67 pages), leather carrying case with secure lock, 25 record forms, and all other test materials.

Time: (30–45) minutes.
Author: Guerry M. Peavy.
Publisher: Psychological Assessment Resources, Inc.
Cross References: For reviews by Joan C. Ballard and Lawrence J. Ryan, see 14:349.

[2265]
The Severity and Acuity of Psychiatric Illness Scales—Adult Version.
Purpose: Designed to assess the severity and acuity of psychiatric illness in adult mental health service recipients.
Population: Adults.
Publication Date: 1998.
Scores, 6: Severity (Complexity Indicator, Probability of Admission, Total), Acuity (Clinical Status, Nursing Status, Total).
Administration: Individual.
Price Data, 2002: $75 per starter kit including training manual (52 pages), 10 reusable Severity item booklets, 25 Severity scale rating sheets, 10 reusable Acuity item booklets, and 25 Acuity scale rating sheets; $18 per 10 Severity scale item booklets; $15 per 25 Severity scale rating sheets; $18 per 10 Acuity scale item booklets; $15 per 25 Acuity scale rating sheets; $120per training manual.
Time: (5) minutes.
Comments: Computer versions available; two scales (Severity and Acuity) can be used separately or together; results to be used as an "integrated outcomes-management and decision-support system for assisting treatment decision-making"; ratings are done by caregivers about clients/patients.
Author: John S. Lyons.
Publisher: The Psychological Corporation.
Cross References: For reviews by Mark J. Atkinson and Roger A. Boothroyd, see 14:350.

[2266]
Sex-Role Egalitarianism Scale.
Purpose: "Developed to measure attitudes toward the equality of men and women."
Population: High school to adult.
Publication Date: 1993.
Acronym: SRES.
Scores, 6: Marital Roles, Parental Roles, Employment Roles, Social-Interpersonal-Heterosexual Roles, Educational Roles, Total.
Administration: Group or individual.
Price Data, 2001: $33.50 per examination kit including manual (1993, 58 pages), 10 question-and-answer documents, and 10 profile sheets; $26 per test manual; $38 per 25 Form B question-and-answer documents; $25 per 25 Form K Research Forms; $10–$12 (depending on volume) per 25 profile sheets; $11.50–$14.50 (depending on volume) per 25 Short Form BB

or KK Question-and-answer sheets; $29 per researcher's kit including one each of manual, Form B question-and-answer documents, Research Form, Form B profile sheet, and one each of Form BB and KK Short Forms.
Time: (25–35) minutes.
Comments: Two full forms, B and K; two abbreviated forms, BB and KK.
Authors: Lynda A. King and Daniel W. King.
Publisher: Sigma Assessment Systems, Inc.
Cross References: See T5:2389 (1 reference); for a review by Carol Collins, see 13:285.

[2267]

Sexometer.

Purpose: Designed to measure one's sex information.
Population: Adolescents and adults.
Publication Dates: 1974–1988.
Scores: Total score only.
Administration: Group.
Manual: No manual.
Price Data, 2002: $1 per scale.
Time: [20] minutes.
Comments: Supplementary article available.
Author: Panos D. Bardis.
Publisher: Donna Bardis.
Cross References: See 8:353 (1 reference).

[2268]

Sexual Adaptation and Functioning Test.

Purpose: Designed "as an aid in the planning of psychotherapeutic intervention techniques and to gain insight into an individual's sexual adaptation and sexual functioning."
Population: White adults ages 16 and over.
Publication Dates: 1985–1986.
Acronym: SAFT.
Scores: Total score only.
Administration: Individual.
Restricted Distribution: Distribution restricted to psychologists registered with the South African Medical and Dental Council.
Foreign Language Edition: Afrikaans edition available.
Price Data: Available from publisher.
Time: (90–100) minutes.
Comments: Projective test; self-administered using audiotaped instructions.
Author: Louise Olivier.
Publisher: Human Sciences Research Council [South Africa].

[2269]

Sexual Adjustment Inventory.

Purpose: "Designed to identify sexually deviate and paraphiliac behavior."
Population: People accused or convicted of sexual offenses.

Publication Date: 1991.
Acronym: SAI.
Scores: 13 scales: Test Item Truthfulness, Sex Item Truthfulness, Sexual Adjustment, Child Molest, Sexual Assault, Exhibitionism, Incest, Alcohol, Drugs, Violence, Antisocial, Distress, Judgment.
Administration: Group.
Forms, 2: Adult, Juvenile.
Price Data: Available from publisher.
Time: (35–40) minutes.
Comments: Both computer version and paper-pencil format are scored using IBM-PC compatibles.
Author: Risk & Needs Assessment, Inc.
Publisher: Risk & Needs Assessment, Inc.
Cross References: For reviews by Richard F. Farmer and Sheila Mehta, see 14:351.

[2270]

Sexual Communication Inventory.

Purpose: Designed to help couples develop their skills for communicating about sexual matters in their relationship.
Population: Premarital and marital counselees.
Publication Date: 1980.
Acronym: SCI.
Scores: Overall score.
Administration: Group.
Price Data, 1993: $.75 per inventory; $2 per manual (6 pages).
Time: (20) minutes
Author: Millard J. Bienvenu.
Publisher: Millard J. Bienvenu, Northwest Publications.
Cross References: For a review by Richard B. Stuart, see 9:1118.

[2271]

Sexual Violence Risk-20.

Purpose: Designed as a "method" (not a test or scale) of assessing an individual's risk for committing sexual violence.
Population: Individuals suspected to be at-risk for committing sexual violence.
Publication Dates: 1997–1998.
Acronym: SVR-20.
Scores: Not scored; ratings in five areas: Psychosocial Adjustment, Sexual Offenses, Future Plans, Other Considerations, Summary Risk Rating.
Administration: Individual.
Price Data, 1999: $44 per kit including manual (1998, 99 pages) and 50 coding sheets; $32 per manual; $19 per 50 coding sheets.
Time: Administration time not reported.
Comments: "Designed to assist evaluations of risk for sexual violence"; administration and coding by trained professionals only; rating done by the professional about a client/offender.

Authors: Douglas P. Boer, Stephen P. Hart, P. Randall Kropp, and Christopher D. Webster.
Publisher: British Columbia Institute Against Family Violence.

[2272]
Sexuality Experience Scales.

Purpose: To be used in sex counseling as an aid in interviewing, diagnosis of sexual dysfunction, and evaluation of therapy, as well as in research.
Population: Adults.
Publication Date: 1981.
Acronym: SES.
Scores: 4 scales: Sexual Morality, Psychosexual Stimulation, Sexual Motivation, Attraction to Marriage.
Administration: Group.
Editions, 2: Female, Male.
Price Data: Available from publisher.
Time: Administration time not reported.
Authors: J. Frenken and P. Vennix.
Publisher: Swets Test Publishers [The Netherlands].
Cross References: See T5:2396 (1 reference) and T4:2449 (2 references).

[2273]
SF-36 Health Survey.

Purpose: Designed as a "survey of general health concepts."
Population: Ages 14 and older.
Publication Dates: 1989–1993.
Acronym: SF-36.
Scores: 8 scales: Physical Functioning, Role-Physical, Bodily Pain, General Health, Vitality, Social Functioning, Role-Emotional, Mental Health.
Administration: Group.
Price Data: Available from publisher; administration and scoring software available from CogniSyst, Inc.
Time: Administration time not reported.
Author: John E. Ware, Jr.
Publisher: The Health Institute, New England Medical Center.
Cross References: For reviews by Ashraf Kagee and Nathaniel J. Pallone, see 14:352; see also T5:2397 (1 reference).

[2274]
Shapes Analysis Test.

Purpose: Designed as a test of spatial perception.
Population: Ages 14 and over.
Publication Date: 1972.
Acronym: SAT.
Scores, 3: 2-Dimensional, 3-Dimensional, Total.
Administration: Group.
Price Data, 2001: £21 per 19 booklets; £35 per 50 answer sheets; £10 per manual (20 pages); £15 per specimen set.
Time: 25(35) minutes.

Authors: A. W. Heim, K. P. Watts, and V. Simmonds.
Publisher: The Test Agency Limited [England].
Cross References: For a review by Charles T. Myers, see 8:1046 (2 references).

[2275]
Shapiro Control Inventory.

Purpose: Designed to "categorize, refine, and articulate a person's state of consciousness regarding control."
Population: Ages 14–88.
Publication Date: 1994.
Acronym: SCI.
Scores, 9: General Domain (Overall Sense of Control, Positive Sense of Control, Negative Sense of Control), Modes of Control (Positive Assertive, Positive Yielding, Negative Assertive, Negative Yielding), Domain-Specific Sense of Control, Overall Desire for Control.
Administration: Group or individual.
Price Data: Available from publisher.
Foreign Language Editions: Spanish, Japanese, and Polish editions under development.
Time: (20–30) minutes.
Author: Deane H. Shapiro, Jr.
Publisher: Behaviordata, Inc.
Cross References: See T5:2399 (1 reference); for reviews by Wesley E. Sime and Claudia R. Wright, see 13:286.

[2276]
Ship Destination Test.

Purpose: Constructed to measure "general reasoning."
Population: Grades 9 and over.
Publication Dates: 1955–1956.
Scores: Total score only.
Administration: Group.
Price Data: Available from publisher.
Time: 15(20) minutes.
Authors: Paul R. Christensen and J. P. Guilford.
Publisher: Charlotte Mackley [No reply from publisher; status unknown].
Cross References: See T5:2401 (1 reference) and T2:457 (13 references); for a review by William B. Schrader, see 6:500 (8 references); for a review by C. J. Adcock, see 5:383.

[2277]
Shipley Institute of Living Scale.

Purpose: "Designed to assess general intellectual functioning in adults and adolescents and to aid in detecting cognitive impairment in individuals with normal original intelligence."
Population: Ages 14 and over.
Publication Dates: 1939–1986.
Acronym: SILS.

Scores, 6: Vocabulary, Abstraction, Combined Total, Conceptual Quotient, Abstraction Quotient, Estimated WAIS or WAIS-R IQ.

Administration: Group.

Price Data, 2002: $105 per complete kit including 100 test forms, hand-scoring key, 2 AutoScore™ test forms, and manual (1986, 100 pages); $19.95 per hand-scoring key; $38.50 per 100 test forms; $42.50 per 25 AutoScore™ test forms; $47.50 per manual; $245 per 25-use IBM Shipley microcomputer disk (PC with DOS).

Time: 20 minutes.

Comments: Formerly called Shipley-Hartford Retreat Scale for Measuring Intellectual Impairment and Shipley-Institute of Living Scale for Measuring Intellectual Impairment.

Authors: Walter C. Shipley (test and original manual) and Robert A. Zachary (revised manual).

Publisher: Western Psychological Services.

Cross References: See T5:2402 (71 references) and T4:2453 (63 references); for a review by William L. Deaton, see 11:360 (56 references); see also 9:1122 (13 references), T3:2179 (64 references), 8:677 (39 references), and T2:1380 (34 references); for a review by Aubrey J. Yates, see 7:138 (21 references); see also P:244 (38 references), 6:173 (13 references), and 5:111 (23 references); for reviews by E. J. G. Bradford, William A. Hunt, and Margaret Ives, see 3:95 (25 references).

[2278]
Shoplifting Inventory.

Purpose: "Designed to evaluate people charged or convicted of shoplifting."

Population: Shoplifting offenders.

Publication Date: 1995.

Acronym: SI.

Scores: 9 scales: Truthfulness, Entitlement, Shoplifting, Antisocial, Peer Pressure, Self-Esteem, Impulsiveness, Alcohol, Drugs.

Administration: Group.

Price Data: Available from publisher.

Time: (35) minutes.

Comments: Both computer version and paper-pencil format are scored on IBM-PC compatibles.

Author: Risk & Needs Assessment, Inc.

Publisher: Risk & Needs Assessment, Inc.

Cross References: For reviews by G. Gage Kingsbury and Kwong-Liem Karl Kwan, see 14:353.

[2279]
Shorr Imagery Test.

Purpose: "Designed to elicit and score the degree of conflict in the visual images projected by the subject."

Population: College students and adults.

Publication Dates: 1974–1977.

Acronym: SIT.

Scores, 6: Item scores in 5 areas (Human, Animal, Inanimate, Botanical, Others) plus Total score for Conflict.

Administration: Individual.

Price Data: Available from publisher.

Time: (15–40) minutes.

Comments: For information for Group Shorr Imagery Test, see 1100.

Author: Joseph E. Shorr.

Publisher: Institute for Psychoimagination Therapy.

[2280]
Short Category Test, Booklet Format.

Purpose: A sensitive indicator of brain damage measuring an individual's ability to solve problems requiring careful observation, development of organizing principles, and responsiveness to feedback.

Population: Ages 15 and over.

Publication Dates: 1986–1987.

Acronym: SCT.

Scores: Total score only.

Subtests, 5: 1, 2, 3, 4, 5.

Administration: Individual.

Price Data, 2002: $175 per complete kit including 100 answer sheets, set of stimulus cards, and manual (1987, 40 pages); $115 per set of stimulus cards, 5 booklets (1986, 20 cards per booklet); $22.50 per 100 answer sheets; $45 per manual.

Time: (15–30) minutes.

Comments: Revision of the Halstead-Reitan Category Test.

Authors: Linda Wetzel and Thomas J. Boll.

Publisher: Western Psychological Services.

Cross References: See T5:2405 (1 reference); for reviews by Scott W. Brown and Hope J. Hartman, see 11:361.

[2281]
Short Employment Tests, Second Edition.

Purpose: "Measures verbal, numerical, and clerical skills."

Population: Adults.

Publication Dates: 1951–1993.

Acronym: SET.

Scores, 4: Verbal, Numerical, Clerical, Total.

Administration: Group or individual.

Forms, 4: 1, 2, 3, 4.

Price Data, 2002: $81 per 25 test booklets (specify test and form) including directions for administering, test booklets, and key; $26 per keys; $43 per examination kit including 1 booklet per test and manual (1993, 71 pages) (Form 1); $47 per examination kit (Forms 2, 3, 4); $285 per 100 test booklets (specify test and form) including directions for administering booklet and key; $45 per manual.

Time: 5(10) minutes.

Comments: Distribution of Form 1 restricted to banks that are members of the American Banking Association.
Authors: George K. Bennett and Marjorie Gelink.
Publisher: The Psychological Corporation.
Cross References: For reviews by Caroline Manuele-Adkins and by Bert W. Westbrook and Michael C. Hansen, see 13:287; see also T4:2456 (3 references); for reviews by Samuel Juni, Ronald Baumanis, and Leonard J. West of an earlier edition, see 9:1124 (1 reference); see also T3:2180 (1 reference); for reviews by Ronald N. Taylor and Paul W. Thayer, see 8:1037 (4 references); see also T2:2151 (6 references); for a review by Leonard W. Ferguson, see 6:1045 (9 references); for a review by P. L. Mellenbruch, see 5:854 (16 references).

[2282]
Short Tests of Clerical Ability.

Purpose: Designed to measure aptitudes and abilities in tasks common to various office jobs.
Population: Applicants for office positions.
Publication Dates: 1959–1997.
Acronym: STCA.
Administration: Individual or group.
Price Data, 2002: $73 per start-up kit including 25 test booklets and examiner's manual (specify Arithmetic, Business Vocabulary, Checking, Coding, Directions—Oral and Written, Filing, or Language); $54 per 25 test booklets (specify test; quantity discounts available); price information available from publisher for Quanta Computer Administration and Scoring software (Windows); $73 per Quanta start-up kit including examiner's manual, 25 administrations and scoring, and oral directions sheet (does not include Quanta software).
Author: Science Research Associates.
Publisher: Reid London House.

   a) ARITHMETIC.
   Scores, 3: Computation, Business Arithmetic, Total.
   Time: 6 minutes.
   b) BUSINESS VOCABULARY.
   Time: 5 minutes.
   c) CHECKING.
   Time: 5 minutes.
   d) CODING.
   Time: 5 minutes.
   e) DIRECTIONS—ORAL AND WRITTEN.
   Time: 5 minutes.
   f) FILING.
   Time: 5 minutes.
   g) LANGUAGE.
   Time: 5 minutes.
Cross References: For reviews by Lorraine D. Eyde and Dean R. Malsbary, see 8:1039 (1 reference);

for reviews by Philip H. Kriedt and Paul W. Thayer, see 6:1046.

[2283]
Shortened Edinburgh Reading Test.

Purpose: Designed as a survey measure of children's reading skills in the upper primary school, and as a screening instrument to detect children who might need remedial help in reading.
Population: Ages 10-0 to 11-6.
Publication Date: 1985.
Scores, 5: Vocabulary, Syntax, Comprehension, Retention, General Reading Quotient.
Administration: Group.
Price Data, 2002: £15.99 per 20 test booklets; £16.99 per manual; £15.99 per specimen set.
Time: (40–45) minutes.
Author: The Godfrey Thomson Unit, University of Edinburgh.
Publisher: Hodder & Stoughton [England].
Cross References: For reviews by Douglas K. Smith and Betsy Waterman, see 14:354.

[2284]
Silver Drawing Test of Cognition and Emotion [Third Edition Revised].

Purpose: Designed as a nonverbal measure of ability in three areas of cognition: sequential concepts, spatial concepts, and association and formation of concepts; and to screen for depression.
Population: Ages 5 and over.
Publication Dates: 1983–1998.
Acronym: SDT.
Scores, 5: Predictive Drawing, Drawing from Observation, Drawing from Imagination, Self-Image, Projection.
Administration: Individual or group.
Price Data, 2001: $10 per set of 10 test booklets, layout sheet, and scoring forms; $32 per manual (1996, 147 pages); $15 per manual entitled "Updating the Silver Drawing Test and Draw A Story Manuals" (1998, 32 pages).
Foreign Language Edition: Brazilian translation and standardization available.
Time: (12–15) minutes.
Comments: Revision of Silver Drawing Test of Cognitive Skills and Adjustment.
Author: Rawley Silver.
Publisher: Ablin Press Distributors.
Cross References: For reviews by Terry Overton and Janet V. Smith, see 14:355; see also T4:2462 (1 reference); for reviews by Kevin D. Crehan and Annie W. Ward of an earlier edition, see 11:362; for reviews by Clinton I. Chase and David J. Mealor of the original edition, see 10:333.

[2285]
Singer-Loomis Type Deployment Inventory.

Purpose: Designed to assess "personality factors that may help an individual in self-understanding and in utilizing skills, talents, and abilities, so as to better deal with interactions between oneself and the environment."
Population: High school and college and adults.
Publication Dates: 1984–1997.
Acronym: SL-TDI.
Scores: Profile of 8 scores: Introverted, Extroverted for each of 4 functions (Thinking, Feeling, Sensing, Intuition), plus Extraversion, Introversion, Judging, Perceiving.
Administration: Group.
Price Data: Available from publisher.
Time: (30–40) minutes.
Comments: Self-report type profile based on Jung's typology.
Authors: June Singer, Mary Loomis, Elizabeth Kirkhart (revision), and Larry Kirkhart (revision).
Publisher: Moving Boundaries, Inc.
Cross References: For reviews by Joni R. Hays and Kevin Lanning, see 14:356; for a review by Richard B. Stuart of the earlier edition, see 10:334 (1 reference).

[2286]
SIPOAS: Styles in Perception of Affect Scale.

Purpose: "A personality scale measuring the ability to respond to the subtle, changing physical cues arising from the body's response to perceptions, memories and associations, and to integrate them into optimal emotional and behavioral response."
Population: Age 18 to adult.
Publication Date: 1995.
Acronym: SIPOAS.
Scores: 3 styles: BB (Based on Body), EE (Emphasis on Evaluation), LL (Looking to Logic).
Administration: Individual or group.
Price Data, 2002: $20 per 25 copies of questionnaire including scoring template with scoring criteria (can be mechanically reproduced); $22.50 per complete research report (203 pages); $14.25 per administration/interpretation manual.
Time: [20–30] minutes.
Comments: Paper-and-pencil test; may be completed by the individual or administered by an assistant to an individual or group. Can be used to determine predominant styles, which is helpful for selecting the optimal psychotherapeutic modality and for predicting therapy outcome. Also has application in marital therapy and in personnel and organizational decision making, and may have application in legal justice settings such as jury selection, witness coaching, child custody and probation/parole issues.
Author: Michael Bernet.
Publisher: Institute for Somat Awareness.

Cross References: For reviews by Brian F. Bolton and S. Alvin Leung, see 14:357.

[2287]
Situational Attitude Scale.

Purpose: "Measures the attitudes of whites toward blacks."
Population: College and adults.
Publication Dates: c1969–1972.
Acronym: SAS.
Scores, 11: 10 situation scores, Total.
Administration: Group.
Forms, 2: A, B.
Price Data: Available from publisher.
Time: Untimed.
Authors: William E. Sedlacek and Glenwood C. Brooks, Jr.
Publisher: University of Maryland, University Counseling Center [No reply from publisher; status unknown].
Cross References: See T5:2413 (1 reference) and T4:2466 (2 references); for reviews by Ralph Mason Dreger and Marvin E. Shaw, see 8:678 (1 reference); see also T2:1381 (3 references).

[2288]
Situational Confidence Questionnaire.

Purpose: Designed to help clients identify high-risk drinking relapse situations.
Population: Adult alcoholics.
Publication Dates: 1987–1988.
Administration: Group.
Editions, 2: Computerized, print.
Authors: Helen M. Annis and J. Martin Graham.
Publisher: Centre for Addiction and Mental Health [Canada].
a) SITUATIONAL CONFIDENCE QUESTIONNAIRE.
Acronym: SCQ-39.
Scores, 9: Unpleasant Emotions/Frustrations, Physical Discomfort, Social Problems at Work, Social Tension, Pleasant Emotions, Positive Social Situations, Urges and Temptations, Testing Personal Control, Average.
Price Data, 2002: C$14.75 per 25 questionnaires; C$13.50 per user's guide (1988, 49 pages); C$25 per specimen set including user's guide and 25 questionnaires.
Time: (10–15) minutes.
b) ALCOHOL CONFIDENCE QUESTIONNAIRE.
Acronym: ACQ-16.
Scores: Total score only.
Time: Administration time not reported.
Comments: Brief version of the Situational Confidence Questionnaire; test items listed in SCQ user's guide.

Cross References: See T5:2414 (7 references); for reviews by Merith Cosden and Cecil R. Reynolds, see 13:288 (4 references); see also T4:2467 (1 reference).

[2289]
Situational Leadership® .

Purpose: Designed to identify successful leaders as "those who can adapt their behavior to meet the demands of their own unique situation."
Population: Managers, leaders, administrators, supervisors, and staff.
Publication Dates: 1973–1998.
Acronym: SL.
Administration: Group.
Manual: No manual.
Price Data: Available from publisher.
Time: Administration time not reported.
Comments: Related programs, Situational Leadership Simulator and Situational Leadership: Leveraging Human Performance, and Situational Leadership One-Day, also available.
Authors: Paul Hersey and Ron Campbell.
Publisher: Leadership Studies, Inc.

a) LEADER EFFECTIVENESS AND ADAPTABILITY.
Publication Dates: 1973–1998.
Acronym: LEAD.
Comments: Ratings of self and others.
Forms, 2: LEAD Self, LEAD Other.
b) READINESS STYLE MATCH.
Publication Date: 1979.
Acronym: RSM.
Scores: Ratings in 4 areas: Major Objectives, Readiness, Integration of Style and Readiness, Readiness Style Match Matrix.
Forms, 2: Staff Member Rating Form, Manager Rating Form.
c) READINESS SCALE.
Publication Date: 1977.
Acronym: MS.
Scores: 2 scores (Task Readiness, Psychological Readiness) for each of 5 major objectives or responsibilities.
Forms, 2: Self Rating Form, Manager Rating Form.
d) POWER PERCEPTION PROFILE.
Publication Date: 1979–1998.
Acronym: PPP.
Scores, 7: Coercive, Connection, Expert, Information, Legitimate, Referent, Reward.
Forms, 2: Perception of Self, Perception of Other.
e) LEADERSHIP SCALE.
Publication Date: 1980–1997.
Acronym: LS.

Scores: 2 scores (Total Task-Behavior, Total Relationship-Behavior) for each of 5 major objectives or responsibilities.
Forms, 2: Staff Member Form, Manager Form.
Cross References: For reviews by Bruce J. Eberhardt and Sheldon Zedeck, see 9:1133.

[2290]
Situational Preference Inventory.

Purpose: "Designed to assess individual styles of social interaction."
Population: Grades 9–16 and adults.
Publication Dates: 1968–1973.
Acronym: SPI.
Scores, 3: Cooperational, Instrumental, Analytic.
Administration: Group.
Price Data: Available from publisher.
Time: (10–15) minutes.
Comments: Self-administered.
Author: Carl N. Edwards.
Publisher: Carl N. Edwards.
Cross References: See T2:1382 (2 references).

[2291]
Six Factor Personality Questionnaire.

Purpose: Designed as a measure of six personality dimensions or broad factors.
Population: Adults.
Publication Date: 2000.
Acronym: SFPQ.
Scores, 6: Extraversion, Agreeableness, Independence, Openness to Experience, Methodicalness, Industriousness.
Administration: Individual or group.
Price Data, 2001: $56 per examination kit including manual (2000, 68 pages); $30.50–$34.50 per 25 test booklets; $20–$23 per Quick Answer Score sheets; $10–$12 per 25 profile forms, $34 per manual; $99 per SigmaSoft SFPQ for Windows (software); $48–$56 (depending on volume) per 10 machine-scorable answer sheets and coupons for basic report; $99 per software package including disks, software manual for Windows, test manual, and 10 coupons for computer reports.
Time: (20) minutes.
Authors: Douglas N. Jackson, Sampo V. Paunonen, and Paul F. Tremblay.
Publisher: Sigma Assessment Systems, Inc.

[2292]
Sixteen Personality Factor (16PF®) Questionnaire, Fifth Edition.

Purpose: Designed to measure personality traits.
Population: Ages 16 and over.
Publication Dates: 1949–2002.
Acronym: 16PF.

Scores, 24: 16 primary factor scores: Warm vs. Reserved (A), Abstract-Reasoning vs. Concrete-Reasoning (B), Emotionally Stable vs. Reactive (C), Dominant vs. Deferential (E), Lively vs. Serious (F), Rule-Conscious vs. Expedient (G), Socially Bold vs. Shy (H), Sensitive vs. Utilitarian (I), Vigilant vs. Trusting (L), Abstracted vs. Grounded (M), Private vs. Forthright (N), Apprehensive vs. Self-Assured (0), Open to Change vs. Traditional (Q1), Self-Reliant vs. Group-Oriented (Q2), Perfectionistic vs. Tolerates Disorder (Q3), Tense vs. Relaxed (Q4); 5 global factor scores: Extraverted vs. Introverted (EX), High Anxiety vs. Low Anxiety (AX), Tough-Minded vs. Receptive (TM), Independent vs. Accommodating (IN), Self-Controlled vs. Unrestrained (SC); 3 response style indices: Impression Management (IM), Infrequency (INF), Acquiescence (ACQ).

Administration: Group or individual.

Price Data, 2002: $115 per complete kit including 10 test booklets, 25 answer sheets, 25 individual record forms, scoring keys, administrator's manual (2002, 162 pages), and one prepaid processing certificate for a basic interpretive report (BIR); $18 per 10 test booklets; $28 per scoring keys and norms table; $15 per 25 answer sheets; $10 per 25 individual record forms; $44 per administrator's manual; $47 per trial packet including test booklet, answer sheet, administrator's manual, and certificate for a Basic Interpretive Report (BIR); $11–$30 for Basic Interpretive Report including profiles, scores, and descriptive comments; $7.50–$30 per Basic Score Report (includes scores only); $65 per technical manual (1994, 279 pages).

Time: (35–50) minutes.

Comments: Computer administration, interpretive reports, and scoring available.

Authors: Raymond B. Cattell, A. Karen S. Cattell, and Heather E. P. Cattell.

Publisher: Institute for Personality and Ability Testing, Inc.

a) 16PF BASIC SCORE REPORT.

Comments: Most concise 16PF report.

b) 16PF DATA SUMMARY REPORT.

Comments: Developed to provide standard output for researchers providing profiles on individual test takers as well as group average profile.

c) 16PF BASIC INTERPRETIVE REPORT.

Comments: A multipurpose, computerized interpretation of the 16PF providing the basic 16 personality scores and other information about characteristics relevant to personal and vocational counseling.

d) 16PF TEAMWORK DEVELOPMENT REPORT.

Comments: Intended to evaluate personality implications for performance in teamwork settings, for development of either individual and/or teams.

e) 16PF PERSONAL CAREER DEVELOPMENT PROFILE.

Comments: Facilitates consulting with clients on how their personal strengths can lead to personal and career success.

f) 16PF HUMAN RESOURCE DEVELOPMENT REPORT.

Comments: Assesses leadership and management potential by analyzing the personality dimensions associated with success in a broad range of managerial settings, and projecting how the examinee might be expected to function.

g) 16PF CATTELL COMPREHENSIVE PERSONALITY INTERPRETATION.

Comments: Provides 8–10 pages of comprehensive narrative covering a number of diverse areas of functioning and offering multi-trait combinations and interactions to provide an in-depth understanding of the client's whole personality. The narrative also discusses therapeutic considerations and approaches.

h) 16PF KARSON CLINICAL REPORT.

Comments: Provides 2–3 pages of descriptive narrative intended for professional use only. Contains sections describing basic areas of functioning, including: emotional adjustment, interpersonal issues, self-control, cognitive style, and areas to explore in couseling.

i) 16PF COUPLE'S COUNSELING REPORT.

Comments: A computer-interpreted report for paired 16PF profiles that examines the personality organization of two people, and compares the profiles; uses 16PF items plus additional questions about relationship history and satisfaction.

j) 16PF INDIVIDUALIZED STRESS MANAGEMENT PROGRAM.

Comments: An assessment and training package using 16PF data plus a stress evaluation inventory to yield a computer-generated, book-length report providing an individualized prescription plan for participants in a stress management program.

Cross References: See T5:2417 (43 references); for reviews by Mary J. McLellan and Pamela Carrington Rotto, see 12:354 (38 references); see also T4:2470 (140 references); for reviews of an earlier edition by James N. Butcher and Marvin Zuckerman, see 9:1136 (67 references); see also T3:2208 (182 references); for reviews by Bruce M. Bloxam, Brian F. Bolton, and James A. Walsh, see 8:679 (619 references); see also T2:1383 (244 references); for reviews by Thomas J. Bouchard, Jr. and Leonard G. Rorer, see 7:139 (295 references); see also P:245 (249 references); for a review by Maurice Lorr, see 6:174 (81 references); for a review by C. J. Adcock, see 5:112 (21 references); for reviews by Charles M. Harsh, Ardie Lubin, and J. Richard Wittenborn, see 4:87 (8 references).

16PF Adolescent Personality Questionnaire.

Purpose: Designed to "measure normal personality of adolescents, problem-solving abilities, and preferred work activities."

Population: Ages 11–22.

Publication Date: 2001.

Acronym: APQ.

Scores: 21 scales: Primary Personality Factor Scales (Warmth, Reasoning, Emotional Stability, Dominance, Liveliness, Rule-Consciousness, Social Boldness, Sensitivity, Vigilance, Abstractedness, Privateness, Apprehension, Openness to Change, Self-Reliance, Perfectionism, Tension), Global Factor Scales (Extraversion, Anxiety, Tough-Mindedness, Independence, Self-Control); plus a ranking of Work Activity Preferences (Manual, Scientific, Artistic, Helping, Sales/Management, and Procedural), Personal Discomfort (Discouragement, Worry, Poor Body Image, Overall Discomfort), "Getting in Trouble" (Anger or Aggression, Problems with Authority, Alcohol or Drugs, Overall Trouble), Context (Home or School), Coping/Managing Difficulty, Impression Management, Missing Responses, Control Responses, Predicted Grade Point Average.

Administration: Group or individual.

Price Data: Available from publisher.

Time: (65) minutes; untimed.

Comments: Computerized scoring and interpretive reports available (APQ Guidance Report and APQ Psychological Report); optional Life's Difficulties section provides an opportunity for the youth to indicate particular problems in areas known to be problematic for adolescents, making the APQ appropriate for screening and for introducing sensitive topics in a counseling setting.

Author: J. M. Schuerger.

Publisher: Institute for Personality and Ability Testing, Inc.

[2294]
16PF® Human Resource Development Report.

Purpose: Assesses an individual's management potential and style, provides insights into the individual's personality, and focuses on five management dimensions frequently identified in research on successful managers.

Population: Managerial candidates.

Publication Dates: 1982–1997.

Acronym: HRDR.

Scores: 5 management dimensions: Leadership, Interaction with Others, Decision-Making Abilities, Initiative, Personal Adjustment; 16 primary factor scores; 5 global factor scores.

Administration: Group or individual.

Price Data, 2002: $343 per introductory kit including test booklet, answer sheet, prepaid processing form to receive Human Resource Development Report, and user's guide (1997, 55 pages); $18 per 10 reusable test booklets; $15 per 25 machine-scorable answer sheets; $30 per user's guide; $16 to $30 per Human Resource Development Report available from publisher scoring service.

Time: 35–50 minutes.

Comments: Based on the Sixteen Personality Factor Questionnaire (2292); mail-in, fax, on-site software, and Net Assess internet delivery options available; can be generated from 4th or 5th edition of 16PF questionnaire.

Author: IPAT staff.

Publisher: Institute for Personality and Ability Testing, Inc.

Cross References: For reviews by S. Alvin Leung and Mary A. Lewis, see 11:169.

[2295]
16PF® Personal Career Development Profile.

Purpose: A consulting tool designed to provide insight into a person's behavioral and career strengths; "commonly used as part of personnel selection and job placement programs, career transition consulting, and career and personal life planning."

Population: Ages 16 and over.

Publication Dates: 1977–2000.

Acronym: PCDP.

Scores: 6 Narrative paragraphs: Problem-Solving Resources, Patterns for Coping with Stressful Conditions, Interpersonal Interaction Styles, Organizational Role and Work-Setting Preferences, Career Activity Interests, Personal Career Life-Style Effectiveness Considerations, plus 7 score summary pages.

Administration: Group or individual.

Parts, 3: Narrative Paragraphs, Occupational Data, Score Profile Pages.

Price Data, 2002: $41 per introductory kit with PCDP+ including Technical & Interpretive Manual (2000, 114 pages), test booklet, answer sheet, and prepaid processing form for one individual to receive both the PCDP and PCDP+; $38 per manual; $16 to $30 per PCDP report; $18 to $30 per PCDP+ report; $25 per Self-Motivated Career Planning Guide.

Foreign Language Edition: Australian English adaptation available; information regarding other non-English-language adaptations available from publisher.

Time: 35–50 minutes.

Comments: Computer-interpreted report of the Sixteen Personality Factor Questionnaire; PCDP+ is available as optional supplement to the PCDP; mail-in, fax, on-site software, and NetAssess internet delivery options available.

Author: Verne Walter.
Publisher: Institute for Personality and Ability Testing, Inc.
Cross References: For a review by Kevin M. Mossholder, see 9:939.

[2296]
16PF Select.

Purpose: A shorter version of the 16PF Fifth Edition personality measure, which was designed for personnel selection.
Population: Ages 16 and over.
Publication Dates: 1949–1999.
Acronym: 16PF Select.
Scores, 12: Warmth, Calmness, Dominance, Liveliness, Rule-Consciousness, Social Boldness, Trust, Imagination, Self-Assuredness, Openness, Self-Reliance, Organization.
Administration: Individual or group.
Price Data, 2002: $33 per introductory kit including manual (1999, 75 pages), dimension specification form, questionnaire/answer sheet booklet and prepaid mail-in report processing certificate; $30 per manual; $30 per 10 questionnaire/answer sheet booklets; $15 to $30 per report.
Time: (20) minutes (untimed).
Comments: A shorter version of the 16PF Fifth Edition (2292).
Authors: Raymond B. Cattell, A. Karen S. Cattell, Heather E. P. Cattell, and Mary L. Kelly.
Publisher: Institute for Personality and Ability Testing, Inc.
Cross References: For information about the complete 16PF see T5:2417 (43 references); for reviews of an earlier edition of the 16PF by Mary J. McLellan and Pamela Carrington Rotto, see 12:354 (38 references); see also T4:2470 (140 references); for reviews by James N. Butcher and Marvin Zuckerman, see 9:1136 (67 references); see also T3:2208 (182 references); for reviews by Bruce M. Bloxam, Brian F. Bolton, and James A. Walsh, see 8:679 (619 references); see also T2:1383 (244 references); for reviews of an earlier edition by Thomas J. Bouchard, Jr. and Leonard G. Rorer, see 7:139 (295 references); see also P:245 (249 references); for a review by Maurice Lorr, see 6:174 (81 references); for a review by C. J. Adcock, see 5:112 (21 references); for reviews by Charles M. Harsh, Ardie Lubin, and J. Richard Wittenborn, see 4:87 (8 references).

[2297]
Skills and Attributes Inventory.

Purpose: Assesses the relative importance of job-related skills and attributes for a position as well as the degree to which an individual possesses those skills and attributes.
Population: Non-management positions.
Publication Dates: 1976–1979.

Acronym: SAI.
Scores, 13: General Functioning Intelligence, Visual Acuity, Visual and Coordination Skills, Physical Coordination, Mechanical Skills, Graphic and Clerical Skills, General Clerical Skills, Leadership Ability, Tolerance in Interpersonal Relations, Organization Identification, Conscientiousness and Reliability, Efficiency Under Stress, Solitary Work.
Administration: Individual or group.
Forms, 2: Ability Rating, Importance Rating.
Price Data, 2002: $101 per start-up kit (specify Importance or Ability) including 25 test booklets, 25 score sheets, and interpretation and research manual; $54 per 25 test booklets (specify Importance or Ability); $31 per 25 score sheets; $28 per interpretation and research manual.
Time: No limit (approximately 30–45 minutes).
Author: Melany E. Baehr.
Publisher: Reid London House.
Cross References: For a review by Lenore W. Harmon, see 9:1137.

[2298]
Skills Assessment Module.

Purpose: To assess a student's affective, cognitive, and manipulative strengths and weaknesses in relation to vocational skills required in various training programs within a school system.
Population: Average, handicapped, and disadvantaged vocational training school students ages 14-18.
Publication Dates: 1985–2000.
Acronym: SAM.
Scores, 13: Digital Discrimination, Clerical Verbal, Motor Coordination, Clerical Numerical, Following Written Directions, Finger Dexterity, Aiming, Reading a Ruler (Measurement), Manual Dexterity, Form Perception, Spatial Perception, Color Discrimination, Following Diagrammed Instructions.
Administration: Individual in part.
Price Data, 2002: $2,995 for complete test including all subtests.
Time: (90-150) minutes.
Comments: Module includes Career Development ITEP software, Basic Skills Locater Test (261), Learning Styles Inventory (1410), Auditory Directions Screen, Voc-Ties Interest Survey, and 13 hands on performance work samples.
Author: Michele Rosinek.
Publisher: Piney Mountain Press, Inc.
Cross References: For reviews by Jean Powell Kirnan and Wilbur L. Layton, see 11:364.

[2299]
Skills Inventory for Teams.

Purpose: To aid early intervention practitioners to "evaluate their ability to work as part of a team."

Population: Early intervention practitioners.
Publication Dates: 1978–1992.
Acronym: SIFT.
Scores, 12: Clarity of Purpose, Cohesion, Clarity of Roles, Communication, Use of Resources, Decision Making/Problem Solving, Responsibility Implementation, Conflict Resolution, View of Family Role, Evaluation, External Support, Internal Support.
Administration: Group.
Price Data: Price information for administration guide and inventory (1992, 66 pages) available from publisher.
Time: Administration time not reported.
Comments: Previously called Skills Inventory for Teachers; self-administered inventory.
Authors: Corinne Garland, Adrienne Frank, Deana Buck, and Patti Seklemian.
Publisher: Child Development Resources.
Cross References: For reviews by Robert Johnson and E. Lea Witta, see 13:289.

[2300]
SkillScan for Management Development.

Purpose: "A 360-degree diagnostic feedback tool that helps field managers understand how they can be more effective managers, and helps organizations understand the strengths and weaknesses of their managers."
Population: Sales managers.
Publication Date: 1994.
Scores: 8 Tasks: Staffing (Recruiting and Selecting), Training, Field Office Development, Administration, Performance Management (Supervision), Business Management, Sales Assistance, Management Development; 12 Behaviors: Communicating, Counseling, Planning, Delegating, Coordinating, Team Building, Supporting, Rewarding, Motivating, Networking, Monitoring, Problem Solving and Decision Making; 5 Personal Attributes: Ethics and Professionalism, Stress Tolerance, Achievement Motivation, Self Improvement, Other Orientation.
Administration: Individual or group.
Forms, 2: Form O (Assessment by Others) and Form S (Self-Assessment by the Manager).
Price Data, 1996: $110 per SkillScan kit including 1 Form S and 7 Form O questionnaires, instructions, and 8 postage-paid envelopes addressed to LIMRA; $3 per additional Form O questionnaire and envelope; $10 per manual (no publication date, 25 pages).
Time: Administration time not reported.
Comments: Replacement for the Management Development Profile (T4:1507); Manager development workshops available.
Author: LIMRA International.
Publisher: LIMRA International.
Cross References: For reviews by Kurt F. Geisinger and Patricia H. Wheeler, see 14:358; for a review by

Richard M. Wolf of the Management Development Profile, see 12:225.

[2301]
SKILLSCOPE®.

Purpose: Assesses managerial strengths and developmental needs from managers and coworkers perspectives.
Population: Managers.
Publication Dates: 1988–1997.
Scores: 15 Skill Areas: Getting Information, Communication, Taking Action, Risk Taking, Administration, Conflict Management, Relationships, Selecting/Developing, Influencing, Flexibility, Knowledge of Job, Energy/Drive, Time Management, Coping With Pressure, Self-Management.
Administration: Group.
Price Data, 2002: $55 per 1–10 complete sets including 9 survey instruments, a feedback report, a development planning guide, and trainer's guide (2000, 17 pages).
Time: [20–30} minutes.
Comments: SKILLSCOPE questionnaires are returned to the Center for Creative Leadership for confidential scoring; managers are rated by self and by coworkers.
Author: Robert E. Kaplan.
Publisher: Center for Creative Leadership.
Cross References: For a review by Linda F. Wightman, see 12:355.

[2302]
Slingerland College-Level Screening for the Identification of Language Learning Strengths and Weaknesses.

Purpose: Developed to screen for strengths and weaknesses in language learning.
Population: College or college graduates.
Publication Date: 1991.
Scores, 10: Visual to Kinesthetic-Motor I, Visual to Kinesthetic-Motor II, Visual Perception-Memory, Visual Discrimination, Visual Perception and Memory to Kinesthetic-Motor, Auditory to Visual-Kinesthetic I, Auditory to Visual-Kinesthetic II, Auditory to Visual, Comprehension, Auditory to Kinesthetic.
Administration: Group.
Price Data: Available from publisher.
Time: (45–50) minutes.
Comments: Upward extension of the Slingerland Screening Tests (2303).
Author: Carol Murray.
Publisher: Carol Murray (the author) [No reply from publisher; status unknown].
Cross References: For reviews by Mary Anne Bunda and Thomas W. Guyette, see 12:356; see T4:2478 (2 references).

[2303]
Slingerland Screening Tests for Identifying Children with Specific Language Disability.

Purpose: "To screen from among a group of children those with potential language difficulties and those with already present specific language disabilities who are in need of special attention."

Population: Grades 1–2.5, 2.5–3.5, 3.5–4, 5-6.

Publication Dates: 1962–1984.

Administration: Group (Echolalia test individually administered).

Subtests, 8 or 9: Copying-Chart, Copying-Page, Visual Perception-Memory, Visual Discrimination, Visual Perception-Memory with Kinesthetic Memory, Auditory Recall, Auditory Sounds, Auditory Association, Orientation (Form D only); plus individual Echolalia test.

Price Data, 2001: $6 per Slingerland Reliability and Validity Study technical manual (1980, 24 pages).

Author: Beth H. Slingerland.

Publisher: Educators Publishing Service, Inc.

a) FORMS A, B, C, REVISED EDITION.

Population: Grades 1–2.5, 2.5–3.5, 3.5–4.

Publication Dates: 1962–1970.

Scores, 13 (8 tests): Visual Copying Far Point, Visual Copying Near Point, Total, Visual Perception-Memory, Visual Discrimination, Visual Perception-Memory with Kinesthetic Memory, Auditory Recall (Letters, Numbers, Spelling), Auditory Discrimination of Sounds, Auditory-Visual Association, Total Errors (excluding Visual Copying), Total Errors plus Self-Corrections and Poor Formations.

Price Data, 2001: $29.65 per 12 tests (A, B, or C); $5.35 per directions for administration (A, B, or C); $18.75 per cards and charts (A, B, or C); $16 per teacher's manual ('70, 172 pages); $10.65 per specimen set including manual and one each of above tests; quantity discounts available.

Time: 56(66) minutes in 2 or 3 sessions.

Authors: Revisions by Beth H. Slingerland and Alice S. Ansara.

1) *Form A.*

Population: Grades 1–2.5.

2) *Form B.*

Population: Grades 2.5–3.5.

3) *Form C.*

Population: Grades 3.5–4.

b) FORM D.

Population: Grades 5–6.

Publication Date: 1974.

Scores, 14 (9 tests): Visual Copying Far Point, Visual Copying Near Point, Total, Visual Perception-Memory, Visual Discrimination, Visual Perception-Memory with Kinesthetic Memory, Auditory Recall (Letters, Numbers, Spelling), Auditory Discrimination of Sounds, Auditory-Visual Association, Auditory Perception and Individual Orientation, Total Errors (excluding Visual Copying), Total Errors and Confusions.

Price Data: $22.20 per 12 tests and 12 summary sheets; $20.35 per cards and charts including directions for administration and scoring; $12.65 per teacher's manual; $12.65 per specimen set including teacher's manual, Form D test, summary sheet, and list of material needed; quantity discounts available.

Time: (110–125) minutes in 2 sessions.

Cross References: See T4:2478 (2 references); for reviews by Martin Fujiki and Elisabeth H. Wiig, see 9:1141 (4 references); see also T3:2214 (2 references); for an excerpted review by Barton B. Proger, see 8:446 (3 references); see also T2:989 (4 references); for reviews by Evelyn Deno and Joseph M. Wepman of *a*, see 7:969 (3 references).

[2304]
Slosson Full-Range Intelligence Test.

Purpose: Constructed as a "quick estimate of general cognitive ability."

Population: Ages 5–21.

Publication Dates: 1988–2002.

Acronym: S-FRIT.

Scores, 8: General Cognition (Full-Range Intelligence Quotient, Rapid Cognitive Index, Best g Index), Cognitive Subdomains (Verbal Index, Abstract Index, Quantitative Index, Memory Index, Performance Index).

Administration: Individual.

Forms, 2: Item Profiles/Score Summaries Form, Brief Score Form.

Price Data, 2002: $110 per complete kit including examiner's manual (1994, 80 pages), normative/technical manual (1994, 93 pages), picture book, 50 motor response forms, 50 brief score forms, and 50 item profiles/score summaries: $38 per 50 forms (specify Motor response, brief score, or item profiles/score summaries); $70 per examiner's manual; $40 per normative/technical manual; $26.50 per picture book.

Time: (20–35) minutes.

Authors: Bob Algozzine, Ronald C. Eaves, Lester Mann, H. Robert Vance, and Steven W. Slosson (Brief Score Form).

Publisher: Slosson Educational Publications, Inc.

Cross References: For reviews by Gerald S. Hanna and Gerald Tindal, see 14:359.

[2305]
Slosson Intelligence Test [2002 Edition].

Purpose: Designed for use as a "quick estimate of general verbal cognitive ability."

Population: Ages 4-0 and over.
Publication Dates: 1961–2002.
Acronym: SIT-R.
Scores: Total score only.
Administration: Individual.
Price Data, 2002: $95 per complete kit including 50 test forms, manual (1991, 45 pages), and norms tables/technical manual (1991, 39 pages); $27 per 50 test forms; $40 per norms tables/technical manual; $40 per manual.
Time: (10-20) minutes.
Authors: Richard L. Slosson, Charles L. Nicholson (revision), and Terry H. Hibpshman (revision).
Publisher: Slosson Educational Publications, Inc.
Cross References: See T5:2432 (33 references); for reviews by Randy W. Kamphaus and T. Steuart Watson, see 12:358 (16 references); see also T4:2482 (43 references); for reviews by Thomas Oakland and William M. Reynolds of an earlier edition , see 9:1142 (11 references); see also T3:2217 (82 references), 8:227 (62 references), and T2:524 (12 references); for reviews by Philip Himelstein and Jane V. Hunt, see 7:424 (31 references).

[2306]
Slosson Oral Reading Test—Revised.

Purpose: Designed as a "quick estimate to target word recognition levels for children and adults."
Population: Preschool–adult.
Publication Dates: 1963–2002.
Acronym: SORT-R.
Scores: Total score only.
Administration: Individual.
Price Data, 2002: $60 per complete kit; $40 per manual (1990, 38 pages); $26 per 50 score sheets; $14 per spiral-bound word lists; $7 per large print word lists.
Special Editions: Large print edition available for individuals with visual handicaps.
Time: (3–5) minutes.
Comments: Grade equivalent (GE) and age equivalent (AE) scores are also available.
Authors: Richard L. Slosson and Charles L. Nicholson.
Publisher: Slosson Educational Publications, Inc.
Cross References: See T5:2433 (4 references); for reviews by Steven R. Shaw and Carol E. Westby, see 12:359 (4 references); see T4:2483 (16 references), T3:2218 (15 references), T2:1688 (5 references), and 6:844.

[2307]
Smedley Hand Dynamometer.

Purpose: Developed to "measure the muscular torque (grip) of the hand and forearm."
Population: Ages 6–18.
Publication Dates: [1920–1953].

Scores: Total score only.
Administration: Individual.
Price Data, 2001: $215 per hand dynamometer.
Time: Administration time not reported.
Author: F. Smedley.
Publisher: Stoelting Co.
Cross References: See T2:1901 (10 references).

[2308]
Smell Identification Test™ [Revised].

Purpose: Designed to measure an individual's ability to "identify a number of odorants at the suprathreshold level."
Population: People 5 years and up with suspected olfactory dysfunction.
Publication Dates: 1981–1995.
Acronym: SIT; UPSIT.
Scores: Total score only.
Administration: Individual.
Price Data, 1998: $169.50 per introductory/combination package including 50 Pocket Smell Tests, 3 Smell Identification Tests, administration manual (1995, 51 pages), and scoring keys; $26.95 per Smell Identification Test; $135 per Pocket Smell Test (75 Pocket Smell Tests); $12.95 per Cross-Cultural Smell Identification Test (must order at least 10); $19.50 per administration manual with scoring keys; $14.95 per Picture Identification Test; $3.50 per scoring key for Smell Identification Test, Picture Identification Test, or Cross-Cultural Smell Identification Test.
Time: [10–15] minutes.
Comments: A 40-item forced-choice questionnaire; also known as University of Pennsylvania Smell Identification Test; for use only by individuals "professionally engaged in the scientific or medical evaluation of smell function"; related versions include the Pocket Smell Test, the Cross-Cultural Smell Identification Test, and the Picture Identification Test (equivalent to the SIT except stimuli are pictures rather than odors).
Author: Richard L. Doty.
Publisher: Sensonics, Inc.
Cross References: For a review by Ralph G. Leverett, see 14:360; see also T5:2437 (4 references).

[2309]
Smit-Hand Articulation and Phonology Evaluation.

Purpose: Designed to assess a child's level of phonology.
Population: Ages 3–9.
Publication Date: 1997.
Acronym: SHAPE.
Scores, 11: Total, Weak Syllable Deletion, Final Consonant Deletion, Reduction of /lrw/ Clusters, Reduction of /s/ Clusters, Stopping of Initial Fricatives, Voicing of Initial Voiceless Obstruents, Fronting of

Velars, Depalatalization, Gliding of Liquid Singletons, Vocalization of Liquids.

Administration: Individual.

Price Data, 2002: $132.50 per kit including 10 record booklets, 10 autoscore answer forms, manual (63 pages), and 1 picture set; $29.50 per 10 record booklets; $18.50 per 10 autoscore forms; $35 per manual; $65 per picture set.

Time: (30) minutes.

Authors: Ann B. Smit and Linda Hand.

Publisher: Western Psychological Services.

Cross References: For reviews by David P. Hurford and Ralph G. Leverett, see 14:361.

[2310]
Smoker Complaint Scale.

Purpose: Designed to measure changes in physiological/emotional/craving states as a function of smoking cessation.

Population: Persons quitting smoking.

Publication Date: 1984.

Acronym: SCS.

Scores: Total score and item scores only.

Administration: Individual or group.

Manual: No manual.

Price Data: Instrument now available without charge from publisher.

Time: (1-5) minutes.

Comments: Self-administered.

Author: Nina G. Schneider.

Publisher: Nina G. Schneider, Ph.D.

Cross References: See T5:2440 (1 reference).

[2311]
Snijders-Oomen Non-Verbal Intelligence Test—Revised.

Purpose: Developed as an untimed, nonverbal test of intelligence.

Publication Dates: 1939–1997.

Administration: Individual.

Price Data: Available from publisher.

Foreign Language Edition: Dutch and German editions available.

Comments: Administered in pantomime (for hearing impaired) or orally.

Publisher: Swets Test Publishers [The Netherlands].

a) SNIJDERS-OOMEN NON-VERBAL INTELLIGENCE SCALE FOR YOUNG CHILDREN.

Population: Dutch children ages 2-6 to 7-0.

Acronym: SON-R 2 1/2–7.

Scores, 6: Sorting, Mosaic, Combination, Memory, Copying, Total.

Time: (45–50) minutes.

Comments: Also called Non-Verbal Intelligence Scale S.O.N. 2 1/2–7.

Authors: J. T. Snijders and N. Snijders-Oomen.

b) SON-R.

Population: Dutch children ages 5-6 to 17-0.

Acronym: SON-R 5 1/2–17.

Scores, 8: Categories, Mosaics, Hidden Pictures, Patterns, Situations, Analogies, Stories, Total.

Time: (60–120) minutes.

Comments: Revised version of the SON-'58 and SSON; older versions out-of-print.

Authors: J. T. Snijders, P. J. Tellegen, J. A. Laros, N. Snijders-Oomen (test), and M. A. H. Huijnen (test).

Cross References: See T5:2441 (2 references) and T4:2491 (2 references); for reviews by Douglas K. Detterman and Timothy Z. Keith of an earlier edition, see 9:1146; see also T3:2221 (1 reference) and T2:512 (5 references); for a review by J. S. Lawes of the 1958 edition, see 6:529 (2 references).

[2312]
Social Adjustment Scale—Self Report.

Purpose: Designed to assess "the ability of an individual to adapt to, and derive satisfaction from, their social roles."

Population: Age 17 and older..

Publication Date: 1999.

Acronym: SAS-SR.

Scores: 7 areas: Work, Social and Leisure Activities, Relations with Extended Family, Primary Relationship, Parenthood, Family Life, Economic.

Administration: Group.

Price Data, 2002: $102 per complete kit including 25 interview guides, 25 QuikScore™ forms, and manual; $27 per 10 question booklets; $38 per 25 QuikScore™ forms; $48 per manual; $55 per specimen set including 3 interview guides, 3 QuikScore™ forms, and manual.

Foreign Language Editions: Available in Afrikaans, Cantonese, Czech, Danish, Dutch, Finnish, French (European), French-Canadian, German, Greek, Hebrew, Hungarian, Italian, Japanese, Mandarin, Norwegian, Portuguese, Russian, Spanish (European), Spanish (South American), and Swedish.

Time: (15–20) minutes.

Author: Myrna Weissmann.

Publisher: Multi-Health Systems, Inc.

[2313]
Social and Prevocational Information Battery—Revised.

Purpose: "To assess knowledge of certain skills and competencies regarded as important for the community adjustment of students with mild mental retardation."

Population: Mildly mentally retarded students in Grades 7–12.

Publication Dates: 1975–1986.

Acronym: SPIB-R.

Scores, 10: Purchasing Habits, Budgeting, Banking, Job Related Behavior, Job Search Skills, Home Management, Health Care, Hygiene and Grooming, Functional Signs, Total.
Administration: Group.
Price Data: Available from publisher.
Time: (20–30) minutes per test.
Comments: Orally administered.
Authors: Andrew S. Halpern, Larry K. Irvin, and Arden W. Munkres (design).
Publisher: CTB/McGraw-Hill.
Cross References: See T4:2492 (1 reference); for reviews by Terry Overton and Terry A. Stinnett, see 11:367; for reviews by M. Harry Daniels and Carol Kehr Tittle of an earlier edition, see 9:1147; see also T3:2224 (7 references); for a review by C. Edward Meyers of the original edition, see 8:984 (2 references).

[2314]
Social Behavior Assessment Inventory.

Purpose: Assesses social skill levels in students.
Population: Grades K–9.
Publication Dates: 1978–1992.
Acronym: SBAI.
Scores, 30: Environmental Behaviors (Care for the Environment, Dealing with Emergencies, Lunchroom Behavior, Movement Around Environment), Interpersonal Behaviors (Accepting Authority, Coping with Conflict, Gaining Attention, Greeting Others, Helping Others, Making Conversation, Organized Play, Positive Attitude Toward Others, Playing Informally, Property: Own and Others), Self-Related Behaviors (Accepting Consequences, Ethical Behavior, Expressing Feelings, Positive Attitude Toward Self, Responsible Behavior, Self-Care), Task-Related Behaviors (Asking and Answering Questions, Attending Behavior, Classroom Discussion, Completing Tasks, Following Directions, Group Activities, Independent Work, On-Task Behavior, Performing Before Others, Quality of Work).
Administration: Individual or group.
Price Data: Available from publisher for complete kit including Social Skills in the Classroom–2nd ed., manual (1992, 34 pages), and 25 rating booklets.
Time: (30–45) minutes.
Comments: Observations made by teacher or trained paraprofessional.
Authors: Thomas M. Stephens and Kevin D. Arnold.
Publisher: Psychological Assessment Resources, Inc.
Cross References: See T5:2444 (1 reference); for reviews by Kathryn A. Hess and David MacPhee, see 12:361; see also T4:2493 (1 reference); for a review by Ronald S. Drabman of an earlier edition, see 9:1148; see also T3:2226 (1 reference).

[2315]
Social Competence and Behavior Evaluation, Preschool Edition.

Purpose: "Designed to assess patterns of social competence, affective expression, and adjustment difficulties."
Population: Children aged 30 months to 76 months.
Publication Date: 1995.
Acronym: SCBE.
Scores: 8 Basic scales (Depressive-Joyful, Anxious-Secure, Angry-Tolerant, Isolated-Integrated, Aggressive-Calm, Egotistical-Prosocial, Oppositional-Cooperative, Dependent-Autonomous); 4 Summary scales (Social Competence, Internalizing Problems, Externalizing Problems, General Adaptation).
Administration: Group.
Price Data, 2002: $79.95 per complete kit including 25 AutoScore™ forms and manual (67 pages); $38 per 25 AutoScore™ forms; $45 per manual.
Time: (15) minutes.
Comments: Ratings by teachers or other child care professionals.
Authors: Peter J. LaFreniere and Jean E. Dumas.
Publisher: Western Psychological Services.
Cross References: For reviews by Ronald A. Madle and G. Michael Poteat, see 14:362.

[2316]
Social-Emotional Dimension Scale.

Purpose: Provides a means for rating nonacademic student behaviors "which may be judged by teachers as problems in the classroom setting."
Population: Ages 5.5–18.5.
Publication Date: 1986.
Acronym: SEDS.
Scores: 6 scores (Avoidance of Peer Interaction, Aggressive Interaction, Avoidance of Teacher Interaction, Inappropriate Behavior, Depressive Reaction, Physical/Fear Reaction) plus a Behavior Quotient and a Behavior Observation Web.
Administration: Individual.
Price Data, 2001: $76 per complete kit including 50 profile/examiner record forms and examiner's manual (54 pages); $39 per 50 profile/examiner record forms; $39 per examiner's manual.
Time: Administration time not reported.
Comments: Behavior checklist for ratings by school personnel.
Authors: Jerry B. Hutton and Timothy G. Roberts.
Publisher: PRO-ED.
Cross References: For a review by Jean Powell Kirnan, see 11:368.

[2317]
Social Phobia and Anxiety Inventory.

Purpose: Constructed for assessment of the "somatic, cognitive and behavioral aspects of social phobia."

Population: Ages 14 and older.
Publication Date: 1996.
Acronym: SPAI.
Scores, 3: Social Phobia, Agoraphobia, Difference.
Administration: Individual or group.
Price Data, 2002: $60 per complete kit including manual and 25 QuikScore™ forms; $30 per 25 QuikScore™ forms; $30 per manual; $40 per specimen set including manual and 3 QuikScore™ forms.
Time: (15) minutes.
Comments: Self-report.
Authors: Samuel M. Turner, Deborah C. Beidel, and Constance V. Dancu.
Publisher: Multi-Health Systems, Inc.
Cross References: For reviews by George Engelhard, Jr. and Delores D. Walcott, see 14:363.

[2318]
Social Phobia & Anxiety Inventory for Children.

Purpose: "Assesses the frequency and range of social fears and anxiety in children and adolescents."
Population: Ages 8–14.
Publication Date: 1998.
Acronym: SPAI-C.
Scores: Total score only.
Administration: Group.
Price Data, 2002: $60 per complete kit; $30 per 25 QuikScore™ Forms; $37 per manual (1998, 50 pages), $38 per specimen set.
Time: (20–30) minutes.
Comments: Self-report; also available as a Windows compatible computer program with a decremented counter; "has been translated into several languages."
Authors: Deborah C. Beidel, Samuel M. Turner, and Tracy L. Morris.
Publisher: Multi-Health Systems, Inc.

[2319]
Social Reticence Scale.

Purpose: To assess an individual's shyness.
Population: High school and college and adults.
Publication Date: 1986.
Acronym: SRTS.
Scores: Total score only.
Administration: Individual or group.
Price Data, 2001: $25 per sampler set including test booklet, scoring key, and manual; $125 per permission set including sampler set and permission to reproduce 200 administrations of the test.
Time: (5-10) minutes.
Authors: Warren H. Jones and Stephen Briggs.
Publisher: Mind Garden, Inc.
Cross References: See T4:2499 (1 reference); for reviews by Owen Scott, III and William K. Wilkinson, see 11:370 (1 reference).

[2320]
Social Skills Inventory, Research Edition.

Purpose: "To assess basic social communication skills."
Population: Ages 14 and over reading at or above the eighth grade level.
Publication Date: 1989.
Acronym: SSI.
Scores, 7: Emotional Expressivity, Emotional Sensitivity, Emotional Control, Social Expressivity, Social Sensitivity, Social Control, Total.
Administration: Group and individual.
Price Data, 2001: $57.80 per 25 test booklets; $12.30 per scoring key; $58 per 25 answer sheets; $30.60 per manual (21 pages), $47.50 per preview kit including item booklet, non-prepaid answer sheet, scoring key, and manual; scoring service offered by publisher.
Time: (30–45) minutes.
Comments: Test booklet title is Self-Description Inventory; self-administered.
Author: Ronald E. Riggio.
Publisher: Consulting Psychologists Press, Inc.
Cross References: See T5:2451 (4 references) and T4:2501 (4 references); for reviews by Judith C. Conger and Susan M. Sheridan, see 11:371 (3 references).

[2321]
Social Skills Rating System.

Purpose: Constructed to screen and classify children suspected of having social behavior problems and to assist in the development of appropriate interventions for identified children.
Publication Date: 1990.
Acronym: SSRS.
Administration: Individual or group.
Price Data, 2002: $159.95 per preschool/elementary levels starter set including 10 copies of each form and level questionnaires, 10 assessment-intervention records, and manual (207 pages); $177.95 per secondary level starter set; $26.95 per 30 questionnaires (select level and form); $36.95 per 30 assessment-intervention records; $68.95 per manual.
Time: (15–25) minutes.
Comments: Ratings by teachers and parents as well as student self-ratings; expanded version of the Teacher Ratings of Social Skills; hand scored or computer scores; computer-scored report options: individual or group summary reports, teacher and parent letters, suggested intervention activities.
Authors: Frank M. Gresham and Stephen N. Elliott.
Publisher: American Guidance Service, Inc.
   a) PRESCHOOL.
      Population: Ages 3-0 to 4-11.
      Scores, 6: Social Skills, Cooperation, Assertion, Problem Behaviors, Internalizing, Externalizing.
      Forms, 2: Parent, Teacher.

b) ELEMENTARY.
Population: Grades K–6.
Scores, 11: Social Skills, Cooperation, Assertion, Responsibility, Empathy, Self-Control, Problem Behaviors, Externalizing, Internalizing, Hyperactivity, Academic Competence.
Forms, 3: Student, Parent, Teacher.
Comments: Forms for all grades completed by parent and teacher; those for Grades 3–6 also completed by student.
c) SECONDARY.
Population: Grades 7–12.
Scores, 3: Same as *b* above except no Hyperactivity subscale.
Forms, 3: Same as *b* above.
Cross References: See T5:2452 (24 references); for reviews by Kathryn M. Benes and Michael Furlong and Mitchell Karno, see 12:362 (10 references); see also T4:2502 (4 references).

[2322]
Social Styles Analysis.
Purpose: Constructed to identify a person's social style of presentation and interaction.
Population: Adults.
Publication Date: 1989.
Scores: 4 categories: Analytical, Driver, Amiable, Expressive.
Administration: Group.
Editions, 2: Self, Other.
Manual: No manual.
Price Data: Price information available from publisher for package for self analysis (5.25-inch or 3.5-inch diskette); package for other analyses (5.25-inch or 3.5-inch diskette).
Time: Administration time not reported.
Comments: IBM microcomputer necessary for scoring.
Author: Wilson Learning Corporation.
Publisher: Jossey-Bass, A Wiley Company.
Cross References: For a review by C. Dale Carpenter, see 11:372.

[2323]
Socio-Sexual Knowledge-Attitudes Assessment Tool—Revised.
Purpose: Designed to assess sexual knowledge and attitudes of individuals with developmental disabilities.
Population: Developmentally disabled adults (ages 15–adult), can be used with other adults.
Publication Dates: 1976–2002.
Acronym: SSKAAT-R.
Scores, 7: Anatomy, Women's Bodies and Women's Knowledge of Men, Men's Bodies and Men's Knowledge of Women, Intimacy, Pregnancy/Childbirth and Child Rearing, Birth Control and STDs, Sexual Boundaries.

Administration: Individual.
Price Data, 2002: $225 per complete kit including easel, stimulus cards, 25 forms, and manual (2002); $100 per easel; $45 per stimulus cards; $55 per 25 record forms; $35 per manual.
Time: (45–60) minutes.
Comments: Criterion or norm referenced.
Author: Stoelting Co.
Publisher: Stoelting Co.
Cross References: For a review by Edward S. Herold of an earlier edition, see 9:1152; see T3:2237 (1 reference).

[2324]
Softball Skills Test.
Purpose: "To improve teaching and evaluation of softball skills."
Population: Grades 5–12 and college.
Publication Date: 1991.
Scores, 4: Batting, Fielding Ground Balls, Overhand Throwing, Baserunning.
Administration: Individual.
Price Data, 2001: $14 per manual (64 pages).
Time: Administration time not reported.
Author: Roberta E. Rikli, Editor.
Publisher: American Association for Active Lifestyles and Fitness.
Cross References: For a review by Don Sebolt, see 12:363.

[2325]
Solid Geometry: National Achievement Tests.
Purpose: To measure achievement in solid geometry.
Population: High school students.
Publication Dates: 1958–1960.
Scores: Total score only.
Administration: Group.
Forms, 2: A, B.
Price Data: Available from publisher.
Time: 40 minutes.
Comments: No specific manual; combined manual (1958, 12 pages) for this test and following tests: Plane Trigonometry (1918), Plane Geometry (1917), and First Year Algebra Test (1003).
Authors: Ray Webb and Julius H. Hlavaty (manual).
Publisher: Psychometric Affiliates.
Cross References: For a review by Sheldon S. Myers, see 6:653.

[2326]
The Sort-A-Sentence Test.
Purpose: Designed to assess reading comprehension.
Population: Ages 7–15.
Publication Date: 2002.
Scores: Total score only.

Administration: Group.
Forms, 2: A, B.
Price Data, 2002: £19.45 per introductory set including administrative manual (7 pages), scoring key, and 25 Form A test booklets; £3 per manual and 3.5-inch disk scoring key; £10.45 per 25 test booklets (Form A or B); technical manual available upon request.
Time: (25) minutes.
Author: Alan Brimer.
Publisher: Educational Evaluations [England].

[2327]
Sources of Stress Scale [2001 Revision].

Purpose: Designed as "an instrument to identify origins of perceived and current anxiety, to quantify the intensity of such stressors, and to determine the pattern of such perceptions for predictions and subsequent interventions."
Population: High school and adults.
Publication Dates: 1986–2001.
Acronym: S.O.S.S.
Scores, 16: Personal Relationships, Finances/Money, Field Experiences, Myself, Academic Activities, Time Management, College Life, Health, Changes, Personal Life, The Future, Friends, High School, Family Issues, Children, Spouse/Partner.
Administration: Group.
Forms, 5: Graduate Students, High School Students, Family, Young Adults, Senior Citizens.
Price Datam 2002: $20 per 25 scales; $.40 per answer sheet; $20 per test manual (2001, 32 pages); $.30 per scoring scale.
Time: [5–15] minutes per scale.
Comments: Self-rating scale.
Authors: Louise M. Soares and Anthony T. Soares.
Publisher: SOARES Associates.

[2328]
South African Written Language Test.

Purpose: To evaluate the written language ability of English-speaking pupils.
Population: South African pupils in Grade II to Standard 5.
Publication Date: 1981.
Acronym: SAWLT.
Scores, 7: Total Words, Total Sentences, Words per Sentence, Sentence Complexity, Correctness, Abstract-Concrete Content, Total.
Administration: Group.
Price Data: Available from publisher.
Time: (30–35) minutes.
Comments: Adaptation of Die Suid-Afrikaanse Skryftaaltoets.
Authors: Marita Brink, Italia Boninelli, and Jan Vorster.

Publisher: Human Sciences Research Council [South Africa].

[2329]
The Southern California Ordinal Scales of Development.

Purpose: To provide "differential assessment of educational needs and abilities."
Population: Multihandicapped, developmentally delayed, and learning disabled children.
Publication Dates: 1977–1985.
Acronym: SCOSD.
Scores: 6 scales: Cognition, Communication, Social-Affective Behavior, Practical Abilities, Fine Motor Abilities, Gross Motor Abilities.
Administration: Individual.
Price Data, 2002: $130 per complete instrument.
Time: (60–120) minutes per scale.
Comments: A Piagetian-based assessment system.
Authors: Donald I. Ashurst, Elaine Bamberg, Julika Barrett, Ann Bisno, Artice Burke, David C. Chambers, Jean Fentiman, Ronald Kadish, Mary Lou Mitchell, Lambert Neeley, Todd Thorne, and Doris Wents.
Publisher: Foreworks.
Cross References: See T5:2459 (1 reference); for reviews by Cameron J. Camp and Arlene C. Rosenthal, see 10:338.

[2330]
Space Relations (Paper Puzzles).

Purpose: Developed as an assessment of mechanical aptitude.
Population: Ages 17 and over.
Publication Dates: 1984–1996.
Scores: Total score only.
Administration: Group.
Price Data, 2002: $91 per start-up kit including 25 test booklets, score key, and interpretation and research manual; $54 per 25 tests; $28 per interpretation and research manual; $20 per score key.
Time: [9] minutes.
Authors: L. L. Thurstone and T. E. Jeffrey.
Publisher: Reid London House.

[2331]
Space Thinking (Flags).

Purpose: To measure the ability to visualize a stable figure, drawing or diagram when it is moved into different positions.
Population: Industrial employees.
Publication Dates: 1959–1984.
Scores: Total score only.
Administration: Individual or group.
Price Data, 2002: $91 per start-up kit including 25 test booklets, score key, and interpretation and research manual; $54 per 25 test booklets (quantity discounts

available); $20 per score key; $28 per interpretation and research manual.

Time: 5 minutes.

Authors: L. L. Thurstone and T. E. Jeffrey.

Publisher: Reid London House.

Cross References: See T4:2515 (1 reference), T3:898 (1 reference), and T2:2245 (1 reference); for a review by I. Macfarlane Smith, see 6:1086.

[2332]
Spadafore Attention Deficit Hyperactivity Disorder Rating Scale.

Purpose: Designed "to examine the wide range of behaviors that are frequently associated with ADHD symptoms."

Population: Ages 5–19.

Publication Date: 1997.

Acronym: S-ADHD-RS.

Scores, 4: Impulsivity/Hyperactivity, Attention, Social Adjustment, ADHD Index.

Administration: Individual.

Price Data, 2002: $80 per test kit including 25 scoring protocols, 25 observation forms, 25 medication tracking forms, and manual (80 pages); $25 per 25 scoring protocols; $15 per 25 observation forms; $10 per 25 medication tracking forms; $25 per manual.

Time: Untimed.

Comments: Rating scale to be completed by classroom teachers about a child; also included in kit: behavioral observation form and medication monitoring form.

Authors: Gerald J. Spadafore and Sharon J. Spadafore.

Publisher: Academic Therapy Publications.

Cross References: For reviews by Scott T. Meier and Judy Oehler-Stinnett, see 14:364.

[2333]
Spadafore Diagnostic Reading Test.

Purpose: Constructed to assess decoding and comprehension skills in reading.

Population: Grades 1–12 and adults.

Publication Date: 1983.

Acronym: SDRT.

Scores, 15: 3 performance levels (Independent, Instructional, Frustration) for each of 5 subtests (Decoding [Word Recognition, Oral Reading], Comprehension [Oral Reading, Silent Reading, Listening]).

Administration: Individual.

Price Data, 2002: $65 per complete kit including test plates, 10 test booklets, and manual (60 pages); $28 per set of test plates; $15 per 10 test booklets; $17 per manual; $17 per specimen set.

Time: (30–60) minutes.

Comments: "Criterion-referenced."

Author: Gerald J. Spadafore.

Publisher: Academic Therapy Publications.

Cross References: See T4:2516 (1 reference); for a review by James R. Sanders and Blaine R. Worthen, see 9:1159.

[2334]
Spanish Assessment of Basic Education, Second Edition.

Purpose: "Designed to measure achievement in the basic skills ... with students for whom Spanish is the language of instruction."

Population: Grades 1.0–1.9, 1.6–2.9, 2.6–3.9, 3.6–4.9, 4.6–6.9, 6.6–8.9.

Publication Dates: 1991–1994.

Acronym: SABE/2.

Administration: Group.

Price Data, 2002: $18.35 per 35 practice tests (select level); $50.75 per 100 student diagnostic profiles (select level); $18.35 per 35 parent reports (select level); $2.05 per class record sheet; $17.30 per examiner's manual (1991, 41–57 pages) (select level); $21.60 per user's guide (1991, 64 pages); $23.75 per technical report (1994, 43 pages); $17.30 per norms book (1994, 159 pages); scoring service available from publisher.

Author: CTB Macmillan/McGraw-Hill.

Publisher: CTB/McGraw-Hill.

a) LEVEL 1.

Population: Grades 1.0–1.9.

Scores, 11: Word Attack, Vocabulary, Reading Comprehension, Mechanics, Expression, Mathematics Computation, Mathematics Concepts and Applications, Total Reading, Total Mathematics, Total Language, Total Battery.

Price Data: $179.25 per 35 scannable test books.

Time: (205) minutes.

b) LEVEL 2.

Population: Grades 1.6–2.9.

Scores: Same as *a* above.

Price Data: Same as *a* above.

Time: (219) minutes.

c) LEVEL 3.

Population: Grades 2.6–3.9.

Scores: Same as *a* above.

Price Data: Same as *a* above.

Time: (255) minutes.

d) LEVEL 4.

Population: Grades 3.6–4.9.

Scores, 12: Vocabulary, Reading Comprehension, Spelling, Mechanics, Expression, Mathematics Computation, Mathematics Concepts and Applications, Study Skills, Total Reading, Total Mathematics, Total Language, Total Battery.

Price Data: $140.40 per 35 reusable test books; $52.95 per 50 answer sheets (for CompuScan® or handscoring); $56.15 per set of 3 handscoring stencils.

Time: (249) minutes.

e) LEVEL 5.
Population: Grades 4.6–6.9.
Scores: Same as *d* above.
Price Data: Same as *d* above.
Time: (260) minutes.
f) LEVEL 6.
Population: Grades 6.6–8.9.
Scores: Same as *d* above.
Price Data: Same as *d* above.
Time: (259) minutes.
Cross References: For reviews by Maria Prendes Lintel and Emelia C. Lopez, see 13:291.

[2335]
A Spanish Computerized Adaptive Placement Exam.

Purpose: Designed to assist appropriate placement into college-level Spanish courses.
Population: College students.
Publication Dates: 1986–1988.
Acronym: S-CAPE.
Scores: Total score only.
Administration: Individual.
Price Data: Available from publisher.
Time: (20–25) minutes.
Comments: IBM-PC or compatible computer necessary for administration.
Authors: Jerry W. Larson and Kim L. Smith.
Publisher: Brigham Young University, Humanities Research Center.
Cross References: For reviews by G. Gage Kingsbury and Steven L. Wise, see 12:364.

[2336]
Spanish/English Reading Comprehension Test [Revised].

Purpose: Designed to "determine the degrees of bilingualism."
Population: Grades 1–6.
Publication Dates: 1974–1993.
Scores: Total score and grade level equivalents.
Administration: Group or individual.
Forms, 2: English, Spanish.
Price Data, 1999: $20 per packet including manual (1993, 42 pages) and 1 English and 1 Spanish rating/answer sheet (permission to copy answer sheets is included).
Time: (30) minutes.
Comments: Spanish Reading based on Mexican curriculum materials; English Reading based on U.S.A. curriculum materials; English Reading Comprehension Test is translated from the Spanish version; pretesting and posttesting used.
Author: Steve Moreno.
Publisher: Moreno Educational Co.

Cross References: For reviews by Esteban L. Olmedo and David T. Sanchez, see 9:1161.

[2337]
Spanish Structured Photographic Expressive Language Test.

Purpose: Assessment of "the monolingual or bilingual child's generation of specific morphological and syntactical structures."
Population: Ages 3-0 to 5-11, 4-0 to 9-5.
Publication Date: 1989.
Acronym: SPELT.
Scores: Item scores only.
Administration: Individual.
Time: Administration time not reported.
Comments: The design of the Spanish SPELT tests is patterned after the original SPELT-II and SPELT-P (9:1198), however, it is not a direct translation of them. Many of the grammatical structures in the English edition were not able to be translated into Spanish. When necessary, to allow for differences in the two languages, grammatical structures were either deleted or added.
Authors: Ellen O'Hara Werner and Janet Dawson Kresheck.
Publisher: Janelle Publications, Inc.
a) SPANISH STRUCTURED PHOTOGRAPHIC EXPRESSIVE LANGUAGE TEST-II.
Population: Ages 4-0 to 9-5.
Acronym: SPELT-II.
Price Data, 1998: $99 per 10 response forms, 50 color photographs, and manual (1989, 39 pages); $20 per 50 response forms.
b) SPANISH STRUCTURED PHOTOGRAPHIC EXPRESSIVE LANGUAGE TEST-PRESCHOOL.
Population: Ages 3-0 to 5-11.
Acronym: SPELT-P.
Price Data: $89 per 10 response forms, 37 color photographs, and manual (1989, 34 pages); $12 per 50 response forms.
Cross References: For a review by Ronald B. Gillam and Linda S. Day, see 11:373; for a review by Joan D. Berryman of the original SPELT, see 9:1198 (2 references).

[2338]
SPAR Spelling and Reading Tests, Third Edition.

Purpose: Designed as a "group test of literacy."
Population: Ages 7-0 to 12-11 years.
Publication Dates: 1976–1998.
Acronym: SPAR.
Scores, 2: Reading Total Score, Spelling Total Score.
Administration: Group.
Parts, 2: Reading Test, Spelling Test.

Price Data, 2002: £7.99 per 20 For A or Form B; £9.99 per manual (1976, 32 pages) including photocopiable version of spelling test; £4.99 per scoring template (A or B); £11.99 per specimen set including 1 copy each of Test Forms A and B, and manual.
Time: 13 minutes for Spelling Test; (20–25) minutes for Reading Test.
Comments: Reading Test is available in parallel Forms (A and B); Spelling Test is created from three parallel banks of items found in the manual.
Author: Dennis Young.
Publisher: Hodder & Stoughton Educational [England].
Cross References: For reviews by Timothy Z. Keith and Brenda A. Stevens, see 14:365; see also T5:2467 (1 reference); for reviews by Cleborne D. Maddux and William R. Merz of the second edition, see 12:365 (2 references); see also T4:2520 (3 references); for reviews by J. Douglas Ayers of earlier editions of the Spelling Test and the Reading Test, see 8:76 and 8:742.

[2339]
Spatial Awareness Skills Program Test.

Purpose: Constructed to identify "children whose spatial awareness skills are developing more slowly than expected" and provide "information about how to remedy a deficit."
Population: Ages 4–10.
Publication Date: 1999.
Acronym: SASP Test.
Scores: Total score only.
Administration: Individual.
Price Data, 2001: $99 per complete kit; $39 per test booklets.
Time: (5) minutes.
Comments: Previously titled Test of Visual Analysis Skills (T5:2721); designed to be used with the Spatial Awareness Skills Program (SASP) Curriculum; criterion-referenced.
Author: Jerome Rosner.
Publisher: PRO-ED.

[2340]
Spatial Orientation Memory Test.

Purpose: "Assesses the development of a child's ability to retain and recall the orientation of visually presented forms."
Population: Ages 5–10.
Publication Dates: 1971–1985.
Scores: Total score only.
Administration: Individual.
Forms, 2: Form 1, Form 2.
Price Data, 2002: $78 per complete kit including stimulus cards (1971, 44 cards), 25 score sheets (1985,

2 pages), and manual (1975, 4 pages); $19.50 per pad of 100 score sheets; $16 per manual.
Time: (10) minutes.
Comments: Orally administered.
Authors: Joseph M. Wepman and Dainis Turaids.
Publisher: Western Psychological Services.
Cross References: For reviews by Deborah Erickson and Nora M. Thompson, see 11:374 (1 reference); see also T3:2251 (2 references).

[2341]
Speaking Proficiency English Assessment Kit.

Purpose: "To assess the English speaking proficiency of people who are not native speakers of English."
Population: Nonnative speakers of English.
Publication Date: 1996.
Acronym: SPEAK.
Scores: Total score only.
Administration: Individual.
Price Data: Available from publisher.
Time: (20) minutes.
Comments: Produced by the Test of English as a Foreign Language Program.
Author: Educational Testing Service.
Publisher: Educational Testing Service.

[2342]
Speech and Language Evaluation Scale.

Purpose: "Designed for in-school screening and referral of students with speech and language problems."
Population: Ages 4.5–18.
Publication Dates: 1989–1990.
Acronym: SLES.
Scores, 6: Speech (Articulation, Voice, Fluency), Language (Form, Content, Pragmatics).
Administration: Individual.
Price Data, 2002: $125 per complete kit including 50 pre-referral checklist forms, 50 pre-referral intervention strategies documentation forms, technical manual (1989, 47 pages), 50 rating forms, and Speech and Language Classroom Intervention Manual (1990, 205 pages); $27 per 50 pre-referral checklist forms; $27 per 50 pre-referral intervention strategies documentation forms; $14 per technical manual; $31 per 50 rating forms; $24 per Speech and Language Intervention Manual; $20 per computerized quick score (DOS).
Time: (15-20) minutes.
Comments: Ratings by teachers.
Authors: Diane R. Fressola, Sandra Cipponeri-Hoerchler, Jacquelyn S. Hagan, Steven B. McDannold, Jacqueline Meyer (manual), and Stephen B. McCarney (technical manual).
Publisher: Hawthorne Educational Services, Inc.
Cross References: For reviews by Katharine G. Butler and Penelope K. Hall, see 12:367.

[2343]
Speech-Ease Screening Inventory (K–1).

Purpose: "Designed to screen the articulation, language development," and auditory comprehension of kindergartners and first-graders.
Population: Grades K–1.
Publication Date: 1985.
Scores: Item scores only in 5 areas (Articulation, Language Association, Auditory Recall, Vocabulary, Basic Concepts) and in 4 optional areas (Auditory, Similarities and Differences, Language Sample, Linguistic Relationships) plus 5 observational ratings (Voice Quality, Fluency, Syntax, Oral-Peripheral, Hearing).
Administration: Individual.
Price Data, 2001: $109 per complete kit; $29 per 100 screening forms; $23 per 50 summary sheets (specify kindergarten or first grade); $39 per manual (32 pages).
Time: (7–10) minutes.
Authors: Teryl Pigott, Jane Barry, Barbara Hughes, Debra Eastin, Patricia Titus, Harriett Stensel, Kathleen Metcalf, and Belinda Porter.
Publisher: PRO-ED.
Cross References: For reviews by Kris L. Baack and Eleanor E. Sanford, see 12:368.

[2344]
Speech Evaluation of the Patient with a Tracheostomy Tube.

Purpose: Designed to help speech-language pathologists "assess the potential of an adult patient with an artificial airway to use a device that promotes phonation."
Population: Adults with artificial airways.
Publication Dates: 1994–1997.
Scores: 6 evaluative areas: Current Airway Assessment Information, Ventilation Status, Nutritional and Swallowing Status, Clinical Observations/Assessment, Patient Goals, Recommendations.
Administration: Individual.
Price Data, 2002: $48 per kit including manual (1997, 124 pages) and reproducible diagrams and laminated evaluation report form.
Time: Administration time not reported.
Comments: Not a standardized test but author provides clinical recommendations based on the information provided on a patient's report form.
Author: Nancy Conway.
Publisher: Imaginart International, Inc.

[2345]
Speech Perception Instructional Curriculum and Evaluation.

Purpose: "Designed to provide a guide for developing listening skills in severely and profoundly deaf children."

Population: Hearing-impaired individuals ages 3–12.
Publication Date: 1995.
Acronym: SPICE.
Scores: Rates total of 16 goals within 4 categories: Detection (Detects Speech, Indicates Onset and Termination of Speech), Suprasegmental Perception (Discriminates between 2 Stimuli Differing in Duration/Stress/and/or Intonation, Identifies Among 3 Stimuli Differing in Duration/Stress/and/or Intonation, Identifies Among 4 Stimuli Differing in Duration/Stress/and/or Intonation, Differentiates Stimuli With Similar Duration but Differing in Stress and/or Intonation; Identifies Among Sentences Differing Only in Duration of Key Words, Vowels and Consonants (Identifies Among Six Sounds, Identifies Words of Similar Duration and Differing in Vowels and/or Consonants, Identifies Monosyllables With the Same Consonants and Differing Vowels; Engages in Discussion About a Familiar Topic, Engages in Connected Discourse Tracking), Connected Speech (Identifies Key Words in the Context of Sentences, Practiced Sentences, Converses Using Picture Context, Engaged in Discussion About a Familiar Topic, Engages in Connected Discourse Tracking.
Administration: Individual.
Price Data, 2001: $350 per complete kit including manual (221 pages), rating forms, box of 16 toys for listening activities, 374 illustrated word and sentence cards, auditory training screen, instructional videotape.
Time: Administration time not reported.
Comments: Informally documents present auditory skill level, helps identify instructional objectives; instructional videotape contains 18 teaching segments; can be adapted for individuals over age 12 through adult.
Authors: Jean S. Moog, Julia J. Biedenstein, and Lisa S. Davidson.
Publisher: Central Institute for the Deaf.

[2346]
Spelling Test: National Achievement Tests.

Purpose: Assesses achievement in the spelling of common words.
Population: Grades 3–4, 5–8, 7–9, 10–12.
Publication Dates: 1936–1957.
Scores: Total score only.
Administration: Group.
Manual: No manual.
Price Data: Available from publisher.
Time: (25) minutes.
Comments: 1956–1957 tests identical to tests copyrighted 1939.
Authors: Robert K. Speer and Samuel Smith.
Publisher: Psychometric Affiliates.
Cross References: For a review by James A. Fitzgerald, see 5:230; for a review by W. J. Osburn, see 1:1161.

[2347]
Spiritual Well-Being Scale.

Purpose: "Developed as a general indicator of the subjective state of religious and existential well-being."
Population: Adults.
Publication Dates: 1982–1991.
Acronym: SWBS.
Scores, 3: Religious Well-Being, Existential Well-Being, Total Spiritual Well-Being.
Administration: Individual or group.
Price Data, 2001: $20 per specimen set including scale, manual (1991, 6 pages), bibliography, and scoring and research information; $2.25 or less per scale; volume discounts and student discounts available.
Time: (10–15) minutes.
Comments: Even-numbered items produce Existential Well-Being Scale (EWB); odd-numbered items produce Religious Well-Being Scale (RWB).
Authors: Craig W. Ellison and Raymond F. Paloutzian.
Publisher: Life Advance, Inc.
Cross References: See T5:2474 (1 reference); for reviews by Ayres D'Costa and Patricia Schoenrade, see 12:369 (1 reference); see also T4:2529 (1 reference).

[2348]
Sports Emotion Test.

Purpose: "Designed to show how an athlete responds affectively to a competition."
Population: High school through adult athletes.
Publication Dates: 1980–1983.
Acronym: SET.
Scores, 24: 4 scores (Intensity, Concentration, Anxiety, Physical Readiness) for 6 different points in time (24 Hours Before, At Breakfast, Just Before, After Start, At Peak, Something Wrong).
Administration: Group.
Price Data: License to reproduce for Ph.D.s and Ed.D.s available from publisher.
Time: (10-20) minutes.
Authors: E. R. Oetting and C. W. Cole (profile).
Publisher: E. R. Oetting, Colorado State University.
Cross References: For reviews by Robert D. Brown and Robert P. Markley, see 10:339.

[2349]
Spousal Assault Risk Assessment Guide.

Purpose: "Helps criminal justice professionals predict the likelihood of domestic violence."
Population: Individuals suspected of or being treated for spousal or family-related assault.
Publication Date: 1999.
Acronym: SARA.
Scores: Total score only.
Administration: Individual.

Price Data, 2002: : $55 per complete kit including 25 assessment forms and manual; $23 per 25 assessment forms; $28 per manual; $30 per specimen set including 3 assessment forms and manual.
Time: Administration time not reported.
Comments: Completed by clinician/rater (criminal justice professional) after all available sources of information from suspect/offender, victim, etc. are gathered.
Authors: P. Randall Kropp, Stephen D. Hart, Christopher D. Webster, and Derek Eaves.
Publisher: Multi-Health Systems, Inc.

[2350]
Standard Progressive Matrices [Australian Edition].

Purpose: "Intended as a test of non-verbal reasoning ability."
Population: Students in years 3–11 (ages 8.3 to 17.2).
Publication Dates: 1955–1989.
Scores: Total score only.
Administration: Group.
Price Data: Available from publisher.
Time: 20(25) minutes.
Comments: 1986 Australian norms are based on the 1958 version of the test; norms are available for timed and for untimed administration.
Authors: Marion M. deLemos (manual) and J. C. Raven (test).
Publisher: Australian Council for Educational Research Ltd. [Australia].
Cross References: See T5:2477 (1 reference); for information on all editions of the Progressive Matrices, see 9:1007 (67 references), T3:1914 (200 references), 8:200 (190 references), T2:439 (122 references), and 7:376 (194 references); for a review by Morton Bortner, see 6:490 (78 references); see also 5:370 (62 references); for reviews by Charlotte Banks, W. D. Wall, and George Westby, see 4:314 (32 references); for reviews by Walter C. Shipley and David Wechsler of the 1938 edition, see 3:258 (13 references); for a review by T. J. Keating, see 2:1417 (8 references).

[2351]
Standard Progressive Matrices, New Zealand Standardization.

Purpose: Designed as a measure of nonverbal reasoning skills.
Population: New Zealand children ages 8–15 and adults.
Publication Date: 1985.
Acronym: SPM.
Scores: Total score only.
Administration: Group.
Price Data: Available from publisher.
Time: 30 minutes.

Authors: J. Raven (manual), J. C. Raven (manual), J. H. Court (manual), and New Zealand Council for Educational Research.

Publisher: New Zealand Council for Educational Research [New Zealand].

Cross References: See T5:2478 (2 references); for information on all editions of the Progressive Matrices, see 9:1007 (67 references), T3:1914 (200 references), 8:200 (190 references), T2:439 (122 references), and 7:376 (194 references); for a review by Morton Bortner, see 6:490 (78 references); see also 5:370 (62 references); for reviews by Charlotte Banks, W. D. Wall, and George Westby, see 4:314 (32 references); for reviews by Walter C. Shipley and David Wechsler of the 1938 edition, see 3:258 (13 references); for a review by T. J. Keating, see 2:1417 (8 references).

[2352]
The Standard Timing Model.

Purpose: "Designed to simulate the motions, functions and operations of automatic production machines" for use in selection, evaluation, and training of employees.

Population: Mechanics.

Publication Date: 1971.

Scores: 4 tasks: Cam "F" Retarded, Rod "C" Lengthened 1/16 inch, Rod "E" Shortened 1/16 inch Spring "E" Disconnected at Lever "E", Cam "D" Retarded.

Administration: Individual.

Price Data: Available from publisher.

Time: [60] minutes.

Author: Scientific Management Techniques, Inc.

Publisher: Scientific Management Techniques, Inc. [No reply from publisher; status unknown].

Cross References: For reviews by Sami Gulgoz and Gary L. Marco, see 12:370.

[2353]
Standardized Bible Content Tests.

Purpose: Aims to assess "general familiarity with the Bible."

Population: Bible college students.

Publication Dates: 1956–1993.

Acronym: SBCT.

Scores: Total score only.

Administration: Group.

Forms, 6: A (Bible Major), B (Bible Major), G, H, HS (mini-test), GS (mini-test).

Price Data, 2001: $1 per test booklet [$75 per 100]; $.40 per mini- test booklet [$30 per 100]; $.10 per answer sheet; $2 per scoring key; $1 per instructions; $5 per manual.

Time: 45(50) minutes.

Comments: Special form (Form SP) available for administration in missionary organizations, Christian high schools, and churches; information concerning foreign language editions available from publisher.

Author: Commission on Professional Development of the Accrediting Association of Bible Colleges.

Publisher: Accrediting Association of Bible Colleges.

Cross References: See 7:651 (1 reference).

[2354]
Standardized Reading Inventory, Second Edition.

Purpose: "Designed primarily to assess children's independent, instructional, and frustration reading levels in word recognition and comprehension skills."

Population: Ages 6-0 to 14-6.

Publication Dates: 1986–1999.

Acronym: SCR-2.

Scores, 4: Passage, Comprehension, Word Accuracy, Vocabulary in Context, Reading Quotient.

Administration: Individual.

Forms, 2: A, B.

Price Data, 2001: $224 per complete kit including manual (1999, 134 pages), story book, 25 each Forms A and B vocabulary sheets, 25 each Forms A and B record booklets, and 50 profile scoring forms; $13 per 25 vocabulary sheets (specify form); $49 per 25 record booklets (specify form); $21 per 50 profile scoring forms; $39 per story book; $47 per examiner's manual.

Time: (30–90) minutes.

Comments: Second Edition is norm-referenced.

Author: Phyllis L. Newcomer.

Publisher: PRO-ED.

Cross References: For reviews by Alan Solomon and Brenda A. Stevens, see 14:366; for reviews by Kenneth W. Howell and Cleborne D. Maddux of the original edition, see 10:340.

[2355]
Standardized Test of Computer Literacy and Computer Anxiety Index (Version AZ), Revised.

Purpose: To measure general computer literacy and identify students who have computer-related anxieties.

Population: Students in introductory computer literacy courses.

Publication Date: 1984.

Acronym: STCL and CAIN.

Administration: Group.

Price Data: Available from publisher.

Authors: Michael Simonson, Mary Montag (manual and achievement test), and Matt Maurer (manual and anxiety survey).

Publisher: Iowa State University Research Foundation, Inc. [No reply from publisher; status unknown].

a) STANDARDIZED TEST OF COMPUTER LITERACY (VERSION AZ), REVISED.

Purpose: Measures achievement in computer literacy.

Scores, 3: Computer Systems, Computer Applications, Computer Programming.
Time: 90(105) minutes.
Comments: May be administered in one session or in separate sessions for each of 3 sections.
b) COMPUTER ANXIETY INDEX.
Time: Administration time not reported.
Comments: Test booklet title is Computer Opinion Survey.
Cross References: For reviews by Ron Edwards and Kevin L. Moreland, see 10:341.

[2356]
Stanford Achievement Test—Abbreviated Version—8th Edition.

Purpose: "Measures student achievement in reading, mathematics, language, spelling, study skills, science, social science, and listening."
Population: Primary (1.5–4.5), Intermediate (4.5–7.5), Advanced (7.5–9.9), TASK (9.0–12.9).
Publication Dates: 1989–1992.
Administration: Group.
Price Data, 2002: $52 per examination kit (for preview only) including complete battery test booklet, directions for administering, practice test with directions (Primary 1 through Advanced 2 only), and hand-scorable answer document (Primary 3 through TASK 3 only); $29 per 25 complete/partial battery hand-scorable test booklets; $21 per copy of directions for administration (specify level); $7.50 per copy of class records; $64 per fall or spring national norms booklet (1988), and $103 per SAT abbreviated national norms booklet (1991).
Comments: For fall testing, the publisher recommends the use of the previous grade level test.
Author: The Psychological Corporation.
Publisher: The Psychological Corporation.
a) PRIMARY 1.
Population: Grades 1.5–2.5.
Scores, 12: Word Study Skills, Word Reading, Reading Comprehension, Total Reading, Language/English, Spelling, Listening, Concepts of Number, Mathematics Computation, Mathematics Applications, Total Mathematics, Environment.
Price Data: $156 per 25 complete battery Type 2 machine-scorable test booklets; $129 per 25 hand-scorable test booklets; $39.80 for keys for hand scoring (hand scoring requires Norms Booklets) complete/partial battery hand-scorable test booklets (Primary 1–Primary 3).
Time: 167 minutes for Partial battery; 187 minutes for Basic battery; 210 minutes for Complete battery.
b) PRIMARY 2.
Population: Grades 2.5–3.5.

Scores, 12: Word Study Skills, Reading Vocabulary, Reading Comprehension, Total Reading, Language/English, Spelling, Listening, Concepts of Numbers, Mathematics Computation, Mathematics Applications, Total Mathematics, Environment.
Price Data: Same as *a* above.
Time: 160 minutes for Partial battery; 180 minutes for Basic battery; 203 minutes for Complete battery.
c) PRIMARY 3.
Population: Grades 3.5–4.5.
Scores, 16: Word Study Skills, Reading Vocabulary, Reading Comprehension, Total Reading, Language Mechanics, Language Expression, Total Language, Study Skills, Spelling, Listening, Concepts of Number, Mathematics Computation, Mathematics Applications, Total Mathematics, Science, Social Science.
Price Data: $156 per 25 complete battery machine-scorable test booklets; $129 per 25 complete battery hand-scorable test booklets; $156 per 25 Type 2 partial battery machine-scorable test booklets; $129 per 25 partial battery hand-scorable test booklets; $129 per 25 complete battery reusable test booklets; $129 per 25 partial battery reusable test booklets; $117 per 100 complete/partial battery Type 2 machine-scorable answer folders; $29 per 25 Form J complete/partial battery hand-scorable answer folders; $46 per keys for hand scoring complete battery hand-scorable answer folders (Primary 3–TASK 3).
Time: 152 minutes for Partial battery; 197 minutes for Basic battery; 233 minutes for Complete battery.
d) INTERMEDIATE 1–3.
Population: Grades 4.5–7.5.
Scores, 15: Reading Vocabulary, Reading Comprehension, Total Reading, Language Mechanics, Language Expression, Total Language, Study Skills, Spelling, Listening, Concepts of Numbers, Mathematics Computation, Mathematics Applications, Total Mathematics, Science, Social Science.
Price Data: $129 per 25 complete battery reusable test booklets; $128 per 25 partial battery reusable test booklets; $117 per 100 complete/partial battery Type 2 machine-scorable answer folders; $29 per 25 Form J complete/partial battery hand-scorable answer folders; $46 per keys for hand scoring complete battery hand-scorable answer folders (Primary 3–TASK 3); see c above for additional price information.
Time: 142 minutes for Partial battery; 187 minutes for Basic battery; 223 minutes for Complete battery.

e) ADVANCED 1–2.
Population: Grades 7–8.
Scores, 15: Reading Vocabulary, Reading Comprehension, Total Reading, Language Mechanics, Language Expression, Total Language, Study Skills, Spelling, Listening, Concepts of Numbers, Mathematics Computation, Mathematics Applications, Total Mathematics, Science, Social Science.
Price Data: Same as *d* above.
Time: 142 minutes for Partial battery; 186 minutes for Basic battery; 222 minutes for Complete battery.
f) TASK 1–3.
Population: Grades 9–12.
Scores, 9: Reading Vocabulary, Reading Comprehension, Total Reading, Language/English, Study Skills, Spelling, Mathematics, Science, Social Science.
Price Data: $118 per 25 complete battery reusable test booklets; $117 per 100 complete/partial battery Type 2 machine-scorable answer folders; $29 per 25 Form J complete/partial battery hand-scorable answer folders.
Time: 95 minutes for Partial battery; 119 minutes for Basic battery; 155 minutes for Complete battery.
Cross References: See T5:2483 (1 reference); for reviews by Stephen N. Elliott, James A. Wollack, and Kevin L. Moreland, see 12:371.

[2357]
Stanford Achievement Test, Ninth Edition.

Purpose: Measures student achievement in reading, language, spelling, study skills, listening, mathematics, science, and social science.
Population: Grades K.0–13.0.
Publication Dates: 1923–1997.
Acronym: Stanford 9.
Forms, 5: Multiple Choice (Complete Battery, Form S; Complete Battery, Form SA; Basic Battery, Form S; Abbreviated Battery, Form S); Open-Ended.
Administration: Group.
Levels, 13: Stanford Early School Achievement Test 1, Stanford Early School Achievement Test 2, Primary 1, Primary 2, Primary 3, Intermediate 1, Intermediate 2, Intermediate 3, Advanced 1, Advanced 2, Stanford Test of Academic Skills 1, Stanford Test of Academic Skills 2, Stanford Test of Academic Skills 3.
Comments: A variety of assessment options are available including full-length and abbreviated batteries, customized content modules (with locally developed items), and open-ended assessments.
Author: Harcourt Brace Educational Measurement.
Publisher: Harcourt Educational Measurement.

a) STANFORD EARLY SCHOOL ACHIEVEMENT TEST 1.
Population: Grades K.0–K.5.
Acronym: SESAT 1.
Scores, 6: Reading (Sounds and Letters, Word Reading, Total Reading), Mathematics, Listening to Words and Stories, Environment.
Price Data, 2002: $36 per Exam Kits (Forms S and SA) including Complete Battery Test Booklet, Directions for Administering, and Practice Test with Directions (SESAT 1 through Advanced 2 only), separate Answer Document (Primary 3–TASK 3 only), open-ended Assessment Preview Brochure (Primary 1–TASK 3 only), and Reviewer's Edition; $18 per 25 Practice Tests, Form S; $110.75 per 25 Complete Battery Type 1 Machine-Scorable Test Booklets (Forms S and SA); $89 per 25 Complete Battery Hand-Scorable Test Booklets, Form S; $37 per Side-by-Side Keys for Scoring Hand-Scorable Booklets, Forms S and SA (hand-scoring requires Norms Books); $30 per Response Keys, Forms S and SA; $75 per Norms Book including scoring tables for both Multiple-Choice and Open-Ended Assessments (all levels; separate Norms Book published for fall and spring); $14 per Directions for Administering (Forms S and SA); $22 per 25 Understanding Test Results, appropriate for all forms and batteries; $6 per Class Record, appropriate for all forms and batteries; $7.50 per 25 Stanford Markers for all levels, appropriate for all forms and batteries; $23.50 per Compendium of Instructional Objectives, Forms S and SA, all levels; $25.90 per Strategies for Instruction: A Handbook of Performance Activities, appropriate for all forms and batteries; $35 per Guide for Organizational Planning, all levels, appropriate for all forms and batteries; $20.50 per Guide for Classroom Planning, appropriate for all forms and batteries; $6 per Directions for Administering Practice Tests, Forms S and SA; $67 per Technical Data Report for all levels, Forms S and SA.
Time: (105) minutes for Basic Battery; (135) minutes for Complete Battery.
b) STANFORD EARLY SCHOOL ACHIEVEMENT TEST 2.
Population: Grades K.5–1.5.
Acronym: SESAT 2.
Scores, 7: Reading (Sounds and Letters, Word Reading, Sentence Reading, Total Reading), Mathematics, Listening to Words and Stories, Environment.
Price Data: Same as *a* above.
Time: (140) minutes for Basic Battery; (170) minutes for Complete Battery.
c) PRIMARY 1.
Population: Grades 1.5–2.5.

1) *Multiple-Choice and Abbreviated Multiple-Choice.*

Scores, 11: Reading (Word Study Skills, Word Reading, Reading Comprehension, Total Reading), Mathematics (Mathematics: Problem Solving, Mathematics: Procedures, Total Mathematics), Language Form S, Spelling, Listening, Environment.

Price Data: Same as *a* above; $36 per Exam Kit, Multiple-Choice Assessment Abbreviated Battery, Form S including Abbreviated Battery Test Booklet, Directions for Administering, Practice Test with Directions and Open-Ended Assessment Preview Brochure; $18 per 25 Practice Tests, Form S; $105 per 25 Multiple-Choice Abbreviated Battery Type 1 Machine-Scorable Test Booklets, Form S; $29.50 per Multiple-Choice Abbreviated Battery Response Keys, Form S; $6 per Directions for Administering Practice Tests, Form S; $12 per Directions for Administering, Form S.

Time: (260) minutes for Basic Battery; (290) minutes for Complete Battery; (143) minutes for Abbreviated Battery.

2) *Open-Ended.*

Scores, 4: Reading, Mathematics, Science, Social Science.

Price Data: Same as *a* above; $10.50 per Open-Ended Reading Exam Kit including Open-Ended Test Booklet and Directions for Administering; $10.50 per Open-Ended Mathematics Exam Kit including Open-Ended Test Booklet and Directions for Administering; $10.50 per Open-Ended Science Exam Kit including Open-Ended Test Booklet and Directions for Administering; $10.50 per Open-Ended Social Science Exam Kit including Open-Ended Test Booklet and Directions for Administering; $25.50 per 25 Open-Ended Reading Test Booklets, Form S including Directions for Administering; $25.50 per 25 Open-Ended Mathematics Test Booklets, Form S including Directions for Administering; $25.50 per 25 Open-Ended Science Test Booklets, Form S including Directions for Administering; $25.50 per 25 Open-Ended Social Science Test Booklets, Form S including Directions for Administering; $22 per Scoring Guide for Open-Ended Reading Assessment; $22 per Scoring Guide for Open-Ended Mathematics Assessment; $22 per Scoring Guide for Open-Ended Science Assessment; $22 per Scoring Guide for Open-Ended Social Science Assessment; $8 per Directions for Administer-

ing Open-Ended Reading Assessment; $8 per Directions for Administering Open-Ended Mathematics Assessment; $8 per Directions for Administering Open-Ended Science Assessment; $8 per Directions for Administering Open-Ended Social Science Assessment.

Time: (50) minutes.

d) PRIMARY 2.

Population: Grades 2.5–3.5.

1) *Multiple-Choice and Abbreviated Multiple-Choice.*

Scores, 11: Reading (Word Study Skills, Reading Vocabulary, Reading Comprehension, Total), Mathematics (Mathematics: Problem Solving, Mathematics: Procedures, Total), Language Form S, Spelling, Listening, Environment.

Price Data: Same as *a* and *c*1 above.

Time: (260) minutes for Basic Battery; (290) minutes for Complete Battery; (137) minutes for Abbreviated Battery.

2) *Open-Ended.*

Scores, 4: Reading, Mathematics, Science, Social Science.

Price Data: Same as *a* and *c*2 above.

Time: (50) minutes.

e) PRIMARY 3.

Population: Grades 3.5–4.5.

1) *Multiple-Choice and Abbreviated Multiple-Choice.*

Scores, 11: Reading (Reading Vocabulary, Reading Comprehension, Total), Mathematics (Mathematics: Problem Solving, Mathematics: Procedures, Total), Language Form S, Spelling, Listening, Science, Social Science.

Price Data: Same as *a* and *c*1 above; $110 per 25 Complete Battery Hand-Scorable Test Booklets, including Science and Social Science, Form S subtests; $110 per 25 Complete Battery Reusable Test Booklets, Form S, including Science and Social Science subtests; $110 per 25 Complete Battery Reusable Test Booklets, Form SA, including Alternate Language, Science, and Social Science subtests (does not include separate Spelling and Study Skills subtests); $86 per 25 Abbreviated Battery Reusable Test Booklets, Form S; $51 per Stencil Keys for Scoring Hand-Scorable Answer Documents, Form S; $44 per Overlay Keys for Scoring Machine-Scorable Answer Documents, Form S; $81 per 100 Complete Battery Type 1 Machine-Scorable Answer Documents, Forms S and SA; $1,040 per 1,250 Continuous Form Type 1 Machine-Scorable Answer Documents, Form

S; $27 per 25 Hand-Scorable Answer Folders, Form S; $67 per 100 Abbreviated Battery Type 1 Machine-Scorable Answer Documents, Form S.

Time: (250) minutes for Basic Battery; (300) minutes for Complete Battery; (123) minutes for Abbreviated Battery.

2) *Open-Ended.*

Scores, 5: Reading, Mathematics, Science, Social Science, Writing.

Price Data: Same as *a* and *c2* above; $11 per Writing Exam Kit including 1 Prompt each of Descriptive, Narrative, Expository, and Persuasive, Directions for Administering, and Response Form; $25.50 per Writing Prompts: Descriptive, Form S including 25 Writing Prompts, 25 Response Forms, and Directions for Administering; $25.50 per Writing Prompts: Narrative, Form S including 25 Writing Prompts, 25 Response Forms, and Directions for Administering); $25.50 per Writing Prompts: Expository, Form S including 25 Writing prompts, 25 Response Forms, and Directions for Administering; $24 per Writing Prompts: Persuasive, Form S including 25 Writing Prompts, 25 Response Forms, and Directions for Administering; $22 per Manual for Interpreting Writing Assessment, all forms and levels; $8 per Directions for Administering, Descriptive, Form S; $8 per Directions for Administering, Narrative, Form S; $8 per Directions for Administering, Expository, Form S; $8 per Directions for Administering, Persuasive, Form S.

Time: (50) minutes.

f) INTERMEDIATE 1.

Population: Grades 4.5–5.5.

1) *Multiple-Choice and Abbreviated Multiple-Choice.*

Scores, 12: Reading (Reading Vocabulary, Reading Comprehension, Total); Mathematics (Mathematics: Problem Solving, Mathematics: Procedures, Total), Language Form S, Spelling, Study Skills, Listening, Science, Social Science.

Price Data: Same as *a*, *c1*, and *e1* above.

Time: (275) minutes for Basic Battery; (325) minutes for Complete Battery; (121) minutes for Abbreviated Battery.

2) *Open-Ended.*

Scores, 5: Same as *e2* above.

Price Data: Same as *a*, *c2*, and *e2* above.

Time: (50) minutes.

g) INTERMEDIATE 2.

Population: Grades 5.5–6.5.

1) *Multiple-Choice and Abbreviated Multiple-Choice.*

Scores, 12: Same as *f1* above.

Price Data: Same as *a*, *c1*, and *e1* above.

Time: (275) minutes for Basic Battery; (325) minutes for Complete Battery; (121) minutes for Abbreviated Battery.

2) *Open-Ended.*

Scores, 5: Same as *e2* above.

Price Data: Same as *a*, *c2*, and *e2* above.

Time: (50) minutes.

h) INTERMEDIATE 3.

Population: Grades 6.5–7.5.

1) *Multiple-Choice and Abbreviated Multiple-Choice.*

Scores, 12: Same as *f1* above.

Price Data: Same as *a*, *c1*, and *e1* above.

Time: (275) minutes for Basic Battery; (325) minutes for Complete Battery; (121) minutes for Abbreviated Battery.

2) *Open-Ended.*

Scores, 5: Same as *e2* above.

Price Data: Same as *a*, *c2*, and *e2* above.

Time: (50) minutes.

i) ADVANCED 1.

Population: Grades 7.5–8.5.

1) *Multiple-Choice and Abbreviated Multiple-Choice.*

Scores, 12: Same as *f1* above.

Price Data: Same as *a*, *c1*, and *e2* above; $25.90 each per Strategies for Instruction: A Handbook of Performance Activities for Reading, Mathematics, Language/Spelling/Listening, and/or Science/Social Science.

Time: (270) minutes for Basic Battery; (320) minutes for Complete Battery; (120) minutes for Abbreviated Battery.

2) *Open-Ended.*

Scores, 5: Same as *e2* above.

Price Data: Same as *a*, *c2*, and *e2* above.

Time: (50) minutes.

j) ADVANCED 2.

Population: Grades 8.5–9.9.

1) *Multiple-Choice and Abbreviated Multiple-Choice.*

Scores, 12: Same as *f1* above.

Price Data: Same as *a*, *c1*, *e1*, and *i1* above.

Time: (270) minutes for Basic Battery; (320) minutes for Complete Battery; (119) minutes for Abbreviated Battery.

2) *Open-Ended.*

Scores, 5: Same as *e2* above.

Price Data: Same as *a*, *c2*, and *e2* above.

Time: (50) minutes.

k) STANFORD TEST OF ACADEMIC SKILLS 1.

Population: Grades 9.0–9.9.

Acronym: TASK 1.

1) *Multiple-Choice and Abbreviated Multiple-Choice.*

Scores, 9: Reading (Reading Vocabulary, Reading Comprehension, Total), Mathematics, Language Form S, Spelling, Study Skills, Science, Social Science.

Price Data: Same as *a*, *c*1, *e*1, and *i*1 above; $105 per 25 Complete Battery Reusable Test Booklets, Form S including Science and Social Science subtests; $105 per Complete Battery Reusable Test Booklets, Form SA including Alternate Language, Science, and Social Science subtests (does not include separate Spelling and Study Skills subtests).

Time: (185) minutes for Basic Battery; (225) minutes for Complete Battery; (95) minutes for Abbreviated Battery.

2) *Open-Ended.*

Scores, 5: Same as *e*2 above.

Price Data: Same as *a*, *c*2, and *e*2 above.

Time: (50) minutes.

l) STANFORD TEST OF ACADEMIC SKILLS 2.

Population: Grades 10.0–10.9.

Acronym: TASK 2.

1) *Multiple-Choice and Abbreviated Multiple-Choice.*

Scores, 9: Same as *k*1 above.

Price Data: Same as *a*, *c*1, *e*1, *i*1, and *k*1 above.

Time: Same as *k*1 above.

2) *Open-Ended.*

Scores, 5: Same as *e*2 above.

Price Data: Same as *a*, *c*2, and *e*2 above.

Time: (50) minutes.

m) STANFORD TEST OF ACADEMIC SKILLS 3.

Population: Grades 11.0–13.0.

Acronym: TASK 3.

1) *Multiple-Choice and Abbreviated Multiple-Choice.*

Scores, 9: Same as *k*1 above.

Price Data: Same as *a*, *c*1, *e*1, *i*1, and *k*1 above.

Time: Same as *k*1 above.

2) *Open-Ended.*

Scores, 5: Same as *e*2 above.

Price Data: Same as *a*, *c*2, and *e*2 above.

Time: (50) minutes.

Cross References: See T5:2484 (15 references); for reviews by Ronald A. Berk and Thomas M. Haladyna, see 13:292 (80 references). For reviews of the Stanford Achievement Test—Abbreviated—8th Edition by Stephen N. Elliott and James A. Wollack and by Kevin L. Moreland, see 12:371; for information on an earlier edition of the Stanford Achievement Test, see T4:2551 (44 references); for reviews by Frederick G. Brown and Howard Stoker, see 11:377 (78 references); for reviews by Mark L. Davison and Michael J. Subkoviak and Frank H. Farley of the 1982 Edition, see 9:1172 (19 references); see also T3:2286 (80 references); for reviews by Robert L. Ebel and A. Harry

Passow and an excerpted review by Irvin J. Lehmann of the 1973 edition, see 8:29 (51 references); see also T2:36 (87 references); for an excerpted review by Peter F. Merenda of the 1964 edition, see 7:25 (44 references); for a review by Miriam M. Bryan and an excerpted review by Robert E. Stake (with J. Thomas Hastings), see 6:26 (13 references); for a review by N. L. Gage of an earlier edition, see 5:25 (19 references); for reviews by Paul R. Hanna (with Claude E. Norcross) and Virgil E. Herrick, see 4:25 (20 references); for reviews by Walter W. Cook and Ralph C. Preston, see 3:18 (33 references). For reviews of subtests, see 9:1173 (1 review), 9:1174 (1 review), 9:1175 (1 review), 8:291 (2 reviews), 8:745 (2 reviews), 7:209 (2 reviews), 7:527 (1 review), 7:708 (1 review), 7:802 (1 review), 7:895 (1 review), 6:637 (1 review), 5:656 (2 reviews), 5:698 (2 reviews), 5:799 (1 review), 4:419 (1 review), 4:555 (1 review), 4:593 (2 reviews), 3:503 (1 review), and 3:595 (1 review); for a review of the Stanford Test of Academic Skills [1982 Edition] by John C. Ory, see 9:1182; see also T3:2298 (3 references); for reviews by Clinton I. Chase and Robert L. Thorndike of an earlier edition, see 8:31.

[2358]
Stanford-Binet Intelligence Scale, Fourth Edition.

Purpose: Designed as "an instrument for measuring cognitive abilities that provides an analysis of pattern as well as the overall level of an individual's cognitive development."

Population: Ages 2–adult.

Publication Dates: 1916–1986.

Acronym: S-B.

Scores, 20: Verbal Reasoning (Vocabulary, Comprehension, Absurdities, Verbal Relations, Total), Abstract/Visual Reasoning (Pattern Analysis, Copying, Matrices, Paper Folding and Cutting, Total), Quantitative Reasoning (Quantitative, Number Series, Equation Building, Total), Short-Term Memory (Bead Memory, Memory for Sentences, Memory for Digits, Memory for Objects, Total), Total.

Administration: Individual.

Price Data: Available from publisher.

Time: Administration time varies.

Comments: Third revision still available.

Authors: Robert L. Thorndike, Elizabeth P. Hagen, Jerome M. Sattler, Elizabeth A. Delaney (Examiner's Handbook), and Thomas F. Hopkins (Examiner's Handbook).

Publisher: Riverside Publishing.

Foreign Adaptation: Australian adaptation available from Australian Council for Educational Research Ltd., 19 Prospect Hill Road, Private Bag 55, Camberwell, Melvourne 3124, Australia. Australian adaptations include a manual supplement, stick-on labels for all modified test items, and an Australian record booklet.

Cross References: See T5:2485 (245 references) and T4:2553 (120 references); for reviews by Anne Anastasi and Lee J. Cronbach, see 10:342 (89 references); see also 9:1176 (41 references), T3:2289 (203 references), 8:229 (176 references), and T2:525 (428 references); for a review by David Freides, see 7:425 (258 references); for a review by Elizabeth D. Fraser and excerpted reviews by Benjamin Balinski, L. B. Birch, James Maxwell, Marie D. Neale, and Julian C. Stanley, see 6:536 (110 references); for reviews by Mary R. Haworth and Norman D. Sundberg of the second revision, see 5:413 (121 references); for a review by Boyd R. McCandless, see 4:358 (142 references); see also 3:292 (217 references); for excerpted reviews by Cyril Burt, Grace H. Kent, and M. Krugman, see 2:1420 (132 references); for reviews by Francis W. Maxfield, J. W. M. Rothney, and F. L. Wells, see 1:1062.

[2359]
Stanford Diagnostic Mathematics Test, Fourth Edition.

Purpose: Designed to measure "competence in the basic concepts and skills that are prerequisite to problem solving in mathematics."

Publication Dates: 1976–1996.

Acronym: SDMT.

Administration: Group.

Parts, 2: Multiple Choice, Free Response.

Forms: 1 for Red, Orange, and Green levels; 2 (J, K) for Purple, Brown, and Blue levels.

Price Data, 2002: $37.50 per examination kit including multiple-choice test booklet and free-response test booklet (specify level) and directions for administering for each, answer document, practice test and practice test directions for administering, and ruler/marker; $17 per 25 practice tests and directions (specify level); $112 per 25 machine-scorable multiple-choice test booklets (specify Red, Orange, or Green level); $76 per 25 hand-scorable multiple-choice test booklets (specify Red, Orange, or Green level), directions for administering, and class record; $76 per 25 free-response test booklets (specify Red, Orange, or Green level) and directions for administering; $112 per hand-scorable multiple-choice/free-response combination kit including 25 hand-scorable multiple-choice test booklets and directions for administering, 25 free-response test booklets and directions for administering, and class record (specify Red, Orange, or Green level); $139 per machine-scorable multiple-choice/free response combination kit including 25 machine-scorable multiple-choice test booklets and directions for administering and 25 free-response test booklets and directions for administering (specify Red, Orange, or Green level); $76 per 25 reusable multiple-choice test booklets and directions for administering (specify Purple, Brown,

or Blue level and Form J or K); $76 per 25 free response test booklets and directions for administering (specify Purple, Brown, or Blue level and Form J or K); $112 per reusable multiple-choice/free-response combination kit including 25 reusable multiple-choice test booklets and directions for administering and 25 free-response test booklets and directions for administering (specify Purple, Brown, or Blue level and Form J or K); $15 per set of response keys for multiple-choice tests (specify level and form); $16 per side-by-side keys for hand-scorable test booklets including blackline master of student record form (specify Red, Orange, or Green level); $15.50 per scoring guide for free-response tests including blackline master of student record form (specify level and form); $22 per stencil keys for hand-scorable answer documents (specify Purple, Brown, or Blue level and Form J or K); $30 per 25 hand-scorable answer documents with blackline master of student record form and class record (specify Purple, Brown, or Blue level); $38 per 25 Purple/Brown/Blue level machine-scorable answer documents type I; $6.50 per 25 ruler/markers; $52 per Fall (1996, 166 pages) or Spring (1996, 166 pages) multilevel norms booklet; $22 per teacher's manual for interpreting (specify Level Red/Orange [1996, 61 pages], Green/Purple [1996, 64 pages], or Brown/Blue [1996, 63 pages]); $10 per directions for administering (specify multiple-choice or free-response, and Level Red, Orange, Green, or Purple/Brown/Blue); $6.50 per practice test directions for administering (specify Red, Orange, Green, Purple, or Brown Level); $6.50 per class record (specify Red, Orange, Green, or Purple/Brown/Blue level); price information for various scoring services available from publisher.

Author: Harcourt Brace Educational Measurement.

Publisher: Harcourt Educational Measurement.

a) RED LEVEL.

Population: GRADES 1.5–2.5.

Scores, 9: Concepts and Applications (Number Systems and Numeration, Patterns and Functions, Graphs and Tables, Problem Solving, Geometry and Measurement, Total), Computation (Addition of Whole Numbers, Subtraction of Whole Numbers, Total).

Time: 65 minutes for multiple choice; 90 minutes for free response.

b) ORANGE LEVEL.

Population: Grades 2.5–3.5.

Scores, 9: Same as for Red level.

Time: Same as for Red level.

c) GREEN LEVEL.

Population: Grades 3.5–4.5.

Scores, 11: Concepts and Applications (Number Systems and Numeration, Patterns and Functions, Graphs and Tables, Problem Solving, Geometry and Measurement, Total), Computation (Addition of Whole Numbers, Subtraction of

Whole Numbers, Multiplication of Whole Numbers, Division of Whole Numbers, Total).
Time: Same as for Red level.
d) PURPLE LEVEL.
Population: Grades 4.5–6.5.
Scores, 12: Concepts and Applications (Number Systems and Numeration, Statistics and Probability, Graphs and Tables, Problem Solving, Geometry and Measurement, Patterns and Functions [free response only], Total), Computation (Addition of Whole Numbers, Subtraction of Whole Numbers, Multiplication of Whole Numbers, Division of Whole Numbers, Total).
Time: 65 minutes for multiple choice; 80 minutes for free response.
e) BROWN LEVEL.
Population: Grades 6.5–8.9.
Scores, 15: Concepts and Applications (Number Systems and Numeration, Patterns and Functions [free response only], Statistics and Probability, Graphs and Tables, Problem Solving, Geometry and Measurement, Total), Computation (Addition and Subtraction of Whole Numbers, Multiplication of Whole Numbers [multiple choice only], Division of Whole Numbers [multiple choice only], Multiplication and Division of Whole Numbers [free response only], Operations with Fractions and Mixed Numbers, Operations with Decimals and Percents, Equations, Total).
Time: Same as Purple level.
f) BLUE LEVEL.
Population: Grades 9.0–13.0.
Scores, 12: Concepts and Applications (Number Systems and Numeration, Patterns and Functions [free response only], Statistics and Probability, Graphs and Tables, Problem Solving, Geometry and Measurement, Total), Computation (Operations with Whole Numbers, Operations with Fractions and Mixed Numbers, Operations with Decimals and Percents, Equations, Total).
Time: Same as Purple level.
Cross References: See T5:2486 (3 references); for reviews by Irvin J. Lehmann, Philip Nagy, and G. Michael Poteat, see 13:293; see also T4:2554 (5 references); for reviews by Bruce G. Rogers and Lorrie A. Shepard of an earlier edition, see 9:1177 (2 references); see also T3:2291 (1 reference); for reviews by Glenda Lappan and Larry Souder, see 8:292.

[2360]
Stanford Diagnostic Reading Test, Fourth Edition.
Purpose: "Intended to diagnose students' strengths and weaknesses in the major components of the reading process."
Publication Dates: 1978–1996.

Acronym: SDRT4.
Administration: Group.
Forms, 2: J, K (for Purple, Brown, and Blue levels).
Price Data, 2002: $37.50 per examination kit including multiple-choice test booklet and directions for administering, practice test and directions for administering, answer document, class record form, Reading Questionnaire, Reading Strategies Survey, Story Retelling (Story and Response Form), and directions for each (specify level); $17 per 25 practice tests and directions for administering (specify Red, Orange, Green, Purple, or Brown level); $111 per 25 machine-scorable test booklets type 1 and directions for administering (specify Red, Orange, or Green level); $76 per 25 hand-scorable test booklets, directions for administering, and class record (specify Red, Orange, or Green level); $76 per 25 reusable test booklets and directions for administering (specify level and form); $37.50 per 25 Reading Questionnaires and directions for administering (specify level and form); $37.50 per 25 Reading Strategies Surveys and directions for administering (specify Level Red/Orange, Green/Purple, or Brown/Blue); $44.50 per Story Retelling manual (1995, 15 pages) and 25 Story and Response forms (specify Level Red/Orange, Green/Purple, or Brown/Blue); $37.50 per 25 machine-scorable answer documents type 1 (for Purple/Brown/Blue levels); $30 per 25 hand-scorable answer documents with blackline master of student record form and class record (for Purple/Brown/Blue levels); $15 per side-by-side keys for hand-scorable test booklets including blackline master of student record form (specify Red, Orange, or Green level); $15 per response keys (specify Purple, Brown, or Blue level and Form J or K); $22 per stencil keys for hand-scorable answer documents (specify Purple, Brown, or Blue level and Form J or K); $6.50 per class record (specify Level Red, Orange, Green, or Purple/Brown/Blue); $6.90 per 25 row markers; $52 per Fall or Spring Multilevel norms booklet (1996, 103 pages); $22 per teacher's manual for interpreting (specify Level Red/Orange [1996, 67 pages], Green/Purple [1996, 68 pages], or Brown/Blue [1996, 62 pages]); $10 per test directions for administering (specify Level Red, Orange, Green, or Purple/Brown/Blue); $6.50 per practice test directions for administering (specify Level Red, Orange, Green, Purple, or Brown); $6.50 per Reading Questionnaire directions for administering; $6.50 per Reading Strategies Survey directions for administering; $9 per Story Retelling manual; price information for scoring services available from publisher.
Authors: Bjorn Karlsen and Eric F. Gardner.
Publisher: Harcourt Educational Measurement.
a) RED LEVEL.
Population: Grades 1.5–2.5.
Scores, 19: Phonetic Analysis (Consonants-Single, Consonants-Blends, Consonants-Digraphs,

Consonants Total, Vowels-Short, Vowels-Long, Vowels Total, Total), Vocabulary (Word Reading, Listening Vocabulary, Nouns, Verbs, Others, Total), Comprehension (Sentences, Riddles, Cloze, Total), Paragraphs with Questions.
Time: 105(110) minutes.
b) ORANGE LEVEL.
Population: Grades 2.5–3.5.
Scores, 19: Phonetic Analysis (Consonants-Single, Consonants-Blends, Consonants-Digraphs, Consonants Total, Vowels-Short, Vowels-Long, Vowels Total, Total), Vocabulary (Listening Vocabulary, Reading Vocabulary, Synonyms, Classification, Total), Comprehension (Cloze, Total), Paragraphs with Questions, Recreational Reading, Textual Reading, Functional Reading.
Time: 100(105) minutes.
c) GREEN LEVEL.
Population: Grades 3.5–4.5.
Scores, 25: Phonetic Analysis (Consonants-Single, Consonants-Blends, Consonants-Digraphs, Consonants Total, Vowels-Short, Vowels-Long, Vowels-Other, Vowels Total, Total), Vocabulary (Listening Vocabulary, Reading Vocabulary, Synonyms, Classification, Word Parts, Content Area Words, Total), Comprehension, Paragraphs with Questions, Recreational Reading, Textual Reading, Functional Reading, Initial Understanding, Interpretation, Critical Analysis and Reading Strategies.
Time: 100(105) minutes.
d) PURPLE LEVEL.
Population: Grades 4.5–6.5.
Scores, 16: Vocabulary (Reading Vocabulary, Synonyms, Classification, Word Parts, Content Area Words, Total), Comprehension, Paragraphs with Questions, Recreational Reading, Textual Reading, Functional Reading, Initial Understanding, Interpretation, Critical Analysis, Reading Strategies, Scanning.
Time: 85(90) minutes.
e) BROWN LEVEL.
Population: Grades 6.5–8.9.
Scores, 16: Same as Purple Level.
Time: 85(90) minutes.
f) BLUE LEVEL.
Population: Grades 9.0–12.9.
Scores, 16: Same as Purple Level.
Time: 85(90) minutes.
Cross References: See T5:2487 (19 references); for reviews by George Engelhard, Jr. and by Mark E. Swerdlik and Jayne E. Bucy, see 13:294 (9 references); see also T4:2555 (24 references); for reviews by Robert J. Tierney and James E. Ysseldyke of an earlier edition, see 9:1178 (7 references); see also T3:2292 (15 references); for a review by Bryon H. Van Roekel, see 8:777

(13 references); see T2:1651 (2 references); for a review by Lawrence M. Kasdon of Levels 1–2 of an earlier edition, see 7:725 (3 references).

[2361]
Stanford Early School Achievement Test, Third Edition.

Purpose: Measures school achievement.
Population: Grades K.0–K.5, K.5–1.5.
Publication Dates: 1969–1991.
Acronym: SESAT.
Administration: Group.
Forms, 2: J, L.
Price Data, 2002: $185 per 25 machine-scorable tests (Type 1, Form J; Type 2, Form L) (scored by publisher) (select level); $23.90 per 25 practice tests and one directions for administering (select level); $7.50 per class record form; $35.50 per 25 previews for parents (select level); $21 per administration directions (select level and form); $7.50 per administration directions for practice test (select level); $67.50 per norms booklet (1988, Form J Only; 1991, Forms J and L) (select level); $47 per coordinator's handbook; $51.50 per examination kit including test booklet, administration directions, and practice test with directions (select level and form).
Comments: Downward extension of the Stanford Achievement Test Series.
Author: The Psychological Corporation.
Publisher: The Psychological Corporation.
a) LEVEL 1.
Population: Grades K.0–K.5.
Scores, 8: Sounds and Letters, Word Reading, Total, Mathematics, Listening to Words and Stories, Total for Basic Battery, Environment, Total for Complete Battery.
Price Data: $185 per 25 machine-scorable test booklets (Type 1, Form J; Type 2, Form L); $119 per 25 hand-scorable test booklets (select form); $175 per set of scoring keys (select form).
Time: (190) minutes over 9 sessions.
b) LEVEL 2.
Population: Grades K.5–1.5.
Scores, 9: Sounds and Letters, Word Reading, Sentence Reading, Total, Mathematics, Listening to Words and Stories, Basic Battery Total, Environment, Complete Battery Total.
Price Data: $185 per 25 machine-scorable test booklets (Type 1, Form J; Type 2, Form L); $126 per 25 hand-scorable test booklets (select form); $175 per set of scoring keys (select form).
Time: (225) minutes over 9 sessions.
Cross References: See T5:2488 (10 references) and T4:2556 (2 references); for reviews by Phillip L. Ackerman and C. Dale Carpenter, see 11:378 (8 references); for a review by Mary J. Allen of an earlier

edition, see 9:1179 (1 reference); see also T3:2293 (9 references); for a review by Courtney B. Cazden of an earlier edition, see 8:30 (6 references); see also T2:38 (1 reference); for reviews by Elizabeth Hagen and William A. Mehrens of Level 1, see 7:28.

[2362]
Stanford Writing Assessment Program, Third Edition.

Purpose: Provides for the direct assessment of written expression in four modes: Descriptive, Narrative, Expository, and Persuasive.
Population: Grades 3–12.
Publication Dates: 1982–1997.
Scores: 4 writing modes: Descriptive, Narrative, Expository, Persuasive.
Administration: Group.
Levels, 9: Primary 3, Intermediate 1, Intermediate 2, Intermediate 3, Advanced 1, Advanced 2, TASK 1, TASK 2, TASK 3.
Forms, 2: S, T (Form T is a secure form).
Price Data, 2002: $25.50 per 25 writing prompts, 25 response forms, and Directions for Administering (specify Descriptive, Narrative, Expository, or Persuasive); $8 per Directions for Administering (specify Descriptive, Narrative, Expository, or Persuasive); $11 per writing exam kit including 1 prompt each of Descriptive, Narrative, Expository and Persuasive, 1 Directions for Administering, 1 response form, and Reviewer's Edition; $75 per norms book; $22 per manual for interpreting (1997, 70 pages) (all forms and levels); scoring prices available from publisher.
Time: (50) minutes.
Comments: Holistic and analytic scoring available; computer scoring available; Form T is a secure form; Third edition provides information about student strengths and weaknesses, which can assist in instructional planning.
Authors: Harcourt Brace Educational Measurement.
Publisher: Harcourt Educational Measurement.
Cross References: For reviews by Linda Crocker and Sharon H. deFur, see 14:367; for reviews by Philip Nagy and Wayne H. Slater of an earlier editions, see 13:295.

[2363]
The Stanton Profile.

Purpose: Designed to provide "pre-employment personality and attitudinal pre-employment assessments."
Population: Employment applicants.
Publication Dates: 1987–1995.
Scores, 6: 4 content scores (Work Motivation, Adaptability/Flexibility, Service Orientation, Trustworthiness), 2 validity checks (Social Desirability Bias, Infrequent Response Patterns).
Administration: Group or individual.

Manual: No manual.
Price Data: Available from the publisher.
Time: Untimed, generally requiring approximately 20 minutes.
Author: William G. Harris.
Publisher: Pinkerton Services Group.

[2364]
The Stanton Survey and the Stanton Survey Phase II.

Purpose: Provides indications of previous counterproductive work behavior and attitudes toward honesty.
Population: Applicants for employment.
Publication Dates: 1964–1995.
Scores: Total score only.
Administration: Individual or group.
Price Data: Available from publisher.
Time: Untimed.
Comments: Available in hard copy or via telephonic IVR.
Authors: Carl S. Klump, Homer B. C. Reed, Jr., and Sherwood Perman.
Publisher: Pinkerton Services Group.
    a) THE STANTON SURVEY.
    b) THE STANTON SURVEY PHASE II.
Cross References: For reviews by H. C. Ganguli and Kenneth G. Wheeler, see 9:1185. (An additional review by William G. Harris is available electronically from the Buros Institute national database: available from SilverPlatter and from Tests Reviews Online via the Buros webpage.)

[2365]
STAR Early Literacy.

Purpose: A computer-adaptive test that "can be useful for evaluating literacy development overall and in seven broad literacy domains."
Population: Prekindergarten–Grade 3.
Publication Date: 2001.
Scores, 8: Graphophonemic Knowledge, General Reading, Phonemic Awareness, Phonics, Comprehension, Structural Analysis, Vocabulary, Scaled Score.
Administration: Individual.
Price Data, 2001: $1,995 per single-computer license kit (up to 40 students) including software manual (71 pages), installation guide (48 pages), technical manual (126 pages), CD-ROM with pre-test instructions, mouse training, practice assessment, actual assessment questions, quick reference card, and 12-month support plan; $3,995 per school site license (network-ready, up to 200 students, expansions available); expansion prices available from publisher.
Time: (13) minutes.
Comments: Also provides domain score and skill score; classifies students into one of three stages of reading development (emergent, transitional, probable

reader); includes software allowing teacher to generate reports; may be administered up to 10 times per year; uses the same database as other software from the same company. System requirements are Windows or Macintosh, CD-ROM drive, mouse, 640x480 monitor, 256 color monitor, sound card, 24 MB RAM, 310 MB hard drive, Power PC or greater and System 7.5.5 or higher (Macintosh) or 133 MHz Pentium and Windows 95 or higher (Windows).

Author: Renaissance Learning, Inc.
Publisher: Renaissance Learning, Inc.

[2366]
STAR Math™.

Purpose: Designed as a computer-adaptive math test and database to place students at the appropriate math level.
Population: Grades 3–12.
Publication Dates: 1998–2001.
Scores: Total score only.
Administration: Individual.
Price Data, 2001: $1,499 per school license for up to 200 students, including installation guide, software manual, Quick Reference card, technical manual, 1-year Expert Support Plan, and Pre-Test Instruction Kit; $499 per single-computer license, Quick Reference card, software manual, installation guide, and technical manual; 1-year Expert Support Plan, and Pre-Test Instruction Kit.
Time: Untimed, (15) minutes.
Comments: Available for Macintosh and Windows computers; manuals are included in PDF format on CD-ROM; can be repeated at no extra cost through school year to track growth.
Author: Renaissance Learning, Inc.
Publisher: Renaissance Learning, Inc.

[2367]
STAR Reading Version 2.2.

Purpose: A computer-adaptive reading test and database "allowing teachers to ... [quickly] assess students' reading abilities."
Population: Grades 1–12.
Publication Dates: 1996–2001.
Scores: Total score only.
Administration: Individual.
Price Data, 2001: $499 per single-computer license kit (up to 40 students) including Software Manual, Installation Guide, CD-ROM (which also includes technical manual), pre-test instructions, quick reference card, and 12-month support plan; $1,499 per network-wide license kit (up to 200 students, expansions available); for expansion prices contact publisher (800) 338-4204.
Time: (10) minutes.
Comments: Revision of STAR Reading; provides grade equivalents, percentile scores, and instructional reading level; includes software allowing teacher to

generate diagnostic reports; may be administered up to 5 times per year; version 2.0 uses the same database as other software from the same company. System requirement: Windows or Macintosh, CD-ROM drive, mouse, 640x480 monitor, 256 color monitor, 8 MB RAM, 25 MB drive space, System 7.1 or higher (Macintosh) or Windows 3.1 or higher and MS-DOS version 3.3 or higher.
Author: Renaissance Learning, Inc.
Publisher: Renaissance Learning, Inc.
Cross References: For reviews by Theresa Volpe-Johnstone and Sandra Ward of the original edition, see 14:368.

[2368]
STAR Supplementary Tests of Achievement in Reading.

Purpose: "Designed to supplement the assessments that teachers make about their pupils' progress and achievement in reading."
Population: Ages 8–13.
Publication Date: 2001.
Administration: Group.
Levels, 2: STAR Test (4–6), STAR Test (7–9).
Forms, 2: A, B.
Price Data, 2002: NZ$38.70 per specimen set (specify level) including teacher's manual (35 pages), 1 test booklet each of Forms A and B, 1 set answer keys each of Forms A and B; NZ$9.90 per 10 test booklets (specify Form A or B, specify level); NZ$9 per photocopiable masters answer key (Level 4–6, specify Form A or B); NZ$9 per photocopiable masters marking key (Level 7–9, specify Form A or B).
Comments: Normed on children living in New Zealand.
Author: Warwick B. Elley.
Publisher: New Zealand Council for Educational Research [New Zealand].

a) STAR TEST (4–6).
   Scores, 4: Word Recognition, Sentence Comprehension, Paragraph Comprehension, Vocabulary Range.
   Time: 20(35) minutes.
b) STAR TEST (7–9).
   Scores, 6: Word Recognition, Sentence Comprehension, Paragraph Comprehension, Vocabulary Range, The Language of Advertising, Reading Different Genres or Styles of Writing.
   Time: 30(45) minutes.

[2369]
START—Strategic Assessment of Readiness for Training.

Purpose: Designed to diagnose adult's learning strengths and weaknesses.
Population: Adults.

Publication Date: 1994.
Acronym: START.
Scores, 8: Anxiety, Attitude, Motivation, Concentration, Identifying Important Information, Knowledge Acquisition Strategies, Monitoring Learning, Time Management.
Administration: Group.
Price Data, 1996: $19.95 per user's manual (21 pages); $9.95 per assessment and learner's guide (volume discounts available).
Time: (15) minutes.
Comments: Self-administered; self-scored.
Authors: Claire E. Weinstein and David R. Palmer.
Publisher: H & H Publishing Co., Inc.
Cross References: For reviews by Phillip L. Ackerman and Patricia A. Bachelor, see 14:369.

[2370]
State-Trait Anger Expression Inventory-2.
Purpose: "Designed to measure the experience, expression, and control of anger for adolescents and adults."
Population: Ages 16 and over.
Publication Dates: 1988–1999.
Acronym: STAXI-2.
Scores, 12: State Anger Scale (Feeling Angry, Feel like Expressing Anger Verbally, Feel like Expressing Anger Physically, Total), Trait Anger Scale (Angry Temperament, Angry Reaction, Total), Angry Expression and Anger Control Scales (Anger Expression—Out, Anger Expression—In, Anger Control—Out, Anger Control—In), Anger Expression Index.
Administration: Group or individual.
Price Data: Available from publisher.
Time: (12–15) minutes.
Author: Charles D. Spielberger.
Publisher: Psychological Assessment Resources, Inc.
Cross References: See T5:2496 (6 references); for reviews by David J. Pittenger and Alan J. Raphael of the Revised Research Edition, see 13:296 (52 references); see also T4:2562 (12 references); for reviews by Bruce H. Biskin and Paul Retzlaff of the STAXI-Research Edition, see 11:379 (8 references).

[2371]
State-Trait Anxiety Inventory for Children.
Purpose: Designed "as a research tool for the study of anxiety in elementary school children."
Population: Grades 4–6.
Publication Dates: 1970–1973.
Acronym: STAIC.
Scores, 2: State Anxiety, Trait Anxiety.
Administration: Group.
Price Data: Available from publisher.
Time: (20) minutes.

Comments: Downward extension of State-Trait Anxiety Inventory (2372); title on test is "How-I-Feel Questionnaire"; self-administering.
Authors: Charles D. Spielberger, C. Drew Edwards, Robert E. Lushene, Joseph Montuori, Denna Platzek.
Publisher: Mind Garden, Inc.
Cross References: See T5:2498 (78 references), T4:2564 (58 references), and T3:2301 (15 references); for a review by Norman S. Endler, see 8:684 (19 references); see also T2:1392 (2 references).

[2372]
State-Trait Anxiety Inventory.
Purpose: Designed to assess anxiety as an emotional state (S-Anxiety) and individual differences in anxiety proneness as a personality trait (T-Anxiety).
Population: Grades 9–16 and adults.
Publication Dates: 1968–1984.
Acronym: STAI.
Scores, 2: State Anxiety, Trait Anxiety.
Administration: Group.
Forms, 2: X, Y.
Parts, 2: 2 parts for each form labeled Form 1 (State), Form 2 (Trait).
Price Data: Available from publisher.
Foreign Language Edition: Spanish edition available.
Time: (10–20) minutes.
Comments: Title on test is Self-Evaluation Questionnaire.
Authors: Charles D. Spielberger; Form Y and manual prepared in collaboration with R. L. Gorsuch, R. Lushene, P. R. Vagg, and G. A. Jacobs.
Publisher: Mind Garden, Inc.
Cross References: See T5:2497 (680 references), T4:2563 (646 references), 9:1186 (158 references), and T3:2300 (277 references); for reviews by Ralph Mason Dreger and Edward S. Katkin, see 8:683 (268 references); see also T2:1391 (45 references) and 7:141 (20 references).

[2373]
State Trait-Depression Adjective Check Lists.
Purpose: "To measure both state and trait depression mood and feelings."
Population: Ages 14 and over.
Publication Dates: 1967–2002.
Acronym: ST-DACL.
Scores, 6: State-Positive Mood, State-Negative Mood, State Mood-Total, Trait-Positive Mood, Trait-Negative Mood, Trait Mood-Total.
Administration: Group.
Forms, 4: 1, 2, A-B, C-D.
Price Data: Price information available from publisher for introductory kit including manual (2002,

83 pages), 25 forms 1 & 2, 25 forms C-D and 25 profile forms.
Time: (4–8) minutes per list.
Comments: Developed from the Depression Adjective Check List.
Author: Bernard Lubin.
Publisher: EdITS/Educational and Industrial Testing Service.
Cross References: See T5:2499 (1 reference); for reviews by Andres Barona and by Janet F. Carlson and Betsy Waterman of an earlier edition, see 13:297 (21 references); see also T4:742 (79 references), 9:315 (21 references), T3:681 (46 references), 8:536 (20 references), and T2:1154 (2 references); for reviews of the earlier edition by Leonard D. Goodstein and Douglas M. McNair, see 7:65 (3 references); see also P:57 (4 references).

[2374]
Stephens Oral Language Screening Test.

Purpose: To screen children "for potential problems in syntax and/or articulation associated with their production of standard American English dialects."
Population: Prekindergarten-grade 1.
Publication Date: 1977.
Acronym: SOLST.
Scores, 2: Syntax, Articulation.
Administration: Individual.
Price Data: Available from publisher.
Time: (9) minutes.
Author: M. Irene Stephens.
Publisher: Interim Publishers [No reply from publisher; status unknown].
Cross References: See 9:1193 (2 references).

[2375]
The Stieglitz Informal Reading Inventory: Assessing Reading Behaviors from Emergent to Advanced Levels.

Purpose: Designed to provide educators with information about students' reading behaviors.
Population: Grades 1–9.
Publication Date: 1992.
Acronym: SIRI.
Scores, 7: Graded Words in Context (Independent, Instructional, Frustration), Graded Reading Passages (Word Recognition, Oral Comprehension, Prior Knowledge, Interest).
Administration: Individual.
Price Data: Available from publisher.
Time: (20–30) minutes.
Author: Ezra L. Stieglitz.
Publisher: Allyn & Bacon.
Cross References: For reviews by Koressa Kutsick Malcolm and Stephanie Stein, see 13:298.

[2376]
Stirling Eating Disorder Scales.

Purpose: Developed as a comprehensive measure of anorexia and bulimia.
Population: Adolescents and adults.
Publication Dates: 1995–1996.
Acronym: SEDS.
Scores: 8 scales: Anorexic Dietary Cognitions, Anorexic Dietary Behavior, Bulimic Dietary Cognitions, Bulimic Dietary Behavior, Perceived External Control, Low Assertiveness, Low Self-Esteem, Self-Directed Hostility.
Administration: Individual.
Price Data, 2002: $94.46 per complete kit including scales, profile forms, and manual (1995, 33 pages).
Time: (30) minutes.
Authors: Gwenllian-Jane Williams and Kevin G. Power.
Publisher: The Psychological Corporation Europe [United Kingdom].

[2377]
Stoelting Brief Nonverbal Intelligence Test.

Purpose: Designed as a nonverbal, nonlanguage measure of cognitive functions.
Population: Ages 6-0 to 20-11.
Publication Date: 1999.
Acronym: S-BIT.
Scores, 7: Figure Ground, Form Completion, Sequential Order, Repeated Patterns, S-BIT IQ, Visualization, Fluid Reasoning.
Administration: Individual.
Price Data, 2001: $295 per complete kit including 20 record forms, examiner's manual (1999, 191 pages), easel book, and response cards; $20 per 20 record forms; $50 per examiner's manual; $170 per easel book; $35 per carrying case; $70 per response cards.
Time: (25) minutes.
Authors: Gale H. Roid and Lucy J. Miller.
Publisher: Stoelting Co.

[2378]
Stokes/Gordon Stress Scale.

Purpose: Developed to measure stressors in healthy individuals over age 65.
Population: Healthy individuals over age 65.
Publication Date: 1987.
Acronym: SGSS.
Scores: Total stress score.
Administration: Group.
Price Data: Available from publisher.
Time: (15–30) minutes.
Comments: Self-administered in person or by mail.
Authors: Shirlee A. Stokes and Susan E. Gordon.
Publisher: Lienhard School of Nursing.

Cross References: For a review by Sharon L. Weinberg, see 13:299; see also T4:2572 (1 reference).

[2379]
Strategic Decision Making Inventory.

Purpose: Designed as a guide to business managers to help them think strategically in their decision making process (deciding how to decide).
Population: Business managers.
Publication Date: 1983.
Scores, 2: Flexibility, Appropriateness.
Administration: Group.
Price Data, 2002: $8.95 per inventory; minimum of 20 (volume discounts available).
Time: [15–20] minutes.
Comments: Self-administered; self-scored.
Author: Herbert S. Kindler.
Publisher: The Center for Management Effectiveness, Inc.

[2380]
Strength Deployment Inventory.

Purpose: Designed to assess "personal strengths in relating to others" under two conditions: when things are going well, and when there is conflict.
Population: Adults.
Publication Dates: 1973–1996.
Acronym: SDI.
Scores: 7 Motivational Values Systems: (Altruistic-Nurturing, Assertive-Directing, Analytic-Autonomizing, Flexible-Cohering, Assertive-Nurturing, Judicious-Competing, Cautious-Supporting); 13 scores reflecting progression through stages of conflict.
Administration: Group or individual.
Price Data, 2001: $22 per Premier Edition including Standard Edition of the Strength Deployment Inventory, interpretive cards, and 2 exercises; Portrait of Personal Strengths and Portrait of Overdone Strengths; $5.50 per either Portrait available separately: $10 per Standard Edition; $14 per Component Edition including interpretive cards; $30 per manual (1996, 146 pages).
Foreign Language Editions: Standard Edition available in French, Swedish, and Spanish; Premier Edition available in Swedish and Dutch.
Time: (20–40) minutes for Standard Edition; (20–40) minutes per exercise in Premier Edition.
Comments: Self-scorable; for corporate (e.g., team building), clinical (e.g., relationship counseling), and career development (e.g., outplacement and welfare-to-work) uses; Feedback Edition uses self-rating and ratings of a significant other person.
Author: Elias H. Porter.
Publisher: Personal Strengths Publishing.
Cross References: For a review by Frederick T. L. Leong, see 14:371.

[2381]
Stress Audit.

Purpose: "Samples the magnitude and types of stress [and stress symptoms] experienced by the respondent and assesses relative vulnerability to stress."
Population: Adults.
Publication Dates: 1983–1987.
Scores, 16: Situational (Family, Individual Roles, Social Being, Environment, Financial, Work/School), Symptom (Muscular System, Parasympathetic Nervous System, Sympathetic Nervous System, Emotional, Cognitive System, Endocrine, Immune System), Vulnerability, Total Situational Stress, Total Symptoms.
Administration: Group.
Price Data: Available from publisher.
Time: [20–30] minutes.
Comments: Self-administered; v5.0 is available in paper-and-pencil format (optically scannable for computer scoring and interpretation), PC format (computer administration, scoring, and interpretation), and on the World Wide Web (http://www.bbinst.org/).
Authors: Lyle H. Miller, Alma Dell Smith, and Bruce L. Mehler (manual only).
Publisher: Biobehavioral Sciences.
Cross References: For a review by Rolf A. Peterson, see 10:347.

[2382]
Stress in General Scale.

Purpose: Designed as a global measure of job stress.
Population: Employees.
Publication Date: 1992.
Acronym: SIG.
Scores: Total score only.
Administration: Individual or group.
Price Data, 2001: $20 per 100 test booklets; $1 per scoring key.
Time: Administration time not reported.
Comments: Previously listed with the Job Descriptive Index (1290).
Authors: Patricia C. Smith, William K. Balzer, Gail H. Ironson, Karen B. Paul, Bob Hayes, Sarah Moore-Hirschl, Luis Fernando Parra.
Publisher: Bowling Green State University, Department of Psychology.

[2383]
Stress Index for Parents of Adolescents.

Purpose: Designed to assess the level of stress in parents of adolescents.
Population: Parents of 11–19-year-olds.
Publication Date: 1998.
Scores, 11: Adolescent Domain (Moodiness/Emotional Lability, Social Isolation/Withdrawal, Delinquency/Antisocial, Failure to Achieve or Persevere), Parent Domain (Life Restrictions, Relationship with

Spouse/Partner, Social Alienation, Incompetence/Guilt), Adolescent-Parent Relationship Domain, Life Stressors, Total Parenting Stress.
Administration: Group or individual.
Price Data: Available from publisher for introductory kit including 25 reusable item booklets, 25 handscorable answer sheet/profile forms, and professional manual (70 pages).
Time: (20) minutes.
Authors: Peter L. Sheras, and Richard R. Abidin.
Publisher: Psychological Assessment Resources, Inc.
Cross References: For reviews by Elizabeth L. Jones and Susan M. Swearer, see 14:372.

[2384]
Stress Indicator & Health Planner.

Purpose: "Assists people to identify their present health practices, pinpoint problem areas and plan for improved health, productivity and well-being."
Population: Adults.
Publication Dates: 1990–1993.
Acronym: SIHP.
Scores, 10: Physical Distress, Psychological Distress, Behavioral Distress, Total Distress Assessment, Interpersonal Stress Assessment, Nutritional Assessment, Health Assessment, Total Wellness Assessment, Time-Stress Assessment, Occupational Stress Assessment.
Administration: Group.
Price Data, 1993: $12 per test booklet; $12 per Professional's Guide (1993, 12 pages); $15 per Releasing Relaxation: Mind and Body audiotape.
Time: (30) minutes for Basic; (180–360) minutes for Facilitated/Advanced.
Comments: Self-administered and self-scored.
Authors: Gwen Faulkner and Terry Anderson.
Publisher: Consulting Resource Group International, Inc.
Cross References: For reviews by Dennis C. Harper and Barbara L. Lachar, see 13:300.

[2385]
Stress Management Questionnaire [Revised].

Purpose: Identifies how one responds to life stressors and copes with stress.
Population: Adults and adolescents.
Publication Dates: 1980–1999.
Acronym: SMQ.
Scores, 11: Warning Signs (Hostility/Anger, Perfectionism, Time Orientation, Disappointment, Negative Mood, Underachievement, Tension), Stress Effects (Physical, Live Work Satisfaction), Stressors (Life Events, Hassles)
Administration: Group or individual.
Forms, 2: Participant, Companion.
Price Data, 2001: $14 per questionnaire (discounts available).

Time: (20–25) minutes.
Comments: Manual title is "Stressmaster Trainer's Manual"; questionnaire completed by self and by a close companion; self-scored.
Author: James C. Petersen.
Publisher: The Assessment and Development Centre.
Cross References: For a review by Jayne E. Stake of an earlier version, see 10:348.

[2386]
Stress Processing Report.

Purpose: Enables individuals to identify, understand and change their reactions to stress, thereby improving their receptivity to organizational change.
Population: Adults.
Publication Date: 1994.
Acronym: SPR.
Scores: 19 domains: Self (Self-Image, Past View, Control, Approval, Growth, Effectiveness), Others (Inclusion, Interpersonal, Intimacy, Trust), Process (Receptiveness, Synergy, Cooperation, Time Orientation, Time Utilization), Goals (Satisfaction, Directedness, Expectations, Future View).
Administration: Individual or group.
Price Data: Price data for test materials including Self-Development Guide and Leader's Guide available from publisher.
Time: Administration time not reported.
Author: Human Synergistics International.
Publisher: Human Synergistics International.

[2387]
Stress Profile.

Purpose: Developed "to provide a brief yet comprehensive stress and health risk assessment."
Population: Adults.
Publication Date: 1999.
Scores, 16: Stress, Health Habits, Exercise, Rest/Sleep, Eating/Nutrition, Prevention, ARC Item Cluster, Social Support Network, Type A Behavior, Cognitive Hardiness, Coping Style, Positive Appraisal, Negative Appraisal, Threat Minimization, Problem Focus, Psychological Well-Being.
Administration: Group.
Price Data, 2002: $105 per kit including 25 AutoScore' forms, manual (63 pages), 1 reusable administration booklet, and a 2-use disk for on-site computer scoring and interpretation; $39.50 per 25 AutoScore' forms to be used with administration booklet; $45 per manual; $22.50 per 25 disposable administration booklets; $49.95 per 5 reusable administration booklets (quantity discounts available); prices for WPS Test Report mail-in service, disks, and FAX service available from publisher.
Time: (20–25) minutes.

Comments: Can be administered and scored by hand or by computer.
Author: Kenneth M. Nowack.
Publisher: Western Psychological Services.

[2388]
Stress Resiliency Profile.

Purpose: Designed to identify some ways individuals unintentionally contribute to their own stress levels.
Population: Employees.
Publication Date: 1992.
Acronym: SRP.
Scores, 3: Deficiency Focusing, Necessitating, Skill Recognition.
Administration: Group or individual.
Price Data, 2001: $8.50 per test booklet/manual (23 pages).
Time: (15) minutes.
Comments: Self-administered and self-scored.
Authors: Kenneth W. Thomas and Walter G. Tymon, Jr.
Publisher: Consulting Psychologists Press, Inc.
Cross References: For reviews by John A. Mills and William R. Merz, Sr., see 13:301.

[2389]
Stromberg Dexterity Test.

Purpose: "Developed as an aid in choosing workers for jobs which require speed and accuracy of arm and hand movement."
Population: Trade school and adults.
Publication Dates: 1945–1981.
Acronym: SDT.
Scores: Total score only.
Administration: Individual.
Price Data, 2002: $614 per complete set including all necessary equipment and manual (1981, 12 pages) in case; $19 per manual.
Time: (5–10) minutes.
Author: Eleroy L. Stromberg.
Publisher: The Psychological Corporation.
Cross References: See T3:2317 (2 references) and T2:2235 (8 references); for a review by Julian C. Stanley, see 4:755 (1 reference).

[2390]
Strong Interest Inventory® [1994].

Purpose: Designed to "identify general areas of interests as well as specific activities and occupations" for further exploration.
Population: Ages 16 and over.
Publication Dates: 1927–1994.
Acronym: Strong.
Scores, 267: 6 General Occupational Themes: Realistic, Investigative, Artistic, Social, Enterprising, Conventional; 25 Basic Interest Scales: Realistic (Agriculture, Nature, Military Activities, Athletics, Mechanical Activities), Investigative (Science, Mathematics, Medical Science), Artistic (Music/Dramatics, Art, Applied Arts, Writing, Culinary Arts), Social (Teaching, Social Service, Medical Service, Religious Activities), Enterprising (Public Speaking, Law/Politics, Merchandising, Sales, Organizational Management), Conventional (Data Management, Computer Activities, Office Services); 211 Occupational Scales: Accountant (female, male), Actuary (f, m), Advertising Executive (f, m), Agribusiness Manager (m), Architect (f, m), Artist/Commercial (f, m), Artist/Fine (f, m), Art Teacher (f, m), Athletic Trainer (f, m), Audiologist (f, m), Auto Mechanic (f, m), Banker (f, m), Biologist (f, m), Bookkeeper (f, m), Broadcaster (f, m), Business Education Teacher (f, m), Buyer (f, m), Carpenter (f, m), Chef (f, m), Chemist (f, m), Child Care Provider (f), Chiropractor (f, m), College Professor (f, m), Community Service Organization Director (f, m), Computer Programmer/Systems Analyst (f, m), Corporate Trainer (f, m), Credit Manager (f, m), Dental Assistant (f), Dental Hygienist (f), Dentist (f, m), Dietitian (f, m), Elected Public Official (f, m), Electrician (f, m), Elementary School Teacher (f, m), Emergency Medical Technician (f, m), Engineer (f, m), English Teacher (f, m), Farmer (f, m), Flight Attendant (f, m), Florist (f, m), Food Service Manager (f, m), Foreign Language Teacher (f, m), Forester (f, m), Gardener/Groundskeeper (f, m), Geographer (f, m), Geologist (f, m), Hair Stylist (f, m), High School Counselor (f, m), Home Economics Teacher (f), Horticultural Worker (f, m), Housekeeping & Maintenance Supervisor (f, m), Human Resources Director (f, m), Interior Decorator (f, m), Investments Manager (f, m), Lawyer (f, m), Librarian (f, m), Life Insurance Agent (f, m), Marketing Executive (f, m), Mathematician (f, m), Mathematics Teacher (f, m), Medical Illustrator (f, m), Medical Records Technician (f, m), Medical Technician (f, m), Medical Technologist (f, m), Military Enlisted Personnel (f, m), Military Officer (f, m), Minister (f, m), Musician (f, m), Nurse/Licensed Practical (f, m), Nurse/Registered (f, m), Nursing Home Administrator (f, m), Occupational Therapist (f, m), Optician (f, m), Optometrist (f, m), Paralegal (f, m), Parks and Recreation Coordinator (f, m), Pharmacist (f, m), Photographer (f, m), Physical Education Teacher (f, m), Physical Therapist (f, m), Physician (f, m), Physicist (f, m), Plumber (m), Police Officer (f, m), Psychologist (f, m), Public Administrator (f, m), Public Relations Director (f, m), Purchasing Agent (f, m), Radiologic Technologist (f, m), Realtor (f, m), Reporter (f, m), Research & Development Manager (f, m), Respiratory Therapist (f, m), Restaurant Manager (f, m), School Administrator (f, m), Science Teacher (f, m), Secretary (f), Small Business Owner (f, m), Social Science Teacher (f, m), Social Worker (f, m), Sociologist (f, m), Special Education Teacher (f, m),

Speech Pathologist (f, m), Store Manager (f, m), Technical Writer (f, m), Translator (f, m), Travel Agent (f, m), Veterinarian (f, m), Vocational Agriculture Teacher (f, m); 4 Personal Style Scales: Work Style, Learning Environment, Leadership Style, Risk Taking/Adventure; 27 Administrative Indexes: Total Response, Infrequent Response, Response Percentages (Like, Indifferent, Dislike) for each of 8 inventory sections (Occupations, School Subjects, Activities, Leisure Activities, Types of People, Characteristics, Preferences: Activities, Preferences: Work), Total for all parts.

Administration: Group.

Price Data, 2001: $75 per 10 prepaid profile combined item booklet/answer sheets; $235 per 10 prepaid interpretive report combined item booklet/answer sheets; $72 per Strong Applications and Technical Guide (1994, 425 pages); $18.95 per Strong Profile preview kit including prepaid profile item booklet/answer sheet and client booklet; $23.10 per Strong interpretive report preview kit including prepaid interpretive item booklet/answer sheet and client booklet; $40 per 10 client booklets; $163 per 10 prepaid professional report combined item booklet/answer sheets; $26.50 per Strong Professional report preview kit including prepaid professional item booklet/answer sheet and booklet; $75 per 10 prepaid Strong Profile, High School Edition combined item booklet/answer sheets; $10.75 per Strong Profile, High School Edition preview kit including prepaid High School profile item booklet/answer sheet and client booklet; $75 per 10 prepaid Strong college item booklet/answer sheets; $10.75 per Strong college preview kit.

Time: (35–40) minutes.

Comments: Scoring options: Prepaid (mail-in) and CPP software system (price data available from publisher); administration also available via CPP software system and the internet: Strong Interest Inventory and Skills Confidence Inventory, Strong and MBTI Career Report, and Strong and MBTI Entrepreneur Report also available from publisher.

Authors: Edward K. Strong, Jr. (original inventory), David P. Campbell (test and manual revision), Lenore W. Harmon (applications and technical guide), Jo-Ida C. Hansen (applications and technical guide), Fred H. Borgen (applications and technical guide), and Allen L. Hammer (applications and technical guide).

Publisher: Consulting Psychologists Press, Inc.

Cross References: See T5:1790 (19 references); for reviews by John Christian Busch and by Blaine R. Worthen and Perry Sailor of the Fourth Edition, see 12:374 (43 references); see also T4:2581 (64 references); for reviews by Wilbur L. Layton and Bert W. Westbrook, see 9:1195 (17 references); see also T3:2318 (99 references); for reviews by John O. Crites, Robert H. Dolliver, Patricia W. Lunneborg, and excerpted reviews by Richard W. Johnson, David P. Campbell,

and Jean C. Steinhauer, see 8:1023 (289 references, these references are for SVIB-M, SBIV-W, and SCII). For references on the Strong Vocational Interest Blank For Men, see T2:2212 (133 references); for reviews by Martin R. Katz and Charles J. Krauskopf and excerpted reviews by David P. Campbell and John W. M. Rothney, see 7:1036 (485 references); for reviews by Alexander W. Astin and Edward J. Furst, see 6:1070 (189 references); see also 5:868 (153 references); for reviews by Edward S. Bordin and Elmer D. Hinckley, see 4:747 (98 references): see also 3:647 (102 references); for reviews by Harold D. Carter, John G. Darley, and N. W. Morton, see 2:1680 (71 references); for a review by John G. Darley, see 1:1178. For references on the Strong Vocational Interest Blank For Women, see T2:2213 (30 references); for reviews by Dorothy M. Clendenen and Barbara A. Kirk, see 7:1037 (92 references); see also 6:1071 (12 references) and 5:869 (19 references); for a review by Gwendolen Schneidler Dickson, see 3:649 (38 references); for a review by Ruth Strang, see 2:1681 (10 references); for a review by John G. Darley, see 1:1179.

[2391]
Stroop Color and Word Test.

Purpose: Designed "for the evaluation of brain dysfunction or for an evaluation of psychopathology in general."

Population: Ages 7 and over.

Publication Date: 1978.

Scores, 3: Word, Color, Color-Word.

Administration: Group.

Price Data, 2001: $85 per complete kit including manual (97 pages), and 25 test forms; $35 per 25 test forms; $305 per manual; (technical supplement available with kit purchase without additional cost); $80 per Spanish version including manual and 25 test forms.

Foreign Language Edition: Spanish version available.

Time: 2.25(5) minutes.

Comments: Publisher advises that children's version will be published in 2002.

Author: Charles J. Golden.

Publisher: Stoelting Co.

Cross References: See T5:2516 (122 references) and T4:2582 (40 references); for reviews by James R. Evans and George W. Hynd, see 9:1196 (15 references); see also T3:2319 (1 reference).

[2392]
Stroop Neuropsychological Screening Test.

Purpose: Provides "an efficient and sensitive neuropsychological screening measure based on the Stroop procedure."

Population: Ages 18 and over.

Publication Date: 1989.

Acronym: SNST.
Scores, 2: Color, Color-Word.
Administration: Individual.
Price Data: Available from publisher.
Time: 4(9) minutes.
Authors: Max R. Trenerry, Bruce Crosson, James DeBoe, and William R. Leber.
Publisher: Psychological Assessment Resources, Inc.
Cross References: See T5:2517 (8 references) and T4:2583 (3 references); for reviews by Manfred J. Meier and Cecil R. Reynolds, see 11:382 (1 reference).

[2393]
Structure of Intellect Learning Abilities Test.

Purpose: "Designed to assess a wide variety of cognitive abilities or factors of intelligence in children and adults."
Population: Preschool–adult.
Publication Dates: 1975–1985.
Acronym: SOI-LA.
Administration: Group or individual.
Price Data, 2002: $215 per complete kit including 10 standard test booklets (5 Form A and 5 Form B), set of scoring keys, set of stimulus cards, 10 worksheets/profiles, and manual (1985, 165 pages); $24.50 per 5 standard test booklets (specify Form A or B); $40 per scoring keys for Forms A, B, and G; $78 per manual (1985, 165 pages).
Authors: Mary Meeker, Robert Meeker, and Gale H. Roid (manual).
Publisher: Western Psychological Services.
   a) FORM A.
   Population: Grade 2–adult.
   Scores: 26 subtests in 5 test areas: Cognition (Cognition of Figural Units, Cognition of Figural Classes, Cognition of Figural Systems, Cognition of Figural Transformations, Cognition of Symbolic Relations, Cognition of Symbolic Systems, Cognition of Semantic Units, Cognition of Semantic Relations, Cognition of Semantic Systems), Memory (Memory of Figural Units, Memory of Symbolic Units—Visual, Memory of Symbolic Systems—Visual, Memory of Symbolic Units—Auditory, Memory of Symbolic Systems—Auditory, Memory of Symbolic Implications), Evaluation (Evaluation of Figural Units, Evaluation of Figural Classes, Evaluation of Symbolic Classes, Evaluation of Symbolic Systems), Convergent Production (Convergent Production of Figural Units, Convergent Production of Symbolic Systems, Convergent Production of Symbolic Transformations, Convergent Production of Symbolic Implications), and Divergent Production (Divergent Production of Figural Units, Divergent Production of Semantic Units, Divergent Production of Symbolic Relations) yielding 14 general ability scores:

Cognition, Memory, Evaluation, Convergent Production, Divergent Production, Figural, Symbolic, Semantic, Units, Classes, Relations, Systems, Transformations, Implications.
   Time: (150–180) minutes.
   b) FORM B.
   Purpose: Alternative to Form A.
   c) GIFTED SCREENING FORM (FORM G).
   Population: Grade 2–adult.
   Subtests, 12: From Form A which best predict gifted status.
   Price Data: $26 per 5 test booklets.
   Time: (60–90) minutes.
   d) PRIMARY FORM (FORM P).
   Population: Grades K–3.
   Subtests, 11: Similar to Form A, 5 measuring figural abilities, 3 measuring symbolic abilities, and 3 measuring semantic abilities.
   Price Data: $27.50 per 5 test booklets; $45 per scoring key.
   Time: (60–90) minutes.
   Comments: Formerly called Process and Diagnostic Screening Test.
Cross References: See T5:2518 (4 references); for reviews by Jack A. Cummings and Dianna L. Newman, see 10:349 (5 references); for reviews by William E. Coffman and Donald A. Leton of an earlier form, see 9:1197 (2 references); see also T3:2320 (2 references).

[2394]
Structured Clinical Inverview for DSM-IV Axis I Disorders: Clinician Version.

Purpose: Constructed as "a semistructured interview for making the major DSM-IV Axis I diagnoses."
Population: Psychiatric or general medical patients ages 18 or older.
Publication Date: 1997.
Acronym: SCID-CV.
Scores, 6: Mood Episodes, Psychotic Symptoms, Psychotic Disorders, Mood Disorders, Substance Use Disorders, Anxiety and Other Disorders.
Administration: Individual.
Price Data, 2002: $91 per complete kit including user's guide (138 pages), administration booklet (84 pages), and 5 score sheets; $32 per packet of 5 score sheets; $38 per user's guide; $35 per administration booklet.
Time: (45–90) minutes.
Comments: Shortened, clinician version of the Structured Clinical interview for DSM-IV Axis I Disorders: Research Version.
Authors: Michael B. First, Robert L. Spitzer, Miriam Gibbon, and Janet B. W. Williams.
Publisher: American Psychiatric Publishing, Inc.

Cross References: For reviews by Paul D. Werner and Thomas A. Widiger, see 14:373; see also T5:2519 (56 references).

[2395]
Structured Clinical Interview for DSM-IV Axis II Personality Disorders.

Purpose: Designed as "a semistructured diagnostic interview for assessing the 10 DSM-IV Axis II personality disorders as well as Depressive Personality Disorder and Passive-Aggressive Personality Disorder."
Population: Adults receiving psychiatric or general medical care.
Publication Date: 1997.
Acronym: SCID-II.
Scores, 13: Avoidant, Dependent, Obsessive-Compulsive, Passive-Aggressive, Depressive, Paranoid, Schizotypal, Schizoid, Histrionic, Narcissistic, Borderline, Antisocial, Not Otherwise Specified.
Administration: Individual.
Price Data, 2002: $58 per complete kit including user's guide and packet of 5 interviews and questionnaire; $32 per 5 interviews and questionnaires; $39 per user's guide.
Time: Administration time not reported.
Comments: Also includes optional, self-report SCID-II Personality Questionnaire.
Authors: Michael B. First, Miriam Gibbon, Robert L. Spitzer, Janet B. W. Williams, and Lorna Smith Benjamin.
Publisher: American Psychiatric Publishing, Inc.
Cross References: For reviews by Paul A. Arbisi and Suzanne G. Martin, see 14:374; see also T5:2520 (25 references).

[2396]
Structured Clinical Interview for DSM-IV Dissociative Disorders—Revised.

Purpose: "Can be used to assess dissociative symptoms and disorders in subjects with a variety of psychiatric illnesses."
Population: Adults with psychiatric illnesses.
Publication Dates: 1985–1994.
Acronym: SCID-D-R
Scores, 5: Amnesia, Depersonalization, Derealization, Identity Confusion, Identity Alteration.
Administration: Individual.
Price Data, 2002: $31.95 per 5 tests.
Time: Administration time not reported.
Comments: Composed of both closed and open-ended questions and does not provide quantitative information regarding a subject; can be used as part of an overall battery of psychiatric diagnostic instruments, or can be administered independently.
Author: Marlene Steinberg.
Publisher: American Psychiatric Publishing, Inc.

[2397]
Structured Interview for Disorders of Extreme Stress & Traumatic Antecedents Questionnaire—Self Report.

Purpose: Designed to assist "in the initial assessment, treatment planning, and progress measurement of clients potentially affected with Post Traumatic Stress Disorder."
Population: Adults potentially affected with Post Traumatic Stress Disorder.
Publication Date: 1999.
Administration: Individual.
Price Data: Available from publisher.
Time: Administration time not reported.
Comments: Computerized.
Author: Bessel A. van der Kolk.
Publisher: Multi-Health Systems, Inc.
  a) STRUCTURED INTERVIEW FOR DISORDERS OF EXTREME STRESS.
  Acronym: SIDES.
  Scores, 9: Affect Regulation, Modulation of Anger, Self Destructiveness, Suicide Preoccupation, Sexual Involvement, Risk Taking, Amnesia, Transient Dissociative Episodes, Depersonalization.
  b) TRAUMATIC ANTECEDENTS QUESTIONNAIRE—SELF REPORT.
  Acronym: TAQ-S.
  Scores, 10: Competence, Safety, Neglect, Separation, Family Secrets, Conflict Resolution, Physical Trauma, Sexual Trauma, Witnessing Trauma, Exposure to Drugs.

[2398]
Structured Interview for the Five-Factor Model of Personality.

Purpose: Designed "to assess personality using the Five-Factor Model."
Population: Ages 18 and above.
Publication Date: 1997.
Acronym: SIFFM.
Scores, 35: Neuroticism (Anxiety, Hostility, Depression, Self-Consciousness, Impulsiveness, Vulnerability, Total), Extraversion (Warmth, Gregariousness, Assertiveness, Activity, Excitement-Seeking, Positive Emotions, Total), Openness to Experience (Fantasy, Aesthetics, Feelings, Actions, Ideas, Values, Total), Agreeableness (Trust, Straightforwardness, Altruism, Compliance, Modesty, Tender-Mindedness, Total), Conscientiousness (Competence, Order, Dutifulness, Achievement-Striving, Self-Discipline, Deliberation, Total).
Administration: Individual.
Price Data: Available from publisher for introductory kit including 25 interview booklets and professional manual (85 pages).

Time: (60) minutes.
Authors: Timothy J. Trull and Thomas A. Widiger.
Publisher: Psychological Assessment Resources, Inc.

[2399]
Structured Interview of Reported Symptoms.

Purpose: Designed to "detect malingering and other forms of feigning of psychological symptoms."
Population: Ages 18 and over.
Publication Dates: 1986–1992.
Acronym: SIRS.
Scores, 13: Primary Scales (Rare Symptoms, Symptom Combinations, Improbable and Absurd Symptoms, Subtle Symptoms, Blatant Symptoms, Severity of Symptoms, Selectivity of Symptoms, Reported vs. Observed Symptoms), Supplementary Scales (Direct Appraisal of Honesty, Defensive Symptoms, Symptom Onset and Resolution, Overly Specified Symptoms, Inconsistency of Symptoms).
Administration: Individual.
Price Data: Available from publisher for complete kit including manual (1992, 47 pages) and 10 interview booklets.
Time: [45–60] minutes.
Authors: Richard Rogers, R. Michael Bagby, and Susan E. Dickens.
Publisher: Psychological Assessment Resources, Inc.
Cross References: For reviews by David N. Dixon and Ronald J. Ganellen, see 12:375.

[2400]
Structured Photographic Articulation Test II Featuring Dudsberry.

Purpose: Designed to assess children's articulation and phonological skills.
Population: Ages 3–9 years.
Publication Dates: 1989–2001.
Acronym: SPAT-D II.
Scores: Total score only.
Administration: Individual.
Price Data: Available from publisher.
Time: Administration time not reported.
Comments: Forty photographs are used to assess 59 singleton consonants and 10 consonant blends; revision of the Structured Photographic Articulation Test Featuring Dudsberry (SPAT-D); earlier edition still available.
Authors: Janet I. Dawson and Patricia J. Tattersall.
Publisher: Janelle Publications, Inc.
Cross References: For reviews by Clinton W. Bennett and Susan Felsenfeld of the earlier edition, see 12:376.

[2401]
Structured Photographic Expressive Language Test.

Purpose: Designed "to assess ... production of expressive morphology and syntax."
Publication Date: 1983.
Acronym: SPELT II.
Scores: Total score only.
Administration: Individual.
Comments: Includes a system of alternative response structures for assessment of the Black population.
Authors: Ellen O'Hara Werner and Janet Dawson Kresheck.
Publisher: Janelle Publications, Inc.

a) STRUCTURED PHOTOGRAPHIC EXPRESSIVE LANGUAGE TEST—PRESCHOOL.
Population: Ages 3-0 to 5-11.
Acronym: SPELT-P.
Price Data, 1998: $89 per complete kit including 37 color photos, 10 response forms, and manual (27 pages); $8 per 50 response forms; $12 per 50 articulation forms.
Time: (3–10) minutes.

b) STRUCTURED PHOTOGRAPHIC EXPRESSIVE LANGUAGE TEST—II.
Population: Ages 4-0 to 9-5.
Acronym: SPELT-II.
Price Data: $99 per complete kit including 50 color photos, 10 response forms, and manual (51 pages); $20 per 50 response forms.
Time: (15–25) minutes.
Cross References: See T5:2524 (13 references) and T4:2588 (1 reference); for a review by Joan D. Berryman, see 9:1198 (2 references).

[2402]
Student Adaptation to College Questionnaire.

Purpose: "Designed to assess how well a student is adapting to the demands of the college experience."
Population: College freshmen.
Publication Date: 1989.
Acronym: SACQ.
Scores, 5: Academic Adjustment, Social Adjustment, Personal Emotional Adjustment, Attachment, Full Scale.
Administration: Group or individual.
Price Data, 2002: $95 per complete kit including 25 hand-scorable questionnaires and manual (76 pages) plus 2 prepaid mail-in answer sheets for computer scoring and interpretation; $39.50 per 25 hand-scorable questionnaires; $45 per manual; $13 per computer-scored mail-in answer sheet (quantity discounts available); $175 per IBM computer disk (25 uses).
Time: (20) minutes.
Authors: Robert W. Baker and Bohdan Siryk.
Publisher: Western Psychological Services.
Cross References: See T5:2525 (13 references) and T4:2590 (9 references); for a review by E. Jack Asher, Jr., see 11:383 (4 references).

[2403]
Student Adjustment Inventory.

Purpose: Designed as "an instrument for identifying common affective-social problems."
Population: Upper elementary, junior high, senior high, and beginning college students.
Publication Dates: 1975–1989.
Acronym: SAI.
Scores, 7: Self-Esteem, Group Interaction, Self-Discipline, Communication, Energy/Effort, Learning/Studying, Attitude Towards Learning Environment.
Administration: Group or individual.
Price Data, 2002: $34 per report kit including manual (1989, 23 pages), 2 reusable test booklets, 5 answer sheets, and processing of 5 mail-in reports; $10 per 10 reusable test booklets; $8 per 50 answer sheets; $10 per manual; $5.45-$6.35 per mail-in report; $225 per SAI microcomputer version per 50 administrations (IBM 3.5-inch disk).
Time: (20–30) minutes.
Comments: Available in pencil and paper or microcomputer versions.
Author: James R. Barclay.
Publisher: MetriTech, Inc.
Cross References: For reviews by Philip Ash and Mark J. Benson, see 12:377.

[2404]
Student Behavior Survey.

Purpose: A multidimensional assessment to rate behavior and classroom performance to reflect the presence of problems in emotional and behavioral adjustment.
Population: Ages 5–18.
Publication Date: 2000.
Acronym: SBS.
Scores: 11 scales: Academic Performance, Academic Habits, Social Skills, Parent Participation, Health Concerns, Emotional Distress, Unusual Behavior, Social Problems, Verbal Aggression, Physical Aggression, Behavior Problems.
Administration: Individual.
Price Data, 2002: $78 per introductory kit including 25 AutoScore™ answer/profile forms and manual (72 pages); $29.95 per 25 AutoScore™ answer/profile forms; $52.50 per manual.
Time: Untimed.
Comments: Ratings by teachers.
Authors: David Lachar, Sabine A. Wingenfeld, Rex B. Kline, and Christian P. Gruber.
Publisher: Western Psychological Services.

[2405]
Student Developmental Task and Lifestyle Inventory.

Purpose: "Assisting students in understanding their own development and establishing goals and plans to shape their own futures."

Population: College students ages 17–24.
Publication Date: 1987.
Acronym: SDTLI.
Scores, 12: Establishing and Clarifying Purpose Task (Educational Involvement Subtask, Career Planning Subtask, Life Management Subtask, Lifestyle Planning Subtask, Cultural Participation Subtask), Developing Mature Interpersonal Relationships Task (Peer Relationships Subtask, Tolerance Subtask, Emotional Autonomy Subtask), Academic Autonomy Task, Salubrious Lifestyle Scale, Intimacy Scale, Response Bias Scale.
Administration: Group.
Price Data, 1997: $50 per 50 reusable test booklets; $25 per 50 answer sheets; $25 per 50 Understanding and Using the SDTLI: A Guide for Students (6 pages); $10 per manual (50 pages).
Time: (30-40) minutes.
Comments: Revision of the Student Developmental Task Inventory, Revised, Second Edition.
Authors: Roger B. Winston, Jr., Theodore K. Miller, and Judith S. Prince.
Publisher: Student Development Associates, Inc.
Cross References: See T5:2527 (17 references) and T4:2592 (9 references); for reviews by Mary Henning-Stout and Willam D. Porterfield, see 11:384 (13 references); for reviews by Fred H. Borgen and Steven D. Brown of the Second Edition, see 9:1199 (5 references).

[2406]
Student Evaluation Scale.

Purpose: To assess children's academic and social-emotional behaviors.
Population: Grades 1–12.
Publication Date: 1970.
Acronym: SES.
Scores, 3: Educational Response, Social Emotional Response, Total.
Administration: Individual.
Price Data, 2002: $6.75 per 25 rating forms; $6.75 per 25 profiles; $5 per specimen set including manual (4 pages).
Time: Administration time not reported.
Comments: Ratings by teachers.
Authors: William T. Martin and Sue Martin.
Publisher: Psychologists and Educators, Inc.

[2407]
Student Goals Exploration.

Purpose: "Designed to help researchers better understand the academic goals of college students."
Population: College.
Publication Date: 1990.
Acronym: SGE.
Scores: 46 scales in 7 sections: Goals in Attending College (Prepare for Career and/or Graduate Profes-

sional School, Acquire a General Education, Nondirected), Educational Purpose (Social Change, Effective Thinking, Systematic Instruction, Vocational Orientation, Personal Enrichment, Great Ideas, Values Clarification), General Academic Orientation (Develop Creativity, Increase Self-Understanding, Improve Speaking Skills, Improve Reasoning Skills, Develop a Life Philosophy, Understand the World Around Me, Work for Social Causes, Develop Scientific Inquiry Skills, Prepare for a Career, Gain Expertise, Develop Human Relations, Improve Numerical Ability, Understand Cultural Diversity, Value Learning for Its Own Sake, Improve Basic Skills), Subject-Specific Goals (English, History, Sociology, Psychology, Biology, Mathematics, Fine Arts, Romance Languages, Introductory Business, Universally Endorsed), Feelings About Studying (Goal Time Frame [Long-Range], Goal Time Frame [Short-Range], Goal Clarity, Goal Source [Expectations], Goal Source [Self], Expectations and Study Skills (Self-Confident Scholar, Anxious Student), Types of Activities Scales (Relates and Applies Coursework, Interacts About Coursework, Explores Beyond Assignments, Concentrates on Task).

Administration: Group.

Forms, 6: Version IR-1 (to be completed early in academic term); Version IR-2 (to be completed late in academic term); Version IR-M (for students who have chosen a field of study); Version CR-1 ("examines goals that students bring to their college courses"); Version CR-2 ("examines students' goals as they complete college courses"); Version CR-M ("examines goals that students hope to achieve in their chosen major").

Price Data: Price information available from publisher for user's manual (Institutional Research Guide, 1991, 149 pages; Classroom Research Guide, 1991, 117 pages) and 300 forms.

Time: (45) minutes for SGE-IR version; (30) minutes for SGE-CR version.

Authors: Joan S. Stark, Malcolm A. Lowther, Kathleen M. Shaw, and Paula L. Sossen.

Publisher: National Center for Research to Improve Postsecondary Teaching and Learning.

Cross References: For reviews by Robert D. Brown and by Steven R. Shaw and Nicholas Benson, see 13:302.

[2408]
Student Instructional Report II.

Purpose: Provides a means for students to "describe and assess their courses and instruction."
Population: College teachers.
Publication Dates: 1971–1996.
Acronym: SIR II.
Scores: 45 item scores plus up to 10 optional locally prepared items.
Administration: Group.
Price Data: Available from publisher.

Time: (10–15) minutes.
Comments: Ratings and background data by students concerning the instructor, course, and student.
Author: Educational Testing Service.
Publisher: Educational Testing Service.
Cross References: See T5:2531 (3 references), T4:2597 (1 reference), and T3:2334 (3 references); for reviews by Frank Costin and William C. McGaghie of the earlier edition, see 8:398 (16 references); see also T2:894 (1 reference).

[2409]
Student Opinion Inventory, Revised Edition.

Purpose: To assess students' opinions concerning many facets of the school and to "solicit students' recommendations for improvement."
Population: Grades 5–12.
Publication Dates: 1974–1995.
Scores: 4 subscales: Quality of the Instructional Program, Support for Student Learning, School Climate/Environment for Learning, Student Activities/Intervention in School.
Administration: Group.
Parts, 2: A (Likert-scale items), B (customize up to 20 local questions).
Price Data, 1998: $15 per 25 inventories; $6.50 per manual (1995, 26 pages).
Time: (35–40) minutes.
Author: National Study of School Evaluation.
Publisher: National Study of School Evaluation.
Cross References: See T3:2335 (1 reference).

[2410]
Student Rights Scales.

Purpose: Designed to determine student and teacher perceptions of student rights in junior and senior high school.
Population: Grades 7–12.
Publication Dates: 1982–1986.
Acronym: SRS.
Scores, 5: General Rights, Due Process, Academic Self Determination, Freedom of Expression, Personal Conduct.
Administration: Group.
Price Data: Available from publisher.
Time: Administration time not reported.
Comments: For research use only.
Author: Thomas R. Oaster.
Publisher: Thomas R. Oaster.
Cross References: For reviews by Steven W. Lee and David Moshman, see 10:351.

[2411]
Student Self-Concept Scale.

Purpose: Designed as a "multidimensional self-report measure of self-concept and related psychological constructs."

Population: Grades 3–12.
Publication Date: 1993.
Acronym: SSCS.
Scores, 13: Self-Confidence (Self-Image, Academic, Social, Lie, Composite), Importance (Self-Image, Academic, Social, Lie), Outcome Confidence (Self-Image, Academic, Social, Composite).
Administration: Group.
Levels, 2: Grades 3–6, grades 7–12.
Price Data, 2002: $35.95 per 25 record booklets (specify Level 1 or Level 2); $49.95 per manual (82 pages).
Time: (20–30) minutes.
Authors: Frank M. Gresham, Stephen N. Elliott, and Sally E. Evans-Fernandez.
Publisher: American Guidance Service, Inc.
Cross References: For reviews by Jeri Benson and Frederick T. L. Leong, see 13:303.

[2412]
Student Styles Questionnaire™.

Purpose: "Designed to detect individual differences students display in their preferences, temperaments, and personal styles."
Population: Ages 8–13.
Publication Date: 1996.
Acronym: SSQ.
Scores, 8: Extroverted, Introverted, Practical, Imaginative, Thinking, Feeling, Organized, Flexible.
Administration: Group or individual.
Price Data, 2002: $98 per starter kit including manual (241 pages), classroom applications booklet, 5 Ready Score™ answer documents, and question booklet; $66 per 25 question booklets; $35 per 25 Ready Score™ answer documents; $18 per 25 record forms; $75 per manual; $22 per classroom applications booklet; $107 per microcomputer kit including 3.5-inch diskette, user's guide, and 25 record forms (Windows only).
Time: (30) minutes.
Authors: Thomas Oakland, Joseph Glutting, and Connie Horton.
Publisher: The Psychological Corporation.
Cross References: For reviews by Gregory Schraw and Jay R. Stewart, see 14:375.

[2413]
Student Talent and Risk Profile.

Purpose: To identify talented students as well as students "at-risk" for counseling, guidance, and special teaching strategies.
Population: Grades 5–12.
Publication Date: 1990.
Acronym: STAR Profile.
Scores, 7: Academic Performance, Creativity, Artistic Potential, Leadership, Emotional Maturity, Educational Orientation, At Risk.

Administration: Group.
Price Data: Available from publisher.
Time: (60–65) minutes.
Comments: Revision of Biographical Inventory Form U.
Author: Institute for Behavioral Research in Creativity.
Publisher: Institute for Behavioral Research in Creativity [No reply from publisher; status unknown].
Cross References: For reviews by Barbara Kerr and John W. Shepard, see 12:378; for reviews by Christopher Borman and Courtland C. Lee of Biographical Inventory Form U, see 9:150.

[2414]
Student-Teacher Relationship Scale.

Purpose: "Quantitative measure of student-teacher interactions," "designed to identify ... relationships that could benefit from intervention and support."
Population: Teachers of preschool through Grade 3 students.
Publication Date: 2001.
Acronym: STRS.
Scores, 4: Conflict, Closeness, Dependency, Total.
Administration: Group or Individual.
Price Data, 2001: $90 per introductory kit including professional manual (58 pages), and 50 response forms; $60 per 50 response forms; $40 per professional manual.
Time: (5–10) minutes per individual; (10–15) minutes per group.
Comments: Intended to inform consultation and intervention efforts as part of the Student, Teachers, and Relationship Support (STARS) program.
Author: Robert C. Pianta.
Publisher: Psychological Assessment Resources, Inc.

[2415]
Study Attitudes and Methods Survey [Revised Short Form].

Purpose: "Developed to measure non-cognitive factors associated with success in school."
Population: Junior high, high school, college.
Publication Dates: 1972–1985.
Acronym: SAMS.
Scores, 6: Academic Interest-Love of Learning, Academic Drive-Conformity, Study Methods, Study Anxiety, Manipulation, Alienation Toward Authority.
Administration: Group.
Price Data, 1998: $13.50 per 25 machine-scoring booklets and answer sheets [$47.50 per 100, $223.50 per 500]; $4.75 per 25 profile and interpretation guides (specify high school or college norms); $14.75 per set of hand-scoring keys; $7.75 per specimen set including test booklet, answer sheet, profile sheet, and manual (1988, 12 pages); $4 per manual.

Time: (20–25) minutes.
Authors: William B. Michael, Joan J. Michael, and Wayne S. Zimmerman.
Publisher: EdITS/Educational and Industrial Testing Service.
Cross References: For reviews by Robert G. Harrington and Kenneth A. Kiewra, see 14:376; see also T5:2538 (1 reference), T4:2604 (6 references), and T3:2340 (2 references); for reviews by Allen Berger and John W. Lombard of an earlier edition, see 8:818 (6 references); see also T2:1766 (4 references).

[2416]
Study of Values: British Edition, 1965.

Purpose: "Aims to measure the relative importance of six basic interests or motives in personality."
Population: College and adults.
Publication Date: 1965.
Acronym: SOV.
Scores, 6: Theoretical, Economic, Aesthetic, Social, Political, Religious.
Administration: Group.
Price Data: Price information available from publisher for test booklets and manual (microfiche) (20 pages).
Time: (20) minutes.
Comments: Self-administering; adaptation of Study of Values: A Scale for Measuring the Dominant Interests in Personality, Third Edition.
Authors: Original test by Gordon W. Allport, Philip E. Vernon, and Gardner Lindzey; adaptation by Sylvia Richardson.
Publisher: NFER-Nelson Publishing Co., Ltd. [England].
Cross References: See T5:2539 (1 reference), T3:2344 (2 references), T2:1404 (4 references), and P:259A.

[2417]
Study Process Questionnaire.

Purpose: "To assess the extent to which a tertiary student at college or university endorses different approaches to learning and the more important motives and strategies comprising those approaches."
Population: College students.
Publication Dates: 1985–1987.
Acronym: SPQ.
Scores, 10: Surface Motive, Surface Strategy, Deep Motive, Deep Strategy, Achieving Motive, Achieving Strategy, Surface Approach, Deep Approach, Achieving Approach, Deep-Achieving Approach.
Administration: Individual or group.
Price Data, 2002: A$11.50 per 10 questionnaires, A$7.69 per 10 answer sheets; A$5.50 per score key; A$34.10 per monograph entitled Student Approaches to Learning and Studying (1987, 151 pages); A$29.80 per manual (1987, 44 pages); A$51.80 per starter set.

Time: 20(40) minutes.
Comments: Secondary counterpart of the Learning Process Questionnaire (1402).
Author: John Biggs.
Publisher: Australian Council for Educational Research Ltd. [Australia].
Cross References: See T5:2540 (8 references) and T4:2608 (1 reference); for a review by Cathy W. Hall, see 11:389 (2 references). For a review by Robert D. Brown of both the Learning Process Questionnaire and the Study Process Questionnaire and a review by Cathy W. Hall of the Learning Process Questionnaire, see 11:202.

[2418]
Stuttering Prediction Instrument for Young Children.

Purpose: Designed to "measure severity and predict chronicity."
Population: Ages 3–8.
Publication Date: 1981.
Acronym: SPI.
Scores, 5: Reactions, Part-Word Repetitions, Prolongations, Frequency, Total.
Administration: Individual.
Price Data, 2001: $86 per complete kit including 50 tests, picture plates, and manual (45 pages); $39 per 50 test forms; $49 per manual with picture plates.
Time: Administration time not reported.
Comments: Information taken from parent interview, observation and tape recording of the child's speech, and analysis of the tape recording.
Author: Glyndon D. Riley.
Publisher: PRO-ED.
Cross References: See T5:2542 (2 references) and T4:2612 (1 reference).

[2419]
Stuttering Severity Instrument for Children and Adults, Third Edition.

Purpose: "Measures stuttering severity for both children and adults."
Population: School-age children and adults.
Publication Dates: 1980–1994.
Acronym: SSI-3.
Scores, 8: Frequency, Duration, Physical Concomitants (Distracting Sounds, Facial Grimaces, Head Movements, Movements of the Extremities, Total), Total.
Administration: Individual.
Forms, 2: Reading, Nonreading.
Price Data, 2001: $94 per complete kit; $39 per 50 test record and frequency computation forms; $54 per examiner's manual (1994, 48 pages) and picture plates.
Time: Administration time not reported.
Comments: Tape recorder necessary for speech sample.

Author: Glyndon D. Riley.
Publisher: PRO-ED.
Cross References: See T5:2543 (3 references); for reviews by Ronald B. Gillam and Rebecca McCauley, see 13:304 (21 references); see also T4:2613 (5 references).

[2420]
Stycar Vision Tests.

Purpose: Designed "to assess visual competence during infancy and early childhood."
Population: Normal and handicapped children 6 months and over.
Publication Dates: 1958–1981.
Acronym: SVT.
Administration: Individual.
Price Data, 1999: £210 per complete kit; £25 per manual (1981, 53 pages).
Author: Mary D. Sheridan.
Publisher: NFER-Nelson Publishing Co., Ltd. [England].
a) MINIATURE TOYS TEST.
Population: Nonspeaking handicapped children mental ages 21 months and over who are unable to recognize letters.
Publication Dates: 1958–1976.
Price Data: £11 per 25 record forms; £27.50 per set of toys (A); £25 per set of toys (B).
Time: [5–10] minutes.
b) GRADED BALLS TEST.
Population: Ages 6–30 months (also handicapped children with mental ages within this range).
Publication Dates: 1968–1976.
Price Data: Record forms same as for *a*; £25 per set of graded balls and rods.
Time: [5] minutes.
c) AGES 3, 4–5.
Publication Dates: 1958–1976.
Levels, 2: 5-letter booklet for 3-year-olds, 7-letter booklet for 4-5-year-olds.
Price Data: £11 per 25 record forms for charts and card tests; £25 per set of distant vision cards and 9 letter cards; £35 per envelope of cards.
Time: [5–10] minutes.
d) AGES 5–7.
Publication Dates: 1958–1976.
Price Data: Record forms same as for *c*; Set C must be purchased to obtain 9-letter key card.
Time: (4) minutes.
e) PANDA TEST.
Population: Severely visually handicapped children ages 6-30 months (also handicapped children with mental ages within this range).
Publication Dates: 1973–1976.
Price Data: £27.50 per set of test cards; £45 per set of plastic letters.
Time: [10] minutes.

Cross References: See T5:2544 (1 reference), T3:2350 (1 reference), 8:884 (8 references), and T2:1931 (5 references).

[2421]
Style of Learning and Thinking.

Purpose: To indicate a student's learning strategy and brain hemisphere preference in problem solving.
Population: Grades K–5, 6–12.
Publication Date: 1988.
Acronym: SOLAT.
Scores, 3: Whole Brain, Left Brain, Right Brain.
Administration: Group.
Forms, 2: Elementary, Youth.
Price Data, 2002: $48.15 per starter set including administrator's manual (46 pages), and 35 questionnaires (specify form); $33.90 per 35 questionnaires (specify form); $16.15 per administrator's manual; $19.50 per sample set including manual and 1 each of Elementary and youth Form questionnaires.
Time: [30-40] minutes.
Comments: Self-scored.
Author: E. Paul Torrance.
Publisher: Scholastic Testing Service, Inc.
Cross References: See T5:2545 (6 references); for reviews by Kenneth A. Kiewra and Damian McShane and by Donald U. Robertson and Virginia L. Brown, see 11:390 (2 references).

[2422]
Styles of Conflict Inventory.

Purpose: "Designed to aid in the assessment of couples' conflict."
Population: Heterosexual couples.
Publication Dates: 1992–1993.
Acronym: SCI.
Scores, 6: Appraisal of Conflict, Styles of Conflict, Comparison of Partners' Styles of Conflict, Differences Between Behaviors and Perceptions, Critical Items, Total.
Administration: Group.
Price Data, 2001: $60.75 per preview kit including manual (1993, 83 pages), and prepaid combined item booklet/answer sheet; $129 per 10 prepaid combined item booklet/answer sheet; $48.66 per manual.
Time: (15–20) minutes.
Comments: Self-administered test; mail-in scoring.
Author: Michael E. Metz.
Publisher: Consulting Psychologists Press, Inc.
Cross References: For reviews by Julie A. Allison and Judy L. Elliott, see 13:305.

[2423]
Styles of Leadership Survey.

Purpose: Assesses individual leadership skills under a variety of conditions.
Population: Adults.

Publication Dates: 1968-1995.
Scores, 5: Philosophy, Planning and Goal Setting, Implementation, Performance and Evaluation, Total.
Administration: Group.
Price Data, 2001: $8.95 per instrument.
Time: Untimed.
Comments: Self-administered survey.
Authors: Jay Hall, Jerry B. Harvey, and Martha S. Williams.
Publisher: Teleometrics International.
Cross References: See T5:2547 (1 reference); for reviews by Kenneth N. Anchor and Norman Sundberg, see 12:379 (1 reference); see T3:2351 (1 reference); for a review by Abraham K. Korman of [Styles of Leadership and Management], see 8:1185 (8 references).

[2424]
Styles of Management Inventory.
Purpose: Assesses individual management style under a variety of conditions.
Population: Adults.
Publication Dates: 1964-2000.
Scores, 5: Philosophy, Planning and Goal Setting, Implementation, Performance Evaluation, Total.
Administration: Group.
Price Data, 2001: $8.95 per instrument.
Time: Untimed.
Comments: Self-administered survey.
Authors: Jay Hall, Jerry B. Harvey, and Martha S. Williams.
Publisher: Teleometrics International.
Cross References: For reviews by Richard W. Faunce and Linda F. Wightman, see 12:380; see T3:2351 (1 reference); for a review by Abraham K. Korman of [Styles of Leadership and Management], see 8:1185 (8 references).

[2425]
Styles of Teamwork Inventory.
Purpose: Assess individual feelings about working in teams and the behaviors one typically employs in work-team situations.
Population: Individuals whose work responsibilities require work-team cooperation.
Publication Dates: 1963-1995.
Acronym: STI.
Scores, 5: Synergistic, Compromise, Win-Lose, Yield-Lose, Lose-Leave.
Administration: Group.
Price Data, 2001: $8.95 per instrument.
Time: Administration time not reported.
Comments: Based on Team Behaviors Model of analysis of individual behaviors in a team setting; self ratings; self scored; formerly called Group Encounter Survey (T3:1014).
Author: Jay Hall.

Publisher: Teleometrics International.
Cross References: See 8:1048 (2 references).

[2426]
Substance Abuse Life Circumstance Evaluation.
Purpose: "Designed to assess alcohol and drug use/abuse behavior, as well as the role that attitude and stress may play in this use/abuse."
Population: Adults.
Publication Date: 1988.
Acronym: SALCE.
Scores, 6: Test-Taking Attitude, Life Circumstance Evaluation, Drinking Evaluation Category, Alcohol Addiction Evaluation, Drug Use Evaluation, Summary Score.
Administration: Individual or group.
Manual: No manual.
Price Data: Available from publisher.
Time: (20) minutes.
Comments: Self-administered; computer scored, IBM compatible with either DOS or Windows required; provides both DSM-IV classification and ASAM patient placement criteria.
Author: ADE Incorporated.
Publisher: ADE Incorporated.
Cross References: For a review by Anita M. Hubley, see 14:377.

[2427]
Substance Abuse Relapse Assessment.
Purpose: Designed to help develop relapse prevention goals and monitor treatment progress.
Population: Adolescents and adults.
Publication Date: 1993.
Acronym: SARA.
Scores: 4 parts: Substance Abuse Behavior, Antecedents of Substance Abuse, Consequences of Substance Abuse, Responses to Slips and Relapses.
Administration: Individual.
Price Data: Available from publisher for introductory kit including 25 interview record forms, 25 each of 3 relapse prevention planning forms, and manual (31 pages) with stimulus card.
Time: (60) minutes.
Authors: Lawrence Schonfeld, Roger Peters, and Addis Dolente.
Publisher: Psychological Assessment Resources, Inc.
Cross References: For reviews by Michael G. Kavan and Jeffrey S. Rain, see 13:306.

[2428]
Substance Abuse Screening Test.
Purpose: "Designed to screen-out those students who are unlikely to have a substance abuse problem."

Population: Ages 13–adult.
Publication Date: 1993.
Acronym: SAST.
Scores: Total Level of Risk.
Administration: Group.
Forms, 2: Response Form, Observation Report.
Price Data, 2002: $56 per complete kit including 50 Response Forms, 50 Observation Reports, and manual (34 pages); $21 per 50 Response Forms; $21 per 50 Observation Reports; $29 per manual.
Time: (5) minutes.
Authors: Terry Hibpshman and Sue Larson.
Publisher: Slosson Educational Publications, Inc.
Cross References: For reviews by Mary Lou Kelley and Mariela C. Shirley, see 13:307.

[2429]
The Substance Abuse Subtle Screening Inventory—3.

Purpose: Designed to "identify individuals who have a high probability of having a substance dependence disorder."
Population: Ages 18–73.
Publication Dates: 1983–1997.
Acronym: SASSI-3.
Scores: 10 subscales: Face Valid Alcohol, Face Valid Other Drugs, Symptoms, Obvious Attributes, Subtle Attributes, Defensiveness, Supplemental Addiction Measure, Family vs. Controls, Correctional, Random Answering Pattern.
Administration: Individual or group.
Price Data: Available from publisher.
Time: [15] minutes.
Comments: May be administered as paper-and-pencil instrument with hand scoring or scoring by optical scanning, computer administered, or via audio-tape for people with special needs regarding vision or literacy.
Author: Glenn A. Miller.
Publisher: The SASSI Institute.
Cross References: See T5:2553 (6 references); for reviews by Barbara Kerr and Nicholas A. Vacc of an earlier edition, see 12:381 (1 reference); see also T4:2623 (1 reference).

[2430]
Substance Use Disorders Diagnostic Schedule-IV.

Purpose: "Designed to elicit information related to the diagnosis of substance use disorders."
Population: Adults suspected of abusing alcohol or drugs.
Publication Dates: 1995–2001.
Acronym: SUDDS-IV.
Scores: Number of Current Dependence Symptoms in Past Year, Number of Current Dependence Catego-

ries, Number of Current Abuse Symptoms in Past Year, Number of Current Abuse Categories for 10 Substance Categories (Alcohol, Marijuana, Cocaine, Sedatives/Tranquilizers, Stimulants, Heroin/Other Opioids, Hallucinogens, PCP, Inhalants, Other/Mixed), DSM-IV Psychoactive Substance Use Disorder Diagnosis Codes (Dependence, Abuse), Ratings for Stress, Depression and Anxiety Screens.
Administration: Individual.
Price Data: Available from publisher.
Time: (30–45) minutes.
Comments: Structured diagnostic interview; also available as a computer-administered interview; designed primarily to provide comprehensive diagnostic information for substance use disorders according to DSM-IV criteria; provides information for patient placement according to American Society of Addiction Medicine criteria.
Authors: Norman G. Hoffmann and Patricia Ann Harrison.
Publisher: Evince Clinical Assessments.
Cross References: For reviews by Andres Barona and Steven I. Pfeiffer of an earlier edition, see 13:308 (2 references).

[2431]
Subsumed Abilities Test.

Purpose: Designed "to determine an individual's or group's ability to learn or to use a previously learned written language, system of mathematics, coding system, or other visual symbol system."
Population: Ages 9 and over.
Publication Dates: 1957–1984.
Acronym: SAT.
Scores, 5: Recognition, Abstraction, Conceptualization, Total (Demonstrated Abilities), Potential Abilities.
Administration: Individual or group.
Price Data, 2001: $69 per test package; $39.50 per manual (1963, 12 pages) and manuals supplement (1984, 17 pages); $19 per key-tabulation sheet package; $46.50 per specimen set.
Time: 30(40) minutes.
Comments: Subtitle on manual is A Measure of Learning Efficiency.
Author: Joseph R. Sanders.
Publisher: Martin M. Bruce, Ph.D.
Cross References: See T2:582 (2 references); for a review by Naomi Stewart, see 6:560.

[2432]
Suffolk Reading Scale.

Purpose: "To provide a standardized measure of reading attainment and to monitor the progress of individuals and groups."
Population: Ages 6–12.

Publication Dates: 1986–1987.
Scores: Total score only.
Administration: Group.
Levels: 3 overlapping levels: Level 1 (ages 6–7), Level 2 (ages 8–10), Level 3 (ages 10–12); 2 parallel forms: A, B.
Price Data: Price information available from publisher for test booklets (Level 1A, Level 1B, Level 2A, Level 2B, Level 3A, or Level 3B), Level 3 answer sheets, and Teacher's Guide (1987, 48 pages); scoring service for Level 3 offered by publisher.
Time: (35–45) minutes per level.
Author: Fred Hagley.
Publisher: NFER-Nelson Publishing Co., Ltd. [England].
Cross References: See T5:2556 (3 references); for reviews by Robert B. Cooter, Jr. and Richard Lehrer, see 11:392.

[2433]
Suicidal Ideation Questionnaire.

Purpose: To measure suicidal ideation.
Population: Grades 7–9, 10–12.
Publication Dates: 1987–1988.
Acronym: SIQ.
Scores: Total Suicidal Ideation.
Administration: Individual or group.
Levels, 2: SIQ (senior high school), SIQ-JR (junior high school).
Price Data: Available from publisher for introductory kit including manual (1988, 47 pages), 25 each SIQ and SIQ-JR hand-scorable answer sheets, and scoring keys for SIQ and SIQ-JR; $34 per 25 hand-scorable answer sheets (specify SIQ or SIQ-JR).
Time: (5–10) minutes.
Author: William M. Reynolds.
Publisher: Psychological Assessment Resources, Inc.
Cross References: See T5:2556 (11 references) and T4:2627 (1 reference); for reviews by James C. Carmer and Collie W. Conoley, see 11:393 (2 references).

[2434]
Suicide Intervention Response Inventory [Revised].

Purpose: Designed to assess "the paraprofessional's ability to select an appropriate response to the self-destructive client."
Population: Mental health paraprofessionals.
Publication Dates: 1980–1997.
Acronym: SIRI.
Scores: Total score only.
Administration: Group.
Price Data: Available from publisher.
Time: (15) minutes.
Author: Robert A. Neimeyer.

Publisher: Robert A. Neimeyer, Ph.D.
Cross References: See T5:2558 (3 references).

[2435]
Suicide Probability Scale.

Purpose: Designed to "measure an individual's self-reported attitudes and behaviors which have a bearing on suicide risk."
Population: Ages 14 and over.
Publication Date: 1982.
Acronym: SPS.
Scores, 5: Hopelessness, Suicide Ideation, Negative Self-Evaluations, Hostility, Total.
Administration: Group or individual.
Price Data, 2002: $95 per kit including 25 tests, 25 profiles, and manual (73 pages plus test and profile); $36 per 25 tests; $29.95 per 100 profiles; $44 per manual; $220 per microcomputer disk (IBM, 25 uses); $15 per 100 answer sheets for use with disk; $10.50 per FAX Service scoring charge.
Time: (5–10) minutes.
Authors: John G. Cull and Wayne S. Gill.
Publisher: Western Psychological Services.
Cross References: See T5:2559 (13 references) and T4:2629 (6 references); for a review by Stephen L. Golding, see 9:1210.

[2436]
Super's Work Values Inventory—Revised.

Purpose: Assesses relative importance of selected attributes of occupations and jobs.
Population: Middle school through adult.
Publication Date: 2001.
Acronym: WVI-R.
Scores, 12: Achievement, Co-Workers, Creativity, Income, Independence, Lifestyle, Mental Challenge, Prestige, Security, Supervision, Work Environment, Variety.
Administration: Individual or group.
Price Data: Available from publisher.
Time: (15–20) minutes.
Comments: Online administration; instant scoring; with Kuder Career Search (1354) and Kuder Skills Assessment (1357), plus the Kuder Electronic Career Portfolio, constitutes the Kuder Career Planning System.
Authors: Donald E. Super; revised by Donald G. Zytowski.
Publisher: National Career Assessment Services, Inc.
Cross References: See T4:2998 (9 references) and T3:2567 (17 references); for an excerpted review by Frederick Brown of an earlier edition, see 8:1030 (52 references); see also T2:2221 (12 references); for reviews by Ralph F. Berdie and David V. Tiedeman, and an excerpted review by John W. French, see 7:1042 (33 references).

[2437]
Supervisory Behavior Description Questionnaire.

Purpose: "Designed to measure the behavior patterns of supervisory and management personnel on two major dimensions of leadership: 'Consideration' and 'Structure.'"
Population: Supervisors and prospective supervisors.
Publication Dates: 1970–1996.
Acronym: SBD.
Scores, 2: Consideration, Structure.
Administration: Group.
Price Data: Available from publisher.
Time: [20] minutes.
Comments: Paper-and-pencil or computer administration available.
Author: Edwin A. Fleishman.
Publisher: Reid London House.

[2438]
Supervisory Inventory on Communication.

Purpose: Designed to assess supervisor's knowledge of certain principles, facts, and techniques of communication.
Population: Supervisors and prospective supervisors.
Publication Dates: 1965–1979.
Acronym: SIC.
Scores: Total score only.
Administration: Group.
Price Data, 2001: $40 per 20 SIC tests and answer booklets; $5 per instructor's manual (1979, 11 pages); $10 per specimen set (including test, answer booklet, manual and leader's guide).
Time: (20) minutes.
Author: Donald L. Kirkpatrick.
Publisher: Donald L. Kirkpatrick.
Cross References: For a review by Joyce L. Carbonell, see 9:1211; see also 7:1152 (1 reference).

[2439]
Supervisory Inventory on Human Relations.

Purpose: Designed to assess supervisors' knowledge of human relations principles, facts, and techniques.
Population: Supervisors and prospective supervisors.
Publication Dates: 1960–1982.
Acronym: SIHR.
Scores: Total score only.
Administration: Group.
Price Data, 2001: $40 per 20 tests and answer booklets; $5 per instructor's manual (1982, 12 pages); $10 per specimen set (including test, answer booklet, and manual).
Time: (15–20) minutes.
Authors: Donald L. Kirkpatrick and Earl Planty (test).
Publisher: Donald L. Kirkpatrick.
Cross References: See T2:2463 (1 reference); for a review by Seymour Levy of the original edition, see 6:1193 (1 reference).

[2440]
Supervisory Practices Test, Revised.

Purpose: "Designed to aid in appraising supervisory ability and potential."
Population: Supervisors.
Publication Dates: 1957–1984.
Acronym: SPT.
Scores: Total score only.
Administration: Group.
Price Data, 2001: $55.95 per specimen set; $94.20 per test package; $52.65 per manual (1974, 14 pages), manuals supplement (1984, 17 pages), and norms supplement; $35.40 per profile sheet package; $3.75 per key.
Foreign Language Editions: French, German, and Spanish editions available.
Time: (20–30) minutes.
Author: Martin M. Bruce.
Publisher: Martin M. Bruce, Ph.D.
Cross References: See T3:2363 (1 reference), T2:2466 (2 references), and 6:1194 (4 references); for reviews by Clifford E. Jurgensen and Mary Ellen Oliverio, see 5:955.

[2441]
Supervisory Reading Test—Form A.

Purpose: "To measure the reading skills required for supervisors."
Population: Adults.
Publication Date: 1992.
Scores: Total score only.
Administration: Group.
Price Data, 2002: $200 per complete kit including 10 reusable test booklets, 100 answer sheets, manual (10 pages), and scoring key.
Time: (30) minutes.
Author: Roland T. Ramsay.
Publisher: Ramsay Corporation.
Cross References: For reviews by Judith A. Monsaas and Robert Wall, see 13:259.

[2442]
Supervisory Simulator.

Purpose: "Designed to assess supervisory skills of first-level supervisors and/or forepersons independent of any particular job classification; may be used for selection and/or career development."
Population: First-level supervisors and/or forepersons.
Publication Dates: 1991–2002.
Acronym: SupSim.
Scores, 3: Leadership/Decision Making, Team Relations, Total.
Administration: Group or individual.
Forms, 4: Public and private sector forms include Standard Version, Police Version, Fire Version, and Transportation Version.

Restricted Distribution: Clients must pay a one-time overhead/sign-up fee of $200.
Price Data, 2002: $130 per candidate for rental/scoring and bar chart; $70 for optional Supervisory Simulator Career Development Report.
Time: (75) minutes.
Author: Richard C. Joines.
Publisher: Management & Personnel Systems, Inc.

[2443]
Supervisory Skills Inventory.

Purpose: Developed to assess a supervisor's day-to-day, on-the-job behavior as seen by self and collectively by five other people.
Population: First-line supervisors.
Publication Date: 1982.
Acronym: SSI.
Scores: 2 scores (Self, Other) in 12 supervisory skill areas: Setting Goals, Planning and Organizing, Directing and Delegating, Solving Problems, Enforcing Work Rules, Relating to and Supporting Staff, Maintaining and Controlling Materials and Equipment, Building Teams, Assuring Safety, Evaluating Performance, Training and Coaching, Reacting to Stress, plus 5 summary perception scores.
Administration: Group.
Forms, 2: Self-Description, Description by Others.
Price Data: Available from publisher.
Comments: Administered to supervisor and 4 or 5 workers.
Author: Human Synergistics International.
Publisher: Human Synergistics International.

[2444]
SUP'R Star Profiles.

Purpose: Designed to identify an individual's dominant personality type.
Population: Adults.
Publication Date: 1994.
Scores: 4 personality types: Self-Reliant, Upbeat, Patient, Reasoning.
Administration: Group.
Price Data, 1994: $5.95 per test; price information for user's guide available from publisher.
Time: (15–20) minutes.
Author: James H. Brewer.
Publisher: Associated Consultants in Education.
Cross References: For reviews by Jeffrey B. Brookings and Carol Collins, see 13:309.

[2445]
Survey Ballot for Industry.

Purpose: Designed "specifically as the psychological measuring instrument for economical assessment of job satisfaction levels of worker groups."
Population: Employee groups.

Publication Date: No date.
Scores, 11: Job Security, Welfare Interest, Supervision, Working Conditions, Co-Workers, Pay, Freedom of Communication, Management Good Intent, Management Good Judgment, Company Effect on Happiness, Total Satisfaction.
Administration: Group.
Price Data, 2001: $4 per specimen set.
Time: Administration time not reported.
Author: W. A. Kerr.
Publisher: Psychometric Affiliates.

[2446]
Survey of Employee Access.

Purpose: Measures effective managerial behavior.
Population: Adults.
Publication Dates: 1989–2000.
Acronym: SEA.
Scores, 5: Access to the Problem, Access to People, Access to Information and Resources, Access to Emotional/Procedural Supports, Access to Solution.
Administration: Group.
Price Data, 2001: $7.95 per instrument.
Time: Untimed.
Comments: Self-administered survey.
Author: Jay Hall.
Publisher: Teleometrics International.
Cross References: For reviews by Marcia J. Belcher and Robert Fitzpatrick, see 12:383.

[2447]
Survey of Functional Adaptive Behaviors.

Purpose: To assess an individual's skill level of adaptive behavior.
Population: Ages 16 and over.
Publication Date: 1986.
Acronym: SFAB.
Scores, 5: Residential Living Skills, Daily Living Skills, Academic Skills, Vocational Skills, SFAB Total Score.
Administration: Individual.
Manual: No manual.
Price Data, 2002: $49.75 per 25 surveys.
Authors: Jack G. Dial, Carolyn Mezger, Theresa Massey, Steve Carter, and Lawrence T. McCarron.
Publisher: McCarron-Dial Systems.
Cross References: For reviews by Steven W. Lee and Steven I. Pfeiffer, see 11:404.

[2448]
Survey of Influence Effectiveness.

Purpose: "Designed to help business and government professionals determine how they are at influencing others with integrity."
Population: Business and government professionals.
Publication Date: 1994.
Administration: Group.

Forms, 2: Self, Other.

Manual: No Manual.

Price Data, 2002: $49 per set including question-naires and answer sheets for 1 self-assessment, 6 others, 6 customers, and 1 feedback report.

Time: [30] minutes.

Comments: Computer scored and interpreted by publisher; can be administered online via the Internet.

Author: Terry R. Bacon.

Publisher: Lore International Institute.

a) SELF FORM.

Scores, 4: Influence Tactic Frequency, Influence Tactic Appropriateness, Influence Tactic Skills and Effectiveness, Source of Power.

Comments: 10 Influence tactics are measured and reported.

b) OTHER FORM.

Scores, 7: Positive Influence Tactic Frequency, Negative Influence Tactic Frequency, Influence Tactic Appropriateness, Influence Tactic Skills and Effectiveness, Overall Influence Assessment, Sources of Power Recommendations.

Comments: A 128-item rating form.

[2449]
Survey of Interpersonal Values.

Purpose: Designed to measure certain values involving an individual's relationships with others.

Population: Individuals in a variety of occupations and job levels.

Publication Dates: 1960–1993.

Acronym: SIV.

Scores, 6: Support, Conformity, Recognition, Independence, Benevolence, Leadership.

Administration: Individual or group.

Price Data, 2002: $163 per start-up kit including 25 test booklets, 100 profile sheets, scoring stencil, and examiner's manual; $64 per 25 test booklets (quantity discounts available); $70 per 100 profile sheets; $20 per scoring stencil; $28 per examiner's manual.

Time: No limit (approximately 15 minutes).

Author: Leonard V. Gordon.

Publisher: Reid London House.

Cross References: See T5:2581 (3 references), T4:2653 (3 references), and T3:2366 (14 references); for reviews by John D. Black and Allan L. LaVoie, see 8:688 (51 references); see also T2:1407 (78 references) and P:261 (48 references); for reviews by Lee J. Cronbach, Leonard D. Goodstein, and John K. Hemphill and an excerpted review by Laurence Siegel, see 6:184 (12 references).

[2450]
Survey of Management Practices.

Purpose: To assess a manager's organizational practices, and whether they enhance employee productivity.

Population: Subordinates of managers.

Publication Dates: 1987–1995.

Acronym: SMP.

Scores, 12: Dimension I (Management Values, Support Structure, Managerial Credibility, Total), Dimension II (Impact, Relevance, Community, Total), Dimension III (Task Environment, Social Context, Problem Solving, Total).

Administration: Group.

Price Data, 2001: $7.95 per instrument.

Time: Administration time not reported.

Comments: Manager behavior rated by subordinates.

Author: Jay Hall.

Publisher: Teleometrics International.

[2451]
Survey of Organizational Climate.

Purpose: To assess an individual's opinion of his/her organizational climate.

Population: Employees.

Publication Dates: 1977–1985.

Scores, 12: Clarity of Goals, Job Interest and Challenge, Rewards and Satisfactions, Standards of Excellence, Degree of Responsibility, Personal Development, Working Relationships, Advancement/Mobility, Job Security, Management's Credibility, Personnel Policies and Procedures, Self-Confidence.

Administration: Group or individual.

Manual: No manual.

Price Data: Price information available from publisher for kit including 20 copies of survey, 20 answer sheets, and 20 interpretation sheets.

Time: (20) minutes.

Comments: Self-scored.

Author: Training House, Inc.

Publisher: Training House, Inc.

Cross References: For a review by Charles K. Parsons, see 11:406.

[2452]
Survey of Organizational Culture.

Purpose: Identification of organizational purpose and mission, perception of customers, and interrelationships of organization members.

Population: Employees of organizations.

Publication Dates: 1987–1989.

Acronym: SOC.

Scores: 15 scales: Culture (Orientation to Customers, Orientation to Employees, Orientation to Stakeholders, Impact of Mission, Managerial Depth, Decision Level/Autonomy, Communication/Openness, Human Scale, Incentive/Motivation, Cooperation/Competition, Organizational Congruence, Behavior Under Pressure, Theory-S/Theory-T, 13 Scales Aggregated), Job Characteristics (Job Satisfaction, Organizational Commitment).

Administration: Group.
Editions, 2: Select Items, Professional.
Manual: No manual.
Price Data: Available from publisher.
Time: (20–25) minutes.
Authors: Robert W. Tucker and Walt J. McCoy.
Publisher: Human Services Resource Group [No reply from publisher; status unknown].
Cross References: For a review by Bertram C. Sippola, see 11:407.

[2453]
Survey of Personal Values.

Purpose: To "measure certain critical values that help to determine the manner in which individuals cope with the problems of everyday living."
Population: Individuals in a variety of occupations, high school and college students.
Publication Dates: 1964–1992.
Acronym: SPV.
Scores, 6: Practical Mindedness, Achievement, Variety, Decisiveness, Orderliness, Goal Orientation.
Administration: Individual or group.
Price Data, 2002: $163 per start-up kit including 25 test booklets, 100 profile sheets, scoring stencil, and examiner's manual: $64 per 25 test booklets (quantity discount available); $70 per 100 profile sheets; $20 per scoring stencil; $28 per examiner's manual.
Time: No limit (approximately 15 minutes).
Author: Leonard V. Gordon.
Publisher: Reid London House.
Cross References: For reviews by William P. Erchul and Rodney L. Lowman, see 10:354; see also T3:2370 (5 references) and T2:1409 (5 references); for a review by Gene V Glass, see 7:148 (6 references); see also P:263 (3 references).

[2454]
Survey of Student Assessment of Study Behaviors.

Purpose: Designed to help students understand their current study behaviors.
Population: Grades 6–13.
Publication Date: 1991.
Scores, 6: Positive Attitudes, Useful Work Habits, Efficient Learning Tools, Good Comprehension, High Performance Writing, Effective Test Taking.
Administration: Individual.
Price Data, 2001: $3 per survey.
Time: Administration time not reported.
Comments: Self-report survey.
Author: The Cambridge Stratford Study Skills Institute.
Publisher: The Cambridge Stratford Study Skills Institute.

[2455]
Survey of Teenage Readiness and Neurodevelopmental Status.

Purpose: "Provides an overview of an adolescent's own perceptions of his or her functioning and performance strategies across a variety of neurocognitive and psychosocial domains."
Population: Ages 13–19.
Publication Date: 2001.
Acronym: STRANDS.
Scores, 13: Attention, Memory, Sequencing, Language, Visual Processing, Motor Functions, Organization and Strategies, Higher-Order Cognition, School Skills, School Life, Social Life, School and Work Preferences, Reasons.
Administration: Individual.
Price Data, 2002: $81.15 per complete set including manual for administration, scoring and interpretation (114 pages), 12 student questionnaires (15 pages), 12 student interview booklets (30 pages), and 12 profile sheets; $21.85 per specimen set including manual for administration, scoring, and interpretation, 1 student questionnaire, and 1 student interview booklet; $19.75 per manual; $68.65 per 12 pair of student questionnaires and student interview booklets; $5.75 per 12 profile sheets (quantity discounts available).
Time: (40) minutes for Student Interview; (20) minutes for Student Questionnaire.
Comments: Examines the relationship between metacognitive knowledge and actual strategic behavior; consists of 2 parts: structured clinical student interview (closed- and open-ended questions), student-completed questionnaire.
Authors: Melvin D. Levine and Stephen R. Hooper.
Publisher: Educators Publishing Service.

[2456]
Survey of Work Styles.

Purpose: A "measure of six components of the Type A behavior pattern."
Population: Adults.
Publication Dates: 1987–1998.
Acronym: SWS.
Scores, 8: Impatience, Anger, Time Urgency, Work Involvement, Job Dissatisfaction, Competitiveness, Scale A, Total.
Administration: Group or individual.
Price Data, 2001: $74 per research test kit including manual, 2nd edition (1993, 22 pages), 25 hand-scorable question-and-answer documents, 25 scoring sheets, and one set of templates; $15 per test manual; $16 per 25 question-and-answer documents; $12 per 25 scoring sheets; $14 per set of four templates; $12 per machine-scorable question-and-answer document for a Developmental Report; $7 per machine-scorable question-and-answer document for a Basic Report; $99 per

software package including disks, software manual for Windows, test manual, and 10 coupons for computer reports.
Time: (15–20) minutes.
Authors: Douglas N. Jackson and Anna Mavrogiannis Gray.
Publisher: Sigma Assessment Systems, Inc.
Cross References: See T5:2592 (1 reference); for a review by Peggy A. Hicks, see 13:311 (1 reference); see also T4:2664 (1 reference).

[2457]
Survey of Work Values, Revised, Form U.

Purpose: Constructed to identify attitudes toward work.
Population: Employees.
Publication Dates: 1975–1976.
Scores, 6: Social Status, Activity Preference, Upward Striving, Attitude Toward Earnings, Pride in Work, Job Involvement.
Administration: Group.
Manual: No manual.
Price Data, 2001: $21 per 100 test booklets; $5 per 100 answer sheets; $5 per 100 hand-scoring sheets; general instructions, free.
Time: [15] minutes.
Author: Bowling Green State University.
Publisher: Bowling Green State University, Department of Psychology.
Cross References: For reviews by Julie A. Allison and H. John Bernardin and Donna K. Cooke, see 12:383 (1 reference); see also T4:2665 (1 reference).

[2458]
Surveys of Research Administration and Environment.

Purpose: Designed "to gather both facts and opinions on a variety of factors related to the jobs of scientists, engineers, and technicians."
Population: Research and engineering and scientific firms.
Publication Dates: 1959–1960.
Scores: No scores.
Administration: Group.
Price Data: Available from publisher.
Author: Morris I. Stein.
Publisher: The Mews Press.
a) STEIN SURVEY FOR ADMINISTRATION.
Population: Supervisors and administrators.
Comments: Also part of Technical Personnel Recruiting Inventory (2499).
Time: (30–40) minutes.
b) STEIN RESEARCH ENVIRONMENTAL SURVEY.
Population: Research and technical personnel.
Time: (90–120) minutes.

[2459]
Swanson-Cognitive Processing Test.

Purpose: Designed to assess "different aspects of mental processing ability and potential."
Population: Ages 5 to adult.
Publication Date: 1996.
Acronym: S-CPT.
Scores: 11 subtest scores: Rhyming Words, Visual Matrix, Auditory Digit Sequence, Mapping and Directions, Story Retelling, Picture Sequence, Phrase Recall, Spatial Organization, Semantic Association, Semantic Categorization, Nonverbal Sequence; 3 composite scores: Semantic, Episodic, Total; 4 component scores: Auditory, Visual, Prospective, Retrospective; 4 supplementary scores: Strategy Efficiency Index, Processing Difference Index, Instructional Efficiency Index, Stability Index.
Administration: Individual.
Price Data, 2001: $194 per complete kit including manual (183 pages), 25 profile/examiner record booklets, picture book, card decks, and strategy cards in storage box; $59 per 25 profile/examiner record booklets; $49 per manual; $24 per picture book; $49 per card deck; $19 per strategy cards.
Time: (120) minutes.
Author: H. Lee Swanson.
Publisher: PRO-ED.
Cross References: See T5:2596 (1 reference); for reviews by Carolyn M. Callahan and Ralph F. Darr, Jr., see 13:312.

[2460]
Swassing-Barbe Modality Kit.

Purpose: To identify an individual's "most efficient learning mode."
Population: Children and adults.
Publication Dates: 1979–2002.
Scores, 4: Visual, Auditory, Kinesthetic, Total.
Administration: Individual.
Price Data, 2002: $213.32 per complete kit ($159.99 school price); $4.99 per 100 scoring sheets.
Time: (20–25) minutes.
Comments: Also known as Zaner-Bloser Modality Index.
Author: Walter B. Barbe and Raymond H. Swassing.
Publisher: Zaner-Bloser Educational Publishers.
Cross References: See T4:2669 (1 reference); for a review by Barbara A. Kerr and Roberta S. Myers, see 9:1219.

[2461]
Symbol Digit Modalities Test.

Purpose: Designed as an early screening of cerebral dysfunction.
Population: Ages 8 and over.
Publication Date: 1973.

Acronym: SDMT.
Scores: Total score only.
Administration: Group or individual.
Forms, 2: Written, Oral.
Price Data, 2002: $72 per complete kit including 25 WPS AutoScore™ test forms and manual (10 pages plus test); $38 per 25 AutoScore™ test forms; $37.50 per manual.
Time: 1.5(10) minutes.
Author: Aaron Smith.
Publisher: Western Psychological Services.
Cross References: See T5:2599 (43 references), T4:2671 (20 references), and T3:2380 (2 references); for reviews by Brad S. Chissom and James C. Reed, see 8:878; see also T2:1889 (4 references).

[2462]
Symbolic Play Test, Second Edition.

Purpose: Developed to assess early concept formation and symbolization based on a child's spontaneous non-verbal play.
Population: Ages 1–3.
Publication Dates: 1976–1988.
Scores: Total score only.
Administration: Individual.
Price Data, 1999: £145 per complete set including toys, 25 record forms, and manual (1988, 39 pages); £14.50 per 25 record forms; £25 per manual.
Time: (10–15) minutes.
Authors: Marianne Lowe and Anthony J. Costello.
Publisher: NFER-Nelson Publishing Co., Ltd. [England].
Cross References: See T5:2601 (3 references); for reviews by Anthony W. Paolitto and Harvey N. Switzky, see 12:384; see also T4:2673 (2 references) and T3:2383 (1 reference).

[2463]
Symptom Assessment—45 Questionnaire.

Purpose: Designed as a "brief yet comprehensive general assessment of psychiatric symptomalogy."
Population: Ages 13 and over, reading at the 6th grade level or higher.
Publication Dates: 1996–1998.
Acronym: SA-45.
Scores, 11: 9 subscales (Anxiety, Depression, Hostility, Interpersonal Sensitivity, Obsessive-Compulsive, Paranoid Ideation, Phobic Anxiety, Psychoticism, Somatization), 2 composite scores (Global Severity Index, Positive Symptom Total).
Administration: Group.
Price Data, 2002: $53 per complete kit including technical manual and 25 Quikscore forms; $27 per 25 Quikscore forms; $32 per technical manual; $35 per specimen set including technical manual and 3 Quikscore forms.

Time: (10–15) minutes.
Comments: Derived from the original Symptom Checklist—90 (SCL-90; 2464); self-report inventory.
Authors: Strategic Advantage, Inc. and Mark Marush.
Publisher: Multi-Health Systems, Inc.
Cross References: For reviews by William M. Reynolds and Chockalingam Viswesvaran, see 14:378.

[2464]
Symptom Checklist-90-Revised.

Purpose: "Designed primarily to reflect the psychological symptom patterns of psychiatric and medical patients," as well as nonpatients.
Population: Adults and adolescents age 13 and older.
Publication Date: 1975.
Acronym: SCL-90-R®.
Scores: 9 primary symptom dimensions: Somatization, Obsessive-Compulsive, Interpersonal Sensitivity, Depression, Anxiety, Hostility, Phobic Anxiety, Paranoid Ideation, Psychoticism; plus 3 indices of distress: Global Severity Index, Positive Symptom Distress Index, Positive Symptom Total.
Administration: Group or individual.
Price Data, 2002: $111 per hand-scoring starter kit including manual, 50 answer sheets, 50 profile forms, 2 worksheets, and answer keys (specify Nonpatient Adult, Nonpatient Adolescent, Outpatient Psychiatric, or Inpatient Psychiatric); $41 per 50 hand-scoring answer sheets; $22.25 per 50 profile forms and 2 worksheets (specify Nonpatient Adult, Nonpatient Adolescent, Outpatient Psychiatric, or Inpatient Psychiatric); $23,59 per answer keys; $30 per manual; price information for Interpretive Report and Profile Report scoring and software available from publisher.
Time: (12–15) minutes.
Comments: Self-report test; companion clinician and observer rating forms also available.
Author: Leonard R. Derogatis.
Publisher: NCS Assessments (Minnetonka).
Cross References: See T5:2603 (593 references) and T4:2674 (318 references); for reviews by Jerome D. Pauker and Robert W. Payne, see 9:1082 (61 references); see also T3:2100 (13 references).

[2465]
Syracuse Dynamic Assessment for Birth to Three.

Purpose: "A play-based assessment instrument ... used to determine eligibility for intervention services."
Population: Birth to 3 years.
Publication Date: 1998.
Acronym: SDA.
Scores: Assesses 6 primary developmental domains: Neuromotor (NM), Sensory-Perceptual (SP), Cognitive (C), Language (L), Social-Emotional (SE), Adaptive Behavior.

Administration: Individual.
Price Data, 2002: $599 per complete kit including examiner's and observer's manual (281 pages), 12 observation forms, 12 Early Play record forms, 12 Later Play record forms, toy kit, and carrying case.
Time: (30–60) minutes.
Comments: 2 major components: Child and Family Information Guides, Developmental Play-Focused Assessment; 3 record forms: Observations (35 behavior ratings), Play Development in the First Year (ages birth to 12 months; 86 behavior ratings), Later Play Development (ages 13–36 months; 147 behavior ratings); all forms are reproducible.
Authors: Gail L. Ensher, Tasia P. Bobish, Eric F. Gardner, Cynthia A. Michaels, Katharine G. Butler, Daniel J. Foertschi, and Christine Cooper.
Publisher: Imaginart International, Inc.

[2466]
System for Testing and Evaluation of Potential.

Purpose: "To evaluate managerial and professional personnel."
Population: Managerial and professional personnel.
Publication Dates: 1986–1995.
Acronym: LH-STEP.
Administration: Group or individual.
Price Data, 2002: $287 per job analysis kit including 10 job analysis questionnaires, computer scoring, individual and composite reports, and a recommendation regarding which LH-STEP battery to use.
Author: Human Resources Center, The University of Chicago.
Publisher: Reid London House.
　a) LH-STEP (STANDARD REPORT).
　Scores: 6 ratings: Potential Estimates (Executive, Middle Manager, Supervisors and Nonsupervisory Professionals), Job Skills (Executive, Middle Manager, Supervisors and Nonsupervisory Professionals); 39 scores: Predictor Profile: (School Achievement, Drive, Vocational Satisfaction, Financial Responsibility, General Family Responsibility, Leadership, Relaxation Pursuits, Non-Verbal Reasoning, Word Fluency, Vocabulary, Closure Flexibility, Creative Potential, Sales Aptitude, Personal Insight, Extroversion, Emotional Responsiveness, Self-Reliance, Ability to Work Under Pressure, Level of Stress Response, Internal Adjustment, External Adjustment, Social Adjustment, General Adjustment), Job Skills: Organization (Setting Organizational Objectives, Financial Planning and Review, Improving Work Procedures and Practices, Interdepartmental Coordination), Leadership (Developing and Implementing Technical Ideas, Judgment and Decision Making, Developing Group Coop-

eration and Teamwork, Coping With Difficulties and Emergencies, Promoting Safety Attitudes and Practices, Communications), Human Resources (Developing Employee Potential, Supervisory Practices, Self-Development and Improvement, Personnel Practices), Community (Promoting Community/Organization Relations, Handling Outside Contacts).
　Price Data: $230 or less per battery.
　Time: (190–210) minutes.
　b) LH-STEP (EXTENDED REPORT).
　Scores: 6 ratings: same as LH-STEP Standard Report; 63 scores: same as LH-STEP Standard Report, plus Calm, Cautious, Composed, Decisive, Demonstrative, Even-Tempered, Persevering, Seeks Company, Self-Confident, Serious, Steady Worker, Talkative, Reaction Time to Verbal Stimuli, Reaction Time to Color Stimuli, Dominance, Independence, Autonomous Work Environment, Pressure Performance, Energy Level, Speed of Reaction, Ideational Spontaneity, Theoretical Interests, Artistic Interests, Mechanical Interests; 12 tests: Managerial and Professional Job Functions Inventory for Ability, Experience and Background Inventory, Word Fluency, Temperament Comparator, Vocabulary Inventory, Non-Verbal Reasoning, Sales Inventory, Cree Questionnaire, The Press Test, Closure Flexibility, EMO Questionnaire, Management Style Questionnaire.
　Price Data: $230 or less per battery.
　Time: (190–210) minutes.

[2467]
System of Multicultural Pluralistic Assessment.

Purpose: Designed as "a comprehensive system for assessing the level at which children function in cognitive abilities, perceptual motor abilities, and adaptive behavior."
Population: Ages 5–11.
Publication Dates: 1977–1978.
Acronym: SOMPA.
Administration: Individual.
Price Data, 2002: $327 per basic kit including parent interview manual (1977, 150 pages), 25 parent interview record forms, 6 ABIC scoring keys, student assessment manual (1978, 125 pages), 25 student assessment record forms, 25 profile folders, and technical manual (1979, 164 pages).
Foreign Language Edition: Spanish edition available.
Authors: Jane R. Mercer and June F. Lewis.
Publisher: The Psychological Corporation.
　a) STUDENT ASSESSMENT.
　Population: Ages 5–11.

Publication Date: 1978.

Scores: 6 instruments: Physical Dexterity Tasks, Bender Visual Motor Gestalt Test, Weight by Height, Visual Acuity (Snellen Test), Auditory Acuity (audiometer), WISC-R (WPPSI for children under 6 years).

Price Data: $209 per SOMPA student assessment kit including 25 record forms, 25 profile folders, and manual.

Time: (60) minutes, several test sessions should be scheduled.

Comments: The following instruments are not available in the SOMPA test kit and must be obtained by the tester: Bender Gestalt, Snellen Test, audiometer, WISC-R, or WPPSI.

b) PARENT INTERVIEW.

Population: Parents.

Publication Date: 1977.

Scores: 3 instruments: Sociocultural Scales, Adaptive Behavior Inventory for Children (ABIC), Health History Inventory.

Price Data: $265 per SOMPA parent interview kit including 25 record forms, 25 profile folders, and manual.

Cross References: See T5:2606 (5 references) and T4:2676 (11 references); for reviews by Lloyd G. Humphreys, Cecil R. Reynolds, and Jonathan Sandoval, see 9:1222 (6 references).

[2468]

Systematic Screening for Behavior Disorders.

Purpose: To screen and identify students at risk for developing serious behavior problems.

Population: Grades K–6.

Publication Dates: 1990–1992.

Acronym: SSBD.

Administration: Individual and group.

Price Data, 2002: $195 per complete kit including technical manual (1992, 80 pages), user's guide (1992, 151 pages), observer training manual (1992, 136 pages), videotape, and 25 sets of classroom screening forms.

Authors: Hill M. Walker and Herbert H. Severson.

Publisher: Sopris West.

a) STAGE I.

Scores: 2 rankings: Internalizing, Externalizing.

Time: (30–45) minutes.

Comments: Rankings by teacher.

b) STAGE II.

Scores, 6: 3 scores: Total Critical Events, Total Adaptive Behavior, Total Maladaptive Behavior in two areas: Internalizing, Externalizing.

Time: (30–45) minutes.

Comments: Ratings by teachers.

c) STAGE III.

Scores, 11: Academic Engaged Time (Total); Peer Social Behavior (Social Engagement, Partici-

pation, Parallel Play, Alone, No Code, Social Interaction, Negative Interaction, Positive Interaction, Total Positive Behavior, Total Negative Behavior).

Administration: Individual and group.

Time: (60–90) minutes.

Comments: Observations by trained staff member.

Cross References: See T5:2607 (1 reference); for reviews by Mary Lou Kelley and by Leland C. Zlomke and Robert Spies, see 13:313.

[2469]

Systems Analysis Aptitude Test.

Purpose: "Measures aptitude for business systems design using a real-life problem."

Population: Applicants for computer systems analyst position.

Publication Date: 1973.

Acronym: SAAT.

Administration: Group.

Restricted Distribution: Restricted to employers of systems analysts, not available to school personnel.

Price Data, 2001: $465 per candidate.

Time: (240) minutes.

Comments: Detailed report on system designed by each candidate.

Author: Jack M. Wolfe.

Publisher: Rose Wolfe Family Partnership LLP [Canada].

[2470]

Systems Programming Aptitude Test.

Purpose: "To evaluate the aptitude and potential of systems programming candidates of all experience levels, for work in all types of systems programming tasks."

Population: Systems programmers.

Publication Date: 1979.

Acronym: SPAT.

Administration: Group.

Price Data, 2001: $440 per person.

Time: Untimed.

Comments: Detailed report provided on each candidate.

Author: Jack M. Wolfe.

Publisher: Rose Wolfe Family Partnership LLP [Canada].

Cross References: For reviews by Samuel Juni and David Marshall, see 10:356.

[2471]

T.A. Survey.

Purpose: "Evaluates an individual's trust attitudes which predict trust performance."

Population: Employees.
Publication Dates: 1970–1981.
Scores: Total score only.
Administration: Group or individual.
Price Data: Price information available from publisher for surveys and yearly license fee.
Time: (15) minutes.
Comments: Also called Trustworthiness Attitude Survey.
Authors: Alan L. Strand and others.
Publisher: Predictive Surveys Corporation.
Cross References: For reviews by John K. Butler, Jr. and Denise M. Rousseau, see 9:1223.

[2472]
Tapping Students' Science Beliefs: A Resource for Teaching and Learning.

Purpose: Designed to "assess the belief students have about certain natural phenomena and permits appropriate learning experiences to be planned."
Population: Primary grade level students.
Publication Date: 1993.
Acronym: TSSB.
Scores, 5: Skateboard News, What Happened Last Night, The Day We Cooked Pancakes in School, Children's Week, Our School Garden.
Administration: Group.
Price Data, 2002: A$43.95 per complete kit including manual (77 pages), 5 unit tests with 1 student score sheet and 1 group profile sheet per unit.
Time: (30) minutes per unit.
Authors: Brian Doig and Ray Adams.
Publisher: Australian Council for Educational Research Ltd. [Australia].
Cross References: For reviews by Jerrilyn V. Andrews and James P. Van Haneghan, see 13:314.

[2473]
The Tapping Test: A Predictor of Typing and Other Tapping Operations.

Purpose: Measures the student's ability to learn typing.
Population: High school.
Publication Dates: 1959–1970.
Acronym: TARC.
Scores: Total score only.
Administration: Group.
Price Data: Available from publisher.
Time: [30] minutes.
Authors: John C. Flanagan, Grace Fivars (manual), Shirley A. Tuska (manual), and Carol F. Hershey (manual).
Publisher: Grace Fivars.
Cross References: See T2:796 (3 references); for reviews by Ray G. Price and Henry Weitz, see 6:52 (2 references).

[2474]
Target Mathematics Tests.

Purpose: Designed "to provide achievement tests which reflect the content of the National Curriculum in Mathematics" in Great Britain.
Population: Levels 2–5, 2–6.
Publication Date: 1993.
Scores: Total score only.
Administration: Group.
Forms, 2: Test 4, Test 5.
Price Data, 2002: £9.99 per 20 test booklets (specify test); £9.99 per manual; £10.99 per specimen set.
Time: [30] minutes.
Author: D. Young.
Publisher: Hodder & Stoughton Educational [England].
Cross References: For reviews by Kevin D. Crehan and Gerald E. DeMauro, see 14:380.

[2475]
Tasks of Emotional Development Test.

Purpose: Assesses "the emotional and social adjustment of children" by means of projective techniques.
Population: Ages 6–11, 12–18.
Publication Dates: 1960–1971.
Acronym: TED.
Scores: LATENCY: 5 scores: (Perception, Outcome, Affect, Motivation, Spontaneity) in each of 12 areas (Peer Socialization, Trust, Aggression Toward Peers, Attitudes For Learning, Respect For Property of Others, Separation From Mother Figure, Identification With Same-Sex Parent, Acceptance of Siblings, Acceptance of Need-Frustration, Acceptance of Parents' Affection to One Another, Orderliness and Responsibility, Self-Image); ADOLESCENCE: 5 scores in each of 13 areas: Same as for Latency plus Heterosexual Socialization.
Administration: Individual.
Levels, 2: Latency (Ages 6–11); Adolescence (Ages 12–18).
Price Data: Available from publisher.
Time: [30–40] minutes.
Authors: Haskel Cohen and Geraldine Rickard Weil.
Publisher: Massachusetts School of Professional Psychology/T.E.D. Test.
Cross References: See T5:2614 (2 references) and T4:2686 (1 reference); for excerpted reviews by Edward Earl Gates, C. H. Ammons, and R. B. Ammons, see 8:691 (7 references); see also T2:1517 (2 references) and P:481 (1 reference).

[2476]
TAT Analysis Sheet.

Purpose: "Tool to facilitate interpretation and analysis of the TAT protocol."

Population: Ages 4 and over.
Publication Date: 1974.
Scores, 19: Section I (Hero or Heroine, General Theme, Dependency Needs, Specific Drives, Views of Special Figures, Trends and Similarities), Section II (Depression, Mania, Paranoid Ideation, Antisocial Reaction, Schizoid Personality, Paranoid Personality, Anxiety, Conversion Reactions, Obsessive-Compulsive, Schizophrenia, Simple Schizophrenia, Paranoid Schizophrenia, Summary).
Administration: Individual.
Manual: No manual.
Price Data, 2002: $15 per 25 analysis forms; $4.50 per specimen set.
Time: (10–20) minutes.
Author: John A. Blazer.
Publisher: Psychologists and Educators, Inc.

[2477]
TAV Selection System.

Purpose: Constructed to measure "interpersonal reactions" for use in vocational selection and counseling.
Population: Adults.
Publication Dates: 1963–1968.
Acronym: TAV.
Administration: Group.
Price Data: Available from publisher.
Time: (180) minutes for the battery, (15–20) minutes for any one test.
Comments: Self-administered.
Author: R. R. Morman.
Publisher: TAV Selection System.
    a) TAV ADJECTIVE CHECKLIST.
    Scores, 3: Toward People (T), Away from People (A), Versus People (V).
    b) TAV JUDGMENTS.
    Scores, 3: Same as *a* above.
    c) TAV PERSONAL DATA.
    Scores, 3: Same as *a* above.
    d) TAV PREFERENCES.
    Scores, 3: Same as *a* above.
    e) TAV PROVERBS AND SAYINGS.
    Scores, 3: Same as *a* above.
    f) TAV SALESMAN REACTIONS.
    Scores, 3: Same as *a* above.
    g) TAV MENTAL AGILITY.
    Scores, 3: Follow Directions and Carefulness, Weights and Balances, Verbal Comprehension.
Cross References: For a review by Robert G. Demaree, see 8:986 (1 reference); see also T2:2113 (3 references); for an excerpted review by John O. Crites, see 7:983 (1 reference); see also P:263A (11 references).

[2478]
The Taylor-Helmstadter Pair Comparison Scale of Aesthetic Judgment.

Purpose: Constructed to assess aesthetic judgment.
Population: Ages 4 and over.
Publication Dates: 1973–1976.
Scores: Total score only.
Administration: Group.
Price Data: Available from publisher.
Time: [20–30] minutes.
Comments: Two carousel slide projectors necessary for administration.
Author: Anne P. Taylor.
Publisher: Anne P. Taylor.
Cross References: See T3:2395 (1 reference).

[2479]
Taylor-Johnson Temperament Analysis [2002 Edition].

Purpose: Designed to "measure a number of ... personality variables or attitudes and behavioral tendencies which influence personal, social, marital, parental, family, scholastic, and vocational adjustment."
Population: Ages 11 and up.
Publication Dates: 1941–2002.
Acronym: T-JTA.
Scores, 11: Nervous vs. Composed, Depressive vs. Light-Hearted, Active-Social vs. Quiet, Expressive-Responsive vs. Inhibited, Sympathetic vs. Indifferent, Subjective vs. Objective, Dominant vs. Submissive, Hostile vs. Tolerant, Self-Disciplined vs. Impulsive, Total, Attitude.
Administration: Group.
Forms, 4: Regular Edition (criss-cross and self-report forms); Form "S" for Adolescents (criss-cross and self-report).
Price Data, 2002: $195 per complete kit (for handscoring); $110 per computer scoring package (for use with mail-in scoring service); $60 per secondary materials module; $99 per test manual; $43 per handbook.
Time: Untimed.
Comments: Can be used as a self-report questionnaire or as a tool for obtaining perceptions of another person (criss-cross form); Form S can be used with adolescents or with adults with poor reading skills; 2002 Edition based upon new 2002 norms.
Authors: Original edition by Roswell H. Johnson, revision by Robert M. Taylor, Lucile P. Morrison (manual), W. Lee Morrison (statistical consultant), and Richard C. Romoser (statistical consultant).
Publisher: Psychological Publications, Inc.
Cross References: For reviews by Michael J. Sporakowski and Stephen E. Trotter of the 1996 Edition, see 14:381; for reviews by Jeffrey A. Jenkins and

Barbara J. Kaplan of an earlier edition, see 13:315; see also T4:2690 (3 references); for reviews by Cathy W. Hall and Paul McReynolds, see 10:357; see also T3:2396 (1 reference) and T2:840 (3 references); for a review by Robert F. Stahmann, see 8:692 (18 references); for a review by Donald L. Mosher of an earlier edition, see 7:572 (1 reference); see also P:264 (3 references) and 6:130 (10 references); for a review by Albert Ellis of the original edition, see 4:62 (6 references); for a review by H. Meltzer of the original edition, see 3:57.

[2480]
TD (Tardive Dyskinesia) Monitor.

Purpose: "Measures the presence and severity of the tardive dyskinesia movements."
Population: Patients receiving chronic neuroleptic maintenance.
Publication Date: 1992.
Acronym: TD Monitor.
Scores: Total score only.
Administration: Individual.
Price Data, 2002: $95 per complete kit including 25 Modified AIMS QuikScore™ forms, 25 Modified Webster QuikScore™ forms, 25 TD Monitor history forms, and manual; $20 per 25 QuikScore™ forms (specify Modified Webster or Modified AIMS); $30 per 25 history forms; $36 per manual; $40 per specimen set including 1 Modified AIMS QuikScore™ form, 1 Modified Webster QuikScore™ form, 1 history form, and manual.
Time: Administration time not reported.
Comments: Includes the Modified Webster Scale of Parkinsonism and centers around the Modified Abnormal Involuntary Movement Scale.
Author: William M. Glazer.
Publisher: Multi-Health Systems, Inc.

[2481]
Teacher Assessment of Grammatical Structures.

Purpose: "Developed to evaluate a child's understanding and use of the grammatical structures of English and to suggest a sequence for teaching these structures."
Population: Ages 2–4, 5–9, 9 and over.
Publication Date: 1983.
Acronym: TAGS.
Scores: 3 ratings: Imitated, Prompted, Spontaneous Production.
Administration: Individual.
Price Data, 2002: $12 per 25 rating forms per level; $19.95 per manual (203 pages).
Time: Administration time not reported.
Comments: Ratings are based on informal administration in classroom or therapy setting.

Authors: Jean S. Moog and Victoria J. Kozak.
Publisher: Central Institute for the Deaf.
  a) TAGS-P, PRE-SENTENCE LEVEL.
  Population: Ages up to 6 years for hearing-impaired children, ages 2–4 for language-impaired children.
  Comments: Assesses receptive and expressive skills.
  b) TAGS-S, SIMPLE-SENTENCE LEVEL.
  Population: Ages 5–9 years for hearing-impaired children, ages 3 and over for language-impaired children.
  Comments: Assesses expressive skills.
  c) TAGS-C, COMPLEX SENTENCE LEVEL.
  Population: Ages 8 and over for hearing-impaired children, ages 3.5 and over for language-impaired children.
Cross References: See T5:2620 (1 reference) and T4:2691 (1 reference); for reviews by Elizabeth M. Prather and Kenneth G. Shipley, see 10:358 (1 reference).

[2482]
Teacher Observation Scales for Identifying Children with Special Abilities.

Purpose: Designed as an assessment instrument for identifying gifted children, tailored to be culturally appropriate for use in New Zealand.
Population: Junior and middle primary school.
Publication Date: 1996.
Scores, 5: Learning Characteristics, Social Leadership Characteristics, Creative Thinking Characteristics, Self-Determination Characteristics, Motivational Characteristics.
Administration: Individual.
Price Data, 2001: NZ$12.60 per 20 observation scales; $12.60 per teacher's handbook (9 pages).
Time: Administration time not reported.
Authors: Don McAlpine and Neil Reid.
Publisher: New Zealand Council for Educational Research [New Zealand].
Cross References: For reviews by Ira Stuart Katz and Kenneth A. Kiewra, see 14:382.

[2483]
Teacher Opinion Inventory, Revised Edition.

Purpose: To assess teachers' opinions concerning many facets of the school, to "compile teachers' recommendations for improvement," and to provide "data to guide the school's professional staff in decision making relative to program development."
Population: Elementary and secondary school teachers.
Publication Dates: 1975–1995.
Scores: 4 subscales: Quality of the Instructional Program, Support for Student Learning, School Climate/

Environment for Learning, School Organization and Administration.
Administration: Group.
Parts, 2: A (Likert-scale items), B (customize up to 20 local questions).
Price Data, 1998: $15 per 25 inventories; $6.50 per Administrator's Manual (1995, 26 pages).
Time: Untimed.
Author: National Study of School Evaluation.
Publisher: National Study of School Evaluation.

[2484]
Teacher Opinionaire on Democracy.

Purpose: Intended as "an objective measure of educational philosophy."
Population: Teachers.
Publication Date: 1949.
Scores: Total score only.
Administration: Group.
Forms, 2: G, H.
Price Data: Available from publisher.
Time: Administration time not reported.
Authors: Enola Ledbetter and Theodore F. Lentz.
Publisher: Lentz Peace Research Laboratory [No reply from publisher; status unknown].
Cross References: See T2:901 (2 references); for reviews by George W. Hartmann and C. Robert Pace, see 4:805.

[2485]
Teacher Performance Assessment [1999 Revision].

Purpose: "Developed to provide both an objective assessment and a self-assessment of classroom instructional activities from individuals who work in different roles and who make different contributions to the schools."
Population: Teachers, student teachers, and classroom assistants.
Publication Dates: 1991–2000.
Acronym: TPA.
Scores, 3: Performance Assessment, Self-Assessment, Reflected Self-Assessment.
Administration: Group.
Forms, 8: Classroom Teachers, Substitute Teachers, Field Associates, Internship I, Internship II, Student Teachers, Classroom Aides, Residents; plus supervisor forms for each.
Price Data, 2002: $20 per 25 scales (specify form); $.40 per answer sheet; $.50 per customized booklet; $15 per manual (2000, 19 pages); $.30 per scale for scoring.
Time: (15) minutes.
Authors: Louise M. Soares and Anthony T. Soares.
Publisher: SOARES Associates.

[2486]
Teacher Values Inventory.

Purpose: Measures "teacher's preferences and opinions."
Population: Teachers.
Publication Dates: 1980–1981.
Acronym: TVI.
Scores, 6: Theoretical, Economic, Aesthetic, Social, Political, Religious.
Administration: Group.
Price Data: Available from publisher.
Foreign Language Edition: Hindi version also available.
Time: Administration time not reported.
Authors: Harbhajan L. Singh and S. P. Ahluwalia.
Publisher: National Psychological Corporation [India] [No reply from publisher; status unknown].

[2487]
Teacher's Handbook of Diagnostic Inventories, Second Edition.

Purpose: Developed "to assess the learning needs of individual students."
Population: Grades K–8.
Publication Dates: 1974–1979.
Scores: 4 areas: Spelling, Reading, Handwriting, Arithmetic.
Administration: Individual.
Price Data: Available from publisher.
Authors: Philip H. Mann, Patricia A. Suiter, and Rose Marie McClung.
Publisher: Allyn & Bacon.

[2488]
Teacher's Handbook of Diagnostic Screening, Second Edition.

Purpose: Provides teachers with a series of screening tests to facilitate the assessment of readiness and the identification of preferred learning modalities.
Population: Ages 4, 6, and over.
Publication Dates: 1974–1979.
Scores: 18 areas: Visual Motor, Visual Figure-Ground, Visual Discrimination, Visual Closure, Visual Memory, Auditory Discrimination, Auditory Closure, Auditory Memory (Sentences), Alphabet-Speech (Auditory-Visual Association), Visual Language Classification, Visual Language Association, Auditory Language Classification, Auditory Language Association, Manual Language Expression, Speech, Verbal Language Expression, Written Language Expression, Non-Verbal Language.
Administration: Individual.
Price Data: Available from publisher.
Comments: 2 levels; one form used for both levels.

Authors: Philip H. Mann, Patricia A. Suiter, and Rose Marie McClung.
Publisher: Allyn & Bacon.
Cross References: For a review by J. Manuel Casas, see 9:1229.

[2489]
Teaching Resource and Assessment of Critical Skills.

Purpose: Designed to assist decision making about an individual's skills and potential to live in an unsupervised setting.
Population: People with special needs.
Publication Date: 1989.
Acronym: TRACS.
Scores: Unscored.
Administration: Individual.
Price Data, 1998: $124 per program including resource, assessment and skill log booklets, user's guide (49 pages), master forms, and audio tape.
Time: Administration time not reported.
Authors: Lauren Meiklejohn and Mark Rice.
Publisher: Program Development Associates.

[2490]
Team Competency Assessment.

Purpose: Designed to "evaluate the level at which a team is performing on ten team competencies."
Population: Team members.
Publication Date: Not dated.
Scores, 11: Committing to a Team Approach, Communicating Effectively Within Teams, Utilizing Team Member Abilities, Resolving Team Conflicts, Creating a Shared Team Purpose, Planning for Results, Making Meetings Work, Evaluating Team Process and Performance, Making Team Decisions by Consensus, Solving Team Problems, Climate.
Administration: Group.
Price Data, 1997: $25 per assessment disk; $69.95 per administrator's manual (includes reporting diskette); $10 per performance skills team preview.
Time: Administration time not reported.
Comments: A 65-item questionnaire; can be computer administered, scored, and interpreted (requiring IBM Windows compatible) or available in pencil-paper format; can be used separately or as one component of a team skills workshop.
Author: Human Technology, Inc.
Publisher: Human Resource Development Press.

[2491]
Team-Development Inventory.

Purpose: "A means by which work-team members can give each other feedback concerning how they are working together."
Population: Work-team members.
Publication Date: 1982.

Acronym: TDI.
Scores, 8: Each team member rank orders all members on 8 dimensions: Participation, Collaboration, Flexibility, Sensitivity, Risk Taking, Commitment, Facilitation, Openness.
Administration: Group.
Price Data: Price information available from publisher for kit including 10 instruments, 10 handouts, and facilitator's guide (16 pages).
Time: (35–50) minutes.
Author: John E. Jones.
Publisher: Jossey-Bass, A Wiley Company.

[2492]
Team Development Survey.

Purpose: A brief assessment tool for work teams.
Population: Work team members.
Publication Date: 1992.
Acronym: TDS.
Scores, 12: Clear Purpose, Informality, Participation, Listening, Civilized Disagreement, Consensus Decisions, Open Communication, Clear Roles and Work Assignments, Shared Leadership, External Relations, Style Diversity, Self-Assessment.
Administration: Group.
Price Data, 2001: $38.50 per materials for 10 team members and leaders guide (18 pages).
Time: Administration time not reported.
Author: Glenn M. Parker.
Publisher: Consulting Psychologists Press, Inc.
Cross References: For reviews by Gregory J. Cizek and Lynn R. Offermann, see 13:316.

[2493]
Team Effectiveness Survey.

Purpose: Designed to assess process issues associated with team dynamics.
Population: Team members.
Publication Dates: 1968–1996.
Acronym: TES.
Scores: 4 scores for each team member: Exposure, Feedback, Defensive, Supportive, plus Total Team Effectiveness score.
Administration: Group.
Price Data, 2001: $8.95 per instrument.
Time: Administration time not reported.
Author: Jay Hall.
Publisher: Teleometrics International.
Cross References: For reviews by Gregory H. Dobbins and Harrison G. Gough, see 12:388; for a review by William G. Mollenkopf of an earlier version, see 8:1055.

[2494]
The Team Leadership Practices Inventory.

Purpose: Focuses on the behaviors and actions of high-performing teams and self-directed work groups.
Population: Managers.

Publication Date: 1992.
Acronym: LPI.
Scores, 15: 3 scores: Self-Average, Team-Average, Total in each of 5 areas: Challenging the Process, Inspiring a Shared Vision, Enabling Others to Act, Modeling the Way, Encouraging the Heart.
Administration: Group.
Price Data: Price information available from publisher for trainer's package including 3 booklets, self-assessment, and observer and trainer's manual (47 pages); deluxe trainer's package including the leadership challenge, self-assessment and analysis, and trainer's manual; IBM scoring program including manual (12 pages); instrument and participant's manual.
Time: (20–140) minutes.
Comments: Self-scored inventory.
Authors: James M. Kouzes and Barry Z. Posner.
Publisher: Jossey-Bass, A Wiley Company.
Cross References: For reviews by Jeffrey B. Brookings and William J. Waldron, see 13:317.

[2495]
Team Process Diagnostic.

Purpose: To analyze and classify group processes according to their implications for member and team effectiveness.
Population: Individuals whose work responsibilities require work-team cooperation.
Publication Dates: 1974–1989.
Scores: 9 clusters in 3 modes: Problem Solving (Integrative, Content-Bound, Process-Bound), Fight (Perceptual Difference, Status-Striving, Frustration), Flight (Fear, Indifference, Powerlessness).
Administration: Group.
Price Data: Price information available from publisher for instrument (1989, 21 pages).
Time: Administration time not reported.
Comments: Team associate ratings, self ratings, self scored.
Author: Jay Hall.
Publisher: Teleometrics International.
Cross References: For a review by Lawrence A. Aleamoni, see 11:416.

[2496]
Teamness Index.

Purpose: To "survey ... conditions of work and the array of feelings that might exist among two or more people as they seek to work together."
Population: Individuals whose work responsibilities require work-team cooperation.
Publication Dates: 1988–1995.
Scores: Item scores only.
Administration: Group.
Price Data, 2001: $8.95 per instrument.
Time: Administration time not reported.

Comments: Self-ratings; self-scored.
Author: Jay Hall.
Publisher: Teleometrics International.
Cross References: For reviews by Barbara Lachar and Frederick T. L. Leong, see 11:417.

[2497]
Teamwork Appraisal Survey.

Purpose: To assess "an associate's feelings about working in teams and the behaviors he or she employs in work-team situations."
Population: Individuals whose work responsibilities require work-team cooperation.
Publication Date: 1987.
Acronym: TAS.
Scores, 5: Synergistic, Compromise, Win-Lose, Yield-Lose, Lose-Leave.
Administration: Group.
Price Data: Price information available from publisher for instrument (24 pages).
Time: Administration time not reported.
Comments: Based on Team Behaviors Model of analysis of individual behaviors in a team setting; work associates rate each other's behavior.
Author: Jay Hall.
Publisher: Teleometrics International.

[2498]
Teamwork-KSA Test.

Purpose: Designed to "measure the essential knowledge, skills, and abilities that are predictive of working effectively in teams."
Population: Adults (industry).
Publication Date: 1994.
Scores: 7 subscales: Conflict Resolution, Collaborative Problem Solving, Communication, Interpersonal Skills, Goal Setting and Performance Management, Planning and Task Coordination, Self-Management Skills, plus Overall Score.
Administration: Group or individual.
Price Data, 2002: $127 per 10 tests; $28 per examiner's manual (1994, 23 pages); price data for scoring software available from publisher.
Time: [30–40] minutes.
Comments: Paper-and-pencil or computer administered.
Authors: Michael J. Stevens and Michael A. Campion.
Publisher: Reid London House.

[2499]
Technical Personnel Recruiting Inventory.

Purpose: Intended for use in research and development within industrial organizations; also for use in hiring.
Population: Research, engineering, and scientific firms.

Publication Dates: 1959–1960.
Scores: Item scores only.
Administration: Group.
Price Data: Available from publisher.
Author: Morris I. Stein.
Publisher: The Mews Press.
   a) INDIVIDUAL QUALIFICATION FORM.
   Population: Supervisors.
   Comments: For description of available position.
   b) PERSONAL DATA FORM FOR SCIENTIFIC, ENGINEERING, AND TECHNICAL PERSONNEL.
   Population: Job applicants.
   c) STEIN SURVEY FOR ADMINISTRATORS.
   Population: Administrators.
   Time: (30-40) minutes.
   Comments: Description of company's research environment; also part of Surveys of Research Administration and Environment (2458).
Cross References: For additional information, see 6:1167.

[2500]
Technical Support Staff Selector.

Purpose: To measure knowledge and aptitude for technical support positions.
Population: Candidates for the position of technical support.
Publication Date: 1994.
Acronym: TECHSUP.
Scores: Total Score, Narrative Evaluation, Ranking, Recommendation.
Administration: Group.
Price Data, 2001: $400 per candidate; quantity discounts available.
Time: (80) minutes.
Comments: Scored by publisher; must be proctored.
Author: Bruce A. Winrow.
Publisher: Walden Personnel Performance, Inc.

[2501]
Technical Test Battery.

Purpose: "Designed for occupational selection and placement."
Population: Technical job applicants and incumbents entry level to professional.
Publication Date: 1990.
Acronym: TTB.
Scores: Total score only for each of 9 tests.
Administration: Individual or group.
Price Data: Available from publisher.
Comments: Subtests available as separates.
Author: Saville & Holdsworth Ltd.
Publisher: SHL Group plc [United Kingdom].
   a) FOLLOWING INSTRUCTIONS (VTS1).
   Time: 20(25) minutes.

   b) NUMERICAL COMPUTATION (NT2).
   Time: 10(15) minutes.
   c) MECHANICAL COMPREHENSION (MT4).
   Time: 15(20) minutes.
   d) NUMERICAL ESTIMATION (NTS2).
   Time: 10(15) minutes.
   e) MECHANICAL COMPREHENSION (MTS3).
   Time: 15(20) minutes.
   f) FAULT FINDING (FTS4).
   Time: 20(25) minutes.
   g) DIAGRAMMATIC THINKING (DTS6).
   Time: 20(25) minutes.
   h) SPATIAL REASONING (ST7).
   Time: 20(25) minutes.
   i) DIAGRAMMATIC REASONING (DT8).
   Time: 15(20) minutes.
Cross References: For a review by Sami Gulgoz, see 11:419.

[2502]
Technical Test Battery [British Edition].

Purpose: Assess vocational skills and abilities.
Population: Apprentice and technical personnel.
Publication Dates: 1979–1982.
Acronym: TTB.
Administration: Group.
Restricted Distribution: Persons who have completed the publisher's training course or members of the Division of Occupational Psychology of the British Psychological Society.
Price Data: Available from publisher.
Comments: Subtests available as separates.
Authors: David Hawkey, Peter Saville, Robert Page (MT4), and Gill Nyfield (manual).
Publisher: SHL Group plc [United Kingdom].
   a) LEVEL 1.
   Purpose: "Basic skills and comprehension."
   Publication Dates: 1979–1981.
      1) Verbal Comprehension.
      Acronym: VT 1.
      Time: 10(15) minutes.
      2) Numerical Computation.
      Acronym: NT 2.
      Time: 10(15) minutes.
      3) Visual Estimation.
      Acronym: ET 3.
      Time: 10(15) minutes.
      4) Mechanical Comprehension.
      Acronym: MT 4.
      Time: 15(20) minutes.
   b) LEVEL 2.
   Purpose: "Higher older reasoning and analytical skills."
   Publication Dates: 1979–1981.
      1) Verbal Reasoning.
      Acronym: VT 5.
      Time: 10(15) minutes.

2) *Numerical Reasoning.*
Acronym: NT 6.
Time: 10(15) minutes.
3) *Spatial Reasoning.*
Acronym: ST 7.
Time: 20(25) minutes.
4) *Diagrammatic Reasoning.*
Acronym: DT 8.
Time: 15(20) minutes.
5) *Spatial Recognition* (optional test for Levels 1 and 2).
Acronym: ST 9.
Time: 15(20) minutes.

[2503]
Technology and Internet Assessment.

Purpose: Designed to determine strengths and weaknesses in eight areas related to computer, Internet, and information skills.
Population: Middle school, high school, and college students, potential and existing employees.
Publication Date: 1999.
Acronym: TIA.
Scores, 8: Use of Technology, Specific Computer Skills, Acquisition of Technology Knowledge, Basic Internet Knowledge, Internet Information Skills, Adapting to Technological Change, Impact of Technology, Ethics of Technology.
Administration: Individual or group.
Price Data, 1999: $3 per test (100 copies or less); $2.50 per test (over 100 copies); user's manual free.
Time: (20–30) minutes.
Comments: Administration and results via World Wide Web.
Author: Michael Ealy.
Publisher: H & H Publishing Co., Inc.

[2504]
Telemarketing Staff Selector.

Purpose: To evaluate the necessary knowledge and skills needed for the position of telemarketing representative.
Population: Candidates for the position of telemarketing representative.
Publication Date: 1997.
Scores: Total Score, Narrative Evaluation, Ranking, Recommendation.
Administration: Group.
Price Data, 2001: $150 per candidate; quantity discounts available.
Time: (81) minutes.
Comments: Scored by publisher; must be proctored.
Author: Walden Personnel Performance, Inc.
Publisher: Walden Personnel Performance, Inc.

[2505]
TEMAS (Tell-Me-A-Story).

Purpose: Identifies "both strengths and deficits in cognitive, affective, and intrapersonal and interpersonal functioning."
Population: Ages 5–18.
Publication Dates: 1986–1988.
Acronym: TEMAS.
Scores, 34: Quantitative Scales (Cognitive Functions [Reaction Time, Total Time, Fluency, Total Omissions], Personality Functions [Interpersonal Relations, Aggression, Anxiety/Depression, Achievement Motivation, Delay of Gratification, Self-Concept, Sexual Identity, Moral Judgment, Reality Testing], Affective Functions [Happy, Sad, Angry, Fearful]), Qualitative Indicators (Affective Functions [Neutral, Ambivalent, Inappropriate Affect], Cognitive Functions [Conflict, Sequencing, Imagination, Relationships, Total Transformations, Inquiries, Omissions and Transformations scores for each of the following: Main Character, Secondary Character, Event, Setting]).
Administration: Individual.
Forms, 2: Short, Long.
Versions, 2: Minority, Nonminority.
Price Data, 2002: $265 per complete kit including nonminority stimulus cards (1986, 36 cards), minority stimulus cards (1986, 36 cards), 25 record booklets, administration instruction card, and manual (1988, 166 pages); $89 per set of stimulus cards; $19.95 per 25 record booklets; $12 per administration instruction card; $62.50 per manual.
Time: (45–60) minutes (short form); (120) minutes (long form).
Authors: Giuseppe Costantino, Robert G. Malgady (manual and record booklet), and Lloyd H. Rogler (manual).
Publisher: Western Psychological Services.
Cross References: See T5:2647 (2 references) and T4:2716 (1 reference); for a review by William Steve Lang, see 11:422.

[2506]
Temperament Comparator.

Purpose: "Designed to assess the relatively permanent temperament traits which are characteristic of an individual's behavior."
Population: Managers, supervisors, salespeople, and other higher-level professionals.
Publication Dates: 1958–1996.
Acronym: TC.
Scores, 15: Trait Scores (Calm, Cautious, Decisive, Demonstrative, Composed, Even-Tempered, Persevering, Seeks Company, Self-Confident, Serious, Steady Worker, Talkative), Factor Scores (Extroversive/Impulsive vs. Introvertive/Cautious, Emotionally Respon-

sive vs. Non-Emotionally Controlled, Self-Reliant/Self-Oriented vs. Dependent/Group Oriented).
Administration: Individual or group.
Price Data, 2002: $99 per start-up kit including 25 test booklets, 25 score sheets, and interpretation and research manual; $54 per 25 test booklets (quantity discounts available); $29 per 25 score sheets; $28 per interpretation and research manual.
Time: No limit (approximately 15 minutes).
Author: Melany E. Baehr.
Publisher: Reid London House.
Cross References: See T5:2648 (1 reference); for reviews by Paul M. Muchinsky and Aharon Tziner, see 9:1234; see also T2:1413 (1 reference); for reviews by Lawrence J. Stricker and Robert L. Thorndike, see 6:187 (1 reference).

[2507]
Temperament Inventory.

Purpose: Designed to measure a set of four genetically determined temperaments.
Population: College and adults.
Publication Dates: 1977–1980.
Acronym: TI.
Scores, 4: Phlegmatic, Sanguine, Choleric, Melancholy.
Administration: Group.
Price Data: Available from publisher.
Foreign Language Editions: French, German, and Spanish.
Time: Administration time not reported.
Authors: Robert J. Cruise and W. Peter Blitchington.
Publisher: Andrews University Press.
  a) [GROUP EDITION].
  Publication Date: 1977.
  b) UNDERSTANDING YOUR TEMPERAMENT.
  Publication Date: 1979.
  Comments: For self-administering, self-scoring, and self-interpreting the scores from a Christian viewpoint.
Cross References: For reviews by Allan L. Lavoie and Paul McReynolds, see 9:1235 (1 reference); see also T3:2411 (1 reference).

[2508]
Tennessee Self-Concept Scale, Second Edition.

Purpose: Designed as a multidimensional self-concept assessment instrument.
Population: Ages 7 to 90.
Publication Dates: 1964–1996.
Acronym: TSCS: 2.
Scores, 15: Validity scores (Inconsistent Responding, Self-Criticism, Faking Good, Response Distribution); Summary scores (Total Self-Concept, Conflict); Self-Concept scales (Physical, Moral, Personal, Family,

Social, Academic/Work); Supplementary scores (Identity, Satisfaction, Behavior).
Administration: Group.
Price Data, 2002: $110 per complete kit including 24 AutoScore™ answer forms (12 for adults and 12 for children), manual (1996, 141 pages), and a 2-use disk and 2 PC answer sheets for on-site computer scoring and interpretation; $41.50 per 20 AutoScore™ forms (specify Adult of Child); $15 per 10 Spanish Research edition answer sheets (specify Adult or Child); $13.50 per mail-in answer sheet (specify Adult or Child); $245 per 25-use disk (PC with Windows; specify Adult or Child form); $15 per 100 answer sheets for use with disk; $10.50 per FAX Service Scoring; $55 per manual.
Time: (10–20) minutes.
Comments: Self-administered; WPS TEST REPORT Service available for computerized scoring and test interpretation.
Authors: William H. Fitts and W. L. Warren.
Publisher: Western Psychological Services.
  a) TSCS:2 ADULT FORM.
  Population: Ages 13 and older.
  b) TSCS:2 CHILD FORM.
  Population: Ages 7–14.
  c) TSCS:2 SHORT FORM.
  Population: Adults (13 and older); child (7–14).
  Comments: The Short Form consists of the first 20 items on the adult and child forms.
Cross References: See T5:2652 (12 references); for reviews by Ric Brown and John Hattie, see 13:320 (41 references); see also T4:2723 (32 references); for reviews by Francis X. Archambault, Jr. and E. Thomas Dowd, see 11:424 (89 references); see also 9:1236 (60 references), T3:2413 (120 references), 8:693 (384 references), and T2:1415 (80 references); for reviews by Peter M. Bentler and Richard M. Suinn and an excerpted review by John O. Crites of an earlier edition, see 7:151 (88 references); see also P:266 (30 references).

[2509]
Tennis Skills Test Manual.

Purpose: Designed to assess essential skills needed to play tennis.
Population: High school and college.
Publication Date: 1989.
Scores, 3: Ground Stroke, Serve, Volley.
Administration: Individual.
Price Data, 2001: $14 per manual (50 pages).
Time: Administration time not reported.
Authors: Larry Hensley, Graham Hatcher, Gloria Hook, Paul Hook, Carolyn Lehr, and Jacqueline Shick.
Publisher: American Association for Active Lifestyles and Fitness.

Cross References: For reviews by Claude A. Sandy and William A. Stock, see 12:390; see also T4:2724 (1 reference).

[2510]
TerraNova, The Second Edition.

Purpose: "A comprehensive, modular series offering multiple measures of both English- and Spanish-language student achievement."
Population: Grades K–12.
Publication Dates: 1997–2002.
Administration: Group.
Levels, 12: 10 (Kindergarten), 11 (Grade 1), 12 (Grade 2), 13 (Grade 3), 14 (Grade 4), 15 (Grade 5), 16 (Grade 6), 17 (Grade 7), 18 (Grade 8), 19 (Grade 9), 20 (Grade 10), 21/22 (Grades 11, 12).
Forms, 2: C, D. (2 forms of the Plus Tests also available).
Price Data, 2002: $47.70 per Teacher's Guide to TerraNova, The Second Edition (2000, 320 pages), quantity discount available; $47.70 per Technical Bulletin (2002, 310 pages), CD-ROM version only; $31.80 per Pre-Publication Technical Bulletin (82 pages), CD-ROM version only; $5.85 per Assessment Accommodations Supplement (17 pages); $2.10 per class record sheet for hand scoring; $42.40 per norms book including student diagnostic profile, CD-ROM with all norms tables (Fall, Winter, or Spring, specify season).
Foreign Language and Other Special Editions: Available in English and Spanish editions (Supera); Braille and large print editions available.
Time: Administration time varies by test and level.
Comments: Also called California Achievement Test, Sixth Edition (CAT6); total remake of the TerraNova (T5:2654) including all new items and thematic content, new norms; TerraNova, The Second Edition, Forms C and D are designed as parallel test forms to the Comprehensive Tests of Basic Skills (CTBS; 1997) Forms A and B; Basic Battery, Basic Multiple Assessments measure only Reading, Language, Mathematics; Survey, Complete Battery, Multiple Assessments measure Reading, Language, Mathematics, Science, Social Studies; Plus Tests measure additional skills (Word Analysis, Vocabulary, Language Mechanics, Spelling, Mathematics Computation); tests may be administered alone or in any combination; 2 formats: paper and pencil, CD-ROM; both Windows and Macintosh versions available; system requirements for Windows: 486 processor or faster, Windows 95 or later, 20 MB hard disk; system requirements for Macintosh: Power Macintosh, Apple OS 7.5.3 or later, 60 MB hard disk; also requires 6 MB RAM, CD-ROM drive, Adobe Acrobat Reader 4.0 or later; full-service scoring available through publisher; reports and data available on CD-ROM; electronic report delivery available; information regarding numerous customized and packaged scoring and reporting services available from publisher; optional locator tests available to assist teachers in identifying appropriate testing level for individual students; optional practice activities available to help familiarize students with test-taking mechanics, item formats, test design elements; website (www.ctb.com) provides sample test questions and answers, information about instructional strategies, report interpretation for teachers, parents, administrators, students.
Author: CTB/McGraw-Hill.
Publisher: CTB/McGraw-Hill.

a) CAT SURVEY AND SURVEY WITH PLUS.
Purpose: Designed to "yield norm-referenced and some curriculum-referenced information in a minimum of testing time."
Price Data: $107.05 per 25 consumable Survey test books (Levels 12–13, specify level) including manipulatives, and Test Directions for Teachers; $42.95 per 25 consumable Plus test books for use with Survey (Levels 12–13, specify level) including manipulatives, and Test Directions for Teachers; $93.30 per 25 reusable Survey test books (Levels 14–21/22, specify level); $36.05 per 25 reusable Plus test books for use with Survey (Levels 14–21/22, specify level); $44.50 per 50 Survey CompuScan answer sheets (Levels 14–21/22) including Plus answer grid; $1,125 per 1,250 continuous form (Trans-Optic) answer sheets for precoding (Levels 14–21/22) including Plus answer grid; $635 per 2,500 student information sheets; $59.35 per 2 Survey or Survey with Plus acetate scoring stencils (Levels 14–21/22); $7.40 per 30 Survey ancillary pieces additional manipulatives (Levels 12–13); $11.65 per 50 Survey ancillary pieces additional manipulatives (Levels 14–22); $17.50 per Test Directions for Teachers (Levels 12–22, specify level); Basic Service scoring: $3.51 per Basic Survey book (Levels 12–13); $2.05 per Survey answer sheet (Levels 14–21/22); $3.89 per Survey with Plus book (Levels 12–13); $2.43 per Survey with Plus answer sheet; $59.95 per Survey accommodation kit (Levels 12–22, specify level).
Comments: Provides norm-referenced scores; all items use selected-response format.
Time: Varies by level; Reading and Language Arts: 60–80(70–90) minutes; Mathematics: 35–40(45–50) minutes; Science, Social Studies: 20–25(30–35) minutes each; 135–170(155–190) minutes total; 215–235(260–280) minutes total with Plus tests.

1) Levels 12–13.
Population: Grades 2–3.
Scores: 5 Survey scores (Reading, Language, Mathematics, Science, Social Studies); 5 Plus

scores (Vocabulary, Language Mechanics, Spelling, Mathematics Computation, Word Analysis).

2) *Levels 14–21/22.*

Population: Grades 4–12.

Scores: 5 Survey scores (Reading, Language, Mathematics, Science, Social Studies); 4 Plus scores (Vocabulary, Language Mechanics, Spelling, Mathematics Computation).

b) CAT COMPLETE BATTERY AND COMPLETE BATTERY PLUS.

Purpose: "Generates norm-referenced achievement scores and a full complement of objective-mastery scores."

Price Data: $138.85 per 25 consumable Complete Battery test books (Levels 10–13, specify level); $143.10 per 25 consumable Complete Battery Plus test books (Levels 11–13, specify level); $103.90 per 25 reusable Complete Battery test books (Levels 14–21/22, specify level); $112.35 per 25 reusable Complete Battery Plus test books (Levels 14–21/22, specify level); $44.50 per 50 complete Battery CompuScan answer sheets (Levels 14–21/22) including Plus grid; $1,125 per 1,250 continuous form (Trans-Optic) answer sheets for precoding (Levels 14–21/22) including Plus answer grid; $635 per 2,500 student information sheets; $59.35 per 3 Complete Battery Plus acetate scoring stencils (Levels 14–21/22); $7.40 per 30 Battery ancillary pieces additional manipulatives (Levels 12–13); $11.65 per 50 Battery ancillary pieces additional manipulatives (Levels 14–21/22); $17.50 per additional Test Directions for Teachers (Levels 10–21/22, specify level); Basic Service scoring: $3.51 per Complete Battery book (Level 10–13); $2.05 per Complete Battery answer sheet (Levels 14–21/22); $3.89 per Complete Battery Plus book (Levels 11–13); $2.43 per Complete Battery Plus answer sheet; $59.95 per Complete Battery accommodation kit (Levels 10–22, specify level),

Comments: Combines Survey items with additional selected-response items; yields detailed diagnostic information; provides norm-referenced scores.

Time: Varies by level; Reading and Language Arts: 55–100(65–110) minutes; Mathematics: 40–70(50–80) minutes; Science, Social Studies: 20–40(30–50) minutes each; 95–250(115–270) minutes total; 95–315(140–360) minutes total with Plus tests.

1) *Level 10.*

Population: Kindergarten.

Scores: 3 Complete Battery scores (Reading, Language, Mathematics); 2 Plus scores (Language Mechanics, Spelling).

2) *Level 11.*

Population: Grade 1.

Scores: 5 Complete Battery scores (Reading, Language, Mathematics, Science, Social Studies); 2 Plus scores (Language Mechanics, Spelling).

3) *Levels 12 and 13.*

Population: Grades 2–3.

Scores: 5 Complete Battery scores (Reading, Language, Mathematics, Science, Social Studies); 5 Plus scores (Language Mechanics, Spelling, Vocabulary, Mathematics Computation, Word Analysis).

4) *Levels 14–21/22.*

Population: Grades 4–12.

Scores: 5 Complete Battery scores (Reading, Language, Mathematics, Science, Social Studies); 4 Plus scores (Language Mechanics, Spelling, Vocabulary, Mathematics Computation).

c) CAT BASIC BATTERY AND BASIC BATTERY PLUS.

Purpose: Designed to "provide the same information as the Complete Battery, targeting the basic areas of reading, language arts, and mathematics."

Price Data: $131.45 per 25 consumable Basic Battery test books (Levels 11–13, specify level) including manipulatives, and Test Directions for Teachers; $42.95 per 25 consumable Plus test books for use with Basic Battery (Levels 11–13, specify level) including manipulatives, and Test Directions for Teachers; $102.80 per 25 reusable Basic Battery test books (Levels 14–21/22, specify level); $36.05 per 25 reusable Plus test books for use with Basic Battery (Levels 14–21/22, specify level); $44.50 per 50 Basic Battery CompuScan answer sheets (Levels 14–21/22) including Plus answer grid; $1,125 per 1,250 continuous form (Trans-Optic) answer sheets for precoding (Levels 14–21/22) including Plus answer grid; $635 per 2,500 student information sheets; $59.35 per 3 Basic Battery or Basic Battery with Plus acetate scoring stencils (Levels 14–21/22); $7.40 per 30 ancillary pieces additional manipulatives (Levels 12–13); $11.65 per 50 ancillary pieces additional manipulatives (Levels 14–21/22); $17.50 per additional Test Directions for Teachers (Levels 10–21/22, specify level); Basic Service scoring: $3.51 per Basic Battery book (Levels 10–13); $2.05 per Basic Battery answer sheet (Levels 14–21/22); $3.89 per Basic Battery Plus book (Levels 11–13); $2.43 per Basic Battery Plus answer sheet.

Comments: Reading/Language Arts and Mathematics tests same as for Complete Battery.

Time: Varies by level; 55–100(65–110) minutes for Reading and Language Arts, 40–70(50–80) minutes for Mathematics, 95–170(140–215) minutes total; 170(215) minutes total with Plus tests.

    1) *Levels 10 and 11.*
Population: Kindergarten–Grade 1.
Scores: 3 Basic Battery scores (Reading, Language, Mathematics); 2 Plus scores (Language Mechanics, Spelling).

    2) *Levels 12 and 13.*
Population: Grades 2–3.
Scores: 3 Basic Battery scores (Reading, Language, Mathematics); 5 Plus scores (Language Mechanics, Spelling, Vocabulary, Mathematics Computation, Word Analysis).

    3) *Levels 14–21/22.*
Population: Grades 4–12.
Scores: 3 Basic Battery scores (Reading, Language, Mathematics); 4 Plus scores (Language Mechanics, Spelling, Vocabulary, Mathematics Computation).

d) CAT MULTIPLE ASSESSMENTS AND MULTIPLE ASSESSMENTS WITH PLUS.
Purpose: Designed "to provide data on students' problem solving and reading skills."
Price Data: $143.10 per 25 consumable scannable CAT Multiple Assessments test books (Levels 11–21/22, specify level); $42.95 per 25 consumable Plus test books for use with Multiple Assessments (Levels 11–13, specify level); $36.05 per 25 reusable Plus test books for use with Multiple Assessments (Levels 14–21/22, specify level); all test book sets include manipulatives and Test Directions for Teachers; $15.90 per scoring guide for CTBS Multiple Assessments (Levels 11–21/22, specify level); $95.40 per Multiple Assessments scoring guide (CD-ROM, Levels 11–21/22); $19.10 per 30 Multiple Assessments ancillary pieces additional manipulatives (Levels 11–21/22); $17.50 per additional Test Directions for Teachers (Levels 11–21/22, specify level); Basic Service scoring: $11.88 per Multiple Assessment (all levels); $12.26 per Multiple Assessment with Plus (all levels); $59.95 per Multiple Assessments accommodation kit (Levels 11–22, specify level).
Comments: Combines selected-response items from Survey with constructed-response items allowing students to produce their own short and extended responses; constructed-response items scanned electronically, hand scored by publisher; produces norm-referenced and curriculum-referenced scores.
Time: Reading and Language Arts: 100–120(110–130) minutes; Mathematics: 50–90(60–100) minutes; Science: 45–60(55–70) minutes; Social Studies: 45–65(55–75) minutes; 240–335(280–375) minutes total; 290–400(355–465) minutes total with Plus tests.

    1) *Level 11.*
Population: Grade 1.
Scores: 5 Multiple Assessments scores (Reading, Language, Mathematics, Science, Social Studies); 3 Plus scores (Vocabulary, Mathematics Computation, Word Analysis).

    2) *Levels 12 and 13.*
Population: Grades 2–3.
Scores: 5 Multiple Assessments scores (Reading, Language, Mathematics, Science, Social Studies); 5 Plus scores (Vocabulary, Mathematics Computation, Language Mechanics, Spelling, Word Analysis).

    3) *Levels 14–21/22.*
Population: Grades 4–12.
Scores: 5 Multiple Assessments scores (Reading, Language, Mathematics, Science, Social Studies); 4 Plus scores (Vocabulary, Mathematics Computation, Language Mechanics, Spelling).

e) CAT BASIC MULTIPLE ASSESSMENTS AND BASIC MULTIPLE ASSESSMENTS PLUS.
Price Data: Available from publisher.
Time: Varies by level; 150–210(195–255) minutes total; 200–275(245–320) minutes total with Plus tests.
Comments: Includes both selected-response and constructed-response items; selected-response items scored electronically; constructed-response items hand scored by publisher; Reading/Language Arts and Mathematics tests same as for Complete Multiple Assessments.

    1) *Level 11.*
Population: Grade 1.
Scores: 3 Basic Multiple Assessment scores (Reading, Language Arts, Mathematics); 3 Plus scores (Vocabulary, Mathematics Computation, Word Analysis).

    2) *Levels 12–21/22.*
Population: Grades 2–12.
Scores: 3 Basic Multiple Assessment scores (Reading, Language Arts, Mathematics); 5 Plus scores (Vocabulary, Mathematics Computation, Language Mechanics, Spelling, Word Analysis).

f) TERRANOVA ALGEBRA TEST.
Purpose: "Measures how students use algebraic processes to manipulate expressions and model mathematical situations."
Population: Students in grades 7–12 who have completed Algebra I.
Scores: Available from publisher.
Price Data: $75.25 per 25 test books; $57.25 per 50 answer sheets; $11.65 per additional Test Directions for Teachers; $1,430 per 2,500 continuous form answer sheets; $25 per Technical

Resource manual; $28 per Algebra specimen set including test book, answer sheet, and test directions); Basic Service scoring: $1.84 per Algebra answer sheet; $1.35 per Algebra individual report; $0.81 per Algebra summary report; $3.60 per Algebra Plan 1 including Basic Service scoring, Algebra individual report, and Algebra summary report.

Comments: Results are reported separately from those of TerraNova, The Second Edition.

Time: 45(50) minutes.

g) SUPERA.

Purpose: "The Spanish-language version of the assessment series, offering multiple measures of student achievement."

Population: Grades 1–10.

Levels, 9: 11, 12, 13, 14, 15, 16, 17, 18, 19/20.

Scores: 3 Supera scores (Reading, Language Arts, Mathematics); 5 Plus scores (Word Analysis, Vocabulary, Language Mechanics, Spelling, Mathematics Computation).

Price Data: $36.70 per Teacher's Guide; $17.30 per Norms Book (specify Fall or Spring); $43.45 per Test Coordinator's Handbook; $20 per Supera Technical Report disk; $10.80 per Handbook of Instructional Objectives (specify Survey, Multiple Assessments, or Plus Edition).

Comments: Uses Spanish "common to all dialects"; designed as a parallel test form of English TerraNova tests; separate norms "allow comparison with either Spanish- or English-speaking peers"; Custom Assessments (Evaluaciones Desarolladas a su Preferencia) also available.

1) *SUPERA Survey (Evaluaciones Esenciales) and Survey Plus.*

Price Data: $152.25 per 30 consumable test books (Levels 11–13, specify level); $119.90 per 30 reusable test books (Levels 14–19/20, specify level); $45.35 per 50 CompuScan answer sheets (Levels 14–20); $34.05 per 25 SCOREZE answer sheets (Levels 14–20); $2,268 per 2,500 continuous form answer sheets (Levels 14–20); $39.95 per scoring stencil (Levels 14–20, specify level); $41.05 per 30 Supera Plus consumable test books (Levels 11–13, specify level); $41.05 per 30 Supera Plus reusable test books (Levels 14–20, specify level); $45.35 per 50 CompuScan Plus answer sheets (Levels 14–20); $1,145 per 1,250 continuous form Plus answer sheets (Levels 14–20); $34.05 per 25 Supera Plus SCOREZE answer sheets (Levels 14–20, specify level).

Time: Reading/Language Arts test: 110–160(155–205) minutes; Mathematics test: 70–100(115–145) minutes; Supera Plus tests: 25–30 minutes for Word Analysis, 20–40 minutes for Vocabulary tests, 25–35 minutes for Language Mechanics tests, 20–25 minutes for Spelling tests, 25–30 minutes for Mathematics Computation tests.

2) *SUPERA Multiple Assessments (Evaluaciones Multiples) and Multiple Assessments Plus.*

Price Data: $126.35 per 30 consumable scannable test books (specify level); $16.20 per scoring guide (specify level).

h) PERFORMANCE ASSESSMENTS.

Purpose: "Available for educators who wish to use extended open-ended assignments."

Population: Grades 3–12.

Levels, 6: 13/14, 14/15, 16/17, 17/18, 19/20, 21/22.

Scores, 10: 6 Communication Arts strands (Establish Understanding, Explore Meaning, Extend Meaning and Examine Strategies, Evaluate Critically, Write Effectively, Write Fluently); 4 Mathematics Competencies (Problem Solving, Communication, Reasoning, Data and Information Processing).

Comments: Open-ended response items require students to "move through a series of activities culminating in a final product or summative activity."

Price Data: $88 per 30 consumable test books including test directions (Communication Arts or Mathematics, specify level); $6.35 per scoring guide (Communication Arts or Mathematics, specify level); $10.60 per additional copy of test directions (Communication Arts or Mathematics, specify level); $36.55 per 30 test materials and accessories for practice activities (Communication Arts or Mathematics, specify level); $79.50 per Communication Arts video cassette (specify level).

Cross References: For reviews by Judith A. Monsaas and Anthony J. Nitko of an earlier edition, see 14:383; for information on the Comprehensive Tests of Basic Skills, see T5:665 (95 references); see also T4:623 (23 references); for reviews by Kenneth D. Hopkins and M. David Miller of the CTBS, see 11:81 (70 references); for reviews by Robert L. Linn and Lorrie A. Shepard of an earlier form, see 9:258 (29 references); see also T3: 551 (59 references); for reviews by Warren G. Findley and Anthony J. Nitko of an earlier edition, see 8:12 (13 references); see also T2:11 (1 reference); for reviews by J. Stanley Ahmann and Frederick G. Brown and excerpted reviews by Brooke B. Collison and Peter A. Taylor (rejoinder by Verna White) of Forms Q and R, see 7:9. For reviews of subtests of earlier editions, see 8:721 (1 review), 8:825 (1 review), 7:685 (1 review), 7:514 (2 reviews), and 7:778 (1 review).

[2511]
Test Anxiety Profile.
Purpose: Constructed to measure "how much anxiety a person generally experiences in different types of testing situations."
Population: Grades 9–12 and college.
Publication Date: 1980.
Acronym: TAP.
Scores, 12: 2 anxiety scores (Feeling of Anxiety, Thought Interference) for 6 different situations (Multiple Choice Test, Time-Limit Test, "Pop" Quiz, Essay Test, Giving Talk, Math Test).
Administration: Group.
Price Data: License to reproduce for Ph.D.s or Ed.D.s available from publisher.
Time: (20) minutes.
Authors: E. R. Oetting, C. W. Cole (test), and J. L. Deffenbacher (manual).
Publisher: E. R. Oetting, Colorado State University.
Cross References: See T4:2725 (2 references); for reviews by Steven D. Brown and John P. Galassi, see 9:1237.

[2512]
Test Attitude Inventory.
Purpose: "Developed to measure individual differences in test anxiety as a situation-specific personality trait."
Population: High school and college students.
Publication Dates: 1977–1980.
Acronym: TAI.
Scores, 3: Worry, Emotionality, Total.
Administration: Group.
Price Data: Available from publisher.
Time: (5–10) minutes.
Comments: Self-report inventory of test anxiety; title of manual is Test Anxiety Inventory.
Author: Charles D. Spielberger.
Publisher: Mind Garden, Inc.
Cross References: See T5:2656 (25 references) and T4:2726 (16 references); for reviews by John P. Galassi and Thomas R. Knapp, see 9:1238 (3 references); see also T3:2417 (2 references).

[2513]
Test for Auditory Comprehension of Language—Third Edition.
Purpose: Designed as a measure of receptive spoken vocabulary, grammar, and syntax.
Population: Ages 3-0 to 9-11.
Publication Dates: 1973–1999.
Acronym: TACL-3.
Scores, 4: Vocabulary, Grammatical Morphemes, Elaborated Phrases and Sentences, Total.
Administration: Individual.

Price Data, 2001: $254 per complete kit; $79 per manual (1999, 117 pages); $129 per picture book; $39 per 25 profile/examiner record booklets.
Time: (15–25) minutes.
Author: Elizabeth Carrow-Woolfolk.
Publisher: PRO-ED.
Cross References: For reviews by Ramasamy Manikam and Christine Novak, see 14:384; see also T5:2657 (37 references) and T4:2727 (20 references); for reviews by Nicholas W. Bankson and William O. Haynes of an earlier edition, see 10:363; see also T3:2472 (25 references); for reviews by John T. Hatten and Huberto Molina of an earlier edition, see 8:454 (6 references); see also T2:997A (2 references).

[2514]
Test for Colour-Blindness.
Purpose: To identify congenital color vision deficiency.
Population: Ages 4 and over.
Publication Dates: 1917–1970.
Scores: Total score only.
Administration: Individual.
Price Data: Available from distributor.
Time: Administration time not reported.
Author: Shinobu Ishihara.
Publisher: Graham-Field (U.S. Distributor) [No reply from distributor; status unknown].
Cross References: See T5:2658 (2 references), T4:2729 (3 references), T3:2419 (1 reference), T2:1932 (29 references), 7:882 (13 references), and 6:962 (58 references).

[2515]
Test for Creative Thinking—Drawing Production.
Purpose: "Meant to be a screening instrument which allows for a first rough, simple, and economic assessment of a person's creative potential."
Population: Age 4–adult.
Publication Date: 1996.
Acronym: TCT-DP.
Scores, 15: Continuations, Completions, New Elements, Connections Made with Lines, Connections that Contribute to a Theme, Boundary-Breaking Being Fragment—Dependent, Perspective, Humour/Affectivity/Emotionality/Expressive Power of the Drawing, Unconventionality A—Uncoventional Manipulation, Unconventionality B—Symbolic/Abstract/Fictional, Unconventionality C—Symbol-Figure-Combinations, Unconventionality D—Nonstereotypical Utilization of Given Fragments/Figures, Speed, Total.
Administration: Group.
Forms, 2: A, B.
Price Data: Available from publisher.
Time: (30) minutes.

Authors: Klaus K. Urban and Hans G. Jellen.
Publisher: Swets Test Publishers [The Netherlands].
Cross References: For reviews by Alice J. Corkill and William Steve Lang, see 14:385.

[2516]
Test for Examining Expressive Morphology.

Purpose: "Developed to help clinicians evaluate expressive morpheme development with children whose language skills range from three to eight years of age."
Population: Ages 3-0 to 8-12.
Publication Date: 1983.
Acronym: TEEM.
Scores, 7: (6 morphemes plus 1 age level approximation): Present Progressives, Plurals, Possessives, Past Tenses, Third-Person Singulars, Derived Adjectives, Total.
Administration: Individual.
Price Data, 1999: $36 per complete kit including manual (43 pages), test booklet, and 25 scoring forms; $15 per 25 scoring forms.
Time: (5–7) minutes.
Authors: Kenneth G. Shipley, Terry A. Stone, and Marlene B. Sue.
Publisher: Communication Skill Builders—A Division of The Psychological Corporation.
Cross References: See T5:2660 (4 references) and T4:2730 (1 reference); for reviews by Doris V. Allen and Janice A. Dole, see 10:364.

[2517]
Test for Oral Language Production.

Purpose: "Provides measures for 16 facets of language production."
Population: Ages 4-6 to 10-5.
Publication Date: 1980.
Acronym: TOLP.
Scores, 16: Word per T-Unit, Type-Token Ratio, Adverbs per T-Unit, Prepositions per T-Unit, Co-Verbs per T-Unit, Deletions per T-Unit, Substitutions per T-Unit, Permutations per T-Unit, Incomplete T-Units per T-Unit, Sentence Structure Corrections per T-Unit, Choice-of-Word Corrections per T-Unit, Word Repetitions per T-Unit, Labels per T-Unit, Nonsense per T-Unit, Abstract-Concreteness Index, Total Number of Words.
Administration: Individual.
Price Data: Available from publisher.
Time: [90–100] minutes.
Author: Jan Vorster.
Publisher: Human Sciences Research Council [South Africa].

[2518]
Test for the Reception of Grammar.

Purpose: "Designed to assess understanding of grammatical contrasts in English."

Population: Ages 4–12 years and also dysphasic adults.
Publication Dates: 1983–1989.
Acronym: TROG.
Scores, 21: Noun, Verb, Adjective, Two Element Combination, Negative, Three Element Combination, Singular/Plural Personal Pronoun, Reversible Active, Masculine/Feminine Personal Pronoun, Singular/Plural Noun Inflection, Comparative/Absolute, Reversible Passive, In and On, Postmodified Subject, X But Not Y, Above and Below, Not Only X But Also Y, Relative Clause, Neither X nor Y, Embedded Sentence, Total.
Administration: Individual.
Price Data, 1998: £70 per test kit including 25 test forms, manual, stimulus book, and cards.
Time: (10–20) minutes.
Comments: An 80-item, orally administered, multiple-choice test; "suitable for American as well as British subjects."
Author: Dorothy Bishop.
Publisher: Dorothy Bishop [England].
Cross References: See T5:2662 (8 references).

[2519]
Test Lessons in Primary Reading, Second Enlarged and Revised Edition.

Purpose: "Designed to evaluate students' reading progress and thinking skills."
Population: Children.
Publication Date: 1980.
Scores: Item scores only.
Administration: Group.
Price Data, 2002: $3.95 per lesson booklet; $2.95 per teacher's manual/answer key (17 pages).
Time: Administration time not reported.
Authors: William A. McCall and Mary Lourita Harby.
Publisher: Teachers College Press.

[2520]
Test of Academic Achievement Skills— Reading, Arithmetic, Spelling, and Listening Comprehension.

Purpose: Measures a child's reading, arithmetic, spelling, and listening comprehension skills.
Population: Ages 4-0 to 12-0.
Publication Date: 1989.
Scores, 6: Spelling, Total Reading (Letter/Word Identification, Listening Comprehension, Total), Arithmetic, Total.
Administration: Individual.
Price Data: Not available.
Time: (15–25) minutes.
Author: Morrison F. Gardner.
Publisher: Psychological & Educational Publications, Inc.

Cross References: For reviews by C. Dale Carpenter and Steve Graham, see 13:321.

[2521]
Test of Academic Performance.

Purpose: Developed to assess achievement in four curriculum areas: Mathematics, Spelling, Reading, and Writing.
Population: Grades K–12.
Publication Date: 1989.
Acronym: TOAP.
Scores, 6: Basic subtests (Mathematics, Spelling, Reading Recognition, Reading Comprehension), Optional subtests (Written Composition, Copying Rate).
Administration: Individual and group.
Price Data, 2002: $119 per complete set including examiner's manual (182 pages), 25 student response forms, 25 record forms, and package of four reading stimulus cards; $75 per examine's manual; $43 per 25 student response forms and record forms.
Time: (20–45) minutes.
Authors: Wayne Adams, Lynn Erb, and David Sheslow.
Publisher: The Psychological Corporation.
Cross References: For reviews by Steve Graham and Cleborne D. Maddux, see 13:222.

[2522]
Test of Adolescent/Adult Word Finding.

Purpose: Developed to assess word finding skills.
Population: Ages 12–80.
Publication Date: 1990.
Acronym: TAWF.
Scores: 5 sections (Picture Naming: Nouns, Sentence Completion Naming, Description Naming, Picture Naming: Verbs, Category Naming) yielding 4 scores: Accuracy, Comprehension, Item Response Time, Word Finding Profile.
Administration: Individual.
Forms, 2: Complete, Brief.
Price Data, 2001: $229 per complete kit including test book, 25 response booklets, examiner's manual (204 pages), and technical manual (121 pages); $36 per 25 response forms; $119 per test book; $49 per examiner's manual; $49 per technical manual.
Time: (20-30) minutes for complete test; [10] minutes for brief test.
Comments: Upward extension of the Test of Word Finding (2571); speed can be measured in actual or estimated Item Response Time; tape recorder and stopwatch required on Section 1 only when using Actual Item Response Time Option.
Author: Diane J. German.
Publisher: PRO-ED.
Cross References: See T5:2667 (1 reference); for reviews by Ronald B. Gillam and Richard E. Harding, see 12:391.

[2523]
Test of Adolescent and Adult Language, Third Edition.

Purpose: Designed "(a) to identify adolescents and adults whose scores are significantly below those of their peers and who might need interventions designed to improve language proficiency; (b) to determine areas of relative strength and weakness across language abilities; (c) to document overall progress in language development as a consequence of intervention programs; and (d) to serve as a measure for research efforts designed to investigate language characteristics of adolescents and adults."
Population: Ages 12-0 to 24-11.
Publication Dates: 1980–1994.
Acronym: TOAL-3.
Scores, 8: 8 subtest scores (Listening/Vocabulary, Listening/Grammar, Speaking/Vocabulary, Speaking/Grammar, Reading/Vocabulary, Reading/Grammar, Writing/Vocabulary, Writing/Grammar); 10 composite scores (Listening, Speaking, Reading, Writing, Spoken Language, Written Language, Vocabulary, Grammar, Receptive Language, Expressive Language).
Administration: Individual and group.
Price Data, 2001: $172 per complete kit including 50 answer booklets, 10 test booklets, 50 summary/profile sheets, and examiner's manual (1994, 111 pages); $54 per 50 answer booklets; $34 per 10 test booklets; $34 per 50 summary/profile sheets; $49 per examiner's manual; $79 per IBM software scoring system.
Time: (60–180) minutes.
Authors: Donald D. Hammill, Virginia L. Brown, Stephen C. Larsen, and J. Lee Wiederholt.
Publisher: PRO-ED.
Cross References: See T5:2668 (7 references); for reviews by John MacDonald and Roger A. Richards, see 13:323 (6 references); see also T4:2738 (9 references); for reviews by Allen Jack Edwards and David A. Shapiro of an earlier edition, see 10:365; for a review by Robert T. Williams of an earlier edition, see 9:1243.

[2524]
Test of Articulation in Context.

Purpose: Designed to "examine a student's phonological abilities in the contest of spontaneous conversation, and can be used to screen, predict change, diagnose and assess a student's phonological progress following treatment."
Population: Preschool through elementary-school-aged children.
Publication Date: 1998.
Acronym: TAC.
Scores, 4: Sound Production, Speech Mechanism, Intelligibility, Adverse Effect on Educational Performance.
Administration: Individual.

Price Data, 2002: $119 per kit including 25 response forms, 4 laminated test boards, manual (45 pages), and canvas carrying bag.
Time: Untimed.
Author: Teresa Lanphere.
Publisher: Imaginart International, Inc.
Cross References: For a review by Thomas W. Guyette, see 14:386.

[2525]
Test of Attitude Toward School.

Purpose: To assess a student's attitude toward school.
Population: Boys in grades 1, 3, 5.
Publication Dates: 1973–1984.
Acronym: TAS.
Scores, 2: Scholastic Attitude Score, Evaluation by the Teacher.
Administration: Individual.
Price Data, 2001: $20 per set of 16 drawings; $49.95 per 25 teacher questionnaires (1984, 3 pages); $18 per manual (1984, 116 pages).
Time: Administration time not reported.
Comments: Projective test.
Authors: Guy Thibaudeau, Cathy Ingram-LeBlanc (translation from French), and Michael Dewson (verification of technical terms).
Publisher: Institute of Psychological Research, Inc. [Canada].
Cross References: For a review by Bert A. Goldman, see 11:425.

[2526]
Test of Auditory Analysis Skills.

Purpose: Constructed to assess "a child's auditory perceptual skills."
Population: Children.
Publication Dates: 1975–1993.
Acronym: TAAS.
Scores: Total score only.
Administration: Individual.
Manual: No manual (Directions on each form).
Price Data, 2002: $16 per 50 test forms.
Time: Administration time not reported.
Comments: "Criterion-referenced"; may be used in conjunction with the Test of Visual Analysis Skills (T5:2721); test is reproduced from author's book Helping Children Overcome Learning Difficulties (1993, Walker Publishing Company, New York).
Author: Jerome Rosner.
Publisher: Academic Therapy Publications.
Cross References: See T5:2671 (3 references); for reviews by Allan O. Diefendorf and Kathy S. Kessler and by Rick Lindskog of the earlier edition, see 11:426.

[2527]
Test of Auditory Comprehension.

Purpose: Designed to be used for the selection of auditory training objectives and measurement of progress in comprehension.
Population: Hearing impaired ages 4–17.
Publication Dates: 1976–1981.
Acronym: TAC.
Scores, 10: Linguistic vs. Nonlinguistic, Linguistic/Human Nonlinguistic/Environmental, Stereotypic Messages, Single Element Core Noun Vocabulary, Recalls Two Critical Elements, Recalls Four Critical Elements, Sequences Three Events, Recalls Five Details, Sequences Three Events With Competing Message, Recalls Five Details With Competing Message.
Administration: Individual.
Price Data: Publisher advises in April 2002 that test is now out of print although support materials (score sheets, tapes, curriculum, etc. will remain available for several years).
Time: (30) minutes.
Comments: Test administered by cassette tape.
Author: Audiologic Services and Southwest School for the Hearing Impaired, Office of the Los Angeles County Superintendent of Schools.
Publisher: Foreworks.
Cross References: See T5:2672 (2 references) and T4:2741 (7 references); for a review by James R. Cox, see 9:1246.

[2528]
Test of Auditory-Perceptual Skills.

Purpose: "To measure a child's functioning in various areas of auditory perception."
Population: Ages 4–12.
Publication Date: 1985.
Acronym: TAPS.
Scores, 7: Auditory Number Memory, Auditory Sentence Memory, Auditory Word Memory, Auditory Interpretation of Directions, Auditory Word Discrimination, Auditory Processing (Thinking and Reasoning), Hyperactivity Index.
Administration: Individual.
Price Data: Not available.
Foreign Language Edition: Spanish version available.
Time: (15–25) minutes.
Comments: The Hyperactivity Index is a parental questionnaire developed by C. Keith Connors.
Author: Morrison F. Gardner.
Publisher: Psychological & Educational Publications, Inc.
Cross References: For reviews by Annabel J. Cohen and by Anne R. Kessler and Jaclyn B. Spitzer, see 13:324 (2 references).

[2529]

Test of Children's Language: Assessing Aspects of Spoken Language, Reading, and Writing.

Purpose: "Designed to measure important aspects of spoken language, reading, and writing."
Population: Ages 5–0 to 8–11.
Publication Date: 1996.
Acronym: TOCL.
Scores, 11: 7 Component Scores (Spoken Language, Knowledge of Print, Word Recognition, Reading Comprehension, Writing Skills, Writing From Memory, Original Writing); 4 Combined Scores (Spoken Language Quotient, Reading Quotient, Writing Quotient, Total Language Quotient).
Administration: Individual.
Price Data, 2001: $144 per complete kit including manual (62 pages), "A Visit with Mr. Turtle" storybook, story picture sheet, 25 student workbooks, and 25 profile/examiner record forms in storage box; $39 per 25 student workbooks; $44 per 25 profile/examiner record forms; $49 per manual; $5 per storybook picture sheet; $12 per "A Visit with Mr. Turtle" storybook.
Time: (30–40) minutes.
Authors: Edna Barenbaum and Phyllis Newcomer.
Publisher: PRO-ED.
Cross References: For reviews by Steve Graham and Richard M. Wolf, see 14:387.

[2530]

Test of Creativity.

Purpose: To gain a quick measure of a person's creativity.
Population: Adolescents and adults.
Publication Date: 1994.
Scores: Total score only.
Administration: Group.
Manual: No manual.
Price Data: Price information available from publisher for tests including self-assessment, answer sheet and feedback, and Types of Creativity.
Time: 35(40) minutes.
Comments: Self-administered, self-scored.
Author: Training House, Inc.
Publisher: Training House, Inc.

[2531]

Test of Early Language Development, Third Edition.

Purpose: Designed to measure the early development of spoken language in the areas of receptive and expressive language, syntax, and semantics.
Population: Ages 2-0 to 7-11.
Publication Dates: 1981–1999.

Acronym: TELD-3.
Scores, 3: Receptive Language, Expressive Language, Spoken Language Quotient.
Administration: Individual.
Forms, 2: A, B.
Price Data, 2001: $264 per complete kit; $74 per manual (1999, 159 pages); $64 per Picture Book; $39 each per profile /Examiner Record booklet; $54 per manipulatives.
Time: (15–40) minutes.
Authors: Wayne P. Hresko, D. Kim Reid, and Donald D. Hammill.
Publisher: PRO-ED.
Cross References: For reviews by Sherwyn P. Morreale and Hoi K. Suen, see 14:388; see also T5:2680 (19 references) and T4:2749 (6 references); for reviews by Javaid Kaiser and David A. Shapiro of an earlier edition, see 12:393 (4 references); for reviews by Janice Arnold Dale and Elizabeth M. Prather of an earlier edition, see 9:1250 (1 reference).

[2532]

Test of Early Mathematics Ability, Second Edition.

Purpose: To "identify those children who are significantly behind or ahead of their peers in the development of mathematical thinking."
Population: Ages 3-0 to 8-11.
Publication Dates: 1983–1990.
Acronym: TEMA-2.
Scores: Total score only.
Administration: Individual.
Price Data, 2001: $169 per complete kit; $49 per picture book; $39 per 25 profile/record forms; $39 per Assessment Probes and Instructional Activities manual; $46 per examiner's manual (1990, 48 pages).
Time: (20) minutes.
Authors: Herbert P. Ginsburg and Arthur J. Baroody.
Publisher: PRO-ED.
Cross References: See T5:2681 (2 references); for reviews by Jerry Johnson and Joyce R. McLarty, see 11:428 (1 reference); for a review by David P. Lindeman of an earlier edition, see 9:1252.

[2533]

Test of Early Reading Ability—Deaf or Hard of Hearing.

Purpose: Designed to measure "children's ability to attribute meaning to printed symbols, their knowledge of the alphabet and its functions, and their knowledge of the conventions of print."
Population: Deaf and hard of hearing children ages 3-0 to 13-11.
Publication Date: 1991.
Acronym: TERA-D/HH.
Scores: Total score only.

Administration: Individual.

Forms, 2: A, B.

Price Data, 2001: $179 per complete kit including picture book, 25 Form A and 25 Form B profile/ examiner record forms, and manual (49 pages); $49 per picture book; $39 per 25 profile/examiner record forms (select Form A or B); $59 per manual.

Time: (20–30) minutes.

Comments: Adaptation of the Test of Early Reading Ability-2 (2534).

Authors: D. Kim Reid, Wayne P. Hresko, Donald D. Hammill, and Susal Wiltshire.

Publisher: PRO-ED.

Cross References: For reviews by Barbara A. Rothlisberg and Esther Stavrou Toubanos, see 12:394.

[2534]

Test of Early Reading Ability, Third Edition.

Purpose: Designed to "assess children's mastery of early developing reading skills."

Population: Ages 3-6 to 8-6.

Publication Dates: 1981–2001.

Acronym: TERA-3.

Scores, 3: Alphabet, Conventions, Meaning.

Administration: Individual.

Forms, 2: A, B.

Price Data, 2001: $229 per complete kit including examiner's manual (2001, 127 pages), 2 picture books (Form A and Form B), 25 profile/examiner record Forms A, and 25 profile/examiner record Forms B; $79 per examiner's manual; $54 per picture book (specify Form A or Form B); $24 per 25 profile/examiner record forms (specify Form A or Form B).

Time: (30) minutes.

Authors: D. Kim Reid, Wayne P. Hresko, and Donald D. Hammill.

Publisher: PRO-ED.

Cross References: See T5:2682 (13 references) and T4:2751 (2 references); for reviews by Michael D. Beck and Robert W. Hiltonsmith of an earlier edition, see 11:429 (1 reference); for reviews by Isabel L. Beck and Janet A. Norris of the original edition, see 9:1253.

[2535]

Test of Early Written Language, Second Edition.

Purpose: "Measures early writing ability in children."

Population: Ages 3–0 to 10–11.

Publication Dates: 1988–1996.

Acronym: TEWL-2.

Scores, 3: Basic Writing, Contextual Writing, Global Writing.

Administration: Individual or group.

Forms, 2: A, B.

Price Data, 2001: $159 per complete kit including manual (1996, 116 pages), 10 each Form A and Form B student workbooks, 10 each Form A and Form B profile/record booklets in storage box; $39 per 10 student workbooks (specify Form A or B); $19 per 10 profile/record booklets (specify Form A or B); $49 per manual.

Time: (30–45) minutes.

Authors: Wayne P. Hresko, Shelley R. Herron, and Pamela K. Peak.

Publisher: PRO-ED.

Cross References: For reviews by David P. Hurford and Michael S. Trevisan, see 13:326; for a review by Patricia Wheeler of an earlier edition, see 11:430.

[2536]

Test of Economic Knowledge, Second Edition.

Purpose: Measures knowledge of economic concepts.

Population: Grades 7–9.

Publication Date: 1987.

Acronym: TEK.

Scores: Total score only.

Administration: Group.

Forms, 2: A, B.

Price Data, 2001: $19.95 per 25 test booklets (specify Form A or B); $14.95 per examiner's manual (61 pages).

Time: (40) minutes.

Comments: "Designed to replace the Junior High School Test of Economics."

Authors: William B. Walstad and John C. Soper.

Publisher: National Council on Economic Education.

Cross References: For reviews by William A. Mehrens and Anthony J. Nitko, see 11:431.

[2537]

Test of Economic Literacy, Third Edition.

Purpose: Designed to "evaluate a student's performance and make decisions about economics instruction at the senior high school level."

Population: Grades 11–12.

Publication Dates: 1978–2001.

Acronym: TEL.

Scores: Total score only.

Administration: Group.

Forms, 2: A, B.

Price Data, 2001: $22.95 per 25 test booklets (specify Form A or B); $17.95 per examiner's manual (2001, 75 pages), which includes scoring keys and a model answer sheet (may be duplicated locally).

Time: (40-50) minutes.

Authors: William B. Walstad and Ken Rebeck.

Publisher: National Council on Economic Education.

Cross References: See T5:2686 (2 references); for reviews by Jennifer J. Fager and Dan Wright of an earlier edition, see 12:395; for a review by Anna S. Ochoa, see 9:1256; see also T2:1968 (19 references); for reviews by Edward J. Furst and Christine H. McGuire, and an excerpted review by Robert L. Ebel, see 7:901 (10 references).

[2538]
Test of English for International Communication (TOEIC).

Purpose: To evaluate the English proficiency of those whose native language is not English.
Population: Adult nonnative speakers of English.
Publication Dates: 1980–1999.
Acronym: TOEIC.
Scores, 3: Listening Comprehension, Reading Comprehension, Total.
Administration: Group.
Price Data, 1999: Price varies for Secure and institutional Programs; price data available from publisher; ICS Program: $175 (plus S & H) per 5 test booklets and answer sheets, audiocassette, and test administration manual (1998, 26 pages); volume discounts available.
Time: (120) minutes.
Comments: Secure Program administered on set dates and scored by TOEIC program office; Institutional and ICS Program administered by the client on-site and/or by TOEIC representative; one-half of test (100 questions) administered by audiocassette tape recording; separate answer sheet.
Author: Educational Testing Service.
Publisher: The Chauncey Group International.
Cross References: For reviews by Dan Douglas and Roger A. Richards, see 11:432.

[2539]
Test of Gross Motor Development—Second Edition.

Purpose: To "measure gross motor abilities that develop early in life."
Population: Ages 3–10.
Publication Dates: 1985–2000.
Acronym: TGMD-2.
Scores, 2: Locomotor, Object Control.
Administration: Individual.
Price Data, 2001: $96 per kit including 50 profile/examiner record booklets, and examiner's manual (2000, 69 pages) in a sturdy storage box; $49 per 50 profile/examiner record booklets; $49 per manual.
Time: (15–20) minutes.
Author: Dale A. Ulrich.
Publisher: PRO-ED.
Cross References: See T5:2689 (2 references) and T4:2762 (2 references); for reviews by Linda K.

Bunker and Ron Edwards of an earlier edition, see 10:370.

[2540]
Test of Inference Ability in Reading Comprehension.

Purpose: "Designed to provide diagnostic information about the inference ability of students."
Population: Grades 6–8.
Publication Dates: 1987–1989.
Scores: Total score only.
Administration: Group.
Forms, 2: Multiple-choice, Constructed-response.
Price Data: Price information available from publisher for tests (specify multiple-choice or constructed-response), manual (1989, 24 pages), and technical report (1989, 58 pages).
Time: (40–45) minutes per form.
Authors: Linda M. Phillips and Cynthia C. Patterson (multiple-choice format).
Publisher: Linda M. Phillips [Canada].
Cross References: For reviews by Douglas K. Smith and Robert Wall, see 13:327.

[2541]
Test of Initial Literacy.

Purpose: To provide teachers with diagnostic information about children who have difficulty with reading and writing.
Population: Ages 7–12.
Publication Date: 1989.
Acronym: TOIL.
Scores, 9: Letter Matching, Word Matching, Copying, Grammatical Punctuation, Orthographic Punctuation, Spelling of Homophones, Spelling, Style, Free Writing.
Administration: Group.
Price Data: Price information available from publisher for test booklets and for teacher's set including test booklet and manual (1989, 39 pages).
Time: Untimed.
Comment: Complements Reading Ability Series.
Authors: Anne Kispal, Alison Tate, Tom Gorman, and Chris Whetton.
Publisher: NFER-Nelson Publishing Co., Ltd. [England].
Cross References: For reviews by Jerrilyn V. Andrews and Cleborne D. Maddux, see 11:434.

[2542]
Test of Interpersonal Competence for Employment.

Purpose: Designed to assess social interaction skills necessary for job tenure for mentally retarded adults.
Population: Mildly retarded adolescents and adults.

Publication Date: 1986.

Acronym: TICE.

Scores, 6: Handling Criticism and Correction, Requesting Assistance, Following Instructions, Cooperative Work Behavior, Handling of Teasing and Provocation, Resolving Personal Concerns.

Administration: Group.

Price Data, 2000: $99 per set including teaching guide and script (56 pages).

Time: (60) minutes.

Authors: Gilbert Foss, Doug Cheney, and Michael Bullis.

Publisher: James Stanfield Co., Inc.

[2543]
Test of Kindergarten/First Grade Readiness Skills.

Purpose: "To assess a child's readiness for kindergarten or for first grade."

Population: Ages 3–6 to 7–0.

Publication Date: 1987.

Acronym: TKFGRS.

Scores, 3: Reading, Spelling, Arithmetic.

Administration: Individual.

Price Data: Not available.

Time: (20–25) minutes.

Author: Karen Gardner Codding.

Publisher: Psychological & Educational Publications, Inc.

Cross References: For reviews by D. Joe Olmi and J. Steven Welsh, see 13:328.

[2544]
Test of Language Competence—Expanded Edition.

Purpose: "To evaluate delays in the emergence of linguistic competence and in the use of semantic, syntactic, and pragmatic strategies."

Publication Dates: 1985–1989.

Acronym: TLC-Expanded.

Scores: 5 subtest scores: Ambiguous Sentences, Listening Comprehension: Making Inferences, Oral Expression: Recreating Speech Acts, Figurative Language, Remembering Word Pairs (supplemental subtest for Level 2 only), plus 4 composite scores: Expressing Intents, Interpreting Intents, Screening Composite, TLC-Expanded Composite.

Administration: Individual.

Price Data, 2002: $405 per complete kit with briefcase including 25 Level 1 & 2 record forms, Level 1 & 2 stimulus manuals, administration manual (1989, 311 pages), technical manual (1989, 98 pages; $359 per complete kit without briefcase; $99 per administration manual; $73 per technical manual.

Time: (60-70) minutes per level.

Authors: Elisabeth H. Wiig and Wayne Secord.

Publisher: The Psychological Corporation.

a) LEVEL 1.

Population: Ages 5 through 18.

Price Data: $45 per 25 record forms; $69 per stimulus manual.

b) LEVEL 2.

Population: Ages 5 through 18.

Price Data: $45 per 25 record forms; $69 per stimulus manual.

Cross References: See T5:2693 (10 references); for reviews by Dolores Kluppel Vetter and Carol E. Westby, see 11:435 (1 reference).

[2545]
Test of Language Development—Intermediate, Third Edition.

Purpose: To determine strengths and weaknesses in language skills.

Population: Ages 8-0 to 12-11.

Publication Dates: 1977–1997.

Acronym: TOLD-I:3.

Scores, 12: General Intelligence/Aptitude Quotient, Spoken Language Quotient (SLQ), Listening Quotient (LiQ), Speaking Quotient (SpA), Semantics Quotient (SeQ), Syntax Quotient (SyQ), Sentence Combining (SC), Picture Vocabulary (PV), Word Ordering (WO), Generals (GL), Grammatic Comprehension (GC), Malapropism (MP).

Administration: Individual

Price Data, 2001: $174 per complete kit; $39 per profile/examiner record forms; $74 per examiner's manual; $64 per picture book; $98 per PRO-SCORE system (Mac or Windows).

Time: (30–60) minutes.

Comments: Primary edition also available.

Authors: Donald D. Hammill and Phyllis L. Newcomer.

Publisher: PRO-ED.

Cross References: For reviews by David P. Hurford and Pat Mirenda, see 14:389; see also T5:2694 (27 references) and T4:2767 (7 references); for reviews by Rebecca McCauley and Kenneth G. Shipley of the TOLD-I:2, see 11:436 (5 references). For a review by Doris V. Allen of an earlier version of the entire Test of Language Development, see 9:1261 (5 references).

[2546]
Test of Language Development—Primary, Third Edition.

Purpose: To determine children's specific strengths and weaknesses in language skills.

Population: Ages 4-0 to 8-11.

Publication Dates: 1977–1997.

Acronym: TOLD-P:3.

Scores, 15: Subtests (Picture Vocabulary, Relational Vocabulary, Oral Vocabulary, Grammatic Understanding, Sentence Imitation, Grammatic Completion, Word Discrimination [Optional], Phoenemic Analysis [Optional], Word Articulation [Optional]); Composites (Listening, Organizing, Speaking, Semantics, Syntax, Spoken Language).
Administration: Individual.
Parts, 2: Subtests, Composites.
Price Data, 2001: $289 per complete kit; $54 per profile/examiner record forms; $79 per examiner's manual; $109 per picture book; $98 per PRO-SCORE systems (Mac or Windows).
Time: (60) minutes.
Comments: Intermediate edition also available; orally administered; examiners need formal training in assessment; PRO-SCORE Computer Scoring System available for Macintosh, Windows, and DOS (1998).
Authors: Phyllis L. Newcomer and Donald D. Hammill.
Publisher: PRO-ED.
Cross References: For reviews by Ronald A. Madle and Gabrielle Stutman, see 14:390; see also T5:2695 (72 references) and T4:2768 (21 references); for reviews by Linda Crocker and Carol E. Westby of a previous edition, see 11:437 (20 references).

[2547]
Test of Mathematical Abilities for Gifted Students.
Purpose: "Designed to identify students who have talent or giftedness in mathematics."
Population: Ages 6–12.
Publication Date: 1998.
Acronym: TOMAGS.
Scores: Total score only.
Administration: Group or individual.
Levels, 2: Primary, Intermediate.
Price Data, 2001: $149 per complete kit including manual (53 pages), 25 each Primary Level and Intermediate Level student booklets, and 25 each Primary Level and Intermediate Level profile/scoring sheets; $39 per 25 student booklets (specify level); $14 per 25 profile/scoring sheets (specify level); $49 per manual.
Time: (30–60) minutes.
Authors: Gail R. Ryser and Susan K. Johnsen.
Publisher: PRO-ED.
Cross References: For reviews by Robert B. Frary and Delwyn L. Harnisch, see 14:391.

[2548]
Test of Mathematical Abilities, Second Edition.
Purpose: "A measure of math ability."
Population: Ages 8-0 to 18-11.
Publication Dates: 1984–1994.

Acronym: TOMA-2.
Scores, 6: Vocabulary, Computation, General Information, Story Problems, Attitude Toward Math, Total.
Administration: Group.
Price Data, 2001: $89 per complete kit including 25 profile/record forms and examiner's manual (1994, 51 pages); $44 per 25 profile/record forms; $47 per examiner's manual.
Time: (120–130) minutes.
Authors: Virginia L. Brown, Mary E. Cronin, and Elizabeth McEntire.
Publisher: PRO-ED.
Cross References: For reviews by Delwyn L. Harnisch and Rosemary Sutton, see 13:329 (1 reference); for a review by Mark L. Davison of the earlier edition, see 9:1263.

[2549]
Test of Mechanical Concepts.
Purpose: "Designed to measure an individual's ability to visualize and understand basic mechanical relationships."
Population: Applicants for industrial positions.
Publication Dates: 1976–1995.
Scores, 4: Mechanical Interrelationships, Mechanical Tools and Devices, Spatial Relations, Total.
Administration: Individual or group.
Forms, 2: A, B.
Price Data, 2002: $106 per start-up kit including 25 test booklets (specify Form A or Form B) and examiner's manual; $91 per 25 test booklets (quantity discounts available; specify Form A or Form B); $28 per examiner's manual.
Time: No limit (approximately 35–45 minutes).
Comments: Previously listed as SRA Test of Mechanical Concepts.
Author: Science Research Associates.
Publisher: Reid London House.
Cross References: See T5:2700 (1 reference); for reviews by Lorraine D. Eyde and Lyle F. Schoenfeldt, see 8:1045.

[2550]
Test of Memory and Learning.
Purpose: For "evaluating children or adolescents referred for learning disabilities, traumatic brain injury, neurological diseases, serious emotional disturbance, Attention Deficit-Hyperactivity Disorder."
Population: Ages 5 to 19.
Publication Date: 1994.
Acronym: TOMAL.
Scores, 25: 9 Verbal subtest scores (Memory for Stories, Word Selective Reminding, Object Recall, Digits Forward, Paired Recall, Letters Forward, Digits Backward, Letters Backward, Total); 7 Nonverbal subtest scores (Facial Memory, Visual Selective Re-

minding, Abstract Visual Memory, Visual Sequential Memory, Memory for Location, Manual Imitation, Total); 4 composite scores (Verbal Memory Index, Nonverbal Memory Index, Composite Memory Index, Delayed Recall Index); 5 Delayed Recall scores (Memory for Stories, Facial Memory, Word Selective Reminding, Visual Selective Reminding, Total).

Administration: Individual.

Price Data, 2001: $214 per complete kit including examiner's manual (105 pages), picture book, 25 record forms and administration booklets, 25 supplementary analysis forms, facial memory picture book, 15 facial memory chips, visual selective reminding test board, and a set of delayed recall cue cards; $49 per examiner's manual; $64 per picture book; $44 per 25 record forms and administration booklets; $14 per 25 supplementary analysis forms; $29 per facial memory picture book; $7 per visual selective reminding test board; $17 per delayed cue card set.

Time: (40–45) minutes.

Authors: Cecil R. Reynolds and Erin D. Bigler.

Publisher: PRO-ED.

Cross References: For reviews by Karen Geller and Susan J. Maller, see 13:330 (1 reference).

[2551]
Test of Memory Malingering.

Purpose: To "assist neuropsychologists in discriminating between bona fide memory-impaired patients and malingerers."

Population: Ages 16 to 84.

Publication Date: 1996.

Acronym: TOMM.

Scores: Total score only.

Administration: Individual

Price Data, 2002: $100 per complete kit including manual (55 pages), 25 recording forms, and 1 set of stimulus booklets; $21 per 25 recording forms; $53 per set of 3 stimulus booklets; $37 per manual; $60 per Computer Program for Windows™ including user's manual, software manual, and 3 uses.

Time: (15) minutes.

Comments: Self-completed; Windows™ computer software available on CD or 3.5-inch disk to administer, score, and report results of TOMM.

Author: Tom N. Tombaugh.

Publisher: Multi-Health Systems, Inc.

Cross References: For reviews by M. Allan Cooperstein and Romeo Vitelli, see 14:392.

[2552]
Test of Minimal Articulation Competence.

Purpose: Assesses articulation performance in children and adults.

Population: Ages 3 to adult.

Publication Date: 1981.

Acronym: T-MAC.

Scores, 3: Vowel/Diphthong, Consonant, Total.

Administration: Individual.

Parts, 3: Complete Test, Screening Test, Rapid Screening Test.

Price Data, 2002: $119 per complete program including Examiner's Manual and 25 record forms; $46 per 25 record forms; $80 per examiner's manual including administration, scoring, and interpretation information.

Time: Administration time not reported.

Author: Wayne Secord.

Publisher: The Psychological Corporation.

Cross References: See T5:2703 (2 referfences); for a review by Barbara W. Hodson, see 9:1264.

[2553]
Test of Nonverbal Intelligence, Third Edition.

Purpose: "Developed to assess aptitude, intelligence, abstract reasoning, and problem solving in a completely language-free format."

Population: Ages 6-0 through 89-11.

Publication Dates: 1982–1997.

Acronym: TONI-3.

Scores: Total score only.

Administration: Individual.

Price Data, 2001: $249 per complete kit including manual (1997, 160 pages), picture book, and 50 each Form A and Form B answer booklets and record forms; $39 per 50 answer booklet and record forms (specify Form A or B); $109 per picture book; $66 per manual.

Time: (15–20) minutes.

Authors: Linda Brown, Rita J. Sherbenou, and Susan K. Johnsen.

Publisher: PRO-ED.

Cross References: For a review by Jeffrey A. Atlas, see 14:393; see also T5:2704 (47 references) and T4:2775 (10 references); for reviews by Kevin K. Murphy and T. Steuart Watson of the Second Edition, see 11:439 (9 references); for reviews by Philip M. Clark and Samuel T. Mayo of the original edition, see 9:1266.

[2554]
Test of Oral Structures and Functions.

Purpose: "Assesses oral structures and motor integrity during verbal and nonverbal oral functioning."

Population: Ages 7–Adults.

Publication Dates: 1986–2002.

Acronym: TOSF.

Scores, 16: Speech Survey (Articulation, Rate/Prosody, Fluency, Voice, Total); Verbal Oral Functioning (Resonance, Balance, Sequenced Syllables, Mixed Syllable Sequence, Sequenced Vowels, Sequenced Syllable Rates, Total); Nonverbal Oral Functions (Isolated

Functioning, Sequenced Functioning); Survey of Orofacial Structures; History-Behavioral Survey.
Administration: Individual.
Price Data, 2002: $85 per complete kit including manual (36 pages), 25 test booklets, finger cots, tongue blades, penlight, and balloons; $35 per examiner's manual; $40 per 25 test booklets; $8 per oroscope penlight.
Time: (20) minutes.
Author: Gary J. Vitali.
Publisher: Slosson Educational Publications, Inc.
Cross References: See T5:2706 (2 references); for reviews by Ronald B. Gillam and Roger L. Towne, see 12:397.

[2555]
Test of Perceptual Organization.

Purpose: "Designed to measure (1) abstract reasoning, (2) psychomotor functioning, and (3) the ability to follow specific, exacting instructions in an accurate manner."
Population: "Normals and psychiatric patients ages 12 and over."
Publication Dates: 1967–1970.
Acronym: TPO.
Scores: Total score only.
Administration: Group.
Price Data, 2002: $40 per examiner set including 25 tests, 25 profiles, scoring key, and manual (1970, 24 pages); $15 per 25 tests; $2.75 per scoring key; $8.25 per 25 profiles; $6.75 per manual; $9 per specimen set including manual, forms, and scoring key.
Time: 10(15) minutes.
Comments: Formerly called Test of Abstract Reasoning.
Author: William T. Martin.
Publisher: Psychologists and Educators, Inc.
Cross References: For reviews by A. Ralph Hakstian and Robert C. Nichols, and an excerpted review by Barton B. Proger, see 8:203, see also 7:390 (1 reference).

[2556]
Test of Phonological Awareness.

Purpose: "Measures young children's awareness of individual sounds in words."
Population: Ages 5–8.
Publication Date: 1994.
Acronym: TOPA.
Scores: Total score only.
Administration: Group.
Editions, 2: Kindergarten, Early Elementary.
Price Data, 2001: $149 per complete kit including examiner's manual (38 pages), 25 kindergarten student booklets, 25 early elementary student booklets, 25 kindergarten profile/examiner forms, and 25 early elemen-

tary profile/examiner forms; $49 per examiner's manual; $39 per 25 student booklets (specify kindergarten or early elementary); $14 per 25 profile/examiner forms (specify kindergarten or early elementary).
Time: (15–20) minutes.
Authors: Joseph K. Torgesen and Brian R. Bryant.
Publisher: PRO-ED.
Cross References: For reviews by Steven H. Long and Rebecca McCauley, see 13:333 (3 references).

[2557]
Test of Pragmatic Language.

Purpose: Designed "to provide an in-depth screening of the effectiveness and appropriateness of a student's pragmatic, or social, language skills."
Population: Ages 5-0 to 13-11.
Publication Date: 1992.
Acronym: TOPL.
Scores, 3: Listening Skills, Speaking Skills, Total.
Administration: Individual.
Price Data, 2001: $134 per complete kit; $49 per examiner's manual (35 pages); $49 per picture book; $39 per 25 profile/examiner record forms.
Time: (45) minutes.
Authors: Diana Phelps-Terasaki and Trisha Phelps-Gunn.
Publisher: PRO-ED.
Cross References: For reviews by Salvador Hector Ochoa and William K. Wilkinson, see 12:398.

[2558]
Test of Pretend Play.

Purpose: To assess symbolic play, conceptual development, and use of symbols.
Population: Ages 1–6.
Publication Dates: 1997–1998.
Acronym: ToPP.
Scores: Scores for 4 sections (Self With Everyday Objects, Toy and Non-representational Material, Representational Toy Alone, Self Alone), and Total Score.
Administration: Individual.
Price Data, 2002: $451.27 per complete kit including record forms, toy components (e.g., doll, bowl, brown stick, cotton wool), and manual (1997, 58 pages).
Time: (45) minutes.
Authors: Vicky Lewis and Jill Boucher.
Publisher: The Psychological Corporation Europe [United Kingdom].

[2559]
Test of Problem Solving.

Purpose: Designed to assess children's everyday thinking and reasoning skills.
Population: Ages 6–12.
Publication Date: 1984.
Acronym: TOPS.

Scores, 6: Explaining Inferences, Determining Causes, Negative Why Questions, Determining Solutions, Avoiding Problems, Total.
Administration: Individual.
Price Data: Available from publisher.
Time: (20–25) minutes.
Authors: Linda Zachman, Carol Jorgensen, Rosemary Huisingh, and Mark Barrett.
Publisher: LinguiSystems, Inc. [No reply from publisher; status unknown].
Cross References: See T5:2710 (8 references).

[2560]
Test of Reading Comprehension, Third Edition.
Purpose: Designed to "quantify the reading comprehension ability of individuals."
Population: Ages 7-0 to 17-11.
Publication Dates: 1978–1995.
Acronym: TORC-3.
Scores: 9 subtests: General Vocabulary, Syntactic Similarities, Paragraph Reading, Sentence Sequencing, Supplementary (Mathematics Vocabulary, Social Studies Vocabulary, Science Vocabulary, Reading the Directions of Schoolwork), Reading Comprehension Quotient.
Administration: Group or individual.
Price Data, 2001: $159 per complete kit including 10 student booklets, 50 answer sheets and subtest 8, 50 profiles, and manual (1995, 91 pages) in storage box; $34 per 10 student booklets; $39 per 50 answer sheets and subtest 8; $39 per 50 profiles; $49 per manual.
Time: (60) minutes.
Authors: Virginia L. Brown, Donald D. Hammill, and J. Lee Wiederholt.
Publisher: PRO-ED.
Cross References: See T5:2712 (1 reference); for reviews by Felice J. Green and Carole Perlman, see 13:334 (3 references); see also T4:2785 (3 references); for reviews by James A. Poteet and Robert J. Tierney of an earlier edition, see 10:372 (4 references); for reviews by Brendon John Bartlett and Joyce Hood of the original edition, see 9:1270; see also T3:2456 (1 reference).

[2561]
Test of Retail Sales Insight.
Purpose: "Developed ... primarily for assessing the degree of knowledge that an individual has in relation to retail selling."
Population: Retail clerks and students.
Publication Dates: 1960–1971.
Acronym: TRSI.
Scores, 6: Sales Knowledge, Customer Motivation, Merchandise Procurement, Sales Promotion, Sales Closure, Total.

Administration: Group.
Price Data, 2002: $27.50 per 25 reusable test booklets; $6.75 per scoring key; $6.75 per 25 answer sheets; $8.25 per 25 profiles; $6.75 per manual (1971, 18 pages); $9 per specimen set (manual, forms, keys not included).
Time: (30) minutes.
Comments: Self-administered; earlier form called Test of Sales Insight.
Author: Russell N. Cassel.
Publisher: Psychologists and Educators, Inc.

[2562]
Test of Sensory Functions in Infants.
Purpose: Developed to measure "sensory processing and reactivity in infants."
Population: Infants ages 4–18 months with regulatory disorders or developmental delays.
Publication Date: 1989.
Acronym: TSFI.
Scores, 6: Reactivity to Tactile Deep Pressure, Adaptive Motor Functions, Visual-Tactile Integration, Ocular-Motor Control, Reactivity to Vestibular Stimulation, Total.
Administration: Individual.
Price Data, 2002: $175 per complete kit including set of test materials, 100 administration and scoring forms, and manual (45 pages) in carrying case; $25 per 100 administration and scoring forms; $38.50 per manual.
Time: (20) minutes.
Authors: Georgia A. DeGangi and Stanley I. Greenspan.
Publisher: Western Psychological Services.
Cross References: See T5:2715 (1 reference); for a review by Mark Albanese, see 11:441.

[2563]
Test of Social Insight.
Purpose: Designed to "appraise the characteristic mode of reaction the individual uses in resolving interpersonal (social) problems."
Population: Grades 6–12, 13–16 and adults.
Publication Dates: 1959-1984.
Acronym: TSI.
Scores, 6: Withdrawal, Passivity, Cooperation, Competition, Aggression, Total.
Administration: Group.
Levels, 2: Youth Edition, Adult Edition.
Price Data, 2001: $90 per test package; $56.40 per manual (1963, 19 pages) and manual supplement (1984, 19 pages); $93.50 per IBM answer sheet/profile sheet package; $43.20 per set of IBM scoring stencils.
Time: [20–25] minutes.
Author: Russell N. Cassel.

Publisher: Martin M. Bruce, Ph.D.
Cross References: See T3:2461 (1 reference) and T2: 1419 (3 references). For reviews by John D. Black and John Pierce-Jones, and an excerpted review by Edward S. Bordin, see 6:190 (4 references).

[2564]
Test of Spoken English.
Purpose: Measures nonnative speakers' ability to produce understandable English speech.
Population: Nonnative speakers of English.
Publication Dates: 1979–1999.
Acronym: TSE.
Score: Holistic score taking into consideration communicative competence comprising Linguistic, Discourse, Functional, and Sociolinguistic competence.
Administration: Group.
Price Data: Examination fee per candidate available from publisher.
Time: (20–25) minutes.
Comments: Test administered 12 times annually at TSE centers (domestic and foreign) established by publisher; cassette or 3/4 ips test tape and 5-inch reel necessary for administration.
Author: International Language Programs, Educational Testing Service.
Publisher: Educational Testing Service.
Cross References: See T5:2717 (1 reference); for reviews by Michael J. Subkoviak and Kikumi K. Tatsuoka, see 9:1273.

[2565]
Test of Understanding in College Economics, Third Edition.
Purpose: To measure college students' understanding of college economics.
Population: Introductory economics students.
Publication Dates: 1967–1991.
Acronym: TUCE III.
Scores: Total score only.
Administration: Group.
Editions, 2: Microeconomics, Macroeconomics.
Price Data, 2001: $19.95 per 25 test booklets (specify Macroeconomics or Microeconomics); $14.85 per examiner's manual (1991, 46 pages), which includes scoring keys.
Time: (45) minutes per test.
Author: Phillip Saunders.
Publisher: National Council on Economic Education.
Cross References: For reviews by Joseph C. Ciechalski and Jennifer J. Fager, see 13:335; see also T2:1970 (10 references); for a review by Christine H. McGuire of an earlier edition, see 7:902.

[2566]
Test of Variables of Attention (Version 7.03).
Purpose: "Developed to assess attention and impulse control."
Population: Ages 4–80.
Publication Dates: 1988–1996.
Acronym: TOVA.
Administration: Individual.
Price Data: Available from publisher.
Time: (21.6) minutes.
Comments: Computer administered via separate or combined software; IBM and Macintosh versions available.
Authors: Lawrence M. Greenberg, Clifford L. Corman, and Carol L. Kindschi.
Publisher: Universal Attention Disorders, Inc.
a) T.O.V.A. VISUAL.
Scores, 4: Commission, Omission, Response Time, Response Time Variability and Signal Detection.
b) T.O.V.A. AUDITORY.
Scores: Same as *a* above.
Cross References: For reviews by Sandra Loew and by Susan C. Whiston and Harrison Kane, see 14:394; see also T5:2720 (2 references); for reviews by Rosa A. Hagin and Peter Della Bella and by Margot B. Stein of an earlier edition, see 13:336 (1 reference).

[2567]
Test of Visual-Motor Integration.
Purpose: Designed to measure the ability of visual and motor skills.
Population: Ages 4 through 17.
Publication Date: 1996.
Acronym: TVMI.
Scores: Total score only.
Administration: Individual or group.
Price Data, 2001: $116 per complete kit including manual (75 pages) and 50 summary/response forms in storage box; $69 per 50 summary/response forms; $49 per manual.
Time: (20) minutes.
Authors: Donald D. Hammill, Nils A. Pearson, and Judith K. Voress.
Publisher: PRO-ED.
Cross References: For a review by Deborah Erickson, see 14:395; see also T5:2722 (1 reference).

[2568]
Test of Visual-Motor Skills.
Purpose: To assess a child's visual-motor functioning.
Population: Ages 2–13.
Publication Date: 1986.
Acronym: TVMS.
Scores: Total score only.

Administration: Group or individual.
Price Data: Not available.
Time: (3–5) minutes.
Author: Morrison F. Gardner.
Publisher: Psychological & Educational Publications, Inc.
Cross References: For reviews by Deborah Erickson and Janet E. Spector, see 13:337 (2 references); see also T4:2791 (1 reference).

[2569]
Test of Visual-Perceptual Skills (Non-Motor).

Purpose: Constructed to "determine a child's visual-perceptual strengths and weaknesses."
Population: Ages 4–12.
Publication Date: 1982.
Acronym: TVPS.
Scores: 7 areas: Visual Discrimination, Visual Memory, Visual-Spatial Relationships, Visual Form Constancy, Visual Sequential Memory, Visual Figure-Ground, Visual Closure.
Administration: Individual.
Price Data: Available from publisher.
Time: (7–15) minutes.
Author: Morrison F. Gardner.
Publisher: Psychological & Educational Publications, Inc.
Cross References: See T5:2724 (13 references); for reviews by Nancy A. Busch-Rossnagel and Joseph W. Denison, see 9:1276.

[2570]
Test of Word Finding in Discourse.

Purpose: Designed to assess children's word-finding skills in discourse.
Population: Ages 6-6 to 12-11.
Publication Date: 1991.
Acronym: TWFD.
Scores, 2: Productivity Index, Word-Finding Behaviors Index.
Administration: Individual.
Price Data, 2001: $106 per complete test including manual (173 pages) and 25 test record forms; $29 per 25 test record forms; $79 per manual.
Time: (15–20) minutes.
Author: Diane J. German.
Publisher: PRO-ED.
Cross References: For reviews by James Dean Brown and Rebecca J. Kopriva, see 12:399; see also T4:2800 (1 reference).

[2571]
Test of Word Finding, Second Edition.

Purpose: Designed as a diagnostic tool for the assessment of children's word finding skills.

Population: Ages 4–12.
Publication Dates: 1986–2000.
Acronym: TWF-2.
Scores, 11: 8 scores for Standardized Assessment (Picture Naming: Nouns, Sentence Completion Naming, Picture Naming: Verbs, Picture Naming: Categories, Comprehension Check for Picture Naming: Nouns, Comprehension Check for Sentence Completion Naming, Comprehension Check for Picture Naming: Verbs, Comprehension Check for Picture Naming: Categories); 5 scores for Informal Assessment (Delayed Response Procedure, Secondary Characteristics Tally, Phonemic Cueing Procedure, Imitation Procedure, Response Analysis for Nouns).
Administration: Individual.
Levels, 3: Preprimary, Primary, Intermediate.
Forms, 2: Standardized Assessment, Informal Assessment.
Price Data, 2001: $339 per complete kit; $10 per Preprimary profile/examiner record forms; $17 per Primary/Intermediate profile/examiner record forms; $79 per examiner's manual (2000, 194 pages); $129 per picture book 1; $94 per picture book 2.
Time: (20–30) minutes.
Author: Diane J. German.
Publisher: PRO-ED.
Cross References: See T5:2725 (10 references); for reviews by Sharon L. Weinberg and Susan Ellis Weisman of an earlier edition, see 11:443 (1 reference); for reviews by Mavis Donahue and Priscilla A. Drum of an earlier edition, see 10:373.

[2572]
Test of Word Knowledge.

Purpose: Developed to "assess a student's skill in the reception and expression of … semantics."
Population: Ages 5–17.
Publication Dates: 1991–1992.
Acronym: TOWK.
Scores, 11: Expressive Vocabulary, Receptive Vocabulary, Word Opposites, Word Definitions, Synonyms, Multiple Contexts, Figurative Usage, Conjunctions and Transition Words, Receptive Composite, Expressive Composite, Total.
Administration: Individual.
Levels, 2: Ages 5–8, Ages 8–17.
Price Data, 2002: $169 per complete kit including stimulus manual, examiner's manual (118 pages), and 12 record forms; $99 per stimulus manual; $69 per examiner's manual; $32 per 12 record forms.
Time: (31) minutes for Level 1; (65) minutes for Level 2.
Authors: Elisabeth H. Wiig and Wayne Secord.
Publisher: The Psychological Corporation.
Cross References: See T5:2727 (1 reference); for a review by Rick Lindskog, see 13:338 (3 references).

[2573]
Test of Word Reading Efficiency.

Purpose: Constructed as a "measure of an individual's ability to pronounce printed words accurately and fluently."

Population: Ages 6-0 to 24-11.

Publication Date: 1999.

Acronym: TOWRE.

Scores, 3: Sight Word Efficiency, Phonemic Decoding Efficiency, Total Word Reading Efficiency.

Administration: Individual.

Forms, 2: A, B.

Price Data, 2001: $119 per complete kit including manual (115 pages), 25 each Forms A and B record booklets, and 1 each Forms A and B word cards; $24 per 25 record booklets (specify form); $14 per word cards (specify form); $49 per manual.

Time: (5–8) minutes.

Authors: Joseph K. Torgesen, Richard K. Wagner, and Carol A. Rashotte.

Publisher: PRO-ED.

[2574]
Test of Work Competency and Stability.

Purpose: Developed to "measure psychological capacity for work."

Population: Ages 21 and over.

Publication Dates: 1959–1961.

Acronym: TWCS.

Scores, 9 to 11: Negative (Questionnaire, Tremometer, Time for P.A.I., Total), Positive (Tapping, Digits Backward, Picture Arrangement, Total), Level of Work Competency, Mirror Tracing (optional), Digit Symbol (optional).

Administration: Individual.

Price Data, 2001: $350 per complete kit; $10 per 25 record blanks; $10 per 25 interview questionnaire sheets; $6 per 25 mirror tracing patterns; $6 per 25 tapping patterns; $75 per mirror tracing apparatus; $18 per manual (1959, 59 pages).

Foreign Language Edition: French edition available.

Time: (30–40) minutes.

Comments: Stopwatch necessary for administration.

Author: A. Gaston Leblanc.

Publisher: Institute of Psychological Research, Inc. [Canada].

Cross References: For a review by Jerome D. Pauker, see 8:695; see also T2:1420 (1 reference) and 6:191 (2 references).

[2575]
Test of Written English.

Purpose: "Designed to measure a student's performance in written English."

Population: Grades 1–6.

Publication Date: 1979.

Acronym: TWE.

Scores, 4: Capitalization, Punctuation, Written Expression, Total.

Administration: Individual.

Price Data, 2002: $50 per test kit including manual (95 pages) and 50 test forms; $25 per 50 test forms; $19 per manual; $25 per specimen set.

Time: (10–20) minutes.

Comments: Can be adapted for administration to small groups if subjects can read; separate answer sheets (test forms) must be used.

Authors: Velma R. Andersen and Sheryl K. Thompson.

Publisher: Academic Therapy Publications.

Cross References: See T5:2729 (3 references); for reviews by James A. Poteet and Robert E. Shafer, see 9:1277.

[2576]
Test of Written Expression.

Purpose: Constructed as a "norm-referenced test of writing."

Population: Ages 6-6 to 14-11.

Publication Date: 1995.

Acronym: TOWE.

Scores, 2: Items, Essay.

Administration: Individual or group.

Price Data, 2001: $129 per complete kit including manual (58 pages), 25 profile/examiner record forms, and 25 student booklets in storage box; $39 per 25 student booklets; $44 per profile/examiner record forms; $49 per examiner's manual.

Time: (60) minutes.

Authors: Ron McGhee, Brian R. Bryant, Stephen C. Larsen, and Diane M. Rivera.

Publisher: PRO-ED.

Cross References: For reviews by Mildred Murray-Ward and Carole Perlman, see 13:339 (1 reference).

[2577]
Test of Written Language—Third Edition.

Purpose: Designed to "(a) identify students who perform significantly more poorly than their peers in writing and who as a result need special help; (b) determine a student's particular strengths and weaknesses in various writing abilities; (c) document a student's progress in a special writing program; and conduct research in writing."

Population: Ages 7-6 to 17-11.

Publication Dates: 1978–1996.

Acronym: TOWL-3.

Scores: 8 subtest scores (Vocabulary, Spelling, Style, Logical Sentences, Sentence Combining, Contextual Conventions, Contextual Language, Story Construc-

tion) plus 3 composite scores (Contrived Writing, Spontaneous Writing, Overall Writing).
Administration: Individual or group.
Forms, 2: A, B.
Price Data, 2001: $179 per complete kit including manual (1996, 134 pages), 25 student response booklets Form A, 25 student response booklets Form B, and 50 profile/story scoring forms in storage box; $44 per 25 A or B student response booklets; $39 per 50 profile/story scoring forms; $56 per manual; $98 per Windows or Macintosh PRO-SCORE System; $89 per IBM DOS PRO-SCORE System.
Time: (90) minutes.
Authors: Donald D. Hammill and Stephen C. Larsen.
Publisher: PRO-ED.
Cross References: See T5:2731 (8 references); for reviews by Joe B. Hansen and by Jayne E. Bucy and Mark E. Swerdlik, see 13:340 (16 references); see also T4:2804 (2 references); for reviews by Stephen L. Benton and Joseph M. Ryan of an earlier edition, see 11:444 (6 references); for reviews by Edward A. Polloway and Robert T. Williams of the original edition, see 9:1278.

[2578]
Test of Written Spelling, Fourth Edition.

Purpose: Designed to assess students' spelling abilities.
Population: Ages 6-0 to 18-11.
Publication Dates: 1976–1999.
Acronym: TWS-4.
Scores: Total score only.
Administration: Group.
Price Data, 2001: $79 per complete kit including manual (1999, 59 pages) and 50 answer sheets; $47 per examiner's manual; $34 per 50 answer sheets.
Time: (15) minutes.
Authors: Stephen C. Larsen, Donald D. Hammill, and Louisa C. Moats.
Publisher: PRO-ED.
Cross References: See T5:2732 (2 references); for reviews by Alfred P. Longo and Hoi K. Suen of an earlier edition, see 13:341 (5 references); see also T4:2805 (4 references); for reviews by Deborah B. Erickson and Ruth M. Noyce of an earlier edition, see 10:374; for reviews by John M. Bradley and Deborah B. Erickson of an earlier edition, see 9:1279.

[2579]
Test on Appraising Observations.

Purpose: Designed to test one aspect of critical thinking: judging credibility.
Population: Grade 10 to adult.
Publication Dates: 1983–1990.
Administration: Group.
Price Data: Available from publisher.

Authors: Stephen P. Norris (multiple-choice format and constructed-response format) and Ruth King (multiple-choice format).
Publisher: Faculty of Education, Memorial University of Newfoundland [Canada].
 a) MULTIPLE-CHOICE FORMAT.
 Publication Date: 1983.
 Scores: Total score only.
 Parts, 2: A, B.
 Time: (40–45) minutes.
 b) CONSTRUCTED-RESPONSE VERSION.
 Publication Date: 1986.
 Scores, 2: Answer-Choice, Justification.
 Time: (40–45) minutes.
Cross References: For reviews by Michael Kane and Jeffrey K. Smith, see 13:342; see also T4:2806 (1 reference).

[2580]
Tests for Everyday Living.

Purpose: Designed to "measure achievement in the life skill area."
Population: Junior and senior high school.
Publication Date: 1979.
Acronym: TEL.
Scores, 8: 7 subtest scores (Purchasing Habits, Banking, Budgeting, Health Care, Home Management, Job Search Skills, Job Related Behavior) plus Total.
Administration: Group.
Price Data: Available from publisher.
Time: (20–30) minutes per test, recommended to administer 2 tests per session in 3 sessions.
Comments: Designed for oral administration in order to eliminate reading ability as a determinant of performance.
Authors: Andrew S. Halpern, Larry K. Irvin, and Janet T. Landman.
Publisher: CTB/McGraw-Hill.
Cross References: For a review by William A. Mehrens, see 9:1281; see also T3:2473 (1 reference).

[2581]
Tests of Achievement and Proficiency™, Forms K, L, and M.

Purpose: Designed to "provide a comprehensive and objective measure of students' progress in a high school curriculum."
Population: Grades 9–12.
Publication Dates: 1978–1996.
Acronym: TAP™.
Forms, 3: K, L, M; 2 batteries: Complete and Survey.
Administration: Group.
Levels, 4: 15, 16, 17, 18.
Price Data: Available from publisher.

Special Editions: Braille and large-print editions available.
Authors: Dale P. Scannell, Oscar M. Haugh, Brenda H. Loyd, and C. Frederick Risinger.
Publisher: Riverside Publishing.

a) COMPLETE BATTERY.
Scores, 15: Vocabulary, Reading Comprehension, Written Expression, Math Concepts and Problem Solving, Math Computation [optional], Social Studies, Science, Information Processing, Reading Total, Math Total, Core Total, Composite, plus Advance Skills Scores for reading, language, and mathematics.
Time: (255) minutes; (275) minutes with optional test.

b) SURVEY BATTERY.
Scores, 10: Reading (Vocabulary, Comprehension, Total), Written Expression, Math Concepts and Problem Solving, Math Computation [optional], Total, plus Advanced Skills Scores for reading, language, and mathematics.
Time: (90) minutes; (100) minutes with optional test.

Cross References: For reviews by Susan M. Brookhart and Darrell L. Sabers, see 14:396; see also T5:2735 (1 reference), T4:2810 (1 reference), and 11:445 (4 references); for a review by Elaine Clark of Forms G and H, see 10:375 (2 references); for reviews by John M. Keene, Jr. and James L. Wardrop of an earlier form, see 9:1282.

[2582]
Tests of Achievement in Basic Skills: Mathematics.

Purpose: To assess mathematics achievement.
Population: Preschool-kindergarten, Grades 1, 2, 3–4, 4–6, 7–9, 10–adult.
Publication Dates: 1970–1976.
Acronym: TABS-M.
Administration: Group.
Price Data, 1998: $13.50 per 30 tests (specify Level K, 1, 2, or A and Form 1 or 2); $13.50 per 35 tests (specify Level B, C, or D and Form 1 or 2); $5.75 per 35 answer sheets; $3.50 per hand-scoring keys (specify Level A, B, C, or D); $30 per manual K (1976, 11 pages) and 30 tests; $4.50 per specimen set (specify level); price data for Individualized Mathematics Program (IMP) materials available from publisher.
Time: (45–70) minutes.
Comments: May be used separately or as part of instructional Individualized Mathematics Program (IMP); "criterion-referenced tests"; 18-69 item scores, each item measuring a specific objective, and part and total scores; separate answer sheets (Digitek) must be used with Levels B–D.

Authors: James C. Young and Robert R. Knapp (Level C manuals).
Publisher: EdITS/Educational and Industrial Testing Service.

a) LEVEL K.
Population: Preschool-kindergarten.
Publication Date: 1974.
Scores: 18 item scores in 3 areas: Arithmetic Skills, Geometry-Measurement, Modern Concepts.

b) LEVEL 1.
Population: Grade 1.
Publication Date: 1974.
Scores: 36 item scores in 3 areas: same as *a* above.

c) LEVEL 2.
Population: Grade 2.
Publication Date: 1974.
Scores: 41 item scores in 3 areas: same as *a* above.

d) LEVEL A.
Population: Grades 3–4.
Publication Date: 1973.
Scores: 49 item scores in 3 areas: same as *a* above.

e) LEVEL B.
Population: Grades 4–6.
Publication Dates: 1972–1973.
Scores: 73 items and total scores in 3 areas: same as *a* above, plus Total.

f) LEVEL C.
Population: Grades 7–9.
Publication Dates: 1970–1971.
Scores: 68 items and total scores in 3 areas: same as *e* above.

g) LEVEL D.
Population: Grades 10-12.
Publication Dates: 1972–1976.
Scores: 47 items and total scores in 2 areas: Arithmetic Skills, Arithmetic Application, plus Total.

Cross References: For reviews by James Braswell and C. Alan Riedesel, and an excerpted review by Barton B. Proger, see 8:293 (2 references); see also 7:492 (1 reference).

[2583]
Tests of Adult Basic Education, Forms 7 & 8.

Purpose: Designed to measure achievement of basic skills commonly found in adult basic education curricula and taught in instructional programs.
Acronym: TABE.
Administration: Group.
Levels, Editions, and Parts: 2 Forms: 7 & 8, each with 2 editions: Complete Battery and Survey, and 5 Levels: L, E, M, D, A.

Price Data, 2002: $46.80 per 25 Practice exercise and Locator Test booklets; $39.40 per 25 Complete Battery Test booklets Level L; $83.75 per 25 Complete Battery and Survey Test books E, M, D, and A; $23.30 per large print edition Practice Exercise and Locator Test; $23.30 per large print Complete Battery Test book Level L; $49.25 per large print edition Complete Battery or Survey Tests Levels E, M, D, or A; $47.95 per 25 answer sheets; $29.50 per 25 hand-scorable SCOREZE answer sheets; $23.60 per 25 machine-scorable answer sheets—Scantron Option 2; $24 per 50 CompuScan 48-column Practice Exercise and Locator Test or Survey Levels E, M, D, A; $46.20 per 50 CompuScan 48-column Complete Battery Levels E, M, D, or A; $17.50 per scoring stencil for hand-scoring CompuScan answer sheets for Practice Exercise and Locator Test stencil and Survey Levels E, M, D, A; $34.45 per scoring stencil for hand-scoring CompuScan answer sheets for Complete Battery; $18.60 per word list; $31 per 25 marker item booklets; $12.85 per 25 individual diagnostic profiles Complete Battery and Survey Levels E, M, D, A; $42.55 per test user's handbook; $15.40 per norms book, Form 7 & 8 (1995, 90 pages); $2.85 per group record sheet; $17.50 per technical report (1996, 72 pages); $15.40 per Complete Battery or Survey manual; $22.15 per 25 examinee record book Level L.

Foreign Language Edition and Other Special Editions: Form 7 is available in a large print edition; TABE Español is available.

Comments: Level L is the same for both the Complete Battery and the Survey editions; an interview checklist, a word list to assist determination of appropriate TABE level, and an Individual Diagnostic Profile are available; a Practice Exercise is available in the same booklet as the Locator Test.

Author: CTB/McGraw-Hill.

Publisher: CTB/McGraw-Hill.

a) FORMS 7 & 8.

Population: Adults in Adult Basic Education programs, vocational-technical centers, and correctional facilities, first and second year college students.

Publication Dates: 1957–1996.

Scores: Level L: 3 scores: Pre-Reading, Reading Skills, Total Reading; Levels E, M, D, and A: 7 scores: Reading, Math Computation, Applied Math, Total Mathematics (Math Computation plus Applied Math), Language, Total Battery, Spelling.

Price Data: $39.40 per 25 Level L Test books; $83.75 per 25 Level E, M, D, or A test books; $23.30 per large print edition test book, Level L; $49.25 per large print edition test book, Levels E, M, D, or A; $47.95 per 25 large print answer sheets; $29.50 per 25 hand-scorable SCOREZE

answer sheets; $46.20 per 50 CompuScan 48-column answer sheets; $34.45 per scoring stencil for hand-scoring CompuScan answer sheets; $12.85 per 25 individual diagnostic profiles; $15.40 per manual (1994, 63 pages).

Time: 154–164 (209) minutes for Levels E, M, D, and A; 35 (65) minutes for Level L.

1) *Locator Test.*

Purpose: "Used to determine the appropriate level of TABE to administer to each examinee."

Scores, 3: Reading, Mathematics, Language (optional).

Time: (35–40) minutes for Reading and Mathematics; (50–55) minutes for Reading, Mathematics, and Language.

b) SURVEY FORM.

Population: Adults in Adult Basic Education programs, vocational-technical centers, and correctional facilities, second year college students.

Publication Dates: 1987–1996.

Scores: Level L: 3 scores: Pre-Reading, Reading Skills, Total Reading; Levels E, M, D, and A: 5 scores: Reading, Mathematics Computation, Applied Mathematics, Language, Spelling.

Price Data: $83.75 per 25 test books; $49.25 per large print test book; $47.95 per 50 large print answer sheets; $29.50 per 25 hand-scorable SCOREZE answer sheets; $24 per 50 machine-scorable answer sheets or CompuScan 48-column answer sheets; $17.50 per survey stencil for hand-scoring CompuScan answer sheets; $15.40 per manual (1994, 36 pages).

Time: (112) minutes.

1) *Locator Test* (same as *a*1 above).

Cross References: For reviews by Michael D. Beck and Bruce G. Rogers, see 13:343; for reviews by Robert W. Lissitz and Steven J. Osterlind of an earlier edition, see 11:446 (2 references); for reviews by Thomas F. Donlon and Norman E. Gronlund of an earlier edition, see 8:33 (1 reference); for a review by A. N. Hieronymus and an excerpted review by S. Alan Cohen of an earlier edition, see 7:32.

[2584]
Tests of Adult Basic Education Work-Related Foundation Skills.

Purpose: "To provide pre-instructional information about an examinee's level of achievement on basic skills, ... to identify areas of weakness ... measure growth, ... and involve the examinee in appraising his or her learning needs to assist ... [in preparing] an instructional program to meet the examinee's individual needs."

Population: Adults in vocational/technical programs, students in adult basic education programs 2-year colleges, and secondary school ROP & JTPA programs.

Publication Dates: 1994–1996.

Acronym: TABE WF.

Scores, 6: Reading, Math Computation, Applied Math, Total Mathematics (Math Computation and Applied Math), Language, Total Battery.

Administration: Group.

Forms, 4: General, Business/Office, Health, Trade/Technical.

Price Data, 2002: $33.65 per review kit including general test book, trade/technical test book, health test book, business/office test book, examiner's manual (1994, 30 pages), and individual diagnostic profile; $54 per manual and 25 locator tests; $83.40 per manual and general trade technical, health, or business/office test book; $24.50 per 25 locator test SCOREZE answer sheets; $29 per general trade/technical, health, or business/office SCOREZE answer sheets; $28.80 per 50 CompuScan answer sheets; $23.95 per 50 Scantron Opt. 2 answer sheets; $12.75 per 25 individual diagnostic profiles; $17.40 per handscoring stencil; $2.85 per group record sheet; $15.80 per examiner's manual; $15.30 per norms book; $14.25 per technical bulletin; $14.25 per technical report (1996, 33 pages) for use with this test and the TABE Work-Related Problem Solving available from publisher.

Time: 120(160) minutes.

Author: CTB Macmillan/McGraw-Hill.

Publisher: CTB/McGraw-Hill.

Cross References: For reviews by Kurt F. Geisinger and Jeffrey A. Jenkins, see 13:344.

[2585]
Tests of Adult Basic Education Work-Related Problem Solving.

Purpose: "Designed to help employers, educators, and training professionals diagnose how an examinee deals with the different aspects of problem solving."

Population: Students in secondary schools, vocational education programs, adult basic education programs, and junior colleges, and employees in industry.

Publication Dates: 1994–1996.

Acronym: TABE-PS.

Scores, 5: Competency scores (Employs Reading and Math Skills to Identify and Define a Problem, Examines Situations Using Problem-Solving Techniques, Makes Decisions About Possible Solutions, Evaluates Outcomes and Effects of Implementing Solutions), Total Number Correct Score.

Administration: Group.

Forms, 2: 7, 8.

Price Data, 2002: $16.80 per review kit including examiner's manual/scoring guide (1994, 56 pages), and test book; $50.65 per 25 test books with 1 manual; $29.70 per 25 practice exercises; $12.90 per 25 handscorable individual diagnostic profiles; $24 per 50 machine-scorable individual diagnostic profiles; $15.50

per examiner's manual/scoring guide; $14.25 per technical report (1996, 33 pages) for use with this test and the TABE Work-Related Foundation Skills available from publisher.

Time: 70(75) minutes for Form 7; 60(65) minutes for Form 8.

Comments: May be administered alone or in conjunction with other TABE materials; test includes a Practice Exercise which was included in the norming studies and so should be administered along with the test; includes Individual Diagnostic Profile, and Interview/Interest Questionnaire.

Author: CTB Macmillan/McGraw-Hill.

Publisher: CTB/McGraw-Hill.

Cross References: For reviews by Gale M. Morrison and Jerry Tindal, see 13:345.

[2586]
Tests of Basic Experiences 2.

Purpose: Designed to measure children's readiness to engage in a number of academic activities.

Population: PreK–beginning of Grade 1, end of K–end of Grade 1.

Publication Dates: 1970–1979.

Acronym: TOBE/2.

Subtests, 4: Language, Mathematics, Science, Social Studies.

Administration: Group.

Levels, 2: K, L.

Price Data, 2002: $203.80 per instructional activities kit; $16.70 per norms and technical data (1979, 61 pages); $2.70 per additional class evaluation records; $14.40 per Spanish directions; $32 per 30 individual evaluation records.

Time: (40–50) minutes per test for each level.

Comments: Revision of still-in-print Tests of Basic Experiences; no reading by examinees; Spanish directions available for both levels.

Author: Margaret H. Moss.

Publisher: CTB/McGraw-Hill.

a) LEVEL K.

Population: PreK–end of Grade 1.

Price Data: $82.70 per 30 of each hand-scored subtest; $32 per 30 practice tests; $15 per examiner's manual (1978, 44 pages).

Comments: Hand-scored test booklets for each test; combined CompuScan machine-scored test booklets for Language and Mathematics tests.

b) LEVEL L.

Population: End of K–end of Grade 1.

Price Data: Same as *a* above.

Comments: Hand-scored test booklets for each test; combined CompuScan test booklets for Language and Mathematics tests.

Cross References: See 9:1283 (1 reference) and T3:2478 (7 references); for a review by Esther E.

Diamond and excerpted reviews by Steven Thurber and Barton B. Proger of an earlier edition, see 8:34 (8 references); for a review by Courtney B. Cazdan of an earlier complete edition, see 7:33. For a review by Stephen M. Koziol, Jr. of the Language test, see 8:59; for a review by Leroy G. Callahan of the Mathematics test, see 8:294; for a review by Arlen R. Gullickson of the Science test, see 8:860.

[2587]
Tests of General Educational Development [the GED Tests].

Purpose: To "assess skills representative of the typical outcomes of a traditional high school education" for the purpose of awarding a secondary school level (GED) diploma.

Population: Candidates for high school equivalency diplomas.

Publication Dates: 1944–1998.

Acronym: GED Tests.

Scores, 6: Writing Skills, Social Studies, Science, Interpreting Literature and the Arts, Mathematics, Total.

Administration: Group or individual.

Forms: 17 U.S. English Operational (secure) full-length forms available; 8 U.S. English forms available of Official GED Practice test (7 nonsecure half-length test, 1 nonsecure full-length test).

Price Data, 1998: Operational (secure) forms not available for purchase and are available only to and administered at Official GED Testing Centers; Official GED Practice Tests half-length (available from Steck-Vaughn Co., (800) 531-5015): $37.50 per 10 test batteries; $15.98 per set of 50 universal machine-scorable answer sheets; $12.98 per set of 10 self-scoring answer sheets (for use with half-length practice test U.S. English Form CC only); full-length U.S. English practice test: $36 per set of 5; $14.91 per set of 25 corresponding answer sheets; $24.20 per administrator's set including teacher's manual ('89, 203 pages), scoring materials, and conversion tables, available in U.S. English half-length, U.S. English full-length, Spanish, or French; $40.50 per 10 Spanish-language edition batteries (or $.88 for one test and one univrsal answer sheet); $15.98 per 50 Spanish-language universal answer sheets; $40.50 per 10 French-language edition batteries (or $4.88 for one test and one universal answer sheet); $15.98 per 50 French-language universal answer sheets; $13.80 per 1 Large Print practice test (U.S. English only) and universal answer sheet; $47.87 per 1 audiocassette practice test (U.S. English only) with large print reference copy. Canadian English practice test batteries (2 forms) available from Gage Publishing Ltd., (416) 293-8141: C27.50 per 10 batteries (avalable singly at C$4.98 each); C$13.68 per 50 Canadian English universal answer sheets; C$25.99 per Canadian English administrator's set. U.S. English (4 forms) and Canadian English (2 forms) computer-delivered practice tests available on CD-ROM through NTC/Contemporary Publishing, (800) 621-1918; outside the U.S., Canada, and their territories through Sylvan Learning Systems (800) 627-4276.

Foreign Language and Special Editions: Operational (secure) full length GED batteries: Canadian English (6 forms), Spanish (3 forms), French (2 forms), and U.S. English large print (3 forms), audiocassettte (2 forms), and Braille (2 forms) available. Computer-delivered U.S. English-language tests available only outside U.S., Canada, and their territories. Official GED Practice Tests: Canadian English, Spanish, French, U.S. English large print, and audiocassette.

Time: 120 minutes for Writing Skills, 85 minutes for Social Studies, 95 minutes for Science, 65 minutes for Interpreting Literature and the Arts, 90 minutes for Mathematics [all times are for Operational (secure) forms) of the tests and do not include time required to give and clarify verbal test-taking instructions].

Comments: Tests administered throughout the year at official GED centers; tests originated in 1942 for granting high school/college credit for veterans, in mid-1950s GED program extended to all non-high school graduates; extensive 1988 revisions include addition of essay component to Writing Skills test and increased emphasis on higher order cognitive skills (e.g., application, analysis/evaluation, and math problem solving) throughout the battery; new tests scheduled for release in September 2001.

Author: General Educational Development Testing Service of the American Council on Education.

Publisher: General Educational Development Testing Service of the American Council on Education.

Cross References: See T4:2816 (2 references); for reviews by Bruce G. Rogers and Michael S. Trevisan, see 11:447 (2 references); for reviews by J. Stanley Ahmann and A. Harry Passow, see 9:1284 (1 reference); see also T3:2485 (2 references), 8:35 (20 references), and 7:34 (21 references); for a review by Robert J. Solomon of earlier forms, see 5:29 (39 references); for a review by Gustav J. Froehlich, see 4:26 (27 references); for reviews by Herbert S. Conrad and Warren G. Findley, see 3:20 (11 references). For reviews by Charlotte W. Croon of an earlier form of the expression subtest, see 3:122; for reviews by W. E. Hall and C. Robert Pace of an earlier form of the social studies reading subtest, see 3:528.

[2588]
Tests of Reading Comprehension.

Purpose: "They aim at assessing the extent to which readers are able to obtain meaning from text."

Population: Grades 3–7, 6–10.

Publication Date: 1987.
Acronym: TORCH.
Scores, 14: Grasshoppers, The Bear Who Liked Hugging People, Lizards Love Eggs, Getting Better, Feeding Puff, Shocking Things/Earthquakes!, The Swamp-creature, The Cats, A Horse of Her Own, Iceberg Towing, The Accident, The Killer Smog of London, I Want to be Andy, The Red Ace of Spades.
Administration: Individual or group.
Levels: 2 overlapping test booklets: A, B.
Price Data, 2002: A$75.90 per complete kit including test booklet A, test booklet B, 16 answer sheets, set of photocopy master sheets, and manual (84 pages); A$26.35 per manual.
Time: Untimed.
Comments: "Content-referenced" and/or "norm-referenced."
Authors: Leila Mossenson, Peter Hill, and Geoffrey Masters.
Publisher: Australian Council for Educational Research Ltd. [Australia].
Cross References: See T5:2743 (3 references) and T4:2817 (1 reference); for reviews by Robert B. Cooter, Jr. and Diane J. Sawyer, see 11:448.

[2589]
TestWell: Health Risk Appraisal.

Purpose: "Designed to provide an awareness of how current behaviors and physical health measurements impact health risks."
Population: Adults ages 18–60 with a minimum of 10th grade education.
Publication Date: 1992.
Scores, 5: Appraised Age, Achievable Age, Positive Lifestyle Behaviors, Top 10 Risks of Death, Suggestions for Improvement.
Administration: Group.
Manual: No manual.
Price Data, 1998: $7 per individual National Wellness Institute scoring; $40 per group report.
Time: (20) minutes.
Comments: Scoring by National Wellness Institute; individual and group reports available.
Author: National Wellness Institute, Inc.
Publisher: National Wellness Institute, Inc.
Cross References: For reviews by Barbara L. Lachar and Steven G. LoBello, see 13:346.

[2590]
TestWell: Wellness Inventory for Windows.

Purpose: Designed to promote awareness of wellness.
Population: Adults with a minimum of 10th grade education.
Publication Date: 1992.
Scores, 11: Physical Fitness and Nutrition, Social Awareness, Medical Self-Care, Spirituality and Values, Emotional Management, Intellectual Wellness, Environmental Wellness, Safety, Occupational Wellness, Sexuality and Emotional Awareness, Total.
Administration: Group.
Manual: No manual.
Price Data, 1998: $399 per interactive version, single user license; $249.95 per interactive version, multiuser license; $695 per group/batch version; $.50 per group/batch entry questionnaire booklet; $750 per reproduction rights (educational institutions only); $395 per scanner support capability.
Time: (20) minutes.
Comments: Requires IBM or compatible computer hardware.
Author: National Wellness Institute, Inc.
Publisher: National Wellness Institute, Inc.
Cross References: For reviews by William W. Deardorff and Theodore L. Hayes, see 13:347; see also T4:2821 (1 reference).

[2591]
TestWell: Wellness Inventory for Windows—College Version.

Purpose: "Designed to address lifestyle choices facing today's college students."
Population: College students.
Publication Date: 1993.
Scores, 11: Physical Fitness, Nutrition, Social Awareness, Self-Care and Safety, Emotional and Sexuality, Intellectual Wellness, Environmental Wellness, Emotional Management, Occupational Wellness, Spirituality and Values, Total.
Administration: Group.
Price Data, 1998: $399 per interactive version, single user license; $599 per interactive version, multiuser license; $695 per group/batch version; $.50 per group/ batch entry questionnaire booklet; $750 per reproduction rights (for educational institutions only); $395 per scanner support capability.
Time: (20) minutes.
Author: National Wellness Institute, Inc.
Publisher: National Wellness Institute, Inc.
Cross References: For reviews by David L. Bolton and Richard E. Harding, see 13:348.

[2592]
Thanatometer.

Purpose: Measures attitudes concerning death.
Population: Adults.
Publication Date: 1986.
Scores: Total score only.
Administration: Group or individual.
Manual: No manual.
Price Data, 2002: $1 per scale.
Time: [5-10] minutes.
Comments: Supplementary article available.

Author: Panos D. Bardis.
Publisher: Donna Bardis.

[2593]
Thematic Apperception Test.

Purpose: "A method of revealing to the trained interpreter some of the dominant drives, emotions, sentiments, complexes and conflicts of a personality."
Population: Ages 4 and over.
Publication Dates: 1935–1943.
Acronym: TAT.
Scores: Total score only.
Administration: Individual.
Price Data: Available from publisher.
Time: 100(200) minutes in 2 sessions 1 day apart.
Author: Henry A. Murray.
Publisher: Harvard University Press.
Cross References: See T5:2749 (87 references), T4:2824 (107 references), 9:1287 (51 references), and T3:2491 (105 references); for a review by Jon D. Swartz, see 8:697 (241 references); see also T2:1519 (231 references); for a review by Richard H. Dana and Leonard D. Eron, see 7:181 (297 references); see also P:484 (339 references); for a review by C. J. Adcock, see 6:245 (287 references); for reviews by Leonard D. Eron and Arthur R. Jensen, see 5:164 (311 references); for a review by Arthur L. Benton, see 4:136 (198 references); for reviews by Arthur L. Benton, Julian Rotter, and J. R. Wittenborn and an excerpted review, see 3:103 (102 references).

[2594]
Theological School Inventory.

Purpose: Assesses motivation for entering the ministry.
Population: Incoming seminary students.
Publication Dates: 1962–1972.
Acronym: TSI.
Scores, 12: Definiteness, Natural Leading, Special Leading, Concept of the Call, Flexibility, Acceptance by Others, Intellectual Concern, Self-Fulfillment, Leadership Success, Evangelistic Witness, Social Reform, Service to Persons.
Administration: Group.
Price Data: Available from publisher.
Time: Administration time not reported.
Authors: James E. Dittes, Frederick Kling, Ellery Pierson, and Harry DeWire.
Publisher: Ministry Inventories.
Cross References: See T2:1028 (7 references) and P:273 (5 references).

[2595]
Therapy Attitude Inventory.

Purpose: Provides ratings of parental satisfaction with training in the behavioral management of their children.

Population: Parents.
Publication Date: 1974.
Scores: Total score only.
Administration: Individual.
Price Data, 1994: No charge for first copy; may photocopy for research or clinical use.
Time: (5) minutes.
Author: Sheila Eyberg.
Publisher: Sheila M. Eyberg (the author) [No reply from publisher; status unknown].
Cross References: See T5:2752 (2 references) and T4:2827 (1 reference); for a review by Terry B. Gutkin, see 9:1289 (2 references); see also T3:2494 (1 reference).

[2596]
Thinking Creatively in Action and Movement.

Purpose: "Designed to sample . . . creative thinking abilities of preschool children."
Population: Ages 3–8.
Publication Date: 1981.
Acronym: TCAM.
Scores, 3: Fluency, Originality, Imagination.
Administration: Individual.
Price Data, 2002: $43.20 per 20 tests and manual/ scoring guide (34 pages); $23.40 per manual; $23.15 per sample set; $6.35 per booklet for scoring service.
Time: (10–30) minutes.
Author: E. Paul Torrance.
Publisher: Scholastic Testing Service, Inc.
Cross References: See T5:2754 (5 references) and T4:2829 (2 references); for reviews by Joseph S. Renzulli and James O. Rust, see 9:1290.

[2597]
Thinking Creatively With Sounds and Words, Research Edition.

Purpose: Developed to assess creative thinking.
Population: Grades 3–12, adults.
Publication Date: 1973.
Acronym: TCSW.
Scores, 2: Sounds and Images, Onomatopoeia and Images.
Administration: Group.
Levels, 2: I, II.
Forms, 2: A, B.
Price Data, 2002: $37.65 per complete kit including 20 test booklets (specify level and form) and manual/scoring guide (20 pages); $37.65 per cassette; $15.25 per manual/scoring guide; $15.30 per norms/technical manual (65 pages); $18 per sample set; $7.05 per booklet for scoring service of the SI or the OI; $10.05 per booklet for scoring service of both the SI and OI.
Time: (30–35) minutes for each test.

Authors: E. Paul Torrance, Joe Khatena, and Bert F. Cunnington (except technical manual).
Publisher: Scholastic Testing Service, Inc.
Cross References: See T5:2755 (2 references) and T4:2830 (5 references); for a review by Lynn H. Fox, see 9:1291 (3 references); see also T3:2496 (5 references); for reviews by Philip M. Clark and Mary Lee Smith, see 8:248 (6 references); see also T2:587 (17 references).

[2598]
Thomas Concept Inventory of Core Strengths.

Purpose: "To identify eight patterns of human strengths."
Population: Managers and adults in organizational settings.
Publication Dates: 1977–1982.
Acronym: TCICS.
Scores: Core Strengths.
Administration: Group.
Forms, 2: A (1977, 2 pages, for self-ratings), B (1977, 2 pages, for ratings by up to 5 others).
Restricted Distribution: Restricted to Thomas Concept Certified Professionals, Certified Teachers, and approved researchers.
Price Data, 2001: Scoring service, $40 per analysis of core strengths (1982, 2 page computer report plus 17 pages of interpretive materials); $2.50 per sample analysis; $6 per manual (1978, 35 pages); $20 per website version.
Time: (10) minutes.
Comments: Form C available for research purposes; ratings by self and others.
Authors: J. W. Thomas, Clyde C. Mayo (manual), and T. J. Thomas (interpretive materials).
Publisher: Thomas Concept.

[2599]
Thomas-Kilmann Conflict Mode Instrument.

Purpose: Designed to assess "an individual's behavior in conflict situations."
Population: Managers.
Publication Date: 1974.
Acronym: TKI.
Scores, 5: Competing, Collaborating, Compromising, Avoiding, Accommodating.
Administration: Group or individual.
Price Data, 2001: $9 per instrument (16 pages including test and general information).
Time: [15] minutes.
Comments: Self-administered, self-scored, online at skillsone.com.
Authors: Kenneth W. Thomas and Ralph H. Kilmann.

Publisher: Consulting Psychologists Press, Inc.
Cross References: See T5:2756 (2 references); for reviews by Richard E. Harding and Ronn Johnson, see 10:377 (4 references).

[2600]
Thurstone Temperament Schedule.

Purpose: Measures personality traits related to job performance.
Population: Variety of occupations from entry-level to management.
Publication Dates: 1949–1991.
Acronym: TTS.
Scores, 6: Active, Impulsive, Dominant, Stable, Sociable, Reflective.
Administration: Individual or group.
Price Data, 2002: $75 per start-up kit including 25 test booklets and examiner's manual; $56 per 25 test booklets (quantity discount available); $28 per examiner's manual.
Time: No limit (approximately 15–20 minutes).
Comments: Administered via paper and pencil; hand-scored carbon format.
Author: L. L. Thurstone.
Publisher: Reid London House.
Cross References: See T5:2757 (1 reference), T4:2833 (6 references), T3:2499 (2 references), T2:1423 (32 references), P:277 (20 references), and 6:192 (17 references); for a review by Neil J. Van Steenberg, see 5:118 (12 references); for reviews by Hans J. Eysenck, Charles M. Harsh, and David G. Ryans, and an excerpted review by Laurance F. Shaffer, see 4:93.

[2601]
Thurstone Test of Mental Alertness.

Purpose: Measures general mental ability to learn and comprehend.
Population: Wide variety of occupations.
Publication Dates: 1943–1998.
Acronym: TMA.
Scores, 3: Quantitative, Linguistic, Total.
Administration: Individual or group.
Forms, 2: A, B.
Price Data, 2002: $86 per start-up kit including 25 test booklets and examiner's manual (specify Form A or Form B); $68 per 25 test booklets (quantity discounts available; specify Form A or Form B); $28 per examiner's manual; price data available from publisher for Quanta computer administration and scoring software (@indows); $86 per Quanta start-up kit including examiner's manual, 25 administrations and scoring (does not include Quanta software).
Time: 20 minutes.
Authors: Thelma Gwinn Thurstone and L. L. Thurstone.
Publisher: Reid London House.

Cross References: See T5:2758 (1 reference) and T2:469 (5 references); for a review by Robert D. North, see 7:392 (4 references); for a review by Joshua A. Fishman, see 5:391; see also 4:326 (3 references); for reviews by Anne Anastasi and Emily T. Burr of an earlier edition, see 3:265.

[2602]
Tiffany Control Scales.

Purpose: Designed to evaluate personality problems related to one's experience of control across different situations.
Population: Adolescents and adults.
Publication Dates: 1985–1999.
Acronym: TCS.
Scores, 16: Control from Self/Internal, Control over Self, Control over the Environment, Control from the Environment, Coping Index, Passive/Assertive/Aggressive Index, Extratensive/Intratensive Index, Repression, Expressive, Self-Directed, Non-Self-Directed, and 5 other measures.
Administration: Individual or group.
Editions, 2: Paper and pencil, computer administered.
Price Data, 2001: $12.50 per 25 paper and pencil tests; $495.95 per computer edition, unlimited use; $50 per limited use edition (5 uses); demo and sample report are free; $25 per test for mail-in scoring; $19.95 per manual (1999, 83 pages).
Time: [20] minutes for Standard TCS; varies when customized.
Comments: For research or clinical use or in employment screening; may be customized to fit examiner's needs; self-rating instrument; scoring and interpretation by computer.
Authors: Donald W. Tiffany and Phyllis G. Tiffany.
Publisher: Psychological Growth Associates, Inc.
Cross References: For a review by Brian F. Bolton, see 14:397.

[2603]
The Time of Your Life.

Purpose: Constructed as a self-assessment tool to provide "insight" into time management.
Population: Employees.
Publication Date: 1988.
Scores: Total score only.
Administration: Group or individual.
Price Data: Price available from publisher for complete kit including 20 inventories and 20 scoring and interpretation sheets.
Time: [30] minutes.
Comments: Self-administered, self-scored.
Author: Training House, Inc.
Publisher: Training House, Inc.

Cross References: For reviews by Ralph F. Darr, Jr. and Richard W. Faunce, see 12:400.

[2604]
Time Perception Inventory.

Purpose: Measures perceptions of time use including degree of personal concern about time usage and frame of reference (past, present, future) used.
Population: Students in time management courses.
Publication Dates: 1976–1987.
Scores, 4: Time Effectiveness, Orientation (Past, Present, Future).
Administration: Group.
Price Data, 2002: $38.50 per complete kit including 10 inventories and manual (1987,8 pages); $24.50 per 10 inventories, including profile; $16.50 per manual.
Time: Administration time not reported.
Comments: Manual has been revised; self-administered.
Author: Albert A. Canfield.
Publisher: Western Psychological Services.
Cross References: For a review by Douglas J. McRae, see 11:449.

[2605]
Time Problems Inventory.

Purpose: Identifies reasons people waste time.
Population: Management and administrative personnel.
Publication Dates: 1980–1987.
Scores, 4: Priorities, Planning, Delegation, Self-Discipline.
Administration: Group.
Price Data, 2002: $38.50 per complete kit including 10 inventories and manual (1987, 8 pages); $24.50 per 10 inventories (1987); $16.50 per manual.
Time: (20–25) minutes.
Comments: Manual has been revised; self-administered.
Author: Albert A. Canfield.
Publisher: Western Psychological Services.
Cross References: For reviews by Jeanette N. Cleveland and Lyle F. Schoenfeldt of an earlier edition, see 9:190.

[2606]
Time Use Analyzer.

Purpose: Designed to "clarify the importance of using time effectively in various aspects of life."
Population: Adults.
Publication Dates: 1981–1990.
Scores: 2 scores (Typicalness, Dissatisfaction) for 8 areas: Work, Sleep, Personal, Personal/Family, Community, Family/Home, Education/Development, Recreation/Hobbies.
Administration: Group.

Price Data, 2002: $38.50 per complete kit including manual (1990, 8 pages), and 10 inventories; $24.50 per 10 inventories; $16.50 per manual.
Time: (5–10) minutes.
Comments: May be used alone or in combination with the Time Perception Inventory (2604) and the Time Problems Inventory (2605).
Author: Albert A. Canfield.
Publisher: Western Psychological Services.
Cross References: For a review by JoEllen V. Carlson, see 14:398.

[2607]
Timed Typings for Holidays.
Purpose: To measure typing skill growth, develop fluency, and help reach for new speed goals.
Population: Students in typing classes.
Publication Date: 1988.
Scores: Total score only.
Administration: Group.
Manual: No manual.
Price Data: Price information available from publisher for blackline masters.
Time: (1–5) minutes per writing.
Authors: Berkley H. Rudd and Carol R. Scott.
Publisher: J. Weston Walch, Publisher.

[2608]
TMJ Scale.
Purpose: "Designed to measure the [clinical significance of] symptom patterns of dental patients with temporomandibular joint disorders and orofacial pain."
Population: TM [temporomandibular] dental patients ages 13 and over.
Publication Dates: 1984–1987.
Scores, 10: Physical Domain (Pain Report, Palpation Pain, Perceived Malocclusion, Joint Dysfunction, Range of Motion Limitation, Non-TM Disorder), Psychosocial Domain (Psychological Factors, Stress, Chronicity), Global Scale.
Administration: Individual.
Price Data, 1994: $20 per specimen set including question booklet, manual (1987, 86 pages), and sample report.
Time: (10–15) minutes.
Comments: Self-administered; self-report.
Authors: Stephen R. Levitt, Tom F. Lundeen, and Michael W. McKinney.
Publisher: Pain Resource Center, Inc.
Cross References: For a review by William W. Deardorff, see 12:402; see also T4:2842 (3 references).

[2609]
Toddler and Infant Motor Evaluation.
Purpose: Designed to be used for "diagnostic, comprehensive assessment of children who are suspected to

have motor delays or deviations, the development of appropriate remediation programs, and treatment efficacy research."
Population: Ages 4 months to 3.5 years.
Publication Date: 1994.
Acronym: TIME.
Scores: 5 Primary Subtests: Mobility, Stability, Motor Organization, Social-Emotional, Functional Performance; 3 Clinical Subtests: Quality Rating, Component Analysis Rating, Atypical Positions.
Administration: Individual.
Price Data, 2002: $451 per complete kit including manual (324 pages), 10 record forms, timer, rattle, 2 balls, squeak toy, toy car, 3 containers, toy telephone, 2 shoelaces, 6 blocks, and nylon tote bag; $37.50 per 10 record forms; $137 per manual.
Time: (15–40) minutes.
Comments: Diagnostic assessment tool designed to be used by licensed/highly trained physical and occupational therapists, or appropriately trained adaptive physical educators, special education teachers, or others with expertise in the motor domain; administered utilizing a partnership between parent(s) or caretaker(s) and a trained examiner.
Authors: Lucy J. Miller and Gale H. Roid.
Publisher: Therapy Skill Builders—A Division of The Psychological Corporation.
Cross References: For reviews by Larry M. Bolen and William R. Merz, Sr., see 14:399.

[2610]
The Token Test for Children.
Purpose: Designed to assess receptive language dysfunction.
Population: Ages 3–12.
Publication Date: 1978.
Scores: Total score only.
Administration: Individual.
Parts, 5: I, II, III, IV, V.
Price Data, 2001: $98 per complete kit including 50 scoring forms, 20 tokens, and manual (63 pages); $29 per 20 tokens; $34 per 50 forms; $39 per manual.
Time: (8) minutes.
Author: Frank DiSimoni.
Publisher: PRO-ED.
Cross References: See T5:2768 (43 references) and T4:2846 (24 references); for reviews by William M. Reynolds and John Salvia, see 9:1295 (9 references); see also T3:2509 (1 reference).

[2611]
Tool Room Attendant—Form WCS.
Purpose: "Developed to measure the knowledge and skills required for maintenance jobs."
Population: Applicants for maintenance jobs.
Publication Dates: 1991–1994.

Scores: 10 areas: Electrical, Hydraulics and Pneumatics, Print Reading, Tools/Materials and Equipment, Power Transmission, Pumps and Piping, Rigging, Maintenance Records, Mobile Equipment, Total.
Administration: Group.
Price Data, 2002: $498 per complete kit including manual (1994, 12 pages), scoring key, 10 reusable test booklets, and 100 answer sheets.
Time: (100–120) minutes.
Author: Roland T. Ramsay.
Publisher: Ramsay Corporation.
Cross References: For reviews by Stephen L. Koffler and Eugene (Geno) Pichette, see 13:349.

[2612]
Tooze Braille Speed Test: A Test of Basic Ability in Reading Braille.

Purpose: "A speed test which seeks to give a quick appraisal of the child's ability to read Braille characters."
Population: Students (Ages 7-13) in Grades 1 or 2 Braille.
Publication Date: 1962.
Scores: Total score only.
Administration: Individual.
Price Data: Available from publisher.
Time: 1(5) minutes.
Author: F. H. G. Tooze.
Publisher: Association for the Education and Welfare of the Visually Handicapped [England] [No reply from publisher; status unknown].

[2613]
Torrance Tests of Creative Thinking.

Purpose: To identify and evaluate creative potential.
Population: Grades K through graduate school.
Publication Dates: 1966–1990.
Acronym: TTCT.
Administration: Individual and group.
Price Data, 2002: $42.30 per 20 scoring worksheets, class record, and directions manual/scoring guide (specify Form A or B and Figural or Verbal); $28.40 per norms/technical manual (1974, 80 pages); $18.80 per sample set including Figural and Verbal booklets (specify Form A or B); $6.20 per student for scoring service of Figural; $7.40 per student for scoring service of Verbal.
Author: E. Paul Torrance.
Publisher: Scholastic Testing Service, Inc.
a) VERBAL TEST.
Scores: 3 for equivalent Forms A and B: Fluency, Flexibility, Originality.
Administration: Individual for Grades K to 3.
Price Data: $31 per examiner's kit; $31.75 per manual for scoring and interpreting results (1974, 49 pages; specify Form A or B).
Time: 45(60) minutes.

Comments: Test booklet is titled Thinking Creatively With Words.
b) FIGURAL TEST.
Scores: 4 for equivalent Forms A and B: Fluency, Flexibility, Originality, Elaboration.
Price Data: $16.30 per directions manual (1974, 43–48 pages; specify Form A or B); $30.10 per streamlined scoring guide for Forms A and B (1984, 74 pages).
Time: 30(45) minutes.
Comments: Test booklet is titled Thinking Creatively with Pictures.
Cross References: See T5:2771 (45 references) and T4:2849 (33 references); for reviews by Clinton I. Chase and Donald J. Treffinger, see 9:1296 (20 references); see also T3:2512 (107 references), 8:249 (229 references), and T2:589 (88 references); for reviews by Leonard L. Baird and Robert L. Thorndike, and excerpted reviews by Ralph Hoepfner, John L. Holland, and Michael A. Wallach, see 7:448 (243 references).

[2614]
Tower of London—Drexel University.

Purpose: "An individually administered neuropsychological instrument designed to assess higher order problem-solving, specifically executive planning abilities."
Population: Children and adolescents and adults.
Publication Dates: 1999–2001.
Acronym: TOLDX.
Scores, 7: Total Move Score, Total Correct, Rule Violations, Time Violations, Initiation Time, Execution Time, Total Problem-Solving Time.
Administration: Individual.
Forms, 2: Adult, Child.
Price Data, 2002: $225 per complete kit including 25 child recording forms, 25 adult recording forms, 2 peg boards with beads, and technical manual (2001, 90 pages); $195 per complete child kit (same as complete kit, but child forms only); $195 per complete adult kit (same as complete kit, but adult forms only); $30 per 25 recording forms (specify Child or Adult); $55 per technical manual.
Time: (10–15) minutes.
Authors: William C. Culbertson and Eric A. Zillmer.
Publisher: Multi-Health Systems, Inc.

[2615]
TQ Manager Inventory and Feedback From Others.

Purpose: To access competency from a Total Quality Management style of leadership approach to managing organizations.
Population: Business managers.
Scores, 5: Openness & Trust, Collaboration & Teamwork, Managing By Fact, Recognition & Reward, Learning Organization.

Administration: Group.
Time: Administration not reported.
Authors: Warren H. Schmidt and Jerome P. Finnigan.
Publisher: Consulting Psychologists Press, Inc.
a) TQ MANAGER INVENTORY.
Publication Date: 1994.
Acronym: TQMI.
Price Data, 2001: $8.50 per inventory.
Comments: Self-assessment.
b) TQ MANAGER INVENTORY: FEEDBACK FROM OTHERS.
Publication Date: 1995.
Acronym: TQMO.
Price Data: $6.75 per inventory.
Comments: Feedback from colleagues to business managers.

[2616]
Trade Aptitude Test Battery.

Purpose: "To select prospective pupils for admission to technical institutes and colleges."
Population: First-year South African students in the technical fields.
Publication Dates: 1981–1983.
Acronym: TRAT.
Scores, 16: Dexterity, Co-ordination, Patterns, Components, Classification, Assembly, Computations, Inspection, Graphs, Mechanical Insight, Mathematics, Spatial Perception/2-D, Vocabulary, Figure Series, Woordeskat, Spatial Perception/3-D.
Administration: Group.
Price Data: Available from publisher.
Time: 288(293) minutes.
Comments: Test materials in both English and Afrikaans.
Authors: J. J. Taljaard and J. W. von Mollendorf (test).
Publisher: Human Sciences Research Council [South Africa].

[2617]
Trainer's Assessment of Proficiency (TAP).

Purpose: Constructed as a "self-assessment exercise that measures relative strengths in twelve instructional skills."
Population: Trainers.
Publication Date: 1991.
Acronym: TAP.
Scores, 12: Assessing Needs and Entering Behavior, Setting Objectives and Terminal Behavior, Analyzing Participants and Situations, Eliciting Relevant Responses and Testing, Applying Classroom Facilitation Skills, Forming Questions and Probes Effectively, Maintaining Adult Relationships, Giving Feedback and Reinforcement, Building Toward Transfer of Training, Getting All Learners to Participate, Managing Class-

room Time Effectively, Displaying Good Flow/Logic/Organization.
Administration: Group.
Forms, 2: Long, Short.
Price Data: Available from publisher.
Time: (60) minutes for Short form; (180) minutes for Long form.
Comments: Videocassette recorder necessary for administration of inventory.
Author: Scott B. Parry.
Publisher: Training House, Inc.
Cross References: For reviews by Mark W. Roberts and Daniel E. Vogler, see 12:403.

[2618]
Trait Evaluation Index.

Purpose: "Designed to elicit comprehensive, multi-dimensional appraisals of 'normal' personality dimensions."
Population: College and adults.
Publication Dates: 1967–1984.
Acronym: TEI.
Scores: 29 scores (Social Orientation, Compliance, Benevolence, Elation, Ambition, Motivational Drive, Self-Confidence, Dynamism, Independence, Personal Adequacy, Caution, Self-Organization, Responsibility, Propriety, Courtesy, Verbal Orientation, Intellectual Orientation, Perception, Self-Control, Fairmindedness, Adaptability, Sincerity) plus 4 general supplementary scores (Overall Adjustment, Masculinity, Femininity, Consistency) and 3 supplementary scores for engineers (Employment Stability, Productivity-Creativity, Job Satisfaction).
Administration: Group.
Price Data, 2001: $94.20 per test package; $83.40 per IBM answer/profile sheet package; $46 per set of IBM scoring stencils; $56.40 per manual (1968, 38 pages) and manual supplement (1984, 17 pages); $74.25 per specimen set; $99.50 per German edition test package.
Foreign Language Editions: German edition available.
Time: (30–50) minutes.
Author: Alan R. Nelson.
Publisher: Martin M. Bruce, Ph.D.
Cross References: See T2:1424 (1 reference); for reviews by Harold Borko and Jacob Cohen, see 7:155 (1 reference).

[2619]
The Trait Pleasure-Displeasure Scale.

Purpose: One of three fundamental dimensions of temperament in Mehrabian's Temperament Model; provides a general assessment of psychological adjustment-maladjustment.
Population: Ages 15 and older.

Publication Dates: 1978–1994.
Scores: Total score only.
Administration: Group or individual.
Price Data: Available from publisher for omplete kit including scale, scoring directions, norms manual (1994, 10 pages), and literature review.
Time: (10–15) minutes.
Author: Albert Mehrabian.
Publisher: Albert Mehrabian (the author).
Cross References: For reviews by Thaddeus Rozecki and Chockalingam Viswesvaran, see 13:351 (1 reference).

[2620]
Transdisciplinary Play-Based Assessment, Revised Edition.

Purpose: Constructed as a multidimensional approach to identifying service needs, to developing intervention plans, and to evaluating progress in children.
Population: Children developmentally functioning between infancy and 6 years of age.
Publication Date: 1993.
Acronym: TPBA.
Scores: 4 domains: Cognitive, Social-Emotional, Communication and Language, Sensorimotor Development.
Administration: Individual
Price Data, 2002: $44 per manual (352 pages).
Time: (60–90) minutes.
Comments: Ratings by transdisciplinary team.
Author: Toni W. Linder.
Publisher: Paul H. Brookes Publishing Co., Inc.
Cross References: For reviews by Terry Overton and Gary J. Stainback, see 13:352.

[2621]
Transition Behavior Scale–Second Edition.

Purpose: "Developed to be an educational-relevant measure of predicted success in employment and independent living based upon school personnel's observation of a student's behavior or skills."
Population: Ages 12–18.
Publication Dates: 1989–2000.
Acronym: TBS-2.
Scores, 3: Work-Related, Interpersonal Relations, Social/Community Expectations.
Administration: Group or individual.
Price Data, 2001: $116 per complete kit including 50 school version rating forms, 50 self-report rating forms, school version technical manual (2000, 41 pages), self-report technical manual (2000, 36 pages), and IEP and intervention manual (2000, 188 pages); $33 per 50 school version rating forms; $33 per 50 self-report rating forms; $14 per school version technical manual; $14 per self-report technical manual; $22 per IEP and intervention manual.

Time: (15–20) minutes.
Authors: Stephen B. McCarney and Paul D. Anderson.
Publisher: Hawthorne Educational Services, Inc.
Cross References: For reviews by Martha Blackwell and David O. Herman of the original edition, see 12:404.

[2622]
Transition Competence Battery for Deaf and Hard of Hearing Adolescents and Young Adults.

Purpose: To measure work and social skills necessary to successfully work and live in the community for persons who are deaf and hard of hearing to successfully work and live in the community.
Population: Deaf and hard of hearing adolescents and young adults.
Publication Date: 1993.
Acronym: TCB.
Scores, 6: Job-Seeking Skills, Work Adjustment Skills, Job-Related Social and Interpersonal Skills, Money Management Skills, Health and Home Skills, Community Awareness Skills.
Administration: Group.
Price Data, 2000: $399 per complete set.
Time: (180) minutes.
Comments: In addition to the written form, a video form is also available in which the test is presented in sign language.
Authors: John Reiman, Michael Bullis, and Cheryl Davis.
Publisher: James Stanfield Co., Inc.

[2623]
Transition Planning Inventory.

Purpose: To identify and plan for the comprehensive transition needs of students.
Population: High school and middle school students with disabilities who need future planning.
Publication Date: 1997.
Acronym: TPI.
Scores: Ratings in 9 areas: Employment, Further Education/Training, Daily Living, Leisure Activities, Community Participation, Health, Self-Determination, Communication, Interpersonal Relationships.
Administration: Individual or group.
Forms, 4: Student, Home, School, Profile and Further Assessment Recommendations.
Price Data, 2001: $154 per complete kit; $35 per Administration and Resource Guide (232 pages), $24 per 25 Profile and Further Assessment Recommendations Forms; $24 per 25 School Forms; $24 per 25 Home Forms; $24 per 25 Student Forms; $24 per 25 Spanish Home Forms; $29 per Informal Assessments for Transition Planning.

Foreign Language Edition: Spanish version of Home Form available.
Time: Administration time not reported.
Authors: Gary M. Clark and James R. Patton.
Publisher: PRO-ED.
Cross References: For reviews by Robert K. Gable and by Rosemary E. Sutton and Theresa A. Quigney, see 14:400.

[2624]

Transition-to-Work Inventory: A Job Placement System for Workers with Severe disAbilities.

Purpose: "Designed to assist employers, supported employment counselors, and other transition professionals in identifying the best match between the skills of an individual with disabilities and the requirements of the job."
Population: Individuals with severe disabilities.
Publication Dates: 1995–1996.
Acronym: TWI™.
Scores, 3: Job Analysis Rating, Worker Analysis Rating, Difference Score.
Administration: Individual.
Parts, 2: Job Analysis Scale, Worker Analysis Scale.
Price Data, 2002: $96 per starter kit including user and accommodation manual, 10 job analysis booklets, 25 worker analysis booklets, and 25 profile sheets; $33 per 25 worker analysis booklets; $17 per 10 job analysis booklets; $16 per individual profile sheets; $57 per manual and accommodation guide (1996, 102 pages).
Time: (30–35) minutes per scale.
Comments: Ratings by transition professionals.
Authors: Lee Friedman, Carl Cameron, and Jennifer Fletcher.
Publisher: The Psychological Corporation.
Cross References: For reviews by Chantale Jeanrie and Erich P. Prien, see 14:401.

[2625]

Trauma Symptom Checklist for Children.

Purpose: Designed "to measure acute and chronic posttraumatic stress and related psychological symptomatology."
Population: Ages 8–16.
Publication Date: 1996.
Acronym: TSCC.
Scores: 8 scales: Underresponse, Hyperresponse, Anxiety, Depression, Anger, Posttraumatic Stress, Dissociation, Sexual Concerns.
Administration: Group or individual.
Price Data: Available from publisher.
Time: (15–20) minutes.
Author: John Briere.
Publisher: Psychological Assessment Resources, Inc.

[2626]

Trauma Symptom Inventory.

Purpose: Designed for the "evaluation of acute and chronic posttraumatic symptomatology."
Population: Ages 18 and older.
Publication Date: 1995.
Acronym: TSI.
Scores, 13: Validity Scales (Response Level, Atypical Response, Inconsistent Response); Clinical Scales (Anxious Arousal, Depression, Anger/Irritability, Intrusive Experiences, Defensive Avoidance, Dissociation, Sexual Concerns, Dysfunctional Sexual Behavior, Impaired Self-Reference, Tension Reduction Behavior).
Administration: Group.
Price Data: Available from publisher for complete kit including manual (67 pages), 10 item booklets, 25 hand-scorable answer sheets, and 25 each of male and female profile forms.
Time: (20) minutes.
Comments: Computer scoring system available from publisher.
Author: John Briere.
Publisher: Psychological Assessment Resources, Inc.
Cross References: For reviews by Ephrem Fernandez and Jack E. Gebart-Eaglemont, see 14:402; see also T5:2782 (3 references).

[2627]

Treatment Intervention Inventory.

Purpose: Designed for intake, referral and post-treatment comparisons of adult counseling clients.
Population: Ages 12–18; Adult counseling clients.
Publication Dates: 1991–1997.
Acronym: TII; TII-J.
Scores, 9: Truthfulness, Anxiety, Depression, Self-Esteem, Distress, Family, Alcohol, Drug, Stress Coping Abilities.
Administration: Group.
Levels, 2: Adult, Juvenile.
Price Data: Available from publisher.
Time: (35) minutes Adult; (25–30) minutes Juvenile.
Comments: "A computerized, self-report assessment"; administration by paper and pencil or by computer; computer scored.
Author: Behavior Data Systems Ltd.
Publisher: Behavior Data Systems Ltd.
Cross References: For reviews by Janice G. Murdoch and Linda J. Zimmerman, see 14:403.

[2628]

Triadal Equated Personality Inventory.

Purpose: To measure personality variables.
Population: Adult males.
Publication Dates: 1960–1963.
Acronym: TEPI.

Scores, 22: Dominance, Self-Confidence, Decisiveness, Independence, Toughness, Suspiciousness, Conscientiousness, Introversion, Restlessness, Solemnity, Foresight, Industriousness, Warmth, Enthusiasm, Conformity, Inventiveness, Persistence, Sex Drive, Recognition Drive, Cooperativeness, Humility-Tolerance, Self-Control.
Administration: Group.
Price Data: Available from publisher.
Time: (50–120) minutes.
Author: Research Staff, United Consultants.
Publisher: Psychometric Affiliates.
Cross References: For a review by Jacob Cohen, see 7:156.

[2629]
Triage Assessment for Addictive Disorders.
Purpose: "Designed to cover diagnostic information for current dependence or abuse of alcohol and drugs."
Population: Adults.
Publication Dates: 1995–2000.
Acronym: TAAD.
Scores, 2: Abuse, Dependence.
Administration: Individual
Price Data: Available from publisher.
Time: (10) minutes.
Comments: Structured interview; screens for DSM-IV diagnostic criteria, providing an estimate of the likelihood that an individual meets the criteria for abuse or dependency; covers current problems only; can be administered by paraprofessionals.
Author: Norman G. Hoffmann.
Publisher: Evince Clinical Assessments.

[2630]
Tutor Evaluation and Self-Assessment Tool.
Purpose: "A structured profile that evaluates tutors' effectiveness … to improve growth and development."
Population: Tutors of all subjects and grade levels.
Publication Date: 1996.
Acronym: TESAT.
Scores, 12: Greeting, Identification of Task, Breaking the Task into Parts, Identification of Thought Process, Setting Agenda, Addressing the Task, Tutee Summary of Content, Tutee Summary of Underlying Process, Confirmation, What Next?, Arranging and Planning Next Session, Closing.
Administration: Group.
Price Data, 2001: $198 per 100 TESATs, quantity discount available; $64.95 (+$3.50 shipping) per Tutor Trainer's Manual (64 pages); $85 per transparency set, $23.95 per Master Tutor Guidebook (124 pages) (quantities up to 29); $16.95 per Master Tutor Guidebook (quantities of 30 or more); Orders of 100 or more Master Tutor Guidebooks include free Tutor Trainer's Manual, transparency set, and 100 tests.

Time: Untimed.
Comments: Administered in paper-and-pencil format only using carbonated compilation and scoring sheets; ranks tutors into one of four skill categories (outstanding, proficient, adequate, needs improvement) for each of 12 steps of the "Tutor Cycle," based on the author's tutoring model; can be completed by tutor for self-assessment or by other evaluator.
Author: Ross B. MacDonald.
Publisher: The Cambridge Stratford Study Skills Institute.

[2631]
Typing 5.
Purpose: Assesses typing skills.
Population: Administrative assistants, secretaries, and any position requiring typing ability.
Publication Date: 1975.
Scores, 2: Speed, Accuracy.
Administration: Individual or group.
Price Data, 1998: $70.50 per start-up kit (specify Form A, B, or C) including 25 test booklets, 25 practice sheets, and examiner's manual; $44 per 25 test booklets (specify Form A, B, or C; quantity discounts available); $14.75 per 25 practice sheets (quantity discounts available); $19.75 per examiner's manual.
Time: 5 minutes per test.
Comments: Previously listed as SRA Typing 5.
Author: Science Research Associates.
Publisher: Reid London House (No reply from publisher; status unknown).
    a) FORM A—TYPING SPEED.
    b) FORM B—BUSINESS LETTER.
    c) FORM C—NUMERICAL.
Cross References: For reviews by Charles J. Cranny and Lawrence W. Erickson, see 8:1035.

[2632]
The Uncritical Inference Test.
Purpose: "Helps students learn to distinguish between observations and inferences."
Population: Adolescents and adults.
Publication Dates: 1955–1982.
Scores: Total score only.
Administration: Group.
Manual: No manual.
Price Data, 2001: $.75 per test (minimum order of 10 tests).
Time: Administration time not reported.
Author: William V. Haney.
Publisher: International Society for General Semantics.

[2633]
Understanding and Managing Stress.
Purpose: Assesses stress level and health-related behaviors.

Population: Adults.
Publication Date: 1989.
Scores: Continuum of risk scores (low, medium, high) for each of 22 areas: Changes on the Job/Total, Changes on the Job/High-Impact, Changes in Personal Life/Total, Changes in Personal Life/High-Impact, Chronic Stressful Conditions on the Job, Chronic Stressful Conditions in Personal Life, Strain Response, Psychological Outlook, General Lifestyle/Importance to Health, General Lifestyle/Present Effectiveness, Social Support, Nutritional Habits and Awareness/Total, Physical Exercise Habits and Awareness, Drinking Habits, Behavioral Habits, Tobacco, Systolic Blood Pressure Reading, Diastolic Blood Pressure Reading, Total Cholesterol, High-Density Lipoprotein (HDL) Level, Ratio of Total Cholesterol to HDL, Triglyceride Level.
Administration: Group.
Price Data: Price information available from publisher for handbook (64 pages).
Time: Administration time not reported.
Comments: Self-administered, self-scored.
Author: John D. Adams.
Publisher: Jossey-Bass, A Wiley Company.
Cross References: For reviews by William J. Waldron and by William K. Wilkinson and Christopher P. Migotsky, see 12:405.

[2634]
Understanding Communication.

Purpose: Developed "to measure comprehension of verbal material in the form of short sentences and phrases."
Population: Variety of occupations.
Publication Dates: 1959–1992.
Scores: Total score only.
Administration: Individual of group.
Price Data, 2002: $91 per start-up kit including 25 test booklets, score key, and interpretation and research manual; $54 per 25 test booklets (quantity discounts available); $20 per score key; $28 per interpretation and research manual.
Time: 15 minutes.
Author: Thelma Gwinn Thurstone.
Publisher: Reid London House.
Cross References: See T4:2864 (1 reference) and T2:1747 (1 reference); for reviews by C. E. Jurgensen and Donald E. P. Smith, see 6:840.

[2635]
Uniform Child Custody Evaluation System.

Purpose: Constructed as a "uniform child custody evaluation procedure."
Population: Professionals involved in custody evaluation.
Publication Date: 1994.

Acronym: UCCES.
Scores: No scores.
Administration: Individual.
Forms, 25: General Data and Administrative Forms (UCCES Checklist, Initial Referral Form, Chronological Record of all Case Contacts Form, Case Notes Form, Consent for Psychological Services to Child(ren) Form, Authorization to Release Information Form, Suitability for Joint Custody Checklist, Collateral Interview Form, Consent for Evaluation of Minor(s) Form, UCCES Summary Chart), Parent Forms (Parent's Family/Personal History Questionnaire, Parent Interview Form, Parenting Abilities Checklist, Suitability for Joint Custody Interview, Analysis of Response Validity Checklist, Behavioral Observations of Parent-Child Interaction Form, Home Visit Observation Form, Agreement Between Parent and Evaluator Form, Explanation of Custody Evaluation Procedures for Parents and Attorneys), Child Forms (Child History Questionnaire, Child Interview Form, Child Abuse Interview Form, Abuse/Neglect Checklist, Child's Adjustment to Home and Community Checklist, Parent-Child Goodness of Fit Observation Form and Checklist).
Price Data: Available from publisher for complete kit including manual (47 pages), 2 sets of Parent Forms, 2 sets of Child Forms, and 1 set of Administrative and Data Forms.
Time: Administration time not reported.
Authors: Harry L. Munsinger and Kevin W. Karlson.
Publisher: Psychological Assessment Resources, Inc.
Cross References: For a review by Steven Zucker, see 13:353.

[2636]
Universal Nonverbal Intelligence Test™.

Purpose: "Designed to provide a ... fair measure of the general intelligence and cognitive abilities of children and adolescents ... who may be disadvantaged by traditional verbal and language-loaded measures."
Population: Ages 5–17.
Publication Date: 1998.
Acronym: UNIT™.
Scores, 11: Symbolic Memory, Cube Design, Spatial Memory, Analogic Reasoning, Object Memory, Mazes, Memory Quotient, Reasoning Quotient, Symbolic Quotient, Nonsymbolic Quotient, Full Scale IQ.
Administration: Individual.
Forms: Abbreviated Battery, Standard Battery, Extended Battery.
Price Data: Available from publisher.
Time: (10–15) minutes, Abbreviated Battery; (30) minutes, Standard Battery; (45) minutes, Extended Battery.
Authors: Bruce A. Bracken and R. Steve McCallum.
Publisher: Riverside Publishing.

Cross References: For a review by Deborah L. Bandalos, see 14:404.

[2637]
University Residence Environment Scale [Revised].

Purpose: Designed to "assess the social climate of university student living groups."
Population: University students and staff.
Publication Dates: 1974–1988.
Acronym: URES.
Scores, 10: Involvement, Emotional Support, Independence, Traditional Social Orientation, Competition, Academic Achievement, Intellectuality, Order and Organization, Student Influence, Innovation.
Administration: Group.
Forms, 4: Real (R), Ideal (I), Expectations (E), Short (S).
Price Data, 2001: $25 per sampler set including manual, test booklet (Forms R, I, E, and S), scoring key, and profile sheet; $125 per permission set.
Time: Administration time not reported.
Comments: Part of the Social Climate Scales (T5:2445).
Author: Rudolf H. Moos.
Publisher: Mind Garden, Inc.
Cross References: For reviews by Barbara A. Rothlisberg and Theresa G. Siskind, see 14:405; see also T4:2865 (8 references) and T3:2534 (3 references); for reviews by Fred H. Borgen and James V. Mitchell, Jr. of an earlier edition, see 8:700 (12 references).

[2638]
Useful Field of View.

Purpose: Designed as a "computer-administered and computer-scored test of visual attention," which may be used to help predict the degree to which a person may perform some everyday activities, such as driving a motor vehicle, safely.
Population: Adults.
Publication Date: 1998.
Acronym: UFOV.
Scores, 3: Central Vision and Processing Speed, Divided Attention, Selective Attention.
Administration: Individual.
Price Data, 1998: $130 per complete kit including user's manual (106 pages), reference card, CD, and use counter.
Time: (15) minutes.
Comments: Microsoft Windows 95 required with video card and CD ROM drive; not for use with laptops.
Authors: Karlene K. Ball and Daniel L. Roenker.
Publisher: The Psychological Corporation.

[2639]
Utah Test of Language Development—3.

Purpose: To assess listening (comprehension) and speaking (expression).
Population: Ages 3-0 to 9-11.
Publication Dates: 1958–1989.
Acronym: UTLD-3.
Scores, 3: Language Comprehension, Language Expression, Language Quotient.
Administration: Individual.
Price Data, 2001: $119 per complete kit including picture book, 50 profile/examiner record forms, and manual (1989, 36 pages); $54 per administration picture book; $29 per 50 profile/examiner record forms; $39 per manual.
Time: Administration time not reported.
Comments: Revised edition of Utah Test of Language Development; earlier edition called Utah Verbal Language Development Scale.
Author: Merlin J. Mecham.
Publisher: PRO-ED.
Cross References: See T5:2801 (3 references) and T4:2872 (1 reference); for a review by Lynn S. Bliss, see 11:454 (2 references); for reviews by Joan I. Lynch and Michelle Quinn of an earlier edition, see 9:1306 (3 references); see also T3:2541 (5 references) and T2:2097 (4 references); for reviews by Katharine G. Butler and William H. Perkins of an earlier edition, see 7:973.

[2640]
Validity Indicator Profile.

Purpose: "Designed to … evaluate an individual's motivation and effort during cognitive testing."
Population: Ages 18–69.
Publication Date: 1997.
Acronym: VIP.
Scores, 2: Nonverbal Subtest Response Style, Verbal Subtest Response Style.
Administration: Individual.
Price Data, 2002: $33 per test booklet; $19 per 25 answer sheets; $38 per manual; $19 per interpretive report (MICROTEST Q™ scoring); $18 per interpretive report (mail-in scoring); $107 per starter kit including manual, test booklet, 3 answer sheets, and 3 interpretive reports (specify MICROTEST Q™ scoring or mail-in scoring); quantity discounts available for the reports.
Time: (30) minutes.
Comments: Instrument must be scored by computer.
Author: Richard I. Frederick.
Publisher: NCS Assessments (Minnetonka).
Cross References: For reviews by Jack E. Gebart-Eaglemont and Stephen H. Ivens, see 14:406.

[2641]
Values Preference Indicator.

Purpose: "Provides respondents with the tools to examine their values and priorities for the purpose of self-learning, group discussion, team development and gaining insight into corporate culture."
Population: Adults.
Publication Date: 1990.
Acronym: VPI.
Scores, 21: Accomplishment, Acknowledgement, Challenge, Cooperation, Creativity, Expertise, Friendship, Honesty, Independence, Instruction, Intimacy, Organization, Pleasure, Quality, Recognition, Responsibility, Security, Spirituality, Tranquility, Variety, Wealth.
Administration: Group.
Manual: No manual.
Price Data, 1993: $10 per inventory.
Time: (45–60) minutes.
Comments: May be self-administered.
Author: Everett Robinson.
Publisher: Consulting Resource Group International, Inc.

[2642]
The Values Scale, Second Edition.

Purpose: "A cross-cultural measure of values in various life roles."
Population: Junior high school to adult.
Publication Dates: 1986–1989.
Acronym: VS.
Scores, 21: Ability Utilization, Achievement, Advancement, Aesthetics, Altruism, Authority, Autonomy, Creativity, Economic Rewards, Life Style, Personal Development, Physical Activity, Prestige, Risk, Social Interaction, Social Relations, Variety, Working Conditions, Cultural Identity, Physical Prowess, Economic Security.
Administration: Group.
Price Data, 2001: 470 per preview kit including item booklet, prepaid answer sheet, and manual; $62 per 25 reusable test booklets; $38 per 25 non-prepaid answer sheets; $38 per 25 report forms; $59.40 per manual.
Time: (30–45) minutes.
Authors: Dorothy D. Nevill and Donald E. Super.
Publisher: Consulting Psychologists Press, Inc.
Cross References: See T5:2805 (3 references); for reviews by Kathy E. Green and Patricia Schoenrade, see 13:355 (4 references); see also T4:2876 (1 reference); for reviews by Denise M. Rousseau and Robert B. Slaney of an earlier edition, see 10:379.

[2643]
Vasectomy Scale: Attitudes.

Purpose: To measure attitudes toward vasectomy.
Population: Adults.
Publication Dates: 1974–1988.
Scores: Total score only.
Administration: Group.
Manual: No manual.
Price Data, 2002: $1 per scale.
Time: [10] minutes.
Comments: Supplementary article available.
Author: Panos D. Bardis.
Publisher: Donna Bardis.

[2644]
Verbal Form.

Purpose: Designed to measure general ability to learn and comprehend.
Population: Employees in a wide variety of occupations.
Publication Dates: 1946–1984.
Scores, 3: Quantitative, Linguistic, Total.
Administration: Individual or group.
Forms, 2: A, B.
Price Data, 2002: $78 per start-up kit including 25 test booklets (specify Form A or Form B) and examiner's manual; $60 per 25 test booklets (quantity discounts available; specify Form A or Form B); $28 per examiner's manual; price data available from publisher for Quanta computer administration and scoring software (Windows); $78 per Quanta start-up kit including examiner's manual, 25 administrations, and scoring (does not include Quanta software).
Time: 15 minutes.
Comments: Previously listed as SRA Verbal Form.
Authors: Thelma Gwinn Thurstone and L. L. Thurstone.
Publisher: Reid London House.
Cross References: See T4:2542 (3 references), T3:2276 (3 references), T2:452 (1 reference), and 7:383 (2 references); for reviews by W. D. Commins and Willis C. Schaefer, see 4:319.

[2645]
Verbal Motor Production Assessment for Children.

Purpose: "Designed to aid in the systematic assessment of the neuromotor integrity of the motor speech system in children ... [with] speech production disorders."
Population: Speech-disordered children ages 3–12.
Publication Date: 1999.
Acronym: VMPAC.
Scores, 8: Global Motor Control, Focal Oromotor Control, Sequencing, Connected Speech and Language Control, Speech Characteristics, Auditory, Visual, Tactile.
Administration: Individual.
Price Data, 2001: $99 per complete kit including examiner's manual (206 pages), 11 stimulus cards, 15

record forms, and training videotape (45 minutes); $79 per examiner's manual; $28 per 15 record forms; $27 per stimulus cards; $37 per training videotape.
Time: (30) minutes.
Authors: Deborah Hayden and Paula Square.
Publisher: The Psychological Corporation.

[2646]
Verbal Reasoning.

Purpose: To measure the capacity to reason logically based on verbal problems.
Population: Wide variety of occupations and vocational counseling.
Publication Dates: 1958–1961.
Scores: Total score only.
Administration: Individual or group.
Price Data, 2002: $92 per start-up kit including 25 test bookets, score key, and interpretation and research manual (1961, 20 pages); $55 per 25 test booklets (quantity discounts available); $20 per score key; $28 per interpretation and reseach manual (1961, 20 pages).
Time: 15 minutes.
Authors: Raymond J. Corsini and Richard Renck.
Publisher: Reid London House.
Cross References: See T3:2553 (1 reference); for reviews by James E. Kennedy and David G. Ryans, see 6:509.

[2647]
VESPAR: A Verbal and Spatial Reasoning Test.

Purpose: "Designed to measure fluid intelligence in neurological patients."
Population: People "who have suffered physical or cognitive impairments as a result of neurological illness."
Publication Date: 1995.
Acronym: VESPAR.
Scores: Available from publisher.
Administration: Individual.
Price Data, 2001: $198 per multi-part test.
Time: Administration time not reported.
Authors: Dawn W. Langdon and Elizabeth K. Warrington.
Publisher: Psychology Press.

[2648]
Veterinary College Admission Test.

Purpose: Designed to measure general academic ability and scientific knowledge.
Population: Veterinary college applicants.
Publication Dates: 1951–1991.
Acronym: VCAT.
Scores, 6: Verbal Ability, Biology, Chemistry, Quantitative Ability, Reading Comprehension, Composite.
Administration: Group.

Restricted Distribution: Distribution restricted and test administered at licensed testing centers; details may be obtained from publisher.
Price Data: Available from publisher.
Time: 205 minutes.
Comments: Formerly called the Veterinary Aptitude Test.
Author: The Psychological Corporation.
Publisher: The Psychological Corporation.
Cross References: For reviews by James B. Erdmann and Terry A. Stinnett, see 12:406; see T2:2358 (1 reference), 6:1139 (3 references), and 5:957 (3 references).

[2649]
Victoria Symptom Validity Test.

Purpose: "Designed to provide evidence that can help to confirm or disconfirm the validity of an examinee's reported cognitive impairments."
Population: Ages 18 and over.
Publication Date: 1997.
Acronym: VSVT.
Scores, 6: Total Items Correct, Easy Items Correct, Difficult Items Correct, Easy Items Response Latency, Difficult Items Response Latency, Right-Left Preference.
Administration: Individual.
Price Data: Available from publisher for introductory kit including program disk, 3.5-inch disk (10 uses), and professional manual (93 pages).
Time: Administration time not reported.
Comments: Requires IBM of compatible personal computer (80386 required; Pentium recommended) with MS Windows 3.11 or Windows 95; computer administered, scored, and interpreted.
Authors: Daniel Slick, Grace Hopp, Esther Strauss, and Garrie B. Thompson.
Publisher: Psychological Assessment Resources, Inc.
Cross References: For reviews by Stephen J. Freeman and Linda J. Zimmerman, see 14:407.

[2650]
ViewPoint.

Purpose: An assessment of work attitudes designed for use in employee selection.
Population: Applicants for nonexempt or entry-level positions in industries.
Publication Dates: 1998–2001.
Scores: 10 scales: WorkView Total, ServiceView Total, Conscientiousness, Trustworthiness, Managing Work Pressure, Getting Along with Others, Drug/Alcohol Avoidance, Safety Orientation, Carelessness, Faking.
Administration: Group.
Price Data, 2002: Available from publisher for test materials including technical manual (1999, 62 pages),

Technical Report Addendum: A Meta-analysis of the Validity of ViewPoint (2001, 13 pages), and examiner's manual (1998, 43 pages).

Comments: Published in five different forms, each one covering a different combination of work and service attitudes; computerized versions are available.

Authors: W. M. Gibson, M. L. Holcom, S. W. Stang, and W. W. Ruch.

Publisher: Psychological Services, Inc.

a) WORKVIEW 6.
Acronym: W6.
Time: (15–20) minutes.
b) WORKVIEW 4.
Acronym: W4.
Time: (10–15) minutes.
c) SERVICEVIEW.
Acronym: SV.
Time: (10–15) minutes.
d) WORKVIEW 6 + SERVICE.
Acronym: W6SV.
Time: (20–30) minutes.
e) WORKVIEW 4 + SERVICE.
Acronym: W4SV.
Time: (20–25) minutes.

[2651]
Vincent Mechanical Diagrams Test, 1979 Revision.

Purpose: "Assesses the individual's ability to understand the concepts of cog, pulley and lever systems and general mechanical reasoning ability."

Population: Ages 15–adult.
Publication Dates: 1936–1979.
Acronym: VMD.
Scores: Total score only.
Administration: Group.
Price Data: Price information available from publisher for test booklets (1979, 13 pages), answer sheets, marking key, and instruction card (no date, 2 pages).
Time: 12(15) minutes.
Comments: Subtest of NIIP Engineering Selection Test Battery.
Author: National Institute of Industrial Psychology.
Publisher: NFER-Nelson Publishing Co., Ltd. [England].

[2652]
Vineland Adaptive Behavior Scales.

Purpose: To "assess personal and social sufficiency of individuals from birth to adulthood."
Population: Birth through age 18-11 and low-functioning adults, ages 3 through 12-11.
Publication Dates: 1935–1985.
Scores, 13: 3 Communication scores (Receptive, Expressive, Written), 3 Daily Living scores (Personal, Domestic, Community), 3 Socialization scores (Inter-personal Relationships, Play and Leisure Time, Coping Skills), 2 Motor Skills scores (Gross, Fine), Adaptive Behavior Composite, Maladaptive Behavior (optional for Survey and Expanded Forms only).

Administration: Individual.
Foreign Language Edition: Spanish edition available.
Comments: Revision of the Vineland Social Maturity Scale; semistructured interview for Survey and Expanded Forms.
Publisher: American Guidance Service, Inc.

a) INTERVIEW EDITION, SURVEY FORM.
Purpose: General assessment of adaptive strengths and weaknesses.
Population: Birth through age 18-11 and low-functioning adults.
Publication Dates: 1935–1984.
Price Data, 2002: $49.95 per 25 record booklets; $19.95 per 25 reports to parents; $16.95 per Interview Training Audiocassette; $56.95 per manual (1984, 313 pages); $84.95 per starter set including 10 record booklets, manual, and 1 report to parents; $199.95 per scoring and reporting software (DOS version for PCs).
Time: (20–60) minutes.
Authors: Sara S. Sparrow, David A. Balla, and Domenic V. Cicchetti.

b) INTERVIEW EDITION, EXPANDED FORM.
Purpose: Comprehensive assessment of adaptive behavior for program planning.
Population: Birth through age 18-11 and low-functioning adults.
Publication Dates: 1935–1984.
Price Data: $84.95 per 25 item booklets and 25 score summary and profile reports; $19.95 per 25 reports to parents; $30.95 per 25 program planning reports; $116.95 per starter set including 10 item booklets, 10 score summary and profile reports, 1 program planning report, 1 report to parents and manual (1984, 334 pages); $199.95 per scoring and reporting software (DOS version for PCs).
Time: (60–90) minutes.
Authors: Sara S. Sparrow, David A. Balla, and Domenic V. Cicchetti.

c) CLASSROOM EDITION.
Purpose: Assessment of adaptive behavior in the classroom.
Population: Ages 3 through 12-11.
Publication Date: 1985.
Price Data: $46.95 per 25 questionnaire booklets; $19.95 per 25 reports to parents; $54.95 per starter set including 10 questionnaire booklets, manual (1985, 186 pages), and 1 report to parents; $199.95 per scoring and reporting software (DOS version for PCs).

Time: (20) minutes.

Authors: Sara S. Sparrow (test and report), David A. Balla (test and report), Domenic V. Cicchetti (test and report), and Patti L. Harrison (manual).

Cross References: See T5:2813 (156 references) and T4:2882 (62 references); for a review by Jerome M. Sattler, see 10:381 (9 references); for a review by Iris Amos Campbell of the Survey Form and Expanded Form, see 9:1327 (8 references); see also T3:2557 (38 references), 8:703 (23 references), T2:1428 (50 references), P:281 (21 references), 6:194 (20 references), and 5:120 (15 references); for reviews by William M. Cruickshank and Florence M. Teagarden of an earlier edition, see 4:94 (21 references); for reviews by C. M. Louttit and John W. M. Rothney and an excerpted review, see 3:107 (58 references); for reviews by Paul H. Furfey, Elaine F. Kinder, and Anna S. Starr, see 1:1143.

[2653]
Vineland Social-Emotional Early Childhood Scales.

Purpose: Designed to assess the social and emotional functioning of young children.

Population: Birth to age 5-11.

Publication Date: 1998.

Acronym: SEEC.

Scores, 4: Interpersonal Relationships, Play and Leisure Time, Coping Skills, Composite.

Administration: Individual.

Price Data, 2002: $54.95 per complete kit; $24.95 per 25 record forms; $199.95 for reporting software (Early Childhood Assessment ASSIST).

Foreign Language Edition: Spanish edition available.

Time: (15–25) minutes.

Comments: Administered as a structured oral interview; interviewee should be the person with the most knowledge of the child's social and emotional functioning (e.g., parent, grandparent, legal guardian).

Authors: Sara S. Sparrow, David A. Balla, and Dominic V. Cicchetti.

Publisher: American Guidance Service, Inc.

Cross References: For reviews by Joseph C. Kush and Donald Lee Stovall, see 14:408.

[2654]
A Violence Scale.

Purpose: Designed to measure attitudes toward violence.

Population: Adolescents and adults.

Publication Date: 1973.

Scores: Total score only.

Administration: Group.

Manual: No manual.

Price Data, 2002: $1 per scale.

Time: [10] minutes.

Comments: Supplementary article available.

Author: Panos D. Bardis.

Publisher: Donna Bardis.

Cross References: See 8:704 (1 reference).

[2655]
Visual Analog Mood Scales.

Purpose: Developed for screening for mood disorders and assessment of mood states.

Population: Ages 18 and over.

Publication Dates: 1996–1997.

Acronym: VAMS.

Scores: 8 scales: Afraid, Confused, Sad, Angry, Energetic, Tired, Happy, Tense.

Administration: Group or Individual.

Price Data: Available from publisher for introductory kit including 25 response booklets, professional manual (1997, 48 pages), and metric ruler.

Time: (1–5) minutes.

Comments: Self-administered or administered by examiner.

Author: Robert A. Stern.

Publisher: Psychological Assessment Resources, Inc.

[2656]
The Visual Aural Digit Span Test.

Purpose: Intended as a "standardized test of intersensory integration and short-term memory for school-age children."

Population: Ages 5-6 to 12.

Publication Date: 1977.

Acronym: VADS Test.

Scores, 11: Aural-Oral, Visual-Oral, Aural-Written, Visual-Written, Aural Input, Visual Input, Oral Expression, Written Expression, Intrasensory Integration, Intersensory Integration, Total. Subtests, 4: Aural-Oral, Visual-Oral, Aural-Written, Visual-Written.

Administration: Individual.

Price Data, 2002: $61 per examination kit including 1 package of stimulus cards, Directions for Administering, and 100 visual scoring forms); $34 per 100 visual scoring forms; $83 per manual (1977, 216 pages).

Time: [10–15] minutes.

Author: Elizabeth M. Koppitz.

Publisher: The Psychological Corporation.

Cross References: See T5:2816 (1 reference) and T4:2884 (1 reference); for reviews by H. Lee Swanson and Robert H. Zabel, see 9:1329 (2 references); see also T3:2560 (2 references).

[2657]
Visual Discrimination Test.

Purpose: Measures "ability to discriminate between like non-alphabetic forms."

Population: Ages 5–8.
Publication Date: 1975.
Scores: Total score only.
Administration: Individual.
Price Data, 2002: $19.50 per 100 score sheets; $16 per manual (8 pages); $82.50 per kit including 1 set of reusable stimulus cards, 25 score sheets, and manual.
Time: (5–7) minutes.
Authors: Joseph M. Wepman, Anne Morency, and Marva Seidl.
Publisher: Western Psychological Services.
Cross References: See T4:2885 (3 references); for reviews by Morton Bortner and Mildred H. Huebner, see 8:448.

[2658]
Visual Functioning Assessment Tool.

Purpose: "Assessment of a student's visual functioning in the educational setting."
Population: Visually impaired in grades preschool and over.
Publication Date: 1980.
Acronym: VFAT.
Scores: No scores.
Administration: Individual.
Price Data, 2001: $95 per complete kit; $38 per reproducible recording booklet; $65 per manual (123 pages).
Time: Administration time not reported.
Authors: Kathleen Byrnes Costello, Patricia Pinkney, and Wendy Scheffers.
Publisher: Stoelting Co.

[2659]
Visual Memory Test.

Purpose: Measures "ability to hold in immediate memory visually presented forms of a non-alphabetic nature."
Population: Ages 5–8.
Publication Date: 1975.
Scores: Total score only.
Administration: Individual.
Price Data, 2002: $19.50 per 100 score sheets; $16 per manual (8 pages); $87.50 per kit including 1 set of reusable stimulus cards, 25 score sheets, and manual.
Time: (5–7) minutes.
Authors: Joseph M. Wepman, Anne Morency, and Marva Seidl.
Publisher: Western Psychological Services.
Cross References: See T5:2819 (1 reference) and T4:2887 (1 reference).

[2660]
Visual Search and Attention Test.

Purpose: Constructed to assess "ability to scan accurately and [to] sustain attention on each of four different visual cancellation tasks."

Population: Ages 18 and over.
Publication Dates: 1987–1990.
Acronym: VSAT.
Scores, 3: Left, Right, Total.
Administration: Individual.
Price Data: Available from publisher for complete kit including 25 test booklets and manual (1990, 18 pages).
Time: 4(6) minutes.
Authors: Max R. Trenerry, Bruce Crosson, James DeBoe, and William R. Leber.
Publisher: Psychological Assessment Resources, Inc.
Cross References: See T5:2820 (1 reference); for reviews by Stephen R. Hooper and Wilfred G. Van Gorp, see 12:407.

[2661]
Visual Skills Appraisal.

Purpose: "Developed to assist teachers and other educators, who may not have specialized training in visual skills assessment, to identify visual inefficiencies that affect school performance."
Population: Grades K–4.
Publication Date: 1984.
Acronym: VSA.
Scores: 6 subtests: Pursuits, Scanning, Aligning, Locating, Eye-Hand Coordination, Fixation Unity.
Administration: Individual.
Price Data, 2002: $85 per complete kit including manual (112 pages), stimulus cards, 25 design completion forms, 25 red/green trail forms, 25 score sheets, and red/green glasses; $12 per stimulus cards; $12 per 25 design completion forms, 25 red/green trail forms, or 25 score sheets; $10 per red/green glasses; $27 per manual.
Time: (10–15) minutes.
Authors: Regina G. Richards and Gary S. Oppenheim in consultation with G. N. Getman.
Publisher: Academic Therapy Publications.
Cross References: See 11:456 (1 reference).

[2662]
Vocabulary Test: National Achievement Tests.

Purpose: Measures the student's vocabulary and judgment in the choice of effective words.
Population: Grades 3–8, 7–12.
Publication Dates: 1939–1957.
Scores: Total score only.
Administration: Group.
Price Data: Available from publisher.
Time: (15) minutes.
Authors: Robert K. Speer and Samuel Smith.
Publisher: Psychometric Affiliates.
Cross References: For a review by Clifford Woody, see 3:168.

[2663]
Vocational Adaptation Rating Scales.

Purpose: "To measure maladaptive behavior that is likely to occur in a vocational setting for a mentally retarded worker."

Population: Ages 13–50 (mentally retarded individuals).

Publication Date: 1980.

Acronym: VARS.

Scores: Frequency and Severity scores in 7 areas: Verbal Manners, Communication Skills, Attendance and Punctuality, Interpersonal Behavior, Respect for Property and Rules and Regulations, Grooming and Personal Hygiene, Total.

Administration: Group.

Price Data, 2002: $62.50 per complete kit; $29.95 per rating booklet and 25 profile forms; $35 per manual (31 pages).

Time: (30–40) minutes.

Authors: Robert G. Malgady, Peter R. Barcher, John Davis (test), and George Towner (test).

Publisher: Western Psychological Services.

Cross References: For a review by Michael Ryan, see 9:1334.

[2664]
Vocational Assessment and Curriculum Guide.

Purpose: "Designed to assess and identify skill deficits in terms of competitive employment expectations; to prescribe training goals designed to reduce identified deficits; to evaluate program effectiveness by reassessing the worker after training."

Population: Mentally retarded employees.

Publication Dates: 1982–1993.

Acronym: VACG.

Scores, 10: Attendance/Endurance, Independence, Production, Learning, Behavior, Communication Skills, Social Skills, Grooming/Eating, Reading/Writing, Math.

Administration: Group.

Price Data, 2002: $12 per complete kit including manual (5 pages), 10 test booklets, curriculum guides, and summary profile sheets; $8 per set of 10 extra forms.

Time: (15–20) minutes.

Authors: Frank R. Rusch, Richard P. Schutz, Dennis E. Mithaug, Jeffrey E. Stewart, and Deanna K. Mar.

Publisher: Exceptional Education.

Cross References: For reviews by Hinsdale Bernard and Gerald R. Schneck, see 13:356; see also T4:2898 (1 reference).

[2665]
Vocational Decision-Making Interview, Revised Edition.

Purpose: Designed to improve the vocational decision making of people with learning and other disabilities.

Population: People with learning and other disabilities, including vision impairments, limited academic skills, limited English-language proficiency, or with displaced workers and people in substance abuse programs.

Publication Dates: 1993–1999.

Acronym: VDMI.

Scores, 3: Decision-Making Readiness, Employment Readiness, Self-Appraisal.

Administration: Individual.

Price Data, 2001: $24.95 per 10 assessments; a Tips booklet included free with each 10 assessments; price information for administration manual available from publisher.

Time: (20–40) minutes.

Comments: Not self-administered or self-scored; six-panel foldout; consumable; no other components needed.

Authors: Thomas Czerlinsky, and Shirley K. Chandler.

Publisher: JIST Publishing, Inc.

Cross References: For reviews by Karen T. Carey and Donald W. Tiffany of an earlier version, see 14:409.

[2666]
Vocational Interest, Experience and Skill Assessment (VIESA), 2nd Canadian Edition.

Purpose: Designed to stimulate career exploration.

Population: Grades 8–10, 11–adults.

Publication Dates: 1985–1992.

Acronym: VIESA, 2nd Canadian Edition.

Scores: Scores for Interests, Skills, and Experiences in 4 areas: People, Data, Things, Ideas.

Administration: Group or individual.

Levels, 2: 1, 2.

Price Data, 2001: $55 per 25 guide books and job family charts (specify level); $28.60 per examination kit level 1 & 2; $28.60 per user's handbook.

Time: (40-45) minutes.

Comments: Self-scored inventory of career-related interests, experiences, skills and values, with supporting materials for counselors; adapted from VIESA, U.S. Edition.

Author: ACT Career Planning Services.

Publisher: Nelson Thomson Learning [Canada].

Cross References: For reviews by David J. Bateson and Brenda H. Loyd; see 12:409; for information for VIESA, 2nd Edition, see 9:1338; for a review by Charles J. Krauskopf of an earlier edition, see 8:1025.

[2667]
Vocational Interest Inventory and Exploration Survey (Voc-Ties).

Purpose: Designed to "assess a student's interest in school based training programs" and provide "information about the training area."

Population: Vocational education students.
Publication Dates: 1991–2000.
Scores: 15 vocational training interest areas: Auto Mechanics, Business and Office, Construction, Cosmetology, Drafting, Electromechanics, Electronics, Family and Consumer Science, Food Service, Graphic Arts, Health Services, Horticulture/Agriculture, Marketing, Metals, Technology Education, Home Economics, Technology Education.
Administration: Individual or group.
Price Data, 2002: $595 per media kit including guide, video cassette, software, and answer sheets; $195 per single station version; $495 per multi-station version; $995 per Network version.
Time: (15-20) minutes.
Authors: Nancy L. Scott and Charles Gilbreath.
Publisher: Piney Mountain Press, Inc.
Cross References: For reviews by Larry Cochran and Kevin R. Murphy of an earlier edition, see 12:408.

[2668]
Vocational Interest Inventory—Revised.

Purpose: "Measures the relative strength of an individual's interest in eight occupational areas."
Population: High school juniors and seniors.
Publication Dates: 1981–1993.
Acronym: VII-R.
Scores, 8: Service, Business Contact, Organization, Technical, Outdoor, Science, General Culture, Arts and Entertainment.
Administration: Group.
Price Data, 2002: $69.50 per complete kit including manual (1993, 63 pages), 4 test reports and mail-in answer sheets; $40 per manual; $10.90 (or less) per mail-in answer sheet and test report; $160 or less per VII-R disk (IBM; 25 uses); $15 per 100 answer sheets for use with VII-R disk.
Time: (20–25) minutes.
Comments: Based on Ann Roe's occupational classifications.
Author: Patricia W. Lunneborg.
Publisher: Western Psychological Services.
Cross References: For reviews by David O. Herman and Joseph G. Law, Jr., see 13:357 (2 references); for reviews by Jo-Ida Hansen and Richard W. Johnson of an earlier edition, see 9:1339 (2 references).

[2669]
Vocational Interest Survey for Australia.

Purpose: Designed to "assist Australians facing career decisions by providing an assessment of their vocational interests."
Population: Job applicants.
Publication Dates: 1989–1995.
Acronym: VISA.

Scores, 8: Caring, Culture, Service, Managing, Clerical, Science, Practical, Environmental.
Administration: Group or individual.
Price Data: Available from publisher.
Time: (5–15) minutes.
Author: Robert Pryor.
Publisher: The Psychological Corporation [Australia].

[2670]
Vocational Opinion Index.

Purpose: Constructed to measure "an individual's attitudes, perceptions and motivations that impact on his/her ability to get and/or hold a job."
Population: Disadvantaged trainees in vocational skills programs.
Publication Dates: 1973–1976.
Acronym: VOI.
Scores, 13: Attractions to Work (Overall, Benefits to Children, Benefits to Worker, Better Life Style, Independence), Losses Associated with Work (Overall, Personal Freedom, Time for Family), Barriers to Employment (Medical, Child Care and Family, New Situation and People, Ability to Get and Hold a Job, Transportation).
Administration: Group.
Forms, 2: A, B.
Price Data: Available from publisher.
Foreign Language Edition: Spanish edition available.
Time: (20–40) minutes.
Author: Associates for Research in Behavior, Inc.
Publisher: ARBOR, Inc.

[2671]
Vocational Preference Inventory, 1985 Edition.

Purpose: "To assess personality … also useful for assessing vocational interests."
Population: High school and college and adults.
Publication Dates: 1953–1985.
Acronym: VPI.
Scores: 11 scales: Realistic, Investigative, Social, Conventional, Enterprising, Artistic, Self-Control, Masculinity-Femininity, Status, Infrequency, Acquiescence.
Administration: Individual or group.
Price Data: Available from publisher for complete kit including 50 test booklet/answer sheet/profile combinations, and manual (1985, 36 pages); price information for computer version also available from publisher.
Time: (15–30) minutes.
Author: John L. Holland.
Publisher: Psychological Assessment Resources, Inc.
Cross References: See T5:2835 (28 references) and T4:2910 (9 references); for reviews by John W.

Shepard and Nicholas A. Vacc, see 10:382 (17 references); for reviews by James B. Rounds and Nicholas A. Vacc and James Pickering of an earlier edition, see 9:1342 (19 references); see also T3:2581 (45 references); for an excerpted review by W. Bruce Walsh of an earlier edition, see 8:1028 (175 references); see also T2:1430 (48 references); for reviews by Joseph A. Johnston and Paul R. Lohnes, see 7:157 (39 references); see also P:283 (31 references); for reviews by Robert L. French and H. Bradley Sagen of an earlier edition, see 6:115 (13 references).

[2672]
Voc-Tech Quick Screener.

Purpose: Designed to identify job interests.
Population: Non-college bound high school students and adults.
Publication Dates: 1984–1990.
Acronym: VTQS.
Scores, 14: Administrative Support/Clerical, Agriculture/Animals and Forestry, Construction Trades, Design/Graphics and Communication, Food/Beverage Services, Health Services, Health Technicians, Industrial Production Trades, Marketing/Sales, Mechanical/Craftsmanship Trades, Personal Services, Protective Services, Science/Engineering Technicians, Transportation/Equipment Operators.
Administration: Group.
Price Data: Available from publisher.
Time: (20–25) minutes.
Authors: Robert Kauk and Robert Robinett.
Publisher: CFKR Career Materials [No reply from publisher; status unknown].
Cross References: For reviews by Albert M. Bugaj and Del Eberhardt, see 12:411.

[2673]
A Voice Assessment Protocol for Children and Adults.

Purpose: "Assesses five parameters of the voice: pitch, loudness, quality, breath features, and rate/rhythm."
Population: Children and adults.
Publication Date: 1987.
Scores: 5 assessments: Pitch, Loudness, Quality, Breath Features, Rate/Rhythm.
Administration: Individual.
Price Data, 2001: $59 per complete kit including 25 protocols, audiocassette, and manual (24 pages); $24 per 25 protocols; $14 per audiocassette; $24 per manual.
Time: Administration time not reported.
Author: Rebekah H. Pindzola.
Publisher: PRO-ED.
Cross References: See T5:2837 (1 reference); for a review by Maynard D. Filter, see 11:459.

[2674]
Vulpe Assessment Battery—Revised.

Purpose: Designed as "a comprehensive, process-oriented, criterion-referenced assessment that emphasizes children's functional abilities."
Population: Children functioning between full term birth to six years of age.
Publication Date: 1994.
Acronym: VAB-R.
Scores: 8 scales: Basic Senses and Functions, Gross Motor, Fine Motor, Language, Cognitive Processes and Specific Concepts, Adaptive Behaviors, Activities of Daily Living, Environmental Assessment.
Administration: Individual or group.
Price Data, 2002: $109 per complete kit including manual (1994, 480 pages) and 50 record sheets; $21 per 50 record sheets.
Time: Administration time not reported.
Comments: Ratings by person familiar with the child.
Author: Shirley German Vulpe.
Publisher: Slosson Educational Publications, Inc.
Cross References: For reviews by Theresa Graham and Diane J. Sawyer, see 14:411.

[2675]
Wagner Enneagram Personality Style Scales.

Purpose: Designed "to measure the nine personality styles described by Enneagram."
Population: Ages 15–85.
Publication Date: 1999.
Acronym: WEKPSS.
Scores: 9 scales: The Good Person, The Loving Person, The Effective Person, The Original Person, The Wise Person, The Loyal Person, The Joyful Person, The Powerful Person, The Peaceful Person.
Administration: Group or individual.
Price Data, 2002: $145 per kit including 25 autoscore forms, manual (114 pages), 100 glossary sheets, 100 brief guides to WEPSS results, 2-use disk for on-site computer scoring and interpretation and 2 PC answer sheets; $49.50 per 25 answer forms; $52.50 per manual; $15 per glossary sheet; $15 per brief guide to WEPSS results; $15 per mail-in answer form; $2e0 per 25-use PC scoring disk; $15 per 100 PC answer sheets; $11 per FAX service.
Time: (20–40) minutes.
Comments: Paper-and-pencil or computer administration available.
Author: Jerome P. Wagner.
Publisher: Western Psychological Services.

[2676]
WAIS-R NI.

Purpose: Constructed as a "process approach to neuropsychological assessment of cognitive functions."

Population: Ages 16–74.
Publication Date: 1991.
Scores, 14: Verbal (Information, Comprehension, Arithmetic, Similarities, Digit Span, Vocabulary, Total), Performance (Digit Symbol, Picture Completion, Block Design, Picture Arrangement, Object Assembly, Total), Total.
Administration: Individual.
Price Data, 2002: $541 per complete kit including manual (153 pages), stimulus booklet, sentence arrangement booklet, 25 response booklets, 25 record forms, 3 puzzles/boxes, spatial span board, object assembly layout shield, and 3 Koh's blocks; $1,155 per combination kit including WAIS-R NI complete kit, WAIS-R complete set and attaché case; $31 per 25 digit symbol response booklets; $110 per 25 record forms.
Time: Administration time varies by number of supplemental subtests administered.
Comments: It is necessary to have the Wechsler Adult Intelligence Scale—Revised (WAIS-R; T4:2937) complete set in order to administer WAIS-R NI.
Authors: Edith Kaplan, Deborah Fein, Robin Morris, and Dean C. Delis.
Publisher: The Psychological Corporation.
Cross References: For reviews by Keith Hattrup and David C. S. Richard, see 14:412.

[2677]
Waksman Social Skills Rating Scale.

Purpose: "Developed to assist psychologists, educators, and other clinicians to identify specific and clinically important social skill deficits in children and adolescents."
Population: Grades K-12.
Publication Dates: 1983-1992.
Acronym: WSSRS.
Scores, 3: Aggressive, Passive, Total.
Administration: Individual.
Price Data, 2001: $45 per complete kit including 50 each of male and female forms, and manual (1992, 10 pages); 420 per 25 male or female forms.
Time: Administration time not reported.
Author: Steven A. Waksman.
Publisher: Enrichment Press
Cross References: See T5:2841 (1 reference) and T4:2915 (2 references); for reviews by Harold R. Keller and Ellen McGinnis, see 10:383.

[2678]
Walden Structured Analysis and Design Concepts Proficiency Test.

Purpose: "Evaluates candidate's knowledge of structured analysis and design methodology, as well as commonly used tools and techniques."
Population: Candidates for EDP systems analysts/designers.

Publication Date: 1983.
Scores: Total Score, Narrative Evaluation, Ranking, Recommendation.
Administration: Group.
Price Data, 2001: $140 per candidate.
Time: (45) minutes.
Comments: Scored by publisher; must be proctored; test previously listed as Wolfe-Winrow Structured Analysis and Design Concepts Proficiency Test.
Author: Bruce A. Winrow.
Publisher: Walden Personnel Performance, Inc. [Canada].
Cross References: For reviews by David O. Anderson and Cynthia Ann Druva-Roush, see 11:474.

[2679]
Walker Problem Behavior Identification Checklist.

Purpose: Tool to assist the elementary teacher in "identifying children with behavior problems who should be referred for further evaluation."
Population: Preschool to grade 6.
Publication Dates: 1970–1983.
Acronym: WPBIC.
Scores, 6: Acting Out, Withdrawal, Distractability, Disturbed Peer Relations, Immaturity, Total.
Administration: Group.
Forms, 2: Male, Female.
Price Data, 2002: $78 per complete kit including 200 checklists and profiles (100 each of Male and Female Forms) and manual (1983, 19 pages); $29.50 or less per 100 pads of checklist and profile (specify Male or Female form); $26.50 per manual.
Time: (2–5) minutes.
Author: Hill M. Walker.
Publisher: Western Psychological Services.
Cross References: See T5:2848 (3 references) and T4:2923 (18 references); for a review by F. Charles Mace, see 9:1345 (5 references); see also T3:2585 (17 references) and 7:159 (1 reference).

[2680]
W-APT Programming Aptitude Test.

Purpose: To evaluate the aptitude and potential for computer programming work at all levels of experience.
Population: Programmers and general population.
Publication Date: 1984.
Acronym: W-APT.
Scores: Total score only.
Administration: Group.
Price Data, 2001: $190 per candidate.
Time: (60) minutes.
Comments: Detailed report provided on each candidate.
Author: Jack M. Wolfe.

Publisher: Rose Wolfe Family Partnership LLP [Canada].

[2681]
Ward Atmosphere Scale (Third Edition).

Purpose: Designed to evaluate treatment program social climates in health care settings.
Population: Patients and staff members.
Publication Dates: 1974–1996.
Acronym: WAS.
Scores, 10: Involvement, Support, Spontaneity, Autonomy, Practical Orientation, Personal Problems Orientation, Anger and Aggression, Order and Organization, Program Clarity, Staff Control.
Administration: Group.
Forms, 3: Real, Ideal, Expectations.
Price Data, 2001: $125 per permission set including sampler set plus permission to reproduce up to 200 copies of the instrument; $25 per sampler set including manual (1996, 73 pages), questionnaire/answer sheet, and scoring directions.
Foreign Language Editions: Translations available in Danish, Dutch, Finnish, French, German, Hebrew, Italian, Norwegian, Spanish, and Swedish.
Time: Administration time not reported.
Comments: Used to describe, plan for, and monitor change or improvements in treatment programs by examining patient and staff social climate perceptions.
Author: Rudolph H. Moos.
Publisher: Mind Garden, Inc.
Cross References: For reviews by Ronald A. Berk and Mary Anne Bunda, see 14:413; see also T5:2850 (3 references), T4:2925 (17 references), and T3:2587 (16 references); for a review by Earl S. Taulbee of an earlier edition, see 8:706 (31 references). For a review of the Social Climate Scales, see 8:681.

[2682]
Warehouse/Plant Worker Staff Selector.

Purpose: To assess the intellectual skills needed for the position of plant worker.
Population: Applicants for plant work.
Publication Date: 1991.
Acronym: PLANT.
Scores: Total Score, Narrative Evaluation, Ranking, Recommendation.
Administration: Group.
Price Data, 2001: $95 per candidate; quantity discounts available.
Time: (60) minutes.
Comments: Scored by publisher.
Author: Walden Personnel Performance, Inc.
Publisher: Walden Personnel Performance, Inc. [Canada].

[2683]
Washer Visual Acuity Screening Technique.

Purpose: To assess visual acuity for near and far vision.
Population: Mental ages 2–6 and over.
Publication Date: 1984.
Acronym: WVAST.
Scores, 6: Farpoint (Both Eyes, Right Eye, Left Eye), Nearpoint (Both Eyes, Right Eye, Left Eye).
Administration: Individual.
Price Data, 2002: $87.85 per starter set including manual (15 pages), 20 screening records, symbol cards, stimulus cards, and set of equipment; $14.70 per additional manual; $11.70 per 20 screening records; $76.90 per set of equipment; $22 per sample set.
Time: Administration time not reported.
Comments: Criterion-referenced scores.
Author: Rhonda Wiczer Washer.
Publisher: Scholastic Testing Service, Inc.

[2684]
The Watkins-Farnum Performance Scale: A Standardized Achievement Test for All Band Instruments.

Purpose: Designed to measure performance and progress on a musical instrument.
Population: Music students.
Publication Dates: 1942–1962.
Scores: Total score only.
Administration: Individual.
Forms, 2: A, B.
Price Data: Available from publisher.
Time: [20-30] minutes.
Authors: John G. Watkins and Stephen E. Farnum.
Publisher: Hal Leonard Publishing Corporation.
Cross References: See T2:216 (4 references); for a review by Herbert D. Wing, see 5:253 (2 references); for related reviews, see 3:1228 (4 excerpts).

[2685]
Watson-Barker Listening Test.

Purpose: To measure adult interpersonal listening abilities.
Population: Adults in business, professions, and college.
Publication Dates: 1984–1994.
Scores, 6: Evaluating Message Content, Understanding Meaning in Conversations, Understanding and Remembering Information in Lectures, Evaluating Emotional Meanings in Messages, Following Instructions and Directions, Total.
Administration: Group.
Forms, 3: A (pre-test), B (post-test), Short Form (for demonstration and listening awareness).
Price Data: Available from publisher.
Time: (40) minutes.

Comments: Administered by video tape.
Authors: Kittie W. Watson and Larry L. Barker with Charles Roberts and Patrice Johnson.
Publisher: Jossey-Bass, A Wiley Company.
Cross References: For a review by James R. Clopton, see 10:384.

[2686]
Watson-Barker Listening Test—High School Version.

Purpose: "Designed to assess overall listening ability."
Population: Grades 7–12.
Publication Dates: 1985–1991.
Acronym: HS-WBLT.
Scores, 6: Evaluating Message Content, Understanding Meaning in Conversations, Understanding and Remembering Information in Lectures, Evaluating Emotional Meanings in Messages, Following Instructions and Directions, Total.
Administration: Group.
Forms, 2: A (pre-test) and B (post-test).
Price Data: Price information available from publisher for Form A and B package (including video tape, facilitator's guide [1991, 42 pages], and 20 answer sheets per group [A & B]).
Time: 40 minutes.
Comments: May be self-scored for awareness training; VHS video tape player and 17-inch (minimum size) color TV monitor needed; high school version of Watson-Barker Listening Test (2685).
Authors: Kittie W. Watson, Larry L. Barker, and Charles V. Roberts.
Publisher: SPECTRA Incorporated, Publishers.
Cross References: For reviews by Michael R. Harwell and by Carol Kehr Tittle and Deborah Hecht, see 11:461; for reviews by James R. Clopton and Joseph P. Stokes of the adult version, see 10:384.

[2687]
Watson-Glaser Critical Thinking Appraisal.

Purpose: Constructed to assess critical thinking abilities related to reading comprehension.
Population: Grades 9–12 and college and adults.
Publication Dates: 1942–1980.
Acronym: WGCTA.
Scores, 6: Inference, Recognition of Assumptions, Deduction, Interpretation, Evaluation of Arguments, Total.
Administration: Group or individual.
Forms, 2: A, B.
Price Data, 2002: $119 per 25 test booklets including manual (1980, 17 pages) (select form); $25.50 per set of hand scoring keys (select form); $10 per class record; $34 per manual; $55 per examination kit including Form A and B test booklets, answer document, and manual.

Time: (40–60) minutes.
Comments: Revision of Form YM and ZM.
Authors: Goodwin Watson and Edward M. Glaser.
Publisher: The Psychological Corporation.
Cross References: See T5:2856 (13 references) and T4:2933 (5 references); for reviews by Allen Berger and Gerald C. Helmstadter, see 9:1347 (4 references); see also T3:2594 (15 references), 8:822 (49 references), and T2:1775 (35 references); for excerpted reviews by John O. Crites and G. C. Helmstadtler, see 7:783 (74 references); see also 6:867 (24 references); ffor reviews by Walker H. Hill and Carl I. Hovland of an earlier edition, see 5:700 (8 references); for a review by Robert H. Thouless and an excerpted review by Harold P. Fawcett, see 3:544 (3 references).

[2688]
Watson-Glaser Critical Thinking Appraisal, Form S.

Purpose: Designed to help "select employees for any job requiring careful, analytical thinking."
Population: Adults with at least a ninth grade education.
Publication Date: 1994.
Acronym: WGCTA-S.
Scores: Composite score derived from following content areas: Inference, Recognition of Assumptions, Deduction, Interpretation, Evaluation of Arguments.
Administration: Group or individual.
Price Data, 2002: $55 per examination kit including Form S test booklet, answer document, and manual (87 pages); $97 per 25 test booklets including directions for administering; $36.50 per 25 scannable answer documents; $25.50 per key for hand scoring scannable answer documents; $47.50 per manual; $6.50 per Directions for Administering.
Time: (30–45) minutes.
Comments: Developed as a shorter version of the WGCTA Form A; Form S norms are developed from norms of original WGCTA (2687).
Authors: Goodwin B. Watson and Edward M. Glaser.
Publisher: The Psychological Corporation.
Cross References: See T5:2857 (1 reference); for reviews by Kurt F. Geisinger and Stephen H. Ivens, see 13:358. For information on the original edition of the WGCTA, see T4:2933; for reviews by Allen Berger and Gerald C. Helmstadter, see 9:1347 (4 references); see also T3:2594 (15 references), 8:822 (49 references), and T2:1775 (35 references); for excerpted reviews by John O. Crites and G. C. Helmstadter, see 7:783 (74 references); see also 6:867 (24 references); for reviews by Walker H. Hill and Carl I. Hovland of an earlier edition, see 5:700 (8 references); for a review by Robert H. Thouless and an excerpted review by Harold P. Fawcett, see 3:544 (3 references).

[2689]
Ways of Coping Questionnaire, Research Edition.

Purpose: "To identify the thoughts and actions an individual has used to cope with a specific stressful encounter."

Population: Adults.

Publication Date: 1988.

Scores, 8: Confrontive Coping, Distancing, Self-Controlling, Seeking Social Support, Accepting Responsibility, Escape-Avoidance, Planful Problem-Solving, Positive Reappraisal.

Administration: Group.

Price Data: Available from publisher.

Time: (10–15) minutes.

Comments: Self-administered.

Authors: Susan Folkman and Richard S. Lazarus.

Publisher: Mind Garden, Inc.

Cross References: See T5:2858 (129 references) and T4:2936 (25 references); for reviews by Judith C. Conger and Kathryn D. Hess, see 11:462 (16 references).

[2690]
Wechsler Abbreviated Scale of Intelligence.

Purpose: Designed as a "short and reliable measure of intelligence."

Population: Ages 6–89.

Publication Date: 1999.

Acronym: WASI.

Administration: Individual.

Price Data, 2002: $198 per complete kit; $36 per 25 record forms; $133 per 100 record forms; $92 per stimulus book; $72 per manual (238 pages).

Author: The Psychological Corporation.

Publisher: The Psychological Corporation.

a) TWO SUBTEST FORM.

Scores, 3: Verbal (Vocabulary), Performance (Matrix Reasoning), Full Scale IQ.

Time: (15) minutes.

b) FOUR SUBTEST FORM.

Scores, 7: Verbal (Vocabulary, Similarities), Performance (Block Design, Matrix Reasoning), Verbal IQ, Performance IQ, Full Scale IQ.

Time: (30) minutes.

Cross References: For reviews by Timothy Z. Keith and by Cederick O. Lindskog and Janet V. Smith, see 14:414.

[2691]
Wechsler Adult Intelligence Scale—Third Edition.

Purpose: Designed to assess the intellectual ability of adults.

Population: Ages 16–89.

Publication Dates: 1939–1997.

Acronym: WAIS-III.

Scores, 22: Verbal (Vocabulary, Similarities, Arithmetic, Digit Span, Information, Comprehension, Letter-Number Sequencing, Total), Performance (Picture Completion, Digit Symbol-Coding, Block Design, Matrix Reasoning, Picture Arrangement, Symbol Search, Object Assembly, Mazes, Total), Verbal Comprehension Index, Perceptual Organization Index, Working Memory Index, Processing Speed Index, Total.

Administration: Individual.

Price Data, 2002: $775 per complete set in attaché case; $725 per complete set in box; $43 per 25 response books; $323 per 100 response books; $85 per 25 response forms; $323 per 100 response forms; $88 per administration and scoring manual (1997, 217 pages); $50 per technical manual (1997, 370 pages).

Time: (60–90) minutes.

Author: David Wechsler.

Publisher: The Psychological Corporation.

Cross References: For reviews by Allen K. Hess and Bruce G. Rogers, see 14:415; see also T5:2860 (1422 references) and T4:2937 (1131 references); for reviews by Alan S. Kaufman and Joseph D. Matarazzo of the revised edition, see 9:1348 (291 references); see also T3:2598 (576 references), 8:230 (351 references), and T2:529 (178 references); for reviews by Alvin G. Burstein and Howard B. Lyman of the original edition, see 7:429 (538 references); see also 6:538 (180 references); for reviews by Nancy Bayley and Wilson H. Guertin, see 5:414 (42 references).

[2692]
Wechsler Individual Achievement Test—Second Edition.

Purpose: "A ... measurement tool useful for achievement skills assessment, learning disability diagnosis, special education placement, curriculum planning, and clinical appraisal for preschool children through adults."

Population: Ages 4–85 years.

Publication Dates: 1992–2001.

Acronym: WIAT-II.

Scores, 21: 9 subtests (Word Reading, Pseudoword Decoding, Reading Comprehension, Math Reasoning, Numerical Operations, Listening Comprehension, Oral Expression, Spelling, Written Expression), 4 composite scores (Reading Composite, Written Language Composite, Mathematics Composite, Oral Language Composite), Total Composite, 7 supplemental scores: Reading (Reading Comprehension, Target Words, Reading Speed), Written Expression (Alphabet Writing, Word Fluency, Word Count), Oral Expression (Word Fluency).

Administration: Individual.

Price Data, 2002: $321 per complete kit including stimulus book 1, stimulus book 2, 25 record forms, 25 response booklets, examiner's manual (2001, 193 pages), Scoring and Normative supplement for Grades PreK–12, Scoring and Normative Supplement for College Students and Adults, word cards, audiotape, and bag; $59 per 25 combination record forms/ response booklets; $86 per stimulus book 1 or 2; $11 per word card, pseudoword card, and audiotape; $96 per examiner's manual, Scoring and Normative Supplement for Grades PreK–12, and Scoring and Normative Supplement for College Students and Adults; $50 per administration training video (CD-ROM Windows or Videotape); $125 per WIAT-II Scoring Assistant (CD-ROM Windows); $150 per WISC-III/WIAT-II Scoring Assistant (CD-ROM Windows or Macintosh); $150 per WAIS-III/WMS-III/WIAT-11 Scoring Assistant (CD-ROM Windows); $399 per WIAT-II Kit with WIAT-II Scoring Assistant (CD-ROM Windows); $449 per WIAT-II Kit with WISC-III/WIAT-II Scoring Assistant (CD-ROM Windows); $449 per WIAT-II Kit with WAIS-III/WMS-III/WIAT-II Scoring Assistant (CD-ROM Windows); $398 per WISC-III/WIAT-II Writer or WAIS-III/WMS-III/ WIAT-II Writer (CD-ROM Windows); all software also available in 3.5-inch diskettes.

Time: Comprehensive Battery: (45) minutes for Grades PreK–K; (90) minutes for Grades 1–6; (90–120) minutes for Grades 7–16.

Comments: Subtests may be given individually; includes norms for 2-year and 4-year college students; standardized with Wechsler Intelligence Scale for Children-III (2694), Wechsler Preschool and Primary Scale of Intelligence—Revised (2696), Wechsler Adult Intelligence Scale—Third Edition (2691), and the Process Assessment of the Learner: Test Battery for Reading and Writing (1986); complete battery is composed of fewer tests for Grades PreK and K; manual or computer scoring; 3 software scoring programs available; WIAT-II Scoring Assistant software generates standard scores and error analyses using raw scores; WISC-III/WIAT-II Scoring Assistant (revision of the Scoring Assistant for the Wechsler Scales) includes all capabilities of WIAT-II Scoring Assistant and computes ability-achievement discrepancy analysis using the WISC-III; WAIS-III/WMS-III/WIAT-II Scoring Assistant software (revision of the Scoring Assistant for the Wechsler Scales for Adults) includes all capabilities of WIAT-II Scoring Assistant, computes ability-achievement discrepancy analysis using the WAIS-III, and generates reports; WISC-III/WIAT-II Writer software (revision of the WISC-III Writer) summarizes results, displays results in tabular and graphic formats, generates interpretive report; WAIS-III/WMS-III/WIAT-II Writer software scores and interprets results; system requirements for all software:

Windows 95/98/2000/Me/NT 4.0 Workstation, 100 MHz Pentium processor, 32 MB RAM, 2 MB video card capable of 800 x 600 resolution (256 colors), 20 MB free hard disk space, 3.5-inch floppy drive, 50 MB temporary disk space; WIAT-II PDA Pocket Norms software available, system requirements Palm OS Personal Digital Assistant.

Author: The Psychological Corporation.
Publisher: The Psychological Corporation.
Cross References: See T5:2861 (4 references); for reviews by Terry Ackerman and Steven Ferrara of a previous edition, see 13:359 (17 references).

[2693]
Wechsler Individual Achievement Test—Second Edition Abbreviated.

Purpose: "Identif[ies] and track[s] basic academic skills and intervention needs in children and adults."
Population: Grades K–16; ages 6–85 years.
Publication Date: 2001.
Acronym: WIAT-II-A.
Scores, 4: 3 subtests (Word Reading, Numerical Operations, Spelling), Composite Score.
Administration: Individual.
Price Data, 2002: $130 per test kit including manual (206 pages), combination record forms/response booklets, 2 word cards, and bag; $35 per manual; $48 per 25 combination record forms/response booklets; $15 per set of 2 word cards.
Time: (10–20) minutes.
Comments: Subtests are taken from the WIAT-II (2692); can be used with Wechsler Abbreviated Scale of Intelligence (2690) for a brief cognitive and achievement battery.
Author: The Psychological Corporation.
Publisher: The Psychological Corporation.

[2694]
Wechsler Intelligence Scale for Children— Third Edition.

Purpose: A "measure of a child's intellectual ability."
Population: Ages 6-0 to 16-11.
Publication Dates: 1971–1991.
Acronym: WISC-III.
Scores, 13 to 16: Verbal (Information, Similarities, Arithmetic, Vocabulary, Comprehension, Digit Span [optional], Total); Performance (Picture Completion, Coding, Picture Arrangement, Block Design, Object Assembly, Symbol Search [optional], Mazes [optional], Total), Total.
Administration: Individual.
Price Data, 2002: $700 per complete box kit; $750 per complete kit with attaché or soft-sided case; $84 per manual (1991, 294 pages); $107 per stimulus book; $44 per 25 mazes response booklets; $158 per

100 mazes response booklets; $44 per 25 symbol search response booklets; $$158 per 100 symbol search response booklets; $79 per 25 record forms; $300 per 100 record forms; $235 per 6 object assembly puzzles.
Time: Core subtests: 50–70 minutes; Supplemental: 10–15 minutes.
Author: David Wechsler.
Publisher: The Psychological Corporation.
Cross References: See T5:2862 (740 references); for reviews by Jeffrey P. Braden and Jonathan Sandoval, see 12:412 (409 references); see also T4:2939 (911 references); for reviews by Morton Bortner, Douglas K. Detterman, and by Joseph C. Witt and Frank Gresham of an earlier edition, see 9:1351 (299 references); see also T3:2602 (645 references); for reviews by David Freides and Randolph H. Whitworth, and excerpted reviews by Carol Kehr Tittle and Joseph Petrosko, see 8:232 (548 references); see also T2:533 (230 references); for reviews by David Freides and R. T. Osborne of the original edition, see 7:431 (518 references); for a review by Alvin G. Burnstein, see 6:540 (155 references); for reviews by Elizabeth D. Fraser, Gerald R. Patterson, and Albert I. Rabin, see 5:416 (111 references); for reviews by James M. Anderson, Harold A. Delp, and Boyd R. McCandless, and an excerpted review by Laurance F. Shaffer, see 4:363 (22 references).

[2695]
Weschler Memory Scale III.

Purpose: Designed to "provide a detailed assessment of clinically relevant aspects of memory functioning" using both auditory and visual stimulus.
Population: Ages 16–89 years.
Publication Dates: 1945–1997.
Acronym: WMS-III.
Scores, 22: Six primary subtests yielding 10 scores (Logical Memory I, Logical Memory II, Verbal Paired Associates I, Verbal Paired Associates II, Letter-Numbering Sequencing, Faces I, Faces II, Family Pictures I, Family Pictures II, Spatial Span); five Optional Subtests yielding 6 scores (Information and Orientation, Word Lists I, Word Lists II, Mental Control, Visual Reproduction I, Visual Reproduction II); Five Supplemental Scores (Recall Total, Recognition Total, Copy Total, Discrimination Total, Percent Retention).
Administration: Individual.
Price Data, 2002: $435 per complete kit including administration/norms manual, technical manual, 25 record forms, 25 visual reproduction response booklets, stimulus booklet 1, stimulus booklet 2, and spatial span board, packaged in a portfolio case; $45 per 25 record forms; $26 per 25 visual reproduction response booklets; $77 per administration/norms manual; $50 per technical manual; $68 per portfolio; $54 per video;

$150 per scoring assistant software (CD-ROM windows).
Time: (30–35) minutes for primary subtests.
Comments: "When used in conjunction with the WAIS-III, it is possible to compute ability-memory difference scores"; WAIS-III/WMS-III Writer interpretive report software available for use with IBM or compatible PC with at least 486 processor.
Author: David Wechsler.
Publisher: The Psychological Corporation.
Cross References: For reviews by Erik Carl D'Amato and Cecil R. Reynolds, see 14:416; see also T5:2863 (431 references) and T4:2940 (117 references); for reviews by E. Scott Huebner and Robert C. Reinehr of an earlier edition, see 11:465 (166 references); see also 9:1355 (49 references); T3:2607 (96 references); 8:250 (36 references), T2:592 (70 references), and 6:561 (9 references); for reviews by Ivan Norma Mensh and Joseph Newman of the original version, see 4:364 (6 references); for a review by Kate Levine Kogan, see 3:302 (3 references).

[2696]
Wechsler Preschool and Primary Scale of Intelligence—Revised.

Purpose: Developed "for assessing the intelligence of children."
Population: Ages 3–7.3 years.
Publication Dates: 1949–1989.
Acronym: WPPSI-R.
Scores, 13 to 15: Verbal (Information, Comprehension, Arithmetic, Vocabulary, Similarities, Sentences [optional], Total), Performance (Object Assembly, Geometric Design, Block Design, Mazes, Picture Completion, Animal Pegs [optional], Total), Total.
Administration: Individual.
Price Data, 2002: $53 per 25 maze test books; $18 per 50 geometric design sheets; $102 per set of 14 blocks; $56 per set of 28 animal house pegs; $131 per animal house board; $53 per 25 record forms; $185 per 100 record forms; $22 per object assembly shield; $88 per manual (1989, 239 pages).
Time: [75] minutes.
Author: David Wechsler.
Publisher: The Psychological Corporation.
Cross References: See T5:2864 (146 references) and T4:2941 (38 references); for reviews by Bruce A. Bracken and Jeffery P. Braden, see 11:466 (118 references); for a review by B. J. Freeman of an earlier edition, see 9:1356 (33 references); see also T3:2608 (280 references), 8:234 (84 references), and T2:538 (30 references); for reviews by Dorothy H. Eichorn and A. B. Silverstein, and excerpted reviews by C. H. Ammons and O. A. Oldridge (with E. E. Allison), see 7:434 (56 references).

[2697]
Weidner-Fensch Speech Screening Test.

Purpose: Designed "to be used in screening out children with speech difficulties from those who have normally developed speech."
Population: Grades 1–3.
Publication Date: No date.
Forms, 2: A, B.
Scores: Item scores only.
Administration: Individual.
Price Data, 2001: $4 per specimen set.
Time: (5–10) minutes.
Authors: William E. Weidner and Edwin A. Fensch.
Publisher: Psychometric Affiliates.

[2698]
Weinberg Depression Scale for Children and Adolescents.

Purpose: Designed to detect depression in children and adolescents.
Population: Children and adolescents with at least a 4th grade reading level.
Publication Dates: 1987–1998.
Acronym: WDSCA.
Scores: Total score only.
Administration: Individual.
Price Data, 2001: $98 per complete kit; $43 per examiner's manual (1998, 40 pages); $29 per 50 summary sheets; $29 per 50 student response sheets.
Time: (5) minutes.
Comments: Normed on children diagnosed with major depression, ages 7 to 18; a self-report measure; WDSCA items based in part on the DSM-IV criteria.
Authors: Warren A. Weinberg, Caryn R. Harper, and Graham J. Emslie.
Publisher: PRO-ED.
Cross References: For reviews by Sandra J. Carr and Radhika Krishnamurthy, see 14:417.

[2699]
Weiss Comprehensive Articulation Test.

Purpose: "For making a thorough diagnosis of articulation and its associated parameters."
Population: All ages.
Publication Dates: 1978–1980.
Acronym: WCAT.
Scores, 5: Articulation, Articulation Age, Intelligibility, Stimulability, Number of Misarticulations.
Administration: Individual.
Forms, 2: Nonreading Subjects, Reading Subjects.
Price Data, 2001: $98 per complete kit including picture cards, sentence card, 50 picture response forms, 50 sentence response forms, and manual (1980, 32 pages); $34 per 100 picture response forms; $34 per 100 sentence response forms.
Time: [20] minutes.

Author: Curtis E. Weiss.
Publisher: PRO-ED.
Cross References: See T5:2866 (5 references) and T4:2942 (2 references); for a review by Richard J. Schissel, see 9:1357.

[2700]
WeldTest—Form AC.

Purpose: "Measures knowledge and skills in welding areas."
Population: Welding job applicants.
Publication Dates: 1984–1998.
Scores: 7 areas: Print Reading; Welding/Cutting Torch and Arc Air Cutting; Welder Maintenance and Operation; Tools/Machines/Material and Equipment; Mobile Equipment and Rigging; Production Welding Calculations; Total.
Administration: Group.
Price Data, 1998: $12 per consumable self-scoring booklet; $24.95 per manual (1998, 16 pages).
Time: (60) minutes.
Comments: Self-scoring instrument.
Author: Roland T. Ramsay.
Publisher: Ramsay Corporation.
Cross References: For reviews by John Peter Hudson, Jr. and David C. Roberts, see 13:360.

[2701]
The Wellness Evaluation of Lifestyle.

Purpose: Designed as "an instrument for assessing and planning wellness lifestyles."
Population: Ages 18 and over.
Publication Date: 2001.
Acronym: WEL.
Scores, 20: Spirituality, Self-Regulation (Sense of Worth, Sense of Control, Realistic Beliefs, Emotional Responsiveness, Intellectual Stimulation, Sense of Humor, Nutrition, Exercise, Self-Care, Stress Management, Gender Identity, Culture Identity, Total), Work & Leisure (Work, Leisure), Friendship, Love, Perceived Wellness, Total Wellness.
Administration: Group.
Price Data, 2001: $25 per sampler set including one of each test component, question/answer sheet, manual (32 pages), and scoring directions; $125 per permission set including one copy of instrument and permission to make up to 200 copies.
Time: [20–30] minutes.
Authors: Jane E. Myers, Thomas J. Sweeney, and J. Melvin Witmer.
Publisher: Mind Garden, Inc.

[2702]
Welsh Figure Preference Test.

Purpose: A nonverbal approach to personality measurement and research incorporating the Barron-Welsh Art Scale.

Population: Ages 6 and over.
Publication Dates: 1959–1980.
Acronym: WFPT.
Scores, 27: Don't Like Total, Repeat, Conformance, Barron-Welsh Art Scale, Revised Art Scale, Male-Female, Neuropsychiatric, Children, Movement, 5 Sex-Symbol Scores, and 13 Figure-Structure Preference Scores.
Administration: Group or individual.
Price Data: Available from publisher.
Time: (50) minutes.
Comments: For research use only; self-administering.
Author: George S. Welsh.
Publisher: Mind Garden, Inc.
Cross References: See T5:2869 (1 reference) and T4:2945 (5 references); for a review by Julien Worland, see 9:1360 (1 reference); see also T3:2613 (4 references), T2:1437 (34 references), and P:287 (24 references); for a review by Harold Borko and an excerpted review by Gordon V. Anderson, see 6:197 (20 references); for information for Barron-Welsh Art Scale, see T3:243 (15 references).

[2703]
Wepman's Auditory Discrimination Test, Second Edition.

Purpose: Measures children's ability to hear spoken English accurately, specifically to "discriminate between commonly used phonemes in the English language."
Population: Ages 4-0 to 8-11.
Publication Dates: 1958–1987.
Acronym: ADT.
Scores: Total score yielding Qualitative score, Standard score, Percentile rank.
Administration: Individual.
Forms, 2: 1A, 2A.
Price Data, 2002: $89.50 per complete kit including 200 tests (100 each of Forms 1A and 2A) and manual (1987, 58 pages); $29.95 per 100 tests (specify form); $36.50 per manual.
Time: (15–20) minutes.
Authors: Joseph M. Wepman (test) and William M. Reynolds (manual).
Publisher: Western Psychological Services.
Cross References: See T5:2870 (5 references) and T4:2946 (1 reference); for a review by Mary Pannbacker and Grace Middleton, see 11:467 (5 references); see also T3:226 (31 references), 8:932 (74 references), and T2:2028 (82 references); for a review by Louis M. DiCarlo of the original edition, see 6:940 (2 references).

[2704]
Wesman Personnel Classification Test.

Purpose: Developed to measure verbal reasoning and numerical ability.

Population: Grades 10–12 and applicants and employees.
Publication Dates: 1946–1965.
Acronym: PCT.
Scores, 3: Verbal, Numerical, Total.
Administration: Group or individual.
Forms, 3: A, B, C.
Price Data, 2002: $71 per 25 test booklets including key (specify form) and manual (1965, 28 pages); $33 per examination kit including test booklet, record form, and manual; $259 per 100 test booklets including key and manual (specify form).
Time: 28 minutes.
Author: Alexander G. Wesman.
Publisher: The Psychological Corporation.
Cross References: See T5:2871 (4 references), T4:2947 (5 references), T3:2614 (4 references), and T2:480 (2 references); for a review by Arthur C. MacKinney, and an excerpted review by Jack C. Merwin, see 7:400 (7 references); see also 5:399 (8 references); for reviews by John C. Flanagan and Erwin K. Taylor, see 4:331 (3 references); for an excerpted review, see 3:253.

[2705]
The Wessex Revised Portage Language Checklist.

Purpose: Designed as a guide in the design of individualized teaching activities.
Population: Developmentally delayed and mentally handicapped children mental ages 0–1, 1–2, 2–3, 3–4.
Publication Date: 1983.
Scores: No scores.
Administration: Individual.
Levels, 4: 0–1, 1–2, 2–3, 3–4 in one booklet.
Manual: No manual.
Price Data: Available from publisher.
Authors: Mollie White and Kathy East.
Publisher: NFER-Nelson Publishing Co., Ltd. [England].
Cross References: For reviews by Kenneth L. Sheldon and Lawrence J. Turton, see 9:1361.

[2706]
Western Aphasia Battery.

Purpose: "To evaluate the main clinical aspects of language function" as well as nonverbal skills.
Population: Adolescents and adults with language disorders.
Publication Dates: 1980–1982.
Acronym: WAB.
Scores: 17 obtained subscores which form 7 major scores: Spontaneous Speech, Comprehension, Repetition, Naming, Reading and Writing, Praxis, Construction (optional), plus 2 derived scores: Aphasia Quotient, Cortical Quotient (optional).

Administration: Individual.
Price Data, 2002: $120.50 per complete kit including 25 test booklets, manual (1980, 3 pages), and stimulus cards; $28 per 25 test booklets; $94 per stimulus cards; $20 per manual; $10 each per Koh's blocks (each two-color block: four blocks are required for testing); $31 per 50 answer documents; $360 per Raven's test booklets.
Time: [60–70] minutes.
Comments: Other test materials (e.g., cup, comb, flower) must be supplied by examiner; a computerized record form (1993) is also available (hardware requirements—DOS-based PC/4.0 or higher, 640K RAM, one hard or floppy drive).
Author: Andrew Kertesz.
Publisher: The Psychological Corporation.
Cross References: See T5:2873 (74 references) and T4:2949 (33 references); for a review by Francis J. Pirozzolo, see 9:1362 (1 reference).

[2707]
The Western Personality Inventory.
Purpose: Identifies alcoholics and potential alcoholics and measures extent of alcohol addiction.
Population: Adults.
Publication Dates: 1963–1988.
Acronym: WPI.
Scores, 14: Anxiety, Depressive Fluctuations, Emotional Sensitivity, Resentfulness, Incompleteness, Aloneness, Interpersonal Relations, Total, Regularity of Drinking, Preference for Drinking over Other Activities, Lack of Controlled Drinking, Rationalization of Drinking, Excessive Emotionality, Total.
Administration: Individual or group.
Manual: No manual; use manuals for The Manson Evaluation and The Alcadd Test.
Price Data, 2002: $99.50 per complete kit including 5 AutoScore test forms, 2 prepaid mail-in answer sheets for computer scoring and interpretation, Manson Evaluation Manual, and Alcadd Manual; $32.50 per Manson Evaluation Manual or Alcadd Manual; $9.50 per mail-in answer sheet; $139.50 per IBM microcomputer disk (25 uses).
Time: Administration time not reported.
Comments: Combination of The Manson Evaluation (1500) and The Alcadd Test (136).
Author: Morse P. Manson.
Publisher: Western Psychological Services.

[2708]
Wharton Attitude Survey.
Purpose: A peer group evaluative tool to identify problems in the classroom.
Population: Grades 7–12.
Publication Date: 1978.

Scores: Ratings in 8 areas: Physical Surroundings, Materials, Subject, Teacher, Self, Other Students, Class Disrupters, Other Comments.
Administration: Group.
Price Data: Available from publisher.
Time: (10–15) minutes.
Author: Kenneth Wharton, Jr.
Publisher: Paul S. Amidon & Associates, Inc. [No reply from publisher; status unknown].

[2709]
What Do You Say?
Purpose: Designed as a self-assessment tool to identify communication style and relate it to two basic types of human interactions: parent-child (McGregor's Theory X) and adult-adult (Theory Y).
Population: Employees.
Publication Dates: 1986–1991.
Scores, 4: Empathic, Critical, Searching, Advising.
Administration: Group or individual.
Price Data: Price available from publisher for complete kit including 20 inventories, 20 answer sheets, and 20 interpretation booklets.
Time: [20] minutes administration; [10] minutes scoring; [30–60] minutes interpretation.
Comments: Self-administered, self-scored.
Author: Training House, Inc.
Publisher: Training House, Inc.
Cross References: For reviews by William L. Deaton and Gerald L. Stone, see 12:413.

[2710]
Whisler Strategy Test.
Purpose: "To discover how effective the individual is in drawing on his abilities and knowledges to demonstrate his general competence."
Population: Business and industry.
Publication Dates: 1955–1961.
Scores, 6: 4 direct scores (Number Circled-Boldness, Number Attempted-Speed, Number Right-Accuracy, Net Strategy), and 2 derived scores (Caution, Hypercaution).
Administration: Group.
Price Data: Available from publisher.
Time: (25) minutes.
Comments: Measures "intelligence action" or strategic ability.
Author: Laurence Whisler.
Publisher: Psychometric Affiliates.
Cross References: See T5:2877 (1 reference) and T2:2292 (1 reference); for reviews by Jean Maier Palormo and Paul F. Ross, see 6:1110 (1 reference).

[2711]
Whitaker Index of Schizophrenic Thinking.
Purpose: Measures degrees of schizophrenic thinking.

Population: Mental patients.
Publication Dates: 1973–1980.
Acronym: WIST.
Scores, 4: Similarities, Word Pairs, New Inventions, Total.
Administration: Individual.
Forms, 2: A, B.
Price Data, 2002: $85 per complete kit; $19.95 or less per 25 tests (specify Form A or B); $10.50 per scoring key; $42.50 per manual (1980, 92 pages).
Time: (20) minutes.
Comments: Manual title is Objective Measurement of Schizophrenic Thinking: A Practical and Theoretical Guide to the Whitaker Index of Schizophrenic Thinking.
Author: Leighton C. Whitaker.
Publisher: Western Psychological Services.
Cross References: See T5:2878 (1 reference) and T4:2955 (2 references); for a review by Stephen G. Flanagan, see 11:469 (12 references); see also T3:2620 (20 references); for reviews by Bertram D. Cohen and Robert W. Payne, see 8:710 (4 references).

[2712]

Who Am I?

Purpose: Assesses "a child's readiness for particular types of learning experiences and identifies the levels that children have reached in their understanding and use of conventional symbols and relevant early learning skills."
Population: Preschool–Year 2 in Australian school system.
Publication Date: 1999.
Scores, 4: Copying, Symbols, Drawing, Total.
Administration: Group or individual.
Price Data, 2002: A$49 per specimen set including task booklet, assessment manual (36 pages), and administration instructions; A$25 per 10 task booklets; A$39.95 per assessment manual; A$8 per administration instructions.
Time: (10–20) minutes.
Authors: Marion de Lemos and Brian Doig.
Publisher: Australian Council for Educational Research Ltd. [Australia].

[2713]

Wide Range Achievement Test 3.

Purpose: To measure the skills needed to learn reading, spelling, and arithmetic.
Population: Ages 5–75.
Publication Dates: 1940–1993.
Acronym: WRAT3.
Scores: 3 subtests: Reading, Spelling, Arithmetic.
Administration: Individual in part.
Forms: 2 equivalent forms: Blue, Tan.
Price Data, 1999: $125 per starter set including 25 Blue test forms, 25 Tan test forms, 25 profile/analysis forms, set of 2 plastic cards for Reading/Spelling, and manual (1993, 188 pages) in attache case; $27 per 25 test forms (specify Blue or Tan); $20 per 25 profile/analysis forms; $14 per set of 2 plastic cards for Reading/Spelling; $40 per manual; $32 per attache case.
Time: (15–30) minutes.
Author: Gary S. Wilkinson.
Publisher: Wide Range, Inc.
Cross References: See T5:2879 (237 references); for reviews by Linda Mabry and Annie W. Ward, see 12:414 (111 references); see also T4:2956 (121 references); for reviews by Elaine Clark and Patti L. Harrison, see 10:389 (161 references); for reviews by Paula Matuszek of an earlier edition and Philip A. Saigh of an earlier edition, see 9:1364 (103 references); see also T3:2621 (249 references), 8:37 (117 references), and T2:50 (35 references); for reviews by Jack C. Merwin and Robert L. Thorndike of an earlier edition, see 7:36 (49 references); see also 6:27 (15 references); for reviews by Paul Douglas Courtney, Verner M. Sims, and Louis P. Thorpe of the 1946 edition, see 3:21.

[2714]

Wide Range Assessment of Memory and Learning.

Purpose: "Psychometric instrument which allows the user to evaluate a child's ability to actively learn and memorize a variety of information."
Population: Ages 5 through 17.
Publication Date: 1990.
Acronym: WRAML.
Scores, 4: Verbal Memory Index, Visual Memory Index, Learning Index, General Memory Index.
Administration: Individual.
Price Data, 1999: $345 per complete kit including 25 sets of forms, supplies, and manual (160 pages); $40 per 25 examiner forms; $42 per 25 response forms; $40 per manual.
Time: (45–60) minutes.
Comments: Screening section available on Examiner Form.
Authors: David Sheslow and Wayne Adams.
Publisher: Wide Range, Inc.
Cross References: See T5:2880 (7 references); for reviews by Richard M. Clark and Frederic J. Medway, see 11:470.

[2715]

Wide Range Assessment of Visual Motor Abilities.

Purpose: A standardized assessment of visual-motor, visual-spatial, and fine motor skills.
Population: Ages 3–17 years.
Publication Date: 1995.
Acronym: WRAVMA.

Scores, 4: Fine Motor, Visual-Spatial, Visual-Motor, Visual-Motor Integration Composite.
Administration: Individual.
Price Data, 1999: $40 per manual (151 pages); $48 per 25 drawing or matching forms; $40 per 25 examiner record forms; $50 per pegboard with pegs; $12 per pencil and marker resupply pack; $38 per soft attache case.
Time: (15–30) minutes; (5–10) minutes per subtest.
Comments: Best results when "integrated with data from other standardized tests and clinical observations"; test should be interpreted by "those with graduate or equivalent professional training in cognitive assessment."
Authors: Wayne Adams and David Sheslow.
Publisher: Wide Range, Inc.
Cross References: For reviews by Linda K. Bunker and Keith F. Widaman, see 14:418.

[2716]
Wide Range Intelligence Test.

Purpose: "Designed to measure an individual's cognitive abilities."
Population: Ages 4–85.
Publication Date: 2000.
Acronym: WRIT.
Scores, 7: Verbal (Verbal Analogies, Vocabulary, Total), Visual (Matrices, Diamonds, Total), Total.
Administration: Individual.
Price Data, 2000: $160 per regular introductory kit including diamonds/matrices easel, diamonds in storage case, manual, and 25 examiner forms all packaged in a canvas carrying case; $195 per deluxe introductory kit including same items as above except all packaged in a briefcase; $48 per manual; $35 per 25 examiner forms.
Time: (20–30) minutes.
Authors: Joseph Glutting, Wayne Adams, and David Sheslow.
Publisher: Wide Range, Inc.

[2717]
Wide Range Interest-Opinion Test.

Purpose: Intended as "an inventory of work interests."
Population: Ages 5 and over.
Publication Dates: 1970–1979.
Acronym: WRIOT.
Scores, 26: 18 occupational interests (Art, Literature, Music, Drama, Sales, Management, Office Work, Personal Service, Protective Service, Social Service, Social Science, Biological Science, Physical Science, Number, Mechanics, Machine Operation, Outdoor, Athletics) and 8 vocational attitudes (Sedentariness, Risk, Ambition, Chosen Skill Level, Sex Stereotype, Agreement, Negative Bias, Positive Bias).

Administration: Group.
Price Data, 1999: $150 per complete kit; $30 per picture book; $30 per 50 answer sheets; $48 per scoring stencils; $30 per 50 profile report forms; $40 per manual (1979, 118 pages).
Time: (40–60) minutes.
Authors: Joseph F. Jastak and Sarah Jastak.
Publisher: Wide Range, Inc.
Cross References: See T4:2959 (1 reference); for reviews by Louis M. Hsu and Caroline A. Manuele, see 9:1366; for a review by Donald G. Zytowski, see 8:1029.

[2718]
Wide-Span Reading Test.

Purpose: To assess "a child's skill in decoding printed symbols into meaningful sounds of language, in fitting meanings to groups of sounds, and in construing the structural relationship of meanings in their total semantic and syntactical context."
Population: Ages 7-10 to 14-11.
Publication Dates: 1972–1984.
Scores: Total score only.
Administration: Group.
Forms, 2: A, B.
Price Data: Price information available from publisher for complete kit, and for pupil's booklets (specify Form A or B), answer sheets, manual (1983, 36 pages), and specimen set.
Time: 30(40) minutes.
Author: Alan Brimer.
Publisher: NFER-Nelson Publishing Co., Ltd. [England].
Cross References: See T5:2883 (1 reference); for reviews by Mariam Jean Dreher and Priscilla A. Drum, see 10:390; see also T3:2625 (1 reference); for reviews by David J. Carroll and William Yule, see 8:747.

[2719]
The Wiesen Test of Mechanical Aptitude.

Purpose: Designed to measure mechanical aptitude for purpose of personnel selection.
Population: Applicants (18 years and older) for jobs requiring mechanical aptitude.
Publication Dates: 1997–1999.
Acronym: WTMA.
Scores, 12: Total Score and 11 research scores: Basic Machines, Movement of Simple and Complex Objects, Center of Gravity and Gravity, Basic Electricity/Electronics, Transfer of Heat, Basic Physical Properties of Matter and Materials, Miscellaneous, Academic, Kitchen Objects, Non-Kitchen Objects, Other Everyday Objects.
Administration: Group.
Price Data: Available from publisher.
Time: (30) minutes.

Comments: A 60-item multiple-choice objective test.
Author: Joel P. Wiesen.
Publisher: Psychological Assessment Resources, Inc.
Cross References: For reviews by John M. Enger and Nambury S. Raju, see 14:419.

[2720]
Wife's or Husband's Marriage Questions.

Purpose: Designed as "a comprehensive marriage analysis system."
Population: Husbands, wives.
Publication Date: 1994.
Administration: Individual or group.
Forms, 2: Wife's Marriage Questions, Husband's Marriage Questions.
Manual: No manual.
Price Data, 2001: $10 per 20 forms (specify Husband or Wife).
Time: Administration time not reported.
Author: Allan Roe.
Publisher: Diagnostic Specialists, Inc.

[2721]
Wiig Criterion Referenced Inventory of Language.

Purpose: "Designed to assist speech-language pathologists and special and regular educators in the diagnosis of children with language disorders and language delays."
Population: Ages 4 through 13.
Publication Date: 1990.
Acronym: Wiig CRIL.
Scores: 4 modules: Semantics, Morphology, Syntax, Pragmatics.
Administration: Individual.
Price Data, 2002: $268 per complete kit including Professional's Guide (63 pages), all 4 stimulus manuals and 10 each of all four record forms; price information for the module package (specify Semantics, Morphology, Syntax, or Pragmatics) including stimulus manual and 10 record forms available from publisher; $42 per 20 record forms (specify Semantics, Morphology, Syntax, or Pragmatics).
Time: Untimed.
Author: Elisabeth H. Wiig.
Publisher: The Psychological Corporation.
Cross References: For reviews by Clinton W. Bennett and Judith R. Johnston, see 13:361.

[2722]
Williams Intelligence Test for Children with Defective Vision.

Purpose: "Should discriminate between … degrees of mental ability."
Population: Ages 5–15 (blind and partially sighted).

Publication Date: 1956.
Scores: Total score only.
Administration: Individual.
Price Data: Price information available from publisher for complete kit, record forms, and handbook (54 pages plus fold-out IQ conversion tables).
Time: [60] minutes.
Author: M. Williams.
Publisher: NFER-Nelson Publishing Co., Ltd. [England].
Cross References: See T5:2888 (1 reference) and T2:540 (1 reference); for a review by T. Ernest Newland, see 6:541 (2 references).

[2723]
Wilson Driver Selection Test.

Purpose: Constructed to measure aptitudes related to safe driving.
Population: Prospective motor vehicle operators.
Publication Dates: 1961–1984.
Scores, 7: Visual Attention, Depth Visualization, Recognition of Simple Detail, Recognition of Complex Detail, Eye-Hand Coordination, Steadiness, Total.
Administration: Group.
Price Data, 2001: $95.40 per test package; $3.75 per key; $54.60 per manual (1961, 28 pages) and manual supplement (1984, 17 pages); $58.80 per specimen set.
Time: 26(50) minutes.
Author: Clark L. Wilson.
Publisher: Martin M. Bruce, Ph.D.
Cross References: For reviews by Willard A. Kerr and D. H. Schuster, see 6:1200.

[2724]
Wisconsin Behavior Rating Scale.

Purpose: "A least biased adaptive behavior scale" to "provide adequate assessment, intervention, and evaluation" of severely and profoundly retarded individuals and of persons functioning below the developmental level of 3 years.
Population: Persons functioning below the developmental level of 3 years.
Publication Dates: 1979–1991.
Acronym: WBRS.
Scores, 12: Gross Motor, Fine Motor, Expressive Language, Receptive Language, Play Skills, Socialization, Domestic Activity, Eating, Toileting, Dressing, Grooming, Total.
Administration: Group.
Price Data, 2001: $15 per 25 scales; $50 per 100 scales (1991, 12 pages); $5.00 per specimen set including scale and manual (1983, 30 pages).
Time: (10-15) minutes.
Comments: "The assessment is performed by interviewing informants who are most familiar with the behavior of the person being evaluated."

Authors: Agnes Song, Stephen Jones, Janet Lippert, Karin Metzgen, Jacqueline Miller, and Christopher Borreca.

Publisher: Central Wisconsin Center for the Developmentally Disabled.

Cross References: For reviews by Pat Mirenda and Harvey N. Switzky, see 11:472 (1 reference).

[2725]
Wisconsin Card Sorting Test, Revised and Expanded.

Purpose: "Developed ... as a measure of abstract reasoning among normal adult populations" and "has increasingly been employed as a clinical neuropsychological instrument."

Population: Ages 6.5–89.

Publication Dates: 1981–1993.

Acronym: WCST.

Scores, 11: Number of Trials Administered, Total Number Correct, Total Number of Errors, Perseverative Responses, Perseverative Errors, Nonperseverative Errors, Conceptual Level Responses, Number of Categories Completed, Trials to Complete First Category, Failure to Maintain Set, Learning to Learn.

Administration: Individual.

Price Data: Available from publisher for complete kit including manual (1993, 234 pages), 2 decks of cards, and 25 record booklets; price information also available from publisher for computer version.

Time: (20–30) minutes.

Comments: Additional materials necessary for testing include a pen or pencil and a clipboard.

Authors: Robert K. Heaton, Gordon J. Chelune, Jack L. Talley, Gary G. Kay, and Glenn Curtiss.

Publisher: Psychological Assessment Resources, Inc.

Cross References: For reviews by Elaine Clark and Deborah D. Roman, see 14:420; see also T5:2892 (309 references) and T4:2967 (96 references); for reviews by Byron Egeland and Robert P. Markley of an earlier edition, see 9:1372 (11 references).

[2726]
Wisconsin Card Sorting Test—64 Card Version.

Purpose: "Developed as a measure of abstracted reasoning ability and ability to shift cognitive set."

Population: Ages 6.5–89.

Publication Dates: 1981–2000.

Acronym: WCST-64.

Scores, 10: Total Number Correct, Total Number of Errors, Perseverative Responses, Perseverative Errors, Nonperseverative Errors, Conceptual Level Responses, Number of Categories Completed, Trials to Complete First Category, Failure to Maintain Set, Learning to Learn.

Administration: Individual.

Price Data: Available from publisher for introductory kit including 50 record booklets, manual (2000, 246 pages), and card deck.

Time: Untimed.

Comments: Abbreviated form of the standard 128-card version of the Wisconsin Card Sorting Test (2725).

Authors: Susan K. Kongs, Laetitia L. Thompson, Grant L. Iverson, and Robert K. Heston.

Publisher: Psychological Assessment Resources, Inc.

Cross References: For information on the Wisconsin Card Sorting Test, Revised and Expanded, see T5:2892 (309 references) and T4:2967 (96 references); for reviews by Byron Egeland and Robert P. Markley of an earlier edition, see 9:1372 (11 references).

[2727]
The Wolfe Computer Operator Aptitude Test.

Purpose: Used "to evaluate a candidate's potential for work as a computer operator."

Population: Applicants for computer training or employment.

Publication Dates: 1979–1982.

Acronym: WCOAT.

Scores: Total score only.

Administration: Group.

Price Data, 2001: $165 per candidate.

Foreign Language Edition: French edition available.

Time: (90) minutes.

Comments: Detailed report provided on each candidate.

Author: Jack M. Wolfe.

Publisher: Rose Wolfe Family Partnership LLP [Canada}.

[2728]
Wolfe-Spence Programming Aptitude Test.

Purpose: Designed as a screening test to identify persons who should receive further consideration for hiring or training for programming.

Population: Applicants in computer programming.

Publication Date: 1970.

Scores: Total score and percentile.

Administration: Group.

Price Data, 2001: $180 per candidate.

Time: (120) minutes.

Authors: Jack M. Wolfe and Richard J. Spence.

Publisher: Rose Wolfe Family Partnership LLP [Canada].

[2729]
Wonderlic Basic Skills Test.

Purpose: "A short form measure of adult language and math skills ... designed to measure the job-readiness of teenagers and adults."

Population: Teenagers and adults.
Publication Date: 1994–1998.
Acronym: WBST.
Scores, 9: Test of Verbal Skills (Word Knowledge, Sentence Construction, Information Retrieval, Total), Test of Quantitative Skills (Explicit, Applied, Interpretive, Total), Composite Score.
Subtests, 2: Test of Verbal Skills, Test of Quantitative Skills.
Administration: Group or individual.
Forms: 2 equivalent forms for each subtest: VS-1, VS-2 for Test of Verbal Skills; QS-1, QS-2 for Test of Quantitative Skills.
Price Data, 1998: $85 per 25 tests, manual (1998, 92 pages), and necessary software for either the Verbal or Quantitative subtests; $110 per composite set including 25 Verbal subtests, 25 Quantitative subtests, manual, and necessary software; $120 per User's Manual for Ability-to-Benefit Testing (1998, 86 pages).
Time: (20) minutes for each subtest.
Comments: The Verbal and Quantitative Skills subtests may be administered together or separately, and are available as separate booklets; scoring requires using IBM-compatible PC; the WBST has been approved by the U.S. Department of Education for use in qualifying postsecondary students for Title IV Federal financial assistance and schools using the WBST for this purpose must follow special procedures and guidelines published in the User's Manual for Ability-to-Benefit Testing.
Authors: Eliot R. Long, Victor S. Artese, and Winifred L. Clonts.
Publisher: Wonderlic, Inc.
Cross References: For reviews by Thomas F. Donlon and Gerald S. Hanna, see 13:362.

[2730]
Wonderlic Personnel Test and Scholastic Level Exam.

Purpose: Designed to be used by businesses and schools to measure general cognitive ability in order to determine "how easily individuals can be trained, how well they can adjust and solve problems on the job, and how well satisfied they are likely to be with the demands of the job."
Population: Ages 15 and up.
Publication Dates: 1937–1998.
Acronym: WPS and SLE.
Scores: Total score only.
Administration: Individual or group.
Forms: 6 alternate forms of the WPT, and 4 alternate forms of the SLE.
Price Data, 2000: $1.80 per test.
Foreign Language and Special Editions: Canadian, Swedish, French, Spanish, Tagalog, Viet-

namese, German, Chinese, Portuguese, Japanese, Korean, Russian, large print, braille, and audio editions.
Time: 12 minutes.
Comments: Computer-administered version available; alternate forms exist to reduce risk of retesting with identical form.
Author: Charles Wonderlic.
Publisher: Wonderlic, Inc.
Cross References: For reviews by Kurt F. Geisinger and Gregory Schraw, see 14:421; see also T5:2899 (20 references) and T4:2972 (11 references); for a review by Marcia J. Belcher of an earlier edition, see 11:475 (10 references); for reviews by Frank L. Schmidt and Lyle F. Schoenfeldt, see 9:1385 (8 references); see also T3:2638 (24 references), and T2:482 (10 references); for reviews by Robert C. Droege and John P. Foley, Jr., see 7:401 (28 references); for reviews by N. M. Downie and Marvin D. Dunnette, see 6:513 (17 references); see also 5:400 (59 references); for reviews by H. E. Brogden, Charles D. Flory, and Irving Lorge, see 3:269 (7 references); see also 2:1415 (2 references).

[2731]
Woodcock Diagnostic Reading Battery.

Purpose: "Provides a diagnostic test that assesses reading achievement and important related abilities."
Population: Ages 4 to 90+.
Publication Date: 1997.
Acronym: WDRB.
Scores, 17: Letter-Word Identification, Word Attack, Reading Vocabulary, Passive Comprehension, Incomplete Words, Sound Blending, Oral Vocabulary, Listening Comprehension, Memory for Sentences, Visual Matching, Total Reading, Broad Reading, Basic Reading Skills, Reading Comprehension, Phonological Awareness, Oral Comprehension, Reading Aptitude.
Administration: Individual.
Price Data: Available from publisher.
Time: ((50–60) minutes.
Comments: Battery comprises selected tests from the Woodcock-Johnson® Psycho-Educational Battery—Revised (2732); for educational, clinical, or research purposes; optional to use any combination of the subtests that are relevant to individual subjects.
Author: Richard W. Woodcock.
Publisher: Riverside Publishing.
Cross References: For reviews by D. Joe Olmi and Herbert C. Rudman, see 14:422.

[2732]
Woodcock-Johnson® III.

Purpose: Designed "to provide a co-normed set of tests for measuring general intellectual ability, specific cognitive abilities, scholastic aptitude, oral language, and academic achievement."
Population: Ages 2–90+.

Publication Dates: 1977–2001.

Acronym: WJ III®.

Parts, 2: Tests of Cognitive Abilities, Tests of Achievement.

Administration: Individual.

Price Data: Available from publisher.

Comments: Tests can be administered separately; previous edition was entitled Woodcock-Johnson Psycho-Educational Battery—Revised; can be scored only with the CompuScore® software included or optional Report Writer; minimum system requirements: Microsoft Windows 95/98/NT 4.0, PC with 486 processor, VGA monitor, 16 MB of RAM Windows-supported printer (Windows System) or Apple system 7.5.5–9.0, Macintosh computer with 68020 processor, Macintosh-compatible printer (Macintosh System), 16 MB RAM; 1991 edition still available.

Authors: Richard W. Woodcock, Kevin S. McGrew, Nancy Mather, and Fredrick A. Schrank (Compuscore® and Profiles Program).

Publisher: Riverside Publishing.

a) TESTS OF ACHIEVEMENT.

Scores: 11 Standard Battery (Form A or B) test scores: Letter-Word Identification, Reading, Fluency, Passage Comprehension, Story Recall, Understanding Directions, Calculation, Math Fluency, Applied Problems, Spelling, Writing Fluency, Writing Samples, and 3 Standard Battery Supplemental test scores: Story Recall—Delayed, Handwriting Legibility Scale, Writing Evaluation Scale, plus 6 Standard Battery cluster scores derived from combinations of the above test scores: Broad Reading, Oral Language—Standard, Broad Math, Math Calculation Skills, Broad Written Language, Written Expression, and 4 Supplementary Battery cluster scores: Academic Skills, Academic Fluency, Academic Applications, Total Achievement; 7 Extended Battery (Form A or B) test scores: Word Attack, Reading Vocabulary, Picture Vocabulary, Oral Comprehension, Quantitative Concepts, Editing, Academic Knowledge, and 3 Extended Battery Supplemental test scores: Spelling of Sounds, Sound Awareness, Punctuation & Capitalization, plus 9 Extended Battery cluster scores derived from combinations of standard and extended battery tests: Basic Reading Skills, Reading Comprehension, Oral Language—Extended, Oral Expression, Listening Comprehension, Math Reasoning, Basic Writing Skills, Academic Knowledge, Phoneme/Grapheme Knowledge.

Forms, 2: A, B.

Price Data, 2002: $444 per Achievement Battery (Form A or B) including Achievement Standard and Extended test books, examiner's manual, audio cassette, 25 test records, 25 response booklets, CompuScore® and Profiles Program version 1.1b (Windows and Macintosh), technical manual, and scoring guides; $522.50 per Achievement Battery with leather carrying case (Form A or B); $58 per 25 Achievement test records and subject response booklets (Form A or B).

Time: Approximately (5) minutes per test; (55–65) minutes for Standard Battery.

b) TESTS OF COGNITIVE ABILITIES.

Scores: 10 Standard Battery test scores: Verbal Comprehension, Visual-Auditory Learning, Spatial Relations, Sound Blending, Concept Formation, Visual Matching, Numbers Reversed, Incomplete Words, Auditory Working Memory, Visual-Auditory Learning—Delayed, plus 3 Standard Battery cluster scores: Verbal Ability, Thinking Ability, Cognitive Efficiency, and 10 Extended Battery test scores: General Information, Retrieval Fluency, Picture Recognition, Auditory Attention, Analysis—Synthesis, Decision Speed, Memory for Words, Rapid Picture Naming, Planning, Pair Cancellation plus 3 Extended Battery cluster scores: Verbal Ability, Thinking Ability, Cognitive Efficiency; 16 factor cluster scores: Comprehension—Knowledge, Long-Term Retrieval, Visual-Spatial Thinking, Auditory Processing, Fluid Reasoning, Processing Speed, Short-Term Memory, Quantitative Knowledge, Reading-Writing Ability, Phonemic Awareness, Working Memory, Broad Attention, Cognitive Fluency, Executive Processes, Delayed Recall, Knowledge.

Price Data: $601 per Tests of Cognitive Abilities Battery including Cognitive Standard and Extended test books, examiner's manual, audio cassette, 25 test records, 25 response booklets, 5 Brief Intellectual ability Test Records, CompuScore® and Profiles Program version 1.1b (Windows and Macintosh), technical manual, and scoring guides; $679.50 per Tests of Cognitive Abilities Battery with leather carrying case; $58 per 25 Cognitive test records and subject response booklets; $26.50 per 25 Brief Intellectual Ability Test Records.

Time: Approximately (5) minutes per test; (35–45) minutes per Standard Battery; (90–115) minutes per Extended Battery.

Cross References: See T5:2901 (140 references); for reviews by Jack A. Cummings and by Steven W. Lee and Elaine Flory Stefany of the 1991 edition, see 12:415 (56 references); see also T4:2973 (90 references); for reviews by Jack A. Cummings and Alan S. Kaufman of the 1977 edition, see 9:1387 (6 references); see also T3:2639 (3 references).

[2733]

Woodcock Language Proficiency Battery— Revised.

Purpose: Intended to measure abilities and achievement in oral language, reading, and written language as well as English language competence.
Population: Ages 2–90+.
Publication Dates: 1980–1991.
Acronym: WLPB-R.
Scores, 25: Oral Language (Memory for Sentences, Picture Vocabulary, Oral Vocabulary, Listening Comprehension, Verbal Analogies), Reading (Letter-Word Identification, Passage Comprehension, Work Attack, Reading Vocabulary), Written Language (Dictation, Writing Samples, Proofing, Writing Fluency), Punctuation and Capitalization, Spelling, Usage, Handwriting, Oral Language, Broad Reading, Basic Reading Skills, Reading Comprehension, Broad Written Language, Basic Writing Skills, Written Expression, Broad English Ability.
Administration: Individual.
Price Data: Available from publisher.
Foreign Language Edition: Spanish edition available.
Time: (20-60) minutes.
Comments: Battery is a subset of the tests included in the Woodcock-Johnson® Psycho-Educational Battery—Revised (2732).
Authors: Richard W. Woodcock (English Form); Richard W. Woodcock and Ana F. Muñoz-Sandoval (Spanish Form).
Publisher: Riverside Publishing.
Cross References: See T5:2902 (5 references); for reviews by Irvin J. Lehmann and G. Michael Poteat, see 12:416 (3 references); see also T4:2974 (1 reference); for reviews by Ruth Noyce and Michelle Quinn, see 9:1388.

[2734]

Woodcock-Muñoz Language Survey [Normative Update].

Purpose: "Establishes language proficiency level in English or Spanish."
Population: Ages 4–adults.
Publication Dates: 1993–2001.
Acronym: WMLS Normative Update.
Scores, 7: Picture Vocabulary, Verbal Analogies, Letter-Word Identification, Dictation, Oral Language, Reading-Writing, Broad Ability.
Administration: Individual.
Editions, 2: English language; Spanish language.
Price Data: Available from publisher.
Foreign Language Edition: Available in English and Spanish.
Time: (5) minutes per subtest.

Comments: WMLS Normative Update offers a scoring option with normative information from the Woodcock-Johnson® III (2732). New software and test records are used with the same WMLS test book.
Authors: Richard W. Woodcock and Ana F. Muñoz-Sandoval.
Publisher: Riverside Publishing.
Cross References: For reviews by Linda Crocker and Chi-Wen Kao, see 13:364.

[2735]

Woodcock Reading Mastery Tests—Revised [1998 Normative Update].

Purpose: To measure reading readiness, basic skills, and comprehension.
Population: Kindergarten through adult.
Publication Dates: 1973–1998.
Scores, 11: Readiness Cluster (Visual-Auditory Learning, Letter Identification, Total), Basic Skills Cluster (Word Identification, Word Attack, Total), Reading Comprehension Cluster (Word Comprehension, Passage Comprehension, Total), Total Reading—Full Scale, Total Reading—Short Scale, plus a Supplementary Letter Checklist.
Administration: Individual.
Forms, 2: G, H (includes Reading Achievement tests only).
Price Data, 2002: $367.95 per Form G and Form H combined kit including Form G and Form H test books, 25 each of test records, sample NU Forms, G and H summary record form, pronunciation guide cassette, sample report to parents, and examiner's manual (1998, 214 pages); $466.95 per combined kit with ASSIST scoring software; $251.95 per Form G complete kit including materials in combined kit for Form G only, and G and H summary record form; $246.95 per Form H complete kit including materials in combined kit for Form H only, and G and H summary record form; $345.95 per Form H kit with ASSIST scoring software; $41.95 per 25 test records (specify Form G or Form H); $24.95 per 25 Form G and H summary record forms; $20.95 per 25 reports to parents; $199.95 per ASSIST scoring software (specify IBM PC/XT/AT, PS/2, and compatibles of Apple IIc, enhanced IIe, and IIGS).
Time: (40–45) minutes for entire battery; (15) minutes for Short Scale.
Comments: Test same as 1987 edition but with 1998 norms for grades K–12 and ages 5–22.
Author: Richard W. Woodcock.
Publisher: American Guidance Service, Inc.
Cross References: For reviews by Linda Crocker and Mildred Murray-Ward, see 14:423; see also T5:2905 (123 references) and T4:2976 (34 references); for reviews by Robert B. Cooter, Jr. and Richard M. Jaeger of an earlier edition, see 10:391

(38 references); see also T3:2641 (17 references); for reviews by Carol Anne Dwyer and J. Jaap Tuinman, and excerpted reviews by Alex Bannatyne, Richard L. Allington, Cherry Houck (with Larry A. Harris), and Barton B. Proger of the 1973 edition, see 8:779 (7 references).

[2736]
Word Fluency.

Purpose: Measures ability to produce appropriate words rapidly for fluency in verbal expression.
Population: Positions requiring sharp verbal communication skills.
Publication Dates: 1959–1961.
Scores: Total score only.
Administration: Individual or group.
Price Data, 2002: $73 per start-up kit including 25 test booklets and interpretation and research manual (1959, 30 pages); $54 per 25 test booklets (quantity discounts available); $28 per interpretation and research manual.
Time: 10 minutes.
Author: Human Resource Center, The University of Chicago.
Publisher: Reid London House.
Cross References: See T5:2907 (9 references), T4:2979 (6 references), T3:2645 (1 reference), and T2:594 (2 references); for a review by James E. Kennedy, see 6:562.

[2737]
Word Identification Scale.

Purpose: Designed as "an informal reading survey that allows a teacher to quickly identify" a student's readability level in terms of "decoding and word recognition skills."
Population: Students.
Publication Dates: 1988–1999.
Acronym: WIS.
Scores: Total score only.
Administration: Individual.
Manual: No manual.
Price Data, 2002: $15 per complete set including plasticized word card with instructions and 50 recording forms.
Time: (5–10) minutes.
Author: John Arena.
Publisher: Academic Therapy Publications.

[2738]
Word Meaning Through Listening.

Purpose: Designed "to infer levels of semantic competence through response to receptive language."
Population: Ages 7–16.
Publication Date: 2002.
Scores: Total score only.
Administration: Group.

Forms, 2: A, B.
Price Data, 2002: £7.75 per complete kit including administrative and technical manual (18 pages) with computer disk scoring key and 25 Form A test booklets; £2.30 per manual and 3.5-inch disk scoring key; £5.25 per 25 test booklets (Form A or B).
Time: (20–25) minutes.
Author: Alan Brimer.
Publisher: Educational Evaluations [England].

[2739]
The Word Memory Test.

Purpose: Designed for symptom validity testing—detecting malingering and feigning in comparison to cases of true brain injury and amnesia.
Population: Adults.
Publication Dates: 1995–2000.
Acronym: WMT.
Scores, 5: Immediate Recognition, Delayed Recognition, Multiple Choice, Paired Associates, Free Recall.
Administration: Individual.
Forms, 2: Oral, Computerized.
Price Data, 2002: $300 per complete test including copyable administration forms and unlimited administration/scoring disk; $25 per manual (1996, 132 pages).
Time: (15) minutes.
Comments: Computerized form (C-WMT) self-administered.
Authors: Paul Green, Kevin Astner, and Lyle M. Allen.
Publisher: CogniSyst, Inc.
Cross References: For reviews by M. Allan Cooperstein and Michael P. Gamache, see 14:424.

[2740]
Word Recognition and Phonic Skills.

Purpose: "Designed to give the teacher two assessments of a child's word recognition ability."
Population: Ages 5.0 to 8.6.
Publication Date: 1994.
Acronym: WRaPS.
Scores: Word Recognition.
Administration: Group.
Price Data, 2002: £6.99 per 10 test booklets; £10.99 per diagnostic scoring template; £10.99 per manual (31 pages); £10.99 per specimen set including one copy of test form and manual.
Time: (30) minutes.
Authors: Clifford Carver and David Moseley.
Publisher: Hodder & Stoughton Educational [England].
Cross References: For reviews by Robert G. Harrington and Joyce R. McLarty, see 14:425; see also T5:2910 (1 reference).

[2741]
The WORD Test.

Purpose: Designed to assess expressive vocabulary and semantics.
Population: Ages 7 and over.
Publication Date: 1981.
Scores, 7: Associations, Synonyms, Semantic Absurdities, Antonyms, Definitions, Multiple Definitions, Total.
Administration: Group.
Price Data: Available from publisher.
Time: (20–30) minutes.
Authors: Carol Jorgensen, Mark Barrett, Rosemary Huisingh, and Linda Zachman.
Publisher: LinguiSystems, Inc. [No reply from publisher; status unknown].
Cross References: See T5:2911 (6 references) and T4:2983 (2 references); for reviews by Mavis Donahue and Nambury S. Raju, see 9:1393.

[2742]
Work Adjustment Inventory.

Purpose: "Designed to evaluate adolescents' and young adults' temperament toward work activities, work environments, other employees, and other aspects of work."
Population: Adolescents and young adults.
Publication Date: 1994.
Acronym: WAI.
Scores, 7: Activity, Empathy, Sociability, Assertiveness, Adaptability, Emotionality, WAI Quotient.
Administration: Group or individual.
Price Data, 2001: $86 per complete kit; $39 per record forms; $49 per manual.
Time: (15–20) minutes.
Author: James E. Gilliam.
Publisher: PRO-ED.
Cross References: For reviews by Mark J. Benson and Wayne J. Camara, see 13:365.

[2743]
Work Adjustment Scale.

Purpose: "A measure of a student's behavioral readiness for employment."
Population: Junior and senior high school students.
Publication Date: 1991.
Acronym: WAS.
Scores, 4: Work Related Behavior, Interpersonal Relations, Social/Community Expectations, Total.
Administration: Individual.
Price Data, 1999: $59.50 per complete kit including technical manual (27 pages), 50 rating forms, and intervention manual (171 pages); $12.50 per technical manual; $31 per 50 rating forms; $16 per intervention manual.
Time: (12–15) minutes.

Comments: Ratings by teachers.
Author: Stephen B. McCarney.
Publisher: Hawthorne Educational Services, Inc.
Cross References: For reviews by Ric Brown and Chantale Jeanrie, see 13:366.

[2744]
Work Aspect Preference Scale.

Purpose: "Constructed to assess the qualities of work that individuals consider important to them."
Population: Grades 10–12 and college and adults.
Publication Date: 1983.
Acronym: WAPS.
Scores: 13 scales: Independence, Co-Workers, Self-Development, Creativity, Money, Life Style, Prestige, Altruism, Security, Management, Detachment, Physical Activity, Surroundings.
Administration: Group.
Price Data, 2002: A$16.50 per 10 question booklets; A$5.50 per scoring key; A$7.69 per 10 answer sheets; A$1.05 per profile; A$29.80 per manual (58 pages); A$37.39 per specimen set excluding scoring key.
Time: (10–20) minutes.
Author: Robert Pryor.
Publisher: Australian Council for Educational Research Ltd. [Australia].
Cross References: See T5:2915 (8 references) and T4:2987 (1 reference).

[2745]
Work Attitudes Questionnaire (Version for Research).

Purpose: "Designed to differentiate the 'workaholic' or the Type A personality from the highly committed worker."
Population: Managers.
Publication Dates: 1980–1981.
Acronym: WAQ.
Scores, 3: Work Commitment, Psychological Health, Total.
Administration: Group.
Price Data: Available from publisher.
Time: Administration time not reported.
Authors: Maxene S. Doty and Nancy E. Betz.
Publisher: Marathon Consulting and Press.
Cross References: For a review by Mary L. Tenopyr, see 9:1395.

[2746]
Work Environment Scale, Second Edition.

Purpose: Developed to "measure the social environment of different types of work settings."
Population: Employees and supervisors.
Publication Dates: 1974–1989.
Acronym: WES.

Scores, 10: Involvement, Peer Cohesion, Supervisor Support, Autonomy, Task Orientation, Work Pressure, Clarity, Control, Innovation, Physical Comfort.
Administration: Group.
Forms, 3: Real (R), Ideal (I), Expected (E).
Price Data, 2001: $35.50 per 25 test booklets (Form R); $49.75 per 25 test booklets (select Form I or E); $19.25 per 25 answer sheets; $44 per 25 self-scorable answer sheets; $17 per set of scoring stencils; $8.50 per 25 profiles; $37.50 per 25 interpretive report forms; $48.80 per manual (57 pages); $13.20 per preview kit (nonprepaid).
Time: [15–20] minutes.
Comments: A part of the Social Climate Scales (T5:2445).
Authors: Rudolf H. Moos and Paul N. Insel (tests).
Publisher: Consulting Psychologists Press, Inc.
Cross References: See T5:2917 (5 references); for reviews by Ralph O. Mueller and Eugene P. Sheehan, see 12:417 (6 references); see also T4:2989 (19 references); for a review by Rabindra N. Kanungo, see 9:1398 (1 reference); see also T3:2652 (2 references) and 8:713 (3 references). For a review of the Social Climate Scales, see 8:681.

[2747]
The Work Experience Survey.
Purpose: Designed as a "structured interview protocol for identifying barriers (and possible solutions) to career maintenance" for a disabled person.
Population: "Individuals with disabilities who are either employed or about to begin employment."
Publication Date: 1995.
Acronym: WES.
Scores: Not scored.
Administration: Individual.
Price Data, 1998: $7.50 per 50 surveys; $5 per manual (59 pages).
Time: (30–60) minutes.
Comments: Administered in a face-to-face or telephone interview.
Authors: Richard T. Roessler (survey and manual), Cheryl A. Reed (manual), and Phillip D. Rumrill (manual).
Publisher: The National Center on Employment & Disability.
Cross References: For reviews by Albert M. Bugaj and Lawrence H. Cross, see 14:426.

[2748]
Work Information Inventory.
Purpose: Designed to assess employee morale by utilizing the direction of perception techniques.
Population: Employee groups in industry.
Publication Date: 1958.
Acronym: WII.

Scores: Total score only.
Administration: Group.
Price Data: Available from publisher.
Time: (15) minutes.
Author: Raymond E. Bernberg.
Publisher: Psychometric Affiliates.
Cross References: For additional information and a review by Albert K. Kurtz, see 8:1057.

[2749]
Work Keys Assessments.
Purpose: "For assessing and documenting employability skills."
Population: Grades 9 to adult.
Publication Dates: 1992–1994.
Administration: Individual or group.
Price Data: Available from publisher.
Author: ACT, Inc.
Publisher: ACT, Inc.
a) READING FOR INFORMATION ASSESSMENT.
Purpose: "Measures the learner's skill in reading and understanding work-related instructions and policies."
Scores: Total score only.
Levels: 5 reading skill levels.
Time: (45) minutes.
b) APPLIED MATHEMATICS ASSESSMENT.
Purpose: "Measures the learner's skill in applying mathematical reasoning to work-related problems."
Scores: Total score only.
Levels: 5 mathematics skill levels.
Time: (45) minutes.
c) LISTENING ASSESSMENT.
Purpose: "Measures the learner's skill at listening to and understanding work-related messages."
Scores: Total score only.
Levels: 5 listening skill levels.
Time: [40] minutes.
Comments: Constructed-response; administered via audiotape; hand-scored by ACT.
d) WRITING ASSESSMENT.
Purpose: "Measures the learner's skill at writing work-related messages."
Scores: Total score only.
Levels: 5 writing skill levels.
Time: [40] minutes.
Comments: Constructed-response; administered via audiotape; hand-scored by ACT.
e) LOCATING INFORMATION ASSESSMENT.
Purpose: "Measures the learner's skill in using information taken from workplace graphics such as diagrams, floor plans, tables, forms, graphs, charts, and instrument gauges."

Scores: Total score only.
Levels: 4 information skill levels.
Time: (45) minutes.
f) TEAMWORK ASSESSMENT.
Purpose: "Measures the learner's skill in choosing behaviors and/or actions that simultaneously support team interrelationships and lead toward the accomplishment of work tasks."
Parts: 2.
Scores: Total score only.
Levels: 4 teamwork skill levels.
Time: (62) minutes.
Comments: Administered via videotape.
g) APPLIED TECHNOLOGY ASSESSMENT.
Purpose: "Measures the learner's skill in solving problems of a technological nature."
Scores: Total score only.
Levels: 4 applied technology levels.
Time: (45) minutes.
h) OBSERVATION ASSESSMENT.
Purpose: "Measures the learner's skill in paying attention to instructions and demonstrations, and in noticing details."
Scores: Total score only.
Levels: 4 observation levels.
Time: (60) minutes.
Comments: Administered via videotape.

[2750]
[Work Motivation].

Purpose: Assesses assumptions and practices characterizing attempts to motivate employees, and evaluate employee motivational needs and values.
Population: Managers, employees.
Publication Dates: 1967–2000.
Scores, 5: Basic-Creature Comfort, Safety and Order, Belonging and Affiliation, Ego-Status, Actualization and Self-Expression.
Administration: Group.
Manual: No manual.
Price Data, 2001: $7.95 per instrument.
Time: [15–30] minutes.
Comments: Self-administered inventory.
Authors: Jay Hall and Martha Williams.
Publisher: Teleometrics International.
  a) MANAGEMENT OF MOTIVES INDEX.
  Purpose: Assesses assumptions and practices characterizing attempts to motivate employees.
  Acronym: MMI.
  b) WORK MOTIVATION INVENTORY.
  Purpose: Evaluate employee motivational needs and values.
  Acronym: WMI.
Cross References: See T3:2655 (4 references) and 8:1189 (3 references).

[2751]
Work Motivation Inventory: A Test of Adult Work Motivation.

Purpose: Measures the importance people place on four major goals or values related to career development decisions.
Population: Ages 16–Adult.
Publication Dates: 1985–1987.
Acronym: WMI.
Scores, 5: Bias, Accomplishment, Recognition, Power, Affiliation.
Administration: Group or individual.
Time: (10-15) minutes.
Comments: Self-administered survey; mail-in to publisher for narrative report processing.
Authors: Larry A. Braskamp and Martin L. Maehr.
Publisher: MetriTech, Inc.
  a) WMI NARRATIVE REPORTS.
  Price Data, 2001: $34 per narrative report kit including manual, processing of 5 reports, and 5 pre-paid test booklets; $5.25-$8.25 per narrative report including processing and answer sheets.
  Comments: Oriented to the test taker and features extensive interpretive information and guidelines for applying the test results to the test taker's career and life planning; based on parent program SPECTRUM.
  b) WMI/PC MICROCOMPUTER VERSION.
  Price Data: $49 per introductory kit including manual and 5 report demo disk; $105 per 10 administration disks; $237.50 per 25 administration disks; $400 per 50 administration disks; $14 per manual; $27 per 50 test booklets/answer sheets; $18 per 50 decision model worksheets.
  Comments: Supports both on-line and off-line testing; IBM version only.
Cross References: For reviews by Cyril J. Sadowski and Terry A. Stinnett, see 12:366.

[2752]
Work Orientation and Values Survey.

Purpose: Identifies and categorizes 32 work values, reflecting survey taker's approach to world of work.
Population: Adult and teenage job seekers and career planners.
Publication Date: 2002.
Acronym: WOVS.
Scores, 8: Earnings and Benefits, Working Conditions, Time Orientation, Task Orientation, Mission Orientation, Coworker Relations, Supervisor Relations, Managing Others.
Administration: Group or individual.
Price Data, 2002: $24.95 per 25 inventories including copy of administrator's guide.
Time: (15–20) minutes.

Comments: Self-administered and self-scored.
Author: Robert P. Brady.
Publisher: JIST Publishing, Inc.

[2753]
Work Performance Assessment.

Purpose: Designed to assess "work-related social/interpersonal skills."
Population: Job trainees.
Publication Dates: 1987–1988.
Acronym: WPA.
Scores: 19 supervisory demands: Greet Each Trainee, Direct Trainee to Work Station and Explain Nature of Work, Provide Vague Instructions, Explain Supervisory Error, Provide Detailed Instructions, Observe Trainees Working, Stand Next to Trainee, Create a Distraction, Show New Way to Work, Introduce Time Pressure, Criticize Trainee's Work, Compliment Trainee's Work, Ask Trainees to Switch Tasks, Ask Trainees to Socialize, Direct Trainees to Work Together, Ask Trainees to Criticize Each Other, Ask Trainees to Compliment Each Other, Observe Trainees Completing the Task Together, Socialize with Each Trainee, yielding a Total Score.
Administration: Group.
Price Data, 1993: $5 per manual (1987, 41 pages); $15 per 25 scripts and rating forms.
Time: (60–70) minutes.
Comments: Ratings by supervisor.
Authors: Richard Roessler, Suki Hinman, and Frank Lewis.
Publisher: The National Center on Employment & Disability.
Cross References: For reviews by Caroline Manuele-Adkins and Gerald R. Schneck, see 13:367.

[2754]
Work Personality Index.

Purpose: "Designed to identify personality traits that directly relate to work performance."
Population: High school to adult.
Publication Date: 2001.
Acronym: WPI.
Scores, 17: Teamwork, Concern for Others, Outgoing, Democratic, Attention to Detail, Rule-Following, Dependability, Ambition, Energy, Persistence, Leadership, Innovation, Analytic Thinking, Self-Control, Stress Tolerance, Initiative, Flexibility, and 5 factors—Achievement, Conscientiousness, Social Orientation, Practical Intelligence and Adjustment.
Administration: Group or individual.
Price Data: Available from publisher.
Foreign Language Edition: Available in English and French.
Time: (20–40) minutes.

Comments: May be administered via paper and pencil or on the Internet.
Authors: Donald Macnab and Shawn Bakker.
Publisher: Psychometrics Canada Ltd. [Canada].

[2755]
Work Personality Profile.

Purpose: Designed to "assess fundamental work role requirements that are essential to achievement and maintenance of suitable employment."
Population: Vocational rehabilitation clients.
Publication Date: 1986.
Acronym: WPP.
Scores, 16: Acceptance of Work Role, Ability to Profit from Instruction or Correction, Work Persistence, Work Tolerance, Amount of Supervision Required, Extent Trainee Seeks Assistance from Supervisor, Degree of Comfort or Anxiety with Supervisor, Appropriateness of Personal Relations with Supervisor, Teamwork, Ability to Socialize with Co-Workers, Social Communication Skills, Task Orientation, Social Skills, Work Motivation, Work Conformance, Personal Presentation.
Administration: Individual.
Price Data, 1994: $5 per manual (40 pages); $20 per floppy disk; $7.50 per 50 tests; $10 per 100 tests; $30 per complete set (including manual, diskette, and 50 tests).
Time: (5–10) minutes.
Comments: Observational ratings by vocational evaluators; to be administered after one week (20-30 hours) in evaluation setting; available on diskette.
Authors: Brian Bolton and Richard Roessler.
Publisher: The National Center on Employment & Disability.
Cross References: See T5:2924 (4 references) and T4:2994 (1 reference); for a review by Ralph O. Mueller and Paula J. Dupuy, see 11:476.

[2756]
Work Potential Profile.

Purpose: "Developed as a tool for the initial descriptive assessment of individuals seeking employment."
Population: Ages 16 and older.
Publication Date: 1997.
Scores, 25: Coping (General Satisfaction, Stress and Anxiety, Self-image, Self-discipline, Time Sense/Use, Total), Freedom from Major Barriers (Preoccupation with Health, Agitation/Aggression, Depression/Resentment, Pervasive Distrust/Delusions, Total), Social Resources (Attitude Towards Others, Social Skills, Total), Abilities (Communication and Literacy, Technology Use, Numeracy, Problem Solving, Total), Motivation (Work Motivation, Intrinsic Motivation, Extrinsic Motivation, Need for Status, Total), Physical Abilities.

Administration: Group.
Price Data, 2002: A$150.70 per complete set.
Time: (10–30) minutes.
Author: Helga A. H. Rowe.
Publisher: Australian Council for Educational Research Ltd. [Australia].

[2757]
Work Preference Questionnaire.

Purpose: To determine preferred job activities.
Population: Business and industry.
Publication Date: 1982.
Scores: Weighted combinations of 150 items into 16 dimensions of work: Making Decisions/Communicating and Having Responsibility, Operating Vehicles, Using Machines-Tools-Instruments, Performing Physical Activities, Operating Keyboard and Office Equipment, Monitoring and/or Controlling Equipment and/or Processes, Working Under Uncomfortable Conditions, Working With Art-Decor Entertainment, Performing Supervisory Duties, Performing Estimating Activities, Processing Written Information, Working With Buyers-Customers-Salespersons, Working Under Hazardous Conditions, Performing Paced and/or Repetitive Activities, Working With Aerial and Aquatic Equipment, Catering/Serving/Smelling/Tasting.
Administration: Group.
Price Data: Available from publisher.
Time: Administration time not reported.
Comments: Also known as Work Activity Questionnaire.
Authors: Robert C. Mecham, Alma F. Harris (test), Ernest J. McCormick (test), and P. R. Jenneret (test).
Publisher: PAQ Services, Inc.

[2758]
Work Profile Questionnaire.

Purpose: "Designed to look at work preference, and identify situations in which people are most likely to flourish and be effective."
Population: Job applicants.
Publication Date: 2001.
Acronym: WPQ.
Scores, 5: Communication Style, Emotions, Drive and Determination, Relationships with People, Thinking Style.
Administration: Individual.
Price Data, 2001: £22 per completed questionnaire.
Time: (5) minutes.
Author: Allan Cameron.
Publisher: The Test Agency Limited [England].

[2759]
Work Profile Questionnaire: Emotional Intelligence.

Purpose: "Designed to measure emotional intelligence … and also identifies respondents' preferred [work] team role."
Population: Adults.
Publication Date: 1999.
Acronym: WPQei.
Scores, 8: Self-Awareness, Empathy, Intuition, Emotions, Motivation, Innovation, Social Skills, Emotional Intelligence.
Administration: Group.
Price Data, 2001: £37.50 per technical manual; £85 per 10 self-scoring questionnaire/answer sheet/profile set; £25 per computer-based WPQei Administrator and Narrative Report Generator.
Time: Untimed.
Comments: Based on the Belbin model of work team functioning; can be administered in paper-and-pencil or personal computer format; requires IBM-compatible PC running Microsoft Windows 95/98/NT, 800x600 resolution display with 256 colors, recommends Pentium processor at 90 Mhz or more, 8 Mb RAM.
Author: Allan Cameron.
Publisher: The Test Agency Limited [England].

[2760]
Work Readiness Profile.

Purpose: "Developed as a tool for the initial descriptive assessment of individuals with disabilities."
Population: Older adolescents and adults with disabilities.
Publication Date: 1995.
Scores, 14: Physical Effectiveness (Health, Travel, Movement, Fine Motor Skills, Gross Motor Skills and Strength, Total Average), Personal Effectiveness (Social and Interpersonal, Work Adjustment, Communication Effectiveness, Abilities and Skills, Literacy and Numeracy, Total Average), Hearing, Vision.
Administration: Group.
Price Data, 2002: A$77 per set including manual (64 pages), 10 answer books, 10 group record forms, and 10 individual record forms; A$7.70 per 10 answer books; A$17.60 per 10 group record forms; A$17.60 per 10 individual record forms; A$55 per manual.
Time: (10–15) minutes.
Comments: Self-administered or ratings by informant.
Author: Helga A. H. Rowe.
Publisher: Australian Council for Educational Research Ltd. [Australia].
Cross References: For reviews by Jean Powell Kirnan and S. Alvin Leung, see 14:427.

[2761]
Work Skills Series Production.

Purpose: Designed to measure the ability to understand instructions, work with numbers, and accurately check machine settings visually.
Population: Manufacturing and production employees and prospective employees.
Publication Date: 1990.
Acronym: WSS.
Scores: Total score only for each of 3 tests: Understanding Instructions (VWP1), Working with Numbers (NWP2), Visual Checking (CWP3).
Administration: Individual or group.
Price Data: Available from publisher.
Time: 12 minutes for VWP1; 10 minutes for NWP2; 7 minutes for CWP3; 29(40) minutes for complete battery.
Author: Saville & Holdsworth Ltd.
Publisher: SHL Group plc [United Kingdom].
Cross References: For reviews by Brian Bolton and Wayne J. Camara, see 12:418.

[2762]
Work Team Simulator.

Purpose: "Designed to identify individuals who want to contribute and to play a meaningful role in the success of a work team, independent of any particular job classification."
Population: Team members.
Publication Dates: 1991–2002.
Acronym: WTS.
Scores, 3: Group Decision Making, Team Relations, Total.
Administration: Group or individual.
Forms, 5: Private and public sector forms: Blue Collar Version, White Collar Version, Police Version, Fire Version, Transportation Version.
Restricted Distribution: Clients must pay a one-time overhead/sign-up fee of $100.
Price Data, 2002: $60 per candidate for rental/scoring bar chart, and feedback report.
Time: 75 Minutes.
Author: Richard C. Joines.
Publisher: Management & Personnel Systems, Inc.

[2763]
Work Temperament Inventory.

Purpose: Identifies "personal traits" of the worker that are then matched to suitable occupations.
Population: Workers.
Publication Date: 1993.
Acronym: WTI.
Scores: 12 scales: Directive, Repetitive, Influencing, Variety, Expressing, Judgments, Alone, Stress, Tolerances, Under, People, Measurable.
Administration: Group.

Price Data, 1993: $30 per complete set including manual (39 pages), software, and 50 forms; $5 per manual; $20 per software (5.25-inch disk); $7.50 per 50 forms.
Time: (15–20) minutes.
Authors: Brian Bolton and Jeffrey Brookings.
Publisher: The National Center on Employment & Disability.
Cross References: For reviews by Peter F. Merenda and Alan J. Raphael, see 13:368.

[2764]
Working—Assessing Skills, Habits, and Style.

Purpose: "Designed to assess personal habits, skills, and styles that are associated with a positive work ethic."
Population: High school and college students and potential employees.
Publication Date: 1996.
Scores: 9 competencies: Taking Responsibility, Working in Teams, Persisting, Having A Sense of Quality, Life-Long Learning, Adapting to Change, Problem Solving, Information Processing, Systems Thinking.
Administration: Group.
Price Data, 1996: $4 each for 1–49 instruments, $3.50 each for 50–499; $3 each for 500–1999; $2.50 each for 2000–4999; $2 each for 5000+; technical and applications manuals available upon request (price information available from publisher); user's manual free with each order.
Time: (30–35) minutes.
Comments: Inventory for self-rating; can be self-administered and self-scored.
Authors: Curtis Miles (test and user's manual), Phyllis Grummon (test, user's manual, and technical manual), and Karen M. Maduschke (technical manual).
Publisher: H & H Publishing Co., Inc.
Cross References: For reviews by Wayne Camara and Joyce Meikamp, see 14:429.

[2765]
Working Memory Test Battery for Children.

Purpose: To evaluate working memory in children and young adolescents.
Population: Ages 5–15.
Publication Date: 2001.
Acronym: WMTB-C.
Scores: 9 subtests: Digit Recall, Word List Matching, Word List Recall, Block Recall, Nonword List Recall, Listening Recall, Counting Recall, Mazes Memory, Backward Digit Recall.
Administration: Individual.
Price Data, 2002: $360.20 per complete battery including forms, stimulus books, and manual (183 pages).

Time: (60) minutes.
Authors: Susan Pickering and Sue Gathercole.
Publisher: The Psychological Corporation Europe [United Kingdom].

[2766]
Workplace Skills Survey.

Purpose: Designed to provide "information regarding basic work ethics and employment skills."
Population: Job applicants and employees.
Publication Date: 1998.
Acronym: WSS.
Scores, 7: Communication, Adapting to Change, Problem Solving, Work Ethics, Technological Literacy, Teamwork, Composite.
Administration: Individual or group.
Price Data, 2001: $40 per introductory kit including 5 reusable test booklets, 20 answer/score sheets, and technical manual; $30 per 20 answer/score sheets; $18 per 10 reusable test booklets.
Time: 20 minutes.
Author: Industrial Psychology International, Ltd.
Publisher: Industrial Psychology International, Ltd.

[2767]
Workplace Skills Survey—Form E.

Purpose: Designed to assess students' workplace readiness and employment skills.
Population: Students in school-to-work and vocational programs.
Publication Date: 2000.
Acronym: WSS-Form E.
Scores, 9: Career Planning, Job Attainment, Communication, Adapting and Coping with Change, Problem Solving, Work Ethics, Technological Literacy, Teamwork, Overall.
Administration: Individual or group.
Price Data, 2000: $8 per assessment per student; $6 per manual; $45 per 25 reusable test booklets.
Time: 50 minutes.
Comments: Scoring and analysis provided by publisher.
Author: Industrial Psychology International, Ltd.
Publisher: Industrial Psychology International, Ltd.

[2768]
World Government Scale.

Purpose: Measures attitudes toward world government.
Population: Students.
Publication Date: 1985.
Scores: Total score only.
Administration: Group.
Manual: No manual.
Price Data, 2002: $1 per scale.
Time: [12] minutes.

Comments: Supplementary article available.
Author: Panos D. Bardis.
Publisher: Donna Bardis.

[2769]
World History/Objective Tests.

Purpose: To assess students' general knowledge of world history.
Population: 1, 2 semesters high school.
Publication Dates: 1961–1970.
Scores: Total score only for each of 14 tests: The Earliest Civilizations, The Greeks, The Romans, The Middle Ages, The Bridge to Modern Times, First Semester Examination, The Era of Political Revolutions, The Age of Revolutions Continues, Imperialism/Nationalism/and World War I, Between the Two Great Wars, World War II, The Postwar World, Second Semester Examination, Final Examination.
Administration: Group.
Manual: No manual.
Price Data, 1994: $10.95 per test book including tests and response key.
Time: [50] minutes for unit tests; [60] minutes for other tests.
Comments: Formerly called Objective Tests in World History.
Author: Earl Bridgewater.
Publisher: Perfection Learning Corp.

[2770]
World of Work Inventory.

Purpose: "Designed to assist clients in thinking about themselves in relation to their total environment" in relation to their personal career development.
Population: Ages 13–65+.
Publication Dates: 1970–2001.
Acronym: WOWI.
Scores, 35: Career Interest Activities (17 scores: Public Service, The Sciences, Engineering & Related, Business Relations, Managerial, The Arts, Clerical, Sales, Service, Primary Outdoor, Processing, Machine Work, Bench Work, Structural Work, Mechanical & Electrical Work, Graphic Arts, Mining); Job Satisfaction Indicators (12 scores: Versatile, Adaptable to Repetitive Work, Adaptable to Performing Under Specific Instructions, Dominant, Gregarious, Isolative, Influencing, Self-Controlled, Valuative, Objective, Subjective, Rigorous): Aptitude/Achievement (6 scores: Verbal, Numerical, Abstractions, Spatial-Form, Mechanical/Electrical, Clerical).
Administration: Individual or group.
Price Data, 2001: Online administration: $13 per single profile report; $14 per single profile report with summary; $23 per profile report with interpretative report, and $189 online site license fee; Paper-and-pencil administration: $7 per test booklet; $16 per

single profile report; $25 per profile report with interpretative report answer sheet; $11 per coupon for interpretative report, and $19.95 per interpretation manual (2001, 70 pages).
Time: (60) minutes for online version; (90) minutes for paper-and-pencil short form.
Authors: Gregory P. M. Neidert and Nancy L. Ortman.
Publisher: World of Work, Inc.

[2771]
Worley's ID Profile.

Purpose: Designed to identify temperament.
Population: Ages 6 and over.
Publication Dates: 1995–2000.
Acronym: WIDP.
Scores, 8: 3 profile scores: Social, Leadership, Relationship; 5 behavior scores: Introverted Sanguine, Sanguine, Phlegmatic, Melancholy, Choleric.
Administration: Individual or group.
Forms, 2: Adult and Youth (Ages 6 to 16).
Price Data: Available from publisher.
Foreign Language Editions: Available in English, Spanish, and Portuguese.
Time: (10) minutes.
Author: John W. Worley.
Publisher: Worley's Identity Discovery Profile, Inc.

[2772]
Writing Process Test.

Purpose: "Measures the quality of students' written products."
Population: Grades 2–12.
Publication Dates: 1991–1992.
Acronym: WPT.
Scores, 14: Development [First Pass (Purpose/Focus, Audience, Vocabulary, Style/Tone, Total), Second Pass (Support/Development, Organization/Coherence, Total)], Fluency [Third Pass (Sentence Structure/Variety, Grammar/Usage, Capitalization/Punctuation, Spelling, Total)], Total.
Administration: Group.
Editions, 2: Individual, Classroom.
Price Data, 2001: $174 per complete kit including test manual (1992, 144 pages), technical manual (1992, 40 pages), 25 analytic scales, 25 Form A first draft booklets, and 25 revision booklets; $55 per test manual; $18 per 25 analytic record forms; $19 per 25 first draft booklets; $13 per 25 revision booklets; $16 per scorer folder; $35 per technical manual; $55 per scoring videotape.
Time: [45] minutes (+30 minutes for revision).
Authors: Robin Warden and Thomas A. Hutchinson.
Publisher: PRO-ED.
Cross References: For reviews by Ernest W. Kimmel and Sandra Ward, see 13:369 (1 reference).

[2773]
Writing Quest.

Purpose: Assessment portion of a program designed to "teach students how to score above expectations on the compulsory [Illinois] state writing examination."
Population: Grades 3–12.
Publication Date: 2001.
Scores, 8: 5 writing elements: Focus (Persuasive/Expository, Narrative), Support/Elaboration (Persuasive/Expository, Narrative), Organization (Persuasive/Expository, Narrative), Conventions, Integration.
Administration: Group.
Levels, 3: 1 (Grades 3–5), 2 (Grades 6–8), 3 (Grades 9–12).
Price Data, 2002: $14.95 per workbook, scoring service, report including answer forms for initial writing assignment (specify level); $11.95 per workbook only (specify level); $14 per manual (specify level); quantity discounts available.
Time: Untimed.
Comments: Part of program designed to teach students rules for evaluating and grading persuasive, expository, and narrative modes of writing; students write an initial essay, which is sent to publisher for scoring; publisher provides Score Report with ratings of the 5 writing elements for each student.
Author: John Wick.
Publisher: MetriTech, Inc.

[2774]
The Written Expression Test.

Purpose: To "measure written expression objectively."
Population: Grades 1 to 6.
Publication Dates: 1979–1982.
Acronym: WET.
Scores, 5: Productivity, Mechanics, Handwriting, Maturity, Composite.
Administration: Individual or group.
Price Data: Not available.
Time: (30) minutes.
Authors: Clark Johnson and Sharon Hubly.
Publisher: McClain.
Cross References: See T5:2934 (1 reference); for reviews by Noel Gregg and Lyn Haber, see 10:396.

[2775]
Written Language Assessment.

Purpose: Assesses writing ability.
Population: Grades 3–12.
Publication Date: 1989.
Acronym: WLA.
Scores, 5: General Writing Ability, Productivity, Word Complexity, Readability, Written Language Quotient.
Administration: Group.

Price Data, 2002: $80 per complete kit including 25 each of 3 writing record forms, 25 scoring/profile forms, manual (1989, 111 pages), and hand counter; $18 per 25 each of 3 writing record forms; $23 per 25 scoring/profile forms; $25 per manual; $15 per hand counter; $25 per specimen set.
Time: (45–60) minutes.
Authors: J. Jeffrey Grill and Margaret M. Kirwin.
Publisher: Academic Therapy Publications.
Cross References: See T5:2935 (2 references); for reviews by Stephen Jurs and Mary Ross Moran, see 11:477.

[2776]
Written Language Syntax Test.
Purpose: Designed as a "screening instrument used to provide information on student performance in written language syntax."
Population: Ages 10–17 hearing-impaired.
Publication Date: 1981.
Acronym: WLST.
Scores: Total score only.
Administration: Group or individual.
Levels, 3: 1, 2, 3.
Price Data: Price information available from publisher for tests (specify Level 1, 2, or 3), screening tests, individual data folders, and administrator's package including manual (33 pages) and one copy of each item.
Time: (10–20) minutes for screening test, (40-60) minutes per test.
Comments: Contains "Screening Test" to determine appropriate level for administration.
Author: Sharon R. Berry.
Publisher: Gallaudet University Press.
Cross References: For reviews by Michael W. Casby and Judith R. Johnston, see 9:1404.

[2777]
Yardsticks.
Purpose: "Criterion-referenced tests in mathematics."
Population: Ages 6, 7, 8, 9, 10, 11.
Publication Dates: 1973–1980.
Scores: Objectives-based scores only.
Administration: Group.
Levels, 6: Corresponding to ages.
Price Data: Available from publisher.
Time: Administration time not reported.
Author: NFER-Nelson Publishing Co., Ltd.
Publisher: NFER-Nelson Publishing Co., Ltd. [England].

[2778]
Young Adult Behavior Checklist and Young Adult Self-Report.
Purpose: "Designed to provide standardized descriptions of behavior, feelings, thoughts, and competencies."

Publication Date: 1997.
Scores, 11: Anxious/Depressed, Withdrawn, Somatic Complaints, Thought Problems, Attention Problems, Intrusive, Aggressive Behavior, Delinquent Behavior, Internalizing, Externalizing, Total.
Administration: Group.
Price Data: Available from publisher.
Author: Thomas M. Achenbach.
Publisher: Research Center for Children, Youth, and Families.
   a) YOUNG ADULT BEHAVIOR CHECKLIST.
   Population: Young adults.
   Acronym: YABCL.
   Time: (10–15) minutes.
   Comments: Ratings by parents.
   b) YOUNG ADULT SELF-REPORT.
   Population: Ages 18–30.
   Acronym: YASR.
   Time: (15–20) minutes.
Cross References: For reviews by Patti L. Harrison and Jonathon Sandoval, see 14:430.

[2779]
Young Children's Achievement Test.
Purpose: Designed to help determine early academic abilities.
Population: Ages 4-0 to 7-11.
Publication Date: 2000.
Acronym: YCAT.
Scores, 6: General Information, Reading, Mathematics, Writing, Spoken Language, and Early Achievement Composite.
Administration: Individual.
Price Data, 2001: $179 per complete kit including examiner's manual (154 pages), picture book (48 pages), 25 student response forms, and 25 profile/examiner record booklets; $55 per examiner's manual; $64 per picture book; $24 per 25 student response forms; $39 per 25 profile/examiner record booklets.
Time: (25–45) minutes.
Authors: Wayne P. Hresko, Pamela K. Peak, Shelley R. Herron, and Deanna L. Bridges.
Publisher: PRO-ED.

[2780]
Youth's Inventory—4.
Purpose: Designed to determine "the extent to which the adolescent patient is aware of his or her symptoms" [of adolescent psychopathology], as determined by self-report.
Population: Ages 12–18.
Publication Date: 1999.
Acronym: YI-4.
Scores, 11: AD/HD Inattentive, Hyperactive–Impulsive, Combined, Oppositional Defiant Disorder, Conduct Disorder, Generalized Anxiety Disorder, Major

Depressive Disorder, Dysthymic Disorder, Separation Anxiety Disorder, Eating Problems, Bipolar Disorder.
Administration: Individual.
Price Data, 2001: $75 per deluxe kit including 50 checklists, 50 symptom count score sheets, 50 symptom severity profile score sheets, and manual (1999, 170 pages); $52 per 50 checklists.
Time: [15] minutes.
Authors: Kenneth D. Gadow and Joyce Sprafkin.
Publisher: Checkmate Plus, Ltd.

MMY TEST REVIEWERS

Test descriptions in Tests in Print VI *include cross references to reviews in previous* Mental Measurements Yearbooks *for tests still in print and those reviewers are also listed in the Names Index. This listing of* MMY *Test Reviewers lists all reviewers in the entire* MMY *series. The numbers after the names represent the* Mental Measurements Yearbooks *in which reviews appear.*

Harold H. Abelson, 3
Murray Aborn, 4
Phillip L. Ackerman, 11-14
Terry A. Ackerman, 12-13
Fred L. Adair, 8
Carol Adams, 9
Clifford R. Adams, 6
Elizabeth C. Adams, 4
Georgia S. Adams, 7-8
Gerald R. Adams, 9
Mary Friend Adams, 8
Russell L. Adams, 9-10
Susan F. Adams, 12
C. J. Adcock, 5-7
Dorothy C. Adkins, 3-7
Dan L. Adler, 5
Seymour Adler, 10
Janet G. Afflerbach, 5
Lois G. Afflerbach, 5
Frederick B. Agard, 3
J. Stanley Ahmann, 6-9
Eugene V. Aidman, 14
Lewis R. Aiken, 9, 12
Mary D. Ainsworth, 5
Peter W. Airasian, 8-10
Mark A. Albanese, 11-14
Lewis E. Albright, 6-8
Norma A. Albright, 2
Bruce K. Alcorn, 11-12

John Charles Alderson, 8
Lawrence M. Aleamoni, 8-9, 11-12
Charlene M. Alexander, 12
Ralph A. Alexander, 9
Bob Algozzine, 9
Henry A. Alker, 7-8
Doris V. Allen, 9-10
Lawrence Allen, 9
Mary J. Allen, 9
Nancy L. Allen, 11
Robert M. Allen, 8
Sarah J. Allen, 11-12
Richard L. Allington, 9-10
Julie A. Allison, 12-14
John C. Almack, 1-2
William D. Altus, 4
Jean D. Amberson, 4
Sueann Robinson Ambron, 8
Vera M. Amerson, 3
Anne Anastasi, 1-11
Nicholas Anastasiow, 7-8
Kenneth N. Anchor, 12
Charles V. Anderson, 8
David O. Anderson, 11-13
Howard R. Anderson, 1-7
Irving H. Anderson, 1, 3
James M. Anderson, 3-4, 6
John O. Anderson, 11-12, 14
Kenneth E. Anderson, 4, 6

Robert P. Anderson, 8-9
Jerrilyn. V. Andrews, 11-13
Lawrence Andrus, 2
Harvey A. Andruss, 3
Charles J. Ansorge, 9
Edgar Anstey, 6
Paul A. Arbisi, 12-14
Francis X. Archambault, Jr., 9, 11-12
Robert P. Archer, 11
Joyce A. Arditti, 12
Edward N. Argulewicz, 9
James A. Armentrout, 8
Christian O. Arndt, 2
Dwight L. Arnold, 4-5
Gwen F. Arnold, 4
Edward Aronow, 12
Raoul A. Arreola, 12-14
Judith A. Arter, 9
F. Marion Asche, 12
Philip Ash, 11-14
Ronald A. Ash, 9, 12
E. Jack Asher, Jr., 11
Theodore A. Ashford, 3, 5
Lear Ashmore, 8-9
Alexander W. Astin, 6-7
Carolyn Peluso Atkins, 9
Samuel D. Atkins, 1-2
Mark J. Atkinson, 14
Deborah H. Atlas, 12
Jeffrey A. Atlas, 11-14
Kathryn Hu-Pei Au, 9
Mark W. Aulls, 9
James T. Austin, 9, 11-14
Mary C. Austin, 6
Stephen N. Axford, 11-14
Frederic L. Ayer, 3-4
George W. Ayer, 8
J. Douglas Ayers, 6-8, 11
Glen P. Aylward, 11-14
Kris L. Baack, 12
James C. Babcock, 2
Patricia A. Bachelor, 11-14
Lyle F. Bachman, 11-12
Philip A. Backlund, 13-14
Ellen H. Bacon, 10-11
Beth D. Bader, 12
Andrew R. Baggaley, 5-6
Stephen J. Bagnato, 9
Theresa M. Bahns, 14
Sherry K. Bain, 12, 14
Leonard L. Baird, 7
Janet Baldwin, 12
Thomas S. Baldwin, 7-8, 10
Benjamin Balinsky, 4-5
Rachel S. Ball, 2
Joan C. Ballard, 14
Warren R. Baller, 4-5

Irol W. Balsley, 6
Deborah L. Bandalos, 12, 14
K. Denise Bane, 11
Charlotte E. K. Banks, 4-5
Nicholas W. Bankson, 8-11
Allan G. Barclay, 7
James R. Barclay, 9-10
Benjamin D. Barker, 14
Laura L. B. Barnes, 11-13
Walter Barnes, 1
Janet Barnes-Farrell, 14
David W. Barnett, 10-12
Rita M. Barnett, 12
W. Leslie Barnette, Jr., 8
Andrés Barona, 11, 13
A. S. Barr, 3
Rebecca C. Barr, 7-8
Richard S. Barrett, 6
Thomas C. Barrett, 6
Frank Barron, 5
William M. Bart, 11-12
Brendan John Bartlett, 9
W. L. Bashaw, 7
Alan R. Bass, 8
David J. Bateson, 12
Donald H. Baucom, 9
Ernest A. Bauer, 11-12
Robert H. Bauernfeind, 5-8
Ronald Baumanis, 9
Deborah N. Bauserman, 9
Brent Baxter, 3-5
Ernest Edward Bayles, 1
Nancy Bayley, 2-3, 5
Kenneth L. Bean, 5-6
Robert M. Bear, 3-4
Harold P. Bechtoldt, 4-7
Isabel L. Beck, 9
Michael D. Beck, 11-13
Roland L. Beck, 2-3
Samuel J. Beck, 2, 5
Wesley C. Becker, 6
Ralph C. Bedell, 3, 5
H. R. Beech, 6
Martha C. Beech, 9
Fred S. Beers, 1
Isaac I. Bejar, 8
Marcia J. Belcher, 11
John E. Bell, 4-6
Peter Della Bella, 13
Camilla Persson Benbow, 11
Kathryn M. Benes, 11-12
James K. Benish, 13-14
Albert A. Bennett, 2-3
Clinton W. Bennett, 12-13
George K. Bennett, 3-7
Jeri Benson, 11, 13
Mark J. Benson, 12-13

Nicholas Benson, 13
Philip G. Benson, 9-12
Marsha Bensoussan, 13
Peter M. Bentler, 6-7
Arthur L. Benton, 3-4, 7
Stephen L. Benton, 11-12
H. E. Benz, 2
Ralph F. Berdie, 3-7
Harry D. Berg, 3-8
Paul Conrad Berg, 7
Allen Berger, 7-9
Michael Berger, 8
Peter Miles Berger, 14
Betty Bergstrom, 13
Ronald A. Berk, 9, 12-14
Hinsdale Bernard, 12-13
H. John Bernardin, 9-12
Rita Sloan Berndt, 9-10
Jean-Jacques Bernier, 11-12
Robert G. Bernreuter, 1-4
Frank M. Bernt, 12-14
Joan D. Berryman, 9
Frederick Bessai, 11-14
Emmett A. Betts, 6
William Betz, 1, 3
Charles L. Bickel, 2
John Biggs, 9
Marion A. Bills, 3
Walter V. Bingham, 1
William C. Bingham, 6, 8
L. B. Birch, 6-7
Herbert G. W. Bischoff, 9, 14
Lisa G. Bischoff, 11-14
Bruce H. Biskin, 11-12
Reign H. Bittner, 3-4
Harold H. Bixler, 3-4
Ake Bjerstedt, 5-6
Donald B. Black, 6-7
Hillel Black, 6
John D. Black, 5-6, 8-9
J. M. Blackburn, 2
James H. Blackhurst, 1
E. G. Blackstone, 3
Martha Blackwell, 12
C. B. Blakemore, 6
Emery P. Bliesmer, 6
Lynn S. Bliss, 10-12
Sonya Blixt, 12
Jack Block, 8
Martin E. Block, 12
Paul J. Blommers, 3-6
Benjamin S. Bloom, 3-5, 7
Lisa A. Bloom, 12-13
Bruce M. Bloxom, 7-9
Milton L. Blum, 3-4
James A. Blumenthal, 9
Jack L. Bodden, 7-9

Ann E. Boehm, 9
Larry M. Bolen, 14
Carol A. Boliek, 11
Joan Bollenbacher, 5
Nancy B. Bologna, 12, 14
Brian F. Bolton, 8-9, 11-114
David L. Bolton, 12-13
Guy L. Bond, 2
Stephen J. Boney, 12
Gwyneth M. Boodoo, 9
Ivan A. Booker, 1-4
Daniel R. Boone, 7-8
Roger A. Boothroyd, 12-14
Edward S. Bordin, 3-5
Fred H. Borgen, 7-9
William Borgen, 9
Harold Borko, 6-7
Christopher Borman, 9-10
Walter C. Borman, 8-9
John R. Bormuth, 7
Robert A. Bornstein, 9-12
Morton Bortner, 6, 8-9
Michael D. Botwin, 12
Thomas J. Bouchard, Jr., 7-8
William R. Boulton, 9
Nicholas G. Bountress, 9
John E. Bowers, 6
Gregory J. Boyle, 11-14
J. David Boyle, 12
Bruce A. Bracken, 9-12
Jeffrey P. Braden, 11-12, 14
E. J. G. Bradford, 3-4
John M. Bradley, 9
Robert H. Bradley, 9
Thomas B. Bradley, 9
Francis F. Bradshaw, 1
John C. Brantley, 11
Marla R. Brassard, 9
James Braswell, 7-8
John R. Braun, 7-9
Arthur H. Brayfield, 4-6
W. C. Brenke, 3
Ann Brewington, 3
Ann Brickner, 7
Robert G. Bridgham, 7
M. Alan Brimer, 5-7
Elizabeth L. Bringsjord, 13
Frank W. Broadbent, 9
Stanley L. Brodsky, 8
Linda E. Brody, 10, 12
Hubert E. Brogden, 3-4
Susan M. Brookhart, 12-14
Jeffrey B. Brookings, 13
Nelson Brooks, 1-6
M. Eustace Broom, 2
R. A. Brotemarkle, 3
W. Dale Brotherton, 13

Tony Cellucci, 14
Edward J. Cervenka, 8
Robert W. Ceurvorst, 9
Hester Chadderdon, 1-2, 4
Robert C. Challman, 4, 6-7
E. G. Chambers, 3-5
Carolyn Chaney, 11
Laura H. Chapman, 8
Clinton I. Chase, 7-10
Henry Chauncey, 3, 6
Maurice Chazan, 7
Henry M. Cherrick, 9
Kathleen Barrows Chesterfield, 9
Brad S. Chissom, 7-8
Mary Mathai Chittooran, 13-14
James P. Choca, 13-14
Andrew Christensen, 9
Sandra L. Christenson, 11
Robert Christopher, 14
Edmund P. Churchill, 3
Ruth D. Churchill, 3, 5
Joseph C. Ciechalski, 11-14
Gregory J. Cizek, 11-14
Charles D. Claiborn, 9, 12
Cherry Ann Clark, 5
D. F. Clark, 7
Elaine Clark, 10, 12-14
Gale W. Clark, 5
J. F. Clark, 5
John L. D. Clark, 7-8
John R. Clark, 2
Kenneth E. Clark, 4
Philip M. Clark, 8-9
Richard M. Clark, 9, 11
Willis W. Clark, 6
H. Harrison Clarke, 4
Glen U. Cleeton, 3
W. V. Clemans, 6
Dorothy M. Clendenen, 5-7
Jeanette N. Cleveland, 9
Victor B. Cline, 7
James R. Clopton, 8-10
Richard W. Coan, 6-8
Harriet C. Cobb, 9
Larry R. Cochran, 9-12
Charles N. Cofer, 3-5
William E. Coffman, 3, 5-9, 11
Andrew D. Cohen, 12
Annabel J. Cohen, 12-13
Ashley Cohen, 14
Bertram D. Cohen, 6, 8
Jacob Cohen, 6-8
John Cohen, 3
Libby G. Cohen, 14
S. Alan Cohen, 7
Stephen L. Cohen, 8
Sanford J. Cohn, 9, 14

Theodore Coladarci, 12, 14
Nicholas Colangelo, 10
Debra E. Cole, 12
Nancy S. Cole, 7-9
Thomas R. Coleman, 9
Roberta R. Collard, 7
Carol J. Collins, 13-14
Deborah Collins, 12
Richard Colwell, 7-10
W. D. Commins, 1-4
Andrew L. Comrey, 5, 7-8
Judith C. Conger, 11-12
Collie W. Conoley, 11-13
Jane Close Conoley, 14
Clinton C. Conrad, 2
Herbert S. Conrad, 1-4
Norman A. Constantine, 11-12
Alicia Skinner Cook, 9, 11
John Cook, 7-9
Walter W. Cook, 2-3, 5
Donna K. Cooke, 12
Norma Cooke, 9
William W. Cooley, 6
Clyde H. Coombs, 3
Colin Cooper, 13-14
Mark Cooper, 14
M. Allan Cooperstein, 13-14
Robert B. Cooter, Jr., 10-11
Mary Kay Corbitt, 9
Stephen M. Corey, 1-2
Virginia E. Corgan, 10
Alice J. Corkill, 11-14
Ethel L. Cornell, 1
Merith Cosden, 11-14
Giuseppe Costantino, 9-10
William C. Cottle, 5
Stuart A. Courtis, 1, 4
Douglas Courtney, 3-4
John A. Courtright, 9-10
Andrew A. Cox, 14
James R. Cox, 9
Marion Monroe Cox, 1, 3
Richard C. Cox, 8
John A. Cox, Jr., 5
Hazel M. Crain, 9
Rick Crandall, 8
A. Garr Cranney, 8
Charles J. Cranny, 8
Albert B. Crawford, 2
Douglas H. Crawford, 9
John Crawford, 13
William R. Crawford, 6-7
Kevin D. Crehan, 11-14
Michelle M. Creighton, 11
Diana Crespo, 13
William J. E. Crissy, 4
R. Lenox Criswell, 2

John O. Crites, 6-9
Linda M. Crocker, 9-11, 13-14
Lysle W. Croft, 3-4
Lee J. Cronbach, 3-10
Lawrence A. Crosby, 9
Lawrence H. Cross, 12-13
Susan L. Crowley, 12
Douglas P. Crowne, 6
William M. Cruickshank, 4
Thomas J. Cullen, Jr., 14
Thomas E. Culliton, Jr., 6
Jack A. Cummings, 9-10, 12, 14
Oliver W. Cummings, 9
Rhoda Cummings, 14
Bert P. Cundick, 9-10
Edward E. Cureton, 1-2, 4
Louise W. Cureton, 4
Thomas K. Cureton, 3
William L. Curlette, 11-12
William Curr, 5
Francis D. Curtis, 1-2
Mary E. Curtis, 9
Michael J. Curtis, 9
Stephanie L. Cutlan, 13
Peter A. Dahl, 8
W. Grant Dahlstrom, 4-6, 8
John T. Dailey, 4-5
Edgar Dale, 3
Reginald R. Dale, 5
Fred L. Damarin, 8-9
Rik Carl D'Amato, 11-12, 14
Larry G. Daniel, 12
Mark H. Daniel, 12-14
John C. Daniels, 5
M. Harry Daniels, 9-10
John G. Darley, 1-2
Richard E. Darnell, 8-9
Ralph F. Darr, Jr., 11-13
J. P. Das, 9-10
Jane Dass, 8
John H. Daugherty, 3
James M. Daum, 9
Charles Davidshofer, 9
Brandon Davis, 11, 13
Charlotte Croon Davis, 3-6, 8
D. Russell Davis, 4-5
Edwin W. Davis, 3
Frederick B. Davis, 1-5, 7
Paul C. Davis, 6
Robert A. Davis, 3
Stanley E. Davis, 6
Steven F. Davis, 11-14
Parker Davis, Jr., 3
Mark L. Davison, 9
Helen C. Dawe, 3
Robyn M. Dawes, 8
Carolyn Dawson, 8

Linda S. Day, 11
Ayres G. D'Costa, 11-14
Gary J. Dean, 12-14
Raymond S. Dean, 9, 14
Lester W. Dearborn, 6
William W. Deardorff, 12-13
William L. Deaton, 11-12
R. J. De Ayala, 14
David A. Decoster, 10
James Deese, 5
Sharon H. deFur, 14
Frank P. DeLay, 2
Connie Kubo Della-Piana, 13-14
Gabriel M. Della-Piana, 6, 11
Vincent J. Dell'Orto, 8
Dennis J. Deloria, 7-9
Harold A. Delp, 4
Robert H. Deluty, 9
Randy Demaline, 8
Robert G. Demaree, 4, 7-8
Gerald E. DeMauro, 11-14
Marilyn E. Demorest, 10
George D. Demos, 6
Jennifer Denicolis, 12
Joseph W. Denison, 9
Evelyn Deno, 7
Susan K. Deri, 3
Mayhew Derryberry, 3
Lawrence G. Derthick, 5
Harry R. DeSilva, 2
Lizanne Destefano, 11-12, 14
Douglas K. Detterman, 9
M. Vere DeVault, 7
Edward F. deVillafranca, 8
Anthony J. DeVito, 9
Joseph C. Dewey, 1-2
Michael L. Dey, 9
Robert E. Deysach, 10
Denise M. DeZolt, 11-13
Esther E. Diamond, 8-9, 11-13
Joseph O. Prewitt Diaz, 14
Louis M. DiCarlo, 6
Charles F. Dicken, 6
Gwendolen S. Dickson, 1, 3
Paul B. Diederich, 1-2, 7
Allan O. Diefendorf, 11-12
John S. Diekhoff, 3-5
Thomas E. Dinero, 12
Jonathan G. Dings, 12
Robert L. Dipboye, 8
James Clyde DiPerna, 14
Jean Dirks, 9
David N. Dixon, 9-11-13
Faith Gunning-Dixon, 13-14
Gregory H. Dobbins, 9-10, 12
Keith S. Dobson, 9
Richard F. Docter, 7

Leland K. Doebler, 9
Janice A. Dole, 9-10
Elizabeth J. Doll, 10, 12-14
Robert H. Dolliver, 7-9
George Domino, 7-10, 12-14
Mavis L. Donahue, 9-10
Hei-Ki Dong, 9
Thomas F. Donlon, 8, 13
Jerome E. Doppelt, 4-8
Dan Douglas, 11
Harl R. Douglass, 2-3
E. Thomas Dowd, 9, 11-14
N. M. Downie, 6
John Downing, 8
Kenneth O. Doyle, Jr., 8
Vincent R. D'Oyley, 7
Ronald S. Drabman, 9
Raleigh M. Drake, 2-5
Richard M. Drake, 2-3
Penelope W. Dralle, 12
Ralph Mason Dreger, 8
Arnold Dresden, 1
Paul L. Dressel, 3-8
James Drever, 2
Philip H. Dreyer, 8-9
Laura A. Driscoll, 8
Robert C. Droege, 7
Lee Droegemueller, 14
Priscilla A. Drum, 8-10
Robert J. Drummond, 11-14
Cynthia Ann Druva-Roush, 11-12
Judy R. Dubno, 9, 13
Linda M. DuBois, 9
Philip H. DuBois, 3, 6-7
John H. Duckitt, 9
Curtis Dudley-Marling, 9
Gerald G. Duffy, 7
Lydia A. Duggins, 5
Stanley G. Dulsky, 2-3
Stephen B. Dunbar, 11
Harold B. Dunkel, 2-6
Jack W. Dunlap, 1-3
James A. Dunn, 7
S. S. Dunn, 5-6
Marvin D. Dunnette, 6
Carl J. Dunst, 9-10, 13
Daniel R. Dupecher, 8
Mary M. Dupuis, 9
Paula J. Dupuy, 11
Richard P. Duran, 9
Walter N. Durost, 4-8
David M. Dush, 9
Ralph D. Dutch, 6-8
August Dvorak, 2
Beatrice J. Dvorak, 3
Patricia L. Dwinell, 9
Carol Anne Dwyer, 8

Calvin O. Dyer, 9
Henry S. Dyer, 5-6
Robert Dykstra, 7-8
Norman Eagle, 5, 7-8
Douglas B. Eamon, 9
Maurice J. Eash, 8
Howard Easley, 2
Robert L. Ebel, 4-8
Bruce J. Eberhardt, 9-10
Del Eberhardt, 12
Tim Eck, 12
Allen Jack Edwards, 10, 12
Bateman Edwards, 2
Reginald Edwards, 5
Ron Edwards, 10-11
Byron R. Egeland, 8-9
Stewart Ehly, 10
Lee H. Ehman, 8
Linnea C. Ehri, 9
Jonathan Ehrlich, 11
William J. Eichman, 6-8
Dorothy H. Eichorn, 5-8
Philip Eisenberg, 3
Richard Elardo, 9
Bradley Elison, 12
John Elkins, 9
Arthur S. Ellen, 11
William Eller, 6
Warwick B. Elley, 8
Judy L. Elliott, 13
M. H. Elliott, 3
Robert W. Elliott, 14
Stephen N. Elliott, 9-11
Steven D. Elliott, 9
Albert Ellis, 3-7
Theresa H. Elofson, 12
Susan Embretson (Whitely), 9
Lon L. Emerick, 8
W. G. Emmett, 3-4
Norman S. Endler, 8-9
Brian Engdahl, 14
George Engelhard, Jr., 11-14
Max D. Engelhart, 1-2, 4-6
John M. Enger, 11-14
Bertram Epstein, 4
Jayne H. Epstein, 9
William P. Erchul, 10-11
James B. Erdmann, 11-13
Gerald L. Ericksen, 6-7
Deborah B. Erickson, 9-14
Lawrence W. Erickson, 6-8
Richard C. Erickson, 8, 10
Emanuel E. Ericson, 2
Claire B. Ernhart, 12
Leonard D. Eron, 5-7
Joan Ershler, 11
Anna S. Espenschade, 4-5

Barbara F. Esser, 6-7
Alvin C. Eurich, 1-2
James R. Evans, 9
Beth L. Evard, 9
Alexander Even, 7
Lorraine D. Eyde, 8-9
Julian Fabry, 9, 11-12
Jennifer J. Fager, 12-14
Doreen Ward Fairbank, 12-14
Shauna Faltin, 12
Xitao Fan, 13
Frank H. Farley, 9
Richard F. Farmer, 13-14
Paul R. Farnsworth, 1-3, 5-6
Roger Farr, 7-8
Wiltrud Fassbinder, 14
Ray N. Faulkner, 1-2
Richard W. Faunce, 11-12
Harold P. Fawcett, 2-5
Jay W. Fay, 1
Karen Fay, 13
Ethel M. Feagley, 3
Howard F. Fehr, 4
Elizabeth Fehrer, 3
Henry Feinberg, 1
Candice Feiring, 9-10
Shirley C. Feldmann, 8
Leonard S. Feldt, 5-8
Susan Felsenfeld, 12
Ray Fenton, 12-13
George A. Ferguson, 3-6
Leonard W. Ferguson, 6
Ephrem Fernandez, 13
F. Felicia Ferrara, 14
Steven Ferrara, 11, 13
Robert H. Ferrell, 5
Trenton R. Ferro, 12-14
C. E. Ficken, 2
James A. Field, Jr., 5
Gordon Fifer, 5
Nikola N. Filby, 8
Maynard D. Filter, 11, 14
Amy Finch-Williams, 10
Diane Billings Findley, 11
Warren G. Findley, 2-8
Stefan R. Fink, 8
Louis J. Finkle, 9
Carmen J. Finley, 11-12
Martin A. Fischer, 13
Seymour Fisher, 6
Wayne D. Fisher, 6
Joshua A. Fishman, 5
John L. Fisk, 9
Donald W. Fiske, 5
James A. Fitzgerald, 5
Colleen Fitzmaurice, 10
Anne R. Fitzpatrick, 11

Corine Fitzpatrick, 14
Robert Fitzpatrick, 7-13
Dawn P. Flanagan, 12
John C. Flanagan, 1, 3-4, 6
Rosemary Flanagan, 14
Stephen G. Flanagan, 11
John W. Fleenor, 11-14
Lisa Fleisher, 9
C. M. Fleming, 4
W. G. Fleming, 6
Charles D. Flory, 1, 3
Joseph J. Foley, 8
John P. Foley, Jr., 5-7
Mary O. Folsom, 7
Janet H. Fontaine, 14
Marie C. Fontana, 8
Thomas G. Foran, 1
Donna Ford, 12
Laurie Ford, 11-12
Rex L. Forehand, 9
Bertram R. Forer, 6
Frank J. Fornoff, 6, 8-9
Elaine Forsyth, 3
Robert A. Forsyth, 7-8
Tomlinson Fort, 2
Jim C. Fortune, 11-14
Judson W. Foust, 2
Hanford M. Fowler, 4-5
Raymond D. Fowler, Jr., 7-8
Charles Fox, 2
Glen Fox, 13-14
Hazel M. Fox, 10
Lynn H. Fox, 8-9
Robert A. Fox, 9
Austin C. Frank, 8
Mary Lou Bryant Frank, 14
Thomas T. Frantz, 7-8
Michael D. Franzen, 9
Stephen L. Franzoi, 9
Robert B. Frary, 9, 12-14
Barry J. Fraser, 9
Elizabeth D. Fraser, 5-6
Richard I. Frederick, 14
Wayne A. Frederick, 5
Norman Frederiksen, 3-8
Norman Fredman, 12
B. J. Freeman, 9
Frank S. Freeman, 4-5
Stephen J. Freeman, 14
David Freides, 7-8
J. Joseph Freilinger, 8
Patricia K. Freitag, 13-14
John W. French, 3-8
Joseph L. French, 7
Robert L. French, 6
Sidney J. French, 3
Bruce R. Fretz, 9

Benno G. Fricke, 5-6
Marilyn Friend, 10
David A. Frisbie, 8-9
Clifford P. Froehlich, 4-5
Gustav J. Froehlich, 3-6
Benjamin Fruchter, 5
Edward B. Fry, 6-8
Maurine A. Fry, 9
Douglas H. Fryer, 3
Verne C. Fryklund, 2
Douglas Fuchs, 10
Lynn S. Fuchs, 9-10
Mark H. Fugate, 12-13
Martin Fujiki, 9-10
Solomon M. Fulero, 12, 14
Paul H. Furfey, 1
Michael Furlong, 12-14
Elaine Furniss, 12
Edward J. Furst, 6-8
Robert K. Gable, 9, 11-14
Lena R. Gaddis, 11-13
N. L. Gage, 4-5
Eugene L. Gaier, 5
Rosslyn Gaines, 7
John P. Galassi, 9
Peggy E. Gallaher, 13
Gloria A. Galvin, 10-11
Leann M. Gamache, 12
Michael P. Gamache, 14
Bessie Lee Gambrill, 2
Ronald J. Ganellen, 12-14
H. C. Ganguli, 9
Calvin P. Garbin, 11
Eugene E. Garcia, 9-10
Eric F. Gardner, 4-10
Sol L. Garfield, 7
Alan Garfinkel, 8-9, 11, 13-14
Ruth Garner, 9
Edgar R. Garrett, 7
Henry E. Garrett, 1-5
Jack E. Gebart-Eaglemont, 13-14
Ann L. Gebhardt, 2
Karl W. Gehrkens, 2
Kurt F. Geisinger, 11-14
John Geisler, 13-14
Kenneth E. Gell, 2
Karen Geller, 13
Glenn B. Gelman, 14
Judy Lynn Genshaft, 9
J. Raymond Gerberich, 2-6
Kathryn Clark Gerken, 9-10
Joanne C. Gersten, 8
Maribeth Gettinger, 10
Esther Geva, 9
John J. Geyer, 7-8
Edwin E. Ghiselli, 3
Cecil A. Gibb, 5-7

H. H. Giles, 1-2
Ronald B. Gillam, 11-13
David Gillespie, 14
Jerry S. Gilmer, 12
John W. Gittinger, 5
Gene V Glass, 7-8
Hugh W. Glenn, 14
James R. Glennon, 6
Goldine C. Gleser, 6-9
John A. Glover, 11
Lewis R. Goldberg, 7-8
Charles J. Golden, 9
Stephen L. Golding, 8-9
Bert A. Goldman, 6-7, 11-14
Leo Goldman, 6
Ronald Goldman, 8
Steven H. Goldman, 9
Marcel L. Goldschmid, 7
Diane Goldsmith, 12
Keith Goltry, 2
Ronald H. Good, III, 11
Elizabeth J. Goodacre, 7
Florence L. Goodenough, 2-3
Joan F. Goodman, 9
Clarence J. Goodnight, 7
Leonard D. Goodstein, 6-8
William L. Goodwin, 8
Rodney K. Goodyear, 9
Betty N. Gordon, 9
Edwin Gordon, 7
Hans C. Gordon, 2-3
Leonard V. Gordon, 6-8
John B. Gormly, 9
Elliot L. Gory, 9, 11
Edward Earl Gotts, 9, 14
Harrison G. Gough, 4-9, 11-12
Neil Gourlay, 5
C. Ray Graham, 8
Grace Graham, 1-2
John R. Graham, 11-12
Steve Graham, 9, 11-14
Theresa Graham, 14
Susan L. Graham-Clay, 9
Larry B. Grantham, 12
Vicki, Gratopp, 12
M. Elizabeth Graue, 12
Carol A. Gray, 9
William S. Gray, 1, 3-4
Felice J. Green, 13-14
Kathy E. Green, 12-13
Russel F. Green, 6-7
Edward B. Greene, 3-5
Harry A. Greene, 2-3
Jeffrey H. Greenhaus, 9
Noel Gregg, 10
Frank M. Gresham, 9-13
Konrad Gries, 4-5

Keith Hattrup, 12-14
G. E. Hawkins, 2
David G. Hawkridge, 7-8
Mary R. Haworth, 5-6
Linda White Hawthorne, 9
Edward N. Hay, 3-5
James R. Hayden, 5-6
Steven C. Hayes, 11
Theodore L. Hayes, 13-14
Leslie M. Haynes, 4
Sandra D. Haynes, 13-14
William O. Haynes, 9-10, 12
Joni R. Hays, 14
E. Charles Healey, 10
Kenneth L. Heaton, 4
Martine Hébert, 11-13
Deborah Hecht, 11
Daniel Heck, 14
Natalie L. Hedberg, 11-12
Earle R. Hedrick, 2
David K. Heenan, 5-6
Lloyd H. Heidgerd, 6
Louis J. Heifetz, 10
Edith S. Heil, 10
Louis M. Heil, 2
Alfred B. Heilbrun, Jr., 5-10
Nancy Heilman, 11
Alice W. Heim, 4-7
Harry Heller, 2
William H. Helme, 6
G. C. Helmstadter, 7, 9
John K. Hemphill, 6-7
Carlen Henington, 13-14
V. A. C. Henmon, 1
Martha E. Hennen, 14
James J. Hennessy, 10, 14
Mary Henning-Stout, 10-13
Edwin R. Henry, 4
Stephan A. Henry, 10
William E. Henry, 4-5
William Hered, 6
David O. Herman, 12-13
Patricia Herman, 9
Edward S. Herold, 9
Edwin L. Herr, 9-10
Virgil E. Herrick, 4-5
Allen K. Hess, 9-14
Kathryn D. Hess, 11-12
Robert M. Hess, 12
John R. Hester, 11
William L. Heward, 9
Julia A. Hickman, 10
Peggy A. Hicks, 13
Elfrieda H. Hiebert, 9
A. N. Hieronymus, 5-7
A. Dirk Hightower, 10
E. H. C. Hildebrandt, 3

Scxott Kristian Hill, 14
Walker H. Hill, 5
John R. Hills, 6-9
Robert W. Hiltonsmith, 9, 11-13
Philip Himelstein, 7
Elmer D. Hinckley, 4
C. B. Hindley, 6
Laura Hines, 9
J. Scott Hinkle, 11
Michael D. Hiscox, 9
Marshall S. Hiskey, 6-7
Jean Hoard, 2
James R. Hobson, 2-5
Emil H. Hoch, 8
Elton Hocking, 3-4
James O. Hodges, 8
Barbara W. Hodson, 9
James V. Hoffman, 9
Robert Hogan, 7-10
Thomas P. Hogan, 8, 14
Dorothy E. Holberg, 3
Raymond H. Holden, 7
Candice Haas Hollingsead, 14
Warren S. Holmes, 2
Robert R. Holt, 4
Wayne H. Holtzman, 5, 7
Charles Holzwarth, 2
Susan P. Homan, 9
L. Michael Honaker, 11
Charles H. Honzik, 4
Marjorie P. Honzik, 6-7
Albert B. Hood, 8
Joyce E. Hood, 8-9
Stephen B. Hood, 8
Stephen R. Hooper, 10-14
Kenneth D. Hopkins, 6-9, 11
John L. Horn, 7
Thomas D. Horn, 7-8
John E. Horrocks, 5-6
Clark W. Horton, 2-5
Daniel L. Householder, 8
Charles Houston, 12
Carl I. Hovland, 3-5
Robert W. Howard, 2
Edgar Howarth, 8
George W. Howe, 9
Kenneth W. Howell, 9-10
Robert J. Howell, 10
Duncan Howie, 5
Monica M. Hoye, 3
Cyril J. Hoyt, 4-7
Kenneth B. Hoyt, 6
Louis M. Hsu, 9
Te-Fang Hua, 13
Mary E. Huba, 11
Carl J. Huberty, 7-9
Anita M. Hubley, 13-14

Harry W. Karn, 4
M. Ray Karnes, 4
Mitchell Karno, 12
Lawrence M. Kasdon, 7-9
Walter Kass, 5
Edward S. Katkin, 8
Walter Katkovsky, 6, 11
Ira Stuart Katz, 14
Martin R. Katz, 5-8
Raymond A. Katzell, 3-8
James M. Kauffman, 9
Alan S. Kaufman, 8-10, 13-14
Nadeen L. Kaufman, 9, 13-14
Walter V. Kaulfers, 1-7
Kenneth A. Kavale, 10
Michael G. Kavan, 11-14
Michael J. Kavanagh, 8
T. J. Keating, 2
J. A. Keats, 5-6
John M. Keene, Jr., 9
J. Ward Keesling, 9
Thomas J. Kehle, 9-10
Jerard F. Kehoe, 11
Gertrude Keir, 4
Patricia B. Keith, 12-14
Timothy Z. Keith, 9-10, 12, 14
Thomas Kellaghan, 8
Harold R. Keller, 10, 14
Mary Lou Kelley, 9-14
Truman L. Kelley, 2
Theodore E. Kellogg, 4-5
E. Lowell Kelly, 3-7
William E. Kendall, 6
Katherine G. Keneally, 4
James E. Kennedy, 6-7
Patricia H. Kennedy, 9
Kathryn W. Kenney, 10, 12
Douglas T. Kenny, 5
Leonard Kenowitz, 9
Grace H. Kent, 2-3
Barbara K. Keogh, 8-9
Robert E. Keohane, 2
Newell C. Kephart, 7
Barbara A. Kerr, 9-10, 12
Nancy Kerr, 9
Willard A. Kerr, 3-4, 6-7
Anne R. Kessler, 13
Carol E. Kessler, 14
Kathy S. Kessler, 11-12
Sandra M. Ketrow, 14
Gilbert C. Kettelkamp, 6
Thomas E. Kieren, 8
Kenneth A. Kiewra, 11-14
Edward Kifer, 9
Jeremy Kilpatrick, 7-8
Ernest W. Kimmel, 11, 13-14
Elaine F. Kinder, 1

Glen D. King, 8
John D. King, 12
Joseph E. King, 3
Suzanne King, 12
Forrest A. Kingsbury, 2
G. Gage Kingsbury, 12, 14
Albert J. Kingston, 6-8
Lucien B. Kinney, 2, 4
Richard T. Kinnier, 13
John R. Kinzer, 3
Wayne K. Kirchner, 6
Barbara A. Kirk, 7
Jean Powell Kirnan, 11-14
Karyll Kiser, 12
Philip M. Kitay, 6-7
Helen Kitchens, 13-14
Tom Kitwood, 8
Paul M. Kjeldergaard, 6
Seymour G. Klebanoff, 4
Beverly M. Klecker, 14
Benjamin Kleinmuntz, 6-10
Milton V. Kline, 6
Paul Kline, 7-8
William E. Kline, 7-8
Martin Kling, 7-8
Robert R. Knapp, 7
Samuel J. Knapp, 9
Thomas R. Knapp, 9, 13
Catharine C. Knight, 12
Howard M. Knoff, 9-14
John F. Knutson, 7
William R. Koch, 11-12
Stephen L. Koffler, 12-13
Kate L. Kogan, 3-4
William S. Kogan, 4
Timothy R. Konold, 14
David Kopel, 1-2
Rebecca J. Kopriva, 12
Abraham K. Korman, 8
Stephen M. Koziol, Jr., 8
Ernest J. Kozma, 11
Jack J. Kramer, 9
Jeffrey Kramer, 14
John H. Kranzler, 12, 14
David R. Krathwohl, 5
Thomas R. Kratochwill, 9
Charles J. Krauskopf, 7-8
Carole M. Krauthamer, 12
Roy A. Kress, 7-9
A. C. Krey, 1
Philip H. Kriedt, 6
Leslie H. Krieger, 14
Radhika Krishnamurthy, 14
S. David Kriska, 12
Russell P. Kropp, 5
Damon Krug, 13
Morris Krugman, 3-5

Paul S. Lomax, 3
John W. Lombard, 7-8
Charles J. Long, 12-14
John A. Long, 3
Louis Long, 3
Steven H. Long, 11-13
Andrew Longacre, 2
Alfred P. Longo, 13
Frank M. Loos, 4
Emilia C. Lopez, 13-14
Peter G. Loret, 6
Irving Lorge, 2-3, 5
Margaret F. Lorimer, 6
Maurice Lorr, 5-8
C. M. Louttit, 1-4
Kenneth Lovell, 6-7
Benson P. Low, 9
Jerry M. Lowe, 14
Rodney L. Lowman, 9-10
Brenda H. Loyd, 9, 12
S. Ruben Lozano, 9
Ardie Lubin, 4
William H. Lucio, 6
William H. Lucow, 5
Leslie Eastman Lukin, 13-14
James Lumsden, 5, 8
Robert W. Lundin, 5-7
Clifford E. Lunneborg, 7-8
Patricia W. Lunneborg, 8-9
David T. Lykken, 6-8
Howard B. Lyman, 6-7
Joan I. Lynch, 9-10
Hugh Lytton, 8
Henry S. Maas, 3
Linda Mabry, 12
Gloria Maccow, 13-14
John MacDonald, 13-14
F. Charles Mace, 9-10
Gordon N. MacKenzie, 3-4
Arthur C. MacKinney, 6-8
Karen Mackler, 14
Saunders MacLane, 6
David MacPhee, 11-13
George F. Madaus, 8-9
Faith Madden, 4
Cleborne D. Maddux, 10-14
Ronald A. Madle, 14
Thomas W. Mahan, Jr., 6
Roderick K. Mahurin, 11-12
James Mainwaring, 5
Timothy J. Makatura, 14
Koressa Kutsick Malcolm, 11, 13-14
Julius B. Maller, 1-2
Susan J. Maller, 13-14
George G. Mallinson, 6-8
Jacqueline V. Mallinson, 6-8
Berenice Mallory, 2

Margaret E. Malone, 13-14
Dean R. Malsbary, 8
Jay A. Mancini, 14
Milton M. Mandell, 4
Joseph R. Manduchi, 14
Kenneth J. Manges, 14
Ramasamy Manikam, 14
Lester Mann, 7-9
M. Jacinta Mann, 5
John Manning, 5, 7
Winton H. Manning, 6
Herschel T. Manuel, 2-5
Caroline Manuele-Adkins, 9-10, 12-13
Gregory J. Marchant, 12-14
Gary L. Marco, 11-14
Carol Mardell-Czudnowski, 10
Howard Margolis, 14
Suzanne Markel-Fox, 12
Robert P. Markley, 9-10
Howard J. Markman, 9
Melvin R. Marks, 6
Marc Marschark, 12
Herbert W. Marsh, 9
David Marshall, 10
Brian K. Martens, 10-11
Charles Wm. Martin, 11
Roy P. Martin, 9
Suzanne G. Martin, 14
William E. Martin, Jr., 13
Stanley S. Marzolf, 3
Bertram B. Masia, 6
Carolyn E. Massad, 8
Paul Mastrangelo, 14
Joseph D. Matarazzo, 9-10
Johnny L. Matson, 9
Ross W. Matteson, 4
Paula Matuszek, 9
Francis N. Maxfield, 1-2
James Maxwell, 3-5
Susanna Maxwell, 9
Samuel T. Mayo, 6-9
Arthur B. Mays, 2
James J. Mazza, 10
Charles C. McArthur, 7
John N. McCall, 7
Raymond J. McCall, 5
W. C. McCall, 2
William A. McCall, 2
James M. McCallister, 3
R. Steve McCallum, 9
Susan McCammon, 10
Boyd R. McCandless, 4, 6-7
James J. McCarthy, 7-9
Kevin J. McCarthy, 12, 14
James Leslie McCary, 8
Robert L. McCaul, 2-3
Clara J. McCauley, 2

Rebecca J. McCauley, 11-14
Erin McClure, 12
Scott R. McConnell, 11
Andrew J. McConney, 14
Richard J. McCowan, 14
Sheila C. McCowan, 14
Robert R. McCrae, 9
R. W. McCulloch, 5
Constance M. McCullough, 2-3, 5, 7
Merilee McCurdy, 14
S. P. McCutchen, 1-2
Hiram L. McDade, 9
Arthur S. McDonald, 6
D. W. McElwain, 4-5
William C. McGaghie, 8
Ellen McGinnis, 10
Carol M. McGregor, 14
Kevin S. McGrew, 10
Christine H. McGuire, 5-8
David E. McIntosh, 12
Robert M. McIntyre, 9
Michael G. McKee, 7
William T. McKee, 10
Margaret G. McKim, 3-4
Thomas McKnight, 14
Joyce R. McLarty, 11, 14
Kenneth F. McLaughlin, 6
John McLeish, 4, 7
Mary J. McLellan, 12-14
Jonathon C. McLendon, 6
John McLeod, 8
Robert J. McMahon, 9
Robert F. McMorris, 9-13
Douglas M. McNair, 7-8
Michael McNamara, 12
Sharon McNeely, 12
Malcolm R. McNeil, 10-14
Jeanette McPherrin, 2
John V. McQuitty, 3-4
Louis L. McQuitty, 4
Douglas J. McRae, 11-13
Leija V. McReynolds, 8
Paul McReynolds, 7-10
Damian McShane, 11
Richard A. Meade, 5
Arthur W. Meadows, 5
David J. Mealor, 9-11
I. G. Meddleton, 5
Albert E. Meder, Jr., 5
Maria Del R. Medina-Diaz, 13-14
Frederic J. Medway, 11, 13
Paul E. Meehl, 3
Sheila Mehta, 14
Edwin I. Megargee, 7-8
Howard D. Mehlinger, 7-8
William A. Mehrens, 7-9, 11-13
Sheila Mehta, 13

Manfred J. Meier, 7-9, 11
Norman C. Meier, 2
Scott T. Meier, 12-14
Joyce Meikamp, 14
William B. Meldrum, 1, 3
P. L. Mellenbruch, 5
Gary B. Melton, 9-10, 12
Richard S. Melton, 6, 8
H. Meltzer, 3
David M. Memory, 9
Gerald A. Mendelsohn, 6
Kevin Menefee, 11-12
Robert J. Menges, 8
Ivan N. Mensh, 4
Gerald M. Meredith, 7
Peter F. Merenda, 11-14
Philip R. Merrifield, 6
Jack C. Merwin, 6-8
William R. Merz, Jr., 12-14
Bernadine Meyer, 5
Donald L. Meyer, 6
John H. Meyer, 3
C. Edward Meyers, 8
Marcee J. Meyers, 9
Joan J. Michael, 7
William B. Michael, 4-13
Hillary Michaels, 14
William J. Micheels, 4-5
Grace Middleton, 11
Christopher P. Migotsky, 12
T. R. Miles, 5-6, 8
John E. Milholland, 5-8
C. Dean Miller, 9
Daniel C. Miller, 14
Gloria E. Miller, 10
John K. Miller, 9
Jon F. Miller, 9
Lovick C. Miller, 7-8
M. David Miller, 11-12, 14
Robert B. Miller, 14
Robert J. Miller, 11-14
Sherri K. Miller, 11
Jason Millman, 6-9
Craig N. Mills, 9, 11-12
John A. Mills, 13-14
J. B. Miner, 2
J. H. Minnick, 2
Patricia L. Mirenda, 10-12, 14
Lorenz Misbach, 3
Ronald W. Mitchell, 7
James V. Mitchell, Jr., 7-8
Carolyn Mitchell-Person, 14
Arthur Mittman, 6-8
Glenn Moe, 9
Huberto Molina, 8
William G. Mollenkopf, 3-4, 8
Floyd V. Monaghan, 7

Eason Monroe, 3
Marion Monroe, 1, 3
Judith A. Monsaas, 12-14
Joseph E. Moore, 2-4, 6
Terence Moore, 6
Walter J. Moore, 7
Pamilla Morales, 14
Mary Ross Moran, 11-12
Kevin L. Moreland, 9-14
G. A. V. Morgan, 5-7
Alice E. Moriarty, 7
Claudia J. Morner, 12, 14
Sherwyn P. Morreale, 12-14
John B. Morris, 5
Coleman Morrison, 6
Frances Crook Morrison, 5-6
Gale M. Morrison, 9, 12-13
Nathan Morrison, 3
Thomas F. Morrison, 2
Irving Morrissett, 8
H. T. Morse, 3
N. W. Morton, 1-2, 4
P. L. Morton, 2
Robert G. Morwood, 14
Harold E. Moser, 5
Donald L. Mosher, 7-8
David Moshman, 10
Charles I. Mosier, 2-3
C. Scott Moss, 6
Pamela A. Moss, 9, 11
Kevin W. Mossholder, 9-10
Stephan J. Motowidlo, 8-9
Donald E. Mowrer, 10
Robert R. Mowrer, 10
Paul M. Muchinsky, 9, 12-14
Daniel J. Mueller, 10
Kate Hevner Mueller, 5
Ralph O. Mueller, 11-13
Ann M. Muench, 11
Ina V. S. Mullis, 8
Leo A. Munday, 7
Allyn M. Munger, 6
Janice W. Murdoch, 14
Carolyn Colvin Murphy, 10
Joseph A. Murphy, 7-8
Kevin R. Murphy, 9-12
Wilbur F. Murra, 1-2
Elsie Murray, 4
Mildred Murray-Ward, 13-14
James L. Mursell, 1-3
Bernard I. Murstein, 6-8
Charles T. Myers, 5, 8
Roberta S. Myers, 9
Sheldon S. Myers, 6-7
Dean H. Nafziger, 8, 11
Jack A. Naglieri, 9, 11
Philip Nagy, 12-13

Louis C. Nanassy, 5
Scott A. Napolitano, 14
Doris E. Nason, 8
Diana S. Natalicio, 8-9
Theodor F. Naumann, 6-7
Wendy Naumann, 14
Leo Nedelsky, 5-6
Charles O. Neidt, 5-6
Leah M. Nellis, 14
Edward A. Nelsen, 9
Clarence H. Nelson, 3-8
Jack L. Nelson, 8
Myrna K. Ness, 9
Debra Neubert, 11-12
Charles Neuringer, 8
Andrew F. Newcomb, 9
Theodore Newcomb, 2
Phyllis L. Newcomer, 8-9
Gwendolyn Newkirk, 10
T. Ernest Newland, 6-7
Bernard H. Newman, 7
Dianna L. Newman, 10-13
E. Jean Newman, 13-14
Isadore Newman, 12
Joseph Newman, 4
Kenneth R. Newton, 5
Arthur M. Nezu, 10
William H. Nibbelink, 8
Lois Nichols, 12
David S. Nichols, 9, 11
Robert C. Nichols, 6, 8-9
John Nisbet, 5-7
Stanley D. Nisbet, 4-7
Michael Nissenbaum, 12
Anthony J. Nitko, 8-14
Victor H. Noll, 1-7
Patricia Noller, 9
Claude E. Norcross, 4
Warren T. Norman, 5-7
Janet A. Norris, 9-14
Raymond C. Norris, 5
Robert D. North, 5-7
Paul A. Northrop, 1-2
Christine Novak, 12, 14
Ruth M. Noyce, 9-10
Edward S. Noyes, 2-3
Jum C. Nunnally, 7
Thomas Oakland, 8-9
C. A. Oakley, 2-3
C. O. Oakley, 3
Thomas C. O'Brien, 7-8
John E. Obrzut, 9, 11
Anna S. Ochoa, 8-9
Salvador Hector Ochoa, 12-14
Charles W. Odell, 1-3
Judy Oehler-Stinnett, 10-14
Lynn R. Offermann, 13

Billy T. Ogletree, 13, 14
Kevin E. O'Grady, 9-10
Stephen Olejnik, 11-12, 14
Donald W. Oliver, 6
Mary Ellen Oliverio, 5, 7-8
Esteban L. Olmedo, 9
D. Joe Olmi, 11-14
Carl J. Olson, 7
Deniz S. Ones, 14
Albert C. Oosterhof, 12-13
Don B. Oppenheim, 9
Pedro T. Orata, 2
Michael D. Orlansky, 9
Jacob S. Orleans, 2-6
David B. Orr, 6-7
John C. Ory, 9
Timothy M. Osberg, 11
Agnes E. Osborne, 3
Alan Osborne, 7-8
R. T. Osborne, 7
Worth J. Osburn, 1-2, 4
Stuart Oskamp, 7-8
Alton O'Steen, 2
Steven J. Osterlind, 11-13
Nicki N. Ostrom, 9
Donald P. Oswald, 13
Jay L. Otis, 3-4
Terry Overton, 11-14
Steven V. Owen, 11-14
Gretchen Owens, 14
William A. Owens, 6, 8-9
Robert E. Owens, Jr., 9-10
C. Robert Pace, 3-8
Abbot Packard, 12, 14
Albert G. Packard, 3
Vicki S. Packman, 14
Ellis Batten Page, 6-9
Kathleen D. Paget, 9-10, 13-14
Nathaniel J. Pallone, 14
Ian C. Palmer, 12
Orville Palmer, 5
Osmond E. Palmer, 5-7
Jean M. Palormo, 6
Josephine B. Pane, 7
Mary Pannbacker, 11
Anthony W. Paolitto, 12-14
Anthony M. Paolo, 14
Ila Parasnis, 14
Gino Parisi, 7
Jayne A. Parker, 9
Anna Parsek, 2
Charles K. Parsons, 9-12
A. Harry Passow, 4, 8-9, 11-12
Donald G. Paterson, 2-4
Gerald R. Patterson, 5
Willard W. Patty, 4
Walter Pauk, 7

Jerome D. Pauker, 6-9
Sharon E. Paulson, 13
Renee Pavelski, 14
David A. Payne, 6-7
Douglas S. Payne, 9
Frank D. Payne, 9
Robert W. Payne, 6-9
William G. Peacher, 4
I. Carolyn Pearson, 13-14
Mary Ellen Pearson, 9-11
John Gray Peatman, 2
Elazar J. Pedhazur, 8-9
E. A. Peel, 4-5
Charles W. Pendleton, 8
Douglas A. Penfield, 12
John P. Penna, 8
L. S. Penrose, 3
William H. Perkins, 7
Carole Perlman, 13
Kathleen N. Perret, 5
Barbara Perry-Sheldon, 10
Charles C. Peters, 1
Jerry L. Peters, 10
Charles A. Peterson, 9-10, 12-14
Christopher Peterson, 9
Donald R. Peterson, 6
Francisca Esteban Peterson, 14
Gary W. Peterson, 9
Harold A. Peterson, 7-10
Norman G. Peterson, 9
Reece L. Peterson, 9
Rolf A. Peterson, 8, 10
Shailer Peterson, 3
Julia Pettiette-Doolin, 10
Steven I. Pfeiffer, 9-14
Susanna W. Pflaum, 9
LeAdelle Phelps, 10, 12-13
Roger P. Phelps, 7-8
Gary W. Phillips, 9
S. E. Phillips, 9-10
Theodore G. Phillips, 5-7
Nick J. Piazza, 10
Eugene (Geno) Pichette, 13
James Pickering, 9
Hale C. Pickett, 3
Douglas A. Pidgeon, 5-9
John Pierce-Jones, 5-6
Ellen V. Piers, 6
Wayne C. Piersel, 9-10, 13-14
Myrtle L. Pignatelli, 2
Len Pikaart, 7-8
A. E. G. Pilliner, 5-8
Paul Pimsleur, 6
James W. Pinkney, 9-10, 12-13
Rudolf Pintner, 1
Francis J. Pirozzolo, 9
David J. Pittenger, 13-14

Barbara S. Plake, 9
Gus P. Plessas, 6-9
Lynnette B. Plumlee, 3, 5-7
John Poggio, 14
Joseph G. Ponterotto, 11
Marcel O. Ponton, 13
Robert C. Pooley, 2-7
Mark Pope, 11-12, 14
Donald B. Pope-Davis, 12
Mary S. Poplin, 9
Julia Y. Porter, 14
Lyman W. Porter, 6
James M. Porter, Jr., 3
William D. Porterfield, 11
Stanley D. Porteus, 2
C. Dale Posey, 10
Winifred L. Post, 4-5
G. Michael Poteat, 10-14
James A. Poteet, 9-10
Kenneth E. Poucher, 8
Thomas E. Powell, 11
Stephen Powers, 9
Elizabeth M. Prather, 9-11
Michael W. Pratt, 9
Sheila R. Pratt, 13-14
Norman T. Pratt, Jr., 1-2
Daniel A. Prescott, 1
Joan Preston, 7
Ralph C. Preston, 3-4
H. Vernon Price, 5
Jack Price, 7
Ray G. Price, 3, 6-7
Roy A. Price, 2-3
Erich P. Prien, 13-14
Kristin O. Prien, 14
Hugh F. Priest, 7
George P. Prigatano, 9
M. L. Kellmer Pringle, 4-7
Barry M. Prizant, 11
Glen W. Probst, 7
Barton B. Proger, 8-9
H. Thompson Prout, 9
Richard C. Pugh, 12-13
Earl V. Pullias, 2
Alan C. Purves, 7-8
Joan E. Pynes, 10
Fred Pyrczak, 8
M. Y. Quereshi, 7-8
Theresa A. Quigney, 14
Michelle Quinn, 9
Albert I. Rabin, 4-5, 7
S. Rachman, 6
John A. Radcliffe, 5-6
Rudolf E. Radocy, 12-13
Jeffrey S. Rain, 12-13
Nambury S. Raju, 9, 11-14
Bikkar S. Randhawa, 11-14

John F. Randolph, 3
Earl F. Rankin, 7-8
Alan J. Raphael, 13-14
Evelyn Raskin, 4
Leslie T. Raskind, 10
Michael M. Ravitch, 9
Glen E. Ray, 12
Alton L. Raygor, 6, 8
S. A. Rayner, 5
Mark D. Reckase, 9
James C. Reed, 7-9, 12-14
Michael L. Reed, 9
Homer B. C. Reed, Jr., 8-9
Edwin H. Reeder, 3-4
Jeff Reese, 14
Ronald E. Reeve, 9
William R. Reevy, 6
Barbara A. Reilly, 11-12
David H. Reilly, 9
Robert C. Reinehr, 11-14
Robert A. Reineke, 11-12
Richard J. Reisboard, 8
Ralph M. Reitan, 6-7
Willard E. Reitz, 7
H. H. Remmers, 1, 3, 5
K. Ann Renninger, 9
Joseph S. Renzulli, 9
Harvey Resnick, 9
Paul Retzlaff, 11-14
Cecil R. Reynolds, 9, 11-14
Maynard C. Reynolds, 5
Sharon B. Reynolds, 10
William M. Reynolds, 9, 14
Marvin Reznikoff, 7
James A. Rice, 8
Gilbert J. Rich, 3
David C. Richard, 14
R. Lynn Richards, 10
Roger A. Richards, 5-9, 11, 13-14
T. W. Richards, 4
James M. Richards, Jr., 7-8
J. A. Richardson, 5
M. W. Richardson, 1-2
S. C. Richardson, 5
Bert O. Richmond, 9
James H. Ricks, Jr., 4-6, 8
T. Andrew Ridenour, 13
Paul R. Rider, 2
Stanley E. Ridley, 9
C. Alan Riedesel, 6-8
William Rieman, III, 3-4
Michelle L. Ries, 14
Edward G. Rietz, 5
Henry L. Rietz, 1
Janet Morgan Riggs, 9
Seymour Rigrodsky, 7
Alice R. Rines, 8

Henry D. Rinsland, 1-4
Charlene Rivera, 11
Harry N. Rivlin, 4-5
James P. Rizzo, 6
Oscar H. Roberts, 7
Brent W. Roberts, 14
David C. Roberts, 13
Holland Roberts, 2-6
Mark W. Roberts, 9, 11, 14
Donald U. Robertson, 11
Gary J. Robertson, 9-10, 13
Elizabeth A. Robinson, 9
Eric Robinson, 12
G. Edith Robinson, 7
H. Alan Robinson, 6-8
Helen M. Robinson, 4-7
Richard D. Robinson, 8
Alec Rodger, 2-4
David A. Rodgers, 7
Ronald C. Rodgers, 9
Bruce G. Rogers, 9-14
Carl R. Rogers, 2
Cyril A. Rogers, 5
Frederick R. Rogers, 2
Margaret R. Rogers, 12
Virginia M. Rogers, 7
W. Todd Rogers, 7
Cynthia A. Rohrbeck, 11, 13-14
Samuel Roll, 10
Deborah D. Roman, 12-14
Thomas A. Romberg, 7-8
Leonard G. Rorer, 7
Carl L. Rosen, 7-9
Ephraim Rosen, 4
Gerald A. Rosen, 13
Marvin Rosen, 8
John H. Rosenbach, 7-9
Robert L. Rosenbaum, 8
Jennifer A. Rosenblatt, 13
Sylvia Rosenfield, 9-10
Arlene Coopersmith Rosenthal, 9-11
Nancy L. Roser, 8-9
Benjamin Rosner, 5-7
Jerome Rosner, 7
Alan O. Ross, 6
C. C. Ross, 2-3
Charles S. Ross, 4-5
Paul F. Ross, 6
Myron F. Rosskopf, 5
Michael J. Roszkowski, 9-10, 12-14
Rodney W. Roth, 11
Harold F. Rothe, 4
Robert D. Rothermel, 9
Barbara A. Rothlisberg, 11-14
John W. M. Rothney, 1, 3-7
Julian B. Rotter, 3
Pamela Carrington Rotto, 12

James B. Rounds, 9-10, 12
Byron P. Rourke, 9
Denise M. Rousseau, 9-10
Harold L. Royer, 6
Arthur B. Royse, 5-6
Thaddeus Rozecki, 13
Ronald H. Rozensky, 11
Mary Roznowski, 14
Donald L. Rubin, 11
Stanley I. Rubin, 6
Floyd L. Ruch, 3-4, 6
Giles M. Ruch, 2
Herbert C. Rudman, 9, 12-14
Lawrence M. Rudner, 11-12
Robert Rueda, 10
C. H. Ruedisili, 3
Mabel E. Rugen, 3
David L. Rule, 10
Edward A. Rundqust, 3
William H. Rupley, 9
David H. Russell, 2-4
Harry J. Russell, 2-3
Michael Lee Russell, 13
James O. Rust, 9-10
John Rust, 12
Leo P. Ruth, 8
Roger A. Ruth, 7-8
Joseph M. Ryan, 11
Lawrence J. Ryan, 14
Michael Ryan, 9-10
David G. Ryans, 3-4, 6
Jane A. Rysberg, 9-10
Richard Rystrom, 7-8
Darrell L. Sabers, 8-14
Donna S. Sabers, 13
Everett B. Sackett, 1, 6
Paul R. Sackett, 9
Cyril J. Sadowski, 12-13
H. Bradley Sagen, 6-7
Philip A. Saigh, 9
Perry Sailor, 12
Kenneth Sakauye, 12
Rachel Salisbury, 2
John Salvia, 9
Vincent J. Samar, 11-12, 14
David T. Sanchez, 9
Daryl Sander, 9
C. Sanders, 5
James R. Sanders, 9
Jonathan Sandoval, 9-10, 12-14
Claude A. Sandy, 12
Eleanor E. Sanford, 11-14
Dixie D. Sanger, 9
Toni E. Santmire, 9-10
Janice Santogrossi, 10
H. J. Sants, 6
Bert R. Sappenfield, 5-6

Irwin G. Sarason, 6
Theodore R. Sarbin, 4
Helen Sargent, 4
I. David Satlow, 5
George A. Satter, 3-4
Jerome M. Sattler, 8-10
Richard A. Saudargas, 10
Aulus W. Saunders, 2
David M. Saunders, 11
David R. Saunders, 5
William I. Sauser, Jr., 9-14
Jean-Guy Savard, 7
Diane J. Sawyer, 9-14
Gilbert Sax, 8
Peter Scales, 9
Dale P. Scannell, 9, 11-13
Douglas E. Scates, 1, 3, 5
William L. Schaaf, 4
Willis C. Schaefer, 4
William D. Schafer, 11-14
Joyce Parr Schaie, 8
K. Warner Schaie, 8-9
Susan J. Schenck, 9-10
Johann H. Schepers, 6
Alvin W. Schindler, 1-2, 4
Steven P. Schinke, 10, 12
Richard F. Schmid, 9
Frank L. Schmidt, 8-9, 13
John F. Schmitt, 9
Neal Schmitt, 9, 12-13
Gerald R. Schneck, 13-14
Arnold E. Schneider, 3
Leroy H. Schnell, 2-3
Lyle F. Schoenfeldt, 7-10
Patricia Schoenrade, 12-13
Wiliiam Schofield, 4-6
Fred J. Schonell, 2, 4-5
Richard V. Schowengerdt, 14
William B. Schrader, 4-6
H. E. Schrammel, 1
Fredrick A. Schrank, 9-10
Gregory Schraw, 12, 14
Robert L. Schreiner, 8
Herbert Schueler, 3-6
Douglas G. Schultz, 4, 6-7
Geoffrey F. Schultz, 11
Harold A. Schultz, 4, 6
Dale H. Schunk, 9
Richard Schupbach, 8
Donald H. Schuster, 6-7
Richard E. Schutz, 6-9
Joseph J. Schwab, 3
Gene Schwarting, 9, 12-14
Neil H. Schwartz, 9-10
Mariette Schwarz, 6
Dean M. Schweickhard, 2
Gladys C. Schwesinger, 4

Craig S. Scott, 8
Louise B. Scott, 5
Owen Scott, III, 11
May V. Seagoe, 4
Carl E. Seashore, 2
Harold G. Seashore, 3-6
Virginia Seavey, 3
Don Sebolt, 12
Charles Secolsky, 9
William Seeman, 4
Stanley J. Segal, 6
David Segel, 1, 3-4
Esther F. Segner, 2
S. B. Sells, 5-7
R. B. Selover, 3
Gary B. Seltzer, 11
Boris Semenonoff, 6
Melvin I. Semmel, 7
Trevor E. Sewell, 9
Robert E. Shafer, 9
Laurance F. Shaffer, 3-6
Marcia B. Shaffer, 9-12
Timothy Shanahan, 9, 14
Spencer Shank, 1
Gregory A. Shannon, 11
David A. Shapiro, 10-12
Edward S. Shapiro, 10-11
Stephen Sharp, 8
Marvin E. Shaw, 8
Steven R. Shaw, 12-14
Carleton B. Shay, 7-8
Marion F. Shaycoft, 5-6
Steward M. Shear, 11
Cynthia M. Sheehan, 9
Eugene P. Sheehan, 12-14
Eugene C. Sheeley, 7-9
Linda Jensen Sheffield, 9-10
Kenneth L. Sheldon, 9-10
William D. Sheldon, 4
Sylvia Shellenberger, 9
Ralph L. Shelton, 7-8
John W. Shepard, 10
Lorrie A. Shepard, 8-9
June Ellen Shepherd, 11
James W. Sherbon, 12
Susan M. Sheridan, 11
Bruce Shertzer, 9-10
John C. Sherwood, 6-9
Benjamin Shimberg, 3-4, 6-7, 9
Stanley L. Shinall, 8
Agnes E. Shine, 12
Richard E. Shine, 7
Kenneth G. Shipley, 9-11, 13
Walter C. Shipley, 3
Mariela C. Shirley, 13
Amy H. Shively, 11
Sidney W. Shnayer, 8

Leslie P. Steffe, 7-8
Harry L. Stein, 5-6
Jack M. Stein, 6-7
Margot B. Stein, 13-14
Stephanie Stein, 11-14
Wendy J. Steinberg, 10
William Stephenson, 4-6
F. E. Sterling, 9
Robert J. Sternberg, 9
Brenda A. Stevens, 14
Jay R. Stewart, 13-14
Krista J. Stewart, 9-10
Naomi Stewart, 4-6
Sheldon L. Stick, 9-10
Charles A. Stickland, 4
Harlan J. Stientjes, 11-12
Terry A. Stinnett, 10-14
William A. Stock, 11-12
Howard Stoker, 11
Joseph P. Stokes, 9-10
Clarence R. Stone, 2
Gerald L. Stone, 9-13
L. Joseph Stone, 4-5
Mark Stone, 9
Gary Stoner, 11
Janet M. Stoppard, 9
Donald Lee Stovall, 14
Phillip S. Strain, 9
David Strand, 10
Ruth M. Strang, 1-2, 5
Richard K. Stratton, 12
Christine F. Strauss, 12
Lois T. Strauss, 11
Lawrence J. Stricker, 6, 8
Ruth Strickland, 5
Douglas C. Strohmer, 9
Stanley R. Strong, 8-9
Charles R. Strother, 3-5
J. B. Stroud, 3
Hans H. Strupp, 7
Richard B. Stuart, 9-13
Dewey B. Stuit, 3-4
George W. Sturrock, 5
Gabrielle Stutman, 12-14
Frederick H. Stutz, 3, 5
Michael J. Subkoviak, 9, 11-13
Richard R. Sudweeks, 13
Hoi K. Suen, 11-14
Alan R. Suess, 7-8, 10
Richard M. Suinn, 7
Gail M. Sullivan, 11
Patricia M. Sullivan, 9
W. L. Sumner, 4
Norman D. Sundberg, 5-9, 11-14
Donna L. Sundre, 12-13
Yong H. Sung, 9
Donald E. Super, 3-6, 8

J. P. Sutcliffe, 5
John Sutherland, 5-6
Rosemary E. Sutton, 11-14
Marilyn N. Suydam, 7-9
John G. Svinicki, 10
Edward O. Swanson, 6
H. Lee Swanson, 9
Richard A. Swanson, 7-8
Robert M. Swanson, 8
Robert S. Swanson, 8
Jon D. Swartz, 8-9
Jody L. Swartz-Kulstad, 14
Cabrini S. Swassing, 10
Susan M. Swearer, 14
Mark E. Swerdlik, 9, 11-14
Harvey N. Switzky, 9, 11-12
Percival M. Symonds, 2-5
Hilda Taba, 1-2, 4
Harold Takooshian, 12
Abraham J. Tannenbaum, 6
Kikumi K. Tatsuoka, 9, 11
Maurice Tatsuoka, 11
Earl S. Taulbee, 8
Calvin W. Taylor, 5
Cie Taylor, 9
Erwin K. Taylor, 3-7
Howard R. Taylor, 3-4
Hugh Taylor, 7
John M. Taylor, 10
Ronald N. Taylor, 8
Wallace W. Taylor, 2-3
Florence M. Teagarden, 2-5
Lorene Teegarden, 2
Phyllis Anne Teeter, 9
Auke Tellegen, 8-9
Cathy Fultz Telzrow, 9-10, 12
Mildred C. Templin, 4
Edward A. Tenney, 2
W. Wesley Tennyson, 5
Mary L. Tenopyr, 9-10
James S. Terwilliger, 11-12
Anita S. Tesh, 12-13
E. W. Testut, 11
James B. Tharp, 2, 4
Paul W. Thayer, 6, 8-10
Herbert A. Thelen, 3
William N. Thetford, 6
C. L. Thiele, 2-3
Charles S. Thomas, 1-2
Cleveland A. Thomas, 5
Ruth G. Thomas, 9-10
Albert S. Thompson, 1-2, 4-6
Anton Thompson, 4
Bruce Thompson, 14
Donald Thompson, 12-14
John H. Thompson, 1
Nora M. Thompson, 11-13

John F. Wakefield, 11
Delores D. Walcott, 14
William J. Waldron, 12-14
Helen M. Walker, 1
Robert Wall, 13-14
Shavaun M. Wall, 9
W. D. Wall, 4
S. Rains Wallace, 4-5
Wimburn L. Wallace, 5-8
Norman E. Wallen, 6
Niels G. Waller, 11-14
James A. Walsh, 7-8
W. Bruce Walsh, 7
Edwin Wandt, 4, 7
Sandra J. Wanner, 14
Morey J. Wantman, 4-6
Richard A. Wantz, 10, 12, 14
F. W. Warburton, 4-5
Annie W. Ward, 11-14
Charles F. Ward, 7
Sandra Ward, 13-14
William C. Ward, 7-8
George Wardlow, 10
James L. Wardrop, 8-10
E. M. Waring, 9
David M. Wark, 7
Charles F. Warnath, 6, 8
Neil D. Warren, 3, 5
Willard G. Warrington, 5-7
Ruth W. Washburn, 3
Orest E. Wasyliw, 12, 14
Alan T. Waterman, 2
Betsy Waterman, 13-14
Eugene A. Waters, 2
Everett Waters, 9
John G. Watkins, 6
Marley W. Watkins, 9
Ralph K. Watkins, 2
Richard W. Watkins, 7-8
Betty U. Watson, 9
Goodwin Watson, 1-3
Robert I. Watson, 3
T. Steuart Watson, 11-14
J. Fred Weaver, 5
Terri L. Weaver, 14
Larry Weber, 12
Harold Webster, 5-6
William J. Webster, 7, 9
David Wechsler, 2-3
Thaddeus E. Weckowicz, 8
M. O'Neal Weeks, 9
Zona R. Weeks, 9
Walter L. Wehner, 8-9
Charles C. Weidemann, 1-2
David P. Weikart, 7
Sharon L. Weinberg, 9, 11-13
Annette B. Weinshank, 9

Sheldon A. Weintraub, 7-8
David L. Weis, 9
Susan Ellis Weismer, 11
David J. Weiss, 7-8
Ellen Weissinger, 12-13
Henry Weitz, 3-8
R. A. Weitzman, 9
Carolyn M. Welch, 3
Wayne W. Welch, 8
A. T. Welford, 4
Beth L. Wellman, 3
F. L. Wells, 1-3
J. Steven Welsh, 11, 13
Lesley A. Welsh, 13
Charles Wenar, 9
Tim L. Wentling, 8
Joseph M. Wepman, 7
Emmy E. Werner, 6-7
Paul D. Werner, 13-14
Edgar B. Wesley, 1-4
Alexander G. Wesman, 4-7
Leonard J. West, 7-9
Bert W. Westbrook, 7-9, 11-13
Carol E. Westby, 11-13
George Westby, 4-6
Goran Westergren, 14
Ingela Westergren, 14
Stephanie Western, 12
Alida S. Westman, 8-9, 11-12
Frederick L. Westover, 4
Harry G. Wheat, 2
D. K. Wheeler, 5
Kenneth G. Wheeler, 9
Patricia H. Wheeler, 11-12, 14
Susan C. Whiston, 14
Edward M. White, 8
Howard R. White, 4
Karl R. White, 9
Kenneth V. White, 11
Shirley A. White, 9
Sue White, 9-10
Susan Embretson (Whitely), 9
Sally Anita Whiting, 9
Dean K. Whitla, 6
Carroll A. Whitmer, 2-3
Richard G. Whitten, 13
Randolph H. Whitworth, 8
Lillian A. Whyte, 9
Keith F. Widaman, 14
Thomas A. Widiger, 9, 11, 14
J. Lee Wiederholt, 8-9
Margaret Rogers Wiese, 11
Martin J. Wiese, 12, 14
James D. Wiggins, 9
Jerry S. Wiggins, 6-7, 10
Linda F. Wightman, 11-12
Elisabeth H. Wiig, 9

Richard L. Wikoff, 9-10
Katherine W. Wilcox, 3
Terry M. Wildman, 12
William K. Wilkinson, 10-14
S. S. Wilks, 1-2
Haydn S. Williams, 5
J. Robert Williams, 6
Janice G. Williams, 11-13
Jean M. Williams, 12
John M. Williams, 11
Robert T. Williams, 9-13
David M. Williamson, 13
Edmund G. Williamson, 1-2
Warren W. Willingham, 6
Carl G. Willis, 7-8
Margaret Willis, 2
W. Grant Willis, 11-12
John M. Willits, 3, 5
Victor L. Willson, 8-10, 12
J. Richard Wilmeth, 6
David R. Wilson, 9
Guy M. Wilson, 1-3
James W. Wilson, 7
Robert M. Wilson, 9
Marlene Wadsworth Winell, 9
Herbert D. Wing, 4-6
Hilda Wing, 11-14
Harris Winitz, 8
William L. Winnett, 7
George P. Winship, Jr., 6-7
R. Winterbourn, 5
Carrie L. Winterowd, 14
Robert D. Wirt, 6-7
Steven L. Wise, 9-10, 12
Emory E. Wiseman, 7
Stephen Wiseman, 3, 5
Ernest C. Witham, 2
E. Lea Witla, 13
Joseph C. Witt, 9-10, 12-13
L. Alan Witt, 11–12
J. Richard Wittenborn, 3-4
Donna Wittmer, 12
Paul A. Witty, 3
David L. Wodrich, 9. 14
Kristen Wojcik, 13
Richard M. Wolf, 8-9, 11-14
Dael L. Wolfle, 1-2, 4
Leroy Wolins, 6
James A. Wollack, 12, 14
Myra N. Womble, 13
E. F. Wonderlic, 3

Hugh B. Wood, 2
Michelle Wood, 13
Ray G. Wood, 3
Clifford Woody, 1, 3
D. A. Worcester, 2-4
Edward A. Workman, 9
Julien Worland, 9
Blaine R. Worthen, 7-9, 12-13
F. Lynwood Wren, 3
C. Gilbert Wrenn, 1-2, 5
Benjamin D. Wright, 9
Claudia R. Wright, 11-14
Dan Wright, 9-12
Logan Wright, 11-12
Robert L. Wright, 7
William J. Wright, 8
J. Wayne Wrightstone, 1-3, 5
Jack Wrigley, 5
Thomas A. Wrobel, 11
Michael K. Wynne, 12
Kaoru Yamamoto, 8
Alfred Yates, 5
Aubrey J. Yates, 7
Daniel L. Yazak, 14
Albert H. Yee, 7
Frank R. Yekovich, 9
Tamela Yelland, 12
Dale Yoder, 4
John W. Young, 12, 14
James E. Ysseldyke, 8-12, 14
William Yule, 8
Robert H. Zabel, 9
Peter Zachar, 13-14
Louis C. Zahner, 2-3, 5
Dan Zakay, 9
O. L. Zangwill, 3
John A. Zarske, 9-10
Sheldon Zedeck, 8-9, 11-14
Paul F. Zelhart, 10
Michael J. Zickar, 14
Edwin Ziegfeld, 2-4
Linda J. Zimmerman, 14
Wayne S. Zimmerman, 6-7
Fred Zimring, 9
Joseph E. Zins, 9
Leland C. Zlomke, 10-14
Steven Zucker, 13
Marvin Zuckerman, 9
Donald G. Zytowski, 7-9, 12

INDEX OF TITLES

This title index includes a comprehensive listing of tests currently in print and included in this volume as well as out-of-print (or status unknown) tests that were listed in Tests in Print V *and* The Fourteenth Mental Measurements Yearbook. *Numbers without colons refer to in-print tests included in this volume. Numbers with colons refer to out-of-print tests not listed in this volume; readers interested in these tests are referred to the last volume listing the tests. For example, T5:1826 refers to test 1826 in* Tests in Print V; *14:399 refers to test 399 in* The 14th MMY. *Superseded titles are listed with a cross reference to the present title. All numbers refer to test entries, not to page numbers.*

A. I. Survey, 1

AAMD Adaptive Behavior Scale, see AAMR Adaptive Behavior Scale-School, Second Edition, 3

AAMD-Becker Reading-Free Vocational Interest Inventory, see Reading-Free Vocational Interest Inventory: 2, 2073

AAMR Adaptive Behavior Scale—Residential and Community, Second Edition, 2

AAMR Adaptive Behavior Scale—School, Second Edition, 3

AATG German Test, see National German Examination for High School Students, 1685

AATG National Standardized Testing Program, see National German Examination for High School Students, 1685

The ABC Inventory to Determine Kindergarten and School Readiness, 4

Aberrant Behavior Checklist, 5

Ability Explorer, 14:431

Abortion Scale, 6

Abuse Risk Inventory for Women, Experimental Edition, 7

Academic Advising Inventory, 8

Academic Aptitude Test: Non-Verbal Intelligence: Acorn National Aptitude Tests, 9

Academic Aptitude Test: Verbal Intelligence: Acorn National Aptitude Tests, 10

Academic Competence Evaluation Scales, 11

Academic Freedom Survey, 12

Academic Perceptions Inventory [2000 Revision], 13

Academic Proficiency Battery, 14

Access Management Survey, 16

ACCESS—A Comprehensive Custody Evaluation Standard System, 15

Accounting Aptitude Test, 17

Accounting Clerk Staff Selector, T5:16

Accounting Program Admission Test, 18

ACCUPLACER: Computerized Placement Tests, 19

ACDI-Corrections Version and Corrections Version II, 20

ACER Adult Form B, see ACER Word Knowledge Test, 34

ACER Advanced Test B40, 21

ACER Advanced Test B90: New Zealand Edition, 22

ACER Advanced Test BL-BQ, New Zealand Revision, 23

ACER Advanced Tests AL and AQ (Second Edition) and BL-BQ, 24

ACER Applied Reading Test, 25

ACER Higher Test PL-PQ, New Zealand Revision, 26

ACER Intermediate Test F, 27

ACER Intermediate Test G, 28

ACER Mechanical Comprehension Test, 29

Predictive Screening Test of Articulation, T5:2028

Pre-Kindergarten Screen, 1947

PRE-LAS English, 1948

PreLAS 2000, 1949

Preliminary Diagnostic Questionnaire, T5:2030

Preliminary SAT/National Merit Scholarship Qualifying Test, 1950

Preliminary Scholastic Aptitude Test, a shortened version of the College Board Scholastic Aptitude Test, see Preliminary SAT/National Merit Scholarship Qualifying Test, 1950

Preliminary Test of English as a Foreign Language, 1951

Pre-Literacy Skills Screening, 1952

A Premarital Communication Inventory, 1953

Premier PSB-Reading Comprehension Examination, see PSB Reading Comprehension Examination, 2018

PREPARE/ENRICH, 1954

Pre-Professional Skills Test, see The Praxis Series: Professional Assessments for Beginning Teachers, 1945

Pre-Referral Intervention Manual [Revised and Updated Second Edition], 1955

Preschool and Kindergarten Behavior Scales, 1956

Preschool and Kindergarten Interest Descriptor, 1957

Preschool and Primary Inventory of Phonological Awareness, 1958

Pre-School Behavior Checklist, 1959

The Preschool Behavior Questionnaire, 1960

Preschool Development Inventory, 1961

Preschool Developmental Inventory, see Preschool Development Inventory, 1961

Preschool Developmental Profile, 1962

Preschool Embedded Figures Test, T5:2042

Preschool Evaluation Scale, 1963

Preschool Language Assessment Instrument, 1964

Preschool Language Scale–3, 1965

Preschool Motor Speech Evaluation & Intervention, 1966

Preschool Performance Scale, see CID Preschool Performance Scale, 478

Preschool Screening Instrument, 1967

Preschool Screening System, 1968

The Pre-School Screening Test, 1969

Preschool Screening Test, see Preschool Skills Test, 1970

Preschool Self-Concept Picture Test, T5:2048

Preschool Skills Test, 1970

Present State Examination, 1971

The Press Test, 1972

The Preverbal Assessment-Intervention Profile, see Assessment for Persons Profoundly or Severely Impaired, 195

Pre-Verbal Communication Schedule, 1973

The Prevocational Assessment and Curriculum Guide, 1974

Prevocational Assessment Screen, 1975

Primary Empathic Abilities, see Diplomacy Test of Empathy, 825

The Primary Language Screen, T5:2055

Primary Measures of Music Audiation, 1976

Primary Mechanical Ability Tests, T5:2057

Primary Reading Test 1, see Reading Tests A and BD, 2081

Primary Reading Test 2, see Reading Tests A and BD, 2081

Primary Reading Test, 1977

Primary Test of Cognitive Skills, 1978

Primary Test of Economic Understanding, T5:2060

Principles of Adult Mentoring Inventory, 1979

PrinTest—Forms A-C and B-C, 1980

Prison Inmate Inventory, 1981

Problem Behavior Inventory [Adult & Adolescent Screening Forms], 1982

Problem Experiences Checklist, 1983

Problem-Solving Decision-Making Style Inventory, 1984

The Problem Solving Inventory, 1985

Process and Diagnostic Screening Test, see Structure of Intellect Learning Abilities Test, 2393

Process Assessment of the Learner: Test Battery for Reading and Writing, 1986

Process Technician Test, T5:2066

Production and Maintenance Technician Test—Form A, 1987

Productive Practices Survey, 1988

Productivity Environmental Preference Survey, 1989

Productivity Profile, 1990

Professional and Managerial Position Questionnaire, 1991

Professional Employment Test, 1992

Profile of a School, T5:2073

Profile of Adaptation to Life, 1993

Profile of Adaptation to Life-Clinical Scale, see Profile of Adaptation to Life, 1993

Profile of Adaptation to Life-Holistic Scale, see Profile of Adaptation to Life, 1993

Profile of Aptitude for Leadership, 1994

Profile of Mood States, 1995

Profile of Mood States, Bi-Polar Form, 1996

Profile of Nonverbal Sensitivity, 1997

[Profiles from Rensis Likert Associates, Inc.], T5:2079

Profiles of Organizational Influence Strategies, see Kipnis-Schmidt Profiles of Organizational Influence Strategies, 1343

Profiles of Problem Solving, T5:2080

Program for Assessing Youth Employment Skills, 1998

Program for the Acquisition of Language with the Severely Impaired, T5:2082

Program Quality Assessment, 1999

Program Self-Assessment Service, 2000

Programmer Analyst Aptitude Test [One-Hour Version], 2001

INDEX OF RECENTLY
OUT-OF-PRINT TESTS

The Index of Recently Out-of-Print Tests is a cumulative listing of tests that appeared in Tests in Print III *through* The Fourteenth Mental Measurements Yearbook *but that do not appear in* Tests in Print VI. *The publishers of most of these tests have advised that the tests are now out of print. For some others, status has been unknown for over 10 years and the last known publisher is no longer in business and the tests are not published by a different publisher so out-of-print status has been assumed. The tests in this new index that appeared in* Tests in Print V *and* The Fourteenth Mental Measurements Yearbook *but are not in* Tests in Print VI *are also integrated into the Index of Titles. All numbers refer to test entries, not page numbers. For example, T4:233 refers to test 233 in* Tests in Print IV, *12:121 refers to test 121 in* The 12th MMY, *and 13:301 refers to test 301 in* The 13th MMY.

AAHPER Cooperative Health Education Test, T3:1
AAHPER Cooperative Physical Education Tests, T3:2
AAHPER Sport Skills Tests, T3:4
AAHPER Youth Fitness Test, T3:5
AAHPERD Health Related Physical Fitness Test, 9:2
AAHPERD-Kennedy Foundation Special Fitness Test for the Mentally Retarded, T3:3
Ability Explorer, 14:431
AC Test of Creative Ability, T3:10
Academic Aptitude Test, T3:11
Academic Readiness and End of First Grade Progress Scale, T3:16
Academic Readiness Scale, T3:17
Academic-Technical Aptitude Tests, T4:12
Accounting Clerk Staff Selector, T5:16
ACER Advanced Test N, T3:20
ACER and University of Melbourne Music Evaluation Kit, 9:6
ACER Arithmetic Tests: Standardized for Use in New Zealand, T3:23
ACER Checklists for School Beginners, 9:7
ACER Chemistry Test Item Collection: Year 12 (Chemtic), 9:8
ACER Early School Series, 9:10
ACER Higher Tests, 9:11
ACER Intermediate Test A, T3:29

ACER Intermediate Tests C and D, T3:30
ACER Junior Non-Verbal Test, T3:31
ACER Junior Test A, T3:32
ACER Listening Test, 9:14
ACER Lower Grades General Ability Scale, Second Edition, T3:34
ACER Mathematics Profile Series, 9:15
ACER Mathematics Tests: AM Series, 9:16
ACER Number Test, T3:39
ACER Paragraph Reading Test, 9:18
ACER Physics Unit Tests: Diagnostic Aids, 9:19
ACER Primary Reading Survey Tests, 10:4
ACER Review and Progress Tests in Mathematics, 9:20
ACER Silent Reading Tests: Standardized for Use in New Zealand, T3:44
ACER Speed and Accuracy Tests, T5:31
ACER Spelling Test-Years 3-6, 9:22
ACER Test of Cognitive Ability, 9:23
ACER Test of Learning Ability, T5:32
ACER Test of Reasoning Ability, 12:6
ACER Tests of Basic Skills-Blue Series, 12:7
ACER Word Knowledge Test—Adult Form B, T3:48
Achievement Test in Jewish History, T4:35
Achievement Test-Hebrew Language, T4:36
Achievement Test-Jewish Life and Observances, T4:37

INDEX OF ACRONYMS

This Index of Acronyms refers the reader to the appropriate test in Tests in Print VI. *In some cases tests are better known by their acronyms than by their full titles, and this index can be of substantial help to the person who knows the former but not the latter. Acronyms are only listed if the author or publisher has made substantial use of the acronym in referring to the test, or if the test is widely known by the acronym. A few acronyms are also registered trademarks (e.g., SAT); where this is known to us, only the test with the registered trademark is referenced. There is some danger in the overuse of acronyms, but this index, like all other indexes in this work, is provided to make the task of identifying a test as easy as possible. All numbers refer to test numbers, not page numbers.*

PBCL: Pre-School Behavior Checklist, 1959
PBF: Parent Behavior Form, 1799
PBI: Power Base Inventory, 1937
PBQ: The Preschool Behavior Questionnaire, 1960
PCA: Personal Creativity Assessment, 1850
PCAD: Psychiatric Content Analysis and Diagnosis, 2022
PCAT: Pharmacy College Admission Test, 1895
PCCI: Parent-Child Communication Inventory, 1800
PCDP: 16PF® Personal Career Development Profile, 2295
PCI: A Premarital Communication Inventory, 1953
PCL-R: Hare Psychopathy Checklist–Revised, 1122
PCL:SV: Hare Psychopathy Checklist: Screening Version, 1123
PCRI: Parent-Child Relationship Inventory, 1801
PCT: Wesman Personnel Classification Test, 2704
PDI: Preschool Development Inventory, 1961
PDI-CSI: PDI Employment Inventory and PDI Customer Service Inventory, 1820
PDI-EI: PDI Employment Inventory and PDI Customer Service Inventory, 1820
PDI-IV: Personality Disorder Interview-IV: A Semistructured Interview for the Assessment of Personality Disorders, 1882
PDI-R: Psychiatric Diagnostic Interview—Revised, 2023
PDMS-2: Peabody Developmental Motor Scales—Second Edition, 1821
PDP: Personal Dynamics Profile, 1852
PDQII: Denver Prescreening Developmental Questionnaire II, 766
PDRT: Portland Digit Recognition Test, 1927
PDS: Posttraumatic Stress Diagnostic Scale, 1934
PDS:BIDR: Paulhus Deception Scales: Balanced Inventory of Desirable Responding Version 7, 1818
PEDI: Pediatric Evaluation of Disability Inventory, 1826
PEDS: Parents' Evaluation of Developmental Status, 1810
PEEK: PEEK—Perceptions, Expectations, Emotions, and Knowledge About College, 1830
PEER: Pediatric Examination of Educational Readiness (PEER), 1828
PEERAMID-2: Pediatric Examination of Educational Readiness at Middle Childhood, 1827
PEET: Pediatric Extended Examination at Three (PEET), 1829
PEEX-2: Pediatric Early Elementary Examination (PEEX2), 1825
PEF: Psychiatric Evaluation Form, 2024
PEI: Personal Effectiveness Inventory, 1853
PEI: Personal Experience Inventory, 1854
PEI-A: Personal Experience Inventory for Adults, 1855
PEP: Psycho-Epistemological Profile, 2029
PEP-R: Psychoeducational Profile Revised, 2028

PEPS: Productivity Environmental Preference Survey, 1989
PES: Preschool Evaluation Scale, 1963
PESQ: Personal Experience Screening Questionnaire, 1856
PEST: The Patterned Elicitation Syntax Test with Morphonemic Analysis, 1817
PET: Professional Employment Test, 1992
P/FII: Parent/Family Involvement Index, 1802
PFMAI: Posture and Fine Motor Assessment of Infants, 1935
PHCSCS: Piers-Harris Children's Self-Concept Scale (The Way I Feel About Myself), 1913
PHIQ: Philadelphia Head Injury Questionnaire, 1897
PHSF: PHSF Relations Questionnaire, 1904
PI: Penguin Index, 1832
PI: Personal Stress Inventory, 1870
PIAT-R: Peabody Individual Achievement Test—Revised [1998 Normative Update], 1822
PIC-2: Personality Inventory for Children, Second Edition, 1883
PII: Prison Inmate Inventory, 1981
PIL: The Purpose in Life Test, 2040
PIP: Elementary Program Implementation Profile, 898
PIPA: Preschool and Primary Inventory of Phonological Awareness, 1958
PIQ: Purdue Interest Questionnaire, 2038
PIT: Picture Identification Test, 1910
PIY: Personality Inventory for Youth, 1884
PKBS: Preschool and Kindergarten Behavior Scales, 1956
PKRS: Phelps Kindergarten Readiness Scale, 1896
PKS: Pre-Kindergarten Screen, 1947
PLAB: Phonological Assessment Battery [Standardised Edition], 1900
PLAI: Preschool Language Assessment Instrument, 1964
PLANT: Warehouse/Plant Worker Staff Selector, 2682
PLP: The Clark Wilson Group Multi-Level Feedback Instruments and Development Programs, 480
PLS-3: Preschool Language Scale–3, 1965
PLSS: Pre-Literacy Skills Screening, 1952
P-MAC/ESP: Perceptual-Motor Assessment for Children & Emotional/Behavioral Screening Program, 1841
PME: Outcomes: Planning, Monitoring, Evaluating, 1787
PMI: Power Management Inventory, 1938
PMMA: Primary Measures of Music Audiation, 1976
PMP: Power Management Profile, 1939
PMPQ: Professional and Managerial Position Questionnaire, 1991
PMS: Participative Management Survey, 1814
PMT: Assessment of Individual Learning Style: The Perceptual Memory Task, 204
PNEE: Entrance Examination for Schools of Practical/Vocational Nursing, 933

CLASSIFIED SUBJECT INDEX

The Classified Subject Index classifies all tests included in Tests in Print VI *into 18 major categories: Achievement, Behavior Assessment, Developmental, Education, English and Language, Fine Arts, Foreign Language, Intelligence and General Aptitude, Mathematics, Miscellaneous, Neuropsychological, Personality, Reading, Science, Sensory-Motor, Social Studies, Speech and Hearing, and Vocations. Each category appears in alphabetical order and tests are ordered alphabetically within each category. The Miscellaneous category has 15 subcategories with tests ordered alphabetically within the subcategories. Each test entry includes test title, population for which the test is intended, and the test entry number in* Tests in Print VI. *All numbers refer to test entry numbers, not to page numbers. Brief suggestions for the use of this index are presented in the introduction. Revised definitions of the categories were effective with the* Fourteenth Mental Measurements Yearbook. *Most tests in* TIP VI *have been classified using the new definitions, which are provided below.*

Achievement

Tests that measure acquired knowledge across school subject content areas. Included here are test batteries that measure multiple content areas and individual subject areas not having separate classification categories. (Note: Some batteries include both achievement and aptitude subtests. Such batteries may be classified under the categories of either Achievement or Intelligence and Aptitude depending upon the principal content area.)

See also Fine Arts, Intelligence and General Aptitude, Mathematics, Reading, Science, and Social Studies.

Behavior Assessment

Tests that measure general or specific behavior within educational, vocational, community, or home settings. Included here are checklists, rating scales, and surveys that measure observer's interpretations of behavior in relation to adaptive or social skills, functional skills, and appropriateness or dysfunction within settings/situations.

Developmental

Tests that are designed to assess skills or emerging skills (such as number concepts, conservation, memory, fine motor, gross motor, communication, letter recognition, social competence) of young children (0-7 years) or tests which are designed to assess such skills in severely or profoundly disabled school-aged individuals. Included here are early screeners, developmental surveys/profiles, kindergarten or school readiness tests, early learning profiles, infant development scales, tests of play behavior, social acceptance/social skills; and preschool psychoeducational batteries. Content specific screeners, such as those assessing readiness, are classified by content area (e.g., Reading).

See also Neuropsychological and Sensory-Motor.

Education

General education-related tests, including measures of instructional/school environment, effective schools/teaching, study skills and strategies, learning styles and strategies, school attitudes, educational programs/curriculae, interest inventories, and educational leadership.

Specific content area tests (i.e., science, mathematics, social studies, etc.) are listed by their content area.

English and Language

Tests that measure skills in using or understanding the English language in spoken or written form. Included here are tests of language proficiency, applied literacy, language comprehension/development/proficiency, English skills/proficiency, communication skills, listening comprehension, linguistics, and receptive/expressive vocabulary. (Tests designed to measure the mechanics of speaking or communicating are classified under the category Speech and Hearing.)

Fine Arts

Tests that measure knowledge, skills, abilities, attitudes, and interests within the various areas of fine and performing arts. Included here are tests of aptitude, achievement, creativity/talent/giftedness specific to the Fine Arts area, and tests of aesthetic judgment.

Foreign Languages

Tests that measure competencies and readiness in reading, comprehending, and speaking a language other than English.

Intelligence and General Aptitude

Tests that measure general acquired knowledge, aptitudes, or cognitive ability and those that assess specific aspects of these general categories. Included here are tests of critical thinking skills, nonverbal/verbal reasoning, cognitive abilities/processing, learning potential/aptitude/efficiency, logical reasoning, abstract thinking, creative thinking/creativity; entrance exams and academic admissions tests.

Mathematics

Tests that measure competencies and attitudes in any of the various areas of mathematics (e.g., algebra, geometry, calculus) and those related to general mathematics achievement/proficiency. (Note: Included here are tests that assess personality or affective variables related to mathematics.)

Miscellaneous

Tests that cannot be sorted into any of the current MMY categories as listed and defined above. Included here are tests of handwriting, ethics and morality, religion, driving and safety, health and physical education, environment (e.g., classroom environment, family environment), custody decisions, substance abuse, and addictions. (See also Personality.)

Neuropsychological

Tests that measure neurological functioning or brain-behavior relationships either generally or in relation to specific areas of functioning. Included here are neuropsychological test batteries, questionnaires,

and screening tests. Also included are tests that measure memory impairment, various disorders or decline associated with dementia, brain/head injury, visual attention, digit recognition, finger tapping, laterality, aphasia, and behavior (associated with organic brain dysfunction or brain injury).

See also Developmental, Intelligence and General Aptitude, Sensory-Motor, and Speech and Hearing.

Personality

Tests that measure individuals' ways of thinking, behaving, and functioning within family and society. Included here are projective and apperception tests, needs inventories, anxiety/depression scales; tests assessing substance use/abuse (or propensity for abuse), risk taking behavior, general mental health, emotional intelligence, self-image/-concept/-esteem, empathy, suicidal ideation, schizophrenia, depression/hopelessness, abuse, coping skills/stress, eating disorders, grief, decision-making, racial attitudes; general motivation, attributions, perceptions; adjustment, parenting styles, and marital issues/satisfaction.

For content-specific tests, see subject area categories (e.g., math efficacy instruments are located in Mathematics). Some areas, such as substance abuse, are cross-referenced with the Personality category.

Reading

Tests that measure competencies and attitudes within the broadly defined area of reading. Included here are reading inventories, tests of reading achievement and aptitude, reading readiness/early reading ability, reading comprehension, reading decoding, and oral reading. (Note: Included here are tests that assess personality or affective variables related to reading.)

Science

Tests that measure competencies and attitudes within any of the various areas of science (e.g., biology, chemistry, physics), and those related to general science achievement/proficiency. (Note: Included here are tests that assess personality or affective variables related to science.)

Sensory-Motor

Tests that are general or specific measures of any or all of the five senses and those that assess fine or gross motor skills. Included here are tests of manual dexterity, perceptual skills, visual-motor skills, perceptual-motor skills, movement and posture, laterality preference, sensory integration, motor development, color blindness/discrimination, visual perception/organization, and visual acuity. (Note: See also the categories Neuropsychological and Speech and Hearing.)

Social Studies

Tests that measure competencies and attitudes within the broadly defined area of social studies. Included here are tests related to economics, sociology, history, geography, and political science, and those related to general social studies achievement/proficiency. (Note: Also included here are tests that assess personality or affective variables related to social studies.)

Speech and Hearing

Tests that measure the mechanics of speaking or hearing the spoken word. Included here are tests of articulation, voice fluency, stuttering, speech sound perception/discrimination, auditory discrimination/comprehension, audiometry, deafness, and hearing loss/impairment. (Note: See Developmental, English and Language, Neuropsychological, and Sensory-Motor.)

Vocations

Tests that measure employee skills, behaviors, attitudes, values, and perceptions relative to jobs, employment, and the work place or organizational environment. Included here are tests of management skill/style/competence, leader behavior, careers (development, exploration, attitudes); job- or work-related selection/admission/entrance tests; tests of work adjustment, team or group processes/communication/effectiveness, employability, vocational/occupational interests, employee aptitudes/competencies, and organizational climate.

See also Intelligence and General Aptitude, and Personality and also specific content area categories (e.g., Mathematics, Reading).

ACHIEVEMENT

Academic Competence Evaluation Scales; Grades K-12, Grades 6-12, 2- or 4-year college, see 11

ACER Tests of Basic Skills—Orchid Series; Students, year 4 to 6 in Australian school system, see 33

Achievement Test for Accounting Graduates; Accounting job applicants or employees, see 39

Adult Basic Learning Examination, Second Edition; Adults with less than 12 years of formal schooling, see 88

Ann Arbor Learning Inventory [1996 Edition]; Grades K-1, Grades 2-4, Grades 5-8, see 162

Aprenda®: La prueba de logros en español—Segunda edición; Grades K.5-12.9, see 169

Basic Achievement Skills Individual Screener; Grades 1-12 and post high school, see 250

BRIGANCE® Diagnostic Comprehensive Inventory of Basic Skills, Revised; Ages 5-13, see 341

BRIGANCE® Diagnostic Inventory of Essential Skills; Grade 6-adult, see 343

BRIGANCE® Diagnostic Life Skills Inventory; Grades 2-8, see 344

Bristol Achievement Tests; Ages 8-0 to 11-11, see 349

California Achievement Tests, Fifth Edition; Grades K.0-K.9, K.6-1.6, 1.6-2.2, 1.6-3.2, 2.6-4.2, 3.6-5.2, 4.6-6.2, 5.6-7.2, 6.6-8.2, 7.6-9.2, 8.6-10.2, 9.6-11.2, 10.6-12.9, see 365

Canadian Achievement Survey Tests for Adults; Adults, see 383

Canadian Achievement Tests, Third Edition; Grades 1.6-postsecondary, see 384

Canadian Tests of Basic Skills, Forms K and L; Grades K-2, 3-8, and 9-12, see 389

Closed High School Placement Test; Eighth grade students, see 537

College Basic Academic Subjects Examination; College students having completed the general education component of a college curriculu, see 557

Collegiate Assessment of Academic Proficiency; Freshmen-Seniors in College, see 609

Comprehensive Testing Program III; Grades 1-2, 2-3, 3-4, 4-6, 6-8, 8-12, see 650

Criterion Test of Basic Skills [2000 Edition]; Grades K-8., see 718

CTB Performance Assessment; Grades 2-11, see 728

Developing Skills Checklist; Ages 4-6.8, see 780

Diagnostic Achievement Battery, Third Edition; Ages 6-0 to 14-0, see 804

Diagnostic Achievement Test for Adolescents, Second Edition; Ages 12-0 to 18-11, see 805

Diagnostic Screening Test: Achievement; Grades K-12, see 810

Differential Ability Scales; Ages 2-6 to 17-11, see 816

Differential Aptitude Tests—Australian and New Zealand Editions [Forms V and W]; Grades 8-12, see 817

Differential Aptitude Tests, Fifth Edition; Grades 7-9, grades 10-12 and adults, see 818

Differential Aptitude Tests for Personnel and Career Assessment; Adult, see 819

Early School Assessment; End of prekindergarten to middle of kindergarten, middle of kindergarten to beginning of grade 1, see 866

Educational Abilities Scales; Ages 13-15, see 880

English Test: Municipal Tests: National Achievement Tests; Grades 3-8, see 927

Essential Skills Assessments: Information Skills; Ages 9-14, see 940

Evaluation of Basic Skills; Ages 3 to 18, see 949

BEHAVIOR ASSESSMENT

DEVELOPMENTAL

EDUCATION

ENGLISH AND LANGUAGE

FINE ARTS

Advanced Measures of Music Audiation; Junior high school through college, see 95

Advanced Placement Examination in Art History; High school students desiring credit for college-level courses and admission to advanced courses, see 96

Advanced Placement Examination in Music Theory; High school students desiring credit for college-level courses and admission to advanced courses, see 115

Advanced Placement Examination in Studio Art; High school students desiring credit for college-level courses and admission to advanced courses, see 121

The Farnum String Scale: A Performance Scale for All String Instruments; Grades 7-12, see 984

Group Tests of Musical Abilities; Ages 7–14, see 1105

Harmonic Improvisation Readiness Record and Rhythm Improvisation Readiness Record; Grades 3 through music graduate school, see 1124

Instrument Timbre Preference Test; Grades 4-12, see 1228

Intermediate Measures of Music Audiation; Grades 1-4, see 1236

Iowa Tests of Music Literacy, Revised; Grades 4–12, see 1270

Keynotes Music Evaluation Software Kit; Ages 9–14, see 1331

Measures of Musical Abilities; Ages 7–14, see 1555

Music Achievement Tests 1, 2, 3, and 4; Grades 3–12, see 1674

Musical Aptitude Profile [1995 Revision]; Grades 5–12, see 1675

Musical Aptitude Test; "White people" in standards 1–10 in South African schools, see 1676

Primary Measures of Music Audiation; K-3, see 1976

The Taylor-Helmstadter Pair Comparison Scale of Aesthetic Judgment; Ages 4 and over, see 2478

The Watkins-Farnum Performance Scale: A Standardized Achievement Test for All Band Instruments; Music students, see 2684

FOREIGN LANGUAGES

Advanced Placement Examination in French Language; High school students desiring credit for college-level courses and admission to advanced courses, see 106

Advanced Placement Examination in French Literature; High school students desiring credit for college-level courses and admission to advanced courses, see 107

Advanced Placement Examination in German Language; High school students desiring credit for college-level courses and admission to advanced courses, see 108

Advanced Placement Examination in Latin Literature; High school students desiring credit for college-level courses and admission to advanced courses, see 111

Advanced Placement Examination in Latin (Vergil); High school students desiring credit for college-level courses and admission to advanced courses, see 112

Advanced Placement Examination in Spanish Language; High school students desiring credit for college-level courses and admission to advanced courses, see 118

Advanced Placement Examination in Spanish Literature; High school students desiring credit for college-level courses and admission to advanced courses, see 119

Arabic Proficiency Test; Postsecondary to adult, see 176

Australian Second Language Proficiency Ratings; Adolescents and adults, see 235

The Ber-Sil Spanish Test; Ages 5–12, 13–17, see 307

Bilingual Syntax Measure [medida de Sintaxis Bilingüe]; Grades PK–2, 3–12, see 310

Chinese Proficiency Test; Postsecondary to adults, see 471

CLEP Examination in College-Level French Language, Levels 1 and 2; Persons entering college or already in college, see 492

CLEP Examination in College-Level German Language, Levels 1 and 2; Persons entering college or already in college, see 493

CLEP Examination in College-Level Spanish Language, Levels 1 and 2; Persons entering college or already in college, see 494

College Board Institutional SAT II: Chinese with Listening Subject Test; Entering college freshmen, see 562

College Board Institutional SAT II: French Subject Test; Entering college freshmen, see 564

College Board Institutional SAT II: French with Listening Subject Tests; Entering college freshmen, see 565

College Board Institutional SAT II: German Subject Test; Entering college freshmen, see 566

College Board Institutional SAT II: German with Listening Subject Test; Entering college freshmen, see 567

INTELLIGENCE AND GENERAL APTITUDE

MATHEMATICS

MISCELLANEOUS

ADJUSTMENT/ADAPTIVE FUNCTIONING

ALCOHOL AND SUBSTANCE USE

The American Drug and Alcohol Survey; Schools and school districts, see 147

ASIST: A Structured Addictions Assessment Interview for Selecting Treatment; Adults, see 188

Assessment of Chemical Health Inventory; Adolescents, adults, see 200

Drug Abuse Screening Test; Clients of addiction treatment, see 838

Drug-Taking Confidence Questionnaire; Clients of addiction treatment, see 839

Inventory of Drinking Situations; Ages 18 to 75, see 1253

Inventory of Drug-Taking Situations; Drug or alcohol users, see 1254

Michigan Alcoholism Screening Test; Adults, see 1583

Practical Adolescent Dual Diagnostic Interview; Ages 12–18, see 1941

QUESTS: A Life-Choice Inventory; Grades 9-12, see 2050

Situational Confidence Questionnaire; Adult alcoholics, see 2288

Substance Abuse Relapse Assessment; Adolescents and adults, see 2427

Substance Abuse Screening Test; Ages 13–adult, see 2428

The Substance Abuse Subtle Screening Inventory–3; Ages 18–73, see 2429

Substance Use Disorders Diagnosis Schedule-IV; Adults suspected of abusing alcohol or drugs, see 2430

Triage Assessment for Addictive Disorders; Adults, see 2629

BLIND

Braille Assessment Inventory; Ages 6–18, see 331

Lorimer Braille Recognition Test: A Test of Ability in Reading Braille Contractions; Students (ages 7-13) in grade 2 Braille, see 1451

Tooze Braille Speed Test: A Test of Basic Ability in Reading Braille; Students (Ages 7-13) in Grades 1 or 2 Braille, see 2612

BUSINESS EDUCATION AND RELATIONSHIPS

Alleman Leadership Development Questionnaire; Mentors and proteges, see 141

Alleman Mentoring Activities Questionnaire; Mentors and proteges, see 142

Alleman Relationship Value Questionnaire; Mentors and proteges, see 143

Diagnosing Organizational Culture; Adults, see 803

Dissemination Self-Inventory; Organizations, see 827

Entrepreneurial Style and Success Indicator; Adults, see 934

Group Environment Scale, Second Edition; Group members and leaders, see 1092

I-SPEAK Your Language™: A Survey of Personal Styles; Employees, see 1187

Influence Strategies Exercise; Managers and employees, see 1217

Inventory for Client and Agency Planning; Infant to adult, see 1250

Kilmann-Saxton Culture-Gap Survey [Revised]; Work team members, employees, see 1336

Kipnis-Schmidt Profiles of Organizational Influence Strategies; Organizational members, see 1343

Management of Differences Inventory; Business managers, see 1479

Mentoring Skills Assessment; Mentors, coaches, and mentees, see 1575

Organizational Climate Exercise II; Work groups, see 1777

Organizational Culture Inventory; Organizational members, see 1778

Watson-Barker Listening Test; Adults in business, professions, and college, see 2685

Watson-Barker Listening Test—High School Version; Grades 7-12, see 2686

Whisler Strategy Test; Business and industry, see 2710

Work Environment Scale, Second Edition; Employees and supervisors, see 2746

CRIMINAL JUSTICE

Correctional Institutions Environment Scale, Second Edition; Residents and staff of correctional facilities, see 700

Correctional Policy Inventory: A Survey of Correctional Philosophy and Characteristic Methods of Dealing with Offenders; Correctional managers, see 702

Defendant Questionnaire; Defendants (misdemeanor or felony), see 749

HCR-20: Assessing Risk for Violence; Adults (Psychiatric and Correctional Settings), see 1128

Juvenile Justice Policy Inventory; Juvenile justice professionals, see 1313

The LAW-PSI Adult Life History Questionnaire; Adults, see 1373

The LAW-PSI Child/Adolescent Life History Questionnaire; Children/adolescents, see 1374

The Lawrence Psychological Forensic Examination; Juvenile, criminal, and civil justice clients, see 1377

Level of Service Inventory—Revised: Screening Version; Ages 16 and older, see 1420

The Level of Service Inventory—Revised; Ages 16 and older, see 1421

Multiphasic Sex Inventory; Juvenile males, adult males, see 1669

Prison Inmate Inventory; Prison inmates, see 1981

Rogers Criminal Responsibility Assessment Scales; Criminals, see 2132

Sexual Violence Risk-20; Individuals suspected to be at-risk for committing sexual violence, see 2271

Shoplifting Inventory; Shoplifting offenders, see 2278

A Premarital Communication Inventory; Premarital couples, see 1953

PREPARE/ENRICH; Couples, see 1954

Scale of Marriage Problems: Revised; Couples, see 2182

Sex-Role Egalitarianism Scale; High school to adult, see 2266

Spousal Assault Risk Assessment Guide; Individuals suspected of or being treated for spousal or family-related assault, see 2349

Styles of Conflict Inventory; Heterosexual couples, see 2422

Uniform Child Custody Evaluation System; Professionals involved in custody evaluation, see 2635

Vasectomy Scale: Attitudes; Adults, see 2643

Wife's or Husband's Marriage Questions; Husbands, wives, see 2720

HEALTH AND PHYSICAL EDUCATION

The ANSER System-Aggregate Neurobehavioral Student Health and Educational Review [Revised 1997]; Children ages 3+, suspected of having learning difficulties, see 163

The Arizona Battery for Communication Disorders of Dementia; Alzheimer's patients, see 181

Behavioral Assessment of Pain Questionnaire; Subacute and chronic pain patients, see 293

Coitometer; Adults, see 555

Comprehensive Sex History; Adults, see 644

Cornell Index—Form N2; Ages 14 and over, see 696

Derogatis Interview for Sexual Functioning; Adults, see 771

Eating Inventory; Ages 17 and older, see 874

Erotometer: A Technique for the Measurement of Heterosexual Love; Adults, see 938

Fast Health Knowledge Test, 1986 Revision; High school and college, see 985

Functional Fitness Assessment for Adults over 60 Years, Second Edition; Adults over age 60, see 1023

Health and Daily Living Form, Second Edition; Students ages 12-18, Adults, see 1129

Health Problems Checklist; Adults, see 1136

Health Status Questionnaire 2.0; Ages 14 and older, see 1137

Krantz Health Opinion Survey; College, healthy adults, and chronic disease populations, see 1353

The LAW-PSI Sexual History Questionnaire; Adults, see 1375

Matching Assistive Technology & CHild; Children with disabilities, ages 0–5, see 1516

Medical Ethics Inventory; First year medical students, see 1566

Menometer; Adolescents and adults, see 1570

MILCOM Patient Data Base System; Medical patients, see 1591

Multidimensional Health Profile; Ages 18–90, see 1659

Organic Dysfunction Survey Schedules; Adult clients, see 1772

Pain Assessment Battery, Research Edition; Patients with chronic pain, see 1788

Psychosocial Pain Inventory [Revised]; Adults with chronic pain, see 2034

RAND-36 Health Status Inventory; Adults, see 2062

Rehabilitation Checklist; Adults, see 2090

Rehabilitation Compliance Scale; Severely injured patients ages 17–85 years, see 2091

Sexometer; Adolescents and adults, see 2267

Sexual Adaptation and Functioning Test; White adults ages 16 and over, see 2268

SF-36 Health Survey; Ages 14 and older, see 2273

Softball Skills Test; Grades 5-12 and college, see 2324

Stirling Eating Disorder Scales; Adolescents and adults, see 2376

Stress Indicator & Health Planner; Adults, see 2384

Tennis Skills Test Manual; High school and college, see 2509

Test of Auditory Analysis Skills; Children, see 2526

TestWell: Health Risk Appraisal; Adults ages 18–60 with a minimum of 10th grade education, see 2589

TestWell: Wellness Inventory for Windows; Adults with a minimum of 10th grade education, see 2590

TestWell: Wellness Inventory for Windows—College Version; College students, see 2591

HANDWRITING

Minnesota Handwriting Assessment; Grades 1–2, see 1619

LEARNING DISABILITIES

Achievement Identification Measure; School age children, see 36

Dyslexia Determination Test, Second Edition; Grades 2–12, see 848

Jordan Left-Right Reversal Test—Revised; Ages 5-12, see 1303

Pathways to Independence, Second Edition; Disadvantaged school-aged children and mentally and otherwise handicapped teenagers and adults and rehabilitating brain-damaged and geriatric patients, see 1816

PHILOSOPHY

C-R Opinionaire; Grades 11-16 and adults, see 708

PSYCHOLOGY

Counselor and Client Verbal Response Category Systems; Counselors in training, see 705

The Experiencing Scale; Counselors and counselor trainees, see 960

NEUROPSYCHOLOGICAL

PERSONALITY

READING

SCIENCE

SENSORY-MOTOR

SOCIAL STUDIES

College Board Institutional SAT II: World History Subject Test; Entering college freshmen, see 577

College Board SAT II: American History and Social Studies Subject Test; Candidates for college entrance with one-year American history course at the college-preparatory level, see 581

College Board SAT II: World History Subject Test; Candidates for college entrance, see 601

[Economics/Objective Tests]; 1 semester high school, see 876

Health and Safety Education Test: National Achievement Tests; Grades 3-6, see 1130

Informeter: An International Technique for the Measurement of Political Information; Adults, see 1221

Irenometer; Adults, see 1275

Quick Quizzes for U.S. History Classes; Grades 6-12, see 2056

Test of Economic Knowledge, Second Edition; Grades 7-9, see 2536

Test of Economic Literacy, Third Edition; Grades 11-12, see 2537

Test of Understanding in College Economics, Third Edition; Introductory economics students, see 2565

World Government Scale; Students, see 2768

World History/Objective Tests; 1, 2 semesters high school, see 2769

SPEECH AND HEARING

Arizona Articulation Proficiency Scale, Third Revision; Ages 1-6 through 18-11 years, see 180

Assessing and Teaching Phonological Knowledge; Young children, see 192

The Assessment of Aphasia and Related Disorders, Second Edition; Aphasic patients, ages 5.5–59, see 199

Assessment of Intelligibility of Dysarthric Speech; Adult and adolescent dysarthric speakers, see 205

The Assessment of Phonological Processes—Revised; Ages 3-0 through 12-0, see 209

Auditory Continuous Performance Test; Ages 6 to 11, see 229

Bankson-Bernthal Test of Phonology; Ages 3-9, see 241

Bedside Evaluation of Dysphagia, Revised Edition; Adults neurologically impaired, see 278

Boston Assessment of Severe Aphasia; Aphasic adults, see 327

Children's Articulation Test; Ages 3–11, see 457

CID Phonetic Inventory; Hearing-impaired children, see 476

CID Picture SPINE (SPeech INtelligibility Evaluation); Hearing-impaired children ages 6–13, see 477

Clinical Evaluation of Language Fundamentals—Preschool; Preschool and early elementary, see 529

Clinical Evaluation of Language Fundamentals, Third Edition; Ages 6.0–21.11, see 530

Communication Activities of Daily Living, Second Edition; Aphasic adults, see 617

Communication and Symbolic Behavior Scales; 6 months to 24 months, see 618

Comprehensive Test of Phonological Processing; Ages 5–6, ages 7–24, see 648

Denver Articulation Screening Exam; Ages 2.5 to 7.0, see 763

Denver Audiometric Screening Test; Ages 3–6, see 764

Draw A Person: A Quantitative Scoring System; Ages 5-17, see 833

Dysarthria Examination Battery; Children and adults, see 846

Early Speech Perception Test; Ages 3–6, ages 6–15, see 871

Eckstein Audiometers; All ages, see 875

Examining for Aphasia, Third Edition; Adolescents and adults, see 953

The Fisher-Logemann Test of Articulation Competence; Preschool to adult, see 1005

Fluharty Preschool Speech and Language Screening Test—Second Edition; Ages 3-0 to 6-11, see 1011

Frenchay Dysarthria Assessment; Ages 12 and over, see 1017

Functional Communication Profile; Aphasic adults, see 1022

Goldman Fristoe Test of Articulation—Second Edition; Ages 2–21, see 1054

Goldman-Fristoe-Woodcock Test of Auditory Discrimination; Ages 3-8 years and up, see 1055

Grammatical Analysis of Elicited Language—Pre-Sentence Level; Hearing-impaired children ages 3–6, see 1077

The Hundred Pictures Naming Test; Ages 4-6 to 11-11, see 1184

INteraction CHecklist for Augmentative Communication, Revised Edition; Augmentative system users, see 1232

Joliet 3-Minute Preschool Speech and Language Screen; 2.5–4.5 years, see 1300

Joliet 3-Minute Speech and Language Screen (Revised); Grades K, 2, 5, see 1301

The Jones-Mohr Listening Test; Persons in educational and training programs, see 1302

Khan-Lewis Phonological Analysis—Second Edition; Ages 2-0 to 21-11, see 1333

VOCATIONS

PUBLISHERS DIRECTORY
AND INDEX

This directory and index gives the names and test entry numbers of all publishers represented in Tests *in Print VI. Current addresses are listed for all publishers for which this is known. Those publishers for which a current address is not available are listed as "Address Unknown." This directory and index also provides telephone and FAX numbers and e-mail and Web page addresses for those publishers who responded to our request for this information. Please note that all test numbers refer to test entry numbers, not page numbers. Publishers are an important source of information about catalogs, specimen sets, price changes, test revisions, and other details.*

ABackans DCP, Inc.
566 White Pond Drive
Suite C #178
Akron, OH 44320-1116
Telephone:330-745-4450
FAX: 330-745-4450
E-mail: ABackans@abackans.com
Web URL: http://abackans.com
Tests: 41, 1933

Ablin Press Distributors
700 John Ringling Blvd., #1603
Sarasota, FL 34236-1504
Telephone: 941-361-7521
FAX: 941-363-9505
Tests: 836, 2284

Academic Consulting & Testing Service
P.O. Box 1883
Lake Oswego, OR 97035
Telephone: 503-639-3292
FAX: 503-639-3292
E-mail: HEDSbyACTS@aol.com
Tests: 219, 793, 1397, 1805, 2207

Academic Therapy Publications
20 Commercial Boulevard
Novato, CA 94949-6191
Telephone: 800-422-7249
FAX: 415-883-3720
E-mail: atp@aol.com
Web URL: www.atpub.com
Tests: 162, 248, 718, 832, 939, 963, 1303, 1369, 1400, 1431, 1586, 1650, 1651, 1706, 1947, 1959, 2054, 2055, 2057, 2086, 2332, 2333, 226, 2575, 2661, 2737, 2775

Accrediting Association of Bible Colleges
P.O. Box 780339
Orlando, FL 32878
Telephone: 407-207-0808
FAX: 407-207-0840
E-mail: exdir@aabc.org
Web URL: www.aabc.org
Tests: 2353

ACS DivCHED Examinations Institute
Clemson University
223 Brackett Hall
Box 341913
Clemson, SC 29634-1913
Tests: 43, 44, 45, 46, 47, 48, 49, 50, 51, 52, 53, 54, 55, 56

ACT, Inc.
2201 N. Dodge Street
P.O. Box 168
Iowa City, IA 52243-0168
Telephone: 319-337-1000
FAX: 319-339-3021
Web URL: www.act.org
Tests: 57, 58, 414, 609, 961, 1916, 2749

Gary L. Adams
[address unknown]
Tests: 646, 1719

ADE Incorporated
P.O. Box 660
Clarkston, MI 48347
Tests: 1312, 1692, 2426

Adult Self Expression Scale
c/o John P. Galassi
CB #3500
Peabody Hall
University of North Carolina
Chapel Hill, NC 27599-3500
Tests: 93

AJA Associates
c/o Marchman Psychology
720 South Dubuque
Iowa City, IA 52240
Tests: 1666

The Allington Corporation
P.O. Box 125
Remington, VA 22734
Tests: 1366

Allyn & Bacon
Department 894
160 Gould Street
Needham Heights, MA 02194-2310
Tests: 891, 2375, 2487, 2488

American Association for Active Lifestyles and Fitness
1900 Association Drive
Reston, VA 22091
Telephone: 800-213-7193
FAX: 703-476-9527
E-mail: AAALF@AAHPERD.ORG
Web URL: WWW.AAHPERD.ORG/AAALF/
    AAALF_main.html
Tests: 1023, 2324, 2509

American Association of Teachers of German, Inc.
112 Haddontowne Court, #104
Cherry Hill, NJ 08034-3668
Tests: 1685

American Dental Association
211 East Chicago Avenue, Suite 1846
Chicago, IL 60611-2678
Telephone: 312-440-2684
FAX: 312-487-4105
E-mail: kramerg@ada.org
Web URL: www.ada.org
Tests: 386, 760

American Guidance Service, Inc.
4201 Woodland Road
Circle Pines, MN 55014-1796
Telephone:
800-328-2560
FAX: 651-287-7221
E-mail: agsmail@agsnet
Web URL: www.agsnet.com
Tests: 130, 249, 280, 355, 458, 637, 790, 964, 1054,
    1055, 1098, 1125, 1315, 1316, 1317, 1319, 1321,
    1322, 1323, 1330, 1333, 1654, 1767, 1768, 1822,
    1823, 2074, 2321, 2411, 2652, 2653, 2735

American Management Association
135 West 50th Street
New York, NY 10020
Tests: 146

The American Occupational Therapy Association, Inc.
4720 Montgomery Lane
Bethesda, MD 20814-3425
Tests: 156, 1350

American Printing House for the Blind, Inc.
1839 Frankfort Avenue
P.O. Box 6085
Louisville, KY 40206-0085
Tests: 2145

American Psychiatric Association
1400 K Street, N.W.
Washington, DC 20005
Tests: 2025

American Psychiatric Publishing, Inc.
1400 K Street, NW — Suite 1101
Washington, DC 20005-2403
Telephone: 800-368-5777
FAX: 202-682-6341
E-mail: appi@psych.org
Web URL: www.appi.org
Tests: 463, 629, 2214, 2394, 2395, 2396

Paul S. Amidon & Associates, Inc.
1966 Benson Avenue
St. Paul, MN 55116-3299
Tests: 2708

Dr. Nancy C. Andreasen
Department of Psychiatry
MHCRC, 2911 JPP
200 Hawkins Drive
Iowa City, IA 52242-1057
Telephone: 319-356-4720
FAX: 319-384-5532
E-mail: Katelyn-dasse@uiowa.edu
Web URL: http://iowa-mhcrc.psychiatry.uiowa.edu/
Tests: 638, 2177, 2178, 2179

Andrews University Press
Berrien Springs, MI
49104-1700
Telephone: 616-471-6915
FAX: 616-471-6224
E-mail: aupress@andrews.edu
Web URL: www.andrewsuniversitypress.com
Tests: 2507

ARBOR, Inc.
ARBOR Corporate Center
One West Third Street
Media, PA 19063
Tests: 2670

The Assessment and Development Centre
6890 E. Sunrise Drive, #120-382
Tucson, AZ 85750
Telephone: 520-299-5501
FAX: 520-299-5348
E-mail: stressmaster@qwest.net
Web URL: www.stressmaster.com
Tests: 1806, 2385

The Assessment and Qualifications Alliance (AQA)
Stag Hill House
Guildford, Surrey GU2 7XJ
England
Telephone: +44 1483 506506
FAX: +44 1483 300152
E-mail: gboyden@aqa.org.uk
Web URL: www.aqa.org.uk
Tests: 262

Assessment Enterprises
925 Hayslope Drive
Knoxville, TN 37919
Telephone: 865-690-4498
E-mail: MSTAHL@UTK.EDU
Tests: 1289

Assessment Resource Center
University of Missouri—Columbia
College of Education
2800 Maguire Blvd.
Columbia, MO 65211
Telephone: 800-366-8232
FAX: 573-822-8937
E-mail: collegebase@arc.missouri.edu
Web URL: www.arc.missouri.edu
Tests: 557, 1631

Assessment Systems Corporation
2233 University Avenue, Suite 200
St. Paul, MN 55114-1629
Tests: 1617

Assessment Systems International, Inc.
544 East Ogden Avenue, Suite 700–391
Milwaukee, WI 53202
Telephone: 414-224-1400
FAX: 414-224-1401
E-mail: cspeck@execpc.com
Web URL: www.asi-intl.com
Tests: 1469

Assessment-Intervention Resources
2265 Elysium Avenue
Eugene, OR 97401-4903
Telephone: 541-338-8736
FAX: 541-338-8736
E-mail: kmerrell@oregon.uoregon.edu
Web URL: www.assessment-intervention.com
Tests: 1162, 2211

Associated Consultants in Education
P.O. Box 875
Suffern, NY 10901
Tests: 308, 2444

Association for the Education and Welfare of the
    Visually Handicapped
ATTN: Mrs. S. A. Clamp, Deputy Head
St. Vincent's School for the Blind
Yew Tree Lane, West Derby
West Derby, Liverpool L12 9HN
England
Tests: 1451, 2612

Association of American Colleges and Universities
1818 "R" Street, NW
Washington, DC 20009
Tests: 943

Association of American Medical Colleges
2501 "M" Street, NW, Lobby 26
Washington, DC 20037-1300
Tests: 1565

Athletic Success Institute
2308 Crystal Court
Antioch, CA 94509
Tests: 217

Australian Council for Educational Research Ltd.
19 Prospect Hill Road
Private Bag 55, Camberwell,
Melbourne, Victoria 3124
Australia
Telephone: +61 3 8266 5555
FAX: +61 3 9277 5500
E-mail: sales@acer.edu.au
Web URL: www.acer.edu.au
Tests: 21, 24, 25, 27, 28, 29, 30, 31, 32, 33, 34, 77, 173, 192, 323, 324, 610, 689, 787, 788, 807, 809, 817, 926, 1184, 1186, 1207, 1331, 1402, 1452, 1506, 1509, 1691, 2007, 2008, 2239, 2350, 2358, 2417, 2472, 2588, 2712, 2744, 2756, 2760, 1525

Australian Department of Immigration and Multicultural Affairs
Benjamin Offices
Chan St.
Belconnen, ACT 2617
Australia
Tests: 235

AVIAT
101 North Main
Ann Arbor, MI 48104
Tests: 1097

Ball Foundation
800 Roosevelt Road
Building E, Suite 200
Glen Ellyn, IL 60137-5850
Telephone: 630-469-6270
FAX: 630-469-6279
E-mail: TESTINFO@BALLFOUNDATION.ORG
Web URL: www.ballfoundation.org
Tests: 240

Ballard & Tighe Publishers
P.O. Box 219
Brea, CA 92822
Telephone: 800-321-4332
FAX: 714-255-9828
E-mail: info@ballard-tighe.com
Web URL: www.ballard-tighe.com
Tests: 1189, 1190, 2052

The Barber Center Press, Inc.
136 East Avenue
Erie, PA 16507
Telephone: 814-453-7661
FAX: 814-455-1132
E-mail: gabcmain@drbarbercenter.org
Web URL: www.drbarbercenter.org
Tests: 785

Donna Bardis
2533 Orkney Drive
Toledo, OH 43606
Telephone: 419-535-6146
E-mail: PBARDIS@POP3.UTOLEDO.EDU
Tests: 6, 326, 555, 745, 938, 971, 983, 1079, 1221, 1275, 1570, 1813, 1914, 2094, 2267, 2592, 2643, 2654, 2768

Barrett & Associates, Inc.
500 West Exchange Street
Akron, OH 44302-1428
Telephone: 330-762-2323
E-mail: gbarrett@barrett-associates.com
Web URL: www.barrett-associates.com
Tests: 231

Bay State Psychological Associates
225 Friend Street
Boston, MA 02114
Telephone: 800-438-2772
FAX: 617-367-5888
E-mail: jerry@eri.com
Web URL: www.eri.com
Tests: 916

James R. Beatty
College of Business Administration
San Diego State University
San Diego, CA 92182
Tests: 1226

Lenore Behar
1821 Woodburn Road
Durham, NC 27705
Telephone: 919-489-1888
FAX: 919-489-1832
E-mail: lbehar@psych.mc.duke.edu
Tests: 1960

Behavior Data Systems, Ltd.
P.O. Box 44256
Phoenix, AZ 85064-4256
Tests: 837, 2627

Behavior Science Systems, Inc.
P.O. Box 580274
Minneapolis, MN 55458
Telephone: 612-929-6220
FAX: 360-351-1374
E-mail: ireto001@tc.umn.edu
Tests: 444, 445, 854, 1210, 1870, 1961

Behavioral-Developmental Initiatives
14636 North 55th Street
Scottsdale, AZ 85254
Telephone: 800-405-2313
FAX: 602-494-2688
E-mail: BDI@TEMPERAMENT.COM
Web URL: www.b-di.com
Tests: 421

Behaviordata, Inc.
2166 The Alameda
San Jose, CA 95126-1144
Tests: 2275

The Ber-Sil Co.
3412 Seaglen Drive
Rancho Palos Verdes, CA 90275
Tests: 307

Nancy E. Betz, Ph.D.
104 Townshend
1885 Neil Ave Mall
The Ohio State University
Columbus, OH 43210
Telephone: 614-292-4166
FAX: 614-292-4537
E-mail: betz.3@osu.edu
Web URL: www.psy.ohio-state.edu/betz
Tests: 401

Millard J. Bienvenu, Ph.D.
Northwest Publications
710 Watson Drive
Natchitoches, LA 71457
Tests: 190, 1243, 1252, 1258, 1503, 1795, 1800, 1953, 2241, 2270

Bigby, Havis, & Associates, Inc.
12750 Merit Drive, Suite 660
Dallas, TX 75251
Telephone: 972-233-6055
FAX: 972-233-3154
E-mail: kcapelle@bigby.com
Web URL: www.bigby.com
Tests: 191, 2170, 2229

Bilingual Educational Services, Inc.
2514 South Grand Avenue
Los Angeles, CA 90007-9979
Telephone: 213-749-6213
FAX: 213-749-1820
Tests: 709, 727

Laurence M. Binder, Ph.D.
4900 SW Griffith Dr.
Suite 244
Beaverton, OR 97005
Telephone: 503-626-5246
FAX: 503-626-1686
E-mail: Larry_Binder@msn.com
Tests: 1927

Biobehavioral Sciences
1051 Beacon Street, Suite 101
Brookline, MA 02446-5622
Tests: 2381

Biofeedback Certification Institute of America
10200 W. 44th Avenue, Suite 304
Wheat Ridge, CO 80033-2840
Tests: 313

Dr. Dorothy Bishop
c/o TROG Research Fund
Age and Cognitive Performance Research Centre
University of Manchester
Manchester M13 9PL
England
Web URL: http://epwww.psych.ox.ac.uk/oscci/
Tests: 2518

Blanchard Training & Development, Inc.
125 State Place
Escondido, CA 92025-1398
Tests: 1378

Sidney J. Blatt
Yale University School of Medicine
Department of Psychiatry
25 Park Street
New Haven, CT 06519
Telephone: 203-785-2090
FAX: 203-785-7357
E-mail: sidney.blatt@yale.edu
Tests: 211, 769

Bowling Green State University
JDI Office
Department of Psychology
Bowling Green, OH 43403
Telephone: 419-372-8247
FAX: 419-372-6013
E-mail: JDI_RA@bgnet.bgnet.bgsu.edu
Web URL: www.bgsu.edu/departments/psych/JDI
Tests: 1290, 2102, 2382, 2457

Brador Publications, Inc.
P.O. Box 149
Scotland, CT 06264
Tests: 318, 2076

BrainTrain
727 Twin Ridge Lane
Richmond, VA 23235
Telephone: 804-320-0105
FAX: 804-320-0242
E-mail: ginger@braintrain.com
Web URL: www.braintrain.com
Tests: 1230

Branden Publishing, Co.
17 Station Street
Box 843
Brookline Village
Boston, MA 02147
Tests: 311

Brandon House, Inc.
P.O. Box 240
Bronx, NY 10471
Tests: 127, 889

Brandt Management Group
5909F Willow Oaks Drive
Richmond, VA 23225
Telephone: 804-232-6121
FAX: 804-232-6121
E-mail: jbrandt@vcu.org
Tests: 1438

Patricia Brandt, Ph.D.
Parent Child Nursing
School of Nursing
University of Washington
Seattle, WA 98195
Tests: 1867

Brigham Young University
Humanities Research Center
Foreign Language Testing
Provo, UT 84602
Tests: 2335

British Columbia Institute Against Family Violence
Suite 551
409 Granville Street
Vancouver, British Columbia V6C 1T2
Canada
Tests: 2271

Brookes Publishing Co., Inc.
P.O. Box 10624
Baltimore, MD 21285-0624
Telephone: 800-638-3775
FAX: 410-337-8539
E-mail: custserv@brookespublishing.com
Web URL: www.brookespublishing.com
Tests: 128, 472, 618, 1213, 2620

Brougham Press
P.O. Box 2702
Olathe, KS 66063-0702
Telephone: 800-360-6244
FAX: 913-782-1116
E-mail: CISE@BroughamPress.com
Web URL: www.BroughamPress.com
Tests: 465

Brown and Benchmark Publishers, A division of Wm.
   C. Brown Communications
2460 Kerper Blvd.
Dubuque, IA 52001
Tests: 485

Martin M. Bruce, Ph.D.
22516 Caravelle Circle
Boca Raton, FL 33433-5909
Telephone: 561-393-2428
FAX: 561-362-6185
E-mail: BRUCEPUBL@AOL.COM
Tests: 175, 216, 354,363, 399, 523, 915, 1637, 1844,
   1888, 1924, 2158, 2161, 2166, 2230, 2431, 2440,
   2563, 2618, 2723

Arnold R. Bruhn and Associates
7910 Woodmont Avenue, Suite 1300
Bethesda, MD 20814
Tests: 865

C.P.S., Inc.
P.O. Box 83
Larchmont, NY 10538
Telephone: 914-833-1633
FAX: 914-833-1633
Tests: 456, 887, 2027, 2197, 2251

California Counseling Centers
22797 Barton Road, Suite 200
Grand Terrace, CA 92324
Telephone: 909-885-1000
FAX: 909-885-0500
E-mail: sblphdmpapsy@linkline.com
Tests: 1373, 1374, 1375, 1377

Callier Center for Communication Disorders
University of Texas at Dallas
1966 Inwood Road
Dallas, TX 75235
Tests: 377

Cambridge Center for Behavioral Studies
Publications Department
336 Baker Avenue
Concord, MA 01742
Telephone: 978-369-2227
FAX: 978-369-2227
E-mail: center@behavior.org
Web URL: www.behavior.org
Tests: 291, 1772

The Cambridge Stratford Study Skills Institute
8560 Main Street
Williamsville, NY 14221
Telephone: 800-466-2232
FAX: 716-626-9076
E-mail: cambridges@aol.com
Web URL: www.cambridgesTraTford.com
Tests: 1811, 2454, 2630

Cambridge University Press
110 Midland Avenue
Port Chester, NY 10573-4930
Tests: 1349, 1551, 1695, 1971

Camelot Unlimited
c/o Michael Lavelli
5757 N. Sheridan Road, Suite 13B
Chicago, IL 60660
Tests: 452

Canadian Test Centre
Educational Assessment Services
85 Citizen Court, Suites 7 & 8
Markham, Ontario L6G 1A8
Canada
Tests: 383, 384, 388

Career Research & Testing, Inc.
2081-F Bering Drive
San Jose, CA 95131
Telephone: 408-441-9100
FAX: 408-441-9101
E-mail: TESTS@CAREERTRAINER.COM
Web URL: WWW.CAREERTRAINER.COM
Tests: 419, 1643, 1736, 2101

CASAS
5151 Murphy Canyon Road, Suite 220
San Diego, CA 92123-4339
Telephone: 858-292-2900
FAX: 858-292-2910
E-mail: bwalsh@casas.org
Web URL: WWW.CASAS.ORG
Tests: 631

Center for Applied Linguistics
4646 40th Street, NW
Washington, DC 20016-1859
Telephone: 202-362-0700
FAX: 202-363-7204
E-mail: store@cal.org
Web URL: www.cal.org
Tests: 176, 253, 471, 1922

Center for Architecture and Urban Planning Research
P.O. Box 413
University of Wisconsin—Milwaukee
Milwaukee, WI 53201-0413
Tests: 859

Center for Creative Leadership
One Leadership Place
P.O. Box 26300
Greensboro, NC 27438-6300
Telephone: 336-286-7210
FAX: 336-286-3999
Web URL: www.ccl.org
Tests: 303, 1288, 1332, 1411, 2014, 2301

The Center for Management Effectiveness, Inc.
P.O. Box 1202
Pacific Palisades, CA 90272
Telephone: 310-459-6052
FAX: 310-459-9307
E-mail: info@cmeinc.org
Web URL: www.cmeinc.org
Tests: 1479, 1869, 2125, 2379

Center for Rehabilitation Effectiveness
Boston University
635 Commonwealth Avenue
Boston, MA 02215
Telephone: 617-358-0175
FAX: 612-353-7500
E-mail: smhaley@bu.edu
Web URL: www.bu.edu/cre/
Tests: 1826

Center for the Study of Aging and Human Development
Box 3003
Duke University Medical Center
Durham, NC 27710
Telephone: 919-660-7500
FAX: 919-686-8569
E-mail: betty.ray@duke.edu
Web URL: www.geri.duke.edu
Tests: 1725

Center for the Study of Ethical Development
University of Minnesota
206 Burton Hall
178 Pillsbury Drive, SE
Minneapolis, MN 55455
Telephone: 612-624-0876
FAX: 612-624-8241
E-mail: tich0016@tc.umn.edu
Web URL: www.coled.umn.edu/CSED/default.html
Tests: 751

Center for the Study of Higher Education
The University of Memphis
Memphis, TN 38152
Telephone: 901-678-2775
FAX: 901-678-4291
E-mail: ccseqlib@cc.memphis.edu
Web URL: www.memphis.edu/cshe
Tests: 622

Central Institute for the Deaf
Publications Department
4560 Clayton Avenue
St. Louis, MO 63110
Telephone: 314-977-0133
FAX: 314-977-0016
E-mail: dgushleff@cid.wustl.edu
Web URL: www.cid.wustl.edu
Tests: 476, 477, 871, 1077, 2188, 2345, 2481

Central Wisconsin Center for the Developmentally Disabled
317 Knutson Drive
Madison, WI 53704
Telephone:608-301-9227
FAX: 608-301-9423
E-mail: kesligp@dhfs.state.wi.us
Tests: 2724

Centre for Addiction and Mental Health
Marketing Services
33 Russell Street
Toronto, Ontario M5S 2S1
Canada
Telephone: 416-595-6059
FAX: 416-593-4694
E-mail: marketing@camh.net
Web URL: www.camh.net
Tests: 137, 188, 838, 839, 1253, 1254, 2288

Centreville School
6201 Kennett Pike
Wilmington, DE 19807
Telephone: 302-571-0230
FAX: 302-571-0270
E-mail: language4@home.com
Web URL: www.busstory.com
Tests: 2095

CERAD Administrative Core
Box 3203
Duke University Medical Center
Durham, NC 27710
Telephone: 919-286-6406
FAX: 919-286-9219
E-mail: stric007@mc.duke.edu
Tests: 429

Vicentita M. Cervera, Ed.D.
13 Miller Street
San Francisco Del Monte
Quezon City, 1105
Philippines
Telephone: 411-2673
FAX: 371-6490
E-mail: vcervera@pacific.net.ph
Tests: 996

CFKR Career Materials
11860 Kemper Road, Unit 7
Auburn, CA 95603
Tests: 184, 404, 962, 1147, 1291, 1449, 1463, 2672

Jay L. Chambers, Ph.D.
160 Kendal Dr., #205
Lexington, VA 24450-1790
Telephone: 540-462-3874
E-mail: ibis@alexres.kendal.org
Tests: 1910

The Chauncey Group International
Educational Testing Service
P.O. Box 6604
Princeton, NJ 08541-6604
Tests: 2538

Checkmate Plus, Ltd.
P.O. Box 696
Stony Brook, NY 11790-0696
Telephone: 800-779-4292
FAX: 631-360-3432
E-mail: info@checkmateplus.com
Web URL: www.checkmateplus.com
Tests: 70, 85, 448, 858, 2780

CHECpoint Systems, Inc.
1520 N. Waterman Avenue
San Bernardino, CA 92404
Tests: 254

Child Development Centers of the Bluegrass, Inc.
465 Springhill Drive
Lexington, KY 40503
Tests: 1424

Child Development Resources
P.O. Box 280
Norge, VA 23127-0280
Tests: 1171, 2299

Child Welfare League of America
P.O. Box 2019
Annapolis Jct., MD 20701
Tests: 449, 730, 974

Larry Christensen, Ph.D.
Chair, Department of Psychology
University of South Alabama
6641 Sugar Creek Drive
Mobile, AL 36695
Telephone: 334-460-6321
FAX: 334-460-6320
E-mail: LChriste@usouthal.edu
Tests: 473

Chronicle Guidance Publications, Inc.
66 Aurora Street
Moravia, NY 13118-1190
Tests: 409, 475, 1868

The Clark Wilson Group, Inc.
4900 Nautilus Court N., Suite 220
Boulder, CO 80301-3242
Telephone: 800-537-7249
FAX: 303-581-9326
E-mail: info@clarkwilsongroup.com
Web URL: www.clarkwilsongroup.com
Tests: 480, 2012

Clinical Psychometric Research, Inc.
P.O. Box 619
Riderwood, MD 21139
Telephone: 800-245-0277
FAX: 410-321-6341
E-mail: mdero@aol.com
Web URL: derogatis-tests.com
Tests: 770, 771, 773, 774, 2033

Clinician's View
6007 Osuna Road, NE
Albuquerque, NM 87109
Tests: 945

CogniSyst, Inc.
3937 Nottaway Road
Durham, NC 27707
Telephone: 919-489-1000
FAX: 919-489-0607
E-mail: lyleallen@nc.rr.com
Web URL: www.cognisyst.com
Tests: 658, 1788, 2739

CogScreen LLC
4910 Mass. Ave.
Washington, DC 20016
Tests: 554

The College Board
45 Columbus Avenue
New York, NY 10023-6992
Tests: 19, 96, 97, 98, 99, 100, 101, 102, 103, 104, 105,
106, 107, 108, 109, 110, 111, 112, 113, 114, 115,
116, 117, 118, 119, 120, 121, 122, 123, 124, 125,
558, 559, 560, 561, 562, 563, 564, 565, 566, 567,
568, 569, 570, 571, 572, 573, 574, 575, 576, 577,
578, 579, 580, 581, 582, 583, 584, 585, 586, 587,
588, 589, 590, 591, 592, 593, 594, 595, 596, 597,
598, 599, 600, 601, 602, 2175

Communication Skill Builders—A Division of the Psychological Corporation
19500 Bulverde Road
San Antonio, TX 78259
Tests: 161, 846, 1300, 1301, 1817, 2107, 2516

John D. Cone
Department of Psychology & Family Studies
United States International University
10455 Pomerado Road
San Diego, CA 92131
Tests: 1802, 2041

Consulting Psychologists Press, Inc.
3803 East Bayshore Road
Palo Alto, CA 94303
Telephone: 800-624-1765
FAX: 650-623-9273
E-mail: knw@cpp-db.com
Web URL: www.cpp-db.com
Tests: 72, 290, 315, 372, 398, 405, 484, 683, 686, 900,
    918, 977, 1002, 1091, 1092, 1108, 1109, 1110,
    1336, 1337, 1361, 1391, 1515, 1673, 1677, 1678,
    1679, 1812, 1824, 1832, 1890, 1937, 1985, 2061,
    2133, 2320, 2388, 2390, 2422, 2492, 2599, 2615,
    2642, 2746

Consulting Resource Group International, Inc.
#386 - 200 West Third Street
Sumas, WA 98295-8000
Tests: 934, 1298, 1390, 1873,2168, 2250, 2384, 2641

Creative Learning Press, Inc.
P.O. Box 320
Mansfield Center, CT 06250
Tests: 482, 711, 1408, 2186

Creative Therapeutics, Inc.
155 County Road
P.O. Box 522
Cresskill, NJ 07626-0522
Tests: 1029, 2103

Critical Thinking Books & Software
ATTN: Linda Barbour
P.O. Box 448
Pacific Grove, CA 93950-0448
Telephone: 800-458-4849
FAX: 831-393-3277
E-mail: llb@criticalthinking.com
Web URL: www.criticalthinking.com
Tests: 695

CTB/McGraw-Hill
20 Ryan Ranch Road
Monterey, CA 93940-5703
Tests: 89, 365, 370, 371, 426, 728, 729, 780, 866, 1016,
    1262, 1364, 1365, 1684, 1948, 1949, 1978, 2313,
    2334, 2510, 2580, 2583, 2584, 2586

Curriculum Associates, Inc.
153 Rangeway Road
P.O. Box 2001
North Billerica, MA 01862-0901
Telephone: 800-225-0248
FAX: 800-366-1158
E-mail: cainfo@curriculumassociates.com
Web URL: www.curriculumassociates.com
Tests: 340, 341, 342, 343, 344, 345, 346, 347, 348, 633,
    634, 2105

Dallas Educational Services
P.O. Box 833114
Richardson, TX 75083-3114
Telephone: 972-234-6371
FAX: 972-437-5342
Tests: 742, 2235

Dansk Psykologisk Forlag
Stockholmsgade 29
2100 Kobenhavn O
Copenhagen, Denmark
Telephone: +45 3538 1655
FAX: +45 3538 1665
E-mail: dk-psych@dpf.dk
Web URL: www.dpf.dk
Tests: 243

DBM Publishing
58 South Service Road, Suite #130
Melville, NY 11747
Telephone: 631-752-3789
FAX: 631-756-2571
E-mail: maureen_sullivan@dbm.com
Web URL: www.dbm.com
Tests: 1187

Delaware County Intermediate Unit
Dr. Nicholas A. Spennato
Language Arts Specialist
6th and Olive Streets
Media, PA 19063
Tests: 755

William H. Dennis
Trumbull County Reading Clinic
255 Bonnie Brae Avenue, NE
Warren, OH 44483
Tests: 758, 759

Denver Developmental Materials, Inc.
P.O. Box 371075
Denver, CO 80237-5075
Telephone: 800-419-4729
FAX: 303-355-5622
Tests: 763, 764, 765, 766, 767, 1165

Department of Research Assessment and Training
1051 Riverside Drive, Unit 123
New York, NY 10032
Telephone: 212-543-5536
FAX: 212-543-5386
E-mail: je10@columbia.edu
Tests: 920, 1052, 2024, 2026, 2044, 2195

Development Associates, Inc.
1730 North Lynn Street
Arlington, VA 22209-2023
Telephone: 703-276-0677
FAX: 703-276-0432
E-mail: azehler@DEVASSOc1.COM
Web URL: WWW.DEVASSOC1.COM
Tests: 92

Developmental Reading Distributors
5879 Wyldewood Lakes Ct.
Fort Myers, FL 33919
Tests: 2069

Developmental Therapy Institute, Inc.
P.O. Box 5153
Athens, GA 30604-5153
Tests: 795

The Devine Group, Inc.
4166 Crossgate Lane
Blue Ash, OH 45236
Tests: 802

Diagnostic Counseling Services, Inc.
P.O. Box 6178
Kokomo, IN 46904-6178
Tests: 1655

Diagnostic Specialists, Inc.
1170 North 660 West
Orem, UT 84057
Telephone: 801-225-7698
FAX: 801-229-1944
E-mail: allanroe@earthlink.com
Web URL: www.psychstuff.com
Tests: 440, 632, 644, 645, 2260, 2720

Directional Insight International, Inc.
1111 McKinley Street
Ft. Worth, TX 76126
Telephone: 800-852-2001
FAX: 817-249-6266
E-mail: test@nsightsuccess.com
Web URL: www.nsightsuccess.com
Tests: 1722

Rodney L. Doran, Ph.D.
Professor of Science Education
State University of New York at Buffalo
Department of Learning and Instruction
593 Baldy Hall
Buffalo, NY 14260
Tests: 1566

Dr. Baker Partnership
10 Elgin Rd.
Bournemouth, BH4 9NL
United Kingdom
Telephone: 011-44-1202-763836
FAX: 011-44-1202-761766
Tests: 2089

Dragon Press
127 Sycamore Avenue
Mill Valley, CA 94941-2821
Tests: 457

Dr. Maurice J. Eash, Director
Institute of Learning and Teaching
University of Massachusetts—Boston
Harbor Campus
Boston, MA 02125-3393
Tests: 1786

Eckstein Bros., Inc.
4807 W. 118th Place
Hawthorne, CA 90250
Tests: 875

Ed & Psych Associates
208 West Hamilton Avenue, Suite #122
State College, PA 16801-5218
Telephone: 814-235-9115
FAX: 814-235-9115
Tests: 73

EdITS/Educational and Industrial Testing Service
P.O. Box 7234
San Diego, CA 92167
Tests: 393, 410, 411, 412, 413, 422, 660, 661, 662, 692,
    824, 966, 967, 989, 1307, 1465, 1670, 1790, 1860,
    1861, 1995, 1996, 2204, 2373, 2415, 2582,

Education Associates
P.O. Box 23308
Louisville, KY 40223
Telephone: 800-626-2950
FAX: 502-327-5106
E-mail: stw@e-a-i.com
Web URL: www.educationassociates.com
Tests: 1293

Educational Activities Software
Attn: Alan Stern
P.O. Box 754
Baldwin, NY 11510
Telephone: 1-800-645-2796
FAX: 516-379-7429
E-mail: astern@edact.com
Web URL: www.edact.com
Tests: 177, 1219, 1409

Educational & Industrial Test Services, Ltd.
83 High Street
Hemel Hempstead, Hertfordshire HP1 3AH
England
Telephone: +44 (0) 1442 215521
FAX: +44 (0) 1442 240531
E-mail: POST@MORRISBY.DEMON.CO.UK
Web URL: WWW.MORRISBY.com
Tests: 997, 1220, 1501, 1831

Educational & Psychological Consultants, Inc.
1715 West Worley Street, Suite #A
Columbia, MO 65203-2603
Telephone: 573-446-6232
E-mail: kuncej@missouri.edu
Tests: 1874

Educational Assessment Service, Inc.
W6050 Apple Road
Watertown, WI 53098-3937
Telephone: 920-261-1118
FAX: 920-261-6622
E-mail: srimm@sylviarimm.com
Web URL: www.sylviarimm.com
Tests: 36, 37, 1087, 1093, 1094, 1957

Educational Evaluations
Awre
Newnham, Gloucestershire, GL14 1ET
England
Telephone: 01594 510503
FAX: 01594 510503
Tests: 923, 1212, 1437, 1735, 2083, 2326, 2738

Educational Publications
532 E. Blacklidge
Tucson, AZ 85705
Tests: 1299

Educational Records Bureau
220 East 42nd Street, Suite 100
New York, NY 10017-5006
Telephone: 212-672-9800
FAX: 212-370-4096
E-mail: info@erbtest.org
Web URL: www.erbtest.org
Tests: 650, 937, 1200

Educational Resources, Inc.
8910 West 62nd Terrace
P.O. Box 29160
Shawnee Mission, KS 66201
Telephone: 1-800-292-2273
FAX: 913-362-4627
E-mail: testing@eriworld.com
Web URL: www.eriworld.com
Tests: 1135, 1152, 1724

Educational Studies & Development
1942 Furhman
Muskegon, MI 49441
Tests: 4

Educational Testing Service
Publication Order Services
P.O. Box 6736
Princeton, NJ 08541-6736
Telephone: 609-921-9000
FAX: 609-734-5410
E-mail: etsinfo@ets.org
Web URL: www.ets.org
Tests: 486, 487, 488, 489, 490, 491, 492, 493, 494, 495,
    496, 497, 498, 499, 500, 501, 502, 503, 504, 505,
    506, 507, 508, 509, 510, 511, 512, 513, 514, 515,
    516, 517, 518, 519, 558, 579, 603, 605, 652, 840,
    1012, 1065, 1066, 1067, 1068, 1069, 1070, 1071,
    1072, 1073, 1074, 1075, 1346, 1462, 1683, 1945,
    1950, 1951, 2000, 2206, 2224, 2341, 2408, 2564

Educators Publishing Service, Inc.
31 Smith Place
Cambridge, MA 02138-1089
Telephone: 800-225-5750
FAX: 617-547-0412
E-mail: cpsbooks@epsbooks.com
Web URL: www.epsbooks.com
Tests: 163, 302, 1825, 1827, 1828, 1829, 2111, 2139,
    2140, 2303, 2455

Carl N. Edwards, Ph.D.
P.O. Box 279
Dover, MA 02030
Tests: 2290

Paul Ekman
Human Interaction Library
University of California—San Francisco
401 Parnassus Avenue, Box HIL
San Francisco, CA 94143-0984
FAX: 415-476-7629
Tests: 969

Elbern Publications
P.O. Box 09497
Columbus, OH 43209
Telephone: 614-235-2643
FAX: 614-237-2637
Tests: 277, 2073

Dr. John Eliot
Institute for Child Study
University of Maryland
College Park, MD 20742
Tests: 899

Ellsworth Krebs Associates
3615 130th Avenue, NE
Bellevue, WA 98005-1351
Telephone: 425-883-4762
FAX: 425-883-4762
Tests: 442, 1993

Ellsworth & Vandermeer Press, Ltd.
P.O. Box 68164
Nashville, TN 37206
Tests: 1810

Patricia B. Elmore, Ph.D.
College of Education and Human Services, Dean's
    Office
Mail Code 4624
Southern Illinois University—Carbondale
Carbondale, IL 62901-4624
Telephone: 618-453-2415
FAX: 618-453-1646
E-mail: pbelmore@siu.edu
Web URL: www.siu.edu/~epse1/elmore/
Tests: 288, 435, 1380

Employers' Tests and Services Associates
2246 Ivy Road, Suite 7
Charlottesville, VA 22903-4988
Telephone: 877-932-8378
FAX: 434-293-5885
E-mail: info@etsatests.com
Web URL: www.etsatests.com
Tests: 942, 1036, 1040, 1561, 1562, 1745, 1751, 1847,
    2155

Endeavor Information Systems, Inc.
1317 Livingston Street
Evanston, IL 60201
Tests: 919

Dr. Meryl E. Englander
Professor Emeritus, Counseling & Educational Psy-
    chology
3508 William Court
Bloomington, IN 47401
Telephone: 812-336-2746
E-mail: englande@indiana.edu
Tests: 1201

English Language Institute
University of Michigan
3020 North University Building
1205 North University Avenue
Ann Arbor, MI 48109-1057
Telephone: 734-764-2416
FAX: 734-763-0369
E-mail: melabelium@umich.edu
Web URL: www.lsa.umich.edu/eli/
Tests: 924, 951, 952, 1436, 1584, 1585, 1587

Enhanced Performance Systems, Inc.
1010 University Avenue, Suite 265
San Diego, CA 92103
Telephone: 619-497—0156
FAX: 619-497-0820
E-mail: sagal@enhanced-performance.com
Web URL: www.enhanced-performance.com
Tests: 225

Robert H. Ennis, Ph.D.
495 East Lake Road
Sanibel Island, FL 33957
Telephone: 941-395-1435
E-mail: rhennis@uiuc.edu
Tests: 930

Enrichment Press
5441 SW Macadam Avenue, #206
Portland, OR 97201
Telephone: 503-222-4046
FAX: 503-222-9989
Tests: 1928, 2677

ERISys
Box 1635
Pawtucket, RI 02862
Tests: 1968

Evince Clinical Assessments
Attn. Dr. Norman Hoffmann
P.O. Box 17305
Smithfield, RI 02917
Telephone: 401-231-2993
FAX: 401-231-2055
E-mail: evinceassessment@aol.com
Tests: 90, 296, 1941, 2088, 2430, 2629

Exceptional Education
P.O. Box 15308
Seattle, WA 98155
Telephone: 206-262-9538
FAX: 206-262-9538
Tests: 1974, 2664

Sheila M. Eyberg, Ph.D.
Department of Clinical & Health Psychology
Health Sciences Center
University of Florida
Gainesville, FL 32610
Tests: 844, 2595

Faculty of Education
Memorial University of Newfoundland
St. John's, Newfoundland A1B 3X8
Canada
Tests: 2579

Dr. Charles G. Fast, Publisher
Route 1, Box 54A
Novinger, MO 63559
Tests: 985

Grace Fivars
Psychometric Techniques Associates
5701 Centre Avenue, #511
Pittsburgh, PA 15206-3707
Tests: 533, 2473

Foreworks
Box 82289
Portland, OR 97282
Telephone: 503-653-2614
E-mail: eric@foreworks.com
Web URL: www.foreworks.com
Tests: 2329, 2527

Myles I. Friedman
College of Education
University of South Carolina
Columbia, SC 29208
Tests: 1946

Functional Resources
3905 Huntington Drive
Amarillo, TX 79019-4047
Telephone: 806-353-1114
FAX: 806-353-1114
E-mail: webmaster@winfssi.com
Web URL: http://www.winfssi.com
Tests: 1027

Gallaudet University Press
800 Florida Avenue, NE
Washington, DC 20002-3695
Tests: 2776

GB Software LLC
4607 Perham Road
Corona del Mar, CA 92625
Tests: 2022

Ruth M. Geiman, Ph.D.
1217 Ironwood Drive
Fairborn, OH 45324
Tests: 1042

General Educational Development Testing Service of
    the American Council on Education (GED)
One Dupont Circle, NW Suite 250
Washington, DC 20036-1163
Tests: 2587

Gerontology Center
College of Health and Human Development
The Pennsylvania State University
135 E. Nittung Ave., Suite 405
State College, PA 16801
Telephone: 814-865-1710
FAX: 814-863-9423
E-mail: GERO@psu.edu
Web URL: geron.psu.edu
Tests: 1568

GIA Publications, Inc.
7404 South Mason Avenue
Chicago, IL 60638
Telephone: 708-496-3800
FAX: 708-496-3828
E-mail: custserv@giamusic.com
Web URL: www.giamusic.com
Tests: 95, 1124, 1228, 1236, 1270, 1675, 1976

Robert Gibson & Sons, Glasgow Ltd.
17 Fitzroy Place
Glasgow, Scotland G3 7SF
United Kingdom
Tests: 703, 704, 1326, 1783

Golden Educational Center
857 Lake Blvd.
Redding, CA 96003
Telephone: 800-800-1791
FAX: 530-244-5939
E-mail: info@goldened.com
Web URL: www.goldened.com
Tests: 1231

Gordon Systems, Inc.
P.O. Box 746
DeWitt, NY 13214
Tests: 1057

Robert S. Goyer
Department of Communication
Arizona State University
Tempe, AZ 85287
Tests: 1060

Graham-Field, Inc.
81 Spence
Bayshore, NY 11706
Tests: 2514

Gregorc Associates, Inc.
15 Doubleday Road
P.O. Box 351
Columbia, CT 06237
Telephone: 860-228-0093
FAX: 860-228-0093
Web URL: www.gregorc.com
Tests: 1083

GRM Educational Consultancy
P.O. Box 154
Beecroft, New South Wales 2119
Australia
Tests: 2215

Guglielmino & Associates
734 Marble Way
Boca Raton, FL 33432
Telephone: 561-392-0379
FAX: 561-392-0379
E-mail: lguglielmino@rocketmail.com
Web URL: guglielmino734.com
Tests: 2237

Guilford Publications, Inc.
72 Spring Street
New York, NY 10012
Telephone: 212-431-9800
FAX: 212-966-6708
Web URL: www.guilford.com
Tests: 69

H & H Publishing Co., Inc.
1231 Kapp Drive
Clearwater, FL 33765
Tests: 1395, 1396, 1830, 2369, 2503, 2764

Hahnemann Medical College & Hospital
Department of Mental Health Sciences
230 North Broad Street
Philadelphia, PA 19102
Tests: 1111, 1112, 1542

Harcourt Educational Measurement
19500 Bulverde Road
San Antonio, TX 78259-3701
Telephone: 800-211-8378
FAX: 877-576-1816
Web URL: WWW.HEMWEB.com
Tests: 169, 1050, 1053, 1579, 1680, 1785, 2357, 2359,
2360, 2362

Susan Harter, Ph.D.
University of Denver
Department of Psychology
2155 South Race Street
Denver, CO 80208-0204
Tests: 1908, 2247

Joseph Hartman Consulting Psychology, Inc.
Albanna Office Center
6015 Chester Circle, Suite 113
Jacksonville, FL 32217-2270
Telephone: 904-636-5757
E-mail: jhartman@bellsouth.net
Tests: 2036

Harvard University Press
79 Garden Street
Cambridge, MA 02138
Tests: 2593

Dr. Robert J. Harvey
1030 S. Jefferson Forest Lane
Blacksburg, VA 24060-8984
Tests: 616

Hawthorne Educational Services, Inc.
800 Gray Oak Drive
Columbia, MO 65201
Telephone: 800-542-1673
FAX: 800-442-9509
E-mail: cs@hes-inc.com
Web URL: www.hes-inc.com
Tests: 62, 87, 220, 221, 282, 283, 284, 331, 855, 856,
902, 905, 1047, 1399, 1955, 1963, 2342, 2621,
2743

Hay Group
Hay Resources Direct
116 Huntington Avenue
Boston, MA 02116-5712
Telephone: 800-729-8074
FAX: 617-927-5008
E-mail: Haytrg@haygroup.com
Web URL: www.hayresourcesdirect.haygroup.com
Tests: 67, 542, 904, 1217, 1382, 1403, 1405, 1482,
1494, 1497, 1777, 1877, 2157

The Health Institute
New England Medical Center #345
750 Washington Street
Boston, MA 02111
Tests: 2273

Health Prisms, Inc.
130 Pleasant Pointe Way
Fayetteville, GA 30214
Tests: 687

Mary J. Heppner, Ph.D.
Career Center
305 Noyes Hall
University of Missouri
Columbia, MO 65211
Tests: 418

Herrmann International
794 Buffalo Creek Road
Lake Lure, NC 28746
Tests: 1144

Hester Evaluation Systems, Inc.
2410 SW Granthurst Avenue
Topeka, KS 66611-1274
Telephone: 800-832-3825
FAX: 785-357-4041
E-mail: hester@inlandnet.net
Web URL: www.hestertesting.com
Tests: 1635

High/Scope Educational Research Foundation
600 North River Street
Ypsilanti, MI 48198-2898
Telephone: 734-485-2000
FAX: 734-485-0704
E-mail: info@highscope.org
Web URL: www.highscope.org
Tests: 898, 1151, 1999

Higher Education Research Institute
UCLA Graduate School of Education
405 Hilgard Avenue
3005 Moore Hall
Los Angeles, CA 90024-1521
Tests: 682

Hilson Research, Inc.
P.O. Box 150239
82-28 Abingdon Road
Kew Gardens, NY 11415-0239
Tests: 1154, 1155, 1156, 1157, 1263, 1264

Hodder & Stoughton Educational
Hodder Headline PLC
338 Euston Road
London NW1 3BH
England
Telephone: 0207 873 6000
FAX: 0207 873 6299
E-mail: chas.knight@hodder.co.uk
Web URL: www.hoddertests.co.uk
Tests: 256, 257, 526, 540, 863, 877, 879, 966, 967, 1046, 1061, 1063, 1095, 1096, 1099, 1211, 1525, 1715, 1794, 1816, 1915, 2075, 2171, 2226, 2283, 2338, 2474, 2740

Hogan Assessment Systems, Inc.
P.O. Box 521176
Tulsa, OK 74152
Tests: 1158, 1159, 1649

Hogrefe & Huber Publishers
P.O. Box 2487
Kirkland, WA 98083
Telephone: 800-228-3749
FAX: 425-823-8324
E-mail: HH@HHPUB.COM
Web URL: WWW.HHPUB.COM
Tests: 749, 747, 982, 1791, 2134, 2193

Home Inventory LLC
c/o Lorraine Coulson
13 Saxony Circle
Little Rock, AR 72209
Telephone: 501-565-7627
E-mail: lrcoulson@ualr.edu
Web URL: www.ualr.edu/~crtldept/home4.htm
Tests: 1164

Houghton Mifflin Company
College Division, Education
222 Berkeley Street
Boston, MA 02116-3764
Telephone: 617-351-5000
FAX: 617-351-1134
E-mail: college_educ@hmco.com
Web URL: http://education.college.hmco.com
Tests: 358

Howdah Press
c/o Priscilla S. Hill, Ph.D.
3530 Damien #117
LaVerne, CA 91750
Tests: 1153

Edwina E. Hubert, Ph.D.
313 Wellesley, SE
Albuquerque, NM 87106
Tests: 1416

Nancy Hughes, Ph.D.
University of Kansas
Psychological Clinic
315 Fraser Hall
Lawrence, KS 66045
Tests: 1178

Human Resource Development Press
22 Amherst Road
Amherst, MA 01002–9709
Tests: 431, 626, 668, 781, 1010, 1218, 1311, 1379,
1407, 1471, 1498, 1533, 1775, 1776, 1845, 1850,
1879, 1979, 2490

Human Sciences Research Council
Private Bag X41
Pretoria, 0001
South Africa
Telephone: 012-302-2341
E-mail: NCWClassen@beauty.hsrc.ac.za
Tests: 14, 174, 319, 995, 1145, 1146, 1208, 1244, 1248,
1305, 1310, 1676, 1686, 1709, 1792, 1904, 1912,
2003, 2142, 2208, 2252, 2253, 2268, 2328, 2517,
2616

Human Services Resource Group
College of Business Administration
University of Nebraska—Omaha
Omaha, NE 68182-0048
Tests: 2452

Human Synergistics International
39819 Plymouth Road, C-8020
Plymouth, MI 48170-8020
Telephone: 800-622-7584
FAX: 734-459-5557
E-mail: info@humansyn.com
Web URL: www.humansyn.com
Tests: 146, 1101, 1385, 1429, 1454, 1472, 1778, 1780,
1853, 2386, 2443

Humanics Learning
P.O. Box 7400
Atlanta, GA 30357
Telephone: 404-874-2176
FAX: 404-874-1976
E-mail: humanics@mindspring.com
Web URL: www.humanicslearning.com
Tests: 443, 455, 1183, 1447

I-MED Instructional Materials & Equipment Distributors
1520 Cotner Avenue
Los Angeles, CA 90025
Tests: 848

The IDEA Center
211 South Seth Child Road
Manhattan, KS 66502-3089
Telephone: 800-255-2757
FAX: 785-532-5725
E-mail: IDEA@KSU.EDU
Web URL: WWW.IDEA.KSU.EDU
Tests: 1188, 1191

IDS Publishing Corporation
P.O. Box 389
Worthington, OH 43085
Telephone: 614-885-2323
FAX: 614-885-2323
Web URL: www.idspublishing.com
Tests: 2093

Illinois Critical Thinking Project
Department of Educational Policy Studies
University of Illinois at Urbana-Champaign
360 Education Bldg.
1310 South Sixth Street
Champaign, IL 61820
Tests: 693, 694

Imaginart International, Inc.
307 Arizona Street
Bisbee, AZ 85603
Telephone: 520-432-5741
FAX: 520-432-5134
E-mail: imaginart@compuserve.com
Web URL: www.imaginartonline.com
Tests: 278, 1232, 1966, 2344, 2465, 2524

Indiana University Center for Postsecondary Research
and Planning
1913 East 7th Street
Ashton-Aley Hall, Suite 102
Bloomington, IN 47405-7510
Telephone: 812-856-5824
FAX: 812-856-5150
E-mail: nsse@indiana.edu
Web URL: www.iub.edu/~cseq or www.iub.edu/~nsse
Tests: 606, 607, 1689

Industrial Psychology International, Ltd.
4106 Fieldstone Road
Champaign, IL 61821
Telephone: 800-747-1119
FAX: 217-398-5798
E-mail: iPI@METRITECH.COM
Web URL: WWW.METRITECH.COM
Tests: 707, 1271, 1721, 2766, 2767

Insight Assessment
217 La Cruz Avenue
Millbrae, CA 94030
Telephone: 650-697-5628
FAX: 650-692-0141
E-mail: info@insightassessment.com
Web URL: www.insightassessment.com
Tests: 368, 369

Insight Institute, Inc.
7205 NW Waukomis Drive
Kansas City, MO 64151
Telephone: 800-861-4769
FAX: 816-587-7198
E-mail: handleyp@insightinstitute.com
Web URL: www.insightinstitute.com
Tests: 1222

Institute for Behavioral Research in Creativity
1570 South 1100th East
Salt Lake City, UT 84105
Tests: 314, 883, 2413

The Institute for Matching Person & Technology, Inc.
486 Lake Road
Webster, NY 14580
Telephone: 585-671-3461
FAX: 585-671-3461
E-mail: impt97@aol.com
Web URL: members.aol.com/IMPT97/MPT.html
Tests: 1516, 1518, 2262

Institute for Personality and Ability Testing, Inc.
P.O. Box 1188
Champaign, IL 61824-1188
Telephone: 217-352-4739
FAX: 217-352-9674
E-mail: custserv@ipat.com
Web URL: www.ipat.com
Tests: 467, 527, 630, 731, 868, 956, 1131, 1148, 1372, 2244, 2292, 2293, 2294, 2295, 2296

Institute for Psychoimagination Therapy
c/o Dr. Joseph E. Shorr
179 South Barrington Place
Los Angeles, CA 90049
Tests: 1100, 2279

Institute for Somat Awareness
Michael Bernet, Ph.D.
1270 North Avenue, Suite 1-P
New Rochelle, NY 10804
Telephone: 914-633-1789
FAX: 914-633-3152
E-mail: mBernet@aol.com
Web URL: www.somats.com
Tests: 2286

Institute for the Advancement of Philosophy for Children
Montclair State University
Upper Montclair, NJ 07043
Telephone: 973-655-4277
FAX: 973-655-7834
E-mail: MATKOWSKI@SATURN.MONTCLAIR.EDU
Web URL: www.montclair.edu/pages/iapc/home.html
Tests: 1703

Institute of Psychological Research, Inc.
34 Fleury Street West
Montreal, Quebec H3L 1S9
Canada
Tests: 392, 1714, 2042, 2151, 2525, 2574

Institute of Rehabilitation Medicine
New York University Medical Center
400 East 34th Street
New York, NY 10016
Tests: 1022

Interim Publishers
3900 Scobie Road
Peninsula, OH 44264
Tests: 2374

International Assessment Network
7400 Metro Blvd. Suite #350
Edina, MN 55439
Tests: 1502

International Career Planning Services, Inc.
254 Republic Avenue
Joliet, IL 60435
Tests: 1905

International Forgiveness Institute
P.O. Box 6153
Madison, WI 53716-0153
Telephone: 608-231-9117
E-mail: GAYLEREED6@aol.com
Web URL: www.Forgiveness-institute.org
Tests: 931

International Personnel Management Association
1617 Duke Street
Alexandria, VA 22314
Tests: 1272, 1273, 1274, 2192

International Society for General Semantics
P.O. Box 728
Concord, CA 94522
Telephone: 925-798-0311
FAX: 925-798-0312
E-mail: isgs@generalsemantics.org
Web URL: www.generalsemantics.org
Tests: 2632

International Training Consultants, Inc.
151 Park Avenue
League City, TX 77573
Telephone: 281-557-9372
FAX: 281-557-9223
E-mail: itc@trainingitc.com
Web URL: www.trainingitc.com
Tests: 1413, 1414

Invest Learning
Worldwide Development Headquarters
4660 S. Hagadorn Road, Suite 520
East Lansing, MI 48823-5353
Tests: 172

Iowa State University Research Foundation, Inc.
Child Development Department
101 Child Development Building
Research Laboratories
Ames, IA 50011
Tests: 1266, 1267, 2355

Irvington Publishers, Inc.
R. R. 1, Box 85-1
Lower Mill Road
North Stratford, NH 03590
Tests: 1997

Israel Science Teaching Center
Hebrew University
Jerusalem, 91904
Israel
Tests: 615

James Stanfield Co., Inc.
P.O. Box 41058
Santa Barbara, CA 93140
Telephone: 800-421-6534
FAX: 805-897-1187
E-mail: maindesk@stanfield.com
Web URL: www.stanfield.com
Tests: 621, 2181, 2542, 2622

Janelle Publications, Inc.
P.O. Box 811
1189 Twombley Road
DeKalb, IL 60115
Tests: 2337, 2400, 2401

Jeannette Jansky
120 East 89th Street
New York, NY 10128
Tests: 1281, 1282

JIST Publishing, Inc.
8902 Otis Avenue
Indianapolis, IN 46216-1033
Telephone: 800-648-5478
FAX: 800-547-8329
E-mail: info@jist.com
Web URL: www.jist.com
Tests: 247, 403, 1106, 1203, 1205, 1294, 1417, 1418,
    1759, 1760, 2665, 2752

Jossey-Bass, A Wiley Company
989 Market Street
San Francisco, CA 94103
Tests: 194, 299, 394, 543, 620, 715, 803, 830, 912, 929,
    944, 1247, 1302, 1343, 1387, 1388, 1392, 1401,
    1435, 1440, 1646, 1774, 1835, 1836, 1837, 1984,
    2322, 2491, 1494, 2633, 2685

C. G. Jung Institute of San Francisco
2040 Gough Street
San Francisco, CA 94109
Tests: 1306

Jerome Kagan
Harvard University
33 Kirkland Street
1510 William James Hall
Cambridge, MA 02138
Tests: 1517

Kaplan Early Learning Company
1310 Lewisville-Clemmons Road
Lewisville, NC 27023
Tests: 800, 1393

S. Karger, AG
P.O. Box CH-4009
Allschwilerstrasse, Basel 10
Switzerland
Tests: 614

Warren Keegan Associates Press
210 Stuyvesant Avenue
Rye, NY 10580
Tests: 1324

Keeler Instruments Inc.
456 Parkway
Broomall, PA 19008
Telephone: 610-353-4350
FAX: 610-353-7814
Web URL: www.keelerusa.com
Tests: 479, 2112

Kendall/Hunt Publishing Company
4050 Westmark Drive
P.O. Box 1840
Dubuque, IA 52004-1840
Telephone: 800-228-0810
FAX: 800-772-9165
E-mail: orders@kendallhunt.com
Web URL: WWW.KENDALLHUNT.COM
Tests: 259

Kindergarten Interventions and Diagnostic Services,
    Inc. (KIDS)
1156 Point Vista Road
Denton, TX 76210-3962
Tests: 1338, 1339

Dr. Donald L. Kirkpatrick
1920 Hawthorne Drive
Elm Grove, WI 53122
Telephone: 262-784-8348
FAX: 262-784-7994
E-mail: dleekirk@aol.com
Tests: 1344, 1474, 1475, 1476, 1477, 1478, 2438, 2439

Marjorie H. Klein, Ph.D.
Department of Psychiatry
6001 Research Park Blvd.
Madison, WI 53717
Telephone: 608-263-6066
FAX: 608-265-4008
E-mail: mhklein@falstaff.wisc.edu
Web URL: www.psychiatry.wisc.edu/Faculty/
    FacultyPages/Klein.htm
Tests: 960

Kolbe Corp
3421 N. 44th Street
Phoenix, AZ 85018
Telephone: 602-840-9770
FAX: 602-952-2706
E-mail: info@kolbe.com
Web URL: www.kolbe.com
Tests: 1352

David S. Krantz
Department of Medical and Clinical Psychology
University of the Health Sciences
4301 Jones Bridge Road
Bethesda, MD 20814-4799
E-mail: krantz@bob.usuhs.mil
Tests: 1353

Krieger Publishing Company
P.O. Box 9542
Melbourne, FL 32902-9542
Tests: 84

Ramanath Kundu
Department of Psychology
University of Calcutta
92, Acharya Prafulla Chandra Road
Calcutta 700009
India
Tests: 1359, 1360

Lafayette Instruments
P.O. Box 5729
3700 Sagamore Parkway North
Lafayette, IN 47903
Tests: 1086, 1622, 2131

Rolfe LaForge
83 Homestead Blvd.
Mill Valley, CA 94941
Tests: 1242

Laurent Clerc National Deaf Education Center
KDES PAS-6
Gallaudet University
800 Florida Avenue, NE
Washington, DC 20002
Telephone: 202-651-5340
FAX: 202-651-5708
Web URL: clerccenter.gallaudet.edu
Tests: 1541

Law School Admission Council/Law School Admis-
    sion Service
Box 40
Newtown, PA 18940-0040
Tests: 1376

Leadership Studies, Inc.
230 West Third Avenue
Escondido, CA 92025
Tests: 2289

Lentz Peace Research Laboratory
c/o UM-St. Louis
8001 Natural Bridge Road
St. Louis, MO 63121
Tests: 708, 1181, 1484

Hal Leonard Publishing Corporation
777 West Bluemound Road
P.O. Box 13819
Milwaukee, WI 53213
Tests: 984, 2684

Lienhard School of Nursing
Pace University
Pleasantville/Briarcliff Campus
Bedford Road
Pleasantville, NY 10570
Tests: 2378

Life Advance, Inc.
81 Front Street
Nyack, NY 10960
Telephone: 914-358-2539
E-mail: ellison@alliancesem.edu
Tests: 2347

Life Innovations, Inc.
P.O. Box 190
Minneapolis, MN 55440-0190
Tests: 534, 968, 981, 1796, 1848, 1954

Life Science Associates
One Fenimore Road
Bayport, NY 11705-2115
Telephone:631-472-2111
FAX: 631-472-8140
E-mail: lifesciassoc@pipeline.com
Web URL: lifesciassoc.home.pipeline.com
Tests: 2063

LIMRA International
P.O. Box 208
Hartford, CT 06141-0208
Tests: 197, 416, 2300

LinguiSystems, Inc.
3100 4th Avenue
East Moline, IL 61244-9700
Tests: 1368, 2559, 2741

Lippincott Williams & Wilkins
351 West Camden Street
Baltimore, MD 21201-2436
Telephone: 410-528-4000
FAX: 410-528-8550
E-mail: info@lww.com
Web URL: http://www.llw.com
Tests: 199

Literacy Volunteers of America, Inc.
P.O. Box 6506
Syracuse, NY 13216
Telephone: 315-472-0001
FAX: 315-472-0002
E-mail: info@literacyvolunteers.org
Web URL: www.literacyvolunteers.org
Tests: 922, 2071

Lore International Institute
P.O. Box 1287
1130 Main Avenue
Durango, CO 81301
Telephone: 970-385-4955
FAX: 970-385-4998
E-mail: assessmentcenter@lorenet.com
Web URL: www.lorenet.com
Tests: 433, 541, 1450, 1730, 2160, 2448

Pamela S. Ludolph (Ph.D.)
311 Awixa Road.
Ann Arbor, MI 48104-1811
Tests: 808

James B. Maas
The Center for Improvement of Undergraduate Education
115 Rand Hall
Cornell University
Ithaca, NY 14850
Tests: 697

Charlotte Mackley
483 West 150 S
Springville, UT 84663
Tests: 145, 675, 1446, 2276

Jean D'Arcy Maculaitis, Ph.D.
P.O. Box 3056
Sea Bright, NJ 07760
Tests: 1457

Maddak, Inc.
6 Industrial Road
Pequannock, NJ 07440-1993
Tests: 269, 1445, 2254

Madison Geriatric Research, Education, and Clinical Center
VA Medical Center
2500 Overlook Terrace
Madison, WI 53705
Tests: 207

Management & Personnel Systems, Inc.
2717 North Main Street, #2
Walnut Creek, CA 94596
Telephone: 800-576-7455
FAX: 925-977-8200
E-mail: mpscorp@value.net
Web URL: www.mps-corp.com
Tests: 738, 1039, 2442, 2762

Management Research Group
14 York Street, #301
Portland, ME 04101-4556
Telephone: 207-775-2173
FAX: 207-775-6796
E-mail: info@mrg.com
Web URL: www.mrg.com
Tests: 167, 1202, 1384, 1851, 2159

Management Research Institute, Inc.
11304 Spur Wheel Lane
Potomac, MD 20854
Tests: 1009

Mann Consulting Group
16070 Sunset Blvd. #105
Pacific Palisades, CA 90272
Tests: 1866

Marathon Consulting and Press
797 South Ashburton Road
Columbus, OH 43227-1027
Tests: 705, 748, 1840, 2745

Massachusetts School of Professional Psychology
T.E.D. Test
221 Rivermoor Street
Boston, MA 02132
Telephone: 617-327-6777
FAX: 617-327-4447
E-mail: ce@mspp.edu
Tests: 2475

MAT
Boston University
School of Music
855 Commonwealth Avenue
Boston, MA 02215
Tests: 1674

Mathematical Association of America
American Mathematics Competitions
Titu Andreesen, Director
University of Nebraska—Lincoln
1740 Vine Street
Lincoln, NE 68588-0658
Telephone: 800-527-3690
FAX: 402-472-6087
E-mail: amcinfo@unl.edu
Web URL: www.unl.edu/amc
Tests: 151, 153, 154, 1520

McCann Associates, Inc.
603 Corporate Drive, West
Langhorne, PA 19047
Tests: 719, 720, 721, 722, 776, 998, 1729, 1920

McCarron-Dial Systems
P.O. Box 45628
Dallas, TX 75245
Telephone: 214-634-2863
FAX: 214-634-9970
E-mail: mds@mccarrondial.com
Web URL: mccarrondial.com
Tests: 40, 65, 204, 903, 1535, 1540, 1732, 1841, 2447

McClain
10 Blue Grouse Ridge Road
Littleton, CO 80127-5704
Tests: 2774

Measurement for Human Resources
83 Rouge Au Avenue
Winnipeg, Manitoba R2C 3X5
Canada
Tests: 1737

Albert Mehrabian, Ph.D.
1130 Alta Mesa Road
Monterey, CA 93940
Telephone: 831-649-5710
E-mail: am@kaaj.com
Web URL: www.kaaj.com/psych/scales
Tests: 186, 239, 446, 1543, 1544, 1546, 1553, 1554, 1556, 2049, 2619

Mental Health, Law, and Policy Institute
Simon Fraser University
8888 University Drive
Burnaby, British Columbia V5A 1S6
Canada
Telephone: 604-291-4554
FAX: 604-268-6695
E-mail: mhlpi@sfu.ca
Web URL: www.sfu.ca/psychology/groups/mhlpi
Tests: 1128

Meta Development LLC
4313 Garnet Street
Regina, Saskatchewan S4S 6J8
Canada
Tests: 1596, 1597, 1598, 1600, 1601, 1602, 1603, 1604,
1605, 1606, 1607

Meta-Visions
5076 Queen Victoria Lane
Kalamazoo, MI 49009-7799
Telephone: 616-353-7111
FAX: 616-353-9577
E-mail: JWalkerMI@aol.com
Tests: 1577

MetriTech, Inc.
4106 Fieldstone Road
P.O. Box 6479
Champaign, IL 61826-6479
Telephone: 800-747-4868
FAX: 217-398-5798
E-mail: mtinfo@metritech.com
Web URL: www.metritech.com
Tests: 59, 91, 1224, 1370, 1773, 1403, 2751, 2773

The Mews Press
Box 2052
Amagansett, NY 11930
FAX: 212-475-2428
Tests: 2097, 2458, 2499

MILCOM Systems
A Division of Hollister, Inc.
2000 Hollister Drive
Libertyville, IL 60048
Tests: 1591

Miller & Tyler Limited
Psychological Assessment and Counselling
96 Greenway
London N20 8EJ
England
Telephone: 44-020-8445-7463
FAX: 44-020-8445-0143
Tests: 2141, 2143

Mind Garden, Inc.
1690 Woodside Road, Suite #202
Redwood City, CA 94061
Telephone: 650-261-3500
FAX: 650-261-3505
E-mail: info@mindgarden.com

Web URL: www.mindgarden.com
Tests: 7, 203, 264, 301, 366, 373, 434, 536, 625, 700,
701, 782, 845, 1018, 1126, 1129, 1195, 1519, 1527,
1575, 1592, 1662, 1663, 1664, 1702, 1756, 1779,
2035, 2091, 2210, 2319, 2371, 2372, 2512, 2637,
2681, 2689, 2701, 2702

Ministry Inventories
ATTN: Richard A. Hunt, Ph.D.
Fuller Graduate School of Psychology
180 N. Oakland Avenue
Pasadena, CA 91101
Tests: 1259, 1629, 2594

MKM
401 3rd Street, Suite 1
Rapid City, SD 57701
Tests: 1632, 1633, 1634

Modern Curriculum Press
4350 Equity Drive
Columbus, OH 43216
Tests: 329, 796, 890

Modern Learning Press, Inc.
P.O. Box 167
Rosemont, NJ 08556
Tests: 1044, 1045

Monaco & Associates, Inc.
4125 Gage Center Drive, Suite 204
Topeka, KS 66604
Telephone: 785-272-5501
FAX: 785-272-5152
E-mail: Jmarks@monacoassociates.com
Web URL: www.monacoassociates.com
Tests: 1645

Moreno Educational Co.
P.O. Box 19329
San Diego, CA 91259-0329
Tests: 1769, 2053, 2336

The Morrisby Organisation
83 High Street
Hemel Hempstead, Hertfordshire HP1 3AH
England
Tests: 706, 1641, 1750

Moving Boundaries, Inc.
1375 SW Blaine Court
Gresham, OR 97080
Tests: 2285

Multi-Health Systems, Inc.
P.O. Box 950
North Tonawanda, NY 14120-0950
Telephone: 416-424-1700
FAX: 416-424-1736
E-mail: CUSTOMERSERVICE@MHS.COM
Web URL: www.mhs.com
Tests: 164, 244, 245, 246, 425, 461, 481, 535, 544, 654,
    659, 669, 670, 671, 672, 673, 674, 685, 690, 746,
    843, 975, 993, 1121, 1122, 1123, 1160, 1237, 1283,
    1284, 1394, 1420, 1421, 1532, 1589, 1625, 1657,
    1818, 1932, 2046, 2090, 2214, 2312, 2317, 2318,
    2349, 2397, 2463, 2480, 2551, 2614

Munroe-Meyer Institute for Genetics & Rehabilitation
University of Nebraska Medical Center
985450 Nebraska Medical Center
Omaha, NE 68198-5450
Tests: 1590

Carol Murray
[Address Unknown]
Tests: 2302

National Association of Secondary School Principals
P.O. Box 3250
1904 Association Drive
Reston, VA 22091-1598
Tests: 635, 636, 1406, 2225

National Career Assessment Services, Inc.
601 Visions Parkway
P.O. Box 277
Adel, IA 50003
Telephone: 800-314-8972
FAX: 515-993-5422
E-mail: ncasi@ncasi.com
Web URL: www.ncasi.com or www.kuder.com
Tests: 1354, 1355, 1356, 1357, 2436

National Center for Research to Improve Postsecondary
    Teaching and Learning
2400 School of Education Building
The University of Michigan
Ann Arbor, MI 48109-1259
Tests: 1644, 2407

The National Center on Employment & Disability
P.O. Box 1358
Hot Springs, AR 71902
Tests: 909, 1295, 2747, 2753, 2755, 2763

National Clearinghouse of Rehabilitation Training
    Materials
5202 N. Richmond Hill Drive
Oklahoma State University
Stillwater, OK 74078-4080
Tests: 1763

National Communication Association
1765 N. Street N.W.
Washington, DC 20036
Tests: 193, 627, 680

National Council on Crime & Delinquency
685 Market Street, Suite 620
San Francisco, CA 94105
Tests: 702, 1313

National Council on Economic Education
1140 Avenue of the Americas
New York, NY 10036
Telephone: 212-730-7007
FAX: 212-730-1793
E-mail: econed@ncee.net
Web URL: www.ncee.net
Tests: 251, 2536, 2537, 2565

National Occupational Competency Testing Institute
500 N. Bronson Avenue
Big Rapids, MI 49307-2737
Telephone: 800-334-6283
FAX: 231-796-4699
E-mail: nocti@nocti.org
Web URL: www.nocti.org
Tests: 1710, 1711, 1712

National Psychological Corporation
4/230, Kacheri Ghat
AGRA-4
India
Tests: 2486

National Reading Styles Institute, Inc.
P.O. Box 737
Syosset, NY 11791-0737
Tests: 612, 2077

National Spanish Exam
2051 Mt. Zion Drive
Golden, CO 80401-1737
Telephone: 303-278-1021
FAX: 303-278-6400
E-mail: martha.quiat@mho.net
Web URL: http://viking.valpo.k12.in.us/~cessna/nse/
    index.htm
Tests: 1688

National Study of School Evaluation
1699 E. Woodfield Road, #406
Schaumburg, IL 60173
Tests: 624, 1803, 2409, 2483

National Wellness Institute, Inc.
1300 College Court
P.O. Box 827
Stevens Point, WI 54481-2962
Tests: 1430, 2589, 2590, 2591

NCS Assessments
Sales Department
5605 Green Circle Drive
Minnetonka, MN 55343
Tests: 139, 268, 333, 335, 336, 380, 395, 396, 772, 1034, 1137, 1192, 1260, 1608, 1609, 1610, 1623, 1624, 1789, 1934, 2045, 2059, 2216, 2464, 2640

Robert A. Neimeyer, Ph.D.
Department of Psychology
Memphis State University
Memphis, TN 38152
Telephone: 901-678-4680
FAX: 901-678-2579
E-mail: neimeyer@memphis.edu
Web URL: http://neimeyer.psyc.memphis.edu
Tests: 2434

Nelson Thomson Learning
1120 Birchmount Road
Scarborough, Ontario M1K 5G4
Canada
Telephone: 416-752-9448
FAX: 416-752-9646
E-mail: inquire@nelson.com
Web URL: www.nelson.com
Tests: 385, 387, 389, 1030, 1143, 1784, 2152, 2666

C. H. Nevins Printing Co.
311 Bryn Mawr Island
Bayshore Gardens
Bradenton, FL 34207
Tests: 1089, 1090

New Zealand Council for Educational Research
Education House West
178-182 Willis Street
Box 3237
Wellington 6000
New Zealand
Telephone: 00 64 4 384 7939
FAX: 00 64 4 384 7933
E-mail: jane.dugdale@nzcer.org.nz
Web URL: www.nzcer.org.nz
Tests: 22, 23, 26, 359, 940, 2006, 2009, 2010, 2013, 2351, 2368, 2482

NFER-Nelson Publishing Co., Ltd.
Darville House
2 Oxford Road East
Windsor, Berkshire SL4 1DF
England
Tests: 131, 132, 133, 134, 135, 196, 237, 255, 297, 349, 350, 351, 360, 415, 436, 439, 453, 548, 724, 815, 864, 872, 878, 880, 885, 925, 978, 979, 1026, 1038, 1062, 1064, 1102, 1103, 1104, 1105, 1169, 1309, 1325, 1327, 1367, 1423, 1434, 1443, 1448, 1521, 1522, 1523, 1526, 1528, 1552, 1555, 1578, 1636, 1642, 1682, 1690, 1704, 1705, 1707, 1708, 1718, 1723, 1728, 1738, 1740, 1741, 1864, 1900, 1911, 1942, 1943,1944, 1973, 1977, 2048, 2065, 2068, 2078, 2080, 2081, 2082, 2087, 2116, 2123, 2127, 2198, 2416, 2420, 2432, 2462, 2541, 2651, 2705, 2718, 2722, 2777

Nichols & Molinder Assessments
437 Bowes Drive
Tacoma, WA 98466-7047
Tests: 1669

Noel-Levitz
2101 ACT Circle
Iowa City, IA 52245-9581
Telephone: 319-337-4700
FAX: 319-337-5274
E-mail: info@noellevitz.com
Web URL: www.noellevitz.com
Tests: 608

Norland Software
P.O. Box 84499
Los Angeles, CA 90073-0499
Telephone: 310-825-9689
FAX: 310-825-9689
E-mail: emiller@ucla.edu
Web URL: www.calcaprt.com
Tests: 367

Northern California Neurobehavioral Group, Inc.
909 Hyde Street, Suite #620
San Francisco, CA 94109-4835
Tests: 545

Nova Media, Inc.
1724 N. State
Big Rapids, MI 49307-9073
Telephone: 231-796-4637
FAX: 231-796-4637
E-mail: trund@nov.com
Web URL: www.nov.com
Tests: 2060

NTS Research Corporation
209 Markham Drive
Chapel Hill, NC 27514
Tests: 2245

Dr. Thomas R. Oaster
School of Education
Educational Research & Psychology
University of Missouri—Kansas City
5100 Rockhill Road
Kansas City, MO 64110-2499
Tests: 1726, 2410

Occupational Research Centre
"Highlands" Gravel Path
Berkhamsted, Hertfordshire HP4 2PQ
United Kingdom
Tests: 1345

E. R. Oetting, Ph.D.
Psychology Department
Colorado State University
Fort Collins, CO 80523
Telephone: 970-491-1615
FAX: 970-491-0527
E-mail: goetting@lamar.colostate.edu
Tests: 1742, 1743, 2348, 2511

OPAC (Office Proficiency Assessment & Certification) Testing Software
1321 Howe Avenue
Sacramento, CA 95825
Telephone: 800-999-0438 x 242
FAX: 916-563-7557
E-mail: blane@opac.com
Web URL: www.opac.com
Tests: 1747

Optometry Admission Testing Program
211 East Chicago Avenue, Suite 1846
Chicago, IL 60611-2678
Telephone: 312-440-2684
FAX: 312-587-4105
E-mail: kramerg@ada.org
Tests: 1766

Organizational Measurement Systems Press
P.O. Box 70586
Eugene, OR 97401
Telephone: 541-484-2715
FAX: 541-465-1602
E-mail: Barb-John-Miner@msn.com
Tests: 1613, 1757

Ned Owens, Inc.
629 W. Centerville Road, Suite 201
Garland, TX 75041
Telephone: 972-278-1387
FAX: 972-278-1387
E-mail: nedowens@fni.com
Web URL: www.fni.net/nedowens
Tests: 86, 218

Oxford Psychologists Press, Ltd.
Lambourne House
311-321 Banbury Road
Oxford OX2 7JH
United Kingdom
Tests: 717, 1593, 2064

P.D.P. Press, Inc.
12015 North July Avenue
Hugo, MN 55038
Tests: 2256

Pain Assessment Resources
3312 S. McCarron Blvd., #309
Reno, NV 89509
Telephone: 775-857-4300
FAX: 775-857-4344
E-mail: baplew@aol.com
Web URL: www.painassessmentresources.com
Tests: 293

Pain Resource Center, Inc.
P.O. Box 2836
Durham, NC 27715
Tests: 474, 2608

PAQ Services, Inc.
Data Processing Division
1625 North 1000 East
Logan, UT 84321
Tests: 1285, 1931, 1991, 1757

Pearson Early Learning
P.O. Box 2500
135 South Mt. Zion Road
Lebanon, IN 46052
Tests: 867, 869

Penna Assessment
c/o Penna Change Consulting
The Manor House
Park Road
Stoke Pages, Bucks SL2 4PG
United Kingdom

Telephone: 00 44 1753 784000
FAX: 00 44 1753 784020
E-mail: colin.selby@e-penna.com
Web URL: www.e-penna.com/change
Tests: 213, 214, 215, 1833, 1834

People Focus
Pleasant Hill Executive Park
391 Taylor Blvd., Suite 110
Pleasant Hill, CA 94523-2275
Telephone: 925-676-6265
FAX: 925-676-0519
E-mail: lfogli@peoplefocus.com
Web URL: www.peoplefocus.com
Tests: 2263

Perfection Learning Corp.
10520 New York Avenue
Des Moines, IA 50322
Tests: 148, 149, 876, 1441, 2769

Person-O-Metrics, Inc.
20504 Williamsburg Road
Dearborn Heights, MI 48127
Tests: 947, 2050, 2234

Personal Strengths Publishing
P.O. Box 2605
Carlsbad, CA 92018-2605
Telephone: 800-624-7347
FAX: 760-602-0087
E-mail: mail@PersonalStrengths.com
Web URL: www.PersonalStrengths.com
Tests: 957, 958, 990, 991, 992, 1628, 1876, 1929, 1930, 2380

Personalysis Corporation
5847 San Felipe, Suite 650
Houston, TX 77057-3008
Telephone: 713-784-4421
FAX: 713-784-9909
E-mail: info@personalysis.com
Web URL: www.personalysis.com
Tests: 1886

Personnel Decisions, Inc.
2000 Plaza VII Tower
45 South Seventh Street
Minneapolis, MN 55402-1608
Tests: 1820

Dr. Linda Phillips
Director, Centre for Research on Literacy
Faculty of Educacion
University of Alberta
Edmonton, Alberta T6G 2G5
Canada
Tests: 1540

Phonovisual Products, Inc.
18761 North Frederick
Gaithersburg, MD 20879
Telephone: 800-283-4888
FAX: 240-358-0228
E-mail: Phonovisual@aol.com
Web URL: www.phonovisual.com
Tests: 1902

Dr. Issy Pilowsky
University of Sydney
Department of Psychological Medicine
Camperdown
New South Wales 2006
Australia
Tests: 1194, 1422

Piney Mountain Press, Inc.
P.O. Box 333
Cleveland, GA 30528
Telephone: 800-255-3127
FAX: 800-905-3127
E-mail: cyberguy@alltel.net
Web URL: www.pineymountain.com
Tests: 261, 1410, 1412, 1975, 2298, 2667

Pinkerton Services Group
6100 Fairview Road, Suite 900
Charlotte, NC 28210-3277
Tests: 2363, 2364

Predictive Surveys Corporation
5802 Howard Avenue
LaGrange, IL 60525
Tests: 1, 853, 1887, 2019, 2020, 2471

Prentice-Hall
College Book Division
200 Old Tappan Rd.
Old Tappan, NJ 07675
Tests: 941, 1198, 1199, 1442, 1513, 1754, 1998

Preschool Skills Test
c/o Carol Lepera
P.O. Box 1246
Greenwood, IN 46142
Tests: 1970

Price Systems, Inc.
Box 1818
Lawrence, KS 66044
Telephone: 785-843-7892
FAX: 785-843-0101
E-mail: gprice@ku.edu
Web URL: www.learningstyle.com
Tests: 1404, 1989

PRO-ED
8700 Shoal Creek Blvd.
Austin, TX 78757-6897
Telephone: 800-897-3202
FAX: 512-451-8542
E-mail: proedrd2@aol.com
Web URL: WWW.PROEDINC.COM
Tests: 2, 3, 63, 74, 81, 165, 168, 181, 189, 195, 198,
205, 206, 209, 223, 236, 241, 242, 260, 279, 287,
292, 317, 327, 338, 424, 546, 617, 642, 643, 648,
648, 651, 664, 712, 732, 741, 768, 777, 778, 779,
783, 784, 786, 791, 794, 797, 798, 804, 805, 834,
862, 953, 1005, 1011, 1017, 1021, 1025, 1048,
1049, 1080, 1081, 1082, 1117, 1103, 1238, 1340,
1371, 1398, 1433, 1615, 1639, 1660, 1733, 1771,
1821, 1898, 1901, 1903, 1909, 1952, 1956, 2028,
2067, 2085, 2113, 2122, 2136, 2137, 2138, 2176,
2184, 2185, 2187, 2199, 2217, 2219, 2240, 2316,
2339, 2343, 2354, 2418, 2419, 2459, 2513, 2522,
2523, 2529, 2531, 2532, 2533, 2534, 2535, 2539,
2545, 2546, 2547, 2548, 2550, 2553, 2556, 2557,
2560, 2567, 2570, 2571, 2573, 2576, 2577, 2578,
2610, 2623, 2639, 2673, 2698, 2699, 2742, 2772,
2779

Professional Picture Framers Association
4305 Sarellen Road
Richmond, VA 23231-4311
Tests: 430

Program Development Associates
P.O. Box 2038
Syracuse, NY 13220-2038
Tests: 2489

Psych Press
Level 4 398 Lonsdale Street
Melbourne, VIC 3000
Australia
Tests: 955

Psychogenics, Inc.
490 Oxford Street East
London, Ontario N5Y 3H7
Canada
Telephone: 519-642-1505
FAX: 519-642-1513
E-mail: alvin@execulink.com
Tests: 2072

Psychological Assessment Resources, Inc.
16204 N. Florida Avenue
Lutz, FL 33549-8119
Telephone: 800-331-8378
FAX: 800-727-9329
E-mail: custsupp@parinc.com
Web URL: www.parinc.com
Tests: 75, 80, 82, 83, 94, 286, 325, 328, 337, 339, 397,
400, 417, 437, 447, 454, 459, 468, 528, 549, 550,
553, 556, 611, 676, 678, 688, 750, 757, 775, 789,
822, 873, 906, 911, 965, 1019, 1116, 1136, 1168,
1170, 1235, 1239, 1240, 1251, 1297, 1329, 1426,
1427, 1504, 1557, 1569, 1572, 1573, 1574, 1599,
1616, 1656, 1659, 1661, 1694, 1701, 1739, 1758,
1807, 1809, 1857, 1862, 1863, 1880, 1881, 1882,
1925, 2034, 2104, 2110, 2115, 2118, 2119, 2120,
2121, 2132, 2135, 2146, 2147, 2148, 2238, 2258,
2264, 2314, 2370, 2383, 2392, 2398, 2399, 2414,
2427, 2433, 2625, 2626, 2635, 2649, 2655, 2660,
2671, 2719, 2725, 2726

The Psychological Corporation [Australia]
30–52 Smidmore Street
Marrickville, New South Wales 2204
Australia
Tests: 233, 234, 817, 2669

The Psychological Corporation Europe
Harcourt Place
32 Jamestown Road
London NW1 7BY
United Kingdom
Telephone: 020 7424 4262
FAX: 020 7424 4457
Web URL: www.tpc-international.com
Tests: 469, 847, 849, 851, 1051, 1439, 1647, 1653,
1782, 1899, 1958, 1969, 2149, 2150, 2243, 2376,
2558, 2765

The Psychological Corporation
19500 Bulverde Road
San Antonio, TX 78259
Telephone: 800-211-8378
FAX: 800-232-1223
E-mail: customer_care@harcourt.com
Web URL: www.PsychCorp.com

Tests: 11, 17, 18, 39, 61, 64, 68, 88, 144, 229, 250, 270,
271, 172, 173, 274, 275, 276, 305, 306, 309, 310,
320, 321, 322, 330, 352, 353, 357, 364, 374, 375,
407, 428, 451, 460, 466, 483, 520, 529, 530, 531,
532, 551, 613, 639, 663, 710, 756, 799, 801, 816,
818, 819, 833, 841, 842, 850, 874, 884, 932, 933,
1001, 1004, 1037, 1056, 1058, 1059, 1107, 1119,
1161, 1173, 1197, 1229, 1255, 1314, 1531, 1536,
1537, 1580, 1581, 1588, 1594, 1595, 1611, 1618,
1640, 1665, 1696, 1699, 1781, 1787, 1808, 1894,
1895, 1926, 1964, 1965, 1986, 2037, 2062, 2096,
2109, 2144, 2190, 2191, 2203, 2257, 2265, 2281,
2356, 2361, 2389, 2412, 2467, 2521, 2544, 2552,
2572, 2624, 2638, 2645, 2648, 2656, 2676, 2687,
2688, 2690, 2691, 2692, 2693, 2694, 2695, 2696,
2704, 2706, 2721

Psychological & Educational Publications, Inc.
P.O. Box 520
Hydesville, CA 95547-0520
Tests: 2520, 2528, 2543, 2568, 2569

Psychological Foundations of Education
University of Minnesota
178 Pillsbury Drive, SE
315 Burton Hall
Minneapolis, MN 55455
Tests: 1524

Psychological Growth Associates, Inc.
Products Division
3813 Tiffany Drive
Lawrence, KS 66049
Telephone: 785-841-1141
FAX: 785-749-2190
E-mail: 73204.303@compuserve.com
Tests: 2602

Psychological Publications, Inc.
P.O. Box 3577
Thousand Oaks, CA 91359-0577
Telephone: 800-345-8378
FAX: 805-527-9266
E-mail: TJTA@aol.com
Web URL: www.TJTA.com
Tests: 980, 2479

Psychological Services Bureau, Inc.
2246 Ivy Road, Suite 7
Charlottesville, VA 22903-4988
Telephone: 877-932-8378
FAX: 434-293-5885
E-mail: info@psbtests.com
Web URL: www.psbtests.com
Tests: 2015, 2016, 2017, 2018

Psychological Services, Inc.
100 West Broadway, Suite #1100
Glendale, CA 91210
Telephone: 818-244-0033
FAX: 818-247-7223
Web URL: www.psionline.com
Tests: 910, 999, 1000, 1921, 1992, 2021, 2650

Psychological Test Publications
Scamp's House
107 Pilton Street
Barnstaple, Devon
England
Tests: 1084, 1415

Psychological Test Specialists
Box 9229
Missoula, MT 59807
Telephone: 406-728-1710
E-mail: beheng1@montana.com
Web URL: www.pr-pms.com
Tests: 2058

Psychologists and Educators, Inc.
Sales Division
P.O. Box 513
Chesterfield, MO 63006
Telephone: 636-536-2366
FAX: 314-434-2331
E-mail: psychologistsed@earthlink.net
Tests: 182, 289, 698, 713, 1174, 1175, 1347, 1507,
1508, 1510, 1511, 1764, 1923, 2222, 2233, 2246,
2249, 2259, 2406, 2476, 2555, 2561

Psychology Press
29 West 35th Street
New York, NY 10001
Telephone: 212-216-7800
FAX: 212-643-1430
Web URL: www.psypress.com
Tests: 316, 378, 427, 950, 2030, 2647

Psychology Press, Inc.
P.O. Box 328
Brandon, VT 05733-0328
Telephone: 802-247-8312
FAX: 802-247-8312
E-mail: info@great-ideas.org
Web URL: www.great-ideas.org
Tests: 1896

Psychometric Affiliates
P.O. Box 807
Murfreesboro, TN 37133-0807
Telephone: 615-890-6296
FAX: 615-890-6296
E-mail: jheritage@a1.mtsu.edu
Tests: 9, 10, 12, 140, 150, 152, 155, 178, 179, 521, 604,
623, 665, 726, 733, 734, 735, 825, 888, 894, 908,
927, 928, 946, 948, 970, 972, 986, 987, 988, 1003,
1024, 1035, 1041, 1043, 1088, 1120, 1130, 1133,
1134, 1138, 1150, 1182, 1261, 1286, 1308, 1389,
1425, 1496, 1529, 1545, 1548, 1549, 1550, 1559,
1648, 1749, 1755, 1843, 1906, 1917, 1918, 1940,
2029, 2040, 2079, 2173, 2227, 2325, 2346, 2445,
2628, 2662, 2697, 2710, 1748

Psychometrics Canada Ltd.
7125 - 77 Avenue
Edmonton, Alberta T6B 0B5
Canada
Telephone: 1-800-661-5158
FAX: 780-469-2283
E-mail: info@psychometrics.com
Web URL: www.psychometrics.com
Tests: 1204, 1206, 2754

Psytec, Inc.
P.O. Box 564
DeKalb, IL 60115
Tests: 441

Donald K. Pumroy, Ph.D.
4006 Oliver Street
Hyattsville, MD 20782
Telephone: 301-864-8935
FAX: 301-864-8935
E-mail: dpumroy@earthlink.net
Tests: 1514

Purdue Research Foundation
Attn: William K. Lebold
Educational Research & Information Systems
Engineering and Administration Building
Purdue University
West Lafayette, IN 47907
Tests: 2038

Ramsay Corporation
Boyce Station Offices
1050 Boyce Road
Pittsburgh, PA 15241-3907
Tests: 893, 896, 897, 1132, 1227, 1296, 1459, 1461,
1558, 1564, 1746, 1748, 1980, 1987, 2070, 2441,
2611, 2700

Rehabilitation Research and Training Center on Blind-
ness and Low Vision
Mississippi State University
P.O. Drawer 6189
Mississippi State, MS 39762
Telephone: 662-325-2001
FAX: 662-325-8989
E-mail: rrtc@ra.msstate.edu
Web URL: www.blind.msstate.edu
Tests: 895

Reid London House
One North Dearborn, Suite 1600
Chicago, IL 60602
Tests: 60, 166, 379, 381, 382, 522, 538, 539, 656, 657,
716, 725, 737, 901, 917, 959, 1007, 1008, 1249,
1386, 1485, 1490, 1560, 1563, 1716, 1717, 1731,
1752, 1842, 1849, 1892, 1907, 1972, 2039, 2066,
2154, 2156, 2164, 2282, 2297, 2330, 2331, 2437,
2449, 2453, 2466, 2498, 2506, 2549, 2600, 2601,
2634, 2644, 2646, 2736, 2631

Reid Psychological Systems
153 West Ohio Street
Chicago, IL 60610-4210
Tests: 2092

Reitan Neuropsychology Laboratory/Press
P.O. Box 66080
Tucson, AZ 85728-6080
Telephone: 520-577-2970
FAX: 520-577-2940
E-mail: REITANLABs@AOL.COM
Tests: 1114

Renaissance Learning, Inc.
P.O. Box 8036
2911 Peach Street
Wisconsin Rapids, WI 54495-8036
Telephone: 800-338-4204
FAX: 800-788-1272
E-mail: answers@renlearn.com
Web URL: www.renlearn.com
Tests: 2365, 2366, 2367

Renovex Corporation
1421 Jersey Avenue, N
Minneapolis, MN 55427
Tests: 200

Research Center for Children, Youth, and Families
1 South Prospect Street
Burlington, VT 05401-3456
Telephone: 802-656-8313
FAX: 802-656-2602
E-mail: mail@ASEBA.org
Web URL: www.ASEBA.org
Tests: 35, 420, 2778

Research for Better Schools, Inc.
444 North Third Street
Philadelphia, PA 19123-4107
Telephone: 215-574-9300
FAX: 215-574-0133
E-mail: maguire@rbs.org
Web URL: www.rbs.org
Tests: 202, 212, 823, 2202

Research Press
P.O. Box 9177
Champaign, IL 61826
Telephone: 217-352-3273
FAX: 217-352-1221
E-mail: gs@researchpress.com
Web URL: www.researchpress.com
Tests: 295, 1014, 1172, 1363, 1667

Richmond Products, Inc.
1021 S. Rogers Circle, Suite #6
Boca Raton, FL 33487-2894
Telephone: 561-994-2112
FAX: 561-994-2235
E-mail: RichmndPro@aol.com
Web URL: www.RichmondProducts.com
Tests: 1176

Risk & Needs Assessment, Inc.
P.O. Box 44828
Phoenix, AZ 85064-4828
Tests: 20, 749, 831, 1280, 1981, 2172, 2269, 2278

Riverside Publishing
425 Spring Lake Drive
Itasca, IL 60143-2079
Telephone: 800-323-9540
FAX: 630-467-7192
Web URL: www.riversidepublishing.com
Tests: 265, 266, 267, 281, 312, 438, 547, 743, 806,
1031, 1214, 1233, 1250, 1265, 1268, 1269, 1530,
1614, 1693, 2098, 2128, 2189, 2358, 2581, 2636,
2731, 2732, 2733, 2734

Rocky Mountain Behavioral Science Institute, Inc.
419 Canyon Avenue, Suite 316
Fort Collins, CO 80521
Tests: 147

Kenneth H. Rubin, Ph.D., Director
Center for Study of Families, Relationships & Child
Development
Department of Human Development, 3304 Benjamin
Building
University of Maryland
College Park, MD 20742-1131
Tests: 1919

SAGE Publications
2455 Teller Road
Thousand Oaks, CA 09320
Tests: 1668

Dr. Shourkry D. Saleh
Chairman, Department of Management Sciences
University of Waterloo
Waterloo, Ontario N2L 3G1
Canada
Tests: 1287

The SASSI Institute
201 Camelot Lane
Springville, IN 47462
Telephone: 800-726-0526
FAX: 800-546-7995
E-mail: sassi@sassi.com
Web URL: WWW.SASSI.COM
Tests: 2429

Dr. K. Warner Schaie
Penn State Gerontology Center
105 Henderson S
Penn State University
University Park, PA 16802
Tests: 2194

Ronald R. Schmeck, Ph.D.
Department of Psychology
Southern Illinois University at Carbondale
Carbondale, IL 62901-6502
Tests: 1256

Nina G. Schneider, Ph.D.
Greater LA VA Healthcare, Nicotine Research Unit
Bldg. 210, 2nd Floor, 11301 Wilshire Blvd.
Mail Code: 691/B151D
Los Angeles, CA 90073
Telephone: 310-268-3059
FAX: 310-268-4125
Tests: 2310

Scholastic Testing Service, Inc.
480 Meyer Road
Bensenville, IL 60106-1617
Telephone: 1-800-642-6787
FAX: 630-766-8054
E-mail: stesting@email.com
Web URL: www.ststesting.com
Tests: 537, 640, 684, 860, 881, 1078, 1113, 1149, 1180,
    1334, 1335, 1358, 1547, 1797, 2051, 2130, 2209,
    2421, 2596, 2597, 2613, 2683

Scientific Management Techniques, Inc.
905 Turnpike
Canton, MA 02021
Tests: 2352

SDQ Instruments, Publication Unit
Faculty of Education
University of Western Sydney—MacArthur
P.O. Box 555
Campbelltown,
New South Wales 2560
Australia
Tests: 2236

Search Institute
700 South 3rd Street, Suite 210
Minneapolis, MN 55415-1138
Telephone: 800-888-7828
FAX: 612-376-8956
E-mail: si@search-institute.org
Web URL: www.search-institute.org
Tests: 2223

SEFA (Publications) Ltd.
"The Globe"
4 Great William St.
Stratford-upon-Avon CV37-6RY
England
FAX: +43-2236-29554
E-mail: admin@sefa.org.uk
Web URL: www.sefa.org.uk
Tests: 1444, 2005

Melvin Selzer, M.D.
6967 Paseo Laredo
La Jolla, CA 92037
Telephone: 619-459-1035
Tests: 1583

Sensonics, Inc.
125 White Horse Pike
Haddon Heights, NJ 08035
Tests: 2308

SHL Group plc
The Pavillion
1 Atwell Place
Thames Ditton, Surrey KT7 0NE
United Kingdom
Tests: 126, 238, 723, 935, 1468, 1473, 1734, 1765,
    1893, 2004, 2163, 2501, 2502, 2761

The Sidran Foundation
200 E. Joppa Road, Suite 207
Towson, MD 21286
Tests: 79, 828, 829

Sigma Assessment Systems, Inc.
511 Fort Street, Suite 435
P.O. Box 610984
Port Huron, MI 48061-0984
Telephone: 800-265-1285
FAX: 800-361-9411
E-mail: SIGMA@sigmaassessmentsystems.com
Web URL: www.sigmaassessmentsystems.com
Tests: 187, 258, 402, 423, 681, 1278, 1279, 1383, 1658,
    1885, 2031, 2266, 2291, 2456

Silverwood Enterprises, LLC
P.O. Box 363
Sharon Center, OH 44273
Telephone: 330-239-1646
FAX: 330-239-0250
E-mail: silverasoc@aol.com
Tests: 141, 142, 143, 1139

Jacob O. Sines
207 Black Springs Circle
Iowa City, IA 52246
Tests: 1163

Singular Publishing Group
[Address Unknown]
Tests: 1458

SLACK Incorporated
6900 Grove Road
Thorofare, NJ 08086-9447
Tests: 1612

Slosson Educational Publications, Inc.
P.O. Box 280
East Aurora, NY 14052-0280
Telephone: 888-756-7766
FAX: 800-655-3840
E-mail: slosson@slosson.com
Web URL: www.slosson.com
Tests: 5, 157, 183, 470, 649, 810, 811, 812, 813, 814,
    821, 1341, 2212, 2213, 2218, 2304, 2305, 2306,
    2428, 2554, 2674

SmarterKidsDotCom
15 Crawford
Needham, MA 02494
Tests: 408

SOARES Associates
111 Teeter Rock Road
Trumbull, CT 06611
Telephone: 203-375-5353
FAX: 203-375-2999
E-mail: atsoares@snet.net
Web URL: www.castleconsultants.com
Tests: 13, 2248, 2327, 2485

SOI Systems
45755 Goodpasture Road
P.O. Box D
Vida, OR 97488
Tests: 714, 761, 762, 1567

Sopris West
4093 Specialty Place
Longmont, CO 80504
Telephone: 800-547-6747
FAX: 303-776-5934
E-mail: WWW.SOPRISWEST.COM
Tests: 870, 1223, 1246, 2201, 2468

Southwest Educational Development Laboratory
211 East Seventh Street, Suite 400
Austin, TX 78701-3281
Tests: 827

SPECTRA Inc.
1004 Palmyra Drive
Tega Cay, SC 29706-8539
Tests: 2686

Stanard & Associates, Inc.
309 West Washington Street, Suite 1000
Chicago, IL 60606
Tests: 1687

Stoelting Co.
620 Wheat Lane
Wood Dale, IL 60191
Telephone: 630-860-9700
FAX: 630-860-9775
E-mail: psychtests@stoeltingco.com
Web URL: www.stoeltingco.com/tests
Tests: 285, 478, 1020, 1257, 1292, 1304, 1318, 1320,
    1348, 1351, 1419, 1432, 1576, 1638, 1967, 2228,
    2307, 2323, 2377, 2391, 2658

Student Development Associates, Inc.
110 Crestwood Drive
Athens, GA 30605
Tests: 8, 2405

Clifford H. Swensen
Department of Psychological Sciences
Purdue University
1364 Psychological Sciences Building
West Lafayette, IN 47907-1364
Telephone: 765-496-6977
FAX: 765-496-2670
E-mail: cswensen@psych.purdue.edu
Tests: 2180, 2182

Swets Test Publishers
P.O. Box 820
2160 Sz
Lisse
The Netherlands
Tests: 628, 1015, 2272, 2311, 2515

TAV Selection System
12807 Arminta Street
North Hollywood, CA 91605
Telephone: 818-765-1884
Tests: 2477

Anne P. Taylor
9 Tumble Weed, NW
Albuquerque, NM 87120-1823
Tests: 2478

Taylor & Francis
7625 Empire Drive
Florence, KY 41042
Tests: 222

Teachers College Press
Teachers College
Columbia University
525 W. 120th Street, Box 303
New York, NY 10027
Telephone: 800-575-6566
FAX: 802-864-7626
E-mail: tcpress@tc.columbia.edu
Web URL: www.teacherscollegepress.com
Tests: 210, 552, 857, 976, 1032, 1215, 1534, 2200,
    2519

Teleometrics International
1755 Woodstead Court
The Woodlands, TX 77380-0964
Telephone: 281-367-0060
FAX: 281-292-1324
E-mail: teleo.info@teleometrics.com
Web URL: www.teleometrics.com
Tests: 16, 432, 666, 667, 736, 914, 1196, 1381, 1470,
    1480, 1481, 1484, 1487, 1488, 1492, 1493, 1495,
    1681, 1814, 1846, 1859, 1865, 1891, 1938, 1939,
    1988, 2043, 2047, 2084, 2162, 2165, 2169, 2423,
    2424, 2425, 2446, 2450, 2493, 2495, 2496, 2497,
    2750

The Test Agency Limited
Cray House
Woodlands Road
Henley-on-Thames, Oxfordshire RG9 4AE
England
Telephone: 01491 413413
FAX: 01491 572249
E-mail: info@testagency.com
Web URL: www.testagency.com
Tests: 886, 892, 1085, 1185, 1428, 1486, 1498, 1539,
    1753, 1815, 1936, 2274, 2758, 2759

Test Analysis & Development Corporation
2400 Park Lake Drive
Boulder, CO 80301
Tests: 2242

Toby J. Tetenbaum
Fordham University
113 West 60th Street, Room 1119
New York, NY 10023
Tests: 227

Thames Valley Test Company, Ltd.
7-9 The Green
Flempton
Bury St. Edmunds, Suffolk IP28 6EL
England
Tests: 298, 2126

Therapy Skill Builders—A Division of The Psycho-
    logical Corporation
19500 Bulverde Road
San Antonio, TX 78259
Tests: 677, 852, 1209, 1216, 1619, 1652, 1770, 1935,
    2205, 2609

Thomas Concept
P.O. Box 160220
Austin, TX 78716-0220
Telephone: 512-327-2656
FAX: 512-327-7516 (FAX)
E-mail: info@thomasconcept.com
Web URL: www.thomasconcept.com
Tests: 2598

Touchstone Applied Science Associates (TASA), Inc.
4 Hardscrabble Heights
P.O. Box 382
Brewster, NY 10509-0382
Web URL: WWW.TASA.COM
Tests: 753, 754, 1460

Training House, Inc.
22 Amherst Road
Pelham, MA 01002-9745
Tests: 160, 170, 201, 619, 691, 913, 1225, 1466, 1483,
    1491, 1793, 1858, 1871, 1872, 1990, 1994, 2231,
    2232, 2451, 2530, 2603, 2617, 2709

TRT Associates, Inc.
1579 Monroe Drive, Suite F510
Atlanta, GA 30324
Telephone: 404-406-8781
FAX: 404-873-3959
E-mail: trtbasis@hotmail.com
Web URL: www.mindspring.com/~trtbasis
Tests: 263

Trust Tutoring
912 Thayer Avenue, Suite #205
Silver Spring, MD 20910
Telephone: 301-589-0733
FAX: 301-589-0733 *51
E-mail: HAVIS@EROLS.COM
Web URL: WWW.WDN.COM/TRUST
Tests: 949

21st Century Assessment
P.O. Box 608
South Pasadena, CA 91031–0608
Telephone: 800-374-2100
FAX: 626-441-0614
Web URL: http://www.21stcenturyassessment.com
Tests: 1878

U.S. Department of Labor
Division Chief for Evaluation and Skill Assessment
Office of Policy and Research
200 Constitution Avenue, NW
Washington, DC 20210
Tests: 1761, 1762

United States Military Entrance Processing C︎nmand
ATTN: Operations Directorate
2500 Green Bay Road
North Chicago, IL 60064-3094
Tests: 185

Universal Attention Disorders, Inc.
4281 Katella Avenue, #215
Los Alamitos, CA 90720
Telephone: 800-729-2886
FAX: 714-229-8782
E-mail: info@tovatest.com
Web URL: www.tovatest.com
Tests: 2566

University of Georgia
College of Education
Division for the Education of Exceptional Children
Aderhold Hall
Athens, GA 30602
Tests: 226

University of Maryland
University Counseling Center
Shoemaker Hall
College Park, MD 20742
Tests: 1713, 2032, 2287

University of Michigan Press
839 Greene Street
P.O. Box 1104
Ann Arbor, MI 48106-1104
Telephone: 734-764-4392
FAX: 734-936-0456
E-mail: um.press.bus@umich.edu
Web URL: www.press.umich.edu
Tests: 861, 1962

University of Minnesota Press
Test Division
Mill Place, Suite 290
111 Third Avenue South
Minneapolis, MN 55401-2520
Tests: 1623, 1624, 2196

University of Utah
Department of Psychology—SBS
390 South 1530 East
Salt Lake City, UT 84112-0251
Tests: 2174

Variety Child Learning Center
47 Humphrey Drive
Syosset, NY 11791-4098
Telephone: 516-921-7171
FAX: 516-921-8130
E-mail: JFVPSW@aol.com
Web URL: www.vclc.org
Tests: 1006

Village Publishing
73 Valley Drive
Furlong, PA 18925
Telephone: 800-553-7678
FAX: 215-794-3386
E-mail: VP@custody-vp.com
Web URL: www.custody-vp.com
Tests: 15, 208, 332, 826, 1166, 1798, 1804, 1839

Vocational and Rehabilitation Research Institute
3304 - 33rd Street, NW
Calgary, Alberta T2L 2A6
Canada
Tests: 66

Vocational Psychology Research
N657 Elliott Hall
University of Minnesota—Twin Cities
75 East River Road
Minneapolis, MN 55455-0344
Telephone: 612-625-1367
FAX: 612-626-0345
E-mail: vpr@tc.umn.edu
Web URL: www.psych.umn.edu/psylabs/vpr
Tests: 1620, 1621, 1626, 1627

VORT Corporation
P.O. Box 60880
Palo Alto, CA 94306
Tests: 294, 1140, 1142

J. Weston Walch, Publisher
P.O. Box 658
321 Valley Street
Portland, ME 04104-0658
Tests: 994, 2056, 2607

Walden Personnel Performance, Inc.
4155 Sherbrooke, W #100
Montreal, Quebec H3Z 1K9
Canada
Telephone: 514-989-9555
FAX: 514-989-9934
E-mail: tests@waldentesting.com
Web URL: www.waldentesting.com
Tests: 158, 159, 252, 361, 362, 376, 524, 525, 653, 655,
    679, 739, 744, 954, 1141, 1276, 1277, 1489, 1697,
    1698, 1727, 1819, 2001, 2002, 2011, 2099, 2100,
    2167, 2500, 2504, 2678, 2682

Arthur Weider
552 Laguardia Pl.
New York, NY 10012-1459
Telephone: 212-777-7303
FAX: 212-388-0001
E-mail: AWEIDER2000@msm.com
Web URL: www.realsolutions.org/weider.htm
Tests: 696, 699

Otto Weininger
1033 Bay Street, Suite #204
Toronto, Ontario M5S 3A5
Canada
Telephone: 416-929-2348
FAX: 416-929-3440
Tests: 820

Western Psychological Services
12031 Wilshire Blvd.
Los Angeles, CA 90025-1251
Telephone: 310-478-2061
FAX: 310-478-7838
Web URL: www.wpspublish.com
Tests: 38, 42, 76, 78, 129, 136, 180, 224, 228, 230, 232,
    300, 304, 334, 356, 390, 391, 450, 462, 464, 752,
    792, 835, 907, 921, 973, 1013, 1033, 1115, 1118,
    1167, 1177, 1179, 1234, 1241, 1245, 1328, 1342,
    1362, 1453, 1455, 1456, 1464, 1467, 1499, 1500,
    1505, 1512, 1538, 1571, 1672, 1700, 1720, 1744,
    1801, 1838, 1854, 1855, 1856, 1883, 1884, 1889,
    1897, 1913, 1982, 1983, 2023, 2106, 2108, 2114,
    2117, 2124, 2129, 2153, 2183, 2220, 2221, 2255,
    2261, 2277, 2280, 2309, 2315, 2340, 2387, 2393,
    2402, 2404, 2435, 2461, 2505, 2508, 2562, 2604,
    2605, 2606, 2657, 2659, 2663, 2668, 2675, 2679,
    2703, 2707, 2711

Wide Range, Inc.
P.O. Box 3410
Wilmington, DE 19804-0250
Tests: 71, 2713, 2714, 2715, 2716, 2717

Winslow Research Institute
1933 Windward Point
Discovery Bay, CA 94514
Tests: 1852, 1875

Wintergreen/Orchard House, Inc.
425 Spring Lake Drive
Itasca, IL 60143-2076
Tests: 406, 882, 1028

Rose Wolfe Family Partnership LLP
c/o Walden Personnel Testing & Consulting, Inc.
4115 Sherbrooke, W #100
Montreal, Quebec H3Z 1K9
Canada
Telephone: 514-989-9555
FAX: 514-989-9934
E-mail: ssilver@waldentesting.com
Web URL: www.waldentesting.com
Tests: 171, 2469, 2470, 2680, 2727, 2728

Wonderlic, Inc.
1795 N. Butterfield Road
Libertyville, IL 60048-1238
Tests: 641, 936, 1127, 2729, 2730

Judith Worell, Ph.D.
Educational & Counseling Psychology
245 Dickey Hall
University of Kentucky
Lexington, KY 40506-0017
Telephone: 859-254-0239
FAX: 859-254-0239
E-mail: jpwphd@aol.com
Tests: 1799

World Health Organization
Management of Substance Dependence
Dr. Maristela Monteiro
CH-1211
Geneva 27
Switzerland
Telephone: 41-22-791-4791
FAX: 41-22-791-4851
E-mail: monteirom@who.int
Web URL: www.who.int
Tests: 138

World of Work, Inc.
64 East Broadway Road 175
Tempe, AZ 85282
Tests: 2770

Worley's Identity Discovery Profile, Inc.
44 Farmers Row
Groton, MA 01450-1802
Telephone: 978-448-2047
FAX: 978-448-3910
E-mail: WIDP@worleyid.com
Web URL: www.worleyid.com
Tests: 2771

Zaner-Bloser Educational Publishers
2200 West Fifth Avenue
P.O. Box 16764
Columbus, OH 43216-6764
Web URL: www.zaner-bloser.com
Tests: 2460

INDEX OF NAMES

This index indicates whether a citation refers to authorship of a test or of a test review for a specific test in a previous Mental Measurements Yearbook. *Numbers refer to test entries in* Tests in Print VI, *not to pages. The abbreviations and numbers following the names may be interpreted as follows: "test, 73" indicates authorship of test 73; "rev, 86" is based on information listed in the cross references for a test and indicates authorship of a previous review of test 86.*

Aaron, I. E.: rev, 329, 485, 2076, 2139, 2140
Aarons, M.: test, 237
Aasland, O. G.: test, 138
Abbott-Shim, M. S.: test, 443
Abell, E. L.: rev, 365
Abidin, R. R.: test, 1807, 1809, 2383
Abraham, J. A.: test, 1309
Academic Consulting & Testing Service: test, 219, 1397, 1805, 2207
Academic Freedom Committee, Illinois Division, American Civil Liberties Union: test, 12
Achenbach, T. M.: test, 35, 420, 2778
Achterberg, J.: test, 1131
Ackerman, M. J.: test, 42
Ackerman, P. L.: rev, 225, 1227, 1322, 1520, 2361, 2369
Ackerman, R. J.: test, 41, 1933
Ackerman, T.: rev, 2692
Ackerman, T. A.: rev, 779, 1706
ACS DivCHED Examinations Institute: test, 43, 44, 45, 46, 47, 48, 49, 50, 51, 52, 53, 54, 55, 56
ACT Career Planning Services: test, 2666
ACT, Inc.: test, 57, 58, 414, 609, 961, 1916
Adair, N.: test, 4
Adamovich, B.: test, 2187
Adams, C. R.: test, 1849
Adams, E.: test, 1954
Adams, G. L.: test, 646, 1719
Adams, G. R.: rev, 732
Adams, J. D.: test, 2633

Adams, M. F.: rev, 251
Adams, R.: test, 2472
Adams, R. L.: rev, 1456, 2054, 2087
Adams, W.: test, 2521, 2714, 2715, 2716
Adcock, C. J.: rev, 1008, 1148, 1613, 2276, 2292, 2296, 2593
Adcock, D.: test, 634
Addiction Research Foundation: test, 188
ADE Incorporated: test, 1312, 1692, 2426
Adkins, D. C.: rev, 910
Adkinson, D. R.: test, 1241
Adler, S.: rev, 1835
Adrian, M.: test, 1023
Ahluwalia, S. P.: test, 2486
Ahmann, J. S.: rev, 2510 2587
Aho, M.: test, 2111
Ahrens, J. B.: test, 399
Ahsen, A.: test, 127, 889
Aidman, E. V.: rev, 225, 334
Aiken, L. R.: rev, 33, 57, 2217
Airasian, P. W.: rev, 365, 1268, 2078
Albanese, M.: rev, 1895, 1897, 2015, 2562
Albanese, M. A.: rev, 412, 1127
Alberts, N. F.: test, 14, 1709, 2252
Albin, J. B.: test, 885
Albright, L. E.: rev, 1620, 1626
Alcorn, B. K.: rev, 1431, 1710, 1987
Alden, L. E.: test, 1255
Alderman, N.: test, 298
Aldous, C.: test, 807

Ashmore, L.: rev, 764, 1302
Ashurst, D. I.: test, 2329
Aspell, D. D.: test, 929
Aspell, P. J.: test, 929
Assessment Systems Corporation: test, 1617
The Associated Examining Board: test, 262
Associates for Research in Behavior, Inc.: test, 2670
Association of American Medical Colleges: test, 1565
Astin, A. W.: rev, 605, 2390; test, 682
Astner, K.: test, 2739
Atkins, C. P.: rev, 1817
Atkinson, M. J.: rev, 770, 2265
Atlas, J. A.: rev, 1184, 1206, 2236, 2553
Au, K. H.: rev, 1682
Audiologic Services and Southwest School for the Hearing Impaired, Office of the Los Angeles County Superintendent of Schools: test, 2527
Aukett, A.: test, 2198
Aulls, M. W.: rev, 359
Ault, M. J.: test, 210
Austin, J. T.: rev, 156, 683, 936, 1468, 1543, 1873, 2229
Austin, M. C.: rev, 798
Australian Council for Educational Research: test, 22, 31, 33, 926
Australian Council for Educational Research Ltd.: test, 21, 24, 29, 30, 2008
Australian Council for Educational Research Press: test, 2007
Auvenshine, A. A.: test, 1424
Averbuch, S.: test, 1445
Avery-Smith, W.: test, 852
Avolio, B.: test, 1663
Avolio, B. J.: test, 1662, 1664, 1779
Axford, S. N.: rev, 741, 766, 1159, 1160, 1934
Aycock, D. W.: test, 687
Ayer, G. W.: rev, 118, 119
Ayers, D.: rev, 34
Ayers, J. D.: rev, 662, 2171, 2338
Aylward, G. P.: rev, 647, 816, 1151, 1399; test, 270
Ayres, A. J.: test, 2255
Ayres, D.: test, 1434

Baack, K. L.: rev, 2343
Babich, A.: test, 1410
Babor, T. F.: test, 138
Bachelor, P. A.: rev, 438, 542, 638, 732, 1518, 1710, 2369
Bachiochi, P. D.: test, 1290
Bachman, L. F.: rev, 2085
Backlund, P.: rev, 862, 2009
Backlund, P. A.: rev, 2531
Bacon, E. H.: rev, 59, 1665
Bacon, T. R.: test, 541, 1450, 1730, 2160, 2448
Baddeley, A.: test, 469, 2126
Bader, B. D.: rev, 2055, 2212
Baehr, G. O.: test, 901

Baehr, M. E.: test, 901, 959, 1490, 1731, 1972, 2297, 2506
Bagby, R. M.: test, 2399
Baggaley, A. R.: rev, 845
Bagnato, S. J.: rev, 2105
Bahns, T. M.: rev, 1694
Bailey-Richardson, B.: rev, 84, 2227
Bain, S. K.: rev, 1978, 2095
Baines, K. A.: test, 206
Baird, L. L.: rev, 2613
Baker, J. M.: test, 1806
Baker, R. W.: test, 2402
Baker, R.: test, 2089
Bakker, S.: test, 2754
Baldwin, J.: rev, 760
Baldwin, L.: test, 2203
Baldwin, T. S.: rev, 1710
Balinski, B.: rev, 2358
Balinsky, B.: test, 2230
Ball, B.: test, 793
Ball Foundation: test, 240
Ball, K. K.: test, 2638
Ball, R. S.: rev, 428
Balla, D. A.: test, 2652, 2653
Ballard, J. C.: rev, 357, 2264
Ballard, W. S.: test, 1189
Baltimore County Public Schools Office of Adult Education: test, 1513
Balzer, W. K.: test, 1290, 2382
Bamberg, E.: test, 2329
Bandalos, D. L.: rev, 202, 921, 1063, 2636
Bandelow, B.: test, 1791
Bane, K. D.: rev, 751
Bangs, T. E.: test, 317
Banks, C.: rev, 717, 2064, 2350, 2351
Banks, C. E. K.: rev, 1911
Banks, M. E.: test, 41, 1933
Bankson, N. W.: rev, 1011, 2513; test, 241, 242
Bannatyne, A.: rev, 1055, 1303, 1330, 1822, 2085, 2735
Bannister, D.: test, 1084
Barbe, W. B.: test, 2460
Barber, G. A.: test, 785
Barcher, P. R.: test, 2663
Barclay, A. G.: rev, 799
Barclay, J. R.: rev, 1786; test, 2403
Bardis, P. D.: test, 6, 326, 555, 745, 938, 971, 983, 1079, 1221, 1275, 1570, 1813, 1914, 2094, 2267, 2592, 2643, 2654, 2768
Bardos, A. N.: test, 834, 1034
Barenbaum, E.: test, 2529
Barenbaum, E. M.: test, 768
Barker, B. D.: rev, 1568
Barker, J.: test, 765
Barker, L. L.: test, 1435, 1440, 2685, 2686
Barnard, E. L.: test, 1723, 2068
Barnard, J.: test, 1691

Barnes, H.: test, 1796
Barnes, L. L. B.: rev, 840, 1271, 1518, 1733, 1748, 1809, 1978, 2045
Barnes-Farrell, J.: rev, 1379
Barnett, D. W.: rev, 130, 267, 790
Bar-On, R.: test, 244, 245, 246
Barona, A.: rev, 1336, 2373, 2430
Baroody, A. J.: test, 2532
Barrett, G. V.: test, 231
Barrett, J.: test, 148, 2329
Barrett, J. S.: test, 1428, 1936
Barrett, M.: test, 2559, 2741
Barrett, R. S.: rev, 264
Barriga, A. Q.: test, 1172
Barron, F.: rev, 884
Barron, S. I.: test, 1265
Barry, J.: test, 2343
Barsch, J. R.: test, 248
Bart, W. M.: rev, 237, 345, 1710
Bartlett, B. J.: rev, 1534, 2560
Baruth, L. G.: test, 1347
Bascom, H. L.: test, 980
Bashaw, W. L.: rev, 1265, 1781
Bashford, A.: test, 2028
Bass, B. M.: test, 264, 1662, 1663, 1664, 1779
Bate, M.: test, 196
Bate, S. M.: test, 2082
Bates, E: test, 1458
Bateson, D. J.: rev, 1143, 2666
Battle, J.: test, 732
Baucom, D. H.: rev, 372
Bauer, A. M.: test, 220, 1399
Bauer, E. A.: rev, 226, 906, 2223
Bauernfeind, R. H.: test, 881
Baum, A.: test, 1353
Baumanis, R.: rev, 2281
Bauserman, D. N.: rev, 1423
Bawtree, S.: test, 723, 935, 2004
Bayles, K. A.: test, 181, 1025
Bayley, N.: rev, 1085, 2691; test, 271
Bearley, W. L.: test, 1776
Beattie, B. L.: test, 535
Beatty, J. R.: test, 1226
Beauvais, F.: test, 147
Bechtel, R.: test, 2022
Bechtoldt, H.: rev, 818, 1108
Bechtoldt, H. P.: rev, 305, 1007, 1271
Beck, A. T.: test, 272, 273, 274, 275, 276
Beck, I. L.: rev, 1447, 2534
Beck, J. S.: test, 276
Beck, M. D.: rev, 1330, 1341, 2534, 2583
Beck, S. J.: rev, 373, 2134
Becker, H.: test, 1027
Becker, R. L.: test, 277, 2073
Bedell, R. C.: rev, 1640
Beech, H. R.: rev, 1728
Beech, M. C.: rev, 1185

Beery, K. E.: test, 796, 1231
Beggs, D. L.: test, 288, 435
Begin, L.: test, 387
Behar, L.: test, 1960
Behavior Data Systems Ltd.: test, 837, 2627
Behrns, H.: test, 177
Beidel, D. C.: test, 2317, 2318
Beitchman, J. H.: test, 993
Bejar, I. I.: rev, 310
Belbin, M.: test, 299
Belcher, M. J.: rev, 58, 2446, 2730
Bell, J. E.: rev, 456, 972, 978, 979, 1015
Bell, M. D.: test, 300
Bell, N.: test, 785
Bella, P. D.: rev, 2566
Bellak, L.: rev, 1728; test, 456, 887, 2027, 2251
Bellak, S. S.: test, 456
Bellingrath, E.: test, 553
Bellman, M.: test, 2198
Bem, S. L.: test, 301
Benbow, C. P.: rev, 154, 1528
Bender, L.: test, 304
Bene, E.: test, 978, 979
Benedict, R. H. B.: test, 339, 1168
Benes, K. M.: rev, 297, 969, 1822, 2321
Benish, J. K.: rev, 270, 401, 1235
Benjamin, L. S.: test, 2174, 2395
Bennett, C. W.: rev, 1817, 2400, 2721
Bennett, G. K.: test, 305, 817, 818, 819, 1119, 2281
Ben-Porath, Y. S.: test, 1624
Benson, J.: rev, 1644, 2077, 2411
Benson, M. J.: rev, 973, 2403, 2742
Benson, N.: rev, 2407
Benson, P.: rev, 802
Benson, P. G.: rev, 240, 1064, 1741, 1938, 2167
Bentler, P. M.: rev, 1242, 1579, 1913, 2508; test, 662
Bentley, A.: test, 1555
Bentley, R. R.: rev, 1555
Benton, A. L.: rev, 304, 1623, 2593; test, 306, 1666
Benton, S. L.: rev, 391, 1083, 1195, 2577
Berdie, R. F.: rev, 818, 1007, 2436
Berenson, B. G.: test, 2032
Berg, H. D.: rev, 123
Berge, P. S.: test, 635
Berger, A.: rev, 698, 755, 2415, 2687, 2688
Berger, M.: rev, 2123
Berger, P. M.: rev, 1834
Bergstrom, B.: rev, 1132, 2016
Beringer, M. L.: test, 307
Berk, R. A.: rev, 347, 1569, 2357, 2681; test, 752
Berkay, P. J.: test, 1763
Berke, S.: test, 524
Berlin, L. J.: test, 1964
Bernard, H.: rev, 622, 2664
Bernardin, H. J.: rev, 1378, 1468, 1497, 1757, 2457
Bernberg, R. E.: test, 1182, 2748
Berndt, D. J.: test, 1671, 1672

Berndt, R. S.: rev, 199, 617, 1367
Bernet, M.: test, 2286
Bernier, J. J.: rev, 389, 804
Berninger, V. W.: test, 1986
Bernstein, D. P.: test, 451
Bernt, F.: rev, 1505
Bernt, F. M.: rev, 429, 447, 791
Bernthal, J. E.: test, 241
Berntson, B.: test, 200
Berry, P.: test, 1367
Berry, S. R.: test, 2776
Berryman, C.: test, 226
Berryman, J. D.: rev, 2337, 2401; test, 226
Bers, S. A..: test, 769
Bessai, F.: rev, 667, 964, 1662, 1746, 1823, 2002
Betts, A.: rev, 2140
Betz, N. E.: test, 401, 1527, 2745
Betz, W.: rev, 1308
Beukelman, D. R.: test, 205
Beukes, D. P. M.: test, 1145
Beyer, F. S.: test, 212, 823
Biedenstein, J. J.: test, 2345
Bienvenu, M.: test, 190
Bienvenu, M. J.: test, 1243, 1252, 1258, 1503, 1795, 1800, 1953, 2241, 2270
Bierer, B. A.: test, 1908
Biersdorf, K. C.: test, 2032
Bigby, Havis, & Associates, Inc.: test, 191, 2170, 2229
Biggs, J.: rev, 248, 391; D.: test, 2550
Bigler, E. D.: test, 528
Bigsby, R.: test, 1935
Bilder, R.: test, 955
Billingslea, F. Y.: rev, 304
Bills, M. A.: rev, 10, 60, 521, 1261
Binder, L. M.: test, 1927
Biofeedback Certification Institute of America: test, 313
Birch, L. B.: rev, 389, 923, 2358
Bird, E.: test, 935
Bischoff, H.: rev, 138
Bischoff, H. G. W.: rev, 824
Bischoff, L.: rev, 1810
Bischoff, L. G.: rev, 356, 443, 859, 1171, 1798
Biscoe, M.: test, 1448
Bishop, D.: test, 2518
Biskin, B. H.: rev, 1109, 2370
Bisno, A.: test, 2329
Bittner, R. H.: rev, 1127, 1559
Bjerstedt, A.: rev, 884, 2135
Black, D. D.: test, 2212
Black, J. D.: rev, 2449, 2563
Blackman, J. A.: test, 1829
Blackwell, M.: rev, 1916, 2621
Blackwell, M. W.: rev, 281, 1395
Blakeley, R. W.: test, 2219
Blakemore, C. B.: rev, 304

Blalock, G.: test, 1082
Blanchard, K.: test, 1378
Blank, M.: test, 1964
Blatt, S. J.: test, 211, 769
Blazer, J. A.: test, 2476
Blesch, G.: test, 4
Blinkhorn, S.: test, 126, 1636, 2004
Bliss, L. S.: rev, 241, 2085, 2122, 2639; test, 2218, 2261
Blitchington, W. P.: test, 2507
Blixt, S.: rev, 866, 1406
Bloch, J. S.: test, 1006
Block, J.: rev, 967; test, 366, 373
Block, M. E.: rev, 785
Block-Pedego, A.: test, 2201
Bloom, B. S.: rev, 605
Bloom, L.: rev, 799, 874
Bloom, L. A.: rev, 287
Bloomer, J.: test, 269
Bloomer, R. H.: test, 318, 2076
Bloxam, B. M.: rev, 2292, 2296
Bloxom, B.: rev, 1002, 1861
Blum, L. H.: test, 613
Blum, M.: test, 1473
Blumenthal, J. A.: rev, 1353
Bly, L.: test, 1652
Bobish, T.: test, 2465
Bock, S. J.: test, 189
Bodden, J. L.: rev, 395, 396, 1362
Boder, E.: test, 320
Bodey, W.: test, 787
Boehm, A. E.: rev, 347; test, 321, 322, 552
Boer, D. P.: test, 2271
Boersma, F. J.: test, 1838
Bolen, L. M.: rev, 1653, 2609
Boliek, C. A.: rev, 304, 1615
Boll, T.: test, 460, 792
Boll, T. J.: test, 2280
Bologna, N. B.: rev, 678, 798, 1650, 1666
Bolser, C.: test, 634
Bolton, B.: rev, 91, 156, 277, 372, 1263, 2023, 2761; test, 909, 2755, 2763
Bolton, B. F.: rev, 1877, 2286, 2292, 2296, 2602
Bolton, D. L.: rev, 398, 1224, 1335, 2591
Bolton, S. O.: test, 1232
Bond, D.: test, 324
Bond, G. L.: rev, 841
Bond, N. A., Jr.: test, 845
Boninelli, I.: test, 2328
Bonta, J.: test, 1420
Bonta, J. L.: test, 1421
Boodoo, G. M.: rev, 815
Bookbinder, G. E.: test, 2171
Booker, G.: test, 323, 324
Booker, I. A.: rev, 1693
Boone, D. R.: rev, 199
Booth, J.A. G.: test, 387

Bruner, G. C., II: rev, 1820, 2153
Bruni, J. R., Jr.: test, 1393
Bruning, R.: rev, 753
Bruning, R. H.: rev, 358
Bruns, D.: test, 268
Brush, J. A.: rev, 1025
Bryan, J. E.: rev, 1134
Bryan, M. M.: rev, 365, 2357
Bryant, B. R.: test, 198, 768, 777, 779, 805, 1080, 1081, 1398, 2199, 2556, 2576
Bryant, N. D.: rev, 1032
Bryce, J.: test, 1331
Bryen, D. N.: rev, 2116, 2117
Buccini, E. P.: test, 480
Buck, D.: test, 2299
Buck, J. N.: test, 1177
Buckly, R.: test, 1992
Bucy, J. E.: rev, 2360, 2577
Budd, K. S.: rev, 843, 1126
Budge, G. W. K.: test, 1415
Buehler, J. A.: test, 1306
Buethe, E.: test, 649
Bugaj, A. M.: rev, 172, 1643, 2152, 2672, 2747
Bugbee, A. C.: rev, 1558
Bugbee, A. C., Jr.: rev, 144, 1227, 1766
Buktenica, N. A.: rev, 1226; test, 796
Bullis, M.: test, 621, 2181, 2542, 2622
Bullock, L. M.: test, 281
Bullock, W. B.: test, 162
Bunch, M. B.: rev, 177, 370, 394, 406, 1736, 1887, 1905, 2263
Bunda, M. A.: rev, 1187, 1200, 1739, 1777, 1991, 2302, 2681
Bunker, L. K.: rev, 785, 985, 1590, 2539, 2715
Burdon, B.: test, 233, 234
Burgess, P. W.: test, 298
Burgess, T. C.: rev, 1640
Burgomeister, B. B.: test, 613
Burke, A.: test, 2329
Burke, C. L.: rev, 1031
Burkholder, R.: test, 1806
Burks, H. F.: test, 356
Burley-Allen, M.: test, 619
Burnett, P. C.: rev, 2008, 2108
Burney, D. M.: test, 75
Burnham, L.: test, 1852, 1875
Burns, C. W.: rev, 1303
Burns, M.: rev, 1881, 2035
Burns, M. S.: test, 357
Burns, P. C.: test, 358
Burnside, R. M.: test, 1332
Burnstein, A. G.: rev, 2694
Burr, E. T.: rev, 2601
Burson, S. L., Jr.: rev, 47
Burstein, A. G.: rev, 2134, 2691
Burt, C.: rev, 2358
Burt, M. K.: test, 310

Burton, S. D.: test, 791
Busch, J. C.: rev, 2220, 2390
Busch-Rossnagel, N. A.: rev, 470, 977, 2569
Bush, B. R.: rev, 356
Buss, A. H.: test, 129
Busse, R. T.: rev, 35
Butcher, J. N.: rev, 2292, 2296; test, 364, 1623, 1624
Butler, J. K., Jr.: rev, 1577, 1887, 2471
Butler, K. G.: rev, 205, 2116, 2117, 2342, 2639; test, 2465
Butler, R. J.: test, 2243
Butt, D. S.: rev, 1283, 1284
Bye, R. A.: test, 1265
Byrd, P. B.: test, 1235
Byrd, R. E.: test, 715, 1646
Byrne, M. C.: rev, 1021, 1054, 1371
Bzoch, K. R.: test, 2085

Caballero, J. A.: test, 1183
Cahen, L. S.: rev, 537
Caldarella, P.: test, 1162
Caldwell, B. M.: test, 1164
Calfee, K. H.: rev, 552
Calfee, R.: rev, 1031
Calfee, R. C.: rev, 2080
Callahan, C. M.: rev, 325, 368 1047, 1332, 1334, 2459; test, 2186
Callahan, L. G.: rev, 2586
Calvert, B.: test, 1718
Camara, W.: rev, 408, 2764
Camara, W. J.: rev, 2163, 2168, 2742, 2761
The Cambridge Stratford Study Skills Institute: test, 1811, 2454
Cambridge, The Adult Education Co.: test, 1442
Cambridge, The Adult Education Company, in association with Moravian College, Bethlehem, PA: test, 1198, 1199
Cameron, A.: test, 1471, 2758, 2759
Cameron, C.: test, 2624
Camp, B. W.: rev, 317, 1210, 2189
Camp, C. J.: rev, 207, 1025, 1985, 2329
Camp, L.: test, 1734
Campbell, A.: test, 941
Campbell, B. A.: test, 1907
Campbell, D.: rev, 136, 1500; test, 379, 380, 381, 382
Campbell, D. P.: rev, 1092, 1637, 2390; test, 2390
Campbell, I. A.: rev, 2652
Campbell, J. A.: rev, 47, 99, 499, 1035
Campbell, J. T.: rev, 1173, 1389
Campbell, M. H.: rev, 839, 2121
Campbell, R.: test, 2289
Campbell, R. A.: test, 465
Campbell, T. F.: rev, 1301
Campion, M. A.: test, 2498
Canadian Test Centre, Educational Assessment Services: test, 384, 388
Canadian Test Centre: test, 383

Cancelli, A. A.: rev, 2104; test, 390, 391, 1362, 1889, 2604, 2605, 2606
Canfield, J. S.: test, 390
Canivez, G. L.: rev, 73
Carbo, M.: test, 612, 2077
Carbonell, J. L.: rev, 2438
Cardall, A. J.: test, 392
Carey, K. T.: rev, 2, 195, 420, 479, 1014, 2665
Carey, W. B.: test, 421
Carlson, C.: rev, 974, 2182
Carlson, C. I.: rev, 979, 1840
Carlson, E.: test, 79
Carlson, E. B.: test, 828
Carlson, J.: rev, 17, 18, 39
Carlson, J. E.: rev, 1766
Carlson, J. F.: rev, 273, 746, 823, 1160, 1682, 1839, 2120, 2373
Carlson, J. V.: rev, 342, 1710, 1799, 2606
Carlson, K. A.: rev, 700; test, 423
Carlson, R. D.: rev, 1959
Carlson, T. R.: rev, 2209
Carmer, J. C.: rev, 1557, 2195, 2433
Carney, A. E.: rev, 871
Carney, C. G.: test, 400
Carney, I.: test, 1171
Carney, R. N.: rev, 1336, 2183
Carpenter, C. D.: rev, 205, 1053, 1231, 1365, 2105, 2322, 2361, 2520
Carpenter, D.: rev, 1768
Carr, S. J.: rev, 2176, 2698
Carrington Rotto, P.: rev, 2296
Carroll, B.: test, 425
Carroll, D. J.: rev, 302, 2718; test, 879
Carroll, J. B.: rev, 818, 1007, 1108, 1193, 1587, 630
Carrow-Woolfolk, E.: test, 637, 1767, 1768, 2513
Carter, H. D.: rev, 1261, 2390
Carter, J. A.: test, 705
Carter, S.: test, 2447
Caruso, D. R.: test, 1532
Caruso, J. C.: rev, 1657, 2044
Carver, C.: test, 2740
CASAS: test, 631
Casas, J. M.: rev, 307, 1460, 2488
Casby, M. W.: rev, 2776
Case-Smith, J.: test, 1935
Cashew, V. M.: test, 881
Cashin, W. E.: test, 1191
Caso, A.: test, 311
Cassaretto, F. P.: rev, 47
Cassel, R.: test, 698, 2563
Cassel, R. N.: test, 888, 1389, 2561
Casualty Actuarial Society: test, 151, 153, 154
Catlin, R.: test, 1588
Cattell, A. K. S.: test, 731, 2292, 2296
Cattell, H. E. P.: test, 2292, 2296
Cattell, M. D.: test, 1148
Cattell, P.: rev, 1358; test, 428

Cattell, R. B.: test, 467, 527, 630, 731, 868, 1148, 2292, 2296
Catterson, J. H.: test, 841
Caulley, D. N.: rev, 753
Cautela, J.: test, 1014
Cautela, J. R.: test, 291, 1014, 1772
Cazdan, C. B.: rev, 2586, 2361
Cehen, Y-F.: test, 1191
Cellucci, T.: rev, 837, 1254
Center for Applied Linguistics: test, 176, 253, 470, 1922
Center for Creative Leadership: test, 303
Center for Occupational and Professional Assessment: test, 1012
Center for Studies in Education and Human Development: test, 1541
Center for the Study of Aging and Human Development: test, 1725
Central Institute for the Deaf: test, 478
Centre for Research on Learning and Instruction, University of Edinburgh: test, 2226
Certification Board of the Professional Picture Framers Association: test, 430
Cerullo, F. M.: test, 890
Cervenka, E. J.: rev, 1587
Cervera, V. M.: test, 996
CFKR Career Materials, Inc.: test, 962, 1147, 1449
Chadbourn, R. A.: rev, 1265
Chadbourne, J. W.: test, 167, 1851
Chall, J. S.: test, 806, 2139, 2140
Challman, R. C.: rev, 2135
Chambers, D. C.: test, 2329
Chambers, J. L.: test, 1910
Chandler, S. K.: test, 2665
Chao, C.: test, 1908
Chapin, F. S.: test, 434
Chapman, J. W.: test, 1838
Charles, D.: test, 705
Chartrand, J. M.: test, 405
Chase, C. I.: rev, 652, 1193, 1951, 2284, 2357, 2613
Chauncey, H.: rev, 1269
Chazan, M.: rev, 1307
Chelune, G.: test, 2725
Cheney, D.: test, 2542
Cherrick, H. M.: rev, 760, 1429
Cheseldine, S.: test, 1816
Chesterfield, K. B.: rev, 650
Chevron, E. S.: test, 211
Chew, A. L.: test, 1447
Child Health and Education Study, University of Bristol: test, 879
Child Welfare League of America, Inc.: test, 730
Children's Bureau of Southern California: test, 974
Childs, R.: test, 453, 1753
Chissom, B. S.: rev, 796, 798, 2461
Chittooran, M. M.: rev, 1151, 1654, 1963
Chizmar, J. F.: test, 251

Emmert, V.: test, 1438
Emmett, W. G.: rev, 1358
Emslie, G. J.: test, 2698
Enderby, P. M.: test, 1017
Endicott, J.: test, 920, 1052, 2024, 2026, 2044, 2195
Endler, N. S.: rev, 186, 2371; test, 685, 690, 921
Engdahl, B.: rev, 910
Engel, D.: test, 785
Engelhard, G.: rev, 2317
Engelhard, G., Jr.: rev, 372, 537, 729, 933, 1886, 2360
Engelhart, M. D.: rev, 57, 561, 584, 1069
Engelmann, H. O.: test, 948
Engen, E.: test, 2122
Engen, T.: test, 2122
Enger, J. M.: rev, 153, 809, 864, 1387, 2719
England, G. W.: test, 1626
Englander, M. E.: test, 1201
The English Language Institute of the University of Michigan, Testing and Certification Division: test, 951
English Language Institute of the University of Michigan: test, 952
The English Language Institute Testing and Certification Division: test, 1584, 1585
Ennis, R. H.: test, 694, 695, 930
Enright, R, D.: test, 931
Ensher, G. L.: test, 2465
Epstein, J.: test, 669
Epstein, J. H.: rev, 1913
Epstein, M. H.: test, 292, 2176
Epstein, S.: test, 676, 1661
Erb, L.: test, 2521
Erchul, W. P.: rev, 37, 823, 2453
Erdmann, J. B.: rev, 1376, 2648
Erhardt, D.: test, 670
Erickson, D.: rev, 1216, 1622, 2340, 2567, 2568
Erickson, D. B.: rev, 2578
Erickson, J. G.: test, 640
Erickson, L. W.: rev, 2631
Erickson, R. C.: rev, 1710
Erikson, J.: test, 1214
Erin, J. N.: test, 784
Ernhart, C. B.: rev, 458, 780
Eron, L. D.: rev, 2134, 2593
Ershler, J.: rev, 267
Esonis, S.: test, 1014
Espenschade, A.: rev, 355, 1432
Espey, L.: test, 1468
Estroff, T. W.: test, 1941
Ethington, C. A.: test, 622
Euhardy, R.: test, 207
Evans, A. S.: test, 2015, 2017
Evans, D. R.: test, 2046
Evans, J.: test, 718
Evans, J. J.: test, 298
Evans, J. R.: rev, 2391
Evans-Fernandez, S. E.: test, 2411

Evard, B. L.: rev, 2053
Exner, J. E., Jr.: rev, 373
Eyberg, S.: test, 2595
Eyberg, S. M.: test, 844, 965
Eyde, L. D.: rev, 2192, 2282, 2549
Eysenck, H. J.: rev, 372, 1161, 1415, 1623, 2134, 2600; test, 966, 967
Eysenck, S. B. G.: test, 966, 967, 1307

Fabry, J.: rev, 1572, 1668, 1772
Facione, N. C.: test, 368
Facione, P. A.: test, 368, 369
Fad, K. M.: test, 40
Fager, J. J.: rev, 643, 1191, 1571, 1822, 2537, 2565
Fagin, H. T.: test, 1174, 1175
Fairbank, D. W.: rev, 237, 283, 285, 790, 1962, 1970
Falender, C. A.: test, 1544, 1556
Faltin, S.: rev, 2131
Fan, X.: rev, 643
Fandal, A. W.: test, 1165
Fanjiang, G.: test, 1616
Fardig, D.: test, 2203
Farmer, R. F.: rev, 273, 473, 799, 2357, 2269
Farnsworth, P. R.: rev, 1555
Farnum, S. E.: test, 984, 2684
Farr, B.: test, 1229
Farr, J. M.: test, 1106, 1205
Farr, R.: test, 1229
Farrah, G. A.: test, 2234
Farrell-Holtan, J.: test, 207
Fasiska, E. J.: test, 936
Fassbinder, W.: rev, 1666
Fast, C. G.: test, 985
Faulkner, G.: test, 2384
Faunce, R. W.: rev, 1468, 2424, 2603
Fawcett, A.: test, 847, 1969
Fawcett, A. J.: test, 849, 851
Fawcett, H. P.: rev, 2687, 2688
Fay, K.: rev, 1171
Feil, E. G.: test, 870
Fein, D.: test, 2676
Feinburg, H.: rev, 778
Feiring, C.: rev, 1328
Feldt, L. S.: rev, 497; test, 1269
Felsenfeld, S.: rev, 2400
Feltham, D. W.: test, 2152
Fensch, E. A.: test, 2697
Fenson, L.: test, 1458
Fentiman, J.: test, 2329
Fenton, R.: rev, 375, 2018
Ferguson, G. A.: rev, 133
Ferguson, L. W.: rev, 2281
Fernandez, E.: rev, 268, 274, 1116
Ferrara, F. F.: rev, 1144, 1788
Ferrara, S.: rev, 204, 262, 2692
Ferro, T. R.: rev, 668, 1083, 1845, 1858
Ferry, F.: test, 404, 1291, 1463

Hulin, C. L.: test, 1290, 2102
Hulme, C.: test, 1899
Human Resources Center, The University of Chicago: test, 2466, 2736
Human Resources Development Press, Inc.: test, 1879
Human Sciences Research Council: test, 2253
Human Synergistics: test, 1472, 2443
Human Synergistics International: test, 1852, 2386
Human Technology, Inc.: test, 1845, 2490
Humphreys, G. W.: test, 316
Humphreys, L. G.: rev, 305, 818, 1594, 2467
Hundert, J.: rev, 2005
Hunsicker, A. L.: rev, 136, 1500
Hunt, B. A.: test, 1490
Hunt, J. A.: test, 1629
Hunt, J. V.: rev, 792, 1536, 2305
Hunt, R. A.: test, 1259
Hunt, T.: rev, 1618
Hunt, W. A.: rev, 2277
Hunter, C.: rev, 1056
Hunter, G. W.: rev, 1043
Hunter-Grundin, E.: test, 1185
Huntley, M.: test, 1085
Hurford, D. P.: rev, 531, 754, 1903, 2309, 2535, 2545
Husek, T. R.: rev, 1355
Hutcheson, C.: test, 1407
Hutchings, E. M. J.: test, 879
Hutchings, M. J.: test, 879
Hutchinson, S. M.: rev, 485
Hutchinson, T. A.: test, 2772
Huttenlocher, J.: test, 1978
Hutton, J. B.: test, 2316
Hutzell, R. R.: rev, 1241
Hynd, G. W.: rev, 2391

IDEA Center: test, 1188
Ihilevich, D.: test, 750
Ilg, F. L.: test, 1044
Iliff, A.: test, 126
Iliffe, A.: test, 2004
Illback, R. J.: rev, 1092
Ilmer, S.: test, 130
Impara, J. C.: rev, 2006, 2007, 2017
Inatsuka, T. T.: test, 1140
Inchaurralde, C.: rev, 278, 1300
Industrial Psychology International, Ltd.: test, 1271, 2766, 2767
Ingram, D. E.: test, 235
Ingram-LeBlanc, C.: test, 2525
Innovative Training Systems, Inc.: test, 68
Insel, E.: test, 1219
Insel, P. N.: test, 2746
The Institute for Behavioral Research in Creativity: test, 314, 883, 2413
Integrated Teaching Team: test, 1231
International Assessment Network: test, 1502

International Association of Administrative Professionals: test, 1747
International LearningWorks: test, 541, 1450, 1730
International Personnel Management Association: test, 1272, 1273, 1274
International Testing and Training Programs, Educational Testing Service: test, 2564
Inwald, R.: test, 1155, 1156, 1263, 1264
Inwald, R. E.: test, 1154, 1157
Iona, M.: rev, 116
IPAT Staff: test, 1372, 2294
Ireton, H.: test, 445, 854, 1210, 1870, 1961
Ireton, H. R.: test, 444
Ironson, G. H.: test, 2382
Irvin, L. K.: test, 2313, 2580
Irvin, R. S.: test, 2259
Irwin, J. L.: test, 1290
Irwin, J. V.: test, 1424
Isenberg, D. P.: test, 2035
Isenhart, C.: rev, 1116, 1498, 1512, 1655
Ishihara, S.: test, 2514
Isonio, S.: rev, 2236
Isquith, P. K.: test, 286
Itskowitz, R.: test, 243
Itzkovich, M.: test, 1445
Ivani-Chalian, R.: test, 2126
Ivens, S. H.: rev, 547, 1594, 2640, 2688
Iverson, A. M.: rev, 443, 976
Iverson, G. L.: test, 2726
Iverson, V. S.: test, 472
Ives, M.: rev, 2277
Ivins, R. G.: test, 1897
Iwanicki, E. F.: rev, 810, 812, 813, 814
Iwanicki, E. J.: rev, 811
Izard, J. F.: test, 1525
Izard, J.: test, 32

Jackson, D. N.: rev, 907, 1148, 1546, 1556; test, 187, 258, 402, 1278, 1279, 1383, 1658, 1885, 2291, 2456
Jackson, M. T.: test, 87
Jackson, P.: test, 2013
Jackson, S. E.: test, 1515
Jacobs, E. V.: test, 2200
Jacobs, G. A.: test, 2372
Jaeger, J.: test, 955, 1495
Jaeger, R. M.: rev, 1071, 1198, 2735
James, L. R.: test, 663
Jamison, C. B.: rev, 2111
Jansing, C.: rev, 50
Jansky, J.: test, 1281, 1282
Jarrico, S.: test, 320
Jastak, J. T.: test, 2717
Jastak, S.: test, 2717
Javorsky, D. J.: test, 328
Jaynes, P. A.: rev, 253, 1948
Jeanneret, P. R.: test, 1285, 1931, 1991, 2757

Lackey, J. E.: test, 1024
Lafayette Instrument: test, 1622
Lafferty, J. C.: test, 1101, 1429, 1454, 1778
LaFreniere, P. J.: test, 2315
Lagos, C. J.: test, 304
Lah, M. I.: test, 2144
Lahey, B. B.: test, 639
Laird, J. T.: test, 1625
Lambert, M. E.: rev, 1023, 1651, 1891
Lambert, N.: test, 2, 3, 458
Lambert, N. M.: rev, 66, 977
Lamberti, G.: test, 747
Lamke, T. A.: test, 1143
LaMonica, E. L.: test, 1361
Lampel, A. K.: test, 826
Land, V. C.: test, 925
Landman, J.: test, 1310
Landman, J. T.: test, 2580
Landrus, R.: test, 74
Landy, F. J.: rev, 667
Lane, H. S.: test, 478
Lane, S.: rev, 1268, 2006, 2131
Lang, P. J.: test, 989
Lang, V.: test, 956
Lang, W. S.: rev, 1140, 1334, 1335, 2505, 2515
Langdon, D. W.: test, 2647
Langevald, M. J.: test, 614
Langevin, R.: test, 481
Langley, J. C.: test, 1789
Langley, M. B.: test, 783
Langloois, A.: rev, 421
Langmuir, C. R.: rev, 1446; test, 1894
Langston, J. W.: test, 545
Languis, M.: test, 1406
Lanning, K.: rev, 91, 2285
Lanphere, T.: test, 2524
Lansing, M. D.: test, 2028
Lanyon, R. I.: rev, 434, 625, 966, 1148, 1263, 1609,
    1624, 2060; test, 1659, 2031
LaPointe, L. L.: test, 2067
Lappan, G.: rev, 2359
Lappan, P. A., Jr.: rev, 140, 491, 593
Laros, J. A.: test, 2311
Larrabee, G. J.: test, 678
Larsen, E.: test, 1774
Larsen, S. C.: test, 2523, 2576, 2577, 2578
Larson, J. W.: test, 2335
Larson, S.: test, 2428
Larson, S. L.: test, 649, 1341
Larson-Daugherty, C. A.: rev, 431, 1775
Lavallee, L.: test, 387
Lavee, Y.: test, 968
LaVoie, A. L.: rev, 901, 2449, 2507
Law, J. G., Jr.: rev, 221, 222, 229, 1157, 2668
Law School Admission Council, administered by Law
    School Admission Service: test, 1376
Lawes, J. S.: rev, 2311

Lawless, K. A.: rev, 1187
Lawlis, G. F.: test, 1131
Lawlor, G.: rev, 321
Lawrence, J.: test, 785
Lawrence, S. B.: test, 1373, 1374, 1375, 1377
Lawshe, C. H.: test, 60
Lawshe, C. H., Jr.: rev, 1119
Layton, T. L.: test, 424
Layton, W. L.: rev, 240, 467, 1620, 2298, 2390
Lazarus, A. A.: test, 1667
Lazarus, R. S.: test, 1126t, 2689
Leach, L.: test, 1314
Leafgren, F.: test, 1430
League, R.: test, 2085
Leark, R. A.: rev, 40, 1700, 2049, 2091
Leatherman, R. W.: test, 1413, 1414
Leber, W. R.: test, 2392, 2660
Leblanc, A. G.: test, 2574
LeBold, W. K.: test, 2038
LeBuffe, P. A.: test, 799, 800, 801
Ledbetter, E.: test, 2484
Leder, S. B.: rev, 278, 327, 846, 1017
Lederer, H.: rev, 493
Ledgerwood, R.: rev, 1579
Ledvinka, J.: rev, 1065
Lee, C. C.: rev, 314
Lee, C. K.: test, 1541
Lee, D.: test, 1552
Lee, J. M.: rev, 1269
Lee, R.: test, 1969
Lee, S. G.: rev, 1015
Lee, S. W.: rev, 265, 534, 905, 2410, 2447, 2732
Lefever, D. W.: rev, 365, 1143, 1173, 1271
Legg, S. M.: rev, 1127
Lehman, P. R.: rev, 1228, 1270, 1976
Lehman, P. W.: test, 622
Lehman, R. A. W.: test, 2034
Lehmann, I. J.: rev, 49, 50, 251, 537, 2357, 2359, 2733
Lehr, C.: test, 2509
Lehrer, R.: rev, 2008, 2432
Leigh, J. E.: test, 63, 260, 284
Leiter, M. P.: test, 1515
LeJeune, S. J.: test, 1529
Leland, H.: test, 2, 3
Lemke, S.: test, 1668
Lennon, R. T.: test, 1785
Lentz, F. E., Jr.: rev, 291, 1453
Lentz, T. F.: rev, 1640; test, 708, 2484
Lentz, T. J.: test, 1181
Lenz, J. G.: test, 417
Leonardelli, C. A.: test, 1612
Leong, F. T. L.: rev, 77, 379, 635, 1387, 1388, 1613,
    2380, 2411, 2496
Lepera, C.: test, 1970
Lepley, W. M.: test, 1849
Lesiak, J. L.: test, 794
Lesiak, W. J.: test, 794

Leslie, J.: test, 2301
Lesser, R.: test, 2030
Leton, D. A.: rev, 796, 2393
Letteri, C. A.: test, 1406
Letts, C.: test, 2116
Leung, S. A.: rev, 906 1793, 2084, 2286, 2294, 2760
Leverett, R. G.: rev, 2308, 2309
Levine, M. D.: test, 163, 1825, 1827, 1828, 1829, 2455
Levine, S. C.: test, 1978
Levitt, E. E.: rev, 696, 1625
Levitt, S. R.: test, 474, 2608
Levy, P. M.: rev, 923
Levy, S.: rev, 2439; test, 1844
Lewandowski, M. J.: test, 293
Lewis, D. C.: test, 1423
Lewis, F.: test, 2753
Lewis, J. F.: test, 64, 2467
Lewis, M. A.: rev, 16, 308, 379, 1271, 1387, 1388, 2263, 2294
Lewis, N. D. C.: rev, 953
Lewis, N. P.: rev, 1401, 2014; test, 822, 1333
Lewis, R.: test, 77, 689
Lewis, V.: test, 2558
LHE, Inc.: test, 431
Liau, A. K.: test, 1172
Lieberman, M.: test, 1551
Life Insurance Marketing and Research Association, Inc.: test, 416
Lifton, P. D.: rev, 1002, 1553
Lifton, W. M.: test, 881
Liggett, J.: rev, 133, 1104
Light, H. W.: test, 1431
Lighter, J.: test, 227
Likert, R.: test, 2109
LIMRA International: test, 197, 2300
Lincoln, N.: test, 2127
Lindamood, C. A.: rev, 1861
Lindamood, C. H.: test, 1433
Lindamood, P. C.: test, 1433
Lindeman, D. P.: rev, 2532
Linder, J.: rev, 966
Linder, T. W.: test, 2620
Lindner, S. J.: rev, 215, 1240
Lindquist, E. F.: test, 389, 2123
Lindquist, M. M.: rev, 256, 257
Lindsay, G.: test, 1211
Lindsay, G. A.: test, 1309
Lindsay, N.: test, 1028
Lindskog, C. O.: rev, 59, 2690
Lindskog, R.: rev, 2526, 2572
Lindvall, C. M.: rev, 1269
Lindzey, G.: test, 2416
Lingam, S.: test, 2198
Lingoes, J. C.: rev, 966
Linkenhoker, D.: test, 65
Linn, R. L.: rev, 321, 760, 818, 1268, 1579, 2510

Lintel, M. P.: rev, 169, 265, 2334
Lintereur, G. E.: rev, 1710
Lippa, R.: rev, 301
Lippert, J.: test, 2724
Lippke, B. A.: test, 1903
Liptak, J. J.: test, 247, 403, 1294, 1418
Lisicia, K.: test, 553
Lissitz, R. W.: rev, 151, 2583
Liu, W.: rev, 365
Liu, W. P.: rev, 1376
Lloyd, H. A.: rev, 367, 535
Lloyd, J. W.: rev, 2140
Lloyd, M. C.: test, 1902
Lloyd, P.: test, 1439
LoBello, S. G.: rev, 1038, 1159, 1195, 1985, 2060, 2589
A Local Chapter Committee, American Association of University Professors: test, 970
Locke, A.: test, 1443
Lockhart, W. E.: test, 1586
Loeb, P. A.: test, 1197
Loevinger, J.: rev, 1885
Loew, S.: rev, 2566
Loew, S. A.: rev, 820
Loewenstein Rehabilitation Hospital: test, 1445
Lofquist, L. H.: test, 1620, 1621, 1626, 1627
Logemann, J. A.: test, 1005
Loher, B.: test, 635
Lohnes, P. R.: rev, 395, 396, 1355, 2671
Lohr, N. E.: test, 808
Lombard, J. W.: rev, 2415
London House: test, 916, 1892, 2163
Lonegan, H.: test, 1898, 1952
Lonergan, W. G.: test, 1490
Long, C. J.: rev, 181, 545, 1394, 1588, 1927, 2187
Long, E. R.: test, 2729
Long, S. H.: rev, 618, 2556
Longo, A. P.: rev, 2052, 2578
Longstaff, H. P.: test, 1618
Lonski, A. B.: test, 140
Loomis, M.: test, 2285
Lopez, E. C.: rev, 1189, 2334
Loranger, A. W.: test, 1239, 1758
LORE International Institute: test, 433
Lorge, I.: rev, 1894, 2730; test, 613, 1714
Lorimer, J.: test, 1451
Lorr, M.: rev, 2292, 2296; test, 1245, 1995, 1996
Loth, J.: test, 2195
Loughnana, T.: test, 1506
Louttit, C. M.: rev, 428, 1926, 2652
Lovell, K.: rev, 349, 923
Low, B. P.: rev, 64, 1408
Lowe, J. M.: rev, 626
Lowe, M.: test, 2462
Lowman, R. L.: rev, 1463, 2453
Lowther, M. A.: test, 2407

Morrison, G. M.: rev, 834, 2585
Morrison, L. P.: test, 2479
Morrison, W. L.: test, 980, 2479
Morriss, R.: test, 224
Morrow, R.: test, 694
Morse, D. T.: test, 1334
Morton, N. W.: rev, 305, 2390; test, 309
Morton, R. L.: rev, 179
Morwood, R. G.: rev, 331, 1827
Mos, L. P.: test, 2029
Moseley, D.: test, 2740
Moses, B. S.: test, 449
Mosher, D. L.: rev, 422, 2479
Moshman, D.: rev, 2410
Moss, M. H.: test, 2586
Moss, P. A.: rev, 1199
Mossenson, L.: test, 2588
Mossholder, K. M.: rev, 2295
Mossholder, K. W.: rev, 2244
Mostue, P.: test, 1777
Motowidlo, S. J.: rev, 1487, 2156, 2161
Mowrer, D. E.: rev, 1054, 1333
Moxley, R.: test, 2301
Moyes, I. C. A.: rev, 1971
Moynihan, C.: test, 446
Mu Alpha Theta: test, 151, 153, 154
Muchinsky, P. M.: rev, 910, 936, 1217, 1295, 2506
Mueller, J.: test, 545
Mueller, R. O.: rev, 382, 631, 1761, 2240, 2746, 2755
Muench, A. M.: rev, 212
Mufer, V.: test, 1899
Mulhall, D. J.: test, 1026, 1864
Mullen, E. M.: test, 1654
Mullins, S.: test, 1417
Munday, L. A.: rev, 1376
Munger, A. M.: rev, 716, 1972
Munkres, A. W.: test, 2313
Muñoz-Sandoval, A. F.: test, 265, 312, 2734
Munro, J.: test, 192
Munsinger, H. L.: test, 2635
Murdoch, J. W.: rev, 1583
Murphy, C. C.: rev, 358
Murphy, E.: test, 1673
Murphy, H. D.: rev, 1007
Murphy, J. A.: rev, 107
Murphy, K. K.: rev, 2553
Murphy, K. R.: rev, 382, 1474, 2092, 2667; test, 222
Murray, C.: test, 2302
Murray, E.: rev, 842
Murray, H. A.: test, 2593
Murray-Ward, M.: rev, 1440, 1693, 2576, 2735
Murrell, P. H.: test, 622
Murstein, B. L.: rev, 456
Mutti, M.: test, 2054
Myers, C. T.: rev, 2274
Myers, I. B.: test, 1678, 1679
Myers, J. E.: test, 1756, 2701

Myers, R. S.: rev, 2460
Myers, S. P.: test, 1486
Myers, S. S.: rev, 2325
Myklebust, H. R.: test, 2037
Myles, B. S.: test, 189

Nafziger, D. H.: rev, 212, 1347
Nafziger, D.: rev, 2202
Naglieri, J. A.: rev, 304, 1045, 1537, 1576; test, 743, 799, 800, 801, 833, 834, 1034, 1531, 1680
Nagy, P.: rev, 1406, 2359, 2362
Napolitano, S. A.: rev, 466, 536
Nash, L.: test, 980
Natemeyer, W. E.: test, 1984
National Assessment of Educational Progress: test, 1683
National Association of Secondary School Principals Task Force on Effective School Environments: test, 636
National Association of Secondary School Principals: test, 2225
National Center for Education Statistics: test, 1683
National Computer Systems: test, 1485
National Computer Systems, Inc.: test, 166
National Council of Teachers of Mathematics: test, 151, 153, 154
The National Foundation for Educational Research: test, 255, 1521
National Foundation for Educational Research in England and Wales: test, 1522, 2068, 2078, 2080, 2081
National Institute for Personnel Research of Human Sciences Research Council: test, 319
National Institute of Industrial Psychology: test, 1102, 1103, 1104, 1707, 1708, 2651
National Occupational Competency Testing Institute: test, 1710, 1711, 1712
National Study of School Evaluation: test, 624, 1803, 2409
National Wellness Institute, Inc.: test, 2589, 2590, 2591
Naumann, T. F.: rev, 716, 1685
Naumann, W.: rev, 725, 1659
Navran, L.: test, 1504
NCS London House: test, 737
Neal, W. R., Jr.: test, 226
Neale, M. D.: rev, 2358; test, 1691
Neale, M..: test, 1690
Nedelsky, L.: rev, 116, 1074
Neeley, L.: test, 2329
Neemann, J.: test, 2247
Neeper, R.: test, 639
Neher, W. R.: test, 1646
Nehring, A. D.: test, 1393
Nehring, E. F.: test, 1393
Neidert, G. P. M.: test, 2770
Neidt, C. O.: rev, 365
Neimeyer, R. A.: test, 2434
Neisworth, J. T.: test, 2098

Powers, S.: rev, 1769
Poxon, S. C.: test, 742
Poznanski, E. O.: test, 462
Prather, E. M.: rev, 2481, 2531; test, 2261
Pratt, C.: test, 1509
Pratt, S.: rev, 161, 1371
Pratt, S. R.: rev, 1817
Preminger, J. L.: test, 1393
Prescott, T. E.: test, 2113
Preston, J.: rev, 2042
Preston, R. C.: rev, 2357
Price, G. E.: test, 1404, 1989
Price, L.: test, 899
Price, R. G.: rev, 2473
Priddy, J. M.: test, 1852, 1875
Prien, E. P.: rev, 67, 299, 1777, 2624
Prien, K. O.: rev, 299
Prigitano, G. N.: rev, 1772
Prince, J. S.: test, 2405
Pringle, M. L. K.: rev, 1056, 1911
Pritchard, B.: test, 2080
Prizant, B. M.: rev, 450; test, 618
Proger, B. B.: rev, 180, 321, 1055, 1822, 1965, 2037, 2085, 2303, 2555, 2582, 2586, 2735
PROJECT RHISE, Children's Development Center: test, 2130
Proulx, G.-B.: test, 1314
Prout, H. T.: rev, 2180; test, 906, 1342
Provence, S.: test, 1213, 1214
Pryor, R.: test, 2669, 2744
Psychological Assessment Resources, Inc.: test, 1925
The Psychological Corporation: test, 17, 39, 144, 169, 250, 407, 483, 520, 616, 932, 933, 1037, 1579, 1895, 2356, 2361, 2648, 2692, 2693, 2690
Psychological Services Bureau: test, 1847
Psychological Services Bureau, Inc.: test, 942, 1036, 1040, 1561, 1562, 1745, 1751, 2015, 2018, 2155
Psychological Services, Inc.: test, 999, 1000, 1921
Psychometric Research Unit, The Hatfield Polytechnic: test, 1064
Pugh, J. L.: test, 687
Pugh, R. C.: rev, 144, 323, 380
Pullias, E. V.: rev, 1579
Pumfrey, P. D.: test, 1423
Pumroy, D. K.: test, 1514, 2032
Purdue Research Foundation: test, 2039
Purisch, A. D.: test, 1456
Putnam, F.: test, 79
Putnam, F. W.: test, 828
Pynes, J. E.: rev, 1497
Pyrczak, F.: rev, 1268

Quasha, W. H.: test, 2109
Quay, H. C.: test, 2104
Quellmalz, E. S.: rev, 145, 1945
Quen, N.: test, 1679
Quenk, N. L.: test, 1678

Quereshi, M. Y.: rev, 660, 818, 1108
Quigley, H.: test, 1448
Quigney, T. A.: rev, 2623
Quinby, S. S.: test, 1117
Quinlan, D. M.: test, 211, 769
Quinn, J.: test, 360
Quinn, M.: rev, 2639, 2733

Raban, B.: test, 1212
Rabb, D.: test, 1023
Rabbit, J.: test, 1183
Rabin, A.: rev, 1464
Rabin, A. I.: rev, 456, 2134, 2694
Radcliffe, J. A.: rev, 884, 1059, 1182
Radocy, R. E.: rev, 95, 1270, 1674
Rafferty, J. E.: test, 2144
Rahim, M. A.: test, 2061
Rahmani, L.: test, 1445
Rain, J. S.: rev, 838, 1413, 2427
Raju, N. S.: rev, 213, 1268, 1461, 1980, 2719, 2741
Ramsay, R. T.: test, 893, 896, 897, 1132, 1227, 1296, 1459, 1461, 1558, 1564, 1746, 1748, 1980, 1987, 2070, 2441, 2611, 2700
Ramsberger, G.: test, 327
RAND Health Services Program: test, 1137
Rand, G.: test, 1176
Randhawa, B. S.: rev, 17, 520, 1229, 1617, 1636
Randolph, C.: test, 2096
Randolph, P. L.: test, 1393
Randt, C. T.: test, 2063
Rankin, E. F.: rev, 879
Raphael, A. J.: rev, 677, 2370, 2763
Rashotte, C. A.: test, 648, 2573
Raskin, E.: rev, 561, 584; test, 1091
Rau, N. S.: rev, 2199
Raven, J.: test, 878, 1593, 2064, 2351
Raven, J. C.: test, 717, 1593, 2064, 2350, 2351
Ravitch, M. M.: rev, 1581
Ray, G. E.: rev, 1770
Raychaudhuri, M.: rev, 889
Raygor, A. L.: rev, 2069
Rayne, F. D.: rev, 301
Raynor, A. L.: rev, 1693
Read, M. R.: test, 2023
Reardon, R. C.: test, 417
Reason, R.: test, 1900
Recht, E.: test, 788
Reckase, M. D.: rev, 309
Reed, C. A.: test, 2747
Reed, H. B. C., Jr.: rev, 1821, 2255; test, 2364
Reed, J. C.: rev, 86, 87, 222, 2461
Reed, J. R.: test, 556, 911
Reed, K. G.: test, 705
Reed, M. L.: rev, 965
Reese, J.: rev, 1583
Rehabilitation Research and Training Center on Blindness and Low Vision: test, 895

Smith, P. T.: test, 2126
Smith, R. A.: test, 824
Smith, R. P.: test, 1415
Smith, S.: test, 178, 179, 927, 928, 1043, 1138, 1150, 2079, 2346, 2662
Smith, S. L.: rev, 1513
Smith, T. A.: rev, 1909
Smock, C. D.: rev, 321, 662
Smyth, S.: test, 194
Snaith, R. P.: test, 1169
Snijders, J. T.: test, 2311
Snijders-Oomen, N.: test, 2311
Snow, J. H.: rev, 1303, 1456
Snowling, M.: test, 1899
Snyder, B.: rev, 1662
Snyder, D. K.: test, 1505
Snyder, K.: rev, 617
Soares, A. T.: test, 13, 2248, 2327, 2485
Soares, L. M.: test, 13, 2248, 2327
Society of Actuaries: test, 151, 153, 154
Sodor, A. L.: test, 1903
Sodowsky, G. R.: rev, 619, 830, 1336, 1778
Solly, D. C.: rev, 1535
Solomon, A.: rev, 652, 2354
Solomon, R. H.: rev, 128, 330
Solomon, R. J.: rev, 2587
Somerville, J. A.: test, 328
Sommers, R. K.: rev, 180, 2219
Song, A.: test, 2724
Soper, J. C.: test, 2536, 2537
Sorenson, C.: test, 635
Sorenson, G.: rev, 409
Sores, L. M.: test, 2485
Sosnowski, M.: test, 785
Sossen, P. L.: test, 2407
Sostek, A. M.: rev, 1695
Sotile, M. O.: test, 973
Sotile, W. M.: test, 973
Souder, L.: rev, 2359
Southwest Educational Development Laboratory: test, 827
Spaan, M.: test, 924, 1436, 1587
Spache, G. D.: rev, 841, 1032, 1902
Spadafore, G. J.: test, 2332, 2333
Spadafore, S. J.: test, 2332
Spalding, N. V.: test, 2054
Spaner, S. D.: rev, 921
Spaney, E.: rev, 1265
Spanier, G. B.: test, 843
Spany, E.: rev, 1781
Sparrow, E.: test, 670
Sparrow, S. S.: test, 130, 2652, 2653
Spector, J. E.: rev, 850, 2568
Speech Communication Association: test, 193, 627
Speer, R. F.: test, 1150
Speer, R. K.: test, 178, 179, 927, 928, 1043, 2079, 2346, 2662

Speer, R. V.: test, 1138
Spence, N.: test, 1194
Spence, R. J.: test, 2728
Spencer, D. G.: rev, 1865
Spencer, L. M.: test, 1777
Spenciner, L. J.: rev, 949, 1399
Spennato, N. A.: test, 755
Speroff, B. J.: test, 665, 908
Speth, C.: test, 635
Speyer, H.: rev, 428
Spielberger, C. D.: rev, 989; test, 1297, 2370, 2371, 2372, 2512
Spies, R.: rev, 280, 1928, 2172, 2468
Spiker, D.: rev, 317, 1257, 1770, 2198
Spillane, S. A.: rev, 975, 1042
Spires, H. P.: test, 1540
Spitzberg, B. H.: test, 680
Spitzer, J. B.: rev, 307, 2190, 2528
Spitzer, R. L.: test, 1052, 2024, 2026, 2195, 2214, 2394, 2395
Spivack, G.: test, 1111, 1112, 1542
Spivack, G. M.: rev, 963
Spooncer, F. A.: test, 1095
Sporakowski, M. J.: rev, 977, 1983, 2479
Sprafkin, J.: test, 70, 85, 448, 858, 2780
Sprague, R. L.: test, 59
Spreat, S.: rev, 790
Spreen, O.: rev, 1167
Spreitzer, G. M.: test, 2014
Square, P.: test, 2645
Squires, J.: test, 128
St. Louis, K. O.: test, 1771
Stacey, B. G.: rev, 452
Staff of the Psychological Services Bureau: test, 2016
Stafford, J.: rev, 1050
Stahl, M. J.: rev, 2021; test, 1289
Stahl, S. A.: rev, 192, 259, 1080
Stahmann, R. F.: rev, 422, 1355, 1356, 2479
Stainback, G. J.: rev, 445, 861, 1328, 2620
Stake, J. E.: rev, 170, 1543, 1992, 2250, 2385, 2357
Stamper, L.: test, 1541
Stanard & Associates, Inc.: test, 1687
Stang, S. W.: test, 2650
Stanley, J. C.: rev, 2358, 2389
Stansfield, C.: rev, 1366
Stansfield, C. W.: rev, 312, 1457; test, 253
Stark, J.: rev, 1965, 2116, 2117; test, 950
Stark, J. S.: test, 2407
Stark, R. H.: test, 1924
Starkey, R. I.: test, 1115
Starr, A. S.: rev, 2652; test, 2151
Starr, E. R.: rev, 556, 2059
Starr, R. P.: test, 1534
Steele, J. M.: test, 482
Steer, R. A.: test, 272, 273, 274, 275
Stefany, E. F.: rev, 265, 2732
Stein, M. B.: rev, 466, 2566

Swenson, C. H., Jr.: rev, 2173
Swerdlik, M. E.: rev, 341, 1031, 1785, 1794, 1970, 2360, 2577
Swift, M.: test, 1111, 1112
Switzer, J.: test, 1720
Switzky, H. N.: rev, 62, 294, 784, 2462, 2724
Sykken, D. T.: rev, 373
Symonds, P. M.: rev, 1013, 1849, 2135
Szczepanski, M.: test, 860

Taggart, B.: test, 1180
Taggart, W.: test, 1180
Takooshian, H.: rev, 724
Taleton, R.: test, 1647
Taljaard, J. J.: test, 1912, 2616
Talley, J. L.: test, 459, 2725
Tamir, P.: test, 615
Tannenbaum, A. J.: rev, 731
Tate, A.: test, 2541
Tatsuoka, K.: rev, 1948
Tatsuoka, K. K.: rev, 652, 1951, 2564
Tattersall, P. J.: test, 2400
Taulbee, E. S.: rev, 2681
Taylor, A. P.: test, 2478
Taylor, E. K.: rev, 1618, 1894, 2704, 910; test, 2156
Taylor, E. M.: rev, 1044
Taylor, H. F.: test, 687
Taylor, H. R.: rev, 392
Taylor, J.: test, 349
Taylor, K. M.: test, 401
Taylor, P. A.: rev, 2510
Taylor, R. A.: test, 1424
Taylor, R. L.: test, 198
Taylor, R. M.: test, 980, 2479
Taylor, R. N.: rev, 1487, 2281
Taylor, T. R.: test, 995, 1146, 1208, 2003, 2142
Teagarden, F. M.: rev, 428, 2652
Tearnan, B. H.: test, 293
Teeter, P. A.: rev, 72, 1320
Teitzel, T.: test, 1958
Teleometrics International: test, 2043
Tellegen, A.: rev, 966, 967, 1864; test, 1623, 1624
Tellegen, P.J.: test, 2311
Telzrow, C.: rev, 130
Telzrow, C. F.: rev, 779, 857, 1304
Tenopyr, M. L.: rev, 1356, 2745
Terborg, J. R.: test, 1495
Terman, E. L.: test, 1714
Terwilliger, J. S.: rev, 57
Tesh, A.: rev, 1746, 2015
Tesh, A. S.: rev, 932
The Test Agency: test, 1539
The Test Agency Ltd.: test, 892
Test Development Committees, American Association of Teachers of Spanish and Portuguese: test, 1688

Test Development Unit of the Foundation for Educational Research in England and Wales: test, 1528
Testut, E. W.: rev, 1841, 1973, 2188
Tetenbaum, T. J.: test, 227
Thal, D.: test, 1458
Thayer, P. W.: rev, 1749, 1752, 2109, 2281, 2282
Thetford, W. N.: rev, 1161
Thibaudeau, G.: test, 2525
Thoma, S.: test, 751
Thomas, G. F.: test, 1937
Thomas, G. V.: test, 1882
Thomas, J. W.: test, 2598
Thomas, K. W.: test, 918, 1937, 2388, 2599
Thomas, R.: test, 2203
Thomas, R. G.: rev, 1279, 1618, 1733
Thomas, T. J.: test, 2598
Thompson, B.: rev, 1530
Thompson, D.: rev, 172, 408, 475, 743, 1355, 1736
Thompson, G. B.: test, 2649
Thompson, J. A.: test, 328
Thompson, L. L.: test, 2726
Thompson, N. M.: rev, 529, 2340
Thompson, S. K.: test, 2575
Thomson, L. K.: test, 1350
Thorndike, R. L.: rev, 372, 559, 581, 825, 868, 908, 2357, 2506, 2613, 2713; test, 385, 547, 548, 2358
Thorndike, R. M.: rev, 630
Thorne, T.: test, 2329
Thornton, G.: rev, 1991
Thornton, G. C., III: rev, 1390, 1710, 1845, 1931, 2061
Thorpe, L. P.: rev, 2713
Thorum, A. R.: test, 1021
Thouless, R. H.: rev, 2687, 2688
Thurber, S.: rev, 2586
Thurstone, L. L.: test, 538, 539, 1249, 1563, 1842, 2330, 2331, 2600, 2601, 2644
Thurstone, T. G.: test, 716, 2601, 2634, 2644
Tidwell, P. S.: rev, 1364
Tiedeman, D. V.: rev, 57, 1033, 2436
Tierney, R. J.: rev, 1081, 1693, 2360, 2560
Tiffany, D. W.: rev, 2665; test, 2602
Tiffany, P. G.: test, 2602
Tiffin, J.: test, 60
Tighe, P. L.: test, 1189, 1190
Tindal, G.: rev, 92, 798, 1142 2028, 2304
Tindal, J.: rev, 1223, 2585
Tinker, M. A.: rev, 841, 842
Tinsley, H. E. A.: test, 1621
Tirre, W. C.: rev, 342, 920
Tittle, C. K.: rev, 203, 547, 548, 2313, 2686, 2694
Titus, P.: test, 2343
Tobin, A. R.: test, 2261
Todis, B.: test, 2201
Toglia, J. P.: test, 677
Tollison, C. D.: test, 1789

VanDuser, M. L.: rev, 76
VanGorp, W. G.: rev, 1167, 1456
VanVelsor, E.: test, 2301
Vasa, S. F.: rev, 779, 812
Vater, S.: test, 1214
Vecchio, R. P.: rev, 1127, 1972
Veldman, D. J.: rev, 657
Venable, G. P.: test, 1371
Vennix, P.: test, 2272
Verdi, W.: rev, 1414, 2256
Verhoeve, M.: test, 1279
Vernon, L. N.: test, 1755
Vernon, M. D.: rev, 1690
Vernon, P. E.: rev, 1108, 1148, 1335, 1641; test, 1061, 1063, 1525, 2416
Vernon, P. V.: rev, 713
Vetter, D. K.: rev, 483, 618, 2544
Viglione, D. J., Jr.: rev, 2135
Villanova, P.: rev, 1757
Vincent, D.: test, 815, 2075
Virtual Knowledge: test, 408
Visser, J.: rev, 796
Visser, R. S. H.: test, 628
Viswesvaran, C.: rev, 1352, 2463, 2619
Vitale, B. M.: test, 162
Vitali, G. J.: test, 649, 1341, 2554
Vitelli, R.: rev, 1421, 2551; test, 921
Vogler, D. E.: rev, 912, 2617
Volpe-Johnstone, T.: rev, 1650, 2367
von Mollendorf, J. W.: test, 2616
Von Roekel, B. H.: rev, 2139
Von Staabs, G.: test, 2193
Voress, J. K.: test, 741, 786, 797, 798, 2567
Vorster, J.: test, 2328, 2517
Vulpe, S. G.: test, 2674

Wacker, D. P.: rev, 784
Wagner, E. E.: rev, 2135; test, 1118
Wagner, J. P.: test, 2675
Wagner, R. K.: test, 648, 2573
Waguespack, M. M.: test, 850
Waitley, D.: test, 1852, 1875
Wakefield, J. F.: rev, 715
Waksman, S. A.: test, 1928, 2677
Walcott, D. D.: rev, 2182, 2317
Walden Personnel Performance, Inc.: test, 252, 679, 739, 954, 1277, 2099, 2100, 2167, 2504, 2682
Walden Personnel Testing: test, 1489
Walden Personnel Testing & Training, Inc.: test, 1141
Waldron, W. J.: rev, 1039, 1461, 1469, 2494, 2633
Walker, H. M.: test, 870, 2201, 2468, 2679
Walker, J. A.: test, 1577
Wall, R.: rev, 1739, 2067, 2441, 2540
Wall, S. M.: rev, 2037
Wall, W. D.: rev, 717, 2064, 2350, 2351
Wallace, G.: test, 642

Wallace, M.: test, 2244
Wallace, S. R.: rev, 910, 2161
Wallace, W. L.: rev, 57, 580, 605
Wallach, M. A.: rev, 2613
Wallen, N. E.: rev, 1143
Waller, N. G.: rev, 272, 273, 828, 1263, 2129, 2177, 2196
Walsh, J. A.: rev, 372, 750, 2292, 2296
Walsh, W. B.: rev, 1356, 2671
Walstad, W. B.: test, 2536, 2537
Walter, V.: test, 2244, 2295
Walters, A.: test, 133
Walters, A. S.: test, 1238
Walton, H. N.: test, 848
Wanberg, K. W.: test, 139
Wang, J-J.: test, 1823
Wang, P. L.: test, 1638
Wanner, S. J.: rev, 1435
Wantman, M. J.: rev, 1565
Wantz, R. A.: rev, 1568, 1809, 1974
Ward, A. W.: rev, 1006, 1329, 1820, 2284, 2713
Ward, C. F.: rev, 894
Ward, M. N.: test, 1424
Ward, S.: rev, 1440, 2367, 2772
Warden, R.: test, 2772
Wardrop, J. L.: rev, 365, 1269, 2581
Ware, J. E., Jr.: test, 2273
Wares, B. R.: test, 2168
Waring, E. M.: rev, 1505
Warnath, C.: rev, 889
Warnath, C. F.: rev, 745
Warner, J.: test, 2180, 2182
Warren, N. D.: rev, 710, 1119, 2039; test, 910
Warren, W. L.: test, 129, 1177, 2108, 2508
Warrington, E.: test, 378
Warrington, E. K.: test, 1062, 2087, 2647
Warrington, W. G.: rev, 50
Wasek, P.: test, 2195
Washer, R. W.: test, 2683
Wasyliw, O. E.: rev, 269, 964, 1823, 1927
Waterhouse, S. M. A.: test, 1686
Waterman, B.: rev, 200, 850, 862, 2283, 2373
Waters, D.: test, 1578
Waters, E.: rev, 1044
Watkins, J. G.: test, 2684
Watson, G.: rev, 708; test, 2687
Watson, G. B.: test, 2688
Watson, K. B.: test, 1440
Watson, K. W.: test, 1435, 2685, 2686
Watson, T. S.: rev, 208, 347, 371, 786, 1956, 2305, 2553
Watts, A. F.: test, 925, 2078
Watts, G.: test, 1327
Watts, K. P.: test, 131, 132, 133, 135, 2274
Waugh, R. P.: rev, 1193
Waxman, H. C.: test, 1786
Weatherman, R. F.: test, 1250, 2189

SCORE INDEX

American Literature: 487
Amiable: 2322
Amicability: 372, 1853
Amnesia: 2396, 2397
Amorality: 1624
Amorality (Ma1): 1623
Amount of Supervision Required: 2755
Amphetamines: 1854
Amplia Habilidad Cognitiva: 265
Amplia Habilidad Cognitiva-Escala Extendida: 265
Amusement: 1174
Análisis Síntesis: 265
Analog Electronics: 1227
Analog/Radio: 897
Analogías Verbalis: 265
Analogic Reasoning: 2636
Analogical Reasoning: 1703
Analogies: 131, 388, 877, 1034, 1262, 1718, 2213, 2311
Analysis: 369, 1834
Analysis of Response Validity Checklist: 2635
Analysis of Science Materials: 1269
Analysis of Social Studies Materials: 1269
Analyst: 1246
Analytic: 729, 1406, 1580, 2290
Analytic-Autonomizing: 990, 1628, 2380
Analytic-Autonomizing Motivation: 958
Analytic Thinking: 2754
Analytical: 1206, 1278, 1874, 1905, 2002, 2322
Analytical Chemistry: 45
Analytical Reasoning: 172, 240, 1071
Analytical Reasoning Skills: 159
Analytical Skills: 361, 1403
Analytical Thinker: 1722
Analytical Thinking: 170, 1471
Analyticity: 368
Analyze: 1886
Analyzing: 380
Analyzing and Interpreting Literature: 488
Analyzing Needs: 480
Analyzing Participants and Situations: 2617
Analyzing Problems Using Mathematical Skills and Concepts: 1053
Analyzing the Needs and "Entering Behavior" of the Learner: 201
Anankastic: 1239
Anatomy: 1161, 2323
Anergia: 1932
Anger: 82, 84, 129, 276, 464, 681, 829, 1577, 1624, 1860, 2293, 2456, 2625
Anger and Aggression: 625, 1092, 2681
Anger (ANG): 1623
Anger Control: 75, 86, 218, 1881
Anger Control/Hypersensitivity: 1283
Anger Control-In: 2370
Anger Control-Out: 2370
Anger Control Problems: 674, 2118

Anger Expression-In: 2370
Anger Expression Index: 2370
Anger Expression-Out: 2370
Anger-Hostility: 1995
Anger/Hostility: 973
Anger/Hostility Patterns: 1156
Anger-In: 364
Anger/Irritability: 2626
Anger-Out: 364
Anger/Violence Proneness: 83
Angry: 2505, 2655
Angry Expression and Anger Control Scales: 2370
Angry Hostility: 2110
Angry Reaction: 2370
Angry Temperament: 2370
Angry-Tolerant: 2315
Anhedonia: 461
Anhedonia-Asociality: 2177
Animal: 1100, 1161, 2279
Animal Care: 380, 2073
Animal Halves: 2127
Animal Naming: 199
Animal Pegs: 2696
Animal Service: 395, 396
Animals: 1734
Animals and Interests Test: 1044
Animals and Plants: 1233
Anomalous Concept Test: 1208
Anomalous Figure Test: 1208
Anomalous Responding: 1172
Anorexia: 463
Anorexia Nervosa: 82, 85, 2023
Anorexic Dietary Behavior: 2376
Anorexic Dietary Cognitions: 2376
Answer-Choice: 2579
Answer Choice Frequency: 681
Answering Objections: 480
Antecedents of Substance Abuse: 2427
Anti-Social Attitudes-Acts: 2024
Anti-Social Behavior: 621
Anti-Social Tendencies: 423
Anticipatory Anxiety: 1791
Antisocial: 681, 749, 993, 1239, 1280, 1610, 1758, 1882, 1981, 2172, 2196, 2269, 2278, 2395
Antisocial-Aggressive: 2211
Antisocial/Aggressive: 1162, 1956
Antisocial Attitudes: 1263
Antisocial Behavior: 1453, 1883, 1884, 2118, 2211
Antisocial Behavior Total: 1162
Antisocial Behaviors: 1264, 1512, 1880
Antisocial Features: 1880
Antisocial History: 2092
Antisocial Impulses or Acts: 2026
Antisocial Personality: 164, 2023, 2059
Antisocial Personality Disorder: 85, 296
Antisocial Practices (ASP): 1623
Antisocial Reaction: 2476

Nap Time: 1171
Narcissism: 164, 1758
Narcissistic: 681, 1239, 1610, 1758, 1882, 2196, 2395
Narcotics-Drugs: 2024
Narrative: 1683, 2065, 2362, 2773
Narrative Memory: 1696
Narrative Text: 1053
Narrative Writing: 199, 1053
Narrow/Focused: 225
Nasals: 209
National: 1221
National Sciences Reading: 1684
Natural: 1109
Natural Leading: 2594
Natural Sciences: 14, 386, 518, 605, 760, 1766
Nature: 167, 408, 1709, 1733, 1851, 2390
Nature-Agriculture: 1279
Nature of Man: 1861
Nature/Outdoors: 395, 396, 1192
Navy Enlisted: 396
Near Point Vision: 1538
Near Vision: 1009, 2112
Nearpoint: 2683
Neatness: 328
Necessary Arithmetic Operations Test: 1346
Necessitating: 2388
Need For Achievement: 213, 2259
Need for Affection: 1624
Need for Affection (Hy2): 1623
Need for Attention: 845
Need for Career Information: 405
Need for Control: 225, 1577
Need for Diversion: 845
Need for Freedom: 845
Need for Mental Challenge: 1834
Need for Precision: 845
Need for Psychiatric Referral: 1855
Need for Routine: 549
Need for Self-Evaluation: 1549
Need for Self-Knowledge: 405
Need for Stability: 1834
Need for Status: 1834, 2756
Need for Structure: 1834
Need Satisfaction: 1973
Needs: 1756
Needs Analysis/Assessment/and Planning: 626
Needs and Preferences: 1973
Needs Mobility: 1404, 1989
Needs-Persistence: 2135
Needs Recognition: 2050
Negations: 2122
Negative: 236, 980, 1919, 2518, 2574
Negative Affect: 931, 1571, 1881
Negative Affect/General Distress: 1238
Negative Affectivity: 1656
Negative Appraisal: 2387
Negative Assertive: 2275

Negative Behavior: 931
Negative Bias: 775, 2717
Negative Child: 1886
Negative Cognition: 931
Negative Communication: 1629
Negative Emotions: 1993
Negative Feelings: 1111
Negative Health Habits: 1659
Negative Home Environment: 1129
Negative Image: 1599
Negative Impression: 1611, 1880
Negative Influence Tactic Frequency: 2448
Negative Interaction: 1973, 2468
Negative Life Change Events: 1129
Negative Life Events: 1426, 1427
Negative Mood: 461, 2385
Negative Mood Scale: 293
Negative Narrative Comments: 2201
Negative or No Resolution: 973
Negative Parent: 1886
Negative Peer Relationships: 993
Negative Relationships: 1880
Negative Score Total: 770
Negative Self-Esteem: 461
Negative Self-Evaluations: 2435
Negative Self Image: 2243
Negative Self-Image: 1854, 1855
Negative Sense of Control: 2275
Negative Situations: 1254
Negative-Social: 222
Negative Social Behaviors: 2181
Negative Social Exchange: 1659
Negative Syndrome: 1932
Negative Temperament: 2196
Negative Total: 979
Negative Treatment Indicators: 1624
Negative Treatment Indicators (TRT): 1623
Negative Why Questions: 2559
Negative Yielding: 2275
Negatives: 1371, 1817
Neglect: 437, 1397
Neglect/Abandonment: 973
Negotiating: 1413, 1414
Negotiating Changes: 2012
Negotiating/Searching: 398
Negotiating Skills: 480
Negotiation: 1009, 1469
Neighborhood: 2045
Neighborhood Morale: 623
Neighborhood Observation Behavior Map: 859
Neither X nor Y: 2518
Neologisms: 2179
Neologistic: 199
Nervous vs. Composed: 2479
Nervousness: 1175, 1244, 1904
Net Speed: 1617
Net Strategy: 2710